D1536786

PRESENTED TO

BY:

ON:

Then he said to me,
"These words are faithful and true."

–Revelation 22:6a

A Visual Exploration of the

People, Places, and Things of Scripture

HOLY LAND ILLUSTRATED BIBLE

CSB Text Edition: 2020

With the exception of the articles on pages 1076-1077 and 1104-05, articles come from Biblical Illustrator magazine and are used by permission. A majority of the images and captions come from the same publication as well. See pages 1967-69 for a listing of photographers.

The interior of the *CSB Holy Land Illustrated Bible* was designed and typeset by 2K/DENMARK, using Bible Serif created by 2K/DENMARK, Højbjerg, Denmark. Proofreading was provided by Peachtree Publishing Services, Peachtree City, Georgia.

Binding	*ISBN*
British Tan LeatherTouch	978-1-4300-7042-9
British Tan LeatherTouch Indexed	978-1-4300-7043-6
Ginger LeatherTouch	978-1-4300-7045-0
Ginger LeatherTouch Indexed	978-1-4300-7046-7
Burgundy LeatherTouch	978-1-0877-5794-0
Burgundy LeatherTouch Indexed	978-1-0877-5795-7
Hardcover	978-1-5359-9792-8
Hardcover Mass Market	978-1-0877-1317-5
Premium Black Genuine Leather	978-1-4300-7047-4

Printed in China
3 4 5 7 8 9 10 — 26 25 24 23 22
APFT1166303

HOLY LAND ILLUSTRATED BIBLE

OLD TESTAMENT

NEW TESTAMENT

ADDITIONAL MATERIAL

INTRODUCTION

We all benefit from the efforts and work of those who have gone before us. My dad understood that; he used to say that we all enjoy sitting in the shade of trees that we did not plant. Many products and gadgets that increase our comfort and make our lives easier and better are available because of other people's visions, plans, and hard work. The Bible you hold in your hand is the product and result of many people's dedication to years of hard work and perseverance in fulfilling God's call on their lives.

In 1973, some people had a vision for a resource that would offer in-depth information for the serious student of the Word. After a time of planning and research, a new magazine was birthed, the *Sunday School Lesson Illustrator*. In its first issue, A.V. Washburn who was at the time the secretary of teaching and training of what is now LifeWay Christian Resoures said: "Now we are taking a bold step to express a dream. The *Sunday School Lesson Illustrator* will contain a new world of biblical information for the Sunday School pupil and teacher. . . . It is for those Bible students who are interested in more in-depth information about persons, places, and things."

Nobel Brown, the magazine's first editor, expressed his appreciation to the first contributors: "The most noticeable attribute common to those involved in producing the *Illustrator* has been an enthusiasm translated into a determination to create a significant magazine. Our writers have put aside other demanding duties in order to spend hours of research in preparing each article."

The magazine's name was later changed to *Biblical Illustrator*, yet the purpose of the magazine never changed. Using words and images, maps and charts, *Biblical Illustrator* helped Bible teachers and students gain a deeper understanding into God's Word.

What is the significance of a particular location? How does this event fit in the larger context of Scripture? What was going on in the world at that time? Was there a significance that the initial readers would have understood that we miss, now centuries later? The *CSB Holy Land Illustrated Bible* is filled with helpful articles and images that appeared in the magazine and addressed these questions and more.

As the year 2020 drew to a close, the magazine ceased publication. With this Bible, though, you have the opportunity to continue sitting at the feet of scholars, to enjoy the shade of men and women who have invested their lives as life-long learners of Scripture. Through their efforts, you will discover the culture, customs, people, and practices of the biblical day. The information on these pages can help you understand the message as the original audience did, deepen your understanding of Scripture, and increase your appreciation for the biblical world.

The intent is not to give you minutia or additional tidbits of obscure information. Instead, it is to help you grow in your commitment to both the Word of God and the God of the Word. The Lord promises, "my word that comes from my mouth will not return to me empty, but it will accomplish what I please and will prosper in what I send it to do" (Is 55:11).

We invite you to pore over these pages. Bask in what the Father has to say to you. Allow the articles to draw you into the biblical world. And as you do, we pray you will find yourself refreshed, spiritually renewed, and confident in your growing knowledge of God's Word. So please, find yourself a place in the shade and prepare to be blessed.

G. B. Howell
Content Editor, *Biblical Illustrator*
2002-2020

Features of the *Holy Land Illustrated Bible*

The *Holy Land Illustrated Bible* immerses readers into the world and culture of the Bible through its various features.

Book Introductions

Each book of the Bible opens with an introduction that discusses the book's authorship, setting, and circumstances of writing.

INTRODUCTION TO

GENESIS

Circumstances of Writing

Since pre-Christian times, authorship of the Torah, the first five books of the Bible, has been attributed to Moses, an enormously influential Israelite leader from the second millennium BC with an aristocratic Egyptian background. Even though Genesis is technically anonymous, both the Old and New Testaments unanimously recognize Moses as the Torah's author (Jos 8:35; 2Ch 23:18; Neh 8:1; Mk 12:19,26; Lk 2:22; Rm 10:5; Heb 10:28). At the same time, evidence in Genesis suggests that minor editorial changes dating to ancient times have been inserted into the text. Examples include the mention of "Dan" (14:14), a city that was not named until the days of the judges (Jdg 18:29), and the use of a phrase that assumed the existence of Israelite kings (Gn 36:31).

The Torah (Hb for "law") was seen as one unit until at least the second century BC. Sometime prior to the birth of Christ, the Torah was divided into five separate books, later referred to as the Pentateuch (lit "five vessels"). Genesis, the first book of the Torah, provides both the universal history of humankind and the patriarchal history of the nation of Israel. The first section (chaps. 1–11) is a general history commonly called the "primeval history," showing how all humanity descended from one couple and became sinners. The second section (chaps. 12–50) is a more specific history commonly referred to as the "patriarchal history," focusing on the covenant God made with Abraham and his descendants: Isaac, Jacob, and Jacob's twelve sons. Genesis unfolds God's plan to bless and redeem humanity through Abraham's descendants. The book concludes with the events that led to the Israelites being in the land of Egypt.

Contribution to the Bible

Genesis lays the groundwork for everything else we read and experience in Scripture. Through Genesis we understand where we came from, how we got in the fallen state we are in, and the beginnings of God's gracious work on our behalf. Genesis unfolds God's original purpose for humanity.

Genesis provides the foundation from which we understand God's covenant with Israel that was established with the giving of the Law. For the Israelite community, the stories of the origins of humanity, sin, and the covenant relationship with God helped them understand why God gave them the Law.

Structure

Genesis is chiefly a narrative. From a narrative standpoint, God is the only true hero of the Bible, and the book of Genesis has the distinct privilege of introducing him. God is the first subject of a verb in the book and is mentioned more frequently than any other character in the Bible. The content of the first eleven chapters is distinct from the patriarchal stories in chapters 12–50. The primary literary device is the catchphrase "these are the family records." The phrase is broader in meaning than simply "generation" and refers more to a narrative account. This was a common practice in ancient Near Eastern writings. This phrase also serves as a link between the key person in the previous narrative and the one anticipated in the next section. Genesis could be described as historical genealogy, which ties together creation and human history in one continuum.

Over 1,200

images, maps, and illustrations of the people, places, and artifacts of Scripture to provide a unique and immersive visual reading experience.

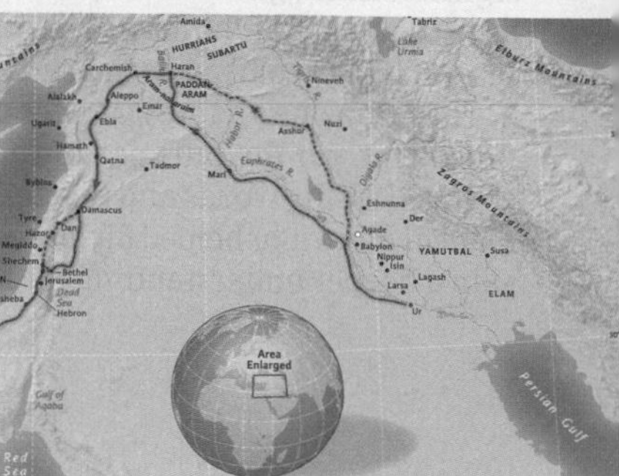

Digging Deeper

More than 40 call-outs that explain a variety of places and artifacts and why they are important to the Bible.

DIGGING DEEPER *Gilgamesh Epic*

The *Gilgamesh Epic*, dating to the seventh century BC, contains a Babylonian record of a worldwide flood. This account was likely borrowed from the *Atrahasis Epic*, which dates to 1800 BC. Portions of *Gilgamesh* have been discovered throughout the Middle East, including the biblical city of Megiddo.

The story tells of a Noah-like figure named Utnapishtim who survived the flood because he was warned by the god Ea to build a boat for his family and many animals. A week of rain swept away the boat, and then it came to rest on Mount Nisir (Kurdistan) where Utnapishtim released several birds that did not return. He then offered sacrifice and was granted immortality.

Some critical scholars say the Bible depends on Babylonian accounts such as *Gilgamesh* since there are noticeable similarities between the stories. However, the mythological message in *Gilgamesh* is absent in the later Genesis description, making it unlikely that the Bible borrowed from the Babylonians. Details of the flood event were distorted as different cultures interpreted the flood through their unique religious beliefs. Supporting this conclusion is the fact that nearly two dozen separate flood accounts exist around the world. Hence the Bible has gotten it right, whereas other accounts mix truth with error.

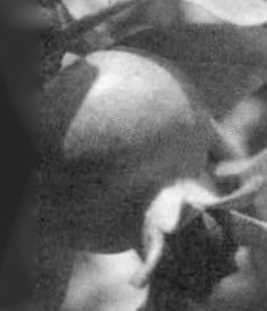

Articles

More than 275 full-length articles provide greater insight and understanding to the world and culture of the Bible.

Ancient Altars

by George H. Shaddix

Relief of a Hittite king and queen before the sacred altar. Dates to 1300 BC.

The simplest altars were constructed of earth built up into a mound. This may have been the type of altar Noah built—and evidently the type Moses later built. Earthen altars were useful, especially for nomadic people. "An earthen altar would not have been very practical for permanently settled people, for the rainy season each year would damage or destroy the altar."[1] Instead, settled people typically used stone to construct altars. These stones were to be natural and not hewn. The stone altar, like the earthen altar, would have no definite shape. The stones would simply be piled on top of one another. Sometimes a single natural rock would serve as an altar (Jdg 6:19–21). So the material the builder used to construct the altar determined its shape.

Scripture appears to make a distinction concerning those who offered sacrifices on each type of altar. Earthen and stone altars were in use before the establishment of the priesthood; therefore, anyone could build an altar wherever they were and could offer a sacrifice (Gn 8:17–20; 22:9–13). With the establishment of the priesthood, people built more elaborate altars, such as those in the tabernacle and the temple. Only here did the priests offer the sacrifices for the people of God.

Most altars were designed for offering sacrifices; however, some seem to have been built as memorials (Ex 17:15–16; Jos 22:26–27).[2]

Altars were not unique to Israel. Other nations also built altars to worship their gods. Archaeologists have uncovered an altar with multiple faces carved into it at Taanach, where Deborah and Barak defeated the Canaanites under Sisera (Jdg 5:19–20).[3] Such adornments were prohibited in Jewish worship. "A striking circular Canaanite altar dating from 2500 BC to 1800 BC was excavated at Megiddo. It was twenty-five feet in diameter and 4 ½ feet high. Four steps led up to the top of the altar."[4] The prohibition in Exodus 20:25–26 against using hewn stone and using steps in conjunction with altars is probably a prohibition against God's people using altars that shared characteristics with the Canaanites' altars.[5] Archaeologists have excavated at Beer-sheba an altar constructed of large hewn stones. This altar has horns on its four corners and dates to the period of the divided kingdom.[6]

The altar was a sacred place in Israel's worship. It represented the presence of God among his people. As offerings were placed on the altar, "the offerings were taken out of man's domain and given to God, and God replied by bestowing blessings (Ex 20:24). Thus the Covenant itself between God and his people was maintained in force, or re-established, upon the altar of sacrifice."[7]

Because the altar was sacred, nothing was to defile it. If, for some reason, it became defiled, it was to be cleansed as it had been in the days of King Hezekiah (2Ch 29:18–19). ✣

Miniature bronze incense burners, probably for domestic use. From Byblos; first century BC–first century AD.

[1] Joel F. Drinkard Jr., "Altar" in *Holman Bible Dictionary* (*HolBD*), ed. Trent C. Butler (Nashville: Holman, 1991), 38. [2] Howard Z. Cleveland, "Altar" in *The New International Dictionary of the Bible*, J. D. Douglas, rev. ed., ed. Merrill C. Tenney (Grand Rapids: Zondervan, 1987), 36. [3] Albert E. Glock, "Taanach" in *The New Encyclopedia of Archaeological Excavations in the Holy Land* (*NEAEHL*), ed. Ephraim Stern (New York: Simon & Schuster, 1993), 4:1431. [4] Drinkard, "Altar," 38. [5] H. M. Wiener, W. S. Caldecott, and C. E. Armerding, "Altar" in *The International Standard Bible Encyclopedia* (*ISBE*), ed. Geoffrey W. Bromiley, vol. 1 (Grand Rapids: Eerdmans, 1979), 101–2. [6] Drinkard, "Altar," 38. [7] Roland de Vaux, *Ancient Israel: Its Life and Institutions* (Grand Rapids: Eerdmans, 1997), 414.

Upper image: One of the best examples of a large stone altar is at Megiddo. The temple complex dates from the time of Abraham. The circular altar is about twenty-five feet in diameter and more than four feet tall. Lower image: Monument, likely an altar, in central area of temple of Echmoun outside of Sidon. Echmoun was the Phoenician god of healing. Temple dates to the seventh century BC.

STUDY BIBLE ARTICLES

BIBLICAL ILLUSTRATOR ARTICLES

DIGGING DEEPER

MAPS AND ILLUSTRATIONS

CONTRIBUTORS

Adkisson, Randall L. Healthy Christian Ministries.
Anderson, Jeff S. Wayland Baptist University.
Andrew, Scott A. Nashville, TN.
Andrews, Stephen J. Midwestern Baptist Theological Seminary.
Arbino, Gary P. Gateway Seminary.
Bergen, Martha S. Hannibal-LaGrange University.
Bergen, Robert D. Hannibal-LaGrange University.
Betts, T. J. The Southern Baptist Theological Seminary.
Beyer, Bryan E. Columbia International University.
Branch, Alan. Midwestern Baptist Theological Seminary.
Browning Jr., Daniel C. William Carey University.
Booth, Steve. Canadian Southern Baptist Seminary.
Booth, Susan. Canadian Southern Baptist Seminary.
Brooks, James A. Bethel Theological Seminary.
Boyd, Timothy N. Kansas-Nebraska Convention of Southern Baptists.
Buescher, Alan Ray. Nashville, TN.
Butler, Trent C. Gallatin, TN.
Byargeon, Rick W. Temple Baptist Church, Ruston, LA.
Caldwell, Daniel P. William Carey University.
Cantrell, Deborah. Houston, TX
Cathey, Joseph R. Dallas Baptist University.
Champy III, Harry D. North Georgia Christian School.
Clendenen, E. Ray. Holman Bible Publishers.
Cole, R. Dennis. New Orleans Baptist Theological Seminary.
Cook III, William F. The Southern Baptist Theological Seminary.
Cox, Ken. New Boston, TX
Crockett Jr., Bennie R. William Carey University.
Davis, Conn. Southern Baptist Believers Church, South Coffeyville, Oklahoma.
Draper, Charles W. Boyce College.
Drinkard Jr., Joel F. Campbellsville University.
Dunn, Mark R. First Baptist Church, Duncanville, TX
Dunston, Robert C. University of the Cumberlands.
Faber, Timothy T. Liberty University.
Fowler, R. D. Bethel Baptist Church, Lincoln, NE.
Garrett, Duane A. The Southern Baptist Theological Seminary.
Goodman, Thomas H. Hillcrest Baptist Church, Austin, TX.
Gregg, D. Larry. Covecraft Consultants.
Gritz, Sharon H. Fort Worth, TX
Hall, Kevin. Oklahoma Baptist University.
Hardin, Gary. Centre, Alabam.
Harris, John L. East Texas Baptist University.
Hays, J. Daniel. Ouachita Baptist University.
Howell Jr., G. B. Lifeway Christian Resources.
Hyatt Jr., Leon. Pineville, LA
Hummel, Scott. William Carey University.
Jenkins, David L. Gilmer, TX
Jones, Robert E. Euclid Avenue Baptist Church, Bristol, VA.
Jones, Roberta Lou. Mid-Continent University.
Kimmitt, Francis X. Bryan College.
Knight, George W. Greenville Presbyterian Theological Seminary.
Knowles, Julie Nall. The Baptist College of Florida.
Kullman, Paul E. College Station, TX
Laird, Dorman. William Carey University.
Lane, Harry A. West Side Baptist Church, Greenwood, SC.
Langston, Scott.
Lanier, David E. Southeastern Baptist Theological Seminary.
Lee, Jerry W.
Lemke, Steve W. New Orleans Baptist Theological Seminary.
Lloyd, R. Raymond. First Baptist Church, Starkville, MS.
Lombard, Becky. Truett McConnell University.
Longino, Byron. New Orleans Baptist Theological Seminary.
Lucas Jr., Roy E. Clear Breek Baptist Bible College.
Mariottini, Claude F. Northern Baptist Theological Seminary.
Matthews, E. LeBron. Eastern Heights Baptist Church, Columbus, GA.
McClain, T. Van. Mid-America Baptist Theological Seminary.
McCoy, Glenn. Eastern New Mexico University.
McWilliams, Warren. Oklahoma Baptist University.
Meier, Janice. Nashville, TN.
Miller, Stephen R. Mid-America Baptist Theological Seminary.
Mitchell, Eric A. Southwestern Baptist Theological Seminary.
Moore, R. Kelvin. Union University.
Moseley, Allan. Southeastern Baptist Theological Seminary.
Mosley, Harold R. New Orleans Baptist Theological Seminary.
Newell, James O. The Baptist College of Florida.

Ortiz, Steven M. Southwestern Baptist Theological Seminary.
Peacock, Kevin C. Canadian Southern Baptist Seminary.
Poulton, Gary M., Virginia Intermont College.
Pouncey, George T. First Baptist Church, Mobile, AL.
Rathel, Mark A. The Baptist College of Florida.
Ray Jr., Charles A. New Orleans Baptist Theological Seminary.
Register, M. Dean. Crosspoint Church, Hattiesburg, MS.
Richards, E. Randolph. Palm Beach Atlantic University.
Roark, C. Mack. Oklahoma Baptist University.
Roberts, Sharon. Nashville, TN.
Robinson, Dale "Geno." First Baptist Church of Fair Oaks, Sacramento, California.
Rodriquez, Seth M. Colorado Christian University.
Shaddix, George H. Dunn's Creek Baptist Church, Echola, AL.
Severance, W. Murray. Nashville, TN.
Simmons, Bob. New Orleans Baptist Theological Seminary.
Smith Jr., Argile A. Parkway Baptist Church, Biloxi, MS.
Stevens, Gerald L. New Orleans Baptist Theological Seminary.
Stewart, Don H. New Orleans Baptist Theological Seminary.
Stewart, Mona. William Carey School of Nursing.
Street, Robert A. Campbellsville University.
Swanson, Philip J. Colts Neck Baptist Church, Colts Neck, NJ.
Tate, Marvin E. The Southern Baptist Theological Seminary.
Taylor, Cecil R. University of Mobile.
Terry, John Mark. The Southern Baptist Theological Seminary.
Tolar, William B. Southwestern Baptist Theological Seminary.
Trammell, Timothy. Dallas Baptist University.
Traylor, John. First Baptist Church, Monroe, LA.
Traylor, Lynn O. Liberty Association, Glasgow, KY.
VanHorn, W. Wayne. Mississippi College.
Wallace, David M. Dallas Baptist University.
Weathers, Robert A. First Baptist Church, Shallotte, NC.
Winslow, Blakeley. North American Mission Board.
Wood, Darryl. First Baptist Church, Vincent, AL.
Wood, Fred M. Preach-Teach Ministries.

INTRODUCTION TO THE CHRISTIAN STANDARD BIBLE

The Bible is God's revelation to humanity. It is our only source for completely reliable information about God, what happens when we die, and where history is headed. The Bible reveals these things because it is God's inspired Word, inerrant in the original manuscripts. Bible translation brings God's Word from the ancient languages (Hebrew, Greek, and Aramaic) into today's world. In dependence on God's Spirit to accomplish this sacred task, the CSB Translation Oversight Committee and Holman Bible Publishers present the Christian Standard Bible.

TEXTUAL BASE OF THE CSB

The textual base for the New Testament (NT) is the Nestle-Aland *Novum Testamentum Graece*, 28th edition, and the United Bible Societies' *Greek New Testament*, 5th corrected edition. The text for the Old Testament (OT) is the *Biblia Hebraica Stuttgartensia*, 4th edition.

Where there are significant differences among Hebrew, Aramaic, or Greek manuscripts, the translators follow what they believe is the original reading and indicate the main alternative(s) in footnotes. The CSB uses the traditional verse divisions found in most Protestant Bibles.

GOALS OF THIS TRANSLATION

- Provide English-speaking people worldwide with an accurate translation in contemporary English.
- Provide an accurate translation for personal study, sermon preparation, private devotions, and memorization.
- Provide a text that is clear and understandable, suitable for public reading, and shareable so that all may access its life-giving message.
- Affirm the authority of Scripture and champion its absolute truth against skeptical viewpoints.

TRANSLATION PHILOSOPHY OF THE CHRISTIAN STANDARD BIBLE

Most discussions of Bible translations speak of two opposite approaches: formal equivalence and dynamic equivalence. This terminology is meaningful, but Bible translations cannot be neatly sorted into these two categories. There is room for another category of translation philosophy that capitalizes on the strengths of the other two.

1. **FORMAL EQUIVALENCE:**
   Often called "word-for-word" (or "literal") translation, the principle of formal equivalence seeks as nearly as possible to preserve the structure of the original language. It seeks to represent each word of the original text with an exact equivalent word in the translation so that the reader can see word for word what the original human author wrote. The merits of this approach include its consistency with the conviction that the Holy Spirit did inspire the very words of Scripture in the original manuscripts. It also provides the English Bible student some access to the structure of the text in the original language. Formal equivalence can achieve accuracy to the degree that English has an exact equivalent for each word and that the grammatical patterns of the original language can be reproduced in understandable English. However, it can sometimes result in awkward, if not incomprehensible, English or in a misunderstanding of the author's intent. The literal rendering of ancient idioms is especially difficult.

2. **DYNAMIC OR FUNCTIONAL EQUIVALENCE:**
   Often called "thought-for-thought" translation, the principle of dynamic equivalence rejects as misguided the attempt to preserve the structure of the original language. It proceeds by extracting the meaning of a text from its form and then translating that meaning so that it makes the same impact on modern readers that the ancient text made on its original readers. Strengths of this approach include a high degree of clarity and readability, especially in places where the original is difficult to render word for word. It also acknowledges that accurate and effective translation may require interpretation. However, the meaning of a text cannot always be neatly separated from its form, nor can it always be precisely determined. A biblical author may have intended multiple meanings, but these may be lost with the elimination of normal structures. In striving for readability, dynamic equivalence also sometimes overlooks and loses some of the less prominent elements of meaning. Furthermore, lack of formal correspondence to the original makes it difficult to verify accuracy and thus can affect the usefulness of the translation for in-depth Bible study.

3. **OPTIMAL EQUIVALENCE:**

In practice, translations are seldom if ever purely formal or dynamic but favor one theory of Bible translation or the other to varying degrees. Optimal equivalence as a translation philosophy recognizes that form cannot always be neatly separated from meaning and should not be changed unless comprehension demands it. The primary goal of translation is to convey the sense of the original with as much clarity as the original text and the translation language permit. Optimal equivalence appreciates the goals of formal equivalence but also recognizes its limitations.

Optimal equivalence starts with an exhaustive analysis of the text at every level (word, phrase, clause, sentence, discourse) in the original language to determine its original meaning and intention (or purpose). Then, relying on the latest and best language tools and experts, the nearest corresponding semantic and linguistic equivalents are used to convey as much of the information and intention of the original text with as much clarity and readability as possible. This process assures the maximum transfer of both the words and the thoughts contained in the original.

The CSB uses optimal equivalence as its translation philosophy. In the many places throughout the Bible where a word-for-word rendering is understandable, a literal translation is used. When a word-for-word rendering might obscure the meaning for a modern audience, a more dynamic translation is used. The Christian Standard Bible places equal value on fidelity to the original and readability for a modern audience, resulting in a translation that achieves both goals.

THE GENDER LANGUAGE USAGE IN BIBLE TRANSLATION

The goal of the translators of the Christian Standard Bible has not been to promote a cultural ideology but to translate the Bible faithfully. Recognizing modern usage of English, the CSB regularly translates the plural of the Greek word *ανθρωπος* ("man") as "people" instead of "men," and occasionally the singular as "one," "someone," or "everyone," when the supporting pronouns in the original languages validate such a translation. While the CSB avoids using "he" or "him" unnecessarily, the translation does not restructure sentences to avoid them when they are in the text.

HISTORY OF THE CSB

After several years of preliminary development, Holman Bible Publishers, the oldest Bible publisher in North America, assembled an international, interdenominational team of one hundred scholars, editors, stylists, and proofreaders, all of whom were committed to biblical inerrancy. Outside consultants and reviewers contributed valuable suggestions from their areas of expertise. Working from the original languages, an executive team of translators edited, polished, and reviewed the final manuscript, which was first published as the Holman Christian Standard Bible (HCSB) in 2004.

A standing committee was also formed to maintain the HCSB translation and look for ways to improve readability without compromising accuracy. As with the original translation team, the committee that prepared this revision of the HCSB, renamed the Christian Standard Bible, is international and interdenominational, comprising evangelical scholars who honor the inspiration and authority of God's written Word.

TRADITIONAL FEATURES FOUND IN THE CSB

In keeping with a long line of Bible publications, the CSB has retained a number of features found in traditional Bibles:

1. Traditional theological vocabulary (for example, *justification, sanctification, redemption*) has been retained since such terms have no other translation equivalent that adequately communicates their exact meaning.
2. Traditional spellings of names and places found in most Bibles have been used to make the CSB compatible with most Bible study tools.
3. Some editions of the CSB will print the words of Christ in red letters to help readers easily locate the spoken words of the Lord Jesus Christ.
4. Descriptive headings, printed above each section of Scripture, help readers quickly identify the contents of that section.
5. OT passages quoted in the NT are indicated. In the CSB, they are set in boldface type.

HOW THE NAMES OF GOD ARE TRANSLATED

The Christian Standard Bible consistently translates the Hebrew names for God as follows:

Hebrew original:	CSB English:
Elohim	God
YHWH (*Yahweh*)	LORD
Adonai	Lord
Adonai Yahweh	Lord GOD
Yahweh Sabaoth	LORD of Armies
El Shaddai	God Almighty

FOOTNOTES

Footnotes are used to show readers how the original biblical language has been understood in the CSB.

1. OLD TESTAMENT (OT) TEXTUAL FOOTNOTES

OT textual notes show important differences among Hebrew (Hb) manuscripts and ancient OT versions, such as the Septuagint and the Vulgate. See the list of abbreviations on page xx for a list of other ancient versions used.

Some OT textual notes (like NT textual notes) give only an alternate textual reading. However, other OT textual notes also give the support for the reading chosen by the editors as well as for the alternate textual reading. For example, the CSB text of Psalm 12:7 reads,

> You, LORD, will guard us;
> you will protect us[A]
> from this generation forever.

The textual footnote for this verse reads,

[A] **12:7** Some Hb mss, LXX; other Hb mss read *him*

The textual note in this example means that there are two different readings found in the Hebrew manuscripts: some manuscripts read *us* and others read *him*. The CSB translators chose the reading *us*, which is also found in the Septuagint (LXX), and placed the other Hebrew reading *him* in the footnote.

Two other kinds of OT textual notes are

Alt Hb tradition reads ____
a variation given by scribes in the Hebrew manuscript tradition (known as *Kethiv/Qere* and *Tiqqune Sopherim* readings)

Hb uncertain
when it is unclear what the original Hebrew text was

2. NEW TESTAMENT (NT) TEXTUAL FOOTNOTES

NT textual notes indicate significant differences among Greek manuscripts (mss) and are normally indicated in one of three ways:

Other mss read ____
Other mss add ____
Other mss omit ____

In the NT, some textual footnotes that use the word "add" or "omit" also have square brackets before and after the corresponding verses in the biblical text. Examples of this use of square brackets are Mark 16:9-20 and John 7:53–8:11.

3. OTHER KINDS OF FOOTNOTES

Lit ____	a more literal rendering in English of the Hebrew, Aramaic, or Greek text
Or ____	an alternate or less likely English translation of the same Hebrew, Aramaic, or Greek text
=	an abbreviation for "it means" or "it is equivalent to"
Hb, Aramaic, Gk	the actual Hebrew, Aramaic, or Greek word is given using equivalent English letters
Hb obscure	the existing Hebrew text is especially difficult to translate
emend(ed) to ____	the original Hebrew text is so difficult to translate that competent scholars have conjectured or inferred a restoration of the original text based on the context, probable root meanings of the words, and uses in comparative languages

In some editions of the CSB, additional footnotes clarify the meaning of certain biblical texts or explain biblical history, persons, customs, places, activities, and measurements. Cross references are given for parallel passages or passages with similar wording, and in the NT, for passages quoted from the OT.

ABBREVIATIONS IN CSB BIBLES

AD	In the year of our Lord
BC	before Christ
c.	century
ca	circa
chap(s).	chapter(s)
cp.	compare
DSS	Dead Sea Scrolls
e.g.	for example
Eng	English
etc.	et cetera
Gk	Greek
Hb	Hebrew
i.e.	that is
Lat	Latin
lit	literal(ly)
LXX	Septuagint—an ancient translation of the Old Testament into Greek
MT	Masoretic Text
NT	New Testament
ms(s)	manuscript(s)
OT	Old Testament
pl.	plural
Ps(s)	Psalm(s)
Sam	Samaritan Pentateuch
sg.	singular
Sym	Symmachus
Syr	Syriac
Tg	Targum
Theod	Theodotian
v./vv.	verse, verses
Vg	Vulgate—an ancient translation of the Bible into Latin
vol(s).	volume(s)

THE OLD TESTAMENT

GENESIS

In southern Israel, the northern Negev Desert where it meets the central plains. The Judean hills rise in the background. Abraham lived for a time in Gerar and Beer-sheba in the Negev.

INTRODUCTION TO

GENESIS

Circumstances of Writing

Since pre-Christian times, authorship of the Torah, the first five books of the Bible, has been attributed to Moses, an enormously influential Israelite leader from the second millennium BC with an aristocratic Egyptian background. Even though Genesis is technically anonymous, both the Old and New Testaments unanimously recognize Moses as the Torah's author (Jos 8:35; 2Ch 23:18; Neh 8:1; Mk 12:19,26; Lk 2:22; Rm 10:5; Heb 10:28). At the same time, evidence in Genesis suggests that minor editorial changes dating to ancient times have been inserted into the text. Examples include the mention of "Dan" (14:14), a city that was not named until the days of the judges (Jdg 18:29), and the use of a phrase that assumed the existence of Israelite kings (Gn 36:31).

The Torah (Hb for "law") was seen as one unit until at least the second century BC. Sometime prior to the birth of Christ, the Torah was divided into five separate books, later referred to as the Pentateuch (lit "five vessels"). Genesis, the first book of the Torah, provides both the universal history of humankind and the patriarchal history of the nation of Israel. The first section (chaps. 1–11) is a general history commonly called the "primeval history," showing how all humanity descended from one couple and became sinners. The second section (chaps. 12–50) is a more specific history commonly referred to as the "patriarchal history," focusing on the covenant God made with Abraham and his descendants: Isaac, Jacob, and Jacob's twelve sons. Genesis unfolds God's plan to bless and redeem humanity through Abraham's descendants. The book concludes with the events that led to the Israelites being in the land of Egypt.

Contribution to the Bible

Genesis lays the groundwork for everything else we read and experience in Scripture. Through Genesis we understand where we came from, how we got in the fallen state we are in, and the beginnings of God's gracious work on our behalf. Genesis unfolds God's original purpose for humanity.

Genesis provides the foundation from which we understand God's covenant with Israel that was established with the giving of the Law. For the Israelite community, the stories of the origins of humanity, sin, and the covenant relationship with God helped them understand why God gave them the Law.

Structure

Genesis is chiefly a narrative. From a narrative standpoint, God is the only true hero of the Bible, and the book of Genesis has the distinct privilege of introducing him. God is the first subject of a verb in the book and is mentioned more frequently than any other character in the Bible. The content of the first eleven chapters is distinct from the patriarchal stories in chapters 12–50. The primary literary device is the catchphrase "these are the family records." The phrase is broader in meaning than simply "generation" and refers more to a narrative account. This was a common practice in ancient Near Eastern writings. This phrase also serves as a link between the key person in the previous narrative and the one anticipated in the next section. Genesis could be described as historical genealogy, which ties together creation and human history in one continuum.

THE CREATION

1 In the beginning God created the heavens and the earth.[A]

2 Now the earth was formless and empty, darkness covered the surface of the watery depths, and the Spirit of God was hovering over the surface of the waters. 3 Then God said, "Let there be light," and there was light. 4 God saw that the light was good, and God separated the light from the darkness. 5 God called the light "day," and the darkness he called "night." There was an evening, and there was a morning: one day.

6 Then God said, "Let there be an expanse between the waters, separating water from water." 7 So God made the expanse and separated the water under the expanse from the water above the expanse. And it was so. 8 God called the expanse "sky."[B] Evening came and then morning: the second day.

9 Then God said, "Let the water under the sky be gathered into one place, and let the dry land appear." And it was so. 10 God called the dry land "earth," and the gathering of the water he called "seas." And God saw that it was good. 11 Then God said, "Let the earth produce vegetation: seed-bearing plants and fruit trees on the earth bearing fruit with seed in it according to their kinds." And it was so. 12 The earth produced vegetation: seed-bearing plants according to their kinds and trees bearing fruit with seed in it according to their kinds. And God saw that it was good. 13 Evening came and then morning: the third day.

14 Then God said, "Let there be lights in the expanse of the sky to separate the day from the night. They will serve as signs for seasons[C] and for days and years. 15 They will be lights in the expanse of the sky to provide light on the earth." And it was so. 16 God made the two great lights — the greater light to rule over the day and the lesser light to rule over the night — as well as the stars. 17 God placed them in the expanse of the sky to provide light on the earth, 18 to rule the day and the night, and to separate light from darkness. And God saw that it was good. 19 Evening came and then morning: the fourth day.

20 Then God said, "Let the water swarm with[D] living creatures, and let birds fly above the earth across the expanse of the sky." 21 So God created the large sea-creatures and every living creature that moves and swarms in the water, according to their kinds. He also created every winged creature according to its kind. And God saw that it was good. 22 God blessed them: "Be fruitful, multiply, and fill the waters of the seas, and let the birds multiply on the earth." 23 Evening came and then morning: the fifth day.

24 Then God said, "Let the earth produce living creatures according to their kinds: livestock, creatures that crawl, and the wildlife of the earth according to their kinds." And it was so. 25 So God made the wildlife of the earth according to their kinds, the livestock according to their kinds, and all the creatures that crawl on the ground according to their kinds. And God saw that it was good.

26 Then God said, "Let us make man[E] in[F] our image, according to our likeness. They will rule the fish of the sea, the birds of the sky, the livestock, the whole earth, and the creatures that crawl[G] on the earth."

27 So God created man in his own image;
he created him in the image of God;
he created them male and female.

28 God blessed them, and God said to them, "Be fruitful, multiply, fill the earth, and subdue it. Rule the fish of the sea, the birds of the sky, and every creature that crawls on the earth." 29 God also said, "Look, I have given you every seed-bearing plant on the surface of the entire earth and every tree whose fruit contains seed. This will be food for you, 30 for all the wildlife of the earth, for every bird of the sky, and for every creature that crawls on the earth — everything having the breath of life in it — I have given[H] every green plant for food." And it was so. 31 God saw all that he had made, and it was very good indeed. Evening came and then morning: the sixth day.

2 So the heavens and the earth and everything in them were completed. 2 On the seventh[I] day God had completed his work that he had done, and he rested[J] on the seventh day from all his work that he had done. 3 God blessed the seventh day and declared it holy, for on it he rested from all his work of creation.

MAN AND WOMAN IN THE GARDEN

4 These are the records of the heavens and the earth, concerning their creation. At the time[K] that the LORD God made the earth and the heavens, 5 no shrub of the field had yet grown on the land,[L] and no plant of the field had yet sprouted, for the LORD God had not made it rain on the land, and there was no man to work the ground. 6 But mist would come up from the earth and water all the ground. 7 Then the LORD God formed the man out of the dust from the ground and breathed the breath of life into his nostrils, and the man became a living being.

8 The LORD God planted a garden in Eden, in the east, and there he placed the man he had formed. 9 The LORD God caused to grow out of the ground every tree pleasing in appearance and good for food, including the tree of life in the middle of the garden, as well as the tree of the knowledge of good and evil.

[A] **1:1** Or *created the universe* [B] **1:8** Or *"heavens."* [C] **1:14** Or *for the appointed times* [D] **1:20** Lit *with swarms of* [E] **1:26** Or *human beings*; Hb *'adam*, also in v. 27 [F] **1:26** Or *as* [G] **1:26** Or *scurry* [H] **1:30** *I have given* added for clarity [I] **2:2** Sam, LXX, Syr read *sixth* [J] **2:2** Or *ceased*, also in v. 3 [K] **2:4** Lit *creation on the day* [L] **2:5** Or *earth*

God "Created": A Word Study

by T. Van McClain

Although all Christians may not agree on the details of how God created the universe and life, all believers would agree that he is the Creator of it all. The Hebrew word to express creation first occurs in Genesis 1:1 and is the word *bara'*.

The first chapter of Genesis uses the verb *bara'* in only three verses. In Genesis 1:1, the context indicates that God created the universe ex nihilo, or "out of nothing." Such action is beyond human capabilities. The writer of Hebrews wrote, "By faith we understand that the universe was created by the word of God, so that what is seen was made from things that are not visible" (Heb 11:3; cf. Ps 33:6,9; Col 1:16). The next two usages of the word *bara'* in Genesis 1 highlight the creation of life. Genesis 1:21 highlights the creation of animal life and 1:27 of human life.

God's creative work did not end with what we see in Genesis. The word *bara'* appears more times in the book of Isaiah than any other Old Testament book, including Genesis. Isaiah promised that the creative work of God would be at work in the coming Messianic Age (Is 4:5). Also, the book of Psalms uses *bara'* in a couple of ways that highlight God's continued creative work. Psalm 102:18 says, "This will be written for a later generation, and a people who have not yet been created will praise the LORD." David prayed, "God, create a clean heart for me and renew a steadfast spirit within me" (Ps 51:10). David's request affirmed his dependency on God's continued creative work. ✜

Partial tablet containing the Mesopotamian creation myth celebrating the god Marduk defeating Tiamat, the goddess of chaos. Marduk created the heavens and the earth from Tiamat's corpse and from her blood created humans to serve the gods. The story dates to the second millennium BC, but the tablet, which came from the library of Ashurbanipal in Nineveh, dates to the seventh century BC.

Overlooking the ruins at the ancient site of Ebla (now called Tell Mardikh) in modern northwest Syria. In the 1970s, archaeologists unearthed thousands of tablets, some containing stories that are similar to the biblical accounts of the flood, the tower of Babylon, and creation. However, the people of Ebla worshiped other gods.

10 A river went[A] out from Eden to water the garden. From there it divided and became the source of four rivers.[B] 11 The name of the first is Pishon, which flows through the entire land of Havilah,[C] where there is gold. 12 Gold from that land is pure;[D] bdellium[E] and onyx[F] are also there. 13 The name of the second river is Gihon, which flows through the entire land of Cush. 14 The name of the third river is Tigris, which runs east of Assyria. And the fourth river is the Euphrates.

15 The LORD God took the man and placed him in the garden of Eden to work it and watch over it. 16 And the LORD God commanded the man, "You are free to eat from any tree of the garden, 17 but you must not eat from the tree of the knowledge of good and evil, for on the day you eat from it, you will certainly die." 18 Then the LORD God said, "It is not good for the man to be alone. I will make a helper corresponding to him." 19 The LORD God formed out of the ground every wild animal and every bird of the sky, and brought each to the man to see what he would call it. And whatever the man called a living creature, that was its name. 20 The man gave names to all the livestock, to the birds of the sky, and to every wild animal; but for the man[G] no helper was found corresponding to him. 21 So the LORD God caused a deep sleep to come over the man, and he slept. God took one of his ribs and closed the flesh at that place. 22 Then the LORD God made the rib he had taken from the man into a woman and brought her to the man. 23 And the man said:

This one, at last, is bone of my bone
and flesh of my flesh;
this one will be called "woman,"
for she was taken from man.

24 This is why a man leaves his father and mother and bonds with his wife, and they become one flesh. 25 Both the man and his wife were naked, yet felt no shame.

THE TEMPTATION AND THE FALL

3 Now the serpent was the most cunning of all the wild animals that the LORD God had made. He said to the woman, "Did God really say, 'You can't eat from any tree in the garden'?"

2 The woman said to the serpent, "We may eat the fruit from the trees in the garden. 3 But about the fruit of the tree in the middle of the garden, God said, 'You must not eat it or touch it, or you will die.'"

4 "No! You will certainly not die," the serpent said to the woman. 5 "In fact, God knows that when[H] you eat it your eyes will be opened and you will be like God, knowing good and evil." 6 The woman saw that the tree was good for food and delightful to look at, and that it was desirable for obtaining wisdom. So she took some of its fruit and ate it; she also gave some to her husband, who was with her, and he ate it. 7 Then the eyes of both of them were opened, and they knew they were naked; so they sewed fig leaves together and made coverings for themselves.

SIN'S CONSEQUENCES

8 Then the man and his wife heard the sound of the LORD God walking in the garden at the time of the evening breeze,[I] and they hid from the LORD God among the trees of the garden. 9 So the LORD God called out to the man and said to him, "Where are you?"

10 And he said, "I heard you[J] in the garden, and I was afraid because I was naked, so I hid."

11 Then he asked, "Who told you that you were naked? Did you eat from the tree that I commanded you not to eat from?"

12 The man replied, "The woman you gave to be with me — she gave me some fruit from the tree, and I ate."

13 So the LORD God asked the woman, "What have you done?"

And the woman said, "The serpent deceived me, and I ate."

14 So the LORD God said to the serpent:

Because you have done this,
you are cursed more than any livestock
and more than any wild animal.
You will move on your belly
and eat dust all the days of your life.
15 I will put hostility between you
and the woman,
and between your offspring
and her offspring.[K]
He will strike your head,
and you will strike his heel.

16 He said to the woman:

I will intensify your labor pains;
you will bear children with painful effort.
Your desire will be for your husband,
yet he will rule over you.

17 And he said to the man, "Because you listened to your wife and ate from the tree about which I commanded you, 'Do not eat from it':

The ground is cursed because of you.
You will eat from it by means of painful labor[L]
all the days of your life.
18 It will produce thorns and thistles for you,
and you will eat the plants of the field.

[A] **2:10** Or *goes* [B] **2:10** Lit *became four heads* [C] **2:11** Or *of the Havilah* [D] **2:12** Lit *good* [E] **2:12** A yellowish, transparent gum resin [F] **2:12** Identity of this precious stone uncertain [G] **2:20** Or *for Adam* [H] **3:5** Lit *on the day* [I] **3:8** Lit *at the wind of the day* [J] **3:10** Lit *the sound of you* [K] **3:15** Lit *your seed and her seed* [L] **3:17** Lit *it through pain*

Eden: All We Know

by Kevin Hall

Tigris River at Diyarbakir, in eastern Turkey.

With the discovery of ancient Near Eastern libraries that contained ancient Akkadian and Sumerian texts, it became common to associate the biblical name "Eden" with the Akkadian term *edinu* (Sumerian, *eden*), meaning "plain, steppe."[1] This explanation of the name made sense to those who thought it likely that Eden was in or around the broad plains of "the land between the rivers," Mesopotamia. More recently, however, Aramaic and Ugaritic studies have yielded evidence associating the name with the idea of a "garden of abundance."[2] This explanation comports well with the basic meaning of the Hebrew term *'eden*, "luxury, delight."

In this context of a region named Eden ("luxury, delight") with a well-watered garden, we can instructively consider ancient Near Eastern parallels. Ancient Near Eastern monarchs such as Assyria's King Sennacherib lavished their capitals with parks and gardens irrigated by springs outside of the city. So if the Bible intends for us to imagine a spring pouring forth from Eden to irrigate a garden or park, then the biblical text describes "a situation that was well known in the ancient world: a sacred spot featuring a spring with an adjoining, well-watered park, stocked with specimens of trees and animals."[3]

The scriptural account of Eden's location is more interested in asserting the "cultural and political centrality" of Eden within the ancient Near Eastern world than with providing a road map for pinpointing Eden's location.[4] ✣

---

[1] Howard N. Wallace, "Eden, Garden of" in *The Anchor Bible Dictionary* (*ABD*), ed. David Noel Freedman (New York: Doubleday, 1992), 2:281–83. [2] J. H. Walton, "Eden, Garden of" in *Dictionary of the Old Testament: Pentateuch* (Downers Grove, IL: InterVarsity, 2003), 202–7. [3] Walton, "Eden," 204. [4] Walton, "Eden."

19 You will eat bread[A] by the sweat of your brow
until you return to the ground,
since you were taken from it.
For you are dust,
and you will return to dust."

[20] The man named his wife Eve[B] because she was
the mother of all the living. [21] The LORD God made
clothing from skins for the man and his wife, and
he clothed them.
[22] The LORD God said, "Since the man has become
like one of us, knowing good and evil, he must not
reach out, take from the tree of life, eat, and live forever." [23] So the LORD God sent him away from the
garden of Eden to work the ground from which he
was taken. [24] He drove the man out and stationed the
cherubim and the flaming, whirling sword east of the
garden of Eden to guard the way to the tree of life.

CAIN MURDERS ABEL

4 The man was intimate with his wife Eve, and
she conceived and gave birth to Cain. She said,
"I have had a male child with the LORD's help."[C] [2] She
also gave birth to his brother Abel. Now Abel became
a shepherd of flocks, but Cain worked the ground. [3] In
the course of time Cain presented some of the land's
produce as an offering to the LORD. [4] And Abel also
presented an offering — some of the firstborn of his
flock and their fat portions. The LORD had regard for
Abel and his offering, [5] but he did not have regard
for Cain and his offering. Cain was furious, and he
looked despondent.
[6] Then the LORD said to Cain, "Why are you furious?
And why do you look despondent? [7] If you do what
is right, won't you be accepted? But if you do not do
what is right, sin is crouching at the door. Its desire
is for you, but you must rule over it."
[8] Cain said to his brother Abel, "Let's go out to the
field."[D] And while they were in the field, Cain attacked
his brother Abel and killed him.
[9] Then the LORD said to Cain, "Where is your brother Abel?"
"I don't know," he replied. "Am I my brother's
guardian?"
[10] Then he said, "What have you done? Your brother's blood cries out to me from the ground! [11] So now
you are cursed, alienated from the ground that
opened its mouth to receive your brother's blood
you have shed.[E] [12] If you work the ground, it will never
again give you its yield. You will be a restless wanderer on the earth."
[13] But Cain answered the LORD, "My punishment[F]
is too great to bear! [14] Since you are banishing me today from the face of the earth, and I must hide from
your presence and become a restless wanderer on
the earth, whoever finds me will kill me."
[15] Then the LORD replied to him, "In that case,[G] whoever kills Cain will suffer vengeance seven times
over." And he placed a mark on Cain so that whoever found him would not kill him. [16] Then Cain went
out from the LORD's presence and lived in the land
of Nod,[H] east of Eden.

THE LINE OF CAIN

[17] Cain was intimate with his wife, and she conceived
and gave birth to Enoch. Then Cain became the builder of a city, and he named the city Enoch after his son.
[18] Irad was born to Enoch, Irad fathered Mehujael,
Mehujael fathered Methushael, and Methushael fathered Lamech. [19] Lamech took two wives for himself,

[A] **3:19** Or *food* [B] **3:20** Lit *Living*, or *Life* [C] **4:1** Lit *the LORD*
[D] **4:8** Sam, LXX, Syr, Vg; MT omits *"Let's go out to the field."*
[E] **4:11** Lit *blood from your hand* [F] **4:13** Or *sin* [G] **4:15** LXX, Syr, Vg
read *"Not so!"* [H] **4:16** Lit *Wandering*

Electrotype copy of gold dagger and elaborate sheath, from Early Dynastic III, 2600–2500 BC.

one named Adah and the other named Zillah. 20 Adah bore Jabal; he was the first[A] of the nomadic herdsmen. 21 His brother was named Jubal; he was the first[A] of all who play the lyre and the flute. 22 Zillah bore Tubal-cain, who made all kinds of bronze and iron tools. Tubal-cain's sister was Naamah.

23 Lamech said to his wives:

Adah and Zillah, hear my voice;
wives of Lamech, pay attention to my words.
For I killed a man for wounding me,
a young man for striking me.
24 If Cain is to be avenged seven times over,
then for Lamech it will be
seventy-seven times!

25 Adam was intimate with his wife again, and she gave birth to a son and named him Seth, for she said, "God has given[B] me another offspring[C] in place of Abel, since Cain killed him." 26 A son was born to Seth also, and he named him Enosh. At that time people began to call on the name of the LORD.

THE LINE OF SETH

5 This is the document containing the family[D] records of Adam.[E] On the day that God created man,[F] he made him in the likeness of God; 2 he created them male and female. When they were created, he blessed them and called them mankind.[G]

3 Adam was 130 years old when he fathered a son in his likeness, according to his image, and named him Seth. 4 Adam lived 800 years after he fathered Seth, and he fathered other sons and daughters. 5 So Adam's life lasted 930 years; then he died.

6 Seth was 105 years old when he fathered Enosh. 7 Seth lived 807 years after he fathered Enosh, and he fathered other sons and daughters. 8 So Seth's life lasted 912 years; then he died.

9 Enosh was 90 years old when he fathered Kenan. 10 Enosh lived 815 years after he fathered Kenan, and he fathered other sons and daughters. 11 So Enosh's life lasted 905 years; then he died.

12 Kenan was 70 years old when he fathered Mahalalel. 13 Kenan lived 840 years after he fathered Mahalalel, and he fathered other sons and daughters. 14 So Kenan's life lasted 910 years; then he died.

15 Mahalalel was 65 years old when he fathered Jared. 16 Mahalalel lived 830 years after he fathered Jared, and he fathered other sons and daughters. 17 So Mahalalel's life lasted 895 years; then he died.

18 Jared was 162 years old when he fathered Enoch. 19 Jared lived 800 years after he fathered Enoch, and he fathered other sons and daughters. 20 So Jared's life lasted 962 years; then he died.

21 Enoch was 65 years old when he fathered Methuselah. 22 And after he fathered Methuselah, Enoch walked with God 300 years and fathered other sons and daughters. 23 So Enoch's life lasted 365 years. 24 Enoch walked with God; then he was not there because God took him.

25 Methuselah was 187 years old when he fathered Lamech. 26 Methuselah lived 782 years after he fathered Lamech, and he fathered other sons and daughters. 27 So Methuselah's life lasted 969 years; then he died.

28 Lamech was 182 years old when he fathered a son. 29 And he named him Noah,[H] saying, "This one will bring us relief from the agonizing labor of our hands, caused by the ground the LORD has cursed." 30 Lamech lived 595 years after he fathered Noah, and he fathered other sons and daughters. 31 So Lamech's life lasted 777 years; then he died.

32 Noah was 500 years old, and he fathered Shem, Ham, and Japheth.

SONS OF GOD AND DAUGHTERS OF MANKIND

6 When mankind began to multiply on the earth and daughters were born to them, 2 the sons of God saw that the daughters of mankind were beautiful, and they took any they chose as wives for themselves. 3 And the LORD said, "My Spirit will not remain[I] with[J] mankind forever, because they are corrupt.[K] Their days will be 120 years." 4 The Nephilim[L] were on the earth both in those days and afterward, when the sons of God came to the daughters of mankind, who bore children to them. They were the powerful men of old, the famous men.

JUDGMENT DECREED

5 When the LORD saw that human wickedness was widespread on the earth and that every inclination of the human mind was nothing but evil all the time, 6 the LORD regretted that he had made man on the earth, and he was deeply grieved. 7 Then the LORD said, "I will wipe mankind, whom I created, off the face of the earth, together with the animals, creatures that crawl, and birds of the sky — for I regret that I made them." 8 Noah, however, found favor with the LORD.

GOD WARNS NOAH

9 These are the family records of Noah. Noah was a righteous man, blameless among his contemporaries; Noah walked with God. 10 And Noah fathered three sons: Shem, Ham, and Japheth.

[A] **4:20,21** Lit *father* [B] **4:25** The Hb word for *given* sounds like the name "Seth." [C] **4:25** Lit *seed* [D] **5:1** Lit *written family* [E] **5:1** Or *mankind* [F] **5:1** Or *Adam, human beings* [G] **5:2** Hb *'adam* [H] **5:29** In Hb, the name *Noah* sounds like "bring us relief." [I] **6:3** Or *strive* [J] **6:3** Or *in* [K] **6:3** Lit *flesh* [L] **6:4** Possibly means "fallen ones"; traditionally, "giants"; Nm 13:31–33

DIGGING DEEPER ***Enuma Elish***

Discovered on clay tablets at the library of Ashurbanipal (see Ezr 4:10) in Nineveh in 1849, the *Enuma Elish* contains the Mesopotamian account of creation and the flood. Composed in Abraham's era sometime around 1800 BC, the *Enuma Elish* offers details similar to those found in Genesis 1–10. It relates the formation of the world, humanity's offense against the gods, and a flood sent by heaven to destroy humanity.

Some critics say the Genesis creation account (written ca 1400 BC) is borrowed from the *Enuma Elish* and other mythical stories that were written beforehand. However, the similarities between Genesis and the earlier accounts are outweighed by the differences. Comparisons reveal that the biblical account is unique, simple, and more historically believable due to its lack of mythological tone. This makes it difficult for critical scholars to argue that the biblical record was borrowed from earlier mythology. Myth always becomes more distorted over time, but never becomes more simplified and historically believable like the Genesis account. Therefore, it is very unlikely that the biblical writers relied on the *Enuma Elish*. The similarities between the two indicate agreement on some basic facts of earth history (e.g., there really was a flood), while the differences indicate the greater historical accuracy of Genesis.

11 Now the earth was corrupt in God's sight, and the earth was filled with wickedness.[A] 12 God saw how corrupt the earth was, for every creature had corrupted its way on the earth. 13 Then God said to Noah, "I have decided to put an end to every creature, for the earth is filled with wickedness because of them; therefore I am going to destroy them along with the earth.

14 "Make yourself an ark of gopher[B] wood. Make rooms in the ark, and cover it with pitch inside and outside. 15 This is how you are to make it: The ark will be 450 feet long, 75 feet wide, and 45 feet high.[C] 16 You are to make a roof,[D] finishing the sides of the ark to within eighteen inches[E] of the roof. You are to put a door in the side of the ark. Make it with lower, middle, and upper decks.

17 "Understand that I am bringing a flood — floodwaters on the earth to destroy every creature under heaven with the breath of life in it. Everything on earth will perish. 18 But I will establish my covenant with you, and you will enter the ark with your sons, your wife, and your sons' wives. 19 You are also to bring into the ark two of all the living creatures, male and female, to keep them alive with you. 20 Two of everything — from the birds according to their kinds, from the livestock according to their kinds, and from the animals that crawl on the ground according to their kinds — will come to you so that you can keep them alive. 21 Take with you every kind of food that is eaten; gather it as food for you and for them." 22 And Noah did this. He did everything that God had commanded him.

ENTERING THE ARK

7 Then the LORD said to Noah, "Enter the ark, you and all your household, for I have seen that you alone are righteous before me in this generation. 2 You are to take with you seven pairs, a male and its female, of all the clean animals, and two of the animals that are not clean, a male and its female, 3 and seven pairs, male and female, of the birds of the sky — in order to keep offspring alive throughout the earth. 4 Seven days from now I will make it rain on the earth forty days and forty nights, and every living thing I have made I will wipe off the face of the earth." 5 And Noah did everything that the LORD commanded him.

6 Noah was six hundred years old when the flood came and water covered the earth. 7 So Noah, his sons, his wife, and his sons' wives entered the ark because of the floodwaters. 8 From the animals that are clean, and from the animals that are not clean, and from the birds and every creature that crawls on the ground, 9 two of each, male and female, came to Noah and entered the ark, just as God had commanded him. 10 Seven days later the floodwaters came on the earth.

THE FLOOD

11 In the six hundredth year of Noah's life, in the second month, on the seventeenth day of the month, on that day all the sources of the vast watery depths burst open, the floodgates of the sky were opened, 12 and the rain fell on the earth forty days and forty nights. 13 On that same day Noah and his three sons, Shem, Ham, and Japheth, entered the ark, along with Noah's wife and his three sons' wives. 14 They entered it with all the wildlife according to their kinds, all livestock according to their kinds, all the creatures that crawl on the earth according to their kinds, every flying creature — all the birds and every winged creature — according to their kinds. 15 Two of every creature that has the breath of life in it came to Noah

[A] **6:11** Or *injustice*, also in v. 13 [B] **6:14** Unknown species of tree; perhaps pine or cypress [C] **6:15** Or *300 cubits long, 50 cubits wide, and 30 cubits high* [D] **6:16** Or *window*, or *hatch*; Hb uncertain [E] **6:16** Lit *to a cubit*

DIGGING DEEPER ***Gilgamesh Epic***

The *Gilgamesh Epic*, dating to the seventh century BC, contains a Babylonian record of a worldwide flood. This account was likely borrowed from the *Atrahasis Epic*, which dates to 1800 BC. Portions of *Gilgamesh* have been discovered throughout the Middle East, including the biblical city of Megiddo.

The story tells of a Noah-like figure named Utnapishtim who survived the flood because he was warned by the god Ea to build a boat for his family and many animals. A week of rain swept away the boat, and then it came to rest on Mount Nisir (Kurdistan) where Utnapishtim released several birds that did not return. He then offered sacrifice and was granted immortality.

Some critical scholars say the Bible depends on Babylonian accounts such as *Gilgamesh* since there are noticeable similarities between the stories. However, the mythological message in *Gilgamesh* is absent in the later Genesis description, making it unlikely that the Bible borrowed from the Babylonians. Details of the flood event were distorted as different cultures interpreted the flood through their unique religious beliefs. Supporting this conclusion is the fact that nearly two dozen separate flood accounts exist around the world. Hence the Bible has gotten it right, whereas other accounts mix truth with error.

and entered the ark. 16 Those that entered, male and female of every creature, entered just as God had commanded him. Then the LORD shut him in.

17 The flood continued for forty days on the earth; the water increased and lifted up the ark so that it rose above the earth. 18 The water surged and increased greatly on the earth, and the ark floated on the surface of the water. 19 Then the water surged even higher on the earth, and all the high mountains under the whole sky were covered. 20 The mountains were covered as the water surged above them more than twenty feet.[A] 21 Every creature perished — those that crawl on the earth, birds, livestock, wildlife, and those that swarm on the earth, as well as all mankind. 22 Everything with the breath of the spirit of life in its nostrils — everything on dry land died. 23 He wiped out every living thing that was on the face of the earth, from mankind to livestock, to creatures that crawl, to the birds of the sky, and they were wiped off the earth. Only Noah was left, and those that were with him in the ark. 24 And the water surged on the earth 150 days.

THE FLOOD RECEDES

8 God remembered Noah, as well as all the wildlife and all the livestock that were with him in the ark. God caused a wind to pass over the earth, and the water began to subside. 2 The sources of the watery depths and the floodgates of the sky were closed, and the rain from the sky stopped. 3 The water steadily receded from the earth, and by the end of 150 days the water had decreased significantly. 4 The ark came to rest in the seventh month, on the seventeenth day of the month, on the mountains of Ararat.

5 The water continued to recede until the tenth month; in the tenth month, on the first day of the month, the tops of the mountains were visible. 6 After forty days Noah opened the window of the ark that he had made, 7 and he sent out a raven. It went back and forth until the water had dried up from the earth. 8 Then he sent out a dove to see whether the water on the earth's surface had gone down, 9 but the dove found no resting place for its foot. It returned to him in the ark because water covered the surface of the whole earth. He reached out and brought it into the ark to himself. 10 So Noah waited seven more days and sent out the dove from the ark again. 11 When the dove came to him at evening, there was a plucked olive leaf in its beak. So Noah knew that the water on the earth's surface had gone down. 12 After he had waited another seven days, he sent out the dove, but it did not return to him again. 13 In the six hundred first year,[B] in the first month, on the first day of the month, the water that had covered the earth was dried up. Then Noah removed the ark's cover and saw that the surface of the ground was drying. 14 By the twenty-seventh day of the second month, the earth was dry.

THE LORD'S PROMISE

15 Then God spoke to Noah, 16 "Come out of the ark, you, your wife, your sons, and your sons' wives with you. 17 Bring out all the living creatures that are with you — birds, livestock, those that crawl on the earth — and they will spread over the earth and be fruitful and multiply on the earth." 18 So Noah, along with his sons, his wife, and his sons' wives, came out. 19 All the animals, all the creatures that crawl, and all the flying creatures — everything that moves on the earth — came out of the ark by their families.

20 Then Noah built an altar to the LORD. He took some of every kind of clean animal and every kind of clean bird and offered burnt offerings on the altar. 21 When the LORD smelled the pleasing aroma, he said to himself, "I will never again curse the ground because of human beings, even though the inclination of the human heart is evil from youth onward. And

[A] **7:20** Lit *surged 15 cubits* [B] **8:13** = of Noah's life

I will never again strike down every living thing as I have done.

22 As long as the earth endures,
seedtime and harvest, cold and heat,
summer and winter, and day and night
will not cease."

GOD'S COVENANT WITH NOAH

9 God blessed Noah and his sons and said to them, "Be fruitful and multiply and fill the earth. 2 The fear and terror of you will be in every living creature on the earth, every bird of the sky, every creature that crawls on the ground, and all the fish of the sea. They are placed under your authority. 3 Every creature that lives and moves will be food for you; as I gave the green plants, I have given you everything. 4 However, you must not eat meat with its lifeblood in it. 5 And I will require a penalty for your lifeblood;[A] I will require it from any animal and from any human; if someone murders a fellow human, I will require that person's life.

6 Whoever sheds human blood,
by humans his blood will be shed,
for God made humans in his image.

7 But you, be fruitful and multiply; spread out over the earth and multiply on it."

8 Then God said to Noah and his sons with him, 9 "Understand that I am establishing my covenant with you and your descendants after you, 10 and with every living creature that is with you — birds, livestock, and all wildlife of the earth that are with you — all the animals of the earth that came out of the ark. 11 I establish my covenant with you that never again will every creature be wiped out by floodwaters; there will never again be a flood to destroy the earth."

12 And God said, "This is the sign of the covenant I am making between me and you and every living creature with you, a covenant for all future generations: 13 I have placed my bow in the clouds, and it will be a sign of the covenant between me and the earth. 14 Whenever I form clouds over the earth and the bow appears in the clouds, 15 I will remember my covenant between me and you and all the living creatures: water will never again become a flood to destroy every creature. 16 The bow will be in the clouds, and I will look at it and remember the permanent covenant between God and all the living creatures on earth." 17 God said to Noah, "This is the sign of the covenant that I have established between me and every creature on earth."

PROPHECIES ABOUT NOAH'S FAMILY

18 Noah's sons who came out of the ark were Shem, Ham, and Japheth. Ham was the father of Canaan. 19 These three were Noah's sons, and from them the whole earth was populated.

20 Noah, as a man of the soil, began by planting[B] a vineyard. 21 He drank some of the wine, became drunk, and uncovered himself inside his tent. 22 Ham, the father of Canaan, saw his father naked and told his two brothers outside. 23 Then Shem and Japheth took a cloak and placed it over both their shoulders, and walking backward, they covered their father's nakedness. Their faces were turned away, and they did not see their father naked.

24 When Noah awoke from his drinking and learned what his youngest son had done to him, 25 he said:

Canaan is cursed.
He will be the lowest of slaves to his brothers.

26 He also said:

Blessed be the LORD, the God of Shem;
Let Canaan be[C] Shem's slave.
27 Let God extend Japheth;[D]
let Japheth dwell in the tents of Shem;
let Canaan be Shem's slave.

28 Now Noah lived 350 years after the flood. 29 So Noah's life lasted 950 years; then he died.

THE TABLE OF NATIONS

10 These are the family records of Noah's sons, Shem, Ham, and Japheth. They also had sons after the flood.

2 Japheth's sons: Gomer, Magog, Madai, Javan, Tubal, Meshech, and Tiras. 3 Gomer's sons: Ashkenaz, Riphath, and Togarmah. 4 And Javan's sons: Elishah, Tarshish, Kittim, and Dodanim.[E] 5 From these descendants, the peoples of the coasts and islands spread out into their lands according to their clans in their nations, each with its own language.

6 Ham's sons: Cush, Mizraim, Put, and Canaan. 7 Cush's sons: Seba, Havilah, Sabtah, Raamah, and Sabteca. And Raamah's sons: Sheba and Dedan.

8 Cush fathered Nimrod, who began to be powerful in the land. 9 He was a powerful hunter in the sight of the LORD. That is why it is said, "Like Nimrod, a powerful hunter in the sight of the LORD." 10 His kingdom started with Babylon, Erech,[F] Accad,[G] and Calneh,[H] in the land of Shinar.[I] 11 From that land he went to Assyria and built Nineveh, Rehoboth-ir, Calah, 12 and Resen, between Nineveh and the great city Calah.

13 Mizraim[J] fathered the people of Lud, Anam, Lehab, Naphtuh, 14 Pathrus, Casluh (the Philistines came from them), and Caphtor.

[A] **9:5** Lit *And your blood belonging to your life I will seek* [B] **9:20** Or *Noah began to be a farmer and planted* [C] **9:26** As a wish or prayer; others interpret the verbs in vv. 26–27 as prophecy: *Canaan will be . . .* [D] **9:27** In Hb, the name *Japheth* sounds like the word "extend." [E] **10:4** Some Hb mss, LXX read *Rodanim*; 1Ch 1:7 [F] **10:10** Or *Uruk* [G] **10:10** Or *Akkad* [H] **10:10** Or *and all of them* [I] **10:10** Or *in Babylonia* [J] **10:13** = Egypt

Ancient Altars

by George H. Shaddix

Relief of a Hittite king and queen before the sacred altar. Dates to 1300 BC.

The simplest altars were constructed of earth built up into a mound. This may have been the type of altar Noah built—and evidently the type Moses later built. Earthen altars were useful, especially for nomadic people. "An earthen altar would not have been very practical for permanently settled people, for the rainy season each year would damage or destroy the altar."[1] Instead, settled people typically used stone to construct altars. These stones were to be natural and not hewn. The stone altar, like the earthen altar, would have no definite shape. The stones would simply be piled on top of one another. Sometimes a single natural rock would serve as an altar (Jdg 6:19–21). So the material the builder used to construct the altar determined its shape.

Scripture appears to make a distinction concerning those who offered sacrifices on each type of altar. Earthen and stone altars were in use before the establishment of the priesthood; therefore, anyone could build an altar wherever they were and could offer a sacrifice (Gn 8:17–20; 22:9–13). With the establishment of the priesthood, people built more elaborate altars, such as those in the tabernacle and the temple. Only here did the priests offer the sacrifices for the people of God.

Most altars were designed for offering sacrifices; however, some seem to have been built as memorials (Ex 17:15–16; Jos 22:26–27).[2]

Altars were not unique to Israel. Other nations also built altars to worship their gods. Archaeologists have uncovered an altar with multiple faces carved into it at Taanach,

Miniature bronze incense burners, probably for domestic use. From Byblos; first century BC–first century AD.

where Deborah and Barak defeated the Canaanites under Sisera (Jdg 5:19–20).[3] Such adornments were prohibited in Jewish worship. "A striking circular Canaanite altar dating from 2500 BC to 1800 BC was excavated at Megiddo. It was twenty-five feet in diameter and 4 ½ feet high. Four steps led up to the top of the altar."[4] The prohibition in Exodus 20:25–26 against using hewn stone and using steps in conjunction with altars is probably a prohibition against God's people using altars that shared characteristics with the Canaanites' altars.[5] Archaeologists have excavated at Beer-sheba an altar constructed of large hewn stones. This altar has horns on its four corners and dates to the period of the divided kingdom.[6]

The altar was a sacred place in Israel's worship. It represented the presence of God among his people. As offerings were placed on the altar, "the offerings were taken out of man's domain and given to God, and God replied by bestowing blessings (Ex 20:24). Thus the Covenant itself between God and his people was maintained in force, or re-established, upon the altar of sacrifice."[7]

Because the altar was sacred, nothing was to defile it. If, for some reason, it became defiled, it was to be cleansed as it had been in the days of King Hezekiah (2Ch 29:18–19). ✣

Upper image: One of the best examples of a large stone altar is at Megiddo. The temple complex dates from the time of Abraham. The circular altar is about twenty-five feet in diameter and more than four feet tall. Lower image: Monument, likely an altar, in central area of temple of Echmoun outside of Sidon. Echmoun was the Phoenician god of healing. Temple dates to the seventh century BC.

---

[1] Joel F. Drinkard Jr., "Altar" in *Holman Bible Dictionary* (*HolBD*), ed. Trent C. Butler (Nashville: Holman, 1991), 38. [2] Howard Z. Cleveland, "Altar" in *The New International Dictionary of the Bible*, J. D. Douglas, rev. ed., ed. Merrill C. Tenney (Grand Rapids: Zondervan, 1987), 36. [3] Albert E. Glock, "Taanach" in *The New Encyclopedia of Archaeological Excavations in the Holy Land* (*NEAEHL*), ed. Ephraim Stern (New York: Simon & Schuster, 1993), 4:1431. [4] Drinkard, "Altar," 38. [5] H. M. Wiener, W. S. Caldecott, and C. E. Armerding, "Altar" in *The International Standard Bible Encyclopedia* (*ISBE*), ed. Geoffrey W. Bromiley, vol. 1 (Grand Rapids: Eerdmans, 1979), 101–2. [6] Drinkard, "Altar," 38. [7] Roland de Vaux, *Ancient Israel: Its Life and Institutions* (Grand Rapids: Eerdmans, 1997), 414.

15 Canaan fathered Sidon his firstborn and Heth,
16 as well as the Jebusites, the Amorites, the Girgashites, 17 the Hivites, the Arkites, the Sinites, 18 the
Arvadites, the Zemarites, and the Hamathites. Afterward the Canaanite clans scattered. 19 The Canaanite
border went from Sidon going toward Gerar as far as
Gaza, and going toward Sodom, Gomorrah, Admah,
and Zeboiim as far as Lasha.

20 These are Ham's sons by their clans, according
to their languages, in their lands and their nations.

21 And Shem, Japheth's older brother, also had sons.
Shem was the father of all the sons of Eber. 22 Shem's
sons were Elam, Asshur, Arpachshad, Lud, and Aram.

23 Aram's sons: Uz, Hul, Gether, and Mash.

24 Arpachshad fathered[A] Shelah, and Shelah fathered Eber. 25 Eber had two sons. One was named
Peleg,[B] for during his days the earth was divided; his
brother was named Joktan. 26 And Joktan fathered
Almodad, Sheleph, Hazarmaveth, Jerah, 27 Hadoram,
Uzal, Diklah, 28 Obal, Abimael, Sheba, 29 Ophir, Havilah,
and Jobab. All these were Joktan's sons. 30 Their settlements extended from Mesha to Sephar, the eastern
hill country.

31 These are Shem's sons by their clans, according
to their languages, in their lands and their nations.

32 These are the clans of Noah's sons, according to
their family records, in their nations. The nations on
earth spread out from these after the flood.

THE TOWER OF BABYLON

11 The whole earth had the same language and
vocabulary. 2 As people migrated from the east,[C]
they found a valley in the land of Shinar and settled
there. 3 They said to each other, "Come, let's make
oven-fired bricks." (They used brick for stone and
asphalt for mortar.) 4 And they said, "Come, let's build
ourselves a city and a tower with its top in the sky.
Let's make a name for ourselves; otherwise, we will
be scattered throughout the earth."

5 Then the LORD came down to look over the city
and the tower that the humans[D] were building. 6 The
LORD said, "If they have begun to do this as one people all having the same language, then nothing they
plan to do will be impossible for them. 7 Come, let's
go down there and confuse their language so that
they will not understand one another's speech." 8 So
from there the LORD scattered them throughout the
earth, and they stopped building the city. 9 Therefore
it is called Babylon,[E,F] for there the LORD confused the
language of the whole earth, and from there the LORD
scattered them throughout the earth.

FROM SHEM TO ABRAM

10 These are the family records of Shem. Shem lived
100 years and fathered Arpachshad two years after the flood. 11 After he fathered Arpachshad, Shem
lived 500 years and fathered other sons and daughters. 12 Arpachshad lived 35 years[G] and fathered Shelah. 13 After he fathered Shelah, Arpachshad lived
403 years and fathered other sons and daughters.
14 Shelah lived 30 years and fathered Eber. 15 After he
fathered Eber, Shelah lived 403 years and fathered
other sons and daughters. 16 Eber lived 34 years and
fathered Peleg. 17 After he fathered Peleg, Eber lived
430 years and fathered other sons and daughters.
18 Peleg lived 30 years and fathered Reu. 19 After he
fathered Reu, Peleg lived 209 years and fathered other
sons and daughters. 20 Reu lived 32 years and fathered
Serug. 21 After he fathered Serug, Reu lived 207 years
and fathered other sons and daughters. 22 Serug lived
30 years and fathered Nahor. 23 After he fathered Nahor, Serug lived 200 years and fathered other sons and
daughters. 24 Nahor lived 29 years and fathered Terah.
25 After he fathered Terah, Nahor lived 119 years and
fathered other sons and daughters. 26 Terah lived 70
years and fathered Abram, Nahor, and Haran.

27 These are the family records of Terah. Terah fathered Abram, Nahor, and Haran, and Haran fathered
Lot. 28 Haran died in his native land, in Ur of the Chaldeans, during his father Terah's lifetime. 29 Abram and
Nahor took wives: Abram's wife was named Sarai,
and Nahor's wife was named Milcah. She was the
daughter of Haran, the father of both Milcah and
Iscah. 30 Sarai was unable to conceive; she did not
have a child.

31 Terah took his son Abram, his grandson Lot (Haran's son), and his daughter-in-law Sarai, his son
Abram's wife, and they set out together from Ur of
the Chaldeans to go to the land of Canaan. But when
they came to Haran, they settled there. 32 Terah lived
205 years and died in Haran.

THE CALL OF ABRAM

12 The LORD said to Abram:
Go from your land,
your relatives,
and your father's house
to the land that I will show you.
2 I will make you into a great nation,
I will bless you,
I will make your name great,
and you will be a blessing.

[A] **10:24** LXX reads *fathered Cainan, and Cainan fathered*; Gn 11:12–13; Lk 3:35–36 [B] **10:25** = Division [C] **11:2** Or *migrated eastward* [D] **11:5** Or *the descendants of Adam* [E] **11:9** Hb *Babel* [F] **11:9** In Hb, the name for "Babylon," *babel* sounds like the word for "confuse," *balal*. [G] **11:12–13** LXX reads *years and fathered Cainan.* **13** *After he fathered Cainan, Arpachshad lived 430 years and fathered other sons and daughters, and he died. Cainan lived 130 years and fathered Shelah. After he fathered Shelah, Cainan lived 330 years and fathered other sons and daughters, and he died*; Gn 10:24; Lk 3:35–36

Reaching the Heavens: A Study of Ancient Towers

by Stephen J. Andrews

The most common Hebrew word translated "tower" is *migdal*. In the New Testament, the Greek word *purgos* occurs four times and refers to a watchtower (Mt 21:33; Mk 12:1) or a building like the tower of Siloam (Lk 13:4; cf. 14:28).

TYPES OF TOWERS

Remains of ancient towerlike structures are scattered widely over the Middle East. Biblical scholars and archaeologists have assigned a variety of functions to such towers. Not counting the metaphorical use of the term, the biblical text readily identifies four functions.[1]

Agricultural Towers—The Bible closely associates some towers with fields, orchards, vineyards, and winepresses (Is 5:2; Mt 21:33; Mk 12:1). Farmers may have used such towers for storing farming tools and supplies. These towers may also have provided a lookout for protecting the crop from wild animals or thieves. In addition, farmhands could live in these structures while working at a distance from their villages.

A typical tower of this type was made of stone and was circular in shape, nine to twelve feet in diameter. The tower created a platform about three feet above the surface of the ground. This may have allowed shepherds to watch over their flocks in the wilderness (2Ch 26:10; metaphorically, Mc 4:8).

Route Markers and Memorials—Stone towers or monuments marked indistinct paths and roads through the desert (Jr 31:21). These were often simple heaps of stones that could reach nine to twelve feet in height.[2] Nomadic herders may also have used these along the migration routes as repositories for food and valuables. Apparently, people also used stone towers or pillars as burial monuments (Gn 35:20; 2Sm 18:18; 2Kg 23:17; Ezk 39:15).

Defensive Towers—Most stone towers were part of a military defense system. Towers served as isolated outposts designed to allow watchmen to forewarn in the event of an enemy's approach (2Kg 17:9; 2Ch 14:7; 27:4). These small independent citadels served as forts or watchtowers from which to oversee traffic along the border roads leading up into the capital (2Kg 9:17; 18:8; 2Ch 27:25). Letter four of the Lachish letters and possibly Jeremiah 6:1 indicate the use of fire signals to communicate the activities of the enemy.[3] Those watching for these fire signals may have done so from the vantage point of a defense tower. Such tower fortifications also provided refuge for exposed settlements in times of attack.[4]

Towers were also important parts of the fortifications of a town or city wall (2Ch 32:5; Neh 3; 12:38–39; Is 2:15). Psalm 48:12 directs the counting of the towers of Zion; Isaiah 33:18 and 1 Chronicles 27:25 indicate that an officer was in charge of towers. Perhaps due to their function or size, some of the towers of Jerusalem had names (Neh 3:1; 12:39; Jr 31:38; Zch 14:10). These towers were distinct from the gates and most likely reinforced the regular city wall at strategic points (2Ch 26:9,15).

Finally, as a defense tower, *migdal* may also refer to a fortified citadel or palace that offered a final place of refuge inside a city. In Judges 9:50–57, Abimelech besieged the city of Thebez and captured it. But the inhabitants fled into the "strong tower" and shut themselves in. The tower of Shechem probably refers to the same type of structure (v. 46). According to the Bible, a citadel also existed at Penuel (Jdg 8:9,17) and Jezreel (2Kg 9:17). Archaeologists have discovered and excavated fortified citadels at Gibeah and Beth-zur.[5]

Watchtower overlooking grain fields near the valley of Lebonah in Israel.

Place Names and Temple Towers—Some scholars suggest that where the word *migdal* occurs with a place name it refers to a fortified town with a temple tower (Gn 35:21; Jos 15:37; Jdg 9:46–49).[6] Consequently, these towns would owe their names to the temple towers that became their prominent landmark during the Middle Bronze and Late Bronze Ages (2200–1200 BC). However, both biblical and archaeological support for this theory exists only for the tower at Migdal-Shechem (Jdg 9:46–49). As mentioned above, Shechem's tower may have been more like a fortified citadel than a temple tower.

The Chogha Zanbil ziggurat near Susa dates to 1250 BC. It was built under the orders of Elam's king Untash-Gal for the worship of Inshoshinak, the Elamite god of the afterlife.

THE TOWER OF BABYLON

The one case where *migdal* most clearly represents a temple tower is in the famous account of the tower of Babylon (or Babel; Gn 11:1–9). The central feature of most Mesopotamian cities was the temple complex or precinct. This area contained both a temple where people worshiped the patron deity and a tower called a ziggurat. The type of material used in its construction and the purpose for which it was built clearly suggest that the tower of Babylon is to be equated with the ziggurat temples of the ancient Near East.[7]

People built ziggurats intending them to be artificial mountains containing stairways from the heavens (the gate of the gods) to earth. These square or rectangular stepped pyramids were designed to enable the gods to come down into the temple on certain ceremonial occasions and bring blessings to the city. The structure provided convenience for the god of the city and for the priest who ministered to the needs of the god.[8] The purpose of the ziggurat was to hold a stairway leading up to a small

Ruins of ancient Shechem including the temple stone (*matstsebah* or "holy stone") and the standing stone, perhaps the one set upright by Joshua.

Using more advanced engineering, this tower at Samarra, Iraq, is taller and narrower than the ancient ziggurats that had been common among the Sumerians. The tower dates to the mid-ninth century AD and is about 170 feet tall.

room at the top of the structure.[9] This room was equipped with a bed and a table. The table was supplied regularly with food. The sole reason for this room was for the deity to refresh himself during his descent to the city.

Most ziggurats were made with a sun-dried brick frame filled with dirt and rubble. Kiln-fired brick with bitumen for mortar finished off the structure, making it waterproof and as durable as stone. Unlike a pyramid, a ziggurat had no internal rooms.

The earliest known ziggurat, at Erech (Gn 10:10), dates to the third millennium BC. It contained a small shrine on a raised platform of clay reinforced with sun-dried bricks and measured 140 feet by 150 feet. The structure was about 30 feet high. The corners were oriented to the cardinal points of the compass. By contrast, the ziggurat at Ur was 200 feet long, 150 feet wide, and 70 feet high, while Entemenanki, the great ziggurat temple of Babylon, was seven stories high.[10]

Builders designed the tower of Babylon to have its "top [or head] in the sky" (Gn 11:4). In Mesopotamian usage, this phrase was reserved almost exclusively for the description of ziggurats.[11] Ostensibly, the tower of Babylon would have been built for God's convenience to come down and see what humankind had accomplished. ✣

---

[1] E. B. Banning, "Towers" in *ABD*, 6:622. [2] Banning, "Towers," 623. [3] W. F. Albright, "Palestinian Inscriptions" in *Ancient Near Eastern Texts Relating to the Old Testament* (*ANET*), ed. James B. Pritchard, 3rd ed. (Princeton: Princeton University Press, 1969), 322. [4] D. Kellerman, "Migdol," *Theological Dictionary of the Old Testament* (*TDOT*), 71. [5] Kellerman, 71. [6] Banning, "Towers," 623–24. [7] John H. Walton, Victor H. Matthews, and Mark W. Chavalas, *The IVP Bible Background Commentary: Old Testament* (Downers Grove, IL: InterVarsity, 2000), 41–42. [8] Walton, *IVP Bible Background*, 42. [9] Photographs of ziggurats may be seen in *The Ancient Near East in Pictures Relating to the Old Testament* (*ANEP2*) ed. James B. Pritchard, 2nd ed. (Princeton: Princeton University Press, 1969), 233–34. An artist's reconstruction of a ziggurat may be found in *Holman Illustrated Bible Dictionary* (*HIBD*, ed. Chad Brand, Charles Draper, Archie England (Nashville: Holman, 2003), 1710. [10] Edward M. Blaiklock, "Ziggurat" in *The New International Dictionary of Biblical Archaeology* (*NIDBA*), ed. E. M. Blaiklock and R. K. Harrison (Grand Rapids: Zondervan, 1983), 484. A photo of the Ur ziggurat may be found in *HIBD*, 1711. [11] Walton, *IVP Bible Background*, 42.

3 I will bless those who bless you,
I will curse anyone who treats you
with contempt,
and all the peoples on earth
will be blessed[A] through you.[B]

4 So Abram went, as the LORD had told him, and Lot went with him. Abram was seventy-five years old when he left Haran. 5 He took his wife, Sarai, his nephew Lot, all the possessions they had accumulated, and the people they had acquired in Haran, and they set out for the land of Canaan. When they came to the land of Canaan, 6 Abram passed through the land to the site of Shechem, at the oak of Moreh. (At that time the Canaanites were in the land.) 7 The LORD appeared to Abram and said, "To your offspring[C] I will give this land." So he built an altar there to the LORD who had appeared to him. 8 From there he moved on to the hill country east of Bethel and pitched his tent, with Bethel on the west and Ai on the east. He built an altar to the LORD there, and he called on the name of the LORD. 9 Then Abram journeyed by stages to the Negev.

ABRAM IN EGYPT

10 There was a famine in the land, so Abram went down to Egypt to stay there for a while because the famine in the land was severe. 11 When he was about to enter Egypt, he said to his wife, Sarai, "Look, I know what a beautiful woman you are. 12 When the Egyptians see you, they will say, 'This is his wife.' They will kill me but let you live. 13 Please say you're my sister so it will go well for me because of you, and my life will be spared on your account." 14 When Abram entered Egypt, the Egyptians saw that the woman was very beautiful. 15 Pharaoh's officials saw her and praised her to Pharaoh, so the woman was taken to Pharaoh's household. 16 He treated Abram well because of her, and Abram acquired flocks and herds, male and female donkeys, male and female slaves, and camels.

17 But the LORD struck Pharaoh and his household with severe plagues because of Abram's wife, Sarai. 18 So Pharaoh sent for Abram and said, "What have you done to me? Why didn't you tell me she was your wife? 19 Why did you say, 'She's my sister,' so that I took her as my wife? Now, here is your wife. Take her and go!" 20 Then Pharaoh gave his men orders about him, and they sent him away with his wife and all he had.

ABRAM AND LOT SEPARATE

13 Abram went up from Egypt to the Negev — he, his wife, and all he had, and Lot with him. 2 Abram was very rich in livestock, silver, and gold. 3 He went by stages from the Negev to Bethel, to the place between Bethel and Ai where his tent had formerly been, 4 to the site where he had built the altar. And Abram called on the name of the LORD there.

5 Now Lot, who was traveling with Abram, also had flocks, herds, and tents. 6 But the land was unable to support them as long as they stayed together, for they had so many possessions that they could not stay together, 7 and there was quarreling between the herdsmen of Abram's livestock and the herdsmen of Lot's livestock. (At that time the Canaanites and the Perizzites were living in the land.)

8 So Abram said to Lot, "Please, let's not have quarreling between you and me, or between your herdsmen and my herdsmen, since we are relatives. 9 Isn't the whole land before you? Separate from me: if you go to the left, I will go to the right; if you go to the right, I will go to the left."

10 Lot looked out and saw that the entire plain[D] of the Jordan as far as Zoar was well watered everywhere like the LORD's garden and the land of Egypt. (This was before the LORD destroyed Sodom and Gomorrah.) 11 So Lot chose the entire plain of the Jordan for himself. Then Lot journeyed eastward, and they separated from each other. 12 Abram lived in the land of Canaan, but Lot lived in the cities on the plain and set up his tent near Sodom. 13 (Now the men of Sodom were evil, sinning immensely[E] against the LORD.)

14 After Lot had separated from him, the LORD said to Abram, "Look from the place where you are. Look north and south, east and west, 15 for I will give you and your offspring[C] forever all the land that you see. 16 I will make your offspring like the dust of the earth, so that if anyone could count the dust of the earth, then your offspring could be counted. 17 Get up and walk around the land, through its length and width, for I will give it to you."

18 So Abram moved his tent and went to live near the oaks of Mamre at Hebron, where he built an altar to the LORD.

ABRAM RESCUES LOT

14 In those days King Amraphel of Shinar, King Arioch of Ellasar, King Chedorlaomer of Elam, and King Tidal of Goiim[F] 2 waged war against King Bera of Sodom, King Birsha of Gomorrah, King Shinab of Admah, and King Shemeber of Zeboiim, as well as the king of Bela (that is, Zoar). 3 All of these came as allies to the Siddim Valley (that is, the Dead Sea). 4 They were subject to Chedorlaomer for twelve years, but in the thirteenth year they rebelled. 5 In the

[A] **12:3** Or *will find blessing* [B] **12:3** Or *will bless themselves by you*
[C] **12:7; 13:15** Lit *seed* [D] **13:10** Lit *circle*; i.e., probably the large round plain where the Jordan River empties into the Dead Sea, also in v. 11
[E] **13:13** Lit *evil and sinful* [F] **14:1** Or *nations*

fourteenth year Chedorlaomer and the kings who were with him came and defeated the Rephaim in Ashteroth-karnaim, the Zuzim in Ham, the Emim in Shaveh-kiriathaim, 6 and the Horites in the mountains of Seir, as far as El-paran by the wilderness. 7 Then they came back to invade En-mishpat (that is, Kadesh), and they defeated the whole territory of the Amalekites, as well as the Amorites who lived in Hazazon-tamar.

8 Then the king of Sodom, the king of Gomorrah, the king of Admah, the king of Zeboiim, and the king of Bela (that is, Zoar) went out and lined up for battle in the Siddim Valley 9 against King Chedorlaomer of Elam, King Tidal of Goiim, King Amraphel of Shinar, and King Arioch of Ellasar — four kings against five. 10 Now the Siddim Valley contained many asphalt pits, and as the kings of Sodom and Gomorrah fled, some fell into them,[A] but the rest fled to the mountains. 11 The four kings took all the goods of Sodom and Gomorrah and all their food and went on. 12 They also took Abram's nephew Lot and his possessions, for he was living in Sodom, and they went on.

13 One of the survivors came and told Abram the Hebrew, who lived near the oaks belonging to Mamre the Amorite, the brother of Eshcol and the brother of Aner. They were bound by a treaty with Abram. 14 When Abram heard that his relative had been taken prisoner, he assembled[B] his 318 trained men, born in his household, and they went in pursuit as far as Dan. 15 And he and his servants deployed against them by night, defeated them, and pursued them as far as Hobah to the north of Damascus. 16 He brought back all the goods and also his relative Lot and his goods, as well as the women and the other people.

MELCHIZEDEK'S BLESSING

17 After Abram returned from defeating Chedorlaomer and the kings who were with him, the king of Sodom went out to meet him in the Shaveh Valley (that is, the King's Valley). 18 Melchizedek, king of Salem,[C] brought out bread and wine; he was a priest to God Most High. 19 He blessed him and said:

Abram is blessed by God Most High,
Creator[D] of heaven and earth,
20 and blessed be God Most High
who has handed over your enemies to you.

And Abram gave him a tenth of everything.

21 Then the king of Sodom said to Abram, "Give me the people, but take the possessions for yourself."

22 But Abram said to the king of Sodom, "I have raised my hand in an oath to the LORD, God Most High, Creator of heaven and earth, 23 that I will not take a thread or sandal strap or anything that belongs to you, so you can never say, 'I made Abram rich.' 24 I will take nothing except what the servants have eaten. But as for the share of the men who came with me — Aner, Eshcol, and Mamre — they can take their share."

THE ABRAHAMIC COVENANT

15 After these events, the word of the LORD came to Abram in a vision:

Do not be afraid, Abram.
I am your shield;
your reward will be very great.

2 But Abram said, "Lord GOD, what can you give me, since I am childless and the heir of my house is Eliezer of Damascus?"[E] 3 Abram continued, "Look, you have given me no offspring, so a slave born in[F] my house will be my heir."

4 Now the word of the LORD came to him: "This one will not be your heir; instead, one who comes from your own body[G] will be your heir." 5 He took him outside and said, "Look at the sky and count the stars, if you are able to count them." Then he said to him, "Your offspring will be that numerous."

6 Abram believed the LORD, and he credited it to him as righteousness.

7 He also said to him, "I am the LORD who brought you from Ur of the Chaldeans to give you this land to possess."

8 But he said, "Lord GOD, how can I know that I will possess it?"

9 He said to him, "Bring me a three-year-old cow, a three-year-old female goat, a three-year-old ram, a turtledove, and a young pigeon."

10 So he brought all these to him, cut them in half, and laid the pieces opposite each other, but he did not cut the birds in half. 11 Birds of prey came down on the carcasses, but Abram drove them away. 12 As the sun was setting, a deep sleep came over Abram, and suddenly great terror and darkness descended on him.

13 Then the LORD said to Abram, "Know this for certain: Your offspring will be resident aliens for four hundred years in a land that does not belong to them and will be enslaved and oppressed.[H] 14 However, I will judge the nation they serve, and afterward they will go out with many possessions. 15 But you will go to your ancestors in peace and be buried at a good old age. 16 In the fourth generation they will return here, for the iniquity of the Amorites has not yet reached its full measure."[I]

[A] **14:10** Sam, LXX; MT reads *fell there* [B] **14:14** Sam; MT reads *poured out* [C] **14:18** = Jerusalem [D] **14:19** Or *Possessor* [E] **15:2** Hb obscure [F] **15:3** Lit *a son of* [G] **15:4** Lit *loins* [H] **15:13** Lit *will serve them and they will oppress them* [I] **15:16** Lit *Amorites is not yet complete*

Ur: The "Capital of the World"

by Scott Hummel

This twenty-four-room house at Ur was reconstructed in the 1990s and dubbed "Abraham's House."

Abram, who would later be known as Abraham, set out from Ur with his entire family.[1] Abram's family was wealthy and included hundreds of servants. Abram headed north along the Euphrates for about a thousand miles until he reached the city of Haran in northern Mesopotamia. Abram's father, Terah, and brother, Nahor, decided to settle in Haran, but Abram obediently answered God's call to leave his country and family to continue to the promised land (Gn 11:31).

The Sumerian civilization at Ur was already ancient by the time of Abram. In fact, the first great civilization in the world was drawing to a close as Abram made his great journey to Canaan.[2] Ur was established about 5000–4000 BC and grew into one of the most important and leading Sumerian cities. Sumer was composed of several, often competing, city-states in southern Mesopotamia. The Sumerians were incredibly inventive and industrious; they invented the wheel, irrigated the desert, built walled cities, and were probably the first to invent writing. Their sixty-based counting system survives today in the measurements of time with sixty minutes in an hour and in the measurements of degrees in a circle.

Ur was an impressive city for its time, rising sixty feet above the plain and covering about 150 acres. In ancient times, the Euphrates River actually flowed through the city of Ur, and the shoreline of the Persian Gulf came farther north than it does today, much closer to the city. Ur was surrounded by massive walls, which were more than seventy-five feet thick at the base and extended about two miles in circumference. Within the walls stood hundreds of homes, reflecting all levels of society from mansions to hovels. The typical homes were two-storied, brick with wood framing, and included a central open courtyard. Thousands of recovered business documents testify to the dynamic economy and far-reaching trade of Ur.

Archaeologist C. L. Woolley's discovery of royal tombs at Ur in the 1920s further demonstrated the wealth, artistic quality, and religious beliefs of the city around 2500 BC, over five hundred years before Abram's birth.[3] While southern Mesopotamia lacked natural resources, political power and trade along the Euphrates River and the Persian Gulf generated the wealth found in the tombs. Extensive irrigation supported flocks and fields of crops, producing a surplus economy. As a result, the royal tombs have produced some of the richest finds in the history of archaeology and demonstrate a remarkably high level of craftsmanship, especially with metalworking. Even though human sacrifice was extremely rare in Mesopotamia, some of the tombs contain the remains of numerous servants who had been ritually killed so they could serve the king in the afterlife.

After centuries of Sumerian domination and prosperity, the Akkadians rose to power about 2350 BC in central Mesopotamia. The Akkadian Empire lasted for nearly 150 years. The Akkadian king Sargon the Great established the world's first empire by controlling all of Mesopotamia from Ur on the Persian Gulf to the Mediterranean Sea. Even though he controlled Sumerian cities politically and militarily, Sargon and later Akkadian kings adopted much of Sumerian culture and religion. Sargon placed Enheduanna, his daughter, as the high priestess of Nanna, the moon god and patron deity of Ur. This established a tradition that lasted nearly 2,000 years.

The whole region fell into a dark age for nearly a century when the Akkadians fell to the Gutian tribes from the east. At the end of this Gutian period, Ur-Nammu, founder of the Third Dynasty of Ur, came to power and restored Sumerian glory and culture. An able general and administrator, Ur-Nammu conquered most of Mesopotamia and then established one of the most prosperous periods in Sumerian history. He expanded international trade, rebuilt temples, repaired irrigation canals, and built numerous ziggurats throughout Mesopotamia. Ur-Nammu even wrote the earliest-known law code. His greatest building achievement was the Great Ziggurat in Ur, which was a huge stepped platform originally rising more than 70 feet high and measuring 200 by 170 feet at its base. A temple stood at the top. The Sumerians viewed the ziggurat as a mountain where the god came down to dwell. The ziggurat was built of a solid core of unbaked bricks surrounded by a skin of baked bricks set with bitumen. The description of the tower of Babylon in the Plain of Shinar (Sumer) in Genesis 11 sounds remarkably similar to the structure of the ziggurat.

Ur's last Sumerian kings tried to hold on to power by slowing the migrations of Amorites into the region and by fortifying Ur, but crop failures, hostility with other Sumerian cities, and the invading Elamites from the east brought the collapse of Ur as a great world power.

Every year for centuries the priests in Ur, recalling the glory days of the past, recited the "Lamentation over the Destruction of Ur," which included these words:

> Ur, my innocent lamb, has been slaughtered. Its good shepherd is gone. . . . Woe! The city and temple are destroyed. O, Nanna, the sanctuary of Ur is destroyed, its people dead.[4]

These words of lament were among the thousands of documents archaeologists uncovered in the city of Ur.

The ziggurat at Ur, discovered by archaeologist Leonard Woolley in the 1920s, measures approximately 200 by 170 feet at the base. Three levels tall, the inner core is mud brick while the outer shell, which is 8 feet thick, is baked brick. At the top was a temple to Nanna, the moon god.

Local Arab tradition holds that Abraham was not from Ur of ancient Mesopotamia but from Sanliurfa, which was just north of Haran. Shown is the Shrine of Abraham at Sanliurfa.

The collapse of the Third Dynasty of Ur in 2004 BC struck Sumerian civilization a mortal blow. Only the Sumerian cities of Isin and Larsa lingered a little longer, but the Amorites, a Semitic people, eventually overwhelmed them as well. Sumerian political control was lost forever and the Sumerian language ceased to be used. Various Amorite dynasties gained control of all the Mesopotamian cities. The most famous of these Amorite kings was Hammurabi of Babylon. It was during this time of transition and migrations that Abram left Ur for the promised land.

UR'S RELIGIOUS IMPORTANCE

In the centuries that followed, the city of Ur remained an important religious and economic center, but its political power was lost. Many nations would later rule over Ur, but each recognized the religious importance of Ur as the center of worship of the moon god, known as Nanna or Sin. When the Persian king Cyrus the Great conquered Babylon in 539 BC, he boasted that "Sin the Nannar [the Semitic and Sumerian names of Ur's chief deity, the moon god] . . . of heaven and earth, with his favorable omen delivered into my hands the four quarters of the world. I returned the gods to their shrines."[5]

This boast was discovered in excavations at Ur and echoes Cyrus's edict to the Jewish exiles in Ezra 1:2: "The Lord, the God of the heavens, has given me all the kingdoms of the earth and has appointed me to build him a house at Jerusalem in Judah."

The Sumerians worshiped hundreds of gods, but each city had a chief deity that represented the city in the divine council. The ancient literature describes the gods behaving much like emotional, petty, political people with great powers. The moon god, Nanna, had power over the night and monthly cycles and was able to see into the dark future.[6] The people of Ur understood it to be their duty to serve and feed the gods through sacrifices and to avoid angering the often abusive gods. They hoped their service resulted in prosperity and the beneficial power of the gods. Since Abram's father worshiped many gods (Jos 24:2), he likely worshiped Nanna, who was also the patron deity of the city of Haran where his family settled after leaving Ur.[7] Abram's spiritual journey from idolatry to the worship of the one true God was a much greater journey than the physical journey from Ur to the promised land.

Although Ur began small, it grew to a magnificent city. However, after the collapse of the Third Dynasty of Ur, the city never rebounded to its former glory. Instead, for generations the city continued to exist as a mere shell of its former self. After about forty-five hundred years of occupation, however, Ur finally did die a quick death—when the Euphrates River changed its course. Without access to the river and with the coast ever farther away, Ur was abandoned and its ruins covered in sand. The great and glorious Sumerian city that seemingly had once been "capital of the world" was no more. ⁘

[1] Biblical scholars contest the location of Abram's Ur. Ancient documents mention several cities by the name of Ur or something similar such as Ure, Uri, and Ura. According to Islamic tradition, Urfa, which is only about twenty miles from Haran, is Abram's Ur. See Cyrus H. Gordon, "Recovering Canaan and Ancient Israel," in *Civilizations of the Ancient Near East* (*CANE*), ed. Jack M. Sasson (Peabody, MA: Hendrickson, 1995, 2006), 3–4:2784. However, Alan R. Millard, "Where Was Abraham's Ur? The Case for the Babylonian City," *Biblical Archaeological Review* (*BAR*) 27.3 (2001): 52–53, 57), and H. W. F. Saggs, "Ur of the Chaldees: A Problem of Identification," *Iraq* 22 (1960): 200–9, both effectively argued for identifying Abram's Ur with Tell el-Muqayyar in southern Mesopotamia. [2] For good summaries of Sumerian civilization and history, see William W. Hallo and William Kelly Simpson, *The Ancient Near East: A History*, 2nd ed. (Fort Worth, TX: Harcourt Brace, 1998); Harriet Crawford, *Sumer and the Sumerians* (Cambridge: Cambridge University Press, 1991); and Samuel Noel Kramer, *The Sumerians: Their History, Culture, and Character* (Chicago: University of Chicago Press, 1963). [3] Woolley discovered more than eighteen hundred tombs, sixteen of which stood out for their wealth and royalty. These tombs date from 2600 to 2400 BC. Cf. C. L. Woolley, *Ur of the Chaldees: A Record of Seven Years of Excavation* (New York: Norton, 1965), 33–89; and Shirley Glubok, ed., *Discovering the Royal Tombs at Ur* (London: Macmillan, 1969), 8; M. J. Selman, "Ur," in *Major Cities of the Biblical World*, ed. R. K. Harrison (Nashville: Thomas Nelson, 1985), 279. [4] "Laments for Ur" in Victor H. Matthews and Don C. Benjamin, *Old Testaments Parallels: Laws and Stories from the Ancient Near East*, 2nd ed. (New York: Paulist, 1997), 237. [5] C. J. Gadd and Leon Legrain, *Ur Excavations, Texts, I: Royal Inscriptions* (London: Trustees of the Two Museums, 1928), 307 (p. 96). See also Selman, "Ur." [6] Alfred J. Hoerth, *Archeology in the Old Testament* (Grand Rapids: Baker, 1998), 66–67. [7] William Osborne, "Ur" in *Dictionary of the Old Testament: Pentateuch*, ed. T. Desmond Alexander and David W. Baker (Downers Grove, IL: InterVarsity, 2003), 875.

Aerial views of the Euphrates River. Abram followed the river when he headed north out of Ur.

17 When the sun had set and it was dark, a smoking
fire pot and a flaming torch appeared and passed
between the divided animals. 18 On that day the LORD
made a covenant with Abram, saying, "I give this
land to your offspring, from the Brook of Egypt to
the great river, the Euphrates River: 19 the land of the
Kenites, Kenizzites, Kadmonites, 20 Hethites, Perizzites, Rephaim, 21 Amorites, Canaanites, Girgashites,
and Jebusites."

HAGAR AND ISHMAEL

16 Abram's wife, Sarai, had not borne any children for him, but she owned an Egyptian slave
named Hagar. 2 Sarai said to Abram, "Since the LORD
has prevented me from bearing children, go to my
slave; perhaps through her I can build a family." And
Abram agreed to what Sarai said. 3 So Abram's wife,
Sarai, took Hagar, her Egyptian slave, and gave her
to her husband, Abram, as a wife for him. This happened after Abram had lived in the land of Canaan
ten years. 4 He slept with[A] Hagar, and she became
pregnant. When she saw that she was pregnant, her
mistress became contemptible to her. 5 Then Sarai
said to Abram, "You are responsible for my suffering![B]
I put my slave in your arms,[C] and when she saw that
she was pregnant, I became contemptible to her. May
the LORD judge between me and you."

6 Abram replied to Sarai, "Here, your slave is in your
power; do whatever you want with her." Then Sarai
mistreated her so much that she ran away from her.

7 The angel of the LORD found her by a spring in the
wilderness, the spring on the way to Shur. 8 He said,
"Hagar, slave of Sarai, where have you come from
and where are you going?"

She replied, "I'm running away from my mistress
Sarai."

9 The angel of the LORD said to her, "Go back to
your mistress and submit to her authority." 10 The
angel of the LORD said to her, "I will greatly multiply your offspring, and they will be too many to
count."

11 The angel of the LORD said to her, "You have conceived and will have a son. You will name him Ishmael,[D] for the LORD has heard your cry of affliction.
12 This man will be like a wild donkey. His hand will be
against everyone, and everyone's hand will be against
him; he will settle near all his relatives."

13 So she named the LORD who spoke to her: "You
are El-roi,"[E] for she said, "In this place, have I actually
seen the one who sees me?"[F] 14 That is why the well is
called Beer-lahai-roi.[G] It is between Kadesh and Bered.

15 So Hagar gave birth to Abram's son, and Abram
named his son (whom Hagar bore) Ishmael. 16 Abram
was eighty-six years old when Hagar bore Ishmael
to him.

COVENANT CIRCUMCISION

17 When Abram was ninety-nine years old, the
LORD appeared to him, saying, "I am God Almighty. Live[H] in my presence and be blameless. 2 I
will set up my covenant between me and you, and I
will multiply you greatly."

3 Then Abram fell facedown and God spoke with
him: 4 "As for me, here is my covenant with you: You
will become the father of many nations. 5 Your name
will no longer be Abram;[I] your name will be Abraham,[J] for I will make you the father of many nations.
6 I will make you extremely fruitful and will make
nations and kings come from you. 7 I will confirm
my covenant that is between me and you and your
future offspring throughout their generations. It is
a permanent covenant to be your God and the God
of your offspring after you. 8 And to you and your
future offspring[K] I will give the land where you are
residing — all the land of Canaan — as a permanent
possession, and I will be their God."

9 God also said to Abraham, "As for you, you and
your offspring after you throughout their generations are to keep my covenant. 10 This is my covenant
between me and you and your offspring after you,
which you are to keep: Every one of your males must
be circumcised. 11 You must circumcise the flesh of
your foreskin to serve as a sign of the covenant between me and you.[L] 12 Throughout your generations,
every male among you is to be circumcised at eight
days old — every male born in your household or
purchased from any foreigner and not your offspring.
13 Whether born in your household or purchased, he
must be circumcised. My covenant will be marked in
your flesh as a permanent covenant. 14 If any male
is not circumcised in the flesh of his foreskin, that
man will be cut off from his people; he has broken
my covenant."

15 God said to Abraham, "As for your wife Sarai,
do not call her Sarai, for Sarah[M] will be her name. 16 I
will bless her; indeed, I will give you a son by her. I
will bless her, and she will produce nations; kings of
peoples will come from her."

17 Abraham fell facedown. Then he laughed and
said to himself, "Can a child be born to a hundred-
year-old man? Can Sarah, a ninety-year-old woman,
give birth?" 18 So Abraham said to God, "If only Ishmael were acceptable[N] to you!"

19 But God said, "No. Your wife Sarah will bear you
a son, and you will name him Isaac.[O] I will confirm

[A] **16:4** Lit *He came to* [B] **16:5** Or *"May my suffering be on you!*
[C] **16:5** Lit *bosom* [D] **16:11** = God Hears [E] **16:13** = God Sees Me
[F] **16:13** Hb obscure [G] **16:14** = Well of the Living One Who Sees Me
[H] **17:1** Or *Walk* [I] **17:5** = The Father Is Exalted [J] **17:5** = Father of a Multitude [K] **17:8** Lit *seed* [L] **17:11** *You* in v. 11 is pl. [M] **17:15** = Princess
[N] **17:18** Lit *alive* [O] **17:19** = He Laughs

my covenant with him as a permanent covenant for
his future offspring. 20 As for Ishmael, I have heard
you. I will certainly bless him; I will make him fruitful
and will multiply him greatly. He will father twelve
tribal leaders, and I will make him into a great nation. 21 But I will confirm my covenant with Isaac,
whom Sarah will bear to you at this time next year."
22 When he finished talking with him, God withdrew[A]
from Abraham.

23 So Abraham took his son Ishmael and those
born in his household or purchased — every male
among the members of Abraham's household — and
he circumcised the flesh of their foreskin on that
very day, just as God had said to him. 24 Abraham was
ninety-nine years old when the flesh of his foreskin
was circumcised, 25 and his son Ishmael was thirteen years old when the flesh of his foreskin was
circumcised. 26 On that very day Abraham and his
son Ishmael were circumcised. 27 And all the men
of his household — whether born in his household
or purchased from a foreigner — were circumcised
with him.

ABRAHAM'S THREE VISITORS

18 The LORD appeared to Abraham at the oaks of
Mamre while he was sitting at the entrance
of his tent during the heat of the day. 2 He looked up,
and he saw three men standing near him. When he
saw them, he ran from the entrance of the tent to
meet them, bowed to the ground, 3 and said, "My lord,
if I have found favor with you, please do not go on
past your servant. 4 Let a little water be brought, that
you may wash your feet and rest yourselves under
the tree. 5 I will bring a bit of bread so that you may
strengthen yourselves. This is why you have passed
your servant's way. Later, you can continue on."

"Yes," they replied, "do as you have said."

6 So Abraham hurried into the tent and said to Sarah, "Quick! Knead three measures[B] of fine flour and
make bread."[C] 7 Abraham ran to the herd and got a
tender, choice calf. He gave it to a young man, who
hurried to prepare it. 8 Then Abraham took curds[D]
and milk, as well as the calf that he had prepared,
and set them before the men. He served[E] them as
they ate under the tree.

SARAH LAUGHS

9 "Where is your wife Sarah?" they asked him.

"There, in the tent," he answered.

10 The LORD said, "I will certainly come back to you
in about a year's time, and your wife Sarah will have
a son!" Now Sarah was listening at the entrance of
the tent behind him.

11 Abraham and Sarah were old and getting on in
years.[F] Sarah had passed the age of childbearing. 12 So
she laughed to herself: "After I am worn out and my
lord is old, will I have delight?"

13 But the LORD asked Abraham, "Why did Sarah
laugh, saying, 'Can I really have a baby when I'm old?'
14 Is anything impossible for the LORD? At the appointed time I will come back to you, and in about a year
she will have a son."

15 Sarah denied it. "I did not laugh," she said, because she was afraid.

But he replied, "No, you did laugh."

ABRAHAM'S PLEA FOR SODOM

16 The men got up from there and looked out over
Sodom, and Abraham was walking with them to see
them off. 17 Then the LORD said, "Should I hide what
I am about to do from Abraham? 18 Abraham is to
become a great and powerful nation, and all the nations of the earth will be blessed through him. 19 For
I have chosen[G] him so that he will command his children and his house after him to keep the way of the
LORD by doing what is right and just. This is how the
LORD will fulfill to Abraham what he promised him."
20 Then the LORD said, "The outcry against Sodom
and Gomorrah is immense, and their sin is extremely serious. 21 I will go down to see if what they have
done justifies the cry that has come up to me. If not,
I will find out."

22 The men turned from there and went toward
Sodom while Abraham remained standing before
the LORD.[H] 23 Abraham stepped forward and said,
"Will you really sweep away the righteous with the
wicked? 24 What if there are fifty righteous people
in the city? Will you really sweep it away instead of
sparing the place for the sake of the fifty righteous
people who are in it? 25 You could not possibly do such
a thing: to kill the righteous with the wicked, treating
the righteous and the wicked alike. You could not
possibly do that! Won't the Judge of the whole earth
do what is just?"

26 The LORD said, "If I find fifty righteous people
in the city of Sodom, I will spare the whole place for
their sake."

27 Then Abraham answered, "Since I have ventured
to speak to my lord — even though I am dust and ashes — 28 suppose the fifty righteous lack five. Will you
destroy the whole city for lack of five?"

He replied, "I will not destroy it if I find forty-five
there."

29 Then he spoke to him again, "Suppose forty are
found there?"

He answered, "I will not do it on account of forty."

[A] **17:22** Lit *went up*, or *ascended* [B] **18:6** Lit *three seahs*; about 21 quarts [C] **18:6** A round, thin, unleavened bread [D] **18:8** Or *butter* [E] **18:8** Lit *was standing by* [F] **18:11** Lit *days* [G] **18:19** Lit *known* [H] **18:22** Alt Hb tradition reads *while the LORD remained standing before Abraham*

Abraham's Travels

by Alan Ray Buescher

Archaeologists care little for wandering nomads; they leave little or no material evidence of their lives for future generations to discover. So likewise with Abraham, who built no cities or buildings, and left no potsherds, tools, or jewelry in garbage dumps or tombs (at least that anyone has discovered). The concept of Abraham as a nomad or seminomad, however, may not survive the test of scriptural scrutiny. Old Testament scholar D. J. Wiseman described Abraham's lifestyle more akin to pastoral nomadism as described in the Mari texts, in which seasonal farming accompanied the herding of flocks and cattle close to towns and cities.[1]

Interior of a Bedouin tent. Continuing still today, Bedouin have a long-established tradition of extending hospitality to travelers and visitors.

Abraham's time in the land of promise significantly illustrates his lifestyle: he spent most of those one hundred years settled in Hebron or in the Negev (in Gerar and Beer-sheba), although he apparently lived in tents rather than permanent structures (e.g., Gn 13:18; 18:1). In the Negev, the area around Beer-sheba provides the only land available for farming without water irrigation, but agriculture did not rank as the primary means of earning a living. The numerous ancient remains discovered at sites in the Negev reveal their main function as caravan stations for trade merchants traveling to and from Egypt.[2]

Perhaps Abraham participated in this trade, which could account partially for his wealth accumulation. He had flocks, cattle, and camels; he also possessed flour for baking (18:6–8), either from farming or via trade with sedentary farmers in nearby settlements. He possessed much silver and gold (13:2), which he earned or inherited from his time spent in Haran. Additionally, he may have accumulated some wealth in Egypt and Canaan through market transactions.

Israeli archaeologist Amihai Mazar believes the archaeological discoveries of the Middle Bronze II

Ruins of Beer-sheba in southern Israel; farmland is in the distance.

Camels grazing in the Judean wilderness.

(MBII) period provide similarities with the patriarchal record in the Bible that cannot be ignored. The Canaanite culture became established primarily along the northern coastal plain and eastward through the valleys of Jezreel and Beth-shean during MBIIA. These Canaanites likely came from the coastal plain around Tyre and also from Aram (modern Syria). Egyptian documents from Byblos as well as documents from Mari during MBIIA contain West Semitic (Amorite) names among the population of Aram and Canaan. One of the Mari texts contains the earliest record of the designation "Canaanite" as one of the population groups of the area. Furthermore, West Semitic or Amorite names correspond closely to Canaanite names.[3]

This Amorite population continued to migrate east into Babylon during MBIIB–C (ca 1800/1750–1550 BC), spreading its culture throughout the northern portion of the Fertile Crescent. During this time, foreign rulers known as the Hyksos came to power in Egypt. These outsiders were none other than Canaanites. Thus a West-Semitic/Amorite/Canaanite culture extended from Egypt, northward along the coastal plain of the promised land, across the Jezreel Valley, and north along the Fertile Crescent to Babylon. This Canaanite influence that began in MBIIA likely could have made a Semitic language the common language of the day for international trade purposes, and it could explain how Abraham communicated with the Egyptians and Abimelech in the Negev. Akkadian, a Semitic language, became the universal language of scribes, priests, and the legal community throughout the ancient Near East by MBIIB–C and likely began its dominance in MBIIA. ✣

[1] D. J. Wiseman, "Abraham Reassessed," in *Essays of the Patriarchal Narratives*, ed. A. R. Millard and D. J. Wiseman (Winona Lake, IN: Eisenbrauns, 1983), 145. [2] A. Reifenberg, *The Struggle between the Desert and the Sown: Rise and Fall of Agriculture in the Levant* (Jerusalem: Publishing Department of the Jewish Agency, 1955), 19. [3] Amihai Mazar, *Archaeology of the Land of the Bible, 10,000–568 BCE* (New York: Doubleday, 1990), 174–89.

Ruins of the palace at Mari in modern Syria. Mari was the capital city of the Amorites from about 2000 to 1750 BC. The palace covered more than six acres and had more than three hundred rooms. One of the most remarkable finds at Mari was the fifteen-thousand-plus texts that detailed everyday life in Mari before its fall. Many of the names on the texts are the same as some from the Old Testament, including Noah, Abram, Laban, Jacob, Benjamin, and Levi.

30 Then he said, "Let my lord not be angry, and I
will speak further. Suppose thirty are found there?"
He answered, "I will not do it if I find thirty there."
31 Then he said, "Since I have ventured to speak to
my lord, suppose twenty are found there?"
He replied, "I will not destroy it on account of
twenty."
32 Then he said, "Let my lord not be angry, and I will
speak one more time. Suppose ten are found there?"
He answered, "I will not destroy it on account of
ten." 33 When the LORD had finished speaking with
Abraham, he departed, and Abraham returned to
his place.

THE DESTRUCTION OF SODOM AND GOMORRAH

19 The two angels entered Sodom in the evening
as Lot was sitting in Sodom's gateway. When
Lot saw them, he got up to meet them. He bowed
with his face to the ground 2 and said, "My lords,
turn aside to your servant's house, wash your feet,
and spend the night. Then you can get up early and
go on your way."
"No," they said. "We would rather spend the night
in the square." 3 But he urged them so strongly that
they followed him and went into his house. He prepared a feast and baked unleavened bread for them,
and they ate.
4 Before they went to bed, the men of the city of
Sodom, both young and old, the whole population,
surrounded the house. 5 They called out to Lot and
said, "Where are the men who came to you tonight?
Send them out to us so we can have sex with them!"
6 Lot went out to them at the entrance and shut
the door behind him. 7 He said, "Don't do this evil, my
brothers. 8 Look, I've got two daughters who haven't
been intimate with a man. I'll bring them out to you,
and you can do whatever you want[A] to them. However, don't do anything to these men, because they have
come under the protection of my roof."
9 "Get out of the way!" they said, adding, "This one
came here as an alien, but he's acting like a judge!
Now we'll do more harm to you than to them." They
put pressure on Lot and came up to break down the
door. 10 But the angels[B] reached out, brought Lot into
the house with them, and shut the door. 11 They struck
the men who were at the entrance of the house, both
young and old, with blindness[C] so that they were unable to find the entrance.
12 Then the angels said to Lot, "Do you have anyone else here: a son-in-law, your sons and daughters,
or anyone else in the city who belongs to you? Get
them out of this place, 13 for we are about to destroy
this place because the outcry against its people is
so great before the LORD, that the LORD has sent us
to destroy it."

DIGGING DEEPER ***Sodom***

Sodom and the other "cities of the plain" (Gn 13:10–12; 19:17–29) were thought by critical scholars to be legendary locations used by the biblical writer to communicate in metaphorical language. This theory has become difficult to sustain due to recent archaeological discoveries unearthed by Dr. Steven Collins at the Tall el-Hammam Excavation Project, located northeast of the Dead Sea and west of Mount Nebo in Jordan. After nearly a dozen seasons of excavation, the data found at the site offers promising evidence supporting the location as biblical Sodom. Pottery, architectural design, and stratigraphy analysis have confirmed that the site is situated in the right time period—the Middle Bronze Age. Tall el-Hammam (Sodom) is also located in the right place. More than forty geographical markers place Sodom on the eastern boundary of the *kikkar*, a circular disklike Jordanian plain, along with the other "cities of the plain" (Gn 19:29; Hb *kikkar*). In addition, Sodom's sister city, Gomorrah (Tall Kafrein), is located a short distance away within the well-watered plain of the Jordan. The location also possesses the right artifacts that reflect obvious catastrophic high-heat indicators. These include a massive destruction layer of ash and debris caused by fire that features pottery melted at temperatures exceeding two thousand degrees Fahrenheit (about the same temperature as volcanic magma), charred human remains, and an occupational gap lasting for at least seven hundred years after the conflagration (see Nm 21:20). Tall el-Hammam meets the geographical markers identified in Genesis 13:1–12 and thus remains an excellent candidate for Sodom's location.

14 So Lot went out and spoke to his sons-in-law,
who were going to marry his daughters. "Get up,"
he said. "Get out of this place, for the LORD is about
to destroy the city!" But his sons-in-law thought he
was joking.
15 At daybreak the angels urged Lot on: "Get up!
Take your wife and your two daughters who are
here, or you will be swept away in the punishment[D]
of the city." 16 But he hesitated. Because of the LORD's
compassion for him, the men grabbed his hand, his
wife's hand, and the hands of his two daughters. They
brought him out and left him outside the city.

[A] **19:8** Lit *do what is good in your eyes* [B] **19:10** Lit *men*, also in v. 12
[C] **19:11** Or *a blinding light* [D] **19:15** Or *iniquity*, or *guilt*

The Invasion of the Kings

by E. LeBron Matthews

Evidence that spearheads were cast, this spearhead and mold date to the time of Abram and Lot.

Abram lived late in the historical period known as the Middle Bronze Age (1800–1600 BC). Bronze was the primary metal used in making tools and weapons in this period. Great upheavals in the populations of Asia Minor and the regions north of Mesopotamia sparked great migrations during this era. No single state dominated Mesopotamia. Power rested in the kings of various city-states.[1]

The land of Canaan had been significantly different at the beginning of the Early Bronze Age (3150–2850 BC). The names of many places identified in the early patriarchal narratives changed over time. Genesis identifies some sites by their later names. For example, Bela was equated with Zoar (Gn 14:2) and the Siddim Valley to the region that was the Dead or Salt Sea (v. 3).[2] Strong urban cultures such as Sodom and Gomorrah developed in this valley.[3] The period was characterized by a high level of material achievement. The fast-spinning potter's wheel was introduced, and metal workers produced a more durable bronze.[4]

At the beginning of the Middle Bronze Age (the time of Abram), Egypt nominally controlled Canaan. Egypt, however, was in trouble. Asiatic people, mostly Semitic, were migrating into the Nile Delta in large numbers. Abram himself had gone there. Unlike Abram, most of these migrants remained in Egypt. The Hyksos, an Egyptian term for these people, would soon gain control of northern Egypt, and the kingdom would separate into two distinct nations. These internal troubles prevented Egypt from military involvement in Canaan.

A coalition of four Mesopotamian kings invaded Canaan. None of the four kings has been identified with extrabiblical historical records. Consequently the episode remains obscure.[5] The coalition consisted of "King Amraphel of Shinar, King Arioch of Ellasar, King Chedorlaomer of Elam, and King Tidal of Goiim" (14:1). Chedorlaomer was their leader. Elam was the southwest region of ancient Persia. Shinar was another name for Babylon.

Certain Canaanite kings had been subjects of Chedorlaomer for twelve years (v. 4) and had paid him an annual tribute. This may have been the result of military conquest or a form of bribery. Whatever the origin of this tribute, when it was due in the thirteenth year, they refused to pay. Therefore Chedorlaomer invaded to reassert his sovereignty over the region. He also may have desired control over the copper mines located in the southern part of the region.[6] Copper and tin were the key ingredients in making bronze.

The Hyksos introduced the chariot into warfare about this time. This new technology was decisive in their conquest of Egypt.[7] Possibly the invading coalition used chariots in their fighting since the kings came from the same area as the Hyksos. But infantry was the primary fighting force in most armies at the time. The most common weapon was the spear. Other weapons included bronze swords and axes. Wood bows and leather slings also were available. Spear tips and arrowheads also were cast in bronze. Shields were constructed of wood and leather. Soldiers did not wear much armor. Battles were bloody encounters of hand-to-hand combat. Fighting continued until one side was destroyed or retreated. Victors frequently executed prisoners or turned them into slaves.

Mining shafts at Timnah in the Arabah, south of the Dead Sea. The kings' withholding tribute from Chedorlaomer meant he lost income from copper, which was produced in abundance in this region. When the kings from the north invaded Canaan, they came through this region.

Genesis lists the kings of the valley's city-states: Bera of Sodom, Birsha of Gomorrah, Shinab of Admah, Shemeber of Zeboiim, and the king of Bela (Zoar) (14:2). All of the names are Amorite.[9] Nothing else is known about them. When the invaders approached, the kings chose to meet them in open battle. Otherwise the kings would have been trapped inside their city walls. So to avoid a siege, their armies formed for battle in the valley. Unfortunately the invading troops defeated them and sacked their cities. Many who survived the battle, though, perished in the numerous tar pits that dotted the landscape. Some made it to the safety of the nearby mountains. Others were taken prisoner. The victorious invaders marched north along the King's Highway. They carried with them the wealth of the conquered cities and an unknown number of captives. Among them was Lot, Abram's nephew.

A wealthy nomad such as Abram retained numerous servants. These servants were expected to fight for him. Abram had 318 men capable of bearing arms (v. 14). He also had made treaties with his neighbors, and they joined forces with Abram. Their force still was likely much smaller than the battle-hardened invaders.

During the initial phase of this military campaign, the invasion force moved south along the King's Highway, the major road between Damascus and the Gulf of Aqaba. They subjugated various towns along the way. The Bible lists these defeated peoples—from the Rephaim in the north to the Horites in the south. The Horites apparently fled to the town of El-paran on the Gulf of Aqaba. The fall of that city brought an end to the first phase of the invasion. Archaeological evidence shows little inhabitation of the area east of the Jordan during the later part of the Middle Bronze Age.[8] This suggests that the invasion destroyed these towns completely.

The second phase involved conquest of territory west of the Jordan River. After capturing El-paran, the invading army turned northwest and attacked the Amalekite city of En-mishpat (Kadesh-barnea). After defeating the Amalekites, the four kings turned back toward the King's Highway and the cities of the valley.

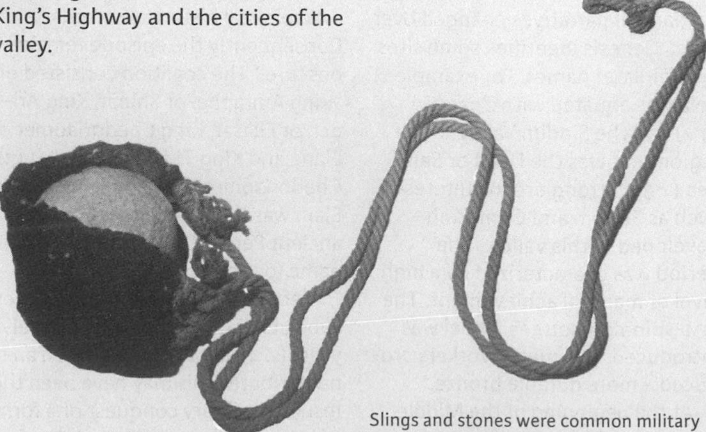
Slings and stones were common military ware in the Middle Bronze Age.

The invaders continued marching home. They would have been slowed by their plunder and captives. Furthermore, the constant fighting would have weakened them physically. Abram shadowed them, moving on a secondary road west of the Jordan. The two roads converged near Damascus.[10] Abram traveled swiftly and set up an ambush, possibly at the Barada Gorge northwest of the city. He attacked at night when the darkness would hide how small his "army" was. His surprise assault created confusion among his enemies. They abandoned their spoils and fled. Abram followed them until he was satisfied they no longer posed a threat. Then he gathered liberated prisoners and captured spoils (vv. 15–16).

According to custom, all of the spoils would have belonged to Abram and his allies. But that was not to be the case. Abram passed the village of Salem (Jerusalem) on his return journey. There he gave the mysterious Melchizedek a tenth of the spoils (vv. 17–21). And Abram's allies took their share of the spoils. But the godly Abram refused to keep any (vv. 23–24).

Abram's victory contributed to his growing influence in the region. Although a resident alien, Abram's vast wealth made him an integral component of the region's economy. His vast flocks offered raw materials for the local textile industry and a convenient food source for the population. His defeat of the invaders added a capable military reputation to his economic power and virtuous character. Subsequently, Canaanite rulers treated him as a peer rather than as an inferior migrant. ✜

---

[1] Joan Oates, *Babylon* (London: Thames & Hudson, 1979), 24. [2] Yohanan Aharoni and Michael Avi-Yonah, *The Macmillan Bible Atlas* (New York: Macmillan, 1977), 24. [3] Derek Kidner, *Genesis*, vol. 1 in Tyndale Old Testament Commentaries (TOTC), ed. D. J. Wiseman (London: Tyndale Press, 1967), 119. [4] A. R. Millard, "The Canaanites," in *Peoples of Old Testament Times*, ed. D. J. Wiseman (Oxford: Clarendon, 1973), 38–39. [5] Aharoni and Avi-Yonah, *Macmillan Bible Atlas*, 24; G. Ernest Wright, *Biblical Archaeology* (Philadelphia: Westminster, 1962), 50–51. [6] Wright, *Biblical Archaeology*, 51. [7] Chaim Herzog and Mordechai Gichon, *Battles of the Bible* (London: Greenhill Books, 1997), 33–34. [8] Harold G. Stigers, *A Commentary on Genesis* (Grand Rapids: Zondervan, 1976), 148. [9] Aharoni and Avi-Yonah, *Macmillan Bible Atlas*, 24. [10] Herzog and Gichon, *Battles*, 34.

Looking north toward Damascus, a major trade route that several biblical persons would have traveled including Paul, Abraham, and Jacob.

[17] As soon as the angels got them outside, one of them[A] said, "Run for your lives! Don't look back and don't stop anywhere on the plain! Run to the mountains, or you will be swept away!"

[18] But Lot said to them, "No, my lords[B] — please. [19] Your servant has indeed found favor with you, and you have shown me great kindness by saving my life. But I can't run to the mountains; the disaster will overtake me, and I will die. [20] Look, this town is close enough for me to flee to. It is a small place. Please let me run to it — it's only a small place, isn't it? — so that I can survive."

[21] And he said to him, "All right,[C] I'll grant your request[D] about this matter too and will not demolish the town you mentioned. [22] Hurry up! Run to it, for I cannot do anything until you get there." Therefore the name of the city is Zoar.[E]

[23] The sun had risen over the land when Lot reached Zoar. [24] Then out of the sky the LORD rained on Sodom and Gomorrah burning sulfur from the LORD. [25] He demolished these cities, the entire plain, all the inhabitants of the cities, and whatever grew on the ground. [26] But Lot's wife looked back and became a pillar of salt.

[27] Early in the morning Abraham went to the place where he had stood before the LORD. [28] He looked down toward Sodom and Gomorrah and all the land of the plain, and he saw that smoke was going up from the land like the smoke of a furnace. [29] So it was, when God destroyed the cities of the plain, he remembered Abraham and brought Lot out of the middle of the upheaval when he demolished the cities where Lot had lived.

THE ORIGIN OF MOAB AND AMMON

[30] Lot departed from Zoar and lived in the mountains along with his two daughters, because he was afraid to live in Zoar. Instead, he and his two daughters lived in a cave. [31] Then the firstborn said to the younger, "Our father is old, and there is no man in the land to sleep with us as is the custom of all the land. [32] Come, let's get our father to drink wine so that we can sleep with him and preserve our father's line." [33] So they got their father to drink wine that night, and the firstborn came and slept with her father; he did not know when she lay down or when she got up.

[34] The next day the firstborn said to the younger, "Look, I slept with my father last night. Let's get him to drink wine again tonight so you can go sleep with him and we can preserve our father's line." [35] That night they again got their father to drink wine, and the younger went and slept with him; he did not know when she lay down or when she got up.

[36] So both of Lot's daughters became pregnant by their father. [37] The firstborn gave birth to a son and named him Moab.[F] He is the father of the Moabites of today. [38] The younger also gave birth to a son, and she named him Ben-ammi.[G] He is the father of the Ammonites of today.

SARAH RESCUED FROM ABIMELECH

20 From there Abraham traveled to the region of the Negev and settled between Kadesh and Shur. While he was staying in Gerar, [2] Abraham said about his wife Sarah, "She is my sister." So King Abimelech of Gerar had Sarah brought to him.

[3] But God came to Abimelech in a dream by night and said to him, "You are about to die because of the woman you have taken, for she is a married woman."[H]

[4] Now Abimelech had not approached her, so he said, "Lord, would you destroy a nation even though it is innocent? [5] Didn't he himself say to me, 'She is my sister'? And she herself said, 'He is my brother.' I did this with a clear conscience[I] and clean[J] hands."

[6] Then God said to him in the dream, "Yes, I know that you did this with a clear conscience.[K] I have also kept you from sinning against me. Therefore I have not let you touch her. [7] Now return the man's wife, for he is a prophet, and he will pray for you and you will live. But if you do not return her, know that you will certainly die, you and all who are yours."

[8] Early in the morning Abimelech got up, called all his servants together, and personally[L] told them all these things, and the men were terrified.

[9] Then Abimelech called Abraham in and said to him, "What have you done to us? How did I sin against you that you have brought such enormous guilt on me and on my kingdom? You have done things to me that should never be done." [10] Abimelech also asked Abraham, "What made you do this?"

[11] Abraham replied, "I thought, 'There is absolutely no fear of God in this place. They will kill me because of my wife.' [12] Besides, she really is my sister, the daughter of my father though not the daughter of my mother, and she became my wife. [13] So when God had me wander from my father's house, I said to her: Show your loyalty to me wherever we go and say about me, 'He's my brother.'"

[14] Then Abimelech took flocks and herds and male and female slaves, gave them to Abraham, and returned his wife Sarah to him. [15] Abimelech said, "Look, my land is before you. Settle wherever you want."[M] [16] And he said to Sarah, "Look, I am giving your brother one thousand pieces of silver. It is a verification

[A] **19:17** LXX, Syr, Vg read *outside, they* [B] **19:18** Or *my Lord*, or *my lord* [C] **19:21** Or *"Look!* [D] **19:21** Lit *I will lift up your face* [E] **19:22** In Hb, the name *Zoar* is related to "small" in v. 20; its previous name was "Bela"; Gn 14:2. [F] **19:37** = From My Father [G] **19:38** = Son of My People [H] **20:3** Lit *is possessed by a husband* [I] **20:5** Lit *with integrity of my heart* [J] **20:5** Lit *cleanness of my* [K] **20:6** Lit *with integrity of your heart* [L] **20:8** Lit *in their ears* [M] **20:15** Lit *Settle in the good in your eyes*

of your honor[A] to all who are with you. You are fully vindicated."

17 Then Abraham prayed to God, and God healed Abimelech, his wife, and his female slaves so that they could bear children, 18 for the LORD had completely closed all the wombs in Abimelech's household on account of Sarah, Abraham's wife.

THE BIRTH OF ISAAC

21 The LORD came to Sarah as he had said, and the LORD did for Sarah what he had promised. 2 Sarah became pregnant and bore a son to Abraham in his old age, at the appointed time God had told him. 3 Abraham named his son who was born to him — the one Sarah bore to him — Isaac. 4 When his son Isaac was eight days old, Abraham circumcised him, as God had commanded him. 5 Abraham was a hundred years old when his son Isaac was born to him.

6 Sarah said, "God has made me laugh, and everyone who hears will laugh with me."[B] 7 She also said, "Who would have told Abraham that Sarah would nurse children? Yet I have borne a son for him[C] in his old age."

HAGAR AND ISHMAEL SENT AWAY

8 The child grew and was weaned, and Abraham held a great feast on the day Isaac was weaned. 9 But Sarah saw the son mocking — the one Hagar the Egyptian had borne to Abraham. 10 So she said to Abraham, "Drive out this slave with her son, for the son of this slave will not be a coheir with my son Isaac!"

11 This was very distressing to[D] Abraham because of his son. 12 But God said to Abraham, "Do not be distressed[E] about the boy and about your slave. Whatever Sarah says to you, listen to her, because your offspring will be traced through Isaac, 13 and I will also make a nation of the slave's son because he is your offspring."

14 Early in the morning Abraham got up, took bread and a waterskin, put them on Hagar's shoulders, and sent her and the boy away. She left and wandered in the Wilderness of Beer-sheba. 15 When the water in the skin was gone, she left the boy under one of the bushes 16 and went and sat at a distance, about a bowshot away, for she said, "I can't bear to watch the boy die!" While she sat at a distance, she[F] wept loudly.

17 God heard the boy crying, and the[G] angel of God called to Hagar from heaven and said to her, "What's wrong, Hagar? Don't be afraid, for God has heard the boy crying from the place where he is. 18 Get up, help the boy up, and grasp his hand, for I will make him a great nation." 19 Then God opened her eyes, and she saw a well. So she went and filled the waterskin and gave the boy a drink. 20 God was with the boy, and he grew; he settled in the wilderness and became an archer. 21 He settled in the Wilderness of Paran, and his mother got a wife for him from the land of Egypt.

ABRAHAM'S COVENANT WITH ABIMELECH

22 At that time Abimelech, accompanied by Phicol the commander of his army, said to Abraham, "God is with you in everything you do. 23 Swear to me by God here and now, that you will not break an agreement with me or with my children and descendants. As I have been loyal to you, so you will be loyal to me and to the country where you are a resident alien."

24 And Abraham said, "I swear it." 25 But Abraham complained to Abimelech because of the well that Abimelech's servants had seized.

26 Abimelech replied, "I don't know who did this thing. You didn't report anything to me, so I hadn't heard about it until today."

27 Abraham took flocks and herds and gave them to Abimelech, and the two of them made a covenant. 28 Abraham separated seven ewe lambs from the flock. 29 And Abimelech said to Abraham, "Why have you separated these seven ewe lambs?"

30 He replied, "You are to accept the seven ewe lambs from me so that this act[H] will serve as my witness that I dug this well." 31 Therefore that place was called Beer-sheba[I] because it was there that the two of them swore an oath. 32 After they had made a covenant at Beer-sheba, Abimelech and Phicol, the commander of his army, left and returned to the land of the Philistines.

33 Abraham planted a tamarisk tree in Beer-sheba, and there he called on the name of the LORD, the Everlasting God. 34 And Abraham lived as an alien in the land of the Philistines for many days.

THE SACRIFICE OF ISAAC

22 After these things God tested Abraham and said to him, "Abraham!"

"Here I am," he answered.

2 "Take your son," he said, "your only son Isaac, whom you love, go to the land of Moriah, and offer him there as a burnt offering on one of the mountains I will tell you about."

3 So Abraham got up early in the morning, saddled his donkey, and took with him two of his young men and his son Isaac. He split wood for a burnt offering

[A] **20:16** Lit *a covering of the eyes* [B] **21:6** Isaac = He Laughs; Gn 17:19 [C] **21:7** Sam, Tg Jonathan; MT omits *him* [D] **21:11** Lit *was very bad in the eyes of* [E] **21:12** Lit *"Let it not be bad in your eyes* [F] **21:16** LXX reads *the boy* [G] **21:17** Or *an* [H] **21:30** Lit *that it* [I] **21:31** = Well of the Oath, or Seven Wells

God's Covenant with Abraham

by Robert D. Bergen

A formal agreement that defined a relationship between two parties in ancient western Asia was known in ancient Hebrew as a *berith*, that is, a covenant or treaty. An agreement of this type could be used to strengthen a relationship between two close friends (Jonathan and David; 1Sm 18:3) or to end a dispute between two unhappy neighbors (Isaac and Abimelech, Jacob and Laban; Gn 26:28; 31:44). The agreement could be between a king and his subjects (David and Israel's elders; 2Sm 5:3) or between two people groups (Israelites and Gibeonites; Jos 9:15). It could embody God-given instructions that people were obligated to follow (God with Israel; Ex 34:10) or express a formal commitment of a group of people to God (Israel and the Lord; 2Kg 11:17). A covenant could even be between God and nonhuman aspects of his creation (God and all living beings; God and the earth; Gn 8:21–22).

Archaeologists have unearthed ancient non-Israelite covenants in the form of cuneiform tablets. These documents, especially those of the Hittite culture found at Alalakh (near Syrian Antioch),[1] provide evidence of formal agreements that were the equivalents of some types of Israelite covenants of the Old Testament period.

TYPES OF TREATIES

Scholars often divide the Old Testament covenants and treaties into two categories, though I personally prefer to add a third. Those established between two people who had roughly the same amount of social power were called *parity treaties*. Many scholars use the term *suzerainty treaty* to refer to agreements that parties with vastly different amounts of social status made. These included agreements a conquering nation made with those they defeated or that God made with people. My third category includes the formal relationships established between God and people or any other aspect of his creation. Each of these treaty types served different purposes and possessed vastly different characteristics.

Parity treaties—those established between social peers—placed requirements on both parties involved. Arrangements of this type could help clarify details of a relationship between two people (see 1Sm 23:17) and establish a framework of clear expectations for both parties (Gn 26:29). As a result, both parties could expect to benefit significantly from this relationship. It might take the form of a marriage commitment (Mal 2:14); a promise to care for another person's family, if needed (1Sm 20:8–16); a trade agreement between nations (1Kg 5:2–12); a mutual assistance treaty between nations (Jos 9:6–15; 10:6–7); or hiring the services of another nation's military forces (1Kg 15:18–19). At the time these agreements were established, participants might have given gifts (see 1Sm 18:4) and shared a lavish meal (Gn 26:30). Biblical examples of this type of treaty include agreements reached between Abraham and Abimelech (Gn 21:22–32), Isaac and Abimelech (26:26–31), Jacob and his father-in-law, Laban (31:44–54), the Israelites and the Gibeonites (Jos 9:6–15), Jonathan and David (1Sm 18:3–4; 20:8–17; 23:16–18), David and Abner (2Sm 3:12–13), David and Israel's ruling elders (2Sam 5:1–3), Solomon and Hiram (1Kg 5:2–12), and King Asa and King Ben-hadad (1Kg 15:18–19). Clearly, Abraham's covenant with God does not fit into the "parity" category, because Abraham could not be expected to provide God with any material or military benefit.

Suzerainty treaties—such as those from Alalakh coming out of

Rising in the distance is the site of ancient Gilgal, just west of the Jordan River. Joshua was camped at Gilgal when the Gibeonites came to make a covenant of peace.

Scene depicts David's covenant with his friend Jonathan (1Sm 18:1–4).

the ancient Hittite kingdom—were agreements that established the conditions for an unequal relationship between two individuals or groups. Conquering kings regularly imposed these on countries they defeated. The party in a position of power would draw up an agreement that provided a disproportionate number of benefits for the victor. These treaties typically contained six distinct elements: (1) a preamble identifying the king who initiated the treaty, (2) a historical prologue providing details of the good things a conquering nation had done for the conquered people and then indicating the conquered nation should be grateful and obedient to the victors, (3) treaty stipulations, (4) a list of gods who supposedly witnessed the treaty, (5) a list of blessings and curses associated with obeying/disobeying the treaty terms, and (6) guidelines for storing the document as well as publicly reading it at prescribed times in the future.[2]

In biblical narratives, the formal arrangements that conquerors made with those they had defeated are similar in fashion. The victorious nations consistently placed heavy financial burdens on those they had conquered—sometimes with exact numbers regarding the size of annual payments to be made to the conqueror. The victors also took strong measures to enforce their demands (see 2Kg 3:4–7; 17:3–5).

A third type of *berith* in the Bible describes formal agreements God made with the nation of Israel, with certain individuals, and with nature. Though scholars usually place these agreements in the category of suzerainty treaty, putting them in a separate category is useful. Perhaps an appropriate term for this God-initiated relationship is *divine covenant*. Divine covenants differ in three significant ways from a classic suzerainty treaty. First and most obviously, they include God as a party in the formal agreement. Second, their purpose was not to impose demands on a conquered group or individual. Third, the benefits directed toward the lesser party—that is, what God offers to the people—far exceed what a conqueror offered in any suzerainty treaty.

GOD'S COVENANT WITH ABRAHAM

By the time the divine covenant had been fully developed between the Lord and Abraham—a process that took many years to complete—both parties had performed several key actions. First, an initiatory act took place when the Lord summoned Abraham to separate from his idol-worshiping family and go to a place of the Lord's choosing (Gn 12:1). Second, a formal covenant ceremony took place. Abraham slaughtered ritually clean mammals and birds and then separated portions of their corpses into two piles. For his part, the Lord symbolically passed between the divided animals (15:17), thereby obligating himself to fulfill the terms of the covenant. Third, Abraham and all males associated with him—his slaves and all future descendants—were required to be circumcised as a sign of submission to the terms of the covenant (17:11–14) and acceptance of Yahweh—the Lord—as their God (v. 7). Finally, Abraham had to pass a test confirming his submission to the Lord of the covenant (22:9–12).

As the benefits of the divine covenant, the Lord made three outstanding promises to Abraham: many descendants, a homeland, and a blessing. ✣

---

[1] J. A. Thompson, *The Ancient Near Eastern Treaties and the Old Testament* (London: Tyndale Press, 1964), 10. [2] Thompson, *Treaties*, 13–14.

Reconstructed well at the entrance to Beer-sheba in southern Israel.

and set out to go to the place God had told him about.
4 On the third day Abraham looked up and saw the
place in the distance. 5 Then Abraham said to his
young men, "Stay here with the donkey. The boy and
I will go over there to worship; then we'll come back
to you." 6 Abraham took the wood for the burnt offering and laid it on his son Isaac. In his hand he took
the fire and the knife, and the two of them walked
on together.
7 Then Isaac spoke to his father Abraham and said,
"My father."

And he replied, "Here I am, my son."

Isaac said, "The fire and the wood are here, but where is the lamb for the burnt offering?"

8 Abraham answered, "God himself will provide[A]
the lamb for the burnt offering, my son." Then the
two of them walked on together.

9 When they arrived at the place that God had
told him about, Abraham built the altar there and
arranged the wood. He bound his son Isaac[B] and
placed him on the altar on top of the wood. 10 Then
Abraham reached out and took the knife to slaughter his son.

11 But the angel of the LORD called to him from heav-
en and said, "Abraham, Abraham!"

He replied, "Here I am."

12 Then he said, "Do not lay a hand on the boy or do
anything to him. For now I know that you fear God,
since you have not withheld your only son from me."
13 Abraham looked up and saw a ram[C] caught in the
thicket by its horns. So Abraham went and took the
ram and offered it as a burnt offering in place of his
son. 14 And Abraham named that place The LORD Will
Provide,[D] so today it is said, "It will be provided[E] on
the LORD's mountain."
15 Then the angel of the LORD called to Abraham
a second time from heaven 16 and said, "By myself I
have sworn," this is the LORD's declaration: "Because
you have done this thing and have not withheld your
only son, 17 I will indeed bless you and make your offspring as numerous as the stars of the sky and the
sand on the seashore. Your offspring will possess the
city gates of their[F] enemies. 18 And all the nations of
the earth will be blessed[G] by your offspring because
you have obeyed my command."

19 Abraham went back to his young men, and they
got up and went together to Beer-sheba. And Abraham settled in Beer-sheba.

[A]**22:8** Lit *see* [B]**22:9** Or *Isaac hand and foot* [C]**22:13** Some Hb mss, Sam, LXX, Syr, Tg; other Hb mss read *saw behind him a ram* [D]**22:14** = *Yahweh-yireh* [E]**22:14** Or *"He will be seen* [F]**22:17** Lit *his* [G]**22:18** Or *will consider themselves blessed*, or *will find blessing*

Zoar

by Harold R. Mosley

Zoar appears alongside Sodom and Gomorrah in the Genesis 19 account of the destruction of those cities. God spared Zoar when he destroyed Sodom and Gomorrah, not because its citizens were more godly, but because it was small (*Zoar* means "small") and Lot had entered the city.

Zoar was located near the southeastern shore of the Dead Sea on the River Zered. The Dead Sea is the lowest place on the surface of the earth, 1,292 feet below sea level. The low elevation and the surrounding mountains cause the Dead Sea to get very little rainfall—fewer than four inches annually.

During the middle ages, Zoar prospered because of the abundance of fresh water nearby. It exported dates, sugar, and indigo. At Madaba, Jordan, a sixth-century AD mosaic map of the Middle East shows Zoar surrounded by palm trees. The modern oasis of Jericho in the valley is a reminder of the productivity possible in the area. The ground is fertile. The climate is ideal for growing crops.

Zoar long ago ceased to exist as a town. The reason for its demise is unclear. Perhaps some catastrophe occurred to upset the city. Or perhaps the water supply failed. Zoar ultimately suffered the fate of Sodom and Gomorrah; it passed into extinction. Zoar sits as the forsaken smaller sister of an infamous group of cities so wicked they were destroyed by "burning sulfur" from heaven (v. 24). ✣

Date palms growing near the Dead Sea.

Bab Edh Dhra, believed by many archaeologists to be ancient Sodom and/or Gomorrah. The scattered black rocks on the ground are an unusual phenomenon in this area of red sandstone.

REBEKAH'S FAMILY

20 Now after these things Abraham was told, "Milcah also has borne sons to your brother Nahor: 21 Uz
his firstborn, his brother Buz, Kemuel the father of
Aram, 22 Chesed, Hazo, Pildash, Jidlaph, and Bethuel."
23 And Bethuel fathered Rebekah. Milcah bore these
eight to Nahor, Abraham's brother. 24 His concubine,
whose name was Reumah, also bore Tebah, Gaham,
Tahash, and Maacah.

SARAH'S BURIAL

23 Now Sarah lived 127 years; these were all the
years of her life. 2 Sarah died in Kiriath-arba
(that is, Hebron) in the land of Canaan, and Abraham
went in to mourn for Sarah and to weep for her.
3 When Abraham got up from beside his dead wife,
he spoke to the Hethites: 4 "I am an alien residing
among you. Give me burial property among you so
that I can bury my dead."[A]
5 The Hethites replied to Abraham,[B] 6 "Listen to us,
my lord. You are a prince of God[C] among us. Bury
your dead in our finest burial place.[D] None of us
will withhold from you his burial place for burying
your dead."
7 Then Abraham rose and bowed down to the Hethites, the people of the land. 8 He said to them, "If you
are willing for me to bury my dead, listen to me and
ask Ephron son of Zohar on my behalf 9 to give me the
cave of Machpelah that belongs to him; it is at the end
of his field. Let him give it to me in your presence, for
the full price, as burial property."
10 Ephron was sitting among the Hethites. So in
the hearing[E] of all the Hethites who came to the gate
of his city, Ephron the Hethite answered Abraham:
11 "No, my lord. Listen to me. I give you the field, and
I give you the cave that is in it. I give it to you in the
sight[F] of my people. Bury your dead."
12 Abraham bowed down to the people of the land
13 and said to Ephron in the hearing of the people of
the land, "Listen to me, if you please. Let me pay the
price of the field. Accept it from me, and let me bury
my dead there."
14 Ephron answered Abraham and said to him,
15 "My lord, listen to me. Land worth four hundred
shekels of silver — what is that between you and me?
Bury your dead." 16 Abraham agreed with Ephron,
and Abraham weighed out to Ephron the silver that
he had agreed to in the hearing of the Hethites: four
hundred standard shekels[G] of silver. 17 So Ephron's
field at Machpelah near Mamre — the field with its
cave and all the trees anywhere within the boundaries of the field — became 18 Abraham's possession
in the sight of all the Hethites who came to the gate of
his city. 19 After this, Abraham buried his wife Sarah
in the cave of the field at Machpelah near Mamre
(that is, Hebron) in the land of Canaan. 20 The field
with its cave passed from the Hethites to Abraham
as burial property.

A WIFE FOR ISAAC

24 Abraham was now old, getting on in years,[H]
and the LORD had blessed him in everything. 2 Abraham said to his servant, the elder of
his household who managed all he owned, "Place
your hand under my thigh, 3 and I will have you
swear by the LORD, God of heaven and God of earth,
that you will not take a wife for my son from the
daughters of the Canaanites among whom I live,
4 but will go to my land and my family to take a wife
for my son Isaac."
5 The servant said to him, "Suppose the woman is
unwilling to follow me to this land? Should I have
your son go back to the land you came from?"
6 Abraham answered him, "Make sure that you
don't take my son back there. 7 The LORD, the God of
heaven, who took me from my father's house and
from my native land, who spoke to me and swore to
me, 'I will give this land to your offspring'[I] — he will
send his angel before you, and you can take a wife
for my son from there. 8 If the woman is unwilling to
follow you, then you are free from this oath to me,
but don't let my son go back there." 9 So the servant
placed his hand under his master Abraham's thigh
and swore an oath to him concerning this matter.
10 The servant took ten of his master's camels, and
with all kinds of his master's goods in hand, he went
to Aram-naharaim, to Nahor's town. 11 At evening, the

[A] **23:4** Lit *dead from before me* [B] **23:5** Lit *Abraham, saying to him* [C] **23:6** Or *a mighty prince* [D] **23:6** Or *finest graves* [E] **23:10** Lit *ears*, also in vv. 13,16 [F] **23:11** Lit *in the eyes of the sons* [G] **23:16** Lit *400 shekels passing to the merchant* [H] **24:1** Lit *days* [I] **24:7** Lit *seed*

A Hittite marriage document, dated 1900–1700 BC.

Human Sacrifice in the Ancient Near East

by David L. Jenkins

At the southeastern tip of the ancient City of David, the Hinnom Valley meets the Kidron Valley.[1] There, the evil kings Ahaz and Manasseh of Judah set up shrines for the pagan god Molech, and people offered children to him in sacrifice (2Ch 28:3; 33:6). "In times of apostasy some Israelites, apparently in desperation, made their children 'go through the fire to Molech'"[2] (see Lv 18:21; 2Kg 23:10). Bible scholars generally assume that such scriptural references point to the sacrifices of children in the valley of Hinnom. Details of the procedure are unclear. "Some contend that the children were thrown into a raging fire. Certain rabbinic writers describe a hollow bronze statue in the form of a human but with the head of an ox. According to the rabbis, children were placed in the structure that was then heated from below. Drums were pounded to drown out the cries of the children."[3]

Throughout history, human sacrifice has served two primary purposes; the first was to provide assistance to someone after death. Archaeologists have unearthed evidence of such practices in Egypt and in other ancient Near Eastern sites; often several servants were interred with a deceased member of a royal family.[4]

The second reason for human sacrifice was to please, communicate with, or appease a deity. Ancient persons believed human blood to be "the sacred life force."[5] Sacrificing a human life was for them, therefore, the ultimate possible offering to their god. Such a sacrifice, they believed, certainly ensured the god's blessing. This second reason seems to be the motivation behind such practices of peoples living in and around ancient Canaan. King Mesha of Moab sacrificed his son in an attempt to persuade his god to help him in battle (2Kg 3:27).

THE PHOENICIANS

Phoenician culture had a strong influence on the ancient Israelites. Phoenician religion was based on

View of the Hinnom Valley, which is on the south side of the ancient City of David. In the Hinnom, Judah's kings Ahaz and Manasseh set up shrines for Molech. Sacrificing children was part of the Molech worship traditions.

Ruins at Dibon, the ancient capital of Moab and the site where archaeologists discovered the Moabite Stone.

The stele of Mesha, also known as the Moabite Stone, tells how Chemosh (the primary god of Moab) helped release Moab's King Mesha from Israelite domination.

fertility rites that were part of Baal worship. Beyond Baal worship practices, the Phoenicians may have influenced the Hebrews to observe rites involving child sacrifice.

In its early history, Carthage, in North Africa, was a Phoenician city-state. Carthage had a particular burial area that covered about 1 ½ acres. At this sacred site, called a *tofet* or *topheth*, archaeologists uncovered about twenty thousand urns that contained the bones and charred remains of infants and small animals. An inscription at the site mentions *mlk*, which many biblical scholars equate with the pagan god Molech.

In Israel, part of the Hinnom Valley was called Topheth in the Old Testament (2Kg 23:10; Jr 7:31–32). This was a place associated with burials and funerary pyres, and where people sacrificed their sons or daughters "in the fire to Molech" (2Kg 23:10). Evidently some of God's people had adopted the Phoenician practice.

THE NABATEANS

The Bible does not mention the Nabateans, yet they exerted a strong influence on the people of Israel during the intertestamental and New Testament eras.[6] Petra (in modern Jordan) was their capital city; they expanded from there into Moab and Edom.

Historians typically depict the Nabateans as a peaceful and civilized people. Their priests, however, evidently sacrificed human lives at the high place of Petra, as well as at other places in their kingdom. "Al Uzza, the morning star goddess [of the Nabateans], is thought to have called for the sacrifice of boys and girls. The philosopher Porphyrius reported that once a year, a boy's throat was cut in a sacrificial ceremony."[7]

THE BIBLICAL CONNECTION

The Bible contains two well-known stories that allude to human sacrifice. Jephthah vowed to the Lord that if he won the war against the Ammonites, the first thing to greet him when he returned home he would offer as a burnt offering. As residents of the region and era often kept small animals inside part of the house for protection from predators, many believe that Jephthah expected a sheep or goat to wander outside as he neared home. This practice and expectation help explain Jephthah's shock and devastation when his only daughter came out of the house

Ruins on Byrsa Hill in Carthage, which is in northern Africa. The sacred precinct at Carthage, the Topheth, covered about 1 ½ acres. Thousands of urns containing the sacrificial, cremated remains of animals and small children have been found there.

to meet him, and thus was to be the offering Jephthah had promised. He clearly had not planned on sacrificing his only daughter. She did not hesitate, though, to encourage her father to fulfill his vow, and, according to the biblical record, he appears to have done so (Jdg 11:29–40).

Genesis 22 records the other story dealing with human sacrifice. God commanded Abraham to offer his son Isaac as a sacrifice. God observed the unquestioning obedience of Abraham and, at the last moment, rescinded the command and provided a ram to be sacrificed as a substitute for Isaac.

God clearly revealed his abhorrence of human sacrifice (Dt 18:9–12). Yet the New Testament lists Abraham and Jephthah as two heroes of the faith (Heb 11:17,32). The apostle Paul urged the Christians in Rome, "present your bodies as a living sacrifice, holy and pleasing to God; this is your true worship" (Rm 12:1). ✣

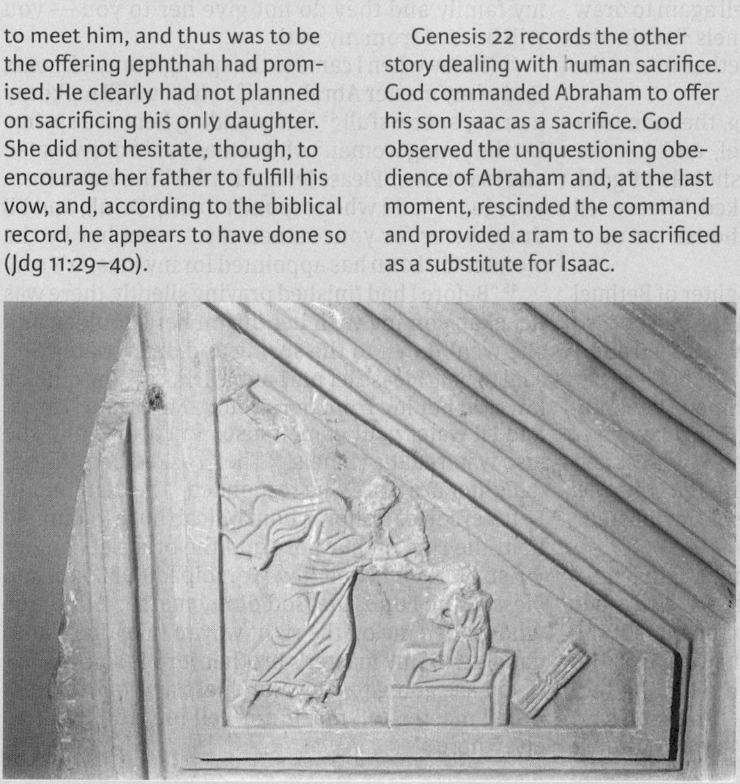

[1] Joseph A. Callaway, "Jerusalem" in *The Biblical World: A Dictionary of Biblical Archaeology*, ed. Charles F. Pfeiffer (Grand Rapids: Baker, 1966), 311. [2] Paul E. Robertson, "Molech" in *HIBD*, 1148. [3] Robertson, "Molech." [4] "Human Sacrifice" in *Encyclopaedia Britannica*, November 21, 2001, www.britannica.com/EBchecked/topic/275881/humansacrifice. [5] "Human Sacrifice." [6] "Nabateans" in *HIBD*, 1166. [7] N. W. Hutchings, *Petra in History and Prophecy* (Oklahoma City: Hearthstone, 1991), 69.

From Ephesus, relief from a Byzantine banister shows Abraham as he was about to offer Isaac.

time when women went out to draw water, he made the camels kneel beside a well outside the town.

12 "LORD, God of my master Abraham," he prayed, "make this happen for me today, and show kindness to my master Abraham. 13 I am standing here at the spring where the daughters of the men of the town are coming out to draw water. 14 Let the girl to whom I say, 'Please lower your water jug so that I may drink,' and who responds, 'Drink, and I'll water your camels also' — let her be the one you have appointed for your servant Isaac. By this I will know that you have shown kindness to my master."

15 Before he had finished speaking, there was Rebekah — daughter of Bethuel son of Milcah, the wife of Abraham's brother Nahor — coming with a jug on her shoulder. 16 Now the girl was very beautiful, a virgin — no man had been intimate with her. She went down to the spring, filled her jug, and came up. 17 Then the servant ran to meet her and said, "Please let me have a little water from your jug."

18 She replied, "Drink, my lord." She quickly lowered her jug to her hand and gave him a drink. 19 When she had finished giving him a drink, she said, "I'll also draw water for your camels until they have had enough to drink."[A] 20 She quickly emptied her jug into the trough and hurried to the well again to draw water. She drew water for all his camels 21 while the man silently watched her to see whether or not the LORD had made his journey a success.

22 As the camels finished drinking, the man took a gold ring weighing half a shekel, and for her wrists two bracelets weighing ten shekels of gold. 23 "Whose daughter are you?" he asked. "Please tell me, is there room in your father's house for us to spend the night?"

24 She answered him, "I am the daughter of Bethuel son of Milcah, whom she bore to Nahor." 25 She also said to him, "We have plenty of straw and feed and a place to spend the night."

26 Then the man knelt low, worshiped the LORD, 27 and said, "Blessed be the LORD, the God of my master Abraham, who has not withheld his kindness and faithfulness from my master. As for me, the LORD has led me on the journey to the house of my master's relatives."

28 The girl ran and told her mother's household about these things. 29 Now Rebekah had a brother named Laban, and Laban ran out to the man at the spring. 30 As soon as he had seen the ring and the bracelets on his sister's wrists, and when he had heard his sister Rebekah's words — "The man said this to me!" — he went to the man. He was standing there by the camels at the spring.

31 Laban said, "Come, you who are blessed by the LORD. Why are you standing out here? I have prepared the house and a place for the camels." 32 So the man came to the house, and the camels were unloaded. Straw and feed were given to the camels, and water was brought to wash his feet and the feet of the men with him.

33 A meal was set before him, but he said, "I will not eat until I have said what I have to say."

So Laban said, "Please speak."

34 "I am Abraham's servant," he said. 35 "The LORD has greatly blessed my master, and he has become rich. He has given him flocks and herds, silver and gold, male and female slaves, and camels and donkeys. 36 Sarah, my master's wife, bore a son to my master in her[B] old age, and he has given him everything he owns. 37 My master put me under this oath: 'You will not take a wife for my son from the daughters of the Canaanites in whose land I live 38 but will go to my father's family and to my clan to take a wife for my son.' 39 But I said to my master, 'Suppose the woman will not come back with me?' 40 He said to me, 'The LORD before whom I have walked will send his angel with you and make your journey a success, and you will take a wife for my son from my clan and from my father's family. 41 Then you will be free from my oath if you go to my family and they do not give her to you — you will be free from my oath.'

42 "Today when I came to the spring, I prayed: LORD, God of my master Abraham, if only you will make my journey successful! 43 I am standing here at a spring. Let the young woman[C] who comes out to draw water, and I say to her, 'Please let me drink a little water from your jug,' 44 and who responds to me, 'Drink, and I'll draw water for your camels also' — let her be the woman the LORD has appointed for my master's son.

45 "Before I had finished praying silently, there was Rebekah coming with her jug on her shoulder, and she went down to the spring and drew water. So I said to her, 'Please let me have a drink.' 46 She quickly lowered her jug from her shoulder and said, 'Drink, and I'll water your camels also.' So I drank, and she also watered the camels. 47 Then I asked her, 'Whose daughter are you?' She responded, 'The daughter of Bethuel son of Nahor, whom Milcah bore to him.' So I put the ring on her nose and the bracelets on her wrists. 48 Then I knelt low, worshiped the LORD, and blessed the LORD, the God of my master Abraham, who guided me on the right way to take the granddaughter of my master's brother for his son. 49 Now, if you are going to show kindness and faithfulness to my master, tell me; if not, tell me, and I will go elsewhere."[D]

[A] **24:19** Lit *they are finished drinking* [B] **24:36** Sam, LXX read *his* [C] **24:43** Or *the virgin* [D] **24:49** Lit *go to the right or to the left*

50 Laban and Bethuel answered, "This is from the LORD; we have no choice in the matter.[A] 51 Rebekah is here in front of you. Take her and go, and let her be a wife for your master's son, just as the LORD has spoken."

52 When Abraham's servant heard their words, he bowed to the ground before the LORD. 53 Then he brought out objects of silver and gold, and garments, and gave them to Rebekah. He also gave precious gifts to her brother and her mother. 54 Then he and the men with him ate and drank and spent the night.

When they got up in the morning, he said, "Send me to my master."

55 But her brother and mother said, "Let the girl stay with us for about ten days. Then she[B] can go."

56 But he responded to them, "Do not delay me, since the LORD has made my journey a success. Send me away so that I may go to my master."

57 So they said, "Let's call the girl and ask her opinion."[C]

58 They called Rebekah and said to her, "Will you go with this man?"

She replied, "I will go." 59 So they sent away their sister Rebekah with the one who had nursed and raised her,[D] and Abraham's servant and his men.

60 They blessed Rebekah, saying to her:

Our sister, may you become
thousands upon ten thousands.
May your offspring possess
the city gates of their[E] enemies.

61 Then Rebekah and her female servants got up, mounted the camels, and followed the man. So the servant took Rebekah and left.

62 Now Isaac was returning from Beer-lahai-roi,[F] for he was living in the Negev region. 63 In the early evening Isaac went out to walk[G] in the field, and looking up he saw camels coming. 64 Rebekah looked up, and when she saw Isaac, she got down from her camel 65 and asked the servant, "Who is that man in the field coming to meet us?"

The servant answered, "It is my master." So she took her veil and covered herself. 66 Then the servant told Isaac everything he had done.

67 And Isaac brought her into the tent of his mother Sarah and took Rebekah to be his wife. Isaac loved her, and he was comforted after his mother's death.

ABRAHAM'S OTHER WIFE AND SONS

25 Abraham had taken[H] another wife, whose name was Keturah, 2 and she bore him Zimran, Jokshan, Medan, Midian, Ishbak, and Shuah. 3 Jokshan fathered Sheba and Dedan. Dedan's sons were the Asshurim, Letushim, and Leummim. 4 And Midian's sons were Ephah, Epher, Hanoch, Abida, and Eldaah. All these were sons of Keturah. 5 Abraham gave everything he owned to Isaac. 6 But Abraham gave gifts to the sons of his concubines, and while he was still alive he sent them eastward, away from his son Isaac, to the land of the East.

ABRAHAM'S DEATH

7 This is the length of Abraham's life:[I] 175 years. 8 He took his last breath and died at a good old age, old and contented,[J] and he was gathered to his people. 9 His sons Isaac and Ishmael buried him in the cave of Machpelah near Mamre, in the field of Ephron son of Zohar the Hethite. 10 This was the field that Abraham bought from the Hethites. Abraham was buried there with his wife Sarah. 11 After Abraham's death, God blessed his son Isaac, who lived near Beer-lahai-roi.

ISHMAEL'S FAMILY RECORDS

12 These are the family records of Abraham's son Ishmael, whom Hagar the Egyptian, Sarah's slave, bore to Abraham. 13 These are the names of Ishmael's sons; their names according to the family records are Nebaioth, Ishmael's firstborn, then Kedar, Adbeel, Mibsam, 14 Mishma, Dumah, Massa, 15 Hadad, Tema, Jetur, Naphish, and Kedemah. 16 These are Ishmael's sons, and these are their names by their settlements and encampments: twelve leaders[K] of their clans.[L] 17 This is the length[M] of Ishmael's life: 137 years. He took his last breath and died, and was gathered to his people. 18 And they[N] settled from Havilah to Shur, which is opposite Egypt as you go toward Asshur.[O] He[P] stayed near[Q] all his relatives.

THE BIRTH OF JACOB AND ESAU

19 These are the family records of Isaac son of Abraham. Abraham fathered Isaac. 20 Isaac was forty years old when he took as his wife Rebekah daughter of Bethuel the Aramean from Paddan-aram and sister of Laban the Aramean. 21 Isaac prayed to the LORD on behalf of his wife because she was childless. The LORD was receptive to his prayer, and his wife Rebekah conceived. 22 But the children inside her struggled with each other, and she said, "Why is this happening to me?"[R] So she went to inquire of the LORD. 23 And the LORD said to her:

[A] **24:50** Lit *we cannot say to you anything bad or good* [B] **24:55** Or *you* [C] **24:57** Lit *mouth* [D] **24:59** Lit *with her wet nurse*; Gn 35:8 [E] **24:60** Lit *his* [F] **24:62** = A Well of the Living One Who Sees Me [G] **24:63** Or *pray*, or *meditate*; Hb obscure [H] **25:1** Or *Abraham took* [I] **25:7** Lit *And these are the days of the years of the life of Abraham that he lived* [J] **25:8** Sam, LXX, Syr read *full of days* [K] **25:16** Or *chieftains* [L] **25:16** Or *peoples* [M] **25:17** Lit *And these are the years* [N] **25:18** LXX, Vg read *he* [O] **25:18** Or *Assyria* [P] **25:18** = Ishmael and his descendants [Q] **25:18** Or *He settled down alongside of* [R] **25:22** Lit *said, "If thus, why this I?"*

Two nations are in your womb;
two peoples will come from you
and be separated.
One people will be stronger than the other,
and the older will serve the younger.

24 When her time came to give birth, there were indeed twins in her womb. 25 The first one came out red-looking,[A] covered with hair[B] like a fur coat, and they named him Esau. 26 After this, his brother came out grasping Esau's heel with his hand. So he was named Jacob.[C] Isaac was sixty years old when they were born.

ESAU SELLS HIS BIRTHRIGHT

27 When the boys grew up, Esau became an expert hunter, an outdoorsman,[D] but Jacob was a quiet man who stayed at home.[E] 28 Isaac loved Esau because he had a taste for wild game, but Rebekah loved Jacob.

29 Once when Jacob was cooking a stew, Esau came in from the field exhausted. 30 He said to Jacob, "Let me eat some of that red stuff, because I'm exhausted." That is why he was also named Edom.[F]

31 Jacob replied, "First sell me your birthright."

32 "Look," said Esau, "I'm about to die, so what good is a birthright to me?"

33 Jacob said, "Swear to me first." So he swore to Jacob and sold his birthright to him. 34 Then Jacob gave bread and lentil stew to Esau; he ate, drank, got up, and went away. So Esau despised his birthright.

THE PROMISE REAFFIRMED TO ISAAC

26 There was another famine in the land in addition to the one that had occurred in Abraham's time. And Isaac went to Abimelech, king of the Philistines, at Gerar. 2 The LORD appeared to him and said, "Do not go down to Egypt. Live in the land that I tell you about; 3 stay in this land as an alien, and I will be with you and bless you. For I will give all these lands to you and your offspring, and I will confirm the oath that I swore to your father Abraham. 4 I will make your offspring as numerous as the stars of the sky, I will give your offspring all these lands, and all the nations of the earth will be blessed[G] by your offspring, 5 because Abraham listened to me and kept my mandate, my commands, my statutes, and my instructions." 6 So Isaac settled in Gerar.

ISAAC'S DECEPTION

7 When the men of the place asked about his wife, he said, "She is my sister," for he was afraid to say "my wife," thinking, "The men of the place will kill me on account of Rebekah, for she is a beautiful woman." 8 When Isaac had been there for some time, Abimelech king of the Philistines looked down from the window and was surprised to see[H] Isaac caressing his wife Rebekah.

9 Abimelech sent for Isaac and said, "So she is really your wife! How could you say, 'She is my sister'?"

Isaac answered him, "Because I thought I might die on account of her."

10 Then Abimelech said, "What have you done to us? One of the people could easily have slept with your wife, and you would have brought guilt on us." 11 So Abimelech warned all the people, "Whoever harms this man or his wife will certainly be put to death."

CONFLICTS OVER WELLS

12 Isaac sowed seed in that land, and in that year he reaped[I] a hundred times what was sown. The LORD blessed him, 13 and the man became rich and kept getting richer until he was very wealthy. 14 He had flocks of sheep, herds of cattle, and many slaves, and the Philistines were envious of him. 15 Philistines stopped up all the wells that his father's servants had dug in the days of his father Abraham, filling them with dirt. 16 And Abimelech said to Isaac, "Leave us, for you are much too powerful for us."[J]

17 So Isaac left there, camped in the Gerar Valley, and lived there. 18 Isaac reopened the wells that had been dug in the days of his father Abraham and that the Philistines had stopped up after Abraham died. He gave them the same names his father had given them. 19 Then Isaac's servants dug in the valley and found a well of spring[K] water there. 20 But the herdsmen of Gerar quarreled with Isaac's herdsmen and said, "The water is ours!" So he named the well Esek[L] because they argued with him. 21 Then they dug another well and quarreled over that one also, so he named it Sitnah.[M] 22 He moved from there and dug another, and they did not quarrel over it. He named it Rehoboth[N] and said, "For now the LORD has made space for us, and we will be fruitful in the land."

THE LORD APPEARS TO ISAAC

23 From there he went up to Beer-sheba, 24 and the LORD appeared to him that night and said, "I am the God of your father Abraham. Do not be afraid, for I am with you. I will bless you and multiply your offspring because of my servant Abraham."

25 So he built an altar there, called on the name of the LORD, and pitched his tent there. Isaac's servants also dug a well there.

[A] **25:25** In Hb, *red-looking* sounds like "Edom"; Gn 32:3. [B] **25:25** In Hb, *hair* sounds like "Seir"; Gn 32:3. [C] **25:26** = He Grasps the Heel [D] **25:27** Lit *a man of the field* [E] **25:27** Lit *man living in tents* [F] **25:30** = Red [G] **26:4** Or *will consider themselves blessed* [H] **26:8** Or *and he looked and behold—* [I] **26:12** Lit *found* [J] **26:16** Or *are more numerous than we are* [K] **26:19** Lit *living* [L] **26:20** = Argument [M] **26:21** = Hostility [N] **26:22** = Open Spaces

COVENANT WITH ABIMELECH

26 Now Abimelech came to him from Gerar with
Ahuzzath his adviser and Phicol the commander of
his army. 27 Isaac said to them, "Why have you come
to me? You hated me and sent me away from you."
28 They replied, "We have clearly seen how the LORD
has been with you. We think there should be an oath
between two parties — between us and you. Let us
make a covenant with you: 29 You will not harm us,
just as we have not harmed you but have done only
what was good to you, sending you away in peace.
You are now blessed by the LORD."
30 So he prepared a banquet for them, and they
ate and drank. 31 They got up early in the morning
and swore an oath to each other.[A] Isaac sent them on
their way, and they left him in peace. 32 On that same
day Isaac's servants came to tell him about the well
they had dug, saying to him, "We have found water!"
33 He called it Sheba.[B] Therefore the name of the city
is still Beer-sheba[C] today.

ESAU'S WIVES

34 When Esau was forty years old, he took as his wives
Judith daughter of Beeri the Hethite, and Basemath
daughter of Elon the Hethite. 35 They made life bitter[D]
for Isaac and Rebekah.

THE STOLEN BLESSING

27 When Isaac was old and his eyes were so weak
that he could not see, he called his older son
Esau and said to him, "My son."
And he answered, "Here I am."
2 He said, "Look, I am old and do not know the day
of my death. 3 So now take your hunting gear, your
quiver and bow, and go out in the field to hunt some
game for me. 4 Then make me a delicious meal that I
love and bring it to me to eat, so that I can bless you
before I die."
5 Now Rebekah was listening to what Isaac said to
his son Esau. So while Esau went to the field to hunt
some game to bring in, 6 Rebekah said to her son Jacob, "Listen! I heard your father talking with your
brother Esau. He said, 7 'Bring me game and make a
delicious meal for me to eat so that I can bless you
in the LORD's presence before I die.' 8 Now, my son,
listen to me and do what I tell you. 9 Go to the flock
and bring me two choice young goats, and I will make
them into a delicious meal for your father — the kind
he loves. 10 Then take it to your father to eat so that
he may bless you before he dies."
11 Jacob answered Rebekah his mother, "Look, my
brother Esau is a hairy man, but I am a man with
smooth skin. 12 Suppose my father touches me. Then
I will be revealed to him as a deceiver and bring a
curse rather than a blessing on myself."
13 His mother said to him, "Your curse be on me, my
son. Just obey me and go get them for me."
14 So he went and got the goats and brought them to
his mother, and his mother made the delicious food
his father loved. 15 Then Rebekah took the best clothes
of her older son Esau, which were in the house, and
had her younger son Jacob wear them. 16 She put the
skins of the young goats on his hands and the smooth
part of his neck. 17 Then she handed the delicious food
and the bread she had made to her son Jacob.
18 When he came to his father, he said, "My father."
And he answered, "Here I am. Who are you, my
son?"
19 Jacob replied to his father, "I am Esau, your firstborn. I have done as you told me. Please sit up and eat
some of my game so that you may bless me."
20 But Isaac said to his son, "How did you ever find
it so quickly, my son?"
He replied, "Because the LORD your God made it
happen for me."
21 Then Isaac said to Jacob, "Please come closer so
I can touch you, my son. Are you really my son Esau
or not?"
22 So Jacob came closer to his father Isaac. When
he touched him, he said, "The voice is the voice of
Jacob, but the hands are the hands of Esau." 23 He did
not recognize him, because his hands were hairy like
those of his brother Esau; so he blessed him. 24 Again
he asked, "Are you really my son Esau?"
And he replied, "I am."
25 Then he said, "Bring it closer to me, and let me
eat some of my son's game so that I can bless you."
Jacob brought it closer to him, and he ate; he brought
him wine, and he drank.
26 Then his father Isaac said to him, "Please come
closer and kiss me, my son." 27 So he came closer
and kissed him. When Isaac smelled[E] his clothes, he
blessed him and said:

Ah, the smell of my son
is like the smell of a field
that the LORD has blessed.
28 May God give to you —
from the dew of the sky
and from the richness of the land —
an abundance of grain and new wine.
29 May peoples serve you
and nations bow in homage to you.
Be master over your relatives;
may your mother's sons bow in homage
to you.
Those who curse you will be cursed,
and those who bless you will be blessed.

[A] **26:31** Lit *swore, each man to his brother* [B] **26:33** Or *Shibah* [C] **26:33** = Well of the Oath [D] **26:35** Lit *And they became bitterness of spirit* [E] **27:27** Lit *smelled the smell of*

"... and Not a Drop to Drink": Water's Effect on Civilization Development

by Claude F. Mariottini

LIFE IN THE DESERT

Isaac moved throughout the land in search of good pasture for his sheep and goats. During times of drought, seminomadic people moved from place to place, as Isaac did, to find water for their flocks. Drought caused disputes between the inhabitants of the cities and seminomads over water rights because the cities also had meadowlands and flocks that needed water.

In Gerar, Isaac planted crops and had an abundant harvest. Because of God's blessing, he became rich and had a large flock and many servants. The Philistines became hostile toward Isaac and expelled him from their city. Banished from a fertile land, Isaac had to dig wells to provide water for his family and flock.

Gerar was a town in the Negev, a desert region in the southern part of Canaan. Gerar was halfway between Beer-sheba and Gaza. Although the annual rainfall in the Negev is insufficient to sustain much agriculture, it rains enough to allow people to maintain small flocks and to provide cultivation of basic crop plants.

The arid areas of Canaan created a challenge to human settlement and to economic development. The natural water supply was too scarce to meet the demands of settled communities. The arid zones of Canaan experienced occasional dry spells, and the lack of rain extended into long-term droughts (Jb 12:15). During these droughts, people suffered, crops failed, and flocks perished (Jr 14:1–3; Hg 1:11).

Because of the harsh climatic nature of arid regions, the need for water is most intense just when water availability by natural precipitation is lacking. This imbalance between water supply and water demand was counterbalanced by the development of other means of providing water, such as wells, cisterns, pools, and water tunnels.

Over the centuries, people settled into the arid and semiarid areas of the ancient Near East and were able to adapt to the harsh conditions of their environment by increasing their water storage capacity and supply. The great civilizations of Mesopotamia and the inhabitants of Canaan and Egypt were able to develop ways of bringing water into their cities. Once water became available beyond the level of subsistence, people built

Water pot dating to the time of Abraham.

The Nile is life sustaining for Egypt. Compare the rich farmland and grazing fields at Luxor with the arid mountains beyond.

Village women carrying water pots.

great cities, thus proving that people can build settlements even in areas with extremely dry conditions. In antiquity, the viability of cities depended on their proximity to water sources.[1]

WATER IN THE ANCIENT NEAR EAST

In Egypt, the main source of water was the Nile River, considered the source of life in ancient Egypt. The waters of the Nile allowed the shores of the river to be easily cultivated (Dt 11:10). The annual flood of the Nile, between July and November, brought a rich silt, called the "black soil," that was deposited on the fields and fertilized the land. Egyptians called this area the Black Land to distinguish it from the Red Land of the desert. The silt the Nile deposited allowed the Egyptians to irrigate the soil and raise different kinds of crops in quantity, including grain (Gn 42:1–2) and vegetables such as cucumbers, melons, leeks, onions, and garlic (Nm 11:5).[2]

On the other side of the ancient Near East, the Tigris and the Euphrates Rivers provided much of the water that aided the development of the ancient Mesopotamian cultures. The word *Mesopotamia* means the land "between the rivers." This section of the ancient Near East is also known as the Fertile Crescent because of its abundant natural resources and the fertile farmland that made possible an increase in food supply and the growth of cities and villages. The area around the Tigris and the Euphrates was the birthplace of the ancient civilizations of the Sumerians, Akkadians, Assyrians, and Babylonians. The rivers' waters, carried by canals, irrigated agricultural fields in the alluvial lands between the rivers.

WATER IN CANAAN

In Canaan, most towns were built on hills, away from the sources of water. Thus the inhabitants of Canaan depended on rains, the morning dew, springs, wadis, brooks, and other sources to supply the physical needs of people, flocks, and land. The people who lived in Canaan developed several ways of supplementing the amount of water available to them.

Springs—Common throughout much of the Holy Land, springs are a natural source of water. In fact, the land of Canaan is described as "a land with streams, springs, and deep water sources, flowing in both valleys and hills" (Dt 8:7). The source of most spring water was the rainfall that seeped into the ground. The amount of water available in a spring varied with the time of the year and the amount of rainfall. Springs furnished sufficient water for communities to use for drinking, irrigation, and watering their flocks. Some cities built canals running from the source of water located outside the city that would bring water into the city.

Pools—In the form of natural or artificial reservoirs, pools collected rainwater for use for drinking, irrigation, and watering flocks. The Bible mentions several pools: of Gibeon (2Sm 2:13), Hebron (4:12), Samaria (1Kg 22:38), Siloam (Jn 9:7), and others. Although the pools held an abundant supply of water, their being open meant evaporation worked against long-term water storage.

Water Tunnels—Some cities built tunnels that went from inside the city, under the walls, to a source of water outside the city. Archaeology has confirmed the existence of water tunnels in Jerusalem, Megiddo, Gibeon, and Hazor.

This water reservoir at Beer-sheba was designed for daily use and times of siege. Five chambers were hewn in the bedrock. Floodwater from a nearby stream was directed into the system through an underground channel. The reservoir held more than 130,000 gallons.

These tunnels were built in a rudimentary fashion by the Canaanites before Israel conquered the land and were vastly improved and expanded during the time of the united monarchy and following. When David became king of Judah, he conquered Jerusalem after Joab used the water shaft to enter the Jebusite city (2Sm 5:8; 1Ch 11:6). The Jebusites cut the water shaft in the limestone rock in the Late Bronze Age to provide access to the Gihon Spring from within the city. The Gihon was the only perennial source of water in Jerusalem.

When Hezekiah, king of Judah, made preparations for war against Sennacherib, king of Assyria, he dug a tunnel under the hill of Ophel (see 2Kg 20:20; 2Ch 32:30). The tunnel served to bring water from the Gihon Spring to a pool inside Jerusalem (Neh 3:15). After the project was completed, an inscription was carved on the rock marking the completion of the project.

The water shaft of Megiddo was built initially by the Canaanites and was improved many times during the period of Israel's monarchy. During Ahab's time (874–853 BC), workers expanded the water system to include an underground passage that led from inside the city to the spring, which was outside the city wall. This water shaft had a flight of steps that led into a tunnel that continued downward as far as the source of the water. The passage was later expanded and deepened so that water flowed back into it and thus provided the city with an underground reservoir that served as a permanent water source for the citizens.[3]

Wells—Another way people who lived in arid areas tried to obtain fresh water was by digging wells. After Isaac left Gerar, he dug five wells, and all of them produced water (Gn 26:18–25,32). People would dig wells to collect water from a subterranean spring. Some cities built deep wells inside the city walls. The depth of the well dictated the size, as deeper wells required a wider opening at the top to prevent collapse of the walls.

Wells were located near major roads, and the water was sold to travelers (Dt 2:6,28). People also dug wells in the wilderness (Gn 16:14), outside a city (24:11), near a city gate (2Sm 23:16), in a field (Gn 29:2), and in a courtyard (2Sm 17:18). At Beth-shemesh, the Canaanites dug a well that remained in use until the end of the northern kingdom. At Gezer, a well dated from the second millennium BC was dug by the Canaanites and was still in use by the time of the Israelites. At Gibeon, a large circular well was reached by a flight of steps into a cave where the water dripped from the rock.[4]

Wells were protected by a wellhead (Gn 29:1–3) or covering (2Sm 17:19) to keep people and animals from falling in. People used leather containers (Gn 21:19), jugs (24:20), or buckets (Jn 4:11) to draw water from the wells. The use of rope and the development of rollers and pulley wheels helped people bring well water to the surface.

Cisterns—Natural sources of water such as perennial rivers and springs are not generally found in most arid areas, and digging for underground water is limited. People who settled in desert areas had to develop the ability to collect and store potable water from runoff during the rainy season. Cisterns provided the solution for storing that rainwater.

Cisterns are artificially constructed reservoirs. Typically bell or bottle-shaped, they differ from wells in that cisterns are filled "by drainage from roofs, streets, or the surface of a slope, or by water channeled from some other source. Wells, on the other hand, might be fed directly from underground springs."[5]

In Canaan, most cisterns were cut into limestone bedrock, which was always porous. Building better cisterns became possible after the discovery during the Early Iron Age (1200 BC) of plasters made of burnt slaked lime that could make the cisterns impermeable. The development of better cisterns contributed to the construction of villages and cities away from the sources of flowing water.[6]

In Canaan, the rainy season, on which the cisterns depended, began in late October and ended in early May. Toward the end of summer, springs and wells either dried up or reduced their flow. When that happened, cisterns and open reservoirs became the only sources of water. Many cisterns were built beside individual houses and fed from roof drainage. These private cisterns were smaller and sunk in the rocks within private boundaries, each owner having his own cistern (2Kg 18:31; Pr 5:15).[7] ✣

[1] Keith Schoville, *Biblical Archaeology in Focus* (Grand Rapids: Baker, 1982), 188. [2] John Ruffle, "Nile River" in *HIBD*, 1191. [3] Amihai Mazar, *Archaeology of the Land of the Bible* (New York: Doubleday, 1992), 479–80. [4] James B. Pritchard, "The Water System at Gibeon," in *Biblical Archaeologist* (*BA*) 19 (1956): 66–75. [5] Archibald C. Dickie and Dorothea W. Harvey, "Cistern" in *ISBE*, 1:702. [6] John Peter Oleson, "Water Works" in *ABD*, 6:887. [7] See "Water Supply" in *The Archaeological Encyclopedia of the Holy Land*, ed. Avraham Negev (Nashville: Thomas Nelson, 1986), 394–96.

The springs at Dan serve as headwaters to the Jordan River.

30 As soon as Isaac had finished blessing Jacob and Jacob had left the presence of his father Isaac, his brother Esau arrived from his hunting. 31 He had also made some delicious food and brought it to his father. He said to his father, "Let my father get up and eat some of his son's game, so that you may bless me."

32 But his father Isaac said to him, "Who are you?"

He answered, "I am Esau your firstborn son."

33 Isaac began to tremble uncontrollably. "Who was it then," he said, "who hunted game and brought it to me? I ate it all before you came in, and I blessed him. Indeed, he will be blessed!"

34 When Esau heard his father's words, he cried out with a loud and bitter cry and said to his father, "Bless me too, my father!"

35 But he replied, "Your brother came deceitfully and took your blessing."

36 So he said, "Isn't he rightly named Jacob?[A] For he has cheated me twice now. He took my birthright, and look, now he has taken my blessing." Then he asked, "Haven't you saved a blessing for me?"

37 But Isaac answered Esau, "Look, I have made him a master over you, have given him all of his relatives as his servants, and have sustained him with grain and new wine. What then can I do for you, my son?"

38 Esau said to his father, "Do you have only one blessing, my father? Bless me too, my father!" And Esau wept loudly.[B]

39 His father Isaac answered him,

Look, your dwelling place will be
away from the richness of the land,
away from the dew of the sky above.
40 You will live by your sword,
and you will serve your brother.
But when you rebel,[C]
you will break his yoke from your neck.

ESAU'S ANGER

41 Esau held a grudge against Jacob because of the blessing his father had given him. And Esau determined in his heart, "The days of mourning for my father are approaching; then I will kill my brother Jacob."

42 When the words of her older son Esau were reported to Rebekah, she summoned her younger son Jacob and said to him, "Listen, your brother Esau is consoling himself by planning to kill you. 43 So now, my son, listen to me. Flee at once to my brother Laban in Haran, 44 and stay with him for a few days until your brother's anger subsides — 45 until your brother's rage turns away from you and he forgets what you have done to him. Then I will send for you and bring you back from there. Why should I lose you both in one day?"

46 So Rebekah said to Isaac, "I'm sick of my life because of these Hethite girls. If Jacob marries someone from around here,[D] like these Hethite girls, what good is my life?"

JACOB'S DEPARTURE

28 So Isaac summoned Jacob, blessed him, and commanded him, "Do not marry a Canaanite girl. 2 Go at once to Paddan-aram, to the house of Bethuel, your mother's father. Marry one of the daughters of Laban, your mother's brother. 3 May God Almighty bless you and make you fruitful and multiply you so that you become an assembly of peoples. 4 May God give you and your offspring the blessing of Abraham so that you may possess the land where you live as a foreigner, the land God gave to Abraham." 5 So Isaac sent Jacob to Paddan-aram, to Laban son of Bethuel the Aramean, the brother of Rebekah, the mother of Jacob and Esau.

6 Esau noticed that Isaac blessed Jacob and sent him to Paddan-aram to get a wife there. When he blessed him, Isaac commanded Jacob, "Do not marry a Canaanite girl." 7 And Jacob listened to his father and mother and went to Paddan-aram. 8 Esau realized that his father Isaac disapproved of the Canaanite women, 9 so Esau went to Ishmael and married, in addition to his other wives, Mahalath daughter of Ishmael, Abraham's son. She was the sister of Nebaioth.

JACOB AT BETHEL

10 Jacob left Beer-sheba and went toward Haran. 11 He reached a certain place and spent the night there because the sun had set. He took one of the stones from the place, put it there at his head, and lay down in that place. 12 And he dreamed: A stairway was set on the ground with its top reaching the sky, and God's angels were going up and down on it. 13 The LORD was standing there beside him,[E] saying, "I am the LORD, the God of your father Abraham and the God of Isaac. I will give you and your offspring the land on which you are lying. 14 Your offspring will be like the dust of the earth, and you will spread out toward the west, the east, the north, and the south. All the peoples on earth will be blessed through you and your offspring. 15 Look, I am with you and will watch over you wherever you go. I will bring you back to this land, for I will not leave you until I have done what I have promised you."

16 When Jacob awoke from his sleep, he said, "Surely the LORD is in this place, and I did not know it."

[A] **27:36** = He Grasps the Heel [B] **27:38** Lit *Esau lifted up his voice and wept* [C] **27:40** Hb obscure [D] **27:46** Lit *someone like these daughters of the land* [E] **28:13** Or *there above it*

Firstborn in the Old Testament

by Susan Booth

Horse pull toy from Greece.

Although primogeniture (giving the elder son preference in inheritance) was standard practice during the time of the patriarchs, centuries passed before Mosaic law codified the right of the firstborn. As "the firstfruits of his [father's] virility," the firstborn son would receive a double portion of the inheritance (Dt 21:17). Mosaic law also linked the theological significance of the firstborn to the exodus. Because the Lord had spared the Israelites by passing over them, heir firstborn—both sons and imals—rightly belonged to God 13:2,14–15). Because the Lord ade human sacrifice, Israelite s redeemed their firstborn offering a substitute 34:20). When the newborn nth old, the father paid ion price of five shekels n 18:16). The Lord also Levites to serve him f the firstborn male every Israelite woman –19).

The firstborn son enjoyed a place of honor and privilege in the family, but he also shouldered a number of responsibilities. As the eldest male, he would inherit a double portion of the estate and the leadership of the household. In a patriarchal society, this meant he would assume complete responsibility for the family's property and prosperity. If necessary, he would represent his family in court and exercise judgment over members of his family. If he became head of the family while his parents were still alive, he assumed responsibility for their physical care and that of his sisters until each sister married.[1]

"His roles included presiding at sacrificial meals celebrated by the family, supervising burials and funerary rites, and serving as kinsman-redeemer."[2] Stepping into the role of patriarch with its greater share of responsibilities may well have been the reason for a firstborn son to receive a greater share of the family resources.[3] ❖

[1] Victor H. Matthews, "Family Relationships" in *Dictionary of the Old Testament: Pentateuch*, ed. T. Desmond Alexander and David W. Baker (Downers Grove, IL: InterVarsity, 2003), 293. [2] John H. Walton, "Genesis" in *Zondervan Illustrated Bible Backgrounds Commentary*, ed. John H. Walton (Grand Rapids: Zondervan, 2009), 106. [3] Walton, "Genesis," 105.

Five-shekel weight from Iron Age III (eighth–sixth c. BC); stone is inscribed with the Hebrew sign for *shekel*.

17 He was afraid and said, "What an awesome place
this is! This is none other than the house of God. This
is the gate of heaven."
18 Early in the morning Jacob took the stone that
was near his head and set it up as a marker. He poured
oil on top of it 19 and named the place Bethel,[A] though
previously the city was named Luz. 20 Then Jacob
made a vow: "If God will be with me and watch over
me during this journey I'm making, if he provides me
with food to eat and clothing to wear, 21 and if I return
safely to my father's family, then the LORD will be my
God. 22 This stone that I have set up as a marker will
be God's house, and I will give to you a tenth of all
that you give me."

JACOB MEETS RACHEL

29 Jacob resumed his journey[B] and went to the
eastern country.[C] 2 He looked and saw a well in
a field. Three flocks of sheep were lying there beside
it because the sheep were watered from this well. But
a large stone covered the opening of the well. 3 The
shepherds would roll the stone from the opening of
the well and water the sheep when all the flocks[D]
were gathered there. Then they would return the
stone to its place over the well's opening.
4 Jacob asked the men at the well, "My brothers!
Where are you from?"
"We're from Haran," they answered.
5 "Do you know Laban, Nahor's grandson?" Jacob
asked them.
They answered, "We know him."
6 "Is he well?" Jacob asked.
"Yes," they said, "and here is his daughter Rachel,
coming with his sheep."
7 Then Jacob said, "Look, it is still broad daylight.
It's not time for the animals to be gathered. Water the
flock, then go out and let them graze."
8 But they replied, "We can't until all the flocks have
been gathered and the stone is rolled from the well's
opening. Then we will water the sheep."
9 While he was still speaking with them, Rachel
came with her father's sheep, for she was a shep-
herdess. 10 As soon as Jacob saw his uncle Laban's
daughter Rachel with his sheep,[E] he went up and
rolled the stone from the opening and watered his
uncle Laban's sheep. 11 Then Jacob kissed Rachel
and wept loudly.[F] 12 He told Rachel that he was her
father's relative, Rebekah's son. She ran and told
her father.

JACOB DECEIVED

13 When Laban heard the news about his sister's son
Jacob, he ran to meet him, hugged him, and kissed
him. Then he took him to his house, and Jacob told
him all that had happened.
14 Laban said to him, "Yes, you are my own flesh
and blood."[G]
After Jacob had stayed with him a month, 15 Laban
said to him, "Just because you're my relative, should
you work for me for nothing? Tell me what your wages should be."
16 Now Laban had two daughters: the older was
named Leah, and the younger was named Rachel.
17 Leah had tender eyes, but Rachel was shapely and
beautiful. 18 Jacob loved Rachel, so he answered Laban, "I'll work for you seven years for your younger
daughter Rachel."
19 Laban replied, "Better that I give her to you than
to some other man. Stay with me." 20 So Jacob worked
seven years for Rachel, and they seemed like only a
few days to him because of his love for her.
21 Then Jacob said to Laban, "Since my time is complete, give me my wife, so I can sleep with[H] her." 22 So
Laban invited all the men of the place and sponsored
a feast. 23 That evening, Laban took his daughter Leah
and gave her to Jacob, and he slept with her. 24 And
Laban gave his slave Zilpah to his daughter Leah as
her slave.
25 When morning came, there was Leah! So he said
to Laban, "What have you done to me? Wasn't it for
Rachel that I worked for you? Why have you deceived
me?"
26 Laban answered, "It is not the custom in our country to give the younger daughter in marriage before
the firstborn. 27 Complete this week of wedding celebration, and we will also give you this younger one in
return for working yet another seven years for me."
28 And Jacob did just that. He finished the week of
celebration, and Laban gave him his daughter Rachel as his wife. 29 And Laban gave his slave Bilhah to
his daughter Rachel as her slave. 30 Jacob slept with
Rachel also, and indeed, he loved Rachel more than
Leah. And he worked for Laban another seven years.

JACOB'S SONS

31 When the LORD saw that Leah was neglected, he
opened her womb; but Rachel was unable to conceive.
32 Leah conceived, gave birth to a son, and named him
Reuben,[I] for she said, "The LORD has seen my affliction; surely my husband will love me now."
33 She conceived again, gave birth to a son, and
said, "The LORD heard that I am neglected and has
given me this son also." So she named him Simeon.[J]

[A] **28:19** = House of God [B] **29:1** Lit *Jacob picked up his feet* [C] **29:1** Lit *the land of the children of the east* [D] **29:3** Sam, some LXX mss read *flocks and the shepherds* [E] **29:10** Lit *with the sheep of Laban his mother's brother* [F] **29:11** Lit *and he lifted his voice and we* [G] **29:14** Lit *my bone and my flesh* [H] **29:21** Lit *can go to* [I] **29:32** = See Son; in Hb, the name *Reuben* sounds like "has seen my affliction. [J] **29:33** In Hb, the name *Simeon* sounds like "has heard."

34 She conceived again, gave birth to a son, and said, "At last, my husband will become attached to me because I have borne three sons for him." Therefore he was named Levi.[A]

35 And she conceived again, gave birth to a son, and said, "This time I will praise the LORD." Therefore she named him Judah.[B] Then Leah stopped having children.

30 When Rachel saw that she was not bearing Jacob any children, she envied her sister. "Give me sons, or I will die!" she said to Jacob.

2 Jacob became angry with Rachel and said, "Am I in the place of God? He has withheld offspring[C] from you!"

3 Then she said, "Here is my maid Bilhah. Go sleep with her, and she'll bear children for me[D] so that through her I too can build a family." 4 So Rachel gave her slave Bilhah to Jacob as a wife, and he slept with her. 5 Bilhah conceived and bore Jacob a son. 6 Rachel said, "God has vindicated me; yes, he has heard me and given me a son," so she named him Dan.[E]

7 Rachel's slave Bilhah conceived again and bore Jacob a second son. 8 Rachel said, "In my wrestlings with God,[F] I have wrestled with my sister and won," and she named him Naphtali.[G]

9 When Leah saw that she had stopped having children, she took her slave Zilpah and gave her to Jacob as a wife. 10 Leah's slave Zilpah bore Jacob a son. 11 Then Leah said, "What good fortune!"[H] and she named him Gad.[I]

12 When Leah's slave Zilpah bore Jacob a second son, 13 Leah said, "I am happy that the women call me happy," so she named him Asher.[J]

14 Reuben went out during the wheat harvest and found some mandrakes in the field. When he brought them to his mother Leah, Rachel asked, "Please give me some of your son's mandrakes."

15 But Leah replied to her, "Isn't it enough that you have taken my husband? Now you also want to take my son's mandrakes?"

"Well then," Rachel said, "he can sleep with you tonight in exchange for your son's mandrakes."

16 When Jacob came in from the field that evening, Leah went out to meet him and said, "You must come with me, for I have hired you with my son's mandrakes." So Jacob slept with her that night.

17 God listened to Leah, and she conceived and bore Jacob a fifth son. 18 Leah said, "God has rewarded me for giving my slave to my husband," and she named him Issachar.[K]

19 Then Leah conceived again and bore Jacob a sixth son. 20 "God has given me a good gift," Leah said. "This time my husband will honor me because I have borne six sons for him," and she named him Zebulun.[L] 21 Later, Leah bore a daughter and named her Dinah.

22 Then God remembered Rachel. He listened to her and opened her womb. 23 She conceived and bore a son, and she said, "God has taken away my disgrace." 24 She named him Joseph[M] and said, "May the LORD add another son to me."

JACOB'S FLOCKS MULTIPLY

25 After Rachel gave birth to Joseph, Jacob said to Laban, "Send me on my way so that I can return to my homeland. 26 Give me my wives and my children that I have worked for, and let me go. You know how hard I have worked for you."

27 But Laban said to him, "If I have found favor with you, stay. I have learned by divination that the LORD has blessed me because of you." 28 Then Laban said, "Name your wages, and I will pay them."

29 So Jacob said to him, "You know how I have served you and how your herds have fared with me. 30 For you had very little before I came, but now your wealth has increased. The LORD has blessed you because of me. And now, when will I also do something for my own family?"

31 Laban asked, "What should I give you?"

And Jacob said, "You don't need to give me anything. If you do this one thing for me, I will continue to shepherd and keep your flock. 32 Let me go through all your sheep today and remove every sheep that is speckled or spotted, every dark-colored sheep among the lambs, and the spotted and speckled among the female goats. Such will be my wages. 33 In the future when you come to check on my wages, my honesty will testify for me. If I have any female goats that are not speckled or spotted, or any lambs that are not black, they will be considered stolen."

34 "Good," said Laban. "Let it be as you have said."

35 That day Laban removed the streaked and spotted male goats and all the speckled and spotted female goats — every one that had any white on it — and every dark-colored one among the lambs, and he placed his sons in charge of them. 36 He put a three-day journey between himself and Jacob. Jacob, meanwhile, was shepherding the rest of Laban's flock.

37 Jacob then took branches of fresh poplar, almond, and plane wood, and peeled the bark, exposing white stripes on the branches. 38 He set the peeled branches in the troughs in front of the sheep — in the water channels where the sheep came to drink. And

[A] **29:34** In Hb, the name *Levi* sounds like "attached to." [B] **29:35** In Hb, the name *Judah* sounds like "praise." [C] **30:2** Lit *the fruit of the womb* [D] **30:3** Lit *bear on my knees* [E] **30:6** In Hb, the name *Dan* sounds like "has vindicated," or "has judged." [F] **30:8** Or *"With mighty wrestlings* [G] **30:8** In Hb, the name *Naphtali* sounds like "my wrestling." [H] **30:11** Alt Hb tradition, LXX, Vg read *"Good fortune has come!"* [I] **30:11** = Good Fortune [J] **30:13** = Happy [K] **30:18** In Hb, the name *Issachar* sounds like "reward." [L] **30:20** In Hb, the name *Zebulun* sounds like "honored." [M] **30:24** = He Adds

A Personal God?

by Dorman Laird

People in ancient Mesopotamia perceived of forces or powers that permeated their world and their daily lives. These forces inhabited the four realms of existence: the heavens, the earth, the seas, and the underworld.[1] People called the forces "gods" because the people knew they could not escape the so-called deities' presence and dominance. Cities and regions often claimed certain deities as their patron gods and built shrines and temples to honor them. People conducted worship to solicit the gods' favor and to drive off demonic forces.

The ancient Mesopotamians also believed in gods and goddesses that claimed an individual or a household as their own domain. Thorkild Jacobsen coined the term *personal god*, which describes "a person's own and special god who stands in a very close relationship to him, and who ensures that his actions will succeed, indeed, that his whole life will be a success."[2] People believed this personal god maintained a close relationship with an individual and his family. The definition of a "personal god," therefore, refers, not to the existence of a god as a person, but to the "belonging of an individual to a particular god."[3]

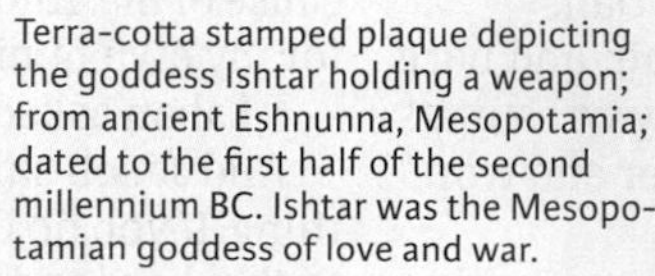

Terra-cotta stamped plaque depicting the goddess Ishtar holding a weapon; from ancient Eshnunna, Mesopotamia; dated to the first half of the second millennium BC. Ishtar was the Mesopotamian goddess of love and war.

Interestingly, the personal gods were rarely given names; rather, they were known by their association with particular individuals or households. In such cases, the personal god's name might be incorporated into the name of the individual whom the god protected; the name of the god was usually El or Ilu.[4] Because people seldom referred to the personal gods by name, one could speculate that this led to the custom of referring to personal gods as "the god of the fathers."

Mesopotamians believed the god or goddess initiated the relationship with an individual. Experiencing good luck or good fortune was an indicator that a person had "acquired a god." Receiving a perceived favorable omen might indicate that a house was about to acquire a god and a bad omen could indicate that "that house will grow poor, [and] will not acquire a god."[5] On occasion, a personal god could be one of the major deities the nation worshiped; usually, though, a personal god was of lesser rank within the pantheon. Even though personal gods adopted individuals, the cultivation of a relationship between the individual and his personal god was the responsibility of the individual and involved religious obligations that were "moral, juridical, and ritual in nature."[6]

The Sumerians believed the higher gods were concerned with more important things than listening to a common man's prayers. "Personal gods were devised as intermediaries between man and the high gods."[7] One ancient Sumerian wisdom text reflects this perspective; it describes a man attempting to move his personal god to intercede before the assembly of the gods. "The main thesis of our poet is that in cases of suffering and adversity, no matter how seemingly unjustified, the victim has but one valid and effective recourse, and that is to continually glorify his god and keep wailing and lamenting before him until he turns a favorable ear to his prayers."[8] In some respects, the cries of the sufferer in the poem resemble the biblical Job's desire for a mediator to plead his case before God.

Rather than portraying a number of personal gods, the Old Testament teaches that the one true God is personal. Explains one scholar:

> By personal, Scripture identifies God as the one who interacts with other persons as a person. God is never presented as some mere abstract concept or impersonal force or power. Rather, He is the all-glorious God who knows, wills, plans, speaks, loves, becomes angry, asks questions, gives commands, listens to praise and prayer, and interacts with His creatures.[9]

This type of shrine reflects temple architecture; its capitals and columns closely resemble some of the architectural elements excavated in archaeological sites. The dove probably represents the goddess Asherah; terra-cotta; ninth–eighth centuries BC; from Jordan. Wealthy families may have used such shrines for household worship.

Also, Scripture describes God as breathing (Gn 2:7). The fact that God is alive, that he creates, and that he redeems fallen humanity fundamentally distinguishes him from the idols of the nations.

Some have attempted to show that the God of Abraham had attributes similar to those of a personal god of ancient Mesopotamia: God was designated the God of the patriarchs; God was always with Abraham wherever he went; God spoke to Abraham and made clear what he had to say; and God made himself visible to Abraham.[10]

The differences between the God of Abraham and the personal gods of ancient Mesopotamia, however, are even more striking than the similarities. For one thing, Yahweh is sovereign over all the nations of the earth. "He is, by his very nature, independent of any state, unlike Ashur, Amnon or Marduk."[11] This fact is evidenced in God's promise that he would give to Abraham the same lands where other gods were worshiped (Gn 15:18–21). Also, Yahweh entered covenants to which he is faithful, in spite of the unfaithfulness of the other party (Jr 31:31–32). Further, the Israelites' worship system was "not the re-enacting of myths about the origin of the world, as in Mesopotamia, nor of nature-myths, as in Canaan."[12] Instead, they worshiped a genuine and personal God who intervened in history.

Perhaps the greatest difference between the personal god imagined by the ancient Mesopotamians and the God of Abraham, Isaac, and Jacob, revealed in history and Scripture, is the fact that God is merciful, gracious, full of truth and goodness, and one who forgives sin. Although he expects obedience from his people, one's relationship to him depends ultimately on God's grace (Ex 34:6–7). ✣

---

[1] Jean-Marc Heimerdinger, "The God of Abraham," *Vox Evangelica* (*VE*) 22 (1992): 41–42. [2] Heimerdinger, "God of Abraham," 43. [3] Heimerdinger, "God of Abraham," 44. [4] Heimerdinger, "God of Abraham." [5] Tammi J. Schneider, *An Introduction to Ancient Mesopotamian Religion* (Grand Rapids: Eerdmans, 2011), 64. [6] Heimerdinger, "God of Abraham," 45. [7] "Ancient Man and His First Civilizations: Sumerian Religion," *Real History Worldwide*, realhistoryww.com/world_history/ancient/Misc/Sumer/Sumerian_Religion.htm. [8] James B. Pritchard, ed., *ANET* with sup., 589. [9] Stephen J. Wellum, "God," in *HIBD* (2015), 652. [10] Heimerdinger, "God of Abraham," 48–49. [11] Heimerdinger, "God of Abraham," 52. [12] Roland de Vaux, *Ancient Israel: Its Life and Institutions* (Grand Rapids: Eerdmans, 1997), 272.

the sheep bred when they came to drink. 39 The flocks
bred in front of the branches and bore streaked,
speckled, and spotted young. 40 Jacob separated the
lambs and made the flocks face the streaked sheep
and the completely dark sheep in Laban's flocks. Then
he set his own stock apart and didn't put them with
Laban's sheep.

41 Whenever the stronger of the flock were breeding, Jacob placed the branches in the troughs, in full
view of the flocks, and they would breed in front of
the branches. 42 As for the weaklings of the flocks,
he did not put out the branches. So it turned out that
the weak sheep belonged to Laban and the stronger
ones to Jacob. 43 And the man became very rich.[A] He
had many flocks, female and male slaves, and camels
and donkeys.

JACOB SEPARATES FROM LABAN

31 Now Jacob heard what Laban's sons were saying: "Jacob has taken all that was our father's
and has built this wealth from what belonged to our
father." 2 And Jacob saw from Laban's face that his
attitude toward him was not the same as before.

3 The LORD said to him, "Go back to the land of your
ancestors and to your family, and I will be with you."

4 Jacob had Rachel and Leah called to the field
where his flocks were. 5 He said to them, "I can see
from your father's face that his attitude toward me is
not the same as before, but the God of my father has
been with me. 6 You know that with all my strength I
have served your father 7 and that he has cheated me
and changed my wages ten times. But God has not let
him harm me. 8 If he said, 'The spotted sheep will be
your wages,' then all the sheep were born spotted.
If he said, 'The streaked sheep will be your wages,'
then all the sheep were born streaked. 9 God has tak-
en away your father's herds and given them to me.

10 "When the flocks were breeding, I saw in a dream
that the streaked, spotted, and speckled males were
mating with the females. 11 In that dream the angel of
God said to me, 'Jacob!' and I said, 'Here I am.' 12 And
he said, 'Look up and see: all the males that are mating
with the flocks are streaked, spotted, and speckled,
for I have seen all that Laban has been doing to you.
13 I am the God of Bethel, where you poured oil on
the stone marker and made a solemn vow to me. Get
up, leave this land, and return to your native land.'"

14 Then Rachel and Leah answered him, "Do we
have any portion or inheritance in our father's family? 15 Are we not regarded by him as outsiders? For
he has sold us and has certainly spent our purchase
price. 16 In fact, all the wealth that God has taken away
from our father belongs to us and to our children. So
do whatever God has said to you."

[A] **30:43** Lit *The man spread out very much, very much*

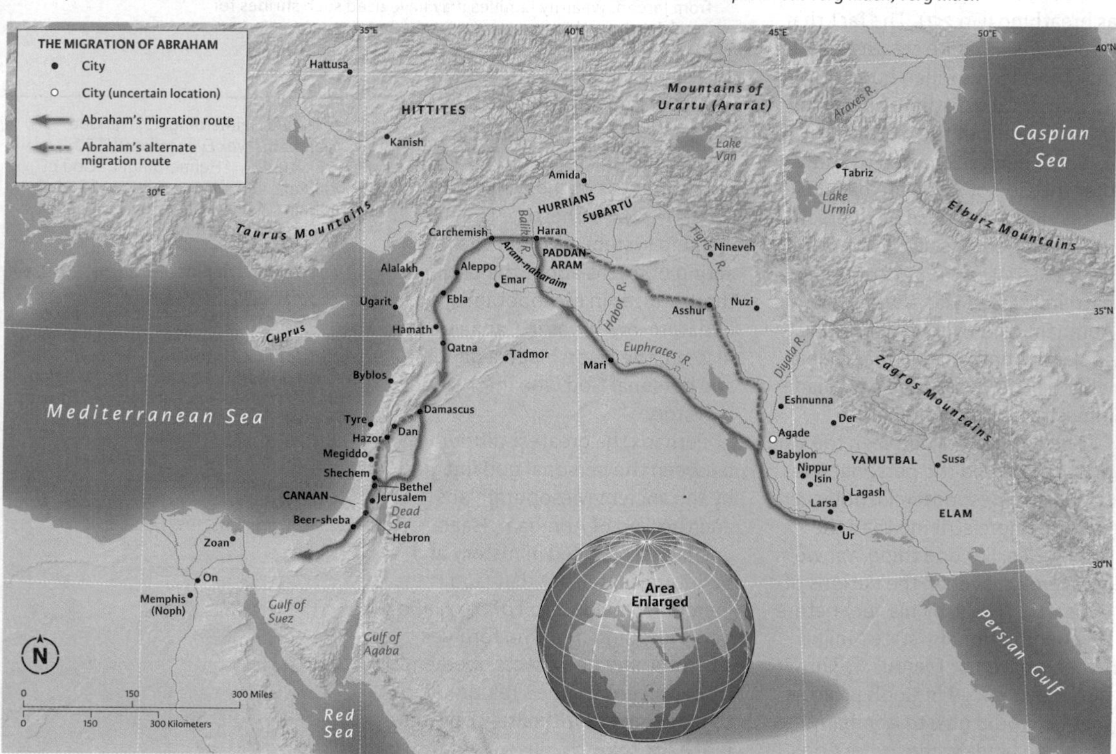

Ancient Marriage Contracts

by Roberta Lou Jones

God planned marriage as a secure relationship between one man and one woman (Mt 19:5–6). Because of human sin, however, matrimony too often includes fear and insecurity. Biblical examples of imperfect marriages include Leah and Rachel, who shared Jacob (Gn 29:18–28). Too often, women were merchandise to buy (Ex 21:7–11) and rewards for military success (Jos 15:16).

Troubled marriages also highlight secular history. The Lipit-Ishtar Law Code (nineteenth c. BC) instructed a man with children by "a harlot from the public square" to provide her grain, oil, and clothing. With common sense, laws prohibited the harlot and the man's wife from living together. Some relationships suggested mere convenience. An Egyptian queen wrote Hittite royalty, "My husband died . . . send me one of your sons, he might become my husband." Lawmakers tried to improve marriage. Hammurabi ruled Babylon from approximately 1728 to 1686 BC. He observed a gadabout wife who neglected her house and husband. Hammurabi commanded someone to throw the woman in water![1] Sadly, problems between husbands and wives frequently overshadowed love and security.

MARRIAGE CONTRACTS

Both verbal and written contracts attempted to stabilize marriages. Although definitions of words varied, many terms and ideas gained wide acceptance in the ancient world.

Bridal gift—The groom's gift to the bride (Gn 34:12).

Mohar—The fathers of the couple discussed the possible marriage. The groom gave a "marriage present," a *mohar*, to the bride's father to show his good intentions, to compensate the bride's family, and to strengthen family ties.

Bride Price—Some scholars interpret the *mohar* as a bride price—a purchase of the bride.

Betrothal Period—If the bride's parents agreed, the couple began their betrothal (engagement) period. Society expected the future groom to exercise servant-leadership and to make loving decisions.[2]

Dowry—The bride's father, or family, contributed the dowry—her possessions. The husband managed the dowry for their mutual benefit. A bride with a good dowry represented a financial and social asset.[3] Caleb gave his daughter a field and springs of water (Jos 15:16–19). Laban offered slaves (Gn 29:24–29).[4]

Ketubah—By the first century BC, Jewish couples chose a written marriage contract, a *ketubah*. Each groom promised a *mohar* if the couple divorced.

Divorce was marital separation. Men could easily divorce their wives. Some cultures offered women this freedom.[5]

SECULAR MARRIAGES

Archaeologists have discovered evidence of marriages in numerous civilizations. History indicates men in Nuzi (2000–1400 BC, Mesopotamia) paid for their brides in livestock, textiles, copper, or silver. Some Nuzi legal contracts allowed delayed payments. Having one wife was the norm—unless the first wife was barren.[6] The Jewish colony of Elephantine (fifth c. BC, Egypt) used papyrus sheets to record marriage contracts. These legal documents mentioned the groom's responsibilities, the bride's dowry, and her personal possessions. Brides listed mirrors, clothing, cosmetic paint, and sandals. The husband agreed to provide the usual food and clothing. In addition, he promised oil for his beloved. (Women in arid Egypt appreciated body oil.)

Slaves also used marriage contracts. Tamut, for instance, mentioned one garment, ointment, a cheap mirror, and possibly sandals in her written agreement. Spoken words were also considered binding. The groom told Tamut's owner, "I have come to you to be given in

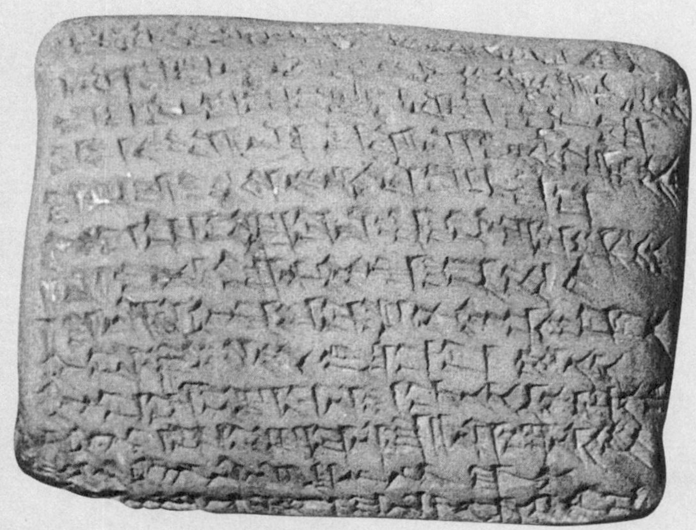

Babylonian marriage contract between Uballitsu-Gula, son of Nabu-nadin-ahi, and Ina-Esagilbanat, daughter of Sumukin; dated 549 BC.

marriage Tamut by name who is your handmaiden. She is my wife, and I her husband from this day and forever."[7]

Zaccur gave his slave Jehoishma a splendid dowry of silver, garments, vessels, and toilet articles. A scribe wrote the contract in the presence of six witnesses.

The fourteenth-century BC world traded horses, exotic animals, chariots, ivory, fancy clothing, precious stones, and gold. In this commercial background, Amenhotep III of Egypt desired another Mitannian princess for his harem. The king of Mitanni demanded a bride price, "without limit, reaching from the earth to the sky." The two rulers exchanged valuable "gifts." Amenhotep sent his ambassador to inspect Princess Taduhepa as a royal Egyptian bridal candidate. The woman passed inspection. So the Mitannian king gave the princess a large dowry, recorded on clay tablets. He begged pagan deities to let the princess be "pleasing to the heart of my brother." Taduhepa and her luxurious items arrived in Egypt where Amenhotep greeted her with great splendor. Thus Mitanni and Egypt arranged a fantastic commercial, political, and romantic venture![8]

BOAZ AND JACOB TAKE WIVES

The marriage of Boaz and Ruth illustrates several Old Testament principles (Ru 4). At the city gate, Boaz received permission from another kinsman to redeem Naomi's inheritance and to marry Ruth. Witnesses watched and listened. Boaz announced he wanted to raise children to honor Naomi's deceased husband (see Dt. 25:5–10). The witnesses responded, "May the LORD make the woman . . . like Rachel and Leah, who together built the house of Israel" (Ru 4:11).

Jacob worked seven years for his uncle Laban, with the verbal agreement to marry beautiful Rachel. Alas, by Laban's trickery, Jacob married the less comely older daughter, Leah. Laban, however, quickly offered Rachel to Jacob as a second wife. Rachel and Leah each received a female slave as partial

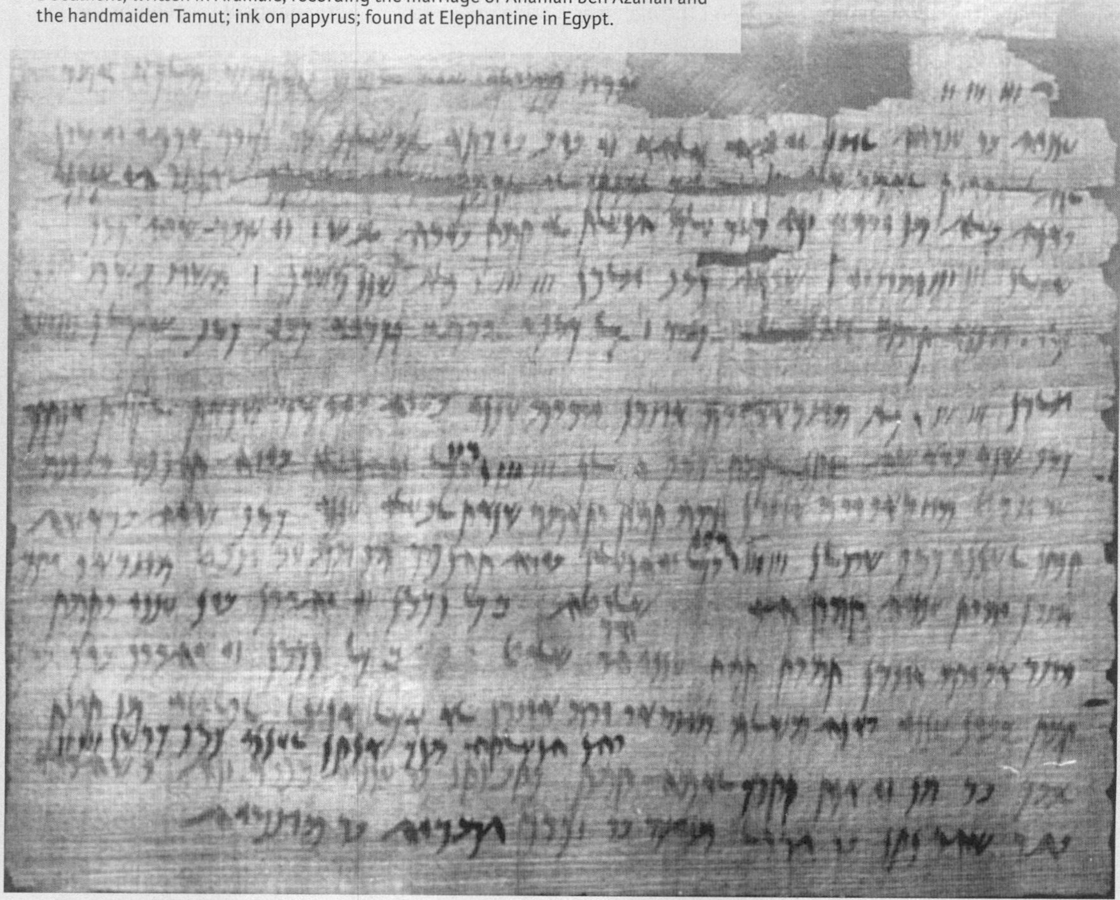

Document, written in Aramaic, recording the marriage of Ananiah ben Azariah and the handmaiden Tamut; ink on papyrus; found at Elephantine in Egypt.

Ruins of Greco-Roman city on Elephantine Island in the Nile. When the Persians ruled Egypt, beginning in 525 BC, a large camp of mercenaries, including Jewish regiments, settled there. The discovery of the Elephantine Papyri has enabled scholars to reconstruct the life of Jewish inhabitants. Most documents deal with legal aspects of marriage, divorce, commerce, and inheritance.

dowry. Jacob toiled another seven years and eventually paid for two bickering wives. He fathered twelve sons and one daughter by his wives and their servants (Gn 27–35).

Despite shortcomings, marriage contracts protected people and property. ❖

[1] "Lipit-Ishtar Law Code," "Suppiluliumas and the Egyptian Queen," and "The Code of Hammurabi" in *ANET*, 1st ed., 159–60, 163, 319, 172, respectively. Hammurabi "reigned 43 years in the first half of the second millennium B.C. His absolute dates are uncertain; his reign began in 1848, 1792, or 1736 B.C." See Gary D. Baldwin and E. Ray Clendenen, "Hammurabi" in *HIBD*, 708. [2] Daniel I. Block, "Marriage and Family in Ancient Israel," in *Marriage and Family in the Biblical World*, ed. Ken M. Campbell (Downers Grove, IL: InterVarsity, 2003), 57–58. [3] Christine Roy Yoder, "The Woman of Substance: A Socioeconomic Reading of Proverbs 31:10-31," *Journal of Biblical Literature* (*JBL*) 122.3 (2002): 432–35, 444. Yoder views Pr 31:10 as a purchase price for a bride, in a culture with marriage being primarily a business transaction. [4] Many terms in marriage contracts varied in meaning. For a discussion of dowry as equivalent to bride-price, see "Dowry" in *HIBD*, 441. [5] John J. Collins, "Marriage, Divorce, and Family in Second Temple Judaism," in *Families in Ancient Israel*, ed. Leo G. Perdue et al. (Louisville: Westminster John Knox, 1997), 113–16. [6] Katarzyna Grosz, "Bridewealth and Dowry in Nuzi," in *Images of Women in Antiquity*, ed. Averil Cameron and Amelie Kuhrt (Detroit: Wayne State University Press, 1983), 199–205. [7] Bezalel Porten, *Archives from Elephantine: The Life of an Ancient Jewish Military Colony* (Berkeley: University of California Press, 1968), 91–92, 206–12, 219–23. [8] George Steindorff and Keith C. Seele (rev. Keith C. Seele), *When Egypt Ruled the East* (Chicago: University of Chicago Press, 1957), 107–9.

17 So Jacob got up and put his children and wives on
the camels. 18 He took all the livestock and possessions
he had acquired in Paddan-aram, and he drove his
herds to go to the land of Canaan, to his father Isaac.
19 When Laban had gone to shear his sheep, Rachel
stole her father's household idols. 20 And Jacob deceived[A] Laban the Aramean, not telling him that he was
fleeing. 21 He fled with all his possessions, crossed the
Euphrates, and headed for[B] the hill country of Gilead.

LABAN OVERTAKES JACOB

22 On the third day Laban was told that Jacob had fled.
23 So he took his relatives with him, pursued Jacob for
seven days, and overtook him in the hill country of
Gilead. 24 But God came to Laban the Aramean in a
dream at night. "Watch yourself!" God warned him.
"Don't say anything to Jacob, either good or bad."

25 When Laban overtook Jacob, Jacob had pitched
his tent in the hill country, and Laban and his relatives
also pitched their tents in the hill country of Gilead.
26 Laban said to Jacob, "What have you done? You
have deceived me and taken my daughters away like
prisoners of war! 27 Why did you secretly flee from
me, deceive me, and not tell me? I would have sent
you away with joy and singing, with tambourines
and lyres, 28 but you didn't even let me kiss my grandchildren and my daughters. You have acted foolishly.
29 I could do you great harm, but last night the God of
your father said to me, 'Watch yourself! Don't say anything to Jacob, either good or bad.' 30 Now you have
gone off because you long for your father's family
— but why have you stolen my gods?"

31 Jacob answered, "I was afraid, for I thought you
would take your daughters from me by force. 32 If
you find your gods with anyone here, he will not
live! Before our relatives, point out anything that is
yours and take it." Jacob did not know that Rachel
had stolen the idols.

33 So Laban went into Jacob's tent, Leah's tent, and
the tents of the two concubines,[C] but he found nothing.
When he left Leah's tent, he went into Rachel's tent.
34 Now Rachel had taken Laban's household idols, put
them in the saddlebag of the camel, and sat on them.
Laban searched the whole tent but found nothing.

35 She said to her father, "Don't be angry, my lord,
that I cannot stand up in your presence; I am having
my period." So Laban searched, but could not find
the household idols.

JACOB'S COVENANT WITH LABAN

36 Then Jacob became incensed and brought charges
against Laban. "What is my crime?" he said to Laban.
"What is my sin, that you have pursued me? 37 You've
searched all my possessions! Have you found anything of yours?[D] Put it here before my relatives and
yours, and let them decide between the two of us.
38 I've been with you these twenty years. Your ewes
and female goats have not miscarried, and I have not
eaten the rams from your flock. 39 I did not bring you
any of the flock torn by wild beasts; I myself bore
the loss. You demanded payment from me for what
was stolen by day or by night. 40 There I was — the
heat consumed me by day and the frost by night, and
sleep fled from my eyes. 41 For twenty years in your
household I served you — fourteen years for your two
daughters and six years for your flocks — and you
have changed my wages ten times! 42 If the God of my
father, the God of Abraham, the Fear of Isaac, had not
been with me, certainly now you would have sent me
off empty-handed. But God has seen my affliction and
my hard work,[E] and he issued his verdict last night."

43 Then Laban answered Jacob, "The daughters are
my daughters; the children, my children; and the
flocks, my flocks! Everything you see is mine! But
what can I do today for these daughters of mine or
for the children they have borne? 44 Come now, let's
make a covenant, you and I. Let it be a witness between the two of us."

45 So Jacob picked out a stone and set it up as a
marker. 46 Then Jacob said to his relatives, "Gather
stones." And they took stones and made a mound,
then ate there by the mound. 47 Laban named the
mound Jegar-sahadutha, but Jacob named it Galeed.[F]

48 Then Laban said, "This mound is a witness between you and me today." Therefore the place was
called Galeed 49 and also Mizpah,[G] for he said, "May
the LORD watch between you and me when we are out
of each other's sight. 50 If you mistreat my daughters
or take other wives, though no one is with us, understand that God will be a witness between you and
me." 51 Laban also said to Jacob, "Look at this mound
and the marker I have set up between you and me.
52 This mound is a witness and the marker is a witness that I will not pass beyond this mound to you,
and you will not pass beyond this mound and this
marker to do me harm. 53 The God of Abraham, and
the gods of Nahor — the gods of their father[H] — will
judge between us." And Jacob swore by the Fear of
his father Isaac. 54 Then Jacob offered a sacrifice on
the mountain and invited his relatives to eat a meal.
So they ate a meal and spent the night on the mountain. 55 Laban got up early in the morning, kissed his
grandchildren and daughters, and blessed them. Then
Laban left to return home.

[A] **31:20** Lit *And he stole the heart of* [B] **31:21** Lit *and set his face to* [C] **31:33** Lit *servants* [D] **31:37** Lit *What have you found from all of the possessions of your house?* [E] **31:42** Lit *and the work of my hands* [F] **31:47** *Jegar-sahadutha* is Aramaic, and *Galeed* is Hb; both names = Mound of Witness [G] **31:49** = Watchtower [H] **31:53** Two Hb mss, LXX omit *the gods of their father*

PREPARING TO MEET ESAU

32 Jacob went on his way, and God's angels met
him. 2 When he saw them, Jacob said, "This
is God's camp." So he called that place Mahanaim.[A]
3 Jacob sent messengers ahead of him to his brother Esau in the land of Seir, the territory of Edom. 4 He
commanded them, "You are to say to my lord Esau,
'This is what your servant Jacob says. I have been
staying with Laban and have been delayed until now.
5 I have oxen, donkeys, flocks, and male and female
slaves. I have sent this message to inform my lord, in
order to seek your favor.' "
6 When the messengers returned to Jacob, they
said, "We went to your brother Esau; he is coming
to meet you — and he has four hundred men with
him." 7 Jacob was greatly afraid and distressed; he
divided the people with him into two camps, along
with the flocks, herds, and camels. 8 He thought, "If
Esau comes to one camp and attacks it, the remaining
one can escape."
9 Then Jacob said, "God of my father Abraham and
God of my father Isaac, the LORD who said to me, 'Go
back to your land and to your family, and I will cause
you to prosper,' 10 I am unworthy of all the kindness
and faithfulness you have shown your servant. Indeed, I crossed over the Jordan with my staff, and now
I have become two camps. 11 Please rescue me from
my brother Esau, for I am afraid of him; otherwise,
he may come and attack me, the mothers, and their
children. 12 You have said, 'I will cause you to prosper,
and I will make your offspring like the sand of the
sea, too numerous to be counted.' "
13 He spent the night there and took part of what he
had brought with him as a gift for his brother Esau:
14 two hundred female goats, twenty male goats, two
hundred ewes, twenty rams, 15 thirty milk camels with
their young, forty cows, ten bulls, twenty female donkeys, and ten male donkeys. 16 He entrusted them to his
slaves as separate herds and said to them, "Go on ahead
of me, and leave some distance between the herds."
17 And he told the first one, "When my brother Esau
meets you and asks, 'Who do you belong to? Where
are you going? And whose animals are these ahead
of you?' 18 then tell him, 'They belong to your servant
Jacob. They are a gift sent to my lord Esau. And look,
he is behind us.' "
19 He also told the second one, the third, and everyone who was walking behind the animals, "Say the
same thing to Esau when you find him. 20 You are also
to say, 'Look, your servant Jacob is right behind us.' "
For he thought, "I want to appease Esau with the gift
that is going ahead of me. After that, I can face him,
and perhaps he will forgive me."
21 So the gift was sent on ahead of him while he
remained in the camp that night. 22 During the night
Jacob got up and took his two wives, his two slave
women, and his eleven sons, and crossed the ford
of Jabbok. 23 He took them and sent them across the
stream, along with all his possessions.

JACOB WRESTLES WITH GOD

24 Jacob was left alone, and a man wrestled with him
until daybreak. 25 When the man saw that he could
not defeat him, he struck Jacob's hip socket as they
wrestled and dislocated his hip. 26 Then he said to
Jacob, "Let me go, for it is daybreak."

[A] **32:2** = Two Camps

The Jabbok River between Jerash and Amman, Jordan.

But Jacob said, "I will not let you go unless you bless me."

27 "What is your name?" the man asked.

"Jacob," he replied.

28 "Your name will no longer be Jacob," he said. "It will be Israel[A] because you have struggled with God and with men and have prevailed."

29 Then Jacob asked him, "Please tell me your name."

But he answered, "Why do you ask my name?" And he blessed him there.

30 Jacob then named the place Peniel,[B] "For I have seen God face to face," he said, "yet my life has been spared." 31 The sun shone on him as he passed by Penuel[C] — limping because of his hip. 32 That is why, still today, the Israelites don't eat the thigh muscle that is at the hip socket: because he struck Jacob's hip socket at the thigh muscle.[D]

JACOB MEETS ESAU

33 Now Jacob looked up and saw Esau coming toward him with four hundred men. So he divided the children among Leah, Rachel, and the two slave women. 2 He put the slaves and their children first, Leah and her children next, and Rachel and Joseph last. 3 He himself went on ahead and bowed to the ground seven times until he approached his brother.

4 But Esau ran to meet him, hugged him, threw his arms around him, and kissed him. Then they wept. 5 When Esau looked up and saw the women and children, he asked, "Who are these with you?"

He answered, "The children God has graciously given your servant." 6 Then the slaves and their children approached him and bowed down. 7 Leah and her children also approached and bowed down, and then Joseph and Rachel approached and bowed down.

8 So Esau said, "What do you mean by this whole procession[E] I met?"

"To find favor with you, my lord," he answered.

9 "I have enough, my brother," Esau replied. "Keep what you have."

10 But Jacob said, "No, please! If I have found favor with you, take this gift from me. For indeed, I have seen your face, and it is like seeing God's face, since you have accepted me. 11 Please take my present that was brought to you, because God has been gracious to me and I have everything I need." So Jacob urged him until he accepted.

12 Then Esau said, "Let's move on, and I'll go ahead of you."

13 Jacob replied, "My lord knows that the children are weak, and I have nursing flocks and herds. If they are driven hard for one day, the whole herd will die. 14 Let my lord go ahead of his servant. I will continue on slowly, at a pace suited to the livestock and the children, until I come to my lord at Seir."

15 Esau said, "Let me leave some of my people with you."

But he replied, "Why do that? Please indulge me,[F] my lord."

16 That day Esau started on his way back to Seir, 17 but Jacob went to Succoth. He built a house for himself and shelters for his livestock; that is why the place was called Succoth.[G]

18 After Jacob came from Paddan-aram, he arrived safely at Shechem in the land of Canaan and camped in front of the city. 19 He purchased a section of the field where he had pitched his tent from the sons of Hamor, Shechem's father, for a hundred pieces of silver.[H] 20 And he set up an altar there and called it God, the God of Israel.[I]

DINAH DEFILED

34 Leah's daughter Dinah, whom Leah bore to Jacob, went out to see some of the young women of the area. 2 When Shechem — son of Hamor the Hivite, who was the region's chieftain — saw her, he took her and raped her. 3 He became infatuated with Jacob's daughter Dinah. He loved the young girl and spoke tenderly to her.[J] 4 "Get me this girl as a wife," he told his father.

5 Jacob heard that Shechem had defiled his daughter Dinah, but since his sons were with his livestock in the field, he remained silent until they returned. 6 Meanwhile, Shechem's father Hamor came to speak with Jacob. 7 Jacob's sons returned from the field when they heard about the incident. They were deeply grieved and very angry, for Shechem had committed an outrage against Israel by raping Jacob's daughter, and such a thing should not be done.

8 Hamor said to Jacob's sons, "My son Shechem has his heart set on your[K] daughter. Please give her to him as a wife. 9 Intermarry with us; give your daughters to us, and take our daughters for yourselves. 10 Live with us. The land is before you. Settle here, move about, and acquire property in it."

11 Then Shechem said to Dinah's father and brothers, "Grant me this favor,[L] and I'll give you whatever you say. 12 Demand of me a high compensation[M] and gift; I'll give you whatever you ask me. Just give the girl to be my wife!"

13 But Jacob's sons answered Shechem and his father Hamor deceitfully because he had defiled their sister Dinah. 14 "We cannot do this thing," they said

[A] **32:28** In Hb, the name *Israel* sounds like "he struggled (with) God." [B] **32:30** = Face of God [C] **32:31** Variant of *Peniel* [D] **32:32** Or *tendon* [E] **33:8** Lit *camp* [F] **33:15** Lit *May I find favor in your eyes* [G] **33:17** = Stalls or Huts [H] **33:19** Lit *100 qesitahs*; the value of this currency is unknown [I] **33:20** = *El-Elohe-Israel* [J] **34:3** Lit *spoke to her heart* [K] **34:8** The Hb word for *your* is pl, showing that Hamor is speaking to Jacob and his sons. [L] **34:11** Lit *"May I find favor in your eyes* [M] **34:12** Or *bride-price*, or *betrothal present*

to them. "Giving our sister to an uncircumcised man
is a disgrace to us. 15 We will agree with you only on
this condition: if all your males are circumcised as we
are. 16 Then we will give you our daughters, take your
daughters for ourselves, live with you, and become
one people. 17 But if you will not listen to us and be
circumcised, then we will take our daughter and go."
18 Their words seemed good to Hamor and his son
Shechem. 19 The young man did not delay doing this,
because he was delighted with Jacob's daughter. Now
he was the most important in all his father's family.
20 So Hamor and his son Shechem went to the gate of
their city and spoke to the men of their city.
21 "These men are peaceful toward us," they said.
"Let them live in our land and move about in it, for
indeed, the region is large enough for them. Let's take
their daughters as our wives and give our daughters
to them. 22 But the men will agree to live with us and
be one people only on this condition: if all our men
are circumcised as they are. 23 Won't their livestock,
their possessions, and all their animals become ours?
Only let's agree with them, and they will live with us."
24 All the men who had come to the city gates listened to Hamor and his son Shechem, and all those
men were circumcised. 25 On the third day, when they
were still in pain, two of Jacob's sons, Simeon and
Levi, Dinah's brothers, took their swords, went into
the unsuspecting city, and killed every male. 26 They
killed Hamor and his son Shechem with their swords,
took Dinah from Shechem's house, and went away.
27 Jacob's sons came to the slaughter and plundered
the city because their sister had been defiled. 28 They
took their flocks, herds, donkeys, and whatever was
in the city and in the field. 29 They captured all their
possessions, dependents, and wives and plundered
everything in the houses.
30 Then Jacob said to Simeon and Levi, "You have
brought trouble on me, making me odious to the inhabitants of the land, the Canaanites and the Perizzites. We are few in number; if they unite against me
and attack me, I and my household will be destroyed."
31 But they answered, "Should he treat our sister
like a prostitute?"

RETURN TO BETHEL

35 God said to Jacob, "Get up! Go to Bethel and
settle there. Build an altar there to the God
who appeared to you when you fled from your brother Esau."
2 So Jacob said to his family and all who were with
him, "Get rid of the foreign gods that are among you.
Purify yourselves and change your clothes. 3 We must
get up and go to Bethel. I will build an altar there to
the God who answered me in my day of distress. He
has been with me everywhere I have gone."
4 Then they gave Jacob all their foreign gods and
their earrings, and Jacob hid them under the oak near
Shechem. 5 When they set out, a terror from God came
over the cities around them, and they did not pursue
Jacob's sons. 6 So Jacob and all who were with him
came to Luz (that is, Bethel) in the land of Canaan.
7 Jacob built an altar there and called the place El-
bethel[A] because it was there that God had revealed
himself to him when he was fleeing from his brother.
8 Deborah, the one who had nursed and raised Rebekah,[B] died and was buried under the oak south of
Bethel. So Jacob named it Allon-bacuth.[C]
9 God appeared to Jacob again after he returned
from Paddan-aram, and he blessed him. 10 God said to
him, "Your name is Jacob; you will no longer be named
Jacob, but your name will be Israel." So he named him
Israel. 11 God also said to him, "I am God Almighty. Be
fruitful and multiply. A nation, indeed an assembly of
nations, will come from you, and kings will descend
from you.[D] 12 I will give to you the land that I gave to
Abraham and Isaac. And I will give the land to your
future descendants." 13 Then God withdrew[E] from him
at the place where he had spoken to him.
14 Jacob set up a marker at the place where he had
spoken to him — a stone marker. He poured a drink
offering on it and poured oil on it. 15 Jacob named the
place where God had spoken with him Bethel.

RACHEL'S DEATH

16 They set out from Bethel. When they were still some
distance from Ephrath, Rachel began to give birth,
and her labor was difficult. 17 During her difficult
labor, the midwife said to her, "Don't be afraid, for
you have another son." 18 With her last breath — for
she was dying — she named him Ben-oni,[F] but his
father called him Benjamin.[G] 19 So Rachel died and
was buried on the way to Ephrath (that is, Bethlehem).
20 Jacob set up a marker on her grave; it is the marker
at Rachel's grave still today.

ISRAEL'S SONS

21 Israel set out again and pitched his tent beyond
the Tower of Eder.[H] 22 While Israel was living in that
region, Reuben went in and slept with his father's
concubine Bilhah, and Israel heard about it.
Jacob had twelve sons:
23 Leah's sons were Reuben (Jacob's firstborn),
Simeon, Levi, Judah,
Issachar, and Zebulun.
24 Rachel's sons were
Joseph and Benjamin.

[A] **35:7** = God of Bethel [B] **35:8** Lit *Deborah, Rebekah's wet nurse*; Gn 24:59 [C] **35:8** = Oak of Weeping [D] **35:11** Lit *will come from your loins* [E] **35:13** Lit *went up* [F] **35:18** = Son of My Sorrow [G] **35:18** = Son of the Right Hand [H] **35:21** Or *beyond Migdal-eder*

25 The sons of Rachel's slave Bilhah
were Dan and Naphtali.
26 The sons of Leah's slave Zilpah
were Gad and Asher.
These are the sons of Jacob, who were born to him
in Paddan-aram.

ISAAC'S DEATH

27 Jacob came to his father Isaac at Mamre in
Kiriath-arba (that is, Hebron), where Abraham and
Isaac had stayed. 28 Isaac lived 180 years. 29 He took his
last breath and died, and was gathered to his people,
old and full of days. His sons Esau and Jacob buried
him.

ESAU'S FAMILY

36 These are the family records of Esau (that
is, Edom). 2 Esau took his wives from the Canaanite women: Adah daughter of Elon the Hethite,
Oholibamah daughter of Anah and granddaughter[A]
of Zibeon the Hivite, 3 and Basemath daughter of Ishmael and sister of Nebaioth. 4 Adah bore Eliphaz to
Esau, Basemath bore Reuel, 5 and Oholibamah bore
Jeush, Jalam, and Korah. These were Esau's sons, who
were born to him in the land of Canaan.
6 Esau took his wives, sons, daughters, and all the
people of his household, as well as his herds, all his
livestock, and all the property he had acquired in Canaan; he went to a land away from his brother Jacob.
7 For their possessions were too many for them to live
together, and because of their herds, the land where
they stayed could not support them. 8 So Esau (that
is, Edom) lived in the mountains of Seir.
9 These are the family records of Esau, father of the
Edomites in the mountains of Seir.
10 These are the names of Esau's sons:
Eliphaz son of Esau's wife Adah,
and Reuel son of Esau's wife Basemath.
11 The sons of Eliphaz were
Teman, Omar, Zepho, Gatam, and Kenaz.
12 Timna, a concubine of Esau's son Eliphaz,
bore Amalek to Eliphaz.
These are the sons of Esau's wife Adah.

13 These are Reuel's sons:
Nahath, Zerah, Shammah, and Mizzah.
These are the sons of Esau's wife Basemath.

14 These are the sons of Esau's wife Oholibamah
daughter of Anah and granddaughter[A]
of Zibeon:
She bore Jeush, Jalam, and Korah to Edom.

15 These are the chiefs among Esau's sons:
the sons of Eliphaz, Esau's firstborn:
chief Teman, chief Omar, chief Zepho, chief
Kenaz,
16 chief Korah,[B] chief Gatam, and chief Amalek.
These are the chiefs descended from Eliphaz
in the land of Edom.
These are the sons of Adah.

17 These are the sons of Reuel, Esau's son:
chief Nahath, chief Zerah, chief Shammah,
and chief Mizzah.
These are the chiefs descended from Reuel
in the land of Edom.
These are the sons of Esau's wife Basemath.

18 These are the sons of Esau's wife Oholibamah:
chief Jeush, chief Jalam, and chief Korah.
These are the chiefs descended
from Esau's wife Oholibamah
daughter of Anah.
19 These are the sons of Esau (that is, Edom),
and these are their chiefs.

SEIR'S FAMILY

20 These are the sons of Seir the Horite,
the inhabitants of the land:
Lotan, Shobal, Zibeon, Anah,
21 Dishon, Ezer, and Dishan.
These are the chiefs among the Horites,
the sons of Seir, in the land of Edom.
22 The sons of Lotan were Hori and Heman.
Timna was Lotan's sister.
23 These are Shobal's sons:
Alvan, Manahath, Ebal, Shepho, and Onam.
24 These are Zibeon's sons: Aiah and Anah.
This was the Anah who found the hot springs[C]
in the wilderness
while he was pasturing the donkeys
of his father Zibeon.
25 These are the children of Anah:
Dishon and Oholibamah daughter of Anah.
26 These are Dishon's sons:
Hemdan, Eshban, Ithran, and Cheran.
27 These are Ezer's sons:
Bilhan, Zaavan, and Akan.
28 These are Dishan's sons: Uz and Aran.

29 These are the chiefs among the Horites:
chief Lotan, chief Shobal, chief Zibeon, chief
Anah,
30 chief Dishon, chief Ezer, and chief Dishan.
These are the chiefs among the Horites,
clan by clan,[D] in the land of Seir.

[A] **36:2,14** Sam, LXX read *Anah son* [B] **36:16** Sam omits *Korah* [C] **36:24** Syr, Vg; Tg reads *the mules*; Hb obscure [D] **36:30** Lit *Horites, for their chiefs*

RULERS OF EDOM

31 These are the kings who reigned in the land
of Edom
before any king reigned over the Israelites:
32 Bela son of Beor reigned in Edom;
the name of his city was Dinhabah.
33 When Bela died, Jobab son of Zerah
from Bozrah reigned in his place.
34 When Jobab died, Husham from the land
of the Temanites reigned in his place.
35 When Husham died, Hadad son of Bedad
reigned in his place.
He defeated Midian in the field of Moab;
the name of his city was Avith.
36 When Hadad died, Samlah from Masrekah
reigned in his place.
37 When Samlah died, Shaul from Rehoboth
on the Euphrates River reigned in his place.
38 When Shaul died, Baal-hanan son of Achbor
reigned in his place.
39 When Baal-hanan son of Achbor died, Hadar[A]
reigned in his place.
His city was Pau, and his wife's name
was Mehetabel
daughter of Matred daughter of Me-zahab.

40 These are the names of Esau's chiefs,
according to their families and their localities,
by their names:
chief Timna, chief Alvah, chief Jetheth,
41 chief Oholibamah, chief Elah, chief Pinon,
42 chief Kenaz, chief Teman, chief Mibzar,
43 chief Magdiel, and chief Iram.
These are Edom's chiefs,
according to their settlements in the land
they possessed.
Esau[B] was father of the Edomites.

JOSEPH'S DREAMS

37 Jacob lived in the land where his father had
stayed, the land of Canaan. 2 These are the family records of Jacob.
At seventeen years of age, Joseph tended sheep
with his brothers. The young man was working with
the sons of Bilhah and Zilpah, his father's wives, and
he brought a bad report about them to their father.
3 Now Israel loved Joseph more than his other sons
because Joseph was a son born to him in his old age,
and he made a long-sleeved robe[C] for him. 4 When his
brothers saw that their father loved him more than
all his brothers, they hated him and could not bring
themselves to speak peaceably to him.
5 Then Joseph had a dream. When he told it to his
brothers, they hated him even more. 6 He said to them,
"Listen to this dream I had: 7 There we were, binding
sheaves of grain in the field. Suddenly my sheaf stood
up, and your sheaves gathered around it and bowed
down to my sheaf."
8 "Are you really going to reign over us?" his brothers asked him. "Are you really going to rule us?" So
they hated him even more because of his dream and
what he had said.
9 Then he had another dream and told it to his
brothers. "Look," he said, "I had another dream, and
this time the sun, moon, and eleven stars were bowing down to me."
10 He told his father and brothers, and his father
rebuked him. "What kind of dream is this that you
have had?" he said. "Am I and your mother and your
brothers really going to come and bow down to the
ground before you?" 11 His brothers were jealous of
him, but his father kept the matter in mind.

JOSEPH SOLD INTO SLAVERY

12 His brothers had gone to pasture their father's
flocks at Shechem. 13 Israel said to Joseph, "Your
brothers, you know, are pasturing the flocks at Shechem. Get ready. I'm sending you to them."
"I'm ready," Joseph replied.
14 Then Israel said to him, "Go and see how your
brothers and the flocks are doing, and bring word
back to me." So he sent him from the Hebron Valley,
and he went to Shechem.
15 A man found him there, wandering in the field,
and asked him, "What are you looking for?"
16 "I'm looking for my brothers," Joseph said. "Can
you tell me where they are pasturing their flocks?"
17 "They've moved on from here," the man said. "I
heard them say, 'Let's go to Dothan.'" So Joseph set
out after his brothers and found them at Dothan.
18 They saw him in the distance, and before he had
reached them, they plotted to kill him. 19 They said
to one another, "Oh, look, here comes that dream
expert![D] 20 So now, come on, let's kill him and throw
him into one of the pits.[E] We can say that a vicious
animal ate him. Then we'll see what becomes of his
dreams!"
21 When Reuben heard this, he tried to save him
from them.[F] He said, "Let's not take his life." 22 Reuben also said to them, "Don't shed blood. Throw him
into this pit in the wilderness, but don't lay a hand
on him" — intending to rescue him from them and
return him to his father.
23 When Joseph came to his brothers, they stripped
off Joseph's robe, the long-sleeved robe that he had
on. 24 Then they took him and threw him into the pit.
The pit was empty, without water.

[A] **36:39** Many Hb mss, Sam, Syr read *Hadad* [B] **36:43** Lit *He Esau* [C] **37:3** Or *an ornate robe*; see 2Sm 13:18,19 [D] **37:19** Lit *comes the lord of the dreams* [E] **37:20** Or *cisterns* [F] **37:21** Lit *their hands*

25 They sat down to eat a meal, and when they looked up, there was a caravan of Ishmaelites coming from Gilead. Their camels were carrying aromatic gum, balsam, and resin, going down to Egypt.

26 Judah said to his brothers, "What do we gain if we kill our brother and cover up his blood? 27 Come on, let's sell him to the Ishmaelites and not lay a hand on him, for he is our brother, our own flesh," and his brothers agreed. 28 When Midianite traders passed by, his brothers pulled Joseph out of the pit and sold him for twenty pieces of silver to the Ishmaelites, who took Joseph to Egypt.

29 When Reuben returned to the pit and saw that Joseph was not there, he tore his clothes. 30 He went back to his brothers and said, "The boy is gone! What am I going to do?"[A] 31 So they took Joseph's robe, slaughtered a male goat, and dipped the robe in its blood. 32 They sent the long-sleeved robe to their father and said, "We found this. Examine it. Is it your son's robe or not?"

33 His father recognized it. "It is my son's robe," he said. "A vicious animal has devoured him. Joseph has been torn to pieces!" 34 Then Jacob tore his clothes, put sackcloth around his waist, and mourned for his son many days. 35 All his sons and daughters tried to comfort him, but he refused to be comforted. "No," he said. "I will go down to Sheol to my son, mourning." And his father wept for him.

36 Meanwhile, the Midianites sold Joseph in Egypt to Potiphar, an officer of Pharaoh and the captain of the guards.

JUDAH AND TAMAR

38 At that time Judah left his brothers and settled near an Adullamite named Hirah. 2 There Judah saw the daughter of a Canaanite named Shua; he took her as a wife and slept with her. 3 She conceived and gave birth to a son, and he named him Er. 4 She conceived again, gave birth to a son, and named him Onan. 5 She gave birth to another son and named him Shelah. It was at Chezib that[B,C] she gave birth to him.

6 Judah got a wife for Er, his firstborn, and her name was Tamar. 7 Now Er, Judah's firstborn, was evil in the LORD's sight, and the LORD put him to death. 8 Then Judah said to Onan, "Sleep with your brother's wife. Perform your duty as her brother-in-law and produce offspring for your brother." 9 But Onan knew that the offspring would not be his, so whenever he slept with his brother's wife, he released his semen on the ground so that he would not produce offspring for his brother. 10 What he did was evil in the LORD's sight, so he put him to death also.

11 Then Judah said to his daughter-in-law Tamar, "Remain a widow in your father's house until my son Shelah grows up." For he thought, "He might die too, like his brothers." So Tamar went to live in her father's house.

12 After a long time[D] Judah's wife, the daughter of Shua, died. When Judah had finished mourning, he and his friend Hirah the Adullamite went up to Timnah to his sheepshearers. 13 Tamar was told, "Your father-in-law is going up to Timnah to shear his sheep." 14 So she took off her widow's clothes, veiled her face, covered herself, and sat at the entrance to Enaim, which is on the way to Timnah. For she saw that, though Shelah had grown up, she had not been given to him as a wife. 15 When Judah saw her, he thought she was a prostitute, for she had covered her face.

16 He went over to her and said, "Come, let me sleep with you," for he did not know that she was his daughter-in-law.

She said, "What will you give me for sleeping with me?"

17 "I will send you a young goat from my flock," he replied.

But she said, "Only if you leave something with me until you send it."

18 "What should I give you?" he asked.

She answered, "Your signet ring, your cord, and the staff in your hand." So he gave them to her and slept with her, and she became pregnant by him. 19 She got up and left, then removed her veil and put her widow's clothes back on.

20 When Judah sent the young goat by his friend the Adullamite in order to get back the items he had left with the woman, he could not find her. 21 He asked the men of the place, "Where is the cult prostitute who was beside the road at Enaim?"

"There has been no cult prostitute here," they answered.

22 So the Adullamite returned to Judah, saying, "I couldn't find her, and besides, the men of the place said, 'There has been no cult prostitute here.'"

23 Judah replied, "Let her keep the items for herself; otherwise we will become a laughingstock. After all, I did send this young goat, but you couldn't find her."

24 About three months later Judah was told, "Your daughter-in-law, Tamar, has been acting like a prostitute, and now she is pregnant."

"Bring her out," Judah said, "and let her be burned to death!"

25 As she was being brought out, she sent her father-in-law this message: "I am pregnant by the man to whom these items belong." And she added, "Examine them. Whose signet ring, cord, and staff are these?"

[A] **37:30** Lit *And I, where am I going?* [B] **38:5** LXX reads *She was at Chezib when* [C] **38:5** Or *He was at Chezib when* [D] **38:12** Lit *And there were many days, and*

Cisterns in the Ancient Near East

by Claude F. Mariottini

Be'er and *bor* are two similar words the Hebrew Bible uses to refer to water sources. The word *be'er* is generally translated as "well," an underground source of water. *Bor* is generally translated "cistern" or "pit." The Joseph story uses *bor* and translates it "pit" (Gn 37:20); the same word is translated "cistern" in the story of Saul seeking David (1Sm 19:22).

Cisterns were common in the ancient Near East and Israel due to the land's dry condition. Canaan was arid. Because of the hot and dry summers, people living in Canaan needed water sources that could provide for their needs throughout the year, especially during the dry months.

Springs were perennial sources of water during the rainless summers. Water from a spring was called "living water." Springs supplied a constant source of water, but in the dry season not enough to provide for a community's needs. In this case, the basic water source for daily use was a cistern.

When people moved away from springs, they had to provide for their needs away from the water source. People in arid places faced hardships related to the lack of water and the limited number of natural water sources. One way to collect water was by digging cisterns. A cistern was an artificial reservoir used for storing water during the dry season and for supplementing a community's water supply.

The rainy season in Canaan was short, lasting from mid-October or early November to the end of April. The fluctuation in precipitation during the rainy season made the development of water collection and storage crucial for the economy of the community, the development of agriculture, feeding the herds and flocks, and private consumption. Cisterns enabled the community to collect rainwater during the rainy season and keep it for the summer months. Cisterns were supplied with water from rooftops and runoff from the hills. People cut channels into the earth to lead street waters into the cisterns.

People dug cisterns mostly out of limestone. Limestone, though, was porous. The water thus seeped slowly through the rocks and the cistern ran dry. In the thirteenth century BC, the inhabitants of the central hills discovered that plaster was impervious to water, and they began plastering the cisterns.

Some cisterns were pear-shaped with a small opening, which allowed them to be covered. The coverings prevented animal, people, or debris from falling in (Ex 21:33–34). Other cisterns were bottle-shaped with a round bottom. These sometimes served as prisons. Cistern capacity varied depending on the community's need. Thousands of small cisterns have been found throughout

Updated, open-air cistern built on the earlier Iron Age cistern site in Amman. David's army defeated the Ammonites at Rabbah, which was later named Philadelphia and then Amman, which is the capital of Jordan.

Water tunnel leading into the cistern at Megiddo. Ahab built the city's water system, including the tunnel and cistern, in the ninth century BC.

Smaller cisterns for private use were usually in one of three typical shapes: bottle, bell, or pear. The length of the neck or shaft leading into the cistern and the size of the cistern itself could vary greatly.

Israel. At Qumran, archaeologists found four large, three medium sized, and four small cisterns.[1]

Using water from runoff required elimination of the impurities, so people put rocks at the bottom of cisterns to catch debris. Also, they drilled holes on one side of the cistern to allow water to go to an adjacent cistern, thus filtering the water as it went from one cistern to another.[2]

CISTERNS IN ISRAEL

At the beginning of the Iron Age (ca 1200 BC), the people who had arrived in the hill country of Canaan dug cisterns on the hills to preserve water, allowing them to live some distance from a spring. This innovation led to the establishment of new settlements away from natural water sources, hence the term "dry farming." The cisterns preserved water during the rainy season so farmers and families could use the water in the dry months.

At the time the Hebrews entered the land of Canaan, three bell-shaped cisterns supplied water to one house compound at Ai. These cisterns were cut into layers of Senonian chalk. The cisterns had small openings, which helped keep out contaminants. The cisterns were closed with a flat, round capstone. A cut along the hill channeled rainwater into the cisterns. These three cisterns were linked together. The water from the first cistern flowed into the second and from the second into the third. The first cistern would collect the sediment so that the water could be filtered into the second and third cisterns.[3]

According to archaeologists, the introduction of cistern technology in the hill country of Canaan allowed people to establish small villages throughout the region. The number and size of the cisterns depended on the number of people in the family or clan and their needs. According to an archaeological report, the number of cisterns in the Negev ran into the thousands. "No Iron II fortress or village could have existed in the Negev without these cisterns of various types, the digging of which is Biblically attested."[4]

THE GOOD WORK OF GOD

When Joseph's brothers threw him into the cistern, it was empty. The empty cistern in the Old Testament carries a negative meaning: In some

Large water cistern built by the paranoid King Herod (37–4 BC) to provide an almost endless supply of fresh water for his palace-fortress at Masada.

At Gergesa, one of the largest basilicas discovered in Israel. Beneath the courtyard of the church, which dates to the fifth–sixth centuries, is a large cistern with two openings. Shown is the reconstructed basalt opening on the south side of the courtyard.

cases, it was a place of imprisonment (Gn 37:20–24; Jr 38:6). The Hebrew word *bor*, rendered as "cistern" in the Joseph story, is translated as "dungeon" or "prison" in Genesis 40:15.

When *bor* is translated as "Pit," the word is associated with death. "Down to the Pit" means "to die" (Ps 28:1). The same word is associated with the entrance of the dead into Sheol: "But you will be brought down to Sheol into the deepest regions of the Pit" (Is 14:15).

Joseph experienced his brothers' betrayal. Because of their actions, he had to suffer. He was put into the *bor*, into the gates of Sheol, by his brothers and by Potiphar. Because God was with Joseph, however, the Lord used the brothers' evil to good use: "You planned evil against me; God planned it for good to bring about the present result—the survival of many people" (Gn 50:20). ✣

[1] Patricia Hidiroglou, "Aqueducts, Basins, and Cisterns: The Water Systems at Qumran," *NEA* 63.3 (2000): 139. [2] Victor H. Matthews, *Manners and Customs in the Bible* (Peabody, MA: Hendrickson, 1991), 46. [3] Joseph A. Callaway, "Village Subsistence: Iron Age Ai and Raddana," in *The Answers Lie Below: Essays in Honor of Lawrence Edmund Toombs* (Lanham, MD: University Press of America, 1984), 55. [4] Nelson Glueck, "An Aerial Reconnaissance of the Negev," *BASOR* 155 (1959): 4.

The Struthion Pool was a water source for the Antonia Fortress in Jerusalem. The original pool, which was likely built by Herod the Great, would hold about eight million gallons of water. In the second century AD, Hadrian turned the pool into a cistern.

26 Judah recognized them and said, "She is more
in the right[A] than I, since I did not give her to my son
Shelah." And he did not know her intimately again.
27 When the time came for her to give birth, there
were twins in her womb. 28 As she was giving birth,
one of them put out his hand, and the midwife took
it and tied a scarlet thread around it, announcing,
"This one came out first." 29 But then he pulled his
hand back, out came his brother, and she said, "What
a breakout you have made for yourself!" So he was
named Perez.[B] 30 Then his brother, who had the scarlet thread tied to his hand, came out, and was named
Zerah.[C]

JOSEPH IN POTIPHAR'S HOUSE

39 Now Joseph had been taken to Egypt. An
Egyptian named Potiphar, an officer of Pharaoh and the captain of the guards, bought him from
the Ishmaelites who had brought him there. 2 The
LORD was with Joseph, and he became a successful man, serving[D] in the household of his Egyptian
master. 3 When his master saw that the LORD was
with him and that the LORD made everything he
did successful, 4 Joseph found favor with his master
and became his personal attendant. Potiphar also
put him in charge of his household and placed all
that he owned under his authority.[E] 5 From the time
that he put him in charge of his household and of
all that he owned, the LORD blessed the Egyptian's
house because of Joseph. The LORD's blessing was
on all that he owned, in his house and in his fields.
6 He left all that he owned under Joseph's authority;[F]
he did not concern himself with anything except
the food he ate.
Now Joseph was well-built and handsome. 7 After
some time his master's wife looked longingly at Joseph and said, "Sleep with me."
8 But he refused. "Look," he said to his master's
wife, "with me here my master does not concern himself with anything in his house, and he has put all
that he owns under my authority.[G] 9 No one in this
house is greater than I am. He has withheld nothing
from me except you, because you are his wife. So
how could I do this immense evil, and how could I
sin against God?"
10 Although she spoke to Joseph day after day, he
refused to go to bed with her.[H] 11 Now one day he went
into the house to do his work, and none of the household servants were there.[I] 12 She grabbed him by his
garment and said, "Sleep with me!" But leaving his
garment in her hand, he escaped and ran outside.

[A] **38:26** Or *more righteous* [B] **38:29** = Breaking Out [C] **38:30** = Brightness of Sunrise; perhaps related to the scarlet thread [D] **39:2** Lit *and he was* [E] **39:4** Lit *owned in his hand* [F] **39:6** Lit *owned in Joseph's hand* [G] **39:8** Lit *owns in my hand* [H] **39:10** Lit *he did not listen to her to lie beside her, to be with her* [I] **39:11** Lit *there in the house*

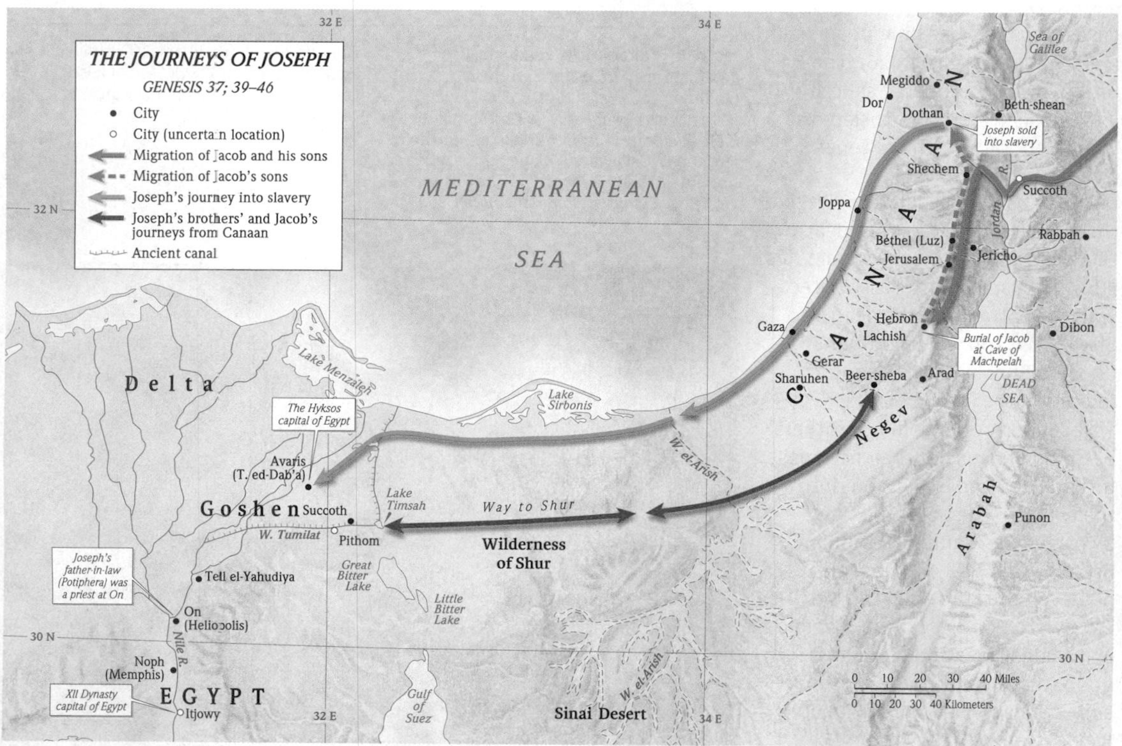

13 When she saw that he had left his garment with her
and had run outside, 14 she called her household servants. "Look," she said to them, "my husband brought
a Hebrew man to make fools of us. He came to me so
he could sleep with me, and I screamed as loud as I
could. 15 When he heard me screaming for help,[A] he
left his garment beside me and ran outside."
16 She put Joseph's garment beside her until his
master came home. 17 Then she told him the same
story: "The Hebrew slave you brought to us came to
make a fool of me, 18 but when I screamed for help,[B]
he left his garment beside me and ran outside."
19 When his master heard the story his wife told
him — "These are the things your slave did to me"
— he was furious 20 and had him thrown into prison,
where the king's prisoners were confined. So Joseph
was there in prison.

JOSEPH IN PRISON

21 But the LORD was with Joseph and extended kindness to him. He granted him favor with the prison
warden. 22 The warden put all the prisoners who were
in the prison under Joseph's authority,[C] and he was
responsible for everything that was done there. 23 The
warden did not bother with anything under Joseph's
authority,[D] because the LORD was with him, and the
LORD made everything that he did successful.

JOSEPH INTERPRETS TWO PRISONERS' DREAMS

40 After this, the king of Egypt's cupbearer
and baker offended their master, the king of
Egypt. 2 Pharaoh was angry with his two officers, the
chief cupbearer and the chief baker, 3 and put them
in custody in the house of the captain of the guards
in the prison where Joseph was confined. 4 The captain of the guards assigned Joseph to them as their
personal attendant, and they were in custody for
some time.[E]
5 The king of Egypt's cupbearer and baker, who
were confined in the prison, each had a dream. Both
had a dream on the same night, and each dream had
its own meaning. 6 When Joseph came to them in the
morning, he saw that they looked distraught. 7 So he
asked Pharaoh's officers who were in custody with
him in his master's house, "Why do you look so sad
today?"
8 "We had dreams," they said to him, "but there is
no one to interpret them."
Then Joseph said to them, "Don't interpretations
belong to God? Tell me your dreams."
9 So the chief cupbearer told his dream to Joseph:
"In my dream there was a vine in front of me. 10 On
the vine were three branches. As soon as it budded,
its blossoms came out and its clusters ripened into
grapes. 11 Pharaoh's cup was in my hand, and I took

Water jar inscribed with the name and blessing of Paser, who was a vizier of Seti I and Ramesses II. A vizier served as the pharaoh's prime minister and high priest.

the grapes, squeezed them into Pharaoh's cup, and
placed the cup in Pharaoh's hand."
12 "This is its interpretation," Joseph said to him.
"The three branches are three days. 13 In just three
days Pharaoh will lift up your head and restore you to
your position. You will put Pharaoh's cup in his hand
the way you used to when you were his cupbearer.
14 But when all goes well for you, remember that I was
with you. Please show kindness to me by mentioning
me to Pharaoh, and get me out of this prison. 15 For
I was kidnapped from the land of the Hebrews, and
even here I have done nothing that they should put
me in the dungeon."[F]
16 When the chief baker saw that the interpretation
was positive, he said to Joseph, "I also had a dream.
Three baskets of white bread were on my head. 17 In
the top basket were all sorts of baked goods for Pharaoh, but the birds were eating them out of the basket
on my head."
18 "This is its interpretation," Joseph replied. "The
three baskets are three days. 19 In just three days Pharaoh will lift up your head — from off you — and
hang you on a tree.[G] Then the birds will eat the flesh
from your body."[H]
20 On the third day, which was Pharaoh's birthday, he gave a feast for all his servants. He elevated[I]
the chief cupbearer and the chief baker among his
servants. 21 Pharaoh restored the chief cupbearer to

[A] **39:15** Lit *he heard that I raised my voice and I screamed* [B] **39:18** Lit *I raised my voice and screamed* [C] **39:22** Lit *prison in the hand of Joseph* [D] **39:23** Lit *anything in his hand* [E] **40:4** Lit *custody days* [F] **40:15** Or *pit, or cistern* [G] **40:19** Or *and impale you on a pole* [H] **40:19** Lit *eat your flesh from upon you* [I] **40:20** Lit *He lifted up the head of*

Camels and Caravans: Joseph's Trip to Egypt

by Deborah Cantrell

Egyptian camel drivers in 1918.

Commerce and trade in the ancient world depended on cross-country caravans and, most important, on the cooperation of camels. Camel domestication probably occurred as early as the third millennium BC in southeast Arabia.[1] The camel, with its ability to travel as far as fifty to sixty miles across the desert in one day, was indispensable to the caravan trade. Camels are especially suited to desert travel with their broad two-toed feet that keep them from sinking in the sand, their nostrils that close to impenetrable slits during a sand storm, and their thickly fringed eyelashes and beetling eyebrows that shield their eyes from the sun. Their teeth are so long that they can chew cactus without the thorns pricking their lips or the roofs of their mouths. Camels will eat almost anything. They grow to seven feet, and adult males of some camel species can weigh a ton.

Ancient camel saddle. The center is the seat; at the four corners are the leather pockets that held wooden braces.

The fat stored in the camel's hump is burned for energy, and the hump diminishes in size as the body fat is depleted. Depending on heat and humidity, a camel requires water only about once every three days and can travel 250 miles between waterings. When a camel does have the opportunity to drink, however, it can consume as much as twenty-eight gallons.[2] Watering an entire camel caravan, therefore, can be an ordeal of many hours. For instance, the approximate time for Rebekah to water the ten camels of Abraham's servant in Genesis 24:19–21 was three hours.

An easy day's travel for a camel is 50 miles, but loaded caravans may

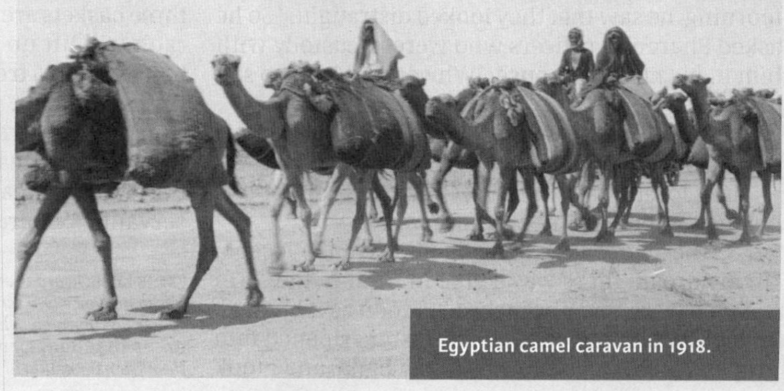
Egyptian camel caravan in 1918.

be slower. On a long journey across the desert, camel caravans average only 4 ½ miles per hour because the camels are kept at a walk. Although camels can carry weight of up to a thousand pounds, this would be highly unusual. A more comfortable load would be about six hundred pounds, twice what a horse would carry and three times more than a typical donkey load.

Camels are inherently irascible. Once loaded, the practice was to walk all day, without stopping, to the next destination because, if allowed to rest, camels sometimes refused to go forward again. And if one tired camel became reluctant and intractable or obnoxious and obdurate, the others frequently joined in the mutiny by refusing to stand or sometimes bucking until they loosened their packs. Their disagreeable temperaments were contagious. Once the caravan began the day, the procession continued, therefore, until evening.

According to the biblical text, Joseph's brothers were sitting down to eat when they saw an Ishmaelite camel caravan from Gilead approaching Dothan, presumably to spend the night.[3] Villages like Dothan and Jezreel were important resting stations for the caravans.[4]

The name Dothan refers to the city and the valley in which the city is located. The valley is dotted with hundreds of rock-cut pits; locals used them as cisterns or for food storage. These rock-cut pits are huge bottled-shaped cavities hewn out of the limestone bedrock; they can be up to forty feet deep.

Once the caravan arrived in Gilead, the hard part of the journey was over. Assuming the caravan began in Saba (modern Yemen), a land known for producing myrrh and frankincense, the traders with their valuable cargo had traveled more than fifteen hundred miles by the time they arrived in Gilead.[5] The camel caravan bearing lavish gifts from the Queen of Sheba to King Solomon in Jerusalem (1Kg 10) probably took about eighty to ninety days.[6]

Gilead, however, was well known for its native-grown medicinal balm extracted from the terebinth tree.[7] This balm was highly prized in Egypt for its healing effectiveness and also used for funerary preparations.

From Dothan to the trading markets at Gaza on the border with Egypt was almost another hundred miles. Assuming the camels traveled forty miles per day over established routes, Joseph's trip from Dothan to Egypt took another two to three days, depending on how long the caravan stopped to rest the camels. ✣

An archaeology student being lowered into a well at Jezreel.

[1] Nigel Groom, *Frankincense and Myrrh: A Study of the Arabian Incense Trade* (London: Longman, 1981), 36–37. [2] Richard W. Bulliet, *The Camel and the Wheel* (New York: Columbia University Press, 1990), 35. [3] Ishmaelites were descendants of Abraham's son by Hagar, the handmaiden of Sarah (Gn 16:15). An Ishmaelite named Obil was in charge of King David's camel herd (1Ch 27:30). [4] For an interesting discussion of archaeological discoveries at Tel Dothan and Jezreel, see Shimon Gibson, Titus Kennedy, and Joel Kramer, "A Note on an Iron Age Four-Horned Altar from Tel Dothan," *Palestine Exploration Quarterly* (*PEQ*) 145.4 (2013): 306–19; and Norma Franklin, "Why Was Jezreel So Important to the Kingdom of Israel?" *The Bible and Interpretation,* November 2013, at www.bibleinterp.com/opeds/2013/11/fra378006.shtml. [5] Bulliet, *Camel*, 77; K. Schippmann, *Ancient South Arabia: From the Queen of Sheba to the Advent of Islam*, trans. Allison Brown (Princeton: Princeton University Press, 2001), 54. [6] Schippmann, *Ancient South Arabia*, 54. [7] Groom, *Frankincense*, 29.

Located between Samaria and Jezreel, Dothan was part of Manasseh's tribal allotment.

his position as cupbearer, and he placed the cup in Pharaoh's hand. 22 But Pharaoh hanged[A] the chief baker, just as Joseph had explained to them. 23 Yet the chief cupbearer did not remember Joseph; he forgot him.

JOSEPH INTERPRETS PHARAOH'S DREAMS

41 At the end of two years Pharaoh had a dream: He was standing beside the Nile, 2 when seven healthy-looking, well-fed cows came up from the Nile and began to graze among the reeds. 3 After them, seven other cows, sickly and thin, came up from the Nile and stood beside those cows along the bank of the Nile. 4 The sickly, thin cows ate the healthy, well-fed cows. Then Pharaoh woke up. 5 He fell asleep and dreamed a second time: Seven heads of grain, plump and good, came up on one stalk. 6 After them, seven heads of grain, thin and scorched by the east wind, sprouted up. 7 The thin heads of grain swallowed up the seven plump, full ones. Then Pharaoh woke up, and it was only a dream.

8 When morning came, he was troubled, so he summoned all the magicians of Egypt and all its wise men. Pharaoh told them his dreams, but no one could interpret them for him.

9 Then the chief cupbearer said to Pharaoh, "Today I remember my faults. 10 Pharaoh was angry with his servants, and he put me and the chief baker in the custody of the captain of the guards. 11 He and I had dreams on the same night; each dream had its own meaning. 12 Now a young Hebrew, a slave of the captain of the guards, was with us there. We told him our dreams, he interpreted our dreams for us, and each had its own interpretation. 13 It turned out just the way he interpreted them to us: I was restored to my position, and the other man was hanged."

14 Then Pharaoh sent for Joseph, and they quickly brought him from the dungeon.[B] He shaved, changed his clothes, and went to Pharaoh.

15 Pharaoh said to Joseph, "I have had a dream, and no one can interpret it. But I have heard it said about you that you can hear a dream and interpret it."

16 "I am not able to," Joseph answered Pharaoh. "It is God who will give Pharaoh a favorable answer."[C]

17 So Pharaoh said to Joseph, "In my dream I was standing on the bank of the Nile, 18 when seven well-fed, healthy-looking cows came up from the Nile and grazed among the reeds. 19 After them, seven other cows — weak, very sickly, and thin — came up. I've never seen such sickly ones as these in all the land of Egypt. 20 Then the thin, sickly cows ate the first seven well-fed cows. 21 When they had devoured them, you could not tell that they had devoured them; their appearance was as bad as it had been before. Then I woke up. 22 In my dream I also saw seven heads of

Decorative faience tile from Egypt depicts a cow grazing among the reeds. Part of Pharaoh's dream involved seven well-fed cows; these represented seven years of plenty.

grain, full and good, coming up on one stalk. 23 After them, seven heads of grain — withered, thin, and scorched by the east wind — sprouted up. 24 The thin heads of grain swallowed the seven good ones. I told this to the magicians, but no one can tell me what it means."

25 Then Joseph said to Pharaoh, "Pharaoh's dreams mean the same thing. God has revealed to Pharaoh what he is about to do. 26 The seven good cows are seven years, and the seven good heads are seven years. The dreams mean the same thing. 27 The seven thin, sickly cows that came up after them are seven years, and the seven worthless heads of grain scorched by the east wind are seven years of famine.

28 "It is just as I told Pharaoh: God has shown Pharaoh what he is about to do. 29 Seven years of great abundance are coming throughout the land of Egypt. 30 After them, seven years of famine will take place, and all the abundance in the land of Egypt will be forgotten. The famine will devastate the land. 31 The abundance in the land will not be remembered because of the famine that follows it, for the famine will be very severe. 32 Since the dream was given twice to Pharaoh, it means that the matter has been determined by God, and he will carry it out soon.

33 "So now, let Pharaoh look for a discerning and wise man and set him over the land of Egypt. 34 Let Pharaoh do this: Let him appoint overseers over the land and take a fifth of the harvest of the land of Egypt during the seven years of abundance.

[A] **40:22** Or *impaled* [B] **41:14** Or *pit*, or *cistern* [C] **41:16** Or *"God will answer Pharaoh with peace of mind."*

35 Let them gather all the excess food during these
good years that are coming. Under Pharaoh's authority, store the grain in the cities, so they may preserve it as food. 36 The food will be a reserve for the
land during the seven years of famine that will take
place in the land of Egypt. Then the country will not
be wiped out by the famine."

JOSEPH EXALTED

37 The proposal pleased Pharaoh and all his servants,
38 and he said to them, "Can we find anyone like this,
a man who has God's spirit[A] in him?" 39 So Pharaoh
said to Joseph, "Since God has made all this known
to you, there is no one as discerning and wise as you
are. 40 You will be over my house, and all my people
will obey your commands.[B] Only I, as king,[C] will be
greater than you." 41 Pharaoh also said to Joseph, "See,
I am placing you over all the land of Egypt." 42 Pharaoh
removed his signet ring from his hand and put it on
Joseph's hand, clothed him with fine linen garments,
and placed a gold chain around his neck. 43 He had
Joseph ride in his second chariot, and servants called
out before him, "Make way!"[D] So he placed him over
all the land of Egypt. 44 Pharaoh said to Joseph, "I am
Pharaoh and no one will be able to raise his hand or
foot in all the land of Egypt without your permission."
45 Pharaoh gave Joseph the name Zaphenath-paneah
and gave him a wife, Asenath daughter of Potiphera,
priest at On.[E] And Joseph went throughout[F] the land
of Egypt.

JOSEPH'S ADMINISTRATION

46 Joseph was thirty years old when he entered the
service of Pharaoh king of Egypt. Joseph left Pharaoh's presence and traveled throughout the land
of Egypt.

47 During the seven years of abundance the land
produced outstanding harvests. 48 Joseph gathered
all the excess food in the land of Egypt during the
seven years and put it in the cities. He put the food
in every city from the fields around it. 49 So Joseph
stored up grain in such abundance — like the sand
of the sea — that he stopped measuring it because it
was beyond measure.

50 Two sons were born to Joseph before the years
of famine arrived. Asenath daughter of Potiphera,
priest at On, bore them to him. 51 Joseph named the
firstborn Manasseh[G] and said, "God has made me
forget all my hardship and my whole family." 52 And
the second son he named Ephraim[H] and said, "God
has made me fruitful in the land of my affliction."

53 Then the seven years of abundance in the land
of Egypt came to an end, 54 and the seven years of
famine began, just as Joseph had said. There was
famine in every land, but in the whole land of Egypt

[A] **41:38** Or *the spirit of the gods*, or *a god's spirit* [B] **41:40** Lit *will kiss your mouth* [C] **41:40** Lit *Only the throne I* [D] **41:43** Or *"Kneel!"* [E] **41:45** Or *Heliopolis*, also in v. 50 [F] **41:45** Or *Joseph gained authority over* [G] **41:51** In Hb, the name *Manasseh* sounds like the verb "forget." [H] **41:52** In Hb, the name *Ephraim* sounds like the word for "fruitful."

Three Egyptian signet rings dating to the New Kingdom Period (1550–1069 BC). Pharaoh removed his ring and placed it on Joseph's finger when he made him vizier of Egypt.

The Egypt Joseph Knew

by Stephen R. Miller

Granite figure of Amenemhet III, who ruled in the Twelfth Dynasty, is shown in the classic pose of a Middle Kingdom official. The dates of his reign (1855–1808 BC) fit the time frame of Joseph's living in Egypt.

According to the early chronology, Jacob entered Egypt about 1876 BC. Since Joseph preceded his father by approximately 25 years (Gn 37:2; 41:46), he arrived about 1900 BC during the reign of Amenemhet II (1929–1895 BC), third pharaoh of Egypt's stable Twelfth Dynasty. Evidence suggests an increase of Asiatics during Amenemhet's time, apparently brought in as household servants. However, Egyptian records indicate that sometimes Asiatics (like Joseph) attained important government posts. Joseph lived for 110 years (50:22), dying about 1805 BC during the reign of Amenemhet III (1842–1797 BC). Amenemhet III's reign marked the zenith of economic prosperity in the Middle Kingdom. Perhaps this is partially due to Joseph's administrative skills and the acquisition of land for the pharaohs during the years of famine (47:20). Statues and other likenesses of these pharaohs have survived, providing a remarkable glimpse into the very faces of people Joseph knew.[1]

EGYPT IN JOSEPH'S TIME

Joseph's Egypt was a fascinating place. The capital of the empire was in the north—near Memphis, about thirty miles south of modern Cairo. The great Nile (the longest river in the world) was abuzz with activity. Large temples and statues were visible throughout the land. The three huge pyramids of Giza and the Sphinx had already weathered the desert sands for more than half a millennium. The Great Pyramid of Khufu rose about 481 feet high, and each of its four sides stretched about 756 feet. This one pyramid contains 2.3 million stone blocks, averaging at least two and a half tons each. Originally covered with gleaming white limestone, the Giza pyramids must have been quite a spectacle. The Greeks designated the Great Pyramid one of the seven Wonders of the Ancient World, and it is the only one that remains.[2]

Religion was a crucial part of Egyptian life. The Egyptians worshiped a myriad of deities. Seven hundred and sixty-five gods decorate the walls of the vestibule leading into the tomb of Thutmose III (1504–1450 BC).[3] Amun (Amun-Re) was hailed as the king of Egypt's gods. Osiris was vital because he was the god of vegetation and the afterlife. The life-giving Nile River was even thought to be Osiris's bloodstream,[4] ironic in light of the first exodus plague—when the river turned to blood (Ex 7:14–25). Other noteworthy gods were Nut (sky goddess), Isis (goddess of mothers and love), Hathor (goddess of love, joy, and sky; portrayed with horns, with cow's ears, or as a cow), Thoth (moon-god and god of writing, sometimes depicted as a baboon!), and various

Drawing on the interior of the tomb of Khnemhotep II at Beni Hasan has what appears to be Hebrew-dressed people on the upper left corner.

Isis wearing a heavy collar with hawk's head terminals and on her head a modius, a symbol of fertility, is surmounted by cow's horns.

sun-gods—Re (or Ra), Aten, and Atum. Egyptians worshiped the pharaohs as the embodiment of the god Horus (represented by a falcon), doubtless the motivation for hauling the millions of tons of stone to build the pharaohs' pyramid tombs.

The Egyptians believed in life after death. If they passed Osiris's examination, they entered a beautiful paradise called the Field of Reeds. If not, their hearts were devoured by the hideous monster Ammit. But those in the Field of Reeds still were not safe. If all earthly memory of a person was lost, the deceased could suffer the Second Death, a permanent annihilation of the spirit. Preservation of the body by mummification and likenesses (tomb paintings, statues) of the deceased were, therefore, necessary to maintain their memory and, in turn, their eternal life. No wonder the pharaohs filled the land with images of themselves: their eternal life depended on it!

During Joseph's day, Egypt led the world culturally. In fact, the twentieth and early nineteenth centuries BC have been designated the apex of Egyptian literature and craftsmanship. Reading and writing were the most important subjects in the schools, and the scribe (the most desired profession in Egypt) spent years mastering the seven hundred signs of Egyptian hieroglyphics. Two great literary works were composed in the Twelfth Dynasty, "The Instructions of Amenemhet" and "The Story of Sinuhe." Jewelry recovered from Middle Kingdom tombs exhibits superb craftsmanship, and tomb paintings show musicians with instruments (e.g., zither, lute, drum, harp, and flute).

Egyptian pottery "soul house," with a portico, two rooms, ventilators on the roof, and stairs to the terrace. Such models were placed on graves. Visitors would place food for the dead in the courtyard. The model also shows the essentials of a town or country house, including an area for food preparation outside, plenty of shade and ventilation, and extra living space on the roof. Dated to the Twelfth Dynasty, about 1990–1800 BC, the time of Joseph.

EVERYDAY LIFE IN JOSEPH'S EGYPT

The vast majority of Egypt's population (perhaps 1.5 million in Joseph's time) lived on the narrow strip of productive land along the Nile. Principal cereal crops were wheat and barley. Rainfall was sparse, and farmers depended on the Nile's inundations to water the land. If the Nile rose too little, famines such as that in Joseph's time could result. Early Egyptian records mention such famines, one lasting seven years.[5] In addition to agricultural activities, scenes on tomb walls depict fishing, hunting, bread making, and brick making, as well as potters, carpenters, decorators, goldsmiths, and sculptors.

Most clothing was made of linen. Men usually were depicted wearing skirtlike garments of varying lengths, and women, ankle-length gowns held up by shoulder straps. Both men and women applied cosmetics heavily, and women were frequently buried with their mirrors. Short hair was the rule, but both sexes often wore wigs. Men were typically clean shaven (Gn 41:14), though images of the pharaohs often depicted them with fake beards. Originally, the Sphinx had a beard.

Mummies from ancient Egypt indicate the average height of women was about five feet, and men, about five feet, five inches. Of course, there were exceptions. Amenhotep II (who may have been the pharaoh of the exodus) was six feet in height, and Senusret III stood six feet six inches tall.[6] Analysis of mummies also reveals that Egyptians suffered from arthritis, tuberculosis, gout, gallstones, tooth decay, and parasites.

The Egyptian diet included bread (mainly from barley), grapes, dates, figs, olives, cabbage, cheese, goat meat, pork, various fowl, and fish. Barley beer and wine (grape, date, or palm) were popular drinks. Sugar cane was introduced later, but the rich could afford honey.

Monogamy was the norm, though nobles and pharaohs could have many wives and a large harem. Ramesses II had eight principal

Figurine of a man plowing; from the Middle Kingdom (2055–1650 BC).

Temple of Isis façade on the island of Philae, at Aswan. Isis was one of the great mother goddesses, the protector of the living and the dead.

wives and fathered more than a hundred children. Love poems suggest people pursued marriages for love, and tomb paintings often portray a husband and wife in loving embrace. Unlike Potiphar's wife (Gn 39:7–19),[7] marriage partners were expected to be faithful. This is underscored by the penalty for adultery: burning or stoning.[8] Egyptian children played games and had toys and dolls. Family pets included dogs and cats.

Following Egyptian custom, both Jacob and Joseph were embalmed or mummified (50:2,26; see article there). In Jacob's case, the entire process for mummification and mourning took seventy days (50:3), a number cited in at least five Egyptian texts and by Herodotus. Joseph died at the age of 110, which was apparently considered the ideal lifespan, for this same age is mentioned in at least twenty-seven Egyptian texts.[9] ✣

[1] According to the late chronology, Joseph lived in Egypt during the latter part of the weak and obscure Thirteenth Dynasty (1782–1650 BC) and in the first part of the Fifteenth Dynasty–Hyksos (1663–1555 BC). Records of the kings of this period are meager. For further study, see Peter A. Clayton, *Chronicle of the Pharaohs: The Reign-by-Reign Record of the Rulers and Dynasties of Ancient Egypt* (London: Thames & Hudson, 1994), 90–4; and Daniel C. Browning Jr. and E. Ray Clendenen, "Hyksos," in *HIBD*, 796–98. [2] Clayton, *Chronicle*, 47; Lorna Oakes and Lucia Gahlin, *Ancient Egypt* (London: Amness, 2003), 66; and http://www.book-of-thoth.com/article_submit/history/alternative-history/the-keys-locks-and-doors-of-thegreat-pyramid.html. [3] Alberto Siliotti, *Guide to the Valley of the Kings* (New York: Barnes & Noble, 1996), 30. [4] John J. Davis, *Moses and the Gods of Egypt: Studies in the Book of Exodus* (Grand Rapids: Baker, 1971), 94. [5] John A. Wilson, trans., "The Tradition of Seven Lean Years in Egypt" and "The Prophecy of Neferti," in *ANET*, 31–2, 444–46. [6] Davis, *Moses and the Gods*, 105; Clayton, *Chronicle*, 84. [7] "The Story of Two Brothers" (ca 1225 BC) tells of an adulteress turning on a young man who spurned her (*ANET*, 23–5). The fictional tale no doubt reflects reality. [8] Joyce Tyldesley, *Judgement of the Pharaoh: Crime and Punishment in Ancient Egypt* (London: Weidenfeld & Nicolson, 2000), 66; A. Rosalie David, *The Egyptian Kingdoms* (New York: Elsevier Phaidon, 1975), 109. [9] John J. Davis, *Paradise to Prison: Studies in Genesis* (Grand Rapids: Baker, 1975), 304. For an example written in the Middle Kingdom period, see "The Instruction of the Vizier Ptah-Hotep," *ANET*, 414.

there was food. 55 When the whole land of Egypt was stricken with famine, the people cried out to Pharaoh for food. Pharaoh told all Egypt, "Go to Joseph and do whatever he tells you." 56 Now the famine had spread across the whole region, so Joseph opened all the storehouses and sold grain to the Egyptians, for the famine was severe in the land of Egypt. 57 Every land came to Joseph in Egypt to buy grain, for the famine was severe in every land.

JOSEPH'S BROTHERS IN EGYPT

42 When Jacob learned that there was grain in Egypt, he said to his sons, "Why do you keep looking at each other? 2 Listen," he went on, "I have heard there is grain in Egypt. Go down there and buy some for us so that we will live and not die." 3 So ten of Joseph's brothers went down to buy grain from Egypt. 4 But Jacob did not send Joseph's brother Benjamin with his brothers, for he thought, "Something might happen to him."

5 The sons of Israel were among those who came to buy grain, for the famine was in the land of Canaan. 6 Joseph was in charge of the country; he sold grain to all its people. His brothers came and bowed down before him with their faces to the ground. 7 When Joseph saw his brothers, he recognized them, but he treated them like strangers and spoke harshly to them.

"Where do you come from?" he asked.

"From the land of Canaan to buy food," they replied.

8 Although Joseph recognized his brothers, they did not recognize him. 9 Joseph remembered his dreams about them and said to them, "You are spies. You have come to see the weakness[A] of the land."

10 "No, my lord. Your servants have come to buy food," they said. 11 "We are all sons of one man. We are honest; your servants are not spies."

12 "No," he said to them. "You have come to see the weakness of the land."

13 But they replied, "We, your servants, were twelve brothers, the sons of one man in the land of Canaan. The youngest is now[B] with our father, and one is no longer living."

14 Then Joseph said to them, "I have spoken:[C] 'You are spies!' 15 This is how you will be tested: As surely as Pharaoh lives, you will not leave this place unless your youngest brother comes here. 16 Send one from among you to get your brother. The rest of you will be imprisoned so that your words can be tested to see if they are true. If they are not, then as surely as Pharaoh lives, you are spies!" 17 So Joseph imprisoned them together for three days.

18 On the third day Joseph said to them, "I fear God — do this and you will live. 19 If you are honest, let one of you[D] be confined to the guardhouse, while the rest of you go and take grain to relieve the hunger of your households. 20 Bring your youngest brother to me so that your words can be confirmed; then you won't die." And they consented to this.

21 Then they said to each other, "Obviously, we are being punished for what we did to our brother. We saw his deep distress when he pleaded with us, but we would not listen. That is why this trouble has come to us."

22 But Reuben replied, "Didn't I tell you not to harm the boy? But you wouldn't listen. Now we must account for his blood!"[E]

23 They did not realize that Joseph understood them, since there was an interpreter between them. 24 He turned away from them and wept. When he turned back and spoke to them, he took Simeon from them and had him bound before their eyes. 25 Joseph then gave orders to fill their containers with grain, return each man's silver to his sack, and give them provisions for their journey. This order was carried out. 26 They loaded the grain on their donkeys and left there.

THE BROTHERS RETURN HOME

27 At the place where they lodged for the night, one of them opened his sack to get feed for his donkey, and he saw his silver there at the top of his bag. 28 He said to his brothers, "My silver has been returned! It's here in my bag." Their hearts sank. Trembling, they turned to one another and said, "What has God done to us?"

29 When they reached their father Jacob in the land of Canaan, they told him all that had happened to them: 30 "The man who is the lord of the country spoke harshly to us and accused us of spying on the country. 31 But we told him, 'We are honest and not spies. 32 We were twelve brothers, sons of the same[F] father. One is no longer living, and the youngest is now with our father in the land of Canaan.' 33 The man who is the lord of the country said to us, 'This is how I will know if you are honest: Leave one brother with me, take food to relieve the hunger of your households, and go. 34 Bring back your youngest brother to me, and I will know that you are not spies but honest men. I will then give your brother back to you, and you can trade in the country.'"

35 As they began emptying their sacks, there in each man's sack was his bag of silver! When they and their father saw their bags of silver, they were afraid. 36 Their father Jacob said to them, "It's me that you make childless. Joseph is gone, and Simeon is gone. Now you want to take Benjamin. Everything happens to me!"

[A] **42:9** Lit *nakedness*, also in v. 12 [B] **42:13** Or *today*, also in v. 32 [C] **42:14** Lit *"That which I spoke to you saying:* [D] **42:19** Lit *your brothers* [E] **42:22** Lit *Even his blood is being sought!"* [F] **42:32** Lit *of our*

Servants in the House of Pharaoh

by Leon Hyatt Jr.

While Joseph was still a slave, the providence of God enabled him to have close contact with three high officers in Pharaoh's court: Potiphar, captain of Pharaoh's guard (Gn 39:1–6a); Pharaoh's chief baker; and Pharaoh's chief cupbearer (40:1–23). The captain of the guard was the head of a highly influential unit of the army, the royal bodyguard. "An oriental monarch's bodyguard consisted of picked men attached to his person and ready to fulfill his pleasure in important and confidential concerns."[1]

Egyptologist Peter Brand wrote, "The royal bakeries were a large institution that baked bread, the staple of the Egyptian diet, in large quantities not just for the king and royal family but for all the people who lived and worked on the royal estate."[2] The chief baker presided over the whole operation, which probably included preparing not just baked goods but every dish for meals.[3]

The name of the cupbearer's position originated in his responsibility to be sure no contamination entered the pharaoh's drink or food; however, the position was of such high trust and responsibility that cupbearers typically became powerful advisers of the pharaoh.[4] The chief cupbearer would have been the leader of all those who served in that highly respected position.

Though a pharaoh was an absolute ruler, with total authority over every aspect of the nation and with power of life and death over everyone in the nation, of necessity he had to rule through various administrators. A vast array of assistants, servants, and slaves assisted each major administrator.

VIZIER

Pharaoh delegated to this officer the power to run the government. The vizier freed the pharaoh to spend the major part of his time performing rituals that were supposed to

Portions of a Stele of the Vizier Naferrenpet, who served during Egypt's Nineteenth Dynasty. This fragment depicts Naferrenpet (left) offering to Ptah of the Valley of the Queens and another deity. Naferrenpet, vizier during the last decade of the reign of Ramesses II, wears the long, high-waisted kilt characteristic of his office, and his head is shaved in the priestly manner.

Egyptian model of a labor scene, painted wood; dated about 2000–1900 BC. The feet of the worker and hoofs of the oxen are driven in the ground; the scene takes place immediately after the withdrawal of floodwaters.

preserve order and harmony in the nation. This included receiving foreign emissaries; deciding the most important court cases; appointing officials; and overseeing the construction of temples, monuments, dams, mausoleums, and other great architectural projects.[5]

Joseph most likely was appointed by Pharaoh to the position of vizier. Pharaoh said that in all the land only he would be greater than Joseph (Gn 41:40), and Joseph's brothers called him "the lord of the country" (42:30,33).[6] His power extended over the entire nation, north and south (41:41–45,55–56). As vizier, Joseph had power to imprison (42:14–20), to determine sentences, and to condemn to slavery (v. 17). Because of the severe drought in Joseph's time, he had to give primary attention to feeding the people.

HIGH PRIESTS

Egyptians considered the pharaoh to be a god; they believed the god Amun-Re united with the pharaoh's father as he conceived the future ruler. As such, the pharaoh was the supreme mediator between the gods and the people and the authority through whom every religious ceremony in the whole land was conducted. In actual practice, the pharaoh was represented by a complicated priestly system that acted in his behalf. The Egyptians believed in many gods and goddesses, some say as many as two thousand; major temples and religious centers were developed for only a relatively small number of the gods. Each major city had its favorite god and temple; a high priest presided over each one.[7] The local high priest in turn supervised a host of lesser priests.[8]

The priests primarily offered sacrifices, conducted religious ceremonies, led religious festivals, practiced fortune-telling and magic, interpreted dreams, and presided over the elaborate rituals and embalmings that accompanied an Egyptian's death and burial. The priesthoods of each different god, however, taught different myths and practiced different rituals that often contradicted each other. The Egyptians were not bothered. They accepted all the different views of the gods and practiced the one or ones that most appealed to them.

Since the high priests were supposed to be acting for the pharaoh, they had tremendous influence on the pharaoh, especially the high priest of the god of the capital city. The pharaoh in turn had great power over the priests, because he provided a salary for each one (47:22). Pharaoh exercised his power over a high priest when he gave the daughter of the high priest of On to Joseph to be his wife (41:45).

GENERAL OF THE ARMY

The pharaoh also was the leader of Egypt's army. Many of the pharaohs planned battle strategies and led armies into battle. Nevertheless, every pharaoh had to have a lead general and a large command structure to train, organize, and deploy the soldiers of his large armies. In Egypt, the army also served as the police for the nation.[9] The lead general often had great influence on the pharaoh, and some were held in great respect and personal affection by their pharaohs.

Limestone wall fragment depicting offering bearers; from Sakkara, Egypt; dated about 2400–2250 BC. The men on the middle register carry birds and ale; in the top row, a priest named Irtyenankh carries a haunch of beef. He is followed by a man who has plucked a sacrificial bird from a cage.

SCRIBES

Though scattered through all of the government departments and other institutions of the nation, another position of high honor and power that was subject to the pharaoh was the scribe, who was highly trained in complicated hieroglyphic writing and without whom Egypt's advanced civilization could not function.[10] The much-treasured legacy of these scribes is the written record they left in tombs, pyramids, and temples, and on objects and scrolls. Without their work, much of what we know about ancient Egypt and its history would have been lost.

Though assisted by officers of high rank and great power and by a great host of lesser officials, the pharaoh of Egypt had absolute authority over appointment, punishment or reward, and removal from office. He actually held in his hands the life and death of everyone. The highest officers and their least assistants were pharaoh's servants and had one concern: pleasing pharaoh. Thus all of Egypt was ultimately the domain of one man. ✣

Padiouiset, an Egyptian priest, offers incense to the sun-god. Dated about 900 BC.

Double ink jars from Egypt's Nineteenth Dynasty, dated about 1280 BC. The inscription indicates the jars belonged to Vizier Paser, called the "Mayor of Thebes" during the reigns of pharaohs Seti I and Ramesses II.

---

[1] Thomas Nicol and Edgar W. Conrad, "Guard" in *ISBE*, 2:578. [2] Peter James Brand, Professor of Egyptology at University of Memphis, in personal correspondence with Leon Hyatt Jr., 21 August 2013. [3] Roland K. Harrison, "Baker" in *ISBE*, 1:404. Two examples of kings of other nations who furnished huge amounts of food for their courts daily: Solomon (1Kg 4:22–23) and Evil-merodach of Babylon (2Kg 25:29–30). [4] Benjamin Reno Downer and Roland K. Harrison, "Cupbearer" in *ISBE*, 1:837. [5] White, *Ancient Egypt* (New York: Crowell, 1953), 47–50. [6] Kenneth A. Kitchen, "Joseph" in *ISBE*, 2:1128. [7] Kenneth A. Kitchen, *The Third Intermediate Period in Egypt* (Warminster, England: Aris & Phillips, 1986), 3–6. [8] White, *Ancient Egypt*, 20–46; Jon Manchip White, *Everyday Life in Ancient Egypt* (New York: Dorset, 1963), 128–42. [9] Cyril Aldred, *The Egyptians*, rev. ed. (London: Thames & Hudson, 1987), 188–92. [10] White, *Everyday Life in Ancient Egypt*, 151–52.

[37] Then Reuben said to his father, "You can kill my
two sons if I don't bring him back to you. Put him in
my care,[A] and I will return him to you."
[38] But Jacob answered, "My son will not go down
with you, for his brother is dead and he alone is left.
If anything happens to him on your journey, you will
bring my gray hairs down to Sheol in sorrow."

DECISION TO RETURN TO EGYPT

43 Now the famine in the land was severe. [2] When
they had used up the grain they had brought
back from Egypt, their father said to them, "Go back
and buy us a little food."
[3] But Judah said to him, "The man specifically
warned us, 'You will not see me again unless your
brother is with you.' [4] If you will send our brother
with us, we will go down and buy food for you. [5] But
if you will not send him, we will not go, for the man
said to us, 'You will not see me again unless your
brother is with you.'"
[6] "Why have you caused me so much trouble?" Israel asked. "Why did you tell the man that you had
another brother?"
[7] They answered, "The man kept asking about us
and our family: 'Is your father still alive? Do you have
another brother?' And we answered him accordingly.
How could we know that he would say, 'Bring your
brother here'?"
[8] Then Judah said to his father Israel, "Send the boy
with me. We will be on our way so that we may live
and not die — neither we, nor you, nor our dependents. [9] I will be responsible for him. You can hold me
personally accountable![B] If I do not bring him back
to you and set him before you, I will be guilty before
you forever. [10] If we had not delayed, we could have
come back twice by now."
[11] Then their father Israel said to them, "If it must be
so, then do this: Put some of the best products of the
land in your packs and take them down to the man
as a gift — a little balsam and a little honey, aromatic
gum and resin, pistachios and almonds. [12] Take twice
as much silver with you. Return the silver that was
returned to you in the top of your bags. Perhaps it
was a mistake. [13] Take your brother also, and go back
at once to the man. [14] May God Almighty cause the
man to be merciful to you so that he will release your
other brother and Benjamin to you. As for me, if I am
deprived of my sons, then I am deprived."

[A] **42:37** Lit *hand* [B] **43:9** Lit *can seek him from my hand*

Dated 2000–1900 BC (patriarchal period), painted Egyptian model of a grain storage unit. Four compartments, each accessible by individual openings in the roof, represented the four attic compartments where grain was actually stored. After correctly interpreting Pharaoh's dream, Joseph secured grain for Egypt before the famine began.

Manasseh, Son of Joseph

by Alan Ray Buescher

While Joseph lived in Egypt, he married Asenath, the daughter of Potiphera, priest at On. Asenath bore two sons with Joseph; the second was Ephraim; the first was Manasseh (Gn 41:51–52; 46:20).

Before his death, Moses allotted land east of the Jordan River to the tribes of Reuben and Gad, and some to Manasseh. The Lord instructed Joshua to divide the land among the tribes according to lot. Manasseh, represented by two half-tribes, received land on the east side of the Jordan that Moses had promised—Gilead and Bashan (Jos 17:1)—and land in the central hill country, north of the area allotted to Ephraim.

Manasseh's land in the central hill country had the city of Shechem at its southern border and continued north to the Jezreel Valley. Taanach and Megiddo, cities located on the southern edge of the Jezreel Valley, provided strategic control of the major trade route between Egypt and Mesopotamia that passed through the land of Canaan.

Ephraim and Manasseh had the largest concentration of Israelite settlements by the time of the monarchy (Iron Age I; 1200–1000 BC).[1] Since the Canaanites maintained control of the Jezreel Valley and the Philistines held the coastal plains during the time of the judges, the land allotted to the sons of Joseph at least provided a foothold in the promised land from which the monarchy would later launch successful military campaigns and lay claim to the land God had given them. Furthermore, the territory of Manasseh contained the three cities that were capitals of the northern kingdom of Israel in later years: Shechem, Tirzah, and Samaria.

God used the location of Ephraim and Manasseh to provide an anchor for the strategic expansion of the Israelite monarchy and control of the international trade route that passed by and through their land. ✣

[1] Amihai Mazar, *Archaeology of the Land of the Bible* (New York: Doubleday, 1990), 335.

The father-in-law of the patriarch Joseph was a priest of On. In Egypt, On was the city later known as Heliopolis. It was a center of worship for the sun god Re. This seventy-foot-tall, red granite obelisk was originally erected in 1600 BC in Heliopolis.

Cattle on the hillside at Bashan, just east of the Sea of Galilee.

Ruins at Dor. Although Dor was located in the tribal territory of East Manasseh, it remained unconquered until King David's reign.

THE RETURN TO EGYPT

15 The men took this gift, double the amount of silver, and Benjamin. They immediately went down to Egypt and stood before Joseph.

16 When Joseph saw Benjamin with them, he said to his steward, "Take the men to my house. Slaughter an animal and prepare it, for they will eat with me at noon." 17 The man did as Joseph had said and brought them to Joseph's house.

18 But the men were afraid because they were taken to Joseph's house. They said, "We have been brought here because of the silver that was returned in our bags the first time. They intend to overpower us, seize us, make us slaves, and take our donkeys." 19 So they approached Joseph's steward[A] and spoke to him at the doorway of the house.

20 They said, "My lord, we really did come down here the first time only to buy food. 21 When we came to the place where we lodged for the night and opened our bags of grain, each one's silver was at the top of his bag! It was the full amount of our silver, and we have brought it back with us. 22 We have brought additional silver with us to buy food. We don't know who put our silver in the bags."

23 Then the steward said, "May you be well. Don't be afraid. Your God and the God of your father must have put treasure in your bags. I received your silver." Then he brought Simeon out to them. 24 The steward brought the men into Joseph's house, gave them water to wash their feet, and got feed for their donkeys. 25 Since the men had heard that they were going to eat a meal there, they prepared their gift for Joseph's arrival at noon. 26 When Joseph came home, they brought him the gift they had carried into the house, and they bowed to the ground before him.

27 He asked if they were well, and he said, "How is your elderly father that you told me about? Is he still alive?"

28 They answered, "Your servant our father is well. He is still alive." And they knelt low and paid homage to him.

29 When he looked up and saw his brother Benjamin, his mother's son, he asked, "Is this your youngest brother that you told me about?" Then he said, "May God be gracious to you, my son." 30 Joseph hurried out because he was overcome with emotion for his brother, and he was about to weep. He went into an inner room and wept there. 31 Then he washed his face and came out. Regaining his composure, he said, "Serve the meal."

32 They served him by himself, his brothers by themselves, and the Egyptians who were eating with him by themselves, because Egyptians could not eat with Hebrews, since that is detestable to them. 33 They were seated before him in order by age, from the firstborn to the youngest. The men looked at each other in astonishment. 34 Portions were served to them from Joseph's table, and Benjamin's portion was five times larger than any of theirs. They drank and became drunk with Joseph.

JOSEPH'S FINAL TEST

44 Joseph commanded his steward, "Fill the men's bags with as much food as they can carry, and put each one's silver at the top of his bag. 2 Put my cup, the silver one, at the top of the youngest one's bag, along with the silver for his grain." So he did as Joseph told him.

3 At morning light, the men were sent off with their donkeys. 4 They had not gone very far from the city when Joseph said to his steward, "Get up. Pursue the men, and when you overtake them, say to them, 'Why have you repaid evil for good? 5 Isn't this the cup that my master drinks from and uses for divination? What you have done is wrong!'"

6 When he overtook them, he said these words to them. 7 They said to him, "Why does my lord say these things? Your servants could not possibly do such a thing. 8 We even brought back to you from the land of Canaan the silver we found at the top of our bags. How could we steal silver or gold from your master's house? 9 If it is found with one of us, your servants, he must die, and the rest of us will become my lord's slaves."

10 The steward replied, "What you have said is right, but only the one who is found to have it will be my slave, and the rest of you will be blameless."

11 So each one quickly lowered his sack to the ground and opened it. 12 The steward searched, beginning with the oldest and ending with the youngest, and the cup was found in Benjamin's sack. 13 Then they tore their clothes, and each one loaded his donkey and returned to the city.

14 When Judah and his brothers reached Joseph's house, he was still there. They fell to the ground before him. 15 "What have you done?" Joseph said to them. "Didn't you know that a man like me could uncover the truth by divination?"

16 "What can we say to my lord?" Judah replied. "How can we plead? How can we justify ourselves? God has exposed your servants' iniquity. We are now my lord's slaves — both we and the one in whose possession the cup was found."

17 Then Joseph said, "I swear that I will not do this. The man in whose possession the cup was found will be my slave. The rest of you can go in peace to your father."

[A] **43:19** Lit *approached the one who was over the house*

Blue faience chalice, mold-made with a lotus design; dated about 1475–1350 BC.

JUDAH'S PLEA FOR BENJAMIN

18 But Judah approached him and said, "My lord, please let your servant speak personally to my lord. Do not be angry with your servant, for you are like Pharaoh. 19 My lord asked his servants, 'Do you have a father or a brother?' 20 and we answered my lord, 'We have an elderly father and a younger brother, the child of his old age. The boy's brother is dead. He is the only one of his mother's sons left, and his father loves him.' 21 Then you said to your servants, 'Bring him to me so that I can see him.' 22 But we said to my lord, 'The boy cannot leave his father. If he were to leave, his father would die.' 23 Then you said to your servants, 'If your younger brother does not come down with you, you will not see me again.'

24 "This is what happened when we went back to your servant my father: We reported to him the words of my lord. 25 But our father said, 'Go again, and buy us a little food.' 26 We told him, 'We cannot go down unless our younger brother goes with us. If our younger brother isn't with us, we cannot see the man.' 27 Your servant my father said to us, 'You know that my wife bore me two sons. 28 One is gone from me — I said he must have been torn to pieces — and I have never seen him again. 29 If you also take this one from me and anything happens to him, you will bring my gray hairs down to Sheol in sorrow.'

30 "So if I come to your servant my father and the boy is not with us — his life is wrapped up with the boy's life — 31 when he sees that the boy is not with us, he will die. Then your servants will have brought the gray hairs of your servant our father down to Sheol in sorrow. 32 Your servant became accountable to my father for the boy, saying, 'If I do not return him to you, I will always bear the guilt for sinning against you, my father.' 33 Now please let your servant remain here as my lord's slave, in place of the boy. Let him go back with his brothers. 34 For how can I go back to my father without the boy? I could not bear to see the grief that would overwhelm my father."

JOSEPH REVEALS HIS IDENTITY

45 Joseph could no longer keep his composure in front of all his attendants,[A] so he called out, "Send everyone away from me!" No one was with him when he revealed his identity to his brothers. 2 But he wept so loudly that the Egyptians heard it, and also Pharaoh's household heard it. 3 Joseph said to his brothers, "I am Joseph! Is my father still living?" But they could not answer him because they were terrified in his presence.

4 Then Joseph said to his brothers, "Please, come near me," and they came near. "I am Joseph, your brother," he said, "the one you sold into Egypt. 5 And now don't be grieved or angry with yourselves for selling me here, because God sent me ahead of you to preserve life. 6 For the famine has been in the land these two years, and there will be five more years without plowing or harvesting. 7 God sent me ahead of you to establish you as a remnant within the land and to keep you alive by a great deliverance.[B] 8 Therefore it was not you who sent me here, but God. He has made me a father to Pharaoh, lord of his entire household, and ruler over all the land of Egypt.

9 "Return quickly to my father and say to him, 'This is what your son Joseph says: "God has made me lord of all Egypt. Come down to me without delay. 10 You can settle in the land of Goshen and be near me — you, your children, and your grandchildren, your flocks, your herds, and all you have. 11 There I will sustain you, for there will be five more years of famine. Otherwise, you, your household, and everything you have will become destitute."' 12 Look! Your eyes and the eyes of my brother Benjamin can see that I'm[C] the one speaking to you. 13 Tell my father about all my glory in Egypt and about all you have seen. And bring my father here quickly."

14 Then Joseph threw his arms around his brother Benjamin and wept, and Benjamin wept on his shoulder. 15 Joseph kissed each of his brothers as he wept,[D] and afterward his brothers talked with him.

[A] **45:1** Lit *all those standing about him* [B] **45:7** Or *keep alive for you many survivors* [C] **45:12** Lit *that my mouth is* [D] **45:15** Lit *brothers, and he wept over them*

THE RETURN FOR JACOB

16 When the news reached Pharaoh's palace, "Joseph's
brothers have come," Pharaoh and his servants were
pleased. 17 Pharaoh said to Joseph, "Tell your brothers,
'Do this: Load your animals and go on back to the land
of Canaan. 18 Get your father and your families, and
come back to me. I will give you the best of the land of
Egypt, and you can eat from the richness of the land.'
19 You are also commanded to tell them, 'Do this: Take
wagons from the land of Egypt for your dependents
and your wives and bring your father here. 20 Do not
be concerned about your belongings, for the best of
all the land of Egypt is yours.' "

21 The sons of Israel did this. Joseph gave them
wagons as Pharaoh had commanded, and he gave
them provisions for the journey. 22 He gave each of
the brothers changes of clothes, but he gave Benjamin three hundred pieces of silver and five changes of clothes. 23 He sent his father the following: ten
donkeys carrying the best products of Egypt and ten
female donkeys carrying grain, food, and provisions
for his father on the journey. 24 So Joseph sent his
brothers on their way, and as they were leaving, he
said to them, "Don't argue[A] on the way."

25 So they went up from Egypt and came to their
father Jacob in the land of Canaan. 26 They said, "Joseph is still alive, and he is ruler over all the land of
Egypt! " Jacob was stunned,[B] for he did not believe
them. 27 But when they told Jacob all that Joseph had
said to them, and when he saw the wagons that Joseph had sent to transport him, the spirit of their
father Jacob revived.

28 Then Israel said, "Enough! My son Joseph is still
alive. I will go to see him before I die."

JACOB LEAVES FOR EGYPT

46 Israel set out with all that he had and came
to Beer-sheba, and he offered sacrifices to
the God of his father Isaac. 2 That night God spoke to
Israel in a vision: "Jacob, Jacob! " he said.

And Jacob replied, "Here I am."

3 God said, "I am God, the God of your father. Do
not be afraid to go down to Egypt, for I will make
you into a great nation there. 4 I will go down with
you to Egypt, and I will also bring you back. Joseph
will close your eyes when you die."[C]

5 Jacob left Beer-sheba. The sons of Israel took their
father Jacob in the wagons Pharaoh had sent to carry
him, along with their dependents and their wives.
6 They also took their cattle and possessions they
had acquired in the land of Canaan. Then Jacob and
all his offspring with him came to Egypt. 7 His sons
and grandsons, his daughters and granddaughters,
indeed all his offspring, he brought with him to Egypt.

JACOB'S FAMILY

8 These are the names of the sons of Israel who came
to Egypt — Jacob and his sons:

Jacob's firstborn: Reuben.

9 Reuben's sons: Hanoch, Pallu, Hezron,
and Carmi.

[A] **45:24** Or *be anxious* [B] **45:26** Lit *Jacob's heart was numb* [C] **46:4** Lit *will put his hand on your eyes*

Harvesting scene in Egypt.

10 Simeon's sons: Jemuel, Jamin, Ohad,
Jachin, Zohar, and Shaul, the son
of a Canaanite woman.
11 Levi's sons: Gershon, Kohath, and Merari.
12 Judah's sons: Er, Onan, Shelah, Perez,
and Zerah; but Er and Onan died in the land
of Canaan.
The sons of Perez were Hezron and Hamul.
13 Issachar's sons: Tola, Puvah,[A] Jashub,[B]
and Shimron.
14 Zebulun's sons: Sered, Elon, and Jahleel.
15 These were Leah's sons born to Jacob
in Paddan-aram, as well as his daughter
Dinah. The total number of persons:[C]
thirty-three.
16 Gad's sons: Ziphion, Haggi, Shuni, Ezbon, Eri,
Arodi, and Areli.
17 Asher's sons: Imnah, Ishvah, Ishvi, Beriah,
and their sister Serah.
Beriah's sons were Heber and Malchiel.
18 These were the sons of Zilpah — whom Laban
gave to his daughter Leah — that she bore
to Jacob: sixteen persons.
19 The sons of Jacob's wife Rachel:
Joseph and Benjamin.
20 Manasseh and Ephraim were born to Joseph
in the land of Egypt. They were born to him
by Asenath daughter of Potiphera, a priest
at On.[D]
21 Benjamin's sons: Bela, Becher, Ashbel, Gera,
Naaman, Ehi, Rosh, Muppim, Huppim,
and Ard.
22 These were Rachel's sons who were born
to Jacob: fourteen persons.
23 Dan's son:[E] Hushim.
24 Naphtali's sons: Jahzeel, Guni, Jezer,
and Shillem.
25 These were the sons of Bilhah, whom Laban
gave to his daughter Rachel. She bore
to Jacob: seven persons.
26 The total number of persons
belonging to Jacob —
his direct descendants,[F] not including
the wives of Jacob's sons — who came
to Egypt: sixty-six.
27 And Joseph's sons who were born to him
in Egypt: two persons.
All those of Jacob's household
who came to Egypt: seventy[G] persons.

JACOB ARRIVES IN EGYPT

28 Now Jacob had sent Judah ahead of him to Joseph
to prepare for his arrival[H] at Goshen. When they came
to the land of Goshen, 29 Joseph hitched the horses to
his chariot and went up to Goshen to meet his father
Israel. Joseph presented himself to him, threw his
arms around him, and wept for a long time.
30 Then Israel said to Joseph, "I'm ready to die now
because I have seen your face and you are still alive!"
31 Joseph said to his brothers and to his father's
family, "I will go up and inform Pharaoh, telling him,
'My brothers and my father's family, who were in the
land of Canaan, have come to me. 32 The men are shepherds; they also raise livestock. They have brought
their flocks and herds and all that they have.' 33 When
Pharaoh addresses you and asks, 'What is your occupation?' 34 you are to say, 'Your servants, both we and
our ancestors, have raised livestock[I] from our youth
until now.' Then you will be allowed to settle in the
land of Goshen, since all shepherds are detestable
to Egyptians."

PHARAOH WELCOMES JACOB

47 So Joseph went and informed Pharaoh: "My
father and my brothers, with their flocks and
herds and all that they own, have come from the land
of Canaan and are now in the land of Goshen."
2 He took five of his brothers and presented them
to Pharaoh. 3 And Pharaoh asked his brothers, "What
is your occupation?"
They said to Pharaoh, "Your servants, both we and
our ancestors, are shepherds." 4 And they said to Pharaoh, "We have come to stay in the land for a while
because there is no grazing land for your servants'
sheep, since the famine in the land of Canaan has
been severe. So now, please let your servants settle
in the land of Goshen."
5 Then Pharaoh said to Joseph, "Now that your
father and brothers have come to you, 6 the land
of Egypt is open before you; settle your father and
brothers in the best part of the land. They can live in
the land of Goshen. If you know of any capable men
among them, put them in charge of my livestock."
7 Joseph then brought his father Jacob and presented him to Pharaoh, and Jacob blessed Pharaoh.
8 Pharaoh said to Jacob, "How many years have you
lived?"
9 Jacob said to Pharaoh, "My pilgrimage has lasted
130 years. My years have been few and hard, and they
have not reached the years of my ancestors during
their pilgrimages." 10 So Jacob blessed Pharaoh and
departed from Pharaoh's presence.
11 Then Joseph settled his father and brothers in
the land of Egypt and gave them property in the best
part of the land, the land of Rameses, as Pharaoh

[A] **46:13** Sam, Syr read *Puah*; 1Ch 7:1 [B] **46:13** Sam, LXX; MT reads *Iob*
[C] **46:15** Lit *All persons his sons and his daughters:* [D] **46:20** Or *Heliopolis*
[E] **46:23** Alt Hb tradition reads *sons:* [F] **46:26** Lit *Jacob who came out from his loins* [G] **46:27** LXX reads *75*; Ac 7:14 [H] **46:28** Lit *to give directions before him* [I] **46:34** Lit *fathers, are men of livestock*

Wheat field beside the Nile Valley at Beni Hasan.

had commanded. 12 And Joseph provided his father,
his brothers, and all his father's family with food for
their dependents.

THE LAND BECOMES PHARAOH'S

13 But there was no food in the entire region, for the
famine was very severe. The land of Egypt and the
land of Canaan were exhausted by the famine. 14 Joseph collected all the silver to be found in the land
of Egypt and the land of Canaan in exchange for the
grain they were purchasing, and he brought the silver to Pharaoh's palace. 15 When the silver from the
land of Egypt and the land of Canaan was gone, all
the Egyptians came to Joseph and said, "Give us food.
Why should we die here in front of you? The silver
is gone!"

16 But Joseph said, "Give me your livestock. Since
the silver is gone, I will give you food in exchange for
your livestock." 17 So they brought their livestock to
Joseph, and he gave them food in exchange for the
horses, the flocks of sheep, the herds of cattle, and
the donkeys. That year he provided them with food
in exchange for all their livestock.

18 When that year was over, they came the next year
and said to him, "We cannot hide from our lord that
the silver is gone and that all our livestock belongs
to our lord. There is nothing left for our lord except
our bodies and our land. 19 Why should we die here
in front of you — both us and our land? Buy us and
our land in exchange for food. Then we with our land
will become Pharaoh's slaves. Give us seed so that
we can live and not die, and so that the land won't
become desolate."

20 In this way, Joseph acquired all the land in Egypt
for Pharaoh, because every Egyptian sold his field
since the famine was so severe for them. The land
became Pharaoh's, 21 and Joseph made the people servants[A] from one end of Egypt to the other. 22 The only
land he did not acquire belonged to the priests, for
they had an allowance from Pharaoh. They ate from
their allowance that Pharaoh gave them; therefore
they did not sell their land.

23 Joseph said to the people, "Understand today that
I have acquired you and your land for Pharaoh. Here
is seed for you. Sow it in the land. 24 At harvest, you are
to give a fifth of it to Pharaoh, and four-fifths will be
yours as seed for the field and as food for yourselves,
your households, and your dependents."

25 "You have saved our lives," they said. "We have
found favor with our lord and will be Pharaoh's
slaves." 26 So Joseph made it a law, still in effect today in the land of Egypt, that a fifth of the produce
belongs to Pharaoh. Only the priests' land does not
belong to Pharaoh.

[A] **47:21** Sam, LXX; MT reads *and he moved the people to the cities*

ISRAEL SETTLES IN GOSHEN

27 Israel settled in the land of Egypt, in the region of
Goshen. They acquired property in it and became
fruitful and very numerous. 28 Now Jacob lived in
the land of Egypt 17 years, and his life span was 147
years. 29 When the time approached for him to die, he
called his son Joseph and said to him, "If I have found
favor with you, put your hand under my thigh and
promise me that you will deal with me in kindness
and faithfulness. Do not bury me in Egypt. 30 When
I rest with my ancestors, carry me away from Egypt
and bury me in their burial place."

Joseph answered, "I will do what you have asked."

31 And Jacob said, "Swear to me." So Joseph swore
to him. Then Israel bowed in thanks at the head of
his bed.[A]

JACOB BLESSES EPHRAIM AND MANASSEH

48 Some time after this, Joseph was told, "Your
father is weaker." So he set out with his two
sons, Manasseh and Ephraim. 2 When Jacob was told,
"Your son Joseph has come to you," Israel summoned
his strength and sat up in bed.

3 Jacob said to Joseph, "God Almighty appeared to
me at Luz in the land of Canaan and blessed me. 4 He
said to me, 'I will make you fruitful and numerous;
I will make many nations come from you, and I will
give this land as a permanent possession to your
future descendants.' 5 Your two sons born to you
in the land of Egypt before I came to you in Egypt
are now mine. Ephraim and Manasseh belong to
me just as Reuben and Simeon do. 6 Children born
to you after them will be yours and will be recorded under the names of their brothers with regard
to their inheritance. 7 When I was returning from
Paddan, to my sorrow Rachel died along the way,
some distance from Ephrath in the land of Canaan.
I buried her there along the way to Ephrath" (that
is, Bethlehem).

8 When Israel saw Joseph's sons, he said, "Who
are these?"

9 And Joseph said to his father, "They are my sons
God has given me here."

So Israel said, "Bring them to me and I will bless
them." 10 Now his eyesight was poor because of old
age; he could hardly[B] see. Joseph brought them to
him, and he kissed and embraced them. 11 Israel said
to Joseph, "I never expected to see your face again, but
now God has even let me see your offspring." 12 Then
Joseph took them from his father's knees and bowed
with his face to the ground.

EPHRAIM'S GREATER BLESSING

13 Then Joseph took them both — with his right hand
Ephraim toward Israel's left, and with his left hand

Rembrandt's depiction of Jacob blessing Joseph's sons, Ephraim and Manasseh, before his death.

Manasseh toward Israel's right — and brought them
to Israel. 14 But Israel stretched out his right hand
and put it on the head of Ephraim, the younger, and
crossing his hands, put his left on Manasseh's head,
although Manasseh was the firstborn. 15 Then he
blessed Joseph and said:

The God before whom my fathers Abraham
  and Isaac walked,
the God who has been my shepherd all my life
  to this day,
16 the angel who has redeemed me
  from all harm —
may he bless these boys.
And may they be called by my name
and the names of my fathers Abraham
  and Isaac,
and may they grow to be numerous
  within the land.

17 When Joseph saw that his father had placed his
right hand on Ephraim's head, he thought it was a
mistake[C] and took his father's hand to move it from
Ephraim's head to Manasseh's. 18 Joseph said to his
father, "Not that way, my father! This one is the firstborn. Put your right hand on his head."

19 But his father refused and said, "I know, my son,
I know! He too will become a tribe,[D] and he too will
be great; nevertheless, his younger brother will be
greater than he, and his offspring will become a pop-
ulous nation."[E] 20 So he blessed them that day, putting

[A] **47:31** Or *Israel worshiped while leaning on the top of his staff*
[B] **48:10** Lit *he was not able to* [C] **48:17** Or *he was displeased*; lit *head, it was bad in his eyes* [D] **48:19** Lit *people* [E] **48:19** Or *a multitude of nations*; lit *a fullness of nations*

Ephraim before Manasseh when he said, "The nation Israel will invoke blessings by you, saying, 'May God make you like Ephraim and Manasseh.'"
21 Israel said to Joseph, "Look, I am about to die, but God will be with you and will bring you back to the land of your fathers.
22 Over and above what I am giving your brothers, I am giving you the one mountain slope[A] that I took from the Amorites with my sword and bow."

JACOB'S LAST WORDS

49 Then Jacob called his sons and said, "Gather around, and I will tell you what will happen to you in the days to come.[B]

2 Come together and listen, sons of Jacob;
listen to your father Israel:

3 Reuben, you are my firstborn,
my strength and the firstfruits of my virility,
excelling in prominence, excelling in power.
4 Turbulent as water, you will not excel,
because you got into your father's bed
and you defiled it — he[C] got into my bed.

5 Simeon and Levi are brothers;
their knives are vicious weapons.
6 May I never enter their council;
may I never join their assembly.
For in their anger they kill men,
and on a whim they hamstring oxen.
7 Their anger is cursed, for it is strong,
and their fury, for it is cruel!
I will disperse them throughout Jacob
and scatter them throughout Israel.

8 Judah, your brothers will praise you.
Your hand will be on the necks
of your enemies;
your father's sons will bow down to you.
9 Judah is a young lion —
my son, you return from the kill.
He crouches; he lies down like a lion
or a lioness — who dares to rouse him?
10 The scepter will not depart from Judah
or the staff from between his feet
until he whose right it is comes[D]
and the obedience of the peoples belongs
to him.
11 He ties his donkey to a vine,
and the colt of his donkey
to the choice vine.
He washes his clothes in wine
and his robes in the blood of grapes.
12 His eyes are darker than wine,
and his teeth are whiter than milk.

13 Zebulun will live by the seashore
and will be a harbor for ships,
and his territory will be next to Sidon.

14 Issachar is a strong donkey
lying down between the saddlebags.[E]
15 He saw that his resting place was good
and that the land was pleasant,
so he leaned his shoulder to bear a load
and became a forced laborer.

16 Dan will judge his people
as one of the tribes of Israel.
17 Dan will be a snake by the road,
a viper beside the path,
that bites the horse's heels
so that its rider falls backward.

18 I wait for your salvation, LORD.

19 Gad will be attacked by raiders,
but he will attack their heels.

20 Asher's[F] food will be rich,
and he will produce royal delicacies.

21 Naphtali is a doe set free
that bears beautiful fawns.

22 Joseph is a fruitful vine,
a fruitful vine beside a spring;
its branches[G] climb over the wall.[H]
23 The archers attacked him,
shot at him, and were hostile toward him.
24 Yet his bow remained steady,
and his strong arms were made agile
by the hands of the Mighty One of Jacob,
by the name of[I] the Shepherd, the Rock
of Israel,
25 by the God of your father who helps you,
and by the Almighty who blesses you
with blessings of the heavens above,
blessings of the deep that lies below,
and blessings of the breasts and the womb.
26 The blessings of your father excel
the blessings of my ancestors[J]
and[K] the bounty of the ancient hills.[H]
May they rest on the head of Joseph,
on the brow of the prince of his brothers.

[A] **48:22** Or *Shechem*, Joseph's burial place; lit *one shoulder* [B] **49:1** Or *in the last days* [C] **49:4** LXX, Syr, Tg read *you* [D] **49:10** Or *until tribute comes to him*, or *until Shiloh comes*, or *until he comes to Shiloh* [E] **49:14** Or *sheep pens* [F] **49:19–20** LXX, Syr, Vg; MT reads *their heel.* **20***From Asher* [G] **49:22** Lit *daughters* [H] **49:22,26** Hb obscure [I] **49:24** Syr, Tg; MT reads *Jacob, from there* [J] **49:26** Or *of the mountains* [K] **49:26** Lit *to*

Egyptian Mummification/ Mourning the Deceased

by Scott Langston and Fred Wood

The belief that each individual possessed a *ka* and a *ba* as aspects of personality compelled Egyptians to preserve the body after death. The *ka* functioned as the "double" of the living person and resided with the individual in the afterlife. The *ba*, often translated as "soul," traveled throughout the underworld but also returned to the deceased each morning. Both of these aspects of a person needed a home for eternity. So it became important to preserve the body as that home. This need, therefore, may have helped produce the development of artificial mummification.[1]

The process as practiced by the ancient Egyptians developed over several centuries. In the early days, called the Old Kingdom (2830–2130 BC), only members of the royalty, especially the king, possessed access to it for their families. By the time of the New Kingdom (1570–1070 BC), the practice extended to almost anyone who desired and could afford it.[2] The process differed according to one's ability to pay.

First, the embalmers removed all the internal organs except the heart. The Egyptians considered the heart necessary to activity in the afterlife. Knowing the internal organs decomposed first, the embalmers mummified them separately. They placed the internal organs in canopic jars in the tomb at the time of the burial. Believing the heart was the seat of intelligence and emotion, the Egyptians left it in the body. Contending the brain had no significant value, they removed it through the nose and discarded it.

Second, the embalmers packed and covered the body with natron, a salty drying agent. They left the body to dry out for forty to fifty days. By this time, the body's moisture had been absorbed, leaving only the hair, skin, and bones. They then stuffed the body cavity with resin, sawdust, or linen to restore the deceased's form and features.

Third, the embalmers wrapped the body in many layers of linen, inserting good luck or protective charms, known as amulets. Since Egyptians considered the scarab beetle the most important good

An open canopic chest revealing alabaster jars sculpted in the likeness of a king.

Model burial of the Late Predynastic period. The body, which is not mummified but desiccated by the dry, hot sand that covered it, is placed on its left side in a contracted position.

Mummy of a priest's wife.

luck piece, embalmers placed it above the heart. The priests recited prayers or incantations at each stage of the wrapping. This often required as many as fifteen days. The final act consisted of putting the body in a shroud or winding sheet. The entire mummification process required about seventy days.

Those in charge of placing the mummy in a decorated coffin also placed prepared furniture, carved statues, games, food, and other items to be buried with the mummy. One final ritual remained, called "The Opening of the Mouth." Egyptians believed this ceremony gave the deceased ability to speak again, eat again, and have full use of his body in the "other world." Having completed the work of embalming and the accompanying rituals, the embalmers sealed the sarcophagus and pronounced it ready for burial.

Unless the person was affluent or of great importance, his funeral resembled one of today but in the context of Egyptian culture. For the poor or anyone not of royalty, funeral services involved little pomp or ceremony. The preparers steeped the body for a short time in bitumen or natron or perhaps even rubbed the body with these substances. They placed his few personal ornaments on it and wrapped it in one piece of linen. To aid him in the nether world, his staff and sandals accompanied him. A few amulets to

Mummification scene in a burial chamber of the catacombs of Kom-El-Shogafa.

help him meet his foe in the grave completed the package.

Not so, the burial of the monarch, his family, or an extremely opulent person. When a king died, the country died symbolically, all the country's inhabitants wept and tore their garments. Religious officials closed the temples. The people abstained from sacrifices and celebrated no festivals for seventy-two days. Men and women went about the streets in great crowds, sometimes as many as two or three hundred with mud on their heads. Knotting their garments below their breasts like girdles, they sang dirges twice daily in praise of the dead. They denied themselves wheat, animal food, wine, and any kind of delicacy or dainty fare.

During this time, no one made use of baths or unguents nor did anyone recline on couches or enjoy the pleasures of sexual love. The people rather continued to sing dirges and spent the days in grief. Meanwhile those preparing the body assembled the paraphernalia necessary for the funeral and placed it in the coffin.

The Scriptures tell us Joseph instructed the physicians in his service to embalm Jacob's body. This varied from ordinary Hebrew custom, but the faithful son planned to fulfill his father's request to carry the body back for burial in the Cave of Machpelah. ✣

A wall painting fragment of mourning women from the tomb of Neb-Amon at Thebes.

---

[1]James E. Harris and Kent R. Weeks, *X-Raying the Pharaohs* (New York: Scribner's Sons, 1973), 76. John Baines and Jaromir Malek, *Atlas of Ancient Egypt* (Oxford: Phaidon, 1984), 226. [2]William J. Murname, "History of Egypt: New Kingdom (DYN. 18–20)," *ABD*, 2:348.

27 Benjamin is a wolf; he tears his prey.
In the morning he devours the prey,
and in the evening he divides the plunder."

28 These are the tribes of Israel, twelve in all, and this is what their father said to them. He blessed them, and he blessed each one with a suitable blessing.

JACOB'S BURIAL INSTRUCTIONS

29 Then he commanded them, "I am about to be gathered to my people. Bury me with my ancestors in the cave in the field of Ephron the Hethite. 30 The cave is in the field of Machpelah near Mamre, in the land of Canaan. This is the field Abraham purchased from Ephron the Hethite as burial property. 31 Abraham and his wife Sarah are buried there, Isaac and his wife Rebekah are buried there, and I buried Leah there. 32 The field and the cave in it were purchased from the Hethites." 33 When Jacob had finished giving charges to his sons, he drew his feet into the bed, took his last breath, and was gathered to his people.

JACOB'S BURIAL

50 Then Joseph, leaning over his father's face, wept and kissed him. 2 He commanded his servants who were physicians to embalm his father. So they embalmed Israel. 3 They took forty days to complete this, for embalming takes that long, and the Egyptians mourned for him seventy days.

4 When the days of mourning were over, Joseph said to Pharaoh's household, "If I have found favor with you, please tell Pharaoh that 5 my father made me take an oath, saying, 'I am about to die. You must bury me there in the tomb that I made for myself in the land of Canaan.' Now let me go and bury my father. Then I will return."

6 So Pharaoh said, "Go and bury your father in keeping with your oath."

7 Then Joseph went to bury his father, and all Pharaoh's servants, the elders of his household, and all the elders of the land of Egypt went with him, 8 along with all Joseph's family, his brothers, and his father's family. Only their dependents, their flocks, and their herds were left in the land of Goshen. 9 Horses and chariots went up with him; it was a very impressive procession. 10 When they reached the threshing floor of Atad, which is across the Jordan, they lamented and wept loudly, and Joseph mourned seven days for his father. 11 When the Canaanite inhabitants of the land saw the mourning at the threshing floor of Atad, they said, "This is a solemn mourning on the part of the Egyptians." Therefore the place is named Abel-mizraim.[A] It is across the Jordan.

12 So Jacob's sons did for him what he had commanded them. 13 They carried him to the land of Canaan and buried him in the cave at Machpelah in the field near Mamre, which Abraham had purchased as burial property from Ephron the Hethite. 14 After Joseph buried his father, he returned to Egypt with his brothers and all who had gone with him to bury his father.

JOSEPH'S KINDNESS

15 When Joseph's brothers saw that their father was dead, they said to one another, "If Joseph is holding a grudge against us, he will certainly repay us for all the suffering we caused him."

16 So they sent this message to Joseph, "Before he died your father gave a command: 17 'Say this to Joseph: Please forgive your brothers' transgression and their sin — the suffering they caused you.' Therefore, please forgive the transgression of the servants of the God of your father." Joseph wept when their message came to him. 18 His brothers also came to him, bowed down before him, and said, "We are your slaves!"

19 But Joseph said to them, "Don't be afraid. Am I in the place of God? 20 You planned evil against me; God planned it for good to bring about the present result — the survival of many people. 21 Therefore don't be afraid. I will take care of you and your children." And he comforted them and spoke kindly to them.[B]

JOSEPH'S DEATH

22 Joseph and his father's family remained in Egypt. Joseph lived 110 years. 23 He saw Ephraim's sons to the third generation; the sons of Manasseh's son Machir were recognized by[C,D] Joseph.

24 Joseph said to his brothers, "I am about to die, but God will certainly come to your aid and bring you up from this land to the land he swore to give to Abraham, Isaac, and Jacob." 25 So Joseph made the sons of Israel take an oath: "When God comes to your aid, you are to carry my bones up from here."

26 Joseph died at the age of 110. They embalmed him and placed him in a coffin in Egypt.

[A] **50:11** = Mourning of Egypt [B] **50:21** Lit *spoke to their hearts*
[C] **50:23** Lit *were born on the knees of* [D] **50:23** Referring to a ritual of adoption or of legitimation; Gn 30:3

EXODUS

Mount Sinai, which the locals refer to as Jebel Musa (meaning "Mountain of Moses").

INTRODUCTION TO

EXODUS

Circumstances of Writing

The book of Exodus does not state who its author was. It does refer to occasions when Moses made a written record of events that took place and of what God had said (17:14; 24:4,7; 34:27–28). The book also contains references to preserving and passing on information. Along with the other four books of the Pentateuch, it has long been considered to be primarily the work of Moses. Moses could have written Exodus at any time during a forty-year time span: after the Israelites finished constructing and dedicating the tabernacle at Mount Sinai, at the start of their second year after leaving Egypt (1445 BC), and before his death in the land of Moab (ca 1406 BC).

Exodus picks up where the Genesis narrative ended, with the death of Joseph around 1805 BC. It quickly moves us forward almost three hundred years to a time when the circumstances of Jacob's descendants had changed in Egypt. The Israelites were serving as slaves during Egypt's Eighteenth Dynasty, probably under the pharaohs Thutmose and Amenhotep II. The Hebrew slaves experienced a miraculous deliverance by God's hand through his servant-leader Moses. The Israelite slavery ended in 1446 BC. The book of Exodus records the events surrounding the exodus from Egypt and the Israelites' first year in the wilderness, including the giving of the law.

The date of the exodus is disputed, but biblical evidence favors 1446 BC. First Kings 6:1 states that the exodus occurred 480 years before Solomon's fourth year as king, established by biblical data combined with Assyrian chronology to be 966 BC. In Judges 11:26, Jephthah said that Israel had been living in regions of Palestine for three hundred years. Jephthah lived around 1100 BC, thus dating the end of the wilderness journey to around 1400 BC.

Contribution to the Bible

Exodus provides the high point of redemptive history in the Old Testament. Many patterns and concepts from Exodus receive attention, further development, and fulfillment elsewhere in Scripture, especially in the past, present, and future work of the Lord Jesus. These include rescue from oppression, provision of sustenance, God's faithfulness to his promises, the self-revelation of God, knowledge of God resulting from his actions, the presence of God, God's glory, efforts required to preserve the knowledge of God, a new identity for people that is based on God's actions, provision for worship, provision for life in community, connection between the reputation of God and his relationship with a group of people, obedience and rebellion, intercession, and gracious forgiveness.

Structure

Exodus is considered a part of the Law, but it is more historical narrative than law. The book is structured around the life and travels of Moses. Sandwiched between the narratives of chapters 1–18 and 32–40 are the establishment of the covenant (chaps. 19–24) and the laws related to the tabernacle and priesthood.

ISRAEL OPPRESSED IN EGYPT

1 These are the names of the sons of Israel who came to Egypt with Jacob; each came with his family:

2 Reuben, Simeon, Levi, and Judah;
3 Issachar, Zebulun, and Benjamin;
4 Dan and Naphtali; Gad and Asher.

5 The total number of Jacob's descendants[A] was seventy;[B] Joseph was already in Egypt.

6 Joseph and all his brothers and all that generation eventually died. 7 But the Israelites were fruitful, increased rapidly, multiplied, and became extremely numerous so that the land was filled with them.

8 A new king, who did not know about Joseph, came to power in Egypt. 9 He said to his people, "Look, the Israelite people are more numerous and powerful than we are. 10 Come, let's deal shrewdly with them; otherwise they will multiply further, and when war breaks out, they will join our enemies, fight against us, and leave the country." 11 So the Egyptians assigned taskmasters over the Israelites to oppress them with forced labor. They built Pithom and Rameses as supply cities for Pharaoh. 12 But the more they oppressed them, the more they multiplied and spread so that the Egyptians came to dread[C] the Israelites. 13 They worked the Israelites ruthlessly 14 and made their lives bitter with difficult labor in brick and mortar and in all kinds of fieldwork. They ruthlessly imposed all this work on them.

15 The king of Egypt said to the Hebrew midwives — the first, whose name was Shiphrah, and the second, whose name was Puah — 16 "When you help the Hebrew women give birth, observe them as they deliver. If the child is a son, kill him, but if it's a daughter, she may live." 17 The midwives, however, feared God and did not do as the king of Egypt had told them; they let the boys live. 18 So the king of Egypt summoned the midwives and asked them, "Why have you done this and let the boys live?"

19 The midwives said to Pharaoh, "The Hebrew women are not like the Egyptian women, for they are vigorous and give birth before the midwife can get to them."

20 So God was good to the midwives, and the people multiplied and became very numerous. 21 Since the midwives feared God, he gave them families. 22 Pharaoh then commanded all his people, "You must throw every son born to the Hebrews into the Nile, but let every daughter live."

MOSES'S BIRTH AND ADOPTION

2 Now a man from the family of Levi married a Levite woman. 2 The woman became pregnant and gave birth to a son; when she saw that he was beautiful,[D] she hid him for three months. 3 But when she could no longer hide him, she got a papyrus basket for him and coated it with asphalt and pitch. She placed the child in it and set it among the reeds by the bank of the Nile. 4 Then his sister stood at a distance in order to see what would happen to him.

5 Pharaoh's daughter went down to bathe at the Nile while her servant girls walked along the riverbank. She saw the basket among the reeds, sent her slave girl, took it, 6 opened it, and saw him, the child — and there he was, a little boy, crying. She felt sorry for him and said, "This is one of the Hebrew boys."

7 Then his sister said to Pharaoh's daughter, "Should I go and call a Hebrew woman who is nursing to nurse the boy for you?"

8 "Go," Pharaoh's daughter told her. So the girl went and called the boy's mother. 9 Then Pharaoh's daughter said to her, "Take this child and nurse him for me, and I will pay your wages." So the woman took the boy and nursed him. 10 When the child grew older, she brought him to Pharaoh's daughter, and he became her son. She named him Moses,[E] "Because," she said, "I drew him out of the water."

MOSES IN MIDIAN

11 Years later,[F] after Moses had grown up, he went out to his own people[G] and observed their forced labor. He saw an Egyptian striking a Hebrew, one of his people. 12 Looking all around and seeing no one, he struck the Egyptian dead and hid him in the sand. 13 The next day he went out and saw two Hebrews fighting. He asked the one in the wrong, "Why are you attacking your neighbor?"[H]

14 "Who made you a commander and judge over us?" the man replied. "Are you planning to kill me as you killed the Egyptian?"

Then Moses became afraid and thought, "What I did is certainly known."

15 When Pharaoh heard about this, he tried to kill Moses. But Moses fled from Pharaoh and went to live in the land of Midian, and sat down by a well.

16 Now the priest of Midian had seven daughters. They came to draw water and filled the troughs to water their father's flock. 17 Then some shepherds arrived and drove them away, but Moses came to their rescue and watered their flock. 18 When they returned to their father Reuel,[I] he asked, "Why have you come back so quickly today?"

19 They answered, "An Egyptian rescued us from the shepherds. He even drew water for us and watered the flock."

[A] **1:5** Lit *of people issuing from Jacob's loins* [B] **1:5** LXX, DSS read *75*; Gn 46:27; Ac 7:14 [C] **1:12** Or *Egyptians loathed* [D] **2:2** Or *healthy* [E] **2:10** The name *Moses* sounds like "drawing out" in Hb and "born" in Egyptian. [F] **2:11** Lit *And it was in those days* [G] **2:11** Lit *his brothers* [H] **2:13** Or *fellow Hebrew* [I] **2:18** Jethro's clan or last name was Reuel; Ex 3:1.

Moses's Early Life

by Philip Swanson

Many comparisons have been made between the birth narrative of Moses in Exodus and that of the Legend of Sargon. Sargon, who later became king of Agade, was delivered to the river because he was the offspring of a priestess who had made vows of chastity and had broken them. As in most of the literature of this kind, the king in the legend was discovered by persons of low rank and carried to safety. The Moses narrative is directly the opposite.[1] Moses's birth is legitimate; a princess of high rank finds the baby; and the identity of the baby is beyond question; he is a Hebrew.

Nonetheless, the facts of Moses's adoption fit well the period of the Nineteenth Dynasty. Mesopotamian law texts have been discovered that relate the procedure for the paid services of a "wet-nurse" until the child reached the age of two or three years.[2] The bulk of Moses's training apparently came through the education system of the Egyptian court (Ac 7:22). That a foreigner would receive the privilege of an education in the royal court is well attested during the rule of the Ramesside kings.[3]

The Egyptians held an elevated view of learning, not for learning's sake, but because education separated the rulers from the ruled.[4] The rigorous schedule for learning began about the age of four[5] and included studies primarily in the areas of writing, reading, mathematics, and the sciences. Writing appears as the most important of the educational requirements.

The order of the day in their studies called for strict discipline. One notable proverb frames the education theory thus: "For the ears of the young are placed on his back, and he hears when he is flogged."[6] The Egyptians possessed a real knowledge of astronomy and provided the world with a usable calendar, in spite of its superstitious elements.[7] Even medicine found its way into the educational curriculum. Strange as it might seem for a people with such an affinity for writing and learning, in general, historical writings have eluded the archaeologist. Annals of the Pharaohs have been found recording the mighty deeds of the king, but no writing of a systematic history of any of the Egyptian periods exists today. Instruction in ethics and good manners, highly valued in the Egyptian world, rounded out the curriculum.[8] Only mathematics, however, escaped the scourge of magic and superstition.[9]

Another area of Egyptian influence in Moses's early life concerns Egyptian religion. Under the New Kingdom (Eighteenth–Twentieth Dynasties), the priesthood became quite powerful and involved in governmental affairs.[10] Some scholars attempt to connect the religious ideas of Moses (particularly monotheism) with the so-called monotheism of the Egyptian pharaoh Akhenaten. In revolt against the priesthood of Thebes, Akhenaten moved the capital city to a location between Thebes and Memphis and named it Akhenaten (modern Tell al-Amarna). The pharaoh proclaimed the god Aten as the "only god, unique and supreme over all the universe."[11] At the same time the pharaoh himself was looked upon as a god.[12] Pharaoh Akhenaten died before the time of Moses, and his efforts at monotheism died with him. Any influence the policies of Akhenaten might have exerted in Egypt would not likely have approached Moses.

Beyond the short-lived element of monotheism, the basic foundation of Egyptian religion remains so different from that of the early Hebrews that any real connection is difficult to make. "Egyptian religion was also practical in outlook. Whether you were a good man or a bad man it supplied you with a gratifying assortment of magical formulae guaranteed to get you by hook or by crook into heaven."[13] The ethical component, so apparent in Hebrew religion, was entirely lacking in the Egyptian system. The idea of sin remained foreign to the Egyptians' religious belief. When the gods punished, the punishment initiated correction to the worshiper who had neglected some facet of the religious ritual prescribed by the priests. The gods, for the most part, existed as immoral men, though a little larger than life.[14]

The student is immediately struck by the veneration of animals, as well. Animals with religious significance include cows, bulls, jackals, cats, lions, crocodiles, baboons, and cobras, as well as a multitude of birds, with the hawk being most prevalent. With astronomy playing an important part in the lives of the Egyptians, the association of gods with the major planets comes as no surprise. Mercury was often connected with the god Seth, Venus with the god Osiris, and Mars, Jupiter, and Saturn with the god Horus.[15] ✣

---

[1] Nahum M. Sarna, *Exploring Exodus: The Heritage of Biblical Israel* (New York: Schocken Books, 1986), 30. [2] Sarna, *Exploring Exodus*, 31–32. [3] Sarna, *Exploring Exodus*, 33. [4] Adolf Erman, *Life in Ancient Egypt*, trans. by H. M. Tirard (New York: Dover, 1971), 328. [5] Sarna, *Exploring Exodus*, 33. [6] Erman, *Life in Egypt*, 331. [7] Erman, *Life in Egypt*, 349–50. [8] Erman, *Life in Egypt*, 164–65. [9] Erman, *Life in Egypt*, 365. [10] Erman, *Life in Egypt*, 104–5. [11] Jack Finegan, *Myth & Mystery: An Introduction to the Pagan Religions of the Biblical World* (Grand Rapids: Baker, 1989), 58. [12] Erman, *Life in Egypt*, 70. [13] Jon E. Manchip White, *Ancient Egypt: Its Culture and History* (New York: Dover, 1970), 36. [14] White, *Ancient Egypt*, 35. [15] Finegan, *Myth & Mystery*, 47.

20 "So where is he?" he asked his daughters. "Why then did you leave the man behind? Invite him to eat dinner."

21 Moses agreed to stay with the man, and he gave his daughter Zipporah to Moses in marriage. 22 She gave birth to a son whom he named Gershom,[A] for he said, "I have been a resident alien in a foreign land."

23 After a long time, the king of Egypt died. The Israelites groaned because of their difficult labor, they cried out, and their cry for help because of the difficult labor ascended to God. 24 God heard their groaning, and God remembered his covenant with Abraham, with Isaac, and with Jacob. 25 God saw the Israelites, and God knew.

MOSES AND THE BURNING BUSH

3 Meanwhile, Moses was shepherding the flock of his father-in-law Jethro,[B] the priest of Midian. He led the flock to the far side of the wilderness and came to Horeb,[C] the mountain of God. 2 Then the angel of the LORD appeared to him in a flame of fire within a bush. As Moses looked, he saw that the bush was on fire but was not consumed. 3 So Moses thought, "I must go over and look at this remarkable sight. Why isn't the bush burning up?"

4 When the LORD saw that he had gone over to look, God called out to him from the bush, "Moses, Moses!"

"Here I am," he answered.

5 "Do not come closer," he said. "Remove the sandals from your feet, for the place where you are standing is holy ground." 6 Then he continued, "I am the God of your father,[D] the God of Abraham, the God of Isaac, and the God of Jacob." Moses hid his face because he was afraid to look at God.

7 Then the LORD said, "I have observed the misery of my people in Egypt, and have heard them crying out because of their oppressors. I know about their sufferings, 8 and I have come down to rescue them from the power of the Egyptians and to bring them from that land to a good and spacious land, a land flowing with milk and honey — the territory of the Canaanites, Hethites, Amorites, Perizzites, Hivites, and Jebusites. 9 So because the Israelites' cry for help has come to me, and I have also seen the way the Egyptians are oppressing them, 10 therefore, go. I am sending you to Pharaoh so that you may lead my people, the Israelites, out of Egypt."

11 But Moses asked God, "Who am I that I should go to Pharaoh and that I should bring the Israelites out of Egypt?"

12 He answered, "I will certainly be with you, and this will be the sign to you that I am the one who sent you: when you bring the people out of Egypt, you will all worship[E] God at this mountain."

13 Then Moses asked God, "If I go to the Israelites and say to them, 'The God of your ancestors has sent me to you,' and they ask me, 'What is his name?' what should I tell them?"

14 God replied to Moses, "I AM WHO I AM.[F] This is what you are to say to the Israelites: I AM has sent me to you." 15 God also said to Moses, "Say this to the Israelites: The LORD, the God of your ancestors, the God of Abraham, the God of Isaac, and the God of Jacob, has sent me to you. This is my name forever; this is how I am to be remembered in every generation.

16 "Go and assemble the elders of Israel and say to them: The LORD, the God of your ancestors, the God of Abraham, Isaac, and Jacob, has appeared to me and said: I have paid close attention to you and to what has been done to you in Egypt. 17 And I have promised you that I will bring you up from the misery of Egypt to the land of the Canaanites, Hethites, Amorites, Perizzites, Hivites, and Jebusites — a land flowing with milk and honey. 18 They will listen to what you say. Then you, along with the elders of Israel, must go to the king of Egypt and say to him: The LORD, the God of the Hebrews, has met with us. Now please let us go on a three-day trip into the wilderness so that we may sacrifice to the LORD our God.

19 "However, I know that the king of Egypt will not allow you to go, even under force from a strong hand. 20 But when I stretch out my hand and strike Egypt with all my miracles that I will perform in it, after that, he will let you go. 21 And I will give these people such favor with the Egyptians that when you go, you will not go empty-handed. 22 Each woman will ask her neighbor and any woman staying in her house for silver and gold jewelry, and clothing, and you will put them on your sons and daughters. So you will plunder the Egyptians."

MIRACULOUS SIGNS FOR MOSES

4 Moses answered, "What if they won't believe me and will not obey me but say, 'The LORD did not appear to you'?"

2 The LORD asked him, "What is that in your hand?"

"A staff," he replied.

3 "Throw it on the ground," he said. So Moses threw it on the ground, it became a snake, and he ran from it. 4 The LORD told Moses, "Stretch out your hand and grab it by the tail." So he stretched out his hand and caught it, and it became a staff in his hand. 5 "This will take place," he continued, "so that they will believe

[A]**2:22** In Hb the name *Gershom* sounds like the phrase "a stranger there." [B]**3:1** Moses's father-in-law's first name was *Jethro*; Ex 2:18. [C]**3:1** = Desolation; another name for Mount Sinai; Dt 4:10,15; 18:16; Mal 4:4 [D]**3:6** Sam, some LXX mss read *fathers*; Ac 7:32 [E]**3:12** Or *serve* [F]**3:14** Or *I AM BECAUSE I AM*, or *I WILL BE WHO I WILL BE*

that the LORD, the God of their ancestors, the God of Abraham, the God of Isaac, and the God of Jacob, has appeared to you."

6 In addition the LORD said to him, "Put your hand inside your cloak." So he put his hand inside his cloak, and when he took it out, his hand was diseased, resembling snow.[A] 7 "Put your hand back inside your cloak," he said. So he put his hand back inside his cloak, and when he took it out, it had again become like the rest of his skin. 8 "If they will not believe you and will not respond to the evidence of the first sign, they may believe the evidence of the second sign. 9 And if they don't believe even these two signs or listen to what you say, take some water from the Nile and pour it on the dry ground. The water you take from the Nile will become blood on the ground."

10 But Moses replied to the LORD, "Please, Lord, I have never been eloquent — either in the past or recently or since you have been speaking to your servant — because my mouth and my tongue are sluggish."[B]

11 The LORD said to him, "Who placed a mouth on humans? Who makes a person mute or deaf, seeing or blind? Is it not I, the LORD? 12 Now go! I will help you speak[C] and I will teach you what to say."

13 Moses said, "Please, Lord, send someone else."[D]

14 Then the LORD's anger burned against Moses, and he said, "Isn't Aaron the Levite your brother? I know that he can speak well. And also, he is on his way now to meet you. He will rejoice when he sees you. 15 You will speak with him and tell him what to say. I will help both you and him to speak[E] and will teach you both what to do. 16 He will speak to the people for you. He will serve as a mouth for you, and you will serve as God to him. 17 And take this staff in your hand that you will perform the signs with."

MOSES'S RETURN TO EGYPT

18 Then Moses went back to his father-in-law, Jethro, and said to him, "Please let me return to my relatives in Egypt and see if they are still living."

Jethro said to Moses, "Go in peace."

19 Now in Midian the LORD told Moses, "Return to Egypt, for all the men who wanted to kill you are dead." 20 So Moses took his wife and sons, put them on a donkey, and returned to the land of Egypt. And Moses took God's staff in his hand.

21 The LORD instructed Moses, "When you go back to Egypt, make sure you do before Pharaoh all the wonders that I have put within your power. But I will harden his heart[F] so that he won't let the people go. 22 And you will say to Pharaoh: This is what the LORD says: Israel is my firstborn son. 23 I told you: Let my son go so that he may worship me, but you refused to let him go. Look, I am about to kill your firstborn son!"

24 On the trip, at an overnight campsite, it happened that the LORD confronted him and intended to put him to death. 25 So Zipporah took a flint, cut off her son's foreskin, threw it at Moses's feet, and said, "You are a bridegroom of blood to me!" 26 So he let him alone. At that time she said, "You are a bridegroom of blood," referring to the circumcision.

REUNION OF MOSES AND AARON

27 Now the LORD had said to Aaron, "Go and meet Moses in the wilderness." So he went and met him at the mountain of God and kissed him. 28 Moses told Aaron everything the LORD had sent him to say, and about all the signs he had commanded him to do. 29 Then Moses and Aaron went and assembled all the elders of the Israelites. 30 Aaron repeated everything the LORD had said to Moses and performed the signs before the people. 31 The people believed, and when they heard that the LORD had paid attention to them and that he had seen their misery, they knelt low and worshiped.

MOSES CONFRONTS PHARAOH

5 Later, Moses and Aaron went in and said to Pharaoh, "This is what the LORD, the God of Israel, says: Let my people go, so that they may hold a festival for me in the wilderness."

2 But Pharaoh responded, "Who is the LORD that I should obey him by letting Israel go? I don't know[G] the LORD, and besides, I will not let Israel go."

3 They answered, "The God of the Hebrews has met with us. Please let us go on a three-day trip into the wilderness so that we may sacrifice to the LORD our God, or else he may strike us with plague or sword."

4 The king of Egypt said to them, "Moses and Aaron, why are you causing the people to neglect their work? Get to your labor!" 5 Pharaoh also said, "Look, the people of the land are so numerous, and you would stop them from their labor."

FURTHER OPPRESSION OF ISRAEL

6 That day Pharaoh commanded the overseers of the people as well as their foremen, 7 "Don't continue to supply the people with straw for making bricks, as before. They must go and gather straw for themselves. 8 But require the same quota of bricks from them as they were making before; do not reduce it. For they are slackers — that is why they are crying out, 'Let us go and sacrifice to our God.' 9 Impose heavier work on the men. Then they will be occupied with it and not pay attention to deceptive words."

[A] **4:6** A reference to whiteness or flakiness of the skin [B] **4:10** Lit *heavy of mouth and heavy of tongue* [C] **4:12** Lit *will be with your mouth* [D] **4:13** Lit *send by the hand of whom you will send* [E] **4:15** Lit *will be with your mouth and with his mouth* [F] **4:21** Or *will make him stubborn* [G] **5:2** Or *recognize*

Papyrus *(Cyperus papyrus)* is a perennial flowering plant that grows abundantly in the marshes along the Nile. Egyptians processed papyrus, making it suitable as a writing surface; additionally, they used it for making sandals, baskets, and even boats.

One often-overlooked Egyptian invention is the development of a paperlike product that made writing easier. This product was produced from the papyrus plant, from which paper gets its name. Papyrus grew abundantly along the banks of the Nile River. To produce the material, the stem of the papyrus plant was cut into strips. Other strips were placed crosswise on them. They were then pressed together and dried, forming sheets.

These sheets were so well made that a number of manuscripts written more than five thousand years ago are still intact. The Egyptians used an ink made by mixing water with soot and vegetable gums on a wooden palette. The writing instrument was a simple reed, trimmed at the end into a tiny brush. The writing made with this primitive ink is still legible. Sheets were often formed into books by gumming the right edge of one sheet to the left edge of the next. This would result in a roll. Some of these rolls were forty yards long.[1]

Egyptian paper became one of the main items of Egyptian foreign trade. The Greeks and the Romans later adopted this writing material. "New Testament manuscripts produced before the fourth century were written exclusively on papyrus; after the fourth century almost all New Testament documents were written on parchment."[2]

The abundance of writing materials allowed the Egyptians to develop one of the earliest school systems in history. The youth of the nobility were educated to provide literate public servants for the pharaoh's bureaucracy. Admission to the school was a great honor and to become an educated man was an important achievement. One extant papyrus states, "Behold, there is no profession that is not governed; it is only the learned man who rules himself."[3] The sculpture of a scribe sitting cross-legged with his papyrus on his lap is one of the most common artifacts of ancient Egypt. ✣

---

[1] Will Durant, *The Story of Civilization Part One: Our Oriental Heritage* (New York: Simon & Schuster, 1942), 171. [2] "Papyrus" in *HolBD*, 1071. [3] Durant, *Civilization*, 170.

10 So the overseers and foremen of the people went
out and said to them, "This is what Pharaoh says: 'I am
not giving you straw. 11 Go get straw yourselves wherever you can find it, but there will be no reduction
at all in your workload.'" 12 So the people scattered
throughout the land of Egypt to gather stubble for
straw. 13 The overseers insisted, "Finish your assigned
work each day, just as you did when straw was provided." 14 Then the Israelite foremen, whom Pharaoh's
slave drivers had set over the people, were beaten
and asked, "Why haven't you finished making your
prescribed number of bricks yesterday or today, as
you did before?"

15 So the Israelite foremen went in and cried for
help to Pharaoh: "Why are you treating your servants this way? 16 No straw has been given to your
servants, yet they say to us, 'Make bricks!' Look, your
servants are being beaten, but it is your own people
who are at fault."

17 But he said, "You are slackers. Slackers! That is
why you are saying, 'Let us go sacrifice to the LORD.'
18 Now get to work. No straw will be given to you,
but you must produce the same quantity of bricks."

19 The Israelite foremen saw that they were in trouble when they were told, "You cannot reduce your
daily quota of bricks." 20 When they left Pharaoh,
they confronted Moses and Aaron, who stood waiting to meet them.

21 "May the LORD take note of you and judge," they
said to them, "because you have made us reek to Pharaoh and his officials — putting a sword in their hand
to kill us!"

22 So Moses went back to the LORD and asked, "Lord,
why have you caused trouble for this people? And
why did you ever send me? 23 Ever since I went in to
Pharaoh to speak in your name he has caused trouble
for this people, and you haven't rescued your people
at all."

6 But the LORD replied to Moses, "Now you will see
what I will do to Pharaoh: because of a strong
hand he will let them go, and because of a strong
hand he will drive them from his land."

GOD PROMISES FREEDOM

2 Then God spoke to Moses, telling him, "I am the LORD.
3 I appeared to Abraham, Isaac, and Jacob as God Almighty, but I was not known to them by my name 'the
LORD.'[A] 4 I also established my covenant with them to
give them the land of Canaan, the land they lived in
as aliens. 5 Furthermore, I have heard the groaning
of the Israelites, whom the Egyptians are forcing to
work as slaves, and I have remembered my covenant.

6 "Therefore tell the Israelites: I am the LORD, and I
will bring you out from the forced labor of the Egyptians and rescue you from slavery to them. I will redeem you with an outstretched arm and great acts of
judgment. 7 I will take you as my people, and I will be
your God. You will know that I am the LORD your God,
who brought you out from the forced labor of the
Egyptians. 8 I will bring you to the land that I swore[B]
to give to Abraham, Isaac, and Jacob, and I will give
it to you as a possession. I am the LORD." 9 Moses told
this to the Israelites, but they did not listen to him
because of their broken spirit and hard labor.

10 Then the LORD spoke to Moses, 11 "Go and tell
Pharaoh king of Egypt to let the Israelites go from
his land."

12 But Moses said in the LORD's presence, "If the
Israelites will not listen to me, then how will Pharaoh listen to me, since I am such a poor speaker?"[C]
13 Then the LORD spoke to Moses and Aaron and gave
them commands concerning both the Israelites and
Pharaoh king of Egypt to bring the Israelites out of
the land of Egypt.

GENEALOGY OF MOSES AND AARON

14 These are the heads of their fathers' families:
The sons of Reuben, the firstborn of Israel:
Hanoch and Pallu, Hezron and Carmi.
These are the clans of Reuben.

15 The sons of Simeon:
Jemuel, Jamin, Ohad, Jachin,
Zohar, and Shaul, the son
of a Canaanite woman.
These are the clans of Simeon.

16 These are the names of the sons of Levi
according to their family records;
Gershon, Kohath, and Merari.
Levi lived 137 years.
17 The sons of Gershon:
Libni and Shimei, by their clans.
18 The sons of Kohath:
Amram, Izhar, Hebron, and Uzziel.
Kohath lived 133 years.
19 The sons of Merari:
Mahli and Mushi.
These are the clans of the Levites
according to their family records.

20 Amram married his father's sister Jochebed,
and she bore him Aaron and Moses.
Amram lived 137 years.
21 The sons of Izhar:
Korah, Nepheg, and Zichri.

[A] **6:3** *LORD* (in small capitals) stands for the personal name of God, which in Hb is *Yahweh*. There is a long tradition of substituting "LORD" for "Yahweh" out of reverence. [B] **6:8** Lit *raised my hand* [C] **6:12** Lit *I have uncircumcised lips*, also in v. 30

The Afterlife: An Egyptian View

by Harold R. Mosley

The pyramids, the complex mummification process, the highly developed funerary rituals, and the writings in the tombs of its people all testify to Egypt's interest in the afterlife.

THE ABODE OF THE GODS

Egyptian religion involved complex and, at times, somewhat contradictory beliefs. Egyptian theology saw the afterlife as the abode of the gods. A person who had died journeyed from this world into the next life. The ideal eternity was one in which the deceased traveled by day with the sun-god Re and returned each night to a well-furnished tomb.[1]

Egyptians viewed the afterlife as a place of abundance. Scenes in tombs often depicted the deceased and his wife working in fields that produced bountifully. Since the tomb usually contained the body of a wealthy person, the deceased did not really expect to be doing manual labor in the fields.[2] However, the depictions do indicate the belief that the afterlife was very similar to the existence in ancient Egypt.

Egyptian theology changed over time. The various gods changed roles and rose or declined in prominence from period to period. The "Pyramid Texts" from pyramids of the late Old Kingdom (ca 2350–2150 BC) constitute the earliest written sources about the afterlife. The kings and queens would ascend into the sky to join the circumpolar stars, seen as "eternal" because they never descended below the horizon. Later beliefs centered on Osiris, the chief god of the afterlife, and Re, the daytime sun. The sun-god traveled across the sky in a boat (the major mode of transportation along the Nile). The goal of the deceased was to journey with Re throughout the afterlife. The numerous models or depictions of boats in tombs reflect this desire.[3]

In the earliest Egyptian theology, the afterlife was available only to kings and nobility. Later the afterlife became accessible to people who could afford the appropriate tools to attain it. The "Pyramid Texts" addressed only kings. The "Coffin Texts," typically written on the interior of wooden coffins, made travel with the sun-god available to individuals who were not nobility. Maps and descriptions of the underworld were inscribed on the bottom of the coffin, to help direct the deceased. Further, the texts contained the proper spells to be quoted at the appropriate times.[4]

THE ESSENCE OF HUMANITY

For ancient Egyptians, three important elements of human beings were *ba*, *ka*, and *akh*. No English

The Step Pyramid at Saqqara is the tomb for Pharaoh Djoser, who ruled about 2667–2648 BC.

From Thebes, a painted wooden shabti box belonging to the priest of Amun Amenhotep. The box contains faience shabtis, dating to the Twenty-first Dynasty (ca 1070–945 BC). Shabtis were small figurines that worked as servants, performing whatever tasks the deceased needed in the afterlife.

equivalents are available for these concepts. The exact nature of these elements changed over time. The *ba*, which is comparable to our notion of personality, was depicted as a stork with a human head. The *ba* could eat and drink as well as speak and move. The deceased person's *ba* allowed him or her to leave the tomb and travel. Providing protection for the *ba* was a primary motivation for tomb building. If, however, the body were destroyed, the *ba* could reside in statues and reliefs that depicted the deceased. In fact, these representations were designed to be substitutes for the body for such an occurrence. Egyptians believed if the *ba* continued to exist on earth, then the person continued to exist in the afterlife.[5]

The *ka* was a person's vital force, depicted graphically as a smaller double of the deceased or in hieroglyphics as two upraised arms. The *ka* resided in the physical body after death, thus the need for preserving the body. Since the *ka* required food and drink, people provided sustenance for it after death. Provisions could consist of actual goods or as carvings, pictures, or writings on the wall. Actual goods could be looted; the pictures would remain.

If the *ba* and the *ka* successfully reunited after death, the result was *akh*. Failing to attain this reunion meant eternal death, that is, the person ceased to exist. The crested ibis was the symbol for *akh*.[6]

For the ancient Egyptian, successful attainment of the afterlife required the preservation of the body. This desire prompted the complex process of mummification. The process reveals beliefs concerning the afterlife. Embalmers removed the brain and discarded it, believing it to be mere filling for the skull. They also removed the various organs, except the heart, and preserved them in jars that accompanied the body. The heart, the most important organ, remained in the body.[7] The deceased required the heart for the judgment called the Weighing of the Heart.

THE WEIGHING OF THE HEART

Osiris, the chief god of the afterlife, presided over the Weighing of the Heart ceremony. The deceased person's heart was placed on one side of the scales; on the opposite side was a feather, which represented standards of truth and justice. If the heart was heavier than the feather (thus representing the presence of sin), it sank and was eaten by Ammit, a composite beast—with a body that was part lion and part hippopotamus and with the head of a crocodile. If the heart and feather balanced, the deceased lived in the afterlife.[8]

The Book of the Dead, however, allowed those who knew various spells to pass the judgment successfully. The Book of the Dead was mainly papyrus sheets with magical spells that helped the dead pass the various dangers of the afterlife. One particular spell had importance for the Weighing of the Heart judgment. This spell consisted of a declaration of innocence that the deceased had not committed a specific set of sins. If the deceased had access to this spell, regardless of whether the person had committed the sins, those sins would be erased. The scales balancing indicated a positive outcome.[9]

Another magic spell that protected the heart involved a heart scarab. This amulet placed over the heart carried an inscription invoking the scarab to prevent the heart from bearing witness against the deceased in judgment.[10]

The emphasis on the *heart* in Egyptian theology may have significance in the plagues of Egypt. The "heart" of Pharaoh was hardened or, as the Hebrew wording occasionally has it, "was heavy." This might be a polemic against Egyptian theology by asserting that God is the One who "weighs the heart."[11] ✣

---

[1] *What Life Was Like on the Banks of the Nile* (Alexandria, VA: Time–Life Books, 1996), 171. Re is also spelled Ra. [2] Lorna Oakes and Lucia Gahlin, *Ancient Egypt* (New York: Barnes & Noble, 2006), 391. [3] John H. Taylor, *Death and the Afterlife in Ancient Egypt* (Chicago: University of Chicago Press, 2001), 25; Oakes and Gahlin, *Ancient Egypt*, 329, 394; Taylor, 28. [4] Oakes and Gahlin, *Ancient Egypt*, 402. [5] Taylor, *Death and the Afterlife*, 20; Oakes and Gahlin, *Ancient Egypt*, 393; Barbara Watterson, *Gods of Ancient Egypt* (Gloucestershire: Sutton, 1996), 68. [6] Oakes and Gahlin, *Ancient Egypt*, 393; Wolfram Grajetzki, *Burial Customs in Ancient Egypt: Life in Death for Rich and Poor* (London: Gerald Duckworth, 2003), 14. [7] Oakes and Gahlin, *Ancient Egypt*, 303. [8] Oakes and Gahlin, *Ancient Egypt*, 394. [9] Carol Andrews, ed., *The Ancient Egyptian Book of the Dead*, trans. Raymond O. Faulkner (Austin: University of Texas Press, 1990), 29; Oakes and Gahlin, *Ancient Egypt*, 395. [10] Oakes and Gahlin, *Ancient Egypt*. [11] The hardening of Pharaoh's heart uses the verb *to make heavy*, as well as the verb *to make strong*, meaning "obstinate."

The papyrus of the scribe Hunefer shows his coming to judgment before Osiris. The heart (represented by the small pot on the left side of the scale) is weighed in the balance against the image of Maat (represented by the feather on the right). Maat represented the Egyptian notion of right or truth. Hunefer is led to the balance by the jackal-headed Anubis, who is also shown adjusting the scales. The monster Ammit, "Devourer of the Dead," crouches beneath the balance so he can swallow the heart, should the weighing indicate the person lived a wicked life. The ibis-headed Thoth, the scribe of the gods, records the outcome.

22 The sons of Uzziel:
Mishael, Elzaphan, and Sithri.
23 Aaron married Elisheba,
daughter of Amminadab and sister
of Nahshon.
She bore him Nadab and Abihu, Eleazar
and Ithamar.
24 The sons of Korah:
Assir, Elkanah, and Abiasaph.
These are the clans of the Korahites.
25 Aaron's son Eleazar married
one of the daughters of Putiel,
and she bore him Phinehas.
These are the heads of the Levite families
by their clans.

26 It was this Aaron and Moses whom the LORD
told, "Bring the Israelites out of the land of Egypt
according to their military divisions." 27 Moses and
Aaron were the ones who spoke to Pharaoh king of
Egypt in order to bring the Israelites out of Egypt.

MOSES AND AARON BEFORE PHARAOH

28 On the day the LORD spoke to Moses in the land of
Egypt, 29 he said to him, "I am the LORD; tell Pharaoh
king of Egypt everything I am telling you."
30 But Moses replied in the LORD's presence, "Since
I am such a poor speaker, how will Pharaoh listen
to me?"

7 The LORD answered Moses, "See, I have made you
like God to Pharaoh, and Aaron your brother will
be your prophet. 2 You must say whatever I command
you; then Aaron your brother must declare it to Pharaoh so that he will let the Israelites go from his land.
3 But I will harden Pharaoh's heart and multiply my
signs and wonders in the land of Egypt. 4 Pharaoh will
not listen to you, but I will put my hand into Egypt
and bring the military divisions of my people the
Israelites out of the land of Egypt by great acts of
judgment. 5 The Egyptians will know that I am the
LORD when I stretch out my hand against Egypt and
bring out the Israelites from among them."
6 So Moses and Aaron did this; they did just as
the LORD commanded them. 7 Moses was eighty
years old and Aaron eighty-three when they spoke
to Pharaoh.
8 The LORD said to Moses and Aaron, 9 "When Pharaoh tells you, 'Perform a miracle,' tell Aaron, 'Take
your staff and throw it down before Pharaoh. It will
become a serpent.'" 10 So Moses and Aaron went in
to Pharaoh and did just as the LORD had commanded.
Aaron threw down his staff before Pharaoh and his
officials, and it became a serpent. 11 But then Pharaoh
called the wise men and sorcerers — the magicians
of Egypt, and they also did the same thing by their
occult practices. 12 Each one threw down his staff, and
it became a serpent. But Aaron's staff swallowed their
staffs. 13 However, Pharaoh's heart was hard, and he
did not listen to them, as the LORD had said.

THE FIRST PLAGUE: WATER TURNED TO BLOOD

14 Then the LORD said to Moses, "Pharaoh's heart is
hard: He refuses to let the people go. 15 Go to Pharaoh
in the morning. When you see him walking out to the
water, stand ready to meet him by the bank of the
Nile. Take in your hand the staff that turned into a
snake. 16 Tell him: The LORD, the God of the Hebrews,
has sent me to tell you: Let my people go, so that they
may worship[A] me in the wilderness. But so far you
have not listened. 17 This is what the LORD says: Here
is how you will know that I am the LORD. Watch. I am
about to strike the water in the Nile with the staff in
my hand, and it will turn to blood. 18 The fish in the
Nile will die, the river will stink, and the Egyptians
will be unable to drink water from it."
19 So the LORD said to Moses, "Tell Aaron: Take
your staff and stretch out your hand over the waters of Egypt — over their rivers, canals, ponds, and
all their water reservoirs — and they will become
blood. There will be blood throughout the land of
Egypt, even in wooden and stone containers."
20 Moses and Aaron did just as the LORD had commanded; in the sight of Pharaoh and his officials, he
raised the staff and struck the water in the Nile, and
all the water in the Nile was turned to blood. 21 The
fish in the Nile died, and the river smelled so bad the
Egyptians could not drink water from it. There was
blood throughout the land of Egypt.
22 But the magicians of Egypt did the same thing by
their occult practices. So Pharaoh's heart was hard,
and he would not listen to them, as the LORD had said.
23 Pharaoh turned around, went into his palace, and
didn't take even this to heart. 24 All the Egyptians
dug around the Nile for water to drink because they
could not drink the water from the river. 25 Seven days
passed after the LORD struck the Nile.

THE SECOND PLAGUE: FROGS

8 Then the LORD said to Moses, "Go in to Pharaoh
and tell him: This is what the LORD says: Let my
people go, so that they may worship me. 2 But if you
refuse to let them go, then I will plague all your territory with frogs. 3 The Nile will swarm with frogs;
they will come up and go into your palace, into your
bedroom and on your bed, into the houses of your
officials and your people, and into your ovens and
kneading bowls. 4 The frogs will come up on you,
your people, and all your officials."

[A] **7:16** Or *serve*; Ex 4:23

Pharaoh's Question: Who Is Yahweh?

by R. Kelvin Moore

The geographical location of the Hebrews caused concern for Pharaoh. The Hebrews lived east of Egypt in Goshen. Most of the Egyptians' enemies came from the east. Pharaoh knew the Hebrews might unite with any enemy that came from the east. Pharaoh also knew this type of union could mean a formidable force on his eastern border. Prudence might have dictated that Pharaoh befriend the Hebrews. Inexplicably and mercilessly, Pharaoh enslaved them! Moses then brought a command from Yahweh to Pharaoh: "Let my people go." Unwilling to relinquish his Hebrew slave labor, Pharaoh asked, "Who is [Yahweh] that I should obey him by letting Israel go? I don't know [Yahweh]" (Ex 5:1-2).[1]

How could Pharaoh not know something of Yahweh, the mighty deity of the Hebrews? The answer probably lies in the same realm that Pharaoh "did not know about Joseph" (1:8). To think that Pharaoh, a man with the best of Egyptian education available to him, did not know his own history and Joseph's part in that history seems outlandish. Rather, he evidently chose to ignore what he knew.

Might the ten plagues be interpreted as the answer to Pharaoh's question?

Some scholars interpret the plagues as striking at the very heart of Egyptian polytheism. The Egyptians, in essence, worshiped the Nile. Its annual flooding irrigated adjacent croplands and made life sustainable in a wasteland of rocks and sand. The Hebrews' God, however, showed his power over the Nile by turning it into blood. Early historical records indicate that Egyptians living in Memphis worshiped the sacred bull, Apis. Destroying the livestock (fifth plague) showed God's power to defeat Apis. The Egyptians worshiped Re, the sun-god. Re wore a disk, symbolizing the sun, as his crown. But the God of the Hebrews made a "darkness over the land of Egypt, a darkness that can be felt" (10:21). Obviously Re did not control the sun after all. The Egyptians viewed Pharaoh as a god. But, the tenth plague records Pharaoh's impotency even to protect his own son's life. So when the plagues came, Egyptian polytheism collapsed.

Loudly and clearly, the plagues answered Pharaoh's question, "Who is Yahweh?" While numerous conclusions might be drawn as to specifically how the plagues answered Pharaoh's question, at least two appear obvious.

The plagues communicated Yahweh's sovereignty. Many in the Old Testament world believed in land-locked deities. Second Kings 5 illustrates that Naaman held to such a belief. Naaman, a Syrian, traveled to the promised land (specifically, Samaria), and Elisha (Yahweh!) healed him of leprosy. Naaman's request appears odd: "please let your servant be given as much soil as a pair of mules can carry" (v. 17). Naaman desired to worship the God who cured his leprosy and believed that physical soil was necessary because gods were land-locked. Perhaps Pharaoh knew about Yahweh but believed that this Yahweh reigned in the land of the Hebrews and not in the land of Egypt. The plagues changed Pharaoh's belief, illustrating Yahweh reigned in Egypt as well as the promised land.

The plagues communicated Yahweh's power. From the earliest accounts, biblical authors present Egypt as one of the most powerful nations in the world. Dating the exodus to about 1450 BC (1Kg 6:1) places it in the time period of what historians refer to as the New Kingdom of Egyptian domination (1539–1075 BC).[2] By the time of Pharaoh Thutmose III (1479–1425 BC), Egypt essentially had become an empire. Geography insulated Egypt from invasions from outsiders. Surrounding deserts proved daunting for most approaching enemies. Only during times of Egyptian weakness or division were enemies able to penetrate successfully. Within this environment one can see Pharaoh arrogantly dismissing the demands of Moses's Yahweh. After all, who could challenge Egyptian supremacy? The plagues changed Pharaoh's belief regarding the power of the Hebrew deity, Yahweh. When the plagues concluded, Pharaoh had the answer to his question, "Who is Yahweh?" ✣

[1] In the CSB, as in most English Bibles, "LORD" in small capital letters represents the Hebrew Tetragrammaton, *YHWH*, which scholars believe may have been pronounced "Yahweh." [2] Herbert B. Huffmon, "Egypt" in *The HarperCollins Bible Dictionary*, ed. Paul J. Achtemeier (New York: HarperCollins, 1996), 272.

Mud brick made with straw and stamped with the cartouche of Ramesses II, who ruled in the Nineteenth Dynasty.

DIGGING DEEPER *Ipuwer Papyrus*

Acquired in 1828, the thirteenth-century BC Ipuwer Papyrus (IP) was translated in 1909 by Alan H. Gardner under the title *The Admonitions of an Egyptian Sage from a Hieratic Papyrus*. The Egyptian scribe, Ipuwer, describes conditions in Egypt that are remarkably similar to those described in the biblical account of the Exodus plagues (Ex 7–11). Ipuwer says the plague is throughout the land (IP 2:5–6; Ex 7:21); the river is blood (IP 7:20; Ex 7:20–21); groaning carries throughout the land (IP 3:14; Ex 12:30); fire mingles with hail (IP 9:23; Ex 9:23–25); trees and herbs are destroyed (IP 6:1; Ex 9:25; 10:15); darkness is in the land (IP 9:11; Ex 10:22); death is widespread (IP 2:13; Ex 6:12; 12:29–30); animals weep and cattle moan (IP 5:53; Ex 9:3); and cattle are left to stray in the field (IP 9:2–3; Ex 9:21). Some Egyptologists believe this papyrus originally dates to the Twelfth Egyptian Dynasty of the Second Intermediate period (ca 1991–1802 BC), in which case the document would be at least 350 years too early to refer to the Exodus plagues. However, the papyrus is currently dated to the thirteenth century BC, which is in range of the biblical exodus. Thus Ipuwer possibly describes the exodus plagues.

5 The LORD then said to Moses, "Tell Aaron: Stretch out your hand with your staff over the rivers, canals, and ponds, and cause the frogs to come up onto the land of Egypt." 6 When Aaron stretched out his hand over the waters of Egypt, the frogs came up and covered the land of Egypt. 7 But the magicians did the same thing by their occult practices and brought frogs up onto the land of Egypt.

8 Pharaoh summoned Moses and Aaron and said, "Appeal to the LORD to remove the frogs from me and my people. Then I will let the people go and they can sacrifice to the LORD."

9 Moses said to Pharaoh, "You may have the honor of choosing. When should I appeal on behalf of you, your officials, and your people, that the frogs be taken away from you and your houses, and remain only in the Nile?"

10 "Tomorrow," he answered.

Moses replied, "As you have said, so that you may know there is no one like the LORD our God, 11 the frogs will go away from you, your houses, your officials, and your people. The frogs will remain only in the Nile." 12 After Moses and Aaron went out from Pharaoh, Moses cried out to the LORD for help concerning the frogs that he had brought against Pharaoh. 13 The LORD did as Moses had said: the frogs in the houses, courtyards, and fields died. 14 They piled them in countless heaps, and there was a terrible odor in the land. 15 But when Pharaoh saw there was relief, he hardened his heart and would not listen to them, as the LORD had said.

THE THIRD PLAGUE: GNATS

16 Then the LORD said to Moses, "Tell Aaron: Stretch out your staff and strike the dust of the land, and it will become gnats[A] throughout the land of Egypt." 17 And they did this. Aaron stretched out his hand with his staff, and when he struck the dust of the land, gnats were on people and animals. All the dust of the land became gnats throughout the land of Egypt. 18 The magicians tried to produce gnats using their occult practices, but they could not. The gnats remained on people and animals.

19 "This is the finger of God," the magicians said to Pharaoh. But Pharaoh's heart was hard, and he would not listen to them, as the LORD had said.

THE FOURTH PLAGUE: SWARMS OF FLIES

20 The LORD said to Moses, "Get up early in the morning and present yourself to Pharaoh when you see him going out to the water. Tell him: This is what the LORD says: Let my people go, so that they may worship[B] me. 21 But if you will not let my people go, then I will send swarms of flies[C] against you, your officials, your people, and your houses. The Egyptians' houses will swarm with flies, and so will the land where they live.[D] 22 But on that day I will give special treatment to the land of Goshen, where my people are living; no flies will be there. This way you will know that I, the LORD, am in the land. 23 I will make a distinction[E] between my people and your people. This sign will take place tomorrow."

24 And the LORD did this. Thick swarms of flies went into Pharaoh's palace and his officials' houses. Throughout Egypt the land was ruined because of the swarms of flies. 25 Then Pharaoh summoned Moses and Aaron and said, "Go sacrifice to your God within the country."

26 But Moses said, "It would not be right[F] to do that, because what we will sacrifice to the LORD our God is detestable to the Egyptians. If we sacrifice what the Egyptians detest in front of them, won't they stone us? 27 We must go a distance of three days into the wilderness and sacrifice to the LORD our God as he instructs us."

28 Pharaoh responded, "I will let you go and sacrifice to the LORD your God in the wilderness, but don't go very far. Make an appeal for me."

[A] **8:16** Perhaps sand fleas or mosquitoes [B] **8:20** Or *serve* [C] **8:21** Or *insects* [D] **8:21** Lit *are* [E] **8:23** LXX, Syr, Vg; MT reads *will place redemption* [F] **8:26** Or *allowable*

29 “As soon as I leave you,” Moses said, “I will appeal to the LORD, and tomorrow the swarms of flies will depart from Pharaoh, his officials, and his people. But Pharaoh must not act deceptively again by refusing to let the people go and sacrifice to the LORD.” 30 Then Moses left Pharaoh’s presence and appealed to the LORD. 31 The LORD did as Moses had said: He removed the swarms of flies from Pharaoh, his officials, and his people; not one was left. 32 But Pharaoh hardened his heart this time also and did not let the people go.

THE FIFTH PLAGUE: DEATH OF LIVESTOCK

9 Then the LORD said to Moses, “Go in to Pharaoh and say to him: This is what the LORD, the God of the Hebrews, says: Let my people go, so that they may worship me. 2 But if you refuse to let them go and keep holding them, 3 then the LORD’s hand will bring a severe plague against your livestock in the field — the horses, donkeys, camels, herds, and flocks. 4 But the LORD will make a distinction between the livestock of Israel and the livestock of Egypt, so that nothing of all that the Israelites own will die.” 5 And the LORD set a time, saying, “Tomorrow the LORD will do this thing in the land.” 6 The LORD did this the next day. All the Egyptian livestock died, but none among the Israelite livestock died. 7 Pharaoh sent messengers who saw that not a single one of the Israelite livestock was dead. But Pharaoh’s heart was hard, and he did not let the people go.

THE SIXTH PLAGUE: BOILS

8 Then the LORD said to Moses and Aaron, “Take handfuls of furnace soot, and Moses is to throw it toward heaven in the sight of Pharaoh. 9 It will become fine dust over the entire land of Egypt. It will become festering boils on people and animals throughout the land of Egypt.” 10 So they took furnace soot and stood before Pharaoh. Moses threw it toward heaven, and it became festering boils on people and animals. 11 The magicians could not stand before Moses because of the boils, for the boils were on the magicians as well as on all the Egyptians. 12 But the LORD hardened Pharaoh’s heart and he did not listen to them, as the LORD had told Moses.

THE SEVENTH PLAGUE: HAIL

13 Then the LORD said to Moses, “Get up early in the morning and present yourself to Pharaoh. Tell him: This is what the LORD, the God of the Hebrews says: Let my people go, so that they may worship me. 14 For this time I am about to send all my plagues against you,[A] your officials, and your people. Then you will know there is no one like me on the whole earth. 15 By now I could have stretched out my hand and struck you and your people with a plague, and you would have been obliterated from the earth. 16 However, I have let you live for this purpose: to show you my power and to make my name known on the whole earth. 17 You are still acting arrogantly against[B] my people by not letting them go. 18 Tomorrow at this time I will rain down the worst hail that has ever occurred in Egypt from the day it was founded until now. 19 Therefore give orders to bring your livestock and all that you have in the field into shelters. Every person and animal that is in the field and not brought inside will die when the hail falls on them.” 20 Those among Pharaoh’s officials who feared the word of the LORD made their servants and livestock flee to shelters, 21 but those who didn’t take to heart the LORD’s word left their servants and livestock in the field.

22 Then the LORD said to Moses, “Stretch out your hand toward heaven and let there be hail throughout the land of Egypt — on people and animals and every plant of the field in the land of Egypt.” 23 So Moses stretched out his staff toward heaven, and the LORD sent thunder and hail. Lightning struck the land, and the LORD rained hail on the land of Egypt. 24 The hail, with lightning flashing through it, was so severe that nothing like it had occurred in the land of Egypt since it had become a nation. 25 Throughout the land of Egypt, the hail struck down everything in the field, both people and animals. The hail beat down every plant of the field and shattered every tree in the field. 26 The only place it didn’t hail was in the land of Goshen, where the Israelites were.

27 Pharaoh sent for Moses and Aaron. “I have sinned this time,” he said to them. “The LORD is the righteous one, and I and my people are the guilty ones. 28 Make an appeal to the LORD. There has been enough of God’s thunder and hail. I will let you go; you don’t need to stay any longer.”

29 Moses said to him, “When I have left the city, I will spread out my hands to the LORD. The thunder will cease, and there will be no more hail, so that you may know the earth[C] belongs to the LORD. 30 But as for you and your officials, I know that you still do not fear the LORD God.”

31 The flax and the barley were destroyed because the barley was ripe[D] and the flax was budding, 32 but the wheat and the spelt were not destroyed since they are later crops.[E]

33 Moses left Pharaoh and the city, and spread out his hands to the LORD. Then the thunder and hail ceased, and rain no longer poured down on the land. 34 When Pharaoh saw that the rain, hail, and thunder

[A] **9:14** Lit *plagues to your heart* [B] **9:17** Or *still obstructing*
[C] **9:29** Or *land* [D] **9:31** Lit *was ears of grain* [E] **9:32** Lit *are late*

had ceased, he sinned again and hardened his heart,
he and his officials. 35 So Pharaoh's heart was hard,
and he did not let the Israelites go, as the LORD had
said through Moses.

THE EIGHTH PLAGUE: LOCUSTS

10 Then the LORD said to Moses, "Go to Pharaoh,
for I have hardened his heart and the hearts of
his officials so that I may do these miraculous signs
of mine among them,[A] 2 and so that you may tell[B] your
son and grandson how severely I dealt with the Egyptians and performed miraculous signs among them,
and you will know that I am the LORD."
3 So Moses and Aaron went in to Pharaoh and told
him, "This is what the LORD, the God of the Hebrews,
says: How long will you refuse to humble yourself
before me? Let my people go, that they may worship
me. 4 But if you refuse to let my people go, then tomorrow I will bring locusts into your territory. 5 They
will cover the surface of the land so that no one will
be able to see the land. They will eat the remainder
left to you that escaped the hail; they will eat every
tree you have growing in the fields. 6 They will fill
your houses, all your officials' houses, and the houses
of all the Egyptians — something your fathers and
grandfathers never saw since the time they occupied the land until today." Then he turned and left
Pharaoh's presence.
7 Pharaoh's officials asked him, "How long must
this man be a snare to us? Let the men go, so that they
may worship the LORD their God. Don't you realize
yet that Egypt is devastated?"
8 So Moses and Aaron were brought back to Pharaoh. "Go, worship the LORD your God," Pharaoh said.
"But exactly who will be going?"
9 Moses replied, "We will go with our young and
with our old; we will go with our sons and with our
daughters, with our flocks and with our herds because we must hold the LORD's festival."
10 He said to them, "The LORD would have to be
with you if I would ever let you and your families
go! Look out — you're heading for trouble. 11 No, go
— just able-bodied men — worship the LORD, since
that's what you want." And they were driven from
Pharaoh's presence.
12 The LORD then said to Moses, "Stretch out your
hand over the land of Egypt, and the locusts will come
up over it and eat every plant in the land, everything
that the hail left." 13 So Moses stretched out his staff
over the land of Egypt, and the LORD sent an east wind
over the land all that day and through the night. By
morning the east wind had brought in the locusts.
14 The locusts went up over the entire land of Egypt
and settled on the whole territory of Egypt. Never
before had there been such a large number of locusts,
and there never will be again. 15 They covered the surface of the whole land so that the land was black, and
they consumed all the plants on the ground and all
the fruit on the trees that the hail had left. Nothing
green was left on the trees or the plants in the field
throughout the land of Egypt.
16 Pharaoh urgently sent for Moses and Aaron and
said, "I have sinned against the LORD your God and
against you. 17 Please forgive my sin once more
and make an appeal to the LORD your God, so that he
will just take this death away from me." 18 Moses left
Pharaoh's presence and appealed to the LORD. 19 Then
the LORD changed the wind to a strong west[C] wind,
and it carried off the locusts and blew them into the
Red Sea. Not a single locust was left in all the territory
of Egypt. 20 But the LORD hardened Pharaoh's heart,
and he did not let the Israelites go.

THE NINTH PLAGUE: DARKNESS

21 Then the LORD said to Moses, "Stretch out your hand
toward heaven, and there will be darkness over the
land of Egypt, a darkness that can be felt." 22 So Moses stretched out his hand toward heaven, and there
was thick darkness throughout the land of Egypt for
three days. 23 One person could not see another, and
for three days they did not move from where they
were. Yet all the Israelites had light where they lived.
24 Pharaoh summoned Moses and said, "Go, worship the LORD. Even your families may go with you;
only your flocks and herds must stay behind."
25 Moses responded, "You must also let us have[D]
sacrifices and burnt offerings to prepare for the LORD
our God. 26 Even our livestock must go with us; not
a hoof will be left behind because we will take some
of them to worship the LORD our God. We will not
know what we will use to worship the LORD until
we get there."
27 But the LORD hardened Pharaoh's heart, and he
was unwilling to let them go. 28 Pharaoh said to him,
"Leave me! Make sure you never see my face again,
for on the day you see my face, you will die."
29 "As you have said," Moses replied, "I will never
see your face again."

THE TENTH PLAGUE: DEATH OF THE FIRSTBORN

11 The LORD said[E] to Moses, "I will bring one more
plague on Pharaoh and on Egypt. After that, he
will let you go from here. When he lets you go,[F] he will
drive you out of here. 2 Now announce to the people
that both men and women should ask their neighbors
for silver and gold items." 3 The LORD gave[G] the people
favor with the Egyptians. In addition, Moses himself

[A] **10:1** Lit *mine in his midst* [B] **10:2** Lit *tell in the ears of* [C] **10:19** Lit *sea* [D] **10:25** Lit *also give in our hand* [E] **11:1** Or *had said* [F] **11:1** Or *go, it will be finished —* [G] **11:3** Or *had given*

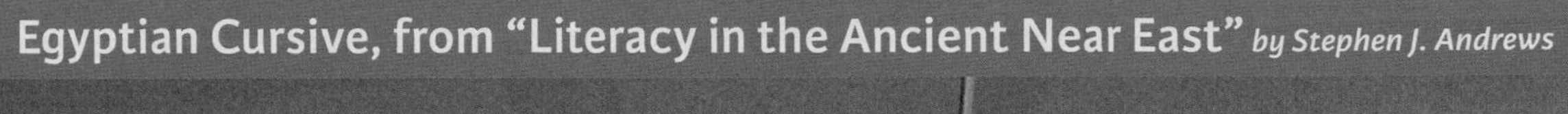

Egyptian Cursive, from "Literacy in the Ancient Near East" *by Stephen J. Andrews*

The Egyptians developed two cursive scripts. They used demotic script mainly for business, legal, and literary purposes, and they used hieratic script primarily for religious texts.

The image above, written on linen, is a copy of the Book of the Dead of Padimin, written in hieratic script; from Akhmim, Egypt; dated after 664 BC. The fragment shown to the right is from Medinet Habu at Luxor. The text, written in demotic script, is a receipt for allotments of grain paid to the northern treasury. ❖

was very highly regarded[A] in the land of Egypt by[B] Pharaoh's officials and the people.

4 So Moses said, "This is what the LORD says: About midnight I will go throughout Egypt, 5 and every firstborn male in the land of Egypt will die, from the firstborn of Pharaoh who sits on his throne to the firstborn of the servant girl who is at the grindstones, as well as every firstborn of the livestock. 6 Then there will be a great cry of anguish through all the land of Egypt such as never was before or ever will be again. 7 But against all the Israelites, whether people or animals, not even a dog will snarl,[C] so that you may know that the LORD makes a distinction between Egypt and Israel. 8 All these officials of yours will come down to me and bow before me, saying: Get out, you and all the people who follow you.[D] After that, I will get out." And he went out from Pharaoh's presence fiercely angry.

9 The LORD said to Moses, "Pharaoh will not listen to you, so that my wonders may be multiplied in the land of Egypt." 10 Moses and Aaron did all these wonders before Pharaoh, but the LORD hardened Pharaoh's heart, and he would not let the Israelites go out of his land.

INSTRUCTIONS FOR THE PASSOVER

12 The LORD said to Moses and Aaron in the land of Egypt, 2 "This month is to be the beginning of months for you; it is the first month of your year. 3 Tell the whole community of Israel that on the tenth day of this month they must each select an animal of the flock according to their fathers' families, one animal per family. 4 If the household is too small for a whole animal, that person and the neighbor nearest his house are to select one based on the combined number of people; you should apportion the animal according to what each will eat. 5 You must have an unblemished animal, a year-old male; you may take it from either the sheep or the goats. 6 You are to keep it until the fourteenth day of this month; then the whole assembly of the community of Israel will slaughter the animals at twilight. 7 They must take some of the blood and put it on the two doorposts and the lintel of the houses where they eat them. 8 They are to eat the meat that night; they should eat it, roasted over the fire along with unleavened bread and bitter herbs. 9 Do not eat any of it raw or cooked in boiling[E] water, but only roasted over fire — its head as well as its legs and inner organs. 10 You must not leave any of it until morning; any part of it left until morning you must burn. 11 Here is how you must eat it: You must be dressed for travel,[F] your sandals on your feet, and your staff in your hand. You are to eat it in a hurry; it is the LORD's Passover.

12 "I will pass through the land of Egypt on that night and strike every firstborn male in the land of Egypt, both people and animals. I am the LORD; I will execute judgments against all the gods of Egypt. 13 The blood on the houses where you are staying will be a distinguishing mark for you; when I see the blood, I will pass over you. No plague will be among you to destroy you when I strike the land of Egypt.

14 "This day is to be a memorial for you, and you must celebrate it as a festival to the LORD. You are to celebrate it throughout your generations as a permanent statute. 15 You must eat unleavened bread for seven days. On the first day you must remove yeast from your houses. Whoever eats what is leavened from the first day through the seventh day must be cut off from Israel. 16 You are to hold a sacred assembly on the first day and another sacred assembly on the seventh day. No work may be done on those days except for preparing what people need to eat — you may do only that.

17 "You are to observe the Festival of Unleavened Bread because on this very day I brought your military divisions out of the land of Egypt. You must observe this day throughout your generations as a permanent statute. 18 You are to eat unleavened bread in the first month, from the evening of the fourteenth day of the month until the evening of the twenty-first day. 19 Yeast must not be found in your houses for seven days. If anyone eats something leavened, that person, whether a resident alien or native of the land, must be cut off from the community of Israel. 20 Do not eat anything leavened; eat unleavened bread in all your homes."[G]

21 Then Moses summoned all the elders of Israel and said to them, "Go, select an animal from the flock according to your families, and slaughter the Passover animal. 22 Take a cluster of hyssop, dip it in the blood that is in the basin, and brush the lintel and the two doorposts with some of the blood in the basin. None of you may go out the door of his house until morning. 23 When the LORD passes through to strike Egypt and sees the blood on the lintel and the two doorposts, he will pass over the door and not let the destroyer enter your houses to strike you.

24 "Keep this command permanently as a statute for you and your descendants. 25 When you enter the land that the LORD will give you as he promised, you are to observe this ceremony. 26 When your children ask you, 'What does this ceremony mean to you?' 27 you are to reply, 'It is the Passover sacrifice to the LORD, for he passed over the houses of the Israelites in Egypt when he struck the Egyptians, and he spared our homes.'" So the people knelt low and worshiped. 28 Then the Israelites went and did this; they did just as the LORD had commanded Moses and Aaron.

[A] **11:3** Lit *was very great* [B] **11:3** Or *in the eyes of* [C] **11:7** Lit *point its tongue* [D] **11:8** Lit *people at your feet* [E] **12:9** Or *or boiled at all in* [F] **12:11** Lit *must have your waist girded* [G] **12:20** Or *settlements*

Pharaoh's Request: Bless Me

by Byron Longino

Pharaoh and his firstborn son, gods according to Egyptian religious beliefs, were helpless, unable to protect themselves and their people from Yahweh. In the minds of many ancient peoples, one of the most important accomplishments of life was obtaining the blessing of a god or gods—even under good circumstances—but especially under bad conditions. People sought blessings for numerous reasons: protection, reproduction, power, healing, or prosperity. Blessings took the form of touchable, visible, and measurable events and experiences. The more powerful one thought the deity to be, the greater the blessing could be; as a result, the stronger one's craving and expectation became for the blessing. Pharaoh asked Moses for a blessing because Pharaoh witnessed the Lord's undeniable and unlimited power when the plagues struck Egypt.[1]

Many "gods" received petitions for blessings from those who lived in the biblical world, but the Old Testament emphatically teaches that the God of the Hebrews alone conferred blessings. He dictated who, how, and when someone received a blessing. Only in God's name could someone bestow a blessing.[2]

Pharaoh reasoned the Lord's power to bless must equal his power to curse; that is, his blessings could offset curses. In the Old Testament, the curses of God had nothing to do with profanity or magical formulas. The idea behind the word *cursed* is "to be regarded lightly."[3] To be cursed referred, therefore, to someone finding himself or herself in a lower position or poorer circumstance than God originally intended due to the person's disobedience.

Pharaoh possessed limited understanding of the ways of God, but he had seen enough of the hand of the Lord and heard enough from the Lord's spokesmen, Moses and Aaron, to know who had the supreme power to bless and curse. The Lord destroyed Pharaoh's ability to ignore him. Now Pharaoh desperately wanted to avoid any more plagues, that is, curses. He thus freed the Hebrews and asked Moses to bless him—to intercede to the Lord for a blessing on his behalf. ✣

A prayer for a blessing over Assyrian houses and temples; cuneiform; dated before 1000 BC. The tablet would have been deposited under the floor at the house's entrance.

[1] Michael L. Brown, "§1385 [*brk*]" (blessed) in *The New International Dictionary of Old Testament Theology and Exegesis* (*NIDOTTE*), ed. Willem A. VanGemeren (Grand Rapids: Zondervan, 1997), 1:758, 761. [2] John N. Oswalt, "§285 [*barak*]" (to bless) in *Theological Wordbook of the Old Testament* (*TWOT*), ed. R. Laird Harris, Gleason L. Archer Jr., and Bruce K. Waltke (Chicago, Moody, 1980), 1:132. [3] Leonard J. Coppes, "§2028 [*qalal*]" (to be slight) in *TWOT*, 2:800–801.

Fragment of a lintel from the Kefar Baram synagogue in Galilee. The Hebrew inscription reads, "May there be peace upon this place and upon all the places of Israel. Joseph the Levite, the son of Levi, put up this lintel. May blessings rest upon his deeds. Shalom."

THE EXODUS

29 Now at midnight the LORD struck every firstborn male in the land of Egypt, from the firstborn of Pharaoh who sat on his throne to the firstborn of the prisoner who was in the dungeon, and every firstborn of the livestock. 30 During the night Pharaoh got up, he along with all his officials and all the Egyptians, and there was a loud wailing throughout Egypt because there wasn't a house without someone dead. 31 He summoned Moses and Aaron during the night and said, "Get out immediately from among my people, both you and the Israelites, and go, worship the LORD as you have said. 32 Take even your flocks and your herds as you asked and leave, and also bless me."

33 Now the Egyptians pressured the people in order to send them quickly out of the country, for they said, "We're all going to die!" 34 So the people took their dough before it was leavened, with their kneading bowls wrapped up in their clothes on their shoulders.

35 The Israelites acted on Moses's word and asked the Egyptians for silver and gold items and for clothing. 36 And the LORD gave the people such favor with the Egyptians that they gave them what they requested. In this way they plundered the Egyptians.

37 The Israelites traveled from Rameses to Succoth, about six hundred thousand able-bodied men on foot, besides their families. 38 A mixed crowd also went up with them, along with a huge number of livestock, both flocks and herds. 39 The people baked the dough they had brought out of Egypt into unleavened loaves, since it had no yeast; for when they were driven out of Egypt, they could not delay and had not prepared provisions for themselves.

40 The time that the Israelites lived in Egypt[A] was 430 years. 41 At the end of 430 years, on that same day, all the LORD's military divisions went out from the land of Egypt. 42 It was a night of vigil in honor of the LORD, because he would bring them out of the land of Egypt. This same night is in honor of the LORD, a night vigil for all the Israelites throughout their generations.

PASSOVER INSTRUCTION

43 The LORD said to Moses and Aaron, "This is the statute of the Passover: no foreigner may eat it. 44 But any slave a man has purchased may eat it, after you have circumcised him. 45 A temporary resident or hired worker may not eat the Passover. 46 It is to be eaten in one house. You may not take any of the meat outside the house, and you may not break any of its bones. 47 The whole community of Israel must celebrate[B] it. 48 If an alien resides among you and wants to observe the LORD's Passover, every male in his household must be circumcised, and then he may participate;[C] he will become like a native of the land. But no uncircumcised person may eat it. 49 The same law will apply to both the native and the alien who resides among you."

50 Then all the Israelites did this; they did just as the LORD had commanded Moses and Aaron. 51 On that same day the LORD brought the Israelites out of the land of Egypt according to their military divisions.

13 The LORD spoke to Moses: 2 "Consecrate every firstborn male to me, the firstborn from every womb among the Israelites, both man and domestic animal; it is mine."

3 Then Moses said to the people, "Remember this day when you came out of Egypt, out of the place of slavery, for the LORD brought you out of here by the strength of his hand. Nothing leavened may be eaten. 4 Today, in the month of Abib,[D] you are going out. 5 When the LORD brings you into the land of the Canaanites, Hethites, Amorites, Hivites, and Jebusites,[E] which he swore to your ancestors that he would give you, a land flowing with milk and honey, you must carry out this ceremony in this month. 6 For seven days you must eat unleavened bread, and on the seventh day there is to be a festival to the LORD. 7 Unleavened bread is to be eaten for those seven days. Nothing leavened may be found among you, and no yeast may be found among you in all your territory. 8 On that day explain to your son, 'This is because of what the LORD did for me when I came out of Egypt.' 9 Let it serve as a sign for you on your hand and as a reminder on your forehead,[F] so that the LORD's instruction may be in your mouth; for the LORD brought you out of Egypt with a strong hand. 10 Keep this statute at its appointed time from year to year.

11 "When the LORD brings you into the land of the Canaanites, as he swore to you and your ancestors, and gives it to you, 12 you are to present to the LORD every firstborn male of the womb. All firstborn offspring of the livestock you own that are males will be the LORD's. 13 You must redeem every firstborn of a donkey with a flock animal, but if you do not redeem it, break its neck. However, you must redeem every firstborn among your sons.

14 "In the future, when your son asks you, 'What does this mean?' say to him, 'By the strength of his hand the LORD brought us out of Egypt, out of the place of slavery. 15 When Pharaoh stubbornly refused to let us go, the LORD killed every firstborn male in the land of Egypt, both the firstborn of humans and the firstborn of livestock. That is why I sacrifice to the LORD all the firstborn of the womb that are males, but

[A] **12:40** LXX, Sam add *and in Canaan* [B] **12:47** Lit *do* [C] **12:48** Lit *may come near to do it* [D] **13:4** March–April; called Nisan in the post-exilic period; Neh 2:1; Est 3:7 [E] **13:5** DSS, Sam, LXX, Syr add *Girgashites* and *Perizzites*; Jos 3:10 [F] **13:9** Lit *reminder between your eyes*

The Hebrew Calendar

by Robert A. Street

The sun and the stars were used to mark the endings and the beginnings of years on a solar calendar. The solar year consists of 365 days and slightly more than eight hours. The moon was used to mark the months. The lunar calendar of twelve months had 29 and 30 days alternately to allow for the lunar cycle of 29 days and slightly more than twelve hours. The ancient Hebrews had to adjust their calendars, just as we do with our leap year. This was accomplished by the addition of a month every two or three years.

The timing of the religious feasts and festivals was specifically noted in the Old Testament. When references are made to these, the dates are connected to specific months, either by the number of the month in the year or by a name. Numbering the months from one to twelve was the most common method. For example, Exodus 12:17–18 sets the Festival of Unleavened Bread in the first month, which was called Abib in the old system (Ex 23:15) and called Nisan after the exile in Babylon (Est 3:7).

The major religious festivals were the foundation for Israel's calendar. During the first month, both Unleavened Bread and Passover were celebrated (Dt 16:1). These celebrations marked the beginning of the new religious year. The oldest liturgical calendars (Ex 23:14–17; 34:18–22) name, in addition to Unleavened Bread, the Festival of Harvest (Firstfruits, Weeks) and the Festival of Ingathering (Shelters, Booths, Tabernacles).[1]

While Unleavened Bread and Passover specifically commemorated the saving grace of God and his redemption of the people of Israel, they are related to the pastoral and agricultural practices of the land of Israel. Unleavened Bread occurred at the beginning of the barley harvest. In its religious function as a remembrance of the exodus, it reminded the people of their hasty departure from bondage when there was no time to let the bread dough rise.

Passover happened at the same time as the birth of new lambs in the spring. In the Passover celebration, the blood of new lambs was smeared on the doorposts in remembrance of the passing over of death in Egypt.

The Festival of Weeks, also known as the Festival of Harvest and Firstfruits (Ex 23:16), was celebrated fifty days after Passover, associated with the wheat harvest in May/June. It was a feast of joy and thanksgiving.

In the fall when the agricultural year was complete, the Festival of Shelters was celebrated during the ingathering of the grapes, olives, and late figs. Religiously, it was a commemoration of the period of wandering in the wilderness after the exodus.

Even though the feasts and festivals of Israel were connected with the agrarian culture, they had religious origins and were deeply meaningful for the faithful. The religious significance outweighed the agrarian associations. ✣

[1] Roland de Vaux, *Social Institutions*, vol. 1 of *Ancient Israel* (New York: McGraw-Hill, 1965), 190.

Tel Gezer, where the Gezer calendar was found.

I redeem all the firstborn of my sons.' 16 So let it be a sign on your hand and a symbol[A] on your forehead, for the LORD brought us out of Egypt by the strength of his hand."

THE ROUTE OF THE EXODUS

17 When Pharaoh let the people go, God did not lead them along the road to the land of the Philistines, even though it was nearby; for God said, "The people will change their minds and return to Egypt if they face war." 18 So he led the people around toward the Red Sea along the road of the wilderness. And the Israelites left the land of Egypt in battle formation.

19 Moses took the bones of Joseph with him, because Joseph had made the Israelites swear a solemn oath, saying, "God will certainly come to your aid; then you must take my bones with you from this place."

20 They set out from Succoth and camped at Etham on the edge of the wilderness. 21 The LORD went ahead of them in a pillar of cloud to lead them on their way during the day and in a pillar of fire to give them light at night, so that they could travel day or night. 22 The pillar of cloud by day and the pillar of fire by night never left its place in front of the people.

14 Then the LORD spoke to Moses: 2 "Tell the Israelites to turn back and camp in front of Pi-hahiroth, between Migdol and the sea; you must camp in front of Baal-zephon, facing it by the sea. 3 Pharaoh will say of the Israelites: They are wandering around the land in confusion; the wilderness has boxed them in. 4 I will harden Pharaoh's heart so that he will pursue them. Then I will receive glory by means of Pharaoh and all his army, and the Egyptians will know that I am the LORD." So the Israelites did this.

THE EGYPTIAN PURSUIT

5 When the king of Egypt was told that the people had fled, Pharaoh and his officials changed their minds about the people and said, "What have we done? We have released Israel from serving us." 6 So he got his chariot ready and took his troops[B] with him; 7 he took six hundred of the best chariots and all the rest of the chariots of Egypt, with officers in each one. 8 The LORD hardened the heart of Pharaoh king of Egypt, and he pursued the Israelites, who were going out defiantly.[C] 9 The Egyptians — all Pharaoh's horses and chariots, his horsemen,[D] and his army — chased after them and caught up with them as they camped by the sea beside Pi-hahiroth, in front of Baal-zephon.

10 As Pharaoh approached, the Israelites looked up and there were the Egyptians coming after them! The Israelites were terrified and cried out to the LORD for help. 11 They said to Moses, "Is it because there are no graves in Egypt that you have taken us away to die in the wilderness? What have you done to us by bringing us out of Egypt? 12 Isn't this what we told you in Egypt: Leave us alone so that we may serve the Egyptians? It would have been better for us to serve the Egyptians than to die in the wilderness."

13 But Moses said to the people, "Don't be afraid. Stand firm and see the LORD's salvation that he will accomplish for you today; for the Egyptians you see today, you will never see again. 14 The LORD will fight for you, and you must be quiet."

ESCAPE THROUGH THE RED SEA

15 The LORD said to Moses, "Why are you crying out to me? Tell the Israelites to break camp. 16 As for you, lift up your staff, stretch out your hand over the sea, and divide it so that the Israelites can go through the sea on dry ground. 17 As for me, I am going to harden the hearts of the Egyptians so that they will go in after them, and I will receive glory by means of Pharaoh, all his army, and his chariots and horsemen. 18 The Egyptians will know that I am the LORD when I receive glory through Pharaoh, his chariots, and his horsemen."

19 Then the angel of God, who was going in front of the Israelite forces, moved and went behind them. The pillar of cloud moved from in front of them and stood behind them. 20 It came between the Egyptian and Israelite forces. There was cloud and darkness, it lit up the night, and neither group came near the other all night long.

21 Then Moses stretched out his hand over the sea. The LORD drove the sea back with a powerful east wind all that night and turned the sea into dry land. So the waters were divided, 22 and the Israelites went through the sea on dry ground, with the waters like a wall to them on their right and their left.

23 The Egyptians set out in pursuit — all Pharaoh's horses, his chariots, and his horsemen — and went into the sea after them. 24 During the morning watch, the LORD looked down at the Egyptian forces from the pillar of fire and cloud, and threw the Egyptian forces into confusion. 25 He caused their chariot wheels to swerve[E,F] and made them drive[G] with difficulty. "Let's get away from Israel," the Egyptians said, "because the LORD is fighting for them against Egypt!"

26 Then the LORD said to Moses, "Stretch out your hand over the sea so that the water may come back on the Egyptians, on their chariots and horsemen." 27 So Moses stretched out his hand over the sea, and at daybreak the sea returned to its normal depth. While

[A] **13:16** Or *phylactery* [B] **14:6** Lit *people* [C] **14:8** Lit *with a raised hand* [D] **14:9** Or *chariot drivers* [E] **14:25** Sam, LXX, Syr read *He bound their chariot wheels* [F] **14:25** Or *fall off* [G] **14:25** Or *and they drove them*

the Egyptians were trying to escape from it, the LORD
threw them into the sea. 28 The water came back and
covered the chariots and horsemen, plus the entire
army of Pharaoh that had gone after them into the
sea. Not even one of them survived.
29 But the Israelites had walked through the sea on
dry ground, with the waters like a wall to them on
their right and their left. 30 That day the LORD saved
Israel from the power of the Egyptians, and Israel saw
the Egyptians dead on the seashore. 31 When Israel
saw the great power that the LORD used against the
Egyptians, the people feared the LORD and believed
in him and in his servant Moses.

ISRAEL'S SONG

15 Then Moses and the Israelites sang this song
to the LORD. They said:
I will sing to the LORD,
for he is highly exalted;
he has thrown the horse
and its rider into the sea.
2 The LORD is my strength and my song;[A]
he has become my salvation.
This is my God, and I will praise him,
my father's God, and I will exalt him.
3 The LORD is a warrior;
the LORD is his name.

4 He threw Pharaoh's chariots
and his army into the sea;
the elite of his officers
were drowned in the Red Sea.
5 The floods covered them;
they sank to the depths like a stone.
6 LORD, your right hand is glorious in power.
LORD, your right hand shattered the enemy.
7 You overthrew your adversaries
by your great majesty.
You unleashed your burning wrath;
it consumed them like stubble.
8 The water heaped up at the blast
from your nostrils;
the currents stood firm like a dam.
The watery depths congealed in the heart
of the sea.
9 The enemy said:
"I will pursue, I will overtake,
I will divide the spoil.
My desire will be gratified at their expense.
I will draw my sword;
my hand will destroy[B] them."
10 But you blew with your breath,
and the sea covered them.
They sank like lead
in the mighty waters.
11 LORD, who is like you among the gods?
Who is like you, glorious in holiness,
revered with praises, performing wonders?
12 You stretched out your right hand,
and the earth swallowed them.
13 With your faithful love,
you will lead the people
you have redeemed;
you will guide them to your holy dwelling
with your strength.

14 When the peoples hear, they will shudder;
anguish will seize the inhabitants of Philistia.
15 Then the chiefs of Edom will be terrified;
trembling will seize the leaders of Moab;
all the inhabitants of Canaan will panic;
16 terror and dread will fall on them.
They will be as still[C] as a stone
because of your powerful arm
until your people pass by, LORD,
until the people whom you purchased[D]
pass by.

17 You will bring them in and plant them
on the mountain of your possession;
LORD, you have prepared the place
for your dwelling;
Lord,[E] your hands have established
the sanctuary.
18 The LORD will reign forever and ever!

19 When Pharaoh's horses with his chariots and
horsemen went into the sea, the LORD brought the
water of the sea back over them. But the Israelites
walked through the sea on dry ground. 20 Then the
prophetess Miriam, Aaron's sister, took a tambourine
in her hand, and all the women came out following
her with tambourines and dancing. 21 Miriam sang
to them:
Sing to the LORD,
for he is highly exalted;
he has thrown the horse
and its rider into the sea.

WATER PROVIDED

22 Then Moses led Israel on from the Red Sea, and
they went out to the Wilderness of Shur. They journeyed for three days in the wilderness without finding water. 23 They came to Marah, but they could
not drink the water at Marah because it was bitter
— that is why it was named Marah.[F] 24 The people
grumbled to Moses, "What are we going to drink?"

[A] **15:2** Or *might* [B] **15:9** Or *conquer* [C] **15:16** Or *silent* [D] **15:16** Or *created* [E] **15:17** Some Hb mss, DSS, Sam, Tg read *LORD* [F] **15:23** = Bitter or Bitterness

by Duane A. Garrett

Egypt's golden age of imperial and military glory was the period known as the New Kingdom (Eighteenth, Nineteenth, and Twentieth Dynasties; 1550–1069 BC). Egypt waged war to the west (Libya), to the south (Nubia), and to the north (the Mitanni Empire of Syria during the Eighteenth Dynasty and the Hittite Empire of Anatolia during the Nineteenth Dynasty). During the Twentieth Dynasty, as Egyptian power waned, Egypt repelled an invasion of "Sea Peoples" from across the Mediterranean Sea. The New Kingdom was also the period in which the exodus occurred.

The Egyptian military machine developed during the wars against the Hyksos, foreigners who dominated northern Egypt 1786–1550 BC. The Egyptians who drove out the Hyksos established the Eighteenth Dynasty and the New Kingdom Era. After expelling the Hyksos, the new Egyptian army did not lay down its arms and go back to the plow. They were a thoroughly militarized society, and they had come to believe that an aggressive foreign policy was the best defense against future humiliation at the hands of foreigners.

SOURCES OF INFORMATION

A primary source of information is the accounts of military successes left by Thutmose III (Eighteenth Dynasty; reigned 1479–1425 BC), Ramesses II (Nineteenth Dynasty; reigned 1279–1213), and Ramesses III (Twentieth Dynasty; reigned 1184–1153 BC). These inscriptions and the accompanying artwork tell us a great deal about Egyptian weapons, tactics, and standard procedures.

Thutmose III left behind accounts of his many campaigns into the land of promise. His most daring exploit was the conquest of the Canaanite city of Megiddo, which had revolted against Egyptian domination with the encouragement of the Syrian city of Kadesh. Thutmose, approaching Megiddo from the southwest, took his army through the narrow Aruna Pass rather than swing around the hills that stood between him and the city. This maneuver forced him to string out his forces, and it could have led to catastrophic defeat. But his enemies were not expecting him to take the narrow pass and made no effort to block it. He surprised them by emerging from the pass and arraying his army for battle before the city gates. Perhaps parts of the Syrian and Canaanite armies were away defending other approaches and did not make it back to the city in time to participate in the battle. At any rate, the forces that did confront Thutmose were defeated outside the gates and had to be hauled up the walls into the city by the inhabitants. Eventually, Megiddo capitulated. In a later campaign, Thutmose carried boats on oxcarts from Byblos to the Euphrates River. Able to move troops up and down the upper part of the river, where it bisected the Mitanni Kingdom, he was able to campaign in the western half of Mitanni and wage war in Syria and Canaan while blocking Mitanni support from coming across the river.

The most famous battle of ancient Egyptian history is that between Ramesses II and his Hittite counterpart, Muwatallis II, at Kadesh on the Orontes River in Syria in about 1274 BC. Driving his army into Syria for an encounter with the Hittites, Ramesses foolishly believed a report from two captured men that the Hittites were still far away.

The Jezreel Valley as seen from atop Megiddo. Controlling Megiddo meant being able to guard the route where the International Coastal Highway entered the valley. The north/south highway linked Egypt to Syria.

(They were in fact concealed behind the city of Kadesh.) The Egyptian army was attacked while its leading units, including the pharaoh, were making camp; the rest of the Egyptian army was still on the march. Pharaoh's forces in the vanguard managed to hold off the enemy until the remainder of his army arrived, and disaster was averted. The battle ended as something of a Hittite victory. (Ramesses failed to take Kadesh, and Egyptian power was confined to the area of Canaan, having been driven from Syria.) Even so, the pharaoh claimed to have won a great victory through his personal prowess in battle.

Recorded on the interior walls of the first hall of the Ramesses II temple at Abu Simbel, Egypt, the massive Egyptian army maneuvers their horses and chariots in preparation for invading Kadesh.

Ramesses III, in the eighth year of his reign, had his greatest victory in a battle fought on the northern frontier of Egypt itself. He repulsed the Sea Peoples, who had attacked Egypt with a combined sea and land invasion. He thus saved Egypt from foreign domination. This great victory included a rare example of a sea battle fought by the ancient Egyptians. They used boats as rapid transports for their troops, but these were mostly river craft used on the Nile for the rapid deployment of forces. But Ramesses had to fight ship-to-ship battles against the Sea Peoples.

Other sources offer information about Egyptian warfare. Horemheb, the last pharaoh of the Eighteenth Dynasty, issued a decree that tells us something about Egyptian military administration. Also, officers in the Egyptian army sometimes had their tombs inscribed with accounts of their bravery in battle. Finally, Egyptian artwork and artifacts, principally from tombs, gives us a better understanding of Egypt's military. Several chariots, for example, were found in tombs.

ORGANIZATION

The pharaoh was the supreme commander of the armed forces and, if he was a vigorous ruler, would personally lead his army into battle. The vizier (the pharaoh's highest-ranking administrator) was in effect his chief of staff, and he might command the army in the field as the pharaoh's representative. Officers were chiefly drawn from the aristocracy; the lowest-ranking officer, perhaps analogous to a lieutenant, was a commander of fifty. Common soldiers were conscripted from the peasant classes (about one man in ten might serve time in the army). Foreigners might also serve in Egypt's army. The army of Ramesses II was organized into four divisions of five thousand men. Each division was named for a god (Ptah, Re, Seth, and Amun), and a fifth division was under the pharaoh's direct command.[1] Divisions were subdivided into smaller units, down to the fifty-man platoon. Chariots were organized into squadrons of twenty-five.

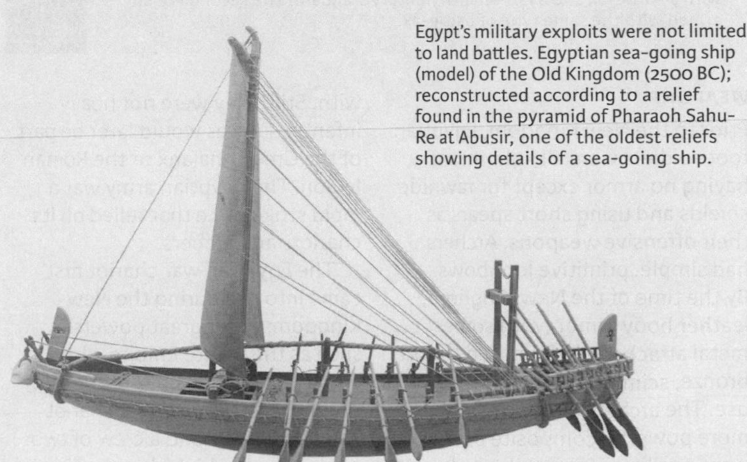

Egypt's military exploits were not limited to land battles. Egyptian sea-going ship (model) of the Old Kingdom (2500 BC); reconstructed according to a relief found in the pyramid of Pharaoh Sahu-Re at Abusir, one of the oldest reliefs showing details of a sea-going ship.

Relief from the funerary temple of Hatshepsut at Thebes. The image depicts two sailors in the royal Egyptian navy. The first sailor is equipped with a battle-ax and a fan-shaped military standard. The second is also armed with the same type of battle-ax.

WEAPONRY

Prior to the New Kingdom, Egyptian foot soldiers were all light infantry, having no armor except for rawhide shields and using short spears as their offensive weapons. Archers had simple, primitive longbows. By the time of the New Kingdom, leather body armor (with some metal attached); helmets; and short, bronze, scimitar-like swords were in use. The archers, now armed with more powerful composite bows, were a military force to be reckoned with. Still, they were not heavy infantry such as would later be part of the Greek phalanx or the Roman legion. The Egyptian army was a rapid strike force that relied on its chariots and archers.

The Egyptian war chariot first came into use during the New Kingdom; other great powers, such as the Hittite Empire, also employed massed chariots at this time. The two-horse war chariot had two wheels and a crew of two: a driver and a shield-bearer. The driver approached the enemy and then fired arrows; he might use a javelin or sword at closer quarters. The chariot was of light wickerwork and designed for speed; it was not armored. The massed chariot attack was meant to terrify the lightly armed foot soldiers who opposed it. Centuries later, when infantry was more heavily armored and was disciplined to hold its ranks, the chariot became obsolete.

Egyptians did not use a cavalry, but employed mounted troops as scouts. Exodus 14:5 suggests such scouts were shadowing the Israelites as they departed. The Bible also indicates that Egyptian infantry set out with the chariot corps in pursuit of the Hebrews (v. 6), but no infantry appear to have been present when the chariots were destroyed at the sea (v. 23). Perhaps they were trailing behind the mounted forces and only arrived after the debacle.

TACTICS

The Egyptian military typically arrayed themselves for battle as a main body with a wing on each side. Such maneuvering, however, would not have been employed while pursuing a large body of refugees, as the Israelites were.

The New Kingdom Egyptians' preferred tactic apparently was to make a rapid strike with their chariot forces. They never developed the slow and methodical art of siege warfare, and evidence from the battles at Megiddo and Kadesh suggests they could be bold to the point of recklessness. This is consonant with what we see in Exodus 14, where they rush into the sea without pausing to ask whether this was a sound idea. Under normal circumstances, the Israelites would have been no match for the Egyptian chariots. Being untrained peasants who only days before had been working as slaves, the Hebrews would have scattered like fallen leaves in a storm before a properly executed Egyptian attack.

VALOR AND MORALE

The Egyptians highly valued personal courage. A soldier who showed valor in battle would be awarded the "golden flies," a military decoration analogous to modern medals for bravery. More than that, he would receive wealth and slaves as his share of the booty. A certain Ahmose son of Abana, on the wall of a rock-cut tomb, left an account of his deeds of valor and of the honors he received while under the service of early Eighteenth Dynasty pharaohs. Another soldier, named Amenemhab, told of his many battles while campaigning with Thutmose III, and he especially made a point of describing how often he was in hand-to-hand combat.[2]

Egyptian commanders also bolstered the morale of their men by speaking of how their gods fought for them. They might call upon Montu, the Egyptian war-god, but during the New Kingdom they extolled the all-conquering power of Amun.

Most importantly, the pharaohs of the New Kingdom personally boosted their troops' and the nation's morale by assuming the role of military hero. Thutmose III, in the Megiddo narrative, is bold and resolute where his general staff is timid and conventional. Ramesses II, in the account of his action at Kadesh, is positively Herculean, single-handedly slaying the enemy hordes while his confused soldiers seek to recover and reorganize themselves. The iconography of the time, portraying the pharaoh as a gigantic figure striding in to vanquish Lilliputian enemies, is the ultimate piece of morale-building propaganda: Egypt is invincible because the pharaoh is invincible.[3]

Relief at Medinet Habu depicts the army of Ramesses III as they prepare for battle with the Sea Peoples.

EGYPTIAN ÉLAN AT THE RED SEA

From the above discussion, one may suggest that a central feature of the New Kingdom Egyptian army, and especially of its chariot corps, was the high value it placed upon élan. This was a particular kind of courage that enabled someone to charge headlong into the thick of battle. It was also a tactic designed to force the outcome of battle by overwhelming the enemy with the sheer audacity of one's attack. Alexander the Great and Napoleon, both great captains, employed this strategy. It was more than a tactic; it was for certain armies their central creed. The New Kingdom Egyptian army belonged in this class. The officially cultivated faith in Amun and his pharaoh, the examples set by Thutmose III at Megiddo and by Ramesses II at Kadesh, the recognition Egyptians gave to the valor of individual soldiers, and the very nature of the war chariot as a weapon of shock attack all suggest that devotion to élan was central to Egypt's military culture. But as a military philosophy, élan had a major drawback, as the Romans under Caesar demonstrated when they were attacked by Gallic warriors rushing madly upon them, screaming and swinging their broadswords. When the legions held their lines in the face of these onslaughts, the élan of the Gauls was quickly transformed into terror and chaotic flight, and Caesar rapidly conquered all of Gaul. Therefore, the Bible credibly describes both the Egyptians' furious rush into the sea and their subsequent panic when they realized God was fighting for Israel (Ex 14:25). ✣

---

[1] The figure of five thousand men per division is based on a comment in Papyrus Anastasi I, but whether that represents the standard size for an Egyptian division at the time is open to question. It may have been smaller. See Anthony J. Spalinger, *War in Ancient Egypt: The New Kingdom* (Oxford: Blackwell, 2005), 149–50. [2] For the inscriptions of Ahmose son of Abana and of Amenemhab, see James Henry Breasted, *Ancient Records of Egypt*, vol. 2 (Chicago: University of Chicago Press, 1906), 3–18, 227–34. [3] For descriptions of the Egyptian military, see esp. Spalinger; also Rosalie David, *Handbook to Life in Ancient Egypt* (New York: Facts on File, 1998), 225–54.

25 So he cried out to the LORD, and the LORD showed him a tree. When he threw it into the water, the water became drinkable.

The LORD made a statute and ordinance for them at Marah, and he tested them there. 26 He said, "If you will carefully obey the LORD your God, do what is right in his sight, pay attention to his commands, and keep all his statutes, I will not inflict any illnesses on you that I inflicted on the Egyptians. For I am the LORD who heals you."

27 Then they came to Elim, where there were twelve springs and seventy date palms, and they camped there by the water.

MANNA AND QUAIL PROVIDED

16 The entire Israelite community departed from Elim and came to the Wilderness of Sin, which is between Elim and Sinai, on the fifteenth day of the second month after they had left the land of Egypt. 2 The entire Israelite community grumbled against Moses and Aaron in the wilderness. 3 The Israelites said to them, "If only we had died by the LORD's hand in the land of Egypt, when we sat by pots of meat and ate all the bread we wanted. Instead, you brought us into this wilderness to make this whole assembly die of hunger!"

4 Then the LORD said to Moses, "I am going to rain bread from heaven for you. The people are to go out each day and gather enough for that day. This way I will test them to see whether or not they will follow my instructions. 5 On the sixth day, when they prepare what they bring in, it will be twice as much as they gather on other days."[A]

6 So Moses and Aaron said to all the Israelites, "This evening you will know that it was the LORD who brought you out of the land of Egypt, 7 and in the morning you will see the LORD's glory because he has heard your complaints about him. For who are we that you complain about us?" 8 Moses continued, "The LORD will give you meat to eat this evening and all the bread you want in the morning, for he has heard the complaints that you are raising against him. Who are we? Your complaints are not against us but against the LORD."

9 Then Moses told Aaron, "Say to the entire Israelite community, 'Come before the LORD, for he has heard your complaints.'" 10 As Aaron was speaking to the entire Israelite community, they turned toward the wilderness, and there in a cloud the LORD's glory appeared.

11 The LORD spoke to Moses, 12 "I have heard the complaints of the Israelites. Tell them: At twilight you will eat meat, and in the morning you will eat bread until you are full. Then you will know that I am the LORD your God."

13 So at evening quail came and covered the camp. In the morning there was a layer of dew all around the camp. 14 When the layer of dew evaporated, there were fine flakes on the desert surface, as fine as frost on the ground. 15 When the Israelites saw it, they asked one another, "What is it?" because they didn't know what it was.

Moses told them, "It is the bread the LORD has given you to eat. 16 This is what the LORD has commanded: 'Gather as much of it as each person needs to eat. You may take two quarts[B] per individual, according to the number of people each of you has in his tent.'"

17 So the Israelites did this. Some gathered a lot, some a little. 18 When they measured it by quarts,[C] the person who gathered a lot had no surplus, and the person who gathered a little had no shortage. Each gathered as much as he needed to eat. 19 Moses said to them, "No one is to let any of it remain until morning." 20 But they didn't listen to Moses; some people left part of it until morning, and it bred worms and stank. Therefore Moses was angry with them.

21 They gathered it every morning. Each gathered as much as he needed to eat, but when the sun grew hot, it melted. 22 On the sixth day they gathered twice as much food, four quarts[D] apiece, and all the leaders of the community came and reported this to Moses. 23 He told them, "This is what the LORD has said: 'Tomorrow is a day of complete rest, a holy Sabbath to the LORD. Bake what you want to bake, and boil what you want to boil, and set aside everything left over to be kept until morning.'"

24 So they set it aside until morning as Moses commanded, and it didn't stink or have maggots in it. 25 "Eat it today," Moses said, "because today is a Sabbath to the LORD. Today you won't find any in the field. 26 For six days you will gather it, but on the seventh day, the Sabbath, there will be none."

27 Yet on the seventh day some of the people went out to gather, but they did not find any. 28 Then the LORD said to Moses, "How long will you[E] refuse to keep my commands and instructions? 29 Understand that the LORD has given you the Sabbath; therefore on the sixth day he will give you two days' worth of bread. Each of you stay where you are; no one is to leave his place on the seventh day." 30 So the people rested on the seventh day.

31 The house of Israel named the substance manna.[F] It resembled coriander seed, was white, and tasted like wafers made with honey. 32 Moses said, "This is what the LORD has commanded: 'Two quarts[G] of it are

[A] **16:5** Lit *as gathering day to day* [B] **16:16** Lit *an omer* [C] **16:18** Lit *by an omer* [D] **16:22** Lit *two omers* [E] **16:28** The Hb word for *you* is pl, referring to the whole nation. [F] **16:31** = what?; Ex 16:15 [G] **16:32** Lit *'A full omer*

What Kind of Tambourine? from "Miriam: All We Know" *by Martha S. Bergen*

After the destruction of the Egyptians in the Red Sea, Miriam took up a tambourine and led the women of Israel in celebration: "Sing to the LORD, for he is highly exalted; he has thrown the horse and its rider into the sea" (Ex 15:21). What kind of tambourine, though, did she use? Was it the freehanded instrument with rows of cymbals, or was it more like a hand drum?

Hebrew uses two different words to describe the two instruments. A *sistrum* typically accompanied ritual ceremonies and was associated with the Egyptian goddess Hathor. Small discs, each with a hole in the middle, hung from the rods. Although these were common in Egypt, this was not the instrument Miriam played.

Miriam played a *toph* (Hb for "tambourine" or "timbrel"), which is thought to have been a wooden or metal hand drum, covered on at least one side with ram or goat skin. A *toph* evidently had no cymbals or discs that jangled. The Hebrew term is onomatopoetic, imitating the instrument's sound. *Toph* drums were the most common musical instruments in ancient times.[1]

Shown are an Egyptian *sistrum* dated 2500 BC and a terra-cotta figurine of a woman playing a *toph*, dated to the ninth century BC. ✣

[1] "Musical Instruments," in *Tyndale Bible Dictionary*, ed. Walter A. Elwell and Philip W. Comfort (Wheaton, IL: Tyndale House, 2001), 925; Ronald F. Youngblood, "[*toph*]," in *TWOT*, 2:978.

to be preserved throughout your generations, so that they may see the bread I fed you in the wilderness when I brought you out of the land of Egypt.' "

33 Moses told Aaron, "Take a container and put two quarts[A] of manna in it. Then place it before the LORD to be preserved throughout your generations." 34 As the LORD commanded Moses, Aaron placed it before the testimony to be preserved.

35 The Israelites ate manna for forty years, until they came to an inhabited land. They ate manna until they reached the border of the land of Canaan. 36 (They used a measure called an omer, which held two quarts.[B])

WATER FROM THE ROCK

17 The entire Israelite community left the Wilderness of Sin, moving from one place to the next according to the LORD's command. They camped at Rephidim, but there was no water for the people to drink. 2 So the people complained to Moses, "Give us water to drink."

"Why are you complaining to me?" Moses replied to them. "Why are you testing the LORD?"

3 But the people thirsted there for water and grumbled against Moses. They said, "Why did you ever bring us up from Egypt to kill us and our children and our livestock with thirst?"

4 Then Moses cried out to the LORD, "What should I do with these people? In a little while they will stone me!"

5 The LORD answered Moses, "Go on ahead of the people and take some of the elders of Israel with you. Take the staff you struck the Nile with in your hand and go. 6 I am going to stand there in front of you on the rock at Horeb; when you hit the rock, water will come out of it and the people will drink." Moses did this in the sight of the elders of Israel. 7 He named the place Massah[C] and Meribah[D] because the Israelites complained, and because they tested the LORD, saying, "Is the LORD among us or not?"

THE AMALEKITES ATTACK

8 At Rephidim, Amalek[E] came and fought against Israel. 9 Moses said to Joshua, "Select some men for us and go fight against Amalek. Tomorrow I will stand on the hilltop with God's staff in my hand."

10 Joshua did as Moses had told him, and fought against Amalek, while Moses, Aaron, and Hur went up to the top of the hill. 11 While Moses held up his hand,[F] Israel prevailed, but whenever he put his hand[F] down, Amalek prevailed. 12 When Moses's hands grew heavy, they took a stone and put it under him, and he sat down on it. Then Aaron and Hur supported his hands, one on one side and one on the other so that his hands remained steady until the sun went down. 13 So Joshua defeated Amalek and his army[G] with the sword.

14 The LORD then said to Moses, "Write this down on a scroll as a reminder and recite it to Joshua: I will completely blot out the memory of Amalek under heaven."

15 And Moses built an altar and named it, "The LORD Is My Banner."[H] 16 He said, "Indeed, my hand is lifted up toward[I] the LORD's throne. The LORD will be at war with Amalek from generation to generation."

JETHRO'S VISIT

18 Moses's father-in-law, Jethro, the priest of Midian, heard about everything that God had done for Moses and for God's people Israel when the LORD brought Israel out of Egypt.

2 Now Jethro, Moses's father-in-law, had taken in Zipporah, Moses's wife, after he had sent her back, 3 along with her two sons, one of whom was named Gershom[J] (because Moses had said, "I have been a resident alien in a foreign land") 4 and the other Eliezer (because he had said, "The God of my father was my helper and rescued me from Pharaoh's sword").[K]

5 Moses's father-in-law, Jethro, along with Moses's wife and sons, came to him in the wilderness where he was camped at the mountain of God. 6 He sent word to Moses, "I, your father-in-law Jethro, am coming to you with your wife and her two sons."

7 So Moses went out to meet his father-in-law, bowed down, and then kissed him. They asked each other how they had been[L] and went into the tent. 8 Moses recounted to his father-in-law all that the LORD had done to Pharaoh and the Egyptians for Israel's sake, all the hardships that confronted them on the way, and how the LORD rescued them.

9 Jethro rejoiced over all the good things the LORD had done for Israel when he rescued them from the power of the Egyptians. 10 "Blessed be the LORD," Jethro exclaimed, "who rescued you from the power of Egypt and from the power of Pharaoh. He has rescued the people from under the power of Egypt! 11 Now I know that the LORD is greater than all gods, because he did wonders when the Egyptians acted arrogantly against Israel."[M]

12 Then Jethro, Moses's father-in-law, brought a burnt offering and sacrifices to God, and Aaron came with all the elders of Israel to eat a meal with Moses's father-in-law in God's presence.

[A] **16:33** Lit *a full omer* [B] **16:36** Lit *(The omer is a tenth of an ephah.)* [C] **17:7** = Testing [D] **17:7** = Quarreling [E] **17:8** A seminomadic people descended from *Amalek*, a grandson of Esau; Gn 36:12 [F] **17:11** Sam, LXX, Syr, Tg, Vg read *hands* [G] **17:13** Or *people* [H] **17:15** = *Yahweh-nissi* [I] **17:16** Or *hand was on*, or *hand was against*; Hb obscure [J] **18:3** In Hb the name *Gershom* sounds like the phrase "a stranger there." [K] **18:4** = My God Is Help [L] **18:7** Lit *other about well-being* [M] **18:11** Hb obscure

The Route of the Exodus: Don't Go By the Way of the Philistines *by Stephen J. Andrews*

Recent archaeological and geographical research in Egypt and Sinai has begun to offer new insights that help identify some of the major stations along the journey.[1] The starting point of the exodus was Rameses, one of the supply cities the Israelites built for Pharaoh (Ex 1:11; 12:37; Nm 33:3). Rameses is generally regarded to be the large archaeological complex at Tell el-Dab'a/Qantir.[2]

Succoth (Ex 12:37), Etham (13:20; Nm 33:6), Pi-hahiroth (Ex 14:2; Nm 33:7), and Migdol may refer to Egyptian forts or military installations in the Wadi Tumilat area. The Wadi Tumilat extends east from the delta region toward Lake Timsah and was a major transportation corridor in biblical times. The two largest sites in the wadi, Tell er-Rataba and Tell el-Maskhuta, have been identified with Pithom (Ex 1:11) and Succoth, but it is uncertain which is which.

The exact location where Israel crossed the sea is unknown and still fervently debated.[3] Options for the site range from Lake Sirbonis in the north near the Mediterranean Sea to the northern edge of the Gulf of Suez.[4] Some texts identify the body of water as "the sea" (14:9,16,21; Nm 33:8); others call it *Yam Suph* or "Sea of Reeds," traditionally translated "Red Sea" in English Bibles (Ex 13:18; 15:4; Nm 33:10).[5] Recent research suggests *Yam Suph* is near modern Lake Ballah in the Gulf of Suez.[6]

ROAD NOT TAKEN

God chose not to lead Israel along the "road to the land of the Philistines" (Ex 13:17). This was a military transit route extending across north Sinai from the eastern Nile Delta to Gaza. The Egyptians called this road the Way of Horus. Its huge fortified headquarters was located at Tell Hebua (ancient Tjaru). Recent excavations there have revealed a massive fort on a narrow strip of land with water on two sides. This installation was designed to be an "ominous obstacle" to those arriving from the east and those leaving from the west.[7] Up to ten smaller fortified way stations protected the route and facilitated the movement of officials, troops, and merchants into and out of Canaan. Archaeologists have found storage areas for weapons, grain silos, and water reservoirs at most of the stations.[8] Large numbers of troops could easily be billeted along the route. God knew that by going this way the Israelites would lose heart and want to return to Egypt (13:17).

THE RED SEA TO MOUNT SINAI

Following the delivery at the Red Sea, Moses led Israel into the Wilderness of Shur, possibly along a southeast direction. Their destination was the mountain (Mount Sinai) where Moses had previously met God (3:12). Scholars debate the location of Mount Sinai and the direction taken to arrive there. Three possible major routes (northern, central, or southern), a few alternative routes, and more than a dozen candidates for Mount Sinai have been identified. The southern route along the eastern coast of the Gulf of Suez with Mount Sinai located at Jebel Musa near the lower tip of

Landforms on the west coast of the Sinai.

Ayun Musa, which translates to the Springs (or Wells) of Moses.

the Sinai Peninsula has traditionally been regarded as the most probable and continues to fit most of the evidence well.

Numbers 33:8–15 lists a total of eight Israelite encampments on the way to Mount Sinai. Their precise locations are unclear. Marah and Elim were associated with water. Two possible candidates for Marah are Bir el-Mura or `Ayun Musa.

Elim contained an abundance of water, shade, and food with twelve springs and seventy date palms (Ex 15:27). Wadi Gharandel with its acacia, tamarisk, and palm trees is possibly Elim.[9] From Elim, the Israelites moved to the Wilderness of Sin, one of seven smaller wildernesses or areas that made up the Sinai Peninsula (16:1).[10] Here God provided manna and quail (16:1–14). Upon leaving, the Israelites moved to several unspecified locations (17:1).

Then the Israelites turned east near the Wadi Feiran, a rising passageway through granite terrain, and headed for Rephidim (17:1).[11] After leaving Rephidim, Moses and the Israelites traveled through the Watiya Pass in the Wilderness of Sinai and probably encamped in the er-Raha plain "in front of the mountain" of God (19:2).[12] Jebel Musa has long been regarded as the location of Mount Sinai, but other possible candidates, Jebel Serbal, Ras Safsaf, and Jebel Katerin, are also nearby.

MOUNT SINAI TO KADESH

After a year's stay, Israel left Mount Sinai and took one of two possible paths. One option followed the route of the Wadi Nasb, which leads gently down to the western coast of the Gulf of Aqaba near modern Dahab. Traveling north along the coast, they passed a network of oases and arrived at Ezion-geber (modern Eilat). The sites of the oases may be reflected in the twenty encampments in Numbers 33:16–35. The other possible path left Mount Sinai and followed the ridgetops farther inland until the travelers came to Ezion-geber.

From Ezion-geber Moses led Israel in a northwesterly direction through the Wilderness of Paran to Kadesh-barnea in the Wilderness of Zin (Nm 20:1; 33:36). The actual location of Kadesh-barnea has been debated, but the modern consensus places it at either `Ain Qudeirat or `Ain Qadis in the northeastern Sinai Peninsula.[13] Both sites contain an

Wadi Gharandel, which may be the location of Elim (Ex 15:27; 16:1).

Vistas of Edomite territory near Petra.

oasis and are less than ten kilometers (six miles) apart. `Ain Qudeirat holds an advantage because it is located at the intersection of two major ancient roads, the route from Edom to Egypt and the road from the Red Sea to the Negev and north to Canaan. This fact may help explain the decision of the Israelites to invade Canaan by way of Arad, since Arad lay north of Kadesh-barnea on this road (Nm 14:39–45; Dt 1:41–46).[14] From here the twelve spies were sent out (Nm 13).

KADESH TO MOAB

When Moses and the Israelites departed from Kadesh through the Wilderness of Zin, the king of Edom denied them passage through the mountains of Edom at Punon to connect with the King's Highway (Nm 20:14–17). They were required to turn south and follow the "way of the Red Sea" through the Arabah to Ezion-geber again (Dt 2:1). From there, they moved northeast again along the fringes of the desert, bypassing Edomite and Moabite military outposts on the "road to the Wilderness of Moab" (v. 8). After they reached the Pisgah highlands, they requested permission to pass through the land of Sihon, king of the Amorites. Sihon attacked and was defeated (Nm 21:18b–30). Then Israel was able to complete its exodus and move on to the plains of Moab to begin the conquest of the promised land. ✣

---

[1] James K. Hoffmeier, *Ancient Israel in Sinai: The Evidence for the Authenticity of the Wilderness Tradition* (Oxford: Oxford University Press, 2005), 89–90. The locations for the sites in this article are based primarily on information in Barry J. Beitzel, *The Moody Atlas of the Bible* (Chicago: Moody, 2009) and Thomas V. Brisco, *Holman Bible Atlas* (Nashville: Broadman & Holman, 1998). [2] Hoffmeier, *Ancient Israel*, 53–58. [3] Hoffmeier, *Ancient Israel*, 75–109. See also Ralph L. Smith, "Red Sea" in *HIBD*, 1369–70. [4] Smith, "Red Sea," 1370. [5] Hoffmeier, *Ancient Israel*, 81–85. [6] Hoffmeier, *Ancient Israel*, 88. [7] Hoffmeier, *Ancient Israel*, 65, 93. [8] Gregory D. Mumford, "Forts, Pharonic Egypt" in *The Encyclopedia of Ancient History*, ed. Roger S. Bagnall et al. (Oxford: Blackwell, 2013), 2729. [9] Hoffmeier, *Ancient Israel*, 162–63. [10] The seven are: Shur, Etham, Sin, Sinai, Paran, Zin, and Kadesh. [11] The campsites beside the Red Sea, Dophkah, and Alush (Nm 33:11–14), are not mentioned in the Exodus account. The locations of these sites are uncertain. See Hoffmeier, *Ancient Israel*, 165 71. [12] Beitzel, *Moody Atlas*, 113. [13] Hoffmeier, *Ancient Israel*, 123–24; See also Joel F. Drinkard Jr., "Kadesh" in *HIBD*, 974–75. [14] Drinkard, "Kadesh," 974.

13 The next day Moses sat down to judge the people, and they stood around Moses from morning until evening. 14 When Moses's father-in-law saw everything he was doing for them he asked, "What is this you're doing for the people? Why are you alone sitting as judge, while all the people stand around you from morning until evening?"

15 Moses replied to his father-in-law, "Because the people come to me to inquire of God. 16 Whenever they have a dispute, it comes to me, and I make a decision between one man and another. I teach them God's statutes and laws."

17 "What you're doing is not good," Moses's father-in-law said to him. 18 "You will certainly wear out both yourself and these people who are with you, because the task is too heavy for you. You can't do it alone. 19 Now listen to me; I will give you some advice, and God be with you. You be the one to represent the people before God and bring their cases to him. 20 Instruct them about the statutes and laws, and teach them the way to live and what they must do. 21 But you should select from all the people able men, God-fearing, trustworthy, and hating dishonest profit. Place them over the people as commanders of thousands, hundreds, fifties, and tens. 22 They should judge the people at all times. Then they can bring you every major case but judge every minor case themselves. In this way you will lighten your load,[A] and they will bear it with you. 23 If you do this, and God so directs you, you will be able to endure, and also all these people will be able to go home satisfied."[B]

24 Moses listened to his father-in-law and did everything he said. 25 So Moses chose able men from all Israel and made them leaders over the people as commanders of thousands, hundreds, fifties, and tens. 26 They judged the people at all times; they would bring the hard cases to Moses, but they would judge every minor case themselves.

27 Moses let his father-in-law go, and he journeyed to his own land.

ISRAEL AT SINAI

19 In the third month from the very day the Israelites left the land of Egypt, they came to the Sinai Wilderness. 2 They traveled from Rephidim, came to the Sinai Wilderness, and camped in the wilderness. Israel camped there in front of the mountain.

3 Moses went up the mountain to God, and the LORD called to him from the mountain: "This is what you must say to the house of Jacob and explain to the Israelites: 4 'You have seen what I did to the Egyptians and how I carried you on eagles' wings and brought you to myself. 5 Now if you will carefully listen to me and keep my covenant, you will be my own possession out of all the peoples, although the whole earth is mine, 6 and you will be my kingdom of priests and my holy nation.' These are the words that you are to say to the Israelites."

7 After Moses came back, he summoned the elders of the people and set before them all these words that the LORD had commanded him. 8 Then all the people responded together, "We will do all that the LORD has spoken." So Moses brought the people's words back to the LORD.

9 The LORD said to Moses, "I am going to come to you in a dense cloud, so that the people will hear when I speak with you and will always believe you." Moses reported the people's words to the LORD, 10 and the LORD told Moses, "Go to the people and consecrate them today and tomorrow. They must wash their clothes 11 and be prepared by the third day, for on the third day the LORD will come down on Mount Sinai in the sight of all the people. 12 Put boundaries for the people all around the mountain and say: Be careful that you don't go up on the mountain or touch its base. Anyone who touches the mountain must be put to death. 13 No hand may touch him;[C] instead he will be stoned or shot with arrows and not live, whether animal or human. When the ram's horn sounds a long blast, they may go up the mountain."

14 Then Moses came down from the mountain to the people and consecrated them, and they washed their clothes. 15 He said to the people, "Be prepared by the third day. Do not have sexual relations with women."

16 On the third day, when morning came, there was thunder and lightning, a thick cloud on the mountain, and a very loud blast from a ram's horn, so that all the people in the camp shuddered. 17 Then Moses brought the people out of the camp to meet God, and they stood at the foot of the mountain. 18 Mount Sinai was completely enveloped in smoke because the LORD came down on it in fire. Its smoke went up like the smoke of a furnace, and the whole mountain shook violently. 19 As the sound of the ram's horn grew louder and louder, Moses spoke and God answered him in the thunder.

20 The LORD came down on Mount Sinai at the top of the mountain. Then the LORD summoned Moses to the top of the mountain, and he went up. 21 The LORD directed Moses, "Go down and warn the people not to break through to see the LORD; otherwise many of them will die. 22 Even the priests who come near the LORD must consecrate themselves, or the LORD will break out in anger against them."

23 Moses responded to the LORD, "The people cannot come up Mount Sinai, since you warned us: Put a boundary around the mountain and consecrate it."

[A] **18:22** Lit *lighten from on you* [B] **18:23** Lit *go to their place in peace*
[C] **19:13** Or *it*

24 And the LORD replied to him, "Go down and come
back with Aaron. But the priests and the people must
not break through to come up to the LORD, or he will
break out in anger against them." 25 So Moses went
down to the people and told them.

THE TEN COMMANDMENTS

20 Then God spoke all these words:
2 I am the LORD your God, who brought you
out of the land of Egypt, out of the place of
slavery.
3 Do not have other gods besides me.
4 Do not make an idol for yourself, whether in
the shape of anything in the heavens above or
on the earth below or in the waters under the
earth. 5 Do not bow in worship to them, and do
not serve them; for I, the LORD your God, am a
jealous God, bringing the consequences of the
fathers' iniquity on the children to the third
and fourth generations of those who hate me,
6 but showing faithful love to a thousand generations of those who love me and keep my
commands.
7 Do not misuse the name of the LORD your God,
because the LORD will not leave anyone unpunished who misuses his name.
8 Remember the Sabbath day, to keep it holy:
9 You are to labor six days and do all your
work, 10 but the seventh day is a Sabbath to
the LORD your God. You must not do any work
— you, your son or daughter, your male or
female servant, your livestock, or the resident
alien who is within your city gates. 11 For the
LORD made the heavens and the earth, the sea,
and everything in them in six days; then he
rested on the seventh day. Therefore the LORD
blessed the Sabbath day and declared it holy.
12 Honor your father and your mother so that
you may have a long life in the land that the
LORD your God is giving you.
13 Do not murder.
14 Do not commit adultery.
15 Do not steal.
16 Do not give false testimony against your
neighbor.
17 Do not covet your neighbor's house. Do not
covet your neighbor's wife, his male or female
servant, his ox or donkey, or anything that belongs to your neighbor.

THE PEOPLE'S REACTION

18 All the people witnessed[A] the thunder and lightning, the sound of the ram's horn, and the mountain
surrounded by smoke. When the people saw it[B] they
trembled and stood at a distance. 19 "You speak to us,
and we will listen," they said to Moses, "but don't let
God speak to us, or we will die."
20 Moses responded to the people, "Don't be afraid,
for God has come to test you, so that you will fear
him and will not[C] sin." 21 And the people remained
standing at a distance as Moses approached the total
darkness where God was.

MOSES RECEIVES ADDITIONAL LAWS

22 Then the LORD told Moses, "This is what you are to
say to the Israelites: You have seen that I have spoken
to you from heaven. 23 Do not make gods of silver to
rival me; do not make gods of gold for yourselves.
24 "Make an earthen altar for me, and sacrifice on
it your burnt offerings and fellowship offerings, your
flocks and herds. I will come to you and bless you in
every place where I cause my name to be remembered. 25 If you make a stone altar for me, do not build
it out of cut stones. If you use your chisel on it, you
will defile it. 26 Do not go up to my altar on steps, so
that your nakedness is not exposed on it.

21 "These are the ordinances that you are to set
before them:

LAWS ABOUT SLAVES

2 "When you buy a Hebrew slave, he is to serve for six
years; then in the seventh he is to leave as a free man[D]
without paying anything. 3 If he arrives alone, he is to
leave alone; if he arrives with[E] a wife, his wife is to
leave with him. 4 If his master gives him a wife and she
bears him sons or daughters, the wife and her children
belong to her master, and the man must leave alone.
5 "But if the slave declares, 'I love my master, my
wife, and my children; I do not want to leave as a free
man,' 6 his master is to bring him to the judges[F] and
then bring him to the door or doorpost. His master
will pierce his ear with an awl, and he will serve his
master for life.
7 "When a man sells his daughter as a concubine,[G]
she is not to leave as the male slaves do. 8 If she is
displeasing to her master, who chose her for himself,
then he must let her be redeemed. He has no right to
sell her to foreigners because he has acted treacherously toward her. 9 Or if he chooses her for his son,
he must deal with her according to the customary
treatment of daughters. 10 If he takes an additional
wife, he must not reduce the food, clothing, or marital
rights of the first wife. 11 And if he does not do these
three things for her, she may leave free of charge,
without any payment.[H]

[A] **20:18** Lit *saw* [B] **20:18** Sam, LXX, Syr, Tg, Vg read *smoke. The people* (or *they*) *were afraid,* [C] **20:20** Lit *that the fear of him may be in you, and you do not* [D] **21:2** Lit *to go forth* [E] **21:3** Lit *he is the husband of* [F] **21:6** Or *to God*; that is, to his sanctuary or court [G] **21:7** Or *servant* [H] **21:11** She doesn't have to pay any redemption price.

LAWS ABOUT PERSONAL INJURY

12 "Whoever strikes a person so that he dies must be
put to death. 13 But if he did not intend any harm,[A] and
yet God allowed it to happen, I will appoint a place
for you where he may flee. 14 If a person schemes and
willfully[B] acts against his neighbor to murder him,
you must take him from my altar to be put to death.

15 "Whoever strikes his father or his mother must
be put to death.

16 "Whoever kidnaps a person must be put to death,
whether he sells him or the person is found in his
possession.

17 "Whoever curses his father or his mother must
be put to death.

18 "When men quarrel and one strikes the other
with a stone or his fist, and the injured man does not
die but is confined to bed, 19 if he can later get up and
walk around outside leaning on his staff, then the one
who struck him will be exempt from punishment.
Nevertheless, he must pay for his lost work time[C] and
provide for his complete recovery.

20 "When a man strikes his male or female slave
with a rod, and the slave dies under his abuse,[D] the
owner must be punished.[E] 21 However, if the slave can
stand up after a day or two, the owner should not be
punished[F] because he is his owner's property.[G]

22 "When men get in a fight and hit a pregnant
woman so that her children are born prematurely
but there is no injury, the one who hit her must be
fined as the woman's husband demands from him,
and he must pay according to judicial assessment. 23 If
there is an injury, then you must give life for life, 24 eye
for eye, tooth for tooth, hand for hand, foot for foot,
25 burn for burn, bruise for bruise, wound for wound.

26 "When a man strikes the eye of his male or female slave and destroys it, he must let the slave go
free in compensation for his eye. 27 If he knocks out
the tooth of his male or female slave, he must let the
slave go free in compensation for his tooth.

28 "When an ox[H] gores a man or a woman to death,
the ox must be stoned, and its meat may not be eaten,
but the ox's owner is innocent. 29 However, if the ox
was in the habit of goring, and its owner has been
warned yet does not restrain it, and it kills a man
or a woman, the ox must be stoned, and its owner
must also be put to death. 30 If instead a ransom is
demanded of him, he can pay a redemption price
for his life in the full amount demanded from him.
31 If it gores a son or a daughter, he is to be dealt with
according to this same law. 32 If the ox gores a male or
female slave, he must give thirty shekels of silver[I] to
the slave's master, and the ox must be stoned.

33 "When a man uncovers a pit or digs a pit, and
does not cover it, and an ox or a donkey falls into
it, 34 the owner of the pit must give compensation;
he must pay to its owner, but the dead animal will
become his.

35 "When a man's ox injures his neighbor's ox and it
dies, they must sell the live ox and divide its proceeds;
they must also divide the dead animal. 36 If, however,
it is known that the ox was in the habit of goring, yet
its owner has not restrained it, he must compensate
fully, ox for ox; the dead animal will become his.

LAWS ABOUT THEFT

22 "When a man steals an ox or a sheep and butch-
ers it or sells it, he must repay five cattle for the
ox or four sheep for the sheep. 2 If a thief is caught in
the act of breaking in, and he is beaten to death, no
one is guilty of bloodshed. 3 But if this happens after
sunrise, the householder is guilty of bloodshed. A
thief must make full restitution. If he is unable, he
is to be sold because of his theft. 4 If what was stolen
— whether ox, donkey, or sheep — is actually found
alive in his possession, he must repay double.

LAWS ABOUT CROP PROTECTION

5 "When a man lets a field or vineyard be grazed in,
and then allows his animals to go and graze in someone else's field, he must repay[J] with the best of his
own field or vineyard.

6 "When a fire gets out of control, spreads to thornbushes, and consumes stacks of cut grain, standing
grain, or a field, the one who started the fire must
make full restitution for what was burned.

LAWS ABOUT PERSONAL PROPERTY

7 "When a man gives his neighbor valuables[G] or goods
to keep, but they are stolen from that person's house,
the thief, if caught, must repay double. 8 If the thief
is not caught, the owner of the house must present
himself to the judges[K] to determine[L] whether or not
he has taken his neighbor's property. 9 In any case
of wrongdoing involving an ox, a donkey, a sheep, a
garment, or anything else lost, and someone claims,
'That's mine,'[M] the case between the two parties is
to come before the judges.[N] The one the judges condemn[O] must repay double to his neighbor.

10 "When a man gives his neighbor a donkey, an ox,
a sheep, or any other animal to care for, but it dies, is
injured, or is stolen, while no one is watching, 11 there
must be an oath before the LORD between the two of
them to determine whether or not he has taken his

[A] **21:13** Lit *he was not lying in wait* [B] **21:14** Or *maliciously* [C] **21:19** Lit *his inactivity* [D] **21:20** Lit *hand* [E] **21:20** Or *must suffer vengeance* [F] **21:21** Or *not suffer vengeance* [G] **21:21; 22:7** Lit *silver* [H] **21:28** Or *a bull, or a steer* [I] **21:32** About one pound of silver [J] **22:5** LXX adds *from his field according to its produce. But if someone lets his animals graze an entire field, he must repay*; DSS, Sam also support this reading. [K] **22:8** Or *to God* [L] **22:8** LXX, Tg, Vg read *swear* [M] **22:9** Lit *That is it* [N] **22:9** Or *before God* [O] **22:9** Or *one whom God condemns*

The Ten Words and Ancient Near Eastern Laws

by Gary P. Arbino

How does ancient Near Eastern law compare to biblical Law, especially those instructions in Exodus 20:1–17—the Ten Words?[1]

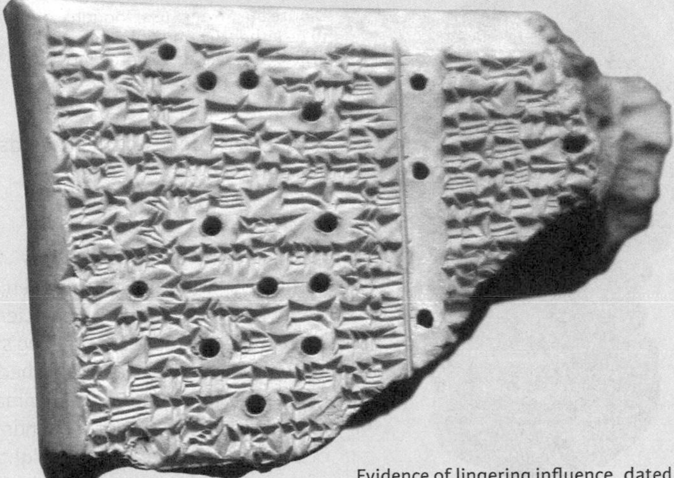

Evidence of lingering influence, dated to about 1,100 years after Hammurabi's original, a fragment of a copy of the Code of Hammurabi from the library of Assyria's King Ashurbanipal.

TOPICS

Biblical regulations and other ancient Near Eastern codes cover many of the same topics—personal injury, sexual relationships and rape, kidnapping, slavery, restitution, inheritance, livestock, boundaries, and construction. Other topics, however, are not in the Torah: loyalty to king and temple, taxation, commerce, wages, fugitives, and the like.

The Ten Words (more commonly called the Ten Commandments) address some major issues common within the ancient Near East—loyalty, family structure and honor, homicide, adultery, theft, perjury, slander, and possibly inappropriate desires. On the other hand, they contain some unique content: loyalty to one God (rather than the king and his divinity), no idols (a completely unique concept in the ancient world), and the radical proposal of a rest day every seven days (rather than working until the next festival).

Within this broad range of topics, however, ancient text writers made no effort to be comprehensive. Correspondingly, the prescriptions in the Torah also do not specifically address all aspects of ancient Israelite life.

The Ur-Nammu Law Code, which is the oldest known law, is from Nippur, Mesopotamia (in modern Iraq). The language is Sumerian; the piece dates to 2112–2095 BC.

TEXTS

What scholars term "laws" in the ancient Near East actually fall within several types of literature: law codes, edicts, treaties, loyalty oaths, and charters for kingship succession. Currently, some one hundred of these official documents have been excavated and translated. While thirty or so originated in Mesopotamia and northern Syria between the years 2500 BC and 1500 BC, more than half come from the Hittite archives of Anatolia (1500–1200 BC). The remaining texts stem from the mid-first millennium: northern Syria (three documents; ca 850 BC), the Neo-Assyrian Empire (about fourteen documents, most are fragmentary; dated 820–627 BC), and Neo-Babylonia (one document; ca 700 BC). Archaeologists and explorers have also discovered hundreds of ancient letters, narratives, and records that illustrate law usage from the ancient world.

PURPOSE

Concern for relationships and seeking to define and govern conduct were the threads connecting these ancient laws. Broadly seen, these relationships are either external, meaning between a king and the people of another land (these called for treaties), or internal, meaning to and/or among the subjects of a king (these called for codes).

The foundational relationship was with the king. Most texts contain an introduction—naming the king, often with his titles, divine selection, attributes, and achievements. These were often in

Diorite bust from Susa; thought to be either Hammurabi or a prince who reigned before him.

first person: "I am Hammurabi, the shepherd, selected by the god Enlil."[2] Always people understood the king to be the giver of the "law," albeit under the direction and charge of his patron deity or deities. The origin of the Ten Words is quite different. Unlike other ancient documents, the narrative context of Exodus 19–21 clearly shows that God personally and vocally gave to the assembled people the initial regulations for conduct: "Then God spoke all these words" (Ex 20:1; see Dt 5:4).

The chief responsibility of ancient kings was to maintain justice—the right relationships within the kingdom and between treaty partners. Standard in ancient legal presentations was the king's statement that he had established justice. "At that time, I, Ur-Namma [Ur-Nammu], . . . king of the lands of Sumer and Akkad, by the might of the god Nanna . . . I established justice in the land."[3] So essential was this responsibility that ancient kings intentionally depicted themselves presiding over cases. Hammurabi stated: "I have inscribed my precious pronouncements upon my stela and set it up. . . . the judgments that I rendered and the verdicts that I gave."[4] Ancient law documents that scholars term "codes" were thus meant to be seen as the concretized specific case rulings that the king made and that he gathered together. These served as both a model for later cases and as proof of the king's justice. Moses and his colleagues also rendered verdicts that were likely codified (Ex 18:13–26; 21:1).

FORM

The presentation of these codified verdicts is overwhelmingly in the form known as "casuistic" or "case law": If/When such happens . . . then this is the consequence. The Old Babylonia Laws of Eshnunna (ca 1725 BC) provide an example: "If an ox gores another ox and thus causes its death, the two ox-owners shall divide the value of the living ox and the carcass of the dead ox. . . . If it gores a slave and thus causes his death, he [the ox owner] shall weigh and deliver fifteen shekels of silver."[5]

Ancient treaties also frequently used this genre for the

The Aleppo Treaty is an agreement between the Hittite king Mursili II and Talmi-sharruma of Aleppo. It regulates future relations between Aleppo and Hatti; dated to 1300 BC.

Ruins at the ancient site of Aleppo, in modern Syria.

stipulations by which each party was to abide. A northern Syrian treaty provided a common obligation: "If a fugitive slave, whether male or female, flees from my country to yours, you must seize him and return him."[6]

Carved into this stone wall is a law code discovered at Gortyn on the island of Crete. It dates to the first half of the fifth century BC and is the earliest known European law code.

Regulations also came in a more absolute form, termed "apodictic": You will do this; you will not do that. Used much more commonly in treaties, but present from the earliest times in law codes, these absolute requirements illustrate the nonnegotiables for the two parties involved. A Hittite treaty (ca 1300 BC) illustrates: "Keep the oath of the king and the hand of the king, and I, My Majesty, will protect you. . . . Do not turn your eyes towards another (land)!"[7] As seen here, sometimes the absolute nature of the apodictic form came with a "rider" that gave either a rationale or a result (here, protection). The Ten Words of Exodus 20 contain both the apodictic form and additional material in four of them (vv. 4,7,8,12).

Both the Covenant Code (20:1–23:33) and the account of Moses's writing the replacement copy of the Ten Words (34:10 26) illustrate that regulations concerning the divine-human relationship (idolatry, festivals, Sabbaths, and sacrifices) and broad standards of social justice for at-risk members of the community (22:21–22; 23:1–3,6–9) are in apodictic form. This makes good sense since the "vertical" and social justice aspects would not usually require additional specificity—no situations existed in which people would allow idolatry or the abuse of a widow.

Although the apodictic form of the Ten Words in Exodus 20 clearly articulates the nonnegotiables of relationships as the people of Yahweh, their placement in the broader context points to a larger structure and intent. They begin with an Introduction of Yahweh and a statement of past benefits (20:2) and stand at the front of a section of mostly casuistic stipulations (21:1–23:19), followed by both promised blessings for adherence and dire warnings for failure (23:20–33) and finally by a ratification ceremony (24:1–11). In addition, witnesses were present (twelve pillars, 24:4; and two tablets—one for each party) and a provision for deposit (in the ark, in the holy of holies/most holy place). Ancient treaties used these structural elements (see "God's Covenant with Abraham" at Gen 17). Importantly, the Ten Words (and what follows) are actually described (Ex 34:2–28; cf. 24:7–8) as *be'rit* (Hb for "covenant"), a particular form of a treaty, and (in 34:29) as the "tablets of the *edut*," a Hebrew word that means "witness" or "testimony" or "obligations" and is a cognate of *adé*, the Akkadian word Assyrians used to describe treaties and loyalty oaths.

Thus the Ten Words are much more than laws. They function as the center of relationships—the initial sections of a treaty (covenant) between Yahweh and his people, one in which he is the true and only Sovereign to whom his subjects owe total allegiance and in whose territory there is a correct and nonnegotiable standard for human actions based on divine justice. ❖

---

[1] Unless indicated otherwise, all Scripture quotations are the writer's translation. For a quick reference of various "legal" terms used in the Old Testament, see Ps 19:7–9. [2] Martha Roth, "The Codes of Hammurabi," in *Canonical Compositions from the Biblical World*, vol. 2 of *The Context of Scripture* (*COS*), ed. William W. Hallo and K. Lawson Younger (Leiden: Brill, 1997), 336. [3] From a third millennium code; Martha Roth, "The Laws of Ur-Namma (Ur-Nammu)" in Hallo and Younger, *COS*, 2:411. [4] Martha Roth, ed., *Law Collections from Mesopotamia and Asia Minor*, 2nd ed., vol. 6 of Writings from the Ancient World (WAW) (Atlanta: Society of Biblical Literature, 1997), 133. [5] Roth, WAW, 6:67. Notice the similarity to the biblical law in Ex 21:32,35. [6] Richard Hess, "The Agreement between Ir-Addu and Niqmepa" in *COS*, 2:330. [7] Notice both the positive and negative absolutes, also seen in the Ten Words. I. Singer, "Treaty between Muršili and Duppi-Tešub" in *COS*, 2:96.

neighbor's property. Its owner must accept the oath, and the other man does not have to make restitution. 12 But if, in fact, the animal was stolen from his custody, he must make restitution to its owner. 13 If it was actually torn apart by a wild animal, he is to bring it as evidence; he does not have to make restitution for the torn carcass.

14 "When a man borrows an animal from his neighbor, and it is injured or dies while its owner is not there with it, the man must make full restitution. 15 If its owner is there with it, the man does not have to make restitution. If it was rented, the loss is covered by[A] its rental price.

LAWS ABOUT SEDUCTION

16 "If a man seduces a virgin who is not engaged, and he sleeps with her, he must certainly pay the bridal price for her to be his wife. 17 If her father absolutely refuses to give her to him, he must pay an amount in silver equal to the bridal price for virgins.

CAPITAL OFFENSES

18 "Do not allow a sorceress to live.

19 "Whoever has sexual intercourse with an animal must be put to death.

20 "Whoever sacrifices to any gods, except the LORD alone, is to be set apart for destruction.

LAWS PROTECTING THE VULNERABLE

21 "You must not exploit a resident alien or oppress him, since you were resident aliens in the land of Egypt.

22 "You must not mistreat any widow or fatherless child. 23 If you do mistreat them, they will no doubt cry to me, and I will certainly hear their cry. 24 My anger will burn, and I will kill you with the sword; then your wives will be widows and your children fatherless.

25 "If you lend silver to my people, to the poor person among you, you must not be like a creditor to him; you must not charge him interest.

26 "If you ever take your neighbor's cloak as collateral, return it to him before sunset. 27 For it is his only covering; it is the clothing for his body.[B] What will he sleep in? And if he cries out to me, I will listen because I am gracious.

RESPECT FOR GOD

28 "You must not blaspheme God[C] or curse a leader among your people.

29 "You must not hold back offerings from your harvest or your vats. Give me the firstborn of your sons. 30 Do the same with your cattle and your flock. Let them stay with their mothers for seven days, but on the eighth day you are to give them to me.

31 "Be my holy people. You must not eat the meat of a mauled animal found in the field; throw it to the dogs.

LAWS ABOUT HONESTY AND JUSTICE

23 "You must not spread a false report. Do not join[D] the wicked to be a malicious witness.

2 "You must not follow a crowd in wrongdoing. Do not testify in a lawsuit and go along with a crowd to pervert justice. 3 Do not show favoritism to a poor person in his lawsuit.

4 "If you come across your enemy's stray ox or donkey, you must return it to him.

5 "If you see the donkey of someone who hates you lying helpless under its load, and you want to refrain from helping it, you must help with it.[E]

6 "You must not deny justice to a poor person among you in his lawsuit. 7 Stay far away from a false accusation. Do not kill the innocent and the just, because I will not justify the guilty. 8 You must not take a bribe, for a bribe blinds the clear-sighted and corrupts the words[F] of the righteous. 9 You must not oppress a resident alien; you yourselves know how it feels to be a resident alien because you were resident aliens in the land of Egypt.

SABBATHS AND FESTIVALS

10 "Sow your land for six years and gather its produce. 11 But during the seventh year you are to let it rest and leave it uncultivated, so that the poor among your people may eat from it and the wild animals may consume what they leave. Do the same with your vineyard and your olive grove.

12 "Do your work for six days but rest on the seventh day so that your ox and your donkey may rest, and the son of your female slave as well as the resident alien may be refreshed.

13 "Pay strict attention to everything I have said to you. You must not invoke the names of other gods; they must not be heard on your lips.[G]

14 "Celebrate a festival in my honor three times a year. 15 Observe the Festival of Unleavened Bread. As I commanded you, you are to eat unleavened bread for seven days at the appointed time in the month of Abib,[H] because you came out of Egypt in that month. No one is to appear before me empty-handed. 16 Also observe the Festival of Harvest[I] with the firstfruits of your produce from what you sow in the field, and observe the Festival of Ingathering[J] at the end of the year, when you gather your produce[K] from the field. 17 Three times a year all your males are to appear before the Lord GOD.

[A] **22:15** Lit *rented, it comes with* [B] **22:27** Lit *skin* [C] **22:28** Or *judges* [D] **23:1** Lit *join hands with* [E] **23:5** Or *load, you must refrain from leaving it to him; you must set it free with him* [F] **23:8** Or *and subverts the cause* [G] **23:13** Lit *mouth* [H] **23:15** March–April; called Nisan in the post-exilic period; Neh 2:1; Est 3:7 [I] **23:16** The *Festival of Harvest* is called Festival of Weeks elsewhere; Ex 34:22. In the NT it is called Pentecost; Ac 2:1. [J] **23:16** The *Festival of Ingathering* is called Festival of Shelters elsewhere; Lv 23:34–36. [K] **23:16** Lit *labors*

18 "You must not offer the blood of my sacrifices
with anything leavened. The fat of my festival offering must not remain until morning.
19 "Bring the best of the firstfruits of your land to
the house of the LORD your God.
"You must not boil a young goat in its mother's
milk.

PROMISES AND WARNINGS

20 "I am going to send an angel before you to protect
you on the way and bring you to the place I have
prepared. 21 Be attentive to him and listen to him. Do
not defy him, because he will not forgive your acts
of rebellion, for my name is in him. 22 But if you will
carefully obey him and do everything I say, then I will
be an enemy to your enemies and a foe to your foes.
23 For my angel will go before you and bring you to the
land of the Amorites, Hethites, Perizzites, Canaanites,
Hivites, and Jebusites, and I will wipe them out. 24 Do
not bow in worship to their gods, and do not serve
them. Do not imitate their practices. Instead, demolish them[A] and smash their sacred pillars to pieces.
25 Serve the LORD your God, and he[B] will bless your
bread and your water. I will remove illnesses from
you. 26 No woman will miscarry or be childless in
your land. I will give you the full number of your days.
27 "I will cause the people ahead of you to feel terror[C]
and will throw into confusion all the nations you come
to. I will make all your enemies turn their backs to you
in retreat.[D] 28 I will send hornets[E] in front of you, and
they will drive the Hivites, Canaanites, and Hethites
away from you. 29 I will not drive them out ahead of
you in a single year; otherwise, the land would become
desolate, and wild animals would multiply against
you. 30 I will drive them out little by little ahead of you
until you have become numerous[F] and take possession
of the land. 31 I will set your borders from the Red Sea
to the Mediterranean Sea,[G] and from the wilderness to
the Euphrates River.[H] For I will place the inhabitants of
the land under your control, and you will drive them
out ahead of you. 32 You must not make a covenant
with them or their gods. 33 They must not remain in
your land, or else they will make you sin against me.
If you serve their gods, it will be a snare for you."

THE COVENANT CEREMONY

24 Then he said to Moses, "Go up to the LORD, you
and Aaron, Nadab, and Abihu, and seventy of Israel's elders, and bow in worship at a distance. 2 Moses
alone is to approach the LORD, but the others are not to
approach, and the people are not to go up with him."
3 Moses came and told the people all the commands
of the LORD and all the ordinances. Then all the people
responded with a single voice, "We will do everything that the LORD has commanded." 4 And Moses
wrote down all the words of the LORD. He rose early
the next morning and set up an altar and twelve pillars for the twelve tribes of Israel at the base of the
mountain. 5 Then he sent out young Israelite men, and
they offered burnt offerings and sacrificed bulls as
fellowship offerings to the LORD. 6 Moses took half
the blood and set it in basins; the other half of the
blood he splattered on the altar. 7 He then took the
covenant scroll and read it aloud to the people. They
responded, "We will do and obey all that the LORD
has commanded."
8 Moses took the blood, splattered it on the people,
and said, "This is the blood of the covenant that the
LORD has made with you concerning all these words."
9 Then Moses went up with Aaron, Nadab, and Abihu, and seventy of Israel's elders, 10 and they saw the
God of Israel. Beneath his feet was something like
a pavement made of lapis lazuli, as clear as the sky
itself. 11 God did not harm[I] the Israelite nobles; they
saw him, and they ate and drank.
12 The LORD said to Moses, "Come up to me on the
mountain and stay there so that I may give you the
stone tablets with the law and commandments I have
written for their instruction."
13 So Moses arose with his assistant Joshua and
went up the mountain of God. 14 He told the elders,
"Wait here for us until we return to you. Aaron and
Hur are here with you. Whoever has a dispute should
go to them." 15 When Moses went up the mountain,
the cloud covered it. 16 The glory of the LORD settled
on Mount Sinai, and the cloud covered it for six days.
On the seventh day he called to Moses from the cloud.
17 The appearance of the LORD's glory to the Israelites
was like a consuming fire on the mountaintop. 18 Moses entered the cloud as he went up the mountain,
and he remained on the mountain forty days and
forty nights.

OFFERINGS TO BUILD THE TABERNACLE

25 The LORD spoke to Moses: 2 "Tell the Israelites
to take an offering for me. You are to take my
offering from everyone who is willing to give. 3 This
is the offering you are to receive from them: gold,
silver, and bronze; 4 blue, purple, and scarlet yarn;
fine linen and goat hair; 5 ram skins dyed red and
fine leather;[J] acacia wood; 6 oil for the light; spices for
the anointing oil and for the fragrant incense; 7 and
onyx[K] along with other gemstones for mounting on
the ephod and breastpiece.[L]

[A] **23:24** Probably the idols [B] **23:25** LXX, Vg read *I* [C] **23:27** Lit *will send terror of me ahead of you* [D] **23:27** Or *I will give your enemies to you by the neck* [E] **23:28** Or *send panic* [F] **23:30** Lit *fruitful* [G] **23:31** Lit *the Sea of the Philistines* [H] **23:31** Lit *the River* [I] **24:11** Lit *not stretch out his hand against* [J] **25:5** Hb obscure [K] **25:7** Or *carnelian* [L] **25:7** Traditionally, *breastplate*

8 "They are to make a sanctuary for me so that I may
dwell among them. 9 You must make it according to
all that I show you — the pattern of the tabernacle as
well as the pattern of all its furnishings.

THE ARK

10 "They are to make an ark of acacia wood, forty-five
inches long, twenty-seven inches wide, and twenty-seven inches high.[A] 11 Overlay it with pure gold; overlay it both inside and out. Also make a gold molding all
around it. 12 Cast four gold rings for it and place them
on its four feet, two rings on one side and two rings
on the other side. 13 Make poles of acacia wood and
overlay them with gold. 14 Insert the poles into the rings
on the sides of the ark in order to carry the ark with
them. 15 The poles are to remain in the rings of the ark;
they must not be removed from it. 16 Put the tablets of[B]
the testimony that I will give you into the ark. 17 Make
a mercy seat of pure gold, forty-five inches long and
twenty-seven inches wide.[C] 18 Make two cherubim of
gold; make them of hammered work at the two ends
of the mercy seat. 19 Make one cherub at one end and
one cherub at the other end. At its two ends, make
the cherubim of one piece with the mercy seat. 20 The
cherubim are to have wings spread out above, covering
the mercy seat with their wings, and are to face one
another. The faces of the cherubim should be toward
the mercy seat. 21 Set the mercy seat on top of the ark
and put the tablets of the testimony that I will give you
into the ark. 22 I will meet with you there above the mercy seat, between the two cherubim that are over the
ark of the testimony; I will speak with you from there
about all that I command you regarding the Israelites.

THE TABLE

23 "You are to construct a table of acacia wood, thirty-six inches long, eighteen inches wide, and twenty-seven inches high.[D] 24 Overlay it with pure gold and
make a gold molding all around it. 25 Make a three-
inch[E] frame all around it and make a gold molding
for it all around its frame. 26 Make four gold rings
for it, and attach the rings to the four corners at its
four legs. 27 The rings should be next to the frame as
holders for the poles to carry the table. 28 Make the
poles of acacia wood and overlay them with gold,
and the table can be carried by them. 29 You are also
to make its plates and cups, as well as its pitchers
and bowls for pouring drink offerings. Make them
out of pure gold. 30 Put the Bread of the Presence on
the table before me at all times.

THE LAMPSTAND

31 "You are to make a lampstand out of pure, hammered gold. It is to be made of one piece: its base
and shaft, its ornamental cups, and its buds[F] and
petals. 32 Six branches are to extend from its sides,
three branches of the lampstand from one side and
three branches of the lampstand from the other side.
33 There are to be three cups shaped like almond blossoms, each with a bud and petals, on one branch, and
three cups shaped like almond blossoms, each with
a bud and petals, on the next branch. It is to be this
way for the six branches that extend from the lampstand. 34 There are to be four cups shaped like almond
blossoms on the lampstand shaft along with its buds
and petals. 35 For the six branches that extend from
the lampstand, a bud must be under the first pair
of branches from it, a bud under the second pair of
branches from it, and a bud under the third pair of
branches from it. 36 Their buds and branches are to
be of one piece.[G] All of it is to be a single hammered
piece of pure gold.

37 "Make its seven lamps, and set them up so that
they illuminate the area in front of it. 38 Its snuffers
and firepans must be of pure gold. 39 The lampstand[H]
with all these utensils is to be made from seventy-five
pounds[I] of pure gold. 40 Be careful to make them according to the pattern you have been shown on the
mountain.

THE TABERNACLE

26 "You are to construct the tabernacle itself with
ten curtains. You must make them of finely
spun linen, and blue, purple, and scarlet yarn, with a
design of cherubim worked into them. 2 Each curtain
should be forty-two feet[J] long and six feet[K] wide; all
the curtains are to have the same measurements.
3 Five of the curtains should be joined together, and
the other five curtains joined together. 4 Make loops
of blue yarn on the edge of the last curtain in the first
set, and do the same on the edge of the outermost
curtain in the second set. 5 Make fifty loops on the
one curtain and make fifty loops on the edge of the
curtain in the second set, so that the loops line up
together. 6 Also make fifty gold clasps and join the
curtains together with the clasps, so that the tabernacle may be a single unit.

7 "You are to make curtains of goat hair for a tent
over the tabernacle; make eleven of these curtains.
8 Each curtain should be forty-five feet[L] long and six
feet wide. All eleven curtains are to have the same
measurements. 9 Join five of the curtains by themselves, and the other six curtains by themselves. Then

[A] **25:10** Lit *two and a half cubits its length, one and a half cubits its width, and one and a half cubits its height* [B] **25:16** *the tablets of* supplied for clarity, also in v. 21 [C] **25:17** Lit *two and a half cubits its length, one and a half cubits its width* [D] **25:23** Lit *two cubits its length, one cubit its width, and one and a half cubits its height* [E] **25:25** Lit *Make it a handbreadth* [F] **25:31** = the outer covering of a flower [G] **25:36** Lit *piece with it* [H] **25:39** Lit *It* [I] **25:39** Lit *a talent* [J] **26:2** Lit *28 cubits* [K] **26:2** Lit *four cubits*, also in v. 8 [L] **26:8** Lit *30 cubits*

fold the sixth curtain double at the front of the tent. 10 Make fifty loops on the edge of one curtain, the outermost in the first set, and make fifty loops on the edge of the corresponding curtain of the second set. 11 Make fifty bronze clasps; put the clasps through the loops and join the tent together so that it is a single unit. 12 As for the flap that remains from the tent curtains, the leftover half curtain is to hang over the back of the tabernacle. 13 What remains along the length of the tent curtains — a half yard[A] on one side and a half yard on the other side — should hang over the sides of the tabernacle on either side to cover it. 14 Make a covering for the tent from ram skins dyed red and a covering of fine leather[B] on top of that.

15 "You are to make upright supports[C] of acacia wood for the tabernacle. 16 Each support is to be fifteen feet[D] long and twenty-seven[E] inches wide. 17 Each support will have two tenons for joining. Do the same for all the supports of the tabernacle. 18 Make the supports for the tabernacle as follows: twenty supports for the south side, 19 and make forty silver bases under the twenty supports, two bases under the first support for its two tenons, and two bases under the next support for its two tenons; 20 twenty supports for the second side of the tabernacle, the north side, 21 along with their forty silver bases, two bases under the first support and two bases under each support; 22 and make six supports for the west side of the tabernacle. 23 Make two additional supports for the two back corners of the tabernacle. 24 They are to be paired at the bottom, and joined together[F] at the top in a single ring. So it should be for both of them; they will serve as the two corners. 25 There are to be eight supports with their silver bases: sixteen bases; two bases under the first support and two bases under each support.

26 "You are to make five crossbars of acacia wood for the supports on one side of the tabernacle, 27 five crossbars for the supports on the other side of the tabernacle, and five crossbars for the supports on the back side of the tabernacle on the west. 28 The central crossbar is to run through the middle of the supports from one end to the other. 29 Then overlay the supports with gold, and make their rings of gold as the holders for the crossbars. Also overlay the crossbars with gold. 30 You are to set up the tabernacle according to the plan for it that you have been shown on the mountain.

31 "You are to make a curtain of blue, purple, and scarlet yarn, and finely spun linen with a design of cherubim worked into it. 32 Hang it on four gold-plated pillars of acacia wood that have gold hooks and that stand on four silver bases. 33 Hang the curtain under the clasps[G] and bring the ark of the testimony there behind the curtain, so the curtain will make a separation for you between the holy place and the most holy place. 34 Put the mercy seat on the ark of the testimony in the most holy place. 35 Place the table outside the curtain and the lampstand on the south side of the tabernacle, opposite the table; put the table on the north side.

36 "For the entrance to the tent you are to make a screen embroidered[H] with blue, purple, and scarlet yarn, and finely spun linen. 37 Make five pillars of acacia wood for the screen and overlay them with gold; their hooks are to be gold, and you are to cast five bronze bases for them.

THE ALTAR OF BURNT OFFERING

27 "You are to construct the altar of acacia wood. The altar must be square, 7 1/2 feet long, and 7 1/2 feet wide;[I] it must be 4 1/2 feet high.[J] 2 Make horns for it on its four corners; the horns are to be of one piece.[K] Overlay it with bronze. 3 Make its pots for removing ashes, and its shovels, basins, meat forks, and firepans; make all its utensils of bronze. 4 Construct a grate for it of bronze mesh, and make four bronze rings on the mesh at its four corners. 5 Set it below, under the altar's ledge,[L] so that the mesh comes halfway up[M] the altar. 6 Then make poles for the altar, poles of acacia wood, and overlay them with bronze. 7 The poles are to be inserted into the rings so that the poles are on two sides of the altar when it is carried. 8 Construct the altar with boards so that it is hollow. They are to make it just as it was shown to you on the mountain.

THE COURTYARD

9 "You are to make the courtyard for the tabernacle. Make hangings for the south side of the courtyard out of finely spun linen, 150 feet[N] long on that side 10 including twenty posts and twenty bronze bases, with silver hooks and silver bands[O] for the posts. 11 And so make hangings 150 feet long for the north side, including twenty posts and their twenty bronze bases, with silver hooks and silver bands for the posts. 12 For the width of the courtyard, make hangings 75 feet[P] long for the west side, including their ten posts and their ten bases. 13 And for the width of the courtyard on the east side toward the sunrise, 75 feet, 14 make hangings 22 1/2 feet[Q] long for one side of the gate, including their three posts and their three bases.

[A] **26:13** Lit *the cubit* [B] **26:14** Hb obscure [C] **26:15** Or *frames*, or *beams* [D] **26:16** Lit *10 cubits* [E] **26:16** Lit *a cubit and a half* [F] **26:24** Lit *and together they are to be complete* [G] **26:33** The *clasps* that join the ten curtains of the tabernacle; Ex 26:6 [H] **26:36** Or *woven* [I] **27:1** Lit *five cubits in length and five cubits in width* [J] **27:1** Lit *wide; and its height three cubits* [K] **27:2** Lit *piece with it* [L] **27:5** Perhaps a *ledge* around the altar on which the priests could stand; Lv 9:22 [M] **27:5** Or *altar's rim, so that the grid comes halfway down* [N] **27:9** Lit *100 cubits*, also in v. 11 [O] **27:10** Or *connecting rods*, also in v. 11 [P] **27:12** Lit *50 cubits*, also in v. 13 [Q] **27:14** Lit *15 cubits*, also in v. 15

The Tabernacle: Its History and Use

by Allan Moseley

As worshipers entered the tabernacle (on the eastern side), the first piece of furniture they encountered was the bronze altar, located in the open space between the entrance to the tabernacle precincts and the entrance to the holy place (Ex 27:38). The bronze altar was a hollow box made of acacia wood and overlaid with bronze. Horns, or protrusions, were on each corner of the bronze altar. Presumably, priests or worshipers tied animals to the horns to secure the animal before killing. The bronze altar was a place of sacrifice, which is fundamental in biblical theology. Sin leads to death. Sacrifices were offered so the sacrificial animals could die in place of the worshipers.

As worshipers moved from the bronze altar through the open-air court of the tabernacle in the direction of the holy place, they encountered the polished bronze basin (Ex 30; 38). The bronze, reflecting beneath the water, allowed the priests who washed their hands to observe whether the water was pure. It would also allow them to see themselves and be reminded of their own need for cleansing. Priests were to wash themselves before they entered the holy place, symbolic of the fact that they were to be cleansed from sin before they were qualified to serve. Some have suggested that the bronze altar communicates the idea of justification, and the bronze basin was for sanctification.

Replica of the tabernacle, erected at Timnah in southern Israel.

As worshipers entered the tent, the golden lampstand was on the left side of the holy place (25:31–40; 37:17–24). The holy place had no windows to allow light to enter, so the lampstand provided light. In the Scriptures, fire and light were evocative of the Lord's presence and direction (3:1–4).

The table of the Bread of the Presence was on the opposite side of the holy place from the lampstand (25:23–30; 37:10–16). The cakes of bread represented the fellowship that God desired to have with all twelve tribes of Israel.

The final piece of furniture in the holy place was the altar of incense (30:1–10; 37:25–29). This altar was on the west side of the holy place, against the curtain that divided the holy place from the most holy place. The horns on this altar presumably were purely ornamental, since no animals were sacrificed on the altar of incense. The smoke of the burning incense, which was to be continual, seems to have represented the prayers of God's people (Ps 141:2; Lk 1:10; Rv 5:8; 8:3–4).[1]

The ark of the covenant was the only furniture in the most holy place. The Lord connected the ark to his presence. He said to Moses, "I will meet with you there" (Ex 25:22). The Lord's presence was associated with a particular space, not a physical object.

God's people constructed the tabernacle and all its furniture in obedience to the Lord's explicit command. He determined where and how he would be worshiped. Pagan religions in the ancient Near East devised worship spaces and rituals that were designed to gain the favor of the gods. However, in the case of the one true God, no person or group has the prerogative to determine how or where he will be worshiped. He commands, and his people worship him accordingly. ✣

---

[1] Walter C. Kaiser Jr., "Exodus" in *The Expositor's Bible Commentary*, ed. Frank E. Gaebelein, vol. 2 (Grand Rapids: Zondervan, 1990), 472–73.

Replica of the table of the Bread of the Presence as it may have appeared in the tabernacle.

Poles and stakes that are in the courtyard of the tabernacle replica, which has been erected at Timna in southern Israel.

15 And make hangings 22 ½ feet long for the other side, including their three posts and their three bases. 16 The gate of the courtyard is to have a 30-foot[A] screen embroidered[B] with blue, purple, and scarlet yarn, and finely spun linen. It is to have four posts and their four bases.

17 "All the posts around the courtyard are to be banded with silver and have silver hooks and bronze bases. 18 The courtyard is to be 150 feet long, 75 feet wide at each end, and 7 ½ feet high,[C] all of it made of finely spun linen. The bases of the posts are to be bronze. 19 All the utensils of the tabernacle for every use and all its tent pegs as well as all the tent pegs of the courtyard are to be made of bronze.

THE LAMPSTAND OIL

20 "You are to command the Israelites to bring you pure oil from crushed olives for the light, in order to keep the lamp burning regularly. 21 In the tent of meeting outside the curtain that is in front of the testimony, Aaron and his sons are to tend the lamp from evening until morning before the LORD. This is to be a permanent statute for the Israelites throughout their generations.

THE PRIESTLY GARMENTS

28 "Have your brother Aaron, with his sons, come to you from the Israelites to serve me as priest — Aaron, his sons Nadab and Abihu, Eleazar and Ithamar. 2 Make holy garments for your brother Aaron, for glory and beauty. 3 You are to instruct all the skilled artisans,[D] whom I have filled with a spirit of wisdom, to make Aaron's garments for consecrating him to serve me as priest. 4 These are the garments that they must make: a breastpiece, an ephod, a robe, a specially woven tunic,[E] a turban, and a sash. They are to make holy garments for your brother Aaron and his sons so that they may serve me as priests. 5 They should use[F] gold; blue, purple, and scarlet yarn; and fine linen.

THE EPHOD

6 "They are to make the ephod of finely spun linen embroidered[B] with gold, and with blue, purple, and scarlet yarn. 7 It must have two shoulder pieces attached to its two edges so that it can be joined together. 8 The artistically woven waistband that is on the ephod[G] must be of one piece,[H] according to the same workmanship of gold, of blue, purple, and scarlet yarn, and of finely spun linen.

9 "Take two onyx stones and engrave on them the names of Israel's sons: 10 six of their names on the first stone and the remaining six names on the second stone, in the order of their birth. 11 Engrave the two stones with the names of Israel's sons as a gem cutter engraves a seal. Mount them, surrounded with gold filigree settings. 12 Fasten both stones on the shoulder pieces of the ephod as memorial stones for the Israelites. Aaron will carry their names on his two shoulders before the LORD as a reminder. 13 Fashion gold filigree settings 14 and two chains of pure gold; you will make them of braided cord work, and attach the cord chains to the settings.

THE BREASTPIECE

15 "You are to make an embroidered breastpiece for making decisions.[I] Make it with the same workmanship as the ephod; make it of gold, of blue, purple, and scarlet yarn, and of finely spun linen. 16 It must be square and folded double, nine inches long and nine inches wide.[J] 17 Place a setting of gemstones[K] on it, four rows of stones:

The first row should be
a row of carnelian, topaz, and emerald;[L]
18 the second row,
a turquoise,[M] a lapis lazuli, and a diamond;[N]
19 the third row,
a jacinth,[E] an agate, and an amethyst;
20 and the fourth row,
a beryl, an onyx, and a jasper.

They should be adorned with gold filigree in their settings. 21 The twelve stones are to correspond to the names of Israel's sons. Each stone must be engraved like a seal, with one of the names of the twelve tribes.

22 "You are to make braided chains[O] of pure gold cord work for the breastpiece. 23 Fashion two gold rings for the breastpiece and attach them to its two corners. 24 Then attach the two gold cords to the two gold rings at the corners of the breastpiece. 25 Attach the other ends of the two cords to the two filigree settings, and in this way attach them to the ephod's shoulder pieces in the front. 26 Make two other gold rings and put them at the two other corners of the breastpiece on the edge that is next to the inner border of the ephod. 27 Make two more gold rings and attach them to the bottom of the ephod's two shoulder pieces on its front, close to its seam,[P] and above the ephod's woven waistband. 28 The artisans are to tie the breastpiece from its rings to the rings of the ephod with a cord of blue yarn, so that the breastpiece is above the ephod's waistband and does not come loose from the ephod.

[A] **27:16** Lit *20-cubit* [B] **27:16; 28:6** Or *woven* [C] **27:18** Lit *be 100 by the cubit, and the width 50 by 50, and the height five cubits* [D] **28:3** Lit *all wise of heart* [E] **28:4,19** Hb obscure [F] **28:5** Lit *receive* [G] **28:8** Lit *waistband of its ephod, which is on it* [H] **28:8** Lit *piece with the ephod* [I] **28:15** Used for determining God's will; Nm 27:21 [J] **28:16** Lit *a span its length and a span its width* [K] **28:17** Many of these stones cannot be identified with certainty. [L] **28:17** Or *beryl* [M] **28:18** Or *malachite*, or *garnet* [N] **28:18** Hb obscure; LXX, Vg read *jasper* [O] **28:22** The same *chains* mentioned in v. 14 [P] **28:27** The place where the *shoulder pieces* join the front of the ephod

29 "Whenever he enters the sanctuary, Aaron is to carry the names of Israel's sons over his heart on the breastpiece for decisions, as a continual reminder before the LORD. 30 Place the Urim and Thummim in the breastpiece for decisions, so that they will also be over Aaron's heart whenever he comes before the LORD. Aaron will continually carry the means of decisions for the Israelites over his heart before the LORD.

THE ROBE

31 "You are to make the robe of the ephod entirely of blue yarn. 32 There should be an opening at its top in the center of it. Around the opening, there should be a woven collar with an opening like that of body armor[A] so that it does not tear. 33 Make pomegranates of blue, purple, and scarlet yarn on its lower hem and all around it. Put gold bells between them all the way around, 34 so that gold bells and pomegranates alternate around the lower hem of the robe. 35 The robe will be worn by Aaron whenever he ministers, and its sound will be heard when he enters the sanctuary before the LORD and when he exits, so that he does not die.

THE TURBAN

36 "You are to make a pure gold medallion and engrave it, like the engraving of a seal: HOLY TO THE LORD. 37 Fasten it to a cord of blue yarn so it can be placed on the turban; the medallion is to be on the front of the turban. 38 It will be on Aaron's forehead so that Aaron may bear the guilt connected with the holy offerings that the Israelites consecrate as all their holy gifts. It is always to be on his forehead, so that they may find acceptance with the LORD.

OTHER PRIESTLY GARMENTS

39 "You are to weave the tunic from fine linen, make a turban of fine linen, and make an embroidered sash. 40 Make tunics, sashes, and headbands for Aaron's sons to give them glory and beauty. 41 Put these on your brother Aaron and his sons; then anoint, ordain,[B] and consecrate them, so that they may serve me as priests. 42 Make them linen undergarments to cover their naked bodies; they must extend from the waist to the thighs. 43 These must be worn by Aaron and his sons whenever they enter the tent of meeting or approach the altar to minister in the sanctuary area, so that they do not incur guilt and die. This is to be a permanent statute for Aaron and for his future descendants.

INSTRUCTIONS ABOUT CONSECRATION

29 "This is what you are to do for them to consecrate them to serve me as priests. Take a young bull and two unblemished rams, 2 with unleavened bread, unleavened cakes mixed with oil, and unleavened wafers coated with oil. Make them out of fine wheat flour, 3 put them in a basket, and bring them in the basket, along with the bull and two rams. 4 Bring Aaron and his sons to the entrance to the tent of meeting and wash them with water. 5 Then take the garments and clothe Aaron with the tunic, the robe for the ephod, the ephod itself, and the breastpiece; fasten the ephod on him with its woven waistband. 6 Put the turban on his head and place the holy diadem on the turban. 7 Take the anointing oil, pour it on his head, and anoint him. 8 You must also bring his sons and clothe them with tunics. 9 Tie the sashes on Aaron and his sons and fasten headbands on them. The priesthood is to be theirs by a permanent statute. This is the way you will ordain Aaron and[C] his sons.

10 "You are to bring the bull to the front of the tent of meeting, and Aaron and his sons must lay their hands on the bull's head. 11 Slaughter the bull before the LORD at the entrance to the tent of meeting. 12 Take some of the bull's blood and apply it to the horns of the altar with your finger; then pour out all the rest of the blood at the base of the altar. 13 Take all the fat that covers the entrails, the fatty lobe of the liver, and the two kidneys with the fat on them, and burn them on the altar. 14 But burn the bull's flesh, its hide, and its waste outside the camp; it is a sin offering.

15 "Take one ram, and Aaron and his sons are to lay their hands on the ram's head. 16 You are to slaughter the ram, take its blood, and splatter it on all sides of the altar. 17 Cut the ram into pieces. Wash its entrails and legs, and place them with its head and its pieces on the altar. 18 Then burn the whole ram on the altar; it is a burnt offering to the LORD. It is a pleasing aroma, a food offering to the LORD.

19 "You are to take the second ram, and Aaron and his sons must lay their hands on the ram's head. 20 Slaughter the ram, take some of its blood, and put it on Aaron's right earlobe, on his sons' right earlobes, on the thumbs of their right hands, and on the big toes of their right feet. Splatter the remaining blood on all sides of the altar. 21 Take some of the blood that is on the altar and some of the anointing oil, and sprinkle them on Aaron and his garments, as well as on his sons and their garments. So he and his garments will be holy, as well as his sons and their garments.

22 "Take the fat from the ram, the fat tail, the fat covering the entrails, the fatty lobe of the liver, the two kidneys and the fat on them, and the right thigh (since this is a ram for ordination[D]); 23 take one loaf of bread, one cake of bread made with oil, and one wafer from the basket of unleavened bread that is

[A] **28:32** Hb obscure [B] **28:41** Lit *anoint them, fill their hand*
[C] **29:9** Lit *you will fill the hand of Aaron and the hand of*; Ex 29:23–24
[D] **29:22** The priest would normally receive the right thigh to be eaten, but here it is burned; Lv 7:32–34.

before the LORD; 24 and put all of them in the hands of Aaron and his[A] sons and present them as a presentation offering before the LORD. 25 Take them from their hands and burn them on the altar on top of the burnt offering, as a pleasing aroma before the LORD; it is a food offering to the LORD.

26 "Take the breast from the ram of Aaron's ordination and present it as a presentation offering before the LORD; it is to be your portion. 27 Consecrate for Aaron and his sons the breast of the presentation offering that is presented and the thigh of the contribution that is lifted up from the ram of ordination. 28 This will belong to Aaron and his sons as a regular portion from the Israelites, for it is a contribution. It will be the Israelites' contribution from their fellowship sacrifices, their contribution to the LORD.

29 "The holy garments that belong to Aaron are to belong to his sons after him, so that they can be anointed and ordained[B] in them. 30 Any priest who is one of his sons and who succeeds him and enters the tent of meeting to minister in the sanctuary must wear them for seven days.

31 "You are to take the ram of ordination and boil its flesh in a holy place. 32 Aaron and his sons are to eat the meat of the ram and the bread that is in the basket at the entrance to the tent of meeting. 33 They must eat those things by which atonement was made at the time of their ordination[C] and consecration. An unauthorized person must not eat them, for these things are holy. 34 If any of the meat of ordination or any of the bread is left until morning, burn what is left over. It must not be eaten because it is holy.

35 "This is what you are to do for Aaron and his sons based on all I have commanded you. Take seven days to ordain them. 36 Sacrifice a bull as a sin offering each day for atonement. Purify[D] the altar when you make atonement for it, and anoint it in order to consecrate it. 37 For seven days you must make atonement for the altar and consecrate it. The altar will be especially holy. Whatever touches the altar will be consecrated.

38 "This is what you are to offer regularly on the altar every day: two year-old lambs. 39 In the morning offer one lamb, and at twilight offer the other lamb. 40 With the first lamb offer two quarts[E] of fine flour mixed with one quart[F] of oil from crushed olives, and a drink offering of one quart of wine. 41 You are to offer the second lamb at twilight. Offer a grain offering and a drink offering with it, like the one in the morning, as a pleasing aroma, a food offering to the LORD. 42 This will be a regular burnt offering throughout your generations at the entrance to the tent of meeting before the LORD, where I will meet you[G] to speak with you. 43 I will also meet with the Israelites there, and that place will be consecrated by my glory. 44 I will consecrate the tent of meeting and the altar; I will also consecrate Aaron and his sons to serve me as priests. 45 I will dwell among the Israelites and be their God. 46 And they will know that I am the LORD their God, who brought them out of the land of Egypt, so that I might dwell among them. I am the LORD their God.

THE INCENSE ALTAR

30 "You are to make an altar for the burning of incense; make it of acacia wood. 2 It must be square, eighteen inches long and eighteen inches wide;[H] it must be thirty-six inches high.[I] Its horns must be of one piece with it. 3 Overlay its top, all around its sides, and its horns with pure gold; make a gold molding all around it. 4 Make two gold rings for it under the molding on two of its sides; put these on opposite sides of it to be holders for the poles to carry it with. 5 Make the poles of acacia wood and overlay them with gold.

6 "You are to place the altar in front of the curtain by the ark of the testimony — in front of the mercy seat that is over the testimony — where I will meet with you. 7 Aaron must burn fragrant incense on it; he must burn it every morning when he tends the lamps. 8 When Aaron sets up the lamps at twilight, he must burn incense. There is to be an incense offering before the LORD throughout your generations. 9 You must not offer unauthorized incense on it, or a burnt or grain offering; you are not to pour a drink offering on it.

10 "Once a year Aaron is to perform the atonement ceremony for the altar. Throughout your generations he is to perform the atonement ceremony for[J] it once a year, with the blood of the sin offering for atonement on the horns. The altar is especially holy to the LORD."

THE ATONEMENT MONEY

11 The LORD spoke to Moses: 12 "When you take a census of the Israelites to register them, each of the men must pay a ransom for his life to the LORD as they are registered. Then no plague will come on them as they are registered. 13 Everyone who is registered must pay half a shekel[K] according to the sanctuary shekel (twenty gerahs to the shekel). This half shekel is a contribution to the LORD. 14 Each man who is registered, twenty years old or more, must give this contribution to the LORD. 15 The wealthy may not give more and the poor may not give less than half a shekel when giving

[A] **29:24** Lit *in the hands of his* [B] **29:29** Lit *him for anointing in them and for filling their hand* [C] **29:33** Lit *made to fill their hand* [D] **29:36** Or *Make a sin offering on* [E] **29:40** Lit *offer a tenth* [F] **29:40** Lit *a fourth of a hin* [G] **29:42** = Moses [H] **30:2** Lit *one cubit its length and one cubit its width* [I] **30:2** Lit *wide; and two cubits its height* [J] **30:10** Or *on* [K] **30:13** A shekel is about two-fifths of an ounce of silver

the contribution to the LORD to atone for[A] your lives. 16 Take the atonement price[B] from the Israelites and use it for the service of the tent of meeting. It will serve as a reminder for the Israelites before the LORD to atone for your lives."

THE BRONZE BASIN

17 The LORD spoke to Moses: 18 "Make a bronze basin for washing and a bronze stand for it. Set it between the tent of meeting and the altar, and put water in it. 19 Aaron and his sons must wash their hands and feet from the basin. 20 Whenever they enter the tent of meeting or approach the altar to minister by burning a food offering to the LORD, they must wash with water so that they will not die. 21 They must wash their hands and feet so that they will not die; this is to be a permanent statute for them, for Aaron and his descendants throughout their generations."

THE ANOINTING OIL

22 The LORD spoke to Moses: 23 "Take for yourself the finest spices: 12 ½ pounds[C] of liquid myrrh, half as much (6 ¼ pounds[D]) of fragrant cinnamon, 6 ¼ pounds of fragrant cane, 24 12 ½ pounds of cassia (by the sanctuary shekel), and a gallon[E] of olive oil. 25 Prepare from these a holy anointing oil, a scented blend, the work of a perfumer; it will be holy anointing oil.

26 "With it you are to anoint the tent of meeting, the ark of the testimony, 27 the table with all its utensils, the lampstand with its utensils, the altar of incense, 28 the altar of burnt offering with all its utensils, and the basin with its stand. 29 Consecrate them and they will be especially holy. Whatever touches them will be consecrated. 30 Anoint Aaron and his sons and consecrate them to serve me as priests.

31 "Tell the Israelites: This will be my holy anointing oil throughout your generations. 32 It must not be used for ordinary anointing on a person's body, and you must not make anything like it using its formula. It is holy, and it must be holy to you. 33 Anyone who blends something like it or puts some of it on an unauthorized person must be cut off from his people."

THE SACRED INCENSE

34 The LORD said to Moses, "Take fragrant spices: stacte, onycha, and galbanum; the spices and pure frankincense are to be in equal measures. 35 Prepare expertly blended incense from these; it is to be seasoned with salt, pure and holy. 36 Grind some of it into a fine powder and put some in front of the testimony in the tent of meeting, where I will meet with you. It must be especially holy to you. 37 As for the incense you are making, you must not make any for yourselves using its formula. It is to be regarded by you as holy — belonging to the LORD. 38 Anyone who makes something like it to smell its fragrance must be cut off from his people."

GOD'S PROVISION OF THE SKILLED WORKERS

31 The LORD also spoke to Moses: 2 "Look, I have appointed by name Bezalel son of Uri, son of Hur, of the tribe of Judah. 3 I have filled him with God's Spirit, with wisdom, understanding, and ability in every craft 4 to design artistic works in gold, silver, and bronze, 5 to cut gemstones for mounting, and to carve wood for work in every craft. 6 I have also selected Oholiab[F] son of Ahisamach, of the tribe of Dan, to be with him. I have put wisdom in the heart of every skilled artisan[G] in order to make all that I have commanded you: 7 the tent of meeting, the ark of the testimony, the mercy seat that is on top of it, and all the other furnishings of the tent — 8 the table with its utensils, the pure gold lampstand with all its utensils, the altar of incense, 9 the altar of burnt offering with all its utensils, the basin with its stand — 10 the specially woven[H] garments, both the holy garments for the priest Aaron and the garments for his sons to serve as priests, 11 the anointing oil, and the fragrant incense for the sanctuary. They must make them according to all that I have commanded you."

OBSERVING THE SABBATH

12 The LORD said to Moses, 13 "Tell the Israelites: You must observe my Sabbaths, for it is a sign between me and you throughout your generations, so that you will know that I am the LORD who consecrates you. 14 Observe the Sabbath, for it is holy to you. Whoever profanes it must be put to death. If anyone does work on it, that person must be cut off from his people. 15 Work may be done for six days, but on the seventh day there must be a Sabbath of complete rest, holy to the LORD. Anyone who does work on the Sabbath day must be put to death. 16 The Israelites must observe the Sabbath, celebrating it throughout their generations as a permanent covenant. 17 It is a sign forever between me and the Israelites, for in six days the LORD made the heavens and the earth, but on the seventh day he rested and was refreshed."

THE TWO STONE TABLETS

18 When he finished speaking with Moses on Mount Sinai, he gave him the two tablets of the testimony, stone tablets inscribed by the finger of God.

[A] **30:15** Or *to ransom*, also in v. 16 [B] **30:16** Lit *the silver of the atonement* [C] **30:23** Lit *500* (shekels), also in v. 24 [D] **30:23** Lit *250* (shekels) [E] **30:24** Lit *a hin* [F] **31:6** LXX, Syr read *Eliab* [G] **31:6** Lit *everyone wise of heart* [H] **31:10** Hb obscure

THE GOLD CALF

32 When the people saw that Moses delayed in
coming down from the mountain, they gathered around Aaron and said to him, "Come, make
gods[A] for us who will go before us because this Moses,
the man who brought us up from the land of Egypt
— we don't know what has happened to him!"
2 Aaron replied to them, "Take off the gold rings
that are on the ears of your wives, your sons, and
your daughters and bring them to me." 3 So all the
people took off the gold rings that were on their ears
and brought them to Aaron. 4 He took the gold from
them, fashioned it with an engraving tool, and made
it into an image of a calf.
Then they said, "Israel, these are your gods,[B] who
brought you up from the land of Egypt!"
5 When Aaron saw this, he built an altar in front of
it and made an announcement: "There will be a festival to the LORD tomorrow." 6 Early the next morning
they arose, offered burnt offerings, and presented
fellowship offerings. The people sat down to eat and
drink, and got up to party.
7 The LORD spoke to Moses: "Go down at once! For
your people you brought up from the land of Egypt
have acted corruptly. 8 They have quickly turned
from the way I commanded them; they have made
for themselves an image of a calf. They have bowed
down to it, sacrificed to it, and said, 'Israel, these
are your gods, who brought you up from the land of
Egypt.'" 9 The LORD also said to Moses, "I have seen
this people, and they are indeed a stiff-necked people. 10 Now leave me alone, so that my anger can burn
against them and I can destroy them. Then I will make
you into a great nation."
11 But Moses sought the favor of the LORD his
God: "LORD, why does your anger burn against your
people you brought out of the land of Egypt with
great power and a strong hand? 12 Why should the
Egyptians say, 'He brought them out with an evil
intent to kill them in the mountains and eliminate
them from the face of the earth'? Turn from your
fierce anger and relent concerning this disaster
planned for your people. 13 Remember your servants
Abraham, Isaac, and Israel — you swore to them by
yourself and declared, 'I will make your offspring
as numerous as the stars of the sky and will give
your offspring all this land that I have promised,
and they will inherit it forever.'" 14 So the LORD relented concerning the disaster he had said he would
bring on his people.
15 Then Moses turned and went down the mountain
with the two tablets of the testimony in his hands.
They were inscribed on both sides — inscribed front
and back. 16 The tablets were the work of God, and the
writing was God's writing, engraved on the tablets.
17 When Joshua heard the sound of the people as
they shouted, he said to Moses, "There is a sound of
war in the camp."
18 But Moses replied,

It's not the sound of a victory cry
and not the sound of a cry of defeat;
I hear the sound of singing!

19 As he approached the camp and saw the calf and
the dancing, Moses became enraged and threw the
tablets out of his hands, smashing them at the base
of the mountain. 20 He took the calf they had made,
burned it up, and ground it to powder. He scattered
the powder over the surface of the water and forced
the Israelites to drink the water.
21 Then Moses asked Aaron, "What did these people
do to you that you have led them into such a grave
sin?"
22 "Don't be enraged, my lord," Aaron replied. "You
yourself know that the people are intent on evil.
23 They said to me, 'Make gods for us who will go
before us because this Moses, the man who brought
us up from the land of Egypt — we don't know what
has happened to him!' 24 So I said to them, 'Whoever
has gold, take it off,' and they gave it to me. When I
threw it into the fire, out came this calf!"
25 Moses saw that the people were out of control,
for Aaron had let them get out of control, making
them a laughingstock to their enemies.[C] 26 And Moses
stood at the camp's entrance and said, "Whoever is for
the LORD, come to me." And all the Levites gathered
around him. 27 He told them, "This is what the LORD,
the God of Israel, says, 'Every man fasten his sword
to his side; go back and forth through the camp from
entrance to entrance, and each of you kill his brother,
his friend, and his neighbor.'" 28 The Levites did as
Moses commanded, and about three thousand men
fell dead that day among the people. 29 Afterward
Moses said, "Today you have been dedicated[D] to the
LORD, since each man went against his son and his
brother. Therefore you have brought a blessing on
yourselves today."
30 The following day Moses said to the people, "You
have committed a grave sin. Now I will go up to the
LORD; perhaps I will be able to atone for your sin."
31 So Moses returned to the LORD and said, "Oh,
these people have committed a grave sin; they have
made a god of gold for themselves. 32 Now if you
would only forgive their sin. But if not, please erase
me from the book you have written."
33 The LORD replied to Moses, "Whoever has sinned
against me I will erase from my book. 34 Now go, lead

[A] **32:1** Or *make a god*, also in v. 23 [B] **32:4** Or *"Israel, this is your god* or *"Israel, this is your God*, also in v. 8 [C] **32:25** Hb obscure
[D] **32:29** Text emended; MT reads *"Today dedicate yourselves*; LXX, Vg read *"Today you have dedicated yourselves*

the people to the place I told you about; see, my angel will go before you. But on the day I settle accounts, I will hold them accountable for their sin." 35 And the LORD inflicted a plague on the people for what they did with the calf Aaron had made.

THE TENT OUTSIDE THE CAMP

33 The LORD spoke to Moses: "Go up from here, you and the people you brought up from the land of Egypt, to the land I promised to Abraham, Isaac, and Jacob, saying: I will give it to your offspring. 2 I will send an angel ahead of you and will drive out the Canaanites, Amorites, Hethites, Perizzites,[A] Hivites, and Jebusites. 3 Go up to a land flowing with milk and honey. But I will not go up with you because you are a stiff-necked people; otherwise, I might destroy you on the way." 4 When the people heard this bad news, they mourned and didn't put on their jewelry.

5 For the LORD said to Moses, "Tell the Israelites: You are a stiff-necked people. If I went up with you for a single moment, I would destroy you. Now take off your jewelry, and I will decide what to do with you." 6 So the Israelites remained stripped of their jewelry from Mount Horeb onward.

7 Now Moses took a tent and pitched it outside the camp, at a distance from the camp; he called it the tent of meeting. Anyone who wanted to consult the LORD would go to the tent of meeting that was outside the camp. 8 Whenever Moses went out to the tent, all the people would stand up, each one at the door of his tent, and they would watch Moses until he entered the tent. 9 When Moses entered the tent, the pillar of cloud would come down and remain at the entrance to the tent, and the LORD would speak with Moses. 10 As all the people saw the pillar of cloud remaining at the entrance to the tent, they would stand up, then bow in worship, each one at the door of his tent. 11 The LORD would speak with Moses face to face, just as a man speaks with his friend, then Moses would return to the camp. His assistant, the young man Joshua son of Nun, would not leave the inside of the tent.

THE LORD'S GLORY

12 Moses said to the LORD, "Look, you have told me, 'Lead this people up,' but you have not let me know whom you will send with me. You said, 'I know you by name, and you have also found favor with me.' 13 Now if I have indeed found favor with you, please teach me your ways, and I will know you, so that I may find favor with you. Now consider that this nation is your people."

14 And he replied, "My presence will go with you, and I will give you rest."

15 "If your presence does not go," Moses responded to him, "don't make us go up from here. 16 How will it be known that I and your people have found favor with you unless you go with us? I and your people will be distinguished by this from all the other people on the face of the earth."

17 The LORD answered Moses, "I will do this very thing you have asked, for you have found favor with me, and I know you by name."

18 Then Moses said, "Please, let me see your glory."

19 He said, "I will cause all my goodness to pass in front of you, and I will proclaim the name 'the LORD' before you. I will be gracious to whom I will be gracious, and I will have compassion on whom I will have compassion." 20 But he added, "You cannot see my face, for humans cannot see me and live." 21 The LORD said, "Here is a place near me. You are to stand on the rock, 22 and when my glory passes by, I will put you in the crevice of the rock and cover you with my hand until I have passed by. 23 Then I will take my hand away, and you will see my back, but my face will not be seen."

NEW STONE TABLETS

34 The LORD said to Moses, "Cut two stone tablets like the first ones, and I will write on them the words that were on the first tablets, which you broke. 2 Be prepared by morning. Come up Mount Sinai in the morning and stand before me on the mountaintop. 3 No one may go up with you; in fact, no one should be seen anywhere on the mountain. Even the flocks and herds are not to graze in front of that mountain."

4 Moses cut two stone tablets like the first ones. He got up early in the morning, and taking the two stone tablets in his hand, he climbed Mount Sinai, just as the LORD had commanded him.

5 The LORD came down in a cloud, stood with him there, and proclaimed his name, "the LORD." 6 The LORD passed in front of him and proclaimed:

The LORD — the LORD is a compassionate and
gracious God, slow to anger and abounding in
faithful love and truth, 7 maintaining faithful
love to a thousand generations, forgiving iniquity, rebellion, and sin. But he will not leave the
guilty unpunished, bringing the consequences of
the fathers' iniquity on the children and grandchildren to the third and fourth generation.

8 Moses immediately knelt low on the ground and worshiped. 9 Then he said, "My Lord, if I have indeed found favor with you, my Lord, please go with us (even though this is a stiff-necked people), forgive our iniquity and our sin, and accept us as your own possession."

[A] **33:2** Sam, LXX add *Girgashites*

COVENANT OBLIGATIONS

10 And the LORD responded, "Look, I am making a
covenant. In the presence of all your people I will
perform wonders that have never been done[A] in the
whole earth or in any nation. All the people you live
among will see the LORD's work, for what I am doing
with you is awe-inspiring. 11 Observe what I command
you today. I am going to drive out before you the
Amorites, Canaanites, Hethites, Perizzites, Hivites,[B]
and Jebusites. 12 Be careful not to make a treaty with
the inhabitants of the land that you are going to enter; otherwise, they will become a snare among you.
13 Instead, you must tear down their altars, smash
their sacred pillars, and chop down their Asherah
poles. 14 Because the LORD is jealous for his reputation, you are never to bow down to another god.[C] He
is a jealous God.

15 "Do not make a treaty with the inhabitants of the
land, or else when they prostitute themselves with
their gods and sacrifice to their gods, they will invite
you, and you will eat their sacrifices. 16 Then you will
take some of their daughters as brides for your sons.
Their daughters will prostitute themselves with their
gods and cause your sons to prostitute themselves
with their gods.

17 "Do not make cast images of gods for yourselves.

18 "Observe the Festival of Unleavened Bread. You
are to eat unleavened bread for seven days at the appointed time in the month of Abib,[D] as I commanded
you, for you came out of Egypt in the month of Abib.

19 "The firstborn male from every womb belongs to
me, including all your male[E,F] livestock, the firstborn
of cattle or sheep. 20 You may redeem the firstborn
of a donkey with a sheep, but if you do not redeem
it, break its neck. You must redeem all the firstborn
of your sons. No one is to appear before me empty-handed.

21 "You are to labor six days but you must rest on
the seventh day; you must even rest during plowing
and harvesting times.

22 "Observe the Festival of Weeks with the firstfruits of the wheat harvest, and the Festival of Ingathering[G] at the turn of the agricultural year. 23 Three
times a year all your males are to appear before the
Lord GOD, the God of Israel. 24 For I will drive out nations before you and enlarge your territory. No one
will covet your land when you go up three times a
year to appear before the LORD your God.

25 "Do not present[H] the blood for my sacrifice with
anything leavened. The sacrifice of the Passover Festival must not remain until morning.

26 "Bring the best firstfruits of your land to the
house of the LORD your God.

"You must not boil a young goat in its mother's
milk."

27 The LORD also said to Moses, "Write down these
words, for I have made a covenant with you and with
Israel based on these words."

28 Moses was there with the LORD forty days and
forty nights; he did not eat food or drink water. He
wrote the Ten Commandments, the words of the covenant, on the tablets.

MOSES'S RADIANT FACE

29 As Moses descended from Mount Sinai — with the
two tablets of the testimony in his hands as he descended the mountain — he did not realize that the
skin of his face shone as a result of his speaking with
the LORD.[I] 30 When Aaron and all the Israelites saw
Moses, the skin of his face shone! They were afraid
to come near him. 31 But Moses called out to them, so
Aaron and all the leaders of the community returned
to him, and Moses spoke to them. 32 Afterward all the
Israelites came near, and he commanded them to do
everything the LORD had told him on Mount Sinai.
33 When Moses had finished speaking with them,
he put a veil over his face. 34 But whenever Moses
went before the LORD to speak with him, he would
remove the veil until he came out. After he came out,
he would tell the Israelites what he had been commanded, 35 and the Israelites would see that Moses's
face[J] was radiant. Then Moses would put the veil over
his face again until he went to speak with the LORD.

THE SABBATH COMMAND

35 Moses assembled the entire Israelite community and said to them, "These are the things
that the LORD has commanded you to do: 2 For six
days work is to be done, but on the seventh day you
are to have a holy day, a Sabbath of complete rest to
the LORD. Anyone who does work on it must be executed. 3 Do not light a fire in any of your homes on
the Sabbath day."

BUILDING THE TABERNACLE

4 Then Moses said to the entire Israelite community,
"This is what the LORD has commanded: 5 Take up an
offering among you for the LORD. Let everyone whose
heart is willing bring this as the LORD's offering: gold,
silver, and bronze; 6 blue, purple, and scarlet yarn; fine
linen and goat hair; 7 ram skins dyed red and fine leather;[F] acacia wood; 8 oil for the light; spices for the anointing oil and for the fragrant incense; 9 and onyx with
gemstones to mount on the ephod and breastpiece.

[A] **34:10** Lit *created* [B] **34:11** DSS, Sam, LXX add *Girgashites*
[C] **34:14** Or *the LORD — his name is Jealous* or *the LORD, being jealous by nature* [D] **34:18** March–April; called Nisan in the post-exilic period; Neh 2:1; Est 3:7 [E] **34:19** LXX, Theod, Vg, Tg read *males*
[F] **34:19; 35:7** Hb obscure [G] **34:22** The *Festival of Ingathering* is called Festival of Shelters elsewhere; Lv 23:34–36. [H] **34:25** Lit *slaughter*
[I] **34:29** Lit *with him* [J] **34:35** Lit *see Moses's face, that the skin of his face*

Literacy in the Ancient Near East

by Stephen J. Andrews

Precuneiform tablet dated about 3300–3200 BC. The tablet was from one of the many administrative archives in the ancient Mesopotamian city of Uruk.

The earliest "written" documents in the ancient Near East were small clay "tablets" used in southern Mesopotamia around 3500–3000 BC. People incised small tokens of various shapes into the clay to record inventories and possibly economic transactions. When the tablets were baked, or left to dry out, they would harden and thus provide a system of accounting that could be checked repeatedly.

By the beginning of the third millennium BC, Sumerians used the idea of incised shapes to create the basis for the earliest known writing system. The shapes became stylized pictures (pictographs) that were cut into soft clay with a stylus. The pictures or signs could represent a single word (logogram), a concept (ideogram), or a syllable (syllabogram) in the Sumerian language. Several such signs could be placed together to represent the spoken language. The Sumerians used a blunt reed as a stylus that left triangular wedge-shaped marks on the tablets. Consequently, this system has come to be known as cuneiform (wedge-shape) writing.

The Sumerians set up specialized scribal schools to train a small portion of the population to write and read cuneiform script on a tablet. The signs went through several stages of simplification. The cuneiform script contained nearly 1,500 distinct signs, although not all of them were in use at the same place or time. The Sumerians also adapted the cuneiform signs to inscribe on stone monuments, such as the Code of Hammurabi.[1]

The Sumerian cuneiform script was later adapted by the Akkadians, a Semitic people who lived in the northern part of the Mesopotamian river valley, to record their spoken language. The Assyrians and Babylonians also used cuneiform script to record their dialects of the Akkadian language. Archaeologists have discovered hundreds of thousands of cuneiform tablets in excavations at sites in modern-day Syria and Iraq. These texts contain a wide range of societal and cultural records: business documents (sales, inventories, deeds); historical annals (royal chronicles, edicts, letters); and religious writings (myths, epics, hymns, prayers). The Hittites, Hurrians, Urartians, Elamites, and other ancient cultures also adopted the cuneiform script.

EGYPTIAN WRITING

Egyptians had also created their own system of writing by the third millennium BC. They designed this for use primarily on public monuments, tombs, and temples. Their picture-signs (pictographs) could be read as words, as ideas, and as phonetic sounds (phonograms) and came to be known as hieroglyphs or sacred letters.[2] Scribes trained to write this formal script, which contained around a thousand distinctive characters.

The Egyptians contributed to literacy by taking the pith of the papyrus plant from the Nile Delta and

Tablet of administrative archives from a temple of Lagash; dated to about 2370 BC; from Tello at ancient Girsu, which is the earliest known Sumerian site. The tablet is a list of offerings made to the gods.

Diorite statue of the Egyptian priest-teacher Ouennefer made to represent a seated scribe; dated to Egypt's Nineteenth–Twentieth Dynasties, about 1295–1070 BC.

creating a thick type of paper for writing. Many copies of the Egyptian magical text, the Book of the Dead, were written on papyrus and placed in coffins.[3] Egyptians later invented two other cursive scripts to simplify the writing process on papyrus for record keeping, inventories, and letters, as well as religious texts and other documents.

The large number of cuneiform and hieroglyph signs restricted literacy to professional scribes who spent considerable time learning their respective systems. The invention of the alphabet early in the second millennium BC changed this situation. The early alphabets were based on consonants only; no vowels were included. Since each letter represented one phonetic unit, each culture needed only twenty to thirty letters to represent most sounds of their individual language. Eventually, this allowed many people to learn to read and write.

The earliest known alphabetic inscriptions came from three specific areas of the ancient Near East. First, several alphabetic inscriptions were discovered at the ruins of Serabit el-Khadem and in the Wadi Maghara in the Sinai Peninsula. These were labeled proto-Sinaitic. Second, similar inscriptions were found at various sites in the southern Levant (countries on the eastern Mediterranean) and were called proto-Canaanite. Third, more recently two inscriptions were found scratched on limestone walls in the Wadi el-Hol in the Egyptian desert west of the Nile. Scholars have dated these last texts to early in the second millennium BC.

The language of these three inscriptions is Semitic in origin.[4] *Semitic* refers to various ancient people groups who lived in southwestern Asia, including the Akkadians, Canaanites, Hebrews, and others. The name comes from Shem, Noah's oldest son (Gn 5:32). The texts contained graffiti and short dedicatory texts and were discovered in locations where Semitic peoples served as soldiers, traders, merchants, and slaves. Scholars regard this Proto-Sinaitic alphabet to be the common ancestor of the Paleo-Hebrew and Phoenician scripts and by extension all other alphabets, including the later Hebrew and Greek alphabets used to write the Bible.[5]

Phoenician and paleo-Hebrew scripts include historical texts such as the Mesha and Tel Dan stelae and the Siloam Tunnel Inscription. Additionally, inscribed pottery shards (ostraca) contain letters, dockets, inventories, and numerous other types of inscribed artifacts.[6] The tenth-century BC Khirbet Qeiyafa inscription (from the Old Testament city of Shaaraim; 1Sm 17:52; 1Ch 4:31) is the earliest inscribed ostracon yet to be discovered within a possible Israelite monarchial context.[7]

IN SCRIPTURE

The Bible presupposes the ability to read and write. God commanded Moses to write down the words of the covenant, among other things (Ex 34:27; cf. 17:14). Moses may have sat cross-legged on the ground with a writing palette in his lap or in front of a small writing table. Several Egyptian reliefs and statues depict the work of the scribe in this manner. He may have had a writing case (Ezk 9:2–3,11) containing pens (Ps 45:1; Jr 8:8), brushes, small sponges as erasers, black and red inks (Jr 36:18), and possibly a scribe's knife (v. 23) to trim the papyrus or parchment.

In 2008, excavators at Khirbet Qeiyafa, biblical Shaaraim, found an ostracon, an ink inscription on a piece of pottery. This inscription is possibly the earliest evidence of Hebrew writing.

The Bible attests to a high level of literacy.[8] The poems and songs in the Psalms demonstrate sophisticated literary style. History offers no definitive information about the number of people in biblical times who were literate. Most in the Bible who could read and write were leaders or professional scribes and secretaries (Dt 17:18; Jos 18:4; 2Kg 10:1; Is 8:1).[9] Yet Moses commanded all Israelites to write God's commandments on the doorposts of their houses (Dt 6:9). ✣

---

[1] E. Ray Clendenen and Jason Zan, "Hammurabi" in *HIBD* (2015), 697–98. [2] I. J. Gelb, *A Study of Writing*, rev. ed. (Chicago: University of Chicago Press, 1963), 72. [3] Daniel C. Browning Jr., Kirk Kilpatrick, and Brian T. Stachowski, "Egypt" in *HIBD* (2015), 468. [4] Christopher A. Rollston, *Writing and Literacy in the World of Ancient Israel* (Atlanta: Society of Biblical Literature, 2010), 12. [5] John Noble Wilford, "Finds in Egypt Date Alphabet in Earlier Era," *New York Times*, 14 November, 1999, nyti.ms/2rhmkdL. [6] See the list in R. Adam Dodd, "Writing," in *HIBD* (2015), 1676–77. [7] Stephen J. Andrews, "The Oldest Attested Hebrew Scriptures and the Khirbet Qeiyafa Inscription," in *The World of Jesus and Early Church: Identity and Interpretation in Early Communities of Faith*, ed. Craig A. Evans (Peabody, MA: Hendrickson, 2011), 153–54. [8] See Dodd, "Writing," 1677–78 for a list of Scripture references. The Bible uses the Hebrew or Greek verbs for "to write" more than four hundred times. [9] Dodd, "Writing," 1678.

From Egypt's Eighteenth Dynasty, a scribe's wooden writing kit, which includes pens and a palette with wells for red and black pigment. Hieroglyphs record that Egyptians considered serving as a king's scribe a badge of honor. Likely from Thebes, dated about 1550–1525 BC.

10 "Let all the skilled artisans[A] among you come and make everything that the LORD has commanded: 11 the tabernacle — its tent and covering, its clasps and supports, its crossbars, its pillars and bases; 12 the ark with its poles, the mercy seat, and the curtain for the screen; 13 the table with its poles, all its utensils, and the Bread of the Presence; 14 the lampstand for light with its utensils and lamps as well as the oil for the light; 15 the altar of incense with its poles; the anointing oil and the fragrant incense; the entryway screen for the entrance to the tabernacle; 16 the altar of burnt offering with its bronze grate, its poles, and all its utensils; the basin with its stand; 17 the hangings of the courtyard, its posts and bases, and the screen for the gate of the courtyard; 18 the tent pegs for the tabernacle and the tent pegs for the courtyard, along with their ropes; 19 and the specially woven[B] garments for ministering in the sanctuary — the holy garments for the priest Aaron and the garments for his sons to serve as priests."

20 Then the entire Israelite community left Moses's presence. 21 Everyone whose heart was moved and whose spirit prompted him came and brought an offering to the LORD for the work on the tent of meeting, for all its services, and for the holy garments. 22 Both men and women came; all who had willing hearts brought brooches, earrings, rings, necklaces, and all kinds of gold jewelry — everyone who presented a presentation offering of gold to the LORD. 23 Everyone who possessed blue, purple, or scarlet yarn, fine linen or goat hair, ram skins dyed red or fine leather,[B] brought them. 24 Everyone making an offering of silver or bronze brought it as a contribution to the LORD. Everyone who possessed acacia wood useful for any task in the work brought it. 25 Every skilled[C] woman spun yarn with her hands and brought it: blue, purple, and scarlet yarn, and fine linen. 26 And all the women whose hearts were moved spun the goat hair by virtue of their skill. 27 The leaders brought onyx and gemstones to mount on the ephod and breastpiece, 28 as well as the spice and oil for the light, for the anointing oil, and for the fragrant incense. 29 So the Israelites brought a freewill offering to the LORD, all the men and women whose hearts prompted them to bring something for all the work that the LORD, through Moses, had commanded to be done.

BEZALEL AND OHOLIAB

30 Moses then said to the Israelites, "Look, the LORD has appointed by name Bezalel son of Uri, son of Hur, of the tribe of Judah. 31 He has filled him with God's Spirit, with wisdom, understanding, and ability in every kind of craft 32 to design artistic works in gold, silver, and bronze, 33 to cut gemstones for mounting, and to carve wood for work in every kind of artistic craft. 34 He has also given[D] both him and Oholiab son of Ahisamach, of the tribe of Dan, the ability to teach others. 35 He has filled them with skill[E] to do all the work of a gem cutter; a designer; an embroiderer[F] in blue, purple, and scarlet yarn and fine linen; and a weaver. They can do every kind of craft and design

36 artistic designs. 1 Bezalel, Oholiab, and all the skilled[G] people are to work based on everything the LORD has commanded. The LORD has given them wisdom and understanding to know how to do all the work of constructing the sanctuary."

2 So Moses summoned Bezalel, Oholiab, and every skilled person in whose heart the LORD had placed wisdom, all whose hearts moved them, to come to the work and do it. 3 They took from Moses's presence all the contributions that the Israelites had brought for the task of making the sanctuary. Meanwhile, the people continued to bring freewill offerings morning after morning.

4 Then all the artisans who were doing all the work for the sanctuary came one by one from the work they were doing 5 and said to Moses, "The people are bringing more than is needed for the construction of the work the LORD commanded to be done."

6 After Moses gave an order, they sent a proclamation throughout the camp: "Let no man or woman make anything else as an offering for the sanctuary." So the people stopped. 7 The materials were sufficient for them to do all the work. There was more than enough.

BUILDING THE TABERNACLE

8 All the skilled artisans[A] among those doing the work made the tabernacle with ten curtains. Bezalel made them of finely spun linen, as well as blue, purple, and scarlet yarn, with a design of cherubim worked into them. 9 Each curtain was forty-two feet[H] long and six feet[I] wide; all the curtains had the same measurements. 10 He joined five of the curtains to each other, and the other five curtains he joined to each other. 11 He made loops of blue yarn on the edge of the last curtain in the first set and did the same on the edge of the outermost curtain in the second set. 12 He made fifty loops on the one curtain and fifty loops on the edge of the curtain in the second set, so that the loops lined up with each other. 13 He also made fifty gold clasps and joined the curtains to each other, so that the tabernacle became a single unit.

[A] **35:10; 36:8** Lit *the wise of heart* [B] **35:19,23** Hb obscure [C] **35:25** Lit *wise of heart* [D] **35:34** Lit *also put in his heart* [E] **35:35** Lit *with wisdom of heart* [F] **35:35** Or *weaver* [G] **36:1** Lit *wise of heart*, also in v. 2 [H] **36:9** Lit *28 cubits* [I] **36:9** Lit *four cubits*, also in v. 15

14 He made curtains of goat hair for a tent over the tabernacle; he made eleven of them. 15 Each curtain was forty-five feet[A] long and six feet wide. All eleven curtains had the same measurements. 16 He joined five of the curtains together, and the other six together. 17 He made fifty loops on the edge of the outermost curtain in the first set and fifty loops on the edge of the corresponding curtain in the second set. 18 He made fifty bronze clasps to join the tent together as a single unit. 19 He also made a covering for the tent from ram skins dyed red and a covering of fine leather[B] on top of it.

20 He made upright supports[C] of acacia wood for the tabernacle. 21 Each support was fifteen feet[D] long and twenty-seven inches[E] wide. 22 Each support had two tenons for joining one to another. He did the same for all the supports of the tabernacle. 23 He made supports for the tabernacle as follows: He made twenty for the south side, 24 and he made forty silver bases to put under the twenty supports, two bases under the first support for its two tenons, and two bases under each of the following supports for their two tenons. 25 For the second side of the tabernacle, the north side, he made twenty supports, 26 with their forty silver bases, two bases under the first support and two bases under each of the following ones. 27 And for the back of the tabernacle, on the west side, he made six supports. 28 He also made two additional supports for the two back corners of the tabernacle. 29 They were paired at the bottom and joined together[F] at the[G] top in a single ring. This is what he did with both of them for the two corners. 30 So there were eight supports with their sixteen silver bases, two bases under each one.

31 He made five crossbars of acacia wood for the supports on one side of the tabernacle, 32 five crossbars for the supports on the other side of the tabernacle, and five crossbars for those at the back of the tabernacle on the west. 33 He made the central crossbar run through the middle of the supports from one end to the other. 34 He overlaid them with gold and made their rings out of gold as holders for the crossbars. He also overlaid the crossbars with gold.

35 Then he made the curtain with blue, purple, and scarlet yarn, and finely spun linen. He made it with a design of cherubim worked into it. 36 He made four pillars of acacia wood for it and overlaid them with gold; their hooks were of gold. And he cast four silver bases for the pillars.

37 He made a screen embroidered[H] with blue, purple, and scarlet yarn, and finely spun linen for the entrance to the tent, 38 together with its five pillars and their hooks. He overlaid the tops of the pillars and their bands with gold, but their five bases were bronze.

MAKING THE ARK

37 Bezalel made the ark of acacia wood, forty-five inches long, twenty-seven inches wide, and twenty-seven inches high.[I] 2 He overlaid it with pure gold inside and out and made a gold molding all around it. 3 He cast four gold rings for it, for its four feet, two rings on one side and two rings on the other side. 4 He made poles of acacia wood and overlaid them with gold. 5 He inserted the poles into the rings on the sides of the ark for carrying the ark.

6 He made a mercy seat of pure gold, forty-five inches long and twenty-seven inches wide.[J] 7 He made two cherubim of gold; he made them of hammered work at the two ends of the mercy seat, 8 one cherub at one end and one cherub at the other end. At each end, he made a cherub of one piece with the mercy seat. 9 They had wings spread out. They faced each other and covered the mercy seat with their wings. The faces of the cherubim were looking toward the mercy seat.

MAKING THE TABLE

10 He constructed the table of acacia wood, thirty-six inches long, eighteen inches wide, and twenty-seven inches high.[K] 11 He overlaid it with pure gold and made a gold molding all around it. 12 He made a three-inch[L] frame all around it and made a gold molding all around its frame. 13 He cast four gold rings for it and attached the rings to the four corners at its four legs. 14 The rings were next to the frame as holders for the poles to carry the table. 15 He made the poles for carrying the table from acacia wood and overlaid them with gold. 16 He also made the utensils that would be on the table out of pure gold: its plates and cups, as well as its bowls and pitchers for pouring drink offerings.

MAKING THE LAMPSTAND

17 Then he made the lampstand out of pure hammered gold. He made it all of one piece: its base and shaft, its ornamental cups, and its buds and petals. 18 Six branches extended from its sides, three branches of the lampstand from one side and three branches of the lampstand from the other side. 19 There were three cups shaped like almond blossoms, each with a bud and petals, on one branch, and three cups shaped like almond blossoms, each with a bud and petals, on the next branch. It was this way for the six branches

[A] **36:15** Lit *30 cubits* [B] **36:19** Hb obscure [C] **36:20** Or *made frames* [D] **36:21** Lit *10 cubits* [E] **36:21** Lit *a cubit and a half* [F] **36:29** Lit *and together they are to be complete* [G] **36:29** Lit *its* [H] **36:37** Or *woven* [I] **37:1** Lit *two and a half cubits its length, one and a half cubits its width, and one and a half cubits its height* [J] **37:6** Lit *two and a half cubits its length and one and a half cubits its width* [K] **37:10** Lit *two cubits its length, one cubit its width, and one and a half cubits its height* [L] **37:12** Lit *a handbreadth* that extended from the lampstand. 20 There were four cups shaped like almond blossoms on the lampstand shaft along with its buds and petals. 21 For the six branches that extended from it, a bud was under the first pair of branches from it, a bud under the second pair of branches from it, and a bud under the third pair of branches from it. 22 Their buds and branches were of one piece with it. All of it was a single hammered piece of pure gold. 23 He also made its seven lamps, snuffers, and firepans of pure gold. 24 He made it and all its utensils of seventy-five pounds[A] of pure gold.

MAKING THE ALTAR OF INCENSE

25 He made the altar of incense out of acacia wood. It was square, eighteen inches long and eighteen inches wide; it was thirty-six inches high.[B] Its horns were of one piece with it. 26 He overlaid it, its top, all around its sides, and its horns with pure gold. Then he made a gold molding all around it. 27 He made two gold rings for it under the molding on two of its sides; he put these on opposite sides of it to be holders for the poles to carry it with. 28 He made the poles of acacia wood and overlaid them with gold.

29 He also made the holy anointing oil and the pure, fragrant, and expertly blended incense.

MAKING THE ALTAR OF BURNT OFFERING

38 Bezalel constructed the altar of burnt offering from acacia wood. It was square, 7 1/2 feet long and 7 1/2 feet wide,[C] and was 4 1/2 feet[D] high. 2 He made horns for it on its four corners; the horns were of one piece with it. Then he overlaid it with bronze.

3 He made all the altar's utensils: the pots, shovels, basins, meat forks, and firepans; he made all its utensils of bronze. 4 He constructed for the altar a grate of bronze mesh under its ledge,[E] halfway up from the bottom. 5 He cast four rings at the four corners of the bronze grate as holders for the poles. 6 He made the poles of acacia wood and overlaid them with bronze. 7 Then he inserted the poles into the rings on the sides of the altar in order to carry it with them. He constructed the altar with boards so that it was hollow.

MAKING THE BRONZE BASIN

8 He made the bronze basin and its stand from the bronze mirrors of the women who served at the entrance to the tent of meeting.

MAKING THE COURTYARD

9 Then he made the courtyard. The hangings on the south side of the courtyard were of finely spun linen, 150 feet[F] long, 10 including their twenty posts and their twenty bronze bases, with silver hooks and silver bands[G] for the posts. 11 The hangings on the north side were also 150 feet long, including their twenty posts and twenty bronze bases. The hooks and bands of the posts were silver. 12 The hangings on the west side were 75 feet[H] long, including their ten posts and their ten bases, with silver hooks and silver bands for the posts. 13 And for the east side toward the sunrise, 75 feet long, 14 the hangings on one side of the gate were 22 1/2 feet,[I] including their three posts and their three bases. 15 It was the same for the other side of the courtyard gate. The hangings were 22 1/2 feet, including their three posts and their three bases. 16 All the hangings around the courtyard were of finely spun linen. 17 The bases for the posts were bronze; the hooks and bands of the posts were silver; and the plating for the tops of the posts was silver. All the posts of the courtyard were banded with silver.

18 The screen for the gate of the courtyard was made of finely spun linen, expertly embroidered[J] with blue, purple, and scarlet yarn. It was 30 feet[K] long, and like the hangings of the courtyard, 7 1/2 feet[L] high.[M] 19 It had four posts with their four bronze bases. Their hooks were silver, and their top plating and their bands were silver. 20 All the tent pegs for the tabernacle and for the surrounding courtyard were bronze.

INVENTORY OF MATERIALS

21 This is the inventory for the tabernacle, the tabernacle of the testimony, that was recorded at Moses's command. It was the work of the Levites under the direction of[N] Ithamar son of Aaron the priest. 22 Bezalel son of Uri, son of Hur, of the tribe of Judah, made everything that the LORD commanded Moses. 23 With him was Oholiab son of Ahisamach, of the tribe of Dan, a gem cutter, a designer, and an embroiderer with blue, purple, and scarlet yarn, and fine linen.

24 All the gold of the presentation offering that was used for the project in all the work on the sanctuary, was 2,193 pounds,[O] according to the sanctuary shekel. 25 The silver from those of the community who were registered was 7,544 pounds,[P] according to the sanctuary shekel — 26 one-fifth of an ounce[Q] per man, that is, half a shekel according to the sanctuary shekel, from everyone twenty years old or more who had crossed over to the registered group, 603,550 men. 27 There were 7,500 pounds[R] of silver used to cast the

[A] **37:24** Lit *a talent* [B] **37:25** Lit *a cubit its length, a cubit its width, and two cubits its height* [C] **38:1** Lit *five cubits its length and five cubits its width* [D] **38:1** Lit *three cubits* [E] **38:4** Or *rim* [F] **38:9** Lit *100 cubits*, also in v. 11 [G] **38:10** Or *connecting rods*, also in vv. 11,17,19,28 [H] **38:12** Lit *50 cubits*, also in v. 13 [I] **38:14** Lit *15 cubits*, also in v. 15 [J] **38:18** Or *woven* [K] **38:18** Lit *20 cubits* [L] **38:18** Lit *five cubits* [M] **38:18** Lit *high in width* [N] **38:21** Lit *Levites by the hand of* [O] **38:24** Lit *29 talents and 730 shekels* [P] **38:25** Lit *100 talents and 1,775 shekels* [Q] **38:26** Lit *a beka* [R] **38:27** Lit *100 talents*

bases of the sanctuary and the bases of the curtain — one hundred bases from 7,500 pounds, 75 pounds[A] for each base. 28 With the remaining 44 pounds[B] he made the hooks for the posts, overlaid their tops, and supplied bands for them.

29 The bronze of the presentation offering totaled 5,310 pounds.[C] 30 He made with it the bases for the entrance to the tent of meeting, the bronze altar and its bronze grate, all the utensils for the altar, 31 the bases for the surrounding courtyard, the bases for the gate of the courtyard, all the tent pegs for the tabernacle, and all the tent pegs for the surrounding courtyard.

MAKING THE PRIESTLY GARMENTS

39 They made specially woven[D] garments for ministry in the sanctuary, and the holy garments for Aaron from the blue, purple, and scarlet yarn, just as the LORD had commanded Moses.

MAKING THE EPHOD

2 Bezalel made the ephod of gold, of blue, purple, and scarlet yarn, and of finely spun linen. 3 They hammered out thin sheets of gold, and he[E] cut threads from them to interweave with the blue, purple, and scarlet yarn, and the fine linen in a skillful design. 4 They made shoulder pieces for attaching it; it was joined together at its two edges. 5 The artistically woven waistband that was on the ephod was of one piece with the ephod, according to the same workmanship of gold, of blue, purple, and scarlet yarn, and of finely spun linen, just as the LORD had commanded Moses.

6 Then they mounted the onyx stones surrounded with gold filigree settings, engraved with the names of Israel's sons as a gem cutter engraves a seal. 7 He fastened them on the shoulder pieces of the ephod as memorial stones for the Israelites, just as the LORD had commanded Moses.

MAKING THE BREASTPIECE

8 He also made the embroidered[F] breastpiece with the same workmanship as the ephod of gold, of blue, purple, and scarlet yarn, and of finely spun linen. 9 They made the breastpiece square and folded double, nine inches long and nine inches wide.[G] 10 They mounted four rows of gemstones[H] on it.

The first row was
a row of carnelian, topaz, and emerald;[I]
11 the second row,
a turquoise,[J] a lapis lazuli, and a diamond;[K]
12 the third row,
a jacinth,[D] an agate, and an amethyst;
13 and the fourth row,
a beryl, an onyx, and a jasper.

They were surrounded with gold filigree in their settings.

14 The twelve stones corresponded to the names of Israel's sons. Each stone was engraved like a seal with one of the names of the twelve tribes.

15 They made braided chains of pure gold cord for the breastpiece. 16 They also fashioned two gold filigree settings and two gold rings and attached the two rings to its two corners. 17 Then they attached the two gold cords to the two gold rings on the corners of the breastpiece. 18 They attached the other ends of the two cords to the two filigree settings, and in this way they attached them to the ephod's shoulder pieces in front. 19 They made two other gold rings and put them at the two other corners of the breastpiece on the edge that is next to the inner border of the ephod. 20 They made two more gold rings and attached them to the bottom of the ephod's two shoulder pieces on its front, close to its seam,[L] above the ephod's woven waistband. 21 Then they tied the breastpiece from its rings to the rings of the ephod with a cord of blue yarn, so that the breastpiece was above the ephod's waistband and did not come loose from the ephod. They did just as the LORD had commanded Moses.

MAKING THE ROBE

22 They made the woven robe of the ephod entirely of blue yarn. 23 There was an opening in the center of the robe like that of body armor[D] with a collar around the opening so that it would not tear. 24 They made pomegranates of finely spun blue, purple, and scarlet yarn[M] on the lower hem of the robe. 25 They made bells of pure gold and attached the bells between the pomegranates, all around the hem of the robe between the pomegranates, 26 a bell and a pomegranate alternating all around the lower hem of the robe[N] to be worn for ministry. They made it just as the LORD had commanded Moses.

THE OTHER PRIESTLY GARMENTS

27 They made the tunics of fine woven linen for Aaron and his sons. 28 They made the turban and the ornate headbands[O] of fine linen, the linen undergarments of finely spun linen, 29 and the sash of finely spun linen expertly embroidered with blue, purple, and scarlet yarn. They did just as the LORD had commanded Moses.

[A] **38:27** Lit *one talent* [B] **38:28** Lit *1,775* (shekels) [C] **38:29** Lit *70 talents and 2,400 shekels* [D] **39:1,12,23** Hb obscure [E] **39:3** Sam, Syr, Tg read *they* [F] **39:8** Or *woven* [G] **39:9** Lit *a span its length and a span its width* [H] **39:10** Many of these stones cannot be identified with certainty. [I] **39:10** Or *beryl* [J] **39:11** Or *malachite*, or *garnet* [K] **39:11** Hb uncertain; LXX, Vg read *jasper* [L] **39:20** The place where the *shoulder pieces* join the front of the ephod [M] **39:24** Sam, LXX, Vg add *and linen* [N] **39:26** Lit *bell and pomegranate, bell and pomegranate, on the hem of the robe around* [O] **39:28** Lit *and the headdresses of headbands*

MAKING THE HOLY DIADEM

30 They made a medallion, the holy diadem, out of pure gold and wrote on it an inscription like the engraving on a seal: HOLY TO THE LORD. 31 They attached a cord of blue yarn to it in order to mount it on the turban, just as the LORD had commanded Moses.

MOSES'S INSPECTION OF THE TABERNACLE

32 So all the work for the tabernacle, the tent of meeting, was finished. The Israelites did everything just as the LORD had commanded Moses. 33 They brought the tabernacle to Moses: the tent with all its furnishings, its clasps, its supports, its crossbars, and its pillars and bases; 34 the covering of ram skins dyed red and the covering of fine leather;[A] the curtain for the screen; 35 the ark of the testimony with its poles and the mercy seat; 36 the table, all its utensils, and the Bread of the Presence; 37 the pure gold lampstand, with its lamps arranged and all its utensils, as well as the oil for the light; 38 the gold altar; the anointing oil; the fragrant incense; the screen for the entrance to the tent; 39 the bronze altar with its bronze grate, its poles, and all its utensils; the basin with its stand; 40 the hangings of the courtyard, its posts and bases, the screen for the gate of the courtyard, its ropes and tent pegs, and all the furnishings for the service of the tabernacle, the tent of meeting; 41 and the specially woven[A] garments for ministering in the sanctuary, the holy garments for the priest Aaron and the garments for his sons to serve as priests. 42 The Israelites had done all the work according to everything the LORD had commanded Moses. 43 Moses inspected all the work they had accomplished. They had done just as the LORD commanded. Then Moses blessed them.

SETTING UP THE TABERNACLE

40 The LORD spoke to Moses: 2 "You are to set up the tabernacle, the tent of meeting, on the first day of the first month.[B] 3 Put the ark of the testimony there and screen off the ark with the curtain. 4 Then bring in the table and lay out its arrangement; also bring in the lampstand and set up its lamps. 5 Place the gold altar for incense in front of the ark of the testimony. Put up the screen for the entrance to the tabernacle. 6 Position the altar of burnt offering in front of the entrance to the tabernacle, the tent of meeting. 7 Place the basin between the tent of meeting and the altar, and put water in it. 8 Assemble the surrounding courtyard and hang the screen for the gate of the courtyard.

9 "Take the anointing oil and anoint the tabernacle and everything in it; consecrate it along with all its furnishings so that it will be holy. 10 Anoint the altar of burnt offering and all its utensils; consecrate the altar so that it will be especially holy. 11 Anoint the basin and its stand and consecrate it.

12 "Then bring Aaron and his sons to the entrance to the tent of meeting and wash them with water. 13 Clothe Aaron with the holy garments, anoint him, and consecrate him, so that he can serve me as a priest. 14 Have his sons come forward and clothe them in tunics. 15 Anoint them just as you anointed their father, so that they may also serve me as priests. Their anointing will serve to inaugurate a permanent priesthood for them throughout their generations."

16 Moses did everything just as the LORD had commanded him. 17 The tabernacle was set up in the first month of the second year, on the first day of the month.[C] 18 Moses set up the tabernacle: He laid its bases, positioned its supports, inserted its crossbars, and set up its pillars. 19 Then he spread the tent over the tabernacle and put the covering of the tent on top of it, just as the LORD had commanded Moses.

20 Moses took the testimony and placed it in the ark, and attached the poles to the ark. He set the mercy seat on top of the ark. 21 He brought the ark into the tabernacle, put up the curtain for the screen, and screened off the ark of the testimony, just as the LORD had commanded him.

22 Moses placed the table in the tent of meeting on the north side of the tabernacle, outside the curtain. 23 He arranged the bread on it before the LORD, just as the LORD had commanded him. 24 He put the lampstand in the tent of meeting opposite the table on the south side of the tabernacle 25 and set up the lamps before the LORD, just as the LORD had commanded him.

26 Moses installed the gold altar in the tent of meeting, in front of the curtain, 27 and burned fragrant incense on it, just as the LORD had commanded him. 28 He put up the screen at the entrance to the tabernacle. 29 He placed the altar of burnt offering at the entrance to the tabernacle, the tent of meeting, and offered the burnt offering and the grain offering on it, just as the LORD had commanded him.

30 He set the basin between the tent of meeting and the altar and put water in it for washing. 31 Moses, Aaron, and his sons washed their hands and feet from it. 32 They washed whenever they came to the tent of meeting and approached the altar, just as the LORD had commanded Moses.

33 Next Moses set up the surrounding courtyard for the tabernacle and the altar and hung a screen for the gate of the courtyard. So Moses finished the work.

THE LORD'S GLORY

34 The cloud covered the tent of meeting, and the glory of the LORD filled the tabernacle. 35 Moses was unable

[A] **39:34,41** Hb obscure [B] **40:2** Lit *on the day of the first month, on the first of the month* [C] **40:17** DSS, Sam, LXX add *of their coming out of Egypt*

to enter the tent of meeting because the cloud rested
on it, and the glory of the LORD filled the tabernacle.
[36] The Israelites set out whenever the cloud was
taken up from the tabernacle throughout all the
stages of their journey. [37] If the cloud was not taken
up, they did not set out until the day it was taken up.
[38] For the cloud of the LORD was over the tabernacle
by day, and there was a fire inside the cloud by night,
visible to the entire house of Israel throughout all the
stages of their journey.

LEVITICUS

Incense burner found in the tomb of a Nubian ruler at Qustul.

INTRODUCTION TO

LEVITICUS

Circumstances of Writing

Although the book of Leviticus is technically anonymous, the evidence from the Bible and from Jewish and Christian traditions attributes it to the lawgiver, Moses (see 18:5 with Rm 10:5). Moses was the chief recipient of God's revelation in the book of Leviticus (1:1; 4:1). Elsewhere, Moses is said to have written down revelation that he received (Ex 24:4; 34:28; Mk 10:4–5; 12:19; Jn 1:45; 5:46). The author of Leviticus was someone well acquainted with the events in the book, and he was knowledgeable of the Sinai Wilderness, making him most likely a firsthand witness.

About one year passed from the time Israel arrived at Mount Sinai until they departed (Ex 19:1; Nm 10:11). During that time, Moses received the covenant from the Lord, erected the tabernacle (Ex 40:17), and received all the instructions in Leviticus and in the early chapters of Numbers. This block of material is the continuous narrative extending from Exodus 19 through Leviticus to Numbers 10:11. Since these events occurred in just one year and yet received the largest amount of space in the books from Exodus through Deuteronomy, Moses showed the special importance of the Sinai revelation to the writing of the Pentateuch. The repeated expression "The LORD spoke to Moses" throughout Leviticus leaves no doubt that its instructions were of divine origin, not the creation of Moses (Lv 4:1; 27:1).

Contribution to the Bible

Leviticus is often neglected because Christians have misunderstood its message and purpose. This was not true of Jesus, who designated "love your neighbor as yourself" (Lv 19:18) as the second-greatest commandment (Mt 22:39). The apostle Paul considered these words the summation of the Mosaic commandments (Rm 13:9; Gl 5:14; see Jms 2:8). The writer of Hebrews relied on the images of Leviticus in describing the person and role of Jesus Christ: sacrifice, the priesthood, and the Day of Atonement (Heb 4:14–10:18). Studying Leviticus gives us a deeper devotion to Jesus Christ, a stronger worship of God, and a better understanding of daily Christian living.

Structure

Leviticus is primarily a collection of laws, with a little historical narrative. The laws contained in Leviticus can be divided into two groups. First are the commands, or apodictic law. These are both positive commands ("You must . . .") and negative commands ("You must not . . ."). The second type of law is casuistic law. These are case laws using an example of what to do if such-and-such happened ("If a man . . ."). Some scholars seek to divide the laws further into civil laws, moral laws, and ceremonial laws, but there is no evidence that the Israelites made such a distinction.

THE BURNT OFFERING

1 Then the LORD summoned Moses and spoke to him from the tent of meeting: 2 "Speak to the Israelites and tell them: When any of you brings an offering to the LORD from the livestock, you may bring your offering from the herd or the flock.

3 "If his offering is a burnt offering from the herd, he is to bring an unblemished male. He will bring it to the entrance to the tent of meeting so that he[A] may be accepted by the LORD. 4 He is to lay his hand on the head of the burnt offering so it can be accepted on his behalf to make atonement for him. 5 He is to slaughter the bull before the LORD; Aaron's sons the priests are to present the blood and splatter it on all sides of the altar that is at the entrance to the tent of meeting. 6 Then he is to skin the burnt offering and cut it into pieces.[B] 7 The sons of Aaron the priest will prepare a fire on the altar and arrange wood on the fire. 8 Aaron's sons the priests are to arrange the pieces, the head, and the fat on top of the burning wood on the altar. 9 The offerer is to wash its entrails and legs with water. Then the priest will burn all of it on the altar as a burnt offering, a food offering, a pleasing aroma to the LORD.

10 "But if his offering for a burnt offering is from the flock, from sheep or goats, he is to present an unblemished male. 11 He will slaughter it on the north side of the altar before the LORD. Aaron's sons the priests will splatter its blood against the altar on all sides. 12 He will cut the animal into pieces with its head and its fat, and the priest will arrange them on top of the burning wood on the altar. 13 But he is to wash the entrails and legs with water. The priest will then present all of it and burn it on the altar; it is a burnt offering, a food offering, a pleasing aroma to the LORD.

14 "If his offering to the LORD is a burnt offering of birds, he is to present his offering from the turtledoves or young pigeons.[C] 15 Then the priest is to bring it to the altar, and will twist off its head and burn it on the altar; its blood should be drained at the side of the altar. 16 He will remove its digestive tract,[D] cutting off the tail feathers, and throw it on the east side of the altar at the place for ashes. 17 He will tear it open by its wings without dividing the bird. Then the priest is to burn it on the altar on top of the burning wood. It is a burnt offering, a food offering, a pleasing aroma to the LORD.

THE GRAIN OFFERING

2 "When anyone presents a grain offering as an offering to the LORD, it is to consist of fine flour. He is to pour olive oil on it, put frankincense on it, 2 and bring it to Aaron's sons the priests. The priest will take a handful of fine flour and oil from it, along with all its frankincense, and will burn this memorial portion of it on the altar, a food offering, a pleasing aroma to the LORD. 3 But the rest of the grain offering will belong to Aaron and his sons; it is the holiest part of the food offerings to the LORD.

4 "When you present a grain offering baked in an oven, it is to be made of fine flour, either unleavened cakes mixed with oil or unleavened wafers coated with oil. 5 If your offering is a grain offering prepared on a griddle, it is to be unleavened bread made of fine flour mixed with oil. 6 Break it into pieces and pour oil on it; it is a grain offering. 7 If your offering is a grain offering prepared in a pan, it is to be made of fine flour with oil. 8 When you bring to the LORD the grain offering made in any of these ways, it is to be presented to the priest, and he will take it to the altar. 9 The priest will remove the memorial portion[E] from the grain offering and burn it on the altar, a food offering, a pleasing aroma to the LORD. 10 But the rest of the grain offering will belong to Aaron and his sons; it is the holiest part of the food offerings to the LORD.

11 "No grain offering that you present to the LORD is to be made with yeast, for you are not to burn[F] any yeast or honey as a food offering to the LORD. 12 You may present them to the LORD as an offering of firstfruits, but they are not to be offered on the altar as a pleasing aroma. 13 You are to season each of your grain offerings with salt; you must not omit from your grain offering the salt of the covenant with your God. You are to present salt with each of your offerings.

14 "If you present a grain offering of firstfruits to the LORD, you are to present fresh heads of grain, crushed kernels, roasted on the fire, for your grain offering of firstfruits. 15 You are to put oil and frankincense on it; it is a grain offering. 16 The priest will then burn some of its crushed kernels and oil with all its frankincense as a food offering to the LORD.

THE FELLOWSHIP OFFERING

3 "If his offering is a fellowship sacrifice, and he is presenting an animal from the herd, whether male or female, he is to present one without blemish before the LORD. 2 He is to lay his hand on the head of his offering and slaughter it at the entrance to the tent of meeting. Then Aaron's sons the priests will splatter the blood on all sides of the altar. 3 He will present part of the fellowship sacrifice as a food offering to the LORD: the fat surrounding the entrails, all the fat that is on the entrails, 4 and the two kidneys with the fat on them at the loins; he will also remove the fatty lobe of the liver with the kidneys. 5 Aaron's sons will

[A] **1:3** Or *it* [B] **1:6** Lit *its pieces*, also in v. 12 [C] **1:14** Or *or pigeons* [D] **1:16** Or *its crop*, or *its crissum* [E] **2:9** Lit *portion of it* [F] **2:11** Some Hb mss, Sam, LXX, Tg read *present*

burn it on the altar along with the burnt offering that is on the burning wood, a food offering, a pleasing aroma to the LORD.

6 "If his offering as a fellowship sacrifice to the LORD is from the flock, he is to present a male or female without blemish. 7 If he is presenting a lamb for his offering, he is to present it before the LORD. 8 He must lay his hand on the head of his offering, then slaughter it before the tent of meeting. Aaron's sons will splatter its blood on all sides of the altar. 9 He will then present part of the fellowship sacrifice as a food offering to the LORD consisting of its fat and the entire fat tail, which he is to remove close to the backbone. He will also remove the fat surrounding the entrails, all the fat on the entrails, 10 the two kidneys with the fat on them at the loins, and the fatty lobe of the liver above the kidneys. 11 Then the priest will burn the food on the altar, as a food offering to the LORD.

12 "If his offering is a goat, he is to present it before the LORD. 13 He must lay his hand on its head and slaughter it before the tent of meeting. Aaron's sons will splatter[A] its blood on all sides of the altar. 14 He will present part of his offering as a food offering to the LORD: the fat surrounding the entrails, all the fat that is on the entrails, 15 and the two kidneys with the fat on them at the loins; he will also remove the fatty lobe of the liver with the kidneys. 16 Then the priest will burn the food on the altar, as a food offering for a pleasing aroma.[B]

"All fat belongs to the LORD. 17 This is a permanent statute throughout your generations, wherever you live: you must not eat any fat or any blood."

THE SIN OFFERING

4 Then the LORD spoke to Moses: 2 "Tell the Israelites: When someone sins unintentionally against any of the LORD's commands and does anything prohibited by them —

3 "If the anointed priest sins, bringing guilt on the people, he is to present to the LORD a young, unblemished bull as a sin[C] offering for the sin he has committed. 4 He is to bring the bull to the entrance to the tent of meeting before the LORD, lay his hand on the bull's head, and slaughter it before the LORD. 5 The anointed priest will then take some of the bull's blood and bring it into the tent of meeting. 6 The priest is to dip his finger in the blood and sprinkle some of it seven times before the LORD in front of the curtain of the sanctuary. 7 The priest is to apply some of the blood to the horns of the altar of fragrant incense that is before the LORD in the tent of meeting. He must pour out the rest of the bull's blood at the base of the altar of burnt offering that is at the entrance to the tent of meeting. 8 He is to remove all the fat from the bull of the sin offering: the fat surrounding the entrails, all the fat that is on the entrails, 9 and the two kidneys with the fat on them at the loins. He will also remove the fatty lobe of the liver with the kidneys, 10 just as the fat is removed from the ox of the fellowship sacrifice. The priest is to burn them on the altar of burnt offering. 11 But the hide of the bull and all its flesh, with its head and legs, and its entrails and waste — 12 all the rest of the bull — he must bring to a ceremonially clean place outside the camp to the ash heap, and must burn it on a wood fire. It is to be burned at the ash heap.

13 "Now if the whole community of Israel errs, and the matter escapes the notice of the assembly, so that they violate any of the LORD's commands and incur guilt by doing what is prohibited, 14 then the assembly must present a young bull as a sin offering. They are to bring it before the tent of meeting when the sin they have committed in regard to the command becomes known. 15 The elders of the community are to lay their hands on the bull's head before the LORD and it is to be slaughtered before the LORD. 16 The anointed priest will bring some of the bull's blood into the tent of meeting. 17 The priest is to dip his finger in the blood and sprinkle it seven times before the LORD in front of the curtain. 18 He is to apply some of the blood to the horns of the altar that is before the LORD in the tent of meeting. He will pour out the rest of the blood at the base of the altar of burnt offering that is at the entrance to the tent of meeting. 19 He is to remove all the fat from it and burn it on the altar. 20 He is to offer this bull just as he did with the bull in the sin offering; he will offer it the same way. So the priest will make atonement on their behalf, and they will be forgiven. 21 Then he will bring the bull outside the camp and burn it just as he burned the first bull. It is the sin offering for the assembly.

22 "When a leader[D] sins and unintentionally violates any of the commands of the LORD his God by doing what is prohibited, and incurs guilt, 23 or someone informs him about the sin he has committed, he is to bring an unblemished male goat as his offering. 24 He is to lay his hand on the head of the goat and slaughter it at the place where the burnt offering is slaughtered before the LORD. It is a sin offering. 25 Then the priest is to take some of the blood from the sin offering with his finger and apply it to the horns of the altar of burnt offering. The rest of its blood he is to pour out at the base of the altar of burnt offering. 26 He must burn all its fat on the altar, like the fat of the fellowship sacrifice. In this way the priest will make atonement on his behalf for that person's sin, and he will be forgiven.

[A] **3:13** Or *dash* [B] **3:16** Sam, LXX add *to the LORD* [C] **4:3** Or *purification* [D] **4:22** Or *ruler*

27 "Now if any of the common people[A] sins unintentionally by violating one of the LORD's commands, does what is prohibited, and incurs guilt, 28 or if someone informs him about the sin he has committed, then he is to bring an unblemished female goat as his offering for the sin that he has committed. 29 He is to lay his hand on the head of the sin offering and slaughter it at the place of the burnt offering. 30 Then the priest is to take some of its blood with his finger and apply it to the horns of the altar of burnt offering. He is to pour out the rest of its blood at the base of the altar. 31 He is to remove all its fat just as the fat is removed from the fellowship sacrifice. The priest is to burn it on the altar as a pleasing aroma to the LORD. In this way the priest will make atonement on his behalf, and he will be forgiven.

32 "Or if the offering that he brings as a sin offering is a lamb, he is to bring an unblemished female. 33 He is to lay his hand on the head of the sin offering and slaughter it as a sin offering at the place where the burnt offering is slaughtered. 34 Then the priest is to take some of the blood of the sin offering with his finger and apply it to the horns of the altar of burnt offering. He is to pour out the rest of its blood at the base of the altar. 35 He is to remove all its fat just as the fat of the lamb is removed from the fellowship sacrifice. The priest will burn it on the altar along with the food offerings to the LORD. In this way the priest will make atonement on his behalf for the sin he has committed, and he will be forgiven.

CASES REQUIRING SIN OFFERINGS

5 "When someone sins in any of these ways:
If he has seen, heard, or known about something he has witnessed, and did not respond to a public call to testify, he will bear his iniquity.
2 Or if someone touches anything unclean — a carcass of an unclean wild animal, or unclean livestock, or an unclean swarming creature — without being aware of it, he is unclean and incurs guilt.
3 Or if he touches human uncleanness — any uncleanness by which one can become defiled — without being aware of it, but later recognizes it, he incurs guilt.
4 Or if someone swears rashly to do what is good or evil — concerning anything a person may speak rashly in an oath — without being aware of it, but later recognizes it, he incurs guilt in such an instance.

5 If someone incurs guilt in one of these cases, he is to confess he has committed that sin. 6 He must bring his penalty for guilt for the sin he has committed to the LORD: a female lamb or goat from the flock as a sin offering. In this way the priest will make atonement on his behalf for his sin.

7 "But if he cannot afford an animal from the flock, then he may bring to the LORD two turtledoves or two young pigeons as penalty for guilt for his sin — one as a sin offering and the other as a burnt offering. 8 He is to bring them to the priest, who will first present the one for the sin offering. He is to twist its head at the back of the neck without severing it. 9 Then he will sprinkle some of the blood of the sin offering on the side of the altar, while the rest of the blood is to be drained out at the base of the altar; it is a sin offering. 10 He will prepare the second bird as a burnt offering according to the regulation. In this way the priest will make atonement on his behalf for the sin he has committed, and he will be forgiven.

11 "But if he cannot afford two turtledoves or two young pigeons, he may bring two quarts[B] of fine flour[C] as an offering for his sin. He must not put olive oil or frankincense on it, for it is a sin offering. 12 He is to bring it to the priest, who will take a handful from it as its memorial portion and burn it on the altar along with the food offerings to the LORD; it is a sin offering. 13 In this way the priest will make atonement on his behalf concerning the sin he has committed in any of these cases, and he will be forgiven. The rest will belong to the priest, like the grain offering."

THE GUILT OFFERING

14 Then the LORD spoke to Moses: 15 "If someone offends by sinning unintentionally in regard to any of the LORD's holy things,[D] he must bring his penalty for guilt to the LORD: an unblemished ram from the flock (based on your assessment of its value in silver shekels, according to the sanctuary shekel) as a guilt offering. 16 He is to make restitution for his sin regarding any holy thing, adding a fifth of its value to it, and give it to the priest. Then the priest will make atonement on his behalf with the ram of the guilt offering, and he will be forgiven.

17 "If someone sins and without knowing it violates any of the LORD's commands concerning anything prohibited, he is guilty, and he will bear his iniquity. 18 He must bring an unblemished ram from the flock according to your assessment of its value as a guilt offering to the priest. Then the priest will make atonement on his behalf for the error he has committed unintentionally, and he will be forgiven. 19 It is a guilt offering; he is indeed guilty before the LORD."

6 The LORD spoke to Moses: 2 "When someone sins and offends the LORD by deceiving his neighbor in regard to a deposit, a security,[E] or a robbery; or defrauds his neighbor; 3 or finds something lost and lies about it; or swears falsely about any of the sinful

[A] 4:27 Lit *the people of the land* [B] 5:11 Lit *one-tenth of an ephah* [C] 5:11 Lit *flour as a sin offering* [D] 5:15 Things dedicated to the LORD [E] 6:2 Or *an investment*

things a person may do — 4 once he has sinned and
acknowledged his guilt — he must return what he
stole or defrauded, or the deposit entrusted to him,
or the lost item he found, 5 or anything else about
which he swore falsely. He will make full restitution
for it and add a fifth of its value to it. He is to pay it
to its owner on the day he acknowledges his guilt.
6 Then he is to bring his guilt offering to the LORD: an
unblemished ram from the flock according to your
assessment of its value as a guilt offering to the priest.
7 In this way the priest will make atonement on his
behalf before the LORD, and he will be forgiven for
anything he may have done to incur guilt."

THE BURNT OFFERING

8 The LORD spoke to Moses: 9 "Command Aaron and
his sons: This is the law of the burnt offering; the
burnt offering itself must remain on the altar's hearth
all night until morning, while the fire of the altar is
kept burning on it. 10 The priest is to put on his linen
robe and linen undergarments.[A] He is to remove the
ashes of the burnt offering the fire has consumed
on the altar, and place them beside the altar. 11 Then
he will take off his garments, put on other clothes,
and bring the ashes outside the camp to a ceremonially clean place. 12 The fire on the altar is to be kept
burning; it must not go out. Every morning the priest
will burn wood on the fire. He is to arrange the burnt
offering on the fire and burn the fat portions from
the fellowship offerings on it. 13 Fire must be kept
burning on the altar continually; it must not go out.

THE GRAIN OFFERING

14 "Now this is the law of the grain offering: Aaron's sons will present it before the LORD in front of
the altar. 15 The priest is to remove a handful of fine
flour and olive oil from the grain offering, with all
the frankincense that is on the offering, and burn
its memorial portion on the altar as a pleasing aroma to the LORD. 16 Aaron and his sons may eat the
rest of it. It is to be eaten in the form of unleavened
bread in a holy place; they are to eat it in the courtyard of the tent of meeting. 17 It must not be baked
with yeast; I have assigned it as their portion from
my food offerings. It is especially holy, like the sin
offering and the guilt offering. 18 Any male among
Aaron's descendants may eat it. It is a permanent
portion[B] throughout your generations from the food
offerings to the LORD. Anything that touches the offerings will become holy."

19 The LORD spoke to Moses: 20 "This is the offering
that Aaron and his sons are to present to the LORD on
the day that he is anointed: two quarts[C] of fine flour
as a regular grain offering, half of it in the morning
and half in the evening. 21 It is to be prepared with oil
on a griddle; you are to bring it well-kneaded. You
are to present it as a grain offering of baked pieces,[D]
a pleasing aroma to the LORD. 22 The priest, who is
one of Aaron's sons and will be anointed to take his
place, is to prepare it. It must be completely burned
as a permanent portion for the LORD. 23 Every grain
offering for a priest will be a whole burnt offering;
it is not to be eaten."

THE SIN OFFERING

24 The LORD spoke to Moses: 25 "Tell Aaron and his
sons: This is the law of the sin offering. The sin offering is most holy and must be slaughtered before
the LORD at the place where the burnt offering is
slaughtered. 26 The priest who offers it as a sin offering will eat it. It is to be eaten in a holy place, in
the courtyard of the tent of meeting. 27 Anything
that touches its flesh will become holy, and if any
of its blood spatters on a garment, then you must
wash that garment[E] in a holy place. 28 A clay pot in
which the sin offering is boiled is to be broken; if it
is boiled in a bronze vessel, it is to be scoured and
rinsed with water. 29 Any male among the priests
may eat it; it is especially holy. 30 But no sin offering
may be eaten if its blood has been brought into the
tent of meeting to make atonement in the holy place;
it must be burned.

THE GUILT OFFERING

7 "Now this is the law of the guilt[F] offering; it is
especially holy. 2 The guilt offering is to be slaughtered at the place where the burnt offering is slaughtered, and the priest is to splatter its blood on all sides
of the altar. 3 The offerer is to present all the fat from
it: the fat tail, the fat surrounding the entrails,[G] 4 and
the two kidneys with the fat on them at the loins; he
will also remove the fatty lobe of the liver with the
kidneys. 5 The priest will burn them on the altar as a
food offering to the LORD; it is a guilt offering. 6 Any
male among the priests may eat it. It is to be eaten in
a holy place; it is especially holy.

7 "The guilt offering is like the sin offering; the
law is the same for both. It belongs to the priest who
makes atonement with it. 8 As for the priest who presents someone's burnt offering, the hide of the burnt
offering he has presented belongs to him; it is the
priest's. 9 Any grain offering that is baked in an oven
or prepared in a pan or on a griddle belongs to the
priest who presents it; it is his. 10 But any grain offering, whether dry or mixed with oil, belongs equally
to all of Aaron's sons.

[A] **6:10** Lit *undergarments on his flesh* [B] **6:18** Or *statute* [C] **6:20** Lit *a tenth of an ephah* [D] **6:21** Hb obscure [E] **6:27** Lit *wash what it spattered on* [F] **7:1** Or *restitution* [G] **7:3** LXX, Sam add *and all the fat that is on the entrails*; Lv 3:3,9,14; 4:8

Sacrificial Animals in Hebrew Worship

by Scott Hummel

Sacrifice was at the heart of Hebrew worship. Sacrifices accompanied daily worship, holidays, dedications, purifications, expressions of thanksgiving, and requests for forgiveness.[1]

The basic procedure of animal sacrifice in Israel involved the worshiper personally presenting the animal at the entrance of the tabernacle (and later at the temple). After laying hands on the animal's head, the worshiper slaughtered the animal and cut it into pieces. In the case of sin and guilt offerings, the worshiper confessed his sins.[2] The priest sprinkled the blood on the altar and arranged the pieces and fat on the altar. In the case of sacrificial birds, the priest killed the birds, sprinkled their blood on the altar and drained the rest at the base of the altar, and placed the birds' bodies on the altar. The priest then made atonement for the worshiper. The priest was responsible for burning the pieces into ashes, maintaining the fire on the altar, and properly disposing of the ashes (Lv 1:2–17; 6:8–7:27). ❖

---

[1] Allen P. Ross, *Holiness to the Lord: A Guide to the Exposition of the Book of Leviticus* (Grand Rapids: Baker Academic, 2002), 73; Victor P. Hamilton, *Handbook on the Pentateuch* (Grand Rapids: Baker Academic, 2005), 233, 238; 2Sm 24:24. [2] Hamilton, *Handbook*, 246.

Limestone horned altar dated to the tenth century BC; from Megiddo.

THE FELLOWSHIP SACRIFICE

11 “Now this is the law of the fellowship sacrifice that someone may present to the LORD: 12 If he presents it for thanksgiving, in addition to the thanksgiving sacrifice, he is to present unleavened cakes mixed with olive oil, unleavened wafers coated with oil, and well-kneaded cakes of fine flour mixed with oil. 13 He is to present as his offering cakes of leavened bread with his thanksgiving sacrifice of fellowship. 14 From the cakes he is to present one portion of each offering as a contribution to the LORD. It will belong to the priest who splatters the blood of the fellowship offering; it is his. 15 The meat of his thanksgiving sacrifice of fellowship must be eaten on the day he offers it; he may not leave any of it until morning.

16 “If the sacrifice he offers is a vow or a freewill offering, it is to be eaten on the day he presents his sacrifice, and what is left over may be eaten on the next day. 17 But what remains of the sacrificial meat by the third day must be burned. 18 If any of the meat of his fellowship sacrifice is eaten on the third day, it will not be accepted. It will not be credited to the one who presents it; it is repulsive. The person who eats any of it will bear his iniquity.[A]

19 “Meat that touches anything unclean must not be eaten; it is to be burned. Everyone who is clean may eat any other meat. 20 But the one who eats meat from the LORD’s fellowship sacrifice while he is unclean, that person must be cut off from his people. 21 If someone touches anything unclean, whether human uncleanness, an unclean animal, or any unclean, abhorrent[B] creature, and eats meat from the LORD’s fellowship sacrifice, that person is to be cut off from his people.”

FAT AND BLOOD PROHIBITED

22 The LORD spoke to Moses: 23 “Tell the Israelites: You are not to eat any fat of an ox, a sheep, or a goat. 24 The fat of an animal that dies naturally or is mauled by wild beasts[C] may be used for any other purpose, but you must not eat it. 25 If anyone eats animal fat from a food offering presented to the LORD, the person who eats it is to be cut off from his people. 26 Wherever you live, you must not eat the blood of any bird or animal. 27 Whoever eats any blood is to be cut off from his people.”

THE PORTION FOR THE PRIESTS

28 The LORD spoke to Moses: 29 “Tell the Israelites: The one who presents a fellowship sacrifice to the LORD is to bring an offering to the LORD from his sacrifice. 30 His own hands will bring the food offerings to the LORD. He will bring the fat together with the breast. The breast is to be presented as a presentation offering before the LORD. 31 The priest is to burn the fat on the altar, but the breast belongs to Aaron and his sons. 32 You are to give the right thigh to the priest as a contribution from your fellowship sacrifices. 33 The son of Aaron who presents the blood of the fellowship offering and the fat will have the right thigh as a portion. 34 I have taken from the Israelites the breast of the presentation offering and the thigh of the contribution from their fellowship sacrifices, and have assigned them to the priest Aaron and to his sons as a permanent portion[D] from the Israelites.”

35 This is the portion from the food offerings to the LORD for Aaron and his sons since the day they were presented to serve the LORD as priests. 36 The LORD commanded this to be given to them by the Israelites on the day he anointed them. It is a permanent portion throughout their generations.

37 This is the law for the burnt offering, the grain offering, the sin offering, the guilt offering, the ordination offering, and the fellowship sacrifice, 38 which the LORD commanded Moses on Mount Sinai on the day he commanded the Israelites to present their offerings to the LORD in the Wilderness of Sinai.

ORDINATION OF AARON AND HIS SONS

8 The LORD spoke to Moses: 2 “Take Aaron, his sons with him, the garments, the anointing oil, the bull of the sin[E] offering, the two rams, and the basket of unleavened bread, 3 and assemble the whole community at the entrance to the tent of meeting.” 4 So Moses did as the LORD commanded him, and the community assembled at the entrance to the tent of meeting. 5 Moses said to them, “This is what the LORD has commanded to be done.”

6 Then Moses presented Aaron and his sons and washed them with water. 7 He put the tunic on Aaron, wrapped the sash around him, clothed him with the robe, and put the ephod on him. He put the woven band of the ephod around him and fastened it to him. 8 Then he put the breastpiece on him and placed the Urim and Thummim into the breastpiece. 9 He also put the turban on his head and placed the gold medallion, the holy diadem, on the front of the turban, as the LORD had commanded Moses.

10 Then Moses took the anointing oil and anointed the tabernacle and everything in it to consecrate them. 11 He sprinkled some of the oil on the altar seven times, anointing the altar with all its utensils, and the basin with its stand, to consecrate them. 12 He poured some of the anointing oil on Aaron’s head and anointed and consecrated him. 13 Then Moses presented Aaron’s sons, clothed them with tunics, wrapped sashes around them, and fastened headbands on them, as the LORD had commanded Moses.

[A] **7:18** Or *will bear his guilt* [B] **7:21** Some Hb mss, Sam, Syr, Tg read *swarming* [C] **7:24** Lit *fat of a carcass or the fat of a mauled beast* [D] **7:34** Or *statute*, also in v. 36 [E] **8:2** Or *purification*

14 Then he brought the bull near for the sin offering, and Aaron and his sons laid their hands on the head of the bull for the sin offering. 15 Then Moses slaughtered it,[A] took the blood, and applied it with his finger to the horns of the altar on all sides, purifying the altar. He poured out the blood at the base of the altar and consecrated it so that atonement can be made on it.[B] 16 Moses took all the fat that was on the entrails, the fatty lobe of the liver, and the two kidneys with their fat, and he burned them on the altar. 17 He burned the bull with its hide, flesh, and waste outside the camp, as the LORD had commanded Moses.

18 Then he presented the ram for the burnt offering, and Aaron and his sons laid their hands on the head of the ram. 19 Moses slaughtered it and[C] splattered the blood on all sides of the altar. 20 Moses cut the ram into pieces and burned the head, the pieces, and the fat, 21 but he washed the entrails and legs with water. He then burned the entire ram on the altar. It was a burnt offering for a pleasing aroma, a food offering to the LORD as he had commanded Moses.

22 Next he presented the second ram, the ram of ordination, and Aaron and his sons laid their hands on the head of the ram. 23 Moses slaughtered it,[D] took some of its blood, and put it on Aaron's right earlobe, on the thumb of his right hand, and on the big toe of his right foot. 24 Moses also presented Aaron's sons and put some of the blood on their right earlobes, on the thumbs of their right hands, and on the big toes of their right feet. Then Moses splattered the blood on all sides of the altar. 25 He took the fat — the fat tail, all the fat that was on the entrails, the fatty lobe of the liver, and the two kidneys with their fat — as well as the right thigh. 26 From the basket of unleavened bread that was before the LORD he took one cake of unleavened bread, one cake of bread made with oil, and one wafer, and placed them on the fat portions and the right thigh. 27 He put all these in the hands of Aaron and his sons and presented them before the LORD as a presentation offering. 28 Then Moses took them from their hands and burned them on the altar with the burnt offering. This was an ordination offering for a pleasing aroma, a food offering to the LORD. 29 He also took the breast and presented it before the LORD as a presentation offering; it was Moses's portion of the ordination ram as the LORD had commanded him.

30 Then Moses took some of the anointing oil and some of the blood that was on the altar and sprinkled them on Aaron and his garments, as well as on his sons and their garments. In this way he consecrated Aaron and his garments, as well as his sons and their garments.

31 Moses said to Aaron and his sons, "Boil the meat at the entrance to the tent of meeting and eat it there with the bread that is in the basket for the ordination offering as I commanded:[E] Aaron and his sons are to eat it. 32 Burn up what remains of the meat and bread. 33 Do not go outside the entrance to the tent of meeting for seven days, until the time your days of ordination are completed, because it will take seven days to ordain you.[F] 34 The LORD commanded what has been done today in order to make atonement for you. 35 You must remain at the entrance to the tent of meeting day and night for seven days and keep the LORD's charge so that you will not die, for this is what I was commanded." 36 So Aaron and his sons did everything the LORD had commanded through Moses.

THE PRIESTLY MINISTRY INAUGURATED

9 On the eighth day Moses summoned Aaron, his sons, and the elders of Israel. 2 He said to Aaron, "Take a young bull for a sin[G] offering and a ram for a burnt offering, both without blemish, and present them before the LORD. 3 And tell the Israelites:[H] Take a male goat for a sin offering; a calf and a lamb, male yearlings without blemish, for a burnt offering; 4 an ox and a ram for a fellowship offering to sacrifice before the LORD; and a grain offering mixed with oil. For today the LORD is going to appear to you."

5 They brought what Moses had commanded to the front of the tent of meeting, and the whole community came forward and stood before the LORD. 6 Moses said, "This is what the LORD commanded you to do, that the glory of the LORD may appear to you." 7 Then Moses said to Aaron, "Approach the altar and sacrifice your sin offering and your burnt offering; make atonement for yourself and the people.[I] Sacrifice the people's offering and make atonement for them, as the LORD commanded."

8 So Aaron approached the altar and slaughtered the calf as a sin offering for himself. 9 Aaron's sons brought the blood to him, and he dipped his finger in the blood and applied it to the horns of the altar. He poured out the blood at the base of the altar. 10 He burned the fat, the kidneys, and the fatty lobe of the liver from the sin offering on the altar, as the LORD had commanded Moses. 11 He burned the flesh and the hide outside the camp.

12 Then he slaughtered the burnt offering. Aaron's sons brought him the blood, and he splattered it on all sides of the altar. 13 They brought him the burnt offering piece by piece, along with the head, and he burned them on the altar. 14 He washed the entrails

[A] **8:14–15** Or *offering, and he slaughtered it.* **15***Then Moses* [B] **8:15** Or *it by making atonement for it* [C] **8:18–19** Or *ram,* **19***and he slaughtered it. Moses* [D] **8:22–23** Or *ram,* **23***and he slaughtered it. Moses*
[E] **8:31** LXX, Syr, Tg read *was commanded*; Ex 29:31–32 [F] **8:33** Lit *because he will fill your hands for seven days* [G] **9:2** Or *purification*
[H] **9:3** Sam, LXX read *elders of Israel* [I] **9:7** LXX reads *and your household*

and the legs and burned them with the burnt offering on the altar.

15 Aaron presented the people's offering. He took the male goat for the people's sin offering, slaughtered it, and made a sin offering with it as he did before. 16 He presented the burnt offering and sacrificed it according to the regulation. 17 Next he presented the grain offering, took a handful of it, and burned it on the altar in addition to the morning burnt offering.

18 Finally, he slaughtered the ox and the ram as the people's fellowship sacrifice. Aaron's sons brought him the blood, and he splattered it on all sides of the altar. 19 They also brought the fat portions from the ox and the ram — the fat tail, the fat surrounding the entrails, the kidneys, and the fatty lobe of the liver — 20 and placed these on the breasts. Aaron burned the fat portions on the altar, 21 but he presented the breasts and the right thigh as a presentation offering before the LORD, as Moses had commanded.[A]

22 Aaron lifted up his hands toward the people and blessed them. He came down after sacrificing the sin offering, the burnt offering, and the fellowship offering. 23 Moses and Aaron then entered the tent of meeting. When they came out, they blessed the people, and the glory of the LORD appeared to all the people. 24 Fire came from the LORD and consumed the burnt offering and the fat portions on the altar. And when all the people saw it, they shouted and fell facedown.

NADAB AND ABIHU

10 Aaron's sons Nadab and Abihu each took his own firepan, put fire in it, placed incense on it, and presented unauthorized fire before the LORD, which he had not commanded them to do. 2 Then fire came from the LORD and consumed them, and they died before the LORD. 3 Moses said to Aaron, "This is what the LORD has spoken:

> I will demonstrate my holiness[B]
> to those who are near me,
> and I will reveal my glory[C]
> before all the people."

And Aaron remained silent.

4 Moses summoned Mishael and Elzaphan, sons of Aaron's uncle Uzziel, and said to them, "Come here and carry your relatives away from the front of the sanctuary to a place outside the camp." 5 So they came forward and carried them in their tunics outside the camp, as Moses had said.

6 Then Moses said to Aaron and his sons Eleazar and Ithamar, "Do not let your hair hang loose and do not tear your clothes, or else you will die, and the LORD will become angry with the whole community. However, your brothers, the whole house of Israel, may weep over the fire that the LORD caused. 7 You must not go outside the entrance to the tent of meeting or you will die, for the LORD's anointing oil is on you." So they did as Moses said.

REGULATIONS FOR PRIESTS

8 The LORD spoke to Aaron: 9 "You and your sons are not to drink wine or beer when you enter the tent of meeting, or else you will die; this is a permanent statute throughout your generations. 10 You must distinguish between the holy and the common, and the clean and the unclean, 11 and teach the Israelites all the statutes that the LORD has given to them through Moses."

12 Moses spoke to Aaron and his remaining sons, Eleazar and Ithamar: "Take the grain offering that is left over from the food offerings to the LORD, and eat it prepared without yeast beside the altar, because it is especially holy. 13 You must eat it in a holy place because it is your portion[D] and your sons' from the food offerings to the LORD, for this is what I was commanded. 14 But you and your sons and your daughters may eat the breast of the presentation offering and the thigh of the contribution in any ceremonially clean place, because these portions have been assigned to you and your children from the Israelites' fellowship sacrifices. 15 They are to bring the thigh of the contribution and the breast of the presentation offering, together with the food offerings of the fat portions, to present as a presentation offering before the LORD. It will belong permanently to you and your children, as the LORD commanded."

16 Then Moses inquired carefully about the male goat of the sin offering, but it had already been burned up. He was angry with Eleazar and Ithamar, Aaron's surviving sons, and asked, 17 "Why didn't you eat the sin offering in the sanctuary area? For it is especially holy, and he has assigned it to you to take away the guilt of the community and make atonement for them before the LORD. 18 Since its blood was not brought inside the sanctuary, you should have eaten it in the sanctuary area, as I commanded."

19 But Aaron replied to Moses, "See, today they presented their sin offering and their burnt offering before the LORD. Since these things have happened to me, if I had eaten the sin offering today, would it have been acceptable in the LORD's sight?" 20 When Moses heard this, it was acceptable to him.[E]

CLEAN AND UNCLEAN LAND ANIMALS

11 The LORD spoke to Moses and Aaron: 2 "Tell the Israelites: You may eat all these kinds of land animals. 3 You may eat any animal with divided hooves and that chews the cud. 4 But among the

[A] **9:21** Some Hb mss, LXX, Sam read *as the LORD commanded Moses*
[B] **10:3** Or *will be treated as holy* [C] **10:3** Or *will be glorified*
[D] **10:13** Or *statute* [E] **10:20** Lit *acceptable in his sight*

Incense in Hebrew Worship

by Ken Cox

An altar for burning incense was part of the furnishings of the tabernacle. When Solomon built the magnificent temple in Jerusalem, a golden altar of incense was in front of the curtain in the holy place (2Ch 4:19). The incense, composed of four equal parts of rare, expensive ingredients, was to be burned exclusively on the altar.

Priests offered incense by placing burning coals from the bronze altar onto the incense altar. The priest would place incense ground into powder upon the coals. The fragrant cloud symbolized Israel's prayers rising constantly before the Lord.[1] The perfume of the offering was a pleasing aroma to fill the temple. As kings and honored house guests were treated with the special aroma of burning incense, likewise the King of kings savored the sweet aroma of the special mixture of incense.[2]

Miniature bronze incense burners, probably for domestic use. From Byblos; first century BC–first century AD.

Incense was burned in one other way on the Day of Atonement. The high priest would carry coals on a censer or fire pan into the most holy place and bring the blood of the sacrifice. Upon entering the most holy place, the priest would place incense on the coals, which came from the bronze altar. The result was a cloud that shielded and provided protection for the priest as he came into the consuming presence of God (Lv 16:12–13).

The improper burning of incense brought immediate punishments. Nadab and Abihu, who were both priests and sons of Aaron, offered "unauthorized fire" in their censers and forfeited their lives (10:1–2).

Incense was to be added to grain offerings that served as fellowship offerings. These "thank offerings" were burned on the altar, the grain and incense together.[3] When grain was presented as a sin offering, incense was not to be added when it was burned. The incense with the thank offerings symbolized the worshiper's gratitude and union with God. The grain the poor offered as a sin offering could not contain incense due to the need of the worshiper to be first restored to communion with God.[4] After the Babylonian exile, the recipe for incense included seven other spices.[5]

In the New Testament, Zechariah, the father of John the Baptist, was the priest who had been selected to offer incense on the altar when he saw the angel that informed him of Elizabeth's miraculous conception. The book of Revelation refers to the smoke of incense as the prayers of God's saints (Rv 5:8; 8:3). ✣

---

[1] C. F. Keil and F. Delitzsch, "The Second Book of Moses (Exodus)," in *The Pentateuch*, vol. 1 of Commentary on the Old Testament (Peabody, MA: Hendrickson, 1996), 457. [2] Immanuel Benzinger et al., "Incense" in *Jewish Encyclopedia* (1906), www.jewishencyclopedia.com/articles/8099-incense. [3] Keil and Delitzsch, "The Third Book of Moses," in *Pentateuch*, 516. [4] Keil and Delitzsch, "Third Book," 529. [5] Roland de Vaux, *Ancient Israel: Its Life and Institutions* (Grand Rapids: Eerdmans, 1997), 432; Benzinger, "Incense."

Replica of one of two incense altars set up in the most holy place in the temple of Arad in southern Israel.

Bronze incense shovel; from Israel; dated to the first or second century AD.

ones that chew the cud or have divided hooves you
are not to eat these:
camels, though they chew the cud,
do not have divided hooves — they are
unclean for you;
5 hyraxes, though they chew the cud,
do not have hooves — they are unclean
for you;
6 hares, though they chew the cud,
do not have hooves — they are unclean
for you;
7 pigs, though they have divided hooves,
do not chew the cud — they are unclean
for you.
8 Do not eat any of their meat or touch their carcasses
— they are unclean for you.

CLEAN AND UNCLEAN AQUATIC ANIMALS

9 "This is what you may eat from all that is in the water: You may eat everything in the water that has fins
and scales, whether in the seas or streams. 10 But these
are to be abhorrent to you: everything in the seas or
streams that does not have fins and scales among all
the swarming things and other living creatures in the
water. 11 They are to remain abhorrent to you; you
must not eat any of their meat, and you must abhor
their carcasses. 12 Everything in the water that does
not have fins and scales will be abhorrent to you.

UNCLEAN BIRDS

13 "You are to abhor these birds. They must not be
eaten because they are abhorrent:
eagles,[A] bearded vultures,
Egyptian vultures,[B] 14 kites,[C]
any kind of falcon,[D]
15 every kind of raven, 16 ostriches,[E]
short-eared owls, gulls,[F]
any kind of hawk,
17 little[G] owls, cormorants,[H]
long-eared owls,[I]
18 barn[J] owls, eagle owls,[K]
ospreys, 19 storks,[L]
any kind of heron,[M]
hoopoes, and bats.

CLEAN AND UNCLEAN FLYING INSECTS

20 "All winged insects that walk on all fours are to be
abhorrent to you. 21 But you may eat these kinds of all
the winged insects that walk on all fours: those that
have jointed legs above their feet for hopping on the
ground. 22 You may eat these:
any kind of locust, katydid, cricket,
and grasshopper.
23 All other winged insects that have four feet are to
be abhorrent to you.

PURIFICATION AFTER TOUCHING DEAD ANIMALS

24 "These will make you unclean. Whoever touches
their carcasses will be unclean until evening, 25 and
whoever carries any of their carcasses is to wash
his clothes and will be unclean until evening. 26 All
animals that have hooves but do not have a divided
hoof and do not chew the cud are unclean for you.
Whoever touches them becomes unclean. 27 All the
four-footed animals that walk on their paws are unclean for you. Whoever touches their carcasses will
be unclean until evening, 28 and anyone who carries
their carcasses is to wash his clothes and will be unclean until evening. They are unclean for you.
29 "These creatures that swarm on the ground are
unclean for you:
weasels,[N] mice,
any kind of large lizard,[O]
30 geckos, monitor lizards,[P]
common lizards,[Q] skinks,[R]
and chameleons.[S]
31 These are unclean for you among all the swarming
creatures. Whoever touches them when they are dead
will be unclean until evening. 32 When any one of
them dies and falls on anything it becomes unclean
— any item of wood, clothing, leather, sackcloth, or
any implement used for work. It is to be rinsed with
water and will remain unclean until evening; then
it will be clean. 33 If any of them falls into any clay
pot, everything in it will become unclean; you are
to break it. 34 Any edible food coming into contact
with that unclean water will become unclean, and
any drinkable liquid in any container will become
unclean. 35 Anything one of their carcasses falls on
will become unclean. If it is an oven or stove, it is to
be smashed; it is unclean and will remain unclean
for you. 36 A spring or cistern containing water will
remain clean, but someone who touches a carcass
in it will become unclean. 37 If one of their carcasses
falls on any seed that is to be sown, it is clean; 38 but
if water has been put on the seed and one of their
carcasses falls on it, it is unclean for you.
39 "If one of the animals that you use for food dies,
anyone who touches its carcass will be unclean until
evening. 40 Anyone who eats some of its carcass is to
wash his clothes and will be unclean until evening.
Anyone who carries its carcass must wash his clothes
and will be unclean until evening.

[A] **11:13** Or *griffon-vultures* [B] **11:13** Or *ospreys*, or *bearded vultures* [C] **11:14** Or *hawks* [D] **11:14** Or *buzzards*, or *hawks* [E] **11:16** Or *eagle owls* [F] **11:16** Or *long-eared owls* [G] **11:17** Or *tawny* [H] **11:17** Or *pelicans* [I] **11:17** Or *ibis* [J] **11:18** Or *little* [K] **11:18** Or *pelicans*, or *horned owls* [L] **11:19** Or *herons* [M] **11:19** Or *cormorants*, or *hawks* [N] **11:29** Or *mole rats*, or *rats* [O] **11:29** Or *of thorn-tailed*, or *dabb lizard*, or *of crocodile* [P] **11:30** Or *spotted lizards*, or *chameleons* [Q] **11:30** Or *geckos*, or *newts*, or *salamanders* [R] **11:30** Or *sand lizards*, or *newts*, or *snails* [S] **11:30** Or *salamanders*, or *moles*

UNCLEAN SWARMING CREATURES

41 “All the creatures that swarm on the earth are abhorrent; they must not be eaten. 42 Do not eat any of the creatures that swarm on the earth, anything that moves on its belly or walks on all fours or on many feet,[A] for they are abhorrent. 43 Do not become contaminated by any creature that swarms; do not become unclean or defiled by them. 44 For I am the LORD your God, so you must consecrate yourselves and be holy because I am holy. Do not defile yourselves by any swarming creature that crawls on the ground. 45 For I am the LORD, who brought you up from the land of Egypt to be your God, so you must be holy because I am holy.

46 “This is the law concerning animals, birds, all living creatures that move in the water, and all creatures that swarm on the ground, 47 in order to distinguish between the unclean and the clean, between the animals that may be eaten and those that may not be eaten.”

PURIFICATION AFTER CHILDBIRTH

12 The LORD spoke to Moses: 2 “Tell the Israelites: When a woman becomes pregnant and gives birth to a male child, she will be unclean seven days, as she is during the days of her menstrual impurity. 3 The flesh of his foreskin must be circumcised on the eighth day. 4 She will continue in purification from her bleeding for thirty-three days. She must not touch any holy thing or go into the sanctuary until completing her days of purification. 5 But if she gives birth to a female child, she will be unclean for two weeks as she is during her menstrual impurity. She will continue in purification from her bleeding for sixty-six days.

6 “When her days of purification are complete, whether for a son or daughter, she is to bring to the priest at the entrance to the tent of meeting a year-old male lamb for a burnt offering, and a young pigeon or a turtledove for a sin[B] offering. 7 He will present them before the LORD and make atonement on her behalf; she will be clean from her discharge of blood. This is the law for a woman giving birth, whether to a male or female. 8 But if she doesn't have sufficient means[C] for a sheep, she may take two turtledoves or two young pigeons, one for a burnt offering and the other for a sin offering. Then the priest will make atonement on her behalf, and she will be clean.”

SKIN DISEASES

13 The LORD spoke to Moses and Aaron: 2 “When a person has a swelling,[D] scab,[E] or spot on the skin of his body, and it may be a serious disease on the skin of his body, he is to be brought to the priest Aaron or to one of his sons, the priests. 3 The priest will examine the sore on the skin of his body. If the hair in the sore has turned white and the sore appears to be deeper than the skin of his body, it is in fact a serious skin disease. After the priest examines him, he must pronounce him unclean. 4 But if the spot on the skin of his body is white and does not appear to be deeper than the skin, and the hair in it has not turned white, the priest will quarantine the stricken person for seven days. 5 The priest will then reexamine him on the seventh day. If he sees that the sore remains unchanged and has not spread on the skin, the priest will quarantine him for another seven days. 6 The priest will examine him again on the seventh day. If the sore has faded and has not spread on the skin, the priest is to pronounce him clean; it is a scab. The person is to wash his clothes and will become clean. 7 But if the scab spreads further on his skin after he has presented himself to the priest for his cleansing, he is to present himself again to the priest. 8 The priest will examine him, and if the scab has spread on the skin, then the priest must pronounce him unclean; he has a serious skin disease.

9 “When a case of serious skin disease may have developed on a person, he is to be brought to the priest. 10 The priest will examine him. If there is a white swelling on the skin that has turned the hair white, and there is a patch of raw flesh in the swelling, 11 it is a chronic serious disease on the skin of his body, and the priest must pronounce him unclean. He need not quarantine him, for he is unclean. 12 But if the skin disease breaks out all over the skin so that it covers all the skin of the stricken person from his head to his feet so far as the priest can see, 13 the priest will look, and if the skin disease has covered his entire body, he is to pronounce the stricken person clean. Since he has turned totally white, he is clean. 14 But whenever raw flesh appears on him, he will be unclean. 15 When the priest examines the raw flesh, he must pronounce him unclean. Raw flesh is unclean; this is a serious skin disease. 16 But if the raw flesh changes[F] and[G] turns white, he is to go to the priest. 17 The priest will examine him, and if the sore has turned white, the priest must pronounce the stricken person clean; he is clean.

18 “When a boil appears on the skin of someone's body and it heals, 19 and a white swelling or a reddish-white spot develops where the boil was, the person is to present himself to the priest. 20 The priest will make an examination, and if the spot seems to be beneath the skin and the hair in it has turned white,

[A] **11:42** Lit *fours, to anything multiplying pairs of feet* [B] **12:6** Or *purification*, also in v. 8 [C] **12:8** Lit *if her hand cannot obtain what is sufficient* [D] **13:2** Or *discoloration* [E] **13:2** Or *rash*, or *eruption* [F] **13:16** Or *recedes* [G] **13:16** Or *flesh again*

the priest must pronounce him unclean; it is a case
of serious skin disease that has broken out in the
boil. 21 But when the priest examines it, if there is
no white hair in it, and it is not beneath the skin but
is faded, the priest will quarantine him seven days.
22 If it spreads further on the skin, the priest must
pronounce him unclean; it is in fact a disease. 23 But
if the spot remains where it is and does not spread,
it is only the scar from the boil. The priest is to pronounce him clean.

24 "When there is a burn on the skin of one's body
produced by fire, and the patch made raw by the burn
becomes reddish-white or white, 25 the priest is to
examine it. If the hair in the spot has turned white
and the spot appears to be deeper than the skin, it
is a serious skin disease that has broken out in the
burn. The priest must pronounce him unclean; it is a
serious skin disease. 26 But when the priest examines
it, if there is no white hair in the spot and it is not beneath the skin but is faded, the priest will quarantine
him seven days. 27 The priest will reexamine him on
the seventh day. If it has spread further on the skin,
the priest must pronounce him unclean; it is in fact
a case of serious skin disease. 28 But if the spot has
remained where it was and has not spread on the
skin but is faded, it is the swelling from the burn.
The priest is to pronounce him clean, for it is only
the scar from the burn.

29 "When a man or woman has a condition on the
head or chin, 30 the priest is to examine the condition. If it appears to be deeper than the skin, and the
hair in it is yellow and sparse, the priest must pronounce the person unclean. It is a scaly outbreak, a
serious skin disease of the head or chin. 31 When the
priest examines the scaly condition, if it does not
appear to be deeper than the skin, and there is no
black hair in it, the priest will quarantine the person
with the scaly condition for seven days. 32 The priest
will reexamine the condition on the seventh day. If
the scaly outbreak has not spread and there is no
yellow hair in it and it does not appear to be deeper
than the skin, 33 the person is to shave himself but not
shave the scaly area. Then the priest will quarantine
the person who has the scaly outbreak for another
seven days. 34 The priest will examine the scaly outbreak on the seventh day, and if it has not spread on
the skin and does not appear to be deeper than the
skin, the priest is to pronounce the person clean. He
is to wash his clothes, and he will be clean. 35 But if
the scaly outbreak spreads further on the skin after
his cleansing, 36 the priest is to examine the person. If
the scaly outbreak has spread on the skin, the priest
does not need to look for yellow hair; the person is
unclean. 37 But if as far as he can see, the scaly outbreak remains unchanged and black hair has grown
in it, then it has healed; he is clean. The priest is to
pronounce the person clean.

38 "When a man or a woman has white spots on
the skin of the body, 39 the priest is to make an examination. If the spots on the skin of the body are dull
white, it is only a rash[A] that has broken out on the
skin; the person is clean.

40 "If a man loses the hair of his head, he is bald,
but he is clean. 41 Or if he loses the hair at his hairline,
he is bald on his forehead, but he is clean. 42 But if
there is a reddish-white condition on the bald head
or forehead, it is a serious skin disease breaking out
on his head or forehead. 43 The priest is to examine
him, and if the swelling of the condition on his bald
head or forehead is reddish-white, like the appearance of a serious skin disease on his body, 44 the man
is afflicted with a serious skin disease; he is unclean.
The priest must pronounce him unclean; the infec-
tion is on his head.

45 "The person who has a case of serious skin disease is to have his clothes torn and his hair hanging
loose, and he must cover his mouth and cry out, 'Unclean, unclean!' 46 He will remain unclean as long as
he has the disease; he is unclean. He must live alone
in a place outside the camp.

CONTAMINATED FABRICS

47 "If a fabric is contaminated with mildew — in wool
or linen fabric, 48 in the warp or weft of linen or wool,
or in leather or anything made of leather — 49 and if
the contamination is green or red in the fabric, the
leather, the warp, the weft, or any leather article, it
is a mildew contamination and is to be shown to the
priest. 50 The priest is to examine the contamination
and quarantine the contaminated fabric for seven
days. 51 The priest is to reexamine the contamination
on the seventh day. If it has spread in the fabric, the
warp, the weft, or the leather, regardless of how
it is used, the contamination is harmful mildew; it
is unclean. 52 He is to burn the fabric, the warp or
weft in wool or linen, or any leather article, which
is contaminated. Since it is harmful mildew it must
be burned.

53 "When the priest examines it, if the contamination has not spread in the fabric, the warp or weft,
or any leather article, 54 the priest is to order whatever is contaminated to be washed and quarantined
for another seven days. 55 After it has been washed,
the priest is to reexamine the contamination. If the
appearance of the contaminated article has not
changed, it is unclean. Even though the contamination has not spread, you must burn the fabric. It is a
fungus[A] on the front or back of the fabric.

[A] 13:39,55 Hb obscure

56 "If the priest examines it, and the contamination has faded after it has been washed, he is to cut the contaminated section out of the fabric, the leather, or the warp or weft. 57 But if it reappears in the fabric, the warp or weft, or any leather article, it has broken out again. You must burn whatever is contaminated. 58 But if the contamination disappears from the fabric, the warp or weft, or any leather article, which have been washed, it is to be washed again, and it will be clean.

59 "This is the law concerning a mildew contamination in wool or linen fabric, warp or weft, or any leather article, in order to pronounce it clean or unclean."

CLEANSING OF SKIN DISEASES

14 The LORD spoke to Moses: 2 "This is the law concerning the person afflicted with a skin disease on the day of his cleansing. He is to be brought to the priest, 3 who will go outside the camp and examine him. If the skin disease has disappeared from the afflicted person,[A] 4 the priest will order that two live clean birds, cedar wood, scarlet yarn, and hyssop be brought for the one who is to be cleansed. 5 Then the priest will order that one of the birds be slaughtered over fresh water in a clay pot. 6 He is to take the live bird together with the cedar wood, scarlet yarn, and hyssop, and dip them all into the blood of the bird that was slaughtered over the fresh water. 7 He will then sprinkle the blood seven times on the one who is to be cleansed from the skin disease. He is to pronounce him clean and release the live bird over the open countryside. 8 The one who is to be cleansed must wash his clothes, shave off all his hair, and bathe with water; he is clean. Afterward he may enter the camp, but he must remain outside his tent for seven days. 9 He is to shave off all his hair again on the seventh day: his head, his beard, his eyebrows, and the rest of his hair. He is to wash his clothes and bathe himself with water; he is clean.

10 "On the eighth day he must take two unblemished male lambs, an unblemished year-old ewe lamb, a grain offering of six quarts[B] of fine flour mixed with olive oil, and one-third of a quart[C] of olive oil. 11 The priest who performs the cleansing will place the person who is to be cleansed, together with these offerings, before the LORD at the entrance to the tent of meeting. 12 The priest is to take one male lamb and present it as a guilt offering, along with the one-third quart of olive oil, and he will present them as a presentation offering before the LORD. 13 He is to slaughter the male lamb at the place in the sanctuary area where the sin offering and burnt offering are slaughtered, for like the sin offering, the guilt offering belongs to the priest; it is especially holy. 14 The priest is to take some of the blood from the guilt offering and put it on the lobe of the right ear of the one to be cleansed, on the thumb of his right hand, and on the big toe of his right foot. 15 Then the priest will take some of the one-third quart of olive oil and pour it into his left palm. 16 The priest will dip his right finger into the oil in his left palm and sprinkle some of the oil with his finger seven times before the LORD. 17 From the oil remaining in his palm the priest will put some on the lobe of the right ear of the one to be cleansed, on the thumb of his right hand, and on the big toe of his right foot, on top of the blood of the guilt offering. 18 What is left of the oil in the priest's palm he is to put on the head of the one to be cleansed. In this way the priest will make atonement for him before the LORD. 19 The priest is to sacrifice the sin offering and make atonement for the one to be cleansed from his uncleanness. Afterward he will slaughter the burnt offering. 20 The priest is to offer the burnt offering and the grain offering on the altar. The priest will make atonement for him, and he will be clean.

21 "But if he is poor and cannot afford these, he is to take one male lamb for a guilt offering to be presented in order to make atonement for him, along with two quarts[D] of fine flour mixed with olive oil for a grain offering, one-third of a quart of olive oil, 22 and two turtledoves or two young pigeons, whatever he can afford, one to be a sin offering and the other a burnt offering. 23 On the eighth day he is to bring these things for his cleansing to the priest at the entrance to the tent of meeting before the LORD. 24 The priest will take the male lamb for the guilt offering and the one-third quart of olive oil, and present them as a presentation offering before the LORD. 25 After he slaughters the male lamb for the guilt offering, the priest is to take some of the blood of the guilt offering and put it on the right earlobe of the one to be cleansed, on the thumb of his right hand, and on the big toe of his right foot. 26 Then the priest will pour some of the oil into his left palm. 27 With his right finger the priest will sprinkle some of the oil in his left palm seven times before the LORD. 28 The priest will also put some of the oil in his palm on the right earlobe of the one to be cleansed, on the thumb of his right hand, and on the big toe of his right foot, on the same place as the blood of the guilt offering. 29 What is left of the oil in the priest's palm he is to put on the head of the one to be cleansed to make atonement for him before the LORD. 30 He is to then sacrifice one type of what he can afford, either the turtledoves or young pigeons, 31 one as a sin offering

[A] **14:3** Lit *the person afflicted with skin disease* [B] **14:10** Lit *three-tenths*; probably three-tenths of an ephah [C] **14:10** Lit *one log*, also in vv. 12,15,21,24 [D] **14:21** Lit *him, and one-tenth*; probably one-tenth of an ephah

and the other as a burnt offering, sacrificing what he can afford together with the grain offering. In this way the priest will make atonement before the LORD for the one to be cleansed. 32 This is the law for someone who has[A] a skin disease and cannot afford the cost of his cleansing."

CLEANSING OF CONTAMINATED OBJECTS

33 The LORD spoke to Moses and Aaron: 34 "When you enter the land of Canaan that I am giving you as a possession, and I place a mildew contamination in a house in the land you possess,[B] 35 the owner of the house is to come and tell the priest: Something like mildew contamination has appeared[C] in my house. 36 The priest must order them to clear the house before he enters to examine the contamination, so that nothing in the house becomes unclean. Afterward the priest will come to examine the house. 37 He will examine it, and if the contamination in the walls of the house consists of green or red indentations[D] that appear to be beneath the surface of the wall, 38 the priest is to go outside the house to its doorway and quarantine the house for seven days. 39 The priest is to return on the seventh day and examine it. If the contamination has spread on the walls of the house, 40 the priest must order that the stones with the contamination be pulled out and thrown into an unclean place outside the city. 41 He is to have the inside of the house completely scraped, and have the plaster[E] that is scraped off dumped in an unclean place outside the city. 42 Then they are to take different stones to replace the former ones and take additional plaster to replaster the house.

43 "If the contamination reappears in the house after the stones have been pulled out, and after the house has been scraped and replastered, 44 the priest is to come and examine it. If the contamination has spread in the house, it is harmful mildew; the house is unclean. 45 It must be torn down with its stones, its beams, and all its plaster, and taken outside the city to an unclean place. 46 Whoever enters the house during any of the days the priest quarantines it will be unclean until evening. 47 Whoever lies down in the house is to wash his clothes, and whoever eats in it is to wash his clothes.

48 "But when the priest comes and examines it, if the contamination has not spread in the house after it was replastered, he is to pronounce the house clean because the contamination has disappeared.[F] 49 He is to take two birds, cedar wood, scarlet yarn, and hyssop to purify the house, 50 and he is to slaughter one of the birds over a clay pot containing fresh water. 51 He will take the cedar wood, the hyssop, the scarlet yarn, and the live bird, dip them in the blood of the slaughtered bird and the fresh water, and sprinkle the house seven times. 52 He will purify the house with the blood of the bird, the fresh water, the live bird, the cedar wood, the hyssop, and the scarlet yarn. 53 Then he is to release the live bird into the open countryside outside the city. In this way he will make atonement for the house, and it will be clean.

54 "This is the law for any skin disease or mildew, for a scaly outbreak, 55 for mildew in clothing or on a house, 56 and for a swelling, scab, or spot, 57 to determine when something is unclean or clean. This is the law regarding skin disease and mildew."

BODILY DISCHARGES

15 The LORD spoke to Moses and Aaron: 2 "Speak to the Israelites and tell them: When any man has a discharge from his member, he is unclean. 3 This is uncleanness of his discharge: Whether his member secretes the discharge or retains it, he is unclean. All the days that his member secretes or retains anything because of his discharge,[G] he is unclean. 4 Any bed the man with the discharge lies on will be unclean, and any furniture he sits on will be unclean. 5 Anyone who touches his bed is to wash his clothes and bathe with water, and he will remain unclean until evening. 6 Whoever sits on furniture that the man with the discharge was sitting on is to wash his clothes and bathe with water, and he will remain unclean until evening. 7 Whoever touches the body[H] of the man with a discharge is to wash his clothes and bathe with water, and he will remain unclean until evening. 8 If the man with the discharge spits on anyone who is clean, he is to wash his clothes and bathe with water, and he will remain unclean until evening. 9 Any saddle the man with the discharge rides on will be unclean. 10 Whoever touches anything that was under him will be unclean until evening, and whoever carries such things is to wash his clothes and bathe with water, and he will remain unclean until evening. 11 If the man with the discharge touches anyone without first rinsing his hands in water, the person who was touched is to wash his clothes and bathe with water, and he will remain unclean until evening. 12 Any clay pot that the man with the discharge touches must be broken, while any wooden utensil is to be rinsed with water.

13 "When the man with the discharge has been cured of it, he is to count seven days for his cleansing, wash his clothes, and bathe his body in fresh water; he will be clean. 14 He must take two turtledoves or two young pigeons on the eighth day, come before the LORD at the entrance to the tent of meeting, and

[A] **14:32** Lit *someone on whom there is* [B] **14:34** Lit *land of your possession* [C] **14:35** Lit *appeared to me* [D] **14:37** Or *eruptions*; Hb obscure [E] **14:41** Lit *dust*, also in v. 42 [F] **14:48** Lit *healed* [G] **15:3** DSS, Sam, LXX; MT omits *he is unclean. All the days that his member secretes or retains anything because of his discharge* [H] **15:7** Or *member*, also in v. 13

RURAL LIFE

The Tall al-'Umayri excavation is part of a larger regional survey and excavation project, the Madaba Plains Project. Comprehensive projects such as this provide us with information about culture, economy, food systems, and environment over a wide geographic area. Unlike excavations that focus on the more urban environments (those often discussed in the biblical text), regional projects let us see a more rural world. Regional projects have shown that more than 80 percent of ancient people lived in rural situations: small towns, villages, and farmsteads. Theirs was a rural agricultural world dependent on the environment; cities were the exception. This knowledge enables us to reconstruct the world of the Bible much more clearly. We begin to see a world quite different from our modern one. With this, not only can we understand the historical narratives more fully, but also we appreciate more acutely the biblical concerns for land ownership (Lv 25; Is 5:8; Mc 2:2) and the depths of faith expressed by Habakkuk (3:17–18).

CITY SIZE

People are surprised to find that almost all cities and villages in the biblical world were so small. 'Umayri illustrates this as well. The Iron Age I (1200–1000 BC) site was only about six acres and probably held fewer than 750 people. The site had an even smaller population during Iron Age II (1000–800) and did not become important again until Iron Age III and into the Babylonian and Persian I eras (800–450 BC) and thus was always small in both area and population.

Cities throughout the Old Testament times likewise were relatively small. They rarely reached 20 acres. Even Jerusalem, at its greatest extent during Jeremiah's day, was only about 125 acres with probably around 25,000 people. Compare that to what you think of when you read "city" in the biblical text. We certainly gain a new appreciation of the Old Testament texts when we resize our views of "cities." Even so, the vast majority of people lived in villages smaller than two acres with populations of fewer than 350 people, usually all related by blood or marriage.

HOUSING AND FAMILY

At the smallest, most foundational level of society, the family, archaeology provides insights. The so-called four-room or pillared house was the most common type of housing unit in Israelite territory during the Iron Age. Excavations at 'Umayri have produced an important example of this two-story structure.

Animals occupied some of the first floor (consider Jephthah's vow in this light, Jdg 11:30–31), while people dwelled on the second floor and roof (Jos 2:8). In these "households," people usually lived with their larger family, the biblical "father's house" (Gn 38:11; Nm 30:3). Each structure probably housed three generations, a man and his wife (or wives) with a couple of adult sons and their wives and children. Often two or three dwellings were joined together as an extended family compound, in which family members could share both labor and benefits. The artifacts themselves establish the types and locations of work activities within the house. These included food preparation, storage, and serving, obviously essential aspects of the household. Archaeologists have also uncovered evidence of textile production, spinning, sewing, and weaving. These finds, which represent the most foundational elements of social and economic organization, certainly illustrate the "noble" wife of Proverbs 31. From the storage vessels unearthed, we understand the nature of the inhabitants' subsistence agricultural economy; they produced and stored enough for their family with little to spare. Finally, the 'Umayri house provides an example of a household shrine, thus giving us knowledge regarding local religious customs (see Micah's household in Jdg 17–18). ❖

Excavation work being conducted at Tall al-Umayri, which is located southwest of Amman, Jordan. The site covered about six acres during Iron Age I (1200–1000 BC).

give them to the priest. 15 The priest is to sacrifice them, one as a sin offering and the other as a burnt offering. In this way the priest will make atonement for him before the LORD because of his discharge.

16 "When a man has an emission of semen, he is to bathe himself completely with water, and he will remain unclean until evening. 17 Any clothing or leather on which there is an emission of semen is to be washed with water, and it will remain unclean until evening. 18 If a man sleeps with a woman and has an emission of semen, both of them are to bathe with water, and they will remain unclean until evening.

19 "When a woman has a discharge, and it consists of blood from her body, she will be unclean because of her menstruation for seven days. Everyone who touches her will be unclean until evening. 20 Anything she lies on during her menstruation will become unclean, and anything she sits on will become unclean. 21 Everyone who touches her bed is to wash his clothes and bathe with water, and he will remain unclean until evening. 22 Everyone who touches any furniture she was sitting on is to wash his clothes and bathe with water, and he will remain unclean until evening. 23 If discharge is on the bed or the furniture she was sitting on, when he touches it he will be unclean until evening. 24 If a man sleeps with her, and blood from her menstruation gets on him, he will be unclean for seven days, and every bed he lies on will become unclean.

25 "When a woman has a discharge of her blood for many days, though it is not the time of her menstruation, or if she has a discharge beyond her period, she will be unclean all the days of her unclean discharge, as she is during the days of her menstruation. 26 Any bed she lies on during the days of her discharge will be like her bed during menstrual impurity; any furniture she sits on will be unclean as in her menstrual period. 27 Everyone who touches them will be unclean; he must wash his clothes and bathe with water, and he will remain unclean until evening. 28 When she is cured of her discharge, she is to count seven days, and after that she will be clean. 29 On the eighth day she must take two turtledoves or two young pigeons and bring them to the priest at the entrance to the tent of meeting. 30 The priest is to sacrifice one as a sin offering and the other as a burnt offering. In this way the priest will make atonement for her before the LORD because of her unclean discharge.

31 "You must keep the Israelites from their uncleanness, so that they do not die by defiling my tabernacle that is among them. 32 This is the law for someone with a discharge: a man who has an emission of semen, becoming unclean by it; 33 a woman who is in her menstrual period; anyone who has a discharge, whether male or female; and a man who sleeps with a woman who is unclean."

THE DAY OF ATONEMENT

16 The LORD spoke to Moses after the death of two of Aaron's sons when they approached the presence of[A] the LORD and died. 2 The LORD said to Moses, "Tell your brother Aaron that he may not come whenever he wants into the holy place behind the curtain in front of the mercy seat on the ark or else he will die, because I appear in the cloud above the mercy seat.

3 "Aaron is to enter the most holy place in this way: with a young bull for a sin offering and a ram for a burnt offering. 4 He is to wear a holy linen tunic, and linen undergarments are to be on his body. He is to tie a linen sash around him and wrap his head with a linen turban. These are holy garments; he must bathe his body with water before he wears them. 5 He is to take from the Israelite community two male goats for a sin offering and one ram for a burnt offering.

6 "Aaron will present the bull for his sin offering and make atonement for himself and his household. 7 Next he will take the two goats and place them before the LORD at the entrance to the tent of meeting. 8 After Aaron casts lots for the two goats, one lot for the LORD and the other for an uninhabitable place,[B,C] 9 he is to present the goat chosen by lot for the LORD and sacrifice it as a sin offering. 10 But the goat chosen by lot for an uninhabitable place is to be presented alive before the LORD to make atonement with it by sending it into the wilderness for an uninhabitable place.

11 "When Aaron presents the bull for his sin offering and makes atonement for himself and his household, he will slaughter the bull for his sin offering. 12 Then he is to take a firepan full of blazing coals from the altar before the LORD and two handfuls of finely ground fragrant incense, and bring them inside the curtain. 13 He is to put the incense on the fire before the LORD, so that the cloud of incense covers the mercy seat that is over the testimony, or else he will die. 14 He is to take some of the bull's blood and sprinkle it with his finger against the east side of the mercy seat; then he will sprinkle some of the blood with his finger before the mercy seat seven times.

15 "When he slaughters the male goat for the people's sin offering and brings its blood inside the curtain, he will do the same with its blood as he did with the bull's blood: He is to sprinkle it against the mercy seat and in front of it. 16 He will make atonement for the most holy place in this way for all their sins because of the Israelites' impurities and rebellious acts.

[A] **16:1** LXX, Tg, Syr, Vg read *they brought strange fire before*; Nm 3:4
[B] **16:8** Lit *for Azazel*, also in vv. 10 (2x),26 [C] **16:8** Traditionally "for the scapegoat"; perhaps a term that means "for the goat that departs," or "for removal," or "for a rough, difficult place," or "for a goat-demon"; Hb obscure, also in vv. 10,26

He will do the same for the tent of meeting that remains among them, because it is surrounded by their impurities. 17 No one may be in the tent of meeting from the time he enters to make atonement in the most holy place until he leaves after he has made atonement for himself, his household, and the whole assembly of Israel. 18 Then he will go out to the altar that is before the LORD and make atonement for it. He is to take some of the bull's blood and some of the goat's blood and put it on the horns on all sides of the altar. 19 He is to sprinkle some of the blood on it with his finger seven times to cleanse and set it apart from the Israelites' impurities.

20 "When he has finished making atonement for the most holy place, the tent of meeting, and the altar, he is to present the live male goat. 21 Aaron will lay both his hands on the head of the live goat and confess over it all the Israelites' iniquities and rebellious acts — all their sins. He is to put them on the goat's head and send it away into the wilderness by the man appointed for the task.[A] 22 The goat will carry all their iniquities into a desolate land, and the man will release it there.

23 "Then Aaron is to enter the tent of meeting, take off the linen garments he wore when he entered the most holy place, and leave them there. 24 He will bathe his body with water in a holy place and put on his clothes. Then he must go out and sacrifice his burnt offering and the people's burnt offering; he will make atonement for himself and for the people. 25 He is to burn the fat of the sin offering on the altar. 26 The man who released the goat for an uninhabitable place is to wash his clothes and bathe his body with water; afterward he may reenter the camp. 27 The bull for the sin offering and the goat for the sin offering, whose blood was brought into the most holy place to make atonement, must be brought outside the camp and their hide, flesh, and waste burned. 28 The one who burns them is to wash his clothes and bathe himself with water; afterward he may reenter the camp.

29 "This is to be a permanent statute for you: In the seventh month, on the tenth day of the month you are to practice self-denial and do no work, both the native and the alien who resides among you. 30 Atonement will be made for you on this day to cleanse you, and you will be clean from all your sins before the LORD. 31 It is a Sabbath of complete rest for you, and you must practice self-denial; it is a permanent statute. 32 The priest who is anointed and ordained[B] to serve as high priest in place of his father will make atonement. He will put on the linen garments, the holy garments, 33 and make atonement for the most holy place. He will make atonement for the tent of meeting and the altar and will make atonement for the priests and all the people of the assembly. 34 This is to be a permanent statute for you, to make atonement for the Israelites once a year because of all their sins." And all this was done as the LORD commanded Moses.

FORBIDDEN SACRIFICES

17 The LORD spoke to Moses: 2 "Speak to Aaron, his sons, and all the Israelites and tell them: This is what the LORD has commanded: 3 Anyone from the house of Israel who slaughters an ox, sheep, or goat in the camp, or slaughters it outside the camp, 4 instead of bringing it to the entrance to the tent of meeting to present it as an offering to the LORD before his tabernacle — that person will be considered guilty.[C] He has shed blood and is to be cut off from his people. 5 This is so the Israelites will bring to the LORD the sacrifices they have been offering in the open country. They are to bring them to the priest at the entrance to the tent of meeting and offer them as fellowship sacrifices to the LORD. 6 The priest will then splatter the blood on the LORD's altar at the entrance to the tent of meeting and burn the fat as a pleasing aroma to the LORD. 7 They must no longer offer their sacrifices to the goat-demons that they have prostituted themselves with. This will be a permanent statute for them throughout their generations.

8 "Say to them: Anyone from the house of Israel or from the aliens who reside among them who offers a burnt offering or a sacrifice 9 but does not bring it to the entrance to the tent of meeting to sacrifice it to the LORD, that person is to be cut off from his people.

EATING BLOOD AND CARCASSES PROHIBITED

10 "Anyone from the house of Israel or from the aliens who reside among them who eats any blood, I will turn[D] against that person who eats blood and cut him off from his people. 11 For the life of a creature is in the blood, and I have appointed it to you to make atonement on the altar for[E] your lives, since it is the lifeblood that makes atonement. 12 Therefore I say to the Israelites: None of you and no alien who resides among you may eat blood.

13 "Any Israelite or alien residing among them, who hunts down a wild animal or bird that may be eaten must drain its blood and cover it with dirt. 14 Since the life of every creature is its blood, I have told the Israelites: You are not to eat the blood of any creature, because the life of every creature is its blood; whoever eats it must be cut off.

15 "Every person, whether the native or the resident alien, who eats an animal that died a natural death or was mauled by wild beasts is to wash his clothes and bathe with water, and he will remain unclean

[A] **16:21** Lit *wilderness in the hand of a ready man* [B] **16:32** Lit *and will fill his hand* [C] **17:4** Lit *tabernacle — blood will be charged against that person* [D] **17:10** Lit *will set my face* [E] **17:11** Or *to ransom*

until evening; then he will be clean. 16 But if he does not wash his clothes and bathe himself, he will bear his iniquity."

PROHIBITED PAGAN PRACTICES

18 The LORD spoke to Moses: 2 "Speak to the Israelites and tell them: I am the LORD your God. 3 Do not follow the practices of the land of Egypt, where you used to live, or follow the practices of the land of Canaan, where I am bringing you. You must not follow their customs. 4 You are to practice my ordinances and you are to keep my statutes by following them; I am the LORD your God. 5 Keep my statutes and ordinances; a person will live if he does them. I am the LORD.

6 "You are not to come near any close relative[A] for sexual intercourse; I am the LORD. 7 You are not to violate the intimacy that belongs to your father and mother.[B] She is your mother; you must not have sexual intercourse with her. 8 You are not to have sex with your father's wife; she is your father's family. 9 You are not to have sexual intercourse with your sister, either your father's daughter or your mother's, whether born at home or born elsewhere. You are not to have sex with her. 10 You are not to have sexual intercourse with your son's daughter or your daughter's daughter, for they are your family.[C] 11 You are not to have sexual intercourse with your father's wife's daughter, who is adopted by[D] your father; she is your sister. 12 You are not to have sexual intercourse with your father's sister; she is your father's close relative. 13 You are not to have sexual intercourse with your mother's sister, for she is your mother's close relative. 14 You are not to violate the intimacy that belongs to[E] your father's brother by approaching his wife to have sexual intercourse; she is your aunt. 15 You are not to have sexual intercourse with your daughter-in-law. She is your son's wife; you are not to have sex with her. 16 You are not to have sexual intercourse with your brother's wife; she is your brother's family. 17 You are not to have sexual intercourse with a woman and her daughter. You are not to marry her son's daughter or her daughter's daughter and have sex with her. They are close relatives; it is depraved. 18 You are not to marry a woman as a rival to her sister and have sexual intercourse with her during her sister's lifetime.

19 "You are not to approach a woman during her menstrual impurity to have sexual intercourse with her. 20 You are not to have sexual intercourse with[F] your neighbor's wife, defiling yourself with her.

21 "You are not to sacrifice any of your children in the fire[G] to Molech. Do not profane the name of your God; I am the LORD. 22 You are not to sleep with a man as with a woman; it is detestable. 23 You are not to have sexual intercourse with[H] any animal, defiling yourself with it; a woman is not to present herself to an animal to mate with it; it is a perversion.

24 "Do not defile yourselves by any of these practices, for the nations I am driving out before you have defiled themselves by all these things. 25 The land has become defiled, so I am punishing it for its iniquity, and the land will vomit out its inhabitants. 26 But you are to keep my statutes and ordinances. You must not commit any of these detestable acts — not the native or the alien who resides among you. 27 For the people who were in the land prior to you have committed all these detestable acts, and the land has become defiled. 28 If you defile the land, it will vomit you out as it has vomited out the nations that were before you. 29 Any person who does any of these detestable practices is to be cut off from his people. 30 You must keep my instruction to not do any of the detestable customs that were practiced before you, so that you do not defile yourselves by them; I am the LORD your God."

LAWS OF HOLINESS

19 The LORD spoke to Moses: 2 "Speak to the entire Israelite community and tell them: Be holy because I, the LORD your God, am holy.

3 "Each of you is to respect his mother and father. You are to keep my Sabbaths; I am the LORD your God. 4 Do not turn to worthless idols or make cast images of gods for yourselves; I am the LORD your God.

5 "When you offer a fellowship sacrifice to the LORD, sacrifice it so that you may be accepted. 6 It is to be eaten on the day you sacrifice it or on the next day, but what remains on the third day must be burned. 7 If any is eaten on the third day, it is a repulsive thing; it will not be accepted. 8 Anyone who eats it will bear his iniquity, for he has profaned what is holy to the LORD. That person is to be cut off from his people.

9 "When you reap the harvest of your land, you are not to reap to the very edge of your field or gather the gleanings of your harvest. 10 Do not strip your vineyard bare or gather its fallen grapes. Leave them for the poor and the resident alien; I am the LORD your God.

11 "Do not steal. Do not act deceptively or lie to one another. 12 Do not swear falsely by my name, profaning the name of your God; I am the LORD.

13 "Do not oppress your neighbor or rob him. The wages due a hired worker must not remain with you

[A] **18:6** Lit *any flesh of his flesh* [B] **18:7** Lit *Do not uncover your father's nakedness and your mother's nakedness* [C] **18:10** Lit *because they are your nakedness* [D] **18:11** Lit *daughter, a relative of* [E] **18:14** Lit *Do not uncover the nakedness of* [F] **18:20** Lit *to give your emission of semen to* [G] **18:21** Lit *to make any of your children pass through the fire* [H] **18:23** Lit *to give your emission to*

until morning. 14 Do not curse the deaf or put a stumbling block in front of the blind, but you are to fear your God; I am the LORD.

15 "Do not act unjustly when deciding a case. Do not be partial to the poor or give preference to the rich; judge your neighbor fairly. 16 Do not go about spreading slander among your people; do not jeopardize[A] your neighbor's life; I am the LORD.

17 "Do not harbor hatred against your brother.[B] Rebuke your neighbor directly, and you will not incur guilt because of him. 18 Do not take revenge or bear a grudge against members of your community, but love your neighbor as yourself; I am the LORD.

19 "You are to keep my statutes. Do not crossbreed two different kinds of your livestock, sow your fields with two kinds of seed, or put on a garment made of two kinds of material.

20 "If a man has sexual intercourse with a woman who is a slave designated for another man, but she has not been redeemed or given her freedom, there must be punishment.[C] They are not to be put to death, because she had not been freed. 21 However, he must bring a ram as his guilt[D] offering to the LORD at the entrance to the tent of meeting. 22 The priest will make atonement on his behalf before the LORD with the ram of the guilt offering for the sin he has committed, and he will be forgiven for the sin he committed.

23 "When you come into the land and plant any kind of tree for food, you are to consider the fruit forbidden.[E] It will be forbidden to you for three years; it is not to be eaten. 24 In the fourth year all its fruit is to be consecrated as a praise offering to the LORD. 25 But in the fifth year you may eat its fruit. In this way its yield will increase for you; I am the LORD your God.

26 "You are not to eat anything with blood in it.[F] You are not to practice divination or witchcraft. 27 You are not to cut off the hair at the sides of your head or mar the edge of your beard. 28 You are not to make gashes on your bodies for the dead or put tattoo marks on yourselves; I am the LORD.

29 "Do not debase[G] your daughter by making her a prostitute, or the land will be prostituted and filled with depravity. 30 Keep my Sabbaths and revere my sanctuary; I am the LORD.

31 "Do not turn to mediums[H] or consult spiritists,[I] or you will be defiled by them; I am the LORD your God.

32 "You are to rise in the presence of the elderly and honor the old. Fear your God; I am the LORD.

33 "When an alien resides with you in your land, you must not oppress him. 34 You will regard the alien who resides with you as the native-born among you. You are to love him as yourself, for you were aliens in the land of Egypt; I am the LORD your God.

35 "Do not be unfair in measurements of length, weight, or volume. 36 You are to have honest balances, honest weights, an honest dry measure,[J] and an honest liquid measure;[K] I am the LORD your God, who brought you out of the land of Egypt. 37 Keep all my statutes and all my ordinances and do them; I am the LORD."

MOLECH WORSHIP AND SPIRITISM

20 The LORD spoke to Moses: 2 "Say to the Israelites: Any Israelite or alien residing in Israel who gives any of his children to Molech must be put to death; the people of the country are to stone him. 3 I will turn[L] against that man and cut him off from his people, because he gave his offspring to Molech, defiling my sanctuary and profaning my holy name. 4 But if the people of the country look the other way when that man[M] gives any of his children to Molech, and do not put him to death, 5 then I will turn against that man and his family, and cut off from their people both him and all who follow[N] him in prostituting themselves with Molech.

6 "Whoever turns to mediums[H] or spiritists[I] and prostitutes himself with them, I will turn against that person and cut him off from his people. 7 Consecrate yourselves and be holy, for I am the LORD your God. 8 Keep my statutes and do them; I am the LORD who sets you apart.

FAMILY AND SEXUAL OFFENSES

9 "If anyone curses his father or mother, he must be put to death. He has cursed his father or mother; his death is his own fault.[O]

10 "If a man commits adultery with a married woman — if he commits adultery with his neighbor's wife — both the adulterer and the adulteress must be put to death. 11 If a man sleeps with his father's wife, he has violated the intimacy that belongs to his father.[P] Both of them must be put to death; their death is their own fault.[Q] 12 If a man sleeps with his daughter-in-law, both of them must be put to death. They have acted perversely; their death is their own fault. 13 If a man sleeps with a man as with a woman, they have both committed a detestable act. They must be put to death; their death is their own fault. 14 If a man marries[R] a woman and her mother, it is depraved. Both he and they must be burned, so that there will be no depravity among you. 15 If a man has sexual intercourse with[S]

[A] **19:16** Lit *not stand against* [B] **19:17** Or *your fellow Israelite* [C] **19:20** Or *compensation* [D] **19:21** Or *restitution* [E] **19:23** Lit *uncircumcised* [F] **19:26** Or *anything over its blood* [G] **19:29** Lit *profane* [H] **19:31; 20:6** Or *spirits of the dead* [I] **19:31; 20:6** Or *familiar spirits* [J] **19:36** Lit *honest ephah* [K] **19:36** Lit *honest hin* [L] **20:3** Lit *will set my face*, also in vv. 5,6 [M] **20:4** Lit *country ever close their eyes from that man when he* [N] **20:5** Lit *prostitute themselves with* [O] **20:9** Lit *his blood on him* [P] **20:11** Lit *has uncovered his father's nakedness* [Q] **20:11** Lit *their blood on them*, also in vv. 12,13,16,27 [R] **20:14** Lit *takes*, also in vv. 17,21 [S] **20:15** Lit *man gives his emission to* an animal, he must be put to death; you are also to kill the animal. 16 If a woman approaches any animal and mates with it, you are to kill the woman and the animal. They must be put to death; their death is their own fault. 17 If a man marries his sister, whether his father's daughter or his mother's daughter, and they have sexual relations,[A] it is a disgrace. They are to be cut off publicly from their people. He has had sexual intercourse with his sister; he will bear his iniquity. 18 If a man sleeps with a menstruating woman and has sexual intercourse with her, he has exposed the source of her flow, and she has uncovered the source of her blood. Both of them are to be cut off from their people. 19 You must not have sexual intercourse with your mother's sister or your father's sister, for it is exposing one's own blood relative; both people will bear their iniquity. 20 If a man sleeps with his aunt, he has violated the intimacy that belongs to his uncle;[B] they will bear their guilt and die childless. 21 If a man marries his brother's wife, it is impurity. He has violated the intimacy that belongs to his brother;[C] they will be childless.

HOLINESS IN THE LAND

22 "You are to keep all my statutes and all my ordinances, and do them, so that the land where I am bringing you to live will not vomit you out. 23 You must not follow the statutes of the nations I am driving out before you, for they did all these things, and I abhorred them. 24 And I promised you: You will inherit their land, since I will give it to you to possess, a land flowing with milk and honey. I am the LORD your God who set you apart from the peoples. 25 Therefore you are to distinguish the clean animal from the unclean one, and the unclean bird from the clean one. Do not become contaminated by any land animal, bird, or whatever crawls on the ground; I have set these apart as unclean for you. 26 You are to be holy to me because I, the LORD, am holy, and I have set you apart from the nations to be mine.

27 "A man or a woman who is[D] a medium or a spiritist must be put to death. They are to be stoned; their death is their own fault."

THE HOLINESS OF THE PRIESTS

21 The LORD said to Moses, "Speak to Aaron's sons, the priests, and tell them: A priest is not to make himself ceremonially unclean for a dead person among his relatives, 2 except for his immediate family: his mother, father, son, daughter, or brother. 3 He may make himself unclean for his unmarried virgin sister in his immediate family. 4 He is not to make himself unclean for those related to him by marriage[E] and so defile himself.

5 "Priests may not make bald spots on their heads, shave the edge of their beards, or make gashes on their bodies. 6 They are to be holy to their God and not profane the name of their God. For they present the food offerings to the LORD, the food of their God, and they must be holy. 7 They are not to marry a woman defiled by prostitution.[F] They are not to marry one divorced by her husband, for the priest is holy to his God. 8 You are to consider him holy since he presents the food of your God. He will be holy to you because I, the LORD who sets you apart, am holy. 9 If a priest's daughter defiles herself by promiscuity,[G] she defiles her father; she must be burned to death.

10 "The priest who is highest among his brothers, who has had the anointing oil poured on his head and has been ordained[H] to wear the clothes, must not dishevel his hair[I] or tear his clothes. 11 He must not go near any dead person or make himself unclean even for his father or mother. 12 He must not leave the sanctuary or he will desecrate the sanctuary of his God, for the consecration of the anointing oil of his God is on him; I am the LORD.

13 "He is to marry a woman who is a virgin. 14 He is not to marry a widow, a divorced woman, or one defiled by prostitution. He is to marry a virgin from his own people, 15 so that he does not corrupt his bloodline[J] among his people, for I am the LORD who sets him apart."

PHYSICAL DEFECTS AND PRIESTS

16 The LORD spoke to Moses: 17 "Tell Aaron: None of your descendants throughout your generations who has a physical defect is to come near to present the food of his God. 18 No man who has any defect is to come near: no man who is blind, lame, facially disfigured, or deformed; 19 no man who has a broken foot or hand, 20 or who is a hunchback or a dwarf,[K] or who has an eye defect, a festering rash, scabs, or a crushed testicle. 21 No descendant of the priest Aaron who has a defect is to come near to present the food offerings to the LORD. He has a defect and is not to come near to present the food of his God. 22 He may eat the food of his God from what is especially holy as well as from what is holy. 23 But because he has a defect, he must not go near the curtain or approach the altar. He is not to desecrate my holy places, for I am the LORD who sets them apart." 24 Moses said this to Aaron and his sons and to all the Israelites.

[A] **20:17** Lit *and he sees her nakedness and she sees his nakedness*
[B] **20:20** Lit *has uncovered his uncle's nakedness* [C] **20:21** Lit *has uncovered his brother's nakedness* [D] **20:27** Lit *is in them* [E] **21:4** Lit *unclean a husband among his people* [F] **21:7** Or *a prostitute, or a defiled woman*
[G] **21:9** Or *prostitution* [H] **21:10** Lit *and one has filled his hand*
[I] **21:10** Or *not uncover his head* [J] **21:15** Lit *not profane his seed*
[K] **21:20** Or *or emaciated*

PRIESTS AND THEIR FOOD

22 The LORD spoke to Moses: 2 "Tell Aaron and his sons to deal respectfully with the holy offerings of the Israelites that they have consecrated to me, so they do not profane my holy name; I am the LORD. 3 Say to them: If any man from any of your descendants throughout your generations is in a state of uncleanness yet approaches the holy offerings that the Israelites consecrate to the LORD, that person will be cut off from my presence; I am the LORD. 4 No man of Aaron's descendants who has a skin disease[A] or a discharge is to eat from the holy offerings until he is clean. Whoever touches anything made unclean by a dead person or by a man who has an emission of semen, 5 or whoever touches any swarming creature that makes him unclean or any person who makes him unclean — whatever his uncleanness — 6 the man who touches any of these will remain unclean until evening and is not to eat from the holy offerings unless he has bathed his body with water. 7 When the sun has set, he will become clean, and then he may eat from the holy offerings, for that is his food. 8 He must not eat an animal that died naturally or was mauled by wild beasts,[B] making himself unclean by it; I am the LORD. 9 They must keep my instruction, or they will be guilty and die because they profane it; I am the LORD who sets them apart.

10 "No one outside a priest's family[C] is to eat the holy offering. A foreigner staying with a priest or a hired worker is not to eat the holy offering. 11 But if a priest purchases someone with his own silver, that person may eat it, and those born in his house may eat his food. 12 If the priest's daughter is married to a man outside a priest's family,[D] she is not to eat from the holy contributions.[E] 13 But if the priest's daughter becomes widowed or divorced, has no children, and returns to her father's house as in her youth, she may share her father's food. But no outsider may share it. 14 If anyone eats a holy offering in error, he is to add a fifth to its value and give the holy offering to the priest. 15 The priests must not profane the holy offerings the Israelites give to the LORD 16 by letting the people eat their holy offerings and having them bear the penalty of restitution. For I am the LORD who sets them apart."

ACCEPTABLE SACRIFICES

17 The LORD spoke to Moses: 18 "Speak to Aaron, his sons, and all the Israelites and tell them: Any man of the house of Israel or of the resident aliens in Israel who presents his offering — whether they present payment of vows or freewill gifts to the LORD as burnt offerings — 19 must offer an unblemished male from the cattle, sheep, or goats in order for you to be accepted. 20 You are not to present anything that has a defect, because it will not be accepted on your behalf.

21 "When a man presents a fellowship sacrifice to the LORD to fulfill a vow or as a freewill offering from the herd or flock, it has to be unblemished to be acceptable; there must be no defect in it. 22 You are not to present any animal to the LORD that is blind, injured, maimed, or has a running sore, festering rash, or scabs; you may not put any of them on the altar as a food offering to the LORD. 23 You may sacrifice as a freewill offering any animal from the herd or flock that has an elongated or stunted limb, but it is not acceptable as a vow offering. 24 You are not to present to the LORD anything that has bruised, crushed, torn, or severed testicles; you must not sacrifice them in your land. 25 Neither you nor[F] a foreigner are to present food to your God from any of these animals. They will not be accepted for you because they are deformed and have a defect."

26 The LORD spoke to Moses: 27 "When an ox, sheep, or goat is born, it is to remain with[G] its mother for seven days; from the eighth day on, it will be acceptable as an offering, a food offering to the LORD. 28 But you are not to slaughter an animal from the herd or flock on the same day as its young. 29 When you offer a thanksgiving sacrifice to the LORD, offer it so that you may be accepted. 30 It is to be eaten on the same day. Do not let any of it remain until morning; I am the LORD.

31 "You are to keep my commands and do them; I am the LORD. 32 You must not profane my holy name; I must be treated as holy among the Israelites. I am the LORD who sets you apart, 33 the one who brought you out of the land of Egypt to be your God; I am the LORD."

HOLY DAYS

23 The LORD spoke to Moses: 2 "Speak to the Israelites and tell them: These are my appointed times, the times of the LORD that you will proclaim as sacred assemblies.

3 "Work may be done for six days, but on the seventh day there is to be a Sabbath of complete rest, a sacred assembly. You are not to do any work; it is a Sabbath to the LORD wherever you live.

4 "These are the LORD's appointed times, the sacred assemblies you are to proclaim at their appointed times. 5 The Passover to the LORD comes in the first month, at twilight on the fourteenth day of the month. 6 The Festival of Unleavened Bread to the LORD is on the fifteenth day of the same month. For seven days you must eat unleavened bread. 7 On the first day you are to hold a sacred assembly; you are not to do any daily work. 8 You are to present a food offering to the LORD for seven days. On the seventh day there will be a sacred assembly; do not do any daily work."

[A] **22:4** Or *has leprosy* or *scale disease* [B] **22:8** Lit *eat a carcass or a mauled beast* [C] **22:10** Lit *"No stranger* [D] **22:12** Lit *to a stranger* [E] **22:12** Lit *the contribution of holy offerings* [F] **22:25** Lit *nor from the hand of* [G] **22:27** Lit *under*

by Joel F. Drinkard Jr.

CLEAN AND UNCLEAN ANIMALS

Clean animals were basically ones that could be eaten and were acceptable as sacrifices. Clearly, domesticated animals (sheep, goats, cattle) could be eaten, but scavengers and predators were forbidden possibly because they shed blood or ate blood. Persons rarely consumed meat during the biblical period; they reserved it for special occasions (see Gn 18:1–8; Lk 15:11–32). The archaeological record provides some limited evidence that the Israelites followed these regulations. The study of animal bones recovered from archaeological excavations shows pig bones are entirely lacking or amazingly rare at Israelite sites but are much more common in non-Israelite sites such as Philistine sites. This evidence supports Israelite avoidance of "unclean" pigs (Lv 11:7).

HYGIENE

Several texts mention washing the body or parts of the body. Since most people in the biblical period walked barefooted or wore sandals, their feet regularly got dirty. Most of the population in ancient Israel lived without bathrooms, which led my former teacher to write concerning an early Israelite house he had excavated at Khirbet Raddana, "There was no bathroom in Ahilud's house. Where did Ahilud's family take baths? They didn't, at least if we define "bath" as soaking in a bathtub, or standing in a shower. Most baths probably consisted of washing the extremities occasionally. And where was the toilet? There wasn't any. Where did people go? Outside. Anywhere."[1] Archaeologists have excavated a few bathrooms and toilets from the Old Testament period, primarily in palaces.

Other archaeological evidence supports bathing among the wealthy elite, especially in the New Testament era. Roman culture had a reputation for their public baths. The Romans also loved the hot springs on both sides of the Jordan River and Dead Sea. From the New Testament period, we find many homes of the wealthy with bathtubs.

RITUAL PURIFICATION

Complete immersion was required for one to be ritually pure (Lv 15:5–10; Nm 19:19). From the New Testament era, one finds numerous examples of immersion baths (Hb *mikveh* or *miqvaot*) in Judea. Some homes of the wealthy excavated in the Jewish Quarter of Jerusalem had ritual baths. Archaeologists unearthed numerous ritual baths at Qumran, leading one scholar to suggest Qumran was a purification center.[2] Some of the ritual baths had two sets of steps, one for going into the bath and the other for exiting. The two sets of steps would prevent contact between those who were unclean entering the bath and those who were leaving purified. Ritual purification was required for anyone entering the temple. In 2004, a large pool was excavated adjacent to the well-known Siloam Pool in Jerusalem. This pool dates between the first century BC and the first century AD on the basis of artifacts found within it. The pool may have been an immersion pool accommodating the many pilgrims coming to temple festivals.[3]

In addition, archaeologists have discovered numerous large stone vessels, probably like the ones used at the wedding in Cana of Galilee (Jn 2:6). Such containers were important because, according to the Mishnah, stone vessels were not susceptible to uncleanness, but pottery vessels were. Likewise, stone plates and platters would not be susceptible to uncleanness. Unclean vessels could not be made clean even with washing, so they had to be broken. Stone vessels, though, could be used over and again.

CONTACT WITH A DEAD BODY

Coming in contact with a corpse or bones brought a seven-day temporary uncleanness (Nm 19:11). Since the decedent's family usually handled burial, contact uncleanness was rather common. Hebrew burial practices do provide some evidence for their understanding of uncleanness related to dead bodies. Secondary burial was a common practice for the biblical period. To be gathered to one's fathers (Jdg 2:10) or to one's people (Gn 25:8) was a literal as well as figurative expression. Hebrews often used rock-cut family tombs to bury

Stone mug that would have been common in Jewish homes because such pieces did not violate any purity laws.

multiple generations of extended families. These tombs could have several burial chambers. The deceased would be placed in one chamber, which was then closed. About a year later, the family would gather the bones and place them in a bone repository with the ancestors.

Numerous examples of such rock-cut burials dating to Old and New Testament periods have been found. A number of ritual baths have been found adjacent to tombs. These ritual baths may have served to purify ones who attended the burial and therefore had secondary impurity from indirect contact with the deceased.[4] Attendees could immerse themselves after the burial and leave ritually purified. Ossuaries, typically carved limestone boxes, were used for secondary burial at the beginning of the New Testament period. Although bones were considered unclean, the stone ossuary would prevent uncleanness by contact with bones because the stone did not become unclean. ✣

[1] Joseph A. Callaway, "A Visit with Ahilud: A Revealing Look at Village Life when Israel First Settled the Promised Land," *BAR* 9.5 (1983): 45. [2] Edwin M. Cook, "What Was Qumran? A Ritual Purification Center," *BAR* 22.6 (1996): 39, 48–51, 73–75. [3] Hershel Shanks, "The Siloam Pool," *BAR* 31.5 (2005): 16–23. [4] Yonatan Adler, "Ritual Baths Adjacent to Tombs: An Analysis of the Archaeological Evidence in Light of the Halakhic Sources," *Journal for the Study of Judaism* (*JSJ*) 40 (2009): 55–73.

About a year after a deceased person had been buried in a cave, relatives would collect the bones and store them in a limestone box called an ossuary. Shown is a child's ossuary excavated from a tomb in Ai.

9 The LORD spoke to Moses: 10 "Speak to the Israelites and tell them: When you enter the land I am giving you and reap its harvest,[A] you are to bring the first sheaf of your harvest to the priest. 11 He will present the sheaf before the LORD so that you may be accepted; the priest is to present it on the day after the Sabbath. 12 On the day you present the sheaf, you are to offer a year-old male lamb[B] without blemish as a burnt offering to the LORD. 13 Its grain offering is to be four quarts[C] of fine flour mixed with oil as a food offering to the LORD, a pleasing aroma, and its drink offering will be one quart[D] of wine. 14 You must not eat bread, roasted grain, or any new grain[E] until this very day, and until you have brought the offering to your God. This is to be a permanent statute throughout your generations wherever you live.

15 "You are to count seven[F] complete weeks[G] starting from the day after the Sabbath, the day you brought the sheaf of the presentation offering. 16 You are to count fifty days until the day after the seventh Sabbath and then present an offering of new grain to the LORD. 17 Bring two loaves of bread from your settlements as a presentation offering, each of them made from four quarts of fine flour, baked with yeast, as firstfruits to the LORD. 18 You are to present with the bread seven unblemished male lambs a year old, one young bull, and two rams. They will be a burnt offering to the LORD, with their grain offerings and drink offerings, a food offering, a pleasing aroma to the LORD. 19 You are also to prepare one male goat as a sin offering, and two male lambs a year old as a fellowship sacrifice. 20 The priest will present the lambs with the bread of firstfruits as a presentation offering before the LORD; the bread and the two lambs will be holy to the LORD for the priest. 21 On that same day you are to make a proclamation and hold a sacred assembly. You are not to do any daily work. This is to be a permanent statute wherever you live throughout your generations. 22 When you reap the harvest of your land, you are not to reap all the way to the edge of your field or gather the gleanings of your harvest. Leave them for the poor and the resident alien; I am the LORD your God."

23 The LORD spoke to Moses: 24 "Tell the Israelites: In the seventh month, on the first day of the month, you are to have a day of complete rest, commemoration, and trumpet blasts — a sacred assembly. 25 You must not do any daily work, but you must present a food offering to the LORD."

26 The LORD again spoke to Moses: 27 "The tenth day of this seventh month is the Day of Atonement. You are to hold a sacred assembly and practice self-denial; you are to present a food offering to the LORD. 28 On this particular day you are not to do any work, for it is a Day of Atonement to make atonement for yourselves before the LORD your God. 29 If any person does not practice self-denial on this particular day, he is to be cut off from his people. 30 I will destroy among his people anyone who does any work on this same day. 31 You are not to do any work. This is a permanent statute throughout your generations wherever you live. 32 It will be a Sabbath of complete rest for you, and you must practice self-denial. You are to observe your Sabbath from the evening of the ninth day of the month until the following evening."

33 The LORD spoke to Moses: 34 "Tell the Israelites: The Festival of Shelters[H] to the LORD begins on the fifteenth day of this seventh month and continues for seven days. 35 There is to be a sacred assembly on the first day; you are not to do any daily work. 36 You are to present a food offering to the LORD for seven days. On the eighth day you are to hold a sacred assembly and present a food offering to the LORD. It is a solemn assembly; you are not to do any daily work.

37 "These are the LORD's appointed times that you are to proclaim as sacred assemblies for presenting food offerings to the LORD, burnt offerings and grain offerings, sacrifices and drink offerings, each on its designated day. 38 These are in addition to the offerings for the LORD's Sabbaths, your gifts, all your vow offerings, and all your freewill offerings that you give to the LORD.

39 "You are to celebrate the LORD's festival on the fifteenth day of the seventh month for seven days after you have gathered the produce of the land. There will be complete rest on the first day and complete rest on the eighth day. 40 On the first day you are to take the product of majestic trees — palm fronds, boughs of leafy trees, and willows of the brook — and rejoice before the LORD your God for seven days. 41 You are to celebrate it as a festival to the LORD seven days each year. This is a permanent statute for you throughout your generations; celebrate it in the seventh month. 42 You are to live in shelters for seven days. All the native-born of Israel must live in shelters, 43 so that your generations may know that I made the Israelites live in shelters when I brought them out of the land of Egypt; I am the LORD your God." 44 So Moses declared the LORD's appointed times to the Israelites.

TABERNACLE OIL AND BREAD

24 The LORD spoke to Moses: 2 "Command the Israelites to bring you pure oil from crushed olives for the light, in order to keep the lamp burning regularly. 3 Aaron is to tend it continually from evening until morning before the LORD outside the curtain of the testimony in the tent of meeting. This

[A] **23:10** = the barley harvest [B] **23:12** Or *a male lamb in its first year* [C] **23:13** Lit *two-tenths of an ephah*, also in v. 17 [D] **23:13** Lit *one-fourth of a hin* [E] **23:14** Grain or bread from the new harvest [F] **23:15** Lit *count; they will be seven* [G] **23:15** Or *Sabbaths* [H] **23:34** Or *Tabernacles*, or *Booths*

is a permanent statute throughout your generations. 4 He must continually tend the lamps on the pure gold lampstand in the LORD's presence.

5 "Take fine flour and bake it into twelve loaves; each loaf is to be made with four quarts.[A] 6 Arrange them in two rows, six to a row, on the pure gold table before the LORD. 7 Place pure frankincense near each row, so that it may serve as a memorial portion for the bread and a food offering to the LORD. 8 The bread is to be set out before the LORD every Sabbath day as a permanent covenant obligation on the part of the Israelites. 9 It belongs to Aaron and his sons, who are to eat it in a holy place, for it is the holiest portion for him from the food offerings to the LORD; this is a permanent rule."

A CASE OF BLASPHEMY

10 Now the son of an Israelite mother and an Egyptian father was[B] among the Israelites. A fight broke out in the camp between the Israelite woman's son and an Israelite man. 11 Her son cursed and blasphemed the Name, and they brought him to Moses. (His mother's name was Shelomith, a daughter of Dibri of the tribe of Dan.) 12 They put him in custody until the LORD's decision could be made clear to them.

13 Then the LORD spoke to Moses: 14 "Bring the one who has cursed to the outside of the camp and have all who heard him lay their hands on his head; then have the whole community stone him. 15 And tell the Israelites: If anyone curses his God, he will bear the consequences of his sin. 16 Whoever blasphemes the name of the LORD must be put to death; the whole community is to stone him. If he blasphemes the Name, he is to be put to death, whether the resident alien or the native.

17 "If a man kills anyone, he must be put to death. 18 Whoever kills an animal is to make restitution for it, life for life. 19 If any man inflicts a permanent injury on his neighbor, whatever he has done is to be done to him: 20 fracture for fracture, eye for eye, tooth for tooth. Whatever injury he inflicted on the person, the same is to be inflicted on him. 21 Whoever kills an animal is to make restitution for it, but whoever kills a person is to be put to death. 22 You are to have the same law for the resident alien and the native, because I am the LORD your God."

23 After Moses spoke to the Israelites, they brought the one who had cursed to the outside of the camp and stoned him. So the Israelites did as the LORD had commanded Moses.

SABBATH YEARS AND JUBILEE

25 The LORD spoke to Moses on Mount Sinai: 2 "Speak to the Israelites and tell them: When you enter the land I am giving you, the land will observe a Sabbath to the LORD. 3 You may sow your field for six years, and you may prune your vineyard and gather its produce for six years. 4 But there will be a Sabbath of complete rest for the land in the seventh year, a Sabbath to the LORD: you are not to sow your field or prune your vineyard. 5 You are not to reap what grows by itself from your crop, or harvest the grapes of your untended vines. It is to be a year of complete rest for the land. 6 Whatever the land produces during the Sabbath year can be food for you — for yourself, your male or female slave, and the hired worker or alien who resides with you. 7 All of its growth may serve as food for your livestock and the wild animals in your land.

8 "You are to count seven sabbatical years, seven times seven years, so that the time period of the seven sabbatical years amounts to forty-nine. 9 Then you are to sound a ram's horn loudly in the seventh month, on the tenth day of the month; you will sound it throughout your land on the Day of Atonement. 10 You are to consecrate the fiftieth year and proclaim freedom in the land for all its inhabitants. It will be your Jubilee, when each of you is to return to his property and each of you to his clan. 11 The fiftieth year will be your Jubilee; you are not to sow, reap what grows by itself, or harvest its untended vines. 12 It is to be holy to you because it is the Jubilee; you may only eat its produce directly from the field.

13 "In this Year of Jubilee, each of you will return to his property. 14 If you make a sale to your neighbor or a purchase from him, do not cheat one another. 15 You are to make the purchase from your neighbor based on the number of years since the last Jubilee. He is to sell to you based on the number of remaining harvest years. 16 You are to increase its price in proportion to a greater amount of years, and decrease its price in proportion to a lesser amount of years, because what he is selling to you is a number of harvests. 17 You are not to cheat one another, but fear your God, for I am the LORD your God.

18 "You are to keep my statutes and ordinances and carefully observe them, so that you may live securely in the land. 19 Then the land will yield its fruit, so that you can eat, be satisfied, and live securely in the land. 20 If you wonder, 'What will we eat in the seventh year if we don't sow or gather our produce?' 21 I will appoint my blessing for you in the sixth year, so that it will produce a crop sufficient for three years. 22 When you sow in the eighth year, you will be eating from the previous harvest. You will be eating this until the ninth year when its harvest comes in.

23 "The land is not to be permanently sold because it is mine, and you are only aliens and temporary

[A] **24:5** Lit *two-tenths of an ephah* [B] **24:10** Lit *went out*

residents on my land.[A] 24 You are to allow the redemption of any land you occupy. 25 If your brother becomes destitute and sells part of his property, his nearest relative may come and redeem what his brother has sold. 26 If a man has no family redeemer, but he prospers[B] and obtains enough to redeem his land, 27 he may calculate the years since its sale, repay the balance to the man he sold it to, and return to his property. 28 But if he cannot obtain enough to repay him, what he sold will remain in the possession of its purchaser until the Year of Jubilee. It is to be released at the Jubilee, so that he may return to his property.

29 "If a man sells a residence in a walled city, his right of redemption will last until a year has passed after its sale; his right of redemption will last a year. 30 If it is not redeemed by the end of a full year, then the house in the walled city is permanently transferred to its purchaser throughout his generations. It is not to be released on the Jubilee. 31 But houses in settlements that have no walls around them are to be classified as open fields. The right to redeem such houses stays in effect, and they are to be released at the Jubilee.

32 "Concerning the Levitical cities, the Levites always have the right to redeem houses in the cities they possess. 33 Whatever property one of the Levites can redeem[C] — a house sold in a city they possess — is to be released at the Jubilee, because the houses in the Levitical cities are their possession among the Israelites. 34 The open pastureland around their cities may not be sold, for it is their permanent possession.

35 "If your brother becomes destitute and cannot sustain himself among[D] you, you are to support him as an alien or temporary resident, so that he can continue to live among you. 36 Do not profit or take interest from him, but fear your God and let your brother live among you. 37 You are not to lend him your silver with interest or sell him your food for profit. 38 I am the LORD your God, who brought you out of the land of Egypt to give you the land of Canaan and to be your God.

39 "If your brother among you becomes destitute and sells himself to you, you must not force him to do slave labor. 40 Let him stay with you as a hired worker or temporary resident; he may work for you until the Year of Jubilee. 41 Then he and his children are to be released from you, and he may return to his clan and his ancestral property. 42 They are not to be sold as slaves,[E] because they are my servants[F] that I brought out of the land of Egypt. 43 You are not to rule over them harshly but fear your God. 44 Your male and female slaves are to be from the nations around you; you may purchase male and female slaves. 45 You may also purchase them from the aliens residing with you, or from their families living among you — those born in your land. These may become your property. 46 You may leave them to your sons after you to inherit as property; you can make them slaves for life. But concerning your brothers, the Israelites, you must not rule over one another harshly.

47 "If an alien or temporary resident living among you prospers, but your brother living near him becomes destitute and sells himself to the alien living among you, or to a member of the resident alien's clan, 48 he has the right of redemption after he has been sold. One of his brothers may redeem him. 49 His uncle or cousin may redeem him, or any of his close relatives from his clan may redeem him. If he prospers, he may redeem himself. 50 The one who purchased him is to calculate the time from the year he sold himself to him until the Year of Jubilee. The price of his sale will be determined by the number of years. It will be set for him like the daily wages of a hired worker. 51 If many years are still left, he must pay his redemption price in proportion to them based on his purchase price. 52 If only a few years remain until the Year of Jubilee, he will calculate and pay the price of his redemption in proportion to his remaining years. 53 He will stay with him like a man hired year by year. A resident alien is not to rule over him harshly in your sight. 54 If he is not redeemed in any of these ways, he and his children are to be released at the Year of Jubilee. 55 For the Israelites are my servants. They are my servants that I brought out of the land of Egypt; I am the LORD your God.

COVENANT BLESSINGS AND DISCIPLINE

26 "Do not make worthless idols for yourselves, set up a carved image or sacred pillar for yourselves, or place a sculpted stone in your land to bow down to it, for I am the LORD your God. 2 Keep my Sabbaths and revere my sanctuary; I am the LORD.

3 "If you follow my statutes and faithfully observe my commands, 4 I will give you rain at the right time, and the land will yield its produce, and the trees of the field will bear their fruit. 5 Your threshing will continue until grape harvest, and the grape harvest will continue until sowing time; you will have plenty of food to eat and live securely in your land. 6 I will give peace to the land, and you will lie down with nothing to frighten you. I will remove dangerous animals from the land, and no sword will pass through your land. 7 You will pursue your enemies, and they will fall before you by the sword. 8 Five of

[A] **25:23** Lit *residents with me* [B] **25:26** Lit *but his hand reaches*
[C] **25:33** Hb obscure [D] **25:35** Lit *and his hand falters with*
[E] **25:42** Lit *sold with a sale of a slave* [F] **25:42** Or *slaves*

you will pursue a hundred, and a hundred of you will pursue ten thousand; your enemies will fall before you by the sword.

9 "I will turn to you, make you fruitful and multiply you, and confirm my covenant with you. 10 You will eat the old grain of the previous year and will clear out the old to make room for the new. 11 I will place my residence[A] among you, and I will not reject you. 12 I will walk among you and be your God, and you will be my people. 13 I am the LORD your God, who brought you out of the land of Egypt, so that you would no longer be their slaves. I broke the bars of your yoke and enabled you to live in freedom.[B]

14 "But if you do not obey me and observe all these commands — 15 if you reject my statutes and despise my ordinances, and do not observe all my commands — and break my covenant, 16 then I will do this to you: I will bring terror on you — wasting disease and fever that will cause your eyes to fail and your life to ebb away. You will sow your seed in vain because your enemies will eat it. 17 I will turn[C] against you, so that you will be defeated by your enemies. Those who hate you will rule over you, and you will flee even though no one is pursuing you.

18 "But if after these things you will not obey me, I will proceed to discipline you seven times for your sins. 19 I will break down your strong pride. I will make your sky like iron and your land like bronze, 20 and your strength will be used up for nothing. Your land will not yield its produce, and the trees of the land will not bear their fruit.

21 "If you act with hostility toward me and are unwilling to obey me, I will multiply your plagues seven times for your sins. 22 I will send wild animals against you that will deprive you of your children, ravage your livestock, and reduce your numbers until your roads are deserted.

23 "If in spite of these things you do not accept my discipline, but act with hostility toward me, 24 then I will act with hostility toward you; I also will strike you seven times for your sins. 25 I will bring a sword against you to execute the vengeance of the covenant. Though you withdraw into your cities, I will send a pestilence among you, and you will be delivered into enemy hands. 26 When I cut off your supply of bread, ten women will bake your bread in a single oven and ration out your bread by weight, so that you will eat but not be satisfied.

27 "And if in spite of this you do not obey me but act with hostility toward me, 28 I will act with furious hostility toward you; I will also discipline you seven times for your sins. 29 You will eat the flesh of your sons; you will eat the flesh of your daughters. 30 I will destroy your high places, cut down your shrines,[D] and heap your lifeless bodies on the lifeless bodies of your idols; I will reject you. 31 I will reduce your cities to ruins and devastate your sanctuaries. I will not smell the pleasing aroma of your sacrifices. 32 I also will devastate the land, so that your enemies who come to live there will be appalled by it. 33 But I will scatter you among the nations, and I will draw a sword to chase after you. So your land will become desolate, and your cities will become ruins.

34 "Then the land will make up for its Sabbath years during the time it lies desolate, while you are in the land of your enemies. At that time the land will rest and make up for its Sabbaths. 35 As long as it lies desolate, it will have the rest it did not have during your Sabbaths when you lived there.

36 "I will put anxiety in the hearts of those of you who survive in the lands of their enemies. The sound of a wind-driven leaf will put them to flight, and they will flee as one flees from a sword, and fall though no one is pursuing them. 37 They will stumble over one another as if fleeing from a sword though no one is pursuing them. You will not be able to stand against your enemies. 38 You will perish among the nations; the land of your enemies will devour you. 39 Those[E] who survive in the lands of your enemies will waste away because of their iniquity; they will also waste away because of their ancestors' iniquities along with theirs.

40 "But when they confess their iniquity and the iniquity of their ancestors — their unfaithfulness that they practiced against me, and how they acted with hostility toward me, 41 and I acted with hostility toward them and brought them into the land of their enemies — and when their uncircumcised hearts are humbled and they make amends for their iniquity, 42 then I will remember my covenant with Jacob. I will also remember my covenant with Isaac and my covenant with Abraham, and I will remember the land. 43 For the land abandoned by them will make up for its Sabbaths by lying desolate without the people, while they make amends for their iniquity, because they rejected my ordinances and abhorred my statutes. 44 Yet in spite of this, while they are in the land of their enemies, I will not reject or abhor them so as to destroy them and break my covenant with them, since I am the LORD their God. 45 For their sake I will remember the covenant with their ancestors, whom I brought out of the land of Egypt in the sight of the nations to be their God; I am the LORD."

46 These are the statutes, ordinances, and laws the LORD established between himself and the Israelites through Moses on Mount Sinai.

[A]**26:11** Or *tabernacle* [B]**26:13** Lit *to walk uprightly* [C]**26:17** Lit *will set my face* [D]**26:30** Or *incense altars* [E]**26:39** Lit *Those of you*

FUNDING THE SANCTUARY

27 The LORD spoke to Moses: 2 "Speak to the Israelites and tell them: When someone makes a special vow to the LORD that involves the assessment of people, 3 if the assessment concerns a male from twenty to sixty years old, your assessment is fifty silver shekels measured by the standard sanctuary shekel. 4 If the person is a female, your assessment is thirty shekels. 5 If the person is from five to twenty years old, your assessment for a male is twenty shekels and for a female ten shekels. 6 If the person is from one month to five years old, your assessment for a male is five silver shekels, and for a female your assessment is three shekels of silver. 7 If the person is sixty years or more, your assessment is fifteen shekels for a male and ten shekels for a female. 8 But if one is too poor to pay the assessment, he is to present the person before the priest and the priest will set a value for him. The priest will set a value for him according to what the one making the vow can afford.

9 "If the vow involves one of the animals that may be brought as an offering to the LORD, any of these he gives to the LORD will be holy. 10 He may not replace it or make a substitution for it, either good for bad, or bad for good. But if he does substitute one animal for another, both that animal and its substitute will be holy.

11 "If the vow involves any of the unclean animals that may not be brought as an offering to the LORD, the animal must be presented before the priest. 12 The priest will set its value, whether high or low; the price will be set as the priest makes the assessment for you. 13 If the one who brought it decides to redeem it, he must add a fifth to the[A] assessed value.

14 "When a man consecrates his house as holy to the LORD, the priest will assess its value, whether high or low. The price will stand just as the priest assesses it. 15 But if the one who consecrated his house redeems it, he must add a fifth to the assessed value, and it will be his.

16 "If a man consecrates to the LORD any part of a field that he possesses, your assessment of value will be proportional to the seed needed to sow it, at the rate of fifty silver shekels for every six bushels[B] of barley seed.[C] 17 If he consecrates his field during the Year of Jubilee, the price will stand according to your assessment. 18 But if he consecrates his field after the Jubilee, the priest will calculate the price for him in proportion to the years left until the next Year of Jubilee, so that your assessment will be reduced. 19 If the one who consecrated the field decides to redeem it, he must add a fifth to the assessed value, and the field will transfer back to him. 20 But if he does not redeem the field or if he has sold it to another man, it is no longer redeemable. 21 When the field is released in the Jubilee, it will be holy to the LORD like a field permanently set apart; it becomes the priest's property.

22 "If a person consecrates to the LORD a field he has purchased that is not part of his inherited landholding, 23 then the priest will calculate for him the amount of the assessment up to the Year of Jubilee, and the person will pay the assessed value on that day as a holy offering to the LORD. 24 In the Year of Jubilee the field will return to the one he bought it from, the original owner. 25 All your assessed values will be measured by the standard sanctuary shekel,[D] twenty gerahs to the shekel.

26 "But no one can consecrate a firstborn of the livestock, whether an animal from the herd or flock, to the LORD, because a firstborn already belongs to the LORD. 27 If it is one of the unclean livestock, it can be ransomed according to your assessment by adding a fifth of its value to it. If it is not redeemed, it can be sold according to your assessment.

28 "Nothing that a man permanently sets apart to the LORD from all he owns, whether a person, an animal, or his inherited landholding, can be sold or redeemed; everything set apart is especially holy to the LORD. 29 No person who has been set apart for destruction is to be ransomed; he must be put to death.

30 "Every tenth of the land's produce, grain from the soil or fruit from the trees, belongs to the LORD; it is holy to the LORD. 31 If a man decides to redeem any part of this tenth, he must add a fifth to its value. 32 Every tenth animal from the herd or flock, which passes under the shepherd's rod, will be holy to the LORD. 33 He is not to inspect whether it is good or bad, and he is not to make a substitution for it. But if he does make a substitution, both the animal and its substitute will be holy; they cannot be redeemed."

34 These are the commands the LORD gave Moses for the Israelites on Mount Sinai.

[A] **27:13** Lit *your*, also in vv. 15,19,23 [B] **27:16** Lit *for a homer* [C] **27:16** Or *grain* [D] **27:25** A *shekel* is about two-fifths of an ounce of silver

NUMBERS

The "Rock of Edom" is located on the edge of the Wilderness of Zin, where the spies set out on their mission.

INTRODUCTION TO

NUMBERS

Circumstances of Writing

Christian scholars have traditionally held that Moses was the author of the Pentateuch, which includes the book of Numbers. As with the other books in the Pentateuch, Numbers is anonymous, but Moses is a central character throughout. Moses kept a journal (33:2), and the phrase "The LORD spoke to Moses" is used thirty-one times. It is possible that a few portions were later added by scribes, such as the reference to Moses's humility (12:3) and the reference to the "Book of the LORD's Wars" (21:14). Moses remains the primary writer.

Numbers continues the historical narrative begun in Exodus. It picks up one month after the close of Exodus (Ex 40:2; Nm 1:1), which is about one year after the Israelites' departure from Egypt. Numbers covers the remaining thirty-nine years of the Israelites' stay in the wilderness, from Sinai to Kadesh, and finally to the plains on the eastern side of the Jordan River.

Contribution to the Bible

Numbers shows us how God responded to the unbelief of the Israelites. There are consequences to our disobedience, but God's grace remains, and his redemptive plan and desire for us will not be stopped. The book of Numbers underscores for us the importance of obedience in the life of a Christian, and Paul reminded us of the value of learning from the way God has worked in the past (Rm 15:4; 1Co 10:6,11).

Structure

Numbers reflects the challenging message of faithfulness. The book consists of seven cycles of material, with the repetition of the following types of material: (1) a statement of the historical setting, (2) reference to the twelve tribes of Israel and their respective leaders, (3) matters related to the priests and Levites, and (4) laws for defining the nature of the faithful community. This book of the Law is primarily narrative with portions of case law interwoven into a vibrant literary fabric.

THE CENSUS OF ISRAEL

1 The LORD spoke to Moses in the tent of meeting in the Wilderness of Sinai, on the first day of the second month of the second year after Israel's departure from the land of Egypt: 2 "Take a census of the entire Israelite community by their clans and their ancestral families,[A] counting the names of every male one by one. 3 You and Aaron are to register those who are twenty years old or more by their military divisions — everyone who can serve in Israel's army.[B] 4 A man from each tribe is to be with you, each one the head of his ancestral family.[C] 5 These are the men who are to assist you:

Elizur son of Shedeur from Reuben;
6 Shelumiel son of Zurishaddai from Simeon;
7 Nahshon son of Amminadab from Judah;
8 Nethanel son of Zuar from Issachar;
9 Eliab son of Helon from Zebulun;
10 from the sons of Joseph:
Elishama son of Ammihud from Ephraim,
Gamaliel son of Pedahzur from Manasseh;
11 Abidan son of Gideoni from Benjamin;
12 Ahiezer son of Ammishaddai from Dan;
13 Pagiel son of Ochran from Asher;
14 Eliasaph son of Deuel[D] from Gad;
15 Ahira son of Enan from Naphtali.

16 These are the men called from the community; they are leaders of their ancestral tribes, the heads of Israel's clans."

17 So Moses and Aaron took these men who had been designated by name, 18 and they assembled the whole community on the first day of the second month. They recorded their ancestry by their clans and their ancestral families, counting one by one the names of those twenty years old or more, 19 just as the LORD commanded Moses. He registered them in the Wilderness of Sinai:

20 The descendants of Reuben, the firstborn of Israel: according to their family records by their clans and their ancestral families, counting one by one the names of every male twenty years old or more, everyone who could serve in the army, 21 those registered for the tribe of Reuben numbered 46,500.

22 The descendants of Simeon: according to their family records by their clans and their ancestral families, those registered counting one by one the names of every male twenty years old or more, everyone who could serve in the army, 23 those registered for the tribe of Simeon numbered 59,300.

24 The descendants of Gad: according to their family records by their clans and their ancestral families, counting the names of those twenty years old or more, everyone who could serve in the army, 25 those registered for the tribe of Gad numbered 45,650.

26 The descendants of Judah: according to their family records by their clans and their ancestral families, counting the names of those twenty years old or more, everyone who could serve in the army, 27 those registered for the tribe of Judah numbered 74,600.

28 The descendants of Issachar: according to their family records by their clans and their ancestral families, counting the names of those twenty years old or more, everyone who could serve in the army, 29 those registered for the tribe of Issachar numbered 54,400.

30 The descendants of Zebulun: according to their family records by their clans and their ancestral families, counting the names of those twenty years old or more, everyone who could serve in the army, 31 those registered for the tribe of Zebulun numbered 57,400.

32 The descendants of Joseph:

The descendants of Ephraim: according to their family records by their clans and their ancestral families, counting the names of those twenty years old or more, everyone who could serve in the army, 33 those registered for the tribe of Ephraim numbered 40,500.

34 The descendants of Manasseh: according to their family records by their clans and their ancestral families, counting the names of those twenty years old or more, everyone who could serve in the army, 35 those registered for the tribe of Manasseh numbered 32,200.

36 The descendants of Benjamin: according to their family records by their clans and their ancestral families, counting the names of those twenty years old or more, everyone who could serve in the army, 37 those registered for the tribe of Benjamin numbered 35,400.

38 The descendants of Dan: according to their family records by their clans and their ancestral families, counting the names of those twenty years old or more, everyone who could

[A] **1:2** Lit *the house of their fathers*, also in vv. 18,20,22,24,26,28,30,32,34,36,38,40,42,45 [B] **1:3** Lit *everyone going out to war in Israel* [C] **1:4** Lit *the house of his fathers*, also in v. 44 [D] **1:14** LXX, Syr read *Reuel*

serve in the army, 39 those registered for the tribe of Dan numbered 62,700.

40 The descendants of Asher: according to their family records by their clans and their ancestral families, counting the names of those twenty years old or more, everyone who could serve in the army, 41 those registered for the tribe of Asher numbered 41,500.

42 The descendants of Naphtali: according to their family records by their clans and their ancestral families, counting the names of those twenty years old or more, everyone who could serve in the army, 43 those registered for the tribe of Naphtali numbered 53,400.

44 These are the men Moses and Aaron registered, with the assistance of the twelve leaders of Israel; each represented his ancestral family. 45 So all the Israelites twenty years old or more, everyone who could serve in Israel's army, were registered by their ancestral families. 46 All those registered numbered 603,550.

DUTIES OF THE LEVITES

47 But the Levites were not registered with them by their ancestral tribe. 48 For the LORD had told Moses, 49 "Do not register or take a census of the tribe of Levi with the other Israelites. 50 Appoint the Levites over the tabernacle of the testimony, all its furnishings, and everything in it. They are to transport the tabernacle and all its articles, take care of it, and camp around it. 51 Whenever the tabernacle is to move, the Levites are to take it down, and whenever it is to stop at a campsite, the Levites are to set it up. Any unauthorized person who comes near it is to be put to death.
52 "The Israelites are to camp by their military divisions, each man with his encampment and under his banner. 53 The Levites are to camp around the tabernacle of the testimony and watch over it, so that no wrath will fall on the Israelite community." 54 The Israelites did everything just as the LORD had commanded Moses.

ORGANIZATION OF THE CAMPS

2 The LORD spoke to Moses and Aaron: 2 "The Israelites are to camp under their respective banners beside the flags of their ancestral families.[A] They are to camp around the tent of meeting at a distance from it:
3 Judah's military divisions will camp on the east side toward the sunrise under their banner. The leader of the descendants of Judah is Nahshon son of Amminadab. 4 His military division numbers 74,600. 5 The tribe of Issachar will camp next to it. The leader of the Issacharites is Nethanel son of Zuar. 6 His military division numbers 54,400. 7 The tribe of Zebulun will be next. The leader of the Zebulunites is Eliab son of Helon. 8 His military division numbers 57,400. 9 The total number in their military divisions who belong to Judah's encampment is 186,400; they will move out first.

10 Reuben's military divisions will camp on the south side under their banner. The leader of the Reubenites is Elizur son of Shedeur. 11 His military division numbers 46,500. 12 The tribe of Simeon will camp next to it. The leader of the Simeonites is Shelumiel son of Zurishaddai. 13 His military division numbers 59,300. 14 The tribe of Gad will be next. The leader of the Gadites is Eliasaph son of Deuel.[B] 15 His military division numbers 45,650. 16 The total number in their military divisions who belong to Reuben's encampment is 151,450; they will move out second.

17 The tent of meeting is to move out with the Levites' camp, which is in the middle of the camps. They are to move out just as they camp, each in his place,[C] with their banners.

18 Ephraim's military divisions will camp on the west side under their banner. The leader of the Ephraimites is Elishama son of Ammihud. 19 His military division numbers 40,500. 20 The tribe of Manasseh will be next to it. The leader of the Manassites is Gamaliel son of Pedahzur. 21 His military division numbers 32,200. 22 The tribe of Benjamin will be next. The leader of the Benjaminites is Abidan son of Gideoni. 23 His military division numbers 35,400. 24 The total in their military divisions who belong to Ephraim's encampment number 108,100; they will move out third.

25 Dan's military divisions will camp on the north side under their banner. The leader of the Danites is Ahiezer son of Ammishaddai. 26 His military division numbers 62,700. 27 The tribe of Asher will camp next to it. The leader of the Asherites is Pagiel son of Ochran. 28 His military division numbers 41,500. 29 The tribe of Naphtali will be next. The leader of the Naphtalites is Ahira son of Enan. 30 His military division numbers 53,400. 31 The total number who belong to Dan's encampment is 157,600; they are to move out last, with their banners."

[A] **2:2** Lit *the house of their fathers*, also in v. 32 [B] **2:14** Some Hb mss, Sam, Vg; other Hb mss read *Reuel* [C] **2:17** Lit *each on his hand*

32 These are the Israelites registered by their ancestral families. The total number in the camps
by their military divisions is 603,550. 33 But the
Levites were not registered among the Israelites,
just as the LORD had commanded Moses.
34 The Israelites did everything the LORD commanded
Moses; they camped by their banners in this way and
moved out the same way, each man by his clan and
by his ancestral family.[A]

AARON'S SONS AND THE LEVITES

3 These are the family records of Aaron and Moses
at the time the LORD spoke with Moses on Mount
Sinai. 2 These are the names of Aaron's sons: Nadab,
the firstborn, and Abihu, Eleazar, and Ithamar. 3 These
are the names of Aaron's sons, the anointed priests,
who were ordained to serve as priests. 4 But Nadab
and Abihu died in the LORD's presence when they
presented unauthorized fire before the LORD in the
Wilderness of Sinai, and they had no sons. So Eleazar
and Ithamar served as priests under the direction of
Aaron their father.
5 The LORD spoke to Moses: 6 "Bring the tribe of
Levi near and present them to the priest Aaron to
assist him. 7 They are to perform duties for[B] him and
the entire community before the tent of meeting by
attending to the service of the tabernacle. 8 They are to
take care of all the furnishings of the tent of meeting
and perform duties for the Israelites by attending to
the service of the tabernacle. 9 Assign the Levites to
Aaron and his sons; they have been assigned exclusively to him[C] from the Israelites. 10 You are to appoint
Aaron and his sons to carry out their priestly responsibilities, but any unauthorized person who comes
near the sanctuary is to be put to death."
11 The LORD spoke to Moses: 12 "See, I have taken the
Levites from the Israelites in place of every firstborn
Israelite from the womb. The Levites belong to me,
13 because every firstborn belongs to me. At the time
I struck down every firstborn in the land of Egypt, I
consecrated every firstborn in Israel to myself, both
man and animal. They are mine; I am the LORD."

THE LEVITICAL CENSUS

14 The LORD spoke to Moses in the Wilderness of
Sinai: 15 "Register the Levites by their ancestral
families[D] and their clans. You are to register every
male one month old or more." 16 So Moses registered them in obedience to the LORD as he had been
commanded:
17 These were Levi's sons by name: Gershon,
Kohath, and Merari. 18 These were the names of
Gershon's sons by their clans: Libni and Shimei.
19 Kohath's sons by their clans were Amram, Izhar, Hebron, and Uzziel. 20 Merari's sons by their
clans were Mahli and Mushi. These were the
Levite clans by their ancestral families.

21 The Libnite clan and the Shimeite clan came from
Gershon; these were the Gershonite clans. 22 Those
registered, counting every male one month old
or more, numbered 7,500. 23 The Gershonite clans
camped behind the tabernacle on the west side,
24 and the leader of the Gershonite families[E] was
Eliasaph son of Lael. 25 The Gershonites' duties at
the tent of meeting involved the tabernacle, the
tent, its covering, the screen for the entrance to the
tent of meeting, 26 the hangings of the courtyard,
the screen for the entrance to the courtyard that
surrounds the tabernacle and the altar, and the
tent ropes — all the work relating to these.

27 The Amramite clan, the Izharite clan, the Hebronite clan, and the Uzzielite clan came from
Kohath; these were the Kohathites. 28 Counting
every male one month old or more, there were
8,600[F] responsible for the duties of[G] the sanctuary. 29 The clans of the Kohathites camped on the
south side of the tabernacle, 30 and the leader of
the families of the Kohathite clans was Eliza-
phan son of Uzziel. 31 Their duties involved the
ark, the table, the lampstand, the altars, the sanctuary utensils that were used with these, and
the screen[H] — and all the work relating to them.
32 The chief of the Levite leaders was Eleazar son
of Aaron the priest; he had oversight of those
responsible for the duties of the sanctuary.

33 The Mahlite clan and the Mushite clan came from
Merari; these were the Merarite clans. 34 Those
registered, counting every male one month old or
more, numbered 6,200. 35 The leader of the families
of the Merarite clans was Zuriel son of Abihail; they
camped on the north side of the tabernacle. 36 The
assigned duties of Merari's descendants involved
the tabernacle's supports, crossbars, pillars, bases,
all its equipment, and all the work related to these,
37 in addition to the posts of the surrounding courtyard with their bases, tent pegs, and ropes.

38 Moses, Aaron, and his sons, who performed
the duties of[I] the sanctuary as a service on
behalf of the Israelites, camped in front of the
tabernacle on the east, in front of the tent of

[A] **2:34** Lit *the house of his fathers* [B] **3:7** Or *to guard*, also in v. 8
[C] **3:9** Some Hb mss, LXX, Sam read *me*; Nm 8:16 [D] **3:15** Lit *the house of their fathers*, also in v. 20 [E] **3:24** Lit *a father's house*, also in vv. 30,35
[F] **3:28** LXX reads *8,300* [G] **3:28** Or *for guarding*, also in v. 32
[H] **3:31** The screen between the most holy place and the holy place; Ex 35:12 [I] **3:38** Or *who guarded*

meeting toward the sunrise. Any unauthorized person who came near it was to be put to death. 39 The total number of all the Levite males one month old or more that Moses and Aaron[A] registered by their clans at the LORD's command was 22,000.

REDEMPTION OF THE FIRSTBORN

40 The LORD told Moses, "Register every firstborn male of the Israelites one month old or more, and list their names. 41 You are to take the Levites for me — I am the LORD — in place of every firstborn among the Israelites, and the Levites' cattle in place of every firstborn among the Israelites' cattle." 42 So Moses registered every firstborn among the Israelites, as the LORD commanded him. 43 The total number of the firstborn males one month old or more listed by name was 22,273.

44 The LORD spoke to Moses again: 45 "Take the Levites in place of every firstborn among the Israelites, and the Levites' cattle in place of their cattle. The Levites belong to me; I am the LORD. 46 As the redemption price for the 273 firstborn Israelites who outnumber the Levites, 47 collect five shekels for each person, according to the standard sanctuary shekel — twenty gerahs to the shekel.[B] 48 Give the silver to Aaron and his sons as the redemption price for those who are in excess among the Israelites."

49 So Moses collected the redemption amount from those in excess of the ones redeemed by the Levites. 50 He collected the silver from the firstborn Israelites: 1,365 shekels[C] measured by the standard sanctuary shekel. 51 He gave the redemption silver to Aaron and his sons in obedience to the LORD, just as the LORD commanded Moses.

DUTIES OF THE KOHATHITES

4 The LORD spoke to Moses and Aaron: 2 "Among the Levites, take a census of the Kohathites by their clans and their ancestral families,[D] 3 men from thirty years old to fifty years old — everyone who is qualified[E] to do work at the tent of meeting.

4 "The service of the Kohathites at the tent of meeting concerns the most holy objects. 5 Whenever the camp is about to move on, Aaron and his sons are to go in, take down the screening curtain, and cover the ark of the testimony with it. 6 They are to place over this a covering made of fine leather,[F] spread a solid blue cloth on top, and insert its poles.

7 "They are to spread a blue cloth over the table of the Presence and place the plates and cups on it, as well as the bowls and pitchers for the drink offering. The regular bread offering is to be on it. 8 They are to spread a scarlet cloth over them, cover them with a covering made of fine leather, and insert the poles in the table.

9 "They are to take a blue cloth and cover the lampstand used for light, with its lamps, snuffers, and firepans, as well as its jars of oil by which they service it. 10 Then they are to place it with all its utensils inside a covering made of fine leather and put them on the carrying frame.

11 "They are to spread a blue cloth over the gold altar, cover it with a covering made of fine leather, and insert its poles. 12 They are to take all the serving utensils they use in the sanctuary, place them in a blue cloth, cover them with a covering made of fine leather, and put them on a carrying frame.

13 "They are to remove the ashes from the bronze altar, spread a purple cloth over it, 14 and place all the equipment on it that they use in serving: the firepans, meat forks, shovels, and basins — all the equipment of the altar. They are to spread a covering made of fine leather over it and insert its poles.[G]

15 "Aaron and his sons are to finish covering the holy objects and all their equipment whenever the camp is to move on. The Kohathites will come and carry them, but they are not to touch the holy objects or they will die. These are the transportation duties of the Kohathites regarding the tent of meeting.

16 "Eleazar, son of Aaron the priest, has oversight of the lamp oil, the fragrant incense, the daily grain offering, and the anointing oil. He has oversight of the entire tabernacle and everything in it, the holy objects and their utensils."[H]

17 Then the LORD spoke to Moses and Aaron: 18 "Do not allow the Kohathite tribal clans to be wiped out from the Levites. 19 Do this for them so that they may live and not die when they come near the most holy objects: Aaron and his sons are to go in and assign each man his task and transportation duty. 20 The Kohathites are not to go in and look at the holy objects as they are covered[I] or they will die."

DUTIES OF THE GERSHONITES

21 The LORD spoke to Moses: 22 "Take a census of the Gershonites also, by their ancestral families and their clans. 23 Register men from thirty years old to fifty years old, everyone who is qualified to perform service, to do work at the tent of meeting. 24 This is the service of the Gershonite clans regarding work and transportation duties: 25 They are to transport the tabernacle curtains, the tent of meeting with its covering

[A] **3:39** Some Hb mss, Sam, Syr omit *and Aaron* [B] **3:47** A shekel is about two-fifths of an ounce of silver [C] **3:50** Over 34 pounds of silver
[D] **4:2** Lit *the house of their fathers*, also in vv. 22,29,34,38,40,42,46
[E] **4:3** Lit *everyone entering the service* [F] **4:6** Hb obscure, also in vv. 8, 10,11,12,14,25 [G] **4:14** Sam, LXX add *They are to take a purple cloth and cover the wash basin and its base. They are to place them in a covering made of fine leather and put them on the carrying frame.*
[H] **4:16** Or *the sanctuary and its furnishings* [I] **4:20** Or *objects, even long enough to swallow,*

and the covering made of fine leather on top of it, the screen for the entrance to the tent of meeting, 26 the hangings of the courtyard, the screen for the entrance at the gate of the courtyard that surrounds the tabernacle and the altar, along with their ropes and all the equipment for their service. They will carry out everything that needs to be done with these items.

27 "All the service of the Gershonites, all their transportation duties and all their other work, is to be done at the command of Aaron and his sons; you are to assign to them all that they are responsible to carry. 28 This is the service of the Gershonite clans at the tent of meeting, and their duties will be under the direction of Ithamar son of Aaron the priest.

DUTIES OF THE MERARITES

29 "As for the Merarites, you are to register them by their clans and their ancestral families. 30 Register men from thirty years old to fifty years old, everyone who is qualified to do the work of the tent of meeting. 31 This is what they are responsible to carry as the whole of their service at the tent of meeting: the supports of the tabernacle, with its crossbars, pillars, and bases, 32 the posts of the surrounding courtyard with their bases, tent pegs, and ropes, including all their equipment and all the work related to them. You are to assign by name the items that they are responsible to carry. 33 This is the service of the Merarite clans regarding all their work at the tent of meeting, under the direction of Ithamar son of Aaron the priest."

CENSUS OF THE LEVITES

34 So Moses, Aaron, and the leaders of the community registered the Kohathites by their clans and their ancestral families, 35 men from thirty years old to fifty years old, everyone who was qualified for work at the tent of meeting. 36 The men registered by their clans numbered 2,750. 37 These were the registered men of the Kohathite clans, everyone who could serve at the tent of meeting. Moses and Aaron registered them at the LORD's command through Moses.

38 The Gershonites were registered by their clans and their ancestral families, 39 men from thirty years old to fifty years old, everyone who was qualified for work at the tent of meeting. 40 The men registered by their clans and their ancestral families numbered 2,630. 41 These were the registered men of the Gershonite clans. At the LORD's command Moses and Aaron registered everyone who could serve at the tent of meeting.

42 The men of the Merarite clans were registered by their clans and their ancestral families, 43 those from thirty years old to fifty years old, everyone who was qualified for work at the tent of meeting. 44 The men registered by their clans numbered 3,200. 45 These were the registered men of the Merarite clans; Moses and Aaron registered them at the LORD's command through Moses.

46 Moses, Aaron, and the leaders of Israel registered all the Levites by their clans and their ancestral families, 47 from thirty years old to fifty years old, everyone who was qualified to do the work of serving at the tent of meeting and transporting it. 48 Their registered men numbered 8,580. 49 At the LORD's command they were registered under the direction of Moses, each one according to his work and transportation duty, and his assignment was as the LORD commanded Moses.

ISOLATION OF THE UNCLEAN

5 The LORD instructed Moses, 2 "Command the Israelites to send away anyone from the camp who is afflicted with a skin disease, anyone who has a discharge, or anyone who is defiled because of a corpse. 3 Send away both male or female; send them outside the camp, so that they will not defile their camps where I dwell among them." 4 The Israelites did this, sending them outside the camp. The Israelites did as the LORD instructed Moses.

COMPENSATION FOR WRONGDOING

5 The LORD spoke to Moses: 6 "Tell the Israelites: When a man or woman commits any sin against another, that person acts unfaithfully toward the LORD and is guilty. 7 The person is to confess the sin he has committed. He is to pay full compensation, add a fifth of its value to it, and give it to the individual he has wronged. 8 But if that individual has no relative to receive compensation, the compensation goes to the LORD for the priest, along with the atonement ram by which the priest will make atonement for the guilty person. 9 Every holy contribution the Israelites present to the priest will be his. 10 Each one's holy contribution is his to give; what each one gives to the priest will be his."

THE JEALOUSY RITUAL

11 The LORD spoke to Moses: 12 "Speak to the Israelites and tell them: If any man's wife goes astray, is unfaithful to him, 13 and sleeps with another,[A] but it is concealed from her husband, and she is undetected, even though she has defiled herself, since there is no witness against her, and she wasn't caught in the act; 14 and if a feeling of jealousy comes over the husband and he becomes jealous because of his wife who has defiled herself — or if a feeling of jealousy comes over him and he becomes jealous of her though she has not defiled herself — 15 then the man is to bring

[A] **5:13** Lit *and man lies with her and has an emission of semen*

his wife to the priest. He is also to bring an offering for her of two quarts[A] of barley flour. He is not to pour oil over it or put frankincense on it because it is a grain offering of jealousy, a grain offering for remembrance to draw attention to guilt.

16 “The priest is to bring her forward and have her stand before the LORD. 17 Then the priest is to take holy water in a clay bowl, take some of the dust from the tabernacle floor, and put it in the water. 18 After the priest has the woman stand before the LORD, he is to let down her hair[B] and place in her hands the grain offering for remembrance, which is the grain offering of jealousy. The priest is to hold the bitter water that brings a curse. 19 The priest will require the woman to take an oath and will say to her, ‘If no man has slept with you, if you have not gone astray and become defiled while under your husband’s authority, be unaffected by this bitter water that brings a curse. 20 But if you have gone astray while under your husband’s authority, if you have defiled yourself and a man other than your husband has slept with you’ — 21 at this point the priest will make the woman take the oath with the sworn curse, and he is to say to her — ‘May the LORD make you into an object of your people’s cursing and swearing when he makes your womb[C] shrivel and your belly swell. 22 May this water that brings a curse enter your stomach, causing your belly to swell and your womb to shrivel.’

“And the woman will reply, ‘Amen, Amen.’

23 “Then the priest is to write these curses on a scroll and wash them off into the bitter water. 24 He will require the woman to drink the bitter water that brings a curse, and it will enter her to cause bitter suffering. 25 The priest is to take the grain offering of jealousy from the woman, present the offering before the LORD, and bring it to the altar. 26 The priest is to take a handful of the grain offering as a memorial portion and burn it on the altar. Afterward, he will require the woman to drink the water.

27 “When he makes her drink the water, if she has defiled herself and been unfaithful to her husband, the water that brings a curse will enter her to cause bitter suffering; her belly will swell, and her womb will shrivel. She will become a curse among her people. 28 But if the woman has not defiled herself and is pure, she will be unaffected and will be able to conceive children.

29 “This is the law regarding jealousy when a wife goes astray and defiles herself while under her husband’s authority, 30 or when a feeling of jealousy comes over a husband and he becomes jealous of his wife. He is to have the woman stand before the LORD, and the priest will carry out all these instructions for her. 31 The husband will be free of guilt, but that woman will bear her iniquity.”

THE NAZIRITE VOW

6 The LORD instructed Moses, 2 “Speak to the Israelites and tell them: When a man or woman makes a special vow, a Nazirite vow, to consecrate himself to the LORD, 3 he is to abstain from wine and beer. He must not drink vinegar made from wine or from beer. He must not drink any grape juice or eat fresh grapes or raisins. 4 He is not to eat anything produced by the grapevine, from seeds to skin, during the period of his consecration.

5 “You must not cut his hair[D] throughout the time of his vow of consecration. He may be holy until the time is completed during which he consecrates himself to the LORD; he is to let the hair of his head grow long. 6 He must not go near a dead body during the time he consecrates himself to the LORD. 7 He is not to defile himself for his father or mother, or his brother or sister, when they die, while the mark of consecration to his God is on his head. 8 He is holy to the LORD during the time of consecration.

9 “If someone suddenly dies near him, defiling his consecrated head, he must shave his head on the day of his purification; he is to shave it on the seventh day. 10 On the eighth day he is to bring two turtledoves or two young pigeons to the priest at the entrance to the tent of meeting. 11 The priest is to offer one as a sin offering and the other as a burnt offering to make atonement on behalf of the Nazirite, since he incurred guilt because of the corpse. On that day he is to consecrate his head again. 12 He is to rededicate his time of consecration to the LORD and to bring a year-old male lamb as a guilt offering. But do not count the initial period of consecration because it became defiled.

13 “This is the law of the Nazirite: On the day his time of consecration is completed, he is to be brought to the entrance to the tent of meeting. 14 He is to present an offering to the LORD of one unblemished year-old male lamb as a burnt offering, one unblemished year-old female lamb as a sin offering, one unblemished ram as a fellowship offering, 15 along with their grain offerings and drink offerings, and a basket of unleavened cakes made from fine flour mixed with oil, and unleavened wafers coated with oil.

16 “The priest is to present these before the LORD and sacrifice the Nazirite’s sin offering and burnt offering. 17 He will also offer the ram as a fellowship sacrifice to the LORD, together with the basket of unleavened bread. Then the priest will offer the accompanying grain offering and drink offering.

[A] **5:15** Lit *a tenth of an ephah* [B] **5:18** Or *to uncover her head*
[C] **5:21** Lit *thigh*, also in vv. 22,27 [D] **6:5** Lit *“A razor is not to pass over his head*

DIGGING DEEPER *Ketef Hinnom Silver Scrolls*

In 1980, while excavating a series of seventh-century BC tombs overlooking the Hinnom Valley in Jerusalem, Gabriel Barkay discovered two tiny silver scrolls on which was inscribed the priestly benediction of Numbers 6:24–26. It reads: "May the LORD bless you and protect you; may the LORD make his face shine on you and be gracious to you; may the LORD look with favor on you and give you peace." Originally rolled up and worn as an amulet, archaeologists unrolled the scrolls and discovered that they measure only four inches when unfurled. Since the scrolls predate the famous Dead Sea Scrolls by four hundred years, they are the oldest-known surviving biblical passages in the world. Experts date them to about 600 BC. The tiny scrolls provide an important evidence for the accuracy and precision of the Old Testament scribal copying process, for manuscripts from much later match this early version of Numbers 6:24–26. Moreover, the ancient Hebrew script contained the oldest reference of the Lord's name (*YHWH*), demonstrating that the tradition of calling God Yahweh and the existence of the Hebrew priestly order did not originate after the Babylonian captivity in the late sixth and fifth centuries BC as some critical scholars have previously argued. Both were early developments, as the silver scrolls prove.

18 "The Nazirite is to shave his consecrated head
at the entrance to the tent of meeting, take the hair
from his head, and put it on the fire under the fellowship sacrifice. 19 The priest is to take the boiled
shoulder from the ram, one unleavened cake from
the basket, and one unleavened wafer, and put them
into the hands of the Nazirite after he has shaved his
consecrated head. 20 The priest is to present them as
a presentation offering before the LORD. It is a holy
portion for the priest, in addition to the breast of the
presentation offering and the thigh of the contribution. After that, the Nazirite may drink wine.
21 "These are the instructions about the Nazirite
who vows his offering to the LORD for his consecration, in addition to whatever else he can afford; he
must fulfill whatever vow he makes in keeping with
the instructions for his consecration."

THE PRIESTLY BLESSING

22 The LORD spoke to Moses: 23 "Tell Aaron and his
sons, 'This is how you are to bless the Israelites. You
should say to them,

24 "May the LORD bless you and protect you;
25 may the LORD make his face shine on you
and be gracious to you;
26 may the LORD look with favor on you[A]
and give you peace."'
27 In this way they will pronounce my name over[B] the
Israelites, and I will bless them."

OFFERINGS FROM THE LEADERS

7 On the day Moses finished setting up the tabernacle, he anointed and consecrated it and all its
furnishings, along with the altar and all its utensils.
After he anointed and consecrated these things, 2 the
leaders of Israel, the heads of their ancestral families,[C]
presented an offering. They were the tribal leaders
who supervised the registration. 3 They brought as
their offering before the LORD six covered carts and
twelve oxen, a cart from every two leaders and an
ox from each one, and presented them in front of
the tabernacle.
4 The LORD said to Moses, 5 "Accept these from them
to be used in the work of the tent of meeting, and give
this offering to the Levites, to each division according
to their service."
6 So Moses took the carts and oxen and gave them
to the Levites. 7 He gave the Gershonites two carts and
four oxen corresponding to their service, 8 and gave
the Merarites four carts and eight oxen corresponding to their service, under the direction of Ithamar
son of Aaron the priest. 9 But he did not give any to
the Kohathites, since their responsibility was service
related to the holy objects carried on their shoulders.
10 The leaders also presented the dedication gift for
the altar when it was anointed. The leaders presented
their offerings in front of the altar. 11 The LORD told
Moses, "Each day have one leader present his offering
for the dedication of the altar."
12 The one who presented his offering on the first
day was Nahshon son of Amminadab from the
tribe of Judah. 13 His offering was one silver dish
weighing 3 1/4 pounds[D] and one silver basin weighing 1 3/4 pounds,[E] measured by the standard sanctuary shekel, both of them full of fine flour mixed
with oil for a grain offering; 14 one gold bowl weighing four ounces,[F] full of incense; 15 one young bull,
one ram, and one male lamb a year old, for a burnt
offering; 16 one male goat for a sin offering; 17 and
two bulls, five rams, five male goats, and five male
lambs a year old, for the fellowship sacrifice. This
was the offering of Nahshon son of Amminadab.

[A] **6:26** Lit *LORD lift his face to you* [B] **6:27** Or *put my name on* [C] **7:2** Lit *the house of their fathers* [D] **7:13** Lit *dish, 130 its shekel-weight*, also in vv. 19,25,31,37,43,49,55,61,67,73,79 [E] **7:13** Lit *70 shekels*, also in vv. 19,25,31,37,43,49,55,61,67,73,79 [F] **7:14** Lit *10* (shekels), also in vv. 20,26,32,38,44,50,56,62,68,74,80,86

18 On the second day Nethanel son of Zuar, leader of Issachar, presented an offering. 19 As his offering, he presented one silver dish weighing 3 1/4 pounds and one silver basin weighing 1 3/4 pounds, measured by the standard sanctuary shekel, both of them full of fine flour mixed with oil for a grain offering; 20 one gold bowl weighing four ounces, full of incense; 21 one young bull, one ram, and one male lamb a year old, for a burnt offering; 22 one male goat for a sin offering; 23 and two bulls, five rams, five male goats, and five male lambs a year old, for the fellowship sacrifice. This was the offering of Nethanel son of Zuar.

24 On the third day Eliab son of Helon, leader of the Zebulunites, presented an offering. 25 His offering was one silver dish weighing 3 1/4 pounds and one silver basin weighing 1 3/4 pounds, measured by the standard sanctuary shekel, both of them full of fine flour mixed with oil for a grain offering; 26 one gold bowl weighing four ounces, full of incense; 27 one young bull, one ram, and one male lamb a year old, for a burnt offering; 28 one male goat for a sin offering; 29 and two bulls, five rams, five male goats, and five male lambs a year old, for the fellowship sacrifice. This was the offering of Eliab son of Helon.

30 On the fourth day Elizur son of Shedeur, leader of the Reubenites, presented an offering. 31 His offering was one silver dish weighing 3 1/4 pounds and one silver basin weighing 1 3/4 pounds, measured by the standard sanctuary shekel, both of them full of fine flour mixed with oil for a grain offering; 32 one gold bowl weighing four ounces, full of incense; 33 one young bull, one ram, and one male lamb a year old, for a burnt offering; 34 one male goat for a sin offering; 35 and two bulls, five rams, five male goats, and five male lambs a year old, for the fellowship sacrifice. This was the offering of Elizur son of Shedeur.

36 On the fifth day Shelumiel son of Zurishaddai, leader of the Simeonites, presented an offering. 37 His offering was one silver dish weighing 3 1/4 pounds and one silver basin weighing 1 3/4 pounds, measured by the standard sanctuary shekel, both of them full of fine flour mixed with oil for a grain offering; 38 one gold bowl weighing four ounces, full of incense; 39 one young bull, one ram, and one male lamb a year old, for a burnt offering; 40 one male goat for a sin offering; 41 and two bulls, five rams, five male goats, and five male lambs a year old, for the fellowship sacrifice. This was the offering of Shelumiel son of Zurishaddai.

42 On the sixth day Eliasaph son of Deuel,[A] leader of the Gadites, presented an offering. 43 His offering was one silver dish weighing 3 1/4 pounds and one silver basin weighing 1 3/4 pounds, measured by the standard sanctuary shekel, both of them full of fine flour mixed with oil for a grain offering; 44 one gold bowl weighing four ounces full of incense; 45 one young bull, one ram, and one male lamb a year old, for a burnt offering; 46 one male goat for a sin offering; 47 and two bulls, five rams, five male goats, and five male lambs a year old, for the fellowship sacrifice. This was the offering of Eliasaph son of Deuel.[A]

48 On the seventh day Elishama son of Ammihud, leader of the Ephraimites, presented an offering. 49 His offering was one silver dish weighing 3 1/4 pounds and one silver basin weighing 1 3/4 pounds, measured by the standard sanctuary shekel, both of them full of fine flour mixed with oil for a grain offering; 50 one gold bowl weighing four ounces, full of incense; 51 one young bull, one ram, and one male lamb a year old, for a burnt offering; 52 one male goat for a sin offering; 53 and two bulls, five rams, five male goats, and five male lambs a year old, for the fellowship sacrifice. This was the offering of Elishama son of Ammihud.

54 On the eighth day Gamaliel son of Pedahzur, leader of the Manassites, presented an offering. 55 His offering was one silver dish weighing 3 1/4 pounds and one silver basin weighing 1 3/4 pounds, measured by the standard sanctuary shekel, both of them full of fine flour mixed with oil for a grain offering; 56 one gold bowl weighing four ounces, full of incense; 57 one young bull, one ram, and one male lamb a year old, for a burnt offering; 58 one male goat for a sin offering; 59 and two bulls, five rams, five male goats, and five male lambs a year old, for the fellowship sacrifice. This was the offering of Gamaliel son of Pedahzur.

60 On the ninth day Abidan son of Gideoni, leader of the Benjaminites, presented an offering. 61 His offering was one silver dish weighing 3 1/4 pounds and one silver basin weighing 1 3/4 pounds, measured by the standard sanctuary shekel, both of them full of fine flour mixed with oil for a grain offering; 62 one gold bowl weighing four ounces, full of incense; 63 one young bull, one ram, and one male lamb a year old, for a burnt offering; 64 one male goat for a sin offering; 65 and two

[A] **7:42,47** LXX, Syr read *Reuel*

bulls, five rams, five male goats, and five male lambs a year old, for the fellowship sacrifice. This was the offering of Abidan son of Gideoni.

66 On the tenth day Ahiezer son of Ammishaddai, leader of the Danites, presented an offering. 67 His offering was one silver dish weighing 3¼ pounds and one silver basin weighing 1¾ pounds, measured by the standard sanctuary shekel, both of them full of fine flour mixed with oil for a grain offering; 68 one gold bowl weighing four ounces, full of incense; 69 one young bull, one ram, and one male lamb a year old, for a burnt offering; 70 one male goat for a sin offering; 71 and two bulls, five rams, five male goats, and five male lambs a year old, for the fellowship sacrifice. This was the offering of Ahiezer son of Ammishaddai.

72 On the eleventh day Pagiel son of Ochran, leader of the Asherites, presented an offering. 73 His offering was one silver dish weighing 3¼ pounds and one silver basin weighing 1¾ pounds, measured by the standard sanctuary shekel, both of them full of fine flour mixed with oil for a grain offering; 74 one gold bowl weighing four ounces, full of incense; 75 one young bull, one ram, and one male lamb a year old, for a burnt offering; 76 one male goat for a sin offering; 77 and two bulls, five rams, five male goats, and five male lambs a year old, for the fellowship sacrifice. This was the offering of Pagiel son of Ochran.

78 On the twelfth day Ahira son of Enan, leader of the Naphtalites, presented an offering. 79 His offering was one silver dish weighing 3¼ pounds and one silver basin weighing 1¾ pounds, measured by the standard sanctuary shekel, both of them full of fine flour mixed with oil for a grain offering; 80 one gold bowl weighing four ounces, full of incense; 81 one young bull, one ram, and one male lamb a year old, for a burnt offering; 82 one male goat for a sin offering; 83 and two bulls, five rams, five male goats, and five male lambs a year old, for the fellowship sacrifice. This was the offering of Ahira son of Enan.

84 This was the dedication gift from the leaders of Israel for the altar when it was anointed: twelve silver dishes, twelve silver basins, and twelve gold bowls. 85 Each silver dish weighed 3¼ pounds,[A] and each basin 1¾ pounds.[B] The total weight of the silver articles was 60 pounds[C] measured by the standard sanctuary shekel. 86 The twelve gold bowls full of incense each weighed four ounces measured by the standard sanctuary shekel. The total weight of the gold bowls was 3 pounds.[D] 87 All the livestock for the burnt offering totaled twelve bulls, twelve rams, and twelve male lambs a year old, with their grain offerings, and twelve male goats for the sin offering. 88 All the livestock for the fellowship sacrifice totaled twenty-four bulls, sixty rams, sixty male goats, and sixty male lambs a year old. This was the dedication gift for the altar after it was anointed.

89 When Moses entered the tent of meeting to speak with the LORD, he heard the voice speaking to him from above the mercy seat that was on the ark of the testimony, from between the two cherubim. He spoke to him that way.

THE LIGHTING IN THE TABERNACLE

8 The LORD spoke to Moses: 2 "Speak to Aaron and tell him: When you set up the lamps, the seven lamps are to give light in front of the lampstand." 3 So Aaron did this; he set up its lamps to give light in front of the lampstand just as the LORD had commanded Moses. 4 This is the way the lampstand was made: it was a hammered work of gold, hammered from its base to its flower petals. The lampstand was made according to the pattern the LORD had shown Moses.

CONSECRATION OF THE LEVITES

5 The LORD spoke to Moses: 6 "Take the Levites from among the Israelites and ceremonially cleanse them. 7 Do this to them for their purification: Sprinkle them with the purification water. Have them shave their entire bodies and wash their clothes, and so purify themselves.

8 "They are to take a young bull and its grain offering of fine flour mixed with oil, and you are to take a second young bull for a sin offering. 9 Bring the Levites before the tent of meeting and assemble the entire Israelite community. 10 Then present the Levites before the LORD, and have the Israelites lay their hands on them. 11 Aaron is to present the Levites before the LORD as a presentation offering from the Israelites, so that they may perform the LORD's work. 12 Next the Levites are to lay their hands on the heads of the bulls. Sacrifice one as a sin offering and the other as a burnt offering to the LORD, to make atonement for the Levites.

13 "You are to have the Levites stand before Aaron and his sons, and you are to present them before the LORD as a presentation offering. 14 In this way you are to separate the Levites from the rest of the Israelites so that the Levites will belong to me. 15 After that the Levites may come to serve at the tent of meeting, once you have ceremonially cleansed them and presented

[A] **7:85** Lit *130* (shekels) [B] **7:85** Lit *70* (shekels) [C] **7:85** Lit *2,400* (shekels) [D] **7:86** Lit *120* (shekels)

them as a presentation offering. 16 For they have been exclusively assigned to me from the Israelites. I have taken them for myself in place of all who come first from the womb, every Israelite firstborn. 17 For every firstborn among the Israelites is mine, both man and animal. I consecrated them to myself on the day I struck down every firstborn in the land of Egypt. 18 But I have taken the Levites in place of every firstborn among the Israelites. 19 From the Israelites, I have given the Levites exclusively to Aaron and his sons to perform the work for the Israelites at the tent of meeting and to make atonement on their behalf, so that no plague will come against the Israelites when they approach the sanctuary."

20 Moses, Aaron, and the entire Israelite community did this to the Levites. The Israelites did everything to them the LORD commanded Moses regarding the Levites. 21 The Levites purified themselves and washed their clothes; then Aaron presented[A] them before the LORD as a presentation offering. Aaron also made atonement for them to cleanse them ceremonially. 22 After that, the Levites came to do their work at the tent of meeting in the presence of Aaron and his sons. So they did to them as the LORD had commanded Moses concerning the Levites.

23 The LORD spoke to Moses: 24 "In regard to the Levites: From twenty-five years old or more, a man enters the service in the work at the tent of meeting. 25 But at fifty years old he is to retire from his service in the work and no longer serve. 26 He may assist his brothers to fulfill responsibilities[B] at the tent of meeting, but he must not do the work. This is how you are to deal with the Levites regarding their duties."

THE SECOND PASSOVER

9 In the first month of the second year after their departure from the land of Egypt, the LORD told Moses in the Wilderness of Sinai, 2 "The Israelites are to observe the Passover at its appointed time. 3 You must observe it at its appointed time on the fourteenth day of this month at twilight; you are to observe it according to all its statutes and ordinances." 4 So Moses told the Israelites to observe the Passover, 5 and they observed it in the first month on the fourteenth day at twilight in the Wilderness of Sinai. The Israelites did everything as the LORD had commanded Moses.

6 But there were some men who were unclean because of a human corpse, so they could not observe the Passover on that day. These men came before Moses and Aaron the same day 7 and said to him, "We are unclean because of a human corpse. Why should we be excluded from presenting the LORD's offering at its appointed time with the other Israelites?"

8 Moses replied to them, "Wait here until I hear what the LORD commands for you."

9 Then the LORD spoke to Moses: 10 "Tell the Israelites: When any one of you or your descendants is unclean because of a corpse or is on a distant journey, he may still observe the Passover to the LORD. 11 Such people are to observe it in the second month, on the fourteenth day at twilight. They are to eat the animal with unleavened bread and bitter herbs; 12 they may not leave any of it until morning or break any of its bones. They must observe the Passover according to all its statutes.

13 "But the man who is ceremonially clean, is not on a journey, and yet fails to observe the Passover is to be cut off from his people, because he did not present the LORD's offering at its appointed time. That man will bear the consequences of his sin.

14 "If an alien resides with you and wants to observe the Passover to the LORD, he is to do it according to the Passover statute and its ordinances. You are to apply the same statute to both the resident alien and the native of the land."

GUIDANCE BY THE CLOUD

15 On the day the tabernacle was set up, the cloud covered the tabernacle, the tent of the testimony, and it appeared like fire above the tabernacle from evening until morning. 16 It remained that way continuously: the cloud would cover it,[C] appearing like fire at night. 17 Whenever the cloud was lifted up above the tent, the Israelites would set out; at the place where the cloud stopped, there the Israelites camped. 18 At the LORD's command the Israelites set out, and at the LORD's command they camped. As long as the cloud stayed over the tabernacle, they camped.

19 Even when the cloud stayed over the tabernacle many days, the Israelites carried out the LORD's requirement and did not set out. 20 Sometimes the cloud remained over the tabernacle for only a few days. They would camp at the LORD's command and set out at the LORD's command. 21 Sometimes the cloud remained only from evening until morning; when the cloud lifted in the morning, they set out. Or if it remained a day and a night, they moved out when the cloud lifted. 22 Whether it was two days, a month, or longer,[D] the Israelites camped and did not set out as long as the cloud stayed over the tabernacle. But when it was lifted, they set out. 23 They camped at the LORD's command, and they set out at the LORD's command. They carried out the LORD's requirement according to his command through Moses.

[A] **8:21** Lit *waved* [B] **8:26** Or *to keep guard* [C] **9:16** LXX, Vg, Syr, Tg read *it by day* [D] **9:22** Or *a year*

TWO SILVER TRUMPETS

10 The LORD spoke to Moses: 2 "Make two trumpets of hammered silver to summon the community and have the camps set out. 3 When both are sounded in long blasts, the entire community is to gather before you at the entrance to the tent of meeting. 4 However, if one is sounded, only the leaders, the heads of Israel's clans, are to gather before you.

5 "When you sound short blasts, the camps pitched on the east are to set out. 6 When you sound short blasts a second time, the camps pitched on the south are to set out. Short blasts are to be sounded for them to set out. 7 When calling the assembly together, you are to sound long blasts, not short ones. 8 The sons of Aaron, the priests, are to sound the trumpets. Your use of these is a permanent statute throughout your generations.

9 "When you enter into battle in your land against an adversary who is attacking you, sound short blasts on the trumpets, and you will be remembered before the LORD your God and be saved from your enemies. 10 You are to sound the trumpets over your burnt offerings and your fellowship sacrifices and on your joyous occasions, your appointed festivals, and the beginning of each of your months. They will serve as a reminder for you before your God: I am the LORD your God."

FROM SINAI TO PARAN

11 During the second year, in the second month on the twentieth day of the month, the cloud was lifted up above the tabernacle of the testimony. 12 The Israelites traveled on from the Wilderness of Sinai, moving from one place to the next until the cloud stopped in the Wilderness of Paran. 13 They set out for the first time according to the LORD's command through Moses.

14 The military divisions of the camp of Judah's descendants with their banner set out first, and Nahshon son of Amminadab was over their divisions. 15 Nethanel son of Zuar was over the division of the tribe of Issachar's descendants, 16 and Eliab son of Helon was over the division of the tribe of Zebulun's descendants. 17 The tabernacle was then taken down, and the Gershonites and the Merarites set out, transporting the tabernacle.

18 The military divisions of the camp of Reuben with their banner set out, and Elizur son of Shedeur was over their divisions. 19 Shelumiel son of Zurishaddai was over the division of the tribe of Simeon's descendants, 20 and Eliasaph son of Deuel[A] was over the division of the tribe of Gad's descendants. 21 The Kohathites then set out, transporting the holy objects; the tabernacle was to be set up before their arrival.

22 Next the military divisions of the camp of Ephraim's descendants with their banner set out, and Elishama son of Ammihud was over their divisions. 23 Gamaliel son of Pedahzur was over the division of the tribe of Manasseh's descendants, 24 and Abidan son of Gideoni was over the division of the tribe of Benjamin's descendants.

25 The military divisions of the camp of Dan's descendants with their banner set out, serving as rear guard for all the camps, and Ahiezer son of Ammishaddai was over their divisions. 26 Pagiel son of Ochran was over the division of the tribe of Asher's descendants, 27 and Ahira son of Enan was over the division of the tribe of Naphtali's descendants. 28 This was the order of march for the Israelites by their military divisions as they set out.

29 Moses said to Hobab, descendant of Reuel the Midianite and Moses's relative by marriage, "We're setting out for the place the LORD promised, 'I will give it to you.' Come with us, and we will treat you well, for the LORD has promised good things to Israel."

30 But he replied to him, "I don't want to go. Instead, I will go to my own land and my relatives."

31 "Please don't leave us," Moses said, "since you know where we should camp in the wilderness, and you can serve as our eyes. 32 If you come with us, whatever good the LORD does for us we will do for you."

33 They set out from the mountain of the LORD on a three-day journey with the ark of the LORD's covenant traveling ahead of them for those three days to seek a resting place for them. 34 Meanwhile, the cloud of the LORD was over them by day when they set out from the camp.

35 Whenever the ark set out, Moses would say:

Arise, LORD!
Let your enemies be scattered,
and those who hate you flee
from your presence.

36 When it came to rest, he would say:

Return, LORD,
to the countless thousands of Israel.

COMPLAINTS ABOUT HARDSHIP

11 Now the people began complaining openly before[B] the LORD about hardship. When the LORD heard, his anger burned, and fire from the LORD blazed among them and consumed the outskirts of the camp. 2 Then the people cried out to Moses, and he prayed to the LORD, and the fire died down. 3 So that place was named Taberah,[C] because the LORD's fire had blazed among them.

[A] **10:20** LXX, Syr read *Reuel* [B] **11:1** Lit *in the ears of* [C] **11:3** = Blaze

COMPLAINTS ABOUT FOOD

4 The riffraff[A] among them had a strong craving for other food. The Israelites wept again and said, "Who will feed us meat? 5 We remember the free fish we ate in Egypt, along with the cucumbers, melons, leeks, onions, and garlic. 6 But now our appetite is gone;[B] there's nothing to look at but this manna!"

7 The manna resembled coriander seed, and its appearance was like that of bdellium.[C] 8 The people walked around and gathered it. They ground it on a pair of grinding stones or crushed it in a mortar, then boiled it in a cooking pot and shaped it into cakes. It tasted like a pastry cooked with the finest oil. 9 When the dew fell on the camp at night, the manna would fall with it.

10 Moses heard the people, family after family, weeping at the entrance of their tents. The LORD was very angry; Moses was also provoked.[D] 11 So Moses asked the LORD, "Why have you brought such trouble on your servant? Why are you angry with me,[E] and why do you burden me with all these people? 12 Did I conceive all these people? Did I give them birth so you should tell me, 'Carry them at your breast, as a nursing mother carries a baby,' to the land that you swore to give their ancestors? 13 Where can I get meat to give all these people? For they are weeping to me, 'Give us meat to eat!' 14 I can't carry all these people by myself. They are too much for me. 15 If you are going to treat me like this, please kill me right now if I have found favor with you, and don't let me see my misery[F] anymore."

SEVENTY ELDERS ANOINTED

16 The LORD answered Moses, "Bring me seventy men from Israel known to you as elders and officers of the people. Take them to the tent of meeting and have them stand there with you. 17 Then I will come down and speak with you there. I will take some of the Spirit who is on you and put the Spirit on them. They will help you bear the burden of the people, so that you do not have to bear it by yourself.

18 "Tell the people: Consecrate yourselves in readiness for tomorrow, and you will eat meat because you wept in the LORD's hearing, 'Who will feed us meat? We were better off in Egypt.' The LORD will give you meat and you will eat. 19 You will eat, not for one day, or two days, or five days, or ten days, or twenty days, 20 but for a whole month — until it comes out of your nostrils and becomes nauseating to you — because you have rejected the LORD who is among you, and wept before him, 'Why did we ever leave Egypt?'"

21 But Moses replied, "I'm in the middle of a people with six hundred thousand foot soldiers, yet you say, 'I will give them meat, and they will eat for a month.' 22 If flocks and herds were slaughtered for them, would they have enough? Or if all the fish in the sea were caught for them, would they have enough?"

23 The LORD answered Moses, "Is the LORD's arm weak?[G] Now you will see whether or not what I have promised will happen to you."

24 Moses went out and told the people the words of the LORD. He brought seventy men from the elders of the people and had them stand around the tent. 25 Then the LORD descended in the cloud and spoke to him. He took some of the Spirit who was on Moses and placed the Spirit on the seventy elders. As the Spirit rested on them, they prophesied, but they never did it again. 26 Two men had remained in the camp, one named Eldad and the other Medad; the Spirit rested on them — they were among those listed, but had not gone out to the tent — and they prophesied in the camp. 27 A young man ran and reported to Moses, "Eldad and Medad are prophesying in the camp."

28 Joshua son of Nun, assistant to Moses since his youth,[H] responded, "Moses, my lord, stop them!"

29 But Moses asked him, "Are you jealous on my account? If only all the LORD's people were prophets and the LORD would place his Spirit on them!" 30 Then Moses returned to the camp along with the elders of Israel.

QUAIL IN THE CAMP

31 A wind sent by the LORD came up and blew quail in from the sea; it dropped them all around the camp. They were flying three feet[I] off[J] the ground for about a day's journey in every direction. 32 The people were up all that day and night and all the next day gathering the quail — the one who took the least gathered sixty bushels[K] — and they spread them out all around the camp.[L]

33 While the meat was still between their teeth, before it was chewed, the LORD's anger burned against the people, and the LORD struck them with a very severe plague. 34 So they named that place Kibroth-hattaavah,[M] because there they buried the people who had craved the meat.

35 From Kibroth-hattaavah the people moved on to Hazeroth[N] and remained there.

MIRIAM AND AARON REBEL

12 Miriam and Aaron criticized Moses because of the Cushite woman he married (for he had married a Cushite woman). 2 They said, "Does the LORD speak only through Moses? Does he not also

[A] **11:4** Or *The mixed multitude*; Hb obscure [B] **11:6** Or *our lives are wasting away*, or *our throat is dry* [C] **11:7** A yellowish, transparent gum resin [D] **11:10** Lit *and it was evil in the eyes of Moses* [E] **11:11** Lit *Why have I not found favor in your eyes* [F] **11:15** Alt Hb tradition reads *your misery* [G] **11:23** Lit *the LORD's arm too short* [H] **11:28** Or *Moses, from his elite young men* [I] **11:31** Lit *two cubits* [J] **11:31** Or *They were three feet deep on* [K] **11:32** Lit *10 homers* [L] **11:32** To dry or cure the meat; 2Sm 17:19; Ezk 26:5,14 [M] **11:34** = Graves of Craving [N] **11:35** = Settlements; Nm 12:16; 33:16–17

speak through us?" And the LORD heard it. 3 Moses was a very humble man, more so than anyone on the face of the earth.

4 Suddenly the LORD said to Moses, Aaron, and Miriam, "You three come out to the tent of meeting." So the three of them went out. 5 Then the LORD descended in a pillar of cloud, stood at the entrance to the tent, and summoned Aaron and Miriam. When the two of them came forward, 6 he said:

"Listen to what I say:
If there is a prophet among you
from the LORD,
I make myself known to him in a vision;
I speak with him in a dream.
7 Not so with my servant Moses;
he is faithful in[A] all my household.
8 I speak with him directly,[B]
openly, and not in riddles;
he sees the form of the LORD.

So why were you not afraid to speak against my servant Moses?" 9 The LORD's anger burned against them, and he left.

10 As the cloud moved away from the tent, Miriam's skin suddenly became diseased, resembling snow.[C] When Aaron turned toward her, he saw that she was diseased 11 and said to Moses, "My lord, please don't hold against us this sin we have so foolishly committed. 12 Please don't let her be like a dead baby[D] whose flesh is half eaten away when he comes out of his mother's womb."

13 Then Moses cried out to the LORD, "God, please heal her!"

14 The LORD answered Moses, "If her father had merely spit in her face, wouldn't she remain in disgrace for seven days? Let her be confined outside the camp for seven days; after that she may be brought back in." 15 So Miriam was confined outside the camp for seven days, and the people did not move on until Miriam was brought back in. 16 After that, the people set out from Hazeroth and camped in the Wilderness of Paran.

SCOUTING OUT CANAAN

13 The LORD spoke to Moses: 2 "Send men to scout out the land of Canaan I am giving to the Israelites. Send one man who is a leader among them from each of their ancestral tribes." 3 Moses sent them from the Wilderness of Paran at the LORD's command. All the men were leaders in Israel. 4 These were their names:

Shammua son of Zaccur from the tribe
of Reuben;
5 Shaphat son of Hori from the tribe of Simeon;
6 Caleb son of Jephunneh from the tribe
of Judah;
7 Igal son of Joseph from the tribe of Issachar;
8 Hoshea son of Nun from the tribe of Ephraim;
9 Palti son of Raphu from the tribe of Benjamin;
10 Gaddiel son of Sodi from the tribe of Zebulun;
11 Gaddi son of Susi from the tribe of Manasseh
(from the tribe of Joseph);
12 Ammiel son of Gemalli from the tribe of Dan;
13 Sethur son of Michael from the tribe of Asher;
14 Nahbi son of Vophsi from the tribe
of Naphtali;
15 Geuel son of Machi from the tribe of Gad.

16 These were the names of the men Moses sent to scout out the land, and Moses renamed Hoshea son of Nun, Joshua.

17 When Moses sent them to scout out the land of Canaan, he told them, "Go up this way to the Negev, then go up into the hill country. 18 See what the land is like, and whether the people who live there are strong or weak, few or many. 19 Is the land they live in good or bad? Are the cities they live in encampments or fortifications? 20 Is the land fertile or unproductive? Are there trees in it or not? Be courageous. Bring back some fruit from the land." It was the season for the first ripe grapes.

21 So they went up and scouted out the land from the Wilderness of Zin[E] as far as Rehob near the entrance to Hamath.[F] 22 They went up through the Negev and came to Hebron, where Ahiman, Sheshai, and Talmai, the descendants of Anak, were living. Hebron was built seven years before Zoan in Egypt. 23 When they came to Eshcol Valley, they cut down a branch with a single cluster of grapes, which was carried on a pole by two men. They also took some pomegranates and figs. 24 That place was called Eshcol[G] Valley because of the cluster of grapes the Israelites cut there. 25 At the end of forty days they returned from scouting out the land.

REPORT ABOUT CANAAN

26 The men went back to Moses, Aaron, and the entire Israelite community in the Wilderness of Paran at Kadesh. They brought back a report for them and the whole community, and they showed them the fruit of the land. 27 They reported to Moses, "We went into the land where you sent us. Indeed it is flowing with milk and honey, and here is some of its fruit. 28 However, the people living in the land are strong, and the cities are large and fortified. We also saw the descendants of Anak there. 29 The Amalekites are living in the land of the Negev; the Hethites, Jebusites, and Amorites

[A] **12:7** Or *is entrusted with* [B] **12:8** Lit *mouth to mouth*
[C] **12:10** A reference to whiteness or flakiness of the skin
[D] **12:12** Alt Hb tradition reads *baby who comes out of our mother's womb and our flesh is half eaten away.* [E] **13:21** Southern border of the promised land [F] **13:21** Or *near Lebo-hamath* [G] **13:24** = Cluster

Spies in the Land

by John L. Harris

With the Israelites encamped in the desert of Paran at the southern border of Canaan, God directed Moses to select twelve men, one from each tribe, "to scout" (Hb *tur*) the land (Nm 13:2).

JOURNEY OF THE SPIES

As directed, the spies left the wilderness of Paran and entered the Negev, traveling through the Wilderness of Zin, probably late in July. These dry and barren areas south of Canaan are bordered by the Wadi Arabah on the east, the Sinai on the south and west, and extend from around Gaza to the western shore of the Dead Sea. In these regions, water is constantly in short supply; the Wilderness of Zin receives fewer than two inches of annual precipitation, and the Negev receives only eight to twelve inches of rain a year.[1] The Negev soil is fine and windblown, and the sparse rain does not absorb but quickly runs off into the wadis. This entire region has an adverse environment for sustaining human life and is mostly unsuitable for cultivation. As the spies journeyed, they would have endured a hot and dry climate. Canaan has only two defined seasons: a hot and dry period (summer) running from mid-June to mid-September and a warm and wet period (winter) running from October to mid-April.

In contrast to the surrounding area of the Negev, the hill country's climate is much more favorable and the area receives abundant rain. The central mountain range and the highlands of Judah receive between twenty and forty inches of annual rainfall, allowing for the collection of water in numerous springs and a greening of the land.[2] The hill country contains rich, red, moisture-absorbing soil and is covered with considerable forests.[3] Referring to this region and its produce, the spies proclaimed the land flowed with "milk and honey" (Nm 13:27).

The spies would have found travel along the central mountain range extremely difficult due to the limestone boulders and occasional cliffs that stood as natural impediments. As the twelve continued northward, they would have followed the ridges and probably would have taken the interregional road known as the Ridge Route or Route of the Patriarchs that ran along the north-south watershed ridge between Hebron and Shechem. Along this route, the spies would have passed the cities of Hormah, Arad, Hebron, Jerusalem, Jericho, Ramah, Gibeon, Bethel, Shiloh, Shechem, Beth-shean, Hazor, Laish (Dan), and Rehob near Lebo-hamath ("the entrance of Hamath").[4] The reference to Lebo-hamath, a city on the east bank of the Orontes River located on one of the main trade routes in the northernmost boundary of Canaan, emphasizes that the scouting mission covered the entire land, a distance of about 250 miles, one way.

The only city singled out for comment was Hebron (meaning "confederacy"), a well-fortified and large town in the hill country of Judah, lying three thousand feet above sea level and twenty miles south of Jerusalem. The fertile land made Hebron a favorable place for farmers and merchants to buy and sell wheat, barley, olives, grapes, pomegranates, and other produce.[5]

The spies were likely intimidated when they saw the fortified cities of the hill country encircled by ramparts that reached "to the heavens"

Modern Shechem taken from the top of Mount Gerizim.

View of the Canaanite city and its protective wall at Arad.

(Dt 1:28; see 3:5) and protected by gates and towers. Not every city in Canaan, however, was fortified and protected by walls. Evidence points to the existence of many open villages in the various regions of Canaan; during this time period, the two forms of settlements, walled and open, coexisted.

Given the search area Moses designated, the spies would have encountered a land that in some areas was densely occupied and in others sparsely inhabited. The Jezreel and Jordan Valleys were densely populated, as were most northern hill regions, but the southern part of upper Galilee and nearly all of lower Galilee were sparsely inhabited.[6]

RETURN AND REPORT OF THE SPIES

After traveling for forty days, the spies returned to Kadesh and informed the people about their findings. The report began positively, but it quickly turned negative. The spies testified that the people who lived in the land were powerful and the cities were large and fortified. Specifically, the spies mentioned the descendants of Anak, the Amalekites, the Hethites, the Jebusites, the Amorites, the Canaanites, and the Nephilim.[7] The sons of Anak were notoriously large warriors who lived in the western region of Canaan in the cities of Gaza, Gath, and Ashdod (Jos 11:21–22). The Amalekites were a nomadic people who lived in the deserts of the southern Negev. The Hethites lived in the Hebron region. The Jebusites lived in and around Jebus (i.e., Jerusalem). The Amorites lived in the hill county, and the Canaanites lived in the lowlands along the seacoast. Some scholars believe that mentioning the Nephilim may have been an exaggeration for rhetorical effect; they were a legendary people thought to be semidivine (Gn 6:1–4).[8] ❖

[1] Carl G. Rasmussen, *Zondervan NIV Atlas of the Bible* (Grand Rapids: Zondervan, 1989), 49, 50. [2] Rasmussen, *NIV Atlas*, 18–19. [3] Yohanan Aharoni, *The Archaeology of the Land of Israel* (Philadelphia: Westminster, 1978), 4–5. [4] Thomas Brisco, *Holman Bible Atlas* (Nashville: Broadman & Holman, 1998), 70; Barry J. Beizel, *The Moody Atlas of Bible Lands* (Chicago: Moody, 1985), 93. [5] Rasmussen, *NIV Atlas*, 42. [6] Amihai Mazar, *Archaeology of the Land of the Bible: 10,000–586 B.C.E.* (New York: Doubleday, 1990), 239; Aharoni, *Archaeology*, 158; Rasmussen, *NIV Atlas*, 34. [7] Timothy R. Ashley, *The Book of Numbers* (Grand Rapids: Eerdmans, 1993), 239. Ashley states, "Amalek was the offspring of Eliphaz son of Esau by the concubine Timna (Gen 36:12)." The Amalekites were constant enemies of Israel. [8] R. K. Harrison, *Numbers: An Exegetical Commentary* (Grand Rapids: Baker, 1992), 209; Ashley, *Numbers*, 243.

live in the hill country; and the Canaanites live by
the sea and along the Jordan."
30 Then Caleb quieted the people in the presence of
Moses and said, "Let's go up now and take possession
of the land because we can certainly conquer it!"
31 But the men who had gone up with him responded, "We can't attack the people because they
are stronger than we are!" 32 So they gave a negative
report to the Israelites about the land they had scouted: "The land we passed through to explore is one that
devours its inhabitants, and all the people we saw
in it are men of great size. 33 We even saw the Nephilim there — the descendants of Anak come from the
Nephilim! To ourselves we seemed like grasshoppers,
and we must have seemed the same to them."

ISRAEL'S REFUSAL TO ENTER CANAAN

14 Then the whole community broke into loud
cries, and the people wept that night. 2 All the
Israelites complained about Moses and Aaron, and
the whole community told them, "If only we had died
in the land of Egypt, or if only we had died in this
wilderness! 3 Why is the LORD bringing us into this
land to die by the sword? Our wives and children
will become plunder. Wouldn't it be better for us to
go back to Egypt?" 4 So they said to one another, "Let's
appoint a leader and go back to Egypt."
5 Then Moses and Aaron fell facedown in front of
the whole assembly of the Israelite community. 6 Joshua son of Nun and Caleb son of Jephunneh, who were
among those who scouted out the land, tore their
clothes 7 and said to the entire Israelite community,
"The land we passed through and explored is an extremely good land. 8 If the LORD is pleased with us, he
will bring us into this land, a land flowing with milk
and honey, and give it to us. 9 Only don't rebel against
the LORD, and don't be afraid of the people of the land,
for we will devour them. Their protection has been
removed from them, and the LORD is with us. Don't
be afraid of them!"
10 While the whole community threatened to stone
them, the glory of the LORD appeared to all the Israelites at the tent of meeting.

GOD'S JUDGMENT OF ISRAEL'S REBELLION

11 The LORD said to Moses, "How long will these people despise me? How long will they not trust in me
despite all the signs I have performed among them?
12 I will strike them with a plague and destroy them.
Then I will make you into a greater and mightier nation than they are."
13 But Moses replied to the LORD, "The Egyptians
will hear about it, for by your strength you brought
up this people from them. 14 They will tell it to the inhabitants of this land. They have heard that you, LORD,
are among these people, how you, LORD, are seen face
to face, how your cloud stands over them, and how
you go before them in a pillar of cloud by day and in
a pillar of fire by night. 15 If you kill this people with
a single blow,[A] the nations that have heard of your
fame will declare, 16 'Since the LORD wasn't able to
bring this people into the land he swore to give them,
he has slaughtered them in the wilderness.'
17 "So now, may my Lord's power be magnified just
as you have spoken: 18 The LORD is slow to anger and
abounding in faithful love, forgiving iniquity and rebellion. But he will not leave the guilty unpunished,
bringing the consequences of the fathers' iniquity
on the children to the third and fourth generation.
19 Please pardon the iniquity of this people, in keeping
with the greatness of your faithful love, just as you
have forgiven them from Egypt until now."
20 The LORD responded, "I have pardoned them as
you requested. 21 Yet as I live and as the whole earth
is filled with the LORD's glory, 22 none of the men who
have seen my glory and the signs I performed in Egypt
and in the wilderness, and have tested me these ten
times and did not obey me, 23 will ever see the land I
swore to give their ancestors. None of those who have
despised me will see it. 24 But since my servant Caleb
has a different spirit and has remained loyal to me, I
will bring him into the land where he has gone, and
his descendants will inherit it. 25 Since the Amalekites and Canaanites are living in the lowlands,[B] turn
back tomorrow and head for the wilderness in the
direction of the Red Sea."
26 Then the LORD spoke to Moses and Aaron: 27 "How
long must I endure this evil community that keeps
complaining about me? I have heard the Israelites'
complaints that they make against me. 28 Tell them:
As I live — this is the LORD's declaration — I will do
to you exactly as I heard you say. 29 Your corpses will
fall in this wilderness — all of you who were registered in the census, the entire number of you twenty
years old or more — because you have complained
about me. 30 I swear that none of you will enter the
land I promised[C] to settle you in, except Caleb son of
Jephunneh and Joshua son of Nun. 31 I will bring your
children whom you said would become plunder into
the land you rejected, and they will enjoy it. 32 But
as for you, your corpses will fall in this wilderness.
33 Your children will be shepherds in the wilderness
for forty years and bear the penalty for your acts of
unfaithfulness until all your corpses lie scattered in
the wilderness. 34 You will bear the consequences of
your iniquities forty years based on the number of
the forty days that you scouted the land, a year for

[A] **14:15** Lit *people as one man* [B] **14:25** Lit *valley* [C] **14:30** Lit *I raised my hand*

each day.[A] You will know my displeasure.[B] 35 I, the LORD, have spoken. I swear that I will do this to the entire evil community that has conspired against me. They will come to an end in the wilderness, and there they will die."

36 So the men Moses sent to scout out the land, and who returned and incited the entire community to complain about him by spreading a negative report about the land — 37 those men who spread the negative report about the land were struck down by the LORD. 38 Only Joshua son of Nun and Caleb son of Jephunneh remained alive of those men who went to scout out the land.

ISRAEL ROUTED

39 When Moses reported these words to all the Israelites, the people were overcome with grief. 40 They got up early the next morning and went up the ridge of the hill country, saying, "Let's go to the place the LORD promised, for we were wrong."

41 But Moses responded, "Why are you going against the LORD's command? It won't succeed. 42 Don't go, because the LORD is not among you and you will be defeated by your enemies. 43 The Amalekites and Canaanites are right in front of you, and you will fall by the sword. The LORD won't be with you, since you have turned from following him."

44 But they dared to go up the ridge of the hill country, even though the ark of the LORD's covenant and Moses did not leave the camp. 45 Then the Amalekites and Canaanites who lived in that part of the hill country came down, attacked them, and routed them as far as Hormah.

LAWS ABOUT OFFERINGS

15 The LORD instructed Moses, 2 "Speak to the Israelites and tell them: When you enter the land I am giving you to settle in, 3 and you make a food offering to the LORD from the herd or flock — either a burnt offering or a sacrifice, to fulfill a vow, or as a freewill offering, or at your appointed festivals — to produce a pleasing aroma for the LORD, 4 the one presenting his offering to the LORD is also to present a grain offering of two quarts[C] of fine flour mixed with a quart[D] of oil. 5 Prepare a quart of wine as a drink offering with the burnt offering or sacrifice of each lamb.

6 "If you prepare a grain offering with a ram, it is to be four quarts[E] of fine flour mixed with a third of a gallon[F] of oil. 7 Also present a third of a gallon of wine for a drink offering as a pleasing aroma to the LORD.

8 "If you prepare a young bull as a burnt offering or as a sacrifice, to fulfill a vow, or as a fellowship offering to the LORD, 9 a grain offering of six quarts[G] of fine flour mixed with two quarts[H] of oil is to be presented with the bull. 10 Also present two quarts of wine as a drink offering. It is a food offering, a pleasing aroma to the LORD. 11 This is to be done for each ox, ram, lamb, or goat. 12 This is how you are to prepare each of them, no matter how many.

13 "Every Israelite is to prepare these things in this way when he presents a food offering as a pleasing aroma to the LORD. 14 When an alien resides with you or someone else is among you and wants to prepare a food offering as a pleasing aroma to the LORD, he is to do exactly as you do throughout your generations. 15 The assembly is to have the same statute for both you and the resident alien as a permanent statute throughout your generations. You and the alien will be alike before the LORD. 16 The same law and the same ordinance will apply to both you and the alien who resides with you."

17 The LORD instructed Moses, 18 "Speak to the Israelites and tell them: After you enter the land where I am bringing you, 19 you are to offer a contribution to the LORD when you eat from the food of the land. 20 You are to offer a loaf from your first batch of dough as a contribution; offer it just like a contribution from the threshing floor. 21 Throughout your generations, you are to give the LORD a contribution from the first batch of your dough.

22 "When you sin unintentionally and do not obey all these commands that the LORD spoke to Moses — 23 all that the LORD has commanded you through Moses, from the day the LORD issued the commands and onward throughout your generations — 24 and if it was done unintentionally without the community's awareness, the entire community is to prepare one young bull for a burnt offering as a pleasing aroma to the LORD, with its grain offering and drink offering according to the regulation, and one male goat as a sin offering. 25 The priest will then make atonement for the entire Israelite community so that they may be forgiven, for the sin was unintentional. They are to bring their offering, a food offering to the LORD, and their sin offering before the LORD for their unintentional sin. 26 The entire Israelite community and the alien who resides among them will be forgiven, since it happened to all the people unintentionally.

27 "If one person sins unintentionally, he is to present a year-old female goat as a sin offering. 28 The priest will then make atonement before the LORD on behalf of the person who acts in error sinning unintentionally, and when he makes atonement for

[A] **14:34** Lit *a day for the year, a day for the year* [B] **14:34** Or *my opposition* [C] **15:4** Lit *a tenth* (of an ephah) [D] **15:4** Lit *a fourth hin*, also in v. 5 [E] **15:6** Lit *two-tenths* (of an ephah) [F] **15:6** Lit *a third hin*, also in v. 7 [G] **15:9** Lit *three-tenths* (of an ephah) [H] **15:9** Lit *a half hin*, also in v. 10

View of Hebron looking toward the south.

The city of Hebron was founded seven years before Zoan (Nm 13:22), which is the city of Tanis in Egypt. As records give information about the founding of Tanis, we can confidently place the founding of Hebron as a city in 1737 BC. Archaeological evidence, however, indicates that the region has been continually inhabited since approximately 3500–3300 BC.

Located about nineteen miles south of Jerusalem in the southern hill country of Judah, Hebron sits on one of the highest points in the hill country, at an elevation of 3,040 feet above sea level. Hebron's original name was Kiriath-arba (Gn 23:2; Jos 20:7), and the original city was in the enviable position of possessing a prolific spring plus extremely fertile soil in the surrounding countryside. For generations, it was an agricultural center of grape and olive oil production.

The archaeological evidence, what little there is of it, generally supports the biblical account. One archaeologist quipped, "Hebron . . . is one of the biblically most important and archaeologically most disappointing sites in Palestine."[1] William F. Albright conducted surveys of the region in the 1920s, and an American expedition dug in the 1960s. Work resumed in the 1980s with the Judean Hills Survey Expedition, sponsored by the Israelis. The political situation there has made archaeological work difficult for the past several decades. Al-Khalil, modern-day Hebron, is part of the West Bank, under Palestinian authority.

Basically two areas of archaeological importance exist in and around Hebron: the ancient city (Tel Hebron) and the traditional tomb of Abraham on a slope opposite the ancient city (Haram al-Khalil). Regarding the ancient city itself, archaeological evidence supports a major settlement of about six to seven acres in the Judean hills dating to the Middle Bronze Age, the period compatible with Abraham and the other ancestors of Israel.[2] This settlement was surrounded by a wall that is partly visible even today. The site was later abandoned temporarily in the Late Bronze Age (the time of the conquest) but was inhabited once again to an even greater capacity in the Iron Age, the period associated with

Interior of the Machpelah in Hebron. Shown are the striped stone-layered cenotaphs, which are not the actual tombs but structures marking the site of the subterranean burial caves. Buried at Machpelah are Abraham and Sarah; Jacob and Leah; and, shown, Rebekah on the left and Isaac on the right. King Herod (37 BC–AD 4) built the structures over the burial caves.

A Herodian building in a remarkable state of preservation, erected by King Herod over the caves of Machpelah at Hebron in Israel. The building was used as a Christian church during the Crusades but was converted to a mosque when Saladin drove out the Crusaders and established the tenets of Islam in the region.

Alabaster bowl from the Middle Bronze Age I (2200–1950 BC), carved in Hebron.

David. A spring in the city continues to provide cold water year-round, a very important commodity in the Judean desert. Today the site of the ancient city overlooks the modern city of Hebron. The Cave of Machpelah (Haram al-Khalil) is also an important archaeological site. For archaeologists, its enormous popularity is also its downfall. The problem is that the monumental structure supposedly built by Herod covers the area, and there has been no systematic excavation of remains under the building. Evidence of several shaft tombs exists, but the structures above the surface prohibit excavation.

One important find regarding Hebron wasn't found in Hebron itself, but on storage jars discovered in and around Jerusalem and Judah.[3] These jars contained seal impressions on their handles. Almost a thousand such impressions are known. These seals are known as *lamelekh* impressions, an expression that means "belonging to the king." One of the jars includes the impression "belonging to the king of Hebron." Because all the *lamelekh* jars were found in the cities involved in the conflict with Sennacherib, scholars generally date the jars to the time of the conflict between Judah and Assyria, around 600 BC. A specific reference like this to a particular city is rare among archaeological finds in Israel. ✜

---

[1] Harry Thomas Frank, *Bible, Archaeology, and Faith* (Nashville: Abingdon, 1971), 127. [2] Avi Ofer, "Hebron," in *NEAEHL*, 2:608; Amihai Mazar, *Archaeology of the Land of the Bible*: 10,000–586 BCE (New York: Doubleday, 1990), 455–58. [3] Mazar, *Archaeology*.

him, he will be forgiven. 29 You are to have the same law for the person who acts in error, whether he is an Israelite or an alien who resides among you.

30 "But the person who acts defiantly,[A] whether native or resident alien, blasphemes the LORD. That person is to be cut off from his people. 31 He will certainly be cut off, because he has despised the LORD's word and broken his command; his guilt remains on him."

SABBATH VIOLATION

32 While the Israelites were in the wilderness, they found a man gathering wood on the Sabbath day. 33 Those who found him gathering wood brought him to Moses, Aaron, and the entire community. 34 They placed him in custody because it had not been decided what should be done to him. 35 Then the LORD told Moses, "The man is to be put to death. The entire community is to stone him outside the camp." 36 So the entire community brought him outside the camp and stoned him to death, as the LORD had commanded Moses.

TASSELS FOR REMEMBRANCE

37 The LORD said to Moses, 38 "Speak to the Israelites and tell them that throughout their generations they are to make tassels for the corners of their garments, and put a blue cord on the tassel at each corner. 39 These will serve as tassels for you to look at, so that you may remember all the LORD's commands and obey them and not prostitute yourselves by following your own heart and your own eyes. 40 This way you will remember and obey all my commands and be holy to your God. 41 I am the LORD your God who brought you out of the land of Egypt to be your God; I am the LORD your God."

KORAH INCITES REBELLION

16 Now Korah son of Izhar, son of Kohath, son of Levi, with Dathan and Abiram, sons of Eliab, and On son of Peleth, sons of Reuben, took 2 two hundred fifty prominent Israelite men who were leaders of the community and representatives in the assembly, and they rebelled against Moses. 3 They came together against Moses and Aaron and told them, "You have gone too far! Everyone in the entire community is holy, and the LORD is among them. Why then do you exalt yourselves above the LORD's assembly?"

4 When Moses heard this, he fell facedown. 5 Then he said to Korah and all his followers, "Tomorrow morning the LORD will reveal who belongs to him, who is set apart, and the one he will let come near him. He will let the one he chooses come near him. 6 Korah, you and all your followers are to do this: take firepans, and tomorrow 7 place fire in them and put incense on them before the LORD. Then the man the LORD chooses will be the one who is set apart. It is you Levites who have gone too far!"

8 Moses also told Korah, "Now listen, Levites! 9 Isn't it enough for you that the God of Israel has separated you from the Israelite community to bring you near to himself, to perform the work at the LORD's tabernacle, and to stand before the community to minister to them? 10 He has brought you near, and all your fellow Levites who are with you, but you are pursuing the priesthood as well. 11 Therefore, it is you and all your followers who have conspired against the LORD! As for Aaron, who is he[B] that you should complain about him?"

12 Moses sent for Dathan and Abiram, the sons of Eliab, but they said, "We will not come! 13 Is it not enough that you brought us up from a land flowing with milk and honey to kill us in the wilderness? Do you also have to appoint yourself as ruler over us? 14 Furthermore, you didn't bring us to a land flowing with milk and honey or give us an inheritance of fields and vineyards. Will you gouge out the eyes of these men? We will not come!"

15 Then Moses became angry and said to the LORD, "Don't respect their offering. I have not taken one donkey from them or mistreated a single one of them." 16 So Moses told Korah, "You and all your followers are to appear before the LORD tomorrow — you, they, and Aaron. 17 Each of you is to take his firepan, place incense on it, and present his firepan before the LORD — 250 firepans. You and Aaron are each to present your firepan also."

18 Each man took his firepan, placed fire in it, put incense on it, and stood at the entrance to the tent of meeting along with Moses and Aaron. 19 After Korah assembled the whole community against them at the entrance to the tent of meeting, the glory of the LORD appeared to the whole community. 20 The LORD spoke to Moses and Aaron, 21 "Separate yourselves from this community so I may consume them instantly."

22 But Moses and Aaron fell facedown and said, "God, God who gives breath to all,[C] when one man sins, will you vent your wrath on the whole community?"

23 The LORD replied to Moses, 24 "Tell the community: Get away from the dwellings of Korah, Dathan, and Abiram."

25 Moses got up and went to Dathan and Abiram, and the elders of Israel followed him. 26 He warned the community, "Get away now from the tents of these wicked men. Don't touch anything that belongs to them, or you will be swept away because of all their

[A] **15:30** Lit *with a high hand* [B] **16:11** Or *Aaron, what has he done* [C] **16:22** Or *God of the spirits of all flesh*

sins." 27 So they got away from the dwellings of Korah, Dathan, and Abiram. Meanwhile, Dathan and Abiram came out and stood at the entrance of their tents with their wives, children, and infants.

28 Then Moses said, "This is how you will know that the LORD sent me to do all these things and that it was not of my own will: 29 If these men die naturally as all people would, and suffer the fate of all, then the LORD has not sent me. 30 But if the LORD brings about something unprecedented, and the ground opens its mouth and swallows them along with all that belongs to them so that they go down alive into Sheol, then you will know that these men have despised the LORD."

31 Just as he finished speaking all these words, the ground beneath them split open. 32 The earth opened its mouth and swallowed them and their households, all Korah's people, and all their possessions. 33 They went down alive into Sheol with all that belonged to them. The earth closed over them, and they vanished from the assembly. 34 At their cries, all the people of Israel who were around them fled because they thought, "The earth may swallow us too!" 35 Fire also came out from the LORD and consumed the 250 men who were presenting the incense.

36 Then the LORD spoke to Moses: 37 "Tell Eleazar son of Aaron the priest to remove the firepans from the burning debris, because they are holy, and scatter the fire far away. 38 As for the firepans of those who sinned at the cost of their own lives, make them into hammered sheets as plating for the altar, for they presented them before the LORD, and the firepans are holy. They will be a sign to the Israelites."

39 So the priest Eleazar took the bronze firepans that those who were burned had presented, and they were hammered into plating for the altar, 40 just as the LORD commanded him through Moses. It was to be a reminder for the Israelites that no unauthorized person outside the lineage of Aaron should approach to offer incense before the LORD and become like Korah and his followers.

41 The next day the entire Israelite community complained about Moses and Aaron, saying, "You have killed the LORD's people!" 42 When the community assembled against them, Moses and Aaron turned toward the tent of meeting, and suddenly the cloud covered it, and the LORD's glory appeared.

43 Moses and Aaron went to the front of the tent of meeting, 44 and the LORD said to Moses, 45 "Get away from this community so that I may consume them instantly." But they fell facedown.

46 Then Moses told Aaron, "Take your firepan, place fire from the altar in it, and add incense. Go quickly to the community and make atonement for them, because wrath has come from the LORD; the plague has begun." 47 So Aaron took his firepan as Moses had ordered, ran into the middle of the assembly, and saw that the plague had begun among the people. After he added incense, he made atonement for the people. 48 He stood between the dead and the living, and the plague was halted. 49 But those who died from the plague numbered 14,700, in addition to those who died because of the Korah incident. 50 Aaron then returned to Moses at the entrance to the tent of meeting, since the plague had been halted.

AARON'S STAFF CHOSEN

17 The LORD instructed Moses, 2 "Speak to the Israelites and take one staff from them for each ancestral tribe,[A] twelve staffs from all the leaders of their tribes.[B] Write each man's name on his staff. 3 Write Aaron's name on Levi's staff, because there is to be one staff for the head of each tribe. 4 Then place them in the tent of meeting in front of the testimony where I meet with you. 5 The staff of the man I choose will sprout, and I will rid myself of the Israelites' complaints that they have been making about you."

6 So Moses spoke to the Israelites, and each of their leaders gave him a staff, one for each of the leaders of their tribes, twelve staffs in all. Aaron's staff was among them. 7 Moses placed the staffs before the LORD in the tent of the testimony.

8 The next day Moses entered the tent of the testimony and saw that Aaron's staff, representing the house of Levi, had sprouted, formed buds, blossomed, and produced almonds! 9 Moses then brought out all the staffs from the LORD's presence to all the Israelites. They saw them, and each man took his own staff. 10 The LORD told Moses, "Put Aaron's staff back in front of the testimony to be kept as a sign for the rebels, so that you may put an end to their complaints before me, or else they will die." 11 So Moses did as the LORD commanded him.

12 Then the Israelites declared to Moses, "Look, we're perishing! We're lost; we're all lost! 13 Anyone who comes near the LORD's tabernacle will die. Will we all perish?"

PROVISION FOR THE PRIESTHOOD

18 The LORD said to Aaron, "You, your sons, and your ancestral family[C] will be responsible for iniquity against the sanctuary. You and your sons will be responsible for iniquity involving your priesthood. 2 But also bring your relatives with you from the tribe of Levi, your ancestral tribe, so they may join you and assist you and your sons in front of the tent of the testimony. 3 They are to perform duties

[A] **17:2** Lit *father's house* [B] **17:2** Lit *the house of their fathers*, also in vv. 3,6 [C] **18:1** Lit *the house of your father*

for you and for the whole tent. They must not come near the sanctuary equipment or the altar; otherwise, both they and you will die. 4 They are to join you and guard the tent of meeting, doing all the work at the tent, but no unauthorized person may come near you.

5 "You are to guard the sanctuary and the altar so that wrath may not fall on the Israelites again. 6 Look, I have selected your fellow Levites from the Israelites as a gift for you, assigned by the LORD to work at the tent of meeting. 7 But you and your sons will carry out your priestly responsibilities for everything concerning the altar and for what is inside the curtain, and you will do that work. I am giving you the work of the priesthood as a gift,[A] but an unauthorized person who comes near the sanctuary will be put to death."

SUPPORT FOR THE PRIESTS AND LEVITES

8 Then the LORD spoke to Aaron, "Look, I have put you in charge of the contributions brought to me. As for all the holy offerings of the Israelites, I have given them to you and your sons as a portion and a permanent statute. 9 A portion of the holiest offerings kept from the fire will be yours; every one of their offerings that they give me, whether the grain offering, sin offering, or guilt offering will be most holy for you and your sons. 10 You are to eat it as a most holy offering.[B] Every male may eat it; it is to be holy to you.

11 "The contribution of their gifts also belongs to you. I have given all the Israelites' presentation offerings to you and to your sons and daughters as a permanent statute. Every ceremonially clean person in your house may eat it. 12 I am giving you all the best of the fresh oil, new wine, and grain, which the Israelites give to the LORD as their firstfruits. 13 The firstfruits of all that is in their land, which they bring to the LORD, belong to you. Every clean person in your house may eat them.

14 "Everything in Israel that is permanently dedicated to the LORD belongs to you. 15 The firstborn of every living thing, human or animal, presented to the LORD belongs to you. But you must certainly redeem a human firstborn, and redeem the firstborn of an unclean animal. 16 You will pay the redemption price for a month-old male according to your assessment: five shekels[C] of silver by the standard sanctuary shekel, which is twenty gerahs.

17 "However, you must not redeem the firstborn of an ox, a sheep, or a goat; they are holy. You are to splatter their blood on the altar and burn their fat as a food offering for a pleasing aroma to the LORD. 18 But their meat belongs to you. It belongs to you like the breast of the presentation offering and the right thigh.

19 "I give to you and to your sons and daughters all the holy contributions that the Israelites present to the LORD as a permanent statute. It is a permanent covenant of salt before the LORD for you as well as your offspring."

20 The LORD told Aaron, "You will not have an inheritance in their land; there will be no portion among them for you. I am your portion and your inheritance among the Israelites.

21 "Look, I have given the Levites every tenth in Israel as an inheritance in return for the work they do, the work of the tent of meeting. 22 The Israelites must never again come near the tent of meeting, or they will incur guilt and die. 23 The Levites will do the work of the tent of meeting, and they will bear the consequences of their iniquity. The Levites will not receive an inheritance among the Israelites; this is a permanent statute throughout your generations. 24 For I have given them the tenth that the Israelites present to the LORD as a contribution for their inheritance. That is why I told them that they would not receive an inheritance among the Israelites."

25 The LORD instructed Moses, 26 "Speak to the Levites and tell them: When you receive from the Israelites the tenth that I have given you as your inheritance, you are to present part of it as an offering to the LORD — a tenth of the tenth. 27 Your offering will be credited to you as if it were your grain from the threshing floor or the full harvest from the winepress. 28 You are to present an offering to the LORD from every tenth you receive from the Israelites. Give some of it to the priest Aaron as an offering to the LORD. 29 You must present the entire offering due the LORD from all your gifts. The best part of the tenth is to be consecrated.

30 "Tell them further: Once you have presented the best part of the tenth, and it is credited to you Levites as the produce of the threshing floor or the winepress, 31 then you and your household may eat it anywhere. It is your wage in return for your work at the tent of meeting. 32 You will not incur guilt because of it once you have presented the best part of it, but you must not defile the Israelites' holy offerings, so that you will not die."

PURIFICATION RITUAL

19 The LORD spoke to Moses and Aaron, 2 "This is the legal statute that the LORD has commanded: Instruct the Israelites to bring you an unblemished red cow that has no defect and has never been yoked. 3 Give it to the priest Eleazar, and he will have it brought outside the camp and slaughtered in his presence. 4 The priest Eleazar is to take some of its blood with his finger and sprinkle it seven times

[A] **18:7** Or *curtain. So you are to perform the service; a gift of your priesthood I grant* [B] **18:10** Or *it in a most holy place* [C] **18:16** A shekel is about two-fifths of an ounce

toward the front of the tent of meeting. 5 The cow is to be burned in his sight. Its hide, flesh, and blood are to be burned along with its waste. 6 The priest is to take cedar wood, hyssop, and crimson yarn, and throw them onto the fire where the cow is burning. 7 Then the priest must wash his clothes and bathe his body in water; after that he may enter the camp, but he will remain ceremonially unclean until evening. 8 The one who burned the cow must also wash his clothes and bathe his body in water, and he will remain unclean until evening.

9 "A man who is clean is to gather up the cow's ashes and deposit them outside the camp in a ceremonially clean place. The ashes will be kept by the Israelite community for preparing the water to remove impurity; it is a sin offering. 10 Then the one who gathers up the cow's ashes must wash his clothes, and he will remain unclean until evening. This is a permanent statute for the Israelites and for the alien who resides among them.

11 "The person who touches any human corpse will be unclean for seven days. 12 He is to purify himself with the water[A] on the third day and the seventh day; then he will be clean. But if he does not purify himself on the third and seventh days, he will not be clean. 13 Anyone who touches a body of a person who has died, and does not purify himself, defiles the tabernacle of the LORD. That person will be cut off from Israel. He remains unclean because the water for impurity has not been sprinkled on him, and his uncleanness is still on him.

14 "This is the law when a person dies in a tent: everyone who enters the tent and everyone who is already in the tent will be unclean for seven days, 15 and any open container without a lid tied on it is unclean. 16 Anyone in the open field who touches a person who has been killed by the sword or has died, or who even touches a human bone, or a grave, will be unclean for seven days. 17 For the purification of the unclean person, they are to take some of the ashes of the burnt sin offering, put them in a jar, and add fresh water to them. 18 A person who is clean is to take hyssop, dip it in the water, and sprinkle the tent, all the furnishings, and the people who were there. He is also to sprinkle the one who touched a bone, a grave, a corpse, or a person who had been killed.

19 "The one who is clean is to sprinkle the unclean person on the third day and the seventh day. After he purifies the unclean person on the seventh day, the one being purified must wash his clothes and bathe in water, and he will be clean by evening. 20 But a person who is unclean and does not purify himself, that person will be cut off from the assembly because he has defiled the sanctuary of the LORD. The water for impurity has not been sprinkled on him; he is unclean. 21 This is a permanent statute for them. The person who sprinkles the water for impurity is to wash his clothes, and whoever touches the water for impurity will be unclean until evening. 22 Anything the unclean person touches will become unclean, and anyone who touches it will be unclean until evening."

WATER FROM THE ROCK

20 The entire Israelite community entered the Wilderness of Zin in the first month, and they[B] settled in Kadesh. Miriam died and was buried there.

2 There was no water for the community, so they assembled against Moses and Aaron. 3 The people quarreled with Moses and said, "If only we had perished when our brothers perished before the LORD. 4 Why have you brought the LORD's assembly into this wilderness for us and our livestock to die here? 5 Why have you led us up from Egypt to bring us to this evil place? It's not a place of grain, figs, vines, and pomegranates, and there is no water to drink!"

6 Then Moses and Aaron went from the presence of the assembly to the doorway of the tent of meeting. They fell facedown, and the glory of the LORD appeared to them. 7 The LORD spoke to Moses, 8 "Take the staff and assemble the community. You and your brother Aaron are to speak to the rock while they watch, and it will yield its water. You will bring out water for them from the rock and provide drink for the community and their livestock."

9 So Moses took the staff from the LORD's presence just as he had commanded him. 10 Moses and Aaron summoned the assembly in front of the rock, and Moses said to them, "Listen, you rebels! Must we bring water out of this rock for you?" 11 Then Moses raised his hand and struck the rock twice with his staff, so that abundant water gushed out, and the community and their livestock drank.

12 But the LORD said to Moses and Aaron, "Because you did not trust me to demonstrate my holiness in the sight of the Israelites, you will not bring this assembly into the land I have given them." 13 These are the Waters of Meribah,[C] where the Israelites quarreled with the LORD, and he demonstrated his holiness to them.

EDOM DENIES PASSAGE

14 Moses sent messengers from Kadesh to the king of Edom, "This is what your brother Israel says, 'You know all the hardships that have overtaken us. 15 Our ancestors went down to Egypt, and we lived in Egypt many years, but the Egyptians treated us and our ancestors badly. 16 When we cried out to the LORD,

[A] **19:12** Or *ashes*; lit *with it* [B] **20:1** Lit *the people* [C] **20:13** = Quarreling

he heard our plea,[A] and sent an angel,[B] and brought
us out of Egypt. Now look, we are in Kadesh, a city
on the border of your territory. 17 Please let us travel
through your land. We won't travel through any field
or vineyard, or drink any well water. We will travel
the King's Highway; we won't turn to the right or the
left until we have traveled through your territory.' "

18 But Edom answered him, "You will not travel
through our land, or we will come out and confront
you with the sword."

19 "We will go on the main road," the Israelites replied to them, "and if we or our herds drink your
water, we will pay its price. There will be no problem;
only let us travel through on foot."

20 Yet Edom insisted, "You may not travel through."
And they came out to confront them with a large
force of heavily-armed people.[C] 21 Edom refused to
allow Israel to travel through their territory, and Israel turned away from them.

AARON'S DEATH

22 After they set out from Kadesh, the entire Israelite
community came to Mount Hor. 23 The LORD said to
Moses and Aaron at Mount Hor on the border of the
land of Edom, 24 "Aaron will be gathered to his people;
he will not enter the land I have given the Israelites,
because you both rebelled against my command at
the Waters of Meribah. 25 Take Aaron and his son
Eleazar and bring them up Mount Hor. 26 Remove
Aaron's garments and put them on his son Eleazar.
Aaron will be gathered to his people and die there."

27 So Moses did as the LORD commanded, and they
climbed Mount Hor in the sight of the whole community. 28 After Moses removed Aaron's garments and
put them on his son Eleazar, Aaron died there on top
of the mountain. Then Moses and Eleazar came down
from the mountain. 29 When the whole community
saw that Aaron had passed away, the entire house of
Israel mourned for him thirty days.

CANAANITE KING DEFEATED

21 When the Canaanite king of Arad, who lived
in the Negev, heard that Israel was coming on
the Atharim road, he fought against Israel and captured some prisoners. 2 Then Israel made a vow to the
LORD, "If you will hand this people over to us, we will
completely destroy their cities." 3 The LORD listened
to Israel's request and handed the Canaanites over
to them, and Israel completely destroyed them and
their cities. So they named the place Hormah.[D]

THE BRONZE SNAKE

4 Then they set out from Mount Hor by way of the Red
Sea to bypass the land of Edom, but the people became impatient because of the journey. 5 The people
spoke against God and Moses: "Why have you led us
up from Egypt to die in the wilderness? There is no
bread or water, and we detest this wretched food!"
6 Then the LORD sent poisonous[E] snakes among the
people, and they bit them so that many Israelites died.

7 The people then came to Moses and said, "We
have sinned by speaking against the LORD and against
you. Intercede with the LORD so that he will take the
snakes away from us." And Moses interceded for
the people.

8 Then the LORD said to Moses, "Make a snake image and mount it on a pole. When anyone who is
bitten looks at it, he will recover." 9 So Moses made
a bronze snake and mounted it on a pole. Whenever
someone was bitten, and he looked at the bronze
snake, he recovered.

JOURNEY AROUND MOAB

10 The Israelites set out and camped at Oboth. 11 They
set out from Oboth and camped at Iye-abarim in the
wilderness that borders Moab on the east. 12 From
there they went and camped at Zered Valley. 13 They
set out from there and camped on the other side of the
Arnon River, in the wilderness that extends from the
Amorite border, because the Arnon was the Moabite
border between Moab and the Amorites. 14 Therefore
it is stated in the Book of the LORD's Wars:

Waheb in Suphah
and the ravines of the Arnon,
15 even the slopes of the ravines
that extend to the site of Ar
and lie along the border of Moab.

16 From there they went to Beer,[F] the well the LORD
told Moses about, "Gather the people so I may give
them water." 17 Then Israel sang this song:

Spring up, well — sing to it!
18 The princes dug the well;
the nobles of the people hollowed it out
with a scepter and with their staffs.

They went from the wilderness to Mattanah,
19 from Mattanah to Nahaliel, from Nahaliel to Bamoth, 20 from Bamoth to the valley in the territory
of Moab near the Pisgah highlands that overlook
the wasteland.[G]

AMORITE KINGS DEFEATED

21 Israel sent messengers to say to King Sihon of the
Amorites, 22 "Let us travel through your land. We
won't go into the fields or vineyards. We won't drink
any well water. We will travel the King's Highway

[A] **20:16** Lit *voice* [B] **20:16** Or *a messenger* [C] **20:20** Lit *with numerous people and a strong hand* [D] **21:3** = Destruction [E] **21:6** Lit *Burning* [F] **21:16** = Well [G] **21:20** Or *overlook Jeshimon*

until we have traveled through your territory." 23 But Sihon would not let Israel travel through his territory. Instead, he gathered his whole army and went out to confront Israel in the wilderness. When he came to Jahaz, he fought against Israel. 24 Israel struck him with the sword and took possession of his land from the Arnon to the Jabbok, but only up to the Ammonite border, because it was fortified.[A]

25 Israel took all the cities and lived in all these Amorite cities, including Heshbon and all its surrounding villages. 26 Heshbon was the city of King Sihon of the Amorites, who had fought against the former king of Moab and had taken control of all his land as far as the Arnon. 27 Therefore the poets[B] say:

Come to Heshbon, let it be rebuilt;
let the city of Sihon be restored.[C]
28 For fire came out of Heshbon,
a flame from the city of Sihon.
It consumed Ar of Moab,
the citizens of Arnon's heights.
29 Woe to you, Moab!
You have been destroyed, people of Chemosh!
He gave up his sons as refugees,
and his daughters into captivity
to Sihon the Amorite king.
30 We threw them down;
Heshbon has been destroyed as far as Dibon.
We caused desolation as far as Nophah,
which reaches as far as Medeba.

31 So Israel lived in the Amorites' land. 32 After Moses sent spies to Jazer, Israel captured its surrounding villages and drove out the Amorites who were there.

33 Then they turned and went up the road to Bashan, and King Og of Bashan came out against them with his whole army to do battle at Edrei. 34 But the LORD said to Moses, "Do not fear him, for I have handed him over to you along with his whole army and his land. Do to him as you did to King Sihon of the Amorites, who lived in Heshbon." 35 So they struck him, his sons, and his whole army until no one was left,[D] and they took possession of his land.

BALAK HIRES BALAAM

22 The Israelites traveled on and camped in the plains of Moab near the Jordan across from Jericho. 2 Now Balak son of Zippor saw all that Israel had done to the Amorites. 3 Moab was terrified of the people because they were numerous, and Moab dreaded the Israelites. 4 So the Moabites said to the elders of Midian, "This horde will devour everything around us like an ox eats up the green plants in the field."

Since Balak son of Zippor was Moab's king at that time, 5 he sent messengers to Balaam son of Beor at Pethor, which is by the Euphrates in the land of his people.[E,F] Balak said to him, "Look, a people has come out of Egypt; they cover the surface of the land and are living right across from me. 6 Please come and put a curse on these people for me because they are more powerful than I am. I may be able to defeat them and drive them out of the land, for I know that those you bless are blessed and those you curse are cursed."

7 The elders of Moab and Midian departed with fees for divination in hand. They came to Balaam and reported Balak's words to him. 8 He said to them, "Spend the night here, and I will give you the answer the LORD tells me." So the officials of Moab stayed with Balaam.

9 Then God came to Balaam and asked, "Who are these men with you?"

10 Balaam replied to God, "Balak son of Zippor, king of Moab, sent this message to me: 11 'Look, a people has come out of Egypt, and they cover the surface of the land. Now come and put a curse on them for me. I may be able to fight against them and drive them away.'"

12 Then God said to Balaam, "You are not to go with them. You are not to curse this people, for they are blessed."

13 So Balaam got up the next morning and said to Balak's officials, "Go back to your land, because the LORD has refused to let me go with you."

14 The officials of Moab arose, returned to Balak, and reported, "Balaam refused to come with us."

15 Balak sent officials again who were more numerous and higher in rank than the others. 16 They came to Balaam and said to him, "This is what Balak son of Zippor says: 'Let nothing keep you from coming to me, 17 for I will greatly honor you and do whatever you ask me. So please come and put a curse on these people for me!'"

18 But Balaam responded to the servants of Balak, "If Balak were to give me his house full of silver and gold, I could not go against the command of the LORD my God to do anything small or great. 19 Please stay here overnight as the others did, so that I may find out what else the LORD has to tell me."

20 God came to Balaam at night and said to him, "Since these men have come to summon you, get up and go with them, but you must only do what I tell you." 21 When he got up in the morning, Balaam saddled his donkey and went with the officials of Moab.

BALAAM'S DONKEY AND THE ANGEL

22 But God was incensed that Balaam was going, and the angel of the LORD took his stand on the path to oppose him. Balaam was riding his donkey, and his two servants were with him. 23 When the donkey

[A] **21:24** LXX reads *because the Ammonite border was Jazer*
[B] **21:27** Lit *ones who speak proverbs* [C] **21:27** Or *firmly founded*
[D] **21:35** Lit *left to him* [E] **22:5** Sam, Vg, Syr read *of the Ammonites*
[F] **22:5** Or *of the Amawites*

saw the angel of the LORD standing on the path with a drawn sword in his hand, she turned off the path and went into the field. So Balaam hit her to return her to the path. 24 Then the angel of the LORD stood in a narrow passage between the vineyards, with a stone wall on either side. 25 The donkey saw the angel of the LORD and pressed herself against the wall, squeezing Balaam's foot against it. So he hit her once again. 26 The angel of the LORD went ahead and stood in a narrow place where there was no room to turn to the right or the left. 27 When the donkey saw the angel of the LORD, she crouched down under Balaam. So he became furious and beat the donkey with his stick.

28 Then the LORD opened the donkey's mouth, and she asked Balaam, "What have I done to you that you have beaten me these three times?"

29 Balaam answered the donkey, "You made me look like a fool. If I had a sword in my hand, I'd kill you now!"

30 But the donkey said, "Am I not the donkey you've ridden all your life until today? Have I ever treated you this way before?"

"No," he replied.

31 Then the LORD opened Balaam's eyes, and he saw the angel of the LORD standing in the path with a drawn sword in his hand. Balaam knelt low and bowed in worship on his face. 32 The angel of the LORD asked him, "Why have you beaten your donkey these three times? Look, I came out to oppose you, because I consider what you are doing to be evil.[A] 33 The donkey saw me and turned away from me these three times. If she had not turned away from me, I would have killed you by now and let her live."

34 Balaam said to the angel of the LORD, "I have sinned, for I did not know that you were standing in the path to confront me. And now, if it is evil in your sight, I will go back."

35 Then the angel of the LORD said to Balaam, "Go with the men, but you are to say only what I tell you." So Balaam went with Balak's officials.

36 When Balak heard that Balaam was coming, he went out to meet him at the Moabite city[B] on the Arnon border at the edge of his territory. 37 Balak asked Balaam, "Did I not send you an urgent summons? Why didn't you come to me? Am I really not able to reward you?"

38 Balaam said to him, "Look, I have come to you, but can I say anything I want? I must speak only the message God puts in my mouth." 39 So Balaam went with Balak, and they came to Kiriath-huzoth.[C] 40 Balak sacrificed cattle, sheep, and goats and sent for Balaam and the officials who were with him.

41 In the morning, Balak took Balaam and brought him to Bamoth-baal.[D] From there he saw the outskirts of the people's camp.

BALAAM'S ORACLES

23 Then Balaam said to Balak, "Build me seven altars here and prepare seven bulls and seven rams for me." 2 So Balak did as Balaam directed, and they offered a bull and a ram on each altar. 3 Balaam said to Balak, "Stay here by your burnt offering while I am gone. Maybe the LORD will meet with me. I will tell you whatever he reveals to me." So he went to a barren hill.

4 God met with him and Balaam said to him, "I have arranged seven altars and offered a bull and a ram on each altar." 5 Then the LORD put a message in Balaam's mouth and said, "Return to Balak and say what I tell you."

6 So he returned to Balak, who was standing there by his burnt offering with all the officials of Moab.

BALAAM'S FIRST ORACLE

7 Balaam proclaimed his poem:

Balak brought me from Aram;
the king of Moab, from the eastern mountains:
"Come, put a curse on Jacob for me;
come, denounce Israel!"
8 How can I curse someone
God has not cursed?
How can I denounce someone the LORD
has not denounced?
9 I see them from the top of rocky cliffs,
and I watch them from the hills.
There is a people living alone;
it does not consider itself among the nations.
10 Who has counted the dust of Jacob
or numbered even one-fourth of Israel?
Let me die the death of the upright;
let the end of my life be like theirs.

11 "What have you done to me?" Balak asked Balaam. "I brought you to curse my enemies, but look, you have only blessed them!"

12 He answered, "Shouldn't I say exactly what the LORD puts in my mouth?"

BALAAM'S SECOND ORACLE

13 Then Balak said to him, "Please come with me to another place where you can see them. You will only see the outskirts of their camp; you won't see all of them. From there, put a curse on them for me." 14 So Balak took him to Lookout Field[E] on top of Pisgah, built seven altars, and offered a bull and a ram on each altar.

15 Balaam said to Balak, "Stay here by your burnt offering while I seek the LORD over there."

[A] **22:32** Lit *because your way is perverse before me* [B] **22:36** Or *at Ir-moab*, or *at Ar of Moab* [C] **22:39** = The City of Streets [D] **22:41** = The High Places of Baal [E] **23:14** Or *to the field of Zophim*

16 The LORD met with Balaam and put a message in his mouth. Then he said, "Return to Balak and say what I tell you."

17 So he returned to Balak, who was standing there by his burnt offering with the officials of Moab. Balak asked him, "What did the LORD say?"

18 Balaam proclaimed his poem:

Balak, get up and listen;
son of Zippor, pay attention to what I say!
19 God is not a man, that he might lie,
or a son of man, that he might change
his mind.
Does he speak and not act,
or promise and not fulfill?
20 I have indeed received a command
to bless;
since he has blessed,[A] I cannot change it.
21 He considers no disaster for Jacob;
he sees no trouble for Israel.[B]
The LORD their God is with them,
and there is rejoicing over the King
among them.
22 God brought them out of Egypt;
he is like the horns of a wild ox for them.[C]
23 There is no magic curse against Jacob
and no divination against Israel.
It will now be said about Jacob and Israel,
"What great things God has done!"
24 A people rise up like a lioness;
they rouse themselves like a lion.
They will not lie down until they devour
the prey
and drink the blood of the slain.

25 Then Balak told Balaam, "Don't curse them and don't bless them!"

26 But Balaam answered him, "Didn't I tell you: Whatever the LORD says, I must do?"

BALAAM'S THIRD ORACLE

27 Again Balak said to Balaam, "Please come. I will take you to another place. Maybe it will be agreeable to God that you can put a curse on them for me there." 28 So Balak took Balaam to the top of Peor, which overlooks the wasteland.[D]

29 Balaam told Balak, "Build me seven altars here and prepare seven bulls and seven rams for me." 30 So Balak did as Balaam said and offered a bull and a ram on each altar.

24 Since Balaam saw that it pleased the LORD to bless Israel, he did not go to seek omens as on previous occasions, but turned[E] toward the wilderness. 2 When Balaam looked up and saw Israel encamped tribe by tribe, the Spirit of God came on him, 3 and he proclaimed his poem:

The oracle of Balaam son of Beor,
the oracle of the man whose eyes
are opened,
4 the oracle of one who hears the sayings
of God,
who sees a vision from the Almighty,
who falls into a trance with his eyes
uncovered:
5 How beautiful are your tents, Jacob,
your dwellings, Israel.
6 They stretch out like river valleys,[F]
like gardens beside a stream,
like aloes the LORD has planted,
like cedars beside the water.
7 Water will flow from his buckets,
and his seed will be by abundant water.
His king will be greater than Agag,
and his kingdom will be exalted.
8 God brought him out of Egypt;
he is like[G] the horns of a wild ox for them.
He will feed on enemy nations
and gnaw their bones;
he will strike them with his arrows.
9 He crouches, he lies down like a lion
or a lioness — who dares to rouse him?
Those who bless you will be blessed,
and those who curse you will be cursed.

10 Then Balak became furious with Balaam, struck his hands together, and said to him, "I summoned you to put a curse on my enemies, but instead, you have blessed them these three times. 11 Now go to your home! I said I would reward you richly, but look, the LORD has denied you a reward."

12 Balaam answered Balak, "Didn't I previously tell the messengers you sent me: 13 If Balak were to give me his house full of silver and gold, I could not go against the LORD's command, to do anything good or bad of my own will? I will say whatever the LORD says. 14 Now I am going back to my people, but first, let me warn you what these people will do to your people in the future."

BALAAM'S FOURTH ORACLE

15 Then he proclaimed his poem:

The oracle of Balaam son of Beor,
the oracle of the man whose eyes are opened;
16 the oracle of one who hears the sayings
of God
and has knowledge from the Most High,
who sees a vision from the Almighty,

[A] **23:20** Sam, LXX read *since I will bless* [B] **23:21** Or *He does not observe sin in Jacob; he does not see wrongdoing in Israel* [C] **23:22** Or *Egypt; they have the horns of a wild ox* [D] **23:28** Or *overlooks Jeshimon* [E] **24:1** Lit *set his face* [F] **24:6** Or *like date palms* [G] **24:8** Or *he has*

Mount Nebo: Its History, Geography, Archaeology, and Significance

by T. J. Betts

Byzantine church atop Mount Nebo.

In Numbers 23:14, Balak the king took Balaam the seer up to "Lookout Field on top of Pisgah" with the intention of having Balaam look down on the camp of the people of Israel and curse them. Deuteronomy 34:1 recounts how God took Moses up to "Mount Nebo, to the top of Pisgah, which faces Jericho" to show him the land he had promised to Abraham and his descendants.

LOCATION AND GEOGRAPHY

In the dry wilderness region of western Jordan, Mount Nebo extends west from Jordan's central plateau, which in biblical times was called the plains of Moab. Even though erosion has been a constant factor in the region, Mount Nebo still rises to a flat top surrounded on all sides by steep slopes. The word *Pisgah* could be another name for it or may be a reference to a prominent peak on it. The mountain is about six miles northwest of Madaba, which was an important settlement on the border of Moab. Additionally, Mount Nebo is about eleven miles from Heshbon, which was at the border between the tribes of Reuben and Gad as the tribes of Israel settled in the promised land. Mount Nebo is almost seventeen miles southeast of Jericho, the great Canaanite stronghold that protected the approach into the land of Canaan from the east. Mount Nebo is about twelve miles east of the mouth of the Jordan River. It is 2,680 feet above sea level and rises about 4,000 feet above the Dead Sea. (The surface of the Dead Sea is the lowest elevation on earth, historically about 1,300 feet below sea level, although it has receded an additional 100-plus feet in the past five decades.) Mount Nebo has two peaks called Siyagha and al-Mukhayyat.[1]

While some have presented other candidates for possible locations of Mount Nebo, three words appear to point to this location as the correct one. First, the word *Neba*, which is the modern word for Nebo, was discovered on one of its ridges. Second, the word *Siaghah* is identical to the Aramaic word *Se'ath*, the word used to translate Nebo in the Targum of Onqelos in Numbers 32:3 where it is called the place of Moses's burial. *Siaghah* is an alternate spelling of the highest summit, Siyagha. Third, the name Tal`at es-Sufa refers to the ascent leading up to the ridge of Mount Nebo from the north. It is related to the Hebrew word *tsuph*, which was part of the Nebo mountain range.[2]

Mount Nebo provides a spectacular view of the region. Beginning the panorama to the north, one may see the eastern side of the highlands of Gilead, which were divided between the tribes of Reuben, Gad, and Manasseh. About fifty miles northwest in Israel, the strategic Beth-shean Valley, which served as an access point from the Jordan River to Israel's inland and the Jezreel Valley, is visible along with the region of ancient Naphtali. To the west, one may view the central mountain range of Judah, including the Mount of Olives; and on the clearest days, one may catch a glimpse of the hills surrounding the eastern side of Jerusalem. To the southwest of Mount Nebo, one can spot Bethlehem and

Mount Nebo as seen from the Jordan River Valley.

the Herodium, one of Herod the Great's magnificent palatial building projects, which lies about three miles south of Bethlehem. Directly south, one can see the Dead Sea toward ancient Zoar.[3]

East of the mountain range where Mount Nebo is located are rolling hills and then beyond them, mostly desert. Southeast of Mount Nebo is the heart of Jordan, the Ard As Sawwan Desert. Just north is the Ard As Sawwan Plain, and north of it is the Syrian Desert.

Pottery excavated at Mount Nebo.

ARCHAEOLOGY AND HISTORY

Excavations at Mount Nebo have uncovered material remains from the biblical era. First, archaeologists have discovered Assyrian-type and Moabite-type pottery in Moabite settlements and tombs. The Judean pottery tradition is also strong, however, pointing to the Judeans who lived in the area as attested in the Old Testament. Second, excavations uncovered Assyrian clay coffins in two of the tombs along with an Assyrian-style cylinder seal.[4] The Assyrian presence in the region is attested in both biblical and extrabiblical texts. At the end of the fourth century AD, a Byzantine church was built on the summit commemorating Moses's encounter with God. In the sixth century, it was enlarged into a basilica full of beautiful mosaics. It was then neglected for many years until the Franciscan Order bought it in 1933. Since then, the Franciscans have excavated and restored much of the church and have also erected other memorials.

One interesting Jewish tradition concerning Mount Nebo comes from the noncanonical book of 2 Maccabees. Numerous caves dot the region, and 2 Maccabees 2:4–8 states that prior to the Babylonian invasion in the sixth century BC, God led Jeremiah to take the tent of the Lord's presence, the altar of incense, and the ark of the covenant to a Mount Nebo. There he discovered a huge cave and hid the sacred pieces. Whether Jeremiah did this or not, this is still part of the story of Mount Nebo.

The mountain likely received its name in honor of the Babylonian god, Nebo or Nabû. Daniel's comrade, Azariah, received the Babylonian name "Abednego" ("servant of Nebo").[5] Given that Assyrians and Babylonians both worshiped this god, the name suggests that the mountain may have been significant to Mesopotamian invaders as they conquered these lands. ✣

---

[1] "Mount Nebo," Tourist Israel: The Guide, 10 May, 2018, www.touristisrael.com/mount-nebo/16954. [2] Henry A. Harper, *The Bible and Modern Discoveries* (London: A. P. Watt, 1895), 139; W. Ewing, "Nebo, Mount," *ISBE*, ed. James Orr (1939). [3] "Mount Nebo," Near East Tourist Agency, 10 May 2018, www.netours.com/content/view/257/30/. [4] Elizabeth Bloch-Smith, *Practices and Beliefs about the Dead* (Sheffield: Sheffield Academic, 1992), 196. [5] Leonard J. Coppes, "§1280 [*nĕbō*]" (*Nebo*, Nebo) in *TWOT*, 545–46. The letter "g" in "Abednego" is most likely an intentional misspelling of this pagan god's name in the Scriptures.

DIGGING DEEPER *Balaam Inscription*

The story of Balaam and his talking donkey (Nm 22:22–40) was viewed skeptically by critical scholars for many decades. It was even doubted that Balaam ever existed. This outlook began to change in 1967 when archaeologists collected a crumbled plaster Aramaic text in the rubble of an ancient building in Deir 'Alla (Jordan). The text contains fifty lines written in faded red and black ink. The inscription reads: "Warnings from the Book of Balaam the son of Beor. He was a seer of the gods" (see Nm 22:5; Jos 24:9). Though the building in which the text was found dates only to the eighth century BC (during the reign of King Uzziah; see Is 6:1), the condition of the plaster and ink of the text itself indicates that it is most likely much older, dating to the time of the biblical Balaam. In addition to Balaam, nearly sixty other Old Testament figures have been historically or archaeologically identified. These include Kings David (1Sm 16:13), Jehu (2Kg 9:2), Omri (1Kg 16:22), Uzziah (Is 6:1), Jotham (2Kg 15:7), Hezekiah (Is 37:1), Jehoiachin (2Ch 36:8), Shalmaneser V (2Kg 17:3), Tiglath-pileser III (1Ch 5:6), Sargon II (Is 20:1), Sennacherib (Is 36:1), Nebuchadnezzar (Dn 2:1), Belshazzar (Dn 5:1), and Cyrus (Is 45:1).

who falls into a trance with his
eyes uncovered:
17 I see him, but not now;
I perceive him, but not near.
A star will come from Jacob,
and a scepter will arise from Israel.
He will smash the forehead[A] of Moab
and strike down[B] all the Shethites.[C]
18 Edom will become a possession;
Seir will become a possession of its enemies,
but Israel will be triumphant.
19 One who comes from Jacob will rule;
he will destroy the city's survivors.

20 Then Balaam saw Amalek and proclaimed his
poem:
Amalek was first among the nations,
but his future is destruction.

21 Next he saw the Kenites and proclaimed his
poem:
Your dwelling place is enduring;
your nest is set in the cliffs.
22 Kain will be destroyed
when Asshur takes you captive.

23 Once more he proclaimed his poem:
Ah, who can live when God does this?
24 Ships will come from the coast
of Kittim;
they will carry out raids against Asshur
and Eber,
but they too will come to destruction.
25 Balaam then arose and went back to his homeland,
and Balak also went his way.

ISRAEL WORSHIPS BAAL

25 While Israel was staying in the Acacia Grove,[D]
the people began to prostitute themselves
with the women of Moab. 2 The women invited them
to the sacrifices for their gods, and the people ate and
bowed in worship to their gods. 3 So Israel aligned
itself with Baal of Peor, and the LORD's anger burned
against Israel. 4 The LORD said to Moses, "Take all the
leaders of the people and execute[E] them in broad
daylight before the LORD so that his burning anger
may turn away from Israel."
5 So Moses told Israel's judges, "Kill each of the men
who aligned themselves with Baal of Peor."

PHINEHAS INTERVENES

6 An Israelite man came bringing a Midianite woman
to his relatives in the sight of Moses and the whole
Israelite community while they were weeping at the
entrance to the tent of meeting. 7 When Phinehas
son of Eleazar, son of Aaron the priest, saw this, he
got up from the assembly, took a spear in his hand,
8 followed the Israelite man into the tent,[F] and drove
it through both the Israelite man and the woman
— through her belly. Then the plague on the Israelites was stopped, 9 but those who died in the plague
numbered twenty-four thousand.
10 The LORD spoke to Moses, 11 "Phinehas son of
Eleazar, son of Aaron the priest, has turned back my
wrath from the Israelites because he was zealous
among them with my zeal,[G] so that I did not destroy
the Israelites in my zeal. 12 Therefore declare: I grant
him my covenant of peace. 13 It will be a covenant of
perpetual priesthood for him and his future descendants, because he was zealous for his God and made
atonement for the Israelites."
14 The name of the slain Israelite man, who was
struck dead with the Midianite woman, was Zimri son of Salu, the leader of a Simeonite family.[H]
15 The name of the slain Midianite woman was Cozbi, the daughter of Zur, a tribal head of a family in
Midian.

[A] **24:17** Or *frontiers* [B] **24:17** Sam reads *and the skulls of*; Jr 48:45 [C] **24:17** Or *Sethites* [D] **25:1** Or *in Shittim* [E] **25:4** Or *impale*, or *hang*, or *expose*; Hb obscure [F] **25:8** Perhaps a tent shrine or bridal tent [G] **25:11** Or *jealousy* [H] **25:14** Lit *a father's house*, also in v. 15

VENGEANCE AGAINST THE MIDIANITES

16 The LORD told Moses, 17 "Attack the Midianites and strike them dead. 18 For they attacked you with the treachery that they used against you in the Peor incident. They did the same in the case involving their sister Cozbi, daughter of the Midianite leader who was killed the day the plague came at Peor."

THE SECOND CENSUS

26 After the plague, the LORD said to Moses and Eleazar son of Aaron the priest, 2 "Take a census of the entire Israelite community by their ancestral families[A] of those twenty years old or more who can serve in Israel's army."

3 So Moses and the priest Eleazar said to them in the plains of Moab by the Jordan across from Jericho, 4 "Take a census of those twenty years old or more, as the LORD had commanded Moses and the Israelites who came out of the land of Egypt."

5 Reuben was the firstborn of Israel.
Reuben's descendants:
the Hanochite clan from Hanoch;
the Palluite clan from Pallu;
6 the Hezronite clan from Hezron;
the Carmite clan from Carmi.
7 These were the Reubenite clans,
and their registered men numbered 43,730.
8 The son of Pallu was Eliab.
9 The sons of Eliab were Nemuel, Dathan,
and Abiram.
(It was Dathan and Abiram, chosen by the
community, who fought against Moses and
Aaron; they and Korah's followers fought
against the LORD. 10 The earth opened its
mouth and swallowed them with Korah, when
his followers died and the fire consumed 250
men. They serve as a warning sign. 11 The sons
of Korah, however, did not die.)

12 Simeon's descendants by their clans:
the Nemuelite clan from Nemuel;
the Jaminite clan from Jamin;
the Jachinite clan from Jachin;
13 the Zerahite clan from Zerah;
the Shaulite clan from Shaul.
14 These were the Simeonite clans,
numbering 22,200 men.

15 Gad's descendants by their clans:
the Zephonite clan from Zephon;
the Haggite clan from Haggi;
the Shunite clan from Shuni;
16 the Oznite clan from Ozni;
the Erite clan from Eri;
17 the Arodite clan from Arod;
the Arelite clan from Areli.
18 These were the Gadite clans numbered
by their registered men: 40,500.

19 Judah's sons included Er and Onan, but
they died in the land of Canaan. 20 Judah's
descendants by their clans:
the Shelanite clan from Shelah;
the Perezite clan from Perez;
the Zerahite clan from Zerah.
21 The descendants of Perez:
the Hezronite clan from Hezron;
the Hamulite clan from Hamul.
22 These were Judah's clans numbered by their
registered men: 76,500.

23 Issachar's descendants by their clans:
the Tolaite clan from Tola;
the Punite clan from Puvah;[B]
24 the Jashubite clan from Jashub;
the Shimronite clan from Shimron.
25 These were Issachar's clans numbered
by their registered men: 64,300.

26 Zebulun's descendants by their clans:
the Seredite clan from Sered;
the Elonite clan from Elon;
the Jahleelite clan from Jahleel.
27 These were the Zebulunite clans numbered
by their registered men: 60,500.

28 Joseph's descendants by their clans
from Manasseh and Ephraim:
29 Manasseh's descendants:
the Machirite clan from Machir.
Machir fathered Gilead;
the Gileadite clan from Gilead.
30 These were Gilead's descendants:
the Iezerite clan from Iezer;
the Helekite clan from Helek;
31 the Asrielite clan from Asriel;
the Shechemite clan from Shechem;
32 the Shemidaite clan from Shemida;
the Hepherite clan from Hepher;
33 Zelophehad son of Hepher had no sons —
only daughters. The names of Zelophehad's
daughters were Mahlah, Noah, Hoglah,
Milcah, and Tirzah.
34 These were Manasseh's clans, numbered
by their registered men: 52,700.
35 These were Ephraim's descendants
by their clans:

[A] **26:2** Lit *the house of their fathers* [B] **26:23** Sam, LXX, Vg, Syr read *Puite clan from Puah*; 1Ch 7:1

the Shuthelahite clan from Shuthelah;
the Becherite clan from Becher;
the Tahanite clan from Tahan.
36 These were Shuthelah's descendants:
the Eranite clan from Eran.
37 These were the Ephraimite clans numbered
by their registered men: 32,500.
These were Joseph's descendants
by their clans.

38 Benjamin's descendants by their clans:
the Belaite clan from Bela;
the Ashbelite clan from Ashbel;
the Ahiramite clan from Ahiram;
39 the Shuphamite clan from Shupham;[A]
the Huphamite clan from Hupham.
40 Bela's descendants from Ard and Naaman:
the Ardite clan from Ard;
the Naamite clan from Naaman.
41 These were the Benjaminite clans numbered
by their registered men: 45,600.

42 These were Dan's descendants by their clans:
the Shuhamite clan from Shuham.
These were the clans of Dan by their clans.
43 All the Shuhamite clans numbered by their
registered men: 64,400.

44 Asher's descendants by their clans:
the Imnite clan from Imnah;
the Ishvite clan from Ishvi;
the Beriite clan from Beriah.
45 From Beriah's descendants:
the Heberite clan from Heber;
the Malchielite clan from Malchiel.
46 And the name of Asher's daughter was Serah.
47 These were the Asherite clans numbered
by their registered men: 53,400.

48 Naphtali's descendants by their clans:
the Jahzeelite clan from Jahzeel;
the Gunite clan from Guni;
49 the Jezerite clan from Jezer;
the Shillemite clan from Shillem.
50 These were the Naphtali clans numbered
by their registered men: 45,400.

51 These registered Israelite men
numbered 601,730.

52 The LORD spoke to Moses, 53 "The land is to be
divided among them as an inheritance based on the
number of names. 54 Increase the inheritance for a
large tribe and decrease it for a small one. Each is to
be given its inheritance according to those who were
registered in it. 55 The land is to be divided by lot; they
will receive an inheritance according to the names
of their ancestral tribes. 56 Each inheritance will be
divided by lot among the larger and smaller tribes."

57 These were the Levites registered
by their clans:
the Gershonite clan from Gershon;
the Kohathite clan from Kohath;
the Merarite clan from Merari.
58 These were the Levite family groups:
the Libnite clan,
the Hebronite clan,
the Mahlite clan,
the Mushite clan,
and the Korahite clan.

Kohath was the ancestor of Amram. 59 The name
of Amram's wife was Jochebed, a descendant of Levi,
born to Levi in Egypt. She bore to Amram: Aaron,
Moses, and their sister Miriam. 60 Nadab, Abihu, Eleazar, and Ithamar were born to Aaron, 61 but Nadab
and Abihu died when they presented unauthorized
fire before the LORD. 62 Those registered were 23,000,
every male one month old or more; they were not
registered among the other Israelites, because no
inheritance was given to them among the Israelites.
63 These were the ones registered by Moses and the
priest Eleazar when they registered the Israelites on
the plains of Moab by the Jordan across from Jericho.
64 But among them there was not one of those who
had been registered by Moses and the priest Aaron
when they registered the Israelites in the Wilderness of Sinai. 65 For the LORD had said to them that
they would all die in the wilderness. None of them
was left except Caleb son of Jephunneh and Joshua
son of Nun.

A CASE OF DAUGHTERS' INHERITANCE

27 The daughters of Zelophehad approached; Zelophehad was the son of Hepher, son of Gilead,
son of Machir, son of Manasseh from the clans of
Manasseh, the son of Joseph. These were the names
of his daughters: Mahlah, Noah, Hoglah, Milcah, and
Tirzah. 2 They stood before Moses, the priest Eleazar,
the leaders, and the entire community at the entrance
to the tent of meeting and said, 3 "Our father died in
the wilderness, but he was not among Korah's followers, who gathered together against the LORD. Instead,
he died because of his own sin, and he had no sons.
4 Why should the name of our father be taken away
from his clan? Since he had no son, give us property
among our father's brothers."

[A] **26:39** Some Hb mss, Sam, LXX, Syr, Tg, Vg; other Hb mss read *Shephupham*

5 Moses brought their case before the LORD, 6 and the LORD answered him, 7 "What Zelophehad's daughters say is correct. You are to give them hereditary property among their father's brothers and transfer their father's inheritance to them. 8 Tell the Israelites: When a man dies without having a son, transfer his inheritance to his daughter. 9 If he has no daughter, give his inheritance to his brothers. 10 If he has no brothers, give his inheritance to his father's brothers. 11 If his father has no brothers, give his inheritance to the nearest relative of his clan, and he will take possession of it. This is to be a statutory ordinance for the Israelites as the LORD commanded Moses."

JOSHUA COMMISSIONED TO SUCCEED MOSES

12 Then the LORD said to Moses, "Go up this mountain of the Abarim range[A] and see the land that I have given the Israelites. 13 After you have seen it, you will also be gathered to your people, as Aaron your brother was. 14 When the community quarreled in the Wilderness of Zin, both of you rebelled against my command to demonstrate my holiness in their sight at the waters." Those were the Waters of Meribah-kadesh[B] in the Wilderness of Zin.

15 So Moses appealed to the LORD, 16 "May the LORD, the God who gives breath to all,[C] appoint a man over the community 17 who will go out before them and come back in before them, and who will bring them out and bring them in, so that the LORD's community won't be like sheep without a shepherd."

18 The LORD replied to Moses, "Take Joshua son of Nun, a man who has the Spirit in him, and lay your hands on him. 19 Have him stand before the priest Eleazar and the whole community, and commission him in their sight. 20 Confer some of your authority on him so that the entire Israelite community will obey him. 21 He will stand before the priest Eleazar who will consult the LORD for him with the decision of the Urim. He and all the Israelites with him, even the entire community, will go out and come back in at his command."

22 Moses did as the LORD commanded him. He took Joshua, had him stand before the priest Eleazar and the entire community, 23 laid his hands on him, and commissioned him, as the LORD had spoken through Moses.

PRESCRIBED OFFERINGS

28 The LORD spoke to Moses, 2 "Command the Israelites and say to them: Be sure to present to me at its appointed time my offering and my food as my food offering, a pleasing aroma to me. 3 And say to them: This is the food offering you are to present to the LORD:

DAILY OFFERINGS

"Each day present two unblemished year-old male lambs as a regular burnt offering. 4 Offer one lamb in the morning and the other lamb at twilight, 5 along with two quarts[D] of fine flour for a grain offering mixed with a quart[E] of olive oil from crushed olives. 6 It is a regular burnt offering established at Mount Sinai for a pleasing aroma, a food offering to the LORD. 7 The drink offering is to be a quart with each lamb. Pour out the offering of beer to the LORD in the sanctuary area. 8 Offer the second lamb at twilight, along with the same kind of grain offering and drink offering as in the morning. It is a food offering, a pleasing aroma to the LORD.

SABBATH OFFERINGS

9 "On the Sabbath day present two unblemished year-old male lambs, four quarts[F] of fine flour mixed with oil as a grain offering, and its drink offering. 10 It is the burnt offering for every Sabbath, in addition to the regular burnt offering and its drink offering.

MONTHLY OFFERINGS

11 "At the beginning of each of your months present a burnt offering to the LORD: two young bulls, one ram, seven male lambs a year old — all unblemished — 12 with six quarts[G] of fine flour mixed with oil as a grain offering for each bull, four quarts of fine flour mixed with oil as a grain offering for the ram, 13 and two quarts[H] of fine flour mixed with oil as a grain offering for each lamb. It is a burnt offering, a pleasing aroma, a food offering to the LORD. 14 Their drink offerings are to be two quarts[I] of wine with each bull, one and a third quarts[J] with the ram, and one quart[K] with each male lamb. This is the monthly burnt offering for all the months of the year. 15 And one male goat is to be offered as a sin offering to the LORD, in addition to the regular burnt offering with its drink offering.

OFFERINGS FOR PASSOVER

16 "The Passover to the LORD comes in the first month, on the fourteenth day of the month. 17 On the fifteenth day of this month there will be a festival; unleavened bread is to be eaten for seven days. 18 On the first day there is to be a sacred assembly; you are not to do any daily work. 19 Present a food offering, a burnt offering to the LORD: two young bulls, one ram, and seven male lambs a year old. Your animals are to be

[A] **27:12** = Mount Nebo; Nm 33:47–48; Dt 32:49; Jr 22:20
[B] **27:14** = Quarreling [C] **27:16** Or *God of the spirits of all flesh*
[D] **28:5** Lit *one-tenth of an ephah* [E] **28:5** Lit *a fourth of a hin*, also in v. 7 [F] **28:9** Lit *two-tenths* (of an ephah), also in vv. 12,20,28
[G] **28:12** Lit *three-tenths* (of an ephah), also in vv. 20,28
[H] **28:13** Lit *one-tenth* (of an ephah), also in vv. 21,29 [I] **28:14** Lit *a half hin* [J] **28:14** Lit *bull, a third hin* [K] **28:14** Lit *a fourth hin*

unblemished. 20 The grain offering with them is to be of fine flour mixed with oil; offer six quarts with each bull and four quarts with the ram. 21 Offer two quarts with each of the seven lambs 22 and one male goat for a sin offering to make atonement for yourselves. 23 Offer these with the morning burnt offering that is part of the regular burnt offering. 24 You are to offer the same food each day for seven days as a food offering, a pleasing aroma to the LORD. It is to be offered with its drink offering and the regular burnt offering. 25 On the seventh day you are to hold a sacred assembly; you are not to do any daily work.

OFFERINGS FOR THE FESTIVAL OF WEEKS

26 "On the day of firstfruits, you are to hold a sacred assembly when you present an offering of new grain to the LORD at your Festival of Weeks; you are not to do any daily work. 27 Present a burnt offering as a pleasing aroma to the LORD: two young bulls, one ram, and seven male lambs a year old, 28 with their grain offering of fine flour mixed with oil, six quarts with each bull, four quarts with the ram, 29 and two quarts with each of the seven lambs, 30 and one male goat to make atonement for yourselves. 31 Offer them with their drink offerings in addition to the regular burnt offering and its grain offering. Your animals are to be unblemished.

FESTIVAL OF TRUMPETS OFFERINGS

29 "You are to hold a sacred assembly in the seventh month, on the first day of the month, and you are not to do any daily work. This will be a day of trumpet blasts for you. 2 Offer a burnt offering as a pleasing aroma to the LORD: one young bull, one ram, seven male lambs a year old — all unblemished — 3 with their grain offering of fine flour mixed with oil, six quarts[A] with the bull, four quarts[B] with the ram, 4 and two quarts[C] with each of the seven male lambs. 5 Also offer one male goat as a sin offering to make atonement for yourselves. 6 These are in addition to the monthly and regular burnt offerings with their prescribed grain offerings and drink offerings. They are a pleasing aroma, a food offering to the LORD.

OFFERINGS FOR THE DAY OF ATONEMENT

7 "You are to hold a sacred assembly on the tenth day of this seventh month and practice self-denial; do not do any work. 8 Present a burnt offering to the LORD, a pleasing aroma: one young bull, one ram, and seven male lambs a year old. All your animals are to be unblemished. 9 Their grain offering is to be of fine flour mixed with oil, six quarts with the bull, four quarts with the ram, 10 and two quarts with each of the seven lambs. 11 Offer one male goat for a sin offering. The regular burnt offering with its grain offering and drink offerings are in addition to the sin offering of atonement.

OFFERINGS FOR THE FESTIVAL OF SHELTERS

12 "You are to hold a sacred assembly on the fifteenth day of the seventh month; you do not do any daily work. You are to celebrate a seven-day festival for the LORD. 13 Present a burnt offering, a food offering, a pleasing aroma to the LORD: thirteen young bulls, two rams, and fourteen male lambs a year old. They are to be unblemished. 14 Their grain offering is to be of fine flour mixed with oil, six quarts with each of the thirteen bulls, four quarts with each of the two rams, 15 and two quarts with each of the fourteen lambs. 16 Also offer one male goat as a sin offering. These are in addition to the regular burnt offering with its grain and drink offerings.

17 "On the second day present twelve young bulls, two rams, and fourteen male lambs a year old — all unblemished — 18 with their grain and drink offerings for the bulls, rams, and lambs, in proportion to their number. 19 Also offer one male goat as a sin offering. These are in addition to the regular burnt offering with its grain and drink and their drink offerings.

20 "On the third day present eleven bulls, two rams, fourteen male lambs a year old — all unblemished — 21 with their grain and drink offerings for the bulls, rams, and lambs, in proportion to their number. 22 Also offer one male goat as a sin offering. These are in addition to the regular burnt offering with its grain and drink offerings.

23 "On the fourth day present ten bulls, two rams, fourteen male lambs a year old — all unblemished — 24 with their grain and drink offerings for the bulls, rams, and lambs, in proportion to their number. 25 Also offer one male goat as a sin offering. These are in addition to the regular burnt offering with its grain and drink offerings.

26 "On the fifth day present nine bulls, two rams, fourteen male lambs a year old — all unblemished — 27 with their grain and drink offerings for the bulls, rams, and lambs, in proportion to their number. 28 Also offer one male goat as a sin offering. These are in addition to the regular burnt offering with its grain and drink offerings.

29 "On the sixth day present eight bulls, two rams, fourteen male lambs a year old — all unblemished — 30 with their grain and drink offerings for the bulls, rams, and lambs, in proportion to their number. 31 Also offer one male goat as a sin offering. These are in addition to the regular burnt offering with its grain and drink offerings.

[A] **29:3** Lit *three-tenths* (of an ephah), also in vv. 9,14 [B] **29:3** Lit *two-tenths* (of an ephah), also in vv. 9,14 [C] **29:4** Lit *one-tenth* (of an ephah), also in vv. 10,15

32 "On the seventh day present seven bulls, two
rams, and fourteen male lambs a year old — all unblemished — 33 with their grain and drink offerings
for the bulls, rams, and lambs, in proportion to their
number. 34 Also offer one male goat as a sin offering.
These are in addition to the regular burnt offering
with its grain and drink offerings.
35 "On the eighth day you are to hold a solemn assembly; you are not to do any daily work. 36 Present
a burnt offering, a food offering, a pleasing aroma
to the LORD: one bull, one ram, seven male lambs a
year old — all unblemished — 37 with their grain and
drink offerings for the bulls, rams, and lambs, in proportion to their number. 38 Also offer one male goat
as a sin offering. These are in addition to the regular
burnt offering with its grain and drink offerings.
39 "Offer these to the LORD at your appointed times
in addition to your vow and freewill offerings, whether burnt, grain, drink, or fellowship offerings." 40 So
Moses told the Israelites everything the LORD had
commanded him.

REGULATIONS ABOUT VOWS

30 Moses told the leaders of the Israelite tribes,
"This is what the LORD has commanded:
2 When a man makes a vow to the LORD or swears
an oath to put himself under an obligation, he must
not break his word; he must do whatever he has
promised.
3 "When a woman in her father's house during her
youth makes a vow to the LORD or puts herself under an obligation, 4 and her father hears about her
vow or the obligation she put herself under, and he
says nothing to her, all her vows and every obligation
she put herself under are binding. 5 But if her father
prohibits her on the day he hears about it, none of
her vows and none of the obligations she put herself
under are binding. The LORD will release her because
her father has prohibited her.
6 "If a woman marries while her vows or the rash
commitment she herself made are binding, 7 and her
husband hears about it and says nothing to her when
he finds out, her vows are binding, and the obligations
she put herself under are binding. 8 But if her husband
prohibits her when he hears about it, he will cancel
her vow that is binding or the rash commitment she
herself made, and the LORD will release her.
9 "Every vow a widow or divorced woman puts
herself under is binding on her.
10 "If a woman in her husband's house has made a
vow or put herself under an obligation with an oath,
11 and her husband hears about it, says nothing to her,
and does not prohibit her, all her vows are binding,
and every obligation she put herself under is binding.
12 But if her husband cancels them on the day he hears
about it, nothing that came from her lips, whether
her vows or her obligation, is binding. Her husband
has canceled them, and the LORD will release her.
13 Her husband may confirm or cancel any vow or any
sworn obligation to deny herself. 14 If her husband
says nothing at all to her from day to day, he confirms
all her vows and obligations, which are binding. He
has confirmed them because he said nothing to her
when he heard about them. 15 But if he cancels them
after he hears about them, he will be responsible for
her commitment."[A]
16 These are the statutes that the LORD commanded
Moses concerning the relationship between a man
and his wife, or between a father and his daughter
in his house during her youth.

WAR WITH MIDIAN

31 The LORD spoke to Moses, 2 "Execute vengeance
for the Israelites against the Midianites. After
that, you will be gathered to your people."
3 So Moses spoke to the people, "Equip some of your
men for war. They will go against Midian to inflict the
LORD's vengeance on them. 4 Send one thousand men
to war from each Israelite tribe." 5 So one thousand
were recruited from each Israelite tribe out of the
thousands[B] in Israel — twelve thousand equipped
for war. 6 Moses sent one thousand from each tribe
to war. They went with Phinehas son of Eleazar the
priest, in whose care were the holy objects and signal trumpets.
7 They waged war against Midian, as the LORD had
commanded Moses, and killed every male. 8 Along
with the others slain by them, they killed the Midianite kings — Evi, Rekem, Zur, Hur, and Reba, the
five kings of Midian. They also killed Balaam son of
Beor with the sword. 9 The Israelites took the Midianite women and their dependents captive, and they
plundered all their cattle, flocks, and property. 10 Then
they burned all the cities where the Midianites lived,
as well as all their encampments, 11 and took away all
the spoils of war and the captives, both people and
animals. 12 They brought the prisoners, animals, and
spoils of war to Moses, the priest Eleazar, and the Israelite community at the camp on the plains of Moab
by the Jordan across from Jericho.
13 Moses, the priest Eleazar, and all the leaders of
the community went to meet them outside the camp.
14 But Moses became furious with the officers, the
commanders of thousands and commanders of hundreds, who were returning from the military campaign. 15 "Have you let every female live?" he asked
them. 16 "Yet they are the ones who, at Balaam's advice,
incited the Israelites to unfaithfulness against the

[A] **30:15** Or *will bear her guilt* [B] **31:5** Or *clans*

LORD in the Peor incident, so that the plague came against the LORD's community. [17] So now, kill every male among the dependents and kill every woman who has gone to bed with a man, [18] but keep alive for yourselves all the young females who have not gone to bed with a man.

[19] "You are to remain outside the camp for seven days. All of you and your prisoners who have killed a person or touched the dead are to purify yourselves on the third day and the seventh day. [20] Also purify everything: garments, leather goods, things made of goat hair, and every article of wood."

[21] Then the priest Eleazar said to the soldiers who had gone to battle, "This is the legal statute the LORD commanded Moses: [22] The gold, silver, bronze, iron, tin, and lead — [23] everything that can withstand fire — you are to pass through fire, and it will be clean. It must still be purified with the purification water. Anything that cannot withstand fire, pass through the water. [24] On the seventh day wash your clothes, and you will be clean. After that you may enter the camp."

[25] The LORD told Moses, [26] "You, the priest Eleazar, and the family heads of the community are to take a count of what was captured, people and animals. [27] Then divide the captives between the troops who went out to war and the entire community. [28] Set aside a tribute for the LORD from what belongs to the fighting men who went out to war: one out of every five hundred people, cattle, donkeys, sheep, and goats. [29] Take the tribute from their half and give it to the priest Eleazar as a contribution to the LORD. [30] From the Israelites' half, take one out of every fifty from the people, cattle, donkeys, sheep, and goats, all the livestock, and give them to the Levites who perform the duties of[A] the LORD's tabernacle."

[31] So Moses and the priest Eleazar did as the LORD commanded Moses. [32] The captives remaining from the plunder the army had taken totaled:

675,000 sheep and goats,
33 72,000 cattle,
34 61,000 donkeys,
35 and 32,000 people, all the females
who had not gone to bed with a man.

[36] The half portion for those who went out to war numbered:

337,500 sheep and goats,
37 and the tribute to the LORD was 675
from the sheep and goats;
38 from the 36,000 cattle,
the tribute to the LORD was 72;
39 from the 30,500 donkeys,
the tribute to the LORD was 61;
40 and from the 16,000 people,
the tribute to the LORD was 32 people.

[41] Moses gave the tribute to the priest Eleazar as a contribution for the LORD, as the LORD had commanded Moses.

[42] From the Israelites' half, which Moses separated from the men who fought, [43] the community's half was:

337,500 sheep and goats,
44 36,000 cattle,
45 30,500 donkeys,
46 and 16,000 people.

[47] Moses took one out of every fifty, selected from the people and the livestock of the Israelites' half. He gave them to the Levites who perform the duties of the LORD's tabernacle, as the LORD had commanded him.

[48] The officers who were over the thousands of the army, the commanders of thousands and of hundreds, approached Moses [49] and told him, "Your servants have taken a census of the fighting men under our command, and not one of us is missing. [50] So we have presented to the LORD an offering of the gold articles each man found — armlets, bracelets, rings, earrings, and necklaces — to make atonement for ourselves before the LORD."

[51] Moses and the priest Eleazar received from them all the articles made out of gold. [52] All the gold of the contribution they offered to the LORD, from the commanders of thousands and of hundreds, was 420 pounds.[B] [53] Each of the soldiers had taken plunder for himself. [54] Moses and the priest Eleazar received the gold from the commanders of thousands and of hundreds and brought it into the tent of meeting as a memorial for the Israelites before the LORD.

TRANSJORDAN SETTLEMENTS

32 The Reubenites and Gadites had a very large number of livestock. When they surveyed the lands of Jazer and Gilead, they saw that the region was a good one for livestock. [2] So the Gadites and Reubenites came to Moses, the priest Eleazar, and the leaders of the community and said, [3] "The territory of Ataroth, Dibon, Jazer, Nimrah, Heshbon, Elealeh, Sebam,[C] Nebo, and Beon, [4] which the LORD struck down before the community of Israel, is good land for livestock, and your servants own livestock." [5] They said, "If we have found favor with you, let this land be given to your servants as a possession. Don't make us cross the Jordan."

[6] But Moses asked the Gadites and Reubenites, "Should your brothers go to war while you stay here? [7] Why are you discouraging the Israelites from crossing into the land the LORD has given them? [8] That's what your ancestors did when I sent them from Kadesh-barnea to see the land. [9] After they went up

[A] **31:30** Or *who protect* [B] **31:52** Lit *16,750 shekels* [C] **32:3** Sam, LXX read *Sibmah* (v. 38); Syr reads *Sebah*

as far as Eshcol Valley and saw the land, they discouraged the Israelites from entering the land the LORD had given them. 10 So the LORD's anger burned that day, and he swore an oath: 11 'Because they did not remain loyal to me, none of the men twenty years old or more who came up from Egypt will see the land I swore to give Abraham, Isaac, and Jacob — 12 none except Caleb son of Jephunneh the Kenizzite and Joshua son of Nun, because they did remain loyal to the LORD.' 13 The LORD's anger burned against Israel, and he made them wander in the wilderness forty years until the whole generation that had done what was evil in the LORD's sight was gone. 14 And here you, a brood of sinners, stand in your ancestors' place adding even more to the LORD's burning anger against Israel. 15 If you turn back from following him, he will once again leave this people in the wilderness, and you will destroy all of them."

16 Then they approached him and said, "We want to build sheep pens here for our livestock and cities for our dependents. 17 But we will arm ourselves and be ready to go ahead of the Israelites until we have brought them into their place. Meanwhile, our dependents will remain in the fortified cities because of the inhabitants of the land. 18 We will not return to our homes until each of the Israelites has taken possession of his inheritance. 19 Yet we will not have an inheritance with them across the Jordan and beyond, because our inheritance will be across the Jordan to the east."

20 Moses replied to them, "If you do this — if you arm yourselves for battle before the LORD, 21 and every one of your armed men crosses the Jordan before the LORD until he has driven his enemies from his presence, 22 and the land is subdued before the LORD — afterward you may return and be free from obligation to the LORD and to Israel. And this land will belong to you as a possession before the LORD. 23 But if you don't do this, you will certainly sin against the LORD; be sure your sin will catch up with you. 24 Build cities for your dependents and pens for your flocks, but do what you have promised."

25 The Gadites and Reubenites answered Moses, "Your servants will do just as my lord commands. 26 Our dependents, wives, livestock, and all our animals will remain here in the cities of Gilead, 27 but your servants are equipped for war before the LORD and will go across to the battle as my lord orders."

28 So Moses gave orders about them to the priest Eleazar, Joshua son of Nun, and the family heads of the Israelite tribes. 29 Moses told them, "If the Gadites and Reubenites cross the Jordan with you, every man in battle formation before the LORD, and the land is subdued before you, you are to give them the land of Gilead as a possession. 30 But if they don't go across with you in battle formation, they must accept land in Canaan with you."

31 The Gadites and Reubenites replied, "What the LORD has spoken to your servants is what we will do. 32 We will cross over in battle formation before the LORD into the land of Canaan, but we will keep our hereditary possession across the Jordan."

33 So Moses gave them — the Gadites, Reubenites, and half the tribe of Manasseh son of Joseph — the kingdom of King Sihon of the Amorites and the kingdom of King Og of Bashan, the land including its cities with the territories surrounding them. 34 The Gadites rebuilt Dibon, Ataroth, Aroer, 35 Atroth-shophan, Jazer, Jogbehah, 36 Beth-nimrah, and Beth-haran as fortified cities, and built sheep pens. 37 The Reubenites rebuilt Heshbon, Elealeh, Kiriathaim, 38 as well as Nebo and Baal-meon (whose names were changed), and Sibmah. They gave names to the cities they rebuilt.

39 The descendants of Machir son of Manasseh went to Gilead, captured it, and drove out the Amorites who were there. 40 So Moses gave Gilead to the clan of Machir son of Manasseh, and they settled in it. 41 Jair, a descendant of Manasseh, went and captured their villages, which he renamed Jair's Villages.[A] 42 Nobah went and captured Kenath with its surrounding villages and called it Nobah after his own name.

WILDERNESS TRAVELS REVIEWED

33 These were the stages of the Israelites' journey when they went out of the land of Egypt by their military divisions under the leadership of Moses and Aaron. 2 At the LORD's command, Moses wrote down the starting points for the stages of their journey; these are the stages listed by their starting points:

3 They traveled from Rameses in the first
month, on the fifteenth day of the month. On
the day after the Passover the Israelites went
out defiantly[B] in the sight of all the Egyptians.
4 Meanwhile, the Egyptians were burying every
firstborn male the LORD had struck down among
them, for the LORD had executed judgment
against their gods. 5 The Israelites traveled from
Rameses and camped at Succoth.
6 They traveled from Succoth and camped at
Etham, which is on the edge of the wilderness.
7 They traveled from Etham and turned back to
Pi-hahiroth, which faces Baal-zephon, and they
camped before Migdol.
8 They traveled from Pi-hahiroth[C] and crossed
through the middle of the sea into the wilderness.

[A] **32:41** Or *renamed Havvoth-jair* [B] **33:3** Lit *with a raised hand*; Ex 14:8
[C] **33:8** Some Hb mss, Sam, Syr, Vg; other Hb mss read *from before Hahiroth*

They took a three-day journey into the
Wilderness of Etham and camped at Marah.
9 They traveled from Marah and came to Elim.
There were twelve springs and seventy date
palms at Elim, so they camped there.
10 They traveled from Elim and camped by the
Red Sea.
11 They traveled from the Red Sea and camped in
the Wilderness of Sin.
12 They traveled from the Wilderness of Sin and
camped in Dophkah.
13 They traveled from Dophkah and camped at
Alush.
14 They traveled from Alush and camped at
Rephidim, where there was no water for the
people to drink.
15 They traveled from Rephidim and camped in
the Wilderness of Sinai.
16 They traveled from the Wilderness of Sinai and
camped at Kibroth-hattaavah.
17 They traveled from Kibroth-hattaavah and
camped at Hazeroth.
18 They traveled from Hazeroth and camped at
Rithmah.
19 They traveled from Rithmah and camped at
Rimmon-perez.
20 They traveled from Rimmon-perez and
camped at Libnah.
21 They traveled from Libnah and camped at
Rissah.
22 They traveled from Rissah and camped at
Kehelathah.
23 They traveled from Kehelathah and camped at
Mount Shepher.
24 They traveled from Mount Shepher and
camped at Haradah.
25 They traveled from Haradah and camped at
Makheloth.
26 They traveled from Makheloth and camped at
Tahath.
27 They traveled from Tahath and camped at Terah.
28 They traveled from Terah and camped at
Mithkah.
29 They traveled from Mithkah and camped at
Hashmonah.
30 They traveled from Hashmonah and camped
at Moseroth.
31 They traveled from Moseroth and camped at
Bene-jaakan.
32 They traveled from Bene-jaakan and camped
at Hor-haggidgad.
33 They traveled from Hor-haggidgad and
camped at Jotbathah.
34 They traveled from Jotbathah and camped at
Abronah.
35 They traveled from Abronah and camped at
Ezion-geber.
36 They traveled from Ezion-geber and camped in
the Wilderness of Zin (that is, Kadesh).
37 They traveled from Kadesh and camped at
Mount Hor on the edge of the land of Edom. 38 At
the LORD's command, the priest Aaron climbed
Mount Hor and died there on the first day of
the fifth month in the fortieth year after the
Israelites went out of the land of Egypt. 39 Aaron
was 123 years old when he died on Mount Hor.
40 At that time the Canaanite king of Arad, who
lived in the Negev in the land of Canaan, heard
the Israelites were coming.
41 They traveled from Mount Hor and camped at
Zalmonah.
42 They traveled from Zalmonah and camped at
Punon.
43 They traveled from Punon and camped at
Oboth.
44 They traveled from Oboth and camped at
Iye-abarim on the border of Moab.
45 They traveled from Iyim[A] and camped at
Dibon-gad.
46 They traveled from Dibon-gad and camped at
Almon-diblathaim.
47 They traveled from Almon-diblathaim and
camped in the Abarim range facing Nebo.
48 They traveled from the Abarim range and
camped on the plains of Moab by the Jordan
across from Jericho. 49 They camped by the
Jordan from Beth-jeshimoth to the Acacia
Meadow[B] on the plains of Moab.

INSTRUCTIONS FOR OCCUPYING CANAAN

50 The LORD spoke to Moses in the plains of Moab by
the Jordan across from Jericho, 51 "Tell the Israelites:
When you cross the Jordan into the land of Canaan,
52 you must drive out all the inhabitants of the land
before you, destroy all their stone images and cast
images, and demolish all their high places. 53 You are
to take possession of the land and settle in it because
I have given you the land to possess. 54 You are to receive the land as an inheritance by lot according to
your clans. Increase the inheritance for a large clan
and decrease it for a small one. Whatever place the
lot indicates for someone will be his. You will receive
an inheritance according to your ancestral tribes.
55 But if you don't drive out the inhabitants of the land
before you, those you allow to remain will become
barbs for your eyes and thorns for your sides; they
will harass you in the land where you will live. 56 And
what I had planned to do to them, I will do to you."

[A] **33:45** A shortened form of Iye-abarim [B] **33:49** Or *to Abel-shittim*

Sheepfolds: Their Construction and Use

by Harold R. Mosley

The sheep of the Bible were probably of the fat-tailed Awassi variety. Ancient paintings and depictions of sheep from across the Middle East indicate this breed was the most common across the area in antiquity. This is also the variety commonly found in the region today. The Awassi sheep are generally white with brown feet and head, although all-white sheep or sheep with a black head and feet are also frequent. All-black, gray, or dappled sheep are much rarer.[1]

Stone-wall sheepfold at Heshbon, east of the Dead Sea, in Moab.

Sheep formed an important component in the area's economy in that the flocks provided milk, yogurt, butter, cheese, and meat as well as wool for clothing and tents. In large part, a person's wealth could be determined by the size of his flocks and herds.[2] Abraham's flocks and herds formed an important part of his wealth (Gn 24:35). Likewise, Job's wealth was measured, among other assets, by his sheep (see Jb 1; 42). In addition to sheep's economic importance, they formed an important part of the worship setting in that they were among the animals designated as sacrifices.

Sheep depend almost entirely on the shepherd for provision and protection. This is especially true at night when the dangers of wild animals and thieves increase. The sheepfold provided a necessary place of refuge. The shepherd would construct a permanent sheepfold as a home base for the sheep. The main enclosure consisted of stones stacked four to six feet high topped with briars and thorn bushes. A low building in the rear of the enclosure afforded shelter from the cold and storms. A watchman would guard the one entrance.[3] The reference in John 10:1–3 has this "gatekeeper" as the background.

Shepherds often led their flocks great distances from home in search of pasture. The picture of the patriarchs is one of a nomadic and seminomadic existence as they led their flocks from field to field seeking pasturage. For example, Abraham crisscrossed the land from Shechem south to Beer-sheba, a distance of some seventy-five miles. The grazing territory for the sheep often included hilly and steep terrain. Visitors to the hills of Israel even today can see trails etched by the feet of countless sheep and goats. Many natural caves and overhangs dot Israel's mountains. These provided temporary refuge when the sheep were away from their permanent enclosure. To construct such a temporary sheepfold, the shepherd built a wall of stones and briars across the mouth of an overhang or cave. The cave's inner recesses afforded refuge from the elements during storms. Or, if the weather was mild, the enclosure provided safety for the animals at the mouth of the cave.[4] The shepherd slept across the entrance to the pen to provide protection.

A group of shepherds sometimes combined their flocks in a single sheepfold at night. In the morning, the shepherds stood apart from each other and called to their sheep. Each shepherd had a unique call. The sheep, recognizing the call of their respective shepherd, followed that voice and separated themselves to their own flock.[5] This practice is behind the statement of Jesus, "My sheep hear my voice . . . and they follow me" (Jn 10:27). In some cases, a shepherd might come to consider a sheep what we would call a pet. Nathan's parable to David concerning David's sin spoke to this relationship (2Sm 12). ✜

[1] Oded Borowski, "Sheep," in *Eerdmans Dictionary of the Bible* (*EDB*), ed. David Noel Freedman (Grand Rapids: Eerdmans, 2000), 1203. This fact has relevance for Genesis 30–31 in the account of Jacob and Laban. [2] Borowski, "Sheep," 1203. [3] Fred H. Wight, *Manners and Customs of Bible Lands* (Chicago: Moody, 1953), 154–55. [4] Wight, *Manners*, 154. [5] George Adam Smith, *The Historical Geography of the Holy Land*, 25th ed. (New York: Ray Long & Richard R. Smith, 1932), 311–12.

BOUNDARIES OF THE PROMISED LAND

34 The LORD spoke to Moses, 2 "Command the
Israelites and say to them: When you enter
the land of Canaan, it will be allotted to you as an
inheritance[A] with these borders:
3 Your southern side will be from the Wilderness
of Zin along the boundary of Edom. Your southern border on the east will begin at the east end
of the Dead Sea. 4 Your border will turn south of
the Scorpions' Ascent,[B] proceed to Zin, and end
south of Kadesh-barnea. It will go to Hazar-
addar and proceed to Azmon. 5 The border will
turn from Azmon to the Brook of Egypt, where it
will end at the Mediterranean Sea.

6 Your western border will be the coastline of
the Mediterranean Sea; this will be your western border.

7 This will be your northern border: From the
Mediterranean Sea draw a line to Mount Hor;
8 from Mount Hor draw a line to the entrance of
Hamath,[C] and the border will reach Zedad. 9 Then
the border will go to Ziphron and end at Hazar-
enan. This will be your northern border.

10 For your eastern border, draw a line from Ha-
zar-enan to Shepham. 11 The border will go down
from Shepham to Riblah east of Ain. It will continue down and reach the eastern slope of the Sea
of Chinnereth.[D] 12 Then the border will go down
to the Jordan and end at the Dead Sea. This will be
your land defined by its borders on all sides."

13 So Moses commanded the Israelites, "This is the
land you are to receive by lot as an inheritance, which
the LORD commanded to be given to the nine and a
half tribes. 14 For the tribe of Reuben's descendants
and the tribe of Gad's descendants have received
their inheritance according to their ancestral families,[E] and half the tribe of Manasseh has received its
inheritance. 15 The two and a half tribes have received
their inheritance across the Jordan east of Jericho,
toward the sunrise."

LEADERS FOR DISTRIBUTING THE LAND

16 The LORD spoke to Moses, 17 "These are the names
of the men who are to distribute the land as an inheritance for you: the priest Eleazar and Joshua son of
Nun. 18 Take one leader from each tribe to distribute
the land. 19 These are the names of the men:
Caleb son of Jephunneh from the tribe of Judah;
20 Shemuel son of Ammihud from the tribe of
Simeon's descendants;
21 Elidad son of Chislon from the tribe of Benjamin;
22 Bukki son of Jogli, a leader from the tribe of
Dan's descendants;
23 from the sons of Joseph:
Hanniel son of Ephod, a leader from the tribe of
Manasseh's descendants,
24 Kemuel son of Shiphtan, a leader from the
tribe of Ephraim's descendants;
25 Eli-zaphan son of Parnach, a leader from the
tribe of Zebulun's descendants;
26 Paltiel son of Azzan, a leader from the tribe of
Issachar's descendants;
27 Ahihud son of Shelomi, a leader from the tribe
of Asher's descendants;
28 Pedahel son of Ammihud, a leader from the
tribe of Naphtali's descendants."
29 These are the ones the LORD commanded to distribute the inheritance to the Israelites in the land
of Canaan.

CITIES FOR THE LEVITES

35 The LORD again spoke to Moses in the plains
of Moab by the Jordan across from Jericho:
2 "Command the Israelites to give cities out of their
hereditary property for the Levites to live in and
pastureland around the cities. 3 The cities will be for
them to live in, and their pasturelands will be for
their herds, flocks, and all their other animals. 4 The
pasturelands of the cities you are to give the Levites
will extend from the city wall five hundred yards[F]
on every side. 5 Measure a thousand yards[G] outside
the city for the east side, a thousand yards for the
south side, a thousand yards for the west side, and
a thousand yards for the north side, with the city in
the center. This will belong to them as pasturelands
for the cities.
6 "The cities you give the Levites will include six
cities of refuge, which you will provide so that the
one who kills someone may flee there; in addition to
these, give forty-two other cities. 7 The total number
of cities you give the Levites will be forty-eight, along
with their pasturelands. 8 Of the cities that you give
from the Israelites' territory, you should take more
from a larger tribe and less from a smaller one. Each
tribe is to give some of its cities to the Levites in proportion to the inheritance it receives."

CITIES OF REFUGE

9 The LORD said to Moses, 10 "Speak to the Israelites
and tell them: When you cross the Jordan into the
land of Canaan, 11 designate cities to serve as cities of
refuge for you, so that a person who kills someone

[A] **34:2** Lit *inheritance — the land of Canaan* [B] **34:4** Lit *of Scorpions*; Jos 15:3; Jdg 1:36 [C] **34:8** Or *to Lebo-hamath* [D] **34:11** = the Sea of Galilee; Jos 12:3; 13:27; Lk 5:1 [E] **34:14** Lit *the house of their fathers* [F] **35:4** Lit *1,000 cubits* [G] **35:5** Lit *2,000 cubits*

unintentionally may flee there. 12 You will have the cities as a refuge from the avenger, so that the one who kills someone will not die until he stands trial before the assembly. 13 The cities you select will be your six cities of refuge. 14 Select three cities across the Jordan and three cities in the land of Canaan to be cities of refuge. 15 These six cities will serve as a refuge for the Israelites and for the alien or temporary resident among them, so that anyone who kills a person unintentionally may flee there.

16 "If anyone strikes a person with an iron object and death results, he is a murderer; the murderer must be put to death. 17 If anyone has in his hand a stone capable of causing death and strikes another person and he dies, the murderer must be put to death. 18 If anyone has in his hand a wooden object capable of causing death and strikes another person and he dies, the murderer must be put to death. 19 The avenger of blood himself is to kill the murderer; when he finds him, he is to kill him. 20 Likewise, if anyone in hatred pushes a person or throws an object at him with malicious intent and he dies, 21 or if in hostility he strikes him with his hand and he dies, the one who struck him must be put to death; he is a murderer. The avenger of blood is to kill the murderer when he finds him.

22 "But if anyone suddenly pushes a person without hostility or throws any object at him without malicious intent 23 or without looking drops a stone that could kill a person and he dies, but he was not his enemy and didn't intend to harm him, 24 the assembly is to judge between the person who kills someone and the avenger of blood according to these ordinances. 25 The assembly is to protect the one who kills someone from the avenger of blood. Then the assembly will return him to the city of refuge he fled to, and he must live there until the death of the high priest who was anointed with the holy oil.

26 "If the one who kills someone ever goes outside the border of the city of refuge he fled to, 27 and the avenger of blood finds him outside the border of his city of refuge and kills him, the avenger will not be guilty of bloodshed, 28 for the one who killed a person was supposed to live in his city of refuge until the death of the high priest. Only after the death of the high priest may the one who has killed a person return to the land he possesses. 29 These instructions will be a statutory ordinance for you throughout your generations wherever you live.

30 "If anyone kills a person, the murderer is to be put to death based on the word of witnesses. But no one is to be put to death based on the testimony of one witness. 31 You are not to accept a ransom for the life of someone who is guilty of murder; he must be put to death. 32 Neither should you accept a ransom for the person who flees to his city of refuge, allowing him to return and live in the land before the death of the high priest.

33 "Do not defile the land where you live, for bloodshed defiles the land, and there can be no atonement for the land because of the blood that is shed on it, except by the blood of the person who shed it. 34 Do not make the land unclean where you live and where I dwell; for I, the LORD, reside among the Israelites."

THE INHERITANCE OF ZELOPHEHAD'S DAUGHTERS

36 The family heads from the clan of the descendants of Gilead — the son of Machir, son of Manasseh — who were from the clans of the sons of Joseph, approached and addressed Moses and the leaders who were heads of the Israelite families. 2 They said, "The LORD commanded my lord to give the land as an inheritance by lot to the Israelites. My lord was further commanded by the LORD to give our brother Zelophehad's inheritance to his daughters. 3 If they marry any of the men from the other Israelite tribes, their inheritance will be taken away from our fathers' inheritance and added to that of the tribe into which they marry. Therefore, part of our allotted inheritance would be taken away. 4 When the Jubilee comes for the Israelites, their inheritance will be added to that of the tribe into which they marry, and their inheritance will be taken away from the inheritance of our ancestral tribe."

5 So Moses commanded the Israelites at the word of the LORD, "What the tribe of Joseph's descendants says is right. 6 This is what the LORD has commanded concerning Zelophehad's daughters: They may marry anyone they like provided they marry within a clan of their ancestral tribe. 7 No inheritance belonging to the Israelites is to transfer from tribe to tribe, because each of the Israelites is to retain the inheritance of his ancestral tribe. 8 Any daughter who possesses an inheritance from an Israelite tribe must marry someone from the clan of her ancestral tribe, so that each of the Israelites will possess the inheritance of his fathers. 9 No inheritance is to transfer from one tribe to another, because each of the Israelite tribes is to retain its inheritance."

10 The daughters of Zelophehad did as the LORD commanded Moses. 11 Mahlah, Tirzah, Hoglah, Milcah, and Noah, the daughters of Zelophehad, married cousins on their father's side. 12 They married men from the clans of the descendants of Manasseh son of Joseph, and their inheritance remained within the tribe of their father's clan.

13 These are the commands and ordinances the LORD commanded the Israelites through Moses in the plains of Moab by the Jordan across from Jericho.

unintentionally may flee there. 12 You will have the
cities as a refuge from the avenger, so that the one
who kills someone will not die until he stands trial
before the assembly. 13 The cities you select will be
your six cities of refuge. 14 Select three cities across
the Jordan and three cities in the land of Canaan to
be cities of refuge. 15 These six cities will serve as a
refuge for the Israelites and for the alien or temporary resident among them, so that anyone who kills
a person unintentionally may flee there.
16 "If anyone strikes a person with an iron object
and death results, he is a murderer; the murderer
must be put to death. 17 If anyone has in his hand a
stone capable of causing death and strikes another
person and he dies, the murderer must be put to death.
18 If anyone has in his hand a wooden object capable of
causing death and strikes another person and he dies,
the murderer must be put to death. 19 The avenger of
blood himself is to kill the murderer; when he finds
him, he is to kill him. 20 Likewise, if anyone in hatred
pushes a person or throws an object at him with malicious intent and he dies, 21 or if in hostility he strikes
him with his hand and he dies, the one who struck him
must be put to death; he is a murderer. The avenger
of blood is to kill the murderer when he finds him.
22 "But if anyone suddenly pushes a person without
hostility or throws any object at him without malicious intent 23 or, without looking, drops a stone that
could kill a person and he dies, but he was not his enemy and didn't intend to harm him, 24 the assembly is
to judge between the person who kills someone and
the avenger of blood according to these ordinances.
25 The assembly is to protect the one who kills someone from the avenger of blood. Then the assembly
will return him to the city of refuge he fled to, and
he must live there until the death of the high priest
who was anointed with the holy oil.
26 "If the one who kills someone ever goes outside
the border of the city of refuge he fled to, 27 and the
avenger of blood finds him outside the border of his
city of refuge and kills him, the avenger will not be
guilty of bloodshed, 28 for the one who killed a person was supposed to live in his city of refuge until
the death of the high priest. Only after the death of
the high priest may the one who has killed a person
return to the land he possesses. 29 These instructions
will be a statutory ordinance for you throughout your
generations wherever you live.
30 "If anyone kills a person, the murderer is to be
put to death based on the word of witnesses. But no
one is to be put to death based on the testimony of one
witness. 31 You are not to accept a ransom for the life
of someone who is guilty of murder; he must be put
to death. 32 Neither should you accept a ransom for
the person who flees to his city of refuge, allowing
him to return and live in the land before the death
of the high priest.
33 "Do not defile the land where you live, for bloodshed defiles the land, and there can be no atonement
for the land because of the blood that is shed on it,
except by the blood of the person who shed it. 34 Do
not make the land unclean where you live and where
I dwell; for I, the LORD, reside among the Israelites."

THE INHERITANCE OF ZELOPHEHAD'S DAUGHTERS

36 The family heads from the clan of the descendants of Gilead — the son of Machir, son of
Manasseh — who were from the clans of the sons
of Joseph, approached and addressed Moses and
the leaders who were heads of the Israelite families.
2 They said, "The LORD commanded my lord to give
the land as an inheritance by lot to the Israelites. My
lord was further commanded by the LORD to give our
brother Zelophehad's inheritance to his daughters.
3 If they marry any of the men from the other Israelite tribes, their inheritance will be taken away from
our fathers' inheritance and added to that of the tribe
into which they marry. Therefore, part of our allotted
inheritance would be taken away. 4 When the Jubilee
comes for the Israelites, their inheritance will be added to that of the tribe into which they marry, and their
inheritance will be taken away from the inheritance
of our ancestral tribe."
5 So Moses commanded the Israelites at the word
of the LORD: "What the tribe of Joseph's descendants
says is right. 6 This is what the LORD has commanded
concerning Zelophehad's daughters: They may marry
anyone they like provided they marry within a clan
of their ancestral tribe. 7 No inheritance belonging to
the Israelites is to transfer from tribe to tribe, because
each of the Israelites is to retain the inheritance of
his ancestral tribe. 8 Any daughter who possesses
an inheritance from an Israelite tribe must marry
someone from the clan of her ancestral tribe, so that
each of the Israelites will possess the inheritance of
his fathers. 9 No inheritance is to transfer from one
tribe to another, because each of the Israelite tribes
is to retain its inheritance."
10 The daughters of Zelophehad did as the LORD
commanded Moses. 11 Mahlah, Tirzah, Hoglah, Milcah, and Noah, the daughters of Zelophehad, married
cousins on their father's side. 12 They married men
from the clans of the descendants of Manasseh son
of Joseph, and their inheritance remained within the
tribe of their father's clan.
13 These are the commands and ordinances the
LORD commanded the Israelites through Moses in
the plains of Moab by the Jordan across from Jericho.

DEUTERONOMY

View toward Israel from Mount Nebo.

INTRODUCTION TO

DEUTERONOMY

Circumstances of Writing

The book itself asserts that Moses is the principal source and author for the material (1:1), as do subsequent Old Testament texts (Jos 1:7–8; 1Kg 2:3; Ezr 3:2) and New Testament texts (Mt 19:7; Ac 3:22; Rm 10:19). This attribution remained virtually unchallenged until the advent of modern rationalism in the seventeenth and eighteenth centuries, but no arguments advanced by this school of thought have successfully overcome the ancient Mosaic tradition.

The exodus probably occurred in 1446 BC, whereupon Israel set out for Canaan, the inheritance God had promised his people. Because of their rebellious spirit, the Israelites were forced to wander in the desert for forty years (Dt 2:7) until at last they arrived in Moab, just opposite Jericho (32:49). It was there that Moses put pen to parchment to compose this farewell treatise (31:9,24).

Contribution to the Bible

Next to the books of Psalms and Isaiah, the New Testament alludes to Deuteronomy more than any other book in the Old Testament. This is true not only in terms of the sheer number of instances but especially in the passages where theological truth seems most to be at issue. Jesus and the apostles considered Deuteronomy of paramount importance to their own teaching about God and his dealings with his chosen people and humanity at large. Jesus in his temptation quoted the book of Deuteronomy three times against Satan (Mt 4:4–10).

Structure

The style of the book of Deuteronomy appears as a series of repetitious, reminiscent, and even irregular exhortations, which is fitting for a collection of Moses's sermons preparing the people for their move into the promised land. The style is also reflective of the typical suzerain-vassal treaties, which could contain a preamble, historical prologue, main provisions, blessings and curses, and plans for continuing the covenant relationship. The book of Deuteronomy could be considered the constitution for the nation of Israel once it was established in the promised land.

INTRODUCTION

1 These are the words Moses spoke to all Israel across the Jordan in the wilderness, in the Arabah opposite Suph,[A] between Paran and Tophel, Laban, Hazeroth, and Di-zahab. 2 It is an eleven-day journey from Horeb to Kadesh-barnea by way of Mount Seir. 3 In the fortieth year, in the eleventh month, on the first of the month, Moses told the Israelites everything the LORD had commanded him to say to them. 4 This was after he had defeated King Sihon of the Amorites, who lived in Heshbon, and King Og of Bashan, who lived in Ashtaroth, at Edrei. 5 Across the Jordan in the land of Moab, Moses began to explain this law, saying:

DEPARTURE FROM HOREB

6 "The LORD our God spoke to us at Horeb: 'You have stayed at this mountain long enough. 7 Resume your journey and go to the hill country of the Amorites and their neighbors in the Arabah, the hill country, the Judean foothills,[B] the Negev and the sea coast — to the land of the Canaanites and to Lebanon as far as the great river, the Euphrates River. 8 See, I have set the land before you. Enter and take possession of the land the LORD swore to give to your ancestors Abraham, Isaac, and Jacob and their future descendants.'

LEADERS FOR THE TRIBES

9 "I said to you at that time: I can't bear the responsibility for you on my own. 10 The LORD your God has so multiplied you that today you are as numerous as the stars of the sky. 11 May the LORD, the God of your ancestors, increase you a thousand times more, and bless you as he promised you. 12 But how can I bear your troubles, burdens, and disputes by myself? 13 Appoint for yourselves wise, understanding, and respected men from each of your tribes, and I will make them your leaders.

14 "You replied to me, 'What you propose to do is good.'

15 "So I took the leaders of your tribes, wise and respected men, and set them over you as leaders: commanders for thousands, hundreds, fifties, and tens, and officers for your tribes. 16 I commanded your judges at that time: Hear the cases between your brothers, and judge rightly between a man and his brother or his resident alien. 17 Do not show partiality when deciding a case; listen to small and great alike. Do not be intimidated by anyone, for judgment belongs to God. Bring me any case too difficult for you, and I will hear it. 18 At that time I commanded you about all the things you were to do.

ISRAEL'S DISOBEDIENCE AT KADESH-BARNEA

19 "We then set out from Horeb and went across all the great and terrible wilderness you saw on the way to the hill country of the Amorites, just as the LORD our God had commanded us. When we reached Kadesh-barnea, 20 I said to you: You have reached the hill country of the Amorites, which the LORD our God is giving us. 21 See, the LORD your God has set the land before you. Go up and take possession of it as the LORD, the God of your ancestors, has told you. Do not be afraid or discouraged.

22 "Then all of you approached me and said, 'Let's send men ahead of us, so that they may explore the land for us and bring us back a report about the route we should go up and the cities we will come to.' 23 The plan seemed good to me, so I selected twelve men from among you, one man for each tribe. 24 They left and went up into the hill country and came to Eshcol Valley, scouting the land. 25 They took some of the fruit from the land in their hands, carried it down to us, and brought us back a report: 'The land the LORD our God is giving us is good.'

26 "But you were not willing to go up. You rebelled against the command of the LORD your God. 27 You grumbled in your tents and said, 'The LORD brought us out of the land of Egypt to hand us over to the Amorites in order to destroy us, because he hates us. 28 Where can we go? Our brothers have made us lose heart,[C] saying: The people are larger and taller than we are; the cities are large, fortified to the heavens. We also saw the descendants of the Anakim there.'

29 "So I said to you: Don't be terrified or afraid of them! 30 The LORD your God who goes before you will fight for you, just as you saw him do for you in Egypt. 31 And you saw in the wilderness how the LORD your God carried you as a man carries his son all along the way you traveled until you reached this place. 32 But in spite of this you did not trust the LORD your God, 33 who went before you on the journey to seek out a place for you to camp. He went in the fire by night and in the cloud by day to guide you on the road you were to travel.

34 "When the LORD heard your[D] words, he grew angry and swore an oath: 35 'None of these men in this evil generation will see the good land I swore to give your ancestors, 36 except Caleb the son of Jephunneh. He will see it, and I will give him and his descendants the land on which he has set foot, because he remained loyal to the LORD.'

37 "The LORD was angry with me also because of you and said, 'You will not enter there either. 38 Joshua son of Nun, who attends you, will enter it. Encourage him, for he will enable Israel to inherit it. 39 Your children, who you said would be plunder, your sons who[E] don't yet know good from evil, will enter there. I will give

[A] **1:1** LXX, Tg, Vg read *the Red Sea* [B] **1:7** Or *the Shephelah*
[C] **1:28** Lit *have melted our hearts* [D] **1:34** Lit *the sound of your*
[E] **1:39** Lit *who today*

them the land, and they will take possession of it. 40 But you are to turn back and head for the wilderness by way of the Red Sea.'

41 "You answered me, 'We have sinned against the LORD. We will go up and fight just as the LORD our God commanded us.' Then each of you put on his weapons of war and thought it would be easy to go up into the hill country.

42 "But the LORD said to me, 'Tell them: Don't go up and fight, for I am not with you to keep you from being defeated by your enemies.' 43 So I spoke to you, but you didn't listen. You rebelled against the LORD's command and defiantly went up into the hill country. 44 Then the Amorites who lived there came out against you and chased you like a swarm of bees. They routed you from Seir as far as Hormah. 45 When you returned, you wept before the LORD, but he didn't listen to your requests or pay attention to you. 46 For this reason you stayed in Kadesh as long as you did.[A]

JOURNEY PAST SEIR

2 "Then we turned back and headed for the wilderness by way of the Red Sea, as the LORD had told me, and we traveled around the hill country of Seir for many days. 2 The LORD then said to me, 3 'You've been traveling around this hill country long enough; turn north. 4 Command the people: You are about to travel through the territory of your brothers, the descendants of Esau, who live in Seir. They will be afraid of you, so be very careful. 5 Don't provoke them, for I will not give you any of their land, not even a foot of it,[B] because I have given Esau the hill country of Seir as his possession. 6 You may purchase food from them, so that you may eat, and buy water from them to drink. 7 For the LORD your God has blessed you in all the work of your hands. He has watched over your journey through this immense wilderness. The LORD your God has been with you these past forty years, and you have lacked nothing.'

JOURNEY PAST MOAB

8 "So we bypassed our brothers, the descendants of Esau, who live in Seir. We turned away from the Arabah road and from Elath and Ezion-geber. We traveled along the road to the Wilderness of Moab. 9 The LORD said to me, 'Show no hostility toward Moab, and do not provoke them to battle, for I will not give you any of their land as a possession, since I have given Ar as a possession to the descendants of Lot.' "

10 The Emim, a great and numerous people as tall as the Anakim, had previously lived there. 11 They were also regarded as Rephaim, like the Anakim, though the Moabites called them Emim. 12 The Horites had previously lived in Seir, but the descendants of Esau drove them out, destroying them completely[C] and settling in their place, just as Israel did in the land of its possession the LORD gave them.

13 "The LORD said, 'Now get up and cross the Zered Valley.' So we crossed the Zered Valley. 14 The time we spent traveling from Kadesh-barnea until we crossed the Zered Valley was thirty-eight years until the entire generation of fighting men had perished from the camp, as the LORD had sworn to them. 15 Indeed, the LORD's hand was against them, to eliminate them from the camp until they had all perished.

JOURNEY PAST AMMON

16 "When all the fighting men had died among the people, 17 the LORD spoke to me, 18 'Today you are going to cross the border of Moab at Ar. 19 When you get close to the Ammonites, don't show any hostility to them or provoke them, for I will not give you any of the Ammonites' land as a possession; I have given it as a possession to the descendants of Lot.' "

20 This too used to be regarded as the land of the Rephaim. The Rephaim lived there previously, though the Ammonites called them Zamzummim, 21 a great and numerous people, tall as the Anakim. The LORD destroyed the Rephaim at the advance of the Ammonites, so that they drove them out and settled in their place. 22 This was just as he had done for the descendants of Esau who lived in Seir, when he destroyed the Horites before them; they drove them out and have lived in their place until now. 23 The Caphtorim, who came from Caphtor,[D] destroyed the Avvites, who lived in villages as far as Gaza, and settled in their place.

DEFEAT OF SIHON THE AMORITE

24 "The LORD also said, 'Get up, move out, and cross the Arnon Valley. See, I have handed the Amorites' King Sihon of Heshbon and his land over to you. Begin to take possession of it; engage[E] him in battle. 25 Today I will begin to put the fear and dread of you on the peoples everywhere under heaven. They will hear the report about you, tremble, and be in anguish because of you.'

26 "So I sent messengers with an offer of peace to King Sihon of Heshbon from the Wilderness of Kedemoth, saying, 27 'Let us travel through your land; we will keep strictly to the highway. We will not turn to the right or the left. 28 You can sell us food in exchange for silver so we may eat, and give us water for silver so we may drink. Only let us travel through on foot, 29 just as the descendants of Esau who live in Seir did for us, and the Moabites who live in Ar, until we cross the Jordan into the land the LORD our God is giving

[A] **1:46** Lit *Kadesh for many days, according to the days you stayed* [B] **2:5** Lit *land as far as the width of a sole of a foot* [C] **2:12** Lit *them before them* [D] **2:23** Probably Crete [E] **2:24** Or *provoke*

The Promised Land: A Crucial Locale

by Ken Cox

Truly a land flowing with milk and honey, the fertile fields of Canaan were a stark contrast to the desert regions of Egypt. Shown, Kishon River from Mount Carmel.

After four decades of living in a barren desert (Dt 1:3), God's chosen people were to live in a fertile region located on highly traveled international caravan routes.

The land of Canaan was a vital location in the ancient world. It formed a strategic land bridge between Europe and Asia to the north and Africa to the south. Within its narrow boundaries were fertile fields, choice pasturage, strategic heights for cities, and well-established commercial trade routes. Surrounding peoples made this land bridge a crucial part of the ancient world. By planting his people in tiny Canaan, God would reveal his truth to the uttermost parts of the earth.[1]

THE REGION AND RESIDENTS

Canaan is part of the region that touches the eastern coasts of the Mediterranean Sea. North of the Mediterranean is Asia Minor, the current country of Turkey. A mountain chain stretches from west of the Black Sea, continues eastward beyond the Caspian Sea, curves to the southeast, and concludes at the Bay of Bengal, east of India. The range stretches north of Asia Minor and Mesopotamia into Asia. These mountains, the Balkans, Caucasus, Elburz, Hindu Kush, and Himalayan ranges, form a northern boundary and curb winter winds to produce a favorable climate for the area south of the range. The Syro-Arabian Desert constitutes a southern boundary to the region. The area that is between the mountains and the southern deserts and that stretches from the Mediterranean Sea to the Persian Gulf forms the biblical world.[2]

The Arabian and Libyan Deserts prohibit population and travel in the largest land area of the region. These deserts and the Mediterranean Sea squeeze the productive land into an agriculturally productive area called the Fertile Crescent. The Fertile Crescent reaches from the Tigris and Euphrates Rivers of Mesopotamia, arches northwest to Haran, west through Syria, southwest through Canaan, and concludes in the agriculturally rich delta and valley of the Nile River.

Civilizations formed in the fertile river valleys throughout this region. In Asia Minor, the Halys River was the site of consolidation for Hittite military power.[3] In Mesopotamia, the Euphrates and Tigris Rivers provided irrigation for farming. In Egypt, the annual floods of the Nile made fertile fields along its course and in the delta.

The Medes, a group of nomadic tribes, became a powerful Mesopotamian presence as they built cities and armies. The dynasties of the pharaohs established Egyptian

Tyre was important to Israel not only because of its harbor but also because of its craftsmen and nearby cedar forests.

monuments to their world-class power by building pyramids and armies. Between the armies of Asia Minor, Mesopotamia, and Egypt lay the land of Canaan.

During years of peace, travelers and traders traversed Canaan. Merchants from Mesopotamia traveled to Egypt and vice versa. Grain from Egypt made its way from the ports of Egypt to the maritime cities of Canaan. From there, Phoenician sailors connected Canaan to the rest of the world.

Conflict also came to the region of Canaan as ambitious pharaohs from Egypt and armies from Mesopotamia met to wage war in the valleys of Canaan. The breaks in the mountains on either side of the Jordan became battlefields for legendary conflicts. Sites such as Megiddo came to be known for battles and became symbols for future conflicts. The climactic battle of evil versus righteousness in Revelation 16:16 occurs in Armageddon (Hb *har*, "hill," plus Megiddo).

Since Canaan was subject to commercial traffic and military encounters, a mixture of peoples ended up living there. The Hethites, Girgashites, Amorites, Canaanites, Perizzites, Hivites, and Jebusites at the time of Joshua's conquest reflect the variety and intermingling of nations after centuries of interchange and conquest.[4] One of the peoples who inhabited part of the region had a long-lasting impact on the land; patriarchal Canaan came to be known as Palestine, a name derived from its Philistine inhabitants.[5]

NATURAL DIVISIONS AND RESOURCES

In addition to being a crossroads for regional powers, Canaan had distinctive qualities within its borders that made it valuable to potential residents. The land promised to Abraham was approximately 150 miles long and 70 miles wide. The eastern and western boundaries of Canaan were the Jordan River and the Mediterranean Sea. Beer-sheba marked the southern border, and Dan was the northern limit. These borders expanded and decreased by military and commercial acquisitions during Israel's history. For instance, after the conquest of Canaan, Israel inhabited the Transjordan Plateau. Over time, several sites in the plateau were lost and regained by Israel's military forces.

Canaan is divided into four contrasting strips of land running north and south, each with unique, desirable traits. Geographical features form the designations for the different areas.

The Coastal Plain—The westernmost strip of land is the coastal plain, which begins at Gaza and continues north to Tyre. This coastal region possesses fertile farmland and is irrigated by springs and seasonal rainfall.[6] Located in the southernmost region of the coastal plain was the plain of Philistia, which was the stronghold of Israel's

perennial enemy, the Philistines. The Philistines recognized the assets of the land and chose it as a home when they migrated from the island of Caphtor (Crete, Am 9:7). The productive farmland contributed to the Philistines' wealth and political power. A major trade route, the Way of the Sea (*Via Maris*), connecting Egypt to Damascus, passed through the Philistine cities of the southwest plain.[7]

Moving north, the fertile plain of Sharon is the next division of the coastal plain. This area runs north from Joppa to Mount Carmel. This entire region was once covered by extensive forests.

Yet farther to the north, the verdant plains of Acco and Esdraelon complete the coastal region. From

Dan marks the northern boundary of Canaan. The springs at Dan are one of the three main sources for the Jordan River.

Tyre to the north, the coastland had natural ports that were manned mostly by Phoenician sailors. The best known of these ports were at Tyre and Sidon.[8]

The Central Hill Country—Moving eastward from the Mediterranean, the central hill country is the second strip of land. A ridge of mountains beginning in the north in Lebanon continues south to Beer-sheba. The mountains cause abrupt climatic changes and provide strategic locations for cities. The western side of the mountain ridge receives seasonal precipitation from atmospheric moisture from the Mediterranean. The resulting fertile hills of Judea are called the Shephelah. These hills ascend to the heights of Hebron and Jerusalem and provide defensible positions for its residents. The hills north of Jerusalem in Samaria are lower in altitude and create openness and accessibility. In peacetime, this convenience encouraged travel and trade. In times of war, however, the lower altitudes made the capital cities difficult to defend. North of Samaria is upper and lower Galilee. This country is suitable for vineyards and provides excellent pasturage for flocks.

Snow covers the peaks of Mount Hermon most months of the year.

On the eastern slopes of the mountains are the wilderness regions of Judea. Since the mountain heights block rainfall in this region, the limited vegetation can sustain only sparse flocks. The arid conditions provide natural defenses against aggressor armies. Near Jerusalem this rugged terrain slopes steeply downward to the Jordan River.

The Jordan River Valley—The third strip of land is the Jordan (or Rift) Valley. This valley is part of a geological rift that begins in Asia Minor and extends south to Victoria Falls in Zambia, Africa.[9] Abundant springs flow from Mount Hermon to form tributaries that empty into the Sea of Galilee, which is nearly seven hundred feet below sea level. The land around the Sea of Galilee is fertile. The Jordan River flows south for about sixty-five miles through dense vegetation and arid wilderness to the lowest body of water on earth, the Dead Sea, about thirteen hundred feet below sea level. Evaporation is the only outlet for all the water draining into the Dead Sea from the Jordan River. This stagnation prevents aquatic life but produces abundant minerals. The water and minerals supplied by the springs, river, and lakes create high demand for this part of Canaan.

The Transjordan Plateau—Yet farther east from the Mediterranean Sea is the fourth strip of land, the Transjordan Plateau. The land rises from the Jordan River Valley and reaches the plateau that extends eastward approximately thirty miles to the Arabian Desert. The fertile land of Bashan and Gilead in the north contrast with the arid heights of Moab and Edom on the southeastern shore of the Dead Sea.[10] Before flowing into the Jordan, rivers irrigate and divide the northern and central Transjordan Plateau. The flocks Israel captured as they began their conquest of Canaan reflect the value of this highly productive region north of the Dead Sea.

Another major trade route of Canaan was located in this strip of land. The King's Highway ran from the Gulf of Aqaba east of the Jordan to Damascus.[11] Caravans traveling to and from Arabia used this highway. ✣

---

[1] J. McKee Adams, *Biblical Backgrounds*, rev. Joseph A. Callaway (Nashville: Broadman, 1965), 25. [2] William Sanford LaSor, David Allan Hubbard, and Frederic William Bush, *Old Testament Survey: The Message, Form, and Background of the Old Testament* (Grand Rapids: Eerdmans, 1996), 619. [3] George L. Kelm, "Hittites and Hivites" in *HolBD*, 655. [4] Adams, *Biblical Backgrounds*, 25. [5] Merrill F. Unger, "Palestine" in *The New Unger's Bible Dictionary*, ed. R. K. Harrison (Chicago: Moody, 1988), 953. [6] Timothy Trammel, "Palestine" in *HolBD*, 1063. [7] LaSor, Hubbard, and Bush, *Old Testament Survey*, 622. [8] LaSor, Hubbard, and Bush, *Old Testament Survey*. [9] LaSor, Hubbard, and Bush, *Old Testament Survey*, 626. [10] Trammel, "Palestine," 1064–68. [11] "Kings Highway" in *HolBD*, 847–48.

us.' 30 But King Sihon of Heshbon would not let us travel through his land, for the LORD your God had made his spirit stubborn and his heart obstinate in order to hand him over to you, as has now taken place.

31 "Then the LORD said to me, 'See, I have begun to give Sihon and his land to you. Begin to take possession of it.' 32 So Sihon and his whole army came out against us for battle at Jahaz. 33 The LORD our God handed him over to us, and we defeated him, his sons, and his whole army. 34 At that time we captured all his cities and completely destroyed the people of every city, including the women and children. We left no survivors. 35 We took only the livestock and the spoil from the cities we captured as plunder for ourselves. 36 There was no city that was inaccessible to[A] us, from Aroer on the rim of the Arnon Valley, along with the city in the valley, even as far as Gilead. The LORD our God gave everything to us. 37 But you did not go near the Ammonites' land, all along the bank of the Jabbok River, the cities of the hill country, or any place that the LORD our God had forbidden.

DEFEAT OF OG OF BASHAN

3 "Then we turned and went up the road to Bashan, and King Og of Bashan came out against us with his whole army to do battle at Edrei. 2 But the LORD said to me, 'Do not fear him, for I have handed him over to you along with his whole army and his land. Do to him as you did to King Sihon of the Amorites, who lived in Heshbon.' 3 So the LORD our God also handed over King Og of Bashan and his whole army to us. We struck him until there was no survivor left. 4 We captured all his cities at that time. There wasn't a city that we didn't take from them: sixty cities, the entire region of Argob, the kingdom of Og in Bashan. 5 All these were fortified with high walls, gates, and bars, besides a large number of rural villages. 6 We completely destroyed them, as we had done to King Sihon of Heshbon, destroying the men, women, and children of every city. 7 But we took all the livestock and the spoil from the cities as plunder for ourselves.

THE LAND OF THE TRANSJORDAN TRIBES

8 "At that time we took the land from the two Amorite kings across the Jordan, from the Arnon Valley as far as Mount Hermon, 9 which the Sidonians call Sirion, but the Amorites call Senir, 10 all the cities of the plateau, Gilead, and Bashan as far as Salecah and Edrei, cities of Og's kingdom in Bashan. 11 (Only King Og of Bashan was left of the remnant of the Rephaim. His bed[B] was made of iron. Isn't it in Rabbah of the Ammonites? It is 13 1/2 feet long and 6 feet wide by a standard measure.[C])

12 "At that time we took possession of this land. I gave to the Reubenites and Gadites the area extending from Aroer by the Arnon Valley, and half the hill country of Gilead along with its cities. 13 I gave to half the tribe of Manasseh the rest of Gilead and all Bashan, the kingdom of Og. The entire region of Argob, the whole territory of Bashan, used to be called the land of the Rephaim. 14 Jair, a descendant of Manasseh, took over the entire region of Argob as far as the border of the Geshurites and Maacathites. He called Bashan by his own name, Jair's Villages,[D] as it is today. 15 I gave Gilead to Machir, 16 and I gave to the Reubenites and Gadites the area extending from Gilead to the Arnon Valley (the middle of the valley was the border) and up to the Jabbok River, the border of the Ammonites. 17 The Arabah and Jordan are also borders from Chinnereth[E] as far as the Sea of the Arabah, the Dead Sea, under the slopes of Pisgah on the east.

18 "I commanded you at that time: The LORD your God has given you this land to possess. All your valiant men will cross over in battle formation ahead of your brothers the Israelites. 19 But your wives, dependents, and livestock — I know that you have a lot of livestock — will remain in the cities I have given you 20 until the LORD gives rest to your brothers as he has to you, and they also take possession of the land the LORD your God is giving them across the Jordan. Then each of you may return to his possession that I have given you.

THE TRANSFER OF ISRAEL'S LEADERSHIP

21 "I commanded Joshua at that time: Your own eyes have seen everything the LORD your God has done to these two kings. The LORD will do the same to all the kingdoms you are about to enter. 22 Don't be afraid of them, for the LORD your God fights for you.

23 "At that time I begged the LORD: 24 Lord GOD, you have begun to show your greatness and your strong hand to your servant, for what god is there in heaven or on earth who can perform deeds and mighty acts like yours? 25 Please let me cross over and see the beautiful land on the other side of the Jordan, that good hill country and Lebanon.

26 "But the LORD was angry with me because of you[F] and would not listen to me. The LORD said to me, 'That's enough! Do not speak to me again about this matter. 27 Go to the top of Pisgah and look to the west, north, south, and east, and see it with your own eyes, for you will not cross the Jordan. 28 But commission Joshua and encourage and strengthen him, for he will cross over ahead of the people and enable them to inherit this land that you will see.' 29 So we stayed in the valley facing Beth-peor.

[A] **2:36** Or *was too high for* [B] **3:11** Or *sarcophagus* [C] **3:11** Lit *nine cubits its length and four cubits its width, by a man's cubit* [D] **3:14** Or *Havvoth-jair* [E] **3:17** = the Sea of Galilee; Jos 12:3; 13:27; Lk 5:1 [F] **3:26** Or *me for your sake*

The Arabah

by David M. Wallace

The historic land of Israel has many diverse physical features. Travelers heading east from the Mediterranean Sea will encounter the coastal plains, the Shephelah region, the Judean hill country, the Jordan Valley, and the eastern plateau.

These five areas run north and south. The two geographical areas that cut across the land westward are the plain of Esdraelon in the north from the Jordan Valley to the Mediterranean at Mount Carmel; and the Negev, from the land south of the Dead Sea west to the River of Egypt. This small region of the world has perhaps more changes in landscape than any other. The region called the Arabah was a significant area in the history of ancient Israel.

The longest and deepest natural depression on earth, known as the Rift Valley, extends from northern Syria to eastern Africa and is one of the most important features in Israel's geography. This natural depression includes the area known as the Arabah.

Peering through "Solomon's Pillars" for an overview of Timnah, an ancient Egyptian mining village in the Arabah.

Arabah is the word used in the Bible to describe all or part of the Great Rift Valley in Israel. It ran from the Sea of Galilee in the north, through the Jordan Valley southward to the Dead Sea, and continued all the way south to the Gulf of Aqaba. In the Bible, the Arabah most commonly refers to the region south of the Dead Sea to Ezion-geber. This was the land of part of Israel's wanderings in the wilderness.

Arabah is a noun and place name that is variously translated in the Bible as "dry," "infertile," "burnt-up," "desert," "wilderness," "valley," and "plain." The place is a wasteland and one of the most desolate and forbidding areas on earth. The root meaning of the word is uncertain, but it most assuredly referred to an arid region.

The Arabah proper begins just south of the Dead Sea and near the Scorpions' Ascent, running through Wadi el-Arabah and terminating at the Gulf of Aqaba. Just south of the Dead Sea the terrain is about 1,300 feet below sea level; it gradually ascends to about 720 feet above sea level before descending to sea level at the gulf, a distance of some 110 miles. Most of the land surrounding the depression of the Arabah is above sea level.

The climate is characterized by hot summers and relatively mild winters. During the summer months of June through September, the daytime temperatures can exceed 120°F (49°C). The average daily temperatures during the winter months of November through March are about 60°F (15.5°C).

Rainfall is sparse, occurring usually in the winter months, with a total annual accumulation of one-half to two inches. After rare thunderstorms, the ground may briefly be covered with grass and flowers, but they will soon die because of the hot sun and dry climate. Due to the lack of precipitation, plants are generally limited to sagebrush, camel thorns, and acacia. However, the areas with more water produce spina-christi trees, which are shaped like umbrellas. Underground water from the highlands on each side makes this desert growth possible. Because the eastern side is higher than the western, it receives more rain. Therefore more erosion comes from the east, created by streams slowly moving dirt, gravel, and sand into the plain.

Just south of the Dead Sea is a wide, barren salt and mudflat area that was once under water. Here the Arabah is 1,275 feet below sea level. It is surrounded by low cliffs. At the base of these cliffs are a few springs that provide some water and produce a fair amount of desert vegetation.

South of the salt and mudflats lies Sela (Petra), rising to three hundred feet above sea level. Sela was an Edomite fortress during the Israelite wanderings. Beyond Sela, the valley widens to as much as twenty-five miles before narrowing again as it slopes downward to the Gulf of Aqaba at Ezion-geber. The entire area has very little vegetation except for occasional oases.

The southern section of the Arabah narrows to only six miles, with steep cliffs on each side. To the east lie the granite mountains of Midian, and to the west is Nubian sandstone terrain.

Another characteristic of the southern Arabah is the distinctive, broad, dried-out mudflats. These mudflats were created by sediment washing into the valley from streams and rain. But because of so little water and drainage, the sediment does not reach the Gulf of Aqaba. This process forms mudflats that are extremely slippery after rain.

An important north-south route, known as the King's Highway, existed in the Arabah during biblical times. The road was controlled by the Edomites and Amorites when the Israelites asked permission to travel it (Nm 20:17).

Along this route were economically important copper mines. Copper ore appears in the sandstone of the southern Arabah, and mining occurred at Punon, Irnahash, and Timnah. Punon is probably the site where Moses raised the bronze serpent (Nm 21:4–9; 33:42–43). Timnah, once called Solomon's mines, was mined by the Egyptians, possibly year-round. Copper and iron were mined at these locations. The Israelites would have avoided the mines when they were fortified by garrisons.

Other important mining and smelting areas were Khirbet en-Nahas, seventeen miles south of the Dead Sea, and Meneiyyeh, twenty-two miles north of the Gulf of Aqaba. Archaeology makes it clear that this area of the Holy Land was one "whose rocks are iron and from whose hills you will mine copper" (Dt 8:9).

The Hebrews lived in and crossed the Arabah while wandering in the wilderness on their way from Egypt to the promised land. Deuteronomy 2:8 tells us that they traveled down the Arabah from Kadesh-barnea to Ezion-geber. They claimed this land (Jos 1–12) and the eastern side of the Jordan River as well (Dt 3:1–20). Then they turned north and traveled through Wadi Yitm to go around the territories of Edom and Moab.

The Arabah lies primarily in the territory of Old Testament Edom.

Pharaoh's Island at the north end of the Gulf of Aqaba near Taba and Elath.

Shepherd with sheep along the Desert Highway between Amman (Rabbah) and Aqaba near Al Qatraneh.

The Edomites based their economy on agriculture and commerce more than on the copper mines of the region. Agriculture was possible in the northeast portion of their territory. Their prosperity depended largely on caravans traveling from India to the Mediterranean Sea over their roads. When Edom controlled the trade routes, their economy was strong, otherwise they lived in decline. A strong army was essential to a healthy economy.

Numbers 20:14–21 tells the story of the Edomites refusing to allow Moses and the Israelites to pass through their territory on the King's Highway. Moses was trying to reach the land east of the Jordan River so they could begin their conquest of the promised land. And because of the threat the Edomite army presented, Israel did not challenge their position. (See also God's directions not to challenge Edom in Dt 2:4–8.) The passage indicates the Arabah had fields, vineyards, and wells from which to drink. Moses and his people were forced to travel northeast around Edom and take a more indirect route to the land "across the Jordan in the wilderness, in the Arabah" (1:1).

The Israelites endured many difficulties during their wanderings in the wilderness of the Arabah. They traveled with donkeys. Camels are never mentioned. After many years in the desert, Israel's wanderings were extended because of the long, forced detour around Edomite and Moabite land in the Arabah. The most suitable land for living was already claimed by the Amalekites in the south and the Edomites and Moabites in northern Arabah.[1]

The land was hot, dry, dusty, and windy. This trip to the promised land was not for the faint of heart. It was a hostile environment at best.

The principal roads in the Arabah provided easier travel and the benefit of finding people with whom to trade for needed goods. However, the Israelites were not always welcome guests (Nm 20:14–21).

Finding water was always a challenge. Besides the occasional oasis, water resources included subterranean reservoirs that could be tapped from the surface and natural open pools along wadis where rainwater collected.

Other challenges included the land's being generally unsuitable for farming. The Israelites used cliffs to provide shelter from wind and storms. Goats were essential to their survival. Goats can live many days without water and show no ill effects. This freed the Israelites to travel long distances without a water source. ✣

---

[1] John Bright, *A History of Israel*, 2nd ed. (Philadelphia: Westminster, 1972), 128.

CALL TO OBEDIENCE

4 "Now, Israel, listen to the statutes and ordinances I am teaching you to follow, so that you may live, enter, and take possession of the land the LORD, the God of your ancestors, is giving you. 2 You must not add anything to what I command you or take anything away from it, so that you may keep the commands of the LORD your God I am giving you. 3 Your eyes have seen what the LORD did at Baal-peor, for the LORD your God destroyed every one of you who followed Baal of Peor. 4 But you who have remained faithful[A] to the LORD your God are all alive today. 5 Look, I have taught you statutes and ordinances as the LORD my God has commanded me, so that you may follow them in the land you are entering to possess. 6 Carefully follow them, for this will show your wisdom and understanding in the eyes of the peoples. When they hear about all these statutes, they will say, 'This great nation is indeed a wise and understanding people.' 7 For what great nation is there that has a god near to it as the LORD our God is to us whenever we call to him? 8 And what great nation has righteous statutes and ordinances like this entire law I set before you today?

9 "Only be on your guard and diligently watch yourselves, so that you don't forget the things your eyes have seen and so that they don't slip from your mind[B] as long as you live. Teach them to your children and your grandchildren. 10 The day you stood before the LORD your God at Horeb, the LORD said to me, 'Assemble the people before me, and I will let them hear my words, so that they may learn to fear me all the days they live on the earth and may instruct their children.' 11 You came near and stood at the base of the mountain, a mountain blazing with fire into the heavens and enveloped in a totally black cloud. 12 Then the LORD spoke to you from the fire. You kept hearing the sound of the words, but didn't see a form; there was only a voice. 13 He declared his covenant to you. He commanded you to follow the Ten Commandments, which he wrote on two stone tablets. 14 At that time the LORD commanded me to teach you statutes and ordinances for you to follow in the land you are about to cross into and possess.

WORSHIPING THE TRUE GOD

15 "Diligently watch yourselves — because you did not see any form on the day the LORD spoke to you out of the fire at Horeb — 16 so you don't act corruptly and make an idol for yourselves in the shape of any figure: a male or female form, 17 or the form of any animal on the earth, any winged creature that flies in the sky, 18 any creature that crawls on the ground, or any fish in the waters under the earth. 19 When you look to the heavens and see the sun, moon, and stars — all the stars in the sky — do not be led astray to bow in worship to them and serve them. The LORD your God has provided them for all people everywhere under heaven. 20 But the LORD selected you and brought you out of Egypt's iron furnace to be a people for his inheritance, as you are today.

21 "The LORD was angry with me on your account. He swore that I would not cross the Jordan and enter the good land the LORD your God is giving you as an inheritance. 22 I won't be crossing the Jordan because I am going to die in this land. But you are about to cross over and take possession of this good land. 23 Be careful not to forget the covenant of the LORD your God that he made with you, and make an idol for yourselves in the shape of anything he has forbidden you. 24 For the LORD your God is a consuming fire, a jealous God.

25 "When you have children and grandchildren and have been in the land a long time, and if you act corruptly, make an idol in the form of anything, and do what is evil in the sight of the LORD your God, angering him, 26 I call heaven and earth as witnesses against you today that you will quickly perish from the land you are about to cross the Jordan to possess. You will not live long there, but you will certainly be destroyed. 27 The LORD will scatter you among the peoples, and you will be reduced to a few survivors[C] among the nations where the LORD your God will drive you. 28 There you will worship man-made gods of wood and stone, which cannot see, hear, eat, or smell. 29 But from there, you will search for the LORD your God, and you will find him when you seek him with all your heart and all your soul. 30 When you are in distress and all these things have happened to you, in the future you will return to the LORD your God and obey him. 31 He will not leave you, destroy you, or forget the covenant with your ancestors that he swore to them by oath, because the LORD your God is a compassionate God.

32 "Indeed, ask about the earlier days that preceded you, from the day God created mankind[D] on the earth and from one end of the heavens to the other: Has anything like this great event ever happened, or has anything like it been heard of? 33 Has a people heard God's voice speaking from the fire as you have, and lived? 34 Or has a god attempted to go and take a nation as his own out of another nation, by trials, signs, wonders, and war, by a strong hand and an outstretched arm, by great terrors, as the LORD your God did for you in Egypt before your eyes? 35 You were shown these things so that you would know that the LORD is God; there is no other besides him. 36 He let

[A] **4:4** Lit *have held on* [B] **4:9** Or *don't depart from your heart*
[C] **4:27** Lit *be left few in number* [D] **4:32** Or *Adam*

The Law: God's Gift to His People

by T. J. Betts

Unlike Israel, other peoples in Israel's day had difficulty discerning the will of their gods. As a result, they resorted to divination, the activity of reading signs and omens as a means of discerning the will of their gods and foretelling the future. Divination involved several practices, such as the analysis of the liver spots of a sacrificed animal (hepatoscopy), the communication with the dead (necromancy), the study of the heavenly bodies (astrology), the mystic reading of water (hydromancy), and the use of a rod, staff, stick, or arrow in order to gain some direction or information (rhabdomancy).[1] ✣

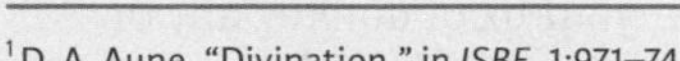

[1] D. A. Aune, "Divination," in *ISBE*, 1:971–74.

Replica of the Code of Hammurabi. Discovered near ancient Susa, it dates from 1750 BC and contains 282 laws. This was the most extensive legal document prior to classical times.

Prologue of the Mesopotamian Law Code of Lipit-Ishtar of Isin; dated to about 1870 BC. Written in Sumerian, this was a forerunner to the Code of Hammurabi.

you hear his voice from heaven to instruct you. He
showed you his great fire on earth, and you heard
his words from the fire. 37 Because he loved your ancestors, he chose their descendants after them and
brought you out of Egypt by his presence and great
power, 38 to drive out before you nations greater and
stronger than you and to bring you in and give you
their land as an inheritance, as is now taking place.
39 Today, recognize and keep in mind that the LORD is
God in heaven above and on earth below; there is no
other. 40 Keep his statutes and commands, which I am
giving you today, so that you and your children after
you may prosper and so that you may live long in the
land the LORD your God is giving you for all time."

CITIES OF REFUGE

41 Then Moses set apart three cities across the Jordan
to the east. 42 Someone could flee there who committed manslaughter, killing his neighbor accidentally
without previously hating him. He could flee to one
of these cities and stay alive: 43 Bezer in the wilderness on the plateau land, belonging to the Reubenites;
Ramoth in Gilead, belonging to the Gadites; or Golan
in Bashan, belonging to the Manassites.

INTRODUCTION TO THE LAW

44 This is the law Moses gave the Israelites. 45 These
are the decrees, statutes, and ordinances Moses
proclaimed to them after they came out of Egypt,
46 across the Jordan in the valley facing Beth-peor
in the land of King Sihon of the Amorites. He lived in
Heshbon, and Moses and the Israelites defeated him
after they came out of Egypt. 47 They took possession
of his land and the land of Og king of Bashan, the two
Amorite kings who were across the Jordan to the east,
48 from Aroer on the rim of the Arnon Valley as far
as Mount Sion (that is, Hermon) 49 and all the Arabah
on the east side of the Jordan as far as the Dead Sea
below the slopes of Pisgah.

THE TEN COMMANDMENTS

5 Moses summoned all Israel and said to them,
"Israel, listen to the statutes and ordinances I am
proclaiming as you hear them today. Learn and follow
them carefully. 2 The LORD our God made a covenant
with us at Horeb. 3 He did not make this covenant with
our ancestors, but with all of us who are alive here
today. 4 The LORD spoke to you face to face from the
fire on the mountain. 5 At that time I was standing
between the LORD and you to report the word[A] of the
LORD to you, because you were afraid of the fire and
did not go up the mountain. And he said:

6 I am the LORD your God, who brought you out
of the land of Egypt, out of the place of slavery.
7 Do not have other gods besides me.
8 Do not make an idol for yourself in the shape
of anything in the heavens above or on the
earth below or in the waters under the earth.
9 Do not bow in worship to them, and do not
serve them, because I, the LORD your God, am
a jealous God, bringing the consequences of
the fathers' iniquity on the children to the
third and fourth generations of those who
hate me, 10 but showing faithful love to a thousand generations of those who love me and
keep my commands.
11 Do not misuse the name of the LORD your God,
because the LORD will not leave anyone unpunished who misuses his name.
12 Be careful to remember the Sabbath day, to
keep it holy as the LORD your God has commanded you. 13 You are to labor six days and
do all your work, 14 but the seventh day is a
Sabbath to the LORD your God. Do not do any
work — you, your son or daughter, your male
or female slave, your ox or donkey, any of
your livestock, or the resident alien who lives
within your city gates, so that your male and
female slaves may rest as you do.
15 Remember that you were a slave in the land
of Egypt, and the LORD your God brought you
out of there with a strong hand and an outstretched arm. That is why the LORD your God
has commanded you to keep the Sabbath day.
16 Honor your father and your mother, as the
LORD your God has commanded you, so that
you may live long and so that you may prosper in the land the LORD your God is giving
you.
17 Do not murder.
18 Do not commit adultery.
19 Do not steal.
20 Do not give dishonest testimony against your
neighbor.
21 Do not covet your neighbor's wife or desire
your neighbor's house, his field, his male or
female slave, his ox or donkey, or anything
that belongs to your neighbor.

THE PEOPLE'S RESPONSE

22 "The LORD spoke these commands in a loud voice
to your entire assembly from the fire, cloud, and total
darkness on the mountain; he added nothing more.
He wrote them on two stone tablets and gave them
to me. 23 All of you approached me with your tribal
leaders and elders when you heard the voice from
the darkness and while the mountain was blazing
with fire. 24 You said, 'Look, the LORD our God has

[A] **5:5** One Hb ms, DSS, Sam, LXX, Syr, Vg read *words*

shown us his glory and greatness, and we have heard
his voice from the fire. Today we have seen that God
speaks with a person, yet he still lives. 25 But now, why
should we die? This great fire will consume us and we
will die if we hear the voice of the LORD our God any
longer. 26 For who out of all humanity has heard the
voice of the living God speaking from the fire, as we
have, and lived? 27 Go near and listen to everything the
LORD our God says. Then you can tell us everything
the LORD our God tells you; we will listen and obey.'

28 "The LORD heard your[A] words when you spoke to
me. He said to me, 'I have heard the words that these
people have spoken to you. Everything they have
said is right. 29 If only they had such a heart to fear
me and keep all my commands always, so that they
and their children would prosper forever. 30 Go and
tell them: Return to your tents. 31 But you stand here
with me, and I will tell you every command — the
statutes and ordinances — you are to teach them,
so that they may follow them in the land I am giving
them to possess.'

32 "Be careful to do as the LORD your God has commanded you; you are not to turn aside to the right or
the left. 33 Follow the whole instruction the LORD your
God has commanded you, so that you may live, prosper, and have a long life in the land you will possess.

THE GREATEST COMMAND

6 "This is the command — the statutes and ordinances — the LORD your God has commanded
me to teach you, so that you may follow them in the
land you are about to enter and possess. 2 Do this so
that you may fear the LORD your God all the days of
your life by keeping all his statutes and commands I
am giving you, your son, and your grandson, and so
that you may have a long life. 3 Listen, Israel, and be
careful to follow them, so that you may prosper and
multiply greatly, because the LORD, the God of your
ancestors, has promised you a land flowing with
milk and honey.

4 "Listen, Israel: The LORD our God, the LORD is one.[B]
5 Love the LORD your God with all your heart, with all
your soul, and with all your strength. 6 These words
that I am giving you today are to be in your heart.
7 Repeat them to your children. Talk about them when
you sit in your house and when you walk along the
road, when you lie down and when you get up. 8 Bind
them as a sign on your hand and let them be a symbol[C]
on your forehead.[D] 9 Write them on the doorposts of
your house and on your city gates.

REMEMBERING GOD THROUGH OBEDIENCE

10 "When the LORD your God brings you into the land
he swore to your ancestors Abraham, Isaac, and Jacob that he would give you — a land with large and
beautiful cities that you did not build, 11 houses full
of every good thing that you did not fill them with,
cisterns that you did not dig, and vineyards and olive
groves that you did not plant — and when you eat
and are satisfied, 12 be careful not to forget the LORD
who brought you out of the land of Egypt, out of the
place of slavery. 13 Fear the LORD your God, worship
him, and take your oaths in his name. 14 Do not follow
other gods, the gods of the peoples around you, 15 for
the LORD your God, who is among you, is a jealous
God. Otherwise, the LORD your God will become angry with you and obliterate you from the face of the
earth. 16 Do not test the LORD your God as you tested
him at Massah. 17 Carefully observe the commands of
the LORD your God, the decrees and statutes he has
commanded you. 18 Do what is right and good in the
LORD's sight, so that you may prosper and so that you
may enter and possess the good land the LORD your
God swore to give your ancestors, 19 by driving out
all your enemies before you, as the LORD has said.

20 "When your son asks you in the future, 'What is
the meaning of the decrees, statutes, and ordinances
that the LORD our God has commanded you?' 21 tell
him, 'We were slaves of Pharaoh in Egypt, but the
LORD brought us out of Egypt with a strong hand.
22 Before our eyes the LORD inflicted great and devastating signs and wonders on Egypt, on Pharaoh,
and on all his household, 23 but he brought us from
there in order to lead us in and give us the land that
he swore to our ancestors. 24 The LORD commanded
us to follow all these statutes and to fear the LORD our
God for our prosperity always and for our preservation, as it is today. 25 Righteousness will be ours if we
are careful to follow every one of these commands
before the LORD our God, as he has commanded us.'

ISRAEL TO DESTROY IDOLATROUS NATIONS

7 "When the LORD your God brings you into the
land you are entering to possess, and he drives
out many nations before you — the Hethites, Girgashites, Amorites, Canaanites, Perizzites, Hivites and
Jebusites, seven nations more numerous and powerful than you — 2 and when the LORD your God delivers them over to you and you defeat them, you must
completely destroy them. Make no treaty with them
and show them no mercy. 3 You must not intermarry
with them, and you must not give your daughters
to their sons or take their daughters for your sons,
4 because they will turn your sons away from me to
worship other gods. Then the LORD's anger will burn
against you, and he will swiftly destroy you. 5 Instead,

[A] **5:28** Lit *the sound of your* [B] **6:4** Or *the LORD is our God; the LORD is one*, or *The LORD is our God, the LORD alone*, or *The LORD our God is one LORD* [C] **6:8** Or *phylactery*; Mt 23:5 [D] **6:8** Lit *symbol between your eyes*

this is what you are to do to them: tear down their altars, smash their sacred pillars, cut down their Asherah poles, and burn their carved images. 6 For you are a holy people belonging to the LORD your God. The LORD your God has chosen you to be his own possession out of all the peoples on the face of the earth.

7 "The LORD had his heart set on you and chose you, not because you were more numerous than all peoples, for you were the fewest of all peoples. 8 But because the LORD loved you and kept the oath he swore to your ancestors, he brought you out with a strong hand and redeemed you from the place of slavery, from the power of Pharaoh king of Egypt. 9 Know that the LORD your God is God, the faithful God who keeps his gracious covenant loyalty for a thousand generations with those who love him and keep his commands. 10 But he directly pays back[A] and destroys those who hate him. He will not hesitate to pay back directly[B] the one who hates him. 11 So keep the command — the statutes and ordinances — that I am giving you to follow today.

12 "If you listen to and are careful to keep these ordinances, the LORD your God will keep his covenant loyalty with you, as he swore to your ancestors. 13 He will love you, bless you, and multiply you. He will bless your offspring,[C] and the produce of your land — your grain, new wine, and fresh oil — the young of your herds, and the newborn of your flocks, in the land he swore to your ancestors that he would give you. 14 You will be blessed above all peoples; there will be no infertile male or female among you or your livestock. 15 The LORD will remove all sickness from you; he will not put on you all the terrible diseases of Egypt that you know about, but he will inflict them on all who hate you. 16 You must destroy all the peoples the LORD your God is delivering over to you and not look on them with pity. Do not worship their gods, for that will be a snare to you.

17 "If you say to yourself, 'These nations are greater than I; how can I drive them out?' 18 do not be afraid of them. Be sure to remember what the LORD your God did to Pharaoh and all Egypt: 19 the great trials that you saw, the signs and wonders, the strong hand and outstretched arm, by which the LORD your God brought you out. The LORD your God will do the same to all the peoples you fear. 20 The LORD your God will also send hornets against them until all the survivors and those hiding from you perish. 21 Don't be terrified of them, for the LORD your God, a great and awesome God, is among you. 22 The LORD your God will drive out these nations before you little by little. You will not be able to destroy them all at once; otherwise, the wild animals will become too numerous for you. 23 The LORD your God will give them over to you and throw them into great confusion until they are destroyed. 24 He will hand their kings over to you, and you will wipe out their names under heaven. No one will be able to stand against you; you will annihilate them. 25 Burn up the carved images of their gods. Don't covet the silver and gold on the images and take it for yourself, or else you will be ensnared by it, for it is detestable to the LORD your God. 26 Do not bring any detestable thing into your house, or you will be set apart for destruction like it. You are to abhor and detest it utterly because it is set apart for destruction.

REMEMBER THE LORD

8 "Carefully follow every command I am giving you today, so that you may live and increase, and may enter and take possession of the land the LORD swore to your ancestors. 2 Remember that the LORD your God led you on the entire journey these forty years in the wilderness, so that he might humble you and test you to know what was in your heart, whether or not you would keep his commands. 3 He humbled you by letting you go hungry; then he gave you manna to eat, which you and your ancestors had not known, so that you might learn that man does not live on bread alone but on every word that comes from the mouth of the LORD. 4 Your clothing did not wear out, and your feet did not swell these forty years. 5 Keep in mind that the LORD your God has been disciplining you just as a man disciplines his son. 6 So keep the commands of the LORD your God by walking in his ways and fearing him. 7 For the LORD your God is bringing you into a good land, a land with streams, springs, and deep water sources, flowing in both valleys and hills; 8 a land of wheat, barley, vines, figs, and pomegranates; a land of olive oil and honey; 9 a land where you will eat food without shortage, where you will lack nothing; a land whose rocks are iron and from whose hills you will mine copper. 10 When you eat and are full, you will bless the LORD your God for the good land he has given you.

11 "Be careful that you don't forget the LORD your God by failing to keep his commands, ordinances, and statutes that I am giving you today. 12 When you eat and are full, and build beautiful houses to live in, 13 and your herds and flocks grow large, and your silver and gold multiply, and everything else you have increases, 14 be careful that your heart doesn't become proud and you forget the LORD your God who brought you out of the land of Egypt, out of the place of slavery. 15 He led you through the great and terrible wilderness with its poisonous[D] snakes and scorpions, a thirsty land where there was no

[A] **7:10** Lit *He pays back to their faces* [B] **7:10** Lit *to pay back to their faces* [C] **7:13** Lit *bless the fruit of your womb* [D] **8:15** Lit *burning*

Educating Children in Ancient Israel

by E. LeBron Matthews

God gave Abraham the responsibility for directing his descendants to an accurate faith. Each new generation passed to subsequent generations both God's promise to become a great nation and the responsibility for loyalty to God. Each generation instructed the next generation in the ancient religion of Israel. The success of each generation varied. At times the worship of the Lord flourished. At other times it seemed to disappear. Yet in every generation, numbers of faithful parents passed down the fundamentals of the faith to their children. The ancient religion never vanished.

Primary responsibility for training children in religious matters remained with the parents. Formal education was limited. Little evidence survives that independent, professional schools existed in Israel. Some young men may have trained in "wisdom" schools similar to those of other ancient cultures. Some scholars have concluded that the book of Proverbs functioned as a textbook for such schools. If indeed these schools existed, only a small select number of adolescent boys attended them. At the heart of their schoolwork was the concept of the "fear of the Lord," which was the natural conclusion of understanding the vast difference between God and humanity.

Unlike other gods of the ancient world, the living God was not represented in a painting or an idol. Israel's God revealed his character and presence through historical activity. Furthermore, he set forth his expectation for human behavior in a written law code. Therefore stories of his nature and his deeds were told over and over. For example, the saga of the exodus from Egypt demonstrated the Lord's power and providence, as well as his mercy and judgment.

The nucleus of Israel's teachings about God was recorded in Deuteronomy 6:4–9. This passage was known as the Shema. *Shema* is a transliteration of the Hebrew imperative commanding the people of Israel to "hear." These verses gave ancient Israel's basic confession of faith. It declared that the Lord was the one true God and that his commandments were compulsory for his people. Later this became the essential statement of the law for Judaism. The enemies of Jesus asked him, "Teacher, which command in the law is the greatest?" He responded by quoting from this passage (Mt 22:34–40).

Fragmentary terra-cotta Ammonite ostracon; from the Baq'ah Valley in Jordan; dated to the Late Iron Age (about 701–586 BC). Although the inscription is incomplete, it does contain the Hebrew word *shema* meaning "hear."

God commanded that the instruction be made indelible by constant repetition. Such repetition was to be more than rote memory. Parents constantly were to demonstrate the lessons to their children by living the instruction before their eyes.

A godly lifestyle afforded numerous opportunities to instruct children on the covenant faith. Two specific examples from Scripture illustrate this point. First was the observance of the Passover celebration (Ex 12:26; 13:8,14). The ritual of this sacred day contrasted greatly with the routine of an ordinary day. Inevitably the peculiar customs of the Passover raised questions in the minds of young children and caused them to ask why. Parents were to grasp these occasions for teaching fundamental truths about God.

A second opportunity was presented by the erection of memorial stones to commemorate the crossing of the Jordan River (Jos 4:6–7,21). Very little imagination is required to see a father and his small son walking along the rocky banks of the river. The boy looks at the stones and concludes that somebody deliberately constructed the pile. He spies an almost identical pile of rocks in the middle of the stream. He turns to his father and asks about them. His father tells the story of his ancestors—one who died in the wilderness because of his lack of faith, and the son of that man, who crossed the Jordan at this very spot. He fought under Joshua against the Canaanites, and God gave great victories. ✣

water. He brought water out of the flint rock for you.
16 He fed you in the wilderness with manna, which
your ancestors had not known, in order to humble
and test you, so that in the end he might cause you
to prosper. 17 You may say to yourself, 'My power
and my own ability have gained this wealth for me,'
18 but remember that the LORD your God gives you
the power to gain wealth, in order to confirm his
covenant he swore to your ancestors, as it is today.
19 If you ever forget the LORD your God and follow
other gods to serve them and bow in worship to
them, I testify against you today that you will certainly perish. 20 Like the nations the LORD is about
to destroy before you, you will perish if you do not
obey the LORD your God.

WARNING AGAINST SELF-RIGHTEOUSNESS

9 "Listen, Israel: Today you are about to cross the
Jordan to enter and drive out nations greater
and stronger than you, with large cities fortified to
the heavens. 2 The people are strong and tall, the descendants of the Anakim. You know about them and
you have heard it said about them, 'Who can stand
up to the sons of Anak?' 3 But understand that today
the LORD your God will cross over ahead of you as a
consuming fire; he will devastate and subdue them
before you. You will drive them out and destroy them
swiftly, as the LORD has told you. 4 When the LORD
your God drives them out before you, do not say to
yourself, 'The LORD brought me in to take possession
of this land because of my righteousness.' Instead, the
LORD will drive out these nations before you because
of their wickedness. 5 You are not going to take possession of their land because of your righteousness
or your integrity. Instead, the LORD your God will
drive out these nations before you because of their
wickedness, in order to fulfill the promise he swore
to your ancestors Abraham, Isaac, and Jacob. 6 Understand that the LORD your God is not giving you this
good land to possess because of your righteousness,
for you are a stiff-necked people.

ISRAEL'S REBELLION AND MOSES'S INTERCESSION

7 "Remember and do not forget how you provoked the
LORD your God in the wilderness. You have been rebelling against the LORD from the day you left the land
of Egypt until you reached this place. 8 You provoked
the LORD at Horeb, and he was angry enough with
you to destroy you. 9 When I went up the mountain to
receive the stone tablets, the tablets of the covenant
the LORD made with you, I stayed on the mountain
forty days and forty nights. I did not eat food or drink
water. 10 On the day of the assembly the LORD gave me
the two stone tablets, inscribed by God's finger. The
exact words were on them, which the LORD spoke to
you from the fire on the mountain. 11 The LORD gave
me the two stone tablets, the tablets of the covenant,
at the end of the forty days and forty nights.

12 "The LORD said to me, 'Get up and go down immediately from here. For your people whom you brought
out of Egypt have acted corruptly. They have quickly
turned from the way that I commanded them; they
have made a cast image for themselves.' 13 The LORD
also said to me, 'I have seen this people, and indeed,
they are a stiff-necked people. 14 Leave me alone, and
I will destroy them and blot out their name under
heaven. Then I will make you into a nation stronger
and more numerous than they.'

15 "So I went back down the mountain, while it was
blazing with fire, and the two tablets of the covenant
were in my hands. 16 I saw how you had sinned against
the LORD your God; you had made a calf image for
yourselves. You had quickly turned from the way
the LORD had commanded for you. 17 So I took hold
of the two tablets and threw them from my hands,
shattering them before your eyes. 18 I fell down like
the first time in the presence of the LORD for forty
days and forty nights; I did not eat food or drink water because of all the sin you committed, doing what
was evil in the LORD's sight and angering him. 19 I
was afraid of the fierce anger the LORD had directed
against you, because he was about to destroy you.
But again the LORD listened to me on that occasion.
20 The LORD was angry enough with Aaron to destroy
him. But I prayed for Aaron at that time also. 21 I took
the sinful calf you had made and burned it. I crushed
it, thoroughly grinding it to powder as fine as dust,
and threw its dust into the stream that came down
from the mountain.

22 "You continued to provoke the LORD at Taberah, Massah, and Kibroth-hattaavah. 23 When the
LORD sent you from Kadesh-barnea, he said, 'Go up
and possess the land I have given you'; you rebelled
against the command of the LORD your God. You did
not believe or obey him. 24 You have been rebelling
against the LORD ever since I have[A] known you.
25 "I fell down in the presence of the LORD forty days
and forty nights because the LORD had threatened to
destroy you. 26 I prayed to the LORD:

Lord GOD, do not annihilate your people, your
inheritance, whom you redeemed through your
greatness and brought out of Egypt with a strong
hand. 27 Remember your servants Abraham,
Isaac, and Jacob. Disregard this people's stubbornness, and their wickedness and sin. 28 Otherwise, those in the land you brought us from will
say, 'Because the LORD wasn't able to bring them
into the land he had promised them, and because

[A] **9:24** Sam, LXX read *since he has*

he hated them, he brought them out to kill them
in the wilderness.' 29 But they are your people,
your inheritance, whom you brought out by your
great power and outstretched arm.

THE COVENANT RENEWED

10 "The LORD said to me at that time, 'Cut two
stone tablets like the first ones and come to
me on the mountain and make a wooden ark. 2 I will
write on the tablets the words that were on the first
tablets you broke, and you are to place them in the
ark.' 3 So I made an ark of acacia wood, cut two stone
tablets like the first ones, and climbed the mountain
with the two tablets in my hand. 4 Then on the day of
the assembly, the LORD wrote on the tablets what had
been written previously, the Ten Commandments that
he had spoken to you on the mountain from the fire.
The LORD gave them to me, 5 and I went back down
the mountain and placed the tablets in the ark I had
made. And they have remained there, as the LORD
commanded me."

6 The Israelites traveled from Beeroth Bene-jaakan[A]
to Moserah. Aaron died and was buried there, and
Eleazar his son became priest in his place. 7 They traveled from there to Gudgodah, and from Gudgodah to
Jotbathah, a land with flowing streams.

8 "At that time the LORD set apart the tribe of Levi to
carry the ark of the LORD's covenant, to stand before
the LORD to serve him, and to pronounce blessings
in his name, as it is today. 9 For this reason, Levi does
not have a portion or inheritance like his brothers;
the LORD is his inheritance, as the LORD your God
told him.

10 "I stayed on the mountain forty days and forty
nights like the first time. The LORD also listened to
me on this occasion; he agreed not to annihilate you.
11 Then the LORD said to me, 'Get up. Continue your
journey ahead of the people, so that they may enter
and possess the land I swore to give their ancestors.'

WHAT GOD REQUIRES

12 "And now, Israel, what does the LORD your God ask
of you except to fear the LORD your God by walking
in all his ways, to love him, and to worship the LORD
your God with all your heart and all your soul? 13 Keep
the LORD's commands and statutes I am giving you
today, for your own good. 14 The heavens, indeed the
highest heavens, belong to the LORD your God, as
does the earth and everything in it. 15 Yet the LORD
had his heart set on your ancestors and loved them.
He chose their descendants after them — he chose
you out of all the peoples, as it is today. 16 Therefore,
circumcise your hearts and don't be stiff-necked any
longer. 17 For the LORD your God is the God of gods and
Lord of lords, the great, mighty, and awe-inspiring
God, showing no partiality and taking no bribe. 18 He
executes justice for the fatherless and the widow, and
loves the resident alien, giving him food and clothing.
19 You are also to love the resident alien, since you
were resident aliens in the land of Egypt. 20 You are
to fear the LORD your God and worship him. Remain
faithful[B] to him and take oaths in his name. 21 He is
your praise and he is your God, who has done for you
these great and awe-inspiring works your eyes have
seen. 22 Your ancestors went down to Egypt, seventy
people in all, and now the LORD your God has made
you numerous, like the stars of the sky.

REMEMBER AND OBEY

11 "Therefore, love the LORD your God and always
keep his mandate and his statutes, ordinances,
and commands. 2 Understand today that it is not your
children who experienced or saw the discipline of
the LORD your God:

His greatness, strong hand, and outstretched
arm; 3 his signs and the works he did in Egypt to
Pharaoh king of Egypt and all his land; 4 what
he did to Egypt's army, its horses and chariots,
when he made the water of the Red Sea flow
over them as they pursued you, and he destroyed them completely;[C] 5 what he did to you in
the wilderness until you reached this place; 6 and
what he did to Dathan and Abiram, the sons of
Eliab the Reubenite, when in the middle of the
whole Israelite camp the earth opened its mouth
and swallowed them, their households, their
tents, and every living thing with them.

7 Your own eyes have seen every great work the LORD
has done.

8 "Keep every command I am giving you today, so
that you may have the strength to cross into and possess the land you are to inherit, 9 and so that you may
live long in the land the LORD swore to your ancestors
to give them and their descendants, a land flowing
with milk and honey. 10 For the land you are entering
to possess is not like the land of Egypt, from which
you have come, where you sowed your seed and irrigated by hand[D] as in a vegetable garden. 11 But the land
you are entering to possess is a land of mountains and
valleys, watered by rain from the sky. 12 It is a land the
LORD your God cares for. He is always watching over
it from the beginning to the end of the year.

13 "If you carefully obey my commands I am giving
you today, to love the LORD your God and worship
him with all your heart and all your soul, 14 I[E] will
provide rain for your land in the proper time, the
autumn and spring rains, and you will harvest your

[A] **10:6** Or *from the wells of Bene-jaakan*, or *from the wells of the Jaakanites* [B] **10:20** Lit *Hold on* [C] **11:4** Lit *to this day* [D] **11:10** Lit *foot* [E] **11:14** DSS, Sam, LXX read *he*

grain, new wine, and fresh oil. 15 I[A] will provide grass
in your fields for your livestock. You will eat and be
satisfied. 16 Be careful that you are not enticed to turn
aside, serve, and bow in worship to other gods. 17 Then
the LORD's anger will burn against you. He will shut
the sky, and there will be no rain; the land will not
yield its produce, and you will perish quickly from
the good land the LORD is giving you.

18 "Imprint these words of mine on your hearts
and minds, bind them as a sign on your hands, and
let them be a symbol[B] on your foreheads.[C] 19 Teach
them to your children, talking about them when
you sit in your house and when you walk along
the road, when you lie down and when you get up.
20 Write them on the doorposts of your house and
on your city gates, 21 so that as long as the heavens
are above the earth, your days and those of your
children may be many in the land the LORD swore to
give your ancestors. 22 For if you carefully observe
every one of these commands I am giving you to
follow — to love the LORD your God, walk in all his
ways, and remain faithful[D] to him — 23 the LORD
will drive out all these nations before you, and you
will drive out nations greater and stronger than you
are. 24 Every place the sole of your foot treads will
be yours. Your territory will extend from the wilderness to Lebanon and from the Euphrates River[E]
to the Mediterranean Sea. 25 No one will be able to
stand against you; the LORD your God will put fear
and dread of you in all the land where you set foot,
as he has promised you.

A BLESSING AND A CURSE

26 "Look, today I set before you a blessing and a curse:
27 there will be a blessing, if you obey the commands
of the LORD your God I am giving you today, 28 and a
curse, if you do not obey the commands of the LORD
your God and you turn aside from the path I command you today by following other gods you have
not known. 29 When the LORD your God brings you
into the land you are entering to possess, you are to
proclaim the blessing at Mount Gerizim and the curse
at Mount Ebal. 30 Aren't these mountains across the
Jordan, beyond the western road in the land of the
Canaanites, who live in the Arabah, opposite Gilgal,
near the oaks[F] of Moreh? 31 For you are about to cross
the Jordan to enter and take possession of the land
the LORD your God is giving you. When you possess it
and settle in it, 32 be careful to follow all the statutes
and ordinances I set before you today.

THE CHOSEN PLACE OF WORSHIP

12 "Be careful to follow these statutes and ordinances in the land that the LORD, the God of
your ancestors, has given you to possess all the days
you live on the earth. 2 Destroy completely all the
places where the nations that you are driving out
worship their gods — on the high mountains, on the
hills, and under every green tree. 3 Tear down their
altars, smash their sacred pillars, burn their Asherah
poles, cut down the carved images of their gods, and
wipe out their names from every[G] place. 4 Don't worship the LORD your God this way. 5 Instead, turn to the
place the LORD your God chooses from all your tribes
to put his name for his dwelling and go there. 6 You
are to bring there your burnt offerings and sacrifices,
your tenths and personal contributions,[H] your vow
offerings and freewill offerings, and the firstborn
of your herds and flocks. 7 You will eat there in the
presence of the LORD your God and rejoice with your
household in everything you do,[I] because the LORD
your God has blessed you.

8 "You are not to do as we are doing here today;
everyone is doing whatever seems right in his own
sight. 9 Indeed, you have not yet come into the resting place and the inheritance the LORD your God is
giving you. 10 When you cross the Jordan and live in
the land the LORD your God is giving you to inherit,
and he gives you rest from all the enemies around
you and you live in security, 11 then the LORD your
God will choose the place to have his name dwell.
Bring there everything I command you: your burnt
offerings, sacrifices, offerings of the tenth, personal
contributions,[J] and all your choice offerings you vow
to the LORD. 12 You will rejoice before the LORD your
God — you, your sons and daughters, your male and
female slaves, and the Levite who is within your city
gates, since he has no portion or inheritance among
you. 13 Be careful not to offer your burnt offerings in
all the sacred places you see. 14 You must offer your
burnt offerings only in the place the LORD chooses in
one of your tribes, and there you must do everything
I command you.

SLAUGHTERING ANIMALS TO EAT

15 "But whenever you want, you may slaughter and
eat meat within any of your city gates, according to
the blessing the LORD your God has given you. Those
who are clean or unclean may eat it, as they would a
gazelle or deer, 16 but you must not eat the blood; pour
it on the ground like water. 17 Within your city gates
you may not eat the tenth of your grain, new wine,
or fresh oil; the firstborn of your herd or flock; any
of your vow offerings that you pledge; your freewill

[A] **11:15** DSS, Sam, LXX read *He* [B] **11:18** Or *phylactery*; Mt 23:5 [C] **11:18** Lit *symbol between your eyes*; Ex 13:16; Dt 6:8 [D] **11:22** Lit *and hold on* [E] **11:24** Some Hb mss, LXX, Tg, Vg read *the great river, the river Euphrates* [F] **11:30** Sam, LXX, Syr, Aq, Sym read *oak*; Gn 12:6 [G] **12:3** Lit *that* [H] **12:6** Lit *and the contributions from your hands* [I] **12:7** Lit *you put your hand to*, also in v. 18 [J] **12:11** Lit *tenth, the contributions from your hands*

offerings; or your personal contributions.[A] 18 You are
to eat them in the presence of the LORD your God at
the place the LORD your God chooses — you, your
son and daughter, your male and female slave, and
the Levite who is within your city gates. Rejoice before the LORD your God in everything you do, 19 and
be careful not to neglect the Levite, as long as you
live in your land.

20 "When the LORD your God enlarges your territory as he has promised you, and you say, 'I want to eat
meat' because you have a strong desire to eat meat,
you may eat it whenever you want. 21 If the place where
the LORD your God chooses to put his name is too far
from you, you may slaughter any of your herd or flock
he has given you, as I have commanded you, and you
may eat it within your city gates whenever you want.
22 Indeed, you may eat it as the gazelle and deer are
eaten; both the clean and the unclean may eat it. 23 But
don't eat the blood, since the blood is the life, and you
must not eat the life with the meat. 24 Do not eat blood;
pour it on the ground like water. 25 Do not eat it, so that
you and your children after you will prosper, because
you will be doing what is right in the LORD's sight.

26 "But you are to take the holy offerings you have
and your vow offerings and go to the place the LORD
chooses. 27 Present the meat and blood of your burnt
offerings on the altar of the LORD your God. The
blood of your other sacrifices is to be poured out
beside the altar of the LORD your God, but you may
eat the meat. 28 Be careful to obey all these things I
command you, so that you and your children after
you may prosper forever, because you will be doing what is good and right in the sight of the LORD
your God.

29 "When the LORD your God annihilates the nations before you, which you are entering to take possession of, and you drive them out and live in their
land, 30 be careful not to be ensnared by their ways
after they have been destroyed before you. Do not
inquire about their gods, asking, 'How did these nations worship their gods? I'll also do the same.' 31 You
must not do the same to the LORD your God, because
they practice every detestable act, which the LORD
hates, for their gods. They even burn their sons and
daughters in the fire to their gods. 32 Be careful to do
everything I command you; do not add anything to
it or take anything away from it.

THE FALSE PROPHET

13 "If a prophet or someone who has dreams arises among you and proclaims a sign or wonder
to you, 2 and that sign or wonder he has promised
you comes about, but he says, 'Let's follow other
gods,' which you have not known, 'and let's worship
them,' 3 do not listen to that prophet's words or to
that dreamer. For the LORD your God is testing you
to know whether you love the LORD your God with
all your heart and all your soul. 4 You must follow the
LORD your God and fear him. You must keep his commands and listen to him; you must worship him and
remain faithful[B] to him. 5 That prophet or dreamer
must be put to death, because he has urged rebellion
against the LORD your God who brought you out of
the land of Egypt and redeemed you from the place
of slavery, to turn you from the way the LORD your
God has commanded you to walk. You must purge
the evil from you.

DON'T TOLERATE IDOLATRY

6 "If your brother, the son of your mother,[C] or your
son or daughter, or the wife you embrace, or your
closest friend secretly entices you, saying, 'Let's go
and worship other gods' — which neither you nor
your ancestors have known, 7 any of the gods of the
peoples around you, near you or far from you, from
one end of the earth to the other — 8 do not yield to
him or listen to him. Show him no pity,[D] and do not
spare him or shield him. 9 Instead, you must kill him.
Your hand is to be the first against him to put him to
death, and then the hands of all the people. 10 Stone
him to death for trying to turn you away from the
LORD your God who brought you out of the land of
Egypt, out of the place of slavery. 11 All Israel will hear
and be afraid, and they will no longer do anything
evil like this among you.

12 "If you hear it said about one of your cities the
LORD your God is giving you to live in, 13 that wicked
men have sprung up among you, led the inhabitants
of their city astray, and said, 'Let's go and worship
other gods,' which you have not known, 14 you are
to inquire, investigate, and interrogate thoroughly.
If the report turns out to be true that this detestable
act has been done among you, 15 you must strike
down the inhabitants of that city with the sword.
Completely destroy everyone in it as well as its livestock with the sword. 16 You are to gather all its spoil
in the middle of the city square and completely burn
the city and all its spoil for the LORD your God. The
city is to remain a mound of ruins forever; it is not
to be rebuilt. 17 Nothing set apart for destruction is
to remain in your hand, so that the LORD will turn
from his burning anger and grant you mercy, show
you compassion, and multiply you as he swore to
your ancestors. 18 This will occur if you obey the
LORD your God, keeping all his commands I am giving you today, doing what is right in the sight of the
LORD your God.

[A] **12:17** Lit *or the contributions from your hands* [B] **13:4** Lit *and hold on*
[C] **13:6** DSS, Sam, LXX read *If the son of your father or the son of your mother* [D] **13:8** Lit *Your eye must not pity him*

FORBIDDEN PRACTICES

14 "You are sons of the LORD your God; do not cut
yourselves or make a bald spot on your head[A]
on behalf of the dead, 2 for you are a holy people belonging to the LORD your God. The LORD has chosen
you to be his own possession out of all the peoples
on the face of the earth.

CLEAN AND UNCLEAN FOODS

3 "You must not eat any detestable thing. 4 These are
the animals you may eat:

oxen, sheep, goats,
5 deer, gazelles, roe deer,
wild goats, ibexes, antelopes,
and mountain sheep.

6 You may eat any animal that has hooves divided in
two and chews the cud.[B] 7 But among the ones that
chew the cud or have divided hooves, you are not
to eat these:

camels, hares, and hyraxes,
though they chew the cud, they do not
have hooves —
they are unclean for you;
8 and pigs, though they have hooves,
they do not chew the cud —
they are unclean for you.

Do not eat their meat or touch their carcasses.
9 "You may eat everything from the water that has
fins and scales, 10 but you may not eat anything that
does not have fins and scales — it is unclean for you.
11 "You may eat every clean bird, 12 but these are the
ones you may not eat:

eagles, bearded vultures,
black vultures, 13 the kites,
any kind of falcon,[C]
14 every kind of raven, 15 ostriches,
short-eared owls, gulls,
any kind of hawk,
16 little owls, long-eared owls,
barn owls, 17 eagle owls,
ospreys, cormorants, 18 storks,
any kind of heron,
hoopoes, and bats.[D]

19 All winged insects are unclean for you; they may not
be eaten. 20 But you may eat every clean flying creature.
21 "You are not to eat any carcass; you may give it
to a resident alien within your city gates, and he may
eat it, or you may sell it to a foreigner. For you are a
holy people belonging to the LORD your God. Do not
boil a young goat in its mother's milk.

A TENTH FOR THE LORD

22 "Each year you are to set aside a tenth of all the produce grown in your fields. 23 You are to eat a tenth of
your grain, new wine, and fresh oil, and the firstborn
of your herd and flock, in the presence of the LORD
your God at the place where he chooses to have his
name dwell, so that you will always learn to fear the
LORD your God. 24 But if the distance is too great for
you to carry it, since the place where the LORD your
God chooses to put his name is too far away from you
and since the LORD your God has blessed you, 25 then
exchange it for silver, take the silver in your hand, and
go to the place the LORD your God chooses. 26 You may
spend the silver on anything you want: cattle, sheep,
goats, wine, beer, or anything you desire. You are to
feast there in the presence of the LORD your God and
rejoice with your family. 27 Do not neglect the Levite
within your city gates, since he has no portion or
inheritance among you.
28 "At the end of every three years, bring a tenth of
all your produce for that year and store it within your
city gates. 29 Then the Levite, who has no portion or
inheritance among you, the resident alien, the fatherless, and the widow within your city gates may come,
eat, and be satisfied. And the LORD your God will bless
you in all the work of your hands that you do.

DEBTS CANCELED

15 "At the end of every seven years you must cancel
debts. 2 This is how to cancel debt: Every creditor[E] is to cancel what he has lent his neighbor. He is
not to collect anything from his neighbor or brother,
because the LORD's release of debts has been proclaimed. 3 You may collect something from a foreigner,
but you must forgive whatever your brother owes you.
4 "There will be no poor among you, however, because the LORD is certain to bless you in the land the
LORD your God is giving you to possess as an inheritance — 5 if only you obey the LORD your God and are
careful to follow every one of these commands I am
giving you today. 6 When the LORD your God blesses
you as he has promised you, you will lend to many
nations but not borrow; you will rule many nations,
but they will not rule you.

LENDING TO THE POOR

7 "If there is a poor person among you, one of your
brothers within any of your city gates in the land the
LORD your God is giving you, do not be hardhearted
or tightfisted toward your poor brother. 8 Instead,
you are to open your hand to him and freely loan
him enough for whatever need he has. 9 Be careful
that there isn't this wicked thought in your heart,
'The seventh year, the year of canceling debts, is near,'

[A] **14:1** Or *forehead* [B] **14:6** The Hb does not specify chewing the cud, but bringing up partially digested food and swallowing it again. [C] **14:13** Some Hb mss, Sam, LXX; other Hb mss, Vg read *the falcon, the various kinds of kite* [D] **14:5–18** The identification of some of these animals is uncertain. [E] **15:2** Lit *owner of a loan of his hand*

and you are stingy toward your poor brother and give
him nothing. He will cry out to the LORD against you,
and you will be guilty. 10 Give to him, and don't have a
stingy heart[A] when you give, and because of this the
LORD your God will bless you in all your work and in
everything you do.[B] 11 For there will never cease to be
poor people in the land; that is why I am commanding you, 'Open your hand willingly to your poor and
needy brother in your land.'

RELEASE OF SLAVES

12 "If your fellow Hebrew, a man or woman, is sold to
you and serves you six years, you must set him free
in the seventh year. 13 When you set him free, do not
send him away empty-handed. 14 Give generously to
him from your flock, your threshing floor, and your
winepress. You are to give him whatever the LORD
your God has blessed you with. 15 Remember that you
were a slave in the land of Egypt and the LORD your
God redeemed you; that is why I am giving you this
command today. 16 But if your slave says to you, 'I
don't want to leave you,' because he loves you and
your family, and is well off with you, 17 take an awl
and pierce through his ear into the door, and he will
become your slave for life. Also treat your female slave
the same way. 18 Do not regard it as a hardship[C] when
you set him free, because he worked for you six years
— worth twice the wages of a hired worker. Then the
LORD your God will bless you in everything you do.

CONSECRATION OF FIRSTBORN ANIMALS

19 "Consecrate to the LORD your God every firstborn
male produced by your herd and flock. You are not
to put the firstborn of your oxen to work or shear
the firstborn of your flock. 20 Each year you and your
family are to eat it before the LORD your God in the
place the LORD chooses. 21 But if there is a defect in the
animal, if it is lame or blind or has any serious defect,
you may not sacrifice it to the LORD your God. 22 Eat
it within your city gates; both the unclean person
and the clean may eat it, as though it were a gazelle
or deer. 23 But you must not eat its blood; pour it on
the ground like water.

THE FESTIVAL OF PASSOVER

16 "Set aside the month of Abib[D] and observe the
Passover to the LORD your God, because the
LORD your God brought you out of Egypt by night in
the month of Abib. 2 Sacrifice to the LORD your God a
Passover animal from the herd or flock in the place
where the LORD chooses to have his name dwell. 3 Do
not eat leavened bread with it. For seven days you are
to eat unleavened bread with it, the bread of hardship — because you left the land of Egypt in a hurry
— so that you may remember for the rest of your life
the day you left the land of Egypt. 4 No yeast is to be
found anywhere in your territory for seven days, and
none of the meat you sacrifice in the evening of the
first day is to remain until morning. 5 You are not to
sacrifice the Passover animal in any of the towns the
LORD your God is giving you. 6 Sacrifice the Passover
animal only at the place where the LORD your God
chooses to have his name dwell. Do this in the evening
as the sun sets at the same time of day you departed
from Egypt. 7 You are to cook and eat it in the place
the LORD your God chooses, and you are to return to
your tents in the morning. 8 Eat unleavened bread for
six days. On the seventh day there is to be a solemn
assembly to the LORD your God; do not do any work.

THE FESTIVAL OF WEEKS

9 "You are to count seven weeks, counting the weeks
from the time the sickle is first put to the standing
grain. 10 You are to celebrate the Festival of Weeks to
the LORD your God with a freewill offering that you
give in proportion to how the LORD your God has
blessed you. 11 Rejoice before the LORD your God in
the place where he chooses to have his name dwell
— you, your son and daughter, your male and female
slave, the Levite within your city gates, as well as the
resident alien, the fatherless, and the widow among
you. 12 Remember that you were slaves in Egypt; carefully follow these statutes.

THE FESTIVAL OF SHELTERS

13 "You are to celebrate the Festival of Shelters for seven
days when you have gathered in everything from your
threshing floor and winepress. 14 Rejoice during your
festival — you, your son and daughter, your male and
female slave, as well as the Levite, the resident alien,
the fatherless, and the widow within your city gates.
15 You are to hold a seven-day festival for the LORD your
God in the place he chooses, because the LORD your
God will bless you in all your produce and in all the
work of your hands, and you will have abundant joy.
16 "All your males are to appear three times a year
before the LORD your God in the place he chooses:
at the Festival of Unleavened Bread, the Festival of
Weeks, and the Festival of Shelters. No one is to appear before the LORD empty-handed. 17 Everyone
must appear with a gift suited to his means, according to the blessing the LORD your God has given you.

APPOINTING JUDGES AND OFFICIALS

18 "Appoint judges and officials for your tribes in all
your towns the LORD your God is giving you. They are
to judge the people with righteous judgment. 19 Do

[A] **15:10** Lit *and let not your heart be grudging* [B] **15:10** Lit *you put your hand to* [C] **15:18** Lit *Let it not be hard in your sight* [D] **16:1** March–April; called Nisan in the post-exilic period; Neh 2:1; Est 3:7

not deny justice or show partiality to anyone. Do not accept a bribe, for it blinds the eyes of the wise and twists the words of the righteous. 20 Pursue justice and justice alone, so that you will live and possess the land the LORD your God is giving you.

FORBIDDEN WORSHIP

21 "Do not set up an Asherah of any kind of wood next to the altar you will build for the LORD your God, 22 and do not set up a sacred pillar; the LORD your God hates them.

17 "Do not sacrifice to the LORD your God an ox or sheep with a defect or any serious flaw, for that is detestable to the LORD your God.

THE JUDICIAL PROCEDURE FOR IDOLATRY

2 "If a man or woman among you in one of your towns that the LORD your God will give you is discovered doing evil in the sight of the LORD your God and violating his covenant 3 and has gone to serve other gods by bowing in worship to the sun, moon, or all the stars in the sky — which I have forbidden — 4 and if you are told or hear about it, then investigate it thoroughly. If the report turns out to be true that this detestable act has been done in Israel, 5 you are to bring out to your city gates that man or woman who has done this evil thing and stone them to death. 6 The one condemned to die is to be executed on the testimony of two or three witnesses. No one is to be executed on the testimony of a single witness. 7 The witnesses' hands are to be the first in putting him to death, and after that, the hands of all the people. You must purge the evil from you.

DIFFICULT CASES

8 "If a case is too difficult for you — concerning bloodshed, lawsuits, or assaults — cases disputed at your city gates, then go up to the place the LORD your God chooses. 9 You are to go to the Levitical priests and to the judge who presides at that time. Ask, and they will give you a verdict in the case. 10 You must abide by the verdict they give you at the place the LORD chooses. Be careful to do exactly as they instruct you. 11 You must abide by the instruction they give you and the verdict they announce to you. Do not turn to the right or the left from the decision they declare to you. 12 The person who acts arrogantly, refusing to listen either to the priest who stands there serving the LORD your God or to the judge, must die. You must purge the evil from Israel. 13 Then all the people will hear about it, be afraid, and no longer behave arrogantly.

APPOINTING A KING

14 "When you enter the land the LORD your God is giving you, take possession of it, live in it, and say, 'I will set a king over me like all the nations around me,' 15 you are to appoint over you the king the LORD your God chooses. Appoint a king from your brothers. You are not to set a foreigner over you, or one who is not of your people. 16 However, he must not acquire many horses for himself or send the people back to Egypt to acquire many horses, for the LORD has told you, 'You are never to go back that way again.' 17 He must not acquire many wives for himself so that his heart won't go astray. He must not acquire very large amounts of silver and gold for himself. 18 When he is seated on his royal throne, he is to write a copy of this instruction for himself on a scroll in the presence of the Levitical priests. 19 It is to remain with him, and he is to read from it all the days of his life, so that he may learn to fear the LORD his God, to observe all the words of this instruction, and to do these statutes. 20 Then his heart will not be exalted above his countrymen, he will not turn from this command to the right or the left, and he and his sons will continue reigning many years[A] in Israel.

PROVISIONS FOR THE LEVITES

18 "The Levitical priests, the whole tribe of Levi, will have no portion or inheritance with Israel. They will eat the LORD's food offerings; that is their[B,C] inheritance. 2 Although Levi has no inheritance among his brothers, the LORD is his inheritance, as he promised him. 3 This is the priests' share from the people who offer a sacrifice, whether it is an ox, a sheep, or a goat; the priests are to be given the shoulder, jaws, and stomach. 4 You are to give him the firstfruits of your grain, new wine, and fresh oil, and the first sheared wool of your flock. 5 For the LORD your God has chosen him and his sons from all your tribes to stand and minister in his name from now on.[D] 6 When a Levite leaves one of your towns in Israel where he was staying and wants to go to the place the LORD chooses, 7 he may serve in the name of the LORD his God like all his fellow Levites who minister there in the presence of the LORD. 8 They will eat equal portions besides what he has received from the sale of the family estate.[E]

OCCULT PRACTICES VERSUS PROPHETIC REVELATION

9 "When you enter the land the LORD your God is giving you, do not imitate the detestable customs of those nations. 10 No one among you is to sacrifice his son or daughter in the fire,[F] practice divination, tell fortunes, interpret omens, practice sorcery, 11 cast spells, consult a medium or a spiritist, or inquire of the dead. 12 Everyone who does these acts is detestable to the LORD, and the LORD your God is driving out the

[A] **17:20** Lit *will lengthen days on his kingdom* [B] **18:1** LXX; MT reads *his* [C] **18:1** Or *his* [D] **18:5** Lit *name all the days* [E] **18:8** Hb obscure [F] **18:10** Lit *to make his son or daughter pass through the fire*

nations before you because of these detestable acts.
13 You must be blameless before the LORD your God.
14 Though these nations you are about to drive out
listen to fortune-tellers and diviners, the LORD your
God has not permitted you to do this.

15 "The LORD your God will raise up for you a prophet like me from among your own brothers. You must
listen to him. 16 This is what you requested from the
LORD your God at Horeb on the day of the assembly
when you said, 'Let us not continue to hear the voice
of the LORD our God or see this great fire any longer,
so that we will not die!' 17 Then the LORD said to me,
'They have spoken well. 18 I will raise up for them a
prophet like you from among their brothers. I will
put my words in his mouth, and he will tell them everything I command him. 19 I will hold accountable
whoever does not listen to my words that he speaks in
my name. 20 But the prophet who presumes to speak
a message in my name that I have not commanded
him to speak, or who speaks in the name of other
gods — that prophet must die.' 21 You may say to yourself, 'How can we recognize a message the LORD has
not spoken?' 22 When a prophet speaks in the LORD's
name, and the message does not come true or is not
fulfilled, that is a message the LORD has not spoken.
The prophet has spoken it presumptuously. Do not
be afraid of him.

CITIES OF REFUGE

19 "When the LORD your God annihilates the nations whose land he is giving you, so that you
drive them out and live in their cities and houses,
2 you are to set apart three cities for yourselves within
the land the LORD your God is giving you to possess.
3 You are to determine the distances[A] and divide the
land the LORD your God is granting you as an inheritance into three regions, so that anyone who commits
manslaughter can flee to these cities.[B]

4 "Here is the law concerning a case of someone
who kills a person and flees there to save his life,
having killed his neighbor accidentally without previously hating him: 5 If, for example, he goes into the
forest with his neighbor to cut timber, and his hand
swings the ax to chop down a tree, but the blade flies
off the handle and strikes his neighbor so that he
dies, that person may flee to one of these cities and
live. 6 Otherwise, the avenger of blood in the heat
of his anger[C] might pursue the one who committed
manslaughter, overtake him because the distance is
great, and strike him dead. Yet he did not deserve to
die,[D] since he did not previously hate his neighbor.
7 This is why I am commanding you to set apart three
cities for yourselves. 8 If the LORD your God enlarges
your territory as he swore to your ancestors, and
gives you all the land he promised to give them —
9 provided you keep every one of these commands I
am giving you today and follow them, loving the LORD
your God and walking in his ways at all times — you
are to add three more cities to these three. 10 In this
way, innocent blood will not be shed, and you will not
become guilty of bloodshed in the land the LORD your
God is giving you as an inheritance. 11 But if someone
hates his neighbor, lies in ambush for him, attacks
him, and strikes him fatally, and flees to one of these
cities, 12 the elders of his city are to send for him, take
him from there, and hand him over to the avenger of
blood and he will die. 13 Do not look on him with pity
but purge from Israel the guilt of shedding innocent
blood, and you will prosper.

BOUNDARY MARKERS

14 "Do not move your neighbor's boundary marker,
established at the start in the inheritance you will
receive in the land the LORD your God is giving you
to possess.

WITNESSES IN COURT

15 "One witness cannot establish any iniquity or sin
against a person, whatever that person has done. A
fact must be established by the testimony of two or
three witnesses.

16 "If a malicious witness testifies against someone
accusing him of a crime, 17 the two people in the dispute are to stand in the presence of the LORD before
the priests and judges in authority at that time. 18 The
judges are to make a careful investigation, and if the
witness turns out to be a liar who has falsely accused
his brother, 19 you must do to him as he intended to
do to his brother. You must purge the evil from you.
20 Then everyone else will hear and be afraid, and they
will never again do anything evil like this among you.
21 Do not show pity: life for life, eye for eye, tooth for
tooth, hand for hand, and foot for foot.

RULES FOR WAR

20 "When you go out to war against your enemies and see horses, chariots, and an army
larger than yours, do not be afraid of them, for the
LORD your God, who brought you out of the land of
Egypt, is with you. 2 When you are about to engage in
battle, the priest is to come forward and address the
army. 3 He is to say to them, 'Listen, Israel: Today you
are about to engage in battle with your enemies. Do
not be cowardly. Do not be afraid, alarmed, or terrified because of them. 4 For the LORD your God is the
one who goes with you to fight for you against your
enemies to give you victory.'

[A] **19:3** Or *to prepare the roads* [B] **19:3** Lit *flee there* [C] **19:6** Lit *heart*
[D] **19:6** Lit *did not have a judgment of death*

Sorcery, Witchcraft, and Divination

by James O. Newell

From Nimrud in ancient Babylon, two leaves from hinged writing boards. The fragments of the original wax are inscribed with a cuneiform text of astrological omens. These omens were intended for the palace of Babylon's king Sargon II at Khorsabad.

Deuteronomy 18:9–18 records the Lord instructing the Israelites about how they were to live once they entered the promised land. Verses 10–11 contain all of the Hebrew words that identified the different methods of foretelling the future and seeking divine guidance for making decisions.[1] These actions were the reason the Lord displaced the Canaanites and gave their land to Israel (v. 12). Punishment for these activities was death (Ex 22:18; Lv 20:27).

The Bible does not record the origin of sorcery, witchcraft, and divination, nor does it provide descriptions of the practices. The writers assumed the reader would understand the actions behind the terms. Curiosity about upcoming events and circumstances was a

Mesopotamian divination text gives instructions for studying animal intestines (usually of sheep) to determine the future.

constant in the ancient Near East. This caused some men to try to develop skills that supposedly allowed them to see into the future.

"The means of divination in the [ancient] Near East are multiple: by prophetic or priestly oracles, dreams, spirits, lots, astrology, the observation of the entrails of a sacrificial animal, the flight of birds, the patterns of oil on water, and the direction of smoke."[2]

Among the Hittites: "Incantation priests probably most often received their payment in the form of leftover ritual materials. For example, in [one tale,] the *Ritual for the Goddess Wishuriyanza*, the magician is allowed to take with her the pottery and utensils that she has used. This is probably the reason that the rituals often call for [massive] amounts of equipment and foodstuffs."[3]

Among the Lyceans, some soothsayers relied on fish. "The diviners would observe the movements of fish, their twists and turns, and interpret these movements in accordance with fixed rules. An alternative procedure is recorded for the 'fish oracle' in the bay of Myra. The procedure there called for a sacrifice of calves to be made to the god, whereupon the flesh was then thrown to the fish. If the fish ate the flesh, the omens were good. If they discarded it and cast it on the shore with their tails, this signified that the god was angry."

Child sacrifice was perhaps the most serious and far-reaching attempt to influence the future by offering such a costly gift to a god in hopes of producing a desired future outcome. The underlying motive of these forbidden practices was the effort "to manipulate or force the 'gods' into certain courses of action."[4] ✤

[1] C. F. Keil and F. Delitzsch, "Deuteronomy," in *The Pentateuch: Three Volumes in One*, vol. 1 in Commentary on the Old Testament in Ten Volumes (Grand Rapids: Eerdmans, repr. ed. 1975), 3:393. [2] Jean-Michel De Tarragon, "Witchcraft, Magic, and Divination in Canaan and Ancient Israel," in *CANE*, 2071. [3] Gabriella Frantz-Szabo, "Hittite Witchcraft, Magic, and Divination," in *CANE*, 2011. [4] Jack S. Deere, "Deuteronomy," in *The Bible Knowledge Commentary: An Exposition of the Scriptures*, ed. J. F. Walvoord and R. B. Zuck (Wheaton, IL: Victor Books, 1985), 1:296.

Model of a sheep's lung, from Nineveh; terra-cotta. In the ancient Near East, a diviner would commonly pronounce an omen based upon his reading of the lungs or liver of a sacrificial sheep. The model's inscription offers instructions for an apprentice who was learning this method of divination.

On the hillside in the distance is the site of ancient En-dor, the home of the medium whom Saul consulted near the end of his life.

5 "The officers are to address the army, 'Has any
man built a new house and not dedicated it? Let him
leave and return home. Otherwise, he may die in battle and another man dedicate it. 6 Has any man planted a vineyard and not begun to enjoy its fruit?[A] Let
him leave and return home. Otherwise he may die
in battle and another man enjoy its fruit.[B] 7 Has any
man become engaged to a woman and not married
her? Let him leave and return home. Otherwise he
may die in battle and another man marry her.' 8 The
officers will continue to address the army and say,
'Is there any man who is afraid or cowardly? Let him
leave and return home, so that his brothers won't lose
heart as he did.'[C] 9 When the officers have finished
addressing the army, they will appoint military commanders to lead it.

10 "When you approach a city to fight against it,
make an offer of peace. 11 If it accepts your offer of
peace and opens its gates to you, all the people found
in it will become forced laborers for you and serve
you. 12 However, if it does not make peace with you
but wages war against you, lay siege to it. 13 When the
LORD your God hands it over to you, strike down all its
males with the sword. 14 But you may take the women,
dependents, animals, and whatever else is in the city
— all its spoil — as plunder. You may enjoy the spoil
of your enemies that the LORD your God has given
you. 15 This is how you are to treat all the cities that
are far away from you and are not among the cities of
these nations. 16 However, you must not let any living
thing survive among the cities of these people the
LORD your God is giving you as an inheritance. 17 You
must completely destroy them — the Hethite, Amorite, Canaanite, Perizzite, Hivite, and Jebusite — as the
LORD your God has commanded you, 18 so that they
won't teach you to do all the detestable acts they do
for their gods, and you sin against the LORD your God.

19 "When you lay siege to a city for a long time,
fighting against it in order to capture it, do not destroy its trees by putting an ax to them, because you
can get food from them. Do not cut them down. Are
trees of the field human, to come under siege by you?
20 But you may destroy the trees that you know do not
produce food. You may cut them down to build siege
works against the city that is waging war against
you, until it falls.

UNSOLVED MURDERS

21 "If a murder victim is found lying in a field in
the land the LORD your God is giving you to
possess, and it is not known who killed him, 2 your
elders and judges are to come out and measure the
distance from the victim to the nearby cities. 3 The
elders of the city nearest to the victim are to get a
young cow that has not been yoked or used for work.
4 The elders of that city will bring the cow down to
a continually flowing stream, to a place not tilled
or sown, and they will break its neck there by the
stream. 5 Then the priests, the sons of Levi, will come
forward, for the LORD your God has chosen them to
serve him and pronounce blessings in his name, and
they are to give a ruling in[D] every dispute and case
of assault. 6 All the elders of the city nearest to the
victim will wash their hands by the stream over the
young cow whose neck has been broken. 7 They will
declare, 'Our hands did not shed this blood; our eyes
did not see it. 8 LORD, wipe away the guilt of your people Israel whom you redeemed, and do not hold the
shedding of innocent blood against them.' Then the
responsibility for bloodshed will be wiped away from
them. 9 You must purge from yourselves the guilt of
shedding innocent blood, for you will be doing what
is right in the LORD's sight.

FAIR TREATMENT OF CAPTURED WOMEN

10 "When you go to war against your enemies and the
LORD your God hands them over to you and you take
some of them prisoner, and 11 if you see a beautiful
woman among the captives, desire her, and want
to take her as your wife, 12 you are to bring her into
your house. She is to shave her head, trim her nails,
13 remove the clothes she was wearing when she was
taken prisoner, live in your house, and mourn for her
father and mother a full month. After that, you may
have sexual relations with her and be her husband,
and she will be your wife. 14 Then if you are not satisfied with her, you are to let her go where she wants,
but you must not sell her or treat her as merchandise,[E]
because you have humiliated her.

THE RIGHT OF THE FIRSTBORN

15 "If a man has two wives, one loved and the other
neglected, and both the loved and the neglected bear
him sons, and if the neglected wife has the firstborn
son, 16 when that man gives what he has to his sons
as an inheritance, he is not to show favoritism to the
son of the loved wife as his firstborn over the firstborn of the neglected wife. 17 He must acknowledge
the firstborn, the son of the neglected wife, by giving
him two shares[F,G] of his estate, for he is the firstfruits
of his virility; he has the rights of the firstborn.

A REBELLIOUS SON

18 "If a man has a stubborn and rebellious son who
does not obey his father or mother and doesn't listen
to them even after they discipline him, 19 his father

[A] **20:6** Lit *not put it to use* [B] **20:6** Lit *man put it to use* [C] **20:8** Lit *brothers' hearts won't melt like his own* [D] **21:5** Lit *and according to their mouth will be* [E] **21:14** Hb obscure [F] **21:17** Lit *him mouth of two*, or *two mouthfuls* [G] **21:17** Or *two-thirds*

and mother are to take hold of him and bring him
to the elders of his city, to the gate of his hometown.
20 They will say to the elders of his city, 'This son of
ours is stubborn and rebellious; he doesn't obey us.
He's a glutton and a drunkard.' 21 Then all the men of
his city will stone him to death. You must purge the
evil from you, and all Israel will hear and be afraid.

DISPLAY OF EXECUTED PEOPLE

22 "If anyone is found guilty of an offense deserving
the death penalty and is executed, and you hang his
body on a tree, 23 you are not to leave his corpse on
the tree overnight but are to bury him that day, for
anyone hung on a tree is under God's curse. You must
not defile the land the LORD your God is giving you
as an inheritance.

CARING FOR YOUR BROTHER'S PROPERTY

22 "If you see your brother Israelite's ox or sheep
straying, do not ignore it; make sure you return it to your brother. 2 If your brother does not live
near you or you don't know him, you are to bring the
animal to your home to remain with you until your
brother comes looking for it; then you can return it
to him. 3 Do the same for his donkey, his garment, or
anything your brother has lost and you have found.
You must not ignore it. 4 If you see your brother's
donkey or ox fallen down on the road, do not ignore
it; help him lift it up.

PRESERVING NATURAL DISTINCTIONS

5 "A woman is not to wear male clothing, and a man is
not to put on a woman's garment, for everyone who
does these things is detestable to the LORD your God.
6 "If you come across a bird's nest with chicks or
eggs, either in a tree or on the ground along the road,
and the mother is sitting on the chicks or eggs, do not
take the mother along with the young. 7 You may take
the young for yourself, but be sure to let the mother
go free, so that you may prosper and live long. 8 If you
build a new house, make a railing around your roof,
so that you don't bring bloodguilt on your house if
someone falls from it. 9 Do not plant your vineyard
with two types of seed; otherwise, the entire harvest,
both the crop you plant and the produce of the vineyard, will be defiled. 10 Do not plow with an ox and a
donkey together. 11 Do not wear clothes made of both
wool and linen. 12 Make tassels on the four corners of
the outer garment you wear.

VIOLATIONS OF PROPER SEXUAL CONDUCT

13 "If a man marries a woman, has sexual relations
with her, and comes to hate her, 14 and accuses her of
shameful conduct, and gives her a bad name, saying,
'I married this woman and was intimate with her,
but I didn't find any evidence of her virginity,' 15 the
young woman's father and mother will take the evidence of her virginity and bring it to the city elders at
the city gate. 16 The young woman's father will say to
the elders, 'I gave my daughter to this man as a wife,
but he hates her. 17 He has accused her of shameful
conduct, saying, "I didn't find any evidence of your
daughter's virginity," but here is the evidence of my
daughter's virginity.' They will spread out the cloth
before the city elders. 18 Then the elders of that city
will take the man and punish him. 19 They will also
fine him a hundred silver shekels and give them to
the young woman's father, because that man gave an
Israelite virgin a bad name. She will remain his wife;
he cannot divorce her as long as he lives. 20 But if this
accusation is true and no evidence of the young woman's virginity is found, 21 they will bring the woman
to the door of her father's house, and the men of her
city will stone her to death. For she has committed an
outrage in Israel by being promiscuous while living in
her father's house. You must purge the evil from you.
22 "If a man is discovered having sexual relations
with another man's wife, both the man who had sex
with the woman and the woman must die. You must
purge the evil from Israel. 23 If there is a young woman
who is a virgin engaged to a man, and another man
encounters her in the city and sleeps with her, 24 take
the two of them out to the gate of that city and stone
them to death — the young woman because she did
not cry out in the city and the man because he has
violated his neighbor's fiancée. You must purge the
evil from you. 25 But if the man encounters an engaged
woman in the open country, and he seizes and rapes
her, only the man who raped her must die. 26 Do nothing to the young woman, because she is not guilty of
an offense deserving death. This case is just like one
in which a man attacks his neighbor and murders
him. 27 When he found her in the field, the engaged
woman cried out, but there was no one to rescue her.
28 If a man encounters a young woman, a virgin who
is not engaged, takes hold of her and rapes her, and
they are discovered, 29 the man who raped her is to
give the young woman's father fifty silver shekels,
and she will become his wife because he violated her.
He cannot divorce her as long as he lives.
30 "A man is not to marry his father's wife; he must
not violate his father's marriage bed.[A]

EXCLUSION AND INCLUSION

23 "No man whose testicles have been crushed
or whose penis has been cut off may enter the
LORD's assembly. 2 No one of illegitimate birth may

[A] **22:30** Lit *not uncover the edge of his father's garment*; Ru 3:9; Ezk 16:8

enter the LORD's assembly; none of his descendants, even to the tenth generation, may enter the LORD's assembly. 3 No Ammonite or Moabite may enter the LORD's assembly; none of their descendants, even to the tenth generation, may ever enter the LORD's assembly. 4 This is because they did not meet you with food and water on the journey after you came out of Egypt, and because Balaam son of Beor from Pethor in Aram-naharaim was hired to curse you. 5 Yet the LORD your God would not listen to Balaam, but he turned the curse into a blessing for you because the LORD your God loves you. 6 Never pursue their welfare or prosperity as long as you live. 7 Do not despise an Edomite, because he is your brother. Do not despise an Egyptian, because you were a resident alien in his land. 8 The children born to them in the third generation may enter the LORD's assembly.

CLEANLINESS OF THE CAMP

9 "When you are encamped against your enemies, be careful to avoid anything offensive. 10 If there is a man among you who is unclean because of a bodily emission during the night, he must go outside the camp; he may not come anywhere inside the camp. 11 When evening approaches, he is to wash with water, and when the sun sets he may come inside the camp. 12 You are to have a place outside the camp and go there to relieve yourself. 13 You are to have a digging tool in your equipment; when you relieve yourself, dig a hole with it and cover up your excrement. 14 For the LORD your God walks throughout your camp to protect you and deliver your enemies to you; so your encampments must be holy. He must not see anything indecent among you or he will turn away from you.

FUGITIVE SLAVES

15 "Do not return a slave to his master when he has escaped from his master to you. 16 Let him live among you wherever he wants within your city gates. Do not mistreat him.

CULT PROSTITUTION FORBIDDEN

17 "No Israelite woman is to be a cult prostitute, and no Israelite man is to be a cult prostitute. 18 Do not bring a female prostitute's wages or a male prostitute's[A] earnings into the house of the LORD your God to fulfill any vow, because both are detestable to the LORD your God.

INTEREST ON LOANS

19 "Do not charge your brother interest on silver, food, or anything that can earn interest. 20 You may charge a foreigner interest, but you must not charge your brother Israelite interest, so that the LORD your God may bless you in everything you do[B] in the land you are entering to possess.

KEEPING VOWS

21 "If you make a vow to the LORD your God, do not be slow to keep it, because he will require it of you, and it will be counted against you as sin. 22 But if you refrain from making a vow, it will not be counted against you as sin. 23 Be careful to do whatever comes from your lips, because you have freely vowed what you promised to the LORD your God.

NEIGHBOR'S CROPS

24 "When you enter your neighbor's vineyard, you may eat as many grapes as you want until you are full, but do not put any in your container. 25 When you enter your neighbor's standing grain, you may pluck heads of grain with your hand, but do not put a sickle to your neighbor's grain.

MARRIAGE AND DIVORCE LAWS

24 "If a man marries a woman, but she becomes displeasing to him because he finds something indecent about her, he may write her a divorce certificate, hand it to her, and send her away from his house. 2 If after leaving his house she goes and becomes another man's wife, 3 and the second man hates her, writes her a divorce certificate, hands it to her, and sends her away from his house or if he dies, 4 the first husband who sent her away may not marry her again after she has been defiled, because that would be detestable to the LORD. You must not bring guilt on the land the LORD your God is giving you as an inheritance.

5 "When a man takes a bride, he must not go out with the army or be liable for any duty. He is free to stay at home for one year, so that he can bring joy to the wife he has married.

SAFEGUARDING LIFE

6 "Do not take a pair of grindstones or even the upper millstone as security for a debt, because that is like taking a life as security.

7 "If a man is discovered kidnapping one of his Israelite brothers, whether he treats him as a slave or sells him, the kidnapper must die. You must purge the evil from you.

8 "Be careful with a person who has a case of serious skin disease, following carefully everything the Levitical priests instruct you to do. Be careful to do as I have commanded them. 9 Remember what the LORD your God did to Miriam on the journey after you left Egypt.

[A] **23:18** Lit *a dog's* [B] **23:20** Lit *you put your hand to*

CONSIDERATION FOR PEOPLE IN NEED

10 "When you make a loan of any kind to your neighbor, do not enter his house to collect what he offers as security. 11 Stand outside while the man you are making the loan to brings the security out to you. 12 If he is a poor man, do not sleep with the garment he has given as security. 13 Be sure to return it[A] to him at sunset. Then he will sleep in it and bless you, and this will be counted as righteousness to you before the LORD your God.

14 "Do not oppress a hired worker who is poor and needy, whether one of your Israelite brothers or one of the resident aliens in a town[B] in your land. 15 You are to pay him his wages each day before the sun sets, because he is poor and depends on them. Otherwise he will cry out to the LORD against you, and you will be held guilty.

16 "Fathers are not to be put to death for their children, and children are not to be put to death for their fathers; each person will be put to death for his own sin. 17 Do not deny justice to a resident alien or fatherless child, and do not take a widow's garment as security. 18 Remember that you were a slave in Egypt, and the LORD your God redeemed you from there. Therefore I am commanding you to do this.

19 "When you reap the harvest in your field, and you forget a sheaf in the field, do not go back to get it. It is to be left for the resident alien, the fatherless, and the widow, so that the LORD your God may bless you in all the work of your hands. 20 When you knock down the fruit from your olive tree, do not go over the branches again. What remains will be for the resident alien, the fatherless, and the widow. 21 When you gather the grapes of your vineyard, do not glean what is left. What remains will be for the resident alien, the fatherless, and the widow. 22 Remember that you were a slave in the land of Egypt. Therefore I am commanding you to do this.

FAIRNESS AND MERCY

25 "If there is a dispute between men, they are to go to court, and the judges will hear their case. They will clear the innocent and condemn the guilty. 2 If the guilty party deserves to be flogged, the judge will make him lie down and be flogged in his presence with the number of lashes appropriate for his crime. 3 He may be flogged with forty lashes, but no more. Otherwise, if he is flogged with more lashes than these, your brother will be degraded in your sight.

4 "Do not muzzle an ox while it treads out grain.

PRESERVING THE FAMILY LINE

5 "When brothers live on the same property[C] and one of them dies without a son, the wife of the dead man may not marry a stranger outside the family. Her brother-in-law is to take her as his wife, have sexual relations with her, and perform the duty of a brother-in-law for her. 6 The first son she bears will carry on the name of the dead brother, so his name will not be blotted out from Israel. 7 But if the man doesn't want to marry his sister-in-law, she is to go to the elders at the city gate and say, 'My brother-in-law refuses to preserve his brother's name in Israel. He isn't willing to perform the duty of a brother-in-law for me.' 8 The elders of his city will summon him and speak with him. If he persists and says, 'I don't want to marry her,' 9 then his sister-in-law will go up to him in the sight of the elders, remove his sandal from his foot, and spit in his face. Then she will declare, 'This is what is done to a man who will not build up his brother's house.' 10 And his family name in Israel will be 'The house of the man whose sandal was removed.'

11 "If two men are fighting with each other, and the wife of one steps in to rescue her husband from the one striking him, and she puts out her hand and grabs his genitals, 12 you are to cut off her hand. Do not show pity.

HONEST WEIGHTS AND MEASURES

13 "Do not have differing weights in your bag, one heavy and one light. 14 Do not have differing dry measures in your house, a larger and a smaller. 15 You must have a full and honest weight, a full and honest dry measure, so that you may live long in the land the LORD your God is giving you. 16 For everyone who does such things and acts unfairly is detestable to the LORD your God.

REVENGE ON THE AMALEKITES

17 "Remember what the Amalekites did to you on the journey after you left Egypt. 18 They met you along the way and attacked all your stragglers from behind when you were tired and weary. They did not fear God. 19 When the LORD your God gives you rest from all the enemies around you in the land the LORD your God is giving you to possess as an inheritance, blot out the memory of Amalek under heaven. Do not forget.

GIVING THE FIRSTFRUITS

26 "When you enter the land the LORD your God is giving you as an inheritance, and you take possession of it and live in it, 2 take some of the first of all the land's produce that you harvest from the land the LORD your God is giving you and put it in a basket. Then go to the place where the LORD your God chooses to have his name dwell. 3 When you come

[A] **24:13** Lit *return what he has given as security* [B] **24:14** Lit *within the city gates* [C] **25:5** Lit *live together*

Establishing Weights and Measures in Ancient Israel

by Claude F. Mariottini

A study of the system of weights and measures of a nation (or "metrology") provides the foundation for understanding some of the factors that shaped the social and economic development of that nation. The systems of weights, measures of length, and measures of capacity in ancient Israel were related to the ancient metrological systems common in Mesopotamia. The ideal condition for trade and commerce in Israel and among ancient Near Eastern nations required an accurate system of weights and measures.

Five-shekel weight from Iron Age III (eighth–sixth centuries BC). The stone is inscribed with the Hebrew sign for *shekel*.

THE METROLOGY OF ANCIENT ISRAEL

In Israel, the demands of the covenant required an honest use of weights and measures since members of the covenant community were to treat one another with respect. Honesty in merchandising is related to the injunction in the Decalogue that prohibits a person to covet that which belongs to another person.[1] This was the reason the laws of holiness in the book of Leviticus urged the Israelites not to defraud each other: "Do not oppress your neighbor or rob him" (Lv 19:13).

The metrology of ancient Israel was derived from systems that originated in Mesopotamia, primarily in Babylon. As early as the third millennium BC, the Babylonians had developed an elaborate system of weights and measures based on the sexagesimal system.[2] Today's division of hours into sixty minutes and minutes into sixty seconds is based on the Babylonian sexagesimal system. Because of commerce and trade, the Babylonian system of weights and measures made its way into Syria and Canaan.

Since the ancient patriarchs of Israel came from Mesopotamia, they possibly brought with them the system of weights and measures they previously used there. However, a reconstruction of this system is difficult. What the Bible has to teach about the metrology of ancient Israel must be adduced from archaeology, the biblical texts, and the literature of the ancient Near East.

Although the people of Israel used a system of weights and measures that was derived from Babylon, Israel's system was not the exact equivalent of the Babylonians'. Israel adapted Babylon's systems to meet its social and economic needs. Any attempt at comparing the biblical standards of weights and measures with contemporary standards is difficult if not impossible, since values change with the passage of time, and modern American and British standards are radically different from Mesopotamian and biblical systems.

From ancient Ur; a carved stone with a handle; likely a weight; dated to Early Dynastic Age III, 2600–2400 BC.

WEIGHTS AND MEASURES IN ISRAEL

The terms Israel used to classify weights and measures came from items in everyday life. They derived measurements of length from the length of the limbs of the human body. The cubit was the distance between the end of one's elbow to the tip of the middle finger (about eighteen inches). The span was measured from the tip of the thumb to the tip of the little finger while both are extended (half a cubit). Only once does the Old Testament use the finger as a unit of measurement (Jr 52:21).

The names the Israelites used for measuring capacities were generally the terms they used for the receptacles that held the provisions. The *omer* (Lv 27:16), a word derived from the Hebrew term for "donkey," refers to a load the animal would carry. The *kor* (1Kg 4:22) was a container to measure flour, wheat, and barley. The *kor* was also a measurement for oil (5:11). The *letek* is a smaller container, equal to half a homer (Hs 3:2).

The Hebrew term *ephah* (Lv 5:11) referred originally to a basket but later came to refer to a measure of flour, barley, and other grains. The *seah* was a container the Israelites used to measure grain (1Sm 25:18, footnote). The *bath* was used to measure liquids such as oil (Ezk 45:14), water (1Kg 7:26), and wine (Is 5:10).

Precious material and metals were weighed on balances with two scales. The weights were made of hard stones called *eben*, a Hebrew word that means "stone" and "weight." These stones were kept in a bag (Dt 25:13; Pr 16:11; Mc 6:11). The Hebrew word that means "to weigh" is *shaqal*, which is the root for the word *shekel*. Thus, the shekel became the basic unit of weight. The value of the shekel was equivalent to the weight of 180 grains of wheat. Three kinds of shekels were in use in the Old Testament era: the king's shekel or the royal standard (2Sm 14:26), the shekel of the sanctuary (Ex 30:13), and the common shekel (Jos 7:21). Genesis 23:16 speaks about the shekel literally "passing to the merchant." Determining the value of this shekel is difficult, however, since many merchants had two kinds of weight, one for buying and one for selling.

Jar from Lachish. Two of the handles are stamped with "lamelekh Hebron," meaning this was something from Hebron that belonged to the king (or his administration). The jar dates from the reign of Hezekiah, about 715–686 BC. The stamp (seal) assured an honest measure.

Because the shekel was the basic measure of weight, determining its value is important.[3] This unit of weight was common to most societies in Mesopotamia. The book of Ezekiel provides the value of the shekel: "The standard unit for weight will be the silver shekel. One shekel will consist of twenty gerahs, and sixty shekels will be equal to one mina" (Ezk 45:12, NLT). Another translation better reflects the Hebrew text: "The shekel is to consist of twenty gerahs. Twenty shekels plus twenty-five shekels plus fifteen shekels equal one mina" (NIV). This division of the mina into three different categories may indicate that people used weights of twenty-five, twenty, and fifteen shekels.

In Exodus 38:25–26, we learn that 603,550 bekas comes to one hundred talents and 1,775 shekels (CSB footnote). According to this information, the value of the shekel of the sanctuary was as follows: one

Bronze lion weight from Nimrud, dated 726–722 BC. The Akkadian inscription on the top reads "Palace of Shalmaneser King." The piece weighs 2,864 grams—about six pounds.

talent was worth sixty minas; one mina was worth fifty shekels; and one shekel was worth two bekas. According to the book of Ezekiel, one talent was worth sixty minas; one mina was worth sixty shekels; and one shekel was worth twenty gerahs. Because Ezekiel was writing while in exile in Babylon, the value of the mina (sixty shekels) corresponds to the value of the mina in Babylon during the exile.

This tablet lists in succession measures of capacity, weights, and measures of area and of length. It probably served as a textbook in schools for teaching the measures and their units, as well as for the writing of numerals. The numerals were written in fractions, units, tens, and sixties, and multiples of these up to theoretical quantities—the highest being the equivalent of more than fourteen million gallons.

LAWS ABOUT WEIGHTS AND MEASURES

Ensuring that systems of weights, measures of length, and measures of capacity were fair required the sanction of authoritative law to make certain the weights and scales people used for buying and selling conformed to a standard set by the community.[4] The law about weights and measures in the book of Deuteronomy was enacted to promote economic honesty in buying and selling. What the law forbade was the practice of employing a double set of stones or weights and different ephahs or dry measures—one used for buying and the other used for selling. Babylonian wisdom literature speaks of merchants who use different sets of weights.[5] Thus the law required that in buying and selling, the people of Israel had to use "a full and honest weight" and accurate ephahs (Dt 25:13–15). A similar law for just balances, just weights, just ephahs, and just hins is in the section of Leviticus commonly known as the Holiness Code (Lv 19:35–36).

Israel's prophets accused the merchants of planning to "reduce the measure while increasing the price and cheat with dishonest scales" (Am 8:5; see Hs 12:7; Mc 6:10-11). Some biblical scholars believe that during his religious and economic reforms at the end of the eighth century BC, King Hezekiah introduced official weights called *lmlk* weights, which helped standardize weights for Judah. The Hebrew word *lmlk* means "belonging to the king." Archaeologists have also uncovered jars, the handles of which bear a *lmlk* stamp. The stamped handles may indicate an attempt to establish uniform volume measurements as well.[6] ✣

[1] Walter C. Kaiser Jr., *Toward Old Testament Ethics* (Grand Rapids: Zondervan, 1983), 136. [2] M. Pierce Matheney, "Weights and Measures," in *HolBD*, 1403. [3] Roland de Vaux, *Ancient Israel* (Grand Rapids: Eerdmans, 1997), 203. [4] De Vaux, *Ancient Israel*, 195. [5] W. G. Lambert, *Babylonian Wisdom Literature* (Winona Lake, IN: Eisenbrauns, 1996), 133, line 108. [6] John Bright, *A History of Israel* (Philadelphia: Westminster, 1981), 283.

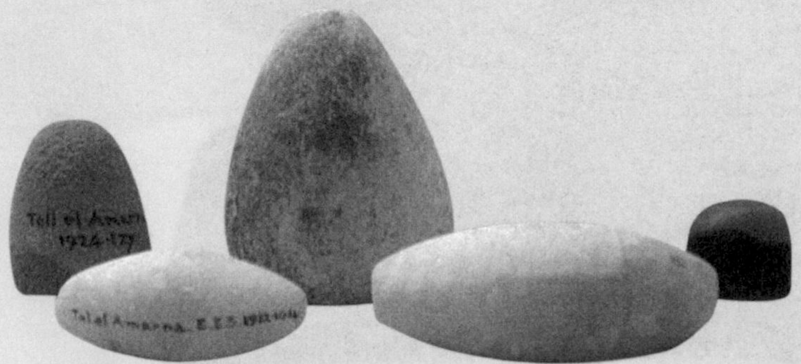

A collection of stone and clay weights from el-Amarna, in Lower Egypt; dated 1350–1320 BC.

TABLE OF WEIGHTS AND MEASURES

Biblical Unit	Language	Biblical Measure	U.S. Equivalent	Metric Equivalent	Various Translations
WEIGHTS					
Gerah	Hebrew	1/20 shekel	1/50 ounce	.6 gram	gerah; oboli
Beka	Hebrew	½ shekel or 10 gerahs	⅕ ounce	5.7 grams	beka; half a shekel; quarter ounce; fifty cents
Pim	Hebrew	⅔ shekel	⅓ ounce	7.6 grams	⅔ of a shekel; quarter
Shekel	Hebrew	2 bekas	⅖ ounce	11.5 grams	shekel; piece; dollar; fifty dollars
Litra (pound)	Greco-Roman	30 shekels	12 ounces	.4 kilogram	pound; pounds
Mina	Hebrew/Greek	50 shekels	1¼ pounds	.6 kilogram	mina; pound
Talent	Hebrew/Greek	3,000 shekels or 60 minas	75 pounds/ 88 pounds	34 kilograms/ 40 kilograms	talent/talents; 100 pounds
LENGTH					
Handbreadth	Hebrew	⅙ cubit or ⅓ span	3 inches	8 centimeters	handbreadth; three inches; four inches
Span	Hebrew	½ cubit or 3 handbreadths	9 inches	23 centimeters	span
Cubit/Pechys	Hebrew/Greek	2 spans	18 inches	.5 meter	cubit/cubits; yard; half a yard; foot
Fathom	Greco-Roman	4 cubits	2 yards	2 meters	fathom; six feet
Kalamos	Greco-Roman	6 cubits	3 yards	3 meters	rod; reed; measuring rod
Stadion	Greco-Roman	⅛ milion or 400 cubits	⅛ mile	185 meters	miles; furlongs; race
Milion	Greco-Roman	8 stadia	1,620 yards	1.5 kilometers	mile
DRY MEASURE					
Xestes	Greco-Roman	½ cab	1⅙ pints	.5 liter	pots; pitchers; kettles; copper pots; copper bowls; vessels of bronze
Cab	Hebrew	1/18 ephah	1 quart	1 liter	cab; kab
Choinix	Greco-Roman	1/18 ephah	1 quart	1 liter	measure; quart
Omer	Hebrew	1/10 ephah	2 quarts	2 liters	omer; tenth of a deal; tenth of an ephah; six pints
Seah/Saton	Hebrew/Greek	⅓ ephah	7 quarts	7.3 liters	measures; pecks; large amounts
Modios	Greco-Roman	4 omers	1 peck or ¼ bushel	9 liters	bushel; bowl; peck
Ephah [Bath]	Hebrew	10 omers	⅗ bushel	22 liters	bushel; peck; deal; part; measure; six pints; seven pints
Lethek	Hebrew	5 ephahs	3 bushels	110 liters	half homer; half sack
Kor [Homer]/ Koros	Hebrew/Greek	10 ephahs	6 bushels or 200 quarts	220 liters/ 525 liters	cor; homer; sack; measures; bushels
LIQUID MEASURE					
Log	Hebrew	1/72 bath	⅓ quart	.3 liter	log; pint; cotulus
Xestes	Greco-Roman	⅛ hin	1⅙ pints	.5 liter	pots; pitchers; kettles; copper bowls; vessels of bronze
Hin	Hebrew	⅙ bath	1 gallon or 4 quarts	4 liters	hin; pints
Bath/Batos	Hebrew/Greek	1 ephah	6 gallons	22 liters	gallon(s); barrels; liquid measures
Metretes	Greco-Roman	10 hins	10 gallons	39 liters	firkins; gallons

before the priest who is serving at that time, say to
him, ‘Today I declare to the LORD your[A] God that I
have entered the land the LORD swore to our ancestors to give us.’
4 “Then the priest will take the basket from you
and place it before the altar of the LORD your God.
5 You are to respond by saying in the presence of the
LORD your God:

> My father was a wandering Aramean. He went
> down to Egypt with a few people and resided
> there as an alien. There he became a great, power-
> ful, and populous nation. 6 But the Egyptians mis-
> treated and oppressed us, and forced us to do hard
> labor. 7 So we called out to the LORD, the God of our
> ancestors, and the LORD heard our cry and saw
> our misery, hardship, and oppression. 8 Then the
> LORD brought us out of Egypt with a strong hand
> and an outstretched arm, with terrifying power,
> and with signs and wonders. 9 He led us to this
> place and gave us this land, a land flowing with
> milk and honey. 10 I have now brought the first of
> the land’s produce that you, LORD, have given me.

You will then place the container before the LORD
your God and bow down to him. 11 You, the Levites,
and the resident aliens among you will rejoice in all
the good things the LORD your God has given you and
your household.

THE TENTH IN THE THIRD YEAR

12 “When you have finished paying all the tenth of
your produce in the third year, the year of the tenth,
you are to give it to the Levites, resident aliens, fatherless children, and widows, so that they may eat
in your towns and be satisfied. 13 Then you will say in
the presence of the LORD your God:

> I have taken the consecrated portion out of my
> house; I have also given it to the Levites, resi-
> dent aliens, fatherless children, and widows,
> according to all the commands you gave me. I
> have not violated or forgotten your commands.
> 14 I have not eaten any of it while in mourning,
> or removed any of it while unclean, or offered
> any of it for the dead. I have obeyed the LORD my
> God; I have done all you commanded me. 15 Look
> down from your holy dwelling, from heaven,
> and bless your people Israel and the land you
> have given us as you swore to our ancestors, a
> land flowing with milk and honey.

COVENANT SUMMARY

16 “The LORD your God is commanding you this day
to follow these statutes and ordinances. Follow them
carefully with all your heart and all your soul. 17 Today
you have affirmed that the LORD is your God and that
you will walk in his ways, keep his statutes, commands, and ordinances, and obey him. 18 And today
the LORD has affirmed that you are his own possession as he promised you, that you are to keep all his
commands, 19 that he will elevate you to praise, fame,
and glory above all the nations he has made, and that
you will be a holy people to the LORD your God as he
promised.”

THE LAW WRITTEN ON STONES

27 Moses and the elders of Israel commanded the
people, “Keep every command I am giving you
today. 2 When you cross the Jordan into the land the
LORD your God is giving you, set up large stones and
cover them with plaster. 3 Write all the words of this
law on the stones after you cross to enter the land
the LORD your God is giving you, a land flowing with
milk and honey, as the LORD, the God of your ancestors, has promised you. 4 When you have crossed the
Jordan, you are to set up these stones on Mount Ebal,
as I am commanding you today, and you are to cover them with plaster. 5 Build an altar of stones there
to the LORD your God — do not use any iron tool on
them. 6 Use uncut stones to build the altar of the LORD
your God and offer burnt offerings to the LORD your
God on it. 7 There you are to sacrifice fellowship offerings, eat, and rejoice in the presence of the LORD
your God. 8 Write clearly all the words of this law on
the plastered stones.”

THE COVENANT CURSES

9 Moses and the Levitical priests spoke to all Israel,
“Be silent, Israel, and listen! This day you have become
the people of the LORD your God. 10 Obey the LORD
your God and follow his commands and statutes I
am giving you today.”
11 On that day Moses commanded the people,
12 “When you have crossed the Jordan, these tribes
will stand on Mount Gerizim to bless the people:
Simeon, Levi, Judah, Issachar, Joseph, and Benjamin.
13 And these tribes will stand on Mount Ebal to deliver the curse: Reuben, Gad, Asher, Zebulun, Dan, and
Naphtali. 14 The Levites will proclaim in a loud voice
to every Israelite:

> 15 ‘The person who makes a carved idol or cast
> image, which is detestable to the LORD, the work
> of a craftsman, and sets it up in secret is cursed.’
> And all the people will reply, ‘Amen!’
> 16 ‘The one who dishonors his father or mother
> is cursed.’
> And all the people will say, ‘Amen!’
> 17 ‘The one who moves his neighbor’s boundary
> marker is cursed.’
> And all the people will say, ‘Amen!’

[A] **26:3** LXX reads *my*

[18] 'The one who leads a blind person astray on the road is cursed.'
And all the people will say, 'Amen!'
[19] 'The one who denies justice to a resident alien, a fatherless child, or a widow is cursed.'
And all the people will say, 'Amen!'
[20] 'The one who sleeps with his father's wife is cursed, for he has violated his father's marriage bed.'[A]
And all the people will say, 'Amen!'
[21] 'The one who has sexual intercourse with any animal is cursed.'
And all the people will say, 'Amen!'
[22] 'The one who sleeps with his sister, whether his father's daughter or his mother's daughter is cursed.'
And all the people will say, 'Amen!'
[23] 'The one who sleeps with his mother-in-law is cursed.'
And all the people will say, 'Amen!'
[24] 'The one who secretly kills his neighbor is cursed.'
And all the people will say, 'Amen!'
[25] 'The one who accepts a bribe to kill an innocent person is cursed.'
And all the people will say, 'Amen!'
[26] 'Anyone who does not put the words of this law into practice is cursed.'
And all the people will say, 'Amen!'

BLESSINGS FOR OBEDIENCE

28 "Now if you faithfully obey the LORD your God and are careful to follow all his commands I am giving you today, the LORD your God will put you far above all the nations of the earth. [2] All these blessings will come and overtake you, because you obey the LORD your God:

3 You will be blessed in the city
and blessed in the country.
4 Your offspring[B] will be blessed,
and your land's produce,
and the offspring of your livestock,
including the young of your herds
and the newborn of your flocks.
5 Your basket and kneading bowl
will be blessed.
6 You will be blessed when you come in
and blessed when you go out.

[7] "The LORD will cause the enemies who rise up against you to be defeated before you. They will march out against you from one direction but flee from you in seven directions. [8] The LORD will grant you a blessing on your barns and on everything you do;[C] he will bless you in the land the LORD your God is giving you. [9] The LORD will establish you as his holy people, as he swore to you, if you obey the commands of the LORD your God and walk in his ways. [10] Then all the peoples of the earth will see that you bear the LORD's name, and they will stand in awe of you. [11] The LORD will make you prosper abundantly with offspring,[D] the offspring of your livestock, and your land's produce in the land the LORD swore to your ancestors to give you. [12] The LORD will open for you his abundant storehouse, the sky, to give your land rain in its season and to bless all the work of your hands. You will lend to many nations, but you will not borrow. [13] The LORD will make you the head and not the tail; you will only move upward and never downward if you listen to the LORD your God's commands I am giving you today and are careful to follow them. [14] Do not turn aside to the right or the left from all the things I am commanding you today, and do not follow other gods to worship them.

CURSES FOR DISOBEDIENCE

[15] "But if you do not obey the LORD your God by carefully following all his commands and statutes I am giving you today, all these curses will come and overtake you:

16 You will be cursed in the city
and cursed in the country.
17 Your basket and kneading bowl will be cursed.
18 Your offspring will be cursed,
and your land's produce,
the young of your herds,
and the newborn of your flocks.
19 You will be cursed when you come in
and cursed when you go out.

[20] The LORD will send against you curses, confusion, and rebuke in everything you do until you are destroyed and quickly perish, because of the wickedness of your actions in abandoning me. [21] The LORD will make pestilence cling to you until he has exterminated you from the land you are entering to possess. [22] The LORD will afflict you with wasting disease, fever, inflammation, burning heat, drought,[E] blight, and mildew; these will pursue you until you perish. [23] The sky above you will be bronze, and the earth beneath you iron. [24] The LORD will turn the rain of your land into falling[F] dust; it will descend on you from the sky until you are destroyed. [25] The LORD will cause you to be defeated before your enemies. You will march out against them from one direction but flee from them in seven directions. You will be an object of horror to all the kingdoms of the earth.

[A] **27:20** Lit *has uncovered the edge of his father's garment*; Ru 3:9; Ezk 16:8 [B] **28:4** Lit *The fruit of your womb*, also in v. 18 [C] **28:8** Lit *you put your hand to*, also in v. 20 [D] **28:11** Lit *abundantly in the fruit of your womb* [E] **28:22** Or *sword* [F] **28:24** Lit *powder and*

26 Your corpses will be food for all the birds of the sky and the wild animals of the earth, with no one to scare them away.

27 "The LORD will afflict you with the boils of Egypt, tumors, a festering rash, and scabies, from which you cannot be cured. 28 The LORD will afflict you with madness, blindness, and mental confusion, 29 so that at noon you will grope as a blind person gropes in the dark. You will not be successful in anything you do. You will only be oppressed and robbed continually, and no one will help you. 30 You will become engaged to a woman, but another man will rape her. You will build a house but not live in it. You will plant a vineyard but not enjoy its fruit. 31 Your ox will be slaughtered before your eyes, but you will not eat any of it. Your donkey will be taken away from you and not returned to you. Your flock will be given to your enemies, and no one will help you. 32 Your sons and daughters will be given to another people, while your eyes grow weary looking for them every day. But you will be powerless to do anything. 33 A people you don't know will eat your land's produce and everything you have labored for. You will only be oppressed and crushed continually. 34 You will be driven mad by what you see. 35 The LORD will afflict you with painful and incurable boils on your knees and thighs — from the sole of your foot to the top of your head.

36 "The LORD will bring you and your king that you have appointed to a nation neither you nor your ancestors have known, and there you will worship other gods, of wood and stone. 37 You will become an object of horror, scorn, and ridicule among all the peoples where the LORD will drive you.

38 "You will sow much seed in the field but harvest little, because locusts will devour it. 39 You will plant and cultivate vineyards but not drink the wine or gather the grapes, because worms will eat them. 40 You will have olive trees throughout your territory but not moisten your skin with oil, because your olives will drop off. 41 You will father sons and daughters, but they will not remain yours, because they will be taken prisoner. 42 Buzzing insects will take possession of all your trees and your land's produce. 43 The resident alien among you will rise higher and higher above you, while you sink lower and lower. 44 He will lend to you, but you won't lend to him. He will be the head, and you will be the tail.

45 "All these curses will come, pursue, and overtake you until you are destroyed, since you did not obey the LORD your God and keep the commands and statutes he gave you. 46 These curses will be a sign and a wonder against you and your descendants forever. 47 Because you didn't serve the LORD your God with joy and a cheerful heart, even though you had an abundance of everything, 48 you will serve your enemies that the LORD will send against you, in famine, thirst, nakedness, and a lack of everything. He will place an iron yoke on your neck until he has destroyed you. 49 The LORD will bring a nation from far away, from the ends of the earth, to swoop down on you like an eagle, a nation whose language you won't understand, 50 a ruthless nation, showing no respect for the old and not sparing the young. 51 They will eat the offspring of your livestock and your land's produce until you are destroyed. They will leave you no grain, new wine, fresh oil, young of your herds, or newborn of your flocks until they cause you to perish. 52 They will besiege you within all your city gates until your high and fortified walls, that you trust in, come down throughout your land. They will besiege you within all your city gates throughout the land the LORD your God has given you.

53 "You will eat your offspring,[A] the flesh of your sons and daughters the LORD your God has given you during the siege and hardship your enemy imposes on you. 54 The most sensitive and refined man among you will look grudgingly at his brother, the wife he embraces, and the rest of his children, 55 refusing to share with any of them his children's flesh that he will eat because he has nothing left during the siege and hardship your enemy imposes on you in all your towns. 56 The most sensitive and refined woman among you, who would not venture to set the sole of her foot on the ground because of her refinement and sensitivity, will begrudge the husband she embraces, her son, and her daughter, 57 the afterbirth that comes out from between her legs and the children she bears, because she will secretly eat them for lack of anything else during the siege and hardship your enemy imposes on you within your city gates.

58 "If you are not careful to obey all the words of this law, which are written in this scroll, by fearing this glorious and awe-inspiring name — the LORD, your God — 59 he will bring wondrous plagues on you and your descendants, severe and lasting plagues, and terrible and chronic sicknesses. 60 He will afflict you again with all the diseases of Egypt, which you dreaded, and they will cling to you. 61 The LORD will also afflict you with every sickness and plague not recorded in the book of this law, until you are destroyed. 62 Though you were as numerous as the stars of the sky, you will be left with only a few people, because you did not obey the LORD your God. 63 Just as the LORD was glad to cause you to prosper and to multiply you, so he will also be glad to cause you to perish and to destroy you. You will be ripped out of the land you

[A] **28:53** Lit *eat the fruit of your womb*

are entering to possess. 64 Then the LORD will scatter you among all peoples from one end of the earth to the other, and there you will worship other gods, of wood and stone, which neither you nor your ancestors have known. 65 You will find no peace among those nations, and there will be no resting place for the sole of your foot. There the LORD will give you a trembling heart, failing eyes, and a despondent spirit. 66 Your life will hang in doubt before you. You will be in dread night and day, never certain of survival. 67 In the morning you will say, 'If only it were evening!' and in the evening you will say, 'If only it were morning!' — because of the dread you will have in your heart and because of what you will see. 68 The LORD will take you back in ships to Egypt by a route that I said you would never see again. There you will sell yourselves to your enemies as male and female slaves, but no one will buy you."

RENEWING THE COVENANT

29 These are the words of the covenant that the LORD commanded Moses to make with the Israelites in the land of Moab, in addition to the covenant he had made with them at Horeb. 2 Moses summoned all Israel and said to them, "You have seen with your own eyes everything the LORD did in Egypt to Pharaoh, to all his officials, and to his entire land. 3 You saw with your own eyes the great trials and those great signs and wonders. 4 Yet to this day the LORD has not given you a mind to understand, eyes to see, or ears to hear. 5 I led you forty years in the wilderness; your clothes and the sandals on your feet did not wear out; 6 you did not eat food or drink wine or beer — so that you might know that I am the LORD your God. 7 When you reached this place, King Sihon of Heshbon and King Og of Bashan came out against us in battle, but we defeated them. 8 We took their land and gave it as an inheritance to the Reubenites, the Gadites, and half the tribe of Manasseh. 9 Therefore, observe the words of this covenant and follow them, so that you will succeed in everything you do.

10 "All of you are standing today before the LORD your God — your leaders, tribes, elders, officials, all the men of Israel, 11 your dependents, your wives, and the resident aliens in your camps who cut your wood and draw your water — 12 so that you may enter into the covenant of the LORD your God, which he is making with you today, so that you may enter into his oath 13 and so that he may establish you today as his people and he may be your God as he promised you and as he swore to your ancestors Abraham, Isaac, and Jacob. 14 I am making this covenant and this oath not only with you, 15 but also with those who are standing here with us today in the presence of the LORD our God and with those who are not here today.

ABANDONING THE COVENANT

16 "Indeed, you know how we lived in the land of Egypt and passed through the nations where you traveled. 17 You saw their abhorrent images and idols made of wood, stone, silver, and gold, which were among them. 18 Be sure there is no man, woman, clan, or tribe among you today whose heart turns away from the LORD our God to go and worship the gods of those nations. Be sure there is no root among you bearing poisonous and bitter fruit. 19 When someone hears the words of this oath, he may consider himself exempt,[A] thinking, 'I will have peace even though I follow my own stubborn heart.' This will lead to the destruction of the well-watered land as well as the dry land. 20 The LORD will not be willing to forgive him. Instead, his anger and jealousy will burn against that person, and every curse written in this scroll will descend on him. The LORD will blot out his name under heaven, 21 and single him out for harm from all the tribes of Israel, according to all the curses of the covenant written in this book of the law.

22 "Future generations of your children who follow you and the foreigner who comes from a distant country will see the plagues of that land and the sicknesses the LORD has inflicted on it. 23 All its soil will be a burning waste of sulfur and salt, unsown, producing nothing, with no plant growing on it, just like the fall of Sodom and Gomorrah, Admah and Zeboiim, which the LORD demolished in his fierce anger. 24 All the nations will ask, 'Why has the LORD done this to this land? Why this intense outburst of anger?' 25 Then people will answer, 'It is because they abandoned the covenant of the LORD, the God of their ancestors, which he had made with them when he brought them out of the land of Egypt. 26 They began to serve other gods, bowing in worship to gods they had not known — gods that the LORD had not permitted them to worship. 27 Therefore the LORD's anger burned against this land, and he brought every curse written in this book on it. 28 The LORD uprooted them from their land in his anger, rage, and intense wrath, and threw them into another land where they are today.' 29 The hidden things belong to the LORD our God, but the revealed things belong to us and our children forever, so that we may follow all the words of this law.

RETURNING TO THE LORD

30 "When all these things happen to you — the blessings and curses I have set before you — and you come to your senses while you are in all the nations where the LORD your God has driven you, 2 and you and your children return to the LORD your God and obey him with all your heart and all

[A] **29:19** Lit *may consider himself blessed in his heart*

your soul by doing[A] everything I am commanding you today, 3 then he will restore your fortunes,[B] have compassion on you, and gather you again from all the peoples where the LORD your God has scattered you. 4 Even if your exiles are at the farthest horizon, he will gather you and bring you back from there. 5 The LORD your God will bring you into the land your ancestors possessed, and you will take possession of it. He will cause you to prosper and multiply you more than he did your ancestors. 6 The LORD your God will circumcise your heart and the hearts of your descendants, and you will love him with all your heart and all your soul so that you will live. 7 The LORD your God will put all these curses on your enemies who hate and persecute you. 8 Then you will again obey him and follow all his commands I am commanding you today. 9 The LORD your God will make you prosper abundantly in all the work of your hands, your offspring,[C] the offspring of your livestock, and the produce of your land. Indeed, the LORD will again delight in your prosperity, as he delighted in that of your ancestors, 10 when you obey the LORD your God by keeping his commands and statutes that are written in this book of the law and return to him with all your heart and all your soul.

CHOOSE LIFE

11 "This command that I give you today is certainly not too difficult or beyond your reach. 12 It is not in heaven so that you have to ask, 'Who will go up to heaven, get it for us, and proclaim it to us so that we may follow it?' 13 And it is not across the sea so that you have to ask, 'Who will cross the sea, get it for us, and proclaim it to us so that we may follow it?' 14 But the message is very near you, in your mouth and in your heart, so that you may follow it. 15 See, today I have set before you life and prosperity, death and adversity. 16 For[D] I am commanding you today to love the LORD your God, to walk in his ways, and to keep his commands, statutes, and ordinances, so that you may live[E] and multiply, and the LORD your God may bless you in the land you are entering to possess. 17 But if your heart turns away and you do not listen and you are led astray to bow in worship to other gods and serve them, 18 I tell you today that you will certainly perish and will not prolong your days in the land you are entering to possess across the Jordan. 19 I call heaven and earth as witnesses against you today that I have set before you life and death, blessing and curse. Choose life so that you and your descendants may live, 20 love the LORD your God, obey him, and remain faithful[F] to him. For he is your life, and he will prolong your days as you live in the land the LORD swore to give to your ancestors Abraham, Isaac, and Jacob."

JOSHUA TAKES MOSES'S PLACE

31 Then Moses continued to speak these[G] words to all Israel, 2 saying, "I am now 120 years old; I can no longer act as your leader.[H] The LORD has told me, 'You will not cross the Jordan.' 3 The LORD your God is the one who will cross ahead of you. He will destroy these nations before you, and you will drive them out. Joshua is the one who will cross ahead of you, as the LORD has said. 4 The LORD will deal with them as he did Sihon and Og, the kings of the Amorites, and their land when he destroyed them. 5 The LORD will deliver them over to you, and you must do to them exactly as I have commanded you. 6 Be strong and courageous; don't be terrified or afraid of them. For the LORD your God is the one who will go with you; he will not leave you or abandon you."

7 Moses then summoned Joshua and said to him in the sight of all Israel, "Be strong and courageous, for you will go with[I] this people into the land the LORD swore to give to their ancestors. You will enable them to take possession of it. 8 The LORD is the one who will go before you. He will be with you; he will not leave you or abandon you. Do not be afraid or discouraged."

9 Moses wrote down this law and gave it to the priests, the sons of Levi, who carried the ark of the LORD's covenant, and to all the elders of Israel. 10 Moses commanded them, "At the end of every seven years, at the appointed time in the year of debt cancellation, during the Festival of Shelters, 11 when all Israel assembles in the presence of the LORD your God at the place he chooses, you are to read this law aloud before all Israel. 12 Gather the people — men, women, dependents, and the resident aliens within your city gates — so that they may listen and learn to fear the LORD your God and be careful to follow all the words of this law. 13 Then their children who do not know the law will listen and learn to fear the LORD your God as long as you live in the land you are crossing the Jordan to possess."

14 The LORD said to Moses, "The time of your death is now approaching. Call Joshua and present yourselves at the tent of meeting so that I may commission him." When Moses and Joshua went and presented themselves at the tent of meeting, 15 the LORD appeared at the tent in a pillar of cloud, and the cloud stood at the entrance to the tent.

16 The LORD said to Moses, "You are about to rest with your ancestors, and these people will soon pros-

[A] **30:2** Lit *soul according to* [B] **30:3** Or *will end your captivity* [C] **30:9** Lit *hands in the fruit of your womb* [D] **30:16** LXX reads *If you obey the commands of the LORD your God that* [E] **30:16** LXX reads *ordinances, then you will live* [F] **30:20** Lit *and hold on* [G] **31:1** Some Hb mss, DSS, LXX, Syr, Vg read *all these* [H] **31:2** Lit *no longer go out or come in* [I] **31:7** Some Hb mss, Sam, Syr, Vg read *you will bring*

titute themselves with the foreign gods of the land
they are entering. They will abandon me and break
the covenant I have made with them. 17 My anger will
burn against them on that day; I will abandon them
and hide my face from them so that they will become
easy prey. Many troubles and afflictions will come to
them. On that day they will say, 'Haven't these troubles
come to us because our God is no longer with us?'
18 I will certainly hide my face on that day because of
all the evil they have done by turning to other gods.
19 Therefore write down this song for yourselves and
teach it to the Israelites; have them sing it,[A] so that this
song may be a witness for me against the Israelites.
20 When I bring them into the land I swore to give
their ancestors, a land flowing with milk and honey,
they will eat their fill and prosper.[B] They will turn
to other gods and worship them, despising me and
breaking my covenant. 21 And when many troubles
and afflictions come to them, this song will testify
against them, because[C] their descendants will not
have forgotten it. For I know what they are prone to
do,[D] even before I bring them into the land I swore
to give them." 22 So Moses wrote down this song on
that day and taught it to the Israelites.

23 The LORD commissioned Joshua son of Nun, "Be
strong and courageous, for you will bring the Israelites into the land I swore to them, and I will be with
you."

MOSES WARNS THE PEOPLE

24 When Moses had finished writing down on a scroll
every single word of this law, 25 he commanded the
Levites who carried the ark of the LORD's covenant,
26 "Take this book of the law and place it beside the
ark of the covenant of the LORD your God so that it
may remain there as a witness against you. 27 For
I know how rebellious and stiff-necked you are. If
you are rebelling against the LORD now, while I am
still alive, how much more will you rebel after I am
dead! 28 Assemble all your tribal elders and officers
before me so that I may speak these words directly to them and call heaven and earth as witnesses
against them. 29 For I know that after my death you
will become completely corrupt and turn from the
path I have commanded you. Disaster will come to
you in the future, because you will do what is evil in
the LORD's sight, angering him with what your hands
have made." 30 Then Moses recited aloud every single
word of this song to the entire assembly of Israel:

SONG OF MOSES

32 Pay attention, heavens, and I will speak;
listen, earth, to the words from my mouth.
2 Let my teaching fall like rain
and my word settle like dew,
like gentle rain on new grass
and showers on tender plants.
3 For I will proclaim the LORD's name.
Declare the greatness of our God!
4 The Rock — his work is perfect;
all his ways are just.
A faithful God, without bias,
he is righteous and true.

5 His people have acted corruptly toward him;
this is their defect[E] — they are not
his children
but a devious and crooked generation.
6 Is this how you repay the LORD,
you foolish and senseless people?
Isn't he your Father and Creator?[F]
Didn't he make you and sustain you?
7 Remember the days of old;
consider the years of past generations.
Ask your father, and he will tell you,
your elders, and they will teach you.
8 When the Most High gave the nations
their inheritance[G]
and divided the human race,
he set the boundaries of the peoples
according to the number of the people
of Israel.[H]
9 But the LORD's portion is his people,
Jacob, his own inheritance.

10 He found him in a desolate land,
in a barren, howling wilderness;
he surrounded him, cared for him,
and protected him as the pupil of his eye.
11 He watches over[I] his nest like an eagle
and hovers over his young;
he spreads his wings, catches him,
and carries him on his feathers.
12 The LORD alone led him,
with no help from a foreign god.
13 He made him ride on the heights of the land
and eat the produce of the field.
He nourished him with honey from the rock
and oil from flinty rock,
14 curds from the herd and milk from the flock,
with the fat of lambs,
rams from Bashan, and goats,
with the choicest grains of wheat;
you drank wine from the finest grapes.[J]

[A] **31:19** Lit *Israelites; put it in their mouths* [B] **31:20** Lit *be fat* [C] **31:21** Lit *because the mouths of* [D] **31:21** Or *know the plans they are devising* [E] **32:5** Or *him; through their fault*; Hb obscure [F] **32:6** Or *Possessor* [G] **32:8** Or *Most High divided the nations* [H] **32:8** One DSS reads *number of the sons of God*; LXX reads *number of the angels of God* [I] **32:11** Or *He stirs up* [J] **32:14** Lit *drank the blood of grapes, fermenting wine*

15 Then[A] Jeshurun[B] became fat and rebelled —
you became fat, bloated, and gorged.
He abandoned the God who made him
and scorned the Rock of his salvation.
16 They provoked his jealousy
with different gods;
they enraged him with detestable practices.
17 They sacrificed to demons, not God,
to gods they had not known,
new gods that had just arrived,
which your ancestors did not fear.
18 You ignored the Rock who gave you birth;
you forgot the God who gave birth to you.

19 When the LORD saw this, he despised them,
angered by his sons and daughters.
20 He said, "I will hide my face from them;
I will see what will become of them,
for they are a perverse generation —
unfaithful children.
21 They have provoked my jealousy
with what is not a god;[C]
they have enraged me with their worthless
idols.
So I will provoke their jealousy
with what is not a people;[D]
I will enrage them with a foolish nation.
22 For fire has been kindled because of
my anger
and burns to the depths of Sheol;
it devours the land and its produce,
and scorches the foundations
of the mountains.

23 "I will pile disasters on them;
I will use up my arrows against them.
24 They will be weak from hunger,
ravaged by pestilence and bitter plague;
I will unleash on them wild beasts with fangs,
as well as venomous snakes that slither
in the dust.
25 Outside, the sword will take their children,
and inside, there will be terror;
the young man and the young woman
will be killed,
the infant and the gray-haired man.

26 "I would have said: I will cut them to pieces[E]
and blot out the memory of them
from mankind,
27 if I had not feared provocation
from the enemy,
or feared that these foes might misunderstand
and say, 'Our own hand has prevailed;
it wasn't the LORD who did all this.'"

28 Israel is a nation lacking sense
with no understanding at all.
29 If only they were wise,
they would comprehend this;
they would understand their fate.
30 How could one pursue a thousand,
or two put ten thousand to flight,
unless their Rock had sold them,
unless the LORD had given them up?
31 But their "rock" is not like our Rock,
as even our enemies concede.
32 For their vine is from the vine of Sodom
and from the fields of Gomorrah.
Their grapes are poisonous;
their clusters are bitter.
33 Their wine is serpents' venom,
the deadly poison of cobras.

34 "Is it not stored up with me,
sealed up in my vaults?
35 Vengeance and retribution belong to me.[F]
In time their foot will slip,
for their day of disaster is near,
and their doom is coming quickly."
36 The LORD will indeed vindicate his people
and have compassion on his servants
when he sees that their strength is gone
and no one is left — slave or free.[G]
37 He will say, "Where are their gods,
the 'rock' they found refuge in?
38 Who ate the fat of their sacrifices
and drank the wine of their drink offerings?
Let them rise up and help you;
let it[H] be a shelter for you.
39 See now that I alone am he;
there is no God but me.
I bring death and I give life;
I wound and I heal.
No one can rescue anyone from my power.
40 I raise my hand to heaven and declare:
As surely as I live forever,
41 when I sharpen my flashing sword,
and my hand takes hold of judgment,
I will take vengeance on my adversaries
and repay those who hate me.
42 I will make my arrows drunk with blood
while my sword devours flesh —
the blood of the slain and the captives,
the heads of the enemy leaders."[I]

[A]**32:15** DSS, Sam, LXX add *Jacob ate his fill;* [B]**32:15** = Upright One, referring to Israel [C]**32:21** Lit *with no gods* [D]**32:21** Lit *with no people* [E]**32:26** LXX reads *will scatter them* [F]**32:35** MT; LXX, reads *On a day of vengeance I will repay.* [G]**32:36** Or *left — even the weak and impaired*; Hb obscure [H]**32:38** Sam, LXX, Tg, Vg read *them* [I]**32:42** Or *the long-haired heads of the enemy*

43 Rejoice, you nations, concerning his people,[A]
for he will avenge the blood of his servants.[B]
He will take vengeance on his adversaries;[C]
he will purify his land and his people.[D]

44 Moses came with Joshua[E] son of Nun and recited all the words of this song in the presence of
the people. 45 After Moses finished reciting all these
words to all Israel, 46 he said to them, "Take to heart
all these words I am giving as a warning to you today,
so that you may command your children to follow
all the words of this law carefully. 47 For they are not
meaningless words to you but they are your life, and
by them you will live long in the land you are crossing
the Jordan to possess."

MOSES'S IMPENDING DEATH

48 On that same day the LORD spoke to Moses, 49 "Go up
Mount Nebo in the Abarim range in the land of Moab,
across from Jericho, and view the land of Canaan I am
giving the Israelites as a possession. 50 Then you will
die on the mountain that you go up, and you will be
gathered to your people, just as your brother Aaron
died on Mount Hor and was gathered to his people.
51 For both of you broke faith with me among the
Israelites at the Waters of Meribath-kadesh in the
Wilderness of Zin by failing to treat me as holy in
their presence. 52 Although from a distance you will
view the land that I am giving the Israelites, you will
not go there."

MOSES'S BLESSINGS

33 This is the blessing that Moses, the man of God,
gave the Israelites before his death. 2 He said:
The LORD came from Sinai
and appeared to them from Seir;
he shone on them from Mount Paran
and came with ten thousand holy ones,[F]
with lightning[G] from his right hand[H]
for them.
3 Indeed he loves the people.[I]
All your[J] holy ones are in your hand,
and they assemble[K] at your feet.
Each receives your words.
4 Moses gave us instruction,
a possession for the assembly of Jacob.
5 So he became King in Jeshurun[L]
when the leaders of the people gathered
with the tribes of Israel.

6 Let Reuben live and not die
though his people become few.
7 He said this about Judah:
LORD, hear Judah's cry and bring him
to his people.
He fights for his cause[M] with his own hands,
but may you be a help against his foes.
8 He said about Levi:
Your Thummim and Urim belong to
your faithful one;[N]
you tested him at Massah
and contended with him at the Waters
of Meribah.
9 He said about his father and mother,
"I do not regard them."
He disregarded his brothers
and didn't acknowledge his sons,
for they kept your word
and maintained your covenant.
10 They will teach your ordinances to Jacob
and your instruction to Israel;
they will set incense before you
and whole burnt offerings on your altar.
11 LORD, bless his possessions,[O]
and accept the work of his hands.
Break the back[P] of his adversaries
and enemies,
so that they cannot rise again.
12 He said about Benjamin:
The LORD's beloved rests[Q] securely on him.
He[R] shields him all day long,
and he rests on his shoulders.[S]
13 He said about Joseph:
May his land be blessed by the LORD
with the dew of heaven's bounty
and the watery depths that lie beneath;
14 with the bountiful harvest from the sun
and the abundant yield of the seasons;
15 with the best products
of the ancient mountains
and the bounty of the eternal hills;
16 with the choice gifts of the land
and everything in it;
and with the favor of him
who appeared[T] in the burning bush.
May these rest on the head of Joseph,
on the brow of the prince of his brothers.

[A] **32:43** LXX reads *Rejoice, you heavens, along with him, and let all the sons of God worship him; rejoice, you nations, with his people, and let all the angels of God strengthen themselves in him*; DSS read *Rejoice, you heavens, along with him, and let all the angels worship him*; Heb 1:6 [B] **32:43** DSS, LXX read *sons* [C] **32:43** DSS, LXX add *and he will repay those who hate him*; v. 41 [D] **32:43** Syr, Tg; DSS, Sam, LXX, Vg read *his people's land* [E] **32:44** LXX, Syr, Vg; MT reads *Hoshea*; Nm 13:8,16 [F] **33:2** LXX reads *Mount Paran with ten thousands from Kadesh* [G] **33:2** Or *fiery law*; Hb obscure [H] **33:2** Or *ones, from his southland to the mountain slopes* [I] **33:3** Or *peoples* [J] **33:3** Lit *his*, or *its* [K] **33:3** Hb obscure [L] **33:5** = Upright One, referring to Israel, also in v. 26 [M] **33:7** Or *He contends for them* [N] **33:8** DSS, LXX read *Give to Levi your Thummim, your Urim to your favored one* [O] **33:11** Or *abilities* [P] **33:11** Or *waist* [Q] **33:12** Or *Let the LORD's beloved rest* [R] **33:12** LXX reads *The Most High* [S] **33:12** Or *and he dwells among his mountain slopes* [T] **33:16** Lit *dwelt*

17 His firstborn bull has[A] splendor,
and horns like[B] those of a wild ox;
he gores all the peoples with them
to the ends of the earth.
Such are the ten thousands of Ephraim,
and such are the thousands of Manasseh.
18 He said about Zebulun:
Rejoice, Zebulun, in your journeys,
and Issachar, in your tents.
19 They summon the peoples to a mountain;
there they offer acceptable sacrifices.
For they draw from the wealth of the seas
and the hidden treasures of the sand.
20 He said about Gad:
The one who enlarges Gad's territory
will be blessed.
He lies down like a lion
and tears off an arm or even a head.
21 He chose the best part for himself,
because a ruler's portion was assigned there
for him.
He came with the leaders of the people;
he carried out the LORD's justice
and his ordinances for Israel.
22 He said about Dan:
Dan is a young lion,
leaping out of Bashan.
23 He said about Naphtali:
Naphtali, enjoying approval,
full of the LORD's blessing,
take[C] possession to the west and the south.
24 He said about Asher:
May Asher[D] be the most blessed of the sons;
may he be the most favored
among his brothers
and dip his foot in olive oil.
25 May the bolts of your gate be iron and bronze,
and your strength last as long as you live.

26 There is none like the God of Jeshurun,
who rides the heavens to your aid,
the clouds in his majesty.
27 The God of old is your dwelling place,
and underneath are the everlasting arms.
He drives out the enemy before you
and commands, "Destroy!"
28 So Israel dwells securely;
Jacob lives untroubled[E]
in a land of grain and new wine;
even his skies drip with dew.
29 How happy you are, Israel!
Who is like you,
a people saved by the LORD?
He is the shield that protects you,
the sword you boast in.
Your enemies will cringe before you,
and you will tread on their backs.[F]

MOSES'S DEATH

34 Then Moses went up from the plains of Moab
to Mount Nebo, to the top of Pisgah, which
faces Jericho, and the LORD showed him all the land:
Gilead as far as Dan, 2 all of Naphtali, the land of
Ephraim and Manasseh, all the land of Judah as far
as the Mediterranean[G] Sea, 3 the Negev, and the plain
in the Valley of Jericho, the City of Palms, as far as
Zoar. 4 The LORD then said to him, "This is the land
I promised Abraham, Isaac, and Jacob, 'I will give it
to your descendants.' I have let you see it with your
own eyes, but you will not cross into it."
5 So Moses the servant of the LORD died there in
the land of Moab, according to the LORD's word. 6 He
buried him[H] in the valley in the land of Moab facing
Beth-peor, and no one to this day knows where his
grave is. 7 Moses was one hundred twenty years old
when he died; his eyes were not weak, and his vitality
had not left him. 8 The Israelites wept for Moses in the
plains of Moab thirty days. Then the days of weeping
and mourning for Moses came to an end.
9 Joshua son of Nun was filled with the spirit of
wisdom because Moses had laid his hands on him.
So the Israelites obeyed him and did as the LORD had
commanded Moses. 10 No prophet has arisen again in
Israel like Moses, whom the LORD knew face to face.
11 He was unparalleled for all the signs and wonders
the LORD sent him to do against the land of Egypt
— to Pharaoh, to all his officials, and to all his land —
12 and for all the mighty acts of power and terrifying
deeds that Moses performed in the sight of all Israel.

[A] **33:17** Some DSS, Sam, LXX, Syr, Vg read *A firstborn bull — he has* [B] **33:17** Lit *and his horns are* [C] **33:23** Sam, LXX, Syr, Vg, Tg read *he will take* [D] **33:24** = Happy or Blessed; Gn 30:13 [E] **33:28** Text emended; MT reads *Jacob's fountain is alone* [F] **33:29** Or *high places* [G] **34:2** Lit *Western* [H] **34:6** Or *he was buried*

JOSHUA

Looking over the Jordan Valley from Old Testament Jericho.

INTRODUCTION TO

JOSHUA

Circumstances of Writing

The author of the book of Joshua is not identified in the Bible and otherwise remains anonymous. If Joshua himself did not originally compose the book that bears his name, it may be presumed that someone who knew him and his exploits recorded the work. There are numerous references throughout Joshua that suggest a final formation of the book after his lifetime. These include the death of Joshua and descriptions of memorials or names that are said to remain "still . . . today" (4:9; 5:9; 6:25; 7:26; 8:28–29; 10:27; 13:13; 14:14; 15:63; 16:10; see 22:17; 23:8).

The accounts in the book of Joshua occur in the period immediately after Moses's death. This was a new generation, not the one that had left Egypt. The story of Joshua is thus set when the nation of Israel first appeared in the land west of the Jordan River—the land that would bear its name. First Kings 6:1 states that the exodus occurred 480 years before Solomon's fourth year as king (966 BC). In Judges 11:26, Jephthah said that Israelites had been living in regions of Israel for 300 years. Jephthah lived around 1100 BC, thus dating the end of the wilderness journey and the beginning of the conquest to around 1400 BC.

Contribution to the Bible

Just as Joshua's leadership begins with the death of Moses, so the book of Joshua follows and completes the book of Deuteronomy. Deuteronomy serves as a means by which the new generation of Israelites renewed their covenant with God. The book of Joshua provides the means by which God fulfilled his part of the covenant. God gave them victories, but each victory required a step of faith. God's provision for the people as their leader and guide bore witness to later generations of the divinely willed leadership for Israel, and his gracious gift of the land showed how the people's faithful fulfillment of the covenant could result in abundant blessing.

Structure

The book of Joshua should be seen as a land grant, similar to the land grants and suzerain treaties of the ancient Near East. The suzerain, who was Israel's God, gave to his people the land that they were meant to receive. There are three major parts to the structure of the land grant.

First is a review of the history and events leading up to the gift of the land. This occurs in chapter 1 with a discussion of what has brought Joshua to this point—the death of Moses. Chapters 2–5 detail the preparation for the acquisition of the gift of the land. Chapters 6–12 describe the battles that were fought as background to the receipt of the land. The second section considers the allotment of the territories to the tribes and families of Israel. The many specific names and towns of this part of the text provide a particularity to the gift that affirms it was an authentic fulfillment of God's promise to his people. The third section is a renewal of the covenant. Here the key parts are the stipulations of the covenant that require loyalty to God alone (24:14–15) and the response of the people that they agree to these demands.

ENCOURAGEMENT OF JOSHUA

1 After the death of Moses the LORD's servant, the LORD spoke to Joshua son of Nun, Moses's assistant: 2 "Moses my servant is dead. Now you and all the people prepare to cross over the Jordan to the land I am giving the Israelites. 3 I have given you every place where the sole of your foot treads, just as I promised Moses. 4 Your territory will be from the wilderness and Lebanon to the great river, the Euphrates River — all the land of the Hittites — and west to the Mediterranean Sea. 5 No one will be able to stand against you as long as you live. I will be with you, just as I was with Moses. I will not leave you or abandon you.

6 "Be strong and courageous, for you will distribute the land I swore to their ancestors to give them as an inheritance. 7 Above all, be strong and very courageous to observe carefully the whole instruction my servant Moses commanded you. Do not turn from it to the right or the left, so that you will have success wherever you go. 8 This book of instruction must not depart from your mouth; you are to meditate on[A] it day and night so that you may carefully observe everything written in it. For then you will prosper and succeed in whatever you do. 9 Haven't I commanded you: be strong and courageous? Do not be afraid or discouraged, for the LORD your God is with you wherever you go."

JOSHUA PREPARES THE PEOPLE

10 Then Joshua commanded the officers of the people, 11 "Go through the camp and tell the people, 'Get provisions ready for yourselves, for within three days you will be crossing the Jordan to go in and take possession of the land the LORD your God is giving you to inherit.'"

12 Joshua said to the Reubenites, the Gadites, and half the tribe of Manasseh, 13 "Remember what Moses the LORD's servant commanded you when he said, 'The LORD your God will give you rest, and he will give you this land.' 14 Your wives, dependents, and livestock may remain in the land Moses gave you on this side of the Jordan. But your best soldiers must cross over in battle formation[B] ahead of your brothers and help them 15 until the LORD gives your brothers rest, as he has given you, and they too possess the land the LORD your God is giving them. You may then return to the land of your inheritance and take possession of what Moses the LORD's servant gave you on the east side of the Jordan."

16 They answered Joshua, "Everything you have commanded us we will do, and everywhere you send us we will go. 17 We will obey you, just as we obeyed Moses in everything. Certainly the LORD your God will be with you, as he was with Moses. 18 Anyone who rebels against your order and does not obey your words in all that you command him, will be put to death. Above all, be strong and courageous!"

SPIES SENT TO JERICHO

2 Joshua son of Nun secretly sent two men as spies from the Acacia Grove,[C] saying, "Go and scout the land, especially Jericho." So they left, and they came to the house of a prostitute named Rahab, and stayed there.

2 The king of Jericho was told, "Look, some of the Israelite men have come here tonight to investigate the land." 3 Then the king of Jericho sent word to Rahab and said, "Bring out the men who came to you and entered your house, for they came to investigate the entire land."

4 But the woman had taken the two men and hidden them. So she said, "Yes, the men did come to me, but I didn't know where they were from. 5 At nightfall, when the city gate was about to close, the men went out, and I don't know where they were going. Chase after them quickly, and you can catch up with them!" 6 But she had taken them up to the roof and hidden them among the stalks of flax that she had arranged on the roof. 7 The men pursued them along the road to the fords of the Jordan, and as soon as they left to pursue them, the city gate was shut.

THE PROMISE TO RAHAB

8 Before the men fell asleep, she went up on the roof 9 and said to them, "I know that the LORD has given you this land and that the terror of you has fallen on us, and everyone who lives in the land is panicking because of you.[D] 10 For we have heard how the LORD dried up the water of the Red Sea before you when you came out of Egypt, and what you did to Sihon and Og, the two Amorite kings you completely destroyed across the Jordan. 11 When we heard this, we lost heart, and everyone's courage failed[E] because of you, for the LORD your God is God in heaven above and on earth below. 12 Now please swear to me by the LORD that you will also show kindness to my father's family, because I showed kindness to you. Give me a sure sign[F] 13 that you will spare the lives of my father, mother, brothers, sisters, and all who belong to them, and save us from death."

14 The men answered her, "We will give our lives for yours. If you don't report our mission, we will show kindness and faithfulness to you when the LORD gives us the land."

15 Then she let them down by a rope through the window, since she lived in a house that was built into the wall of the city. 16 "Go to the hill country so that

[A]1:8 Or *to recite* [B]1:14 Or *over armed* [C]2:1 Or *from Shittim* [D]2:9 Or *land panics at your approach* [E]2:11 Lit *and spirit no longer remained in anyone* [F]2:12 Or *a sign of truth*

the men pursuing you won't find you," she said to
them. "Hide there for three days until they return;
afterward, go on your way."
17 The men said to her, "We will be free from this
oath you made us swear, 18 unless, when we enter the
land, you tie this scarlet cord to the window through
which you let us down. Bring your father, mother,
brothers, and all your father's family into your house.
19 If anyone goes out the doors of your house, his death
will be his own fault, and we will be innocent. But if
anyone with you in the house should be harmed, his
death will be our fault. 20 And if you report our mission, we are free from the oath you made us swear."
21 "Let it be as you say," she replied, and she sent
them away. After they had gone, she tied the scarlet
cord to the window.
22 So the two men went into the hill country and
stayed there three days until the pursuers had returned. They searched all along the way, but did not
find them. 23 Then the men returned, came down from
the hill country, and crossed the Jordan. They went
to Joshua son of Nun and reported everything that
had happened to them. 24 They told Joshua, "The LORD
has handed over the entire land to us. Everyone who
lives in the land is also panicking because of us."[A]

CROSSING THE JORDAN

3 Joshua started early the next morning and left the
Acacia Grove[B] with all the Israelites. They went
as far as the Jordan and stayed there before crossing.
2 After three days the officers went through the camp
3 and commanded the people, "When you see the ark
of the covenant of the LORD your God carried by the
Levitical priests, you are to break camp and follow
it. 4 But keep a distance of about a thousand yards[C]
between yourselves and the ark. Don't go near it, so
that you can see the way to go, for you haven't traveled this way before."
5 Joshua told the people, "Consecrate yourselves,
because the LORD will do wonders among you tomorrow." 6 Then he said to the priests, "Carry the ark of the
covenant and go on ahead of the people." So they carried the ark of the covenant and went ahead of them.
7 The LORD spoke to Joshua: "Today I will begin to exalt you in the sight of all Israel, so they will know that
I will be with you just as I was with Moses. 8 Command
the priests carrying the ark of the covenant: When
you reach the edge of the water,[D] stand in the Jordan."
9 Then Joshua told the Israelites, "Come closer and
listen to the words of the LORD your God." 10 He said,
"You will know that the living God is among you and
that he will certainly dispossess before you the Canaanites, Hethites, Hivites, Perizzites, Girgashites,
Amorites, and Jebusites 11 when the ark of the covenant of the Lord of the whole earth goes ahead of
you into the Jordan. 12 Now choose twelve men from
the tribes of Israel, one man for each tribe. 13 When the
feet[E] of the priests who carry the ark of the LORD, the
Lord of the whole earth, come to rest in the Jordan's
water, its water will be cut off. The water flowing
downstream will stand up in a mass."
14 When the people broke camp to cross the Jordan,
the priests carried the ark of the covenant ahead of
the people. 15 Now the Jordan overflows its banks
throughout the harvest season. But as soon as the
priests carrying the ark reached the Jordan, their
feet touched the water at its edge 16 and the water
flowing downstream stood still, rising up in a mass
that extended as far as[F] Adam, a city next to Zarethan.
The water flowing downstream into the Sea of the
Arabah — the Dead Sea — was completely cut off,
and the people crossed opposite Jericho. 17 The priests
carrying the ark of the LORD's covenant stood firmly
on dry ground in the middle of the Jordan, while all
Israel crossed on dry ground until the entire nation
had finished crossing the Jordan.

THE MEMORIAL STONES

4 After the entire nation had finished crossing
the Jordan, the LORD spoke to Joshua: 2 "Choose
twelve men from the people, one man for each tribe,
3 and command them: Take twelve stones from this
place in the middle of the Jordan where the priests[G]
are standing, carry them with you, and set them down
at the place where you spend the night."
4 So Joshua summoned the twelve men he had selected from the Israelites, one man for each tribe,
5 and said to them, "Go across to the ark of the LORD
your God in the middle of the Jordan. Each of you
lift a stone onto his shoulder, one for each of the Israelite tribes, 6 so that this will be a sign among you.
In the future, when your children ask you, 'What do
these stones mean to you?' 7 you should tell them,
'The water of the Jordan was cut off in front of the
ark of the LORD's covenant. When it crossed the Jordan, the Jordan's water was cut off.' Therefore these
stones will always be a memorial for the Israelites."
8 The Israelites did just as Joshua had commanded
them. The twelve men took stones from the middle
of the Jordan, one for each of the Israelite tribes, just
as the LORD had told Joshua. They carried them to
the camp and set them down there. 9 Joshua also set
up twelve stones in the middle[H] of the Jordan where
the priests who carried the ark of the covenant were
standing. The stones are still there today.

[A] **2:24** Or *land also panics at our approach* [B] **3:1** Or *left Shittim* [C] **3:4** Lit *2,000 cubits* [D] **3:8** Lit *waters of the Jordan* [E] **3:13** Lit *soles of the feet* [F] **3:16** Alt Hb tradition reads *mass at* [G] **4:3** Lit *feet of the priests*, also in v. 9 [H] **4:9** Or *Now Joshua set up the twelve stones that had been in the middle*

The Hittites: A Historical Perspective

by Claude F. Mariottini

Historical and archaeological evidence indicates at least four distinct ethnic groups were known as Hittites or Hethites.[1] The first were called the Hattians. These people lived in Asia Minor in the third millennium BC. Their capital city was Hattusa, and they spoke a distinctive language, which archaeologists call Hattian or Proto-Hittite. The second group known as Hittites was the Indo-European invaders who settled in Asia Minor about 2000 BC and who conquered and assimilated the Hattians into their own culture. They called their kingdom Hatti and spoke a language called Nesian or Hittite. The third known group of Hittites were those who survived the collapse of the Hittite Empire around 1180 BC. With the dissolution of the empire, some Hittite centers of power survived in the region of northern Syria, particularly at Carchemish, Hamath, and Kue. "Syria during the first half of the first millennium BC was ruled by kings of two ethnic groups, called 'Arameans' and 'Hittites.' To distinguish these kingdoms from the second-millennium Anatolian kingdom most scholars today refer to them as 'Neo-Hittites.'"[2] The fourth ethnic group of people known as Hittites were the people who lived in the land of Canaan. While most English translations do not differentiate them, based on recent scholarship the CSB refers to these "sons of Heth" as Hethites.[3]

IN ANATOLIA

Until the end of the nineteenth century, history was relatively silent about the Anatolian Hittites. The oldest-known references to the Hittites were in Egyptian documents. One document refers to the battle of Kadesh on the Orontes between Ramesses II, a pharaoh of the Nineteenth Dynasty of Egypt, and Muwattalis, king of the Hittites.[4] Another reference to the Hittites appears in the Amarna letters. A Hittite king sent this particular letter to Pharaoh Akhenaten on the occasion of Akhenaten's inauguration as the new king of Egypt. The letter has been dated around 1380 BC.[5]

At the beginning of the twentieth century AD, archaeologists began excavating at the ancient Anatolian village of Hattusa, modern Bogazkoy, Turkey. During excavations, archaeologists discovered thousands of cuneiform tablets written in an unknown language. When the language was deciphered, scholars concluded that the Hittite language was not similar to the spoken languages of the ancient Near East. They concluded instead that the Hittite language had the

Discovered among the remains of royal archives of Boyuk Kale at Bogazkoy; the Treaty of Kadesh (dated 1296 BC) is one of the oldest-known peace treaties between ancient countries. The treaty was an alliance between Hattusilis, king of the Hittites, and Egypt's Ramesses II.

Temple gate at Bogazkoy, the lower part of the city complex.

Pair of Hittite deities, silver, dated about 1400–1200 BC. These figures combine Hittite-style features (large head and ears) with Syrian elements (headdress and posture); from Anatolia.

Terra-cotta vase fragment decorated with an image of a deer; from Alishar, which was part of the Hittite Empire; dated 1600–1400 BC.

characteristics of an Indo-European language, meaning those spoken in Europe and the areas in south and southwest Asia into which European peoples migrated and settled.

The Hittites of Anatolia probably came from the Caucasus region, located between the Black and Caspian Seas, at the beginning of the third millennium BC. After arriving, they mixed with the ancient Hattic inhabitants of Anatolia and eventually established an empire that included Anatolia, northern Mesopotamia, and Lebanon.

Several events contributed to bring the demise of the Hittite kingdom in Anatolia. The most important was the appearance of invaders, often identified with the Sea Peoples, about 1200 BC. Hittite documents speak of a naval battle between the Hittites and the Sea Peoples and the burning of Hattusa, the capital of the Hittite Empire. In addition, a severe drought produced famine throughout the kingdom, forcing the Hittite king to ask Egypt for help.

IN CANAAN

With the end of the Hittite Empire in Anatolia, a portion of the population moved into northern Syria, where they continued and preserved Hittite culture. Archaeologists call this group Neo-Hittites. The north Syria Hittites lived in several small city-states, which the Assyrians conquered and incorporated into their vast empire during the ninth and eighth centuries BC. According to 1 Kings 10:29, Solomon exported horses and chariots to the "kings of the Hittites." These Hittite kings were the Neo-Hittite rulers of Carchemish, Hamath, and Kue (Cilicia).[6]

When Joshua was preparing to enter the land of Canaan after Moses's death, the Lord promised Joshua that Israel's territory would include all the land of the Hittites (Jos 1:4). Assyrian documents mention this land north of Canaan, referring to it as Hatti land, the land of the Hittites.

Scholars disagree about the identity of the Hittites/Hethites within Canaan mentioned in the Old Testament. Some scholars believe these people belonged to the group of Hittites from the Anatolian regions. Others see them as native Canaanites, with no connection to the Anatolian Hittites. Those who hold to this second view point to the fact that all those in Canaan mentioned in the Old Testament have Semitic names.[7]

The Table of Nations in Genesis 10 lists Noah's grandson Canaan as the father of Heth, the person many consider to be the ancestor of Canaan's Hethites. The Old Testament indicates that the Hethites lived as far south as Hebron (Gn 23:1–3) and Beer-sheba (26:23–25,33–34). The biblical text shows that the patriarchs and later Israelites had many contacts with the Hethites. After Sarah died, Abraham bought the Cave of Machpelah from the Hethites to bury his wife (23:3); the Hebrew literally reads "sons of Heth." The cave that Abraham bought was located in Hebron, a place also known as Kiriath-arba (23:2), which is in southern Judah. Numbers 13:29, however, indicates the Hethites also lived in the hill country of central Canaan. Esau, Isaac's son, married two Hethite women (Gn 26:34; Ezk 16:3). Solomon, on the other hand, married Anatolian or Syrian Hittite women (1Kg 11:1).

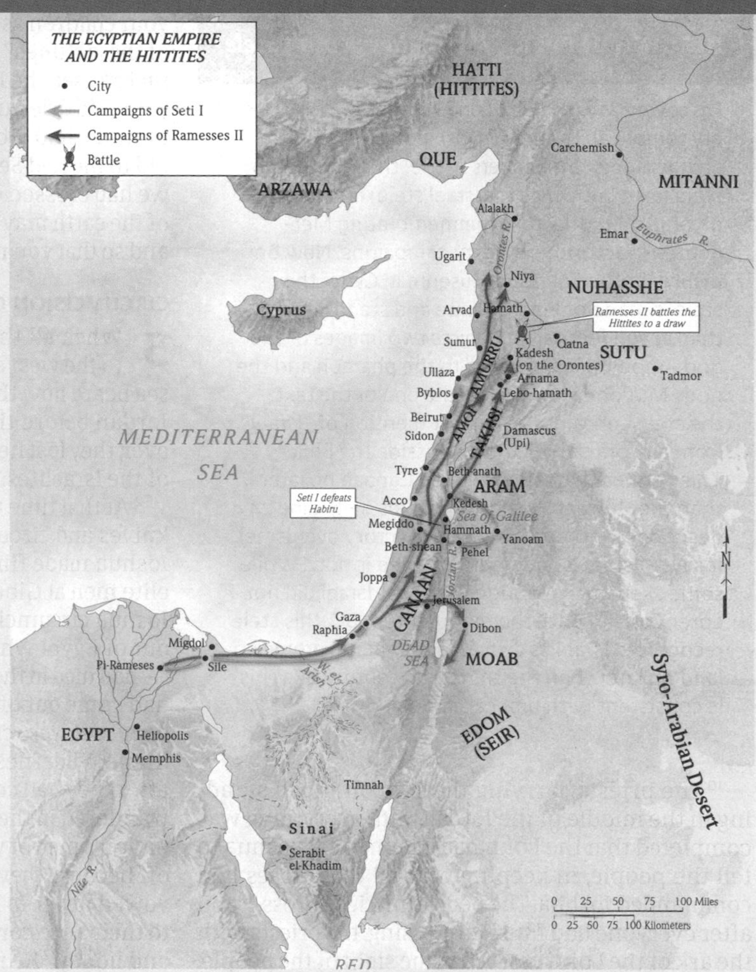

CULTURAL INFLUENCE

Although scholars have disagreed about the extent of legal, cultural, and religious influence the Hittites had on ancient Israel, they generally agree that the Old Testament does reflect one area of Hittite culture: the form of the covenant.

The Hittite Empire from the Late Bronze Age II and III (ca 1400–1200 BC) provides extensive materials that aid us in the study of the covenant traditions of Israel. The most important covenants were international treaties that regulated relationships between two distinct social or political units.

The form of the covenant between God and Israel has many parallels with Hittite treaties. These include (1) a preamble of the covenant in which the Great King identifies himself, (2) a historical prologue in which the Great King tells what he has done, (3) the covenantal stipulations in which the nation binds itself by accepting the covenant's demands, (4) the preservation of the covenant, (5) the public reading of the covenant, (6) the list of witnesses, and (7) the covenantal blessings and curses.

CONCLUSION

The Hittites established a great empire in the second millennium BC in Anatolia. Documents and monuments they left behind reveal that their empire extended as far as Mesopotamia, and yet people knew little of their history and culture until a century ago. The Hethites were among the Canaanites with whom the patriarchs interacted for good and bad. In many ways, the Hittites and Hethites as a people remain enigmatic. Because they are not a single group, some issues regarding their exact identity and origins remain mysteries. Despite these uncertainties, one unquestionable fact remains: these people influenced the history and culture of Israel in many ways. ✣

[1] H. A. Hoffner, "The Hittites and the Hurrians," *People of Old Testament Times*, ed. D. J. Wiseman (Oxford: Clarendon, 1973), 197. [2] Hoffner, "Hittites," 199. [3] Bryant G. Wood, "Hittites and Hethites: A Proposed Solution to an Etymological Conundrum," *Journal of the Evangelical Theological Society* (*JETS*), 54.2 (June 2011), 239–50. [4] John Bright, *A History of Israel* (Louisville: Westminster John Knox, 2000), 113. [5] Aharon Kempinski, "Hittites in the Bible: What Does Archaeology Say?" *BAR* 5.5 (1979): 23–24. [6] Kenneth A. Kitchen, "Hittites" in *NIDBA*, 241. [7] Hoffner, "Hittites and Hurrians," 214.

DIGGING DEEPER *Merneptah Stele*

Discovered within Pharaoh Merneptah's funerary temple at Thebes (Egypt) in 1896 by English archaeologist Sir Flinders Petrie, the Merneptah stele (also known as the Israel stele) is a hieroglyphic memorial text commemorating Merneptah's victorious military campaigns. Now on display at the Egyptian Museum in Cairo, the stele is made of black granite and stands more than seven feet tall. It depicts two images of the god Amon facing outward to the pharaoh and the gods Mut and Horus. Near the end of the text, the stele contains the earliest mention of "Israel" from any official document outside the Bible. This verifies that Israel entered Canaan no later than the thirteenth century BC (Jos 4–5). Line 24 describes Merneptah's military victory over Israel. It says, "Israel is laid waste; its seed is not." While some skeptics have suggested that Israel did not enter Canaan until the ninth century BC, this stele recognizes Israel as a social entity in the promised land no later than the thirteenth century BC. This is consistent with biblical chronology.

10 The priests carrying the ark continued standing in the middle of the Jordan until everything was
completed that the LORD had commanded Joshua to
tell the people, in keeping with all that Moses had
commanded Joshua. The people hurried across, 11 and
after everyone had finished crossing, the priests with
the ark of the LORD crossed in the sight of the people.
12 The Reubenites, Gadites, and half the tribe of Manasseh went in battle formation in front of the Israelites, as Moses had instructed them. 13 About forty
thousand equipped for war crossed to the plains of
Jericho in the LORD's presence.

14 On that day the LORD exalted Joshua in the sight
of all Israel, and they revered him throughout his life,
as they had revered Moses. 15 The LORD told Joshua,
16 "Command the priests who carry the ark of the
testimony to come up from the Jordan."

17 So Joshua commanded the priests, "Come up
from the Jordan." 18 When the priests carrying the
ark of the LORD's covenant came up from the middle
of the Jordan, and their feet[A] stepped out on solid
ground, the water of the Jordan resumed its course,
flowing over all the banks as before.

19 The people came up from the Jordan on the tenth
day of the first month, and camped at Gilgal on the
eastern limits of Jericho. 20 Then Joshua set up in Gilgal the twelve stones they had taken from the Jordan,
21 and he said to the Israelites, "In the future, when
your children ask their fathers, 'What is the meaning
of these stones?' 22 you should tell your children, 'Israel crossed the Jordan on dry ground.' 23 For the LORD
your God dried up the water of the Jordan before you
until you had crossed over, just as the LORD your God
did to the Red Sea, which he dried up before us until
we had crossed over. 24 This is so that all the peoples
of the earth may know that the LORD's hand is strong,
and so that you may always fear the LORD your God."

CIRCUMCISION OF THE ISRAELITES

5 When all the Amorite kings across the Jordan
to the west and all the Canaanite kings near the
sea heard how the LORD had dried up the water of the
Jordan before the Israelites until they had crossed
over, they lost heart and their courage failed because
of the Israelites.

2 At that time the LORD said to Joshua, "Make flint
knives and circumcise the Israelite men again." 3 So
Joshua made flint knives and circumcised the Israelite men at Gibeath-haaraloth.[B] 4 This is the reason
Joshua circumcised them: All the people who came
out of Egypt who were males — all the men of war
— had died in the wilderness along the way after they
had come out of Egypt. 5 Though all the people who
came out were circumcised, none of the people born
in the wilderness along the way were circumcised
after they had come out of Egypt. 6 For the Israelites
wandered in the wilderness forty years until all the
nation's men of war who came out of Egypt had died
off because they did not obey the LORD. So the LORD
vowed never to let them see the land he had sworn
to their ancestors to give us, a land flowing with milk
and honey. 7 He raised up their sons in their place; it
was these Joshua circumcised. They were still uncircumcised, since they had not been circumcised
along the way. 8 After the entire nation had been circumcised, they stayed where they were in the camp
until they recovered. 9 The LORD then said to Joshua,
"Today I have rolled away the disgrace of Egypt from
you." Therefore, that place is still called Gilgal[C] today.

FOOD FROM THE LAND

10 While the Israelites camped at Gilgal on the plains
of Jericho, they observed the Passover on the evening of the fourteenth day of the month. 11 The day
after Passover they ate unleavened bread and roasted grain from the produce of the land. 12 And the
day after they ate from the produce of the land, the
manna ceased. Since there was no more manna for
the Israelites, they ate from the crops of the land of
Canaan that year.

[A] **4:18** Lit *and the soles of the feet of the priests* [B] **5:3** Or *The Hill of Foreskins* [C] **5:9** = to roll

COMMANDER OF THE LORD'S ARMY

13 When Joshua was near Jericho, he looked up and saw a man standing in front of him with a drawn sword in his hand. Joshua approached him and asked, "Are you for us or for our enemies?"

14 "Neither," he replied. "I have now come as commander of the LORD's army."

Then Joshua bowed with his face to the ground in homage and asked him, "What does my lord want to say to his servant?"

15 The commander of the LORD's army said to Joshua, "Remove the sandals from your feet, for the place where you are standing is holy." And Joshua did that.

THE CONQUEST OF JERICHO

6 Now Jericho was strongly fortified because of the Israelites — no one leaving or entering. 2 The LORD said to Joshua, "Look, I have handed Jericho, its king, and its best soldiers over to you. 3 March around the city with all the men of war, circling the city one time. Do this for six days. 4 Have seven priests carry seven ram's-horn trumpets in front of the ark. But on the seventh day, march around the city seven times, while the priests blow the rams' horns. 5 When there is a prolonged blast of the horn and you hear its sound, have all the troops give a mighty shout. Then the city wall will collapse, and the troops will advance, each man straight ahead."

6 So Joshua son of Nun summoned the priests and said to them, "Take up the ark of the covenant and have seven priests carry seven rams' horns in front of the ark of the LORD." 7 He said to the troops, "Move forward, march around the city, and have the armed men go ahead of the ark of the LORD."

8 After Joshua had spoken to the troops, seven priests carrying seven rams' horns before the LORD moved forward and blew the rams' horns; the ark of the LORD's covenant followed them. 9 While the rams' horns were blowing, the armed men went in front of the priests who blew the rams' horns, and the rear guard went behind the ark. 10 But Joshua had commanded the troops, "Do not shout or let your voice be heard. Don't let one word come out of your mouth until the time I say, 'Shout!' Then you are to shout." 11 So the ark of the LORD was carried around the city, circling it once. They returned to the camp and spent the night there.[A]

12 Joshua got up early the next morning. The priests took the ark of the LORD, 13 and the seven priests carrying seven rams' horns marched in front of the ark of the LORD. While the rams' horns were blowing, the armed men went in front of them, and the rear guard went behind the ark of the LORD. 14 On the second day they marched around the city once and returned to the camp. They did this for six days.

DIGGING DEEPER *Ruins of Jericho*

Jericho (Tell es-Sultan) is one of the oldest continuously inhabited cities in the world, dating back to thousands of years before Christ. It is located nine miles north of the Dead Sea and five miles west of the Jordan River adjacent to the arid Judean wilderness to the southwest and the fertile Jordan River Valley to the northeast. Archaeologists undertook four major excavation campaigns at Jericho during the late nineteenth and mid-twentieth centuries. These teams were unable to match the data chronologically with Joshua's conquest of Canaan as recorded in Scripture (Jos 6). However, in 1990 Bryant Wood of the Associates for Biblical Research reevaluated much of the previous data and concluded that Jericho's destruction must have occurred circa 1440 BC, bringing the conquest more in line with the biblical chronology. Wood also identified pieces of evidence that match biblical descriptions of Jericho's destruction. These include collapsed fortification walls (6:20), evidence that this occurred in springtime (2:6; 3:15; 5:10), evidence of fire damage (6:24), evidence of a short siege since the grain stores were not consumed (6:15,20), and evidence that, as the Bible says, the Hebrews were not permitted to use anything (such as grain) found within the city (6:17–18).

15 Early on the seventh day, they started at dawn and marched around the city seven times in the same way. That was the only day they marched around the city seven times. 16 After the seventh time, the priests blew the rams' horns, and Joshua said to the troops, "Shout! For the LORD has given you the city. 17 But the city and everything in it are set apart to the LORD for destruction. Only Rahab the prostitute and everyone with her in the house will live, because she hid the messengers we sent. 18 But keep yourselves from the things set apart, or you will be set apart for destruction. If you[B] take any of those things, you will set apart the camp of Israel for destruction and make trouble for it. 19 For all the silver and gold, and the articles of bronze and iron, are dedicated to the LORD and must go into the LORD's treasury."

20 So the troops shouted, and the rams' horns sounded. When they heard the blast of the ram's horn, the troops gave a great shout, and the wall collapsed. The troops advanced into the city, each man straight ahead, and they captured the city. 21 They completely

[A] **6:11** Lit *at the camp* [B] **6:18** LXX reads *you covet and*; Jos 7:21

The Peoples of Canaan

by Daniel P. Caldwell

A residential area at Ugarit (modern Ras Shamra, Syria). Archaeologists have excavated family houses and public buildings, including two temples, one dedicated to Baal and the other to Dagon. Workers also unearthed numerous administrative and economic documents. By about 1900 BC, the Amorites gained control of Ugarit and held that control until the city collapsed at the end of the Late Bronze Age, about 1200 BC.

As Joshua 3:10 makes plain, the political and cultural makeup of the promised land was diverse and lacking in unity. The Hebrews did not face one common foe. They faced a number of different small city-states, each with its own traditions, people, culture, and gods.

Before the Hebrews came into Canaan, the country was organized around major cities. No one had attempted to organize them into one central unit for times of defense. The book of Joshua describes the kings of these city-states banding together to form alliances (9:1–2; 10:1–5). No one king, however, could influence all of Canaan to unite in opposition to the Hebrews.

The cultural and religious influences of the people of the land did affect the Hebrews when they settled into Canaan. Most of the population lived in rural areas outside of the cities and usually had gardens and farms. It was an agrarian society. The primary crops included grain, grapes, and olives.

Canaanite religion did not differ greatly from those of Assyria and Babylon. The findings of religious texts at Ugarit have shed light on Canaanite religion. One of the distinctive characteristics of the Judeo-Christian religion is the acknowledgment and reverence of only one God. By contrast, religions of the biblical world were polytheistic, acknowledging and worshiping multiple gods.

The Canaanites referred to the chief deity of their pantheon (all the deities of a religion considered collectively) as El. As king of the deities, he was supposedly the creator god and a fertility god and usually depicted as a bull. El lived upon Mount Zaphon (Mount Casius), north of Ugarit.

Figurine from Lachish representing the goddess Astarte; dated from the ninth to seventh centuries BC. Figurines of this type clearly show that many Israelites continued to honor traditional Canaanite deities.

A second Canaanite deity was Athirat, whom the Old Testament refers to as Asherah (plural *asheroth* and *asherim*). While her worship was represented by a wooden object such as a pole, the Old Testament

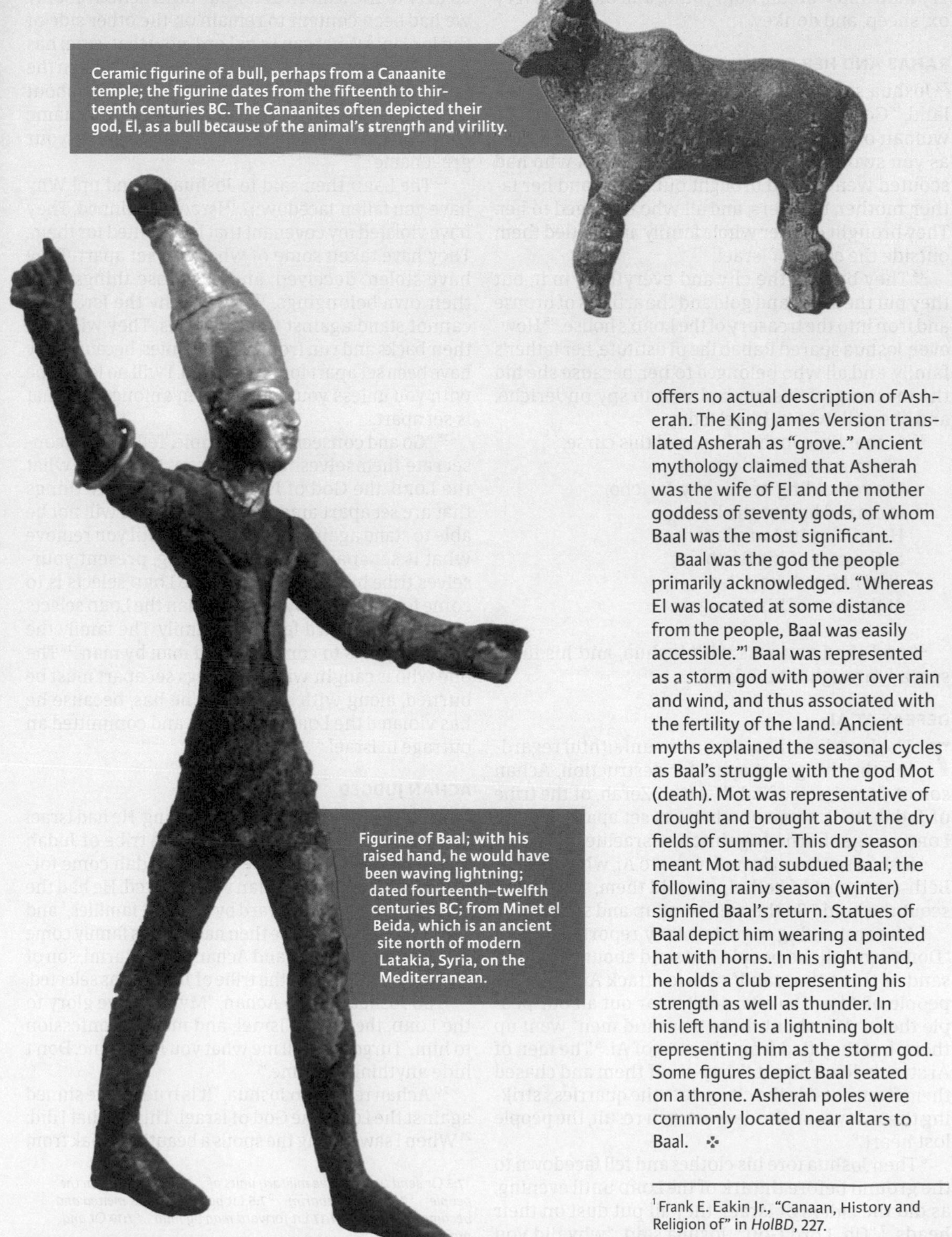

Ceramic figurine of a bull, perhaps from a Canaanite temple; the figurine dates from the fifteenth to thirteenth centuries BC. The Canaanites often depicted their god, El, as a bull because of the animal's strength and virility.

Figurine of Baal; with his raised hand, he would have been waving lightning; dated fourteenth–twelfth centuries BC; from Minet el Beida, which is an ancient site north of modern Latakia, Syria, on the Mediterranean.

offers no actual description of Asherah. The King James Version translated Asherah as "grove." Ancient mythology claimed that Asherah was the wife of El and the mother goddess of seventy gods, of whom Baal was the most significant.

Baal was the god the people primarily acknowledged. "Whereas El was located at some distance from the people, Baal was easily accessible."[1] Baal was represented as a storm god with power over rain and wind, and thus associated with the fertility of the land. Ancient myths explained the seasonal cycles as Baal's struggle with the god Mot (death). Mot was representative of drought and brought about the dry fields of summer. This dry season meant Mot had subdued Baal; the following rainy season (winter) signified Baal's return. Statues of Baal depict him wearing a pointed hat with horns. In his right hand, he holds a club representing his strength as well as thunder. In his left hand is a lightning bolt representing him as the storm god. Some figures depict Baal seated on a throne. Asherah poles were commonly located near altars to Baal. ✣

[1] Frank E. Eakin Jr., "Canaan, History and Religion of" in *HolBD*, 227.

destroyed everything in the city with the sword — every man and woman, both young and old, and every ox, sheep, and donkey.

RAHAB AND HER FAMILY SPARED

22 Joshua said to the two men who had scouted the land, "Go to the prostitute's house and bring the woman out of there, and all who are with her, just as you swore to her." 23 So the young men who had scouted went in and brought out Rahab and her father, mother, brothers, and all who belonged to her. They brought out her whole family and settled them outside the camp of Israel.

24 They burned the city and everything in it, but they put the silver and gold and the articles of bronze and iron into the treasury of the LORD's house. 25 However, Joshua spared Rahab the prostitute, her father's family, and all who belonged to her, because she hid the messengers Joshua had sent to spy on Jericho, and she still lives in Israel today.

26 At that time Joshua imposed this curse:

The man who undertakes
the rebuilding of this city, Jericho,
is cursed before the LORD.
He will lay its foundation
at the cost of his firstborn;
he will finish its gates
at the cost of his youngest.

27 And the LORD was with Joshua, and his fame spread throughout the land.

DEFEAT AT AI

7 The Israelites, however, were unfaithful regarding the things set apart for destruction. Achan son of Carmi, son of Zabdi, son of Zerah, of the tribe of Judah, took some of what was set apart, and the LORD's anger burned against the Israelites.

2 Joshua sent men from Jericho to Ai, which is near Beth-aven, east of Bethel, and told them, "Go up and scout the land." So the men went up and scouted Ai.

3 After returning to Joshua they reported to him, "Don't send all the people, but send about two thousand or three thousand[A] men to attack Ai. Since the people of Ai are so few, don't wear out all our people there." 4 So about three thousand men[B] went up there, but they fled from the men of Ai. 5 The men of Ai struck down about thirty-six of them and chased them from outside the city gate to the quarries,[C] striking them down on the descent. As a result, the people lost heart.[D]

6 Then Joshua tore his clothes and fell facedown to the ground before the ark of the LORD until evening, as did the elders of Israel; they all put dust on their heads. 7 "Oh, Lord GOD," Joshua said, "why did you ever bring these people across the Jordan to hand us over to the Amorites for our destruction? If only we had been content to remain on the other side of the Jordan! 8 What can I say, Lord, now that Israel has turned its back and run from its enemies? 9 When the Canaanites and all who live in the land hear about this, they will surround us and wipe out our name from the earth. Then what will you do about your great name?"

10 The LORD then said to Joshua, "Stand up! Why have you fallen facedown? 11 Israel has sinned. They have violated my covenant that I appointed for them. They have taken some of what was set apart. They have stolen, deceived, and put those things with their own belongings. 12 This is why the Israelites cannot stand against their enemies. They will turn their backs and run from their enemies, because they have been set apart for destruction. I will no longer be with you unless you remove from among you what is set apart.

13 "Go and consecrate the people. Tell them to consecrate themselves for tomorrow, for this is what the LORD, the God of Israel, says: There are things that are set apart among you, Israel. You will not be able to stand against your enemies until you remove what is set apart. 14 In the morning, present yourselves tribe by tribe. The tribe the LORD selects is to come forward clan by clan. The clan the LORD selects is to come forward family by family. The family the LORD selects is to come forward man by man. 15 The one who is caught with the things set apart must be burned, along with everything he has, because he has violated the LORD's covenant and committed an outrage in Israel."

ACHAN JUDGED

16 Joshua got up early the next morning. He had Israel come forward tribe by tribe, and the tribe of Judah was selected. 17 He had the clans of Judah come forward, and the Zerahite clan was selected. He had the Zerahite clan come forward by heads of families,[E] and Zabdi was selected. 18 He then had Zabdi's family come forward man by man, and Achan son of Carmi, son of Zabdi, son of Zerah, of the tribe of Judah, was selected.

19 So Joshua said to Achan, "My son, give glory to the LORD, the God of Israel, and make a confession to him.[F] I urge you, tell me what you have done. Don't hide anything from me."

20 Achan replied to Joshua, "It is true. I have sinned against the LORD, the God of Israel. This is what I did: 21 When I saw among the spoils a beautiful cloak from

[A] **7:3** Or *send two or three military units of* [B] **7:4** Lit *men from the people* [C] **7:5** Or *to Shebarim* [D] **7:5** Lit *people's hearts melted and became like water* [E] **7:17** Lit *forward man by man* [F] **7:19** Or *and praise him*

Babylon,[A] five pounds[B] of silver, and a bar of gold weighing a pound and a quarter,[C] I coveted them and took them. You can see for yourself. They are concealed in the ground inside my tent, with the silver under the cloak." 22 So Joshua sent messengers who ran to the tent, and there was the cloak, concealed in his tent, with the silver underneath. 23 They took the things from inside the tent, brought them to Joshua and all the Israelites, and spread them out in the LORD's presence.

24 Then Joshua and all Israel with him took Achan son of Zerah, the silver, the cloak, and the bar of gold, his sons and daughters, his ox, donkey, and sheep, his tent, and all that he had, and brought them up to the Valley of Achor. 25 Joshua said, "Why have you brought us trouble? Today the LORD will bring you trouble!" So all Israel stoned them[D] to death. They burned their bodies, threw stones on them, 26 and raised over him a large pile of rocks that remains still today. Then the LORD turned from his burning anger. Therefore that place is called the Valley of Achor[E] still today.

CONQUEST OF AI

8 The LORD said to Joshua, "Do not be afraid or discouraged. Take all the troops with you and go attack Ai. Look, I have handed over to you the king of Ai, his people, city, and land. 2 Treat Ai and its king as you did Jericho and its king, except that you may plunder its spoil and livestock for yourselves. Set an ambush behind the city."

3 So Joshua and all the troops set out to attack Ai. Joshua selected thirty thousand of his best soldiers and sent them out at night. 4 He commanded them, "Pay attention. Lie in ambush behind the city, not too far from it, and all of you be ready. 5 Then I and all the people who are with me will approach the city. When they come out against us as they did the first time, we will flee from them. 6 They will come after us until we have drawn them away from the city, for they will say, 'They are fleeing from us as before.' While we are fleeing from them, 7 you are to come out of your ambush and seize the city. The LORD your God will hand it over to you. 8 After taking the city, set it on fire. Follow the LORD's command — see that you do as I have ordered you." 9 So Joshua sent them out, and they went to the ambush site and waited between Bethel and Ai, to the west of Ai. But he spent that night with the troops.

10 Joshua started early the next morning and mobilized them. Then he and the elders of Israel led the people up to Ai. 11 All the troops who were with him went up and approached the city, arriving opposite Ai, and camped to the north of it, with a valley between them and the city. 12 Now Joshua had taken about five thousand men and set them in ambush between Bethel and Ai, to the west of the city. 13 The troops were stationed in this way: the main[F] camp to the north of the city and its rear guard to the west of the city. And that night Joshua went into the valley.

14 When the king of Ai saw the Israelites, the men of the city hurried and went out early in the morning so that he and all his people could engage Israel in battle at a suitable place facing the Arabah. But he did not know there was an ambush waiting for him behind the city. 15 Joshua and all Israel pretended to be beaten back by them and fled toward the wilderness. 16 Then all the troops of Ai were summoned to pursue them, and they pursued Joshua and were drawn away from the city. 17 Not a man was left in Ai or Bethel who did not go out after Israel, leaving the city exposed while they pursued Israel.

18 Then the LORD said to Joshua, "Hold out the javelin in your hand toward Ai, for I will hand the city over to you." So Joshua held out his javelin toward it. 19 When he held out his hand, the men in ambush rose quickly from their position. They ran, entered the city, captured it, and immediately set it on fire.

20 The men of Ai turned and looked back, and smoke from the city was rising to the sky! They could not escape in any direction, and the troops who had fled to the wilderness now became the pursuers. 21 When Joshua and all Israel saw that the men in ambush had captured the city and that smoke was rising from it, they turned back and struck down the men of Ai. 22 Then men in ambush came out of the city against them, and the men of Ai were trapped between the Israelite forces, some on one side and some on the other. They struck them down until no survivor or fugitive remained, 23 but they captured the king of Ai alive and brought him to Joshua.

24 When Israel had finished killing everyone living in Ai who had pursued them into the open country, and when every last one of them had fallen by the sword, all Israel returned to Ai and struck it down with the sword. 25 The total of those who fell that day, both men and women, was twelve thousand — all the people of Ai. 26 Joshua did not draw back his hand that was holding the javelin until all the inhabitants of Ai were completely destroyed. 27 Israel plundered only the cattle and spoil of that city for themselves, according to the LORD's command that he had given Joshua.

28 Joshua burned Ai and left it a permanent ruin, still desolate today. 29 He hung[G] the body of the king of Ai on a tree[H] until evening, and at sunset Joshua commanded that they take his body down from the tree. They threw it down at the entrance of the city gate and put a large pile of rocks over it, which still remains today.

[A] **7:21** Lit *Shinar* [B] **7:21** Lit *200 shekels* [C] **7:21** Lit *50 shekels*
[D] **7:25** Lit *him* [E] **7:26** Or *of Trouble* [F] **8:13** Lit *way: all the*
[G] **8:29** Or *impaled* [H] **8:29** Or *wooden stake*

Jericho: A Strategic Locale

by David L. Jenkins

The base of a round Neolithic tower dated to about 8000 BC. The tower, which measures about twenty-eight feet in diameter at the base and twenty-five feet tall, has an internal staircase. Especially considering that workers had only stone tools, the tower was a remarkable engineering feat.

The word *Jericho* means either "a place of fragrance," maybe referring to the prolific flowers native to the area, or "place of the moon," alluding to this being a site where people worshiped the lunar gods, which they believed controlled the seasons. Jericho has deep roots in the early history of Bible lands and places. Surrounding the ancient city were walls so massive that houses were built upon them (Jos 2:15). The remains of Old Testament and prehistoric Jericho lie beneath a mound known as Tell es-Sultan. This mound is located on the west side of the Jordan Valley, approximately ten miles north of the Dead Sea and four miles west of the Jordan River.

A spring, 'Ain es-Sultan, provides ample water to the site, producing up to a thousand gallons per minute. The spring hydrates an oasis that stretches from Jericho eastward toward the Jordan. This spring and the area's fertile soil attracted settlers from as early as the Mesolithic Age (10,000–8000 BC). The oldest known building on the site dates to about 9250 BC. Unlike other inhabited places from early in the Neolithic Era (8000–4500 BC), Jericho was a walled site. "By 8000 BC a walled town (the world's earliest) of about 10 acres had been built."[1] The wall, constructed of huge stones, stood more than nineteen feet tall. "A massive round tower within the wall was amazingly well constructed. The tower measured 8.5 m [27.9 ft] in diameter and is preserved to a height of 7.7 m [25.3 ft]; it was built with a solid stone core, and a steep stairway led to its top."[2] Jericho has consequently been called the "Citadel of the Neolithic Age."[3] Archaeologists have thus found at Jericho evidence of prehistoric nomads who were hunter-gatherers; later, those who developed a village on the site; and still later, those who established permanent dwellings, farmed the area, and had domesticated animals. Also emerging durling this era was the expansion of human technology. People moved from developing polished stone implements to making crudely fired ceramic vessels. Jericho is the oldest biblical city to show all of these types of progression.[4]

Archaeological evidence indicates the site was abandoned about 4000 BC but began to repopulate about seven hundred years later. By the time of Abraham, Isaac, and Jacob, people in Jericho were living civilized lives. Archaeologists have found at Jericho tombs dated to about 1600 BC, wooden furniture, fine pottery, wooden boxes with inlaid decorations, and basketwork.[5] As the Israelites settled into Canaan, Joshua assigned Jericho to the tribe of Benjamin (Jos 18:21). Even though ancient Jericho was destroyed some time after this, a small settlement remained, assuring the continuity of life in that area.

By the time Jesus encountered Zacchaeus the tax collector there,

Part of the ruins of Herod's palace at Jericho.

no doubt Jericho was more than a small, nondescript village. In fact, Herod the Great had fortified the city and built several new palaces there, naming them after his friends. He retired and died in Jericho. Jericho's, and by extension Zacchaeus's, wealth no doubt came in part from taxes on the salt, sulfur, and bitumen (natural products of the Dead Sea) as they passed through the city. Wealth acquired from this trade likely contributed considerably to the city's many building projects.

The Synoptic Gospels record Jesus's encounter with beggars in Jericho (Mt 20:29–34; Mk 10:46–52; Lk 18:35–43). Beggars would have considered such a prosperous city an ideal place to assure an income for themselves.

Another plus for Jericho was the city's location near a major ford in the Jordan River. This made the city a natural gateway from the Transjordan and the plains of Moab to the region that lay westward beyond the Jordan River (Nm 22:1; 26:3; 31:12; 33:48,50; 35:1; Dt 32:49; Jos 2:1). Situated on the major east-west trade route, Jericho controlled the traffic flow from the Transjordan area into the central hill country. This included the city of Jerusalem, which was approximately fourteen miles southwest of Jericho. To further enhance the importance of Jericho's geographical significance was its location on an important north-south highway that connected the city to Beth-shean to the north. Consequently for an invading army to possess Jericho carried many benefits, including control of the major entrance to western Canaan from the Transjordan, possession of the water rights and oasis-like garden land east of the city, and control of the mineral traffic in the area of the Dead Sea. ❖

[1] Karen Joines and Eric Mitchell, "Jericho" in *HIBD*, 886. [2] Amihai Mazar, *Archaeology of the Land of the Bible 10,000–586 B.C.E.* (New York: Doubleday, 1992), 41. [3] LaMoine F. DeVries, *Cities of the Biblical World* (Peabody, MA: Hendrickson, 1997), 189. [4] Charles F. Pfeiffer, ed., *The Biblical World* (Nashville: Broadman, 1976), 306. [5] Pat Alexander, ed., *The Lion Encyclopedia of the Bible* (Pleasantville, NY: Reader's Digest, 1987), 264.

The Wadi Qelt, a dry riverbed in New Testament Jericho. The wadi ran through the middle of Herod's winter palace complex.

RENEWED COMMITMENT TO THE LAW

30 At that time Joshua built an altar on Mount Ebal to the LORD, the God of Israel, 31 just as Moses the LORD's servant had commanded the Israelites. He built it according to what is written in the book of the law of Moses: an altar of uncut stones on which no iron tool has been used. Then they offered burnt offerings to the LORD and sacrificed fellowship offerings on it. 32 There on the stones, Joshua copied the law of Moses, which he had written in the presence of the Israelites. 33 All Israel — resident alien and citizen alike — with their elders, officers, and judges, stood on either side of the ark of the LORD's covenant facing the Levitical priests who carried it. Half of them were in front of Mount Gerizim and half in front of Mount Ebal, as Moses the LORD's servant had commanded earlier concerning blessing the people of Israel. 34 Afterward, Joshua read aloud all the words of the law — the blessings as well as the curses — according to all that is written in the book of the law. 35 There was not a word of all that Moses had commanded that Joshua did not read before the entire assembly of Israel, including the women, the dependents, and the resident aliens who lived among them.

DECEPTION BY GIBEON

9 When all the kings heard about Jericho and Ai, those who were west of the Jordan in the hill country, in the Judean foothills,[A] and all along the coast of the Mediterranean Sea toward Lebanon — the Hethites, Amorites, Canaanites, Perizzites, Hivites, and Jebusites — 2 they formed a unified alliance to fight against Joshua and Israel.

3 When the inhabitants of Gibeon heard what Joshua had done to Jericho and Ai, 4 they acted deceptively. They gathered provisions[B] and took worn-out sacks on their donkeys and old wineskins, cracked and mended. 5 They wore old, patched sandals on their feet and threadbare clothing on their bodies. Their entire provision of bread was dry and crumbly. 6 They went to Joshua in the camp at Gilgal and said to him and the men of Israel, "We have come from a distant land. Please make a treaty with us."

7 The men of Israel replied to the Hivites, "Perhaps you live among us. How can we make a treaty with you?"

8 They said to Joshua, "We are your servants."

Then Joshua asked them, "Who are you and where do you come from?"

9 They replied to him, "Your servants have come from a faraway land because of the reputation of the LORD your God. For we have heard of his fame, and all that he did in Egypt, 10 and all that he did to the two Amorite kings beyond the Jordan — King Sihon of Heshbon and King Og of Bashan, who was in Ashtaroth. 11 So our elders and all the inhabitants of our land told us, 'Take provisions with you for the journey; go and meet them and say, "We are your servants. Please make a treaty with us." ' 12 This bread of ours was warm when we took it from our houses as food on the day we left to come to you; but see, it is now dry and crumbly. 13 These wineskins were new when we filled them; but see, they are cracked. And these clothes and sandals of ours are worn out from the extremely long journey." 14 Then the men of Israel took some of their provisions, but did not seek the LORD's decision. 15 So Joshua established peace with them and made a treaty to let them live, and the leaders of the community swore an oath to them.

GIBEON'S DECEPTION DISCOVERED

16 Three days after making the treaty with them, they heard that the Gibeonites were their neighbors, living among them. 17 So the Israelites set out and reached the Gibeonite cities on the third day. Now their cities were Gibeon, Chephirah, Beeroth, and Kiriath-jearim. 18 But the Israelites did not attack them, because the leaders of the community had sworn an oath to them by the LORD, the God of Israel. Then the whole community grumbled against the leaders.

19 All the leaders answered them, "We have sworn an oath to them by the LORD, the God of Israel, and now we cannot touch them. 20 This is how we will treat them: we will let them live, so that no wrath will fall on us because of the oath we swore to them." 21 They also said, "Let them live." So the Gibeonites became woodcutters and water carriers for the whole community, as the leaders had promised them.

22 Joshua summoned the Gibeonites and said to them, "Why did you deceive us by telling us you live far away from us, when in fact you live among us? 23 Therefore you are cursed and will always be slaves — woodcutters and water carriers for the house of my God."

24 The Gibeonites answered him, "It was clearly communicated to your servants that the LORD your God had commanded his servant Moses to give you all the land and to destroy all the inhabitants of the land before you. We greatly feared for our lives because of you, and that is why we did this. 25 Now we are in your hands. Do to us whatever you think is right." 26 This is what Joshua did to them: he rescued them from the Israelites, and they did not kill them. 27 On that day he made them woodcutters and water carriers — as they are today — for the community and for the LORD's altar at the place he would choose.

[A] **9:1** Or *the Shephelah* [B] **9:4** Some Hb mss, LXX, Syr, Vg; other Hb mss read *They went disguised as ambassadors*

Ai

by Daniel P. Caldwell

Ruins of Early Bronze Age public buildings atop the acropolis of the ancient city of Ai.

The city of Ai probably began as a village, as did other sites in the surrounding area. During the Early Canaanite I Age, this city became fortified. The logical reason for fortification may have been a dominant nation, such as Egypt, penetrating into the land.[1] At the same time Ai was fortified, other cities in the southern region were also fortified.

An extraordinary structure made of large stones, the wall surrounding the early city of Ai had a width of nineteen feet and a height of about twenty-one feet. The wall encompassed an area of about twenty-seven acres. This made the city considerably larger than Jerusalem (known then as Jebus), which was about eight to ten acres in size at this time in Israel's history.[2] Archaeologists discovered within the early city a large public pool for water collection. The pool, which was "constructed inside the corner of the city wall," held about eighteen hundred to two thousand cubic meters of water. "This would be enough to supplement rainfall and other sources for a population of 2,000 inhabitants."[3] ✣

---

[1] Yohanan Aharoni, *The Archaeology of the Land of Israel*, trans. Anson F. Rainey (Philadelphia: Westminster, 1982), 57.
[2] Aharoni, *Archaeology*, 59. [3] Joseph A. Callaway, "Ai" in *ABD*, 129.

THE DAY THE SUN STOOD STILL

10 Now King Adoni-zedek of Jerusalem heard that Joshua had captured Ai and completely destroyed it, treating Ai and its king as he had Jericho and its king, and that the inhabitants of Gibeon had made peace with Israel and were living among them. 2 So Adoni-zedek and his people were[A] greatly alarmed because Gibeon was a large city like one of the royal cities; it was larger than Ai, and all its men were warriors. 3 Therefore King Adoni-zedek of Jerusalem sent word to King Hoham of Hebron, King Piram of Jarmuth, King Japhia of Lachish, and King Debir of Eglon, saying, 4 "Come up and help me. We will attack Gibeon, because they have made peace with Joshua and the Israelites." 5 So the five Amorite kings — the kings of Jerusalem, Hebron, Jarmuth, Lachish, and Eglon — joined forces, advanced with all their armies, besieged Gibeon, and fought against it.

6 Then the men of Gibeon sent word to Joshua in the camp at Gilgal: "Don't give up on your servants. Come quickly and save us! Help us, for all the Amorite kings living in the hill country have joined forces against us." 7 So Joshua and all his troops, including all his best soldiers, came from Gilgal.

8 The LORD said to Joshua, "Do not be afraid of them, for I have handed them over to you. Not one of them will be able to stand against you."

9 So Joshua caught them by surprise, after marching all night from Gilgal. 10 The LORD threw them into confusion before Israel. He defeated them in a great slaughter at Gibeon, chased them through the ascent of Beth-horon, and struck them down as far as Azekah and Makkedah. 11 As they fled before Israel, the LORD threw large hailstones on them from the sky along the descent of Beth-horon all the way to Azekah, and they died. More of them died from the hail than the Israelites killed with the sword.

12 On the day the LORD gave the Amorites over to the Israelites, Joshua spoke to the LORD in the presence of Israel:

"Sun, stand still over Gibeon,
and moon, over the Valley of Aijalon."
13 And the sun stood still
and the moon stopped
until the nation took vengeance
on its enemies.

Isn't this written in the Book of Jashar?[B]

So the sun stopped
in the middle of the sky
and delayed its setting
almost a full day.

14 There has been no day like it before or since, when the LORD listened to a man, because the LORD fought for Israel. 15 Then Joshua and all Israel with him returned to the camp at Gilgal.

EXECUTION OF THE FIVE KINGS

16 Now the five defeated kings had fled and hidden in the cave at Makkedah. 17 It was reported to Joshua, "The five kings have been found; they are hiding in the cave at Makkedah."

18 Joshua said, "Roll large stones against the mouth of the cave, and station men by it to guard the kings. 19 But as for the rest of you, don't stay there. Pursue your enemies and attack them from behind. Don't let them enter their cities, for the LORD your God has handed them over to you." 20 So Joshua and the Israelites finished inflicting a terrible slaughter on them until they were destroyed, although a few survivors ran away to the fortified cities. 21 The people returned safely to Joshua in the camp at Makkedah. And no one dared to threaten the Israelites.

22 Then Joshua said, "Open the mouth of the cave, and bring those five kings to me out of there." 23 That is what they did. They brought the five kings of Jerusalem, Hebron, Jarmuth, Lachish, and Eglon to Joshua out of the cave. 24 When they had brought the kings to him, Joshua summoned all the men of Israel and said to the military commanders who had accompanied him, "Come here and put your feet on the necks of these kings." So the commanders came forward and put their feet on their necks. 25 Joshua said to them, "Do not be afraid or discouraged. Be strong and courageous, for the LORD will do this to all the enemies you fight."

26 After this, Joshua struck them down and executed them. He hung[C] their bodies on five trees[D] and they were there until evening. 27 At sunset Joshua commanded that they be taken down from the trees and thrown into the cave where they had hidden. Then large stones were placed against the mouth of the cave, and the stones are still there today.

CONQUEST OF SOUTHERN CITIES

28 On that day Joshua captured Makkedah and struck it down with the sword, including its king. He completely destroyed it[E] and everyone in it, leaving no survivors. So he treated the king of Makkedah as he had the king of Jericho.

29 Joshua and all Israel with him crossed from Makkedah to Libnah and fought against Libnah. 30 The LORD also handed it and its king over to Israel. He struck it down, putting everyone in it to the sword, and left no survivors in it. He treated Libnah's king as he had the king of Jericho.

31 From Libnah, Joshua and all Israel with him crossed to Lachish. They laid siege to it and attacked it. 32 The LORD handed Lachish over to Israel, and Joshua captured it on the second day. He struck it down,

[A] **10:2** One Hb ms, Syr, Vg read *So he was* [B] **10:13** Or *of the Upright*
[C] **10:26** Or *impaled* [D] **10:26** Or *wooden stakes*, also in v. 27
[E] **10:28** Some Hb mss read *them*

putting everyone in it to the sword, just as he had done to Libnah. 33 At that time King Horam of Gezer went to help Lachish, but Joshua struck him down along with his people, leaving no survivors.

34 Then Joshua crossed from Lachish to Eglon and all Israel with him. They laid siege to it and attacked it. 35 On that day they captured it and struck it down, putting everyone in it to the sword. He completely destroyed it that day, just as he had done to Lachish.

36 Next, Joshua and all Israel with him went up from Eglon to Hebron and attacked it. 37 They captured it and struck down its king, all its villages, and everyone in it with the sword. He left no survivors, just as he had done at Eglon. He completely destroyed Hebron and everyone in it.

38 Finally, Joshua turned toward Debir and attacked it. And all Israel was with him. 39 He captured it — its king and all its villages. They struck them down with the sword and completely destroyed everyone in it, leaving no survivors. He treated Debir and its king as he had treated Hebron and as he had treated Libnah and its king.

40 So Joshua conquered the whole region — the hill country, the Negev, the Judean foothills,[A] and the slopes — with all their kings, leaving no survivors. He completely destroyed every living being, as the LORD, the God of Israel, had commanded. 41 Joshua conquered everyone from Kadesh-barnea to Gaza, and all the land of Goshen as far as Gibeon. 42 Joshua captured all these kings and their land in one campaign, because the LORD, the God of Israel, fought for Israel. 43 Then Joshua returned with all Israel to the camp at Gilgal.

CONQUEST OF NORTHERN CITIES

11 When King Jabin of Hazor heard this news, he sent a message to: King Jobab of Madon, the kings of Shimron and Achshaph, 2 and the kings of the north in the hill country, the Arabah south of Chinnereth, the Judean foothills,[B] and the Slopes of Dor[C] to the west, 3 the Canaanites in the east and west, the Amorites, Hethites, Perizzites, and Jebusites in the hill country, and the Hivites at the foot of Hermon in the land of Mizpah. 4 They went out with all their armies — a multitude as numerous as the sand on the seashore — along with a vast number of horses and chariots. 5 All these kings joined forces; they came and camped together at the Waters of Merom to attack Israel.

6 The LORD said to Joshua, "Do not be afraid of them, for at this time tomorrow I will cause all of them to be killed before Israel. You are to hamstring their horses and burn their chariots." 7 So Joshua and all his troops surprised them at the Waters of Merom and attacked them. 8 The LORD handed them over to Israel, and they struck them down, pursuing them as far as greater Sidon and Misrephoth-maim, and to the east as far as the Valley of Mizpeh. They struck them down, leaving no survivors. 9 Joshua treated them as the LORD had told him; he hamstrung their horses and burned their chariots.

10 At that time Joshua turned back, captured Hazor, and struck down its king with the sword, because Hazor had formerly been the leader of all these kingdoms. 11 They struck down everyone in it with the sword, completely destroying them; he left no one alive. Then he burned Hazor.

12 Joshua captured all these kings and their cities and struck them down with the sword. He completely destroyed them, as Moses the LORD's servant had commanded. 13 However, Israel did not burn any of the cities that stood on their mounds except Hazor, which Joshua burned. 14 The Israelites plundered all the spoils and cattle of these cities for themselves. But they struck down every person with the sword until they had annihilated them, leaving no one alive. 15 Just as the LORD had commanded his servant Moses, Moses commanded Joshua. That is what Joshua did, leaving nothing undone of all that the LORD had commanded Moses.

SUMMARY OF CONQUESTS

16 So Joshua took all this land — the hill country, all the Negev, all the land of Goshen, the foothills, the Arabah, and the hill country of Israel with its foothills — 17 from Mount Halak, which ascends to Seir, as far as Baal-gad in the Valley of Lebanon at the foot of Mount Hermon. He captured all their kings and struck them down, putting them to death. 18 Joshua waged war with all these kings for a long time. 19 No city made peace with the Israelites except the Hivites who inhabited Gibeon; all of them were taken in battle. 20 For it was the LORD's intention to harden their hearts, so that they would engage Israel in battle, be completely destroyed without mercy, and be annihilated, just as the LORD had commanded Moses.

21 At that time Joshua proceeded to exterminate the Anakim from the hill country — Hebron, Debir, Anab — all the hill country of Judah and of Israel. Joshua completely destroyed them with their cities. 22 No Anakim were left in the land of the Israelites, except for some remaining in Gaza, Gath, and Ashdod.

23 So Joshua took the entire land, in keeping with all that the LORD had told Moses. Joshua then gave it as an inheritance to Israel according to their tribal allotments. After this, the land had rest from war.

[A] **10:40** Or *the Shephelah* [B] **11:2** Or *Shephelah*, also in v. 16
[C] **11:2** Or *and in Naphoth-dor*

Joshua: Leader of the Conquest

by Bryan E. Beyer

Joshua son of Nun played a significant role in God's purpose for Israel. Under his leadership, the Israelites conquered Canaan and divided it among the tribes. Joshua's name means "Yahweh has saved" or "Yahweh is salvation." His name is thus related to the names Isaiah and Hosea, and the name Joshua was Jesus's Hebrew name as well.

Joshua's work essentially involved two purposes: conquer the land of Canaan, and allot it to Israel's tribes. The conquest of Canaan included three major campaigns: a central campaign, a southern campaign, and a northern campaign.[1] These campaigns lasted approximately five to six years altogether; as they concluded, Israel had achieved effective control of Canaan, though some groups of people remained in the land.[2]

After the battle of Jericho, Joshua achieved control of the central plateau without a fight by making a treaty with the deceitful Gibeonites. In doing so, he cut the land in half, isolating northern and southern Canaan. A southern coalition of kings recognized the threat Joshua posed, but Joshua and his army routed the coalition and then extended the battle southward, conquering the major cities and towns. To the north, Jabin king of Hazor assembled another coalition of kings to face Joshua. God again gave Joshua success as Israel's army defeated the coalition and then pressed the battle throughout the northern territory's cities and towns. Israel thus achieved effective control of the promised land.

The Lord gave Joshua many strengths. First, he was a good

Bronze quiver fragment from Urartu. The relief illustrates the Tree of Life flanked by priests.

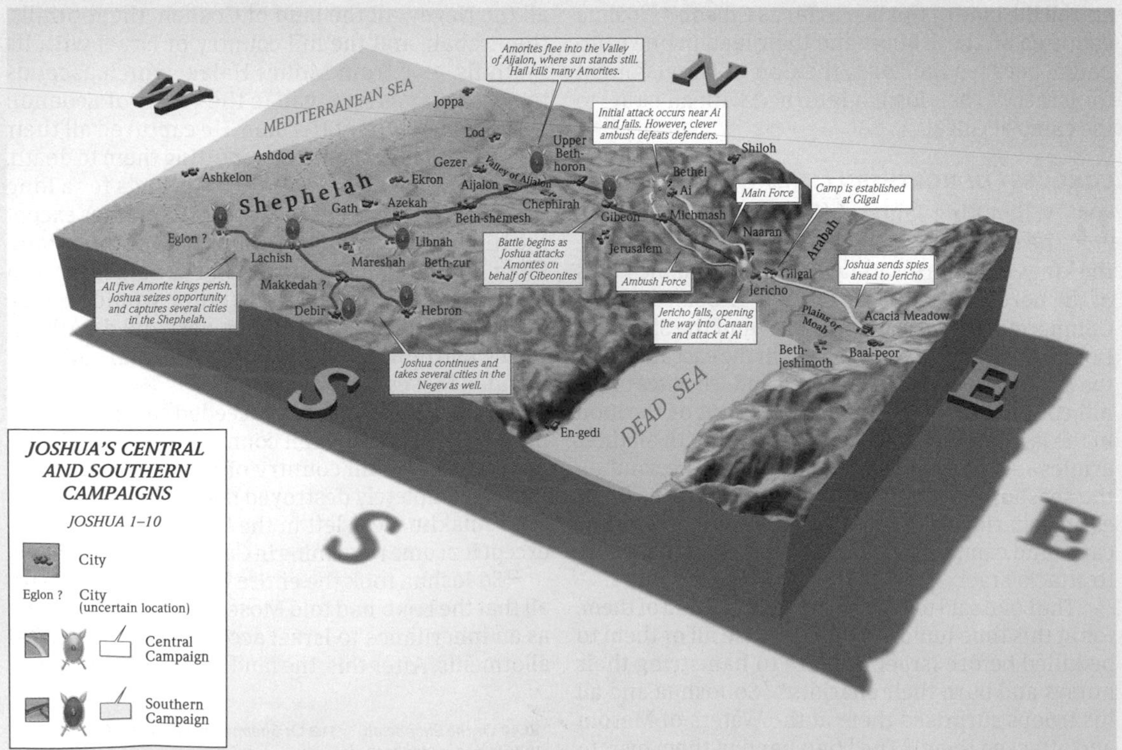

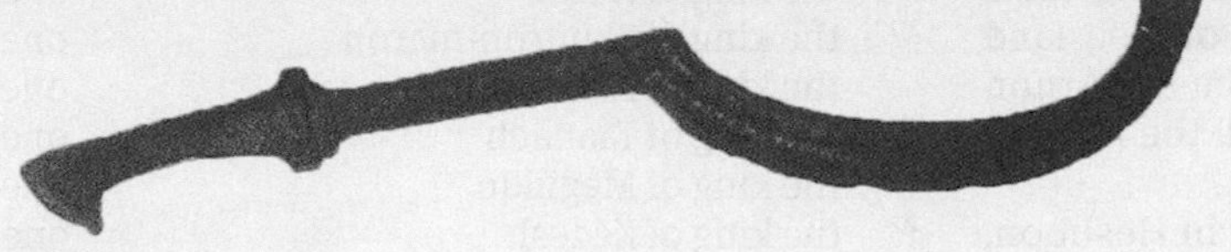

Hittite sickle sword.

Duck bill ax head.

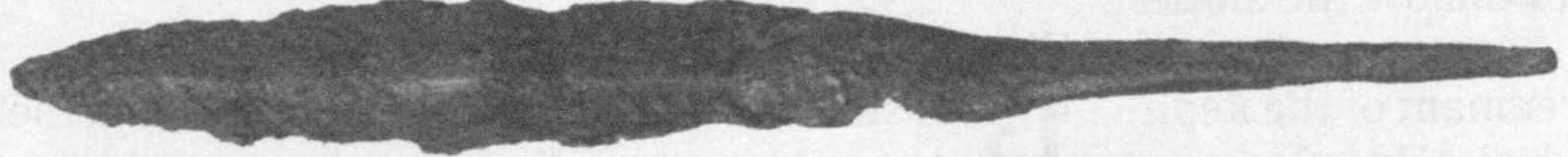

Bronze arrowhead; from Tel Dan; Late Bronze Age (1550–1200 BC).

Chisel ax head.

Bronze Hittite helmet from Urartu.

leader; the people saw God's hand on him and followed him. Second, he was a good general; he remembered the land well from when he surveyed it as one of Israel's twelve spies, and he used his knowledge of the land to help Israel achieve victory. Third, he was a man of faith; he persevered for forty-five years as he awaited the fulfillment of God's promise.[3] He also expressed his faith publicly on many occasions and led the Israelites in renewing their faith pledge to God. ✠

[1] Bill T. Arnold and Bryan E. Beyer, *Encountering the Old Testament: A Christian Survey*, 2nd ed. (Grand Rapids: Baker Academic, 2008), 172–76. [2] Donald H. Madvig, "Joshua" in *The Expositor's Bible Commentary*, ed. Frank E. Gaebelein, vol. 3 (Grand Rapids: Zondervan, 1992), 311. [3] "The time periods referred to in vv. 7 and 10 give us an insight into the period of time covered by most of the Book of Joshua. Israel was sentenced to forty years of wandering in the wilderness after the spies came back with their report (Num 14:33-34). Verse 10 shows that forty-five years had elapsed since the time of this sentence, so the conquest to date had occupied some five years." David M. Howard Jr., *Joshua*, vol. 5 in NAC (1998), 329.

TERRITORY EAST OF THE JORDAN

12 The Israelites struck down the following kings
of the land and took possession of their land
beyond the Jordan to the east and from the Arnon
River to Mount Hermon, including all the Arabah
eastward:
2 King Sihon of the Amorites lived in Heshbon.
He ruled from Aroer on the rim of the Arnon River,
along the middle of the valley, and half of Gilead up
to the Jabbok River (the border of the Ammonites),
3 the Arabah east of the Sea of Chinnereth[A] to the Sea
of Arabah (that is, the Dead Sea), eastward through
Beth-jeshimoth and southward[B] below the slopes
of Pisgah.
4 King Og[C] of Bashan, of the remnant of the Rephaim, lived in Ashtaroth and Edrei. 5 He ruled over
Mount Hermon, Salecah, all Bashan up to the Gesh-
urite and Maacathite border, and half of Gilead to
the border of King Sihon of Heshbon. 6 Moses the
LORD's servant and the Israelites struck them down.
And Moses the LORD's servant gave their land as an
inheritance to the Reubenites, Gadites, and half the
tribe of Manasseh.

TERRITORY WEST OF THE JORDAN

7 Joshua and the Israelites struck down the following kings of the land beyond the Jordan to the
west, from Baal-gad in the Valley of Lebanon to
Mount Halak, which ascends toward Seir (Joshua
gave their land as an inheritance to the tribes of
Israel according to their allotments: 8 the hill country, the Judean foothills,[D] the Arabah, the slopes,
the wilderness, and the Negev — the lands of the
Hethites, Amorites, Canaanites, Perizzites, Hivites,
and Jebusites):

9 the king of Jericho one
the king of Ai, which is next to Bethel one
10 the king of Jerusalem one
the king of Hebron one
11 the king of Jarmuth one
the king of Lachish one
12 the king of Eglon one
the king of Gezer one
13 the king of Debir one
the king of Geder one
14 the king of Hormah one
the king of Arad one
15 the king of Libnah one
the king of Adullam one
16 the king of Makkedah one
the king of Bethel one
17 the king of Tappuah one
the king of Hepher one
18 the king of Aphek one
the king of Lasharon one
19 the king of Madon one
the king of Hazor one
20 the king of Shimron-meron one
the king of Achshaph one
21 the king of Taanach one
the king of Megiddo one
22 the king of Kedesh one
the king of Jokneam in Carmel one
23 the king of Dor in Naphath-dor[E] one
the king of Goiim in Gilgal[F] one
24 the king of Tirzah one
the total number of all kings: thirty-one.

UNCONQUERED LANDS

13 Joshua was now old, advanced in age, and the
LORD said to him, "You have become old, advanced in age, but a great deal of the land remains to
be possessed. 2 This is the land that remains:
All the districts of the Philistines and the Geshurites: 3 from the Shihor east of Egypt to the
border of Ekron on the north (considered to
be Canaanite territory) — the five Philistine
rulers of Gaza, Ashdod, Ashkelon, Gath, and
Ekron, as well as the Avvites 4 in the south; all
the land of the Canaanites, from Arah of the
Sidonians to Aphek and as far as the border of
the Amorites; 5 the land of the Gebalites; and
all Lebanon east from Baal-gad below Mount
Hermon to the entrance of Hamath[G] — 6 all the
inhabitants of the hill country from Lebanon
to Misrephoth-maim, all the Sidonians.
I will drive them out before the Israelites, only distribute the land as an inheritance for Israel, as I have
commanded you. 7 Therefore, divide this land as an
inheritance to the nine tribes and half the tribe of
Manasseh."

THE INHERITANCE EAST OF THE JORDAN

8 With the other half of the tribe of Manasseh, the
Reubenites and Gadites had received the inheritance
Moses gave them beyond the Jordan to the east, just
as Moses the LORD's servant had given them:
9 From Aroer on the rim of the Arnon Valley,
along with the city in the middle of the valley, all
the Medeba plateau as far as Dibon, 10 and all the
cities of King Sihon of the Amorites, who reigned
in Heshbon, to the border of the Ammonites;
11 also Gilead and the territory of the Geshurites
and Maacathites, all Mount Hermon, and all Bashan to Salecah — 12 the whole kingdom of Og in
Bashan, who reigned in Ashtaroth and Edrei; he
was one of the remaining Rephaim.

[A] **12:3** = Galilee [B] **12:3** Or *and from Teman* [C] **12:4** LXX; MT reads *The territory of Og* [D] **12:8** Or *the Shephelah* [E] **12:23** Or *in the Slopes of Dor* [F] **12:23** LXX reads *Galilee* [G] **13:5** Or *to Lebo-hamath*

Moses struck them down and drove them out, 13 but
the Israelites did not drive out the Geshurites and
Maacathites. So Geshur and Maacath still live in Israel today.

14 He did not, however, give any inheritance to the
tribe of Levi. This was their inheritance, just as he
had promised: the food offerings made to the LORD,
the God of Israel.

REUBEN'S INHERITANCE

15 To the tribe of Reuben's descendants by their clans,
Moses gave 16 this as their territory:

From Aroer on the rim of the Arnon Valley, along
with the city in the middle of the valley, the whole
plateau as far as[A] Medeba, 17 with Heshbon and all
its cities on the plateau — Dibon, Bamoth-baal,
Beth-baal-meon, 18 Jahaz, Kedemoth, Mephaath,
19 Kiriathaim, Sibmah, Zereth-shahar on the hill in
the valley, 20 Beth-peor, the slopes of Pisgah, and
Beth-jeshimoth — 21 all the cities of the plateau,
and all the kingdom of King Sihon of the Amorites, who reigned in Heshbon. Moses had killed
him and the chiefs of Midian — Evi, Rekem, Zur,
Hur, and Reba — the princes of Sihon who lived
in the land. 22 Along with those the Israelites put
to death, they also killed the diviner, Balaam son
of Beor, with the sword.

23 The border of the Reubenites was the Jordan and
its plain. This was the inheritance of the Reubenites
by their clans, with the cities and their settlements.

GAD'S INHERITANCE

24 To the tribe of the Gadites by their clans, Moses
gave 25 this as their territory:

Jazer and all the cities of Gilead, and half the
land of the Ammonites to Aroer, near Rabbah; 26 from Heshbon to Ramath-mizpeh and
Betonim, and from Mahanaim to the border
of Debir;[B] 27 in the valley: Beth-haram, Beth-
nimrah, Succoth, and Zaphon — the rest of
the kingdom of King Sihon of Heshbon. Their
land also included the Jordan and its territory
as far as the edge of the Sea of Chinnereth[C] on
the east side of the Jordan.

28 This was the inheritance of the Gadites by their
clans, with the cities and their settlements.

EAST MANASSEH'S INHERITANCE

29 And to half the tribe of Manasseh (that is, to half
the tribe of Manasseh's descendants by their clans)
Moses gave 30 this as their territory:

From Mahanaim through all Bashan — all the
kingdom of King Og of Bashan, including all
of Jair's Villages[D] that are in Bashan — sixty
cities. 31 But half of Gilead, and Og's royal cities
in Bashan — Ashtaroth and Edrei — are for the
descendants of Machir son of Manasseh (that is,
half the descendants of Machir by their clans).

32 These were the portions Moses gave them on
the plains of Moab beyond the Jordan east of Jericho.
33 But Moses did not give a portion to the tribe of Levi.
The LORD, the God of Israel, was their inheritance, just
as he had promised them.

ISRAEL'S INHERITANCE IN CANAAN

14 The Israelites received these portions that the
priest Eleazar, Joshua son of Nun, and the family heads of the Israelite tribes gave them in the land
of Canaan. 2 Their inheritance was by lot as the LORD
commanded through Moses for the nine and a half
tribes, 3 because Moses had given the inheritance to
the two and a half tribes beyond the Jordan. But he
gave no inheritance among them to the Levites. 4 The
descendants of Joseph became two tribes, Manasseh
and Ephraim. No portion of the land was given to the
Levites except cities to live in, along with pasturelands
for their cattle and livestock. 5 So the Israelites did as
the LORD commanded Moses, and they divided the land.

CALEB'S INHERITANCE

6 The descendants of Judah approached Joshua at Gilgal, and Caleb son of Jephunneh the Kenizzite said to
him, "You know what the LORD promised Moses the
man of God at Kadesh-barnea about you and me. 7 I
was forty years old when Moses the LORD's servant
sent me from Kadesh-barnea to scout the land, and
I brought back an honest report. 8 My brothers who
went with me caused the people to lose heart, but I
followed the LORD my God completely. 9 On that day
Moses swore to me, 'The land where you have set foot
will be an inheritance for you and your descendants
forever, because you have followed the LORD my God
completely.'

10 "As you see, the LORD has kept me alive these
forty-five years as he promised, since the LORD spoke
this word to Moses while Israel was journeying in
the wilderness. Here I am today, eighty-five years
old. 11 I am still as strong today as I was the day Moses sent me out. My strength for battle and for daily
tasks[E] is now as it was then. 12 Now give me this hill
country the LORD promised me on that day, because
you heard then that the Anakim are there, as well as
large fortified cities. Perhaps the LORD will be with
me and I will drive them out as the LORD promised."

13 Then Joshua blessed Caleb son of Jephunneh
and gave him Hebron as an inheritance. 14 Therefore,

[A] **13:16** Some Hb mss read *plateau near* [B] **13:26** Or *Lidbir*, or *Lo-debar* [C] **13:27** = Galilee [D] **13:30** Or *all of Havvoth-jair* [E] **14:11** Lit *for going out and coming in*

Hebron still belongs to Caleb son of Jephunneh the
Kenizzite as an inheritance today because he followed
the LORD, the God of Israel, completely. 15 Hebron's
name used to be Kiriath-arba; Arba was the greatest man among the Anakim. After this, the land had
rest from war.

JUDAH'S INHERITANCE

15 Now the allotment for the tribe of the descendants of Judah by their clans was in the southernmost region, south to the Wilderness of Zin and
over to the border of Edom.

2 Their southern border began at the tip of the
Dead Sea on the south bay[A] 3 and went south of
the Scorpions' Ascent, proceeded to Zin, ascended to the south of Kadesh-barnea, passed Hezron, ascended to Addar, and turned to Karka. 4 It
proceeded to Azmon and to the Brook of Egypt
and so the border ended at the Mediterranean
Sea. This is your[B] southern border.

5 Now the eastern border was along the Dead Sea
to the mouth of the Jordan.

The border on the north side was from the bay of
the sea at the mouth of the Jordan. 6 It ascended
to Beth-hoglah, proceeded north of Beth-arabah,
and ascended to the Stone of Bohan son of Reuben. 7 Then the border ascended to Debir from
the Valley of Achor, turning north to the Gilgal
that is opposite the Ascent of Adummim, which
is south of the ravine. The border proceeded to
the Waters of En-shemesh and ended at En-rogel. 8 From there the border ascended Ben Hinnom Valley to the southern Jebusite slope (that
is, Jerusalem) and ascended to the top of the
hill that faces Hinnom Valley on the west, at the
northern end of Rephaim Valley. 9 From the top
of the hill the border curved to the spring of the
Waters of Nephtoah, went to the cities of Mount
Ephron, and then curved to Baalah (that is,
Kiriath-jearim). 10 The border turned westward
from Baalah to Mount Seir, went to the northern slope of Mount Jearim (that is, Chesalon),
descended to Beth-shemesh, and proceeded to
Timnah. 11 Then the border reached to the slope
north of Ekron, curved to Shikkeron, proceeded
to Mount Baalah, went to Jabneel, and ended at
the Mediterranean Sea.

12 Now the western border was the coastline of
the Mediterranean Sea.

This was the boundary of the descendants of Judah
around their clans.

CALEB AND OTHNIEL

13 He gave Caleb son of Jephunneh the following portion among the descendants of Judah based on the
LORD's instruction to Joshua: Kiriath-arba (that is, Hebron; Arba was the father of Anak). 14 Caleb drove out
from there the three sons of Anak: Sheshai, Ahiman,
and Talmai, descendants of Anak. 15 From there he
marched against the inhabitants of Debir, which used
to be called Kiriath-sepher, 16 and Caleb said, "Whoever attacks and captures Kiriath-sepher, I will give my
daughter Achsah to him as a wife." 17 So Othniel son of
Caleb's brother, Kenaz, captured it, and Caleb gave his
daughter Achsah to him as a wife. 18 When she arrived,
she persuaded Othniel to ask her father for a field. As
she got off her donkey, Caleb asked her, "What can I do
for you?" 19 She replied, "Give me a blessing. Since you
have given me land in the Negev, give me the springs
also." So he gave her the upper and lower springs.

JUDAH'S CITIES

20 This was the inheritance of the tribe of the descendants of Judah by their clans.

21 These were the outermost cities of the tribe of
the descendants of Judah toward the border of
Edom in the Negev: Kabzeel, Eder, Jagur, 22 Kinah,
Dimonah, Adadah, 23 Kedesh, Hazor, Ithnan, 24 Ziph,
Telem, Bealoth, 25 Hazor-hadattah, Kerioth-hez-
ron (that is, Hazor), 26 Amam, Shema, Moladah,
27 Hazar-gaddah, Heshmon, Beth-pelet, 28 Hazar-
shual, Beer-sheba, Biziothiah, 29 Baalah, Iim, Ezem,
30 Eltolad, Chesil, Hormah, 31 Ziklag, Madmannah,
Sansannah, 32 Lebaoth, Shilhim, Ain, and Rimmon
— twenty-nine cities in all, with their settlements.

33 In the Judean foothills:[C] Eshtaol, Zorah, Ashnah,
34 Zanoah, En-gannim, Tappuah,[D] Enam, 35 Jarmuth, Adullam, Socoh,[E] Azekah, 36 Shaaraim, Ad-
ithaim, Gederah, and Gederothaim — fourteen
cities, with their settlements; 37 Zenan, Hadashah,
Migdal-gad, 38 Dilan, Mizpeh, Jokthe-el, 39 Lachish, Bozkath, Eglon, 40 Cabbon, Lahmam, Chit-
lish, 41 Gederoth, Beth-dagon, Naamah, and Makkedah — sixteen cities, with their settlements;
42 Libnah, Ether, Ashan, 43 Iphtah, Ashnah, Nezib,
44 Keilah, Achzib, and Mareshah — nine cities,
with their settlements; 45 Ekron, with its surrounding villages and settlements; 46 from Ekron
to the sea, all the cities near Ashdod, with their
settlements; 47 Ashdod, with its surrounding villages and settlements; Gaza, with its surrounding
villages and settlements, to the Brook of Egypt
and the coastline of the Mediterranean Sea.

[A] **15:2** Lit *Sea at the tongue that turns southward* [B] **15:4** LXX reads *their* [C] **15:33** Or *the Shephelah* [D] **15:34** Or *En-gannim-tappuah* [E] **15:35** Or *Adullam-socoh*

[48] In the hill country: Shamir, Jattir, Socoh,
[49] Dannah, Kiriath-sannah (that is, Debir),
[50] Anab, Eshtemoh, Anim, [51] Goshen, Holon, and
Giloh — eleven cities, with their settlements;
[52] Arab, Dumah,[A] Eshan, [53] Janim, Beth-tappuah,
Aphekah, [54] Humtah, Kiriath-arba (that is, Hebron), and Zior — nine cities, with their settlements; [55] Maon, Carmel, Ziph, Juttah, [56] Jezreel,
Jokdeam, Zanoah, [57] Kain, Gibeah, and Timnah
— ten cities, with their settlements; [58] Halhul,
Beth-zur, Gedor, [59] Maarath, Beth-anoth, and
Eltekon — six cities, with their settlements;[B]
[60] Kiriath-baal (that is, Kiriath-jearim), and Rabbah — two cities, with their settlements.

[61] In the wilderness: Beth-arabah, Middin, Secacah, [62] Nibshan, the City of Salt,[C] and En-gedi
— six cities, with their settlements.
[63] But the descendants of Judah could not drive out the Jebusites who lived in Jerusalem. So the Jebusites still live in Jerusalem among the descendants of Judah today.

JOSEPH'S INHERITANCE

16 The allotment for the descendants of Joseph went from the Jordan at Jericho to the Waters of Jericho on the east, through the wilderness ascending from Jericho into the hill country of Bethel. [2] From Bethel it went to Luz and
proceeded to the border of the Archites by Ataroth. [3] It then descended westward to the border of the Japhletites as far as the border of Lower Beth-horon, then to Gezer, and ended at the Mediterranean Sea. [4] So Ephraim and Manasseh, the
sons of Joseph, received their inheritance.

EPHRAIM'S INHERITANCE

[5] This was the territory of the descendants of Ephraim by their clans:
The border of their inheritance went from Ataroth-addar on the east to Upper Beth-horon. [6] In
the north the border went westward from Michmethath; it turned eastward from Taanath-shiloh and passed it east of Janoah. [7] From Janoah it descended to Ataroth and Naarah, and then reached Jericho and went to the Jordan. [8] From Tappuah
the border went westward along the Brook of Kanah and ended at the Mediterranean Sea.

This was the inheritance of the tribe of the descendants of Ephraim by their clans, together with [9] the
cities set apart for the descendants of Ephraim within the inheritance of the descendants of Manasseh — all these cities with their settlements. [10] However, they
did not drive out the Canaanites who lived in Gezer. So the Canaanites still live in Ephraim today, but they are forced laborers.

WEST MANASSEH'S INHERITANCE

17 This was the allotment for the tribe of Manasseh as Joseph's firstborn. Gilead and Bashan were given to Machir, the firstborn of Manasseh and the father of Gilead, because he was a man of war. [2] So the
allotment was for the rest of Manasseh's descendants by their clans, for the sons of Abiezer, Helek, Asriel, Shechem, Hepher, and Shemida. These are the male descendants of Manasseh son of Joseph, by their clans.
[3] Now Zelophehad son of Hepher, son of Gilead, son of Machir, son of Manasseh, had no sons, only daughters. These are the names of his daughters: Mahlah, Noah, Hoglah, Milcah, and Tirzah. [4] They
came before the priest Eleazar, Joshua son of Nun, and the leaders, saying, "The LORD commanded Moses to give us an inheritance among our male relatives." So they gave them an inheritance among their father's brothers, in keeping with the LORD's instruction. [5] As
a result, ten tracts fell to Manasseh, besides the land of Gilead and Bashan, which are beyond the Jordan,[D]
[6] because Manasseh's daughters received an inheritance among his sons. The land of Gilead belonged to the rest of Manasseh's sons.
[7] The border of Manasseh went from Asher to
Michmethath near Shechem. It then went southward toward the inhabitants of En-tappuah.
[8] The region of Tappuah belonged to Manasseh,
but Tappuah itself on Manasseh's border belonged to the descendants of Ephraim. [9] From
there the border descended to the Brook of Kanah; south of the brook, cities belonged to Ephraim among Manasseh's cities. Manasseh's border was on the north side of the brook and ended
at the Mediterranean Sea. [10] Ephraim's territory
was to the south and Manasseh's to the north, with the Sea as its border. They reached Asher on the north and Issachar on the east. [11] Within
Issachar and Asher, Manasseh had Beth-shean, Ibleam, and the inhabitants of Dor with their surrounding villages; the inhabitants of En-dor, Taanach, and Megiddo — the three cities of[E]
Naphath — with their surrounding villages.
[12] The descendants of Manasseh could not possess these cities, because the Canaanites were determined to stay in this land. [13] However, when the Israelites
grew stronger, they imposed forced labor on the Canaanites but did not drive them out completely.

[A] **15:52** Some Hb mss read *Rumah* [B] **15:59** LXX adds *Tekoa, Ephrathah (that is, Bethlehem), Peor, Etam, Culom, Tatam, Sores, Carem, Gallim, Baither, and Manach — eleven cities, with their settlements* [C] **15:62** Or *Ir-hamelach* [D] **17:5** = east of the Jordan River [E] **17:11** LXX, Vg read *the third is*

JOSEPH'S ADDITIONAL INHERITANCE

14 Joseph's descendants said to Joshua, "Why did you
give us only one tribal allotment as an inheritance?
We have many people, because the LORD has been
blessing us greatly."
15 "If you have so many people," Joshua replied to
them, "go to the forest and clear an area for yourselves
there in the land of the Perizzites and the Rephaim,
because Ephraim's hill country is too small for you."
16 But the descendants of Joseph said, "The hill
country is not enough for us, and all the Canaanites
who inhabit the valley area have iron chariots, both
at Beth-shean with its surrounding villages and in
the Jezreel Valley."
17 So Joshua replied to Joseph's family (that is,
Ephraim and Manasseh), "You have many people and
great strength. You will not have just one allotment,
18 because the hill country will be yours also. It is a
forest; clear it and its outlying areas will be yours.
You can also drive out the Canaanites, even though
they have iron chariots and are strong."

LAND DISTRIBUTION AT SHILOH

18 The entire Israelite community assembled at
Shiloh and set up the tent of meeting there.
The land had been subdued before them, 2 but seven
tribes among the Israelites were left who had not
divided up their inheritance. 3 So Joshua asked the
Israelites, "How long will you delay going out to take
possession of the land that the LORD, the God of your
ancestors, gave you? 4 Appoint for yourselves three
men from each tribe, and I will send them out. They
are to go and survey the land, write a description of
it for the purpose of their inheritance, and return to
me. 5 Then they are to divide it into seven portions.
Judah is to remain in its territory in the south and
Joseph's family in their territory in the north. 6 When
you have written a description of the seven portions
of land and brought it to me, I will cast lots for you
here in the presence of the LORD our God. 7 But the
Levites among you do not get a portion, because their
inheritance is the priesthood of the LORD. Gad, Reuben, and half the tribe of Manasseh have taken their
inheritance beyond the Jordan to the east, which
Moses the LORD's servant gave them."
8 As the men prepared to go, Joshua commanded
them[A] to write down a description of the land, saying,
"Go and survey the land, write a description of it, and
return to me. I will then cast lots for you here in Shiloh
in the presence of the LORD." 9 So the men left, went
through the land, and described it by towns in a document of seven sections. They returned to Joshua at
the camp in Shiloh. 10 Joshua cast lots for them at Shiloh in the presence of the LORD where he distributed
the land to the Israelites according to their divisions.

BENJAMIN'S INHERITANCE

11 The lot came up for the tribe of Benjamin's descendants by their clans, and their allotted territory lay between Judah's descendants and Joseph's descendants.
12 Their border on the north side began at the
Jordan, ascended to the slope of Jericho on the
north, through the hill country westward, and
ended at the wilderness around Beth-aven.
13 From there the border went toward Luz, to
the southern slope of Luz (that is, Bethel); it then
went down by Ataroth-addar, over the hill south
of Lower Beth-horon.

14 On the west side, from the hill facing Beth-horon on the south, the border curved, turning
southward, and ended at Kiriath-baal (that is,
Kiriath-jearim), a city of the descendants of Judah. This was the west side of their border.

15 The south side began at the edge of Kiriath-
jearim, and the border extended westward; it
went to the spring at the Waters of Nephtoah.
16 The border descended to the foot of the hill
that faces Ben Hinnom Valley at the northern
end of Rephaim Valley. It ran down Hinnom Valley toward the south Jebusite slope and downward to En-rogel. 17 It curved northward and
went to En-shemesh and on to Geliloth, which is
opposite the Ascent of Adummim, and continued down to the Stone of Bohan son of Reuben.
18 Then it went north to the slope opposite the
Arabah[B] and proceeded into the plains.[C] 19 The
border continued to the north slope of Beth-hoglah and ended at the northern bay of the Dead
Sea, at the southern end of the Jordan. This was
the southern border.

20 The Jordan formed the border on the east side.
This was the inheritance of Benjamin's descendants,
by their clans, according to its surrounding borders.

BENJAMIN'S CITIES

21 These were the cities of the tribe of Benjamin's descendants by their clans:
Jericho, Beth-hoglah, Emek-keziz, 22 Beth-arabah, Zemaraim, Bethel, 23 Avvim, Parah, Ophrah,
24 Chephar-ammoni, Ophni, and Geba — twelve
cities, with their settlements; 25 Gibeon, Ramah,
Beeroth, 26 Mizpeh, Chephirah, Mozah, 27 Rekem,
Irpeel, Taralah, 28 Zela, Haeleph, Jebus[D] (that is,
Jerusalem), Gibeah, and Kiriath[E] — fourteen cities, with their settlements.

[A] **18:8** Lit *the ones going around* [B] **18:18** LXX reads *went northward to Beth-arabah* [C] **18:18** Or *the Arabah* [D] **18:28** Lit *Jebusite* [E] **18:28** LXX, Syr read *Kiriath-jearim*

This was the inheritance for Benjamin's descendants
by their clans.

SIMEON'S INHERITANCE

19 The second lot came out for Simeon, for the
tribe of his descendants by their clans, but
their inheritance was within the inheritance given
to Judah's descendants. 2 Their inheritance included
Beer-sheba (or Sheba), Moladah, 3 Hazar-shual,
Balah, Ezem, 4 Eltolad, Bethul, Hormah, 5 Ziklag,
Beth-marcaboth, Hazar-susah, 6 Beth-lebaoth,
and Sharuhen — thirteen cities, with their
settlements; 7 Ain, Rimmon, Ether, and Ashan
— four cities, with their settlements; 8 and all the
settlements surrounding these cities as far as
Baalath-beer (Ramah in the south[A]).
This was the inheritance of the tribe of Simeon's descendants by their clans. 9 The inheritance of Simeon's descendants was within the territory of Judah's
descendants, because the share for Judah's descendants was too large. So Simeon's descendants received an inheritance within Judah's portion.

ZEBULUN'S INHERITANCE

10 The third lot came up for Zebulun's descendants
by their clans.
The territory of their inheritance stretched as
far as Sarid; 11 their border went up westward
to Maralah, reached Dabbesheth, and met the
brook east of Jokneam. 12 From Sarid, it turned
due east along the border of Chisloth-tabor,
went to Daberath, and went up to Japhia. 13 From
there, it went due east to Gath-hepher and to
Eth-kazin; it extended to Rimmon, curving
around to Neah. 14 The border then circled
around Neah on the north to Hannathon and
ended at Iphtah-el Valley, 15 along with Kattath,
Nahalal, Shimron, Idalah, and Bethlehem —
twelve cities, with their settlements.
16 This was the inheritance of Zebulun's descendants
by their clans, these cities, with their settlements.

ISSACHAR'S INHERITANCE

17 The fourth lot came out for the tribe of Issachar's
descendants by their clans.
18 Their territory went to Jezreel, and included Chesulloth, Shunem, 19 Hapharaim, Shion,
Anaharath, 20 Rabbith, Kishion, Ebez, 21 Remeth,
En-gannim, En-haddah, and Beth-pazzez. 22 The
border reached Tabor, Shahazumah, and Beth-
shemesh, and ended at the Jordan — sixteen
cities, with their settlements.
23 This was the inheritance of the tribe of Issachar's
descendants by their clans, the cities, with their settlements.

ASHER'S INHERITANCE

24 The fifth lot came out for the tribe of Asher's descendants by their clans.
25 Their boundary included Helkath, Hali, Beten,
Achshaph, 26 Allammelech, Amad, and Mishal
and reached westward to Carmel and Shi-
hor-libnath. 27 It turned eastward to Beth-dagon,
reached Zebulun and Iphtah-el Valley, north
toward Beth-emek and Neiel, and went north to
Cabul, 28 Ebron, Rehob, Hammon, and Kanah, as
far as greater Sidon. 29 The boundary then turned
to Ramah as far as the fortified city of Tyre; it
turned back to Hosah and ended at the Mediterranean Sea, including Mahalab, Achzib,[B] 30 Um-
mah, Aphek, and Rehob — twenty-two cities,
with their settlements.
31 This was the inheritance of the tribe of Asher's
descendants by their clans, these cities with their
settlements.

NAPHTALI'S INHERITANCE

32 The sixth lot came out for Naphtali's descendants
by their clans.
33 Their boundary went from Heleph and from
the oak in Zaanannim, including Adami-nekeb
and Jabneel, as far as Lakkum, and ended at the
Jordan. 34 To the west, the boundary turned to
Aznoth-tabor and went from there to Hukkok,
reaching Zebulun on the south, Asher on the
west, and Judah[C] at the Jordan on the east. 35 The
fortified cities were Ziddim, Zer, Hammath,
Rakkath, Chinnereth, 36 Adamah, Ramah, Hazor,
37 Kedesh, Edrei, En-hazor, 38 Iron, Migdal-el, Ho-
rem, Beth-anath, and Beth-shemesh — nineteen
cities, with their settlements.
39 This was the inheritance of the tribe of Naphtali's descendants by their clans, the cities with their
settlements.

DAN'S INHERITANCE

40 The seventh lot came out for the tribe of Dan's descendants by their clans.
41 The territory of their inheritance included Zorah, Eshtaol, Ir-shemesh, 42 Shaalabbin,
Aijalon, Ithlah, 43 Elon, Timnah, Ekron, 44 Elte-
keh, Gibbethon, Baalath, 45 Jehud, Bene-berak,
Gath-rimmon, 46 Me-jarkon, and Rakkon, with
the territory facing Joppa.
47 When the territory of the descendants of Dan
slipped out of their control, they went up and fought
against Leshem, captured it, and struck it down with
the sword. So they took possession of it, lived there,

[A] **19:8** Or *the Negev* [B] **19:29** Or *Sea, in the region of Achzib*
[C] **19:34** LXX omits *Judah*

Chariots: Their Development and Use

by R. Kelvin Moore

A stone manger or feeding trough still in place in the enormous stables of King Ahab's (869–850 BC) "city of chariots" at Megiddo in Israel. Some scholars maintain the stables date to Solomon.

Archaeological evidence indicates the chariot developed in Mesopotamia before 3000 BC and that the Hyksos introduced chariot warfare into Syria and Egypt between 1800 and 1600 BC.[1] The development of the horse-drawn chariot permitted for the first time large empires, such as the Hittite and Assyrian, to dominate.

CHARIOT STYLE AND DEVELOPMENT

Originally, chariots were probably made of light wickerwork and had a boxlike shape. Commonly, the front was curved, the sides straight, with the back open. Oftentimes woven rope comprised the floor—giving the rider(s) a soft and springy footing. An axle with wooden wheels of four, six, or eight spokes supported the carriage.

The chariot's physical appearance developed across the centuries. Eventually, wicker gave way to wood. First to do so, the Philistines fortified their wooden chariots with metal plates (Jos 17:16–18). The advancement of "armor plate" made the Philistine chariot significantly stronger than the lighter, unfortified chariot belonging to the Israelites. Normally chariots were low slung, but Sennacherib introduced the high chariot, the wheels of which were easily a man's height.[2]

The Egyptians revolutionized chariotry. "The Egyptian chariot was probably the finest in the world in Joshua's day."[3] Previous chariots were heavy, difficult to maneuver, and pulled by slow-moving donkeys. Because of the scarcity of wood along the Nile River, Egyptians normally constructed chariots of much lighter wicker. Rather than using donkeys to pull chariots, the Egyptians pulled their chariots with horses. Thus, made of light materials and pulled by horses, the Egyptian chariots possessed greater speed than earlier chariots. The Egyptians also improved the chariot's design. Egyptian chariots had a lower body that gave the chariot a lower center of gravity. This design provided greater stability than the often clumsy predecessor. The rider stood directly over the axle in the Egyptian version. Such design distributed the rider's weight away from the horses to the chariot and placed less stress on the horses. Under the able leadership of Egyptian designers, the chariot developed into an effective military tool that opposing forces greatly feared.

Normally two individuals, a driver and a warrior, rode in military chariots. But a third rider manned Hittite chariots. Chariots that developed after Assyrian King Ashurbanipal (668–629 BC) carried four riders at times. Two horses pulled the chariot, but occasionally historical monuments show a third horse. The

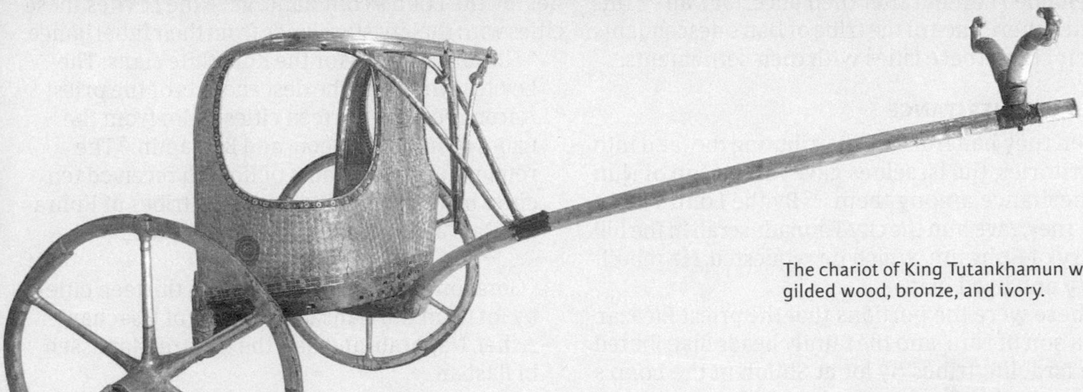

The chariot of King Tutankhamun was gilded wood, bronze, and ivory.

third horse, not actually yoked to the chariot, was a spare.

While mountainous regions rendered the chariot useless, the chariot was a deadly weapon in flat, open terrain. Long, intimidating knives attached to the chariot's wheels shredded enemy soldiers as the chariot raced across the battlefield.

From Antioch of Syria, this orthostat shows two warriors in a chariot. Dates from the eighth century BC. One drove the chariot while the other's hands were free for battle.

CHARIOTS IN ISRAEL

In their early history, the Israelites did not commonly use the chariot. When they initiated the conquest, they found it impossible to defeat the Canaanites in the open plains because of the Canaanite use of the chariot. The agrarian Israelites found themselves at a distinct disadvantage. But with God's help, the military genius Joshua managed to defeat Jabin, king of Hazor, and Jabin's allies in spite of Jabin's powerful chariot force. Joshua launched a surprise attack at the "Waters of Merom" (Jos 11:5). To neutralize Jabin's ominous chariot force, the Israelites hamstrung Jabin's horses, that is, cut the large tendon at the back of the hock.[4]

Because early Israelite chariot usage was rare, the Israelites avoided the great royal highway along the Mediterranean Sea. Instead, they favored the hill country to the east where enemy chariots were less maneuverable and less effective.

During the times of the prophet Samuel and King Saul, the Philistines dominated the Israelites for numerous reasons, chariots being one. The chariot played a key role in the Israelite-Philistine life-and-death struggle,[5] which eventually cost King Saul his life. King David's victories over the Philistines were undoubtedly because he introduced the chariot to the Israelite military.[6] Chariot usage among the Hebrews climaxed with King Ahab, who exceeded both David and Solomon. According to Assyrian records, King Ahab engaged the Assyrians at the battle of Qarqar (853 BC) with two thousand chariots![7]

With the advent of horseback riding by 1000 BC, chariots were no longer the preferred military implement for soldiers and officers. Mounted cavalry replaced chariots as the military instrument of choice. Yet long after the demise of their usefulness in war, chariots continued to be used for hunting and sport racing. ✣

---

[1] Lai Ling Elizabeth Ngan, "Chariots" in *HolBD*, 245. [2] J. W. Wevers, "Chariot" in *The Interpreter's Dictionary of the Bible* (*IDB*), ed. George A Buttrick (Nashville: Abingdon, 1962), 1:553. [3] V. Gilbert Beers, "Canaanite Chariots" in *The Victor Handbook of Bible Knowledge* (Wheaton, IL: Victor Books), 141. [4] William H. Morton, "Joshua" in *Broadman Bible Commentary*, ed. Clifton J. Allen (Nashville: Broadman, 1970), 2:346. [5] John Bright, *A History of Israel*, 3rd ed. (Philadelphia: Westminster, 1981), 185. [6] Wevers, "Chariot," 554. [7] Ngan, "Chariots," 245.

and renamed Leshem after their ancestor Dan. 48 This was the inheritance of the tribe of Dan's descendants by their clans, these cities with their settlements.

JOSHUA'S INHERITANCE

49 When they had finished distributing the land into its territories, the Israelites gave Joshua son of Nun an inheritance among them. 50 By the LORD's command, they gave him the city Timnath-serah in the hill country of Ephraim, which he requested. He rebuilt the city and lived in it.

51 These were the portions that the priest Eleazar, Joshua son of Nun, and the family heads distributed to the Israelite tribes by lot at Shiloh in the LORD's presence at the entrance to the tent of meeting. So they finished dividing up the land.

CITIES OF REFUGE

20 Then the LORD spoke to Joshua, 2 "Tell the Israelites: Select your cities of refuge, as I instructed you through Moses, 3 so that a person who kills someone unintentionally or accidentally may flee there. These will be your refuge from the avenger of blood. 4 When someone flees to one of these cities, stands at the entrance of the city gate, and states his case before the elders of that city, they are to bring him into the city and give him a place to live among them. 5 And if the avenger of blood pursues him, they must not hand the one who committed manslaughter over to him, for he killed his neighbor accidentally and did not hate him beforehand. 6 He is to stay in that city until he stands trial before the assembly and until the death of the high priest serving at that time. Then the one who committed manslaughter may return home to his own city from which he fled."

7 So they designated Kedesh in the hill country of Naphtali in Galilee, Shechem in the hill country of Ephraim, and Kiriath-arba (that is, Hebron) in the hill country of Judah. 8 Across the Jordan east of Jericho, they selected Bezer on the wilderness plateau from Reuben's tribe, Ramoth in Gilead from Gad's tribe, and Golan in Bashan from Manasseh's tribe.

9 These are the cities appointed for all the Israelites and the aliens residing among them, so that anyone who kills a person unintentionally may flee there and not die at the hand of the avenger of blood until he stands before the assembly.

CITIES OF THE LEVITES

21 The Levite family heads approached the priest Eleazar, Joshua son of Nun, and the family heads of the Israelite tribes. 2 At Shiloh, in the land of Canaan, they told them, "The LORD commanded through Moses that we be given cities to live in, with their pasturelands for our livestock." 3 So the Israelites, by the LORD's command, gave the Levites these cities with their pasturelands from their inheritance.

4 The lot came out for the Kohathite clans: The Levites who were the descendants of the priest Aaron received thirteen cities by lot from the tribes of Judah, Simeon, and Benjamin. 5 The remaining descendants of Kohath received ten cities by lot from the clans of the tribes of Ephraim, Dan, and half the tribe of Manasseh.

6 Gershon's descendants received thirteen cities by lot from the clans of the tribes of Issachar, Asher, Naphtali, and half the tribe of Manasseh in Bashan.

7 Merari's descendants received twelve cities for their clans from the tribes of Reuben, Gad, and Zebulun.

8 The Israelites gave these cities with their pasturelands around them to the Levites by lot, as the LORD had commanded through Moses.

CITIES OF AARON'S DESCENDANTS

9 The Israelites gave these cities by name from the tribes of the descendants of Judah and Simeon 10 to the descendants of Aaron from the Kohathite clans of the Levites, because they received the first lot. 11 They gave them Kiriath-arba (that is, Hebron; Arba was the father of Anak) with its surrounding pasturelands in the hill country of Judah. 12 But they gave the fields and settlements of the city to Caleb son of Jephunneh as his possession.

13 They gave to the descendants of the priest Aaron:
Hebron, the city of refuge for the one who commits manslaughter, with its pasturelands, Libnah with its pasturelands, 14 Jattir with its pasturelands, Eshtemoa with its pasturelands, 15 Holon with its pasturelands, Debir with its pasturelands, 16 Ain with its pasturelands, Juttah with its pasturelands, and Beth-shemesh with its pasturelands — nine cities from these two tribes.

17 From the tribe of Benjamin they gave:
Gibeon with its pasturelands, Geba with its pasturelands, 18 Anathoth with its pasturelands, and Almon with its pasturelands — four cities. 19 All thirteen cities with their pasturelands were for the priests, the descendants of Aaron.

CITIES OF KOHATH'S OTHER DESCENDANTS

20 The allotted cities to the remaining clans of Kohath's descendants, who were Levites, came from the tribe of Ephraim. 21 The Israelites gave them:
Shechem, the city of refuge for the one who commits manslaughter, with its pasturelands in

the hill country of Ephraim, Gezer with its pasturelands, 22 Kibzaim with its pasturelands, and
Beth-horon with its pasturelands — four cities.

23 From the tribe of Dan they gave:
Elteke with its pasturelands, Gibbethon with its
pasturelands, 24 Aijalon with its pasturelands,
and Gath-rimmon with its pasturelands — four
cities.

25 From half the tribe of Manasseh they gave:
Taanach with its pasturelands and Gath-rimmon[A] with its pasturelands — two cities.
26 All ten cities with their pasturelands were for the
clans of Kohath's other descendants.

CITIES OF GERSHON'S DESCENDANTS

27 From half the tribe of Manasseh, they gave to the
descendants of Gershon, who were one of the Levite clans:
Golan, the city of refuge for the one who commits manslaughter, with its pasturelands in
Bashan, and Beeshterah with its pasturelands
— two cities.

28 From the tribe of Issachar they gave:
Kishion with its pasturelands, Daberath with its
pasturelands, 29 Jarmuth with its pasturelands, and
En-gannim with its pasturelands — four cities.

30 From the tribe of Asher they gave:
Mishal with its pasturelands, Abdon with its
pasturelands, 31 Helkath with its pasturelands,
and Rehob with its pasturelands — four cities.

32 From the tribe of Naphtali they gave:
Kedesh in Galilee, the city of refuge for the one
who commits manslaughter, with its pasturelands, Hammoth-dor with its pasturelands, and
Kartan with its pasturelands — three cities.
33 All thirteen cities with their pasturelands were for
the Gershonites by their clans.

CITIES OF MERARI'S DESCENDANTS

34 From the tribe of Zebulun, they gave to the clans of
the descendants of Merari, who were the remaining
Levites:
Jokneam with its pasturelands, Kartah with its
pasturelands, 35 Dimnah with its pasturelands,
and Nahalal with its pasturelands — four cities.

36 From the tribe of Reuben they gave:
Bezer with its pasturelands, Jahzah[B] with its pas-
turelands, 37 Kedemoth with its pasturelands, and
Mephaath with its pasturelands — four cities.[C]

38 From the tribe of Gad they gave:
Ramoth in Gilead, the city of refuge for the one
who commits manslaughter, with its pasturelands, Mahanaim with its pasturelands, 39 Heshbon with its pasturelands, and Jazer with its
pasturelands — four cities in all. 40 All twelve
cities were allotted to the clans of Merari's descendants, the remaining Levite clans.

41 Within the Israelite possession there were forty-eight cities in all with their pasturelands for the
Levites. 42 Each of these cities had its own surrounding pasturelands; this was true for all the cities.

THE LORD'S PROMISES FULFILLED

43 So the LORD gave Israel all the land he had sworn
to give their ancestors, and they took possession of it
and settled there. 44 The LORD gave them rest on every
side according to all he had sworn to their ancestors.
None of their enemies were able to stand against
them, for the LORD handed over all their enemies
to them. 45 None of the good promises the LORD had
made to the house of Israel failed. Everything was
fulfilled.

EASTERN TRIBES RETURN HOME

22 Joshua summoned the Reubenites, Gadites,
and half the tribe of Manasseh 2 and told
them, "You have done everything Moses the LORD's
servant commanded you and have obeyed me in
everything I commanded you. 3 You have not deserted your brothers even once this whole time but
have carried out the requirement of the command
of the LORD your God. 4 Now that he has given your
brothers rest, just as he promised them, return to
your homes in your own land that Moses the LORD's
servant gave you across the Jordan. 5 Only carefully obey the command and instruction that Moses
the LORD's servant gave you: to love the LORD your
God, walk in all his ways, keep his commands, be
loyal to him, and serve him with all your heart and
all your soul."
6 Joshua blessed them and sent them on their way,
and they went to their homes. 7 Moses had given territory to half the tribe of Manasseh in Bashan, but
Joshua had given territory to the other half,[D] with
their brothers, on the west side of the Jordan. When
Joshua sent them to their homes and blessed them,
8 he said, "Return to your homes with great wealth: a
huge number of cattle, and silver, gold, bronze, iron,
and a large quantity of clothing. Share the spoil of
your enemies with your brothers."

[A] **21:25** Or *Ibleam* [B] **21:36** Or *Jahaz* [C] **21:36–37** Some Hb mss omit these vv. [D] **22:7** Lit *to his half*

EASTERN TRIBES BUILD AN ALTAR

9 The Reubenites, Gadites, and half the tribe of Manasseh left the Israelites at Shiloh in the land of Canaan
to return to their own land of Gilead, which they
took possession of according to the LORD's command
through Moses. 10 When they came to the region of[A]
the Jordan in the land of Canaan, the Reubenites,
Gadites, and half the tribe of Manasseh built a large,
impressive altar there by the Jordan.

11 Then the Israelites heard it said, "Look, the Reubenites, Gadites, and half the tribe of Manasseh have
built an altar on the frontier of the land of Canaan
at the region of[B] the Jordan, on the Israelite side."
12 When the Israelites heard this, the entire Israelite
community assembled at Shiloh to go to war against
them.

EXPLANATION OF THE ALTAR

13 The Israelites sent Phinehas son of Eleazar the
priest to the Reubenites, Gadites, and half the tribe
of Manasseh, in the land of Gilead. 14 They sent ten
leaders with him — one family leader for each tribe
of Israel. All of them were heads of their ancestral
families among the clans of Israel. 15 They went to the
Reubenites, Gadites, and half the tribe of Manasseh, in
the land of Gilead, and told them, 16 "This is what the
LORD's entire community says: 'What is this treachery you have committed today against the God of
Israel by turning away from the LORD and building
an altar for yourselves, so that you are in rebellion
against the LORD today? 17 Wasn't the iniquity of Peor,
which brought a plague on the LORD's community,
enough for us? We have not cleansed ourselves from
it even to this day, 18 and now would you turn away
from the LORD? If you rebel against the LORD today,
tomorrow he will be angry with the entire community of Israel. 19 But if the land you possess is defiled,
cross over to the land the LORD possesses where the
LORD's tabernacle stands, and take possession of it
among us. But don't rebel against the LORD or against
us by building for yourselves an altar other than the
altar of the LORD our God. 20 Wasn't Achan son of
Zerah unfaithful regarding what was set apart for
destruction, bringing wrath on the entire community of Israel? He was not the only one who perished
because of his iniquity.'"

21 The Reubenites, Gadites, and half the tribe of
Manasseh answered the heads of the Israelite clans,
22 "The Mighty One, God, the LORD! The Mighty One,
God, the LORD![C] He knows, and may Israel also know.
Do not spare us today, if it was in rebellion or treachery against the LORD 23 that we have built for ourselves
an altar to turn away from him. May the LORD himself
hold us accountable if we intended to offer burnt
offerings and grain offerings on it, or to sacrifice fellowship offerings on it. 24 We actually did this from a
specific concern that in the future your descendants
might say to our descendants, 'What relationship do
you have with the LORD, the God of Israel? 25 For the
LORD has made the Jordan a border between us and
you descendants of Reuben and Gad. You have no
share in the LORD!' So your descendants may cause
our descendants to stop fearing the LORD.

26 "Therefore we said: Let's take action and build an
altar for ourselves, but not for burnt offering or sacrifice. 27 Instead, it is to be a witness between us and
you, and between the generations after us, so that we
may carry out the worship of the LORD in his presence
with our burnt offerings, sacrifices, and fellowship
offerings. Then in the future, your descendants will
not be able to say to our descendants, 'You have no
share in the LORD!' 28 We thought that if they said this
to us or to our generations in the future, we would
reply: Look at the replica of the LORD's altar that our
ancestors made, not for burnt offering or sacrifice,
but as a witness between us and you. 29 We would
never ever rebel against the LORD or turn away from
him today by building an altar for burnt offering,
grain offering, or sacrifice, other than the altar of
the LORD our God, which is in front of his tabernacle."

CONFLICT RESOLVED

30 When the priest Phinehas and the community leaders, the heads of Israel's clans who were with him,
heard what the descendants of Reuben, Gad, and
Manasseh had to say, they were pleased. 31 Phinehas
son of Eleazar the priest said to the descendants of
Reuben, Gad, and Manasseh, "Today we know that
the LORD is among us, because you have not committed this treachery against him. As a result, you
have rescued the Israelites from the LORD's power."

32 Then the priest Phinehas son of Eleazar and the
leaders returned from the Reubenites and Gadites in
the land of Gilead to the Israelites in the land of Canaan
and brought back a report to them. 33 The Israelites
were pleased with the report, and they blessed God.
They spoke no more about going to war against them
to ravage the land where the Reubenites and Gadites
lived. 34 So the Reubenites and Gadites named the altar: It[D] is a witness between us that the LORD is God.

JOSHUA'S FAREWELL ADDRESS

23 A long time after the LORD had given Israel rest
from all the enemies around them, Joshua was
old, advanced in age. 2 So Joshua summoned all Israel,
including its elders, leaders, judges, and officers, and
said to them, "I am old, advanced in age, 3 and you

[A] **22:10** Or *to Geliloth by* [B] **22:11** Or *at Geliloth by* [C] **22:22** Or *The LORD is the God of gods! The LORD is the God of gods!* [D] **22:34** Some Hb mss, Syr, Tg read *altar Witness because it*

have seen for yourselves everything the LORD your
God did to all these nations on your account, because
it was the LORD your God who was fighting for you.
4 See, I have allotted these remaining nations to you
as an inheritance for your tribes, including all the
nations I have destroyed, from the Jordan westward
to the Mediterranean Sea. 5 The LORD your God will
force them back on your account and drive them out
before you so that you can take possession of their
land, as the LORD your God promised you.

6 "Be very strong and continue obeying all that is
written in the book of the law of Moses, so that you
do not turn from it to the right or left 7 and so that
you do not associate with these nations remaining
among you. Do not call on the names of their gods or
make an oath to them; do not serve them or bow in
worship to them. 8 Instead, be loyal to the LORD your
God, as you have been to this day.

9 "The LORD has driven out great and powerful nations before you, and no one is able to stand against
you to this day. 10 One of you routed a thousand because the LORD your God was fighting for you, as he
promised.[A] 11 So diligently watch yourselves! Love the
LORD your God! 12 If you ever turn away and become
loyal to the rest of these nations remaining among
you, and if you intermarry or associate with them
and they with you, 13 know for certain that the LORD
your God will not continue to drive these nations
out before you. They will become a snare and a trap
for you, a sharp stick[B] for your sides and thorns in
your eyes, until you disappear from this good land
the LORD your God has given you.

14 "I am now going the way of the whole earth, and
you know with all your heart and all your soul that
none of the good promises the LORD your God made
to you has failed. Everything was fulfilled for you; not
one promise has failed. 15 Since every good thing the
LORD your God promised you has come about, so he
will bring on you every bad thing until he has annihilated you from this good land the LORD your God has
given you. 16 If you break the covenant of the LORD
your God, which he commanded you, and go and serve
other gods, and bow in worship to them, the LORD's
anger will burn against you, and you will quickly disappear from this good land he has given you."

REVIEW OF ISRAEL'S HISTORY

24 Joshua assembled all the tribes of Israel at Shechem and summoned Israel's elders, leaders,
judges, and officers, and they presented themselves
before God. 2 Joshua said to all the people, "This is
what the LORD, the God of Israel, says: 'Long ago your
ancestors, including Terah, the father of Abraham
and Nahor, lived beyond the Euphrates River and
worshiped other gods. 3 But I took your father Abraham from the region beyond the Euphrates River, led
him throughout the land of Canaan, and multiplied
his descendants. I gave him Isaac, 4 and to Isaac I gave
Jacob and Esau. I gave the hill country of Seir to Esau
as a possession.

"'Jacob and his sons, however, went down to Egypt.
5 I sent Moses and Aaron, and I defeated Egypt by
what I did within it, and afterward I brought you
out. 6 When I brought your ancestors out of Egypt
and you reached the Red Sea, the Egyptians pursued
your ancestors with chariots and horsemen as far as
the sea. 7 Your ancestors cried out to the LORD, so he
put darkness between you and the Egyptians, and
brought the sea over them, engulfing them. Your own
eyes saw what I did to Egypt. After that, you lived in
the wilderness a long time.

8 "'Later, I brought you to the land of the Amorites
who lived beyond the Jordan. They fought against
you, but I handed them over to you. You possessed
their land, and I annihilated them before you. 9 Balak
son of Zippor, king of Moab, set out to fight against
Israel. He sent for Balaam son of Beor to curse you,
10 but I would not listen to Balaam. Instead, he repeatedly blessed you, and I rescued you from him.

11 "'You then crossed the Jordan and came to Jericho. Jericho's citizens — as well as the Amorites, Perizzites, Canaanites, Hethites, Girgashites, Hivites, and
Jebusites — fought against you, but I handed them
over to you. 12 I sent hornets[C] ahead of you, and they
drove out the two Amorite kings before you. It was
not by your sword or bow. 13 I gave you a land you did
not labor for, and cities you did not build, though you
live in them; you are eating from vineyards and olive
groves you did not plant.'

THE COVENANT RENEWAL

14 "Therefore, fear the LORD and worship him in sincerity and truth. Get rid of the gods your ancestors
worshiped beyond the Euphrates River and in Egypt,
and worship the LORD. 15 But if it doesn't please you
to worship the LORD, choose for yourselves today:
Which will you worship — the gods your ancestors
worshiped beyond the Euphrates River or the gods
of the Amorites in whose land you are living? As for
me and my family, we will worship the LORD."

16 The people replied, "We will certainly not abandon the LORD to worship other gods! 17 For the LORD
our God brought us and our ancestors out of the land
of Egypt, out of the place of slavery, and performed
these great signs before our eyes. He also protected us
all along the way we went and among all the peoples
whose lands we traveled through. 18 The LORD drove

[A] **23:10** Lit *promised you* [B] **23:13** Or *a whip*; Hb obscure
[C] **24:12** Or *sent terror*

Idolatry: Its Persistent Appeal

by Leon Hyatt Jr.

The southern ridge that overlooks the Hinnom Valley on the south side of Jerusalem; burial caves are located all along the ridge.

The various false gods and goddesses Israel worshiped had differing myths and rituals, but all of them combined in various measures the same elements that pervade virtually every false and deceptive religion. This allows us to consider the appeal of all of them—together.

MAGIC AND MYSTERY

The priests and priestesses of the false religions that fascinated the Israelites practiced various forms of magic, divination, fortune-telling, and spell casting. Casting spells, pronouncing curses, and dispensing favors gained as much fame for the practitioners in the days of Balaam (Nm 22:1–7) as they did for Nostradamus (AD 1503–1566) and Edgar Cayce (AD 1877–1945) in more recent years.

Lament for Dumuzi; Sumerian. In this lament, Dumuzi—"Tammuz" in Scripture (Ezk 8:14–18)—a shepherd-god, is lost to the underworld in a number of myths and is then bewailed by his wife—a motif that became widespread in antiquity, possibly related to the Adonis myth of the classical world.

ILLICIT SEX

In the days of ancient Israel, many of those worshiping false gods tied the change of seasons and the productivity of the land to fertility cults. As part of the fertility rites, the king, representing the major deity of the people, would engage in relations with a temple prostitute or slave, who represented the goddess. The people believed that these illicit actions caused crops to be fruitful and livestock to be productive. In time, priests and priestesses (or temple prostitutes) emulated these actions at various sacred sites, believing they too were ensuring the land's fertility. Adopting these practices, the Israelites built shrines "on every high hill and under every green tree" (1Kg 14:23; see 2Kg 16:4; 2Ch 28:4; Is 57:5; Jr 3:6). Some consisted of a pillar with sexual significance or a female image with exaggerated sexual features (Ex 34:13; Dt 12:3; Jdg 3:7; 1Kg 14:23; 2Kg 17:10; Is 27:9; Jr 17:2). Some such shrines contained small rooms where people could practice sexual perversions.[1]

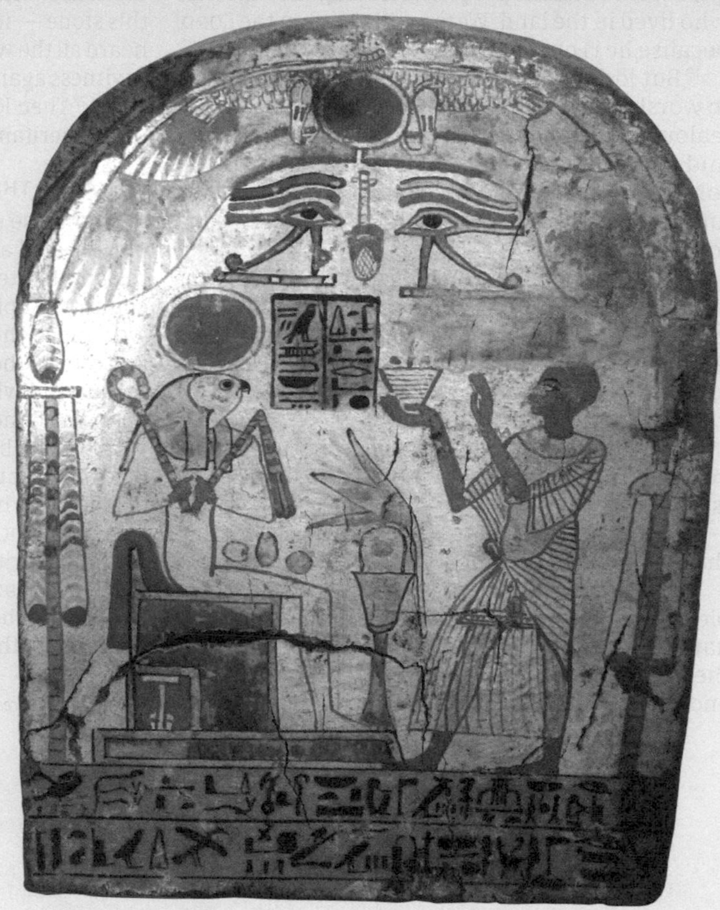

The priest Padiouiset offering incense to the Egyptian sun god Re-Horakhty-Atoum; dated 900 BC.

RIGHTEOUSNESS THROUGH SUFFERING

Man-made religions seem to have a morbid attraction to the idea that gods are more likely to grant a person's wishes if he punishes or harms his body. The best-known example of that practice came when Elijah challenged the priests of Baal to a contest on Mount Carmel. Baal's priests cut themselves, as they raved and danced around their sacrificial bull from morning until evening and received no response from Baal (1Kg 18:26–29).

The most extreme example of that mistaken idea was the use of human sacrifice, especially sacrificing one's own children. Practitioners called it causing the children to "pass through the fire" (see Lv 18:21; 2Kg 16:3; Jr 32:35; Ezk 16:21). Sometimes, a follower of a false god sacrificed a son or a daughter to appease his god's anger or disappointment (2Kg 3:26–27), but more often they did it as a means of obtaining a favor from their god (Jr 32:35; Ezk 16:20–21). In all likelihood, some did it to obtain the additional "benefit" of ridding themselves of unwanted children. In the Hinnom Valley, just south of Jerusalem, the people of Judah even built an idol that they called Topheth, which they used when offering their children as sacrifices to Molech (2Kg 23:10; 2Ch 33:6; Jr 32:35). Rabbinic writers told that Topheth consisted of a hollow statue in the form of a man with a bull's head. Worshipers heated the statue from below and then threw their children inside while drums drowned out the cries of the children.[2] Few practices reveal a more complete misunderstanding of the true God, who is by nature a God of grace, love, and blessing. That fact did nothing to lessen spiritually dead men from being drawn to gods who specialized in suffering and death. ✣

---

[1] Peter C. Craigie and Gerald H. Wilson, "Religions, Canaanite" in *ISBE*, vol. 4 (1988), 100. [2] Roland K. Harrison, "Molech" in *ISBE*, vol. 3 (1986), 401.

out before us all the peoples, including the Amorites who lived in the land. We too will worship the LORD, because he is our God."

19 But Joshua told the people, "You will not be able to worship the LORD, because he is a holy God. He is a jealous God; he will not forgive your transgressions and sins. 20 If you abandon the LORD and worship foreign gods, he will turn against you, harm you, and completely destroy you, after he has been good to you."

21 "No!" the people answered Joshua. "We will worship the LORD."

22 Joshua then told the people, "You are witnesses against yourselves that you yourselves have chosen to worship the LORD."

"We are witnesses," they said.

23 "Then get rid of the foreign gods that are among you and turn your hearts to the LORD, the God of Israel."

24 So the people said to Joshua, "We will worship the LORD our God and obey him."

25 On that day Joshua made a covenant for the people at Shechem and established a statute and ordinance for them. 26 Joshua recorded these things in the book of the law of God; he also took a large stone and set it up there under the oak at the sanctuary of the LORD. 27 And Joshua said to all the people, "You see this stone — it will be a witness against us, for it has heard all the words the LORD said to us, and it will be a witness against you, so that you will not deny your God." 28 Then Joshua sent the people away, each to his own inheritance.

BURIAL OF THREE LEADERS

29 After these things, the LORD's servant, Joshua son of Nun, died at the age of 110. 30 They buried him in his allotted territory at Timnath-serah, in the hill country of Ephraim north of Mount Gaash. 31 Israel worshiped the LORD throughout Joshua's lifetime and during the lifetimes of the elders who outlived Joshua and who had experienced all the works the LORD had done for Israel.

32 Joseph's bones, which the Israelites had brought up from Egypt, were buried at Shechem in the parcel of land Jacob had purchased from the sons of Hamor, Shechem's father, for a hundred pieces of silver.[A] It was an inheritance for Joseph's descendants.

33 And Eleazar son of Aaron died, and they buried him at Gibeah,[B] which had been given to his son Phinehas in the hill country of Ephraim.

[A] **24:32** Lit *a hundred qesitahs* [B] **24:33** = the Hill

JUDGES

The spring of Harod and Gideon Cave, at the foot of Mount Gilboa. By observing how his men drank the water of the stream, Gideon determined which of his soldiers would go to battle against the Midianites.

INTRODUCTION TO

JUDGES

Circumstances of Writing

No author is named in the book of Judges, nor is any indication given of the writer or writers who are responsible for it. The three divisions of the book are on a different footing regarding the sources from which they are drawn. The historical introduction presents a form of the traditional narrative of the conquest of Canaan that is parallel to the book of Joshua. The main portion of the book, comprising the narratives of the judges, appears to be based on oral or written traditions of a local observer.

The period of the Israelite judges lay between the conquest of the promised land under Joshua and the rise of the monarchy with Saul and David. The events described are thus to be dated from the end of the fifteenth century BC to the latter part of the eleventh century BC, a period of around three hundred years. This was a time of social and religious anarchy, characterized by the repeated refrain, "In those days there was no king in Israel; everyone did whatever seemed right to him" (Jdg 17:6; 21:25; see 18:1; 19:1).

We cannot ascertain exactly when the book of Judges was composed. The reference in 18:30 to the fate of Dan at "the time of the exile from the land" suggests a date of final editing after the exile of the northern kingdom by Assyria around 722 BC. Meanwhile, the suggestion that readers could visit the site of Gideon's altar at Ophrah in 6:24 suggests a date prior to the exile of the southern kingdom, Judah, in 586 BC. Its message would have resonated strongly at several points of Israel's history, and it has been argued that it fits well during the dark days of Manasseh (686–642 BC; 2Kg 21:1–18). However, it is not possible to date Judges with precision.

Contribution to the Bible

The book of Judges shows us that the nation of Israel survived the dark days of the judges entirely by the grace of God. In mercy, he sent oppressors as reminders of their rebellion. In mercy, he responded to their cries and raised up deliverers. Judges also illustrates the fundamental problem of the human heart. When God's people forget his saving acts, they go after other gods. Judges also illustrates the link between spiritual commitments and ethical conduct. In the end, the book of Judges illustrates the eternal truth: the Lord will build his kingdom, in spite of our sin and rebellion.

Structure

The book falls into three parts. There is a prologue (1:1–3:6) that deals with the failure of the second generation to press on with the conquest of Canaan. This is followed by a sixfold cycle of sin and salvation (3:7–16:31), which forms the bulk of the book. Finally, there is an appendix (chaps. 17–21) that shows the full effects of total depravity let loose upon the people. This structure demonstrates not only the repetition of patterns of sin and judgment but also negative progress. The midpoint of the narrative is the linked episode involving Gideon and Abimelech, which serves to highlight further the significance of the issue of kingship.

JUDAH'S LEADERSHIP AGAINST THE CANAANITES

1 After the death of Joshua, the Israelites inquired of the LORD, "Who will be the first to fight for us against the Canaanites?"

2 The LORD answered, "Judah is to go. I have handed the land over to him."

3 Judah said to his brother Simeon, "Come with me to my allotted territory, and let's fight against the Canaanites. I will also go with you to your allotted territory." So Simeon went with him.

4 When Judah attacked, the LORD handed the Canaanites and Perizzites over to them. They struck down ten thousand men in Bezek. 5 They found Adoni-bezek in Bezek, fought against him, and struck down the Canaanites and Perizzites.

6 When Adoni-bezek fled, they pursued him, caught him, and cut off his thumbs and big toes. 7 Adoni-bezek said, "Seventy kings with their thumbs and big toes cut off used to pick up scraps[A] under my table. God has repaid me for what I have done." They brought him to Jerusalem, and he died there.

8 The men of Judah fought against Jerusalem, captured it, put it to the sword, and set the city on fire. 9 Afterward, the men of Judah marched down to fight against the Canaanites who were living in the hill country, the Negev, and the Judean foothills.[B] 10 Judah also marched against the Canaanites who were living in Hebron (Hebron was formerly named Kiriath-arba). They struck down Sheshai, Ahiman, and Talmai. 11 From there they marched against the residents of Debir (Debir was formerly named Kiriath-sepher).

12 Caleb said, "Whoever attacks and captures Kiriath-sepher, I will give my daughter Achsah to him as a wife." 13 So Othniel son of Kenaz, Caleb's youngest brother, captured it, and Caleb gave his daughter Achsah to him as his wife.

14 When she arrived, she persuaded Othniel to ask her father for a field. As she got off her donkey, Caleb asked her, "What do you want?" 15 She answered him, "Give me a blessing. Since you have given me land in the Negev, give me springs also." So Caleb gave her both the upper and lower springs.

16 The descendants of the Kenite, Moses's father-in-law, had gone up with the men of Judah from the City of Palms[C] to the Wilderness of Judah, which was in the Negev of Arad. They went to live among the people.

17 Judah went with his brother Simeon, struck the Canaanites who were living in Zephath, and completely destroyed the town. So they named the town Hormah. 18 Judah captured Gaza and its territory, Ashkelon and its territory, and Ekron and its territory. 19 The LORD was with Judah and enabled them to take possession of the hill country, but they could not drive out the people who were living in the plain because those people had iron chariots.

20 Judah gave Hebron to Caleb, just as Moses had promised. Then Caleb drove out the three sons of Anak who lived there.

BENJAMIN'S FAILURE

21 At the same time the Benjaminites did not drive out the Jebusites who were living in Jerusalem. The Jebusites have lived among the Benjaminites in Jerusalem to this day.

SUCCESS OF THE HOUSE OF JOSEPH

22 The house of Joseph also attacked Bethel, and the LORD was with them. 23 They sent spies to Bethel (the town was formerly named Luz). 24 The spies saw a man coming out of the town and said to him, "Please show us how to get into town, and we will show you kindness." 25 When he showed them the way into the town, they put the town to the sword but released the man and his entire family. 26 Then the man went to the land of the Hittites, built a town, and named it Luz. That is its name still today.

FAILURE OF THE OTHER TRIBES

27 At that time Manasseh failed to take possession of Beth-shean and Taanach and their surrounding villages, or the residents of Dor, Ibleam, and Megiddo and their surrounding villages; the Canaanites were determined to stay in this land. 28 When Israel became stronger, they made the Canaanites serve as forced labor but never drove them out completely.

29 At that time Ephraim failed to drive out the Canaanites who were living in Gezer, so the Canaanites have lived among them in Gezer.

30 Zebulun failed to drive out the residents of Kitron or the residents of Nahalol, so the Canaanites lived among them and served as forced labor.

31 Asher failed to drive out the residents of Acco or of Sidon, or Ahlab, Achzib, Helbah, Aphik, or Rehob. 32 The Asherites lived among the Canaanites who were living in the land, because they failed to drive them out.

33 Naphtali did not drive out the residents of Beth-shemesh or the residents of Beth-anath. They lived among the Canaanites who were living in the land, but the residents of Beth-shemesh and Beth-anath served as their forced labor.

34 The Amorites forced the Danites into the hill country and did not allow them to go down into the valley. 35 The Amorites were determined to stay in Har-heres, Aijalon, and Shaalbim. When the house of Joseph got the upper hand, the Amorites were made to serve as forced labor. 36 The territory of the

[A] **1:7** Lit *toes cut off are gathering* [B] **1:9** Or *the Shephelah*
[C] **1:16** = Jericho; Dt 34:3; Jdg 3:13; 2Ch 28:15

Amorites extended from the Scorpions' Ascent, that is from Sela upward.

PATTERN OF SIN AND JUDGMENT

2 The angel of the LORD went up from Gilgal to Bochim and said, "I brought you out of Egypt and led you into the land I had promised to your ancestors. I also said: I will never break my covenant with you. 2 You are not to make a covenant with the inhabitants of this land. You are to tear down their altars. But you have not obeyed me. What have you done? 3 Therefore, I now say: I will not drive out these people before you. They will be thorns[A] in your sides, and their gods will be a trap for you." 4 When the angel of the LORD had spoken these words to all the Israelites, the people wept loudly. 5 So they named that place Bochim[B] and offered sacrifices there to the LORD.

JOSHUA'S DEATH

6 Previously, when Joshua had sent the people away, the Israelites had gone to take possession of the land, each to his own inheritance. 7 The people worshiped the LORD throughout Joshua's lifetime and during the lifetimes of the elders who outlived Joshua. They had seen all the LORD's great works he had done for Israel.

8 Joshua son of Nun, the servant of the LORD, died at the age of 110. 9 They buried him in the territory of his inheritance, in Timnath-heres, in the hill country of Ephraim, north of Mount Gaash. 10 That whole generation was also gathered to their ancestors. After them another generation rose up who did not know the LORD or the works he had done for Israel.

11 The Israelites did what was evil in the LORD's sight. They worshiped the Baals 12 and abandoned the LORD, the God of their ancestors, who had brought them out of Egypt. They followed other gods from the surrounding peoples and bowed down to them. They angered the LORD, 13 for they abandoned him and worshiped Baal and the Ashtoreths.

14 The LORD's anger burned against Israel, and he handed them over to marauders who raided them. He sold them to the enemies around them, and they could no longer resist their enemies. 15 Whenever the Israelites went out, the LORD was against them and brought disaster on them, just as he had promised and sworn to them. So they suffered greatly.

16 The LORD raised up judges, who saved them from the power of their marauders, 17 but they did not listen to their judges. Instead, they prostituted themselves with other gods, bowing down to them. They quickly turned from the way of their ancestors, who had walked in obedience to the LORD's commands. They did not do as their ancestors did. 18 Whenever the LORD raised up a judge for the Israelites, the LORD was with him and saved the people from the power of their enemies while the judge was still alive. The LORD was moved to pity whenever they groaned because of those who were oppressing and afflicting them. 19 Whenever the judge died, the Israelites would act even more corruptly than their ancestors, following other gods to serve them and bow in worship to them. They did not turn from their evil practices or their obstinate ways.

20 The LORD's anger burned against Israel, and he declared, "Because this nation has violated my covenant that I made with their ancestors and disobeyed me, 21 I will no longer drive out before them any of the nations Joshua left when he died. 22 I did this to test Israel and to see whether or not they would keep the LORD's way by walking in it, as their ancestors had." 23 The LORD left these nations and did not drive them out immediately. He did not hand them over to Joshua.

THE LORD TESTS ISRAEL

3 These are the nations the LORD left in order to test all those in Israel who had experienced none of the wars in Canaan. 2 This was to teach the future generations of the Israelites how to fight in battle, especially those who had not fought before. 3 These nations included the five rulers of the Philistines and all of the Canaanites, the Sidonians, and the Hivites who lived in the Lebanese mountains from Mount Baal-hermon as far as the entrance to Hamath.[C] 4 The LORD left them to test Israel, to determine if they would keep the LORD's commands he had given their ancestors through Moses. 5 But they settled among the Canaanites, Hethites, Amorites, Perizzites, Hivites, and Jebusites. 6 The Israelites took their daughters as wives for themselves, gave their own daughters to their sons, and worshiped their gods.

OTHNIEL, THE FIRST JUDGE

7 The Israelites did what was evil in the LORD's sight; they forgot the LORD their God and worshiped the Baals and the Asherahs. 8 The LORD's anger burned against Israel, and he sold them to King Cushan-rishathaim[D] of Aram-naharaim,[E] and the Israelites served him eight years.

9 The Israelites cried out to the LORD. So the LORD raised up Othniel son of Kenaz, Caleb's youngest brother, as a deliverer to save the Israelites. 10 The Spirit of the LORD came on him, and he judged Israel. Othniel went out to battle, and the LORD handed over King Cushan-rishathaim of Aram to him, so that Othniel overpowered him. 11 Then the land had peace for forty years, and Othniel son of Kenaz died.

[A] **2:3** Lit *traps* [B] **2:5** Or *Weeping* [C] **3:3** Or *as Lebo-hamath*
[D] **3:8** Lit *Doubly-Evil* [E] **3:8** = Mesopotamia

How Iron Changed Warfare

by Joseph R. Cathey

Reconstructed copper smelting furnace from Timnah, in southern Israel. The furnace, dating to the twelfth century BC, has a round tuyère (heat-exchange pipe) in the back and a slag pit in the front.

Metals allowed the introduction of technology that undoubtedly changed the entire landscape of the ancient Near East. The refining of metals and the ability to work with them were at the forefront of human technological development. Nowhere is the refining of metals more pronounced than in the areas of religious iconography, tools, and weapons.

Evidence is prevalent from the Neolithic cultures onward illustrating the rise of humans working various metals. As early as the eighth millennium BC, people worked native copper, bitumen, and obsidian into items such as decorative pins, pendants, and religious iconography.[1] Although copper was the earliest metal to be mined, smelted, and cast—due to its prevalence and ease of working—one should not discount meteoric iron. As early as the second millennium BC, the ancient Near East knew and most likely made use of meteoric iron, "the iron from heaven."[2]

The Scriptures witness iron's dramatic rise from humble beginnings. Genesis 4:22 explains that Tubal-cain worked as a metalworker. Some believe that Tubal-cain's metallurgy included weapons as well as agricultural tools.[3]

The shift from bronze to iron came about for reasons of practicality and utility. Although bronze is much easier to work than iron, the necessary element for bronze, namely tin, is extremely rare.[4] Due to an abundance of ore and improvements in smelting, iron became the prevailing utilitarian metal from approximately 1200 to 800 BC.[5] In the Late Bronze Age (period of the judges), iron was not as technically advanced as bronze. Bronze is harder than iron, therefore a bronze knife or sword would keep its edge longer and would not bend or break as readily as iron. The key to the later technological breakthrough with iron was the carburization process by which iron becomes steel.[6] Steel is harder and

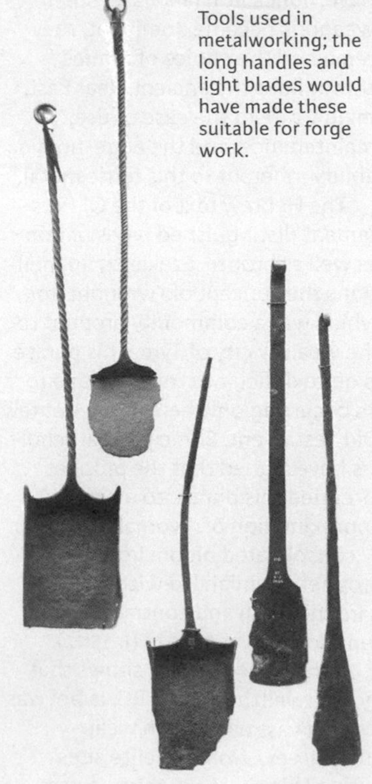

Tools used in metalworking; the long handles and light blades would have made these suitable for forge work.

Arrowheads from Lachish; dated tenth–sixth centuries BC. At the beginning of the Iron Age, iron was scarce and was too valuable to be used for expendable projectile points. Only after the tenth century did it become widespread enough to replace bronze arrowheads with iron ones.

Iron helmet with bronze inlay around the rim; Assyrian; eighth century BC.

stronger than bronze, and it will keep an edge better. The advent of carburized iron (steel) gave a value to iron that it previously did not have.[7] Once iron (and later steel) weapons became dominant, they remained the choice of armies throughout the ancient Near East, mainly due to the ease of use, maintenance, and the edge-holding ability inherent to this ferric metal.[8]

The Hebrew text of the Old Testament distinguished types of iron as well as bronze. Ezekiel 27:19 mentions the concept of "wrought iron," which was a commodity brought to the wealthy city of Tyre. This phrase is quite difficult to translate due to its occurring only here in the Hebrew Old Testament. Some biblical scholars have argued that the prophet intended this phrase to mean an approximation of "workable iron" or a "consolidated bloom iron."[9] The prophet Jeremiah likewise knew of hardened iron and contrasted its superiority over bronze (Jr 15:12).

Archaeology clearly shows that by the twelfth century BC, Israel was making vast use of iron weapons. Surveys from Israelite sites during this era show thirty-seven arrowheads, five knives/blades, five daggers, five spearheads, one spear butt, seven javelin heads, and two lance heads.[10] In contrast, this same survey explored commonly held Philistine sites,[11] which yielded an equally impressive assortment of weapons. As expected, archaeologists uncovered a greater number of Philistines blades—thirteen to the Israelite ten. The infrastructure required for metallurgy was slightly more tilted toward the Philistines' favor than the Israelites. Likewise, the biblical account indicates that the Philistines often fought from the mounted chariot position rather than as dismounted infantry. A cursory examination of the bulk of Israelite weaponry appears to indicate that the Hebrews preferred standoff weapons (metal-tipped arrows, shafts, and lances) that would afford the infantry distance from the chariots.

Judges 4 gives an impressive window into the mind-set of early Israel and their preference for range weapons. The text illustrates the writer's appreciation of Canaanite warfare, namely the iron chariot (see 1:19). The writer explains that Canaan's king Jabin had used his vast numbers of iron chariots to oppress Israel for more than twenty years. Likewise, the Canaanite commander Sisera used nine hundred iron chariots in his battle against Israel. Undoubtedly, the iron chariot was a paradigmatic shift in warfare of the ancient Near East.

The archaeological remains of the first millennium BC have yielded impressive finds associated with chariots of the ancient Near East. The shift in mobile warfare platforms was gradual due to the technology associated with making these war machines. Ancient Egyptian and Asiatic imagery highlights the importance of iron chariots as mobile firing platforms as well as for flanking and harassing dismounted infantry. To find chariots equipped with bow cases, quivers of arrows, axes, and even long swords was not uncommon.[12] Details from Egypt's New Kingdom (1550–1070 BC) have provided ample insights into chariot construction. Elements such as a D-shaped floor (for quick mounting and dismounting), hip-high sides (for shield mounting), and ample storage for battle weapons made the iron chariot a highly desirable commodity.[13] Iron Age chariots eventually spread throughout the entire Near East (Hatti, Egypt, Canaan, Assyria, and Babylon).

As this platform grew, the key to effective deployment was reconciling speed and maneuverability with fire power and security. The bite of iron swords, arrows, javelins, and spears necessitated a triple function within the charioteer corps. Three soldiers were required to effectively fight a concerted battle—a driver, a fighter, and a defender (often depicted as deploying a shield covering the fighter).[14]

Iron and the technology that it brought to the ancient Near East was a double-edged sword. On the one hand, it was a meteoric jump in offensive weapons (sword, arrow, spear, and lance). This advantage was offset, however, by the development and usage of the iron chariot as seen in Judges 1; 4. Truly elements such as geography and maneuverability would hamper the iron chariot in the hill country of Israel. However, once iron weapons became commonplace in the field of martial combat, nations would never again embrace a lesser metal for blood or conquest. ✣

A two-man Assyrian chariot, bearing the sacred standards; from the North-West Palace at Nimrud; dated about 865–860 BC.

[1] See Paul T. Craddock, "Metallurgy: Metallurgy in the Old World" in *The Oxford Companion to Archaeology*, ed. Niel Asher Silberman, 2nd ed. (Oxford: Oxford University Press, 2012), 378. [2] Thoman Zimmermann, Latif Özen, Yakup Kalayci, and Rukiye Akdogan, "The Metal Tablet from Bogazköy-Hattuša: First Archaeometric Impressions," *Journal of Near Eastern Studies* (*JNES*) 69.2 (October 2010): 228–29. [3] See Kenneth A. Matthews, *Genesis 1–11:26*, vol. 1 in NAC (1996), 287. Matthews suggests that Tubal-cain most likely worked meteoric iron. [4] One distinct impediment was the temperature and equipment necessary to smelt ores. For example, to smelt copper, the temperature has to reach no less than 1,981°F and silver, 1,762°F—versus iron at 2,786°F. Even when iron was smelted, it often had to be worked by hammer (e.g., forging) and then shaped in a much more labor-intensive process. [5] See J. D. Muhly, "Metals: Artifacts of the Neolithic, Bronze, and Iron Ages" in *The Oxford Encyclopedia of Archaeology in the Near East* (*OEANE*), ed. Eric M. Meyers (Oxford: Oxford University Press, 1997), 4:13. [6] T. Stech-Wheeler et al., "Iron at Taanach and Early Iron Metallurgy in the Eastern Mediterranean," *American Journal of Archaeology* (*AJA*) 85.3 (1981): 245. [7] James D. Muhly, "How Iron Technology Changed the Ancient World and Gave the Philistines a Military Edge," *BAR* 8.6 (1982): 43–44. [8] Allan C. Emery, "Weapons of the Israelite Monarchy: A Catalogue with Its Linguistic and Cross-Culture Implications" (PhD diss., Harvard University, 1999), 135–55; see M. Heltzer, "Akkadian *ktinnu* and Hebrew *kidon*, 'sword,'" *Journal of Cuneiform Studies* (*JCS*) 41.1 (1989): 65–68. [9] Dan Levene and Beno Rothenberg, "Early Evidence for Steelmaking in the Judaic Sources," *Jewish Quarterly Review* (*JQR*) 92.1–2 (2001): 109–10. [10] Elizabeth Bloch-Smith, "Israelite Ethnicity in Iron I: Archaeology Preserves What Is Remembered and What Is Forgotten in Israel's History," *JBL* 122. 3 (2003): 419. Bloch-Smith restricted the "Israel" sites to the central highlands (Dothan, Bethel, Ai, Khirbet Raddana, Tell en-Nasbeh, Giloh, el-Khadr, Beth Zur, and Tel Beersheve). [11] For example, sites such as Ashdod, Tel Miqne-Ekron, Beth Dagon, Tell el 'Ajjul/Gaza, and Tell Qasile were surveyed. Such sites are commonly within the realm of what is normally associated with the "Philistines." [12] See Joost H. Crouwel, "Chariots in Iron Age Cyprus," *Report of the Department of Antiquities, Cyprus* (1987), 101–18. [13] See Joost Crouwel and Mary Aiken Littauer, "Chariots" in *OEANE*, 485. [14] See Sa-Moon Kang, *Divine War in the Old Testament and in the Ancient Near East* (Berlin: de Gruyter, 1989), 50.

EHUD

12 The Israelites again did what was evil in the LORD's sight. He gave King Eglon of Moab power over Israel, because they had done what was evil in the LORD's sight. 13 After Eglon convinced the Ammonites and the Amalekites to join forces with him, he attacked and defeated Israel and took possession of the City of Palms.[A] 14 The Israelites served King Eglon of Moab eighteen years.

15 Then the Israelites cried out to the LORD, and he raised up Ehud son of Gera, a left-handed Benjaminite,[B] as a deliverer for them. The Israelites sent him with the tribute for King Eglon of Moab.

16 Ehud made himself a double-edged sword eighteen inches long.[C] He strapped it to his right thigh under his clothes 17 and brought the tribute to King Eglon of Moab, who was an extremely fat man. 18 When Ehud had finished presenting the tribute, he dismissed the people who had carried it. 19 At the carved images near Gilgal he returned and said, "King Eglon, I have a secret message for you." The king said, "Silence!" and all his attendants left him. 20 Then Ehud approached him while he was sitting alone in his upstairs room where it was cool. Ehud said, "I have a message from God for you," and the king stood up from his throne. 21 Ehud reached with his left hand, took the sword from his right thigh, and plunged it into Eglon's belly. 22 Even the handle went in after the blade, and Eglon's fat closed in over it, so that Ehud did not withdraw the sword from his belly. And the waste came out.[D] 23 Ehud escaped by way of the porch, closing and locking the doors of the upstairs room behind him.

24 Ehud was gone when Eglon's servants came in. They looked and found the doors of the upstairs room locked and thought he was relieving himself[E] in the cool room. 25 The servants waited until they became embarrassed and saw that he had still not opened the doors of the upstairs room. So they took the key and opened the doors — and there was their lord lying dead on the floor!

26 Ehud escaped while the servants waited. He passed the Jordan near the carved images and reached Seirah. 27 After he arrived, he sounded the ram's horn throughout the hill country of Ephraim. The Israelites came down with him from the hill country, and he became their leader. 28 He told them, "Follow me, because the LORD has handed over your enemies, the Moabites, to you." So they followed him, captured the fords of the Jordan leading to Moab, and did not allow anyone to cross over. 29 At that time they struck down about ten thousand Moabites, all stout and able-bodied men. Not one of them escaped. 30 Moab became subject to Israel that day, and the land had peace for eighty years.

SHAMGAR

31 After Ehud, Shamgar son of Anath became judge. He also delivered Israel, striking down six hundred Philistines with a cattle prod.

DEBORAH AND BARAK

4 The Israelites again did what was evil in the sight of the LORD after Ehud had died. 2 So the LORD sold them to King Jabin of Canaan, who reigned in Hazor. The commander of his army was Sisera who lived in Harosheth of the Nations.[F] 3 Then the Israelites cried out to the LORD, because Jabin had nine hundred iron chariots, and he harshly oppressed them twenty years.

4 Deborah, a prophetess and the wife of Lappidoth, was judging Israel at that time. 5 She would sit under the palm tree of Deborah between Ramah and Bethel in the hill country of Ephraim, and the Israelites went up to her to settle disputes.

6 She summoned Barak son of Abinoam from Kedesh in Naphtali and said to him, "Hasn't the LORD, the God of Israel, commanded you, 'Go, deploy the troops on Mount Tabor, and take with you ten thousand men from the Naphtalites and Zebulunites? 7 Then I will lure Sisera commander of Jabin's army, his chariots, and his infantry at the Wadi Kishon to fight against you, and I will hand him over to you.'"

8 Barak said to her, "If you will go with me, I will go. But if you will not go with me, I will not go."

9 "I will gladly go with you," she said, "but you will receive no honor on the road you are about to take, because the LORD will sell Sisera to a woman." So Deborah got up and went with Barak to Kedesh. 10 Barak summoned Zebulun and Naphtali to Kedesh; ten thousand men followed him, and Deborah also went with him.

11 Now Heber the Kenite had moved away from the Kenites, the sons of Hobab, Moses's father-in-law, and pitched his tent beside the oak tree of Zaanannim, which was near Kedesh.

12 It was reported to Sisera that Barak son of Abinoam had gone up Mount Tabor. 13 Sisera summoned all his nine hundred iron chariots and all the troops who were with him from Harosheth of the Nations to the Wadi Kishon. 14 Then Deborah said to Barak, "Go! This is the day the LORD has handed Sisera over to you. Hasn't the LORD gone before you?" So Barak came down from Mount Tabor with ten thousand men following him.

15 The LORD threw Sisera, all his charioteers, and all his army into a panic before Barak's assault. Sisera

[A] **3:13** = Jericho; Dt 34:3; Jdg 1:16; 2Ch 28:15 [B] **3:15** = son of the right hand [C] **3:16** Lit *sword a gomed in length* [D] **3:22** Or *And Eglon's bowels discharged* [E] **3:24** Lit *was covering his feet* [F] **4:2** Or *Harosheth-ha-goiim,* also in vv. 13,16

left his chariot and fled on foot. 16 Barak pursued the
chariots and the army as far as Harosheth of the Nations, and the whole army of Sisera fell by the sword;
not a single man was left.

17 Meanwhile, Sisera had fled on foot to the tent of
Jael, the wife of Heber the Kenite, because there was
peace between King Jabin of Hazor and the family of
Heber the Kenite. 18 Jael went out to greet Sisera and
said to him, "Come in, my lord. Come in with me. Don't
be afraid." So he went into her tent, and she covered
him with a blanket. 19 He said to her, "Please give me
a little water to drink for I am thirsty." She opened
a container of milk, gave him a drink, and covered
him again. 20 Then he said to her, "Stand at the entrance to the tent. If a man comes and asks you, 'Is
there a man here?' say, 'No.' " 21 While he was sleeping
from exhaustion, Heber's wife, Jael, took a tent peg,
grabbed a hammer, and went silently to Sisera. She
hammered the peg into his temple and drove it into
the ground, and he died.

22 When Barak arrived in pursuit of Sisera, Jael
went out to greet him and said to him, "Come and
I will show you the man you are looking for." So he
went in with her, and there was Sisera lying dead
with a tent peg through his temple!

23 That day God subdued King Jabin of Canaan before the Israelites. 24 The power of the Israelites continued to increase against King Jabin of Canaan until
they destroyed him.

DEBORAH'S SONG

5 On that day Deborah and Barak son of Abinoam sang:

2 When the leaders lead[A] in Israel,
when the people volunteer,
blessed be the LORD.
3 Listen, kings! Pay attention, princes!
I will sing to the LORD;
I will sing praise to the LORD God of Israel.
4 LORD, when you came from Seir,
when you marched from the fields of Edom,
the earth trembled,
the skies poured rain,
and the clouds poured water.
5 The mountains melted before the LORD,
even Sinai,[B] before the LORD, the God of Israel.

6 In the days of Shamgar son of Anath,
in the days of Jael,
the main roads were deserted
because travelers kept to the side roads.
7 Villages were deserted,[C]
they were deserted in Israel,
until I,[D] Deborah, arose,
a mother in Israel.
8 Israel chose new gods,
then there was war in the city gates.
Not a shield or spear was seen
among forty thousand in Israel.
9 My heart is with the leaders of Israel,
with the volunteers of the people.
Blessed be the LORD!
10 You who ride on white[C] donkeys,
who sit on saddle blankets,
and who travel on the road, give praise!
11 Let them tell the righteous acts of the LORD,
the righteous deeds of his villagers in Israel,
with the voices of the singers
at the watering places.[C]

Then the LORD's people went down to the city
gates.
12 "Awake! Awake, Deborah!
Awake! Awake, sing a song!
Arise, Barak,
and take your prisoners,
son of Abinoam!"
13 Then the survivors came down to the nobles;
the LORD's people came down to me[E]
against the warriors.
14 Those with their roots in Amalek[F] came
from Ephraim;
Benjamin came with your people after you.
The leaders came down from Machir,
and those who carry a marshal's staff came
from Zebulun.
15 The princes of Issachar were with Deborah;
Issachar was with Barak;
they were under his leadership[G] in the valley.
There was great searching[H] of heart
among the clans of Reuben.
16 Why did you sit among the sheep pens[I]
listening to the playing of pipes
for the flocks?
There was great searching of heart
among the clans of Reuben.
17 Gilead remained beyond the Jordan.
Dan, why did you linger at the ships?
Asher remained at the seashore
and stayed in his harbors.
18 The people of Zebulun defied death,
Naphtali also, on the heights of the battlefield.

19 Kings came and fought.
Then the kings of Canaan fought

[A] **5:2** Or *the locks of hair are loose* [B] **5:5** Or LORD, *this one of Sinai*
[C] **5:7,10,11** Hb obscure [D] **5:7** Or *you* [E] **5:13** LXX reads *down for him*
[F] **5:14** LXX reads *in the valley* [G] **5:15** Lit *they set out as his feet*
[H] **5:15** Some Hb mss, Syr read *There were great resolves* [I] **5:16** Or *the campfires*

at Taanach by the Waters of Megiddo,
but they did not plunder the silver.
20 The stars fought from the heavens;
the stars fought with Sisera from their paths.
21 The river Kishon swept them away,
the ancient river, the river Kishon.
March on, my soul, in strength!
22 The horses' hooves then hammered —
the galloping, galloping of his[A] stallions.
23 "Curse Meroz," says the angel of the LORD,
"Bitterly curse her inhabitants,
for they did not come to help the LORD,
to help the LORD with the warriors."

24 Most blessed of women is Jael,
the wife of Heber the Kenite;
she is most blessed among
tent-dwelling women.
25 He asked for water; she gave him milk.
She brought him cream in a majestic bowl.
26 She reached for a tent peg,
her right hand, for a workman's hammer.
Then she hammered Sisera —
she crushed his head;
she shattered and pierced his temple.
27 He collapsed, he fell, he lay down between
her feet;
he collapsed, he fell between her feet;
where he collapsed, there he fell — dead.

28 Sisera's mother looked through the window;
she peered through the lattice, crying out:
"Why is his chariot so long in coming?
Why don't I hear the hoofbeats
of his horses?"[B]
29 Her wisest princesses answer her;
she even answers herself:
30 "Are they not finding and dividing the spoil —
a girl or two[C] for each warrior,
the spoil of colored garments for Sisera,
the spoil of an embroidered garment or two
for my neck?"[D]

31 LORD, may all your enemies perish
as Sisera did.[E]
But may those who love him
be like the rising of the sun in its strength.

And the land had peace for forty years.

MIDIAN OPPRESSES ISRAEL

6 The Israelites did what was evil in the sight of the
LORD. So the LORD handed them over to Midian
seven years, 2 and they oppressed Israel. Because of
Midian, the Israelites made hiding places for themselves in the mountains, caves, and strongholds.
3 Whenever the Israelites planted crops, the Midianites, Amalekites, and the people of the east came
and attacked them. 4 They encamped against them
and destroyed the produce of the land, even as far
as Gaza. They left nothing for Israel to eat, as well as
no sheep, ox, or donkey. 5 For the Midianites came
with their cattle and their tents like a great swarm of
locusts. They and their camels were without number,
and they entered the land to lay waste to it. 6 So Israel
became poverty-stricken because of Midian, and the
Israelites cried out to the LORD.
7 When the Israelites cried out to him because of
Midian, 8 the LORD sent a prophet to them. He said
to them, "This is what the LORD God of Israel says:
'I brought you out of Egypt and out of the place of
slavery. 9 I rescued you from the power of Egypt and
the power of all who oppressed you. I drove them
out before you and gave you their land. 10 I said to
you: I am the LORD your God. Do not fear the gods
of the Amorites whose land you live in. But you did
not obey me.'"

THE LORD CALLS GIDEON

11 The angel of the LORD came, and he sat under the
oak that was in Ophrah, which belonged to Joash,
the Abiezrite. His son Gideon was threshing wheat in
the winepress in order to hide it from the Midianites.
12 Then the angel of the LORD appeared to him and
said, "The LORD is with you, valiant warrior."
13 Gideon said to him, "Please, my lord, if the LORD
is with us, why has all this happened? And where
are all his wonders that our ancestors told us about?
They said, 'Hasn't the LORD brought us out of Egypt?'
But now the LORD has abandoned us and handed us
over to Midian."
14 The LORD turned to him and said, "Go in the
strength you have and deliver Israel from the grasp
of Midian. I am sending you!"
15 He said to him, "Please, Lord, how can I deliver
Israel? Look, my family is the weakest in Manasseh,
and I am the youngest in my father's family."
16 "But I will be with you," the LORD said to him.
"You will strike Midian down as if it were one man."
17 Then he said to him, "If I have found favor with
you, give me a sign that you are speaking with me.
18 Please do not leave this place until I return to you.
Let me bring my gift and set it before you."
And he said, "I will stay until you return."
19 So Gideon went and prepared a young goat and
unleavened bread from a half bushel[F] of flour. He
placed the meat in a basket and the broth in a pot.

[A] **5:22** = Sisera's [B] **5:28** Lit *Why have the hoofbeats of his chariots delayed* [C] **5:30** Lit *a womb or two wombs* [D] **5:30** Hb obscure [E] **5:31** Lit *perish in this way* [F] **6:19** Lit *an ephah*

He brought them out and offered them to him under the oak.

20 The angel of God said to him, "Take the meat with the unleavened bread, put it on this stone, and pour the broth on it." So he did that.

21 The angel of the LORD extended the tip of the staff that was in his hand and touched the meat and the unleavened bread. Fire came up from the rock and consumed the meat and the unleavened bread. Then the angel of the LORD vanished from his sight.

22 When Gideon realized that he was the angel of the LORD, he said, "Oh no, Lord GOD! I have seen the angel of the LORD face to face!"

23 But the LORD said to him, "Peace to you. Don't be afraid, for you will not die." 24 So Gideon built an altar to the LORD there and called it The LORD Is Peace.[A] It is still in Ophrah of the Abiezrites today.

GIDEON TEARS DOWN A BAAL ALTAR

25 On that very night the LORD said to him, "Take your father's young bull and a second bull seven years old. Then tear down the altar of Baal that belongs to your father and cut down the Asherah pole beside it. 26 Build a well-constructed altar to the LORD your God on the top of this mound. Take the second bull and offer it as a burnt offering with the wood of the Asherah pole you cut down." 27 So Gideon took ten of his male servants and did as the LORD had told him. But because he was too afraid of his father's family and the men of the city to do it in the daytime, he did it at night.

28 When the men of the city got up in the morning, they found Baal's altar torn down, the Asherah pole beside it cut down, and the second bull offered up on the altar that had been built. 29 They said to each other, "Who did this?" After they made a thorough investigation, they said, "Gideon son of Joash did it."

30 Then the men of the city said to Joash, "Bring out your son. He must die, because he tore down Baal's altar and cut down the Asherah pole beside it."

31 But Joash said to all who stood against him, "Would you plead Baal's case for him? Would you save him? Whoever pleads his case will be put to death by morning! If he is a god, let him plead his own case because someone tore down his altar." 32 That day Gideon was called Jerubbaal, since Joash said, "Let Baal contend with him," because he tore down his altar.

THE SIGN OF THE FLEECE

33 All the Midianites, Amalekites, and people of the east gathered together, crossed over the Jordan, and camped in the Jezreel Valley.

34 The Spirit of the LORD enveloped[B] Gideon, and he blew the ram's horn and the Abiezrites rallied behind him. 35 He sent messengers throughout all of Manasseh, who rallied behind him. He also sent messengers throughout Asher, Zebulun, and Naphtali, who also came to meet him.

36 Then Gideon said to God, "If you will deliver Israel by me, as you said, 37 I will put a wool fleece here on the threshing floor. If dew is only on the fleece, and all the ground is dry, I will know that you will deliver Israel by me, as you said." 38 And that is what happened. When he got up early in the morning, he squeezed the fleece and wrung dew out of it, filling a bowl with water.

39 Gideon then said to God, "Don't be angry with me; let me speak one more time. Please allow me to make one more test with the fleece. Let it remain dry, and the dew be all over the ground." 40 That night God did as Gideon requested: only the fleece was dry, and dew was all over the ground.

GOD SELECTS GIDEON'S ARMY

7 Jerubbaal (that is, Gideon) and all the troops who were with him, got up early and camped beside the spring of Harod. The camp of Midian was north of them, below the hill of Moreh, in the valley. 2 The LORD said to Gideon, "You have too many troops for me to hand the Midianites over to them, or else Israel might elevate themselves over me and say,[C] 'I saved myself.' 3 Now announce to the troops, 'Whoever is fearful and trembling may turn back and leave Mount Gilead.'" So twenty-two thousand of the troops turned back, but ten thousand remained.

4 Then the LORD said to Gideon, "There are still too many troops. Take them down to the water, and I will test them for you there. If I say to you, 'This one can go with you,' he can go. But if I say about anyone, 'This one cannot go with you,' he cannot go." 5 So he brought the troops down to the water, and the LORD said to Gideon, "Separate everyone who laps water with his tongue like a dog. Do the same with everyone who kneels to drink." 6 The number of those who lapped with their hands to their mouths was three hundred men, and all the rest of the troops knelt to drink water. 7 The LORD said to Gideon, "I will deliver you with the three hundred men who lapped and hand the Midianites over to you. But everyone else is to go home." 8 So Gideon sent all the Israelites to their tents but kept the three hundred troops, who took the provisions and their rams' horns. The camp of Midian was below him in the valley.

GIDEON SPIES ON THE MIDIANITE CAMP

9 That night the LORD said to him, "Get up and attack the camp, for I have handed it over to you. 10 But if you are afraid to attack the camp, go down with Purah

[A] **6:24** = *Yahweh-shalom* [B] **6:34** Lit *clothed*; 1Ch 12:18; 2Ch 24:20
[C] **7:2** Lit *brag against me*

The Role of Geography in the Warfare of the Judges

by Eric A. Mitchell

Geography can help determine military strategy. Armies choose a battleground (if possible) to highlight their strengths as well as their enemy's weaknesses. Typically, each side wants the high ground because of its good defensive capabilities. In the Elah Valley battle (where David faced Goliath), the Philistines had the high ground on the hill to the south at Socoh while the Israelites had the high ground on the ridge to the north at a small walled town (likely Shaaraim, Hb for "two gates"; 1Sm 17:52).[1] Saul's choice of encampment north of the Philistines rather than east of them precluded any Philistine advance or retreat. The Philistines were checkmated; if they moved east into the Judean hills or if they returned westward to home, Israel would attack them from the rear—thus Goliath's forty-day challenge (17:16).

Although geography and weather were crucial to victory, they were not the key factor in determining the outcome of Israel's battles. This was evident when Ben-hadad, king of Aram-Damascus, lost a battle against Israel's King Ahab in the mountainous countryside surrounding Samaria (1Kg 20). In consoling the Aramean king, Ben-hadad's advisers commented, "The LORD is a god of the mountains" (v. 28). To counter this wrong view of God, the Lord again brought Israel victory when the Arameans attacked them on the plain. Jonathan's attack on the Philistine garrison is another example of an Israelite victory despite the geography of the battlefield (1Sm 14). In that instance, the Philistines had the high ground. Jonathan literally had to climb a cliff followed by his armor-bearer to reach the Philistines watching from above; however, God used Jonathan to rout the Philistines.

In the battle of Deborah and Barak versus the Canaanites (led by Sisera) in Judges 4–5, geography and weather combine in a unique way. When Israel cried out to God for deliverance from Canaan's king Jabin, his commander Sisera plus his army of troops and chariots were stationed in the valley just east of Megiddo. Deborah the prophetess was judging Israel in the central hill country just north of Jerusalem; Barak was in his hometown of Kedesh in Naphtali, overlooking the southwestern shore of the Sea of Galilee.

God planned the battle. He chose the commander, the troops, the gathering and campsite, the enemy, the battlefield terrain, the plan of attack, the timing, and—as we will see—the weather.

The effect of Sisera's nine hundred iron chariots upon Israel's ranks would have been similar to nine hundred armed and armored Humvees attacking two light infantry divisions today. The chariot in ancient times was not large, usually only about five feet from wheel to wheel and was pulled by one or two horses. They typically carried two warriors, a driver and an archer, both of whom would have a sword. The chariot would also carry javelins for them to throw at the enemy. A chariot charge could have a devastating effect on an infantry, scattering them in the field. Using chariots, soldiers would often dart in, fire arrows point-blank at frontline troops, and then quickly get out of range. Since chariots needed smooth ground, the steep slopes of Mount Tabor (a rounded cone-shaped mountain rising out of the eastern valley of Megiddo) were a good collection point for the nearby tribal warriors and yet safe from chariotry.[2]

With Barak and his ten thousand troops stationed on the slopes of Tabor, God drew the Canaanite chariots and army out across the floodplain of the little Kishon River. The Canaanite chariots would have had to move directly eastward from Megiddo crossing the Kishon and its

Barak stationed his troops on the slopes of Mount Tabor when facing the Canaanites. Mount Tabor rises to about 1,843 feet above sea level.

Kishon River Valley; Sisera gathered his soldiers and nine hundred iron chariots to the Kishon River as he prepared to fight Deborah and Barak.

feeder streams to approach the Israelites at Mount Tabor. Normally the Kishon is not much larger than what we would call a small creek. The Kishon winds its way through the flat valley of Megiddo from southeast to northwest. The valley has only a small exit to the northwest between the slopes of the Carmel mountain range on the southwest and a ridge to the northwest that separated the valley from the coast. Because of this poor drainage, rain would cause the Kishon to overflow its banks, and much of the valley became a swamp. The Canaanites marched out toward Tabor, but when they were in the valley, God sent a surprise attack—a thunderstorm.[3] The Canaanites' heavy iron chariot wheels sank into the soft muddy ground. At that moment, the Canaanites saw the disaster and they turned to flee (5:22). At the same time, Deborah ordered Barak to attack. The Israelite warriors charged down-slope into the bogged-down chariots—a direct reversal of fortunes for the Canaanites. Barak caught the Canaanites in mud that not long before had been solid ground. It was a slaughter.

We would expect that at the moment of attack Barak and his men pulled out their weapons and charged, but the men of Naphtali and Zebulun who rushed down the slopes of Tabor had no spears or shields (see 5:8). This could mean they fought with swords only. First Chronicles 12:33–34 indicates, however, that a Naphtali warrior's normal weaponry was spear and shield and that Zebulun fought with all sorts of weapons. The lack of weapons likely means these men had no regular weapons but had resorted to whatever was available (Jdg 3:31—Shamgar delivered Israel with a cattle prod; Jdg 15—Samson defeated the Philistines with the jawbone of a donkey). Perhaps the Canaanites had banned the Israelites from owning weapons or blacksmithing. A similar situation existed at the end of the period of the judges and beginning of the monarchy, when Saul and Jonathan were the only Israelites with swords when they fought the Philistines (1Sm 13:19–22). In that instance, the Philistines were regulating the blacksmith trade so Israel could not make or sharpen their own weapons or tools. Perhaps the men of Naphtali and Zebulun were using farm implements such as "plows, mattocks, axes, and sickles" (1Sm 13:20). In any case, even though the Canaanites' weaponry overmatched their own, the Israelite forces attacked, pursued, and annihilated the Canaanite army to the last man. ✜

---

[1] This city with two gates was recently discovered by Israeli archaeologist Yosef Garfinkel, Khirbet Qeiyafa Archaeological Project, http://qeiyafa.huji.ac.il/. [2] Thomas Brisco, *Holman Bible Atlas* (Nashville: B&H, 1998), 148. [3] Deborah mentions the rain in several ways in her song about the battle in Judges 5. In verse 4: "the earth trembled"—thunder; "the skies poured"—rain; "the clouds poured"—heavy rain. In verse 20: "the stars fought from the heavens"—divine intervention, perhaps again rain. In verse 21: "The river Kishon swept them away"—flooding.

your servant. 11 Listen to what they say, and then you
will be encouraged to attack the camp." So he went
down with Purah his servant to the outpost of the
troops[A] who were in the camp.
12 Now the Midianites, Amalekites, and all the people of the east had settled down in the valley like a
swarm of locusts, and their camels were as innumerable as the sand on the seashore. 13 When Gideon
arrived, there was a man telling his friend about a
dream. He said, "Listen, I had a dream: a loaf of barley
bread came tumbling into the Midianite camp, struck
a tent, and it fell. The loaf turned the tent upside down
so that it collapsed."
14 His friend answered, "This is nothing less than
the sword of Gideon son of Joash, the Israelite. God
has handed the entire Midianite camp over to him."

GIDEON ATTACKS THE MIDIANITES

15 When Gideon heard the account of the dream and
its interpretation, he bowed in worship. He returned
to Israel's camp and said, "Get up, for the LORD has
handed the Midianite camp over to you." 16 Then he
divided the three hundred men into three companies and gave each of the men a ram's horn in one
hand and an empty pitcher with a torch inside it in
the other hand.
17 "Watch me," he said to them, "and do what I do.
When I come to the outpost of the camp, do as I do.
18 When I and everyone with me blow our rams' horns,
you are also to blow your rams' horns all around
the camp. Then you will say, 'For the LORD and for
Gideon!'"
19 Gideon and the hundred men who were with him
went to the outpost of the camp at the beginning of the
middle watch after the sentries had been stationed.
They blew their rams' horns and broke the pitchers
that were in their hands. 20 The three companies blew
their rams' horns and shattered their pitchers. They
held their torches in their left hands and their rams'
horns to blow in their right hands, and they shouted,
"A sword for the LORD and for Gideon!" 21 Each Israelite
took his position around the camp, and the entire Midianite army began to run, and they cried out as they
fled. 22 When Gideon's men blew their three hundred
rams' horns, the LORD caused the men in the whole
army to turn on each other with their swords. They
fled to Acacia House[B] in the direction of Zererah as far
as the border of Abel-meholah near Tabbath. 23 Then
the men of Israel were called from Naphtali, Asher,
and Manasseh, and they pursued the Midianites.

THE MEN OF EPHRAIM JOIN THE BATTLE

24 Gideon sent messengers throughout the hill country of Ephraim with this message: "Come down to
intercept the Midianites and take control of the watercourses ahead of them as far as Beth-barah and
the Jordan." So all the men of Ephraim were called
out, and they took control of the watercourses as
far as Beth-barah and the Jordan. 25 They captured
Oreb and Zeeb, the two princes of Midian; they killed
Oreb at the rock of Oreb and Zeeb at the winepress
of Zeeb, while they were pursuing the Midianites.
They brought the heads of Oreb and Zeeb to Gideon
across the Jordan.

8 The men of Ephraim said to him, "Why have you
done this to us, not calling us when you went to
fight against the Midianites?" And they argued with
him violently.
2 So he said to them, "What have I done now compared to you? Is not the gleaning of Ephraim better
than the grape harvest of Abiezer? 3 God handed over
to you Oreb and Zeeb, the two princes of Midian. What
was I able to do compared to you?" When he said this,
their anger against him subsided.

GIDEON PURSUES THE KINGS OF MIDIAN

4 Gideon and the three hundred men came to the Jordan and crossed it. They were exhausted but still in
pursuit. 5 He said to the men of Succoth, "Please give
some loaves of bread to the troops under my command,[C] because they are exhausted, for I am pursuing
Zebah and Zalmunna, the kings of Midian."
6 But the princes of Succoth asked, "Are Zebah and
Zalmunna now in your hands that we should give
bread to your army?"
7 Gideon replied, "Very well, when the LORD has
handed Zebah and Zalmunna over to me, I will tear[D]
your flesh with thorns and briers from the wilderness!" 8 He went from there to Penuel and asked the
same thing from them. The men of Penuel answered
just as the men of Succoth had answered. 9 He also
told the men of Penuel, "When I return safely, I will
tear down this tower!"
10 Now Zebah and Zalmunna were in Karkor, and
with them was their army of about fifteen thousand
men, who were all those left of the entire army of the
people of the east. Those who had been killed were
one hundred twenty thousand armed men. 11 Gideon traveled on the caravan route[E] east of Nobah and
Jogbehah and attacked their army while the army felt
secure. 12 Zebah and Zalmunna fled, and he pursued
them. He captured these two kings of Midian and
routed the entire army.
13 Gideon son of Joash returned from the battle
by the Ascent of Heres. 14 He captured a youth from
the men of Succoth and interrogated him. The youth
wrote down for him the names of the seventy-seven

[A] **7:11** Lit *of those who were arranged in companies of 50* [B] **7:22** Or *Beth-shittah* [C] **8:5** Lit *troops at my feet* [D] **8:7** Lit *thresh* [E] **8:11** Lit *on the route of those who live in tents*

leaders and elders of Succoth. 15 Then he went to the men of Succoth and said, "Here are Zebah and Zalmunna. You taunted me about them, saying, 'Are Zebah and Zalmunna now in your power that we should give bread to your exhausted men?' " 16 So he took the elders of the city, and he took some thorns and briers from the wilderness, and he disciplined the men of Succoth with them. 17 He also tore down the tower of Penuel and killed the men of the city.

18 He asked Zebah and Zalmunna, "What kind of men did you kill at Tabor?"

"They were like you," they said. "Each resembled the son of a king."

19 So he said, "They were my brothers, the sons of my mother! As the LORD lives, if you had let them live, I would not kill you." 20 Then he said to Jether, his firstborn, "Get up and kill them." The youth did not draw his sword, for he was afraid because he was still a youth.

21 Zebah and Zalmunna said, "Get up and strike us down yourself, for a man is judged by his strength." So Gideon got up, killed Zebah and Zalmunna, and took the crescent ornaments that were on the necks of their camels.

GIDEON'S LEGACY

22 Then the Israelites said to Gideon, "Rule over us, you as well as your sons and your grandsons, for you delivered us from the power of Midian."

23 But Gideon said to them, "I will not rule over you, and my son will not rule over you; the LORD will rule over you." 24 Then he said to them, "Let me make a request of you: Everyone give me an earring from his plunder." Now the enemy had gold earrings because they were Ishmaelites.

25 They said, "We agree to give them." So they spread out a cloak, and everyone threw an earring from his plunder on it. 26 The weight of the gold earrings he requested was forty-three pounds[A] of gold, in addition to the crescent ornaments and ear pendants, the purple garments on the kings of Midian, and the chains on the necks of their camels. 27 Gideon made an ephod from all this and put it in Ophrah, his hometown. Then all Israel prostituted themselves by worshiping it there, and it became a snare to Gideon and his household.

28 So Midian was subdued before the Israelites, and they were no longer a threat. The land had peace for forty years during the days of Gideon. 29 Jerubbaal (that is, Gideon) son of Joash went back to live at his house.

30 Gideon had seventy sons, his own offspring, since he had many wives. 31 His concubine who was in Shechem also bore him a son, and he named him Abimelech. 32 Then Gideon son of Joash died at a good old age and was buried in the tomb of his father Joash in Ophrah of the Abiezrites.

33 When Gideon died, the Israelites turned and prostituted themselves by worshiping the Baals and made Baal-berith[B] their god. 34 The Israelites did not remember the LORD their God who had rescued them from the hand of the enemies around them. 35 They did not show kindness to the house of Jerubbaal (that is, Gideon) for all the good he had done for Israel.

ABIMELECH BECOMES KING

9 Abimelech son of Jerubbaal went to Shechem and spoke to his uncles and to his mother's whole clan, saying, 2 "Please speak in the hearing of all the citizens of Shechem, 'Is it better for you that seventy men, all the sons of Jerubbaal, rule over you or that one man rule over you?' Remember that I am your own flesh and blood."[C]

3 His mother's relatives spoke all these words about him in the hearing of all the citizens of Shechem, and they were favorable to Abimelech, for they said, "He is our brother." 4 So they gave him seventy pieces of silver from the temple of Baal-berith.[B] Abimelech used it to hire worthless and reckless men, and they followed him. 5 He went to his father's house in Ophrah and killed his seventy brothers, the sons of Jerubbaal, on top of a large stone. But Jotham, the youngest son of Jerubbaal, survived, because he hid. 6 Then all the citizens of Shechem and of Beth-millo gathered together and proceeded to make Abimelech king at the oak of the pillar in Shechem.

JOTHAM'S PARABLE

7 When they told Jotham, he climbed to the top of Mount Gerizim, raised his voice, and called to them:

Listen to me, citizens of Shechem,
and may God listen to you:

8 The trees decided
to anoint a king over themselves.
They said to the olive tree, "Reign over us."
9 But the olive tree said to them,
"Should I stop giving my oil
that people use to honor both God and men,
and rule[D] over the trees?"

10 Then the trees said to the fig tree,
"Come and reign over us."
11 But the fig tree said to them,
"Should I stop giving
my sweetness and my good fruit,
and rule over trees?"

[A] 8:26 Lit *1,700 shekels* [B] 8:33; 9:4 Lit *Baal of the Covenant*, or *Lord of the Covenant* [C] 9:2 Lit *your bone and your flesh* [D] 9:9 Lit *and go to sway*, also in vv. 11,13

12 Later, the trees said to the grapevine,
"Come and reign over us."
13 But the grapevine said to them,
"Should I stop giving my wine
that cheers both God and man,
and rule over trees?"

14 Finally, all the trees said to the bramble,
"Come and reign over us."
15 The bramble said to the trees,
"If you really are anointing me
as king over you,
come and find refuge in my shade.
But if not,
may fire come out from the bramble
and consume the cedars of Lebanon."

16 "Now if you have acted faithfully and honestly
in making Abimelech king, if you have done well by
Jerubbaal and his family, and if you have rewarded him appropriately for what he did — 17 for my
father fought for you, risked his life, and rescued
you from Midian, 18 and now you have attacked my
father's family today, killed his seventy sons on top
of a large stone, and made Abimelech, the son of his
slave woman, king over the citizens of Shechem 'because he is your brother' — 19 so if you have acted
faithfully and honestly with Jerubbaal and his house
this day, rejoice in Abimelech and may he also rejoice
in you. 20 But if not, may fire come from Abimelech
and consume the citizens of Shechem and Beth-millo,
and may fire come from the citizens of Shechem and
Beth-millo and consume Abimelech." 21 Then Jotham
fled, escaping to Beer, and lived there because of his
brother Abimelech.

ABIMELECH'S PUNISHMENT

22 When Abimelech had ruled over Israel three years,
23 God sent an evil spirit between Abimelech and the
citizens of Shechem. They treated Abimelech deceitfully, 24 so that the crime against the seventy sons
of Jerubbaal might come to justice and their blood
would be avenged on their brother Abimelech, who
killed them, and on the citizens of Shechem, who
had helped him kill his brothers. 25 The citizens of
Shechem rebelled against him by putting men in ambush on the tops of the mountains, and they robbed
everyone who passed by them on the road. So this
was reported to Abimelech.

26 Gaal son of Ebed came with his brothers and
crossed into Shechem, and the citizens of Shechem
trusted him. 27 So they went out to the countryside
and harvested grapes from their vineyards. They
trampled the grapes and held a celebration. Then
they went to the house of their god, and as they ate
and drank, they cursed Abimelech. 28 Gaal son of Ebed
said, "Who is Abimelech and who is Shechem that we
should serve him? Isn't he the son of Jerubbaal, and
isn't Zebul his officer? You are to serve the men of
Hamor, the father of Shechem. Why should we serve
Abimelech? 29 If only these people were in my power, I
would remove Abimelech." So he said[A] to Abimelech,
"Gather your army and come out."

30 When Zebul, the ruler of the city, heard the words
of Gaal son of Ebed, he was angry. 31 So he secretly sent
messengers to Abimelech, saying, "Beware! Gaal son of
Ebed and his brothers have come to Shechem and are
turning the city against you.[B] 32 Now tonight, you and
the troops with you, come and wait in ambush in the
countryside. 33 Then get up early, and at sunrise attack
the city. When he and the troops who are with him
come out against you, do to him whatever you can."
34 So Abimelech and all the troops with him got up at
night and waited in ambush for Shechem in four units.

35 Gaal son of Ebed went out and stood at the
entrance of the city gate. Then Abimelech and the
troops who were with him got up from their ambush.
36 When Gaal saw the troops, he said to Zebul, "Look,
troops are coming down from the mountaintops!"
But Zebul said to him, "The shadows of the mountains
look like men to you."

37 Then Gaal spoke again, "Look, troops are coming
down from the central part of the land, and one unit
is coming from the direction of the Diviners' Oak."
38 Zebul replied, "What do you have to say now? You
said, 'Who is Abimelech that we should serve him?'
Aren't these the troops you despised? Now go and
fight them!"

39 So Gaal went out leading the citizens of Shechem
and fought against Abimelech, 40 but Abimelech pursued him, and Gaal fled before him. Numerous bodies
were strewn as far as the entrance of the city gate.
41 Abimelech stayed in Arumah, and Zebul drove Gaal
and his brothers from Shechem.

42 The next day when the people of Shechem[C] went
into the countryside, this was reported to Abimelech.
43 He took the troops, divided them into three companies, and waited in ambush in the countryside. He
looked, and the people were coming out of the city, so
he arose against them and struck them down. 44 Then
Abimelech and the units that were with him rushed
forward and took their stand at the entrance of the
city gate. The other two units rushed against all who
were in the countryside and struck them down. 45 So
Abimelech fought against the city that entire day, captured it, and killed the people who were in it. Then he
tore down the city and sowed it with salt.

[A] **9:29** DSS read *They said*; LXX reads *I would say* [B] **9:31** Hb obscure
[C] **9:42** *of Shechem* supplied for clarity

46 When all the citizens of the Tower of Shechem heard, they entered the inner chamber[A] of the temple of El-berith.[B] 47 Then it was reported to Abimelech that all the citizens of the Tower of Shechem had gathered. 48 So Abimelech and all the troops who were with him went up to Mount Zalmon. Abimelech took his ax in his hand and cut a branch from the trees. He picked up the branch, put it on his shoulder, and said to the troops who were with him, "Hurry and do what you have seen me do." 49 Each of the troops also cut his own branch and followed Abimelech. They put the branches against the inner chamber and set it on fire; about a thousand men and women died, including all the men of the Tower of Shechem.

50 Abimelech went to Thebez, camped against it, and captured it. 51 There was a strong tower inside the city, and all the men, women, and citizens of the city fled there. They locked themselves in and went up to the roof of the tower. 52 When Abimelech came to attack the tower, he approached its entrance to set it on fire. 53 But a woman threw the upper portion of a millstone on Abimelech's head and fractured his skull. 54 He quickly called his armor-bearer and said to him, "Draw your sword and kill me, or they'll say about me, 'A woman killed him.'" So his armor-bearer ran him through, and he died. 55 When the Israelites saw that Abimelech was dead, they all went home.

56 In this way, God brought back Abimelech's evil—the evil that Abimelech had done to his father when he killed his seventy brothers. 57 God also brought back to the men of Shechem all their evil. So the curse of Jotham son of Jerubbaal came upon them.

TOLA AND JAIR

10 After Abimelech, Tola son of Puah, son of Dodo became judge and began to deliver Israel. He was from Issachar and lived in Shamir in the hill country of Ephraim. 2 Tola judged Israel twenty-three years and when he died, was buried in Shamir.

3 After him came Jair the Gileadite, who judged Israel twenty-two years. 4 He had thirty sons who rode on thirty donkeys. They had thirty towns[C] in Gilead, which are still called Jair's Villages[D] today. 5 When Jair died, he was buried in Kamon.

ISRAEL'S REBELLION AND REPENTANCE

6 Then the Israelites again did what was evil in the sight of the LORD. They worshiped the Baals and the Ashtoreths, the gods of Aram, Sidon, and Moab, and the gods of the Ammonites and the Philistines. They abandoned the LORD and did not worship him. 7 So the LORD's anger burned against Israel, and he sold them to the Philistines and the Ammonites. 8 They shattered and crushed the Israelites that year, and for eighteen years they did the same to all the Israelites who were on the other side of the Jordan in the land of the Amorites in Gilead. 9 The Ammonites also crossed the Jordan to fight against Judah, Benjamin, and the house of Ephraim. Israel was greatly oppressed, 10 so they cried out to the LORD, saying, "We have sinned against you. We have abandoned our God and worshiped the Baals."

11 The LORD said to the Israelites, "When the Egyptians, Amorites, Ammonites, Philistines, 12 Sidonians, Amalekites, and Maonites[E] oppressed you, and you cried out to me, did I not deliver you from them? 13 But you have abandoned me and worshiped other gods. Therefore, I will not deliver you again. 14 Go and cry out to the gods you have chosen. Let them deliver you whenever you are oppressed."

15 But the Israelites said, "We have sinned. Deal with us as you see fit; only rescue us today!" 16 So they got rid of the foreign gods among them and worshiped the LORD, and he became weary of Israel's misery.

17 The Ammonites were called together, and they camped in Gilead. So the Israelites assembled and camped at Mizpah. 18 The rulers[F] of Gilead said to one another, "Which man will begin the fight against the Ammonites? He will be the leader of all the inhabitants of Gilead."

JEPHTHAH BECOMES ISRAEL'S LEADER

11 Jephthah the Gileadite was a valiant warrior, but he was the son of a prostitute, and Gilead was his father. 2 Gilead's wife bore him sons, and when they grew up, they drove Jephthah out and said to him, "You will have no inheritance in our father's family, because you are the son of another woman." 3 So Jephthah fled from his brothers and lived in the land of Tob. Then some worthless men joined Jephthah and went on raids with him.

4 Some time later, the Ammonites fought against Israel. 5 When the Ammonites made war with Israel, the elders of Gilead went to get Jephthah from the land of Tob. 6 They said to him, "Come, be our commander, and let's fight the Ammonites."

7 Jephthah replied to the elders of Gilead, "Didn't you hate me and drive me out of my father's family? Why then have you come to me now when you're in trouble?"

8 They answered Jephthah, "That's true. But now we turn to you. Come with us, fight the Ammonites, and you will become leader of all the inhabitants of Gilead."

9 So Jephthah said to them, "If you are bringing me back to fight the Ammonites and the LORD gives them to me, I will be your leader."

[A] **9:46** Or *the crypt*, or *the vault* [B] **9:46** = God of the Covenant
[C] **10:4** LXX; MT reads *donkeys* [D] **10:4** Or *called Havvoth-jair*
[E] **10:12** LXX reads *Midianites* [F] **10:18** Lit *The people, rulers*

Ashtoreth

by Robert A. Street

The Canaanites were nature worshipers, and their gods were intricately connected with the region's cycle of nature. With a climate having a wet season and a dry season, half of the year was fertile with prospering crops. The other half was dry and crops perished. The Canaanites assumed that when their gods were unhappy or separated, the land languished and was barren. Believing the gods responded to actions on earth, Canaanite worship searched for ways to entice the gods to be gracious. How could the Canaanites control the gods who brought the prosperity of the crops and the land? By "proper worship," of course. The Hebrews then bought into the Canaanite way of worship centered on a fertility cult.

So who or what were the gods enticing the Hebrews into apostasy and desertion? Judges 2:13 identifies them as Baal and Ashtaroth. "[Ashtaroth] seems to have become a generic term for the female deities of the Canaanites, and when used with Baal, or Baalim, it was the collective term for pagan deities."[1] Baalim and Ashtaroth are plural nouns. As plural nouns, the terms most likely reference a local manifestation of the Canaanite god Baal and the Canaanite goddess Ashtoreth.[2]

Baal is more familiar to readers of the Old Testament. Scripture, however, does little to explain what exactly took place in the Canaanites' nature worship. To ascertain how the Canaanites understood their gods and goddesses influenced the natural world, we must look to parallels from the ancient Near East. The people of Babylon, Assyria, Ugarit, and Egypt practiced nature worship with similar deities.

Baal was the Canaanite fertility god and god of the storm. Hence, they believed he brought the rains to grow crops. The Ugaritic tablets from Ras Shamra, which date about 1400 BC, describe a relationship between Baal and his goddess consort, wife, and sister.

To further complicate matters, Ashtoreth might have gone by several different names.[3] The multiple names might explain why the book of Judges uses the plural forms. A Greek transliteration of her name is Astarte. Though it is not certain, the people of Ras Shamra may have referred to her as Anat. Another possibility is that she was known as Asherah.[4] Her Babylonian and Assyrian counterpart was Ishtar (or Ashtar). Even if not referring to the same deity, the functions were similar. She was the goddess of fertility, the bringer of life, and even the destroyer of death.

The Old Testament provides no physical description of a god or any pagan deities. History teaches, though, that Astarte (Ashtaroth) was symbolized by a wooden pole, a tree, or even a grove of trees. Not surprisingly, the wooden figures representing Astarte have not survived. Stone and terra-cotta Astarte images and symbols from the ancient Near East, though, have survived. In the fourteenth century BC, Ras Shamra portrayed her in clay and terra-cotta figurines, decorative stone friezes, and even ivory carvings. The stele of Ashtoreth from Beth-shean has a depiction of her. Egyptians depicted her counterpart as a nude goddess. While we cannot know for certain that the disloyal Hebrews knew her in these forms, they did worship a goddess like her in the hopes of guaranteeing the land fertility.

Asherah figurine. Mentioned throughout the Old Testament, Asherah was the primary goddess of Syria and Canaan. The people believed she was the wife of the Canaanite god El and also mother to seventy other gods, the most famous being Baal.

Cultic figurine of Astarte; from Cyprus; dated about 1300 BC.

Terra-cotta stamped relief depicting Ishtar holding her weapon, Eshnunna; from Mesopotamia; dated second millennium BC.

WORSHIP PRACTICES

What exactly was the worship activity that took place and made the apostasy so difficult to remove from Israel and Judah? History provides no actual descriptions of what took place. But perhaps no verse gives better hints about Baal and Astarte worship than Amos 2:7: "A man and his father have sexual relations with the same girl, profaning my holy name."

The religion's worship practice included "sacred" prostitution in which the men had intimate relations with the priestesses of the goddess, and the women, with the priests of the god. The concept behind such action was one of "sympathetic" magic. The devotees of the cult enacted orgiastic rites in worship. "According to a pattern of sympathetic or imitative magic, whereby the worshiper imitates the actions he desires the gods to perform, male and female worshipers engaged in sacred prostitution, supposing thereby to assure the rhythmic cycle of nature."[5] Their actions were in essence saying, "May Baal, the god of the storm, send the rain to fertilize the earth and cause the crops to flourish." The idea was as the gods saw what was on earth, so it went in heaven and vice versa. ✣

---

[1] Bryce N. Sandlin, "Ashtaroth" *Biblical Illustrator* (*BI*) 15.4 (Summer 1989): 18. [2] Sandlin, "Ashtaroth"; Scott Langston, "Ashtaroth" in *HolBD*, 112–13. [3] Jimmy Albright, "Ashtoreth," *BI* 6.1 (Fall 1979): 23–24. [4] "§1718 [`*ashtarot*]" (Ashtaroth) in *TWOT*, 707. See Sandlin, "Ashtaroth," 18–19. [5] James King West, *Introduction to the Old Testament*, 2nd ed. (New York: Macmillan, 1981), 216.

This fifteen-ton lion symbolized the Assyrian goddess Ishtar. A pair of these statues guarded her temple at Nimrud. The statue measures 8 ½ feet tall and 13 feet long.

10 The elders of Gilead said to Jephthah, "The LORD is our witness if we don't do as you say." 11 So Jephthah went with the elders of Gilead. The people made him their leader and commander, and Jephthah repeated all his terms in the presence of the LORD at Mizpah.

JEPHTHAH REJECTS AMMONITE CLAIMS

12 Jephthah sent messengers to the king of the Ammonites, asking, "What do you have against me that you have come to fight me in my land?"

13 The king of the Ammonites said to Jephthah's messengers, "When Israel came from Egypt, they seized my land from the Arnon to the Jabbok and the Jordan. Now restore it peaceably."

14 Jephthah again sent messengers to the king of the Ammonites 15 to tell him, "This is what Jephthah says: Israel did not take away the land of Moab or the land of the Ammonites. 16 But when they came from Egypt, Israel traveled through the wilderness to the Red Sea and came to Kadesh. 17 Israel sent messengers to the king of Edom, saying, 'Please let us travel through your land,' but the king of Edom would not listen. They also sent messengers to the king of Moab, but he refused. So Israel stayed in Kadesh.

18 "Then they traveled through the wilderness and around the lands of Edom and Moab. They came to the east side of the land of Moab and camped on the other side of the Arnon but did not enter into the territory of Moab, for the Arnon was the boundary of Moab.

19 "Then Israel sent messengers to Sihon king of the Amorites, king of Heshbon. Israel said to him, 'Please let us travel through your land to our country,' 20 but Sihon would not trust Israel to pass through his territory. Instead, Sihon gathered all his troops, camped at Jahaz, and fought with Israel. 21 Then the LORD God of Israel handed over Sihon and all his troops to Israel, and they defeated them. So Israel took possession of the entire land of the Amorites who lived in that country. 22 They took possession of all the territory of the Amorites from the Arnon to the Jabbok and from the wilderness to the Jordan.

23 "The LORD God of Israel has now driven out the Amorites before his people Israel, and will you now force us out? 24 Isn't it true that you can have whatever your god Chemosh conquers for you, and we can have whatever the LORD our God conquers for us? 25 Now are you any better than Balak son of Zippor, king of Moab? Did he ever contend with Israel or fight against them? 26 While Israel lived three hundred years in Heshbon and Aroer and their surrounding villages, and in all the cities that are on the banks of the Arnon, why didn't you take them back at that time? 27 I have not sinned against you, but you are doing me wrong by fighting against me. Let the LORD who is the judge decide today between the Israelites and the Ammonites." 28 But the king of the Ammonites would not listen to Jephthah's message that he sent him.

JEPHTHAH'S VOW AND SACRIFICE

29 The Spirit of the LORD came on Jephthah, who traveled through Gilead and Manasseh, and then through Mizpah of Gilead. He crossed over to the Ammonites from Mizpah of Gilead. 30 Jephthah made this vow to the LORD: "If you in fact hand over the Ammonites to me, 31 whoever comes out the doors of my house to greet me when I return safely from the Ammonites will belong to the LORD, and I will offer that person as a burnt offering."

32 Jephthah crossed over to the Ammonites to fight against them, and the LORD handed them over to him. 33 He defeated twenty of their cities with a great slaughter from Aroer all the way to the entrance of Minnith and to Abel-keramim. So the Ammonites were subdued before the Israelites.

34 When Jephthah went to his home in Mizpah, there was his daughter, coming out to meet him with tambourines and dancing! She was his only child; he had no other son or daughter besides her. 35 When he saw her, he tore his clothes and said, "No! Not my daughter! You have devastated me! You have brought great misery on me.[A] I have given my word to the LORD and cannot take it back."

36 Then she said to him, "My father, you have given your word to the LORD. Do to me as you have said, for the LORD brought vengeance on your enemies, the Ammonites." 37 She also said to her father, "Let me do this one thing: Let me wander two months through the mountains with my friends and mourn my virginity."

38 "Go," he said. And he sent her away two months. So she left with her friends and mourned her virginity as she wandered through the mountains. 39 At the end of two months, she returned to her father, and he kept the vow he had made about her. And she had never been intimate with a man. Now it became a custom in Israel 40 that four days each year the young women of Israel would commemorate the daughter of Jephthah the Gileadite.

CONFLICT WITH EPHRAIM

12 The men of Ephraim were called together and crossed the Jordan to Zaphon. They said to Jephthah, "Why have you crossed over to fight against the Ammonites but didn't call us to go with you? We will burn your house with you in it!"

2 Then Jephthah said to them, "My people and I had a bitter conflict with the Ammonites. So I called for you, but you didn't deliver me from their power.

[A] **11:35** Lit *have been among those who trouble me*

3 When I saw that you weren't going to deliver me, I took my life in my own hands and crossed over to the Ammonites, and the LORD handed them over to me. Why then have you come today to fight against me?"

4 Then Jephthah gathered all of the men of Gilead. They fought and defeated Ephraim, because Ephraim had said, "You Gileadites are Ephraimite fugitives in the territories of Ephraim and Manasseh." 5 The Gileadites captured the fords of the Jordan leading to Ephraim. Whenever a fugitive from Ephraim said, "Let me cross over," the Gileadites asked him, "Are you an Ephraimite?" If he answered, "No," 6 they told him, "Please say Shibboleth." If he said, "Sibboleth," because he could not pronounce it correctly, they seized him and executed him at the fords of the Jordan. At that time forty-two thousand from Ephraim died.

7 Jephthah judged Israel six years, and when he died, he was buried in one of the cities of Gilead.[A]

IBZAN, ELON, AND ABDON

8 Ibzan, who was from Bethlehem, judged Israel after Jephthah 9 and had thirty sons. He gave his thirty daughters in marriage to men outside the tribe and brought back thirty wives for his sons from outside the tribe. Ibzan judged Israel seven years, 10 and when he died, he was buried in Bethlehem.

11 Elon, who was from Zebulun, judged Israel after Ibzan. He judged Israel ten years, 12 and when he died, he was buried in Aijalon in the land of Zebulun.

13 After Elon, Abdon son of Hillel, who was from Pirathon, judged Israel. 14 He had forty sons and thirty grandsons, who rode on seventy donkeys. Abdon judged Israel eight years, 15 and when he died, he was buried in Pirathon in the land of Ephraim, in the hill country of the Amalekites.

BIRTH OF SAMSON

13 The Israelites again did what was evil in the LORD's sight, so the LORD handed them over to the Philistines forty years. 2 There was a certain man from Zorah, from the family of Dan, whose name was Manoah; his wife was unable to conceive and had no children. 3 The angel of the LORD appeared to the woman and said to her, "Although you are unable to conceive and have no children, you will conceive and give birth to a son. 4 Now please be careful not to drink wine or beer, or to eat anything unclean; 5 for indeed, you will conceive and give birth to a son. You must never cut his hair,[B] because the boy will be a Nazirite to God from birth, and he will begin to save Israel from the power of the Philistines."

6 Then the woman went and told her husband, "A man of God came to me. He looked like the awe-inspiring angel of God. I didn't ask him where he came from, and he didn't tell me his name. 7 He said to me, 'You will conceive and give birth to a son. Therefore, do not drink wine or beer, and do not eat anything unclean, because the boy will be a Nazirite to God from birth until the day of his death.'"

8 Manoah prayed to the LORD and said, "Please, Lord, let the man of God you sent come again to us and teach us what we should do for the boy who will be born."

9 God listened to Manoah, and the angel of God came again to the woman. She was sitting in the field, and her husband, Manoah, was not with her. 10 The woman ran quickly to her husband and told him, "The man who came to me the other day has just come back!"

11 So Manoah got up and followed his wife. When he came to the man, he asked, "Are you the man who spoke to my wife?"

"I am," he said.

12 Then Manoah asked, "When your words come true, what will be the boy's responsibilities and work?"

13 The angel of the LORD answered Manoah, "Your wife needs to do everything I told her. 14 She must not eat anything that comes from the grapevine or drink wine or beer. And she must not eat anything unclean. Your wife must do everything I have commanded her."

15 "Please stay here," Manoah told him, "and we will prepare a young goat for you."

16 The angel of the LORD said to him, "If I stay, I won't eat your food. But if you want to prepare a burnt offering, offer it to the LORD." (Manoah did not know he was the angel of the LORD.)

17 Then Manoah said to him, "What is your name, so that we may honor you when your words come true?"

18 "Why do you ask my name," the angel of the LORD asked him, "since it is beyond understanding?"

19 Manoah took a young goat and a grain offering and offered them on a rock to the LORD, who did something miraculous[C] while Manoah and his wife were watching. 20 When the flame went up from the altar to the sky, the angel of the LORD went up in its flame. When Manoah and his wife saw this, they fell facedown on the ground. 21 The angel of the LORD did not appear again to Manoah and his wife. Then Manoah realized that it was the angel of the LORD.

22 "We're certainly going to die," he said to his wife, "because we have seen God!"

23 But his wife said to him, "If the LORD had intended to kill us, he wouldn't have accepted the burnt offering and the grain offering from us, and he would not have shown us all these things or spoken to us like this."

[A] **12:7** LXX reads *in his city in Gilead* [B] **13:5** Lit *And a razor is not to go up on his head* [C] **13:19** LXX reads *to the LORD, to the one who works wonders*

24 So the woman gave birth to a son and named him Samson. The boy grew, and the LORD blessed him. 25 Then the Spirit of the LORD began to stir him in the Camp of Dan,[A] between Zorah and Eshtaol.

SAMSON'S RIDDLE

14 Samson went down to Timnah and saw a young Philistine woman there. 2 He went back and told his father and his mother, "I have seen a young Philistine woman in Timnah. Now get her for me as a wife."

3 But his father and mother said to him, "Can't you find a young woman among your relatives or among any of our people? Must you go to the uncircumcised Philistines for a wife?"

But Samson told his father, "Get her for me. She's the right one for me." 4 Now his father and mother did not know this was from the LORD, who wanted the Philistines to provide an opportunity for a confrontation.[B] At that time, the Philistines were ruling Israel.

5 Samson went down to Timnah with his father and mother and came to the vineyards of Timnah. Suddenly a young lion came roaring at him, 6 the Spirit of the LORD came powerfully on him, and he tore the lion apart with his bare hands as he might have torn a young goat. But he did not tell his father or mother what he had done. 7 Then he went and spoke to the woman, because she seemed right to Samson.

8 After some time, when he returned to marry her, he left the road to see the lion's carcass, and there was a swarm of bees with honey in the carcass. 9 He scooped some honey into his hands and ate it as he went along. When he came to his father and mother, he gave some to them and they ate it. But he did not tell them that he had scooped the honey from the lion's carcass.

10 His father went to visit the woman, and Samson prepared a feast there, as young men were accustomed to do. 11 When the Philistines saw him, they brought thirty men to accompany him.

12 "Let me tell you a riddle," Samson said to them. "If you can explain it to me during the seven days of the feast and figure it out, I will give you thirty linen garments and thirty changes of clothes. 13 But if you can't explain it to me, you must give me thirty linen garments and thirty changes of clothes."

"Tell us your riddle," they replied.[C] "Let's hear it."

14 So he said to them:

Out of the eater came something to eat,
and out of the strong came something sweet.

After three days, they were unable to explain the riddle. 15 On the fourth[D] day they said to Samson's wife, "Persuade your husband to explain the riddle to us, or we will burn you and your father's family to death. Did you invite us here to rob us?"

16 So Samson's wife came to him, weeping, and said, "You hate me and don't love me! You told my people the riddle, but haven't explained it to me."

"Look," he said,[E] "I haven't even explained it to my father or mother, so why should I explain it to you?"

17 She wept the whole seven days of the feast, and at last, on the seventh day, he explained it to her, because she had nagged him so much. Then she explained it to her people. 18 On the seventh day, before sunset, the men of the city said to him:

What is sweeter than honey?
What is stronger than a lion?

So he said to them:

If you hadn't plowed with my young cow,
you wouldn't know my riddle now!

19 The Spirit of the LORD came powerfully on him, and he went down to Ashkelon and killed thirty of their men. He stripped them and gave their clothes to those who had explained the riddle. In a rage, Samson returned to his father's house, 20 and his wife was given to one of the men who had accompanied him.

SAMSON'S REVENGE

15 Later on, during the wheat harvest, Samson took a young goat as a gift and visited his wife. "I want to go to my wife in her room," he said. But her father would not let him enter.

2 "I was sure you hated her," her father said, "so I gave her to one of the men who accompanied you. Isn't her younger sister more beautiful than she is? Why not take her instead?"

3 Samson said to them, "This time I will be blameless when I harm the Philistines." 4 So he went out and caught three hundred foxes. He took torches, turned the foxes tail-to-tail, and put a torch between each pair of tails. 5 Then he ignited the torches and released the foxes into the standing grain of the Philistines. He burned the piles of grain and the standing grain as well as the vineyards and olive groves.

6 Then the Philistines asked, "Who did this?"

They were told, "It was Samson, the Timnite's son-in-law, because he took Samson's wife and gave her to his companion." So the Philistines went to her and her father and burned them to death.

7 Then Samson told them, "Because you did this, I swear that I won't rest until I have taken vengeance on you." 8 He tore them limb from limb[F] and then went down and stayed in the cave at the rock of Etam.

[A] **13:25** Or *in Mahaneh-dan* [B] **14:4** *for a confrontation* supplied for clarity [C] **14:13** Lit *replied to him* [D] **14:15** LXX, Syr; MT reads *seventh* [E] **14:16** Lit *said to her* [F] **15:8** Lit *He struck them hip and thigh with a great slaughter*

The Nazirite Vow

by Byron Longino

Remnant of an ancient winepress in the area of Zorah. In the foreground, the deeper part caught the grape juice. The upper part held the grapes while they were being pressed. A trench joins the two sections. An angel appeared to Manoah's wife at Zorah and instructed that she was not to "eat anything that comes from the grapevine or drink wine or beer. And she must not eat anything unclean" (Jdg 13:14).

Numbers 6:1–21 is the only biblical passage that details the requirements of the Nazirite vow. The Hebrew phrase translated "makes a special vow" in Numbers 6:2 emphasizes the commitment of someone strongly devoted to God.[1] Making this Nazirite vow was not an occasional act of consecration. The vow marked the point at which the individual entered a state of total separation "to" the Lord and also a state of separation "from" certain normally permissible community practices and traditions. Women as well as men made Nazirite vows.

Two types of Nazirite vows existed—lifelong and limited. In the first, a parent made the vow or accepted the calling for a yet-to-be-conceived child to be a Nazirite.[2] In the second, the individual made the vow for a limited period of time. This second type was the more common practice; it involved the person voluntarily submitting oneself and making the vow in person.

The Lord commanded Nazirites to abstain from three actions: (1) consuming wine and other grape-related products, (2) cutting their hair, and (3) touching the dead. The three areas of prohibition—diet, appearance, and associations—represented individual areas of life and served as a means to achieve separation and to remain totally devoted to God. The Nazirite regulations required the one under the vow to go beyond the dietary requirements of the Israelite culture in general. The uncut hair provided the visible sign of the Nazirite's state of consecration. All Israelites were to avoid contact with the dead unless the burial of a family member required contact. The person under a Nazirite vow could not even come into contact with a dead loved one (Nm 6:7).

For those who made the Nazirite vow for a limited time, two actions marked the conclusion of the dedicatory period. First, the participant would cut his or her hair. This served as a visual notification of the vow's conclusion. Second, the person would offer gifts to God. These gifts were expensive and expressed the person's total commitment to the Lord during this period of ardent devotion (Nm 6:13–21).

Samson, the Old Testament judge, is the only individual the Bible specifically designates as being a Nazirite. An angel announced to Samson's mother that she would conceive and have a son who would be consecrated to God as a Nazirite. Samson acknowledged his commission as a lifelong Nazirite (Jdg 16:17). However, more than once he violated the prohibition against touching a dead body (a lion, 14:8–9; a donkey, 15:15; and a bowstring made of sinew, 16:7).[3] In his rebellion, he also made friends with a woman who was a Philistine, a sworn enemy of Israel and of Israel's God. He eventually divulged to her that the secret of his strength was his adherence to the restriction against cutting his hair, thus enabling her to violate his Nazirite vow. ✣

---

[1] Ronald B. Allen, "Numbers" in *The Expositor's Bible Commentary*, vol. 2 (Grand Rapids: Zondervan, 1990), 748–49. [2] "Nazirite" in *HolBD*, 1011. [3] Daniel I. Block, *Judges, Ruth*, vol. 6 in NAC, 457–58.

9 The Philistines went up, camped in Judah, and raided Lehi. 10 So the men of Judah said, "Why have you attacked us?"

They replied, "We have come to tie Samson up and pay him back for what he did to us."

11 Then three thousand men of Judah went to the cave at the rock of Etam, and they asked Samson, "Don't you realize that the Philistines rule us? What have you done to us?"

"I have done to them what they did to me," he answered.[A]

12 They said to him, "We've come to tie you up and hand you over to the Philistines."

Then Samson told them, "Swear to me that you yourselves won't kill me."

13 "No," they said,[B] "we won't kill you, but we will tie you up securely and hand you over to them." So they tied him up with two new ropes and led him away from the rock.

14 When he came to Lehi, the Philistines came to meet him shouting. The Spirit of the LORD came powerfully on him, and the ropes that were on his arms and wrists became like burnt flax and fell off. 15 He found a fresh jawbone of a donkey, reached out his hand, took it, and killed a thousand men with it. 16 Then Samson said:

With the jawbone of a donkey
I have piled them in heaps.
With the jawbone of a donkey
I have killed a thousand men.

17 When he finished speaking, he threw away the jawbone and named that place Jawbone Hill.[C] 18 He became very thirsty and called out to the LORD, "You have accomplished this great victory through your servant. Must I now die of thirst and fall into the hands of the uncircumcised?" 19 So God split a hollow place in the ground at Lehi, and water came out of it. After Samson drank, his strength returned, and he revived. That is why he named it Hakkore Spring,[D] which is still in Lehi today. 20 And he judged Israel twenty years in the days of the Philistines.

SAMSON AND DELILAH

16 Samson went to Gaza, where he saw a prostitute and went to bed with her. 2 When the Gazites heard that Samson was there, they surrounded the place and waited in ambush for him all that night at the city gate. They kept quiet all night, saying, "Let's wait until dawn; then we will kill him." 3 But Samson stayed in bed only until midnight. Then he got up, took hold of the doors of the city gate along with the two gateposts, and pulled them out, bar and all. He put them on his shoulders and took them to the top of the mountain overlooking Hebron.

4 Some time later, he fell in love with a woman named Delilah, who lived in the Sorek Valley. 5 The Philistine leaders went to her and said, "Persuade him to tell you[E] where his great strength comes from, so we can overpower him, tie him up, and make him helpless. Each of us will then give you 1,100 pieces of silver."

6 So Delilah said to Samson, "Please tell me, where does your great strength come from? How could someone tie you up and make you helpless?"

7 Samson told her, "If they tie me up with seven fresh bowstrings that have not been dried, I will become weak and be like any other man."

8 The Philistine leaders brought her seven fresh bowstrings that had not been dried, and she tied him up with them. 9 While the men in ambush were waiting in her room, she called out to him, "Samson, the Philistines are here!"[F] But he snapped the bowstrings as a strand of yarn snaps when it touches fire. The secret of his strength remained unknown.

10 Then Delilah said to Samson, "You have mocked me and told me lies! Won't you please tell me how you can be tied up?"

11 He told her, "If they tie me up with new ropes that have never been used, I will become weak and be like any other man."

12 Delilah took new ropes, tied him up with them, and shouted, "Samson, the Philistines are here!" But while the men in ambush were waiting in her room, he snapped the ropes off his arms like a thread.

13 Then Delilah said to Samson, "You have mocked me all along and told me lies! Tell me how you can be tied up."

He told her, "If you weave the seven braids on my head into the fabric on a loom —"[G]

14 She fastened the braids with a pin and called to him, "Samson, the Philistines are here!" He awoke from his sleep and pulled out the pin, with the loom and the web.

15 "How can you say, 'I love you,'" she told him, "when your heart is not with me? This is the third time you have mocked me and not told me what makes your strength so great!"

16 Because she nagged him day after day and pleaded with him until she wore him out,[H] 17 he told her the whole truth and said to her, "My hair has never been cut,[I] because I am a Nazirite to God from birth. If I am shaved, my strength will leave me, and I will become weak and be like any other man."

[A] **15:11** Lit *answered them* [B] **15:13** Lit *said to him* [C] **15:17** Hb *Ramath-lehi* [D] **15:19** = Spring of the One Who Cried Out [E] **16:5** Lit *him and see* [F] **16:9** Lit *are on you*, also in vv. 12,14,20 [G] **16:13–14** LXX reads *loom and fasten them with a pin into the wall and I will become weak and be like any other man."* **14** *And while he was sleeping, Delilah wove the seven braids on his head into the loom.* [H] **16:16** Lit *him and he became short to death* [I] **16:17** Lit *A razor has not gone up on my head*

18 When Delilah realized that he had told her the whole truth, she sent this message to the Philistine leaders: "Come one more time, for he has told me the whole truth." The Philistine leaders came to her and brought the silver with them.

19 Then she let him fall asleep on her lap and called a man to shave off the seven braids on his head. In this way, she made him helpless, and his strength left him. 20 Then she cried, "Samson, the Philistines are here!" When he awoke from his sleep, he said, "I will escape as I did before and shake myself free." But he did not know that the LORD had left him.

SAMSON'S DEFEAT AND DEATH

21 The Philistines seized him and gouged out his eyes. They brought him down to Gaza and bound him with bronze shackles, and he was forced to grind grain in the prison. 22 But his hair began to grow back after it had been shaved.

23 Now the Philistine leaders gathered together to offer a great sacrifice to their god Dagon. They rejoiced and said:

Our god has handed over
our enemy Samson to us.

24 When the people saw him, they praised their god and said:

Our god has handed over to us
our enemy who destroyed our land
and who multiplied our dead.

25 When they were in good spirits,[A] they said, "Bring Samson here to entertain us." So they brought Samson from prison, and he entertained them. They had him stand between the pillars.

26 Samson said to the young man who was leading him by the hand, "Lead me where I can feel the pillars supporting the temple, so I can lean against them." 27 The temple was full of men and women; all the leaders of the Philistines were there, and about three thousand men and women were on the roof watching Samson entertain them. 28 He called out to the LORD, "Lord GOD, please remember me. Strengthen me, God, just once more. With one act of vengeance, let me pay back the Philistines for my two eyes." 29 Samson took hold of the two middle pillars supporting the temple and leaned against them, one on his right hand and the other on his left. 30 Samson said, "Let me die with the Philistines." He pushed with all his might, and the temple fell on the leaders and all the people in it. And those he killed at his death were more than those he had killed in his life.

31 Then his brothers and his father's whole family came down, carried him back, and buried him between Zorah and Eshtaol in the tomb of his father Manoah. So he judged Israel twenty years.

MICAH'S PRIEST

17 There was a man from the hill country of Ephraim named Micah. 2 He said to his mother, "The 1,100 pieces of silver taken from you, and that I heard you place a curse on — here's the silver. I took it."

Then his mother said, "My son, may you be blessed by the LORD!"

3 He returned the 1,100 pieces of silver to his mother, and his mother said, "I personally consecrate the silver to the LORD for my son's benefit to make a carved image and a silver idol.[B] I will give it back to you." 4 So he returned the silver to his mother, and she took five pounds of silver and gave it to a silversmith. He made it into a carved image and a silver idol, and it was in Micah's house.

5 This man Micah had a shrine, and he made an ephod and household idols, and installed one of his sons to be his priest. 6 In those days there was no king in Israel; everyone did whatever seemed right to him.

7 There was a young man, a Levite from Bethlehem in Judah, who was staying within the clan of Judah. 8 The man left the town of Bethlehem in Judah to stay wherever he could find a place. On his way he came to Micah's home in the hill country of Ephraim.

9 "Where do you come from?" Micah asked him.

He answered him, "I am a Levite from Bethlehem in Judah, and I'm going to stay wherever I can find a place."

10 Micah replied,[C] "Stay with me and be my father and priest, and I will give you four ounces of silver a year, along with your clothing and provisions." So the Levite went in 11 and agreed to stay with the man, and the young man became like one of his sons. 12 Micah consecrated the Levite, and the young man became his priest and lived in Micah's house. 13 Then Micah said, "Now I know that the LORD will be good to me, because a Levite has become my priest."

DAN'S INVASION AND IDOLATRY

18 In those days, there was no king in Israel, and the Danite tribe was looking for territory to occupy. Up to that time no territory had been captured by them among the tribes of Israel. 2 So the Danites sent out five brave men from all their clans, from Zorah and Eshtaol, to scout out the land and explore it. They told them, "Go and explore the land."

They came to the hill country of Ephraim as far as the home of Micah and spent the night there. 3 While they were near Micah's home, they recognized the accent of the young Levite. So they went over to him and asked, "Who brought you here? What are you doing in this place? What is keeping you here?"

[A] **16:25** Or *When they were feeling good* [B] **17:3** Or *image and a cast image,* also in v. 4 [C] **17:10** Lit *replied to him*

4 He told them, "This is what Micah has done for me: He has hired me, and I became his priest."

5 Then they said to him, "Please inquire of God for us to determine if we will have a successful journey."

6 The priest told them, "Go in peace. The LORD is watching over the journey you are going on."

7 The five men left and came to Laish. They saw that the people who were there were living securely, in the same way as the Sidonians, quiet and unsuspecting. There was nothing lacking[A] in the land and no oppressive ruler. They were far from the Sidonians, having no alliance with anyone.[B]

8 When the men went back to their relatives at Zorah and Eshtaol, their relatives asked them, "What did you find out?"

9 They answered, "Come on, let's attack them, for we have seen the land, and it is very good. Why wait? Don't hesitate to go and invade and take possession of the land! 10 When you get there, you will come to an unsuspecting people and a spacious land, for God has handed it over to you. It is a place where nothing on earth is lacking." 11 Six hundred Danites departed from Zorah and Eshtaol armed with weapons of war. 12 They went up and camped at Kiriath-jearim in Judah. This is why the place is still called the Camp of Dan[C] today; it is west of Kiriath-jearim. 13 From there they traveled to the hill country of Ephraim and arrived at Micah's house.

14 The five men who had gone to scout out the land of Laish told their brothers, "Did you know that there are an ephod, household gods, and a carved image and a silver idol[D] in these houses? Now think about what you should do." 15 So they detoured there and went to the house of the young Levite at the home of Micah and greeted him. 16 The six hundred Danite men were standing by the entrance of the city gate, armed with their weapons of war. 17 Then the five men who had gone to scout out the land went in and took the carved image, the ephod, the household idols, and the silver idol,[E] while the priest was standing by the entrance of the city gate with the six hundred men armed with weapons of war.

18 When they entered Micah's house and took the carved image, the ephod, the household idols, and the silver idol, the priest said to them, "What are you doing?"

19 They told him, "Be quiet. Keep your mouth shut.[F] Come with us and be a father and a priest to us. Is it better for you to be a priest for the house of one person or for you to be a priest for a tribe and family in Israel?" 20 So the priest was pleased and took the ephod, household idols, and carved image, and went with the people. 21 They prepared to leave, putting their dependents, livestock, and possessions in front of them.

22 After they were some distance from Micah's house, the men who were in the houses near it were mustered and caught up with the Danites. 23 They called to the Danites, who turned to face them, and said to Micah, "What's the matter with you that you mustered the men?"

24 He said, "You took the gods I had made and the priest, and went away. What do I have left? How can you say to me, 'What's the matter with you?'"

25 The Danites said to him, "Don't raise your voice against us, or angry men will attack you, and you and your family will lose your lives." 26 The Danites went on their way, and Micah turned to go back home, because he saw that they were stronger than he was.

27 After they had taken the gods Micah had made and the priest that belonged to him, they went to Laish, to a quiet and unsuspecting people. They killed them with their swords and burned the city. 28 There was no one to rescue them because it was far from Sidon and they had no alliance with anyone. It was in a valley that belonged to Beth-rehob. They rebuilt the city and lived in it. 29 They named the city Dan, after the name of their ancestor Dan, who was born to Israel. The city was formerly named Laish.

30 The Danites set up the carved image for themselves. Jonathan son of Gershom, son of Moses,[G] and his sons were priests for the Danite tribe until the time of the exile from the land. 31 So they set up for themselves Micah's carved image that he had made, and it was there as long as the house of God was in Shiloh.

OUTRAGE IN BENJAMIN

19 In those days, when there was no king in Israel, a Levite staying in a remote part of the hill country of Ephraim acquired a woman from Bethlehem in Judah as his concubine. 2 But she was unfaithful to[H] him and left him for her father's house in Bethlehem in Judah. She was there for four months. 3 Then her husband got up and followed her to speak kindly to her and bring her back. He had his servant with him and a pair of donkeys. So she brought him to her father's house, and when the girl's father saw him, he gladly welcomed him. 4 His father-in-law, the girl's father, detained him, and he stayed with him for three days. They ate, drank, and spent the nights there.

5 On the fourth day, they got up early in the morning and prepared to go, but the girl's father said to his son-in-law, "Have something to eat to keep up your

[A] **18:7** Hb obscure [B] **18:7** MT; some LXX mss, Sym, Old Lat, Syr read *Aram* [C] **18:12** Or *called Mahaneh-dan* [D] **18:14** Or *image, the cast image* [E] **18:17** Or *the cast image*, also in v. 18 [F] **18:19** Lit *Put your hand on your mouth* [G] **18:30** Some Hb mss, LXX, Vg; other Hb mss read *Manasseh* [H] **19:2** LXX reads *was angry with*

Dan Moves North

by Leon Hyatt Jr.

Dan's portion, allotted to the tribe by Joshua and the high priest Eleazar, bordered the Mediterranean Sea between two river systems, the Aijalon/Yarkon and the Sorek. It was an irregular, peanut-shaped territory, up to twenty miles in length and breadth. Along the sea ran a beautiful plain varying from six to twelve miles wide and rising to approximately five hundred feet above sea level.[1] Joppa, the only natural harbor in Israel's territory, was located at the approximate center of Dan's coastline.[2]

The rest of Dan's assigned territory was in the Shephelah, the hill country that lay between the coastal plain and the mountains that paralleled the Jordan Valley. These foothills ranged mostly from five hundred to eight hundred feet high, with none of them higher than fifteen hundred feet.[3] Two wide and productive valleys crossed the Shephelah from east to west in Dan's territory, the Aijalon (Jos 10:12) and the Sorek (Jdg 16:4).

But when their allotted territory "slipped out of their control" (Jos 19:47), they sought an alternative. Laish (Leshem in Jos 19:47) was nominally in the area claimed by the Phoenician city of Sidon, but a river and two mountain ranges separated it from Sidon. The city was virtually independent and had protective alliances with no one. Thus it was easy to conquer and occupy. A contingent of six hundred armed men did so and renamed it Dan. It became the northernmost city in Israel, resulting in the expression "from Dan to Beer-sheba" (Jdg 20:1).

Dan's army hired an idol-worshiping Levite named Jonathan to be the tribe's priest (18:19). Later, when the ten northern tribes rebelled against David's house and chose Jeroboam as their king, Jeroboam set up one of his golden calves in Dan (1Kg 12:28–30).

Archaeologists have located the ruins of ancient Dan and have conducted excavations there for twenty seasons. At the level dated around the beginning of the twelfth century BC, the excavations revealed a drastic change in the city's culture. The Danites' conquest must have occurred at that time. Figurines of Egyptian and Canaanite gods were found near the sanctuary in the level belonging to the Greek period.[4] These finds may suggest that the apostasy started by the Danites continued among Israelites until the overthrow of the whole nation by Rome. ✣

---

[1] J. McKee Adams, *Biblical Backgrounds* (Nashville: Broadman, 1946), 145.
[2] Timothy Trammel, "Joppa," *HolBD*, 811.
[3] Trammel, "Joppa," 4:2762–63. [4] Avraham Biran, "Dan (Place)," *ABD*, 2:12.

The main entrance gate to Dan from the Solomonic period. Shown is a reconstructed canopy and platform for a judge's seat inside the gate.

strength and then you can go." 6 So they sat down and the two of them ate and drank together. Then the girl's father said to the man, "Please agree to stay overnight and enjoy yourself." 7 The man got up to go, but his father-in-law persuaded him, so he stayed and spent the night there again. 8 He got up early in the morning of the fifth day to leave, but the girl's father said to him, "Please keep up your strength." So they waited until late afternoon and the two of them ate. 9 The man got up to go with his concubine and his servant, when his father-in-law, the girl's father, said to him, "Look, night is coming. Please spend the night. See, the day is almost over. Spend the night here, enjoy yourself, then you can get up early tomorrow for your journey and go home."

10 But the man was unwilling to spend the night. He got up, departed, and arrived opposite Jebus (that is, Jerusalem). The man had his two saddled donkeys and his concubine with him. 11 When they were near Jebus and the day was almost gone, the servant said to his master, "Please, why not let us stop at this Jebusite city and spend the night here?"

12 But his master replied to him, "We will not stop at a foreign city where there are no Israelites. Let's move on to Gibeah." 13 "Come on," he said,[A] "let's try to reach one of these places and spend the night in Gibeah or Ramah." 14 So they continued on their journey, and the sun set as they neared Gibeah in Benjamin. 15 They stopped[B] to go in and spend the night in Gibeah. The Levite went in and sat down in the city square, but no one took them into their home to spend the night.

16 In the evening, an old man came in from his work in the field. He was from the hill country of Ephraim, but he was residing in Gibeah where the people were Benjaminites. 17 When he looked up and saw the traveler in the city square, the old man asked, "Where are you going, and where do you come from?"

18 He answered him, "We're traveling from Bethlehem in Judah to the remote hill country of Ephraim, where I am from. I went to Bethlehem in Judah, and now I'm going to the house of the LORD.[C] No one has taken me into his home, 19 although there's straw and feed for the donkeys, and I have bread and wine for me, my concubine, and the servant[D] with us. There is nothing we lack."

20 "Welcome!" said the old man. "I'll take care of everything you need. Only don't spend the night in the square." 21 So he brought him to his house and fed the donkeys. Then they washed their feet and ate and drank. 22 While they were enjoying themselves, all of a sudden, wicked men of the city surrounded the house and beat on the door. They said to the old man who was the owner of the house, "Bring out the man who came to your house so we can have sex with him!"

23 The owner of the house went out and said to them, "Please don't do this evil, my brothers. After all, this man has come into my house. Don't commit this horrible outrage. 24 Here, let me bring out my virgin daughter and the man's concubine now. Abuse them and do whatever you want to them. But don't commit this outrageous thing against this man."

25 But the men would not listen to him, so the man seized his concubine and took her outside to them. They raped her and abused her all night until morning. At daybreak they let her go. 26 Early that morning, the woman made her way back, and as it was getting light, she collapsed at the doorway of the man's house where her master was.

27 When her master got up in the morning, opened the doors of the house, and went out to leave on his journey, there was the woman, his concubine, collapsed near the doorway of the house with her hands on the threshold. 28 "Get up," he told her. "Let's go." But there was no response. So the man put her on his donkey and set out for home.

29 When he entered his house, he picked up a knife, took hold of his concubine, cut her into twelve pieces, limb by limb, and then sent her throughout the territory of Israel. 30 Everyone who saw it said, "Nothing like this has ever happened or has been seen since the day the Israelites came out of the land of Egypt until now.[E] Think it over, discuss it, and speak up!"

WAR AGAINST BENJAMIN

20 All the Israelites from Dan to Beer-sheba and from the land of Gilead came out, and the community assembled as one body before the LORD at Mizpah. 2 The leaders of all the people and of all the tribes of Israel presented themselves in the assembly of God's people: four hundred thousand armed foot soldiers. 3 The Benjaminites heard that the Israelites had gone up to Mizpah.

The Israelites asked, "Tell us, how did this evil act happen?"

4 The Levite, the husband of the murdered woman, answered, "I went to Gibeah in Benjamin with my concubine to spend the night. 5 Citizens of Gibeah came to attack me and surrounded the house at night. They intended to kill me, but they raped my concubine, and she died. 6 Then I took my concubine and cut her in pieces, and sent her throughout Israel's territory, because they have committed a wicked

[A] **19:13** Lit *said to his servant* [B] **19:15** Lit *stopped there* [C] **19:18** LXX reads *to my house* [D] **19:19** Some Hb mss, Syr, Tg, Vg; other Hb mss read *servants* [E] **19:30** LXX reads *until now." He commanded the men he sent out, saying, "You will say this to all the men of Israel: Has anything like this happened since the day the Israelites came out of Egypt until this day?*

outrage in Israel. 7 Look, all of you are Israelites. Give your judgment and verdict here and now."

8 Then all the people stood united and said, "None of us will go to his tent or return to his house. 9 Now this is what we will do to Gibeah: we will attack it. By lot 10 we will take ten men out of every hundred from all the tribes of Israel, and one hundred out of every thousand, and one thousand out of every ten thousand to get provisions for the troops when they go to Gibeah in Benjamin to punish them for all the outrage they committed in Israel."

11 So all the men of Israel gathered united against the city. 12 Then the tribes of Israel sent men throughout the tribe of Benjamin, saying, "What is this evil act that has happened among you? 13 Hand over the wicked men in Gibeah so we can put them to death and purge evil from Israel." But the Benjaminites would not listen to their fellow Israelites. 14 Instead, the Benjaminites gathered together from their cities to Gibeah to go out and fight against the Israelites. 15 On that day the Benjaminites mobilized twenty-six thousand armed men from their cities, besides seven hundred fit young men rallied by the inhabitants of Gibeah. 16 There were seven hundred fit young men who were left-handed among all these troops; all could sling a stone at a hair and not miss.

17 The Israelites, apart from Benjamin, mobilized four hundred thousand armed men, every one an experienced warrior. 18 They set out, went to Bethel, and inquired of God. The Israelites asked, "Who is to go first to fight for us against the Benjaminites?"

And the LORD answered, "Judah will be first."

19 In the morning, the Israelites set out and camped near Gibeah. 20 The men of Israel went out to fight against Benjamin and took their battle positions against Gibeah. 21 The Benjaminites came out of Gibeah and slaughtered twenty-two thousand men of Israel on the field that day. 22 But the Israelite troops rallied and again took their battle positions in the same place where they positioned themselves on the first day. 23 They went up, wept before the LORD until evening, and inquired of him, "Should we again attack our brothers the Benjaminites?"

And the LORD answered, "Fight against them."

24 On the second day the Israelites advanced against the Benjaminites. 25 That same day the Benjaminites came out from Gibeah to meet them and slaughtered an additional eighteen thousand Israelites on the field; all were armed.

26 The whole Israelite army went to Bethel where they wept and sat before the LORD. They fasted that day until evening and offered burnt offerings and fellowship offerings to the LORD. 27 Then the Israelites inquired of the LORD. In those days, the ark of the covenant of God was there, 28 and Phinehas son of Eleazar, son of Aaron, was serving before it. The Israelites asked, "Should we again fight against our brothers the Benjaminites or should we stop?"

The LORD answered, "Fight, because I will hand them over to you tomorrow." 29 So Israel set up an ambush around Gibeah. 30 On the third day the Israelites fought against the Benjaminites and took their battle positions against Gibeah as before. 31 Then the Benjaminites came out against the troops and were drawn away from the city. They began to attack the troops as before, killing about thirty men of Israel on the highways, one of which goes up to Bethel and the other to Gibeah through the open country. 32 The Benjaminites said, "We are defeating them as before."

But the Israelites said, "Let's flee and draw them away from the city to the highways." 33 So all the men of Israel got up from their places and took their battle positions at Baal-tamar, while the Israelites in ambush charged out of their places west of[A] Geba. 34 Then ten thousand fit young men from all Israel made a frontal assault against Gibeah, and the battle was fierce, but the Benjaminites did not know that disaster was about to strike them. 35 The LORD defeated Benjamin in the presence of Israel, and on that day the Israelites slaughtered 25,100 men of Benjamin; all were armed. 36 Then the Benjaminites realized they had been defeated.

The men of Israel had retreated before Benjamin, because they were confident in the ambush they had set against Gibeah. 37 The men in ambush had rushed quickly against Gibeah; they advanced and put the whole city to the sword. 38 The men of Israel had a prearranged signal with the men in ambush: when they sent up a great cloud of smoke from the city, 39 the men of Israel would return to the battle. When Benjamin had begun to strike them down, killing about thirty men of Israel, they said, "They're defeated before us, just as they were in the first battle." 40 But when the column of smoke began to go up from the city, Benjamin looked behind them, and the whole city was going up in smoke.[B] 41 Then the men of Israel returned, and the men of Benjamin were terrified when they realized that disaster had struck them. 42 They retreated before the men of Israel toward the wilderness, but the battle overtook them, and those who came out of the cities[C] slaughtered those between them. 43 They surrounded the Benjaminites, pursued them, and easily overtook them near Gibeah toward the east. 44 There were eighteen thousand men who died from Benjamin; all were warriors. 45 Then Benjamin turned and fled toward the wilderness to Rimmon Rock, and Israel killed five thousand

[A] **20:33** LXX, Syr, Vg; MT reads *places in the plain of*, or *places in the cave of* [B] **20:40** Lit *up to the sky* [C] **20:42** LXX, Vg read *city*

men on the highways. They overtook them at Gidom and struck two thousand more dead.

46 All the Benjaminites who died that day were twenty-five thousand armed men; all were warriors. 47 But six hundred men escaped into the wilderness to Rimmon Rock and stayed there four months. 48 The men of Israel turned back against the other Benjaminites and killed them with their swords — the entire city, the animals, and everything that remained. They also burned all the cities that remained.

BRIDES FOR BENJAMIN

21 The men of Israel had sworn an oath at Mizpah: "None of us will give his daughter to a Benjaminite in marriage." 2 So the people went to Bethel and sat there before God until evening. They wept loudly and bitterly, 3 and cried out, "Why, LORD God of Israel, has it occurred[A] that one tribe is missing in Israel today?" 4 The next day the people got up early, built an altar there, and offered burnt offerings and fellowship offerings. 5 The Israelites asked, "Who of all the tribes of Israel didn't come to the LORD with the assembly?" For a great oath had been taken that anyone who had not come to the LORD at Mizpah would certainly be put to death.

6 But the Israelites had compassion on their brothers, the Benjaminites, and said, "Today a tribe has been cut off from Israel. 7 What should we do about wives for the survivors? We've sworn to the LORD not to give them any of our daughters as wives." 8 They asked, "Which city among the tribes of Israel didn't come to the LORD at Mizpah?" It turned out that no one from Jabesh-gilead had come to the camp and the assembly. 9 For when the roll was called, no men were there from the inhabitants of Jabesh-gilead.

10 The congregation sent twelve thousand brave warriors there and commanded them, "Go and kill the inhabitants of Jabesh-gilead with the sword, including women and dependents. 11 This is what you should do: Completely destroy every male, as well as every woman who has gone to bed with a man." 12 They found among the inhabitants of Jabesh-gilead four hundred young virgins, who had not been intimate with a man, and they brought them to the camp at Shiloh in the land of Canaan.

13 The whole congregation sent a message of peace to the Benjaminites who were at Rimmon Rock. 14 Benjamin returned at that time, and Israel gave them the women they had kept alive from Jabesh-gilead. But there were not enough for them.

15 The people had compassion on Benjamin, because the LORD had made this gap in the tribes of Israel. 16 The elders of the congregation said, "What should we do about wives for those who are left, since the women of Benjamin have been destroyed?" 17 They said, "There must be heirs for the survivors of Benjamin, so that a tribe of Israel will not be wiped out. 18 But we can't give them our daughters as wives." For the Israelites had sworn, "Anyone who gives a wife to a Benjaminite is cursed." 19 They also said, "Look, there's an annual festival to the LORD in Shiloh, which is north of Bethel, east of the highway that goes up from Bethel to Shechem, and south of Lebonah."

20 Then they commanded the Benjaminites, "Go and hide in the vineyards. 21 Watch, and when you see the young women of Shiloh come out to perform the dances, each of you leave the vineyards and catch a wife for yourself from the young women of Shiloh, and go to the land of Benjamin. 22 When their fathers or brothers come to us and protest, we will tell them, 'Show favor to them, since we did not get enough wives for each of them in the battle. You didn't actually give the women to them, so[B] you are not guilty of breaking your oath.'"

23 The Benjaminites did this and took the number of women they needed from the dancers they caught. They went back to their own inheritance, rebuilt their cities, and lived in them. 24 At that time, each of the Israelites returned from there to his own tribe and family. Each returned from there to his own inheritance.

25 In those days there was no king in Israel; everyone did whatever seemed right to him.

[A] **21:3** Lit *has this occurred in Israel* [B] **21:22** Lit *at this time*

RUTH

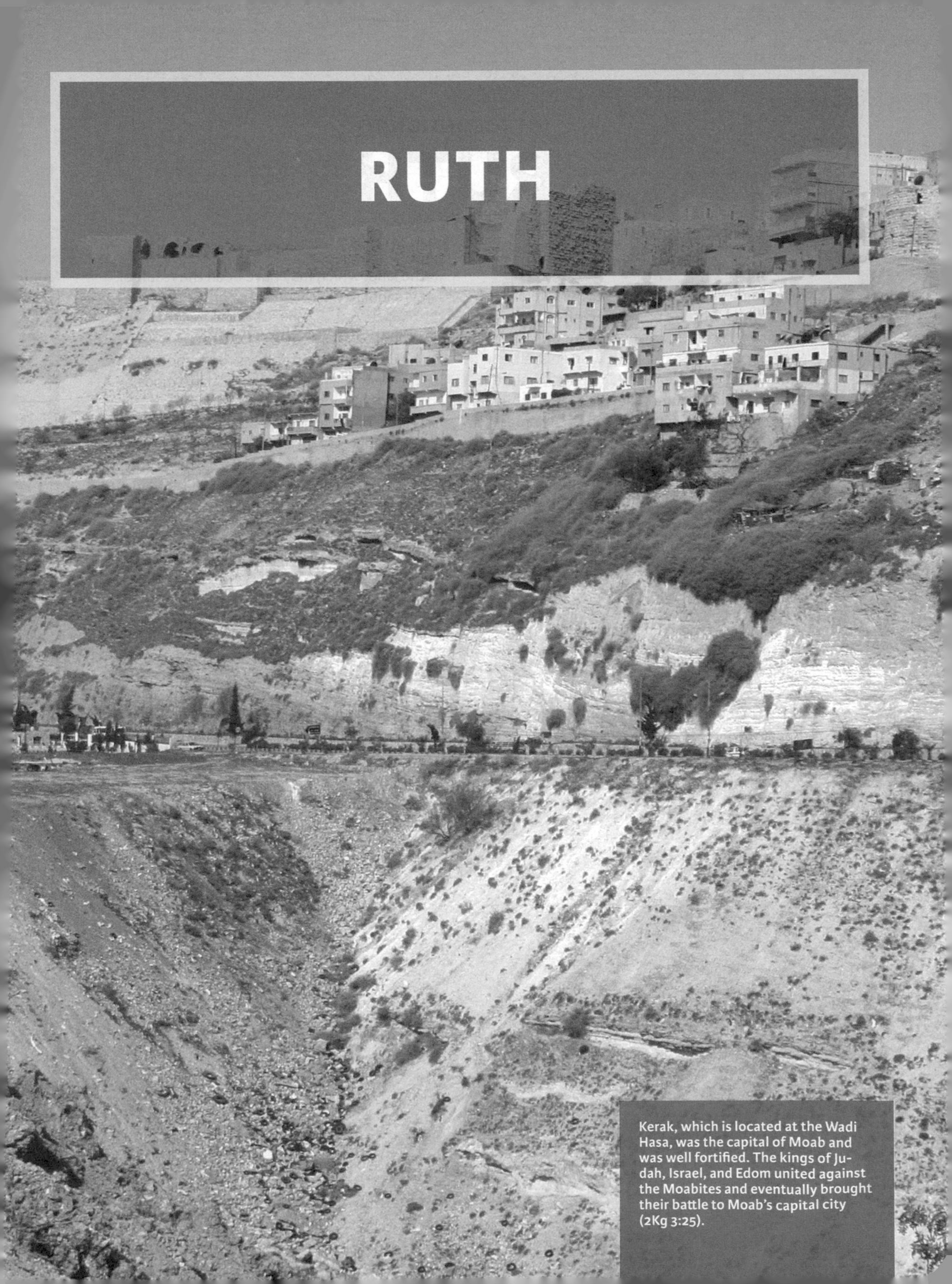

Kerak, which is located at the Wadi Hasa, was the capital of Moab and was well fortified. The kings of Judah, Israel, and Edom united against the Moabites and eventually brought their battle to Moab's capital city (2Kg 3:25).

INTRODUCTION TO

RUTH

Circumstances of Writing

The Talmud attributes the authorship of Ruth to Samuel, but the book itself offers no hint of the identity of its author. We can only speculate about who might have written the book of Ruth, and its provenance and date must be deduced from the internal evidence—language and style, historical allusions, and themes. The family records at the end and the explanation of archaic customs requires a date during or later than the reign of King David (1011–971 BC), though it could have been written as late as after the exile, when the issue of the inclusion of Gentiles once again became pressing.

The book of Ruth is set "during the time of the judges" (1:1), a period of social and religious disorder when "everyone did whatever seemed right to him" (Jdg 17:6). Historically, this era bridged the time between the conquest of the land under Joshua and the rise of King David, whose family records form the conclusion of the book. It is not clear exactly when during the time of the judges the book belongs, but it opens with a famine in the land, which may have been the result of Israel's idolatry.

Contribution to the Bible

Ruth's covenantal faithfulness to her mother-in-law, Naomi, and her God provided a model showing that those who were not ethnic Israelites could be incorporated into the people of God through faith. If Moabites who joined themselves to the Lord could be accepted, there was hope for other Gentiles as well (Is 56:3–7). The book also effectively answered questions that may have been raised over the legitimacy of the Davidic line, given his Moabite roots.

Structure

The book of Ruth is a delightful short story with a classical plot that moves from crisis to complication to resolution. The narrator draws the reader into the minds of the characters (successively Naomi, Ruth, and Boaz), inviting us to identify with their personal anxieties and joys and in the end to celebrate the movement from emptiness and frustration to fulfillment and joy.

NAOMI'S FAMILY IN MOAB

1 During the time[A] of the judges, there was a famine in the land. A man left Bethlehem in Judah
with his wife and two sons to stay in the territory
of Moab for a while. 2 The man's name was Elimelech, and his wife's name was Naomi.[B] The names of
his two sons were Mahlon and Chilion. They were
Ephrathites from Bethlehem in Judah. They entered the fields of Moab and settled there. 3 Naomi's
husband, Elimelech, died, and she was left with
her two sons. 4 Her sons took Moabite women as
their wives: one was named Orpah and the second
was named Ruth. After they lived in Moab about
ten years, 5 both Mahlon and Chilion also died, and
the woman was left without her two children and
without her husband.

RUTH'S LOYALTY TO NAOMI

6 She and her daughters-in-law set out to return from
the territory of Moab, because she had heard in Moab
that the LORD had paid attention to his people's need
by providing them food. 7 She left the place where she
had been living, accompanied by her two daughters-
in-law, and traveled along the road leading back to
the land of Judah.

8 Naomi said to them, "Each of you go back to your
mother's home. May the LORD show kindness to you
as you have shown to the dead and to me. 9 May the
LORD grant each of you rest in the house of a new
husband." She kissed them, and they wept loudly.

10 They said to her, "We insist on returning with
you to your people."

11 But Naomi replied, "Return home, my daughters.
Why do you want to go with me? Am I able to have
any more sons who could become your husbands?
12 Return home, my daughters. Go on, for I am too old
to have another husband. Even if I thought there was
still hope for me to have a husband tonight and to
bear sons, 13 would you be willing to wait for them to
grow up? Would you restrain yourselves from remar-
rying?[C] No, my daughters, my life is much too bitter
for you to share,[D] because the LORD's hand has turned
against me." 14 Again they wept loudly, and Orpah
kissed her mother-in-law, but Ruth clung to her. 15 Naomi said, "Look, your sister-in-law has gone back to
her people and to her gods. Follow your sister-in-law."

16 But Ruth replied:

Don't plead with me to abandon you
or to return and not follow you.
For wherever you go, I will go,
and wherever you live, I will live;
your people will be my people,
and your God will be my God.
17 Where you die, I will die,
and there I will be buried.
May the LORD punish me,
and do so severely,
if anything but death separates you and me.

18 When Naomi saw that Ruth was determined to go
with her, she stopped talking to her.

19 The two of them traveled until they came to Bethlehem. When they entered Bethlehem, the whole
town was excited about their arrival[E] and the local
women exclaimed, "Can this be Naomi?"

20 "Don't call me Naomi. Call me Mara,"[F] she answered, "for the Almighty has made me very bitter. 21 I went away full, but the LORD has brought
me back empty. Why do you call me Naomi, since
the LORD has opposed[G] me, and the Almighty has
afflicted me?"

22 So Naomi came back from the territory of Moab
with her daughter-in-law Ruth the Moabitess. They
arrived in Bethlehem at the beginning of the barley
harvest.

RUTH AND BOAZ MEET

2 Now Naomi had a relative on her husband's side.
He was a prominent man of noble character from
Elimelech's family. His name was Boaz.

2 Ruth the Moabitess asked Naomi, "Will you let
me go into the fields and gather fallen grain behind
someone with whom I find favor?"

Naomi answered her, "Go ahead, my daughter."
3 So Ruth left and entered the field to gather grain
behind the harvesters. She happened to be in the
portion of the field belonging to Boaz, who was from
Elimelech's family.

4 Later, when Boaz arrived from Bethlehem, he said
to the harvesters, "The LORD be with you."

"The LORD bless you," they replied.

5 Boaz asked his servant who was in charge of the
harvesters, "Whose young woman is this?"

6 The servant answered, "She is the young Moabite
woman who returned with Naomi from the territory
of Moab. 7 She asked, 'Will you let me gather fallen
grain among the bundles behind the harvesters?' She
came and has been on her feet since early morning,
except that she rested a little in the shelter."[H]

8 Then Boaz said to Ruth, "Listen, my daughter.[I]
Don't go and gather grain in another field, and don't
leave this one, but stay here close to my female servants. 9 See which field they are harvesting, and follow them. Haven't I ordered the young men not to

[A] **1:1** Lit *In the days of the judging* [B] **1:2** = Pleasant; also in v. 20
[C] **1:13** Lit *marrying a man* [D] **1:13** Lit *daughters, for more bitter to me than you* [E] **1:19** Lit *excited because of them* [F] **1:20** = Bitter; see v. 2
[G] **1:21** LXX, Syr, Vg read *has humiliated* [H] **2:7** LXX reads *morning, and until evening she has not rested in the field a little*; Vg reads *morning until now and she did not return to the house*; Hb uncertain
[I] **2:8** Lit *"Haven't you heard, my daughter?*

Moab: Its History and People

by John Traylor

Ruins at Dibon, which was one of the ancient capital cities of Moab.

Moab was located on the high, fertile plateau immediately east of Judah. It was thus bordered on the west by the lower Jordan River and the Dead Sea. The Arabian Desert formed the eastern border and ended Moab's agricultural zone. At the times of its largest territorial possession, Moab's northern border stretched beyond Heshbon to the hills of Gilead; for most of the time, though, its northern border was the Arnon River (Jdg 11:18). The Zered River, the southern border, separated Moab from Edom.

Interpreters divided Moab into three districts: the area north of the Arnon River, the area south of the Arnon, and the Jordan Valley. From the Jordan River and the Dead Sea, the land moved upward to the east to the plateau that stood three thousand feet above sea level. Both the Zered and the Arnon Rivers flowed from east to west into the Dead Sea. The Arnon Gorge, which at points is seventeen hundred feet deep and two miles wide, discouraged armies from invading Moab proper. The "King's Highway" (Nm 20:17) ran north and south through Moab's heart. However, both the Edomites and the Amorites refused to allow Israel to travel that way (20:17; 21:22). The "road to the Wilderness of Moab" (Dt 2:8), which the Israelites followed, ran north and south between the agricultural zone and the desert.

JOURNEY TO MOAB

"The territory of Moab" (Ru 1:1), literally "the field of Moab," probably refers to the area south of the Arnon River. In their journey, Elimelech and his family would have traveled north from Bethlehem to Jerusalem. Then they would have turned east down to Jericho to cross the Jordan River at its southern tip before it entered the Dead Sea. They would have next climbed the rugged Jordan Valley to "the plains of Moab" where the Israelites camped and received final instructions before crossing the Jordan River into the promised land (Nm 36:13). As Elimelech and his family looked eastward across the rolling pastureland to the desert, they would have seen Mount Nebo, from which God showed Moses the promised land and then buried him in a nearby valley (Dt 34:1–6). Because of the width and the depth of the Arnon Gorge, they probably would have crossed the Arnon as it came out of the desert. When they settled in "the field of Moab," they would have found rich soil with ideal climate and abundant rains in the fall and spring to grow grain and to raise sheep and cattle (Nm 32:1; 2Kg 3:4). They would also have found cisterns, which collected and held rainwater for use in the dry seasons.

Elimelech and his family entered Moab at a time of peaceful relations between the Moabites and the Israelites. But, in their mutual histories, Moab and Israel were often at war with each other, usually over who would possess the land north of the Arnon River.

During the time of the divided kingdom, Omri, who ruled northern

Aerial view of the Wadi Hasa, through which the Zered River flows before emptying into the southern end of the Dead Sea. The Zered River served as the boundary between Moab and its southern neighbor Edom.

Israel, conquered Moab and forced Moab to pay annual tribute of as much as "one hundred thousand lambs and the wool of one hundred thousand rams" (2Kg 3:4). Around 850 BC, however, Moab's king Mesha broke Israel's yoke and retook the land north of the Arnon River. To celebrate his victory, he erected the Moabite stone in Dibon, the city just north of the Arnon in which he was raised. In particular, King Mesha praised the Moabite god Chemosh for delivering the northern kingdom into his hands and for enabling him to fulfill his lifelong dream of Moab once again possessing the land north of the Arnon.

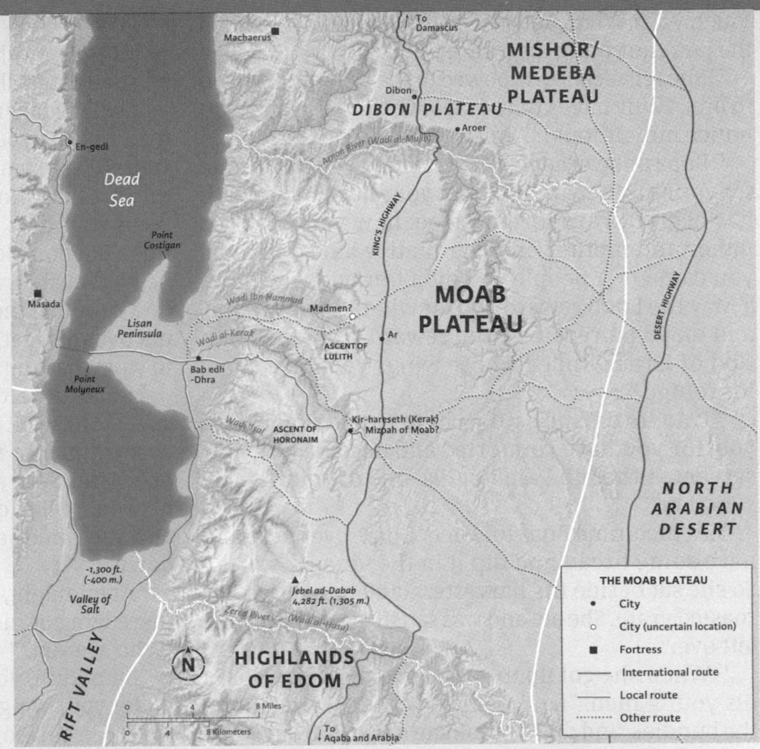

RELIGION OF MOAB

The Bible refers to the Moabites as "the people of Chemosh" (Nm 21:29; Jr 48:46). The Moabite king was thought to be Chemosh's son, and the people were thought to be the god's other sons and daughters. The people believed their national god, Chemosh, ruled through the king and princes. His priests presided over temples dedicated to him; the people sought his forgiveness and favor through such extreme measures as child sacrifice (2Kg 3:27).

The Moabites also worshiped the Baal gods. Indeed, the Israelites joined themselves to these gods with the daughters of Moab at Baal-peor (Nm 25:1–3). These gods supposedly controlled productivity of the land. Through acts of so-called "sacred prostitution," worshipers sought to encourage the Baal gods to mate in the heavens in order to increase crop production as well as animal and human reproduction on the earth. The Moabites probably mingled worship of the Baals with that of Chemosh. ✣

The Arnon River Valley bisected Moab. During the time of the tribal allotments, the Arnon, which flows westward into the Dead Sea (seen right, on the horizon), separated Moab from the territory of Reuben.

touch you? When you are thirsty, go and drink from the jars the young men have filled."

10 She fell facedown, bowed to the ground, and said to him, "Why have I found favor with you, so that you notice me, although I am a foreigner?"

11 Boaz answered her, "Everything you have done for your mother-in-law since your husband's death has been fully reported to me: how you left your father and mother and your native land, and how you came to a people you didn't previously know. 12 May the LORD reward you for what you have done, and may you receive a full reward from the LORD God of Israel, under whose wings you have come for refuge."

13 "My lord," she said, "I have found favor with you, for you have comforted and encouraged your servant, although I am not like one of your female servants."

14 At mealtime Boaz told her, "Come over here and have some bread and dip it in the vinegar sauce." So she sat beside the harvesters, and he offered her roasted grain. She ate and was satisfied and had some left over.

15 When she got up to gather grain, Boaz ordered his young men, "Let her even gather grain among the bundles, and don't humiliate her. 16 Pull out some stalks from the bundles for her and leave them for her to gather. Don't rebuke her." 17 So Ruth gathered grain in the field until evening. She beat out what she had gathered, and it was about twenty-six quarts[A] of barley. 18 She picked up the grain and went into the town, where her mother-in-law saw what she had gleaned. She brought out what she had left over from her meal and gave it to her.

19 Her mother-in-law said to her, "Where did you gather barley today, and where did you work? May the LORD bless the man who noticed you."

Ruth told her mother-in-law whom she had worked with and said, "The name of the man I worked with today is Boaz."

20 Then Naomi said to her daughter-in-law, "May the LORD bless him because he has not abandoned his kindness to the living or the dead." Naomi continued, "The man is a close relative. He is one of our family redeemers."

21 Ruth the Moabitess said, "He also told me, 'Stay with my young men until they have finished all of my harvest.'"

22 So Naomi said to her daughter-in-law Ruth, "My daughter, it is good for you to work[B] with his female servants, so that nothing will happen to you in another field." 23 Ruth stayed close to Boaz's female servants and gathered grain until the barley and the wheat harvests were finished. And she lived with[C] her mother-in-law.

RUTH'S APPEAL TO BOAZ

3 Ruth's mother-in-law Naomi said to her, "My daughter, shouldn't I find rest for you, so that you will be taken care of? 2 Now isn't Boaz our relative? Haven't you been working with his female servants? This evening he will be winnowing barley on the threshing floor. 3 Wash, put on perfumed oil, and wear your best clothes. Go down to the threshing floor, but don't let the man know you are there until he has finished eating and drinking. 4 When he lies down, notice the place where he's lying, go in and uncover his feet, and lie down. Then he will explain to you what you should do."

5 So Ruth said to her, "I will do everything you say."[D] 6 She went down to the threshing floor and did everything her mother-in-law had charged her to do. 7 After Boaz ate, drank, and was in good spirits, he went to lie down at the end of the pile of barley, and she came secretly, uncovered his feet, and lay down.

8 At midnight, Boaz was startled, turned over, and there lying at his feet was a woman! 9 So he asked, "Who are you?"

"I am Ruth, your servant," she replied. "Take me under your wing,[E] for you are a family redeemer."

10 Then he said, "May the LORD bless you, my daughter. You have shown more kindness now than before,[F] because you have not pursued younger men, whether rich or poor. 11 Now don't be afraid, my daughter. I will do for you whatever you say,[G] since all the people in my town[H] know that you are a woman of noble character. 12 Yes, it is true that I am a family redeemer, but there is a redeemer closer than I am. 13 Stay here tonight, and in the morning, if he wants to redeem you, that's good. Let him redeem you. But if he doesn't want to redeem you, as the LORD lives, I will. Now lie down until morning."

14 So she lay down at his feet until morning but got up while it was still dark.[I] Then Boaz said, "Don't let it be known that a[J] woman came to the threshing floor." 15 And he told Ruth, "Bring the shawl you're wearing and hold it out." When she held it out, he shoveled six measures of barley into her shawl, and she[K] went into the town.

16 She went to her mother-in-law, Naomi, who asked her, "What happened,[L] my daughter?"

Then Ruth told her everything the man had done for her. 17 She said, "He gave me these six measures

[A]**2:17** Lit *about an ephah* [B]**2:22** Lit *go out* [C]**2:23** Some Hb mss, Vg read *she returned to* [D]**3:5** Alt Hb tradition reads *say to me* [E]**3:9** Or *"Spread the edge of your garment*; lit *"Spread the wing of your garment*; Ru 2:12 [F]**3:10** Lit *kindness at the last than at the first* [G]**3:11** Some Hb mss, Orig, Syr, Tg, Vg read *say to me* [H]**3:11** Lit *all the gate of my people* [I]**3:14** Lit *up before a man could recognize his companion* [J]**3:14** LXX; MT reads *the* [K]**3:15** Some Hb mss, Aramaic, Syr, Vg; other Hb mss read *he* [L]**3:16** Lit *"Who are you*

The Kinsman Redeemer: His Rights and Responsibilities

by Robert A. Street

English Bibles often translate the Hebrew noun *go'el* as "kinsman" ("family redeemer" in Ru 2:20; 3:9,12; 4:1,14). The word is based on the verb *ga'al* and describes a person who has a familial responsibility. This kinsman's obligation was to protect the family's and clan's interests.[1] Three specific areas of human responsibility are apparent from the use of *go'el* in the Old Testament, those related to property, descendants, and justice. The fourth use of *go'el* is with reference to God as the Redeemer.[2]

PROPERTY

Redemption of property is an important part of Hebrew Law as depicted in stipulations related to the Jubilee Year and to animal sacrifice. The Hebrews were not to sell permanently their family or tribal land (Lv 25:23). The basic concept of the Jubilee Year was the "general return of lands and real property to the original owners or their heirs."[3] Rather than simply focusing on the Jubilee Year, an examination of the kinsman's role proves enlightening. If a brother (family member) sold property, the kinsman was to redeem it (v. 25). If the brother was too poor to care for himself, the kinsman was to "support him" (vv. 35–36). When the brother sold himself into slavery to a foreigner, he was to be redeemed by his brother, his uncle, his cousin, a near kinsman, or, he could even redeem himself—by paying the redemption price (vv. 47–55).

DESCENDANTS

The story of Ruth describes something akin to levirate marriage (see Dt 25:5–10), which emphasized the perpetuation of a bloodline. In this type of marriage, the brother of a deceased man was to marry the widow to perpetuate his brother's name. Though levirate marriage[4] might not properly be part of the kinsman redeemer obligation,[5] it is clearly connected with the Ruth and Boaz narrative.

Boaz was a relative (2:1; Hb *moda`*) of Ruth through her marriage to one of Elimelech's sons. Boaz did not become the *go'el*, the kinsman redeemer, until the end of the story, when he accepted responsibility not only for redeeming the land but also for redeeming Ruth. This marriage was in accord with the concept of levirate marriage, where a kinsman would marry a widow of a relative to ensure the continuance of the relative's name (bloodline) in Israel.

JUSTICE

Limiting the role of the kinsman redeemer to the picture presented in the book of Ruth misses many details about his responsibilities. The most unusual kinsman obligation is related to justice. In Numbers 35:19, the *go'el* is "the avenger of blood" (*go'el ha-dam*). The book of Numbers clearly describes a situation in which a relative is killed and the kinsman's resultant duty is to see that justice was carried out. ✣

---

[1] Jan de Waard and Eugene A. Nida, *A Translator's Handbook on the Book of Ruth* (London: United Bible Societies, 1973), 43. [2] "[*ga'al*]" (redeem) in *A Concise Hebrew and Aramaic Lexicon of the Old Testament*, ed. William L. Holladay (Grand Rapids: Eerdmans, 1971), 52. [3] Roland de Vaux, *Ancient Israel* (Grand Rapids: Eerdmans, 1997), 175. [4] Solomon Schechter and Joseph Jacobs, "Levirate Marriage" in *JE*, www.jewishencyclopedia.com/articles/9859-levirate-marriage. [5] R. Laird Harris, "[*ga'al*]" (redeem) in *TWOT*, 1:144–45.

Field of Boaz, near Bethlehem.

Levirate Marriage and the Book of Ruth

by R. Kelvin Moore

Woman gathering grain at the foot of Herodium, Herod's palace-fortress.

The term translated "levirate" comes from the Latin word *levir*, meaning "brother-in-law."[1] Thus "levirate" refers to an ancient marriage custom that involved an in-law. In addition to Israel, other cultures in the Old Testament world, including Assyrian, Hittite, and Canaanite, practiced some form of levirate marriage.[2] The Old Testament records three passages regarding levirate marriage: Genesis 38; Deuteronomy 25:5–10; and Ruth 3–4. Scholars attempt to explain these three passages in numerous ways. Some interpret Genesis 38 as the oldest of the three passages, followed by Deuteronomy 25 and then Ruth 3–4. Others interpret Ruth 3–4 as the oldest of the three, followed by Genesis 38 and Deuteronomy 25. Regardless, chronology has not provided the key by which these three passages can be explained to everyone's satisfaction. Perhaps an acceptable method to interpret these passages understands Deuteronomy 25:5–10 as a record of the law that spells out levirate marriage. Working on that assumption, Genesis 38 and Ruth 3–4 illustrate the implementation of this law.

Deuteronomy 25:5–10 records the law that spells out levirate marriage, revealing numerous aspects. Levirate marriage stipulated that the brothers live in close geographical proximity: "brothers [who] live on the same property" (v. 5). Deuteronomy 25:5 qualified the brother-in-law as the person responsible to marry the widow: "Her brother-in-law is to take her as his wife." Additionally, this passage maintains that the "first son she bears will carry on the name of the dead brother, so his name will not be blotted out from Israel" (v. 6). Levirate marriage viewed the first son born to the newly married couple as the son of the deceased man. Finally, Deuteronomy 25:7–10 illustrates the optional aspect of levirate marriage in that a brother-in-law could refuse to marry the widow: "I don't want to marry her" (v. 8). But the brother-in-law paid a price in humiliation for his refusal: "then his sister-in-law will go up to him in the sight of the elders . . . and spit in his face" (v. 9).

The events of Genesis 38 record numerous similarities with levirate marriage as found in Deuteronomy 25:5–10. Judah, son of Jacob (Israel), gave Tamar as a wife to his eldest son, Er. Er died sonless, creating a classic need for levirate marriage. Judah did his part and instructed Er's oldest brother, Onan, to "Perform your duty as her brother-in-law" (Gn 38:8). The brothers seem to have lived on the same property, and Onan was the actual brother-in-law. Judah did instruct Onan to produce a child in order to carry on his deceased brother's name. The humiliation aspect remains irrelevant because Genesis 38 reveals nothing of Onan refusing to accept his initial responsibilities. But the parallels end here. When Onan refused to impregnate Tamar, "he [God] put him to death" (v. 10). Levirate marriage stipulated that Judah's youngest son, Shelah, now became the brother-in-law to perpetuate the names of both Er and Onan. But Judah did not instruct Shelah to perform his duty as brother-in-law to Tamar and evidently had no intentions of doing so (v. 14). Eventually Tamar deceived her father-in-law, Judah, and became pregnant by him. In essence, the father-in-law became the man responsible for perpetuating the names of his sons.

THE SITUATION WITH RUTH

The events of Ruth 3–4 adhered to at least one regulation of levirate marriage as found in Deuteronomy 25:5–10. Boaz intended to marry Ruth to "perpetuate the man's name" (Ru 4:5; v. 10 says "deceased man's"), as Deuteronomy 25:6 instructed. But Ruth 3–4 offers numerous atypical characteristics of levirate marriage as outlined in Deuteronomy. Ruth 3–4 does not communicate explicitly that Boaz met the levirate stipulation to "live on the same property," because Naomi had "returned from the territory of Moab" (4:3). Deuteronomy 25:5 maintains that the levirate marriage responsibility fell to the brother-in-law. Boaz was not Ruth's brother-in-law and Deuteronomy 25:5–10 provides no insight regarding the substitution of a more distant relative. Boaz referred to the transferal of property: "Naomi . . . is selling the portion of the field that belonged to our brother Elimelech" (Ru 4:3). Deuteronomy 25:5–10 records no stipulation for property transferal. Whereas Deuteronomy records humiliation for the man who refused to meet levirate marriage obligations, Ruth 4 records no such humiliation (vv. 6–12). Deuteronomy 25 records an important legal aspect to levirate marriage in that the brother-in-law "is to take her as his wife" (v. 5). But the unnamed next-of-kin in Ruth 4 does not appear to have been under any legal obligation to marry Ruth. Furthermore, neither Ruth nor Naomi voiced any concept of a legal right to levirate marriage. Deuteronomy 25:5 instructs the brother-in-law to initiate levirate marriage. But Ruth initiated the contact with Boaz.

Undoubtedly Naomi (and consequently Ruth) found herself in a desperate situation when left "without her two children and without her husband" (Ru 1:5). Readers of the book of Ruth sense anxiety in Naomi's words as she encouraged her daughters-in-law to return home (1:8). In tears, Naomi reminded her daughters-in-law that age prevented her from bearing sons who might marry them (1:11–14). Such desperate measures could explain the presence of Boaz (not a brother-in-law) even though he did not appear to "live on the same property" as Mahlon, Ruth's deceased husband. Such desperate measures could also explain Ruth's boldness in initiating contact with Boaz.

REASONS FOR LEVIRATE MARRIAGE

What purpose did levirate marriage serve? Three purposes are apparent. First, levirate marriage preserved the family estate. Boaz informed the elders and the people of his intentions to marry Ruth in order to "perpetuate the deceased man's name on his property, so that his name will not disappear among his relatives or from the gate of his hometown" (4:10).

Second, levirate marriage preserved the family name. This was an important consideration in the Old Testament era.

Finally, levirate marriage, in prohibiting that a widow be married to an outsider, provided for the widow. Levirate marriage offered the widow some level of security. The Bible records numerous passages regarding widows, including Deuteronomy 14:28–29 and James 1:27. Levirate marriage unambiguously communicates God's concern for widows. While the protection of property inheritance and the perpetuation of the deceased's name constituted real needs, the provision for the widow may have been the most pressing incentive for levirate marriage. God provided for widows, as well as all individuals and groups susceptible to neglect and abuse (Dt 15:12–14; 24:19–22; Mt 25:31–46). ✣

---

[1] David Atkinson, *The Message of Ruth, The Wings of Refuge* (Downers Grove, IL: InterVarsity, 1983), 86. [2] O. J. Baab, "Marriage" in *IDB*, 3:282.

Sealing the Deal in the Ancient Near East

by Robert D. Bergen

"Sealing a deal" in the ancient Near East frequently involved a highly structured ritual that included carefully scripted spoken words, written documentation, the exchange of possessions, or even the shedding of blood. The end result of these commitments was that a change took place—of status, ownership, or obligation.

FORMAL COMMITMENTS: ARCHAEOLOGICAL EVIDENCE

Commitments between People Groups—Old Testament scholars have given their primary attention to treaties coming out of the Hittite Empire of the fifteenth to thirteenth centuries BC. Hittite kings drew up these treaties and imposed them on people groups they defeated in battle. They are of interest to biblical scholars because they possess similarities to the covenant God established with Israel at Mount Sinai.

Hittite suzerainty treaties involved leading representatives of the two nations formally coming together to offer up religious sacrifices and set forth the specific details of the agreement. Included in the meeting were a description of the historical relationship between the nations, a general statement of principles for future conduct, a declaration of the treaty's terms, the invoking of deities to oversee the treaty, and the expression of curses associated with nonfulfillment of the treaty's terms, as well as blessings resulting from fulfillment of the treaty.[1]

Commitments between Individuals—Many different kinds of transactions between individuals, each involving a ritual of some sort, took place in the ancient Near East. Archaeologists have found written contracts that record details about sales and purchases, rentals, labor contracts, business partnerships, loans, mortgages, bankruptcies, and power of attorney. Documented familial transactions included marriage, divorce, adoption, and inheritance. Documentary evidence suggests that the more important of these transactions included certain common elements: the swearing of oaths, the presence of authorized witnesses, and the creation of a record of the transaction in the form of a clay, papyrus, or leather document. As a rule, these documents included the names or cylinder seal impressions of those who witnessed the event.

FORMAL COMMITMENTS: BIBLICAL EVIDENCE

Commitments between People Groups—Like other cultures in the ancient Near East, the Israelites established binding agreements in the form of treaties or covenants with other people groups. At times, people drew up treaties with equal benefits for both parties, known in the world of Old Testament scholarship as parity treaties. At other times, the treaties consisted of one group imposing demands on another (suzerainty treaties). People established parity treaties especially for economic reasons (Israel and Tyre; 1Kg 5:6–12) or for mutual assistance in times of war (Israel and Judah against Moab; 2Kg 3:7). They drew up suzerainty treaties by conquering nations and forcing them on defeated people groups (Israel with Aram and Edom; 2 Sm 8:6,14; 10:19).

Israelites termed the establishment of a covenant "making" or "cutting" the covenant (Gn 21:27). This event, described most fully in

During the reign of Darius I (522–486 BC), cylinder seals regained their popularity. The designs typically depicted military personnel, deities, or animals—some mythological and others real. This seal depicts a Median archer and a soldier in a crested helmet.

Genesis 15:9–18, required the butchering of animals, separating the body parts into two piles, and the responsible parties standing between the divided carcasses while confirming the commitment. This portion of the event symbolically invoked the curse of a horrible death for anyone who broke the agreement.

Certain long-term treaties in the Old Testament were termed "a covenant of salt" (see Nm 18:19; 2Ch 13:5). While this term is never explained, the name is likely derived from a special ritual involving salt that was associated with the enactment of the treaty.

Commitments between Individuals—The Old Testament's legal materials, narratives, wisdom sayings, and prophetic literature all supply useful details describing the rituals and practices that were part of Israel's financial and familial transactions. One of the most detailed illustrations of an interpersonal legal transaction is in Ruth 4.

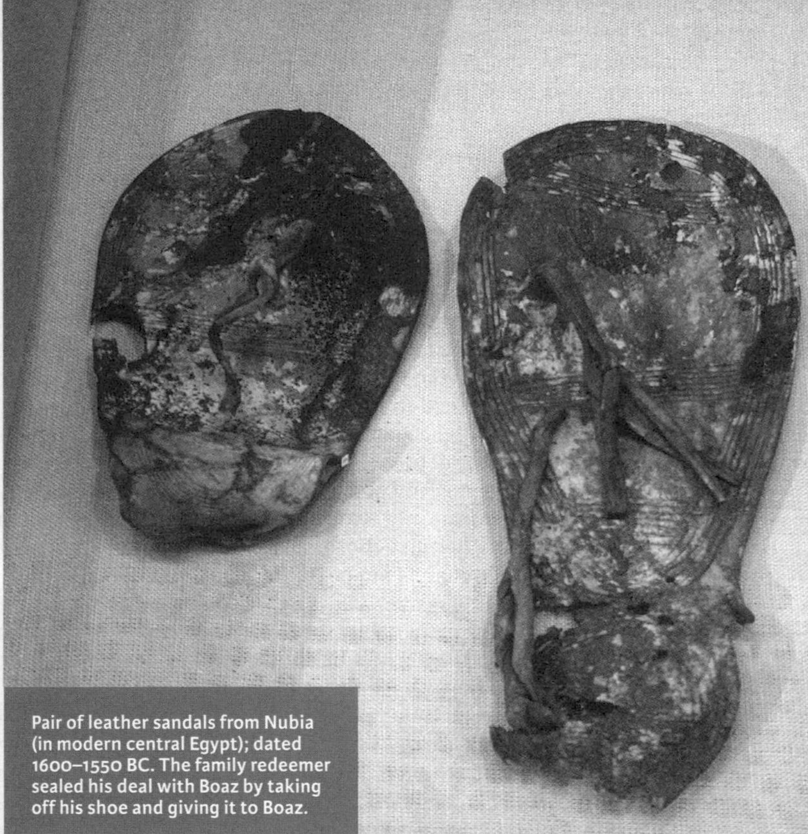

Pair of leather sandals from Nubia (in modern central Egypt); dated 1600–1550 BC. The family redeemer sealed his deal with Boaz by taking off his shoe and giving it to Boaz.

In larger financial transactions, ones involving the transfer of land or slaves to a nonfamily member, for example, four main elements seem to have been involved. First came the gathering of witnesses. Before an important business deal could be worked out, trusted individuals, normally a village's older males, had to be assembled to witness the transaction. Boaz's efforts in a complex deal involving land transfer and acceptance of responsibility for a childless widow clearly demonstrate this (Ru 4:2).

Second came negotiating an agreed-upon purchase price. Disagreements regarding price might exist, but because of the importance of honor within that culture, both the buyer and the seller were expected to avoid humiliating the other person.

Third came the exchange of payment, or at least a good-faith pledge for payment. Coined or printed money did not exist in ancient Israel, so persons usually completed purchases through the transfer of agreed-upon amounts of bronze, silver, or gold weighed out on balance scales (Lv 19:36; Jr 32:9). Sometimes people used grain or animals instead of metal for payment (Gn 38:16–17a; Hs 3:2). If an individual could not make the full payment at the time of the transaction, he was required to provide some sort of collateral or good-faith pledge (Gn 38:17b–18; Ex 22:26) until he could pay the debt (Ezk 18:7). However, collateral could not consist of anything directly connected with a person's existence, livelihood, or dignity (Dt 24:6; Jb 22:6; 24:3).

Fourth came the creation of evidence to verify that the transaction had taken place. The evidence varied according the nature of the transaction and the era in which it occurred. Ruth 4:7 indicates that in Boaz's day, a man redeeming or transferring property would remove one of his sandals and give it to the person making the acquisition or accepting the transfer. This would serve as a "legal attestation of a transfer of goods or rights."[2] In the days of the prophet Jeremiah (early sixth century BC), a similar transaction required the production of two identical documents, signed by witnesses, detailing the sale. One was "tied with straps and sealed for ready verification in the event the ownership was challenged."[3] Both documents were then preserved in a protected earthen storage jar. ✣

---

[1] J. A. Thompson, *The Ancient Near Eastern Treaties and the Old Testament* (London: Tyndale Press, 1964), 16–17. [2] Daniel I. Block, *Judges, Ruth*, vol. 6 in NAC (1999), 718. [3] F. B. Huey Jr., *Jeremiah, Lamentations*, vol. 16 in NAC (1993), 291.

of barley, because he said,[A] 'Don't go back to your mother-in-law empty-handed.'"

18 Naomi said, "My daughter, wait until you find out how things go, for he won't rest unless he resolves this today."

RUTH AND BOAZ MARRY

4 Boaz went to the gate of the town and sat down there. Soon the family redeemer Boaz had spoken about came by. Boaz said, "Come over here[B] and sit down." So he went over and sat down. 2 Then Boaz took ten men of the town's elders and said, "Sit here." And they sat down. 3 He said to the redeemer, "Naomi, who has returned from the territory of Moab, is selling the portion of the field that belonged to our brother Elimelech. 4 I thought I should inform you: Buy it back in the presence of those seated here and in the presence of the elders of my people. If you want to redeem it, do it. But if you do[C] not want to redeem it, tell me so that I will know, because there isn't anyone other than you to redeem it, and I am next after you."

"I want to redeem it," he answered.

5 Then Boaz said, "On the day you buy the field from Naomi, you will acquire[D] Ruth the Moabitess, the wife of the deceased man, to perpetuate the man's name on his property."[E]

6 The redeemer replied, "I can't redeem it myself, or I will ruin my own inheritance. Take my right of redemption, because I can't redeem it."

7 At an earlier period in Israel, a man removed his sandal and gave it to the other party in order to make any matter legally binding concerning the right of redemption or the exchange of property. This was the method of legally binding a transaction in Israel.

8 So the redeemer removed his sandal and said to Boaz, "Buy back the property yourself."

9 Boaz said to the elders and all the people, "You are witnesses today that I am buying from Naomi everything that belonged to Elimelech, Chilion, and Mahlon. 10 I have also acquired Ruth the Moabitess, Mahlon's widow, as my wife, to perpetuate the deceased man's name on his property, so that his name will not disappear among his relatives or from the gate of his hometown. You are witnesses today."

11 All the people who were at the city gate, including the elders, said, "We are witnesses. May the LORD make the woman who is entering your house like Rachel and Leah, who together built the house of Israel. May you be powerful in Ephrathah and your name well known in Bethlehem. 12 May your house become like the house of Perez, the son Tamar bore to Judah, because of the offspring the LORD will give you by this young woman."

13 Boaz took Ruth and she became his wife. He slept with her, and the LORD granted conception to her, and she gave birth to a son. 14 The women said to Naomi, "Blessed be the LORD, who has not left you without a family redeemer today. May his name become well known in Israel. 15 He will renew your life and sustain you in your old age. Indeed, your daughter-in-law, who loves you and is better to you than seven sons, has given birth to him." 16 Naomi took the child, placed him on her lap, and became a mother to him. 17 The neighbor women said, "A son has been born to Naomi," and they named him Obed. He was the father of Jesse, the father of David.

DAVID'S GENEALOGY FROM JUDAH'S SON

18 Now these are the family records of Perez:

Perez fathered Hezron,
19 Hezron fathered Ram,[F]
Ram fathered Amminadab,
20 Amminadab fathered Nahshon,
Nahshon fathered Salmon,
21 Salmon fathered Boaz,
Boaz fathered Obed,
22 Obed fathered Jesse,
and Jesse fathered David.

[A] **3:17** Alt Hb tradition, LXX, Syr, Tg read *said to me* [B] **4:1** Or *said, "Come here Mr. So-and-so* [C] **4:4** Some Hb mss, LXX, Syr, Vg; other Hb mss read *if he does* [D] **4:5** Lit *Naomi and from* [E] **4:5** Alt Hb tradition reads *Naomi, I will have already acquired from Ruth the Moabitess, the wife of the dead man, the privilege of raising up the name of the dead man on his property* [F] **4:19** LXX reads *Aram*; Mt 1:3–4

1 SAMUEL

Azekah, where the Philistine army lined up behind Goliath in opposition to Saul and his army.

INTRODUCTION TO

1 SAMUEL

Circumstances of Writing

Early tradition suggests 1 and 2 Samuel were originally one book. Some scholars believe Samuel was largely responsible for the material up to 1 Samuel 25 and that the prophets Nathan and Gad gave significant input to the rest (based on 1Ch 29:29). This proposal, however, must remain speculative, because the books name no authors. First Samuel 27:6 suggests the book was not completed until perhaps a few generations after the division of the kingdom around 930 BC.

After Israel's conquest of the land during the days of Joshua, Israel entered a time of apostasy. The book of Judges describes recurrences of a cycle with predictable phases. First, the people sinned against the Lord and fell into idolatry. Second, the Lord raised up an adversary to afflict them and turn them back to him. Third, the people cried out to the Lord in repentance. Fourth, the Lord brought deliverance for them through a judge whom he raised up. The book of Judges' famous verse, "In those days there was no king in Israel; everyone did whatever seemed right to him" (21:25), aptly describes the period. The book of 1 Samuel picks up the historical record toward the end of those stormy days.

Contribution to the Bible

The books of 1 and 2 Samuel describe Israel's transition from a loosely organized tribal league under God (a theocracy) to centralized leadership under a king who answered to God (a monarchy). Samuel's life and ministry greatly shaped this period of restructuring as he consistently pointed people back to God.

Saul's rule highlighted the dangers to which the Israelites fell victim as they clamored for a king to lead them. Samuel's warnings fell on deaf ears (1Sm 8:10–20) because God's people were intent on becoming like the nations around them. In the end, they got exactly what they asked for, but they paid a terrible price. Saul's life stands as a warning to trust God's timing for life's provisions.

David's rule testified to the amazing works the Lord could and would do through a life yielded to him. Israel's second king seemed quite aware of God's blessing on his life and displayed a tender heart toward the things of God (2Sm 5:12; 7:1–2; 22:1–51; 23:1–7). Later generations would receive blessing because of David's life (Is 37:35). God's special covenant with David (2Sm 7:1–29) found its ultimate fulfillment in Jesus, the Son of David (Lk 1:32–33). The consequences of David's sin with Bathsheba, however, stand as a warning to all who experience sin's attraction. God holds his children accountable for their actions, and even forgiven sin can have terrible consequences.

Structure

The first seven chapters of 1 Samuel describe Samuel's birth, call, and initial ministry among the Israelites. Chapter 8 is a major turning point as the people ask for a king to rule them "the same as all the other nations have" (v. 5). Chapters 9–12 then describe Saul's selection—at God's direction, yet not his perfect will for the time (12:16–18).

First Samuel 13–31 describes Saul's victories and failures. Saul was a king with great physical stature and military skill (14:47–52), but his heart was not one with the Lord (13:14). His unwillingness to obey the Lord's commands ultimately outweighed his accomplishments, and chapters 16–31 describe his reign's downward spiral. During this time, God raised up David and was preparing him for the day he would succeed Saul—a fact Saul gradually realized (15:28; 24:20–21; 28:17).

HANNAH'S VOW

1 There was a man from Ramathaim-zophim in[A] the hill country of Ephraim. His name was Elkanah son of Jeroham, son of Elihu, son of Tohu, son of Zuph, an Ephraimite. 2 He had two wives, the first named Hannah and the second Peninnah. Peninnah had children, but Hannah was childless. 3 This man would go up from his town every year to worship and to sacrifice to the LORD of Armies at Shiloh, where Eli's two sons, Hophni and Phinehas, were the LORD's priests.

4 Whenever Elkanah offered a sacrifice, he always gave portions of the meat to his wife Peninnah and to each of her sons and daughters. 5 But he gave a double[B] portion to Hannah, for he loved her even though the LORD had kept her from conceiving. 6 Her rival would taunt her severely just to provoke her, because the LORD had kept Hannah from conceiving. 7 Year after year, when she went up to the LORD's house, her rival taunted her in this way. Hannah would weep and would not eat. 8 "Hannah, why are you crying?" her husband, Elkanah, would ask. "Why won't you eat? Why are you troubled? Am I not better to you than ten sons?"

9 On one occasion, Hannah got up after they ate and drank at Shiloh.[C] The priest Eli was sitting on a chair by the doorpost of the LORD's temple. 10 Deeply hurt, Hannah prayed to the LORD and wept with many tears. 11 Making a vow, she pleaded, "LORD of Armies, if you will take notice of your servant's affliction, remember and not forget me, and give your servant a son, I will give him to the LORD all the days of his life, and his hair will never be cut."[D]

12 While she continued praying in the LORD's presence, Eli watched her mouth. 13 Hannah was praying silently, and though her lips were moving, her voice could not be heard. Eli thought she was drunk 14 and said to her, "How long are you going to be drunk? Get rid of your wine!"

15 "No, my lord," Hannah replied. "I am a woman with a broken heart. I haven't had any wine or beer; I've been pouring out my heart before the LORD. 16 Don't think of me as a wicked woman; I've been praying from the depth of my anguish and resentment."

17 Eli responded, "Go in peace, and may the God of Israel grant the request you've made of him."

18 "May your servant find favor with you," she replied. Then Hannah went on her way; she ate and no longer looked despondent.[E]

SAMUEL'S BIRTH AND DEDICATION

19 The next morning Elkanah and Hannah got up early to worship before the LORD. Afterward, they returned home to Ramah. Then Elkanah was intimate with his wife Hannah, and the LORD remembered her. 20 After some time,[F] Hannah conceived and gave birth to a son. She named him Samuel,[G] because she said, "I requested him from the LORD."

21 When Elkanah and all his household went up to make the annual sacrifice and his vow offering to the LORD, 22 Hannah did not go and explained to her husband, "After the child is weaned, I'll take him to appear in the LORD's presence and to stay there permanently."

23 Her husband, Elkanah, replied, "Do what you think is best, and stay here until you've weaned him. May the LORD confirm your[H] word." So Hannah stayed there and nursed her son until she weaned him. 24 When she had weaned him, she took him with her to Shiloh, as well as a three-year-old bull,[I] half a bushel[J] of flour, and a clay jar of wine. Though the boy was still young,[K] she took him to the LORD's house at Shiloh. 25 Then they slaughtered the bull and brought the boy to Eli.

26 "Please, my lord," she said, "as surely as you live, my lord, I am the woman who stood here beside you praying to the LORD. 27 I prayed for this boy, and since the LORD gave me what I asked him for, 28 I now give the boy to the LORD. For as long as he lives, he is given to the LORD." Then he[L] worshiped the LORD there.[M]

HANNAH'S TRIUMPHANT PRAYER

2 Hannah prayed:

My heart rejoices in the LORD;
my horn is lifted up by the LORD.
My mouth boasts over my enemies,
because I rejoice in your salvation.
2 There is no one holy like the LORD.
There is no one besides you!
And there is no rock like our God.
3 Do not boast so proudly,
or let arrogant words come out of your mouth,
for the LORD is a God of knowledge,
and actions are weighed by him.
4 The bows of the warriors are broken,
but the feeble are clothed with strength.
5 Those who are full hire themselves out
for food,
but those who are starving hunger no more.
The woman who is childless gives birth
to seven,
but the woman with many sons pines away.

[A] **1:1** Or *from Ramathaim, a Zuphite from* [B] **1:5** Or *gave only one*; Hb obscure [C] **1:9** LXX adds *and presented herself before the LORD* [D] **1:11** Lit *and no razor will go up on his head* [E] **1:18** Lit *and her face was not to her again* [F] **1:20** Lit *In the turning of the days* [G] **1:20** In Hb, the name *Samuel* sounds like the phrase "requested from God." [H] **1:23** DSS, LXX, Syr; MT reads *his* [I] **1:24** DSS, LXX, Syr; MT reads *Shiloh with three bulls* [J] **1:24** Lit *bull and an ephah* [K] **1:24** Lit *And the youth was a youth* [L] **1:28** DSS read *she*; some Hb mss, Syr, Vg read *they* [M] **1:28** LXX reads *Then she left him there before the LORD*

Barrenness in the Ancient Near East

by Julie Nall Knowles

Pomegranates growing at Byblos in June. Because of their numerous seeds, pomegranates were considered to aid in fertility.

Women produced children, as many as possible, to maintain both lineage and tribe. Children, especially a son, would continue the names of Elkanah's fathers (1 Sm 1:1) and transmit their possessions for years to come.

To hasten conception, Hannah may have used mandrakes—as Leah did (Gn 30:14–17) and the Beloved in Song of Songs: "The mandrakes give off a fragrance. . . . I have treasured them up for you, my love" (7:13). Women ate the mandrakes' roots, long associated with fertility, as "love-apples" and "tied them around their body in order to conceive."[1] Time passed.

Could Hannah have been infertile? One remedy prescribed twenty-one stones on a linen thread tied around a barren woman's neck[2]—reflecting the mystic multiplication of three times seven. Swallowing tabernacle dust mixed with holy water (the "bitter water" ordeal) could result in fertility for a faithful wife (Nm 5:11–31); barren women swallowed dust or dirt as "straight fertility magic."[3] After a while, Elkanah could have divorced Hannah for barrenness. A similar stipulation appears in the Code of Hammurabi (Old Babylonian Empire, ca 1700 BC).[4] However, a marriage agreement between Hannah's and Elkanah's fathers may have required Hannah to find someone to bear children for her husband. An ancient Nuzi Akkadian adoption tablet details such a contract:

> Kelim-ninu has been given in marriage to Shennima. If Kelim-ninu bears (children), Shennima shall not take another wife; but if Kelim-ninu does not bear, Kelim-ninu shall acquire a woman of the land of Lullu as wife for Shennima.[5]

Could Hannah have "acquired" her fellow wife? Anyway, following law and custom accepted across the land, Peninnah arrived. She gave Elkanah both sons and daughters (1Sm 1:4).

The growing family traveled annually to worship in Shiloh, then the home of the ark of the covenant. On each pilgrimage, Peninnah reminded Hannah that she had no children (vv. 6–7). Early Israelites thought illness and tragedies resulted from sin; barrenness was considered

The recipes on this tablet cover barrenness, pregnancy tests, and treatment for gynecological conditions. Dated about 600–400 BC; likely from Babylon.

sin, sickness, and one of the worst of disgraces. Why did Hannah not defend herself?

Possibly, her marriage agreement ordered Hannah to treat a second wife amiably. In Calah, Assyria's ancient capital (near Mosul, Iraq), a lady named Subietu had a contract stating that for no *sons*, Subietu's husband would take a second woman, and it stipulated Subietu's treatment of a "rival":

> Amat-Aštarti . . . gives her daughter Subietu to Milki-ramu, the son of Abdi-Asuzi . . . (most of the text outlines the dowry). If Subietu does not bear sons he shall take a handmaid. . . . She (the wife) shall not curse, strike, nor be furious and treat her (the handmaid) improperly.[6]

A wife's dowry likely prevented many husbands from discarding a barren woman, for the Code of Hammurabi established that if a man discarded his barren wife he had to return to her the dowry he had received when they were married.[7] But Elkanah loved Hannah and continued taking her to Shiloh (vv. 5–8).

Hannah could have stayed home and joined Canaanites as they observed pagan rituals. By joining Baal devotees, "it was believed possible to insure fertility of crops, to secure offspring with divine sanction, or to feel one's self assimilated to the deity."[8] Inscriptions on a tablet from Ugarit, an ancient city on the Mediterranean coast (Ras Shamra, Syria), outline cultic practices; one line translates, "Over the fire, seven times the sweet-voiced youths chant, 'Coriander in milk, mint in butter.'"[9] If this were a dish eaten in a ceremonial meal, could neighbors have invited barren Hannah to join the worship of Baal?

Once, after their sacrificial meal at Shiloh, Hannah abruptly left and hastened to Yahweh's sanctuary. There, she urgently begged God for a son (vv. 9–11). "It is completely in accordance with Eastern custom that Hannah asks not for a child, or children, but for a son."[10] ✣

---

[1] Raphael Patai, *Sex and Family in the Bible and the Middle East* (Garden City, NY: Doubleday, 1959), 74–76. [2] Robert D. Biggs, "Medicine, Surgery, and Public Health in Ancient Mesopotamia" in *CANE*, 3:1917. [3] Patai, *Sex and Family*, 91. [4] W. W. Davies, *The Codes of Hammurabi and Moses* (Cincinnati: Jennings & Graham, 1905), 138 (p. 65). [5] "Documents from the Practice of Law" in *ANET*, 220. [6] John Van Seters, "The Problem of Childlessness in Near Eastern Law and the Patriarchs of Israel," *JBL* 87.4 (1968): 407. [7] Davies, *Codes*, 138. [8] Beatrice A. Brooks, "Fertility Cult Functionaries in the Old Testament," *JBL* 60.3 (1941): 230. [9] This line has been suggested to be a Canaanite pagan ritual forbidden to Israelites, because of the law "You must not boil a young goat in its mother's milk" (Ex 23:19; 34:26; Dt 14:21). However, in this Ugaritic tablet, no animal is being cooked. See Jack M. Sasson, "Should Cheeseburgers Be Kosher?" *Bible Review* (*BRev*) 19.6 (2003): 43. [10] Hans Wilhelm Hertzberg, *I and II Samuel: A Commentary* (Philadelphia: Westminster, 1964), 25.

Taweret was an Egyptian goddess associated with childbirth and is usually shown, as here, in the form of a pregnant hippopotamus with the face of a lion. Dated 664–343 BC.

The Assyrian demon Pazuzu; despite his ferocious appearance, which varied in detail, Pazuzu helped humankind because he was anathema to Lamashtu, the female demon who preyed on women in childbirth. He sometimes appears on amulets directed against her. This head of Pazuzu was probably attached to bedroom furniture.

6 The LORD brings death and gives life;
he sends some down to Sheol, and he raises
others up.
7 The LORD brings poverty and gives wealth;
he humbles and he exalts.
8 He raises the poor from the dust
and lifts the needy from the trash heap.
He seats them with noblemen
and gives them a throne of honor.[A]
For the foundations of the earth are the
LORD's;
he has set the world on them.
9 He guards the steps[B] of his faithful ones,
but the wicked perish in darkness,
for a person does not prevail by his own
strength.
10 Those who oppose the LORD will be shattered;[C]
he will thunder in the heavens against them.
The LORD will judge the ends of the earth.
He will give power to his king;
he will lift up the horn of his anointed.[D]

11 Elkanah went home to Ramah, but the boy served
the LORD in the presence of the priest Eli.

ELI'S FAMILY JUDGED

12 Eli's sons were wicked men; they did not respect
the LORD 13 or the priests' share of the sacrifices from
the people. When anyone offered a sacrifice, the
priest's servant would come with a three-pronged
meat fork while the meat was boiling 14 and plunge
it into the container, kettle, cauldron, or cooking pot.
The priest would claim for himself whatever the meat
fork brought up. This is the way they treated all the
Israelites who came there to Shiloh. 15 Even before the
fat was burned, the priest's servant would come and
say to the one who was sacrificing, "Give the priest
some meat to roast, because he won't accept boiled
meat from you — only raw." 16 If that person said to
him, "The fat must be burned first; then you can take
whatever you want for yourself," the servant would
reply, "No, I insist that you hand it over right now. If
you don't, I'll take it by force!" 17 So the servants' sin
was very severe in the presence of the LORD, because
the men treated the LORD's offering with contempt.
18 Samuel served in the LORD's presence—this
mere boy was dressed in the linen ephod. 19 Each
year his mother made him a little robe and took it to
him when she went with her husband to offer the
annual sacrifice. 20 Eli would bless Elkanah and his
wife: "May the LORD give you children by this woman
in place of the one she[E] has given to the LORD." Then
they would go home.
21 The LORD paid attention to Hannah's need, and
she conceived and gave birth to three sons and two
daughters. Meanwhile, the boy Samuel grew up in
the presence of the LORD.
22 Now Eli was very old. He heard about everything
his sons were doing to all Israel and how they were
sleeping with the women who served at the entrance
to the tent of meeting. 23 He said to them, "Why are
you doing these things? I have heard about your evil
actions from all these people. 24 No, my sons, the news
I hear the LORD's people spreading is not good. 25 If
one person sins against another, God can intercede
for him, but if a person sins against the LORD, who
can intercede for him?" But they would not listen
to their father, since the LORD intended to kill them.
26 By contrast, the boy Samuel grew in stature and in
favor with the LORD and with people.
27 A man of God came to Eli and said to him, "This
is what the LORD says: 'Didn't I reveal myself to your
forefather's family[F] when they were in Egypt and
belonged to Pharaoh's palace? 28 Out of all the tribes
of Israel, I chose your house[G] to be my priests, to
offer sacrifices on my altar, to burn incense, and
to wear an ephod in my presence. I also gave your
forefather's family all the Israelite food offerings.
29 Why, then, do all of you despise my sacrifices and
offerings that I require at the place of worship? You
have honored your sons more than me, by making
yourselves fat with the best part of all of the offerings
of my people Israel.'
30 "Therefore, this is the declaration of the LORD,
the God of Israel: 'I did say that your family and your
forefather's family would walk before me forever.
But now,' this is the LORD's declaration, 'no longer!
For those who honor me I will honor, but those who
despise me will be disgraced. 31 Look, the days are
coming when I will cut off your strength and the
strength of your forefather's family, so that none in
your family will reach old age. 32 You will see distress
in the place of worship, in spite of all that is good in
Israel, and no one in your family will ever again reach
old age. 33 Any man from your family I do not cut off
from my altar will bring grief[H] and sadness to you.
All your descendants will die violently.[I,J] 34 This will
be the sign that will come to you concerning your
two sons Hophni and Phinehas: both of them will
die on the same day.
35 " 'Then I will raise up a faithful priest for myself.
He will do whatever is in my heart and mind. I will
establish a lasting dynasty for him, and he will walk
before my anointed one for all time. 36 Anyone who is

[A] **2:8** DSS, LXX add *He gives the vow of the one who makes a vow and he blesses the years of the just.* [B] **2:9** Lit *feet* [C] **2:10** DSS, LXX read *The LORD shatters those who dispute with him* [D] **2:10** Or *Messiah* [E] **2:20** DSS; MT reads *he* [F] **2:27** Lit *the house of your father* [G] **2:28** Lit *selected him* [H] **2:33** Lit *grief to your eyes* [I] **2:33** DSS, LXX read *die by the sword of men* [J] **2:33** Lit *die men*

left in your family will come and bow down to him for
a piece of silver or a loaf of bread. He will say: Please
appoint me to some priestly office so I can have a
piece of bread to eat.'"

SAMUEL'S CALL

3 The boy Samuel served the LORD in Eli's presence.
In those days the word of the LORD was rare and
prophetic visions were not widespread.
2 One day Eli, whose eyesight was failing, was lying
in his usual place. 3 Before the lamp of God had gone
out, Samuel was lying down in the temple of the LORD,
where the ark of God was located.
4 Then the LORD called Samuel,[A] and he answered,
"Here I am." 5 He ran to Eli and said, "Here I am; you
called me."
"I didn't call," Eli replied. "Go back and lie down."
So he went and lay down.
6 Once again the LORD called, "Samuel!"
Samuel got up, went to Eli, and said, "Here I am;
you called me."
"I didn't call, my son," he replied. "Go back and
lie down."
7 Now Samuel did not yet know the LORD, because
the word of the LORD had not yet been revealed to
him. 8 Once again, for the third time, the LORD called
Samuel. He got up, went to Eli, and said, "Here I am;
you called me."
Then Eli understood that the LORD was calling the
boy. 9 He told Samuel, "Go and lie down. If he calls you,
say, 'Speak, LORD, for your servant is listening.'" So
Samuel went and lay down in his place.
10 The LORD came, stood there, and called as before,
"Samuel, Samuel!"
Samuel responded, "Speak, for your servant is listening."
11 The LORD said to Samuel, "I am about to do something in Israel that will cause everyone who hears
about it to shudder.[B] 12 On that day I will carry out
against Eli everything I said about his family, from
beginning to end. 13 I told him that I am going to
judge his family forever because of the iniquity he
knows about: his sons are cursing God,[C] and he has
not stopped them. 14 Therefore, I have sworn to Eli's
family: The iniquity of Eli's family will never be wiped
out by either sacrifice or offering."
15 Samuel lay down until the morning; then he
opened the doors of the LORD's house. He was afraid
to tell Eli the vision, 16 but Eli called him and said,
"Samuel, my son."
"Here I am," answered Samuel.
17 "What was the message he gave you?" Eli asked.
"Don't hide it from me. May God punish you and do
so severely if you hide anything from me that he told
you." 18 So Samuel told him everything and did not
hide anything from him. Eli responded, "He is the
LORD. Let him do what he thinks is good."
19 Samuel grew. The LORD was with him, and he
fulfilled everything Samuel prophesied.[D] 20 All Israel
from Dan to Beer-sheba knew that Samuel was a confirmed prophet of the LORD. 21 The LORD continued to
appear in Shiloh, because there he revealed himself
4 to Samuel by his word. 1 And Samuel's words
came to all Israel.

THE ARK CAPTURED BY THE PHILISTINES

Israel went out to meet the Philistines in battle and[E]
camped at Ebenezer while the Philistines camped at
Aphek. 2 The Philistines lined up in battle formation
against Israel, and as the battle intensified, Israel was
defeated by the Philistines, who struck down about
four thousand men on the battlefield.
3 When the troops returned to the camp, the elders
of Israel asked, "Why did the LORD defeat us today before the Philistines? Let's bring the ark of the LORD's
covenant from Shiloh. Then it[F] will go with us and save
us from our enemies." 4 So the people sent men to Shiloh to bring back the ark of the covenant of the LORD
of Armies, who is enthroned between the cherubim.
Eli's two sons, Hophni and Phinehas, were there with
the ark of the covenant of God. 5 When the ark of the
covenant of the LORD entered the camp, all the Israelites raised such a loud shout that the ground shook.
6 The Philistines heard the sound of the war cry
and asked, "What's this loud shout in the Hebrews'
camp?" When the Philistines discovered that the ark
of the LORD had entered the camp, 7 they panicked.
"A god has entered their camp!" they said. "Woe to
us! Nothing like this has happened before. 8 Woe to
us! Who will rescue us from these magnificent gods?
These are the gods that slaughtered the Egyptians
with all kinds of plagues in the wilderness. 9 Show
some courage and be men, Philistines! Otherwise,
you'll serve the Hebrews just as they served you. Now
be men and fight!"
10 So the Philistines fought, and Israel was defeated, and each man fled to his tent. The slaughter was
severe — thirty thousand of the Israelite foot soldiers
fell. 11 The ark of God was captured, and Eli's two sons,
Hophni and Phinehas, died.

ELI'S DEATH AND ICHABOD'S BIRTH

12 That same day, a Benjaminite man ran from the
battle and came to Shiloh. His clothes were torn, and
there was dirt on his head. 13 When he arrived, there

[A] **3:4** DSS, LXX read *called, "Samuel! Samuel!"* [B] **3:11** Lit *about it, his two ears will tingle*; Hb obscure [C] **3:13** LXX, Old Lat; MT reads *them* [D] **3:19** Lit *he let none of his words fall to the ground* [E] **4:1** LXX reads *In those days the Philistines gathered together to fight against Israel, and Israel went out to engage them in battle. They* [F] **4:3** Or *he*

Excavating Shiloh: An Interview with Scott Stripling

by Eric A. Mitchell

During the judges period, Shiloh was the central worship site and national meeting place for the people of Israel. Annually the Israelites came to Shiloh to offer sacrifices and to worship God. Shiloh remained the central worship site until God abandoned it and allowed the Philistines to destroy it due to the sins of the people, their leaders, the high priest Eli, and his sons (1Sm. 4; Ps 78; Jr 7:12).

The following is a synopsis of Eric Mitchell's interview with Dr. Scott Stripling.

The fenced area in the center of this photograph may have been the location where the holy place and most holy place once stood. If so, the surrounding areas show excavations in the outer courtyard of the tabernacle.

MITCHELL: Dr. Stripling, what is the significance of Tel Shiloh (Arabic Khirbet Seilun)?

STRIPLING: In Joshua 18:1, after the initial phase of the conquest, which lasted six to seven years, Israel set up the tabernacle at Shiloh, in the tribal territory of Ephraim. Joshua was from the tribe of Ephraim. This became the Israelites' worship center for the next 300–350 years before the Philistines destroyed Shiloh.

MITCHELL: Can you elaborate on the possible location of the tabernacle?

STRIPLING: A large unexcavated building is on the summit, possibly from the Byzantine era, that may preserve remains from the tabernacle beneath it. The ABR (Associates for Biblical Research) excavations look to excavate this building down to bedrock in order to explore this possibility. The tabernacle, however, may have been outside the camp. In 1866, British archaeologist Charles Wilson posited it was on the north side (Option 1). But it could be in a big flat area on the south side (Option 2). Early Christians venerated the south side as the location.

MITCHELL: Is there any evidence of an altar?

STRIPLING: Archaeologists have found only seven horned altars in Israel, and two of them were at Shiloh. Finkelstein found a large Late Bronze Age (1485–1173 BC)

Carved into the bedrock in the northern platform are square postholes, incrementally spaced. Exodus 27:10–16 explains there were twenty pillars that went the length of each side of the tabernacle courtyard, ten pillars the width of the west end, and six pillars on the east end, which allowed room for the linen screened entrance.

The flat area (lower, center), the northern platform, may be the location of the tabernacle or its storerooms.

bone deposit in Area D on the northeast corner of the tell, which he attributes to the Canaanites. The bones, though, are mostly from animals prescribed in the Law for Israelite sacrifices. This indicates that either the Canaanites were already using this as a worship site, or the Israelites deposited bones there. We will do further probing in this area.

MITCHELL: What about material culture—have archaeologists found any Israelite pottery?

STRIPLING: Yes, a lot. Both the Danish and Israeli excavations found an abundance of Israelite storage jars. Finkelstein found them in Area C. He posited these were storage areas for the tabernacle.

MITCHELL: Where did the ancient road approach the tell?

STRIPLING: I think the ancient road ran similar to the modern road going north-south (i.e., a little west of the site). It is more practical that the road probably came up the south side of the tell. But other factors support the other positions too. It would be easier from the south. The reason that is important is that when the young man brought news from the battle of Ebenezer, he went through the city gate to get to Eli, who was beside the road, likely near the entrance to the tabernacle (1Sm 4:12–14). ✣

was Eli sitting on his chair beside the road waiting, because he was anxious about the ark of God. When the man entered the city to give a report, the entire city cried out.

14 Eli heard the outcry and asked, "Why this commotion?" The man quickly came and reported to Eli. 15 At that time Eli was ninety-eight years old, and his eyes didn't move[A] because he couldn't see.

16 The man said to Eli, "I'm the one who came from the battle.[B] I fled from there today."

"What happened, my son?" Eli asked.

17 The messenger answered, "Israel has fled from the Philistines, and also there was a great slaughter among the people. Your two sons, Hophni and Phinehas, are both dead, and the ark of God has been captured." 18 When he mentioned the ark of God, Eli fell backward off the chair by the city gate, and since he was old and heavy, his neck broke and he died. Eli had judged Israel forty years.

19 Eli's daughter-in-law, the wife of Phinehas, was pregnant and about to give birth. When she heard the news about the capture of God's ark and the deaths of her father-in-law and her husband, she collapsed and gave birth because her labor pains came on her. 20 As she was dying,[C] the women taking care of her said, "Don't be afraid. You've given birth to a son!" But she did not respond or pay attention. 21 She named the boy Ichabod,[D] saying, "The glory has departed from Israel," referring to the capture of the ark of God and to the deaths of her father-in-law and her husband. 22 "The glory has departed from Israel," she said, "because the ark of God has been captured."

THE ARK IN PHILISTINE HANDS

5 After the Philistines had captured the ark of God, they took it from Ebenezer to Ashdod, 2 brought it into the temple of Dagon[E] and placed it next to his statue.[F] 3 When the people of Ashdod got up early the next morning, there was Dagon, fallen with his face to the ground before the ark of the LORD. So they took Dagon and returned him to his place. 4 But when they got up early the next morning, there was Dagon, fallen with his face to the ground before the ark of the LORD. This time, Dagon's head and both of his hands were broken off and lying on the threshold. Only Dagon's torso remained.[G] 5 That is why, still today, the priests of Dagon and everyone who enters the temple of Dagon in Ashdod do not step on Dagon's threshold.

6 The LORD's hand was heavy on the people of Ashdod. He terrified the people of Ashdod and its territory and afflicted them with tumors.[H,I] 7 When the people of Ashdod saw what was happening, they said, "The ark of Israel's God must not stay here with us, because his hand is strongly against us and our god Dagon." 8 So they called all the Philistine rulers together and asked, "What should we do with the ark of Israel's God?"

"The ark of Israel's God should be moved to Gath," they replied. So they moved the ark of Israel's God. 9 After they had moved it, the LORD's hand was against the city of Gath, causing a great panic. He afflicted the people of the city, from the youngest to the oldest, with an outbreak of tumors.

10 The people of Gath then sent the ark of God to Ekron, but when it got there, the Ekronites cried out, "They've moved the ark of Israel's God to us to kill us and our people!"[J]

11 The Ekronites called all the Philistine rulers together. They said, "Send the ark of Israel's God away. Let it return to its place so it won't kill us and our people!"[K] For the fear of death pervaded the city; God's hand was oppressing them. 12 Those who did not die were afflicted with tumors, and the outcry of the city went up to heaven.

THE RETURN OF THE ARK

6 When the ark of the LORD had been in Philistine territory for seven months, 2 the Philistines summoned the priests and the diviners and pleaded, "What should we do with the ark of the LORD? Tell us how we can send it back to its place."

3 They replied, "If you send the ark of Israel's God away, do not send it without an offering. Send back a guilt offering to him, and you will be healed. Then the reason his hand hasn't been removed from you will be revealed."[L]

4 They asked, "What guilt offering should we send back to him?"

And they answered, "Five gold tumors and five gold mice corresponding to the number of Philistine rulers, since there was one plague for both you[M] and your rulers. 5 Make images of your tumors and of your mice that are destroying the land. Give glory to Israel's God, and perhaps he will stop oppressing you,[N] your gods, and your land. 6 Why harden your hearts as the Egyptians and Pharaoh hardened theirs? When he afflicted them, didn't they send Israel away, and Israel left?

7 "Now then, prepare one new cart and two milk cows that have never been yoked. Hitch the cows to

[A] **4:15** Lit *his eyes stood*; 1Kg 14:4 [B] **4:16** LXX reads *camp* [C] **4:20** LXX reads *And in her time of delivery, she was about to die* [D] **4:21** = Where Is Glory? [E] **5:2** A Philistine god of the sea, grain, or storm [F] **5:2** Lit *to Dagon* [G] **5:4** LXX; Hb reads *Only Dagon remained on it* [H] **5:6** LXX adds *He brought up mice against them, and they swarmed in their ships. Then mice went up into the land and there was a mortal panic in the city.* [I] **5:6** Perhaps bubonic plague [J] **5:10** DSS, LXX read *"Why have you moved . . . people?"* [K] **5:11** DSS, LXX read *"Why don't you return it to . . . people?"* [L] **6:3** DSS, LXX read *healed, and an atonement shall be made for you. Shouldn't his hand be removed from you?"* [M] **6:4** Some Hb mss, LXX; other Hb mss read *them* [N] **6:5** Lit *will lighten the heaviness of his hand from you*

The Historical Setting for 1 and 2 Samuel

by Robert D. Bergen

The events in the books of 1 and 2 Samuel took place in ancient Israel over a span of about 130 years, from the beginning of the eleventh century BC to the early part of the tenth century BC. At that time the world's approximately fifty million[1] people lived in preindustrial societies; their lives centered on agricultural tasks they performed using primitive tools made mostly of wood and stone and some iron.

THE INTERNATIONAL SCENE

Not all civilizations were equal; those situated in warm climates on fertile land near large rivers had significant advantages, especially if they were surrounded by mountains or deserts. Such surroundings made an enemy's attack difficult. Cultural groups that possessed these favorable sets of circumstances were poised to be superpowers. Within the Old Testament world, three different cultural groups had these ideal natural circumstances: Egypt, Assyria, and Babylon. Israel did not, because it lacked significant natural defenses and had no useful river—the Jordan River lies completely below sea level, and none of the other rivers in its territory have a dependable year-round flow.

The House of David inscription; discovered at Tel Dan in 1994. The stone fragment was part of a stele erected apparently by King Hazael of Damascus commemorating his victory over the house of David some 250 years after David's reign. The highlighted text is the oldest non-biblical reference to David and his kingdom.

Even though Israel had some significant natural disadvantages, it nevertheless managed to become the dominant military and cultural power along the eastern shores of the Mediterranean Sea during the historical period described in 1–2 Samuel. How did this happen? Through a combination of events that took place within and outside of its borders.

Egypt, the once-mighty nation that had enslaved the Israelites and dominated north Africa and western Asia, was experiencing internal dissension that brought to an end what later historians would call the New Kingdom period, a glorious phase of its existence that stretched over half a millennium—from about 1551 to 1070 BC. Conflicts within Egypt during the time of Eli and Samuel caused that nation to slip into a more chaotic phase known as the Third Intermediate period. This phase of its history lasted more than four centuries, from about 1070 to 664 BC.[2] Not until 925 BC, in the fifth year of King Rehoboam of Judah's reign, was an Egyptian king strong enough to project his military strength against Israel (see 1Kg 14:25).

Around 1200 BC, Assyria, whose capital city of Nineveh was located on the Tigris River, was expanding its territorial holdings to the west and north as it attacked the Hittites in what is today modern Turkey.[3] However, Assyria did not continue its expansion southward into Israel or the territories of Israel's immediate neighbors. Around 1100 BC, the Assyrian Empire began to decline, a situation that lasted about seventy-five years. Babylon, situated on the banks of the Euphrates, would

Excavated area of Tell Shiloh (modern Seilun) in Israel. This isolated hill just east of the highway from Bethel to Shechem became a city in the tribe of Ephraim. The tabernacle, along with the ark of the covenant, remained here for four hundred years. Samuel served God at Shiloh as a youth under Eli the priest.

not play a significant role until the seventh century BC.[4] As a result, neither of the ancient superpowers played a role in the events of 1–2 Samuel.

Israel's most troublesome enemy at this time was the Philistines. This people group had been present in Canaan even in the days of Abraham (Gn 21:32), but did not become a military threat to Israel until the days of the judges. The Philistines were responsible for the deaths of several important Israelite figures prior to and during the days of 1–2 Samuel: Samson, Saul, and Jonathan. The Philistines were also the major enemy that David confronted during the early phase of his reign as Israel's king.

THE CULTURAL SETTING

At that time and throughout Old Testament history, Israel was a patriarchal culture. As such, men filled the leadership roles within their clans and exercised the primary social power within the culture. Although women could not have more than one husband simultaneously (polyandry), men might have more than one wife at the same time (polygamy; 1Sm 1:2; 25:43; 2Sm 5:13; 12:8). The cultural justification for this probably related to the need for families to have a male heir. A man might take an additional wife if his first wife was childless (1Sm 1:2,4–8), and kings would have a harem to produce many potential heirs to the throne (2Sm 5:13–16).

The events of 1–2 Samuel took place in the archaeological periods known as Iron Ages I and II (1200–800 BC).[5] As the names imply, iron began to play a strategic role in society during this time. Canaanites had used iron in weaponry for centuries prior to the days of Israel's monarchy (Jos 17:16; Jdg 1:19; 4:3). The Philistines likewise used iron in at least some of their weapons (1Sm 17:7). Evidently, however, the Israelites, who were a relatively impoverished people group, neither had nor used iron in their weapons in the earlier periods of their history. Instead, they used bronze, a much softer metal alloy composed of copper and tin, which melts at a much lower temperature than iron.

Bronze did not require sophisticated smelting techniques—technology that the Israelites lacked as late as the reign of King Saul (1Sm 13:19).

THE RELIGIOUS SETTING

Israel was surrounded by cultures that possessed religious beliefs and practices quite different from the ones God gave at Mount Sinai. Whereas Israel's authorized religion was ethical monotheism centered on the worship of Yahweh, its neighbors were involved in polytheistic fertility cults involving the worship of gods and goddesses, most notably Baal and Ashtoreth (1Sm 12:10). They commonly revered several other gods, each one associated with some significant aspect of nature—heavenly bodies, weather phenomena, geographical features, diseases, or plant and animal life. Additionally, many peoples also practiced a form of ancestor worship in which they would attempt to conjure up the dead and consult them for guidance (Dt 18:11). Some of Israel's neighbors also practiced human sacrifice, causing their children to "pass through the fire" as food for their gods (Lv 18:21; Ezk 23:37).

These practices proved enticing to many Israelites. As a result, during the days of 1–2 Samuel many Israelites supplemented their worship of Yahweh with the worship of other gods. Not surprisingly, they also became involved in pagan practices associated with these other religions. One key event in 1–2 Samuel dealt with the Israelites' struggle to worship only Yahweh (1Sm 7:3–4).

THE GOVERNMENTAL SETTING

One of the most important series of events in 1–2 Samuel involves Israel's transition from tribal government to national government. As 1 Samuel opens, no truly national political leader existed in Israel; executive decisions were made at the clan or tribal level by "elders," the oldest male members of a clan. Regional or national decisions might be made by a group of tribal elders (1Sm 4:3; 8:4), but never by one individual.

However, all that changed as the Philistines continued to threaten Israel and existing political leadership proved inadequate (8:3,20). As a result, a council of elders came together to ask Samuel, the most famous prophet of the eleventh century BC, to appoint a king over them, thus creating for the first time a monarchy in Israel.

Huge changes in Israelite culture resulted from the transition to monarchical rule. Politically the transition meant rule by a single person over all of Israel's tribes and clans. Psychologically it meant people had to think of the state as more important than their clans. Religiously it meant people would be tempted to trust in an earthly king and in the nation's military might more than in God (Ps 20:7). Militarily it meant Israel for the first time would have a permanent army. Though Israel's first standing military force consisted of only a few thousand men (1Sm 13:2), its existence had huge implications. Industrially an army required the development of a manufacturing complex to produce hardware for war (8:12). Financially this meant the development of a national taxation system to pay the expenses of the king and his army (v. 15). Administratively taxation meant the government had to create a system to collect, store, distribute, and account for the income. This led to the construction of government warehouses, which meant more citizens would be taken from the family farms to participate in building and maintaining government projects (v. 16).

The books of 1–2 Samuel chronicle one of the most fascinating and change-filled eras of Israelite history. ✣

[1] "Historical Estimates of World Population," U.S. Census Bureau, accessed 5 August 2009, http://www.census.gov/ipc/www/worldhis.html. [2] Kenneth A. Kitchen, "Egypt, Land of" in *Zondervan Pictorial Encyclopedia of the Bible* (*ZPEB*), ed. Merrill C. Tenney (Grand Rapids: Zondervan, 1975), 2:231–32, 41–44. [3] Howard G. Andersen, "Assyria" in *ZPEB*, 1:374–76. [4] Jeremy Black, ed., *The Atlas of World History*, 2nd ed. (New York: Covent Garden Books, 2005), 222. [5] "Archaeological Periods of Palestine" in *Holman Bible Handbook*, ed. David S. Dockery (Nashville: Holman, 1992), 71.

the cart, but take their calves away and pen them up.
8 Take the ark of the LORD, place it on the cart, and put
the gold objects that you're sending him as a guilt
offering in a box beside the ark. Send it off and let it
go its way. 9 Then watch: If it goes up the road to its
homeland toward Beth-shemesh, it is the LORD who
has made this terrible trouble for us. However, if it
doesn't, we will know that it was not his hand that
punished us — it was just something that happened
to us by chance."

10 The men did this: They took two milk cows,
hitched them to the cart, and confined their calves
in the pen. 11 Then they put the ark of the LORD on the
cart, along with the box containing the gold mice
and the images of their tumors. 12 The cows went
straight up the road to Beth-shemesh. They stayed
on that one highway, lowing as they went; they never strayed to the right or to the left. The Philistine
rulers were walking behind them to the territory of
Beth-shemesh.

13 The people of Beth-shemesh were harvesting
wheat in the valley, and when they looked up and
saw the ark, they were overjoyed to see it. 14 The
cart came to the field of Joshua of Beth-shemesh
and stopped there near a large rock. The people of
the city chopped up the cart and offered the cows as
a burnt offering to the LORD. 15 The Levites removed
the ark of the LORD, along with the box containing
the gold objects, and placed them on the large rock.
That day the people of Beth-shemesh offered burnt
offerings and made sacrifices to the LORD. 16 When
the five Philistine rulers observed this, they returned
to Ekron that same day.

17 As a guilt offering to the LORD, the Philistines had
sent back one gold tumor for each city: Ashdod, Gaza,
Ashkelon, Gath, and Ekron. 18 The number of gold
mice also corresponded to the number of Philistine
cities of the five rulers, the fortified cities and the
outlying villages. The large rock[A] on which the ark
of the LORD was placed is still in the field of Joshua
of Beth-shemesh today.

19 God struck down the people of Beth-shemesh
because they looked inside the ark of the LORD.[B] He
struck down seventy persons.[C] The people mourned
because the LORD struck them with a great slaughter.
20 The people of Beth-shemesh asked, "Who is able to
stand in the presence of the LORD this holy God? To
whom should the ark go from here?"

21 They sent messengers to the residents of Kiriath-
jearim, saying, "The Philistines have returned the ark
of the LORD. Come down and get it."[D]

7 So the people of Kiriath-jearim came for the ark
of the LORD and took it to Abinadab's house on
the hill. They consecrated his son Eleazar to take
care of it.

VICTORY AT MIZPAH

2 Time went by until twenty years had passed since
the ark had been taken to Kiriath-jearim. Then the
whole house of Israel longed for the LORD. 3 Samuel
told them, "If you are returning to the LORD with all
your heart, get rid of the foreign gods and the Ashtoreths that are among you, set your hearts on the
LORD, and worship only him. Then he will rescue
you from the Philistines." 4 So the Israelites removed
the Baals and the Ashtoreths and only worshiped
the LORD.

5 Samuel said, "Gather all Israel at Mizpah, and I
will pray to the LORD on your behalf." 6 When they
gathered at Mizpah, they drew water and poured
it out in the LORD's presence. They fasted that day,
and there they confessed, "We have sinned against
the LORD." And Samuel judged the Israelites at
Mizpah.

7 When the Philistines heard that the Israelites had
gathered at Mizpah, their rulers marched up toward
Israel. When the Israelites heard about it, they were
afraid because of the Philistines. 8 The Israelites said
to Samuel, "Don't stop crying out to the LORD our God
for us, so that he will save us from the Philistines."

9 Then Samuel took a young lamb and offered it as
a whole burnt offering to the LORD. He cried out to
the LORD on behalf of Israel, and the LORD answered
him. 10 Samuel was offering the burnt offering as
the Philistines approached to fight against Israel.
The LORD thundered loudly against the Philistines
that day and threw them into such confusion that
they were defeated by Israel. 11 Then the men of Israel charged out of Mizpah and pursued the Philistines striking them down all the way to a place
below Beth-car.

12 Afterward, Samuel took a stone and set it upright between Mizpah and Shen. He named it Ebenezer,[E] explaining, "The LORD has helped us to
this point." 13 So the Philistines were subdued and[F]
did not invade Israel's territory again. The LORD's
hand was against the Philistines all of Samuel's life.
14 The cities from Ekron to Gath, which they had
taken from Israel, were restored; Israel even rescued their surrounding territories from Philistine
control. There was also peace between Israel and
the Amorites.

15 Samuel judged Israel throughout his life. 16 Every
year he would go on a circuit to Bethel, Gilgal, and
Mizpah and would judge Israel at all these locations.

[A] **6:18** Some Hb mss, LXX, Tg; other Hb mss read *meadow*
[B] **6:19** LXX reads *But the sons of Jeconiah did not rejoice with the men of Beth-shemesh when they saw the ark of the LORD.* [C] **6:19** Some Hb mss, Josephus; other Hb mss read *70 men, 50,000 men* [D] **6:21** Lit *and bring it up to you* [E] **7:12** = Stone of Help [F] **7:13** LXX reads *The LORD humbled the Philistines and they*

17 Then he would return to Ramah because his home
was there, he judged Israel there, and he built an altar
to the LORD there.

ISRAEL'S DEMAND FOR A KING

8 When Samuel grew old, he appointed his sons as
judges over Israel. 2 His firstborn son's name was
Joel and his second was Abijah. They were judges in
Beer-sheba. 3 However, his sons did not walk in his
ways — they turned toward dishonest profit, took
bribes, and perverted justice.
4 So all the elders of Israel gathered together and
went to Samuel at Ramah. 5 They said to him, "Look,
you are old, and your sons do not walk in your ways.
Therefore, appoint a king to judge us the same as all
the other nations have."
6 When they said, "Give us a king to judge us," Samuel considered their demand wrong, so he prayed to
the LORD. 7 But the LORD told him, "Listen to the people
and everything they say to you. They have not rejected
you; they have rejected me as their king. 8 They are doing the same thing to you that they have done to me,[A]
since the day I brought them out of Egypt until this day,
abandoning me and worshiping other gods. 9 Listen to
them, but solemnly warn them and tell them about the
customary rights of the king who will reign over them."
10 Samuel told all the LORD's words to the people
who were asking him for a king. 11 He said, "These are
the rights of the king who will reign over you: He will
take your sons and put them to his use in his chariots,
on his horses, or running in front of his chariots. 12 He
can appoint them for his use as commanders of thousands or commanders of fifties, to plow his ground
and reap his harvest, or to make his weapons of war
and the equipment for his chariots. 13 He can take your
daughters to become perfumers, cooks, and bakers.
14 He can take your best fields, vineyards, and olive orchards and give them to his servants. 15 He can take a
tenth of your grain and your vineyards and give them
to his officials and servants. 16 He can take your male
servants, your female servants, your best cattle,[B] and
your donkeys and use them for his work. 17 He can take
a tenth of your flocks, and you yourselves can become
his servants. 18 When that day comes, you will cry out
because of the king you've chosen for yourselves, but
the LORD won't answer you on that day."
19 The people refused to listen to Samuel. "No!" they
said. "We must have a king over us. 20 Then we'll be
like all the other nations: our king will judge us, go
out before us, and fight our battles."
21 Samuel listened to all the people's words and
then repeated them to the LORD. 22 "Listen to them,"
the LORD told Samuel. "Appoint a king for them."
Then Samuel told the men of Israel, "Each of you,
go back to your city."

SAUL ANOINTED KING

9 There was a prominent man of Benjamin named
Kish son of Abiel, son of Zeror, son of Becorath,
son of Aphiah, son of a Benjaminite. 2 He had a son
named Saul, an impressive young man. There was no
one more impressive among the Israelites than he.
He stood a head taller than anyone else.[C]
3 One day the donkeys of Saul's father Kish wandered off. Kish said to his son Saul, "Take one of the
servants with you and go look for the donkeys."
4 Saul and his servant went through the hill country
of Ephraim and then through the region of Shalishah,
but they didn't find them. They went through the region of Shaalim — nothing. Then they went through
the Benjaminite region but still didn't find them.
5 When they came to the land of Zuph, Saul said
to the servant who was with him, "Come on, let's
go back, or my father will stop worrying about the
donkeys and start worrying about us."
6 "Look," the servant said, "there's a man of God in
this city who is highly respected; everything he says
is sure to come true. Let's go there now. Maybe he'll
tell us which way we should go."
7 "Suppose we do go," Saul said to his servant, "what
do we take the man? The food from our packs is gone,
and there's no gift to take to the man of God. What
do we have?"
8 The servant answered Saul, "Here, I have a little[D]
silver. I'll give it to the man of God, and he will tell us
which way we should go."
9 Formerly in Israel, a man who was going to inquire of God would say, "Come, let's go to the seer,"
for the prophet of today was formerly called the seer.
10 "Good," Saul replied to his servant. "Come on,
let's go." So they went to the city where the man of
God was. 11 As they were climbing the hill to the city,
they found some young women coming out to draw
water and asked, "Is the seer here?"
12 The women answered, "Yes, he is ahead of you.
Hurry, he just now entered the city, because there's a
sacrifice for the people at the high place today. 13 As
soon as you enter the city, you will find him before
he goes to the high place to eat. The people won't eat
until he comes because he must bless the sacrifice; after that, the guests can eat. Go up immediately — you
can find him now." 14 So they went up toward the city.
Saul and his servant were entering the city when
they saw Samuel coming toward them on his way to
the high place. 15 Now the day before Saul's arrival, the
LORD had informed Samuel, 16 "At this time tomorrow I
will send you a man from the land of Benjamin. Anoint
him ruler over my people Israel. He will save them

[A] **8:8** LXX; MT omits *to me* [B] **8:16** LXX; MT reads *young men*
[C] **9:2** Lit *From his shoulder and up higher than any of the people*
[D] **9:8** Lit *a quarter of a shekel* (about a tenth of an ounce)

Royal Personnel in the Ancient Near East

by John L. Harris

In the ancient Near East, the royal court was a vital organization that formed the center of the king's power and government. Surrounding and supporting all ancient Near Eastern kings was an entourage.[1] Typical members of an ancient Near Eastern royal court included high officials responsible for state administration, magicians, astrologers, sorcerers (Ex 7:11; Dn 2:2), servants, waiters, cupbearers (Neh 1:11; 2:1–5), wise men, counselors (Dn 1:3–5), military generals, royal guards, priests, district leaders, scribes, royal secretaries, recorders, concubines, the queen, the queen mother, royal children, singers, and heralds. In Israel, David's royal court included the commander of the army, a recorder, priests, a secretary, the leader of the Cherethites and Pelethites, and David's sons—who were priests (2Sm 8:15–18).[2] Solomon had twelve district governors who supplied provisions for the king and the royal household (1Kg 4:7–19).

Noticeably absent from the lists is the position of "prophet." This seems unusual due to the fact that throughout the ancient Near East, prophets were often connected with the kings and their courts.[3] Early in Israel's history, prophets such as Samuel and Nathan were closely connected to the monarchy. Evidently the prophets served as the king's independent advisers and spiritual guides, rather than as employees of the king in their courts.

Three of the most important high officials were the master of the palace, the royal secretary/scribe, and the royal herald.[4]

In the list of Solomon's officials, Ahishar is "in charge of the palace," or the palace administrator (1Kg 4:6). Second Chronicles 28:7 uses a similar title, "governor of the palace," for Azrikam. Assyrian and Babylonian palace administrators served as the kings' stewards; beyond this, they tended to the royal palace's administrative concerns.[5] In Egypt, the vizier had greater authority. He oversaw all concerns related to the kingdom, including applying his seal to palace documents, supervising all officials, and serving as pharaoh pro tem when the monarch was away.[6] Similarly to the Egyptian vizier, the master of the palace in later Israel had considerable authority. Second Kings 18:18 lists this position of palace administrator first and follows it with the secretary and the historian or recorder. This perhaps indicates that he was the highest-ranking official in the royal court (see Is 22:22).

The second-ranking high official was the royal secretary/scribe; he ranked just below the master of the palace. In the ancient Near East, early scribes were mere copiers, recorders, and clerks, but in time they became influential members of the royal courts who were involved in all public and state affairs. They served as representatives of the kings.[7] Duties typically included drafting royal decrees and providing wise counsel. Further duties of the secretary/scribe "included administering and keeping records of tax collection, forced labor, military activities, commodities, and building projects"[8] (see 2Kg 12:10–11). In Israel, the royal secretary/scribe was an indispensable individual who was multilingual and served as the king's personal assistant and the secretary of state in charge of all royal communications. The sons of David's secretary are mentioned in the same office under Solomon; this could indicate that the position was passed from father to son.

The seated scribe or *accroupi* holding a parchment in his lap. Found at Saqqara, Egypt; Fourth or Fifth Dynasty, 2600–2350 BC, limestone and paint, eyes incrusted with crystal rocks. The scribe's girth indicates the prosperity his job has brought him.

Dated to the ninth century BC, an exterior wall (left) and the residence of the commander of Ahab's chariot forces at Megiddo.

The third-ranking high official was the court historian or recorder (Hb *mazkir*).[9] Although the Bible does not mention the recorder's duties, in Egypt his primary responsibility evidently was to advise Pharaoh on civic concerns.[10] Secondary duties included serving both as the king's public spokesman and as the herald who was in charge of the palace ceremonies and who introduced people.[11]

Outside the high officials, no other member of the royal court was more significant than the queen mother (i.e., the king's mother) or "the great lady" (Hb *gebirah*). People treated her with respect; she held a significant official political position that only the king himself superseded.[12] She held this position independently of the king and retained it after his death. She at times served as the regent herself (1Kgs 11). Not only did she serve as the king's chief adviser, she also could participate in the political, religious, military, and economic affairs of the royal court; could be engaged in international correspondence; and could oppose the king on issues of state.[13] Though powerful, the queen mother could be removed for a serious offense (1Kg 15:11–13).

The royal attendants served the king and the people of importance (1Kg 10:4–5). Eunuchs supervised the royal harem and the royal children. Singers provided entertainment (1Sm 16:14–23). The royal guard provided protection. Officials oversaw the king's clothing and hygiene; cupbearers, bakers, and carvers were in charge of the royal table (Gn 40; 1Kg 10:5). The cupbearer (Hb *mashqeh*, "one who gives drink") was an important and trustworthy officer of high rank; his duty was to ensure the safety of the wine at the king's table. Earning the king's trust, cupbearers could have great influence in royal matters.

The royal court was a reflection of the king's power and character. Entering the king's presence was a serious matter requiring humility (Pr 25:6–7), dignity (1Kg 1:28,31), and proper dress (Est 5:1–2). The respect due the king and his authority was thus associated with his court. ✣

[1] Louis L. Orlin, *Life and Thought in the Ancient Near East* (Ann Arbor: University of Michigan Press, 2008), 24, points to a text from the period of Ur III (ca 2100–2000 BC) that lists the total number of people connected to the royal and temple households at 242. [2] First Chronicles 18:14–17 gives a duplicate list and states, "David's sons were the chief officials at the king's side." [3] Gary V. Smith, "Prophet" in *ISBE*, vol. 3 (1986), 986–1004. [4] The three most important officials of the Egyptian court were the vizier, the royal scribe, and the herald; see Roland de Vaux, *Ancient Israel* (Grand Rapids: Eerdmans, 1997), 132. [5] De Vaux, *Ancient Israel*, 130. [6] De Vaux, *Ancient Israel*. [7] Donald A. Hagner, "Scribes" in *ISBE*, vol. 4 (1988), 359–61; see De Vaux, *Ancient Israel*, 132. [8] Anthony J. Saldarini, "Scribes" in *ABD* 5:1012; see Gerald L. Stevens, "Secretary" in *EDB*, 1178. [9] A. Perry Hancock, "Recorder" in *EDB*, 1113; see Nola J. Opperwall-Galluch, "Recorder" in *ISBE*, 4:58. [10] Hancock, "Recorder," 1113. [11] De Vaux, *Ancient Israel*, 132; Opperwall-Galluch, "Recorder," 58. [12] Linda S. Schearing, "Queen" in *EDB*, 1103; Nola J. Opperwall-Galluch, "Queen Mother" in *ISBE*, 4:7–8; De Vaux, *Ancient Israel*, 117. [13] The Akkadian texts of Ras Shamra indicate the queen mother played a role in the kingdom's political affairs (De Vaux, *Ancient Israel*, 117); Linda S. Schearing, "Queen" in *ADB*, 5:585, says the queen mother's activities "were confined to domestic rather than international matters."

from the Philistines because I have seen the affliction of my people, for their cry has come to me." 17 When Samuel saw Saul, the LORD told him, "Here is the man I told you about; he will govern my people."

18 Saul approached Samuel in the city gate and asked, "Would you please tell me where the seer's house is?"

19 "I am the seer," Samuel answered.[A] "Go up ahead of me to the high place and eat with me today. When I send you off in the morning, I'll tell you everything that's in your heart. 20 As for the donkeys that wandered away from you three days ago, don't worry about them because they've been found. And who does all Israel desire but you and all your father's family?"

21 Saul responded, "Am I not a Benjaminite from the smallest of Israel's tribes and isn't my clan the least important of all the clans of the Benjaminite tribe? So why have you said something like this to me?"

22 Samuel took Saul and his servant, brought them to the banquet hall, and gave them a place at the head of the thirty[B] or so men who had been invited. 23 Then Samuel said to the cook, "Get the portion of meat that I gave you and told you to set aside."

24 The cook picked up the thigh and what was attached to it and set it before Saul. Then Samuel said, "Notice that the reserved piece is set before you. Eat it because it was saved for you for this solemn event at the time I said, 'I've invited the people.'" So Saul ate with Samuel that day. 25 Afterward, they went down from the high place to the city, and Samuel spoke with Saul on the roof.[C]

26 They got up early, and just before dawn, Samuel called to Saul on the roof, "Get up, and I'll send you on your way!" Saul got up, and both he and Samuel went outside. 27 As they were going down to the edge of the city, Samuel said to Saul, "Tell the servant to go on ahead of us, but you stay for a while, and I'll reveal the word of God to you." So the servant went on.

10 Samuel took the flask of oil, poured it out on Saul's head, kissed him, and said, "Hasn't the LORD anointed you ruler over his inheritance?[D] 2 Today when you leave me, you'll find two men at Rachel's Grave at Zelzah in the territory of Benjamin. They will say to you, 'The donkeys you went looking for have been found, and now your father has stopped being concerned about the donkeys and is worried about you, asking: What should I do about my son?'

3 "You will proceed from there until you come to the oak of Tabor. Three men going up to God at Bethel will meet you there, one bringing three goats, one bringing three loaves of bread, and one bringing a clay jar of wine. 4 They will ask how you are and give you two loaves[E] of bread, which you will accept from them.

5 "After that you will come to Gibeah of God where there are Philistine garrisons.[F] When you arrive at the city, you will meet a group of prophets coming down from the high place prophesying. They will be preceded by harps, tambourines, flutes, and lyres. 6 The Spirit of the LORD will come powerfully on you, you will prophesy with them, and you will be transformed. 7 When these signs have happened to you, do whatever your circumstances require[G] because God is with you. 8 Afterward, go ahead of me to Gilgal. I will come to you to offer burnt offerings and to sacrifice fellowship offerings. Wait seven days until I come to you and show you what to do."

9 When Saul turned to leave Samuel, God changed his heart,[H] and all the signs came about that day. 10 When Saul and his servant arrived at Gibeah, a group of prophets met him. Then the Spirit of God came powerfully on him, and he prophesied along with them.

11 Everyone who knew him previously and saw him prophesy with the prophets asked each other, "What has happened to the son of Kish? Is Saul also among the prophets?"

12 Then a man who was from there asked, "And who is their father?"

As a result, "Is Saul also among the prophets?" became a popular saying. 13 Then Saul finished prophesying and went to the high place.

14 Saul's uncle asked him and his servant, "Where did you go?"

"To look for the donkeys," Saul answered. "When we saw they weren't there, we went to Samuel."

15 "Tell me," Saul's uncle asked, "what did Samuel say to you?"

16 Saul told him, "He assured us the donkeys had been found." However, Saul did not tell him what Samuel had said about the matter of kingship.

SAUL RECEIVED AS KING

17 Samuel summoned the people to the LORD at Mizpah 18 and said to the Israelites, "This is what the LORD, the God of Israel, says: 'I brought Israel out of Egypt, and I rescued you from the power of the Egyptians and all the kingdoms that were oppressing you.' 19 But today you have rejected your God, who saves you from all your troubles and afflictions. You said to him, 'You[I] must set a king over us.' Now therefore present yourselves before the LORD by your tribes and clans."

[A] **9:19** Lit *answered Saul* [B] **9:22** LXX reads *70* [C] **9:25** LXX reads *city. They prepared a bed for Saul on the roof, and he slept.* [D] **10:1** LXX adds *And you will reign over the LORD's people, and you will save them from the hand of their enemies all around. And this is the sign to you that the LORD has anointed you ruler over his inheritance.* [E] **10:4** DSS, LXX read *wave offerings* [F] **10:5** Or *governors* [G] **10:7** Lit *do for yourself whatever your hand finds* [H] **10:9** Lit *God turned to him another heart* [I] **10:19** Some Hb mss, LXX, Syr, Vg read *You said, 'No, you*

20 Samuel had all the tribes of Israel come forward, and the tribe of Benjamin was selected. 21 Then he had the tribe of Benjamin come forward by its clans, and the Matrite clan was selected.[A] Finally, Saul son of Kish was selected. But when they searched for him, they could not find him. 22 They again inquired of the LORD, "Has the man come here yet?"

The LORD replied, "There he is, hidden among the supplies."

23 They ran and got him from there. When he stood among the people, he stood a head taller than anyone else.[B] 24 Samuel said to all the people, "Do you see the one the LORD has chosen? There is no one like him among the entire population."

And all the people shouted,[C] "Long live the king!"

25 Samuel proclaimed to the people the rights of kingship. He wrote them on a scroll, which he placed in the presence of the LORD. Then Samuel sent all the people home.

26 Saul also went to his home in Gibeah, and brave men whose hearts God had touched went with him. 27 But some wicked men said, "How can this guy save us?" They despised him and did not bring him a gift, but Saul said nothing.[D,E]

SAUL'S DELIVERANCE OF JABESH-GILEAD

11 Nahash[F] the Ammonite came up and laid siege to Jabesh-gilead. All the men of Jabesh said to him, "Make a treaty with us, and we will serve you."

2 Nahash the Ammonite replied, "I'll make one with you on this condition: that I gouge out everyone's right eye and humiliate all Israel."

3 "Don't do anything to us for seven days," the elders of Jabesh said to him, "and let us send messengers throughout the territory of Israel. If no one saves us, we will surrender to you."

4 When the messengers came to Gibeah, Saul's hometown, and told the terms to the people, all wept aloud. 5 Just then Saul was coming in from the field behind his oxen. "What's the matter with the people? Why are they weeping?" Saul inquired, and they repeated to him the words of the men from Jabesh.

6 When Saul heard these words, the Spirit of God suddenly came powerfully on him, and his anger burned furiously. 7 He took a team of oxen, cut them in pieces, and sent them throughout the territory of Israel by messengers who said, "This is what will be done to the ox of anyone who doesn't march behind Saul and Samuel." As a result, the terror of the LORD fell on the people, and they went out united.

8 Saul counted them at Bezek. There were three hundred thousand[G] Israelites and thirty thousand[H] men from Judah. 9 He told the messengers who had come, "Tell this to the men of Jabesh-gilead: 'Deliverance will be yours tomorrow by the time the sun is hot.'" So the messengers told the men of Jabesh, and they rejoiced.

10 Then the men of Jabesh said to Nahash, "Tomorrow we will come out, and you can do whatever you want to us."

11 The next day Saul organized the troops into three divisions. During the morning watch, they invaded the Ammonite camp and slaughtered them until the heat of the day. There were survivors, but they were so scattered that no two of them were left together.

SAUL'S CONFIRMATION AS KING

12 Afterward, the people said to Samuel, "Who said that Saul should not[I] reign over us? Give us those men so we can kill them!"

13 But Saul ordered, "No one will be executed this day, for today the LORD has provided deliverance in Israel."

14 Then Samuel said to the people, "Come, let's go to Gilgal, so we can renew the kingship there." 15 So all the people went to Gilgal, and there in the LORD's presence they made Saul king. There they sacrificed fellowship offerings in the LORD's presence, and Saul and all the men of Israel rejoiced greatly.

SAMUEL'S FINAL PUBLIC SPEECH

12 Then Samuel said to all Israel, "I have carefully listened to everything you said to me and placed a king over you. 2 Now you can see that the king is leading you. As for me, I'm old and gray, and my sons are here with you. I have led you from my youth until now. 3 Here I am. Bring charges against me before the LORD and his anointed: Whose ox or donkey have I taken? Who have I wronged or mistreated? Who gave me a bribe to overlook something?[J] I will return it to you."

4 "You haven't wronged us, you haven't mistreated us, and you haven't taken anything from anyone," they responded.

5 He said to them, "The LORD is a witness against you, and his anointed is a witness today that you haven't found anything in my hand."

"He is a witness," they said.

[A] **10:21** LXX adds *And he had the Matrite clan come forward, man by man.* [B] **10:23** Lit *people, and he was higher than any of the people from his shoulder and up* [C] **10:24** LXX reads *acknowledged and said* [D] **10:27** DSS add *Nahash king of the Ammonites had been severely oppressing the Gadites and Reubenites. He gouged out the right eye of each of them and brought fear and trembling on Israel. Of the Israelites beyond the Jordan none remained whose right eye Nahash, king of the Ammonites, had not gouged out. But there were seven thousand men who had escaped from the Ammonites and entered Jabesh-gilead.* [E] **10:27** Lit *gift, and he was like a mute person* [F] **11:1** DSS, LXX read *About a month later, Nahash* [G] **11:8** LXX reads *600,000* [H] **11:8** DSS, LXX read *70,000* [I] **11:12** Some Hb mss, LXX; other Hb mss omit *not* [J] **12:3** LXX reads *bribe or a pair of shoes? Testify against me.*

6 Then Samuel said to the people, "The LORD, who appointed Moses and Aaron and who brought your ancestors up from the land of Egypt, is a witness.[A] 7 Now present yourselves, so I may confront you before the LORD about all the righteous acts he has done for you and your ancestors.

8 "When Jacob went to Egypt,[B] your ancestors cried out to the LORD, and he sent them Moses and Aaron, who led your ancestors out of Egypt and settled them in this place. 9 But they forgot the LORD their God, so he handed them over to Sisera commander of the army of Hazor, to the Philistines, and to the king of Moab. These enemies fought against them. 10 Then they cried out to the LORD and said, 'We have sinned, for we abandoned the LORD and worshiped the Baals and the Ashtoreths. Now rescue us from the power of our enemies, and we will serve you.' 11 So the LORD sent Jerubbaal, Barak,[C] Jephthah, and Samuel. He rescued you from the power of the enemies around you, and you lived securely. 12 But when you saw that Nahash king of the Ammonites was coming against you, you said to me, 'No, we must have a king reign over us' — even though the LORD your God is your king.

13 "Now here is the king you've chosen, the one you requested. Look, this is the king the LORD has placed over you. 14 If you fear the LORD, worship and obey him, and if you don't rebel against the LORD's command, then both you and the king who reigns over you will follow the LORD your God. 15 However, if you disobey the LORD and rebel against his command, the LORD's hand will be against you as it was against your ancestors.[D]

16 "Now, therefore, present yourselves and see this great thing that the LORD will do before your eyes. 17 Isn't the wheat harvest today? I will call on the LORD, and he will send thunder and rain so that you will recognize what an immense evil you committed in the LORD's sight by requesting a king for yourselves." 18 Samuel called on the LORD, and on that day the LORD sent thunder and rain. As a result, all the people greatly feared the LORD and Samuel.

19 They pleaded with Samuel, "Pray to the LORD your God for your servants so we won't die! For we have added to all our sins the evil of requesting a king for ourselves."

20 Samuel replied, "Don't be afraid. Even though you have committed all this evil, don't turn away from following the LORD. Instead, worship the LORD with all your heart. 21 Don't turn away to follow worthless[E] things that can't profit or rescue you; they are worthless. 22 The LORD will not abandon his people, because of his great name and because he has determined to make you his own people.

23 "As for me, I vow that I will not sin against the LORD by ceasing to pray for you. I will teach you the good and right way. 24 Above all, fear the LORD and worship him faithfully with all your heart; consider the great things he has done for you. 25 However, if you continue to do what is evil, both you and your king will be swept away."

SAUL'S FAILURE

13 Saul was thirty years[F] old when he became king, and he reigned forty-two years[G] over Israel.[H] 2 He chose three thousand men from Israel for himself: two thousand were with Saul at Michmash and in Bethel's hill country, and one thousand were with Jonathan in Gibeah of Benjamin. He sent the rest of the troops away, each to his own tent.

3 Jonathan attacked the Philistine garrison[I] in Gibeah,[J] and the Philistines heard about it. So Saul blew the ram's horn throughout the land saying, "Let the Hebrews hear!"[K] 4 And all Israel heard the news, "Saul has attacked the Philistine garrison, and Israel is now repulsive to the Philistines." Then the troops were summoned to join Saul at Gilgal.

5 The Philistines also gathered to fight against Israel: three thousand[L] chariots, six thousand horsemen, and troops as numerous as the sand on the seashore. They went up and camped at Michmash, east of Beth-aven.[M]

6 The men of Israel saw that they were in trouble because the troops were in a difficult situation. They hid in caves, in thickets, among rocks, and in holes and cisterns. 7 Some Hebrews even crossed the Jordan to the land of Gad and Gilead.

Saul, however, was still at Gilgal, and all his troops were gripped with fear. 8 He waited seven days for the appointed time that Samuel had set, but Samuel didn't come to Gilgal, and the troops were deserting him. 9 So Saul said, "Bring me the burnt offering and the fellowship offerings." Then he offered the burnt offering.

10 Just as he finished offering the burnt offering, Samuel arrived. So Saul went out to greet him, 11 and Samuel asked, "What have you done?"

Saul answered, "When I saw that the troops were deserting me and you didn't come within the appointed days and the Philistines were gathering at Michmash, 12 I thought, 'The Philistines will now descend on me at Gilgal, and I haven't sought the LORD's favor.' So I forced myself to offer the burnt offering."

[A] **12:6** LXX; MT omits *is a witness* [B] **12:8** LXX reads *"When Jacob and his sons went to Egypt and Egypt humbled them* [C] **12:11** LXX, Syr; MT reads *Bedan*; Jdg 4:6; Heb 11:32 [D] **12:15** LXX *against you and against your king* [E] **12:21** LXX reads *away after empty* [F] **13:1** Some LXX mss; MT reads *was one year* [G] **13:1** Text emended; MT reads *two years* [H] **13:1** Some LXX mss omit v. 1 [I] **13:3** Or *governor*, also in v. 4 [J] **13:3** LXX; MT reads *Geba* [K] **13:3** LXX reads *"The slaves have revolted"* [L] **13:5** One LXX ms, Syr; MT reads *30,000* [M] **13:5** LXX reads *Michmash, opposite Beth-horon to the south*

Rain as Divine Communication

by Steve W. Lemke

Because the people had shifted their trust to an earthly king, Samuel threatened to ask God to send thunder and rain—during the harvest season (1Sm 12:17).

The timing of the thunderstorm—at harvest season—was particularly significant. In the typical weather pattern in the Holy Land, the early rains fall in October–November; this prepares the land for plowing and sowing. The "late rains," which fall from February through March, help crops mature (Jms 5:7; Jr 5:24).[1] Without the early and latter rains, famine would ruin the crops (Jr 14:4). Harvest in Israel typically was in the dry season, between April and September. Even small variations in the typical weather cycle could have disastrous consequences for crops.

Any farmer knows how devastating hail or a severe rainstorm can be at harvest time. For the people in this ancient and agrarian culture, a thunderstorm in harvest season could mean a crop failure and economic disaster. Therefore, Samuel's announcement that God would send a thunderstorm during the wheat harvest terrified the people.

Modern-day readers may have difficulty fully comprehending the impact that the timing of rain or sun has on people whose livelihood is agriculture. Ancient peoples had no refrigeration to keep food fresh and no grocery stores filled with vegetables year-round. Although some crops such as barley and wheat could be stored from year to year, fresh-food crops could not. Even the loss of one year's olive or grape crop was catastrophic. The people had no fall-back option. ✣

[1] "Rain" in *HIBD*, 1362.

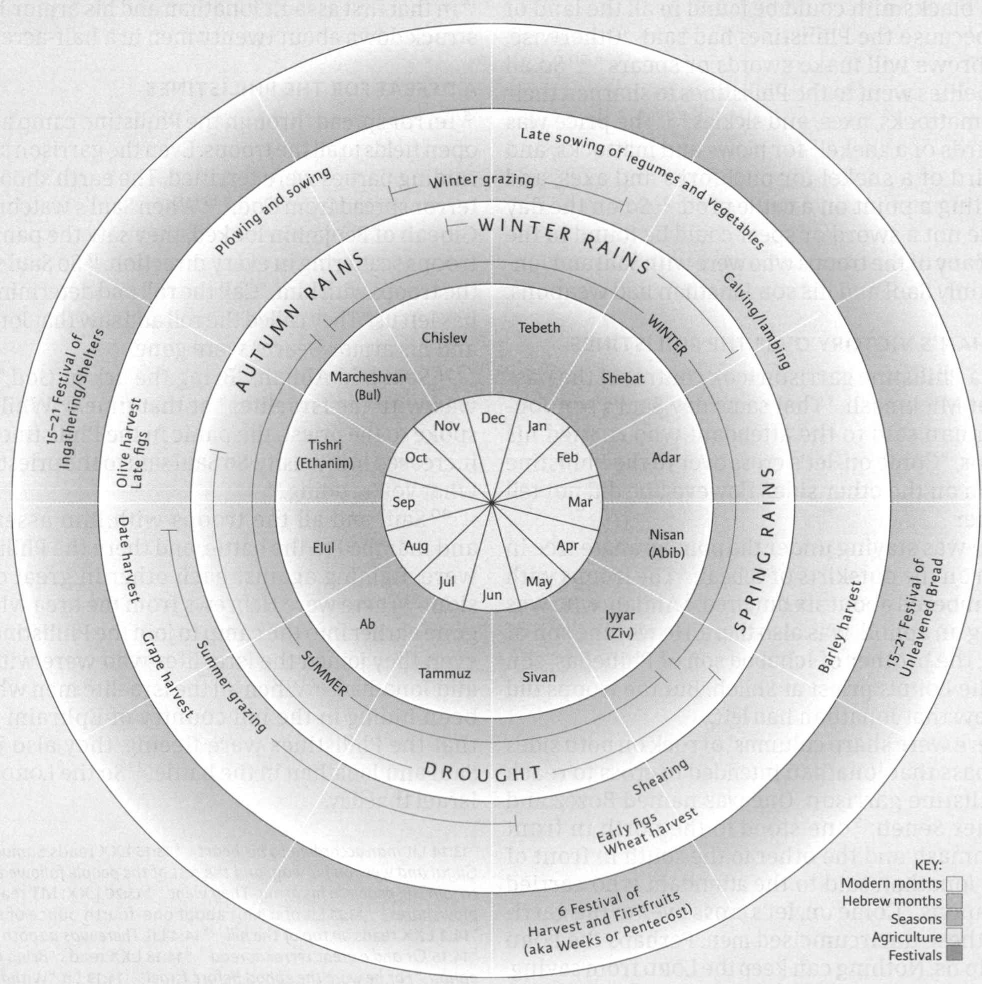

13 Samuel said to Saul, "You have been foolish. You have not kept the command the LORD your God gave you. It was at this time that the LORD would have permanently established your reign over Israel, 14 but now your reign will not endure. The LORD has found a man after his own heart,[A] and the LORD has appointed him as ruler over his people, because you have not done what the LORD commanded." 15 Then Samuel went[B] from Gilgal to Gibeah in Benjamin. Saul registered the troops who were with him, about six hundred men.

16 Saul, his son Jonathan, and the troops who were with them were staying in Geba of Benjamin, and the Philistines were camped at Michmash. 17 Raiding parties went out from the Philistine camp in three divisions. One division headed toward the Ophrah road leading to the land of Shual. 18 The next division headed toward the Beth-horon road, and the last division headed down the border road that looks out over the Zeboim Valley toward the wilderness.

19 No blacksmith could be found in all the land of Israel because the Philistines had said, "Otherwise, the Hebrews will make swords or spears." 20 So all the Israelites went to the Philistines to sharpen their plows, mattocks, axes, and sickles.[C] 21 The price was two-thirds of a shekel[D] for plows and mattocks, and one-third of a shekel for pitchforks and axes, and for putting a point on a cattle prod. 22 So on the day of battle not a sword or spear could be found in the hand of any of the troops who were with Saul and Jonathan; only Saul and his son Jonathan had weapons.

JONATHAN'S VICTORY OVER THE PHILISTINES

23 Now a Philistine garrison took control of the pass at Michmash. **14** 1 That same day Saul's son Jonathan said to the attendant who carried his weapons, "Come on, let's cross over to the Philistine garrison on the other side." However, he did not tell his father.

2 Saul was staying under the pomegranate tree in Migron on the outskirts of Gibeah.[E] The troops with him numbered about six hundred. 3 Ahijah, who was wearing an ephod, was also there. He was the son of Ahitub, the brother of Ichabod son of Phinehas, son of Eli the LORD's priest at Shiloh. But the troops did not know that Jonathan had left.

4 There were sharp columns[F] of rock on both sides of the pass that Jonathan intended to cross to reach the Philistine garrison. One was named Bozez and the other Seneh; 5 one stood to the north in front of Michmash and the other to the south in front of Geba. 6 Jonathan said to the attendant who carried his weapons, "Come on, let's cross over to the garrison of these uncircumcised men. Perhaps the LORD will help us. Nothing can keep the LORD from saving, whether by many or by few."

7 His armor-bearer responded, "Do what is in your heart. Go ahead! I'm completely with you."

8 "All right," Jonathan replied, "we'll cross over to the men and then let them see us. 9 If they say, 'Wait until we reach you,' then we will stay where we are and not go up to them. 10 But if they say, 'Come on up,' then we'll go up, because the LORD has handed them over to us — that will be our sign."

11 They let themselves be seen by the Philistine garrison, and the Philistines said, "Look, the Hebrews are coming out of the holes where they've been hiding!" 12 The men of the garrison called to Jonathan and his armor-bearer. "Come on up, and we'll teach you a lesson!" they said.

"Follow me," Jonathan told his armor-bearer, "for the LORD has handed them over to Israel." 13 Jonathan climbed up using his hands and feet, with his armor-bearer behind him. Jonathan cut them down, and his armor-bearer followed and finished them off. 14 In that first assault Jonathan and his armor-bearer struck down about twenty men in a half-acre field.

A DEFEAT FOR THE PHILISTINES

15 Terror spread through the Philistine camp and the open fields to all the troops. Even the garrison and the raiding parties were terrified. The earth shook, and terror spread from God.[G] 16 When Saul's watchmen in Gibeah of Benjamin looked, they saw the panicking troops scattering in every direction. 17 So Saul said to the troops with him, "Call the roll and determine who has left us." They called the roll and saw that Jonathan and his armor-bearer were gone.

18 Saul told Ahijah, "Bring the ark of God," for it was with the Israelites[H] at that time. 19 While Saul spoke to the priest, the panic in the Philistine camp increased in intensity. So Saul said to the priest, "Stop what you're doing."[I]

20 Saul and all the troops with him assembled and marched to the battle, and there the Philistines were, fighting against each other in great confusion! 21 There were Hebrews from the area who had gone earlier into the camp to join the Philistines, but even they joined the Israelites who were with Saul and Jonathan. 22 When all the Israelite men who had been hiding in the hill country of Ephraim heard that the Philistines were fleeing, they also joined Saul and Jonathan in the battle. 23 So the LORD saved Israel that day.

[A] **13:14** Lit *man according to his heart* [B] **13:15** LXX reads *Samuel left Gilgal and went on his way, and the rest of the people followed Saul to join the people in his army. They went* [C] **13:20** LXX; MT reads *plowshares* [D] **13:21** Lit *of a pim*; about one-fourth ounce of silver [E] **14:2** LXX reads *on top of the hill* [F] **14:4** Lit *There was a tooth* [G] **14:15** Or *and a great terror spread* [H] **14:18** LXX reads *"Bring the ephod." For he wore the ephod before Israel* [I] **14:19** Lit *"Withdraw your hand"*

SAUL'S RASH OATH

The battle extended beyond Beth-aven, 24 and the
men of Israel were worn out that day, for Saul had[A]
placed the troops under an oath: "The man who eats
food before evening, before I have taken vengeance
on my enemies is cursed." So none of the troops tasted any food.
25 Everyone[B] went into the forest, and there was
honey on the ground. 26 When the troops entered the
forest, they saw the flow of honey, but none of them
ate any of it[C] because they feared the oath. 27 However, Jonathan had not heard his father make the
troops swear the oath. He reached out with the end
of the staff he was carrying and dipped it into the
honeycomb. When he ate the honey,[D] he had renewed
energy.[E] 28 Then one of the troops said, "Your father
made the troops solemnly swear, 'The man who eats
food today is cursed,' and the troops are exhausted."
29 Jonathan replied, "My father has brought trouble to the land. Just look at how I have renewed energy[F] because I tasted a little of this honey. 30 How
much better if the troops had eaten freely today from
the plunder they took from their enemies! Then the
slaughter of the Philistines would have been much
greater."
31 The Israelites struck down the Philistines that
day from Michmash all the way to Aijalon. Since the
Israelites were completely exhausted, 32 they rushed
to the plunder, took sheep, goats, cattle, and calves,
slaughtered them on the ground, and ate meat with
the blood still in it. 33 Some reported to Saul, "Look,
the troops are sinning against the LORD by eating
meat with the blood still in it."
Saul said, "You have been unfaithful. Roll a large
stone over here at once." 34 He then said, "Go among
the troops and say to them, 'Let each man bring me
his ox or his sheep. Do the slaughtering here and
then you can eat. Don't sin against the LORD by eating
meat with the blood in it.'" So every one of the troops
brought his ox that night and slaughtered it there.
35 Then Saul built an altar to the LORD; it was the first
time he had built an altar to the LORD.
36 Saul said, "Let's go down after the Philistines
tonight and plunder them until morning. Don't let
even one remain!"
"Do whatever you want," the troops replied.
But the priest said, "Let's approach God here."
37 So Saul inquired of God, "Should I go after the
Philistines? Will you hand them over to Israel?" But
God did not answer him that day.
38 Saul said, "All you leaders of the troops, come
here. Let's investigate[G] how this sin has occurred
today. 39 As surely as the LORD lives who saves Israel,
even if it is because of my son Jonathan, he must die!"
Not one of the troops answered him.
40 So he said to all Israel, "You will be on one side,
and I and my son Jonathan will be on the other side."
And the troops replied, "Do whatever you want."
41 So Saul said to the LORD, "God of Israel, why have
you not answered your servant today? If the unrighteousness is in me or in my son Jonathan, LORD God
of Israel, give Urim; but if the fault is in your people
Israel, give Thummim."[H] Jonathan and Saul were selected, and the troops were cleared of the charge.
42 Then Saul said, "Cast the lot between me and my
son Jonathan," and Jonathan was selected. 43 Saul
commanded him, "Tell me what you did."
Jonathan told him, "I tasted a little honey with the
end of the staff I was carrying. I am ready to die!"
44 Saul declared to him, "May God punish me and
do so severely if you do not die, Jonathan!"
45 But the people said to Saul, "Must Jonathan
die? He accomplished such a great deliverance for
Israel! No, as the LORD lives, not a hair of his head
will fall to the ground, for he worked with God's
help today." So the people redeemed Jonathan, and
he did not die. 46 Then Saul gave up the pursuit of
the Philistines, and the Philistines returned to their
own territory.

SUMMARY OF SAUL'S KINGSHIP

47 When Saul assumed the kingship over Israel, he
fought against all his enemies in every direction:
against Moab, the Ammonites, Edom, the kings of
Zobah, and the Philistines. Wherever he turned, he
caused havoc.[I] 48 He fought bravely, defeated the Amalekites, and rescued Israel from those who plundered them.
49 Saul's sons were Jonathan, Ishvi, and Malchishua. The names of his two daughters were Merab,
his firstborn, and Michal, the younger. 50 The name of
Saul's wife was Ahinoam daughter of Ahimaaz. The
name of the commander of his army was Abner son
of Saul's uncle Ner. 51 Saul's father was Kish. Abner's
father was Ner son of Abiel.
52 The conflict with the Philistines was fierce all of
Saul's days, so whenever Saul noticed any strong or
valiant man, he enlisted him.

SAUL REJECTED AS KING

15 Samuel told Saul, "The LORD sent me to anoint
you as king over his people Israel. Now, listen
to the words of the LORD. 2 This is what the LORD of
Armies says: 'I witnessed[J] what the Amalekites did

[A] **14:24** LXX adds *committed a great act of ignorance and*
[B] **14:25** Lit *All the land* [C] **14:26** Lit *but there was none who raised his hand to his mouth* [D] **14:27** Lit *he returned his hand to his mouth*
[E] **14:27** Lit *his eyes became bright* [F] **14:29** Lit *how my eyes became bright*
[G] **14:38** Lit *know and see* [H] **14:41** LXX; MT reads *said to the LORD, "God of Israel, give us the right decision."* [I] **14:47** LXX reads *he was victorious* [J] **15:2** LXX reads *I will avenge*

to the Israelites when they opposed them along the
way as they were coming out of Egypt. 3 Now go and
attack the Amalekites and completely destroy everything they have. Do not spare them. Kill men and
women, infants and nursing babies, oxen and sheep,
camels and donkeys.' "
4 Then Saul summoned the troops and counted
them at Telaim: two hundred thousand foot soldiers
and ten thousand men from Judah. 5 Saul came to the
city of Amalek and set up an ambush in the wadi. 6 He
warned the Kenites, "Since you showed kindness to
all the Israelites when they came out of Egypt, go on
and leave! Get away from the Amalekites, or I'll sweep
you away with them." So the Kenites withdrew from
the Amalekites.
7 Then Saul struck down the Amalekites from Havilah all the way to Shur, which is next to Egypt. 8 He
captured King Agag of Amalek alive, but he completely destroyed all the rest of the people with the
sword. 9 Saul and the troops spared Agag, and the
best of the sheep, goats, cattle, and choice animals,[A]
as well as the young rams and the best of everything
else. They were not willing to destroy them, but they
did destroy all the worthless and unwanted things.
10 Then the word of the LORD came to Samuel, 11 "I
regret that I made Saul king, for he has turned away
from following me and has not carried out my instructions." So Samuel became angry and cried out
to the LORD all night.
12 Early in the morning Samuel got up to confront
Saul, but it was reported to Samuel, "Saul went to Carmel where he set up a monument for himself. Then
he turned around and went down to Gilgal." 13 When
Samuel came to him, Saul said, "May the LORD bless
you. I have carried out the LORD's instructions."
14 Samuel replied, "Then what is this sound of
sheep, goats, and cattle I hear?"
15 Saul answered, "The troops brought them from
the Amalekites and spared the best sheep, goats, and
cattle in order to offer a sacrifice to the LORD your
God, but the rest we destroyed."
16 "Stop!" exclaimed Samuel. "Let me tell you what
the LORD said to me last night."
"Tell me," he replied.
17 Samuel continued, "Although you once considered yourself unimportant, haven't you become the
leader of the tribes of Israel? The LORD anointed you
king over Israel 18 and then sent you on a mission and
said, 'Go and completely destroy the sinful Amalekites. Fight against them until you have annihilated
them.' 19 So why didn't you obey the LORD? Why did
you rush on the plunder and do what was evil in the
LORD's sight?"
20 "But I did obey the LORD!" Saul answered.[B] "I
went on the mission the LORD gave me: I brought back
King Agag of Amalek, and I completely destroyed
the Amalekites. 21 The troops took sheep, goats, and
cattle from the plunder — the best of what was set
apart for destruction — to sacrifice to the LORD your
God at Gilgal."
22 Then Samuel said:

Does the LORD take pleasure
  in burnt offerings and sacrifices
as much as in obeying the LORD?

Look: to obey is better than sacrifice,
to pay attention is better than the fat of rams.
23 For rebellion is like the sin of divination,
and defiance is like wickedness and idolatry.
Because you have rejected the word
  of the LORD,
he has rejected you as king.

24 Saul answered Samuel, "I have sinned. I have
transgressed the LORD's command and your words.
Because I was afraid of the people, I obeyed them.
25 Now therefore, please forgive my sin and return
with me so I can worship the LORD."
26 Samuel replied to Saul, "I will not return with
you. Because you rejected the word of the LORD, the
LORD has rejected you from being king over Israel." 27 When Samuel turned to go, Saul grabbed the
corner of his robe, and it tore. 28 Samuel said to him,
"The LORD has torn the kingship of Israel away from
you today and has given it to your neighbor who is
better than you. 29 Furthermore, the Eternal One of
Israel does not lie or change his mind, for he is not
man who changes his mind."
30 Saul said, "I have sinned. Please honor me now
before the elders of my people and before Israel.
Come back with me so I can bow in worship to the
LORD your God." 31 Then Samuel went back, following
Saul, and Saul bowed down to the LORD.
32 Samuel said, "Bring me King Agag of Amalek."
Agag came to him trembling,[C] for he thought, "Certainly the bitterness of death has come."[D,E]
33 Samuel declared:

As your sword has made women childless,
so your mother will be childless
  among women.

Then he hacked Agag to pieces before the LORD at
Gilgal.
34 Samuel went to Ramah, and Saul went up to his
home in Gibeah of Saul. 35 Even to the day of his death,
Samuel never saw Saul again. Samuel mourned for
Saul, and the LORD regretted he had made Saul king
over Israel.

[A] **15:9** Lit *and the second ones* [B] **15:20** Lit *answered Samuel*
[C] **15:32** Hb obscure [D] **15:32** LXX reads *"Is death bitter in this way?"*
[E] **15:32** Lit *turned*

SAMUEL ANOINTS DAVID

16 The LORD said to Samuel, "How long are you going to mourn for Saul, since I have rejected him as king over Israel? Fill your horn with oil and go. I am sending you to Jesse of Bethlehem because I have selected for myself a king from his sons."

2 Samuel asked, "How can I go? Saul will hear about it and kill me!"

The LORD answered, "Take a young cow with you and say, 'I have come to sacrifice to the LORD.' 3 Then invite Jesse to the sacrifice, and I will let you know what you are to do. You are to anoint for me the one I indicate to you."

4 Samuel did what the LORD directed and went to Bethlehem. When the elders of the town met him, they trembled[A] and asked, "Do[B] you come in peace?"

5 "In peace," he replied. "I've come to sacrifice to the LORD. Consecrate yourselves and come with me to the sacrifice."[C] Then he consecrated Jesse and his sons and invited them to the sacrifice. 6 When they arrived, Samuel saw Eliab and said, "Certainly the LORD's anointed one is here before him."

7 But the LORD said to Samuel, "Do not look at his appearance or his stature because I have rejected him. Humans do not see what the LORD sees,[D] for humans see what is visible, but the LORD sees the heart."

8 Jesse called Abinadab and presented him to Samuel. "The LORD hasn't chosen this one either," Samuel said. 9 Then Jesse presented Shammah, but Samuel said, "The LORD hasn't chosen this one either." 10 After Jesse presented seven of his sons to him, Samuel told Jesse, "The LORD hasn't chosen any of these." 11 Samuel asked him, "Are these all the sons you have?"

"There is still the youngest," he answered, "but right now he's tending the sheep." Samuel told Jesse, "Send for him. We won't sit down to eat until he gets here." 12 So Jesse sent for him. He had beautiful eyes and a healthy,[E] handsome appearance.

Then the LORD said, "Anoint him, for he is the one." 13 So Samuel took the horn of oil and anointed him in the presence of his brothers, and the Spirit of the LORD came powerfully on David from that day forward. Then Samuel set out and went to Ramah.

DAVID IN SAUL'S COURT

14 Now the Spirit of the LORD had left Saul, and an evil spirit sent from the LORD began to torment him, 15 so Saul's servants said to him, "You see that an evil spirit from God is tormenting you. 16 Let our lord command your servants here in your presence to look for someone who knows how to play the lyre. Whenever the evil spirit from God comes on you, that person can play the lyre, and you will feel better."

17 Then Saul commanded his servants, "Find me someone who plays well and bring him to me."

18 One of the young men answered, "I have seen a son of Jesse of Bethlehem who knows how to play the lyre. He is also a valiant man, a warrior, eloquent, handsome, and the LORD is with him."

19 Then Saul dispatched messengers to Jesse and said, "Send me your son David, who is with the sheep." 20 So Jesse took a donkey loaded with bread, a wineskin, and one young goat and sent them by his son David to Saul. 21 When David came to Saul and entered his service, Saul loved him very much, and David became his armor-bearer. 22 Then Saul sent word to Jesse: "Let David remain in my service, for he has found favor with me." 23 Whenever the spirit from God came on Saul, David would pick up his lyre and play, and Saul would then be relieved, feel better, and the evil spirit would leave him.

DAVID VERSUS GOLIATH

17 The Philistines gathered their forces for war at Socoh in Judah and camped between Socoh and Azekah in Ephes-dammim. 2 Saul and the men of Israel gathered and camped in the Valley of Elah; then they lined up in battle formation to face the Philistines.

3 The Philistines were standing on one hill, and the Israelites were standing on another hill with a ravine between them. 4 Then a champion named Goliath, from Gath, came out from the Philistine camp. He was nine feet, nine inches[F,G] tall 5 and wore a bronze helmet and bronze scale armor that weighed one hundred twenty-five pounds.[H] 6 There was bronze armor on his shins, and a bronze javelin was slung between his shoulders. 7 His spear shaft was like a weaver's beam, and the iron point of his spear weighed fifteen pounds.[I] In addition, a shield-bearer was walking in front of him.

8 He stood and shouted to the Israelite battle formations, "Why do you come out to line up in battle formation?" He asked them, "Am I not a Philistine and are you not servants of Saul? Choose one of your men and have him come down against me. 9 If he wins in a fight against me and kills me, we will be your servants. But if I win against him and kill him, then you will be our servants and serve us." 10 Then the Philistine said, "I defy the ranks of Israel today. Send me a man so we can fight each other!" 11 When Saul and all Israel heard these words from the Philistine, they lost their courage and were terrified.

12 Now David was the son of the Ephrathite from Bethlehem of Judah named Jesse. Jesse had eight

[A] **16:4** LXX reads *were astonished* [B] **16:4** DSS, LXX read *"Seer, do* [C] **16:5** LXX reads *and rejoice with me today* [D] **16:7** LXX reads *God does not see as a man sees* [E] **16:12** Or *ruddy* [F] **17:4** DSS, LXX read *four cubits and a span*; i.e., six and a half feet [G] **17:4** Lit *was six cubits and a span* [H] **17:5** Lit *5,000 shekels* [I] **17:7** Lit *600 shekels*

sons and during Saul's reign was already an old man. 13 Jesse's three oldest sons had followed Saul to the war, and their names were Eliab, the firstborn, Abinadab, the next, and Shammah, the third, 14 and David was the youngest. The three oldest had followed Saul, 15 but David kept going back and forth from Saul to tend his father's flock in Bethlehem.

16 Every morning and evening for forty days the Philistine came forward and took his stand. 17 One day Jesse had told his son David, "Take this half-bushel[A] of roasted grain along with these ten loaves of bread for your brothers and hurry to their camp. 18 Also take these ten portions of cheese to the field commander.[B] Check on the well-being of your brothers and bring a confirmation from them. 19 They are with Saul and all the men of Israel in the Valley of Elah fighting with the Philistines."

20 So David got up early in the morning, left the flock with someone to keep it, loaded up, and set out as Jesse had charged him.

He arrived at the perimeter of the camp as the army was marching out to its battle formation shouting their battle cry. 21 Israel and the Philistines lined up in battle formation facing each other. 22 David left his supplies in the care of the quartermaster and ran to the battle line. When he arrived, he asked his brothers how they were. 23 While he was speaking with them, suddenly the champion named Goliath, the Philistine from Gath, came forward from the Philistine battle line and shouted his usual words, which David heard. 24 When all the Israelite men saw Goliath, they retreated from him terrified.

25 Previously, an Israelite man had declared, "Do you see this man who keeps coming out? He comes to defy Israel. The king will make the man who kills him very rich and will give him his daughter. The king will also make the family of that man's father exempt from paying taxes in Israel."

26 David spoke to the men who were standing with him: "What will be done for the man who kills that Philistine and removes this disgrace from Israel? Just who is this uncircumcised Philistine that he should defy the armies of the living God?"

27 The troops told him about the offer, concluding, "That is what will be done for the man who kills him."

28 David's oldest brother Eliab listened as he spoke to the men, and he became angry with him. "Why did you come down here?" he asked. "Who did you leave those few sheep with in the wilderness? I know your arrogance and your evil heart — you came down to see the battle!"

29 "What have I done now?" protested David. "It was just a question." 30 Then he turned from those beside him to others in front of him and asked about the offer. The people gave him the same answer as before.

31 What David said was overheard and reported to Saul, so he had David brought to him. 32 David said to Saul, "Don't let anyone be discouraged by him; your servant will go and fight this Philistine!"

33 But Saul replied, "You can't go fight this Philistine. You're just a youth, and he's been a warrior since he was young."

34 David answered Saul, "Your servant has been tending his father's sheep. Whenever a lion or a bear came and carried off a lamb from the flock, 35 I went after it, struck it down, and rescued the lamb from its mouth. If it reared up against me, I would grab it by its fur,[C] strike it down, and kill it. 36 Your servant has killed lions and bears; this uncircumcised Philistine will be like one of them, for he has defied the armies of the living God." 37 Then David said, "The LORD who rescued me from the paw of the lion and the paw of the bear will rescue me from the hand of this Philistine."

Saul said to David, "Go, and may the LORD be with you."

38 Then Saul had his own military clothes put on David. He put a bronze helmet on David's head and had him put on armor. 39 David strapped his sword on over the military clothes and tried to walk, but he was not used to them. "I can't walk in these," David said to Saul, "I'm not used to them." So David took them off. 40 Instead, he took his staff in his hand and chose five smooth stones from the wadi and put them in the pouch, in his shepherd's bag. Then, with his sling in his hand, he approached the Philistine.

41 The Philistine came closer and closer to David, with the shield-bearer in front of him. 42 When the Philistine looked and saw David, he despised him because he was just a youth, healthy[D] and handsome. 43 He said to David, "Am I a dog that you come against me with sticks?"[E] Then he cursed David by his gods. 44 "Come here," the Philistine called to David, "and I'll give your flesh to the birds of the sky and the wild beasts!"

45 David said to the Philistine, "You come against me with a sword, spear, and javelin, but I come against you in the name of the LORD of Armies, the God of the ranks of Israel — you have defied him. 46 Today, the LORD will hand you over to me. Today, I'll strike you down, remove your head, and give the corpses[F] of the Philistine camp to the birds of the sky and the wild creatures of the earth. Then all the world will know that Israel has a God, 47 and this whole assembly will know that it is not by sword or by spear that the LORD saves, for the battle is the LORD's. He will hand you over to us."

[A] **17:17** Lit *this ephah* [B] **17:18** Lit *the leader of 1,000* [C] **17:35** LXX reads *throat*; lit *beard* [D] **17:42** Or *ruddy* [E] **17:43** Some LXX mss add *and stones?" And David said, "No! Worse than a dog!"* [F] **17:46** LXX reads *give your limbs and the limbs*

The Goliath Inscription

by Joseph R. Cathey

The Philistine city of Gath (Tell es-Safi), located in the Shephelah, was Goliath's hometown.

The Goliath inscription is a small piece of inscribed tenth–ninth-century BC pottery (*ostracon*; plural *ostraca*). What makes the ostracon significant is that it has an inscription of two Philistine names. Both of the names are very close etymologically to the biblical *Goliath*. The letters of the inscription were Hebrew while the names were Philistine in origin. Archaeologically speaking, this is a significant find because it is one of the earliest Hebrew inscriptions found in a verifiable archaeological context. The popular press and media quickly labeled it the "Goliath inscription."

Archaeologists found the inscription in the 2005 excavation of the ancient city of Gath (Tell es-Safi). Gath lies in the central section of Israel between Jerusalem and Ashkelon. Principally Gath guarded the main north-south route of the Shephelah, which are foothills that run west from the plain toward Gezer in central Israel. Excavations at Gath began in 1899.

Gath shows significant occupation from the early Chalcolithic period (4500–4000 BC) until the modern period (about 1948). Representative archaeological finds from Gath include marked jar handles (some with stamps), figurines, and shekel weights from the end of the Solomonic era.

Archaeologists find ostraca (inscribed pottery) infrequently in Israel today. Most recovered ostraca contain nothing more than a single word, a few letters, or a single letter. Some ostraca have only half of a letter inscribed. What makes this inscription interesting are the names that were inscribed and the place in which it was found. Whoever inscribed the names used Hebrew characters to write out Philistine names.[1] Those who inscribed the ostracon most likely used a sharp pointed instrument. We know from history that the Philistines were actually from the Aegean and thus had Indo-European names. Yet with their migration into Canaan, they slowly began to culturally assimilate the local alphabet (in Hebrew) to express their own unique language. Although the inscription does not actually preserve the name "Goliath," it does preserve names that are similar etymologically.

Dating from the tenth to mid-ninth centuries BC, this shard discovered at Tell es-Safi contains the oldest Philistine inscription ever found and mentions two names remarkably similar to the name Goliath.

The biblical significance of this ostracon is twofold. First, we can definitely say that as early as the tenth–ninth centuries BC the early Hebrew script was used in Israel.[2] This script was used by those in the Philistine city of Gath to designate certain individuals. Second, we can infer from this inscription that individuals with names very similar to the biblical Goliath were familiar to those at Gath. Consequently, having someone named Goliath to reside at Philistine Gath would not have been uncommon. ✣

---

[1] Aren Maeir, "Gath Inscription Evidences Philistine Assimilation," *BAR* 32.2 (2006): 16.
[2] Frank Moore Cross and Lawrence E. Stager, "Cypro-Minoan Inscriptions Found in Ashkelon," *Israel Exploration Journal* (*IEJ*) 56.2 (2006): 150–51.

48 When the Philistine started forward to attack him, David ran quickly to the battle line to meet the Philistine. 49 David put his hand in the bag, took out a stone, slung it, and hit the Philistine on his forehead. The stone sank into his forehead, and he fell facedown to the ground. 50 David defeated the Philistine with a sling and a stone. David overpowered the Philistine and killed him without having a sword. 51 David ran and stood over him. He grabbed the Philistine's sword, pulled it from its sheath, and used it to kill him. Then he cut off his head. When the Philistines saw that their hero was dead, they fled. 52 The men of Israel and Judah rallied, shouting their battle cry, and chased the Philistines to the entrance of the valley and to the gates of Ekron.[A] Philistine bodies were strewn all along the Shaaraim road to Gath and Ekron.

53 When the Israelites returned from the pursuit of the Philistines, they plundered their camps. 54 David took Goliath's[B] head and brought it to Jerusalem, but he put Goliath's weapons in his own tent.

55[C] When Saul had seen David going out to confront the Philistine, he asked Abner the commander of the army, "Whose son is this youth, Abner?"

"Your Majesty, as surely as you live, I don't know," Abner replied.

56 The king said, "Find out whose son this young man is!"

57 When David returned from killing the Philistine, Abner took him and brought him before Saul with the Philistine's head still in his hand. 58 Saul said to him, "Whose son are you, young man?"

"The son of your servant Jesse of Bethlehem," David answered.

DAVID'S SUCCESS

18 When David had finished speaking with Saul, Jonathan was bound to David in close friendship,[D] and loved him as much as he loved himself. 2 Saul kept David with him from that day on and did not let him return to his father's house.

3 Jonathan made a covenant with David because he loved him as much as himself. 4 Then Jonathan removed the robe he was wearing and gave it to David, along with his military tunic, his sword, his bow, and his belt.

5 David marched out with the army and was successful in everything Saul sent him to do. Saul put him in command of the fighting men, which pleased all the people and Saul's servants as well.

6 As the troops were coming back, when David was returning from killing the Philistine, the women came out from all the cities of Israel to meet King Saul, singing and dancing with tambourines, with shouts of joy, and with three-stringed instruments. 7 As they danced, the women sang:

> Saul has killed his thousands,
> but David his tens of thousands.

8 Saul was furious and resented this song. "They credited tens of thousands to David," he complained, "but they only credited me with thousands. What more can he have but the kingdom?" 9 So Saul watched David jealously from that day forward.

SAUL ATTEMPTS TO KILL DAVID

10 The next day an evil spirit sent from God came powerfully on Saul, and he began to rave[E] inside the palace. David was playing the lyre as usual, but Saul was holding a spear, 11 and he threw it, thinking, "I'll pin David to the wall." But David got away from him twice.

12 Saul was afraid of David, because the LORD was with David but had left Saul. 13 Therefore, Saul sent David away from him and made him commander over a thousand men. David led the troops 14 and continued to be successful in all his activities because the LORD was with him. 15 When Saul observed that David was very successful, he dreaded him. 16 But all Israel and Judah loved David because he was leading their troops. 17 Saul told David, "Here is my oldest daughter Merab. I'll give her to you as a wife if you will be a warrior for me and fight the LORD's battles." But Saul was thinking, "I don't need to raise a hand against him; let the hand of the Philistines be against him."

18 Then David responded, "Who am I, and what is my family or my father's clan in Israel that I should become the king's son-in-law?" 19 When it was time to give Saul's daughter Merab to David, she was given to Adriel the Meholathite as a wife.

DAVID'S MARRIAGE TO MICHAL

20 Now Saul's daughter Michal loved David, and when it was reported to Saul, it pleased him. 21 "I'll give her to him," Saul thought. "She'll be a trap for him, and the hand of the Philistines will be against him." So Saul said to David a second time, "You can now be my son-in-law."

22 Saul then ordered his servants, "Speak to David in private and tell him, 'Look, the king is pleased with you, and all his servants love you. Therefore, you should become the king's son-in-law.'"

23 Saul's servants reported these words directly to David, but he replied, "Is it trivial in your sight to become the king's son-in-law? I am a poor commoner."

24 The servants reported back to Saul, "These are the words David spoke."

[A] **17:52** LXX reads *Ashkelon* [B] **17:54** Lit *the Philistine's* [C] **17:55** LXX omits 1Sm 17:55–18:5 [D] **18:1** Lit *the life of Jonathan was bound to the life of David* [E] **18:10** Or *prophesy*

25 Then Saul replied, "Say this to David: 'The king desires no other bride-price except a hundred Philistine foreskins, to take revenge on his enemies.'" Actually, Saul intended to cause David's death at the hands of the Philistines.

26 When the servants reported these terms to David, he was pleased to become the king's son-in-law. Before the wedding day arrived, 27 David and his men went out and killed two hundred[A] Philistines. He brought their foreskins and presented them as full payment to the king to become his son-in-law. Then Saul gave his daughter Michal to David as his wife. 28 Saul realized[B] that the LORD was with David and that his daughter Michal loved him, 29 and he became even more afraid of David. As a result, Saul was David's enemy from then on.

30 Every time the Philistine commanders came out to fight, David was more successful than all of Saul's officers. So his name became well known.

DAVID DELIVERED FROM SAUL

19 Saul ordered his son Jonathan and all his servants to kill David. But Saul's son Jonathan liked David very much, 2 so he told him, "My father, Saul, intends to kill you. Be on your guard in the morning and hide in a secret place and stay there. 3 I'll go out and stand beside my father in the field where you are and talk to him about you. When I see what he says, I'll tell you."

4 Jonathan spoke well of David to his father, Saul. He said to him, "The king should not sin against his servant David. He hasn't sinned against you; in fact, his actions have been a great advantage to you. 5 He took his life in his hands when he struck down the Philistine, and the LORD brought about a great victory for all Israel. You saw it and rejoiced, so why would you sin against innocent blood by killing David for no reason?"

6 Saul listened to Jonathan's advice and swore an oath: "As surely as the LORD lives, David will not be killed." 7 So Jonathan summoned David and told him all these words. Then Jonathan brought David to Saul, and he served him as he did before.

8 When war broke out again, David went out and fought against the Philistines. He defeated them with such great force that they fled from him.

9 Now an evil spirit sent from the LORD came on Saul as he was sitting in his palace holding a spear. David was playing the lyre, 10 and Saul tried to pin David to the wall with the spear. As the spear struck the wall, David eluded Saul, ran away, and escaped that night. 11 Saul sent agents to David's house to watch for him and kill him in the morning. But his wife Michal warned David, "If you don't escape tonight, you will be dead tomorrow!" 12 So she lowered David from the window, and he fled and escaped. 13 Then Michal took the household idol and put it on the bed, placed some goat hair on its head, and covered it with a garment. 14 When Saul sent agents to seize David, Michal said, "He's sick."

15 Saul sent the agents back to see David and said, "Bring him on his bed so I can kill him." 16 When the agents arrived, to their surprise, the household idol was on the bed with some goat hair on its head.

17 Saul asked Michal, "Why did you deceive me like this? You sent my enemy away, and he has escaped!"

She answered him, "He said to me, 'Let me go! Why should I kill you?'"

18 So David fled and escaped and went to Samuel at Ramah and told him everything Saul had done to him. Then he and Samuel left and stayed at Naioth.

19 When it was reported to Saul that David was at Naioth in Ramah, 20 he sent agents to seize David. However, when they saw the group of prophets prophesying with Samuel leading them, the Spirit of God came on Saul's agents, and they also started prophesying. 21 When they reported to Saul, he sent other agents, and they also began prophesying. So Saul tried again and sent a third group of agents, and even they began prophesying. 22 Then Saul himself went to Ramah. He came to the large cistern at Secu and asked, "Where are Samuel and David?"

"At Naioth in Ramah," someone said.

23 So he went to Naioth in Ramah. The Spirit of God also came on him, and as he walked along, he prophesied until he entered Naioth in Ramah. 24 Saul then removed his clothes and also prophesied before Samuel; he collapsed and lay naked all that day and all that night. That is why they say, "Is Saul also among the prophets?"

JONATHAN PROTECTS DAVID

20 David fled from Naioth in Ramah and came to Jonathan and asked, "What have I done? What did I do wrong? How have I sinned against your father so that he wants to take my life?"

2 Jonathan said to him, "No, you won't die. Listen, my father doesn't do anything, great or small, without telling me. So why would he hide this matter from me? This can't be true."

3 But David said, "Your father certainly knows that I have found favor with you. He has said, 'Jonathan must not know of this, or else he will be grieved.'" David also swore, "As surely as the LORD lives and as you yourself live, there is but a step between me and death."

4 Jonathan said to David, "Whatever you say, I will do for you."

[A] **18:27** LXX reads *100* [B] **18:28** Lit *saw and knew*

5 So David told him, "Look, tomorrow is the New Moon, and I'm supposed to sit down and eat with the king. Instead, let me go, and I'll hide in the countryside for the next two nights.[A] 6 If your father misses me at all, say, 'David urgently requested my permission to go quickly to his hometown, Bethlehem, for an annual sacrifice there involving the whole clan.' 7 If he says, 'Good,' then your servant is safe, but if he becomes angry, you will know he has evil intentions. 8 Deal kindly with[B] your servant, for you have brought me into a covenant with you before the LORD. If I have done anything wrong, then kill me yourself; why take me to your father?"

9 "No!" Jonathan responded. "If I ever find out my father has evil intentions against you, wouldn't I tell you about it?"

10 So David asked Jonathan, "Who will tell me if your father answers you harshly?"

11 He answered David, "Come on, let's go out to the countryside." So both of them went out to the countryside. 12 "By the LORD, the God of Israel, I will sound out my father by this time tomorrow or the next day. If I find out that he is favorable toward you, will I not send for you and tell you? 13 If my father intends to bring evil on you, may the LORD punish Jonathan and do so severely if I do not tell you and send you away so you may leave safely. May the LORD be with you, just as he was with my father. 14 If I continue to live, show me kindness[C] from the LORD, but if I die, 15 don't ever withdraw your kindness from my household — not even when the LORD cuts off every one of David's enemies from the face of the earth." 16 Then Jonathan made a covenant with the house of David, saying, "May the LORD hold David's enemies accountable."[D] 17 Jonathan once again swore to David[E] in his love for him, because he loved him as he loved himself.

18 Then Jonathan said to him, "Tomorrow is the New Moon; you'll be missed because your seat will be empty. 19 The following day hurry down and go to the place where you hid on the day this incident began and stay beside the rock Ezel. 20 I will shoot three arrows beside it as if I'm aiming at a target. 21 Then I will send a servant and say, 'Go and find the arrows!' Now, if I expressly say to the servant, 'Look, the arrows are on this side of you — get them,' then come, because as the LORD lives, it is safe for you and there is no problem. 22 But if I say this to the youth, 'Look, the arrows are beyond you!' then go, for the LORD is sending you away. 23 As for the matter you and I have spoken about, the LORD will be a witness[F] between you and me forever." 24 So David hid in the countryside.

At the New Moon, the king sat down to eat the meal. 25 He sat at his usual place on the seat by the wall. Jonathan sat facing him[G] and Abner took his place beside Saul, but David's place was empty. 26 Saul did not say anything that day because he thought, "Something unexpected has happened; he must be ceremonially unclean — yes, that's it, he is unclean."

27 However, the day after the New Moon, the second day, David's place was still empty, and Saul asked his son Jonathan, "Why didn't Jesse's son come to the meal either yesterday or today?"

28 Jonathan answered, "David asked for my permission to go to Bethlehem. 29 He said, 'Please let me go because our clan is holding a sacrifice in the town, and my brother has told me to be there. So now, if I have found favor with you, let me go so I can see my brothers.' That's why he didn't come to the king's table."

30 Then Saul became angry with Jonathan and shouted, "You son of a perverse and rebellious woman! Don't I know that you are siding with Jesse's son to your own shame and to the disgrace of your mother?[H] 31 Every day Jesse's son lives on earth you and your kingship are not secure. Now send for him and bring him to me — he must die!"

32 Jonathan answered his father back, "Why is he to be killed? What has he done?"

33 Then Saul threw his spear at Jonathan to kill him, so he knew that his father was determined to kill David. 34 He got up from the table fiercely angry and did not eat any food that second day of the New Moon, for he was grieved because of his father's shameful behavior toward David.

35 In the morning Jonathan went out to the countryside for the appointed meeting with David. A young servant was with him. 36 He said to the servant, "Run and find the arrows I'm shooting." As the servant ran, Jonathan shot an arrow beyond him. 37 He came to the location of the arrow that Jonathan had shot, but Jonathan called to him and said, "The arrow is beyond you, isn't it?" 38 Then Jonathan called to him, "Hurry up and don't stop!" Jonathan's servant picked up the arrow and returned to his master. 39 He did not know anything; only Jonathan and David knew the arrangement. 40 Then Jonathan gave his equipment to the servant who was with him and said, "Go, take it back to the city."

41 When the servant had gone, David got up from the south side of the stone Ezel, fell facedown to the ground, and paid homage three times. Then he and Jonathan kissed each other and wept with each other, though David wept more.

[A] **20:5** Lit *countryside until the third night* [B] **20:8** Or *Show loyalty to* [C] **20:14** Or *loyalty*, also in v. 15 [D] **20:16** Lit *LORD require it from the hand of David's enemies* [E] **20:17** LXX; MT reads *Jonathan once again made David swear* [F] **20:23** LXX; MT omits *a witness* [G] **20:25** Text emended; MT reads *Jonathan got up* [H] **20:30** Lit *your mother's nakedness*

42 Jonathan then said to David, "Go [illegible]
ance the two of us pledged in the name of [illegible]
when we said, 'The LORD will be a witness b[illegible]
you and me and between my offspring and you[illegible]
spring forever.'" Then David left, and Jonathan we[illegible]
into the city.

DAVID FLEES TO NOB

21 David went to the priest Ahimelech at Nob.
Ahimelech was afraid to meet David, so he said
to him, "Why are you alone and no one is with you?"
2 David answered the priest Ahimelech, "The king
gave me a mission, but he told me, 'Don't let anyone
know anything about the mission I'm sending you
on or what I have ordered you to do.' I have stationed
my young men at a certain place. 3 Now what do you
have on hand? Give me five loaves of bread or whatever can be found."
4 The priest told him, "There is no ordinary bread
on hand. However, there is consecrated bread, but the
young men may eat it[A] only if they have kept themselves from women."
5 David answered him, "I swear that women are
being kept from us, as always when I go out to battle.
The young men's bodies[B] are consecrated even on
an ordinary mission, so of course their bodies are
consecrated today." 6 So the priest gave him the consecrated bread, for there was no bread there except
the Bread of the Presence that had been removed
from the presence of the LORD. When the bread was
removed, it had been replaced with warm bread.
7 One of Saul's servants, detained before the LORD,
was there that day. His name was Doeg the Edomite,
chief of Saul's shepherds.
8 David said to Ahimelech, "Do you have a spear
or sword on hand? I didn't even bring my sword or
my weapons since the king's mission was urgent."
9 The priest replied, "The sword of Goliath the Philistine, whom you killed in the Valley of Elah, is here,
wrapped in a cloth behind the ephod. If you want to
take it for yourself, then take it, for there isn't another one here."
"There's none like it!" David said. "Give it to me."

DAVID FLEES TO GATH

10 David fled that day from Saul's presence and went
to King Achish of Gath. 11 But Achish's servants said
to him, "Isn't this David, the king of the land? Don't
they sing about him during their dances:

Saul has killed his thousands,
but David his tens of thousands?"

12 David took this to heart and became very afraid
of King Achish of Gath, 13 so he pretended to be insane
in their presence. He acted like a madman around
them,[C] scribbling[D] on the doors of the city gate and
letting saliva run down his beard.
14 "Look! You can see the man is crazy," Achish said
to his servants. "Why did you bring him to me? 15 Do I
have such a shortage of crazy people that you brought
[illegible]is one to act crazy around me? Is this one going to
[illegible]e into my house?"

SAUL'[illegible]CREASING PARANOIA

22 So [illegible]vid left Gath and took refuge in the cave
of Ad[illegible]am. When David's brothers and his
father's whole [illegible]mily heard, they went down and
joined him there. [illegible]n addition, every man who was
desperate, in debt, [illegible] discontented rallied around
him, and he became the[illegible] lea[illegible]er. About four hundred
men were with him.
3 From there David went to Mizpeh of Moab where
he said to the king of Moab, "Please let my father and
mother stay with you until I know what God will do
for me." 4 So he left them in the care of the king of
Moab, and they stayed with him the whole time David
was in the stronghold.
5 Then the prophet Gad said to David, "Don't stay
in the stronghold. Leave and return to the land of
Judah." So David left and went to the forest of Hereth.
6 Saul heard that David and his men had been discovered. At that time Saul was in Gibeah, sitting under the tamarisk tree at the high place. His spear
was in his hand, and all his servants were standing
around him. 7 Saul said to his servants, "Listen, men
of Benjamin: Is Jesse's son going to give all of you
fields and vineyards? Do you think he'll make all of
you commanders of thousands and commanders
of hundreds? 8 That's why all of you have conspired
against me! Nobody tells me when my own son makes
a covenant with Jesse's son. None of you cares about
me or tells me that my son has stirred up my own servant to wait in ambush for me, as is the case today."
9 Then Doeg the Edomite, who was in charge of
Saul's servants, answered, "I saw Jesse's son come
to Ahimelech son of Ahitub at Nob. 10 Ahimelech inquired of the LORD for him and gave him provisions.
He also gave him the sword of Goliath the Philistine."

SLAUGHTER OF THE PRIESTS

11 The king sent messengers to summon the priest
Ahimelech son of Ahitub, and his father's whole family, who were priests in Nob. All of them came to the
king. 12 Then Saul said, "Listen, son of Ahitub!"
"I'm at your service, my lord," he said.
13 Saul asked him, "Why did you and Jesse's son
conspire against me? You gave him bread and a

[A] **21:4** DSS; MT omits *may eat it* [B] **21:5** Lit *vessels* [C] **21:13** Lit *madman in their hand* [D] **21:13** LXX reads *drumming*

Excavating Gath: An Interview with Dr. Aren Maeir

Q: What kind of significant finds have you uncovered in these past seasons?

MAEIR: We have many, but I'll mention a couple: (1) The so-called Goliath inscription: a small sherd, dated to the tenth or early ninth century BC, in which two names of non-Semitic, Indo-European origin are written, in an archaic alphabetic script. These names (ALWT and WLT) are somewhat similar to what the original name of Goliath was and serve as a very nice indicator that during the Iron Age IIA (more or less the time of King David) there were people at Gath, the home of Goliath according to the Bible, who had names quite similar to the name Goliath. (2) In the lower city, we discovered a building (probably a temple) in which we found a large stone altar.

Recent excavations at Gath.

Q: Could you please describe this stone altar?

MAEIR: The altar was made of hard limestone. It is the only two-horned altar known in the Levant; others (one or two) have been unearthed at Cyprus. The decorations on the altar are quite similar to those on other Levantine Iron Age altars.

Q: How would you describe the gate?

MAEIR: The gate is located in the middle of the northern side of the lower city, right opposite a water well, which is still in use today; in fact, during the time of the modern Arab village, one of the paths leading up to the village reused the path that ran through the Iron Age gate. It appears that the gate has stone foundations and a brick superstructure.

An aerial view of Tell es-Safi, biblical Gath.

Dr. Maeir with the stone horned altar, which was excavated in 2011. It measures about twenty by twenty by forty inches.

Q: What do the gate and fortification walls tell us about the ancient city of Gath?

Maeir: They tell us that Gath was a large, fortified city during the tenth–ninth centuries BC, probably the strongest city-state in the region at the time. This strong Philistine presence probably meant that the Judahite kingdom could not expand into this region until after Gath's destruction by Hazael king of Aram-Damascus in 830 BC. ✣

The top of the massive city wall, indicated by the rough stones, is visible in the archaeological dig squares.

sword and inquired of God for him, so he could rise up against me and wait in ambush, as is the case today."

14 Ahimelech replied to the king, "Who among all your servants is as faithful as David? He is the king's son-in-law, captain of your bodyguard, and honored in your house. 15 Was today the first time I inquired of God for him? Of course not! Please don't let the king make an accusation against your servant or any of my father's family, for your servant didn't have any idea[A] about all this."

16 But the king said, "You will die, Ahimelech — you and your father's whole family!"

17 Then the king ordered the guards standing by him, "Turn and kill the priests of the LORD because they sided with David. For they knew he was fleeing, but they didn't tell me." But the king's servants would not lift a hand to execute the priests of the LORD.

18 So the king said to Doeg, "Go and execute the priests!" So Doeg the Edomite went and executed the priests himself. On that day, he killed eighty-five men who wore linen ephods. 19 He also struck down Nob, the city of the priests, with the sword — both men and women, infants and nursing babies, oxen, donkeys, and sheep.

20 However, one of the sons of Ahimelech son of Ahitub escaped. His name was Abiathar, and he fled to David. 21 Abiathar told David that Saul had killed the priests of the LORD. 22 Then David said to Abiathar, "I knew that Doeg the Edomite was there that day and that he was sure to report to Saul. I myself am responsible for[B] the lives of everyone in your father's family. 23 Stay with me. Don't be afraid, for the one who wants to take my life wants to take your life. You will be safe with me."

DELIVERANCE AT KEILAH

23 It was reported to David, "Look, the Philistines are fighting against Keilah and raiding the threshing floors."

2 So David inquired of the LORD: "Should I launch an attack against these Philistines?"

The LORD answered David, "Launch an attack against the Philistines and rescue Keilah."

3 But David's men said to him, "Look, we're afraid here in Judah; how much more if we go to Keilah against the Philistine forces!"

4 Once again, David inquired of the LORD, and the LORD answered him, "Go at once to Keilah, for I will hand the Philistines over to you." 5 Then David and his men went to Keilah, fought against the Philistines, drove their livestock away, and inflicted heavy losses on them. So David rescued the inhabitants of Keilah. 6 Abiathar son of Ahimelech fled to David at Keilah, and he brought an ephod with him.

7 When it was reported to Saul that David had gone to Keilah, he said, "God has handed him over to me, for he has trapped himself by entering a town with barred gates." 8 Then Saul summoned all the troops to go to war at Keilah and besiege David and his men.

9 When David learned that Saul was plotting evil against him, he said to the priest Abiathar, "Bring the ephod."

10 Then David said, "LORD God of Israel, your servant has reliable information that Saul intends to come to Keilah and destroy the town because of me. 11 Will the citizens of Keilah hand me over to him? Will Saul come down as your servant has heard? LORD God of Israel, please tell your servant."

The LORD answered, "He will come down."

12 Then David asked, "Will the citizens of Keilah hand me and my men over to Saul?"

"They will," the LORD responded.

13 So David and his men, numbering about six hundred, left Keilah at once and moved from place to place. When it was reported to Saul that David had escaped from Keilah, he called off the expedition. 14 David then stayed in the wilderness strongholds and in the hill country of the Wilderness of Ziph. Saul searched for him every day, but God did not hand David over to him.

A RENEWED COVENANT

15 David was in the Wilderness of Ziph in Horesh when he saw that Saul had come out to take his life. 16 Then Saul's son Jonathan came to David in Horesh and encouraged him in his faith[C] in God, 17 saying, "Don't be afraid, for my father Saul will never lay a hand on you. You yourself will be king over Israel, and I'll be your second-in-command. Even my father Saul knows it is true." 18 Then the two of them made a covenant in the LORD's presence. Afterward, David remained in Horesh, while Jonathan went home.

DAVID'S NARROW ESCAPE

19 Some Ziphites came up to Saul at Gibeah and said, "Isn't it true that David is hiding among us in the strongholds in Horesh on the hill of Hachilah south of Jeshimon? 20 So now, whenever the king wants to come down, let him come down. As for us, we will be glad to hand him over to the king."

21 "May you be blessed by the LORD," replied Saul, "for you have shown concern for me. 22 Go and check again. Investigate[D] where he goes[E] and who has seen him there; they tell me he is extremely cunning. 23 Investigate[F] all the places where he hides. Then come

[A] **22:15** Lit *didn't know a thing, small or large* [B] **22:22** LXX, Syr, Vg; MT reads *I myself turn in* [C] **23:16** Lit *and strengthened his hand* [D] **23:22** Lit *Know and see* [E] **23:22** Lit *watch his place where his foot will be* [F] **23:23** Lit *See and know*

back to me with accurate information, and I'll go with you. If it turns out he really is in the region, I'll search for him among all the clans[A] of Judah." 24 So they went to Ziph ahead of Saul.

Now David and his men were in the wilderness near Maon in the Arabah south of Jeshimon, 25 and Saul and his men went to look for him. When David was told about it, he went down to the rock and stayed in the Wilderness of Maon. Saul heard of this and pursued David there.

26 Saul went along one side of the mountain and David and his men went along the other side. Even though David was hurrying to get away from Saul, Saul and his men were closing in on David and his men to capture them. 27 Then a messenger came to Saul saying, "Come quickly, because the Philistines have raided the land!" 28 So Saul broke off his pursuit of David and went to engage the Philistines. Therefore, that place was named the Rock of Separation. 29 From there David went up and stayed in the strongholds of En-gedi.

DAVID SPARES SAUL

24 When Saul returned from pursuing the Philistines, he was told, "David is in the wilderness near En-gedi." 2 So Saul took three thousand of Israel's fit young men and went to look for David and his men in front of the Rocks of the Wild Goats. 3 When Saul came to the sheep pens along the road, a cave was there, and he went in to relieve himself.[B] David and his men were staying in the recesses of the cave, 4 so they said to him, "Look, this is the day the LORD told you about: 'I will hand your enemy over to you so you can do to him whatever you desire.'" Then David got up and secretly cut off the corner of Saul's robe.

5 Afterward, David's conscience bothered[C] him because he had cut off the corner of Saul's robe.[D] 6 He said to his men, "As the LORD is my witness, I would never do such a thing to my lord, the LORD's anointed. I will never lift my hand against him, since he is the LORD's anointed." 7 With these words David persuaded[E] his men, and he did not let them rise up against Saul.

Then Saul left the cave and went on his way. 8 After that, David got up, went out of the cave, and called to Saul, "My lord the king!" When Saul looked behind him, David knelt low with his face to the ground and paid homage. 9 David said to Saul, "Why do you listen to the words of people who say, 'Look, David intends to harm you'? 10 You can see with your own eyes that the LORD handed you over to me today in the cave. Someone advised me to kill you, but I[F,G] took pity on you and said: I won't lift my hand against my lord, since he is the LORD's anointed. 11 Look, my father! Look at the corner of your robe in my hand, for I cut it off, but I didn't kill you. Recognize[H] that I've committed no crime or rebellion. I haven't sinned against you even though you are hunting me down to take my life.

12 "May the LORD judge between me and you, and may the LORD take vengeance on you for me, but my hand will never be against you. 13 As the old proverb says, 'Wickedness comes from wicked people.' My hand will never be against you. 14 Who has the king of Israel come after? What are you chasing after? A dead dog? A single flea? 15 May the LORD be judge and decide between you and me. May he take notice and plead my case and deliver[I] me from you."

16 When David finished saying these things to him, Saul replied, "Is that your voice, David my son?" Then Saul wept aloud 17 and said to David, "You are more righteous than I, for you have done what is good to me though I have done what is evil to you. 18 You yourself have told me today what good you did for me: when the LORD handed me over to you, you didn't kill me. 19 When a man finds his enemy, does he let him go unharmed?[J] May the LORD repay you with good for what you've done for me today.

20 "Now I know for certain you will be king, and the kingdom of Israel will be established[K] in your hand. 21 Therefore swear to me by the LORD that you will not cut off my descendants or wipe out my name from my father's family." 22 So David swore to Saul. Then Saul went back home, and David and his men went up to the stronghold.

DAVID, NABAL, AND ABIGAIL

25 Samuel died, and all Israel assembled to mourn for him, and they buried him by his home in Ramah. David then went down to the Wilderness of Paran.[L]

2 A man in Maon had a business in Carmel; he was a very rich man with three thousand sheep and one thousand goats and was shearing his sheep in Carmel. 3 The man's name was Nabal, and his wife's name, Abigail. The woman was intelligent and beautiful, but the man, a Calebite, was harsh and evil in his dealings.

4 While David was in the wilderness, he heard that Nabal was shearing sheep, 5 so David sent ten young men instructing them, "Go up to Carmel, and when you come to Nabal, greet him[M] in my name. 6 Then say this: 'Long life to you,[N] and peace to you, peace to your family, and peace to all that is yours. 7 I hear that you are shearing.[O] When your shepherds were with

[A] **23:23** Or *thousands* [B] **24:3** Lit *to cover his feet* [C] **24:5** Lit *David's heart struck* [D] **24:5** Some Hb mss, LXX, Syr, Vg; other Hb mss omit *robe* [E] **24:7** Or *restrained* [F] **24:10** LXX, Syr, Tg; MT reads *she or it* [G] **24:10** Or *my eye* [H] **24:11** Lit *Know and see* [I] **24:15** Lit *render a verdict for* [J] **24:19** Lit *go on a good way* [K] **24:20** Or *will flourish* [L] **25:1** LXX reads *to Maon* [M] **25:5** Or *Nabal, ask him for peace* [N] **25:6** Lit *'To life* [O] **25:7** Lit *you have shearers*

En-gedi: History and Archaeology

by Joel F. Drinkard Jr.

En-gedi is an oasis in a barren area of the Judean wilderness. En-gedi lies along the Wadi Ghar, or Nahal Arugot, also probably to be identified as the Valley of Beracah (2Ch 20:26). This area is desolate with only a few scrub bushes and wild grasses, apart from wadi beds and around the few springs. The limited rainfall provides sparse grazing for the bedouin flocks today, much as it would have in David's day. The many caves along the hillsides provide shelter from midday heat and nighttime cold. They also are the dens for the wild animals of the region, the bears and lions of David's day. Those same caves could provide a hideout for David and his men fleeing from Saul. David would know the region well; he would know which caves would be least noticeable to Saul's army, which would provide the best view of approaches, and which lay near water sources.

En-gedi is the major spring and oasis along the western shore of the Dead Sea. It lies almost midway down the length of the Dead Sea. The name in Hebrew means "Spring of Kids," which fits with the description of the nearby hills as "Rocks of the Wild Goats" (1Sm 24:2). A short distance from the spring is a beautiful waterfall and pool. The available water creates an oasis of lush vegetation in stark contrast to the desolate hills just a few hundred yards away. The immediate area around the spring and waterfall has been inhabited at least since the Chalcolithic period (4000–3200 BC). The Chalcolithic remains include a well-preserved shrine or sanctuary about ninety-five feet by sixty-two feet. The shrine has a wall enclosing a courtyard with two buildings. The larger building to the north is a broad-room structure about sixty-two feet by twenty-two feet. The other building, also a broad-room structure, is on the east and is about twenty-five feet by sixteen feet. The enclosure wall has two gates, the larger one on the south and the smaller one on the northeast. The courtyard has a circular structure in the center about ten feet in diameter, made of small stones. Its function is unknown. Both buildings and gates had doors; the stone sills and hinge holes are still present.

The main building had a niche in the middle of the back wall surrounded by a low wall and had benches on both sides. Apparently sacrifices were made in this building because the floor had pits on both ends filled with burned bones, horns, pottery, and ashes. The excavators suggested that the enclosure was a cult site, perhaps a central sanctuary.[1] About six miles south of En-gedi a major find of the Chalcolithic period was made. A cache of more than four hundred copper-bronze objects were found in a cave in Nahal Mishmar. The cache included "crowns," wands or standards, maces, and chisels suggesting a cultic function for the objects. In addition to the copper-bronze objects, several hematite and hippopotamus tusk objects were found. The objects show superb artistic and technical workmanship. Since no other major sanctuary from the Chalcolithic period has been found in the surrounding region, it is possible that the Nahal Mishmar copper treasure may have belonged to the En-gedi shrine. Perhaps the priests of this shrine took the cult objects to the cave in Nahal Mishmar for safekeeping when they abandoned the site, hoping to return later and retrieve them. They then may have died or been killed before being able to retrieve the objects, and their secret location remained hidden for more than five thousand years until 1961 when the cave was explored.[2] If these objects did belong to the En-gedi shrine, that sanctuary

A view of the mountains of En-gedi with caves that could provide hiding places for fugitives.

would have been the most important one of the Chalcolithic period yet known in Israel. Since the shrine was not destroyed, but was abandoned, the remains would have been prominently visible and could have been known by David three thousand years ago. Perhaps his stronghold at En-gedi was on top of one of the steep hillsides around the sanctuary.

The excavators found no evidence of remains belonging to the time of David at En-gedi. There was a settlement, now called Tel Goren, from the seventh and sixth centuries BC, late in the period of the divided monarchy. This settlement had a number of buildings noted for having large store jars partially sunken into the floors. These buildings were apparently part of an industrial complex that produced perfume and/or medicines. From later periods, Persian through Roman-Byzantine, there is evidence of the cultivation and processing of balsam plants. Belonging to the settlement of the earliest stratum, the seventh century BC, were seals and jar handles bearing Hebrew inscriptions and stone weights with signs indicating one, four, and eight shekels. A royal stamp impression, "of/for the king, [from] Ziph," was found on the handle of a store jar. But there were no Iron I remains that would date to the period of Saul-David-Solomon.

We should not be surprised that archaeologists haven't found a settlement belonging to the time when David fled into this region. He wanted an isolated hiding place, not a built-up community. To hide in a desolate, uninhabited area is much easier. Had there been a settlement, Saul would have known of it. David knew the area; he knew the good hiding places and the sources of water. The many caves in the surrounding hills would provide excellent hiding places.

The Hebrew Bible refers to the strongholds to which David fled throughout the wilderness of Judah. Three times the reference is specifically to "the stronghold" (1Sm 22:4,5; 24:22). Some scholars[3] have suggested "the stronghold" was Masada, the mountain fortress about ten miles south of En-gedi, later made famous by Herod's palace and the zealots' stand against the Romans in AD 66–73. The name *Masada* means "stronghold," and the Hebrew word for "stronghold" used in 1 Samuel is closely related to the name *Masada*. Certainly the top of Masada would be almost impregnable. The flat top hill rises more than a thousand feet from the floor of the Dead Sea Valley, with steep slopes on all sides. Even on the west where Masada has the least rise from the valley below, there is a drop of three hundred feet. The top would also provide a perfect view of all approaches and ample opportunity for a small band of men to escape to one side while an army approached from the opposite direction. Presumably the other strongholds in the wilderness of Judah would have given similar opportunity for escape. Indeed the biblical text describes that type of escape from Saul (23:24–26).

The steep wadi slopes from Qumran south to Masada along the western side of the Dead Sea have been explored by Israeli archaeologists since the 1960s. They discovered numerous caves showing habitation from the Chalcolithic period through the Second Jewish Revolt of AD 132–135. Many of the caves were nearly inaccessible. Steep cliffs with almost sheer drops of 600–750 feet were not uncommon. One of the caves in Nahal Mishmar had Iron I sherds belonging to the time of Saul, David, and Solomon. The archaeologists concluded that for more than five thousand years these caves have provided places of refuge in times of danger—exactly the use David made of these caves and strongholds! ✣

---

[1] Benjamin Mazar, "En-Gedi," *NEAEHL*, 2:405. [2] P. Bar-Adon, "The Nahal Mishmar Caves," *NEAEHL*, 3:822–27. [3] Yohanan Aharoni, *Land of the Bible*, rev. ed. (Louisville: Westminster John Knox, 1979), 290 and n. 9.

us, we did not harass them, and nothing of theirs was
missing the whole time they were in Carmel. 8 Ask
your young men, and they will tell you. So let my
young men find favor with you, for we have come on
a feast[A] day. Please give whatever you have on hand
to your servants and to your son David.'"
9 David's young men went and said all these things
to Nabal on David's behalf,[B] and they waited.[C] 10 Nabal asked them, "Who is David? Who is Jesse's son?
Many slaves these days are running away from their
masters. 11 Am I supposed to take my bread, my water,
and my meat that I butchered for my shearers and
give them to these men? I don't know where they
are from."
12 David's young men retraced their steps. When
they returned to him, they reported all these words.
13 He said to his men, "All of you, put on your swords!"
So each man put on his sword, and David also put on
his sword. About four hundred men followed David
while two hundred stayed with the supplies.
14 One of Nabal's young men informed Abigail, Nabal's wife, "Look, David sent messengers from the
wilderness to greet our master, but he screamed at
them. 15 The men treated us very well. When we were
in the field, we weren't harassed and nothing of ours
was missing the whole time we were living among
them. 16 They were a wall around us, both day and
night, the entire time we were with them herding the
sheep. 17 Now consider carefully[D] what you should do,
because there is certain to be trouble for our master
and his entire family. He is such a worthless fool nobody can talk to him!"
18 Abigail hurried, taking two hundred loaves of
bread, two clay jars of wine, five butchered sheep,
a bushel[E] of roasted grain, one hundred clusters of
raisins, and two hundred cakes of pressed figs, and
loaded them on donkeys. 19 Then she said to her male
servants, "Go ahead of me. I will be right behind you."
But she did not tell her husband, Nabal.
20 As she rode the donkey down a mountain pass
hidden from view, she saw David and his men coming toward her and met them. 21 David had just said,
"I guarded everything that belonged to this man in
the wilderness for nothing. He was not missing anything, yet he paid me back evil for good. 22 May God
punish me[F] and do so severely if I let any of his males[G]
survive until morning."
23 When Abigail saw David, she quickly got off the
donkey and knelt down with her face to the ground
and paid homage to David. 24 She knelt at his feet and
said, "The guilt is mine, my lord, but please let your
servant speak to you directly. Listen to the words
of your servant. 25 My lord should pay no attention
to this worthless fool Nabal, for he lives up to his
name:[H] His name means 'stupid,' and stupidity is all
he knows.[I] I, your servant, didn't see my lord's young
men whom you sent. 26 Now my lord, as surely as the
LORD lives and as you yourself live— it is the LORD
who kept you from participating in bloodshed and
avenging yourself by your own hand—may your
enemies and those who intend to harm my lord be
like Nabal. 27 Let this gift your servant has brought to
my lord be given to the young men who follow my
lord. 28 Please forgive your servant's offense, for the
LORD is certain to make a lasting dynasty for my lord
because he fights the LORD's battles. Throughout your
life, may evil[J] not be found in you.
29 "Someone is pursuing you and intends to take
your life. My lord's life is tucked safely in the place[K]
where the LORD your God protects the living, but
he is flinging away your enemies' lives like stones
from a sling. 30 When the LORD does for my lord all
the good he promised you and appoints you ruler
over Israel, 31 there will not be remorse or a troubled conscience for my lord because of needless
bloodshed or my lord's revenge. And when the LORD
does good things for my lord, may you remember
me your servant."
32 Then David said to Abigail, "Blessed be the LORD
God of Israel, who sent you to meet me today! 33 May
your discernment be blessed, and may you be blessed.
Today you kept me from participating in bloodshed
and avenging myself by my own hand. 34 Otherwise, as
surely as the LORD God of Israel lives, who prevented
me from harming you, if you had not come quickly to
meet me, Nabal wouldn't have had any males[L] left by
morning light." 35 Then David accepted what she had
brought him and said, "Go home in peace. See, I have
heard what you said and have granted your request."
36 Then Abigail went to Nabal, and there he was in
his house, holding a feast fit for a king. Nabal's heart
was cheerful,[M] and he was very drunk, so she didn't
say anything[N] to him until morning light.
37 In the morning when Nabal sobered up,[O] his wife
told him about these events. His heart died[P] and he became a stone. 38 About ten days later, the LORD struck
Nabal dead.
39 When David heard that Nabal was dead, he said,
"Blessed be the LORD who championed my cause
against Nabal's insults and restrained his servant
from doing evil. The LORD brought Nabal's evil deeds
back on his own head."

[A] **25:8** Lit *good* [B] **25:9** Lit *name* [C] **25:9** LXX reads *and he became arrogant* [D] **25:17** Lit *Now know and see* [E] **25:18** Lit *sheep, five seahs* [F] **25:22** LXX; MT reads *David's enemies* [G] **25:22** Lit *of those of his who are urinating against the wall* [H] **25:25** Lit *for as is his name is, so he is* [I] **25:25** Lit *and foolishness is with him* [J] **25:28** Or *trouble* [K] **25:29** Lit *bundle* [L] **25:34** Lit *had anyone urinating against a wall* [M] **25:36** Lit *Nabal's heart was good on him* [N] **25:36** Lit *anything at all* [O] **25:37** Lit *when the wine had gone out of Nabal* [P] **25:37** Lit *Then his heart died within him*

Then David sent messengers to speak to Abigail about marrying him. 40 When David's servants came to Abigail at Carmel, they said to her, "David sent us to bring you to him as a wife."

41 She stood up, paid homage with her face to the ground, and said, "Here I am, your servant, a slave to wash the feet of my lord's servants." 42 Then Abigail got up quickly, and with her five female servants accompanying her, rode on the donkey following David's messengers. And so she became his wife.

43 David also married Ahinoam of Jezreel, and the two of them became his wives. 44 But Saul gave his daughter Michal, David's wife, to Palti son of Laish, who was from Gallim.

DAVID AGAIN SPARES SAUL

26 Then the Ziphites came to Saul at Gibeah saying, "David is hiding on the hill of Hachilah opposite Jeshimon." 2 So Saul, accompanied by three thousand of the fit young men of Israel, went immediately to the Wilderness of Ziph to search for David there. 3 Saul camped beside the road at the hill of Hachilah opposite Jeshimon. David was living in the wilderness and discovered Saul had come there after him. 4 So David sent out spies and knew for certain that Saul had come. 5 Immediately, David went to the place where Saul had camped. He saw the place where Saul and Abner son of Ner, the commander of his army, were lying down. Saul was lying inside the inner circle of the camp with the troops camped around him. 6 Then David asked Ahimelech the Hethite and Joab's brother Abishai son of Zeruiah, "Who will go with me into the camp to Saul?"

"I'll go with you," answered Abishai.

7 That night, David and Abishai came to the troops, and Saul was lying there asleep in the inner circle of the camp with his spear stuck in the ground by his head. Abner and the troops were lying around him. 8 Then Abishai said to David, "Today God has delivered your enemy to you. Let me thrust the spear through him into the ground just once. I won't have to strike him twice!"

9 But David said to Abishai, "Don't destroy him, for who can lift a hand against the LORD's anointed and be innocent?" 10 David added, "As the LORD lives, the LORD will certainly strike him down: either his day will come and he will die, or he will go into battle and perish. 11 However, as the LORD is my witness, I will never lift my hand against the LORD's anointed. Instead, take the spear and the water jug by his head, and let's go."

12 So David took the spear and the water jug by Saul's head, and they went their way. No one saw them, no one knew, and no one woke up; they all remained asleep because a deep sleep from the LORD came over them. 13 David crossed to the other side and stood on top of the mountain at a distance; there was a considerable space between them. 14 Then David shouted to the troops and to Abner son of Ner, "Aren't you going to answer, Abner?"

"Who are you who calls to the king?" Abner asked.

15 David called to Abner, "You're a man, aren't you? Who in Israel is your equal? So why didn't you protect your lord the king when one of the people came to destroy him? 16 What you have done is not good. As the LORD lives, all of you deserve to die[A] since you didn't protect your lord, the LORD's anointed. Now look around; where are the king's spear and water jug that were by his head?"

17 Saul recognized David's voice and asked, "Is that your voice, my son David?"

"It is my voice, my lord and king," David said. 18 Then he continued, "Why is my lord pursuing his servant? What have I done? What crime have I committed? 19 Now, may my lord the king please hear the words of his servant: If it is the LORD who has incited you against me, then may he accept an offering. But if it is people, may they be cursed in the presence of the LORD, for today they have banished me from sharing in the inheritance of the LORD, saying, 'Go and worship other gods.' 20 So don't let my blood fall to the ground far from the LORD's presence, for the king of Israel has come out to search for a single flea, like one who pursues a partridge in the mountains."

21 Saul responded, "I have sinned. Come back, my son David, I will never harm you again because today you considered my life precious. I have been a fool! I've committed a grave error."

22 David answered, "Here is the king's spear; have one of the young men come over and get it. 23 The LORD will repay every man for his righteousness and his loyalty. I wasn't willing to lift my hand against the LORD's anointed, even though the LORD handed you over to me today. 24 Just as I considered your life valuable today, so may the LORD consider my life valuable and rescue me from all trouble."

25 Saul said to him, "You are blessed, my son David. You will certainly do great things and will also prevail." Then David went on his way, and Saul returned home.

DAVID FLEES TO ZIKLAG

27 David said to himself, "One of these days I'll be swept away by Saul. There is nothing better for me than to escape immediately to the land of the Philistines. Then Saul will give up searching for me everywhere in Israel, and I'll escape from him." 2 So David set out with his six hundred men and went over

[A] **26:16** Lit *you are sons of death*

to Achish son of Maoch, the king of Gath. 3 David and
his men stayed with Achish in Gath. Each man had
his family with him, and David had his two wives:
Ahinoam of Jezreel and Abigail of Carmel, Nabal's
widow. 4 When it was reported to Saul that David had
fled to Gath, he no longer searched for him.
5 Now David said to Achish, "If I have found favor
with you, let me be given a place in one of the outlying
towns, so I can live there. Why should your servant
live in the royal city with you?" 6 That day Achish gave
Ziklag to him, and it still belongs to the kings of Judah
today. 7 The length of time that David stayed in Philistine territory amounted to a year and four months.
8 David and his men went up and raided the Geshurites, the Girzites,[A] and the Amalekites. From ancient
times they had been the inhabitants of the region
through Shur as far as the land of Egypt. 9 Whenever
David attacked the land, he did not leave a single person alive, either man or woman, but he took flocks,
herds, donkeys, camels, and clothing. Then he came
back to Achish, 10 who inquired, "Where did you raid
today?"[B]

David replied, "The south country of Judah," "The
south country of the Jerahmeelites," or "The south
country of the Kenites."
11 David did not let a man or woman live to be
brought to Gath, for he said, "Or they will inform on
us and say, 'This is what David did.'" This was David's
custom during the whole time he stayed in the Philistine territory. 12 So Achish trusted David, thinking,
"Since he has made himself repulsive to his people
Israel, he will be my servant forever."

SAUL AND THE MEDIUM

28 At that time, the Philistines gathered their military units into one army to fight against Israel.
So Achish said to David, "You know, of course, that you
and your men must march out in the army[C] with me."
2 David replied to Achish, "Good, you will find out
what your servant can do."

So Achish said to David, "Very well, I will appoint
you as my permanent bodyguard."
3 By this time Samuel had died, all Israel had
mourned for him and buried him in Ramah, his
city, and Saul had removed the mediums and spiritists from the land. 4 The Philistines gathered and
camped at Shunem. So Saul gathered all Israel, and
they camped at Gilboa. 5 When Saul saw the Philistine
camp, he was afraid and his heart pounded. 6 He inquired of the LORD, but the LORD did not answer him
in dreams or by the Urim or by the prophets. 7 Saul
then said to his servants, "Find me a woman who is
a medium, so I can go and consult her."

His servants replied, "There is a woman at En-dor
who is a medium."
8 Saul disguised himself by putting on different
clothes and set out with two of his men. They came
to the woman at night, and Saul said, "Consult a spirit
for me. Bring up for me the one I tell you."
9 But the woman said to him, "You surely know
what Saul has done, how he has cut off the mediums
and spiritists from the land. Why are you setting a
trap for me to get me killed?"
10 Then Saul swore to her by the LORD: "As surely
as the LORD lives, no punishment will come to you[D]
from this."
11 "Who is it that you want me to bring up for you?"
the woman asked.

"Bring up Samuel for me," he answered.
12 When the woman saw Samuel, she screamed,
and then she asked Saul, "Why did you deceive me?
You are Saul!"
13 But the king said to her, "Don't be afraid. What
do you see?"

"I see a spirit form[E] coming up out of the earth,"
the woman answered.
14 Then Saul asked her, "What does he look like?"

"An old man is coming up," she replied. "He's wearing a robe." Then Saul knew that it was Samuel, and
he knelt low with his face to the ground and paid
homage.
15 "Why have you disturbed me by bringing me up?"
Samuel asked Saul.

"I'm in serious trouble," replied Saul. "The Philistines are fighting against me and God has turned
away from me. He doesn't answer me anymore, either
through the prophets or in dreams. So I've called on
you to tell me what I should do."
16 Samuel answered, "Since the LORD has turned
away from you and has become your enemy, why are
you asking me? 17 The LORD has done[F] exactly what
he said through me: The LORD has torn the kingship
out of your hand and given it to your neighbor David. 18 You did not obey the LORD and did not carry
out his burning anger against Amalek; therefore the
LORD has done this to you today. 19 The LORD will also
hand Israel over to the Philistines along with you. Tomorrow you and your sons will be with me,[G] and the
LORD will hand Israel's army over to the Philistines."
20 Immediately, Saul fell flat on the ground. He was
terrified by Samuel's words and was also weak because he had not eaten anything all day and all night.
21 The woman came over to Saul, and she saw that he
was terrified and said to him, "Look, your servant
has obeyed you. I took my life in my hands and did

[A] **27:8** Alt Hb tradition reads *Gezerites* [B] **27:10** Some Hb mss, Syr, Tg; LXX, Vg, DSS read *"Against whom did you raid today?"*
[C] **28:1** DSS, LXX read *battle* [D] **28:10** Or *lives, you will not incur guilt*
[E] **28:13** Or *a god*, or *a divine being* [F] **28:17** Some Hb, some LXX mss, Vg read *done to you* [G] **28:19** LXX reads *sons will fall*

what you told me to do. 22 Now please listen to your
servant. Let me set some food in front of you. Eat and
it will give you strength so you can go on your way."
23 He refused, saying, "I won't eat," but when his
servants and the woman urged him, he listened to
them. He got up off the ground and sat on the bed.
24 The woman had a fattened calf at her house, and
she quickly slaughtered it. She also took flour, kneaded it, and baked unleavened bread. 25 She served it to
Saul and his servants, and they ate. Afterward, they
got up and left that night.

PHILISTINES REJECT DAVID

29 The Philistines brought all their military units
together at Aphek while Israel was camped
by the spring in Jezreel. 2 As the Philistine leaders
were passing in review with their units of hundreds
and thousands, David and his men were passing in
review behind them with Achish. 3 Then the Philistine commanders asked, "What are these Hebrews
doing here?"

Achish answered the Philistine commanders, "That
is David, servant of King Saul of Israel. He has been
with me a considerable period of time.[A] From the day
he defected until today, I've found no fault with him."
4 The Philistine commanders, however, were enraged with Achish and told him, "Send that man back
and let him return to the place you assigned him. He
must not go down with us into battle only to become
our adversary during the battle. What better way
could he ingratiate himself with his master than with
the heads of our men? 5 Isn't this the David they sing
about during their dances:

> Saul has killed his thousands,
> but David his tens of thousands?"

6 So Achish summoned David and told him, "As
the LORD lives, you are an honorable man. I think it
is good[B] to have you fighting[C] in this unit with me,
because I have found no fault in you from the day
you came to me until today. But the leaders don't
think you are reliable. 7 Now go back quietly and you
won't be doing anything the Philistine leaders think
is wrong."
8 "But what have I done?" David replied to Achish.
"From the first day I entered your service until today,
what have you found against your servant to keep
me from going to fight against the enemies of my
lord the king?"
9 Achish answered David, "I'm convinced that you
are as reliable as an angel of God. But the Philistine
commanders have said, 'He must not go into battle
with us.' 10 So get up early in the morning, you and
your masters' servants who came with you.[D] When
you've all gotten up early, go as soon as it's light." 11 So
David and his men got up early in the morning to return to the land of the Philistines. And the Philistines
went up to Jezreel.

DAVID'S DEFEAT OF THE AMALEKITES

30 David and his men arrived in Ziklag on the
third day. The Amalekites had raided the Negev and attacked and burned Ziklag. 2 They also had
kidnapped the women and everyone[E] in it from youngest to oldest. They had killed no one but had carried
them off as they went on their way.
3 When David and his men arrived at the town,
they found it burned. Their wives, sons, and daughters had been kidnapped. 4 David and the troops with
him wept loudly until they had no strength left to
weep. 5 David's two wives, Ahinoam the Jezreelite
and Abigail the widow of Nabal the Carmelite, had
also been kidnapped. 6 David was in an extremely
difficult position because the troops talked about
stoning him, for they were all very bitter over the
loss of their sons and daughters. But David found
strength in the LORD his God.
7 David said to the priest Abiathar son of Ahimelech, "Bring me the ephod." So Abiathar brought it
to him, 8 and David asked the LORD, "Should I pursue
these raiders? Will I overtake them?"

The LORD replied to him, "Pursue them, for you
will certainly overtake them and rescue the people."
9 So David and the six hundred men with him went.
They came to the Wadi Besor, where some stayed behind. 10 David and four hundred of the men continued
the pursuit, while two hundred stopped because they
were too exhausted to cross the Wadi Besor.
11 David's men found an Egyptian in the open country and brought him to David. They gave him some
bread to eat and water to drink. 12 Then they gave him
some pressed figs and two clusters of raisins. After
he ate he revived, for he hadn't eaten food or drunk
water for three days and three nights.
13 Then David said to him, "Who do you belong to?
Where are you from?"

"I'm an Egyptian, the slave of an Amalekite man,"
he said. "My master abandoned me when I got sick
three days ago. 14 We raided the south country of the
Cherethites, the territory of Judah, and the south
country of Caleb, and we burned Ziklag."
15 David then asked him, "Will you lead me to these
raiders?"

He said, "Swear to me by God that you won't kill
me or turn me over to my master, and I will lead you
to them."

[A] **29:3** Hb obscure [B] **29:6** Lit *It was good in my eyes* [C] **29:6** Lit *you going out and coming in* [D] **29:10** LXX adds *and go to the place I appointed you to. Don't take this evil matter to heart, for you are good before me.* [E] **30:2** LXX; MT omits *and everyone*

16 So he led him, and there were the Amalekites,
spread out over the entire area, eating, drinking, and
celebrating because of the great amount of plunder
they had taken from the land of the Philistines and
the land of Judah. 17 David slaughtered them from
twilight until the evening of the next day. None of
them escaped, except four hundred young men who
got on camels and fled.
18 David recovered everything the Amalekites had
taken; he also rescued his two wives. 19 Nothing of
theirs was missing from the youngest to the oldest,
including the sons and daughters, and all the plunder the Amalekites had taken. David got everything
back. 20 He took all the flocks and herds, which were
driven ahead of the other livestock, and the people
shouted, "This is David's plunder!"
21 When David came to the two hundred men who
had been too exhausted to go with him and had been
left at the Wadi Besor, they came out to meet him and
to meet the troops with him. When David approached
the men, he greeted them, 22 but all the corrupt and
worthless men among those who had gone with David argued, "Because they didn't go with us, we will
not give any of the plunder we recovered to them
except for each man's wife and children. They may
take them and go."
23 But David said, "My brothers, you must not do
this with what the LORD has given us. He protected us
and handed over to us the raiders who came against
us. 24 Who can agree to your proposal? The share of
the one who goes into battle is to be the same as the
share of the one who remains with the supplies. They
will share equally." 25 And it has been so from that day
forward. David established this policy[A] as a law and
an ordinance for Israel and it still continues today.
26 When David came to Ziklag, he sent some of the
plunder to his friends, the elders of Judah, saying,
"Here is a gift for you from the plunder of the LORD's
enemies." 27 He sent gifts[B] to those in Bethel, in Ramoth of the Negev, and in Jattir; 28 to those in Aroer,
in Siphmoth, and in Eshtemoa; 29 to those in Racal,
in the towns of the Jerahmeelites, and in the towns
of the Kenites; 30 to those in Hormah, in Bor-ashan,
and in Athach; 31 to those in Hebron, and to those in
all the places where David and his men had roamed.

THE DEATH OF SAUL AND HIS SONS

31 The Philistines fought against Israel, and Israel's men fled from them and were killed on
Mount Gilboa. 2 The Philistines pursued Saul and his
sons and killed his sons, Jonathan, Abinadab, and
Malchishua. 3 When the battle intensified against
Saul, the archers found him and severely wounded
him.[C] 4 Then Saul said to his armor-bearer, "Draw
your sword and run me through with it, or these
uncircumcised men will come and run me through
and torture me!" But his armor-bearer would not do
it because he was terrified. Then Saul took his sword
and fell on it. 5 When his armor-bearer saw that Saul
was dead, he also fell on his own sword and died with
him. 6 So on that day, Saul died together with his three
sons, his armor-bearer, and all his men.
7 When the men of Israel on the other side of the
valley and on the other side of the Jordan saw that
Israel's men had fled and that Saul and his sons were
dead, they abandoned the cities and fled. So the Philistines came and settled in them.
8 The next day when the Philistines came to strip
the slain, they found Saul and his three sons dead
on Mount Gilboa. 9 They cut off Saul's head, stripped
off his armor, and sent messengers throughout the
land of the Philistines to spread the good news in the
temples of their idols and among the people. 10 Then
they put his armor in the temple of the Ashtoreths
and hung his body on the wall of Beth-shan.
11 When the residents of Jabesh-gilead heard what
the Philistines had done to Saul, 12 all their brave men
set out, journeyed all night, and retrieved the body
of Saul and the bodies of his sons from the wall of
Beth-shan. When they arrived at Jabesh, they burned
the bodies there. 13 Afterward, they took their bones
and buried them under the tamarisk tree in Jabesh
and fasted seven days.

[A] **30:25** *this policy* supplied for clarity [B] **30:27** *He sent gifts* supplied for clarity [C] **31:3** LXX reads *and he was wounded under the ribs*

The Philistines at War

by R. Kelvin Moore

History, archaeology, and the Bible reveal much about the Philistines and their methods in war. The Philistine army consisted of highly trained, one might conclude, professional soldiers.[1] The Israelites were little more than farmers and shepherds.[2] The Philistines' well-organized army stood in stark contrast to the loose-knit Israelite tribal system.

A portion of the Philistines' army fought in chariots drawn by two horses with a driver and two warriors.[3] The infantry fought in formations of four men armed with long straight swords and spears. All four soldiers were equipped with round shields.[4] Philistine archers used powerful bows with metal arrows rather than stone or wood.

Assuming Goliath was not abnormal except for his stature,[5] a battle-ready Philistine soldier wore a bronze helmet, a coat of mail, and leg protectors.[6] His spear was large and heavy, possibly a "loop javelin."[7] His sword may have been a scimitar.[8] The first weapon mentioned in 1 Samuel 17:45, the "sword," was the double-edged pointed sword used for thrusting. The Philistines were well acquainted with the psychological side of warfare. Their warriors wore plumed or feathered headdresses, which added height to their physical appearance. The professional soldier of the Philistine army, armed with the latest military implements of the day, was overmatched for the poorly armed and poorly trained Israelites.

The Philistine military's effectiveness coerced the Israelites into a guerrilla-type warfare (2Sm 5:23). The Philistine army was large (1Sm 13:5); David's, by comparison, was small. The Philistine army used heavy armor. Without heavy armor, the Israelites moved quickly in a "slash and dash" strategy. The Philistines preferred fighting in the plains where their chariots were most effective. The Israelites preferred to fight in the hills rendering the chariot useless.[9] ✣

---

[1] LaMoine DeVries, "Philistines, The" in *HolBD*, 1108; Richard A. Gabriel, *The Military History of Ancient Israel* (Westport, CT: Praeger, 2003), 25. [2] V. Gilbert Beers, *The Victor Handbook of Bible Knowledge* (Wheaton, IL: Victor Books, 1981), 138. [3] William Sanford LaSor, "Philistines" in *ISBE*, vol. 3 (1986), 844. [4] LaSor, "Philistines." [5] See John Bright, *A History of Israel*, 3rd ed. (Philadelphia: Westminster, 1981), 185: "Goliath's armor (1 Sam. 17:5-7) was probably unusual only for its bulk. . . . As for [Goliath's] sword, there was 'none like it' (1 Sam. 21:9)."

[6] Edward E. Hindson, *The Philistines and the Old Testament* (Grand Rapids: Baker, 1971), 154: Goliath looked like "a typical Aegean warrior." [7] Hindson, *Philistines.* [8] Bierling, 148. In addition to "javelin," Francis Brown, S. R. Driver, and Charles A. Briggs, *The New Brown, Driver, and Briggs Hebrew and English Lexicon of the Old Testament* (Lafayette, IN: Associated Publishers and Authors, 1981), 475, offers "dart." See "כִּידוֹן." [9] Beers, *Victor Handbook*, 139.

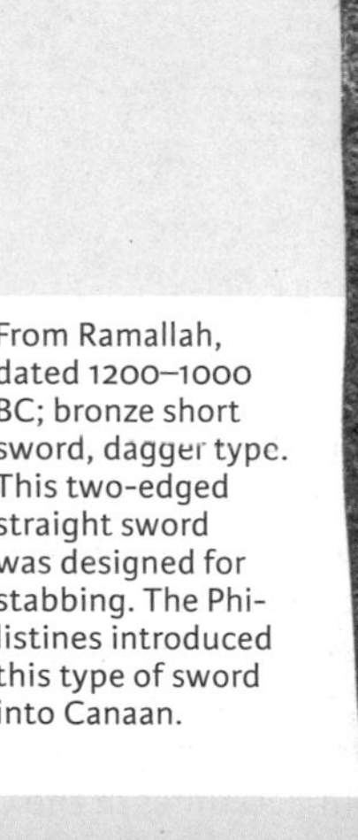

From Ramallah, dated 1200–1000 BC; bronze short sword, dagger type. This two-edged straight sword was designed for stabbing. The Philistines introduced this type of sword into Canaan.

Mount Gilboa was the location for King Saul's final battle against the Philistines. They killed three of his sons: Jonathan, Abinadab, and Malchishua.

by E. LeBron Matthews

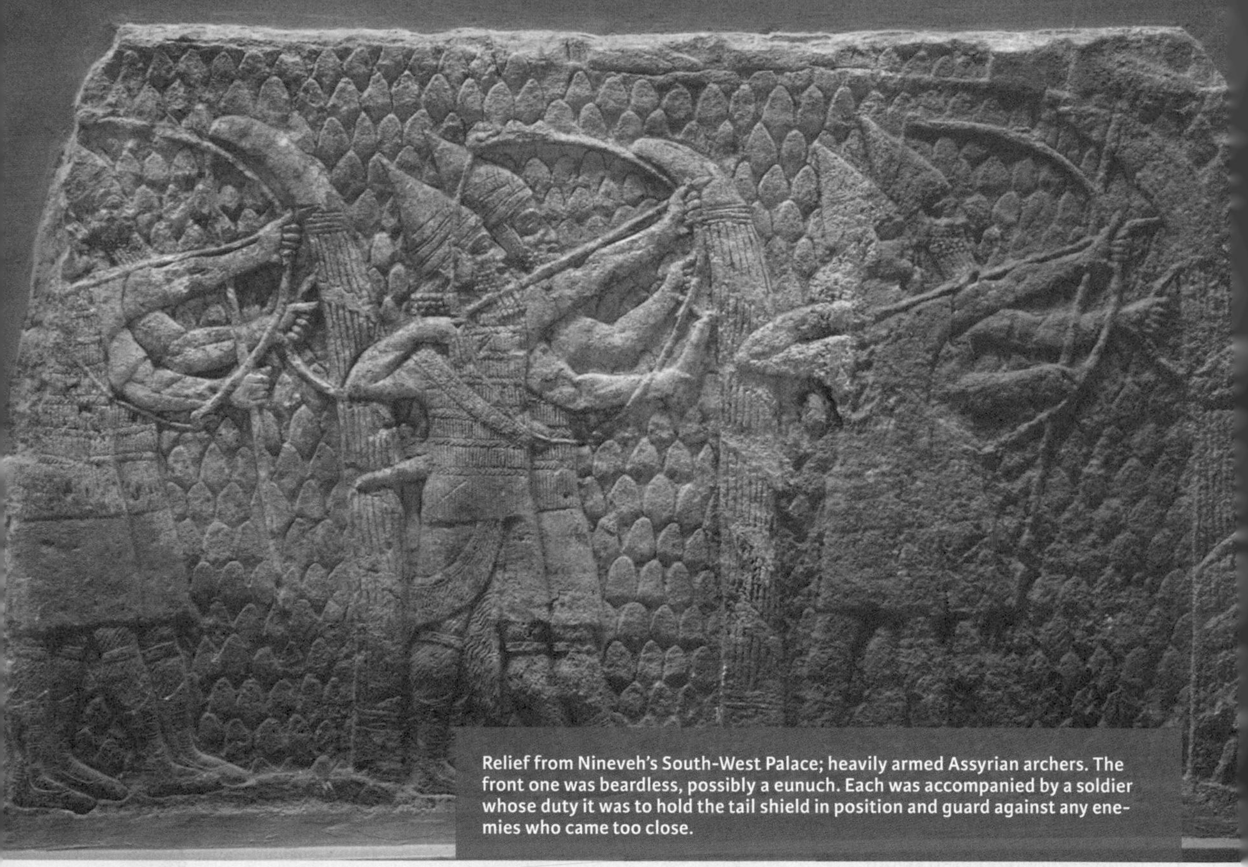

Relief from Nineveh's South-West Palace; heavily armed Assyrian archers. The front one was beardless, possibly a eunuch. Each was accompanied by a soldier whose duty it was to hold the tail shield in position and guard against any enemies who came too close.

The Hebrew phrase rendered *armor-bearer* literally means "the one carrying his equipment." The word for *equipment* designated a wide variety of items, including containers, tools, weapons, musical instruments, and even jewelry. It occurs about 320 times in the Old Testament and is rendered into English according to the context.[1] The translation "armor-bearer" is derived from a soldier's equipment. The primary task assigned to these soldiers seems to have been carrying the king's or commander's armor, shield, extra weapons, and baggage. However, Goliath was assigned a shield-bearer (1Sm 17:7). Thus, extraordinary warriors could receive similar assistance.

One of the armor-bearer's duties was positioning a shield to protect his assigned superior. This allowed elite warriors such as Goliath to use both hands with long-range weapons such as javelins or arrows. As combat turned into hand-to-hand fighting, the warrior could exchange these weapons for the shield and sword. The armor-bearer then took the bow and unexpended projectiles. On the battlefield, kings and other army commanders faced the same risks as common soldiers. Consequently the armor-bearer enabled the commander to be ready to defend himself if necessary, and yet move freely between units under his command. At times armor-bearers killed wounded enemy soldiers left on the battlefield.[2]

Living four centuries in Egypt without question influenced the military Israel developed during and after the exodus. The Egyptian army began to employ armor during that period, primarily on the army's ranking officers.[3] Private soldiers still dressed in short linen kilts and carried an elongated shield crafted from wood and leather.[4] Egyptian chariot archers wore a mail coat made of 450 bronze scales stitched together in overlapping rows.[5]

Jonathan's armor-bearer was an experienced professional soldier. The Hebrew word for attendant in 1 Samuel 14:6 commonly refers to adolescent boys. However, the term had a specific military connotation. It denoted experienced warriors as opposed to militia.[6] This suggests that armor-bearers had proven their ability in combat. The commander entrusted his life to these attendants. In the brutal warfare of the ancient world, an army commander's death often also meant the subsequent extermination of his army and even entire villages of his people. Being an armor-bearer, therefore, was a crucial responsibility.

When Saul became king, Israel did not have a professional army. It relied on mustering the military-age men during a crisis. In Saul's initial campaigns, certain soldiers emerged as being dependable and capable. So the king selected three thousand of these to serve permanently. He organized this force into two units. Two thousand men served directly under him; the rest were under the command of his eldest son, Jonathan. This force became the nucleus of a standing army. Their task was to defend the kingdom until the tribal contingents could be mobilized.

Jonathan and his armor-bearer unexpectedly attacked a Philistine outpost and killed twenty men. Panic gripped the entire Philistine force, and Israel won an important victory. The incident demonstrates the extreme loyalty and bravery of the armor-bearer. When Jonathan proposed that the two men—by themselves—attack a much larger body of Philistines, the armor-bearer readily agreed to go. Most soldiers would have likely considered this a suicide mission with no possibility for success. Jonathan's armor-bearer, though, never hesitated.

David became Saul's "armor-bearer" (1Sm 16:21). His responsibilities seem limited to playing the harp. So the term may have a more restrictive application in this case. Nevertheless, it retains three very significant attributes of the armor-bearer. First, David was entrusted with the well-being of the king and, by extension the nation. Second, he had proven experience at the task assigned to him. And third, the position created a close, personal relationship with his superior. ✣

---

[1] K.-M. Beyse, "יִלְכּ" (*keli*; container, tool, weapon) in *Theological Dictionary of the Old Testament* (*TDOT*), ed. G. Johannes Botterweck and Helmer Ringgren, trans. John T. Willis et al., vol. 7 (Grand Rapids: Eerdmans, 1995), 169–75. [2] Daniel C. Fredericks, "Arms and Armor" in *HIBD*, 116; William White Jr., "Armor-bearer" in *ZPEB*, 1:321. [3] Barbara Mertz, *Red Land, Black Land: Daily Life in Ancient Egypt*, rev. ed. (New York: Dodd, Mead, 1978), 142–43. [4] *What Life Was Like on the Banks of the Nile: Egypt 3050–30 BC* (Alexandria, VA: Time-Life Books, 1996), 124. [5] *What Life Was Like*, 125. [6] H. F. Fuhs, "רַעַנ, naar; הָרֲעַנ, naarah; םיִרוּעְנ neurim, תוֹרֻעְנ neurot, רַעֹנ noar" in *TDOT*, vol. 4 (1998), 482.

2 SAMUEL

South of the City of David, base of a wall that was about 10 feet wide; dated to Middle Bronze Age (2220–1550 BC). The Assyrians destroyed the wall in 701 BC.

INTRODUCTION TO

2 SAMUEL

Circumstances of Writing

Early tradition suggests 1 and 2 Samuel were originally one book. Some scholars believe Samuel was largely responsible for the material up to 1 Samuel 25 and that the prophets Nathan and Gad gave significant input to the rest (based on 1Ch 29:29). This proposal, however, must remain speculative, because the books name no authors. First Samuel 27:6 suggests the book was not completed until perhaps a few generations after the division of the kingdom around 930 BC.

After Israel's conquest of the land during the days of Joshua, Israel entered a time of apostasy. The book of Judges describes recurrences of a cycle with predictable phases. First, the people sinned against the Lord and fell into idolatry. Second, the Lord raised up an adversary to afflict them and turn them back to him. Third, the people cried out to the Lord in repentance. Fourth, the Lord brought deliverance for them through a judge whom he raised up. The book of Judges' famous verse, "In those days there was no king in Israel; everyone did whatever seemed right to him" (21:25), aptly describes the period. The book of 1 Samuel picks up the historical record toward the end of those stormy days.

Contribution to the Bible

The books of 1 and 2 Samuel describe Israel's transition from a loosely organized tribal league under God (a theocracy) to centralized leadership under a king who answered to God (a monarchy). Samuel's life and ministry greatly shaped this period of restructuring as he consistently pointed people back to God.

Saul's rule highlighted the dangers to which the Israelites fell victim as they clamored for a king to lead them. Samuel's warnings fell on deaf ears (1Sm 8:10–20) because God's people were intent on becoming like the nations around them. In the end, they got exactly what they asked for, but they paid a terrible price. Saul's life stands as a warning to trust God's timing for life's provisions.

David's rule testified to the amazing works the Lord could and would do through a life yielded to him. Israel's second king seemed quite aware of God's blessing on his life and displayed a tender heart toward the things of God (2Sm 5:12; 7:1–2; 22:1–51; 23:1–7). Later generations would receive blessing because of David's life (Is 37:35). God's special covenant with David (2Sm 7:1–29) found its ultimate fulfillment in Jesus, the Son of David (Lk 1:32–33). The consequences of David's sin with Bathsheba, however, stand as a warning to all who experience sin's attraction. God holds his children accountable for their actions, and even forgiven sin can have terrible consequences.

Structure

Second Samuel 1–4 describes the struggle for Israel's throne that began with Saul's death. David was anointed king by the men of Judah (2:4), but Abner anointed Ish-bosheth, Saul's oldest surviving son, as king over Israel (2:8–9). A two-year civil war resulted in Ish-bosheth's death and in David's becoming king over all Israel.

Second Samuel 5–24 presents highlights of David's reign. God established a special covenant with David, promising to establish the throne of his kingdom forever (7:1–29). David's sin with Bathsheba, however, brought disastrous consequences to his reign and became a turning point in 2 Samuel. In the end, David's repentance confirmed his designation as a man after God's heart, but his sin showed that even the king is not above breaking God's laws.

RESPONSES TO SAUL'S DEATH

1 After the death of Saul, David returned from
defeating the Amalekites and stayed at Ziklag
two days. 2 On the third day a man with torn clothes
and dust on his head came from Saul's camp. When
he came to David, he fell to the ground and paid
homage. 3 David asked him, "Where have you come
from?"
He replied to him, "I've escaped from the Israelite
camp."
4 "What was the outcome? Tell me," David asked
him.
"The troops fled from the battle," he answered.
"Many of the troops have fallen and are dead. Also,
Saul and his son Jonathan are dead."
5 David asked the young man who had brought
him the report, "How do you know Saul and his son
Jonathan are dead?"
6 "I happened to be on Mount Gilboa," he replied,
"and there was Saul, leaning on his spear. At that very
moment the chariots and the cavalry were closing
in on him. 7 When he turned around and saw me,
he called out to me, so I answered: I'm at your service. 8 He asked me, 'Who are you?' I told him: I'm
an Amalekite. 9 Then he begged me, 'Stand over me
and kill me, for I'm mortally wounded,[A] but my life
still lingers.' 10 So I stood over him and killed him
because I knew that after he had fallen he couldn't
survive. I took the crown that was on his head and
the armband that was on his arm, and I've brought
them here to my lord."
11 Then David took hold of his clothes and tore
them, and all the men with him did the same. 12 They
mourned, wept, and fasted until the evening for those
who died by the sword — for Saul, his son Jonathan,
the LORD's people, and the house of Israel.
13 David inquired of the young man who had
brought him the report, "Where are you from?"
"I'm the son of a resident alien," he said. "I'm an
Amalekite."
14 David questioned him, "How is it that you were
not afraid to lift your hand to destroy the LORD's
anointed?" 15 Then David summoned one of his servants and said, "Come here and kill him!" The servant
struck him, and he died. 16 For David had said to the
Amalekite, "Your blood is on your own head because
your own mouth testified against you by saying, 'I
killed the LORD's anointed.'"
17 David sang the following lament for Saul and his
son Jonathan, 18 and he ordered that the Judahites be
taught The Song of the Bow. It is written in the Book
of Jashar:[B]

19 The splendor of Israel lies slain
on your heights.
How the mighty have fallen!
20 Do not tell it in Gath,
don't announce it in the marketplaces
of Ashkelon,
or the daughters of the Philistines will rejoice,
and the daughters of the uncircumcised
will celebrate.
21 Mountains of Gilboa,
let no dew or rain be on you,
or fields of offerings,[C]
for there the shield of the mighty
was defiled —
the shield of Saul, no longer anointed with oil.
22 Jonathan's bow never retreated,
Saul's sword never returned unstained,[D]
from the blood of the slain,
from the flesh[E] of the mighty.
23 Saul and Jonathan,
loved and delightful,
they were not parted in life or in death.
They were swifter than eagles,
stronger than lions.
24 Daughters of Israel, weep for Saul,
who clothed you in scarlet,
with luxurious things,
who decked your garments
with gold ornaments.
25 How the mighty have fallen in the thick
of battle!
Jonathan lies slain on your heights.
26 I grieve for you, Jonathan, my brother.
You were such a friend to me.
Your love for me was more wondrous
than the love of women.
27 How the mighty have fallen
and the weapons of war have perished!

DAVID, KING OF JUDAH

2 Some time later, David inquired of the LORD:
"Should I go to one of the towns of Judah?"
The LORD answered him, "Go."
Then David asked, "Where should I go?"
"To Hebron," the LORD replied.
2 So David went there with his two wives, Ahinoam
the Jezreelite and Abigail, the widow of Nabal the
Carmelite. 3 In addition, David brought the men who
were with him, each one with his family, and they
settled in the towns near Hebron. 4 Then the men of
Judah came, and there they anointed David king over
the house of Judah. They told David, "It was the men
of Jabesh-gilead who buried Saul."
5 David sent messengers to the men of Jabesh-gilead and said to them, "The LORD bless you because

[A] **1:9** LXX reads *for terrible darkness has taken hold of me*
[B] **1:18** Or *of the Upright* [C] **1:21** LXX reads *firstfruits* [D] **1:22** Lit *empty*
[E] **1:22** Lit *fat*

Why Anoint?

by Robert C. Dunston

Relief of Horus and Ptah anointing the king; outside the first pylon (the first entrance building) at the temple of Sobek and Haroeris in Kom Ombo, Egypt.

Anointing involved smearing or pouring oil on a person or an object. People typically used olive oil; at times they also used oils from plants, nuts, and fish. Sometimes they mixed the oils with aromatic spices (Ex 30:22–25).[1]

People used anointing for various common purposes. Naomi instructed Ruth to anoint herself with oil before meeting Boaz (Ru 3:3). Anointing with oil was also used for medicinal purposes (Is 1:6) and when preparing a body for burial (Mk 16:1). The word *anoint* also occurs referring to oiling a shield (Is 21:5), painting a house (Jr 22:14), and coating unleavened bread with oil (Lv 2:4).[2]

Although people anointed for everyday purposes, the Bible most often speaks of anointing in the context of setting an object or person apart for God. Such objects or persons then fulfilled a special function in the worship or service of God.

After Jacob had his vision of the stairway reaching from earth to heaven, he set up a stone as a marker and anointed it (Gn 28:18). Anointing indicated the stone was not simply a marker, but a holy reminder of a holy event and God's presence. Moses anointed the tabernacle, the altar, the basin and stand, and all the vessels used in worship, setting them apart from everyday use (Ex 40:9–11). Someone who broke a pot could not go to the tabernacle and borrow a vessel for cooking a meal or storing water. Those vessels exclusively served a religious function. The tabernacle, the altar, and the vessels were holy, set apart for worshiping God. The act of anointing them with oil indicated their holiness and their separation from common use.

Moses also anointed his brother Aaron and Aaron's sons to be priests (Ex 40:12–15). This anointing not only set Aaron and his sons apart, but also initiated a permanent priesthood. Following this tradition, the Israelites continued to anoint the priest and especially the high priest, as he came to serve in this important office and function (Lv 21:10–12). Only one instance exists of a biblical prophet being anointed and that is Elijah's anointing of Elisha to succeed him (1Kg 19:16). Yet other prophets considered themselves anointed as well, although by God's Spirit rather than by human agency (Is 61:1).

Most references to the anointing of persons are to the anointing of kings. A prophet alone might anoint the new king as when Samuel anointed Saul (1Sm 10:1) and David (16:13). In some cases, the people anointed the new king. David had already been anointed by Samuel, but following Saul's death the people of Judah anointed David as king (2Sm 2:4). Later the elders of the other Israelite tribes anointed David as their king too (5:3).

The Hittites anointed their kings as part of their enthronement ceremony. The act conferred on the new leader the right and power to rule. The Assyrians and Babylonians did not anoint their kings. In Egypt, the new pharaoh did not receive anointing, but he anointed his high officials into office. Among the Hittites and in Egypt, anointing indicated an individual's elevation to a particular office with the accompanying authority to execute the role.[3]

In the Old Testament, the anointing of a king indicated his new position, but it seems also to have indicated that God had conveyed "power and ability to perform the function for which one was being anointed. It further designated that the person had been chosen by God (1 Sam 9:16), and so kings in particular could be referred to as 'the Lord's anointed' (24:6)."[4] As the Spirit of the Lord entered the judges so that they could deliver their people (Jdg 3:10; 6:34), so the ceremony of anointing symbolized the Spirit of the Lord entering the king and empowering him to lead God's people in God's ways (1Sm 16:13).

As someone God chose and set apart for his service, the anointed king represented the Lord in a special way. To honor the king was to honor God. To disrespect the king was to disrespect God. Twice David had the opportunity to kill Saul and become king (1Sm 24:1–22; 26:1–25), but each time he refused. David respected Saul as God's anointed for as long as Saul lived.

Isaiah foretold that the Lord would use "his anointed" (Is 45:1) to bring the Jews back from Babylonian captivity. Another—the Messiah, God's anointed One—would ultimately come and sit on David's throne and rule with perfect justice and righteousness (9:6–7). ✤

---

[1] Mike Mitchell, "Anoint, Anointed" in *HIBD*, 70. [2] Klaus Seybold, "שָׁמַח ,שָׁמַחִי" (*mashach*, to anoint; *mashiach*, anointed one) in *TDOT* vol. 9 (1998), 45. [3] Franz Hesse, "χρίω" (*chrio*, to smear or anoint) in *Theological Dictionary of the New Testament* (*TDNT*), ed. Gerhard Friedrich, trans. Geoffrey W. Bromiley, vol. 9 (Grand Rapids: Eerdmans, 1974), 496–97. [4] Timothy B. Cargal, "Anoint" in *EDB*, 66.

you have shown this kindness to Saul your lord when
you buried him. 6 Now, may the LORD show kindness
and faithfulness to you, and I will also show the same
goodness to you because you have done this deed.
7 Therefore, be strong[A] and valiant, for though Saul
your lord is dead, the house of Judah has anointed
me king over them."

8 Abner son of Ner, commander of Saul's army, took
Saul's son Ish-bosheth[B,C] and moved him to Mahanaim. 9 He made him king over Gilead, Asher, Jezreel,
Ephraim, Benjamin — over all Israel. 10 Saul's son
Ish-bosheth was forty years old when he became
king over Israel; he reigned for two years. The house
of Judah, however, followed David. 11 The length of
time that David was king in Hebron over the house
of Judah was seven years and six months.

12 Abner son of Ner and soldiers of Ish-bosheth son
of Saul marched out from Mahanaim to Gibeon. 13 So
Joab son of Zeruiah and David's soldiers marched out
and met them by the pool of Gibeon. The two groups
took up positions on opposite sides of the pool.

14 Then Abner said to Joab, "Let's have the young
men get up and compete in front of us."

"Let them get up," Joab replied.

15 So they got up and were counted off — twelve
for Benjamin and Ish-bosheth son of Saul, and
twelve from David's soldiers. 16 Then each man
grabbed his opponent by the head and thrust his
sword into his opponent's side so that they all died
together. So this place, which is in Gibeon, is named
Field of Blades.[D]

17 The battle that day was extremely fierce, and Abner and the men of Israel were defeated by David's
soldiers. 18 The three sons of Zeruiah were there: Joab,
Abishai, and Asahel. Asahel was a fast runner, like
one of the wild gazelles. 19 He chased Abner and did
not turn to the right or the left in his pursuit of him.
20 Abner glanced back and said, "Is that you, Asahel?"

"Yes it is," Asahel replied.

21 Abner said to him, "Turn to your right or left, seize
one of the young soldiers, and take whatever you
can get from him." But Asahel would not stop chasing him. 22 Once again, Abner warned Asahel, "Stop
chasing me. Why should I strike you to the ground?
How could I ever look your brother Joab in the face?"

23 But Asahel refused to turn away, so Abner hit
him in the stomach with the butt of his spear. The
spear went through his body, and he fell and died
right there. As they all came to the place where Asahel had fallen and died, they stopped, 24 but Joab and
Abishai pursued Abner. By sunset, they had gone as
far as the hill of Ammah, which is opposite Giah on
the way to the wilderness of Gibeon.

25 The Benjaminites rallied to Abner; they formed
a unit and took their stand on top of a hill. 26 Then
Abner called out to Joab, "Must the sword devour
forever? Don't you realize this will only end in bitterness? How long before you tell the troops to stop
pursuing their brothers?"

27 "As God lives," Joab replied, "if you had not spoken up, the troops wouldn't have stopped pursuing
their brothers until morning." 28 Then Joab blew the
ram's horn, and all the troops stopped; they no longer
pursued Israel or continued to fight. 29 So Abner and
his men marched through the Arabah all that night.
They crossed the Jordan, marched all morning,[E] and
arrived at Mahanaim.

30 When Joab had turned back from pursuing Abner, he gathered all the troops. In addition to Asahel,
nineteen of David's soldiers were missing, 31 but they
had killed 360 of the Benjaminites and Abner's men.
32 Afterward, they carried Asahel to his father's tomb
in Bethlehem and buried him. Then Joab and his men
marched all night and reached Hebron at dawn.

CIVIL WAR

3 During the long war between the house of Saul
and the house of David, David was growing stronger and the house of Saul was becoming weaker.

2 Sons were born to David in Hebron:

His firstborn was Amnon,
by Ahinoam the Jezreelite;
3 his second was Chileab,
by Abigail, the widow of Nabal the Carmelite;
the third was Absalom,
son of Maacah the daughter of King Talmai
of Geshur;
4 the fourth was Adonijah,
son of Haggith;
the fifth was Shephatiah,
son of Abital;
5 the sixth was Ithream,
by David's wife Eglah.

These were born to David in Hebron.

6 During the war between the house of Saul and the
house of David, Abner kept acquiring more power in
the house of Saul. 7 Now Saul had a concubine whose
name was Rizpah daughter of Aiah, and Ish-bosheth
questioned Abner, "Why did you sleep with my father's concubine?"

8 Abner was very angry about Ish-bosheth's accusation. "Am I a dog's head[F] who belongs to Judah?"
he asked. "All this time I've been loyal to the family
of your father Saul, to his brothers, and to his friends
and haven't betrayed you to David, but now you accuse me of wrongdoing with this woman! 9 May God

[A] **2:7** Lit *Therefore, strengthen your hands* [B] **2:8** Some LXX mss read *Ishbaal*; 1Ch 8:33; 9:39 [C] **2:8** = Man of Shame [D] **2:16** Or *Helkath-hazzurim* [E] **2:29** Or *marched through the Bithron* [F] **3:8** = a despised person

punish Abner and do so severely if I don't do for David what the LORD swore to him: 10 to transfer the kingdom from the house of Saul and establish the throne of David over Israel and Judah from Dan to Beer-sheba." 11 Ish-bosheth did not dare respond to Abner because he was afraid of him.

12 Abner sent messengers as his representatives to say to David, "Whose land is it? Make your covenant with me, and you can be certain I am on your side to turn all Israel over to you."

13 David replied, "Good, I will make a covenant with you. However, there's one thing I require of you: You will not see my face unless you first bring Saul's daughter Michal when you come to see me."

14 Then David sent messengers to say to Ish-bosheth son of Saul, "Give me back my wife Michal. I was engaged to her for the price of a hundred Philistine foreskins."

15 So Ish-bosheth sent someone to take her away from her husband, Paltiel son of Laish. 16 Her husband followed her, weeping all the way to Bahurim. Abner said to him, "Go back." So he went back.

THE ASSASSINATION OF ABNER

17 Abner conferred with the elders of Israel: "In the past you wanted David to be king over you. 18 Now take action, because the LORD has spoken concerning David: 'Through my servant David I will save my people Israel from the power of the Philistines and the power of all Israel's enemies.' "

19 Abner also informed the Benjaminites and went to Hebron to inform David about all that was agreed on by Israel and the whole house of Benjamin. 20 When Abner and twenty men came to David at Hebron, David held a banquet for him and his men.

21 Abner said to David, "Let me now go and I will gather all Israel to my lord the king. They will make a covenant with you, and you will reign over all you desire." So David dismissed Abner, and he went in peace.

22 Just then David's soldiers and Joab returned from a raid and brought a large amount of plundered goods with them. Abner was not with David in Hebron because David had dismissed him, and he had gone in peace. 23 When Joab and his whole army arrived, Joab was informed, "Abner son of Ner came to see the king, the king dismissed him, and he went in peace."

24 Joab went to the king and said, "What have you done? Look here, Abner came to you. Why did you dismiss him? Now he's getting away. 25 You know that Abner son of Ner came to deceive you and to find out about your military activities[A] and everything you're doing." 26 Then Joab left David and sent messengers after Abner. They brought him back from the well[B] of Sirah, but David was unaware of it. 27 When Abner returned to Hebron, Joab pulled him aside to the middle of the city gate, as if to speak to him privately, and there Joab stabbed him in the stomach. So Abner died in revenge for the death of Asahel,[C] Joab's brother.

28 David heard about it later and said, "I and my kingdom are forever innocent before the LORD concerning the blood of Abner son of Ner. 29 May it hang over Joab's head and his father's whole family, and may the house of Joab never be without someone who has a discharge or a skin disease, or a man who can only work a spindle,[D] or someone who falls by the sword or starves." 30 Joab and his brother Abishai killed Abner because he had put their brother Asahel to death in the battle at Gibeon.

31 David then ordered Joab and all the people who were with him, "Tear your clothes, put on sackcloth, and mourn over Abner." And King David walked behind the coffin.[E]

32 When they buried Abner in Hebron, the king wept aloud at Abner's tomb. All the people wept, 33 and the king sang a lament for Abner:

Should Abner die as a fool dies?
34 Your hands were not bound,
your feet not placed in bronze shackles.
You fell like one who falls victim to criminals.

And all the people wept over him even more.

35 Then they came to urge David to eat food while it was still day, but David took an oath: "May God punish me and do so severely if I taste bread or anything else before sunset!" 36 All the people took note of this, and it pleased them. In fact, everything the king did pleased them. 37 On that day all the troops and all Israel were convinced that the king had no part in the killing of Abner son of Ner.

38 Then the king said to his soldiers, "You must know that a great leader has fallen in Israel today. 39 As for me, even though I am the anointed king, I have little power today. These men, the sons of Zeruiah, are too fierce for me. May the LORD repay the evildoer according to his evil!"

THE ASSASSINATION OF ISH-BOSHETH

4 When Saul's son Ish-bosheth heard that Abner had died in Hebron, he gave up,[F] and all Israel was dismayed. 2 Saul's son had two men who were leaders of raiding parties: one named Baanah and the other Rechab, sons of Rimmon the Beerothite of the Benjaminites. Beeroth is also considered part of Benjamin, 3 and the Beerothites fled to Gittaim and still reside there as aliens today.

[A] **3:25** Lit *your going out and your coming in* [B] **3:26** Or *cistern* [C] **3:27** Lit *And he died for the blood of Asahel* [D] **3:29** LXX reads *who uses a crutch* [E] **3:31** Or *the bier*; lit *the bed* [F] **4:1** Lit *his hands dropped*

4 Saul's son Jonathan had a son whose feet were crippled. He was five years old when the report about Saul and Jonathan came from Jezreel. His nanny picked him up and fled, but as she was hurrying to flee, he fell and became lame. His name was Mephibosheth.

5 Rechab and Baanah, the sons of Rimmon the Beerothite, set out and arrived at Ish-bosheth's house during the heat of the day while the king was taking his midday nap. 6 They entered the interior of the house as if to get wheat and stabbed him in the stomach. Then Rechab and his brother Baanah escaped. 7 They had entered the house while Ish-bosheth was lying on his bed in his bedroom and stabbed and killed him. They removed his head, took it, and traveled by way of the Arabah all night. 8 They brought Ish-bosheth's head to David at Hebron and said to the king, "Here's the head of Ish-bosheth son of Saul, your enemy who intended to take your life. Today the LORD has granted vengeance to my lord the king against Saul and his offspring."

9 But David answered Rechab and his brother Baanah, sons of Rimmon the Beerothite, "As the LORD lives, the one who has redeemed my life from every distress, 10 when the person told me, 'Look, Saul is dead,' he thought he was a bearer of good news, but I seized him and put him to death at Ziklag. That was my reward to him for his news! 11 How much more when wicked men kill a righteous man in his own house on his own bed! So now, should I not require his blood from you and purge you from the earth?"

12 So David gave orders to the young men, and they killed Rechab and Baanah. They cut off their hands and feet and hung their bodies by the pool in Hebron, but they took Ish-bosheth's head and buried it in Abner's tomb in Hebron.

DAVID, KING OF ISRAEL

5 All the tribes of Israel came to David at Hebron and said, "Here we are, your own flesh and blood.[A] 2 Even while Saul was king over us, you were the one who led us out to battle and brought us back. The LORD also said to you, 'You will shepherd my people Israel, and you will be ruler over Israel.'"

3 So all the elders of Israel came to the king at Hebron. King David made a covenant with them at Hebron in the LORD's presence, and they anointed David king over Israel.

4 David was thirty years old when he began his reign; he reigned forty years. 5 In Hebron he reigned over Judah seven years and six months, and in Jerusalem he reigned thirty-three years over all Israel and Judah.

6 The king and his men marched to Jerusalem against the Jebusites who inhabited the land. The Jebusites had said to David, "You will never get in here. Even the blind and lame can repel you" thinking, "David can't get in here."

7 Yet David did capture the stronghold of Zion, that is, the city of David. 8 He said that day, "Whoever attacks the Jebusites must go through the water shaft to reach the lame and the blind who are despised by David."[B] For this reason it is said, "The blind and the lame will never enter the house."[C]

9 David took up residence in the stronghold, which he named the city of David. He built it up all the way around from the supporting terraces inward. 10 David became more and more powerful, and the LORD God of Armies was with him. 11 King Hiram of Tyre sent envoys to David; he also sent cedar logs, carpenters, and stonemasons, and they built a palace for David. 12 Then David knew that the LORD had established him as king over Israel and had exalted his kingdom for the sake of his people Israel.

13 After he arrived from Hebron, David took more concubines and wives from Jerusalem, and more sons and daughters were born to him. 14 These are the names of those born to him in Jerusalem: Shammua, Shobab, Nathan, Solomon, 15 Ibhar, Elishua, Nepheg, Japhia, 16 Elishama, Eliada, and Eliphelet.

17 When the Philistines heard that David had been anointed king over Israel, they all went in search of David, but he heard about it and went down to the stronghold. 18 So the Philistines came and spread out in Rephaim Valley.

19 Then David inquired of the LORD: "Should I attack the Philistines? Will you hand them over to me?"

The LORD replied to David, "Attack, for I will certainly hand the Philistines over to you."

20 So David went to Baal-perazim and defeated them there and said, "Like a bursting flood, the LORD has burst out against my enemies before me." Therefore, he named that place The Lord Bursts Out.[D] 21 The Philistines abandoned their idols there, and David and his men carried them off.

22 The Philistines came up again and spread out in Rephaim Valley. 23 So David inquired of the LORD, and he answered, "Do not attack directly, but circle around behind them and come at them opposite the balsam trees. 24 When you hear the sound of marching in the tops of the balsam trees, act decisively, for then the LORD will have gone out ahead of you to strike down the army of the Philistines." 25 So David did exactly as the LORD commanded him, and he struck down the Philistines all the way from Geba to Gezer.

[A] **5:1** Lit *your bone and your flesh* [B] **5:8** Alt Hb tradition, LXX, Tg, Syr read *who despise David* [C] **5:8** Or *temple*, or *palace* [D] **5:20** Or *Baal-perazim*; 2Sm 6:8; 1Ch 13:11

DAVID MOVES THE ARK

6 David again assembled all the fit young men in Israel: thirty thousand. 2 He and all his troops set out to bring the ark of God from Baale-judah.[A] The ark bears the Name, the name of the LORD of Armies who is enthroned between the cherubim. 3 They set the ark of God on a new cart and transported it from Abinadab's house, which was on the hill. Uzzah and Ahio,[B] sons of Abinadab, were guiding the cart 4 and brought it with the ark of God from Abinadab's house on the hill. Ahio walked in front of the ark. 5 David and the whole house of Israel were dancing before the LORD with all kinds of fir wood instruments,[C] lyres, harps, tambourines, sistrums,[D] and cymbals.

6 When they came to Nacon's threshing floor, Uzzah reached out to the ark of God and took hold of it because the oxen had stumbled. 7 Then the LORD's anger burned against Uzzah, and God struck him dead on the spot for his irreverence, and he died there next to the ark of God. 8 David was angry because of the LORD's outburst against Uzzah, so he named that place Outburst Against Uzzah,[E] as it is today. 9 David feared the LORD that day and said, "How can the ark of the LORD ever come to me?" 10 So he was not willing to bring the ark of the LORD to the city of David; instead, he diverted it to the house of Obed-edom of Gath. 11 The ark of the LORD remained in his house three months, and the LORD blessed Obed-edom and his whole family.

12 It was reported to King David, "The LORD has blessed Obed-edom's family and all that belongs to him because of the ark of God." So David went and had the ark of God brought up from Obed-edom's house to the city of David with rejoicing. 13 When those carrying the ark of the LORD advanced six steps, he sacrificed an ox and a fattened calf. 14 David was dancing[F] with all his might before the LORD wearing a linen ephod. 15 He and the whole house of Israel were bringing up the ark of the LORD with shouts and the sound of the ram's horn. 16 As the ark of the LORD was entering the city of David, Saul's daughter Michal looked down from the window and saw King David leaping and dancing before the LORD, and she despised him in her heart.

17 They brought the ark of the LORD and set it in its place inside the tent David had pitched for it. Then David offered burnt offerings and fellowship offerings in the LORD's presence. 18 When David had finished offering the burnt offering and the fellowship offerings, he blessed the people in the name of the LORD of Armies. 19 Then he distributed a loaf of bread, a date cake, and a raisin cake to each one in the entire Israelite community, both men and women. Then all the people went home.

20 When David returned home to bless his household, Saul's daughter Michal came out to meet him. "How the king of Israel honored himself today!" she said. "He exposed himself today in the sight of the slave girls of his subjects like a vulgar person would expose himself."

21 David replied to Michal, "It was before the LORD who chose me over your father and his whole family to appoint me ruler over the LORD's people Israel. I will dance before the LORD, 22 and I will dishonor myself and humble myself even more.[G,H] However, by the slave girls you spoke about, I will be honored." 23 And Saul's daughter Michal had no child to the day of her death.

THE LORD'S COVENANT WITH DAVID

7 When the king had settled into his palace and the LORD had given him rest on every side from all his enemies, 2 the king said to the prophet Nathan, "Look, I am living in a cedar house while the ark of God sits inside tent curtains."

3 So Nathan told the king, "Go and do all that is on your mind, for the LORD is with you."

4 But that night the word of the LORD came to Nathan: 5 "Go to my servant David and say, 'This is what the LORD says: Are you to build me a house to dwell in? 6 From the time I brought the Israelites out of Egypt until today I have not dwelt in a house; instead, I have been moving around with a tent as my dwelling. 7 In all my journeys with all the Israelites, have I ever spoken a word to one of the tribal leaders of Israel, whom I commanded to shepherd my people Israel, asking: Why haven't you built me a house of cedar?'

8 "So now this is what you are to say to my servant David: 'This is what the LORD of Armies says: I took you from the pasture, from tending the flock, to be ruler over my people Israel. 9 I have been with you wherever you have gone, and I have destroyed all your enemies before you. I will make a great name for you like that of the greatest on the earth. 10 I will designate a place for my people Israel and plant them, so that they may live there and not be disturbed again. Evildoers will not continue to oppress them as they have done 11 ever since the day I ordered judges to be over my people Israel. I will give you rest from all your enemies.

"'The LORD declares to you: The LORD himself will make a house for you. 12 When your time comes and you rest with your ancestors, I will raise up after you your descendant, who will come from your body, and I will establish his kingdom. 13 He is the one who will build a house for my name, and I will establish the

[A] **6:2** = Kiriath-jearim in 1Sm 7:1; 1Ch 13:6; 2Ch 1:4 [B] **6:3** Or *And his brothers* [C] **6:5** DSS, LXX read *with tuned instruments with strength, with songs*; 1Ch 13:8 [D] **6:5** = an Egyptian percussion instrument [E] **6:8** Or *Perez-uzzah*; 2Sm 5:20 [F] **6:14** Or *whirling* [G] **6:22** LXX reads *more and I will be humble in your eyes* [H] **6:22** Lit *more and I will be humble in my own eyes*

The Origins of the Monarchy in Israel

by Claude F. Mariottini

The monarchy was an anomaly and a late development in Israel. Israel became a nation when Yahweh delivered her from the oppression in Egypt. Israel was born a free nation in order to express God's justice and faithful love among the nations. Israel was a special nation, a community of free citizens in which the people would always remember that they had been slaves in Egypt, and the remembrance of that event would influence their treatment of each other and of the stranger in their midst. However, something happened after Joshua's death that caused the chaotic situation in the days of the judges. Those who at one time were oppressed, and whose God was known as the "God of the oppressed," were willing now to establish the kind of government from which they sought to escape.

Basalt orthostat image depicting the Aramean king Barrekup worshiping the Divine Emblems, shown in the upper-right corner.

The clans of Israel were willing to give up their individual autonomy to establish a form of government that created and promoted social inequality and social oppression among its population. Why were the people willing to give up so much in order to support a king who, like a Canaanite king, would force them to plow and to reap for him, who would tax their property and their crops, and who would exact their services as slaves and servants (1Sm 8:11–18)?

Two reasons can be adduced to explain the antimonarchic feelings in Israel. The first reason was the belief that kingship would jeopardize God's rule. In the ancient Near East, monarchy was a sacred institution and the king was highly exalted by the community and often honored as a god. The rejection of hereditary kingship in Israel was based on the idea that such a view of kingship was contrary to Israel's theocratic traditions.

The second reason for the antimonarchic feelings was that ancient Israelite society was organized as a patriarchal system that gave much power to the leaders of the clans. From its beginning, Israel was a tribal society, a nation composed of twelve tribes, each named after one of the sons of Jacob. A tribe was composed of several clans, and a clan was composed of several families. Traditionally the political decisions among the tribes were made by the representatives of each tribe who were selected from among the leaders of the clans. In times of community crisis, the elders of the tribes would come together and make decisions that were binding on all the tribes. In case of national crisis, several tribes would unite to fight against a common enemy, and God would raise up a leader from among the people who would lead them to war against the oppressors. The judges who appear in the book of Judges were military leaders who led the tribes in their struggle against the foreign nations that oppressed Israel. Once the struggle ended and the danger diminished, the tribes would again revert to their traditional distributed political patterns. Early Israel resisted the establishment of a central government and refused to elect a person to be the king of the entire nation. The imposition of kingship would bring a radical change in the basic structure of Israelite society. Monarchy would shift the power of decision away from the tribes and from their clan leaders to an individual, who in turn would make decisions that would affect the whole nation.

In spite of any opposition, the monarchy was established in Israel. The emergence of the state reshaped Israelite society; it abolished many of the old traditions of the community and created new ones. Even with Samuel's warning (1Sm 8:10–18), the people believed that the benefits derived from the monarchy outweighed the inequities and the cruelties brought about by the state.

The Mediterranean Sea from Ashkelon, which was a coastal city of the Philistines.

A bronze bottle from Tel Siron dating from the mid-seventh century BC. The bottle is engraved with an account of the works done by Amminadab, king of the Ammonites.

Whenever a community is faced with a serious struggle for survival, it will seek to centralize its power and resources in order to fight against a common enemy. These conflicts can be external—such as wars—or internal—such as revolts and insurrections. The most serious threat to Israel's survival during the times of the judges was the Philistines' desire for supremacy in Canaan. As early as the time of Shamgar, one of the judges of Israel (Jdg 3:31), and the days of Samson (Jdg 15:20), the Philistines were already menacing Israel. Although during his lifetime Shamgar was able to deliver Israel from Philistine oppression, Samson failed to do so. By Samuel's time, the Philistines had become Israel's most dangerous and persistent enemies and were established in the coastal area of Canaan as a federation of five cities: Gaza, Ashdod, Ashkelon, Gath, and Ekron (Jos 13:3). Samson's victories over them were not sufficient to remove the threat posed to the community. The Philistines' victory at Aphek, the conquest of the ark, and the destruction of Shiloh (1Sm 4:1–11; Jr 7:12–14) reemphasized the perceived need for a stronger centralized power that would be equal to the Philistine military organization.[1]

The Philistine menace was based on their superior military power over Israel and their control of the production and use of iron. The Philistines' military power was the result of their use of chariots and superior weapons of war (1Sm 13:19–22).[2] Initially with Egypt's consent, the Philistines established themselves in Canaan, seeking to extend their control over most of the Canaanite city-states as well as over Israel. By the time Israel elected Saul as king, the Philistines had expanded their control to Geba (1Sm 13:3), Ziklag (1Sm 27:5–6), and Bethlehem (2Sm 23:14). The rules and regulations imposed by the Philistines on Israel reflect the Philistines' desire to control Israel's economy. Such a control would have been disastrous for Israel. Control of Israel's agricultural and pastoral life by the Philistines would have meant not only the end of formal independence for the tribes but also the impoverishment of Israel's predominantly peasant population. Philistine conquest of Israel would have opened the way for the drafting of Israelite men to fight under Philistine command and the drafting of Israelite manpower for state labor either to serve on building projects or to serve the Philistines' agricultural needs.

The result of this Philistine domination would have been for Israel a reestablishment of her condition of bondage under the Egyptian pharaoh. The nation was also beset by attacks of the Moabites, Canaanites, Midianites, and Ammonites. Faced with a struggle for survival, the members of the tribes came to Samuel at Ramah, asking for a king who would form a militaristic, centralized government, with a monopoly on the use of force in order to fight against the enemy.

Because of perceived political necessity, internal problems, and external pressures, the clans of Israel first delegated power to the judges, then centralized power in the hands of Saul, and finally institutionalized power under David. ✣

[1] John Bright, *A History of Israel* (Louisville: Westminster John Knox, 2000), 186.
[2] LaMoine DeVries, "Philistines, The" in *HolBD*, 1108.

DIGGING DEEPER *House of David Inscription*

When the ancients wanted to make a permanent, public proclamation, they would inscribe a message in a stone object known as a *stele* and then erect it in a prominent location so everyone could read it. While excavating at Tel Dan in northern Israel in 1993, Avraham Biran uncovered an early eighth-century BC Aramaic stele that was likely erected by King Hazael of Syria, an enemy of Israel (2Kg 8:7–15; 10:32). The inscription is a valuable piece of evidence that establishes the reliability of the biblical descriptions of several kings of Judah, Israel, and Syria, including Ahab (1Kg 16:28), Joram (2Kg 8:16), Ahaz (2Kg 15:38), and Ben-hadad (1Kg 15:20; 2Kg 8:15). However, the most striking part of the stele is that it contains the Aramaic phrase "house of David" (*bytdwd* or *Beth-David*) which is the first known reference to David and his dynasty outside the Bible (2Sm 7:1–29; Zch 12:8,10). Since its discovery, critical scholars have attempted to argue that the phrase refers to a place rather than a person named David. This theory has not been well received; there is no biblical or extrabiblical evidence for a *place* named "house of David."

throne of his kingdom forever. 14 I will be his father, and he will be my son. When he does wrong, I will discipline him with a rod of men and blows from mortals. 15 But my faithful love will never leave him as it did when I removed it from Saul, whom I removed from before you. 16 Your house and kingdom will endure before me[A] forever, and your throne will be established forever.' "

17 Nathan reported all these words and this entire vision to David.

DAVID'S PRAYER OF THANKSGIVING

18 Then King David went in, sat in the LORD's presence, and said,

Who am I, Lord GOD, and what is my house that you have brought me this far? 19 What you have done so far[B] was a little thing to you, Lord GOD, for you have also spoken about your servant's house in the distant future. And this is a revelation[C] for mankind, Lord GOD. 20 What more can David say to you? You know your servant, Lord GOD. 21 Because of your word and according to your will, you have revealed all these great things to your servant.

22 This is why you are great, Lord GOD. There is no one like you, and there is no God besides you, as all we have heard confirms. 23 And who is like your people Israel? God came to one nation on earth in order to redeem a people for himself, to make a name for himself, and to perform for them[D] great and awesome acts,[E] driving out nations and their gods before your people you redeemed for yourself from Egypt. 24 You established your people Israel to be your own people forever, and you, LORD, have become their God.

25 Now, LORD God, fulfill the promise forever that you have made to your servant and his house. Do as you have promised, 26 so that your name will be exalted forever, when it is said, "The LORD of Armies is God over Israel." The house of your servant David will be established before you 27 since you, LORD of Armies, God of Israel, have revealed this to your servant when you said, "I will build a house for you." Therefore, your servant has found the courage to pray this prayer to you. 28 Lord GOD, you are God; your words are true, and you have promised this good thing to your servant. 29 Now, please bless your servant's house so that it will continue before you forever. For you, Lord GOD, have spoken, and with your blessing your servant's house will be blessed forever.

DAVID'S VICTORIES

8 After this, David defeated the Philistines, subdued them, and took Metheg-ammah[F] from Philistine control.[G] 2 He also defeated the Moabites, and after making them lie down on the ground, he measured them off with a cord. He measured every two cord lengths of those to be put to death and one full length of those to be kept alive. So the Moabites became David's subjects and brought tribute.

3 David also defeated Hadadezer son of Rehob, king of Zobah, when he went to restore his control at the Euphrates River. 4 David captured seventeen hundred horsemen[H] and twenty thousand foot soldiers from him, and he hamstrung all the horses and kept a hundred chariots.[I]

5 When the Arameans of Damascus came to assist King Hadadezer of Zobah, David struck down twenty-two thousand Aramean men. 6 Then he placed garrisons in Aram of Damascus, and the Arameans became David's subjects and brought tribute. The LORD made David victorious wherever he went.

[A] **7:16** Some Hb mss, LXX, Syr; other Hb mss read *you* [B] **7:19** Lit *Yet this* [C] **7:19** Or *custom*, or *instruction* [D] **7:23** Some Hb mss, Tg, Vg, Syr; other Hb mss read *you* [E] **7:23** LXX; MT reads *acts for your land* [F] **8:1** Or *took control of the mother city*; Hb obscure [G] **8:1** LXX reads *them, and David took tribute out of the hand of the Philistines* [H] **8:4** LXX, DSS read *1,000 chariots and 7,000 horsemen* [I] **8:4** Or *chariot horses*

7 David took the gold shields of Hadadezer's officers and brought them to Jerusalem. 8 King David also took huge quantities of bronze from Betah[A] and Berothai, Hadadezer's cities.

9 When King Toi of Hamath heard that David had defeated the entire army of Hadadezer, 10 he sent his son Joram to King David to greet him and to congratulate him because David had fought against Hadadezer and defeated him, for Toi and Hadadezer had fought many wars. Joram had items of silver, gold, and bronze with him. 11 King David also dedicated these to the LORD, along with the silver and gold he had dedicated from all the nations he had subdued — 12 from Edom,[B] Moab, the Ammonites, the Philistines, the Amalekites, and the spoil of Hadadezer son of Rehob, king of Zobah.

13 David made a reputation for himself when he returned from striking down eighteen thousand Edomites[C] in Salt Valley.[D] 14 He placed garrisons throughout Edom, and all the Edomites were subject to David. The LORD made David victorious wherever he went.

15 So David reigned over all Israel, administering justice and righteousness for all his people.

16 Joab son of Zeruiah was over the army;
Jehoshaphat son of Ahilud was
court historian;
17 Zadok son of Ahitub and Ahimelech
son of Abiathar were priests;
Seraiah was court secretary;
18 Benaiah son of Jehoiada was over the
Cherethites and the Pelethites;
and David's sons were chief officials.[E]

DAVID'S KINDNESS TO MEPHIBOSHETH

9 David asked, "Is there anyone remaining from the family of Saul I can show kindness to for Jonathan's sake?" 2 There was a servant of Saul's family named Ziba. They summoned him to David, and the king said to him, "Are you Ziba?"

"I am your servant," he replied.

3 So the king asked, "Is there anyone left of Saul's family that I can show the kindness of God to?"

Ziba said to the king, "There is still Jonathan's son who was injured in both feet."

4 The king asked him, "Where is he?"

Ziba answered the king, "You'll find him in Lo-debar at the house of Machir son of Ammiel." 5 So King David had him brought from the house of Machir son of Ammiel in Lo-debar.

6 Mephibosheth son of Jonathan son of Saul came to David, fell facedown, and paid homage. David said, "Mephibosheth!"

"I am your servant," he replied.

7 "Don't be afraid," David said to him, "since I intend to show you kindness for the sake of your father Jonathan. I will restore to you all your grandfather Saul's fields, and you will always eat meals at my table."

8 Mephibosheth paid homage and said, "What is your servant that you take an interest in a dead dog like me?"

9 Then the king summoned Saul's attendant Ziba and said to him, "I have given to your master's grandson all that belonged to Saul and his family. 10 You, your sons, and your servants are to work the ground for him, and you are to bring in the crops so your master's grandson will have food to eat. But Mephibosheth, your master's grandson, is always to eat at my table." Now Ziba had fifteen sons and twenty servants.

11 Ziba said to the king, "Your servant will do all my lord the king commands."

So Mephibosheth ate at David's[F] table just like one of the king's sons. 12 Mephibosheth had a young son whose name was Mica. All those living in Ziba's house were Mephibosheth's servants. 13 However, Mephibosheth lived in Jerusalem because he always ate at the king's table. His feet had been injured.

WAR WITH THE AMMONITES

10 Some time later, the king of the Ammonites died, and his son Hanun became king in his place. 2 Then David said, "I'll show kindness to Hanun son of Nahash, just as his father showed kindness to me."

So David sent his emissaries to console Hanun concerning his father. However, when they arrived in the land of the Ammonites, 3 the Ammonite leaders said to Hanun their lord, "Just because David has sent men with condolences for you, do you really believe he's showing respect for your father? Instead, hasn't David sent his emissaries in order to scout out the city, spy on it, and demolish it?" 4 So Hanun took David's emissaries, shaved off half their beards, cut their clothes in half at the hips, and sent them away.

5 When this was reported to David, he sent someone to meet them, since they were deeply humiliated. The king said, "Stay in Jericho until your beards grow back; then return."

6 When the Ammonites realized they had become repulsive to David, they hired twenty thousand foot soldiers from the Arameans of Beth-rehob and Zobah, one thousand men from the king of Maacah, and twelve thousand men from Tob.

7 David heard about it and sent Joab and all the elite troops. 8 The Ammonites marched out and lined up in battle formation at the entrance to the city gate

[A] **8:8** Some LXX mss, Syr read *Tebah* [B] **8:12** Some Hb mss, LXX, Syr; other Hb mss read *Aram*; 1Ch 18:11 [C] **8:13** Some Hb mss, LXX, Syr; other Hb mss read *Arameans*; 1Ch 18:12 [D] **8:13** = the Dead Sea region [E] **8:18** LXX; MT reads *were priests*; 1Ch 18:17 [F] **9:11** LXX; Syr reads *the king's*; Vg reads *your*; MT reads *my*

Who Were the Arameans?

by Joel F. Drinkard Jr.

First, *where* were the Arameans? They were in Syria and Mesopotamia—both in many English translations and in history. So, *who* were the Arameans? The Arameans were the neighbors of Israel to the north and east, primarily east of the Jordan River and the Rift Valley as far as the Middle Euphrates and its tributaries.

The Arameans were Semitic tribes who were closely related to the Israelites. The Aramaic language the Arameans spoke was a Semitic language closely related to Hebrew. Abraham was living in Aram when God called him to go to Canaan (Gn 11:31–12:1). Abraham's brother, Nahor, Isaac's wife Rebekah, and Jacob's wives Leah and Rachel all lived in Aram.

The Arameans occupied much of the territory that linked trade and commerce between Egypt and Assyria-Babylon. They lived north of Canaan-Israel and east of Phoenicia. The primary god of the Arameans was Hadad, a storm god. The Arameans eventually became strong enough that they controlled much of the region of eastern Syria and Assyria. Partly because of this expansion and partly because their language was alphabetic (unlike the cuneiform-syllabic languages of Assyria and Babylon), Aramaic became a common language of trade and commerce as well as diplomacy during the Assyrian and Babylonian empires of the late eighth to sixth centuries BC. Aramaic then became the lingua franca for almost all the Near East during the Persian and Hellenistic periods.[1] Aramaic and Greek were the two primary languages of the New Testament era throughout the Near East.

The earliest specific mention of the Arameans was in Assyrian texts dated to the time of Tiglath-pileser I (reigned 1115–1077 BC). He fought against the Arameans and defeated them from Tadmor (Palmyra) in modern Syria as far as Babylonia.[2] By this time, the Arameans were spread from central Syria eastward across the Euphrates River at least as far as the Babylonian territory. The Assyrian texts describe the Arameans both as pastoral tribal groups and also as ones who dwelled in towns or villages.

The Arameans mentioned in 2 Kings 5 were those who lived west of the Euphrates in what is modern Syria. They never formed a unified nation. Instead they had a series of

Ruins at Tadmor (known in English as Palmyra); located in the central Syrian desert, Tadmor was an important stop for travelers and caravans along the route from Mesopotamia westward. Tiglath-pileser I defeated the Arameans at Tadmor.

Aramean debt contract established before four witnesses. The contract states a man borrowed twenty-seven silver shekels from Bait' el-Yada', leaving him a slave as deposit; dates to about 570 BC, the thirty-fourth year of Nebuchadnezzar's reign; from Aleppo.

independent city-states, including Aram-Damascus. David occupied Aram-Damascus (2 Sm 8:6), and it remained under Israel's control during his reign. Rezon recaptured Damascus from Solomon.

Ben-hadad II (who is probably also named Hadadezer) along with Israel's king Ahab fought against Assyria's king Shalmaneser III at the battle of Qarqar in 853 BC. Ben-Hadad II had twelve hundred chariots, twelve hundred cavalry, and twenty thousand soldiers in the battle; Ahab had two thousand chariots and ten thousand soldiers.[3] As prophesied by both Elijah and Elisha, Hazael assassinated Ben-Hadad in 842 BC and became king (1Kg 19:15; 2Kg 8:13). Hazael is most likely the Aramean king in the Tel Dan stele. In the stele's inscription, the king claims to have killed both the kings of Israel and Judah, Joram and Ahaziah.[4] During Hazael's reign, Aram-Damascus reached its greatest extent east of the Jordan and subjugated Israel and Judah (2Kg 12–13). Tiglath-pileser III (reigned 744–727 BC) conquered the Arameans of Damascus in 732 BC, and the Arameans ceased to be a political force in Syria. ✜

[1] Benjamin Mazar, "The Aramean Empire and Its Relations with Israel," *BA* 25.4 (1962): 111. [2] James B. Prichard, ed., *ANET*, 3rd ed. with sup., 275. [3] Pritchard, *ANET*, 278–79. [4] William M. Schniedewind, "Tel Dan Stela: New Light on Aramaic and Jehu's Revolt," *BASOR* 302 (1996): 75–79; Matthew J. Suriano, "The Apology of Hazael: A Literary and Historical Analysis of the Tel Dan Inscription," *JNES* 66.3 (2007): 163–76.

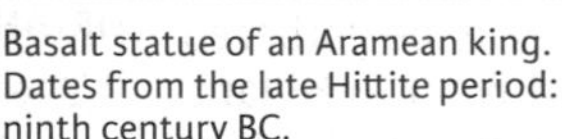

Basalt statue of an Aramean king. Dates from the late Hittite period: ninth century BC.

Bedouin tent and herd near Sheikh Mizken (translated "leader of the poor people") in Syria. Some Arameans were rural tent dwellers; others lived in cities.

while the Arameans of Zobah and Rehob and the men of Tob and Maacah were in the field by themselves. 9 When Joab saw that there was a battle line in front of him and another behind him, he chose some of Israel's finest young men and lined up in formation to engage the Arameans. 10 He placed the rest of the forces under the command of his brother Abishai. They lined up in formation to engage the Ammonites.

11 "If the Arameans are too strong for me," Joab said, "then you will be my help. However, if the Ammonites are too strong for you, I'll come to help you. 12 Be strong! Let's prove ourselves strong for our people and for the cities of our God. May the LORD's will be done."[A]

13 Joab and his troops advanced to fight against the Arameans, and they fled before him. 14 When the Ammonites saw that the Arameans had fled, they too fled before Abishai and entered the city. So Joab withdrew from the attack against the Ammonites and went to Jerusalem.

15 When the Arameans saw that they had been defeated by Israel, they regrouped. 16 Hadadezer sent messengers to bring the Arameans who were beyond the Euphrates River, and they came to Helam with Shobach, commander of Hadadezer's army, leading them.

17 When this was reported to David, he gathered all Israel, crossed the Jordan, and went to Helam. Then the Arameans lined up to engage David in battle and fought against him. 18 But the Arameans fled before Israel, and David killed seven hundred of their charioteers and forty thousand foot soldiers.[B] He also struck down Shobach commander of their army, who died there. 19 When all the kings who were Hadadezer's subjects saw that they had been defeated by Israel, they made peace with Israel and became their subjects. After this, the Arameans were afraid to ever help the Ammonites again.

DAVID'S ADULTERY WITH BATHSHEBA

11 In the spring when kings march out to war, David sent Joab with his officers and all Israel. They destroyed the Ammonites and besieged Rabbah, but David remained in Jerusalem.

2 One evening David got up from his bed and strolled around on the roof of the palace. From the roof he saw a woman bathing — a very beautiful woman. 3 So David sent someone to inquire about her, and he said, "Isn't this Bathsheba, daughter of Eliam and wife of Uriah the Hethite?"[C]

4 David sent messengers to get her, and when she came to him, he slept with her. Now she had just been purifying herself from her uncleanness. Afterward, she returned home. 5 The woman conceived and sent word to inform David, "I am pregnant."

6 David sent orders to Joab: "Send me Uriah the Hethite." So Joab sent Uriah to David. 7 When Uriah came to him, David asked how Joab and the troops were doing and how the war was going. 8 Then he said to Uriah, "Go down to your house and wash your feet." So Uriah left the palace, and a gift from the king followed him. 9 But Uriah slept at the door of the palace with all his master's servants; he did not go down to his house.

10 When it was reported to David, "Uriah didn't go home," David questioned Uriah, "Haven't you just come from a journey? Why didn't you go home?"

11 Uriah answered David, "The ark, Israel, and Judah are dwelling in tents, and my master Joab and his soldiers[D] are camping in the open field. How can I enter my house to eat and drink and sleep with my wife? As surely as you live and by your life, I will not do this!"

12 "Stay here today also," David said to Uriah, "and tomorrow I will send you back." So Uriah stayed in Jerusalem that day and the next. 13 Then David invited Uriah to eat and drink with him, and David got him drunk. He went out in the evening to lie down on his cot with his master's servants, but he did not go home.

URIAH'S DEATH ARRANGED

14 The next morning David wrote a letter to Joab and sent it with Uriah. 15 In the letter he wrote:

> Put Uriah at the front of the fiercest fighting,
> then withdraw from him so that he is struck
> down and dies.

16 When Joab was besieging the city, he put Uriah in the place where he knew the best enemy soldiers were. 17 Then the men of the city came out and attacked Joab, and some of the men from David's soldiers fell in battle; Uriah the Hethite also died.

18 Joab sent someone to report to David all the details of the battle. 19 He commanded the messenger, "When you've finished telling the king all the details of the battle — 20 if the king's anger gets stirred up and he asks you, 'Why did you get so close to the city to fight? Didn't you realize they would shoot from the top of the wall? 21 At Thebez, who struck Abimelech son of Jerubbesheth?[E,F] Didn't a woman drop an upper millstone on him from the top of the wall so that he died? Why did you get so close to the wall?' — then say, 'Your servant Uriah the Hethite is dead also.'" 22 Then the messenger left.

When he arrived, he reported to David all that Joab had sent him to tell. 23 The messenger reported to David, "The men gained the advantage over us

[A] **10:12** Lit *the LORD do what is good in his eyes* [B] **10:18** Some LXX mss; MT reads *horsemen*; 1Ch 19:18 [C] **11:3** DSS add *Joab's armor-bearer* [D] **11:11** Lit *servants* [E] **11:21** LXX reads *Jerubbaal* [F] **11:21** = Gideon

and came out against us in the field, but we counterattacked right up to the entrance of the city gate. 24 However, the archers shot down on your servants from the top of the wall, and some of the king's servants died. Your servant Uriah the Hethite is also dead."

25 David told the messenger, "Say this to Joab: 'Don't let this matter upset you because the sword devours all alike. Intensify your fight against the city and demolish it.' Encourage him."

26 When Uriah's wife heard that her husband, Uriah, had died, she mourned for him.[A] 27 When the time of mourning ended, David had her brought to his house. She became his wife and bore him a son. However, the LORD considered what David had done to be evil.

NATHAN'S PARABLE AND DAVID'S REPENTANCE

12 So the LORD sent Nathan to David. When he arrived, he said to him:

> There were two men in a certain city, one rich and the other poor. 2 The rich man had very large flocks and herds, 3 but the poor man had nothing except one small ewe lamb that he had bought. He raised her, and she grew up with him and with his children. From his meager food she would eat, from his cup she would drink, and in his arms she would sleep. She was like a daughter to him. 4 Now a traveler came to the rich man, but the rich man could not bring himself to take one of his own sheep or cattle to prepare for the traveler who had come to him. Instead, he took the poor man's lamb and prepared it for his guest.[B]

5 David was infuriated with the man and said to Nathan, "As the LORD lives, the man who did this deserves to die! 6 Because he has done this thing and shown no pity, he must pay four lambs for that lamb."

7 Nathan replied to David, "You are the man! This is what the LORD God of Israel says: 'I anointed you king over Israel, and I rescued you from Saul. 8 I gave your master's house to you and your master's wives into your arms,[C] and I gave you the house of Israel and Judah, and if that was not enough, I would have given you even more. 9 Why then have you despised the LORD's command by doing what I consider[D] evil? You struck down Uriah the Hethite with the sword and took his wife as your own wife — you murdered him with the Ammonite's sword. 10 Now therefore, the sword will never leave your house because you despised me and took the wife of Uriah the Hethite to be your own wife.'

11 "This is what the LORD says, 'I am going to bring disaster on you from your own family: I will take your wives and give them to another[E] before your very eyes, and he will sleep with them in broad daylight.[F] 12 You acted in secret, but I will do this before all Israel and in broad daylight.'"[G]

13 David responded to Nathan, "I have sinned against the LORD."

Then Nathan replied to David, "And the LORD has taken away your sin; you will not die. 14 However, because you treated[H] the LORD with such contempt in this matter, the son born to you will die." 15 Then Nathan went home.

THE DEATH OF BATHSHEBA'S SON

The LORD struck the baby that Uriah's wife had borne to David, and he became deathly ill. 16 David pleaded with God for the boy. He fasted, went home, and spent the night lying on the ground. 17 The elders of his house stood beside him to get him up from the ground, but he was unwilling and would not eat anything with them.

18 On the seventh day the baby died. But David's servants were afraid to tell him the baby was dead. They said, "Look, while the baby was alive, we spoke to him, and he wouldn't listen to us. So how can we tell him the baby is dead? He may do something desperate."

19 When David saw that his servants were whispering to each other, he guessed that the baby was dead. So he asked his servants, "Is the baby dead?"

"He is dead," they replied.

20 Then David got up from the ground. He washed, anointed himself, changed his clothes, went to the LORD's house, and worshiped. Then he went home and requested something to eat. So they served him food, and he ate.

21 His servants asked him, "Why have you done this? While the baby was alive, you fasted and wept, but when he died, you got up and ate food."

22 He answered, "While the baby was alive, I fasted and wept because I thought, 'Who knows? The LORD may be gracious to me and let him live.' 23 But now that he is dead, why should I fast? Can I bring him back again? I'll go to him, but he will never return to me."

THE BIRTH OF SOLOMON

24 Then David comforted his wife Bathsheba; he went to her and slept with her. She gave birth to a son and named[I] him Solomon.[J] The LORD loved him, 25 and he sent a message through the prophet Nathan, who named[K] him Jedidiah,[L] because of the LORD.

[A] **11:26** Lit *her husband* [B] **12:4** Lit *for the man who had come to him* [C] **12:8** Lit *bosom* [D] **12:9** Alt Hb tradition reads *what he considers* [E] **12:11** Or *to your neighbor* [F] **12:11** Lit *in the eyes of this sun* [G] **12:12** Lit *and before the sun* [H] **12:14** Alt Hb tradition, one LXX ms; MT reads *treated the enemies of*; DSS read *treated the word of* [I] **12:24** Alt Hb tradition reads *he named* [J] **12:24** In Hb, the name *Solomon* sounds like "peace." [K] **12:25** Or *prophet to name* [L] **12:25** = Beloved of the LORD

Adultery: The "Great Sin"

by Dorman Laird

From Eshnunna, statue of a seated Mesopotamian prince. The Laws of Eshnunna dealt with marital relationships and other domestic and civic matters.

ADULTERY IN ANCIENT ISRAEL

David and all Israel had been warned about the gravity of the sin of adultery. Not only was this act condemned in the Ten Commandments and in the other sexual laws of the Pentateuch, but from the time of Abraham adultery was labeled a "great sin" (Hb *chata'ah gedolah*). Abraham had journeyed to the land of Gerar and told Abimelech, the king, that Sarah was his sister, thinking that someone might slay him in order to take Sarah for a wife. Abimelech believed Abraham and took Sarah for his own wife innocently, but providentially did not "touch her" (Gn 20:6). God warned Abimelech in a dream that Sarah was actually Abraham's wife. In his rebuke of Abraham, Abimelech thought of how close he had come to committing adultery with Sarah and asked Abraham why he had brought on Abimelech and his nation a "great sin" ("enormous guilt" in v. 9).[1] When Abimelech restored Sarah to Abraham, he greatly rewarded them in order to remove any curses and divine judgments against Abimelech and the people of Gerar.

Generations later, the Pentateuch included adultery in a list of sexual crimes that would defile the land of Israel and cause the land to "vomit out its inhabitants" (Lv 18:20–25). God's standards had not changed.

The reasons for the severity of the sin of adultery are not explicitly stated in the Old Testament.[2] Obviously this sin was an assault on the integrity of the family and a violation of the ideal marital state that God expressed to Adam and Eve (Gn 2:24). Other suggestions center on the patrilineal nature of Israelite society and the divine directive that property was never to be removed from one tribe to another (Nm 36:7). Mistaken paternity could lead to the bequeathal of the family inheritance to an illegitimate heir.[3] Whatever might have been the social, religious, and economic factors behind the strong condemnation of adultery in Scriptures, Israel saw adultery as a crime worthy of the death of both parties (Dt 22:22).

THE "GREAT SIN" IN THE ANCIENT NEAR EAST

Ancient Israel was not alone in the view of adultery as the "great sin." Evidence has come to light indicating that other nations of the ancient Near East shared this opinion. Four ancient Egyptian marriage contracts, one dating around 850 BC, labeled adultery as the "great sin." The phrase in the Egyptian documents is similar to that in Genesis 20:9.[4] Further, another ancient Egyptian text, "The Story of Two Brothers," tells the story of two brothers who were working in the field at planting time. When they ran short of seed, the older brother sent the younger one to the village to get more seed. The younger brother found his brother's wife alone at home, fixing her hair. The woman tried to seduce her brother-in-law, but he refused her saying, "What . . . is this great crime which you have said to me? Don't say it to me again!"[5]

Archaeologists have also found references to adultery as the "great sin" among the Akkadian documents of Ugarit in northern Syria. One of the texts, which dates to about 1245 BC, tells of the king's wife, in whom was found a fault. Her action forced her to flee Ugarit to take refuge in her native land of Amurru. In interpreting details of the record, scholars have consistently designated the queen's indiscretion as the "great sin," adultery.[6]

Other ancient laws dealt with repercussions and extenuating circumstances related to adultery. Among the Hittites, a law stated that a man who seized a woman in the mountains was singularly guilty and would be killed. But if the act occurred in her house, the woman was to blame and would be killed. A husband who found his wife and another man in the act of adultery could kill them both without punishment.[7] Likewise, a Middle Assyrian law allowed a husband to kill his wife and a man if the husband caught the two committing adultery.[8] A similar stipulation was also in the Code of Hammurabi.[9]

Still other ancient Near Eastern law codes helped to clarify the concept of adultery. One of the Laws of Eshnunna in Mesopotamia (dated to 1950 BC) dealt with a case in which a man might be kidnapped or otherwise forcibly separated from his wife for an extended time. If his wife had become another man's wife because of the extended absence, the law gave guidelines on whether the first husband could reclaim her if he returned home. Another of the Laws of Eshnunna dealt with a husband's voluntary abandonment of his wife and how that might affect another man's right to marry her.[10] Similar laws regarding the husband's extended absence or abandonment were a regular part of Middle Assyrian law codes.[11]

Interpreters have found parallels between the ancient Near Eastern documents and the Old Testament references and laws about adultery.[12] Similarities in phrasing, the variety of extenuating circumstances, degrees of punishment or lack thereof, and other factors give evidence that ancient societies and peoples shared a general consensus that adultery was the "great sin." Even though the nations that were contemporaries of ancient Israel undermined their own laws by worshiping fertility gods, tacitly accepting harlotry, practicing polygamy, and demonstrating generally low moral standards, they saw the need to prohibit violations of marriage contracts. Whether instinctively or by experience, they apparently understood that the stability of a nation depended on a careful ordering of society and that the safeguarding of the nuclear family was essential to the endurance of a nation. ❖

---

[1] Five times, the Old Testament uses the phrase "great sin," this one time in respect to adultery. The other four instances refer to idolatry ("grave sin" in Ex 32:21,30,31; "immense sin" in 2Kg 17:21). This reflects the Old Testament's likening Israel's idolatrous practices to the nation committing adultery. See Jacob J. Rabinowitz, "The 'Great Sin' in Ancient Egyptian Marriage Contracts," *JNES* 18.1 (1959): 73. [2] Elaine Adler Goodfriend, "Adultery" in *ABD*, 1:82. [3] Goodfriend, "Adultery." [4] Rabinowitz, "Great Sin," 73. [5] "Egyptian Myths, Tales, and Mortuary Texts" in *ANET*, 3rd ed. with sup.; 24. [6] W. L. Moran, "The Scandal of the 'Great Sin' at Ugarit," *JNES* 18.4 (1959): 280–81; Carole Roche, "The Lady of Ugarit," *NEA* 63.4 (2000): 214–15. [7] "The Hittite Laws" in *ANET*, 196. [8] "The Middle Assyrian Laws" in *ANET*, 181. [9] "The Code of Hammurabi" in *ANET*, 171. [10] "The Laws of Eshnunna" in *ANET*, 162. [11] "The Middle Assyrian Laws" in *ANET*, 183. [12] Rabinowitz, "Great Sin," 73.

Statue depicting either Hammurabi or a prince who served him.

CAPTURE OF THE CITY OF RABBAH

26 Joab fought against Rabbah of the Ammonites and captured the royal fortress. 27 Then Joab sent messengers to David to say, "I have fought against Rabbah and have also captured its water supply. 28 Now therefore, assemble the rest of the troops, lay siege to the city, and capture it. Otherwise I will be the one to capture the city, and it will be named after me." 29 So David assembled all the troops and went to Rabbah; he fought against it and captured it. 30 He took the crown from the head of their king,[A] and it was placed on David's head. The crown weighed seventy-five pounds[B] of gold, and it had a precious stone in it. In addition, David took away a large quantity of plunder from the city. 31 He removed the people who were in the city and put them to work with saws, iron picks, and iron axes, and to labor at brickmaking. He did the same to all the Ammonite cities. Then he and all his troops returned to Jerusalem.

AMNON RAPES TAMAR

13 Some time passed. David's son Absalom had a beautiful sister named Tamar, and David's son Amnon was infatuated with her. 2 Amnon was frustrated to the point of making himself sick over his sister Tamar because she was a virgin, but it seemed impossible to do anything to her. 3 Amnon had a friend named Jonadab, a son of David's brother Shimeah. Jonadab was a very shrewd man, 4 and he asked Amnon, "Why are you, the king's son, so miserable every morning? Won't you tell me?"

Amnon replied, "I'm in love with Tamar, my brother Absalom's sister."

5 Jonadab said to him, "Lie down on your bed and pretend you're sick. When your father comes to see you, say to him, 'Please let my sister Tamar come and give me something to eat. Let her prepare a meal in my presence so I can watch and eat from her hand.'"

6 So Amnon lay down and pretended to be sick. When the king came to see him, Amnon said to him, "Please let my sister Tamar come and make a couple of cakes in my presence so I can eat from her hand."

7 David sent word to Tamar at the palace: "Please go to your brother Amnon's house and prepare a meal for him."

8 Then Tamar went to his house while Amnon was lying down. She took dough, kneaded it, made cakes in his presence, and baked them. 9 She brought the pan and set it down in front of him, but he refused to eat. Amnon said, "Everyone leave me!" And everyone left him. 10 "Bring the meal to the bedroom," Amnon told Tamar, "so I can eat from your hand." Tamar took the cakes she had made and went to her brother Amnon's bedroom. 11 When she brought them to him to eat, he grabbed her and said,[C] "Come sleep with me, my sister!"

12 "Don't, my brother!" she cried. "Don't disgrace me, for such a thing should never be done in Israel. Don't commit this outrage! 13 Where could I ever go with my humiliation? And you — you would be like one of the outrageous fools in Israel! Please, speak to the king, for he won't keep me from you." 14 But he refused to listen to her, and because he was stronger than she was, he disgraced her by raping her.

15 So Amnon hated Tamar with such intensity that the hatred he hated her with was greater than the love he had loved her with. "Get out of here!" he said.

16 "No," she cried,[D] "sending me away is much worse than the great wrong you've already done to me!"

But he refused to listen to her. 17 Instead, he called to the servant who waited on him, "Get this away from me, throw her out, and bolt the door behind her!" 18 Amnon's servant threw her out and bolted the door behind her. Now Tamar was wearing a long-sleeved[E] robe, because this is what the king's virgin daughters wore. 19 Tamar put ashes on her head and tore the long-sleeved robe she was wearing. She put her hand on her head and went away crying out.

20 Her brother Absalom said to her, "Has your brother Amnon been with you? Be quiet for now, my sister. He is your brother. Don't take this thing to heart." So Tamar lived as a desolate woman in the house of her brother Absalom.

ABSALOM MURDERS AMNON

21 When King David heard about all these things, he was furious.[F] 22 Absalom didn't say anything to Amnon, either good or bad, because he hated Amnon since he disgraced his sister Tamar.

23 Two years later, Absalom's sheepshearers were at Baal-hazor near Ephraim, and Absalom invited all the king's sons. 24 Then he went to the king and said, "Your servant has just hired sheepshearers. Will the king and his servants please come with your servant?"

25 The king replied to Absalom, "No, my son, we should not all go, or we would be a burden to you." Although Absalom urged him, he wasn't willing to go, though he did bless him.

26 "If not," Absalom said, "please let my brother Amnon go with us."

The king asked him, "Why should he go with you?" 27 But Absalom urged him, so he sent Amnon and all the king's sons.[G]

[A] **12:30** LXX reads *of Milcom*; some emend to *Molech*; 1Kg 11:5,33 [B] **12:30** Lit *a talent* [C] **13:11** Lit *said to her* [D] **13:16** Lit *she said to him* [E] **13:18** Or *ornate*; Gn 37:3 [F] **13:21** LXX, DSS add *but he did not grieve the spirit of Amnon his son, for he loved him because he was his firstborn*; 1Kg 1:6 [G] **13:27** LXX adds *And Absalom prepared a feast like a royal feast.*

28 Now Absalom commanded his young men, "Watch Amnon until he is in a good mood from the wine. When I order you to strike Amnon, then kill him. Don't be afraid. Am I not the one who has commanded you? Be strong and valiant!" 29 So Absalom's young men did to Amnon just as Absalom had commanded. Then all the rest of the king's sons got up, and each fled on his mule.

30 While they were on the way, a report reached David: "Absalom struck down all the king's sons; not even one of them survived!" 31 In response the king stood up, tore his clothes, and lay down on the ground, and all his servants stood by with their clothes torn.

32 But Jonadab, son of David's brother Shimeah, spoke up: "My lord must not think they have killed all the young men, the king's sons, because only Amnon is dead. In fact, Absalom has planned this[A] ever since the day Amnon disgraced his sister Tamar. 33 So now, my lord the king, don't take seriously the report that says all the king's sons are dead. Only Amnon is dead."

34 Meanwhile, Absalom had fled. When the young man who was standing watch looked up, there were many people coming from the road west of him from the side of the mountain.[B] 35 Jonadab said to the king, "Look, the king's sons have come! It's exactly like your servant said." 36 Just as he finished speaking, the king's sons entered and wept loudly. Then the king and all his servants also wept very bitterly. 37 But Absalom fled and went to Talmai son of Ammihud, king of Geshur. And David mourned for his son[C] every day.

38 After Absalom had fled to Geshur and had been there three years, 39 King David[D] longed to go to Absalom, for David had finished grieving over Amnon's death.

ABSALOM RESTORED TO DAVID

14 Joab son of Zeruiah realized that the king's mind was on Absalom. 2 So Joab sent someone to Tekoa to bring a wise woman from there. He told her, "Pretend to be in mourning: dress in mourning clothes and don't put on any oil. Act like a woman who has been mourning for the dead for a long time. 3 Go to the king and speak these words to him." Then Joab told her exactly what to say.[E]

4 When the woman from Tekoa came[F] to the king, she fell facedown to the ground, paid homage, and said, "Help me, Your Majesty!"

5 "What's the matter?" the king asked her.

"Sadly, I am a widow; my husband died," she said. 6 "Your servant had two sons. They were fighting in the field with no one to separate them, and one struck the other and killed him. 7 Now the whole clan has risen up against your servant and said, 'Hand over the one who killed his brother so we may put him to death for the life of the brother he murdered. We will eliminate the heir!' They would extinguish my one remaining ember by not preserving my husband's name or posterity on earth."

8 The king told the woman, "Go home. I will issue a command on your behalf."

9 Then the woman of Tekoa said to the king, "My lord the king, may any blame be on me and my father's family, and may the king and his throne be innocent."

10 "Whoever speaks to you," the king said, "bring him to me. He will not trouble you again!"

11 She replied, "Please, may the king invoke the LORD your God, so that the avenger of blood will not increase the loss, and they will not eliminate my son!"

"As the LORD lives," he vowed, "not a hair of your son will fall to the ground."

12 Then the woman said, "Please, may your servant speak a word to my lord the king?"

"Speak," he replied.

13 The woman asked, "Why have you devised something similar against the people of God? When the king spoke as he did about this matter, he has pronounced his own guilt. The king has not brought back his own banished one. 14 We will certainly die and be like water poured out on the ground, which can't be recovered. But God would not take away a life; he would devise plans so that the one banished from him does not remain banished.

15 "Now therefore, I've come to present this matter to my lord the king because the people have made me afraid. Your servant thought: I must speak to the king. Perhaps the king will grant his servant's request. 16 The king will surely listen in order to keep his servant from the grasp of this man who would eliminate both me and my son from God's inheritance. 17 Your servant thought: May the word of my lord the king bring relief, for my lord the king is able to discern the good and the bad like the angel of God. May the LORD your God be with you."

18 Then the king answered the woman, "I'm going to ask you something; don't conceal it from me!"

"Let my lord the king speak," the woman replied.

19 The king asked, "Did Joab put you up to[G] all this?"

The woman answered. "As you live, my lord the king, no one can turn to the right or left from all my lord the king says. Yes, your servant Joab is the one who gave orders to me; he told your servant exactly what to say.[H] 20 Joab your servant has done this to address the issue indirectly,[I] but my lord has

[A] **13:32** Lit *In fact, it was established on the mouth of Absalom*
[B] **13:34** LXX adds *And the watchman came and reported to the king saying, "I see men on the Horonaim road on the side of the mountain."*
[C] **13:37** Probably Amnon [D] **13:39** DSS, LXX, Tg read *David's spirit*
[E] **14:3** Lit *Joab put the words into her mouth* [F] **14:4** Some Hb mss, LXX, Syr, Tg, Vg; other Hb mss read *spoke* [G] **14:19** Lit *"Is the hand of Joab in* [H] **14:19** Lit *he put all these words into the mouth of your servant*
[I] **14:20** Lit *to go around the face of the matter*

wisdom like the wisdom of the angel of God, knowing everything on earth."

21 Then the king said to Joab, "I hereby grant this request. Go, bring back the young man Absalom."

22 Joab fell with his face to the ground in homage and blessed the king. "Today," Joab said, "your servant knows I have found favor with you, my lord the king, because the king has granted the request of your servant."

23 So Joab got up, went to Geshur, and brought Absalom to Jerusalem. 24 However, the king added, "He may return to his house, but he may not see my face." So Absalom returned to his house, but he did not see the king.[A]

25 No man in all Israel was as handsome and highly praised as Absalom. From the sole of his foot to the top of his head, he did not have a single flaw. 26 When he shaved his head — he shaved it at the end of every year because his hair got so heavy for him that he had to shave it off — he would weigh the hair from his head and it would be five pounds[B] according to the royal standard.

27 Three sons were born to Absalom, and a daughter named Tamar, who was a beautiful woman. 28 Absalom resided in Jerusalem two years but never saw the king. 29 Then Absalom sent for Joab in order to send him to the king, but Joab was unwilling to come to him. So he sent again, a second time, but he still would not come. 30 Then Absalom said to his servants, "See, Joab has a field right next to mine, and he has barley there. Go and set fire to it!" So Absalom's servants set the field on fire.[C]

31 Then Joab came to Absalom's house and demanded, "Why did your servants set my field on fire?"

32 "Look," Absalom explained to Joab, "I sent for you and said, 'Come here. I want to send you to the king to ask: Why have I come back from Geshur? I'd be better off if I were still there.' So now, let me see the king. If I am guilty, let him kill me."

33 Joab went to the king and told him. So David summoned Absalom, who came to the king and paid homage with his face to the ground before him. Then the king kissed Absalom.

ABSALOM'S REVOLT

15 After this, Absalom got himself a chariot, horses, and fifty men to run before him. 2 He would get up early and stand beside the road leading to the city gate. Whenever anyone had a grievance to bring before the king for settlement, Absalom called out to him and asked, "What city are you from?" If he replied, "Your servant is from one of the tribes of Israel," 3 Absalom said to him, "Look, your claims are good and right, but the king does not have anyone to listen to you." 4 He added, "If only someone would appoint me judge in the land. Then anyone who had a grievance or dispute could come to me, and I would make sure he received justice." 5 When a person approached to pay homage to him, Absalom reached out his hand, took hold of him, and kissed him. 6 Absalom did this to all the Israelites who came to the king for a settlement. So Absalom stole the hearts of the men of Israel.

7 When four[D] years had passed, Absalom said to the king, "Please let me go to Hebron to fulfill a vow I made to the LORD. 8 For your servant made a vow when I lived in Geshur of Aram, saying, 'If the LORD really brings me back to Jerusalem, I will worship the LORD in Hebron.'"[E]

9 "Go in peace," the king said to him. So he went to Hebron.

10 Then Absalom sent agents throughout the tribes of Israel with this message: "When you hear the sound of the ram's horn, you are to say, 'Absalom has become king in Hebron!'"

11 Two hundred men from Jerusalem went with Absalom. They had been invited and were going innocently, for they did not know the whole situation. 12 While he was offering the sacrifices, Absalom sent for David's adviser Ahithophel the Gilonite, from his city of Giloh. So the conspiracy grew strong, and the people supporting Absalom continued to increase.

13 Then an informer came to David and reported, "The hearts of the men of Israel are with Absalom."

14 David said to all the servants with him in Jerusalem, "Get up. We have to flee, or we will not escape from Absalom! Leave quickly, or he will overtake us quickly, heap disaster on us, and strike the city with the edge of the sword."

15 The king's servants said to the king, "Whatever my lord the king decides, we are your servants." 16 Then the king set out, and his entire household followed him. But he left behind ten concubines to take care of the palace. 17 So the king set out, and all the people followed him. They stopped at the last house 18 while all his servants marched past him. Then all the Cherethites, the Pelethites, and the people of Gath — six hundred men who came with him from there — marched past the king.

19 The king said to Ittai of Gath, "Why are you also going with us? Go back and stay with the new king since you're both a foreigner and an exile from your homeland. 20 Besides, you only arrived yesterday; should I make you wander around with us today while I go wherever I can? Go back and take your

[A] **14:24** Lit *king's face* [B] **14:26** Lit *200 shekels* [C] **14:30** DSS, LXX add *So Joab's servants came to him with their clothes torn and said, "Absalom's servants have set the field on fire!"* [D] **15:7** Some LXX mss, Syr, Vg; other LXX mss, MT read *40* [E] **15:8** Some LXX mss; MT omits *in Hebron*

brothers with you. May the LORD show you[A] kindness and faithfulness."

21 But in response, Ittai vowed to the king, "As the LORD lives and as my lord the king lives, wherever my lord the king is, whether it means life or death, your servant will be there!"

22 "March on," David replied to Ittai. So Ittai of Gath marched past with all his men and the dependents who were with him. 23 Everyone in the countryside was weeping loudly while all the people were marching out of the city. As the king was crossing the Kidron Valley, all the people were marching past on the road that leads to the wilderness.

24 Zadok was also there, and all the Levites with him were carrying the ark of the covenant of God. They set the ark of God down, and Abiathar offered sacrifices[B] until the people had finished marching past. 25 Then the king instructed Zadok, "Return the ark of God to the city. If I find favor with the LORD, he will bring me back and allow me to see both it and its[C] dwelling place. 26 However, if he should say, 'I do not delight in you,' then here I am — he can do with me whatever pleases him."[D]

27 The king also said to the priest Zadok, "Look,[E] return to the city in peace and your two sons with you: your son Ahimaaz and Abiathar's son Jonathan. 28 Remember, I'll wait at the fords[F] of the wilderness until word comes from you to inform me." 29 So Zadok and Abiathar returned the ark of God to Jerusalem and stayed there.

30 David was climbing the slope of the Mount of Olives, weeping as he ascended. His head was covered, and he was walking barefoot. All of the people with him covered their heads and went up, weeping as they ascended.

31 Then someone reported to David, "Ahithophel is among the conspirators with Absalom."

"LORD," David pleaded, "please turn the counsel of Ahithophel into foolishness!"

32 When David came to the summit where he used to worship God, Hushai the Archite was there to meet him with his robe torn and dust on his head. 33 David said to him, "If you go away with me, you'll be a burden to me, 34 but if you return to the city and tell Absalom, 'I will be your servant, Your Majesty! Previously, I was your father's servant, but now I will be your servant,' then you can counteract Ahithophel's counsel for me. 35 Won't the priests Zadok and Abiathar be there with you? Report everything you hear from the palace to the priests Zadok and Abiathar. 36 Take note: their two sons are there with them—Zadok's son Ahimaaz and Abiathar's son Jonathan. Send them to tell me everything you hear." 37 So Hushai, David's personal adviser, entered Jerusalem just as Absalom was entering the city.

ZIBA HELPS DAVID

16 When David had gone a little beyond the summit,[G] Ziba, Mephibosheth's servant, was right there to meet him. He had a pair of saddled donkeys loaded with two hundred loaves of bread, one hundred clusters of raisins, one hundred bunches of summer fruit, and a clay jar of wine. 2 The king said to Ziba, "Why do you have these?"

Ziba answered, "The donkeys are for the king's household to ride, the bread and summer fruit are for the young men to eat, and the wine is for those to drink who become exhausted in the wilderness."

3 "Where is your master's grandson?" the king asked.

"Why, he's staying in Jerusalem," Ziba replied to the king, "for he said, 'Today, the house of Israel will restore my grandfather's kingdom to me.'"

4 The king said to Ziba, "All that belongs to Mephibosheth is now yours!"

"I bow before you," Ziba said. "May I find favor with you, my lord the king!"

SHIMEI CURSES DAVID

5 When King David got to Bahurim, a man belonging to the family of the house of Saul was just coming out. His name was Shimei son of Gera, and he was yelling curses as he approached. 6 He threw stones at David and at all the royal[H] servants, the people and the warriors on David's right and left. 7 Shimei said as he cursed, "Get out, get out, you man of bloodshed, you wicked man! 8 The LORD has paid you back for all the blood of the house of Saul in whose place you became king, and the LORD has handed the kingdom over to your son Absalom. Look, you are in trouble because you're a man of bloodshed!"

9 Then Abishai son of Zeruiah said to the king, "Why should this dead dog curse my lord the king? Let me go over and remove his head!"

10 The king replied, "Sons of Zeruiah, do we agree on anything? He curses me this way because the LORD[I] told him, 'Curse David!' Therefore, who can say, 'Why did you do that?'" 11 Then David said to Abishai and all his servants, "Look, my own son, my own flesh and blood,[J] intends to take my life — how much more now this Benjaminite! Leave him alone and let him curse me; the LORD has told him to. 12 Perhaps the LORD will see my affliction[K] and restore goodness to me instead of Shimei's curses today." 13 So David and his men

[A] **15:20** LXX; MT omits Lit *May the LORD show you* [B] **15:24** Or *Abiathar went up* [C] **15:25** Or *his* [D] **15:26** Lit *me what is good in his eyes* [E] **15:27** LXX; MT reads *"Are you a seer?* [F] **15:28** Alt Hb tradition reads *plains* [G] **16:1** = Mount of Olives [H] **16:6** Lit *all King David's* [I] **16:10** Alt Hb tradition reads *If he curses, and if the LORD* [J] **16:11** Lit *son who came from my belly* [K] **16:12** Some Hb mss, LXX, Syr, Vg; one Hb tradition reads *iniquity*; alt Hb tradition reads *eyes*; another Hb tradition reads *will look with his eye*

King's Privileges or King's Crimes?

by Jeff S. Anderson

Were ancient Near Eastern monarchs held to personal standards of morality in keeping with the laws of their nations? A great wealth of textual material exists that relates to kingship in the ancient Near East, which could help to answer this question.

Although formal legal similarities existed among Israel's neighbors regarding the expectations of the king, the extent to which the king followed these standards obviously was not the same in every society. Evidence also exists that some of Israel's neighbors had a tendency to deify their own kings.

From textual and iconographic data, it is clear that the king was the central symbol of the social system for the nation. In the ancient Near East, the king was primarily in power to establish order. In most nations, he served as warrior, judge, and even priest. As warrior, he was to protect the state from external enemies and internal threats. As judge, he was to guarantee order by administrating justice and equity. As priests, Israel's neighboring monarchs fulfilled the wishes of the gods and were the earthly representatives of the divine realm. Easily the people took the short step from affirming that the gods set the king in place to upholding the conviction that the king himself carried divine prerogatives.

Fragments of the third-oldest known law code. It was promulgated by Lipit-Ishtar, king of Isin, about 1870 BC and was a forerunner of the Code of Hammurabi. The laws written in Sumerian cover a variety of subjects.

The vast literary evidence—particularly that from the prologues and epilogues of ancient Near Eastern law codes—demonstrates a remarkably consistent expectation of the monarch.[1] These law codes provide the clearest evidence that the king had the responsibility of establishing and maintaining the divine order. The king issued the laws for the nation, stood as the authority to enforce penalties for violating those laws, and threatened punishment for any who might attempt to change the laws in any way.

From around 1800 BC, ancient Babylon provides one example of how a particular Near Eastern king related to the law. The prologue to the Code of Hammurabi, a legal code promulgated by a Babylonian king, states that, as king, Hammurabi was responsible to establish law and justice in the land. He was to "cause justice to prevail in Babylon, to destroy wicked and evil, to stop the strong from oppressing the weak, and to rule like the sun over blackheaded people."[2] The epilogue concludes with a number of powerful curses against anyone who might break the laws in Hammurabi's Code. Consequently,

Hammurabi was the purveyor and the enforcer of the laws of the land.

Old Testament legal codes take this expectation a surprising step further. In them, the king himself was accountable to faithfully observe the requirements of God's law. He was not merely responsible for promulgating the laws of the land for others to follow. The king was to have his own copy of the law on a scroll so he could read it every single day and thus abide by it. Finally, he was not to be above his countrymen in terms of keeping the law but was himself accountable to it. Thus subordination to the law was the great equalizer in Israelite society—no matter what one's position might have been. Practically, however, the Old Testament indicates that Israelite monarchs violated these commands.

In Genesis 12, Abraham lied and said Sarah was his sister. Abraham's actions demonstrate his fear about the king's power to do exactly as David later did with Uriah's wife. The question, therefore, is not whether kings had the capabilities to do such evils. They most certainly did. The question is whether they were accountable for such actions.

The highly stratified Near Eastern social structure, which obviously existed in Babylon, consisted of an urban society with a noble class, an artisan class, and a slave class. Different penalties existed for violations of the law—based on one's social status. Consequently, the king's limited power likely did not allow for a fair measure of democracy for the lower classes.

In the biblical account of David's adultery, the prophet Nathan squarely condemned David for his sinful actions. Middle Assyrian laws allowed payment of restitution to a wronged husband in the case of adultery.[3] David could have easily forced Uriah to demand only symbolic reparation for the king's violation of Uriah's wife. Instead, his solution went to the opposite extreme.

The story of David's coveting Uriah's wife and the account of Ahab's coveting Naboth's vineyard have some striking parallels.[4] Both kings encountered a prophet, and in both cases these monarchs were accountable to the law's standards.

Although other monarchies may have allowed their kings to commit immoral behavior and may have seen it as a privilege, God's law for Israel held the action as a punishable offense—even for a king. ❖

[1] The literary examples come from sources such as the law codes of Lipit-Ishtar and Hammurabi and from royal Sumerian hymns and Egyptian royal inscriptions. [2] Celia Brewer Marshall, *A Guide through the Old Testament* (Louisville: Westminster John Knox, 1989), 58. [3] Baruch Halpern, *David's Secret Demons* (Grand Rapids: Eerdmans, 2001), 93. Victor Hamilton, *Handbook on the Historical Books* (Grand Rapids: Eerdmans, 2001), 330.

Chalk bathtub from the eleventh century BC from the sanctuary of Aphrodite.

proceeded along the road as Shimei was going along
the ridge of the hill opposite him. As Shimei went,
he cursed David, threw stones at him, and kicked up
dust. 14 Finally, the king and all the people with him
arrived[A] exhausted, so they rested there.

ABSALOM'S ADVISERS

15 Now Absalom and all the Israelites came to Jerusalem. Ahithophel was also with him. 16 When David's
friend Hushai the Archite came to Absalom, Hushai
said to Absalom, "Long live the king! Long live the
king!"

17 "Is this your loyalty to your friend?" Absalom
asked Hushai. "Why didn't you go with your friend?"

18 "Not at all," Hushai answered Absalom. "I am on
the side of the one that the LORD, this people, and all the
men of Israel have chosen. I will stay with him. 19 Furthermore, whom will I serve if not his son? As I served
in your father's presence, I will also serve in yours."

20 Then Absalom said to Ahithophel, "Give me your
advice. What should we do?"

21 Ahithophel replied to Absalom, "Sleep with your
father's concubines whom he left to take care of the
palace. When all Israel hears that you have become
repulsive to your father, everyone with you will be
encouraged."[B] 22 So they pitched a tent for Absalom
on the roof, and he slept with his father's concubines
in the sight of all Israel.

23 Now the advice Ahithophel gave in those days
was like someone asking about a word from God
— such was the regard that both David and Absalom

17 had for Ahithophel's advice. 1 Ahithophel said
to Absalom, "Let me choose twelve thousand
men, and I will set out in pursuit of David tonight. 2 I
will attack him while he is weary and discouraged,[C]
throw him into a panic, and all the people with him
will scatter. I will strike down only the king 3 and bring
all the people back to you. When everyone returns
except the man you're looking for, all[D] the people will
be at peace." 4 This proposal seemed right to Absalom
and all the elders of Israel.

5 Then Absalom said, "Summon Hushai the Archite
also. Let's hear what he has to say as well."

6 So Hushai came to Absalom, and Absalom told
him, "Ahithophel offered this proposal. Should we
carry out his proposal? If not, what do you say?"

7 Hushai replied to Absalom, "The advice Ahithophel has given this time is not good." 8 Hushai continued, "You know your father and his men. They are
warriors and are desperate like a wild bear robbed of
her cubs. Your father is an experienced soldier who
won't spend the night with the people. 9 He's probably already hiding in one of the caves[E] or some other
place. If some of our troops fall[F] first, someone is sure
to hear and say, 'There's been a slaughter among the
people who follow Absalom.' 10 Then, even a brave
man with the heart of a lion will lose heart[G] because
all Israel knows that your father and the valiant men
with him are warriors. 11 Instead, I advise that all Israel from Dan to Beer-sheba — as numerous as the
sand by the sea — be gathered to you and that you
personally go into battle. 12 Then we will attack David wherever we find him, and we will descend on
him like dew on the ground. Not even one will be
left—neither he nor any of the men with him. 13 If he
retreats to some city, all Israel will bring ropes to that
city, and we will drag its stones[H] into the valley until
not even a pebble can be found there." 14 Since the
LORD had decreed that Ahithophel's good advice be
undermined in order to bring about Absalom's ruin,
Absalom and all the men of Israel said, "The advice of
Hushai the Archite is better than Ahithophel's advice."

DAVID INFORMED OF ABSALOM'S PLANS

15 Hushai then told the priests Zadok and Abiathar,
"This is what[I] Ahithophel advised Absalom and the
elders of Israel, and this is what[J] I advised. 16 Now
send someone quickly and tell David, 'Don't spend
the night at the wilderness ford,[K] but be sure to cross
over the Jordan,[L] or the king and all the people with
him will be devoured.'"

17 Jonathan and Ahimaaz were staying at En-rogel,
where a servant girl would come and pass along information to them. They in turn would go and inform
King David, because they dared not be seen entering
the city. 18 However, a young man did see them and
informed Absalom. So the two left quickly and came
to the house of a man in Bahurim. He had a well in
his courtyard, and they climbed down into it. 19 Then
his wife took the cover, placed it over the mouth of
the well, and scattered grain on it so nobody would
know anything.

20 Absalom's servants came to the woman at the
house and asked, "Where are Ahimaaz and Jonathan?"

"They passed by toward the water,"[M] the woman
replied to them. The men searched but did not find
them, so they returned to Jerusalem.

21 After they had gone, Ahimaaz and Jonathan
climbed out of the well and went and informed King
David. They told him, "Get up and immediately ford
the river, for Ahithophel has given this advice against
you." 22 So David and all the people with him got up

[A] **16:14** LXX adds *at the Jordan* [B] **16:21** Lit *father, the hands of everyone with you will be strong* [C] **17:2** Lit *and weak of hands* [D] **17:3** LXX reads *to you as a bride returns to her husband. You seek the life of only one man, and all* [E] **17:9** Or *pits*, or *ravines* [F] **17:9** Lit *And it will be when a falling on them at* [G] **17:10** Lit *melt* [H] **17:13** Lit *drag it* [I] **17:15** Lit *"Like this and like this* [J] **17:15** Lit *and like this and like this* [K] **17:16** Some Hb mss; MT reads *plains* [L] **17:16** *the Jordan* supplied for clarity [M] **17:20** Or *brook*; Hb obscure

and crossed the Jordan. By daybreak, there was no
one who had not crossed the Jordan.
23 When Ahithophel realized that his advice had
not been followed, he saddled his donkey and set out
for his house in his hometown. He set his house in
order and hanged himself. So he died and was buried
in his father's tomb.
24 David had arrived at Mahanaim by the time Absalom crossed the Jordan with all the men of Israel.
25 Now Absalom had appointed Amasa over the army in
Joab's place. Amasa was the son of a man named Ithra[A]
the Israelite;[B] Ithra had married Abigail daughter of
Nahash.[C] Abigail was a sister to Zeruiah, Joab's mother.
26 And Israel and Absalom camped in the land of Gilead. 27 When David came to Mahanaim, Shobi son of
Nahash from Rabbah of the Ammonites, Machir son
of Ammiel from Lo-debar, and Barzillai the Gileadite
from Rogelim 28 brought beds, basins,[D] and pottery
items. They also brought wheat, barley, flour, roasted grain, beans, lentils,[E] 29 honey, curds, sheep, goats,
and cheese[F] from the herd for David and the people
with him to eat. They had reasoned, "The people must
be hungry, exhausted, and thirsty in the wilderness."

ABSALOM'S DEFEAT

18 David reviewed his troops and appointed commanders of thousands and of hundreds over
them. 2 He then sent out the troops, a third under Joab,
a third under Joab's brother Abishai son of Zeruiah,
and a third under Ittai of Gath. The king said to the
troops, "I must also march out with you."
3 "You must not go!" the people pleaded. "If we have
to flee, they will not pay any attention to us. Even if
half of us die, they will not pay any attention to us because you are worth[G] ten thousand of us. Therefore,
it is better if you support us from the city."
4 "I will do whatever you think is best," the king replied to them. So he stood beside the city gate while all
the troops marched out by hundreds and thousands.
5 The king commanded Joab, Abishai, and Ittai, "Treat
the young man Absalom gently for my sake." All the
people heard the king's orders to all the commanders
about Absalom.
6 Then David's forces marched into the field to engage Israel in battle, which took place in the forest
of Ephraim. 7 Israel's army was defeated by David's
soldiers, and the slaughter there was vast that day
— twenty thousand dead. 8 The battle spread over
the entire area, and that day the forest claimed more
people than the sword.

ABSALOM'S DEATH

9 Absalom was riding on his mule when he happened
to meet David's soldiers. When the mule went under
the tangled branches of a large oak tree, Absalom's
head was caught fast in the tree. The mule under him
kept going, so he was suspended in midair.[H] 10 One of
the men saw him and informed Joab. He said, "I just
saw Absalom hanging in an oak tree!"
11 "You just saw him!" Joab exclaimed.[I] "Why didn't
you strike him to the ground right there? I would have
given you ten silver pieces[J] and a belt!"
12 The man replied to Joab, "Even if I had the weight
of a thousand pieces of silver[K] in my hand, I would not
raise my hand against the king's son. For we heard
the king command you, Abishai, and Ittai, 'Protect the
young man Absalom for me.'[L] 13 If I had jeopardized
my own[M] life — and nothing is hidden from the king
— you would have abandoned me."
14 Joab said, "I'm not going to waste time with you!"
He then took three spears[N] in his hand and thrust
them into Absalom's chest. While Absalom was still
alive in the oak tree, 15 ten young men who were Joab's
armor-bearers surrounded Absalom, struck him,
and killed him. 16 Joab blew the ram's horn, and the
troops broke off their pursuit of Israel because Joab
restrained them. 17 They took Absalom, threw him into
a large pit in the forest, and raised up a huge mound
of stones over him. And all Israel fled, each to his tent.
18 When he was alive, Absalom had taken a pillar
and raised it up for himself in the King's Valley, since
he thought, "I have no son to preserve the memory
of my name." So he named the pillar after himself. It
is still called Absalom's Monument today.
19 Ahimaaz son of Zadok said, "Please let me run
and tell the king the good news that the LORD has
vindicated him by freeing him from his enemies."
20 Joab replied to him, "You are not the man to take
good news today. You may do it another day, but today you aren't taking good news, because the king's
son is dead." 21 Joab then said to a Cushite, "Go tell the
king what you have seen." The Cushite bowed to Joab
and took off running.
22 However, Ahimaaz son of Zadok persisted and
said to Joab, "No matter what, please let me also run
behind the Cushite!"
Joab replied, "My son, why do you want to run since
you won't get a reward?"[O]
23 "No matter what, I want to run!"
"Then run!" Joab said to him. So Ahimaaz ran by
way of the plain and outran the Cushite.

[A] **17:25** Or *Jether* [B] **17:25** Some LXX mss read *Ishmaelite* [C] **17:25** Some LXX mss read *Jesse* [D] **17:28** LXX reads *brought 10 embroidered beds with double coverings, 10 vessels* [E] **17:28** LXX, Syr; MT adds *roasted grain* [F] **17:29** Hb obscure [G] **18:3** Some Hb mss, LXX, Vg; other Hb mss read *because there would now be about* [H] **18:9** Lit *was between heaven and earth* [I] **18:11** Lit *Joab said to the man who told him* [J] **18:11** About four ounces of silver [K] **18:12** About 25 pounds of silver [L] **18:12** Some Hb mss, LXX, Tg, Vg; other Hb mss read *'Protect, whoever, the young man Absalom'*; Hb obscure [M] **18:13** Alt Hb tradition reads *jeopardized his* [N] **18:14** Lit *rods* [O] **18:22** Or *you have no good news?*

24 David was sitting between the city gates when
the watchman went up to the roof of the city gate and
over to the wall. The watchman looked out and saw a
man running alone. 25 He called out and told the king.
The king said, "If he's alone, he bears good news."
As the first runner came closer, 26 the watchman
saw another man running. He called out to the gatekeeper, "Look! Another man is running alone!"
"This one is also bringing good news," said the king.
27 The watchman said, "The way the first man runs
looks to me like the way Ahimaaz son of Zadok runs."
"This is a good man; he comes with good news,"
the king commented.
28 Ahimaaz called out to the king, "All is well," and
paid homage to the king with his face to the ground.
He continued, "Blessed be the LORD your God! He
delivered up the men who rebelled against my lord
the king."
29 The king asked, "Is the young man Absalom all
right?"
Ahimaaz replied, "When Joab sent the king's servant and your servant, I saw a big disturbance, but I
don't know what it was."
30 The king said, "Move aside and stand here." So
he stood to one side.
31 Just then the Cushite came and said, "May my
lord the king hear the good news: The LORD has vindicated you today by freeing you from all who rise
against you!"
32 The king asked the Cushite, "Is the young man
Absalom all right?"
The Cushite replied, "I wish that the enemies of my
lord the king, along with all who rise up against you
with evil intent, would become like that young man."
33 The king was deeply moved and went up to the
chamber above the city gate and wept. As he walked,
he cried, "My son Absalom! My son, my son Absalom! If only I had died instead of you, Absalom, my
son, my son!"

DAVID'S KINGDOM RESTORED

19 It was reported to Joab, "The king is weeping.
He's mourning over Absalom." 2 That day's
victory was turned into mourning for all the troops
because on that day the troops heard, "The king is
grieving over his son." 3 So they returned to the city
quietly that day like troops come in when they are humiliated after fleeing in battle. 4 But the king covered
his face and cried loudly, "My son Absalom! Absalom,
my son, my son!"
5 Then Joab went into the house to the king and said,
"Today you have shamed all your soldiers — those
who saved your life as well as your sons, your wives,
and your concubines — 6 by loving your enemies and
hating those who love you! Today you have made it
clear that the commanders and soldiers mean nothing
to you. In fact, today I know that if Absalom were alive
and all of us were dead, it would be fine with you![A]
7 "Now get up! Go out and encourage[B] your soldiers,
for I swear by the LORD that if you don't go out, not a
man will remain with you tonight. This will be worse
for you than all the trouble that has come to you from
your youth until now!"
8 So the king got up and sat in the city gate, and all
the people were told, "Look, the king is sitting in the
city gate." Then they all came into the king's presence.
Meanwhile, each Israelite had fled to his tent. 9 People throughout all the tribes of Israel were arguing
among themselves, saying, "The king rescued us from
the grasp of our enemies, and he saved us from the
grasp of the Philistines, but now he has fled from the
land because of Absalom. 10 But Absalom, the man we
anointed over us, has died in battle. So why do you
say nothing about restoring the king?"
11 King David sent word to the priests Zadok and
Abiathar: "Say to the elders of Judah, 'Why should you
be the last to restore the king to his palace? The talk
of all Israel has reached the king at his house. 12 You
are my brothers, my flesh and blood.[C] So why should
you be the last to restore the king?' 13 And tell Amasa,
'Aren't you my flesh and blood?[D] May God punish me
and do so severely if you don't become commander
of my army from now on instead of Joab!'"
14 So he won over[E] all the men of Judah, and they
unanimously sent word to the king: "Come back,
you and all your servants." 15 Then the king returned.
When he arrived at the Jordan, Judah came to Gilgal
to meet the king and escort him across the Jordan.
16 Shimei son of Gera, the Benjaminite from Bahurim, hurried down with the men of Judah to meet
King David. 17 There were a thousand men from Benjamin with him. Ziba, an attendant from the house
of Saul, with his fifteen sons and twenty servants
also rushed down to the Jordan ahead of the king.
18 They forded the Jordan to bring the king's household across and do whatever the king desired.[F]
When Shimei son of Gera crossed the Jordan, he
fell facedown before the king 19 and said to him, "My
lord, don't hold me guilty, and don't remember your
servant's wrongdoing on the day my lord the king
left Jerusalem. May the king not take it to heart. 20 For
your servant knows that I have sinned. But look! Today I am the first one of the entire house of Joseph
to come down to meet my lord the king."
21 Abishai son of Zeruiah asked, "Shouldn't Shimei
be put to death for this, because he cursed the LORD's
anointed?"

[A] **19:6** Lit *be right in your eyes* [B] **19:7** Lit *speak to the heart of* [C] **19:12** Lit *my bone and my flesh* [D] **19:13** Lit *my bone and my flesh?* [E] **19:14** Lit *he turned the heart of* [F] **19:18** Lit *do what is good in his eyes*

Joab: A Man after His Own Heart

by T. Van McClain

Part of the underground water tunnel that leads from inside the city of Jerusalem to an outside water source. At the end of the tunnel is a 43 ½-foot shaft that drops down to the Gihon Spring. The tunnel system provided the people of Jerusalem access to water, even when the city was under attack from outsiders.

Scripture describes David as a man after God's own heart (1Sm 13:14). Joab could aptly be described as a man who was after *his* own heart.

Joab was the son of David's sister Zeruiah. Her three exceptional sons were Abishai, Joab, and Asahel. Abner, an enemy general, reluctantly killed Asahel in self-defense (2Sm 2:19–23). Abner later came over to David's side, but Joab murdered him treacherously. David clearly disavowed some of Joab's actions, but he did not deal with Joab for his crimes.

Joab became commander of David's army due to his bravery in the capture of the city of Jerusalem. Joab proved himself a proficient warrior and commander in a battle against Ammonite and Aramean forces (10:6–14). When King David fell into sin with Bathsheba, Joab assisted the king in his murderous plot to end the life of Uriah the Hittite. Second Samuel 12:26–31 describes Joab conquering Rabbah, the capital city of the Ammonites; apparently he wanted to honor King David by allowing him the privilege of leading the army into the city. Was this an act of respect to David? Actually, his actions could have been a way of both showing respect and protecting his position.

David's son Absalom killed his brother Amnon in revenge for raping his sister, then he fled the country. Joab was instrumental in reconciling Absalom with his father, David. However, Absalom then attempted to usurp the throne. In a later battle, Joab put Absalom to death, running spears through his heart while Absalom hung by his hair in a tree—although David had clearly indicated he did not want Absalom to die. David mourned for Absalom, but Joab convinced him to refrain from mourning. In a bid to gain the confidence of those who had followed Absalom and Amasa, David offered Amasa command of the army in place of Joab. Amasa accepted the offer, and in jealousy, Joab would later murder Amasa.

Joab did show some wisdom in advising King David not to take a census, but Joab was overruled and the census was taken (chap. 24). As a consequence of David's sin, a great pestilence came upon Israel.

Joab did show loyalty to David at times and offered sound advice, but Joab was a man who followed his own heart and did not seek after God's heart. As a result, he received his just reward (1Kg 2:34). ✣

The forest of Ephraim where Joab disobeyed King David's command to spare Absalom's life.

22 David answered, "Sons of Zeruiah, do we agree
on anything? Have you become my adversary today? Should any man be killed in Israel today? Am I
not aware that today I'm king over Israel?" 23 So the
king said to Shimei, "You will not die." Then the king
gave him his oath.

24 Mephibosheth, Saul's grandson, also went down
to meet the king. He had not taken care of his feet,
trimmed his mustache, or washed his clothes from
the day the king left until the day he returned safely.
25 When he came from Jerusalem to meet the king,
the king asked him, "Mephibosheth, why didn't you
come with me?"

26 "My lord the king," he replied, "my servant Ziba
betrayed me. Actually your servant said, 'I'll saddle
the donkey for myself[A] so that I may ride it and go
with the king' — for your servant is lame. 27 Ziba slandered your servant to my lord the king. But my lord
the king is like the angel of God, so do whatever you
think best.[B] 28 For my grandfather's entire family deserves death from my lord the king, but you set your
servant among those who eat at your table. So what
further right do I have to keep on making appeals
to the king?"

29 The king said to him, "Why keep on speaking
about these matters of yours? I hereby declare: you
and Ziba are to divide the land."

30 Mephibosheth said to the king, "Instead, since
my lord the king has come to his palace safely, let
Ziba take it all!"

31 Barzillai the Gileadite had come down from Rogelim and accompanied the king to the Jordan River
to see him off at the Jordan. 32 Barzillai was a very old
man — eighty years old — and since he was a very
wealthy man, he had provided for the needs of the
king while he stayed in Mahanaim.

33 The king said to Barzillai, "Cross over with me,
and I'll provide for you[C] at my side in Jerusalem."

34 Barzillai replied to the king, "How many years of
my life are left that I should go up to Jerusalem with
the king? 35 I'm now eighty years old. Can I discern
what is pleasant and what is not? Can your servant
taste what he eats or drinks? Can I still hear the voice
of male and female singers? Why should your servant
be an added burden to my lord the king? 36 Since your
servant is only going with the king a little way across
the Jordan, why should the king repay me with such
a reward? 37 Please let your servant return so that I
may die in my own city near the tomb of my father
and mother. But here is your servant Chimham; let
him cross over with my lord the king. Do for him what
seems good to you."[D]

38 The king replied, "Chimham will cross over with
me, and I will do for him what seems good to you, and
whatever you desire from me I will do for you." 39 So
all the people crossed the Jordan, and then the king
crossed. The king kissed Barzillai and blessed him,
and Barzillai returned to his home.

40 The king went on to Gilgal, and Chimham went
with him. All the troops of Judah and half of Israel's
escorted the king. 41 Suddenly, all the men of Israel came to the king. They asked him, "Why did our
brothers, the men of Judah, take you away secretly
and transport the king and his household across the
Jordan, along with all of David's men?"

42 All the men of Judah responded to the men of
Israel, "Because the king is our relative. Why does
this make you angry? Have we ever eaten anything
of the king's or been honored at all?"[E]

43 The men of Israel answered the men of Judah,
"We have ten shares in the king, so we have a greater
claim to David than you. Why then do you despise us?
Weren't we the first to speak of restoring our king?"
But the words of the men of Judah were harsher than
those of the men of Israel.

SHEBA'S REVOLT

20 Now a wicked man, a Benjaminite named Sheba son of Bichri, happened to be there. He blew
the ram's horn and shouted:

> We have no portion in David,
> no inheritance in Jesse's son.
> Each man to his tent,[F] Israel!

2 So all the men of Israel deserted David and followed
Sheba son of Bichri, but the men of Judah from the
Jordan all the way to Jerusalem remained loyal to
their king.

3 When David came to his palace in Jerusalem, he
took the ten concubines he had left to take care of the
palace and placed them under guard. He provided for
them, but he was not intimate with them. They were
confined until the day of their death, living as widows.

4 The king said to Amasa, "Summon the men of
Judah to me within three days and be here yourself."
5 Amasa went to summon Judah, but he took longer
than the time allotted him. 6 So David said to Abishai,
"Sheba son of Bichri will do more harm to us than
Absalom. Take your lord's soldiers and pursue him,
or he will find fortified cities and elude us."[G]

7 So Joab's men, the Cherethites, the Pelethites, and
all the warriors marched out under Abishai's command;[H] they left Jerusalem to pursue Sheba son of
Bichri. 8 They were at the great stone in Gibeon when
Amasa joined them. Joab was wearing his uniform and

[A] **19:26** LXX, Syr, Vg read *said to him, 'Saddle the donkey for me*
[B] **19:27** Lit *do what is good in your eyes* [C] **19:33** LXX reads *for your old age*; Ru 4:15 [D] **19:37** Lit *what is good in your eyes*, also in v. 38
[E] **19:42** LXX reads *king's or has he given us a gift or granted us a portion*
[F] **20:1** Alt Hb tradition reads *gods* [G] **20:6** Lit *and snatch away our eyes*
[H] **20:7** Lit *out following him*

over it was a belt around his waist with a sword in its
sheath. As he approached, the sword fell out. 9 Joab
asked Amasa, "Are you well, my brother?" Then with
his right hand Joab grabbed Amasa by the beard to
kiss him. 10 Amasa was not on guard against the sword
in Joab's hand, and Joab stabbed him in the stomach
with it and spilled his intestines out on the ground.
Joab did not stab him again, and Amasa died.

Joab and his brother Abishai pursued Sheba son
of Bichri. 11 One of Joab's young men had stood over
Amasa saying, "Whoever favors Joab and whoever
is for David, follow Joab!" 12 Now Amasa had been
writhing in his blood in the middle of the highway,
and the man had seen that all the troops stopped. So
he moved Amasa from the highway to the field and
threw a garment over him because he realized that
all those who encountered Amasa were stopping.
13 When he was removed from the highway, all the
men passed by and followed Joab to pursue Sheba
son of Bichri.

14 Sheba passed through all the tribes of Israel to
Abel of Beth-maacah. All the Berites[A] came together
and followed him. 15 Joab's troops came and besieged
Sheba in Abel of Beth-maacah. They built a siege ramp
against the outer wall of the city. While all the troops
with Joab were battering the wall to make it collapse,
16 a wise woman called out from the city, "Listen! Listen! Please tell Joab to come here and let me speak
with him."

17 When he had come near her, the woman asked,
"Are you Joab?"

"I am," he replied.

"Listen to the words of your servant," she said to
him.

He answered, "I'm listening."

18 She said, "In the past they used to say, 'Seek counsel in Abel,' and that's how they settled disputes. 19 I am
one of the peaceful and faithful in Israel, but you're
trying to destroy a city that is like a mother in Israel. Why would you devour the LORD's inheritance?"

20 Joab protested: "Never! I would never devour or
demolish! 21 That is not the case. There is a man named
Sheba son of Bichri, from the hill country of Ephraim,
who has rebelled against King David. Deliver this one
man, and I will withdraw from the city."

The woman replied to Joab, "Watch! His head will
be thrown over the wall to you." 22 The woman went
to all the people with her wise counsel, and they cut
off the head of Sheba son of Bichri and threw it to
Joab. So he blew the ram's horn, and they dispersed
from the city, each to his own tent. Joab returned to
the king in Jerusalem.

23 Joab commanded the whole army of Israel;
Benaiah son of Jehoiada was over the
Cherethites and Pelethites;
24 Adoram[B] was over forced labor;
Jehoshaphat son of Ahilud was court
historian;
25 Sheva was court secretary;
Zadok and Abiathar were priests;
26 and in addition, Ira the Jairite was David's
priest.

JUSTICE FOR THE GIBEONITES

21 During David's reign there was a famine for
three successive years, so David inquired[C] of
the LORD. The LORD answered, "It is due to Saul and to
his bloody family, because he killed the Gibeonites."
2 The Gibeonites were not Israelites but rather a
remnant of the Amorites. The Israelites had taken an
oath concerning them, but Saul had tried to kill them
in his zeal for the Israelites and Judah. So David summoned the Gibeonites and spoke to them. 3 He asked
the Gibeonites, "What should I do for you? How can
I make atonement so that you will bring a blessing
on[D] the LORD's inheritance?"

4 The Gibeonites said to him, "We are not asking
for silver and gold from Saul or his family, and we
cannot put anyone to death in Israel."

"Whatever you say, I will do for you," he said.

5 They replied to the king, "As for the man who annihilated us and plotted to destroy us so we would not
exist within the whole territory of Israel, 6 let seven
of his male descendants be handed over to us so we
may hang[E] them in the presence of the LORD at Gibeah
of Saul, the LORD's chosen."

The king answered, "I will hand them over."

7 David spared Mephibosheth, the son of Saul's son
Jonathan, because of the oath of the LORD that was
between David and Jonathan, Saul's son. 8 But the
king took Armoni and Mephibosheth, who were the
two sons whom Rizpah daughter of Aiah had borne
to Saul, and the five sons whom Merab[F] daughter of
Saul had borne to Adriel son of Barzillai the Meholathite 9 and handed them over to the Gibeonites. They
hanged[G] them on the hill in the presence of the LORD;
the seven of them died together. They were executed
in the first days of the harvest at the beginning of the
barley harvest.[H]

THE BURIAL OF SAUL'S FAMILY

10 Rizpah, Aiah's daughter, took sackcloth and spread
it out for herself on the rock from the beginning of
the harvest[I] until the rain poured down from heaven

[A] **20:14** LXX, Vg read *Bichrites* [B] **20:24** Some Hb mss, LXX, Syr read *Adoniram*; 1Kg 4:6; 5:14 [C] **21:1** Lit *sought the face of* [D] **21:3** Lit *will bless* [E] **21:6** Or *impale*, or *expose* [F] **21:8** Some Hb mss, LXX, Syr, Tg; other Hb mss read *Michal* [G] **21:9** Or *impaled*, or *exposed*, also in v. 13 [H] **21:9** = March–April [I] **21:10** = April to October

on the bodies. She kept the birds of the sky from them
by day and the wild animals by night.
11 When it was reported to David what Saul's concubine Rizpah daughter of Aiah had done, 12 he went and
got the bones of Saul and his son Jonathan from the
citizens of Jabesh-gilead. They had stolen them from
the public square of Beth-shan where the Philistines
had hung the bodies the day the Philistines killed Saul
at Gilboa. 13 David had the bones brought from there.
They gathered up the bones of Saul's family who had
been hanged 14 and buried the bones of Saul and his
son Jonathan at Zela in the land of Benjamin in the
tomb of Saul's father Kish. They did everything the
king commanded. After this, God was receptive to
prayer for the land.

THE PHILISTINE GIANTS

15 The Philistines again waged war against Israel. David went down with his soldiers, and they fought the
Philistines, but David became exhausted. 16 Then Ish-
bi-benob, one of the descendants of the giant,[A] whose
bronze spear weighed about eight pounds[B] and who
wore new armor, intended to kill David. 17 But Abishai
son of Zeruiah came to his aid, struck the Philistine,
and killed him. Then David's men swore to him, "You
must never again go out with us to battle. You must
not extinguish the lamp of Israel."
18 After this, there was another battle with the Philistines at Gob. At that time Sibbecai the Hushathite
killed Saph, who was one of the descendants of the
giant.
19 Once again there was a battle with the Philistines
at Gob, and Elhanan son of Jaare-oregim the Bethle-
hemite killed[C] Goliath of Gath. The shaft of his spear
was like a weaver's beam.
20 At Gath there was still another battle. A huge
man was there with six fingers on each hand and
six toes on each foot — twenty-four in all. He, too,
was descended from the giant. 21 When he taunted
Israel, Jonathan, son of David's brother Shimei,
killed him.
22 These four were descended from the giant in
Gath and were killed by David and his soldiers.

DAVID'S SONG OF THANKSGIVING

22 David spoke the words of this song to the
LORD on the day the LORD rescued him from
the grasp of all his enemies and from the grasp of
Saul. 2 He said:

The LORD is my rock, my fortress,
and my deliverer,
3 my God,[D] my rock where I seek refuge.
My shield, the horn of my salvation,
my stronghold, my refuge,
and my Savior, you save me from violence.
4 I called to the LORD, who is worthy of praise,
and I was saved from my enemies.
5 For the waves of death engulfed me;
the torrents of destruction terrified me.
6 The ropes of Sheol entangled me;
the snares of death confronted me.

7 I called to the LORD in my distress;
I called to my God.
From his temple he heard my voice,
and my cry for help reached his ears.
8 Then the earth shook and quaked;
the foundations of the heavens[E] trembled;
they shook because he burned with anger.
9 Smoke rose from his nostrils,
and consuming fire came from his mouth;
coals were set ablaze by it.[F]
10 He bent the heavens and came down,
total darkness beneath his feet.
11 He rode on a cherub and flew,
soaring[G] on the wings of the wind.
12 He made darkness a canopy around him,
a gathering[H] of water and thick clouds.
13 From the radiance of his presence,
blazing coals were ignited.
14 The LORD thundered from heaven;
the Most High made his voice heard.
15 He shot arrows and scattered them;
he hurled lightning bolts and routed them.
16 The depths of the sea became visible,
the foundations of the world were exposed
at the rebuke of the LORD,
at the blast of the breath of his nostrils.

17 He reached down from on high
and took hold of me;
he pulled me out of deep water.
18 He rescued me from my powerful enemy
and from those who hated me,
for they were too strong for me.
19 They confronted me in the day
of my calamity,
but the LORD was my support.
20 He brought me out to a spacious place;
he rescued me because he delighted in me.

21 The LORD rewarded me
according to my righteousness;
he repaid me
according to the cleanness of my hands.

[A] **21:16** Or *Raphah*, also in vv. 18,20,22 [B] **21:16** Lit *300* (shekels) [C] **21:19** 1Ch 20:5 adds *the brother of* [D] **22:3** LXX, Ps 18:2 read *my God*; MT reads *God of* [E] **22:8** Some Hb mss, Syr, Vg read *mountains*; Ps 18:7 [F] **22:9** Or *him* [G] **22:11** Some Hb mss; other Hb mss, Syr, Tg read *he was seen* [H] **22:12** Or *sieve*, or *mass*; Hb obscure

22 For I have kept the ways of the LORD
and have not turned from my God
to wickedness.
23 Indeed, I let all his ordinances guide me[A]
and have not disregarded his statutes.
24 I was blameless before him
and kept myself from my iniquity.
25 So the LORD repaid me
according to my righteousness,
according to my cleanness[B] in his sight.

26 With the faithful
you prove yourself faithful,
with the blameless
you prove yourself blameless,
27 with the pure
you prove yourself pure,
but with the crooked
you prove yourself shrewd.
28 You rescue an oppressed people,
but your eyes are set against the proud —
you humble them.
29 LORD, you are my lamp;
the LORD illuminates my darkness.
30 With you I can attack a barricade,[C]
and with my God I can leap over a wall.
31 God — his way is perfect;
the word of the LORD is pure.
He is a shield to all who take refuge in him.

32 For who is God besides the LORD?
And who is a rock? Only our God.
33 God is my strong refuge;[D]
he makes my way perfect.[E]
34 He makes my feet like the feet of a deer
and sets me securely on the[F] heights.[G]
35 He trains my hands for war;
my arms can bend a bow of bronze.
36 You have given me the shield
of your salvation;
your help[H] exalts me.
37 You make a spacious place beneath me
for my steps,
and my ankles do not give way.
38 I pursue my enemies and destroy them;
I do not turn back until they are wiped out.
39 I wipe them out and crush them,
and they do not rise;
they fall beneath my feet.
40 You have clothed me with strength
for battle;
you subdue my adversaries beneath me.
41 You have made my enemies retreat
before me;[I]
I annihilate those who hate me.
42 They look, but there is no one
to save them —
they look to the LORD, but he does not
answer them.
43 I pulverize them like dust of the earth;
I crush them and trample them like mud
in the streets.

44 You have freed me from the feuds
among my people;
you have preserved me as head of nations;
a people I had not known serve me.
45 Foreigners submit to me cringing;
as soon as they hear, they obey me.
46 Foreigners lose heart
and come trembling from their fortifications.

47 The LORD lives — blessed be my rock!
God, the rock of my salvation, is exalted.
48 God — he grants me vengeance
and casts down peoples under me.
49 He frees me from my enemies.
You exalt me above my adversaries;
you rescue me from violent men.

50 Therefore I will give thanks to you among
the nations, LORD;
I will sing praises about your name.
51 He is a tower of salvation for[J] his king;
he shows loyalty to his anointed,
to David and his descendants forever.

DAVID'S LAST WORDS

23 These are the last words of David:
The declaration of David son of Jesse,
the declaration of the man raised on high,[K]
the one anointed by the God of Jacob.
This is the most delightful of Israel's songs.
2 The Spirit of the LORD spoke through me,
his word was on my tongue.
3 The God of Israel spoke;
the Rock of Israel said to me,
"The one who rules the people with justice,
who rules in the fear of God,
4 is like the morning light when the sun rises
on a cloudless morning,
the glisten of rain on sprouting grass."

[A] **22:23** Lit *Indeed, all his ordinances have been in front of me*
[B] **22:25** LXX, Syr, Vg read *to the cleanness of my hands*; Ps 18:24
[C] **22:30** Or *a ridge*, or *raiders* [D] **22:33** DSS, some LXX mss, Syr, Vg read *God clothes me with strength*; Ps 18:32 [E] **22:33** Some LXX mss, Syr; MT reads *he sets free the blameless his way*; Hb obscure
[F] **22:34** LXX; some Hb mss read *my*; other Hb mss read *his*
[G] **22:34** Or *on my high places* [H] **22:36** LXX reads *humility*; Ps 18:35
[I] **22:41** Lit *you gave me the neck of my enemies* [J] **22:51** DSS read *he gives great victory to* [K] **23:1** Or *raised up by the high God*

Music in David's Time

by Becky Lombard

For Hebrews in the centuries before Christ, music was a vehicle for the worshiper to experience supernatural moments with God (1Sm 10:5–6; 16:23; 2Kg 3:14–16).

There were two worship traditions in the Old Testament. First, worship was spontaneous and ecstatic, exemplified in the above passages. Much religious poetry and music was improvised in response to events in the lives of worshipers. After the Israelites were delivered from the Egyptians, Moses and Miriam led in celebration that was poetic, vocal, and instrumental (Ex 15:1–21). The song they sang was repetitive, involving much physical movement and rhythm.

Worship could also be professional and formal.[1] David led in the organization of worship leader teams who were trained and well skilled at leading and performing music in the temple. The opening ceremony for the temple was a musical spectacular (2Ch 5:12–13).

In Hebrew worship of the tenth century, Scripture was not spoken. It was chanted or sung to melody. This was to honor the sanctity of Scripture, setting it apart from the conversations of daily life.[2] Harmony was not used. Voices and instruments performed the same melody, with each performer adding embellishments. There are some indications that drones under the melody might have been common. The spirit was exuberant and most scholars believe it to have been quite loud. The instruments used to accompany and help create this heterophonic sound included string (harp, lyre), wind (ram's horn, trumpet), and percussion (tambourine, cymbals, rattles).

Some implications concerning performance style can be drawn from poetry texts. Many psalms have heading designations that indicate who was to perform the poetry. Several are delineated as repertoire for specific musician

The remains of this lyre were found in the king's grave (Tomb 789) located near that of Sub-ad (Pu-abi) in the royal cemetery at Ur.

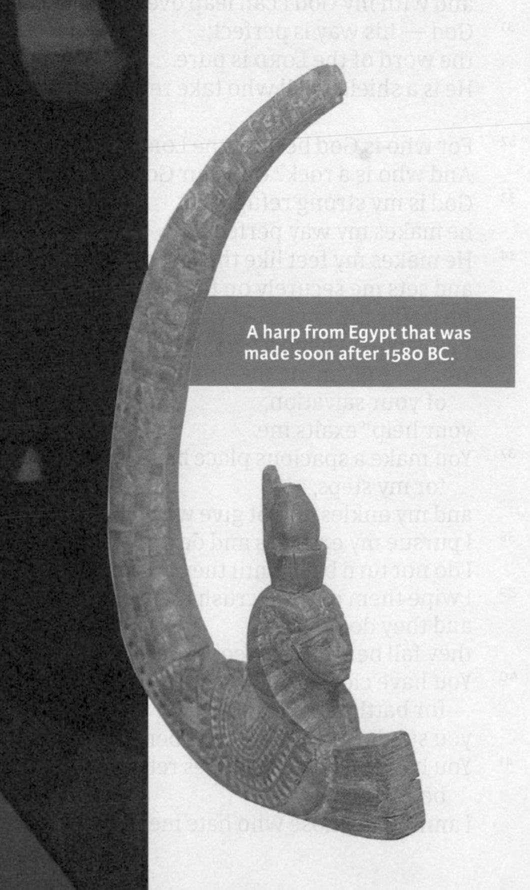

A harp from Egypt that was made soon after 1580 BC.

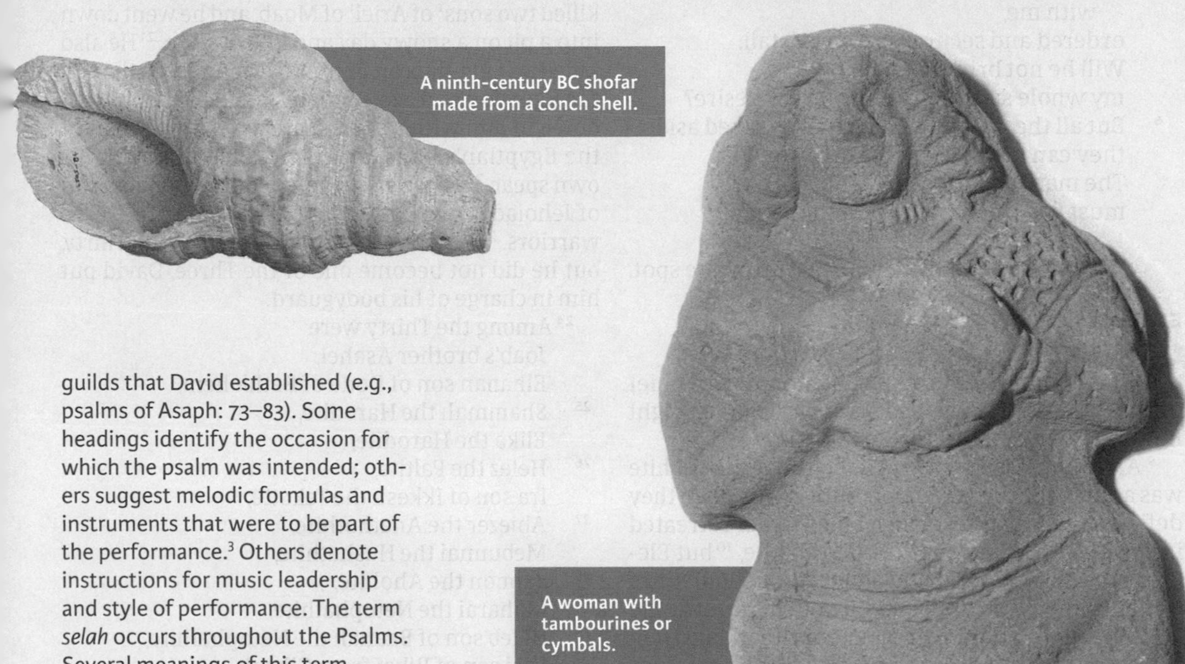

A ninth-century BC shofar made from a conch shell.

A woman with tambourines or cymbals.

guilds that David established (e.g., psalms of Asaph: 73–83). Some headings identify the occasion for which the psalm was intended; others suggest melodic formulas and instruments that were to be part of the performance.[3] Others denote instructions for music leadership and style of performance. The term *selah* occurs throughout the Psalms. Several meanings of this term have been conjectured. The most commonly accepted theory is that it indicated some sort of pause, probably a musical interlude between verses of the text.

One musicological scholar has asserted that the various symbols and marks that appear over and under letters throughout Hebrew Scriptures are a form of musical notation. (Scholars have generally considered these marks to be accent marks or punctuation.) Using the musical interpretation of these marks, a system of notation has been devised and some transcription and recording of melodies accomplished.[4]

The structure of the poetry is also important in understanding how Israelites worshiped through music. Psalms were written with textual parallelism in which a statement was followed by a restatement of the same idea using different words. This textual style was conducive to musical performance. It allowed for *responsorial* performance where the worship leader sang the first statement and a group of singers responded with the reiteration. Style of writing also allowed *antiphonal* performance where two groups alternated singing the text. Several psalms use a repeated refrain that allowed for a *litany* in which the congregation could respond with each repetition (e.g., Ps 136).

There was no rhyme scheme to Hebrew poetry. The syllable accents within a line were inconsistent and did not allow an even meter as does our music today. There were strong and weak accents within the lines of poetry, and the rhythm of these textual inflections probably guided the rhythm of the music as opposed to any kind of steady beat. The melodic formulas would also have accommodated these irregular poetry lines.[5] ✣

[1] Donald P. Hustad, *Jubilate II: Church Music in Worship and Renewal* (Carol Stream, IL: Hope, 1993), 131–32. [2] Andrew Wilson-Dickson, *The Story of Christian Music* (Minneapolis: Fortress, 1996), 23. [3] Wilson-Dickson, *Story*, 20. [4] Suzanne Haik-Vantoura, *The Music of the Bible Revealed*, trans. Dennis Weber (Berkeley, CA: BIBAL, 1991). [5] Wilson-Dickson, *Story*, 21.

5 Is it not true my house is with God?
For he has established a permanent covenant
with me,
ordered and secured in every detail.
Will he not bring about
my whole salvation and my every desire?
6 But all the wicked are like thorns raked aside;
they can never be picked up by hand.
7 The man who touches them
must be armed with iron and the shaft
of a spear.
They will be completely burned up on the spot.

EXPLOITS OF DAVID'S WARRIORS

8 These are the names of David's warriors:
Josheb-basshebeth the Tahchemonite was chief
of the officers.[A] He wielded his spear[B] against eight
hundred men that he killed at one time.
9 After him, Eleazar son of Dodo son of an Ahohite
was among the three warriors with David when they
defied the Philistines. The men of Israel retreated
in the place they had gathered for battle, 10 but Eleazar stood his ground and attacked the Philistines
until his hand was tired and stuck to his sword. The
LORD brought about a great victory that day. Then
the troops came back to him, but only to plunder
the dead.
11 After him was Shammah son of Agee the Hararite. The Philistines had assembled in formation
where there was a field full of lentils. The troops fled
from the Philistines, 12 but Shammah took his stand
in the middle of the field, defended it, and struck
down the Philistines. So the LORD brought about a
great victory.
13 Three of the thirty leading warriors went down
at harvest time and came to David at the cave of Adullam, while a company of Philistines was camping
in Rephaim Valley. 14 At that time David was in the
stronghold, and a Philistine garrison was at Bethlehem. 15 David was extremely thirsty[C] and said, "If
only someone would bring me water to drink from
the well at the city gate of Bethlehem!" 16 So three of
the warriors broke through the Philistine camp and
drew water from the well at the gate of Bethlehem.
They brought it back to David, but he refused to drink
it. Instead, he poured it out to the LORD. 17 David said,
"LORD, I would never do such a thing! Is this not the
blood of men who risked their lives?" So he refused to
drink it. Such were the exploits of the three warriors.
18 Abishai, Joab's brother and son of Zeruiah, was
leader of the Three.[D] He wielded his spear against
three hundred men and killed them, gaining a reputation among the Three. 19 Was he not more honored
than the Three? He became their commander even
though he did not become one of the Three.
20 Benaiah son of Jehoiada was the son of a brave
man from Kabzeel, a man of many exploits. Benaiah
killed two sons[E] of Ariel[F] of Moab, and he went down
into a pit on a snowy day and killed a lion. 21 He also
killed an Egyptian, an impressive man. Even though
the Egyptian had a spear in his hand, Benaiah went
down to him with a staff, snatched the spear out of
the Egyptian's hand, and then killed him with his
own spear. 22 These were the exploits of Benaiah son
of Jehoiada, who had a reputation among the three
warriors. 23 He was the most honored of the Thirty,
but he did not become one of the Three. David put
him in charge of his bodyguard.
24 Among the Thirty were
Joab's brother Asahel,
Elhanan son of Dodo of Bethlehem,
25 Shammah the Harodite,
Elika the Harodite,
26 Helez the Paltite,
Ira son of Ikkesh the Tekoite,
27 Abiezer the Anathothite,
Mebunnai the Hushathite,
28 Zalmon the Ahohite,
Maharai the Netophathite,
29 Heleb son of Baanah the Netophathite,
Ittai son of Ribai from Gibeah
of the Benjaminites,
30 Benaiah the Pirathonite,
Hiddai from the wadis of Gaash,[G]
31 Abi-albon the Arbathite,
Azmaveth the Barhumite,
32 Eliahba the Shaalbonite,
the sons of Jashen,
Jonathan son of[H] 33 Shammah
the Hararite,
Ahiam son of Sharar the Hararite,
34 Eliphelet son of Ahasbai
son of the Maacathite,
Eliam son of Ahithophel the Gilonite,
35 Hezro the Carmelite,
Paarai the Arbite,
36 Igal son of Nathan from Zobah,
Bani the Gadite,
37 Zelek the Ammonite,
Naharai the Beerothite, the armor-bearer
for Joab son of Zeruiah,
38 Ira the Ithrite,
Gareb the Ithrite,
39 and Uriah the Hethite.
There were thirty-seven in all.

[A] **23:8** Some Hb mss, LXX read *Three* [B] **23:8** Some Hb mss; other Hb mss, LXX read *He was Adino the Eznite* [C] **23:15** Lit *And David craved* [D] **23:18** Some Hb mss, Syr read *the Thirty* [E] **23:20** LXX; MT omits *sons* [F] **23:20** Or *two warriors* [G] **23:30** Or *from Nahale-gaash* [H] **23:32** Some LXX mss; MT omits *son of*; 1Ch 11:34

Threshing Floors

by J. Mark Terry

Wooden winnowing fan from Egypt's New Kingdom. Employed in pairs, these fans were used to throw the trodden grain into the air for the breeze to separate the chaff from the grain.

Threshing floor at Zaatara, outside Bethlehem. After winnowing barley on the threshing floor at Bethlehem, Boaz fell asleep. He awakened to find Ruth lying at his feet.

The farmers in ancient Israel raised several types of grain. The Old Testament mentions wheat (Gn 30:14), spelt (an inferior type of wheat, Ex 9:32), barley (v. 31), and millet (Ezk 4:9). The King James Version usually employs the word translated "corn" for all types of grain, but the translators did not have in mind the corn (maize) that is grown in North America.[1]

Threshing is the process of separating the kernels of grain from the husks. Normally the Israelites threshed their grain on a threshing floor. The threshing floor (Hb *goren*) was a level surface in the open air. It could be either smoothed stone or hard-packed earth. Usually the threshing floor was circular in shape and about fifty feet in diameter with a stone border to keep the grain inside. Most floors were located on the outskirts of the village or town, often on a hilltop. The Hebrews preferred to place their threshing floors on hilltops so the wind would blow away the chaff. Some floors were privately owned, like those of Atad (Gn 50:10) and Araunah (2Sm 24:16), but most floors belonged to the community.[2]

Threshing time was a time for community celebration. Normally the workers cut the grain in the field with sickles, leaving some stalks on the margins of the field for the poor. Once the grain was cut, the harvesters gathered the grain into bundles or sheaves. The workers then transported the sheaves to the threshing floor. A small amount of grain might be threshed by flailing the grain on the threshing floor. Sometimes the grain would be threshed by walking an ox over the grain. More often, the thresher would use a sledge (Jb 41:30) or a cart (sometimes called a wheel; Is 28:27). The threshing board (Is 41:15) was made of wooden planks nailed together with rocks or metal objects attached to the bottom. Usually oxen or horses pulled the sledge across the grain again and again. The farmer often piled stones or stood on the sledge to make it heavier. Somewhat later the Hebrews used a threshing cart or wheel (Pr 20:26). This was a metal roller that threshed the grain more efficiently.

During the threshing, the farmer would turn the sheaves over frequently with a wooden "fork." This enabled the breeze to blow some of the chaff away. After threshing was complete, workers would then winnow the grain. This involved putting the grain into large shallow baskets and tossing the grain into the air. Again, the purpose was to allow the wind to blow away the chaff. The chaff was burned, and the grain was stored in underground silos or in clay jars until it was needed.[3]

The process of threshing took several days. While the threshing proceeded, someone would sleep on the threshing floor to guard the grain, lest robbers come to steal it. Boaz was doing just that when Ruth came to the floor and slept at his feet (Ru 3:7–8). ✣

---

[1] See "Grain" in *HIBD*, 680. [2] L. G. Herr, "Thresh; Threshing" in *ISBE*, vol. 4 (1988), 844; and Nelson B. Baker, "Threshing" and "Threshing Floor" in *Wycliffe Bible Encyclopedia*, ed. Charles F. Pfeiffer, Howard. F. Vos, and John Rea (Chicago: Moody, 1975), 1701. [3] Baker, "Threshing."

DAVID'S MILITARY CENSUS

24 The LORD's anger burned against Israel again, and he stirred up David against them to say, "Go, count the people of Israel and Judah."

2 So the king said to Joab, the commander of his army, "Go through all the tribes of Israel from Dan to Beer-sheba and register the troops so I can know their number."

3 Joab replied to the king, "May the LORD your God multiply the troops a hundred times more than they are — while my lord the king looks on! But why does my lord the king want to do this?"

4 Yet the king's order prevailed over Joab and the commanders of the army. So Joab and the commanders of the army left the king's presence to register the troops of Israel.

5 They crossed the Jordan and camped in Aroer, south of the town in the middle of the valley, and then proceeded toward Gad and Jazer. 6 They went to Gilead and to the land of the Hittites[A] and continued on to Dan-jaan and around to Sidon. 7 They went to the fortress of Tyre and all the cities of the Hivites and Canaanites. Afterward, they went to the Negev of Judah at Beer-sheba.

8 When they had gone through the whole land, they returned to Jerusalem at the end of nine months and twenty days. 9 Joab gave the king the total of the registration of the troops. There were eight hundred thousand valiant armed men[B] from Israel and five hundred thousand men from Judah.

10 David's conscience troubled him after he had taken a census of the troops. He said to the LORD, "I have sinned greatly in what I've done. Now, LORD, because I've been very foolish, please take away your servant's guilt."

DAVID'S PUNISHMENT

11 When David got up in the morning, the word of the LORD had come to the prophet Gad, David's seer: 12 "Go and say to David, 'This is what the LORD says: I am offering you three choices. Choose one of them, and I will do it to you.'"

13 So Gad went to David, told him the choices, and asked him, "Do you want three[C] years of famine to come on your land, to flee from your foes three months while they pursue you, or to have a plague in your land three days? Now, consider carefully[D] what answer I should take back to the one who sent me."

14 David answered Gad, "I have great anxiety. Please, let us fall into the LORD's hands because his mercies are great, but don't let me fall into human hands."

15 So the LORD sent a plague on Israel from that morning until the appointed time, and from Dan to Beer-sheba seventy thousand men died. 16 Then the angel extended his hand toward Jerusalem to destroy it, but the LORD relented concerning the destruction and said to the angel who was destroying the people, "Enough, withdraw your hand now!" The angel of the LORD was then at the threshing floor of Araunah[E] the Jebusite.

17 When David saw the angel striking the people, he said to the LORD, "Look, I am the one who has sinned; I am the one[F] who has done wrong. But these sheep, what have they done? Please, let your hand be against me and my father's family."

DAVID'S ALTAR

18 Gad came to David that day and said to him, "Go up and set up an altar to the LORD on the threshing floor of Araunah the Jebusite." 19 David went up in obedience to Gad's command, just as the LORD had commanded. 20 Araunah looked down and saw the king and his servants coming toward him, so he went out and paid homage to the king with his face to the ground.

21 Araunah said, "Why has my lord the king come to his servant?"

David replied, "To buy the threshing floor from you in order to build an altar to the LORD, so the plague on the people may be halted."

22 Araunah said to David, "My lord the king may take whatever he wants[G] and offer it. Here are the oxen for a burnt offering and the threshing sledges and ox yokes for the wood. 23 Your Majesty, Araunah gives everything here to the king." Then he said to the king, "May the LORD your God accept you."

24 The king answered Araunah, "No, I insist on buying it from you for a price, for I will not offer to the LORD my God burnt offerings that cost me nothing." David bought the threshing floor and the oxen for twenty ounces[H] of silver. 25 He built an altar to the LORD there and offered burnt offerings and fellowship offerings. Then the LORD was receptive to prayer for the land, and the plague on Israel ended.

[A] **24:6** LXX; MT reads *of Tahtim-hodshi*; Hb obscure [B] **24:9** Lit *men of valor drawing the sword* [C] **24:13** LXX; MT reads *seven*; 1Ch 21:12 [D] **24:13** Lit *Now, know and see* [E] **24:16** = Ornan in 1Ch 21:15–28; 2Ch 3:1 [F] **24:17** LXX reads *shepherd* [G] **24:22** Lit *take what is good in his eyes* [H] **24:24** Lit *50 shekels*

1 KINGS

Site in Sinai referred to as Elijah's basin. Tradition claims Elijah stayed here after he fled from Jezebel. Here God spoke to Elijah in a soft whisper.

INTRODUCTION TO

1 KINGS

Circumstances of Writing

Scholars cannot identify the authors of any portions of 1 Kings. Traditional guesses such as Samuel and Jeremiah lack evidence, although a prominent worshiper of the Lord like Jeremiah would have been influential in the circles that produced these books. Since the books of 1 and 2 Kings clearly incorporated many earlier documents, the complete authorship would include all writers who contributed to the source documents of this work. At some point, the Holy Spirit worked in the human authors to authenticate the inspired, inerrant books of 1 and 2 Kings. The final stage of composition or compilation had to come after the release of Jehoiachin from Babylonian imprisonment (ca 562 BC). That edition may have added only a postscript to a work completed years earlier, or it may have involved significant additions.

The history recorded in 1 and 2 Kings covers approximately 410 years. First Kings begins around 970 BC with the death of King David; 2 Kings ends around 560 BC with the release of King Jehoiachin from prison. During this time, the nation of Israel split into two kingdoms (930 BC), and both kingdoms went into exile (Israel in 722 BC and Judah in 587 BC).

Contribution to the Bible

For the Bible writers, history could not have existed without God's purposes. This makes all history theological. The books of 1 and 2 Kings interpreted Hebrew history in light of Old Testament covenant theology. The Babylonian exile created the need for this work of historical apologetics. The exiles needed to explain the failure of the religious program established by the sovereign God. In the Deuteronomistic History—Joshua, Judges, 1 and 2 Samuel, and 1 and 2 Kings—this failure was consistently explained as the failures of the people to live up to their part of the covenant.

Structure

The organizing principle of 1 and 2 Kings is not story or narrative. Kings is unique because the basic structural units were the formulaic royal records. Formal openers (1Kg 15:9–10) and closers (1Kg 15:23–24) usually identify the boundaries of the record of an individual monarch. Then the writer could insert other types of literature before, between, and after the openers and closers: narratives, prayers, descriptions, and so forth. But the most important element was the evaluation of the ruler's faithfulness to the covenant (15:11–15). All of these materials made up a history of covenant obedience and disobedience.

DAVID'S LAST DAYS

1 Now King David was old and advanced in age.
Although they covered him with bedclothes, he
could not get warm. 2 So his servants said to him,
"Let us[A] search for a young virgin for my lord the
king. She is to attend the king and be his caregiver.
She is to lie by your side so that my lord the king
will get warm." 3 They searched for a beautiful girl
throughout the territory of Israel; they found Abishag
the Shunammite[B] and brought her to the king. 4 The
girl was of unsurpassed beauty, and she became the
king's caregiver. She attended to him, but he was not
intimate with[C] her.

ADONIJAH'S BID FOR POWER

5 Adonijah son of Haggith kept exalting himself, saying, "I will be king!" He prepared chariots, cavalry, and
fifty men to run ahead of him.[D] 6 But his father had
never once infuriated him by asking, "Why did you
do that?" In addition, he was quite handsome and
was born after Absalom. 7 He conspired[E] with Joab
son of Zeruiah and with the priest Abiathar. They
supported Adonijah, 8 but the priest Zadok, Benaiah
son of Jehoiada, the prophet Nathan, Shimei, Rei,
and David's royal guard[F] did not side with Adonijah.

9 Adonijah sacrificed sheep, goats, cattle, and fattened cattle near the stone of Zoheleth, which is next
to En-rogel. He invited all his royal brothers and all
the men of Judah, the servants of the king, 10 but he
did not invite the prophet Nathan, Benaiah, the royal
guard, or his brother Solomon.

NATHAN'S AND BATHSHEBA'S APPEALS

11 Then Nathan said to Bathsheba, Solomon's mother,
"Have you not heard that Adonijah son of Haggith has
become king and our lord David does not know it?
12 Now please come and let me advise you. Save your
life and the life of your son Solomon. 13 Go, approach
King David and say to him, 'My lord the king, did you
not swear to your servant: Your son Solomon is to
become king after me, and he is the one who is to sit
on my throne? So why has Adonijah become king?'
14 At that moment, while you are still there speaking with the king, I'll come in after you and confirm
your words."

15 So Bathsheba went to the king in his bedroom.
Since the king was very old, Abishag the Shunammite was attending to him. 16 Bathsheba knelt low
and paid homage to the king, and he asked, "What
do you want?"

17 She replied, "My lord, you swore to your servant
by the LORD your God, 'Your son Solomon is to become
king after me, and he is the one who is to sit on my
throne.' 18 Now look, Adonijah has become king. And,[G]
my lord the king, you didn't know it. 19 He has lavishly
sacrificed oxen, fattened cattle, and sheep. He invited
all the king's sons, the priest Abiathar, and Joab the
commander of the army, but he did not invite your
servant Solomon. 20 Now, my lord the king, the eyes
of all Israel are on you to tell them who will sit on the
throne of my lord the king after him. 21 Otherwise,
when my lord the king rests with his ancestors, I
and my son Solomon will be regarded as criminals."

22 At that moment, while she was still speaking
with the king, the prophet Nathan arrived, 23 and it
was announced to the king, "The prophet Nathan
is here." He came into the king's presence and paid
homage to him with his face to the ground.

24 "My lord the king," Nathan said, "did you say,
'Adonijah is to become king after me, and he is the
one who is to sit on my throne'? 25 For today he went
down and lavishly sacrificed oxen, fattened cattle,
and sheep. He invited all the sons of the king, the
commanders of the army, and the priest Abiathar.
And look! They're eating and drinking in his presence, and they're saying, 'Long live King Adonijah!'
26 But he did not invite me — me, your servant —
or the priest Zadok or Benaiah son of Jehoiada or
your servant Solomon. 27 I'm certain my lord the king
would not have let this happen without letting your
servant[H] know who will sit on my lord the king's
throne after him."

SOLOMON CONFIRMED KING

28 King David responded by saying, "Call in Bathsheba for me." So she came into the king's presence
and stood before him. 29 The king swore an oath and
said, "As the LORD lives, who has redeemed my life
from every difficulty, 30 just as I swore to you by the
LORD God of Israel: Your son Solomon is to become
king after me, and he is the one who is to sit on my
throne in my place, that is exactly what I will do this
very day."

31 Bathsheba knelt low with her face to the ground,
paying homage to the king, and said, "May my lord
King David live forever!"

32 King David then said, "Call in the priest Zadok,
the prophet Nathan, and Benaiah son of Jehoiada
for me." So they came into the king's presence. 33 The
king said to them, "Take my servants with you, have
my son Solomon ride on my own mule, and take him
down to Gihon. 34 There, the priest Zadok and the
prophet Nathan are to anoint him as king over Israel. You are to blow the ram's horn and say, 'Long live

[A] **1:2** Lit *them* [B] **1:3** Shunem was a town in the hill country of Issachar at the foot of Mt. Moreh; Jos 19:17–18. [C] **1:4** Lit *he did not know* [D] **1:5** Heralds announcing his procession [E] **1:7** Lit *His words were* [F] **1:8** Lit *David's warriors* [G] **1:18** Some Hb mss, LXX, Vg, Syr; other Hb mss read *And now* [H] **1:27** Some Hb mss, LXX; alt Hb tradition reads *servants*

King Solomon!' 35 You are to come up after him, and
he is to come in and sit on my throne. He is the one
who is to become king in my place; he is the one I
have commanded to be ruler over Israel and Judah."
36 "Amen," Benaiah son of Jehoiada replied to the
king. "May the LORD, the God of my lord the king, so
affirm it. 37 Just as the LORD was with my lord the king,
so may he[A] be with Solomon and make his throne
greater than the throne of my lord King David."
38 Then the priest Zadok, the prophet Nathan, Benaiah son of Jehoiada, the Cherethites, and the Pelethites went down, had Solomon ride on King David's
mule, and took him to Gihon. 39 The priest Zadok took
the horn of oil from the tabernacle and anointed
Solomon. Then they blew the ram's horn, and all the
people proclaimed, "Long live King Solomon!" 40 All
the people went up after him, playing flutes and rejoicing with such a great joy that the earth split open
from the sound.[B]

ADONIJAH HEARS OF SOLOMON'S CORONATION

41 Adonijah and all the invited guests who were with
him heard the noise as they finished eating. Joab
heard the sound of the ram's horn and said, "Why is
the town in such an uproar?" 42 He was still speaking
when Jonathan son of Abiathar the priest, suddenly
arrived. Adonijah said, "Come in, for you are an important man, and you must be bringing good news."
43 "Unfortunately not," Jonathan answered him.
"Our lord King David has made Solomon king. 44 And
with Solomon, the king has sent the priest Zadok, the
prophet Nathan, Benaiah son of Jehoiada, the Cherethites, and the Pelethites, and they have had him ride
on the king's mule. 45 The priest Zadok and the prophet Nathan have anointed him king in Gihon. They have
gone up from there rejoicing. The town has been in
an uproar; that's the noise you heard. 46 Solomon has
even taken his seat on the royal throne.
47 "The king's servants have also gone to congratulate our lord King David, saying, 'May your God make
the name of Solomon more well known than your
name, and may he make his throne greater than your
throne.' Then the king bowed in worship on his bed.
48 And the king went on to say this: 'Blessed be the
LORD God of Israel! Today he has provided one to sit
on my throne, and I am a witness.'"[C]
49 Then all of Adonijah's guests got up trembling
and went their separate ways. 50 Adonijah was afraid
of Solomon, so he got up and went to take hold of the
horns of the altar.
51 It was reported to Solomon, "Look, Adonijah
fears King Solomon, and he has taken hold of the
horns of the altar, saying, 'Let King Solomon first[D]
swear to me that he will not kill his servant with the
sword.'"
52 Then Solomon said, "If he is a man of character,
not a single hair of his will fall to the ground, but if
evil is found in him, he dies." 53 So King Solomon sent
for him, and they took him down from the altar. He
came and paid homage to King Solomon, and Solomon said to him, "Go to your home."

DAVID'S DYING INSTRUCTIONS TO SOLOMON

2 As the time approached for David to die, he ordered his son Solomon, 2 "As for me, I am going
the way of all of the earth. Be strong and be a man,
3 and keep your obligation to the LORD your God to
walk in his ways and to keep his statutes, commands,
ordinances, and decrees. This is written in the law of
Moses, so that you will have success in everything you
do and wherever you turn, 4 and so that the LORD will
fulfill his promise that he made to me: 'If your sons
take care to walk faithfully before me with all their
heart and all their soul, you will never fail to have a
man on the throne of Israel.'
5 "You also know what Joab son of Zeruiah did to
me and what he did to the two commanders of Israel's
army, Abner son of Ner and Amasa son of Jether. He
murdered them in a time of peace to avenge blood
shed in war. He spilled that blood on his own waistband and on the sandals of his feet.[E] 6 Act according
to your wisdom, and do not let his gray head descend
to Sheol in peace.
7 "Show kindness to the sons of Barzillai the Gileadite and let them be among those who eat at your
table because they supported me when I fled from
your brother Absalom.
8 "Keep an eye on Shimei son of Gera, the Benjaminite from Bahurim who is with you. He uttered
malicious curses against me the day I went to Mahanaim. But he came down to meet me at the Jordan
River, and I swore to him by the LORD, 'I will never kill
you with the sword.' 9 So don't let him go unpunished,
for you are a wise man. You know how to deal with
him to bring his gray head down to Sheol with blood."
10 Then David rested with his ancestors and was
buried in the city of David. 11 The length of time David
reigned over Israel was forty years: he reigned seven
years in Hebron and thirty-three years in Jerusalem.
12 Solomon sat on the throne of his father David, and
his kingship was firmly established.

ADONIJAH'S FOOLISH REQUEST

13 Now Adonijah son of Haggith came to Bathsheba,
Solomon's mother. She asked, "Do you come peacefully?"

[A] **1:37** Alt Hb tradition reads *so he will* [B] **1:40** LXX reads *the land resounded with their noise* [C] **1:48** Lit *and my eyes are seeing* [D] **1:51** Some Hb mss, LXX, Syr, Vg read *today* [E] **2:5** LXX, Old Lat read *on my waistband and . . . my feet*; v. 31

"Peacefully," he replied, 14 and then asked, "May I talk with you?"[A]

"Go ahead," she answered.

15 "You know the kingship was mine," he said. "All Israel expected me to be king, but then the kingship was turned over to my brother, for the LORD gave it to him. 16 So now I have just one request of you; don't turn me down."[B]

She said to him, "Go on."

17 He replied, "Please speak to King Solomon since he won't turn you down. Let him give me Abishag the Shunammite as a wife."

18 "Very well," Bathsheba replied. "I will speak to the king for you."

19 So Bathsheba went to King Solomon to speak to him about Adonijah. The king stood up to greet her, bowed to her, sat down on his throne, and had a throne placed for the king's mother. So she sat down at his right hand.

20 Then she said, "I have just one small request of you. Don't turn me down."

"Go ahead and ask, mother," the king replied, "for I won't turn you down."

21 So she said, "Let Abishag the Shunammite be given to your brother Adonijah as a wife."

22 King Solomon answered his mother, "Why are you requesting Abishag the Shunammite for Adonijah? Since he is my elder brother, you might as well ask the kingship for him, for the priest Abiathar, and for Joab son of Zeruiah."[C] 23 Then King Solomon took an oath by the LORD: "May God punish me and do so severely if Adonijah has not made this request at the cost of his life. 24 And now, as the LORD lives — the one who established me, seated me on the throne of my father David, and made me a dynasty as he promised — I swear Adonijah will be put to death today!" 25 Then King Solomon dispatched Benaiah son of Jehoiada, who struck down Adonijah, and he died.

ABIATHAR'S BANISHMENT

26 The king said to the priest Abiathar, "Go to your fields in Anathoth. Even though you deserve to die, I will not put you to death today, since you carried the ark of the Lord GOD in the presence of my father David and you suffered through all that my father suffered." 27 So Solomon banished Abiathar from being the LORD's priest, and it fulfilled the LORD's prophecy he had spoken at Shiloh against Eli's family.

JOAB'S EXECUTION

28 The news reached Joab. Since he had supported Adonijah but not Absalom, Joab fled to the LORD's tabernacle and took hold of the horns of the altar. 29 It was reported to King Solomon, "Joab has fled to the LORD's tabernacle and is now beside the altar."

Then Solomon sent[D] Benaiah son of Jehoiada and told him, "Go and strike him down!"

30 So Benaiah went to the tabernacle and said to Joab, "This is what the king says: 'Come out!'"

But Joab said, "No, for I will die here."

So Benaiah took a message back to the king, "This is what Joab said, and this is how he answered me."

31 The king said to him, "Do just as he says. Strike him down and bury him in order to remove from me and from my father's family the blood that Joab shed without just cause. 32 The LORD will bring back his own blood on his head because he struck down two men more righteous and better than he, without my father David's knowledge. With his sword, Joab murdered Abner son of Ner, commander of Israel's army, and Amasa son of Jether, commander of Judah's army. 33 The responsibility for their deaths will come back to Joab and to his descendants[E] forever, but for David, his descendants, his dynasty, and his throne, there will be peace from the LORD forever."

34 Benaiah son of Jehoiada went up, struck down Joab, and put him to death. He was buried at his house in the wilderness. 35 Then the king appointed Benaiah son of Jehoiada in Joab's place over the army, and he appointed the priest Zadok in Abiathar's place.

SHIMEI'S BANISHMENT AND EXECUTION

36 Then the king summoned Shimei and said to him, "Build a house for yourself in Jerusalem and live there, but don't leave there and go anywhere else. 37 On the day you do leave and cross the Kidron Valley, know for sure that you will certainly die. Your blood will be on your own head."

38 Shimei said to the king, "The sentence is fair; your servant will do as my lord the king has spoken." And Shimei lived in Jerusalem for a long time.

39 But then, at the end of three years, two of Shimei's slaves ran away to Achish son of Maacah, king of Gath. Shimei was informed, "Look, your slaves are in Gath." 40 So Shimei saddled his donkey and set out to Achish at Gath to search for his slaves. He went and brought them back from Gath.

41 It was reported to Solomon that Shimei had gone from Jerusalem to Gath and had returned. 42 So the king summoned Shimei and said to him, "Didn't I

[A] **2:14** Lit *then said, "I have a word for you."* [B] **2:16** Lit *don't make me turn my face* [C] **2:22** LXX, Vg, Syr read *kingship for him, and on his side are Abiathar the priest and Joab son of Zeruiah* [D] **2:29** LXX adds *Joab a message: "What is the matter with you, that you have fled to the altar?" And Joab replied, "Because I feared you, I have fled to the Lord." And Solomon the king sent* [E] **2:33** Lit *Their blood will return on the head of Joab and on the head of his seed*

make you swear by the LORD and warn you, saying, 'On the day you leave and go anywhere else, know for sure that you will certainly die'? And you said to me, 'The sentence is fair; I will obey.' 43 So why have you not kept the LORD's oath and the command that I gave you?" 44 The king also said, "You yourself know all the evil that you did to my father David. Therefore, the LORD has brought back your evil on your head, 45 but King Solomon will be blessed, and David's throne will remain established before the LORD forever."

46 Then the king commanded Benaiah son of Jehoiada, and he went out and struck Shimei down, and he died. So the kingdom was established in Solomon's hand.

THE LORD APPEARS TO SOLOMON

3 Solomon made an alliance[A] with Pharaoh king of Egypt by marrying Pharaoh's daughter. Solomon brought her to the city of David until he finished building his palace, the LORD's temple, and the wall surrounding Jerusalem. 2 However, the people were sacrificing on the high places, because until that time a temple for the LORD's name had not been built. 3 Solomon loved the LORD by walking in the statutes of his father David, but he also sacrificed and burned incense on the high places.

4 The king went to Gibeon to sacrifice there because it was the most famous high place. He offered a thousand burnt offerings on that altar. 5 At Gibeon the LORD appeared to Solomon in a dream at night. God said, "Ask. What should I give you?"

6 And Solomon replied, "You have shown great and faithful love to your servant, my father David, because he walked before you in faithfulness, righteousness, and integrity.[B] You have continued this great and faithful love for him by giving him a son to sit on his throne, as it is today.

7 "LORD my God, you have now made your servant king in my father David's place. Yet I am just a youth with no experience in leadership.[C] 8 Your servant is among your people you have chosen, a people too many to be numbered or counted. 9 So give your servant a receptive heart to judge your people and to discern between good and evil. For who is able to judge this great people of yours?"

10 Now it pleased the Lord that Solomon had requested this. 11 So God said to him, "Because you have requested this and did not ask for long life[D] or riches for yourself, or the death[E] of your enemies, but you asked discernment for yourself to administer justice, 12 I will therefore do what you have asked. I will give you a wise and understanding heart, so that there has never been anyone like you before and never will be again. 13 In addition, I will give you what you did not ask for: both riches and honor, so that no king will be your equal during your entire life. 14 If you walk in my ways and keep my statutes and commands just as your father David did, I will give you a long life."

15 Then Solomon woke up and realized it had been a dream. He went to Jerusalem, stood before the ark of the Lord's covenant, and offered burnt offerings and fellowship offerings. Then he held a feast for all his servants.

SOLOMON'S WISDOM

16 Then two women who were prostitutes came to the king and stood before him. 17 One woman said, "Please, my lord, this woman and I live in the same house, and I had a baby while she was in the house. 18 On the third day after I gave birth, she also had a baby and we were alone. No one else[F] was with us in the house; just the two of us were there. 19 During the night this woman's son died because she lay on him. 20 She got up in the middle of the night and took my son from my side while your servant was asleep. She laid him in her arms, and she put her dead son in my arms. 21 When I got up in the morning to nurse my son, I discovered he was dead. That morning, when I looked closely at him I realized that he was not the son I gave birth to."

22 "No," the other woman said. "My son is the living one; your son is the dead one."

The first woman said, "No, your son is the dead one; my son is the living one." So they argued before the king.

23 The king replied, "This woman says, 'This is my son who is alive, and your son is dead,' but that woman says, 'No, your son is dead, and my son is alive.'" 24 The king continued, "Bring me a sword." So they brought the sword to the king. 25 And the king said, "Cut the living boy in two and give half to one and half to the other."

26 The woman whose son was alive spoke to the king because she felt great compassion[G] for her son. "My lord, give her the living baby," she said, "but please don't have him killed!"

But the other one said, "He will not be mine or yours. Cut him in two!"

27 The king responded, "Give the living baby to the first woman, and don't kill him. She is his mother." 28 All Israel heard about the judgment the king had given, and they stood in awe of the king because they saw that God's wisdom was in him to carry out justice.

[A] **3:1** Lit *Solomon made himself a son-in-law* [B] **3:6** Lit *and uprightness of heart with you* [C] **3:7** Lit *am a little youth and do not know to go out or come in* [D] **3:11** Lit *for many days* [E] **3:11** Lit *life* [F] **3:18** Lit *No stranger* [G] **3:26** Lit *because her compassion grew hot*

Solomon's Foreign Wives and Their Gods

by Alan Branch

The most obvious indicator of Solomon's unfaithfulness to God is his unparalleled participation in polygamy. For Solomon, polygamy was initially a form of political expediency and a method for forging alliances with surrounding nations. While other Old Testament men engaged in polygamy, Solomon's excessive wealth and political power allowed him to entertain an unrestrained appetite for more women, a lack of discipline that corresponded to his ill-advised foray into supporting paganism.

Solomon imported the worship of foreign gods into Jerusalem and established places for pagan worship on the Mount of Olives (1Kg 11:7). In so doing, he engaged in religious syncretism, an attempt to reconcile the contradictory beliefs between monotheistic Yahwism and the polytheistic teachings of surrounding nations. The writer of Kings listed four pagan gods that Solomon's foreign wives enticed the aging king to worship—Ashtoreth, Milcom, Chemosh, and Molech (vv. 1–13).

Winged lion on the side of the throne of Ashtoreth in the temple of Echmoun. This temple complex was for worship of Echmoun, the Phoenician god of healing. Temple dates to the seventh century BC.

ASHTORETH

The Old Testament is unequivocally opposed to goddess worship and uses several terms to critique the practice of worshiping ancient goddesses. Because these terms look and sound familiar, they can be somewhat confusing. First Kings 11:5 says, "Solomon followed Ashtoreth, the goddess of the Sidonians." Ashtoreth can be easily confused with either the terms *Asherah* or *Asherim* mentioned elsewhere in Scripture. In Canaanite mythology, the highest deities were El and his wife, Asherah. The Hebrew word *Asherim* is the plural form of Asherah and refers to various symbols of the goddess Asherah. Among the seventy children of El and Asherah were the god Baal and the goddess Ashtoreth, both of whom were the focus of popular devotion. People commonly considered Ashtoreth to be the wife of Baal and identified her with a widely popular goddess in the ancient Near East known by either of the names Ashtart (Phoenician) or Astarte (Greek). In the ancient Near East, the goddess that people knew by the names Ashtoreth, Ashtart, or Astarte was associated with love and war. The Hebrew word *Ashtoreth* is actually a way of showing contempt and condemnation for worship of this goddess since "Ashtoreth" is formed by taking the consonants for Ashtart and combining them with the vowels from the Hebrew word for shame, *bosheth*.[1]

Stele of the Moabite warrior god, likely Kamosh (spelled "Chemosh" in the Old Testament), brandishing a weapon. Although the lack of provenance information makes dating imprecise, the style indicates 1200–800 BC. The clothing and hair reflect an Egyptian influence.

Understanding the goddess worship condemned in Scripture is also confusing because some cultures blended the goddesses Asherah and Ashtoreth into one. Devotees of Canaanite religion in different places and different periods felt free to arrange the pantheon according to their own preferences.[2] The late Old Testament scholar William F. Albright summarized the complexity of the relationship between these goddesses: "The goddesses Ashtaroth [Ashtoreth] and Asherah seem to interchange repeatedly in the Hebrew Bible, where both are mentioned with Baal."[3] Due to this interplay between the goddesses Asherah and Ashtoreth, the reference to "Ashtoreth, the goddess of the Sidonians" in 1 Kings 11 may be either a way of saying this was the goddess Ashtoreth from the Canaanite pantheon or, more broadly, a generic way of saying Solomon initiated officially sanctioned Canaanite goddess worship.

People almost always associated goddess worship, whether under the name Asherah or Ashtoreth, with fertility cults. Deuteronomy 23:17 warns, "No Israelite woman is to be a cult prostitute, and no Israelite man is to be a cult prostitute." Ritual prostitution was part of the entire complex of beliefs associated with veneration of the male god Baal and his various goddess consorts. Evidently the goddess worship Solomon sanctioned entailed this sort of prostitution several centuries later. Second Kings 23:7 says that Josiah "tore down the houses of the male cult prostitutes that were in the LORD's temple, in which the women were weaving tapestries for Asherah."

MILCOM

The Old Testament teaches that Milcom was the Ammonites' patron deity. The name "Milcom" was a deliberate Hebrew scribal misvocalization of the god's name,[4] a pronunciation the Hebrew scribes apparently created to slander the Ammonites' national deity. Some modern translations consider the name "Milcom" to be an allusion to the god Molech. For example, the NIV translates "Milcom" as "Molek" in 1 Kings 11:5. The CSB translates "Molech" in 1 Kings 11:7 as "Milcom." These different translations reflect ongoing debate concerning the possibility that Milcom and Molech are different names for the same god, with Milcom being the Ammonite version of Molech worship. Supporting this view is the fact that both the names "Milcom" and "Molech" come from the Hebrew word *melek*, which means "king."[5] The account of Josiah's reforms in 2 Kings 23:10–14 seems to differentiate between Molech and Milcom as separate entities. With this in mind, 1 Kings 11:5 may be a reference to veneration of Milcom as king of the gods within the Ammonite pantheon.[6]

CHEMOSH

Chemosh was the Moabites' patron deity. The Old Testament calls the Moabites the "people of Chemosh" (Nm 21:29; Jr 48:46). Additionally, the inscription on the Moabite Stone mentions Moab's King Mesha attributing his victory over Israel to Chemosh.[7] Although the specifics of Chemosh worship are somewhat obscure, evidence indicates the Moabites especially venerated Chemosh as a war god. In fact, the Moabite Stone "is most emphatic on [Chemosh's] intervention and specific guidance in times of war."[8]

MOLECH

First Kings 11:7 says that Solomon built a place of worship for "Molech the abomination of the people of

At Hazor, under the modern shelter is the high place or altar area, erected during Solomon's time. Such structures gave evidence of syncretistic worship practices.

Ammon" (NKJV). As mentioned above, the CSB translates "Molech" as "Milcom" here, though the CSB translator's footnote indicates the word is literally "Molech." We can easily imagine the Ammonites incorporating Molech worship into their polytheistic pantheon, adding the worship of Molech to their practice of venerating their primary god, Milcom. Their being two separate deities helps us understand Josiah destroying places of worship dedicated to both Milcom and Molech. Thus 1 Kings 11 may in fact be differentiating between two separate gods, Molech and Milcom.

Scholars have debated about the specific god or practices condemned under the title "Molech" in the Old Testament. A vocal minority insists that references to "Molech" in the Old Testament are not references to a particular god, but to the practice of child sacrifice.[9] The majority opinion, though, explains Molech as an underworld deity who was appeased or worshiped through human sacrifice, particularly the sacrifice of children.[10] Ancient worshipers closely related Molech to a cult of the dead. Leviticus 18:21 specifically condemned worshiping him: "You are not to make any of your children pass through the fire to Molech" (CSB footnote). ✣

---

[1] Scott Langston, "Ashtaroth" in *HIBD*, 127. [2] Bryce N. Sandlin, "Ashtaroth," *BI* 15.4 (Summer 1989): 19. [3] William Foxwell Albright, *Archaeology and the Religion of Israel*, 5th ed. (Louisville: Westminster John Knox, 1968), 74. [4] Richard D. Patterson and Hermann J. Austel, *1, 2 Kings*, vol. 4 in The Expositor's Bible Commentary (Grand Rapids: Zondervan, 1988), 245. [5] E. Ray Clendenen, "Religious Background of the Old Testament," in *Foundations for Biblical Interpretation*, ed. David S. Dockery, Kenneth A. Mathews, and Robert B. Sloan (Nashville: Broadman & Holman, 1994), 298. [6] See "Milcom" in *HIBD*, 1124. [7] "The Moabite Stone" in *The Ancient Near East*, ed. James B. Pritchard (Princeton: Princeton University Press, 1955), 1:209–10. [8] Gerald L. Mattingly, "Chemosh" in *ABD*, 1:897. [9] For example, Stephen J. Andrews, "Molech" in *Mercer Dictionary of the Bible* (*MDB*), ed. Watson E. Mills (Macon, GA: Mercer University Press, 1990), 580–81. [10] See Richard S. Hess, *Israelite Religions: An Archaeological and Biblical Survey* (Grand Rapids: Baker Academic, 2007), 101–2.

SOLOMON'S OFFICIALS

4 King Solomon reigned over all Israel, 2 and these were his officials:

Azariah son of Zadok, priest;
3 Elihoreph and Ahijah the sons of Shisha, secretaries;
Jehoshaphat son of Ahilud, court historian;
4 Benaiah son of Jehoiada, in charge of the army;
Zadok and Abiathar, priests;
5 Azariah son of Nathan, in charge of the deputies;
Zabud son of Nathan, a priest and adviser to the king;
6 Ahishar, in charge of the palace;
and Adoniram son of Abda, in charge of forced labor.

7 Solomon had twelve deputies for all Israel. They provided food for the king and his household; each one made provision for one month out of the year. 8 These were their names:

Ben-hur, in the hill country of Ephraim;
9 Ben-deker, in Makaz, Shaalbim, Beth-shemesh, and Elon-beth-hanan;
10 Ben-hesed, in Arubboth (he had Socoh and the whole land of Hepher);
11 Ben-abinadab, in all Naphath-dor (Taphath daughter of Solomon was his wife);
12 Baana son of Ahilud, in Taanach, Megiddo, and all Beth-shean which is beside Zarethan below Jezreel, from Beth-shean to Abel-meholah, as far as the other side of Jokmeam;
13 Ben-geber, in Ramoth-gilead (he had the villages of Jair son of Manasseh, which are in Gilead, and he had the region of Argob, which is in Bashan, sixty great cities with walls and bronze bars);
14 Ahinadab son of Iddo, in Mahanaim;
15 Ahimaaz, in Naphtali (he also had married a daughter of Solomon — Basemath);
16 Baana son of Hushai, in Asher and Bealoth;
17 Jehoshaphat son of Paruah, in Issachar;
18 Shimei son of Ela, in Benjamin;
19 Geber son of Uri, in the land of Gilead, the country of King Sihon of the Amorites and of King Og of Bashan.

There was one deputy in the land of Judah.[A]

SOLOMON'S PROVISIONS

20 Judah and Israel were as numerous as the sand by the sea; they were eating, drinking, and rejoicing. 21 Solomon ruled all the kingdoms from the Euphrates River to the land of the Philistines and as far as the border of Egypt. They offered tribute and served Solomon all the days of his life.

22 Solomon's provisions for one day were 180 bushels[B] of fine flour and 360 bushels[C] of meal, 23 ten fattened cattle, twenty range cattle, and a hundred sheep and goats, besides deer, gazelles, roebucks, and penfed poultry,[D] 24 for he had dominion over everything west of the Euphrates from Tiphsah to Gaza and over all the kings west of the Euphrates. He had peace on all his surrounding borders. 25 Throughout Solomon's reign, Judah and Israel lived in safety from Dan to Beer-sheba, each person under his own vine and his own fig tree. 26 Solomon had forty thousand[E] stalls of horses for his chariots, and twelve thousand horsemen. 27 Each of those deputies for a month in turn provided food for King Solomon and for everyone who came to King Solomon's table. They neglected nothing. 28 Each man brought the barley and the straw for the chariot teams and the other horses to the required place according to his assignment.[F]

SOLOMON'S WISDOM AND LITERARY GIFTS

29 God gave Solomon wisdom, very great insight, and understanding as vast as the sand on the seashore. 30 Solomon's wisdom was greater than the wisdom of all the people of the East, greater than all the wisdom of Egypt. 31 He was wiser than anyone — wiser than Ethan the Ezrahite, and Heman, Calcol, and Darda, sons of Mahol. His reputation extended to all the surrounding nations.

32 Solomon spoke 3,000 proverbs, and his songs numbered 1,005. 33 He spoke about trees, from the cedar in Lebanon to the hyssop growing out of the wall. He also spoke about animals, birds, reptiles, and fish. 34 Emissaries of all peoples, sent by every king on earth who had heard of his wisdom, came to listen to Solomon's wisdom.

HIRAM'S BUILDING MATERIALS

5 King Hiram of Tyre sent his emissaries to Solomon when he heard that he had been anointed king in his father's place, for Hiram had always been friends with David.

2 Solomon sent this message to Hiram: 3 "You know my father David was not able to build a temple for the name of the LORD his God. This was because of the warfare all around him until the LORD put his enemies under his feet. 4 The LORD my God has now given me rest on every side; there is no enemy or misfortune. 5 So I plan to build a temple for the name of the LORD my God, according to what the LORD promised my father David: 'I will put your son on your throne in your place, and he will build the temple for my name.'

[A] **4:19** LXX; MT omits *of Judah* [B] **4:22** Lit *30 cors* [C] **4:22** Lit *60 cors* [D] **4:23** Hb obscure [E] **4:26** 2Ch 9:25 reads *4,000 stalls* [F] **4:28** Lit *judgment*

DIGGING DEEPER ***House of Yahweh Inscription***

Prior to the 1960s, critical scholars questioned whether Solomon's temple really existed as the Bible describes (1Kg 6; 9:15). This skepticism began to change when Yohanan Aharoni led a team of archaeologists to Tel Arad, twenty miles northeast of the ancient city of Beer-sheba. During his excavations from 1962 to 1967, Aharoni unearthed several pieces of pottery (ostraca) that were inscribed with the Hebrew phrase *Bayit Yahweh* ("house of Yahweh"). Dating from the eighth to sixth centuries BC, the shards most likely refer to Solomon's temple in Jerusalem. In 1997, a second Hebrew inscription surfaced from an unknown location. It appears to be a receipt for silver donated to Solomon's temple project. The likely date range of this receipt is from the ninth to the seventh centuries BC. It reads: ". . . silver of Tarshish for the house (or temple) of Yahweh—3 shekels" (1Kg 10:22,27). In light of such evidences, most scholars now agree that the biblical descriptions of Solomon's temple are accurate, while there is ongoing debate about the temple's precise location and function.

6 "Therefore, command that cedars from Lebanon be cut down for me. My servants will be with
your servants, and I will pay your servants' wages
according to whatever you say, for you know that
not a man among us knows how to cut timber like
the Sidonians."
7 When Hiram heard Solomon's words, he rejoiced
greatly and said, "Blessed be the LORD today! He has
given David a wise son to be over this great people!"
8 Then Hiram sent a reply to Solomon, saying, "I have
heard your message; I will do everything you want
regarding the cedar and cypress timber. 9 My servants
will bring the logs down from Lebanon to the sea, and
I will make them into rafts to go by sea to the place
you indicate. I will break them apart there, and you
can take them away. You then can meet my needs by
providing my household with food."
10 So Hiram provided Solomon with all the cedar
and cypress timber he wanted, 11 and Solomon provided Hiram with one hundred twenty thousand
bushels[A] of wheat as food for his household and
one hundred twenty thousand gallons[B] of oil from
crushed olives. Solomon did this for Hiram year after year.
12 The LORD gave Solomon wisdom, as he had promised him. There was peace between Hiram and Solomon, and the two of them made a treaty.

SOLOMON'S WORKFORCE

13 Then King Solomon drafted forced laborers from
all Israel; the labor force numbered thirty thousand men. 14 He sent ten thousand to Lebanon each
month in shifts; one month they were in Lebanon,
two months they were at home. Adoniram was in
charge of the forced labor. 15 Solomon had seventy
thousand porters and eighty thousand stonecutters
in the mountains, 16 not including his thirty-three
hundred[C] deputies in charge of the work. They supervised the people doing the work. 17 The king commanded them to quarry large, costly stones to lay
the foundation of the temple with dressed stones.
18 So Solomon's builders and Hiram's builders, along
with the Gebalites, quarried the stone and prepared
the timber and stone for the temple's construction.

BUILDING THE TEMPLE

6 Solomon began to build the temple for the LORD
in the four hundred eightieth year after the Israelites came out of the land of Egypt, in the fourth year
of his reign over Israel, in the month of Ziv, which is
the second month.[D] 2 The temple that King Solomon
built for the LORD was ninety feet[E] long, thirty feet[F]
wide, and forty-five feet[G] high. 3 The portico in front
of the temple sanctuary was thirty feet long extending across the temple's width, and fifteen feet deep[H]
in front of the temple. 4 He also made windows with
beveled frames[I] for the temple.
5 He then built a chambered structure[J] along the
temple wall, encircling the walls of the temple, that
is, the sanctuary and the inner sanctuary. And he
made side chambers[K] all around. 6 The lowest chamber was 7½ feet[L] wide, the middle was 9 feet[M] wide,
and the third was 10½ feet[N] wide. He also provided
offset ledges for the temple all around the outside so
that nothing would be inserted into the temple walls.
7 The temple's construction used finished stones cut
at the quarry so that no hammer, chisel, or any iron
tool was heard in the temple while it was being built.
8 The door for the lowest[O] side chamber was on the
right side of the temple. They[P] went up a stairway[I] to
the middle chamber, and from the middle to the third.
9 When he finished building the temple, he paneled it
with boards and planks of cedar. 10 He built the chambers along the entire temple, joined to the temple with
cedar beams; each story was 7½ feet high.

[A]**5:11** Lit *20,000 cors* [B]**5:11** LXX reads *20,000 baths*; MT reads *20 cors*
[C]**5:16** Some LXX mss read *3,600*; 2Ch 2:2,18 [D]**6:1** April–May
[E]**6:2** Lit *60 cubits* [F]**6:2** Lit *20 cubits*, also in vv. 3,16,20 [G]**6:2** Lit *30 cubits* [H]**6:3** Lit *10 cubits wide* [I]**6:4,8** Hb obscure [J]**6:5** Lit *built the temple of chamber* [K]**6:5** Lit *made ribs* or *sides* [L]**6:6** Lit *five cubits*, also in vv. 10,24 [M]**6:6** Lit *six cubits* [N]**6:6** Lit *seven cubits*
[O]**6:8** LXX, Tg; MT reads *middle* [P]**6:8** = People

11 The word of the LORD came to Solomon: 12 "As for this temple you are building — if you walk in my statutes, observe my ordinances, and keep all my commands by walking in them, I will fulfill my promise to you, which I made to your father David. 13 I will dwell among the Israelites and not abandon my people Israel."

14 When Solomon finished building the temple,[A] 15 he paneled the interior temple walls with cedar boards; from the temple floor to the surface of the ceiling he overlaid the interior with wood. He also overlaid the floor with cypress boards. 16 Then he lined thirty feet of the rear of the temple with cedar boards from the floor to the surface of the ceiling,[B] and he built the interior as an inner sanctuary, the most holy place. 17 The temple, that is, the sanctuary in front of the most holy place,[C] was sixty feet[D] long. 18 The cedar paneling inside the temple was carved with ornamental gourds and flower blossoms. Everything was cedar; not a stone could be seen.

19 He prepared the inner sanctuary inside the temple to put the ark of the LORD's covenant there. 20 The interior of the sanctuary was thirty feet long, thirty feet wide, and thirty feet high; he overlaid it with pure gold. He also overlaid the cedar altar. 21 Next, Solomon overlaid the interior of the temple with pure gold, and he hung[E] gold chains across the front of the inner sanctuary and overlaid it with gold. 22 So he added the gold overlay to the entire temple until everything was completely finished, including the entire altar that belongs to the inner sanctuary.

23 In the inner sanctuary he made two cherubim 15 feet[F] high out of olive wood. 24 One wing of the first cherub was 7 1/2 feet long, and the other wing was 7 1/2 feet long. The wingspan was 15 feet from tip to tip. 25 The second cherub also was 15 feet; both cherubim had the same size and shape. 26 The first cherub's height was 15 feet and so was the second cherub's. 27 Then he put the cherubim inside the inner temple. Since their wings were spread out, the first one's wing touched one wall while the second cherub's wing touched the other[G] wall, and in the middle of the temple their wings were touching wing to wing. 28 He also overlaid the cherubim with gold.

29 He carved all the surrounding temple walls with carved engravings — cherubim, palm trees, and flower blossoms — in the inner and outer sanctuaries. 30 He overlaid the temple floor with gold in both the inner and the outer sanctuaries.

31 For the entrance of the inner sanctuary, he made olive wood doors. The pillars of the doorposts were five-sided.[H] 32 The two doors were made of olive wood. He carved cherubim, palm trees, and flower blossoms on them and overlaid them with gold, hammering gold over the cherubim and palm trees. 33 In the same way, he made four-sided[H] olive wood doorposts for the sanctuary entrance. 34 The two doors were made of cypress wood; the first door had two folding sides, and the second door had two folding panels. 35 He carved cherubim, palm trees, and flower blossoms on them and overlaid them with gold applied evenly over the carving. 36 He built the inner courtyard with three rows of dressed stone and a row of trimmed cedar beams.

37 The foundation of the LORD's temple was laid in Solomon's fourth year in the month of Ziv. 38 In his eleventh year in the month of Bul, which is the eighth month,[I] the temple was completed in every detail and according to every specification. So he built it in seven years.

SOLOMON'S PALACE COMPLEX

7 Solomon completed his entire palace complex after thirteen years of construction. 2 He built the House of the Forest of Lebanon. It was one hundred fifty feet[J] long, seventy-five feet[K] wide, and forty-five feet[L] high on four rows of cedar pillars, with cedar beams on top of the pillars. 3 It was paneled above with cedar at the top of the chambers that rested on forty-five pillars, fifteen per row. 4 There were three rows of window frames, facing each other[M] in three tiers.[N] 5 All the doors and doorposts had rectangular frames, the openings facing each other[O] in three tiers. 6 He made the hall of pillars seventy-five feet long and forty-five feet wide. A portico was in front of the pillars, and a canopy with pillars[H] was in front of them. 7 He made the Hall of the Throne where he would judge — the Hall of Judgment. It was paneled with cedar from the floor to the rafters.[P] 8 Solomon's own palace where he would live, in the other courtyard behind the hall, was of similar construction. And he made a house like this hall for Pharaoh's daughter, his wife.[Q]

9 All of these buildings were of costly stones, cut to size and sawed with saws on the inner and outer surfaces, from foundation to coping and from the outside to the great courtyard. 10 The foundation was made of large, costly stones twelve and fifteen feet[R] long. 11 Above were also costly stones, cut to size, as well as cedar wood. 12 Around the great courtyard, as well as the inner courtyard of the LORD's temple and

[A] **6:11–14** LXX omits these vv. [B] **6:16** LXX; MT omits *of the ceiling*; 1Kg 6:15 [C] **6:17** Lit *front of me*; Hb obscure [D] **6:17** Lit *40 cubits* [E] **6:21** Lit *he caused to pass across* [F] **6:23** Lit *10 cubits*, also in vv. 24,25,26 [G] **6:27** Lit *the second* [H] **6:31,33; 7:6** Hb obscure [I] **6:38** = October–November [J] **7:2** Lit *100 cubits* [K] **7:2** Lit *50 cubits*, also in v. 6 [L] **7:2** Lit *30 cubits*, also in vv. 6,23 [M] **7:4** Lit *frames, window to window* [N] **7:4** Lit *three times*; = at 3 different places, also in v. 5 [O] **7:5** Lit *frames, opposing window to window* [P] **7:7** Syr, Vg; MT reads *floor* [Q] **7:8** Lit *daughter he had taken* [R] **7:10** Lit *ten cubits and eight cubits*

The Archaeology of David and Solomon

by Steven M. Ortiz

Solomonic gate and casemate walls at Tel Hazor.

Does the archaeological data have anything to say about the development of a kingdom during the reigns of David and Solomon? In other words, do archaeologists find evidence for a centralized authority during the tenth century BC?

Four areas of archaeological data provide evidence for David: settlement data, monumental architecture, Jerusalem and the temple, and inscriptions.

Shifts in settlement between the eleventh and tenth centuries BC are dramatic. Remains at more than three hundred small villages and towns found throughout the hill country of Samaria and Judah illustrate evidence of a tribal or chiefdom social structure. During the tenth century, the picture changes; no longer do we have hundreds of small villages, but we start to see a process of urbanization, city planning, and centralized authority. Archaeologists have associated this type of settlement pattern to a centralized authority—such as a king, who would control the region from a capital. A king set up centers, building towns and networks to unify his kingdom. While these settlements do not prove that David existed, they do suggest evidence of major changes in the social fabric of society, and these major changes suggest a central authority figure such as a king.

In addition, archaeologists can look at the individual cities to determine evidence of a shift from tribes to a state. Archaeologists and historians commonly identify an abundance of monumental building activity with a state. In the tenth century BC and following, many cities underwent drastic change. Builders constructed major fortifications such as city walls, ramparts, and multiple-entry city gates. Well-planned cities with sewage systems, water storage works, organized streets, and public areas became common. Government and public buildings such as large pillared storehouses, stables, and palaces made their appearances. One of the classic case studies of the archaeology of David and Solomon includes the six-chambered gates found at Hazor, Megiddo, and Gezer. The biblical text in 1 Kings 9:15 summarizes Solomon's activities and records that he constructed major fortifications at Hazor, Megiddo, and Gezer. This has become a classic case study in biblical archaeology of connecting a biblical text with the stones on the ground, as the similarity between these gate complexes evidences a relationship. Further, protoaeolic capitals dating from the tenth century BC have been found in the archaeological record from the north down to Judah. These large rectangular capitals are well-carved stones used for palatial edifices, something that would not be found in simple villages.

Naturally when we think of the archaeology of David and Solomon, we need to address the question of Jerusalem and the temple. Unfortunately archaeologists working in Jerusalem have not found much archaeological evidence for David. Realistically, we should expect not to find much! Jerusalem is a living city, having been continually occupied through most of its history. Today not much area is available to the spade of the archaeologist. Most excavations are chance occurrences as a parking lot gets repaved or a sewer is fixed. Jerusalem sat on a hill; the city was frequently destroyed, rebuilt, and repaired. This means that archaeological remains from the tenth century would have been destroyed throughout that history. In spite of these difficulties, archaeologists have found public structures that date to the tenth century such as the Stepped-Stone Structure, as well as a recently discovered public structure popularly reported as possibly being King David's palace.

Looking for the temple that Solomon built would be foolish. It was surely dismantled in the Babylonian destruction, and any evidence would have been removed during the rebuilding by Nehemiah and especially by Herod the Great.

All the archaeological data coalesced illustrates that the social revolution that occurred during the tenth century can only be attributed to a centralized authority such as a king. Archaeologists have felt safe in assuming that while we do not have the name David or Solomon associated with any of these activities, they are the likely candidates.

The lack of any name association changed, however, with the discovery of the "house of David" inscription found at Tel Dan. The Tel Dan inscription is a stela commemorating victories by an Aramean king bragging that he smote the "house of David." Now we have archaeological evidence for the name David. ❖

the portico of the temple, were three rows of dressed stone and a row of trimmed cedar beams.

13 King Solomon had Hiram[A] brought from Tyre. 14 He was a widow's son from the tribe of Naphtali, and his father was a man of Tyre, a bronze craftsman. Hiram had great skill, understanding, and knowledge to do every kind of bronze work. So he came to King Solomon and carried out all his work.

THE BRONZE PILLARS

15 He cast two bronze pillars, each 27 feet[B] high and 18 feet[C] in circumference.[D] 16 He also made two capitals of cast bronze to set on top of the pillars; 7 1/2 feet[E] was the height of the first capital, and 7 1/2 feet was also the height of the second capital. 17 The capitals on top of the pillars had gratings of latticework, wreaths[F] made of chainwork — seven for the first capital and seven for the second.

18 He made the pillars with two encircling rows of pomegranates on the one grating to cover the capital on top; he did the same for the second capital. 19 And the capitals on top of the pillars in the portico were shaped like lilies, six feet[G] high. 20 The capitals on the two pillars were also immediately above the rounded surface next to the grating, and two hundred pomegranates were in rows encircling each[H] capital. 21 He set up the pillars at the portico of the sanctuary: he set up the right pillar and named it Jachin;[I] then he set up the left pillar and named it Boaz.[J] 22 The tops of the pillars were shaped like lilies. Then the work of the pillars was completed.

THE BASIN

23 He made the cast metal basin,[K] 15 feet[L] from brim to brim, perfectly round. It was 7 1/2 feet high and 45 feet in circumference. 24 Ornamental gourds encircled it below the brim, ten every half yard,[M] completely encircling the basin. The gourds were cast in two rows when the basin was cast. 25 It stood on twelve oxen, three facing north, three facing west, three facing south, and three facing east. The basin was on top of them and all their hindquarters were toward the center. 26 The basin was three inches[N] thick, and its rim was fashioned like the brim of a cup or of a lily blossom. It held eleven thousand gallons.[O]

THE BRONZE WATER CARTS

27 Then he made ten bronze water carts.[P] Each water cart was 6 feet long, 6 feet wide, and 4 1/2 feet[Q] high. 28 This was the design of the carts: They had frames; the frames were between the cross-pieces, 29 and on the frames between the cross-pieces were lions, oxen, and cherubim. On the cross-pieces there was a pedestal above, and below the lions and oxen were wreaths of hanging[R] work. 30 Each cart had four bronze wheels with bronze axles. Underneath the four corners of the basin were cast supports, each next to a wreath. 31 And the water cart's opening inside the crown on top was eighteen inches[S] wide. The opening was round, made as a pedestal twenty-seven inches[T] wide. On it were carvings, but their frames were square, not round. 32 There were four wheels under the frames, and the wheel axles were part of the water cart; each wheel was twenty-seven inches[U] tall. 33 The wheels' design was similar to that of chariot wheels: their axles, rims, spokes, and hubs were all of cast metal. 34 Four supports were at the four corners of each water cart; each support was one piece with the water cart. 35 At the top of the cart was a band nine inches[V] high encircling it; also, at the top of the cart, its braces and its frames were one piece with it. 36 He engraved cherubim, lions, and palm trees on the plates of its braces and on its frames, wherever each had space, with encircling wreaths. 37 In this way he made the ten water carts using the same casting, dimensions, and shape for all of them.

BRONZE BASINS AND OTHER UTENSILS

38 Then he made ten bronze basins — each basin held 220 gallons[W] and each was six feet wide — one basin for each of the ten water carts. 39 He set five water carts on the right side of the temple and five on the left side. He put the basin near the right side of the temple toward the southeast. 40 Then Hiram made the basins, the shovels, and the sprinkling basins.

COMPLETION OF THE BRONZE WORKS

So Hiram finished all the work that he was doing for King Solomon on the LORD's temple: 41 two pillars; bowls for the capitals that were on top of the two pillars; the two gratings for covering both bowls of the capitals that were on top of the pillars; 42 the four hundred pomegranates for the two gratings (two rows of pomegranates for each grating covering both capitals' bowls on top of the pillars); 43 the ten water carts; the ten basins on the water carts; 44 the basin; the twelve oxen underneath the basin; 45 and the pots, shovels, and sprinkling basins. All the utensils that Hiram made for King Solomon at the LORD's temple were made of burnished bronze. 46 The king had them cast in clay molds in the Jordan Valley between

[A] 7:13 = Huram in 2Ch 4:11 [B] 7:15 Lit *18 cubits* [C] 7:15 Lit *12 cubits* [D] 7:15 LXX adds *and the thickness of the pillar was four fingers hollowed and similarly the second pillar* [E] 7:16 Lit *five cubits*, also in v. 23 [F] 7:17 Lit *tassels* [G] 7:19 Lit *four cubits*, also in vv. 27,38 [H] 7:20 Lit *encircling the second* [I] 7:21 = He Will Establish [J] 7:21 = In Him Is Strength [K] 7:23 Lit *sea* [L] 7:23 Lit *10 cubits* [M] 7:24 Lit *10 per cubit* [N] 7:26 Lit *a handbreadth* [O] 7:26 Lit *2,000 baths* [P] 7:27 Lit *bronze stands* [Q] 7:27 Lit *three cubits* [R] 7:29 Or *hammered-down* [S] 7:31 Lit *a cubit* [T] 7:31 Lit *one and a half cubits* [U] 7:32 Lit *was one and a half cubits* [V] 7:35 Lit *half a cubit* [W] 7:38 Lit *40 baths*

Succoth and Zarethan. 47 Solomon left all the utensils
unweighed because there were so many; the weight
of the bronze was not determined.

COMPLETION OF THE GOLD FURNISHINGS

48 Solomon also made all the equipment in the LORD's
temple: the gold altar; the gold table that the Bread
of the Presence was placed on; 49 the pure gold lampstands in front of the inner sanctuary, five on the
right and five on the left; the gold flowers, lamps,
and tongs; 50 the pure gold ceremonial bowls, wick
trimmers, sprinkling basins, ladles,[A] and firepans;
and the gold hinges for the doors of the inner temple
(that is, the most holy place) and for the doors of the
temple sanctuary.

51 So all the work King Solomon did in the LORD's
temple was completed. Then Solomon brought in
the consecrated things of his father David — the silver, the gold, and the utensils — and put them in the
treasuries of the LORD's temple.

SOLOMON'S DEDICATION OF THE TEMPLE

8 At that time Solomon assembled the elders of Israel, all the tribal heads and the ancestral leaders
of the Israelites before him at Jerusalem in order to
bring the ark of the LORD's covenant from the city
of David, that is Zion. 2 So all the men of Israel were
assembled in the presence of King Solomon in the
month of Ethanim, which is the seventh month,[B] at
the festival.

3 All the elders of Israel came, and the priests picked
up the ark. 4 The priests and the Levites brought the
ark of the LORD, the tent of meeting, and the holy
utensils that were in the tent. 5 King Solomon and
the entire congregation of Israel, who had gathered
around him and were with him in front of the ark,
were sacrificing sheep, goats, and cattle that could
not be counted or numbered, because there were
so many. 6 The priests brought the ark of the LORD's
covenant to its place, into the inner sanctuary of the
temple, to the most holy place beneath the wings of
the cherubim. 7 For the cherubim were spreading
their wings over[C] the place of the ark, so that the
cherubim covered the ark and its poles from above.
8 The poles were so long that their ends were seen
from the holy place in front of the inner sanctuary,
but they were not seen from outside the sanctuary;
they are still there today. 9 Nothing was in the ark except the two stone tablets that Moses had put there
at Horeb,[D] where the LORD made a covenant with the
Israelites when they came out of the land of Egypt.

10 When the priests came out of the holy place, the
cloud filled the LORD's temple, 11 and because of the
cloud, the priests were not able to continue ministering, for the glory of the LORD filled the temple.

12 Then Solomon said:

The LORD said that he would dwell
in total darkness.
13 I have indeed built an exalted temple for you,
a place for your dwelling forever.

14 The king turned around and blessed the entire congregation of Israel while they were standing. 15 He
said:

Blessed be the LORD God of Israel!
He spoke directly to my father David,
and he has fulfilled the promise
by his power.
He said,
16 "Since the day I brought my people Israel
out of Egypt,
I have not chosen a city to build a temple in
among any of the tribes of Israel,
so that my name would be there.
But I have chosen David to rule
my people Israel."
17 My father David had his heart set
on building a temple for the name of the LORD,
the God of Israel.
18 But the LORD said to my father David,
"Since your heart was set on building a temple
for my name,
you have done well to have this desire.[E]
19 Yet you are not the one to build it;
instead, your son, your own offspring,
will build it for my name."
20 The LORD has fulfilled what he promised.
I have taken the place of my father David,
and I sit on the throne of Israel,
as the LORD promised.
I have built the temple for the name of the
LORD, the God of Israel.
21 I have provided a place there for the ark,
where the LORD's covenant is
that he made with our ancestors
when he brought them out of the land
of Egypt.

SOLOMON'S PRAYER

22 Then Solomon stood before the altar of the LORD in
front of the entire congregation of Israel and spread
out his hands toward heaven. 23 He said:

LORD God of Israel,
there is no God like you
in heaven above or on earth below,
who keeps the gracious covenant
with your servants who walk before you
with all their heart.

[A] **7:50** Or *dishes*, or *spoons*; lit *palms* [B] **8:2** = September–October [C] **8:7** LXX; MT reads *toward* [D] **8:9** = Sinai [E] **8:18** Lit *well because it was with your heart*

24 You have kept what you promised
to your servant, my father David.
You spoke directly to him
and you fulfilled your promise by your power
as it is today.
25 Therefore, LORD God of Israel,
keep what you promised
to your servant, my father David:
You will never fail to have a man
to sit before me on the throne of Israel,
if only your sons take care to walk before me
as you have walked before me.
26 Now LORD[A] God of Israel,
please confirm what you promised
to your servant, my father David.

27 But will God indeed live on earth?
Even heaven, the highest heaven,
cannot contain you,
much less this temple I have built.
28 Listen[B] to your servant's prayer
and his petition,
LORD my God,
so that you may hear the cry and the prayer
that your servant prays before you today,
29 so that your eyes may watch over this temple
night and day,
toward the place where you said,
"My name will be there,"
and so that you may hear the prayer
that your servant prays toward this place.
30 Hear the petition of your servant
and your people Israel,
which they pray toward this place.
May you hear in your dwelling place in heaven.
May you hear and forgive.

31 When a man sins against his neighbor
and is forced to take an oath,[C]
and he comes to take an oath
before your altar in this temple,
32 may you hear in heaven and act.
May you judge your servants,
condemning the wicked man by bringing
what he has done on his own head
and providing justice for the righteous
by rewarding him according to
his righteousness.

33 When your people Israel are defeated
before an enemy,
because they have sinned against you,
and they return to you and praise your name,
and they pray and plead with you
for mercy in this temple,
34 may you hear in heaven
and forgive the sin of your people Israel.
May you restore them to the land
you gave their ancestors.

35 When the skies are shut and there is no rain,
because they have sinned against you,
and they pray toward this place
and praise your name,
and they turn from their sins
because you are afflicting them,
36 may you hear in heaven
and forgive the sin of your servants
and your people Israel,
so that you may teach them to walk on
the good way.
May you send rain on your land
that you gave your people for an inheritance.

37 When there is famine in the land,
when there is pestilence,
when there is blight or mildew, locust
or grasshopper,
when their enemy besieges them
in the land and its cities,[D]
when there is any plague or illness,
38 every prayer or petition
that any person or that all your people Israel
may have —
they each know their own affliction[E] —
as they spread out their hands
toward this temple,
39 may you hear in heaven, your dwelling place,
and may you forgive, act, and give to
everyone
according to all their ways, since you know
each heart,
for you alone know every human heart,
40 so that they may fear you
all the days they live on the land
you gave our ancestors.

41 Even for the foreigner who is not
of your people Israel
but has come from a distant land
because of your name —
42 for they will hear of your great name,
strong hand, and outstretched arm,
and will come and pray toward this temple —
43 may you hear in heaven, your dwelling place,
and do according to all the foreigner asks.

[A] **8:26** Some Hb mss, LXX, Syr, Tg, Vg, 2Ch 6:16; other Hb mss omit *LORD* [B] **8:28** Lit *Turn* [C] **8:31** Lit *and he lifts a curse against him to curse him* [D] **8:37** Lit *land of its gates* [E] **8:38** Lit *know in his heart of a plague*

Then all peoples of earth will know
your name,
to fear you as your people Israel do
and to know that this temple I have built
bears your name.

44 When your people go out to fight
against their enemies,[A]
wherever you send them,
and they pray to the LORD
in the direction of the city you have chosen
and the temple I have built for your name,
45 may you hear their prayer and petition
in heaven
and uphold their cause.

46 When they sin against you —
for there is no one who does not sin —
and you are angry with them
and hand them over to the enemy,
and their captors deport them
to the enemy's country —
whether distant or nearby —
47 and when they come to their senses[B]
in the land where they were deported
and repent and petition you
in their captors' land:
"We have sinned and done wrong;
we have been wicked,"
48 and when they return to you
with all their heart and all their soul
in the land of their enemies
who took them captive,
and when they pray to you in the direction
of their land
that you gave their ancestors,
the city you have chosen,
and the temple I have built for your name,
49 may you hear in heaven, your dwelling place,
their prayer and petition and uphold
their cause.
50 May you forgive your people
who sinned against you
and all their rebellions[C] against you,
and may you grant them compassion
before their captors,
so that they may treat them compassionately.
51 For they are your people
and your inheritance;
you brought them out of Egypt,
out of the middle of an iron furnace.
52 May your eyes be open
to your servant's petition
and to the petition of your people Israel,
listening to them whenever they call to you.
53 For you, Lord GOD, have set them apart
as your inheritance
from all peoples of the earth,
as you spoke through your servant Moses
when you brought our ancestors
out of Egypt.

SOLOMON'S BLESSING

54 When Solomon finished praying this entire prayer
and petition to the LORD, he got up from kneeling before the altar of the LORD, with his hands spread out
toward heaven, 55 and he stood and blessed the whole
congregation of Israel with a loud voice: 56 "Blessed
be the LORD! He has given rest to his people Israel
according to all he has said. Not one of all the good
promises he made through his servant Moses has
failed. 57 May the LORD our God be with us as he was
with our ancestors. May he not abandon us or leave
us 58 so that he causes us to be devoted[D] to him, to
walk in all his ways, and to keep his commands, statutes, and ordinances, which he commanded our ancestors. 59 May my words with which I have made my
petition before the LORD be near the LORD our God
day and night. May he uphold his servant's cause and
the cause of his people Israel, as each day requires.
60 May all the peoples of the earth know that the
LORD is God. There is no other! 61 Be wholeheartedly
devoted to the LORD our God to walk in his statutes
and to keep his commands, as it is today."
62 The king and all Israel with him were offering
sacrifices in the LORD's presence. 63 Solomon offered
a sacrifice of fellowship offerings to the LORD: twenty-two thousand cattle and one hundred twenty thousand sheep and goats. In this manner the king and all
the Israelites dedicated the LORD's temple.
64 On the same day, the king consecrated the middle
of the courtyard that was in front of the LORD's temple
because that was where he offered the burnt offering,
the grain offering, and the fat of the fellowship offerings, since the bronze altar before the LORD was too
small to accommodate the burnt offerings, the grain
offerings, and the fat of the fellowship offerings.
65 Solomon and all Israel with him — a great assembly, from the entrance of Hamath[E] to the Brook
of Egypt — observed the festival at that time in the
presence of the LORD our God, seven days, and seven
more days — fourteen days.[F] 66 On the fifteenth day[G]
he sent the people away. So they blessed the king and
went to their homes[H] rejoicing and with happy hearts

[A] **8:44** Some Hb mss, some ancient versions, 2Ch 6:34; other Hb mss read *enemy* [B] **8:47** Lit *they return to their heart* [C] **8:50** Lit *rebellions that they have rebelled* [D] **8:58** Lit *causes our hearts to be inclined* [E] **8:65** Or *from Lebo-hamath* [F] **8:65** Temple dedication lasted seven days, and the Festival of Shelters lasted seven days. [G] **8:66** Lit *the eighth day* [H] **8:66** Lit *tents*

for all the goodness that the LORD had done for his servant David and for his people Israel.

THE LORD'S RESPONSE

9 When Solomon finished building the temple of the LORD, the royal palace, and all that Solomon desired to do, 2 the LORD appeared to Solomon a second time just as he had appeared to him at Gibeon. 3 The LORD said to him:

> I have heard your prayer and petition you have made before me. I have consecrated this temple you have built, to put[A] my name there forever; my eyes and my heart will be there at all times.
>
> 4 As for you, if you walk before me as your father David walked, with a heart of integrity and in what is right, doing everything I have commanded you, and if you keep my statutes and ordinances, 5 I will establish your royal throne over Israel forever, as I promised your father David: You will never fail to have a man on the throne of Israel.
>
> 6 If you or your sons turn away from following me and do not keep my commands — my statutes that I have set before you — and if you go and serve other gods and bow in worship to them, 7 I will cut off Israel from the land I gave them, and I will reject[B] the temple I have sanctified for my name. Israel will become an object of scorn and ridicule among all the peoples. 8 Though this temple is now exalted,[C] everyone who passes by will be appalled and will scoff.[D] They will say, "Why did the LORD do this to this land and this temple?" 9 Then they will say, "Because they abandoned the LORD their God who brought their ancestors out of the land of Egypt. They held on to other gods and bowed in worship to them and served them. Because of this, the LORD brought all this ruin on them."

KING HIRAM'S TWENTY TOWNS

10 At the end of twenty years, during which Solomon had built the two houses, the LORD's temple and the royal palace — 11 King Hiram of Tyre having supplied him with cedar and cypress logs and gold for his every wish — King Solomon gave Hiram twenty towns in the land of Galilee. 12 So Hiram went out from Tyre to look over the towns that Solomon had given him, but he was not pleased with them. 13 So he said, "What are these towns you've given me, my brother?" So he called them the Land of Cabul,[E] as they are still called today. 14 Now Hiram had sent the king nine thousand pounds[F] of gold.

SOLOMON'S FORCED LABOR

15 This is the account of the forced labor that King Solomon had imposed to build the LORD's temple, his own palace, the supporting terraces, the wall of Jerusalem, and Hazor, Megiddo, and Gezer. 16 Pharaoh king of Egypt had attacked and captured Gezer. He then burned it, killed the Canaanites who lived in the city, and gave it as a dowry to his daughter, Solomon's wife. 17 Then Solomon rebuilt Gezer, Lower Beth-horon, 18 Baalath, Tamar[G,H] in the Wilderness of Judah, 19 all the storage cities that belonged to Solomon, the chariot cities, the cavalry cities, and whatever Solomon desired to build in Jerusalem, Lebanon, or anywhere else in the land of his dominion.

20 As for all the peoples who remained of the Amorites, Hethites, Perizzites, Hivites, and Jebusites, who were not Israelites — 21 their descendants who remained in the land after them, those whom the Israelites were unable to destroy completely — Solomon imposed forced labor on them; it is still this way today. 22 But Solomon did not consign the Israelites to slavery; they were soldiers, his servants, his commanders, his captains, and commanders of his chariots and his cavalry. 23 These were the deputies who were over Solomon's work: 550 who supervised the people doing the work.

SOLOMON'S OTHER ACTIVITIES

24 Pharaoh's daughter moved from the city of David to the house that Solomon had built for her; he then built the terraces.

25 Three times a year Solomon offered burnt offerings and fellowship offerings on the altar he had built for the LORD, and he burned incense with them in the LORD's presence. So he completed the temple.

26 King Solomon put together a fleet of ships at Ezion-geber, which is near Eloth on the shore of the Red Sea in the land of Edom. 27 With the fleet, Hiram sent his servants, experienced seamen, along with Solomon's servants. 28 They went to Ophir and acquired gold there — sixteen tons[I] — and delivered it to Solomon.

THE QUEEN OF SHEBA

10 The queen of Sheba heard about Solomon's fame connected with the name of the LORD and came to test him with difficult questions. 2 She came to Jerusalem with a very large entourage, with camels bearing spices, gold in great abundance, and

[A] **9:3** Or *by putting* [B] **9:7** Lit *send from my presence* [C] **9:8** Some ancient versions read *temple will become a ruin* [D] **9:8** Lit *hiss* [E] **9:13** = Like Nothing [F] **9:14** Lit *120 talents* [G] **9:18** Alt Hb traditions, LXX, Syr, Tg, Vg read *Tadmor*; 2Ch 8:4 [H] **9:18** Tamar was a city in southern Judah; Ezk 47:19; 48:28. [I] **9:28** Lit *420 talents*

precious stones. She came to Solomon and spoke
to him about everything that was on her mind. 3 So
Solomon answered all her questions; nothing was
too difficult for the king to explain to her. 4 When the
queen of Sheba observed all of Solomon's wisdom, the
palace he had built, 5 the food at his table, his servants'
residence, his attendants' service and their attire, his
cupbearers, and the burnt offerings he offered at the
LORD's temple, it took her breath away.

6 She said to the king, "The report I heard in my own
country about your words and about your wisdom
is true. 7 But I didn't believe the reports until I came
and saw with my own eyes. Indeed, I was not even
told half. Your wisdom and prosperity far exceed
the report I heard. 8 How happy are your men.[A] How
happy are these servants of yours, who always stand
in your presence hearing your wisdom. 9 Blessed be
the LORD your God! He delighted in you and put you
on the throne of Israel, because of the LORD's eternal
love for Israel. He has made you king to carry out
justice and righteousness."

10 Then she gave the king four and a half tons[B] of
gold, a great quantity of spices, and precious stones.
Never again did such a quantity of spices arrive as
those the queen of Sheba gave to King Solomon.

11 In addition, Hiram's fleet that carried gold from
Ophir brought from Ophir a large quantity of almug[C]
wood and precious stones. 12 The king made the almug
wood into steps for the LORD's temple and the king's
palace and into lyres and harps for the singers. Never
before did such almug wood arrive, and the like has
not been seen again.

13 King Solomon gave the queen of Sheba her every
desire — whatever she asked — besides what he had
given her out of his royal bounty. Then she, along with
her servants, returned to her own country.

SOLOMON'S WEALTH

14 The weight of gold that came to Solomon annually
was twenty-five tons,[D] 15 besides what came from
merchants, traders' merchandise, and all the Arabian
kings and governors of the land.

16 King Solomon made two hundred large shields
of hammered gold; fifteen pounds[E] of gold went into
each shield. 17 He made three hundred small shields
of hammered gold; nearly four pounds[F] of gold went
into each shield. The king put them in the House of
the Forest of Lebanon.

18 The king also made a large ivory throne and overlaid it with fine gold. 19 The throne had six steps; there
was a rounded top at the back of the throne, armrests
on either side of the seat, and two lions standing beside the armrests. 20 Twelve lions were standing there
on the six steps, one at each end. Nothing like it had
ever been made in any other kingdom.

21 All of King Solomon's drinking cups were gold,
and all the utensils of the House of the Forest of Lebanon were pure gold. There was no silver, since it
was considered as nothing in Solomon's time, 22 for
the king had ships of Tarshish at sea with Hiram's
fleet, and once every three years the ships of Tarshish would arrive bearing gold, silver, ivory, apes,
and peacocks.[G]

23 King Solomon surpassed all the kings of the
world in riches and in wisdom. 24 The whole world
wanted an audience with Solomon to hear the wisdom that God had put in his heart. 25 Every man would
bring his annual tribute: items[H] of silver and gold,
clothing, weapons,[I] spices, and horses and mules.

26 Solomon accumulated 1,400 chariots and 12,000
horsemen and stationed them in the chariot cities
and with the king in Jerusalem. 27 The king made silver as common in Jerusalem as stones, and he made
cedar as abundant as sycamore in the Judean foothills. 28 Solomon's horses were imported from Egypt
and Kue.[J] The king's traders bought them from Kue
at the going price. 29 A chariot was imported from
Egypt for fifteen pounds[K] of silver, and a horse for
four pounds.[L] In the same way, they exported them to
all the kings of the Hittites and to the kings of Aram
through their agents.

SOLOMON'S UNFAITHFULNESS TO GOD

11 King Solomon loved many foreign women in
addition to Pharaoh's daughter: Moabite, Ammonite, Edomite, Sidonian, and Hittite women 2 from
the nations about which the LORD had told the Israelites, "You must not intermarry with them, and
they must not intermarry with you, because they
will turn your heart away to follow their gods." To
these women Solomon was deeply attached[M] in love.
3 He had seven hundred wives who were princesses
and three hundred who were concubines, and they
turned his heart away.

4 When Solomon was old, his wives turned his
heart away to follow other gods. He was not wholeheartedly devoted to the LORD his God, as his father
David had been. 5 Solomon followed Ashtoreth, the
goddess of the Sidonians, and Milcom, the abhorrent
idol of the Ammonites. 6 Solomon did what was evil
in the LORD's sight, and unlike his father David, he
did not remain loyal to the LORD.

7 At that time, Solomon built a high place for Chemosh, the abhorrent idol of Moab, and for Milcom,[N]

[A] **10:8** LXX, Syr read *your wives* [B] **10:10** Lit *120 talents*
[C] **10:11** = algum in 2Ch 2:8; 9:10–11 [D] **10:14** Lit *666 talents*
[E] **10:16** Lit *600* (shekels) [F] **10:17** Lit *three minas* [G] **10:22** Or *baboons*
[H] **10:25** Or *vessels*, or *weapons* [I] **10:25** Or *fragrant balsam*
[J] **10:28** = Cilicia [K] **10:29** Lit *600 shekels* [L] **10:29** Lit *150 shekels*
[M] **11:2** Lit *Solomon clung* [N] **11:7** Lit *Molech*

Gezer: Gateway to Jerusalem

Steven M. Ortiz

Gezer was an important city in the biblical period. It has become well known in biblical archaeology due to the existence of a major gate system that is similar to gates found at Hazor and Megiddo—archaeological evidence that illuminates a small reference to the building projects of King Solomon. First Kings 9:15 states that after building the temple, his palace, and Jerusalem, Solomon rebuilt "Hazor, Megiddo, and Gezer." Most scholars believe Solomon chose these three important cities because they guarded key regions of the kingdom. The city of Gezer is located on a main juncture of the Via Maris. It guarded the Aijalon Valley and the route from the coast up to Jerusalem and the Judean Hills. Someone wanting to attack Jerusalem first had to take out Gezer, as it served as the last sentinel to protect Jerusalem from the coast.

People recognized Gezer's importance even before Solomon fortified the city. Several Egyptian sources mentioned Gezer as various Egyptian pharaohs conquered the city and bragged about the conquest in campaign reports. The conquest of the city is mentioned in: (1) the annals of Thutmose III (about 1468 BC); (2) the Amarna Letters, which describe it as a vassal city of Egypt during the fourteenth century BC; and (3) the Merneptah Stele, which contains the first mention of Israel outside the Bible.

The biblical city of Gezer is identified as Tell el-Jezer, about halfway between the modern cities of Tel Aviv and Jerusalem. It is a thirty-three-acre mound located in the foothills of Judah. In addition to the historical sources, the site is well known due to several archaeological expeditions. Two major excavations were carried out in 1902–1909 by R. A. S. Macalister and in 1964–1973 by William G. Dever and Joe D. Seger. Smaller excavations were conducted by Alan Rowe (1934) and Dever (1984, 1990).

The mound of Gezer was initially occupied around 3500 BC. The settlement continued to grow until it was a walled city during the Middle Bronze Age (about 2000–1500 BC) when major fortifications (gate, tower, and protective sloping bank or *glacis*) were built and the "High Place" was founded. This is typical for all major Canaanite cities during the Patriarchal period. Gezer was a major Canaanite city-state throughout the second millennium BC. The city was destroyed (about 1500 BC) and rebuilt during the Late Bronze Age when it came under Egyptian dominance as evidenced by several palaces and residences.

Dr. Harold Mosley digging at Gezer. To the right and waist high is a dark horizontal line just below the Solomonic casemate construction, thought to be the burn layer of 1 Kings 9:16–17.

During the Israelite conquest and settlement, Gezer played an important role as one of the leaders in a coalition against Joshua. Although the king of Gezer organized a large coalition of kings and their cities to go against the Israelites, Joshua defeated the king of Gezer as well as the Canaanite coalition (Jos 10:33). In spite of the victory by Joshua's forces, Gezer remained in Canaanite hands throughout the period of the Judges (Jos 16:10; Jdg 1:29) even though it formed the boundary for Ephraim's tribal allotment (Jos 16:3) and was assigned as a Levitical city (21:21). David fought against the Philistines near Gezer (2Sm 5:25; 1Ch 20:4). These texts of the early Israelite state formation clearly show that Gezer sat on the border between the tribes up in the hill country and the Philistines on the coast. Archaeological evidence confirms this picture from the biblical text.

Gezer came into Israelite hands by a conquest by the Egyptian pharaoh, who gave it to Solomon as a dowry for his marriage to Pharaoh's daughter (1Kg 9:16). Most scholars associate Siamun as Solomon's Egyptian father-in-law. Archaeology has confirmed that the city was destroyed at this time and immediately upon the destruction is evidence of major construction activity: a four-entryway monumental city gate, a palace, a casemate wall, a water storage system, public buildings, and guardrooms.

A boundary stone at Gezer. The inscription reads in Greek, *Alkiou*, and in Hebrew, *Techem Gezer*, meaning, "Belonging to Alkios, Boundary of Gezer." This is one of thirteen such boundary stones that have been found at Gezer.

Pharaoh Shishak (about 950–925 BC) destroyed the city. Archaeological evidence shows the city was rebuilt and experienced another destruction at the hands of the Assyrians in 733 BC. An inscription and relief of Tiglath-pileser III (eighth c. BC) mentions this Assyrian conquest. The city had minor occupation until the Persian period. Gezer became known as Gazara in the Hellenistic period and became an important city for the Hasmonean rulers. During the New Testament period, the major city moved north across the valley, and is probably the Emmaus of the Gospel accounts.

The ancient site of Gezer is so important for biblical history that a major excavation project was initiated in 2006 to investigate the site. Archaeological research continues to illustrate that the events recorded in Scripture are based on actual historical events of the kings of Israel and Judah. ❖

the abhorrent idol of the Ammonites, on the hill across from Jerusalem. 8 He did the same for all his foreign wives, who were burning incense and offering sacrifices to their gods.

9 The LORD was angry with Solomon, because his heart had turned away from the LORD, the God of Israel, who had appeared to him twice. 10 He had commanded him about this, so that he would not follow other gods, but Solomon did not do what the LORD had commanded.

11 Then the LORD said to Solomon, "Since you have done this[A] and did not keep my covenant and my statutes, which I commanded you, I will tear the kingdom away from you and give it to your servant. 12 However, I will not do it during your lifetime for the sake of your father David; I will tear it out of your son's hand. 13 Yet I will not tear the entire kingdom away from him. I will give one tribe to your son for the sake of my servant David and for the sake of Jerusalem that I chose."

SOLOMON'S ENEMIES

14 So the LORD raised up Hadad the Edomite as an enemy against Solomon. He was of the royal family in Edom. 15 Earlier, when David was in Edom, Joab, the commander of the army, had gone to bury the dead and had struck down every male in Edom. 16 For Joab and all Israel had remained there six months, until he had killed every male in Edom. 17 Hadad fled to Egypt, along with some Edomites from his father's servants. At the time Hadad was a small boy. 18 Hadad and his men set out from Midian and went to Paran. They took men with them from Paran and went to Egypt, to Pharaoh king of Egypt, who gave Hadad a house, ordered that he be given food, and gave him land. 19 Pharaoh liked Hadad so much[B] that he gave him a wife, the sister of his own wife, Queen Tahpenes. 20 Tahpenes's sister gave birth to Hadad's son Genubath. Tahpenes herself weaned him in Pharaoh's palace, and Genubath lived there along with Pharaoh's sons.

21 When Hadad heard in Egypt that David rested with his ancestors and that Joab, the commander of the army, was dead, Hadad said to Pharaoh, "Let me leave, so I may go to my own country."

22 But Pharaoh asked him, "What do you lack here with me for you to want to go back to your own country?"

"Nothing," he replied, "but please let me leave."

23 God raised up Rezon son of Eliada as an enemy against Solomon. Rezon had fled from his master King Hadadezer of Zobah 24 and gathered men to himself. He became leader of a raiding party when David killed the Zobaites. He[C] went to Damascus, lived there, and became king in Damascus. 25 Rezon was Israel's enemy throughout Solomon's reign, adding to the trouble Hadad had caused. He reigned over Aram[D] and loathed Israel.

26 Now Solomon's servant, Jeroboam son of Nebat, was an Ephraimite from Zeredah. His widowed mother's name was Zeruah. Jeroboam rebelled against Solomon, 27 and this is the reason he rebelled against the king: Solomon had built the supporting terraces and repaired the opening in the wall of the city of his father David. 28 Now the man Jeroboam was capable, and Solomon noticed the young man because he was getting things done. So he appointed him over the entire labor force of the house of Joseph.

29 During that time, the prophet Ahijah the Shilonite met Jeroboam on the road as Jeroboam came out of Jerusalem. Now Ahijah had wrapped himself with a new cloak, and the two of them were alone in the open field. 30 Then Ahijah took hold of the new cloak he had on, tore it into twelve pieces, 31 and said to Jeroboam, "Take ten pieces for yourself, for this is what the LORD God of Israel says: 'I am about to tear the kingdom out of Solomon's hand. I will give you ten tribes, 32 but one tribe will remain his for the sake of my servant David and for the sake of Jerusalem, the city I chose out of all the tribes of Israel. 33 For they have abandoned me; they have bowed down to Ashtoreth, the goddess of the Sidonians, to Chemosh, the god of Moab, and to Milcom, the god of the Ammonites. They have not walked in my ways to do what is right in my sight and to carry out my statutes and my judgments as his father David did.

34 " 'However, I will not take the whole kingdom from him but will let him be ruler all the days of his life for the sake of my servant David, whom I chose and who kept my commands and my statutes. 35 I will take ten tribes of the kingdom from his son and give them to you. 36 I will give one tribe to his son, so that my servant David will always have a lamp[E] before me in Jerusalem, the city I chose for myself to put my name there. 37 I will appoint you, and you will reign as king over all you want, and you will be king over Israel.

38 " 'After that, if you obey all I command you, walk in my ways, and do what is right in my sight in order to keep my statutes and my commands as my servant David did, I will be with you. I will build you a lasting dynasty just as I built for David, and I will give you Israel. 39 I will humble David's descendants, because of their unfaithfulness, but not forever.' "[F]

40 Therefore, Solomon tried to kill Jeroboam, but he fled to Egypt, to King Shishak of Egypt, where he remained until Solomon's death.

[A] **11:11** Lit *"Since this was with you* [B] **11:19** Lit *Hadad found much favor in Pharaoh's eyes* [C] **11:24** LXX; Hb reads *They* [D] **11:25** Some Hb mss, LXX, Syr read *Edom* [E] **11:36** Or *dominion* [F] **11:38–39** LXX omits *and I will give . . . but not forever*

SOLOMON'S DEATH

41 The rest of the events of Solomon's reign, along with
all his accomplishments and his wisdom, are written in the Book of Solomon's Events. 42 The length of
Solomon's reign in Jerusalem over all Israel totaled
forty years. 43 Solomon rested with his ancestors and
was buried in the city of his father David. His son Rehoboam became king in his place.

THE KINGDOM DIVIDED

12 Then Rehoboam went to Shechem, for all Israel had gone to Shechem to make him king.
2 When Jeroboam son of Nebat heard about it, he
stayed in Egypt, where he had fled from King Solomon's presence. Jeroboam stayed in Egypt.[A] 3 But
they summoned him, and Jeroboam and the whole
assembly of Israel came and spoke to Rehoboam:
4 "Your father made our yoke harsh. You, therefore,
lighten your father's harsh service and the heavy
yoke he put on us, and we will serve you."
5 Rehoboam replied, "Go away for three days and
then return to me." So the people left. 6 Then King Rehoboam consulted with the elders who had served
his father Solomon when he was alive, asking, "How
do you advise me to respond to this people?"
7 They replied, "Today if you will be a servant to this
people and serve them, and if you respond to them
by speaking kind words to them, they will be your
servants forever."
8 But he rejected the advice of the elders who had
advised him and consulted with the young men who
had grown up with him and attended him. 9 He asked
them, "What message do you advise that we send back
to this people who said to me, 'Lighten the yoke your
father put on us'?"
10 The young men who had grown up with him told
him, "This is what you should say to this people who
said to you, 'Your father made our yoke heavy, but
you, make it lighter on us!' This is what you should
tell them: 'My little finger is thicker than my father's
waist! 11 Although my father burdened you with a
heavy yoke, I will add to your yoke; my father disciplined you with whips, but I will discipline you with
barbed whips.'"[B]
12 So Jeroboam and all the people came to Rehoboam on the third day, as the king had ordered: "Return
to me on the third day." 13 Then the king answered
the people harshly. He rejected the advice the elders
had given him 14 and spoke to them according to the
young men's advice: "My father made your yoke
heavy, but I will add to your yoke; my father disciplined you with whips, but I will discipline you with
barbed whips."
15 The king did not listen to the people, because this
turn of events came from the LORD to carry out his
word, which the LORD had spoken through Ahijah
the Shilonite to Jeroboam son of Nebat. 16 When all
Israel saw that the king had not listened to them, the
people answered him:

> What portion do we have in David?
> We have no inheritance in the son of Jesse.
> Israel, return to your tents;
> David, now look after your own house!

So Israel went to their tents, 17 but Rehoboam reigned
over the Israelites living in the cities of Judah.
18 Then King Rehoboam sent Adoram,[C] who was
in charge of forced labor, but all Israel stoned him to
death. King Rehoboam managed to get into the chariot and flee to Jerusalem. 19 Israel is still in rebellion
against the house of David today.

REHOBOAM IN JERUSALEM

20 When all Israel heard that Jeroboam had come
back, they summoned him to the assembly and made
him king over all Israel. No one followed the house of
David except the tribe of Judah alone. 21 When Rehoboam arrived in Jerusalem, he mobilized one hundred
eighty thousand fit young soldiers from the entire
house of Judah and the tribe of Benjamin to fight
against the house of Israel to restore the kingdom
to Rehoboam son of Solomon. 22 But the word of God

DIGGING DEEPER *Tel Dan*

Dan, Israel's northernmost city in ancient times, was previously known as the territory of Laish (Jdg 18:7,14). Its name changed to Dan because the Israelite tribe of Dan fought and expelled the area's occupants in the late thirteenth century BC (18:29). Modern excavations of the site by Avraham Biran have confirmed that Laish existed during the time when Abraham pursued the northern kings in order to free his nephew Lot from captivity (Gn 14:1–24). Of particular interest at Tel Dan is an arched mud-brick gate that dates to approximately 2000 BC. This is the only intact example of such an ancient gate; given that it dates to Abraham's era, it is likely that Abraham himself passed through it while visiting Dan (14:14). Several pagan altars have been found in Dan, including the altar erected for calf worship by Jeroboam I in the tenth century BC (1Kg 12:25–33) which made Bethel and Dan the centers of pagan idolatry for the northern tribes, just as the Bible describes (v. 29).

[A] **12:2** LXX, Vg read *Jeroboam returned from Egypt*; 2Ch 10:2
[B] **12:11** Lit *with scorpions*, also in v. 14 [C] **12:18** LXX reads *Adoniram*; 1Kg 4:6; 5:14

came to Shemaiah, the man of God: 23 "Say to Rehoboam son of Solomon, king of Judah, to the whole house of Judah and Benjamin, and to the rest of the people, 24 'This is what the LORD says: You are not to march up and fight against your brothers, the Israelites. Each of you return home, for this situation is from me.' "

So they listened to the word of the LORD and went back according to the word of the LORD.

JEROBOAM'S IDOLATRY

25 Jeroboam built Shechem in the hill country of Ephraim and lived there. From there he went out and built Penuel. 26 Jeroboam said to himself, "The kingdom might now return to the house of David. 27 If these people regularly go to offer sacrifices in the LORD's temple in Jerusalem, the heart of these people will return to their lord, King Rehoboam of Judah. They will kill me and go back to the king of Judah." 28 So the king sought advice.

Then he made two golden calves, and he said to the people, "Going to Jerusalem is too difficult for you. Israel, here are your gods[A] who brought you up from the land of Egypt." 29 He set up one in Bethel, and put the other in Dan. 30 This led to sin; the people walked in procession before one of the calves all the way to Dan.[B]

31 Jeroboam also made shrines[C] on the high places and made priests from the ranks of the people who were not Levites. 32 Jeroboam made a festival in the eighth month on the fifteenth day of the month, like the festival in Judah. He offered sacrifices on the altar; he made this offering in Bethel to sacrifice to the calves he had made. He also stationed the priests in Bethel for the high places he had made. 33 He offered sacrifices on[D] the altar he had set up in Bethel on the fifteenth day of the eighth month. He chose this month on his own. He made a festival for the Israelites, offered sacrifices on the altar, and burned incense.

JUDGMENT ON JEROBOAM

13 A man of God came, however, from Judah to Bethel by the word of the LORD while Jeroboam was standing beside the altar to burn incense. 2 The man of God cried out against the altar by the word of the LORD: "Altar, altar, this is what the LORD says, 'A son will be born to the house of David, named Josiah, and he will sacrifice on you the priests of the high places who are burning incense on you. Human bones will be burned on you.' " 3 He gave a sign that day. He said, "This is the sign that the LORD has spoken: 'The altar will now be ripped apart, and the ashes that are on it will be poured out.' "

4 When the king heard the message that the man of God had cried out against the altar at Bethel, Jeroboam stretched out his hand from the altar and said, "Arrest him!" But the hand he stretched out against him withered, and he could not pull it back to himself. 5 The altar was ripped apart, and the ashes poured from the altar, according to the sign that the man of God had given by the word of the LORD.

6 Then the king responded to the man of God, "Plead for the favor of the LORD your God and pray for me so that my hand may be restored to me." So the man of God pleaded for the favor of the LORD, and the king's hand was restored to him and became as it had been at first.

7 Then the king declared to the man of God, "Come home with me, refresh yourself, and I'll give you a reward."

8 But the man of God replied, "If you were to give me half your house, I still wouldn't go with you, and I wouldn't eat food or drink water in this place, 9 for this is what I was commanded by the word of the LORD: 'You must not eat food or drink water or go back the way you came.' " 10 So he went another way; he did not go back by the way he had come to Bethel.

THE OLD PROPHET AND THE MAN OF GOD

11 Now a certain old prophet was living in Bethel. His son[E] came and told him all the deeds that the man of God had done that day in Bethel. His sons also told their father the words that he had spoken to the king. 12 Then their father asked them, "Which way did he go?" His sons had seen[F] the way taken by the man of God who had come from Judah. 13 Then he said to his sons, "Saddle the donkey for me." So they saddled the donkey for him, and he got on it. 14 He followed the man of God and found him sitting under an oak tree. He asked him, "Are you the man of God who came from Judah?"

"I am," he said.

15 Then he said to him, "Come home with me and eat some food."

16 But he answered, "I cannot go back with you or accompany you; I will not eat food or drink water with you in this place. 17 For a message came to me by the word of the LORD: 'You must not eat food or drink water there or go back by the way you came.' "

18 He said to him, "I am also a prophet like you. An angel spoke to me by the word of the LORD: 'Bring him back with you to your house so that he may eat food and drink water.' " The old prophet deceived him, 19 and the man of God went back with him, ate food in his house, and drank water.

[A] **12:28** Or *here is your God*, or *here is your god* [B] **12:30** Some LXX mss read *calves to Bethel and the other to Dan* [C] **12:31** Lit *a house* [D] **12:33** Or *He went up to* [E] **13:11** Some Hb mss, LXX, Syr, Vg read *sons* [F] **13:12** LXX, Syr, Tg, Vg read *sons showed him*

20 While they were sitting at the table, the word of
the LORD came to the prophet who had brought him
back, 21 and the prophet cried out to the man of God
who had come from Judah, "This is what the LORD says:
'Because you rebelled against the LORD's command
and did not keep the command that the LORD your
God commanded you — 22 but you went back and
ate food and drank water in the place that he said to
you, "Do not eat food and do not drink water" — your
corpse will never reach the grave of your ancestors.' "
23 So after he had eaten food and after he had drunk,
the old prophet saddled the donkey for the prophet
he had brought back. 24 When he left,[A] a lion attacked[B]
him along the way and killed him. His corpse was
thrown on the road, and the donkey was standing
beside it; the lion was standing beside the corpse too.
25 There were men passing by who saw the corpse
thrown on the road and the lion standing beside it,
and they went and spoke about it in the city where
the old prophet lived. 26 When the prophet who had
brought him back from his way heard about it, he
said, "He is the man of God who disobeyed the LORD's
command. The LORD has given him to the lion, and it
has mauled and killed him, according to the word of
the LORD that he spoke to him."
27 Then the old prophet instructed his sons, "Saddle
the donkey for me." They saddled it, 28 and he went
and found the corpse thrown on the road with the
donkey and the lion standing beside the corpse. The
lion had not eaten the corpse or mauled the donkey.
29 So the prophet lifted the corpse of the man of God
and laid it on the donkey and brought it back. The
old prophet came into the city to mourn and to bury
him. 30 Then he laid the corpse in his own grave, and
they mourned over him, "Oh, my brother!"
31 After he had buried him, he said to his sons,
"When I die, bury me in the grave where the man of
God is buried; lay my bones beside his bones, 32 for
the message that he cried out by the word of the LORD
against the altar in Bethel and against all the shrines
of the high places in the cities of Samaria is certain
to happen."
33 Even after this, Jeroboam did not repent of his
evil way but again made priests for the high places
from the ranks of the people. He ordained whoever
so desired it, and they became priests of the high
places. 34 This was the sin that caused the house of
Jeroboam to be cut off and obliterated from the face
of the earth.

DISASTER ON THE HOUSE OF JEROBOAM

14 At that time Abijah son of Jeroboam became
sick. 2 Jeroboam said to his wife, "Go disguise
yourself, so they won't know that you're Jeroboam's
wife, and go to Shiloh. The prophet Ahijah is there; it
was he who told about me becoming king over this
people. 3 Take with you ten loaves of bread, some
cakes, and a jar of honey, and go to him. He will tell
you what will happen to the boy."
4 Jeroboam's wife did that: she went to Shiloh and
arrived at Ahijah's house. Ahijah could not see; he
was blind[C] due to his age. 5 But the LORD had said to
Ahijah, "Jeroboam's wife is coming soon to ask you
about her son, for he is sick. You are to say such and
such to her. When she arrives, she will be disguised."
6 When Ahijah heard the sound of her feet entering
the door, he said, "Come in, wife of Jeroboam! Why
are you disguised? I have bad news for you. 7 Go tell
Jeroboam, 'This is what the LORD God of Israel says:
I raised you up from among the people, appointed
you ruler over my people Israel, 8 tore the kingdom
away from the house of David, and gave it to you. But
you were not like my servant David, who kept my
commands and followed me with all his heart, doing
only what is right in my sight. 9 You behaved more
wickedly than all who were before you. In order to
anger me, you have proceeded to make for yourself
other gods and cast images, but you have flung me
behind your back. 10 Because of all this, I am about to
bring disaster on the house of Jeroboam:

I will wipe out all of Jeroboam's males,[D]
both slave and free,[E] in Israel;
I will sweep away the house of Jeroboam
as one sweeps away dung until it is all gone!
11 Anyone who belongs to Jeroboam and dies
in the city,
the dogs will eat,
and anyone who dies in the field,
the birds[F] will eat,
for the LORD has spoken!'

12 "As for you, get up and go to your house. When
your feet enter the city, the boy will die. 13 All Israel
will mourn for him and bury him. He alone out of Jeroboam's house will be given a proper burial because
out of the house of Jeroboam something favorable to
the LORD God of Israel was found in him. 14 The LORD
will raise up for himself a king over Israel, who will
wipe out the house of Jeroboam. This is the day, yes,[G]
even today! 15 For the LORD will strike Israel so that
they will[H] shake as a reed shakes in water. He will
uproot Israel from this good soil that he gave to their
ancestors. He will scatter them beyond the Euphrates
because they made their Asherah poles, angering the

[A] **13:23-24** LXX reads *donkey, and he turned* **24***and left, and*
[B] **13:24** Lit *met* [C] **14:4** Lit *see, for his eyes stood*; 1Sm 4:15
[D] **14:10** Lit *eliminate Jeroboam's one who urinates against the wall*
[E] **14:10** Or *males, even the weak and impaired*; Hb obscure
[F] **14:11** Lit *birds of the sky* [G] **14:14** Hb obscure [H] **14:15** *so that they will* supplied for clarity

The Golden Calves at Dan and Bethel

by Conn Davis

The predecessor to Jeroboam's two calves was the golden calf in the wilderness that Aaron built after the exodus from Egypt. Aaron and Jeroboam used remarkably similar language after building their golden calves: "Israel, these are/here are your gods, who brought you up from the land of Egypt" (Ex 32:4,8; 1Kg 12:28).

From Mesopotamia to Egypt to India, residents of the region have historically used the bull/calf image for religious practices. They have understood the calf as a pedestal or base on which their gods rested. The greatest example in the Old Testament was the Canaanite idol Baal, which sometimes existed as a bull. Israel lived in a constant state of spiritual crisis because of their syncretistic worship of Baal while attempting obedience to the Almighty God of their covenant. The classic confrontation between Elijah and the prophets of Baal on Mount Carmel witnessed to this tragic situation.

The Egyptian and Canaanite backgrounds of calf worship are significant, for Israel had extensive interaction with both cultures. The ancient Egyptian capital of Memphis became a religious center for the worship of the Apis bull. This idol represented strength and fertility. Likewise, the Canaanites perceived Baal as a symbol of fertility and strength, and as a storm-god.[1]

A bronze bull found in Antioch of Syria (Antakya, Turkey). Dates possibly from the ninth–eighth centuries BC.

JEROBOAM'S CALVES

Some scholars believe that Jeroboam I built his two calves to symbolize the invisible God as either standing or enthroned on the calf.[2] According to this view, the two shrines rivaled the ark of the covenant with its mercy seat on which God resided.

For the calves' placement, Dan and Bethel were strategic geographic locations. Dan was on Israel's extreme northern border; Bethel was on the southern edge, only twelve miles north of Jerusalem. Furthermore, Bethel had a rich spiritual tradition with historic connections to Abraham and Jacob.

ARCHAEOLOGICAL FINDINGS

Archaeologists have found little evidence of Jeroboam's shrine at Bethel. However, the Israeli archaeologist Avraham Biran discovered important remains from Dan. He excavated a limestone block platform or high place that Jeroboam built.[3] The main section of this rectangular-shaped worship area measured about sixty by twenty-five feet.

Biran believed that this sanctuary was the remains of the "shrines on the high places" built with the golden calf (1Kg 12:31). The destruction of Jeroboam's shrine at Dan probably occurred when Ben-hadad of Syria attacked Dan and other towns of northern Israel about 885 BC.

Part of the Canaanite high place and altar complex at Dan in northern Israel; dated to the thirteenth–twelfth centuries BC.

Found in Royal Graves at Ur, this gold bull's head is from the sounding box of a harp from the tomb of Queen Pu-abi (formerly read as Sub-ad). The originals were in the Iraq Museum, Baghdad.

Another Israeli archaeologist, Amihai Mazar, excavated an important related site in the hills of Samaria close to Dothan. He described the find of a circular worship area approximately fifty-two hundred square feet. His most crucial discovery was a unique bronze figurine of a bull, about seven inches in length and five inches in height. He analyzed the metal composition of the small image as being 92 percent copper, 4 percent lead, and 4 percent tin. Moreover, he dated the high place/worship area and the bull figurine to the time of the judges, 1200 BC. Archaeologists refer to this type of bull image as a zebu bull because of a hump on its back and other features. The zebu bull originated in India and spread to the ancient Near East by 3000 BC.[4]

The best biblical descriptions of the construction of idols such as these calves comes from select passages in Isaiah and Jeremiah (Is 40:18–20; 44:9–17; 46:6–7; Jr 10:3–5). The two basic building methods involved the skills of a carpenter and a metalsmith/craftsman. The carpenter took the wood from a cedar or oak tree and carved an image known as a carved or graven image. The metalsmith then covered or lined the wood image with gold. In the second method, a metalsmith formed gold or metal into a mold in a fire and hammered it into final shape—a cast or molten image. Second Kings 17:16 describes the two calves as "cast images." ✜

---

[1] See K. A. Kitchen, "Golden Calf" in *The Illustrated Bible Dictionary* (Wheaton, IL: Tyndale House, 1980), 1:226. [2] John Bright, *A History of Israel*, 2nd ed. (Philadelphia: Westminster, 1972), 234. [3] Avraham Biran, "Tel Dan," *BA* 43.3 (Summer 1980): 175. [4] Amihai Mazar, "The Bull Site," *BASOR* 247 (Summer 1982): 27,29,32–33.

LORD. 16 He will give up Israel because of Jeroboam's sins that he committed and caused Israel to commit."

17 Then Jeroboam's wife got up and left and went to Tirzah. As she was crossing the threshold of the house, the boy died. 18 He was buried, and all Israel mourned for him, according to the word of the LORD he had spoken through his servant the prophet Ahijah.

19 As for the rest of the events of Jeroboam's reign, how he waged war and how he reigned, note that they are written in the Historical Record of Israel's Kings. 20 The length of Jeroboam's reign was twenty-two years. He rested with his ancestors, and his son Nadab became king in his place.

JUDAH'S KING REHOBOAM

21 Now Rehoboam, Solomon's son, reigned in Judah. Rehoboam was forty-one years old when he became king; he reigned seventeen years in Jerusalem, the city where the LORD had chosen from all the tribes of Israel to put his name. Rehoboam's mother's name was Naamah the Ammonite.

22 Judah did what was evil in the LORD's sight. They provoked him to jealous anger more than all that their ancestors had done with the sins they committed. 23 They also built for themselves high places, sacred pillars, and Asherah poles on every high hill and under every green tree; 24 there were even male cult prostitutes in the land. They imitated all the detestable practices of the nations the LORD had dispossessed before the Israelites.

25 In the fifth year of King Rehoboam, King Shishak of Egypt went to war against Jerusalem. 26 He seized the treasuries of the LORD's temple and the treasuries of the royal palace. He took everything. He took all the gold shields that Solomon had made. 27 King Rehoboam made bronze shields to replace them and committed them into the care of the captains of the guards[A] who protected the entrance to the king's palace. 28 Whenever the king entered the LORD's temple, the guards would carry the shields, then they would take them back to the armory.[B]

29 The rest of the events of Rehoboam's reign, along with all his accomplishments, are written about in the Historical Record of Judah's Kings. 30 There was war between Rehoboam and Jeroboam throughout their reigns. 31 Rehoboam rested with his ancestors and was buried with his ancestors in the city of David. His mother's name was Naamah the Ammonite. His son Abijam[C] became king in his place.

JUDAH'S KING ABIJAM

15 In the eighteenth year of Israel's King Jeroboam son of Nebat, Abijam became king over Judah, 2 and he reigned three years in Jerusalem. His mother's name was Maacah daughter[D] of Abishalom.

3 Abijam walked in all the sins his father before him had committed, and he was not wholeheartedly devoted to the LORD his God as his ancestor David had been. 4 But for the sake of David, the LORD his God gave him a lamp[E] in Jerusalem by raising up his son after him and by preserving Jerusalem. 5 For David did what was right in the LORD's sight, and he did not turn aside from anything he had commanded him all the days of his life, except in the matter of Uriah the Hethite.

6 There had been war between Rehoboam and Jeroboam all the days of Rehoboam's life. 7 The rest of the events of Abijam's reign, along with all his accomplishments, are written in the Historical Record of Judah's Kings. There was also war between Abijam and Jeroboam. 8 Abijam rested with his ancestors and was buried in the city of David. His son Asa became king in his place.

JUDAH'S KING ASA

9 In the twentieth year of Israel's King Jeroboam, Asa became king of Judah, 10 and he reigned forty-one years in Jerusalem. His grandmother's[F] name was Maacah daughter of Abishalom.

11 Asa did what was right in the LORD's sight, as his ancestor David had done. 12 He banished the male cult prostitutes from the land and removed all of the idols that his ancestors had made. 13 He also removed his grandmother[G] Maacah from being queen mother because she had made an obscene image of Asherah. Asa chopped down her obscene image and burned it in the Kidron Valley. 14 The high places were not taken away, but Asa was wholeheartedly devoted to the LORD his entire life. 15 He brought his father's consecrated gifts and his own consecrated gifts into the LORD's temple: silver, gold, and utensils.

16 There was war between Asa and King Baasha of Israel throughout their reigns. 17 Israel's King Baasha went to war against Judah. He built Ramah in order to keep anyone from leaving or coming to King Asa of Judah. 18 So Asa withdrew all the silver and gold that remained in the treasuries of the LORD's temple and the treasuries of the royal palace and gave it to his servants. Then King Asa sent them to Ben-hadad son of Tabrimmon son of Hezion king of Aram who lived in Damascus, saying, 19 "There is a treaty between me and you, between my father and your father. Look, I have sent you a gift of silver and gold. Go and break your treaty with King Baasha of Israel so that he will withdraw from me."

20 Ben-hadad listened to King Asa and sent the commanders of his armies against the cities of Israel. He attacked Ijon, Dan, Abel-beth-maacah, all

[A] **14:27** Lit *the runners* [B] **14:28** Lit *the chamber of the runners* [C] **14:31** = Abijah in 2Ch 13 [D] **15:2** Possibly granddaughter, also in v. 10; 2Ch 13:2 [E] **15:4** Or *dominion* [F] **15:10** Lit *mother's* [G] **15:13** Lit *mother*

Abel-beth-maacah: Its History and Significance

by Eric A. Mitchell

Abel-beth-maacah (Tell Abil el-Qameh).

Several towns in ancient Israel have the name of Abel (meaning "meadow") accompanied by a modifier indicating a distinction about the location. Those in the Old Testament are Abel-mizraim, "meadow/mourning of Egypt," located at Atad on the eastern side of the Jordan River and north of the Dead Sea, which was where the Egyptians traveled with Joseph to mourn Jacob's death (Gn 50:11); Abel-shittim, "the Acacia Meadow" located across the Jordan River from Jericho (Nm 33:49); Abel-keramim, "meadow/plain of vineyards," in the Transjordan near Amman (Jdg 11:33); and Abel-meholah, "meadow of the dance," which was likely located in the Jordan Valley south of Beth-shean (1Kg 19:16).

Abel-beth-maacah (also called Abel of Beth-maacah) means "meadow of the house of Maacah," perhaps designating the town as the Abel that lies in the ancient region of the Aramean tribe of Maacah.[1] This twenty-five-acre site is located 4 ½ miles west of Tel Dan, a mile south of the modern Israeli border with Lebanon; and is 21 miles east of Tyre and 43 miles southwest of Damascus. By the end of the judges period, this was an Aramean border region with Phoenicians to the west and north and Israelites to the south.[2]

During the Late Iron I period (1200–1100 BC), the Aramean clan of Maacah controlled the kingdom of Geshur. This territory was just north of Israel and south of Mount Hermon from the Transjordan across the Golan Heights into the Jordan Valley north of the Sea of Galilee.[3]

RESOURCES

Abel-beth-maacah had all four basic resources required for a good city location in ancient times: (1) for protection, an elevated location with sloping sides, (2) water, (3) agricultural fields, and (4) a nearby route for income-producing trade. Nestled next to the Lebanon

Excavated buildings dated to the late eleventh–early tenth centuries BC; between the upper and lower mounds, on the east side of the tel.

range on its west, which separates Israel and Jordan, the site is on a plateau fourteen hundred feet above sea level and overlooks the Huleh Valley to the south. Archaeologist William Dever described the site as sitting on a "grassy knoll above the falls at the headwaters of one of the sources of the Jordan."[3] The ancient city's tel rises an imposing forty-nine feet above the surrounding fields.

Abel-beth-maacah strategically controlled a significant ancient crossing point for two major routes: first, a trade route from Mesopotamia to Egypt through Lebanon's Beqa'a Valley to its north, and second, an east-west route from Damascus and the Transjordan across the Golan Heights (just south of Mount Hermon) to Abel-beth-maacah and then north and west to Tyre or Sidon. The surrounding agricultural fields were a rich resource. The fields to its north and east rise in elevation toward the north.[4]

ARCHAEOLOGICAL EXCAVATIONS

Only recently have the first-ever excavations occurred at Abel-beth-maacah, which is known locally as Tell Abil el-Qameh. Naama Yahalom-Mack and Nava Panitz-Cohen of Jerusalem's Hebrew University are jointly leading the excavations with Robert Mullins of Azusa Pacific University. The excavations have taken place from 2013 to 2017.[5]

The surveys have revealed many ancient sites within three miles of Abil el-Qameh, which indicates a regional habitation from the Early Bronze to Ottoman periods. The site itself is an oval, stretching north to south with a three-acre upper tel on the northern end that is another thirty-two feet higher than the southern (lower) tel. Current excavations have revealed occupation on the lower tel in the Middle Bronze (2400–1500 BC), Late Bronze (1500–1200), and Iron Age I (1200–1000) after which the lower city was abandoned. The upper acropolis of the city continued in use, however, from Iron Age II to the Hellenistic period (1000–ca 334 BC).[6]

A Benjaminite, named Sheba the son of Bichri, blew a trumpet and called all Israel to reject David's rule. David immediately gave orders to find or capture Sheba and quell the revolt. Sheba had run to the most distant city in Israelite territory from Jerusalem—Abel-beth-maacah. Joab and his men cast a siege ramp against the city to attack it, but a wise woman declared that Abel was

As seen from Abel-beth-maacah, mountains of Lebanon rise in the distance.

Cooking installation excavated at Abel-beth-maacah; shown are two silos, each measuring more than five feet in diameter. Archaeologists excavated from them ash, bones, and pottery. The indentation in the front left was likely a cooking pit. Ceramic ovens would have been located on the raised platform in the back left corner of this same room. The installation dates to the Middle Bronze Age II (1950–1550 BC), the time of the patriarchs.

known as a place of wisdom. She called her city "a mother in Israel" (a city with "daughter" villages; 2Sm 20:18–19). The woman convinced the people of the city to behead Sheba and throw his head over the wall to Joab. Politically for David, having a loyal Aramean city kill the rebellious Benjaminite was better than David's own men killing him. ❖

[1] W. G. Dever, "Abel-Beth-Ma'acah: Northern Gateway of Ancient Israel" in *The Archaeology of Jordan and Other Studies*, ed. L. T. Geraty and L. G. Herr (Berrien Springs, MI: Andrews University Press, 1986), 208–10. [2] Nava Panitz-Cohen, Robert A. Mullins, and Ruham Bonfil, "Northern Exposure: Launching Excavations at Tell Abil el-Qameh (Abel Beth Maacah)," *Strata: Bulletin of the Anglo-Israel Archaeological Society* 31 (2013): 27–28. Tel Abel Beth Maacah Excavations, abel-beth-maacah.org/index.php/about. [3] Dever, "Abel-Beth-Ma'acah," 214. Nava Panitz-Cohen, R. A. Mullins, and R. Bonfil, "Second Preliminary Report of the Excavations at Tell Abil el-Qameh (Abel Beth Maacah)," *Strata* 33 (2015): 55–56. Cf. B. Mazar, "Geshur and Maacah," *JBL* 80 (March 1961): 16–28. [4] Dever, "Abel-Beth-Ma'acah," 210. [5] Dever, "Abel-Beth-Ma'acah," 210–11, 217. [6] Dever, "Abel-Beth-Ma'acah," 216; cf. Tel Abel Beth Maacah Excavations, abel-beth-maacah.org/index.php/staff/core-staff.

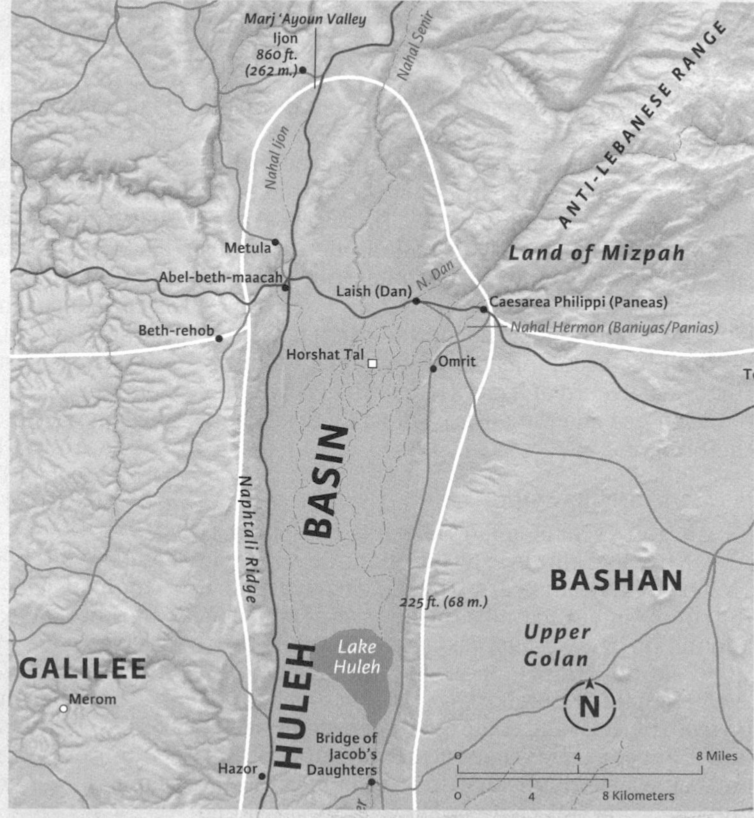

The location of Abel-beth-maacah in the northern Huleh Basin.

Chinnereth, and the whole land of Naphtali. 21 When Baasha heard about it, he quit building Ramah and stayed in Tirzah. 22 Then King Asa gave a command to everyone without exception in Judah, and they carried away the stones of Ramah and the timbers Baasha had built it with. Then King Asa built Geba of Benjamin and Mizpah with them.

23 The rest of all the events of Asa's reign, along with all his might, all his accomplishments, and the cities he built, are written in the Historical Record of Judah's Kings. But in his old age he developed a disease in his feet. 24 Then Asa rested with his ancestors and was buried in the city of his ancestor David. His son Jehoshaphat became king in his place.

ISRAEL'S KING NADAB

25 Nadab son of Jeroboam became king over Israel in the second year of Judah's King Asa; he reigned over Israel two years. 26 Nadab did what was evil in the LORD's sight and walked in the ways of his father and the sin he had caused Israel to commit.

27 Then Baasha son of Ahijah of the house of Issachar conspired against Nadab, and Baasha struck him down at Gibbethon of the Philistines while Nadab and all Israel were besieging Gibbethon. 28 In the third year of Judah's King Asa, Baasha killed Nadab and reigned in his place.

29 When Baasha became king, he struck down the entire house of Jeroboam. He did not leave Jeroboam any survivors but[A] destroyed his family according to the word of the LORD he had spoken through his servant Ahijah the Shilonite. 30 This was because Jeroboam had angered[B] the LORD God of Israel by the sins he had committed and had caused Israel to commit.

31 The rest of the events of Nadab's reign, along with all his accomplishments, are written in the Historical Record of Israel's Kings. 32 There was war between Asa and King Baasha of Israel throughout their reigns.

ISRAEL'S KING BAASHA

33 In the third year of Judah's King Asa, Baasha son of Ahijah became king over all Israel, and he reigned in Tirzah twenty-four years. 34 He did what was evil in the LORD's sight and walked in the ways of Jeroboam and the sin he had caused Israel to commit.

16 Now the word of the LORD came to Jehu son of Hanani against Baasha: 2 "Because I raised you up from the dust and made you ruler over my people Israel, but you have walked in the ways of Jeroboam and have caused my people Israel to sin, angering me with their sins, 3 take note: I will eradicate Baasha and his house, and I will make your house like the house of Jeroboam son of Nebat:

4 Anyone who belongs to Baasha and dies
in the city,
the dogs will eat,
and anyone who is his and dies in the field,
the birds[C] will eat."

5 The rest of the events of Baasha's reign, along with all his accomplishments and might, are written in the Historical Record of Israel's Kings. 6 Baasha rested with his ancestors and was buried in Tirzah. His son Elah became king in his place. 7 But through the prophet Jehu son of Hanani the word of the LORD also had come against Baasha and against his house because of all the evil he had done in the LORD's sight. His actions angered the LORD, and Baasha's house became like the house of Jeroboam, because he had struck it down.

ISRAEL'S KING ELAH

8 In the twenty-sixth year of Judah's King Asa, Elah son of Baasha became king over Israel, and he reigned in Tirzah two years.

9 His servant Zimri, commander of half his chariots, conspired against him while Elah was in Tirzah getting drunk in the house of Arza, who was in charge of the household at Tirzah. 10 In the twenty-seventh year of Judah's King Asa, Zimri went in and struck Elah down, killing him. Then Zimri became king in his place.

11 When he became king, as soon as he was seated on his throne, Zimri struck down the entire house of Baasha. He did not leave a single male,[D] including his kinsmen and his friends. 12 So Zimri destroyed the entire house of Baasha, according to the word of the LORD he had spoken against Baasha through the prophet Jehu. 13 This happened because of all the sins of Baasha and those of his son Elah, which they committed and caused Israel to commit, angering the LORD God of Israel with their worthless idols.

14 The rest of the events of Elah's reign, along with all his accomplishments, are written in the Historical Record of Israel's Kings.

ISRAEL'S KING ZIMRI

15 In the twenty-seventh year of Judah's King Asa, Zimri became king for seven days in Tirzah. Now the troops were encamped against Gibbethon of the Philistines. 16 When these troops heard that Zimri had not only conspired but had also struck down the king, then all Israel made Omri, the army commander, king over Israel that very day in the camp. 17 Omri along with all Israel marched up from Gibbethon and

[A] **15:29** Lit *Jeroboam anyone breathing until he* [B] **15:30** Lit *provoked in the provocation of* [C] **16:4** Lit *birds of the sky* [D] **16:11** Lit *leave him one who urinates against the wall*

besieged Tirzah. [18] When Zimri saw that the city was captured, he entered the citadel of the royal palace and burned it down over himself. He died [19] because of the sin he committed by doing what was evil in the LORD's sight and by walking in the ways of Jeroboam and the sin he caused Israel to commit.

[20] The rest of the events of Zimri's reign, along with the conspiracy that he instigated, are written in the Historical Record of Israel's Kings. [21] At that time the people of Israel were divided: half the people followed Tibni son of Ginath, to make him king, and half followed Omri. [22] However, the people who followed Omri proved stronger than those who followed Tibni son of Ginath. So Tibni died and Omri became king.

ISRAEL'S KING OMRI

[23] In the thirty-first year of Judah's King Asa, Omri became king over Israel, and he reigned twelve years. He reigned six years in Tirzah, [24] then he bought the hill of Samaria from Shemer for 150 pounds[A] of silver, and he built up the hill. He named the city he built Samaria[B] based on the name Shemer, the owner of the hill.

[25] Omri did what was evil in the LORD's sight; he did more evil than all who were before him. [26] He walked in all the ways of Jeroboam son of Nebat in every respect and continued in his sins that he caused Israel to commit, angering the LORD God of Israel with their worthless idols. [27] The rest of the events of Omri's reign, along with his accomplishments and the might he exercised, are written in the Historical Record of Israel's Kings. [28] Omri rested with his ancestors and was buried in Samaria. His son Ahab became king in his place.

ISRAEL'S KING AHAB

[29] Ahab son of Omri became king over Israel in the thirty-eighth year of Judah's King Asa; Ahab son of Omri reigned over Israel in Samaria twenty-two years. [30] But Ahab son of Omri did what was evil in the LORD's sight more than all who were before him. [31] Then, as if following the sin of Jeroboam son of Nebat were not enough, he married Jezebel, the daughter of Ethbaal king of the Sidonians, and then proceeded to serve Baal and bow in worship to him. [32] He set up an altar for Baal in the temple of Baal that he had built in Samaria. [33] Ahab also made an Asherah pole. Ahab did more to anger the LORD God of Israel than all the kings of Israel who were before him.

[34] During his reign, Hiel the Bethelite built Jericho. At the cost of Abiram his firstborn, he laid its foundation, and at the cost of Segub his youngest, he finished its gates, according to the word of the LORD he had spoken through Joshua son of Nun.

ELIJAH ANNOUNCES FAMINE

17 Now Elijah the Tishbite, from the Gilead settlers,[C] said to Ahab, "As the LORD God of Israel lives, in whose presence I stand, there will be no dew or rain during these years except by my command!"

[2] Then the word of the LORD came to him: [3] "Leave here, turn eastward, and hide at the Wadi Cherith where it enters the Jordan. [4] You are to drink from the wadi. I have commanded the ravens to provide for you there."

[5] So he proceeded to do what the LORD commanded. Elijah left and lived at the Wadi Cherith where it enters the Jordan. [6] The ravens kept bringing him bread and meat in the morning and in the evening, and he would drink from the wadi. [7] After a while, the wadi dried up because there had been no rain in the land.

ELIJAH AND THE WIDOW

[8] Then the word of the LORD came to him: [9] "Get up, go to Zarephath that belongs to Sidon and stay there. Look, I have commanded a woman who is a widow to provide for you there." [10] So Elijah got up and went to Zarephath. When he arrived at the city gate, there was a widow gathering wood. Elijah called to her and said, "Please bring me a little water in a cup and let me drink." [11] As she went to get it, he called to her and said, "Please bring me a piece of bread in your hand."

[12] But she said, "As the LORD your God lives, I don't have anything baked — only a handful of flour in the jar and a bit of oil in the jug. Just now, I am gathering a couple of sticks in order to go prepare it for myself and my son so we can eat it and die."

[13] Then Elijah said to her, "Don't be afraid; go and do as you have said. But first make me a small loaf from it and bring it out to me. Afterward, you may make some for yourself and your son, [14] for this is what the LORD God of Israel says, 'The flour jar will not become empty and the oil jug will not run dry until the day the LORD sends rain on the surface of the land.'"

[15] So she proceeded to do according to the word of Elijah. Then the woman, Elijah, and her household ate for many days. [16] The flour jar did not become empty, and the oil jug did not run dry, according to the word of the LORD he had spoken through[D] Elijah.

THE WIDOW'S SON RAISED

[17] After this, the son of the woman who owned the house became ill. His illness got worse until he stopped breathing. [18] She said to Elijah, "Man of God, what do you have against me? Have you come to call attention to my iniquity so that my son is put to death?"

[A] **16:24** Lit *for two talents* [B] **16:24** = Belonging to Shemer's Clan
[C] **17:1** LXX reads *from Tishbe of Gilead* [D] **17:16** Lit *by the hand of*

19 But Elijah said to her, "Give me your son." So he
took him from her arms, brought him up to the upstairs room where he was staying, and laid him on
his own bed. 20 Then he cried out to the LORD and said,
"LORD my God, have you also brought tragedy on the
widow I am staying with by killing her son?" 21 Then
he stretched himself out over the boy three times. He
cried out to the LORD and said, "LORD my God, please
let this boy's life come into him again!"

22 So the LORD listened to Elijah, and the boy's life
came into him again, and he lived. 23 Then Elijah took
the boy, brought him down from the upstairs room
into the house, and gave him to his mother. Elijah
said, "Look, your son is alive."

24 Then the woman said to Elijah, "Now I know you
are a man of God and the LORD's word from your
mouth is true."

ELIJAH'S MESSAGE TO AHAB

18 After a long time, the word of the LORD came to
Elijah in the third year: "Go and present yourself to Ahab. I will send rain on the surface of the
land." 2 So Elijah went to present himself to Ahab.

The famine was severe in Samaria. 3 Ahab called for
Obadiah, who was in charge of the palace. Obadiah
was a man who greatly feared the LORD 4 and took a
hundred prophets and hid them, fifty men to a cave,
and provided them with food and water when Jezebel
slaughtered the LORD's prophets. 5 Ahab said to Obadiah, "Go throughout the land to every spring and to
every wadi. Perhaps we'll find grass so we can keep
the horses and mules alive and not have to destroy
any cattle." 6 They divided the land between them in
order to cover it. Ahab went one way by himself, and
Obadiah went the other way by himself.

7 While Obadiah was walking along the road, Elijah
suddenly met him. When Obadiah recognized him,
he fell facedown and said, "Is it you, my lord Elijah?"

8 "It is I," he replied. "Go tell your lord, 'Elijah is
here!'"[A]

9 But Obadiah said, "What sin have I committed,
that you are handing your servant over to Ahab to
put me to death? 10 As the LORD your God lives, there
is no nation or kingdom where my lord has not sent
someone to search for you. When they said, 'He is not
here,' he made that kingdom or nation swear they
had not found you.

11 "Now you say, 'Go tell your lord, "Elijah is here!"'
12 But when I leave you, the Spirit of the LORD may
carry you off to some place I don't know. Then when
I go report to Ahab and he doesn't find you, he will
kill me. But I, your servant, have feared the LORD from
my youth. 13 Wasn't it reported to my lord what I did
when Jezebel slaughtered the LORD's prophets? I hid
a hundred of the prophets of the LORD, fifty men to
a cave, and I provided them with food and water.
14 Now you say, 'Go tell your lord, "Elijah is here!"'
He will kill me!"

15 Then Elijah said, "As the LORD of Armies lives, in
whose presence I stand, today I will present myself
to Ahab."

16 Obadiah went to meet Ahab and told him. Then
Ahab went to meet Elijah. 17 When Ahab saw Elijah,
Ahab said to him, "Is that you, the one ruining Israel?"

18 He replied, "I have not ruined Israel, but you and
your father's family have, because you have abandoned the LORD's commands and followed the Baals.
19 Now summon all Israel to meet me at Mount Carmel, along with the 450 prophets of Baal and the 400
prophets of Asherah who eat at Jezebel's table."

ELIJAH AT MOUNT CARMEL

20 So Ahab summoned all the Israelites and gathered the prophets at Mount Carmel. 21 Then Elijah
approached all the people and said, "How long will
you waver between two opinions?[B] If the LORD is God,
follow him. But if Baal, follow him." But the people
didn't answer him a word.

22 Then Elijah said to the people, "I am the only
remaining prophet of the LORD, but Baal's prophets
are 450 men. 23 Let two bulls be given to us. They are
to choose one bull for themselves, cut it in pieces,
and place it on the wood but not light the fire. I will
prepare the other bull and place it on the wood but
not light the fire. 24 Then you call on the name of your
god, and I will call on the name of the LORD. The God
who answers with fire, he is God."

All the people answered, "That's fine."

25 Then Elijah said to the prophets of Baal, "Since
you are so numerous, choose for yourselves one bull
and prepare it first. Then call on the name of your god
but don't light the fire."

26 So they took the bull that he gave them, prepared
it, and called on the name of Baal from morning until noon, saying, "Baal, answer us!" But there was no
sound; no one answered. Then they danced[C] around
the altar they had made.

27 At noon Elijah mocked them. He said, "Shout
loudly, for he's a god! Maybe he's thinking it over;
maybe he has wandered away;[D] or maybe he's on the
road. Perhaps he's sleeping and will wake up!" 28 They
shouted loudly, and cut themselves with knives and
spears, according to their custom, until blood gushed
over them. 29 All afternoon they kept on raving until
the offering of the evening sacrifice, but there was
no sound; no one answered, no one paid attention.

[A] **18:8** The Hb words translated *'Elijah is here'* also mean *'Look, my God is the LORD'* [B] **18:21** Lit *you hobble on two crutches?* [C] **18:26** Or *hobbled* [D] **18:27** Or *has turned aside*; possibly to relieve himself

Elijah: A Man of God

by Robert C. Dunston

Elijah came from Tishbe, a village of uncertain location, in the area of Gilead east of the Jordan River. During Elijah's time, Gilead comprised a forested, sparsely settled area of the northern kingdom of Israel. Since "Tishbite" is so similar to the Hebrew word for "settler," Elijah's identification as a Tishbite may describe him more as a settler in Gilead than as an inhabitant of a particular village.[1]

Elijah's ministry occurred during the reigns of Ahab (874–853 BC) and Ahaziah (853–852 BC), both kings of the northern kingdom. A good economy had enabled Omri to build a capital city of Samaria. Omri also created a stable government that allowed him to pass his kingship peacefully to Ahab.[2]

Ahab married Jezebel, a princess from the Phoenician city of Tyre. Ahab and Jezebel's marriage cemented ties between the northern kingdom and Phoenicia, provided expanded opportunities for trade, and created an alliance against the expanding power and influence of Damascus. As Solomon had done before him, Ahab allowed his wife Jezebel to worship her gods; he built a temple in Samaria to Baal and set up an Asherah pole (1Kg 16:31–33).

Baal's followers worshiped him as the storm-god who brought rains, and thus fertility, to the land and as the one who provided for the agricultural needs. Baal worshipers believed that during the annual dry season, their deity was trapped in the land of the dead unable to return without help. Baal worship involved fertility rites and ritualistic prostitution as the people sought, through sympathetic magic, to coax Baal's sister and lover Anat to go to the underworld and rescue him. Worshipers wrote stories about the deity that suggested Baal "could go on a journey, fall asleep, or even resort to bloody self-mutilation."[3] Baal prophets sometimes employed mutilation in an effort to get his attention (18:27–28).

In Elijah's initial confrontation with Ahab, Elijah prophesied God would withhold rain and dew for the next several years. God intended the extended drought to underscore Baal's inability to free himself from death and provide for people's needs and to demonstrate the one true God's living reality and power (17:1). ✣

[1] Simon J. DeVries, *1 Kings*, vol. 12 in Word Biblical Commentary (WBC) (Waco, TX: Word Books, 1985), 216. [2] Paul R. House, *1, 2 Kings*, vol. 8 in NAC, 203, 212, 242. [3] House, *1, 2 Kings*, 220.

Dated to Iron Age II (1000–800 BC), a small ceramic juglet made of gray-black clay. This piece has a widening neck opening and a handle that attaches at the rim. One of the miracles associated with Elijah involved the Lord providing an unending supply of oil, which sustained a widow and her son during a severe drought (1Kg 17:9–16).

The fifth-century monastery of St. George, along the northern bank of the Wadi Qelt. Tradition holds that the ravens fed Elijah here.

30 Then Elijah said to all the people, "Come near me." So all the people approached him. Then he repaired the LORD's altar that had been torn down: 31 Elijah took twelve stones — according to the number of the tribes of the sons of Jacob, to whom the word of the LORD had come, saying, "Israel will be your name" — 32 and he built an altar with the stones in the name of the LORD. Then he made a trench around the altar large enough to hold about four gallons.[A,B] 33 Next, he arranged the wood, cut up the bull, and placed it on the wood. He said, "Fill four water pots with water and pour it on the offering to be burned and on the wood." 34 Then he said, "A second time!" and they did it a second time. And then he said, "A third time!" and they did it a third time. 35 So the water ran all around the altar; he even filled the trench with water.

36 At the time for offering the evening sacrifice, the prophet Elijah approached the altar and said, "LORD, the God of Abraham, Isaac, and Israel, today let it be known that you are God in Israel and I am your servant, and that at your word I have done all these things. 37 Answer me, LORD! Answer me so that this people will know that you, the LORD, are God and that you have turned their hearts back."

38 Then the LORD's fire fell and consumed the burnt offering, the wood, the stones, and the dust, and it licked up the water that was in the trench. 39 When all the people saw it, they fell facedown and said, "The LORD, he is God! The LORD, he is God!"

40 Then Elijah ordered them, "Seize the prophets of Baal! Do not let even one of them escape." So they seized them, and Elijah brought them down to the Wadi Kishon and slaughtered them there. 41 Elijah said to Ahab, "Go up, eat and drink, for there is the sound of a rainstorm."

42 So Ahab went to eat and drink, but Elijah went up to the summit of Carmel. He bent down on the ground and put his face between his knees. 43 Then he said to his servant, "Go up and look toward the sea."

So he went up, looked, and said, "There's nothing."

Seven times Elijah said, "Go back."

44 On the seventh time, he reported, "There's a cloud as small as a man's hand coming up from the sea."

Then Elijah said, "Go and tell Ahab, 'Get your chariot ready and go down so the rain doesn't stop you.'"

45 In a little while, the sky grew dark with clouds and wind, and there was a downpour. So Ahab got in his chariot and went to Jezreel. 46 The power of the LORD was on Elijah, and he tucked his mantle under his belt and ran ahead of Ahab to the entrance of Jezreel.

ELIJAH'S JOURNEY TO HOREB

19 Ahab told Jezebel everything that Elijah had done and how he had killed all the prophets with the sword. 2 So Jezebel sent a messenger to Elijah, saying, "May the gods punish me and do so severely if I don't make your life like the life of one of them by this time tomorrow!"

3 Then Elijah became afraid[C] and immediately ran for his life. When he came to Beer-sheba that belonged to Judah, he left his servant there, 4 but he went on a day's journey into the wilderness. He sat down under a broom tree and prayed that he might die. He said, "I have had enough! LORD, take my life, for I'm no better than my ancestors." 5 Then he lay down and slept under the broom tree.

Suddenly, an angel touched him. The angel told him, "Get up and eat." 6 Then he looked, and there at his head was a loaf of bread baked over hot stones, and a jug of water. So he ate and drank and lay down again. 7 Then the angel of the LORD returned for a second time and touched him. He said, "Get up and eat, or the journey will be too much for you." 8 So he got up, ate, and drank. Then on the strength from that food, he walked forty days and forty nights to Horeb, the mountain of God. 9 He entered a cave there and spent the night.

ELIJAH'S ENCOUNTER WITH THE LORD

Suddenly, the word of the LORD came to him, and he said to him, "What are you doing here, Elijah?"

10 He replied, "I have been very zealous for the LORD God of Armies, but the Israelites have abandoned your covenant, torn down your altars, and killed your prophets with the sword. I alone am left, and they are looking for me to take my life."

11 Then he said, "Go out and stand on the mountain in the LORD's presence."

At that moment, the LORD passed by. A great and mighty wind was tearing at the mountains and was shattering cliffs before the LORD, but the LORD was not in the wind. After the wind there was an earthquake, but the LORD was not in the earthquake. 12 After the earthquake there was a fire, but the LORD was not in the fire. And after the fire there was a voice, a soft whisper. 13 When Elijah heard it, he wrapped his face in his mantle and went out and stood at the entrance of the cave.

Suddenly, a voice came to him and said, "What are you doing here, Elijah?"

14 "I have been very zealous for the LORD God of Armies," he replied, "but the Israelites have abandoned your covenant, torn down your altars, and killed your prophets with the sword. I alone am left, and they're looking for me to take my life."

15 Then the LORD said to him, "Go and return by the way you came to the Wilderness of Damascus. When you arrive, you are to anoint Hazael as king

[A] **18:32** LXX reads *trench containing two measures of seed*
[B] **18:32** Lit *altar corresponding to a house of two seahs of seed*
[C] **19:3** Some Hb mss, LXX, Syr, Vg; other Hb mss read *He saw*

over Aram. 16 You are to anoint Jehu son of Nimshi
as king over Israel and Elisha son of Shaphat from
Abel-meholah as prophet in your place. 17 Then Jehu
will put to death whoever escapes the sword of Hazael, and Elisha will put to death whoever escapes the
sword of Jehu. 18 But I will leave seven thousand in
Israel — every knee that has not bowed to Baal and
every mouth that has not kissed him."

ELISHA'S APPOINTMENT AS ELIJAH'S SUCCESSOR

19 Elijah left there and found Elisha son of Shaphat as
he was plowing. Twelve teams of oxen were in front of
him, and he was with the twelfth team. Elijah walked
by him and threw his mantle over him. 20 Elisha left
the oxen, ran to follow Elijah, and said, "Please let me
kiss my father and mother, and then I will follow you."

"Go on back," he replied, "for what have I done
to you?"

21 So he turned back from following him, took the
team of oxen, and slaughtered[A] them. With the oxen's
wooden yoke and plow, he cooked the meat and gave
it to the people, and they ate. Then he left, followed
Elijah, and served him.

VICTORY OVER BEN-HADAD

20 Now King Ben-hadad of Aram assembled his
entire army. Thirty-two kings, along with
horses and chariots, were with him. He marched up,
besieged Samaria, and fought against it. 2 He sent
messengers into the city to King Ahab of Israel and
said to him, "This is what Ben-hadad says: 3 'Your silver and your gold are mine! And your best wives and
children are mine as well!'"

4 Then the king of Israel answered, "Just as you say,
my lord the king: I am yours, along with all that I have."

5 The messengers then returned and said, "This
is what Ben-hadad says: 'I have sent messengers to
you, saying, "You are to give me your silver, your gold,
your wives, and your children." 6 But at this time tomorrow I will send my servants to you,[B] and they will
search your palace and your servants' houses. They
will lay their hands on and take away whatever is
precious to you.'"

7 Then the king of Israel called for all the elders of
the land and said, "Recognize[C] that this one is only
looking for trouble, for he demanded my wives, my
children, my silver, and my gold, and I didn't turn
him down."

8 All the elders and all the people said to him, "Don't
listen or agree."

9 So he said to Ben-hadad's messengers, "Say to
my lord the king, 'Everything you demanded of your
servant the first time, I will do, but this thing I cannot do.'" So the messengers left and took word back
to him.

10 Then Ben-hadad sent messengers to him and
said, "May the gods punish me and do so severely if
Samaria's dust amounts to a handful for each of the
people who follow me."

11 The king of Israel answered, "Say this: 'Don't let
the one who puts on his armor boast like the one
who takes it off.'"

12 When Ben-hadad heard this response, while he
and the kings were drinking in their quarters,[D] he
said to his servants, "Take your positions." So they
took their positions against the city.

13 A prophet approached King Ahab of Israel and
said, "This is what the LORD says: 'Do you see this
whole huge army? Watch, I am handing it over to
you today so that you may know that I am the LORD.'"

14 Ahab asked, "By whom?"

And the prophet said, "This is what the LORD says:
'By the young men of the provincial leaders.'"

Then he asked, "Who is to start the battle?"

He said, "You."

15 So Ahab mobilized the young men of the provincial leaders, and there were 232. After them he mobilized all the Israelite troops: 7,000. 16 They marched
out at noon while Ben-hadad and the thirty-two kings
who were helping him were getting drunk in their
quarters. 17 The young men of the provincial leaders
marched out first. Then Ben-hadad sent out scouts,
and they reported to him, saying, "Men are marching
out of Samaria."

18 So he said, "If they have marched out in peace,
take them alive, and if they have marched out for
battle, take them alive."

19 The young men of the provincial leaders and the
army behind them marched out from the city, 20 and
each one struck down his opponent. So the Arameans
fled and Israel pursued them, but King Ben-hadad of
Aram escaped on a horse with the cavalry. 21 Then the
king of Israel marched out and attacked the cavalry
and the chariots. He inflicted a severe slaughter on
Aram.

22 The prophet approached the king of Israel and
said to him, "Go and strengthen yourself, then consider carefully[E] what you should do, for in the spring
the king of Aram will attack you."

23 Now the king of Aram's servants said to him,
"Their gods are gods of the hill country. That's why
they were stronger than we were. Instead, we should
fight with them on the plain; then we will certainly
be stronger than they are. 24 Also do this: remove
each king from his position and appoint captains in
their place. 25 Raise another army for yourself like the
army you lost — horse for horse, chariot for chariot

[A] **19:21** Or *sacrificed* [B] **20:6** Lit *take all the delight of your eyes*
[C] **20:7** Lit *"Know and see* [D] **20:12** Lit *booths*, also in v. 16
[E] **20:22** Lit *then know and see*

— and let's fight with them on the plain; and we will certainly be stronger than they are." The king listened to them and did it.

26 In the spring, Ben-hadad mobilized the Arameans and went up to Aphek to battle Israel. 27 The Israelites mobilized, gathered supplies, and went to fight them. The Israelites camped in front of them like two little flocks of goats, while the Arameans filled the landscape.

28 Then the man of God approached and said to the king of Israel, "This is what the LORD says: 'Because the Arameans have said, "The LORD is a god of the mountains and not a god of the valleys," I will hand over all this whole huge army to you. Then you will know that I am the LORD.'"

29 They camped opposite each other for seven days. On the seventh day, the battle took place, and the Israelites struck down the Arameans — one hundred thousand foot soldiers in one day. 30 The ones who remained fled into the city of Aphek, and the wall fell on those twenty-seven thousand remaining men.

Ben-hadad also fled and went into an inner room in the city. 31 His servants said to him, "Consider this: we have heard that the kings of the house of Israel are merciful kings. So let's put sackcloth around our waists and ropes around our heads, and let's go out to the king of Israel. Perhaps he will spare your life."

32 So they dressed with sackcloth around their waists and ropes around their heads, went to the king of Israel, and said, "Your servant Ben-hadad says, 'Please spare my life.'"

So he said, "Is he still alive? He is my brother."

33 Now the men were looking for a sign of hope, so they quickly picked up on this[A] and responded, "Yes, it is your brother Ben-hadad."

Then he said, "Go and bring him."

So Ben-hadad came out to him, and Ahab had him come up into the chariot. 34 Then Ben-hadad said to him, "I restore to you the cities that my father took from your father, and you may set up marketplaces for yourself in Damascus, like my father set up in Samaria."

Ahab responded, "On the basis of this treaty, I release you." So he made a treaty with him and released him.

AHAB REBUKED BY THE LORD

35 One of the sons of the prophets said to his fellow prophet by the word of the LORD, "Strike me!" But the man refused to strike him.

36 He told him, "Because you did not listen to the LORD, mark my words: When you leave me, a lion will kill you." When he left him, a lion attacked and killed him.

37 The prophet found another man and said to him, "Strike me!" So the man struck him, inflicting a wound. 38 Then the prophet went and waited for the king on the road. He disguised himself with a bandage over his eyes. 39 As the king was passing by, he cried out to the king and said, "Your servant marched out into the middle of the battle. Suddenly, a man turned aside and brought someone to me and said, 'Guard this man! If he is ever missing, it will be your life in place of his life, or you will weigh out seventy-five pounds[B] of silver.' 40 But while your servant was busy here and there, he disappeared."

The king of Israel said to him, "That will be your sentence; you yourself have decided it."

41 He quickly removed the bandage from his eyes. The king of Israel recognized that he was one of the prophets. 42 The prophet said to him, "This is what the LORD says: 'Because you released from your hand the man I had set apart for destruction, it will be your life in place of his life and your people in place of his people.'" 43 The king of Israel left for home resentful and angry, and he entered Samaria.

AHAB AND NABOTH'S VINEYARD

21 Some time passed after these events. Naboth the Jezreelite had a vineyard; it was in Jezreel next to the palace of King Ahab of Samaria. 2 So Ahab spoke to Naboth, saying, "Give me your vineyard so I can have it for a vegetable garden, since it is right next to my palace. I will give you a better vineyard in its place, or if you prefer, I will give you its value in silver."

3 But Naboth said to Ahab, "As the LORD is my witness, I will never give my ancestors' inheritance to you."

4 So Ahab went to his palace resentful and angry because of what Naboth the Jezreelite had told him. He had said, "I will not give you my ancestors' inheritance." He lay down on his bed, turned his face away, and didn't eat any food.

5 Then his wife Jezebel came to him and said to him, "Why are you so upset that you refuse to eat?"

6 "Because I spoke to Naboth the Jezreelite," he replied. "I told him, 'Give me your vineyard for silver, or if you wish, I will give you a vineyard in its place.' But he said, 'I won't give you my vineyard!'"

7 Then his wife Jezebel said to him, "Now, exercise your royal power over Israel. Get up, eat some food, and be happy. For I will give you the vineyard of Naboth the Jezreelite." 8 So she wrote letters in Ahab's name and sealed them with his seal. She sent the letters to the elders and nobles who lived with Naboth in his city. 9 In the letters, she wrote:

[A] **20:33** Some Hb mss, alt Hb tradition, LXX; other Hb mss read *they hastened and caught hold; "Is this it?"* [B] **20:39** Lit *a talent*

DIGGING DEEPER *King Hezekiah's Seal*

To certify their letters as authentic and authoritative, ancient kings would press their signet rings into a moist lump of clay and then affix the lump to a string that was used to bind a rolled-up papyrus document. It was customary for ancient royal families and their servants to possess such seals (1Kg 21:6–8,25), including King Hezekiah (late eighth century BC) and his servants. To date, archaeologists have collected three of Hezekiah's clay impressions. Known as *bullae*, the impressions measure approximately a half inch wide and read: "Belonging to Hezekiah, [son of] Ahaz, king of Judah." One particular bulla had been baked and hardened, thus preserving in clear detail the twenty-seven-hundred-year-old Hebrew script and a two-winged dung beetle design that originated in Egypt and was often used by the Phoenicians. In addition to Hezekiah's, archaeologists have identified nearly two dozen of his servant's impressions and those of other biblical figures, including Jeremiah's scribe Baruch (Jr 36:4), King Ahaz (2Kg 16; Is 7), Jerahmeel (Jr 36:26), Gemariah (Jr 36:10–12,25), Jehucal (Jr 37:3; 38:1), Gedaliah (Jr 38:1), Pedaiah (1Ch 3:18–19), Amariah (2Ch 31:15), and Shema, the servant of Jeroboam II (2Kg 14:23–25).

Proclaim a fast and seat Naboth at the head of the people. 10 Then seat two wicked men opposite him and have them testify against him, saying, "You have cursed God and the king!" Then take him out and stone him to death.

11 The men of his city, the elders and nobles who lived in his city, did as Jezebel had sent word to them, just as it was written in the letters she had sent them. 12 They proclaimed a fast and seated Naboth at the head of the people. 13 The two wicked men came in and sat opposite him. Then the wicked men testified against Naboth in the presence of the people, saying, "Naboth has cursed God and the king!" So they took him outside the city and stoned him to death with stones. 14 Then they sent word to Jezebel: "Naboth has been stoned to death."

15 When Jezebel heard that Naboth had been stoned to death, she said to Ahab, "Get up and take possession of the vineyard of Naboth the Jezreelite who refused to give it to you for silver, since Naboth isn't alive, but dead." 16 When Ahab heard that Naboth was dead, he got up to go down to the vineyard of Naboth the Jezreelite to take possession of it.

THE LORD'S JUDGMENT ON AHAB

17 Then the word of the LORD came to Elijah the Tishbite: 18 "Get up and go to meet King Ahab of Israel, who is in Samaria. He's in Naboth's vineyard, where he has gone to take possession of it. 19 Tell him, 'This is what the LORD says: Have you murdered and also taken possession?' Then tell him, 'This is what the LORD says: In the place where the dogs licked up Naboth's blood, the dogs will also lick up your blood!'"

20 Ahab said to Elijah, "So, my enemy, you've found me, have you?"

He replied, "I have found you because you devoted yourself to do what is evil in the LORD's sight. 21 This is what the LORD says:[A] 'I am about to bring disaster on you and will eradicate your descendants:

I will wipe out all of Ahab's males,[B]
both slave and free,[C] in Israel;

22 I will make your house like the house of Jeroboam son of Nebat and like the house of Baasha son of Ahijah, because you have angered me and caused Israel to sin.' 23 The LORD also speaks of Jezebel: 'The dogs will eat Jezebel in the plot of land[D] at Jezreel:

24 Anyone who belongs to Ahab and dies
in the city, the dogs will eat,
and anyone who dies in the field, the birds[E]
will eat.'"

25 Still, there was no one like Ahab, who devoted himself to do what was evil in the LORD's sight, because his wife Jezebel incited him. 26 He committed the most detestable acts by following idols as the Amorites had, whom the LORD had dispossessed before the Israelites.

27 When Ahab heard these words, he tore his clothes, put sackcloth over his body, and fasted. He lay down in sackcloth and walked around subdued. 28 Then the word of the LORD came to Elijah the Tishbite: 29 "Have you seen how Ahab has humbled himself before me? I will not bring the disaster during his lifetime, because he has humbled himself before me. I will bring the disaster on his house during his son's lifetime."

JEHOSHAPHAT'S ALLIANCE WITH AHAB

22 There was a lull of three years without war between Aram and Israel. 2 However, in the third year, King Jehoshaphat of Judah went to visit the king of Israel. 3 The king of Israel had said to his servants, "Don't you know that Ramoth-gilead is ours,

[A] **21:21** LXX; MT omits *This is what the LORD says* [B] **21:21** Lit *eliminate Ahab's one who urinates against the wall* [C] **21:21** Or *males, even the weak and impaired*; Hb obscure [D] **21:23** Some Hb mss, Syr, Tg, Vg, 2Kg 9:36; other Hb mss, LXX read *the rampart* [E] **21:24** Lit *birds of the sky*

What was the allure of Baal throughout the Old Testament era for the Israelites—the people of Yahweh? As seen in the actions of Elijah and Josiah (1Kg 18–19; 2Kg 23), God's people made dramatic strides from time to time to abolish Baal worship. Yet Baalism in its many forms constantly reared its ugly head to tempt the Israelites to abandon the Lord to worship the fertility gods.

Fertility worship took two forms among the Israelites. The first was golden calf worship. The calf Aaron made portrayed a young bull, which was one of the figures under which Baal was worshiped throughout the ancient Near East. "A young bull [was] the symbol of strength and virility . . . and was pictured in Canaanite epics as mating with heifers to produce calves."[1] The people identified the golden calf as "your gods, who brought you up from the land of Egypt" (Ex 32:4). After the people ate and drank, they "got up to party" (v. 6). Partying included ritual sexual activities inducing the deities to ensure fertility for the worshipers' fields and families. The roots of this type of worship are found in the ancient Baal cultic practices.

The damning nature of calf worship was that it reduced the Lord to an image, identified him with the fertility gods, and put his implied approval on the licentious worship by which people would act out in his name the lusts of their flesh.

The people abandoned the Lord and "worshiped Baal and the Ashtoreths" (Jdg 2:13). Ashtoreth was "worshiped . . . as the consort of Baal, depicted in the nude with horns on her head, and was thus a member of the fertility cult."[2] The Ashtoreths may refer to the figures of Ashtoreth located at the various Baal shrines. These images are sometimes called "Asherah" or an "Asherah pole" (Dt 16:21; Jdg 6:25; 2Kg 23:6,13–14), after Asherah, the Canaanite fertility goddess, who was thought to be the mother of Baal.

Baalism took over the northern kingdom with the ascension of Ahab to the throne. When Ahab married Jezebel, the daughter of Ethbaal, king of the Sidonians, Baalism became the state religion along with the calf worship of Jeroboam (1Kg 16:31–33). As seen in the contest to determine who is God, both Baal and his consort had prophets who taught the doctrines of the fertility cult and facilitated the people in their licentious worship (18:19).

Hezekiah took major steps to purge Baalism from the southern kingdom and to lead the people to serve only the Lord (vv. 1–6). But Hezekiah's son Manasseh sealed the doom of the southern kingdom by erasing Hezekiah's reforms and plunging the nation deeper into fertility worship, including child sacrifice and every form of divination (21:1–6).

In the end, Baalism and its attendant evils led God to reject Israel and to destroy Judah and Jerusalem (2Kg 17:6–7,16–18; 21:3,11–12).

BAAL'S ENDURING APPEAL

The name Baal means "lord, possessor." Baal was worshiped as "the Lord of heaven" in contrast with the Lord God of Israel who is the true

This figurine likely represents the Canaanite god Baal in the role of warrior; bronze figure with silver overlay; dates 1400–1200 BC; from Tyre.

High place, or bema (right) and altar at Tel Dan. The structure dates to the time of Jeroboam II (eighth century BC) and replaced an earlier structure erected by Jeroboam son of Nebat in the tenth century BC. The area served as a sacred place for a thousand years, until the end of the Roman period. Dan was a site dedicated to syncretistic worship; Jeroboam set up a golden calf that represented Yahweh.

Greek silver coin known as a stater of the Satrap Mazaios, showing Baal, who was the official god of Tarsus; issued about 350 BC.

"LORD, the God of the heavens" (Ezr 1:2; Neh 1:5). Baal is variously pictured as the sun-god and the storm-god. A favorite image portrays him with a lightning bolt in one hand, a mace in the other hand, and a helmet with horns. Baal was thought to be the giver of life who provided the winter rains, the spring mist, and the summer dew. On the other hand, Baal was thought to take life away by withholding the rain and sending the fierce summer heat that brought drought and death. At such times, worshipers sacrificed their children along with animals to placate Baal's anger and to restore his favor (2Kg 21:6; Jr 19:5).[3]

What was the allure of Baal? People by their nature are religious. They will worship someone or something. Baalism provided religion without the moral demands of the Lord. Also Baalism claimed to provide the fertility needed in an agricultural society through the means of satisfying the lusts of the flesh. Through their own sexual relations at the altar of Baal and those of the priests and priestesses, the people sought to use sympathetic magic to entice Baal and his female consort to mate in heaven and thereby produce on earth the needed fertility in crop life, animal life, and human life. "To ensure her fertility in marriage, a young lady would sit in the gate of the Baal shrine for seven days to engage in prostitution with the priests and/or strangers."[4] These practices took away their hearts and led to their doom (Hs 4:8–14). ✠

---

[1]John H. Traylor, *Bible Book Study for Adult Teachers* (Nashville: The Sunday School Board, 1979), 158–59. [2]"Ashtoreth" in *ISBE*, vol. 1 (1979), 320. [3]See "Baal" in *HolBD*, 138; Taylor Ray Ellison, "Baal, God of Thunder," 30 May 2006, www.touregypt.net/featurestories/baal.htm. [4]Testaments of the Twelve Patriarchs, "The Testament of Judah concerning Fortitude, and Love of Money, and Fornication" 4.12.

but we're doing nothing to take it from the king of
Aram?" 4 So he asked Jehoshaphat, "Will you go with
me to fight Ramoth-gilead?"
Jehoshaphat replied to the king of Israel, "I am as
you are, my people as your people, my horses as your
horses." 5 But Jehoshaphat said to the king of Israel,
"First, please ask what the LORD's will is."
6 So the king of Israel gathered the prophets,
about four hundred men, and asked them, "Should
I go against Ramoth-gilead for war or should I refrain?"
They replied, "March up, and the Lord will hand it
over to the king."
7 But Jehoshaphat asked, "Isn't there a prophet of
the LORD here anymore? Let's ask him."
8 The king of Israel said to Jehoshaphat, "There is
still one man who can inquire of the LORD, but I hate
him because he never prophesies good about me, but
only disaster. He is Micaiah son of Imlah."
"The king shouldn't say that!" Jehoshaphat replied.
9 So the king of Israel called an officer and said,
"Hurry and get Micaiah son of Imlah!"
10 Now the king of Israel and King Jehoshaphat of
Judah, clothed in royal attire, were each sitting on his
own throne. They were on the threshing floor at the
entrance to the gate of Samaria, and all the prophets
were prophesying in front of them. 11 Then Zedekiah
son of Chenaanah made iron horns and said, "This
is what the LORD says: 'You will gore the Arameans
with these until they are finished off.'" 12 And all the
prophets were prophesying the same: "March up to
Ramoth-gilead and succeed, for the LORD will hand
it over to the king."

MICAIAH'S MESSAGE OF DEFEAT

13 The messenger who went to call Micaiah instructed
him, "Look, the words of the prophets are unanimously favorable for the king. So let your words be
like theirs, and speak favorably."
14 But Micaiah said, "As the LORD lives, I will say
whatever the LORD says to me."
15 So he went to the king, and the king asked him,
"Micaiah, should we go to Ramoth-gilead for war, or
should we refrain?"
Micaiah told him, "March up and succeed. The
LORD will hand it over to the king."
16 But the king said to him, "How many times must I
make you swear not to tell me anything but the truth
in the name of the LORD?"
17 So Micaiah said:
I saw all Israel scattered on the hills
like sheep without a shepherd.
And the LORD said,
"They have no master;
let everyone return home in peace."
18 So the king of Israel said to Jehoshaphat, "Didn't
I tell you he never prophesies good about me, but
only disaster?"
19 Then Micaiah said, "Therefore, hear the word of
the LORD: I saw the LORD sitting on his throne, and
the whole heavenly army was standing by him at
his right hand and at his left hand. 20 And the LORD
said, 'Who will entice Ahab to march up and fall at
Ramoth-gilead?' So one was saying this and another
was saying that.
21 "Then a spirit came forward, stood in the LORD's
presence, and said, 'I will entice him.'
22 "The LORD asked him, 'How?'
"He said, 'I will go and become a lying spirit in the
mouth of all his prophets.'
"Then he said, 'You will certainly entice him and
prevail. Go and do that.'
23 "You see, the LORD has put a lying spirit into the
mouth of all these prophets of yours, and the LORD
has pronounced disaster against you."
24 Then Zedekiah son of Chenaanah came up, hit
Micaiah on the cheek, and demanded, "Did[A] the Spirit
of the LORD leave me to speak to you?"
25 Micaiah replied, "You will soon see when you go
to hide in an inner chamber on that day."
26 Then the king of Israel ordered, "Take Micaiah
and return him to Amon, the governor of the city, and
to Joash, the king's son, 27 and say, 'This is what the
king says: Put this guy in prison and feed him only
a little bread and water[B] until I come back safely.'"
28 But Micaiah said, "If you ever return safely, the
LORD has not spoken through me." Then he said, "Listen, all you people!"[C]

AHAB'S DEATH

29 Then the king of Israel and Judah's King Jehoshaphat went up to Ramoth-gilead. 30 But the king of
Israel said to Jehoshaphat, "I will disguise myself and
go into battle, but you wear your royal attire." So the
king of Israel disguised himself and went into battle.
31 Now the king of Aram had ordered his thirty-two
chariot commanders, "Do not fight with anyone at
all[D] except the king of Israel."
32 When the chariot commanders saw Jehoshaphat, they shouted, "He must be the king of Israel!"
So they turned to fight against him, but Jehoshaphat
cried out. 33 When the chariot commanders saw that
he was not the king of Israel, they turned back from
pursuing him.
34 But a man drew his bow without taking special aim and struck the king of Israel through the
joints of his armor. So he said to his charioteer, "Turn

[A] **22:24** Lit *"Which way did* [B] **22:27** Lit *him on bread of oppression and water of oppression* [C] **22:28** LXX omits *Then he said, "Listen, all you people!"* [D] **22:31** Lit *with small or with great*

around and take me out of the battle,[A] for I am badly wounded!" 35 The battle raged throughout that day, and the king was propped up in his chariot facing the Arameans. He died that evening, and blood from his wound flowed into the bottom of the chariot. 36 Then the cry rang out in the army as the sun set, declaring:

Each man to his own city,
and each man to his own land!

37 So the king died and was brought to Samaria. They buried the king in Samaria. 38 Then someone washed the chariot at the pool of Samaria. The dogs licked up his blood, and the prostitutes bathed in it, according to the word of the LORD that he had spoken.

39 The rest of the events of Ahab's reign, along with all his accomplishments, including the ivory palace he built, and all the cities he built, are written in the Historical Record of Israel's Kings. 40 Ahab rested with his ancestors, and his son Ahaziah became king in his place.

JUDAH'S KING JEHOSHAPHAT

41 Jehoshaphat son of Asa became king over Judah in the fourth year of Israel's King Ahab. 42 Jehoshaphat was thirty-five years old when he became king; he reigned twenty-five years in Jerusalem. His mother's name was Azubah daughter of Shilhi. 43 He walked in all the ways of his father Asa; he did not turn away from them but did what was right in the LORD's sight. However, the high places were not taken away;[B] the people still sacrificed and burned incense on the high places. 44 Jehoshaphat also made peace with the king of Israel.

45 The rest of the events of Jehoshaphat's reign, along with the might he exercised and how he waged war, are written in the Historical Record of Judah's Kings. 46 He eradicated from the land the rest of the male cult prostitutes who were left from the days of his father Asa. 47 There was no king in Edom; a deputy served as king. 48 Jehoshaphat made ships of Tarshish to go to Ophir for gold, but they did not go because the ships were wrecked at Ezion-geber. 49 At that time, Ahaziah son of Ahab said to Jehoshaphat, "Let my servants go with your servants in the ships," but Jehoshaphat was not willing. 50 Jehoshaphat rested with his ancestors and was buried with them in the city of his ancestor David. His son Jehoram became king in his place.

ISRAEL'S KING AHAZIAH

51 Ahaziah son of Ahab became king over Israel in Samaria in the seventeenth year of Judah's King Jehoshaphat, and he reigned over Israel two years. 52 He did what was evil in the LORD's sight. He walked in the ways of his father, in the ways of his mother, and in the ways of Jeroboam son of Nebat, who had caused Israel to sin. 53 He served Baal and bowed in worship to him. He angered the LORD God of Israel just as his father had done.

[A] **22:34** LXX; MT reads *camp* [B] **22:43** LXX, Syr, Vg read *he did not remove the high places*

2 KINGS

Countryside as seen from Ahab's capital city of Samaria.

INTRODUCTION TO

2 KINGS

Circumstances of Writing

Scholars cannot identify the authors of any portions of 2 Kings. Traditional guesses such as Samuel and Jeremiah lack evidence, although a prominent worshiper of the Lord, such as Jeremiah, would have been influential in the circles that produced these books. Since the books of 1 and 2 Kings clearly incorporated many earlier documents, the complete authorship would include all writers who contributed to the source documents of this work. At some point, the Holy Spirit worked in the human authors to authenticate the inspired, inerrant books of 1 and 2 Kings. The final stage of composition or compilation had to come after the release of Jehoiachin from Babylonian imprisonment (ca 562 BC). That edition may have added only a postscript to a work completed years earlier, or it may have involved significant additions.

The history recorded in 1 and 2 Kings covers approximately 410 years. First Kings begins around 970 BC with the death of King David; 2 Kings ends around 560 BC with the release of King Jehoiachin from prison. During this time, the nation of Israel split into two kingdoms (930 BC), and both kingdoms went into exile (Israel in 722 BC and Judah in 587 BC).

Contribution to the Bible

For the Bible writers, history could not have existed without God's purposes. This makes all history theological. The books of 1 and 2 Kings interpreted Hebrew history in light of Old Testament covenant theology. The Babylonian exile created the need for this work of historical apologetics. The exiles needed to explain the failure of the religious program established by the sovereign God. In the Deuteronomistic History—Joshua, Judges, 1 and 2 Samuel, and 1 and 2 Kings—this failure was consistently explained as the failures of the people to live up to their part of the covenant.

Structure

The organizing principle of 1 and 2 Kings is not story or narrative. Kings is unique because the basic structural units were the formulaic royal records. Formal openers (1Kg 15:9–10) and closers (1Kg 15:23–24) usually identify the boundaries of the record of a particular monarch. Then the writer could insert other types of literature before, between, and after the openers and closers: narratives, prayers, descriptions, and so forth. But the most important element was the evaluation of the ruler's faithfulness to the covenant (1Kg 15:11–15). All of these materials made up a history of covenant obedience and disobedience.

AHAZIAH'S SICKNESS AND DEATH

1 After Ahab's death, Moab rebelled against Israel.
2 Ahaziah had fallen through the latticed window
of his upstairs room in Samaria and was injured. So
he sent messengers, instructing them, "Go inquire of
Baal-zebub,[A] the god of Ekron, whether I will recover
from this injury."
3 But the angel of the LORD said to Elijah the Tishbite, "Go and meet the messengers of the king of Samaria and say to them, 'Is it because there is no God
in Israel that you are going to inquire of Baal-zebub,
the god of Ekron? 4 Therefore, this is what the LORD
says: You will not get up from your sickbed; you will
certainly die.'" Then Elijah left.
5 The messengers returned to the king, who asked
them, "Why have you come back?"
6 They replied, "A man came to meet us and said,
'Go back to the king who sent you and declare to
him, "This is what the LORD says: Is it because there
is no God in Israel that you're sending these men to
inquire of Baal-zebub, the god of Ekron? Therefore,
you will not get up from your sickbed; you will certainly die."'"
7 The king asked them, "What sort of man came up
to meet you and spoke those words to you?"
8 They replied, "A hairy man with a leather belt
around his waist."
He said, "It's Elijah the Tishbite."
9 So King Ahaziah sent a captain with his fifty men
to Elijah. When the captain went up to him, he was
sitting on top of the hill. He announced, "Man of God,
the king declares, 'Come down!'"
10 Elijah responded to the captain, "If I am a man of
God, may fire come down from heaven and consume
you and your fifty men." Then fire came down from
heaven and consumed him and his fifty men.
11 So the king sent another captain with his fifty men to Elijah. He took in the situation[B] and announced, "Man of God, this is what the king says:
'Come down immediately!'"
12 Elijah responded, "If I am a man of God, may fire
come down from heaven and consume you and your
fifty men." So a divine fire[C] came down from heaven
and consumed him and his fifty men.
13 Then the king sent a third captain with his fifty men. The third captain went up and fell on his
knees in front of Elijah and begged him, "Man of God,
please let my life and the lives of these fifty servants
of yours be precious to you. 14 Already fire has come
down from heaven and consumed the first two captains with their companies, but this time let my life
be precious to you."
15 The angel of the LORD said to Elijah, "Go down
with him. Don't be afraid of him." So he got up and
went down with him to the king.
16 Then Elijah said to King Ahaziah, "This is what
the LORD says: 'Because you have sent messengers
to inquire of Baal-zebub, the god of Ekron — is it
because there is no God in Israel for you to inquire
of his will? — you will not get up from your sickbed;
you will certainly die.'"
17 Ahaziah died according to the word of the LORD
that Elijah had spoken. Since he had no son, Joram[D]
became king in his place. This happened in the second
year of Judah's King Jehoram son of Jehoshaphat.[E]
18 The rest of the events of Ahaziah's reign, along with
his accomplishments, are written in the Historical
Record of Israel's Kings.[F]

ELIJAH IN THE WHIRLWIND

2 The time had come for the LORD to take Elijah up
to heaven in a whirlwind. Elijah and Elisha were
traveling from Gilgal, 2 and Elijah said to Elisha, "Stay
here; the LORD is sending me on to Bethel."
But Elisha replied, "As the LORD lives and as you
yourself live, I will not leave you." So they went down
to Bethel.
3 Then the sons of the prophets who were at Bethel
came out to Elisha and said, "Do you know that the
LORD will take your master away from you today?"
He said, "Yes, I know. Be quiet."
4 Elijah said to him, "Elisha, stay here; the LORD is
sending me to Jericho."
But Elisha said, "As the LORD lives and as you yourself live, I will not leave you." So they went to Jericho.
5 Then the sons of the prophets who were in Jericho
came up to Elisha and said, "Do you know that the
LORD will take your master away from you today?"
He said, "Yes, I know. Be quiet."
6 Elijah said to him, "Stay here; the LORD is sending
me to the Jordan."
But Elisha said, "As the LORD lives and as you yourself
live, I will not leave you." So the two of them went on.
7 Fifty men from the sons of the prophets came and
stood observing them at a distance while the two of
them stood by the Jordan. 8 Elijah took his mantle,
rolled it up, and struck the water, which parted to
the right and left. Then the two of them crossed over
on dry ground. 9 When they had crossed over, Elijah
said to Elisha, "Tell me what I can do for you before I
am taken from you."
So Elisha answered, "Please, let me inherit two
shares of your spirit."
10 Elijah replied, "You have asked for something
difficult. If you see me being taken from you, you will
have it. If not, you won't."

[A] 1:2 = Lord of the Flies [B] 1:11 Lit *He answered* [C] 1:12 Lit *a fire of God* [D] 1:17 Lit *Jehoram*; 2Kg 8:16 [E] 1:17 LXX omits *in the second year . . . Jehoshaphat* [F] 1:18 LXX adds 4 more vv. here similar to 2Kg 3:1–3.

11 As they continued walking and talking, a chariot of fire with horses of fire suddenly appeared and separated the two of them. Then Elijah went up into heaven in the whirlwind. 12 As Elisha watched, he kept crying out, "My father, my father, the chariots and horsemen of Israel!"

ELISHA SUCCEEDS ELIJAH

When he could see him no longer, he took hold of his own clothes, tore them in two, 13 picked up the mantle that had fallen off Elijah, and went back and stood on the bank of the Jordan. 14 He took the mantle Elijah had dropped, and he struck the water. "Where is the LORD God of Elijah?" he asked. He struck the water himself, and it parted to the right and the left, and Elisha crossed over.

15 When the sons of the prophets from Jericho who were observing saw him, they said, "The spirit of Elijah rests on Elisha." They came to meet him and bowed down to the ground in front of him.

16 Then the sons of the prophets said to Elisha, "Since there are fifty strong men here with your servants, please let them go and search for your master. Maybe the Spirit of the LORD has carried him away and put him on one of the mountains or into one of the valleys."

He answered, "Don't send them."

17 However, they urged him to the point of embarrassment, so he said, "Send them." They sent fifty men, who looked for three days but did not find him. 18 When they returned to him in Jericho where he was staying, he said to them, "Didn't I tell you not to go?"

19 The men of the city said to Elisha, "My lord can see that even though the city's location is good, the water is bad and the land unfruitful."

20 He replied, "Bring me a new bowl and put salt in it."

After they had brought him one, 21 Elisha went out to the spring, threw salt in it, and said, "This is what the LORD says: 'I have healed this water. No longer will death or unfruitfulness result from it.'" 22 Therefore, the water still remains healthy today according to the word that Elisha spoke.

23 From there Elisha went up to Bethel. As he was walking up the path, some small boys came out of the city and jeered at him, chanting, "Go up, baldy! Go up, baldy!" 24 He turned around, looked at them, and cursed them in the name of the LORD. Then two female bears came out of the woods and mauled forty-two of the children. 25 From there Elisha went to Mount Carmel, and then he returned to Samaria.

ISRAEL'S KING JORAM

3 Joram son of Ahab became king over Israel in Samaria during the eighteenth year of Judah's King Jehoshaphat, and he reigned twelve years. 2 He did what was evil in the LORD's sight, but not like his father and mother, for he removed the sacred pillar of Baal his father had made. 3 Nevertheless, Joram clung to the sins that Jeroboam son of Nebat had caused Israel to commit. He did not turn away from them.

MOAB'S REBELLION AGAINST ISRAEL

4 King Mesha of Moab was a sheep breeder. He used to pay the king of Israel one hundred thousand lambs and the wool of one hundred thousand rams, 5 but when Ahab died, the king of Moab rebelled against the king of Israel. 6 So King Joram marched out from Samaria at that time and mobilized all Israel. 7 Then he sent a message to King Jehoshaphat of Judah: "The king of Moab has rebelled against me. Will you go with me to fight against Moab?"

Jehoshaphat said, "I will go. I am as you are, my people as your people, my horses as your horses."

8 He asked, "Which route should we take?"

He replied, "The route of the Wilderness of Edom."

9 So the king of Israel, the king of Judah, and the king of Edom set out. After they had traveled their indirect route for seven days, they had no water for the army or the animals with them.

10 Then the king of Israel said, "Oh no, the LORD has summoned these three kings, only to hand them over to Moab."

11 But Jehoshaphat said, "Isn't there a prophet of the LORD here? Let's inquire of the LORD through him."

One of the servants of the king of Israel answered, "Elisha son of Shaphat, who used to pour water on Elijah's hands, is here."

12 Jehoshaphat affirmed, "The word of the LORD is with him." So the king of Israel and Jehoshaphat and the king of Edom went to him.

13 However, Elisha said to King Joram of Israel, "What do we have in common? Go to the prophets of your father and your mother!"

But the king of Israel replied, "No, because it is the LORD who has summoned these three kings to hand them over to Moab."

14 Elisha responded, "By the life of the LORD of Armies, before whom I stand: If I did not have respect for King Jehoshaphat of Judah, I wouldn't look at you; I would not take notice of you. 15 Now, bring me a musician."

While the musician played, the LORD's hand came on Elisha. 16 Then he said, "This is what the LORD says: 'Dig ditch after ditch in this wadi.' 17 For the LORD says, 'You will not see wind or rain, but the wadi will be filled with water, and you will drink — you and your cattle and your animals.' 18 This is easy in the LORD's sight. He will also hand Moab over to you. 19 Then you will attack every fortified city and every

During the historical period covered by 1 and 2 Kings, approximately 970–586 BC, the prophets, priests, and kings led their covenant people at various times and in different ways. Of these three groups, the kings assumed the greatest leadership role due to the coercive nature of political power when aligned with military force, not to mention the people's voluntary submission in asking for a king. The priests performed religious duties related to the temple or other shrines. The individual prophets were active in inverse proportion to the righteous actions of the kings. When the kings sinned against the Lord by violating his covenant instruction, the prophets appeared to confront the kings and to pronounce judgment if repentance did not ensue.[1]

Fig tree in modern Anathoth, hometown of Jeremiah, about three miles northeast of Jerusalem.

THE PROPHETS

During this period, Israel witnessed three types of prophets: the individual prophets, who confronted the sins of kings and people; the institutional prophets, who basically served as "yes-men" for the kings; and the prophetic guilds, called twelve times in 1 and 2 Kings "the sons of the prophets" (2Kg 2:5). A group of "the sons of the prophets" resided at Bethel and another at Jericho (vv. 3,5). The latter group had at least fifty men (v. 7). Some of "the sons of the prophets" were married (4:1). We know little else of these groups except their submission to the preeminence of Elisha.

Noteworthy individual prophets featured in 1 and 2 Kings include Ahijah, Jehu, Elijah, Elisha, Micaiah, and Isaiah. By far the most important prophets of 1 and 2 Kings were Elijah and Elisha, whose stories dominate from 1 Kings 17 through 2 Kings 13. God commissioned these individual prophets to denounce the sins of the kings and their people and to warn them of the grave consequences for their covenant violations as stipulated in the Law.

THE PRIESTS

The priesthood originally held an important place in the covenant community. The priests were responsible for maintaining the religious shrines, whether the tabernacle in the wilderness or the temple in Jerusalem.[2] The priests also had to educate the covenant people in the instruction Moses received on Mount Sinai (called the Torah). Historically however, the priesthood became an establishment answerable to the king.

THE KINGS

The most significant theological truth about the period of the kings is that only nine of the forty-one kings "did what was right in the LORD's sight" (1Kg 15:5). The most notable example of these good kings was David. He became the proverbial measuring stick by which all other kings were assessed. When the Lord informed Jeroboam he would be king of Israel, Ahijah the prophet commended him to do what was right "as my servant David did" (11:38). ✣

In Jordan, this area west of Ajloun is called Mar Elias, which is Arabic for St. Elijah. Tradition has long associated this area with Tishbe, hometown of Elijah.

[1] See Paul R. House, *1, 2 Kings*, vol. 8 in NAC.
[2] R. Laird Harris, "Priests" in *HIBD*, 1328.

choice city. You will cut down every good tree and
stop up every spring. You will ruin every good piece
of land with stones."
20 About the time for the grain offering the next
morning, water suddenly came from the direction
of Edom and filled the land.
21 All Moab had heard that the kings had come up
to fight against them. So all who could bear arms,
from the youngest to the oldest, were summoned
and took their stand at the border. 22 When they got
up early in the morning, the sun was shining on the
water, and the Moabites saw that the water across
from them was red like blood. 23 "This is blood!" they
exclaimed. "The kings have crossed swords[A] and
their men have killed one another. So, to the spoil,
Moab!"
24 However, when the Moabites came to Israel's
camp, the Israelites attacked them, and they fled from
them. So Israel went into the land attacking the Moabites. 25 They would destroy the cities, and each of
them would throw a stone to cover every good piece
of land. They would stop up every spring and cut
down every good tree. This went on until only the
buildings of Kir-hareseth were left. Then men with
slings surrounded the city and attacked it.
26 When the king of Moab saw that the battle was
too fierce for him, he took seven hundred swordsmen
with him to try to break through to the king of Edom,
but they could not do it. 27 So he took his firstborn son,
who was to become king in his place, and offered him
as a burnt offering on the city wall. Great wrath was
on the Israelites, and they withdrew from him and
returned to their land.

THE WIDOW'S OIL MULTIPLIED

4 One of the wives of the sons of the prophets cried
out to Elisha, "Your servant, my husband, has
died. You know that your servant feared the LORD.
Now the creditor is coming to take my two children
as his slaves."
2 Elisha asked her, "What can I do for you? Tell me,
what do you have in the house?"
She said, "Your servant has nothing in the house
except a jar of oil."
3 Then he said, "Go out and borrow empty containers from all your neighbors. Do not get just a few.
4 Then go in and shut the door behind you and your
sons, and pour oil into all these containers. Set the
full ones to one side." 5 So she left.
After she had shut the door behind her and her
sons, they kept bringing her containers, and she kept
pouring. 6 When they were full, she said to her son,
"Bring me another container."
But he replied, "There aren't any more." Then the
oil stopped.
7 She went and told the man of God, and he said,
"Go sell the oil and pay your debt; you and your sons
can live on the rest."

THE SHUNAMMITE WOMAN'S HOSPITALITY

8 One day Elisha went to Shunem. A prominent woman who lived there persuaded him to eat some food.
So whenever he passed by, he stopped there to eat.
9 Then she said to her husband, "I know that the one
who often passes by here is a holy man of God, 10 so
let's make a small, walled-in upper room and put a
bed, a table, a chair, and a lamp there for him. Whenever he comes, he can stay there."

THE SHUNAMMITE WOMAN'S SON

11 One day he came there and stopped at the upstairs
room to lie down. 12 He ordered his attendant Gehazi,
"Call this Shunammite woman." So he called her and
she stood before him.
13 Then he said to Gehazi, "Say to her, 'Look, you've
gone to all this trouble for us. What can we do for
you? Can we speak on your behalf to the king or to
the commander of the army?'"
She answered, "I am living among my own people."
14 So he asked, "Then what should be done for her?"
Gehazi answered, "Well, she has no son, and her
husband is old."
15 "Call her," Elisha said. So Gehazi called her, and
she stood in the doorway. 16 Elisha said, "At this time
next year you will have a son in your arms."
Then she said, "No, my lord. Man of God, do not lie
to your servant."
17 The woman conceived and gave birth to a son
at the same time the following year, as Elisha had
promised her.

THE SHUNAMMITE'S SON RAISED

18 The child grew and one day went out to his father
and the harvesters. 19 Suddenly he complained to his
father, "My head! My head!"
His father told his servant, "Carry him to his mother." 20 So he picked him up and took him to his mother.
The child sat on her lap until noon and then died.
21 She went up and laid him on the bed of the man of
God, shut him in, and left.
22 She summoned her husband and said, "Please
send me one of the servants and one of the donkeys,
so I can hurry to the man of God and come back again."
23 But he said, "Why go to him today? It's not a New
Moon or a Sabbath."
She replied, "It's all right."
24 Then she saddled the donkey and said to her
servant, "Go fast; don't slow the pace for me unless I

[A] **3:23** Or *have been laid waste*

The Moabite Stone: Its Biblical and Historical Significance

by R. Dennis Cole

French missionary F. A. Klein reportedly discovered the Moabite Stone, also called the Mesha stele, in 1868 in the town of Dhiban (equivalent to ancient Dibon). Struggles between the Europeans and local bedouins over the possession of this 4-foot tall and 2 ½-foot wide basalt stone inscription resulted in its being broken into several pieces. Eventually the fragments were pieced together and the original text was restored so it could be translated and interpreted.

The Bible records that Moab's King Mesha rebelled against the Israelite overlords after the death of the infamous King Ahab (2Kg 1:1; 3:4–27).

The region of Moab had originally come under the dominion of the Israelites through David's conquests (2Sm 8:2; 1Ch 18:2). The Israelites seemingly lost control of the territory, however, during the Israelite wars between Jeroboam I and Rehoboam. Several decades later, King Omri restored Israel's dominion over the region of Moab around 880 BC. The Bible does not mention this latter fact. It is directly referenced, though, in the so-called Moabite Stone, the monumental stele (inscribed standing stone) of Mesha, king of Moab. The inscription begins: "I am Mesha, son of Chemosh— . . . king of Moab, the Dibonite. My father was king over Moab thirty years and I became king after my father."[1] This important archaeological find illuminates these and other facets of the relationship between ancient Israel and Moab.

The Moabite Stone, also called the Mesha Stele, stands about forty-nine inches tall and is about thirty-one inches wide and fourteen inches thick.

A vista of Moabite territory near the ancient city of Balu.

The numerous caves at Ataroth provided protection and later burial places for its inhabitants.

The inscription recounts Mesha honoring Chemosh, Moab's patron god, by building a sacred altar complex in his palace in Dibon. Mesha credited Chemosh for delivering him from his oppressors and giving him victory over all his adversaries. Mesha also tore down the altar erected during the time of King David. The text goes on to recount how, after his successful revolt against Israel and the construction of the worship complex in Dibon, Mesha continued to honor Chemosh through conquests and numerous building projects. The inscription mentions several cities formerly held by Israel and originally allocated to the tribe of Gad, including Dibon, Ataroth, and Aroer (Nm 32:34–36). Against the critics of the Bible and its historical credibility, this text echoes how the biblical account records real geographical information of that era in history. Typical of ancient Near Eastern annals, the Mesha stele records the lofty boasting and exaggeration of a king who perceived his might came from such a god as Chemosh. One should likewise read the records of the Arameans, Assyrians, Egyptians, and Babylonians with a critical eye, discerning the verifiable truth amidst the lengthy texts of those periods.

On the Moabite Stone, Mesha reported how Moab had served Israel for thirty years since King Omri conquered this region, a fact not included in 1 Kings.

The writer of Kings downplayed Omri's international fame. Nevertheless, the highly fortified walls and "ivory palaces" of Ahab and the later kings of Israel in Samaria were internationally renowned. Even after Omri, Ahab, and their dynasty had been replaced in the Jehu purge, the kingdom continued to be known as the kingdom of Omri, or *Bit Umri* (house of Omri) in Assyrian documents.

Ruins at biblical Aroer, which was an ancient Moabite settlement on the north bank of the Arnon River. The inscription on the Moabite Stone says: "I built Aroer and made the highway in the Arnon."

Ruins at Dibon, which for a while served as the ancient capital of Moab.

The Mesha stele contributes details to the story of the crucial period in Israel's history after Ahab's death while also confirming the veracity of the biblical account. ✣

[1] Clyde E. Fant and Mitchell G. Reddish, *Lost Treasures of the Bible* (Grand Rapids: Eerdmans, 2008), 99.

A HISTORICAL SNAPSHOT OF ISRAEL AND MOAB THROUGH THE LENS OF SCRIPTURE AND THE MOABITE STONE

King David gained control over Moab.	Solomon maintained control over Moab, took a Moabite wife, and honored Chemosh, the chief Moabite god.	After Solomon's death and after the kingdom divided, Moab became part of the northern kingdom. Evidently, though, the Moabites eventually broke away.	Israel's King Omri regained control over the Moabites. Omri's son Ahab continued to dominate Moab. Israel dominated Moab for about thirty years.	King Mesha of Moab paid tribute to Ahab. After Ahab died, Mesha led a successful revolt against Israel and gained independence for Moab.
2Sm 8:2; 1Ch 18:2	1Kg 11:1,7		The Moabite Stone	2Kg 3:4–27 and the Moabite Stone

tell you." 25 So she came to the man of God at Mount Carmel.

When the man of God saw her at a distance, he said to his attendant Gehazi, "Look, there's the Shunammite woman. 26 Run out to meet her and ask, 'Are you all right? Is your husband all right? Is your son all right?' "

And she answered, "It's all right."

27 When she came up to the man of God at the mountain, she clung to his feet. Gehazi came to push her away, but the man of God said, "Leave her alone — she is in severe anguish, and the LORD has hidden it from me. He hasn't told me."

28 Then she said, "Did I ask my lord for a son? Didn't I say, 'Do not lie to me?' "

29 So Elisha said to Gehazi, "Tuck your mantle under your belt, take my staff with you, and go. If you meet anyone, don't stop to greet him, and if a man greets you, don't answer him. Then place my staff on the boy's face."

30 The boy's mother said to Elisha, "As the LORD lives and as you yourself live, I will not leave you." So he got up and followed her.

31 Gehazi went ahead of them and placed the staff on the boy's face, but there was no sound or sign of life, so he went back to meet Elisha and told him, "The boy didn't wake up."

32 When Elisha got to the house, he discovered the boy lying dead on his bed. 33 So he went in, closed the door behind the two of them, and prayed to the LORD. 34 Then he went up and lay on the boy: he put mouth to mouth, eye to eye, hand to hand. While he bent down over him, the boy's flesh became warm. 35 Elisha got up, went into the house, and paced back and forth. Then he went up and bent down over him again. The boy sneezed seven times and opened his eyes.

36 Elisha called Gehazi and said, "Call the Shunammite woman." He called her and she came. Then Elisha said, "Pick up your son." 37 She came, fell at his feet, and bowed to the ground; she picked up her son and left.

THE DEADLY STEW

38 When Elisha returned to Gilgal, there was a famine in the land. The sons of the prophets were sitting before him. He said to his attendant, "Put on the large pot and make stew for the sons of the prophets."

39 One went out to the field to gather herbs and found a wild vine from which he gathered as many wild gourds as his garment would hold. Then he came back and cut them up into the pot of stew, but they were unaware of what they were.[A]

40 They served some for the men to eat, but when they ate the stew they cried out, "There's death in the pot, man of God!" And they were unable to eat it.

41 Then Elisha said, "Get some flour." He threw it into the pot and said, "Serve it for the people to eat." And there was nothing bad in the pot.

THE MULTIPLIED BREAD

42 A man from Baal-shalishah came to the man of God with his sack full of[B] twenty loaves of barley bread from the first bread of the harvest. Elisha said, "Give it to the people to eat."

43 But Elisha's attendant asked, "What? Am I to set this before a hundred men?"

"Give it to the people to eat," Elisha said, "for this is what the LORD says: 'They will eat, and they will have some left over.' " 44 So he set it before them, and as the LORD had promised, they ate and had some left over.

NAAMAN'S DISEASE HEALED

5 Naaman, commander of the army for the king of Aram, was a man important to his master and highly regarded because through him, the LORD had given victory to Aram. The man was a valiant warrior, but he had a skin disease.

2 Aram had gone on raids and brought back from the land of Israel a young girl who served Naaman's wife. 3 She said to her mistress, "If only my master were with the prophet who is in Samaria, he would cure him of his skin disease."

4 So Naaman went and told his master what the girl from the land of Israel had said. 5 Therefore, the king of Aram said, "Go, and I will send a letter with you to the king of Israel."

So he went and took with him 750 pounds[C] of silver, 150 pounds[D] of gold, and ten sets of clothing. 6 He brought the letter to the king of Israel, and it read:

> When this letter comes to you, note that I have sent you my servant Naaman for you to cure him of his skin disease.

7 When the king of Israel read the letter, he tore his clothes and asked, "Am I God, killing and giving life, that this man expects me to cure a man of his skin disease? Recognize[E] that he is only picking a fight with me."

8 When Elisha the man of God heard that the king of Israel had torn his clothes, he sent a message to the king: "Why have you torn your clothes? Have him come to me, and he will know there is a prophet in Israel." 9 So Naaman came with his horses and chariots and stood at the door of Elisha's house.

10 Then Elisha sent him a messenger, who said, "Go wash seven times in the Jordan and your skin will be restored and you will be clean."

[A] **4:39** *of what they were* added for clarity [B] **4:42** Or *with some heads of fresh grain and* [C] **5:5** Lit *10 talents* [D] **5:5** Lit *6,000 shekels* [E] **5:7** Lit *Know and see*

11 But Naaman got angry and left, saying, "I was telling myself: He will surely come out, stand and call on
the name of the LORD his God, and wave his hand over
the place and cure the skin disease. 12 Aren't Abana
and Pharpar, the rivers of Damascus, better than all
the waters of Israel? Couldn't I wash in them and be
clean?" So he turned and left in a rage.
13 But his servants approached and said to him, "My
father, if the prophet had told you to do some great
thing, would you not have done it? How much more
should you do it when he only tells you, 'Wash and be
clean'?" 14 So Naaman went down and dipped himself
in the Jordan seven times, according to the command
of the man of God. Then his skin was restored and
became like the skin of a small boy, and he was clean.
15 Then Naaman and his whole company went back
to the man of God, stood before him, and declared,
"I know there's no God in the whole world except
in Israel. Therefore, please accept a gift from your
servant."
16 But Elisha said, "As the LORD lives, in whose presence I stand, I will not accept it." Naaman urged him
to accept it, but he refused.
17 Naaman responded, "If not, please let your servant be given as much soil as a pair of mules can carry,
for your servant will no longer offer a burnt offering
or a sacrifice to any other god but the LORD. 18 However, in a particular matter may the LORD pardon your
servant: When my master, the king of Aram, goes into
the temple of Rimmon to bow in worship while he is
leaning on my arm,[A] and I have to bow in the temple
of Rimmon — when I bow[B] in the temple of Rimmon,
may the LORD pardon your servant in this matter."
19 So he said to him, "Go in peace."

GEHAZI'S GREED PUNISHED

After Naaman had traveled a short distance from
Elisha, 20 Gehazi, the attendant of Elisha the man of
God, thought, "My master has let this Aramean Naaman off lightly by not accepting from him what he
brought. As the LORD lives, I will run after him and
get something from him."
21 So Gehazi pursued Naaman. When Naaman saw
someone running after him, he got down from the
chariot to meet him and asked, "Is everything all right?"
22 Gehazi said, "It's all right. My master has sent me
to say, 'I have just now discovered that two young men
from the sons of the prophets have come to me from
the hill country of Ephraim. Please give them seventy-five pounds[C] of silver and two sets of clothing.'"
23 But Naaman insisted, "Please, accept one hundred fifty pounds."[D] He urged Gehazi and then packed
one hundred fifty pounds of silver in two bags with
two sets of clothing. Naaman gave them to two of
his attendants who carried them ahead of Gehazi.
24 When Gehazi came to the hill,[E] he took the gifts
from them and deposited them in the house. Then
he dismissed the men, and they left.
25 Gehazi came and stood by his master. "Where
did you go, Gehazi?" Elisha asked him.
He replied, "Your servant didn't go anywhere."
26 "And my heart didn't go[F] when the man got down
from his chariot to meet you," Elisha said. "Is this a
time to accept silver and clothing, olive orchards and
vineyards, flocks and herds, and male and female
slaves? 27 Therefore, Naaman's skin disease will cling
to you and your descendants forever." So Gehazi went
out from his presence diseased, resembling snow.[G]

THE FLOATING AX HEAD

6 The sons of the prophets said to Elisha, "Please
notice that the place where we live under your
supervision[H] is too small for us. 2 Please let us go to
the Jordan where we can each get a log and can build
ourselves a place to live there."
"Go," he said.
3 Then one said, "Please come with your servants."
"I'll come," he answered.
4 So he went with them, and when they came to the
Jordan, they cut down trees. 5 As one of them was cutting down a tree, the iron ax head fell into the water,
and he cried out, "Oh, my master, it was borrowed!"
6 Then the man of God asked, "Where did it fall?"
When he showed him the place, the man of God
cut a piece of wood, threw it there, and made the
iron float. 7 Then he said, "Pick it up." So he reached
out and took it.

THE ARAMEAN WAR

8 When the king of Aram was waging war against
Israel, he conferred with his servants, "My camp will
be at such and such a place."
9 But the man of God sent word to the king of Israel:
"Be careful passing by this place, for the Arameans
are going down there." 10 Consequently, the king of
Israel sent word to the place the man of God had told
him about. The man of God repeatedly[I] warned the
king, so the king would be on his guard.
11 The king of Aram was enraged because of this
matter, and he called his servants and demanded
of them, "Tell me, which one of us is for the king of
Israel?"
12 One of his servants said, "No one, my lord the
king. Elisha, the prophet in Israel, tells the king of
Israel even the words you speak in your bedroom."

[A] **5:18** Lit *worship, and he leans on my hand* [B] **5:18** LXX, Vg read *when he bows himself* [C] **5:22** Lit *a talent* [D] **5:23** Lit *two talents* [E] **5:24** Or *citadel* [F] **5:26** Or *"Did not my heart go* [G] **5:27** A reference to whiteness or flakiness of the skin [H] **6:1** Lit *we are living before you* [I] **6:10** Lit *not once and not twice*

13 So the king said, "Go and see where he is, so I can
send men to capture him."
When he was told, "Elisha is in Dothan," 14 he sent
horses, chariots, and a massive army there. They went
by night and surrounded the city.
15 When the servant of the man of God got up early
and went out, he discovered an army with horses and
chariots surrounding the city. So he asked Elisha, "Oh,
my master, what are we to do?"
16 Elisha said, "Don't be afraid, for those who are
with us outnumber those who are with them."
17 Then Elisha prayed, "LORD, please open his eyes
and let him see." So the LORD opened the servant's
eyes, and he saw that the mountain was covered with
horses and chariots of fire all around Elisha.
18 When the Arameans came against him, Elisha
prayed to the LORD, "Please strike this nation with
blindness."[A] So he struck them with blindness, according to Elisha's word. 19 Then Elisha said to them,
"This is not the way, and this is not the city. Follow me,
and I will take you to the man you're looking for." And
he led them to Samaria. 20 When they entered Samaria, Elisha said, "LORD, open these men's eyes and let
them see." So the LORD opened their eyes, and they
saw that they were in the middle of Samaria.
21 When the king of Israel saw them, he said to Elisha, "Should I kill them, should I kill them, my father?"
22 Elisha replied, "Don't kill them. Do you kill those
you have captured with your sword or your bow? Set
food and water in front of them so they can eat and
drink and go to their master."
23 So he prepared a big feast for them. When they
had eaten and drunk, he sent them away, and they
went to their master. The Aramean raiders did not
come into Israel's land again.

THE SIEGE OF SAMARIA

24 Some time later, King Ben-hadad of Aram brought
all his military units together and marched up and
laid siege to Samaria. 25 So there was a severe famine
in Samaria, and they continued the siege against it
until a donkey's head sold for thirty-four ounces[B] of
silver, and a cup[C] of dove's dung[D] sold for two ounces[E] of silver.
26 As the king of Israel was passing by on the wall,
a woman cried out to him, "My lord the king, help!"
27 He answered, "If the LORD doesn't help you,
where can I get help for you? From the threshing
floor or the winepress?" 28 Then the king asked her,
"What's the matter?"
She said, "This woman said to me, 'Give up your
son, and we will eat him today. Then we will eat my
son tomorrow.' 29 So we boiled my son and ate him,
and I said to her the next day, 'Give up your son, and
we will eat him,' but she has hidden her son."
30 When the king heard the woman's words, he tore
his clothes. Then, as he was passing by on the wall,
the people saw that there was sackcloth under his
clothes next to his skin. 31 He announced, "May God
punish me and do so severely if the head of Elisha son
of Shaphat remains on his shoulders today."
32 Elisha was sitting in his house, and the elders
were sitting with him. The king sent a man ahead
of him, but before the messenger got to him, Elisha
said to the elders, "Do you see how this murderer has
sent someone to remove my head? Look, when the
messenger comes, shut the door to keep him out. Isn't
the sound of his master's feet behind him?"
33 While Elisha was still speaking with them, the
messenger[F] came down to him. Then he said, "This
disaster is from the LORD. Why should I wait for the
LORD any longer?"
7 Elisha replied, "Hear the word of the LORD! This
is what the LORD says: 'About this time tomorrow
at Samaria's gate, six quarts[G] of fine flour will sell for
a half ounce of silver[H] and twelve quarts[I] of barley
will sell for a half ounce of silver.'"
2 Then the captain, the king's right-hand man,[J] responded to the man of God, "Look, even if the LORD
were to make windows in heaven, could this really
happen?"
Elisha announced, "You will in fact see it with your
own eyes, but you won't eat any of it."
3 Now four men with a skin disease were at the
entrance to the city gate. They said to each other,
"Why just sit here until we die? 4 If we say, 'Let's go
into the city,' we will die there because the famine is
in the city, but if we sit here, we will also die. So now,
come on. Let's surrender to the Arameans' camp. If
they let us live, we will live; if they kill us, we will die."
5 So the diseased men got up at twilight to go to the
Arameans' camp. When they came to the camp's edge,
they discovered that no one was there, 6 for the Lord[K]
had caused the Aramean camp to hear the sound of
chariots, horses, and a large army. The Arameans
had said to each other, "The king of Israel must have
hired the kings of the Hittites and the kings of Egypt
to attack us." 7 So they had gotten up and fled at twilight, abandoning their tents, horses, and donkeys.
The camp was intact, and they had fled for their lives.
8 When these diseased men came to the edge of the
camp, they went into a tent to eat and drink. Then they
picked up the silver, gold, and clothing and went off
and hid them. They came back and entered another

[A] **6:18** Or *a blinding light* [B] **6:25** Lit *for 80*; "shekels" is assumed
[C] **6:25** Lit *a fourth of a kab* [D] **6:25** Or *seedpods*, or *wild onions*
[E] **6:25** Lit *for five*; "shekels" is assumed [F] **6:33** Some emend to *king*
[G] **7:1** Lit *a seah*, also in vv. 16,18 [H] **7:1** Lit *for a shekel*, also in vv. 16,18
[I] **7:1** Lit *two seahs*, also in vv. 16,18 [J] **7:2** Lit *captain, upon whose hand the king leaned*, also in v. 17 [K] **7:6** Some Hb mss read *LORD*

Elisha: His Life and Mission

by Fred M. Wood

Elisha first appeared as the son of an apparently well-to-do farmer (1Kg 19:19–21). His home, Abel-meholah, was in a rich, agricultural district of Manasseh. Being last in a group of twelve men, each following his plow, suggests he was the overseer.

Since the Bible nowhere records the anointing of a prophet with oil in a formal ceremony, we should understand Elijah's casting his mantle upon the younger man as the official act. The mantle was a prophet's distinctive garb. Later, when Elijah was taken into heaven, his mantle fell to Elisha.

When Elijah was about to be taken up in the chariot of fire, fifty men from the school of the prophets followed closely behind but did not cross the Jordan with the two prophets. Who were these younger men, these "sons of the prophets"? Possibly they were associated with a guild or brotherhood of prophets. They apparently lived some type of communal life, although they were not celibate. They looked to Elisha as their possible tutor when Elijah left.

Elisha's prayer to be heir of his teacher's spirit and power (2Kg 2:9) should not be considered a selfish request. True, in Jewish law, the older son was entitled to a double portion of his father's possessions. Elisha, however, meant more than this type of boon. He wanted the strength of Elijah's gentleness, which was probably to a large extent a product of Elijah's Horeb experience. The gift Elisha sought was the spirit of vision and insight.

How does one evaluate a person such as Elisha, especially compared with his mentor, Elijah? Elijah was wilderness oriented, rugged, and austere. Elisha ministered to civilized life; his dress, manners, and appearance resembled other citizens. Elijah was a prophet of vengeance—sudden, fierce, and overwhelming. Elisha's ministry majored on mercy and restoration. Many of Elijah's miracles were designed to execute wrath. Most of Elisha's miracles brought benefit and healing. Elisha delivered his most powerful sermons through his life of service. ✣

Statue of the Canaanite god Baal. Like his predecessor Elijah, Elisha diligently worked to keep his people faithful to God.

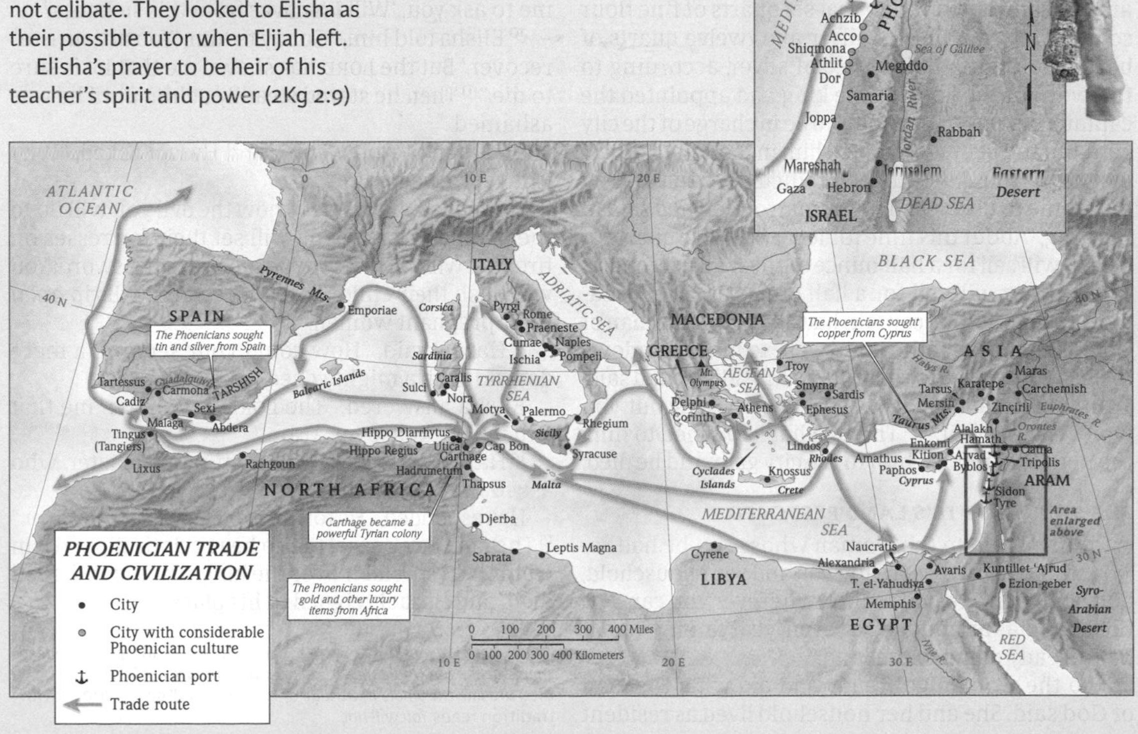

tent, picked things up, and hid them. 9 Then they said to each other, "We're not doing what is right. Today is a day of good news. If we are silent and wait until morning light, our punishment will catch up with us. So let's go tell the king's household."

10 The diseased men came and called to the city's gatekeepers and told them, "We went to the Aramean camp and no one was there — no human sounds. There was nothing but tethered horses and donkeys, and the tents were intact." 11 The gatekeepers called out, and the news was reported to the king's household.

12 So the king got up in the night and said to his servants, "Let me tell you what the Arameans have done to us. They know we are starving, so they have left the camp to hide in the open country, thinking, 'When they come out of the city, we will take them alive and go into the city.' "

13 But one of his servants responded, "Please, let messengers take five of the horses that are left in the city. Their fate is like the entire Israelite community who will die,[A] so let's send them and see."

14 The messengers took two chariots with horses, and the king sent them after the Aramean army, saying, "Go and see." 15 So they followed them as far as the Jordan. They saw that the whole way was littered with clothes and equipment the Arameans had thrown off in their haste. The messengers returned and told the king.

16 Then the people went out and plundered the Aramean camp. It was then that six quarts of fine flour sold for a half ounce of silver and twelve quarts of barley sold for a half ounce of silver, according to the word of the LORD. 17 The king had appointed the captain, his right-hand man, to be in charge of the city gate, but the people trampled him in the gate. He died, just as the man of God had predicted when the king had come to him. 18 When the man of God had said to the king, "About this time tomorrow twelve quarts of barley will sell for a half ounce of silver and six quarts of fine flour will sell for a half ounce of silver at Samaria's gate," 19 this captain had answered the man of God, "Look, even if the LORD were to make windows in heaven, could this really happen?" Elisha had said, "You will in fact see it with your own eyes, but you won't eat any of it." 20 This is what happened to him: the people trampled him in the city gate, and he died.

THE SHUNAMMITE'S LAND RESTORED

8 Elisha said to the woman whose son he had restored to life, "Get ready, you and your household, and go live as a resident alien wherever you can. For the LORD has announced a seven-year famine, and it has already come to the land."

2 So the woman got ready and did what the man of God said. She and her household lived as resident aliens in the land of the Philistines for seven years. 3 When the woman returned from the land of the Philistines at the end of seven years, she went to appeal to the king for her house and field.

4 The king had been speaking to Gehazi, the attendant of the man of God, saying, "Tell me all the great things Elisha has done."

5 While he was telling the king how Elisha restored the dead son to life, the woman whose son he had restored to life came to appeal to the king for her house and field. So Gehazi said, "My lord the king, this is the woman and this is the son Elisha restored to life."

6 When the king asked the woman, she told him the story. So the king appointed a court official for her, saying, "Restore all that was hers, along with all the income from the field from the day she left the country until now."

ARAM'S KING HAZAEL

7 Elisha came to Damascus while King Ben-hadad of Aram was sick, and the king was told, "The man of God has come here." 8 So the king said to Hazael, "Take a gift with you and go meet the man of God. Inquire of the LORD through him, 'Will I recover from this sickness?' "

9 Hazael went to meet Elisha, taking with him a gift: forty camel-loads of all the finest products of Damascus. When he came and stood before him, he said, "Your son, King Ben-hadad of Aram, has sent me to ask you, 'Will I recover from this sickness?' "

10 Elisha told him, "Go say to him, 'You are sure to[B] recover.' But the LORD has shown me that he is sure to die." 11 Then he stared steadily at him until he was ashamed.

The man of God wept, 12 and Hazael asked, "Why is my lord weeping?"

He replied, "Because I know the evil you will do to the people of Israel. You will set their fortresses on fire. You will kill their young men with the sword. You will dash their children to pieces. You will rip open their pregnant women."

13 Hazael said, "How could your servant, a mere dog, do such a mighty deed?"

Elisha answered, "The LORD has shown me that you will be king over Aram."

14 Hazael left Elisha and went to his master, who asked him, "What did Elisha say to you?"

He responded, "He told me you are sure to recover." 15 The next day Hazael took a heavy cloth, dipped it in water, and spread it over the king's face. Ben-hadad died, and Hazael reigned in his place.

[A] **7:13** Some Hb mss, LXX, Syr, Vg; other Hb mss read *left in it. Indeed, they are like the whole multitude of Israel that are left in it; indeed, they are like the whole multitude of Israel who will die.* [B] **8:10** Alt Hb tradition reads *You will not*

JUDAH'S KING JEHORAM

16 In the fifth year of Israel's King Joram son of Ahab,
Jehoram[A] son of Jehoshaphat became king of Judah,
replacing his father.[B] 17 He was thirty-two years old
when he became king, and he reigned eight years
in Jerusalem. 18 He walked in the ways of the kings
of Israel, as the house of Ahab had done, for Ahab's
daughter was his wife. He did what was evil in the
LORD's sight. 19 For the sake of his servant David,
the LORD was unwilling to destroy Judah, since he
had promised to give a lamp[C] to David and his sons
forever.
20 During Jehoram's reign, Edom rebelled against
Judah's control and appointed their own king. 21 So
Jehoram crossed over to Zair with all his chariots.
Then at night he set out to attack the Edomites who
had surrounded him and the chariot commanders,
but his troops fled to their tents. 22 So Edom is still in
rebellion against Judah's control today. Libnah also
rebelled at that time.
23 The rest of the events of Jehoram's reign, along
with all his accomplishments, are written in the Historical Record of Judah's Kings. 24 Jehoram rested
with his ancestors and was buried with his ancestors
in the city of David, and his son Ahaziah became king
in his place.

JUDAH'S KING AHAZIAH

25 In the twelfth year of Israel's King Joram son of
Ahab, Ahaziah son of Jehoram became king of Judah. 26 Ahaziah was twenty-two years old when he
became king, and he reigned one year in Jerusalem.
His mother's name was Athaliah, granddaughter of
Israel's King Omri. 27 He walked in the ways of the
house of Ahab and did what was evil in the LORD's
sight like the house of Ahab, for his father had married into[D] the house of Ahab.
28 Ahaziah went with Joram son of Ahab to fight
against King Hazael of Aram in Ramoth-gilead, and
the Arameans wounded Joram. 29 So King Joram returned to Jezreel to recover from the wounds that the
Arameans had inflicted on him in Ramoth-gilead[E]
when he fought against Aram's King Hazael. Then
Judah's King Ahaziah son of Jehoram went down to
Jezreel to visit Joram son of Ahab since Joram was ill.

JEHU ANOINTED AS ISRAEL'S KING

9 The prophet Elisha called one of the sons of the
prophets and said, "Tuck your mantle under
your belt, take this flask of oil with you, and go to
Ramoth-gilead. 2 When you get there, look for Jehu
son of Jehoshaphat, son of Nimshi. Go in, get him
away from his colleagues, and take him to an inner
room. 3 Then take the flask of oil, pour it on his head,
and say, 'This is what the LORD says: "I anoint you king
over Israel."' Open the door and escape. Don't wait."
4 So the young prophet[F] went to Ramoth-gilead.
5 When he arrived, the army commanders were
sitting there, so he said, "I have a message for you,
commander."
Jehu asked, "For which one of us?"
He answered, "For you, commander."
6 So Jehu got up and went into the house. The young
prophet poured the oil on his head and said, "This is
what the LORD God of Israel says: 'I anoint you king
over the LORD's people, Israel. 7 You are to strike down
the house of your master Ahab so that I may avenge
the blood shed by the hand of Jezebel — the blood of
my servants the prophets and of all the servants of the
LORD. 8 The whole house of Ahab will perish, and I will
wipe out all of Ahab's males,[G] both slave and free,[H] in
Israel. 9 I will make the house of Ahab like the house of
Jeroboam son of Nebat and like the house of Baasha
son of Ahijah. 10 The dogs will eat Jezebel in the plot
of land at Jezreel — no one will bury her.'" Then the
young prophet opened the door and escaped.
11 When Jehu came out to his master's servants,
they asked, "Is everything all right? Why did this crazy
person come to you?"
Then he said to them, "You know the sort and their
ranting."
12 But they replied, "That's a lie! Tell us!"
So Jehu said, "He talked to me about this and that
and said, 'This is what the LORD says: I anoint you
king over Israel.'"
13 Each man quickly took his garment and put it
under Jehu on the bare steps.[I] They blew the ram's
horn and proclaimed, "Jehu is king!"
14 Then Jehu son of Jehoshaphat, son of Nimshi,
conspired against Joram. Joram and all Israel had
been at Ramoth-gilead on guard against King Hazael
of Aram. 15 But King Joram had returned to Jezreel
to recover from the wounds that the Arameans had
inflicted on him when he fought against Aram's King
Hazael. Jehu said, "If you commanders wish to make
me king,[J] then don't let anyone escape from the city
to go tell about it in Jezreel."

JEHU KILLS JORAM AND AHAZIAH

16 Jehu got into his chariot and went to Jezreel since
Joram was laid up there and King Ahaziah of Judah
had gone down to visit Joram. 17 Now the watchman
was standing on the tower in Jezreel. He saw Jehu's
mob approaching and shouted, "I see a mob!"

[A] **8:16** = The LORD is Exalted [B] **8:16** Lit *Judah; Jehoshaphat had been king of Judah* [C] **8:19** Or *dominion* [D] **8:27** Lit *for he was related by marriage to* [E] **8:29** Lit *Ramah* [F] **9:4** Or *the young man, the attendant of the prophet* [G] **9:8** Lit *wipe out Ahab's one who urinates against a wall* [H] **9:8** Or *males, even the weak and impaired*; Hb obscure [I] **9:13** Lit *on the bones of the steps* [J] **9:15** Lit *"If your desire exists*

Joram responded, "Choose a rider and send him to meet them and have him ask, 'Do you come in peace?'"

18 So a horseman went to meet Jehu and said, "This is what the king asks: 'Do you come in peace?'"

Jehu replied, "What do you have to do with peace? Fall in behind me."

The watchman reported, "The messenger reached them but hasn't started back."

19 So he sent out a second horseman, who went to them and said, "This is what the king asks: 'Do you come in peace?'"

Jehu answered, "What do you have to do with peace? Fall in behind me."

20 Again the watchman reported, "He reached them but hasn't started back. Also, the driving is like that of Jehu son of Nimshi — he drives like a madman."

21 "Get the chariot ready!" Joram shouted, and they got it ready. Then King Joram of Israel and King Ahaziah of Judah set out, each in his own chariot, and met Jehu at the plot of land of Naboth the Jezreelite. 22 When Joram saw Jehu he asked, "Do you come in peace, Jehu?"

He answered, "What peace can there be as long as there is so much prostitution and sorcery from your mother Jezebel?"

23 Joram turned around and fled, shouting to Ahaziah, "It's treachery, Ahaziah!"

24 Then Jehu drew his bow and shot Joram between the shoulders. The arrow went through his heart, and he slumped down in his chariot. 25 Jehu said to Bidkar his aide, "Pick him up and throw him on the plot of ground belonging to Naboth the Jezreelite. For remember when you and I were riding side by side behind his father Ahab, and the LORD uttered this pronouncement against him: 26 'As surely as I saw the blood of Naboth and the blood of his sons yesterday' — this is the LORD's declaration — 'so will I repay you on this plot of land' — this is the LORD's declaration. So now, according to the word of the LORD, pick him up and throw him on the plot of land."

27 When King Ahaziah of Judah saw what was happening, he fled up the road toward Beth-haggan. Jehu pursued him, shouting, "Shoot him too!" So they shot him in his chariot[A] at Gur Pass near Ibleam, but he fled to Megiddo and died there. 28 Then his servants carried him to Jerusalem in a chariot and buried him in his ancestors' tomb in the city of David. 29 It was in the eleventh year of Joram son of Ahab that Ahaziah had become king over Judah.

JEHU KILLS JEZEBEL

30 When Jehu came to Jezreel, Jezebel heard about it, so she painted her eyes, fixed her hair,[B] and looked down from the window. 31 As Jehu entered the city gate, she said, "Do you come in peace, Zimri, killer of your master?"

32 He looked up toward the window and said, "Who is on my side? Who?" Two or three eunuchs looked down at him, 33 and he said, "Throw her down!" So they threw her down, and some of her blood splattered on the wall and on the horses, and Jehu rode over her.

34 Then he went in, ate and drank, and said, "Take care of this cursed woman and bury her, since she's a king's daughter." 35 But when they went out to bury her, they did not find anything but the skull, the feet, and the hands. 36 So they went back and told him, and he said, "This fulfills the LORD's word that he spoke through his servant Elijah the Tishbite: 'In the plot of land at Jezreel, the dogs will eat Jezebel's flesh. 37 Jezebel's corpse will be like manure on the surface of the ground in the plot of land at Jezreel so that no one will be able to say: This is Jezebel.'"

JEHU KILLS THE HOUSE OF AHAB

10 Since Ahab had seventy sons in Samaria, Jehu wrote letters and sent them to Samaria to the rulers of Jezreel, to the elders, and to the guardians of Ahab's sons,[C] saying:

> 2 Your master's sons are with you, and you have chariots, horses, a fortified city, and weaponry, so when this letter arrives 3 select the most qualified[D] of your master's sons, set him on his father's throne, and fight for your master's house.

4 However, they were terrified and reasoned, "Look, two kings couldn't stand against him; how can we?"

5 So the overseer of the palace, the overseer of the city, the elders, and the guardians sent a message to Jehu: "We are your servants, and we will do whatever you tell us. We will not make anyone king. Do whatever you think is right."[E]

6 Then Jehu wrote them a second letter, saying:

> If you are on my side, and if you will obey me, bring me the heads of your master's sons[F] at this time tomorrow at Jezreel.

All seventy of the king's sons were being cared for by the city's prominent men. 7 When the letter came to them, they took the king's sons and slaughtered all seventy, put their heads in baskets, and sent them to Jehu at Jezreel. 8 When the messenger came and told him, "They have brought the heads of the king's sons," the king said, "Pile them in two heaps at the entrance of the city gate until morning."

[A] **9:27** LXX, Syr, Vg; MT omits *So they shot him* [B] **9:30** Lit *made her head pleasing* [C] **10:1** LXX; MT reads *of Ahab* [D] **10:3** Lit *the good and the upright* [E] **10:5** Lit *Do what is good in your eyes* [F] **10:6** Lit *heads of the men of the sons of your master*

9 The next morning when he went out and stood at the gate, he said to all the people, "You are innocent. It was I who conspired against my master and killed him. But who struck down all these? 10 Know, then, that not a word the LORD spoke against the house of Ahab will fail, for the LORD has done what he promised through his servant Elijah." 11 So Jehu killed all who remained of the house of Ahab in Jezreel — all his great men, close friends, and priests — leaving him no survivors.

12 Then he set out and went to Samaria. On the way, while he was at Beth-eked of the Shepherds, 13 Jehu met the relatives of King Ahaziah of Judah and asked, "Who are you?"

They answered, "We're Ahaziah's relatives. We've come down to greet the king's sons and the queen mother's sons."

14 Then Jehu ordered, "Take them alive." So they took them alive and then slaughtered them at the pit of Beth-eked — forty-two men. He didn't spare any of them.

15 When he left there, he found Jehonadab son of Rechab coming to meet him. He greeted him and then asked, "Is your heart one with mine?"[A]

"It is," Jehonadab replied.

Jehu said, "If it is,[B] give me your hand."

So he gave him his hand, and Jehu pulled him up into the chariot with him. 16 Then he said, "Come with me and see my zeal for the LORD!" So he let him ride with him in his chariot. 17 When Jehu came to Samaria, he struck down all who remained from the house of Ahab in Samaria until he had annihilated his house, according to the word of the LORD spoken to Elijah.

DIGGING DEEPER ***The Black Obelisk of Shalmaneser III***

In the mid-twentieth century, archaeologist A. H. Layard became famous due to his excavations in the old Assyrian Empire around Nineveh. Concentrating his efforts at Calah, Layard in 1846 discovered a black stone obelisk written in cuneiform that stands 6.7 feet tall. Known as the Black Obelisk of Shalmaneser III, the stone depicts the tribute of silver and gold "Jehu son of Omri" paid to Assyrian King Shalmaneser III (859–825 BC; see 2Kg 10:31). Though Shalmaneser III is not mentioned in the Bible (he is not to be confused with Shalmaneser IV; 2Kg 17:3), Layard's obelisk provides information about the time preceding Jehu's death, when much of Israel's northern territory was conquered by pagan invaders (2Kg 10:32–36). Some critical scholars assumed that the obelisk indicated the Bible is wrong since the Bible does not identify Jehu (841–814 BC; 2Kgs 9–10) as the direct son of Omri (reigned 885–874 BC). However, the problem may be resolved by understanding the obelisk's "son of Omri" to be an eponym referring to the "house" or "lineage" of Omri (1Kg 16:15–28), in which case the obelisk doesn't imply that Jehu was Omri's son.

JEHU KILLS THE BAAL WORSHIPERS

18 Then Jehu brought all the people together and said to them, "Ahab served Baal a little, but Jehu will serve him a lot. 19 Now, therefore, summon to me all the prophets of Baal, all his servants, and all his priests. None must be missing, for I have a great sacrifice for Baal. Whoever is missing will not live." However, Jehu was acting deceptively in order to destroy the servants of Baal. 20 Jehu commanded, "Consecrate a solemn assembly for Baal." So they called one.

21 Then Jehu sent messengers throughout all Israel, and all the servants of Baal[C] came; no one failed to come. They entered the temple of Baal, and it was filled from one end to the other. 22 Then he said to the custodian of the wardrobe, "Bring out the garments for all the servants of Baal." So he brought out their garments.

23 Then Jehu and Jehonadab son of Rechab entered the temple of Baal, and Jehu said to the servants of Baal, "Look carefully to see that there are no servants of the LORD here among you — only servants of Baal." 24 Then they went in to offer sacrifices and burnt offerings.

Now Jehu had stationed eighty men outside, and he warned them, "Whoever allows any of the men I am placing in your hands to escape will forfeit his life for theirs." 25 When he finished offering the burnt offering, Jehu said to the guards and officers, "Go in and kill them. Don't let anyone out." So they struck them down with the sword. Then the guards and officers threw the bodies out and went into the inner room of the temple of Baal. 26 They brought out the pillar of the temple of Baal and burned it, 27 and they tore down the pillar of Baal. Then they tore down the temple of Baal and made it a latrine — which it still is today.

EVALUATION OF JEHU'S REIGN

28 Jehu eliminated Baal worship from Israel, 29 but he did not turn away from the sins that Jeroboam son of Nebat had caused Israel to commit — worshiping the

[A] **10:15** Lit *heart upright like my heart is with your heart*
[B] **10:15** LXX, Syr, Vg; MT reads *mine?" Jehonadab said, "It is and it is*
[C] **10:21** LXX adds *— all his priests and all his prophets —*

Jezebel Unveiled

by Julie Nall Knowles

The writer of 2 Kings (9:37) so hated Ahab's foreign wife that he cleverly punctuated the Hebrew *yzbl* so her name would be pronounced like their word "dung-heap" (a crude epithet): *'i-zebul* ("Where is the prince [Baal]?") became *'i-zebel* ("Where is the dung?").

Jezebel married Ahab to seal a diplomatic union between the monarch of Israel and her father Ithobaal (biblical Ethbaal), who in 887 BC usurped the throne of Tyre, the island-city known as a fortress.

Two years later, a commander named Omri seized control of Israel. For Omri's new city on the hill of Samaria, Ithobaal probably garnered more trade than Hiram, the Tyrian king who helped build Solomon's temple. Meanwhile, brutal Ashurnasirpal II ruled expanding Assyria, and Israel became a buffer between the eastern threat and the sea. To secure their alliance, Ithobaal either suggested to Omri that his daughter marry Israel's crown prince or negotiated directly with Ahab after he became king.

In that day, princesses were moved like pawns in a political game. Conquerors demanded families as tribute (1Kg 20:3)—one king of Tyre took "his daughters, his nieces, and his son across the channel to the Assyrian king."[1] Monarchs gave their daughters to officers (1Kg 4:11,15) or friendly rulers (2Sm 3:3; 1Kg 3:1; 11:1). Diplomatic wives functioned as envoys of their parents' states—royal harems competed for markets to exchange goods and services from their homeland.[2]

Prosperous and powerful, Tyre stood on a resplendent island "perfect in beauty" (Ezk 27:3) with a magnificent temple to the rain-god Baal. "There I saw it," wrote Herodotus, "there were two pillars, one of refined gold, one of emerald, a great pillar that shone in the nighttime."[3] Tyrian engineers may have copied these columns as Jachin and Boaz for the temple in Jerusalem (2Ch 3:17); similar pillars may have been erected for Baal's temple that Ahab built in Samaria (1Kg 16:32). According to Josephus, Ithobaal was a priest of the fertility goddess Astarte (Ashtoreth),[4] so Ahab provided for that worship as well (16:33).

A daughter of both a priest and a king would extend substantial foreign influence. Heathen personnel at Jezebel's table (1Kg 18:19) conceivably came with her. All of them were prepared to proselytize Israel. Tyre sold many luxuries—purple dye, wares in precious metal, carvings of ivory, even exotic monkeys (1Kg 10:22). As her homeland's agent, Jezebel may have decorated Israel's palace in such Phoenician-style ivories that it was labeled Ahab's "ivory house."

Monumental stairs located at the top of ancient Samaria, a city whose name was later changed to Sebaste. The steps, which may be located near the site of Ahab's palace, were actually part of a temple built during the reign of Septimus Severus (AD 193–211). Samaria served as capital of the Northern Kingdom of Israel.

Looking toward the Mediterranean Sea, Roman columns sit on ancient foundations at Tyre, Jezebel's hometown.

Ahab seems to have fallen for her completely. "That her looks may not have been Semitic is more than likely."[5] With common cosmetics—cochineal rouge accenting lips and cheeks (Sg 4:3), galena making eyes appear larger (Jr 4:30; Ezk 23:40), henna on nails and flowers in her hair[6]—Jezebel must have created a considerable stir. Though Ahab had a harem (1Kg 20:3–7), another woman is never named. Besides, Jezebel was educated and efficient.

While temple prostitution honored Astarte, Baalism supported human offerings (Jr 19:5; 32:35); Yahwism forbade both practices. Surely someone protested the deaths at Jericho. Jezebel may have countered by eliminating many Yahwist prophets (1Kg 18:4,13)—or she may have created places for her court mouthpieces.

As the Chronicler retold Jezebel's story, he identified Israel's apostasy with sexual promiscuity. Jezebel advanced temple prostitution that bewitched many Israelites, much as she had charmed Ahab.

In her closing performance, Jezebel played neither whore nor witch, but a queen. Israel's *gebirah* (queen mother) could have rallied popular support by a royal appearance. Accordingly, Jezebel applied cosmetics—emphasized eyes with bluish-gray paint called *puk*[7]—and arranged her hair, covering it with a fine fabric "wrapped turban style."[8] Like a regent, she placed herself at a window of her palace in Jezreel. When her son's murderer Jehu arrived, Jezebel taunted Jehu by calling him "Zimri," another assassin who had a short reign. At Jehu's command, Jezebel was hurled down from the window to the pavement. Her blood splattered as he drove over her lifeless body (2Kg 9:30–33). ✣

---

[1] Richard S. Hanson, *Tyrian Influence in the Upper Galilee* (Cambridge, MA: ASOR, 1980), 10. [2] Victor H. Matthews and Don C. Benjamin, *Social World of Ancient Israel, 1250–587 BCE* (Peabody, MA: Hendrickson, 1993), 165. [3] Herodotus, *Histories* 2.44. [4] Josephus, *Against Apion* 1.18. [5] Norah Lofts, *Women in the Old Testament: Twenty Psychological Portraits* (New York: Macmillan, 1949), 143. [6] Edith Deen, *The Bible's Legacy for Womanhood* (New York: Doubleday, 1969), 128–29. [7] Victor H. Matthews, *Manners and Customs in the Bible*, rev. ed. (Peabody, MA: Hendrickson, 1991), 122. [8] Deen, *Bible's Legacy*, 129.

gold calves that were in Bethel and Dan. 30 Nevertheless, the LORD said to Jehu, "Because you have done well in carrying out what is right in my sight and have done to the house of Ahab all that was in my heart, four generations of your sons will sit on the throne of Israel."

31 Yet Jehu was not careful to follow the instruction of the LORD God of Israel with all his heart. He did not turn from the sins that Jeroboam had caused Israel to commit.

32 In those days the LORD began to reduce the size of Israel. Hazael defeated the Israelites throughout their territory 33 from the Jordan eastward: the whole land of Gilead — the Gadites, the Reubenites, and the Manassites — from Aroer which is by the Arnon Valley through Gilead to Bashan.[A]

34 The rest of the events of Jehu's reign, along with all his accomplishments and all his might, are written in the Historical Record of Israel's Kings. 35 Jehu rested with his ancestors and was buried in Samaria. His son Jehoahaz became king in his place. 36 The length of Jehu's reign over Israel in Samaria was twenty-eight years.

ATHALIAH USURPS THE THRONE

11 When Athaliah, Ahaziah's mother, saw that her son was dead, she proceeded to annihilate all the royal heirs. 2 Jehosheba, who was King Jehoram's daughter and Ahaziah's sister, secretly rescued Joash son of Ahaziah from among the king's sons who were being killed and put him and the one who nursed him in a bedroom. So he was hidden from Athaliah and was not killed. 3 Joash was in hiding with her in the LORD's temple six years while Athaliah reigned over the land.

ATHALIAH OVERTHROWN

4 In the seventh year, Jehoiada sent for the commanders of hundreds, the Carites, and the guards. He had them come to him in the LORD's temple, where he made a covenant with them and put them under oath. He showed them the king's son 5 and commanded them, "This is what you are to do: A third of you who come on duty on the Sabbath are to provide protection for the king's palace. 6 A third are to be at the Foundation[B] Gate and a third at the gate behind the guards. You are to take turns providing protection for the palace.[C]

7 "Your two divisions that go off duty on the Sabbath are to provide the king protection at the LORD's temple. 8 Completely surround the king with weapons in hand. Anyone who approaches the ranks is to be put to death. Be with the king in all his daily tasks."[D]

9 So the commanders of hundreds did everything the priest Jehoiada commanded. They each brought their men — those coming on duty on the Sabbath and those going off duty — and came to the priest Jehoiada. 10 The priest gave to the commanders of hundreds King David's spears and shields that were in the LORD's temple. 11 Then the guards stood with their weapons in hand surrounding the king — from the right side of the temple to the left side, by the altar and by the temple.

12 Jehoiada brought out the king's son, put the crown on him, gave him the testimony,[E] and made him king. They anointed him and clapped their hands and cried, "Long live the king!"

13 When Athaliah heard the noise from the guard and the crowd, she went out to the people at the LORD's temple. 14 She looked, and there was the king standing by the pillar according to the custom. The commanders and the trumpeters were by the king, and all the people of the land were rejoicing and blowing trumpets. Athaliah tore her clothes and screamed "Treason! Treason!"

15 Then the priest Jehoiada ordered the commanders of hundreds in charge of the army, "Take her out between the ranks, and put to death by the sword anyone who follows her," for the priest had said, "She is not to be put to death in the LORD's temple." 16 So they arrested her, and she went through the horse entrance to the king's palace, where she was put to death.

JEHOIADA'S REFORMS

17 Then Jehoiada made a covenant between the LORD, the king, and the people that they would be the LORD's people and another covenant between the king and the people.[F] 18 So all the people of the land went to the temple of Baal and tore it down. They smashed its altars and images to pieces, and they killed Mattan, the priest of Baal, at the altars.

Then Jehoiada the priest appointed guards for the LORD's temple. 19 He took the commanders of hundreds, the Carites, the guards, and all the people of the land, and they brought the king from the LORD's temple. They entered the king's palace by way of the guards' gate. Then Joash sat on the throne of the kings. 20 All the people of the land rejoiced, and the city was quiet, for they had put Athaliah to death by the sword in the king's palace.

JUDAH'S KING JOASH

21 Joash[G] was seven years old when he became king.

12 1 In the seventh year of Jehu, Joash became king, and he reigned forty years in Jerusalem. His mother's name was Zibiah; she was from Beer-sheba.

[A] **10:33** Lit *Arnon Valley and Gilead and Bashan* [B] **11:6** See 2Ch 23:5; MT here reads *Sur* [C] **11:6** Hb obscure [D] **11:8** Lit *king when he goes out and when he comes in* [E] **11:12** Or *him the copy of the covenant*, or *him a diadem*, or *him jewels* [F] **11:17** Some Gk versions, 2Ch 23:16 omit *and another covenant between the king and the people* [G] **11:21** = The LORD Has Bestowed

2 Throughout the time the priest Jehoiada instructed him, Joash did what was right in the LORD's sight. 3 Yet the high places were not taken away; the people continued sacrificing and burning incense on the high places.

REPAIRING THE TEMPLE

4 Then Joash said to the priests, "All the dedicated silver brought to the LORD's temple, census silver, silver from vows, and all silver voluntarily given for the LORD's temple — 5 each priest is to take it from his assessor[A] and repair whatever damage is found in the temple."[B]

6 But by the twenty-third year of the reign of King Joash, the priests had not repaired the damage[C] to the temple. 7 So King Joash called the priest Jehoiada and the other priests and asked, "Why haven't you repaired the temple's damage? Since you haven't, don't take any silver from your assessors; instead, hand it over for the repair of the temple." 8 So the priests agreed that they would receive no silver from the people and would not be the ones to repair the temple's damage.

9 Then the priest Jehoiada took a chest, bored a hole in its lid, and set it beside the altar on the right side as one enters the LORD's temple; the priests who guarded the threshold put into the chest all the silver that was brought to the LORD's temple. 10 Whenever they saw there was a large amount of silver in the chest, the king's secretary and the high priest would go bag up and tally the silver found in the LORD's temple. 11 Then they would give the weighed silver to those doing the work — those who oversaw the LORD's temple. They in turn would pay it out to those working on the LORD's temple — the carpenters, the builders, 12 the masons, and the stonecutters — and would use it to buy timber and quarried stone to repair the damage to the LORD's temple and for all expenses for temple repairs.

13 However, no silver bowls, wick trimmers, sprinkling basins, trumpets, or any articles of gold or silver were made for the LORD's temple from the contributions[D] brought to the LORD's temple. 14 Instead, it was given to those doing the work, and they repaired the LORD's temple with it. 15 No accounting was required from the men who received the silver to pay those doing the work, since they worked with integrity. 16 The silver from the guilt offering and the sin offering was not brought to the LORD's temple since it belonged to the priests.

ARAMEAN INVASION OF JUDAH

17 At that time King Hazael of Aram marched up and fought against Gath and captured it. Then he planned to attack Jerusalem. 18 So King Joash of Judah took all the items consecrated by himself and by his ancestors — Judah's kings Jehoshaphat, Jehoram, and Ahaziah — as well as all the gold found in the treasuries of the LORD's temple and in the king's palace, and he sent them to King Hazael of Aram. Then Hazael withdrew from Jerusalem.

JOASH ASSASSINATED

19 The rest of the events of Joash's reign, along with all his accomplishments, are written in the Historical Record of Judah's Kings. 20 Joash's servants conspired against him and attacked him at Beth-millo on the road that goes down to Silla. 21 It was his servants Jozabad[E] son of Shimeath and Jehozabad son of Shomer who attacked him. He died and they buried him with his ancestors in the city of David, and his son Amaziah became king in his place.

ISRAEL'S KING JEHOAHAZ

13 In the twenty-third year of Judah's King Joash son of Ahaziah, Jehoahaz son of Jehu became king over Israel in Samaria, and he reigned seventeen years. 2 He did what was evil in the LORD's sight and followed the sins that Jeroboam son of Nebat had caused Israel to commit; he did not turn away from them. 3 So the LORD's anger burned against Israel, and he handed them over to King Hazael of Aram and to his son Ben-hadad during their reigns.

4 Then Jehoahaz sought the LORD's favor, and the LORD heard him, for he saw the oppression the king of Aram inflicted on Israel. 5 Therefore, the LORD gave Israel a deliverer, and they escaped from the power of the Arameans. Then the people of Israel returned to their former way of life,[F] 6 but they didn't turn away from the sins that the house of Jeroboam had caused Israel to commit. Jehoahaz continued them, and the Asherah pole also remained standing in Samaria. 7 Jehoahaz did not have an army left, except for fifty horsemen, ten chariots, and ten thousand foot soldiers, because the king of Aram had destroyed them, making them like dust at threshing.

8 The rest of the events of Jehoahaz's reign, along with all his accomplishments and his might, are written in the Historical Record of Israel's Kings. 9 Jehoahaz rested with his ancestors, and he was buried in Samaria. His son Jehoash[G] became king in his place.

ISRAEL'S KING JEHOASH

10 In the thirty-seventh year of Judah's King Joash, Jehoash son of Jehoahaz became king over Israel

[A] 12:5 Hb obscure [B] 12:5 Lit *repair the breach of the temple wherever there is found a breach* [C] 12:6 Lit *breach* in 2Kg 12:5–12
[D] 12:13 Lit *silver* [E] 12:21 Some Hb mss, LXX read *Jozacar*; 2Ch 24:26 reads *Zabad* [F] 13:5 Lit *Israel dwelt in their tents as formerly*
[G] 13:9 Lit *Joash*

in Samaria, and he reigned sixteen years. [11] He did what was evil in the LORD's sight. He did not turn away from all the sins that Jeroboam son of Nebat had caused Israel to commit, but he continued them.

[12] The rest of the events of Jehoash's reign, along with all his accomplishments and the power he had to wage war against Judah's King Amaziah, are written in the Historical Record of Israel's Kings. [13] Jehoash rested with his ancestors, and Jeroboam sat on his throne. Jehoash was buried in Samaria with the kings of Israel.

ELISHA'S DEATH

[14] When Elisha became sick with the illness from which he died, King Jehoash of Israel went down and wept over him and said, "My father, my father, the chariots and horsemen of Israel!"

[15] Elisha responded, "Get a bow and arrows." So he got a bow and arrows. [16] Then Elisha said to the king of Israel, "Grasp the bow." So the king grasped it, and Elisha put his hands on the king's hands. [17] Elisha said, "Open the east window." So he opened it. Elisha said, "Shoot!" So he shot. Then Elisha said, "The LORD's arrow of victory, yes, the arrow of victory over Aram. You are to strike down the Arameans in Aphek until you have put an end to them."

[18] Then Elisha said, "Take the arrows!" So he took them. Then Elisha said to the king of Israel, "Strike the ground!" So he struck the ground three times and stopped. [19] The man of God was angry with him and said, "You should have struck the ground five or six times. Then you would have struck down Aram until you had put an end to them, but now you will strike down Aram only three times." [20] Then Elisha died and was buried.

Now Moabite raiders used to come into the land in the spring of the year. [21] Once, as the Israelites were burying a man, suddenly they saw a raiding party, so they threw the man into Elisha's tomb. When he touched Elisha's bones, the man revived and stood up!

GOD'S MERCY ON ISRAEL

[22] King Hazael of Aram oppressed Israel throughout the reign of Jehoahaz, [23] but the LORD was gracious to them, had compassion on them, and turned toward them because of his covenant with Abraham, Isaac, and Jacob. He was not willing to destroy them. Even now he has not banished them from his presence.

[24] King Hazael of Aram died, and his son Ben-hadad became king in his place. [25] Then Jehoash son of Jehoahaz took back from Ben-hadad son of Hazael the cities that Hazael had taken in war from Jehoash's father Jehoahaz. Jehoash defeated Ben-hadad three times and recovered the cities of Israel.

JUDAH'S KING AMAZIAH

14 In the second year of Israel's King Jehoash[A] son of Jehoahaz,[B] Amaziah son of Joash became king of Judah. [2] He was twenty-five years old when he became king, and he reigned twenty-nine years in Jerusalem. His mother's name was Jehoaddan;[C] she was from Jerusalem. [3] He did what was right in the LORD's sight, but not like his ancestor David. He did everything his father Joash had done. [4] Yet the high places were not taken away, and the people continued sacrificing and burning incense on the high places.

[5] As soon as the kingdom was firmly in his grasp, Amaziah killed his servants who had killed his father the king. [6] However, he did not put the children of the killers to death, as it is written in the book of the law of Moses where the LORD commanded, "Fathers are not to be put to death because of children, and children are not to be put to death because of fathers; instead, each one will be put to death for his own sin."

[7] Amaziah killed ten thousand Edomites in Salt Valley. He took Sela in battle and called it Joktheel, which is still its name today. [8] Amaziah then sent messengers to Jehoash son of Jehoahaz, son of Jehu, king of Israel, and challenged him: "Come, let's meet face to face."

[9] King Jehoash of Israel sent word to King Amaziah of Judah, saying, "The thistle in Lebanon once sent a message to the cedar in Lebanon, saying, 'Give your daughter to my son as a wife.' Then a wild animal in Lebanon passed by and trampled the thistle. [10] You have indeed defeated Edom, and you have become overconfident.[D] Enjoy your glory and stay at home. Why should you stir up such trouble that you fall — you and Judah with you?"

[11] But Amaziah would not listen, so King Jehoash of Israel advanced. He and King Amaziah of Judah met face to face at Beth-shemesh that belonged to Judah. [12] Judah was routed before Israel, and each man fled to his own tent. [13] King Jehoash of Israel captured Judah's King Amaziah son of Joash,[E] son of Ahaziah, at Beth-shemesh. Then Jehoash went to Jerusalem and broke down two hundred yards[F] of Jerusalem's wall from the Ephraim Gate to the Corner Gate. [14] He took all the gold and silver, all the articles found in the LORD's temple and in the treasuries of the king's palace, and some hostages. Then he returned to Samaria.

JEHOASH'S DEATH

[15] The rest of the events of Jehoash's reign, along with his accomplishments, his might, and how he waged war against King Amaziah of Judah, are written in the

[A] **14:1** Lit *Joash*, also in vv. 23,27 [B] **14:1** Lit *Joahaz* [C] **14:2** Alt Hb tradition, some Hb mss, Syr, Tg, Vg, 2Ch 25:1; other Hb mss, LXX read *Jehoaddin* [D] **14:10** Lit *and your heart has lifted you* [E] **14:13** Lit *Jehoash* [F] **14:13** Lit *400 cubits*

Historical Record of Israel's Kings. 16 Jehoash rested
with his ancestors, and he was buried in Samaria
with the kings of Israel. His son Jeroboam became
king in his place.

AMAZIAH'S DEATH

17 Judah's King Amaziah son of Joash lived fifteen
years after the death of Israel's King Jehoash son of
Jehoahaz. 18 The rest of the events of Amaziah's reign
are written in the Historical Record of Judah's Kings.
19 A conspiracy was formed against him in Jerusalem,
and he fled to Lachish. However, men were sent after him to Lachish, and they put him to death there.
20 They carried him back on horses, and he was buried
in Jerusalem with his ancestors in the city of David.
21 Then all the people of Judah took Azariah,[A] who
was sixteen years old, and made him king in place of
his father Amaziah. 22 After Amaziah the king rested
with his ancestors, Azariah rebuilt Elath[B] and restored it to Judah.

ISRAEL'S KING JEROBOAM

23 In the fifteenth year of Judah's King Amaziah son
of Joash, Jeroboam son of Jehoash became king of
Israel in Samaria, and he reigned forty-one years.
24 He did what was evil in the LORD's sight. He did not
turn away from all the sins Jeroboam son of Nebat
had caused Israel to commit.
25 He restored Israel's border from Lebo-hamath as
far as the Sea of the Arabah, according to the word
the LORD, the God of Israel, had spoken through
his servant, the prophet Jonah son of Amittai from
Gath-hepher. 26 For the LORD saw that the affliction
of Israel was very bitter for both slaves and free people.[C] There was no one to help Israel. 27 The LORD had
not said he would blot out the name of Israel under
heaven, so he delivered them by the hand of Jeroboam son of Jehoash.
28 The rest of the events of Jeroboam's reign —
along with all his accomplishments, the power he
had to wage war, and how he recovered for Israel
Damascus and Hamath, which had belonged to Judah[D] — are written in the Historical Record of Israel's Kings. 29 Jeroboam rested with his ancestors,
the kings of Israel. His son Zechariah became king
in his place.

JUDAH'S KING AZARIAH

15 In the twenty-seventh year of Israel's King Jeroboam, Azariah[E] son of Amaziah became king
of Judah. 2 He was sixteen years old when he became
king, and he reigned fifty-two years in Jerusalem. His
mother's name was Jecoliah; she was from Jerusalem. 3 Azariah did what was right in the LORD's sight
just as his father Amaziah had done. 4 Yet the high
places were not taken away; the people continued
sacrificing and burning incense on the high places.
5 The LORD afflicted the king, and he had a serious
skin disease until the day of his death. He lived in
quarantine,[F] while Jotham, the king's son, was over
the household governing the people of the land.
6 The rest of the events of Azariah's reign, along
with all his accomplishments, are written in the Historical Record of Judah's Kings. 7 Azariah rested with
his ancestors and was buried with his ancestors in
the city of David. His son Jotham became king in
his place.

ISRAEL'S KING ZECHARIAH

8 In the thirty-eighth year of Judah's King Azariah,
Zechariah son of Jeroboam reigned over Israel in
Samaria for six months. 9 He did what was evil in the
LORD's sight as his predecessors had done. He did not
turn away from the sins Jeroboam son of Nebat had
caused Israel to commit.
10 Shallum son of Jabesh conspired against Zechariah. He struck him down publicly,[G] killed him, and
became king in his place. 11 As for the rest of the events
of Zechariah's reign, they are written in the Historical
Record of Israel's Kings. 12 The word of the LORD that
he spoke to Jehu was, "Four generations of your sons
will sit on the throne of Israel," and it was so.

ISRAEL'S KING SHALLUM

13 In the thirty-ninth year of Judah's King Uzziah,[H]
Shallum son of Jabesh became king; he reigned in
Samaria a full month. 14 Then Menahem son of Gadi
came up from Tirzah to Samaria and struck down
Shallum son of Jabesh there. He killed him and became king in his place. 15 As for the rest of the events
of Shallum's reign, along with the conspiracy that he
formed, they are written in the Historical Record of
Israel's Kings.

ISRAEL'S KING MENAHEM

16 At that time, starting from Tirzah, Menahem attacked Tiphsah, all who were in it, and its territory
because they wouldn't surrender. He ripped open all
the pregnant women.
17 In the thirty-ninth year of Judah's King Azariah,
Menahem son of Gadi became king over Israel, and
he reigned ten years in Samaria. 18 He did what was
evil in the LORD's sight. Throughout his reign, he did
not turn away from the sins Jeroboam son of Nebat
had caused Israel to commit.

[A] **14:21** = Uzziah in 2Ch 26:1 [B] **14:22** = Eloth in 2Ch 26:2
[C] **14:26** Hb obscure [D] **14:28** Lit *recovered Damascus and for Judah in Israel*; Hb obscure [E] **15:1** = Uzziah in 2Ch 26:3 [F] **15:5** Lit *in a house of exemption from duty* [G] **15:10** Some LXX mss read *down at Ibleam*; Hb uncertain [H] **15:13** = Azariah, also in vv. 30,32,34

The Life of Jeroboam II

by Claude F. Mariottini

Jeroboam II carried on Joash's policies of aggressive expansion of Israel's borders. He was able to contain Syrian invasion by conquering their capital, Damascus. The restoration of the borders of Israel, "from Lebo-hamath as far as the Sea of the Arabah" (2Kg 14:25), was a return to the ideal boundaries of Israel that existed in the days of Solomon (1Kg 8:65).[1] Jeroboam's conquests were made possible because of Assyria's weakness and its involvement with military campaigns elsewhere in its empire. With the absence of Assyria in Israel, the door was wide open for Jeroboam to step in and restore Israel's boundaries to the ideal borders of the Solomonic era.

The recovery of territory that Israel had lost brought a great flow of wealth back into the northern kingdom. With the increase of territory came the increase of revenue brought in by trade and taxation. Israel controlled many of the important trade routes and as such was receiving the tolls of the caravans that used those routes. The standard of living in Israel improved. The economic prosperity was good; John Bright said that no living Israelite could remember better times.[2]

According to Amos, people were able to build better houses, "houses of cut stone" (Am 5:11). The rich people had summer and winter houses. The description Amos provided of a banquet scene within one of these palatial abodes clearly describes the prosperous life of many Israelites in the eighth century BC.

With the increase of commercial activities in Israel, wealth poured into the country. Great fortunes were quickly made, the arts flourished, and the cities began to grow in number and size. Beneath all this glamour and wealth there was a disastrous by-product caused by increased economic prosperity: the gap between the rich and poor became more pronounced. The wealthier classes imported new comforts and enjoyed undreamed-of luxuries. The poor profited little from the new commercial relations for they had no capital to invest. The prophet Amos's message is addressed to a group "who are steadily driving the landed peasantry away from their earlier solid independence into the condition of serfs. The small farmer no longer owned his own land; he was a tenant of an urban class to whom he must pay a rental for the use of the land, a rental that was often the lion's share of the grain which the land produced."[3]

The presentation by the writer of 2 Kings of the religious life during Jeroboam's reign was not positive. Spiritually, Israel was in a deep depression. Over the years, Israel had been slipping away from God, and under Jeroboam's leadership, the spiritual decay of the nation was at an all-time high. Under Jeroboam, the nation of Israel was militarily strong but spiritually weak. ✣

[1] Yohanan Aharoni and Michael Avi-Yonah, *The Macmillan Bible Atlas* (New York: Macmillan, 1968), 89. [2] John Bright, *A History of Israel* (Philadelphia: Westminster, 1983), 259. [3] James L. Mays, *Amos* (Philadelphia: Westminster, 1969), 94.

An aerial view of modern Damascus.

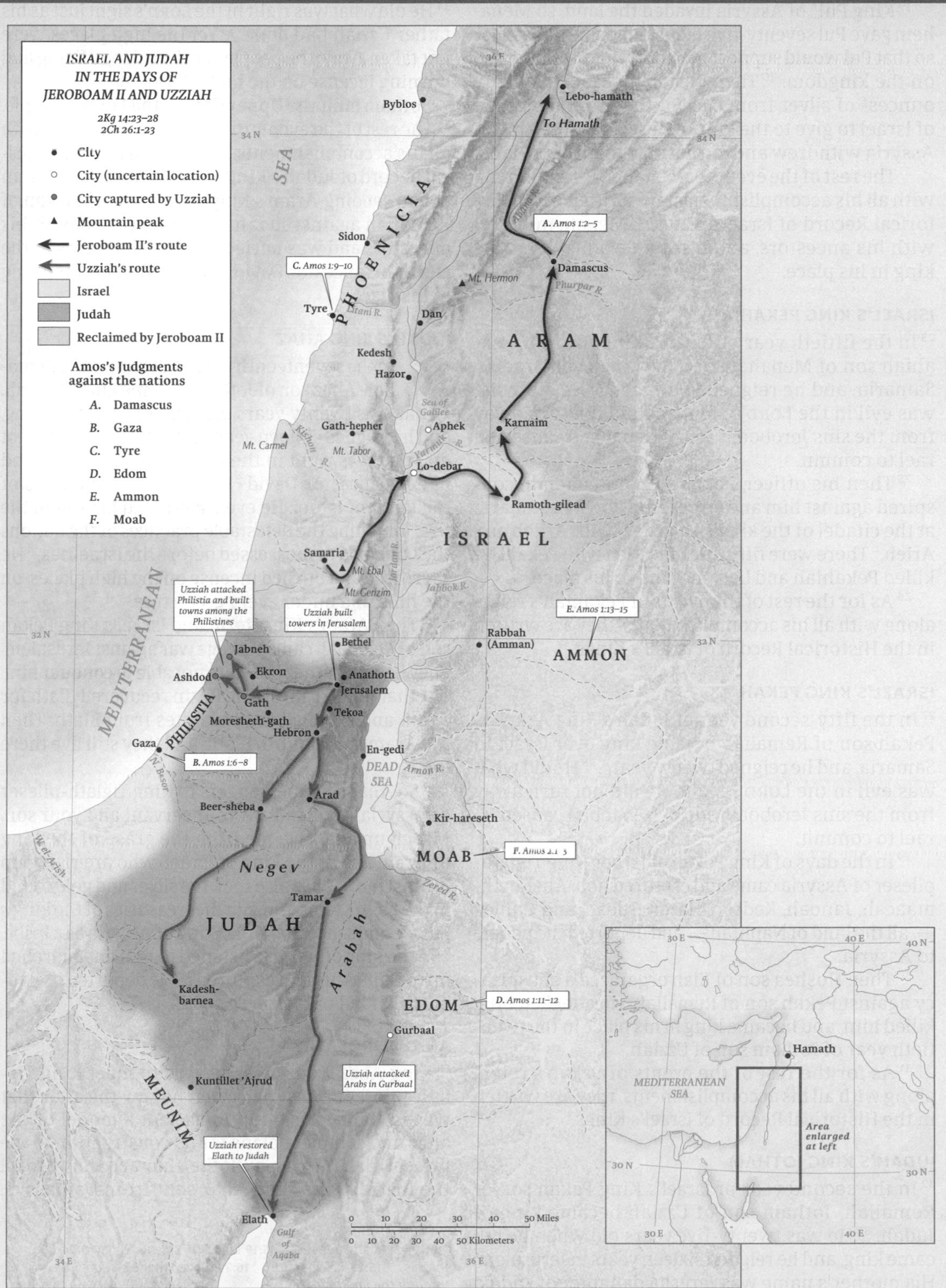

ISRAEL AND JUDAH IN THE DAYS OF JEROBOAM II AND UZZIAH
2Kg 14:23–28
2Ch 26:1-23
City
City (uncertain location)
City captured by Uzziah
Mountain peak
Jeroboam II's route
Uzziah's route
Israel
Judah
Reclaimed by Jeroboam II
Amos's Judgments against the nations
A. Damascus
B. Gaza
C. Tyre
D. Edom
E. Ammon
F. Moab
Byblos
Lebo-hamath
To Hamath
34 N
SEA
PHOENICIA
A. Amos 1:2–5
Sidon
Damascus
C. Amos 1:9–10
Mt. Hermon
Pharpar R.
Tyre
Litani R.
Dan
ARAM
Kedesh
Hazor
Sea of Galilee
Gath-hepher
Aphek
Karnaim
Kishon R.
Mt. Carmel
Mt. Tabor
Yarmuk R.
Lo-debar
Ramoth-gilead
ISRAEL
Samaria
Mt. Ebal
Mt. Gerizim
Jordan R.
Jabbok R.
MEDITERRANEAN
Uzziah attacked Philistia and built towns among the Philistines
Uzziah built towers in Jerusalem
E. Amos 1:13–15
32 N
Bethel
Rabbah (Amman)
AMMON
Jabneh
Ekron
Ashdod
Anathoth
Jerusalem
Gath
Tekoa
Moresheth-gath
Hebron
PHILISTIA
Gaza
En-gedi
N. Besor
B. Amos 1:6–8
DEAD SEA
Arnon R.
Arad
Beer-sheba
Kir-hareseth
W. el-Arish
MOAB
F. Amos 2:1–3
Negev
Zered R.
Tamar
JUDAH
Arabah
Kadesh-barnea
EDOM
D. Amos 1:11–12
Gurbaal
Uzziah attacked Arabs in Gurbaal
Kuntillet 'Ajrud
MEUNIM
Uzziah restored Elath to Judah
Elath
Gulf of Aqaba
0 10 20 30 40 50 Miles
0 10 20 30 40 50 Kilometers
34 E
36 E
30 E
40 E
40 N
Hamath
MEDITERRANEAN SEA
Area enlarged at left
30 N

19 King Pul[A] of Assyria invaded the land, so Menahem gave Pul seventy-five thousand pounds[B] of silver so that Pul would support him to strengthen his grasp on the kingdom. 20 Then Menahem exacted twenty ounces[C] of silver from each of the prominent men of Israel to give to the king of Assyria. So the king of Assyria withdrew and did not stay there in the land.

21 The rest of the events of Menahem's reign, along with all his accomplishments, are written in the Historical Record of Israel's Kings. 22 Menahem rested with his ancestors, and his son Pekahiah became king in his place.

ISRAEL'S KING PEKAHIAH

23 In the fiftieth year of Judah's King Azariah, Pekahiah son of Menahem became king over Israel in Samaria, and he reigned two years. 24 He did what was evil in the LORD's sight and did not turn away from the sins Jeroboam son of Nebat had caused Israel to commit.

25 Then his officer, Pekah son of Remaliah, conspired against him and struck him down in Samaria at the citadel of the king's palace — with Argob and Arieh.[D] There were fifty Gileadite men with Pekah. He killed Pekahiah and became king in his place.

26 As for the rest of the events of Pekahiah's reign, along with all his accomplishments, they are written in the Historical Record of Israel's Kings.

ISRAEL'S KING PEKAH

27 In the fifty-second year of Judah's King Azariah, Pekah son of Remaliah became king over Israel in Samaria, and he reigned twenty years. 28 He did what was evil in the LORD's sight. He did not turn away from the sins Jeroboam son of Nebat had caused Israel to commit.

29 In the days of King Pekah of Israel, King Tiglath-pileser of Assyria came and captured Ijon, Abel-beth-maacah, Janoah, Kedesh, Hazor, Gilead, and Galilee — all the land of Naphtali — and deported the people to Assyria.

30 Then Hoshea son of Elah organized a conspiracy against Pekah son of Remaliah. He attacked him, killed him, and became king in his place in the twentieth year of Jotham son of Uzziah.

31 As for the rest of the events of Pekah's reign, along with all his accomplishments, they are written in the Historical Record of Israel's Kings.

JUDAH'S KING JOTHAM

32 In the second year of Israel's King Pekah son of Remaliah, Jotham son of Uzziah became king of Judah. 33 He was twenty-five years old when he became king, and he reigned sixteen years in Jerusalem. His mother's name was Jerusha daughter of Zadok. 34 He did what was right in the LORD's sight just as his father Uzziah had done. 35 Yet the high places were not taken away; the people continued sacrificing and burning incense on the high places.

Jotham built the Upper Gate of the LORD's temple. 36 The rest of the events of Jotham's reign, along with all his accomplishments, are written in the Historical Record of Judah's Kings. 37 In those days the LORD began sending Aram's King Rezin and Pekah son of Remaliah against Judah. 38 Jotham rested with his ancestors and was buried with his ancestors in the city of his ancestor David. His son Ahaz became king in his place.

JUDAH'S KING AHAZ

16 In the seventeenth year of Pekah son of Remaliah, Ahaz son of Jotham became king of Judah. 2 Ahaz was twenty years old when he became king, and he reigned sixteen years in Jerusalem. He did not do what was right in the sight of the LORD his God like his ancestor David 3 but walked in the ways of the kings of Israel. He even sacrificed his son in the fire,[E] imitating the detestable practices of the nations the LORD had dispossessed before the Israelites. 4 He sacrificed and burned incense on the high places, on the hills, and under every green tree.

5 Then Aram's King Rezin and Israel's King Pekah son of Remaliah came to wage war against Jerusalem. They besieged Ahaz but were not able to conquer him. 6 At that time Aram's King Rezin recovered Elath for Aram and expelled the Judahites from Elath. Then the Arameans came to Elath, and they still live there today.

7 So Ahaz sent messengers to King Tiglath-pileser of Assyria, saying, "I am your servant and your son. March up and save me from the grasp of the king of Aram and of the king of Israel, who are rising up against me." 8 Ahaz also took the silver and gold found in the LORD's temple and in the treasuries of the king's palace and sent them to the king of Assyria as a bribe. 9 So the king of Assyria listened to him and marched up to Damascus and captured it. He deported its people to Kir but put Rezin to death.

AHAZ'S IDOLATRY

10 King Ahaz went to Damascus to meet King Tiglath-pileser of Assyria. When he saw the altar that was in Damascus, King Ahaz sent a model of the altar and complete plans for its construction to the priest Uriah. 11 Uriah built the altar according to all the instructions King Ahaz sent from Damascus.

[A] **15:19** = Tiglath-pileser [B] **15:19** Lit *1,000 talents* [C] **15:20** Lit *50 shekels* [D] **15:25** Hb obscure [E] **16:3** Lit *even made his son pass through the fire*

Therefore, by the time King Ahaz came back from Damascus, the priest Uriah had completed it. 12 When the king came back from Damascus, he saw the altar. Then he approached the altar and ascended it.[A] 13 He offered his burnt offering and his grain offering, poured out his drink offering, and splattered the blood of his fellowship offerings on the altar. 14 He took the bronze altar that was before the LORD in front of the temple between his altar and the LORD's temple, and put it on the north side of his altar.

15 Then King Ahaz commanded the priest Uriah, "Offer on the great altar the morning burnt offering, the evening grain offering, and the king's burnt offering and his grain offering. Also offer the burnt offering of all the people of the land, their grain offering, and their drink offerings. Splatter on the altar all the blood of the burnt offering and all the blood of sacrifice. The bronze altar will be for me to seek guidance."[B] 16 The priest Uriah did everything King Ahaz commanded.

17 Then King Ahaz cut off the frames of the water carts[C] and removed the bronze basin from each of them. He took the basin[D] from the bronze oxen that were under it and put it on a stone pavement. 18 To satisfy the king of Assyria, he removed from the LORD's temple the Sabbath canopy they had built in the palace, and he closed the outer entrance for the king.

AHAZ'S DEATH

19 The rest of the events of Ahaz's reign, along with his accomplishments, are written in the Historical Record of Judah's Kings. 20 Ahaz rested with his ancestors and was buried with his ancestors in the city of David, and his son Hezekiah became king in his place.

ISRAEL'S KING HOSHEA

17 In the twelfth year of Judah's King Ahaz, Hoshea son of Elah became king over Israel in Samaria, and he reigned nine years. 2 He did what was evil in the LORD's sight, but not like the kings of Israel who preceded him.

3 King Shalmaneser of Assyria attacked him, and Hoshea became his vassal and paid him tribute. 4 But the king of Assyria caught Hoshea in a conspiracy: He had sent envoys to So king of Egypt and had not paid tribute to the king of Assyria as in previous years.[E] Therefore the king of Assyria arrested him and put him in prison. 5 The king of Assyria invaded the whole land, marched up to Samaria, and besieged it for three years.

THE FALL OF SAMARIA

6 In the ninth year of Hoshea, the king of Assyria captured Samaria. He deported the Israelites to Assyria and settled them in Halah, along the Habor (Gozan's river), and in the cities of the Medes.

WHY ISRAEL FELL

7 This disaster happened because the people of Israel sinned against the LORD their God who had brought them out of the land of Egypt from the power of Pharaoh king of Egypt and because they worshiped[F] other gods. 8 They lived according to the customs of the nations that the LORD had dispossessed before the Israelites and according to what the kings of Israel did. 9 The Israelites secretly did things[G] against the LORD their God that were not right. They built high places in all their towns from watchtower to fortified city. 10 They set up for themselves sacred pillars and Asherah poles on every high hill and under every green tree. 11 They burned incense there on all the high places just like the nations that the LORD had driven out before them had done. They did evil things, angering the LORD. 12 They served idols, although the LORD had told them, "You must not do this." 13 Still, the LORD warned Israel and Judah through every prophet and every seer, saying, "Turn from your evil ways and keep my commands and statutes according to the whole law I commanded your ancestors and sent to you through my servants the prophets."

14 But they would not listen. Instead they became obstinate like[H] their ancestors who did not believe the LORD their God. 15 They rejected his statutes and his covenant he had made with their ancestors and the warnings he had given them. They followed worthless idols and became worthless themselves, following the surrounding nations the LORD had commanded them not to imitate.

16 They abandoned all the commands of the LORD their God. They made cast images for themselves, two calves, and an Asherah pole. They bowed in worship to all the stars in the sky and served Baal. 17 They sacrificed their sons and daughters in the fire[I] and practiced divination and interpreted omens. They devoted themselves to do what was evil in the LORD's sight and angered him.

18 Therefore, the LORD was very angry with Israel, and he removed them from his presence. Only the tribe of Judah remained. 19 Even Judah did not keep the commands of the LORD their God but lived according to the customs Israel had practiced. 20 So the LORD rejected all the descendants of Israel, punished them, and handed them over to plunderers until he had banished them from his presence.

[A] **16:12** Or *and offered on it:* [B] **16:15** Hb obscure [C] **16:17** Lit *the stands* [D] **16:17** Lit *sea* [E] **17:4** Lit *as year by year* [F] **17:7** Lit *feared* [G] **17:9** Or *Israelites spoke words* [H] **17:14** Lit *they stiffened their neck like the neck of* [I] **17:17** Lit *They made their sons and daughters pass through the fire*

Samaria: Its Rise and Fall

by Gary P. Arbino

First Kings 16 tells of King Omri founding Samaria, the new capital city of the northern kingdom of Israel. Recent analysis of data from excavations in the twentieth century has illustrated a complex early occupational history for the site.[1] Examining the archaeology and the biblical text together indicates that the site was occupied in Iron Age I (1200–1000 BC), abandoned, and then transferred to Shemer as a family estate.

Countryside as seen from Ahab's capital city of Samaria.

The site, itself imposing, was an excellent military and commercial choice for a capital. The hill of Samaria rises to about fourteen hundred feet above sea level and dominates the surrounding countryside, including important trade routes, which it overlooks. Valleys surround it on three sides, making it defensible. Strategically located within the heart of the northern kingdom, Samaria controlled Israel. The one thing the site lacked was a good water supply; a stone water system was created to solve this deficiency.

Most of the excavations focusing on the Iron Age II (1000–800 BC) have centered on the acropolis, only a small portion of the city.[2] Here archaeologists have uncovered a citadel measuring about two hundred by one hundred yards. The citadel is an enclosure surrounded by a casemate (double) wall system. The casemate fortifications are impressive; the masonry bears a marked similarity to the highly skilled Phoenician craftsmanship from the era. Inside the citadel were a palace, storerooms, public buildings, and courtyards with rectangular pools (see 1Kg 22:38). The citadel was decorated in the high style befitting an international capital. Hundreds of beautiful Syrian-style ivory fragments, depicting both local and Egyptian motifs and accented with gold foil, were found

Phoenician ivory from Nimrud depicts two seated figures; ninth–eighth centuries BC.

both at Samaria and at the Assyrian cities of Arslan Tash and Nimrud, where they were probably taken as spoils when Samaria was captured late in the eighth century. First Kings 22:39 and Amos 6:4 mention this lavish decoration, which had become a symbol of the nobility's utter lack of compassion for and abuse of the poor. While international connections and commerce do not necessitate religious infidelity, at Samaria they were part of the overall situation that the biblical writers chastised. Even the dishes were opulent. A beautiful and delicate high-quality red-burnished pottery is known as "Samaria ware" because archaeologists first found it in this city. Although they later found this same pottery in other cities, the finest pieces were in ancient Samaria.

The grandness of the place was, sadly, paralleled by a decline in absolute allegiance to

Dated to the eighth century BC, one of the decorative ivories found at Samaria. The figure represented a palm tree.

From ancient Hadatu (now Arslan Tash, Syria). After conquering Hadatu, Assyria established a new palace there and decorated the palace's Phoenician and Aramean furniture with ivories.

Yahweh. Interestingly, the biblical text never says Omri participated in the worship of Baal specifically, something stated for most all later members of the dynasty (1Kg 16:31; 22:53); yet his policies and treaties clearly paved the way for this to become a "legal" religion in Israel. Omri's son Ahab built a Baal temple in Samaria for his new Phoenician queen, Jezebel, who became the local patron of the religion (16:32).

Excavators recovered some sixty-three potsherds with writing on them (known as *ostraca*) from the citadel of Samaria. These record shipments of oil and wine and seem to be tax receipts. As evidenced by the types of names found on these documents, they also clearly reflect the syncretistic nature of the population of Samaria during Iron Age II: the names honored both Yahweh and Baal.

Fortifications at Samaria.

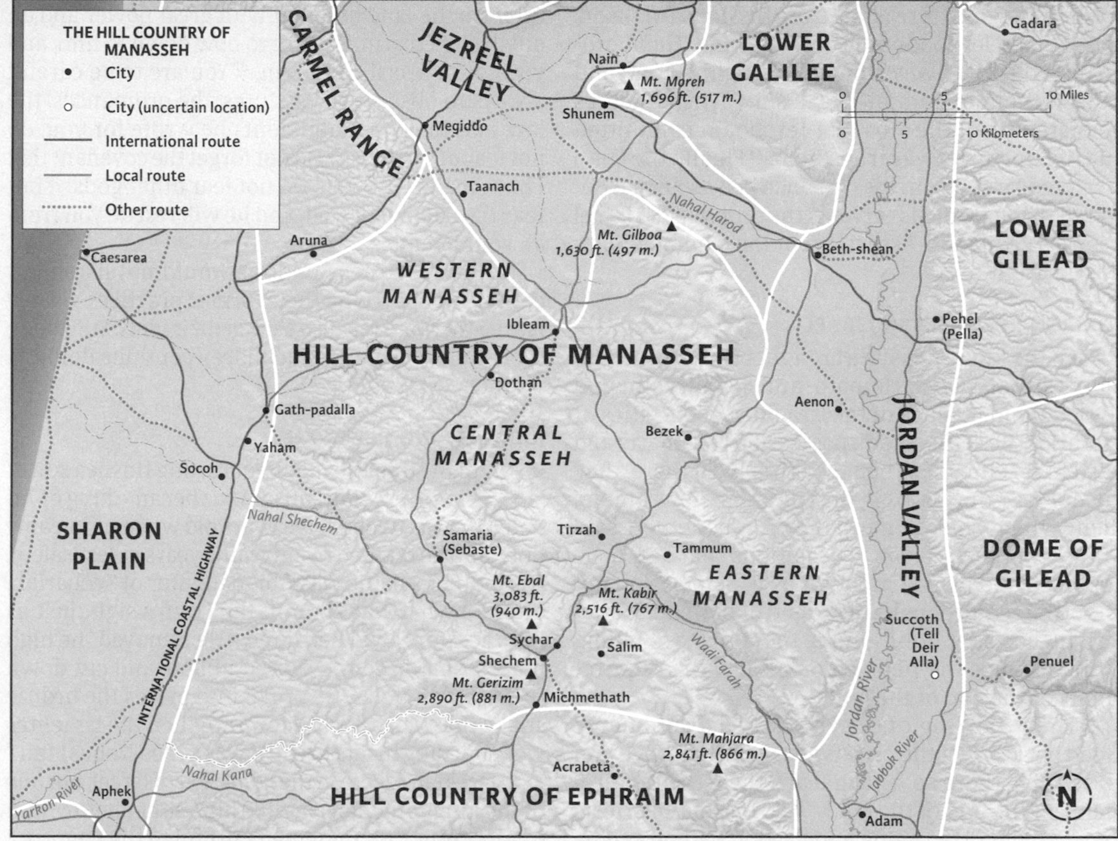

Archaeology shows that following his purge and removal of the Omride rulers, King Jehu also worked on building Samaria. He continued the cosmopolitan quality of the capital. Samaria reached its zenith during Jeroboam II's long and powerful reign (782–753 BC).

Over the course of more than a decade, Assyria chipped away at the northern kingdom, finally capturing the capital. Comparisons of the Assyrian documents and archaeological evidence with the biblical record have resulted in ongoing debates in the academic community about the details of Assyria taking Samaria.[3] What is now clear is that Samaria was not destroyed, but by 720 BC was in Assyrian hands. Much of Samaria's population, especially the nobility and a contingent of the Israelite chariot corps, had been deported to other parts of the empire. In their place, new peoples were moved in. The new inhabitants of Samaria worshiped both Yahweh and the gods of their homelands. The mixing of Israelite bloodlines formed the basis for the tension between those of the north, later known as Samaritans, and those from Judah, later known as Jews. This complex situation comes to full flower by the time of Jesus and is reflected in the New Testament. ✣

[1] Ron Tappy, "Samaria" in *OEANE*, 4:463–67; Nahman Avigad, "Samaria (City)" in *NEAEHL*, 4:1300–1310. [2] See Avigad, "Samaria"; James D. Purvis, "Samaria (City)" in *ABD*, 5:914–21. [3] Ron E. Tappy, "The Final Years of Israelite Samaria: Toward a Dialogue between Texts and Archaeology," in *"Up to the Gates of Ekron": Essays on the Archaeology and History of the Eastern Mediterranean in Honor of Seymour Gitin*, ed. Sidnie White Crawford (Jerusalem: W. F. Albright Institute of Archaeological Research and Israel Exploration Society, 2007), 258–79.

SUMMARY OF ISRAEL'S HISTORY

21 When the LORD tore Israel from the house of David, Israel made Jeroboam son of Nebat king. Then Jeroboam led Israel away from following the LORD and caused them to commit grave sin. 22 The Israelites persisted in all the sins that Jeroboam committed and did not turn away from them. 23 Finally, the LORD removed Israel from his presence just as he had declared through all his servants the prophets. So Israel has been exiled to Assyria from their homeland to this very day.

FOREIGN REFUGEES IN ISRAEL

24 Then the king of Assyria brought people from Babylon, Cuthah, Avva, Hamath, and Sepharvaim and settled them in place of the Israelites in the cities of Samaria. The settlers took possession of Samaria and lived in its cities. 25 When they first lived there, they did not fear the LORD. So the LORD sent lions among them, which killed some of them. 26 The settlers said to the king of Assyria, "The nations that you have deported and placed in the cities of Samaria do not know the requirements of the god of the land. Therefore he has sent lions among them that are killing them because the people don't know the requirements of the god of the land."

27 Then the king of Assyria issued a command: "Send back one of the priests you deported. Have him go and live there so he can teach them the requirements of the god of the land." 28 So one of the priests they had deported came and lived in Bethel, and he began to teach them how they should fear the LORD.

29 But the people of each nation were still making their own gods in the cities where they lived and putting them in the shrines of the high places that the people of Samaria had made. 30 The men of Babylon made Succoth-benoth, the men of Cuth made Nergal, the men of Hamath made Ashima, 31 the Avvites made Nibhaz and Tartak, and the Sepharvites burned their children in the fire to Adrammelech and Anammelech, the gods of Sepharvaim. 32 They feared the LORD, but they also made from their ranks priests for the high places, who were working for them at the shrines of the high places. 33 They feared the LORD, but they also worshiped their own gods according to the practice of the nations from which they had been deported.

34 They are still observing the former practices to this day. None of them fear the LORD or observe the statutes and ordinances, the law and commandments that the LORD had commanded the descendants of Jacob, whom he had given the name Israel. 35 The LORD made a covenant with Jacob's descendants and commanded them, "Do not fear other gods; do not bow in worship to them; do not serve them; do not sacrifice to them. 36 Instead fear the LORD, who brought you up from the land of Egypt with great power and an outstretched arm. You are to bow down to him, and you are to sacrifice to him. 37 You are to be careful always to observe the statutes, the ordinances, the law, and the commandments he wrote for you; do not fear other gods. 38 Do not forget the covenant that I have made with you. Do not fear other gods, 39 but fear the LORD your God, and he will rescue you from all your enemies."

40 However, these nations would not listen but continued observing their former practices. 41 They feared the LORD but also served their idols. Still today, their children and grandchildren continue doing as their ancestors did.

JUDAH'S KING HEZEKIAH

18 In the third year of Israel's King Hoshea son of Elah, Hezekiah son of Ahaz became king of Judah. 2 He was twenty-five years old when he became king, and he reigned twenty-nine years in Jerusalem. His mother's name was Abi[A] daughter of Zechariah. 3 He did what was right in the LORD's sight just as his ancestor David had done. 4 He removed the high places, shattered the sacred pillars, and cut down the Asherah poles. He broke into pieces the bronze snake that Moses made, for until then the Israelites were burning incense to it. It was called Nehushtan.[B]

5 Hezekiah relied on the LORD God of Israel; not one of the kings of Judah was like him, either before him or after him. 6 He remained faithful to the LORD and did not turn from following him but kept the commands the LORD had commanded Moses.

7 The LORD was with him, and wherever he went he prospered. He rebelled against the king of Assyria and did not serve him. 8 He defeated the Philistines as far as Gaza and its borders, from watchtower to fortified city.

REVIEW OF ISRAEL'S FALL

9 In the fourth year of King Hezekiah, which was the seventh year of Israel's King Hoshea son of Elah, Assyria's King Shalmaneser marched against Samaria and besieged it. 10 The Assyrians captured it at the end of three years. In the sixth year of Hezekiah, which was the ninth year of Israel's King Hoshea, Samaria was captured. 11 The king of Assyria deported the Israelites to Assyria and put them in Halah, along the Habor (Gozan's river), and in the cities of the Medes, 12 because they did not listen to the LORD their God but violated his covenant — all he had commanded Moses the servant of the LORD. They did not listen, and they did not obey.

[A] **18:2** = Abijah in 2Ch 29:1 [B] **18:4** = A Bronze Thing

SENNACHERIB'S INVASION

13 In the fourteenth year of King Hezekiah, Assyria's King Sennacherib attacked all the fortified cities of Judah and captured them. 14 So King Hezekiah of Judah sent word to the king of Assyria at Lachish: "I have done wrong; withdraw from me. Whatever you demand from me, I will pay." The king of Assyria demanded eleven tons[A] of silver and one ton[B] of gold from King Hezekiah of Judah. 15 So Hezekiah gave him all the silver found in the LORD's temple and in the treasuries of the king's palace.

16 At that time Hezekiah stripped the gold from the doors of the LORD's sanctuary and from the doorposts he had overlaid and gave it to the king of Assyria.

17 Then the king of Assyria sent the field marshal, the chief of staff, and his royal spokesman, along with a massive army, from Lachish to King Hezekiah at Jerusalem. They advanced and came to Jerusalem, and[C] they took their position by the aqueduct of the upper pool, by the road to the Launderer's Field. 18 They called for the king, but Eliakim son of Hilkiah, who was in charge of the palace, Shebnah the court secretary, and Joah son of Asaph, the court historian, came out to them.

THE ROYAL SPOKESMAN'S SPEECH

19 Then the royal spokesman said to them, "Tell Hezekiah this is what the great king, the king of Assyria, says: 'What are you relying on?[D] 20 You think mere words are strategy and strength for war. Who are you now relying on so that you have rebelled against me? 21 Now look, you are relying on Egypt, that splintered reed of a staff that will pierce the hand of anyone who grabs it and leans on it. This is what Pharaoh king of Egypt is to all who rely on him. 22 Suppose you say to me, "We rely on the LORD our God." Isn't he the one whose high places and altars Hezekiah has removed, saying to Judah and to Jerusalem, "You must worship at this altar in Jerusalem"?'

23 "So now, make a bargain with my master the king of Assyria. I'll give you two thousand horses if you're able to supply riders for them! 24 How then can you drive back a single officer among the least of my master's servants? How can you rely on Egypt for chariots and for horsemen? 25 Now, have I attacked this place to destroy it without the LORD's approval? The LORD said to me, 'Attack this land and destroy it.' "

26 Then Eliakim son of Hilkiah, Shebnah, and Joah said to the royal spokesman, "Please speak to your servants in Aramaic, since we understand it. Don't speak with us in Hebrew[E] within earshot of the people on the wall."

27 But the royal spokesman said to them, "Has my master sent me to speak these words only to your master and to you? Hasn't he also sent me to the men who sit on the wall, destined with you to eat their own excrement and drink their own urine?"

28 The royal spokesman stood and called out loudly in Hebrew: "Hear the word of the great king, the king of Assyria. 29 This is what the king says: 'Don't let Hezekiah deceive you; he can't rescue you from my power. 30 Don't let Hezekiah persuade you to rely on the LORD by saying, "Certainly the LORD will rescue us! This city will not be handed over to the king of Assyria." '

31 "Don't listen to Hezekiah, for this is what the king of Assyria says: 'Make peace[F] with me and surrender to me. Then each of you may eat from his own vine and his own fig tree, and each may drink water from his own cistern 32 until I come and take you away to a land like your own land — a land of grain and new wine, a land of bread and vineyards, a land of olive trees and honey — so that you may live and not die. But don't listen to Hezekiah when he misleads you, saying, "The LORD will rescue us." 33 Has any of the gods of the nations ever rescued his land from the power of the king of Assyria? 34 Where are the gods of Hamath and Arpad? Where are the gods of Sepharvaim, Hena, and Ivvah?[G] Have they rescued Samaria from my power? 35 Who among all the gods of the lands has rescued his land from my power? So will the LORD rescue Jerusalem from my power?' "

36 But the people kept silent; they did not answer him at all, for the king's command was, "Don't answer him." 37 Then Eliakim son of Hilkiah, who was in charge of the palace, Shebna the court secretary, and Joah son of Asaph, the court historian, came to Hezekiah with their clothes torn and reported to him the words of the royal spokesman.

HEZEKIAH SEEKS ISAIAH'S COUNSEL

19 When King Hezekiah heard their report, he tore his clothes, covered himself with sackcloth, and went into the LORD's temple. 2 He sent Eliakim, who was in charge of the palace, Shebna the court secretary, and the leading priests, who were covered with sackcloth, to the prophet Isaiah son of Amoz. 3 They said to him, "This is what Hezekiah says: 'Today is a day of distress, rebuke, and disgrace, for children have come to the point of birth, but there is no strength to deliver them. 4 Perhaps the LORD your God will hear all the words of the royal spokesman, whom his master the king of Assyria sent to mock the living God, and will rebuke him for the words

[A] **18:14** Lit *300 talents* [B] **18:14** Lit *30 talents* [C] **18:17** LXX, Syr, Vg; MT reads *and came and* [D] **18:19** Lit *'What is this trust which you trust* [E] **18:26** Lit *Judahite*, also in v. 28 [F] **18:31** Lit *a blessing* [G] **18:34** Some LXX mss, Old Lat read *Sepharvaim? Where are the gods of the land of Samaria?*

that the LORD your God has heard. Therefore, offer a
prayer for the surviving remnant.' "
5 So the servants of King Hezekiah went to Isaiah,
6 who said to them, "Tell your master, 'The LORD says
this: Don't be afraid because of the words you have
heard, with which the king of Assyria's attendants
have blasphemed me. 7 I am about to put a spirit in
him, and he will hear a rumor and return to his own
land, where I will cause him to fall by the sword.' "

SENNACHERIB'S DEPARTING THREAT

8 When the royal spokesman heard that the king
of Assyria had pulled out of Lachish, he left and
found him fighting against Libnah. 9 The king had
heard concerning King Tirhakah of Cush, "Look, he
has set out to fight against you." So he again sent
messengers to Hezekiah, saying, 10 "Say this to King
Hezekiah of Judah: 'Don't let your God, on whom you
rely, deceive you by promising that Jerusalem will
not be handed over to the king of Assyria. 11 Look, you
have heard what the kings of Assyria have done to all
the countries: They completely destroyed them. Will
you be rescued? 12 Did the gods of the nations that
my predecessors destroyed rescue them — nations
such as Gozan, Haran, Rezeph, and the Edenites in
Telassar? 13 Where is the king of Hamath, the king
of Arpad, the king of the city of[A] Sepharvaim, Hena,
or Ivvah?' "

HEZEKIAH'S PRAYER

14 Hezekiah took the letter from the messengers'
hands, read it, then went up to the LORD's temple,
and spread it out before the LORD. 15 Then Hezekiah
prayed before the LORD:

LORD God of Israel, enthroned between the
cherubim, you are God — you alone — of all
the kingdoms of the earth. You made the heavens and the earth. 16 Listen closely, LORD, and
hear; open your eyes, LORD, and see. Hear the
words that Sennacherib has sent to mock the
living God. 17 LORD, it is true that the kings of
Assyria have devastated the nations and their
lands. 18 They have thrown their gods into the
fire, for they were not gods but made by human hands — wood and stone. So they have
destroyed them. 19 Now, LORD our God, please
save us from his power so that all the kingdoms
of the earth may know that you, LORD, are God
— you alone.

GOD'S ANSWER THROUGH ISAIAH

20 Then Isaiah son of Amoz sent a message to Hezekiah: "The LORD, the God of Israel says, 'I have heard
your prayer to me about King Sennacherib of Assyria.'
21 This is the word the LORD has spoken against him:

Virgin Daughter Zion
despises you and scorns you;
Daughter Jerusalem
shakes her head behind your back.
22 Who is it you mocked and blasphemed?
Against whom have you raised your voice
and lifted your eyes in pride?
Against the Holy One of Israel!
23 You have mocked the Lord[B] through[C]
your messengers.
You have said, 'With my many chariots
I have gone up to the heights
of the mountains,
to the far recesses of Lebanon.
I cut down its tallest cedars,
its choice cypress trees.
I came to its farthest outpost,
its densest forest.
24 I dug wells
and drank water in foreign lands.
I dried up all the streams of Egypt
with the soles of my feet.'

25 Have you not heard?
I designed it long ago;
I planned it in days gone by.
I have now brought it to pass,
and you have crushed fortified cities
into piles of rubble.
26 Their inhabitants have become powerless,
dismayed, and ashamed.
They are plants of the field,
tender grass,
grass on the rooftops,
blasted by the east wind.[D]

27 But I know your sitting down,
your going out and your coming in,
and your raging against me.
28 Because your raging against me
and your arrogance have reached my ears,
I will put my hook in your nose
and my bit in your mouth;
I will make you go back
the way you came.

29 "This will be the sign for you: This year you will
eat what grows on its own, and in the second year
what grows from that. But in the third year sow
and reap, plant vineyards and eat their fruit. 30 The
surviving remnant of the house of Judah will again
take root downward and bear fruit upward. 31 For a

[A] 19:13 Or *king of Lair,* [B] 19:23 Many mss read *LORD* [C] 19:23 Lit *by the hand of* [D] 19:26 DSS; MT reads *blasted before standing grain*; Is 37:27

remnant will go out from Jerusalem, and survivors,
from Mount Zion. The zeal of the LORD of Armies will
accomplish this.

32 Therefore, this is what the LORD says
about the king of Assyria:
He will not enter this city,
shoot an arrow here,
come before it with a shield,
or build up a siege ramp against it.
33 He will go back
the way he came,
and he will not enter this city.
This is the LORD's declaration.
34 I will defend this city and rescue it
for my sake and for the sake of my
servant David."

DEFEAT AND DEATH OF SENNACHERIB

35 That night the angel of the LORD went out and struck
down one hundred eighty-five thousand in the camp
of the Assyrians. When the people got up the next
morning — there were all the dead bodies! 36 So King
Sennacherib of Assyria broke camp and left. He returned home and lived in Nineveh.
37 One day, while he was worshiping in the temple
of his god Nisroch, his sons Adrammelech and Sharezer struck him down with the sword and escaped to
the land of Ararat. Then his son Esar-haddon became
king in his place.

HEZEKIAH'S ILLNESS AND RECOVERY

20 In those days Hezekiah became terminally
ill. The prophet Isaiah son of Amoz came and
said to him, "This is what the LORD says: 'Set your
house in order, for you are about to die; you will
not recover.' "
2 Then Hezekiah turned his face to the wall and
prayed to the LORD, 3 "Please, LORD, remember how I
have walked before you faithfully and wholeheartedly and have done what pleases you."[A] And Hezekiah
wept bitterly.
4 Isaiah had not yet gone out of the inner courtyard when the word of the LORD came to him: 5 "Go
back and tell Hezekiah, the leader of my people,
'This is what the LORD God of your ancestor David
says: I have heard your prayer; I have seen your
tears. Look, I will heal you. On the third day from
now you will go up to the LORD's temple. 6 I will add
fifteen years to your life. I will rescue you and this
city from the grasp of the king of Assyria. I will
defend this city for my sake and for the sake of my
servant David.' "
7 Then Isaiah said, "Bring a lump of pressed figs."
So they brought it and applied it to his infected skin,
and he recovered.
8 Hezekiah had asked Isaiah, "What is the sign that
the LORD will heal me and that I will go up to the
LORD's temple on the third day?"
9 Isaiah said, "This is the sign to you from the LORD
that he will do what he has promised: Should the
shadow go ahead ten steps or go back ten steps?"
10 Then Hezekiah answered, "It's easy for the shadow to lengthen ten steps. No, let the shadow go back
ten steps." 11 So the prophet Isaiah called out to the
LORD, and he brought the shadow[B] back the ten steps
it had descended on the stairway of Ahaz.[C]

HEZEKIAH'S FOLLY

12 At that time Merodach-baladan[D] son of Baladan, king
of Babylon, sent letters and a gift to Hezekiah since he
heard that he had been sick. 13 Hezekiah listened to
the letters and showed the envoys his whole treasure
house — the silver, the gold, the spices, and the precious oil — and his armory, and everything that was
found in his treasuries. There was nothing in his palace
and in all his realm that Hezekiah did not show them.
14 Then the prophet Isaiah came to King Hezekiah
and asked him, "Where did these men come from and
what did they say to you?"
Hezekiah replied, "They came from a distant country, from Babylon."
15 Isaiah asked, "What have they seen in your palace?"
Hezekiah answered, "They have seen everything
in my palace. There isn't anything in my treasuries
that I didn't show them."
16 Then Isaiah said to Hezekiah, "Hear the word of
the LORD: 17 'Look, the days are coming when everything in your palace and all that your predecessors
have stored up until today will be carried off to Babylon; nothing will be left,' says the LORD. 18 'Some of
your descendants — who come from you, whom you
father — will be taken away, and they will become
eunuchs[E] in the palace of the king of Babylon.' "
19 Then Hezekiah said to Isaiah, "The word of the
LORD that you have spoken is good," for he thought,
"Why not, if there will be peace and security during
my lifetime?"

HEZEKIAH'S DEATH

20 The rest of the events of Hezekiah's reign, along
with all his might and how he made the pool and the
tunnel and brought water into the city, are written
in the Historical Record of Judah's Kings. 21 Hezekiah rested with his ancestors, and his son Manasseh
became king in his place.

[A] **20:3** Lit *what is good in your eyes* [B] **20:11** Lit *shadow on the steps*
[C] **20:11** Tg, Vg; DSS read *on the steps of Ahaz's roof chamber*; Is 38:8
[D] **20:12** Some Hb mss, LXX, Syr, Tg, some Vg mss, Is 39:1; other Hb
mss read *Berodach-baladan* [E] **20:18** Or *court officials*

It Happened at Lachish

by Scott Hummel

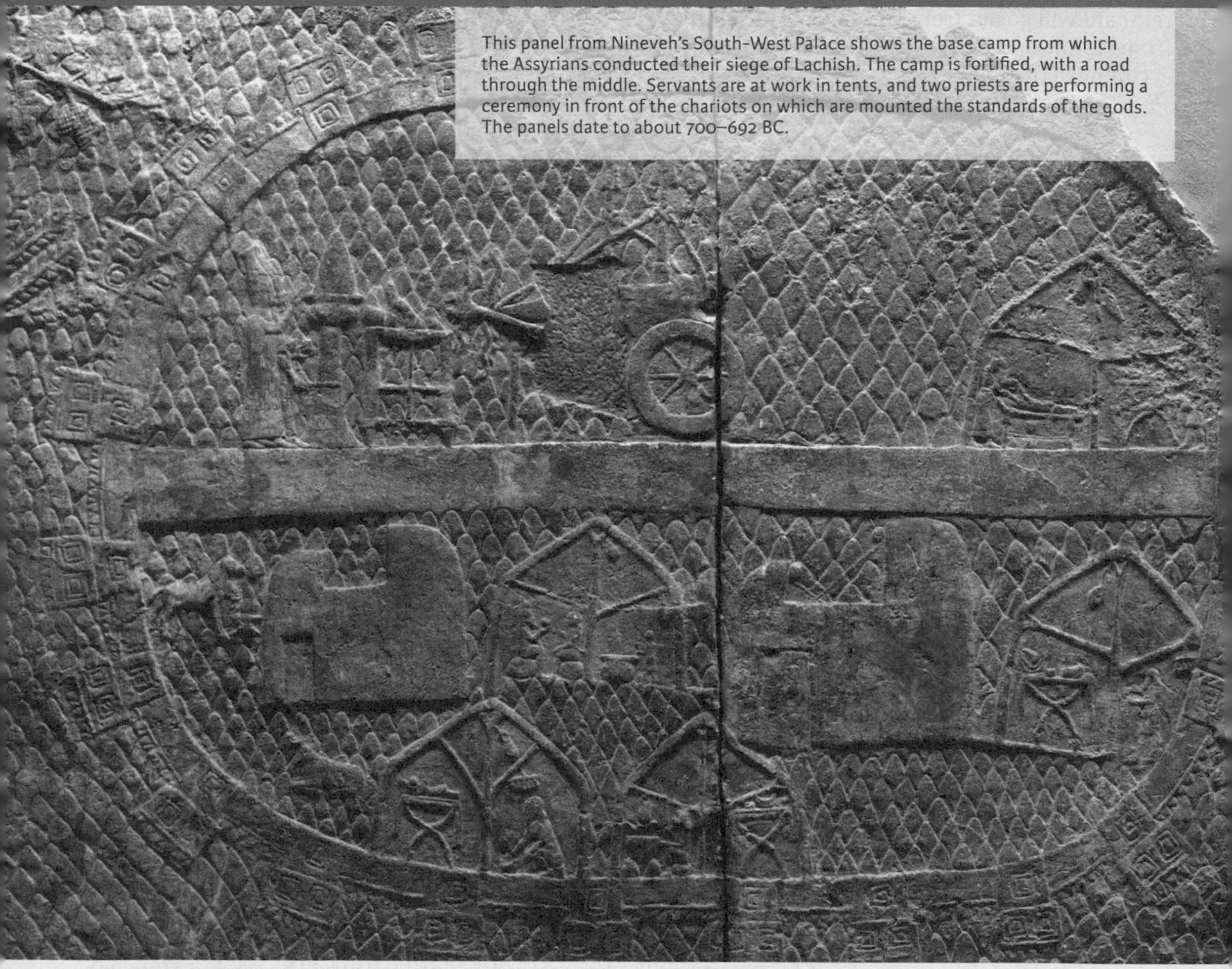

This panel from Nineveh's South-West Palace shows the base camp from which the Assyrians conducted their siege of Lachish. The camp is fortified, with a road through the middle. Servants are at work in tents, and two priests are performing a ceremony in front of the chariots on which are mounted the standards of the gods. The panels date to about 700–692 BC.

Lachish (Tell ed-Duweir) was about twenty acres in size, making it one of the largest in Canaan, on par with cities such as Jericho and Jerusalem.[1] Lachish was strategically located about thirty-five miles southwest of Jerusalem near the main road leading from the southern coastal plain into the central mountains. The earliest-known mention of Lachish was in the Ebla commercial texts (ca 2400 BC) and then in the Amarna letters (ca 1350 BC), which include correspondence between Egypt and Canaanite cities.[2]

After Joshua's conquest, Lachish was assigned to the tribe of Judah (Jos 15:39), but it remained abandoned through the period of the judges.[3] During the divided monarchy, Judah's King Rehoboam fortified Lachish as a part of his southern defense. The fortifications failed to stop Pharaoh Shishak's invasion (ca 925 BC) in which he ravaged both Israel and Judah.[4]

Ruins of shops along the main street at Lachish. Locals call the site Tell ed-Duweir, Arabic for "small round," likely a description of the hill. The tell rises about sixty-three feet above the surrounding land.

After destroying the northern kingdom of Israel (722 BC), Assyria's King Sennacherib in 701 BC attacked Judean cities, including Lachish, which was a major administrative center and military fortification second only to Jerusalem in size (2Kg 18:13–37).[5] Sennacherib proudly recorded his Judean campaign in his annals:

> Because Hezekiah of Judah did not submit to my yoke, I laid siege to forty-six of his fortified cities and walled forts and to the countless villages in their vicinity. I conquered them using earthen ramps and battering rams. These siege engines were supported by infantry who tunneled under the walls. . . . I imprisoned Hezekiah in Jerusalem like a bird in a cage.[6]

Reconstructed gate at Lachish

At Lachish, Sennacherib's army faced massive fortifications and a formidable defense with its double-walled defensive system, twenty-foot-thick walls, an outer gate protected by towers, and a large six-chambered inner gate. Even after the walls were breached, a fortified palace dominated the center of the city. Any army less skilled or determined than the Assyrians would likely have been repelled.[7]

To breach the outer walls, the Assyrians built a ramp fifty-two feet high, using nineteen thousand tons of stone.[8] In response, the defenders built a counter ramp, but it failed to prevent the breach as evidenced by hundreds of arrowheads, armor scales, sling stones, and helmets found inside Lachish.[9] On the western slope of the city, a mass grave held over fifteen hundred skeletons.[10]

While Sennacherib had to settle for commemorating the destruction of Lachish instead of Jerusalem, he proudly displayed the siege and conquest of Lachish in minute detail on the wall of his palace in Nineveh. The Lachish reliefs are seventy feet long and provide invaluable information about the sequence of events, detailed images of Lachish's defenses, Assyrian siege techniques, armor types, various weapons, chariots, and Assyrian cruelty to the Israelite captives.[11] Because so much of the material evidence has been

Part of the ruins of the palace at Lachish. Originally a Canaanite fortress-city, Lachish came under Israelite control in the tenth century BC. Still heavily fortified, Lachish served as one of Judah's largest cities before it fell to the Assyrians in 701 BC.

destroyed by time, if not for the Lachish reliefs much less would be known about military equipment, armor, weapon, and chariot design. By revealing stages of the conquest, the reliefs help explain even the Assyrians' battle tactics. With the biblical narrative, Sennacherib's annals, the Lachish reliefs, and the archaeological evidence, the battle for Lachish is one of the best-recorded events in all the ancient Near East.[12]

Sennacherib's destruction of Lachish was so complete that the site remained abandoned for half a century. As the Assyrian Empire began to collapse, Judah's King Josiah exerted independence over his territory, including the reoccupation and refortification of Lachish.[13] But Lachish was a shadow of its former self, so it stood no chance of surviving the Babylonian onslaught in 587 BC.

The Lachish letters provide a chilling eyewitness testimony of the panic of the days immediately preceding Nebuchadnezzar's conquest of Lachish. Twenty-one *ostraca* (pieces of pottery with writing on them) or letters were discovered in a room adjacent to the city gate and form one of the largest collections of Jewish documents from the period of the monarchy.[14] Letter 3 describes the correspondence between Yaush, a military commander, and his subordinate, Hoshayahu, including orders, accusations of insubordination, intelligence reports, and intercepted letters. In Letter 4, Yaush writes, "This letter certifies to my commanding officer that I remain on duty to carry out your orders to keep the signal fire burning at Lachish because the fire at Azekah has been put out."[15]

For more than a century Lachish lay in ruins, until Jews resettled it (Neh 11:30). It belonged, however, to Idumea instead of Judah.[16] A Persian official resided in a palace built on the platform of the earlier Israelite palace-fort until regional governance was relocated to the city of Mareshah in the early Hellenistic period.[17] "During the Maccabean wars, Lachish was destroyed for the last time (ca 150 BC)."[18] ✣

---

[1] V. R. Gold and K. N. Schoville, "Lachish" in *ISBE*, vol. 3 (1986), 59; H. G. M. Williamson, "Lachish" in *Dictionary of the Old Testament Historical Books*, ed. Bill T. Arnold and H. G. M. Williamson (Downers Grove, IL: InterVarsity, 2005), 635. The city would later cover more than thirty acres. George Kelm, *Escape to Conflict: A Biblical and Archaeological Approach to the Hebrew Exodus and Settlement in Canaan* (Fort Worth, TX: IAR, 1991), 173. The excavations of Lachish by David Ussishkin from 1973 to 1994 provide the most comprehensive archaeological information about Lachish. [2] Gold and Schoville, "Lachish," 56; Paul F. Jacobs, "Lachish" in *EDB* (2000), 781. [3] Gold and Schoville, "Lachish," 57. [4] Williamson, "Lachish," 635; Gold and Schoville, "Lachish," 58; 2Ch 12:1–12. [5] Amihai Mazar, *Archaeology of the Land of the Bible 10,000–586 BCE*, vol. 1 in Anchor Bible Reference Library (ABRL) (New York: Doubleday, 1990), 427, 432. The large number of storage jars stamped *lmlk* ("to the king") demonstrate Hezekiah's administrative and logistical preparations. [6] "Annals of Sennacherib" in Victor H. Matthews and Don C. Benjamin, *Old Testament Parallels*, 3rd ed. (New York: Paulist, 2006), 191–92. [7] B. S. J. Isserlin, *The Israelites* (London: Thames & Hudson, 1998), 202; Philip J. King and Lawrence E. Stager, *Life in Biblical Israel* (Louisville: Westminster John Knox, 2001), 249. [8] Ephraim Stern, *Archaeology of the Land of the Bible: The Assyrian, Babylonian, and Persian Periods (732–332 BCE)* vol. 2 in ABRL (2001), 6. The siege ramp at Lachish is the only known example of an Assyrian ramp. Mazar, *Archaeology*, 432; Williamson, "Lachish," 638. [9] Stern, *Archaeology*, 6; Alfred J. Hoerth, *Archaeology and the Old Testament* (Grand Rapids: Baker, 1998), 350. [10] King and Stager, *Life*, 250. [11] Hoerth, *Archaeology*, 350; Stern, *Archaeology*, 5; David Ussishkin, "The 'Lachish Reliefs' and the City of Lachish," *IEJ* 30 (1980): 174–95. The reliefs are on display in the British Museum. [12] Mazar, *Archaeology*, 432. [13] Gold and Schoville, "Lachish," 58. [14] Stern, *Archaeology*, 149; Hoerth, *Archaeology*, 364; Mazar, *Archaeology*, 434–35. [15] Matthews and Benjamin, *Old Testament Parallels*, 203. [16] Jerome Murphy-O'Connor, *The Holy Land: An Oxford Archaeological Guide from Earliest Times to 1700*, 4th ed. (Oxford: Oxford University Press, 1998), 316; Gold and Schoville, "Lachish," 58. [17] Gold and Schoville, "Lachish," 58; Williamson, "Lachish," 638. [18] Gold and Schoville, "Lachish," 58; Murphy-O'Connor, *Holy Land*, 316.

Sling stones found at Lachish. Sling stones, uniformly carved from flint, could be aimed with deadly accuracy (see Jdg 20:16; 1Sm 25:29; 2Ch 26:14).

Rising in the distance is ancient Lachish, which was the last fortress to fall before Jerusalem fell to the Babylonians in 586 BC. The citadel sat atop the hill, in the center.

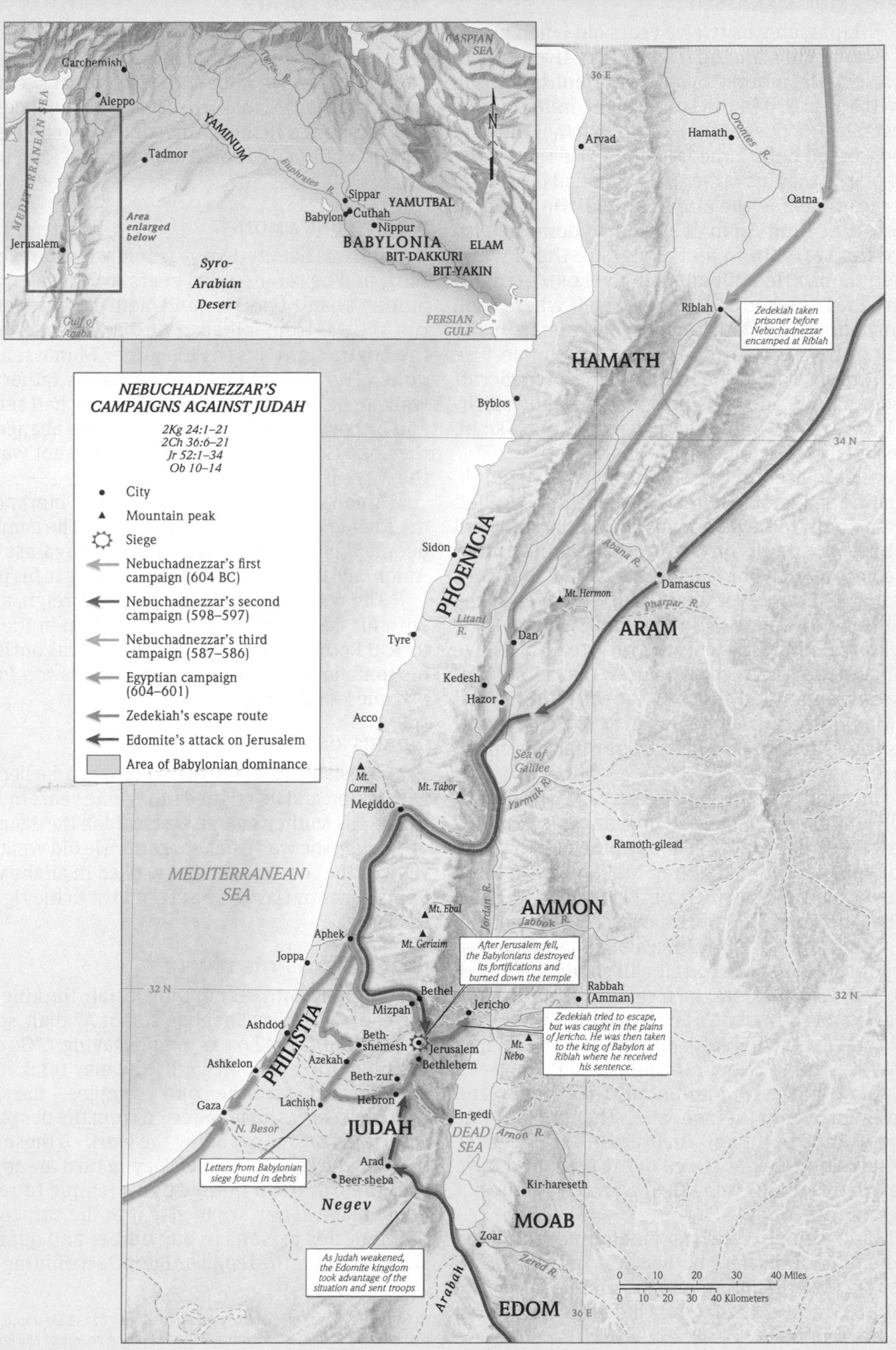
NEBUCHADNEZZAR'S CAMPAIGNS AGAINST JUDAH
2Kg 24:1–21
2Ch 36:6–21
Jr 52:1–34
Ob 10–14
City
Mountain peak
Siege
Nebuchadnezzar's first campaign (604 BC)
Nebuchadnezzar's second campaign (598–597)
Nebuchadnezzar's third campaign (587–586)
Egyptian campaign (604–601)
Zedekiah's escape route
Edomite's attack on Jerusalem
Area of Babylonian dominance
Carchemish
Aleppo
Tadmor
MEDITERRANEAN SEA
YAMINUM
Tigris R.
Euphrates R.
CASPIAN SEA
Sippar
Babylon
Cuthah
Nippur
YAMUTBAL
BABYLONIA
ELAM
BIT-DAKKURI
BIT-YAKIN
Jerusalem
Area enlarged below
Syro-Arabian Desert
Gulf of Aqaba
PERSIAN GULF
N
Arvad
Hamath
Orontes R.
Qatna
36 E
Riblah
Zedekiah taken prisoner before Nebuchadnezzar encamped at Riblah
HAMATH
Byblos
34 N
PHOENICIA
Sidon
Abana R.
Damascus
Mt. Hermon
Pharpar R.
Litani R.
Tyre
Dan
ARAM
Kedesh
Hazor
Acco
Sea of Galilee
Mt. Carmel
Mt. Tabor
Yarmuk R.
Megiddo
Ramoth-gilead
MEDITERRANEAN SEA
Jordan R.
AMMON
Mt. Ebal
Jabbok R.
Aphek
Mt. Gerizim
After Jerusalem fell, the Babylonians destroyed its fortifications and burned down the temple
Joppa
32 N
Bethel
Rabbah (Amman)
Mizpah
Jericho
Ashdod
Zedekiah tried to escape, but was caught in the plains of Jericho. He was then taken to the king of Babylon at Riblah where he received his sentence.
PHILISTIA
Beth-shemesh
Jerusalem
Mt. Nebo
Azekah
Ashkelon
Bethlehem
Beth-zur
Lachish
Hebron
Gaza
En-gedi
N. Besor
JUDAH
DEAD SEA
Arnon R.
Arad
Letters from Babylonian siege found in debris
Beer-sheba
Kir-hareseth
Negev
MOAB
Zoar
As Judah weakened, the Edomite kingdom took advantage of the situation and sent troops
Zered R.
Arabah
EDOM
0 10 20 30 40 Miles
0 10 20 30 40 Kilometers

JUDAH'S KING MANASSEH

21 Manasseh was twelve years old when he became king, and he reigned fifty-five years in Jerusalem. His mother's name was Hephzibah. 2 He did what was evil in the LORD's sight, imitating the detestable practices of the nations that the LORD had dispossessed before the Israelites. 3 He rebuilt the high places that his father Hezekiah had destroyed and reestablished the altars for Baal. He made an Asherah, as King Ahab of Israel had done; he also bowed in worship to all the stars in the sky and served them. 4 He built altars in the LORD's temple, where the LORD had said, "Jerusalem is where I will put my name." 5 He built altars to all the stars in the sky in both courtyards of the LORD's temple. 6 He sacrificed his son in the fire,[A] practiced witchcraft and divination, and consulted mediums and spiritists. He did a huge amount of evil in the LORD's sight, angering him.

7 Manasseh set up the carved image of Asherah, which he made, in the temple that the LORD had spoken about to David and his son Solomon: "I will establish my name forever in this temple and in Jerusalem, which I have chosen out of all the tribes of Israel. 8 I will never again cause the feet of the Israelites to wander from the land I gave to their ancestors if only they will be careful to do all I have commanded them — the whole law that my servant Moses commanded them." 9 But they did not listen; Manasseh caused them to stray so that they did worse evil than the nations the LORD had destroyed before the Israelites.

10 The LORD said through his servants the prophets, 11 "Since King Manasseh of Judah has committed all these detestable acts — worse evil than the Amorites who preceded him had done — and by means of his idols has also caused Judah to sin, 12 this is what the LORD God of Israel says: 'I am about to bring such a disaster on Jerusalem and Judah that everyone who hears about it will shudder.[B] 13 I will stretch over Jerusalem the measuring line used on Samaria and the mason's level used on the house of Ahab, and I will wipe Jerusalem clean as one wipes a bowl — wiping it and turning it upside down. 14 I will abandon the remnant of my inheritance and hand them over to their enemies. They will become plunder and spoil to all their enemies, 15 because they have done what is evil in my sight and have angered me from the day their ancestors came out of Egypt until today.' "

16 Manasseh also shed so much innocent blood that he filled Jerusalem with it from one end to another. This was in addition to his sin that he caused Judah to commit, so that they did what was evil in the LORD's sight.

MANASSEH'S DEATH

17 The rest of the events of Manasseh's reign, along with all his accomplishments and the sin that he committed, are written in the Historical Record of Judah's Kings. 18 Manasseh rested with his ancestors and was buried in the garden of his own house, the garden of Uzza. His son Amon became king in his place.

JUDAH'S KING AMON

19 Amon was twenty-two years old when he became king, and he reigned two years in Jerusalem. His mother's name was Meshullemeth daughter of Haruz; she was from Jotbah. 20 He did what was evil in the LORD's sight, just as his father Manasseh had done. 21 He walked in all the ways his father had walked; he served the idols his father had served, and he bowed in worship to them. 22 He abandoned the LORD God of his ancestors and did not walk in the ways of the LORD.

23 Amon's servants conspired against him and put the king to death in his own house. 24 The common people[C] killed all who had conspired against King Amon, and they made his son Josiah king in his place.

25 The rest of the events of Amon's reign, along with his accomplishments, are written in the Historical Record of Judah's Kings. 26 He was buried in his tomb in the garden of Uzza, and his son Josiah became king in his place.

JUDAH'S KING JOSIAH

22 Josiah was eight years old when he became king, and he reigned thirty-one years in Jerusalem. His mother's name was Jedidah the daughter of Adaiah; she was from Bozkath. 2 He did what was right in the LORD's sight and walked in all the ways of his ancestor David; he did not turn to the right or the left.

JOSIAH REPAIRS THE TEMPLE

3 In the eighteenth year of King Josiah, the king sent the court secretary Shaphan son of Azaliah, son of Meshullam, to the LORD's temple, saying, 4 "Go up to the high priest Hilkiah so that he may total up the silver brought into the LORD's temple — the silver the doorkeepers have collected from the people. 5 It is to be given to those doing the work — those who oversee the LORD's temple. They in turn are to give it to the workmen in the LORD's temple to repair the damage. 6 They are to give it to the carpenters, builders, and masons to buy timber and quarried stone to repair the temple. 7 But no accounting is to

[A] **21:6** Lit *He made his son pass through the fire* [B] **21:12** Lit *about it, his two ears will tingle*; Hb obscure [C] **21:24** Lit *The people of the land*

be required from them for the silver given to them
since they work with integrity."

THE BOOK OF THE LAW FOUND

8 The high priest Hilkiah told the court secretary
Shaphan, "I have found the book of the law in the
LORD's temple," and he gave the book to Shaphan,
who read it.
9 Then the court secretary Shaphan went to the
king and reported,[A] "Your servants have emptied out
the silver that was found in the temple and have giv-
en it to those doing the work — those who oversee
the LORD's temple." 10 Then the court secretary Shaphan told the king, "The priest Hilkiah has given me
a book," and Shaphan read it in the presence of the
king.
11 When the king heard the words of the book of
the law, he tore his clothes. 12 Then he commanded
the priest Hilkiah, Ahikam son of Shaphan, Achbor
son of Micaiah, the court secretary Shaphan, and the
king's servant Asaiah, 13 "Go and inquire of the LORD
for me, for the people, and for all Judah about the
words in this book that has been found. For great is
the LORD's wrath that is kindled against us because
our ancestors have not obeyed the words of this book
in order to do everything written about us."

HULDAH'S PROPHECY OF JUDGMENT

14 So the priest Hilkiah, Ahikam, Achbor, Shaphan,
and Asaiah went to the prophetess Huldah, wife of
Shallum son of Tikvah, son of Harhas, keeper of the
wardrobe. She lived in Jerusalem in the Second District. They spoke with her.
15 She said to them, "This is what the LORD God
of Israel says: Say to the man who sent you to me,
16 'This is what the LORD says: I am about to bring disaster on this place and on its inhabitants, fulfilling[B]
all the words of the book that the king of Judah has
read, 17 because they have abandoned me and burned
incense to other gods in order to anger me with all
the work of their hands. My wrath will be kindled
against this place, and it will not be quenched.' 18 Say
this to the king of Judah who sent you to inquire of
the LORD: 'This is what the LORD God of Israel says: As
for the words that you heard, 19 because your heart
was tender and you humbled yourself before the
LORD when you heard what I spoke against this place
and against its inhabitants, that they would become
a desolation and a curse, and because you have torn
your clothes and wept before me, I myself have heard'
— this is the LORD's declaration. 20 'Therefore, I will
indeed gather you to your ancestors, and you will be
gathered to your grave in peace. Your eyes will not
see all the disaster that I am bringing on this place.' "
Then they reported[C] to the king.

COVENANT RENEWAL

23 So the king sent messengers, and they gathered
all the elders of Judah and Jerusalem to him.
2 Then the king went to the LORD's temple with all the
men of Judah and all the inhabitants of Jerusalem, as
well as the priests and the prophets — all the people from the youngest to the oldest. He read in their
hearing all the words of the book of the covenant
that had been found in the LORD's temple. 3 Next, the
king stood by the pillar[D] and made a covenant in the
LORD's presence to follow the LORD and to keep his
commands, his decrees, and his statutes with all his
heart and with all his soul in order to carry out the
words of this covenant that were written in this book;
all the people agreed to[E] the covenant.

JOSIAH'S REFORMS

4 Then the king commanded the high priest Hilkiah
and the priests of the second rank and the doorkeepers to bring out of the LORD's sanctuary all the
articles made for Baal, Asherah, and all the stars in
the sky. He burned them outside Jerusalem in the
fields of the Kidron and carried their ashes to Bethel. 5 Then he did away with the idolatrous priests the
kings of Judah had appointed to burn incense at the
high places in the cities of Judah and in the areas
surrounding Jerusalem. They had burned incense
to Baal, and to the sun, moon, constellations, and
all the stars in the sky. 6 He brought out the Asherah
pole from the LORD's temple to the Kidron Valley
outside Jerusalem. He burned it at the Kidron Valley,
beat it to dust, and threw its dust on the graves of the
common people.[F] 7 He also tore down the houses of
the male cult prostitutes that were in the LORD's temple, in which the women were weaving tapestries[G]
for Asherah.
8 Then Josiah brought all the priests from the cities of Judah, and he defiled the high places from
Geba to Beer-sheba, where the priests had burned
incense. He tore down the high places of the city
gates at the entrance of the gate of Joshua the governor of the city (on the left at the city gate). 9 The
priests of the high places, however, did not come
up to the altar of the LORD in Jerusalem; instead,
they ate unleavened bread with their fellow priests.
10 He defiled Topheth, which is in Ben Hinnom Valley, so that no one could sacrifice his son or daughter
in the fire[H] to Molech. 11 He did away with the horses that the kings of Judah had dedicated to the sun.
They had been at the entrance of the LORD's temple

[A] **22:9** Lit *and returned a word to the king and said* [B] **22:16** *fulfilling* supplied for clarity [C] **22:20** Lit *returned a word* [D] **23:3** 2Ch 34:31 reads *platform* [E] **23:3** Lit *people took a stand in* [F] **23:6** Lit *the sons of the people* [G] **23:7** Or *clothing* [H] **23:10** Lit *could make his son or daughter pass through the fire*

DIGGING DEEPER *Babylonian Chronicles*

The Babylonian Chronicles are an assortment of cuneiform tablets that describe important events transpiring between the eighth and third centuries BC. One particular chronicle covers the period between 605 and 594 BC, recording the military exploits of Babylonian King Nebuchadnezzar II (605–562 BC) and his invasion of Jerusalem (2Kg 23). It recounts how in 605 BC Nebuchadnezzar was crowned king after the death of his father, Nabopolassar. The Chronicles say that by 599 BC Nebuchadnezzar's army advanced to Syria, continued westward to Judea, arriving there in March 597 BC. Once there, he invaded Jerusalem, took captive King Jehoiachin (609–597 BC), and crowned his replacement King Zedekiah (597–586 BC; 2Kg 24:10–20). Robert Koldeway discovered supporting evidence for these events in the Babylonian ration records (595 BC), for they document the amount of food rations given to Jehoiachin and his royal family while in captivity (2Kgs 24:8–16). Additionally, hastily inscribed shards known as the Lachish letters record Israel's desperate pleas in the hours immediately before Babylonian forces overwhelmed Israel's military outposts some twenty-five miles outside Jerusalem. These strong archaeological evidences support the biblical record describing Jerusalem's final days under siege by Nebuchadnezzar.

in the precincts by the chamber of Nathan-melech,
the eunuch. He also burned the chariots of the sun.
12 The king tore down the altars that the kings of
Judah had made on the roof of Ahaz's upper chamber.
He also tore down the altars that Manasseh had made
in the two courtyards of the LORD's temple. Then he
smashed them[A] there and threw their dust into the
Kidron Valley. 13 The king also defiled the high places that were across from Jerusalem, to the south of
the Mount of Destruction, which King Solomon of
Israel had built for Ashtoreth, the abhorrent idol
of the Sidonians; for Chemosh, the abhorrent idol
of Moab; and for Milcom, the detestable idol of the
Ammonites. 14 He broke the sacred pillars into pieces,
cut down the Asherah poles, then filled their places
with human bones.
15 He even tore down the altar at Bethel and the
high place that had been made by Jeroboam son of
Nebat, who caused Israel to sin. He burned the high
place, crushed it to dust, and burned the Asherah.
16 As Josiah turned, he saw the tombs there on the
mountain. He sent someone to take the bones out of
the tombs, and he burned them on the altar. He defiled
it according to the word of the LORD proclaimed by
the man of God[B] who proclaimed these things. 17 Then
he said, "What is this monument I see?"
The men of the city told him, "It is the tomb of the
man of God who came from Judah and proclaimed
these things that you have done to the altar at Bethel."
18 So he said, "Let him rest. Don't let anyone disturb
his bones." So they left his bones undisturbed with
the bones of the prophet who came from Samaria.
19 Josiah also removed all the shrines of the high
places that were in the cities of Samaria, which the
kings of Israel had made to anger the LORD. Josiah did
the same things to them that he had done at Bethel.
20 He slaughtered on the altars all the priests of those
high places, and he burned human bones on the altars. Then he returned to Jerusalem.

PASSOVER OBSERVED

21 The king commanded all the people, "Observe the
Passover of the LORD your God as written in the book
of the covenant." 22 No such Passover had ever been
observed from the time of the judges who judged
Israel through the entire time of the kings of Israel
and Judah. 23 But in the eighteenth year of King Josiah, the LORD's Passover was observed in Jerusalem.

FURTHER ZEAL FOR THE LORD

24 In addition, Josiah eradicated the mediums, the
spiritists, household idols, images, and all the abhorrent things that were seen in the land of Judah and
in Jerusalem. He did this in order to carry out the
words of the law that were written in the book that
the priest Hilkiah found in the LORD's temple. 25 Before him there was no king like him who turned to
the LORD with all his heart and with all his soul and
with all his strength according to all the law of Moses,
and no one like him arose after him.
26 In spite of all that, the LORD did not turn from
the fury of his intense burning anger, which burned
against Judah because of all the affronts with which
Manasseh had angered him. 27 For the LORD had said,
"I will also remove Judah from my presence just as I
have removed Israel. I will reject this city Jerusalem,
that I have chosen, and the temple about which I said,
'My name will be there.'"

JOSIAH'S DEATH

28 The rest of the events of Josiah's reign, along with
all his accomplishments, are written in the Historical
Record of Judah's Kings. 29 During his reign, Pharaoh

[A] **23:12** Text emended; MT reads *he ran from* [B] **23:16** LXX adds *when Jeroboam stood by the altar of the feast. And he turned and raised his eyes to the tomb of the man of God*

The Woman Huldah, drawn from "Prophetesses in Ancient Israel" *by Sharon Roberts*

Model of Herod's Temple in Jerusalem as it appeared in Jesus's day. At the bottom left of the picture is a porch with steps and two sets of double doors known as the Huldah Gates.

In ancient Israel, a wife addressed her husband as *baal* (master) or *adon* (lord) (e.g., Gn 18:12; Jdg 19:26; Am 4:1). This form of address was comparable to that used by a slave to his master. The wife held the status of a minor and, according to the Decalogue (Ex 20:17; Dt 5:21), was listed as one of her husband's possessions. She could not inherit from her husband, nor could a daughter from her father unless there were no male heirs. For a woman's vow to be valid, it had to be witnessed and accepted by a male relative (Nm 30). Whereas the husband could repudiate the wife, she could not initiate divorce. Also, the heavy household duties fell to her: tending flocks, cooking meals, spinning cloth, working the fields.

Despite these conditions, Israelite women were granted a certain level of consideration. They fared better than their counterparts in Assyria, who were treated as beasts of burden, but their lot was slightly worse than that of Babylonian and Egyptian women. Whereas an Israelite could sell his daughters and his slaves, he could not sell his wife. He could divorce her, but the letter of repudiation restored her freedom. The wife also retained part ownership of the *mohar* (money paid by the fiancé to the bride's father) and the dowry received from her parents. A woman's work in the household earned respect from the other family members. This respect increased with the birth of the first child, especially if the child was a boy. Children were expected to obey and revere their mother.

Sometimes, in unusual circumstances, women became influential in religious and political life. Biblical writers referred to Miriam, Deborah, Huldah, and Noadiah, each of whom fulfilled the prophetic role in ancient Israel. The only prophetess to be mentioned during the period of the monarchy was Huldah (2Kg 22:14–20; 2Ch 34:22–28). Josiah, after discovering the book of the law in the temple, sent his advisers to her. Their inquiries were met with an immediate answer: the nation would be judged for its disobedience of God. The fulfillment of this prophecy was postponed, however, due to the nationwide revival initiated by Josiah.

As the wife of Shallum, the king's wardrobe keeper, Huldah was automatically placed in close proximity to the king. His high opinion of her is evidenced by his immediate response. She was a contemporary of Jeremiah, and the two may even have been related. Huldah headed an academy in Jerusalem (2Kg 22:14) and, according to the Talmud (Middot 1:3), the temple's Huldah Gate formerly led to the schoolhouse. ✣

Neco king of Egypt marched up to help the king of
Assyria at the Euphrates River. King Josiah went to
confront him, and at Megiddo when Neco saw him he
killed him. 30 From Megiddo his servants carried his
dead body in a chariot, brought him into Jerusalem,
and buried him in his own tomb. Then the common
people[A] took Jehoahaz son of Josiah, anointed him,
and made him king in place of his father.

JUDAH'S KING JEHOAHAZ

31 Jehoahaz was twenty-three years old when he became king, and he reigned three months in Jerusalem.
His mother's name was Hamutal daughter of Jeremiah; she was from Libnah. 32 He did what was evil in the
LORD's sight just as his ancestors had done. 33 Pharaoh
Neco imprisoned him at Riblah in the land of Hamath to keep him from reigning in Jerusalem, and he
imposed on the land a fine of seventy-five hundred
pounds[B] of silver and seventy-five pounds[C] of gold.

JUDAH'S KING JEHOIAKIM

34 Then Pharaoh Neco made Eliakim son of Josiah
king in place of his father Josiah and changed Eliakim's name to Jehoiakim. But Neco took Jehoahaz and
went to Egypt, and he died there. 35 So Jehoiakim gave
the silver and the gold to Pharaoh, but at Pharaoh's
command he taxed the land to give it. He exacted the
silver and the gold from the common people, each according to his assessment, to give it to Pharaoh Neco.

36 Jehoiakim was twenty-five years old when he
became king, and he reigned eleven years in Jerusalem. His mother's name was Zebidah daughter of
Pedaiah; she was from Rumah. 37 He did what was
evil in the LORD's sight just as his ancestors had done.

JEHOIAKIM'S REBELLION AND DEATH

24 During Jehoiakim's reign, King Nebuchadnezzar of Babylon attacked. Jehoiakim became
his vassal for three years, and then he turned and
rebelled against him. 2 The LORD sent Chaldean, Aramean, Moabite, and Ammonite raiders against Jehoiakim. He sent them against Judah to destroy it,
according to the word of the LORD he had spoken
through his servants the prophets. 3 Indeed, this happened to Judah at the LORD's command to remove
them from his presence. It was because of the sins
of Manasseh, according to all he had done, 4 and also
because of all the innocent blood he had shed. He had
filled Jerusalem with innocent blood, and the LORD
was not willing to forgive.

5 The rest of the events of Jehoiakim's reign, along
with all his accomplishments, are written in the Historical Record of Judah's Kings. 6 Jehoiakim rested
with his ancestors, and his son Jehoiachin became
king in his place.

7 Now the king of Egypt did not march out of his
land again, for the king of Babylon took everything
that had belonged to the king of Egypt, from the
Brook of Egypt to the Euphrates River.

JUDAH'S KING JEHOIACHIN

8 Jehoiachin was eighteen years old when he became
king, and he reigned three months in Jerusalem. His
mother's name was Nehushta daughter of Elnathan;
she was from Jerusalem. 9 He did what was evil in the
LORD's sight just as his father had done.

DEPORTATIONS TO BABYLON

10 At that time the servants of King Nebuchadnezzar
of Babylon marched up to Jerusalem, and the city
came under siege. 11 King Nebuchadnezzar of Babylon
came to the city while his servants were besieging
it. 12 King Jehoiachin of Judah, along with his mother, his servants, his commanders, and his officials,[D]
surrendered to the king of Babylon.

So the king of Babylon took him captive in the
eighth year of his reign. 13 He also carried off from
there all the treasures of the LORD's temple and the
treasures of the king's palace, and he cut into pieces
all the gold articles that King Solomon of Israel had
made for the LORD's sanctuary, just as the LORD had
predicted. 14 He deported all Jerusalem and all the
commanders and all the best soldiers — ten thousand captives including all the craftsmen and metalsmiths. Except for the poorest people of the land,
no one remained.

15 Nebuchadnezzar deported Jehoiachin to Babylon. He took the king's mother, the king's wives, his
officials, and the leading men of the land into exile
from Jerusalem to Babylon. 16 The king of Babylon
brought captive into Babylon all seven thousand
of the best soldiers and one thousand craftsmen
and metalsmiths — all strong and fit for war. 17 And
the king of Babylon made Mattaniah, Jehoiachin's[E]
uncle, king in his place and changed his name to
Zedekiah.

JUDAH'S KING ZEDEKIAH

18 Zedekiah was twenty-one years old when he became king, and he reigned eleven years in Jerusalem.
His mother's name was Hamutal daughter of Jeremiah; she was from Libnah. 19 Zedekiah did what was
evil in the LORD's sight just as Jehoiakim had done.
20 Because of the LORD's anger, it came to the point in
Jerusalem and Judah that he finally banished them
from his presence. Then Zedekiah rebelled against
the king of Babylon.

[A] **23:30** Lit *the people of the land*, also in v. 35 [B] **23:33** Lit *100 talents*
[C] **23:33** Lit *one talent* [D] **24:12** Or *eunuchs* [E] **24:17** Lit *his*

Scene depicting the fall of Lachish; this decorated the walls of Nineveh's South-West Palace. The scene depicts siege engines ascending a man-made ramp. The battering ram is ramming against the tower at the city gate.

CONDITIONS BEFORE THE FALL

The Chaldeans were a people group who migrated into southeastern Mesopotamia between 1000 and 900 BC. Over time, they gained control of the region of Babylonia. People began to refer to them both as Chaldeans and Babylonians. The Chaldeans continued to grow in power, so that by the eighth century BC they were the chief rivals of the Assyrians,

Wall panel showing Sargon II (left) receiving a high official, probably his son and thus the next king of Assyria, Sennacherib.

The Babylonian Chronicles cover the years 605–595 BC. They begin by telling the story of the battle of Carchemish, when Nebuchadnezzar finally routed the Egyptian forces in Syria, and record the extension of Babylonian power to the Mediterranean. They record Ashkelon being captured in 604 and Babylon's first capture of Jerusalem in 598 BC.

the then-dominant world power. During Assyria's dominance, the Chaldeans served as allies of Judah against the Assyrians. With the fall of the Assyrians and the rise of the Neo-Babylonian Empire, however, Judah came under the rule of the Chaldeans, becoming a vassal state in 604–603 BC.[1]

When the Babylonians suffered defeat at the Egyptian border in 601 BC, Judah under King Jehoiakim revolted. Judah's independence, though, was short lived; in 598 the Babylonians under Nebuchadnezzar besieged Jerusalem. The Babylonians deported King Jehoiachin (Jehoiakim's son), the royal family, and ten thousand citizens.

Nebuchadnezzar placed Zedekiah (Jehoiachin's uncle) on the throne of Judah. Expecting Egyptian support, Zedekiah rebelled. Nebuchadnezzar swiftly responded, conquering Judah's fortress-cities and besieging Jerusalem. The Babylonians captured Jerusalem in 586 BC, burned the city, and destroyed the temple.

THE BABYLONIAN STRATEGY

The primary means of capturing a city in biblical times was a siege. This involved surrounding the city with an army and cutting the city off from food, water, and other resources. If successful, this tactic typically led to the eventual surrender of the city to the attackers.

Armies used various methods to harass a besieged city. They built ramps around the city wall and placed mobile towers against the walls. The towers allowed attackers to shoot at the defenders or send projectiles, including torches, down into the city. Attackers would weaken the city's wall by setting fires at its base and/or digging tunnels under it. Ladders enabled attackers to scale the wall. Further, soldiers used battering rams to break through city gates.[2] Jeremiah records that the Jerusalem inhabitants defended their city in part by tearing down some of their houses in order to construct defenses against the siege works (Jr 33:4).

Nebuchadnezzar's forces penetrated the city only after they breached a spot in the walls. After breaching a city's wall, the conquering army typically pillaged and burned the city (2Kg 14:12–14; 25:9–11).[3]

CONDITIONS DURING THE FALL

Archaeological excavations in the area of Jerusalem now known as the Jewish Quarter uncovered four ancient latrines. At least one dates to the time of Nebuchadnezzar's destruction of the city in 586 BC. Analysis of the contents reveals that the inhabitants of the city had stopped eating their normal diet and instead were eating backyard plants; in other words, whatever they found growing wild inside the city.

Archaeological excavations have uncovered large stones scattered where the walls once stood and houses that had been reduced to charred ruins. Smashed pottery littered the area. Archaeologists also recovered arrowheads in the houses and at the northern sections of the city fortifications.

CONDITIONS AFTER THE FALL

The Babylonians punished peoples who continued to revolt by exiling them to distant areas of the kingdom. After destroying Jerusalem, Nebuchadnezzar deported a significant number of Judeans to Babylonia (2Kg 25:8–21). This was the third deportation. The first occurred in 605 BC, when Daniel and other nobles from Judah were taken into exile. The second deportation in 597 BC included King Jehoiachin, the royal family, seven thousand warriors, and one thousand metalsmiths and craftsmen (24:10–16). A fourth deportation occurred in 582 BC (Jr 52:30).

The Babylonians demolished Jerusalem and other major sites—but they did not totally destroy Judah. The Babylonians allowed some people to remain to work the land (Jr 52:16). The people who remained worshiped in the temple ruins. ✣

Foundation cylinder with the record of public works of Nebuchadnezzar II; dated 604–562 BC. The cylinder was found in the temple foundations in the ancient Sumerian city of Marad. The inscription mentions walls, water supply, towers, and temples, and contains his prayers for riches and a long reign.

[1] The paragraphs in this section are based on the article by Tony M. Martin, "Chaldea" in *HIBD*, 276. [2] "Siegeworks" in *HIBD*, 1500. [3] Victor Matthews, *The Cultural World of the Bible: An Illustrated Guide to Manners and Customs*, 4th ed. (Grand Rapids: Baker Academic, 2015), 162.

NEBUCHADNEZZAR'S SIEGE OF JERUSALEM

25 In the ninth year of Zedekiah's reign, on the tenth day of the tenth month, King Nebuchadnezzar of Babylon advanced against Jerusalem with his entire army. They laid siege to the city and built a siege wall against it all around. 2 The city was under siege until King Zedekiah's eleventh year.

3 By the ninth day of the fourth month the famine was so severe in the city that the common people had no food. 4 Then the city was broken into, and all the warriors fled at night by way of the city gate between the two walls near the king's garden, even though the Chaldeans surrounded the city. As the king made his way along the route to the Arabah, 5 the Chaldean army pursued him and overtook him in the plains of Jericho. Zedekiah's entire army left him and scattered. 6 The Chaldeans seized the king and brought him up to the king of Babylon at Riblah, and they passed sentence on him. 7 They slaughtered Zedekiah's sons before his eyes. Finally, the king of Babylon blinded Zedekiah, bound him in bronze chains, and took him to Babylon.

JERUSALEM DESTROYED

8 On the seventh day of the fifth month — which was the nineteenth year of King Nebuchadnezzar of Babylon — Nebuzaradan, the captain of the guards, a servant of the king of Babylon, entered Jerusalem. 9 He burned the LORD's temple, the king's palace, and all the houses of Jerusalem; he burned down all the great houses. 10 The whole Chaldean army with the captain of the guards tore down the walls surrounding Jerusalem. 11 Nebuzaradan, the captain of the guards, deported the rest of the people who remained in the city, the deserters who had defected to the king of Babylon, and the rest of the population. 12 But the captain of the guards left some of the poorest of the land to be vinedressers and farmers.

13 Now the Chaldeans broke into pieces the bronze pillars of the LORD's temple, the water carts, and the bronze basin,[A] which were in the LORD's temple, and carried the bronze to Babylon. 14 They also took the pots, shovels, wick trimmers, dishes, and all the bronze articles used in the priests' service. 15 The captain of the guards took away the firepans and sprinkling basins — whatever was gold or silver.

16 As for the two pillars, the one basin, and the water carts that Solomon had made for the LORD's temple, the weight of the bronze of all these articles was beyond measure. 17 One pillar was twenty-seven feet[B] tall and had a bronze capital on top of it. The capital, encircled by a grating and pomegranates of bronze, stood five feet[C] high. The second pillar was the same, with its own grating.

18 The captain of the guards also took away Seraiah the chief priest, Zephaniah the priest of the second rank, and the three doorkeepers. 19 From the city he took a court official[D] who had been appointed over the warriors; five trusted royal aides[E] found in the city; the secretary of the commander of the army, who enlisted the people of the land for military duty; and sixty men from the common people[F] who were found within the city. 20 Nebuzaradan, the captain of the guards, took them and brought them to the king of Babylon at Riblah. 21 The king of Babylon put them to death at Riblah in the land of Hamath. So Judah went into exile from its land.

GEDALIAH MADE GOVERNOR

22 King Nebuchadnezzar of Babylon appointed Gedaliah son of Ahikam, son of Shaphan, over the rest of the people he left in the land of Judah. 23 When all the commanders of the armies — they and their men — heard that the king of Babylon had appointed Gedaliah, they came to Gedaliah at Mizpah. The commanders included Ishmael son of Nethaniah, Johanan son of Kareah, Seraiah son of Tanhumeth the Netophathite, and Jaazaniah son of the Maacathite — they and their men. 24 Gedaliah swore an oath to them and their men, assuring them, "Don't be afraid of the servants of the Chaldeans. Live in the land and serve the king of Babylon, and it will go well for you."

25 In the seventh month, however, Ishmael son of Nethaniah, son of Elishama, of the royal family, came with ten men and struck down Gedaliah, and he died. Also, they killed the Judeans and the Chaldeans who were with him at Mizpah. 26 Then all the people, from the youngest to the oldest, and the commanders of the army, left and went to Egypt, for they were afraid of the Chaldeans.

JEHOIACHIN PARDONED

27 On the twenty-seventh day of the twelfth month of the thirty-seventh year of the exile of Judah's King Jehoiachin, in the year Evil-merodach became king of Babylon, he pardoned King Jehoiachin of Judah and released him[G] from prison. 28 He spoke kindly to him and set his throne over the thrones of the kings who were with him in Babylon. 29 So Jehoiachin changed his prison clothes, and he dined regularly in the presence of the king of Babylon for the rest of his life. 30 As for his allowance, a regular allowance was given to him by the king, a portion for each day, for the rest of his life.

[A] **25:13** Lit *sea* [B] **25:17** Lit *18 cubits* [C] **25:17** Lit *three cubits*
[D] **25:19** Or *eunuch* [E] **25:19** Lit *five men who look on the king's face*
[F] **25:19** Lit *the people of the land* [G] **25:27** *and released him* supplied for clarity

1 CHRONICLES

Relief showing Tiglath-pileser III of Assyria from the Central Palace of Nimrud.

INTRODUCTION TO

1 CHRONICLES

Circumstances of Writing

An ancient tradition ascribes the authorship of Chronicles to Ezra. The author must have lived sometime after the return of the Jews to Israel from the Babylonian exile. He also had a strong interest in the reimplementation of the law and the temple, and he must have had access to historical records. All of these criteria suit Ezra, and this identification is corroborated by the fact that the last verses of Chronicles are the first verses of the book of Ezra. However, since the book does not explicitly claim Ezra for its author, in these notes we will refer to him simply as the Chronicler.

The books of 1 and 2 Chronicles include extensive genealogies from the time of Adam and take the reader up to the period of the nation's exile and restoration. First Chronicles gives us the genealogies and focuses on the reign of King David. Second Chronicles focuses on all the kings who followed David up to the exile and restoration. It covers the same time period as 1 and 2 Kings, but 2 Chronicles focuses exclusively on the kings of Judah. The content of the books necessitates that they were written sometime after the return from the exile, perhaps the middle of the fifth century BC.

Contribution to the Bible

Chronicles brings together many dimensions of biblical revelation, such as historical events (as recounted in Genesis through Kings), temple ritual (as prescribed in Leviticus), sin and judgment (as preached by the prophets), and even some psalms. Because a recurring theme is that God will always accept people who return to him no matter how wicked they may have been, it has been called, perhaps a little whimsically, "The Gospel According to Ezra." The books of 1 and 2 Chronicles give us the big picture of Old Testament history, capturing the Davidic covenant in light of Israel's history back to Adam and pointing to the eternal continuation of that covenant through the reign of the Messiah.

Structure

The Hebrew Bible divides its books into three categories: the Law, the Prophets, and the Writings. In this arrangement, the books of Samuel and Kings are counted among the Prophets, whereas Chronicles belongs to the Writings. This classification may be partially due to the fact that Chronicles repeats information, such as the genealogies of Genesis and the histories of the kings of Judah from the books of Samuel and Kings. Still the Chronicler uses this repeated content to support his own point, and he also adds a lot of information that we find in Chronicles alone. He limits his discussion of the various kings almost entirely to those of Judah, the southern kingdom.

FROM ADAM TO ABRAHAM

1 Adam, Seth, Enosh,
2 Kenan, Mahalalel, Jared,
3 Enoch, Methuselah, Lamech,
4 Noah, Noah's sons:[A]
Shem, Ham, and Japheth.

5 Japheth's sons: Gomer, Magog, Madai, Javan,
Tubal, Meshech, and Tiras.
6 Gomer's sons: Ashkenaz, Riphath,[B] and Togarmah.
7 Javan's sons: Elishah, Tarshish, Kittim, and
Rodanim.[C]

8 Ham's sons: Cush, Mizraim,[D] Put, and Canaan.
9 Cush's sons: Seba, Havilah, Sabta, Raama, and
Sabteca.
Raama's sons: Sheba and Dedan.
10 Cush fathered Nimrod, who was the first to
become a great warrior on earth.
11 Mizraim fathered the people of Lud, Anam,
Lehab, Naphtuh, 12 Pathrus, Casluh (the
Philistines came from them), and Caphtor.
13 Canaan fathered Sidon as his firstborn and
Heth, 14 as well as the Jebusites, Amorites,
Girgashites, 15 Hivites, Arkites, Sinites,
16 Arvadites, Zemarites, and Hamathites.

17 Shem's sons: Elam, Asshur, Arpachshad, Lud,
Aram, Uz, Hul, Gether, and Meshech.
18 Arpachshad fathered Shelah, and Shelah
fathered Eber. 19 Two sons were born to Eber. One
of them was named Peleg[E] because the earth was
divided during his lifetime, and the name of his
brother was Joktan. 20 Joktan fathered Almodad,
Sheleph, Hazarmaveth, Jerah, 21 Hadoram, Uzal,
Diklah, 22 Ebal, Abimael, Sheba, 23 Ophir, Havilah,
and Jobab. All of these were Joktan's sons.

24 Shem, Arpachshad, Shelah,
25 Eber, Peleg, Reu,
26 Serug, Nahor, Terah,
27 and Abram (that is, Abraham).

ABRAHAM'S DESCENDANTS

28 Abraham's sons: Isaac and Ishmael.

29 These are their family records: Nebaioth,
Ishmael's firstborn, Kedar, Adbeel, Mibsam,
30 Mishma, Dumah, Massa, Hadad, Tema, 31 Jetur,
Naphish, and Kedemah.
These were Ishmael's sons.

32 The sons born to Keturah, Abraham's
concubine: Zimran, Jokshan, Medan, Midian,
Ishbak, and Shuah.
Jokshan's sons: Sheba and Dedan.
33 Midian's sons: Ephah, Epher, Hanoch, Abida,
and Eldaah.
All of these were Keturah's descendants.

34 Abraham fathered Isaac.
Isaac's sons: Esau and Israel.
35 Esau's sons: Eliphaz, Reuel, Jeush, Jalam, and
Korah.
36 Eliphaz's sons: Teman, Omar, Zephi, Gatam,
and Kenaz; and by Timna, Amalek.[F]
37 Reuel's sons: Nahath, Zerah, Shammah, and
Mizzah.

THE EDOMITES

38 Seir's sons: Lotan, Shobal, Zibeon, Anah,
Dishon, Ezer, and Dishan.
39 Lotan's sons: Hori and Homam. Timna was
Lotan's sister.
40 Shobal's sons: Alian, Manahath, Ebal, Shephi,
and Onam.
Zibeon's sons: Aiah and Anah.
41 Anah's son: Dishon.
Dishon's sons: Hamran, Eshban, Ithran, and
Cheran.
42 Ezer's sons: Bilhan, Zaavan, and Jaakan.
Dishan's sons: Uz and Aran.

43 These were the kings who reigned in the land
of Edom
before any king reigned over the Israelites:
Bela son of Beor.
Bela's town was named Dinhabah.
44 When Bela died, Jobab son of Zerah
from Bozrah reigned in his place.
45 When Jobab died, Husham
from the land of the Temanites
reigned in his place.
46 When Husham died, Hadad son of Bedad,
who defeated Midian in the territory
of Moab, reigned in his place.
Hadad's town was named Avith.
47 When Hadad died, Samlah from Masrekah
reigned in his place.
48 When Samlah died, Shaul from Rehoboth
on the Euphrates River reigned
in his place.
49 When Shaul died, Baal-hanan son of Achbor
reigned in his place.
50 When Baal-hanan died, Hadad reigned
in his place.

[A] **1:4** LXX; MT omits *Noah's sons* [B] **1:6** Some Hb mss, LXX, Vg; other Hb mss read *Diphath*; Gn 10:3 [C] **1:7** Some Hb mss, Syr read *Dodanim*; Gn 10:4 [D] **1:8** = Egypt [E] **1:19** = Division [F] **1:36** LXX; MT reads *and Timna and Amalek*; Gn 36:12

Hadad's city was named Pai, and his wife's
name was Mehetabel
daughter of Matred, daughter of Me-zahab.
51 Then Hadad died.

Edom's chiefs: Timna, Alvah,[A] Jetheth,
52 Oholibamah, Elah, Pinon, 53 Kenaz, Teman,
Mibzar, 54 Magdiel, and Iram.
These were Edom's chiefs.

ISRAEL'S SONS

2 These were Israel's sons:
Reuben, Simeon, Levi,
Judah, Issachar, Zebulun,
2 Dan, Joseph, Benjamin,
Naphtali, Gad, and Asher.

JUDAH'S DESCENDANTS

3 Judah's sons: Er, Onan, and Shelah. These three were born to him by Bath-shua the Canaanite woman. Er, Judah's firstborn, was evil in the LORD's sight, so he put him to death. 4 Judah's daughter-in-law Tamar bore Perez and Zerah to him. Judah had five sons in all.

5 Perez's sons: Hezron and Hamul.
6 Zerah's sons: Zimri, Ethan, Heman, Calcol, and Dara[B] — five in all.
7 Carmi's son: Achar,[C] who brought trouble on Israel when he was unfaithful by taking the things set apart for destruction.
8 Ethan's son: Azariah.
9 Hezron's sons, who were born to him: Jerahmeel, Ram, and Chelubai.[D]

10 Ram fathered Amminadab, and Amminadab fathered Nahshon, a leader of Judah's descendants.
11 Nahshon fathered Salma, and Salma fathered Boaz.
12 Boaz fathered Obed, and Obed fathered Jesse.
13 Jesse fathered Eliab, his firstborn; Abinadab was born second, Shimea third, 14 Nethanel fourth, Raddai fifth, 15 Ozem sixth, and David seventh. 16 Their sisters were Zeruiah and Abigail. Zeruiah's three sons: Abishai, Joab, and Asahel. 17 Amasa's mother was Abigail, and his father was Jether the Ishmaelite.

18 Caleb son of Hezron had children by his wife Azubah and by Jerioth. These were Azubah's sons: Jesher, Shobab, and Ardon. 19 When Azubah died, Caleb married Ephrath, and she bore Hur to him. 20 Hur fathered Uri, and Uri fathered Bezalel. 21 After this, Hezron slept with the daughter of Machir the father of Gilead. Hezron had married her when he was sixty years old, and she bore Segub to him. 22 Segub fathered Jair, who possessed twenty-three towns in the land of Gilead. 23 But Geshur and Aram captured[E] Jair's Villages[F] along with Kenath and its surrounding villages — sixty towns. All these were the descendants of Machir father of Gilead. 24 After Hezron's death in Caleb-ephrathah, his wife Abijah bore[G] Ashhur to him. He was the father of Tekoa.

25 The sons of Jerahmeel, Hezron's firstborn: Ram, his firstborn, Bunah, Oren, Ozem, and Ahijah. 26 Jerahmeel had another wife named Atarah, who was the mother of Onam.
27 The sons of Ram, Jerahmeel's firstborn: Maaz, Jamin, and Eker.
28 Onam's sons: Shammai and Jada.
Shammai's sons: Nadab and Abishur. 29 Abishur's wife was named Abihail, who bore Ahban and Molid to him.
30 Nadab's sons: Seled and Appaim. Seled died without children.
31 Appaim's son: Ishi.
Ishi's son: Sheshan.
Sheshan's descendant: Ahlai.
32 The sons of Jada, brother of Shammai: Jether and Jonathan. Jether died without children.
33 Jonathan's sons: Peleth and Zaza. These were the descendants of Jerahmeel.
34 Sheshan had no sons, only daughters, but he did have an Egyptian servant whose name was Jarha. 35 Sheshan gave his daughter in marriage to his servant Jarha, and she bore Attai to him.

36 Attai fathered Nathan, and Nathan fathered Zabad.
37 Zabad fathered Ephlal, and Ephlal fathered Obed.
38 Obed fathered Jehu, and Jehu fathered Azariah.
39 Azariah fathered Helez, and Helez fathered Elasah.
40 Elasah fathered Sismai, and Sismai fathered Shallum.
41 Shallum fathered Jekamiah, and Jekamiah fathered Elishama.

42 The sons of Caleb brother of Jerahmeel: Mesha, his firstborn, fathered Ziph, and Mareshah, his second son,[H] fathered Hebron.

[A] **1:51** Alt Hb tradition reads *Aliah* [B] **2:6** Some Hb mss, LXX, Syr, Tg, Vg read *Darda*; 1Kg 4:31 [C] **2:7** = Trouble; Achan in Jos 7:1,16–26 [D] **2:9** = Caleb [E] **2:23** Lit *took from them* [F] **2:23** Or *captured Havvoth-jair* [G] **2:24** LXX, Vg read *death, Caleb slept with Ephrath (Hezron's wife was Abijah) and she bore* [H] **2:42** Lit *and the sons of Mareshah*

43 Hebron's sons: Korah, Tappuah, Rekem, and
Shema.
44 Shema fathered Raham, who fathered
Jorkeam, and Rekem fathered Shammai.
45 Shammai's son was Maon, and Maon fathered
Beth-zur.
46 Caleb's concubine Ephah was the mother of
Haran, Moza, and Gazez. Haran fathered Gazez.
47 Jahdai's sons: Regem, Jotham, Geshan, Pelet,
Ephah, and Shaaph.
48 Caleb's concubine Maacah was the mother of
Sheber and Tirhanah. 49 She was also the mother
of Shaaph, Madmannah's father, and of Sheva,
the father of Machbenah and Gibea. Caleb's
daughter was Achsah.
50 These were Caleb's descendants.

The sons of Hur, Ephrathah's firstborn:
Shobal fathered Kiriath-jearim;
51 Salma fathered Bethlehem,
and Hareph fathered Beth-gader.

52 These were the descendants of Shobal the
father of Kiriath-jearim: Haroeh, half of the Manahathites,[A] 53 and the families of Kiriath-jearim
— the Ithrites, Puthites, Shumathites, and Mish-
raites. The Zorathites and Eshtaolites descended
from these.

54 Salma's descendants: Bethlehem, the Netophathites, Atroth-beth-joab, and half of the
Manahathites, the Zorites, 55 and the families
of scribes who lived in Jabez — the Tirathites,
Shimeathites, and Sucathites. These are the Kenites who came from Hammath, the father of
Rechab's family.

DAVID'S DESCENDANTS

3 These were David's sons who were born to him
in Hebron:
Amnon was the firstborn, by Ahinoam of
Jezreel;
Daniel was born second, by Abigail of Carmel;
2 Absalom son of Maacah, daughter of King
Talmai of Geshur, was third;
Adonijah son of Haggith was fourth;
3 Shephatiah, by Abital, was fifth;
and Ithream, by David's wife Eglah, was sixth.
4 Six sons were born to David in Hebron, where
he reigned seven years and six months, and he
reigned in Jerusalem thirty-three years.
5 These sons were born to him in Jerusalem:
Shimea, Shobab, Nathan, and Solomon. These
four were born to him by Bath-shua daughter of
Ammiel.
6 David's other sons: Ibhar, Elishua,[B] Eliphelet,
7 Nogah, Nepheg, Japhia, 8 Elishama, Eliada, and
Eliphelet — nine sons.
9 These were all David's sons, with their sister
Tamar, in addition to the sons by his concubines.

JUDAH'S KINGS

10 Solomon's son was Rehoboam;
his son was Abijah, his son Asa,
his son Jehoshaphat, 11 his son Jehoram,[C,D]
his son Ahaziah, his son Joash,
12 his son Amaziah, his son Azariah,
his son Jotham, 13 his son Ahaz,
his son Hezekiah, his son Manasseh,
14 his son Amon, and his son Josiah.
15 Josiah's sons:
Johanan was the firstborn, Jehoiakim second,
Zedekiah third, and Shallum fourth.
16 Jehoiakim's sons:
his sons Jeconiah and Zedekiah.

DAVID'S LINE AFTER THE EXILE

17 The sons of Jeconiah the captive:
his sons Shealtiel, 18 Malchiram, Pedaiah,
Shenazzar, Jekamiah, Hoshama, and Nedabiah.
19 Pedaiah's sons: Zerubbabel and Shimei.
Zerubbabel's sons: Meshullam and Hananiah,
with their sister Shelomith; 20 and five others
— Hashubah, Ohel, Berechiah, Hasadiah, and
Jushab-hesed.
21 Hananiah's descendants: Pelatiah, Jeshaiah,
and the sons of Rephaiah, Arnan, Obadiah, and
Shecaniah.[E]
22 The son[F] of Shecaniah: Shemaiah.
Shemaiah's sons: Hattush, Igal, Bariah, Neariah,
and Shaphat — six.
23 Neariah's sons: Elioenai, Hizkiah, and Azrikam
— three.
24 Elioenai's sons: Hodaviah, Eliashib, Pelaiah,
Akkub, Johanan, Delaiah, and Anani — seven.

JUDAH'S DESCENDANTS

4 Judah's sons: Perez, Hezron, Carmi, Hur, and
Shobal.
2 Reaiah son of Shobal fathered Jahath, and
Jahath fathered Ahumai and Lahad.
These were the families of the Zorathites.
3 These were Etam's sons:[G] Jezreel, Ishma, and
Idbash, and their sister was named Hazzelelponi.
4 Penuel fathered Gedor, and Ezer fathered
Hushah.

[A] **2:52** Lit *Manuhoth* [B] **3:6** Lit *Elishama*; 2Sm 5:15; 1Ch 14:5
[C] **3:11** Lit *Joram* [D] **3:11** = The LORD is Exalted [E] **3:21** LXX reads
*Jeshaiah, his son Rephaiah, his son Arnan, his son Obadiah, and his son
Shecaniah* [F] **3:22** LXX; MT reads *sons* [G] **4:3** LXX; MT reads *father*

DIGGING DEEPER *Khirbet Qeiyafa*

Some critical scholars, such as Israel Finkelstein and Neil Asher Silberman, describe King David as a tribal chieftain who ruled over a loosely associated group of small villages lacking urbanization, fortifications, or centralized authority. However, recent excavations such as the one at Khirbet Qeiyafa conducted by Yosef Garfinkel and Saar Ganor of the Hebrew University tell a different story about David's kingdom. This late eleventh- or early tenth-century-BC city was in existence during David's reign. It was located near the Elah Valley, where David faced Goliath, and possessed massive fortifications resembling those discovered at Gezer and Hazor. In addition, pottery samples, dwellings, and huge architectural features found there do not appear in the Philistine cities—making it an unlikely Philistine location. Furthermore, objects unearthed at Qeiyafa reveal an inhabitant diet consistent with that of the Israelites; notably, there are no pig bones there, though pork was a common staple of Philistine cultures. The evidence discovered at Khirbet Qeiyafa has delivered a substantial blow to the chieftain theory, revealing that David was indeed an urbanized king who possessed the resources and technology to construct fortified cities boasting massive architectural features. It is unlikely a mere chief could have accomplished such a task. Garfinkel and Ganor suggest the location is part of David's network of administrative sites. Qeiyafa sported a two-gate construction. This rare feature would make it possible to identify the city as biblical Shaaraim, meaning "two gates" (1Ch 4:31). Alternatively, Gershon Galil of the University of Haifa identifies the city as David's administrative location, Netaim (v. 23).

These were the sons of Hur, Ephrathah's
firstborn and the father of Bethlehem:
5 Ashhur fathered Tekoa and had two wives,
Helah and Naarah.
6 Naarah bore Ahuzzam, Hepher, Temeni, and
Haahashtari to him. These were Naarah's sons.
7 Helah's sons: Zereth, Zohar,[A] and Ethnan. 8 Koz
fathered Anub, Zobebah,[B] and the families of
Aharhel son of Harum.

9 Jabez[C] was more honored than his brothers. His
mother named him Jabez and said, "I gave birth to
him in pain."
10 Jabez called out to the God of Israel, "If only you
would bless me, extend my border, let your hand be
with me, and keep me from harm, so that I will not
experience pain."[D] And God granted his request.
11 Chelub brother of Shuhah fathered Mehir,
who was the father of Eshton. 12 Eshton fathered
Beth-rapha, Paseah, and Tehinnah the father of
Irnahash. These were the men of Recah.
13 Kenaz's sons: Othniel and Seraiah.
Othniel's sons: Hathath and Meonothai.[E]
14 Meonothai fathered Ophrah,
and Seraiah fathered Joab, the ancestor of those in
the Craftsmen's Valley,[F] for they were craftsmen.
15 The sons of Caleb son of Jephunneh: Iru, Elah,
and Naam.
Elah's son: Kenaz.
16 Jehallelel's sons: Ziph, Ziphah, Tiria, and
Asarel.
17 Ezrah's sons: Jether, Mered, Epher, and Jalon.
Mered's wife Bithiah gave birth to Miriam,
Shammai, and Ishbah the father of Eshtemoa.
18 These were the sons of Pharaoh's daughter
Bithiah; Mered had married her. His Judean wife
gave birth to Jered the father of Gedor, Heber
the father of Soco, and Jekuthiel the father of
Zanoah. 19 The sons of Hodiah's wife, the sister of
Naham: the father of Keilah the Garmite and the
father of Eshtemoa the Maacathite.
20 Shimon's sons: Amnon, Rinnah, Ben-hanan,
and Tilon.
Ishi's sons: Zoheth and Ben-zoheth.

21 The sons of Shelah son of Judah: Er the father of
Lecah, Laadah the father of Mareshah, the families of the guild[G] of linen workers at Beth-ashbea,
22 Jokim, the men of Cozeba; and Joash and Saraph,
who married Moabites[H] and returned to Lehem.[I]
These names are from ancient records. 23 They
were the potters and residents of Netaim and Gederah. They lived there in the service of the king.

SIMEON'S DESCENDANTS

24 Simeon's sons: Nemuel, Jamin, Jarib, Zerah,
and Shaul;
25 Shaul's sons: his son Shallum, his son Mibsam,
and his son Mishma.
26 Mishma's sons: his son Hammuel, his son
Zaccur, and his son Shimei.

27 Shimei had sixteen sons and six daughters, but
his brothers did not have many children, so their
whole family did not become as numerous as the

[A] **4:7** Alt Hb tradition reads *Izhar* [B] **4:8** Or *Hazzobebah* [C] **4:9** In Hb, the name *Jabez* sounds like "he causes pain." [D] **4:10** Or *not cause any pain* [E] **4:13** LXX, Vg; MT omits *and Meonothai* [F] **4:14** Or *the Ge-harashim* [G] **4:21** Lit *house* [H] **4:22** Or *who ruled over Moab* [I] **4:22** Tg, Vg; MT reads *and Jashubi Lehem*

Judeans. 28 They lived in Beer-sheba, Moladah, Hazar-shual, 29 Bilhah, Ezem, Tolad, 30 Bethuel, Hormah, Ziklag, 31 Beth-marcaboth, Hazar-susim, Beth-biri, and Shaaraim. These were their cities until David became king. 32 Their villages were Etam, Ain, Rimmon, Tochen, and Ashan — five cities, 33 and all their surrounding villages as far as Baal. These were their settlements, and they kept a genealogical record for themselves.

34 Meshobab, Jamlech, Joshah son of Amaziah,
35 Joel, Jehu son of Joshibiah, son of Seraiah, son of Asiel,
36 Elioenai, Jaakobah, Jeshohaiah, Asaiah, Adiel, Jesimiel, Benaiah, 37 and Ziza son of Shiphi, son of Allon, son of Jedaiah, son of Shimri, son of Shemaiah —

38 these mentioned by name were leaders in their families. Their ancestral houses increased greatly. 39 They went to the entrance of Gedor, to the east side of the valley to seek pasture for their flocks. 40 They found rich, good pasture, and the land was broad, peaceful, and quiet, for some Hamites had lived there previously.

41 These who were recorded by name came in the days of King Hezekiah of Judah, attacked the Hamites' tents and the Meunites who were found there, and set them apart for destruction, as they are today. Then they settled in their place because there was pasture for their flocks. 42 Now five hundred men from these sons of Simeon went with Pelatiah, Neariah, Rephaiah, and Uzziel, the descendants of Ishi, as their leaders to Mount Seir. 43 They struck down the remnant of the Amalekites who had escaped, and they still live there today.

REUBEN'S DESCENDANTS

5 These were the sons of Reuben the firstborn of Israel. He was the firstborn, but his birthright was given to the sons of Joseph son of Israel, because Reuben defiled his father's bed. He is not listed in the genealogy according to birthright. 2 Although Judah became strong among his brothers and a ruler came from him, the birthright was given to Joseph.

3 The sons of Reuben, Israel's firstborn:
Hanoch, Pallu, Hezron, and Carmi.
4 Joel's sons: his son Shemaiah,
his son Gog, his son Shimei,
5 his son Micah, his son Reaiah,
his son Baal, 6 and his son Beerah.

Beerah was a leader of the Reubenites, and King Tiglath-pileser[A] of Assyria took him into exile. 7 His relatives by their families as they are recorded in their family records:

Jeiel the chief, Zechariah,
8 and Bela son of Azaz,
son of Shema, son of Joel.

They settled in Aroer as far as Nebo and Baal-meon. 9 They also settled in the east as far as the edge of the desert that extends to the Euphrates River, because their herds had increased in the land of Gilead. 10 During Saul's reign they waged war against the Hagrites, who were defeated by their power. And they lived in their tents throughout the region east of Gilead.

GAD'S DESCENDANTS

11 The sons of Gad lived next to them in the land of Bashan as far as Salecah:
12 Joel the chief, Shapham the second in command, Janai, and Shaphat in Bashan.
13 Their relatives according to their ancestral houses: Michael, Meshullam, Sheba, Jorai, Jacan, Zia, and Eber — seven.
14 These were the sons of Abihail son of Huri,
son of Jaroah, son of Gilead,
son of Michael, son of Jeshishai,
son of Jahdo, son of Buz.
15 Ahi son of Abdiel, son of Guni, was head of their ancestral family.[B] 16 They lived in Gilead, in Bashan and its surrounding villages, and throughout the pasturelands of Sharon. 17 All of them were registered in the genealogies during the reigns of Judah's King Jotham and Israel's King Jeroboam.

18 The descendants of Reuben and Gad and half the tribe of Manasseh had 44,760 warriors who could serve in the army — men who carried shield and sword, drew the bow, and were trained for war. 19 They waged war against the Hagrites, Jetur, Naphish, and Nodab. 20 They received help against these enemies because they cried out to God in battle, and the Hagrites and all their allies were handed over to them. He was receptive to their prayer because they trusted in him. 21 They captured the Hagrites' livestock — fifty thousand of their camels, two hundred fifty thousand sheep, and two thousand donkeys — as well as one hundred thousand people. 22 Many of the Hagrites were killed because it was God's battle. And they lived there in the Hagrites' place until the exile.

HALF THE TRIBE OF MANASSEH

23 The descendants of half the tribe of Manasseh settled in the land from Bashan to Baal-hermon (that is, Senir or Mount Hermon); they were numerous.

[A] 5:6 LXX; MT reads *Tilgath-pilneser* [B] 5:15 Lit *the house of their fathers*, also in v. 24

[24] These were the heads of their ancestral families:
Epher, Ishi, Eliel, Azriel, Jeremiah, Hodaviah, and
Jahdiel. They were valiant warriors, famous men,
and heads of their ancestral houses. [25] But they were
unfaithful to the God of their ancestors. They prostituted themselves with the gods of the nations[A] God
had destroyed before them. [26] So the God of Israel
roused the spirit of King Pul (that is, Tiglath-pileser[B])
of Assyria, and he took the Reubenites, Gadites, and
half the tribe of Manasseh into exile. He took them
to Halah, Habor, Hara, and Gozan's river, where they
are until today.

THE LEVITES

6 Levi's sons: Gershom,[C] Kohath, and Merari.
[2] Kohath's sons: Amram, Izhar, Hebron,
and Uzziel.
[3] Amram's children: Aaron, Moses, and Miriam.
Aaron's sons: Nadab, Abihu, Eleazar,
and Ithamar.
[4] Eleazar fathered Phinehas;
Phinehas fathered Abishua;
[5] Abishua fathered Bukki;
Bukki fathered Uzzi;
[6] Uzzi fathered Zerahiah;
Zerahiah fathered Meraioth;
[7] Meraioth fathered Amariah;
Amariah fathered Ahitub;
[8] Ahitub fathered Zadok;
Zadok fathered Ahimaaz;
[9] Ahimaaz fathered Azariah;
Azariah fathered Johanan;
[10] Johanan fathered Azariah, who served as
priest in the temple that Solomon built in
Jerusalem;
[11] Azariah fathered Amariah;
Amariah fathered Ahitub;
[12] Ahitub fathered Zadok;
Zadok fathered Shallum;
[13] Shallum fathered Hilkiah;
Hilkiah fathered Azariah;
[14] Azariah fathered Seraiah;
and Seraiah fathered Jehozadak.
[15] Jehozadak went into exile when the LORD sent
Judah and Jerusalem into exile at the hands
of Nebuchadnezzar.

[16] Levi's sons: Gershom, Kohath, and Merari.
[17] These are the names of Gershom's sons: Libni
and Shimei.
[18] Kohath's sons: Amram, Izhar, Hebron
and Uzziel.
[19] Merari's sons: Mahli and Mushi.
These are the Levites' families according to
their fathers:
[20] Of Gershom: his son Libni,
his son Jahath, his son Zimmah,
[21] his son Joah, his son Iddo,
his son Zerah, and his son Jeatherai.
[22] Kohath's sons: his son Amminadab,
his son Korah, his son Assir,
[23] his son Elkanah, his son Ebiasaph,
his son Assir, [24] his son Tahath,
his son Uriel, his son Uzziah,
and his son Shaul.
[25] Elkanah's sons: Amasai and Ahimoth,
[26] his son Elkanah, his son Zophai,
his son Nahath, [27] his son Eliab,
his son Jeroham, and his son Elkanah.
[28] Samuel's sons: his firstborn Joel,[D]
and his second son Abijah.
[29] Merari's sons: Mahli, his son Libni,
his son Shimei, his son Uzzah,
[30] his son Shimea, his son Haggiah,
and his son Asaiah.

THE MUSICIANS

[31] These are the men David put in charge of the music
in the LORD's temple after the ark came to rest there.
[32] They ministered with song in front of the tabernacle, the tent of meeting, until Solomon built the LORD's
temple in Jerusalem, and they performed their task
according to the regulations given to them. [33] These
are the men who served with their sons.
From the Kohathites: Heman the singer,
son of Joel, son of Samuel,
[34] son of Elkanah, son of Jeroham,
son of Eliel, son of Toah,
[35] son of Zuph, son of Elkanah,
son of Mahath, son of Amasai,
[36] son of Elkanah, son of Joel,
son of Azariah, son of Zephaniah,
[37] son of Tahath, son of Assir,
son of Ebiasaph, son of Korah,
[38] son of Izhar, son of Kohath,
son of Levi, son of Israel.

[39] Heman's relative was Asaph, who stood
at his right hand:
Asaph son of Berechiah, son of Shimea,
[40] son of Michael, son of Baaseiah,
son of Malchijah, [41] son of Ethni,
son of Zerah, son of Adaiah,
[42] son of Ethan, son of Zimmah,
son of Shimei, [43] son of Jahath,
son of Gershom, son of Levi.

[A] **5:25** Lit *the peoples of the land* [B] **5:26** LXX; MT reads *Tilgath-pilneser* [C] **6:1** In Hb Levi's son's name is spelled "Gershon" here and many other places [D] **6:28** Some LXX mss, Syr, Arabic; other Hb mss omit *Joel*; 1Sm 8:2

44 On the left, their relatives were Merari's sons:
Ethan son of Kishi, son of Abdi,
son of Malluch, 45 son of Hashabiah,
son of Amaziah, son of Hilkiah,
46 son of Amzi, son of Bani,
son of Shemer, 47 son of Mahli,
son of Mushi, son of Merari,
son of Levi.

AARON'S DESCENDANTS

48 Their relatives, the Levites, were assigned to all
the service of the tabernacle, God's temple. 49 But
Aaron and his sons did all the work of the most holy
place. They presented the offerings on the altar of
burnt offerings and on the altar of incense to make
atonement for Israel according to all that Moses the
servant of God had commanded.

50 These are Aaron's sons: his son Eleazar,
his son Phinehas, his son Abishua,
51 his son Bukki, his son Uzzi,
his son Zerahiah, 52 his son Meraioth,
his son Amariah, his son Ahitub,
53 his son Zadok, and his son Ahimaaz.

THE SETTLEMENTS OF THE LEVITES

54 These were the places assigned to Aaron's descendants from the Kohathite family for their settlements in their territory, because the first lot was
for them. 55 They were given Hebron in the land of
Judah and its surrounding pasturelands, 56 but the
fields and settlements around the city were given
to Caleb son of Jephunneh. 57 Aaron's descendants
were given:
Hebron (a city of refuge), Libnah and its pasturelands, Jattir, Eshtemoa and its pasturelands,
58 Hilen[A] and its pasturelands, Debir and its
pasturelands, 59 Ashan and its pasturelands, and
Beth-shemesh and its pasturelands. 60 From the
tribe of Benjamin they were given Geba and its
pasturelands, Alemeth and its pasturelands, and
Anathoth and its pasturelands. They had thirteen towns in all among their families.

61 To the rest of the Kohathites, ten towns from half
the tribe of Manasseh were assigned by lot.
62 The Gershomites were assigned thirteen towns
from the tribes of Issachar, Asher, Naphtali, and Manasseh in Bashan according to their families.
63 The Merarites were assigned by lot twelve
towns from the tribes of Reuben, Gad, and Zebulun
according to their families. 64 So the Israelites gave
these towns and their pasturelands to the Levites.
65 They assigned by lot the towns named above from
the tribes of the descendants of Judah, Simeon, and
Benjamin.

66 Some of the families of the Kohathites were given
towns from the tribe of Ephraim for their territory:
67 Shechem (a city of refuge) with its pasturelands in the hill country of Ephraim, Gezer and
its pasturelands, 68 Jokmeam and its pasturelands, Beth-horon and its pasturelands, 69 Aijalon and its pasturelands, and Gath-rimmon and
its pasturelands. 70 From half the tribe of Manasseh, Aner and its pasturelands, and Bileam
and its pasturelands were given to the rest of the
families of the Kohathites.

71 The Gershomites received:
Golan in Bashan and its pasturelands, and Ashtaroth and its pasturelands from the families of
half the tribe of Manasseh. 72 From the tribe of
Issachar they received Kedesh and its pasturelands, Daberath and its pasturelands, 73 Ramoth
and its pasturelands, and Anem and its pasturelands. 74 From the tribe of Asher they received
Mashal and its pasturelands, Abdon and its
pasturelands, 75 Hukok and its pasturelands, and
Rehob and its pasturelands. 76 From the tribe of
Naphtali they received Kedesh in Galilee and its
pasturelands, Hammon and its pasturelands,
and Kiriathaim and its pasturelands.

77 The rest of the Merarites received:
From the tribe of Zebulun they received Rimmo-
no and its pasturelands and Tabor and its pasturelands. 78 From the tribe of Reuben across the
Jordan at Jericho, to the east of the Jordan, they
received Bezer in the desert and its pasturelands,
Jahzah and its pasturelands, 79 Kedemoth and
its pasturelands, and Mephaath and its pasturelands. 80 From the tribe of Gad they received Ramoth in Gilead and its pasturelands, Mahanaim
and its pasturelands, 81 Heshbon and its pasturelands, and Jazer and its pasturelands.

ISSACHAR'S DESCENDANTS

7 Issachar's sons: Tola, Puah, Jashub, and
Shimron — four.
2 Tola's sons: Uzzi, Rephaiah, Jeriel, Jahmai,
Ibsam, and Shemuel, the heads of their
ancestral families.[B] During David's reign, 22,600
descendants of Tola were recorded as valiant
warriors in their family records.
3 Uzzi's son: Izrahiah.
Izrahiah's sons: Michael, Obadiah, Joel, Isshiah.
All five of them were chiefs. 4 Along with them,
they had 36,000 troops for battle according to

[A] 6:58 Some Hb mss, LXX; other Hb mss read *Hilez* [B] 7:2 Lit *the house of their fathers*, also in vv. 4,7,9,40

Tiglath-pileser III: Rebuilder of Assyria

by Stephen J. Andrews

Ancient Assyrian records confirm that actually three kings with this name existed: Tiglath-pileser I (ca 1116–1076 BC), Tiglath-pileser II (ca 940 BC), and Tiglath-pileser III (745–727 BC). Some historians attribute the founding of the Neo-Assyrian Empire to Tiglath-pileser III.[1] He played a significant role in the last fateful days of the kingdom of Israel.

USURPER TO THE THRONE

History says nothing about the birth and upbringing of Tiglath-pileser III. Assyrian records state that a rebellion occurred in the capital city of Calah (modern Nimrud, Iraq) two months before Tiglath-pileser became king. Two Assyrian documents give conflicting accounts of the identity of his father. Tiglath-pileser may have been of royal birth and possibly a high-ranking official or military officer. Most scholars believe he was not in the direct royal line but actually a usurper who took advantage of a political crisis to stage a coup d'état for the Assyrian throne.[2]

Tiglath-pileser's name in Akkadian, Tukulti-apil-Esharra, means "my trust [is] in the heir of [the temple of] Esharra."[3] Since Esharra was the temple dedicated to the god Ashur, the "heir" in the name is the god Ninurta, the firstborn son of Ashur. Thus Tiglath-pileser's name essentially means "my trust is in the god Ninurta." The Bible calls him Tiglath-pileser (2Kg 15:29; 16:7,10), Tilgath-pilneser (1Ch 5:6,26; 2Ch 28:20, NASB), and Pul (2Kg 15:19; 1Ch 5:26). Pul is a shortened form of *apil*, the Akkadian word for "son" or "heir." A number of Aramaic sources also referred to Tiglath-pileser.[4]

MIGHTY WARRIOR

Tiglath-pileser came to power at a time when Assyrian power had greatly diminished. He faced powerful enemies on the north, south, and east. He reorganized the army and carried out administrative reforms aimed at strengthening his own royal authority and reducing the power of the Assyrian aristocracy.[5]

Like previous kings, Tiglath-pileser led yearly campaigns in an effort to reestablish the Assyrian Empire. He proved to be a formidable general who, in the eighteen years of his reign, effectively changed the balance of power in the ancient Near East. The inscriptions Tiglath-pileser left at Calah and other places attest to his many victories.[6] He routed the army of Urartu, the powerful nation on his north, and defeated Babylonia on the south. Tiglath-pileser also campaigned along the Tigris River and Zagros Mountains to the east and the Mediterranean Sea on the west. He defeated the northern states of Syria and marched on Aram-Damascus, Transjordan, and northern Israel. He placed a gold statue of himself in Gaza and set up a commemorative stele as far south as the "Brook of Egypt."[7]

EMPIRE BUILDER

Assyrian kings had often raided and plundered neighboring states. Some had occasionally reached as far as the Mediterranean. But none had taken an active hand in annexing or incorporating any of the territories west of the Euphrates into the Assyrian Empire. Tiglath-pileser III dramatically changed this pattern.

Tiglath-pileser III conquered Babylonia and established himself as its king. He defeated the states of northern Syria and annexed them into his empire, including the territories of Aram-Damascus, Transjordan, and northern Israel. Tyre, Sidon, Samaria, Judah, and the rest of the smaller kingdoms and city-states became vassals and were obliged to provide tribute. Under Tiglath-pileser's policy of annexation, Assyria

Basalt relief orthostats from a doorway portraying the classes of the Assyrian army. This Neo-Assyrian piece is from the period of Tiglath-pileser III.

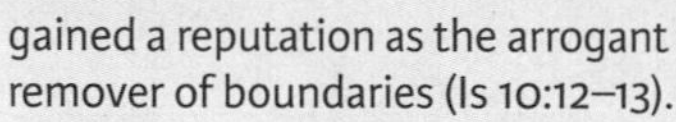

gained a reputation as the arrogant remover of boundaries (Is 10:12–13).

Although he was not the first Assyrian king to do so, Tiglath-pileser III was the first Neo-Assyrian king to practice mass deportation on a grand scale.[8] Entire villages and districts such as the Galilee district were depopulated.[9] Tiglath-pileser carried out unprecedented "two-way" deportations by resettling hundreds of thousands in distant regions (1Ch 5:6,26) and then replacing them by force with persons from still other regions. Assyrian bas-reliefs show parents carrying possessions on their shoulders and grasping their children by the hand. Men are shown walking in long files with their wives following in carts or riding on horses or donkeys.[10] Supposedly, Assyrian deportation suppressed national political loyalties, repopulated abandoned regions, developed agriculture and economic growth, and supplied troops and laborers.[11] Royal governors received instructions to provide the deportees with food and protection. They were not slaves; they paid taxes; they were given civil rights; and some even rose to important posts in the government.[12] Although Tiglath-pileser

An Assyrian inscription in basalt dating from the eighth century BC. Found at Tavle village in Turkey.

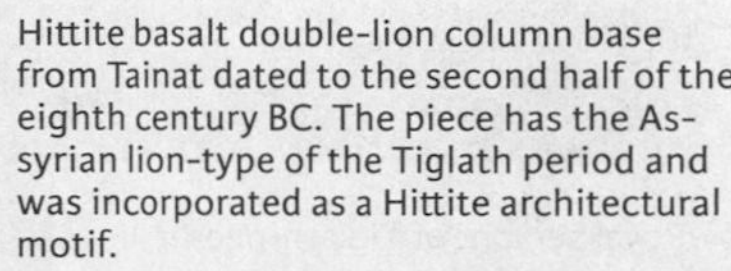

Hittite basalt double-lion column base from Tainat dated to the second half of the eighth century BC. The piece has the Assyrian lion-type of the Tiglath period and was incorporated as a Hittite architectural motif.

Royal servant of Tiglath-pileser III.

counted them as the people of Assyria[13] and treated them as his own citizens, these actions did not lessen the pain and suffering of forced deportations.

Since Tiglath-pileser's main interest was rebuilding the Assyrian Empire, he spent little time on building projects. At Calah he did erect a new palace at the edge of the Tigris River. Imported woods and precious metals decorated the palace. Huge stone slabs lined the palace walls. These slabs contained incised cuneiform, bas-reliefs, and depictions of Tiglath-pileser's victories and conquests.[14]

POLITICAL RELATIONS

Like other Assyrian kings before him, Tiglath-pileser III turned his eyes toward the Mediterranean coast fairly early in his reign. There he encountered the kings of Israel and Judah. The Bible records various details of the ensuing conflicts. Unfortunately, the fragmented inscriptions of Tiglath-pileser III provide only a partial picture of his encounters with the people and leaders of Israel and Judah.

Uzziah?—Two texts of Tiglath-pileser III mention an Azriyau whom the Assyrians defeated in 738 BC. Unfortunately, the name of Azriyau's country is broken off. Several scholars have suggested that this Azriyau is none other than Uzziah of Judah (also known as Azariah). But the Bible does not confirm this fact, and the issue must remain unsettled.[15]

Menahem—The Annals of Tiglath-pileser mention tribute money Menahem of Samaria paid in 738 BC.[16] This may refer to the payment mentioned in 2 Kings 15:19. Possibly, as a usurper to the throne of Israel, Menahem had to pay the heavy fine and then likely continued to provide a regular yearly tribute as referred to in the Annals.

Pekah—Two years into the reign of Pekahiah the son of Menahem, Pekah the son of Remaliah, another usurper, assassinated Pekahiah and seized the throne. According to 2 Kings 15:29, Tiglath-pileser campaigned against the confederacy led by Rezin of Damascus and Pekah of Israel and took the cities of Ijon, Abel-beth-maacah, Janoah, Kedesh, and Hazor. He also took Gilead, Galilee, and the land of Naphtali. In the aftermath, Tiglath-pileser deported the Israelites to Assyria and annexed most of the country.

According to 2 Kings 15:30, Hoshea son of Elah assassinated Pekah and assumed the throne. One of the summary inscriptions of Tiglath-pileser III also confirms the removal of Pekah from the throne of Israel during the campaign of 733–732 BC. In the inscription, Tiglath-pileser claimed that he directly installed Hoshea as king of Israel.[17]

Hoshea—One other possible synchronism between Hoshea and Tiglath-pileser may exist. Another summary inscription of Tiglath-pileser III contains language suggesting that Hoshea, or one of his representatives, made a trip to Sarrabani in Mesopotamia in 731 BC to pay tribute and do obeisance. The Bible does not record this trip. Was it possible that Hoshea's control over the state of Samaria was so unstable that such a trip was necessary? Or was Hoshea perceived as less than loyal to the Assyrian crown? Nine years later, just prior to the beginning of the siege of Samaria, Shalmaneser V arrested Hoshea for treason (2Kg 17:4).[18]

Ahaz—According to 2 Kings 16:5–9, Pekah of Israel and Rezin of Aram-Damascus attacked Ahaz, king of Judah. Their combined forces laid siege to Jerusalem and threatened to replace Ahaz on the throne with a usurper, the son of Tabeel (Is 7:1–6).

Ahaz responded by seeking help from Tiglath-pileser III. What happened next seems to have been a fairly standard pattern for Assyrian diplomacy and expansion. Ahaz sent a pledge of fidelity, a grievance, a distressed call for help, and a bribe (2Kg 16:7–8). Tiglath-pileser III responded by attacking Damascus, deporting its inhabitants, and executing Rezin (v. 9).

The bribe worked. Ahaz, however, got more than he bargained for. Tiglath-pileser came to his aid, but he also subjugated Ahaz as a vassal. One of the summary inscriptions of Tiglath-pileser lists Ahaz among the many tribute-bearing kings from Syro-Palestine.[19] The payment of tribute listed in the inscription is not necessarily the same as the bribe Ahaz sent (see 2Kg 16:8). The Assyrians expected regular tribute from their vassals, and Ahaz would be treated no differently. ✣

---

[1] George Roux, *Ancient Iraq*, 3rd ed. (New York: Penguin Books, 1992), 305. [2] See the summary in A. K. Grayson, "Assyria: Tiglath-Pileser III to Sargon II (744–705 BC)" in Cambridge Ancient History (CAH), ed. J. Boardman et al., 2nd ed., vol. 3, part 2 (Cambridge: Cambridge University Press, 1991), 73–74. [3] Knut L. Tallqvist, *Assyrian Personal Names* (Hildesheim: Georg Olms Verlagsbuchhhandlung, 1966), 233–34. [4] Ludwig Koehler and Walter Baumgartner, *The Hebrew and Aramaic Lexicon of the Old Testament* (*HALOT*), trans. M. E. J. Richardson, study edition (Leiden: Brill, 2001), 1687. [5] Roux, *Ancient Iraq*, 305–6, 347–48. [6] See H. Tadmor, *The Inscriptions of Tiglath-Pileser III King of Assyria* (Jerusalem: Israel Academy of Sciences and Humanities, 1994). Excerpts from the inscriptions are in J. B. Pritchard, *ANET*, 282–84. [7] Tadmor, *Inscriptions*, 9. [8] Bustenay Oded, *Mass Deportation and Deportees in the Neo-Assyrian Empire* (Wiesbaden: Dr. Ludwig Reichert Verlag, 1979), 21. [9] Zvi Gal, "Israel in Exile: Deserted Galilee Testifies to Assyrian Conquest of the Northern Kingdom," *BAR* 24.3 (1998): 48–53. See K. L. Younger Jr., "The Deportation of the Israelites," *JBL* 117 (1998): 201–27. [10] Oded, *Mass Deportation*, plates I–VI. [11] Oded, *Mass Deportation*, 41–74. [12] Roux, *Ancient Iraq*, 307–8; Oded, *Mass Deportation*, 87–89. [13] Oded, *Mass Deportation*, 82, 87, 89. [14] Grayson, "Assyria," 83–84. [15] Tadmor, *Inscriptions*, 273–76. See H. Tadmor, "Azriyau of Yaudi" in *Scripta Hierosolymitana*, ed. Chaim Rabin, vol. 8 (Jerusalem: Magnes, 1961), 232–71. [16] Pritchard, *ANET*, 283. [17] Pritchard, *ANET*, 284; Tadmor, *Inscriptions*, 277. [8] Tadmor, *Inscriptions*, 189, 278. [19] Tadmor, *Inscriptions*, 171, 277.

the family records of their ancestral families, for they had many wives and children. 5 Their tribesmen who were valiant warriors belonging to all the families of Issachar totaled 87,000 in their genealogies.

BENJAMIN'S DESCENDANTS

6 Three of Benjamin's sons: Bela, Becher, and Jediael.
7 Bela's sons: Ezbon, Uzzi, Uzziel, Jerimoth, and Iri — five. They were valiant warriors and heads of their ancestral families; 22,034 were listed in their genealogies.
8 Becher's sons: Zemirah, Joash, Eliezer, Elioenai, Omri, Jeremoth, Abijah, Anathoth, and Alemeth; all these were Becher's sons. 9 Their family records were recorded according to the heads of their ancestral families — 20,200 valiant warriors.
10 Jediael's son: Bilhan.
Bilhan's sons: Jeush, Benjamin, Ehud, Chenaanah, Zethan, Tarshish, and Ahishahar. 11 All these sons of Jediael listed by family heads were valiant warriors; there were 17,200 who could serve in the army. 12 Shuppim and Huppim were sons of Ir, and the Hushim were the sons of Aher.

NAPHTALI'S DESCENDANTS

13 Naphtali's sons: Jahziel, Guni, Jezer, and Shallum — Bilhah's sons.

MANASSEH'S DESCENDANTS

14 Manasseh's sons through his Aramean concubine: Asriel and Machir the father of Gilead. 15 Machir took wives from Huppim and Shuppim. The name of his sister was Maacah. Another descendant was named Zelophehad, but he had only daughters.
16 Machir's wife Maacah gave birth to a son, and she named him Peresh. His brother was named Sheresh, and his sons were Ulam and Rekem.
17 Ulam's son: Bedan. These were the sons of Gilead son of Machir, son of Manasseh. 18 His sister Hammolecheth gave birth to Ishhod, Abiezer, and Mahlah.
19 Shemida's sons: Ahian, Shechem, Likhi, and Aniam.

EPHRAIM'S DESCENDANTS

20 Ephraim's sons: Shuthelah, and his son Bered,
his son Tahath, his son Eleadah,
his son Tahath, 21 his son Zabad,
his son Shuthelah, also Ezer, and Elead.

The men of Gath, born in the land, killed them because they went down to raid their cattle. 22 Their father Ephraim mourned a long time, and his relatives[A] came to comfort him. 23 He slept with his wife, and she conceived and gave birth to a son. So he named him Beriah, because there had been misfortune in his home.[B] 24 His daughter was Sheerah, who built Lower and Upper Beth-horon and Uzzen-sheerah,

25 his son Rephah,[C] his son Resheph,
his son Telah, his son Tahan,
26 his son Ladan, his son Ammihud,
his son Elishama, 27 his son Nun,
and his son Joshua.

28 Their holdings and settlements were Bethel and its surrounding villages; Naaran to the east, Gezer and its villages to the west, and Shechem and its villages as far as Ayyah and its villages, 29 and along the borders of the descendants of Manasseh, Beth-shean, Taanach, Megiddo, and Dor with their surrounding villages. The sons of Joseph son of Israel lived in these towns.

ASHER'S DESCENDANTS

30 Asher's sons: Imnah, Ishvah, Ishvi, and Beriah, with their sister Serah.
31 Beriah's sons: Heber, and Malchiel, who fathered Birzaith.
32 Heber fathered Japhlet, Shomer, and Hotham, with their sister Shua.
33 Japhlet's sons: Pasach, Bimhal, and Ashvath. These were Japhlet's sons.
34 Shemer's sons: Ahi, Rohgah, Hubbah, and Aram.
35 His brother Helem's sons: Zophah, Imna, Shelesh, and Amal.
36 Zophah's sons: Suah, Harnepher, Shual, Beri, Imrah, 37 Bezer, Hod, Shamma, Shilshah, Ithran, and Beera.
38 Jether's sons: Jephunneh, Pispa, and Ara.
39 Ulla's sons: Arah, Hanniel, and Rizia.
40 All these were Asher's descendants. They were the heads of their ancestral families, chosen men, valiant warriors, and chiefs among the leaders. The number of men listed in their genealogies for military service was 26,000.

BENJAMIN'S DESCENDANTS

8 Benjamin fathered Bela, his firstborn; Ashbel was born second, Aharah third, 2 Nohah fourth, and Rapha fifth.

[A] **7:22** Or *his brothers* [B] **7:23** In Hb, the name *Beriah* sounds like "in misfortune." [C] **7:25** Probably Ephraim's son

3 Bela's sons: Addar, Gera, Abihud,[A] 4 Abishua,
Naaman, Ahoah, 5 Gera, Shephuphan, and
Huram.
6 These were Ehud's sons, who were the heads
of the families living in Geba and who were
deported to Manahath: 7 Naaman, Ahijah, and
Gera. Gera deported them and was the father of
Uzza and Ahihud.
8 Shaharaim had sons in the territory of Moab
after he had divorced his wives Hushim and
Baara. 9 His sons by his wife Hodesh: Jobab, Zibia,
Mesha, Malcam, 10 Jeuz, Sachia, and Mirmah.
These were his sons, family heads. 11 He also had
sons by Hushim: Abitub and Elpaal.
12 Elpaal's sons: Eber, Misham, and Shemed who
built Ono and Lod and its surrounding villages,
13 Beriah and Shema, who were the family
heads of Aijalon's residents and who drove out
the residents of Gath, 14 Ahio,[B] Shashak, and
Jeremoth.
15 Zebadiah, Arad, Eder, 16 Michael, Ishpah, and
Joha were Beriah's sons.
17 Zebadiah, Meshullam, Hizki, Heber, 18 Ishmerai,
Izliah, and Jobab were Elpaal's sons.
19 Jakim, Zichri, Zabdi, 20 Elienai, Zillethai, Eliel,
21 Adaiah, Beraiah, and Shimrath were Shimei's
sons.
22 Ishpan, Eber, Eliel, 23 Abdon, Zichri, Hanan,
24 Hananiah, Elam, Anthothijah, 25 Iphdeiah, and
Penuel were Shashak's sons.
26 Shamsherai, Shehariah, Athaliah,
27 Jaareshiah, Elijah, and Zichri were Jeroham's
sons.
28 These were family heads, chiefs according to
their family records; they lived in Jerusalem.

29 Jeiel[C] fathered Gibeon and lived in Gibeon.
His wife's name was Maacah. 30 Abdon was
his firstborn son, then Zur, Kish, Baal, Nadab,
31 Gedor, Ahio, Zecher, 32 and Mikloth who
fathered Shimeah. These also lived opposite
their relatives in Jerusalem, with their other
relatives.
33 Ner fathered Kish, Kish fathered Saul, and Saul
fathered Jonathan, Malchishua, Abinadab, and
Esh-baal.[D]
34 Jonathan's son was Merib-baal,[E] and
Merib-baal fathered Micah.
35 Micah's sons: Pithon, Melech, Tarea, and
Ahaz.
36 Ahaz fathered Jehoaddah, Jehoaddah fathered
Alemeth, Azmaveth, and Zimri, and Zimri
fathered Moza.
37 Moza fathered Binea. His son was Raphah, his
son Elasah, and his son Azel.
38 Azel had six sons, and these were their names:
Azrikam, Bocheru, Ishmael, Sheariah, Obadiah,
and Hanan. All these were Azel's sons.
39 His brother Eshek's sons: Ulam was his
firstborn, Jeush second, and Eliphelet third.
40 Ulam's sons were valiant warriors and
archers.[F] They had many sons and grandsons
— 150 of them.
All these were among Benjamin's sons.

AFTER THE EXILE

9 All Israel was registered in the genealogies that
are written in the Book of the Kings of Israel. But
Judah was exiled to Babylon because of their unfaithfulness. 2 The first to live in their towns on their own
property again were Israelites, priests, Levites, and
temple servants.
3 These people from the descendants of Judah,
Benjamin, Ephraim, and Manasseh settled in
Jerusalem:
4 Uthai son of Ammihud, son of Omri, son of
Imri, son of Bani, a descendant[G] of Perez son of
Judah;
5 from the Shilonites:
Asaiah the firstborn and his sons;
6 and from the descendants of Zerah:
Jeuel and their relatives — 690 in all.

7 The Benjaminites: Sallu son of Meshullam, son
of Hodaviah, son of Hassenuah;
8 Ibneiah son of Jeroham;
Elah son of Uzzi, son of Michri;
Meshullam son of Shephatiah, son of Reuel, son
of Ibnijah;
9 and their relatives according to their family
records — 956 in all. All these men were heads
of their ancestral families.[H]

10 The priests: Jedaiah; Jehoiarib; Jachin;
11 Azariah son of Hilkiah, son of Meshullam, son
of Zadok, son of Meraioth, son of Ahitub, the
chief official of God's temple;
12 Adaiah son of Jeroham, son of Pashhur, son of
Malchijah;
Maasai son of Adiel, son of Jahzerah, son
of Meshullam, son of Meshillemith, son of
Immer;
13 and their relatives, the heads of their ancestral
families — 1,760 in all. They were capable men
employed in the ministry of God's temple.

[A] **8:3** Or *Gera father of Ehud*; Jdg 3:15 [B] **8:13–14** LXX reads *Gath* **14** *and their brother* [C] **8:29** LXX; MT omits *Jeiel*; 1Ch 9:35 [D] **8:33** = Man of Baal [E] **8:34** = Baal Contends [F] **8:40** Lit *valiant ones who string the bow* [G] **9:4** Lit *Bani, from the sons* [H] **9:9** Lit *the house of their fathers*, also in vv. 13,19

Polygamy in the Ancient World

by Kevin Hall

To establish what might have been common practice regarding polygamy in the ancient Near East is difficult because most ancient literature, including the Bible, profiles and highlights the lives of uncommon people, most of whom were either royalty or at least relatively wealthy. Among the biblical polygamists mentioned above, Elkanah is the most typical or common Israelite, and his wife Hannah is apparently one of only two wives. The other notable biblical polygamists were either relatively prosperous (Abraham, Jacob) or leaders on par with typical ancient kings (Gideon, David). So while we can easily and confidently state that polygamy was widely practiced in the ancient world, knowing how common the practice actually was is quite difficult, if not impossible.[1] Given the economic advantages of a large family in ancient agricultural life, we can be reasonably certain that polygamy would have been common among men who could support more than one wife. Since women had a shorter life expectancy than men, due in part to the perils of childbirth, a man who could support more than one wife could increase the fertility of his household.[2] Nevertheless, most literary evidence for polygamy throughout the ancient world points to the practice among the elite men of society.

POLITICAL POLYGAMY

In the cases of David and Solomon, the practice of polygamy had a decidedly political aim and advantage. In the ancient Near East, treaties between kings and other important figures were often sealed with the marriage of one ruler's daughter into the household of another ruler. This practice is demonstrated in the infamous example of the marriage of Ahab, the king of Israel, to Jezebel, a Phoenician princess. The marriage represented the political and economic ties that Ahab's father, Omri (widely considered one of the most powerful kings of Israel), had established years earlier with the commercially powerful king of Phoenicia.

Not surprisingly, therefore, David and Solomon, each a king of a united Israel and Judah, engaged in political polygamy. This is precisely what God's people requested earlier when they found themselves under threat from the Philistines' coalition of kings; they asked the Lord for a king "like all the other nations" (1Sm 8:20; see v.5). Speaking through Samuel, the Lord warned his people that in asking for such a king, they would be rejecting him as King and turning to a model of kingship that would enslave them. As expected, the two most beloved kings of Israel imitated the practices of the kings of the other nations, including politically advantageous marriages. Ironically, King Solomon's first wife was Pharaoh's daughter (1Kg 3:1)!

Though the practice of political polygamy is glaringly on display in Solomon's kingdom, the practice began with David. The early chapters of 2 Samuel describe David's consolidation of power as he began his reign as king over Judah and eventually became king over a united Israel and Judah. Twice the Bible reports on the growing household of this rising king. Of the six sons born to the new king of Judah while in his first capital of Hebron, each has a different mother. And though the information about the lineage of these women is incomplete, the indication is that these six mothers of David's first six sons provided David with strategic alliances and connections; his multiple marriages were part and parcel of his kingdom building (2Sm 3:2–5).[3] As David moved his capital to Jerusalem, he added more women to his household and in time, additional children (5:13–16).

Terra-cotta figurine of a pregnant woman; this type of fertility figurine was common in Israel and Judah in the Iron Age. The prominence of the figurines and their exaggerated feminine features has caused speculation about whether people believed the figurines could affect fertility and pregnancy.

KINGDOM BUILDING

A strange and tragic episode involving one of David's sons demonstrates the strategic significance of the women of David's dynasty. The episode also clarifies the fact that David's polygamy typified common practices among ancient rulers. Those practices were based on then-current common cultural assumptions, one of which claimed that multiple wives solidified kingdoms. How do we see that played out? David's third son, Absalom, whose mother was daughter of the king of Geshur (2Sm 3:3), revolted against David. After driving David from the capital, Absalom sought advice from one of his advisers. His goal was to solidify his control over David's kingdom and strengthen the resolve of those who had joined him in revolt. The advice Absalom received makes no sense apart from the logic of the common ancient practice of political polygamy. The adviser instructed Absalom to take the women of David's house that had been left behind to care for the palace and to have relations with them. He did so on the roof of the palace for all to see. The people understood this sort of conduct as evidence of Absalom's power over David's kingdom. This entire episode gives us a glimpse into an ancient mindset that David and the other kings of Israel and Judah held; indeed they had become what the people had asked for—a king "like all the other nations." Polygamy of this type was just one facet of this development.[4]

No wonder then that David's son Solomon, kingdom builder par excellence, pursued this kingdom-building practice with such vigor. By the end of his time on the throne, Solomon had married women from most of the kingdoms surrounding Israel. ✠

---

[1] Victor P. Hamilton, "Marriage (Old Testament and Ancient Near East)" in *ABD*, 4:559–69. [2] Jon L. Berquist, "Marriage" in *EDB*, 861–62. [3] See the discussion in Robert D. Bergen, *1, 2 Samuel*, vol. 7 in NAC (1996), 305–6. [4] Hamilton, "Marriage," 4:560, cites a document from ancient Ugarit as evidence that "Ugarit shared with Israel the concept that marriage to a former king's wife, or even his concubines, bestowed legitimacy on an aspirant who otherwise had no claim to the throne."

Dr. Harold Mosley digging at Gezer. Pharaoh attacked and captured Gezer, burned it down and gave it as a dowry to his daughter, Solomon's wife. To the right and waist high is a dark horizontal line just below the Solomonic casemate construction, thought to be the burn layer.

14 The Levites: Shemaiah son of Hasshub, son of Azrikam, son of Hashabiah of the Merarites;
15 Bakbakkar, Heresh, Galal, and Mattaniah, son of Mica, son of Zichri, son of Asaph;
16 Obadiah son of Shemaiah, son of Galal, son of Jeduthun;
and Berechiah son of Asa, son of Elkanah who lived in the settlements of the Netophathites.

17 The gatekeepers: Shallum, Akkub, Talmon, Ahiman, and their relatives.
Shallum was their chief; 18 he was previously stationed at the King's Gate on the east side.
These were the gatekeepers from the camp of the Levites.
19 Shallum son of Kore, son of Ebiasaph, son of Korah and his relatives from his ancestral family, the Korahites, were assigned to guard the thresholds of the tent.[A] Their ancestors had been assigned to the LORD's camp as guardians of the entrance. 20 In earlier times Phinehas son of Eleazar had been their leader, and the LORD was with him. 21 Zechariah son of Meshelemiah was the gatekeeper at the entrance to the tent of meeting.

22 The total number of those chosen to be gatekeepers at the thresholds was 212. They were registered by genealogy in their settlements. David and the seer Samuel had appointed them to their trusted positions. 23 So they and their sons were assigned as guards to the gates of the LORD's temple, which had been the tent-temple. 24 The gatekeepers were on the four sides: east, west, north, and south. 25 Their relatives came from their settlements at fixed times to be with them seven days, 26 but the four chief gatekeepers, who were Levites, were entrusted with the rooms and the treasuries of God's temple. 27 They spent the night in the vicinity of God's temple, because they had guard duty and were in charge of opening it every morning.

28 Some of them were in charge of the utensils used in worship. They would count them when they brought them in and when they took them out. 29 Others were put in charge of the furnishings and all the utensils of the sanctuary, as well as the fine flour, wine, oil, incense, and spices. 30 Some of the priests' sons mixed the spices. 31 A Levite called Mattithiah, the firstborn of Shallum the Korahite, was entrusted with baking the bread.[B] 32 Some of the Kohathites' relatives were responsible for preparing the rows of the Bread of the Presence every Sabbath.

33 The singers, the heads of the Levite families, stayed in the temple chambers and were exempt from other tasks because they were on duty day and night. 34 These were the heads of the Levite families, chiefs according to their family records; they lived in Jerusalem.

SAUL'S FAMILY

35 Jeiel fathered Gibeon and lived in Gibeon.
His wife's name was Maacah. 36 Abdon was his firstborn son, then Zur, Kish, Baal, Ner, Nadab, 37 Gedor, Ahio, Zechariah, and Mikloth. 38 Mikloth fathered Shimeam. These also lived opposite their relatives in Jerusalem with their other relatives.
39 Ner fathered Kish, Kish fathered Saul, and Saul fathered Jonathan, Malchishua, Abinadab, and Esh-baal.
40 Jonathan's son was Merib-baal, and Merib-baal fathered Micah.
41 Micah's sons: Pithon, Melech, Tahrea, and Ahaz.[C]
42 Ahaz fathered Jarah;
Jarah fathered Alemeth, Azmaveth, and Zimri;
Zimri fathered Moza.
43 Moza fathered Binea.
His son was Rephaiah, his son Elasah, and his son Azel.
44 Azel had six sons, and these were their names: Azrikam, Bocheru, Ishmael, Sheariah, Obadiah, and Hanan. These were Azel's sons.

THE DEATH OF SAUL AND HIS SONS

10 The Philistines fought against Israel, and Israel's men fled from them. Many were killed on Mount Gilboa. 2 The Philistines pursued Saul and his sons and killed his sons Jonathan, Abinadab, and Malchishua. 3 When the battle intensified against Saul, the archers spotted him and severely wounded him. 4 Then Saul said to his armor-bearer, "Draw your sword and run me through with it, or these uncircumcised men will come and torture me." But his armor-bearer would not do it because he was terrified. Then Saul took his sword and fell on it. 5 When his armor-bearer saw that Saul was dead, he also fell on his own sword and died. 6 So Saul and his three sons died — his whole house died together.

7 When all the men of Israel in the valley saw that the army had fled and that Saul and his sons were dead, they abandoned their cities and fled. So the Philistines came and settled in them.

8 The next day when the Philistines came to strip the slain, they found Saul and his sons dead on Mount Gilboa. 9 They stripped Saul, cut off his head, took his armor, and sent messengers throughout the land

[A] **9:19** = the temple [B] **9:31** Lit *with things prepared in pans*
[C] **9:41** LXX, Syr, Tg, Vg, Arabic; MT omits *and Ahaz*; 1Ch 8:35

of the Philistines to spread the good news to their idols and the people. 10 Then they put his armor in the temple of their gods and hung his skull in the temple of Dagon.

11 When all Jabesh-gilead heard of everything the Philistines had done to Saul, 12 all their brave men set out and retrieved the body of Saul and the bodies of his sons and brought them to Jabesh. They buried their bones under the oak[A] in Jabesh and fasted seven days.

13 Saul died for his unfaithfulness to the LORD because he did not keep the LORD's word. He even consulted a medium for guidance, 14 but he did not inquire of the LORD. So the LORD put him to death and turned the kingdom over to David son of Jesse.

DAVID'S ANOINTING AS KING

11 All Israel came together to David at Hebron and said, "Here we are, your own flesh and blood.[B] 2 Even previously when Saul was king, you were leading Israel out to battle and bringing us back. The LORD your God also said to you, 'You will shepherd my people Israel, and you will be ruler over my people Israel.' "

3 So all the elders of Israel came to the king at Hebron. David made a covenant with them at Hebron in the LORD's presence, and they anointed David king over Israel, in keeping with the LORD's word through Samuel.

DAVID'S CAPTURE OF JERUSALEM

4 David and all Israel marched to Jerusalem (that is, Jebus); the Jebusites who inhabited the land were there. 5 The inhabitants of Jebus said to David, "You will never get in here." Yet David did capture the stronghold of Zion, that is, the city of David.

6 David said, "Whoever is the first to kill a Jebusite will become chief commander." Joab son of Zeruiah went up first, so he became the chief.

7 Then David took up residence in the stronghold; therefore, it was called the city of David. 8 He built up the city all the way around, from the supporting terraces to the surrounding parts, and Joab restored the rest of the city. 9 David steadily grew more powerful, and the LORD of Armies was with him.

EXPLOITS OF DAVID'S WARRIORS

10 The following were the chiefs of David's warriors who, together with all Israel, strongly supported him in his reign to make him king according to the LORD's word about Israel. 11 This is the list of David's warriors:

Jashobeam son of Hachmoni was chief of the Thirty;[C] he wielded his spear against three hundred and killed them at one time.

DIGGING DEEPER *Ruins of the City of David*

David began his reign as king of Israel soon after his thirtieth birthday. David ruled in Hebron for seven years and six months (2Sm 5:4–5) and then led the Israelites to Jerusalem (then known as Jebus). At Jerusalem, he conquered the stronghold of the Jebusites (1Ch 11:4–6) and renamed the territory the "city of David" (v. 7). The small piece of land became the administrative headquarters after David "built up the city all the way around, from the supporting terraces to the surrounding parts, and Joab restored the rest of the city" (v. 8). Today the city is located south of the Temple Mount platform and west of the Kidron Valley adjacent to the Mount of Olives. In 2005, archaeologist Eilat Mazar announced that she had uncovered a large stone structure which she believed was the palace of King David. Subsequent discoveries at the site have supported Mazar's claim. These include pottery, architecture dating to the tenth century BC, and clay seals bearing the names of Jehucal (or Jucal) son of Shelemiah (Jr 37:3; 38:1) and Gedaliah son of Pashhur (38:1–6), the infamous enemies of the prophet Jeremiah.

12 After him, Eleazar son of Dodo the Ahohite was one of the three warriors. 13 He was with David at Pas-dammim when the Philistines had gathered there for battle. There was a portion of a field full of barley, where the troops had fled from the Philistines. 14 But Eleazar and David[D] took their stand in the middle of the field and defended it. They killed the Philistines, and the LORD gave them a great victory.

15 Three of the thirty chief men went down to David, to the rock at the cave of Adullam, while the Philistine army was encamped in Rephaim Valley. 16 At that time David was in the stronghold, and a Philistine garrison was at Bethlehem. 17 David was extremely thirsty[E] and said, "If only someone would bring me water to drink from the well at the city gate of Bethlehem!" 18 So the Three broke through the Philistine camp and drew water from the well at the gate of Bethlehem. They brought it back to David, but he refused to drink it. Instead, he poured it out to the LORD. 19 David said, "I would never do such a thing in the presence of my God! How can I drink the blood of these men who risked their lives?" For they brought it at the risk of their lives. So he would not drink it. Such were the exploits of the three warriors.

[A] **10:12** Or *terebinth*, or *large tree* [B] **11:1** Lit *your bone and your flesh*
[C] **11:11** Alt Hb tradition reads *Three* [D] **11:14** Lit *But they*
[E] **11:17** Lit *And David craved*

20 Abishai, Joab's brother, was the leader of the
Three.[A] He raised his spear against three hundred
men and killed them, gaining a reputation among
the Three. 21 He was more honored than the Three
and became their commander even though he did
not become one of the Three.
22 Benaiah son of Jehoiada was the son of a brave
man[B] from Kabzeel, a man of many exploits. Benaiah
killed two sons of Ariel of Moab,[C] and he went down
into a pit on a snowy day and killed a lion. 23 He also
killed an Egyptian who was seven and a half feet
tall.[D] Even though the Egyptian had a spear in his
hand like a weaver's beam, Benaiah went down to
him with a staff, snatched the spear out of the Egyptian's hand, and then killed him with his own spear.
24 These were the exploits of Benaiah son of Jehoiada,
who had a reputation among the three warriors. 25 He
was the most honored of the Thirty, but he did not
become one of the Three. David put him in charge
of his bodyguard.
26 The best soldiers were
Joab's brother Asahel,
Elhanan son of Dodo of Bethlehem,
27 Shammoth the Harorite,
Helez the Pelonite,
28 Ira son of Ikkesh the Tekoite,
Abiezer the Anathothite,
29 Sibbecai the Hushathite,
Ilai the Ahohite,
30 Maharai the Netophathite,
Heled son of Baanah the Netophathite,
31 Ithai son of Ribai from Gibeah
of the Benjaminites,
Benaiah the Pirathonite,
32 Hurai from the wadis of Gaash,
Abiel the Arbathite,
33 Azmaveth the Baharumite,
Eliahba the Shaalbonite,
34 the sons of[E] Hashem the Gizonite,
Jonathan son of Shagee the Hararite,
35 Ahiam son of Sachar the Hararite,
Eliphal son of Ur,
36 Hepher the Mecherathite,
Ahijah the Pelonite,
37 Hezro the Carmelite,
Naarai son of Ezbai,
38 Joel the brother of Nathan,
Mibhar son of Hagri,
39 Zelek the Ammonite,
Naharai the Beerothite, the armor-bearer
for Joab son of Zeruiah,
40 Ira the Ithrite,
Gareb the Ithrite,
41 Uriah the Hethite,
Zabad son of Ahlai,
42 Adina son of Shiza the Reubenite, chief
of the Reubenites, and thirty with him,
43 Hanan son of Maacah,
Joshaphat the Mithnite,
44 Uzzia the Ashterathite,
Shama and Jeiel the sons of Hotham
the Aroerite,
45 Jediael son of Shimri and his brother Joha
the Tizite,
46 Eliel the Mahavite,
Jeribai and Joshaviah, the sons of Elnaam,
Ithmah the Moabite,
47 Eliel, Obed, and Jaasiel the Mezobaite.

DAVID'S FIRST SUPPORTERS

12 The following were the men who came to David at Ziklag while he was still banned from
the presence of Saul son of Kish. They were among
the warriors who helped him in battle. 2 They were
archers who could use either the right or left hand,
both to sling stones and shoot arrows from a bow.
They were Saul's relatives from Benjamin:
3 Their chief was Ahiezer son of Shemaah the
Gibeathite.
Then there was his brother Joash;
Jeziel and Pelet sons of Azmaveth;
Beracah, Jehu the Anathothite;
4 Ishmaiah the Gibeonite, a warrior among the
Thirty and a leader over the Thirty;
Jeremiah, Jahaziel, Johanan, Jozabad the
Gederathite;
5 Eluzai, Jerimoth, Bealiah, Shemariah,
Shephatiah the Haruphite;
6 Elkanah, Isshiah, Azarel, Joezer, and
Jashobeam, the Korahites;
7 and Joelah and Zebadiah, the sons of Jeroham
from Gedor.

8 Some Gadites defected to David at his stronghold
in the desert. They were valiant warriors, trained for
battle, expert with shield and spear. Their faces were
like the faces of lions, and they were as swift as gazelles on the mountains.
9 Ezer was the chief, Obadiah second, Eliab third,
10 Mishmannah fourth, Jeremiah fifth,
11 Attai sixth, Eliel seventh,
12 Johanan eighth, Elzabad ninth,
13 Jeremiah tenth, and Machbannai eleventh.
14 These Gadites were army commanders; the least
of them was a match for a hundred, and the greatest
of them for a thousand. 15 These are the men who

[A] 11:20 Syr reads *Thirty* [B] 11:22 Or *was a valiant man* [C] 11:22 Or *He killed two Moabite warriors* [D] 11:23 Lit *who measured five cubits* [E] 11:34 LXX omits *the sons of*; 2Sm 23:32

by Gary P. Arbino

In a brilliant strategic move, David decided to capture a Canaanite stronghold in Judah's hill country for his capital. The city was known as Jebus in the time of David (Jdg 19:10–11; 1Ch 11:4–5), but also as *Urusalim* in the Amarna letters of the fourteenth century BC.

A FORTIFIED CITY

The Canaanite city encompassed the twelve-acre spur of hill south of what became the Temple Mount. The hill was bounded on the west by "the valley" (later known as the Tyropoeon) and on the east by the Kidron Valley. The hill extends about two thousand feet and slopes down toward the south. The two valleys join at the southern tip of what would later become the city of David. As Psalm 125:2 poetically notes, the city is situated on the lowest of the local hills.

From the taunts recorded in 2 Samuel 5:6 and 1 Chronicles 11:5, the Jebusite inhabitants felt very secure in their stronghold, called in Hebrew the *Metsudat Tsion* or "stronghold of Zion" (2Sm 5:7). This stronghold was probably located at the northern end of the town near its highest and most vulnerable point.

On the eastern slope of the hill, archaeologists have uncovered a massive architectural feature known as the Stepped-Stone Structure. This terraced mantle of stone courses laid over a substructure of terraces, rib walls, and fill extends down the slope at least 120 feet from the crest of the hill. Its full extent has not yet been determined. From its size and position, this is often considered to be the supporting foundation for the *Metsudat Tsion*, reused by David after his capture of the city.

In addition to the fortress on the north, fortification walls surrounded Jebus. Archaeologists have uncovered little if any of the western wall system from the tenth century. Possibly a structure exposed in the nineteenth century could be a western gate from this period. On the east side of the city, it seems that a Middle Bronze Age (2200–1550 BC) wall continued to be used throughout the Late Bronze and Iron Ages (1550–586 BC). This wall, measuring some eight feet thick, was located halfway up the east slope at the top of a steep rock outcrop. Near the northern extent of this wall, below the Stepped-Stone Structure, famed archaeologist Kathleen Kenyon excavated what appears to be a gate in the wall.

STRATEGIC LOCATION

After reigning for more than seven years in his own tribal territory at Hebron, David needed to expand his influence (2Sm 5:1–5). Jebus was centrally located between his tribe, Judah, and the rest of the tribes. Although assigned to the Benjaminites (the tribe of David's former rival, Saul), no tribe had yet possessed it. Located on the border between Judah and Benjamin (Jos 15:8), the city was attacked years earlier by the Judahites (v. 63; Jdg 1:8) who could not hold the city, and so it was given to the Benjaminites (Jos 18:28) who also could not keep it (Jdg 1:21). The city remained a Jebusite enclave until the time of David, thus making it a perfect centralized capital city, one he could make his own city.

WATER FOR THE CITY

So David and his mighty men, his personal army, besieged Jebus. The biblical text notes that Joab became the commander of David's army when he took charge of the attack of Jebus. He accomplished this by going through the *tsinnor*, often translated as "water shaft" (1Ch 11:6; 2Sm 5:8). Most biblical scholars assume this means he climbed up a shaft in the water system near the Gihon Spring on the east slope of the city, entered the city, and let the Israelite army into the city. This spring, named for its intermittent "gushing" (Gihon is derived from a Hebrew root meaning "to gush"), is the only perennial water supply in the city of David.

Recently archaeologists have discovered two massive fortification towers and a deep pool at the spring and dated them to the Middle Bronze Age (2200–1550 BC).[1] These are outside of the Middle Bronze Age walls but seem to have been connected to the walls and possibly accessed by Kenyon's gate. Archaeologists have agreed that these walls were still in use during the days of the Jebusites and David. Certainly the spring was still used. A tunnel provided additional, more secure access to the spring. Commonly

A segment of the city wall in Jerusalem dating to the First Temple period (1000–586 BC). This section of the wall, which protected the north side of Jerusalem, is almost twenty-three feet wide and more than two hundred feet long.

Remains of the Stepped-Stone Structure.

referred to as Warren's Shaft, this tunnel, carved from the soft limestone, crossed under the city walls and gave hidden access to the spring pool. Until recently, the tunnel appeared to end in a forty-foot natural vertical shaft where people would lower jugs to get water. This shaft was long thought to have been Joab's *tsinnor*. Recent excavations, however, indicate the vertical section was not exposed during the time of David and Joab, rather the tunnel connected to a cave whose mouth opened at the pool. So we do not know what exactly Joab's *tsinnor* was, but it does seem to have something to do with a water channel.

DAVID'S CAPITAL

Regardless of the precise method, David had taken the city with his army and so in effect it was his spoil of war, his personal stronghold. Thus David had shrewdly created a fortified capital city that was not the possession of any tribe yet was centrally located.

According to 2 Samuel 5:9 and 1 Chronicles 11:8, David and Joab immediately began improvements to the city. Although Joab could be credited with restoring the city to life (an allusion to residential restoration?), David would receive credit for building the northern end of town, the fortress and palace areas, including the area "from the *millo*."

The term *millo* seems to mean an in-filled area, and many take this to mean a terrace system (1Ch 11:8). If this is the case, then the *millo* may refer to the terrace and fills used to extend the city northward toward the Temple Mount. Since David actually purchased the Temple Mount and placed the ark shrine there (2Sm 6; 24; 1Ch 21–22), we could reasonably conclude that he would begin filling in the space between the city of David and the Temple Mount. David's placement of the ark in the city of David was an important step in the creation of this as his capital city. Clearly David showed his loyalty to God in this act. On another level, we see his vision and political and religious acumen as he solidified for himself and the people his role as God's chosen and then solidified Jerusalem for Israel's capital (2Sm 6).

In 2 Samuel 5:11, we read that David also built a palace for himself. According to verse 17, David had to go down to reach the *Metsudat Tsion*. If this fortress sat atop the Stepped-Stone Structure, then we would need to look upslope to the north to find the palace. Recently renowned archaeologist Eilat Mazar has uncovered monumental architecture in this area that she dates to the early Iron Age II (1000–900 BC), the time of David. Given its six-to-eight-foot-wide walls, Mazar calls her find the "Large-Stone Structure." Mazar connects her finds to a short section of casemate wall (a typically Israelite wall style) uncovered nearby by Kenyon as well as some ashlar blocks (large, square-cut stones) and a proto-Aeolic column capital (decorative architectural remains, often found associated with Iron Age royal buildings) discovered downslope. Evaluating her findings, Mazar cautiously argued that her structure comprises the foundations of David's royal palace.[2]

The palace would have been an imposing building at the highest part of town. It would have served as the reception hall for emissaries to the young kingdom (2Sm 8:9–10) and housed the royal family (5:13–16). From there, David's wife Michal could look down on the procession bringing the ark into town (6:16), and David could look down on his city across the rooftops and see Bathsheba bathing (11:2). In his palace, David could even keep an eye on his last remaining potential rival from Saul's house (2Sm 9).

David's rebuilding of the Jebusite city also included residential areas. Recent excavations have uncovered houses inside the city wall on the east slope. These houses are constructed into the mantle of the Stepped-Stone Structure. Some archaeologists date these houses to the time of David.[3] These domestic units are solidly built and are located just below the stronghold and the palace area. These may have been the houses of David's officials and elite soldiers (8:15–18; see 1Ch 11:10–47). Just below the Middle Bronze Age (2200–1550 BC) wall on the east slope, the Israeli archaeologist Yigal Shiloh excavated another residential neighborhood. This domestic area, outside the city walls, was unprotected and poorly constructed, with some evidence of household religious activity.[4] The difference between houses inside and outside the walls may illustrate some social stratification in David's Jerusalem. The Bible also records that the nobility owned estates outside the city walls (2Sm 14:30–31).

David's Jerusalem was his stronghold, a city small in size but complete with royal and administrative architecture, fortifications, a complex water supply, socially diverse domestic areas, and nearby agricultural lands. ✣

---

[1] Ronny Reich and Eli Shukron, "Light at the End of the Tunnel: Warren's Shaft Theory of David's Conquest Shattered," *BAR* 25.1 (1999): 22–33, 72. [2] Eilat Mazar, "Did I Find King David's Palace?" *BAR* 32.1 (2006): 16–27, 70. [3] Jane Cahill, "Jerusalem in David and Solomon's Time: It Really Was a Major City in the Tenth Century BCE," *BAR* 30.6 (2004): 26–27. [4] D. T. Ariel and A. De Groot, "The Iron Age Extramural Occupation at the City of David and Additional Observations on the Siloam Channel," in *Excavations at the City of David*, vol. 5, ed. D. T. Ariel, Qedem 40 (Jerusalem: Hebrew University, 2000), 155–69.

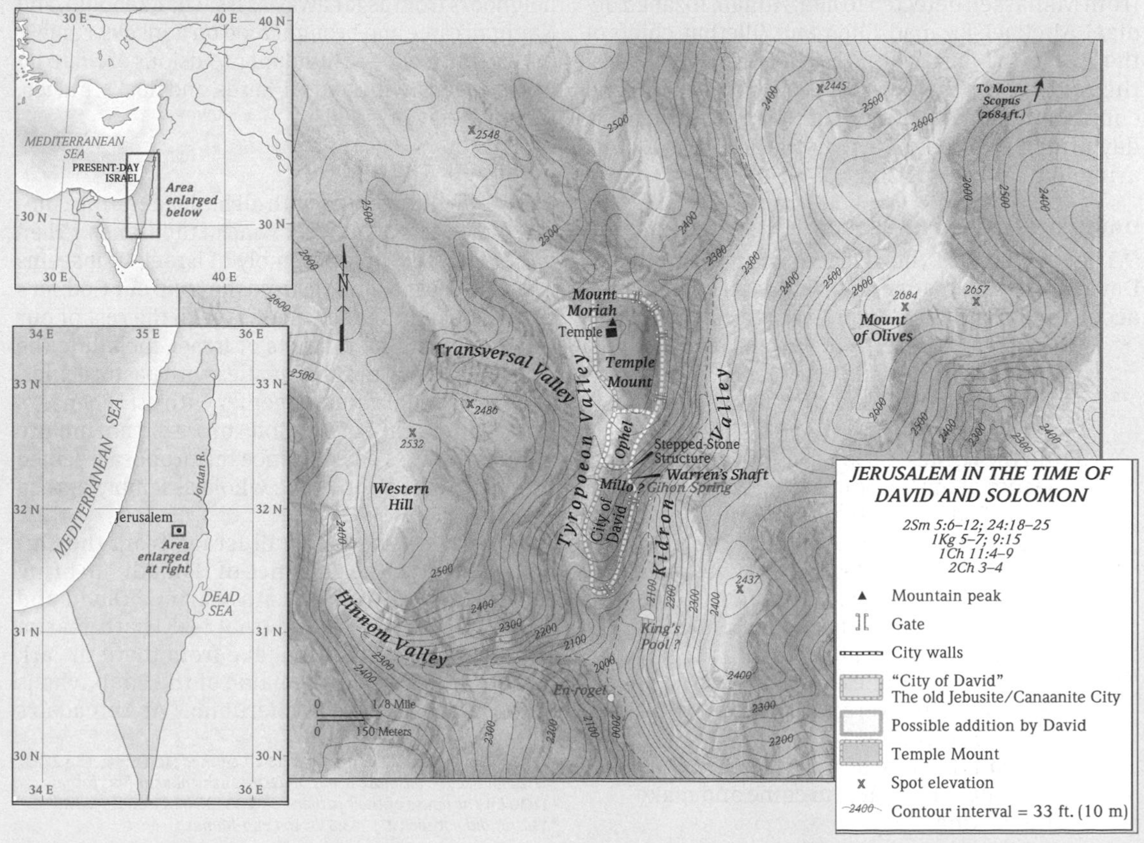

crossed the Jordan in the first month[A] when it was
overflowing all its banks, and put to flight all those
in the valleys to the east and to the west.
16 Other Benjaminites and men from Judah also
went to David at the stronghold. 17 David went out
to meet them and said to them, "If you have come in
peace to help me, my heart will be united with you,
but if you have come to betray me to my enemies even
though my hands have done no wrong, may the God
of our ancestors look on it and judge."
18 Then the Spirit enveloped[B] Amasai, chief of the
Thirty, and he said:

We are yours, David,
we are with you, son of Jesse!
Peace, peace to you,
and peace to him who helps you,
for your God helps you.

So David received them and made them leaders of
his troops.
19 Some Manassites defected to David when he
went with the Philistines to fight against Saul. However, they did not help the Philistines because the
Philistine rulers sent David away after a discussion.
They said, "It will be our heads if he defects to his
master Saul." 20 When David went to Ziklag, some men
from Manasseh defected to him: Adnah, Jozabad, Jediael, Michael, Jozabad, Elihu, and Zillethai, chiefs of
thousands in Manasseh. 21 They helped David against
the raiders, for they were all valiant warriors and
commanders in the army. 22 At that time, men came
day after day to help David until there was a great
army, like an army of God.[C]

DAVID'S SOLDIERS IN HEBRON

23 The numbers of the armed troops who came to
David at Hebron to turn Saul's kingdom over to him,
according to the LORD's word, were as follows:

24 From the Judahites: 6,800 armed troops bearing shields and spears.
25 From the Simeonites: 7,100 valiant warriors ready for war.
26 From the Levites: 4,600 27 in addition to Jehoiada, leader of the house of Aaron, with 3,700 men; 28 and Zadok, a young valiant warrior, with 22 commanders from his ancestral family.[D]
29 From the Benjaminites, the relatives of Saul: 3,000 (up to that time the majority of the Benjaminites maintained their allegiance to the house of Saul).
30 From the Ephraimites: 20,800 valiant warriors who were famous men in their ancestral families.[E]
31 From half the tribe of Manasseh: 18,000 designated by name to come and make David king.
32 From the Issacharites, who understood the times and knew what Israel should do: 200 chiefs with all their relatives under their command.
33 From Zebulun: 50,000 who could serve in the army, trained for battle with all kinds of weapons of war, with one purpose to help David.[F]
34 From Naphtali: 1,000 commanders accompanied by 37,000 men with shield and spear.
35 From the Danites: 28,600 trained for battle.
36 From Asher: 40,000 who could serve in the army, trained for battle.
37 From across the Jordan — from the Reubenites, Gadites, and half the tribe of Manasseh: 120,000 men equipped with all the military weapons of war.

38 All these warriors, lined up in battle formation,
came to Hebron wholeheartedly determined to make
David king over all Israel. All the rest of Israel was also
of one mind to make David king. 39 They spent three
days there eating and drinking with David, for their
relatives had provided for them. 40 In addition, their
neighbors from as far away as Issachar, Zebulun, and
Naphtali came and brought food on donkeys, camels,
mules, and oxen — abundant provisions of flour, fig
cakes, raisins, wine and oil, herds, and flocks. Indeed,
there was joy in Israel.

DAVID AND THE ARK

13 David consulted with all his leaders, the commanders of hundreds and of thousands. 2 Then
he said to the whole assembly of Israel, "If it seems
good to you, and if this is from the LORD our God, let's
spread out and send the message to the rest of our
relatives in all the districts of Israel, including the
priests and Levites in their cities with pasturelands,
that they should gather together with us. 3 Then let's
bring back the ark of our God, for we did not inquire
of him[G] in Saul's days." 4 Since the proposal seemed
right to all the people, the whole assembly agreed
to do it.
5 So David assembled all Israel, from the Shihor of Egypt to the entrance of Hamath,[H] to bring
the ark of God from Kiriath-jearim. 6 David and
all Israel went to Baalah (that is, Kiriath-jearim
that belongs to Judah) to take from there the ark
of God, which bears the name of the LORD who is
enthroned between the cherubim. 7 At Abinadab's

[A] **12:15** = Nisan (March–April) [B] **12:18** Lit *clothed*; Jdg 6:34; 2Ch 24:20
[C] **12:22** Or *like the ultimate army* [D] **12:28** Lit *the house of his father*
[E] **12:30** Lit *the house of their fathers* [F] **12:33** LXX; MT omits *David*
[G] **13:3** Or *did not seek it* [H] **13:5** Or *to Lebo-hamath*

house they set the ark of God on a new cart. Uzzah and Ahio[A] were guiding the cart.

8 David and all Israel were dancing with all their might before God with songs and with lyres, harps, tambourines, cymbals, and trumpets. 9 When they came to Chidon's threshing floor, Uzzah reached out to hold the ark because the oxen had stumbled. 10 Then the LORD's anger burned against Uzzah, and he struck him dead because he had reached out to the ark. So he died there in the presence of God.

11 David was angry because of the LORD's outburst against Uzzah, so he named that place Outburst Against Uzzah,[B] as it is still named today. 12 David feared God that day and said, "How can I ever bring the ark of God to me?" 13 So David did not bring the ark of God home[C] to the city of David; instead, he diverted it to the house of Obed-edom of Gath. 14 The ark of God remained with Obed-edom's family in his house for three months, and the LORD blessed his family and all that he had.

GOD'S BLESSING ON DAVID

14 King Hiram of Tyre sent envoys to David, along with cedar logs, stonemasons, and carpenters to build a palace for him. 2 Then David knew that the LORD had established him as king over Israel and that his kingdom had been exalted for the sake of his people Israel.

3 David took more wives in Jerusalem, and he became the father of more sons and daughters. 4 These are the names of the children born to him in Jerusalem: Shammua, Shobab, Nathan, Solomon, 5 Ibhar, Elishua, Elpelet, 6 Nogah, Nepheg, Japhia, 7 Elishama, Beeliada, and Eliphelet.

8 When the Philistines heard that David had been anointed king over all Israel, they all went in search of David; when David heard of this, he went out to face them. 9 Now the Philistines had come and raided in Rephaim Valley, 10 so David inquired of God, "Should I attack the Philistines? Will you hand them over to me?"

The LORD replied, "Attack, and I will hand them over to you."

11 So the Israelites went up to Baal-perazim, and David defeated the Philistines there. Then David said, "Like a bursting flood, God has used me to burst out against my enemies." Therefore, they named that place The Lord Bursts Out.[D] 12 The Philistines abandoned their idols there, and David ordered that they be burned in the fire.

13 Once again the Philistines raided in the valley. 14 So David again inquired of God, and God answered him, "Do not pursue them directly. Circle around them and attack them opposite the balsam trees. 15 When you hear the sound of marching in the tops of the balsam trees, then go out to battle, for God will have gone out ahead of you to strike down the army of the Philistines." 16 So David did as God commanded him, and they struck down the Philistine army from Gibeon to Gezer. 17 Then David's fame spread throughout the lands, and the LORD caused all the nations to be terrified of him.

THE ARK COMES TO JERUSALEM

15 David built houses for himself in the city of David, and he prepared a place for the ark of God and pitched a tent for it. 2 Then David said, "No one but the Levites may carry the ark of God, because the LORD has chosen them to carry the ark of the LORD and to minister before him forever."

3 David assembled all Israel at Jerusalem to bring the ark of the LORD to the place he had prepared for it. 4 Then he gathered together the descendants of Aaron and the Levites:

5 From the Kohathites, Uriel the leader and 120 of his relatives; 6 from the Merarites, Asaiah the leader and 220 of his relatives; 7 from the Gershomites,[E] Joel the leader and 130 of his relatives; 8 from the Elizaphanites, Shemaiah the leader and 200 of his relatives; 9 from the Hebronites, Eliel the leader and 80 of his relatives; 10 from the Uzzielites, Amminadab the leader and 112 of his relatives.

11 David summoned the priests Zadok and Abiathar and the Levites Uriel, Asaiah, Joel, Shemaiah, Eliel, and Amminadab. 12 He said to them, "You are the heads of the Levite families. You and your relatives must consecrate yourselves so that you may bring the ark of the LORD God of Israel to the place I have prepared for it. 13 For the LORD our God burst out in anger against us because you Levites were not with us the first time, for we didn't inquire of him about the proper procedures." 14 So the priests and the Levites consecrated themselves to bring up the ark of the LORD God of Israel. 15 Then the Levites carried the ark of God the way Moses had commanded according to the word of the LORD: on their shoulders with the poles.

16 Then David told the leaders of the Levites to appoint their relatives as singers and to have them raise their voices with joy accompanied by musical instruments — harps, lyres, and cymbals. 17 So the Levites appointed Heman son of Joel; from his relatives, Asaph son of Berechiah; and from their relatives the Merarites, Ethan son of Kushaiah. 18 With them were their relatives second in rank: Zechariah, Jaaziel,[F] Shemiramoth, Jehiel, Unni, Eliab, Benaiah, Maaseiah, Mattithiah, Eliphelehu, Mikneiah, and the gatekeepers Obed-edom and Jeiel. 19 The singers Heman, Asaph, and Ethan were to sound the bronze cymbals;

[A] **13:7** Or *And his brothers* [B] **13:11** Or *Perez-uzzah* [C] **13:13** Lit *to himself* [D] **14:11** Or *Baal-perazim* [E] **15:7** = Gershonites [F] **15:18** Some Hb mss, LXX; other Hb mss read *Zechariah son and Jaaziel*

20 Zechariah, Aziel, Shemiramoth, Jehiel, Unni, Eliab,
Maaseiah, and Benaiah were to play harps according
to *Alamoth*[A] 21 and Mattithiah, Eliphelehu, Mikneiah,
Obed-edom, Jeiel, and Azaziah were to lead the music
with lyres according to the *Sheminith*. 22 Chenaniah,
the leader of the Levites in music, was to direct the
music because he was skillful. 23 Berechiah and Elkanah were to be gatekeepers for the ark. 24 The priests,
Shebaniah, Joshaphat, Nethanel, Amasai, Zechariah,
Benaiah, and Eliezer, were to blow trumpets before
the ark of God. Obed-edom and Jehiah were also to
be gatekeepers for the ark.

25 David, the elders of Israel, and the commanders of thousands went with rejoicing to bring the
ark of the covenant of the LORD from the house of
Obed-edom. 26 Because God helped the Levites who
were carrying the ark of the covenant of the LORD,
with God's help, they sacrificed seven bulls and sev-
en rams.

27 Now David was dressed in a robe of fine linen,
as were all the Levites who were carrying the ark, as
well as the singers and Chenaniah, the music leader
of the singers. David also wore a linen ephod. 28 So all
Israel brought up the ark of the covenant of the LORD
with shouts, the sound of the ram's horn, trumpets,
and cymbals, and the playing of harps and lyres. 29 As
the ark of the covenant of the LORD was entering the
city of David, Saul's daughter Michal looked down
from the window and saw King David leaping[B] and
dancing, and she despised him in her heart.

16 They brought the ark of God and placed it inside the tent David had pitched for it. Then
they offered burnt offerings and fellowship offerings
in God's presence. 2 When David had finished offering the burnt offerings and the fellowship offerings,
he blessed the people in the name of the LORD. 3 Then
he distributed to each and every Israelite, both men
and women, a loaf of bread, a date cake, and a raisin cake.

4 David appointed some of the Levites to be ministers before the ark of the LORD, to celebrate the LORD
God of Israel, and to give thanks and praise to him.
5 Asaph was the chief and Zechariah was second to
him. Jeiel, Shemiramoth, Jehiel, Mattithiah, Eliab,
Benaiah, Obed-edom, and Jeiel played the harps and
lyres, while Asaph sounded the cymbals 6 and the
priests Benaiah and Jahaziel blew the trumpets regularly before the ark of the covenant of God.

DAVID'S PSALM OF THANKSGIVING

7 On that day David decreed for the first time that
thanks be given to the LORD by Asaph and his relatives:

8 Give thanks to the LORD; call on his name;
proclaim his deeds among the peoples.
9 Sing to him; sing praise to him;
tell about all his wondrous works!
10 Boast in his holy name;
let the hearts of those who seek the LORD
rejoice.
11 Seek the LORD and his strength;
seek his face always.
12 Remember the wondrous works he has done,
his wonders, and the judgments
he has pronounced,[C]
13 you offspring of Israel his servant,
Jacob's descendants — his chosen ones.

14 He is the LORD our God;
his judgments govern the whole earth.
15 Remember his covenant forever —
the promise he ordained for a thousand
generations,
16 the covenant he made with Abraham,
swore[D] to Isaac,
17 and confirmed to Jacob as a decree,
and to Israel as a permanent covenant:
18 "I will give the land of Canaan to you
as your inherited portion."

19 When they[E] were few in number,
very few indeed, and resident aliens
in Canaan
20 wandering from nation to nation
and from one kingdom to another,
21 he allowed no one to oppress them;
he rebuked kings on their behalf:
22 "Do not touch my anointed ones
or harm my prophets."

23 Let the whole earth sing to the LORD.
Proclaim his salvation from day to day.
24 Declare his glory among the nations,
his wondrous works among all peoples.

25 For the LORD is great and highly praised;
he is feared above all gods.
26 For all the gods of the peoples are
worthless idols,
but the LORD made the heavens.
27 Splendor and majesty are before him;
strength and joy are in his place.
28 Ascribe to the LORD, families of the peoples,
ascribe to the LORD glory and strength.
29 Ascribe to the LORD the glory of his name;
bring an offering and come before him.

[A] **15:20** This may refer to a high pitch, perhaps a tune sung by soprano voices; the Hb word means "young women"; Ps 46 title [B] **15:29** Or *whirling* [C] **16:12** Lit *judgments of his mouth* [D] **16:16** Lit *and his oath* [E] **16:19** One Hb ms, LXX, Vg; other Hb mss read *you*

David and the Philistines

by Marvin E. Tate

Terra-cotta anthropoid coffin lid from Lachish gives evidence that the Philistines continued to use distinctive burial methods that reflected their Anatolian and Aegean heritage.

PHILISTINES' HISTORY

The Philistines were in the land of Canaan long before David was born. Many today still use their name to refer to David's land, for "Palestine" is derived from "Philistine." We first read about them in the fifth year of Pharaoh Ramesses III (reigned 1184–1153 BC), who repulsed a land and sea invasion of his western borders by the Libyans. The Peleset (Philistines) and Tjekker were among the Libyan's allies.[1] Three years later, Ramesses had to deal with another effort to invade Egypt. This time a mixed group from the north, including the Peleset, took a position at Amor (probably in Syria) after victories in areas that had been part of the Hittite Empire. The invaders came with their military equipment, plus oxcarts loaded with women, children, and goods. They were prepared to occupy and settle in new lands.

The land invaders and sea raiders who attacked Egypt during this period are known as the Sea Peoples. The Sea Peoples were Indo-European groups from the Aegean islands, Cyprus, and Asia Minor. They appeared in the areas of the eastern Mediterranean and Asia Minor during the times of great turmoil and movement that marked the end of the Bronze Age and the beginnings of the Iron Age (1200–1100 BC).

The precise origin of the Philistines, however, eludes our present knowledge.[2] Old Testament references link them with Caphtor (Jr 47:4; Am 9:7). Most biblical scholars identify Caphtor with the island of Crete. The Kapturi or Kaptara of cuneiform texts and the Keftiu of Egyptian texts support this view. However, no certain archaeological evidence exists to associate the Philistines with Crete, though pottery and other items do relate them to Cyprus. The Philistine use of iron suggests an association with the Hittites in Asia Minor, as does the Philistine use of a three-man chariot similar to that of the Hittites.[3] The explanation for this uncertainty may lie in the likely possibility that people came to use the term *Caphtor* in the broad sense to refer to the Cretan-Aegean world.[4] Before moving into Crete and other Aegean areas, the Philistines may have lived on mainland Greece and even lands farther away.

In any case, the Philistines were part of the powerful movement of the Sea Peoples toward Egypt and Israel. The major area of their settlement in Israel was the southern coastal plain and adjacent territory, specifically in what came to be known as the five Philistine cities (Gaza, Ashkelon, Ashdod, Gath, and Ekron; see Jos 13:3; Jdg 3:3). We do not know the circumstances of their settlement in this region. Some Philistines probably were there before the battles of the Sea Peoples with Ramesses III.

The Philistine presence was not confined, however, to five towns on the southern coastal plain. We know they lived in other places as well, such as Megiddo and Beth-shean (see 1Sm 31:8,12). The Philistines seem to have formed a horseshoe-shaped ring of towns and dominion around the Israelite tribes settled in the central highlands.[5]

The exact nature of the Philistine establishment in the land of Israel is still historically blurred, but evidence points toward a military aristocracy operating as feudal lords under a declining Egyptian influence.[6] The Philistines seem to have adapted themselves to the long-established Canaanite city-state system. These city-states apparently were organized in an essentially feudal way. The pharaohs of Egypt, sometimes with great force, held overall dominion, but usually without a highly efficient administrative system or much direct supervision. The Egyptians depended on native rulers to exercise control over the city-states, allowing the rulers considerable autonomy so long as they performed satisfactorily and paid the necessary tribute. The Egyptian presence helped stabilize the political and economic situation and generally was advantageous to the local Canaanite rulers. These rulers in turn depended on vassals who were given smaller towns and grants of land and who were expected to support the ruler to whom they owed their vassalage. The vassals, of course, exacted payments of various sorts and support from landowners and peasants under them.

The Philistine-Canaanite feudal system probably is reflected in the accounts of David's relationship with the Philistines through Achish, who is called "king of Gath" (1Sm 27:2–3). Achish likely was a Canaanite vassal king of the Philistines, who ruled Gath and surrounding towns (such as Ziklag) that were under Philistine vassalage.[7]

PHILISTINES, DAVID, AND ISRAEL

The Old Testament use of "Philistine" is rather broad. Various texts use the term to refer to the Philistines proper, others to similar and associated groups.[8] The Old Testament narratives tell of repeated sharp conflict between the Philistines and the Israelites. The accounts of Samson in Judges 13–16 reflect both the interaction and the conflict between the two groups. According to Judges 14:4, "At that time, the Philistines were ruling Israel."

The Philistines' location in the relatively well supplied and compact area of the southern coastal plain provided a base that was fairly easily defended. Their presence in one way or another up the coastal areas, through the Esdraelon and Jezreel Valleys, and into the Jordan Valley formed a kind of "horse collar" around the Israelite tribes in the central highlands that cut them off from the tribes in Galilee and at least interfered with relationships with tribes across the Jordan.

The Philistines' technology gave them significant military and economic superiority over the Israelites.[9] The Philistines had acquired skill in iron-working (probably from the Hittites) and used iron weapons and chariots. They also used heavily armed infantry, sometimes in single combat as illustrated in David's killing the well-armed Philistine champion Goliath (1Sm 17). In addition to man-to-man combat, the Philistines used mobile strike forces of well-organized raiders to

Waterfront at Crete. Known in the Old Testament as Caphtor, Crete was the likely home to the Philistines (Am 9:7).

move into Israelite territory (see 1Sm 13:17–18; 14:15).[10] We see evidence of the Philistines' economic superiority in the short summary in 1 Samuel 13:19–23, which informs us that there was no ironsmith in the land of Israel. The Israelites had to depend on the Philistines for agricultural implements of various types. We also read of Philistine use of gold in 1 Samuel 6.

The Philistines' economic advantage must have been enhanced by their experience and activity as sea and land traders. Their control of roads probably influenced the Philistine drive against the Israelites. Evidently the Philistines saw the Israelites as a serious threat to trade in the Jordan Valley and the Transjordan.

The Philistine push for control of the land had been so successful that by the time David came to young manhood, Israel was fighting for survival as a people. Gaining the upper hand was essential if Israel was going to retain any significant degree of self-rule and economic well-being. Fortunately for David, he was able to begin his career in the midst of Saul's considerable success. David emerged as a warrior fighting with Saul's forces to break the Philistine grip on the central highlands and to maintain the Israelite positions (1Sm 17–18). David's success led to a tragic break of relationship with Saul and to his flight to the Negev, where he began guerrilla operations against both Saul and the Philistines (23:1–13). Eventually, however, he secured a base of operations at Ziklag and a more favorable frame of authority by accepting vassalage to Achish at Gath (21:10–15; 27:1–7).

This arrangement apparently gave David a safer and stronger basis for his activities and permitted him to develop his leadership so that he was ready to rise to power after Saul's death. As a vassal, David raided hostile groups in the Negev and gave presents from the plunder to the elders of Judah who ruled in the area (30:26–31), while his overlord Achish was allowed to believe that he was making himself very unacceptable to the Israelites (27:8–12).

The Philistine rulers did not trust David enough to allow him to take a direct part in the final battle with Saul (29:1–11). However, David's move to Hebron and his anointing there as Judah's king almost certainly was carried out with their tacit approval.[11] They may not have trusted David fully, but they must have considered favorably the establishment of one of their vassals in a rival kingship to that of the heirs of Saul's kingdom (Abner and Ish-bosheth, 2Sm 2:1–11). They would have viewed this development as giving them access to valuable territory and as stabilizing their southern flank.

When David became the king of "all the tribes of Israel," however, the situation changed, and the Philistines lost no time in going after him (2Sm 5:1–5,17–21). They attacked in the Rephaim Valley near Jerusalem in an effort to separate David from the northern tribes. They failed, and David defeated them at Baal-perazim. This began a major power shift in Israel's favor. Subsequently David forced the Philistines back inside their traditional territory on the coastal plain (5:22–25) and continued to expand his kingdom until it became a sizable empire. However, he never conquered the Philistine heartland on the coastal plain, and Philistia endured alongside the Israelite states for centuries, until its independent existence was ended by the Babylonians in 604 BC.

David's success appears to have been due, in part at least, to his adoption of some Philistine tactics and policies. He seems to have beaten the Philistines with their own methods of warfare, using tough, professional, and mobile strike forces rather than large unwieldy forces used by the Canaanite city-states and to some extent by Saul. Evidently he reversed the situation at Gath, taking it out of the control of the Philistines (1Ch 18:1), and made Achish his vassal (at the beginning of the reign of Solomon, Achish was still king at Gath; 1Kg 2:39–41).

David's use of professional mercenary soldiers, along with elite groups of superior fighters (note "the Thirty" in 2Sm 23:18–39), is especially striking. Clearly, he did not depend mainly on the farmer militia from the tribes but on his own troops and commanders (like Benaiah) who owed their positions solely to him. Among these troops were six hundred men from Gath, under their commander Ittai (2Sm 15:17–22), who supported David during Absalom's revolt. The Cherethites and Pelethites (named with the six hundred men from Gath in 15:18) are cited repeatedly in association with David. Their presence was decisive in bringing Solomon to the throne after David finally made up his mind about his successor (2Sm 8:18; 20:7,23; 1Kg 1:38–40,44; 1Ch 18:17). These two groups may have been Philistines or closely related to them. ✣

---

[1] For the history of this period in Egypt, see R. O. Faulkner, "Egypt: From the Inception of the Nineteenth Dynasty to the Death of Rameses III" in CAH, vol. 2, part 2, 241–51; R. D. Barnett, "The Sea Peoples" in CAH, vol. 2, part 2, 359–78. [2] For a good review of the theories, see Roland de Vaux, *The Early History of Israel*, trans. David Smith (Philadelphia: Westminster, 1978), 503–10; also Barnett, "Sea Peoples." [3] See Yigael Yadin, *The Art of Warfare in Biblical Lands* (New York: McGraw-Hill, 1963), 2–250. [4] Barnett, "Sea Peoples," 375; Frederick W. Bush, "Caphtor" in *ISBE*, vol. 1 (1979), 610–11. [5] G. Ernst Wright, "Fresh Evidence for the Philistine Story," *BA* 29.3 (1966): 70–78. [6] Norman K. Gottwald, *The Tribes of Yahweh* (Maryknoll, NY: Orbis, 1979), 410–14. [7] Argued by Hanna E. Kassis, "Gath and the Structure of the 'Philistine' Society," *JBL* 84 (1965), 259–71, and accepted by Gottwald, *Tribes*, 413. [8] K. A. Kitchen, "The Philistines" in *Peoples of Old Testament Times*, ed. D. J. Wiseman (Oxford: Clarendon, 1973), 57. [9] Gottwald, *Tribes*, 414–17. [10] Gottwald, *Tribes*, 415. [11] Martin Noth, *The History of Israel*, trans. Stanley Godman (New York: Harper, 1958), 162.

Worship the LORD
in the splendor of his holiness;
30 let the whole earth tremble before him.

The world is firmly established;
it cannot be shaken.
31 Let the heavens be glad and the earth rejoice,
and let them say among the nations,
"The LORD reigns!"
32 Let the sea and all that fills it resound;
let the fields and everything in them exult.
33 Then the trees of the forest will shout for joy
before the LORD,
for he is coming to judge the earth.

34 Give thanks to the LORD, for he is good;
his faithful love endures forever.
35 And say, "Save us, God of our salvation;
gather us and rescue us from the nations
so that we may give thanks to your holy name
and rejoice in your praise.
36 Blessed be the LORD God of Israel
from everlasting to everlasting."
Then all the people said, "Amen" and "Praise the LORD."

37 So David left Asaph and his relatives there before
the ark of the LORD's covenant to minister regularly
before the ark according to the daily requirements.
38 He assigned Obed-edom and his[A] sixty-eight relatives. Obed-edom son of Jeduthun and Hosah were
to be gatekeepers. 39 David left the priest Zadok and
his fellow priests before the tabernacle of the LORD
at the high place in Gibeon 40 to offer burnt offerings
regularly, morning and evening, to the LORD on the
altar of burnt offerings and to do everything that
was written in the law of the LORD, which he had
commanded Israel to keep. 41 With them were Heman,
Jeduthun, and the rest who were chosen and designated by name to give thanks to the LORD — for his
faithful love endures forever. 42 Heman and Jeduthun
had with them trumpets and cymbals to play and
musical instruments of God. Jeduthun's sons were
at the city gate.

43 Then all the people went home, and David returned home to bless his household.

THE LORD'S COVENANT WITH DAVID

17 When David had settled into his palace, he said
to the prophet Nathan, "Look! I am living in a
cedar house while the ark of the LORD's covenant is
under tent curtains."

2 So Nathan told David, "Do all that is on your mind,
for God is with you."

3 But that night the word of God came to Nathan:
4 "Go to David my servant and say, 'This is what the
LORD says: You are not the one to build me a house to
dwell in. 5 From the time I brought Israel out of Egypt
until today I have not dwelt in a house; instead, I have
moved from one tent site to another, and from one
tabernacle location to another.[B] 6 In all my journeys
throughout Israel, have I ever spoken a word to even
one of the judges of Israel, whom I commanded to
shepherd my people, asking: Why haven't you built
me a house of cedar?'

7 "So now this is what you are to say to my servant
David: 'This is what the LORD of Armies says: I took
you from the pasture, from tending the flock, to be
ruler over my people Israel. 8 I have been with you
wherever you have gone, and I have destroyed all
your enemies before you. I will make a name for you
like that of the greatest on the earth. 9 I will designate
a place for my people Israel and plant them, so that
they may live there and not be disturbed again. Evildoers will not continue to oppress them as they have
done 10 ever since the day I ordered judges to be over
my people Israel. I will also subdue all your enemies.

"'Furthermore, I declare to you that the LORD himself will build a house for you. 11 When your time
comes to be with your ancestors, I will raise up after you your descendant, who is one of your own
sons, and I will establish his kingdom. 12 He is the one
who will build a house for me, and I will establish his
throne forever. 13 I will be his father, and he will be my
son. I will not remove my faithful love from him as I
removed it from the one who was before you. 14 I will
appoint him over my house and my kingdom forever,
and his throne will be established forever.'"

15 Nathan reported all these words and this entire
vision to David.

DAVID'S PRAYER OF THANKSGIVING

16 Then King David went in, sat in the LORD's presence, and said,

Who am I, LORD God, and what is my house that
you have brought me this far? 17 This was a little
thing to you,[C] God, for you have spoken about
your servant's house in the distant future. You
regard me as a man of distinction,[D] LORD God.
18 What more can David say to you for honoring
your servant? You know your servant. 19 LORD,
you have done this whole great thing, making
known all these great promises for the sake of
your servant and according to your will. 20 LORD,
there is no one like you, and there is no God besides you, as all we have heard confirms. 21 And
who is like your people Israel? God, you came
to one nation on earth to redeem a people for
yourself, to make a name for yourself through

[A] **16:38** LXX, Syr, Vg; Hb reads *their* [B] **17:5** Lit *I was from tent to tent and from tabernacle* [C] **17:17** Lit *thing in your eyes* [D] **17:17** Hb obscure

great and awesome works by driving out nations
before your people you redeemed from Egypt.
22 You made your people Israel your own people
forever, and you, LORD, have become their God.

23 Now, LORD, let the word that you have spoken concerning your servant and his house be
confirmed forever, and do as you have promised.
24 Let your name be confirmed and magnified
forever in the saying, "The LORD of Armies, the
God of Israel, is God over Israel." May the house
of your servant David be established before
you. 25 Since you, my God, have revealed to[A]
your servant that you will build him a house,
your servant has found courage to pray in your
presence. 26 LORD, you indeed are God, and you
have promised this good thing to your servant.
27 So now, you have been pleased to bless your
servant's house that it may continue before you
forever. For you, LORD, have blessed it, and it is
blessed forever.

DAVID'S MILITARY CAMPAIGNS

18 After this, David defeated the Philistines, subdued them, and took Gath and its surrounding
villages from Philistine control. 2 He also defeated
the Moabites, and they became David's subjects and
brought tribute.
3 David also defeated King Hadadezer of Zobah at
Hamath when he went to establish his control at the
Euphrates River. 4 David captured one thousand chariots, seven thousand horsemen, and twenty thousand
foot soldiers from him, hamstrung all the horses, and
kept a hundred chariots.[B]
5 When the Arameans of Damascus came to assist
King Hadadezer of Zobah, David struck down twenty-two thousand Aramean men. 6 Then he placed
garrisons[C] in Aram of Damascus, and the Arameans
became David's subjects and brought tribute. The
LORD made David victorious wherever he went.
7 David took the gold shields carried by Hadadezer's officers and brought them to Jerusalem. 8 From
Tibhath and Cun, Hadadezer's cities, David also took
huge quantities of bronze, from which Solomon
made the bronze basin,[D] the pillars, and the bronze
articles.
9 When King Tou of Hamath heard that David had
defeated the entire army of King Hadadezer of Zobah,
10 he sent his son Hadoram to King David to greet him
and to congratulate him because David had fought
against Hadadezer and defeated him, for Tou and
Hadadezer had fought many wars. Hadoram brought
all kinds of gold, silver, and bronze items. 11 King David also dedicated these to the LORD, along with the
silver and gold he had carried off from all the nations
— from Edom, Moab, the Ammonites, the Philistines,
and the Amalekites.
12 Abishai son of Zeruiah struck down eighteen
thousand Edomites in the Salt Valley. 13 He put garrisons in Edom, and all the Edomites were subject
to David. The LORD made David victorious wherever
he went.
14 So David reigned over all Israel, administering
justice and righteousness for all his people.

15 Joab son of Zeruiah was over the army;
Jehoshaphat son of Ahilud was
court historian;
16 Zadok son of Ahitub and Ahimelech[E]
son of Abiathar were priests;
Shavsha was court secretary;
17 Benaiah son of Jehoiada was over the
Cherethites and the Pelethites;
and David's sons were the chief officials
at the king's side.

WAR WITH THE AMMONITES

19 Some time later, King Nahash of the Ammonites died, and his son became king in his place.
2 Then David said, "I'll show kindness to Hanun son of
Nahash, because his father showed kindness to me."
So David sent messengers to console him concerning his father. However, when David's emissaries arrived in the land of the Ammonites to console him,
3 the Ammonite leaders said to Hanun, "Just because
David has sent men with condolences for you, do you
really believe he's showing respect for your father?
Instead, haven't his emissaries come in order to scout
out, overthrow, and spy on the land?" 4 So Hanun took
David's emissaries, shaved them, cut their clothes in
half at the hips, and sent them away.
5 It was reported to David about his men, so he sent
messengers to meet them, since the men were deeply
humiliated. The king said, "Stay in Jericho until your
beards grow back; then return."
6 When the Ammonites realized they had made
themselves repulsive to David, Hanun and the
Ammonites sent thirty-eight tons[F] of silver to hire
chariots and horsemen from Aram-naharaim, Aram-
maacah, and Zobah. 7 They hired thirty-two thousand
chariots and the king of Maacah with his army, who
came and camped near Medeba. The Ammonites also
came together from their cities for the battle.
8 David heard about this and sent Joab and all
the elite troops. 9 The Ammonites marched out and
lined up in battle formation at the entrance of the city
while the kings who had come were in the field by

[A]**17:25** Lit *have uncovered the ear of* [B]**18:4** Or *chariot horses*
[C]**18:6** Some Hb mss, LXX, Vg; other Hb mss omit *garrisons*; 2Sm 8:6
[D]**18:8** Lit *sea* [E]**18:16** Some Hb mss, LXX, Syr, Vg; other Hb mss read *Abimelech*; 2Sm 8:17 [F]**19:6** Lit *1,000 talents*

themselves. 10 When Joab saw that there was a battle line in front of him and another behind him, he chose some of Israel's finest young men[A] and lined up in formation to engage the Arameans. 11 He placed the rest of the forces under the command of his brother Abishai. They lined up in formation to engage the Ammonites.

12 "If the Arameans are too strong for me," Joab said, "then you'll be my help. However, if the Ammonites are too strong for you, I'll help you. 13 Be strong! Let's prove ourselves strong for our people and for the cities of our God. May the LORD's will be done."[B]

14 Joab and the people with him approached the Arameans for battle, and they fled before him. 15 When the Ammonites saw that the Arameans had fled, they likewise fled before Joab's brother Abishai and entered the city. Then Joab went to Jerusalem.

16 When the Arameans realized that they had been defeated by Israel, they sent messengers to summon the Arameans who were beyond the Euphrates River. They were led by Shophach, the commander of Hadadezer's army.

17 When this was reported to David, he gathered all Israel and crossed the Jordan. He came up to the Arameans and lined up against them. When David lined up to engage them, they fought against him. 18 But the Arameans fled before Israel, and David killed seven thousand of their charioteers and forty thousand foot soldiers. He also killed Shophach, commander of the army. 19 When Hadadezer's subjects saw that they had been defeated by Israel, they made peace with David and became his subjects. After this, the Arameans were never willing to help the Ammonites again.

CAPTURE OF THE CITY OF RABBAH

20 In the spring[C] when kings march out to war, Joab led the army and destroyed the Ammonites' land. He came to Rabbah and besieged it, but David remained in Jerusalem. Joab attacked Rabbah and demolished it. 2 Then David took the crown from the head of their king,[D,E] and it was placed on David's head. He found that the crown weighed seventy-five pounds[F] of gold, and there was a precious stone in it. In addition, David took away a large quantity of plunder from the city. 3 He brought out the people who were in it and put them to work with saws,[G] iron picks, and axes.[H] David did the same to all the Ammonite cities. Then he and all his troops returned to Jerusalem.

THE PHILISTINE GIANTS

4 After this, a war broke out with the Philistines at Gezer. At that time Sibbecai the Hushathite killed Sippai, a descendant of the Rephaim,[I] and the Philistines were subdued.

5 Once again there was a battle with the Philistines, and Elhanan son of Jair killed Lahmi the brother of Goliath of Gath. The shaft of his spear was like a weaver's beam.

6 There was still another battle at Gath where there was a man of extraordinary stature with six fingers on each hand and six toes on each foot — twenty-four in all. He, too, was descended from the giant.[J] 7 When he taunted Israel, Jonathan son of David's brother Shimei killed him.

8 These were the descendants of the giant in Gath killed by David and his soldiers.

DAVID'S MILITARY CENSUS

21 Satan[K] rose up against Israel and incited David to count the people of Israel. 2 So David said to Joab and the commanders of the troops, "Go and count Israel from Beer-sheba to Dan and bring a report to me so I can know their number."

3 Joab replied, "May the LORD multiply the number of his people a hundred times over! My lord the king, aren't they all my lord's servants? Why does my lord want to do this? Why should he bring guilt on Israel?"

4 Yet the king's order prevailed over Joab. So Joab left and traveled throughout Israel and then returned to Jerusalem. 5 Joab gave the total troop registration to David. In all Israel there were one million one hundred thousand armed men[L] and in Judah itself four hundred seventy thousand armed men. 6 But he did not include Levi and Benjamin in the count because the king's command was detestable to him. 7 This command was also evil in God's sight, so he afflicted Israel.

8 David said to God, "I have sinned greatly because I have done this thing. Now, please take away your servant's guilt, for I've been very foolish."

DAVID'S PUNISHMENT

9 Then the LORD instructed Gad, David's seer, 10 "Go and say to David, 'This is what the LORD says: I am offering you three choices. Choose one of them for yourself, and I will do it to you.' "

11 So Gad went to David and said to him, "This is what the LORD says: 'Take your choice: 12 three years of famine, or three months of devastation by your foes with the sword of your enemy overtaking you, or three days of the sword of the LORD — a plague on

[A] **19:10** Lit *Israel's choice ones* [B] **19:13** Lit *the LORD do what is good in his eyes* [C] **20:1** Lit *At the time of the return of the year* [D] **20:2** LXX, Vg read *of Milcom* [E] **20:2** = Molech; 1Kg 11:5,7 [F] **20:2** Lit *a talent* [G] **20:3** Text emended; MT reads *and sawed them with the saw*; 2Sm 12:31 [H] **20:3** Text emended; MT reads *saws*; 2Sm 12:31 [I] **20:4** Or *the Rephaites* [J] **20:6** Or *Raphah*, also in v. 8 [K] **21:1** Or *An adversary*; Jb 1:6; Zch 3:1–2 [L] **21:5** Lit *men drawing the sword*

the land, the angel of the LORD bringing destruction to the whole territory of Israel.' Now decide what answer I should take back to the one who sent me."

13 David answered Gad, "I'm in anguish. Please, let me fall into the LORD's hands because his mercies are very great, but don't let me fall into human hands."

14 So the LORD sent a plague on Israel, and seventy thousand Israelite men died. 15 Then God sent an angel to Jerusalem to destroy it, but when the angel was about to destroy the city,[A] the LORD looked, relented concerning the destruction, and said to the angel who was destroying the people, "Enough, withdraw your hand now!" The angel of the LORD was then standing at the threshing floor of Ornan[B] the Jebusite.

16 When David looked up and saw the angel of the LORD standing between earth and heaven, with his drawn sword in his hand stretched out over Jerusalem, David and the elders, covered in sackcloth, fell facedown. 17 David said to God, "Wasn't I the one who gave the order to count the people? I am the one who has sinned and acted very wickedly. But these sheep, what have they done? LORD my God, please let your hand be against me and against my father's family, but don't let the plague be against your people."

DAVID'S ALTAR

18 So the angel of the LORD ordered Gad to tell David to go and set up an altar to the LORD on the threshing floor of Ornan the Jebusite. 19 David went up at Gad's command spoken in the name of the LORD.

20 Ornan was threshing wheat when he turned and saw the angel. His four sons, who were with him, hid. 21 David came to Ornan, and when Ornan looked and saw David, he left the threshing floor and bowed to David with his face to the ground.

22 Then David said to Ornan, "Give me this threshing-floor plot so that I may build an altar to the LORD on it. Give it to me for the full price, so the plague on the people may be stopped."

23 Ornan said to David, "Take it! My lord the king may do whatever he wants.[C] See, I give the oxen for the burnt offerings, the threshing sledges for the wood, and the wheat for the grain offering — I give it all."

24 King David answered Ornan, "No, I insist on paying the full price, for I will not take for the LORD what belongs to you or offer burnt offerings that cost me nothing."

25 So David gave Ornan fifteen pounds of gold[D] for the plot. 26 He built an altar to the LORD there and offered burnt offerings and fellowship offerings. He called on the LORD, and he answered him with fire from heaven on the altar of burnt offering.

27 Then the LORD spoke to the angel, and he put his sword back into its sheath. 28 At that time, David offered sacrifices there when he saw that the LORD answered him at the threshing floor of Ornan the Jebusite. 29 The tabernacle of the LORD, which Moses made in the wilderness, and the altar of burnt offering were at the high place in Gibeon, 30 but David could not go before it to inquire of God, because he was terrified of the sword of the LORD's angel.

22 1 Then David said, "This is the house of the LORD God, and this is the altar of burnt offering for Israel."

DAVID'S PREPARATIONS FOR THE TEMPLE

2 So David gave orders to gather the resident aliens that were in the land of Israel, and he appointed stonecutters to cut finished stones for building God's house. 3 David supplied a great deal of iron to make the nails for the doors of the gates and for the fittings, together with an immeasurable quantity of bronze, 4 and innumerable cedar logs because the Sidonians and Tyrians had brought a large quantity of cedar logs to David. 5 David said, "My son Solomon is young and inexperienced, and the house that is to be built for the LORD must be exceedingly great and famous and glorious in all the lands. Therefore, I will make provision for it." So David made lavish preparations for it before his death.

6 Then he summoned his son Solomon and charged him to build a house for the LORD God of Israel. 7 "My son," David said to Solomon, "It was in my heart to build a house for the name of the LORD my God, 8 but the word of the LORD came to me: 'You have shed much blood and waged great wars. You are not to build a house for my name because you have shed so much blood on the ground before me. 9 But a son will be born to you; he will be a man of rest. I will give him rest from all his surrounding enemies, for his name will be Solomon,[E] and I will give peace and quiet to Israel during his reign. 10 He is the one who will build a house for my name. He will be my son, and I will be his father. I will establish the throne of his kingdom over Israel forever.'

11 "Now, my son, may the LORD be with you, and may you succeed in building the house of the LORD your God, as he said about you. 12 Above all, may the LORD give you insight and understanding when he puts you in charge of Israel so that you may keep the law of the LORD your God. 13 Then you will succeed if you carefully follow the statutes and ordinances

[A] **21:15** Lit *but as he was destroying* [B] **21:15-28** = Araunah in 2Sm 24:16-24 [C] **21:23** Lit *do what is good in his eyes* [D] **21:25** Lit *600 shekels of gold by weight* [E] **22:9** In Hb, the name *Solomon* sounds like "peace."

Ancient Threshing Floors

by Paul E. Kullman

A properly constructed threshing floor requires either a flat rocky area or hard compacted soil with a surface free of loose dust. The preferred site was typically on an elevated area near the edge of town. The winds, which naturally occur on a raised geographical elevation, helped the winnowing operation be productive. Being able to take advantage of the prevailing winds actually determined the threshing floor's exact location. Each threshing floor would be constructed in about a fifty-foot-diameter circle with a "crown" in the center, a raised area that helped shed rainwater.[1] If the crown did not occur naturally, workers would use the abundant stone supply and build up the center of the floor with stone pavers and sand joint filler.

AGRICULTURE

The threshing floor method of harvesting a crop occurred at a common gathering location for the ancient agrarian society. Several farmers, or the whole village, would share a threshing floor. This is one of the earliest forms of a business cooperative, where pieces of the operation provided communal benefit to the local economy.

At Samaria, this threshing floor is still used by the locals.

(Similarly, communities often shared winepresses.)

The purpose of a threshing floor is quite simple. Farmers of the ancient Near East would harvest grain crops, load them into flat carts pulled by draft animals (usually oxen or donkeys), and deliver the grain to a threshing floor. Workers unloaded and sorted the grain for processing. The larger sheaves were spread out uniformly on the ground and crushed by animals treading on them or cart wheels being driven over them (Is 28:27–28). Farmers would also use another tool of threshing known as the "threshing sledge."[2] A driver, riding atop a sledge, would direct animals to pull a heavy timber with embedded stones or iron teeth across the harvested grain. Once the harvest was broken up, laborers used the winnowing fork to toss stalks into the wind to separate chaff from the kernels. The kernel, the valuable part of the food product, would fall to the ground, allowing laborers to gather it for storage or market.

The harvest for barley and wheat occurs in the spring and requires many laborers to process. Therefore, the need for an abundance of laborers required families and the community to join together to help bring economic success to a village or small town.[3] After the threshing operation was complete, the threshing floor held an important and valuable commodity, one that the locals had to protect from theft (1Sm 23:1).

SYMBOLISM

The Bible uses the term *threshing floor* many times in both a symbolic and literal sense with the agrarian usage being the latter. The threshing floor was frequently a place that symbolized spiritual significance and blessing (Nm 18:27–32; Jdg 6:11–40). For instance, Gideon used the threshing floor as the location for a divine miracle—laying out his fleece. Also, the law speaks of its usage. Concerning the slave who has fulfilled his term of servitude, Deuteronomy 15:14 says, "Give generously to him from your flock, your threshing floor, and your winepress. You are to give him whatever the Lord your God has blessed you with." The threshing floor was the symbolic source of the sacrifice that worshipers gave back to the Lord out of thanksgiving for his divine blessings (Nm 15:20; Dt 16:13). Likewise, the threshing sledge was a symbol of brute force in the judgment of nations or people groups or for victory over Israel's enemies (Is 41:15–16; Am 1:3). The Lord used a harvesting metaphor to speak of judging Babylon, who was "like a threshing floor" at the time of her "harvest." This was a euphemism for his judgment (Jr 51:33).

John the Baptist used a threshing floor metaphor to describe the coming Messiah and what Jesus would do regarding spiritual judgment (Mt 3:12). The chaff that separates from the barley and wheat sheaves is deemed useless and destined for the fire, but the valued wheat is gathered and stored in the barn. Sometimes the chaff was gathered and sold as fuel for baking ovens. Likewise, farmers sold the prized wheat kernels to customers for baking bread. This metaphor is a strong visual illustration, as chaff represents the unsaved sent to the fire while the kernels are the saved who are a valuable part of the harvest. ✠

---

[1] "Threshing Floor" in *Wycliffe Biblical Dictionary*, ed. Charles F. Pfeiffer, Howard F. Vos, and John Rea (Peabody, MA: Hendrickson, 2003), 1701. [2] "Threshing Sledge" in *The Baker Illustrated Bible Dictionary*, ed. Tremper Longman III (Grand Rapids: Baker, 2013), 1630. [3] F. Nigel Hepper, "Agriculture" in *HolBD*, 24–25.

the LORD commanded Moses for Israel. Be strong and courageous. Don't be afraid or discouraged.

14 "Notice I have taken great pains to provide for the house of the LORD — 3,775 tons of gold, 37,750 tons of silver,[A] and bronze and iron that can't be weighed because there is so much of it. I have also provided timber and stone, but you will need to add more to them. 15 You also have many workers: stonecutters, masons, carpenters, and people skilled in every kind of work 16 in gold, silver, bronze, and iron — beyond number. Now begin the work, and may the LORD be with you."

17 Then David ordered all the leaders of Israel to help his son Solomon: 18 "The LORD your God is with you, isn't he? And hasn't he given you rest on every side? For he has handed the land's inhabitants over to me, and the land has been subdued before the LORD and his people. 19 Now determine in your mind and heart to seek the LORD your God. Get started building the LORD God's sanctuary so that you may bring the ark of the LORD's covenant and the holy articles of God to the temple that is to be built for the name of the LORD."

THE DIVISIONS OF THE LEVITES

23 When David was old and full of days, he installed his son Solomon as king over Israel. 2 Then he gathered all the leaders of Israel, the priests, and the Levites. 3 The Levites thirty years old or more were counted; the total number of men was thirty-eight thousand by headcount. 4 "Of these," David said, "twenty-four thousand are to be in charge of the work on the LORD's temple, six thousand are to be officers and judges, 5 four thousand are to be gatekeepers, and four thousand are to praise the LORD with the instruments that I have made for worship."

6 Then David divided them into divisions according to Levi's sons: Gershom,[B] Kohath, and Merari.

7 The Gershonites: Ladan and Shimei.

8 Ladan's sons: Jehiel was the first, then Zetham, and Joel — three.

9 Shimei's sons: Shelomoth, Haziel, and Haran — three. Those were the heads of the families of Ladan.

10 Shimei's sons: Jahath, Zizah,[C] Jeush, and Beriah. Those were Shimei's sons — four.

11 Jahath was the first and Zizah was the second; however, Jeush and Beriah did not have many sons, so they became one family[D] and received a single assignment.

12 Kohath's sons: Amram, Izhar, Hebron, and Uzziel — four.

13 Amram's sons: Aaron and Moses.

Aaron, along with his descendants, was set apart forever to consecrate the most holy things, to burn incense in the presence of the LORD, to minister to him, and to pronounce blessings in his name forever. 14 As for Moses the man of God, his sons were named among the tribe of Levi.

15 Moses's sons: Gershom and Eliezer.

16 Gershom's sons: Shebuel was first.

17 Eliezer's sons were Rehabiah, first; Eliezer did not have any other sons, but Rehabiah's sons were very numerous.

18 Izhar's sons: Shelomith was first.

19 Hebron's sons: Jeriah was first, Amariah second, Jahaziel third, and Jekameam fourth.

20 Uzziel's sons: Micah was first, and Isshiah second.

21 Merari's sons: Mahli and Mushi.

Mahli's sons: Eleazar and Kish.

22 Eleazar died having no sons, only daughters. Their cousins, the sons of Kish, married them.

23 Mushi's sons: Mahli, Eder, and Jeremoth — three.

24 These were the descendants of Levi by their ancestral families[E] — the family heads, according to their registration by name in the headcount — twenty years old or more, who worked in the service of the LORD's temple. 25 For David said, "The LORD God of Israel has given rest to his people, and he has come to stay in Jerusalem forever. 26 Also, the Levites no longer need to carry the tabernacle or any of the equipment for its service" — 27 for according to the last words of David, the Levites twenty years old or more were to be counted — 28 "but their duty will be to assist the descendants of Aaron with the service of the LORD's temple, being responsible for the courts and the chambers, the purification of all the holy things, and the work of the service of God's temple — 29 as well as the rows of the Bread of the Presence, the fine flour for the grain offering, the wafers of unleavened bread, the baking,[F] the mixing, and all measurements of volume and length. 30 They are also to stand every morning to give thanks and praise to the LORD, and likewise in the evening. 31 Whenever burnt offerings are offered to the LORD on the Sabbaths, New Moons, and appointed festivals, they are to offer them regularly in the LORD's presence according to the number prescribed for them. 32 They are to carry out their responsibilities for the tent of meeting, for the holy place, and for their relatives, the descendants of Aaron, in the service of the LORD's temple."

[A] **22:14** Lit *100,000 talents of gold and 1,000,000 talents of silver* [B] **23:6** Lit *Gershon* [C] **23:10** LXX, Vg; MT reads *Zina* [D] **23:11** Lit *a father's house* [E] **23:24** Lit *the house of their fathers* [F] **23:29** Lit *the griddle*

Royal Succession in the Ancient Near East

by T. J. Betts

People of the ancient Near East understood kingship to have both divine and human significance that affected everyone to some degree. For this reason, the concept of royal succession was an important concern for every nation.

CONTRIBUTING FACTORS

Different factors led to the establishment of kingship in the ancient Near East. First, in Israel's case, enemies were a threat. The Philistines had become a threat to every tribe of Israel. The elders of the tribes, therefore, approached God's prophet, Samuel, and demanded that he appoint them a king, someone who could lead them to victory over their common enemy. The people were willing to submit to a king's rule and taxation so they could have a king who would "judge" them, "go out before" them, and "fight" their "battles" (1Sm 8:1–20). They desired to have a person—a human ruler like other nations had—to protect them.

A second reason for desiring a king is mentioned above: the need for someone to "judge" them. Tribes had leaders that judged the people within the tribe. As trade and commerce grew between various tribes and groups in the ancient Near East, the people realized they needed a centralized power to administrate business transactions and ensure security in economic pursuits and acquisitions. A significant portion of the Code of Hammurabi pertains to commercial law. The need for the administration of commerce may have been a primary reason for the development of city-states in Mesopotamia. Each city-state had a king who ruled the city and the surrounding area. Agricultural endeavors transpired outside the walls of the city; these provided food and other necessities for everyone. Outlying farmers and herdsmen also served as an early warning system of approaching enemies. The city itself provided a place for the people to do business, a place of safety should enemies invade, and a king to oversee all these concerns.

A third probable reason for the development of kingship came as a result of a chieftain conquering adjacent territories. By subjugating various tribes or groups, the chieftain established his kingdom.

DIVINE CONNECTION

Simply put, the role of kings in the ancient Near East was to ensure the protection of their subjects and provide for their economic rights and needs. However, these responsibilities were only by-products of what was most important about kingship in the ancient Near East—the king's divine origins and his relationship to the divine. For instance, the

From Abydos, Egypt; part of one of the king lists in the temples of Ramesses II and his father Seti I.

Dated to about 1800 BC, a partial copy of the Sumerian King List, compiled originally around 2050 BC.

Egyptians believed the pharaohs were gods, sons of Re, and manifestations of Horus. The pharaohs were earthly mediators of the blessings of the gods. Every religious and secular activity, therefore, related to the pharaoh.[1] Mesopotamian kings claimed that the gods, especially their patron god, established their rule. Early on, they appeared to be "priest-kings," but as kingdoms grew, kings became increasingly secular. Nonetheless, they often kept their attachment to the cult by appointing their sons and daughters as the high priests and priestesses of the patron gods.[2] Divine election guaranteed the king's authority as he took the throne.[3]

Deuteronomy 17:15 indicates that Yahweh divinely elected the legitimate kings of Israel and Judah. These kings were to be God's servants for their nations. Israel's and Judah's kings were responsible for keeping Yahweh's covenant and for leading their nations to do the same. If the kings were faithful to Yahweh, then he would bless them as they reigned (1Kg 2:1–4). Failure to do so resulted in harsh punishment. For some, this failure resulted in the end of their dynasties, as with Jeroboam I (13:33–34).

CRITERIA

The succession of kings in the ancient Near East appears to have been based upon two and sometimes three criteria. The first criterion was an appeal to royal lineage of the father's throne,[4] normally made by the eldest son. At one point in the Eighteenth Dynasty of Egypt, however, the royal bloodline had no son to take the throne. In this case, the daughters continued the royal lineage even though their husbands became pharaohs. When her husband died, however, Hatshepsut, one of the daughters, in effect laid claim to the throne and for about twenty years ruled Egypt as a pharaoh would.[5]

The second appeal for kingship in the ancient Near East was to divine election.[6] First Samuel 18–20 describes the relationship between Saul, the first king of Israel; Jonathan, his oldest son; and David. Jonathan loved David, but Saul saw David as a rival and threat to the throne. He clearly expressed this sentiment to Jonathan, saying, "Every day Jesse's son lives on earth you and your kingship are not secure" (20:31). Saul assumed his oldest son should be heir to the throne. Nevertheless, the criterion of divine election outweighed the appeal to royal blood in this instance. God rejected Saul and his dynasty because of his sin. David's being "a man after [God's] own heart" means that God chose David as king (13:13–14).

Sometimes a third qualification was necessary. If the nation was a vassal state, then authorization from the king of the suzerain nation was required. On occasion, the suzerain king decided who would be king. For instance, King Nebuchadnezzar took Judah's King Jehoiachin into Babylonian captivity and set Jehoiachin's uncle, Zedekiah, in his place (2Kg 24:15–17).

Of course coups and assassinations occurred in the ancient Near East. One such incident happened in Judah when King Ahaziah was assassinated. His mother, Athaliah, saw it as an opportunity to grab power and had her own sons and grandsons murdered so she could have the throne to herself. Unaware that Joash, Ahaziah's toddler son, had escaped and was secretly being raised by the high priest, she reigned for six years until the high priest anointed Joash king and had Athaliah put to death amidst her cries of "treason" (11:1–16). To make the transition easier, years before their deaths some kings, like those in Hammurabi's dynasty, elevated their oldest sons to the throne alongside them establishing a coregency so that the son's reign would be solidly established at the passing of his father. ✣

[1] H. W. Fairman, "The Kingship Rituals of Egypt," in *Myth, Ritual, and Kingship*, ed. S. H. Hooke (Oxford: Oxford University Press, 1958), 75–76. [2] William H. Stiebing Jr., *Ancient Near Eastern History and Culture* (New York: Addison-Wesley Longman, 2003), 51. [3] Tomoo Ishida, *The Royal Dynasties in Ancient Israel* (Berlin: de Gruyter, 1977), 25. [4] Ishida, *Royal Dynasties.* [5] Eugene H. Merrill, *Kingdom of Priests*, 2nd ed. (Grand Rapids: Baker, 2008), 76, 78. Merrill suggests Hatshepsut raised Moses. [6] Ishida, *Royal Dynasties*, 25.

Yariris (right), regent king of Carchemesh (reigned ca 815–790 BC), is leading by the hand Kamanis (left), the young prince and heir to the throne. Kamanis is already holding in his right hand a mace, which symbolized his authority. The inscription reads, "This is statue of Yariris. This is Kamanis. . . . I took him by the hand to set him over the temple when he was a child."

THE DIVISIONS OF THE PRIESTS

24 The divisions of the descendants of Aaron were as follows: Aaron's sons were Nadab, Abihu, Eleazar, and Ithamar. 2 But Nadab and Abihu died before their father, and they had no sons, so Eleazar and Ithamar served as priests. 3 Together with Zadok from the descendants of Eleazar and Ahimelech from the descendants of Ithamar, David divided them according to the assigned duties of their service. 4 Since more leaders were found among Eleazar's descendants than Ithamar's, they were divided accordingly: sixteen heads of ancestral families[A] were from Eleazar's descendants, and eight heads of ancestral families were from Ithamar's. 5 They were assigned by lot, for there were officers of the sanctuary and officers of God among both Eleazar's and Ithamar's descendants.

6 The secretary, Shemaiah son of Nethanel, a Levite, recorded them in the presence of the king and the officers, the priest Zadok, Ahimelech son of Abiathar, and the heads of families of the priests and the Levites. One ancestral family[B] was taken for Eleazar, and then one for Ithamar.

7 The first lot fell to Jehoiarib, the second
to Jedaiah,
8 the third to Harim, the fourth to Seorim,
9 the fifth to Malchijah, the sixth to Mijamin,
10 the seventh to Hakkoz, the eighth to Abijah,
11 the ninth to Jeshua, the tenth to Shecaniah,
12 the eleventh to Eliashib, the twelfth to Jakim,
13 the thirteenth to Huppah, the fourteenth
to Jeshebeab,
14 the fifteenth to Bilgah, the sixteenth to Immer,
15 the seventeenth to Hezir, the eighteenth
to Happizzez,
16 the nineteenth to Pethahiah, the twentieth
to Jehezkel,
17 the twenty-first to Jachin, the twenty-second
to Gamul,
18 the twenty-third to Delaiah, and the
twenty-fourth to Maaziah.

19 These had their assigned duties for service when they entered the LORD's temple, according to their regulations, which they received from their ancestor Aaron, as the LORD God of Israel had commanded him.

THE REST OF THE LEVITES

20 As for the rest of Levi's sons:
from Amram's sons: Shubael;
from Shubael's sons: Jehdeiah.
21 From Rehabiah:
from Rehabiah's sons: Isshiah was the first.
22 From the Izharites: Shelomoth;
from Shelomoth's sons: Jahath.
23 Hebron's[C] sons:
Jeriah the first, Amariah the second,
Jahaziel the third, and Jekameam the fourth.
24 From Uzziel's sons: Micah;
from Micah's sons: Shamir.
25 Micah's brother: Isshiah;
from Isshiah's sons: Zechariah.
26 Merari's sons: Mahli and Mushi,
and from his sons, Jaaziah his son.[D]
27 Merari's sons, by his son Jaaziah:[E]
Shoham, Zaccur, and Ibri.
28 From Mahli: Eleazar, who had no sons.
29 From Kish, from Kish's sons: Jerahmeel.
30 Mushi's sons: Mahli, Eder, and Jerimoth.

Those were the descendants of the Levites according to their ancestral families.[F]
31 They also cast lots the same way as their relatives the descendants of Aaron did in the presence of King David, Zadok, Ahimelech, and the heads of the families of the priests and Levites — the family heads and their younger brothers alike.

THE LEVITICAL MUSICIANS

25 David and the officers of the army also set apart some of the sons of Asaph, Heman, and Jeduthun, who were to prophesy accompanied by lyres, harps, and cymbals. This is the list of the men who performed their service:

2 From Asaph's sons:
Zaccur, Joseph, Nethaniah, and Asarelah, sons of
Asaph, under Asaph's authority, who prophesied
under the authority of the king.
3 From Jeduthun: Jeduthun's sons:
Gedaliah, Zeri, Jeshaiah, Shimei,[G] Hashabiah,
and Mattithiah — six — under the authority
of their father Jeduthun, prophesying to the
accompaniment of lyres, giving thanks and
praise to the LORD.
4 From Heman: Heman's sons:
Bukkiah, Mattaniah, Uzziel, Shebuel, Jerimoth,
Hananiah, Hanani, Eliathah, Giddalti,
Romamti-ezer, Joshbekashah, Mallothi, Hothir,
and Mahazioth.
5 All these sons of Heman, the
king's seer, were given by the promises of God
to exalt him,[H] for God had given Heman fourteen
sons and three daughters.

6 All these men were under their own fathers' authority for the music in the LORD's temple, with

[A] **24:4** Lit *house of fathers* [B] **24:6** Lit *father's house* [C] **24:23** Some Hb mss, some LXX mss; other Hb mss omit *Hebron's*; 1Ch 23:19 [D] **24:26** Or *Mushi; Jaaziah's sons: Beno.* [E] **24:27** Or *sons, Jaaziah: Beno,* [F] **24:30** Lit *the house of their fathers* [G] **25:3** One Hb ms, LXX; other Hb mss omit *Shimei* [H] **25:5** Lit *by the words of God to lift a horn*

cymbals, harps, and lyres for the service of God's temple. Asaph, Jeduthun, and Heman were under the king's authority. 7 They numbered 288 together with their relatives who were all trained and skillful in music for the LORD. 8 They cast lots for their duties, young and old alike, teacher as well as pupil.

9 The first lot for Asaph fell to Joseph,
his sons, and his relatives — 12[A]
to Gedaliah the second: him,
his relatives, and his sons — 12
10 the third to Zaccur, his sons,
and his relatives — 12
11 the fourth to Izri,[B] his sons,
and his relatives — 12
12 the fifth to Nethaniah, his sons,
and his relatives — 12
13 the sixth to Bukkiah, his sons,
and his relatives — 12
14 the seventh to Jesarelah, his sons,
and his relatives — 12
15 the eighth to Jeshaiah, his sons,
and his relatives — 12
16 the ninth to Mattaniah, his sons,
and his relatives — 12
17 the tenth to Shimei, his sons,
and his relatives — 12
18 the eleventh to Azarel,[C] his sons,
and his relatives — 12
19 the twelfth to Hashabiah, his sons,
and his relatives — 12
20 the thirteenth to Shubael, his sons,
and his relatives — 12
21 the fourteenth to Mattithiah, his sons,
and his relatives — 12
22 the fifteenth to Jeremoth, his sons,
and his relatives — 12
23 the sixteenth to Hananiah, his sons,
and his relatives — 12
24 the seventeenth to Joshbekashah,
his sons, and his relatives — 12
25 the eighteenth to Hanani, his sons,
and his relatives — 12
26 the nineteenth to Mallothi, his sons,
and his relatives — 12
27 the twentieth to Eliathah, his sons,
and his relatives — 12
28 the twenty-first to Hothir, his sons,
and his relatives — 12
29 the twenty-second to Giddalti, his sons,
and his relatives — 12
30 the twenty-third to Mahazioth, his sons,
and his relatives — 12
31 and the twenty-fourth to Romamti-ezer,
his sons, and his relatives — 12.

THE LEVITICAL GATEKEEPERS

26 The following were the divisions of the gatekeepers:

From the Korahites: Meshelemiah son of Kore,
one of the sons of Asaph.
2 Meshelemiah had sons:
Zechariah the firstborn, Jediael the second,
Zebadiah the third, Jathniel the fourth,
3 Elam the fifth, Jehohanan the sixth,
and Eliehoenai the seventh.
4 Obed-edom also had sons:
Shemaiah the firstborn, Jehozabad the second,
Joah the third, Sachar the fourth,
Nethanel the fifth, 5 Ammiel the sixth,
Issachar the seventh, and Peullethai the eighth,
for God blessed him.
6 Also, to his son Shemaiah were born sons who
ruled their ancestral families[D] because they
were strong, capable men.
7 Shemaiah's sons: Othni, Rephael, Obed, and
Elzabad; his relatives Elihu and Semachiah were
also capable men. 8 All of these were among the
sons of Obed-edom with their sons and relatives;
they were capable men with strength for the
work — sixty-two from Obed-edom.
9 Meshelemiah also had sons and relatives who
were capable men — eighteen.
10 Hosah, from the Merarites, also had sons:
Shimri the first (although he was not the
firstborn, his father had appointed him as the
first), 11 Hilkiah the second, Tebaliah the third,
and Zechariah the fourth. The sons and relatives
of Hosah were thirteen in all.

12 These divisions of the gatekeepers, under their leading men, had duties for ministering in the LORD's temple, just as their relatives did. 13 They cast lots for each temple gate according to their ancestral families, young and old alike.
14 The lot for the east gate fell to Shelemiah.[E] They also cast lots for his son Zechariah, an insightful counselor, and his lot came out for the north gate. 15 Obed-edom's was the south gate, and his sons' lot was for the storehouses; 16 it was the west gate and the gate of Shallecheth on the ascending highway for Shuppim and Hosah.
There were guards stationed at every watch. 17 There were six Levites each day[F] on the east, four each day on the north, four each day on the south, and two pair at the storehouses. 18 As for the court on the west, there were four at the highway and two

[A]**25:9** LXX; MT lacks *his sons, and his relatives — 12* [B]**25:11** Variant of Zeri [C]**25:18** Variant of Uzziel [D]**26:6** Lit *the house of their fathers*, also in v. 13 [E]**26:14** Variant of Meshelemiah [F]**26:17** LXX; MT omits *each day*

at the court. 19 Those were the divisions of the gatekeepers from the descendants of the Korahites and
Merarites.

THE LEVITICAL TREASURERS AND OTHER OFFICIALS

20 From the Levites, Ahijah was in charge of the treasuries of God's temple and the treasuries of what had
been dedicated. 21 From the sons of Ladan, who were
the descendants of the Gershonites through Ladan
and were the family heads belonging to Ladan the
Gershonite: Jehieli. 22 The sons of Jehieli, Zetham and
his brother Joel, were in charge of the treasuries of
the LORD's temple.

23 From the Amramites, the Izharites, the Hebronites, and the Uzzielites: 24 Shebuel, a descendant of
Moses's son Gershom, was the officer in charge of
the treasuries. 25 His relatives through Eliezer: his
son Rehabiah, his son Jeshaiah, his son Joram, his
son Zichri, and his son Shelomith.[A] 26 This Shelomith
and his relatives were in charge of all the treasuries of
what had been dedicated by King David, by the family
heads who were the commanders of thousands and
of hundreds, and by the army commanders. 27 They
dedicated part of the plunder from their battles for
the repair of the LORD's temple. 28 All that the seer
Samuel, Saul son of Kish, Abner son of Ner, and Joab
son of Zeruiah had dedicated, along with everything
else that had been dedicated, were in the care of Shelomith and his relatives.

29 From the Izrahites: Chenaniah and his sons had
duties outside the temple[B] as officers and judges
over Israel. 30 From the Hebronites: Hashabiah and
his relatives, 1,700 capable men, had assigned duties in Israel west of the Jordan for all the work of
the LORD and for the service of the king. 31 From the
Hebronites: Jerijah was the head of the Hebronites,
according to the family records of his ancestors.
A search was made in the fortieth year of David's
reign and strong, capable men were found among
them at Jazer in Gilead. 32 There were among Jerijah's
relatives 2,700 capable men who were family heads.
King David appointed them over the Reubenites, the
Gadites, and half the tribe of Manasseh as overseers
in every matter relating to God and the king.

DAVID'S SECULAR OFFICIALS

27 This is the list of the Israelites, the family heads,
the commanders of thousands and the commanders of hundreds, and their officers who served
the king in every matter to do with the divisions that
were on rotated military duty each month throughout[C] the year. There were 24,000 in each division:

2 Jashobeam son of Zabdiel was in charge of the
first division, for the first month; 24,000 were in
his division. 3 He was a descendant of Perez and
chief of all the army commanders for the first
month.

4 Dodai the Ahohite was in charge of the division
for the second month, and Mikloth was the
leader; 24,000 were in his division.

5 The third army commander, as chief for the
third month, was Benaiah son of the priest
Jehoiada; 24,000 were in his division. 6 This
Benaiah was a mighty man among the Thirty
and over the Thirty, and his son Ammizabad was
in charge[D] of his division.

7 The fourth commander, for the fourth month,
was Joab's brother Asahel, and his son Zebadiah
was commander after him; 24,000 were in his
division.

8 The fifth, for the fifth month, was the
commander Shamhuth the Izrahite; 24,000 were
in his division.

9 The sixth, for the sixth month, was Ira son of
Ikkesh the Tekoite; 24,000 were in his division.

10 The seventh, for the seventh month, was Helez
the Pelonite from the descendants of Ephraim;
24,000 were in his division.

11 The eighth, for the eighth month, was Sibbecai
the Hushathite, a Zerahite; 24,000 were in his
division.

12 The ninth, for the ninth month, was Abiezer
the Anathothite, a Benjaminite; 24,000 were in
his division.

13 The tenth, for the tenth month, was Maharai
the Netophathite, a Zerahite; 24,000 were in his
division.

14 The eleventh, for the eleventh month, was
Benaiah the Pirathonite from the descendants of
Ephraim; 24,000 were in his division.

15 The twelfth, for the twelfth month, was Heldai
the Netophathite, of Othniel's family;[E] 24,000
were in his division.

16 The following were in charge of the tribes of
Israel:
For the Reubenites, Eliezer son of Zichri was the
chief official;
for the Simeonites, Shephatiah son of Maacah;
17 for the Levites, Hashabiah son of Kemuel; for
Aaron, Zadok;
18 for Judah, Elihu, one of David's brothers; for
Issachar, Omri son of Michael;
19 for Zebulun, Ishmaiah son of Obadiah;
for Naphtali, Jerimoth son of Azriel;

[A] **26:25** Or *Shelomoth*, also in vv. 26,28 [B] **26:29** *the temple* added for clarity [C] **27:1** Lit *that came in and went out month by month for all months of* [D] **27:6** LXX; MT omits *in charge* [E] **27:15** Lit *belonging to Othniel*

20 for the Ephraimites, Hoshea son of Azaziah;
for half the tribe of Manasseh, Joel son of Pedaiah;
21 for half the tribe of Manasseh in Gilead, Iddo
son of Zechariah;
for Benjamin, Jaasiel son of Abner;
22 for Dan, Azarel son of Jeroham.
Those were the leaders of the tribes of Israel.

23 David didn't count the men aged twenty or under, for the LORD had said he would make Israel as
numerous as the stars of the sky. 24 Joab son of Zeruiah began to count them, but he didn't complete
it. There was wrath against Israel because of this
census, and the number was not entered in the Historical Record[A] of King David.

25 Azmaveth son of Adiel was in charge of the
king's storehouses.
Jonathan son of Uzziah was in charge of the
storehouses in the country, in the cities, in the
villages, and in the fortresses.
26 Ezri son of Chelub was in charge of those who
worked in the fields tilling the soil.
27 Shimei the Ramathite was in charge of the
vineyards.
Zabdi the Shiphmite was in charge of the
produce of the vineyards for the wine cellars.
28 Baal-hanan the Gederite was in charge of the
olive and sycamore trees in the Judean foothills.[B]
Joash was in charge of the stores of olive oil.
29 Shitrai the Sharonite was in charge of the
herds that grazed in Sharon, while Shaphat son
of Adlai was in charge of the herds in the valleys.
30 Obil the Ishmaelite was in charge of the camels.
Jehdeiah the Meronothite was in charge of the
donkeys.
31 Jaziz the Hagrite was in charge of the flocks.
All these were officials in charge of King David's
property.

32 David's uncle Jonathan was a counselor; he was
a man of understanding and a scribe. Jehiel son of
Hachmoni attended[C] the king's sons. 33 Ahithophel
was the king's counselor. Hushai the Archite was the
king's friend. 34 After Ahithophel came Jehoiada son
of Benaiah, then Abiathar. Joab was the commander
of the king's army.

DAVID COMMISSIONS SOLOMON TO BUILD THE TEMPLE

28 David assembled all the leaders of Israel in Jerusalem: the leaders of the tribes, the leaders
of the divisions in the king's service, the commanders of thousands and the commanders of hundreds,
and the officials in charge of all the property and
cattle of the king and his sons, along with the court
officials, the fighting men, and all the best soldiers.
2 Then King David rose to his feet and said, "Listen to
me, my brothers and my people. It was in my heart
to build a house as a resting place for the ark of the
LORD's covenant and as a footstool for our God. I had
made preparations to build, 3 but God said to me, 'You
are not to build a house for my name because you are
a man of war and have shed blood.'

4 "Yet the LORD God of Israel chose me out of all
my father's family to be king over Israel forever.
For he chose Judah as leader, and from the house
of Judah, my father's family, and from my father's
sons, he was pleased to make me king over all Israel.
5 And out of all my sons — for the LORD has given
me many sons — he has chosen my son Solomon
to sit on the throne of the LORD's kingdom over Israel. 6 He said to me, 'Your son Solomon is the one
who is to build my house and my courts, for I have
chosen him to be my son, and I will be his father. 7 I
will establish his kingdom forever if he perseveres
in keeping my commands and my ordinances as he
is doing today.'

8 "So now in the sight of all Israel, the assembly
of the LORD, and in the hearing of our God, observe
and follow all the commands of the LORD your God
so that you may possess this good land and leave it as
an inheritance to your descendants forever.

9 "As for you, Solomon my son, know the God of
your father, and serve him wholeheartedly and with
a willing mind, for the LORD searches every heart and
understands the intention of every thought. If you
seek him, he will be found by you, but if you abandon
him, he will reject you forever. 10 Realize now that the
LORD has chosen you to build a house for the sanctuary. Be strong, and do it."

11 Then David gave his son Solomon the plans for
the portico of the temple and its buildings, treasuries, upstairs rooms, inner rooms, and a room for the
mercy seat. 12 The plans contained everything he had
in mind[D] for the courts of the LORD's house, all the
surrounding chambers, the treasuries of God's house,
and the treasuries for what is dedicated. 13 Also included were plans for the divisions of the priests
and the Levites; all the work of service in the LORD's
house; all the articles of service of the LORD's house;
14 the weight of gold for all the articles for every kind
of service; the weight of all the silver articles for
every kind of service; 15 the weight of the gold lampstands and their gold lamps, including the weight
of each lampstand and its lamps; the weight of each
silver lampstand and its lamps, according to the service of each lampstand; 16 the weight of gold for each

[A] **27:24** LXX; MT reads *the number of the Historical Record*
[B] **27:28** Or *the Shephelah* [C] **27:32** Lit *was with* [D] **28:12** Or *he received from the Spirit*

Building Temples in the Ancient Near East

by Joel F. Drinkard Jr.

A temple was God's house or God's palace. The temple was theologically understood as God's dwelling place on earth. In the case of the Jerusalem temple, the division of the entire structure of the temple grounds into precincts of increasing holiness as one approached the most holy place represented one's coming ever closer to God's presence.

Temples were closely associated with kingship in the Bible and in the ancient Near East. Temples were built by kings, by empire builders. A temple became one of the marks of a successful king, especially one establishing a new dynasty; he built a house/palace for himself and his dynasty, and he built a house/palace for his god. The king would often honor his god for giving him the kingdom by building a temple for that god. Each successive king in a dynasty did not necessarily build a new temple, but many kings would renovate, restore, or make additions to a temple after their ascension to the throne or after some significant event. Just one ancient Near Eastern example will illustrate this point. According to the Mesha stele, King Mesha of Moab built a high place for Kemosh (the Moabite deity; Chemosh, CSB) in Qarho because Kemosh had saved him from all his enemies (lines 3–4). In addition, Mesha later in the stele mentioned building a palace ("king's house," line 23) for himself.

The same pattern of temple building is found in Israel/Judah. While there were certainly earlier shrines and sanctuaries built for God prior to the monarchy, it was only with the rise of David and Solomon that the temple was built. David began and Solomon consolidated the kingdom. One mark of their achievement included the building of both a temple and a palace.

Following the division of the kingdom into Israel and Judah after Solomon's death, Jeroboam I of Israel built his own temples at Dan and Bethel, both the sites of earlier shrines (1Kg 12:26–33). Again the rationale was simple; a separate kingdom needed its own temples.

In terms of biblical and archaeological data, the Solomonic temple undoubtedly had Phoenician influence. Along with Israelite workers (many of whom were forced laborers, 1Kg 5:13–17), Solomon also employed Phoenician workers of King Hiram of Tyre (1Kg 5:6). Solomon also employed an Israelite-Phoenician artisan, Hiram of Tyre (not King Hiram of Tyre) whose father was Phoenician and mother was an Israelite, to do *all* the bronze work for the temple (1Kg 7:13–47).

Since the primary workers mentioned for wood and metal were Phoenician, and since most of the decorative features were either carved in wood or cast in metal, it seems obvious that most of the artwork for the temple would have Phoenician influence.

Surely the temple was a magnificent structure, but Solomon's palace was much larger. The entire temple could easily fit in just one part of the palace: the "House of the Forest of Lebanon" was one hundred cubits long, fifty cubits wide, and thirty cubits high (ca 150 by 75 by 45 feet, 1Kg 7:2). Actually two temples could fit in this one structure side by side and still have almost enough room for two more temples turned sideways behind them. In terms of

The remains of an Israelite temple at Arad.

actual floor space, the temple covered twelve hundred square cubits, or about twenty-seven hundred square feet; the House of the Forest of Lebanon covered five thousand square cubits or about 11,250 square feet. Somewhat like St. George's Chapel at Windsor Castle, the temple, size-wise, was rather small in the royal palace complex.

The temple was undoubtedly constructed of the fine ashlar masonry associated with monumental architecture during the monarchy. Ashlar masonry is characterized by quite large stones, finely dressed faces, and at times a decorative boss on the outer face. Although no remains of the Solomonic temple have been found (if such exist, they would likely be found beneath the platform of the Herodian temple, which *also* serves as the platform for Haram es-Sharif, where the Dome of the Rock sits today). Such masonry, apparently belonging to the time of Solomon, has been found in major structures at Megiddo, Hazor, and Gezer, all sites the Bible describes as major cities Solomon built or rebuilt. In addition, fine examples of slightly later, ninth-century ashlar masonry have been found at Samaria and elsewhere, apparently reflecting the building activity of Omri or Ahab.

One area where we might expect native Israelite influence is in the stonework of the temple. The text does specify that the stoneworkers were Israelite (1Kg 5:15–18). And we do find, from a later period, unique to Israelite and Moabite-Ammonite sites, the carved stone capitals variously known as proto-Ionic, proto-Aeolic, or volute capitals. These capitals, which stood on top of pier walls, are carved with large volutes, probably representing palm trees or the Tree of Life. Several of these stone capitals have been found at Megiddo and are attributed to Solomonic construction. Although no such capitals have been found in Jerusalem of the Solomonic period, and only one has been found in Jerusalem, these capitals clearly belong to monumental and/or royal structures. Certainly the temple would have had monumental architecture of this sort along with the ashlar masonry.

The most holy place in the Israelite temple at Arad. The most holy place here is square, the same as at the temple in Jerusalem.

The temple building itself was based on a fairly common long-room plan known throughout the ancient Near East. Basically the temple had three parts: the porch, the inner room, also called the nave, and the holy of holies or most holy place. From Middle Bronze and Late Bronze Age temples in Canaan and Syria, we find similar floor plans. Temples at Shechem, Megiddo, Hazor, and farther north at Ebla have related, but clearly not identical, floor plans. The most significant aspect of these temples was a direct access (and direct view) from the outside through the inner room to the niche or most holy place. Most of these temples had an inner room or nave that was longer than wide, called a long-room temple. Several of these temples also had pillars or columns in front, reminding one of the two pillars, Jachin and Boaz.

While these other temples have somewhat similar floor plans, the Solomonic temple had certain distinctive features. Clearly the Solomonic temple was not just a copy of some existing temple. In particular, the most holy place was larger and was described as a perfect cube. For many of the Canaanite and Syrian examples, the most holy place was a small niche in which, apparently, the image of the deity was placed. In the Israelite cult, there was no image of God; the ark of the covenant served as the symbol of God's presence.

The one example of an Israelite temple that has been discovered is the small sanctuary at Arad. Although the inner room was of a broad-room (wider than it is long) plan rather than the long room of the Solomonic temple, the Arad temple does preserve a square-shaped most holy place. It also had two incense altars just outside the most holy place. In addition, two flat stone slabs are outside the nave, probably bases for columns or pillars corresponding to Jachin and Boaz at the Solomonic temple. And in the courtyard beyond the nave, there was an altar of sacrifice made of unhewn stones as prescribed in Exodus 20:25. This sanctuary gives clear evidence of the Israelites' temple-building practices. The excavator attributed the earliest phase of this temple to the time of Solomon, and the latest, when the sanctuary was covered over and made inaccessible in Josiah's reform. ✣

table for the rows of the Bread of the Presence and the silver for the silver tables; 17 the pure gold for the forks, sprinkling basins, and pitchers; the weight of each gold dish; the weight of each silver bowl; 18 the weight of refined gold for the altar of incense; and the plans for the chariot of[A] the gold cherubim that spread out their wings and cover the ark of the LORD's covenant.

19 David concluded, "By the LORD's hand on me, he enabled me to understand everything in writing, all the details of the plan."[B]

20 Then David said to his son Solomon, "Be strong and courageous, and do the work. Don't be afraid or discouraged, for the LORD God, my God, is with you. He won't leave you or abandon you until all the work for the service of the LORD's house is finished. 21 Here are the divisions of the priests and the Levites for all the service of God's house. Every willing person of any skill will be at your disposal for the work, and the leaders and all the people are at your every command."

CONTRIBUTIONS FOR BUILDING THE TEMPLE

29 Then King David said to all the assembly, "My son Solomon — God has chosen him alone — is young and inexperienced. The task is great because the building will not be built for a human but for the LORD God. 2 So to the best of my ability I've made provision for the house of my God: gold for the gold articles, silver for the silver, bronze for the bronze, iron for the iron, and wood for the wood, as well as onyx, stones for mounting,[C] antimony,[D] stones of various colors, all kinds of precious stones, and a great quantity of marble. 3 Moreover, because of my delight in the house of my God, I now give my personal treasures of gold and silver for the house of my God over and above all that I've provided for the holy house: 4 100 tons[E] of gold (gold of Ophir) and 250 tons[F] of refined silver for overlaying the walls of the buildings, 5 the gold for the gold work and the silver for the silver, for all the work to be done by the craftsmen. Now who will volunteer to consecrate himself to the LORD today?"

6 Then the leaders of the households, the leaders of the tribes of Israel, the commanders of thousands and of hundreds, and the officials in charge of the king's work gave willingly. 7 For the service of God's house they gave 185 tons[G] of gold and 10,000 gold coins,[H] 375 tons[I] of silver, 675 tons[J] of bronze, and 4,000 tons[K] of iron. 8 Whoever had precious stones gave them to the treasury of the LORD's house under the care of Jehiel the Gershonite. 9 Then the people rejoiced because of their leaders' willingness to give, for they had given to the LORD wholeheartedly. King David also rejoiced greatly.

DAVID'S PRAYER

10 Then David blessed the LORD in the sight of all the assembly. David said,

May you be blessed, LORD God of our father Israel,
from eternity to eternity. 11 Yours, LORD, is the
greatness and the power and the glory and the
splendor and the majesty, for everything in the
heavens and on earth belongs to you. Yours, LORD,
is the kingdom, and you are exalted as head over
all. 12 Riches and honor come from you, and you
are the ruler of everything. Power and might
are in your hand, and it is in your hand to make
great and to give strength to all. 13 Now therefore,
our God, we give you thanks and praise your
glorious name.

14 But who am I, and who are my people, that we
should be able to give as generously as this? For
everything comes from you, and we have given
you only what comes from your own hand.[L]
15 For we are aliens and temporary residents
in your presence as were all our ancestors.
Our days on earth are like a shadow, without
hope. 16 LORD our God, all this wealth that we've
provided for building you a house for your
holy name comes from your hand; everything
belongs to you. 17 I know, my God, that you test
the heart and that you are pleased with what is
right. I have willingly given all these things with
an upright heart, and now I have seen your people who are present[M] here giving joyfully and[N]
willingly to you. 18 LORD God of Abraham, Isaac,
and Israel, our ancestors, keep this desire forever in the thoughts of the hearts of your people,
and confirm their hearts toward you. 19 Give my
son Solomon an undivided heart to keep and to
carry out all your commands, your decrees, and
your statutes, and to build the building for which
I have made provision.

20 Then David said to the whole assembly, "Blessed be the LORD your God." So the whole assembly praised the LORD God of their ancestors. They knelt low and paid homage to the LORD and the king.

21 The following day they offered sacrifices to the LORD and burnt offerings to the LORD: a thousand bulls, a thousand rams, and a thousand lambs, along with their drink offerings, and sacrifices in

[A] **28:18** Or *chariot, that is*; Ps 18:10; Ezk 1:5,15 [B] **28:19** Hb obscure [C] **29:2** Or *mosaic* [D] **29:2** In Hb, the word *antimony* is similar to "turquoise"; Ex 28:18. [E] **29:4** Lit *3,000 talents* [F] **29:4** Lit *7,000 talents* [G] **29:7** Lit *5,000 talents* [H] **29:7** Or *drachmas*, or *darics* [I] **29:7** Lit *10,000 talents* [J] **29:7** Lit *18,000 talents* [K] **29:7** Lit *100,000 talents* [L] **29:14** Lit *and from your hand we have given to you* [M] **29:17** Lit *found* [N] **29:17** Or *now with joy I've seen your people who are present here giving* abundance for all Israel. [22] They ate and drank with great joy in the LORD's presence that day.

THE ENTHRONEMENT OF SOLOMON

Then, for a second time, they made David's son Solomon king; they anointed him[A] as the LORD's ruler, and Zadok as the priest. [23] Solomon sat on the LORD's throne as king in place of his father David. He prospered, and all Israel obeyed him. [24] All the leaders and the mighty men, and all of King David's sons as well, pledged their allegiance to King Solomon. [25] The LORD highly exalted Solomon in the sight of all Israel and bestowed on him such royal majesty as had not been bestowed on any king over Israel before him.

A SUMMARY OF DAVID'S LIFE

[26] David son of Jesse was king over all Israel. [27] The length of his reign over Israel was forty years; he reigned in Hebron for seven years and in Jerusalem for thirty-three. [28] He died at a good old age, full of days, riches, and honor, and his son Solomon became king in his place. [29] As for the events of King David's reign, from beginning to end, note that they are written in the Events of the Seer Samuel, the Events of the Prophet Nathan, and the Events of the Seer Gad, [30] along with all his reign, his might, and the incidents that affected him and Israel and all the kingdoms of the surrounding lands.

[A] **29:22** LXX, Tg, Vg; MT omits *him*

2 CHRONICLES

Panel of glazed bricks depicting a lion. These images decorated the Processional Way in Babylon, connecting the temple of Marduk with the temple of Akitu. Dated to the reign of Nebuchadnezzar II (605–562 BC).

INTRODUCTION TO

2 CHRONICLES

Circumstances of Writing

An ancient tradition ascribes the authorship of Chronicles to Ezra. The author must have lived sometime after the return of the Jews to Israel from the Babylonian exile. He also had a strong interest in the reimplementation of the law and the temple, and he must have had access to historical records. All of these criteria suit Ezra, and this identification is corroborated by the fact that the last verses of Chronicles are the first verses of the book of Ezra. However, since the book does not explicitly claim Ezra for its author, in these notes we will refer to him simply as the Chronicler.

The books of 1 and 2 Chronicles include extensive genealogies from the time of Adam and take the reader up to the period of the nation's exile and restoration. Second Chronicles focuses on all the kings who followed David up to the exile and restoration. It covers the same time period as 1 and 2 Kings, but 2 Chronicles focuses exclusively on the kings of Judah. The content of the books necessitates that they were written sometime after the return from the exile, perhaps the middle of the fifth century BC.

Contribution to the Bible

Chronicles brings together many dimensions of biblical revelation, such as historical events (as recounted in Genesis through Kings), temple ritual (as prescribed in Leviticus), sin and judgment (as preached by the prophets), and even some psalms. Because a recurring theme is that God will always accept people who return to him no matter how wicked they may have been, it has been called, perhaps a little whimsically, "The Gospel According to Ezra." The books of 1 and 2 Chronicles give us the big picture of Old Testament history, capturing the Davidic covenant in light of Israel's history back to Adam and pointing to the eternal continuation of that covenant through the reign of the Messiah.

Structure

The Hebrew Bible divides its books into three categories: the Law, the Prophets, and the Writings. In this arrangement, the books of Samuel and Kings are counted among the Prophets, whereas Chronicles belongs to the Writings. This classification may be partially due to the fact that Chronicles repeats information, such as the genealogies of Genesis and the histories of the kings of Judah from the books of Samuel and Kings. Still the Chronicler uses this repeated content to support his own point, and he also adds a lot of information that we find in Chronicles alone. He limits his discussion of the various kings almost entirely to those of Judah, the southern kingdom.

SOLOMON'S REQUEST FOR WISDOM

1 Solomon son of David strengthened his hold on his kingdom. The LORD his God was with him and highly exalted him. 2 Then Solomon spoke to all Israel, to the commanders of thousands and of hundreds, to the judges, and to every leader in all Israel — the family heads. 3 Solomon and the whole assembly with him went to the high place that was in Gibeon because God's tent of meeting, which the LORD's servant Moses had made in the wilderness, was there. 4 Now David had brought the ark of God from Kiriath-jearim to the place[A] he had set up for it, because he had pitched a tent for it in Jerusalem, 5 but he put[B] the bronze altar, which Bezalel son of Uri, son of Hur, had made, in front of the LORD's tabernacle. Solomon and the assembly inquired of him[C] there. 6 Solomon offered sacrifices there in the LORD's presence on the bronze altar at the tent of meeting; he offered a thousand burnt offerings on it.

7 That night God appeared to Solomon and said to him, "Ask. What should I give you?"

8 And Solomon said to God, "You have shown great and faithful love to my father David, and you have made me king in his place. 9 LORD God, let your promise to my father David now come true. For you have made me king over a people as numerous as the dust of the earth. 10 Now grant me wisdom and knowledge so that I may lead these people, for who can judge this great people of yours?"

11 God said to Solomon, "Since this was in your heart, and you have not requested riches, wealth, or glory, or for the life of those who hate you, and you have not even requested long life, but you have requested for yourself wisdom and knowledge that you may judge my people over whom I have made you king, 12 wisdom and knowledge are given to you. I will also give you riches, wealth, and glory, unlike what was given to the kings who were before you, or will be given to those after you." 13 So Solomon went to Jerusalem from[D] the high place that was in Gibeon in front of the tent of meeting, and he reigned over Israel.

SOLOMON'S HORSES AND WEALTH

14 Solomon accumulated 1,400 chariots and 12,000 horsemen, which he stationed in the chariot cities and with the king in Jerusalem. 15 The king made silver and gold as common in Jerusalem as stones, and he made cedar as abundant as sycamore in the Judean foothills. 16 Solomon's horses came from Egypt and Kue.[E] The king's traders would get them from Kue at the going price. 17 A chariot could be imported from Egypt for fifteen pounds[F] of silver and a horse for nearly four pounds.[G] In the same way, they exported them to all the kings of the Hittites and to the kings of Aram through their agents.

SOLOMON'S LETTER TO HIRAM

2 Solomon decided to build a temple for the name of the LORD and a royal palace for himself, 2 so he assigned 70,000 men as porters, 80,000 men as stonecutters in the mountains, and 3,600 as supervisors over them.

3 Then Solomon sent word to King Hiram[H] of Tyre:

Do for me what you did for my father David. You sent him cedars to build him a house to live in. 4 Now I am building a temple for the name of the LORD my God in order to dedicate it to him for burning fragrant incense before him, for displaying the rows of the Bread of the Presence continuously, and for sacrificing burnt offerings for the morning and the evening, the Sabbaths and the New Moons, and the appointed festivals of the LORD our God. This is ordained for Israel permanently. 5 The temple that I am building will be great, for our God is greater than any of the gods. 6 But who is able to build a temple for him, since even heaven and the highest heaven cannot contain him? Who am I then that I should build a temple for him except as a place to burn incense before him? 7 Therefore, send me an artisan who is skilled in engraving to work with gold, silver, bronze, and iron, and with purple, crimson, and blue yarn. He will work with the artisans who are with me in Judah and Jerusalem, appointed by my father David. 8 Also, send me cedar, cypress, and algum[I] logs from Lebanon, for I know that your servants know how to cut the trees of Lebanon. Note that my servants will be with your servants 9 to prepare logs for me in abundance because the temple I am building will be great and wondrous. 10 I will give your servants, the woodcutters who cut the trees, one hundred twenty thousand bushels[J] of wheat flour, one hundred twenty thousand bushels of barley, one hundred twenty thousand gallons[K] of wine, and one hundred twenty thousand gallons of oil.

HIRAM'S REPLY

11 Then King Hiram of Tyre wrote a letter[L] and sent it to Solomon:

Because the LORD loves his people, he set you over them as king.

12 Hiram also said:

Blessed be the LORD God of Israel, who made the heavens and the earth! He gave King David a

[A] **1:4** Vg; MT omits *the place* [B] **1:5** Some Hb mss, Tg, Syr; other Hb mss, LXX, Vg read *but there was* [C] **1:5** Or *it* [D] **1:13** LXX, Vg; MT reads *to* [E] **1:16** = Cilicia [F] **1:17** Lit *600 shekels* [G] **1:17** Lit *150 shekels* [H] **2:3** Some Hb mss, LXX, Syr, Vg; other Hb mss read *Huram*; 2Sm 5:11; 1Kg 5:1–2 [I] **2:8** = almug in 1Kg 10:11–12 [J] **2:10** Lit *20,000 cors* [K] **2:10** Lit *20,000 baths* [L] **2:11** Lit *Tyre said in writing*

wise son with insight and understanding, who
will build a temple for the LORD and a royal palace for himself. 13 I have now sent Huram-abi,[A] a
skillful man who has understanding. 14 He is the
son of a woman from the daughters of Dan. His
father is a man of Tyre. He knows how to work
with gold, silver, bronze, iron, stone, and wood,
with purple, blue, crimson yarn, and fine linen.
He knows how to do all kinds of engraving and
to execute any design that may be given him. I
have sent him to be with your artisans and the
artisans of my lord, your father David. 15 Now, let
my lord send the wheat, barley, oil, and wine to
his servants as promised. 16 We will cut logs from
Lebanon, as many as you need, and bring them
to you as rafts by sea to Joppa. You can then take
them up to Jerusalem.

SOLOMON'S WORKFORCE

17 Solomon took a census of all the resident alien
men in the land of Israel, after the census that his father David had conducted, and the total was 153,600.
18 Solomon made 70,000 of them porters, 80,000
stonecutters in the mountains, and 3,600 supervisors to make the people work.

BUILDING THE TEMPLE

3 Then Solomon began to build the LORD's temple
in Jerusalem on Mount Moriah where the LORD[B]
had appeared to his father David, at the site David
had prepared on the threshing floor of Ornan[C] the
Jebusite. 2 He began to build on the second day of the
second month in the fourth year of his reign. 3 These
are Solomon's foundations[D] for building God's temple: the length[E] was ninety feet,[F] and the width thirty
feet.[G] 4 The portico, which was across the front extending across the width of the temple, was thirty feet
wide; its height was thirty feet;[H] he overlaid its inner
surface with pure gold. 5 The larger room[I] he paneled with cypress wood, overlaid with fine gold, and
decorated with palm trees and chains. 6 He adorned
the temple with precious stones for beauty, and the
gold was the gold of Parvaim. 7 He overlaid the temple — the beams, the thresholds, its walls and doors
— with gold, and he carved cherubim on the walls.

THE MOST HOLY PLACE

8 Then he made the most holy place; its length corresponded to the width of the temple, 30 feet, and
its width was 30 feet. He overlaid it with forty-five
thousand pounds[J] of fine gold. 9 The weight of the
nails was twenty ounces[K] of gold, and he overlaid
the ceiling with gold.
10 He made two cherubim of sculptured work, for
the most holy place, and he overlaid them with gold.
11 The overall length of the wings of the cherubim was
30 feet: the wing of one was 7 1/2 feet,[L] touching the
wall of the room; its other wing was 7 1/2 feet, touching the wing of the other cherub. 12 The wing of the
other[M] cherub was 7 1/2 feet, touching the wall of the
room; its other wing was 7 1/2 feet, reaching the wing
of the other cherub. 13 The wingspan of these cherubim was 30 feet. They stood on their feet and faced
the larger room.[N]
14 He made the curtain of blue, purple, and crimson
yarn and fine linen, and he wove cherubim into it.

THE BRONZE PILLARS

15 In front of the temple he made two pillars, each
27 feet[O] high. The capital on top of each was 7 1/2 feet
high. 16 He had made chainwork in the inner sanctuary and also put it on top of the pillars. He made a
hundred pomegranates and fastened them into the
chainwork. 17 Then he set up the pillars in front of
the sanctuary, one on the right and one on the left.
He named the one on the right Jachin[P] and the one
on the left Boaz.[Q]

THE ALTAR AND BASINS

4 He made a bronze altar 30 feet[R] long, 30 feet wide,
and 15 feet[S] high.
2 Then he made the cast metal basin,[T] 15 feet from
brim to brim, perfectly round. It was 7 1/2 feet[U] high
and 45 feet[V] in circumference. 3 The likeness of oxen[W]
was below it, completely encircling it, ten every half
yard,[X] completely surrounding the basin. The oxen
were cast in two rows when the basin was cast. 4 It
stood on twelve oxen, three facing north, three facing
west, three facing south, and three facing east. The
basin was on top of them and all their hindquarters
were toward the center. 5 The basin was three inches[Y] thick, and its rim was fashioned like the brim of
a cup or a lily blossom. It could hold eleven thousand
gallons.[Z]
6 He made ten basins for washing and he put five
on the right and five on the left. The parts of the burnt
offering were rinsed in them, but the basin was used
by the priests for washing.

[A] **2:13** Lit *Huram my father* [B] **3:1** LXX; Tg reads *the angel of the LORD*; MT reads *he* [C] **3:1** = Araunah in 2Sm 24:16–24 [D] **3:3** Tg reads *The measurements which Solomon decreed* [E] **3:3** Lit *length — cubits in the former measure —* [F] **3:3** Lit *60 cubits* [G] **3:3** Lit *20 cubits*, also in vv. 4,8,11,13 [H] **3:4** LXX, Syr; MT reads *120 cubits* [I] **3:5** Lit *The house* [J] **3:8** Lit *600 talents* [K] **3:9** Lit *50 shekels* [L] **3:11** Lit *five cubits*, also in vv. 12,15 [M] **3:12** Syr, Vg; MT reads *the one* [N] **3:13** Lit *the house* [O] **3:15** Syr reads *18 cubits* (27 feet); Hb reads *35 cubits* (52 1/2 feet) [P] **3:17** = He Will Establish [Q] **3:17** = Strength Is in Him [R] **4:1** Lit *20 cubits* [S] **4:1** Lit *10 cubits*, also in v. 2 [T] **4:2** Lit *sea* [U] **4:2** Lit *five cubits* [V] **4:2** Lit *30 cubits* [W] **4:3** = gourds in 1Kg 7:24 [X] **4:3** Lit *10 per cubit* [Y] **4:5** Lit *a handbreadth* [Z] **4:5** Text emended; MT reads *3,000 baths* in 1Kg 7:26

Moriah: Its Biblical and Historical Significance

by Gary P. Arbino

In Genesis 22:2 God told Abram to go "to the land of The Moriah" to "one of the mountains about which I will tell you."[1] So we turn to our *Holman Bible Atlas*[2] and look in the gazetteer and notice that it has no entry for "the land of The Moriah." In fact, a search of our concordance proves that "the land of The Moriah" is never mentioned again in the Bible. It is also never mentioned in any extrabiblical text. So where, exactly, was this place?

Turning back to Genesis 22, we get some clues. Verse 4 says that on "the third day" of the journey from Beer-sheba in the Negev wilderness, Abram saw his destination. Enough of the day remained to allow him and Isaac to reach the mountain God chose and return to the others who had traveled with them. So, assuming a spry old man and three youth could probably cover anywhere from 15 to 45 miles a day, they traveled between 45 and 115 miles. We are not told which direction.

Verse 2 tells us that "The Moriah" is characterized by mountains. The main ancient Greek version, the *Septuagint,* points to the mountainous nature of the Moriah. Rather than simply transliterating "The Moriah," the Septuagint uses a phrase that in English reads "the lofty land." Thus "The Moriah" may simply have been a popular early name for the range of highlands along the west side of the Jordan Valley.

Unlike our modern English versions, all of the ancient translations of the Bible translate the word *Moriah*. Since Hebrew proper names rarely take definite articles, translators did not use "The Moriah" as a proper name; they therefore thought the term needed to be translated.

One option holds that *Moriah* came from the Hebrew word for "teach" (*yoreh*). Some of the rabbis thus felt the phrase "the land of the teaching" reflected that this was the place from which all teaching went into the world. Interestingly a place name with "teach" in it is in another important spot in the Abraham narrative. The first time God spoke to Abram in Canaan, he did so at the oaks of "Moreh" (Gn 12:6).

The Aramaic translations (Targumim) and several rabbinic sources read the original word as deriving from *yera'*, the Hebrew word meaning "fear/worship." They thus translate the phrase as "the land of the worship," a reference to Abraham's sacrifice.

Several ancient Greek versions, the Samaritan Pentateuch, and the Latin Vulgate translate *Moriah* as "vision"; "the land of the vision." This derives from understanding the word as coming from the verb *ra'ah*, meaning "to see." This is also a meaning within chapter 22 itself, as mentioned above in Abraham's naming of the site.

According to verse 14, Abram named the place Yahweh *yir'eh*, meaning "Yahweh is seen" or

Two monks overlook the Kidron Valley from the ancient city of David. The background shows that Jerusalem was a city built on and in the hills.

A close-up of the ruins of the Samaritan temple on Mount Gerizim that John Hyrcanus the Hasmonean king destroyed in 128 BC. Mount Gerizim is the place the Samaritans believe Abraham went to offer Isaac.

"Yahweh has provided."[3] The verse makes a reference to a popular saying: "it is said, 'In the mountain of Yahweh it will be seen/provided [*yera'eh*].'" Later generations ("to this day") would connect this particular mountain to "the mountain of Yahweh." In the Old Testament, this is the name applied to Zion (Jerusalem) because of the temple (Ps 24:3; Is 2:3; Zch 8:3).

While Genesis makes no specific connection, Israelites later connected Moriah with the Temple Mount and Solomon's temple, built around 950 BC and destroyed by the Babylonians in 586 BC.

If Abraham was at the place where Solomon's temple would later be located, he not only saw Jerusalem but would actually have built the altar for sacrificing Isaac either in or quite near the city. The site of the temple was just north of the Jebusite city (later called "the city of David") on the upper part of the same ridge. The Egyptian Execration texts from the eighteenth–nineteenth centuries BC already referred to the city as Urushalimu. If one assumes that Salem is a shortened name for Jerusalem in the Melchizedek narrative (Gn 14:18–20), it was evidently a thriving town with a "king." However, Genesis 22 never mentions this city, which is a bit odd if this important story takes place in or near it and Abram knew its king.

In 2 Chronicles 3:1, a verse not paralleled in the earlier book of Kings, the writer joins several lines of detail about the site of the temple, seemingly drawing from Genesis 22, 2 Samuel 24, and

1 Chronicles 21–22. Chronicles indicates that Solomon built the temple on "Mount Moriah" but does not explicitly mention Abraham or the events of Genesis 22. Instead the focus is on *David's* role in the temple. The text refers to Mount Moriah as the place (1) where Yahweh appeared to David—perhaps implying it supersedes Yahweh's appearance to Abraham; (2) which David himself chose—ignoring Abraham; and (3) where, on the threshing floor of Ornan the Jebusite, David built an altar—perhaps to be seen as supplanting Abraham's.

During the Second Temple period (515 BC–AD 70), people promoted the idea that the mountain of Abraham was connected to a single "Mount Moriah." This was the same as the "mountain of Yahweh" (Zion) where David decided to build the temple, where Solomon actually built it, and where Zerubbabel built the second temple. These links are affirmed by other Second Temple period Jewish texts such as the *Jewish Antiquities* by Josephus, *Jubilees*, the *Genesis Apocryphon*, and the Targum of Jonathan.

MOUNT MORIAH TODAY

Today when you visit the site of Mount Moriah (the Temple Mount or Haram es-Sharif) you are standing on the platform King Herod enlarged to forty-five acres, but the building you see is the Dome of the Rock. Caliph Abd-al-Malik built this magnificent golden-domed structure between AD 688 and 691; it remains substantially unaltered to this day. This building was erected on or near the spot of a Roman temple to Jupiter, which itself was built on the remains of Herod's temple. Surrounding this monument (not specifically a "mosque") are numerous other examples of Islamic-period architecture (AD 638–1917), the most notable of which is the Al-Aqsa Mosque (originally built between AD 709 and 715) in the southwest corner of the mount. There are no remains from either the Byzantine Christian period (AD 330–638; they left the mount as an empty holy space) or from the Roman period following the destruction of Herod's temple in AD 70.

Surviving materials from the Second Temple complex (including Herod's rebuild) are largely limited to the enclosure wall that surrounds the platform. A visitor today can take the underground Western Wall Tunnel walk along the wall where remains from Hasmonean (165–63 BC) and Herodian (63 BC–AD 70) architecture are visible. Most notable is the "master course" of huge, beautifully dressed building stones (the largest is 41 feet long, 11 1/2 feet high, and 15 feet wide, estimated to weigh six hundred tons) used by Herod's builders. Along the south wall, you can walk up the wide Herodian temple staircase. The eastern face of the enclosure wall reveals the seams between Herod's additions and the earlier construction. While nothing remains from the first (Solomon's) temple, several later structures on the mount have been traditionally related to Solomon. Centrally, the "Rock" inside the Dome is purportedly the site of Abraham's altar on Moriah, the place of the most holy place for the temple, and the spot from which Muslims believe Muhammad ascended to heaven after his night visit to Jerusalem. ✣

---

[1] Author's literal translation. [2] Many of the specific geographic and chronological references in this article are from Thomas Brisco, *Holman Bible Atlas* (Nashville: Holman Reference, 1998). [3] The Hebrew *yir'eh* is usually translated "see" in verses 2 and 14, and "provided" in the context of verse 8—like the English phrase "see to it."

THE LAMPSTANDS, TABLES, AND COURTS

7 He made the ten gold lampstands according to their specifications and put them in the sanctuary, five on the right and five on the left. 8 He made ten tables and placed them in the sanctuary, five on the right and five on the left. He also made a hundred gold bowls.

9 He made the courtyard of the priests and the large court, and doors for the court. He overlaid the doors with bronze. 10 He put the basin on the right side, toward the southeast. 11 Then Huram[A] made the pots, the shovels, and the bowls.

COMPLETION OF THE BRONZE FURNISHINGS

So Huram finished doing the work that he was doing for King Solomon in God's temple: 12 two pillars; the bowls and the capitals on top of the two pillars; the two gratings for covering both bowls of the capitals that were on top of the pillars; 13 the four hundred pomegranates for the two gratings (two rows of pomegranates for each grating covering both capitals' bowls on top of the pillars). 14 He also made the water carts[B] and the basins on the water carts. 15 The one basin and the twelve oxen underneath it, 16 the pots, the shovels, the forks, and all their utensils — Huram-abi[C] made them for King Solomon for the LORD's temple. All these were made of polished bronze. 17 The king had them cast in clay molds in the Jordan Valley between Succoth and Zeredah. 18 Solomon made all these utensils in such great abundance that the weight of the bronze was not determined.

COMPLETION OF THE GOLD FURNISHINGS

19 Solomon also made all the equipment in God's temple: the gold altar; the tables on which to put the Bread of the Presence; 20 the lampstands and their lamps of pure gold to burn in front of the inner sanctuary according to specifications; 21 the flowers, lamps, and gold tongs — of purest gold; 22 the wick trimmers, sprinkling basins, ladles,[D] and firepans — of purest gold; and the entryway to the temple, its inner doors to the most holy place, and the doors of the temple sanctuary — of gold.

5 So all the work Solomon did for the LORD's temple was completed. Then Solomon brought the consecrated things of his father David — the silver, the gold, and all the utensils — and put them in the treasuries of God's temple.

PREPARATIONS FOR THE TEMPLE DEDICATION

2 At that time Solomon assembled at Jerusalem the elders of Israel — all the tribal heads, the ancestral chiefs of the Israelites — in order to bring the ark of the covenant of the LORD up from the city of David, that is, Zion. 3 So all the men of Israel were assembled in the king's presence at the festival; this was in the seventh month.[E]

4 All the elders of Israel came, and the Levites picked up the ark. 5 They brought up the ark, the tent of meeting, and the holy utensils that were in the tent. The priests and the Levites brought them up. 6 King Solomon and the entire congregation of Israel who had gathered around him were in front of the ark sacrificing sheep, goats, and cattle that could not be counted or numbered because there were so many. 7 The priests brought the ark of the LORD's covenant to its place, into the inner sanctuary of the temple, to the most holy place, beneath the wings of the cherubim. 8 And the cherubim spread their wings over the place of the ark so that the cherubim formed a cover above the ark and its poles. 9 The poles were so long that their ends were seen from the holy place[F] in front of the inner sanctuary, but they were not seen from outside; they are still there today. 10 Nothing was in the ark except the two tablets that Moses had put in it at Horeb,[G] where the LORD had made a covenant with the Israelites when they came out of Egypt.

11 Now all the priests who were present had consecrated themselves regardless of their divisions. When the priests came out of the holy place, 12 the Levitical singers dressed in fine linen and carrying cymbals, harps, and lyres were standing east of the altar, and with them were 120 priests blowing trumpets. The Levitical singers were descendants of Asaph, Heman, and Jeduthun and their sons and relatives. 13 The trumpeters and singers joined together to praise and thank the LORD with one voice. They raised their voices, accompanied by trumpets, cymbals, and musical instruments, in praise to the LORD:

For he is good;
his faithful love endures forever.

The temple, the LORD's temple, was filled with a cloud. 14 And because of the cloud, the priests were not able to continue ministering, for the glory of the LORD filled God's temple.

SOLOMON'S DEDICATION OF THE TEMPLE

6 Then Solomon said:
The LORD said he would dwell
in total darkness,
2 but I have built an exalted temple for you,
a place for your dwelling forever.

[A] 4:11 = Hiram in 1Kg 7:13,40,45 [B] 4:14 Lit *the stands* [C] 4:16 Lit *Huram my father* [D] 4:22 Or *dishes*, or *spoons*; lit *palms* [E] 5:3 = Tishri (September–October) [F] 5:9 Some Hb mss, LXX; other Hb mss read *the ark*; 1Kg 8:8 [G] 5:10 = Sinai

[3] Then the king turned and blessed the entire congregation of Israel while they were standing. [4] He said:

Blessed be the LORD God of Israel!
He spoke directly to my father David,
and he has fulfilled the promise
by his power.
He said,
5 "Since the day I brought my people Israel
out of the land of Egypt,
I have not chosen a city to build a temple in
among any of the tribes of Israel,
so that my name would be there,
and I have not chosen a man
to be ruler over my people Israel.
6 But I have chosen Jerusalem
so that my name will be there,
and I have chosen David
to be over my people Israel."

7 My father David had his heart set
on building a temple for the name of the LORD,
the God of Israel.
8 However, the LORD said to my father David,
"Since it was your desire to build a temple
for my name,
you have done well to have this desire.
9 Yet, you are not the one to build the temple,
but your son, your own offspring,
will build the temple for my name."
10 So the LORD has fulfilled
what he promised.
I have taken the place of my father David
and I sit on the throne of Israel, as the
LORD promised.
I have built the temple for the name of the
LORD, the God of Israel.
11 I have put the ark there,
where the LORD's covenant is
that he made with the Israelites.

SOLOMON'S PRAYER

[12] Then Solomon stood before the altar of the LORD in front of the entire congregation of Israel and spread out his hands. [13] For Solomon had made a bronze platform 7 1/2 feet[A] long, 7 1/2 feet wide, and 4 1/2 feet[B] high and put it in the court. He stood on it, knelt down in front of the entire congregation of Israel, and spread out his hands toward heaven. [14] He said:

LORD God of Israel,
there is no God like you
in heaven or on earth,
who keeps his gracious covenant
with your servants who walk before you
with all their heart.
15 You have kept what you promised
to your servant, my father David.
You spoke directly to him,
and you fulfilled your promise
by your power,
as it is today.
16 Therefore, LORD God of Israel,
keep what you promised
to your servant, my father David:
"You will never fail to have a man
to sit before me on the throne of Israel,
if only your sons take care to walk
in my Law
as you have walked before me."
17 Now, LORD God of Israel, please confirm
what you promised to your servant David.

18 But will God indeed live on earth
with humans?
Even heaven, the highest heaven,
cannot contain you,
much less this temple I have built.
19 Listen[C] to your servant's prayer
and his petition,
LORD my God,
so that you may hear the cry and the prayer
that your servant prays before you,
20 so that your eyes watch over this temple
day and night,
toward the place where you said
you would put your name;
and so that you may hear the prayer
your servant prays toward this place.
21 Hear the petitions of your servant
and your people Israel,
which they pray toward this place.
May you hear in your dwelling place
in heaven.
May you hear and forgive.

22 If a man sins against his neighbor
and is forced to take an oath[D]
and he comes to take an oath
before your altar in this temple,
23 may you hear in heaven and act.
May you judge your servants,
condemning the wicked man
by bringing
what he has done on his own head
and providing justice for the righteous
by rewarding him according to
his righteousness.

[A] **6:13** Lit *five cubits* [B] **6:13** Lit *three cubits* [C] **6:19** Lit *Turn* [D] **6:22** Lit *and he lifts a curse against him to curse him*

24 If your people Israel are defeated
before an enemy,
because they have sinned against you,
and they return to you and praise your name,
and they pray and plead for mercy
before you in this temple,
25 may you hear in heaven
and forgive the sin of your people Israel.
May you restore them to the land
you gave them and their ancestors.

26 When the skies are shut and there is no rain
because they have sinned against you,
and they pray toward this place
and praise your name,
and they turn from their sins
because you are afflicting[A] them,
27 may you hear in heaven
and forgive the sin of your servants
and your people Israel,
so that you may teach them the good way
they should walk in.
May you send rain on your land
that you gave your people for an inheritance.

28 When there is famine in the land,
when there is pestilence,
when there is blight or mildew, locust
or grasshopper,
when their enemies besiege them
in the land and its cities,[B,C]
when there is any plague or illness,
29 every prayer or petition
that any person or that all your people Israel
may have —
they each know their own affliction[D]
and suffering —
as they spread out their hands
toward this temple,
30 may you hear in heaven, your dwelling place,
and may you forgive and give to everyone[E]
according to all their ways, since you know
each heart,
for you alone know the human heart,
31 so that they may fear you
and walk in your ways
all the days they live on the land
you gave our ancestors.

32 Even for the foreigner who is not of
your people Israel
but has come from a distant land
because of your great name
and your strong hand and outstretched arm:
when he comes and prays toward this temple,
33 may you hear in heaven in your dwelling place,
and do all the foreigner asks you.
Then all the peoples of the earth will know
your name,
to fear you as your people Israel do
and know that this temple I have built
bears your name.

34 When your people go out to fight against
their enemies,
wherever you send them,
and they pray to you
in the direction of this city you have chosen
and the temple that I have built for your name,
35 may you hear their prayer and petition
in heaven
and uphold their cause.

36 When they sin against you —
for there is no one who does not sin —
and you are angry with them
and hand them over to the enemy,
and their captors deport them
to a distant or nearby country,
37 and when they come to their senses
in the land where they were deported
and repent and petition you
in their captors' land,
saying, "We have sinned and done wrong;
we have been wicked,"
38 and when they return to you with all
their mind and all their heart
in the land of their captivity
where they were taken captive,
and when they pray in the direction
of their land
that you gave their ancestors,
and the city you have chosen,
and toward the temple I have built
for your name,
39 may you hear their prayer and petitions
in heaven,
your dwelling place,
and uphold their cause.[F]
May you forgive your people
who sinned against you.

40 Now, my God,
please let your eyes be open
and your ears attentive
to the prayer of this place.

[A] **6:26** LXX, Vg; MT reads *answering*; 1Kg 8:35 [B] **6:28** Lit *land of its gates* [C] **6:28** Lit *if his* (Israel's) *enemies besiege him in the land of his gates*; Jos 2:7; Jdg 16:2–3 [D] **6:29** Lit *plague* [E] **6:30** Lit *give for the man* [F] **6:39** Lit *and do their judgment*, or *justice*

41 Now therefore:

Arise, LORD God, come to your resting place,
you and your powerful ark.
May your priests, LORD God, be clothed
with salvation,
and may your faithful people rejoice
in goodness.
42 LORD God, do not reject your anointed one;[A]
remember your servant David's acts of
faithful love.

THE DEDICATION CEREMONIES

7 When Solomon finished praying, fire descended from heaven and consumed the burnt offering and the sacrifices, and the glory of the LORD filled the temple. 2 The priests were not able to enter the LORD's temple because the glory of the LORD filled the temple of the LORD. 3 All the Israelites were watching when the fire descended and the glory of the LORD came on the temple. They bowed down on the pavement with their faces to the ground. They worshiped and praised the LORD:

For he is good,
for his faithful love endures forever.

4 The king and all the people were offering sacrifices in the LORD's presence. 5 King Solomon offered a sacrifice of twenty-two thousand cattle and one hundred twenty thousand sheep and goats. In this manner the king and all the people dedicated God's temple. 6 The priests and the Levites were standing at their stations. The Levites had the musical instruments of the LORD, which King David had made to give thanks to the LORD — "for his faithful love endures forever" — when he offered praise with them. Across from the Levites, the priests were blowing trumpets, and all the people were standing. 7 Since the bronze altar that Solomon had made could not accommodate the burnt offering, the grain offering, and the fat of the fellowship offerings, Solomon first consecrated the middle of the courtyard that was in front of the LORD's temple and then offered the burnt offerings and the fat of the fellowship offerings there.

8 So Solomon and all Israel with him — a very great assembly, from the entrance to Hamath[B] to the Brook of Egypt — observed the festival at that time for seven days. 9 On the eighth day[C] they held a solemn assembly, for the dedication of the altar lasted seven days and the festival seven days. 10 On the twenty-third day of the seventh month he sent the people home,[D] rejoicing and with happy hearts for the goodness the LORD had done for David, for Solomon, and for his people Israel.

11 So Solomon finished the LORD's temple and the royal palace. Everything that had entered Solomon's heart to do for the LORD's temple and for his own palace succeeded.

THE LORD'S RESPONSE

12 Then the LORD appeared to Solomon at night and said to him:

I have heard your prayer and have chosen this place for myself as a temple of sacrifice. 13 If I shut the sky so there is no rain, or if I command the grasshopper to consume the land, or if I send pestilence on my people, 14 and my people, who bear my name, humble themselves, pray and seek my face, and turn from their evil ways, then I will hear from heaven, forgive their sin, and heal their land. 15 My eyes will now be open and my ears attentive to prayer from this place. 16 And I have now chosen and consecrated this temple so that my name may be there forever; my eyes and my heart will be there at all times.

17 As for you, if you walk before me as your father David walked, doing everything I have commanded you, and if you keep my statutes and ordinances, 18 I will establish your royal throne, as I promised your father David: You will never fail to have a man ruling in Israel.

19 However, if you turn away and abandon my statutes and my commands that I have set before you and if you go and serve other gods and bow in worship to them, 20 then I will uproot Israel from the soil that I gave them, and this temple that I have sanctified for my name I will banish from my presence; I will make it an object of scorn and ridicule among all the peoples. 21 As for this temple, which was exalted, everyone who passes by will be appalled and will say, "Why did the LORD do this to this land and this temple?" 22 Then they will say, "Because they abandoned the LORD God of their ancestors who brought them out of the land of Egypt. They clung to other gods and bowed in worship to them and served them. Because of this, he brought all this ruin on them."

SOLOMON'S LATER BUILDING PROJECTS

8 At the end of twenty years during which Solomon had built the LORD's temple and his own palace — 2 Solomon had rebuilt the cities Hiram[E] gave him and settled Israelites there — 3 Solomon

[A] **6:42** Some Hb mss, LXX; other Hb mss read *ones*; Ps 132:10
[B] **7:8** Or *from Lebo-hamath* [C] **7:9** = the day after the festival, or the 15th day [D] **7:10** Lit *people to their tents* [E] **8:2** = the king of Tyre

went to Hamath-zobah and seized it. 4 He built Tadmor in the wilderness along with all the storage cities that he built in Hamath. 5 He built Upper Beth-horon and Lower Beth-horon — fortified cities with walls, gates, and bars — 6 Baalath, all the storage cities that belonged to Solomon, all the chariot cities, the cavalry cities, and everything Solomon desired to build in Jerusalem, Lebanon, or anywhere else in the land of his dominion.

7 As for all the peoples who remained of the Hethites, Amorites, Perizzites, Hivites, and Jebusites, who were not from Israel — 8 their descendants who remained in the land after them, those the Israelites had not completely destroyed — Solomon imposed forced labor on them; it is this way today. 9 But Solomon did not consign the Israelites to be slaves for his work; they were soldiers, commanders of his captains, and commanders of his chariots and his cavalry. 10 These were King Solomon's deputies: 250 who supervised the people.

11 Solomon brought the daughter of Pharaoh from the city of David to the house he had built for her, for he said, "My wife must not live in the house[A] of King David of Israel because the places the ark of the LORD has come into are holy."

PUBLIC WORSHIP ESTABLISHED AT THE TEMPLE

12 At that time Solomon offered burnt offerings to the LORD on the LORD's altar he had made in front of the portico. 13 He followed the daily requirement for offerings according to the commandment of Moses for Sabbaths, New Moons, and the three annual appointed festivals: the Festival of Unleavened Bread, the Festival of Weeks, and the Festival of Shelters. 14 According to the ordinances of his father David, he appointed the divisions of the priests over their service, of the Levites over their responsibilities to offer praise and to minister before the priests following the daily requirement, and of the gatekeepers by their divisions with respect to each temple gate, for this had been the command of David, the man of God. 15 They did not turn aside from the king's command regarding the priests and the Levites concerning any matter or concerning the treasuries. 16 All of Solomon's work was carried out from the day the foundation was laid for the LORD's temple until it was finished. So the LORD's temple was completed.

SOLOMON'S FLEET

17 At that time Solomon went to Ezion-geber and to Eloth on the seashore in the land of Edom. 18 So Hiram[B] sent ships to him by his servants along with crews of experienced seamen. They went with Solomon's servants to Ophir, took from there seventeen tons[C] of gold, and delivered it to King Solomon.

THE QUEEN OF SHEBA

9 The queen of Sheba heard of Solomon's fame, so she came to test Solomon with difficult questions at Jerusalem with a very large entourage, with camels bearing spices, gold in abundance, and precious stones. She came to Solomon and spoke with him about everything that was on her mind. 2 So Solomon answered all her questions; nothing was too difficult for Solomon to explain to her. 3 When the queen of Sheba observed Solomon's wisdom, the palace he had built, 4 the food at his table, his servants' residence, his attendants' service and their attire, his cupbearers and their attire, and the burnt offerings he offered at the LORD's temple, it took her breath away.

5 She said to the king, "The report I heard in my own country about your words and about your wisdom is true. 6 But I didn't believe their reports until I came and saw with my own eyes. Indeed, I was not even told half of your great wisdom! You far exceed the report I heard. 7 How happy are your men.[D] How happy are these servants of yours, who always stand in your presence hearing your wisdom. 8 Blessed be the LORD your God! He delighted in you and put you on his throne as king for the LORD your God. Because your God loved Israel enough to establish them forever, he has set you over them as king to carry out justice and righteousness."

9 Then she gave the king four and a half tons[E] of gold, a great quantity of spices, and precious stones. There never were such spices as those the queen of Sheba gave to King Solomon. 10 In addition, Hiram's servants and Solomon's servants who brought gold from Ophir also brought algum wood and precious stones. 11 The king made the algum wood into walkways for the LORD's temple and for the king's palace and into lyres and harps for the singers. Never before had anything like them been seen in the land of Judah.

12 King Solomon gave the queen of Sheba her every desire, whatever she asked — far more than she had brought the king. Then she, along with her servants, returned to her own country.

SOLOMON'S WEALTH

13 The weight of gold that came to Solomon annually was twenty-five tons,[F] 14 besides what was brought by the merchants and traders. All the Arabian kings and governors of the land also brought gold and silver to Solomon.

15 King Solomon made two hundred large shields of hammered gold; 15 pounds[G] of hammered gold went into each shield. 16 He made three hundred small

[A] **8:11** LXX reads *city* [B] **8:18** Lit *Huram* [C] **8:18** Lit *450 talents*
[D] **9:7** LXX, Old Lat read *wives*; 1Kg 10:8 [E] **9:9** Lit *120 talents*
[F] **9:13** Lit *666 talents* [G] **9:15** Lit *600* (shekels)

Solomon in All His Splendor

by E. LeBron Matthews

In the steps Solomon took to secure his throne, he demonstrated wisdom and leadership.

In the ancient world, bloody purges were common aftermaths of a new king's coronation. To consolidate power, a new monarch frequently eliminated potential rivals, including members of the royal family. After David's death, Solomon also eliminated potential troublemakers. But unlike many kings of his time, Solomon's order to put Adonijah to death was neither vindictive nor unwarranted. It followed clear evidence that his half brother still entertained hope of becoming king. The deaths of Joab and Shimei reflected Solomon's willingness to listen to the advice of others. His father had instructed him to execute both men.

Solomon cemented an alliance with Egypt by marrying Pharaoh's daughter. The union may have seemed impressive; historically Egypt had been the world's great superpower. But Egypt now existed in name only. During the Twenty-first Dynasty, Egypt was in reality a group of independent states held together by trade and title.[1]

The true significance of Solomon's marriage to an Egyptian princess was the political recognition it provided. The loose confederation of Israelite tribes that David had forged into a tenuous kingdom had become a political state equal to its neighbors, including mythical Egypt. The importance of this cannot be overstated. Only a generation earlier, the stability of Israel was threatened. A victorious Philistine coalition had defeated Israel's army and occupied considerable territory west of the Jordan River. Under Solomon, the entire region between the Sinai Peninsula in the south and Syria in the north and between the Mediterranean Sea to the west and the Arabian Desert to the east was under Israel's control. The marriage to an Egyptian princess signified international respect for Solomon's power and prestige.

In ancient Israel, people commonly identified themselves by their tribal affiliation. Solomon reorganized his kingdom into political units called districts rather than maintaining the old tribal confederation. While the move was politically expedient, it ultimately weakened the unity of the nation by removing the tribal identity of its citizens. As a result, unrest in the tribes increased. The scars of his father's civil wars did not heal. But initially the reorganization likely produced a jubilant atmosphere of fresh hope that is common to political change and innovation. Its bureaucracy established the image of a strong and efficient administration.

Solomon aggressively pursued public works projects such as construction of his palace and Yahweh's temple. The infrastructure of Israel improved. Public buildings provided an object of national pride. The temple would serve as the heart of Israel's religion for centuries.

Solomon established further foreign political alliances, especially with Hiram of Tyre. These alliances resulted in peaceful relations with Israel's neighbors. Peace benefited both the economy and the society. Furthermore, the Phoenicians were seafaring traders who provided access to a larger world market.[2] Archaeological evidence suggests that Phoenician merchants set up business throughout Israel. They were joined by merchants from Arabia who brought spices, incense, and gold overland.[3] However, Israel's role in international trade at this time seems mainly to have been in importation, as little evidence exists that they shipped large quantities of materials outside the kingdom.

The early years of the reign of Solomon were known as Israel's Golden Age. It was a time of peace and prosperity. Cultural achievements expanded. The king gained a reputation for his proverbs. In part this was due to his patronage of wisdom literature and his establishment of schools to educate Israel's adolescent boys. Formal education and literary progress produced works such as those recorded in the biblical books of Proverbs and Song of Songs. Solomon in all his splendor was a ruler worthy of allegiance. ✣

Tyre, a Phoenician coastal city and home to a major seaport, was vitally involved with Israel in international commerce. King Hiram of Tyre formed a mutually beneficial trade alliance with both David and Solomon. Shown, a Phoenician jug found at Tyre.

---

[1] George Steindorff and Keith C. Seele, *When Egypt Ruled the East*, rev. ed. (Chicago, University of Chicago Press, 1957), 270, 275; John A. Wilson, *The Culture of Ancient Egypt* (Chicago: University of Chicago Press, 1951), 289–92, 320. [2] Glenn E. Markoe, *The Phoenicians, Peoples of the Past* (Berkeley: University of California Press, 2000), 33–35, 94, 129; D. R. Ap-Thomas, "The Phoenicians," *Peoples of Old Testament Times* (Oxford: Oxford University Press, 1973), 273–81. [3] B. S. J. Isserlin, *The Israelites* (London: Thames & Hudson, 1998), 185–87.

shields of hammered gold; 7 1/2 pounds[A] of gold went into each shield. The king put them in the House of the Forest of Lebanon.

17 The king also made a large ivory throne and overlaid it with pure gold. 18 The throne had six steps; there was a footstool covered in gold for the throne, armrests on either side of the seat, and two lions standing beside the armrests. 19 Twelve lions were standing there on the six steps, one at each end. Nothing like it had ever been made in any other kingdom.

20 All of King Solomon's drinking cups were gold, and all the utensils of the House of the Forest of Lebanon were pure gold. There was no silver, since it was considered as nothing in Solomon's time, 21 for the king's ships kept going to Tarshish with Hiram's servants, and once every three years the ships of Tarshish would arrive bearing gold, silver, ivory, apes, and peacocks.[B]

22 King Solomon surpassed all the kings of the world in riches and wisdom. 23 All the kings of the world wanted an audience with Solomon to hear the wisdom God had put in his heart. 24 Each of them would bring his own gift — items[C] of silver and gold, clothing, weapons,[D,E] spices, and horses and mules — as an annual tribute.

25 Solomon had four thousand stalls for horses and chariots, and twelve thousand horsemen. He stationed them in the chariot cities and with the king in Jerusalem. 26 He ruled over all the kings from the Euphrates River to the land of the Philistines and as far as the border of Egypt. 27 The king made silver as common in Jerusalem as stones, and he made cedar as abundant as sycamore in the Judean foothills. 28 They were bringing horses for Solomon from Egypt and from all the countries.

SOLOMON'S DEATH

29 The remaining events of Solomon's reign, from beginning to end, are written in the Events of the Prophet Nathan, the Prophecy of Ahijah the Shilonite, and the Visions of the Seer Iddo concerning Jeroboam son of Nebat. 30 Solomon reigned in Jerusalem over all Israel for forty years. 31 Solomon rested with his ancestors and was buried in the city of his father David. His son Rehoboam became king in his place.

THE KINGDOM DIVIDED

10 Then Rehoboam went to Shechem, for all Israel had gone to Shechem to make him king. 2 When Jeroboam son of Nebat heard about it — for he was in Egypt where he had fled from King Solomon's presence — Jeroboam returned from Egypt. 3 So they summoned him. Then Jeroboam and all Israel came and spoke to Rehoboam: 4 "Your father made our yoke harsh. Therefore, lighten your father's harsh service and the heavy yoke he put on us, and we will serve you."

5 Rehoboam replied, "Return to me in three days." So the people left.

6 Then King Rehoboam consulted with the elders who had attended his father Solomon when he was alive, asking, "How do you advise me to respond to this people?"

7 They replied, "If you will be kind to this people and please them by speaking kind words to them, they will be your servants forever."

8 But he rejected the advice of the elders who had advised him, and he consulted with the young men who had grown up with him, the ones attending him. 9 He asked them, "What message do you advise we send back to this people who said to me, 'Lighten the yoke your father put on us'?"

10 Then the young men who had grown up with him told him, "This is what you should say to the people who said to you, 'Your father made our yoke heavy, but you, make it lighter on us!' This is what you should say to them: 'My little finger is thicker than my father's waist! 11 Now therefore, my father burdened you with a heavy yoke, but I will add to your yoke; my father disciplined you with whips, but I, with barbed whips.'"[F]

12 So Jeroboam and all the people came to Rehoboam on the third day, just as the king had ordered, saying, "Return to me on the third day." 13 Then the king answered them harshly. King Rehoboam rejected the elders' advice 14 and spoke to them according to the young men's advice, saying, "My father made your yoke heavy,[G] but I will add to it; my father disciplined you with whips, but I, with barbed whips."

15 The king did not listen to the people because the turn of events came from God, in order that the LORD might carry out his word that he had spoken through Ahijah the Shilonite to Jeroboam son of Nebat.

16 When all Israel saw[H] that the king had not listened to them, the people answered the king:

> What portion do we have in David?
> We have no inheritance in the son of Jesse.
> Israel, each to your tent;
> David, look after your own house now!

So all Israel went to their tents. 17 But as for the Israelites living in the cities of Judah, Rehoboam reigned over them.

18 Then King Rehoboam sent Hadoram,[I] who was in charge of the forced labor, but the Israelites stoned

[A] **9:16** Lit *300 (shekels)* [B] **9:21** Or *baboons* [C] **9:24** Or *vessels*, or *weapons* [D] **9:24** LXX reads *resin* [E] **9:24** Or *fragrant balsam*
[F] **10:11** Lit *with scorpions*, also in v. 14 [G] **10:14** Some Hb mss, LXX; other Hb mss read *I will make your yoke heavy*; 1Kg 12:14
[H] **10:16** Some Hb mss, LXX; other Hb mss omit *saw*; 1Kg 12:16
[I] **10:18** = Adoram in 1Kg 12:18

him to death. However, King Rehoboam managed to get into his chariot to flee to Jerusalem. 19 Israel is in rebellion against the house of David until today.

REHOBOAM IN JERUSALEM

11 When Rehoboam arrived in Jerusalem, he mobilized the house of Judah and Benjamin — one hundred eighty thousand fit young soldiers — to fight against Israel to restore the reign to Rehoboam. 2 But the word of the LORD came to Shemaiah, the man of God: 3 "Say to Rehoboam son of Solomon, king of Judah, to all Israel in Judah and Benjamin, and to the rest of the people, 4 'This is what the LORD says: You are not to march up and fight against your brothers. Each of you return home, for this incident has come from me.' "

So they listened to what the LORD said and turned back from going against Jeroboam.

JUDAH'S KING REHOBOAM

5 Rehoboam stayed in Jerusalem, and he fortified cities[A] in Judah. 6 He built up Bethlehem, Etam, Tekoa, 7 Beth-zur, Soco, Adullam, 8 Gath, Mareshah, Ziph, 9 Adoraim, Lachish, Azekah, 10 Zorah, Aijalon, and Hebron, which are fortified cities in Judah and in Benjamin. 11 He strengthened their fortifications and put leaders in them with supplies of food, oil, and wine. 12 He also put large shields and spears in each and every city to make them very strong. So Judah and Benjamin were his.

13 The priests and Levites from all their regions throughout Israel took their stand with Rehoboam, 14 for the Levites left their pasturelands and their possessions and went to Judah and Jerusalem, because Jeroboam and his sons refused to let them serve as priests of the LORD. 15 Jeroboam appointed his own priests for the high places, the goat-demons, and the golden calves he had made. 16 Those from every tribe of Israel who had determined in their hearts to seek the LORD their God followed the Levites to Jerusalem to sacrifice to the LORD, the God of their ancestors. 17 So they strengthened the kingdom of Judah and supported Rehoboam son of Solomon for three years, because they walked in the ways of David and Solomon for three years.

18 Rehoboam married Mahalath, daughter of David's son Jerimoth and of Abihail daughter of Jesse's son Eliab. 19 She bore sons to him: Jeush, Shemariah, and Zaham. 20 After her, he married Maacah daughter[B] of Absalom. She bore Abijah, Attai, Ziza, and Shelomith to him. 21 Rehoboam loved Maacah daughter of Absalom more than all his wives and concubines. He acquired eighteen wives and sixty concubines and was the father of twenty-eight sons and sixty daughters.

22 Rehoboam appointed Abijah son of Maacah as chief, leader among his brothers, intending to make him king. 23 Rehoboam also showed discernment by dispersing some of his sons to all the regions of Judah and Benjamin and to all the fortified cities. He gave them plenty of provisions and sought many wives for them.

SHISHAK'S INVASION

12 When Rehoboam had established his sovereignty and royal power, he abandoned the law of the LORD — he and all Israel with him. 2 Because they were unfaithful to the LORD, in the fifth year of King Rehoboam, King Shishak of Egypt went to war against Jerusalem 3 with 1,200 chariots, 60,000 cavalrymen, and countless people who came with him from Egypt — Libyans, Sukkiim, and Cushites. 4 He captured the fortified cities of Judah and came as far as Jerusalem.

5 Then the prophet Shemaiah went to Rehoboam and the leaders of Judah who were gathered at Jerusalem because of Shishak. He said to them, "This is what the LORD says: You have abandoned me; therefore, I have abandoned you to Shishak."

6 So the leaders of Israel and the king humbled themselves and said, "The LORD is righteous."

7 When the LORD saw that they had humbled themselves, the LORD's message came to Shemaiah: "They have humbled themselves; I will not destroy them but will grant them a little deliverance. My wrath will not be poured out on Jerusalem through Shishak. 8 However, they will become his servants so that they may recognize the difference between serving me and serving the kingdoms of other lands."

9 So King Shishak of Egypt went to war against Jerusalem. He seized the treasuries of the LORD's temple and the treasuries of the royal palace. He took everything. He took the gold shields that Solomon had made. 10 King Rehoboam made bronze shields to replace them and committed them into the care of the captains of the guards[C] who protected the entrance to the king's palace. 11 Whenever the king entered the LORD's temple, the guards would carry the shields and take them back to the armory.[D] 12 When Rehoboam humbled himself, the LORD's anger turned away from him, and he did not destroy him completely. Besides that, conditions were good in Judah.

REHOBOAM'S LAST DAYS

13 King Rehoboam established his royal power in Jerusalem. Rehoboam was forty-one years old when he became king, and he reigned seventeen years in

[A] **11:5** Lit *he built cities for a fortress* [B] **11:20** Possibly *granddaughter*, also in v. 21; 2Ch 13:2 [C] **12:10** Lit *the runners* [D] **12:11** Lit *the chamber of the runners*

Egypt's Influence on the Divided Kingdom

by Ken Cox

Egypt exerted no significant religious influence on Israel and Judah through its complex array of gods and idols.[1] Yet, after being harbored in Egypt, Jeroboam instituted calf worship in Israel (1Kg 12:28–29). However, the more prominent apostasy through Baal and Ashtoreth worship Israel borrowed from Canaanite neighbors.[2]

One of Egypt's exports during the divided kingdom period was papyrus writing material. Using papyrus grown along the Nile, the Egyptians processed, layered, and stuck the plant stems together to form scrolls. These scrolls were common both as writing material in ancient Egypt and for production of biblical scrolls in Canaan. Baruch, the scribe, used papyrus scrolls to record the prophecies of Jeremiah. Israel duplicated this technology by planting papyrus in Galilee for parchment production.[3]

Jacob's descendants in the promised land were sandwiched between the military and commercial powers of Assyria, Babylon, and Aram to the north and Egypt to the south. The narrow land bridge of Canaan connected the nations that often moved through their borders.[4] Egypt's primary influences on the divided kingdom were as a threatening military power or an unreliable ally.[5]

God's Word prohibited the tribes of Israel from relying on Egypt for military support. Deuteronomy 17:14–20 describes the character of Israel's future kings. The Lord forbade the kings to return to Egypt to acquire horses. Scriptures had portrayed Egypt as a place of darkness and bondage. God's power of salvation had lovingly delivered his people from the stranglehold of Egyptian power. God's people, therefore, were not to return to Egypt after the exodus. They were to trust in God, not political allies, for their security.

King Solomon broke this commandment. Israel's alliance with Egypt, though, was short-lived. Pharaoh Shishak antagonized Solomon during the final years of Solomon's reign by granting refuge to Jeroboam.[6] After Solomon's death, Jeroboam likely requested permission to return to Canaan where he incited a rebellion against the newly enthroned King Rehoboam.

Pharaoh Shishak's enmity was not limited to harboring Jeroboam. After Israel divided, in the fifth year of Rehoboam's reign, Shishak attacked Jerusalem and carried off the treasures of the temple (1Kg 14:25–26). This Egyptian victory is recorded on the walls of the temple in Karnak.[7] Shishak took the gold shields Solomon had made for his personal guard.

Nile River crossing to Beni Hasan. Vegetation forms a ribbon of green on either side of the river.

When Pharaoh Neco's forces killed Judah's King Josiah, Pharaoh was leading his Egyptian army north, toward Damascus, to aid his allies in Assyria. Babylon was rising as a world power after the fall of Nineveh in 612 BC. Babylon's King Nebuchadnezzar defeated Pharaoh Neco at Carchemish in 605 BC.[8]

After Egypt's defeat at Carchemish, Jerusalem was in a tug of war between Babylon and Egypt. Pharaoh Hophra wanted to reestablish domination of Judah and attempted to halt Babylon's final siege of Jerusalem.[9] Hophra's intervention in Judah was unsuccessful, and in 586 BC the Babylonians devastated Jerusalem. ✣

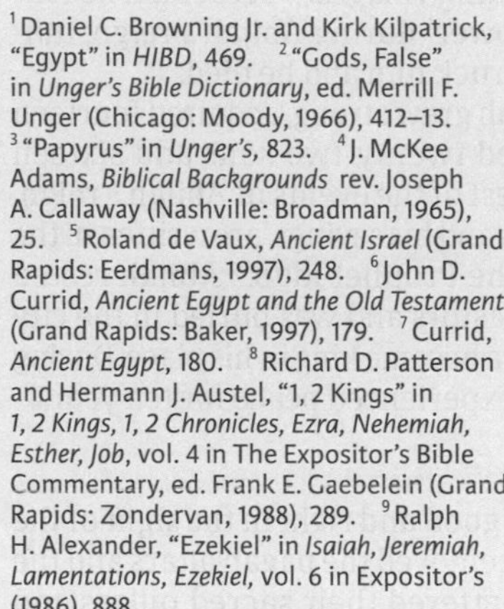

The Serapeum at Saqqara was the burial place for sacred bulls, which the ancient Egyptians worshiped as the incarnations of Ptah, their god of creation. After the division of the kingdom, King Jeroboam brought calf worship in Israel.

---

[1] Daniel C. Browning Jr. and Kirk Kilpatrick, "Egypt" in *HIBD*, 469. [2] "Gods, False" in *Unger's Bible Dictionary*, ed. Merrill F. Unger (Chicago: Moody, 1966), 412–13. [3] "Papyrus" in *Unger's*, 823. [4] J. McKee Adams, *Biblical Backgrounds* rev. Joseph A. Callaway (Nashville: Broadman, 1965), 25. [5] Roland de Vaux, *Ancient Israel* (Grand Rapids: Eerdmans, 1997), 248. [6] John D. Currid, *Ancient Egypt and the Old Testament* (Grand Rapids: Baker, 1997), 179. [7] Currid, *Ancient Egypt*, 180. [8] Richard D. Patterson and Hermann J. Austel, "1, 2 Kings" in *1, 2 Kings, 1, 2 Chronicles, Ezra, Nehemiah, Esther, Job*, vol. 4 in The Expositor's Bible Commentary, ed. Frank E. Gaebelein (Grand Rapids: Zondervan, 1988), 289. [9] Ralph H. Alexander, "Ezekiel" in *Isaiah, Jeremiah, Lamentations, Ezekiel*, vol. 6 in Expositor's (1986), 888.

At the Karnak Temple in Egypt; interior of the Bubastite portal. The inscriptions brag of Shishak's military campaigns against Israel and Judah, during which he claims to have destroyed 156 towns and villages.

Jerusalem, the city the LORD had chosen from all the tribes of Israel to put his name. Rehoboam's mother's name was Naamah the Ammonite. 14 Rehoboam did what was evil, because he did not determine in his heart to seek the LORD.

15 The events of Rehoboam's reign, from beginning to end, are written in the Events of the Prophet Shemaiah and of the Seer Iddo concerning genealogies. There was war between Rehoboam and Jeroboam throughout their reigns. 16 Rehoboam rested with his ancestors and was buried in the city of David. His son Abijah[A] became king in his place.

JUDAH'S KING ABIJAH

13 In the eighteenth year of Israel's King Jeroboam, Abijah[A] became king over Judah, 2 and he reigned three years in Jerusalem. His mother's name was Micaiah[B] daughter of Uriel; she was from Gibeah.

There was war between Abijah and Jeroboam. 3 Abijah set his army of warriors in order with four hundred thousand fit young men. Jeroboam arranged his mighty army of eight hundred thousand fit young men in battle formation against him. 4 Then Abijah stood on Mount Zemaraim, which is in the hill country of Ephraim, and said, "Jeroboam and all Israel, hear me. 5 Don't you know that the LORD God of Israel gave the kingship over Israel to David and his descendants forever by a covenant of salt? 6 But Jeroboam son of Nebat, a servant of Solomon son of David, rose up and rebelled against his lord. 7 Then worthless and wicked men gathered around him to resist Rehoboam son of Solomon when Rehoboam was young, inexperienced, and unable to assert himself against them.

8 "And now you are saying you can assert yourselves against the LORD's kingdom, which is in the hand of one of David's sons. You are a vast number and have with you the golden calves that Jeroboam made for you as gods.[C] 9 Didn't you banish the priests of the LORD, the descendants of Aaron and the Levites, and make your own priests like the peoples of other lands do? Whoever comes to ordain himself with a young bull and seven rams may become a priest of what are not gods.

10 "But as for us, the LORD is our God. We have not abandoned him; the priests ministering to the LORD are descendants of Aaron, and the Levites serve at their tasks. 11 They offer a burnt offering and fragrant incense to the LORD every morning and every evening, and they set the rows of the Bread of the Presence on the ceremonially clean table. They light the lamps of the gold lampstand every evening. We are carrying out the requirements of the LORD our God, while you have abandoned him. 12 Look, God and his priests are with us at our head. The trumpets are ready to sound the charge against you. Israelites, don't fight against the LORD God of your ancestors, for you will not succeed."

13 Now Jeroboam had sent an ambush around to advance from behind them. So they were in front of Judah, and the ambush was behind them. 14 Judah turned and discovered that the battle was in front of them and behind them, so they cried out to the LORD. Then the priests blew the trumpets, 15 and the men of Judah raised the battle cry. When the men of Judah raised the battle cry, God routed Jeroboam and all Israel before Abijah and Judah. 16 So the Israelites fled before Judah, and God handed them over to them. 17 Then Abijah and his people struck them with a mighty blow, and five hundred thousand fit young men of Israel were killed. 18 The Israelites were subdued at that time. The Judahites succeeded because they depended on the LORD, the God of their ancestors.

19 Abijah pursued Jeroboam and captured some cities from him: Bethel, Jeshanah, and Ephron,[D] along with their surrounding villages. 20 Jeroboam no longer retained his power[E] during Abijah's reign; ultimately, the LORD struck him and he died.

21 However, Abijah grew strong, acquired fourteen wives, and fathered twenty-two sons and sixteen daughters. 22 The rest of the events of Abijah's reign, along with his ways and his sayings, are written in the

14 Writing of the Prophet Iddo. 1 Abijah rested with his ancestors and was buried in the city of David. His son Asa became king in his place. During his reign the land experienced peace for ten years.

JUDAH'S KING ASA

2 Asa did what was good and right in the sight of the LORD his God. 3 He removed the pagan altars and the high places. He shattered their sacred pillars and chopped down their Asherah poles. 4 He told the people of Judah to seek the LORD God of their ancestors and to carry out the instruction and the commands. 5 He also removed the high places and the shrines[F] from all the cities of Judah, and the kingdom experienced peace under him.

6 Because the land experienced peace, Asa built fortified cities in Judah. No one made war with him in those days because the LORD gave him rest. 7 So he said to the people of Judah, "Let's build these cities and surround them with walls and towers, with doors and bars. The land is still ours because we sought the LORD our God. We sought him and he gave us rest on every side." So they built and succeeded.

[A] **12:16; 13:1** = Abijam in 1Kg 14:31–15:8 [B] **13:2** LXX, Syr, Arabic read *Maacah*; 1Kg 15:2; 2Ch 11:22 [C] **13:8** Or *God*; 1Kg 12:28 [D] **13:19** Alt Hb tradition reads *Ephrain* [E] **13:20** Lit *He did not restrain the power of Jeroboam* [F] **14:5** Or *incense altars*

THE CUSHITE INVASION

8 Asa had an army of three hundred thousand from Judah bearing large shields and spears, and two hundred eighty thousand from Benjamin bearing regular shields and drawing the bow. All these were valiant warriors. 9 Then Zerah the Cushite came against them with an army of one million men and three hundred[A] chariots. They came as far as Mareshah. 10 So Asa marched out against him and lined up in battle formation in Zephathah Valley at Mareshah.

11 Then Asa cried out to the LORD his God, "LORD, there is no one besides you to help the mighty and those without strength. Help us, LORD our God, for we depend on you, and in your name we have come against this large army. LORD, you are our God. Do not let a mere mortal hinder you."

12 So the LORD routed the Cushites before Asa and before Judah, and the Cushites fled. 13 Then Asa and the people who were with him pursued them as far as Gerar. The Cushites fell until they had no survivors, for they were crushed before the LORD and his army. So the people of Judah carried off a great supply of loot. 14 Then they attacked all the cities around Gerar because the terror of the LORD was on them. They also plundered all the cities, since there was a great deal of plunder in them. 15 They also attacked the tents of the herdsmen and captured many sheep and camels. Then they returned to Jerusalem.

REVIVAL UNDER ASA

15 The Spirit of God came on Azariah son of Oded. 2 So he went out to meet Asa and said to him, "Asa and all Judah and Benjamin, hear me. The LORD is with you when you are with him. If you seek him, he will be found by you, but if you abandon him, he will abandon you. 3 For many years Israel has been without the true God, without a teaching priest, and without instruction, 4 but when they turned to the LORD God of Israel in their distress and sought him, he was found by them. 5 In those times there was no peace for those who went about their daily activities because the residents of the lands had many conflicts. 6 Nation was crushed by nation and city by city, for God troubled them with every possible distress. 7 But as for you, be strong; don't give up,[B] for your work has a reward."

8 When Asa heard these words and the prophecy of Azariah son of Oded the prophet, he took courage and removed the abhorrent idols from the whole land of Judah and Benjamin and from the cities he had captured in the hill country of Ephraim. He renovated the altar of the LORD that was in front of the portico of the LORD's temple. 9 Then he gathered all Judah and Benjamin, as well as those from the tribes of Ephraim, Manasseh, and Simeon who were residing among them, for they had defected to him from Israel in great numbers when they saw that the LORD his God was with him.

10 They were gathered in Jerusalem in the third month of the fifteenth year of Asa's reign. 11 At that time they sacrificed to the LORD seven hundred cattle and seven thousand sheep and goats from all the plunder they had brought. 12 Then they entered into a covenant to seek the LORD God of their ancestors with all their heart and all their soul. 13 Whoever would not seek the LORD God of Israel would be put to death, young or old,[C] man or woman. 14 They took an oath to the LORD in a loud voice, with shouting, with trumpets, and with rams' horns. 15 All Judah rejoiced over the oath, for they had sworn it wholeheartedly. They had sought him with all sincerity, and he was found by them. So the LORD gave them rest on every side.

16 King Asa also removed Maacah, his grandmother,[D] from being queen mother because she had made an obscene image of Asherah. Asa chopped down her obscene image, then crushed it and burned it in the Kidron Valley. 17 The high places were not taken away from Israel; nevertheless, Asa was wholeheartedly devoted his entire life.[E] 18 He brought his father's consecrated gifts and his own consecrated gifts into God's temple: silver, gold, and utensils.

19 There was no war until the thirty-fifth year of Asa's reign.

ASA'S TREATY WITH ARAM

16 In the thirty-sixth year of Asa, Israel's King Baasha went to war against Judah. He built Ramah in order to keep anyone from leaving or coming to King Asa of Judah. 2 So Asa brought out the silver and gold from the treasuries of the LORD's temple and the royal palace and sent it to Aram's King Ben-hadad, who lived in Damascus, saying, 3 "There's a treaty between me and you, between my father and your father. Look, I have sent you silver and gold. Go break your treaty with Israel's King Baasha so that he will withdraw from me."

4 Ben-hadad listened to King Asa and sent the commanders of his armies to the cities of Israel. They attacked Ijon, Dan, Abel-maim,[F] and all the storage cities[G] of Naphtali. 5 When Baasha heard about it, he quit building Ramah and stopped his work. 6 Then King Asa brought all Judah, and they carried away the stones of Ramah and the timbers Baasha had built it with. Then he built Geba and Mizpah with them.

[A] **14:9** Syr, Arabic read *30,000* [B] **15:7** Lit *don't let your hands drop* [C] **15:13** Or *insignificant or great* [D] **15:16** Lit *mother*; 1Kg 15:2; 2Ch 11:22 [E] **15:17** Lit *wholehearted all his days* [F] **16:4** *Abel-beth-maacah* in 1Kg 15:20 [G] **16:4** = all Chinnereth in 1Kg 15:20

by Kevin C. Peacock

Part of the restored mosaic floor at the synagogue in Hammath Tiberias. The image depicts the Torah ark, menorahs, incense shovels, shofars, lulavs, and ethrogs; dated fourth–fifth centuries AD.

Bronze figurine of a trumpeter; from Anatolia; dated eighth–sixth centuries BC.

Of the musical instruments the Old Testament names, the shofar, or ram's horn, is the most frequent. Sometimes translated as "trumpet," the shofar is the only biblical instrument used in synagogues today. Many who hear a shofar have difficulty terming it as a "musical" instrument. Its musical qualities are limited to only two or three harmonic overtones, making it difficult for any melodies, and clear tonality is almost nonexistent. With its high shrill sound, the shofar was ideal as a noise maker.

KINDS OF TRUMPETS

Horns or trumpets in the Bible were of two types, those made of animal horn and those of metal. The Hebrew terms *yobel*, *qeren*, and *shofar* were used interchangeably. *Yobel* ("ram"; Ex 19:13; Jos 6:5), usually translated as "horn," refers to a shofar (Jos 6:4,6; see Ex 19:13,16). The term *Jubilee* is named after *yobel* (Lv 25:13), a celebration beginning with sounding of the ram's horn (v. 9). Jubal, the inventor of musical instruments (Gn 4:21), seems to carry the same name as the ram. *Qeren* ("horn"; 1Ch 25:5 , CSB footnote) is the literal horn of an animal (Gn 22:13; Ps 22:21) from which the musical instrument was made. It is used once as a synonym for shofar (*qeren hayyobel*, "the horn of the ram"; Jos 6:5). The related Aramaic term *qarna* is in Daniel 3:5,7.[1]

The other type of trumpet was made from hammered metal (Nm 10:1–2), usually bronze, copper, gold, or silver.[2] This *chatsotsrah* was described by Josephus[3] and shown on ancient coins and artwork as a straight tube with a mouthpiece and a flared end. Those used in temple service were always made of silver and were blown by the priests and Levites. These were used in sacrificial ceremony (1Ch 15:24), in war (Nm 31:6), and in royal coronations (2Kg 11:14) in much the same way as the shofar.

CONSTRUCTION AND TONES

Shofars are still made today as in ancient times. The horn of any kosher animal except a cow is suitable, but the preferred horn is that of a ram, the animal Abraham sacrificed in the place of Isaac (Gn 22:1–14).[4] Some shofars are left in their natural curved shape, but craftsmen often use steam or heat to soften the horn to straighten it. Then they will bend the wide end, forming a right angle. A hole bored at the point into the natural hollow allows the trumpeter to blow it like a bugle.[5]

The Hebrew Old Testament records two different horn sounds: *teqa'* ("a trumpet blast") and *teru'ah* ("a shout"). Rabbinic tradition defined the *teqa'* as a long sustained lower tone that ended abruptly and the *teru'ah* as a higher trill or series of notes. The rabbis added a third sound comprising three connected short notes, the *shevarim*. These three patterns are combined into sequences, making a phrase of thirty notes that may be repeated several times.[6] This prescribed pattern of different pitches, lengths of tone, and staccato and legato articulation were designed to imitate a sobbing or wailing sound of the human voice.

The Septuagint employed the Greek term *salpinx* ("trumpet") to translate both *chatsotsrah* and *shofar*, making no distinction between the two. The New Testament refers simply to a "trumpet" eleven times, with no differentiation of horn or metal.[7] ✣

---

[1] Daniel A. Foxvog and Anne D. Kilmer, "Music" in *ISBE*, vol. 3 (1986), 439. [2] Foxvog and Kilmer, "Music," 439. [3] Josephus, *Jewish Antiquities* 3.12.6. [4] Lawrence H. Schiffman, "Shophar" in *Harper's Bible Dictionary*, ed. Paul J. Achtemeier (San Francisco: Harper & Row, 1985), 947. [5] J. A. Thompson, *Handbook of Life in Bible Times* (Downers Grove, IL: InterVarsity, 1986), 255. [6] Dennis F. McCorkle, "Shofar or Ram's Horn," *The Music of the Bible* (2007), www.musicofthebible.com. [7] Foxvog and Kilmer, "Music," 446.

HANANI'S REBUKE OF ASA

7 At that time, the seer Hanani came to King Asa of Judah and said to him, "Because you depended on the king of Aram and have not depended on the LORD your God, the army of the king of Aram has escaped from you. 8 Were not the Cushites and Libyans a vast army with many chariots and horsemen? When you depended on the LORD, he handed them over to you. 9 For the eyes of the LORD roam throughout the earth to show himself strong for those who are wholeheartedly devoted to him. You have been foolish in this matter. Therefore, you will have wars from now on." 10 Asa was enraged with the seer and put him in prison[A] because of his anger over this. And Asa mistreated some of the people at that time.

ASA'S DEATH

11 Note that the events of Asa's reign, from beginning to end, are written in the Book of the Kings of Judah and Israel. 12 In the thirty-ninth year of his reign, Asa developed a disease in his feet, and his disease became increasingly severe. Yet even in his disease he didn't seek the LORD but only the physicians. 13 Asa rested with his ancestors; he died in the forty-first year of his reign. 14 He was buried in his own tomb that he had made for himself in the city of David. They laid him out in a coffin that was full of spices and various mixtures of prepared ointments; then they made a great fire in his honor.

JUDAH'S KING JEHOSHAPHAT

17 His son Jehoshaphat became king in his place and strengthened himself against Israel. 2 He stationed troops in every fortified city of Judah and set garrisons in the land of Judah and in the cities of Ephraim that his father Asa had captured.

3 Now the LORD was with Jehoshaphat because he walked in the former ways of his ancestor David.[B] He did not seek the Baals 4 but sought the God of his father and walked by his commands, not according to the practices of Israel. 5 So the LORD established the kingdom in his hand. Then all Judah brought him tribute, and he had riches and honor in abundance. 6 He took great pride in the LORD's ways, and he again removed the high places and Asherah poles from Judah.

JEHOSHAPHAT'S EDUCATIONAL PLAN

7 In the third year of his reign, Jehoshaphat sent his officials — Ben-hail,[C] Obadiah, Zechariah, Nethanel, and Micaiah — to teach in the cities of Judah. 8 The Levites with them were Shemaiah, Nethaniah, Zebadiah,[D] Asahel, Shemiramoth, Jehonathan, Adonijah, Tobijah, and Tob-adonijah; the priests, Elishama and Jehoram, were with these Levites. 9 They taught throughout Judah, having the book of the LORD's instruction with them. They went throughout the towns of Judah and taught the people.

10 The terror of the LORD was on all the kingdoms of the lands that surrounded Judah, so they didn't fight against Jehoshaphat. 11 Some of the Philistines also brought gifts and silver as tribute to Jehoshaphat, and the Arabs brought him flocks: 7,700 rams and 7,700 male goats.

JEHOSHAPHAT'S MILITARY MIGHT

12 Jehoshaphat grew stronger and stronger. He built fortresses and storage cities in Judah 13 and carried out great works in the towns of Judah. He had fighting men, valiant warriors, in Jerusalem. 14 These are their numbers according to their ancestral families.[E] For Judah, the commanders of thousands:

Adnah the commander and three hundred
thousand valiant warriors with him;
15 next to him, Jehohanan the commander and
two hundred eighty thousand with him;
16 next to him, Amasiah son of Zichri, the
volunteer of the LORD, and two hundred
thousand valiant warriors with him;
17 from Benjamin, Eliada, a valiant warrior, and
two hundred thousand with him armed
with bow and shield;
18 next to him, Jehozabad and one hundred
eighty thousand with him equipped
for war.

19 These were the ones who served the king, besides those he stationed in the fortified cities throughout all Judah.

JEHOSHAPHAT'S ALLIANCE WITH AHAB

18 Now Jehoshaphat had riches and honor in abundance, and he made an alliance with Ahab through marriage.[F] 2 Then after some years, he went down to visit Ahab in Samaria. Ahab slaughtered many sheep, goats, and cattle for him and for the people who were with him, and he persuaded him to attack Ramoth-gilead, 3 for Israel's King Ahab asked Judah's King Jehoshaphat, "Will you go with me to Ramoth-gilead?"

He replied to him, "I am as you are, my people as your people; we will be with you in the battle." 4 But Jehoshaphat said to the king of Israel, "First, please ask what the LORD's will is."

5 So the king of Israel gathered the prophets, four hundred men, and asked them, "Should we go to Ramoth-gilead for war or should I refrain?"

[A] **16:10** Lit *the house of stocks* [B] **17:3** Some Hb mss, LXX omit *David* [C] **17:7** = Son of Power [D] **17:8** Some Hb mss, Syr, Tg, Arabic read *Zechariah* [E] **17:14** Lit *the house of their fathers* [F] **18:1** Lit *made himself a son-in-law to Ahab*; 1Kg 3:1; Ezr 9:14

They replied, "March up, and God will hand it over
to the king."
6 But Jehoshaphat asked, "Isn't there a prophet of
the LORD here anymore? Let's ask him."
7 The king of Israel said to Jehoshaphat, "There is
still one man who can inquire of the LORD, but I hate
him because he never prophesies good about me, but
only disaster. He is Micaiah son of Imlah."
"The king shouldn't say that," Jehoshaphat replied.
8 So the king of Israel called an officer and said,
"Hurry and get Micaiah son of Imlah!"
9 Now the king of Israel and King Jehoshaphat of
Judah, clothed in royal attire, were each sitting on his
own throne. They were sitting on the threshing floor
at the entrance to Samaria's gate, and all the prophets
were prophesying in front of them. 10 Then Zedekiah
son of Chenaanah made iron horns and said, "This
is what the LORD says: You will gore the Arameans
with these until they are finished off." 11 And all the
prophets were prophesying the same, saying, "March
up to Ramoth-gilead and succeed, for the LORD will
hand it over to the king."

MICAIAH'S MESSAGE OF DEFEAT

12 The messenger who went to call Micaiah instructed him, "Look, the words of the prophets are unanimously favorable for the king. So let your words be
like theirs, and speak favorably."
13 But Micaiah said, "As the LORD lives, I will say
whatever my God says."[A]
14 So he went to the king, and the king asked him,
"Micaiah, should we go to Ramoth-gilead for war, or
should I[B] refrain?"
Micaiah said, "March up and succeed, for they will
be handed over to you."
15 But the king said to him, "How many times must I
make you swear not to tell me anything but the truth
in the name of the LORD?"
16 So Micaiah said:

I saw all Israel scattered on the hills
like sheep without a shepherd.
And the LORD said,
"They have no master;
let each return home in peace."

17 So the king of Israel said to Jehoshaphat, "Didn't
I tell you he never prophesies good about me, but
only disaster?"
18 Then Micaiah said, "Therefore, hear the word of
the LORD. I saw the LORD sitting on his throne, and
the whole heavenly army was standing at his right
hand and at his left hand. 19 And the LORD said, 'Who
will entice King Ahab of Israel to march up and fall at
Ramoth-gilead?' So one was saying this and another
was saying that.
20 "Then a spirit came forward, stood before the
LORD, and said, 'I will entice him.'
"The LORD asked him, 'How?'
21 "So he said, 'I will go and become a lying spirit in
the mouth of all his prophets.'
"Then he said, 'You will entice him and also prevail.
Go and do that.'
22 "Now, you see, the LORD has put a lying spirit into
the mouth of[C] these prophets of yours, and the LORD
has pronounced disaster against you."
23 Then Zedekiah son of Chenaanah came up, hit
Micaiah on the cheek, and demanded, "Which way
did the spirit from the LORD leave me to speak to
you?"
24 Micaiah replied, "You will soon see when you go
to hide in an inner chamber on that day."
25 Then the king of Israel ordered, "Take Micaiah and return him to Amon, the governor of the
city, and to Joash, the king's son, 26 and say, 'This is
what the king says: Put this guy in prison and feed
him only a little bread and water[D] until I come back
safely.'"
27 But Micaiah said, "If you ever return safely, the
LORD has not spoken through me." Then he said, "Listen, all you people!"

AHAB'S DEATH

28 Then the king of Israel and Judah's King Jehoshaphat went up to Ramoth-gilead. 29 But the king of
Israel said to Jehoshaphat, "I will disguise myself
and go into battle, but you wear your royal attire." So
the king of Israel disguised himself, and they went
into battle.
30 Now the king of Aram had ordered his chariot
commanders, "Do not fight with anyone at all[E] except
the king of Israel."
31 When the chariot commanders saw Jehoshaphat, they shouted, "He must be the king of Israel!"
So they turned to attack him, but Jehoshaphat cried
out and the LORD helped him. God drew them away
from him. 32 When the chariot commanders saw
that he was not the king of Israel, they turned back
from pursuing him.
33 But a man drew his bow without taking special aim and struck the king of Israel through the
joints of his armor. So he said to the charioteer, "Turn
around and take me out of the battle,[F] for I am badly wounded!" 34 The battle raged throughout that
day, and the king of Israel propped himself up in his
chariot facing the Arameans until evening. Then he
died at sunset.

[A] **18:13** LXX, Vg add *to me*; 1Kg 22:14 [B] **18:14** LXX reads *we*; 1Kg 22:15 [C] **18:22** Some Hb mss, LXX, Syr, Vg add *all*; 1Kg 22:23 [D] **18:26** Lit *him on bread of oppression and water of oppression* [E] **18:30** Lit *with small or with great* [F] **18:33** LXX, Vg; MT reads *camp*

JEHU'S REBUKE OF JEHOSHAPHAT

19 King Jehoshaphat of Judah returned to his home in Jerusalem in peace. 2 Then Jehu son of the seer Hanani went out to confront him[A] and said to King Jehoshaphat, "Do you help the wicked and love those who hate the LORD? Because of this, the LORD's wrath is on you. 3 However, some good is found in you, for you have eradicated the Asherah poles from the land and have determined in your heart to seek God."

JEHOSHAPHAT'S REFORMS

4 Jehoshaphat lived in Jerusalem, and once again he went out among the people from Beer-sheba to the hill country of Ephraim and brought them back to the LORD, the God of their ancestors. 5 He appointed judges in all the fortified cities of the land of Judah, city by city. 6 Then he said to the judges, "Consider what you are doing, for you do not judge for a man, but for the LORD, who is with you in the matter of judgment. 7 And now, may the terror of the LORD be on you. Watch what you do, for there is no injustice or partiality or taking bribes with the LORD our God."

8 Jehoshaphat also appointed in Jerusalem some of the Levites and priests and some of the Israelite family heads for deciding the LORD's will and for settling disputes of the residents of[B] Jerusalem. 9 He commanded them, saying, "In the fear of the LORD, with integrity, and wholeheartedly, you are to do the following: 10 For every dispute that comes to you from your brothers who dwell in their cities — whether it regards differences of bloodguilt, law, commandment, statutes, or judgments — you are to warn them, so they will not incur guilt before the LORD and wrath will not come on you and your brothers. Do this, and you will not incur guilt.

11 "Note that Amariah, the chief priest, is over you in all matters related to the LORD, and Zebadiah son of Ishmael, the ruler of the house of Judah, in all matters related to the king, and the Levites are officers in your presence. Be strong; may the LORD be with those who do what is good."

WAR AGAINST EASTERN ENEMIES

20 After this, the Moabites and Ammonites, together with some of the Meunites,[C] came to fight against Jehoshaphat. 2 People came and told Jehoshaphat, "A vast number from beyond the Dead Sea and from Edom[D] has come to fight against you; they are already in Hazazon-tamar" (that is, En-gedi). 3 Jehoshaphat was afraid, and he resolved to seek the LORD. Then he proclaimed a fast for all Judah, 4 who gathered to seek the LORD. They even came from all the cities of Judah to seek him.

JEHOSHAPHAT'S PRAYER

5 Then Jehoshaphat stood in the assembly of Judah and Jerusalem in the LORD's temple before the new courtyard. 6 He said:

LORD, God of our ancestors, are you not the God who is in heaven, and do you not rule over all the kingdoms of the nations? Power and might are in your hand, and no one can stand against you. 7 Are you not our God who drove out the inhabitants of this land before your people Israel and who gave it forever to the descendants of Abraham your friend? 8 They have lived in the land and have built you a sanctuary in it for your name and have said, 9 "If disaster comes on us — sword or judgment, pestilence or famine — we will stand before this temple and before you, for your name is in this temple. We will cry out to you because of our distress, and you will hear and deliver."

10 Now here are the Ammonites, Moabites, and the inhabitants of Mount Seir. You did not let Israel invade them when Israel came out of the land of Egypt, but Israel turned away from them and did not destroy them. 11 Look how they repay us by coming to drive us out of your possession that you gave us as an inheritance. 12 Our God, will you not judge them? For we are powerless before this vast number that comes to fight against us. We do not know what to do, but we look to you.[E]

GOD'S ANSWER

13 All Judah was standing before the LORD with their dependents, their wives, and their children. 14 In the middle of the congregation, the Spirit of the LORD came on Jahaziel (son of Zechariah, son of Benaiah, son of Jeiel, son of Mattaniah, a Levite from Asaph's descendants), 15 and he said, "Listen carefully, all Judah and you inhabitants of Jerusalem, and King Jehoshaphat. This is what the LORD says: 'Do not be afraid or discouraged because of this vast number, for the battle is not yours, but God's. 16 Tomorrow, go down against them. You will see them coming up the Ascent of Ziz, and you will find them at the end of the valley facing the Wilderness of Jeruel. 17 You do not have to fight this battle. Position yourselves, stand still, and see the salvation of the LORD. He is with you, Judah and Jerusalem. Do not be afraid or discouraged. Tomorrow, go out to face them, for the LORD is with you.' "

[A] **19:2** Lit *to his face* [B] **19:8** LXX, Vg; MT reads *disputes and they returned to* [C] **20:1** LXX; MT reads *Ammonites*; 2Ch 26:7
[D] **20:2** Some Hb mss, Old Lat; other Hb mss read *Aram*
[E] **20:12** Lit *but on you our eyes*

A Prophet's Royal Influence

by D. Larry Gregg

Somewhat more than three thousand years ago, two figures began to emerge from the context of ancient Israel's religious, political, and social fabric. One figure was the prophet (Hb *nabi*); the other was the king (Hb *melek*). From the time of Israel's judges (ca 1200–1000 BC) through the fall of Jerusalem to the Babylonians (ca 586 BC), the cooperation and conflict between these two figures is one of the lenses through which we see Israel's story of faith unfold.

Prophets and kings emerged in Israel's cultural history as an ancient Semitic people transitioned from nomadic tribalism to sedentary national identity. The formal anointing of Saul son of Kish as Israel's first king (1Sm 9–10) around 1020–1000 BC marked a new era. Before a tumultuous century had passed, the role of king as tribal war leader had developed into that of hereditary ancient Near Eastern monarch. Against this backdrop, the classic Israelite prophet emerged as the monarch's counterpart, confidant, conscience, and challenger.

Although individuals such as Nathan, Elijah, and Elisha stand apart as the prophetic voice of Yahweh, they did not function as absolutely solitary figures. Nathan appears to have been at least a semiofficial court prophet under David. While he emerged from nowhere in the biblical narrative, Nathan functioned harmoniously over time with the monarchy in the announcement of the Davidic dynasty (2Sm 7:1–17) and the determination of Solomon as David's successor (1Kg 1:1–40). This harmony does not appear to have been interrupted even by Nathan's denunciation of David for his adultery with Bathsheba and the subsequent murder of Uriah (2Sm 12:1–25).

Phrygian terra-cotta jug with cut beaked spout; seventh–sixth centuries BC. Prophets anointed kings with oil, possibly using this type of container.

What distinguished these personalities in contrast to their contemporaries, who also bore the title of *nabi*, was their independence. While closely associated with their respective monarchical protagonists, they were not institutionally "housebroken." Their ears were attuned to the voice of Yahweh and their mouths told forth the pronouncements of God. This set them apart from sycophantic court prophets of the time who simply uttered what the king wanted to hear. First Kings 22 clearly brings this conflict into focus as Micaiah, one of the prophets associated with Elijah, pronounced God's truth before Ahab of Israel and Jehoshaphat of Judah.

Generations later, in the literary prophets, the emphasis shifted from focus specifically on the monarch to focus on the nation as a corporate entity. While voices such as those of Isaiah, Hosea, Amos, and Jeremiah set their oracles in the context of the reigns of specific kings, their messages directly addressed a people who failed to be faithful to Israel's covenant relationship with Yahweh. In many cases, the prophet appears as God's prosecuting attorney in a covenant lawsuit (Hb *rib*) against the nation (see Is 1:2–3; Jr 2:4–13; Mc 6:1–8). Hosea announced, "Hear the word of the Lord, people of Israel, for the Lord has a case [*rib*] against the inhabitants of the land" (4:1). ✣

Hellenistic site at Tell Sandahannah. This was the Old Testament Moresheth-gath, home of Micah, the eighth-century-BC prophet.

18 Then Jehoshaphat knelt low with his face to the ground, and all Judah and the inhabitants of Jerusalem fell down before the LORD to worship him. 19 Then the Levites from the sons of the Kohathites and the Korahites stood up to praise the LORD God of Israel shouting loudly.

VICTORY AND PLUNDER

20 In the morning they got up early and went out to the wilderness of Tekoa. As they were about to go out, Jehoshaphat stood and said, "Hear me, Judah and you inhabitants of Jerusalem. Believe in the LORD your God, and you will be established; believe in his prophets, and you will succeed." 21 Then he consulted with the people and appointed some to sing for the LORD and some to praise the splendor of his holiness. When they went out in front of the armed forces, they kept singing:[A]

> Give thanks to the LORD,
> for his faithful love endures forever.

22 The moment they began their shouts and praises, the LORD set an ambush against the Ammonites, Moabites, and the inhabitants of Mount Seir who came to fight against Judah, and they were defeated. 23 The Ammonites and Moabites turned against the inhabitants of Mount Seir and completely annihilated them. When they had finished with the inhabitants of Seir, they helped destroy each other.

24 When Judah came to a place overlooking the wilderness, they looked for the large army, but there were only corpses lying on the ground; nobody had escaped. 25 Then Jehoshaphat and his people went to gather the plunder. They found among them[B] an abundance of goods on the bodies[C] and valuable items. So they stripped them until nobody could carry any more. They were gathering the plunder for three days because there was so much. 26 They assembled in the Valley of Beracah[D] on the fourth day, for there they blessed the LORD. Therefore, that place is still called the Valley of Beracah today.

27 Then all the men of Judah and Jerusalem turned back with Jehoshaphat their leader, returning joyfully to Jerusalem, for the LORD enabled them to rejoice over their enemies. 28 So they came into Jerusalem to the LORD's temple with harps, lyres, and trumpets.

29 The terror of God was on all the kingdoms of the lands when they heard that the LORD had fought against the enemies of Israel. 30 Then Jehoshaphat's kingdom was quiet, for his God gave him rest on every side.

SUMMARY OF JEHOSHAPHAT'S REIGN

31 Jehoshaphat became king over Judah. He was thirty-five years old when he became king, and he reigned twenty-five years in Jerusalem. His mother's name was Azubah daughter of Shilhi. 32 He walked in the ways of Asa his father; he did not turn away from it but did what was right in the LORD's sight. 33 However, the high places were not taken away; the people had not yet set their hearts on the God of their ancestors.

34 The rest of the events of Jehoshaphat's reign from beginning to end are written in the Events of Jehu son of Hanani, which is recorded in the Book of Israel's Kings.

JEHOSHAPHAT'S FLEET OF SHIPS

35 After this, Judah's King Jehoshaphat made an alliance with Israel's King Ahaziah, who was guilty of wrongdoing. 36 Jehoshaphat formed an alliance with him to make ships to go to Tarshish, and they made the ships in Ezion-geber. 37 Then Eliezer son of Dodavahu of Mareshah prophesied against Jehoshaphat, saying, "Because you formed an alliance with Ahaziah, the LORD has broken up what you have made." So the ships were wrecked and were not able to go to Tarshish.

JEHORAM BECOMES KING OVER JUDAH

21 Jehoshaphat rested with his ancestors and was buried with his ancestors in the city of David. His son Jehoram[E] became king in his place. 2 He had brothers, sons of Jehoshaphat: Azariah, Jehiel, Zechariah, Azariah, Michael, and Shephatiah; all these were the sons of King Jehoshaphat of Judah.[F] 3 Their father had given them many gifts of silver, gold, and valuable things, along with fortified cities in Judah, but he gave the kingdom to Jehoram because he was the firstborn. 4 When Jehoram had established himself over his father's kingdom, he strengthened his position by killing with the sword all his brothers as well as some of the princes of Israel.

JUDAH'S KING JEHORAM

5 Jehoram was thirty-two years old when he became king, and he reigned eight years in Jerusalem. 6 He walked in the ways of the kings of Israel, as the house of Ahab had done, for Ahab's daughter was his wife. He did what was evil in the LORD's sight, 7 but for the sake of the covenant the LORD had made with David, he was unwilling to destroy the house of David since the LORD had promised to give a lamp[G] to David and to his sons forever.

8 During Jehoram's reign, Edom rebelled against Judah's control and appointed their own king. 9 So Jehoram crossed into Edom with his commanders and all his chariots. Then at night he set out to attack the Edomites who had surrounded him and the chariot

[A] **20:21** Lit *saying* [B] **20:25** LXX reads *found cattle* [C] **20:25** Some Hb mss, Old Lat, Vg read *goods, garments* [D] **20:26** = Blessing [E] **21:1** = Joram [F] **21:2** Some Hb mss, LXX, Syr, Vg, Arabic; other Hb mss read *Israel* [G] **21:7** Or *dominion*

commanders. 10 And now Edom is still in rebellion
against Judah's control today. Libnah also rebelled
at that time against his control because he had abandoned the LORD, the God of his ancestors. 11 Jehoram
also built high places in the hills[A] of Judah, and he
caused the inhabitants of Jerusalem to prostitute
themselves, and he led Judah astray.

ELIJAH'S LETTER TO JEHORAM

12 Then a letter came to Jehoram from the prophet
Elijah, saying:

> This is what the LORD, the God of your ancestor
> David says: "Because you have not walked in the
> ways of your father Jehoshaphat or in the ways
> of King Asa of Judah 13 but have walked in the
> ways of the kings of Israel, have caused Judah
> and the inhabitants of Jerusalem to prostitute
> themselves like the house of Ahab prostituted
> itself, and also have killed your brothers, your
> father's family, who were better than you, 14 the
> LORD is now about to strike your people, your
> sons, your wives, and all your possessions with a
> horrible affliction. 15 You yourself will be struck
> with many illnesses, including a disease of the
> intestines, until your intestines come out day
> after day because of the disease."

JEHORAM'S LAST DAYS

16 The LORD roused the spirit of the Philistines and the
Arabs who lived near the Cushites to attack Jehoram.
17 So they went to war against Judah and invaded
it. They carried off all the possessions found in the
king's palace and also his sons and wives; not a son
was left to him except Jehoahaz,[B] his youngest son.
18 After all these things, the LORD afflicted him in
his intestines with an incurable disease. 19 This continued day after day until two full years passed. Then
his intestines came out because of his disease, and
he died from severe[C] illnesses. But his people did not
hold a fire in his honor like the fire in honor of his
predecessors.
20 Jehoram was thirty-two years old when he became king; he reigned eight years in Jerusalem. He
died to no one's regret[D] and was buried in the city of
David but not in the tombs of the kings.

JUDAH'S KING AHAZIAH

22 Then the inhabitants of Jerusalem made Ahaziah, his youngest son, king in his place, because the troops that had come with the Arabs to
the camp had killed all the older sons.[E] So Ahaziah
son of Jehoram became king of Judah. 2 Ahaziah was
twenty-two[F] years old when he became king, and he
reigned one year in Jerusalem. His mother's name
was Athaliah, granddaughter[G] of Omri.
3 He walked in the ways of the house of Ahab, for
his mother gave him evil advice. 4 So he did what was
evil in the LORD's sight like the house of Ahab, for they
were his advisers after the death of his father, to his
destruction. 5 He also followed their advice and went
with Joram[H] son of Israel's King Ahab to fight against
King Hazael of Aram, in Ramoth-gilead. The Arameans[I]
wounded Joram, 6 so he returned to Jezreel to recover
from the wounds they inflicted on him in Ramoth-gilead[J] when he fought against King Hazael of Aram. Then
Judah's King Ahaziah[K] son of Jehoram went down to
Jezreel to visit Joram son of Ahab since Joram was ill.
7 Ahaziah's downfall came from God when he went
to Joram. When Ahaziah arrived, he went out with Joram to meet Jehu son of Nimshi, whom the LORD had
anointed to destroy the house of Ahab. 8 So when Jehu
executed judgment on the house of Ahab, he found
the rulers of Judah and the sons of Ahaziah's brothers who were serving Ahaziah, and he killed them.
9 Then Jehu looked for Ahaziah, and Jehu's soldiers
captured him (he was hiding in Samaria). So they
brought Ahaziah to Jehu, and they killed him. The
soldiers buried him, for they said, "He is the grandson of Jehoshaphat who sought the LORD with all his
heart." So no one from the house of Ahaziah had the
strength to rule the kingdom.

ATHALIAH USURPS THE THRONE

10 When Athaliah, Ahaziah's mother, saw that her son
was dead, she proceeded to annihilate all the royal
heirs[L] of the house of Judah. 11 Jehoshabeath,[M] the
king's daughter, rescued Joash son of Ahaziah from
the king's sons who were being killed and put him
and the one who nursed him in a bedroom. Now Jehoshabeath was the daughter of King Jehoram and the
wife of the priest Jehoiada. Since she was Ahaziah's
sister, she hid Joash from Athaliah so that she did not
kill him. 12 He was hiding with them in God's temple
for six years while Athaliah reigned over the land.

ATHALIAH OVERTHROWN

23 Then, in the seventh year, Jehoiada summoned
his courage and took the commanders of hundreds into a covenant with him: Azariah son of Jeroham, Ishmael son of Jehohanan, Azariah son of Obed,
Maaseiah son of Adaiah, and Elishaphat son of Zichri.
2 They made a circuit throughout Judah. They gathered the Levites from all the cities of Judah and the
family heads of Israel, and they came to Jerusalem.

[A] **21:11** Some Hb mss, LXX, Vg read *cities* [B] **21:17** LXX, Syr, Tg read *Ahaziah* [C] **21:19** Lit *evil* [D] **21:20** Lit *He walked in no desirability* [E] **22:1** Lit *the former ones* [F] **22:2** Some LXX mss, Syr; MT reads *42*; 2Kg 8:26 [G] **22:2** Lit *daughter* [H] **22:5** = Jehoram [I] **22:5** Lit *Rammites* [J] **22:6** Lit *in Ramah* [K] **22:6** Some Hb mss, LXX, Syr, Vg; other Hb mss read *Azariah* [L] **22:10** Lit *seed* [M] **22:11** = Jehosheba; 2Kg 11:2

Jezreel: Military Headquarters of the Northern Kingdom of Israel

by Deborah O'Daniel Cantrell

Ruins of Tel Jezreel.

Jezreel, a site in northern Israel, is famously known as the hometown of Naboth and his disputed vineyard. Additionally, it was the place where Jehu's chariot horses trampled Jezebel to death when he usurped the throne (1Kg 21:1–16; 2Kg 9:30–37). Even more significant, it was key to ancient Israel's military defense for more than a hundred years.

Samaria was evidently proving to be a difficult capital city to protect and less than satisfactory as a military headquarters. That the enemy could so easily come to the gates of Samaria placed the entire nation in constant risk. The Israelite rulers eventually realized Samaria's vulnerability, both strategically and possibly economically.

Near the close of Ahab's reign, or possibly during that of his son Joram, the Israelite rulers apparently moved their military headquarters from Samaria to Jezreel—about thirty miles north. This command post was less than two hours from Samaria by chariot or on horseback. Located on the Via Maris (Way of the Sea), the great international highway from Assyria to Egypt, and at the narrowest point of the expansive Jezreel Valley, Jezreel was an ideal launching pad for an attack against Israel's enemies to the northeast, whether the Arameans or the Assyrians. Jezreel was also situated at the northern end of the Way of the Patriarchs, the local north-south route from Jezreel via Dothan to Samaria. Thus Jezreel was ideally situated to protect Samaria from invading armies. Economically Jezreel, on the edge of the well-watered fertile Jezreel Valley, could provide grain and pasturage to feed thousands of horses.

The most important component of Israel's army was its horses. A strong chariotry was essential to success; care of the horses was, therefore, a primary concern. During the famine in Samaria, King Ahab personally went in search of pasturage for his army horses and mules. To sustain military horses required three things: water, food (grain and fodder), and training. Jezreel supplied all of these needs.

The walled compound at Jezreel covered some eleven acres. "A rock-cut moat surrounded the enclosure on all sides, except the northeastern, where the wall and ramp extended along the edge of the steep slope of the ridge. . . . The impressive moat is unique in this period, and indicates the particular strength of the fortifications and the importance of the enclosure."[1] Jezreel had a large, smooth, flat surface area, 948 feet long by 515 feet wide, ideal for working on training maneuvers with the horses inside the safety of the walls. Entrance to the compound was via a chambered gate, which allowed the rapid hitching and unhitching of several chariots at once. At the gate, a bridge or drawbridge over the moat allowed access to the city.

Jezreel has its own perennial spring, the spring of Jezreel; nearby is the spring of Harod (Jdg 7:1; 1Sm 29:1). These provided adequate water for thousands of horses. And Jezreel, on the edge of the fertile agricultural plain of the Jezreel Valley, never had to worry about the growing or shipping of grain to feed livestock. In fact, archaeologists have excavated more than one hundred rock-cut bottle-shaped pits at Jezreel. Some of these pits were for water storage, but many were originally silos for grain, wine, and other perishables. Grain could, therefore, easily be stored in sufficient quantities, not only to feed the horses year-round, but also to be transported to soldiers in distant battlefields. In this way, hundreds or even thousands of horses and warriors could be easily cared for and maintained in and around Jezreel.

Tactically, Jezreel served as a superior lookout site and proved to be an excellent vantage point for detecting incoming horses and chariotry (2Kg 9:17–21). This is still evident today, as ancient Jezreel overlooks the valley and beyond to the mountains over the Jordan. With Jezreel as the military depot for the Israelite army, Samaria, which had vital fighting chariotry units, was well protected. An enemy would first have to conquer Jezreel before it could proceed to the capital. ✤

[1] David Ussishkin and John Woodhead, "Jezreel (Yitze'el), Tel" in *NEAEHL*, 5:1838.

Omri, Ahab's father, purchased the hill of Samaria and built Israel's capital there. Shown are the ruins of Ahab's palace in Samaria.

3 Then the whole assembly made a covenant with the king in God's temple. Jehoiada said to them, "Here is the king's son! He will reign, just as the LORD promised concerning David's sons. 4 This is what you are to do: a third of you, priests and Levites who are coming on duty on the Sabbath, are to be gatekeepers. 5 A third are to be at the king's palace, and a third are to be at the Foundation Gate, and all the troops will be in the courtyards of the LORD's temple. 6 No one is to enter the LORD's temple but the priests and those Levites who serve; they may enter because they are holy, but all the people are to obey the requirement of the LORD. 7 The Levites are to completely surround the king with weapons in hand. Anyone who enters the temple is to be put to death. Accompany the king in all his daily tasks."[A]

8 So the commanders of hundreds did everything the priest Jehoiada commanded. They each brought their men — those coming on duty on the Sabbath and those going off duty on the Sabbath — for the priest Jehoiada did not release the divisions. 9 The priest Jehoiada gave to the commanders of hundreds King David's spears, shields, and quivers[B] that were in God's temple. 10 Then he stationed all the troops with their weapons in hand surrounding the king — from the right side of the temple to the left side, by the altar and by the temple.

11 They brought out the king's son, put the crown on him, gave him the testimony, and made him king. Jehoiada and his sons anointed him and cried, "Long live the king!"

12 When Athaliah heard the noise from the troops, the guards, and those praising the king, she went to the troops in the LORD's temple. 13 As she looked, there was the king standing by his pillar[C] at the entrance. The commanders and the trumpeters were by the king, and all the people of the land were rejoicing and blowing trumpets while the singers with musical instruments were leading the praise. Athaliah tore her clothes and screamed, "Treason! Treason!"

14 Then the priest Jehoiada sent out the commanders of hundreds, those in charge of the army, saying, "Take her out between the ranks, and put anyone who follows her to death by the sword," for the priest had said, "Don't put her to death in the LORD's temple." 15 So they arrested her, and she went by the entrance of the Horse Gate to the king's palace, where they put her to death.

JEHOIADA'S REFORMS

16 Then Jehoiada made a covenant between himself, the king, and the people that they would be the LORD's people. 17 So all the people went to the temple of Baal and tore it down. They smashed its altars and images and killed Mattan, the priest of Baal, at the altars. 18 Then Jehoiada put the oversight of the LORD's temple into the hands of the Levitical priests, whom David had appointed over the LORD's temple, to offer burnt offerings to the LORD as it is written in the law of Moses, with rejoicing and song ordained by[D] David. 19 He stationed gatekeepers at the gates of the LORD's temple so that nothing unclean could enter for any reason. 20 Then he took with him the commanders of hundreds, the nobles, the governors of the people, and all the people of the land and brought the king down from the LORD's temple. They entered the king's palace through the Upper Gate and seated the king on the throne of the kingdom. 21 All the people of the land rejoiced, and the city was quiet, for they had put Athaliah to death by the sword.

JUDAH'S KING JOASH

24 Joash was seven years old when he became king, and he reigned forty years in Jerusalem. His mother's name was Zibiah; she was from Beer-sheba. 2 Throughout the time of the priest Jehoiada, Joash did what was right in the LORD's sight. 3 Jehoiada acquired two wives for him, and he was the father of sons and daughters.

REPAIRING THE TEMPLE

4 Afterward, Joash took it to heart to renovate the LORD's temple. 5 So he gathered the priests and Levites and said, "Go out to the cities of Judah and collect silver from all Israel to repair the temple of your God as needed year by year, and do it quickly."

However, the Levites did not hurry. 6 So the king called Jehoiada the high priest and said, "Why haven't you required the Levites to bring from Judah and Jerusalem the tax imposed by the LORD's servant Moses and the assembly of Israel for the tent of the testimony? 7 For the sons of that wicked Athaliah broke into the LORD's temple and even used the sacred things of the LORD's temple for the Baals."

8 At the king's command a chest was made and placed outside the gate of the LORD's temple. 9 Then a proclamation was issued in Judah and Jerusalem that the tax God's servant Moses imposed on Israel in the wilderness be brought to the LORD. 10 All the leaders and all the people rejoiced, brought the tax, and put it in the chest until it was full. 11 Whenever the chest was brought by the Levites to the king's overseers, and when they saw that there was a large amount of silver, the king's secretary and the high priest's deputy came and emptied the chest, picked

[A] **23:7** Lit *king when he comes in and when he goes out* [B] **23:9** Or *spears and large and small shields* [C] **23:13** LXX reads *post* [D] **23:18** Lit *song on the hands of*

it up, and returned it to its place. They did this daily and gathered the silver in abundance. 12 Then the king and Jehoiada gave it to those in charge of the labor on the LORD's temple, who were hiring stonecutters and carpenters to renovate the LORD's temple, also blacksmiths and coppersmiths to repair the LORD's temple.

13 The workmen did their work, and through them the repairs progressed. They restored God's temple to its specifications and reinforced it. 14 When they finished, they presented the rest of the silver to the king and Jehoiada, who made articles for the LORD's temple with it — articles for ministry and for making burnt offerings, and ladles[A] and articles of gold and silver. They regularly offered burnt offerings in the LORD's temple throughout Jehoiada's life.

JOASH'S APOSTASY

15 Jehoiada died when he was old and full of days; he was 130 years old at his death. 16 He was buried in the city of David with the kings because he had done what was good in Israel with respect to God and his temple.

17 However, after Jehoiada died, the rulers of Judah came and paid homage to the king. Then the king listened to them, 18 and they abandoned the temple of the LORD, the God of their ancestors, and served the Asherah poles and the idols. So there was wrath against Judah and Jerusalem for this guilt of theirs. 19 Nevertheless, he sent them prophets to bring them back to the LORD; they admonished them, but the people would not listen.

20 The Spirit of God enveloped[B] Zechariah son of Jehoiada the priest. He stood above the people and said to them, "This is what God says, 'Why are you transgressing the LORD's commands so that you do not prosper? Because you have abandoned the LORD, he has abandoned you.' " 21 But they conspired against him and stoned him at the king's command in the courtyard of the LORD's temple. 22 King Joash didn't remember the kindness that Zechariah's father Jehoiada had extended to him, but killed his son. While he was dying, he said, "May the LORD see and demand an account."

ARAMEAN INVASION OF JUDAH

23 At the turn of the year, an Aramean army attacked Joash. They entered Judah and Jerusalem and destroyed all the leaders of the people among them and sent all the plunder to the king of Damascus. 24 Although the Aramean army came with only a few men, the LORD handed over a vast army to them because the people of Judah had abandoned the LORD, the God of their ancestors. So they executed judgment on Joash.

JOASH ASSASSINATED

25 When the Arameans saw that Joash had many wounds, they left him. His servants conspired against him, and killed him on his bed, because he had shed the blood of the sons of the priest Jehoiada. So he died, and they buried him in the city of David, but they did not bury him in the tombs of the kings.

26 Those who conspired against him were Zabad, son of the Ammonite woman Shimeath, and Jehozabad, son of the Moabite woman Shimrith.[C] 27 The accounts concerning his sons, the many divine pronouncements about him, and the restoration of God's temple are recorded in the Writing of the Book of the Kings. His son Amaziah became king in his place.

JUDAH'S KING AMAZIAH

25 Amaziah became king when he was twenty-five years old, and he reigned twenty-nine years in Jerusalem. His mother's name was Jehoaddan; she was from Jerusalem. 2 He did what was right in the LORD's sight but not wholeheartedly.

3 As soon as the kingdom was firmly in his grasp,[D] he executed his servants who had killed his father the king. 4 However, he did not put their children to death, because — as it is written in the Law, in the book of Moses, where the LORD commanded — "Fathers are not to die because of children, and children are not to die because of fathers, but each one will die for his own sin."

AMAZIAH'S CAMPAIGN AGAINST EDOM

5 Then Amaziah gathered Judah and assembled them according to ancestral families,[E] according to commanders of thousands, and according to commanders of hundreds. He numbered those twenty years old or more for all Judah and Benjamin. He found there to be three hundred thousand fit young men who could serve in the army, bearing spear and shield. 6 Then for 7,500 pounds[F] of silver he hired one hundred thousand valiant warriors from Israel.

7 However, a man of God came to him and said, "King, do not let Israel's army go with you, for the LORD is not with Israel — all the Ephraimites. 8 But if you go with them, do it! Be strong for battle! But God will make you stumble before the enemy, for God has the power to help or to make one stumble."

9 Then Amaziah said to the man of God, "What should I do about the 7,500 pounds of silver I gave to Israel's division?"

The man of God replied, "The LORD is able to give you much more than this."

[A] **24:14** Or *dishes*, or *spoons*; lit *palms* [B] **24:20** Lit *clothed* [C] **24:26** = Shomer in 2Kg 12:21 [D] **25:3** LXX, Syr; MT reads *was strong on him*; 1Kg 14:4 [E] **25:5** Lit *house of fathers* [F] **25:6** Lit *100 talents*, also in v. 9

10 So Amaziah released the division that came to him from Ephraim to go home. But they got very angry with Judah and returned home in a fierce rage. 11 Amaziah strengthened his position and led his people to the Salt Valley. He struck down ten thousand Seirites,[A] 12 and the Judahites captured ten thousand alive. They took them to the top of a cliff where they threw them off, and all of them were dashed to pieces. 13 As for the men of the division that Amaziah sent back so they would not go with him into battle, they raided the cities of Judah from Samaria to Beth-horon, struck down three thousand of their people, and took a great deal of plunder.

14 After Amaziah came from the attack on the Edomites, he brought the gods of the Seirites and set them up as his gods. He worshiped before them and burned incense to them. 15 So the LORD's anger was against Amaziah, and he sent a prophet to him, who said, "Why have you sought a people's gods that could not rescue their own people from you?"

16 While he was still speaking to him, the king asked, "Have we made you the king's counselor? Stop, why should you lose your life?"

So the prophet stopped, but he said, "I know that God intends to destroy you, because you have done this and have not listened to my advice."

AMAZIAH'S WAR WITH ISRAEL'S KING JEHOASH

17 King Amaziah of Judah took counsel and sent word to Jehoash[B] son of Jehoahaz, son of Jehu, king of Israel, and challenged him: "Come, let's meet face to face."

18 King Jehoash of Israel sent word to King Amaziah of Judah, saying, "The thistle in Lebanon sent a message to the cedar in Lebanon, saying, 'Give your daughter to my son as a wife.' Then a wild animal in Lebanon passed by and trampled the thistle. 19 You have said, 'Look, I[C] have defeated Edom,' and you have become overconfident[D] that you will get glory. Now stay at home. Why stir up such trouble so that you fall and Judah with you?"

20 But Amaziah would not listen, for this turn of events was from God in order to hand them over to their enemies because they went after the gods of Edom. 21 So King Jehoash of Israel advanced. He and King Amaziah of Judah met face to face at Beth-shemesh that belonged to Judah. 22 Judah was routed before Israel, and each man fled to his own tent. 23 King Jehoash of Israel captured Judah's King Amaziah son of Joash, son of Jehoahaz,[E] at Beth-shemesh. Then Jehoash took him to Jerusalem and broke down two hundred yards[F] of Jerusalem's wall from the Ephraim Gate to the Corner Gate.[G] 24 He took all the gold, silver, all the utensils that were found with Obed-edom in God's temple, the treasures of the king's palace, and the hostages. Then he returned to Samaria.

AMAZIAH'S DEATH

25 Judah's King Amaziah son of Joash lived fifteen years after the death of Israel's King Jehoash son of Jehoahaz. 26 The rest of the events of Amaziah's reign, from beginning to end, are written in the Book of the Kings of Judah and Israel.

27 From the time Amaziah turned from following the LORD, a conspiracy was formed against him in Jerusalem, and he fled to Lachish. However, men were sent after him to Lachish, and they put him to death there. 28 They carried him back on horses and buried him with his ancestors in the city of Judah.[H]

JUDAH'S KING UZZIAH

26 All the people of Judah took Uzziah,[I] who was sixteen years old, and made him king in place of his father Amaziah. 2 After Amaziah the king rested with his ancestors, Uzziah rebuilt Eloth[J] and restored it to Judah.

3 Uzziah was sixteen years old when he became king, and he reigned fifty-two years in Jerusalem. His mother's name was Jecoliah; she was from Jerusalem. 4 He did what was right in the LORD's sight just as his father Amaziah had done. 5 He sought God throughout the lifetime of Zechariah, the teacher of the fear[K] of God. During the time that he sought the LORD, God gave him success.

UZZIAH'S EXPLOITS

6 Uzziah went out to wage war against the Philistines, and he tore down the wall of Gath, the wall of Jabneh, and the wall of Ashdod. Then he built cities in the vicinity of Ashdod and among the Philistines. 7 God helped him against the Philistines, the Arabs that live in Gur-baal, and the Meunites. 8 The Ammonites[L] paid tribute to Uzziah, and his fame spread as far as the entrance of Egypt, for God made him very powerful. 9 Uzziah built towers in Jerusalem at the Corner Gate, the Valley Gate, and the corner buttress, and he fortified them. 10 Since he had many cattle both in the Judean foothills[M] and the plain, he built towers in the desert and dug many wells. And since he was a lover of the soil, he had farmers and vinedressers in the hills and in the fertile lands.[N]

11 Uzziah had an army equipped for combat that went out to war by division according to their assignments, as recorded by Jeiel the court secretary and Maaseiah the officer under the authority of

[A] **25:11** = Edomites, also in v. 14 [B] **25:17** Lit *Joash* [C] **25:19** Some LXX mss, Old Lat, Tg, Vg; MT reads *you* [D] **25:19** Lit *and your heart has lifted you* [E] **25:23** = Ahaziah in 2Kg 14:13 [F] **25:23** Lit *400 cubits* [G] **25:23** Some Hb mss; other Hb mss read *to Happoneh* [H] **25:28** Some Hb mss read *city of David* [I] **26:1** = Azariah in 2Kg 14:21 [J] **26:2** LXX, Syr, Vg read *Elath* [K] **26:5** Some Hb mss, LXX, Syr, Tg, Arabic; other Hb mss, Vg read *visions* [L] **26:8** LXX reads *Meunites* [M] **26:10** Or *the Shephelah* [N] **26:10** Or *in Carmel*

In the City Gate

by Joel F. Drinkard Jr.

Gates in Iron Age Israel (1200–586 BC) routinely had two or more sets of pier walls creating chambers on each side of the gateway. The most common patterns were two, four, or six chambers. The number of chambers does not seem to be related to size of the site, the chronology within Iron Age Israel, or location (Israel or Judah or neighboring states). Instead the number of chambers seems to depend on the topography of the site and the use made of the gate complex. Most gates at major sites in Israel and surrounding lands were made entirely of stone, or had stone lower courses and mud brick above. Pier walls were typically about six feet wide, chambers about nine feet wide and fifteen to eighteen feet deep. And the gates often had towers on either side. At a number of sites, inner and outer gates have been discovered.[1]

Gates were not just entryways into and out of cities and towns, but they certainly did provide entry and egress. The gate complex was at the center of activity for the city. Obviously gates had a defensive purpose of offering protection to the citizens inside. As such, the gate complex often had military installations associated with it. The gate complex included the entryway doors (Neh 6:1; 7:1), towers (2Ch 26:9), and gate bars (Jdg 16:3; 2Ch 8:5) that could be put in place to secure the town.

Benches were located in the chambers and immediately inside and outside the gate at many sites including Beer-sheba,[2] Gezer,[3] and Tel Dan.[4] Such benches are often related to biblical texts that speak of "sitting in the city gate" (2Sm 19:8). However, these benches vary in height from about six inches to more than thirty inches, some too low to sit on, others too high, and others too narrow. In these instances, the bench was probably a shelf on which items could be placed.

In addition, many major business and social activities took place at the gate complex. An open plaza (Hb *rechob*, "street, square, plaza"; Gn 19:2; Jdg 19:15; 2Sm 21:12) was often located just inside or outside the gate. The plaza was the marketplace where merchants offered their goods, and the people would gather to buy and sell. It was the equivalent of today's mall and farmer's market all in one. Archaeologists have excavated such plazas at Beer-sheba,[5] Tel Dan,[6] and other sites. The market or plaza was a natural gathering place. In such a plaza, Hezekiah spoke to the assembled people to encourage them at the time of Sennacherib's attack (2Ch 32:6). Likewise, Ezra read the book of the law to the assembled people in the plaza of the Water Gate of Jerusalem (Neh 8:1,3). Since many benches in gate chambers were unsuited for sitting and the gate chambers were often quite small, to what did the idea of "sitting in the city gate" refer? Most likely it referred to sitting anywhere in the gate complex, either just inside or just outside the gate, but especially in the plaza. Lot was "in Sodom's gateway" (Gn 19:1), probably in the plaza area, since this is where the angels proposed to spend the night (v. 2). It is also where the Levite sat with his concubine when he was going to spend the night at Gibeah (Jdg 19:15).

Not all such plazas were inside the gate. There is at least one reference to "streets" or "bazaars" (Hb *chuts*), which were located outside the gate (1Kg 20:34; the basic meaning of *chuts* is "outside"). The late Israeli archaeologist Avraham Biran interpreted such structures excavated outside the gate at Tel Dan as the *chuts*.[7] Again their location close to the gate makes perfect sense. They are the place merchants would offer goods for sale. A location just inside or just outside the city gates is convenient, readily accessible, and also easily kept under the watchful eye of officials to prevent trouble. Another place associated with the gate and just outside the city is a threshing floor. The kings of Israel and Judah held a summit meeting seated on their thrones at the threshing floor at the entrance to the gate of Samaria (1Kg 22:10). Like the bazaars, the threshing floor would be a large open public space, perfect for a public meeting.

The rebuilt fortress atop a hill overlooking the Canaanite city of Arad. Although Arad dates back to about 4000 BC, the fortress was built in the time of Solomon and David. Characteristically, towers were on either side of the city gate.

Reconstructed judgment seat in the entrance gate of Dan. The left front base stone is original.

The gate complex thus was the place persons gathered and transacted business. Abraham negotiated to purchase the field and burial cave for Sarah (Gn 23:10–16) at the city gate of Hebron (or Kiriath-arba). Similarly, Boaz negotiated for the purchase of Elimelech's property including the hand of Ruth in marriage (Ru 4:1–12) at the gate of Bethlehem.

High places or sanctuaries were associated with city gates during the Iron Age. Josiah broke down the high places of the city gate as part of his religious reform (2Kg 23:8). Archaeologists have discovered city-gate sanctuaries at Tel Dan and Bethsaida. The Iron Age gate complex at Bethsaida had at least seven stele, which were worshiped in the high places in the city-gate complex.[8] One just to the right of the gate had a couple of steps leading up to a basalt basin for libation offerings. A stele with a bovine-headed deity sat above the libation area. At Tel Dan, four sets of standing stones (Hb *matseboth*) have been discovered in the gate complex.[9]

Biblical references to "justice in the city gates" refers to justice dispensed in or near the gate complex. Because the gate complex was the place the people gathered for business and socialization, and because it was a place of public assembly for reading the law and encouraging the people, it was also the expected place for holding court. Accusations were made in public, the trial took place in public, and the decision was given in a public place. So also the sentence was carried out in public (Am 5:15; see Dt 17:5; 21:18–21; 22:23–24).

In 2 Samuel 19:7–8, the larger context can help readers visualize the gate complex where David was sitting. Before the battle between David's forces and Absalom's forces, David stood "beside the city gate" as the army marched out (2Sm 18:4). He was probably standing just outside the gate, reviewing the troops. He then is described as "sitting between the [two] city gates" when a watchman went up to the roof of the gate and saw a runner bringing news of the battle (v. 24). The description suggests Mahanaim had an inner and outer gate, such as ones found at Beer-sheba, Tel Dan, Megiddo, and elsewhere. When David heard that Absalom had been killed, he "went up to the chamber above the city gate" and wept (v. 33). The upper chamber would either be a second story or a rooftop room of the gate complex. Finally, David got up from his mourning and "sat in the city gate"; when the people heard that "the king is sitting in the city gate," all the people came before the king (19:8). So the gate at Mahanaim had an inner and outer gate, a second story or roof room, and a place for the king to sit between the inner and outer gates. At Tel Dan, excavators discovered a platform in the open area between the inner and outer gates. The platform originally had a canopy over it. The excavator suggests that the platform was the location of a seat for the king, a visiting dignitary, or a deity. That reconstructed platform may help people today visualize where David sat for the people to come before him. On a throne in the plaza of Mahanaim, David was reacclaimed as king by the people after the army had successfully put down Absalom's rebellion. ✣

[1] See drawing, Ze'ev Herzog, "Tel Beersheba," in *NEAEHL*, 1:167. [2] Herzog, "Tel Beersheba," 171. [3] William Dever, "Gezer" in *NEAEHL*, 2:503, 505. [4] Avraham Biran, "Dan" in *NEAEHL*, 1:329–30; Avraham Biran, "Sacred Spaces," *BAR* 24.5 (1998): 38–45. [5] Herzog, "Tel Beersheba," 167, 171–72. [6] Biran, "Dan," 329–30; Biran, "Sacred Spaces," 41, 44–45, 70. [7] Biran, "Dan"; Biran, "Sacred Spaces." [8] Rami Arav, Richard A. Freund, and John F. Shroder Jr., "Bethsaida Rediscovered," *BAR* 26.1 (2000): 44–56; Rami Arav, email message, October 15, 2009; and Tina Haettner Blomquist, *Gates and Gods* (Stockholm: Almqvist & Wicksell, 1999), 50–57. [9] Biran, "Sacred Spaces," 44–45; Blomquist, 57–67.

View of the gate complex at Dan shows the massive walls of the towers at the entrance. Ruins of benches and a threshold are also located at the gate. Buttresses reinforced the support for the walls at the tower and gate.

DIGGING DEEPER *King Uzziah's Burial Plaque*

First noticed by E. L. Sukenik when he examined a display at the Russian Convent on the Mount of Olives in the early 1930s, this first-century-AD burial plaque contains Hebrew script written with Aramaic characteristics identifying the eighth-century-BC biblical King Uzziah, also known as Azariah (2Kg 15:27; 2Ch 26). The Bible says Uzziah overstepped his royal office by offering incense in the temple. This right was forbidden to anyone except the priests according to Mosaic law (Nm 3:10; 16:39–40; 2Ch 26:16). As a result of his disobedience, Uzziah contracted leprosy and was isolated until the day he died (2Kg 15:5,27; 2Ch 26:21–23). The first-century plaque appears to be a copy from an earlier memorial inscription. It reads: "To this place were brought the bones of Uzziah, king of Judah, do not open!" The plaque may indicate that Uzziah's bones were transferred from his original tomb to a different location and reburied in a small bone-box known as an ossuary. The confirmation of Uzziah's existence here and in other extrabiblical sources such as Flavius Josephus (*Jewish Antiquities* 9.10.4) strengthens the case for the biblical descriptions of King Uzziah.

Hananiah, one of the king's commanders. 12 The total number of family heads was 2,600 valiant warriors. 13 Under their authority was an army of 307,500 equipped for combat, a powerful force to help the king against the enemy. 14 Uzziah provided the entire army with shields, spears, helmets, armor, bows, and slingstones. 15 He made skillfully designed devices in Jerusalem to shoot arrows and catapult large stones for use on the towers and on the corners. So his fame spread even to distant places, for he was wondrously helped until he became strong.

UZZIAH'S DISEASE

16 But when he became strong, he grew arrogant, and it led to his own destruction. He acted unfaithfully against the LORD his God by going into the LORD's sanctuary to burn incense on the incense altar. 17 The priest Azariah, along with eighty brave priests of the LORD, went in after him. 18 They took their stand against King Uzziah and said, "Uzziah, you have no right to offer incense to the LORD — only the consecrated priests, the descendants of Aaron, have the right to offer incense. Leave the sanctuary, for you have acted unfaithfully! You will not receive honor from the LORD God."

19 Uzziah, with a firepan in his hand to offer incense, was enraged. But when he became enraged with the priests, in the presence of the priests in the LORD's temple beside the altar of incense, a skin disease broke out on his forehead. 20 Then Azariah the chief priest and all the priests turned to him and saw that he was diseased on his forehead. They rushed him out of there. He himself also hurried to get out because the LORD had afflicted him. 21 So King Uzziah was diseased to the time of his death. He lived in quarantine[A] with a serious skin disease and was excluded from access to the LORD's temple, while his son Jotham was over the king's household governing the people of the land.

22 Now the prophet Isaiah son of Amoz wrote about the rest of the events of Uzziah's reign, from beginning to end. 23 Uzziah rested with his ancestors, and he was buried with his ancestors in the burial ground of the kings' cemetery, for they said, "He has a skin disease." His son Jotham became king in his place.

JUDAH'S KING JOTHAM

27 Jotham was twenty-five years old when he became king, and he reigned sixteen years in Jerusalem. His mother's name was Jerushah daughter of Zadok. 2 He did what was right in the LORD's sight just as his father Uzziah had done. In addition, he didn't enter the LORD's sanctuary, but the people still behaved corruptly.

3 Jotham built the Upper Gate of the LORD's temple, and he built extensively on the wall of Ophel. 4 He also built cities in the hill country of Judah and fortresses and towers in the forests. 5 He waged war against the king of the Ammonites. He overpowered the Ammonites, and that year they gave him 7,500 pounds[B] of silver, 60,000 bushels[C] of wheat, and 60,000 bushels of barley. They paid him the same in the second and third years. 6 So Jotham strengthened his position because he did not waver in obeying[D] the LORD his God.

7 As for the rest of the events of Jotham's reign, along with all his wars and his ways, note that they are written in the Book of the Kings of Israel and Judah. 8 He was twenty-five years old when he became king, and he reigned sixteen years in Jerusalem. 9 Jotham rested with his ancestors and was buried in the city of David. His son Ahaz became king in his place.

JUDAH'S KING AHAZ

28 Ahaz was twenty years old when he became king, and he reigned sixteen years in Jerusalem. He did not do what was right in the LORD's sight like his ancestor David, 2 for he walked in the

[A] **26:21** Lit *in a house of exemption from duty* [B] **27:5** Lit *100 talents* [C] **27:5** Lit *10,000 cors* [D] **27:6** Lit *he established his ways before*

ways of the kings of Israel and made cast images of the Baals. 3 He burned incense in Ben Hinnom Valley and burned his children in[A] the fire, imitating the detestable practices of the nations the LORD had dispossessed before the Israelites. 4 He sacrificed and burned incense on the high places, on the hills, and under every green tree.

5 So the LORD his God handed Ahaz over to the king of Aram. He attacked him and took many captives to Damascus.

Ahaz was also handed over to the king of Israel, who struck him with great force: 6 Pekah son of Remaliah killed one hundred twenty thousand in Judah in one day — all brave men — because they had abandoned the LORD God of their ancestors. 7 An Ephraimite warrior named Zichri killed the king's son Maaseiah, Azrikam governor of the palace, and Elkanah who was second to the king. 8 Then the Israelites took two hundred thousand captives from their brothers — women, sons, and daughters. They also took a great deal of plunder from them and brought it to Samaria.

9 A prophet of the LORD named Oded was there. He went out to meet the army that came to Samaria and said to them, "Look, the LORD God of your ancestors handed them over to you because of his wrath against Judah, but you slaughtered them in a rage that has reached heaven. 10 Now you plan to reduce the people of Judah and Jerusalem, male and female, to slavery. Are you not also guilty before the LORD your God? 11 Listen to me and return the captives you took from your brothers, for the LORD's burning anger is on you."

12 So some men who were leaders of the Ephraimites — Azariah son of Jehohanan, Berechiah son of Meshillemoth, Jehizkiah son of Shallum, and Amasa son of Hadlai — stood in opposition to those coming from the war. 13 They said to them, "You must not bring the captives here, for you plan to bring guilt on us from the LORD to add to our sins and our guilt. For we have much guilt, and burning anger is on Israel."

14 The army left the captives and the plunder in the presence of the officers and the congregation. 15 Then the men who were designated by name took charge of the captives and provided clothes for their naked ones from the plunder. They clothed them, gave them sandals, food and drink, dressed their wounds, and provided donkeys for all the feeble. The Israelites brought them to Jericho, the City of Palms, among their brothers. Then they returned to Samaria.

16 At that time King Ahaz asked the king of Assyria for help. 17 The Edomites came again, attacked Judah, and took captives. 18 The Philistines also raided the cities of the Judean foothills[B] and the Negev of Judah. They captured and occupied Beth-shemesh, Aijalon, and Gederoth, as well as Soco, Timnah, and Gimzo with their surrounding villages. 19 For the LORD humbled Judah because of King Ahaz of Judah,[C] who threw off restraint in Judah and was unfaithful to the LORD. 20 Then King Tiglath-pileser[D] of Assyria came against Ahaz; he oppressed him and did not give him support. 21 Although Ahaz plundered the LORD's temple and the palace of the king and of the rulers and gave the plunder to the king of Assyria, it did not help him.

22 At the time of his distress, King Ahaz himself became more unfaithful to the LORD. 23 He sacrificed to the gods of Damascus which had defeated him; he said, "Since the gods of the kings of Aram are helping them, I will sacrifice to them so that they will help me." But they were the downfall of him and of all Israel.

24 Then Ahaz gathered up the utensils of God's temple, cut them into pieces, shut the doors of the LORD's temple, and made himself altars on every street corner in Jerusalem. 25 He made high places in every city of Judah to offer incense to other gods, and he angered the LORD, the God of his ancestors.

AHAZ'S DEATH

26 As for the rest of his deeds and all his ways, from beginning to end, they are written in the Book of the Kings of Judah and Israel. 27 Ahaz rested with his ancestors and was buried in the city, in Jerusalem, but they did not bring him into the tombs of the kings of Israel. His son Hezekiah became king in his place.

JUDAH'S KING HEZEKIAH

29 Hezekiah was twenty-five years old when he became king, and he reigned twenty-nine years in Jerusalem. His mother's name was Abijah[E] daughter of Zechariah. 2 He did what was right in the LORD's sight just as his ancestor David had done.

3 In the first year of his reign, in the first month, he opened the doors of the LORD's temple and repaired them. 4 Then he brought in the priests and Levites and gathered them in the eastern public square. 5 He said to them, "Hear me, Levites. Consecrate yourselves now and consecrate the temple of the LORD, the God of your ancestors. Remove everything impure from the holy place. 6 For our ancestors were unfaithful and did what is evil in the sight of the LORD our God. They abandoned him, turned their faces away from the LORD's dwelling place, and turned their backs on him.[F] 7 They also closed the doors of the portico, extinguished the lamps, did not burn incense, and did not offer burnt offerings in the holy place of the

[A] **28:3** LXX, Syr, Tg read *and passed his children through* [B] **28:18** Or *the Shephelah* [C] **28:19** Some Hb mss; other Hb mss read *Israel* [D] **28:20** Text emended; MT reads *Tilgath-pilneser*; 1Ch 5:6,26 [E] **29:1** = Abi in 2Kg 18:2 [F] **29:6** Lit *and they gave the back of the neck*

God of Israel. 8 Therefore, the wrath of the LORD was
on Judah and Jerusalem, and he made them an object
of terror, horror, and mockery,[A] as you see with your
own eyes. 9 Our fathers fell by the sword, and our sons,
our daughters, and our wives are in captivity because
of this. 10 It is in my heart now to make a covenant
with the LORD, the God of Israel so that his burning
anger may turn away from us. 11 My sons, don't be
negligent now, for the LORD has chosen you to stand
in his presence, to serve him, and to be his ministers
and burners of incense."

CLEANSING THE TEMPLE

12 Then the Levites stood up:
Mahath son of Amasai and Joel son of Azariah
from the Kohathites;
Kish son of Abdi and Azariah son of Jehallelel
from the Merarites;
Joah son of Zimmah and Eden son of Joah
from the Gershonites;
13 Shimri and Jeuel from the Elizaphanites;
Zechariah and Mattaniah from the Asaphites;
14 Jehiel[B] and Shimei from the Hemanites;
Shemaiah and Uzziel from the Jeduthunites.
15 They gathered their brothers together, consecrated
themselves, and went according to the king's command by the words of the LORD to cleanse the LORD's
temple.
16 The priests went to the entrance of the LORD's
temple to cleanse it. They took all the unclean things
they found in the LORD's sanctuary to the courtyard of
the LORD's temple. Then the Levites received them and
took them outside to the Kidron Valley. 17 They began
the consecration on the first day of the first month,
and on the eighth day of the month they came to the
portico of the LORD's temple. They consecrated the
LORD's temple for eight days, and on the sixteenth
day of the first month they finished.
18 Then they went inside to King Hezekiah and said,
"We have cleansed the whole temple of the LORD, the
altar of burnt offering and all its utensils, and the
table for the rows of the Bread of the Presence and
all its utensils. 19 We have set up and consecrated all
the utensils that King Ahaz rejected during his reign
when he became unfaithful. They are in front of the
altar of the LORD."

RENEWAL OF TEMPLE WORSHIP

20 King Hezekiah got up early, gathered the city officials, and went to the LORD's temple. 21 They brought
seven bulls, seven rams, seven lambs, and seven male
goats as a sin offering for the kingdom, for the sanctuary, and for Judah. Then he told the descendants of
Aaron, the priests, to offer them on the altar of the
LORD. 22 So they slaughtered the bulls, and the priests
received the blood and splattered it on the altar. They
slaughtered the rams and splattered the blood on
the altar. They slaughtered the lambs and splattered
the blood on the altar. 23 Then they brought the goats
for the sin offering right into the presence of the
king and the congregation, who laid their hands on
them. 24 The priests slaughtered the goats and put
their blood on the altar for a sin offering, to make
atonement for all Israel, for the king said that the
burnt offering and sin offering were for all Israel.
25 Hezekiah stationed the Levites in the LORD's
temple with cymbals, harps, and lyres according to
the command of David, Gad the king's seer, and the
prophet Nathan. For the command was from the LORD
through his prophets. 26 The Levites stood with the instruments of David, and the priests with the trumpets.
27 Then Hezekiah ordered that the burnt offering
be offered on the altar. When the burnt offerings
began, the song of the LORD and the trumpets began,
accompanied by the instruments of King David of
Israel. 28 The whole assembly was worshiping, singing the song, and blowing the trumpets — all this
continued until the burnt offering was completed.
29 When the burnt offerings were completed, the king
and all those present with him bowed down and worshiped. 30 Then King Hezekiah and the officials told
the Levites to sing praise to the LORD in the words
of David and of the seer Asaph. So they sang praises
with rejoicing and knelt low and worshiped.
31 Hezekiah concluded, "Now you are consecrated[C] to the LORD. Come near and bring sacrifices and
thanksgiving offerings to the LORD's temple." So the
congregation brought sacrifices and thanksgiving
offerings, and all those with willing hearts brought
burnt offerings. 32 The number of burnt offerings the
congregation brought was seventy bulls, one hundred rams, and two hundred lambs; all these were for
a burnt offering to the LORD. 33 Six hundred bulls and
three thousand sheep and goats were consecrated.
34 However, since there were not enough priests,
they weren't able to skin all the burnt offerings, so
their Levite brothers helped them until the work was
finished and until the priests consecrated themselves.
For the Levites were more conscientious[D] to consecrate themselves than the priests were. 35 Furthermore, the burnt offerings were abundant, along with
the fat of the fellowship offerings and with the drink
offerings for the burnt offering.
So the service of the LORD's temple was established.
36 Then Hezekiah and all the people rejoiced over
how God had prepared the people, for it had come
about suddenly.

[A] **29:8** Lit *hissing* [B] **29:14** Alt Hb tradition reads *Jehuel* [C] **29:31** Lit *Now you have filled your hands* [D] **29:34** Lit *upright of heart*; Ps 32:11; 64:10

CELEBRATION OF THE PASSOVER

30 Then Hezekiah sent word throughout all Israel and Judah, and he also wrote letters to Ephraim and Manasseh to come to the LORD's temple in Jerusalem to observe the Passover of the LORD, the God of Israel. 2 For the king and his officials and the entire congregation in Jerusalem decided to observe the Passover of the LORD in the second month, 3 because they were not able to observe it at the appropriate time. Not enough of the priests had consecrated themselves, and the people hadn't been gathered together in Jerusalem. 4 The proposal pleased the king and the congregation, 5 so they affirmed the proposal and spread the message throughout all Israel, from Beer-sheba to Dan, to come to observe the Passover of the LORD, the God of Israel in Jerusalem, for they hadn't observed it often,[A] as prescribed.[B]

6 So the couriers went throughout Israel and Judah with letters from the hand of the king and his officials, and according to the king's command, saying, "Israelites, return to the LORD, the God of Abraham, Isaac, and Israel so that he may return to those of you who remain, who have escaped the grasp of the kings of Assyria. 7 Don't be like your ancestors and your brothers who were unfaithful to the LORD, the God of their ancestors so that he made them an object of horror as you yourselves see. 8 Don't become obstinate[C] now like your ancestors did. Give your allegiance[D] to the LORD, and come to his sanctuary that he has consecrated forever. Serve the LORD your God so that he may turn his burning anger away from you, 9 for when you return to the LORD, your brothers and your sons will receive mercy in the presence of their captors and will return to this land. For the LORD your God is gracious and merciful; he will not turn his face away from you if you return to him."

10 The couriers traveled from city to city in the land of Ephraim and Manasseh as far as Zebulun, but the inhabitants[E] laughed at them and mocked them. 11 But some from Asher, Manasseh, and Zebulun humbled themselves and came to Jerusalem. 12 Also, the power of God was at work in Judah to unite them[F] to carry out the command of the king and his officials by the word of the LORD.

13 A very large assembly of people was gathered in Jerusalem to observe the Festival of Unleavened Bread in the second month. 14 They proceeded to take away the altars that were in Jerusalem, and they took away the incense altars and threw them into the Kidron Valley. 15 They slaughtered the Passover lamb on the fourteenth day of the second month. The priests and Levites were ashamed, and they consecrated themselves and brought burnt offerings to the LORD's temple. 16 They stood at their prescribed posts, according to the law of Moses, the man of God. The priests splattered the blood received from the Levites, 17 for there were many in the assembly who had not consecrated themselves, and so the Levites were in charge of slaughtering the Passover lambs for every unclean person to consecrate the lambs to the LORD. 18 A large number of the people — many from Ephraim, Manasseh, Issachar, and Zebulun — were ritually unclean, yet they had eaten the Passover contrary to what was written. But Hezekiah had interceded for them, saying, "May the good LORD provide atonement on behalf of 19 whoever sets his whole heart on seeking God, the LORD, the God of his ancestors, even though not according to the purification rules of the sanctuary." 20 So the LORD heard Hezekiah and healed the people. 21 The Israelites who were present in Jerusalem observed the Festival of Unleavened Bread seven days with great joy, and the Levites and the priests praised the LORD day after day with loud instruments. 22 Then Hezekiah encouraged[G] all the Levites who performed skillfully before the LORD. They ate at the appointed festival for seven days, sacrificing fellowship offerings and giving thanks to the LORD, the God of their ancestors.

23 The whole congregation decided to observe seven more days, so they observed seven days with joy, 24 for King Hezekiah of Judah contributed one thousand bulls and seven thousand sheep for the congregation. Also, the officials contributed one thousand bulls and ten thousand sheep for the congregation, and many priests consecrated themselves. 25 Then the whole assembly of Judah with the priests and Levites, the whole assembly that came from Israel, the resident aliens who came from the land of Israel, and those who were living in Judah, rejoiced. 26 There was great rejoicing in Jerusalem, for nothing like this was known since the days of Solomon son of David, the king of Israel.

27 Then the priests and the Levites stood to bless the people, and God heard them, and their prayer came into his holy dwelling place in heaven.

REMOVAL OF IDOLATRY

31 When all this was completed, all Israel who had attended went out to the cities of Judah and broke up the sacred pillars, chopped down the Asherah poles, and tore down the high places and altars throughout Judah and Benjamin, as well as in Ephraim and Manasseh, to the last one.[H] Then all the Israelites returned to their cities, each to his own possession.

[A] **30:5** Or *in great numbers* [B] **30:5** Lit *often, according to what is written* [C] **30:8** Lit *Don't stiffen your neck* [D] **30:8** Lit *hand* [E] **30:10** Lit *but they* [F] **30:12** Lit *to give them one heart* [G] **30:22** Lit *spoke to the heart of* [H] **31:1** Lit *Manasseh, until finishing*

OFFERINGS FOR LEVITES

2 Hezekiah reestablished the divisions of the priests and Levites for the burnt offerings and fellowship offerings, for ministry, for giving thanks, and for praise in the gates of the camp of the LORD, each division corresponding to his service among the priests and Levites. 3 The king contributed[A] from his own possessions for the regular morning and evening burnt offerings, the burnt offerings of the Sabbaths, of the New Moons, and of the appointed feasts, as written in the law of the LORD. 4 He told the people who lived in Jerusalem to give a contribution for the priests and Levites so that they could devote their energy to the law of the LORD. 5 When the word spread, the Israelites gave liberally of the best of the grain, new wine, fresh oil, honey, and of all the produce of the field, and they brought in an abundance, a tenth of everything. 6 As for the Israelites and Judahites who lived in the cities of Judah, they also brought a tenth of the herds and flocks, and a tenth of the dedicated things that were consecrated to the LORD their God. They gathered them into large piles. 7 In the third month they began building up the piles, and they finished in the seventh month. 8 When Hezekiah and his officials came and viewed the piles, they blessed the LORD and his people Israel.

9 Hezekiah asked the priests and Levites about the piles. 10 The chief priest Azariah, of the household of Zadok, answered him, "Since they began bringing the offering to the LORD's temple, we have been eating and are satisfied and there is plenty left over because the LORD has blessed his people; this abundance is what is left over."

11 Hezekiah told them to prepare chambers in the LORD's temple, and they prepared them. 12 The offering, the tenth, and the dedicated things were brought faithfully. Conaniah the Levite was the officer in charge of them, and his brother Shimei was second. 13 Jehiel, Azaziah, Nahath, Asahel, Jerimoth, Jozabad, Eliel, Ismachiah, Mahath, and Benaiah were deputies under the authority of Conaniah and his brother Shimei by appointment of King Hezekiah and of Azariah the chief official of God's temple.

14 Kore son of Imnah the Levite, the keeper of the East Gate, was over the freewill offerings to God to distribute the contribution to the LORD and the consecrated things. 15 Eden, Miniamin, Jeshua, Shemaiah, Amariah, and Shecaniah in the cities of the priests were to distribute it faithfully under his authority to their brothers by divisions, whether large or small. 16 In addition, they distributed it to males registered by genealogy three[B] years old and above; to all who would enter the LORD's temple for their daily duty, for their service in their responsibilities according to their divisions. 17 They distributed also to those recorded by genealogy of the priests by their ancestral families[C] and the Levites twenty years old and above, by their responsibilities in their divisions; 18 to those registered by genealogy — with all their dependents, wives, sons, and daughters — of the whole assembly (for they had faithfully consecrated themselves as holy); 19 and to the descendants of Aaron, the priests, in the common fields of their cities, in each and every city. There were men who were registered by name to distribute a portion to every male among the priests and to every Levite recorded by genealogy.

20 Hezekiah did this throughout all Judah. He did what was good and upright and true before the LORD his God. 21 He was diligent in every deed that he began in the service of God's temple, in the instruction and the commands, in order to seek his God, and he prospered.

SENNACHERIB'S INVASION

32 After Hezekiah's faithful deeds, King Sennacherib of Assyria came and entered Judah. He laid siege to the fortified cities and intended[D] to break into them. 2 Hezekiah saw that Sennacherib had come and that he planned[E] war on Jerusalem, 3 so he consulted with his officials and his warriors about stopping up the water of the springs that were outside the city, and they helped him. 4 Many people gathered and stopped up all the springs and the stream that flowed through the land; they said, "Why should the kings of Assyria come and find abundant water?" 5 Then Hezekiah strengthened his position by rebuilding the entire broken-down wall and heightening the towers and the other outside wall. He repaired the supporting terraces of the city of David, and made an abundance of weapons and shields.

6 He set military commanders over the people and gathered the people in the square of the city gate. Then he encouraged them,[F] saying, 7 "Be strong and courageous! Don't be afraid or discouraged before the king of Assyria or before the large army that is with him, for there are more with us than with him. 8 He has only human strength,[G] but we have the LORD our God to help us and to fight our battles." So the people relied on the words of King Hezekiah of Judah.

SENNACHERIB'S SERVANT'S SPEECH

9 After this, while King Sennacherib of Assyria with all his armed forces besieged[H] Lachish, he sent his servants to Jerusalem against King Hezekiah of Judah

[A]**31:3** Lit *The king's portion* [B]**31:16** Or *30*; 1Ch 23:3 [C]**31:17** Lit *by the house of their fathers* [D]**32:1** Lit *said to himself* [E]**32:2** Lit *that his face was for* [F]**32:6** Lit *he spoke to their hearts* [G]**32:8** Lit *With him an arm of flesh* [H]**32:9** Lit *with his dominion was against*

and against all those of Judah who were in Jerusalem, saying, [10] "This is what King Sennacherib of Assyria says: 'What are you relying on that you remain in Jerusalem under siege? [11] Isn't Hezekiah misleading you to give you over to death by famine and thirst when he says, "The LORD our God will keep us from the grasp of the king of Assyria"? [12] Didn't Hezekiah himself remove his high places and his altars and say to Judah and Jerusalem, "You must worship before one altar, and you must burn incense on it"?

[13] " 'Don't you know what I and my predecessors have done to all the peoples of the lands? Have any of the national gods of the lands been able to rescue their land from my power? [14] Who among all the gods of these nations that my predecessors completely destroyed was able to rescue his people from my power, that your God should be able to deliver you from my power? [15] So now, don't let Hezekiah deceive you, and don't let him mislead you like this. Don't believe him, for no god of any nation or kingdom has been able to rescue his people from my power or the power of my predecessors. How much less will your God rescue you from my power!' "

[16] His servants said more against the LORD God and against his servant Hezekiah. [17] He also wrote letters to mock the LORD, the God of Israel, saying against him:

> Just like the national gods of the lands that did not rescue their people from my power, so Hezekiah's God will not rescue his people from my power.

[18] Then they called out loudly in Hebrew[A] to the people of Jerusalem, who were on the wall, to frighten and discourage them in order that he might capture the city. [19] They spoke against the God of Jerusalem like they had spoken against the gods of the peoples of the earth, which were made by human hands.

DELIVERANCE FROM SENNACHERIB

[20] King Hezekiah and the prophet Isaiah son of Amoz prayed about this and cried out to heaven, [21] and the LORD sent an angel who annihilated every valiant warrior, leader, and commander in the camp of the king of Assyria. So the king of Assyria returned in disgrace to his land. He went to the temple of his god, and there some of his own children struck him down with the sword.

[22] So the LORD saved Hezekiah and the inhabitants of Jerusalem from the power of King Sennacherib of Assyria and from the power of all others. He gave them rest[B] on every side. [23] Many were bringing an offering to the LORD to Jerusalem and valuable gifts to King Hezekiah of Judah, and he was exalted in the eyes of all the nations after that.

HEZEKIAH'S ILLNESS AND PRIDE

[24] In those days Hezekiah became sick to the point of death, so he prayed to the LORD, who spoke to him and gave him a miraculous sign. [25] However, because his heart was proud, Hezekiah didn't respond according to the benefit that had come to him. So there was wrath on him, Judah, and Jerusalem. [26] Then Hezekiah humbled himself for the pride of his heart — he and the inhabitants of Jerusalem — so the LORD's wrath didn't come on them during Hezekiah's lifetime.

HEZEKIAH'S WEALTH AND WORKS

[27] Hezekiah had abundant riches and glory, and he made himself treasuries for silver, gold, precious stones, spices, shields, and every desirable item. [28] He made warehouses for the harvest of grain, new wine, and fresh oil, and stalls for all kinds of cattle, and pens for flocks. [29] He made cities for himself, and he acquired vast numbers of flocks and herds, for God gave him abundant possessions.

[30] This same Hezekiah blocked the upper outlet of the water from the Gihon Spring and channeled it smoothly downward and westward to the city of David. Hezekiah succeeded in everything he did. [31] When the ambassadors of Babylon's rulers were sent[C] to him to inquire about the miraculous sign that happened in the land, God left him to test him and discover what was in his heart.

HEZEKIAH'S DEATH

[32] As for the rest of the events of Hezekiah's reign and his deeds of faithful love, note that they are written in the Visions of the Prophet Isaiah son of Amoz, and in the Book of the Kings of Judah and Israel. [33] Hezekiah rested with his ancestors and was buried on the ascent to the tombs of David's descendants. All Judah and the inhabitants of Jerusalem paid him honor at his death. His son Manasseh became king in his place.

JUDAH'S KING MANASSEH

33 Manasseh was twelve years old when he became king, and he reigned fifty-five years in Jerusalem. [2] He did what was evil in the LORD's sight, imitating the detestable practices of the nations that the LORD had dispossessed before the Israelites. [3] He rebuilt the high places that his father Hezekiah had torn down and reestablished the altars for the Baals. He made Asherah poles, and he bowed in worship to all the stars in the sky and served them. [4] He built altars in the LORD's temple, where the LORD had said, "Jerusalem is where my name will remain forever." [5] He built altars to all the stars in the sky in both

[A] **32:18** Lit *Judahite* [B] **32:22** Lit *He led them*; Ps 23:2 [C] **32:31** LXX, Tg, Vg; MT reads *of Babylon sent*

DIGGING DEEPER *Hezekiah's Tunnel and the Siloam Inscription*

According to 2 Chronicles 32:30 and 2 Kings 20:20, King Hezekiah (reigned 726–697 BC) of Jerusalem constructed a tunnel to channel water from the Gihon spring, which was exposed outside the city gates, into a pool located within Jerusalem's walls (Is 22:9–11). Hezekiah was concerned for the city's vulnerable water supply in light of the impending Assyrian invasion (2Ch 32:2–5; Is 36–39). In 1838, American explorer Edward Robinson discovered Hezekiah's Tunnel (commonly known as the Siloam Tunnel) around the year 1800. It measured more than seventeen hundred feet in length. Nearly fifty years after Robinson's discovery, a group of youths discovered an ancient Hebrew inscription associated with Hezekiah's Tunnel. It dated to the eighth century BC and is now known as the Siloam Inscription. It tells of the final dramatic moments as two groups of workmen advanced toward one another from each end of the tunnel. It reads: "And on the day of the breakthrough the stonecutters struck each man towards his fellow, ax against ax, and the waters flowed from the source to the pool, for 1,200 cubits."

courtyards of the LORD's temple. 6 He passed his sons
through the fire in Ben Hinnom Valley. He practiced
witchcraft, divination, and sorcery, and consulted
mediums and spiritists. He did a huge amount of evil
in the LORD's sight, angering him.
7 Manasseh set up a carved image of the idol, which
he had made, in God's temple that God had spoken
about to David and his son Solomon: "I will establish
my name forever[A] in this temple and in Jerusalem,
which I have chosen out of all the tribes of Israel. 8 I
will never again remove the feet of the Israelites from
the land where I stationed your[B] ancestors, if only
they will be careful to do all I have commanded them
through Moses — all the law, statutes, and judgments."
9 So Manasseh caused Judah and the inhabitants of
Jerusalem to stray so that they did worse evil than the
nations the LORD had destroyed before the Israelites.

MANASSEH'S REPENTANCE

10 The LORD spoke to Manasseh and his people, but
they didn't listen. 11 So he brought against them the
military commanders of the king of Assyria. They
captured Manasseh with hooks, bound him with
bronze shackles, and took him to Babylon. 12 When
he was in distress, he sought the favor of the LORD his
God and earnestly humbled himself before the God of
his ancestors. 13 He prayed to him, and the LORD was
receptive to his prayer. He granted his request and
brought him back to Jerusalem, to his kingdom. So
Manasseh came to know that the LORD is God.
14 After this, he built the outer wall of the city of
David from west of Gihon in the valley to the entrance
of the Fish Gate; he brought it around Ophel, and he
heightened it considerably. He also placed military
commanders in all the fortified cities of Judah.
15 He removed the foreign gods and the idol from
the LORD's temple, along with all the altars that he
had built on the mountain of the LORD's temple and
in Jerusalem, and he threw them outside the city. 16 He
built[C] the altar of the LORD and offered fellowship
and thanksgiving sacrifices on it. Then he told Judah
to serve the LORD, the God of Israel. 17 However, the
people still sacrificed at the high places, but only to
the LORD their God.

MANASSEH'S DEATH

18 The rest of the events of Manasseh's reign, along
with his prayer to his God and the words of the seers
who spoke to him in the name of the LORD, the God of
Israel, are written in the Events of Israel's Kings. 19 His
prayer and how God was receptive to his prayer, and
all his sin and unfaithfulness and the sites where he
built high places and set up Asherah poles and carved
images before he humbled himself, they are written
in the Events of Hozai. 20 Manasseh rested with his
ancestors, and he was buried in his own house. His
son Amon became king in his place.

JUDAH'S KING AMON

21 Amon was twenty-two years old when he became
king, and he reigned two years in Jerusalem. 22 He did
what was evil in the LORD's sight, just as his father
Manasseh had done. Amon sacrificed to all the carved
images that his father Manasseh had made, and he
served them. 23 But he did not humble himself before
the LORD like his father Manasseh humbled himself;
instead, Amon increased his guilt.
24 So his servants conspired against him and put
him to death in his own house. 25 The common people[D]
killed all who had conspired against King Amon, and
they made his son Josiah king in his place.

JUDAH'S KING JOSIAH

34 Josiah was eight years old when he became
king, and he reigned thirty-one years in Jerusalem. 2 He did what was right in the LORD's sight

[A] **33:7** LXX, Syr, Tg, Vg; 2Kg 21:7; MT reads *name for Elom* [B] **33:8** LXX, Syr, Vg read *land I gave to their*; 2Kg 21:8 [C] **33:16** Some Hb mss, Syr, Tg, Arabic; other Hb mss, LXX, Vg read *restored* [D] **33:25** Lit *The people of the land*

and walked in the ways of his ancestor David; he did not turn aside to the right or the left.

JOSIAH'S REFORM

3 In the eighth year of his reign, while he was still a youth, Josiah began to seek the God of his ancestor David, and in the twelfth year he began to cleanse Judah and Jerusalem of the high places, the Asherah poles, the carved images, and the cast images. 4 Then in his presence the altars of the Baals were torn down, and he chopped down the shrines[A] that were above them. He shattered the Asherah poles, the carved images, and the cast images, crushed them to dust, and scattered them over the graves of those who had sacrificed to them. 5 He burned the bones of the priests on their altars. So he cleansed Judah and Jerusalem. 6 He did the same in the cities of Manasseh, Ephraim, and Simeon, and as far as Naphtali and on their surrounding mountain shrines.[B] 7 He tore down the altars, and he smashed the Asherah poles and the carved images to powder. He chopped down all the shrines throughout the land of Israel and returned to Jerusalem.

JOSIAH'S REPAIR OF THE TEMPLE

8 In the eighteenth year of his reign, in order to cleanse the land and the temple, Josiah sent Shaphan son of Azaliah, along with Maaseiah the governor of the city and the court historian Joah son of Joahaz, to repair the temple of the LORD his God.

9 So they went to the high priest Hilkiah and gave him the silver brought into God's temple. The Levites and the doorkeepers had collected it from Manasseh, Ephraim, and from the entire remnant of Israel, and from all Judah, Benjamin, and the inhabitants of Jerusalem. 10 They gave it to those doing the work — those who oversaw the LORD's temple. They gave it to the workmen who were working in the LORD's temple, to repair and restore the temple; 11 they gave it to the carpenters and builders and also used it to buy quarried stone and timbers — for joining and making beams — for the buildings that Judah's kings had destroyed.

12 The men were doing the work with integrity. Their overseers were Jahath and Obadiah, Levites from the Merarites, and Zechariah and Meshullam from the Kohathites as supervisors. The Levites were all skilled with musical instruments. 13 They were also over the porters and were supervising all those doing the work task by task. Some of the Levites were secretaries, officers, and gatekeepers.

THE RECOVERY OF THE BOOK OF THE LAW

14 When they brought out the silver that had been deposited in the LORD's temple, the priest Hilkiah found the book of the law of the LORD written by the hand of Moses. 15 Consequently, Hilkiah told the court secretary Shaphan, "I have found the book of the law in the LORD's temple," and he gave the book to Shaphan.

16 Shaphan took the book to the king, and also reported, "Your servants are doing all that was placed in their hands. 17 They have emptied out the silver that was found in the LORD's temple and have given it to the overseers and to those doing the work." 18 Then the court secretary Shaphan told the king, "The priest Hilkiah gave me a book," and Shaphan read from it in the presence of the king.

19 When the king heard the words of the law, he tore his clothes. 20 Then he commanded Hilkiah, Ahikam son of Shaphan, Abdon son of Micah, the court secretary Shaphan, and the king's servant Asaiah, 21 "Go and inquire of the LORD for me and for those remaining in Israel and Judah, concerning the words of the book that was found. For great is the LORD's wrath that is poured out on us because our ancestors have not kept the word of the LORD in order to do everything written in this book."

HULDAH'S PROPHECY OF JUDGMENT

22 So Hilkiah and those the king had designated[C] went to the prophetess Huldah, the wife of Shallum son of Tokhath, son of Hasrah, keeper of the wardrobe. She lived in Jerusalem in the Second District. They spoke with her about this.

23 She said to them, "This is what the LORD God of Israel says: Say to the man who sent you to me, 24 'This is what the LORD says: I am about to bring disaster on this place and on its inhabitants, fulfilling[D] all the curses written in the book that they read in the presence of the king of Judah, 25 because they have abandoned me and burned incense to other gods so as to anger me with all the works of their hands. My wrath will be poured out on this place, and it will not be quenched.' 26 Say this to the king of Judah who sent you to inquire of the LORD: 'This is what the LORD God of Israel says: As for the words that you heard, 27 because your heart was tender and you humbled yourself before God when you heard his words against this place and against its inhabitants, and because you humbled yourself before me, and you tore your clothes and wept before me, I myself have heard' — this is the LORD's declaration. 28 'I will indeed gather you to your ancestors, and you will be gathered to your grave in peace. Your eyes will not see all the disaster that I am bringing on this place and on its inhabitants.' "

Then they reported to the king.

[A] **34:4** Lit *incense altars*, also in v. 7 [B] **34:6** One Hb tradition reads *Naphtali with their swords*; alt Hb tradition, Syr, Vg read *Naphtali, the ruins all around*; Hb obscure [C] **34:22** LXX; MT omits *designated* [D] **34:24** *fulfilling* supplied for clarity

AFFIRMATION OF THE COVENANT BY JOSIAH AND THE PEOPLE

29 So the king sent messengers and gathered all the elders of Judah and Jerusalem. 30 The king went up to the LORD's temple with all the men of Judah and the inhabitants of Jerusalem, as well as the priests and the Levites — all the people from the oldest to the youngest. He read in their hearing all the words of the book of the covenant that had been found in the LORD's temple. 31 Then the king stood at his post and made a covenant in the LORD's presence to follow the LORD and to keep his commands, his decrees, and his statutes with all his heart and with all his soul in order to carry out the words of the covenant written in this book.

32 He had all those present in Jerusalem and Benjamin agree[A] to it. So all the inhabitants of Jerusalem carried out the covenant of God, the God of their ancestors.

33 So Josiah removed everything that was detestable from all the lands belonging to the Israelites, and he required all who were present in Israel to serve the LORD their God. Throughout his reign they did not turn aside from following the LORD, the God of their ancestors.

JOSIAH'S PASSOVER OBSERVANCE

35 Josiah observed the LORD's Passover and slaughtered the Passover lambs on the fourteenth day of the first month. 2 He appointed the priests to their responsibilities and encouraged them to serve in the LORD's temple. 3 He said to the Levites who taught all Israel the holy things of the LORD, "Put the holy ark in the temple built by Solomon son of David king of Israel. Since you do not have to carry it on your shoulders, now serve the LORD your God and his people Israel.

4 "Organize your ancestral families[B] by your divisions according to the written instruction of King David of Israel and that of his son Solomon. 5 Serve in the holy place by the groupings of the ancestral families[C] for your brothers, the lay people,[D] and according to the division of the Levites by family. 6 Slaughter the Passover lambs, consecrate yourselves, and make preparations for your brothers to carry out the word of the LORD through Moses."

7 Then Josiah donated thirty thousand sheep, lambs, and young goats, plus three thousand cattle from his own possessions, for the Passover sacrifices for all the lay people who were present.

8 His officials also donated willingly for the people, the priests, and the Levites. Hilkiah, Zechariah, and Jehiel, chief officials of God's temple, gave twenty-six hundred Passover sacrifices and three hundred cattle for the priests. 9 Conaniah and his brothers Shemaiah and Nethanel, and Hashabiah, Jeiel, and Jozabad, officers of the Levites, donated five thousand Passover sacrifices for the Levites, plus five hundred cattle.

10 So the service was established; the priests stood at their posts and the Levites in their divisions according to the king's command. 11 Then they slaughtered the Passover lambs, and while the Levites were skinning the animals, the priests splattered the blood[E] they had been given.[F] 12 They removed the burnt offerings so that they might be given to the groupings of the ancestral families[G] of the lay people to offer to the LORD, according to what is written in the book of Moses; they did the same with the cattle. 13 They roasted the Passover lambs with fire according to regulation. They boiled the holy sacrifices in pots, kettles, and bowls; and they quickly brought them to the lay people. 14 Afterward, they made preparations for themselves and for the priests, since the priests, the descendants of Aaron, were busy offering up burnt offerings and fat until night. So the Levites made preparations for themselves and for the priests, the descendants of Aaron.

15 The singers, the descendants of Asaph, were at their stations according to the command of David, Asaph, Heman, and Jeduthun the king's seer. Also, the gatekeepers were at each temple gate. None of them left their tasks because their Levite brothers had made preparations for them.

16 So all the service of the LORD was established that day for observing the Passover and for offering burnt offerings on the altar of the LORD, according to the command of King Josiah. 17 The Israelites who were present in Judah also observed the Passover at that time and the Festival of Unleavened Bread for seven days. 18 No Passover had been observed like it in Israel since the days of the prophet Samuel. None of the kings of Israel ever observed a Passover like the one that Josiah observed with the priests, the Levites, all Judah, the Israelites who were present in Judah, and the inhabitants of Jerusalem. 19 In the eighteenth year of Josiah's reign, this Passover was observed.

JOSIAH'S LAST DEEDS AND DEATH

20 After all this that Josiah had prepared for the temple, King Neco of Egypt marched up to fight at Carchemish by the Euphrates, and Josiah went out to confront him. 21 But Neco sent messengers to him, saying, "What is the issue between you and me, king of Judah? I have not come against you today[H] but I am fighting another dynasty.[I] God told me to hurry.

[A] **34:32** Lit *take a stand.* [B] **35:4** Lit *the house of your fathers* [C] **35:5** Lit *the house of the fathers* [D] **35:5** Lit *the sons of the people,* also in vv. 7,12,13 [E] **35:11** LXX, Vg, Tg; MT omits *blood* [F] **35:11** Lit *splattered from their hand* [G] **35:12** Lit *house of fathers* [H] **35:21** LXX, Syr, Tg, Vg; MT reads *Not against you, you today* [I] **35:21** Lit *house*

Statutes, Commandments, Judgments, and Testimonies

by Phillip Swanson

The concept of law was not unique among the Hebrews. Nearly every civilization produced its own law codes. Several existing law codes that preceded the biblical law have assisted scholars in interpreting the biblical law. The Code of Hammurabi, among the better-known ancient law codes, dates to the second millennium BC. Hammurabi's code, representing almost three hundred paragraphs of text, outlined the duties of his citizens and other matters of civil concern to the population.

Archaeologists have unearthed Sumerian law codes of the Mesopotamian Kings Ur-Namma, Lipit-Ishtar, and Eshnunna from the third millennium BC. Other ancient Near Eastern law codes, more coincidental with the biblical period, include Hittite laws (fourteenth century BC), Assyrian laws (twelfth century BC), and Neo-Babylonian laws (seventh–sixth century BC).[1] However, the entire sweep of the biblical concept of law does not exhibit the same legal/judicial connotation expressed by the ancient law codes noted above or in current Western culture. Biblical law exhibits a certain religious overtone expected in Holy Scripture. Consequently, portions of biblical law address matters of ritualistic purity, morally correct behavior, and regulations for sacrifice and the tithe, as well as criminal behavior.[2] ✣

[1] Dale Patrick, *Old Testament Law* (Atlanta: John Knox, 1985), 28–30. [2] H. Cazelles, "Ten Commandments" in *Interpreter's Dictionary of the Bible: Supplementary Volume* (*IDBSup*), ed. Keith Crim (Nashville: Abingdon, 1976), 875.

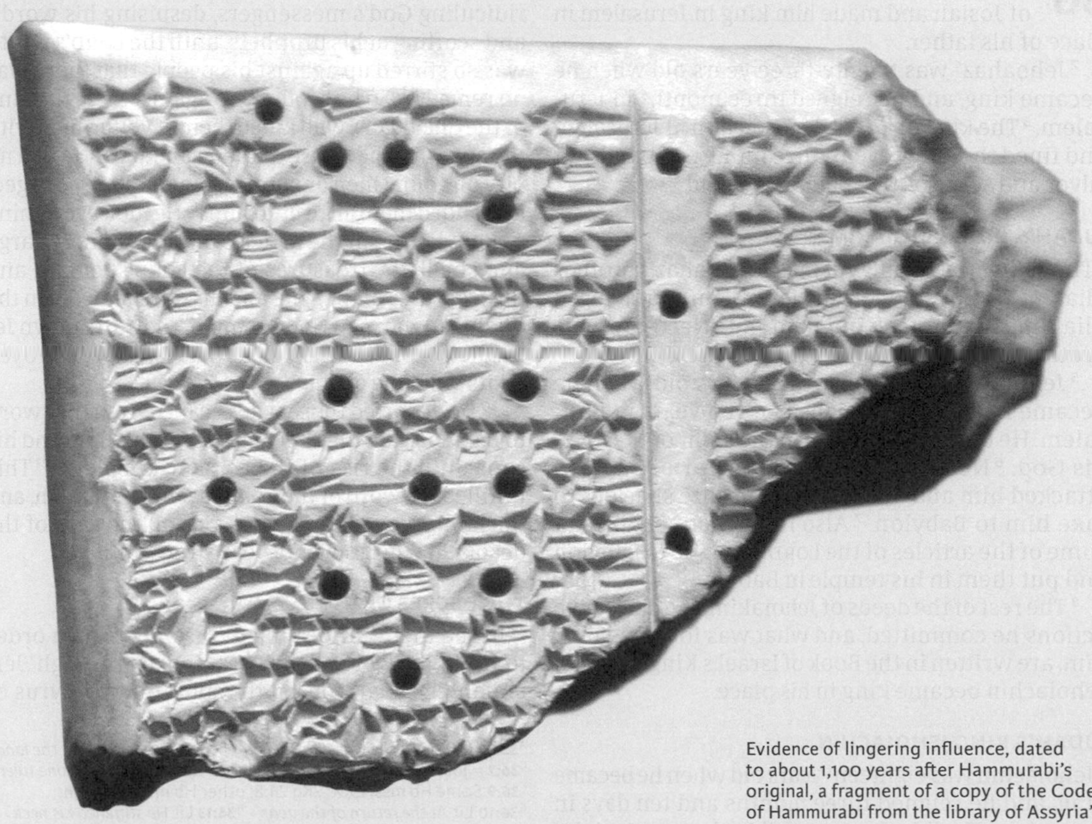

Evidence of lingering influence, dated to about 1,100 years after Hammurabi's original, a fragment of a copy of the Code of Hammurabi from the library of Assyria's King Assurbanipal.

Stop opposing God who is with me; don't make him destroy you!"

22 But Josiah did not turn away from him; instead, in order to fight with him he disguised himself.[A] He did not listen to Neco's words from the mouth of God, but went to the Valley of Megiddo to fight. 23 The archers shot King Josiah, and he said to his servants, "Take me away, for I am severely wounded!" 24 So his servants took him out of the war chariot, carried him in his second chariot, and brought him to Jerusalem. Then he died, and they buried him in the tomb of his ancestors. All Judah and Jerusalem mourned for Josiah. 25 Jeremiah chanted a dirge over Josiah, and all the male and female singers still speak of Josiah in their dirges today. They established them as a statute for Israel, and indeed they are written in the Dirges.

26 The rest of the events of Josiah's reign, along with his deeds of faithful love according to what is written in the law of the LORD, 27 and his words, from beginning to end, are written in the Book of the Kings of Israel and Judah.

JUDAH'S KING JEHOAHAZ

36 Then the common people[B] took Jehoahaz son of Josiah and made him king in Jerusalem in place of his father.

2 Jehoahaz[C] was twenty-three years old when he became king, and he reigned three months in Jerusalem. 3 The king of Egypt deposed him in Jerusalem and fined the land seventy-five hundred pounds[D] of silver and seventy-five pounds[E] of gold.

JUDAH'S KING JEHOIAKIM

4 Then King Neco of Egypt made Jehoahaz's brother Eliakim king over Judah and Jerusalem and changed Eliakim's name to Jehoiakim. But Neco took his brother Jehoahaz and brought him to Egypt.

5 Jehoiakim was twenty-five years old when he became king, and he reigned eleven years in Jerusalem. He did what was evil in the sight of the LORD his God. 6 Now King Nebuchadnezzar of Babylon attacked him and bound him in bronze shackles to take him to Babylon. 7 Also Nebuchadnezzar took some of the articles of the LORD's temple to Babylon and put them in his temple in Babylon.

8 The rest of the deeds of Jehoiakim, the detestable actions he committed, and what was found against him, are written in the Book of Israel's Kings. His son Jehoiachin became king in his place.

JUDAH'S KING JEHOIACHIN

9 Jehoiachin was eighteen[F] years old when he became king, and he reigned three months and ten days in Jerusalem. He did what was evil in the LORD's sight. 10 In the spring[G] Nebuchadnezzar sent for him and brought him to Babylon along with the valuable articles of the LORD's temple. Then he made Jehoiachin's brother Zedekiah king over Judah and Jerusalem.

JUDAH'S KING ZEDEKIAH

11 Zedekiah was twenty-one years old when he became king, and he reigned eleven years in Jerusalem. 12 He did what was evil in the sight of the LORD his God and did not humble himself before the prophet Jeremiah at the LORD's command. 13 He also rebelled against King Nebuchadnezzar who had made him swear allegiance by God. He became obstinate[H] and hardened his heart against returning to the LORD, the God of Israel. 14 All the leaders of the priests and the people multiplied their unfaithful deeds, imitating all the detestable practices of the nations, and they defiled the LORD's temple that he had consecrated in Jerusalem.

THE DESTRUCTION OF JERUSALEM

15 But the LORD, the God of their ancestors sent word against them by the hand of his messengers, sending them time and time again, for he had compassion on his people and on his dwelling place. 16 But they kept ridiculing God's messengers, despising his words, and scoffing at his prophets, until the LORD's wrath was so stirred up against his people that there was no remedy. 17 So he brought up against them the king of the Chaldeans, who killed their fit young men with the sword in the house of their sanctuary. He had no pity on young men or young women, elderly or aged; he handed them all over to him. 18 He took everything to Babylon — all the articles of God's temple, large and small, the treasures of the LORD's temple, and the treasures of the king and his officials. 19 Then the Chaldeans burned God's temple. They tore down Jerusalem's wall, burned all its palaces, and destroyed all its valuable articles.

20 He deported those who escaped from the sword to Babylon, and they became servants to him and his sons until the rise of the Persian[I] kingdom. 21 This fulfilled the word of the LORD through Jeremiah, and the land enjoyed its Sabbath rest all the days of the desolation until seventy years were fulfilled.

THE DECREE OF CYRUS

22 In the first year of King Cyrus of Persia, in order to fulfill the word of the LORD spoken through[J] Jeremiah, the LORD roused the spirit of King Cyrus of

[A] **35:22** LXX reads *he was determined* [B] **36:1** Lit *the people of the land* [C] **36:2** = Joahaz, also in v. 4 [D] **36:3** Lit *100 talents* [E] **36:3** Lit *one talent* [F] **36:9** Some Hb mss, LXX; 2Kg 24:8; other Hb mss read *eight* [G] **36:10** Lit *At the return of the year* [H] **36:13** Lit *He stiffened his neck* [I] **36:20** LXX reads *Median* [J] **36:22** Lit *LORD by the mouth of*

From Nebuchadnezzar to Cyrus II

by Joseph R. Cathey

Assyria had ruled the ancient Near East for centuries. By 640 BC, this mighty nation-state was at its apex. Thirty years later, the great empire of Assyria was no more—collapsing under its own weight of bloated bureaucracy and constant warfare. The heavy demands of paying tribute money, the psychology of terror, and the mass deportations only encouraged other nation-states to revolt at the most opportune time. Assyria's King Ashurbanipal (reigned ca 668–627 BC) suppressed a rebellion in the ancient city of Arvad (in modern western Syria) as well as submitted Hamath, Phoenicia, and Nariri to his vassalage.[1]

For the next half century, Assyria would effectively lose control of the western province of Judah. During this time period, peoples in the north (Urartu), south (Babylon), and west (Syria) would revolt against Assyria's reign.[2] One could argue that during this time the people of Judah sowed the seeds that led to the nation's downfall.

RISE OF AN EMPIRE

For Judah, the seventh century BC was a tumultuous time in which the nation witnessed great upheavals politically, geographically, and theologically. Perhaps the seminal event that foreshadowed the conquering of Judah occurred in 605 BC. Nebuchadnezzar II, the Neo-Babylonian prince-regent and military commander, had broken the Assyrian yoke and effectively conquered the Egyptians at Carchemish. The Babylonians pushed the Egyptians to the south—back to their homeland—and placed the northern territories (such as Syria and the northern Mediterranean coast) under Babylonian hegemony. After his father's death, Nebuchadnezzar II took the throne. During this time of transition and confusion, Egypt as well as Judah took the opportunity to revolt against Babylon.[3]

As early as 601 BC, Nebuchadnezzar had reasserted control over Egypt and effectively pushed the nation back across the Sinai. As the Babylonian king pressed southward, he encountered marked resistance from southern independent city-states. Perhaps the greatest resistance was that of Judah. Nebuchadnezzar promptly set his sights on the errant state. The Babylonians were quick to implement exile as a form of punishment to any wayward nation; Judah would not be spared.[4] At issue in Judah were three disparate political factions vying for kingship. Jeremiah clearly delineates these three factions—one, pro-Egyptian; the second, pro-Babylonian; and the third, for an independent Judah.

REBELLION OF A NATION

Judah's king Jehoiakim (608–598 BC) gave in to the pro-Egyptian party and sought favor and military support from Egypt. Egypt, though, could not save Judah this time. Nebuchadnezzar surrounded Jerusalem and deported the intelligentsia and royalty and took vast treasures (2Kg 24:8–17).

In the interim period from 597 to 587 BC, Babylon experienced a

The Cyrus Cylinder describes in Babylonian cuneiform script Cyrus II capturing Babylon (in 539 BC), restoring a temple in honor of the Babylonian god Marduk, and encouraging previously captured peoples to return to their homelands so they could worship their gods. Cyrus's decree mirrors the details of Ezra 1:1–11.

rebellion at home—possibly instigated by their own military officers. Judah took this opportune time to once again revolt against their Babylonian overlords and assert their independence. The nation of Judah once again allied with Egypt via Pharaoh Hophra and stood against the mighty Babylon.

Under Nebuchadnezzar's leadership, the Babylonian army left a path of destruction as it besieged and/or destroyed nearly every fortified city in central Judah—before finally razing Jerusalem in 586 BC. The archaeological record confirms both the total destruction and the fact that many of the cities were not rebuilt for several years.[5]

RESTORATION OF A PEOPLE

Under the direction of Cyrus, Gobryas (a Persian general) took Babylon; by the end of October 539 BC, the capital was in Persian hands. While Cyrus ceded the title "king of Babylon" to his son Cambyses II, he took the more traditional Mesopotamian designation "king of the lands" for himself. Cyrus instituted a policy of tolerance toward other religions and issued an edict that released captured peoples, including the Jews (Ezr 1:2–4; 6:3–5).

The Persians also differed from the Assyrians in terms of cultural sensitivities to conquered peoples. While the Assyrians had been interested in integrating conquered peoples into the military machinery of the state, the Persians allowed conquered peoples certain freedoms (worship of their own gods, religious peculiarities, along with cultural sensitivities). As long as they continued to offer tribute and supplied what the Persians requested, they could stay in their homelands. If, however, the conquered peoples did not meet the Persians' demands, instead of freedom, they

Brick with a Babylonian inscription that reads: "Cyrus, king of the world, king of Anshan, son of Cambyses, king of Anshan. The great gods delivered all the lands into my hand, and I made this land to dwell in peace."

The Audience Palace of Cyrus the Great had these jambs. This one has a figure of a bull-man and a fish-man. These figures may represent Cyrus's religious tolerance.

faced deportation to Persia. Deportees were always under strong Persian rule.

Once coming to power, Cyrus allowed the Jews to return to their homeland. His motives may not have been altogether altruistic. He may have wanted the Jews back in their homeland so they could serve as a buffer between Persia and Egypt. In any case, Sheshbazzar the prince of Judah accompanied the first Babylonian exiles back to Judah in 538 BC to begin restoration of the temple. ✣

---

[1] A. K. Grayson, *Assyrian Rulers of the Early First Millennium BC (858–745 BC)* (Toronto: University of Toronto Press, 2002), 211. [2] William W. Hallo and William Kelly Simpson, *The Ancient Near East: A History*, 2nd ed. (New York: Harcourt Brace, 1998), 140–41. [3] Marc Van De Mieroop, *A History of the Ancient Near East: ca. 3000–323 BC* (Malden, MA: Blackwell, 2007), 276–77. [4] See James D. Purvis and Eric M. Myeres, "Exile and Return: From the Babylonian Destruction to the Reconstruction of the Jewish State," in *Ancient Israel: From Abraham to the Roman Destruction of the Temple*, ed. Hershel Shanks (Washington, DC: Biblical Archaeology Society, 1999), 201–2. [5] John Bright, *A History of Israel*, 4th ed. (Louisville: Westminster John Knox, 2000), 344–45; Dan Bahat, "Jerusalem" in *OEANE*, 226–28.

Persia to issue a proclamation throughout his entire
kingdom and also to put it in writing:
23 This is what King Cyrus of Persia says: The
LORD, the God of the heavens, has given me all
the kingdoms of the earth and has appointed me
to build him a temple at Jerusalem in Judah. Any
of his people among you may go up, and may the
LORD his God be with him.

EZRA

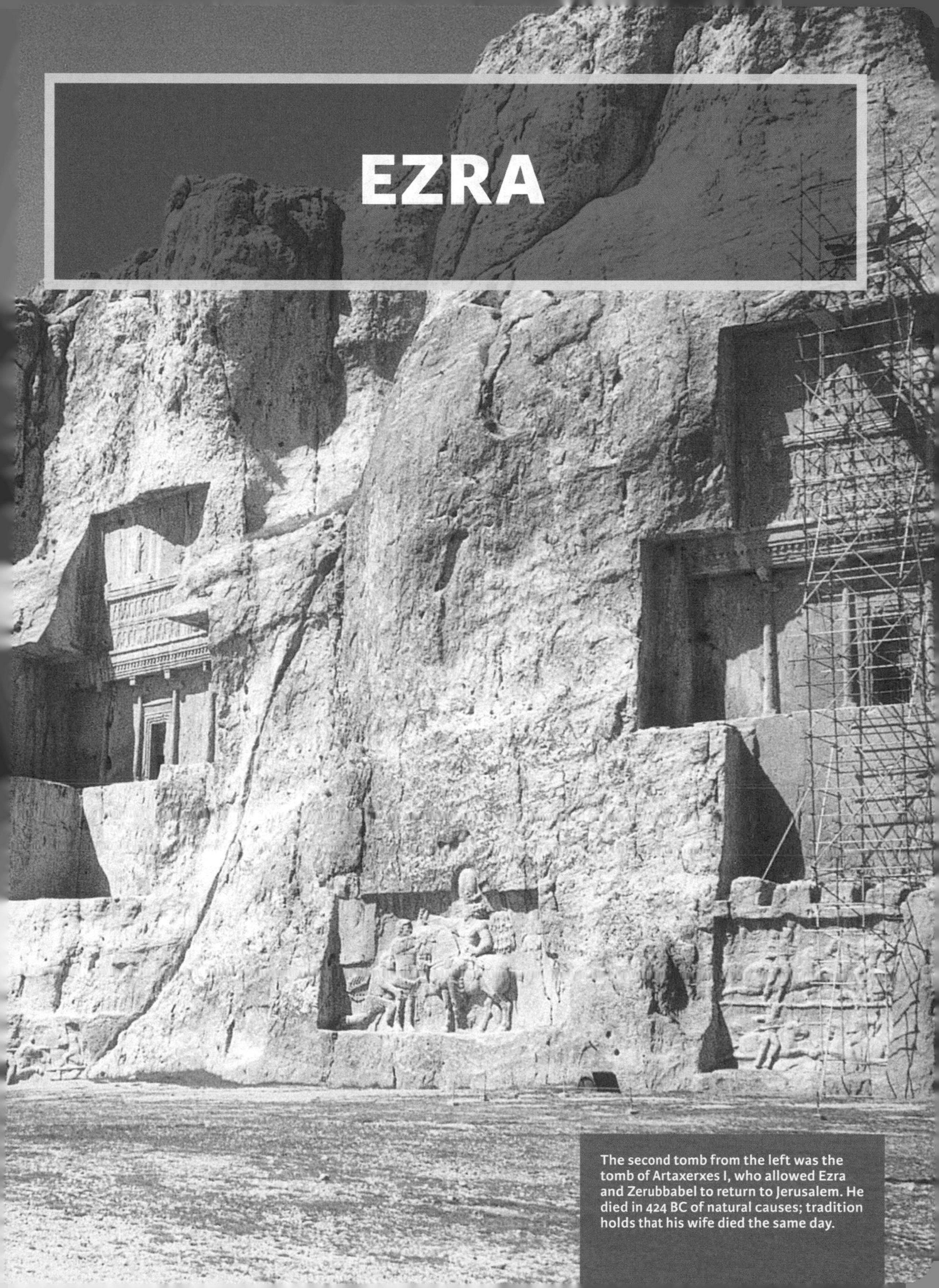

The second tomb from the left was the tomb of Artaxerxes I, who allowed Ezra and Zerubbabel to return to Jerusalem. He died in 424 BC of natural causes; tradition holds that his wife died the same day.

INTRODUCTION TO

EZRA

Circumstances of Writing

Ezra and Nehemiah are anonymous. Ancient Jewish sources usually credit Ezra as the author of Ezra–Nehemiah. More likely Ezra–Nehemiah was written by the "Chronicler," the person (or persons) responsible for 1 and 2 Chronicles. Not only is Ezra–Nehemiah linked to Chronicles at its introduction (Ezr 1:1–2 = 2Ch 36:22–23), but it also shares many similarities in language, terminology, themes, and perspective.

It is probably safe to assume that Ezra–Nehemiah was written soon after the conclusion of Nehemiah's ministry. Most likely the book was written no later than 400 BC.

In Ezra–Nehemiah, it is clear that Ezra came to Jerusalem first, probably in 458 BC, and that Nehemiah followed him thirteen years later, probably in 445 BC. Nehemiah made no mention of Ezra, his ministry, or his reforms. Ezra and Nehemiah appear together in only two texts (Neh 8:9; 12:36). The two events in which Ezra and Nehemiah were together were significant. In Nehemiah 8, the context is the reading of the law to the people; in Nehemiah 12, the two joyous processions walking around the city walls in the dedication ceremony include Ezra (v. 36) and Nehemiah (v. 38).

Contribution to the Bible

The events that occurred in Ezra and Nehemiah, the rebuilt temple, the stabilizing of Jerusalem, and the Jewish community that developed, all played key roles in the life and ministry of Jesus recorded in the Gospels. The rebuilt temple may have paled in comparison to the temple that Solomon built, but it would serve the Jews for centuries until Christ removed the need for a physical temple.

Structure

Ezra was written in two related but distinct languages—Hebrew and Aramaic. The Hebrew sections generally reflect the style of the postexilic era with some evidence of the impact of Aramaic on the language. Aramaic, a Semitic language similar to Hebrew, occurs in two sections in the book of Ezra (4:8–6:18; 7:12–26). During the Persian period (ca 540–330 BC), Aramaic was the official language of diplomacy and commerce.

Ezra is similar to Samuel and Kings, and especially Chronicles, in that many sources were used in its composition. These include two major types of sources. Much of Ezra consists of material from the Ezra Memoir. The Ezra Memoir, written mostly in the first person, includes Ezra 7–10, along with Nehemiah 8 and probably chapter 9; embedded in this memoir are lists and records from other sources used by Ezra. Ezra also contains many lists, genealogies, inventories, letters, and census records throughout the book. For a community attempting to reestablish itself after the disaster of 586 BC and the subsequent exile to Babylon, this material was crucial in reordering its life together.

THE DECREE OF CYRUS

1 In the first year of King Cyrus of Persia, in order
to fulfill the word of the LORD spoken through
Jeremiah, the LORD roused the spirit of King Cyrus to
issue a proclamation throughout his entire kingdom
and to put it in writing:

2 This is what King Cyrus of Persia says: "The
LORD, the God of the heavens, has given me all
the kingdoms of the earth and has appointed
me to build him a house at Jerusalem in Judah.
3 Any of his people among you, may his God be
with him, and may he go to Jerusalem in Judah
and build the house of the LORD, the God of
Israel, the God who is in Jerusalem. 4 Let every
survivor, wherever he resides, be assisted by the
men of that region with silver, gold, goods, and
livestock, along with a freewill offering for the
house of God in Jerusalem."

RETURN FROM EXILE

5 So the family heads of Judah and Benjamin, along
with the priests and Levites — everyone whose spirit God had roused — prepared to go up and rebuild
the LORD's house in Jerusalem. 6 All their neighbors
supported them[A] with silver articles, gold, goods,
livestock, and valuables, in addition to all that was
given as a freewill offering. 7 King Cyrus also brought
out the articles of the LORD's house that Nebuchadnezzar had taken from Jerusalem and had placed in
the house of his gods. 8 King Cyrus of Persia had them
brought out under the supervision of Mithredath the
treasurer, who counted them out to Sheshbazzar the
prince of Judah. 9 This was the inventory:

30 gold basins, 1,000 silver basins,
29 silver knives, 10 30 gold bowls,
410 various[B] silver bowls,
and 1,000 other articles.

11 The gold and silver articles totaled 5,400. Sheshbazzar brought all of them when the exiles went up from
Babylon to Jerusalem.

THE EXILES WHO RETURNED

2 These now are the people of the province who
came from those captive exiles King Nebuchadnezzar of Babylon[C] had deported to Babylon. They
returned to Jerusalem and Judah, each to his own
town. 2 They came with Zerubbabel, Jeshua, Nehemiah, Seraiah, Reelaiah, Mordecai, Bilshan, Mispar,
Bigvai, Rehum, and Baanah.

The number of the Israelite men included[D]

3 Parosh's descendants 2,172
4 Shephatiah's descendants 372
5 Arah's descendants 775
6 Pahath-moab's descendants:
Jeshua's and Joab's descendants 2,812
7 Elam's descendants 1,254
8 Zattu's descendants 945
9 Zaccai's descendants 760
10 Bani's descendants 642
11 Bebai's descendants 623
12 Azgad's descendants 1,222
13 Adonikam's descendants 666
14 Bigvai's descendants 2,056
15 Adin's descendants 454
16 Ater's descendants: of Hezekiah 98
17 Bezai's descendants 323
18 Jorah's descendants 112
19 Hashum's descendants 223
20 Gibbar's descendants 95
21 Bethlehem's people 123
22 Netophah's men 56
23 Anathoth's men 128
24 Azmaveth's people 42
25 Kiriatharim's, Chephirah's,
and Beeroth's people 743
26 Ramah's and Geba's people 621
27 Michmas's men 122
28 Bethel's and Ai's men 223
29 Nebo's people 52
30 Magbish's people 156
31 the other Elam's people 1,254
32 Harim's people 320
33 Lod's, Hadid's, and Ono's people 725
34 Jericho's people 345
35 Senaah's people 3,630

36 The priests included
Jedaiah's descendants of
the house of Jeshua 973
37 Immer's descendants 1,052
38 Pashhur's descendants 1,247
39 and Harim's descendants 1,017

40 The Levites included
Jeshua's and Kadmiel's descendants
from Hodaviah's descendants 74

41 The singers included
Asaph's descendants 128

42 The gatekeepers' descendants included
Shallum's descendants, Ater's descendants,
Talmon's descendants,
Akkub's descendants,
Hatita's descendants,
Shobai's descendants, in all 139

[A] 1:6 Lit *strengthened their hands* [B] 1:10 Or *similar*
[C] 2:1 Nebuchadnezzar reigned 605–562 BC [D] 2:2 Lit *the men of the people of Israel*

Jerusalem Before the Return

by Jerry Lee

Looking across the Kidron Valley toward the Temple Mount in Jerusalem. Today the Temple Mount is dominated by the Dome of the Rock, which is the gold-domed building in the foreground.

John Bright estimated Judah's population as possibly 125,000 even after the deportation of exiles in 597 BC. At that time, ten thousand exiles were marched away to Babylon (2Kg 24:14). The population was reduced further by the execution of leading citizens, additional deportations in 586 and 582 BC (Jr 52:28–30), and flights of groups to the safety of surrounding areas until the number of inhabitants dwindled to "scarcely above 20,000 even after the first exiles had returned" in 536 BC.[1]

A month after Jerusalem's fall, Nebuzaradan began the systematic destruction of Jerusalem. The Babylonians defiled the temple with a pagan feast and then dismantled, looted, and burned it. They systematically destroyed the houses of the city and broke down the walls. No significant ruins of any building dating prior to 586 BC have been discovered by archaeologists. Only floors remain and a portion of the city's wall.

The inhabitants were driven from Jerusalem. All governmental buildings were razed. The Babylonians set up a government at Mizpah, about eight miles north of Jerusalem. Many prominent political and military leaders fled to Egypt for safety. One group of such people forced Jeremiah to accompany them to Egypt.

The Babylonians were thorough in their destruction. They razed all of Judah's fortified cities. Debir, Lachish, Beth-shemesh, and others were destroyed. Some cities were not reoccupied until many years later.[2] The people subsisted among such ashes and destruction.

The kingdom was but a fraction of its former glory. The borders were severely reduced. The northern border was below Bethel, and the southern boundary did not reach Hebron. The vast Negev (south) had been occupied by the Idumeans who pressed northward as far as Hebron. These were former Edomites who had been thrust from their land by increasing hordes of Arabians. On the east, the Jordan River was the boundary; to the west, the mountain area near the Mediterranean was the boundary. Michael Avi-Yonah declared that the reduced kingdom was about twenty-five miles north to south and about thirty-two miles from east to west, making it about eight hundred square miles. Of that, at least a third would be unproductive desert and mountains.[3]

The Babylonians forced the leading citizens and artisans into exile. The poorer and lower classes of society remained in the land. Peasants were left to cultivate the lands and fields. They had to cultivate the crops to keep from starving to death and to pay tribute imposed by Babylon on Judah. That the people left in the land were poor probably reflected Babylon's policy to stifle nationalism. With a vacuum of leadership, these people who had such limited experience became community leaders.

Many families were disrupted or destroyed. Doubtless many orphaned children wandered aimlessly. Many people suddenly became widows or widowers. Biblical injunctions on choosing a mate were ignored. As the children grew up without religious guidance, and as other people entered the land, they began to intermarry. When Ezra returned, he found intermarriage with pagans to be a major problem. Even the high priest's grandson was married to Sanballat's daughter (Neh 13:28). Consequently the people even lost the proficiency to speak Hebrew. Instead, they spoke various languages. Ultimately Aramaic from Babylon became a common language. The inhabitants' knowledge of God's Word was limited. They were not even aware of basic standards taught in God's Word.

Economically the people were devastated. They lived, apparently, on limited means. They had no money or inclination to begin building programs to improve their status. In addition, they were impoverished by inflation (Hg 1:6). What they did earn was like putting something into a purse with holes in it. The inhabitants eked out a living, but they lived in poverty.

Such a devastating defeat by the Babylonians raised serious religious questions about Yahweh's status. The people may have thought that if Yahweh was an all-powerful God, why did he allow his land and people to be devoured by foreigners? Consequently many of the pagan cults began to flourish. Those who lived through the Babylonian holocaust wondered if they should not serve other gods. Like those who forced Jeremiah to flee with them to Egypt, many probably turned to worship the "queen of heaven," Astarte/Artemis, again. Other pagan gods also were worshiped by many. A form of Yahwism remained, but it was diluted and polluted with syncretism as the people worshiped other gods.

Some of the people still adored the Temple Mount and offered some sacrifices on a makeshift altar in the ruins. They even fasted to commemorate the fall and burning of the city and temple. They also remembered Gedaliah's death with a fast. However, little attention was given to the Word of God. No wonder Jeremiah depicted these inhabitants as "bad figs" to be despised (Jr 24:8).

The good figs were taken away into captivity. In Babylon, they sought to preserve their sacred books that spoke of Yahweh's holiness and unfailing love. They developed worship cells that became the synagogue movement in which God's Word was studied and faith in God was nurtured. They also kept alive the hope that was ultimately fulfilled in their liberation by Cyrus and their freedom to return to the land.

When the exiles returned, they were shocked by the apostasy and lethargy of those who had remained in the land. Nevertheless, those returning began to rally and inspire the many discouraged and despairing inhabitants. Leaders such as Ezra and Nehemiah demanded that God's instructions regarding marriage, tithing, and worship be obeyed. Gradually but surely the people reconsecrated themselves to God's service and began to rebuild. They became the people through whom God would send the Messiah. ✣

---

[1] John Bright, *A History of Israel*, 3rd ed. (Philadelphia: Westminster, 1981), 344. [2] Bright, *History of Israel*. [3] Michael Avi-Yonah, *The Holy Land: From the Persia II Period to the Arab Conquests* (Grand Rapids: Baker, 1966), 19.

The northern Negev where it meets the central plains. During the exile, the vast Negev (south) had been occupied by the Idumeans, who pressed northward as far as Hebron.

[43] The temple servants included
Ziha's descendants, Hasupha's descendants,
Tabbaoth's descendants,
[44] Keros's descendants,
Siaha's descendants, Padon's descendants,
45 Lebanah's descendants,
Hagabah's descendants,
Akkub's descendants, [46] Hagab's descendants,
Shalmai's[A] descendants, Hanan's descendants,
47 Giddel's descendants, Gahar's descendants,
Reaiah's descendants, [48] Rezin's descendants,
Nekoda's descendants, Gazzam's descendants,
49 Uzza's descendants, Paseah's descendants,
Besai's descendants, [50] Asnah's descendants,
Meunim's[B] descendants,
Nephusim's[C] descendants,
51 Bakbuk's descendants,
Hakupha's descendants,
Harhur's descendants,
[52] Bazluth's descendants,
Mehida's descendants, Harsha's descendants,
53 Barkos's descendants, Sisera's descendants,
Temah's descendants, [54] Neziah's descendants,
and Hatipha's descendants.

[55] The descendants of Solomon's servants included
Sotai's descendants,
Hassophereth's descendants,
Peruda's descendants, [56] Jaalah's descendants,
Darkon's descendants, Giddel's descendants,
57 Shephatiah's descendants,
Hattil's descendants,
Pochereth-hazzebaim's descendants,
and Ami's descendants.
58 All the temple servants
and the descendants
of Solomon's servants 392.

[59] The following are those who came from Tel-
melah, Tel-harsha, Cherub, Addan, and Immer but
were unable to prove that their ancestral families[D]
and their lineage were Israelite:
60 Delaiah's descendants,
Tobiah's descendants,
Nekoda's descendants 652
[61] and from the descendants of the priests: the descendants of Hobaiah, the descendants of Hakkoz,
the descendants of Barzillai — who had taken a wife
from the daughters of Barzillai the Gileadite and who
bore their name. [62] These searched for their entries
in the genealogical records, but they could not be
found, so they were disqualified from the priesthood.
[63] The governor ordered them not to eat the most holy
things until there was a priest who could consult the
Urim and Thummim.

64 The whole combined assembly
numbered 42,360
65 not including their 7,337 male
and female servants,
and their 200 male and female singers.
66 They had 736 horses, 245 mules,
67 435 camels, and 6,720 donkeys.

GIFTS FOR THE WORK

[68] After they arrived at the LORD's house in Jerusalem,
some of the family heads gave freewill offerings for
the house of God in order to have it rebuilt on its
original site. [69] Based on what they could give, they
gave 61,000 gold coins,[E] 6,250 pounds[F] of silver, and
100 priestly garments to the treasury for the project.
[70] The priests, Levites, singers, gatekeepers, temple
servants, and some of the people settled in their
towns, and the rest of Israel settled in their towns.

SACRIFICE RESTORED

3 When the seventh month arrived, and the Israelites were in their towns, the people gathered
as one in Jerusalem. [2] Jeshua son of Jozadak and his
brothers the priests along with Zerubbabel son of
Shealtiel and his brothers began to build the altar of
Israel's God in order to offer burnt offerings on it,
as it is written in the law of Moses, the man of God.
[3] They set up the altar on its foundation and offered
burnt offerings for the morning and evening on it to
the LORD even though they feared the surrounding
peoples. [4] They celebrated the Festival of Shelters as
prescribed, and offered burnt offerings each day,
based on the number specified by ordinance for each
festival day. [5] After that, they offered the regular burnt
offering and the offerings for the beginning of each
month[G] and for all the LORD's appointed holy occasions, as well as the freewill offerings brought to[H]
the LORD.

[6] On the first day of the seventh month they began
to offer burnt offerings to the LORD, even though the
foundation of the LORD's temple had not yet been laid.
[7] They gave money to the stonecutters and artisans,
and gave food, drink, and oil to the people of Sidon
and Tyre, so they would bring cedar wood from Lebanon to Joppa by sea, according to the authorization
given them by King Cyrus of Persia.

REBUILDING THE TEMPLE

[8] In the second month of the second year after they
arrived at God's house in Jerusalem, Zerubbabel son

[A] **2:46** Alt Hb tradition reads *Shamlai's* [B] **2:50** Alt Hb tradition reads *Meinim's* [C] **2:50** Alt Hb tradition reads *Nephisim's* [D] **2:59** Lit *that the house of their fathers* [E] **2:69** Or *drachmas*, or *darics* [F] **2:69** Lit *5,000 minas* [G] **3:5** Lit *for the new moons* [H] **3:5** Lit *well as those of everyone making a freewill offering to*

Ancient Lebanon

by John Traylor

Like Solomon before him (1Kg 5:6), Zerubbabel arranged for cedar wood to be imported from Lebanon for the construction of the temple (Ezr 3:7). Lebanon is on the eastern end of the Mediterranean Sea immediately west of Syria and north of modern Israel. The land is rectangular in shape and divides itself into four sections running parallel to the coast. From west to east, the sections are the Coastal Plain, the Lebanon Mountains, the Valley of Lebanon, and the Anti-Lebanon Mountains.

Generally speaking, the southern border of Lebanon in the Old Testament era would have run from Mount Carmel on the coast across to Mount Hermon on the southern tip of the Anti-Lebanon Mountains. The northern border would have extended above Arvad on the coast over to the Euphrates River. The Coastal Plain is narrow, never more than about four miles wide with mountain spurs at times pushing into the sea.

Entryway into the Baalbek Temple, which is in the Beqaa Valley of Lebanon. During the Roman period, the city became an important center for the worship of Jupiter, Mercury, and Venus.

PEOPLE AND NAME

The name "Lebanon" comes from a Hebrew verb meaning "be white," probably because of its snow-covered mountain peaks (Jr 18:14).[1] The ancient Lebanese were Canaanites. Sidon, who established the city of Sidon, was Canaan's firstborn (Gn 10:15,19). Canaan was called "the land of merchants" (Ezk 17:4).

The Greeks spoke of Lebanon's Coastal Plain as "Phoenicia" (Ac 11:19) and its inhabitants as "Phoenicians." The Greek term for "Phoenicia" marks the coastal area as a land of dates or palm trees. The Greek term *phoinix* means "date palm" or "red-purple."[2] The Phoenicians were called "purple people," because they extracted and exported purple dye from the murex snail that inhabited the sea's coastal waters. Scholars debate whether the Phoenicians developed the alphabet called by their name, but they certainly distributed the alphabet through trade activities with the world of their day.

MAJOR CITIES

Major Lebanese cities mentioned in the Bible in order of appearance are Sidon, Hamath, Tyre, Zarephath, Arvad, and Gebal (Gn 10:19; Nm 13:21; Jos 19:29; 1Kg 17:9; Ezk 27:8,9). All of these cities were on the Coastal Plain except Hamath, which was in the northern interior on the Orontes River. Hamath was both a city and a regional area (Nm 13:21). Some take Baal-gad (Jos 13:5) to be Baalbek,

Rock strip marking the site of the ancient port of Sidon.

which was a key center of pagan worship in the Valley of Lebanon.[3] As seen in the cases of Hiram king of Tyre, Toi king of Hamath, and Ethbaal king of the Sidonians, these cities were city-states (2Sm 5:11; 8:9; 1Kg 16:31).

Gebal is on the northwest Phoenician coast and was occupied as far back as about 5000 BC.[4] Its inhabitants were called Gebalites (Jos 13:5). Like Tyre and Sidon, Gebal was a thriving maritime center. The Greek name for Gebal was "Byblos," their name for book, because the Gebalites exported the Egyptian papyrus plant, which people used for making books. Ultimately "Byblos" came to mean "Bible," a term for many papyrus books.

CROSSROADS OF INVADING ARMIES

Lebanon was at the crossroads of the ancient world and was the corridor through which world armies marched to and from battles. To celebrate their victories, some kings erected monuments at Dog River Pass, which cuts through the Coastal Plain to the sea about seven miles north of Beirut. Egypt's Ramesses II began the practice around 1240 BC, when he erected a monument on the south face of the pass to celebrate his victory over the Hittites at the battle of Kadesh. In the decade of 680–670 BC, Assyria's King Esarhaddon overran Sidon and Tyre and conquered Egypt. He positioned a monument depicting himself next to that of Ramesses II, apparently to show Assyria as being superior to Egypt. In addition to devastating Tyre, Babylon's King Nebuchadnezzar crushed the Egyptians

Found at Tyre and dated to the first century BC, a two-handled cup with a grapevine design. This piece of lead-glazed earthenware was made from a mold.

Housing area at Tyre containing ruins from many time periods, from the Iron Age through the Byzantine Empire.

Site of the citadel at Hamath. Located between the modern Syrian cities of Homs and Aleppo on the Orontes River, Hamath shows evidence of occupation to the Neolithic Age. At times, Hamath served as the northern boundary of ancient Israel. The Hebrew word *hamath* means "fortress."

and the Assyrians at the battle of Carchemish (605 BC). He erected his monument on the north face of the pass. Cyrus king of Persia conquered Babylon but erected no monument.

RELIGION

As in the case of other Canaanites, the worship of Baal and his female consort, Asherah, dominated the religion of ancient Lebanon. People believed Baal to be the god of fertility. Worshipers along with the priests and priestesses would engage in so-called sacred prostitution to encourage the gods to mate in heaven to produce fertility on earth among human, animal, and vegetable life (Hs 4:13). Worship could involve child sacrifice (Jr 19:5). Baalism multiplied in the northern kingdom when Israel's King Ahab married Jezebel the daughter of Ethbaal, king of the Sidonians (1Kg 16:31). Jezebel attempted to make Baalism the religion of Israel. ✜

[1] William Sanford LaSor, "Lebanon" in *ISBE* vol. 3 (1986), 98. [2] Mario Liverani, "Phoenicia" in *ISBE*, 3:853. [3] "Baal-gad" in *HolBD*, 139. [4] Adrianus Van Selms, "Gebal" in *ISBE*, vol. 2 (1982), 420.

of Shealtiel, Jeshua son of Jozadak, and the rest of their brothers, including the priests, the Levites, and all who had returned to Jerusalem from the captivity, began to build. They appointed the Levites who were twenty years old or more to supervise the work on the LORD's house. 9 Jeshua with his sons and brothers, Kadmiel with his sons, and the sons of Judah[A] and of Henadad, with their sons and brothers, the Levites, joined together to supervise those working on the house of God.

TEMPLE FOUNDATION COMPLETED

10 When the builders had laid the foundation of the LORD's temple, the priests, dressed in their robes and holding trumpets, and the Levites descended from Asaph, holding cymbals, took their positions to praise the LORD, as King David of Israel had instructed. 11 They sang with praise and thanksgiving to the LORD: "For he is good; his faithful love to Israel endures forever." Then all the people gave a great shout of praise to the LORD because the foundation of the LORD's house had been laid.

12 But many of the older priests, Levites, and family heads, who had seen the first temple, wept loudly when they saw the foundation of this temple, but many others shouted joyfully. 13 The people could not distinguish the sound of the joyful shouting from that of the[B] weeping, because the people were shouting so loudly. And the sound was heard far away.

OPPOSITION TO REBUILDING THE TEMPLE

4 When the enemies of Judah and Benjamin heard that the returned exiles[C] were building a temple for the LORD, the God of Israel, 2 they approached Zerubbabel and the family heads and said to them, "Let us build with you, for we also worship your God and have been sacrificing to him[D] since the time King Esar-haddon of Assyria brought us here."

3 But Zerubbabel, Jeshua, and the other heads of Israel's families answered them, "You may have no part with us in building a house for our God, since we alone will build it for the LORD, the God of Israel, as King Cyrus, the king of Persia has commanded us." 4 Then the people who were already in the land[E] discouraged[F] the people of Judah and made them afraid to build. 5 They also bribed officials to act against them to frustrate their plans throughout the reign of King Cyrus of Persia and until the reign of King Darius of Persia.

OPPOSITION TO REBUILDING THE CITY

6 At the beginning of the reign of Ahasuerus, the people who were already in the land wrote an accusation against the residents of Judah and Jerusalem. 7 During the time of King Artaxerxes of Persia, Bishlam, Mithredath, Tabeel and the rest of his colleagues wrote to King Artaxerxes. The letter was written in Aramaic and translated.[G]

8 Rehum the chief deputy and Shimshai the scribe wrote a letter to King Artaxerxes concerning Jerusalem as follows:

> 9 From Rehum[H] the chief deputy, Shimshai the scribe, and the rest of their colleagues — the judges and magistrates[I] from Tripolis, Persia, Erech, Babylon, Susa (that is, the people of Elam),[J] 10 and the rest of the peoples whom the great and illustrious Ashurbanipal[K] deported and settled in the cities of Samaria and the region west of the Euphrates River.

11 This is the text of the letter they sent to him:

> To King Artaxerxes from your servants, the men from the region west of the Euphrates River:
>
> 12 Let it be known to the king that the Jews who came from you have returned to us at Jerusalem. They are rebuilding that rebellious and evil city, finishing its walls, and repairing its foundations. 13 Let it now be known to the king that if that city is rebuilt and its walls are finished, they will not pay tribute, duty, or land tax, and the royal revenue[J] will suffer. 14 Since we have taken an oath of loyalty to the king,[L] and it is not right for us to witness his dishonor, we have sent to inform the king 15 that a search should be made in your predecessors' record books. In these record books you will discover and verify that the city is a rebellious city, harmful to kings and provinces. There have been revolts in it since ancient times. That is why this city was destroyed. 16 We advise the king that if this city is rebuilt and its walls are finished, you will not have any possession west of the Euphrates.

ARTAXERXES'S REPLY

17 The king sent a reply to his chief deputy Rehum, Shimshai the scribe, and the rest of their colleagues living in Samaria and elsewhere in the region west of the Euphrates River:

> Greetings.
>
> 18 The letter you sent us has been translated and read[M] in my presence. 19 I issued a decree and a search was conducted. It was discovered that

[A] **3:9** Or *Hodaviah*; Neh 7:43; 1 Esdras 5:58 [B] **3:13** Lit *the people* [C] **4:1** Lit *the sons of the exile* [D] **4:2** Alt Hb tradition reads *have not been sacrificing* [E] **4:4** Lit *people of the land*, also in v. 6 [F] **4:4** Lit *weakened the hands of* [G] **4:7** Ezr 4:8–6:18 is written in Aramaic. [H] **4:9** Lit *Then Rehum* [I] **4:9** Or *ambassadors* [J] **4:9,13** Aramaic obscure [K] **4:10** Lit *Osnappar* [L] **4:14** Lit *have eaten the salt of the palace* [M] **4:18** Or *been read clearly*

this city has had uprisings against kings since
ancient times, and there have been rebellions
and revolts in it. 20 Powerful kings have also
ruled over Jerusalem and exercised authority
over the whole region west of the Euphrates
River, and tribute, duty, and land tax were paid to
them. 21 Therefore, issue an order for these men
to stop, so that this city will not be rebuilt until
a further decree has been pronounced by me.
22 See that you not neglect this matter. Otherwise,
the damage will increase and the royal interests[A]
will suffer.

23 As soon as the text of King Artaxerxes's letter
was read to Rehum, Shimshai the scribe, and their
colleagues, they immediately went to the Jews in
Jerusalem and forcibly stopped them.

REBUILDING OF THE TEMPLE RESUMED

24 Now the construction of God's house in Jerusalem
had stopped and remained at a standstill until the
second year of the reign of King Darius of Persia.
5 1 But when the prophets Haggai and Zechariah
son of Iddo prophesied to the Jews who were in
Judah and Jerusalem, in the name of the God of Israel
who was over them, 2 Zerubbabel son of Shealtiel and
Jeshua son of Jozadak began to rebuild God's house
in Jerusalem. The prophets of God were with them,
helping them.
3 At that time Tattenai the governor of the region
west of the Euphrates River, Shethar-bozenai, and
their colleagues came to the Jews and asked, "Who
gave you the order to rebuild this temple and finish
this structure?"[B] 4 They also asked them, "What are
the names of the workers[C] who are constructing this
building?" 5 But God was watching[D] over the Jewish
elders. These men wouldn't stop them until a report
was sent to Darius, so that they could receive written
instructions about this matter.

THE LETTER TO DARIUS

6 This is the text of the letter that Tattenai the governor of the region west of the Euphrates River, Shethar-bozenai, and their colleagues, the officials in the
region, sent to King Darius. 7 They sent him a report,
written as follows:

To King Darius:

All greetings.

8 Let it be known to the king that we went to the
house of the great God in the province of Judah.
It is being built with cut[E] stones, and its beams
are being set in the walls. This work is being
done diligently and succeeding through the
people's efforts. 9 So we questioned the elders
and asked, "Who gave you the order to rebuild
this temple and finish this structure?" 10 We also
asked them for their names, so that we could
write down the names of their leaders for your
information.

11 This is the reply they gave us:

We are the servants of the God of the heavens
and earth, and we are rebuilding the temple that
was built many years ago, which a great king of
Israel built and finished. 12 But since our ancestors angered the God of the heavens, he handed
them over to King Nebuchadnezzar of Babylon,
the Chaldean, who destroyed this temple and
deported the people to Babylon. 13 However, in the
first year of King Cyrus of Babylon, he issued a
decree to rebuild the house of God. 14 He also took
from the temple in Babylon the gold and silver
articles of God's house that Nebuchadnezzar had
taken from the temple in Jerusalem and carried
them to the temple in Babylon. He released them
from the temple in Babylon to a man named
Sheshbazzar, the governor by the appointment
of King Cyrus. 15 Cyrus told him, "Take these articles, put them in the temple in Jerusalem, and let
the house of God be rebuilt on its original site."
16 Then this same Sheshbazzar came and laid the
foundation of God's house in Jerusalem. It has
been under construction from that time until
now, but it has not been completed.

17 So if it pleases the king, let a search of the
royal archives[F] in Babylon be conducted to see
if it is true that a decree was issued by King
Cyrus to rebuild the house of God in Jerusalem.
Let the king's decision regarding this matter be
sent to us.

DARIUS'S SEARCH

6 King Darius gave the order, and they searched in
the library of Babylon in the archives.[G] 2 But it was
in the fortress of Ecbatana in the province of Media
that a scroll was found with this record written on it:
3 In the first year of King Cyrus, he issued a decree concerning the house of God in Jerusalem:

Let the house be rebuilt as a place for offering
sacrifices, and let its original foundations be

[A] **4:22** Lit *the kings* [B] **5:3** Or *finish its furnishings*, also in v. 9 [C] **5:4** One Aramaic ms, LXX, Syr; MT reads *Then we told them exactly what the names of the men were* [D] **5:5** Lit *But the eye of their God was* [E] **5:8** Or *huge* [F] **5:17** Lit *treasure house* [G] **6:1** Lit *Babylon where the treasures were stored*

Zerubbabel's Temple

by Conn Davis

The pinnacle of the temple at Jerusalem as seen from the southwest across the Kidron Valley. The marked change in the style of stonework along this vertical line clearly shows the smooth, precisely cut stones of Herod's extension to the temple platform on the southwest. The rougher, more pronounced stones along the wall to the north most likely are stones dating to Solomon's time that were reset by Zerubbabel after the Israelites' return from exile. This corner is called Zerubbabel's Marking.

ISRAEL'S FIRST TEMPLE

King Solomon completed the first temple for worship in ancient Israel about 960 BC. He established the temple when the monarchy and the nation were united and mighty. Solomon's construction was remarkable for the thousands of workers involved in seven years of building activity. The temple was not only the national worship center but served as the most visible symbol of divine blessings upon the government.

The temple remained central to Jewish worship, even into the time of the divided monarchy. Worship in this first temple was inconsistent, though. Some kings refused to reverence the Lord.

This magnificent and luxurious temple existed for nearly four centuries until the Babylonian destruction of 586 BC. Nebuchadnezzar and his army burned this temple to the ground and took all the precious metal vessels and contents to Babylonia.

Forty-seven years later, the Persian Empire replaced Babylonia as the dominant world power in 539 BC. The Persians, much like the Greeks and Romans after them, governed with benevolent style. They instituted progressive reforms such as local provincial rule, paved roads, postal service, and coinage. Cyrus II, the first Persian king, issued a famous proclamation, which was recorded in cuneiform on the Cyrus Cylinder.[1] This edict allowed the return of the Jews from exile to Jerusalem to rebuild their temple (2Ch 36:22–23; Ezr 1:1–4). A second proclamation (520 BC), this one by Darius the Great, confirmed and sustained the initial decree of Cyrus. Moreover, Darius commanded Persian political officials in the province to support the rebuilding efforts of the temple (Ezr 6).

ISRAEL'S SECOND TEMPLE

Because of Zerubbabel's leadership role in the reconstruction project (Hg 1:14), this second house of worship came to be called Zerubbabel's temple. It required four years to complete. The project had the unusual support of the Persian rulers plus two prominent Old Testament prophets, Haggai and Zechariah.

The return of almost fifty thousand Jews (Ezr 2:64–65) marked the first time in recorded history that a conquered people had survived captivity and the loss of their homeland.[2] With unprecedented legal, financial, and moral support from Persian leaders, the Jews began to renew themselves in nation building.

The material wealth and economic prosperity of Solomon's golden age were replaced by severe economic and social conditions after the 586 BC destruction of Jerusalem. This affected the building project. The second temple lacked the impressive quality and grandeur of the first. Nevertheless, masons and carpenters used large cuts of limestone rock and cedar wood to complete their task (6:4). The stonemasons relied on hammers and wooden pegs to break the rocks from quarries. They made individual building stones using picks.[3] When the cut stones and cedar lumber were ready, skilled laborers from the Levites, including the clans of Jeshua, Kadmiel, Judah, and Henadad (3:9), rebuilt the new temple. Using Levites for this task was not without precedent. The Levites had historically been responsible for the operation and maintenance of the temple. From the time of David and Solomon, a large group of Levites had been assigned to temple construction.

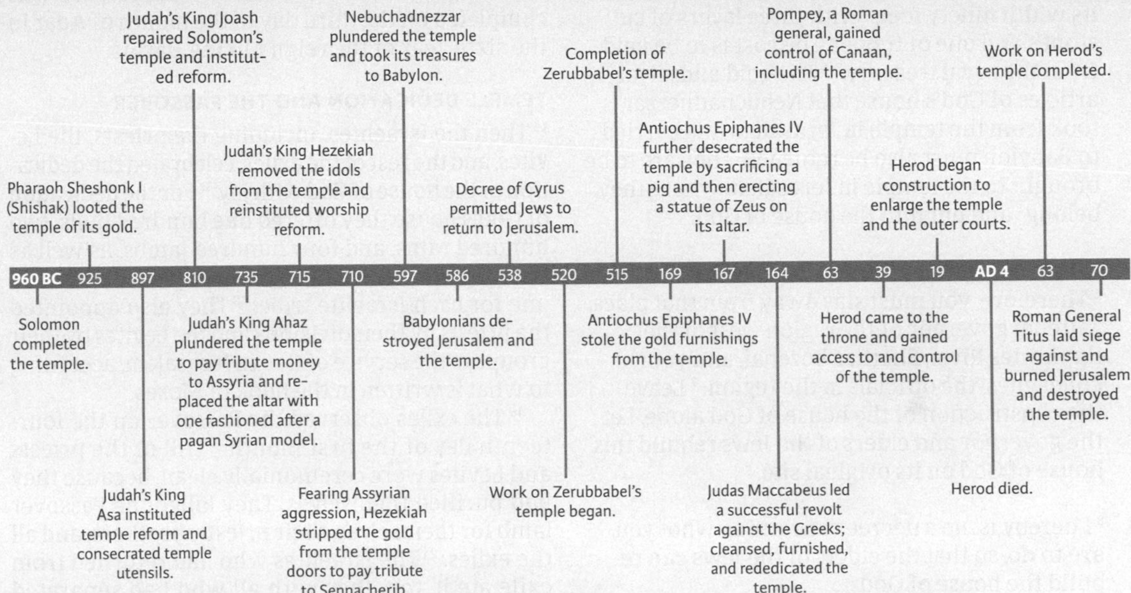

Although not as impressive as Solomon's temple, Zerubbabel's temple was not void of splendor. Greek and Roman contacts and references provide historical evidence that the second temple was well constructed and rich in its contents.[4] Cyrus authorized the release of all the gold and silver vessels Nebuchadnezzar had stolen. Thus the returning Jews brought with them to Jerusalem and to the temple more than five thousand precious metal vessels, including chests, bowls, lampstands, and knives (1:9–11).

Zerubbabel's temple followed the basic rectangular design of Solomon's temple with three areas: the vestibule and entrance, the holy area or sanctuary, and the most holy place where the ark had resided. The first and second temples essentially had the same interior dimensions: sixty cubits long by thirty cubits high by twenty cubits wide, approximately one hundred-by-fifty-by-thirty-five feet. Without the existence of the ark, the symbol of the dwelling presence of God, worship focus shifted to the large sanctuary area, the holy area, known in Hebrew as the *heikal*.

In 515 BC—seventy years after the destruction of Solomon's temple—the Jews completed in Jerusalem a new temple. The restored nation of Jews had their worship center. Their faith and devotion to the God of their covenant were rekindled. Zerubbabel's temple endured for almost five hundred years until Herod the Great rebuilt it as the third temple in 19 BC. ✠

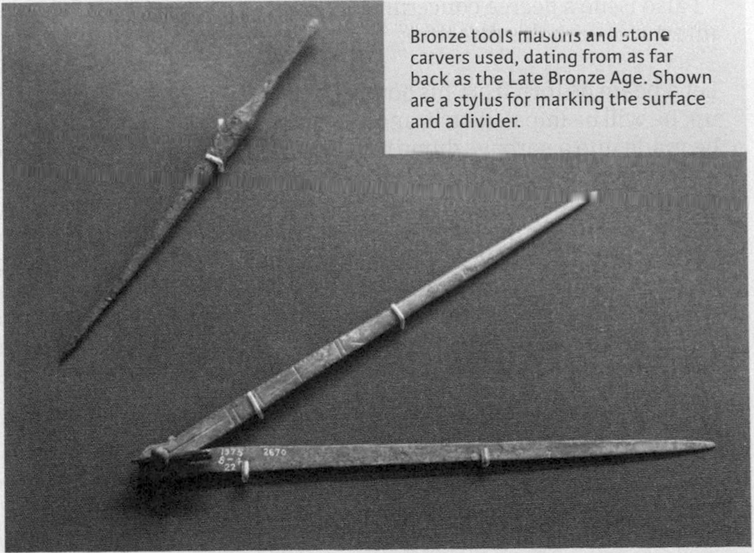
Bronze tools masons and stone carvers used, dating from as far back as the Late Bronze Age. Shown are a stylus for marking the surface and a divider.

---

[1] Jack Finegan, *Light from the Ancient Past: The Archaeological Background of the Hebrew-Christian Religion*, 2nd ed. (Princeton: Princeton University Press, 1959), 218, fig. 86. For a translation of the Cyrus Cylinder text, see *ANET*, 315–16. [2] *A Historical Atlas of the Jewish People*, ed. Eli Barnavi (New York: Alfred Knopf, 1992), 28. [3] *Nelson's New Illustrated Bible Dictionary*, ed. Ronald Youngblood (Nashville: Thomas Nelson, 1995), 921. [4] Roland de Vaux, *Ancient Israel* (New York: McGraw-Hill, 1965), 324–25.

retained.[A] Its height is to be ninety feet[B] and its width ninety feet, 4 with three layers of cut[C] stones and one of timber. The cost is to be paid from the royal treasury.[D] 5 The gold and silver articles of God's house that Nebuchadnezzar took from the temple in Jerusalem and carried to Babylon must also be returned. They are to be brought to the temple in Jerusalem where they belong[E] and put into the house of God.

DARIUS'S DECREE

6 Therefore, you must stay away from that place, Tattenai governor of the region west of the Euphrates River, Shethar-bozenai, and your[F] colleagues, the officials in the region. 7 Leave the construction of the house of God alone. Let the governor and elders of the Jews rebuild this house of God on its original site.

8 I hereby issue a decree concerning what you are to do, so that the elders of the Jews can rebuild the house of God:

The cost is to be paid in full to these men out of the royal revenues from the taxes of the region west of the Euphrates River, so that the work will not stop. 9 Whatever is needed — young bulls, rams, and lambs for burnt offerings to the God of the heavens, or wheat, salt, wine, and oil, as requested by the priests in Jerusalem — let it be given to them every day without fail, 10 so that they can offer sacrifices of pleasing aroma to the God of the heavens and pray for the life of the king and his sons.

11 I also issue a decree concerning any man who interferes with this directive:

Let a beam be torn from his house and raised up; he will be impaled on it, and his house will be made into a garbage dump because of this offense. 12 May the God who caused his name to dwell there overthrow any king or people who dares[G] to harm or interfere with this house of God in Jerusalem. I, Darius, have issued the decree. Let it be carried out diligently.

13 Then Tattenai governor of the region west of the Euphrates River, Shethar-bozenai, and their colleagues diligently carried out what King Darius had decreed. 14 So the Jewish elders continued successfully with the building under the prophesying of Haggai the prophet and Zechariah son of Iddo. They finished the building according to the command of the God of Israel and the decrees of Cyrus, Darius, and King Artaxerxes of Persia. 15 This house was completed on the third day of the month of Adar in the sixth year of the reign of King Darius.

TEMPLE DEDICATION AND THE PASSOVER

16 Then the Israelites, including the priests, the Levites, and the rest of the exiles, celebrated the dedication of the house of God with joy. 17 For the dedication of God's house they offered one hundred bulls, two hundred rams, and four hundred lambs, as well as twelve male goats as a sin offering for all Israel — one for each Israelite tribe. 18 They also appointed the priests by their divisions and the Levites by their groups to the service of God in Jerusalem, according to what is written in the book of Moses.

19 The exiles observed the Passover on the fourteenth day of the first month. 20 All of the priests and Levites were ceremonially clean, because they had purified themselves. They killed the Passover lamb for themselves, their priestly brothers, and all the exiles. 21 The Israelites who had returned from exile ate it, together with all who had separated themselves from the uncleanness of the Gentiles of the land[H] in order to worship the LORD, the God of Israel. 22 They observed the Festival of Unleavened Bread for seven days with joy, because the LORD had made them joyful, having changed the Assyrian king's attitude toward them, so that he supported them[I] in the work on the house of the God of Israel.

EZRA'S ARRIVAL

7 After these events, during the reign of King Artaxerxes of Persia, Ezra —

Seraiah's son, Azariah's son,
Hilkiah's son, 2 Shallum's son,
Zadok's son, Ahitub's son,
3 Amariah's son, Azariah's son,
Meraioth's son, 4 Zerahiah's son,
Uzzi's son, Bukki's son,
5 Abishua's son, Phinehas's son,
Eleazar's son, the chief priest
Aaron's son

6 — came up from Babylon. He was a scribe skilled in the law of Moses, which the LORD, the God of Israel, had given. The king had granted him everything he requested because the hand of the LORD his God was on him. 7 Some of the Israelites, priests, Levites, singers, gatekeepers, and temple servants accompanied him to Jerusalem in the seventh year of King Artaxerxes.

[A] **6:3** Lit *be brought forth* [B] **6:3** Lit *60 cubits* [C] **6:4** Or *huge* [D] **6:4** Lit *the king's house* [E] **6:5** Lit *Jerusalem, to its place,* [F] **6:6** Lit *their* [G] **6:12** Lit *who stretches out its hand* [H] **6:21** Lit *land to them* [I] **6:22** Lit *strengthened their hands*

8 Ezra[A] came to Jerusalem in the fifth month, during the seventh year of the king. 9 He began the journey from Babylon on the first day of the first month
and arrived in Jerusalem on the first day of the fifth
month since the gracious hand of his God was on him.
10 Now Ezra had determined in his heart to study the
law of the LORD, obey it, and teach its statutes and
ordinances in Israel.

LETTER FROM ARTAXERXES

11 This is the text of the letter King Artaxerxes gave to
Ezra the priest and scribe, an expert in matters of the
LORD's commands and statutes for Israel:[B]
12 Artaxerxes, king of kings, to Ezra the priest, an
expert in the law of the God of the heavens:

Greetings.

13 I issue a decree that any of the Israelites in my
kingdom, including their priests and Levites,
who want to go to Jerusalem, may go with you.
14 You are sent by the king and his seven counselors to evaluate Judah and Jerusalem according to the law of your God, which is in your
possession. 15 You are also to bring the silver and
gold the king and his counselors have willingly given to the God of Israel, whose dwelling is
in Jerusalem, 16 and all the silver and gold you
receive throughout the province of Babylon,
together with the freewill offerings given by
the people and the priests to the house of their
God in Jerusalem. 17 Then you are to be diligent
to buy with this money bulls, rams, and lambs,
along with their grain and drink offerings, and
offer them on the altar at the house of your God
in Jerusalem. 18 You may do whatever seems
best to you and your brothers with the rest of
the silver and gold, according to the will of your
God. 19 Deliver to the God of Jerusalem all the
articles given to you for the service of the house
of your God. 20 You may use the royal treasury[C]
to pay for anything else needed for the house of
your God.

21 I, King Artaxerxes, issue a decree to all the
treasurers in the region west of the Euphrates
River:

Whatever Ezra the priest, an expert in the law
of the God of the heavens, asks of you must be
provided in full, 22 up to 7,500 pounds[D] of silver,
500 bushels[E] of wheat, 550 gallons[F] of wine, 550
gallons of oil, and salt without limit.[G] 23 Whatever is commanded by the God of the heavens
must be done diligently for the house of the God
of the heavens, so that wrath will not fall on the
realm of the king and his sons. 24 Be advised that
you do not have authority to impose tribute,
duty, and land tax on any priests, Levites, singers,
doorkeepers, temple servants, or other servants
of this house of God.

25 And you, Ezra, according to[H] God's wisdom
that you possess, appoint magistrates and judges to judge all the people in the region west of
the Euphrates who know the laws of your God
and to teach anyone who does not know them.
26 Anyone who does not keep the law of your
God and the law of the king, let the appropriate judgment be executed against him, whether
death, banishment, confiscation of property, or
imprisonment.

27 Blessed be the LORD, the God of our ancestors,
who has put it into the king's mind to glorify the
house of the LORD in Jerusalem, 28 and who has shown
favor to me before the king, his counselors, and all
his powerful officers. So I took courage because I
was strengthened by the hand of the LORD my God,[I]
and I gathered Israelite leaders to return with me.

[A] **7:8** LXX, Syr, Vg read *They* [B] **7:11** Ezr 7:12–26 is written in Aramaic. [C] **7:20** Lit *the king's house* [D] **7:22** Lit *100 talents* [E] **7:22** Lit *100 cors* [F] **7:22** Lit *100 baths* [G] **7:22** Lit *without instruction* [H] **7:25** Lit *to your* [I] **7:28** Lit *because the hand of the LORD my God was on me*

DIGGING DEEPER *Silver Bowl of Artaxerxes I*

Royal families in the ancient Near East would customarily fashion special tablewares that would help demonstrate the nation's wealth and power. The silver bowl of Persian King Artaxerxes I was likely created from a single piece of silver, and it served as part of his royal decorations. Artaxerxes I reigned 464–424 BC and is mentioned in Ezra 7–8. The cuneiform inscription visible around the rim lists additional biblical figures such as Xerxes (also known as Ahasuerus; Est 1:1–19) and Darius I (522–486 BC) mentioned in the books of Ezra (4:5,24), Haggai (1:1,15; 2:10), and Zechariah (1:1,7; 7:1). The cuneiform inscription translates as "Artaxerxes, the great king, king of kings, king of countries, son of Xerxes the king, of Xerxes [who was] son of Darius the king, the Achaemenian, in whose house this silver drinking-cup [was] made." Additionally, several tombs of Persian rulers such as Cyrus the Great (Is 45:1) and Artaxerxes I have been located in various areas of modern Iran, confirming the Bible's accuracy.

Who Was Artaxerxes?

by T. Van McClain

In one of the most famous battles of ancient history, Xerxes defeated the Spartans of Greece at the battle of Thermopylae in 480 BC. This Xerxes was likely the king of Persia who was the husband of the biblical Esther. Xerxes had another wife named Amestris. Queen Amestris was probably the same as Vashti in the book of Esther, since the word Vashti can mean "the best" or "the beloved."[1] The third son of Xerxes and Amestris was named Artaxerxes I Longimanus.

Artaxerxes I Longimanus was the king of Persia from 465 to 424 BC. Artaxerxes means "kingdom of righteousness" or "kingdom of justice" and Longimanus means "longhanded."[2] The Greek scholar Plutarch said Artaxerxes's right hand was longer than his left. Plutarch also claimed that Artaxerxes was "preeminent among the kings of Persia for gentleness and magnanimity."[3] Artaxerxes's character contrasts with that of his parents—whose reputations for immorality and brutality long outlived them. Artaxerxes is important to Bible students because of his connection to Ezra and Nehemiah. He permitted Ezra to leave Persia and visit Jerusalem in 458 BC, and he authorized his cupbearer Nehemiah for a mission to Jerusalem in 445 BC.[4]

THE RISE OF ARTAXERXES I

Artaxerxes may have shown kindness to Ezra and Nehemiah, but his reign began in intrigue and assassination. The historical sources relate that a powerful royal official named Artabanus had King Xerxes killed in his bedchamber and blamed it on Darius, the eldest son of Xerxes. After some months, the eighteen-year-old Artaxerxes then killed Darius. Eventually Artaxerxes determined that Artabanus was behind the assassination plot and put him to death also. Artaxerxes would later defeat another older brother, Hystaspes, in battle. Hystaspes was a satrap or governor in Bactria who rebelled against his brother's rule.[5]

THE REIGN OF ARTAXERXES I

With a young king on the throne and his army occupied or having been weakened with threats to the kingdom by Hystaspes, 461–460 BC seemed a propitious time to the Egyptians to rebel against Persian rule. The Persians would suffer reversals at the beginning of the war; completely subduing Egyptian forces would take about ten years—with Athens and its navy as an ally to the Egyptians in the rebellion.

The accusations of the foes of the Jews, as described in Ezra 4:7–23, would have been of particular concern to the Persian

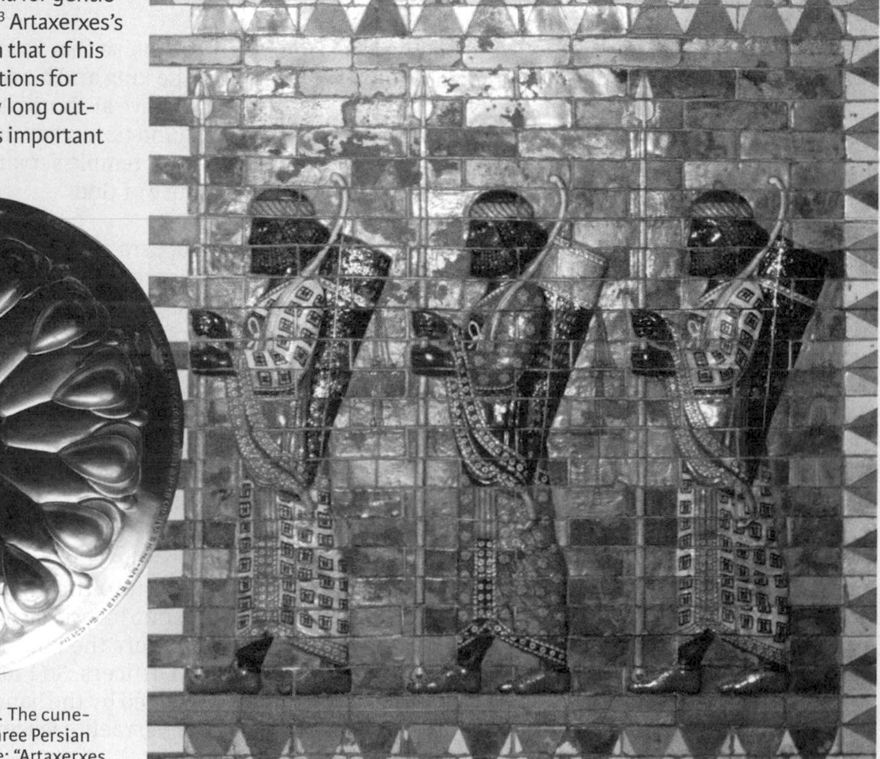

Silver bowl; fifth century BC. The cuneiform inscription refers to three Persian kings mentioned in the Bible: "Artaxerxes, the great king, king of kings, king of countries, son of Xerxes the king, of Xerxes, son of Darius the king, the Achaemenian, in whose house this drinking cup was made."

From the palace at Susa, relief of a bodyguard of the Persian King Artaxerxes II; dated 404 to 358 BC.

monarch given the fact that Persian forces would have to travel through Israel to quell the rebellion in Egypt. People accused the Jews of being rebellious and evil; they further claimed that tax revenue would suffer if the Jews completed their rebuilding of the city of Jerusalem and its walls. Artaxerxes then stopped the rebuilding of the city.

Eventually Artaxerxes allowed the Jews under Ezra to return to Israel with the king's blessing. Perhaps the king realized that any kindness he showed to Israel would result in a loyal buffer state between his forces and the rebellious Egyptians.[6] Of course, the real reason the king looked favorably on Ezra and his mission to Israel was because God's hand was on Ezra (Ezr 7:6).

The Persian general Megabyzus, who had ended the rebellion of Egypt, was satrap of Syria for a time but eventually rebelled against Artaxerxes. He was finally reconciled to the Persian monarch. Later, though, Artaxerxes sent Megabyzus into exile for shooting a lion before the king could do so while the two were on a hunting expedition. After some time in exile, he would again be restored to favor.[7]

By the time Artaxerxes granted Nehemiah the liberty to return to Israel in 445 BC, the Egyptian revolt and the subsequent rebellion of Megabyzus would have long been over. Moreover, the war between Persia and the Greek city-states apparently came to a halt or truce about 449 BC with the Peace of Callias.[8]

In about 425–424 BC, Artaxerxes died of natural causes—which was a rarity among Persian kings.[9] The relative stability and peacefulness Artaxerxes exhibited in his reign are in accord with what the Scriptures say about him. If he was as generous to his other subjects as he was to the Jews, then one should not be surprised that he had such little opposition to his reign.

One should also not be surprised at Artaxerxes's generosity as he encouraged Ezra and Nehemiah with protection and financial support. Both biblical and extrabiblical sources indicate Persian kings were tolerant of other religions, "actively supported the temple-worship of the gods of their subjects, [and] contributed to the building of their temples."[10] ✣

Alabaster vase that honors King Xerxes I; dated 485 to 465 BC. Inscription says: "Xerxes, the Great King." The inscription is in Egyptian, Old Persian, Elamite, and Neo-Babylonian languages and written in hieroglyphics and cuneiform.

---

[1] G. H. Wilson, "Vashti" in *ISBE*, vol. 4 (1988), 966. [2] "Artaxerxes" in *HIBD*, 120. [3] Plutarch, *Artaxerxes* 1. [4] This writer presupposes the traditional date of the arrival of Ezra and Nehemiah in Israel. See Eugene H. Merrill, *Kingdom of Priests: A History of Old Testament Israel*, 2nd ed. (Grand Rapids: Baker Academic, 2008), 514–18. [5] Edwin M. Yamauchi, *Persia and the Bible* (Grand Rapids: Baker, 1990), 248. [6] Yamauchi, *Persia*, 250, n. 39. [7] Yamauchi, *Persia*, 250. [8] Yamauchi, *Persia*, 252. [9] Yamauchi, *Persia*, 278. [10] G. B. Gray and M. Cary, "The Reign of Darius" in *The Persian Empire and the West*, vol. 4 in CAH, 187.

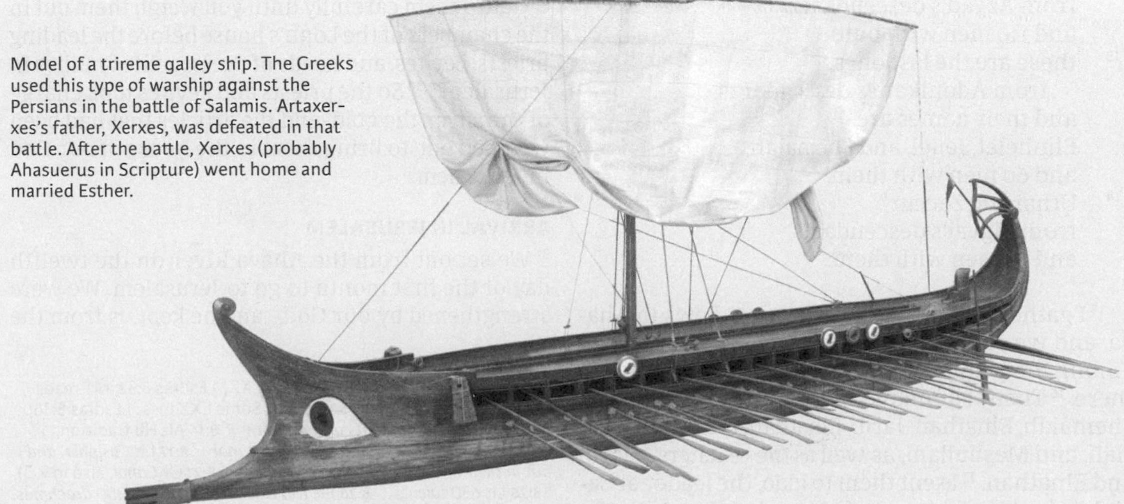

Model of a trireme galley ship. The Greeks used this type of warship against the Persians in the battle of Salamis. Artaxerxes's father, Xerxes, was defeated in that battle. After the battle, Xerxes (probably Ahasuerus in Scripture) went home and married Esther.

THOSE RETURNING WITH EZRA

8 These are the family heads and the genealogical
records of those who returned with me from
Babylon during the reign of King Artaxerxes:

2 Gershom, from Phinehas's descendants;
Daniel, from Ithamar's descendants;
Hattush, from David's descendants,
3 who was of Shecaniah's descendants;
Zechariah, from Parosh's descendants,
and 150 men[A] with him who were registered
by genealogy;
4 Eliehoenai son of Zerahiah
from Pahath-moab's descendants,
and 200 men with him;
5 Shecaniah[B] son of Jahaziel
from Zattu's descendants,
and 300 men with him;
6 Ebed son of Jonathan
from Adin's descendants,
and 50 men with him;
7 Jeshaiah son of Athaliah
from Elam's descendants,
and 70 men with him;
8 Zebadiah son of Michael
from Shephatiah's descendants,
and 80 men with him;
9 Obadiah son of Jehiel
from Joab's descendants,
and 218 men with him;
10 Shelomith[C] son of Josiphiah
from Bani's descendants,
and 160 men with him;
11 Zechariah son of Bebai
from Bebai's descendants,
and 28 men with him;
12 Johanan son of Hakkatan
from Azgad's descendants,
and 110 men with him;
13 these are the last ones,
from Adonikam's descendants,
and their names are
Eliphelet, Jeuel, and Shemaiah,
and 60 men with them;
14 Uthai and Zaccur[D]
from Bigvai's descendants,
and 70 men with them.

15 I gathered them at the river[E] that flows to Ahava, and we camped there for three days. I searched
among the people and priests, but found no Levites
there. 16 Then I summoned the leaders: Eliezer, Ariel,
Shemaiah, Elnathan, Jarib, Elnathan, Nathan, Zechariah, and Meshullam, as well as the teachers Joiarib
and Elnathan. 17 I sent them to Iddo, the leader at Casiphia, with a message for[F] him and his brothers, the
temple servants at Casiphia, that they should bring
us ministers for the house of our God. 18 Since the
gracious hand of our God was on us, they brought us
Sherebiah — a man of insight from the descendants
of Mahli, a descendant of Levi son of Israel — along
with his sons and brothers, 18 men, 19 plus Hashabiah,
along with Jeshaiah, from the descendants of Merari, and his brothers and their sons, 20 men. 20 There
were also 220 of the temple servants, who had been
appointed by David and the leaders for the work of
the Levites. All were identified by name.

PREPARING TO RETURN

21 I proclaimed a fast by the Ahava River,[G] so that we
might humble ourselves before our God and ask him
for a safe journey for us, our dependents, and all our
possessions. 22 I did this because I was ashamed to ask
the king for infantry and cavalry to protect us from enemies during the journey, since we had told him, "The
hand of our God is gracious to all who seek him, but
his fierce anger is against all who abandon him." 23 So
we fasted and pleaded with our God about this, and he
was receptive to our prayer.

24 I selected twelve of the leading priests, along
with Sherebiah, Hashabiah, and ten of their brothers. 25 I weighed out to them the silver, the gold, and
the articles — the contribution for the house of our
God that the king, his counselors, his leaders, and
all the Israelites who were present had offered. 26 I
weighed out to them 24 tons[H] of silver, silver articles weighing 7,500 pounds,[I] 7,500 pounds of gold,
27 twenty gold bowls worth a thousand gold coins,[J]
and two articles of fine gleaming bronze, as valuable
as gold. 28 Then I said to them, "You are holy to the
LORD, and the articles are holy. The silver and gold are
a freewill offering to the LORD God of your ancestors.
29 Guard them carefully until you weigh them out in
the chambers of the LORD's house before the leading
priests, Levites, and heads of the Israelite families in
Jerusalem." 30 So the priests and Levites took charge
of the silver, the gold, and the articles that had been
weighed out, to bring them to the house of our God
in Jerusalem.

ARRIVAL IN JERUSALEM

31 We set out from the Ahava River on the twelfth
day of the first month to go to Jerusalem. We were
strengthened by our God,[K] and he kept us from the

[A] **8:3** Or *males*; also in vv. 4–14 [B] **8:5** LXX, 1 Esdras 8:32; MT reads *the descendants of Shecaniah* [C] **8:10** Some LXX mss, 1 Esdras 8:36; MT reads *the descendants of Shelomith* [D] **8:14** Alt Hb tradition, some LXX mss read *Zabud* [E] **8:15** Or *canal* [F] **8:17** Lit *Casiphia, and I put in their mouth the words to speak to* [G] **8:21** Or *Canal*, also in v. 31 [H] **8:26** Lit *650 talents* [I] **8:26** Lit *100 talents* [J] **8:27** Or *1,000 drachmas*, or *1,000 darics* [K] **8:31** Lit *The hand of our God was on us*

grasp of the enemy and from ambush along the way.
32 So we arrived at Jerusalem and rested there for
three days. 33 On the fourth day the silver, the gold,
and the articles were weighed out in the house of
our God into the care of the priest Meremoth son
of Uriah. Eleazar son of Phinehas was with him. The
Levites Jozabad son of Jeshua and Noadiah son of
Binnui were also with them. 34 Everything was verified by number and weight, and the total weight was
recorded at that time.

35 The exiles who had returned from the captivity
offered burnt offerings to the God of Israel: twelve
bulls for all Israel, ninety-six rams, and seventy-sev-
en lambs, along with twelve male goats as a sin offering. All this was a burnt offering for the LORD.
36 They also delivered the king's edicts to the royal
satraps and governors of the region west of the Euphrates, so that they would support the people and
the house of God.

ISRAEL'S INTERMARRIAGE

9 After these things had been done, the leaders
approached me and said, "The people of Israel, the priests, and the Levites have not separated
themselves from the surrounding peoples whose
detestable practices are like those of the Canaanites,
Hethites, Perizzites, Jebusites, Ammonites, Moabites, Egyptians, and Amorites. 2 Indeed, the Israelite
men[A] have taken some of their daughters as wives
for themselves and their sons, so that the holy seed
has become mixed with the surrounding peoples.
The leaders[B] and officials have taken the lead in
this unfaithfulness!" 3 When I heard this report, I
tore my tunic and robe, pulled out some of the hair
from my head and beard, and sat down devastated.

EZRA'S CONFESSION

4 Everyone who trembled at the words of the God of
Israel gathered around me, because of the unfaithfulness of the exiles, while I sat devastated until the
evening offering. 5 At the evening offering, I got up
from my time of humiliation, with my tunic and robe
torn. Then I fell on my knees and spread out my hands
to the LORD my God. 6 And I said:

> My God, I am ashamed and embarrassed to lift
> my face toward you, my God, because our iniq-
> uities are higher than our heads and our guilt
> is as high as the heavens. 7 Our guilt has been
> terrible from the days of our ancestors until the
> present. Because of our iniquities we have been
> handed over, along with our kings and priests,
> to the surrounding kings, and to the sword,
> captivity, plundering, and open shame, as it
> is today. 8 But now, for a brief moment, grace
> has come from the LORD our God to preserve a
> remnant for us and give us a stake in his holy
> place. Even in our slavery, God has given us a
> little relief and light to our eyes. 9 Though we
> are slaves, our God has not abandoned us in
> our slavery. He has extended grace to us in the
> presence of the Persian kings, giving us relief,
> so that we can rebuild the house of our God and
> repair its ruins, to give us a wall in Judah and
> Jerusalem.

10 Now, our God, what can we say in light of[C] this?
For we have abandoned the commands 11 you
gave through your servants the prophets, saying,
"The land you are entering to possess is an impure land. The surrounding peoples have filled it
from end to end with their uncleanness by their
impurity and detestable practices. 12 So do not
give your daughters to their sons in marriage or
take their daughters for your sons. Never pursue their welfare or prosperity, so that you will
be strong, eat the good things of the land, and
leave it as an inheritance to your sons forever."
13 After all that has happened to us because of
our evil deeds and terrible guilt — though you,
our God, have punished us less than our iniquities deserve and have allowed us to survive[D] —
14 should we break your commands again and
intermarry with the peoples who commit these
detestable practices? Wouldn't you become so
angry with us that you would destroy us, leaving neither remnant nor survivor? 15 LORD God
of Israel, you are righteous, for we survive as a
remnant today. Here we are before you with our
guilt, though no one can stand in your presence
because of this.

SENDING AWAY FOREIGN WIVES

10 While Ezra prayed and confessed, weeping and
falling facedown before the house of God, an
extremely large assembly of Israelite men, women,
and children gathered around him. The people also
wept bitterly. 2 Then Shecaniah son of Jehiel, an Elamite, responded to Ezra, "We have been unfaithful to
our God by marrying foreign women from the surrounding peoples, but there is still hope for Israel in
spite of this. 3 Therefore, let's make a covenant before
our God to send away all the foreign wives and their
children, according to the counsel of my lord and of
those who tremble at the command of our God. Let it
be done according to the law. 4 Get up, for this matter
is your responsibility, and we support you. Be strong
and take action!"

[A] **9:2** Lit *they* [B] **9:2** Lit *hand of the leaders* [C] **9:10** Lit *say after*
[D] **9:13** Lit *and gave us a remnant like this*

Ezra: Scribe and Priest

by Robert C. Dunston

Although dating later than Ezra, these split-rib bronze pens were used with carbon ink to write on papyrus, parchment, or wooden leaf tablets. More common would have been pens made of reed, quill, bone, or ivory.

The pottery inkwell held ink made of one part gum water to three parts carbon black. Gum-based inks do better on papyrus; gallic inks are better for parchment.

Although a priest, Ezra served as a scribe. Scribes were court officials who held varying levels of authority. Artaxerxes I of Persia appointed Ezra as a scribe and charged him with governing Judah according to God's law (Ezr 7:14,25). Ezra's knowledge of and ability to teach God's law added a dimension to the term *scribe* that became dominant in later Judaism. A Jewish scribe possessed knowledge of God's law and the ability to interpret and apply the law in any situation. Ezra was described as "skilled" (v. 6), a term originally referring to a scribe's ability to write quickly and accurately but later used to refer to a scribe's wisdom and experience. While probably not the first in the long line of Jewish scholars who copied, studied, interpreted, and taught the law, Ezra certainly was one of the greatest Jewish scribes.[1]

EZRA'S TIMES

The Persian King Artaxerxes I sent Ezra to Jerusalem. Artabanus, who likely served as captain of the royal guard, had assassinated Artaxerxes's father, Xerxes I, in August 465 BC and then accused Xerxes's eldest son, Darius, of the murder. Artaxerxes killed Darius, seized the throne, and enjoyed a long rule (464–424 BC). In 460 BC, Egypt, aided by Athens, rebelled against Artaxerxes. Artaxerxes regained control of Egypt in 454 BC, but he was forced to submit to a humiliating treaty with the Greeks in 448 BC.[2]

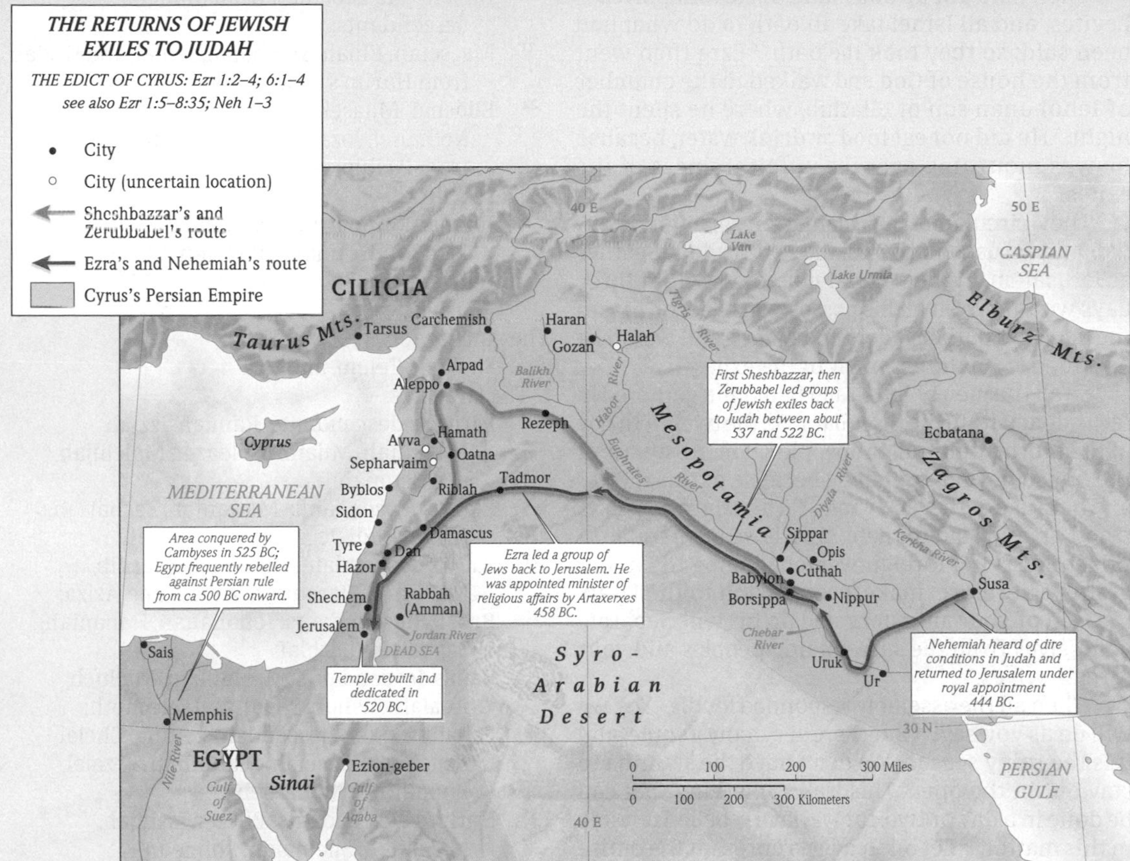

Conditions in Judah remained difficult. Judah had never recovered from the decimation of its economy and population resulting from the Babylonian conquest. Although some Jews had returned from Babylonian exile and joined the descendants of those who had never left Judah, the population in Jerusalem and Judah remained small (Neh 11:1–2). Jerusalem's wall was in disrepair with gaping holes. Although worship continued in the rebuilt temple, the people were dispirited; faithfulness to God seemed a low priority. For most, making a living proved difficult. The people needed hope and direction.

With unrest in Egypt, Artaxerxes needed to keep adjoining provinces, such as Judah, satisfied, loyal, and peaceful. Sending Ezra to Jerusalem to support worship and to ensure the Jews followed their law worked to Artaxerxes's advantage.[3] In addition, the Jews needed someone to renew their faith and spirit. God worked through Ezra to extend Artaxerxes's role and to call God's people to faithful obedience. ✣

[1] Joseph Blenkinsopp, *Ezra-Nehemiah*, Old Testament Library (OTL) (Philadelphia: Westminster, 1988), 136–37; Mervin Breneman, *Ezra, Nehemiah, Esther*, vol. 10 in NAC (1993), 127–28; Robert North, "Ezra" in *ABD*, 726; H. G. M. Williamson, *Ezra, Nehemiah*, vol. 19 in WBC (1985), 92. [2] Breneman, *Ezra*, 23; G. Byrns Coleman, "Artaxerxes" in *MDB*, 65. [3] Breneman, *Ezra*, 24; Coleman, "Artaxerxes," 65.

5 Then Ezra got up and made the leading priests,
Levites, and all Israel take an oath to do what had
been said; so they took the oath. 6 Ezra then went
from the house of God and walked to the chamber
of Jehohanan son of Eliashib, where he spent the
night.[A] He did not eat food or drink water, because
he was mourning over the unfaithfulness of the
exiles.

7 They circulated a proclamation throughout Judah and Jerusalem that all the exiles should gather
at Jerusalem. 8 Whoever did not come within three
days would forfeit all his possessions,[B] according to
the decision of the leaders and elders, and would be
excluded from the assembly of the exiles.

9 So all the men of Judah and Benjamin gathered in
Jerusalem within the three days. On the twentieth day
of the ninth month, all the people sat in the square at
the house of God, trembling because of this matter
and because of the heavy rain. 10 Then the priest Ezra
stood up and said to them, "You have been unfaithful by marrying foreign women, adding to Israel's
guilt. 11 Therefore, make a confession to the LORD,
the God of your ancestors, and do his will. Separate
yourselves from the surrounding peoples and your
foreign wives."

12 Then all the assembly responded loudly, "Yes, we
will do as you say! 13 But there are many people, and
it is the rainy season. We don't have the stamina to
stay out in the open. This isn't something that can
be done in a day or two, for we have rebelled terribly
in this matter. 14 Let our leaders represent the entire
assembly. Then let all those in our towns who have
married foreign women come at appointed times,
together with the elders and judges of each town, in
order to avert the fierce anger of our God concerning[C] this matter." 15 Only Jonathan son of Asahel and
Jahzeiah son of Tikvah opposed this, with Meshullam
and Shabbethai the Levite supporting them.

16 The exiles did what had been proposed. The
priest Ezra selected men[D] who were family heads,
all identified by name, to represent[E] their ancestral
families.[F] They convened on the first day of the tenth
month to investigate the matter, 17 and by the first day
of the first month they had dealt with all the men who
had married foreign women.

THOSE MARRIED TO FOREIGN WIVES

18 The following were found to have married foreign
women from the descendants of the priests:
from the descendants of Jeshua son of Jozadak
and his brothers: Maaseiah, Eliezer, Jarib, and
Gedaliah. 19 They pledged[G] to send their wives
away, and being guilty, they offered a ram from
the flock for their guilt;

20 Hanani and Zebadiah from Immer's
descendants;
21 Maaseiah, Elijah, Shemaiah, Jehiel, and Uzziah
from Harim's descendants;
22 Elioenai, Maaseiah, Ishmael,
Nethanel, Jozabad, and Elasah
from Pashhur's descendants.

23 The Levites:
Jozabad, Shimei, Kelaiah (that is Kelita),
Pethahiah, Judah, and Eliezer.

24 The singers:
Eliashib.
The gatekeepers:
Shallum, Telem, and Uri.

25 The Israelites:
Parosh's descendants: Ramiah, Izziah,
Malchijah, Mijamin, Eleazar, Malchijah,[H]
and Benaiah;
26 Elam's descendants: Mattaniah, Zechariah,
Jehiel, Abdi, Jeremoth, and Elijah;
27 Zattu's descendants: Elioenai, Eliashib,
Mattaniah, Jeremoth, Zabad, and Aziza;
28 Bebai's descendants: Jehohanan, Hananiah,
Zabbai, and Athlai;
29 Bani's descendants: Meshullam, Malluch,
Adaiah, Jashub, Sheal, and Jeremoth;
30 Pahath-moab's descendants: Adna, Chelal,
Benaiah, Maaseiah, Mattaniah, Bezalel,
Binnui, and Manasseh;
31 Harim's descendants: Eliezer, Isshijah,
Malchijah, Shemaiah, Shimeon,
32 Benjamin, Malluch, and Shemariah;
33 Hashum's descendants: Mattenai, Mattattah,
Zabad, Eliphelet, Jeremai, Manasseh, and
Shimei;

34 Bani's descendants: Maadai, Amram,
Uel, 35 Benaiah, Bedeiah, Cheluhi, 36 Vaniah,
Meremoth, Eliashib, 37 Mattaniah, Mattenai,
Jaasu, 38 Bani, Binnui, Shimei, 39 Shelemiah,
Nathan, Adaiah, 40 Machnadebai, Shashai,
Sharai, 41 Azarel, Shelemiah, Shemariah,
42 Shallum, Amariah, and Joseph;

43 Nebo's descendants: Jeiel, Mattithiah, Zabad,
Zebina, Jaddai, Joel, and Benaiah.

44 All of these had married foreign women, and some
of the wives had given birth to children.

[A] **10:6** 1 Esdras 9:2, Syr; MT, Vg read *he went* [B] **10:8** Lit *would set apart all his possessions for destruction* [C] **10:14** Some Hb mss, LXX, Vg; other Hb mss read *until* [D] **10:16** 1 Esdras 9:16, Syr; MT, Vg read *priest and men were selected* [E] **10:16** Lit *name, for* [F] **10:16** Lit *the house of their fathers* [G] **10:19** Lit *gave their hand* [H] **10:25** Some LXX mss, 1 Esdras 9:26 read *Hashabiah*

NEHEMIAH

Herod's Gate in Jerusalem received its name from pilgrims visiting the city who (erroneously) thought the entrance led directly to Herod's palace. Though originally L-shaped, the entrance was rebuilt as a projection from the wall. The entrance gives direct entry into the Old City.

INTRODUCTION TO

NEHEMIAH

Circumstances of Writing

Ezra and Nehemiah are anonymous. Ancient Jewish sources usually credit Ezra as the author of Ezra–Nehemiah. More likely Ezra–Nehemiah was written by the "Chronicler," the person (or persons) responsible for 1 and 2 Chronicles. Not only is Ezra–Nehemiah linked to Chronicles at its introduction (Ezr 1:1–2 = 2Ch 36:22–23), it also shares many similarities in language, terminology, themes, and perspective.

It is probably safe to assume that Ezra–Nehemiah was written soon after the conclusion of Nehemiah's ministry. Most likely the book was written no later than 400 BC.

In Ezra–Nehemiah, it is clear that Ezra came to Jerusalem first, probably in 458 BC, and that Nehemiah followed him thirteen years later, probably in 445 BC. Nehemiah made no mention of Ezra, his ministry, or his reforms. Ezra and Nehemiah appear together in only two texts (Neh 8:9; 12:36). The two events in which Ezra and Nehemiah were together were significant. In Nehemiah 8, the context is the reading of the law to the people; in Nehemiah 12, the two joyous processions walking around the city walls in the dedication ceremony include Ezra (v. 36) and Nehemiah (v. 38).

Contribution to the Bible

The events that occurred in Ezra and Nehemiah, the rebuilt temple, the stabilizing of Jerusalem, and the Jewish community that developed, all played key roles in the life and ministry of Jesus recorded in the Gospels. The rebuilt temple may have paled in comparison to the temple that Solomon built, but it would serve the Jews for centuries until Christ removed the need for a physical temple.

Structure

Nehemiah is similar to Samuel and Kings, and especially Chronicles, in that many sources were used in its composition. These include two major types of sources. Much of Nehemiah consists of material from the Nehemiah Memoir. The composition of the Nehemiah Memoir is regarded as including chapters 1–7 as well as 11–13. But here also Nehemiah incorporated lists and records in his memoir. Nehemiah also contains many lists, genealogies, inventories, letters, and census records throughout the book. For a community attempting to reestablish itself after the disaster of 586 BC and the subsequent exile to Babylon, this material was crucial in reordering its life together.

1 The words of Nehemiah son of Hacaliah:

NEWS FROM JERUSALEM

During the month of Chislev in the twentieth year, when I was in the fortress city of Susa, 2 Hanani, one of my brothers, arrived with men from Judah, and I questioned them about Jerusalem and the Jewish remnant that had survived the exile. 3 They said to me, "The remnant in the province, who survived the exile, are in great trouble and disgrace. Jerusalem's wall has been broken down, and its gates have been burned."

NEHEMIAH'S PRAYER

4 When I heard these words, I sat down and wept. I mourned for a number of days, fasting and praying before the God of the heavens. 5 I said,

> LORD, the God of the heavens, the great and awe-inspiring God who keeps his gracious covenant with those who love him and keep his commands, 6 let your eyes be open and your ears be attentive to hear your servant's prayer that I now pray to you day and night for your servants, the Israelites. I confess the sins[A] we have committed against you. Both I and my father's family have sinned. 7 We have acted corruptly toward you and have not kept the commands, statutes, and ordinances you gave your servant Moses. 8 Please remember what you commanded your servant Moses: "If you are unfaithful, I will scatter you among the peoples. 9 But if you return to me and carefully observe my commands, even though your exiles were banished to the farthest horizon,[B] I will gather them from there and bring them to the place where I chose to have my name dwell." 10 They are your servants and your people. You redeemed them by your great power and strong hand. 11 Please, Lord, let your ear be attentive to the prayer of your servant and to that of your servants who delight to revere your name. Give your servant success today, and grant him compassion in the presence of this man.[C]

At the time, I was the king's cupbearer.

NEHEMIAH SENT TO JERUSALEM

2 During the month of Nisan in the twentieth year of King Artaxerxes, when wine was set before him, I took the wine and gave it to the king. I had never been sad in his presence, 2 so the king said to me, "Why do you look so sad, when you aren't sick? This is nothing but sadness of heart."

I was overwhelmed with fear 3 and replied to the king, "May the king live forever! Why should I[D] not be sad when the city where my ancestors are buried lies in ruins and its gates have been destroyed by fire?"

4 Then the king asked me, "What is your request?"

So I prayed to the God of the heavens 5 and answered the king, "If it pleases the king, and if your servant has found favor with you, send me to Judah and to the city where my ancestors are buried,[E] so that I may rebuild it."

6 The king, with the queen seated beside him, asked me, "How long will your journey take, and when will you return?" So I gave him a definite time, and it pleased the king to send me.

7 I also said to the king, "If it pleases the king, let me have letters written to the governors of the region west of the Euphrates River, so that they will grant me safe passage until I reach Judah. 8 And let me have a letter written to Asaph, keeper of the king's forest, so that he will give me timber to rebuild the gates of the temple's fortress, the city wall, and the home where I will live."[F] The king granted my requests, for the gracious hand of my God was on me.

9 I went to the governors of the region west of the Euphrates and gave them the king's letters. The king had also sent officers of the infantry and cavalry with me. 10 When Sanballat the Horonite and Tobiah the Ammonite official heard that someone had come to pursue the prosperity of the Israelites, they were greatly displeased.

PREPARING TO REBUILD THE WALLS

11 After I arrived in Jerusalem and had been there three days, 12 I got up at night and took a few men with me. I didn't tell anyone what my God had laid on my heart to do for Jerusalem. The only animal I took[G] was the one I was riding. 13 I went out at night through the Valley Gate toward the Serpent's[H] Well and the Dung Gate, and I inspected the walls of Jerusalem that had been broken down and its gates that had been destroyed by fire. 14 I went on to the Fountain Gate and the King's Pool, but farther down it became too narrow for my animal to go through. 15 So I went up at night by way of the valley and inspected the wall. Then heading back, I entered through the Valley Gate and returned. 16 The officials did not know where I had gone or what I was doing, for I had not yet told the Jews, priests, nobles, officials, or the rest of those who would be doing the work. 17 So I said to them, "You see the trouble we are in. Jerusalem lies in ruins and its gates have been burned. Come, let's rebuild Jerusalem's wall, so that we will no longer be a disgrace." 18 I told them how the gracious hand of my God had been on me, and what the king had said to me.

[A] **1:6** Lit *sins of the Israelites* [B] **1:9** Lit *skies* [C] **1:11** = the king
[D] **2:3** Lit *my face* [E] **2:5** Lit *city, the house of the graves of my fathers,*
[F] **2:8** Lit *enter* [G] **2:12** Lit *animal with me* [H] **2:13** Or *Dragon's*

The King's Cupbearer

by Kevin C. Peacock

The royal cupbearer was a high-ranking officer in an ancient Near Eastern court. The king trusted the cupbearer to usher important guests into his presence and keep away undesirables. By tasting the wine before the king did, the cupbearer daily placed his life on the line for his sovereign and thus gained much respect and gratitude. Standing next to the king and always being ready to serve meant that the cupbearer overheard most all of the king's conversations and thus was required to be trustworthy and able to keep confidences. Such confidential relations many times endeared the cupbearer to the king, making him one of the most influential (and many times most wealthy) people in the land.[1]

The Hebrew term *masqeh* is usually translated "cupbearer" and is related to the verb root *saqah* ("to drink"). Technically *masqeh* is a causative participle and literally means "one giving drink." This term occurs twelve times in the Old Testament in the sense of "cupbearer."[2] Rabshakeh was the spokesman for the Assyrian emperor Sennacherib (2Kg 18:17–19:18; Is 36:2–37:8). *Rabshakeh* was a civil title, not his proper name. It comes from the Akkadian term *rab-shaqu*, meaning "chief cupbearer." He was a trusted official of the king, a "governor" or even "prime minister."[3]

CUPBEARERS IN THE ANCIENT NEAR EAST

Herodotus described the office of royal cupbearer as an honor "of very particular distinction" in Persia.[4] Xenophon described the duties of a cupbearer in the royal court of the Medes. He described the cupbearer as "handsome," and having the role of introducing persons to the king and keeping others out. He poured and served the wine to the king with great skill, tasting it first, in order to guard against poisoning.[5]

Ancient artwork depicts royal cupbearers in Egypt, Sumer, Assyria, Canaan, and Persia. Many pictures display a figure standing next to the king with a cup, a bottle, a fan, or a flyswatter in hand, attending to the king's needs. In ancient Egypt, many cupbearers were foreigners who became confidants and favorites of the king. As such, they held considerable political influence.[6] Pharaoh's cupbearer is described as "the chief cupbearer" (Gn 40:2), denoting a larger group of these officials of which he was the leader. The apocryphal book of Tobit described Ahikar the chief cupbearer in the Assyrian court of Esar-haddon. He

The bottom of this bronze bowl was indented at the center, which allowed the user to hold it comfortably in one hand. Persian; fifth–fourth centuries BC.

was "keeper of the signet, and in charge of administration of the accounts, for Esarhaddon had appointed him second to himself" (Tobit 1:22 RSV). In later Persian history the cupbearer sometimes held more influence than the king himself.[7]

NEHEMIAH, THE KING'S CUPBEARER

Artaxerxes I, son of Xerxes I, ruled Persia from 465 to 424 BC. Nehemiah served as Artaxerxes's cupbearer. What did this role mean for this devout Israelite?

Nehemiah served the king. Nehemiah selected wines to the king's liking and served them in the most appealing way.[8] He was a constant companion to the king and no doubt was a listening ear and confidant. Nehemiah, who was possibly quite handsome (see Dn 1:4), had the poise, dignity, and self-presentation needed for the role. When Nehemiah requested to return to Jerusalem to rebuild the city, the king's first question was, "How long will your journey take, and when will you return?" (Neh 2:6). The king apparently had become quite attached to Nehemiah.

Nehemiah was a man of proven trustworthiness. Tasting the wine (and probably the food) for poison, Nehemiah daily risked his life for the king. Standing between the king and death, Nehemiah became a trusted and proven companion. As such, the king even noticed when Nehemiah's face was downfallen (2:2). In the ancient Near East, many times these courtiers were eunuchs, thus they could be trusted around the king's harem (see Est 1:10–11). Because of this, some have proposed that because Nehemiah served in the presence of the queen (Neh 2:6), he must have been a eunuch. This, however, is by no means certain and is based mainly on conjecture rather than evidence in the text.[9] Regardless, the king trusted Nehemiah with his own life.

Nehemiah was probably quite wealthy. He was a man of considerable financial ability (Neh 5:8–19) who was even able to refuse part of his governor's support package (vv. 14,18). Considering the number of people the king regularly fed around his table (vv. 17–18), Nehemiah's personal service to the king must have been financially rewarding.

Nehemiah was a man of great influence with an insider's education in governance. Court servants were usually well trained in court etiquette (see Dn 1:4). As one with close access to the king, Nehemiah overheard much of the business of the kingdom. Few individuals had as much power, and fewer had a better education. Nehemiah would need such governing skills in his future ministry in Judah.

Before God compelled him into service to his people and homeland, Nehemiah was not looking to leave his job. Few had the kind of lucrative position that Nehemiah enjoyed, thus he was making quite a sacrifice in leaving the role. But in the news of the catastrophe of his own people and his beloved city, Nehemiah heard God's call into service. Rebuilding the walls of Jerusalem and reordering the community of God's chosen people was a ministry for which God had uniquely prepared Nehemiah through his position and training. ✣

Partly gilded, fluted silver rhyton with winged griffin protome; about fifth century BC. This originally held wine. It was made in two parts. A pair of holes in the chest acted as the pourer.

---

[1] B. R. Downer and R. K. Harrison, "Cupbearer" in *ISBE*, vol. 1 (1979), 837. [2] See Edwin M. Yamauchi, "Was Nehemiah the Cupbearer a Eunuch?" *Zeitschrift für die alttestamentliche Wissenschaft* (*ZAW*) 92 (1980), 132. [3] Robert H. O'Connell, "sqh" in *NIDOTTE*, 1:233. [4] Herodotus, *Histories* 3.34. [5] Xenophon, *Cyropaedia* 1.100.3.8-9. [6] K. A. Kitchen, "Cupbearer" in *New Bible Dictionary*, ed. J. D. Douglas (Leicester: Inter-Varsity, 1982), 255. [7] A. T. Olmstead, *History of the Persian Empire* (Chicago: University of Chicago Press, 1948), 217–18. [8] Josephus, *Jewish Antiquities* 16.8.1; Xenophon, *Cyropaedia* 1.100.3.8. [9] Olmstead, 314–15. Two ancient versions of the Septuagint (Vaticanus and Sinaiticus) have *eunouchos*, "eunuch," in the place of the more accepted reading *oinochoos*, "cupbearer," but this may be merely a spelling error. See Yamauchi, "Was Nehemiah?" 132–42, for a full-fledged argument on the matter.

They said, "Let's start rebuilding," and their hands
were strengthened[A] to do this good work.
19 When Sanballat the Horonite, Tobiah the Ammonite official, and Geshem the Arab heard about
this, they mocked and despised us, and said, "What is
this you're doing? Are you rebelling against the king?"
20 I gave them this reply, "The God of the heavens is
the one who will grant us success. We, his servants,
will start building, but you have no share, right, or
historic claim in Jerusalem."

REBUILDING THE WALLS

3 The high priest Eliashib and his fellow priests
began rebuilding the Sheep Gate. They dedicated
it and installed its doors. After building the wall to
the Tower of the Hundred and the Tower of Hananel,
they dedicated it. 2 The men of Jericho built next to
Eliashib, and next to them Zaccur son of Imri built.

FISH GATE

3 The sons of Hassenaah built the Fish Gate. They built
it with beams and installed its doors, bolts, and bars.
4 Next to them Meremoth son of Uriah, son of Hakkoz,
made repairs. Beside them Meshullam son of Berechiah, son of Meshezabel, made repairs. Next to them
Zadok son of Baana made repairs. 5 Beside them the
Tekoites made repairs, but their nobles did not lift a
finger to help[B] their supervisors.

OLD GATE, BROAD WALL, AND TOWER OF THE OVENS

6 Joiada son of Paseah and Meshullam son of Besode-
iah repaired the Old[C] Gate. They built it with beams and
installed its doors, bolts, and bars. 7 Next to them the
repairs were done by Melatiah the Gibeonite, Jadon
the Meronothite, and the men of Gibeon and Mizpah,
who were under the authority[D] of the governor of the
region west of the Euphrates River. 8 After him Uzziel
son of Harhaiah, the goldsmith, made repairs, and
next to him Hananiah son of the perfumer made repairs. They restored Jerusalem as far as the Broad Wall.
9 Next to them Rephaiah son of Hur, ruler of half the
district of Jerusalem, made repairs. 10 After them Jedaiah son of Harumaph made repairs across from his
house. Next to him Hattush the son of Hashabneiah
made repairs. 11 Malchijah son of Harim and Hasshub
son of Pahath-moab made repairs to another section,
as well as to the Tower of the Ovens. 12 Beside him
Shallum son of Hallohesh, ruler of half the district
of Jerusalem, made repairs — he and his daughters.

VALLEY GATE, DUNG GATE, AND FOUNTAIN GATE

13 Hanun and the inhabitants of Zanoah repaired the
Valley Gate. They rebuilt it and installed its doors,
bolts, and bars, and repaired five hundred yards[E] of
the wall to the Dung Gate. 14 Malchijah son of Rechab,
ruler of the district of Beth-haccherem, repaired the
Dung Gate. He rebuilt it and installed its doors, bolts,
and bars.
15 Shallun[F] son of Col-hozeh, ruler of the district
of Mizpah, repaired the Fountain Gate. He rebuilt it
and roofed it. Then he installed its doors, bolts, and
bars. He also made repairs to the wall of the Pool of
Shelah near the king's garden, as far as the stairs that
descend from the city of David.
16 After him Nehemiah son of Azbuk, ruler of half the
district of Beth-zur, made repairs up to a point opposite
the tombs of David, as far as the artificial pool and the
House of the Warriors. 17 Next to him the Levites made
repairs under Rehum son of Bani. Beside him Hashabiah, ruler of half the district of Keilah, made repairs
for his district. 18 After him their fellow Levites made
repairs under Binnui[G] son of Henadad, ruler of half
the district of Keilah. 19 Next to him Ezer son of Jeshua, ruler of Mizpah, made repairs to another section
opposite the ascent to the armory at the Angle.

THE ANGLE, WATER GATE, AND TOWER ON OPHEL

20 After him Baruch son of Zabbai[H] diligently repaired
another section, from the Angle to the door of the
house of the high priest Eliashib. 21 Beside him Meremoth son of Uriah, son of Hakkoz, made repairs to
another section, from the door of Eliashib's house to
the end of his house. 22 And next to him the priests
from the surrounding area made repairs.
23 After them Benjamin and Hasshub made repairs
opposite their house. Beside them Azariah son of
Maaseiah, son of Ananiah, made repairs beside his
house. 24 After him Binnui son of Henadad made repairs to another section, from the house of Azariah
to the Angle and the corner. 25 Palal son of Uzai made
repairs opposite the Angle and tower that juts out
from the king's upper palace,[I] by the courtyard of the
guard. Beside him Pedaiah son of Parosh 26 and the
temple servants living on Ophel made repairs opposite the Water Gate toward the east and the tower that
juts out. 27 Next to him the Tekoites made repairs to
another section from a point opposite the great tower
that juts out, as far as the wall of Ophel.

HORSE GATE, INSPECTION GATE, AND SHEEP GATE

28 Each of the priests made repairs above the Horse
Gate, each opposite his own house. 29 After them Zadok son of Immer made repairs opposite his house.

[A] **2:18** Lit *they put their hands* [B] **3:5** Lit *not bring their neck to the work of* [C] **3:6** Or *Jeshanah* [D] **3:7** Or *Mizpah, the seat* [E] **3:13** Lit *1,000 cubits* [F] **3:15** Some Hb mss, Syr read *Shallum* [G] **3:18** Some Hb mss, Syr, LXX; Neh 3:24; other Hb mss, Vg read *Bavvai* [H] **3:20** Alt Hb tradition, Vg read *Zaccai*; Ezr 2:9 [I] **3:25** Or *and the upper tower that juts out from the palace*

Enemies of Rebuilding Jerusalem

by Jerry W. Lee

Nehemiah's Adversaries

by David L. Jenkins

When Nehemiah, the cupbearer of Artaxerxes (464–424 BC), arrived in Jerusalem in 444 BC, he had royal orders from the Persian monarch to rebuild the walls of the city. Without walls, Jerusalem could not attain its preexilic status, strength, and significance. To rebuild the walls was a noble task, but many people were opposed to such efforts.

Sanballat apparently was the leader of the opposition. Sanballat was an official of the Persian monarchy with a primary responsibility for Samaria and the surrounding area. Samaria's domain extended far beyond the city to include the geographical area reaching to a few miles north of Jerusalem.

The name *Sanballat* is derived from an Akkadian word *Sin-uballit,* meaning "Sin (the moon-god) has given life."[1] Because of his location near Jerusalem, his relationships with prestigious religious officials in Jerusalem, and his associates, the name may have been an assumed name designed to curry favor and support from the Persian monarchy. Sanballat established a ruling dynasty that was to last for several centuries. Since his sons were named Delaiah and Shelemiah, Sanballat apparently was familiar with Yahweh worship and may have considered himself a worshiper of Yahweh.[2] Both sons' names end with "iah," an implied reference to Yahweh. A papyrus dating from the time of Darius I mentions "Sanballat the governor of Samaria."[3] Although the Scriptures never refer to him by that title, the manner in which Sanballat approached Nehemiah implied they were equals in position and authority (Neh 6:2).[4] Later Samaritan rulers by the name of Sanballat issued coins discovered in present-day Jordan at Jerash. Josephus wrote of a Sanballat who built the Samaritan temple on Mount Gerizim and who, at the right time, switched his allegiance from Persia to Greece and Alexander the Great.[5]

Sanballat's associate Tobiah was an Ammonite official. Tobiah was probably appointed by the Persian king to oversee the affairs of the Ammonites who lived east of the Jordan River. Tobiah's name indicates that he was familiar with temple worship. His name meant "Yahweh is good." He is mentioned fourteen times in Nehemiah, but normally he is listed second to Sanballat. He married into a prominent Jewish family and was afforded the favor of storage space in the temple area. Nehemiah later rescinded that privilege and ejected him from the temple.

Geshem the Arabian was another ally to Sanballat. He was an influential Arab who, with his son, ruled over a federation of Arabian tribes in North Africa. His name meant "rain storm."[6] He is mentioned only three times, but he vigorously opposed Nehemiah's building efforts. The word *Gashmu* may be another name given to him. His name has been found on a silver bowl in Egypt's eastern delta and in an ancient Arabian inscription testifying to his significance.[7]

Sanballat was called the Horonite. Such a name indicated his geographical association. While some may suggest that he originally came from Haran, such an identification would necessitate emending the biblical text. Some students have suggested that he was a Moabite from Horonaim in Moab. The best suggestion is that he was from Beth-horon, which was the name of two adjacent villages, Upper Beth-horon and

Old Testament Ashdod—one of the five principal Philistine cities.

Overview of the ruins of the Samaritan temple on Mount Gerizim. The temple was destroyed in 128 BC. This temple was built by the family of Sanballat, who was mentioned in the book of Nehemiah.

Lower Beth-horon, in the territory that formerly belonged to the tribe of Ephraim (1Ch 7:24; 2Ch 8:5). In Nehemiah's day, this area, only about ten miles northwest of Jerusalem, was included in the region of Samaria.[8]

Other adversaries specified were the Arabs, Ammonites, and Ashdodites (Neh 4:7). Arabia extended out into the desert east of the Jordan River. Ashdod was a seaport on the Mediterranean below Joppa. Ammon was the mountainous territory to the east of the Jordan River. Its center was the ancient city of Rabbah. This may suggest a reason for their vehement opposition to Nehemiah's construction project.

From one's perspective in Jerusalem, the areas loom large and were located to the east, west, north, and south. From Persia's perspective, however, the entire region was seen probably as distant lands sharing common boundaries and common interests. Persia's major concern would be that the territory remained relatively peaceful and produced the stipulated taxes when due.

Several factors probably were behind the vicious opposition to Nehemiah's rebuilding project. Apparently Sanballat's position as governor of Samaria would be jeopardized by a restored Jerusalem. His location at Beth-horon would indicate that his position as governor of Samaria would extend fairly near to Jerusalem. The success of Nehemiah's plans would curtail Sanballat's influence over the territory near Jerusalem.

Another factor seemed to be power politics. Sanballat, Geshem, and Tobiah all enjoyed a limited hegemony into Judah and over Jerusalem. Without walls, the city needed to accommodate their presence and power. A strong city surrounded by walls would be able to exercise influence and control over an extensive area. That would cut severely into the power base of Nehemiah's adversaries. They did not want that to occur. Should Nehemiah successfully reconstruct the walls, his position as governor of the region would be enhanced at their expense.

Another factor undoubtedly was economics. Trade routes came from the west from Ashdod through Jerusalem. Those routes continued into the Arabian Desert. North-south

Obverse and reverse of a Samaritan coin that mentions Sanballat. We do not know which Sanballat this coin represents. Regardless, finding this coin in Jordan would suggest that Sanballat's kingdom was not limited to a district on the west side of the Jordan, but stretched to a considerable territory on the east side of the Jordan as well.

trade routes linking Egypt and Persia passed through Judah. A strong city serving as the capital of the region would claim its share of revenue from the traders and caravans using the trade routes. Apparently Nehemiah's adversaries had been able to profit from commerce in the region, but that income would be curtailed, or would disappear. Instead of going to them, the revenue would be funneled into Jerusalem, which would become richer and stronger.

Another factor leading to their opposition may have been Nehemiah's exclusion of non-Jews from the politics and religion of Jerusalem. His attitude toward foreigners may have alienated these adversaries. After the Assyrian conquest of Samaria in 721 BC, homogenization took place. People left in the northern kingdom's territory intermarried with other nationalities who were brought in by the Assyrians. With Jerusalem's fall in 587 BC, people in the lower socioeconomic level began to marry outside their own people and religion. The entire area was experiencing this general mixture of various nationalities. In exile, however, the Jews saw the need to maintain their distinctiveness. When Nehemiah arrived at Jerusalem, he did not accommodate himself to the inclusiveness of other political officials. He demanded a strict exclusiveness that threatened the status quo. Nehemiah's adversaries may well have been offended by such an attitude. They determined to be his undoing.

Since Nehemiah refused to have anything to do with the other political officials in the region (Sanballat, Tobiah, and Geshem), they used psychological, physical, and legal means to thwart Nehemiah's efforts. When intimidation, sarcasm, and brute force failed, Nehemiah's enemies hired councilors to write slanderous accusations against Nehemiah to the Persian monarch. Nehemiah's enemies were able to employ certain prophets such as Shemaiah and Noadiah. These prophets attempted to get Nehemiah to act foolishly to discredit him. Nehemiah saw through their charades and rejected them. When all efforts failed, Nehemiah's enemies sought to assassinate him.

The enemies of the rebuilding of Jerusalem failed in their efforts. By God's grace and through Nehemiah's personal strength of character, example, and sacrifice, Nehemiah led the people to complete the wall. ❖

---

[1] Jerry Vardaman, "Sanballat the Horonite," *BI* (Fall 1995), 63. [2] John Arthur Thompson, "Sanballat" in *ISBE*, vol. 4 (1988), 320. [3] "Aramaic Letters" in *ANET*, 492. [4] H. G. M. Williamson, *Ezra, Nehemiah*, vol. 16 in WBC (1985), 182. [5] Josephus, *Jewish Antiquities* 11.8. [6] J. J. Reeve, "Geshem" in *ISBE*, vol. 2 (1982), 449. [7] C. E. Armerding and R K. Harrison, "Nehemiah" in *ISBE*, vol. 3 (1988), 514. [8] C. F. Keil and F. Delitzsch, "Nehemiah" in *1 & 2 Kings, 1 & 2 Chronicles, Ezra, Nehemiah, Esther*, vol. 3 in Commentary on the Old Testament in Ten Volumes (Grand Rapids: Eerdmans, 1976), 168; "Beth-horon" in *HIBD*, 193.

And beside him Shemaiah son of Shecaniah, guard of
the East Gate, made repairs. 30 Next to him Hananiah
son of Shelemiah and Hanun the sixth son of Zalaph
made repairs to another section.
After them Meshullam son of Berechiah made repairs opposite his room. 31 Next to him Malchijah,
one of the goldsmiths, made repairs to the house of
the temple servants and the merchants, opposite the
Inspection[A] Gate, and as far as the upstairs room on
the corner. 32 The goldsmiths and merchants made
repairs between the upstairs room on the corner
and the Sheep Gate.

PROGRESS IN SPITE OF OPPOSITION

4 When Sanballat heard that we were rebuilding
the wall, he became furious. He mocked the Jews
2 before his colleagues and the powerful men[B] of Samaria and said, "What are these pathetic Jews doing?
Can they restore it by themselves? Will they offer sacrifices? Will they ever finish it? Can they bring these
burnt stones back to life from the mounds of rubble?"
3 Then Tobiah the Ammonite, who was beside him,
said, "Indeed, even if a fox climbed up what they are
building, he would break down their stone wall!"
4 Listen, our God, for we are despised. Make their
insults return on their own heads and let them be
taken as plunder to a land of captivity. 5 Do not cover
their guilt or let their sin be erased from your sight,
because they have angered[C] the builders.
6 So we rebuilt the wall until the entire wall was
joined together up to half its height, for the people
had the will to keep working.
7 When Sanballat, Tobiah, and the Arabs, Ammonites, and Ashdodites heard that the repair to the walls
of Jerusalem was progressing and that the gaps were
being closed, they became furious. 8 They all plotted
together to come and fight against Jerusalem and
throw it into confusion. 9 So we prayed to our God
and stationed a guard because of them day and night.
10 In Judah, it was said:[D]

The strength of the laborer fails,
since there is so much rubble.
We will never be able
to rebuild the wall.

11 And our enemies said, "They won't realize it[E] until we're among them and can kill them and stop the
work." 12 When the Jews who lived nearby arrived,
they said to us time and again,[F] "Everywhere you turn,
they attack[G] us." 13 So I stationed people behind the
lowest sections of the wall, at the vulnerable areas. I
stationed them by families with their swords, spears,
and bows. 14 After I made an inspection, I stood up and
said to the nobles, the officials, and the rest of the people, "Don't be afraid of them. Remember the great and
awe-inspiring Lord, and fight for your countrymen,
your sons and daughters, your wives and homes."

SWORD AND TROWEL

15 When our enemies heard that we knew their
scheme and that God had frustrated it, every one
of us returned to his own work on the wall. 16 From
that day on, half of my men did the work while the
other half held spears, shields, bows, and armor. The
officers supported all the people of Judah, 17 who
were rebuilding the wall. The laborers who carried
the loads worked with one hand and held a weapon
with the other. 18 Each of the builders had his sword
strapped around his waist while he was building, and
the one who sounded the ram's horn was beside me.
19 Then I said to the nobles, the officials, and the rest
of the people, "The work is enormous and spread out,
and we are separated far from one another along the
wall. 20 Wherever you hear the sound of the ram's
horn, rally to us there. Our God will fight for us!" 21 So
we continued the work, while half of the men were
holding spears from daybreak until the stars came
out. 22 At that time, I also said to the people, "Let everyone and his servant spend the night inside Jerusalem,
so that they can stand guard by night and work by
day." 23 And I, my brothers, my servants, and the men
of the guard with me never took off our clothes. Each
carried his weapon, even when washing.[H]

SOCIAL INJUSTICE

5 There was a widespread outcry from the people
and their wives against their Jewish countrymen.
2 Some were saying, "We, our sons, and our daughters
are numerous. Let us get grain so that we can eat and
live." 3 Others were saying, "We are mortgaging our
fields, vineyards, and homes to get grain during the
famine." 4 Still others were saying, "We have borrowed
money to pay the king's tax on our fields and vineyards. 5 We and our children are just like our countrymen and their children, yet we are subjecting our
sons and daughters to slavery. Some of our daughters
are already enslaved, but we are powerless[I] because
our fields and vineyards belong to others."
6 I became extremely angry when I heard their outcry and these complaints. 7 After seriously considering
the matter, I accused the nobles and officials, saying
to them, "Each of you is charging his countrymen interest." So I called a large assembly against them 8 and
said, "We have done our best to buy back our Jewish
countrymen who were sold to foreigners, but now
you sell your own countrymen, and we have to buy

[A] **3:31** Or *Muster* [B] **4:2** Or *the army* [C] **4:5** Or *provoked you in front of* [D] **4:10** Lit *Judah said* [E] **4:11** Lit *won't know or see* [F] **4:12** Lit *us 10 times* [G] **4:12** Or *again from every place, "You must return to* [H] **4:23** Lit *Each his weapon the water* [I] **5:5** Lit *but there is not the power in our hand*

them back." They remained silent and could not say
a word. 9 Then I said, "What you are doing isn't right.
Shouldn't you walk in the fear of our God and not invite the reproach of our foreign enemies? 10 Even I, as
well as my brothers and my servants, have been lending them money and grain. Please, let's stop charging
this interest.[A] 11 Return their fields, vineyards, olive
groves, and houses to them immediately, along with
the percentage[B] of the money, grain, new wine, and
fresh oil that you have been assessing them."

12 They responded, "We will return these things
and require nothing more from them. We will do
as you say."

So I summoned the priests and made everyone
take an oath to do this. 13 I also shook the folds of my
robe and said, "May God likewise shake from his
house and property everyone who doesn't keep this
promise. May he be shaken out and have nothing!"

The whole assembly said, "Amen," and they praised
the LORD. Then the people did as they had promised.

GOOD AND BAD GOVERNORS

14 Furthermore, from the day King Artaxerxes appointed me to be their governor in the land of Judah
— from the twentieth year until his thirty-second
year, twelve years — I and my associates never ate
from the food allotted to the governor. 15 The governors who preceded me had heavily burdened the
people, taking from them food and wine as well as a
pound[C] of silver. Their subordinates also oppressed
the people, but because of the fear of God, I didn't do
this. 16 Instead, I devoted myself to the construction
of this wall, and all my subordinates were gathered
there for the work. We didn't buy any land.

17 There were 150 Jews and officials, as well as
guests from the surrounding nations at my table.
18 Each[D] day, one ox, six choice sheep, and some fowl
were prepared for me. An abundance of all kinds of
wine was provided every ten days. But I didn't demand the food allotted to the governor, because the
burden on the people was so heavy.

19 Remember me favorably, my God, for all that I
have done for this people.

ATTEMPTS TO DISCOURAGE THE BUILDERS

6 When Sanballat, Tobiah, Geshem the Arab, and
the rest of our enemies heard that I had rebuilt
the wall and that no gap was left in it — though at
that time I had not installed the doors in the city gates
— 2 Sanballat and Geshem sent me a message: "Come,
let's meet together in the villages of[E] the Ono Valley."
They were planning to harm me.

3 So I sent messengers to them, saying, "I am doing
important work and cannot come down. Why should
the work cease while I leave it and go down to you?"
4 Four times they sent me the same proposal, and I
gave them the same reply.

5 Sanballat sent me this same message a fifth time
by his aide, who had an open letter in his hand. 6 In it
was written:

> It is reported among the nations — and Geshem[F]
> agrees — that you and the Jews plan to rebel.
> This is the reason you are building the wall.
> According to these reports, you are to become
> their king 7 and have even set up the prophets in
> Jerusalem to proclaim on your behalf, "There is
> a king in Judah." These rumors will be heard by
> the king. So come, let's confer together.

8 Then I replied to him, "There is nothing to these
rumors you are spreading; you are inventing them
in your own mind." 9 For they were all trying to intimidate us, saying, "They will drop their hands from[G]
the work, and it will never be finished."

But now, my God, strengthen my hands.

ATTEMPTS TO INTIMIDATE NEHEMIAH

10 I went to the house of Shemaiah son of Delaiah,
son of Mehetabel, who was restricted to his house.
He said:

> Let's meet at the house of God,
> inside the temple.
> Let's shut the temple doors
> because they're coming to kill you.
> They're coming to kill you tonight![H]

11 But I said, "Should a man like me run away? How can
someone like me enter the temple and live? I will not
go." 12 I realized that God had not sent him, because of
the prophecy he spoke against me. Tobiah and Sanballat had hired him. 13 He was hired, so that I would
be intimidated, do as he suggested, sin, and get a bad
reputation, in order that they could discredit me.

14 My God, remember Tobiah and Sanballat for
what they have done, and also the prophetess Noadiah and the other prophets who wanted to intimidate me.

THE WALL COMPLETED

15 The wall was completed in fifty-two days, on the
twenty-fifth day of the month Elul. 16 When all our
enemies heard this, all the surrounding nations were
intimidated and lost their confidence,[I] for they realized that this task had been accomplished by our
God.

17 During those days, the nobles of Judah sent many
letters to Tobiah, and Tobiah's letters came to them.

[A] **5:10** Or *us forgive these debts* [B] **5:11** Lit *hundred* [C] **5:15** Lit *40 shekels* [D] **5:18** Lit *And that which was prepared each* [E] **6:2** Or *together at Kephirim in* [F] **6:6** Lit *Gashmu* [G] **6:9** Or *will give up on* [H] **6:10** Or *by night* [I] **6:16** Lit *and fell greatly in their eyes*

18 For many in Judah were bound by oath to him, since
he was a son-in-law of Shecaniah son of Arah, and his
son Jehohanan had married the daughter of Meshullam son of Berechiah. 19 These nobles kept mentioning Tobiah's good deeds to me, and they reported my
words to him. And Tobiah sent letters to intimidate me.

THE EXILES RETURN

7 When the wall had been rebuilt and I had the doors
installed, the gatekeepers, singers, and Levites
were appointed. 2 Then I put my brother Hanani in
charge of Jerusalem, along with Hananiah, commander of the fortress, because he was a faithful man who
feared God more than most. 3 I said to them, "Do not
open the gates of Jerusalem until the sun is hot, and
let the doors be shut and securely fastened while the
guards are on duty. Station the citizens of Jerusalem as
guards, some at their posts and some at their homes."
4 The city was large and spacious, but there were few
people in it, and no houses had been built yet. 5 Then
my God put it into my mind to assemble the nobles,
the officials, and the people to be registered by genealogy. I found the genealogical record of those who
came back first, and I found the following written in it:
6 These are the people of the province who went up
among the captive exiles deported by King Nebuchadnezzar of Babylon. Each of them returned to Jerusalem
and Judah, to his own town. 7 They came with Zerubbabel,
Jeshua, Nehemiah, Azariah, Raamiah, Nahamani, Mordecai, Bilshan, Mispereth, Bigvai, Nehum, and Baanah.

The number of the Israelite men included[A]

8 Parosh's descendants 2,172
9 Shephatiah's descendants 372
10 Arah's descendants 652
11 Pahath-moab's descendants:
Jeshua's and Joab's descendants 2,818
12 Elam's descendants 1,254
13 Zattu's descendants 845
14 Zaccai's descendants 760
15 Binnui's descendants 648
16 Bebai's descendants 628
17 Azgad's descendants 2,322
18 Adonikam's descendants 667
19 Bigvai's descendants 2,067
20 Adin's descendants 655
21 Ater's descendants: of Hezekiah 98
22 Hashum's descendants 328
23 Bezai's descendants 324
24 Hariph's descendants 112
25 Gibeon's[B] descendants 95
26 Bethlehem's and Netophah's men 188
27 Anathoth's men 128
28 Beth-azmaveth's men 42
29 Kiriath-jearim's, Chephirah's, and Beeroth's men 743
30 Ramah's and Geba's men 621
31 Michmas's men 122
32 Bethel's and Ai's men 123
33 the other Nebo's men 52
34 the other Elam's people 1,254
35 Harim's people 320
36 Jericho's people 345
37 Lod's, Hadid's, and Ono's people 721
38 Senaah's people 3,930.

39 The priests included
Jedaiah's descendants
of the house of Jeshua 973
40 Immer's descendants 1,052
41 Pashhur's descendants 1,247
42 Harim's descendants 1,017.

43 The Levites included
Jeshua's descendants: of Kadmiel
Hodevah's descendants 74.

44 The singers included
Asaph's descendants 148.

45 The gatekeepers included
Shallum's descendants,
Ater's descendants,
Talmon's descendants,
Akkub's descendants,
Hatita's descendants,
Shobai's descendants 138.

46 The temple servants included
Ziha's descendants, Hasupha's descendants,
Tabbaoth's descendants,
47 Keros's descendants,
Sia's descendants, Padon's descendants,
48 Lebanah's descendants,
Hagabah's descendants,
Shalmai's descendants,
49 Hanan's descendants,
Giddel's descendants, Gahar's descendants,
50 Reaiah's descendants, Rezin's descendants,
Nekoda's descendants,
51 Gazzam's descendants,
Uzza's descendants, Paseah's descendants,
52 Besai's descendants,
Meunim's descendants,
Nephishesim's[C] descendants,
53 Bakbuk's descendants,
Hakupha's descendants,
Harhur's descendants,

[A] 7:7 Lit *the men of the people of Israel* [B] 7:25 = Gibbar's in Ezr 2:20
[C] 7:52 Alt Hb tradition reads *Nephushesim's*

Jewish Nobility

by Robert C. Dunston

The Hebrew noun translated as "nobles" may derive from an Arabic root meaning "be or become free." Modern Hebrew uses the same Hebrew word translated as "nobles" to describe free individuals. Some biblical scholars doubt that Arabic, Aramaic, and Modern Hebrew reflect the earlier understanding of the Hebrew word, but others disagree, believing the Hebrew noun used in the Old Testament also carried the meaning of "free." Thus the "nobles" referred not to a class of hereditary, titled leaders possibly related to the royal family, but to a group of free citizens possessing rights and influence others did not enjoy. Isaiah condemned those who bought the land of poorer families and created vast estates worked by hired servants or slaves (Is 5:8–10). The group Isaiah condemned probably formed the nobles, a group of wealthy landowners and merchants who enjoyed a freedom from debt and indentured service not experienced by other Israelites.[1]

A reasonable case can be made for the development of such a group. David's conquests and Solomon's alliances provided opportunity for individuals to share in the wealth that came to the royal court. Princes not likely to become king certainly could have profited from their family connections as could other highly placed people in the royal court. By virtue of their importance to the economy, the nobles would have gained significant influence and could have become important leaders alongside the elders. Nebuchadnezzar could easily have wanted to deport these people to Babylon along with political leaders to create a leadership vacuum in Judah, as well as to ensure Babylonia controlled the economy. Some of the nobles who remained in Jerusalem probably joined with Zedekiah in his rebellion seeking to regain their economic power. When Nebuchadnezzar captured Zedekiah and killed his sons, the nobles may have been executed for their part in the rebellion. In Nehemiah's time, wealth and economic power continued to provide influence, giving the nobles rights not enjoyed by the general populace and marking them as leaders among the people. ✣

[1] "חרר" ("be or become free") in Francis Brown, S. R. Driver, and Charles A. Briggs, *The Brown-Driver-Briggs Hebrew and English Lexicon* (Peabody, MA: Hendrickson, 1996), 359; Robert North, "Palestine, Administration of (Judean Officials)," in *ABD*, 5:88.

A letter written to an Assyrian merchant in Cappadocia in about 1850 BC.

54 Bazlith's descendants, Mehida's descendants,
Harsha's descendants,
55 Barkos's descendants,
Sisera's descendants, Temah's descendants,
56 Neziah's descendants, Hatipha's descendants.

57 The descendants of Solomon's servants included
Sotai's descendants,
Sophereth's descendants,
Perida's descendants,
58 Jaala's descendants,
Darkon's descendants, Giddel's descendants,
59 Shephatiah's descendants,
Hattil's descendants,
Pochereth-hazzebaim's descendants,
Amon's descendants.

60 All the temple servants
and the descendants of Solomon's servants
392.

61 The following are those who came from Tel-
melah, Tel-harsha, Cherub, Addon, and Immer, but
were unable to prove that their ancestral families[A]
and their lineage were Israelite:
62 Delaiah's descendants,
Tobiah's descendants,
and Nekoda's descendants 642
63 and from the priests: the descendants of Hobaiah,
the descendants of Hakkoz, and the descendants of
Barzillai — who had taken a wife from the daughters
of Barzillai the Gileadite and who bore their name.
64 These searched for their entries in the genealogical
records, but they could not be found, so they were
disqualified from the priesthood. 65 The governor
ordered them not to eat the most holy things until
there was a priest who could consult the Urim and
Thummim.
66 The whole combined assembly numbered
42,360
67 not including their 7,337 male
and female servants,
as well as their 245 male and female singers.
68 They had 736 horses, 245 mules,[B]
69 435 camels, and 6,720 donkeys.

70 Some of the family heads contributed to the project. The governor gave 1,000 gold coins,[C] 50 bowls, and
530 priestly garments to the treasury. 71 Some of the
family heads gave 20,000 gold coins and 2,200 silver
minas to the treasury for the project. 72 The rest of
the people gave 20,000 gold coins, 2,000 silver minas,
and 67 priestly garments. 73 The priests, Levites, gatekeepers, temple singers, some of the people, temple
servants, and all Israel settled in their towns.

PUBLIC READING OF THE LAW

When the seventh month came and the Israelites
8 had settled in their towns, 1 all the people gathered together at the square in front of the Water
Gate. They asked the scribe Ezra to bring the book of
the law of Moses that the LORD had given Israel. 2 On
the first day of the seventh month, the priest Ezra
brought the law before the assembly of men, women,
and all who could listen with understanding. 3 While
he was facing the square in front of the Water Gate,
he read out of it from daybreak until noon before the
men, the women, and those who could understand.
All the people listened attentively[D] to the book of
the law. 4 The scribe Ezra stood on a high wooden
platform made for this purpose. Mattithiah, Shema,
Anaiah, Uriah, Hilkiah, and Maaseiah stood beside
him on his right; to his left were Pedaiah, Mishael,
Malchijah, Hashum, Hash-baddanah, Zechariah, and
Meshullam. 5 Ezra opened the book in full view of all
the people, since he was elevated above everyone. As
he opened it, all the people stood up. 6 Ezra blessed
the LORD, the great God, and with their hands uplifted all the people said, "Amen, Amen!" Then they
knelt low and worshiped the LORD with their faces
to the ground.
7 Jeshua, Bani, Sherebiah, Jamin, Akkub, Shabbethai, Hodiah, Maaseiah, Kelita, Azariah, Jozabad, Hanan, and Pelaiah, who were Levites,[E] explained the
law to the people as they stood in their places. 8 They
read out of the book of the law of God, translating
and giving the meaning so that the people could understand what was read. 9 Nehemiah the governor,
Ezra the priest and scribe, and the Levites who were
instructing the people said to all of them, "This day
is holy to the LORD your God. Do not mourn or weep."
For all the people were weeping as they heard the
words of the law. 10 Then he said to them, "Go and eat
what is rich, drink what is sweet, and send portions
to those who have nothing prepared, since today is
holy to our Lord. Do not grieve, because the joy of
the LORD is your strength."[F] 11 And the Levites quieted all the people, saying, "Be still, since today is holy.
Don't grieve." 12 Then all the people began to eat and
drink, send portions, and have a great celebration,
because they had understood the words that were
explained to them.

FESTIVAL OF SHELTERS OBSERVED

13 On the second day, the family heads of all the people, along with the priests and Levites, assembled
before the scribe Ezra to study the words of the law.

[A] **7:61** Lit *the house of their fathers* [B] **7:68** Some Hb mss, LXX; Ezr 2:66; other Hb mss omit v. 68 [C] **7:70** Or *drachmas*, or *darics*; also in vv. 71,72 [D] **8:3** Lit *The ears of all the people listened* [E] **8:7** Vg, 1 Esdras 9:48; MT reads *Pelaiah and the Levites* [F] **8:10** Or *stronghold*

Postexilic Hebrew Worship Practices

by G. B. Howell Jr.

WORSHIP BEFORE THE EXILE

For centuries, Hebrew worship had centered on Solomon's temple in Jerusalem. Daily sacrifices marked the sacred activities. Annual celebrations focused on national feasts and festivals: Passover, Unleavened Bread, Trumpets, Weeks (or Harvest or Pentecost), Shelters (or Tabernacles or Booths), and the Day of Atonement.[1] The priesthood developed into a hierarchy with three grades: Levites or temple servers; priests, descendants of Zadok; and the high priest, who annually entered the most holy place.

Throughout its history, worship became for the people of God an increasingly nationalistic ritual. Judah was not merely a civil state, but a religious community centered on the national altar in Jerusalem. Individual responsibility faded. The annual sacrifices became calls for forgiveness for the national sins, rather than a call for personal repentance. With the centralization of worship at the temple in Jerusalem, the call for individual or even community-based sacrifice was practically silent.

Yet worship was celebrated with fanfare and faithfulness for those at the temple in Jerusalem. "The maintenance of this sanctuary with its priests became the first and [principal] duty of the community."[2] These traditions came to an abrupt halt, however, when Babylon seized Jerusalem and took its citizenry into captivity in 586 BC.

WORSHIP DURING THE EXILE

Two unexpected events occurred during the Hebrew exile that set the stage for postexilic worship changes. First, God appeared in his glory in a foreign land. Hebrew understanding before the exile was that Yahweh would reveal himself only in Jerusalem. With Jerusalem being a distant memory, the book of Psalms expressed the exiles' sense of spiritual alienation: "By the rivers of Babylon—there we sat down and wept when we remembered Zion. . . . How can we sing the LORD's song on foreign soil?" (137:1,4). God, however, did the unexpected. He showed up in Babylon. The glory of God appeared in the land of the Chaldeans (Ezk 1:1,28).

Second, the exiles found they could practice some aspects of Jewish worship without all of the temple traditions. "As no sacrificial feasts could be held in the foreign land . . . [the worshiping community] had to renounce more and more every material and sacramental support, and greater attention had to be given to the spiritual and the intangible."[3] For a people whose identity had been inseparably tied to a land and a national temple, the loss of

Menorah carved on basalt found inside the synagogue at Qasrin.

Synagogue at Qasrin, northeast of the Sea of Galilee. The synagogue's door frame is about 4½ feet wide and 8 feet tall. It is composed of sculpted bands with a flat architrave, a convex frieze, and a cornice with an egg-and-dart design. The lintel has a relief of a wreath tied in a Hercules knot, flanked by two pomegranates and two amphorae. The entire synagogue measured about 49 by 55 feet.

both could have stifled all expressions of Hebrew worship. Instead, during the captivity, the exiles began to stress with renewed vigor certain aspects of their religious traditions: keeping the Sabbath and practicing circumcision. These traditions allowed the people of Israel to maintain their individuality, to nurture a sense of community, and to express both to the Babylonians and to Yahweh their allegiance to God. Additionally the exiles began to place a renewed emphasis on the Scriptures. This emphasis proved to be a foreshadowing of worship changes implemented during the postexilic period.

WORSHIP AFTER THE EXILE

In 539 BC, Babylon fell to the Persians. Persia's King Cyrus issued a decree in 538 BC that captives should return to their homelands. Part of his motivation was to allow the exiles to worship in their own temples back home. About 516 BC, Zerubbabel's Jerusalem temple was complete. The temple provided the Jews with a national worship center and an internationally recognized status.[4] With flair and enthusiasm, Israel dedicated its new temple. Afterward, the Israelites celebrated Passover and the Feast of Unleavened Bread (Ezr 6:15–22). Expectations, however, did not match reality.

Worship in the new temple lacked fervor. The limited resources of the returning exiles meant the new temple lacked the splendor of Solomon's temple. Disappointment and disillusionment crippled morale. "Although the temple was rebuilt and worship, priestly sacrifices, and pilgrimages were reestablished at [the temple], the enthusiasm was never to be of the same intensity."[5]

When Ezra came from Babylon, he exhibited a profound devotion to God. Nehemiah recorded Ezra standing on a platform and reading the book of the law "from daybreak until noon" (Neh 8:3–4). Ezra's actions that day served as a catalyst to bring reform to Hebrew worship.

Postexilic worship was characterized by two dramatic changes. First, worship placed a new emphasis on the Torah. This emphasis on the law became the most important distinguishing characteristic of postexilic Hebrew worship. The result of the new emphasis on the Scriptures was far reaching. Rather than depending

Since the ark of the covenant was gone, worship in postexilic Judaism lacked a focal worship article for the sanctuary. The golden lampstand may have gained prominence as a symbol of the Lord's presence (Zch 4:1–14). Later images support this notion. The item is included in this first-century column capital from a synagogue in Capernaum.

on priests to offer sacrifices, worshipers wanted scribes and teachers ("rabbis") to instruct them in the law. The new leader of worship was not the one who could lead with burnt offerings but the one who could define and interpret the law and its applications in an understandable manner. "To fill this need there arose a class of scribes who devoted themselves to the study of the law and passed their learning on to their disciples."[6]

The second major shift in Hebrew worship was not in the method but in the location. Temple worship was difficult, if not impossible, for Jews living far from Jerusalem. The need for the law to be read and taught in individual communities became increasingly evident. In all likelihood, this was one of the factors that led to the rise and growing popularity of the synagogue in postexilic Judaism.

History is unclear about when and why synagogical worship began. But most scholars conclude that the synagogue was a by-product of the exile. Many Jews elected to remain in Persia, even after the proclamation of the Cyrus edict. Such a response would indicate they had found a way to have their religious needs met, even in a foreign land. They evidently had grown comfortable offering worship to God away from the Jerusalem temple.

Synagogues also became a common part of Hebrew worship for the Jews who did return to their homeland. The synagogue offered a meaningful worship experience to the masses. Worship in the synagogue contained no elaborate ritual or sacrificial systems. Worship for the first time focused on reading and meditating on Scripture rather than sacrifice. Synagogical worship consisted of three primary parts; "reading of the Scriptures, in which God spoke to man; prayer and praise, in which man spoke to God; and an address, in which man spoke to his fellow man."[7] Each of these divisions consisted of multiple actions.

Several specific actions from synagogical worship were present in Ezra's actions on the day he read from the Torah. Whether Ezra learned these practices during the exile and imported them to Jerusalem or whether the Jews adopted Ezra's practices as the norm for synagogical worship is unclear. The synagogical worship elements that Ezra and the people demonstrated that day were

- assembly;
- request for a reading from the Torah;
- opening of the Torah-scroll;
- standing by the people;
- blessing of the community;
- response of the community;
- prostration;
- sermon;
- reading of the Torah;
- oral Targum [interpretation];
- exhortation;
- departure.[8]

The merging of a new emphasis on Scriptures and the introduction of local houses of worship became the hallmark of postexilic worship. For Jews scattered throughout the region, emphasis on the Torah replaced the necessity of pilgrimages to and rituals at the Jerusalem temple. And local rabbis became the worship leaders for most families, rather than temple priests.

So by the close of the Old Testament era, Jews had two alternatives for worship. One focused on the temple with the presented feast for the senses. The production included elaborate rituals, ceremonies, and sacrificial offerings. The alternative centered on the more simple and convenient local experience of prayer, praise, and preaching.

Worship in the synagogue proved to be amazingly effective and popular. The synagogue became, by the time of Christ, the most important religious institution for the Jews' everyday life. Further, synagogical worship, with its emphasis on Scriptures, was probably the greatest influencing factor in the development of Christian worship in the emerging New Testament church. ❖

[1] Hobart H. Freeman, "Festivals of Israel," in *The Biblical Foundations of Christian Worship*, ed. Robert E. Webber (Peabody, MA: Hendrickson, 1993), 185–93. [2] Ilion T. Jones, *A Historical Approach to Evangelical Worship* (New York: Abingdon, 1954), 28. [3] Hans-Joachim Kraus, *Worship in Israel: A Cultic History of the Old Testament*, trans. Geoffrey Buswell (Richmond: John Knox, 1966), 229–30. [4] John Bright, *A History of Israel* (Louisville: Westminster John Knox, 2000), 378. [5] Ralph P. Martin, "Worship" in *ISBE*, vol. 4 (1988), 1122. [6] Bright, *History*, 437. [7] Ernest F. Scott, *The Nature of the Early Church* (New York: Scribner's Sons, 1941), 72. [8] H. G. M. Williamson, *Ezra, Nehemiah*, vol. 16 in WBC (1985), 281.

14 They found written in the law how the LORD had
commanded through Moses that the Israelites should
dwell in shelters during the festival of the seventh
month. 15 So they proclaimed and spread this news
throughout their towns and in Jerusalem, saying,
"Go out to the hill country and bring back branches
of olive, wild olive, myrtle, palm, and other leafy trees
to make shelters, just as it is written." 16 The people
went out, brought back branches, and made shelters
for themselves on each of their rooftops and courtyards, the court of the house of God, the square by
the Water Gate, and the square by the Ephraim Gate.
17 The whole community that had returned from exile
made shelters and lived in them. The Israelites had
not celebrated like this from the days of Joshua son
of Nun until that day. And there was tremendous joy.
18 Ezra[A] read out of the book of the law of God every
day, from the first day to the last. The Israelites celebrated the festival for seven days, and on the eighth
day there was a solemn assembly, according to the
ordinance.

NATIONAL CONFESSION OF SIN

9 On the twenty-fourth day of this month the Israelites assembled; they were fasting, wearing
sackcloth, and had put dust on their heads. 2 Those of
Israelite descent separated themselves from all foreigners, and they stood and confessed their sins and
the iniquities of their ancestors. 3 While they stood
in their places, they read from the book of the law of
the LORD their God for a fourth of the day and spent
another fourth of the day in confession and worship
of the LORD their God. 4 Jeshua, Bani, Kadmiel, Shebaniah, Bunni, Sherebiah, Bani, and Chenani stood
on the raised platform built for the Levites and cried
out loudly to the LORD their God. 5 Then the Levites
— Jeshua, Kadmiel, Bani, Hashabneiah, Sherebiah,
Hodiah, Shebaniah, and Pethahiah — said, "Stand
up. Blessed be the LORD your God from everlasting
to everlasting."

Blessed be your glorious name,
and may it be exalted above all blessing
and praise.

6 You,[B] LORD, are the only God.[C]
You created the heavens,
the highest heavens with all their stars,
the earth and all that is on it,
the seas and all that is in them.
You give life to all of them,
and all the stars of heaven worship you.

7 You, the LORD,
are the God who chose Abram
and brought him out of Ur
of the Chaldeans,
and changed his name to Abraham.

8 You found his heart faithful in your sight,
and made a covenant with him
to give the land of the Canaanites,
Hethites, Amorites, Perizzites,
Jebusites, and Girgashites —
to give it to his descendants.
You have fulfilled your promise,
for you are righteous.

9 You saw the oppression of our ancestors
in Egypt
and heard their cry at the Red Sea.

10 You performed signs and wonders
against Pharaoh,
all his officials, and all the people
of his land,
for you knew how arrogantly they treated
our ancestors.
You made a name for yourself
that endures to this day.

11 You divided the sea before them,
and they crossed through it on dry ground.
You hurled their pursuers into the depths
like a stone into raging water.

12 You led them with a pillar of cloud by day,
and with a pillar of fire by night,
to illuminate the way they should go.

13 You came down on Mount Sinai,
and spoke to them from heaven.
You gave them impartial ordinances,
reliable instructions,
and good statutes and commands.

14 You revealed your holy Sabbath to them,
and gave them commands, statutes,
and instruction
through your servant Moses.

15 You provided bread from heaven
for their hunger;
you brought them water from the rock
for their thirst.
You told them to go in and possess the land
you had sworn[D] to give them.

16 But our ancestors acted arrogantly;
they became stiff-necked and did not listen
to your commands.

17 They refused to listen
and did not remember your wonders
you performed among them.
They became stiff-necked and appointed
a leader
to return to their slavery in Egypt.[E]

[A] **8:18** Some Hb mss, Syr read *They* [B] **9:6** LXX reads *And Ezra said: You* [C] **9:6** Lit *are alone* [D] **9:15** Lit *lifted your hand* [E] **9:17** Some Hb mss, LXX; other Hb mss read *in their rebellion*

But you are a forgiving God,
gracious and compassionate,
slow to anger and abounding in faithful love,
and you did not abandon them.
18 Even after they had cast an image of a calf
for themselves and said,
"This is your god who brought you
out of Egypt,"
and they had committed terrible blasphemies,
19 you did not abandon them in the wilderness
because of your great compassion.
During the day the pillar of cloud
never turned away from them,
guiding them on their journey.
And during the night the pillar of fire
illuminated the way they should go.
20 You sent your good Spirit to instruct them.
You did not withhold your manna
from their mouths,
and you gave them water for their thirst.
21 You provided for them in the wilderness
forty years,
and they lacked nothing.
Their clothes did not wear out,
and their feet did not swell.

22 You gave them kingdoms and peoples
and established boundaries for them.
They took possession
of the land of King Sihon[A] of Heshbon
and of the land of King Og of Bashan.
23 You multiplied their descendants
like the stars of the sky
and brought them to the land
you told their ancestors to go in and possess.
24 So their descendants went in and possessed
the land:
You subdued the Canaanites who inhabited
the land before them
and handed their kings and the surrounding
peoples over to them,
to do as they pleased with them.
25 They captured fortified cities and fertile land
and took possession of well-supplied houses,
cisterns cut out of rock, vineyards,
olive groves, and fruit trees in abundance.
They ate, were filled,
became prosperous, and delighted
in your great goodness.

26 But they were disobedient and rebelled
against you.
They flung your law behind their backs
and killed your prophets
who warned them
in order to turn them back to you.
They committed terrible blasphemies.
27 So you handed them over to their enemies,
who oppressed them.
In their time of distress, they cried out to you,
and you heard from heaven.
In your abundant compassion
you gave them deliverers, who rescued them
from the power of their enemies.
28 But as soon as they had relief,
they again did what was evil in your sight.
So you abandoned them to the power
of their enemies,
who dominated them.
When they cried out to you again,
you heard from heaven and rescued them
many times in your compassion.
29 You warned them to turn back to your law,
but they acted arrogantly
and would not obey your commands.
They sinned against your ordinances,
which a person will live by if he does them.
They stubbornly resisted,[B]
stiffened their necks, and would not obey.
30 You were patient with them for many years,
and your Spirit warned them
through your prophets,
but they would not listen.
Therefore, you handed them over
to the surrounding peoples.
31 However, in your abundant compassion,
you did not destroy them or abandon them,
for you are a gracious
and compassionate God.

32 So now, our God — the great, mighty,
and awe-inspiring God who keeps
his gracious covenant —
do not view lightly all the hardships
that have afflicted us,
our kings and leaders,
our priests and prophets,
our ancestors and all your people,
from the days of the Assyrian kings until today.
33 You are righteous concerning all
that has happened to us,
because you have acted faithfully,
while we have acted wickedly.
34 Our kings, leaders, priests, and ancestors
did not obey your law
or listen to your commands
and warnings you gave them.

[A] **9:22** One Hb ms, LXX; other Hb mss, Vg read *of Sihon, even the land of the king* [B] **9:29** Lit *They gave a stubborn shoulder*

35 When they were in their kingdom,
with your abundant goodness that
you gave them,
and in the spacious and fertile land you set
before them,
they would not serve you or turn
from their wicked ways.

36 Here we are today,
slaves in the land you gave our ancestors
so that they could enjoy its fruit
and its goodness.
Here we are — slaves in it!
37 Its abundant harvest goes to the kings
you have set over us,
because of our sins.
They rule over our bodies
and our livestock as they please.
We are in great distress.

ISRAEL'S VOW OF FAITHFULNESS

38 In view of all this, we are making a binding agreement in writing on a sealed document containing the
names of our leaders, Levites, and priests.

10 Those whose seals were on the document were
the governor Nehemiah son of Hacaliah,
and Zedekiah,
2 Seraiah, Azariah, Jeremiah,
3 Pashhur, Amariah, Malchijah,
4 Hattush, Shebaniah, Malluch,
5 Harim, Meremoth, Obadiah,
6 Daniel, Ginnethon, Baruch,
7 Meshullam, Abijah, Mijamin,
8 Maaziah, Bilgai, and Shemaiah.
These were the priests.

9 The Levites were
Jeshua son of Azaniah,
Binnui of the sons of Henadad, Kadmiel,
10 and their brothers
Shebaniah, Hodiah, Kelita, Pelaiah, Hanan,
11 Mica, Rehob, Hashabiah,
12 Zaccur, Sherebiah, Shebaniah,
13 Hodiah, Bani, and Beninu.

14 The heads of the people were
Parosh, Pahath-moab, Elam, Zattu, Bani,
15 Bunni, Azgad, Bebai,
16 Adonijah, Bigvai, Adin,
17 Ater, Hezekiah, Azzur,
18 Hodiah, Hashum, Bezai,
19 Hariph, Anathoth, Nebai,
20 Magpiash, Meshullam, Hezir,
21 Meshezabel, Zadok, Jaddua,
22 Pelatiah, Hanan, Anaiah,
23 Hoshea, Hananiah, Hasshub,
24 Hallohesh, Pilha, Shobek,
25 Rehum, Hashabnah, Maaseiah,
26 Ahijah, Hanan, Anan,
27 Malluch, Harim, Baanah.

28 The rest of the people — the priests, Levites,
gatekeepers, singers, and temple servants, along with
their wives, sons, and daughters, everyone who is
able to understand and who has separated themselves from the surrounding peoples to obey the
law of God — 29 join with their noble brothers and
commit themselves with a sworn oath[A] to follow the
law of God given through God's servant Moses and
to obey carefully all the commands, ordinances, and
statutes of the LORD our Lord.

DETAILS OF THE VOW

30 We will not give our daughters in marriage to
the surrounding peoples and will not take their
daughters as wives for our sons.

31 When the surrounding peoples bring merchandise or any kind of grain to sell on the
Sabbath day, we will not buy from them on the
Sabbath or a holy day. We will also leave the land
uncultivated in the seventh year and will cancel
every debt.

32 We will impose the following commands on
ourselves:

To give an eighth of an ounce of silver[B] yearly
for the service of the house of our God: 33 the
bread displayed before the LORD,[C] the daily
grain offering, the regular burnt offering, the
Sabbath and New Moon offerings, the appointed festivals, the holy things, the sin offerings
to atone for Israel, and for all the work of the
house of our God.

34 We have cast lots among the priests, Levites,
and people for the donation of wood by our
ancestral families[D] at the appointed times each
year. They are to bring the wood to our God's
house to burn on the altar of the LORD our God,
as it is written in the law.

35 We will bring the firstfruits of our land and
of every fruit tree to the LORD's house year by
year. 36 We will also bring the firstborn of our
sons and our livestock, as prescribed by the law,

[A] **10:29** Lit *and enter in a curse and in an oath* [B] **10:32** Lit *give one-third of a shekel* [C] **10:33** Lit *rows of bread* [D] **10:34** Lit *the house of our fathers*

Life after the Exile

by T. Van McClain

After the Persians conquered Babylon, King Cyrus issued a decree allowing the Jewish people to return to Jerusalem. The Babylonians had destroyed the city and the temple, and the city walls were in disrepair.

Some have wondered if this return from exile actually happened. An archaeological artifact, the Cyrus Cylinder, provides corroboration of Cyrus decreeing that the Jews could return to their homeland (see 2Ch 36). Persia's King Cyrus II reigned 550–530 BC and produced the cylinder chronicling some of the events of his reign. While the cylinder's text does not mention Jerusalem or the Jews by name, it does indicate that King Cyrus had a tolerant policy toward conquered peoples and offered to restore their religious sanctuaries. According to the cylinder, King Cyrus made the following claim regarding holy cities "whose sanctuaries had been in ruins over a long period, the gods whose abode is in the midst of them, I returned to their places and housed them in lasting abodes. I gathered together all their inhabitants and restored to them their dwellings."[1] This return from exile actually occurred. Surely the Jews' hearts were filled with joy as they realized this was a fulfillment of Jeremiah's prophecy from God to return the people of Israel to their promised land after seventy years of captivity (Jr 29:10; see 25:11–12).

Of course, their new life was different from what they experienced under the Davidic kingship. The Davidic kingship had ended; in its stead, a governor the Persians appointed ruled over the Jews. The returnees had to answer to their Persian rulers and seek their approval before beginning any building projects.

The Jews had the freedom to reinstitute the worship of Yahweh, celebrating the appointed feasts and Sabbaths as the Torah commanded; but had they really learned to refrain from idolatry? Some Jews

A pottery figure of a foreigner who came to Judah while the Jews were in captivity in Babylon. Aramaic writing on the base of the figure suggests the individual had a Mediterranean background. One of the problems the returnees faced was the reaction of those who had inhabited the land while the Jews were in captivity.

did; they became overzealous of the law, adding to the Lord's commandments, perhaps with the desire never to return to idolatry. These were the forerunners of the Pharisees. In contrast, others intermarried with their pagan neighbors, probably for financial or political reasons. The wives from these other nations introduced foreign deities, and the children of these unions turned to idolatry.

The Jews returned to their homeland in three waves, and God's hand was evident in each one. Zerubbabel, who was the leader of the tribe of Judah, led the first wave in 538 BC. This Zerubbabel was also a descendant of King David and of the imprisoned king named Jehoiachin (Jeconiah).

The returnees found the temple in ruins, homes devastated, and Jerusalem's walls in shambles.

Interior of a reconstructed four-room house typical of those found in ancient Israel.

WHERE TO LIVE

Many of the returnees lived in Jerusalem. Since farming was the most common vocation, others lived in the surrounding country, close to Jerusalem. The apportionment of property likely was based on genealogical considerations (as inheritance of property was based on tribal affiliation), deeds, or other documentation of family ownership that may have been preserved. Other property assignments would have been based on the personal recollections of those old enough to remember their former homes and on the guidance and decisions Zerubbabel and his associates made. Of course, some people's previous homes or farms may have been inhabited by those currently residing in the Jerusalem area. If so, the returning Jews likely had to find someplace else to live.

When the Babylonians destroyed Jerusalem, they took many of the Jews captive. Some Jews who remained in the land, however, later abandoned their homes and fled to Egypt. Thus the homes of many Jews, if not destroyed, had fallen into disrepair. Restoring all of these homes was a huge challenge.

According to 2 Kings 17:24, the Assyrians (who had conquered Israel in 722 BC) brought in foreigners from Babylon and other areas to live in the land of Israel. Many of these people likely settled in the area of Judah after the Jews were taken into captivity. The Assyrians took one of the Jewish priests into captivity but later returned him to Bethel, in Israel. In spite of his presence, idolatry continued among the inhabitants. They claimed to worship Yahweh but had a bent toward idolatry. As a result, they did not fear God (2Kg 17:34). This mixed group of people would be called "Samaritans." These people opposed the Jews' rebuilding work. Ezra's and Nehemiah's later attempts to lead the Hebrew men to divorce their pagan wives further drove a wedge between the Jews and their neighbors.

In 458 BC, Ezra led a second group of Jews back to the land of Israel with the blessing of Persia's king. Many Jews in Israel had intermarried with the pagan people around them.

The nation was in danger of reverting to idolatry. Doing so would mean facing God's judgment again. A leader named Shecaniah proposed a solution for the intermarriage problem; he suggested the Jewish men divorce their pagan wives. Shecaniah indicated he and others would support Ezra in calling the people to make this difficult decision (Ezr 10:2–4).

Ezra led the people to make this covenant. Intermarriage with foreigners was not forbidden if that person had come to faith in Yahweh. The resultant revival of true worship that Ezra led was exceptional—albeit short-lived. Within a generation of Ezra, the intermarriage with pagans and the resulting idolatry would again be an issue.

Excavations in Jerusalem unearthed this base of a small tower and a portion of Nehemiah's wall.

JEWISH GOVERNMENT

How would living under a foreign king's rule compare with life under a national king? Before the Babylonian exile, the Jews had lived under the rule of their own kings for about 450 years. The king was accountable to God. After returning to their homeland, the Jews lived under the rule of a governor whom the king of Persia appointed; the governor answered to the king. Evidence of this change was apparent when the Jews' enemies persuaded the Persian king to halt the Jews' work on the temple for seventeen years during Zerubbabel's governorship. The Persian monarch did provide the Jews a great deal of religious freedom during this time, but the Jews did not have political autonomy.

CHANGING RELIGIOUS PRACTICES

One of the greatest changes in Jewish religious practices during and after the exile was the growth and prominence of the synagogue. While in captivity, the Jews were unable to worship at the temple, so they met in smaller groups and worshiped under the leading of rabbis.

Additionally, the Jews likely adopted the Aramaic language as long as they were in Babylon, although they continued to study Hebrew. As a result, Hebrew may have not been the Jews' native language after the exile.

Two factors indicate that the priests likely had greater authority in Israel after the exile: the loss of a centralized ruler and the rise of the synagogues' importance. The fortunes of the Jews therefore depended on the character of the priest. Joshua (or Jeshua) the son of Jehozadak (or Jozadak), who returned as high priest after the exile, found favor with God (Zch 3; 6:9–14); however, some of his sons married foreign women (Ezr 10:18). Such priestly misconduct seemed to be rampant, as both Nehemiah and Malachi had to address the priests' sins (Neh 13:4–9; Mal 1:6–2:9). The priests' loss of respect for God led to the people's loss of respect for him as well. One result was that people neglected tithing (Neh 13:10–13; Mal 3:7–12). ✣

---

[1] Bill T. Arnold and Bryan E. Beyer, eds., *Readings from the Ancient Near East: Primary Sources for Old Testament Study* (Grand Rapids: Baker Academic, 2002), 148–49.

and will bring the firstborn of our herds and flocks to the house of our God, to the priests who serve in our God's house. [37] We will bring a loaf from our first batch of dough to the priests at the storerooms of the house of our God. We will also bring the firstfruits of our grain offerings, of every fruit tree, and of the new wine and fresh oil. A tenth of our land's produce belongs to the Levites, for the Levites are to collect the one-tenth offering in all our agricultural towns. [38] A priest from Aaron's descendants is to accompany the Levites when they collect the tenth, and the Levites are to take a tenth of this offering to the storerooms of the treasury in the house of our God. [39] For the Israelites and the Levites are to bring the contributions of grain, new wine, and fresh oil to the storerooms where the articles of the sanctuary are kept and where the priests who minister are, along with the gatekeepers and singers. We will not neglect the house of our God.

RESETTLING JERUSALEM

11 Now the leaders of the people stayed in Jerusalem, and the rest of the people cast lots for one out of ten to come and live in Jerusalem, the holy city, while the other nine-tenths remained in their towns. [2] The people blessed all the men who volunteered to live in Jerusalem.

[3] These are the heads of the province who stayed in Jerusalem (but in the villages of Judah each lived on his own property in their towns — the Israelites, priests, Levites, temple servants, and descendants of Solomon's servants — [4] while some of the descendants of Judah and Benjamin settled in Jerusalem):

Judah's descendants:

Athaiah son of Uzziah, son of Zechariah, son of Amariah, son of Shephatiah, son of Mahalalel, of Perez's descendants; [5] and Maaseiah son of Baruch, son of Col-hozeh, son of Hazaiah, son of Adaiah, son of Joiarib, son of Zechariah, a descendant of the Shilonite. [6] The total number of Perez's descendants, who settled in Jerusalem, was 468 capable men.

[7] These were Benjamin's descendants:

Sallu son of Meshullam, son of Joed, son of Pedaiah, son of Kolaiah, son of Maaseiah, son of Ithiel, son of Jeshaiah, [8] and after him Gabbai and Sallai: 928. [9] Joel son of Zichri was the officer over them, and Judah son of Hassenuah was second in command over the city.

[10] The priests:

Jedaiah son of Joiarib, Jachin, and [11] Seraiah son of Hilkiah, son of Meshullam, son of Zadok, son of Meraioth, son of Ahitub, the chief official of God's temple, [12] and their relatives who did the work at the temple: 822. Adaiah son of Jeroham, son of Pelaliah, son of Amzi, son of Zechariah, son of Pashhur, son of Malchijah [13] and his relatives, the heads of families: 242. Amashsai son of Azarel, son of Ahzai, son of Meshillemoth, son of Immer, [14] and their relatives, capable men: 128. Zabdiel son of Haggedolim, was their chief.

[15] The Levites:

Shemaiah son of Hasshub, son of Azrikam, son of Hashabiah, son of Bunni; [16] and Shabbethai and Jozabad, from the heads of the Levites, who supervised the work outside the house of God; [17] Mattaniah son of Mica, son of Zabdi, son of Asaph, the one[A] who began the thanksgiving in prayer; Bakbukiah, second among his relatives; and Abda son of Shammua, son of Galal, son of Jeduthun. [18] All the Levites in the holy city: 284.

[19] The gatekeepers:

Akkub, Talmon, and their relatives, who guarded the city gates: 172.

[20] The rest of Israel, the priests, and the Levites were in all the villages of Judah, each on his own inherited property. [21] The temple servants lived on Ophel; Ziha and Gishpa supervised the temple servants.

THE LEVITES AND PRIESTS

[22] The leader of the Levites in Jerusalem was Uzzi son of Bani, son of Hashabiah, son of Mattaniah, son of Mica, of the descendants of Asaph, who were singers for the service of God's house. [23] There was, in fact, a command of the king regarding them, and an ordinance regulating the singers' daily tasks. [24] Pethahiah son of Meshezabel, of the descendants of Zerah son of Judah, was the king's agent[B] in every matter concerning the people.

[25] As for the farming settlements with their fields:
Some of Judah's descendants lived in
Kiriath-arba
and Dibon and their surrounding villages,
and Jekabzeel and its settlements;

[A] **11:17** Lit *the head* [B] **11:24** Lit *was at the king's hand*

26 in Jeshua, Moladah, Beth-pelet,
27 Hazar-shual, and Beer-sheba
and its surrounding villages;
28 in Ziklag and Meconah and its surrounding
villages;
29 in En-rimmon, Zorah, Jarmuth, and
30 Zanoah and Adullam with their settlements;
in Lachish with its fields and Azekah
and its surrounding villages.
So they settled from Beer-sheba
to Hinnom Valley.

31 Benjamin's descendants:
from Geba,[A] Michmash, Aija,
and Bethel and its surrounding villages,
32 Anathoth, Nob, Ananiah,
33 Hazor, Ramah, Gittaim,
34 Hadid, Zeboim, Neballat,
35 Lod, and Ono, in Craftsmen's Valley.
36 Some of the Judean divisions of Levites were
in Benjamin.

12 These are the priests and Levites who went
up with Zerubbabel son of Shealtiel and with
Jeshua:
Seraiah, Jeremiah, Ezra,
2 Amariah, Malluch, Hattush,
3 Shecaniah, Rehum, Meremoth,
4 Iddo, Ginnethoi, Abijah,
5 Mijamin, Maadiah, Bilgah,
6 Shemaiah, Joiarib, Jedaiah,
7 Sallu, Amok, Hilkiah, Jedaiah.
These were the heads of the priests and their relatives
in the days of Jeshua.
8 The Levites:
Jeshua, Binnui, Kadmiel,
Sherebiah, Judah, and Mattaniah —
he and his relatives were in charge
of the songs of praise.
9 Bakbukiah, Unni,[B] and their relatives stood
opposite them in the services.
10 Jeshua fathered Joiakim,
Joiakim fathered Eliashib,
Eliashib fathered Joiada,
11 Joiada fathered Jonathan,
and Jonathan fathered Jaddua.[C]

12 In the days of Joiakim, the heads of the priestly
families were
Meraiah of Seraiah,
Hananiah of Jeremiah,
13 Meshullam of Ezra,
Jehohanan of Amariah,
14 Jonathan of Malluchi,
Joseph of Shebaniah,
15 Adna of Harim,
Helkai of Meraioth,
16 Zechariah of Iddo,
Meshullam of Ginnethon,
17 Zichri of Abijah,
Piltai of Moadiah, of Miniamin,
18 Shammua of Bilgah,
Jehonathan of Shemaiah,
19 Mattenai of Joiarib,
Uzzi of Jedaiah,
20 Kallai of Sallai,
Eber of Amok,
21 Hashabiah of Hilkiah,
and Nethanel of Jedaiah.

22 In the days of Eliashib, Joiada, Johanan, and
Jaddua, the heads of the families of the Levites and
priests were recorded while Darius the Persian ruled.
23 Levi's descendants, the family heads, were recorded in the Book of the Historical Events during the
days of Johanan son of Eliashib. 24 The heads of the
Levites — Hashabiah, Sherebiah, and Jeshua son of
Kadmiel, along with their relatives opposite them
— gave praise and thanks, division by division, as
David the man of God had prescribed. 25 This included Mattaniah, Bakbukiah, and Obadiah. Meshullam,
Talmon, and Akkub were gatekeepers who guarded
the storerooms at the city gates. 26 These served in
the days of Joiakim son of Jeshua, son of Jozadak,
and in the days of Nehemiah the governor and Ezra
the priest and scribe.

DEDICATION OF THE WALL

27 At the dedication of the wall of Jerusalem, they sent
for the Levites wherever they lived and brought them
to Jerusalem to celebrate the joyous dedication with
thanksgiving and singing accompanied by cymbals,
harps, and lyres. 28 The singers gathered from the region around Jerusalem, from the settlements of the
Netophathites, 29 from Beth-gilgal, and from the fields
of Geba and Azmaveth, for they had built settlements
for themselves around Jerusalem. 30 After the priests
and Levites had purified themselves, they purified
the people, the city gates, and the wall.
31 Then I brought the leaders of Judah up on top of
the wall, and I appointed two large processions that
gave thanks. One went to the right on the wall, toward
the Dung Gate. 32 Hoshaiah and half the leaders of Judah followed, 33 along with Azariah, Ezra, Meshullam,
34 Judah, Benjamin, Shemaiah, Jeremiah, 35 and some
of the priests' sons with trumpets, and Zechariah
son of Jonathan, son of Shemaiah, son of Mattaniah,

[A] 11:31 Or *descendants from Geba lived in* [B] 12:9 Alt Hb tradition reads *Unno* [C] 12:10–11 These men were high priests.

son of Micaiah, son of Zaccur, son of Asaph followed
36 as well as his relatives — Shemaiah, Azarel, Milalai,
Gilalai, Maai, Nethanel, Judah, and Hanani, with the
musical instruments of David, the man of God. Ezra
the scribe went in front of them. 37 At the Fountain
Gate they climbed the steps of the city of David on
the ascent of the wall and went above the house of
David to the Water Gate on the east.
38 The second thanksgiving procession went to the
left, and I followed it with half the people along the
top of the wall, past the Tower of the Ovens to
the Broad Wall, 39 above the Ephraim Gate, and by
the Old Gate, the Fish Gate, the Tower of Hananel,
and the Tower of the Hundred, to the Sheep Gate.
They stopped at the Gate of the Guard. 40 The two
thanksgiving processions stood in the house of God.
So did I and half of the officials accompanying me,
41 as well as the priests:

Eliakim, Maaseiah, Miniamin,
Micaiah, Elioenai, Zechariah,
and Hananiah, with trumpets;
42 and Maaseiah, Shemaiah, Eleazar,
Uzzi, Jehohanan, Malchijah, Elam, and Ezer.

Then the singers sang, with Jezrahiah as the leader. 43 On that day they offered great sacrifices and
rejoiced because God had given them great joy. The
women and children also celebrated, and Jerusalem's
rejoicing was heard far away.

SUPPORT OF THE LEVITES' MINISTRY

44 On that same day men were placed in charge of
the rooms that housed the supplies, contributions,
firstfruits, and tenths. The legally required portions
for the priests and Levites were gathered from the village fields, because Judah was grateful to the priests
and Levites who were serving. 45 They performed the
service of their God and the service of purification,
along with the singers and gatekeepers, as David and
his son Solomon had prescribed. 46 For long ago, in
the days of David and Asaph, there were heads[A] of
the singers and songs of praise and thanksgiving to
God. 47 So in the days of Zerubbabel and Nehemiah, all
Israel contributed the daily portions for the singers
and gatekeepers. They also set aside daily portions
for the Levites, and the Levites set aside daily portions
for Aaron's descendants.

NEHEMIAH'S FURTHER REFORMS

13 At that time the book of Moses was read publicly to[B] the people. The command was found
written in it that no Ammonite or Moabite should
ever enter the assembly of God, 2 because they did
not meet the Israelites with food and water. Instead,
they hired Balaam against them to curse them, but
our God turned the curse into a blessing. 3 When they
heard the law, they separated all those of mixed descent from Israel.
4 Now before this, the priest Eliashib had been put
in charge of the storerooms of the house of our God.
He was a relative[C] of Tobiah 5 and had prepared a large
room for him where they had previously stored the
grain offerings, the frankincense, the articles, and the
tenths of grain, new wine, and fresh oil prescribed
for the Levites, singers, and gatekeepers, along with
the contributions for the priests.
6 While all this was happening, I was not in Jerusalem, because I had returned to King Artaxerxes of
Babylon in the thirty-second year of his reign. It was
only later that I asked the king for a leave of absence
7 so I could return to Jerusalem. Then I discovered the
evil that Eliashib had done on behalf of Tobiah by
providing him a room in the courts of God's house.
8 I was greatly displeased and threw all of Tobiah's
household possessions out of the room. 9 I ordered
that the rooms be purified, and I had the articles of
the house of God restored there, along with the grain
offering and frankincense. 10 I also found out that because the portions for the Levites had not been given,
each of the Levites and the singers performing the
service had gone back to his own field. 11 Therefore,
I rebuked the officials, asking, "Why has the house
of God been neglected?" I gathered the Levites and
singers together and stationed them at their posts.
12 Then all Judah brought a tenth of the grain, new
wine, and fresh oil into the storehouses. 13 I appointed
as treasurers over the storehouses the priest Shelemiah, the scribe Zadok, and Pedaiah of the Levites,
with Hanan son of Zaccur, son of Mattaniah to assist
them, because they were considered trustworthy.
They were responsible for the distribution to their
colleagues.
14 Remember me for this, my God, and don't erase
the deeds of faithful love I have done for the house
of my God and for its services.
15 At that time I saw people in Judah treading winepresses on the Sabbath. They were also bringing in
stores of grain and loading them on donkeys, along
with wine, grapes, and figs. All kinds of goods were
being brought to Jerusalem on the Sabbath day. So I
warned them against selling food on that day. 16 The
Tyrians living there were importing fish and all kinds
of merchandise and selling them on the Sabbath to
the people of Judah in Jerusalem.
17 I rebuked the nobles of Judah and said to them,
"What is this evil you are doing — profaning the Sabbath day? 18 Didn't your ancestors do the same, so that
our God brought all this disaster on us and on this

[A] **12:46** Alt Hb tradition reads *there was a head* [B] **13:1** Lit *read in the ears of* [C] **13:4** Or *an associate*

The Jerusalem Gates

by Gary P. Arbino

Gates and Gatekeepers

by Scott Hummel

As seen from Gethsemane, the Eastern or Golden Gate, showing the Kidron Valley rising up to the city walls. This gate, on the eastern side of the city, was constructed in the post-Byzantine period. To prevent the Messiah from entering Jerusalem through this gate, the Muslims sealed it during the mid-1500s.

The book of Nehemiah mentions a total of twelve different gates around the city of Jerusalem. Situating these twelve gates physically is difficult.

The first and last gates in Nehemiah's circuit were in the northern wall, probably originally built by Judah's King Manasseh (reigned 696–642 BC; see 2Ch 33:14). The Sheep Gate stood just east of the fortress created by the Hananel and Meah/Hundred towers at the northwestern corner of the temple enclosure (Neh 12:39). It probably exited to an animal market. Rebuilt and consecrated by a priestly family (3:1), this gate was perhaps also sacral—bringing in animal sacrifices for the temple. Archaeological evidence for the Sheep Gate might be found in an underground passage, known in later literature as the Tadi Gate.[1] The Gate of the Guard (or Prison Gate) was located between the Sheep Gate and the northeast corner of the wall (v. 39). Functionally, this gate seems to be connected to the court of the guard (Jr 37–39), which was positioned at the southern part of the temple

Jerusalem's Zion Gate, so named because it is situated on Mount Zion. Some also call it David's Gate, because the traditional tomb of David faces the gate. This gate was constructed in AD 1540.

compound. The absence of archaeological evidence makes a precise placement impossible.

Located along the western wall, a short distance south from the Hananel Tower, the Fish Gate was probably so named because the fish markets were outside of it. Zephaniah 1:10–11 indicates that it was a focus of Babylon's attack. Given the number of crews Nehemiah assigned to this area (Neh 3:2–8), destruction here evidently was severe. A short distance south stood the "Old" Gate. Difficult to translate, the gate name could mean that it led into the "old city" or that it led out to the Mishneh. The next gate, the Ephraim Gate, is not mentioned in chapter 3 but is situated by chapter 12. Named for the road that led north to Ephraim, it was probably near the juncture where the Broad Wall enclosing the Mishneh joined the wall surrounding the Solomonic city (3:8; cf. 2Kg 14:13). Associated with this gate was a plaza (Neh 8:16). No archaeological evidence has been found for these three gates.

South of the Ephraim Gate stood the Valley Gate, the main city gate. About five hundred yards farther south along a section of wall that sustained only minor damage was the Dung Gate (Hb *ashpot*, "rubbish"). Although no archaeological evidence has yet been unearthed for the Persian-period Dung Gate, its location somewhere near the southern tip of the city of David is certain (2:13–15; 12:31,37). It had open access to the Hinnom Valley rubbish heaps, hence its name and use. Just to the north and east of the Dung Gate was the Fountain Gate (or Spring Gate). According to Nehemiah (2:14–15; 3:15; 12:37), this gate (not yet found) was associated with a set of stairs, now excavated, that led upslope into the city of David. Archaeologists also excavated a series of water channels connected to these stairs. The channels ran from the Gihon Spring, about three hundred yards up the valley. These channels and their overflow drainage probably created a spring or fountain of sorts near the gate, hence its name.

Nehemiah lists twelve work crews along the eastern wall between the Fountain and Water Gates (3:16–26). This large number suggests that these fortifications had suffered extensive damage (2:14–15). Archaeologists confirm that the wall line was moved upslope in this area to the crest of the hill during the Persian period. Recent excavations have shown evidence of late Iron Age fortifications around the Gihon Spring, the likely location for the Water Gate.[2] Two towers (3:26–27) protecting the spring and a pool have been discovered. We

The Lions' Gate is also called St. Stephen's Gate, because Stephen may have been martyred in this region. This is the only gate currently open on the east side of the Old City of Jerusalem. The gate opens to the Kidron Valley, east of Jerusalem.

The Dung Gate was used for disposal of garbage and refuse. Beyond the gate is the Hinnom Valley and Silwan, where Jerusalem's original inhabitants settled. [Neh 2:13; 3:13; 12:31]

assume these towers were part of the Water Gate complex, left intact by the Babylonians or repaired by earlier returnees to Jerusalem. This configuration would have left an open space between the Persian walls upslope and the Water Gate in the Kidron Valley. This then was the "square" (Hb *rehov*, "open space") where Ezra read the Torah during the rededication ceremony (8:1–15).

Lack of archaeological evidence prevents the final two gates on the circuit from being reasonably located. The Horse Gate was in the eastern external wall somewhere near the southern part of the temple complex (Jr 31:40). Additional internal gates brought the horses from the Horse Gate into the stable areas (2Kg 11:16). Finally, the Muster Gate, also translated as "Inspection" or *Miphqad* (Neh 3:31), was situated in the eastern wall between the Horse Gate and the northeastern

Herod's Gate in Jerusalem received its name from pilgrims visiting the city who (erroneously) thought the entrance led directly to Herod's palace. Though originally L-shaped, the entrance was rebuilt as a projection from the wall. The entrance gives direct entry into the Old City.

A view of the Damascus Gate. This is the most massive and ornate of all the gates in Jerusalem. The road from this gate leads to Shechem and then to Damascus. Recent excavations have uncovered an ancient Roman entrance beneath the gate. [Neh 3:32]

Jaffa Gate; for centuries this was the only entrance into the city from the west. Its Arabic name means "Gate of Hebron," as the main road to Hebron started at this gate.

corner. The name is difficult to translate and is not used elsewhere. It is possible that it is the same as the Benjamin Gate (Jr 17:19; 37:13; 38:7; Zch 14:10) leading north from Jerusalem.

GATEKEEPERS

Because the gate was the most vulnerable part of the wall, the gate had to be well fortified and designed to restrict access. The doors were made of wood and iron nails (1Ch 22:3; Neh 2:8). To reduce the chance of fire, some doors were plated with bronze (Ps 107:16).[3] Double doors were necessary because the gate had to be wide enough to allow a chariot through. When the doors were closed, they were "barred" from the inside with a wooden, bronze, or iron-plated bar (1Kg 4:13; Nah 3:13). "Wooden posts braced the doors, and the doors pivoted in stone sockets"[4] (see Jdg 16:2–3).

While some gates had only two chambers, one on each side of the entrance, the classical Israelite gate was either four or six chambered. For example, the Solomonic gates at Megiddo, Hazor, and Gezer were all six-chambered gates (1Kg 9:15).[5] Benches lined the inside of each chamber, which formed a small room where the guards could lodge. Each pair of chambers had its own doors, which attackers had to breach successively.[6] Towers usually flanked each side of the gate and watchmen stood on the roof of the gate (2Sm 18:24).[7] All this made the gate complex a veritable fortress.

For greater security, many of the large cities built an outer gate complex. This could trap invaders between the outer and inner gates. By forcing a sharp right turn, it created indirect access to the gate, forced the invaders to expose their right side, which was not protected by their shields, and made it more difficult to set up battering rams and siege towers against the gates (Ezk 21:22).[8]

The gates were only as secure as the gatekeepers were courageous and trustworthy (1Ch 9:22).[9] They served as watchmen and reported news and potential danger (2Sm 18:24). They guarded the nearby storehouses, opened and shut the gates each day, kept the city gates shut during the Sabbath, and defended the gates during assault (Neh 7:3; 12:25; 13:19).

The temple gatekeepers not only protected the temple, they "ministered" in the gates and assisted with the sacrifices (2Ch 31:2; Neh 13:22; Ezk 44:11). They protected the temple treasures and accounted for the temple utensils (1Ch 9:17–28). During his reforms, Josiah called upon the gatekeepers to rid the temple of idols (2Kg 23:4).

As far back as the time of the tabernacle, the gatekeepers were a special class of Levites (1Ch 9:19). As such, they enjoyed the Levitical privileges such as receiving support from the tithes imposed on Israelites (Neh 10:39; 12:47; 13:5) and exemption from taxes (Ezr 7:24). The priests and Levites, including the gatekeepers, performed their responsibilities between the ages of thirty and fifty (Nm 4:3). Even in exile away from Jerusalem and the temple, they maintained their identity as gatekeepers from one generation to the next.

The gatekeepers were organized into a hierarchical structure with a chief gatekeeper (1Ch 9:17) and a captain in charge of each gate (2Kg 7:17). The divisions of gatekeepers were assigned to specific gates, sometimes by casting lots and sometimes by royal appointment (1Ch 26:12–19; 2Ch 35:15). The number of gatekeepers is recorded as high as 4,000, but during the time of Nehemiah only 172 served (1Ch 23:3; Neh 11:19). In times of emergency, non-Levitical gatekeepers could be assigned to guard the city gates, as Nehemiah did when threatened by the Samaritans, Arabs, Ammonites, and Ashdodites (Neh 7:3).

City gates served contrasting purposes, restricting access for military purposes while providing access for commerce and communication. Since everyone entered through the gates, the courtyards and squares adjacent to them were centers for public life and markets.

Parties settled disputes and trials in the city gates (Dt 21:19; 22:15). For example, Boaz legally redeemed Ruth in the city gate (Ru 4:1–11). Citizens brought their disputes before the city elders or even the king who administered justice from his throne, which was sometimes in the city gate (2Sm 15:2; 1Kg 22:10). Immediately following a verdict, punishment was carried out publicly at the gates (Dt 17:5; Jr 20:2). The prophets demanded "justice at the city gate" (Am 5:15; see Zch 8:16).[10]

Religious assemblies gathered at the gates and in the courtyards of the gates. When the people gathered to hear Ezra read the law, they gathered in the square before the Water Gate (Neh 8:3). Later, in observance of the Feast of Shelters (or Tabernacles or Booths), the people made and lived in their shelters "on each of their rooftops and courtyards, the court of the house of God, the square by the Water Gate, and the square by the Ephraim Gate" (v. 16). ✣

---

[1] Leen and Kathleen Ritmeyer, *Jerusalem in the Time of Nehemiah* (Jerusalem: Carta, 2005), 25–28. [2] See Ronny Reich and Eli Shukron, "Light at the End of the Tunnel," *BAR* 25.1 (1999), 22–33; Hershel Shanks, "2700-Year-Old Tower Found?" *BAR* 26.5 (2000), 39–41. [3] Philip J. King and Lawrence E. Stager, *Life in Biblical Israel* (Louisville: Westminster John Knox, 2001), 234. [4] King and Stager, *Life*, 236. [5] Alfred J. Hoerth, *Archaeology and the Old Testament* (Grand Rapids: Baker Academic, 1998), 287; King and Stager, *Life*, 236. [6] Hoerth, *Archaeology and the Old Testament*, 286; King and Stager, *Life*, 236. [7] Roland de Vaux, *Ancient Israel* (Grand Rapids: Eerdmans, 1961), 234; Ephraim Stern, *Archaeology of the Land of the Bible: The Assyrian, Babylonian, and Persian Periods (732–332 BCE)*, vol. 2 in ABRL (2001), 466–67. [8] De Vaux, *Ancient Israel*, 234; King and Stager, *Life*, 234. [9] Gary A. Lee, "Gatekeeper" in *ISBE*, vol. 2 (1982), 409. [10] De Vaux, *Ancient Israel*, 152.

Looking through the six-chambered gate at Megiddo. Located on the northern side of the city, the gate overlooks the valley, about 160 feet below.

city? And now you are rekindling his anger against
Israel by profaning the Sabbath!"
19 When shadows began to fall on the city gates of
Jerusalem just before the Sabbath, I gave orders that
the city gates be closed and not opened until after the
Sabbath. I posted some of my men at the gates, so that
no goods could enter during the Sabbath day. 20 Once
or twice the merchants and those who sell all kinds
of goods camped outside Jerusalem, 21 but I warned
them, "Why are you camping in front of the wall? If
you do it again, I'll use force[A] against you." After that
they did not come again on the Sabbath. 22 Then I instructed the Levites to purify themselves and guard
the city gates in order to keep the Sabbath day holy.

Remember me for this also, my God, and look on
me with compassion according to the abundance of
your faithful love.

23 In those days I also saw Jews who had married
women from Ashdod, Ammon, and Moab. 24 Half of
their children spoke the language of Ashdod or the
language of one of the other peoples but could not
speak Hebrew.[B] 25 I rebuked them, cursed them, beat
some of their men, and pulled out their hair. I forced
them to take an oath before God and said, "You must
not give your daughters in marriage to their sons or
take their daughters as wives for your sons or yourselves! 26 Didn't King Solomon of Israel sin in matters
like this? There was not a king like him among many
nations. He was loved by his God, and God made him
king over all Israel, yet foreign women drew him into
sin. 27 Why then should we hear about you doing all
this terrible evil and acting unfaithfully against our
God by marrying foreign women?" 28 Even one of the
sons of Jehoiada, son of the high priest Eliashib, had
become a son-in-law to Sanballat the Horonite. So I
drove him away from me.

29 Remember them, my God, for defiling the priesthood as well as the covenant of the priesthood and
the Levites.

30 So I purified them from everything foreign and
assigned specific duties to each of the priests and
Levites. 31 I also arranged for the donation of wood
at the appointed times and for the firstfruits.

Remember me, my God, with favor.

[A] **13:21** Lit *again, I will send a hand* [B] **13:24** Lit *Judahite*

ESTHER

Pictured on the right is the entrance to the harem building, restored, at Persepolis. With its impressive architecture, Persepolis was the last capital of the Persian Empire; it was located in what is now Iran.

INTRODUCTION TO

ESTHER

Circumstances of Writing

As in most Old Testament books, the author of this book is unknown. In the Jewish Talmud, it is suggested that the members of the Great Synagogue wrote the book. However, it is hard to imagine this prestigious group of religious scholars writing a book that mentions the Persian king 190 times but never mentions God. Many early writers, Jewish as well as Christian, suggested Mordecai as the author.

Background: The story of Esther is rooted in the historical situation of King Xerxes (Ahasuerus), who ruled as king of Persia from 486 to 465 BC.

Mid-twentieth century critical scholars tended to date the book late, even into the second century BC. However, most now argue for an earlier date. The discovery of the Dead Sea Scrolls in 1947 showed that the Hebrew of Esther was very different from the Hebrew of the first century BC. Also, there are no Greek words in the text of Esther, which would suggest that it was written before Alexander the Great's conquest (ca 333 BC) made Greek the language of the region. Most likely the book was written in the fourth century BC.

The book gives every indication of being a historical narrative. For that reason, the alleged historical anomalies in the text raise for many interpreters problems in accepting the historicity of the story. While it is regrettable not to have any extant extrabiblical confirmation of the main characters in the story (Esther, Haman, Mordecai), several points must be considered.

First, there are few extant Persian records for the reign of Xerxes; thus very few historical figures are known from this time. Moreover, the Greek writers, especially Herodotus, were writing their history particularly as it related to the Greeks—not as court historians for the Persians—thus their material is selective and would leave unmentioned many significant figures. Second, the absence of extrabiblical evidence does not mean these people did not exist. Third, while there is no positive extrabiblical confirmation of these individuals, they appear in an account that even ardent critics acknowledge as being remarkably accurate in its description of the Persian era.

Contribution to the Bible

Without ever mentioning God directly, the book of Esther underscores the providence of God. God's promise to give the Jews an eternal ruler remained in place, even in the face of threatened annihilation. Esther shows us that many Jews remained faithful to their God even in exile. They kept their identity as God's people through the synagogues that developed as the centers of the Jewish community wherever Jews settled. The synagogues would later play a significant role as the gospel spread throughout the Roman Empire, for these served as natural starting places for the deliverance of the gospel in the towns visited by the apostles (e.g., Ac 9:20; 17:1–2; 18:19; 19:8).

Structure

The Hebrew of the Masoretic Text used as the basis for the Christian Standard Bible is a fairly straightforward text. It is written in a form of late biblical Hebrew common to the postexilic era and found in other biblical books of that time, such as Chronicles, Ezra-Nehemiah, and Daniel. Like Ezra-Nehemiah, Esther shows the growing influence of Aramaic in its grammar and vocabulary, as well as the presence of many Persian words.

VASHTI ANGERS THE KING

1 These events took place during the days of Ahasuerus, who ruled 127 provinces from India to Cush. 2 In those days King Ahasuerus reigned from his royal throne in the fortress at Susa. 3 He held a feast in the third year of his reign for all his officials and staff, the army of Persia and Media, the nobles, and the officials from the provinces. 4 He displayed the glorious wealth of his kingdom and the magnificent splendor of his greatness for a total of 180 days.

5 At the end of this time, the king held a week-long banquet in the garden courtyard of the royal palace for all the people, from the greatest to the least, who were present in the fortress of Susa. 6 White and blue linen hangings were fastened with fine white and purple linen cords to silver rods on marble[A] columns. Gold and silver couches were arranged on a mosaic pavement of red feldspar,[B] marble, mother-of-pearl, and precious stones.

7 Drinks were served in an array of gold goblets, each with a different design. Royal wine flowed freely, according to the king's bounty. 8 The drinking was according to royal decree: "There are no restrictions." The king had ordered every wine steward in his household to serve whatever each person wanted. 9 Queen Vashti also gave a feast for the women of King Ahasuerus's palace.

10 On the seventh day, when the king was feeling good from the wine, Ahasuerus commanded Mehuman, Biztha, Harbona, Bigtha, Abagtha, Zethar, and Carkas — the seven eunuchs who personally served him — 11 to bring Queen Vashti before him with her royal crown. He wanted to show off her beauty to the people and the officials, because she was very beautiful. 12 But Queen Vashti refused to come at the king's command that was delivered by his eunuchs. The king became furious and his anger burned within him.

THE KING'S DECREE

13 The king consulted the wise men who understood the times,[C] for it was his normal procedure to confer with experts in law and justice. 14 The most trusted ones[D] were Carshena, Shethar, Admatha, Tarshish, Meres, Marsena, and Memucan. They were the seven officials of Persia and Media who had personal access to the king and occupied the highest positions in the kingdom. 15 The king asked, "According to the law, what should be done with Queen Vashti, since she refused to obey King Ahasuerus's command that was delivered by the eunuchs?"

16 Memucan said in the presence of the king and his officials, "Queen Vashti has wronged not only the king, but all the officials and the peoples who are in every one of King Ahasuerus's provinces. 17 For the queen's action will become public knowledge to all the women and cause them to despise their husbands and say, 'King Ahasuerus ordered Queen Vashti brought before him, but she did not come.' 18 Before this day is over, the noble women of Persia and Media who hear about the queen's act will say the same thing to all the king's officials, resulting in more contempt and fury.

19 "If it meets the king's approval, he should personally issue a royal decree. Let it be recorded in the laws of the Persians and the Medes, so that it cannot be revoked: Vashti is not to enter King Ahasuerus's presence, and her royal position is to be given to another woman who is more worthy than she. 20 The decree the king issues will be heard throughout his vast kingdom, so all women will honor their husbands, from the greatest to the least."

21 The king and his counselors approved the proposal, and he followed Memucan's advice. 22 He sent letters to all the royal provinces, to each province in its own script and to each ethnic group in its own language, that every man should be master of his own house and speak in the language of his own people.

THE SEARCH FOR A NEW QUEEN

2 Some time later, when King Ahasuerus's rage had cooled down, he remembered Vashti, what she had done, and what was decided against her. 2 The king's personal attendants suggested, "Let a search be made for beautiful young virgins for the king. 3 Let the king appoint commissioners in each province of his kingdom, so that they may gather all the beautiful young virgins to the harem at the fortress of Susa. Put them under the supervision of Hegai, the king's eunuch, keeper of the women, and give them the required beauty treatments. 4 Then the young woman who pleases the king will become queen instead of Vashti." This suggestion pleased the king, and he did accordingly.

5 In the fortress of Susa, there was a Jewish man named Mordecai son of Jair, son of Shimei, son of Kish, a Benjaminite. 6 Kish[E] had been taken into exile from Jerusalem with the other captives when King Nebuchadnezzar of Babylon took King Jeconiah of Judah into exile. 7 Mordecai was the legal guardian of his cousin[F] Hadassah (that is, Esther), because she had no father or mother. The young woman had a beautiful figure and was extremely good-looking. When her father and mother died, Mordecai had adopted her as his own daughter.

8 When the king's command and edict became public knowledge and when many young women were gathered at the fortress of Susa under Hegai's

[A] **1:6** Or *alabaster* [B] **1:6** Or *of porphyry* [C] **1:13** Or *understood propitious times* [D] **1:14** Lit *Those near him* [E] **2:6** Lit *He* [F] **2:7** Lit *uncle's daughter*

Susa in the Days of Queen Esther

by Daniel C. Browning Jr.

In the middle of the sixth century BC, the Persian Empire overtook the Neo-Babylonian Empire. Shortly after coming to power, Cyrus the Great formed the Persian Empire by uniting the kingdoms of the Medes and the Persians. Cyrus took Babylon in 539 BC and in the following year issued an edict allowing the Jews to return to Jerusalem and rebuild their temple (Ezr 1:1–4).

While many Jews returned to their homeland, many did not, and so a diaspora (meaning "scattered") community of Jews continued in the area around Babylon. These Jews, now free, began to conduct commerce and settle in other cities, including those in Persia to the east of Babylonia. Primary among the Persian cities was Susa, where the story of Esther occurred in the fifth century BC.

ARCHAEOLOGY AND HISTORY

Susa (Hb *Shushan*) is identified with the town of Shush, a collection of mounds on a natural extension of Mesopotamia into southwest Persia, modern Iran. This region, ancient Susiana, was sometimes under the control of the dominant state of southern Mesopotamia, sometimes independent, and sometimes part of the large Persian states. Susa was usually its capital.

After the British made a brief investigation of the area in 1851, the French excavated Susa almost continuously from 1884 until the Iranian revolution halted all foreign activity in 1979. Excavations revealed that Susa was occupied without major interruption from about 4200 BC until the Mongol invasions of the thirteenth century AD.[1]

Early occupation at Susa paralleled the development of civilization in neighboring Mesopotamia. Susa, sharing the Uruk culture of southern Mesopotamia in the mid-fourth millennium BC, developed sculpture, wheel-turned pottery, and an accounting convention using tokens enclosed in a clay envelope—an important step in the development of cuneiform writing. Breaking from Mesopotamia after 3200 BC, Susa produced its own still-undeciphered abstract symbols called Proto-Elamite. By 2800 BC, Susa was back in the Mesopotamian sphere as an essentially Sumerian city-state. Sargon the Great controlled Susa as part of his Semitic Empire from 2350 BC. When that empire failed early in the twenty-second century, though, the city became part of the Elamite kingdom of Awan, only to be reconquered by Shulgi, a powerful Sumerian king of Ur. About 2000 BC, Elamite and Susianan invaders destroyed Ur and its empire.[2] As the Elamite civilization took shape, Susa was integrated as a major center, so that the first ruler of the Sukkalmah Dynasty (ca 1970–1500 BC) called himself "King of Anshan and of Susa."[3]

Elam reached its cultural and political peak in the Middle Elamite period (ca 1500–1100 BC), and Susiana became increasingly Elamite in language and religion. A new capital replaced Susa around 1500 BC, but Susa regained its prominence about

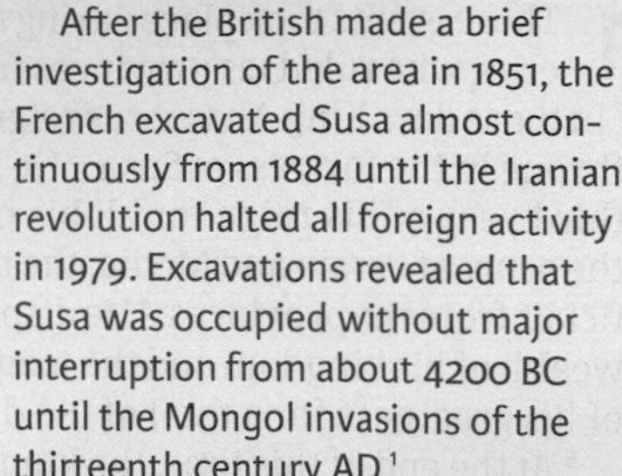

A glazed brick frieze representing the Persian Royal Guard, from the palace of Darius at Susa; dated to the sixth century BC.

The tomb of Cyrus the Great, which bore the following inscription: "Mortal! I am Cyrus, son of Cambyses, who founded the Persian Empire, and was Lord of Asia. Grudge me not, then, my monument."

1200 BC under the Shutrukid kings. This dynasty conquered Babylon, from which they looted several iconic monuments of Mesopotamia, including the Naram-Sin stele and the stele of Hammurabi, containing his famous law code.[4] A French archaeological team discovered these iconic Mesopotamian monuments on the Susa Acropolis about 1900, near the lavishly rebuilt temple of Susa's chief god, Inshushinak.[5] This brief Shutrukid Empire collapsed about 1100 BC, and all of Elam entered a dark age with almost no written records until late in the eighth century BC.

When Elam reemerged into the light of history in 743 BC, Susa was one of three capitals of the later Neo-Elamite kings who found themselves in a struggle against Assyria, the prevailing Mesopotamian power. The Elamites were often allied with Babylon in the latter's frequent attempts to rebel from Assyrian domination. For example, Elam supported the Chaldean Merodach-baladan (Is 39:1) in his bids for Babylonian freedom against the Assyrian Kings Sargon II and Sennacherib. The last great Assyrian king, Ashurbanipal, effectively destroyed Elamite power and pillaged Susa in 646 BC. Ezra 4:9–10 reports that "Osnapper"—apparently Ashurbanipal—deported Elamites of Susa and settled them in the region of Samaria. Meanwhile, the plateau of Persia was consumed by the growing Median and Persian kingdoms, and a modest Elamite kingdom was reestablished around 625 BC at Susa.

In a vision dated to about 552 BC, Daniel saw himself at Susa, at the Ulai Canal (Dn 8:1–2,16). The vision began with a two-horned ram that surely represented the Persian Empire (also called the Achaemenid Empire). The Persian Empire was created with Cyrus the Great uniting the Medes and the Persians in 550 BC. Cyrus took Susa in 539 BC, just before his capture of Babylon that made the Persians masters of the Near East. This was the Cyrus who ended the exile of the Jews with his edict in 538 BC (Ezr 1:2–4).

IN ESTHER'S DAY

Cyrus and his son Cambyses II may have used Susa some during their reigns, but the vast majority of the Persian remains on the site date to the reigns of Darius I the Great

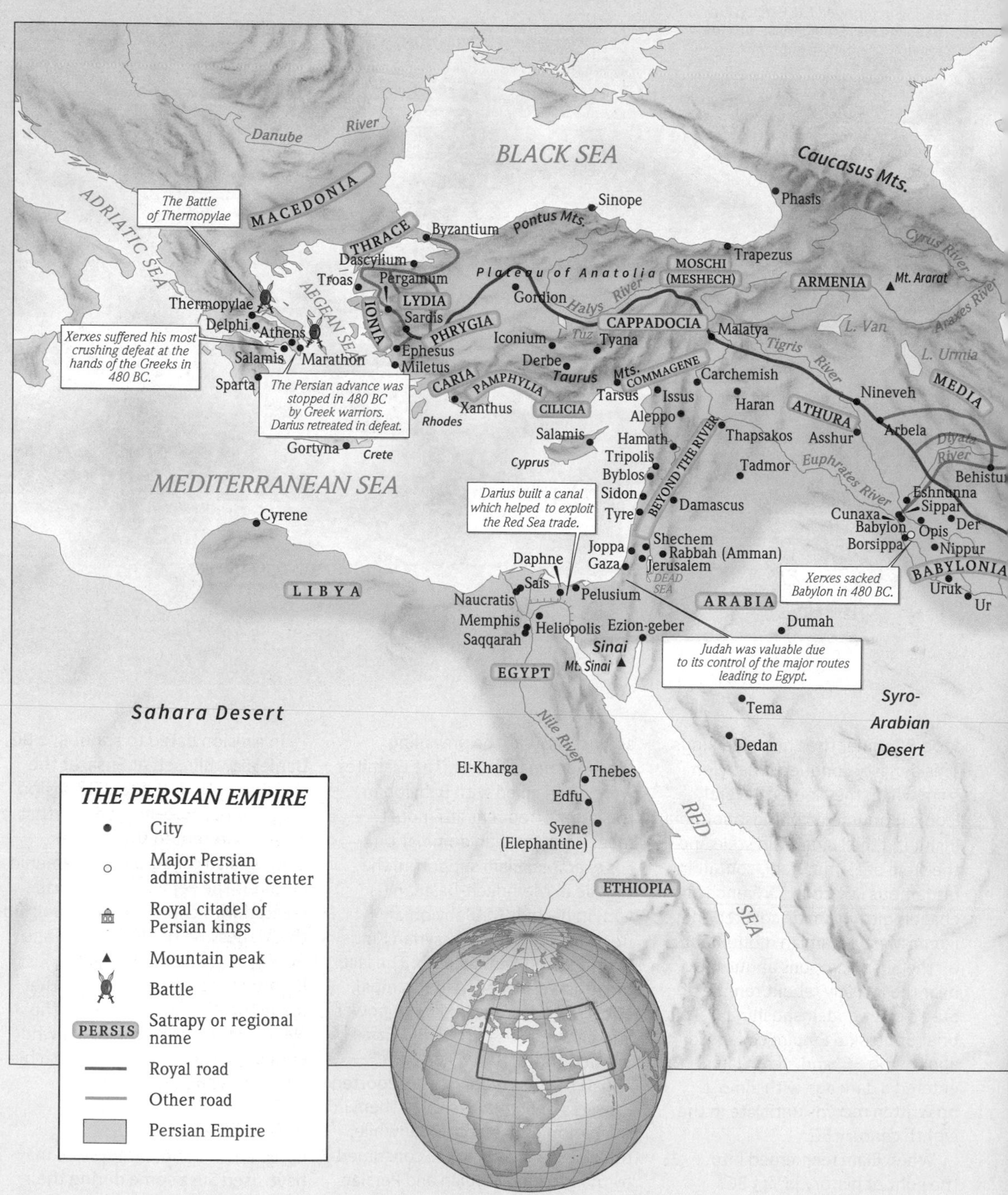
THE PERSIAN EMPIRE
City
Major Persian administrative center
Royal citadel of Persian kings
Mountain peak
Battle
PERSIS Satrapy or regional name
Royal road
Other road
Persian Empire
BLACK SEA
MEDITERRANEAN SEA
Danube River
Caucasus Mts.
ADRIATIC SEA
AEGEAN SEA
The Battle of Thermopylae
Xerxes suffered his most crushing defeat at the hands of the Greeks in 480 BC.
The Persian advance was stopped in 480 BC by Greek warriors. Darius retreated in defeat.
Darius built a canal which helped to exploit the Red Sea trade.
Judah was valuable due to its control of the major routes leading to Egypt.
Xerxes sacked Babylon in 480 BC.
MACEDONIA
THRACE
LYDIA
IONIA
PHRYGIA
CARIA
PAMPHYLIA
CILICIA
CAPPADOCIA
COMMAGENE
MOSCHI (MESHECH)
ARMENIA
MEDIA
ATHURA
BEYOND THE RIVER
ARABIA
BABYLONIA
LIBYA
EGYPT
ETHIOPIA
Sinope
Phasis
Byzantium
Pontus Mts.
Trapezus
Cyrus River
Mt. Ararat
Araxes River
Dascylium
Troas
Pergamum
Plateau of Anatolia
Gordion
Halys River
Thermopylae
Delphi
Athens
Salamis
Marathon
Sparta
Sardis
Ephesus
Miletus
Iconium
L. Tuz
Tyana
Malatya
L. Van
Tigris River
L. Urmia
Derbe
Taurus Mts.
Tarsus
Carchemish
Issus
Nineveh
Xanthus
Rhodes
Aleppo
Haran
Arbela
Salamis
Hamath
Thapsakos
Asshur
Diyala River
Gortyna
Crete
Cyprus
Tripolis
Byblos
Tadmor
Euphrates River
Behistun
Sidon
Damascus
Eshnunna
Sippar
Tyre
Cunaxa
Babylon
Opis
Der
Cyrene
Shechem
Borsippa
Nippur
Joppa
Rabbah (Amman)
Gaza
Jerusalem
Dead Sea
Daphne
Sais
Pelusium
Uruk
Ur
Naucratis
Memphis
Heliopolis
Ezion-geber
Dumah
Saqqarah
Sinai
Mt. Sinai
Sahara Desert
Tema
Syro-Arabian Desert
Nile River
Dedan
El-Kharga
Thebes
Edfu
Syene (Elephantine)
RED SEA

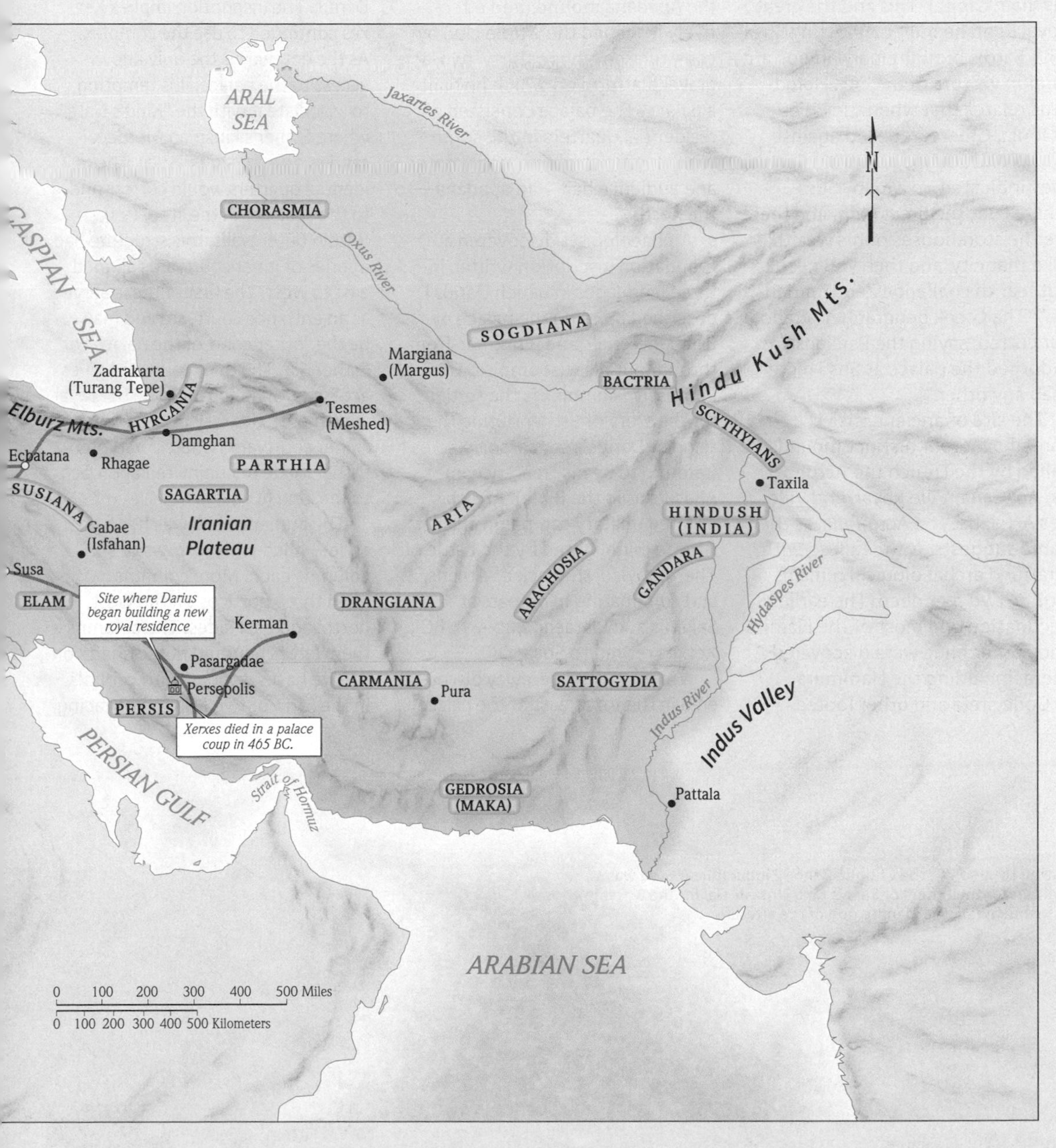
ARAL SEA
Jaxartes River
CHORASMIA
CASPIAN SEA
Oxus River
SOGDIANA
Hindu Kush Mts.
Margiana (Margus)
BACTRIA
Zadrakarta (Turang Tepe)
HYRCANIA
Tesmes (Meshed)
Elburz Mts.
Damghan
SCYTHYIANS
Ecbatana
Rhagae
PARTHIA
Taxila
SUSIANA
SAGARTIA
HINDUSH (INDIA)
Gabae (Isfahan)
Iranian Plateau
ARIA
ARACHOSIA
GANDARA
Susa
Hydaspes River
ELAM
Site where Darius began building a new royal residence
DRANGIANA
Kerman
Pasargadae
Persepolis
CARMANIA
Pura
SATTOGYDIA
Indus River
Indus Valley
PERSIS
Xerxes died in a palace coup in 465 BC.
PERSIAN GULF
Strait of Hormuz
GEDROSIA (MAKA)
Pattala
ARABIAN SEA
0 100 200 300 400 500 Miles
0 100 200 300 400 500 Kilometers
N

(522–486 BC) or Artaxerxes II (404–359 BC).[6] Darius made Susa his main capital. This and the great Royal Road he built connecting Susa with Sardis brought many important foreign visitors to the city. Herodotus relates that when the cities of Ionia, Greece, rebelled against Darius and sought help from Sparta, they indicated on a map "Susa where lives the great king, and there are the storehouses of his wealth; take that city, and then you need not fear to challenge Zeus for riches."[7] The Greek geographer Strabo concurred, saying the Persians "adorned the palace at Susa more than any other."[8]

The site of ancient Susa is spread over four distinct mounds, called by the French the Acropolis, Apadana, Ville Royal, and Ville des Artisans. The Acropolis, as the name suggests, is the tallest, with stratified archaeological remains eighty-two feet deep. The earliest occupation and most of the Elamite and earlier finds were discovered there, including the Hammurabi Code stele and other looted Mesopotamian treasures.[9] North of the Acropolis, Darius I created the Apadana mound (and effectively reshaped the whole city) by constructing a huge thirty-two-acre gravel platform on which he built a palace. The palace consisted of residential quarters in the south with an official government center and audience hall—an apadana—to the north.[10]

Archaeologists discovered a foundation inscription written in three languages in which Darius I described building the palace by using materials and workmen from throughout his vast empire. This impressive complex is the setting for the story of Esther during the reign of Darius's successor, Xerxes I (referred to by his Hebrew name Ahasuerus in the Bible). After his ill-fated military campaign against Greece (highlighted by the battle of Thermopylae, the sack of Athens, and culminating in defeats at Salamis and Plataeai, 480–479 BC), Xerxes retired to Susa.

A monumental gateway discovered in the 1970s east of the palace complex contains inscriptions of Xerxes, attributing its construction to Darius. The inscription implies Xerxes continued to use the complex. As the gateway is the only known access to the palace, it is tempting to associate it with the "King's Gate" where Esther's kinsman Mordecai sat (Est 2:19,21; 5:9,13; 6:10). The residential quarters would correspond to the "palace" in the story (5:1). Within outer walls, this structure had a series of inner courtyards aligned east to west. The first of these served as an entrance courtyard and may be the "outer court of the palace" of Esther 6:4. The third courtyard gives access to what appear to be the royal apartments and may thus be the "inner courtyard" where a nervous Esther made her uninvited approach to the king (4:11; 5:1).[11]

The audience hall was hypostyle—filled with six rows of six columns each. More columns filled three porticos on the west, north, and east sides. The columns themselves featured fluted shafts on square bases, topped with capitals in the form of two bull torsos facing

Dating to 1250 BC, the Chogha Zanbil Ziggurat near Susa was built under the orders of Elam's King Untash-Gal for the worship of Inshushinak, the Elamite god of the afterlife.

Elamite inscription from Susa details Shilhak-Inshushinak conquering lower Babylonia. Shilhak-Inshushinak, king of Anshan and Susa (ca 1150–1120 BC), built many monuments honoring the god of Susa.

in opposite directions. They rose sixty-five feet, an achievement unparalleled in the ancient world. The entire palace, residence, and apadana were decorated exclusively with glazed brickwork depicting mythical animals and figures of the immortals, the elite guard troops of the king.[12]

The royal parts of the city, consisting of the Acropolis, Apadana, and Ville Royal mounds, were enclosed in an impressive city wall. A canal diverted from the Chaour River on the west ran along the north and east sides of the royal enclosure, separating it from the unfortified lower city to the east, represented by the fourth mound, the Ville des Artisans. These distinct parts of the city may be reflected in the text of Esther, where "the fortress of Susa" (9:6,11,12) can refer to the royal walled section, while "Susa" without further qualification (vv. 13–15) may indicate the lower city.[13]

LATER SUSA

Susa's importance as a capital ended with the conquests of Alexander the Great, although the city continued to exist and prosper under Hellenistic, Parthian, Sassanian, and Islamic rule. It was finally abandoned in the thirteenth century AD. Nevertheless, Susa has been and remains a site of pilgrimage for Jews, Christians, Muslims, and Mandeans who venerate a medieval structure now enclosed in a mosque as the tomb of the prophet Daniel. While the Tomb of Daniel has been known from at least the seventh century AD,[14] Susa has no shrine that is associated with Queen Esther. ✣

---

[1] Holly Pittman, "Susa," in *OEANE*, 5:106–7. [2] Pierre de Miroschedji, "Susa" in *ABD*, 6:243. [3] François Vallat, "Elam (Place)" in *ABD*, 2:424–25. [4] Pittman, "Susa," 109. [5] Miroschedji, "Susa," 243. [6] Pittman, "Susa," 109. [7] Herodotus, *Histories* 5.49. [8] Strabo, *Geography* 15.3. [9] Edwin M. Yamauchi, *Persia and the Bible* (Grand Rapids: Baker, 1990), 282–85. [10] Pittman, "Susa," 109. [11] Miroschedji, "Susa," 244. [12] Roman Ghirshman, *Persia: From the Origins to Alexander the Great*, trans. Stuart Gilbert and James Emmons (London: Thames & Hudson, 1964), 138–42. [13] Miroschedji, "Susa," 244. [14] Sylvia A. Matheson, *Persia: An Archaeological Guide* (Park Ridge, NJ: Noyes, 1973), 150.

supervision, Esther was taken to the palace, into the supervision of Hegai, keeper of the women. 9 The young woman pleased him and gained his favor so that he accelerated the process of the beauty treatments and the special diet that she received. He assigned seven hand-picked female servants to her from the palace and transferred her and her servants to the harem's best quarters.

10 Esther did not reveal her ethnicity or her family background, because Mordecai had ordered her not to make them known. 11 Every day Mordecai took a walk in front of the harem's courtyard to learn how Esther was doing and to see what was happening to her.

12 During the year before each young woman's turn to go to King Ahasuerus, the harem regulation required her to receive beauty treatments with oil of myrrh for six months and then with perfumes and cosmetics for another six months. 13 When the young woman would go to the king, she was given whatever she requested to take with her from the harem to the palace. 14 She would go in the evening, and in the morning she would return to a second harem under the supervision of the king's eunuch Shaashgaz, keeper of the concubines. She never went to the king again, unless he desired her and summoned her by name.

ESTHER BECOMES QUEEN

15 Esther was the daughter of Abihail, the uncle of Mordecai who had adopted her as his own daughter. When her turn came to go to the king, she did not ask for anything except what Hegai, the king's eunuch, keeper of the women, suggested. Esther gained favor in the eyes of everyone who saw her.

16 She was taken to King Ahasuerus in the palace in the tenth month, the month Tebeth, in the seventh year of his reign. 17 The king loved Esther more than all the other women. She won more favor and approval from him than did any of the other virgins. He placed the royal crown on her head and made her queen in place of Vashti. 18 The king held a great banquet for all his officials and staff. It was Esther's banquet. He freed his provinces from tax payments and gave gifts worthy of the king's bounty.

MORDECAI SAVES THE KING

19 When the virgins were gathered a second time, Mordecai was sitting at the King's Gate. 20 Esther still did not reveal her family background or her ethnicity, as Mordecai had directed. She obeyed Mordecai's orders, as she always had while he raised her.

21 During those days while Mordecai was sitting at the King's Gate, Bigthan and Teresh, two of the king's eunuchs who guarded the entrance, became infuriated and planned to assassinate[A] King Ahasuerus. 22 When Mordecai learned of the plot, he reported it to Queen Esther, and she told the king on Mordecai's behalf. 23 When the report was investigated and verified, both men were hanged on the gallows. This event was recorded in the Historical Record in the king's presence.

HAMAN'S PLAN TO KILL THE JEWS

3 After all this took place, King Ahasuerus honored Haman, son of Hammedatha the Agagite. He promoted him in rank and gave him a higher position than all the other officials. 2 The entire royal staff at the King's Gate bowed down and paid homage to Haman, because the king had commanded this to be done for him. But Mordecai would not bow down or pay homage. 3 The members of the royal staff at the King's Gate asked Mordecai, "Why are you disobeying the king's command?" 4 When they had warned him day after day and he still would not listen to them, they told Haman in order to see if Mordecai's actions would be tolerated, since he had told them he was a Jew.

5 When Haman saw that Mordecai was not bowing down or paying him homage, he was filled with rage. 6 And when he learned of Mordecai's ethnic identity, it seemed repugnant to Haman to do away with[B] Mordecai alone. He planned to destroy all of Mordecai's people, the Jews, throughout Ahasuerus's kingdom.

7 In the first month, the month of Nisan, in King Ahasuerus's twelfth year, the *pur* — that is, the lot — was cast before Haman for each day in each month, and it fell on the twelfth month, the month Adar. 8 Then Haman informed King Ahasuerus, "There is one ethnic group, scattered throughout the peoples in every province of your kingdom, keeping themselves separate. Their laws are different from everyone else's and they do not obey the king's laws. It is not in the king's best interest to tolerate them. 9 If the king approves, let an order be drawn up authorizing their destruction, and I will pay 375 tons of silver to[C] the officials for deposit in the royal treasury."

10 The king removed his signet ring from his hand and gave it to Haman son of Hammedatha the Agagite, the enemy of the Jews. 11 Then the king told Haman, "The money and people are given to you to do with as you see fit."

12 The royal scribes were summoned on the thirteenth day of the first month, and the order was written exactly as Haman commanded. It was intended for the royal satraps, the governors of each of the provinces, and the officials of each ethnic group and

[A] **2:21** Lit *and they sought to stretch out a hand against* [B] **3:6** Lit *to stretch out a hand against* [C] **3:9** Lit *will weigh 10,000 silver talents on the hands of*

Royal Persian Architecture

by Paul E. Kullman

The Achaemenid dynasty ruled Persia from the time of Cyrus I to Darius III (550–330 BC). This period produced some of the best ancient architectural design, which was produced under the leadership of four prominent kings—Cyrus the Great, Darius I, Xerxes I, and Artaxerxes I. Beginning with Cyrus (reigned 559–530 BC), the ability to construct beautiful and complex royal palace projects taught other empires that would follow how it is done. Cyrus acquired the best craftsmen to build magnificent structures; these rivaled structures in other empires in size, detail, and quality of construction technique. Darius I (reigned 522–486 BC) would take up the work of building great royal projects and later his son Xerxes I (486–465 BC) would do likewise. The book of Esther calls Xerxes I "Ahasuerus."

ROYAL PALACES

Once Cyrus defeated the Babylonians in 539 BC, a centuries-long capital improvement campaign began. His first major building project was in Pasargadae, the original ancient Persian capital (550–530 BC). This included the freestanding capital, citadel, palace, and eventually his tomb. These were "garden pavilion" arrangements constructed of large cut stone (some without mortar) reinforced with swallowtail lead and iron clamps and dowels,[1] which was revolutionary for stone reinforcement at that time.

After the death of Cyrus's son Cambyses, Darius I took the throne and ascended to the role of chief Persian developer in design and construction of great palaces. The primary locations for these palaces were Persepolis (ceremonial capital) and Susa (winter capital). A third capital, Ecbatana (summer capital), was captured when Cyrus defeated the Medes in 550 BC. The Median King Deioces constructed the original palace and citadel here. This capital location would serve most of the Achaemenid rulers for several centuries, but Persian design influence was limited.

Persepolis—In 518 BC, Darius I initiated the building of the Persepolis complex with the palace set on an expansive flat rock table located some fifty feet above the surrounding plains. The ongoing construction project was entrusted to Xerxes I and later his son, Artaxerxes I. Completion took sixty years.[2] Each ruler added various new spaces and renovations during their respective reigns. This royal complex has extensive ruins, which architects and engineers have widely studied.

The palace project initiated another construction detail, the use of decorative reliefs. Some of the most elaborate and best-detailed reliefs dated to as early as 700 BC and were discovered in Khorsabad (in modern Iraq).[3] Although the Assyrians used the method of engraved stone reliefs on their interior walls, the Persians perfected this method of design with intricate quality detailing on the stairway façades and exterior walls at Persepolis.[4] Throughout the palace, reliefs depicted the procession of rulers, soldiers, and servants along with various animal images at key locations. The creation of these magnificent stone reliefs gave Persian royalty identification to the building that other kings would look to replicate.

Model of the Apadana, which was part of the capital at Susa. The Apadana featured a large meeting hall and portico.

Winged human-headed bull decorative carving that was part of the column capital on the frame to the Gate of All Nations at Persepolis. The roof's support beams fit between the carved figures.

Susa—The book of Esther documents the palace in Susa as its setting. Originally built by Darius, this palace, much like Persepolis, was completed by Xerxes I.

At Susa, builders performed deep and laborious excavation of the rocky soil in order to build the foundation platform, which was supported by retaining walls, column plinths, and massive amounts of gravel fill and rubble material. The builders spared no expense, importing cedar (from Lebanon), teak (from the Zagros Mountains), and quality natural stone (from western Persia). Craftsmen from vassal provinces such as Ionia, Babylon, and Assyria brought time-tested building methods from their native lands. Magnificently detailed reliefs and friezes, used previously at Persepolis, were integrated into the buildings at Susa. Interior walls decorated with colorful polychromatic glazed tile told various stories of the empire.

PALACE DESIGN AND CONSTRUCTION

Archaeological discoveries show that ancient Persian building was a direct contributor to the betterment of civilization through its rich heritage of architectural design. While restored and reused ruins are not as extensive in Persia (modern Iran) as in other ancient sites in Turkey, Egypt, and Greece, they do exist.

Egyptian, Assyrian, and Babylonian architecture established unique design styles in their respective eras. The ancient Persians, however, were the ones who created, refined, and incorporated complex material methodologies into an eclectic design style that defined architecture over the next two millennia. Modern architects and structural engineers still research these projects to learn the finer design techniques that their ancient colleagues used. The techniques include the use of the hypostyle hall plan, the extensive use of double column capitals with unique bull or horse heads, squinches, bell-shaped column bases, protruding stone surrounds at door and window jambs and lintels, cornices, plinths, barrel vaults, and dome roofs. Wide stone-paved stairways and sloped ramparts provided access to various floor levels. Ruins indicate that floor finishes had a variety of colored paved brick, smooth stone, and marble.

Structural stone columns designed for spatial efficiency supported heavy timber roof framing, which in turn transferred the building's total weight, called the dead load weight, into the subfloor foundation column plinths and subsurface compacted rocky soil. Integrating ancient techniques, the builders used dried mud bricks and stone for thick exterior walls that separated spaces from multiple gatehouse vestibules for pedestrian access to the large hypostyle halls at Persepolis. The Apadana space alone was 250 feet square with thirty-six 50-foot columns with centerline spacing of 27 feet by 27 feet as well as the Throne Hall of One Hundred Columns—each 37 feet high.[5] These were adjacent to smaller upper-level apartments, storerooms, the harem, and the treasury.

While Esther 1:6 gives detail to the opulent fabric furnishings, precious metals and stones, and

A colossal Persian column capital from the Apadana at Susa (Hb *Shushan*). It boasts a unique engineering design that secured the huge roof and ceiling timbers between the neck and head of two stylized bulls. They date to the reign of Darius I (522–486 BC).

abundance of exquisite materials used at the Susa palace, the focus of the story of Esther is on her struggle as a Jewish young woman in a pagan land. These surroundings served as the backdrop for Queen Esther and her relationship with the king. The palace was a place of security for her.

For centuries, the extraordinarily massive thick exterior and interior wall design and construction provided fortification against attacks. Although well designed and superbly constructed, the best of Persian architecture and design, however, could not hold back the armies of Alexander the Great, which conquered Susa in 331 BC. ✤

---

[1] Sir Banister Fletcher, *A History of Architecture*, ed. Dan Cruickshank, 20th ed. (Burlington, MA: Architectural Press, 1996), 93. [2] Edwin M. Yamauchi, "Persians" in *Peoples of the Old Testament World*, ed. Alfred J. Hoerth, Gerald L. Mattingly, and Edwin M. Yamauchi (Grand Rapids: Baker, 1994), 121. [3] J. A. Thompson, *The Bible and Archaeology* (Grand Rapids: Eerdmans, 1977), 197. [4] John Julius Norwich, ed., *Great Architecture of the World* (New York: Bonanza, 1982), 44. [5] Fletcher, *History of Architecture*, 93–97.

Xerxes I: His Life and Times

by Joseph R. Cathey

Xerxes, known in the book of Esther as Ahasuerus, was one of the last great Achaemenid (Persian) kings. He was the son of Darius I, and grandson of Cyrus the Great, under whose power the Achaemenids expanded their geopolitical hegemony up to the city-states of Greece. Xerxes was born around 518 BC to Darius and his queen Atossa. The majority of biblical references to Xerxes are in the book of Esther; the others are in Ezra 4:6 and Daniel 9:1. The events recorded in Esther most likely took place between the completion of the rebuilt temple under Haggai and the return of the exiles under Ezra (515–458 BC).[1]

HIS FATHER'S BATTLE

The battle that was to define Xerxes was not one he began but one he fought against the Greeks to avenge his father's defeat. The Persians had added vast territories under King Darius I's rule. After brutally suppressing opponents at home, Darius turned his attention to a convincing show of strength in the ancient Near East. In the east, he subjugated northwest India; in the west, he pacified various Aegean islands. However, this pacification of the Greek border took four long, bloody years and ended with the Greeks defeating Persia at Marathon in 490 BC.[2] Afterward, Darius's anger "against the Athenians . . . waxed still fiercer, and he became more than ever eager to lead an army against Greece."[3] Darius died, however, before he could mount an offensive against the Greeks.

Shortly before Darius's death, a revolt broke out in Egypt. Darius sent Xerxes to quell the disturbance in 485 BC. In a year's time, Xerxes had laid siege to Egypt, confiscated temple items, and imposed harsh new taxes. Quickly he besieged Babylon and devastated the temple of Marduk. Once these two nations were pacified, Xerxes set his sights on the rebellious Greek city-states.

HIS BATTLE

To preserve the memory of his father, Xerxes determined to completely conquer the Greeks. The plan Xerxes unfolded to the Persian military aristocracy was nothing short of total war. Ancient historians list forty-six nations that supplied men for combat when Persia invaded Greece.[4] Xerxes's naval forces were not as vast as the land contingent but were nonetheless quite impressive. The Persian monarch reportedly put to sea no fewer than twelve hundred manned ships from various nations. At the time of his campaign, Xerxes fielded the largest land and naval contingent in the ancient world.

Xerxes left his capital city likely around April 481 BC; he assembled his full land contingent in the fall of that same year at Critalla, about four hundred miles east of Sardis. After wintering in Sardis, Xerxes set his sights on what he believed to be the weakest link in his campaign—Hellespont. Under Xerxes's command, the Persian army did what everybody believed to be impossible; they bridged the strait at Hellespont and crossed from the city of Abydos on the southeastern side to the town of Sestos on the opposite side.[5] Once across the strait, Xerxes's army marched to Thermopylae, which was a Greek term meaning "the Hot Gates."

Thermopylae was located in a narrow pass between the mountains of central Greece and an adjacent gulf inlet. The Spartans fought valiantly. Opposing Xerxes, Leonidas, king of the city-state of Sparta, "made his gallant stand on a hill" overlooking the pass.[6] Fighting beside Leonidas were three hundred

A calcite jar dated 486 to 465 BC. The jar is inscribed "Xerxes, Great King of Persia" in Old Persian, Elamite, Babylonian, and Egyptian scripts. This was Xerxes's gift to Artemisia, queen of Caria, who provided ships and helped in the fight when Xerxes was preparing for and carrying out his invasion of Greece in 480 BC.

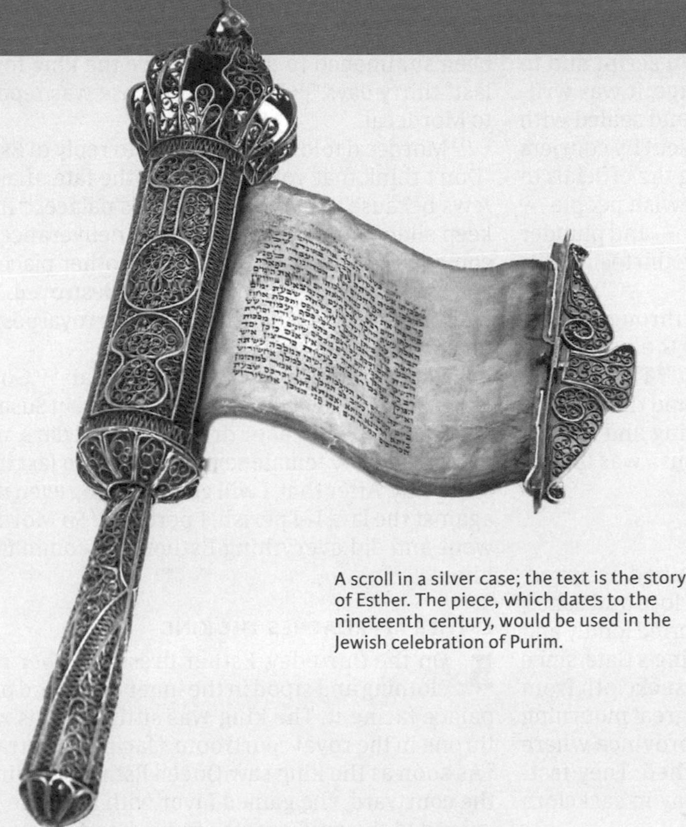

A scroll in a silver case; the text is the story of Esther. The piece, which dates to the nineteenth century, would be used in the Jewish celebration of Purim.

Spartan soldiers (his select royal guard) and about seven thousand hoplite soldiers from surrounding Greek city-states. They killed wave after wave of Persian soldiers in the pass. This small contingent of dedicated Greek warriors killed twenty thousand Persian soldiers and Xerxes's two half brothers. After two days of fighting, a Greek traitor came to Xerxes and told him of a path that bypassed the Hot Gates. Some of Xerxes's soldiers followed the path and came secretly behind the Greek army, trapping them from the front and the rear. All but one of the three hundred Spartans died at Thermopylae.

After Thermopylae, the Greeks, emboldened, rallied under the leadership of Themistocles, a Greek navy strategist, by engaging the Persian navy at the Straits of Salamis. Employing unconventional tactics, the Greek navy scored a decisive victory against the much larger Persian navy. Xerxes's battles against the Greeks at Thermopylae and the island of Salamis were perhaps *the* two pivotal battles in the west.

The defeat at Salamis caused a demoralized Xerxes to retreat back across the strait at Hellespont and leave his general behind to continue the battle. Seeking repose, Xerxes returned to his winter home at Susa.

HIS STORY—AND ESTHER

How does Xerxes fit with details in the book of Esther? Chronologically Xerxes may have planned and presented his battle plans to the Persian military aristocracy during the 180 days that he showed off his wealth, as described in Esther 1. The battles at Thermopylae and Salamis likely occurred between the events of Esther 1 and 2. The search for a replacement queen (2:1–4) also could have occurred after Xerxes's defeat at Salamis and his subsequent retreat to Susa. Finally, Xerxes's "large tax . . . may readily have followed the exhaustion of the royal treasury by [his] disastrous expedition into Greece" (10:1).[7]

The book of Esther's characterization of Xerxes is similar to what the ancient historians said. Esther characterizes Xerxes as "a bumbling, inept figure who becomes an object of mocking."[8] This type of characterization is the same as Herodotus describing the monarch's petulant flight after his loss at Salamis. Esther's vivid description of Xerxes as dependent upon his advisers (1:12–14) is consistent with the monarch's delegation of power to his generals after his defeat in Greece. Aeschylus, the Greek playwright of Athens, portrays the end of Xerxes as inextricably bound to prideful ambition. "The Greek playwright's critique of the megalomaniacal ego of the Persian kings resonates with a similar evaluation of the Persian monarchy found in the book of Esther."[9] In the end, twenty years after ascending the throne, Xerxes was assassinated by Artabanus—the captain of his bodyguard. ✣

---

[1] See Mervin Breneman, *Ezra, Nehemiah, Esther*, vol. 10 in NAC (1993), 278. [2] Edwin M. Yamauchi, "Persians" in *Peoples of the Old Testament World*, ed. Alfred Hoerth, Gerald L. Mattingly, and Edwin M. Yamauchi (Grand Rapids: Baker, 1997), 114–15. [3] Herodotus, *Histories* 7.1. [4] Herodotus, *Histories* 9.27. [5] F. Maurice, "The Size of the Army of Xerxes in the Invasion of Greece 480 BC," *Journal of Hellenic Studies* (*JHS*) 50 (1930): 211; N. G. L. Hammond and L. J. Roseman, "The Construction of Xerxes' Bridge over the Hellespont," *JHS* 116 (1996): 88–107. [6] Edwin M. Yamauchi, *Persia and the Bible* (Grand Rapids: Baker, 1990), 204–5. [7] "Xerxes" in *Cyclopedia of Biblical, Theological, and Ecclesiastical Literature*, ed. John McClintock and James Strong, vol. 2 (New York: Harper, 1887), 1001. [8] See Karen H. Jobes, "Esther 1: Book of" in *Dictionary of the Old Testament: Wisdom, Poetry & Writings*, ed. Tremper Longman III and Peter Enns (Downers Grove, IL: IVP Academic, 2008), 163. [9] Karen H. Jobes, "Esther 2: Extrabiblical Background" in *Dictionary of the Old Testament: Wisdom, Poetry & Writings*, ed. Tremper Longman III and Peter Enns (Downers Grove, IL: IVP Academic, 2008), 171–72.

written for each province in its own script and to each ethnic group in its own language. It was written in the name of King Ahasuerus and sealed with the royal signet ring. 13 Letters were sent by couriers to each of the royal provinces telling the officials to destroy, kill, and annihilate all the Jewish people — young and old, women and children — and plunder their possessions on a single day, the thirteenth day of Adar, the twelfth month.[A]

14 A copy of the text, issued as law throughout every province, was distributed to all the peoples so that they might get ready for that day. 15 The couriers left, spurred on by royal command, and the law was issued in the fortress of Susa. The king and Haman sat down to drink, while the city of Susa was in confusion.

MORDECAI APPEALS TO ESTHER

4 When Mordecai learned all that had occurred, he tore his clothes, put on sackcloth and ashes, went into the middle of the city, and cried loudly and bitterly. 2 He went only as far as the King's Gate, since the law prohibited anyone wearing sackcloth from entering the King's Gate. 3 There was great mourning among the Jewish people in every province where the king's command and edict reached. They fasted, wept, and lamented, and many lay in sackcloth and ashes.

4 Esther's female servants and her eunuchs came and reported the news to her, and the queen was overcome with fear. She sent clothes for Mordecai to wear so that he would take off his sackcloth, but he did not accept them. 5 Esther summoned Hathach, one of the king's eunuchs who attended her, and dispatched him to Mordecai to learn what he was doing and why.[B] 6 So Hathach went out to Mordecai in the city square in front of the King's Gate. 7 Mordecai told him everything that had happened as well as the exact amount of money Haman had promised to pay the royal treasury for the slaughter of the Jews.

8 Mordecai also gave him a copy of the written decree issued in Susa ordering their destruction, so that Hathach might show it to Esther, explain it to her, and command her to approach the king, implore his favor, and plead with him personally for her people. 9 Hathach came and repeated Mordecai's response to Esther.

10 Esther spoke to Hathach and commanded him to tell Mordecai, 11 "All the royal officials and the people of the royal provinces know that one law applies to every man or woman who approaches the king in the inner courtyard and who has not been summoned — the death penalty — unless the king extends the gold scepter, allowing that person to live. I have not been summoned to appear before the king for the last[C] thirty days." 12 Esther's response was reported to Mordecai.

13 Mordecai told the messenger to reply to Esther, "Don't think that you will escape the fate of all the Jews because you are in the king's palace. 14 If you keep silent at this time, relief and deliverance will come to the Jewish people from another place, but you and your father's family will be destroyed. Who knows, perhaps you have come to your royal position for such a time as this."

15 Esther sent this reply to Mordecai: 16 "Go and assemble all the Jews who can be found in Susa and fast for me. Don't eat or drink for three days, night or day. I and my female servants will also fast in the same way. After that, I will go to the king even if it is against the law. If I perish, I perish." 17 So Mordecai went and did everything Esther had commanded him.

ESTHER APPROACHES THE KING

5 On the third day, Esther dressed in her royal clothing and stood in the inner courtyard of the palace facing it. The king was sitting on his royal throne in the royal courtroom,[D] facing its entrance. 2 As soon as the king saw Queen Esther standing in the courtyard, she gained favor with him. The king extended the gold scepter in his hand toward Esther, and she approached and touched the tip of the scepter.

3 "What is it, Queen Esther?" the king asked her. "Whatever you want, even to half the kingdom, will be given to you."

4 "If it pleases the king," Esther replied, "may the king and Haman come today to the banquet I have prepared for them."

5 The king said, "Hurry, and get Haman so we can do as Esther has requested." So the king and Haman went to the banquet Esther had prepared.

6 While drinking the[E] wine, the king asked Esther, "Whatever you ask will be given to you. Whatever you want, even to half the kingdom, will be done."

7 Esther answered, "This is my petition and my request: 8 If I have found favor in the eyes of the king, and if it pleases the king to grant my petition and perform my request, may the king and Haman come to the banquet I will prepare for them. Tomorrow I will do what the king has asked."

9 That day Haman left full of joy and in good spirits.[F] But when Haman saw Mordecai at the King's Gate, and Mordecai didn't rise or tremble in fear at his presence, Haman was filled with rage toward

[A] **3:13** LXX adds the text of Ahasuerus's letter here. [B] **4:5** Lit *what is this and why is this* [C] **4:11** Lit *king these* [D] **5:1** Lit *house* [E] **5:6** Lit *During the banquet of* [F] **5:9** Lit *left rejoicing and good of heart*

When Approaching the King of Persia

by Martha S. Bergen

Throughout human history, leaders in society have set high expectations for how others were to behave toward them. While specifics varied from society to society, leaders have always demanded that others treat them with the loftiest levels of respect and honor. Rulers considered themselves important—in some cases like the Egyptian pharaohs, even as gods—and required others to view them as supremely important as well. This expectation was certainly the case in ancient Persia, the largest empire during the Old Testament period.

One of the Amarna tablets; this letter from the Canaanite prince Shuwardata to a pharaoh dates to the middle of the fourteenth century BC. In this letter, Shuwardata says that "seven times seven times [he] falls on his stomach" at the king's feet. Further, he explains that he and Abdu-Heba had fought against the leader of Apiru.

Historical records relating to the Achaemenid dynasty—a family of Persian rulers that included Cyrus the Great (550–530 BC); Darius I (522–486 BC); Xerxes I, known in the Bible as Ahasuerus (486–465 BC); Artaxerxes I (464–424 BC); and others[1]—provide modern researchers with only limited information regarding courtly life in ancient Persia. What information we do have comes primarily from the ancient Greek historians Herodotus, Xenophon, and Strabo, and from the Bible. Nevertheless, these accounts clearly show that courtly practices in the Persian kingdom were in keeping with those of royal courts in other parts of the Old Testament world.

Royal courts in the ancient Near East were established as parallels to the royal court of the heavenly realm. They understood their god to be the supreme ruler of heaven; kings were the supreme authorities in their respective kingdoms. Recognizing this parallel between the heavenly and earthly kingdoms helps us gain insights into ancient Near Eastern courtly traditions by examining biblical descriptions of proper behavior in the presence of God.

When people were in the presence of God, they were expected to bow down and show reverence (2Ch 7:3; 20:18). Likewise, the subjects of earthly kings had to bow down before their rulers (1Kg 1:31; 1Ch 21:21), sometimes to the point of extremity. For example, in an Amarna tablet, the Canaanite official Abdu-Heba told the pharaoh, "At the two feet of the king, my lord, seven times and seven times I fall."[2] Even royal officials who represented the king could demand that subjects bow before them; Absalom's encounter with an unnamed Israelite reflects this (2Sm 15:5). This is even more directly evident in the biblical account of Mordecai's refusal to bow down before Haman, King Xerxes's top official. Mordecai's behavior was considered so offensive to Haman that he determined to kill not only Mordecai, but also all of the Jews throughout the kingdom (Est 3:1–6).

Just as God limited those who could come before him, so earthly kings also would not allow just anyone to appear before them. Information on imperial courts related to the Achaemenid rulers provides insight into ancient Persia's courtly expectations. While the imperial court consisted of many people, the king himself lived a relatively secluded life. Herodotus mentioned that certain representatives of Persia's six noblest clans, thought to be relatives of the six men who helped Darius I bring down the usurper Gaumata, enjoyed the privilege of unrestricted access to the king.[3] This limitation on who would be in regular attendance before the king is probably reflected in Esther 1, where King Xerxes is feasting and drinking with "Carshena, Shethar,

Admatha, Tarshish, Meres, Marsena, and Memucan. They were the seven officials of Persia and Media who had personal access to the king and occupied the highest positions in the kingdom" (v. 14).

Within royal courts of the ancient Near East, only a few women could have access to the king. Within ancient Israel, the queen mother had special rights. According to 1 Kings 2:19, Solomon prepared a special throne for his mother and had it located immediately to the right of his own. In ancient Persia, evidence suggests that the king's mother and primary wife could enter his presence without being summoned.[4] If this is the case, the account of Esther's bold appearance before her husband, King Xerxes, may indicate that she did not consider herself his primary wife. Perhaps she reached this conclusion based on the fact that she had not been summoned to the king's chamber for the previous thirty days (4:11).

Just as access to the Lord in the most holy place was strictly forbidden, no one was permitted to see the king without his approval. According to Numbers 4:20, the Kohathites were not to enter certain parts of the tabernacle or look upon, even for a moment, the sacred objects, or they would die. Hebrews 9:7 states that only the high priest could enter the most holy place, once a year. In the Persian court of Esther's day, an unauthorized person attempting to approach the king would be executed unless the king granted a special dispensation. In the case of Esther, King Xerxes granted such a dispensation, signified by the custom of extending to her his gold scepter.

In the religion of ancient Israel, the way a person dressed when appearing before the Lord mattered. The entire Israelite congregation was commanded to wash their garments prior to their meeting with the Lord at Mount Sinai (Ex 19:10). All Israelite priests were required to wear clothing of fine linen; the high priest wore clothing woven with gold and adorned with semiprecious stones (28:1–43). Reflections of these clothing requirements associated with the heavenly court are in two locations in the book of Esther. In her most crucial appearance before King Xerxes, Esther "dressed in her royal clothing" as she "stood in the inner courtyard of the palace" (Est 5:1). Esther's appearance in her finest apparel is particularly understandable when viewed in light of an incident describing her relative, Mordecai. When he heard the news of Haman's wicked decree to kill the Jews, Mordecai tore his clothes in grief and put on sackcloth and ashes. Because he was wearing sackcloth, he could go only as far as the King's Gate, "since the law

Xerxes's throne hall, which was also known as the Hall of One Hundred Columns, at Persepolis. Xerxes used this hall primarily as a reception hall for hosting foreign dignitaries.

prohibited anyone wearing sackcloth from entering the King's Gate" (4:1–2). These Persian customs had their counterpart in ancient Egypt where Joseph was required to shave his head and change his clothes prior to appearing before Pharaoh, having been summoned from prison to interpret Pharaoh's dreams (Gn 41:14).

Besides proper clothing, courtly manner also dictated one's proper demeanor and facial expression. The book of Nehemiah has an example of this tradition. Nehemiah, cupbearer to King Artaxerxes I, appeared before the king with a sad expression on his face. Though Nehemiah's sadness was understandable in light of a report he had received from his brother about Jerusalem's condition, he knew his life was in danger because his countenance violated courtly protocol (Neh 2:2–3). ✣

[1] Mervin Breneman, *Ezra, Nehemiah, Esther*, vol. 10 in NAC (1993), 17. [2] James B. Pritchard, ed., *The Ancient Near East: An Anthology of Texts and Pictures* (Princeton: Princeton University Press, 2011), 438. [3] Herodotus, *Histories* 3.84; Muhammad A. Dandamayev, "Courts and Courtiers: In the Median and Achaemenid Periods" in *Encyclopaedia Iranica* (*EIr*), ed. Ehsan Yarshater, 15 December 1993, www.iranicaonline.org/articles/courts-and-courtiers-i. [4] Dandamayev, "Courts and Courtiers."

Limestone relief depicting a Persian servant carrying a dish; the figure was one in a procession bringing food or drink to the banquet ceremony known as the March of Nations. From the palace of Xerxes at Persepolis, in modern southwestern Iran.

Mordecai. 10 Yet Haman controlled himself and went home. He sent for his friends and his wife Zeresh to join him. 11 Then Haman described for them his glorious wealth and his many sons. He told them all how the king had honored him and promoted him in rank over the other officials and the royal staff. 12 "What's more," Haman added, "Queen Esther invited no one but me to join the king at the banquet she had prepared. I am invited again tomorrow to join her with the king. 13 Still, none of this satisfies me since I see Mordecai the Jew sitting at the King's Gate all the time."

14 His wife Zeresh and all his friends told him, "Have them build a gallows seventy-five feet[A] tall. Ask the king in the morning to hang Mordecai on it. Then go to the banquet with the king and enjoy yourself." The advice pleased Haman, so he had the gallows constructed.

MORDECAI HONORED BY THE KING

6 That night sleep escaped the king, so he ordered the book recording daily events to be brought and read to the king. 2 They found the written report of how Mordecai had informed on Bigthana and Teresh, two of the king's eunuchs who guarded the entrance, when they planned to assassinate King Ahasuerus. 3 The king inquired, "What honor and special recognition have been given to Mordecai for this act?"

The king's personal attendants replied, "Nothing has been done for him."

4 The king asked, "Who is in the court?" Now Haman was just entering the outer court of the palace to ask the king to hang Mordecai on the gallows he had prepared for him.

5 The king's attendants answered him, "Haman is there, standing in the court."

"Have him enter," the king ordered. 6 Haman entered, and the king asked him, "What should be done for the man the king wants to honor?"

Haman thought to himself, "Who is it the king would want to honor more than me?" 7 Haman told the king, "For the man the king wants to honor: 8 Have them bring a royal garment that the king himself has worn and a horse the king himself has ridden, which has a royal crown on its head. 9 Put the garment and the horse under the charge of one of the king's most noble officials. Have them clothe the man the king wants to honor, parade him on the horse through the city square, and call out before him, 'This is what is done for the man the king wants to honor.'"

10 The king told Haman, "Hurry, and do just as you proposed. Take a garment and a horse for Mordecai the Jew, who is sitting at the King's Gate. Do not leave out anything you have suggested."

11 So Haman took the garment and the horse. He clothed Mordecai and paraded him through the city square, calling out before him, "This is what is done for the man the king wants to honor."

12 Then Mordecai returned to the King's Gate, but Haman hurried off for home, mournful and with his head covered. 13 Haman told his wife Zeresh and all his friends everything that had happened. His advisers and his wife Zeresh said to him, "Since Mordecai is Jewish, and you have begun to fall before him, you won't overcome him, because your downfall is certain." 14 While they were still speaking with him, the king's eunuchs arrived and rushed Haman to the banquet Esther had prepared.

HAMAN IS EXECUTED

7 The king and Haman came to feast[B] with Esther the queen. 2 Once again, on the second day while drinking wine, the king asked Esther, "Queen Esther, whatever you ask will be given to you. Whatever you seek, even to half the kingdom, will be done."

3 Queen Esther answered, "If I have found favor with you, Your Majesty, and if the king is pleased, spare my life; this is my request. And spare my people; this is my desire. 4 For my people and I have been sold to destruction, death, and annihilation. If we had merely been sold as male and female slaves, I would have kept silent. Indeed, the trouble wouldn't be worth burdening the king."

5 King Ahasuerus spoke up and asked Queen Esther, "Who is this, and where is the one who would devise such a scheme?"[C]

6 Esther answered, "The adversary and enemy is this evil Haman."

Haman stood terrified before the king and queen. 7 The king arose in anger and went from where they were drinking wine to the palace garden.[D] Haman remained to beg Queen Esther for his life because he realized the king was planning something terrible for him. 8 Just as the king returned from the palace garden to the banquet hall,[E] Haman was falling on the couch where Esther was reclining. The king exclaimed, "Would he actually violate the queen while I am in the house?" As soon as the statement left the king's mouth, they covered Haman's face.

9 Harbona, one of the king's eunuchs, said, "There is a gallows seventy-five feet[A] tall at Haman's house that he made for Mordecai, who gave the report that saved[F] the king."

The king said, "Hang him on it."

10 They hanged Haman on the gallows he had prepared for Mordecai. Then the king's anger subsided.

[A] **5:14; 7:9** Lit *50 cubits* [B] **7:1** Lit *drink* [C] **7:5** Lit *who would fill his heart to do this* [D] **7:7** Lit *the garden of the house*, also in v. 8 [E] **7:8** Or *the house of wine* [F] **7:9** Lit *who spoke good for*

Roles and Responsibilities of Persian Queens

by Mona Stewart

Kings had absolute power and their word was law. Queens had a major role and were second in rank only to the king. Kings often sought their wisdom in decision making. Polygamy was common; kings had large harems. Persian lineage was a requirement to become a Persian queen. Esther could not have become a queen had Mordecai not told her to keep her Jewish roots secret. Children born to concubines could not inherit the throne. Marriages often took place among relatives, even between brother and sister. Persians did not consider this improper or immoral, but a way to keep the bloodline pure.

Many queens were indeed evil. The first Greek historian to write about Persia, Herodotus, relates how queens often killed anyone who might have stood in their way—including royal children. He further reported that the ancient Persians had no temples or gods other than nature. They worshiped the sun, moon, sky, earth, fire, wind, and water.[1] The story was told that when Xerxes's wife Amestris reached old age, she buried alive fourteen sons of notable Persians as a thank-offering to the god of the nether world.[2]

Queens were secluded from the public and were often unaware of the world outside the palace. They lived in luxury, employed many maids and servants, and had their own royal guards. The queen's wardrobe consisted of royal robes and a crown.

Persians honored and revered women. Queens as well as noble women led military armies, owned land, and received equal pay for equal work. Many Persian women were both beautiful and strong. Queens were allowed to oversee property and supervise large workforces. They practiced hospitality by hosting banquets for the noble women. Their influence was felt throughout the empire. When Xerxes was informed that a woman named Artemisia, commander of a ship, had destroyed an enemy ship, he remarked, "My men have become women, and my women men."[3]

Museums house ancient objects that would have been common in the royal households of Persia, items such as rugs, jewelry, pottery, textiles, art, and golden dinnerware. Further, they display women's hairpieces and makeup, including eyeliners and red dye used for rouge and lip color. Archaeologists have also excavated intricately designed perfume bottles. Doubtless each of these items would have been familiar to Queen Esther. ✣

[1] Herodotus, *Histories* 1.131. [2] Herodotus, *Histories* 7.114. [3] Herodotus, *Histories* 8.88.

Relief at Persepolis depicting the king, likely Darius the Great, seated on his throne. Dressed in full regalia, the king would have been receiving visiting dignitaries.

ESTHER INTERVENES FOR THE JEWS

8 That same day King Ahasuerus awarded Queen Esther the estate of Haman, the enemy of the Jews. Mordecai entered the king's presence because Esther had revealed her relationship to Mordecai. 2 The king removed his signet ring he had recovered from Haman and gave it to Mordecai, and Esther put him in charge of Haman's estate.

3 Then Esther addressed the king again. She fell at his feet, wept, and begged him to revoke the evil of Haman the Agagite and his plot he had devised against the Jews. 4 The king extended the gold scepter toward Esther, so she got up and stood before the king.

5 She said, "If it pleases the king and I have found favor with him, if the matter seems right to the king and I am pleasing in his eyes, let a royal edict be written. Let it revoke the documents the scheming Haman son of Hammedatha the Agagite wrote to destroy the Jews who are in all the king's provinces. 6 For how could I bear to see the disaster that would come on my people? How could I bear to see the destruction of my relatives?"

7 King Ahasuerus said to Esther the queen and to Mordecai the Jew, "Look, I have given Haman's estate to Esther, and he was hanged on the gallows because he attacked[A] the Jews. 8 Write in the king's name whatever pleases you concerning the Jews, and seal it with the royal signet ring. A document written in the king's name and sealed with the royal signet ring cannot be revoked."

9 On the twenty-third day of the third month — that is, the month Sivan — the royal scribes were summoned. Everything was written exactly as Mordecai commanded for the Jews, to the satraps, the governors, and the officials of the 127 provinces from India to Cush. The edict was written for each province in its own script, for each ethnic group in its own language, and to the Jews in their own script and language.

10 Mordecai wrote in King Ahasuerus's name and sealed the edicts with the royal signet ring. He sent the documents by mounted couriers, who rode fast horses bred in the royal stables.

11 The king's edict gave the Jews in each and every city the right to assemble and defend themselves, to destroy, kill, and annihilate every ethnic and provincial army hostile to them, including women and children, and to take their possessions as spoils of war. 12 This would take place on a single day throughout all the provinces of King Ahasuerus, on the thirteenth day of the twelfth month, the month Adar.

13 A copy of the text, issued as law throughout every province, was distributed to all the peoples so the Jews could be ready to avenge themselves against their enemies on that day. 14 The couriers rode out in haste on their royal horses at the king's urgent command. The law was also issued in the fortress of Susa.

15 Mordecai went from the king's presence clothed in royal blue and white, with a great gold crown and a purple robe of fine linen. The city of Susa shouted and rejoiced, 16 and the Jews celebrated[B] with gladness, joy, and honor. 17 In every province and every city where the king's command and edict reached, gladness and joy took place among the Jews. There was a celebration and a holiday.[C] And many of the ethnic groups of the land professed themselves to be Jews because fear of the Jews had overcome them.

VICTORIES OF THE JEWS

9 The king's command and law went into effect on the thirteenth day of the twelfth month, the month Adar. On the day when the Jews' enemies had hoped to overpower them, just the opposite happened. The Jews overpowered those who hated them. 2 In each of King Ahasuerus's provinces the Jews assembled in their cities to attack those who intended to harm them.[D] Not a single person could withstand them; fear of them fell on every nationality.

3 All the officials of the provinces, the satraps, the governors, and the royal civil administrators[E] aided the Jews because they feared Mordecai. 4 For Mordecai exercised great power in the palace, and his fame spread throughout the provinces as he became more and more powerful.

5 The Jews put all their enemies to the sword, killing and destroying them. They did what they pleased to those who hated them. 6 In the fortress of Susa the Jews killed and destroyed five hundred men, 7 including Parshandatha, Dalphon, Aspatha, 8 Poratha, Adalia, Aridatha, 9 Parmashta, Arisai, Aridai, and Vaizatha. 10 They killed these ten sons of Haman son of Hammedatha, the enemy of the Jews. However, they did not seize[F] any plunder.

11 On that day the number of people killed in the fortress of Susa was reported to the king. 12 The king said to Queen Esther, "In the fortress of Susa the Jews have killed and destroyed five hundred men, including Haman's ten sons. What have they done in the rest of the royal provinces? Whatever you ask will be given to you. Whatever you seek will also be done."

13 Esther answered, "If it pleases the king, may the Jews who are in Susa also have tomorrow to carry out today's law, and may the bodies of Haman's ten sons be hung on the gallows." 14 The king gave the orders for this to be done, so a law was announced in Susa,

[A] **8:7** Lit *stretched out his hand against* [B] **8:16** Lit *had light* [C] **8:17** Lit *good day* [D] **9:2** Lit *cities to send out a hand against the seekers of their evil* [E] **9:3** Lit *and those who do the king's work*; Est 3:9 [F] **9:10** Lit *not put their hands on*, also in vv. 15,16

The Feast of Purim

by Dorman Laird

Figurine of two girls playing knuckle bones. The bones, each of whose six faces was different, could be used as dice.

Pur means "lot," and *Purim*, the word for which the feast is named, means "lots." Casting of the *pur* was done to ascertain a favorable day for Haman to carry out his scheme to annihilate all the Jews in Persia.[1]

As the events of the book of Esther unfolded, Esther requested that Ahasuerus reverse the previous orders that Haman had given about killing the Jews. Ahasuerus told the Jews to rise up on that chosen day and put to death all the officials who had intended to slay them (Est 8:11). The next day even in the king's palace at Susa (Shushan) others who were involved in the plot were put to death (9:15).

The modern celebration of Purim is a two-day festival that celebrates these two days of deliverance of the Jews. The happy festival is held near the end of winter in February.[2] Several symbols are involved. Three-cornered pastries filled with poppy seeds are eaten. The three corners are a reminder of the shape of Haman's hat and the banquet attended by three people, while the poppy seeds represent God's promise to multiply Abraham's seed like the grains of earth.[3] When the scroll of Esther is read in the synagogues, all the people are supposed to yell and stamp their feet or shake noisemakers to drown out Haman's name when it is mentioned.[4] Also Jews give alms to the poor and exchange gifts with relatives and friends during Purim.[5] ✣

[1] Larry Walker, "Festivals" in *HIBD*, 572.
[2] Barbara E. Organ, *Judaism for Gentiles* (N. Richland Hills, TX: BIBAL, 1996), 61.
[3] Sidney L. Markowitz, *Jewish Religion, History, Ethics, and Culture* (Secaucus, NJ: Citadel Press, 1982), 195. [4] Organ, *Judaism*.
[5] Markowitz, *Jewish Religion*.

Dice were made of different materials; shown is one made of steatite and the other of bone.

and they hung the bodies of Haman's ten sons. 15 The Jews in Susa assembled again on the fourteenth day of the month of Adar and killed three hundred men in Susa, but they did not seize any plunder.

16 The rest of the Jews in the royal provinces assembled, defended themselves, and gained relief from their enemies. They killed seventy-five thousand[A] of those who hated them, but they did not seize any plunder. 17 They fought on the thirteenth day of the month of Adar and rested on the fourteenth, and it became a day of feasting and rejoicing.

18 But the Jews in Susa had assembled on the thirteenth and the fourteenth days of the month. They rested on the fifteenth day of the month, and it became a day of feasting and rejoicing. 19 This explains why the rural Jews who live in villages observe the fourteenth day of the month of Adar as a time of rejoicing and feasting. It is a holiday when they send gifts to one another.

20 Mordecai recorded these events and sent letters to all the Jews in all of King Ahasuerus's provinces, both near and far. 21 He ordered them to celebrate the fourteenth and fifteenth days of the month of Adar every year 22 because during those days the Jews gained relief from their enemies. That was the month when their sorrow was turned into rejoicing and their mourning into a holiday. They were to be days of feasting, rejoicing, and of sending gifts to one another and to the poor.

23 So the Jews agreed to continue the practice they had begun, as Mordecai had written them to do. 24 For Haman son of Hammedatha the Agagite, the enemy of all the Jews, had plotted against the Jews to destroy them. He cast the *pur* — that is, the lot — to crush and destroy them. 25 But when the matter was brought before the king, he commanded by letter that the evil plan Haman had devised against the Jews return on his own head and that he should be hanged with his sons on the gallows. 26 For this reason these days are called Purim, from the word *pur*. Because of all the instructions in this letter as well as what they had witnessed and what had happened to them, 27 the Jews bound themselves, their descendants, and all who joined with them to a commitment that they would not fail to celebrate these two days each and every year according to the written instructions and according to the time appointed. 28 These days are remembered and celebrated by every generation, family, province, and city, so that these days of Purim will not lose their significance in Jewish life[B] and their memory will not fade from their descendants.

29 Queen Esther, daughter of Abihail, along with Mordecai the Jew, wrote this second letter with full authority to confirm the letter about Purim. 30 He sent letters with assurances of peace and security[C] to all the Jews who were in the 127 provinces of the kingdom of Ahasuerus, 31 in order to confirm these days of Purim at their proper time just as Mordecai the Jew and Esther the queen had established them and just as they had committed themselves and their descendants to the practices of fasting and lamentation. 32 So Esther's command confirmed these customs of Purim, which were then written into the record.

MORDECAI'S FAME

10 King Ahasuerus imposed a tax throughout the land even to the farthest shores.[D] 2 All of his powerful and magnificent accomplishments and the detailed account of Mordecai's great rank with which the king had honored him, have they not been written in the Book of the Historical Events of the Kings of Media and Persia? 3 Mordecai the Jew was second only to King Ahasuerus. He was famous among the Jews and highly esteemed by many of his relatives. He continued to pursue prosperity for his people and to speak for the well-being of all his descendants.

[A] **9:16** Some LXX mss read *10,107*; other LXX mss read *15,000*
[B] **9:28** LXX reads *will be celebrated into all times* [C] **9:30** Or *of peace and faithfulness* [D] **10:1** Or *imposed forced labor on the land and the coasts of the sea*

JOB

From Egypt's Thirteenth Dynasty (1794–1648 BC); faience on terracotta. When he answered Job, God said, "Look at Behemoth, which I made along with you" (Jb 40:15). Although scholars have offered different interpretations of what Behemoth was, the most common suggestion has been the hippopotamus.

INTRODUCTION TO

JOB

Circumstances of Writing

The author of Job is unknown, but he was a learned man whose knowledge embraced the heavens (Jb 22:12; 38:32–33) and earth (26:7–8; 28:9–11; 37:11,16). His knowledge touched on foreign lands (28:16,19), various products (6:19), and human professions (7:6; 9:26; 18:8–10; 28:1–11). He was familiar with plants (14:7–9) and animals (4:10–11; 38:39–39:30; 40:15–41:34). He was a wise man, familiar with traditional wisdom (6:5–6; 17:5; 28:12,28), but was above all a man of spiritual sensitivity (1:1,5,8; 2:3; 14:14–15; 16:11–21; 19:23–27; 23:10; 34:26–28; 40:1–5; 42:1–6). He was doubtless an Israelite as confirmed by his frequent use of God's covenant name (Yahweh, usually rendered as "the Lord").

The story of Job is set in the patriarchal period. In that era, wealth consisted of the possession of cattle and servants. Like other Old Testament patriarchal family heads, Job performed priestly duties, including offering sacrifices for his family. Like the patriarchs, Job lived to be more than a hundred years old. Geographically, the action took place in the northern Arabian Peninsula, in the land of Uz (1:1), often associated with Edom. Job's three friends also had Edomite or southern associations, as did the young Elihu.

Although Job is set in the patriarchal period, its date of writing is unknown. Jewish tradition places the authorship of Job in the time of Moses.

Contribution to the Bible

The book of Job teaches that suffering comes to everyone, the righteous and unrighteous alike. God does not always keep the righteous from danger or suffering. Ultimately God controls all of life's situations, including limiting the power of Satan. God's comfort and strength are always available to the trusting soul.

Although the book of Job does take note of the problem of suffering, it focuses more on the nature of human conduct before a sovereign and holy God. In harmony with the rest of Scripture, the book teaches that even a consistent practice of religion is insufficient without a genuine heart relationship with God (Dt 6:4–6; Ps 86:11–12; Mt 22:37). The answer to life's problems and goals lies in a proper reverence for him who is perfect in all his being and actions. Man needs not just to confess God but to surrender everything to him. By letting him truly be God in every area of life, a person will find him sufficient.

Structure

The writer was a skilled storyteller, artistically characterizing the distinctions between the protagonist (Job), antagonist (Satan), and literary foils (the three friends and Elihu). The characterization demonstrates that God himself is the ultimate protagonist (or "hero") of the story. Satan was as much challenging God as Job's piety. Although Job's three "comforters" applied traditional wisdom to Job's situation, each did it in a different way. Eliphaz, the rationalist, reasoned with Job (Jb 15:17–18); Bildad, the apologist, sought to defend God (25:1–6); and Zophar acted much like a prosecutor (11:1–6). The youthful Elihu served as a mediating influence, to prepare for the divine speeches that follow (33:23–26). The writer constructed a well-developed plot built around dramatic dialogue. The fact that he related the account of Job's test in story form does not mean that Job was not a real person who underwent a real test.

JOB AND HIS FAMILY

1 There was a man in the country of Uz named Job. He was a man of complete integrity, who feared God and turned away from evil. [2] He had seven sons and three daughters. [3] His estate included seven thousand sheep and goats, three thousand camels, five hundred yoke of oxen, five hundred female donkeys, and a very large number of servants. Job was the greatest man among all the people of the east.

[4] His sons used to take turns having banquets at their homes. They would send an invitation to their three sisters to eat and drink with them. [5] Whenever a round of banqueting was over, Job would send for his children and purify them, rising early in the morning to offer burnt offerings for[A] all of them. For Job thought, "Perhaps my children have sinned, having cursed God in their hearts." This was Job's regular practice.

SATAN'S FIRST TEST OF JOB

[6] One day the sons of God came to present themselves before the LORD, and Satan[B] also came with them. [7] The LORD asked Satan, "Where have you come from?"

"From roaming through the earth," Satan answered him, "and walking around on it."

[8] Then the LORD said to Satan, "Have you considered my servant Job? No one else on earth is like him, a man of perfect integrity, who fears God and turns away from evil."

[9] Satan answered the LORD, "Does Job fear God for nothing? [10] Haven't you placed a hedge around him, his household, and everything he owns? You have blessed the work of his hands, and his possessions have increased in the land. [11] But stretch out your hand and strike everything he owns, and he will surely curse you to your face."

[12] "Very well," the LORD told Satan, "everything he owns is in your power. However, do not lay a hand on Job himself." So Satan left the LORD's presence.

[13] One day when Job's sons and daughters were eating and drinking wine in their oldest brother's house, [14] a messenger came to Job and reported, "While the oxen were plowing and the donkeys grazing nearby, [15] the Sabeans swooped down and took them away. They struck down the servants with the sword, and I alone have escaped to tell you!"

[16] He was still speaking when another messenger came and reported, "God's fire fell from heaven. It burned the sheep and the servants and devoured them, and I alone have escaped to tell you!"

[17] That messenger was still speaking when yet another came and reported, "The Chaldeans formed three bands, made a raid on the camels, and took them away. They struck down the servants with the sword, and I alone have escaped to tell you!"

[18] He was still speaking when another messenger came and reported, "Your sons and daughters were eating and drinking wine in their oldest brother's house. [19] Suddenly a powerful wind swept in from the desert and struck the four corners of the house. It collapsed on the young people so that they died, and I alone have escaped to tell you!"

[20] Then Job stood up, tore his robe, and shaved his head. He fell to the ground and worshiped, [21] saying:

Naked I came from my mother's womb,
and naked I will leave this life.[C]
The LORD gives, and the LORD takes away.
Blessed be the name of the LORD.

[22] Throughout all this Job did not sin or blame God for anything.[D]

SATAN'S SECOND TEST OF JOB

2 One day the sons of God came again to present themselves before the LORD, and Satan also came with them to present himself before the LORD. [2] The LORD asked Satan, "Where have you come from?"

"From roaming through the earth," Satan answered him, "and walking around on it."

[3] Then the LORD said to Satan, "Have you considered my servant Job? No one else on earth is like him, a man of perfect integrity, who fears God and turns away from evil. He still retains his integrity, even though you incited me against him, to destroy him for no good reason."

[4] "Skin for skin!" Satan answered the LORD. "A man will give up everything he owns in exchange for his life. [5] But stretch out your hand and strike his flesh and bones, and he will surely curse you to your face."

[6] "Very well," the LORD told Satan, "he is in your power; only spare his life." [7] So Satan left the LORD's presence and infected Job with terrible boils from the soles of his feet to the top of his head. [8] Then Job took a piece of broken pottery to scrape himself while he sat among the ashes.

[9] His wife said to him, "Are you still holding on to your integrity? Curse God and die!"

[10] "You speak as a foolish woman speaks," he told her. "Should we accept only good from God and not adversity?" Throughout all this Job did not sin in what he said.[E]

JOB'S THREE FRIENDS

[11] Now when Job's three friends — Eliphaz the Temanite, Bildad the Shuhite, and Zophar the Naamathite — heard about all this adversity that had happened to him, each of them came from his home. They met

[A] **1:5** Lit *for the number of* [B] **1:6** Or *the adversary* [C] **1:21** Lit *will return there*; Ps 139:13,15 [D] **1:22** Lit *or ascribe blame to God* [E] **2:10** Lit *sin with his lips*

together to go and sympathize with him and comfort
him. [12] When they looked from a distance, they could
barely recognize him. They wept aloud, and each man
tore his robe and threw dust into the air and on his
head. [13] Then they sat on the ground with him seven
days and nights, but no one spoke a word to him because they saw that his suffering was very intense.

JOB'S OPENING SPEECH

3 After this, Job began to speak and cursed the day
he was born. [2] He said:

3 May the day I was born perish,
and the night that said,
"A boy is conceived."
4 If only that day had turned to darkness!
May God above not care about it,
or light shine on it.
5 May darkness and gloom reclaim it,
and a cloud settle over it.
May what darkens the day terrify it.
6 If only darkness had taken that night away!
May it not appear[A] among the days of the year
or be listed in the calendar.[B]
7 Yes, may that night be barren;
may no joyful shout be heard in it.
8 Let those who curse days
condemn it,
those who are ready to rouse Leviathan.
9 May its morning stars grow dark.
May it wait for daylight but have none;
may it not see the breaking[C] of dawn.
10 For that night did not shut
the doors of my mother's womb,
and hide sorrow from my eyes.

11 Why was I not stillborn;
why didn't I die as I came from the womb?
12 Why did the knees receive me,
and why were there breasts for me to nurse?
13 Now I would certainly be lying down in peace;
I would be asleep.
Then I would be at rest
14 with the kings and counselors of the earth,
who rebuilt ruined cities for themselves,
15 or with princes who had gold,
who filled their houses with silver.
16 Or why was I not hidden
like a miscarried child,
like infants who never see daylight?
17 There the wicked cease to make trouble,
and there the weary find rest.
18 The captives are completely at rest;
they do not hear a taskmaster's voice.
19 Both small and great are there,
and the slave is set free from his master.

20 Why is light given to one burdened with grief,
and life to those whose existence is bitter,
21 who wait for death, but it does not come,
and search for it more than
for hidden treasure,
22 who are filled with much joy
and are glad when they reach the grave?
23 Why is life given to a man whose path is hidden,
whom God has hedged in?
24 I sigh when food is put before me,[D]
and my groans pour out like water.
25 For the thing I feared has overtaken me,
and what I dreaded has happened to me.
26 I cannot relax or be calm;
I have no rest, for turmoil has come.

FIRST SERIES OF SPEECHES
ELIPHAZ SPEAKS

4 Then Eliphaz the Temanite replied:
2 Should anyone try to speak with you
when you are exhausted?
Yet who can keep from speaking?
3 Indeed, you have instructed many
and have strengthened weak hands.
4 Your words have steadied the one
who was stumbling
and braced the knees that were buckling.
5 But now that this has happened to you,
you have become exhausted.
It strikes you, and you are dismayed.
6 Isn't your piety your confidence,
and the integrity of your life[E] your hope?
7 Consider: Who has perished when he
was innocent?
Where have the honest[F] been destroyed?
8 In my experience, those who plow injustice
and those who sow trouble reap the same.
9 They perish at a single blast from God
and come to an end by the breath
of his nostrils.
10 The lion may roar and the fierce lion growl,
but the teeth of young lions are broken.
11 The strong lion dies if it catches no prey,
and the cubs of the lioness are scattered.

12 A word was brought to me in secret;
my ears caught a whisper of it.
13 Among unsettling thoughts from visions
in the night,
when deep sleep comes over men,
14 fear and trembling came over me
and made all my bones shake.

[A] **3:6** LXX, Syr, Tg, Vg; MT reads *rejoice* [B] **3:6** Lit *or enter the number of months* [C] **3:9** Lit *the eyelids* [D] **3:24** Or *My sighing serves as my food* [E] **4:6** Lit *ways* [F] **4:7** Or *the upright*, or *those with integrity*

Job's Friends: Models of Compassion?

by J. Mark Terry

ELIPHAZ

Eliphaz's name means "God is victorious." He made his home in Teman, a town in Edom. Edom lies between the southern border of Israel and the Gulf of Aqaba. Later the descendants of Esau settled there. In the book of Job, Eliphaz always spoke first. This indicates that he was the oldest and most prominent of the three men. The Scriptures provide no details about his life or family. He was the kindest of the three friends. Before coming to see Job, Eliphaz had had a dream that affected him greatly (4:12–21) and likely set the tone for all three of his speeches. Eliphaz believed that all suffering was punishment for sin. Therefore, in Eliphaz's mind, because Job was suffering greatly, he must have sinned grievously against God.

Eliphaz was a good man, a man of upright character and sympathy. Were he not kind and sympathetic, he would not have traveled many miles to see his friend. Still, his narrow and limited understanding of human suffering led him to misdiagnose Job's problem. When Job rejected his argument, Eliphaz responded with hateful words.[1]

The Nabonidus stele was discovered in the city of Tema in Arabia. Eliphaz, described as being a Temanite, may have been from Tema.

BILDAD

Bildad's name may mean "son of Hadad," but this is not certain. Bildad lived in Shuah. The location of Shuah is unknown, but ancient Akkadian documents mention a district called Suhu, which was on the middle Euphrates River in what is now Iraq.[2]

As with Eliphaz, the Bible gives no information about Bildad's family. Most Bible commentators believe he was younger than Eliphaz, as it was customary for the oldest person to speak first. Bildad was a consummate traditionalist (8:8–10). He expressed amazement that Job would question the traditional belief that suffering is the result of sin.

ZOPHAR

Zophar's name may mean "young bird" or "little bird." He came from Naamah. Although Naamah was almost certainly east of the Jordan River, its exact location is still not known. The fact that Zophar spoke third suggests he was the youngest of the friends. He valued common sense and found no delight in many words (11:2). He showed little patience with Job. Like his friends, Zophar focused on Job's disobedience as the cause of his suffering. He went further than the friends, though, by suggesting that God had reduced Job's punishment.

The Bible says Eliphaz, Bildad, and Zophar came to comfort Job. How well did they do? Job declared that they were "miserable comforters" (16:2). Surely they meant well, but they made Job feel even worse than he had before their arrival. ✣

[1] H. L. Ellison, "Eliphaz" in *ISBE*, vol. 2 (1982), 69. [2] John E. Hartley, *The Book of Job*, New International Commentary on the Old Testament (Grand Rapids: Eerdmans, 1988), 86.

15 I felt a draft[A] on my face,
and the hair on my body stood up.
16 A figure stood there,
but I could not recognize its appearance;
a form loomed before my eyes.
I heard a whispering voice:
17 "Can a mortal be righteous before God?
Can a man be more pure than his Maker?"
18 If God puts no trust in his servants
and he charges his angels with foolishness,[B]
19 how much more those who dwell
in clay houses,
whose foundation is in the dust,
who are crushed like a moth!
20 They are smashed to pieces from dawn to dusk;
they perish forever while no one notices.
21 Are their tent cords not pulled up?
They die without wisdom.

5 Call out! Will anyone answer you?
Which of the holy ones will you turn to?
2 For anger kills a fool,
and jealousy slays the gullible.
3 I have seen a fool taking root,
but I immediately pronounced a curse
on his home.
4 His children are far from safety.
They are crushed at the city gate,
with no one to rescue them.
5 The hungry consume his harvest,
even taking it out of the thorns.[C]
The thirsty[D] pant for his children's wealth.
6 For distress does not grow out of the soil,
and trouble does not sprout from the ground.
7 But humans are born for trouble
as surely as sparks fly upward.

8 However, if I were you, I would appeal to God
and would present my case to him.
9 He does great and unsearchable things,
wonders without number.
10 He gives rain to the earth
and sends water to the fields.
11 He sets the lowly on high,
and mourners are lifted to safety.
12 He frustrates the schemes of the crafty
so that they[E] achieve no success.
13 He traps the wise in their craftiness
so that the plans of the deceptive
are quickly brought to an end.
14 They encounter darkness by day,
and they grope at noon
as if it were night.
15 He saves the needy from their sharp words[F]
and from the clutches of the powerful.
16 So the poor have hope,
and injustice shuts its mouth.
17 See how happy is the person whom
God corrects;
so do not reject the discipline
of the Almighty.
18 For he wounds but he also bandages;
he strikes, but his hands also heal.
19 He will rescue you from six calamities;
no harm will touch you in seven.
20 In famine he will redeem you from death,
and in battle, from the power of the sword.
21 You will be safe from slander[G]
and not fear destruction when it comes.
22 You will laugh at destruction and hunger
and not fear the land's wild creatures.
23 For you will have a covenant with the stones
of the field,
and the wild animals will be at peace
with you.
24 You will know that your tent is secure,
and nothing will be missing when you inspect
your home.
25 You will also know that your offspring
will be many
and your descendants like the grass
of the earth.
26 You will approach the grave in full vigor,
as a stack of sheaves is gathered in its season.

27 We have investigated this, and it is true!
Hear it and understand it for yourself.

JOB'S REPLY TO ELIPHAZ

6 Then Job answered:
2 If only my grief could be weighed
and my devastation placed with it
on the scales.
3 For then it would outweigh the sand
of the seas!
That is why my words are rash.
4 Surely the arrows of the Almighty
have pierced[H] me;
my spirit drinks their poison.
God's terrors are arrayed against me.
5 Does a wild donkey bray over fresh grass
or an ox low over its fodder?
6 Is bland food eaten without salt?
Is there flavor in an egg white?[C]
7 I refuse to touch them;
they are like contaminated food.

[A] **4:15** Or *a spirit* [B] **4:18** Or *error*; Hb obscure [C] **5:5; 6:6** Hb obscure
[D] **5:5** Aq, Sym, Syr, Vg; MT reads *snares* [E] **5:12** Lit *their hands*
[F] **5:15** Lit *from the sword of their mouth*; Ps 55:21; 59:7 [G] **5:21** Lit *be hidden from the whip of the tongue* [H] **6:4** Lit *Almighty are in*

8 If only my request would be granted
and God would provide what I hope for:
9 that he would decide to crush me,
to unleash his power and cut me off!
10 It would still bring me comfort,
and I would leap for joy in unrelenting pain
that I have not denied[A] the words
of the Holy One.

11 What strength do I have, that I should
continue to hope?
What is my future, that I should be patient?
12 Is my strength that of stone,
or my flesh made of bronze?
13 Since I cannot help myself,
the hope for success has been banished
from me.

14 A despairing man should receive loyalty
from his friends,[B]
even if he abandons the fear of the Almighty.
15 My brothers are as treacherous as a wadi,
as seasonal streams that overflow
16 and become darkened[C] because of ice,
and the snow melts into them.
17 The wadis evaporate in warm weather;
they disappear from their channels
in hot weather.
18 Caravans turn away from their routes,
go up into the desert, and perish.
19 The caravans of Tema look for these streams.
The traveling merchants of Sheba hope
for them.
20 They are ashamed because they
had been confident of finding water.
When they arrive there, they are disappointed.
21 So this is what you have now become to me.[D]
When you see something dreadful,
you are afraid.
22 Have I ever said, "Give me something"
or "Pay a bribe for me from your wealth"
23 or "Deliver me from the enemy's hand"
or "Redeem me from the hand
of the ruthless"?

24 Teach me, and I will be silent.
Help me understand what I did wrong.
25 How painful honest words can be!
But what does your rebuke prove?
26 Do you think that you can disprove my words
or that a despairing man's words are
mere wind?
27 No doubt you would cast lots
for a fatherless child
and negotiate a price to sell your friend.
28 But now, please look at me;
I will not lie to your face.
29 Reconsider; don't be unjust.
Reconsider; my righteousness is still the issue.
30 Is there injustice on my tongue
or can my palate not taste disaster?

7 Isn't each person consigned to forced labor
on earth?
Are not his days like those of a hired worker?
2 Like a slave he longs for shade;
like a hired worker he waits for his pay.
3 So I have been made to inherit months
of futility,
and troubled nights have been assigned to me.
4 When I lie down I think,
"When will I get up?"
But the evening drags on endlessly,
and I toss and turn until dawn.
5 My flesh is clothed with maggots
and encrusted with dirt.[E]
My skin forms scabs[F] and then oozes.

6 My days pass more swiftly
than a weaver's shuttle;
they come to an end without hope.
7 Remember that my life is but a breath.
My eye will never again see anything good.
8 The eye of anyone who looks on me
will no longer see me.
Your eyes will look for me, but I will be gone.
9 As a cloud fades away and vanishes,
so the one who goes down to Sheol will never
rise again.
10 He will never return to his house;
his hometown will no longer remember[G] him.

11 Therefore I will not restrain my mouth.
I will speak in the anguish of my spirit;
I will complain in the bitterness of my soul.
12 Am I the sea[H] or a sea monster,
that you keep me under guard?
13 When I say, "My bed will comfort me,
and my couch will ease my complaint,"
14 then you frighten me with dreams,
and terrify me with visions,
15 so that I prefer strangling[I] —
death rather than life in this body.[J]
16 I give up! I will not live forever.
Leave me alone, for my days are a breath.[K]

[A] **6:10** Lit *hidden* [B] **6:14** Lit *To the despairing his friend loyalty* [C] **6:16** Or *turbid* [D] **6:21** Alt Hb tradition reads *So you have now become nothing* [E] **7:5** Or *and dirty scabs* [F] **7:5** Lit *skin hardens* [G] **7:10** Lit *know* [H] **7:12** Or *the sea god* [I] **7:15** Or *suffocation* [J] **7:15** Lit *than my bones* [K] **7:16** Or *are futile*

17 What is a mere human, that you think
so highly of him
and pay so much attention to him?
18 You inspect him every morning,
and put him to the test every moment.
19 Will you ever look away from me,
or leave me alone long enough to swallow?[A]
20 If I have sinned, what have I done to you,
Watcher of humanity?
Why have you made me your target,
so that I have become a burden to you?[B]
21 Why not forgive my sin
and pardon my iniquity?
For soon I will lie down in the grave.
You will eagerly seek me, but I will be gone.

BILDAD SPEAKS

8 Then Bildad the Shuhite replied:
2 How long will you go on saying these things?
Your words are a blast of wind.
3 Does God pervert justice?
Does the Almighty pervert what is right?
4 Since your children sinned against him,
he gave them over to their rebellion.
5 But if you earnestly seek God
and ask the Almighty for mercy,
6 if you are pure and upright,
then he will move even now on your behalf
and restore the home where
your righteousness dwells.
7 Then, even if your beginnings were modest,
your final days will be full of prosperity.

8 For ask the previous generation,
and pay attention to what
their ancestors discovered,
9 since we were born only yesterday and know
nothing.
Our days on earth are but a shadow.
10 Will they not teach you and tell you
and speak from their understanding?
11 Does papyrus grow where
there is no marsh?
Do reeds flourish without water?
12 While still uncut shoots,
they would dry up quicker than
any other plant.
13 Such is the destiny[C] of all who forget God;
the hope of the godless will perish.
14 His source of confidence is fragile;[D]
what he trusts in is a spider's web.
15 He leans on his web, but it doesn't stand firm.
He grabs it, but it does not hold up.
16 He is a well-watered plant in the sunshine;
his shoots spread out over his garden.
17 His roots are intertwined around a pile
of rocks.
He looks for a home among the stones.
18 If he is uprooted[E] from his place,
it will deny knowing him, saying,
"I never saw you."
19 Surely this is the joy of his way of life;
yet others will sprout from the dust.
20 Look, God does not reject a person
of integrity,
and he will not support[F] evildoers.
21 He will yet fill your mouth with laughter
and your lips with a shout of joy.
22 Your enemies will be clothed with shame;
the tent of the wicked will no longer exist.

JOB'S REPLY TO BILDAD

9 Then Job answered:
2 Yes, I know what you've said is true,
but how can a person be justified
before God?
3 If one wanted to take him to court,
he could not answer God[G] once
in a thousand times.
4 God is wise and all-powerful.
Who has opposed him
and come out unharmed?
5 He removes mountains
without their knowledge,
overturning them in his anger.
6 He shakes the earth from its place
so that its pillars tremble.
7 He commands the sun not to shine
and seals off the stars.
8 He alone stretches out the heavens
and treads on the waves of the sea.[H]
9 He makes the stars: the Bear,[I] Orion,
the Pleiades, and the constellations[J]
of the southern sky.
10 He does great and unsearchable things,
wonders without number.
11 If he passed by me, I wouldn't see him;
if he went by, I wouldn't recognize him.
12 If he snatches something,
who can stop[K] him?
Who can ask him, "What are you doing?"
13 God does not hold back his anger;
Rahab's assistants cringe in fear
beneath him!

[A] **7:19** Lit *swallow my saliva?* [B] **7:20** Alt Hb tradition, LXX; MT, Vg read *myself* [C] **8:13** Lit *Such are the ways* [D] **8:14** Or *cut off*; Hb obscure [E] **8:18** Or *destroyed* [F] **8:20** Lit *grasp the hand of* [G] **9:3** Or *court, God would not answer him* [H] **9:8** Or *and walks on the back of the sea god* [I] **9:9** Or *Aldebaran* [J] **9:9** Or *chambers* [K] **9:12** Or *dissuade*

14 How then can I answer him
or choose my arguments against him?
15 Even if I were in the right,
I could not answer.
I could only beg my Judge for mercy.
16 If I summoned him and he answered me,
I do not believe he would pay attention to
what I said.
17 He batters me with a whirlwind
and multiplies my wounds without cause.
18 He doesn't let me catch my breath
but fills me with bitter experiences.
19 If it is a matter of strength, look, he is
the powerful one!
If it is a matter of justice, who can
summon him?[A]
20 Even if I were in the right, my own mouth
would condemn me;
if I were blameless, my mouth would
declare me guilty.

21 Though I am blameless,
I no longer care about myself;
I renounce my life.
22 It is all the same. Therefore I say,
"He destroys both the blameless
and the wicked."
23 When catastrophe[B] brings sudden death,
he mocks the despair of the innocent.
24 The earth[C] is handed over to the wicked;
he blindfolds[D] its judges.
If it isn't he, then who is it?

25 My days fly by faster than a runner;[E]
they flee without seeing any good.
26 They sweep by like boats made of papyrus,
like an eagle swooping down on its prey.
27 If I said, "I will forget my complaint,
change my expression, and smile,"
28 I would still live in terror of all my pains.
I know you will not acquit me.
29 Since I will be found guilty,
why should I struggle in vain?
30 If I wash myself with snow,
and cleanse my hands with lye,
31 then you dip me in a pit of mud,
and my own clothes despise me!

32 For he is not a man like me, that I can
answer him,
that we can take each other to court.
33 There is no mediator between us,
to lay his hand on both of us.
34 Let him take his rod away from me
so his terror will no longer frighten me.
35 Then I would speak and not fear him.
But that is not the case; I am on my own.

10 I am disgusted with my life.
I will give vent to my complaint
and speak in the bitterness of my soul.
2 I will say to God,
"Do not declare me guilty!
Let me know why you prosecute me.
3 Is it good for you to oppress,
to reject the work of your hands,
and favor[F] the plans of the wicked?
4 Do you have eyes of flesh,
or do you see as a human sees?
5 Are your days like those of a human,
or your years like those of a man,
6 that you look for my iniquity
and search for my sin,
7 even though you know that I am not wicked
and that there is no one who can rescue
from your power?

8 "Your hands shaped me and formed me.
Will you now turn and destroy me?
9 Please remember that you formed me like clay.
Will you now return me to dust?
10 Did you not pour me out like milk
and curdle me like cheese?
11 You clothed me with skin and flesh,
and wove me together with bones
and tendons.
12 You gave me life and faithful love,
and your care has guarded my life.

13 "Yet you concealed these thoughts
in your heart;
I know that this was your hidden plan:[G]
14 if I sin, you would notice,[H]
and would not acquit me of my iniquity.
15 If I am wicked, woe to me!
And even if I am righteous, I cannot lift up
my head.
I am filled with shame
and have drunk deeply of[I] my affliction.
16 If I am proud,[J] you hunt me like a lion
and again display your miraculous power
against me.
17 You produce new witnesses[K] against me
and multiply your anger toward me.
Hardships assault me, wave after wave.[L]

[A] **9:19** LXX; MT reads *me* [B] **9:23** Or *whip*; Hb obscure [C] **9:24** Or *land* [D] **9:24** Lit *covers the faces of* [E] **9:25** = a royal messenger [F] **10:3** Lit *shine on* [G] **10:13** Lit *was with you* [H] **10:14** Lit *notice me* [I] **10:15** Or *and look at* [J] **10:16** Lit *If he lifts up* [K] **10:17** Or *You bring fresh troops* [L] **10:17** Lit *Changes and a host are with me*

18 "Why did you bring me out of the womb?
I should have died and never been seen.
19 I wish[A] I had never existed
but had been carried from the womb
to the grave.
20 Are my days not few? Stop it![B]
Leave me alone, so that I can smile a little
21 before I go to a land of darkness and gloom,
never to return.
22 It is a land of blackness
like the deepest darkness,
gloomy and chaotic,
where even the light is like[C] the darkness."

ZOPHAR SPEAKS

11 Then Zophar the Naamathite replied:
2 Should this abundance of words
go unanswered
and such a talker[D] be acquitted?
3 Should your babbling put others to silence,
so that you can keep on ridiculing
with no one to humiliate you?
4 You have said, "My teaching is sound,
and I am pure in your sight."
5 But if only God would speak
and open his lips against you!
6 He would show you the secrets of wisdom,
for true wisdom has two sides.
Know then that God has chosen to overlook
some of your iniquity.

7 Can you fathom the depths of God
or discover the limits of the Almighty?
8 They are higher than the heavens — what can
you do?
They are deeper than Sheol — what can
you know?
9 Their measure is longer than the earth
and wider than the sea.

10 If he passes by and throws someone in prison
or convenes a court, who can stop him?
11 Surely he knows which people are worthless.
If he sees iniquity, will he not take note of it?
12 But a stupid person will gain understanding
as soon as a wild donkey is born a human!

13 As for you, if you redirect your heart
and spread out your hands to him in prayer —
14 if there is iniquity in your hand, remove it,
and don't allow injustice to dwell
in your tents —
15 then you will hold your head high,
free from fault.
You will be firmly established and unafraid.
16 For you will forget your suffering,
recalling it only as water that has flowed by.
17 Your life will be brighter than noonday;
its darkness[E] will be like the morning.
18 You will be confident, because there is hope.
You will look carefully about and lie down
in safety.

19 You will lie down with no one to frighten you,
and many will seek your favor.
20 But the sight of the wicked will fail.
Their way of escape will be cut off,
and their only hope is their last breath.

JOB'S REPLY TO ZOPHAR

12 Then Job answered:
2 No doubt you are the people,
and wisdom will die with you!
3 But I also have a mind like you;
I am not inferior to you.
Who doesn't know the things you are
talking about?[F]

4 I am a laughingstock to my[G] friends,
by calling on God, who answers me.[H]
The righteous and blameless man is
a laughingstock.
5 The one who is at ease holds calamity
in contempt
and thinks it is prepared for those whose feet
are slipping.
6 The tents of robbers are safe,
and those who trouble God are secure;
God holds them in his hands.[I]

7 But ask the animals, and they will
instruct you;
ask the birds of the sky, and they will tell you.
8 Or speak to the earth,
and it will instruct you;
let the fish of the sea inform you.
9 Which of all these does not know
that the hand of the LORD has done this?
10 The life of every living thing is in his hand,
as well as the breath of all humanity.
11 Doesn't the ear test words
as the palate tastes food?
12 Wisdom is found with the elderly,
and understanding comes with long life.

[A] **10:19** Lit *As if* [B] **10:20** Alt Hb tradition reads *Will he not leave my few days alone?* [C] **10:22** Lit *chaotic, and shines as* [D] **11:2** Lit *a man of lips* [E] **11:17** Text emended; MT reads *noonday; you are dark, you* [F] **12:3** Lit *With whom are not such things as these?* [G] **12:4** Lit *his* [H] **12:4** Lit *him* [I] **12:6** Or *secure; to those who bring their god in their hands*

Legal Concepts in the Book of Job

by Harry D. Champy III

An illustrated animal fable from Egypt's Twentieth Dynasty (1186–1069 BC). The mouse, a caricature of an impressive magistrate, has risen from his seat and leans gravely on his staff, while his bailiff, the cat, inflicts punishment on the boy prisoner. On the back of the ostracon, the artist has scribbled in hieratic a caption: "The cat and mouse bring the bad boy to court."

Job used many words that would cause the Hebrew reader to think of a legal setting—the equivalent of using words like *prosecute*, *indictment*, *plaintiff*, or *attorney* today. Job was well acquainted with the legal process. He had sat in the gate and administered justice (Jb 29:7–17). As his friends were probably "colleagues," the book sounds like a conversation between lawyers or judges who naturally used forensic words to describe their ordinary experiences. This legal theme then became the framework of the entire book.

Earthly justice, as Job's friends demonstrated, is imperfect because humans have limited knowledge and make generalizations. Job took his claim directly to God and trusted in his heavenly Redeemer. Then Job's summons was answered. God spoke to Job from a whirlwind and bombarded him with numerous questions (38:1–41:34). Acknowledging that God was all powerful, Job retracted his legal claim (42:6).

13 Wisdom and strength belong to God;
counsel and understanding are his.
14 Whatever he tears down cannot be rebuilt;
whoever he imprisons cannot be released.
15 When he withholds water, everything
dries up,
and when he releases it, it destroys the land.
16 True wisdom and power belong to him.
The deceived and the deceiver are his.
17 He leads counselors away barefoot
and makes judges go mad.
18 He releases the bonds[A] put on by kings
and fastens a belt around their waists.
19 He leads priests away barefoot
and overthrows established leaders.
20 He deprives trusted advisers of speech
and takes away the elders' good judgment.
21 He pours out contempt on nobles
and disarms[B] the strong.
22 He reveals mysteries from the darkness
and brings the deepest darkness into the light.
23 He makes nations great, then destroys them;
he enlarges nations, then leads them away.
24 He deprives the world's leaders of reason,
and makes them wander
in a trackless wasteland.
25 They grope around in darkness without light;
he makes them stagger like a drunkard.

13 Look, my eyes have seen all this;
my ears have heard and understood it.
2 Everything you know, I also know;
I am not inferior to you.
3 Yet I prefer to speak to the Almighty
and argue my case before God.
4 You use lies like plaster;
you are all worthless healers.
5 If only you would shut up
and let that be your wisdom!

6 Hear now my argument,
and listen to my defense.[C]
7 Would you testify unjustly on God's behalf
or speak deceitfully for him?
8 Would you show partiality to him
or argue the case in his defense?
9 Would it go well if he examined you?
Could you deceive him as you would deceive
a man?
10 Surely he would rebuke you
if you secretly showed partiality.
11 Would God's majesty not terrify you?
Would his dread not fall on you?
12 Your memorable sayings are proverbs of ash;
your defenses are made of clay.

13 Be quiet,[D] and I will speak.
Let whatever comes happen to me.
14 I will put[E] myself at risk[F]
and take my life in my own hands.
15 Even if he kills me, I will hope in him.[G]
I will still defend my ways before him.
16 Yes, this will result in my deliverance,
for no godless person can appear
before him.
17 Pay close attention to my words;
let my declaration ring in your ears.
18 Now then, I have prepared my case;
I know that I am right.
19 Can anyone indict me?
If so, I will be silent and die.

20 Only grant these two things to me, God,
so that I will not have to hide
from your presence:
21 remove your hand from me,
and do not let your terror frighten me.
22 Then call, and I will answer,
or I will speak, and you can respond to me.
23 How many iniquities and sins
have I committed?[H]
Reveal to me my transgression and sin.
24 Why do you hide your face
and consider me your enemy?
25 Will you frighten a wind-driven leaf?
Will you chase after dry straw?
26 For you record bitter accusations against me
and make me inherit the iniquities
of my youth.
27 You put my feet in the stocks
and stand watch over all my paths,
setting a limit for the soles[I] of my feet.

28 A person wears out like something rotten,
like a moth-eaten garment.

14 Anyone born of woman
is short of days and full of trouble.
2 He blossoms like a flower, then withers;
he flees like a shadow and does not last.
3 Do you really take notice of one like this?
Will you bring me into judgment against you?[J]
4 Who can produce something pure from what
is impure?
No one!

[A] **12:18** Text emended; MT reads *discipline* [B] **12:21** Lit *and loosens the belt of* [C] **13:6** Lit *to the claims of my lips* [D] **13:13** Lit *quiet before me* [E] **13:14** LXX; MT reads *Why do I put* [F] **13:14** Lit *I take my flesh in my teeth* [G] **13:15** Some Hb mss read *I will be without hope* [H] **13:23** Lit *sins are to me* [I] **13:27** Lit *paths. You mark a line around the roots* [J] **14:3** LXX, Syr, Vg read *him*

5 Since a person's days are determined
and the number of his months depends
on you,
and since you have set[A] limits he cannot pass,
6 look away from him and let him rest
so that he can enjoy his day
like a hired worker.

7 There is hope for a tree:
If it is cut down, it will sprout again,
and its shoots will not die.
8 If its roots grow old in the ground
and its stump starts to die in the soil,
9 the scent of water makes it thrive
and produce twigs like a sapling.
10 But a person dies and fades away;
he breathes his last — where is he?
11 As water disappears from a lake
and a river becomes parched and dry,
12 so people lie down never to rise again.
They will not wake up until the heavens are
no more;
they will not stir from their sleep.

13 If only you would hide me in Sheol
and conceal me until your anger passes.
If only you would appoint a time for me
and then remember me.
14 When a person dies, will he
come back to life?
If so, I would wait all the days of my struggle
until my relief comes.
15 You would call, and I would answer you.
You would long for the work of your hands.
16 For then you would count my steps
but would not take note of my sin.
17 My rebellion would be sealed up in a bag,
and you would cover over my iniquity.

18 But as a mountain collapses and crumbles
and a rock is dislodged from its place,
19 as water wears away stones
and torrents wash away the soil
from the land,
so you destroy a man's hope.
20 You completely overpower him, and he
passes on;
you change his appearance
and send him away.
21 If his sons receive honor,
he does not know it;
if they become insignificant, he is unaware
of it.
22 He feels only the pain of his own body
and mourns only for himself.

SECOND SERIES OF SPEECHES

ELIPHAZ SPEAKS

15 Then Eliphaz the Temanite replied:
2 Does a wise man answer
with empty[B] counsel
or fill himself[C] with the hot east wind?
3 Should he argue with useless talk
or with words that serve no good purpose?
4 But you even undermine the fear of God
and hinder meditation before him.
5 Your iniquity teaches you what to say,
and you choose the language of the crafty.
6 Your own mouth condemns you, not I;
your own lips testify against you.

7 Were you the first human ever born,
or were you brought forth before the hills?
8 Do you listen in on the council of God,
or have a monopoly on wisdom?
9 What do you know that we don't?
What do you understand that is not clear to us?
10 Both the gray-haired and the elderly are
with us —
older than your father.
11 Are God's consolations not enough for you,
even the words that deal gently with you?
12 Why has your heart misled you,
and why do your eyes flash
13 as you turn your anger[D] against God
and allow such words to leave your mouth?

14 What is a mere human, that he should be pure,
or one born of a woman, that he
should be righteous?
15 If God puts no trust in his holy ones
and the heavens are not pure in his sight,
16 how much less one who is revolting
and corrupt,
who drinks injustice like water?

17 Listen to me and I will inform you.
I will describe what I have seen,
18 what the wise have declared and
not concealed,
that came from their ancestors,
19 to whom alone the land was given
when no foreigner passed among them.
20 A wicked person writhes in pain all his days,
throughout the number of years reserved
for the ruthless.
21 Dreadful sounds fill his ears;
when he is at peace, a robber attacks him.

[A] **14:5** Lit *set his* [B] **15:2** Lit *windy*; Jb 16:3 [C] **15:2** Lit *his belly*
[D] **15:13** Or *spirit*

22 He doesn't believe he will return
from darkness;
he is destined for the sword.
23 He wanders about for food, asking,
"Where is it?"
He knows the day of darkness is at hand.
24 Trouble and distress terrify him,
overwhelming him like a king prepared
for battle.
25 For he has stretched out his hand against God
and has arrogantly opposed the Almighty.
26 He rushes headlong at him
with his thick, studded shields.
27 Though his face is covered with fat[A]
and his waistline bulges with it,
28 he will dwell in ruined cities,
in abandoned houses destined to become
piles of rubble.
29 He will no longer be rich; his wealth
will not endure.
His possessions[B] will not increase in the land.
30 He will not escape from the darkness;
flames will wither his shoots,
and by the breath of God's mouth,
he will depart.
31 Let him not put trust in worthless things,
being led astray,
for what he gets in exchange
will prove worthless.
32 It will be accomplished before his time,
and his branch will not flourish.
33 He will be like a vine that drops
its unripe grapes
and like an olive tree that sheds its blossoms.
34 For the company of the godless will have
no children,
and fire will consume the tents of those
who offer bribes.
35 They conceive trouble and give birth to evil;
their womb prepares deception.

JOB'S REPLY TO ELIPHAZ

16 Then Job answered:
2 I have heard many things like these.
You are all miserable comforters.
3 Is there no end to your empty[C] words?
What provokes you that you
continue testifying?
4 If you were in my place I could also talk
like you.
I could string words together against you
and shake my head at you.
5 Instead, I would encourage you with my mouth,
and the consolation from my lips
would bring relief.
6 If I speak, my suffering is not relieved,
and if I hold back, does any of it leave me?
7 Surely he[D] has now exhausted me.
You have devastated my entire family.
8 You have shriveled me up[E] — it has become
a witness;
my frailty rises up against me and testifies
to my face.
9 His anger tears at me, and he harasses me.
He gnashes his teeth at me.
My enemy pierces me with his eyes.
10 They open their mouths against me
and strike my cheeks with contempt;
they join themselves together
against me.
11 God hands me over to the unjust;[F]
he throws me to the wicked.
12 I was at ease, but he shattered me;
he seized me by the scruff of the neck
and smashed me to pieces.
He set me up as his target;
13 his archers[G] surround me.
He pierces my kidneys without mercy
and pours my bile on the ground.
14 He breaks through my defenses again
and again;[H]
he charges at me like a warrior.

15 I have sewn sackcloth over my skin;
I have buried my strength[I] in the dust.
16 My face has grown red with weeping,
and darkness covers my eyes,
17 although my hands are free from violence
and my prayer is pure.

18 Earth, do not cover my blood;
may my cry for help find no resting place.
19 Even now my witness is in heaven,
and my advocate is in the heights!
20 My friends scoff at me
as I weep before God.
21 I wish that someone might argue for a man
with God
just as anyone[J] would for a friend.
22 For only a few years will pass
before I go the way of no return.

17 My spirit is broken.
My days are extinguished.
A graveyard awaits me.

[A] **15:27** Lit *with his fat* [B] **15:29** Text emended; MT reads *Their gain* [C] **16:3** Lit *windy*; Jb 15:2 [D] **16:7** Or *it* [E] **16:8** Or *have seized me*; Hb obscure [F] **16:11** LXX, Vg; MT reads *to a boy* [G] **16:13** Or *arrows* [H] **16:14** Lit *through me, breach on breach* [I] **16:15** Lit *horn* [J] **16:21** Lit *a son of man*

2 Surely mockers surround[A] me,
and my eyes must gaze at their rebellion.

3 Accept my pledge! Put up security for me.
Who else will be my sponsor?[B]
4 You have closed their minds to understanding,
therefore you will not honor them.
5 If a man denounces his friends for a price,
the eyes of his children will fail.

6 He has made me an object of scorn
to the people;
I have become a man people spit at.[C]
7 My eyes have grown dim from grief,
and my whole body has become
but a shadow.
8 The upright are appalled at this,
and the innocent are roused
against the godless.
9 Yet the righteous person will hold to his way,
and the one whose hands are clean
will grow stronger.
10 But come back and try again, all of you.[D]
I will not find a wise man among you.

11 My days have slipped by;
my plans have been ruined,
even the things dear to my heart.
12 They turned night into day
and made light seem near in the face
of darkness.
13 If I await Sheol as my home,
spread out my bed in darkness,
14 and say to corruption, "You are my father,"
and to the maggot, "My mother" or "My sister,"
15 where then is my hope?
Who can see any hope for me?
16 Will it go down to the gates of Sheol,
or will we descend together to the dust?

BILDAD SPEAKS

18 Then Bildad the Shuhite replied:
2 How long until you stop talking?
Show some sense, and then we can talk.
3 Why are we regarded as cattle,
as stupid in your sight?
4 You who tear yourself in anger[E] —
should the earth be abandoned
on your account,
or a rock be removed from its place?

5 Yes, the light of the wicked is extinguished;
the flame of his fire does not glow.
6 The light in his tent grows dark,
and the lamp beside him is put out.
7 His powerful stride is shortened,
and his own schemes trip him up.
8 For his own feet lead him into a net,
and he strays into its mesh.
9 A trap catches him by the heel;
a noose seizes him.
10 A rope lies hidden for him on the ground,
and a snare waits for him along the path.
11 Terrors frighten him on every side
and harass him at every step.
12 His strength is depleted;
disaster lies ready for him to stumble.[F]
13 Parts of his skin are eaten away;
death's firstborn consumes his limbs.
14 He is ripped from the security of his tent
and marched away to the king of terrors.
15 Nothing he owned remains in his tent.
Burning sulfur is scattered over his home.
16 His roots below dry up,
and his branches above wither away.
17 All memory of him perishes from the earth;
he has no name anywhere.[G]
18 He is driven from light to darkness
and chased from the inhabited world.
19 He has no children or descendants
among his people,
no survivor where he used to live.
20 Those in the west are appalled at his fate,
while those in the east tremble in horror.
21 Indeed, such is the dwelling of the unjust man,
and this is the place of the one who does not
know God.

JOB'S REPLY TO BILDAD

19 Then Job answered:
2 How long will you torment me
and crush me with words?
3 You have humiliated me ten times now,
and you mistreat[H] me without shame.
4 Even if it is true that I have sinned,
my mistake concerns only[I] me.
5 If you really want to appear superior to me
and would use my disgrace as evidence
against me,
6 then understand that it is God
who has wronged me
and caught me in his net.

7 I cry out, "Violence!" but get no response;
I call for help, but there is no justice.

[A] **17:2** Lit *are with* [B] **17:3** Or *Who is there that will shake hands with me?* [C] **17:6** Lit *become a spitting to the faces* [D] **17:10** Some Hb mss, LXX, Vg; other Hb mss read *them* [E] **18:4** Lit *He who tears himself in his anger* [F] **18:12** Or *disaster hungers for him* [G] **18:17** Or *name in the streets* [H] **19:3** Hb obscure [I] **19:4** Lit *mistake lives with*

8 He has blocked my way so that I cannot
pass through;
he has veiled my paths with darkness.
9 He has stripped me of my honor
and removed the crown from my head.
10 He tears me down on every side so that
I am ruined.[A]
He uproots my hope like a tree.
11 His anger burns against me,
and he regards me as one of his enemies.
12 His troops advance together;
they construct a ramp[B] against me
and camp around my tent.

13 He has removed my brothers from me;
my acquaintances have abandoned me.
14 My relatives stop coming by,
and my close friends have forgotten me.
15 My house guests[C] and female servants
regard me as a stranger;
I am a foreigner in their sight.
16 I call for my servant, but he does not answer,
even if I beg him with my own mouth.
17 My breath is offensive to my wife,
and my own family[D] finds me repulsive.
18 Even young boys scorn me.
When I stand up, they mock me.
19 All of my best friends[E] despise me,
and those I love have turned against me.
20 My skin and my flesh cling to my bones;
I have escaped with only the skin of my teeth.

21 Have mercy on me, my friends, have mercy,
for God's hand has struck me.
22 Why do you persecute me as God does?
Will you never get enough of my flesh?

23 I wish that my words were written down,
that they were recorded on a scroll
24 or were inscribed in stone forever
by an iron stylus and lead!
25 But I know that my Redeemer lives,[F]
and at the end he will stand on the dust.
26 Even after my skin has been destroyed,[G]
yet I will see God in[H] my flesh.
27 I will see him myself;
my eyes will look at him, and not as a stranger.[I]
My heart longs[J] within me.

28 If you say, "How will we pursue him,
since the root of the problem lies with him?"[K]
29 then be afraid of the sword,
because wrath brings punishment
by the sword,
so that you may know there is a judgment.

ZOPHAR SPEAKS

20 Then Zophar the Naamathite replied:
2 This is why my unsettling thoughts
compel me to answer,
because I am upset![L]
3 I have heard a rebuke that insults me,
and my understanding[M] makes me reply.

4 Don't you know that ever since antiquity,
from the time a human was placed on earth,
5 the joy of the wicked has been brief
and the happiness of the godless has lasted
only a moment?
6 Though his arrogance reaches heaven,
and his head touches the clouds,
7 he will vanish forever like his own dung.
Those who know[N] him will ask,
"Where is he?"
8 He will fly away like a dream and never
be found;
he will be chased away like a vision
in the night.
9 The eye that saw him will see him no more,
and his household will no longer see him.
10 His children will beg from[O] the poor,
for his own hands must give back his wealth.
11 His frame may be full of youthful vigor,
but it will lie down with him in dust.

12 Though evil tastes sweet in his mouth
and he conceals it under his tongue,
13 though he cherishes it and will not let it go
but keeps it in his mouth,
14 yet the food in his stomach turns
into cobras' venom inside him.
15 He swallows wealth but must vomit it up;
God will force it from his stomach.
16 He will suck the poison of cobras;
a viper's fangs[P] will kill him.
17 He will not enjoy the streams,
the rivers flowing with honey and curds.
18 He must return the fruit of his labor
without consuming it;
he doesn't enjoy the profits
from his trading.
19 For he oppressed and abandoned the poor;
he seized a house he did not build.

[A] **19:10** Lit *gone* [B] **19:12** Lit *they raise up their way* [C] **19:15** Or *The resident aliens in my household* [D] **19:17** Lit *and the sons of my belly* [E] **19:19** Lit *of the men of my council* [F] **19:25** Or *know my living Redeemer* [G] **19:26** Lit *skin which they destroyed*, or *skin they destroyed in this way* [H] **19:26** Or *apart from* [I] **19:27** Or *not a stranger* [J] **19:27** Lit *My kidneys grow faint* [K] **19:28** Some Hb mss, LXX, Vg; other Hb mss read *me* [L] **20:2** Lit *because of my feeling within me* [M] **20:3** Lit *and a spirit from my understanding* [N] **20:7** Lit *have seen* [O] **20:10** Or *children must compensate* [P] **20:16** Lit *tongue*

20 Because his appetite is never satisfied,[A]
he does not let anything he desires escape.
21 Nothing is left for him to consume;
therefore, his prosperity will not last.
22 At the height of his success[B] distress will come
to him;
the full weight of misery[C] will crush him.
23 When he fills his stomach,
God will send his burning anger against him,
raining it down on him while he is eating.[D]
24 If he flees from an iron weapon,
an arrow from a bronze bow will pierce him.
25 He pulls it out of his back,
the flashing tip out of his liver.[E]
Terrors come over him.
26 Total darkness is reserved for his treasures.
A fire unfanned by human hands
will consume him;
it will feed on what is left in his tent.
27 The heavens will expose his iniquity,
and the earth will rise up against him.
28 The possessions in his house will be removed,
flowing away on the day of God's anger.
29 This is the wicked person's lot from God,
the inheritance God ordained for him.

JOB'S REPLY TO ZOPHAR

21 Then Job answered:
2 Pay close attention to my words;
let this be the consolation you offer.
3 Bear with me while I speak;
then after I have spoken, you may
continue mocking.

4 As for me, is my complaint against a human
being?
Then why shouldn't I be impatient?
5 Look at me and shudder;
put your hand over your mouth.
6 When I think about it, I am terrified
and my body trembles in horror.
7 Why do the wicked continue to live,
growing old and becoming powerful?
8 Their children are established while they are
still alive,[F]
and their descendants, before their eyes.
9 Their homes are secure and free of fear;
no rod from God strikes them.
10 Their bulls breed without fail;
their cows calve and do not miscarry.
11 They let their little ones run
around like lambs;
their children skip about,
12 singing to the tambourine and lyre
and rejoicing at the sound of the flute.
13 They spend[G] their days in prosperity
and go down to Sheol in peace.
14 Yet they say to God, "Leave us alone!
We don't want to know your ways.
15 Who is the Almighty, that we should serve him,
and what will we gain by pleading with him?"
16 But their prosperity is not of their own doing.
The counsel of the wicked is far from me!

17 How often is the lamp of the wicked put out?
Does disaster[H] come on them?
Does he apportion destruction in his anger?
18 Are they like straw before the wind,
like chaff a storm sweeps away?
19 God reserves a person's punishment
for his children.
Let God repay the person himself, so that
he may know it.
20 Let his own eyes see his demise;
let him drink from the Almighty's wrath!
21 For what does he care about his family once
he is dead,
when the number of his months has run out?

22 Can anyone teach God knowledge,
since he judges the exalted ones?[I]
23 One person dies in excellent health,[J]
completely secure[K] and at ease.
24 His body is[L] well fed,[M]
and his bones are full of marrow.[N]
25 Yet another person dies with a bitter soul,
having never tasted prosperity.
26 But they both lie in the dust,
and worms cover them.

27 I know your thoughts very well,
the schemes by which you would wrong me.
28 For you say, "Where now is
the nobleman's house?"
and "Where are the tents the wicked lived in?"
29 Have you never consulted those who travel
the roads?
Don't you accept their reports?[O]
30 Indeed, the evil person is spared from the day
of disaster,
rescued from the day of wrath.

[A] **20:20** Lit *Because he does not know ease in his stomach* [B] **20:22** Lit *In the fullness of his excess* [C] **20:22** Some Hb mss, LXX, Vg; other Hb mss read *the hand of everyone in misery* [D] **20:23** Text emended; MT reads *him, against his flesh* [E] **20:25** Or *gallbladder* [F] **21:8** Lit *established before them with them* [G] **21:13** Alt Hb tradition reads *fully enjoy* [H] **21:17** Lit *their disaster* [I] **21:22** Probably angels [J] **21:23** Lit *in bone of his perfection* [K] **21:23** Text emended; MT reads *health, all at ease* [L] **21:24** Or *His sides are*; Hb obscure [M] **21:24** Lit *is full of milk* [N] **21:24** Lit *and the marrow of his bones is watered* [O] **21:29** Lit *signs*

31 Who would denounce his behavior
to his face?
Who would repay him for what he has done?
32 He is carried to the grave,
and someone keeps watch over his tomb.
33 The dirt on his grave is[A] sweet to him.
Everyone follows behind him,
and those who go before him are
without number.

34 So how can you offer me
such futile comfort?
Your answers are deceptive.

THIRD SERIES OF SPEECHES

ELIPHAZ SPEAKS

22 Then Eliphaz the Temanite replied:
2 Can a man be of any use to God?
Can even a wise man be of use to him?
3 Does it delight the Almighty if you
are righteous?
Does he profit if you perfect your behavior?

4 Does he correct you and take you to court
because of your piety?
5 Isn't your wickedness abundant
and aren't your iniquities endless?
6 For you took collateral from your brothers
without cause,
stripping off their clothes and leaving them
naked.
7 You gave no water to the thirsty
and withheld food from the famished,
8 while the land belonged to a powerful man
and an influential man lived on it.
9 You sent widows away empty-handed,
and the strength of the fatherless
was[B] crushed.
10 Therefore snares surround you,
and sudden dread terrifies you,
11 or darkness, so you cannot see,
and a flood of water covers you.

12 Isn't God as high as the heavens?
And look at the highest stars — how lofty
they are!
13 Yet you say, "What does God know?
Can he judge through total darkness?
14 Clouds veil him so that he cannot see,
as he walks on the circle of the sky."
15 Will you continue on the ancient path
that wicked men have walked?
16 They were snatched away before their time,
and their foundations were washed away
by a river.
17 They were the ones who said to God,
"Leave us alone!"
and "What can the Almighty do to us?"[C]
18 But it was he who filled their houses
with good things.
The counsel of the wicked is far from me!
19 The righteous see this and rejoice;
the innocent mock them, saying,
20 "Surely our opponents are destroyed,
and fire has consumed what they left behind."

21 Come to terms with God and be at peace;
in this way[D] good will come to you.
22 Receive instruction from his mouth,
and place his sayings in your heart.
23 If you return to the Almighty, you will
be renewed.
If you banish injustice from your tent
24 and consign your gold to the dust,
the gold of Ophir to the stones in the wadis,
25 the Almighty will be your gold
and your finest silver.
26 Then you will delight in the Almighty
and lift up your face to God.
27 You will pray to him, and he will hear you,
and you will fulfill your vows.
28 When you make a decision, it will be
carried out,[E]
and light will shine on your ways.
29 When others are humiliated and you say,
"Lift them up,"
God will save the humble.[F]
30 He will even rescue the guilty one,
who will be rescued by the purity
of your hands.

JOB'S REPLY TO ELIPHAZ

23 Then Job answered:
2 Today also my complaint is bitter.[G]
His[H] hand is heavy despite my groaning.
3 If only I knew how to find him,
so that I could go to his throne.
4 I would plead my case before him
and fill my mouth with arguments.
5 I would learn how[I] he would answer me;
and understand what he would say to me.
6 Would he prosecute me forcefully?
No, he would certainly pay attention to me.
7 Then an upright man could reason with him,
and I would escape from my Judge[J] forever.

[A] **21:33** Lit *The clods of the wadi are* [B] **22:9** LXX, Syr, Vg, Tg read *you have* [C] **22:17** LXX, Syr; MT reads *them* [D] **22:21** Lit *peace; by them* [E] **22:28** Lit *out for you* [F] **22:29** Lit *bowed of eyes* [G] **23:2** Syr, Tg, Vg; MT reads *rebellion* [H] **23:2** LXX, Syr; MT reads *My* [I] **23:5** Lit *the words* [J] **23:7** Or *judgment*

8 If I go east, he is not there,
and if I go west, I cannot perceive him.
9 When he is at work to the north, I cannot
see him;
when he turns south, I cannot find him.
10 Yet he knows the way I have taken;[A]
when he has tested me, I will emerge
as pure gold.
11 My feet have followed in his tracks;
I have kept to his way and not turned aside.
12 I have not departed from the commands
from his lips;
I have treasured[B] the words from his mouth
more than my daily food.

13 But he is unchangeable; who can oppose him?
He does what he desires.
14 He will certainly accomplish
what he has decreed for me,
and he has many more things like these
in mind.[C]
15 Therefore I am terrified in his presence;
when I consider this, I am afraid of him.
16 God has made my heart faint;
the Almighty has terrified me.
17 Yet I am not destroyed[D] by the darkness,
by the thick darkness that covers my face.

24 Why does the Almighty not reserve times
for judgment?
Why do those who know him never see
his days?
2 The wicked displace boundary markers.
They steal a flock and provide pasture for it.
3 They drive away the donkeys owned
by the fatherless
and take the widow's ox as collateral.
4 They push the needy off the road;
the poor of the land are forced into hiding.
5 Like wild donkeys in the wilderness,
the poor go out to their task of foraging for food;
the desert provides nourishment
for their children.
6 They gather their fodder in the field
and glean the vineyards of the wicked.
7 Without clothing, they spend the night naked,
having no covering against the cold.
8 Drenched by mountain rains,
they huddle against[E] the rocks, shelterless.
9 The fatherless infant is snatched
from the breast;
the nursing child of the poor is seized
as collateral.[F]
10 Without clothing, they wander about naked.
They carry sheaves but go hungry.
11 They crush olives in their presses;[G]
they tread the winepresses, but go thirsty.
12 From the city, men[H] groan;
the mortally wounded cry for help,
yet God pays no attention to this crime.

13 The wicked are those who rebel against the light.
They do not recognize its ways
or stay on its paths.
14 The murderer rises at dawn
to kill the poor and needy,
and by night he becomes a thief.
15 The adulterer's eye watches for twilight,
thinking, "No eye will see me,"
and he covers his face.
16 In the dark they break[I] into houses;
by day they lock themselves in,[J]
never experiencing the light.
17 For the morning is like darkness to them.
Surely they are familiar with the terrors
of darkness!

18 They float[K] on the surface of the water.
Their section of the land is cursed,
so that they never go to their vineyards.
19 As dry ground and heat snatch away
the melted snow,
so Sheol steals those who have sinned.
20 The womb forgets them;
worms feed on them;
they are remembered no more.
So injustice is broken like a tree.
21 They prey on[L] the childless woman
who is unable to conceive,
and do not deal kindly with the widow.
22 Yet God drags away[M] the mighty by his power;
when he rises up, they have no assurance of life.
23 He gives them a sense of security, so they
can rely on it,
but his eyes watch over their ways.
24 They are exalted for a moment, then gone;
they are brought low and shrivel up
like everything else.[N]
They wither like heads of grain.

25 If this is not true, then who can prove me
a liar
and show that my speech is worthless?

[A] **23:10** Lit *way with me* [B] **23:12** LXX, Vg read *treasured in my bosom* [C] **23:14** Lit *these with him* [D] **23:17** Or *silenced* [E] **24:8** Lit *they embrace* [F] **24:9** Text emended; MT reads *breast; they seize collateral against the poor* [G] **24:11** Lit *olives between their rows* [H] **24:12** One Hb ms, Syr read *the dying* [I] **24:16** Lit *dig* [J] **24:16** Lit *they seal for themselves* [K] **24:18** Lit *are insignificant* [L] **24:21** LXX, Tg read *They harm* [M] **24:22** Or *God prolongs the life of* [N] **24:24** LXX reads *like a mallow plant in the heat*

Livestock as Wealth in the Old Testament Era

by Julie Nall Knowles

Relief from the palace of King Tiglath-pileser III (744–727 BC) shows sheep and goats, captured during a military campaign, being driven back to the Assyrian camp.

Twin pottery jars in the form of bulls. Old Hittite era (1680–1500 BC), from Bogazkoy.

SHEEP, GOATS, AND CATTLE

Domesticated near the Caspian Sea, broadtail sheep appear on a bowl of Uruk III (ca 3000 BC) and centuries later on wall reliefs completed for Tiglath-pileser III (ca 745–727 BC).[1] Sheep became the most important livestock for capital investment in Israel. Job's seven thousand represented great wealth; powerful Nabal had three thousand to shear in Carmel (1Sm 25:2). As well as providing income from food, milk, wool, and felt, sheep were a medium of exchange; for example, Tyre and Damascus traded with wool (Ezk 27:18); King Mesha of Moab paid Israel tribute with wool and lambs (2Kg 3:4).

Other sheep-rearing tribes probably held grazing rights in Job's "land of Uz." Canaanite and Perizzite herdsmen shared pastures near Bethel and Ai (Gn 13:7) and could not welcome herds

Frieze of a dairy scene from Tell al-Ubaid, Egypt. It shows two men transferring liquid from one container to another, probably storing butter. Another man has a large container, presumably containing milk. From about 2500 BC.

belonging to Abram and Lot. In remote pastures, shepherds corralled livestock at night in rough forts for protection. Sheep held an important role in local economies. Jacob disputed with Laban over wages (31:38–41), using wording of Old Babylonian herding contracts to remind his father-in-law that he owned considerably fewer animals than the 20 percent normally due a shepherd.[2]

Evidence from Jericho dating to about 7000 BC indicated that goats may be the earliest domesticated livestock. On a vase fragment from about 3000 BC found near Baghdad, a person feeds two goats that have curved horns. In fact, the ram-in-the-thicket goat of Genesis 22:13 may have been like one from Ur with horns twisted into a corkscrew.[3] Goats were suited to mountainous territory and hot, dry regions; they provided meat and a steady supply of milk. Merchandise from goat hair and hides included clothing, carpets, tents, and even leather for boats used on rivers.[4]

Agriculture developed in river valleys and with it animal husbandry. With five hundred yoke of oxen, what a field Job cultivated! In Mesopotamia, several breeds of cattle—piebald, horned/hornless, and humped zebu from India—served as draft animals. As Job owned more than a thousand head of cattle, his family could have eaten veal, a wealthy indulgence (Am 6:4). Job probably prospered significantly in cattle trading. A statue found at Megiddo shows a certain Thuthotep with Asian cattle; he may have represented Egypt in shipments of cattle and merchandise.[5] Warriors took cattle as booty; this happened at Ai (Jos 8:27) and when the Sabeans ravaged Job's fields (Jb 1:14–15).

DONKEYS AND CAMELS

Caravan traders, the Sabeans may have seized Job's donkeys as the more valuable plunder. Domesticated in the Nile Valley, donkeys helped transport Abram's entourage from Egypt to the promised land (Gn 12:16–13:5). Evidence indicates donkeys were being bred at Lahav in southern Israel at the same time trade networks through the region were being developed.[6] Either or both of these occurrences could have links to Abram as he came into Canaan. Also a Twelfth Dynasty Beni Hasan tomb painting shows Israelites entering Egypt with donkeys transporting packs.[7] To own a donkey seemed necessary for minimal existence (Jb 24:3); successful merchants used many in their caravans. All Jewish classes—men, women, and children—rode donkeys; rulers chose white donkeys (Jdg 5:10).

Horse bit with cheek pieces in the form of winged goats.

Perhaps the most amicable animal, its peaceful nature emphasizes the image of Israel's coming Messiah, riding on a donkey (Zch 9:9). More donkeys were brought from Babylon than any other livestock (Ezr 2:66–67). Some may have been acquired in business, for in the Old Assyrian trade, shares could include donkeys.[8] As described by Herodotus, caravan drivers who brought donkeys to the river enjoyed a rather unique commerce:

The boats which come down the river to Babylon are circular, and made of skins. . . . Each vessel has a live ass on board; those of larger size have more than one. When they reach Babylon, the cargo is landed and offered for sale; after which the men break up their boats . . . and loading their asses with the skins, set off on their way back to Armenia.[9]

The marauders who stole Job's cattle probably took his camels to southern Babylonia, their territory. Domesticated in Arabia, the "ass of the south" had tonic effects on Mesopotamian commerce. A camel's feet accommodate arid soil, and the ability to subsist on little food and water helps camels to carry loads over deserts. As slow breeders, however, herds have low growth, which may have given impetus to obtain stock by raiding.[10]

Job did not have an excessive number of camels. Aristotle reported, "Some of the inhabitants of Upper Asia have as many as three thousand camels."[11]

Cuneiform lists and seals show the Bactrian camel (two-humped), but caravan travelers preferred the faster dromedary (one-humped). Some owners bought goods and sold them again, repeating the process going back. Others arranged to deliver merchandise to another to take farther, the first receiving cargo for return. A merchant's letters might ask that goods be delivered to bearers.

HORSES AND MULES

King Solomon's merchants obtained horses and chariots from Egypt and other horses from Cilicia and traded with Hittite and Aramean states (1Kg 10:28–29). The horses came from those domesticated in northern Persian mountains. Along with chariots, horses (the "ass of the north") reached Egypt during Hyksos domination of the area. During Thutmose III's campaign to crush the Hyksos in Israel, a war story tells how an Egyptian commander besieging Joppa asked the defenders to let his horses be brought inside the city, "because outside they are vulnerable." General Djehuty then took Joppa, having saved his horses.[12] This story illustrates the advantage horses gave in military campaigns.

Successive writers regarded the horse as a battle animal. For warfare every kingdom had charioteer corps. For his thousands of horses and chariots King Solomon built stables in "chariot cities" (1Kg 9:19).

Frieze of a dairy scene from Tell al-Ubaid, Egypt. One image depicts a cow being milked. A separate scene (on page 729) shows two men transferring liquid from one container to another, probably storing butter. Another man has a large container—presumably containing milk. From about 2500 BC.

Although not specifically named as such, Hazor, Megiddo, and Gezer (v. 15) may have been home to both Solomon's chariots and horsemen. The so-called Solomon's stables excavated at Megiddo caused great excitement when discovered. Yet the doorways and aisles are too narrow to easily accommodate horses. So although Megiddo may have been a "chariot city," excavations have yet to unearth Solomon's authentic stables at the site. King Sargon II of Assyria (722–705 BC) found an Israelite royal stable and well-fed horses, and other Assyrian documents mention "king's stables" for horses and mules.[13]

Because crossbreeding was forbidden (Lv 19:19), the Israelites bought mules (cross of a donkey and a horse). Those ridden by King David's sons (2Sm 13:29) may have come from Tyre, which traded in horses and mules with Beth-togarmah in Cilicia (Ezk 27:14). The art of mule breeding probably developed there, in the Hittites' homeland, which was famous for breeding and training chariot horses. The Hittites also likely bred the superior mules royalty and many wealthy people commonly rode.

On mountain paths mules are sure-footed and can carry much cargo, so mules traveled the northern caravan routes. Of the livestock Jews brought from Babylon, only 3 percent were mules (Ezr 2:66–67). Their owners could have been like the Murashus of Nippur who prospered during the exile[14] and could afford expensive mules. Apparently, the returning Jews did not have sheep, goats, and oxen, but these animals could be bought in Israel. ✣

---

[1] Frederick E. Zeuner, *A History of Domesticated Animals* (New York: Harper & Row, 1963), 173. [2] J. J. Finkelstein, "An Old Babylonian Herding Contract and Genesis 31:38 f.," *Journal of the American Oriental Society* (*JAOS*) 88 (1968): 35. [3] Zeuner, *History*, 133–39. [4] Georges Contenau, *Everyday Life in Babylon and Assyria* (New York: St. Martin's, 1954), 48. [5] Amihai Mazar, *Archaeology of the Land of the Bible, 10,000–586 BCE*, vol. 1 in ABRL,187. [6] Brian Hesse, "Animal Husbandry and Human Diet in the Ancient Near East" in CANE, vol. 1 (1990), 216. [7] Mazar, *Archaeology*, 187. [8] Mogens Trolle Larsen, "Partnerships in the Old Assyrian Trade," *Iraq* 39 (1977): 135. [9] Herodotus, *Histories* 1.194. [10] Hesse, "Animal Husbandry," 217. [11] Aristotle, *History of Animals* 9:50. [12] T. C. Mitchell, *The Bible in the British Museum* (New York: Paulist, 2004), 38. [13] Yigael Yadin, "In Defense of the Stables at Megiddo," *BAR* 2.5 (1976): 22. [14] Contenau, *Everyday Life*, 85.

BILDAD SPEAKS

25 Then Bildad the Shuhite replied:
2 Dominion and dread belong to him,
the one who establishes harmony
in his heights.
3 Can his troops be numbered?
Does his light not shine on everyone?
4 How can a human be justified before God?
How can one born of woman be pure?
5 If even the moon does not shine
and the stars are not pure in his sight,
6 how much less a human, who is a maggot,
a son of man,[A] who is a worm!

JOB'S REPLY TO BILDAD

26 Then Job answered:
2 How you have helped the powerless
and delivered the arm that is weak!
3 How you have counseled the unwise
and abundantly provided insight!
4 With whom did you speak these words?
Whose breath came out of your mouth?

5 The departed spirits tremble
beneath the waters and all that inhabit them.
6 Sheol is naked before God,
and Abaddon has no covering.
7 He stretches the northern skies
over empty space;
he hangs the earth on nothing.
8 He wraps up the water in his clouds,
yet the clouds do not burst beneath its weight.
9 He obscures the view of his throne,
spreading his cloud over it.
10 He laid out the horizon on the surface
of the waters
at the boundary between light and darkness.
11 The pillars that hold up the sky tremble,
astounded at his rebuke.
12 By his power he stirred the sea,
and by his understanding he crushed Rahab.
13 By his breath the heavens gained
their beauty;
his hand pierced the fleeing serpent.[B]
14 These are but the fringes of his ways;
how faint is the word we hear of him!
Who can understand his mighty thunder?

27 Job continued his discourse, saying:
2 As God lives, who has deprived me
of justice,
and the Almighty who has made me bitter,
3 as long as my breath is still in me
and the breath from God remains
in my nostrils,
4 my lips will not speak unjustly,
and my tongue will not utter deceit.
5 I will never affirm that you are right.
I will maintain my integrity[C] until I die.
6 I will cling to my righteousness and never
let it go.
My conscience will not accuse me as long as
I live!

7 May my enemy be like the wicked
and my opponent like the unjust.
8 For what hope does the godless person have
when he is cut off,
when God takes away his life?
9 Will God hear his cry
when distress comes on him?
10 Will he delight in the Almighty?
Will he call on God at all times?
11 I will teach you about God's power.
I will not conceal what the Almighty
has planned.[D]
12 All of you have seen this for yourselves,
why do you keep up this empty talk?

13 This is a wicked man's lot from God,
the inheritance the ruthless receive
from the Almighty.
14 Even if his children increase,
they are destined for the sword;
his descendants will never
have enough food.
15 Those who survive him will be buried
by the plague,
yet their widows will not weep for them.
16 Though he piles up silver like dust
and heaps up fine clothing like clay —
17 he may heap it up, but the righteous
will wear it,
and the innocent will divide up his silver.
18 The house he built is like a moth's cocoon
or a shelter set up by a watchman.
19 He lies down wealthy, but will
do so no more;
when he opens his eyes, it is gone.
20 Terrors overtake him like a flood;
a storm wind sweeps him away at night.
21 An east wind picks him up, and he is gone;
it carries him away from his place.
22 It blasts at him without mercy,
while he flees desperately from its force.
23 It claps its hands at him
and scoffs at him from its place.

[A] **25:6** Or *a mere mortal* [B] **26:13** = Leviathan [C] **27:5** Lit *will not remove my integrity from me* [D] **27:11** Lit *what is with the Almighty*

A HYMN TO WISDOM

28 Surely there is a mine for silver
and a place where gold is refined.
2 Iron is taken from the ground,
and copper is smelted from ore.
3 A miner puts an end to the darkness;
he probes[A] the deepest recesses
for ore in the gloomy darkness.
4 He cuts a shaft far from human habitation,
in places unknown to those who walk
above ground.
Suspended far away from people,
the miners swing back and forth.
5 Food may come from the earth,
but below the surface the earth
is transformed as by fire.
6 Its rocks are a source of lapis lazuli,
containing flecks of gold.
7 No bird of prey knows that path;
no falcon's eye has seen it.
8 Proud beasts have never walked on it;
no lion has ever prowled over it.
9 The miner uses a flint tool
and turns up ore from the root
of the mountains.
10 He cuts out channels in the rocks,
and his eyes spot every treasure.
11 He dams up the streams from flowing[B]
so that he may bring to light what is hidden.

12 But where can wisdom be found,
and where is understanding located?
13 No one can know its value,[C]
since it cannot be found in the land
of the living.
14 The ocean depths say, "It's not in me,"
while the sea declares, "I don't have it."
15 Gold cannot be exchanged for it,
and silver cannot be weighed out for its price.
16 Wisdom cannot be valued in the gold of Ophir,
in precious onyx or lapis lazuli.
17 Gold and glass do not compare with it,
and articles of fine gold cannot be exchanged
for it.
18 Coral and quartz are not worth mentioning.
The price of wisdom is beyond pearls.
19 Topaz from Cush cannot compare with it,
and it cannot be valued in pure gold.

20 Where then does wisdom come from,
and where is understanding located?
21 It is hidden from the eyes of every living thing
and concealed from the birds of the sky.
22 Abaddon and Death say,
"We have heard news of it with our ears."
23 But God understands the way to wisdom,
and he knows its location.
24 For he looks to the ends of the earth
and sees everything under the heavens.
25 When God fixed the weight of the wind
and distributed the water by measure,
26 when he established a limit[D] for the rain
and a path for the lightning,
27 he considered wisdom and evaluated it;
he established it and examined it.
28 He said to mankind,
"The fear of the Lord—that is wisdom.
And to turn from evil is understanding."

JOB'S FINAL CLAIM OF INNOCENCE

29 Job continued his discourse, saying:
2 If only I could be as in months gone by,
in the days when God watched over me,
3 when his lamp shone above my head,
and I walked through darkness by his light!
4 I would be as I was in the days of my youth
when God's friendship rested on my tent,
5 when the Almighty was still with me
and my children were around me,
6 when my feet were bathed in curds
and the rock poured out streams
of oil for me!

7 When I went out to the city gate
and took my seat in the town square,
8 the young men saw me and withdrew,
while older men stood to their feet.
9 City officials stopped talking
and covered their mouths with their hands.
10 The noblemen's voices were hushed,
and their tongues stuck to the roof
of their mouths.
11 When they heard me, they blessed me,
and when they saw me, they spoke well
of me.[E]
12 For I rescued the poor who cried out for help,
and the fatherless child who had no one
to support him.
13 The dying blessed me,
and I made the widow's heart rejoice.
14 I clothed myself in righteousness,
and it enveloped me;
my just decisions were like a robe
and a turban.
15 I was eyes to the blind
and feet to the lame.

[A]**28:3** Lit *probes all* [B]**28:11** LXX, Vg read *He explores the sources of the streams* [C]**28:13** LXX reads *way* [D]**28:26** Or *decree*
[E]**29:11** Lit *When an ear heard, it called me blessed, and when an eye saw, it testified for me*

16 I was a father to the needy,
and I examined the case of the stranger.
17 I shattered the fangs of the unjust
and snatched the prey from his teeth.

18 So I thought, "I will die in my own nest
and multiply my days as the sand.[A]
19 My roots will have access to water,
and the dew will rest on my branches all night.
20 My whole being will be refreshed within me,
and my bow will be renewed in my hand."

21 Men listened to me with expectation,
waiting silently for my advice.
22 After a word from me they did not
speak again;
my speech settled on them like dew.
23 They waited for me as for the rain
and opened their mouths as for
spring showers.
24 If I smiled at them, they couldn't believe it;
they were thrilled at[B] the light
of my countenance.
25 I directed their course and presided as chief.
I lived as a king among his troops,
like one who comforts those who mourn.

30 But now they mock me,
men younger than I am,
whose fathers I would have refused to put
with my sheep dogs.
2 What use to me was the strength
of their hands?
Their vigor had left them.
3 Emaciated from poverty and hunger,
they gnawed the dry land,
the desolate wasteland by night.
4 They plucked mallow[C] among the shrubs,
and the roots of the broom tree were
their food.
5 They were banished from human society;
people shouted at them
as if they were thieves.
6 They are living on the slopes of the wadis,
among the rocks and in holes in the ground.
7 They bray among the shrubs;
they huddle beneath the thistles.
8 Foolish men, without even a name.
They were forced to leave the land.

9 Now I am mocked by their songs;
I have become an object of scorn to them.
10 They despise me and keep their distance
from me;
they do not hesitate to spit in my face.
11 Because God has loosened my[D] bowstring
and oppressed me,
they have cast off restraint in my presence.
12 The rabble[E] rise up at my right;
they trap[F] my feet
and construct their siege ramp[G] against me.
13 They tear up my path;
they contribute to my destruction,
without anyone to help them.
14 They advance as through a gaping breach;
they keep rolling in through the ruins.
15 Terrors are turned loose against me;
they chase my dignity away like the wind,
and my prosperity has passed by like a cloud.

16 Now my life is poured out before me,
and days of suffering have seized me.
17 Night pierces my bones,
but my gnawing pains never rest.
18 My clothing is distorted with great force;
he chokes me by the neck of my garment.[E]
19 He throws me into the mud,
and I have become like dust and ashes.

20 I cry out to you for help, but you do not
answer me;
when I stand up, you merely look at me.
21 You have turned against me with cruelty;
you harass me with your strong hand.
22 You lift me up on the wind and make me
ride it;
you scatter me in the storm.
23 Yes, I know that you will lead me to death —
the place appointed for all who live.

24 Yet no one would stretch out his hand
against a ruined person[H]
when he cries out to him for help
because of his distress.
25 Have I not wept for those who have fallen
on hard times?
Has my soul not grieved for the needy?
26 But when I hoped for good, evil came;
when I looked for light, darkness came.
27 I am churning within[I] and cannot rest;
days of suffering confront me.
28 I walk about blackened, but not by the sun.[J]
I stood in the assembly and cried out for help.
29 I have become a brother to jackals
and a companion of ostriches.

[A] **29:18** Or *as the phoenix* [B] **29:24** Lit *they did not cast down* [C] **30:4** Or *saltwort* [D] **30:11** Alt Hb tradition, LXX, Vg read *his* [E] **30:12,18** Hb obscure [F] **30:12** Lit *stretch out* [G] **30:12** Lit *and raise up their destructive paths* [H] **30:24** Lit *a heap of ruins* [I] **30:27** Lit *My bowels boil* [J] **30:28** Or *walk in sunless gloom*

Archaeologists tell us that ancient peoples used six different metals: gold, copper, and iron in earlier times and later silver, lead, and tin. Ancient peoples also used three alloys (combinations of metals): electrum (gold and silver), bronze (copper and tin), and later brass (copper and zinc).[1] Each played important parts in ancient cultures, both as a measure of wealth and for their value in making tools, weapons, and utensils. People smelted each of the metals from ore, which meant they searched diligently for ore's sources.

COPPER

Peoples of Bible times prized copper because they could easily fashion it into many different objects. Copper ore was found throughout the Fertile Crescent (the modern Middle East), and its availability led to widespread use. Copper is not hard or durable. Ancient artisans thus combined copper with tin to make bronze. Translators render the same Hebrew word (*nechosheth*) as "copper" or "bronze." Bronze came into such wide use that archaeologists refer to the period from 3150 to 1200 BC as the Bronze Age. The Old Testament refers to bronze doors, fetters, helmets, armor, and swords (1Sm 17:5–6; 2Ch 33:11; Is 45:2).

The New Testament writers mention copper (referring to coins, Mt 10:9); John used the same Greek word (*chalkos*) to describe "brass" (Rv 18:12). The Greek language also used *chalkos* to refer to bronze (9:20). This multiuse of these Hebrew and Greek terms has caused some confusion in English Bible translations about whether the writer was referring to bronze or brass. History helps clarify.

Hand- and footholds that allowed miners to descend into the shaft below to retrieve copper; at Timnah, in southern Israel.

The Romans first began producing brass (an alloy of copper and zinc) about 20 BC, roughly four hundred years after the last Old Testament prophet. Strictly speaking, therefore, brass was not known or used in Old Testament times. The King James Version of the Old Testament contains many references to brass. More modern Bible translations use the word *bronze* rather than *brass*. Of course, copper is a common element in both bronze and brass.[2]

GOLD

The Bible refers to gold more than any other metal. The scarcity of gold ore increased its value in ancient times, just as is true today. Peoples of the ancient Near East valued gold for its beauty and luster. Because gold is malleable, goldsmiths of

Bible times used it to make jewelry and ornaments. Craftsmen used gold in constructing the tabernacle, Solomon's temple, and many of the utensils used in each (Ex 35–39; 1Kg 6–7). Biblical texts often use the word *gold* to describe anything beautiful, valuable, or pure.[3]

IRON

The Iron Age (1200–586 BC) followed the Bronze Age. The ancients prized iron because it was harder than bronze, and iron tools and weapons proved more durable. God promised his children that they would find iron in the land of Canaan (Dt 8:9). This was

Large roundel with a winged lion in the center. Unearthed at Ecbatana, the capital city of the Medes. Similar objects found in this same area are marked as belonging to Persia's King Artaxerxes II (reigned 404–358 BC), who built a summer palace in Ecbatana.

Lead pipe with stone sleeve sockets that would have joined the pieces of pipe; unearthed beneath the temple of Artemis, the primary goddess of Ephesus.

a demonstration of God's blessing and the richness of the land. The Israelites, like other peoples of the region, used iron to make jewelry; but they especially made plows, axes, picks, swords, and spears from iron. An army with iron weapons had a technological advantage over an enemy using bronze weapons. The Philistines possessed and exploited this advantage over the Israelites, at least for a time (Jdg 1:19; 1Sm 13:19–22). Biblical writers used "iron" as a symbol of hardness and judgment (Ps 2:9; Rv 2:27).[4]

SILVER

Ancient civilizations knew of and used silver from early times. The Bible often mentions gold and silver together, and both became symbols of wealth (Gn 13:2; Zph 1:18; Hg 2:8). As the nation of Israel prospered, the amount of silver in use increased. By the time of Solomon, silver was so common that people used it like money. Though the Israelites did not use coins during the monarchy (1050–586 BC), they used weights of silver—shekels, talents, and minas—as units of exchange (Gn 23:15–16; Ex 21:32; Neh 7:72; Is 7:23).[5] Determining the exact equivalent weights in modern systems of measurement is quite difficult, as the weights varied somewhat in ancient times. However, the *Holman Illustrated Bible Dictionary* provides these estimates: A shekel weighed about 2/5 of an ounce; a mina weighed 1 1/4 pounds; and a talent weighed 75 pounds.[6] Peoples of the ancient Near East also used silver for jewelry, idols, and items for their temples.

LEAD

Ancient prospectors found lead deposits in Egypt and Asia Minor. Often silver was derived from the smelting of lead (Jr 6:27–30). The Romans used lead to make water pipes and coins.

TIN

The biblical writers seldom mention tin. The ancients valued it, though, because they could mix it with copper to make bronze (Nm 31:22; Ezk 22:18,20). ✣

---

[1]W. Gordon Brown, "Minerals and Metals" in *Wycliffe Bible Encyclopedia*, ed. Charles F. Pfeiffer, Howard F. Vos, and John Rea (Chicago: Moody, 1975), 2:1121–22. [2]Daniel C. Browning Jr., "Minerals and Metals" in *HIBD*, 1131; A. Stewart and J. Ruffle, "Mining and Metals" in *New Bible Dictionary* (*NBD3*), ed. D. R. W. Wood, Howard Marshall, J. D. Douglas, and N. Hillyer, 3rd ed. (Downers Grove, IL: InterVarsity, 1996), 768. [3]Stewart and Ruffle, "Mining and Metals," 767–68; Browning, "Minerals and Metals," 1131. [4]Tim Turnham, "Iron" in *HIBD*, 834–35; Stewart and Ruffle, "Mining and Metals," 768. [5]Browning, "Minerals and Metals," 1132. [6]M. Pierce Matheney, "Weights and Measures" in *HIBD*, 1666.

Hand-operated drill dated about 3150 to 2200 BC, the Early Bronze Age; from Syria. The operator would slide the crossbar up and down the central rotating rod, causing it to spin. The stone weight helped stabilize the drill.

30 My skin blackens and flakes off,[A]
and my bones burn with fever.
31 My lyre is used for mourning
and my flute for the sound of weeping.

31 I have made a covenant with my eyes.
How then could I look at a young woman?[B]
2 For what portion would I have
from God above,
or what inheritance from the Almighty
on high?
3 Doesn't disaster come to the unjust
and misfortune to evildoers?
4 Does he not see my ways
and number all my steps?

5 If I have walked in falsehood
or my foot has rushed to deceit,
6 let God weigh me on accurate scales,
and he will recognize my integrity.

7 If my step has turned from the way,
my heart has followed my eyes,
or impurity has stained my hands,
8 let someone else eat what I have sown,
and let my crops be uprooted.

9 If my heart has gone astray over a woman
or I have lurked at my neighbor's door,
10 let my own wife grind grain for another man,
and let other men sleep with[C] her.
11 For that would be a disgrace;
it would be an iniquity deserving punishment.
12 For it is a fire that consumes down
to Abaddon;
it would destroy my entire harvest.

13 If I have dismissed the case of my male
or female servants
when they made a complaint against me,
14 what could I do when God stands up to judge?
How should I answer him when he calls me
to account?
15 Did not the one who made me in the womb
also make them?
Did not the same God form us both
in the womb?

16 If I have refused the wishes of the poor
or let the widow's eyes go blind,
17 if I have eaten my few crumbs alone
without letting the fatherless eat any of it —
18 for from my youth, I raised him as his father,
and since the day I was born[D] I guided
the widow —
19 if I have seen anyone dying for lack of clothing
or a needy person without a cloak,
20 if he[E] did not bless me
while warming himself with the fleece
from my sheep,
21 if I ever cast my vote[F] against a fatherless child
when I saw that I had support in the city gate,
22 then let my shoulder blade fall from my back,
and my arm be pulled from its socket.
23 For disaster from God terrifies me,
and because of his majesty I could not do
these things.

24 If I placed my confidence in gold
or called fine gold my trust,
25 if I have rejoiced because my wealth is great
or because my own hand has acquired
so much,
26 if I have gazed at the sun when it was shining
or at the moon moving in splendor,
27 so that my heart was secretly enticed
and I threw them a kiss,[G]
28 this would also be an iniquity
deserving punishment,
for I would have denied God above.

29 Have I rejoiced over my enemy's distress,
or become excited when trouble came
his way?
30 I have not allowed my mouth to sin
by asking for his life with a curse.
31 Haven't the members of my household said,
"Who is there who has not had enough to eat
at Job's table?"
32 No stranger had to spend the night
on the street,
for I opened my door to the traveler.
33 Have I covered my transgressions
as others do[H]
by hiding my iniquity in my heart
34 because I greatly feared the crowds
and because the contempt of the clans
terrified me,
so I grew silent and would not go outside?

35 If only I had someone to hear my case!
Here is my signature; let the Almighty
answer me.
Let my Opponent compose his indictment.
36 I would surely carry it on my shoulder
and wear it like a crown.

[A] **30:30** Lit *blackens away from me* [B] **31:1** Or *a virgin* [C] **31:10** Lit *men kneel down over* [D] **31:18** Lit *and from my mother's womb* [E] **31:20** Lit *his loins* [F] **31:21** Lit *I raise my hand* [G] **31:27** Lit *and my hand kissed my mouth* [H] **31:33** Or *as Adam*

37 I would give him an account
of all my steps;
I would approach him like a prince.

38 If my land cries out against me
and its furrows join in weeping,
39 if I have consumed its produce
without payment
or shown contempt for its tenants,[A]
40 then let thorns grow instead of wheat
and stinkweed instead of barley.

The words of Job are concluded.

ELIHU'S ANGRY RESPONSE

32 So these three men quit answering Job, because he was righteous in his own eyes. 2 Then
Elihu son of Barachel the Buzite from the family of
Ram became angry. He was angry at Job because he
had justified himself rather than God. 3 He was also
angry at Job's three friends because they had failed
to refute him and yet had condemned him.[B]
4 Now Elihu had waited to speak to Job because
they were all older than he. 5 But when he saw that
the three men could not answer Job, he became angry.
6 So Elihu son of Barachel the Buzite replied:

I am young in years,
while you are old;
therefore I was timid and afraid
to tell you what I know.
7 I thought that age should speak
and maturity should teach wisdom.
8 But it is the spirit in a person—
the breath from the Almighty—
that gives anyone understanding.
9 It is not only the old who are wise
or the elderly who understand
how to judge.
10 Therefore I say, "Listen to me.
I too will declare what I know."
11 Look, I waited for your conclusions;
I listened to your insights
as you sought for words.
12 I paid close attention to you.
Yet no one proved Job wrong;
not one of you refuted his arguments.
13 So do not claim, "We have found wisdom;
let God deal with him, not man."
14 But Job has not directed his argument to me,
and I will not respond to him
with your arguments.

15 Job's friends are dismayed and can
no longer answer;
words have left them.
16 Should I continue to wait now that
they are silent,
now that they stand there
and no longer answer?
17 I too will answer;[C]
yes, I will tell what I know.
18 For I am full of words,
and my spirit[D] compels me to speak.
19 My heart[E] is like unvented wine;
it is about to burst like new wineskins.
20 I must speak so that I can find relief;
I must open my lips and respond.
21 I will be partial to no one,
and I will not give anyone an undeserved title.
22 For I do not know how to give such titles;
otherwise, my Maker would remove me
in an instant.

ELIHU CONFRONTS JOB

33 But now, Job, pay attention to my speech,
and listen to all my words.
2 I am going to open my mouth;
my tongue will form words on my palate.
3 My words come from my upright heart,
and my lips speak with sincerity
what they know.
4 The Spirit of God has made me,
and the breath of the Almighty gives me life.
5 Refute me if you can.
Prepare your case against me;
take your stand.
6 I am just like you before God;
I was also pinched off from a piece of clay.
7 Fear of me should not terrify you;
no pressure from me should weigh you down.

8 Surely you have spoken in my hearing,
and I have heard these very[F] words:
9 "I am pure, without transgression;
I am clean and have no iniquity.
10 But he finds reasons to oppose me;
he regards me as his enemy.
11 He puts my feet in the stocks;
he stands watch over all my paths."

12 But I tell you that you are wrong in this matter,
since God is greater than man.
13 Why do you take him to court
for not answering anything a person asks?[G]
14 For God speaks time and again,
but a person may not notice it.

[A] **31:39** Lit *or caused the breath of its tenants to breathe out*
[B] **32:3** Alt Hb tradition reads *condemned God* [C] **32:17** Lit *answer my part* [D] **32:18** Lit *and the spirit of my belly* [E] **32:19** Lit *belly* [F] **33:8** Lit *heard a sound of* [G] **33:13** Lit *court, for he does not answer all his words*

15 In a dream, a vision in the night,
when deep sleep comes over people
as they slumber on their beds,
16 he uncovers their ears
and terrifies them[A] with warnings,
17 in order to turn a person from his actions
and suppress the pride of a person.
18 God spares his soul from the Pit,
his life from crossing the river of death.[B]
19 A person may be disciplined on his bed
with pain
and constant distress in his bones,
20 so that he detests bread,
and his soul despises his favorite food.
21 His flesh wastes away to nothing,[C]
and his unseen bones stick out.
22 He draws near to the Pit,
and his life to the executioners.
23 If there is an angel on his side,
one mediator out of a thousand,
to tell a person what is right for him[D]
24 and to be gracious to him and say,
"Spare him from going down to the Pit;
I have found a ransom,"
25 then his flesh will be healthier[E] than
in his youth,
and he will return to the days
of his youthful vigor.
26 He will pray to God, and God will delight
in him.
That person will see his face with a shout
of joy,
and God will restore his righteousness to him.
27 He will look at men and say,
"I have sinned and perverted what was right;
yet I did not get what I deserved.[F]
28 He redeemed my soul from going down
to the Pit,
and I will continue to see the light."
29 God certainly does all these things
two or three times to a person
30 in order to turn him back from the Pit,
so he may shine with the light of life.
31 Pay attention, Job, and listen to me.
Be quiet, and I will speak.
32 But if you have something to say,[G] answer me;
speak, for I would like to justify you.
33 If not, then listen to me;
be quiet, and I will teach you wisdom.

34 Then Elihu continued,[H] saying:
2 Hear my words, you wise ones,
and listen to me, you knowledgeable ones.
3 Doesn't the ear test words
as the palate tastes food?
4 Let us judge for ourselves what is right;
let us decide together what is good.
5 For Job has declared, "I am righteous,
yet God has deprived me of justice.
6 Would I lie about my case?
My wound[I] is incurable,
though I am without transgression."
7 What man is like Job?
He drinks derision like water.
8 He keeps company with evildoers
and walks with wicked men.
9 For he has said, "A man gains nothing
when he becomes God's friend."

10 Therefore listen to me, you men
of understanding.
It is impossible for God to do wrong,
and for the Almighty to act unjustly.
11 For he repays a person according to his deeds,
and he gives him what his conduct deserves.[J]
12 Indeed, it is true that God does not act wickedly
and the Almighty does not pervert justice.
13 Who gave him authority over the earth?
Who put him in charge of the entire world?
14 If he put his mind to it
and withdrew the spirit and breath he gave,
15 every living thing would perish together
and mankind would return to the dust.

16 If you have understanding, hear this;
listen to what I have to say.
17 Could one who hates justice govern the world?
Will you condemn the mighty Righteous One,
18 who says to a king, "Worthless man!"
and to nobles, "Wicked men!"?
19 God is not partial to princes
and does not favor the rich over the poor,
for they are all the work of his hands.
20 They die suddenly in the middle of the night;
people shudder, then pass away.
Even the mighty are removed without effort.

21 For his eyes watch over a man's ways,
and he observes all his steps.
22 There is no darkness, no deep darkness,
where evildoers can hide.
23 God does not need to examine
a person further,
that one should[K] approach him in court.

[A] **33:16** LXX; MT reads *and seals* [B] **33:18** Or *from perishing by the sword* [C] **33:21** Lit *away from sight* [D] **33:23** Or *to vouch for a person's uprightness* [E] **33:25** Hb obscure [F] **33:27** Lit *and the same was not to me* [G] **33:32** Lit *If there are words* [H] **34:1** Lit *answered* [I] **34:6** Lit *arrow* [J] **34:11** Lit *and like a path of a man, he causes him to find* [K] **34:23** Some emend to *God has not appointed a time for man to*

24 He shatters the mighty
without an investigation
and sets others in their place.
25 Therefore, he recognizes their deeds
and overthrows them by night, and they
are crushed.
26 In full view of the public,[A]
he strikes them for their wickedness,
27 because they turned aside from following him
and did not understand any of his ways
28 but caused the poor to cry out to him,
and he heard the outcry of the needy.
29 But when God is silent, who can declare
him guilty?
When he hides his face, who can see him?
Yet he watches over both individuals
and nations,
30 so that godless men should not rule
or ensnare the people.

31 Suppose someone says to God,
"I have endured my punishment;
I will no longer act wickedly.
32 Teach me what I cannot see;
if I have done wrong, I won't do it again."
33 Should God repay you on your terms
when you have rejected his?
You must choose, not I!
So declare what you know.
34 Reasonable men will say to me,
along with the wise men who hear me,
35 "Job speaks without knowledge;
his words are without insight."
36 If only Job were tested to the limit,
because his answers are like those
of wicked men.
37 For he adds rebellion to his sin;
he scornfully claps in our presence,
while multiplying his words against God.

35 Then Elihu continued, saying:
2 Do you think it is just when you say,
"I am righteous before God"?
3 For you ask, "What does it profit you,[B]
and what benefit comes to me,
if I do not sin?"
4 I will answer you
and your friends with you.
5 Look at the heavens and see;
gaze at the clouds high above you.
6 If you sin, how does it affect God?
If you multiply your transgressions,
what does it do to him?
7 If you are righteous, what do you give him,
or what does he receive from your hand?
8 Your wickedness affects a person like yourself,
and your righteousness, a son of man.[C]
9 People cry out because of severe oppression;
they shout for help because of the power
of the mighty.
10 But no one asks, "Where is God my Maker,
who provides us with songs in the night,
11 who gives us more understanding
than the animals of the earth
and makes us wiser than the birds
of the sky?"
12 There they cry out, but he does not answer,
because of the pride of evil people.
13 Indeed, God does not listen to empty cries,
and the Almighty does not take note of it —
14 how much less when[D] you complain[E]
that you do not see him,
that your case is before him
and you are waiting for him.
15 But now, because God's anger does not punish
and he does not pay attention
to transgression,[F]
16 Job opens his mouth in vain
and multiplies words without knowledge.

36 Then Elihu continued, saying:
2 Be patient with me a little longer, and I will
inform you,
for there is still more to be said
on God's behalf.
3 I will get my knowledge from a distant place
and ascribe justice to my Maker.
4 Indeed, my words are not false;
one who has complete knowledge is with you.

5 Yes, God is mighty, but he despises no one;
he understands all things.[G]
6 He does not keep the wicked alive,
but he gives justice to the oppressed.
7 He does not withdraw his gaze
from the righteous,
but he seats them forever
with enthroned kings,
and they are exalted.

8 If people are bound with chains
and trapped by the cords of affliction,
9 God tells them what they have done
and how arrogantly they have transgressed.
10 He opens their ears to correction
and tells them to repent from iniquity.

[A] **34:26** Lit *In a place of spectators* [B] **35:3** Some emend to *me* [C] **35:8** Or *a mere mortal* [D] **35:14** Or *how then can* [E] **35:14** Lit *say* [F] **35:15** LXX, Vg; MT reads *folly, or arrogance*; Hb obscure [G] **36:5** Lit *he is mighty in strength of heart*

11 If they listen and serve him,
they will end their days in prosperity
and their years in happiness.
12 But if they do not listen,
they will cross the river of death[A]
and die without knowledge.

13 Those who have a godless heart
harbor anger;
even when God binds them, they do not cry
for help.
14 They die in their youth;
their life ends among male cult prostitutes.
15 God rescues the afflicted by their affliction;
he instructs them by their torment.

16 Indeed, he lured you from the jaws[B]
of distress
to a spacious and unconfined place.
Your table was spread with choice food.
17 Yet now you are obsessed with the judgment
due the wicked;
judgment and justice have seized you.
18 Be careful that no one lures you with riches;[C]
do not let a large ransom[D] lead you astray.
19 Can your wealth[E] or all your physical exertion
keep you from distress?
20 Do not long for the night
when nations will disappear
from their places.
21 Be careful that you do not turn to iniquity,
for that is why you have been tested
by[F] affliction.

22 Look, God shows himself exalted by his power.
Who is a teacher like him?
23 Who has appointed his way for him,
and who has declared, "You have
done wrong"?
24 Remember that you should praise his work,
which people have sung about.
25 All mankind has seen it;
people have looked at it from a distance.
26 Yes, God is exalted beyond our knowledge;
the number of his years cannot be counted.
27 For he makes waterdrops evaporate;[G]
they distill the rain into its[H] mist,
28 which the clouds pour out
and shower abundantly on mankind.
29 Can anyone understand how the clouds
spread out
or how the thunder roars
from God's pavilion?
30 See how he spreads his lightning around him
and covers the depths of the sea.
31 For he judges the nations with these;
he gives food in abundance.
32 He covers his hands with lightning
and commands it to hit its mark.
33 The[I] thunder declares his presence;[J]
the cattle also, the approaching storm.

37 My heart pounds at this
and leaps from my chest.[K]
2 Just listen to his thunderous voice
and the rumbling that comes
from his mouth.
3 He lets it loose beneath the entire sky;
his lightning to the ends of the earth.

4 Then there comes a roaring sound;
God thunders with his majestic voice.
He does not restrain the lightning
when his rumbling voice is heard.
5 God thunders wondrously with his voice;
he does great things that
we cannot comprehend.
6 For he says to the snow, "Fall to the earth,"
and the torrential rains,
his mighty torrential rains,
7 serve as his sign to all mankind,
so that all men may know his work.
8 The wild animals enter their lairs
and stay in their dens.
9 The windstorm comes from its chamber,
and the cold from the driving north winds.
10 Ice is formed by the breath of God,
and watery expanses are frozen.
11 He saturates clouds with moisture;
he scatters his lightning through them.
12 They swirl about,
turning round and round at his direction,
accomplishing everything
he commands them
over the surface of the inhabited world.
13 He causes this to happen for punishment,
for his land, or for his faithful love.

14 Listen to this, Job.
Stop and consider God's wonders.
15 Do you know how God directs his clouds
or makes their lightning flash?
16 Do you understand how the clouds float,
those wonderful works of him who has
perfect knowledge?

[A] **36:12** Or *will perish by the sword* [B] **36:16** Lit *from a mouth of narrowness* [C] **36:18** Or *you into mockery* [D] **36:18** Or *bribe* [E] **36:19** Or *cry for help* [F] **36:21** Or *for you have preferred this to* [G] **36:27** Lit *he draws in waterdrops* [H] **36:27** Or *his* [I] **36:33** Lit *His*, or *Its* [J] **36:33** Lit *thunder announces concerning him* or *it* [K] **37:1** Lit *from its place*

17 You whose clothes get hot
when the south wind brings calm to the land,
18 can you help God spread out the skies
as hard as a cast metal mirror?
19 Teach us what we should say to him;
we cannot prepare our case because of
our darkness.
20 Should he be told that I want to speak?
Can a man speak when he is confused?
21 Now no one can even look at the sun
after a wind has swept through and cleared
the sky.
22 Out of the north he comes, shrouded
in a golden glow;
awesome majesty surrounds him.
23 The Almighty — we cannot reach him —
he is exalted in power!
He will not violate justice and
abundant righteousness,
24 therefore, men fear him.
He does not look favorably on any
who are wise in heart.

THE LORD SPEAKS

38 Then the LORD answered Job from the whirlwind. He said:
2 Who is this who obscures my counsel
with ignorant words?
3 Get ready to answer me like a man;
when I question you, you will inform me.
4 Where were you when I established the earth?
Tell me, if you have[A] understanding.
5 Who fixed its dimensions?
Certainly you know!
Who stretched a measuring line across it?
6 What supports its foundations?
Or who laid its cornerstone
7 while the morning stars sang together
and all the sons of God shouted for joy?

8 Who enclosed the sea behind doors
when it burst from the womb,
9 when I made the clouds its garment
and total darkness its blanket,[B]
10 when I determined its boundaries[C]
and put its bars and doors in place,
11 when I declared, "You may come this far,
but no farther;
your proud waves stop here"?

12 Have you ever in your life commanded
the morning
or assigned the dawn its place,
13 so it may seize the edges of the earth
and shake the wicked out of it?
14 The earth is changed as clay is by a seal;
its hills stand out like the folds of a garment.
15 Light[D] is withheld from the wicked,
and the arm raised in violence is broken.

16 Have you traveled to the sources of the sea
or walked in the depths of the oceans?
17 Have the gates of death been revealed to you?
Have you seen the gates of deep darkness?
18 Have you comprehended the extent
of the earth?
Tell me, if you know all this.

19 Where is the road to the home of light?
Do you know where darkness lives,
20 so you can lead it back to its border?
Are you familiar with the paths to its home?
21 Don't you know? You were already born;
you have lived so long![E]
22 Have you entered the place where the snow
is stored?
Or have you seen the storehouses of hail,
23 which I hold in reserve for times of trouble,
for the day of warfare and battle?
24 What road leads to the place where light
is dispersed?[F]
Where is the source of the east wind
that spreads across the earth?

25 Who cuts a channel for the flooding rain
or clears the way for lightning,
26 to bring rain on an uninhabited land,
on a desert with no human life,[G]
27 to satisfy the parched wasteland
and cause the grass to sprout?
28 Does the rain have a father?
Who fathered the drops of dew?
29 Whose womb did the ice come from?
Who gave birth to the frost of heaven
30 when water becomes as hard as stone,[H]
and the surface of the watery depths
is frozen?

31 Can you fasten the chains of the Pleiades
or loosen the belt of Orion?
32 Can you bring out the constellations[I]
in their season
and lead the Bear[J] and her cubs?
33 Do you know the laws of heaven?
Can you impose its[K] authority on earth?

[A] **38:4** Lit *know* [B] **38:9** Lit *swaddling clothes* [C] **38:10** Lit *I broke my statute on it* [D] **38:15** Lit *Their light* [E] **38:21** Lit *born; the number of your days is great* [F] **38:24** Or *where lightning is distributed* [G] **38:26** Lit *no man in it* [H] **38:30** Lit *water hides itself as the stone* [I] **38:32** Or *Mazzaroth*; Hb obscure [J] **38:32** Or *lead Aldebaran* [K] **38:33** Or *God's*

34 Can you command[A] the clouds
so that a flood of water covers you?
35 Can you send out lightning bolts, and they go?
Do they report to you, "Here we are"?

36 Who put wisdom in the heart[B]
or gave the mind understanding?
37 Who has the wisdom to number the clouds?
Or who can tilt the water jars of heaven
38 when the dust hardens like cast metal
and the clods of dirt stick together?

39 Can you hunt prey for a lioness
or satisfy the appetite of young lions
40 when they crouch in their dens
and lie in wait within their lairs?
41 Who provides the raven's food
when its young cry out to God
and wander about for lack of food?

39 Do you know when mountain goats
give birth?
Have you watched the deer in labor?
2 Can you count the months they are pregnant[C]
so you can know the time they give birth?
3 They crouch down to give birth to their young;
they deliver their newborn.[D]
4 Their offspring are healthy and grow up
in the open field.
They leave and do not return.[E]

5 Who set the wild donkey free?
Who released the swift donkey
from its harness?
6 I made the desert its home,
and the salty wasteland its dwelling.
7 It scoffs at the noise of the village
and never hears the shouts of a driver.
8 It roams the mountains for its pastureland,
searching for anything green.
9 Would the wild ox be willing to serve you?
Would it spend the night
by your feeding trough?
10 Can you hold the wild ox to a furrow
by its harness?
Will it plow the valleys behind you?
11 Can you depend on it because its strength
is great?
Would you leave it to do your hard work?
12 Can you trust the wild ox to harvest your grain
and bring it to your threshing floor?

13 The wings of the ostrich flap joyfully,
but are her feathers and plumage
like the stork's?[F]
14 She abandons her eggs on the ground
and lets them be warmed in the sand.
15 She forgets that a foot may crush them
or that some wild animal may trample them.
16 She treats her young harshly, as if
they were not her own,
with no fear that her labor may have been
in vain.
17 For God has deprived her of wisdom;
he has not endowed her with understanding.
18 When she proudly[F] spreads her wings,
she laughs at the horse and its rider.

19 Do you give strength to the horse?
Do you adorn his neck with a mane?[F]
20 Do you make him leap like a locust?
His proud snorting fills one with terror.
21 He paws[G] in the valley and rejoices
in his strength;
he charges into battle.[H]
22 He laughs at fear, since he is afraid of nothing;
he does not run from the sword.
23 A quiver rattles at his side,
along with a flashing spear and a javelin.
24 He charges ahead[I] with trembling rage;
he cannot stand still at the sound of the
ram's horn.
25 When the ram's horn blasts,
he snorts defiantly.[J]
He smells the battle from a distance;
he hears the officers' shouts
and the battle cry.

26 Does the hawk take flight
by your understanding
and spread its wings to the south?
27 Does the eagle soar at your command
and make its nest on high?
28 It lives on a cliff where it spends the night;
its stronghold is on a rocky crag.
29 From there it searches for prey;
its eyes penetrate the distance.
30 Its brood gulps down blood,
and where the slain are, it is there.

40 The LORD answered Job:
2 Will the one who contends
with the Almighty correct him?
Let him who argues with God give an answer.[K]

[A]**38:34** Lit *lift up your voice to* [B]**38:36** Or *the inner self*; Ps 51:6 [C]**39:2** Lit *months they fulfill* [D]**39:3** Or *they send away their labor pains* [E]**39:4** Lit *return to them* [F]**39:13,18,19** Hb obscure [G]**39:21** LXX, Syr; MT reads *They dig* [H]**39:21** Lit *he goes out to meet the weaponry* [I]**39:24** Lit *He swallows the ground* [J]**39:25** Lit *he says, "Aha!"* [K]**40:2** Lit *God respond to it*

Sun, Moon, and Stars as Imagery and Symbolism

by Harry D. Champy III

Roman-era mosaic depicts a chariot drawn by four horses. In the chariot is a personification of the sun with the word *ORIENS* (east), suggesting that the sun is carried along each morning in its horse-drawn chariot to begin the day.

CHRONOLOGICAL USE

Astronomical observations helped keep track of time. According to Genesis 1:14–19, God created two great lights, the sun and the moon. These lights were "signs" ("to separate light from darkness") for festivals (marking appointed times), days (cycle of light and darkness), and years (cycle of days).

The month was measured by the visible cycle of the moon. The same Hebrew word meant "month" and "new moon." Mesopotamia and Egypt, the first great cultural centers, both used lunar calendars.

The year was the largest basic unit of time. Some ancient civilizations used the lunar year, which was based on the cycles of the moon. Others used the solar year, which was based on Earth's rotation around the sun. For those using the lunar calendar, adjustments were necessary to harmonize with the solar year. The Egyptians devised a unique way of harmonizing the two calendars, using the yearly rising of the star Sirius. This heliacal rising of Sirius was on the same solar date every year and marked the new year and the yearly rising of the Nile.[1]

AGRICULTURAL USE

Because writing developed after agriculture, no written records exist to explain how the first farmers decided when to plant. Observation of seasonal weather and trial and error must have played vital roles. In Egypt and Mesopotamia, the agricultural season followed the yearly flooding of the rivers. Celestial indicators of time helped the people predict when the flooding would occur.

The Sumerian "farmer's almanac" contained instructions from a farmer to his son. The work began with the yearly flooding of the fields in May or June and ended with harvest in April or May.[2] The Gezer calendar, a student's practice tablet found in Israel, more explicitly tied agricultural activities to the twelve months of the year: two for the vine and olive harvest, two for sowing, two for spring pasture, one for flax pulling, one for barley harvest, one for wheat harvest, two for pruning, and one for summer fruit.[3]

NAVIGATIONAL USE

The earliest Mesopotamian and Egyptian cultures developed around rivers, using them for fishing, irrigation, and transportation. The Phoenicians—Canaanites living in Tyre and Sidon on the northeastern coast of the Mediterranean—mastered open-sea navigation. First-century Greek historian Strabo described their reputation:

The Sidonians, according to tradition, are skilled in many beautiful arts . . . besides this they are philosophers in the sciences of astronomy and arithmetic, having begun their studies with practical calculations and with night-sailings, for each of these branches of knowledge concerns the merchant and the shipowner.[4]

Knowing the location and movement of specific stars and constellations was necessary for navigation.[5]

The Phoenicians helped Solomon build a national fleet that sailed from harbors on the Red Sea. This fleet used Phoenician methods of celestial navigation to bring gold and other exotic treasures from Ophir, probably in Arabia or India (1Kg 9–10).

Stone tablet showing Shamash, the Mesopotamian sun-god, seated under an awning and holding the rod and ring that symbolized divine authority. His seat is supported by bull-men, who open the gates of dawn. The symbols of the sun, moon, and Venus are above him, but they are dwarfed by another sun symbol. The larger symbol is supported above an altar by two of the god's attendants. Babylon's King Nabu-apla-iddina, who ruled in the ninth century BC, is shown being assisted by an interceding god and goddess as he approaches from the left.

RELIGIOUS USE

The Mesopotamians and Egyptians deified the sun, moon, and stars. The Mesopotamians called the sun Shamash, the judge of heaven and earth. The Egyptians worshiped the sun as Re, the creator; Horus, the manifestation of Re's order; and Amun, "the All." Further, Egyptians considered Pharaoh to be the embodiment of Horus, ruling for him on earth. Honoring their moon gods, the Mesopotamians worshiped Sin—and the Egyptians, Thoth. Because the moon was essential for calculating time, Thoth was also the Egyptian god of knowledge. Many ancient peoples considered the stars to be divine because they did not set; they never perished.[6]

PROPHETIC USE

Many ancient cultures believed these divine celestial bodies influenced the fate of humans. Such divination blossomed in Mesopotamia, especially among the Babylonians. The Babylonian Venus tablets tracked the appearances of the planet Venus. Another set of Babylonian tablets, the Enuma Anu Enlil, contains various celestial omens; twenty-three tablets offer information about just the moon.[7]

During the reign of the Neo-Babylonian, or Chaldean, Nabunasir (ca 747 BC), the term *Chaldean* became synonymous with the term *astronomer*.[8] Daniel used the term *Chaldean* as a type of diviner (Dn 2:2; 3:8; 4:7; 5:7). The wise men in Matthew 2 were probably similar diviners, but they received a message from the true God.

USE FOR GOD'S PEOPLE

The ancients used the sun, moon, and stars to establish measurements

Tablet 56 of the seventy Babylonian Venus tablets; dedicated to observing planets, stars that move themselves across the sky, and comets. The tablet contains omens related to stars, and the position of the moon, planets, and constellations.

of time, to mark the agricultural seasons, and to guide sea travel. They worshiped these celestial bodies and looked to them to divine the will of the gods. While the Israelites shared the first three uses, the Israelites were forbidden to worship any other god or to make an image of anything on earth or in the heavens (Ex 20:3–5). ✣

---

[1] H. W. F. Saggs, *Civilization before Greece and Rome* (New Haven, CT: Yale University Press, 1989), 231. [2] Samuel Noah Kramer, *History Begins at Sumer* (London: Thames & Hudson, 1958), 105–9. [3] Bill T. Arnold and Bryan E. Beyer, eds., *Readings from the Ancient Near East* (Grand Rapids: Baker Academic, 2002), 171. [4] Strabo, *Geography* 16.2.24. [5] Robert R. Steiglitz, "Long-Distance Seafaring in the Ancient Near East," *BA* 47.3 (1984): 141–42. [6] A. Leo Oppenheim, *Ancient Mesopotamia: Portrait of a Dead Civilization* (Chicago: University of Chicago Press, 1964), 195; Stephen Quirke and Jeffrey Spencer, eds., *The British Museum Book of Ancient Egypt* (New York: Thames & Hudson, 1992), 60–65. [7] William W. Hallo and William Kelly Simpson, *The Ancient Near East: A History* (New York: Harcourt Brace Jovanovich, 1971), 168; Joan Oates, *Babylon* (London: Thames & Hudson, 1979), 179. [8] Hallo and Simpson, *Ancient Near East*, 144.

Large boundary stone, called a *kudurru*, depicting Babylon's King Melishipak II (1186–1172 BC); discovered in Susa. Melishipak, with his hand before his mouth as a sign of respectful prayer, is introducing his daughter to the Mesopotamian goddess Nannaya. The symbols of three main celestial gods are in the sky: the star of Ishtar; the sun of Shamash; and the crescent of Sin, the moon-god. The text calls for the earth to produce gifts for the king and his daughter.

3 Then Job answered the LORD:
4 I am so insignificant. How can I answer you?
I place my hand over my mouth.
5 I have spoken once, and I will not reply;
twice, but now I can add nothing.

6 Then the LORD answered Job from the whirlwind:
7 Get ready to answer me like a man;
When I question you, you will inform me.
8 Would you really challenge my justice?
Would you declare me guilty
to justify yourself?
9 Do you have an arm like God's?
Can you thunder with a voice like his?

10 Adorn yourself with majesty and splendor,
and clothe yourself with honor and glory.
11 Pour out your raging anger;
look on every proud person and humiliate him.
12 Look on every proud person and humble him;
trample the wicked where they stand.[A]
13 Hide them together in the dust;
imprison them in the grave.[B]
14 Then I will confess to you
that your own right hand can deliver you.

15 Look at Behemoth,
which I made along with you.
He eats grass like cattle.
16 Look at the strength of his back[C]
and the power in the muscles of his belly.
17 He stiffens his tail like a cedar tree;
the tendons of his thighs are woven
firmly together.
18 His bones are bronze tubes;
his limbs are like iron rods.
19 He is the foremost of God's works;
only his Maker can draw the sword
against him.
20 The hills yield food for him,
while all sorts of wild animals play there.
21 He lies under the lotus plants,
hiding in the protection[D] of marshy reeds.
22 Lotus plants cover him with their shade;
the willows by the brook surround him.
23 Though the river rages, Behemoth is unafraid;
he remains confident, even if
the Jordan surges up to his mouth.
24 Can anyone capture him while he looks on,[E]
or pierce his nose with snares?

41 Can you pull in Leviathan with a hook
or tie his tongue down with a rope?
2 Can you put a cord[F] through his nose
or pierce his jaw with a hook?
3 Will he beg you for mercy
or speak softly to you?
4 Will he make a covenant with you
so that you can take him as a slave forever?
5 Can you play with him like a bird
or put him on a leash[G] for your girls?
6 Will traders bargain for him
or divide him among the merchants?
7 Can you fill his hide with harpoons
or his head with fishing spears?
8 Lay a[H] hand on him.
You will remember the battle
and never repeat it!
9 Any hope of capturing him proves false.
Does a person not collapse at the very sight
of him?
10 No one is ferocious enough
to rouse Leviathan;
who then can stand against me?
11 Who confronted me,
that I should repay him?
Everything under heaven belongs to me.

12 I cannot be silent about his limbs,
his power, and his graceful proportions.
13 Who can strip off his outer covering?
Who can penetrate his double layer
of armor?[I]
14 Who can open his jaws,[J]
surrounded by those terrifying teeth?
15 His pride is in his rows of scales,
closely sealed together.
16 One scale is so close to another[K]
that no air can pass between them.
17 They are joined to one another,
so closely connected[L] they cannot
be separated.
18 His snorting[M] flashes with light,
while his eyes are like the rays[N] of dawn.
19 Flaming torches shoot from his mouth;
fiery sparks fly out!
20 Smoke billows from his nostrils
as from a boiling pot or burning reeds.
21 His breath sets coals ablaze,
and flames pour out of his mouth.
22 Strength resides in his neck,
and dismay dances before him.
23 The folds of his flesh are joined together,
solid as metal[O] and immovable.

[A] **40:12** Lit *wicked in their place* [B] **40:13** Lit *together; bind their faces in the hidden place* [C] **40:16** Or *waist* [D] **40:21** Lit *plants, in the hiding place* [E] **40:24** Lit *capture it in its eyes* [F] **41:2** Lit *reed* [G] **41:5** Lit *or bind him* [H] **41:8** Lit *your* [I] **41:13** LXX; MT reads *double bridle* [J] **41:14** Lit *open the doors of his face* [K] **41:16** Lit *One by one they approach* [L] **41:17** Lit *another; they cling together and* [M] **41:18** Or *sneezing* [N] **41:18** Lit *eyelids* [O] **41:23** Lit *together, hard on him*

Job's Daughters

by T. Van McClain

At the end of Job's life, he was again blessed with seven sons and three daughters. The Scriptures do not give the names of the sons, but it does introduce us to the three daughters, who were named Jemimah, Keziah, and Keren-happuch. The question naturally arises, why were the names given?

Jemimah's name probably means "dove," based on an Arabic root. Doves were known for their gentle cooing and their innocent and peaceful nature. The word *dove* could have also referred to the daughter's beautiful eyes, "dove's eyes." It was also common to use the word *dove* as a term of endearment (Sg 2:14; 5:2; 6:9).

Keziah refers to cassia, a precious fragrance similar to cinnamon. Cassia was considered one of the finest of spices and was used in making holy anointing oil (Ex 30:24–25). Its value is indicated by its listing among the spices traded by Tyre in Ezekiel 27:19. Cassia was mixed with myrrh and aloes as a fragrance for the king's garments in Psalm 45:8. Job named his second daughter after a most pleasant and precious perfume.

Keren-happuch means "horn of antimony" or "horn of stibnite," a sulfide mineral, and refers to a paint or dye with which females tinged their eyelashes. The use of this eye shadow was culturally acceptable. It made a woman's eyes appear larger and accentuated her beauty.

Job gave these daughters a portion of his estate with his sons, which was also very unusual (Jb 42:15). Normally with the Hebrews, the daughters did not receive any inheritance, unless a father had no sons. The fact that Job gave these three daughters a portion of the inheritance shows the great love and regard he had for them. ✣

Polychrome glass two-handled cosmetic jar with wide neck from Memphis, Egypt; dates 1350 to 1300 BC. The name of one of Job's daughters, Keren-happuch, refers to a dye women used as eye shadow.

24 His heart is as hard as a rock,
as hard as a lower millstone!
25 When Leviathan rises, the mighty[A]
are terrified;
they withdraw because of his thrashing.
26 The sword that reaches him will have
no effect,
nor will a spear, dart, or arrow.
27 He regards iron as straw,
and bronze as rotten wood.
28 No arrow can make him flee;
slingstones become like stubble to him.
29 A club is regarded as stubble,
and he laughs at the sound of a javelin.
30 His undersides are jagged potsherds,
spreading the mud like a threshing sledge.
31 He makes the depths seethe
like a cauldron;
he makes the sea like an ointment jar.
32 He leaves a shining wake behind him;[B]
one would think the deep had gray hair!
33 He has no equal on earth —
a creature devoid of fear!
34 He surveys everything that is haughty;
he is king over all the proud beasts.[C]

JOB REPLIES TO THE LORD

42 Then Job replied to the LORD:
2 I[D] know that you can do anything
and no plan of yours can be thwarted.
3 You asked, "Who is this who conceals
my counsel with ignorance?"
Surely I spoke about things I did not
understand,
things too wondrous for me to[E] know.
4 You said, "Listen now, and I will speak.
When I question you, you will inform me."
5 I had heard reports about you,
but now my eyes have seen you.
6 Therefore, I reject my words and am sorry
for them;
I am dust and ashes.[F,G]

7 After the LORD had finished speaking[H] to Job, he
said to Eliphaz the Temanite, "I am angry with you
and your two friends, for you have not spoken the
truth about me, as my servant Job has. 8 Now take
seven bulls and seven rams, go to my servant Job,
and offer a burnt offering for yourselves. Then my
servant Job will pray for you. I will surely accept his
prayer and not deal with you as your folly deserves.
For you have not spoken the truth about me, as my
servant Job has." 9 Then Eliphaz the Temanite, Bildad
the Shuhite, and Zophar the Naamathite went and did
as the LORD had told them, and the LORD accepted
Job's prayer.

GOD RESTORES JOB

10 After Job had prayed for his friends, the LORD restored his fortunes and doubled his previous possessions. 11 All his brothers, sisters, and former acquaintances came to him and dined with him in his house.
They sympathized with him and comforted him concerning all the adversity the LORD had brought on
him. Each one gave him a piece of silver[I] and a gold
earring.

12 So the LORD blessed the last part of Job's life more
than the first. He owned fourteen thousand sheep
and goats, six thousand camels, one thousand yoke
of oxen, and one thousand female donkeys. 13 He also
had seven sons and three daughters. 14 He named his
first daughter Jemimah, his second Keziah, and his
third Keren-happuch. 15 No women as beautiful as
Job's daughters could be found in all the land, and
their father granted them an inheritance with their
brothers.

16 Job lived 140 years after this and saw his children
and their children to the fourth generation. 17 Then
Job died, old and full of days.

[A] **41:25** Or *the divine beings* [B] **41:32** Lit *a path* [C] **41:34** Lit *the children of pride* [D] **42:2** Alt Hb tradition reads *You* [E] **42:3** Lit *me, and I did not* [F] **42:6** LXX reads *I despise myself and melt; I consider myself dust and ashes* [G] **42:6** Lit *I reject and I relent, concerning dust and ashes* [H] **42:7** Lit *speaking these words* [I] **42:11** Lit *a qesitah*; the value of this currency is unknown

PSALMS

From a synagogue at Gaza, a mosaic dating from AD 508 depicting King David playing the lyre. David's association with music is a prominent motif in Scripture.

INTRODUCTION TO

PSALMS

Circumstances of Writing

Because the book is a collection of many different psalms written over a long time, there is not just one author for this collection. By far the most common designation in the titles is "Of David," which may refer to David as the author of those psalms. David's role as a musician in Saul's court (1Sm 16:14–23) as well as his many experiences as a shepherd, a soldier, and a king make him a likely candidate for writing many of these psalms.

The problem is that the mention of his name in the titles consists of an ambiguous Hebrew construction. It is nothing more than a preposition attached to David's name. The preposition could be translated as "written by," "belonging to," "for," or "about." This does nothing more than relate the psalms bearing that title to David in some way but not necessarily naming him as author. The translation "Of David" accurately conveys this same ambiguity.

Other titles include the designations of Solomon (Pss 72; 172), Asaph (Pss 50; 70–83), the sons of Korah (Pss 42; 44–49), Ethan (Ps 89), Heman son of Korah (Ps 88), and Moses (Ps 90). All of these use the same Hebrew preposition that appears with David's name and therefore have the same ambiguity about authorship. In the case of Asaph, although he was one of David's chief musicians (1Ch 6:39), the name itself became associated with a group of musicians bearing the same name (Ezr 2:40–41). This might explain why an apparently postexilic psalm (Ps 74) includes the title "Of Asaph."

The book of Psalms consists of many different hymns and prayers composed by individuals but used by the community. If one were to take the names in the titles as authors, the date of composition ranges from the time of Moses (fifteenth century BC) to a time following the exile (sixth century BC or later). Some of the titles do contain historical information that might indicate the setting of the composition, although even this (like the authorship) is ambiguous. They might not refer to the date of composition but to the setting of its contents, being composed sometime after the events had taken place. This is a more likely scenario since some of these psalms describe life-threatening situations, where composing a psalm in the heat of the moment would not have been a top priority. In many cases, these psalms include thanksgiving sections as well, showing that they were written after God had answered the prayers.

Contribution to the Bible

The relationship between God's activities in the lives of his people and their responses to them is the most significant contribution of this book. God never spoke directly in any of the psalms, as he often did in the narratives and prophets. Therefore, they are written from the human perspective as authors work their way through various life situations. The struggle to understand how God's attributes, particularly his sovereignty and goodness, relate to life experiences is a major theme in the collection. These words are from people who had not lost their faith in God, although they might have been tempted to at times (Ps 73). They wrestled with how God was dealing with them personally and as a community.

Structure

The book of Psalms is, from first to last, a book of poetry. Hebrew poetry lacks rhyme and regular meter but uses parallelism wherein two (or three) lines are balanced and complete a thought. Some parallelism is synonymous, where the second line echoes the first. Antithetic parallelism uses a contrast between the two segments, and in synthetic parallelism the second segment completes the idea in the first segment.

The psalms can be divided into classes. There are hymns (Pss 145–150) and songs of thanksgiving (Pss 30–32). Psalms of lament (Pss 38–39) are prayers or cries to God on the occasion of distressful situations. Royal psalms (Pss 2; 110) are concerned with the earthly king of Israel. Enthronement psalms (Pss 96; 98) celebrate the kingship of the Lord. Penitential psalms (Pss 32; 38; 51) express contrition and repentance, and wisdom or didactic psalms (Pss 19; 119) tend to be proverbial.

BOOK I (Psalms 1–41)

THE TWO WAYS

1 How happy is the one who does not
walk in the advice of the wicked
or stand in the pathway with sinners
or sit in the company of mockers!
2 Instead, his delight is in the
LORD's instruction,
and he meditates on it day and night.
3 He is like a tree planted beside flowing
streams[A]
that bears its fruit in its season,
and its leaf does not wither.
Whatever he does prospers.

4 The wicked are not like this;
instead, they are like chaff that the wind
blows away.
5 Therefore the wicked will not stand up in
the judgment,
nor sinners in the assembly of the righteous.

6 For the LORD watches over the way
of the righteous,
but the way of the wicked leads to ruin.

CORONATION OF THE SON

2 Why do the nations rage
and the peoples plot in vain?
2 The kings of the earth take their stand,
and the rulers conspire together
against the LORD and his Anointed One:[B]
3 "Let's tear off their chains
and throw their ropes off of us."

4 The one enthroned[C] in heaven laughs;
the Lord ridicules them.
5 Then he speaks to them in his anger
and terrifies them in his wrath:
6 "I have installed my king
on Zion, my holy mountain."

7 I will declare the LORD's decree.
He said to me, "You are my Son;[D]
today I have become your Father.
8 Ask of me,
and I will make the nations your inheritance
and the ends of the earth your possession.
9 You will break them with an iron scepter;
you will shatter them like pottery."

10 So now, kings, be wise;
receive instruction, you judges of the earth.
11 Serve the LORD with reverential awe
and rejoice with trembling.
12 Pay homage to[E] the Son or he will be angry
and you will perish in your rebellion,[F]
for his anger may ignite at any moment.
All who take refuge in him are happy.

CONFIDENCE IN TROUBLED TIMES

3 *A psalm of David when he fled from his son Absalom.*

1 LORD, how my foes increase!
There are many who attack me.
2 Many say about me,
"There is no help for him in God." *Selah*

3 But you, LORD, are a shield around me,
my glory, and the one who lifts up my head.
4 I cry aloud to the LORD,
and he answers me from his holy mountain.
Selah

5 I lie down and sleep;
I wake again because the LORD
sustains me.
6 I will not be afraid of thousands of people
who have taken their stand against me
on every side.

7 Rise up, LORD!
Save me, my God!
You strike all my enemies on the cheek;
you break the teeth of the wicked.
8 Salvation belongs to the LORD;
may your blessing be on your people. *Selah*

A NIGHT PRAYER

4 *For the choir director: with stringed instruments. A psalm of David.*

1 Answer me when I call,
God, who vindicates me.[G]
You freed me from affliction;
be gracious to me and hear my prayer.

2 How long, exalted ones,[H] will my honor
be insulted?
How long will you love what is worthless
and pursue a lie? *Selah*
3 Know that the LORD has set apart
the faithful for himself;
the LORD will hear when I call to him.
4 Be angry[I] and do not sin;
reflect in your heart while on
your bed and be silent. *Selah*

[A] **1:3** Or *beside irrigation channels* [B] **2:2** Or *anointed one* [C] **2:4** Lit *who sits* [D] **2:7** Or *son*, also in v. 12 [E] **2:12** Lit *Kiss* [F] **2:12** Lit *perish in the way* [G] **4:1** Or *God of my righteousness* [H] **4:2** Lit *long, sons of a man* [I] **4:4** Or *Tremble*

Psalms: An Overview

by Francis X. Kimmitt

The essential function of the Psalter was for use in worship by ancient Israel. The Levitical musicians and singers performed many of the psalms and led the congregation to sing God's praises.[1] Israelites sang many of the psalms on the pilgrimages (the songs of ascents), at the high festivals (*Hallel* psalms) or at the various times when they came to the temple to offer sacrifices or pray.[2] The lament psalms, which comprise a significant portion of the Psalter, were also a regular part of the prayers of petition the people used when they gathered to pray in the sanctuary.[3] Much as the psalms are used today, they were used in the public and private worship of the people of God, singing and praying to him, offering praises, petitions, and thanksgivings for who he is and for all that he has done.

The Psalter is divided into Books I through V, with each book ending in a doxology of praise. The fivefold division appears to be from as early as the first century BC, as rabbinic scholars have explained.[4] Books I and II reflect the history of Israel's united monarchy. Book III focuses on the events of the divided kingdoms and the fall of Judah and Israel to Babylon and Assyria, respectively. Book IV remembers the Babylonian exile, but it also holds out the hope of restoration and faith in the Lord who reigns. Book V "celebrates the community of faith's restoration to the land and the sovereignty of God over them."[5] Psalm 119, the celebration of the Torah, plays an important role in the re-formation of the postexilic community. ✣

---

[1] Mark D. Futato, "The Book of Psalms" in *Psalms, Proverbs*, vol. 7 in Cornerstone Biblical Commentary (Carol Stream, IL: Tyndale House, 2009), 6. [2] Allen P. Ross, *A Commentary on the Psalms, Volume 1 (1–41)* (Grand Rapids: Kregel, 2011), 148. [3] Ross, *Commentary*, 149. [4] Nancy deClaisse-Walford, Rolf A. Jacobson, and Beth LaNeel Tanner, *The Book of Psalms* (Grand Rapids: Eerdmans, 2014), 26. [5] DeClaisse-Walford, Jacobson, and Tanner, *Psalms*, 38.

The Great Psalms Scroll from Cave 11 at Qumran on the northwest shore of the Dead Sea. In 1956, a Bedouin discovered six scrolls in Cave 11, the largest and most extensive of these was the Great Psalms Scroll.

5 Offer sacrifices in righteousness[A]
and trust in the LORD.

6 Many are asking, "Who can show us
anything good?"
Let the light of your face shine on us, LORD.

7 You have put more joy in my heart
than they have when their grain
and new wine abound.

8 I will both lie down and sleep in peace,
for you alone, LORD, make me live in safety.

THE REFUGE OF THE RIGHTEOUS

5 *For the choir director: with the flutes. A psalm of David.*

1 Listen to my words, LORD;
consider my sighing.
2 Pay attention to the sound of my cry,
my King and my God,
for I pray to you.

3 In the morning, LORD, you hear my voice;
in the morning I plead my case to you
and watch expectantly.

4 For you are not a God who delights
in wickedness;
evil cannot dwell with you.
5 The boastful cannot stand in your sight;
you hate all evildoers.
6 You destroy those who tell lies;
the LORD abhors violent and treacherous
people.

7 But I enter your house
by the abundance of your faithful love;
I bow down toward your holy temple
in reverential awe of you.
8 LORD, lead me in your righteousness
because of my adversaries;
make your way straight before me.

9 For there is nothing reliable in what they say;
destruction is within them;
their throat is an open grave;
they flatter with their tongues.
10 Punish them, God;
let them fall by their own schemes.
Drive them out because of
their many crimes,
for they rebel against you.

11 But let all who take refuge in you rejoice;
let them shout for joy forever.
May you shelter them,
and may those who love your name boast
about you.
12 For you, LORD, bless the righteous one;
you surround him with favor like a shield.

A PRAYER FOR MERCY

6 *For the choir director: with stringed instruments, according to* Sheminith. *A psalm of David.*

1 LORD, do not rebuke me in your anger;
do not discipline me in your wrath.
2 Be gracious to me, LORD, for I am weak;[B]
heal me, LORD, for my bones are shaking;
3 my whole being is shaken with terror.
And you, LORD — how long?

4 Turn, LORD! Rescue me;
save me because of your faithful love.
5 For there is no remembrance of you in death;
who can thank you in Sheol?

6 I am weary from my groaning;
with my tears I dampen my bed
and drench my couch every night.
7 My eyes are swollen from grief;
they grow old because of all my enemies.

8 Depart from me, all evildoers,
for the LORD has heard the sound
of my weeping.
9 The LORD has heard my plea for help;
the LORD accepts my prayer.
10 All my enemies will be ashamed and shake
with terror;
they will turn back and suddenly be disgraced.

PRAYER FOR JUSTICE

7 A Shiggaion *of David, which he sang to the LORD concerning the words of Cush, a Benjaminite.*

1 LORD my God, I seek refuge in you;
save me from all my pursuers and rescue me,
2 or they[C] will tear me like a lion,
ripping me apart with no one to rescue me.

3 LORD my God, if I have done this,
if there is injustice on my hands,
4 if I have done harm to one at peace with me
or have plundered[D] my adversary
without cause,
5 may an enemy pursue and overtake me;
may he trample me to the ground
and leave my honor in the dust. *Selah*

[A] **4:5** Or *Offer right sacrifices* [B] **6:2** Or *sick* [C] **7:2** Lit *he* [D] **7:4** Or *me and have spared*

6 Rise up, LORD, in your anger;
lift yourself up against the fury
of my adversaries;
awake for me;[A]
you have ordained a judgment.
7 Let the assembly of peoples gather
around you;
take your seat on high over it.
8 The LORD judges the peoples;
vindicate me, LORD,
according to my righteousness
and my integrity.

9 Let the evil of the wicked come to an end,
but establish the righteous.
The one who examines the thoughts
and emotions[B]
is a righteous God.
10 My shield is with God,
who saves the upright in heart.
11 God is a righteous judge
and a God who shows his wrath every day.

12 If anyone does not repent,
he will sharpen his sword;
he has strung his bow and made it ready.
13 He has prepared his deadly weapons;
he tips his arrows with fire.

14 See, the wicked one is pregnant with evil,
conceives trouble, and gives birth to deceit.
15 He dug a pit and hollowed it out
but fell into the hole he had made.
16 His trouble comes back on his own head;
his own violence comes down on top
of his head.

17 I will thank the LORD for his righteousness;
I will sing about the name of the LORD
Most High.

GOD'S GLORY, HUMAN DIGNITY

8 *For the choir director: on the* Gittith. *A psalm of David.*

1 LORD, our Lord,
how magnificent is your name
throughout the earth!

You have covered the heavens
with your majesty.[C]
2 From the mouths of infants and
nursing babies,
you have established a stronghold[D]
on account of your adversaries
in order to silence the enemy and the avenger.

3 When I observe your heavens,
the work of your fingers,
the moon and the stars,
which you set in place,
4 what is a human being
that you remember him,
a son of man[E] that you look after him?
5 You made him little less than God[F,G]
and crowned him with glory and honor.
6 You made him ruler over the works
of your hands;
you put everything under his feet:
7 all the sheep and oxen,
as well as the animals in the wild,
8 the birds of the sky,
and the fish of the sea
that pass through the currents of the seas.

9 LORD, our Lord,
how magnificent is your name
throughout the earth!

CELEBRATION OF GOD'S JUSTICE

9 *For the choir director: according to* Muth-labben. *A psalm of David.*

1 I will thank the LORD with all my heart;
I will declare all your wondrous works.
2 I will rejoice and boast about you;
I will sing about your name, Most High.

3 When my enemies retreat,
they stumble and perish before you.
4 For you have upheld my just cause;
you are seated on your throne
as a righteous judge.
5 You have rebuked the nations:
You have destroyed the wicked;
you have erased their name
forever and ever.
6 The enemy has come to eternal ruin;
you have uprooted the cities,
and the very memory of them has perished.

7 But the LORD sits enthroned forever;
he has established his throne for judgment.
8 And he judges the world
with righteousness;
he executes judgment on the nations
with fairness.
9 The LORD is a refuge for the persecuted,
a refuge in times of trouble.

[A] **7:6** LXX reads *awake, Lord my God* [B] **7:9** Lit *examines hearts and kidneys* [C] **8:1** Lit *earth, which has set your splendor upon the heavens* [D] **8:2** LXX reads *established praise* [E] **8:4** Or *a mere mortal* [F] **8:5** LXX reads *angels* [G] **8:5** Or *heavenly beings*; Hb *Elohim*

Crowns Fit for a King

by Roberta Lou Jones

STYLES OF CROWNS

Designers showed great creativity in making crowns for important people. Many ancient crowns resembled caps. Assyrian kings often ruled in embroidered, jewel-studded cloth turbans. Persian royalty wore skullcaps with rosettes and jewels. Egyptian pharaohs frequently added to their crowns images of the highly poisonous cobra. Another type of crown originated from simple cloth or leather headbands. Craftsmen borrowed the headband idea and made crowns of gold, silver, and copper.[1] Monarchs in the biblical world seemed to search constantly for suitable royal headgear to express their power and position.

Queen Puabi (or Shubad) lived in Ur about 2500 BC. Her headband-style crown included gold wreaths with dangling willow and beech leaves. Chains of blue lapis lazuli and orange-red carnelian beads added even more splendor.[2]

WORDS FOR CROWN

Scholars often translate the Hebrew words *kether* and *atarah* as "crown." Both words suggest circular headpieces. Additionally, the Hebrew word *nezer* can be translated "crown" and implies dedication or service to God. *Atarah*, *nezer*, and *kether* can be translated with words synonymous with "crown." For instance, in the CSB, the medallion that Moses attached to Aaron's turban was called a "diadem" (*nezer*; Lv 8:9). In Ezekiel 23:42, common men flattered women by putting "tiaras" (*atarah*) on their heads.

CROWNS IN SURPRISING PLACES

In 1962, archaeologists explored the Nahal Mishmar caves near the Dead Sea. The agile adventurers used ropes and ladders to scale down a high cliff to a cave entrance. The archaeologists discovered grain, leather sandals, woven straw platters, and pottery. They also found a

A silver tetradrachma coin shows a radiant crown, which was a diadem with spikes. This coin, likely showing Antiochus VI (145–142 BC), has six spikes. Other coins show as many as fourteen.

surprising cache of metal objects, including ten copper crowns. The archaeologists called this place Cave of the Treasure. Likely, a fertility cult used the crowns in religious rituals during the Chalcolithic Period (4000–3150 BC).[3]

Hammurabi became king of Babylon sometime between 1848 and 1736 BC. He arranged a rock pillar, about seven feet tall, inscribed with 282 laws. That diorite stele is now known as the Code of Hammurabi. The pillar showed Shamash (the sun-god) and Hammurabi wearing regal clothing and crowns.

The tomb of Egyptian King Tutankhamun (ca 1361 BC) contained an ornate wooden chair. This throne shimmered with gold, colored glazes, and precious stones. Two winged serpents, both wearing crowns, formed the arms of Tutankhamun's throne. Each chair leg ended in a carved lion's paw. The front panel of the back of the throne showed the royal couple wearing elaborate crowns. His crown included numerous images of the royal cobra. Surely the spreading snake heads properly terrified the king's enemies.[4]

THE CROWN OF PSALM 8

King David meditated on God's great name. Then the former shepherd boy considered the moon and stars. David pondered, "What is a human being that you remember him" (Ps 8:1–4). The answer: "You made him little less than God and crowned him with glory and honor" (v. 5). The psalmist continued, "You made him ruler over the works of your hands" (v. 6). How are we rulers? Humanity represents God as Ruler over all created things. Therefore, the Creator of the world honors human beings by crowning them as his authorized representatives. ✣

---

[1] John Rea, "Crown" in *Wycliffe Bible Dictionary*, ed. Charles F. Pfeiffer, Howard F. Vos, and John Rea (Peabody, MA: Hendrickson, 1998), 405–7.
[2] P. R. S. Moorey, *UR "of the Chaldees": A Revised and Updated Edition of Sir Leonard Woolley's Excavations at Ur* (Ithaca, NY: Cornell University Press, 1982), 60–77.
[3] *Encyclopedia of Archaeological Excavations in the Holy Land* (*EAEHL*), ed. Michael Avi-Yonah and Ephraim Stern, English ed., vol. 3 (Englewood Cliffs, NJ: Prentice-Hall, 1977), 683–90. See P. Bar-Adon, "Expedition C–The Cave of the Treasure," *IEJ* 12.3–4 (1962): 215–26; Isaac Gilead, "Religio-Magic Behavior in the Chalcolithic Period of Palestine," in *Aharon Kempinski Memorial Volume*, ed. Eliezer D. Oren and Shmuel Ahituv (Israel: Ben-Gurion University of the Negev Press, 2002), 103–22. [4] Howard Carter and A. C. Mace, *The Tomb of Tut-ankh-Amen* (London: Cassell, 1930), 46–47, 118–19, 206–7, plates 2, 24, 62, 63.

Replica of a statue in Diana's temple at Ephesus. Her crown, called a castle crown, is made to resemble the city of Ephesus.

10 Those who know your name trust in you
because you have not abandoned
those who seek you, LORD.

11 Sing to the LORD, who dwells in Zion;
proclaim his deeds among the nations.
12 For the one who seeks an accounting
for bloodshed remembers them;
he does not forget the cry of the oppressed.

13 Be gracious to me, LORD;
consider my affliction at the hands of those
who hate me.
Lift me up from the gates of death,
14 so that I may declare all your praises.
I will rejoice in your salvation
within the gates of Daughter Zion.

15 The nations have fallen into the pit they made;
their foot is caught in the net
they have concealed.
16 The LORD has made himself known;
he has executed justice,
snaring the wicked
by the work of their hands. *Higgaion. Selah*

17 The wicked will return to Sheol —
all the nations that forget God.
18 For the needy will not always be forgotten;
the hope of the oppressed[A] will not perish
forever.

19 Rise up, LORD! Do not let
mere humans prevail;
let the nations be judged in your presence.
20 Put terror in them, LORD;
let the nations know they are
only humans. *Selah*

NEED FOR GOD'S JUSTICE

10 LORD,[B,C] why do you stand so far away?
Why do you hide in times of trouble?
2 In arrogance the wicked relentlessly pursue
their victims;
let them be caught in the schemes
they have devised.

3 For the wicked one boasts about
his own cravings;
the one who is greedy curses[D] and despises
the LORD.
4 In all his scheming,
the wicked person arrogantly thinks,[E]
"There's no accountability,
since there's no God."

5 His ways are always secure;[F]
your lofty judgments have no effect on him;[G]
he scoffs at all his adversaries.
6 He says to himself, "I will never be moved —
from generation to generation I will be
without calamity."
7 Cursing, deceit, and violence fill his mouth;
trouble and malice are under his tongue.
8 He waits in ambush near settlements;
he kills the innocent in secret places.
His eyes are on the lookout for the helpless;
9 he lurks in secret like a lion in a thicket.
He lurks in order to seize a victim;
he seizes a victim and drags him in his net.
10 So he is oppressed and beaten down;
helpless people fall because of the wicked
one's strength.
11 He says to himself, "God has forgotten;
he hides his face and will never see."

12 Rise up, LORD God! Lift up your hand.
Do not forget the oppressed.
13 Why has the wicked person despised God?
He says to himself, "You will not demand
an account."
14 But you yourself have seen trouble and grief,
observing it in order to take the matter
into your hands.
The helpless one entrusts himself to you;
you are a helper of the fatherless.
15 Break the arm of the wicked, evil person,
until you look for his wickedness,
but it can't be found.

16 The LORD is King forever and ever;
the nations will perish from his land.
17 LORD, you have heard the desire
of the humble;
you will strengthen their hearts.
You will listen carefully,
18 doing justice for the fatherless
and the oppressed
so that mere humans from the earth
may terrify them no more.

REFUGE IN THE LORD

11 *For the choir director. Of David.*
I have taken refuge in the LORD.
How can you say to me,
"Escape to the mountains[H] like a bird!

[A]**9:18** Alt Hb tradition reads *humble* [B]**10:1** Some Hb mss, LXX connect Pss 9–10. [C]**10:1** Together Pss 9–10 form a partial acrostic. [D]**10:3** Or *he blesses the greedy* [E]**10:4** Lit *wicked according to the height of his nose* [F]**10:5** Or *prosperous* [G]**10:5** Lit *judgments are away from in front of him* [H]**11:1** Lit *your mountain*

2 For look, the wicked string bows;
they put their arrows on bowstrings
to shoot from the shadows at the upright
in heart.
3 When the foundations are destroyed,
what can the righteous do?"

4 The LORD is in his holy temple;
the LORD—his throne is in heaven.
His eyes watch;
his gaze[A] examines everyone.[B]
5 The LORD examines the righteous,
but he hates the wicked
and[C] those who love violence.
6 Let him rain burning coals[D] and sulfur
on the wicked;
let a scorching wind be the portion
in their cup.
7 For the LORD is righteous; he loves
righteous deeds.
The upright will see his face.

OPPRESSION BY THE WICKED

12 *For the choir director: according to* Sheminith. *A psalm of David.*

1 Help, LORD, for no faithful one remains;
the loyal have disappeared
from the human race.[E]
2 They lie to one another;
they speak with flattering lips
and deceptive hearts.
3 May the LORD cut off all flattering lips
and the tongue that speaks boastfully.
4 They say, "Through our tongues
we have power;
our lips are our own — who can be
our master?"

5 "Because of the devastation of the needy
and the groaning of the poor,
I will now rise up," says the LORD.
"I will provide safety for the one
who longs for it."

6 The words of the LORD
are pure words,
like silver refined in an earthen furnace,
purified seven times.

7 You, LORD, will guard us;[F]
you will protect us[G] from this generation
forever.
8 The wicked prowl[H] all around,
and what is worthless is exalted
by the human race.

A PLEA FOR DELIVERANCE

13 *For the choir director. A psalm of David.*

How long, LORD? Will you
forget me forever?
How long will you hide your face
from me?
2 How long will I store up anxious concerns[I]
within me,
agony in my mind every day?
How long will my enemy dominate me?

3 Consider me and answer, LORD my God.
Restore brightness to my eyes;
otherwise, I will sleep in death.
4 My enemy will say, "I have triumphed
over him,"
and my foes will rejoice
because I am shaken.

5 But I have trusted in your faithful love;
my heart will rejoice in your deliverance.
6 I will sing to the LORD
because he has treated me generously.

A PORTRAIT OF SINNERS

14 *For the choir director. Of David.*

The fool says in his heart,
"There's no God."
They are corrupt; they do vile deeds.
There is no one who does good.
2 The LORD looks down from heaven
on the human race[J]
to see if there is one who is wise,
one who seeks God.
3 All have turned away;
all alike have become corrupt.
There is no one who does good,
not even one.

4 Will evildoers never understand?
They consume my people
as they consume bread;
they do not call on the LORD.

5 Then[K] they will be filled with dread,
for God is with those who are[L] righteous.
6 You sinners frustrate the plans
of the oppressed,
but the LORD is his refuge.

[A] **11:4** Lit *eyelids* [B] **11:4** Or *examines the descendants of Adam* [C] **11:5** Or *righteous and the wicked, and he hates* [D] **11:6** Sym; MT reads *rain snares, fire* [E] **12:1** Or *the descendants of Adam,* also in v. 8 [F] **12:7** Some Hb mss, LXX, Jer; other Hb mss read *them* [G] **12:7** Some Hb mss, LXX; other Hb mss read *him* [H] **12:8** Lit *walk about* [I] **13:2** Or *up counsels* [J] **14:2** Or *the descendants of Adam* [K] **14:5** Or *There* [L] **14:5** Lit *with the generation of the*

7 Oh, that Israel's deliverance would come
from Zion!
When the LORD restores the fortunes
of his people,[A]
let Jacob rejoice, let Israel be glad.

A DESCRIPTION OF THE GODLY

15 *A psalm of David.*
LORD, who can dwell in your tent?
Who can live on your holy mountain?

2 The one who lives blamelessly,
practices righteousness,
and acknowledges the truth in his heart —
3 who does not slander with his tongue,
who does not harm his friend
or discredit his neighbor,
4 who despises the one rejected by the LORD[B]
but honors those who fear the LORD,
who keeps his word whatever the cost,
5 who does not lend his silver at interest
or take a bribe against the innocent —
the one who does these things will never
be shaken.

CONFIDENCE IN THE LORD

16 A Miktam *of David.*
Protect me, God, for I take refuge in you.
2 I[C] said to the LORD, "You are my Lord;
I have nothing good besides you."[D]
3 As for the holy people who are in the land,
they are the noble ones.
All my delight is in them.
4 The sorrows of those who take another god
for themselves will multiply;
I will not pour out their drink offerings
of blood,
and I will not speak their names with my lips.

5 LORD, you are my portion[E]
and my cup of blessing;
you hold my future.
6 The boundary lines have fallen for me
in pleasant places;
indeed, I have a beautiful inheritance.

7 I will bless the LORD who counsels me —
even at night when my thoughts trouble me.[F]
8 I always let the LORD guide me.[G]
Because he is at my right hand,
I will not be shaken.

9 Therefore my heart is glad
and my whole being rejoices;
my body also rests securely.
10 For you will not abandon me to Sheol;
you will not allow your faithful one to see decay.
11 You reveal the path of life to me;
in your presence is abundant joy;
at your right hand are eternal pleasures.

A PRAYER FOR PROTECTION

17 *A prayer of David.*
LORD, hear a just cause;
pay attention to my cry;
listen to my prayer —
from lips free of deceit.
2 Let my vindication come from you,
for you see what is right.
3 You have tested my heart;
you have examined me at night.
You have tried me and found nothing evil;
I have determined that my mouth will not sin.[H]
4 Concerning what people do:
by the words from your lips
I have avoided the ways of the violent.
5 My steps are on your paths;
my feet have not slipped.

6 I call on you, God,
because you will answer me;
listen closely to me; hear what I say.
7 Display the wonders of your faithful love,
Savior of all who seek refuge
from those who rebel against your right hand.[I]
8 Protect me as the pupil of your eye;
hide me in the shadow of your wings
9 from[J] the wicked who treat me violently,[K]
my deadly enemies who surround me.

10 They are uncaring;[L]
their mouths speak arrogantly.
11 They advance against me;[M]
now they surround me.
They are determined[N]
to throw me to the ground.
12 They are[O] like a lion eager to tear,
like a young lion lurking in ambush.

13 Rise up, LORD!
Confront him; bring him down.
With your sword, save me from the wicked.

[A] **14:7** Or *restores his captive people* [B] **15:4** Lit *in his eyes the rejected is despised* [C] **16:2** Some Hb mss, LXX, Syr, Jer; other Hb mss read *You* [D] **16:2** Or *"Lord, my good; there is none besides you."* [E] **16:5** Or *allotted portion* [F] **16:7** Or *at night my heart instructs me* [G] **16:8** Lit *I place the LORD in front of me always* [H] **17:3** Or *evil; my mouth will not sin* [I] **17:7** Or *love, you who save with your right hand those seeking refuge from adversaries* [J] **17:9** Lit *from the presence of* [K] **17:9** Or *who plunder me* [L] **17:10** Lit *have closed up their fat* [M] **17:11** Vg; MT reads *Our steps* [N] **17:11** Lit *They set their eyes* [O] **17:12** Lit *He is*

14 With your hand, LORD, save me from men,
from men of the world
whose portion is in this life:
You fill their bellies with what you have
in store;
their sons are satisfied,
and they leave their surplus to their children.

15 But I will see your face in righteousness;
when I awake, I will be satisfied
with your presence.[A]

PRAISE FOR DELIVERANCE

18 *For the choir director. Of the servant of the LORD, David, who spoke the words of this song to the LORD on the day the LORD rescued him from the grasp of all his enemies and from the power of Saul. He said:*

1 I love you, LORD, my strength.
2 The LORD is my rock,
my fortress, and my deliverer,
my God, my rock where I seek refuge,
my shield and the horn of my salvation,
my stronghold.
3 I called to the LORD, who is worthy of praise,
and I was saved from my enemies.

4 The ropes of death were wrapped around me;
the torrents of destruction terrified me.
5 The ropes of Sheol entangled me;
the snares of death confronted me.
6 I called to the LORD in my distress,
and I cried to my God for help.
From his temple he heard my voice,
and my cry to him reached his ears.

7 Then the earth shook and quaked;
the foundations of the mountains trembled;
they shook because he burned with anger.
8 Smoke rose from his nostrils,
and consuming fire came from his mouth;
coals were set ablaze by it.[B]
9 He bent the heavens and came down,
total darkness beneath his feet.
10 He rode on a cherub and flew,
soaring on the wings of the wind.
11 He made darkness his hiding place,
dark storm clouds his canopy around him.
12 From the radiance of his presence,
his clouds swept onward with hail
and blazing coals.
13 The LORD thundered from[C] heaven;
the Most High made his voice heard.[D]
14 He shot his arrows and scattered them;
he hurled[E] lightning bolts and routed them.
15 The depths of the sea became visible,
the foundations of the world were exposed,
at your rebuke, LORD,
at the blast of the breath of your nostrils.

16 He reached down from on high
and took hold of me;
he pulled me out of deep water.
17 He rescued me from my powerful enemy
and from those who hated me,
for they were too strong for me.
18 They confronted me in the day
of my calamity,
but the LORD was my support.
19 He brought me out to a spacious place;
he rescued me because he delighted in me.

20 The LORD rewarded me
according to my righteousness;
he repaid me
according to the cleanness of my hands.
21 For I have kept the ways of the LORD
and have not turned from my God
to wickedness.
22 Indeed, I let all his ordinances guide me[F]
and have not disregarded his statutes.
23 I was blameless toward him
and kept myself from my iniquity.
24 So the LORD repaid me
according to my righteousness,
according to the cleanness of my hands
in his sight.

25 With the faithful
you prove yourself faithful,
with the blameless
you prove yourself blameless,
26 with the pure
you prove yourself pure,
but with the crooked
you prove yourself shrewd.
27 For you rescue an oppressed people,
but you humble those with haughty eyes.
28 LORD, you light my lamp;
my God illuminates my darkness.
29 With you I can attack a barricade,[G]
and with my God I can leap over a wall.

30 God — his way is perfect;
the word of the LORD is pure.
He is a shield to all who take refuge in him.

[A] **17:15** Lit *form* [B] **18:8** Or *him* [C] **18:13** Some Hb mss, LXX, Tg, Jer; other Hb mss read *in* [D] **18:13** Some Hb mss read *voice, with hail and blazing coals* [E] **18:14** Or *multiplied* [F] **18:22** Lit *Indeed, all his ordinances have been in front of me* [G] **18:29** Or *a ridge*, or *raiders*

31 For who is God besides the LORD?
And who is a rock? Only our God.
32 God — he clothes me with strength
and makes my way perfect.
33 He makes my feet like the feet of a deer
and sets me securely on the heights.[A]
34 He trains my hands for war;
my arms can bend a bow of bronze.
35 You have given me the shield
of your salvation;
your right hand upholds me,
and your humility exalts me.
36 You make a spacious place beneath me
for my steps,
and my ankles do not give way.

37 I pursue my enemies and overtake them;
I do not turn back until they are wiped out.
38 I crush them, and they cannot get up;
they fall beneath my feet.
39 You have clothed me with strength
for battle;
you subdue my adversaries beneath me.
40 You have made my enemies retreat
before me;[B]
I annihilate those who hate me.
41 They cry for help, but there is no one
to save them —
they cry to the LORD, but he does not
answer them.
42 I pulverize them like dust before the wind;
I trample them[C] like mud in the streets.

43 You have freed me from the feuds
among the people;
you have appointed me the head of nations;
a people I had not known serve me.
44 Foreigners submit to me cringing;
as soon as they hear they obey me.
45 Foreigners lose heart
and come trembling from their fortifications.

46 The LORD lives — blessed be my rock!
The God of my salvation is exalted.
47 God — he grants me vengeance
and subdues peoples under me.
48 He frees me from my enemies.
You exalt me above my adversaries;
you rescue me from violent men.
49 Therefore I will give thanks to you among
the nations, LORD;
I will sing praises about your name.
50 He gives great victories to his king;
he shows loyalty to his anointed,
to David and his descendants forever.

THE WITNESS OF CREATION AND SCRIPTURE

19 *For the choir director. A psalm of David.*
The heavens declare the glory of God,
and the expanse proclaims the work
of his hands.
2 Day after day they pour out speech;
night after night
they communicate knowledge.[D]
3 There is no speech; there are no words;
their voice is not heard.
4 Their message[E] has gone out to the whole earth,
and their words to the ends of the world.

In the heavens he has pitched a tent for the sun.
5 It is like a bridegroom coming from his home;
it rejoices like an athlete running a course.
6 It rises from one end of the heavens
and circles to their other end;
nothing is hidden from its heat.

7 The instruction of the LORD is perfect,
renewing one's life;
the testimony of the LORD is trustworthy,
making the inexperienced wise.
8 The precepts of the LORD are right,
making the heart glad;
the command of the LORD is radiant,
making the eyes light up.
9 The fear of the LORD is pure,
enduring forever;
the ordinances of the LORD are reliable
and altogether righteous.
10 They are more desirable than gold —
than an abundance of pure gold;
and sweeter than honey
dripping from a honeycomb.
11 In addition, your servant is warned by them,
and in keeping them there is
an abundant reward.

12 Who perceives his unintentional sins?
Cleanse me from my hidden faults.
13 Moreover, keep your servant from willful sins;
do not let them rule me.
Then I will be blameless
and cleansed from blatant rebellion.
14 May the words of my mouth
and the meditation of my heart
be acceptable to you,
LORD, my rock and my Redeemer.

[A] **18:33** Or *on my high places* [B] **18:40** Or *You gave me the necks of my enemies* [C] **18:42** Some Hb mss, LXX, Syr, Tg; other Hb mss read *I poured them out* [D] **19:2** Or *Day to day pours out speech, and night to night communicates knowledge* [E] **19:4** LXX, Sym, Syr, Vg; MT reads *line*

DELIVERANCE IN BATTLE

20 *For the choir director. A psalm of David.*
May the LORD answer you in a day of trouble;
may the name of Jacob's God protect you.
2 May he send you help from the sanctuary
and sustain you from Zion.
3 May he remember all your offerings
and accept your burnt offering. *Selah*

4 May he give you what your heart desires
and fulfill your whole purpose.
5 Let us shout for joy at your victory
and lift the banner in the name of our God.
May the LORD fulfill all your requests.

6 Now I know that the LORD gives victory
to his anointed;
he will answer him from his holy heaven
with mighty victories from his right hand.
7 Some take pride in chariots, and others
in horses,
but we take pride in the name of the LORD
our God.
8 They collapse and fall,
but we rise and stand firm.
9 LORD, give victory to the king!
May he[A] answer us on the day that we call.

THE KING'S VICTORY

21 *For the choir director. A psalm of David.*
LORD, the king finds joy in your strength.
How greatly he rejoices in your victory!
2 You have given him his heart's desire
and have not denied the request
of his lips. *Selah*
3 For you meet him with rich blessings;
you place a crown of pure gold on his head.
4 He asked you for life, and you gave it to him —
length of days forever and ever.
5 His glory is great through your victory;
you confer majesty and splendor on him.
6 You give him blessings forever;
you cheer him with joy in your presence.
7 For the king relies on the LORD;
through the faithful love of the Most High
he is not shaken.

8 Your hand will capture all your enemies;
your right hand will seize those who hate you.
9 You will make them burn
like a fiery furnace when you appear;
the LORD will engulf them in his wrath,
and fire will devour them.
10 You will wipe their progeny from the earth
and their offspring from the human race.[B]
11 Though they intend to harm[C] you
and devise a wicked plan, they will not prevail.
12 Instead, you will put them to flight
when you ready your bowstrings to shoot
at them.

13 Be exalted, LORD, in your strength;
we will sing and praise your might.

FROM SUFFERING TO PRAISE

22 *For the choir director: according to "The Deer of the Dawn." A psalm of David.*
1 My God, my God, why have you
abandoned me?
Why are you so far from my deliverance
and from my words of groaning?
2 My God, I cry by day, but you do not answer,
by night, yet I have no rest.
3 But you are holy,
enthroned on the praises of Israel.
4 Our ancestors trusted in you;
they trusted, and you rescued them.
5 They cried to you and were set free;
they trusted in you and were not disgraced.

6 But I am a worm and not a man,
scorned by mankind and despised by people.
7 Everyone who sees me mocks me;
they sneer[D] and shake their heads:
8 "He relies on[E] the LORD;
let him save him;
let the LORD[F] rescue him,
since he takes pleasure in him."

9 It was you who brought me out of the womb,
making me secure at my mother's breast.
10 I was given over to you at birth;[G]
you have been my God
from my mother's womb.

11 Don't be far from me, because distress is near
and there's no one to help.

12 Many bulls surround me;
strong ones of Bashan encircle me.
13 They open their mouths against me —
lions, mauling and roaring.
14 I am poured out like water,
and all my bones are disjointed;
my heart is like wax,
melting within me.

[A] **20:9** Or *LORD, save. May the king* [B] **21:10** Or *the descendants of Adam* [C] **21:11** Lit *they stretch out harm against* [D] **22:7** Lit *separate with the lip* [E] **22:8** Or *Rely on* [F] **22:8** Lit *let him* [G] **22:10** Lit *was cast on you from the womb*

15 My strength is dried up like baked clay;
my tongue sticks to the roof of my mouth.
You put me into the dust of death.
16 For dogs have surrounded me;
a gang of evildoers has closed in on me;
they pierced[A] my hands and my feet.
17 I can count all my bones;
people[B] look and stare at me.
18 They divided my garments among themselves,
and they cast lots for my clothing.

19 But you, LORD, don't be far away.
My strength, come quickly to help me.
20 Rescue my life from the sword,
my only life[C] from the power of these dogs.
21 Save me from the lion's mouth,
from the horns of wild oxen.

You answered me![D]
22 I will proclaim your name to my brothers
and sisters;
I will praise you in the assembly.
23 You who fear the LORD, praise him!
All you descendants of Jacob, honor him!
All you descendants of Israel, revere him!
24 For he has not despised or abhorred
the torment of the oppressed.
He did not hide his face from him
but listened when he cried to him for help.

25 I will give praise in the great assembly
because of you;
I will fulfill my vows
before those who fear you.[E]
26 The humble will eat and be satisfied;
those who seek the LORD will praise him.
May your hearts live forever!

27 All the ends of the earth will remember
and turn to the LORD.
All the families of the nations
will bow down before you,
28 for kingship belongs to the LORD;
he rules the nations.
29 All who prosper on earth will eat
and bow down;
all those who go down to the dust
will kneel before him —
even the one who cannot preserve his life.
30 Their descendants will serve him;
the next generation will be told
about the Lord.
31 They will come and declare his righteousness;
to a people yet to be born
they will declare what he has done.

THE GOOD SHEPHERD

23 *A psalm of David.*
The LORD is my shepherd;
I have what I need.
2 He lets me lie down in green pastures;
he leads me beside quiet waters.
3 He renews my life;
he leads me along the right paths[F]
for his name's sake.
4 Even when I go through the darkest valley,[G]
I fear no danger,
for you are with me;
your rod and your staff — they comfort me.

5 You prepare a table before me
in the presence of my enemies;
you anoint my head with oil;
my cup overflows.
6 Only goodness and faithful love
will pursue me
all the days of my life,
and I will dwell in[H] the house of the LORD
as long as I live.[I]

THE KING OF GLORY

24 *A psalm of David.*
The earth and everything in it,
the world and its inhabitants,
belong to the LORD;
2 for he laid its foundation on the seas
and established it on the rivers.

3 Who may ascend the mountain of the LORD?
Who may stand in his holy place?
4 The one who has clean hands
and a pure heart,
who has not appealed to[J] what is false,
and who has not sworn deceitfully.
5 He will receive blessing from the LORD,
and righteousness[K] from the God
of his salvation.
6 Such is the generation of those
who inquire of him,
who seek the face of the God of Jacob.[L] *Selah*

7 Lift up your heads, you gates!
Rise up, ancient doors!
Then the King of glory will come in.

[A] **22:16** Some Hb mss, LXX, Syr; other Hb mss read *me; like a lion* [B] **22:17** Lit *they* [C] **22:20** Lit *my only one* [D] **22:21** Or *oxen you rescued me* [E] **22:25** Lit *him* [F] **23:3** Or *me in paths of righteousness* [G] **23:4** Or *the valley of the shadow of death* [H] **23:6** LXX, Sym, Syr, Tg, Vg, Jer; MT reads *will return to* [I] **23:6** Lit *LORD for length of days*; traditionally *LORD forever* [J] **24:4** Lit *not lifted up his soul to* [K] **24:5** Or *vindication* [L] **24:6** LXX; some Hb mss, Syr read *seek your face, God of Jacob*; some Hb mss read *seek your face, Jacob*

8 Who is this King of glory?
The LORD, strong and mighty,
the LORD, mighty in battle.
9 Lift up your heads, you gates!
Rise up, ancient doors!
Then the King of glory will come in.
10 Who is he, this King of glory?
The LORD of Armies,
he is the King of glory. *Selah*

DEPENDENCE ON THE LORD

25 *Of David.*
LORD, I appeal to you.[A]
2 My God, I trust in you.
Do not let me be disgraced;
do not let my enemies gloat over me.
3 No one who waits for you
will be disgraced;
those who act treacherously without cause
will be disgraced.

4 Make your ways known to me, LORD;
teach me your paths.
5 Guide me in your truth and teach me,
for you are the God of my salvation;
I wait for you all day long.
6 Remember, LORD, your compassion
and your faithful love,
for they have existed from antiquity.[B]
7 Do not remember the sins of my youth
or my acts of rebellion;
in keeping with your faithful love,
remember me
because of your goodness, LORD.

8 The LORD is good and upright;
therefore he shows sinners the way.
9 He leads the humble in what is right
and teaches them his way.
10 All the LORD's ways show faithful love
and truth
to those who keep his covenant and decrees.
11 LORD, for the sake of your name,
forgive my iniquity, for it is immense.

12 Who is this person who fears the LORD?
He will show him the way
he should choose.
13 He will live a good life,
and his descendants will inherit the land.[C]
14 The secret counsel of the LORD
is for those who fear him,
and he reveals his covenant to them.
15 My eyes are always on the LORD,
for he will pull my feet out of the net.

16 Turn to me and be gracious to me,
for I am alone and afflicted.
17 The distresses of my heart increase;[D]
bring me out of my sufferings.
18 Consider my affliction and trouble,
and forgive all my sins.
19 Consider my enemies;
they are numerous,
and they hate me violently.
20 Guard me and rescue me;
do not let me be disgraced,
for I take refuge in you.
21 May integrity and what is right
watch over me,
for I wait for you.

22 God, redeem Israel, from all
its distresses.

PRAYER FOR VINDICATION

26 *Of David.*
Vindicate me, LORD,
because I have lived with integrity
and have trusted in the LORD
without wavering.
2 Test me, LORD, and try me;
examine my heart and mind.
3 For your faithful love guides me,[E]
and I live by your truth.

4 I do not sit with the worthless
or associate with hypocrites.
5 I hate a crowd of evildoers,
and I do not sit with the wicked.
6 I wash my hands in innocence
and go around your altar, LORD,
7 raising my voice in thanksgiving
and telling about your wondrous works.

8 LORD, I love the house where you dwell,
the place where your glory resides.
9 Do not destroy me along with sinners,
or my life along with men of bloodshed
10 in whose hands are evil schemes
and whose right hands are filled
with bribes.

11 But I live with integrity;
redeem me and be gracious to me.
12 My foot stands on level ground;
I will bless the LORD in the assemblies.

[A] **25:1** Or *To you, LORD, I lift up my soul* [B] **25:6** Or *everlasting*
[C] **25:13** Or *earth* [D] **25:17** Or *Relieve the distresses of my heart*
[E] **26:3** Lit *love is in front of my eyes*

Valleys and Pastures: A Geographical Overview of Ancient Israel *by R. Dennis Cole*

The land contained within the classical borders from Dan to Beer-sheba and from the Mediterranean Sea to the Jordan River is a relatively small territory that covers an area of fewer than seventy-five hundred square miles. This land of great theological importance is just a little bigger than the state of New Jersey and much smaller than the great powers that surrounded it. Agriculturally only about 20 percent of Israel is arable land; about half is semiarid to arid.[1] Much of the most-arid land is rocky and hilly. The arable farmlands are located primarily along the coastal plains and the inland valleys—farmlands that were and are some of the most productive in the world. The descriptive phrase of Israel as the "least of the nations" (Dt 7:7, writer's translation) applied to its population, territory, and military might; Israel's strength, power, and source of blessing was God and his faithful love for his people.

LAND OF CONTRASTS

The territory of ancient Israel was positioned in the southern half of the land bridge that connected Africa and Asia, and between the regions of the ancient empires of Egypt to the southwest, the Hittites to the north, and the Assyrians and Babylonians to the east and northeast. The terrain to ancient Israel ranges from the tree-covered mountainous northern highlands of upper Galilee, Mount Carmel, and the Golan Heights to the barren rocky wilderness areas of the Dead Sea, Negev, and Arabah in the south. Along the Mediterranean coastal plains of Philistia, Sharon, and Acco are rolling sand dunes and lush farmlands occasionally cut by small streams such as the Lachish, Sorek, Yarkon, and Kishon. Most of these streams begin in the mountains of Judah, Samaria, and Galilee, bringing replenishing soils and nutrients to the valleys from the foothills (biblical Shephelah) to the inland coastal plains.

Israel's climate likewise is a study of contrasts from the well-watered regions of the north and west to the parched and rocky desert areas of the Dead Sea and the Negev. With a latitude parallel to the southern USA (Savannah, Georgia = Tel Aviv), the temperatures reflect these variations with summer highs ranging from the upper 80s and low 90s in the coastal northwest around Acco, to the 110 to 120-degree range around the Dead Sea to and the southern Negev. Rainfall variations also reflect the changing terrain, with extremely low annual amounts in the lower Negev and Dead Sea regions (less than three inches); the northern areas around Dan and Metulla receive up to forty inches.

Fields and cropland in northern Israel near Mount Hermon.

Most of the rainfall comes from November through April.

At the heart of the land's geological makeup is its limestone core of various hardness levels ranging from the strikingly hard chert and flint to the softer chalky limestone. The cavernous areas in the heart of the Judean, Samarian, and Galilean mountains contain large underground aquifers, which intermittently erupt into springs along the perimeters of the various valleys, even in the more deserted areas of the Dead Sea and Negev. Examples of these springs (names beginning with En- or Ein- both translate as "spring" or "spring of") include such famous regions as En-gedi (where David hid from Saul), to En-harod ("the spring of Harod," where God directed Gideon to choose his army), to Ein-feshkha (near Qumran at the Dead Sea).

LONGITUDINAL ZONES

Israel's geography and its environs divide into six distinctive longitudinal (north-south) zones, with one major diagonal valley, the Jezreel Valley, which separates the Galilee region in the north from the hills of Samaria. First, in the west, is the coastal plain along the Mediterranean Sea. The coastal plain consists of some sand dunes along the shorelines and rich farmlands inland. Elevations extend upward to three hundred feet or more. Traditionally this zone has been divided into three major sections: (1) the Acco plain in the north extending from the Lebanon border to the Mount Carmel ridge, which extends almost to the Mediterranean; (2) the Sharon plain, extending from Mount Carmel to the Yarkon River, near modern Tel Aviv; and (3) the Philistine plain, extending from the Yarkon southward to the northeast Sinai. The coastal plains' farmlands extend inland as little as two miles near Mount Carmel to as much as thirty miles in the southern Philistine plain. Flowing through these coastal plains are the rivers and streams such as the Sorek, Lachish, and Hadera, which typically have their origins in the hill country.

The second zone is the Shephelah, a term that describes the "foothills" or "lowlands" between the coastal plain and the mountains of Judah. This distinctive geological zone, with elevations reaching a thousand feet, is cut by several valleys. The valleys provided the strategic buffer between the Philistines and the tribes of Judah and Simeon. Cities such as Gezer in the Aijalon Valley, Timnah and Beth-shemesh in the Sorek Valley, Azekah and Shaaraim in the Elah Valley, and Lachish in the Lachish Valley, were often fortified for the protection of Judah's heartland, namely Jerusalem, Hebron, and other major cities.

East of the Shephelah, the third north-south zone is the central hill country, a ridge of mountains extending from north of Beer-sheba, in the south, to Mount Carmel and Mount Gilboa overlooking the Jezreel Valley. Elevations around Hebron and Mounts Ebal and Gerizim reach three thousand feet or more. North of the Jezreel Valley are the mountains of upper and lower Galilee, with elevations in upper Galilee reaching almost four thousand feet at Mount Merom. These mountain highlands form the watershed for

Overlooking the Aijalon Valley from the ruins at Gezer. On the right-center of the image are the remains of a Canaanite tower. It joins a wall, under the footbridge; dated to the time of the patriarchs.

Looking westward from atop the ruins of Jericho. Beyond the greenery is the Jordan Valley.

the "early" (late October–December) and "late" (January–March) rains that the Bible describes.

Deep beneath the surface in the honey-combed limestone of the mountains are huge natural aquifers, which erupt into springs along the flanks of the valleys and flow through the Shephelah and into the coastal plains. The rich farmlands of the valleys such as the Sorek functioned as the "breadbasket" for the kingdom of Judah in the Old Testament era. Capital cities such as Jerusalem of Judah and Samaria in the north were located strategically in the central mountains. The pasturage and still waters described in Psalm 23 would be typically located in these hills and the valleys of the Shephelah. Rainfall amounts here were at their peak for growing grasses and other forage plants, and here springs would puddle, providing still waters for the timid sheep.

East of the peak in the central mountains was the fourth zone, the wilderness of Judah and Samaria. Here the rainfall amounts drop off dramatically as one heads eastward toward the deep geological rift of the Jordan Valley, our fifth longitudinal zone. Average annual rainfall in Jerusalem is around twenty-five inches. Fifteen miles east in Jericho, this drops to about five inches or less. Near the southern end of the Dead Sea, the amount is two inches or less. The arid nature of the wilderness and valley zones decrease as one heads northward up the Jordan Valley from the Dead Sea. The Jordan Valley is part of one of the deepest geological rifts in the earth's surface, reaching 1,380 feet below mean sea level today. Due to heavy use of fresh-water irrigation by persons on both sides of the Jordan, the level of the Dead Sea has been dropping steadily, about one hundred feet in the past fifty years.[2] The desert valley south of the Dead Sea, the Arabah, gradually rises to more than one thousand feet above sea level before descending to the Red Sea finger of the Gulf of Aqaba (Eilat). West of the Arabah is the Negev ("southern") region, which extends south of the Beer-sheba Valley and into the Sinai.

East of the Jordan Valley is the sixth zone, the Transjordan (or Eastern) Plateau, with elevations reaching to around four thousand feet, bounded on the north by Mount Hermon (elev. ca 9,100 feet) and reaching southward through what was ancient Edom. The aquifers of Mount Hermon, which erupt into numerous springs such as those at Caesarea Philippi, Dan, and Ijon, form the upper Jordan River in the Huleh Basin. From Mount Hermon and through the Golan Heights region east of the Huleh Basin are the volcanically enriched soils that provided lush farming opportunities throughout ancient and into modern times. South of the Golan, which is separated from Gilead by the Yarmuk River, are the rich soils and mountain highlands of the ancient territories of the Ammonites and Moabites; to the south are the more desertlike regions of the Edomites. ✣

---

[1] *Israel's Agriculture* (Tel Aviv: Israel Export & International Cooperation Institute, n.d.), 8. [2] Stephanie Pappas, "Could the Dead Sea Completely Vanish?" *LiveScience*, 6 December 2011, www.livescience.com/17324-dead-sea-completely-vanish.html.

Crusader ruins at Acco in northern Israel. During the time of the conquest, Acco was tribal territory allotted to Asher. Yet "Asher failed to drive out the residents of Acco" and some other cities (Jdg 1:31).

MY STRONGHOLD

27 *Of David.*

The LORD is my light and my salvation —
whom should I fear?
The LORD is the stronghold of my life —
whom should I dread?
2 When evildoers came against me to devour
my flesh,
my foes and my enemies stumbled and fell.
3 Though an army deploys against me,
my heart will not be afraid;
though a war breaks out against me,
I will still be confident.

4 I have asked one thing from the LORD;
it is what I desire:
to dwell in the house of the LORD
all the days of my life,
gazing on the beauty of the LORD
and seeking him in his temple.
5 For he will conceal me in his shelter
in the day of adversity;
he will hide me under the cover of his tent;
he will set me high on a rock.
6 Then my head will be high
above my enemies around me;
I will offer sacrifices in his tent with shouts
of joy.
I will sing and make music to the LORD.

7 LORD, hear my voice when I call;
be gracious to me and answer me.
8 My heart says this about you:
"Seek[A] his face."
LORD, I will seek your face.
9 Do not hide your face from me;
do not turn your servant away in anger.
You have been my helper;
do not leave me or abandon me,
God of my salvation.
10 Even if my father and mother abandon me,
the LORD cares for me.

11 Because of my adversaries,
show me your way, LORD,
and lead me on a level path.
12 Do not give me over to the will of my foes,
for false witnesses rise up against me,
breathing violence.

13 I am certain that I will see the LORD's goodness
in the land of the living.
14 Wait for the LORD;
be strong, and let your heart be courageous.
Wait for the LORD.

MY STRENGTH

28 *Of David.*

LORD, I call to you;
my rock, do not be deaf to me.
If you remain silent to me,
I will be like those going down to the Pit.
2 Listen to the sound of my pleading
when I cry to you for help,
when I lift up my hands
toward your holy sanctuary.

3 Do not drag me away with the wicked,
with the evildoers,
who speak in friendly ways
with their neighbors
while malice is in their hearts.
4 Repay them according to what
they have done —
according to the evil of their deeds.
Repay them according to the work
of their hands;
give them back what they deserve.
5 Because they do not consider
what the LORD has done
or the work of his hands,
he will tear them down and not rebuild them.

6 Blessed be the LORD,
for he has heard the sound of my pleading.
7 The LORD is my strength and my shield;
my heart trusts in him, and I am helped.
Therefore my heart celebrates,
and I give thanks to him with my song.

8 The LORD is the strength of his people;[B]
he is a stronghold of salvation
for his anointed.
9 Save your people, bless your possession,
shepherd them, and carry them forever.

THE VOICE OF THE LORD

29 *A psalm of David.*

Ascribe to the LORD, you heavenly beings,[C]
ascribe to the LORD glory and strength.
2 Ascribe to the LORD the glory due his name;
worship the LORD
in the splendor of his holiness.[D]

3 The voice of the LORD is above the waters.
The God of glory thunders —
the LORD, above the vast water,

[A] **27:8** The command is pl in Hb [B] **28:8** Some Hb mss, LXX, Syr; other Hb mss read *strength for them* [C] **29:1** Or *you sons of gods,* or *you sons of mighty ones* [D] **29:2** Or *in holy attire,* or *in holy appearance*

4 the voice of the LORD in power,
the voice of the LORD in splendor.
5 The voice of the LORD breaks the cedars;
the LORD shatters the cedars of Lebanon.
6 He makes Lebanon skip like a calf,
and Sirion, like a young wild ox.
7 The voice of the LORD flashes
flames of fire.
8 The voice of the LORD shakes
the wilderness;
the LORD shakes the wilderness of Kadesh.
9 The voice of the LORD makes the deer
give birth[A]
and strips the woodlands bare.

In his temple all cry, "Glory!"

10 The LORD sits enthroned over the flood;
the LORD sits enthroned, King forever.
11 The LORD gives his people strength;
the LORD blesses his people with peace.

JOY IN THE MORNING

30 *A psalm; a dedication song for the house. Of David.*

1 I will exalt you, LORD,
because you have lifted me up
and have not allowed my enemies
to triumph over me.
2 LORD my God,
I cried to you for help, and you healed me.
3 LORD, you brought me up from Sheol;
you spared me from among those
going down[B] to the Pit.

4 Sing to the LORD, you his faithful ones,
and praise his holy name.
5 For his anger lasts only a moment,
but his favor, a lifetime.
Weeping may stay overnight,
but there is joy in the morning.

6 When I was secure, I said,
"I will never be shaken."
7 LORD, when you showed your favor,
you made me stand like a strong mountain;
when you hid your face, I was terrified.
8 LORD, I called to you;
I sought favor from my Lord:
9 "What gain is there in my death,
if I go down to the Pit?
Will the dust praise you?
Will it proclaim your truth?
10 LORD, listen and be gracious to me;
LORD, be my helper."
11 You turned my lament into dancing;
you removed my sackcloth
and clothed me with gladness,
12 so that I can sing to you and not be silent.
LORD my God, I will praise you forever.

A PLEA FOR PROTECTION

31 *For the choir director. A psalm of David.*

LORD, I seek refuge in you;
let me never be disgraced.
Save me by your righteousness.
2 Listen closely to me; rescue me quickly.
Be a rock of refuge for me,
a mountain fortress to save me.
3 For you are my rock and my fortress;
you lead and guide me
for your name's sake.
4 You will free me from the net
that is secretly set for me,
for you are my refuge.
5 Into your hand I entrust my spirit;
you have redeemed me,[C] LORD, God of truth.

6 I[D] hate those who are devoted
to worthless idols,
but I trust in the LORD.
7 I will rejoice and be glad in your faithful love
because you have seen my affliction.
You know the troubles of my soul
8 and have not handed me over to the enemy.
You have set my feet in a spacious place.

9 Be gracious to me, LORD,
because I am in distress;
my eyes are worn out from frustration —
my whole being[E] as well.
10 Indeed, my life is consumed with grief
and my years with groaning;
my strength has failed
because of my iniquity,[F]
and my bones waste away.
11 I am ridiculed by all my adversaries
and even by my neighbors.
I am dreaded by my acquaintances;
those who see me in the street run from me.
12 I am forgotten: gone from memory
like a dead person — like broken pottery.
13 I have heard the gossip of many;
terror is on every side.
When they conspired against me,
they plotted to take my life.

[A] **29:9** Or *the oaks shake* [B] **30:3** Some Hb mss, LXX, Theod, Orig, Syr; other Hb mss, Aq, Sym, Tg, Jer read *from going down* [C] **31:5** Or *spirit. Redeem me* [D] **31:6** One Hb ms, LXX, Syr, Vg, Jer read *You* [E] **31:9** Lit *my soul and my belly* [F] **31:10** LXX, Syr, Sym read *affliction*

14 But I trust in you, LORD;
I say, "You are my God."
15 The course of my life is in your power;
rescue me from the power of my enemies
and from my persecutors.
16 Make your face shine on your servant;
save me by your faithful love.
17 LORD, do not let me be disgraced when I call
on you.
Let the wicked be disgraced;
let them be quiet[A,B] in Sheol.
18 Let lying lips
that arrogantly speak against the righteous
in proud contempt be silenced.

19 How great is your goodness,
which you have stored up for those
who fear you.
In the presence of everyone[C] you have acted
for those who take refuge in you.
20 You hide them in the protection
of your presence;
you conceal them in a shelter
from human schemes,
from quarrelsome tongues.
21 Blessed be the LORD,
for he has wondrously shown his faithful love
to me
in a city under siege.
22 In my alarm I said,
"I am cut off from your sight."
But you heard the sound of my pleading
when I cried to you for help.

23 Love the LORD, all his faithful ones.
The LORD protects the loyal,
but fully repays the arrogant.
24 Be strong, and let your heart be courageous,
all you who put your hope in the LORD.

THE JOY OF FORGIVENESS

32 *Of David. A* Maskil.
How joyful is the one
whose transgression is forgiven,
whose sin is covered!
2 How joyful is a person whom
the LORD does not charge with iniquity
and in whose spirit is no deceit!

3 When I kept silent, my bones became brittle
from my groaning all day long.
4 For day and night your hand was heavy
on me;
my strength was drained[D]
as in the summer's heat. *Selah*
5 Then I acknowledged my sin to you
and did not conceal my iniquity.
I said, "I will confess my transgressions
to the LORD,"
and you forgave the guilt of my sin. *Selah*

6 Therefore let everyone who is faithful
pray to you immediately.[E]
When great floodwaters come,
they will not reach him.
7 You are my hiding place;
you protect me from trouble.
You surround me with joyful shouts
of deliverance. *Selah*

8 I will instruct you and show you the way to go;
with my eye on you, I will give counsel.
9 Do not be like a horse or mule,
without understanding,
that must be controlled with bit and bridle
or else it will not come near you.

10 Many pains come to the wicked,
but the one who trusts in the LORD
will have faithful love surrounding him.
11 Be glad in the LORD and rejoice,
you righteous ones;
shout for joy,
all you upright in heart.

PRAISE TO THE CREATOR

33 Rejoice in the LORD, you righteous ones;
praise from the upright is beautiful.
2 Praise the LORD with the lyre;
make music to him with a ten-stringed harp.
3 Sing a new song to him;
play skillfully on the strings,
with a joyful shout.

4 For the word of the LORD is right,
and all his work is trustworthy.
5 He loves righteousness and justice;
the earth is full of the LORD's unfailing love.

6 The heavens were made by the word
of the LORD,
and all the stars, by the breath of his mouth.
7 He gathers the water of the sea into a heap;[F]
he puts the depths into storehouses.
8 Let the whole earth fear the LORD;
let all the inhabitants of the world
stand in awe of him.

[A] **31:17** LXX reads *brought down* [B] **31:17** Or *them wail* [C] **31:19** Or *of the descendants of Adam* [D] **32:4** Hb obscure [E] **32:6** Lit *you at a time of finding* [F] **33:7** LXX, Tg, Syr, Vg, Jer read *sea as in a bottle*

9 For he spoke, and it came into being;
he commanded, and it came into existence.

10 The LORD frustrates the counsel
of the nations;
he thwarts the plans of the peoples.
11 The counsel of the LORD stands forever,
the plans of his heart from generation
to generation.
12 Happy is the nation whose God is the LORD —
the people he has chosen to be
his own possession!

13 The LORD looks down from heaven;
he observes everyone.
14 He gazes on all the inhabitants of the earth
from his dwelling place.
15 He forms the hearts of them all;
he considers all their works.
16 A king is not saved by a large army;
a warrior will not be rescued
by great strength.
17 The horse is a false hope for safety;
it provides no escape by its great power.

18 But look, the LORD keeps his eye on those
who fear him —
those who depend on his faithful love
19 to rescue them from death
and to keep them alive in famine.

20 We wait for the LORD;
he is our help and shield.
21 For our hearts rejoice in him
because we trust in his holy name.
22 May your faithful love rest on us, LORD,
for we put our hope in you.

THE LORD DELIVERS THE RIGHTEOUS

34 *Concerning David, when he pretended to be insane in the presence of Abimelech, who drove him out, and he departed.*

1 I will bless the LORD at all times;
his praise will always be on my lips.
2 I will boast in the LORD;
the humble will hear and be glad.
3 Proclaim the LORD's greatness with me;
let us exalt his name together.

4 I sought the LORD, and he answered me
and rescued me from all my fears.
5 Those who look to him are[A] radiant with joy;
their faces will never be ashamed.
6 This poor man cried, and the LORD heard him
and saved him from all his troubles.
7 The angel of the LORD encamps
around those who fear him, and rescues them.

8 Taste and see that the LORD is good.
How happy is the person who takes refuge
in him!
9 You who are his holy ones, fear the LORD,
for those who fear him lack nothing.
10 Young lions[B] lack food and go hungry,
but those who seek the LORD
will not lack any good thing.

11 Come, children, listen to me;
I will teach you the fear of the LORD.
12 Who is someone who desires life,
loving a long life to enjoy what is good?
13 Keep your tongue from evil
and your lips from deceitful speech.
14 Turn away from evil and do what is good;
seek peace and pursue it.

15 The eyes of the LORD are on the righteous,
and his ears are open to their cry for help.
16 The face of the LORD is set
against those who do what is evil,
to remove[C] all memory of them
from the earth.
17 The righteous[D] cry out, and the LORD hears,
and rescues them from all their troubles.
18 The LORD is near the brokenhearted;
he saves those crushed in spirit.

19 One who is righteous has many adversities,
but the LORD rescues him from them all.
20 He protects all his bones;
not one of them is broken.
21 Evil brings death to the wicked,
and those who hate the righteous
will be punished.
22 The LORD redeems the life of his servants,
and all who take refuge in him will not
be punished.

PRAYER FOR VICTORY

35 *Of David.*
Oppose my opponents, LORD;
fight those who fight me.
2 Take your shields — large and small —
and come to my aid.
3 Draw the spear and javelin
against my pursuers,
and assure me, "I am your deliverance."

[A] **34:5** Some Hb mss, LXX, Aq, Syr, Jer read *Look to him and be* [B] **34:10** LXX, Syr, Vg read *The rich* [C] **34:16** Or *cut off* [D] **34:17** Lit *They*

Our Forgiving God: Unique among Ancient Religions?

by Blakeley Winslow

Model of a scene from the Egyptian Book of the Dead: Isty is brought before the gods and goddesses who will judge her. To prove her virtue, Isty recites the Negative Confession. Instead of asking for forgiveness for her sins, she'll tell the gods all the terrible things she did not do.

All religions must address the need for restitution between God and humanity when sin occurs. But as Psalm 32 highlights, the ancient Jews envisioned their God's forgiving nature in a markedly different manner from their Near Eastern peers. Its message mirrors one of the distinctive and revolutionary concepts of ancient Judaism: God desires a personal relationship with his children.

IN OTHER RELIGIONS

Judaism and other ancient Near Eastern religions professed profoundly different worldviews. The foundational teaching that "Yahweh is one" clearly demarcated Judaism from the elaborate polytheistic hierarchies of the Egyptians, Babylonians, Assyrians, Philistines, and Canaanites. Yahweh thus related to his people on a unique ethical plane, to which other ancient Near Eastern belief systems offer no clear parallel. The ancient Israelites had God alone, and with him alone did they contend when they sinned. By contrast, when these other ancient peoples sought forgiveness, they had to contend with a whole host of deities.

In fact, many of ancient Israel's contemporaries honored their gods not so much for the particular deity's own essential nature but for whatever prosperity or wealth he or she could bestow in return. Forgiveness often entailed regaining the gods' favor rather than truly repenting from wrongdoing. Ancient Egyptians, for example, believed their gods showed mercy because the people provided care for the deities' likenesses. Egyptians believed their gods' "existence was ultimately dependent upon the existence of mortals."[1] In contrast, the Old Testament prophets constantly stressed that people should worship God for his inherent nature and not merely for a material blessing he might grant. Furthermore, Yahweh demanded ethical living. Genuine worship and ethical living were far more important to him than sacrifices (Am 5:21–24). Egyptian prayers, conversely, often took the form of spiritual bartering in which priests would make offerings to the gods in exchange for tangible favors.[2] As a result, Egyptians were usually more interested either in gaining material treasures from the gods or avoiding divine punishment, rather than receiving the purely spiritual gifts of forgiveness and restoration, for which David longed in Psalm 32.

Turning to the religious customs of the Canaanites, we find further contrasts. Like their Jewish neighbors, Canaanites at times employed a system of animal sacrifices to atone for sin. But their penitential practices also included the occasional child sacrifice, something Yahweh abhorred and Scripture expressly forbade (Lv 18:21). The Canaanites made their offerings both in hopes of gaining forgiveness and of obtaining material boons including good harvests and fortune in war. The Jews' emphasis on being restored in a relationship with their God, either on a national or personal level, was not a focus for the Canaanites. The Canaanites possessed a cyclical belief system, inherently tied to the changing seasons and unexplainable occurrences in nature, while the Jews worshiped a profoundly historical God who stood above nature and over all human affairs.

Other ancient Mesopotamian cultures, including the Sumerians and the Babylonians, never engaged in anything like the true atoning sacrifices to gain divine forgiveness that the Old Testament describes frequently. Other ancient religions employed other methods for dealing with sin,[3] including rituals similar to exorcisms, intended solely to alleviate divine anger and requiring neither confession of wrongdoing nor repentance.

PSALM 32

Turning to Psalm 32, we find the Jewish religion teaches that the soul-cleansing forgiveness God offers requires only a true and heartfelt spirit of repentance. Deceiving God about one's sinfulness will only cause further grief. Confession of sin, before both God and others whom we might have wronged, is a way of life that must be practiced daily. Old Testament law does not represent a mere list of obligations that persons should meet in order to appease God. Instead, it involves a comprehensive code of ethical teachings, which address all possible dimensions of life.[4] Thus the ancient Jews engaged the question of sin and forgiveness in a much more thorough and systematic way than did any of their peers.

While the Old Testament prophets always featured as a central theme fidelity to the law, they were equally concerned that an inward spirit of repentance accompanied the outward rituals related to seeking forgiveness.[5] Judaism established a revolutionary concept of a personal accountability to God. ✣

Gypsum copy of an eighth-century relief with an inscription in Hittite hieroglyphics portraying the Hittite King Warpalawas Urpalla (right) paying homage to a vegetation god. The Hittites believed social sins, such as murder or theft, could be cleansed by participating in religious rituals, but the guilty party would still receive punishment.

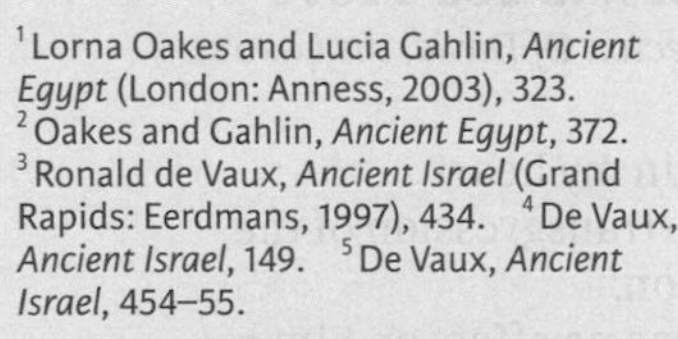

[1] Lorna Oakes and Lucia Gahlin, *Ancient Egypt* (London: Anness, 2003), 323.
[2] Oakes and Gahlin, *Ancient Egypt*, 372.
[3] Ronald de Vaux, *Ancient Israel* (Grand Rapids: Eerdmans, 1997), 434. [4] De Vaux, *Ancient Israel*, 149. [5] De Vaux, *Ancient Israel*, 454–55.

On Crete, the temple of Egyptian Gods at Gortyn was one of five temples dedicated to pagan gods on the island. This one was dedicated to the Egyptian deities: Isis, Serapis, and Hermes-Anubis. The temple had a space where worshipers went through purification rites; small niches in the walls held statues of the gods. Egyptian worship included honoring the deities in exchange for the gods' good favor.

4 Let those who intend to take my life
be disgraced and humiliated;
let those who plan to harm me
be turned back and ashamed.
5 Let them be like chaff in the wind,
with the angel of the LORD driving them away.
6 Let their way be dark and slippery,
with the angel of the LORD pursuing them.
7 They hid their net for me without cause;
they dug a pit for me without cause.
8 Let ruin come on him unexpectedly,
and let the net that he hid ensnare him;
let him fall into it — to his ruin.

9 Then I will rejoice in the LORD;
I will delight in his deliverance.
10 All my bones will say,
"LORD, who is like you,
rescuing the poor from one too strong for him,
the poor or the needy from one
who robs him?"

11 Malicious witnesses come forward;
they question me about things I do not know.
12 They repay me evil for good,
making me desolate.
13 Yet when they were sick,
my clothing was sackcloth;
I humbled myself with fasting,
and my prayer was genuine.[A]
14 I went about mourning as if for my friend
or brother;
I was bowed down with grief,
like one mourning for a mother.
15 But when I stumbled, they gathered in glee;
they gathered against me.
Assailants I did not know
tore at me and did not stop.
16 With godless mockery[B]
they gnashed their teeth at me.

17 Lord, how long will you look on?
Rescue me from their ravages;
rescue my precious life from the young lions.
18 I will praise you in the great assembly;
I will exalt you among many people.
19 Do not let my deceitful enemies rejoice over me;
do not let those who hate me without cause
wink at me maliciously.
20 For they do not speak in friendly ways,
but contrive fraudulent schemes[C]
against those who live peacefully in the land.
21 They open their mouths wide against me
and say,
"Aha, aha! We saw it!"[D]
22 You saw it, LORD; do not be silent.
Lord, do not be far from me.
23 Wake up and rise to my defense,
to my cause, my God and my Lord!
24 Vindicate me, LORD my God,
in keeping with your righteousness,
and do not let them rejoice over me.
25 Do not let them say in their hearts,
"Aha! Just what we wanted."
Do not let them say,
"We have swallowed him up!"
26 Let those who rejoice at my misfortune
be disgraced and humiliated;
let those who exalt themselves over me
be clothed with shame and reproach.

27 Let those who want my vindication
shout for joy and be glad;
let them continually say,
"The LORD be exalted.
He takes pleasure in his servant's well-being."
28 And my tongue will proclaim
your righteousness,
your praise all day long.

HUMAN WICKEDNESS AND GOD'S LOVE

36 *For the choir director. Of David, the LORD's servant.*

1 An oracle within my heart
concerning the transgression of the
wicked person:
Dread of God has no effect on him.[E]
2 For with his flattering opinion of himself,
he does not discover and hate
his iniquity.
3 The words from his mouth are malicious
and deceptive;
he has stopped acting wisely
and doing good.
4 Even on his bed he makes malicious plans.
He sets himself on a path that is not good,
and he does not reject evil.

5 LORD, your faithful love reaches to heaven,
your faithfulness to the clouds.
6 Your righteousness is
like the highest mountains,
your judgments like the deepest sea.
LORD, you preserve people and animals.
7 How priceless your faithful love is, God!
People take refuge in the shadow
of your wings.

[A] **35:13** Lit *prayer returned to my chest* [B] **35:16** Hb obscure
[C] **35:20** Lit *but devise fraudulent words* [D] **35:21** Lit *Our eyes saw!*
[E] **36:1** Lit *There is no dread of God in front of his eyes*

8 They are filled from the abundance
of your house.
You let them drink from
your refreshing stream.
9 For the wellspring of life is with you.
By means of your light we see light.

10 Spread your faithful love over those
who know you,
and your righteousness over the upright
in heart.
11 Do not let the foot of the arrogant
come near me
or the hand of the wicked drive me away.
12 There! The evildoers have fallen.
They have been thrown down and cannot rise.

INSTRUCTION IN WISDOM

37 *Of David.*
Do not be agitated by evildoers;
do not envy those who do wrong.
2 For they wither quickly like grass
and wilt like tender green plants.

3 Trust in the LORD and do what is good;
dwell in the land and live securely.[A]
4 Take delight in the LORD,
and he will give you your heart's desires.

5 Commit your way to the LORD;
trust in him, and he will act,
6 making your righteousness shine like the dawn,
your justice like the noonday.

7 Be silent before the LORD and wait expectantly
for him;
do not be agitated by one who prospers
in his way,
by the person who carries out evil plans.

8 Refrain from anger and give up your rage;
do not be agitated — it can only bring harm.
9 For evildoers will be destroyed,
but those who put their hope in the LORD
will inherit the land.

10 A little while, and the wicked person will be
no more;
though you look for him, he will not be there.
11 But the humble will inherit the land
and will enjoy abundant prosperity.

12 The wicked person schemes
against the righteous
and gnashes his teeth at him.
13 The Lord laughs at him
because he sees that his day is coming.

14 The wicked have drawn the sword and strung
the[B] bow
to bring down the poor and needy
and to slaughter those whose way is upright.
15 Their swords will enter their own hearts,
and their bows will be broken.

16 The little that the righteous person has is better
than the abundance of many wicked people.
17 For the arms of the wicked will be broken,
but the LORD supports the righteous.

18 The LORD watches over the blameless
all their days,
and their inheritance will last forever.
19 They will not be disgraced in times of adversity;
they will be satisfied in days of hunger.

20 But the wicked will perish;
the LORD's enemies, like the glory
of the pastures,
will fade away —
they will fade away like smoke.

21 The wicked person borrows
and does not repay,
but the righteous one is gracious and giving.
22 Those who are blessed by the LORD will inherit
the land,
but those cursed by him will be destroyed.

23 A person's steps are established by the LORD,
and he takes pleasure in his way.
24 Though he falls, he will not be overwhelmed,
because the LORD supports him with his hand.

25 I have been young and now I am old,
yet I have not seen the righteous abandoned
or his children begging for bread.
26 He is always generous, always lending,
and his children are a blessing.

27 Turn away from evil, do what is good,
and settle permanently.
28 For the LORD loves justice
and will not abandon his faithful ones.
They are kept safe forever,
but the children of the wicked
will be destroyed.

[A] **37:3** Or *and cultivate faithfulness*, or *and befriend faithfulness*
[B] **37:14** Lit *their*

29 The righteous will inherit the land
and dwell in it permanently.

30 The mouth of the righteous utters wisdom;
his tongue speaks what is just.
31 The instruction of his God is in his heart;
his steps do not falter.

32 The wicked one lies in wait for the righteous
and intends to kill him;
33 the LORD will not leave him
in the power of the wicked one
or allow him to be condemned
when he is judged.

34 Wait for the LORD and keep his way,
and he will exalt you to inherit the land.
You will watch when the wicked
are destroyed.

35 I have seen a wicked, violent person
well-rooted,[A] like a flourishing native tree.
36 Then I[B] passed by and noticed he was gone;
I searched for him, but he could not be found.

37 Watch the blameless and observe the upright,
for the person of peace will have a future.[C]
38 But transgressors will all be eliminated;
the future of the wicked will be destroyed.

39 The salvation of the righteous is
from the LORD,
their refuge in a time of distress.
40 The LORD helps and delivers them;
he will deliver them from the wicked
and will save them
because they take refuge in him.

PRAYER OF A SUFFERING SINNER

38 *A psalm of David to bring remembrance.*

LORD, do not punish me in your anger
or discipline me in your wrath.
2 For your arrows have sunk into me,
and your hand has pressed down on me.

3 There is no soundness in my body
because of your indignation;
there is no health[D] in my bones
because of my sin.
4 For my iniquities have flooded over my head;
they are a burden too heavy for me to bear.
5 My wounds are foul and festering
because of my foolishness.
6 I am bent over and brought very low;
all day long I go around in mourning.
7 For my insides are full of burning pain,
and there is no soundness in my body.
8 I am faint and severely crushed;
I groan because of the anguish of my heart.

9 Lord, my every desire is in front of you;
my sighing is not hidden from you.
10 My heart races, my strength leaves me,
and even the light of my eyes has faded.[E]
11 My loved ones and friends stand back
from my affliction,
and my relatives stand at a distance.
12 Those who intend to kill me set traps,
and those who want to harm me threaten
to destroy me;
they plot treachery all day long.

13 I am like a deaf person; I do not hear.
I am like a speechless person
who does not open his mouth.
14 I am like a man who does not hear
and has no arguments in his mouth.
15 For I put my hope in you, LORD;
you will answer me, my Lord, my God.
16 For I said, "Don't let them rejoice over me —
those who are arrogant toward me
when I stumble."
17 For I am about to fall,
and my pain is constantly with me.
18 So I confess my iniquity;
I am anxious because of my sin.
19 But my enemies are vigorous and powerful;[F]
many hate me for no reason.
20 Those who repay evil for good
attack me for pursuing good.

21 LORD, do not abandon me;
my God, do not be far from me.
22 Hurry to help me,
my Lord, my salvation.

THE FLEETING NATURE OF LIFE

39 *For the choir director, for Jeduthun. A psalm of David.*

1 I said, "I will guard my ways
so that I may not sin with my tongue;
I will guard my mouth with a muzzle
as long as the wicked are in my presence."
2 I was speechless and quiet;
I kept silent, even from speaking good,
and my pain intensified.

[A] **37:35** Hb obscure [B] **37:36** LXX, Syr, Vg, Jer; MT reads *he* [C] **37:37** Or *posterity*, also in v. 38 [D] **38:3** Hb *shalom* [E] **38:10** Or *and the light of my eyes — even that is not with me* [F] **38:19** Or *numerous*

3 My heart grew hot within me;
as I mused, a fire burned.
I spoke with my tongue:
4 "LORD, make me aware of my end
and the number of my days
so that I will know how short-lived I am.
5 In fact, you have made my days just
inches long,
and my life span is as nothing to you.
Yes, every human being stands as
only a vapor. *Selah*
6 Yes, a person goes about
like a mere shadow.
Indeed, they rush around in vain,
gathering possessions
without knowing who will get them.

7 "Now, Lord, what do I wait for?
My hope is in you.
8 Rescue me from all my transgressions;
do not make me the taunt of fools.
9 I am speechless; I do not open my mouth
because of what you have done.
10 Remove your torment from me.
Because of the force of your hand I am
finished.
11 You discipline a person with punishment
for iniquity,
consuming like a moth what is precious
to him;
yes, every human being is only
a vapor. *Selah*

12 "Hear my prayer, LORD,
and listen to my cry for help;
do not be silent at my tears.
For I am here with you as an alien,
a temporary resident like all my ancestors.
13 Turn your angry gaze from me
so that I may be cheered up
before I die and am gone."

THANKSGIVING AND A CRY FOR HELP

40 *For the choir director. A psalm of David.*

I waited patiently for the LORD,
and he turned to me and heard my cry
for help.
2 He brought me up from a desolate[A] pit,
out of the muddy clay,
and set my feet on a rock,
making my steps secure.
3 He put a new song in my mouth,
a hymn of praise to our God.
Many will see and fear,
and they will trust in the LORD.

4 How happy is anyone
who has put his trust in the LORD
and has not turned to the proud
or to those who run after lies!
5 LORD my God, you have done many things —
your wondrous works and your plans for us;
none can compare with you.
If I were to report and speak of them,
they are more than can be told.

6 You do not delight in sacrifice and offering;
you open my ears to listen.[B]
You do not ask for a whole burnt offering
or a sin offering.
7 Then I said, "See, I have come;
in the scroll it is written about me.
8 I delight to do your will, my God,
and your instruction is deep within me."

9 I proclaim righteousness
in the great assembly;
see, I do not keep my mouth closed[C] —
as you know, LORD.
10 I did not hide your righteousness in my heart;
I spoke about your faithfulness and salvation;
I did not conceal your constant love and truth
from the great assembly.

11 LORD, you do not[D] withhold your compassion
from me.
Your constant love and truth will always
guard me.
12 For troubles without number
have surrounded me;
my iniquities have overtaken me; I am unable
to see.
They are more than the hairs of my head,
and my courage leaves me.
13 LORD, be pleased to rescue me;
hurry to help me, LORD.

14 Let those who intend to take my life
be disgraced and confounded.
Let those who wish me harm
be turned back and humiliated.
15 Let those who say to me, "Aha, aha!"
be appalled because of their shame.

16 Let all who seek you rejoice and be glad in you;
let those who love your salvation
continually say,
"The LORD is great!"

[A] **40:2** Or *watery* [B] **40:6** Lit *you hollow out ears for me* [C] **40:9** Lit *not restrain my lips* [D] **40:11** Or *LORD, do not*

17 I am oppressed and needy;
may the Lord think of me.
You are my helper and my deliverer;
my God, do not delay.

VICTORY IN SPITE OF BETRAYAL

41 *For the choir director. A psalm of David.*
Happy is one who is considerate of the poor;
the LORD will save him in a day of adversity.
2 The LORD will keep him and preserve him;
he will be blessed in the land.
You will not give him over to the desire
of his enemies.
3 The LORD will sustain him on his sickbed;
you will heal him on the bed where he lies.

4 I said, "LORD, be gracious to me;
heal me, for I have sinned against you."
5 My enemies speak maliciously about me:
"When will he die and be forgotten?"
6 When one of them comes to visit,
he speaks deceitfully;
he stores up evil in his heart;
he goes out and talks.
7 All who hate me whisper together about me;
they plan to harm me.
8 "Something awful has overwhelmed him,[A]
and he won't rise again from where he lies!"
9 Even my friend[B] in whom I trusted,
one who ate my bread,
has raised his heel against me.

10 But you, LORD, be gracious to me
and raise me up;
then I will repay them.
11 By this I know that you delight in me:
my enemy does not shout in triumph over me.
12 You supported me because of my integrity
and set me in your presence forever.

13 Blessed be the LORD God of Israel,
from everlasting to everlasting.
Amen and amen.

BOOK II (Psalms 42–72)

LONGING FOR GOD

42 *For the choir director. A* Maskil *of the sons of Korah.*
1 As a deer longs for flowing streams,
so I long for you, God.
2 I thirst for God, the living God.
When can I come and appear before God?
3 My tears have been my food day and night,
while all day long people say to me,
"Where is your God?"
4 I remember this as I pour out my heart:
how I walked with many,
leading the festive procession to the house
of God,
with joyful and thankful shouts.

5 Why, my soul, are you so dejected?
Why are you in such turmoil?
Put your hope in God, for I will still praise him,
my Savior and my God.
6 I[C] am deeply depressed;
therefore I remember you from the land
of Jordan
and the peaks of Hermon, from Mount Mizar.
7 Deep calls to deep in the roar
of your waterfalls;
all your breakers and your billows have swept
over me.
8 The LORD will send his faithful love by day;
his song will be with me in the night —
a prayer to the God of my life.

9 I will say to God, my rock,
"Why have you forgotten me?
Why must I go about in sorrow
because of the enemy's oppression?"
10 My adversaries taunt me,
as if crushing my bones,
while all day long they say to me,
"Where is your God?"
11 Why, my soul, are you so dejected?
Why are you in such turmoil?
Put your hope in God, for I will still praise him,
my Savior and my God.

43[D] Vindicate me, God, and champion my cause
against an unfaithful nation;
rescue me from the deceitful
and unjust person.
2 For you are the God of my refuge.
Why have you rejected me?
Why must I go about in sorrow
because of the enemy's oppression?

3 Send your light and your truth; let them lead me.
Let them bring me to your holy mountain,
to your dwelling place.
4 Then I will come to the altar of God,
to God, my greatest joy.
I will praise you with the lyre,
God, my God.

[A] **41:8** Lit *"A thing of worthlessness has been poured into him*
[B] **41:9** Lit *Even a man of my peace* [C] **42:5–6** Some Hb mss, LXX, Syr; other Hb mss read *him, the salvation of his presence.* [6] *My God, I*
[D] **43** Many Hb mss connect Pss 42 and 43

5 Why, my soul, are you so dejected?
Why are you in such turmoil?
Put your hope in God, for I will still praise him,
my Savior and my God.

ISRAEL'S COMPLAINT

44 *For the choir director. A* Maskil *of the sons of Korah.*

1 God, we have heard with our ears —
our ancestors have told us —
the work you accomplished in their days,
in days long ago:
2 In order to plant them,
you displaced the nations by your hand;
in order to settle them,
you brought disaster on the peoples.
3 For they did not take the land
by their sword —
their arm did not bring them victory —
but by your right hand, your arm,
and the light of your face,
because you were favorable toward them.

4 You are my King, my God,
who ordains[A] victories for Jacob.
5 Through you we drive back our foes;
through your name we trample
our enemies.
6 For I do not trust in my bow,
and my sword does not bring me victory.
7 But you give us victory over our foes
and let those who hate us be disgraced.
8 We boast in God all day long;
we will praise your name forever. *Selah*

9 But you have rejected and humiliated us;
you do not march out with our armies.
10 You make us retreat from the foe,
and those who hate us
have taken plunder for themselves.
11 You hand us over to be eaten like sheep
and scatter us among the nations.
12 You sell your people for nothing;
you make no profit from selling them.
13 You make us an object of reproach
to our neighbors,
a source of mockery and ridicule to those
around us.
14 You make us a joke among the nations,
a laughingstock[B] among the peoples.
15 My disgrace is before me all day long,
and shame has covered my face,
16 because of the taunts[C] of the scorner
and reviler,
because of the enemy and avenger.

17 All this has happened to us,
but we have not forgotten you
or betrayed your covenant.
18 Our hearts have not turned back;
our steps have not strayed from your path.
19 But you have crushed us in a haunt
of jackals
and have covered us with deepest darkness.
20 If we had forgotten the name of our God
and spread out our hands to a foreign god,
21 wouldn't God have found this out,
since he knows the secrets of the heart?
22 Because of you we are being put to death
all day long;
we are counted as sheep to be slaughtered.

23 Wake up, LORD! Why are you sleeping?
Get up! Don't reject us forever!
24 Why do you hide
and forget our affliction and oppression?
25 For we have sunk down to the dust;
our bodies cling to the ground.
26 Rise up! Help us!
Redeem us because of your faithful love.

A ROYAL WEDDING SONG

45 *For the choir director: according to "The Lilies." A* Maskil *of the sons of Korah. A love song.*

1 My heart is moved by a noble theme
as I recite my verses to the king;
my tongue is the pen of a skillful writer.
2 You are the most handsome of men;[D]
grace flows from your lips.
Therefore God has blessed you forever.

3 Mighty warrior, strap your sword at your side.
In your majesty and splendor —
4 in your splendor ride triumphantly
in the cause of truth, humility, and justice.
May your right hand show your awe-inspiring
acts.
5 Your sharpened arrows pierce the hearts
of the king's enemies;
the peoples fall under you.

6 Your throne, God, is[E] forever and ever;
the scepter of your kingdom is a scepter
of justice.
7 You love righteousness and hate wickedness;
therefore God, your God, has anointed you
with the oil of joy
more than your companions.

[A] **44:4** LXX, Syr, Aq; MT reads *King, God; ordain* [B] **44:14** Lit *shaking of the head* [C] **44:16** Lit *voice* [D] **45:2** Or *of the descendants of Adam* [E] **45:6** Or *Your divine throne is*, or *Your throne is God's*

8 Myrrh, aloes, and cassia perfume
all your garments;
from ivory palaces harps bring you joy.
9 Kings' daughters are
among your honored women;
the queen, adorned with gold from Ophir,
stands at your right hand.

10 Listen, daughter, pay attention and consider:
Forget your people and your father's house,
11 and the king will desire your beauty.
Bow down to him, for he is your lord.
12 The daughter of Tyre, the wealthy people,
will seek your favor with gifts.

13 In her chamber, the royal daughter
is all glorious,
her clothing embroidered with gold.
14 In colorful garments she is led to the king;
after her, the virgins, her companions,
are brought to you.
15 They are led in with gladness and rejoicing;
they enter the king's palace.

16 Your sons will succeed your ancestors;
you will make them princes
throughout the land.
17 I will cause your name to be remembered
for all generations;
therefore the peoples will praise you forever
and ever.

GOD OUR REFUGE

46 *For the choir director. A song of the sons of Korah. According to* Alamoth.

1 God is our refuge and strength,
a helper who is always found
in times of trouble.
2 Therefore we will not be afraid,
though the earth trembles
and the mountains topple
into the depths of the seas,
3 though its water roars and foams
and the mountains quake with its turmoil.
Selah

4 There is a river —
its streams delight the city of God,
the holy dwelling place of the Most High.
5 God is within her; she will not be toppled.
God will help her when the morning dawns.
6 Nations rage, kingdoms topple;
the earth melts when he lifts his voice.
7 The LORD of Armies is with us;
the God of Jacob is our stronghold. *Selah*

8 Come, see the works of the LORD,
who brings devastation on the earth.
9 He makes wars cease throughout the earth.
He shatters bows and cuts spears to pieces;
he sets wagons ablaze.
10 "Stop fighting, and know that I am God,
exalted among the nations,
exalted on the earth."
11 The LORD of Armies is with us;
the God of Jacob is our stronghold. *Selah*

GOD OUR KING

47 *For the choir director. A psalm of the sons of Korah.*

1 Clap your hands, all you peoples;
shout to God with a jubilant cry.
2 For the LORD, the Most High,
is awe-inspiring,
a great King over the whole earth.
3 He subdues peoples under us
and nations under our feet.
4 He chooses for us our inheritance —
the pride of Jacob, whom he loves. *Selah*

5 God ascends among shouts of joy,
the LORD, with the sound of a ram's horn.
6 Sing praise to God, sing praise;
sing praise to our King, sing praise!
7 Sing a song of wisdom,[A]
for God is King of the whole earth.

8 God reigns over the nations;
God is seated on his holy throne.
9 The nobles of the peoples have assembled
with the people of the God of Abraham.
For the leaders[B] of the earth belong to God;
he is greatly exalted.

ZION EXALTED

48 *A song. A psalm of the sons of Korah.*

The LORD is great and highly praised
in the city of our God.
His holy mountain, 2 rising splendidly,
is the joy of the whole earth.
Mount Zion — the summit of Zaphon —
is the city of the great King.
3 God is known as a stronghold
in its citadels.

4 Look! The kings assembled;
they advanced together.
5 They looked and froze with fear;
they fled in terror.

[A] 47:7 Or *Sing a* maskil [B] 47:9 Lit *shields*

6 Trembling seized them there,
agony like that of a woman in labor,
7 as you wrecked the ships of Tarshish
with the east wind.

8 Just as we heard, so we have seen
in the city of the LORD of Armies,
in the city of our God;
God will establish it forever. *Selah*
9 God, within your temple,
we contemplate your faithful love.
10 Like your name, God, so your praise
reaches to the ends of the earth;
your right hand is filled with justice.
11 Mount Zion is glad.
Judah's villages[A] rejoice
because of your judgments.

12 Go around Zion, encircle it;
count its towers,
13 note its ramparts; tour its citadels
so that you can tell a future generation:
14 "This God, our God forever and ever —
he will always lead us."[B]

MISPLACED TRUST IN WEALTH

49 *For the choir director. A psalm of the sons of Korah.*

1 Hear this, all you peoples;
listen, all who inhabit the world,
2 both low and high,
rich and poor together.
3 My mouth speaks wisdom;
my heart's meditation brings understanding.
4 I turn my ear to a proverb;
I explain my riddle with a lyre.

5 Why should I fear in times of trouble?
The iniquity of my foes surrounds me.
6 They trust in their wealth
and boast of their abundant riches.
7 Yet these cannot redeem a person[C]
or pay his ransom to God —
8 since the price of redeeming him is too costly,
one should forever stop trying[D] —
9 so that he may live forever
and not see the Pit.

10 For one can see that the wise die;
the foolish and stupid also pass away.
Then they leave their wealth to others.
11 Their graves are their permanent homes,[E]
their dwellings from generation
to generation,
though they have named estates
after themselves.
12 But despite his assets,[F] mankind will not last;
he is like the animals that perish.

13 This is the way of those who are arrogant,
and of their followers,
who approve of their words.[G] *Selah*
14 Like sheep they are headed for Sheol;
Death will shepherd them.
The upright will rule over them
in the morning,
and their form will waste away in Sheol,[H]
far from their lofty abode.
15 But God will redeem me
from the power of Sheol,
for he will take me. *Selah*

16 Do not be afraid when a person gets rich,
when the wealth[I] of his house increases.
17 For when he dies, he will take nothing at all;
his wealth will not follow him down.
18 Though he blesses himself
during his lifetime —
and you are acclaimed when you do well
for yourself —
19 he will go to the generation of his ancestors;
they will never see the light.
20 Mankind, with his assets
but without understanding,
is like the animals that perish.

GOD AS JUDGE

50 *A psalm of Asaph.*

The Mighty One, God,[J] the LORD, speaks;
he summons the earth
from the rising of the sun to its setting.
2 From Zion, the perfection of beauty,
God appears in radiance.[K]
3 Our God is coming; he will not be silent!
Devouring fire precedes him,
and a storm rages around him.
4 On high, he summons heaven and earth
in order to judge his people:
5 "Gather my faithful ones to me,
those who made a covenant with me
by sacrifice."
6 The heavens proclaim his righteousness,
for God is the Judge. *Selah*

[A] **48:11** Lit *daughters* [B] **48:14** Some Hb mss, LXX; other Hb mss read *over death* [C] **49:7** Or *Certainly he cannot redeem himself*, or *Yet he cannot redeem a brother* [D] **49:8** Or *costly, it will cease forever* [E] **49:11** LXX, Syr, Tg; MT reads *Their inner thought is that their houses are eternal* [F] **49:12** Or *honor* [G] **49:13** Lit *and after them with their mouth they were pleased* [H] **49:14** Hb obscure [I] **49:16** Or *glory*, also in v. 17 [J] **50:1** Or *The God of gods* [K] **50:2** Or *God shines forth*

7 "Listen, my people, and I will speak;
I will testify against you, Israel.
I am God, your God.
8 I do not rebuke you for your sacrifices
or for your burnt offerings,
which are continually before me.
9 I will not take a bull from your household
or male goats from your pens,
10 for every animal of the forest is mine,
the cattle on a thousand hills.
11 I know every bird of the mountains,
and the creatures of the field are mine.
12 If I were hungry, I would not tell you,
for the world and everything in it is mine.
13 Do I eat the flesh of bulls
or drink the blood of goats?
14 Offer a thanksgiving sacrifice to God,
and pay your vows to the Most High.
15 Call on me in a day of trouble;
I will rescue you, and you will honor me."

16 But God says to the wicked:
"What right do you have to recite
my statutes
and to take my covenant on your lips?
17 You hate instruction
and fling my words behind you.
18 When you see a thief,
you make friends with him,
and you associate with adulterers.
19 You unleash your mouth for evil
and harness your tongue for deceit.
20 You sit, maligning your brother,
slandering your mother's son.
21 You have done these things, and I kept silent;
you thought I was just like you.
But I will rebuke you
and lay out the case before you.[A]

22 "Understand this, you who forget God,
or I will tear you apart,
and there will be no one to rescue you.
23 Whoever offers a thanksgiving sacrifice
honors me,
and whoever orders his conduct,
I will show him the salvation of God."

A PRAYER FOR RESTORATION

51 *For the choir director. A psalm of David, when the prophet Nathan came to him after he had gone to Bathsheba.*

1 Be gracious to me, God,
according to your faithful love;
according to your abundant compassion,
blot out my rebellion.
2 Completely wash away my guilt
and cleanse me from my sin.
3 For I am conscious of my rebellion,
and my sin is always before me.
4 Against you — you alone — I have sinned
and done this evil in your sight.
So you are right when you pass sentence;
you are blameless when you judge.
5 Indeed, I was guilty when I was born;
I was sinful when my mother conceived me.

6 Surely you desire integrity in the inner self,
and you teach me wisdom deep within.
7 Purify me with hyssop, and I will be clean;
wash me, and I will be whiter than snow.
8 Let me hear joy and gladness;
let the bones you have crushed rejoice.
9 Turn your face away[B] from my sins
and blot out all my guilt.

10 God, create a clean heart for me
and renew a steadfast[C] spirit within me.
11 Do not banish me from your presence
or take your Holy Spirit from me.
12 Restore the joy of your salvation to me,
and sustain me by giving me a willing spirit.
13 Then I will teach the rebellious your ways,
and sinners will return to you.

14 Save me from the guilt of bloodshed, God —
God of my salvation —
and my tongue will sing of your righteousness.
15 Lord, open my lips,
and my mouth will declare your praise.
16 You do not want a sacrifice, or I would give it;
you are not pleased with a burnt offering.
17 The sacrifice pleasing to God is[D]
a broken spirit.
You will not despise a broken
and humbled heart, God.

18 In your good pleasure, cause Zion to prosper;
build the walls of Jerusalem.
19 Then you will delight in righteous sacrifices,
whole burnt offerings;
then bulls will be offered on your altar.

GOD JUDGES THE PROUD

52 *For the choir director. A* Maskil *of David. When Doeg the Edomite went and reported to Saul, telling him, "David went to Ahimelech's house."*

1 Why boast about evil, you hero!
God's faithful love is constant.

[A] **50:21** Lit *lay it out before your eyes* [B] **51:9** Lit *Hide your face* [C] **51:10** Or *right* [D] **51:17** Lit *The sacrifices of God are*

2 Like a sharpened razor,
your tongue devises destruction,
working treachery.
3 You love evil instead of good,
lying instead of speaking truthfully. *Selah*
4 You love any words that destroy,
you treacherous tongue!

5 This is why God will bring you down forever.
He will take you, ripping you
out of your tent;
he will uproot you from the land
of the living. *Selah*
6 The righteous will see and fear,
and they will derisively say about that hero,[A]
7 "Here is the man
who would not make God his refuge,
but trusted in the abundance
of his riches,
taking refuge in his destructive behavior."

8 But I am like a flourishing olive tree
in the house of God;
I trust in God's faithful love forever and ever.
9 I will praise you forever for what
you have done.
In the presence of your faithful people,
I will put my hope in your name,
for it is good.

A PORTRAIT OF SINNERS

53 *For the choir director: on* Mahalath. A Maskil *of David.*

1 The fool says in his heart, "There's no God."
They are corrupt, and they do vile deeds.
There is no one who does good.
2 God looks down from heaven
on the human race[B]
to see if there is one who is wise,
one who seeks God.
3 All have turned away;
all alike have become corrupt.
There is no one who does good,
not even one.

4 Will evildoers never understand?
They consume my people
as they consume bread;
they do not call on God.
5 Then they will be filled with dread —
dread like no other —
because God will scatter
the bones of those who besiege you.
You will put them to shame,
for God has rejected them.
6 Oh, that Israel's deliverance would come
from Zion!
When God restores the fortunes
of his people,[C]
let Jacob rejoice, let Israel be glad.

PRAYER FOR DELIVERANCE

54 *For the choir director: with stringed instruments.* A Maskil *of David. When the Ziphites went and said to Saul, "Is David not hiding among us?"*

1 God, save me by your name,
and vindicate me by your might!
2 God, hear my prayer;
listen to the words from my mouth.
3 For strangers rise up against me,
and violent men intend to kill me.
They do not let God guide them.[D] *Selah*

4 God is my helper;
the Lord is the sustainer of my life.[E]
5 He will repay my adversaries for their evil.
Because of your faithfulness, annihilate them.

6 I will sacrifice a freewill offering to you.
I will praise your name, LORD,
because it is good.
7 For he has rescued me from every trouble,
and my eye has looked down on my enemies.

BETRAYAL BY A FRIEND

55 *For the choir director: with stringed instruments.* A Maskil *of David.*

1 God, listen to my prayer
and do not hide from my plea for help.
2 Pay attention to me and answer me.
I am restless and in turmoil
with my complaint,
3 because of the enemy's words,[F]
because of the pressure[G] of the wicked.
For they bring down disaster on me
and harass me in anger.

4 My heart shudders within me;
terrors of death sweep over me.
5 Fear and trembling grip me;
horror has overwhelmed me.
6 I said, "If only I had wings like a dove!
I would fly away and find rest.
7 How far away I would flee;
I would stay in the wilderness. *Selah*

[A] **52:6** Lit *about him* [B] **53:2** Or *the descendants of Adam* [C] **53:6** Or *restores his captive people* [D] **54:3** Lit *They do not set God in front of them* [E] **54:4** Or *is with those who sustain my life* [F] **55:3** Lit *voice* [G] **55:3** Or *threat, or oppression*

Was David's Adultery a Crime?

by Seth M. Rodriquez

From Persepolis in modern Iran; limestone lintel that formed the top of a window in a structure the original excavator called the Harem of King Xerxes; dated 486–465 BC. Persepolis was the last capital of the Persian Empire. After they were not chosen, women who were potential wives for Xerxes entered his harem.

From a legal standpoint, was David's adultery with Bathsheba a crime? Did Israelite law permit the king to take the wife of another man? If David's action was a crime within the nation of Israel, would that have been true if he were the king of another nation? In other words, did ancient Near Eastern cultures permit (or even expect) a king to take another man's wife?

LAW CODES

In ancient Israel, the law of Moses was the law of the land. As king, David was accountable to follow these laws. In Israelite society, the law for the king was no different than the law for the common citizen. David's adultery was a crime.

What about other nations in the ancient Near East? How did they view adultery? The common mindset in the ancient Near East permitted a man to have sexual relations with an unmarried woman but not with a married one.[1] For example, in Middle Assyrian law, a man would be punished for adultery only if he knew the woman was married, but would be innocent if he did not.[2] Cult prostitution in the ancient world would be another example of culturally permissible sexual activity outside of marriage.

On the other hand, having sexual relations with a married woman was widely condemned in the ancient Near East on moral, spiritual, and sometimes legal grounds. For instance, the Book of the Dead tells of a recently deceased Egyptian trying to gain access to a blessed afterlife by confessing before the gods that he had not committed adultery with another man's wife.[3] Similarly, people in Mesopotamia believed their gods were angered by adultery.[4]

Similar to ancient Israel, the death penalty was a common punishment for adultery in other nations. The man alone, the woman alone, or both together could be executed, depending on the situation. In the Egyptian fable Tale of the Two Brothers, a husband kills his wife for trying to seduce his brother.[5] In the Code of Hammurabi, the couple caught in the act of adultery are both sentenced to death and thrown into water; under different circumstances, only the woman was sentenced to death.[6] Hittite law made similar distinctions of who received the death penalty in certain situations. At other times, the death penalty was not imposed.[7] Mutilation, shaving the hair, or public floggings were other punishments inflicted on those who committed adultery in the ancient Near East.[8]

ROYAL EXPECTATIONS

What about the king? Did ancient Near Eastern cultures hold the king to the same standards of sexual conduct as everyone else? Evidence indicates the king's sexual activities received special consideration. Although the Mosaic law prohibited Hebrew kings from accumulating concubines and multiple wives (Dt 17:17), other ancient Near Eastern cultures expected their kings to do so. For example, when Persia's King Xerxes was looking for a new wife after divorcing Vashti, he did not look for one woman but instead gathered together a group of women. In turn, each would spend the night with the king. He then chose one to be the queen, and added the rest to his harem (Est 2:1–14).

From the limited information we have on the topic, the same moral standards seem to have applied to the king as to the commoner. Although the king was expected to have sexual relations with multiple women, taking the wife of another man was shameful. Direct evidence of the mind-set of ancient kings comes from the stories of the patriarchs. When Abraham allowed Pharaoh to take Sarah as a wife, Pharaoh was appalled when he found out that Sarah was actually Abraham's wife (Gn 12:14–20). Taking another man's wife clearly was not an acceptable practice, even for Pharaoh himself. The later story involving Sarah and Abimelech, king of Gerar, reflects the same mind-set (20:2–18). When God confronted Abimelech in a dream for taking Sarah from Abraham, Abimelech pled his innocence because he did not know the true nature of Abraham and Sarah's relationship. Abimelech's mind-set was the same as Pharaoh's; he did not believe he had the right to take another man's wife, even though he was king. A few chapters later, a Philistine king whom Isaac encountered expressed a similar moral standard (26:6–11).

Indirect evidence comes from ancient law codes and the book of Esther. As stated above, Mesopotamian and Hittite law codes condemned adultery and punished the offenders. Since the kings were responsible for setting the laws of the land, these laws are evidence that they themselves opposed adultery. In Esther 2:1–4, Xerxes gathered a group of "young virgins" from which to select a wife. The Hebrew term means "young marriageable woman" and often refers to unmarried women;[9] married women apparently were not included in Xerxes's roundup.

Gerar is on the border of Canaanite territory between Gaza and Beer-sheba. Gerar's King Abimelech took Sarah, not knowing she was Abraham's wife. The Lord revealed the truth to Abimelech in a dream before the king had been intimate with Sarah.

Although a king in the ancient Near East was expected to have sexual relations with numerous women, the available evidence strongly suggests that kings did not normally take other men's wives for themselves. Although no available laws from the ancient Near East specifically address this situation, the general mind-set in both biblical and extrabiblical sources indicates that having sexual relations with another man's wife was viewed as morally wrong.[10] Thus, even when David is judged by the accepted standards of surrounding pagan nations, his adultery with Bathsheba was reprehensible. ✣

---

[1] Bruce Wells, "Sex Crimes in the Laws of the Hebrew Bible," *NEA* 78.4 (2015): 294–95. [2] Middle Assyrian Law Code, Tablet A: A14 in *ANET* with sup., 181; Edwin M. Yamauchi, "Adultery" in *Dictionary of Daily Life in Biblical & Post-Biblical Antiquity*, ed. Edwin M. Yamauchi and Marvin R. Wilson, vol. 1 (Peabody, MA: Hendrickson, 2014). [3] Pnina Galpaz-Feller, "Private Lives and Public Censure—Adultery in Ancient Egypt and Biblical Israel," *NEA* 67.3 (2004): 155. [4] Yamauchi, "Adultery." [5] Galpaz-Feller, "Private Lives," 154–55. [6] Code of Hammurabi §129, 133–33a in *ANET*, 171. [7] Hittite Law 197. See Samuel Greengus, *Laws in the Bible and in Early Rabbinic Collections: The Legal Legacy of the Ancient Near East* (Eugene, OR: Cascade, 2011), 61. [8] Yamauchi, "Adultery." [9] Bruce K. Waltke, "§295a [*betula*]" (virgin) in *TWOT*, 1:137–38. [10] Yamauchi, "Adultery."

8 I would hurry to my shelter
from the raging wind and the storm."

9 Lord, confuse[A] and confound their speech,[B]
for I see violence and strife in the city;
10 day and night they make the rounds
on its walls.
Crime and trouble are within it;
11 destruction is inside it;
oppression and deceit never leave
its marketplace.

12 Now it is not an enemy who insults me —
otherwise I could bear it;
it is not a foe who rises up against me —
otherwise I could hide from him.
13 But it is you, a man who is my peer,
my companion and good friend!
14 We used to have close fellowship;
we walked with the crowd into the house
of God.

15 Let death take them by surprise;
let them go down to Sheol alive,
because evil is in their homes
and within them.
16 But I call to God,
and the LORD will save me.
17 I complain and groan morning, noon,
and night,
and he hears my voice.
18 Though many are against me,
he will redeem me from my battle unharmed.
19 God, the one enthroned from long ago,
will hear and will humiliate them *Selah*
because they do not change
and do not fear God.

20 My friend acts violently
against those at peace with him;
he violates his covenant.
21 His buttery words are smooth,
but war is in his heart.
His words are softer than oil,
but they are drawn swords.

22 Cast your burden on the LORD,
and he will sustain you;
he will never allow the righteous to be shaken.

23 God, you will bring them down
to the Pit of destruction;
men of bloodshed and treachery
will not live out half their days.
But I will trust in you.

A CALL FOR GOD'S PROTECTION

56 *For the choir director: according to "A Silent Dove Far Away."* A Miktam *of David. When the Philistines seized him in Gath.*

1 Be gracious to me, God, for a man is
trampling me;
he fights and oppresses me all day long.
2 My adversaries trample me all day,
for many arrogantly fight against me.[C]

3 When I am afraid,
I will trust in you.
4 In God, whose word I praise,
in God I trust; I will not be afraid.
What can mere mortals do to me?

5 They twist my words all day long;
all their thoughts against me are evil.
6 They stir up strife,[D] they lurk,
they watch my steps
while they wait to take my life.
7 Will they escape in spite of such sin?
God, bring down the nations in wrath.

8 You yourself have recorded my wanderings.[E]
Put my tears in your bottle.
Are they not in your book?
9 Then my enemies will retreat on the day
when I call.
This I know: God is for me.

10 In God, whose word I praise,
in the LORD, whose word I praise,
11 in God I trust; I will not be afraid.
What can mere humans do to me?

12 I am obligated by vows[F] to you, God;
I will make my thanksgiving sacrifices to you.
13 For you rescued me from death,
even my feet from stumbling,
to walk before God in the light of life.

PRAISE FOR GOD'S PROTECTION

57 *For the choir director: "Do Not Destroy."* A Miktam *of David. When he fled before Saul into the cave.*

1 Be gracious to me, God, be gracious to me,
for I take refuge in you.
I will seek refuge in the shadow
of your wings
until danger passes.

[A] **55:9** Or *destroy* [B] **55:9** Lit *and divide their tongue* [C] **56:2** Or *many fight against me, O exalted one,* or *many fight against me from the heights* [D] **56:6** Or *They attack* [E] **56:8** Or *misery* [F] **56:12** Lit *On me the vows*

2 I call to God Most High,
to God who fulfills his purpose for me.[A]
3 He reaches down from heaven and saves me,
challenging the one who tramples me. *Selah*
God sends his faithful love and truth.
4 I am surrounded by lions;
I lie down among devouring lions —
people whose teeth are spears and arrows,
whose tongues are sharp swords.
5 God, be exalted above the heavens;
let your glory be over the whole earth.
6 They prepared a net for my steps;
I was despondent.
They dug a pit ahead of me,
but they fell into it! *Selah*

7 My heart is confident, God, my heart
is confident.
I will sing; I will sing praises.
8 Wake up, my soul!
Wake up, harp and lyre!
I will wake up the dawn.
9 I will praise you, Lord, among the peoples;
I will sing praises to you among the nations.
10 For your faithful love is as high as
the heavens;
your faithfulness reaches the clouds.
11 God, be exalted above the heavens;
let your glory be over the whole earth.

A CRY AGAINST INJUSTICE

58 *For the choir director: "Do Not Destroy."*
A Miktam *of David.*

1 Do you really speak righteously,
you mighty ones?[B]
Do you judge people fairly?
2 No, you practice injustice in your hearts;
with your hands you weigh out violence
in the land.

3 The wicked go astray from the womb;
liars wander about from birth.
4 They have venom like the venom of a snake,
like the deaf cobra that stops up its ears,
5 that does not listen to the sound
of the charmers
who skillfully weave spells.

6 God, knock the teeth out of their mouths;
LORD, tear out the young lions' fangs.
7 May they vanish like water that flows by;
may they aim their blunted arrows.[C]
8 Like a slug that moves along in slime,
like a woman's miscarried child,
may they not see the sun.
9 Before your pots can feel the heat of
the thorns —
whether green or burning —
he will sweep them away.[D]
10 The righteous one will rejoice
when he sees the retribution;
he will wash his feet in the blood of the wicked.
11 Then people will say,
"Yes, there is a reward for the righteous!
There is a God who judges on earth!"

GOD OUR STRONGHOLD

59 *For the choir director: "Do Not Destroy."*
A Miktam *of David. When Saul sent agents to watch the house and kill him.*

1 Rescue me from my enemies, my God;
protect me from those who rise up
against me.
2 Rescue me from evildoers,
and save me from men of bloodshed.
3 Because look, LORD, they set an ambush
for me.
Powerful men attack me,
but not because of any sin or rebellion
of mine.
4 For no fault of mine,
they run and take up a position.
Awake to help me, and take notice.
5 LORD God of Armies, you are the God of Israel.
Rise up to punish all the nations;
do not show favor to any wicked traitors.
Selah

6 They return at evening, snarling like dogs
and prowling around the city.
7 Look, they spew from their mouths —
sharp words from[E] their lips.
"For who," they say, "will hear?"
8 But you laugh at them, LORD;
you ridicule all the nations.
9 I will keep watch for you, my[F] strength,
because God is my stronghold.
10 My faithful God[G] will come to meet me;
God will let me look down on my adversaries.

11 Do not kill them; otherwise, my people
will forget.
By your power, make them homeless wanderers
and bring them down,
Lord, our shield.

[A] **57:2** Or *who avenges me* [B] **58:1** Or *Can you really speak righteousness in silence?* [C] **58:7** Hb obscure [D] **58:9** Or *thorns, he will sweep it away, whether raw or cooking* [E] **59:7** Lit *swords are on* [F] **59:9** Some Hb mss, LXX, Vg, Tg; other Hb mss read *his* [G] **59:10** Alt Hb tradition reads *My God in his faithful love*

12 For the sin of their mouths and the words of
their lips,
let them be caught in their pride.
They utter curses and lies.
13 Consume them in fury;
consume them until they are gone.
Then people will know throughout[A] the earth
that God rules over Jacob. *Selah*

14 And they return at evening,
snarling like dogs
and prowling around the city.
15 They scavenge for food;
they growl if they are not satisfied.

16 But I will sing of your strength
and will joyfully proclaim
your faithful love in the morning.
For you have been a stronghold for me,
a refuge in my day of trouble.
17 To you, my strength, I sing praises,
because God is my stronghold —
my faithful God.

PRAYER IN DIFFICULT TIMES

60 *For the choir director: according to "The Lily of Testimony." A* Miktam *of David for teaching. When he fought with Aram-naharaim and Aram-zobah, and Joab returned and struck Edom in Salt Valley, killing twelve thousand.*

1 God, you have rejected us;
you have broken us down;
you have been angry. Restore us![B]
2 You have shaken the land and split it open.
Heal its fissures, for it shudders.
3 You have made your people
suffer hardship;
you have given us wine to drink
that made us stagger.
4 You have given a signal flag to those
who fear you,
so that they can flee before the archers.[C] *Selah*
5 Save with your right hand, and answer me,
so that those you love may be rescued.

6 God has spoken in his sanctuary:[D]
"I will celebrate!
I will divide up Shechem.
I will apportion the Valley of Succoth.
7 Gilead is mine, Manasseh is mine,
and Ephraim is my helmet;
Judah is my scepter.
8 Moab is my washbasin.
I throw my sandal on Edom;
I shout in triumph over Philistia."
9 Who will bring me to the fortified city?
Who will lead me to Edom?
10 God, haven't you rejected us?
God, you do not march out with our armies.
11 Give us aid against the foe,
for human help is worthless.
12 With God we will perform valiantly;
he will trample our foes.

SECURITY IN GOD

61 *For the choir director: on stringed instruments. Of David.*

1 God, hear my cry;
pay attention to my prayer.
2 I call to you from the ends of the earth
when my heart is without strength.
Lead me to a rock that is high above me,
3 for you have been a refuge for me,
a strong tower in the face of the enemy.
4 I will dwell in your tent forever
and take refuge under the shelter
of your wings. *Selah*

5 God, you have heard my vows;
you have given a heritage
to those who fear your name.
6 Add days to the king's life;
may his years span many generations.
7 May he sit enthroned before God forever.
Appoint faithful love and truth
to guard him.
8 Then I will continually sing of your name,
fulfilling my vows day by day.

TRUST IN GOD ALONE

62 *For the choir director: according to Jeduthun. A psalm of David.*

1 I am at rest in God alone;
my salvation comes from him.
2 He alone is my rock and my salvation,
my stronghold; I will never be shaken.

3 How long will you threaten a man?
Will all of you attack[E]
as if he were a leaning wall
or a tottering fence?
4 They only plan to bring him down
from his high position.
They take pleasure in lying;
they bless with their mouths,
but they curse inwardly. *Selah*

[A] **59:13** Lit *know to the ends of* [B] **60:1** Or *Turn back to us*
[C] **60:4** Or *can rally before the archers, or can rally because of the truth*
[D] **60:6** Or *has promised by his holy nature* [E] **62:3** Some Hb mss read *you be struck down*

5 Rest in God alone, my soul,
for my hope comes from him.
6 He alone is my rock and my salvation,
my stronghold; I will not be shaken.
7 My salvation and glory depend on God,
my strong rock.
My refuge is in God.
8 Trust in him at all times, you people;
pour out your hearts before him.
God is our refuge. *Selah*

9 Common people are only a vapor;
important people, an illusion.
Together on a scale,
they weigh less than[A] a vapor.
10 Place no trust in oppression
or false hope in robbery.
If wealth increases,
don't set your heart on it.

11 God has spoken once;
I have heard this twice:
strength belongs to God,
12 and faithful love belongs to you, Lord.
For you repay each according to his works.

PRAISE GOD WHO SATISFIES

63 *A psalm of David. When he was in the Wilderness of Judah.*

1 God, you are my God; I eagerly seek you.
I thirst for you;
my body faints for you
in a land that is dry, desolate, and without water.
2 So I gaze on you in the sanctuary
to see your strength and your glory.

3 My lips will glorify you
because your faithful love is better than life.
4 So I will bless you as long as I live;
at your name, I will lift up my hands.
5 You satisfy me as with rich food;[B]
my mouth will praise you with joyful lips.

6 When I think of you as I lie on my bed,
I meditate on you during the night watches
7 because you are my helper;
I will rejoice in the shadow of your wings.
8 I follow close to you;
your right hand holds on to me.

9 But those who intend to destroy my life
will go into the depths of the earth.
10 They will be given over to the power
of the sword;
they will become a meal for jackals.

11 But the king will rejoice in God;
all who swear by him will boast,
for the mouths of liars will be shut.

PROTECTION FROM EVILDOERS

64 *For the choir director. A psalm of David.*

God, hear my voice when I am in anguish.
Protect my life from the terror of the enemy.
2 Hide me from the scheming of wicked people,
from the mob of evildoers,
3 who sharpen their tongues like swords
and aim bitter words like arrows,
4 shooting from concealed places
at the blameless.
They shoot at him suddenly and are not afraid.
5 They adopt[C] an evil plan;
they talk about hiding traps and say,
"Who will see them?"[D]
6 They devise crimes and say,
"We have perfected a secret plan."
The inner man and the heart are mysterious.

7 But God will shoot them with arrows;
suddenly, they will be wounded.
8 They will be made to stumble;
their own tongues work against them.
All who see them will shake their heads.
9 Then everyone will fear
and will tell about God's work,
for they will understand what he has done.

10 The righteous one rejoices in the LORD
and takes refuge in him;
all those who are upright in heart
will offer praise.

GOD'S CARE FOR THE EARTH

65 *For the choir director. A psalm of David. A song.*

1 Praise is rightfully yours,[E]
God, in Zion;
vows to you will be fulfilled.
2 All humanity will come to you,
the one who hears prayer.
3 Iniquities overwhelm me;
only you can atone for our rebellions.
4 How happy is the one you choose
and bring near to live in your courts!
We will be satisfied with the goodness
of your house,
the holiness of your temple.[F]

[A] **62:9** Lit *they go up more than* [B] **63:5** Lit *with fat and fatness* [C] **64:5** Or *They strengthen themselves with* [D] **64:5** Or *it* [E] **65:1** Or *Praise is silence to you*, or *Praise awaits you* [F] **65:4** Or *house, your holy temple*

5 You answer us in righteousness,
with awe-inspiring works,
God of our salvation,
the hope of all the ends of the earth
and of the distant seas.
6 You establish the mountains by your power;
you are robed with strength.
7 You silence the roar of the seas,
the roar of their waves,
and the tumult of the nations.
8 Those who live far away are awed
by your signs;
you make east and west shout for joy.

9 You visit the earth and water it abundantly,
enriching it greatly.
God's stream is filled with water,
for you prepare the earth in this way,
providing people with grain.
10 You soften it with showers and bless
its growth,
soaking its furrows and leveling its ridges.
11 You crown the year with your goodness;
your carts overflow with plenty.[A]
12 The wilderness pastures overflow,
and the hills are robed with joy.
13 The pastures are clothed with flocks
and the valleys covered with grain.
They shout in triumph; indeed, they sing.

PRAISE FOR GOD'S MIGHTY ACTS

66 *For the choir director. A song. A psalm.*
Let the whole earth shout joyfully to God!
2 Sing about the glory of his name;
make his praise glorious.
3 Say to God, "How awe-inspiring are your works!
Your enemies will cringe before you
because of your great strength.
4 The whole earth will worship you
and sing praise to you.
They will sing praise to your name." *Selah*

5 Come and see the wonders of God;
his acts for humanity[B] are awe-inspiring.
6 He turned the sea into dry land,
and they crossed the river on foot.
There we rejoiced in him.
7 He rules forever by his might;
he keeps his eye on the nations.
The rebellious should not
exalt themselves. *Selah*
8 Bless our God, you peoples;
let the sound of his praise be heard.
9 He keeps us alive[C]
and does not allow our feet to slip.
10 For you, God, tested us;
you refined us as silver is refined.
11 You lured us into a trap;
you placed burdens on our backs.
12 You let men ride over our heads;
we went through fire and water,
but you brought us out to abundance.[D]

13 I will enter your house with burnt offerings;
I will pay you my vows
14 that my lips promised
and my mouth spoke during my distress.
15 I will offer you fattened sheep
as burnt offerings,
with the fragrant smoke of rams;
I will sacrifice bulls with goats. *Selah*

16 Come and listen, all who fear God,
and I will tell what he has done for me.
17 I cried out to him with my mouth,
and praise was on my tongue.
18 If I had been aware of malice in my heart,
the Lord would not have listened.
19 However, God has listened;
he has paid attention to the sound
of my prayer.
20 Blessed be God!
He has not turned away my prayer
or turned his faithful love from me.

ALL WILL PRAISE GOD

67 *For the choir director: with stringed instruments. A psalm. A song.*
1 May God be gracious to us
and bless us;
may he make his face shine upon us *Selah*
2 so that your way may be known on earth,
your salvation among all nations.

3 Let the peoples praise you, God;
let all the peoples praise you.
4 Let the nations rejoice and shout for joy,
for you judge the peoples with fairness
and lead the nations on earth. *Selah*
5 Let the peoples praise you, God,
let all the peoples praise you.

6 The earth has produced its harvest;
God, our God, blesses us.
7 God will bless us,
and all the ends of the earth
will fear him.

[A] **65:11** Lit *your paths drip with fat* [B] **66:5** Or *for the descendants of Adam* [C] **66:9** Lit *He sets our soul in life* [D] **66:12** Or *a place of satisfaction*

GOD'S MAJESTIC POWER

68 *For the choir director. A psalm of David. A song.*

1 God arises. His enemies scatter,
and those who hate him flee
from his presence.
2 As smoke is blown away,
so you blow them away.
As wax melts before the fire,
so the wicked are destroyed before God.
3 But the righteous are glad;
they rejoice before God and celebrate with joy.

4 Sing to God! Sing praises to his name.
Exalt him who rides on the clouds[A] —
his name is the LORD[B] — and celebrate
before him.
5 God in his holy dwelling is
a father of the fatherless
and a champion of widows.
6 God provides homes for those
who are deserted.
He leads out the prisoners to prosperity,[C]
but the rebellious live in a scorched land.

7 God, when you went out before your people,
when you marched through the desert, *Selah*
8 the earth trembled and the skies poured rain
before God, the God of Sinai,[D]
before God, the God of Israel.
9 You, God, showered abundant rain;
you revived your inheritance
when it languished.
10 Your people settled in it;
God, you provided for the poor
by your goodness.

11 The Lord gave the command;
a great company of women brought
the good news:
12 "The kings of the armies flee — they flee!"
She who stays at home divides the spoil.
13 While[E] you lie among the sheep pens,[F]
the wings of a dove are covered with silver,
and its feathers with glistening gold.
14 When the Almighty scattered kings in the land,
it snowed on Zalmon.[G]

15 Mount Bashan is God's towering mountain;
Mount Bashan is a mountain of many peaks.
16 Why gaze with envy, you mountain peaks,
at the mountain God desired for his abode?
The LORD will dwell there forever!
17 God's chariots are tens of thousands,
thousands and thousands;
the Lord is among them in the sanctuary[H]
as he was at Sinai.
18 You ascended to the heights,
taking away captives;
you received gifts from[I] people,
even from the rebellious,
so that the LORD God might dwell there.[J]

19 Blessed be the Lord!
Day after day he bears our burdens;
God is our salvation. *Selah*
20 Our God is a God of salvation,
and escape from death belongs to the LORD
my Lord.
21 Surely God crushes the heads of his enemies,
the hairy brow of one who goes on
in his guilty acts.
22 The Lord said, "I will bring them back
from Bashan;
I will bring them back from the depths
of the sea
23 so that your foot may wade[K] in blood
and your dogs' tongues may have their share
from the enemies."
24 People have seen your procession, God,
the procession of my God,
my King, in the sanctuary.
25 Singers lead the way,
with musicians following;
among them are young women
playing tambourines.
26 Bless God in the assemblies;
bless the LORD from the fountain of Israel.
27 There is Benjamin, the youngest, leading them,
the rulers of Judah in their assembly,[L]
the rulers of Zebulun, the rulers of Naphtali.

28 Your God has decreed your strength.
Show your strength, God,
you who have acted on our behalf.
29 Because of your temple at Jerusalem,
kings will bring tribute to you.
30 Rebuke the beast in the reeds,
the herd of bulls with the calves
of the peoples.
Trample underfoot those with bars of silver.[M]
Scatter the peoples who take pleasure in war.

[A] **68:4** Or *rides through the desert* [B] **68:4** Hb *Yah* [C] **68:6** Or *prisoners with joyous music*; Hb uncertain [D] **68:8** Or *God, this one of Sinai* [E] **68:13** Or *If* [F] **68:13** Or *the campfires*, or *the saddlebags*; Hb obscure [G] **68:14** Or *Black Mountain* [H] **68:17** Or *in holiness*, also in v. 24 [I] **68:18** Lit *among* [J] **68:18** Or *even those rebelling against the LORD God's living there*; Hb obscure [K] **68:23** LXX, Syr read *dip* [L] **68:27** Hb obscure [M] **68:30** Or *peoples, trampling on those who take pleasure in silver*, or *peoples, trampling on the bars of silver*, or *peoples, who trample each other for bars of silver*

31 Ambassadors will come[A] from Egypt;
Cush will stretch out its hands to God.
32 Sing to God, you kingdoms of the earth;
sing praise to the Lord, *Selah*
33 to him who rides in the ancient,
highest heavens.
Look, he thunders with his powerful voice!
34 Ascribe power to God.
His majesty is over Israel;
his power is among the clouds.
35 God, you are awe-inspiring in your sanctuaries.
The God of Israel gives power and strength
to his people.
Blessed be God!

A PLEA FOR RESCUE

69 *For the choir director: according to "The Lilies." Of David.*

1 Save me, God,
for the water has risen to my neck.
2 I have sunk in deep mud, and there is
no footing;
I have come into deep water,
and a flood sweeps over me.
3 I am weary from my crying;
my throat is parched.
My eyes fail, looking for my God.
4 Those who hate me without cause
are more numerous than the hairs
of my head;
my deceitful enemies, who would destroy me,
are powerful.
Though I did not steal, I must repay.

5 God, you know my foolishness,
and my guilty acts are not hidden from you.
6 Do not let those who put their hope in you
be disgraced because of me,
Lord GOD of Armies;
do not let those who seek you
be humiliated because of me,
God of Israel.
7 For I have endured insults because of you,
and shame has covered my face.
8 I have become a stranger to my brothers
and a foreigner to my mother's sons
9 because zeal for your house
has consumed me,
and the insults of those who insult you
have fallen on me.
10 I mourned and fasted,
but it brought me insults.
11 I wore sackcloth as my clothing,
and I was a joke to them.
12 Those who sit at the city gate talk about me,
and drunkards make up songs about me.

13 But as for me, LORD,
my prayer to you is for a time of favor.
In your abundant, faithful love, God,
answer me with your sure salvation.
14 Rescue me from the miry mud;
don't let me sink.
Let me be rescued from those who hate me
and from the deep water.
15 Don't let the floodwaters sweep over me
or the deep swallow me up;
don't let the Pit close its mouth over me.
16 Answer me, LORD,
for your faithful love is good.
In keeping with your abundant compassion,
turn to me.
17 Don't hide your face from your servant,
for I am in distress.
Answer me quickly!
18 Come near to me and redeem me;
ransom me because of my enemies.

19 You know the insults I endure —
my shame and disgrace.
You are aware of all my adversaries.
20 Insults have broken my heart,
and I am in despair.
I waited for sympathy,
but there was none;
for comforters, but found no one.
21 Instead, they gave me gall for my food,
and for my thirst
they gave me vinegar to drink.

22 Let their table set before them be a snare,
and let it be a trap for their allies.
23 Let their eyes grow too dim to see,
and let their hips continually quake.
24 Pour out your rage on them,
and let your burning anger overtake them.
25 Make their fortification desolate;
may no one live in their tents.
26 For they persecute the one you struck
and talk about the pain of those you wounded.
27 Charge them with crime on top of crime;
do not let them share in your righteousness.
28 Let them be erased from the book of life
and not be recorded with the righteous.

29 But as for me — poor and in pain —
let your salvation protect me, God.

[A] **68:31** Or *They bring red cloth*, or *They bring bronze*

30 I will praise God's name with song
and exalt him with thanksgiving.
31 That will please the LORD more than an ox,
more than a bull with horns and hooves.
32 The humble will see it and rejoice.
You who seek God, take heart!
33 For the LORD listens to the needy
and does not despise
his own who are prisoners.

34 Let heaven and earth praise him,
the seas and everything that moves in them,
35 for God will save Zion
and build up[A] the cities of Judah.
They will live there and possess it.
36 The descendants of his servants
will inherit it,
and those who love his name will live in it.

A CALL FOR DELIVERANCE

70 *For the choir director. Of David. To bring remembrance.*

1 God, hurry to rescue me.
LORD, hurry to help me!
2 Let those who seek to kill me
be disgraced and confounded;
let those who wish me harm
be turned back and humiliated.
3 Let those who say, "Aha, aha!"
retreat because of their shame.

4 Let all who seek you rejoice and be glad
in you;
let those who love your salvation
continually say, "God is great!"
5 I am oppressed and needy;
hurry to me, God.
You are my help and my deliverer;
LORD, do not delay.

GOD'S HELP IN OLD AGE

71 LORD, I seek refuge in you;
let me never be disgraced.
2 In your justice, rescue and deliver me;
listen closely to me and save me.
3 Be a rock of refuge for me,
where I can always go.
Give the command to save me,
for you are my rock and fortress.
4 Deliver me, my God, from the power
of the wicked,
from the grasp of the unjust and oppressive.
5 For you are my hope, Lord GOD,
my confidence from my youth.
6 I have leaned on you from birth;
you took me from my mother's womb.
My praise is always about you.
7 I am like a miraculous sign to many,
and you are my strong refuge.
8 My mouth is full of praise
and honor to you all day long.

9 Don't discard me in my old age.
As my strength fails, do not abandon me.
10 For my enemies talk about me,
and those who spy on me plot together,
11 saying, "God has abandoned him;
chase him and catch him,
for there is no one to rescue him."
12 God, do not be far from me;
my God, hurry to help me.
13 May my adversaries be disgraced
and destroyed;
may those who intend to harm me
be covered with disgrace and humiliation.
14 But I will hope continually
and will praise you more and more.
15 My mouth will tell about your righteousness
and your salvation all day long,
though I cannot sum them up.
16 I come because of the mighty acts
of the Lord GOD;
I will proclaim your righteousness,
yours alone.

17 God, you have taught me from my youth,
and I still proclaim your wondrous works.
18 Even while I am old and gray,
God, do not abandon me,
while I proclaim your power
to another generation,
your strength to all who are to come.
19 Your righteousness reaches
the heights, God,
you who have done great things;
God, who is like you?
20 You caused me to experience
many troubles and misfortunes,
but you will revive me again.
You will bring me up again,
even from the depths of the earth.
21 You will increase my honor
and comfort me once again.
22 Therefore, I will praise you with a harp
for your faithfulness, my God;
I will sing to you with a lyre,
Holy One of Israel.

[A] **69:35** Or *and rebuild*

With Harp and Lyre: Musical Instruments in the Old Testament *by Becky Lombard*

The Israelites understood that God both ordained and enabled music. They viewed music as coming from the Lord and longed for their music to return to him as the fragrance of the incense.

Music was formational in the life, work, and worship of the Israelite community. After the parting of the Red Sea, Miriam took up her tambourine and sang of the Lord's rescue and strength (Ex 15). Joshua and those he led used music to topple the walls of Jericho (Jos 6). Deborah and Barak sang of God's victory in battle (Jdg 5). Saul's life changed when he met prophets accompanied by men playing harps, tambourines, flutes, and lyres (1Sm 10).

Lists of musical instruments appear regularly in the Old Testament narrative. The first appears in Genesis 4:21, which introduces Jubal, "the first of all who play the lyre and the flute." Some ensemble listings are small groups, like that in Psalm 92—"with a ten-stringed harp and the music of a lyre" (v. 3). Others are quite extensive. David's appointed orchestra of Levites included harps, lyres, cymbals, trumpets, and ram's horns (1Ch 15:16–16:5). Old Testament passages often pair the harp and lyre, which had wide usage in the ancient Near East (1Kg 10:12; 1Ch 13:8; Pss 81:2; 108:2; 150:3).

Old Testament instruments fall into three major categories—string, percussion, and wind. Though we have no original instruments through archaeological studies, we can look at pottery, drawings, and clay figures from the biblical era in Israel and surrounding areas.

STRINGED INSTRUMENTS

Harp—The harp's construction resembled an archer's bow. Strings stretched across a curved wooden frame or across two pieces of wood joined at a right angle. Each string sounded a single pitch and was larger than the strings of the lyre. According to the Talmud, harp strings were made with sheep intestines and sounded louder than those of the lyre.

Lyre—The lyre was the most common stringed instrument of biblical times. Though today we typically think of David as a harpist, he actually played a lyre. Its wooden construction was typically a sound box with two upright arms attached. Strings stretched from a crosspiece and spanned the arms to the sound box. A fingerboard made it possible for strings to play multiple pitches.[1] The lyre was always an instrument of joy. When the occasion for joy ceased, the lyres were put away and remained silent (Ps 137:2). Prophets

Close-up scene on the Standard of Ur. A singer and a man playing the lyre are entertaining the king, who is banqueting with his friends (not shown).

Basalt relief showing musicians playing tambourines and lyres. From the palace of the Hittite King Barrekup at ancient Zinjirli-Sam'al (in modern southeastern Turkey); dates from the late Hittite period, eighth century BC.

From Thebes, Egypt, restored wooden harp with a spade-shaped sounding board. Such harps were in use in Egypt from the time of the Old Kingdom (2700–2160 BC); this one probably dates from the New Kingdom (ca 1300 BC).

warned that if the people continued in sin, they would be punished and the lyre would no longer be heard (Ezk 26:13).

From the general region of the Holy Land, drawings remain that show Semitic people playing the lyre. One of these drawings shows captives playing the lyre under the eye of the Assyrian guard. In this instance the players are using their hands to play. Evidence indicates people used their hands when playing instrumental pieces but used the plectrum (a pick made of wood or bone) when accompanying voices.[2]

PERCUSSION INSTRUMENTS

Bell—Bells were attached to the hem of Aaron's priestly robe (Ex 28:33–35). The bells of biblical times likely resembled small rattles with a pellet or clapper. Archaeologists have found many bells of that description, made of bronze, in sites in Israel.

Cymbal—Cymbals first appear in Scripture during the time of David, in the procession that moved the ark to Jerusalem. They were the only percussion instruments included in the temple instruments that David specified (1Ch 15:16). David appointed Heman, Asaph, and Ethan to sound the cymbals, a Levitical position of much distinction and privilege. Cymbals were probably used to accompany singing with other instruments, to draw God's attention to the worshipers, and to signal the beginnings of singing in services of worship.

Made of bronze, the twin cymbals were shaped like saucers. The centers were pierced for finger rings made of iron or wire. Questions remain as to whether they were used horizontally or vertically. They were

Clay plaque depicting a musician; from Mesopotamia. Music was a regular part of temple rituals, burial ceremonies, and festival celebrations. Individuals also played music for entertainment.

sounded by striking one against the other or by touching their rims together. Depending on the performance method, the sound of cymbals ranged from light tinkling to a dull clash.[3]

Tambourine—The tambourine was probably a small hand-drum. Archaeologists think it probably did not have the "jingles" attached like our modern tambourine. In Scripture, women often played this instrument as they sang and danced with joy. Many clay figures holding the small hand-drum date from biblical time.[4]

WIND INSTRUMENTS

Flute—Scholars have varied opinions about the words that most English Bibles translate as "flute." Some use the word "pipe" to describe the flute. Early models were hollow reed pipes with finger holes. With the larger ensembles of temple music, the "pipe" used was probably a stronger-toned reed. These louder instruments probably consisted of two pipes strung together creating a double pipe, each fingered by a different hand. Bronze and clay artifacts from Israel and likely from the Old Testament era portray individuals playing these instruments.[5]

Trumpet—Trumpets of Old Testament times were fashioned of straight tubes of metal with bell-shaped ends. People used bronze trumpets in secular settings and silver ones for sacred occasions. Unlike our modern trumpets, these had no valves. This limited to three or four the number of tones that the instrument could make. The sound they emitted was probably not very lovely but, in the minds of the people, it was loud enough to bring the attention of God in heaven down to man on earth.

Trumpet players generally performed in pairs or larger groups. In 2 Chronicles 5:12–13, when the Levites brought the ark of the covenant into the temple from the city of David, priests blew 120 trumpets, joining singers, more trumpets, cymbals, and other instruments. Only the priestly descendants of Aaron could play trumpets for sacred occasions (Nm 10:8) and in war (2Ch 13:12). Players sounded trumpets for numerous events in Old Testament life: to summon Israelites to the tent of meeting, to signal to Israelites to break camp, as a remembrance of God's presence among his people, to sound an alarm in warfare, on holidays and at the beginning of the new moon, over sacrifices and burnt offerings, when the ark was moved to Jerusalem, at the dedications of the first and second temples, and to join other instruments of praise.[6]

Shofar—English Bibles often translate the Hebrew term *shofar* as "trumpet" to refer to an instrument made from the ram's horn. Some scholars believe the significance of the ram's horn was rooted in the importance of the sacrificial ram that God provided Abraham as he obediently began to offer Isaac. The shofar was a ritual and warfare trumpet. It was used to signal and give commands, as well as sound the alarm. When the Israelites blasted the shofar and shouted, the wall of Jericho tumbled. It is the only biblical instrument still in use today in its original form.[7]

Musical instruments of the Old Testament are many and varied. Our understanding and knowledge of them is also widely dispersed and varied. Though we have no sound or musical notation from the era to narrow our understanding, what we can piece together is an understanding of the character of the sound, the symbolism of the music as it sounded, and something of the cultural setting in the biblical world. ✣

[1] Richard Leonard, "Musical Instruments in Scripture" in *The Biblical Foundations of Christian Worship,* vol. 1 in The Complete Library of Christian Worship, ed. Robert E. Webber (Peabody, MA: Hendrickson, 1993), 237. [2] Ovid R. Sellers, "Musical Instruments of Israel," *BA* 4.3 (1941): 38–39. [3] Ivor H. Jones, "Music and Musical Instruments" in *ABD*, 4:935; Alfred Sendrey, *Music in the Social and Religious Life of Antiquity* (Rutherford, NJ: Fairleigh Dickinson University Press, 1974), 99, 205–206. [4] Jeremy Montagu, *Musical Instruments of the Bible* (Lanham, MD: Scarecrow Press, 2002), 16–18. [5] Montagu, *Musical Instruments*, 47. [6] Sendrey, *Music*, 189–91. [7] Montagu, *Musical Instruments*, 19–23.

Bronze wheeled stand dated to the thirteenth or twelfth century BC. Decorated with scenes that depict a seated harp-player approached by a musician and a serving boy; on the back, a winged sphinx. From Cyprus.

23 My lips will shout for joy
when I sing praise to you
because you have redeemed me.
24 Therefore, my tongue will proclaim
your righteousness all day long,
for those who intend to harm me
will be disgraced and confounded.

A PRAYER FOR THE KING

72 *Of Solomon.*
God, give your justice to the king
and your righteousness to the king's son.
2 He will judge your people with righteousness
and your afflicted ones with justice.
3 May the mountains bring well-being[A]
to the people
and the hills, righteousness.
4 May he vindicate the afflicted
among the people,
help the poor,
and crush the oppressor.

5 May they fear you[B] while the sun endures
and as long as the moon,
throughout all generations.
6 May the king be like rain that falls
on the cut grass,
like spring showers that water the earth.
7 May the righteous[C] flourish in his days
and well-being abound
until the moon is no more.

8 May he rule from sea to sea
and from the Euphrates
to the ends of the earth.
9 May desert tribes kneel before him
and his enemies lick the dust.
10 May the kings of Tarshish
and the coasts and islands bring tribute,
the kings of Sheba and Seba offer gifts.
11 Let all kings bow in homage to him,
all nations serve him.

12 For he will rescue the poor who cry out
and the afflicted who have no helper.
13 He will have pity on the poor and helpless
and save the lives of the poor.
14 He will redeem them from oppression
and violence,
for their lives are[D] precious[E] in his sight.

15 May he live long!
May gold from Sheba be given to him.
May prayer be offered for him continually,
and may he be blessed all day long.
16 May there be plenty of grain in the land;
may it wave on the tops of the mountains.
May its crops be like Lebanon.
May people flourish in the cities
like the grass of the field.
17 May his name endure forever;
as long as the sun shines,
may his fame increase.
May all nations be blessed by him
and call him blessed.

18 Blessed be the LORD God, the God of Israel,
who alone does wonders.
19 Blessed be his glorious name forever;
the whole earth is filled with his glory.
Amen and amen.
20 The prayers of David son of Jesse are concluded.

BOOK III (Psalms 73–89)

GOD'S WAYS VINDICATED

73 *A psalm of Asaph.*
God is indeed good to Israel,
to the pure in heart.
2 But as for me, my feet almost slipped;
my steps nearly went astray.
3 For I envied the arrogant;
I saw the prosperity of the wicked.

4 They have an easy time until they die,[F]
and their bodies are well fed.[G]
5 They are not in trouble like others;
they are not afflicted like most people.
6 Therefore, pride is their necklace,
and violence covers them like a garment.
7 Their eyes bulge out from fatness;
the imaginations of their hearts run wild.
8 They mock, and they speak maliciously;
they arrogantly threaten oppression.
9 They set their mouths against heaven,
and their tongues strut across the earth.
10 Therefore his people turn to them[H]
and drink in their overflowing words.[I]
11 The wicked say, "How can God know?
Does the Most High know everything?"
12 Look at them — the wicked!
They are always at ease,
and they increase their wealth.

13 Did I purify my heart
and wash my hands in innocence for nothing?

[A] **72:3** Or *peace*, also in v. 7 [B] **72:5** LXX reads *May he continue* [C] **72:7** Some Hb mss, LXX, Syr, Jer read *May righteousness* [D] **72:14** Lit *their blood is* [E] **72:14** Or *valuable* [F] **73:4** Lit *For there are no pangs to their death* [G] **73:4** Lit *fat* [H] **73:10** Lit *turn here* [I] **73:10** Lit *and waters of fullness are drained by them*

14 For I am afflicted all day long
and punished every morning.
15 If I had decided to say these things aloud,
I would have betrayed your people.[A]
16 When I tried to understand all this,
it seemed hopeless[B]
17 until I entered God's sanctuary.
Then I understood their destiny.
18 Indeed, you put them in slippery places;
you make them fall into ruin.
19 How suddenly they become a desolation!
They come to an end, swept away by terrors.
20 Like one waking from a dream,
Lord, when arising, you will despise
their image.

21 When I became embittered
and my innermost being[C] was wounded,
22 I was stupid and didn't understand;
I was an unthinking animal toward you.
23 Yet I am always with you;
you hold my right hand.
24 You guide me with your counsel,
and afterward you will take me up in glory.[D]
25 Who do I have in heaven but you?
And I desire nothing on earth but you.
26 My flesh and my heart may fail,
but God is the strength[E] of my heart,
my portion forever.
27 Those far from you will certainly perish;
you destroy all who are unfaithful to you.
28 But as for me, God's presence is my good.
I have made the Lord GOD my refuge,
so I can tell about all you do.

PRAYER FOR ISRAEL

74 *A Maskil of Asaph.*
Why have you rejected us forever, God?
Why does your anger burn
against the sheep of your pasture?
2 Remember your congregation,
which you purchased long ago
and redeemed as the tribe
for your own possession.
Remember Mount Zion where you dwell.
3 Make your way[F] to the perpetual ruins,
to all that the enemy has destroyed
in the sanctuary.
4 Your adversaries roared in the meeting place
where you met with us.[G]
They set up their emblems as signs.
5 It was like men in a thicket of trees,
wielding axes,
6 then smashing all the carvings
with hatchets and picks.
7 They set your sanctuary on fire;
they utterly[H] desecrated
the dwelling place of your name.
8 They said in their hearts,
"Let's oppress them relentlessly."
They burned every place throughout the land
where God met with us.[I]
9 There are no signs for us to see.
There is no longer a prophet.
And none of us knows how long
this will last.
10 God, how long will the enemy mock?
Will the foe insult your name forever?
11 Why do you hold back your hand?
Stretch out[J] your right hand
and destroy them!

12 God my King is from ancient times,
performing saving acts on the earth.
13 You divided the sea with your strength;
you smashed the heads
of the sea monsters in the water;
14 you crushed the heads of Leviathan;
you fed him to the creatures of the desert.
15 You opened up springs and streams;
you dried up ever-flowing rivers.
16 The day is yours, also the night;
you established the moon and the sun.
17 You set all the boundaries of the earth;
you made summer and winter.

18 Remember this: the enemy has mocked
the LORD,
and a foolish people has insulted your name.
19 Do not give to beasts the life of your dove;[K]
do not forget the lives
of your poor people forever.
20 Consider the covenant,
for the dark places of the land
are full of violence.
21 Do not let the oppressed turn away
in shame;
let the poor and needy praise your name.
22 Rise up, God, champion your cause!
Remember the insults
that fools bring against you all day long.
23 Do not forget the clamor of your adversaries,
the tumult of your opponents that goes up
constantly.

[A] **73:15** Lit *betrayed the generation of your sons* [B] **73:16** Lit *it was trouble in my eyes* [C] **73:21** Lit *my kidneys* [D] **73:24** Or *will receive me with honor* [E] **73:26** Lit *rock* [F] **74:3** Lit *Lift up your steps* [G] **74:4** Lit *in your meeting place* [H] **74:7** Lit *they to the ground* [I] **74:8** Lit *every meeting place of God in the land* [J] **74:11** Lit *From your bosom* [K] **74:19** One Hb ms, LXX, Syr read *life that praises you*

GOD JUDGES THE WICKED

75 *For the choir director: "Do Not Destroy." A psalm of Asaph. A song.*

1 We give thanks to you, God;
we give thanks to you, for your name is near.
People tell about your wondrous works.

2 "When I choose a time,
I will judge fairly.
3 When the earth and all its inhabitants shake,
I am the one who steadies its pillars. *Selah*
4 I say to the boastful, 'Do not boast,'
and to the wicked, 'Do not lift up your horn.
5 Do not lift up your horn against heaven[A]
or speak arrogantly.'"

6 Exaltation does not come
from the east, the west, or the desert,
7 for God is the Judge:
He brings down one and exalts another.
8 For there is a cup in the LORD's hand,
full of wine blended with spices, and he pours
from it.
All the wicked of the earth will drink,
draining it to the dregs.

9 As for me, I will tell about him forever;
I will sing praise to the God of Jacob.

10 "I will cut off all the horns of the wicked,
but the horns of the righteous will be
lifted up."

GOD, THE POWERFUL JUDGE

76 *For the choir director: with stringed instruments. A psalm of Asaph. A song.*

1 God is known in Judah;
his name is great in Israel.
2 His tent is in Salem,
his dwelling place in Zion.
3 There he shatters the bow's flaming arrows,
the shield, the sword, and the weapons of war.
Selah

4 You are resplendent and majestic
coming down from the mountains of prey.
5 The brave-hearted have been plundered;
they have slipped into their final sleep.
None of the warriors was able to lift a hand.
6 At your rebuke, God of Jacob,
both chariot and horse lay still.

7 And you — you are to be feared.[B]
When you are angry,
who can stand before you?
8 From heaven you pronounced judgment.
The earth feared and grew quiet
9 when God rose up to judge
and to save all the lowly of the earth. *Selah*
10 Even human wrath will praise you;
you will clothe yourself
with the wrath that remains.[C]

11 Make and keep your vows
to the LORD your God;
let all who are around him bring tribute
to the awe-inspiring one.[D]
12 He humbles the spirit of leaders;
he is feared by the kings of the earth.

CONFIDENCE IN A TIME OF CRISIS

77 *For the choir director: according to Jeduthun. Of Asaph. A psalm.*

1 I cry aloud to God,
aloud to God, and he will hear me.
2 I sought the Lord in my day of trouble.
My hands were continually lifted up
all night long;
I refused to be comforted.
3 I think of God; I groan;
I meditate; my spirit becomes weak. *Selah*

4 You have kept me from closing my eyes;
I am troubled and cannot speak.
5 I consider days of old,
years long past.
6 At night I remember my music;
I meditate in my heart, and my spirit ponders.

7 "Will the Lord reject forever
and never again show favor?
8 Has his faithful love ceased forever?
Is his promise at an end for all generations?
9 Has God forgotten to be gracious?
Has he in anger withheld his compassion?"
Selah

10 So I say, "I am grieved
that the right hand of the Most High
has changed."[C]
11 I will remember the LORD's works;
yes, I will remember your ancient wonders.
12 I will reflect on all you have done
and meditate on your actions.

13 God, your way is holy.
What god is great like God?

[A]**75:5** Lit *horn to the height* [B]**76:7** Or *are awe-inspiring*
[C]**76:10; 77:10** Hb obscure [D]**76:11** Or *tribute with awe*

14 You are the God who works wonders;
you revealed your strength
among the peoples.
15 With power you redeemed your people,
the descendants of Jacob and Joseph. *Selah*

16 The water saw you, God.
The water saw you; it trembled.
Even the depths shook.
17 The clouds poured down water.
The storm clouds thundered;
your arrows flashed back and forth.
18 The sound of your thunder was
in the whirlwind;
lightning lit up the world.
The earth shook and quaked.
19 Your way went through the sea
and your path through the vast water,
but your footprints were unseen.
20 You led your people like a flock
by the hand of Moses and Aaron.

LESSONS FROM ISRAEL'S PAST

78 *A* Maskil *of Asaph.*
My people, hear my instruction;
listen to the words from my mouth.
2 I will declare wise sayings;
I will speak mysteries from the past —
3 things we have heard and known
and that our ancestors have passed down
to us.
4 We will not hide them from their children,
but will tell a future generation
the praiseworthy acts of the LORD,
his might, and the wondrous works
he has performed.
5 He established a testimony in Jacob
and set up a law in Israel,
which he commanded our ancestors
to teach to their children
6 so that a future generation —
children yet to be born — might know.
They were to rise and tell their children
7 so that they might put their confidence in God
and not forget God's works,
but keep his commands.
8 Then they would not be like their ancestors,
a stubborn and rebellious generation,
a generation whose heart was not loyal
and whose spirit was not faithful to God.

9 The Ephraimite archers turned back
on the day of battle.
10 They did not keep God's covenant
and refused to live by his law.
11 They forgot what he had done,
the wondrous works he had shown them.
12 He worked wonders in the sight of
their ancestors
in the land of Egypt, the territory of Zoan.
13 He split the sea and brought them across;
the water stood firm like a wall.
14 He led them with a cloud by day
and with a fiery light throughout the night.
15 He split rocks in the wilderness
and gave them drink as abundant as the depths.
16 He brought streams out of the stone
and made water flow down like rivers.

17 But they continued to sin against him,
rebelling in the desert against the Most High.
18 They deliberately[A] tested God,
demanding the food they craved.
19 They spoke against God, saying,
"Is God able to provide food in the wilderness?
20 Look! He struck the rock and water gushed out;
torrents overflowed.
But can he also provide bread
or furnish meat for his people?"
21 Therefore, the LORD heard
and became furious;
then fire broke out against Jacob,
and anger flared up against Israel
22 because they did not believe God
or rely on his salvation.
23 He gave a command to the clouds above
and opened the doors of heaven.
24 He rained manna for them to eat;
he gave them grain from heaven.
25 People[B] ate the bread of angels.[C]
He sent them an abundant supply of food.
26 He made the east wind blow in the skies
and drove the south wind by his might.
27 He rained meat on them like dust,
and winged birds like the sand of the seas.
28 He made them fall in the camp,
all around the tents.
29 The people ate and were completely satisfied,
for he gave them what they craved.
30 Before they had turned from
what they craved,
while the food was still in their mouths,
31 God's anger flared up against them,
and he killed some of their best men.
He struck down Israel's fit young men.

32 Despite all this, they kept sinning
and did not believe his wondrous works.

[A]**78:18** Lit *in their heart* [B]**78:25** Lit *Man* [C]**78:25** Lit *mighty ones*

33 He made their days end in futility,
their years in sudden disaster.
34 When he killed some of them,
the rest began to seek him;
they repented and searched for God.
35 They remembered that God was their rock,
the Most High God, their Redeemer.
36 But they deceived him with their mouths,
they lied to him with their tongues,
37 their hearts were insincere toward him,
and they were unfaithful to his covenant.
38 Yet he was compassionate;
he atoned for their iniquity
and did not destroy them.
He often turned his anger aside
and did not unleash[A] all his wrath.
39 He remembered that they were only flesh,
a wind that passes and does not return.

40 How often they rebelled against him
in the wilderness
and grieved him in the desert.
41 They constantly tested God
and provoked the Holy One of Israel.
42 They did not remember his power shown
on the day he redeemed them from the foe,
43 when he performed his miraculous signs
in Egypt
and his wonders in the territory of Zoan.
44 He turned their rivers into blood,
and they could not drink from their streams.
45 He sent among them swarms of flies,
which fed on them,
and frogs, which devastated them.
46 He gave their crops to the caterpillar
and the fruit of their labor to the locust.
47 He killed their vines with hail
and their sycamore fig trees with a flood.
48 He handed over their livestock to hail
and their cattle to lightning bolts.
49 He sent his burning anger against them:
fury, indignation, and calamity —
a band of deadly messengers.[B]
50 He cleared a path for his anger.
He did not spare them from death
but delivered their lives to the plague.
51 He struck all the firstborn in Egypt,
the first progeny of the tents of Ham.
52 He led his people out like sheep
and guided them like a flock
in the wilderness.
53 He led them safely, and they were not afraid;
but the sea covered their enemies.
54 He brought them to his holy territory,
to the mountain his right hand acquired.
55 He drove out nations before them.
He apportioned their inheritance by lot
and settled the tribes of Israel in their tents.

56 But they rebelliously tested
the Most High God,
for they did not keep his decrees.
57 They treacherously turned away
like their ancestors;
they became warped like a faulty bow.
58 They enraged him with their high places
and provoked his jealousy
with their carved images.
59 God heard and became furious;
he completely rejected Israel.
60 He abandoned the tabernacle at Shiloh,
the tent where he resided among mankind.
61 He gave up his strength to captivity
and his splendor to the hand of a foe.
62 He surrendered his people to the sword
because he was enraged with his heritage.
63 Fire consumed his chosen young men,
and his young women had no wedding songs.[C]
64 His priests fell by the sword,
and the widows could not lament.

65 The Lord awoke as if from sleep,
like a warrior from the effects of wine.
66 He beat back his foes;
he gave them lasting disgrace.
67 He rejected the tent of Joseph
and did not choose the tribe of Ephraim.
68 He chose instead the tribe of Judah,
Mount Zion, which he loved.
69 He built his sanctuary like the heights,
like the earth that he established forever.
70 He chose David his servant
and took him from the sheep pens;
71 he brought him from tending ewes
to be shepherd over his people Jacob —
over Israel, his inheritance.
72 He shepherded them with a pure heart
and guided them with his skillful hands.

FAITH AMID CONFUSION

79 *A psalm of Asaph.*
God, the nations have invaded
your inheritance,
desecrated your holy temple,
and turned Jerusalem into ruins.
2 They gave the corpses of your servants
to the birds of the sky for food,

[A] **78:38** Or *stir up* [B] **78:49** Or *angels* [C] **78:63** Lit *virgins were not praised*

the flesh of your faithful ones
to the beasts of the earth.
3 They poured out their blood
like water all around Jerusalem,
and there was no one to bury them.
4 We have become an object of reproach
to our neighbors,
a source of mockery and ridicule
to those around us.

5 How long, LORD? Will you be angry forever?
Will your jealousy keep burning like fire?
6 Pour out your wrath on the nations
that don't acknowledge you,
on the kingdoms that don't call on your name,
7 for they have devoured Jacob
and devastated his homeland.
8 Do not hold past iniquities[A] against us;
let your compassion come to us quickly,
for we have become very weak.

9 God of our salvation, help us,
for the glory of your name.
Rescue us and atone for our sins,
for your name's sake.
10 Why should the nations ask,
"Where is their God?"
Before our eyes,
let vengeance for the shed blood
of your servants
be known among the nations.
11 Let the groans of the prisoners reach you;
according to your great power,
preserve those condemned to die.

12 Pay back sevenfold to our neighbors
the reproach they have hurled at you, Lord.
13 Then we, your people, the sheep
of your pasture,
will thank you forever;
we will declare your praise
to generation after generation.

A PRAYER FOR RESTORATION

80 *For the choir director: according to "The Lilies." A testimony of Asaph. A psalm.*

1 Listen, Shepherd of Israel,
who leads Joseph like a flock;
you who sit enthroned between the cherubim,
shine 2 on Ephraim,
Benjamin, and Manasseh.
Rally your power and come to save us.
3 Restore us, God;
make your face shine on us,
so that we may be saved.

4 LORD God of Armies,
how long will you be angry
with your people's prayers?
5 You fed them the bread of tears
and gave them a full measure[B]
of tears to drink.
6 You put us at odds with our neighbors;
our enemies mock us.
7 Restore us, God of Armies;
make your face shine on us, so that we
may be saved.

8 You dug up a vine from Egypt;
you drove out the nations and planted it.
9 You cleared a place for it;
it took root and filled the land.
10 The mountains were covered by its shade,
and the mighty cedars[C] with its branches.
11 It sent out sprouts toward the Sea[D]
and shoots toward the River.[E]

12 Why have you broken down its walls
so that all who pass by pick its fruit?
13 Boars from the forest tear at it
and creatures of the field feed on it.
14 Return, God of Armies.
Look down from heaven and see;
take care of this vine,
15 the root[F] your right hand planted,
the son[G] that you made strong for yourself.
16 It was cut down and burned;
they[H] perish at the rebuke of your countenance.
17 Let your hand be with the man
at your right hand,
with the son of man
you have made strong for yourself.
18 Then we will not turn away from you;
revive us, and we will call on your name.
19 Restore us, LORD, God of Armies;
make your face shine on us, so that we may
be saved.

A CALL TO OBEDIENCE

81 *For the choir director: on the* Gittith. *Of Asaph.*

Sing for joy to God our strength;
shout in triumph to the God of Jacob.
2 Lift up a song — play the tambourine,
the melodious lyre, and the harp.
3 Blow the ram's horn on the day of our feasts[I]
during the new moon
and during the full moon.

[A] **79:8** Or *hold the sins of past generations* [B] **80:5** Lit *a one-third measure* [C] **80:10** Lit *the cedars of God* [D] **80:11** = the Mediterranean [E] **80:11** = the Euphrates [F] **80:15** Hb obscure [G] **80:15** Or *shoot* [H] **80:16** Or *may they* [I] **81:3** Lit *feast*

4 For this is a statute for Israel,
an ordinance of the God of Jacob.
5 He set it up as a decree for Joseph
when he went throughout[A] the land of Egypt.

I heard an unfamiliar language:
6 "I relieved his shoulder from the burden;
his hands were freed from carrying
the basket.
7 You called out in distress, and I rescued you;
I answered you from the thundercloud.
I tested you at the Waters of Meribah. *Selah*
8 Listen, my people, and I will admonish you.
Israel, if you would only listen to me!
9 There must not be a strange god among you;
you must not bow down to a foreign god.
10 I am the LORD your God,
who brought you up from the land of Egypt.
Open your mouth wide, and I will fill it.

11 "But my people did not listen to my voice;
Israel did not obey me.
12 So I gave them over to their stubborn hearts
to follow their own plans.
13 If only my people would listen to me
and Israel would follow my ways,
14 I would quickly subdue their enemies
and turn my hand against their foes."
15 Those who hate the LORD
would cower to him;
their doom would last forever.
16 But he would feed Israel[B] with the best wheat.
"I would satisfy you with honey from the rock."

A PLEA FOR RIGHTEOUS JUDGMENT

82 *A psalm of Asaph.*
God stands in the divine assembly;
he pronounces judgment among the gods:[C]
2 "How long will you judge unjustly
and show partiality to the wicked? *Selah*
3 Provide justice for the needy
and the fatherless;
uphold the rights of the oppressed
and the destitute.
4 Rescue the poor and needy;
save them from the power of the wicked."

5 They do not know or understand;
they wander in darkness.
All the foundations of the earth are shaken.

6 I said, "You are gods;
you are all sons of the Most High.
7 However, you will die like humans
and fall like any other ruler."

8 Rise up, God, judge the earth,
for all the nations belong to you.

PRAYER AGAINST ENEMIES

83 *A song. A psalm of Asaph.*
God, do not keep silent.
Do not be deaf, God; do not be quiet.
2 See how your enemies make an uproar;
those who hate you have acted arrogantly.[D]
3 They devise clever schemes
against your people;
they conspire against your treasured ones.
4 They say, "Come, let's wipe them out
as a nation
so that Israel's name will no longer
be remembered."
5 For they have conspired with one mind;
they form an alliance[E] against you —
6 the tents of Edom and the Ishmaelites,
Moab and the Hagrites,
7 Gebal, Ammon, and Amalek,
Philistia with the inhabitants of Tyre.
8 Even Assyria has joined them;
they lend support[F] to the sons of Lot.[G] *Selah*

9 Deal with them as you did with Midian,
as you did with Sisera
and Jabin at the Kishon River.
10 They were destroyed at En-dor;
they became manure for the ground.
11 Make their nobles like Oreb and Zeeb,
and all their tribal leaders like Zebah
and Zalmunna,
12 who said, "Let's seize God's pastures
for ourselves."

13 Make them like tumbleweed, my God,
like straw before the wind.
14 As fire burns a forest,
as a flame blazes through mountains,
15 so pursue them with your tempest
and terrify them with your storm.
16 Cover their faces with shame
so that they will seek your name, LORD.
17 Let them be put to shame
and terrified forever;
let them perish in disgrace.
18 May they know that you alone —
whose name is the LORD —
are the Most High over the whole earth.

[A] **81:5** Or *he gained authority over* [B] **81:16** Lit *him* [C] **82:1** Or *the heavenly beings*, or *the earthly rulers*; Hb *elohim* [D] **83:2** Lit *have lifted their head* [E] **83:5** Lit *they cut a covenant* [F] **83:8** Lit *they are an arm* [G] **83:8** = Moab and Ammon

LONGING FOR GOD'S HOUSE

84 *For the choir director: on the* Gittith. *A psalm of the sons of Korah.*

1 How lovely is your dwelling place,
LORD of Armies.
2 I long and yearn
for the courts of the LORD;
my heart and flesh cry out
for[A] the living God.

3 Even a sparrow finds a home,
and a swallow, a nest for herself
where she places her young —
near your altars, LORD of Armies,
my King and my God.
4 How happy are those who reside
in your house,
who praise you continually. *Selah*

5 Happy are the people whose strength is
in you,
whose hearts are set on pilgrimage.
6 As they pass through the Valley of Baca,[B]
they make it a source of spring water;
even the autumn rain will cover it
with blessings.[C]
7 They go from strength to strength;
each appears before God in Zion.

8 LORD God of Armies, hear my prayer;
listen, God of Jacob. *Selah*
9 Consider our shield,[D] God;
look on the face of your anointed one.

10 Better a day in your courts
than a thousand anywhere else.
I would rather stand at the threshold
of the house of my God
than live in the tents of wicked people.
11 For the LORD God is a sun and shield.
The LORD grants favor and honor;
he does not withhold the good
from those who live with integrity.
12 Happy is the person who trusts in you,
LORD of Armies!

RESTORATION OF FAVOR

85 *For the choir director. A psalm of the sons of Korah.*

1 LORD, you showed favor to your land;
you restored the fortunes of Jacob.[E]
2 You forgave your people's guilt;
you covered all their sin. *Selah*
3 You withdrew all your fury;
you turned from your burning anger.

4 Return to us, God of our salvation,
and abandon your displeasure with us.
5 Will you be angry with us forever?
Will you prolong your anger for all generations?
6 Will you not revive us again
so that your people may rejoice in you?
7 Show us your faithful love, LORD,
and give us your salvation.

8 I will listen to what God will say;
surely the LORD will declare peace
to his people, his faithful ones,
and not let them go back to foolish ways.
9 His salvation is very near those who fear him,
so that glory may dwell in our land.

10 Faithful love and truth will join together;
righteousness and peace will embrace.
11 Truth will spring up from the earth,
and righteousness will look down from heaven.
12 Also, the LORD will provide what is good,
and our land will yield its crops.
13 Righteousness will go before him
to prepare the way for his steps.

LAMENT AND PETITION

86 *A prayer of David.*

Listen, LORD, and answer me,
for I am poor and needy.
2 Protect my life, for I am faithful.
You are my God; save your servant who trusts
in you.
3 Be gracious to me, Lord,
for I call to you all day long.
4 Bring joy to your servant's life,
because I appeal to you, Lord.

5 For you, Lord, are kind and ready to forgive,
abounding in faithful love to all who call
on you.
6 LORD, hear my prayer;
listen to my cries for mercy.
7 I call on you in the day of my distress,
for you will answer me.

8 Lord, there is no one like you among the gods,
and there are no works like yours.
9 All the nations you have made
will come and bow down before you, Lord,
and will honor your name.
10 For you are great and perform wonders;
you alone are God.

[A] **84:2** Or *flesh shout for joy to* [B] **84:6** Or *Valley of Tears* [C] **84:6** Or *pools* [D] **84:9** = the king [E] **85:1** Or *restored Jacob from captivity*

11 Teach me your way, LORD,
and I will live by your truth.
Give me an undivided mind to fear
your name.
12 I will praise you with all my heart,
Lord my God,
and will honor your name forever.
13 For your faithful love for me is great,
and you rescue my life from the depths
of Sheol.

14 God, arrogant people have attacked me;
a gang of ruthless men intends to kill me.
They do not let you guide them.[A]
15 But you, Lord, are a compassionate
and gracious God,
slow to anger and abounding in faithful love
and truth.
16 Turn to me and be gracious to me.
Give your strength to your servant;
save the son of your female servant.
17 Show me a sign of your goodness;
my enemies will see and be put to shame
because you, LORD, have helped
and comforted me.

ZION, THE CITY OF GOD

87 *A psalm of the sons of Korah. A song.*
The city he founded[B] is
on the holy mountains.
2 The LORD loves Zion's city gates
more than all the dwellings of Jacob.
3 Glorious things are said about you,
city of God. *Selah*

4 "I will make a record of those who know me:
Rahab, Babylon, Philistia, Tyre, and Cush —
each one was born there."
5 And it will be said of Zion,
"This one and that one were born in her."
The Most High himself will establish her.
6 When he registers the peoples,
the LORD will record,
"This one was born there." *Selah*
7 Singers and dancers[C] alike will say,[D]
"My whole source of joy is[E] in you."

A CRY OF DESPERATION

88 *A song. A psalm of the sons of Korah. For the choir director: according to* Mahalath Leannoth. *A* Maskil *of Heman the Ezrahite.*
1 LORD, God of my salvation,
I cry out before you day and night.
2 May my prayer reach your presence;
listen to my cry.
3 For I have had enough troubles,
and my life is near Sheol.
4 I am counted among those going down to the Pit.
I am like a man without strength,
5 abandoned[F] among the dead.
I am like the slain lying in the grave,
whom you no longer remember,
and who are cut off from your care.[G]

6 You have put me in the lowest part of the Pit,
in the darkest places, in the depths.
7 Your wrath weighs heavily on me;
you have overwhelmed me with all
your waves. *Selah*
8 You have distanced my friends from me;
you have made me repulsive to them.
I am shut in and cannot go out.
9 My eyes are worn out from crying.
LORD, I cry out to you all day long;
I spread out my hands to you.

10 Do you work wonders for the dead?
Do departed spirits rise up
to praise you? *Selah*
11 Will your faithful love be declared in the grave,
your faithfulness in Abaddon?
12 Will your wonders be known in the darkness
or your righteousness in the land of oblivion?

13 But I call to you for help, LORD;
in the morning my prayer meets you.
14 LORD, why do you reject me?
Why do you hide your face from me?
15 From my youth,
I have been suffering and near death.
I suffer your horrors; I am desperate.
16 Your wrath sweeps over me;
your terrors destroy me.
17 They surround me like water all day long;
they close in on me from every side.
18 You have distanced loved one and neighbor
from me;
darkness is my only friend.[H]

PERPLEXITY ABOUT GOD'S PROMISES

89 *A* Maskil *of Ethan the Ezrahite.*
I will sing about the LORD's
faithful love forever;
I will proclaim your faithfulness to all
generations
with my mouth.

[A] **86:14** Lit *They do not set you in front of them* [B] **87:1** Lit *His foundation* [C] **87:7** Or *musicians* [D] **87:7** Or *As they dance they will sing* [E] **87:7** Lit *"All my springs are* [F] **88:5** Or *set free* [G] **88:5** Or *hand* [H] **88:18** Or *from me, my friends. Oh darkness!*

2 For I will declare,
"Faithful love is built up forever;
you establish your faithfulness in the heavens."

3 The LORD said,
"I have made a covenant with my chosen one;
I have sworn an oath to David my servant:
4 'I will establish your offspring forever
and build up your throne for all generations.' "
Selah

5 LORD, the heavens praise your wonders —
your faithfulness also —
in the assembly of the holy ones.
6 For who in the skies can compare
with the LORD?
Who among the heavenly beings[A] is
like the LORD?
7 God is greatly feared in the council
of the holy ones,
more awe-inspiring than[B]
all who surround him.
8 LORD God of Armies,
who is strong like you, LORD?
Your faithfulness surrounds you.
9 You rule the raging sea;
when its waves surge, you still them.
10 You crushed Rahab like one who is slain;
you scattered your enemies
with your powerful arm.
11 The heavens are yours; the earth also is yours.
The world and everything in it —
you founded them.
12 North and south — you created them.
Tabor and Hermon shout for joy at your name.
13 You have a mighty arm;
your hand is powerful;
your right hand is lifted high.
14 Righteousness and justice are the foundation
of your throne;
faithful love and truth go before you.
15 Happy are the people who know
the joyful shout;
LORD, they walk in the light from your face.
16 They rejoice in your name all day long,
and they are exalted by your righteousness.
17 For you are their magnificent strength;
by your favor our horn is exalted.
18 Surely our shield[C] belongs to the LORD,
our king to the Holy One of Israel.

19 You once spoke in a vision
to your faithful ones
and said, "I have granted help to a warrior;
I have exalted one chosen[D] from the people.
20 I have found David my servant;
I have anointed him with my sacred oil.
21 My hand will always be with him,
and my arm will strengthen him.
22 The enemy will not oppress[E] him;
the wicked will not afflict him.
23 I will crush his foes before him
and strike those who hate him.
24 My faithfulness and love will be with him,
and through my name
his horn will be exalted.
25 I will extend his power to the sea
and his right hand to the rivers.
26 He will call to me, 'You are my Father,
my God, the rock of my salvation.'
27 I will also make him my firstborn,
greatest of the kings of the earth.
28 I will always preserve my faithful love for him,
and my covenant with him will endure.
29 I will establish his line forever,
his throne as long as heaven lasts.[F]
30 If his sons abandon my instruction
and do not live by my ordinances,
31 if they dishonor my statutes
and do not keep my commands,
32 then I will call their rebellion
to account with the rod,
their iniquity with blows.
33 But I will not withdraw
my faithful love from him
or betray my faithfulness.
34 I will not violate my covenant
or change what my lips have said.
35 Once and for all
I have sworn an oath by my holiness;
I will not lie to David.
36 His offspring will continue forever,
his throne like the sun before me,
37 like the moon, established forever,
a faithful witness in the sky."
Selah

38 But you have spurned and rejected him;
you have become enraged with your anointed.
39 You have repudiated the covenant
with your servant;
you have completely dishonored his crown.[G]
40 You have broken down all his walls;
you have reduced his fortified cities to ruins.
41 All who pass by plunder him;
he has become an object of ridicule
to his neighbors.

[A] **89:6** Or *the angels*, or *the sons of the mighty* [B] **89:7** Or *ones, revered by* [C] **89:18** = the king [D] **89:19** Or *exalted a young man* [E] **89:22** Or *not exact tribute from* [F] **89:29** Lit *as days of heaven* [G] **89:39** Lit *have dishonored his crown to the ground*

42 You have lifted high the right hand of his foes;
you have made all his enemies rejoice.
43 You have also turned back his sharp sword
and have not let him stand in battle.
44 You have made his splendor[A] cease
and have overturned his throne.
45 You have shortened the days of his youth;
you have covered him with shame. *Selah*

46 How long, LORD? Will you hide forever?
Will your anger keep burning like fire?
47 Remember how short my life is.
Have you created everyone for nothing?
48 What courageous person can live and
never see death?
Who can save himself from the power
of Sheol? *Selah*
49 Lord, where are the former acts
of your faithful love
that you swore to David in your faithfulness?
50 Remember, Lord, the ridicule
against your servants —
in my heart I carry abuse from all
the peoples —
51 how your enemies have ridiculed, LORD,
how they have ridiculed every step
of your anointed.

52 Blessed be the LORD forever.
Amen and amen.

BOOK IV (Psalms 90–106)

ETERNAL GOD AND MORTAL MAN

90 *A prayer of Moses, the man of God.*
Lord, you have been our refuge[B]
in every generation.
2 Before the mountains were born,
before you gave birth to the earth and the world,
from eternity to eternity, you are God.

3 You return mankind to the dust,
saying, "Return, descendants of Adam."
4 For in your sight a thousand years
are like yesterday that passes by,
like a few hours of the night.
5 You end their lives;[C] they sleep.
They are like grass that grows
in the morning —
6 in the morning it sprouts and grows;
by evening it withers and dries up.

7 For we are consumed by your anger;
we are terrified by your wrath.
8 You have set our iniquities before you,
our secret sins in the light of your presence.
9 For all our days ebb away under your wrath;
we end our years like a sigh.
10 Our lives last[D] seventy years
or, if we are strong, eighty years.
Even the best of them are[E] struggle
and sorrow;
indeed, they pass quickly and we fly away.
11 Who understands the power of your anger?
Your wrath matches the fear that is due you.
12 Teach us to number our days carefully
so that we may develop wisdom
in our hearts.[F]

13 LORD — how long?
Turn and have compassion on your servants.
14 Satisfy us in the morning
with your faithful love
so that we may shout with joy and be glad
all our days.
15 Make us rejoice for as many days
as you have humbled us,
for as many years as we have seen adversity.
16 Let your work be seen by your servants,
and your splendor by their children.
17 Let the favor of the Lord our God be on us;
establish for us the work of our hands —
establish the work of our hands!

THE PROTECTION OF THE MOST HIGH

91 The one who lives under the protection
of the Most High
dwells in the shadow of the Almighty.

2 I will say[G] concerning the LORD, who is
my refuge and my fortress,
my God in whom I trust:
3 He himself will rescue you from the bird trap,
from the destructive plague.
4 He will cover you with his feathers;
you will take refuge under his wings.
His faithfulness will be a protective shield.
5 You will not fear the terror of the night,
the arrow that flies by day,
6 the plague that stalks in darkness,
or the pestilence that ravages at noon.
7 Though a thousand fall at your side
and ten thousand at your right hand,
the pestilence will not reach you.
8 You will only see it with your eyes
and witness the punishment of the wicked.

[A] **89:44** Hb obscure [B] **90:1** Some Hb mss, LXX; other Hb mss read *dwelling place* [C] **90:5** Or *You overwhelm them*; Hb obscure [D] **90:10** Lit *The days of our years in them* [E] **90:10** LXX, Tg, Syr, Vg read *Even their span is*; Hb obscure [F] **90:12** Or *develop a heart of wisdom* [G] **91:1–2** LXX, Syr, Jer read [2]*Almighty, saying,* or [2]*Almighty, he will say*

9 Because you have made the LORD —
my refuge,
the Most High — your dwelling place,
10 no harm will come to you,
no plague will come near your tent.
11 For he will give his angels orders
concerning you,
to protect you in all your ways.
12 They will support you with their hands
so that you will not strike your foot
against a stone.
13 You will tread on the lion and the cobra;
you will trample the young lion
and the serpent.

14 Because he has his heart set on me,
I will deliver him;
I will protect him because he knows
my name.
15 When he calls out to me, I will answer him;
I will be with him in trouble.
I will rescue him and give him honor.
16 I will satisfy him with a long life
and show him my salvation.

GOD'S LOVE AND FAITHFULNESS

92 *A psalm. A song for the Sabbath day.*
It is good to give thanks to the LORD,
to sing praise to your name, Most High,
2 to declare your faithful love in the morning
and your faithfulness at night,
3 with a ten-stringed harp[A]
and the music of a lyre.

4 For you have made me rejoice, LORD,
by what you have done;
I will shout for joy
because of the works of your hands.
5 How magnificent are your works, LORD,
how profound your thoughts!
6 A stupid person does not know,
a fool does not understand this:
7 though the wicked sprout like grass
and all evildoers flourish,
they will be eternally destroyed.
8 But you, LORD, are exalted forever.
9 For indeed, LORD, your enemies —
indeed, your enemies will perish;
all evildoers will be scattered.
10 You have lifted up my horn
like that of a wild ox;
I have been anointed[B] with the finest oil.
11 My eyes look at my enemies;
when evildoers rise against me,
my ears hear them.

12 The righteous thrive like a palm tree
and grow like a cedar tree in Lebanon.
13 Planted in the house of the LORD,
they thrive in the courts of our God.
14 They will still bear fruit in old age,
healthy and green,
15 to declare, "The LORD is just;
he is my rock,
and there is no unrighteousness in him."

GOD'S ETERNAL REIGN

93 The LORD reigns! He is robed in majesty;
the LORD is robed,
enveloped in strength.
The world is firmly established;
it cannot be shaken.
2 Your throne has been established
from the beginning;[C]
you are from eternity.
3 The floods have lifted up, LORD,
the floods have lifted up their voice;
the floods lift up their pounding waves.
4 Greater than the roar of a huge torrent —
the mighty breakers of the sea —
the LORD on high is majestic.

5 LORD, your testimonies
are completely reliable;
holiness adorns your house
for all the days to come.

THE JUST JUDGE

94 LORD, God of vengeance —
God of vengeance, shine!
2 Rise up, Judge of the earth;
repay the proud what they deserve.
3 LORD, how long will the wicked —
how long will the wicked celebrate?

4 They pour out arrogant words;
all the evildoers boast.
5 LORD, they crush your people;
they oppress your heritage.
6 They kill the widow and the resident alien
and murder the fatherless.
7 They say, "The LORD doesn't see it.
The God of Jacob doesn't pay attention."

8 Pay attention, you stupid people!
Fools, when will you be wise?
9 Can the one who shaped the ear not hear,
the one who formed the eye not see?

[A] **92:3** Or *ten-stringed instrument and a harp* [B] **92:10** Syr reads *you have anointed me* [C] **93:2** Lit *from then*

10 The one who instructs nations,
the one who teaches mankind knowledge —
does he not discipline?
11 The LORD knows the thoughts of mankind;
they are futile.

12 LORD, how happy is anyone you discipline
and teach from your law
13 to give him relief from troubled times
until a pit is dug for the wicked.
14 The LORD will not leave his people
or abandon his heritage,
15 for the administration of justice will again
be righteous,
and all the upright in heart will follow[A] it.

16 Who stands up for me against the wicked?
Who takes a stand for me against evildoers?
17 If the LORD had not been my helper,
I would soon rest in the silence of death.
18 If I say, "My foot is slipping,"
your faithful love will support me, LORD.
19 When I am filled with cares,
your comfort brings me joy.

20 Can a corrupt throne be your ally,
a throne that makes evil laws?
21 They band together against the life
of the righteous
and condemn the innocent to death.
22 But the LORD is my refuge;
my God is the rock of my protection.
23 He will pay them back for their sins
and destroy them for their evil.
The LORD our God will destroy them.

WORSHIP AND WARNING

95 Come, let's shout joyfully to the LORD,
shout triumphantly to the rock
of our salvation!
2 Let's enter his presence with thanksgiving;
let's shout triumphantly to him in song.

3 For the LORD is a great God,
a great King above all gods.
4 The depths of the earth are in his hand,
and the mountain peaks are his.
5 The sea is his; he made it.
His hands formed the dry land.

6 Come, let's worship and bow down;
let's kneel before the LORD our Maker.
7 For he is our God,
and we are the people of his pasture,
the sheep under his care.[B]
Today, if you hear his voice:
8 Do not harden your hearts as at Meribah,
as on that day at Massah in the wilderness
9 where your ancestors tested me;
they tried me, though they had seen what I did.
10 For forty years I was disgusted
with that generation;
I said, "They are a people whose hearts
go astray;
they do not know my ways."
11 So I swore in my anger,
"They will not enter my rest."

KING OF THE EARTH

96 Sing a new song to the LORD;
let the whole earth sing to the LORD.
2 Sing to the LORD, bless his name;
proclaim his salvation from day to day.
3 Declare his glory among the nations,
his wondrous works among all peoples.

4 For the LORD is great and is highly praised;
he is feared above all gods.
5 For all the gods of the peoples
are worthless idols,
but the LORD made the heavens.
6 Splendor and majesty are before him;
strength and beauty are in his sanctuary.

7 Ascribe to the LORD, you families
of the peoples,
ascribe to the LORD glory and strength.
8 Ascribe to the LORD the glory of his name;
bring an offering and enter his courts.
9 Worship the LORD in the splendor
of his holiness;
let the whole earth tremble before him.

10 Say among the nations, "The LORD reigns.
The world is firmly established; it cannot
be shaken.
He judges the peoples fairly."
11 Let the heavens be glad and the earth rejoice;
let the sea and all that fills it resound.
12 Let the fields and everything
in them celebrate.
Then all the trees of the forest will shout
for joy
13 before the LORD, for he is coming —
for he is coming to judge the earth.
He will judge the world with righteousness
and the peoples with his faithfulness.

[A] **94:15** Or *heart will support*; lit *heart after* [B] **95:7** Lit *sheep of his hand*

God as "King" in Ancient Israel

by T. Van McClain

The ancient Israelites sang, "The Lord reigns! He is robed in majesty" (Ps 93:1). In what way did God reign in ancient Israel?

The covenant God made with Israel at Sinai closely resembles the suzerain/vassal Hittite covenants of the late second millennium BC.[1] The suzerain or king would write the treaty and proclaim the stipulations the vassals or citizens had to follow. The very form of the covenant made at Sinai underscored the kingship of God, and Exodus 19:5–6 goes even further by calling Israel a kingdom of priests.

Since the kingdom of the Lord was often equated with the kingdom of Judah, many could not fathom Judah ever falling. The people of Babylon would have boasted that Judah's falling to Babylon proved that Marduk, the chief deity of Babylon, was greater than the God of Israel—but Judah knew better. Yahweh, their King, had predicted the fall of Judah due to the sin and idolatry of the Judeans. Judah fell because of the power of the true God, not because of Marduk. ✣

[1] J. Walton, *Ancient Israelite Literature in Its Cultural Context* (Grand Rapids: Zondervan, 1989), 107.

Onyx scepter from about 600 BC.

THE MAJESTIC KING

97 The LORD reigns! Let the earth rejoice;
let the many coasts and islands be glad.

2 Clouds and total darkness surround him;
righteousness and justice are the foundation
of his throne.
3 Fire goes before him
and burns up his foes on every side.
4 His lightning lights up the world;
the earth sees and trembles.
5 The mountains melt like wax
at the presence of the LORD —
at the presence of the Lord of the whole earth.

6 The heavens proclaim his righteousness;
all the peoples see his glory.

7 All who serve carved images,
those who boast in worthless idols, will be
put to shame.
All the gods[A] must worship him.

8 Zion hears and is glad,
Judah's villages[B] rejoice
because of your judgments, LORD.
9 For you, LORD,
are the Most High over the whole earth;
you are exalted above all the gods.

10 You who love the LORD, hate evil!
He protects the lives of his faithful ones;
he rescues them from the power of
the wicked.
11 Light dawns[C,D] for the righteous,
gladness for the upright in heart.
12 Be glad in the LORD, you righteous ones,
and give thanks to his holy name.[E]

PRAISE THE KING

98 *A psalm.*
Sing a new song to the LORD,
for he has performed wonders;
his right hand and holy arm
have won him victory.
2 The LORD has made his victory known;
he has revealed his righteousness
in the sight of the nations.
3 He has remembered his love
and faithfulness to the house of Israel;
all the ends of the earth
have seen our God's victory.

4 Let the whole earth shout to the LORD;
be jubilant, shout for joy, and sing.
5 Sing to the LORD with the lyre,
with the lyre and melodious song.
6 With trumpets and the blast
of the ram's horn
shout triumphantly
in the presence of the LORD, our King.

7 Let the sea and all that fills it,
the world and those who live in it,
resound.
8 Let the rivers clap their hands;
let the mountains shout together for joy
9 before the LORD,
for he is coming to judge the earth.
He will judge the world righteously
and the peoples fairly.

THE KING IS HOLY

99 The LORD reigns! Let the peoples tremble.
He is enthroned between the cherubim.
Let the earth quake.
2 The LORD is great in Zion;
he is exalted above all the peoples.
3 Let them praise your great
and awe-inspiring name.
He is holy.

4 The mighty King loves justice.
You have established fairness;
you have administered justice
and righteousness in Jacob.
5 Exalt the LORD our God;
bow in worship at his footstool.
He is holy.

6 Moses and Aaron were
among his priests;
Samuel also was among those calling on
his name.
They called to the LORD
and he answered them.
7 He spoke to them in a pillar of cloud;
they kept his decrees and the statutes
he gave them.
8 LORD our God, you answered them.
You were a forgiving God to them,
but an avenger of their sinful actions.

9 Exalt the LORD our God;
bow in worship at his holy mountain,
for the LORD our God is holy.

[A] **97:7** LXX, Syr read *All his angels*; Heb 1:6 [B] **97:8** Lit *daughters* [C] **97:11** One Hb ms, LXX, some ancient versions read *rises to shine*; Ps 112:4 [D] **97:11** Lit *Light is sown* [E] **97:12** Lit *to the memory of his holiness*

BE THANKFUL

100 *A psalm of thanksgiving.*
Let the whole earth shout triumphantly
to the LORD!
2 Serve the LORD with gladness;
come before him with joyful songs.
3 Acknowledge that the LORD is God.
He made us, and we are his[A]—
his people, the sheep of his pasture.
4 Enter his gates with thanksgiving
and his courts with praise.
Give thanks to him and bless his name.
5 For the LORD is good, and his faithful love
endures forever;
his faithfulness, through all generations.

A VOW OF INTEGRITY

101 *A psalm of David.*
I will sing of faithful love and justice;
I will sing praise to you, LORD.
2 I will pay attention to the way of integrity.
When will you come to me?
I will live with a heart of integrity
in my house.
3 I will not let anything worthless guide me.[B]
I hate the practice of transgression;
it will not cling to me.
4 A devious heart will be far from me;
I will not be involved with[C] evil.

5 I will destroy anyone
who secretly slanders his neighbor;
I cannot tolerate anyone
with haughty eyes or an arrogant heart.
6 My eyes favor the faithful of the land
so that they may sit down with me.
The one who follows the way of integrity
may serve me.
7 No one who acts deceitfully
will live in my palace;
the one who tells lies
will not be retained here to guide me.[D]
8 Every morning I will destroy
all the wicked of the land,
wiping out all evildoers from the LORD's city.

AFFLICTION IN LIGHT OF ETERNITY

102 *A prayer of a suffering person who is weak and pours out his lament before the LORD.*
1 LORD, hear my prayer;
let my cry for help come before you.
2 Do not hide your face from me in my day
of trouble.
Listen closely to me;
answer me quickly when I call.
3 For my days vanish like smoke,
and my bones burn like a furnace.
4 My heart is suffering, withered like grass;
I even forget to eat my food.
5 Because of the sound of my groaning,
my flesh sticks to my bones.
6 I am like an eagle owl,
like a little owl among the ruins.
7 I stay awake;
I am like a solitary bird on a roof.
8 My enemies taunt me all day long;
they ridicule and use my name as a curse.
9 I eat ashes like bread
and mingle my drinks with tears
10 because of your indignation and wrath;
for you have picked me up
and thrown me aside.
11 My days are like a lengthening shadow,
and I wither away like grass.

12 But you, LORD, are enthroned forever;
your fame endures to all generations.
13 You will rise up and have compassion
on Zion,
for it is time to show favor to her —
the appointed time has come.
14 For your servants take delight
in its stones
and favor its dust.

15 Then the nations will fear the name
of the LORD,
and all the kings of the earth your glory,
16 for the LORD will rebuild Zion;
he will appear in his glory.
17 He will pay attention to the prayer
of the destitute
and will not despise their prayer.

18 This will be written for a later generation,
and a people who have not yet been created
will praise the LORD:
19 He looked down from his holy heights —
the LORD gazed out from heaven to earth —
20 to hear a prisoner's groaning,
to set free those condemned to die,[E]
21 so that they might declare
the name of the LORD in Zion
and his praise in Jerusalem
22 when peoples and kingdoms are assembled
to serve the LORD.

[A] **100:3** Alt Hb tradition, some Hb mss, LXX, Syr, Vg read *and not we ourselves* [B] **101:3** Lit *I will not put a worthless thing in front of my eyes* [C] **101:4** Lit *not know* [D] **101:7** Lit *be established in front of my eyes* [E] **102:20** Lit *free sons of death*

Waterfalls and Wadis: Water Imagery in the Psalms

by R. Kelvin Moore

God's people needed no one to remind them of their dependence on water. The Hebrews lived in an agrarian society. Two distinct climatic factors characterized the promised land: drought and dryness.[1] The Hebrews lived in a constant threat of drought. Water and the deficiency of water each portrayed dramatic, understandable, and meaningful images for the Hebrews.

Israel received rain in only two periods of the year. The early rains fall in October and November, the latter rains in February and March. During these two rainy seasons, previously dry riverbeds (wadis) could suddenly become swollen in heavy downpours. The potential flood could have been disconcerting. David comforted himself with a reminder that God led him beside quiet waters.

Because rain of any significance rarely fell outside of the two rainy seasons, drought was a dangerous reality in Israel. The writer of Psalm 42:1–2 understood a lack of water: "As a deer longs for flowing streams, so I long for you, God. I thirst for God, the living God." Because they knew about drought, the original hearers of Psalm 42 would have understood the fear and panic the deer experienced. Modern readers can visualize an unfortunate animal, in Psalm 42 a deer, frantically searching for water during a drought. The animal sought water because its life depended on finding it.

The only mention of waterfalls in Scripture is in this same psalm (42:7). Rather than telling of refreshment and enjoyment, the psalmist described raging torrents of despair that had overwhelmed him.

Psalm 98 records another image of water. Maybe during a rainy season the writer observed the Jordan River, white-capped with rushing water. To the psalmist, the crashing waters, rising and falling, may have mimicked hands clapping together.

The Jordan waters rushing would have been a common sight for the

The Jabbok River, in the region of Gilead, flows westward into the Jordan River.

psalmist. The Hebrew word for *Jordan* means "the descender," a reflection of the river's significant drop. Beginning at two hundred feet above sea level at Mount Hermon, the water drops to more than thirteen hundred feet below sea level at its terminus, the Dead Sea. For those in the promised land, the Jordan is indeed the descender.

People living in areas of abundant annual rainfall, areas where droughts are rare, may have difficulty appreciating the imagery of water throughout the book of Psalms (and Scripture). But the metaphor created a powerful, unmistakable image for the Old Testament Hebrews. ✣

---

[1] "Rain" in *Dictionary of Biblical Imagery*, ed. Leland Ryken, James C. Wilhoit, Tremper Longman III (Downers Grove, IL: InterVarsity, 1998), 694.

The Banias Waterfall and River. This fall is fed by water from the spring near the Cave of Pan. It is a major source for the Jordan River.

23 He has broken my[A] strength in midcourse;
he has shortened my days.
24 I say, "My God, do not take me
in the middle of my life![B]
Your years continue through all generations.
25 Long ago you established the earth,
and the heavens are the work of your hands.
26 They will perish, but you will endure;
all of them will wear out like clothing.
You will change them like a garment,
and they will pass away.
27 But you are the same,
and your years will never end.
28 Your servants' children will dwell securely,
and their offspring will be established
before you."

THE FORGIVING GOD

103 *Of David.*
My soul, bless the LORD,
and all that is within me, bless his holy name.
2 My soul, bless the LORD,
and do not forget all his benefits.

3 He forgives all your iniquity;
he heals all your diseases.
4 He redeems your life from the Pit;
he crowns you with faithful love
and compassion.
5 He satisfies you[C] with good things;
your youth is renewed like the eagle.

6 The LORD executes acts of righteousness
and justice for all the oppressed.
7 He revealed his ways to Moses,
his deeds to the people of Israel.
8 The LORD is compassionate and gracious,
slow to anger and abounding in faithful love.
9 He will not always accuse us
or be angry forever.
10 He has not dealt with us as our sins deserve
or repaid us according to our iniquities.

11 For as high as the heavens are above
the earth,
so great is his faithful love
toward those who fear him.
12 As far as the east is from the west,
so far has he removed
our transgressions from us.
13 As a father has compassion on his children,
so the LORD has compassion on those
who fear him.
14 For he knows what we are made of,
remembering that we are dust.
15 As for man, his days are like grass —
he blooms like a flower of the field;
16 when the wind passes over it, it vanishes,
and its place is no longer known.[D]
17 But from eternity to eternity
the LORD's faithful love is toward
those who fear him,
and his righteousness
toward the grandchildren
18 of those who keep his covenant,
who remember to observe his precepts.
19 The LORD has established his throne
in heaven,
and his kingdom rules over all.

20 Bless the LORD,
all his angels of great strength,
who do his word,
obedient to his command.
21 Bless the LORD, all his armies,
his servants who do his will.
22 Bless the LORD, all his works
in all the places where he rules.
My soul, bless the LORD!

GOD THE CREATOR

104 My soul, bless the LORD!
LORD my God, you are very great;
you are clothed with majesty and splendor.
2 He wraps himself in light
as if it were a robe,
spreading out the sky like a canopy,
3 laying the beams of his palace
on the waters above,
making the clouds his chariot,
walking on the wings of the wind,
4 and making the winds his messengers,[E]
flames of fire his servants.

5 He established the earth on its foundations;
it will never be shaken.
6 You covered it with the deep
as if it were a garment;
the water stood above the mountains.
7 At your rebuke the water fled;
at the sound of your thunder
they hurried away —
8 mountains rose and valleys sank[F] —
to the place you established for them.
9 You set a boundary they cannot cross;
they will never cover the earth again.

[A] **102:23** Some Hb mss, LXX read *his* [B] **102:24** Lit *my days* [C] **103:5** Lit *satisfies your ornament*; Hb obscure [D] **103:16** Lit *place no longer knows it* [E] **104:4** Or *angels* [F] **104:7–8** Or *away. They flowed over the mountains and went down valleys*

10 He causes the springs to gush into the valleys;
they flow between the mountains.
11 They supply water for every wild beast;
the wild donkeys quench their thirst.
12 The birds of the sky live beside the springs;
they make their voices heard
among the foliage.
13 He waters the mountains from his palace;
the earth is satisfied by the fruit of your labor.

14 He causes grass to grow for the livestock
and provides crops for man to cultivate,
producing food from the earth,
15 wine that makes human hearts glad —
making his face shine with oil —
and bread that sustains human hearts.

16 The trees of the LORD flourish,[A]
the cedars of Lebanon that he planted.
17 There the birds make their nests;
storks make their homes in the pine trees.
18 The high mountains are for the wild goats;
the cliffs are a refuge for hyraxes.

19 He made the moon to mark the[B] festivals;[C]
the sun knows when to set.
20 You bring darkness, and it becomes night,
when all the forest animals stir.
21 The young lions roar for their prey
and seek their food from God.
22 The sun rises; they go back
and lie down in their dens.
23 Man goes out to his work
and to his labor until evening.

24 How countless are your works, LORD!
In wisdom you have made them all;
the earth is full of your creatures.[D]
25 Here is the sea, vast and wide,
teeming with creatures beyond number —
living things both large and small.
26 There the ships move about,
and Leviathan, which you formed
to play there.

27 All of them wait for you
to give them their food at the right time.
28 When you give it to them,
they gather it;
when you open your hand,
they are satisfied with good things.
29 When you hide your face,
they are terrified;
when you take away their breath,
they die and return to the dust.
30 When you send your breath,[E]
they are created,
and you renew the surface of the ground.

31 May the glory of the LORD endure forever;
may the LORD rejoice in his works.
32 He looks at the earth, and it trembles;
he touches the mountains,
and they pour out smoke.
33 I will sing to the LORD all my life;
I will sing praise to my God while I live.
34 May my meditation be pleasing to him;
I will rejoice in the LORD.
35 May sinners vanish from the earth
and wicked people be no more.
My soul, bless the LORD!
Hallelujah!

GOD'S FAITHFULNESS TO HIS PEOPLE

105 Give thanks to the LORD, call on his name;
proclaim his deeds among the peoples.
2 Sing to him, sing praise to him;
tell about all his wondrous works!
3 Boast in his holy name;
let the hearts of those who seek the LORD rejoice.
4 Seek the LORD and his strength;
seek his face always.
5 Remember the wondrous works he has done,
his wonders, and the judgments
he has pronounced,[F]
6 you offspring of Abraham his servant,
Jacob's descendants — his chosen ones.

7 He is the LORD our God;
his judgments govern the whole earth.
8 He remembers his covenant forever,
the promise he ordained
for a thousand generations —
9 the covenant he made with Abraham,
swore[G] to Isaac,
10 and confirmed to Jacob as a decree
and to Israel as a permanent covenant:
11 "I will give the land of Canaan to you
as your inherited portion."

12 When they were few in number,
very few indeed,
and resident aliens in Canaan,
13 wandering from nation to nation
and from one kingdom to another,
14 he allowed no one to oppress them;
he rebuked kings on their behalf:

[A]**104:16** Lit *are satisfied* [B]**104:19** Lit *moon for* [C]**104:19** Or *the appointed times* [D]**104:24** Lit *possessions* [E]**104:30** Or *Spirit* [F]**105:5** Lit *judgments of his mouth* [G]**105:9** Lit *and his oath*

Who Were the Canaanites?

by Trent C. Butler

Scene of Amenhotep II and his Asiatic campaign. A stele describing this campaign by Amenhotep II has the earliest Egyptian text mentioning the Canaanites.

Sarcophagus fragment depicting a Phoenician shepherd (fifth–fourth centuries BC).

In the narrowest sense of the word, *Canaanite* originally referred to the people living on the northwestern Mediterranean seacoast of Phoenicia (Nm 13:29). Centuries later the Phoenicians came to refer to themselves as Canaanites. In a wider meaning of the term, *Canaanites* referred to the persons living in the valleys and hills throughout Canaan (Nm 14:25,45; Dt 11:30). They were one of several ethnic groups Israel confronted in the land (Jos 3:10; 9:1; 11:3). Apparently, Canaan proper stopped at the Jordan River. Gilead and other lands east of the Jordan River were not part of Canaan (Jos 22:9–10,32).

God's purpose in the exodus was to take his people back to the land of promise (Ex 3:8), famed for its fruitfulness (v. 17), so they would obey him and let him be their God (Lv 18:3; 25:38). God's promise and its fulfillment became a central part of Israel's worship (Ps 105:11; cf. Ac 13:19).

As they prepared to enter the land of Canaan, Israel had one God-given goal—to exterminate the Canaanites (Dt 20:17). But the Israelites succumbed to the false belief that because the Canaanites dwelt in the land long before the Israelites, they must have known the secrets to its fertility and blessing—worshiping the high god Baal, the master of storms and fertility. If military success with Yahweh was good, they reasoned, then adding some agricultural and fertility success with Canaan's gods could only make things better (3:6–7). Such constant temptation lasted into the postexilic period with Ezra (Ezr 9:1).

ANCIENT NEAR EASTERN TEXTS

Texts from the ancient Near East give us additional information about Canaanites and Baal. Canaan appears in texts from Mari, Alalakh, Ugarit, and Amarna and in the Egyptian Merneptah stele. These affirm that the geographical and ethnic names were known long before Joshua.

Mention of Baal goes back to Egyptian execration texts from about 1800 BC and back to texts from the Syrian city of Ebla after 1500 BC. Most information comes from the texts found at Ugarit on the Syrian coast of the Mediterranean Sea. These texts and artistic renderings closely associated Baal with thunder and lightning and with battle against Yam, the god of the sea. Baal's partner was the goddess Anath. She joined him in battle against Mot, the god of the dead. Defeat of Yam brought Baal the title "King of the Gods." Baal's entrance into Mot's underworld brought temporary death for Baal and for the crops of Canaan until Anath rescued Baal, restoring fertility.

Astarte is another, infrequently mentioned consort of Baal in the Ugaritic materials. In the Bible, she appears often in the forms of Asherah, Ashtoreth, or the plural form Ashtaroth.

Canaanite worshipers believed the local king represented the major god. Sacrifices formed the central worship rites as well as serving as the means of expiating sins and provided opportunities for social gatherings. Annual agricultural festivals included sacred meals and renewal of religious and political commitments.

Politically Egypt controlled Canaan and took advantage of its geographical location to control international trade routes. The Amarna letters indicate that local city-state kings or governors paid homage and taxes to the Egyptian pharaoh and fought among themselves for local control. From 3500 to about 2000 BC, about twenty city-states dominated, but most had populations of fewer than two thousand. Megiddo, Laish (or Dan), and Ai were the largest cities in this period. Around 2300 BC, Egypt's Old Kingdom collapsed. So did Canaan's cities, so that only a very small population remained.

The Middle Bronze Age (2000–1550 BC) brought trade growth to Phoenicia and population growth in Canaanite cities. Canaanite population thus reached about 140,000. The majority of the population were farmers living outside the major cities, providing food for each family and for the king and his elite administrators. Foreign trading brought in specialty items, including fine garments and pottery and metal goods. Hazor was the dominant city with a population possibly reaching

Standing stones (Hb *masseboth*); these mark the likely site of Canaanite worship in Megiddo.

20,000. The hill country remained basically unpopulated. New siege weapons, chariots, and composite bows helped advance military technology and forced cities to build massive defensive walls. Just before 1550 BC, various armies and causes destroyed most of these cities.

The Late Bronze Age (1550–1200 BC) is the apparent time of the exodus and conquest of Canaan. The region became a battlefield among the Hittites to the north, the Hurrian Mitanni to the northeast, and the Egyptians to the south. Canaanites suffered as they paid taxes, were forced to join enemy military ranks, and even became slaves, particularly to the Egyptians. From about 1425 to 1350 BC, Egypt had peace from its wars but continued to tax and enslave the people of Canaan, cutting its population in half to about seventy thousand. Shortly after 1300, Pharaoh Ramesses II suffered defeat by the Hittites at Kadesh and turned his ire again against the Canaanites.[1]

After 1300 BC, Egyptian control tightened with more troops and more Egyptian outposts in Canaan and more taxes for the Canaanites. The hill country and the area east of the Jordan had few settlements or people.

Egyptian rule brought the Canaanites poverty and hardship. Only the Egyptian-selected rulers in the twenty or so city-states had any luxuries. People not belonging to the ruling elite in Canaan had few choices. The few talented people became artisans, creating items demanded by the elite. Otherwise, a Canaanite became a farmer on land he did not own, paying much of his crop to the aristocratic or royal property owner or became a nomadic shepherd following sheep and goats to pasture lands, occasionally settling down near or in a village.

The opening years of the Iron Age (1200–1000 BC) changed the situation. Egypt withdrew. The Hittite Empire collapsed. The highland or hill country population increased radically, growing, for example, from 5 sites in the tribe of Ephraim to 115 sites.[2] Canaanites (and Israelites) gained freedom to govern themselves. Droughts and famines set people on the move, looking for better living conditions. Included were the Sea Peoples coming from Sicily, Cyprus, and Crete. One group of Sea Peoples settled on the southern Mediterranean coast. They became the Philistines, the major challengers of ancient Israel.

ARCHAEOLOGICAL EXCAVATIONS

Archaeological excavations show much about Canaanite daily life. One result surprises: "The strong continuance of Late Bronze Age material culture into Iron Age I can

support Israel's presence in the land prior to 1200 and their acceptance of much of the material culture. . . . The proposition that certain traits distinguish Israelite from Canaanite settlements is highly questionable."[3] Thus daily life remained much the same for Canaanites and Israelites, even down to the way they built four-room houses and made collar-rimmed jars. Archaeologists cannot distinguish between Israelite settlements and Canaanite ones.

Israel's major distinction lay in its official religion. Yet its insistence on a centralized worship and its refusal to use material images of God leave little behind for archaeologists to find. Similarly, stories such as those of Rahab (Jos 2) and the Gibeonites (Jos 9) present only two of what probably were many cases of foreigners joining with Israel and bringing with them "Canaanite" artistry and skills.[4]

Excavations have shown that Canaanite religion was dynamic and varied in nature, with different types of worship structures from rural high places to urban temples to funeral sites where the Canaanites worshiped their ancestors. Standing stones or *masseboth* played an important role in many worship sites as did Egyptian obelisks. Archaeologists found that large Canaanite cities had multiple temples, and certain sites served as regional worship centers with professional staffs. The temple courtyard led to the most holy place and had altars for burnt offerings. The courtyard often had workshops for temple metalworkers and potters who produced sacred objects for use in worship. These included ceramic vessels, small statues—especially of female figurines used in fertility and funeral practices—bronze cymbals, small stone statues of gods and goddesses, clay masks, and various types of jewelry and ornaments.[5]

What became of the Canaanites? History offers no solid details. Evidently they were not destroyed in war or taken captive. Many Bible scholars believe instead they eventually were assimilated into other people groups in the area. Although they ceased to exist as a separate people, their influences on religion and culture continued throughout the Old Testament era. ✣

[1] Information and population figures cited above, from K. L. Noll, *Canaan and Israel in Antiquity: An Introduction* (London: Sheffield Academic, 2001), 83–116. [2] Israel Finkelstein, *The Archaeology of the Israelite Settlement* (Jerusalem: Israel Exploration Society, 1988), 186. "An influx of settlers overran the region" (187). [3] Alfred J. Hoerth, *Archaeology and the Old Testament* (Grand Rapids: Baker Academic, 1998), 216. [4] See Richard S. Hess, "Early Israel in Canaan: A Survey of Recent Evidence and Interpretation" in *Israel's Past in Recent Research: Essays on Israelite Historiography*; ed. V. Philips Long. Sources for Biblical and Theological Studies 7 (Winona Lake, IN: Eisenbrauns, 1999), 498–512; originally published in *PEQ* 125 (1993), 125–42. [5] Beth Alpert Nakhai, "Canaanite Religion" in *Near Eastern Archaeology: A Reader*, ed. Suzanne Richard (Winona Lake, IN: Eisenbrauns, 2003), 343–48.

Palace ruins at Ebla (later known as Tel Mardikh). Ebla was the dynastic capital of the region. Excavations at Ebla uncovered thousands of cuneiform tablets dating to the Middle Bronze Age (ca 2000 BC). Several refer to names of cities and persons mentioned in the Bible. Further, many of the texts offer information about worship practices and beliefs related to the Canaanite god Baal. The name Ebla means "white rock"—likely a reference to the limestone on which the city was built.

15 "Do not touch my anointed ones,
or harm my prophets."

16 He called down famine against the land
and destroyed the entire food supply.
17 He had sent a man ahead of them —
Joseph, who was sold as a slave.
18 They hurt his feet with shackles;
his neck was put in an iron collar.
19 Until the time his prediction came true,
the word of the LORD tested him.
20 The king sent for him and released him;
the ruler of peoples set him free.
21 He made him master of his household,
ruler over all his possessions —
22 binding[A] his officials at will
and instructing his elders.

23 Then Israel went to Egypt;
Jacob lived as an alien in the land of Ham.[B]
24 The LORD[C] made his people very fruitful;
he made them more numerous than their foes,
25 whose hearts he turned to hate his people
and to deal deceptively with his servants.
26 He sent Moses his servant,
and Aaron, whom he had chosen.
27 They performed his miraculous signs
among them
and wonders in the land of Ham.
28 He sent darkness, and it became dark —
for did they not defy his commands?
29 He turned their water into blood
and caused their fish to die.
30 Their land was overrun with frogs,
even in their royal chambers.
31 He spoke, and insects came —
gnats throughout their country.
32 He gave them hail for rain,
and lightning throughout their land.
33 He struck their vines and fig trees
and shattered the trees of their territory.
34 He spoke, and locusts came —
young locusts without number.
35 They devoured all the vegetation in their land
and consumed the produce of their land.
36 He struck all the firstborn in their land,
all their first progeny.

37 Then he brought Israel out with silver
and gold,
and no one among his tribes stumbled.
38 Egypt was glad when they left,
for the dread of Israel[D] had fallen on them.
39 He spread a cloud as a covering
and gave a fire to light up the night.
40 They asked, and he brought quail
and satisfied them with bread from heaven.
41 He opened a rock, and water gushed out;
it flowed like a stream in the desert.
42 For he remembered his holy promise
to Abraham his servant.
43 He brought his people out with rejoicing,
his chosen ones with shouts of joy.
44 He gave them the lands of the nations,
and they inherited
what other peoples had worked for.

45 All this happened
so that they might keep his statutes
and obey his instructions.
Hallelujah!

ISRAEL'S UNFAITHFULNESS TO GOD

106 Hallelujah!
Give thanks to the LORD, for he is good;
his faithful love endures forever.
2 Who can declare the LORD's mighty acts
or proclaim all the praise due him?
3 How happy are those who uphold justice,
who practice righteousness at all times.

4 Remember me, LORD,
when you show favor to your people.
Come to me with your salvation
5 so that I may enjoy the prosperity
of your chosen ones,
rejoice in the joy of your nation,
and boast about your heritage.

6 Both we and our ancestors have sinned;
we have done wrong and have acted wickedly.
7 Our ancestors in Egypt did not grasp
the significance of your wondrous works
or remember your many acts of faithful love;
instead, they rebelled by the sea — the Red Sea.
8 Yet he saved them for his name's sake,
to make his power known.
9 He rebuked the Red Sea, and it dried up;
he led them through the depths as through
a desert.
10 He saved them from the power of the adversary;
he redeemed them from the power
of the enemy.
11 Water covered their foes;
not one of them remained.
12 Then they believed his promises
and sang his praise.

[A] **105:22** LXX, Syr, Vg read *teaching* [B] **105:23** = Egypt, also in v. 27
[C] **105:24** Lit *He* [D] **105:38** Lit *them*

13 They soon forgot his works
and would not wait for his counsel.
14 They were seized with craving in the wilderness
and tested God in the desert.
15 He gave them what they asked for,
but sent a wasting disease among them

16 In the camp they were envious of Moses
and of Aaron, the LORD's holy one.
17 The earth opened up and swallowed Dathan;
it covered the assembly of Abiram.
18 Fire blazed throughout their assembly;
flames consumed the wicked.

19 At Horeb they made a calf
and worshiped the cast metal image.
20 They exchanged their glory[A,B]
for the image of a grass-eating ox.
21 They forgot God their Savior,
who did great things in Egypt,
22 wondrous works in the land of Ham,[C]
awe-inspiring acts at the Red Sea.
23 So he said he would have destroyed them —
if Moses his chosen one
had not stood before him in the breach
to turn his wrath away from destroying them.

24 They despised the pleasant land
and did not believe his promise.
25 They grumbled in their tents
and did not listen to the LORD.
26 So he raised his hand against them
with an oath
that he would make them fall in the desert
27 and would disperse their descendants[D]
among the nations,
scattering them throughout the lands.

28 They aligned themselves with Baal of Peor
and ate sacrifices offered to lifeless gods.[E]
29 They angered the LORD with their deeds,
and a plague broke out against them.
30 But Phinehas stood up and intervened,
and the plague was stopped.
31 It was credited to him as righteousness
throughout all generations to come.

32 They angered the LORD at the Waters
of Meribah,
and Moses suffered[F] because of them,
33 for they embittered his spirit,[G]
and he spoke rashly with his lips.

34 They did not destroy the peoples
as the LORD had commanded them
35 but mingled with the nations
and adopted their ways.
36 They served their idols,
which became a snare to them.
37 They sacrificed their sons and daughters
to demons.
38 They shed innocent blood —
the blood of their sons and daughters
whom they sacrificed to the idols of Canaan;
so the land became polluted with blood.
39 They defiled themselves by their actions
and prostituted themselves by their deeds.

40 Therefore the LORD's anger burned
against his people,
and he abhorred his own inheritance.
41 He handed them over to the nations;
those who hated them ruled over them.
42 Their enemies oppressed them,
and they were subdued under their power.
43 He rescued them many times,
but they continued to rebel deliberately
and were beaten down by their iniquity.

44 When he heard their cry,
he took note of their distress,
45 remembered his covenant with them,
and relented according to the abundance
of his faithful love.
46 He caused them to be pitied
before all their captors.

47 Save us, LORD our God,
and gather us from the nations,
so that we may give thanks to your holy name
and rejoice in your praise.

48 Blessed be the LORD God of Israel,
from everlasting to everlasting.
Let all the people say, "Amen!"
Hallelujah!

BOOK V (Psalms 107–150)

THANKSGIVING FOR GOD'S DELIVERANCE

107 Give thanks to the LORD,
for he is good;
his faithful love endures forever.
2 Let the redeemed of the LORD proclaim
that he has redeemed them from the power
of the foe

[A]106:20 Alt Hb tradition reads *his glory*, or *my glory* [B]106:20 = God [C]106:22 = Egypt [D]106:27 Syr; MT reads *would make their descendants fall* [E]106:28 Lit *sacrifices for dead ones* [F]106:32 Lit *and it was evil for Moses* [G]106:33 Some Hb mss, LXX, Syr, Jer; other Hb mss read *they rebelled against his Spirit*

3 and has gathered them from the lands —
from the east and the west,
from the north and the south.

4 Some wandered in the desolate wilderness,
finding no way to a city where they could live.
5 They were hungry and thirsty;
their spirits failed[A] within them.
6 Then they cried out to the LORD
in their trouble;
he rescued them from their distress.
7 He led them by the right path
to go to a city where they could live.
8 Let them give thanks to the LORD
for his faithful love
and his wondrous works for all humanity.
9 For he has satisfied the thirsty
and filled the hungry with good things.

10 Others sat in darkness and gloom[B] —
prisoners in cruel chains —
11 because they rebelled
against God's commands
and despised the counsel of the Most High.
12 He broke their spirits[C] with hard labor;
they stumbled, and there was no one to help.
13 Then they cried out to the LORD
in their trouble;
he saved them from their distress.
14 He brought them out of darkness and gloom
and broke their chains apart.
15 Let them give thanks to the LORD
for his faithful love
and his wondrous works for all humanity.
16 For he has broken down the bronze gates
and cut through the iron bars.

17 Fools suffered affliction
because of their rebellious ways
and their iniquities.
18 They loathed all food
and came near the gates of death.
19 Then they cried out to the LORD
in their trouble;
he saved them from their distress.
20 He sent his word and healed them;
he rescued them from their traps.
21 Let them give thanks to the LORD
for his faithful love
and his wondrous works for all humanity.
22 Let them offer thanksgiving sacrifices
and announce his works with shouts of joy.

23 Others went to sea in ships,
conducting trade on the vast water.
24 They saw the LORD's works,
his wondrous works in the deep.
25 He spoke and raised a stormy wind
that stirred up the waves of the sea.[D]
26 Rising up to the sky, sinking down
to the depths,
their courage[E] melting away in anguish,
27 they reeled and staggered like a drunkard,
and all their skill was useless.
28 Then they cried out to the LORD
in their trouble,
and he brought them out of their distress.
29 He stilled the storm to a whisper,
and the waves of the sea were hushed.
30 They rejoiced when the waves grew quiet.
Then he guided them to the harbor
they longed for.
31 Let them give thanks to the LORD
for his faithful love
and his wondrous works for all humanity.
32 Let them exalt him in the assembly
of the people
and praise him in the council of the elders.

33 He turns rivers into desert,
springs into thirsty ground,
34 and fruitful land into salty wasteland,
because of the wickedness of its inhabitants.
35 He turns a desert into a pool,
dry land into springs.
36 He causes the hungry to settle there,
and they establish a city
where they can live.
37 They sow fields and plant vineyards
that yield a fruitful harvest.
38 He blesses them, and they multiply greatly;
he does not let their livestock decrease.

39 When they are diminished and are humbled
by cruel oppression and sorrow,
40 he pours contempt on nobles
and makes them wander
in a trackless wasteland.
41 But he lifts the needy out of their suffering
and makes their families multiply
like flocks.
42 The upright see it and rejoice,
and all injustice shuts its mouth.

43 Let whoever is wise pay attention
to these things
and consider the LORD's acts of faithful love.

[A] **107:5** Lit *their soul fainted* [B] **107:10** Or *the shadow of death*, also in v. 14 [C] **107:12** Lit *hearts* [D] **107:25** Lit *of it* [E] **107:26** Lit *souls*

A PLEA FOR VICTORY

108 *A song. A psalm of David.*
My heart is confident, God;
I will sing; I will sing praises
with the whole of my being.[A]
2 Wake up, harp and lyre!
I will wake up the dawn.
3 I will praise you, LORD, among the peoples;
I will sing praises to you among the nations.
4 For your faithful love is higher than the heavens,
and your faithfulness reaches to the clouds.
5 God, be exalted above the heavens,
and let your glory be over the whole earth.
6 Save with your right hand and answer me
so that those you love may be rescued.

7 God has spoken in his sanctuary:[B]
"I will celebrate!
I will divide up Shechem.
I will apportion the Valley of Succoth.
8 Gilead is mine, Manasseh is mine,
and Ephraim is my helmet;
Judah is my scepter.
9 Moab is my washbasin;
I throw my sandal on Edom.
I shout in triumph over Philistia."

10 Who will bring me to the fortified city?
Who will lead me to Edom?
11 God, haven't you rejected us?
God, you do not march out with our armies.
12 Give us aid against the foe,
for human help is worthless.
13 With God we will perform valiantly;
he will trample our foes.

PRAYER AGAINST AN ENEMY

109 *For the choir director. A psalm of David.*
God of my praise, do not be silent.
2 For wicked and deceitful mouths open
against me;
they speak against me with lying tongues.
3 They surround me with hateful words
and attack me without cause.
4 In return for my love they accuse me,
but I continue to pray.[C]
5 They repay me evil for good,
and hatred for my love.

6 Set a wicked person over him;
let an accuser[D] stand at his right hand.
7 When he is judged, let him be found guilty,
and let his prayer be counted as sin.
8 Let his days be few;
let another take over his position.
9 Let his children be fatherless
and his wife a widow.
10 Let his children wander as beggars,
searching for food far[E]
from their demolished homes.
11 Let a creditor seize all he has;
let strangers plunder what he has worked for.
12 Let no one show him kindness,
and let no one be gracious
to his fatherless children.
13 Let the line of his descendants be cut off;
let their name be blotted out
in the next generation.
14 Let the iniquity of his fathers
be remembered before the LORD,
and do not let his mother's sin
be blotted out.
15 Let their sins[F] always remain
before the LORD,
and let him remove[G] all memory of them
from the earth.

16 For he did not think to show kindness,
but pursued the suffering, needy,
and brokenhearted
in order to put them to death.
17 He loved cursing — let it fall on him;
he took no delight in blessing — let it be far
from him.
18 He wore cursing like his coat —
let it enter his body like water
and go into his bones like oil.
19 Let it be like a robe he wraps around himself,
like a belt he always wears.
20 Let this be the LORD's payment
to my accusers,
to those who speak evil against me.

21 But you, LORD, my Lord,
deal kindly with me for your name's sake;
because your faithful love is good, rescue me.
22 For I am suffering and needy;
my heart is wounded within me.
23 I fade away like a lengthening shadow;
I am shaken off like a locust.
24 My knees are weak from fasting,
and my body is emaciated.[H]
25 I have become an object of ridicule
to my accusers;[I]
when they see me, they shake their heads
in scorn.

[A]108:1 Lit *praises, even my glory* [B]108:7 Or *has promised by his holy nature* [C]109:4 Lit *but I, prayer* [D]109:6 Or *adversary* [E]109:10 LXX reads *beggars, driven far* [F]109:15 Lit *Let them* [G]109:15 Or *cut off* [H]109:24 Lit *denied from fat* [I]109:25 Lit *to them*

26 Help me, LORD my God;
save me according to your faithful love
27 so they may know that this is your hand
and that you, LORD, have done it.
28 Though they curse, you will bless.
When they rise up, they will be put to shame,
but your servant will rejoice.
29 My accusers will be clothed with disgrace;
they will wear their shame like a cloak.
30 I will fervently thank the LORD
with my mouth;
I will praise him in the presence of many.
31 For he stands at the right hand of the needy
to save him from those who would
condemn him.

THE PRIESTLY KING

110 *A psalm of David.*
This is the declaration of the LORD
to my Lord:
"Sit at my right hand
until I make your enemies your footstool."
2 The LORD will extend your mighty scepter
from Zion.
Rule[A] over your surrounding[B] enemies.
3 Your people will volunteer
on your day of battle.[C]
In holy splendor, from the womb of the dawn,
the dew of your youth belongs to you.[D]
4 The LORD has sworn an oath and will not
take it back:
"You are a priest forever
according to the pattern of Melchizedek."

5 The Lord is at your right hand;
he will crush kings on the day of his anger.
6 He will judge the nations, heaping up corpses;
he will crush leaders over the entire world.
7 He will drink from the brook by the road;
therefore, he will lift up his head.

PRAISE FOR THE LORD'S WORKS

111 Hallelujah![E]
I will praise the LORD with all my heart
in the assembly of the upright
and in the congregation.
2 The LORD's works are great,
studied by all who delight in them.
3 All that he does is splendid and majestic;
his righteousness endures forever.
4 He has caused his wondrous works
to be remembered.
The LORD is gracious and compassionate.
5 He has provided food for those who fear him;
he remembers his covenant forever.
6 He has shown his people the power
of his works
by giving them the inheritance of the nations.
7 The works of his hands are truth and justice;
all his instructions are trustworthy.
8 They are established forever and ever,
enacted in truth and in uprightness.
9 He has sent redemption to his people.
He has ordained his covenant forever.
His name is holy and awe-inspiring.

10 The fear of the LORD is the beginning
of wisdom;
all who follow his instructions[F] have
good insight.
His praise endures forever.

THE TRAITS OF THE RIGHTEOUS

112 Hallelujah![E]
Happy is the person who fears the LORD,
taking great delight in his commands.
2 His descendants will be powerful in the land;
the generation of the upright will be blessed.
3 Wealth and riches are in his house,
and his righteousness endures forever.
4 Light shines in the darkness for the upright.
He is gracious, compassionate, and righteous.
5 Good will come to the one
who lends generously
and conducts his business fairly.
6 He will never be shaken.
The righteous one will be remembered forever.
7 He will not fear bad news;
his heart is confident, trusting in the LORD.
8 His heart is assured; he will not fear.
In the end he will look in triumph on his foes.
9 He distributes freely to the poor;
his righteousness endures forever.
His horn will be exalted in honor.

10 The wicked one will see it and be angry;
he will gnash his teeth in despair.
The desire of the wicked leads to ruin.

PRAISE TO THE MERCIFUL GOD

113 Hallelujah!
Give praise, servants of the LORD;
praise the name of the LORD.
2 Let the name of the LORD be blessed
both now and forever.
3 From the rising of the sun to its setting,
let the name of the LORD be praised.

[A] **110:2** One Hb ms, LXX, Tg read *You will rule* [B] **110:2** Lit *Rule in the midst of your* [C] **110:3** Lit *power* [D] **110:3** Hb obscure [E] **111:1; 112:1** The lines of this poem form an acrostic. [F] **111:10** Lit *follow them*

4 The LORD is exalted above all the nations,
his glory above the heavens.
5 Who is like the LORD our God —
the one enthroned on high,
6 who stoops down to look
on the heavens and the earth?
7 He raises the poor from the dust
and lifts the needy from the trash heap
8 in order to seat them with nobles —
with the nobles of his people.
9 He gives the childless woman a household,
making her the joyful mother of children.
Hallelujah!

GOD'S DELIVERANCE OF ISRAEL

114 When Israel came out of Egypt —
the house of Jacob from a people
who spoke a foreign language —
2 Judah became his sanctuary,
Israel, his dominion.

3 The sea looked and fled;
the Jordan turned back.
4 The mountains skipped like rams,
the hills, like lambs.
5 Why was it, sea, that you fled?
Jordan, that you turned back?
6 Mountains, that you skipped like rams?
Hills, like lambs?

7 Tremble, earth, at the presence of the Lord,
at the presence of the God of Jacob,
8 who turned the rock into a pool,
the flint into a spring.

GLORY TO GOD ALONE

115 Not to us, LORD, not to us,
but to your name give glory
because of your faithful love, because of
your truth.
2 Why should the nations say,
"Where is their God?"
3 Our God is in heaven
and does whatever he pleases.

4 Their idols are silver and gold,
made by human hands.
5 They have mouths but cannot speak,
eyes, but cannot see.
6 They have ears but cannot hear,
noses, but cannot smell.
7 They have hands but cannot feel,
feet, but cannot walk.
They cannot make a sound
with their throats.
8 Those who make them are[A] just like them,
as are all who trust in them.

9 Israel,[B] trust in the LORD!
He is their help and shield.
10 House of Aaron, trust in the LORD!
He is their help and shield.
11 You who fear the LORD, trust in the LORD!
He is their help and shield.
12 The LORD remembers us and will bless us.
He will bless the house of Israel;
he will bless the house of Aaron;
13 he will bless those who fear the LORD —
small and great alike.

14 May the LORD add to your numbers,
both yours and your children's.
15 May you be blessed by the LORD,
the Maker of heaven and earth.
16 The heavens are the LORD's,[C]
but the earth he has given to the human race.
17 It is not the dead who praise the LORD,
nor any of those descending into the silence
of death.
18 But we will bless the LORD,
both now and forever.
Hallelujah!

THANKS TO GOD FOR DELIVERANCE

116 I love the LORD because he has heard
my appeal for mercy.
2 Because he has turned his ear to me,
I will call out to him as long as I live.

3 The ropes of death were wrapped
around me,
and the torments of Sheol overcame me;
I encountered trouble and sorrow.
4 Then I called on the name of the LORD:
"LORD, save me!"

5 The LORD is gracious and righteous;
our God is compassionate.
6 The LORD guards the inexperienced;
I was helpless, and he saved me.
7 Return to your rest, my soul,
for the LORD has been good to you.
8 For you, LORD, rescued me from death,
my eyes from tears,
my feet from stumbling.
9 I will walk before the LORD
in the land of the living.

[A] **115:8** Or *May those who make them become* [B] **115:9** Some Hb mss, LXX, Syr read *House of Israel* [C] **115:16** Lit *the LORD's heavens*

10 I believed, even when I said,
"I am severely oppressed."
11 In my alarm I said,
"Everyone is a liar."

12 How can I repay the LORD
for all the good he has done for me?
13 I will take the cup of salvation
and call on the name of the LORD.
14 I will fulfill my vows to the LORD
in the presence of all his people.

15 The death of his faithful ones
is valuable in the LORD's sight.
16 LORD, I am indeed your servant;
I am your servant, the son
of your female servant.
You have loosened my bonds.

17 I will offer you a thanksgiving sacrifice
and call on the name of the LORD.
18 I will fulfill my vows to the LORD
in the presence of all his people,
19 in the courts of the LORD's house —
within you, Jerusalem.
Hallelujah!

UNIVERSAL CALL TO PRAISE

117 Praise the LORD, all nations!
Glorify him, all peoples!
2 For his faithful love to us is great;
the LORD's faithfulness endures forever.
Hallelujah!

THANKSGIVING FOR VICTORY

118 Give thanks to the LORD, for he is good;
his faithful love endures forever.
2 Let Israel say,
"His faithful love endures forever."
3 Let the house of Aaron say,
"His faithful love endures forever."
4 Let those who fear the LORD say,
"His faithful love endures forever."

5 I called to the LORD in distress;
the LORD answered me
and put me in a spacious place.[A]
6 The LORD is for me; I will not be afraid.
What can a mere mortal do to me?
7 The LORD is my helper;
therefore, I will look in triumph on those
who hate me.

8 It is better to take refuge in the LORD
than to trust in humanity.
9 It is better to take refuge in the LORD
than to trust in nobles.

10 All the nations surrounded me;
in the name of the LORD I destroyed them.
11 They surrounded me, yes, they surrounded me;
in the name of the LORD I destroyed them.
12 They surrounded me like bees;
they were extinguished like a fire
among thorns;
in the name of the LORD I destroyed them.
13 They[B] pushed me hard to make me fall,
but the LORD helped me.
14 The LORD is my strength and my song;
he has become my salvation.

15 There are shouts of joy and victory
in the tents of the righteous:
"The LORD's right hand performs valiantly!
16 The LORD's right hand is raised.
The LORD's right hand performs valiantly!"
17 I will not die, but I will live
and proclaim what the LORD has done.
18 The LORD disciplined me severely
but did not give me over to death.

19 Open the gates of righteousness for me;
I will enter through them
and give thanks to the LORD.
20 This is the LORD's gate;
the righteous will enter through it.
21 I will give thanks to you
because you have answered me
and have become my salvation.
22 The stone that the builders rejected
has become the cornerstone.
23 This came from the LORD;
it is wondrous in our sight.
24 This is the day the LORD has made;
let's rejoice and be glad in it.

25 LORD, save us!
LORD, please grant us success!
26 He who comes in the name
of the LORD is blessed.
From the house of the LORD we bless you.
27 The LORD is God and has given us light.
Bind the festival sacrifice with cords
to the horns of the altar.
28 You are my God, and I will give you thanks.
You are my God; I will exalt you.
29 Give thanks to the LORD, for he is good;
his faithful love endures forever.

[A] **118:5** Or *answered me with freedom* [B] **118:13** Lit *You*

DELIGHT IN GOD'S WORD

א Aleph

119 How[A] happy are those whose way
is blameless,
who walk according to the LORD's
instruction!
2 Happy are those who keep his decrees
and seek him with all their heart.
3 They do nothing wrong;
they walk in his ways.
4 You have commanded that your precepts
be diligently kept.
5 If only my ways were committed
to keeping your statutes!
6 Then I would not be ashamed
when I think about all your commands.
7 I will praise you with an upright heart
when I learn your righteous judgments.
8 I will keep your statutes;
never abandon me.

ב Beth

9 How can a young man keep his way pure?
By keeping your[B] word.
10 I have sought you with all my heart;
don't let me wander from your commands.
11 I have treasured your word in my heart
so that I may not sin against you.
12 LORD, may you be blessed;
teach me your statutes.
13 With my lips I proclaim
all the judgments from your mouth.
14 I rejoice in the way revealed by
your decrees
as much as in all riches.
15 I will meditate on your precepts
and think about your ways.
16 I will delight in your statutes;
I will not forget your word.

ג Gimel

17 Deal generously with your servant
so that I might live;
then I will keep your word.
18 Open my eyes so that I may contemplate
wondrous things from your instruction.
19 I am a resident alien on earth;
do not hide your commands from me.
20 I am continually overcome
with longing for your judgments.
21 You rebuke the arrogant,
the ones under a curse,
who wander from your commands.
22 Take insult and contempt away from me,
for I have kept your decrees.
23 Though princes sit together speaking
against me,
your servant will think about your statutes;
24 your decrees are my delight
and my counselors.

ד Daleth

25 My life is down in the dust;
give me life through your word.
26 I told you about my life,
and you answered me;
teach me your statutes.
27 Help me understand
the meaning of your precepts
so that I can meditate on your wonders.
28 I am weary[C] from grief;
strengthen me through your word.
29 Keep me from the way of deceit
and graciously give me your instruction.
30 I have chosen the way of truth;
I have set your ordinances before me.
31 I cling to your decrees;
LORD, do not put me to shame.
32 I pursue the way of your commands,
for you broaden my understanding.[D]

ה He

33 Teach me, LORD, the meaning[E] of your statutes,
and I will always keep them.[F]
34 Help me understand your instruction,
and I will obey it
and follow it with all my heart.
35 Help me stay on the path of your commands,
for I take pleasure in it.
36 Turn my heart to your decrees
and not to dishonest profit.
37 Turn my eyes
from looking at what is worthless;
give me life in your ways.[G]
38 Confirm what you said to your servant,
for it produces reverence for you.
39 Turn away the disgrace I dread;
indeed, your judgments are good.
40 How I long for your precepts!
Give me life through your righteousness.

ו Waw

41 Let your faithful love come to me, LORD,
your salvation, as you promised.
42 Then I can answer the one who taunts me,
for I trust in your word.

[A] **119:1** The stanzas of this poem form an acrostic. [B] **119:9** Or *keeping it according to your* [C] **119:28** Or *I weep* [D] **119:32** Lit *you enlarge my heart* [E] **119:33** Lit *way* [F] **119:33** Or *will keep it as my reward* [G] **119:37** Some Hb mss, Tg read *word*

43 Never take the word of truth
from my mouth,
for I hope in your judgments.
44 I will always obey your instruction,
forever and ever.
45 I will walk freely in an open place
because I study your precepts.
46 I will speak of your decrees before kings
and not be ashamed.
47 I delight in your commands,
which I love.
48 I will lift up my hands to your commands,
which I love,
and will meditate on your statutes.

ז Zayin

49 Remember your word to your servant;
you have given me hope through it.
50 This is my comfort in my affliction:
Your promise has given me life.
51 The arrogant constantly ridicule me,
but I do not turn away
from your instruction.
52 LORD, I remember your judgments
from long ago
and find comfort.
53 Fury seizes me because of the wicked
who reject your instruction.
54 Your statutes are the theme of my song
during my earthly life.[A]
55 LORD, I remember your name in the night,
and I obey your instruction.
56 This is my practice:
I obey your precepts.

ח Cheth

57 The LORD is my portion;[B]
I have promised to keep your words.
58 I have sought your favor with all my heart;
be gracious to me according to
your promise.
59 I thought about my ways
and turned my steps back to your decrees.
60 I hurried, not hesitating
to keep your commands.
61 Though the ropes of the wicked
were wrapped around me,
I did not forget your instruction.
62 I rise at midnight to thank you
for your righteous judgments.
63 I am a friend to all who fear you,
to those who keep your precepts.
64 LORD, the earth is filled with
your faithful love;
teach me your statutes.

ט Teth

65 LORD, you have treated your servant well,
just as you promised.
66 Teach me good judgment and discernment,
for I rely on your commands.
67 Before I was afflicted I went astray,
but now I keep your word.
68 You are good, and you do what is good;
teach me your statutes.
69 The arrogant have smeared me with lies,
but I obey your precepts with all my heart.
70 Their hearts are hard and insensitive,
but I delight in your instruction.
71 It was good for me to be afflicted
so that I could learn your statutes.
72 Instruction from your lips is better for me
than thousands of gold and silver pieces.

י Yod

73 Your hands made me and formed me;
give me understanding
so that I can learn your commands.
74 Those who fear you will see me and rejoice,
for I put my hope in your word.
75 I know, LORD, that your judgments are just
and that you have afflicted me fairly.
76 May your faithful love comfort me
as you promised your servant.
77 May your compassion come to me
so that I may live,
for your instruction is my delight.
78 Let the arrogant be put to shame
for slandering me with lies;
I will meditate on your precepts.
79 Let those who fear you,
those who know your decrees, turn to me.
80 May my heart be blameless
regarding your statutes
so that I will not be put to shame.

כ Kaph

81 I long for your salvation;
I put my hope in your word.
82 My eyes grow weary
looking for what you have promised;
I ask, "When will you comfort me?"
83 Though I have become like a wineskin dried
by smoke,
I do not forget your statutes.
84 How many days must your servant wait?
When will you execute judgment
on my persecutors?

[A] **119:54** Lit *song in the house of my sojourning* [B] **119:57** Lit *You are my portion, LORD*

85 The arrogant have dug pits for me;
they violate your instruction.
86 All your commands are true;
people persecute me with lies — help me!
87 They almost ended my life on earth,
but I did not abandon your precepts.
88 Give me life in accordance with
your faithful love,
and I will obey the decree you have spoken.

ל Lamed

89 LORD, your word is forever;
it is firmly fixed in heaven.
90 Your faithfulness is for all generations;
you established the earth,
and it stands firm.
91 Your judgments stand firm today,
for all things are your servants.
92 If your instruction had not been my delight,
I would have died in my affliction.
93 I will never forget your precepts,
for you have given me life through them.
94 I am yours; save me,
for I have studied your precepts.
95 The wicked hope to destroy me,
but I contemplate your decrees.
96 I have seen a limit to all perfection,
but your command is without limit.

מ Mem

97 How I love your instruction!
It is my meditation all day long.
98 Your command makes me wiser
than my enemies,
for it is always with me.
99 I have more insight than all my teachers
because your decrees are my meditation.
100 I understand more than the elders
because I obey your precepts.
101 I have kept my feet from every evil path
to follow your word.
102 I have not turned from your judgments,
for you yourself have instructed me.
103 How sweet your word is to my taste —
sweeter than honey in my mouth.
104 I gain understanding from your precepts;
therefore I hate every false way.

נ Nun

105 Your word is a lamp for my feet
and a light on my path.
106 I have solemnly sworn
to keep your righteous judgments.
107 I am severely afflicted;
LORD, give me life according to your word.
108 LORD, please accept my freewill offerings
of praise,
and teach me your judgments.
109 My life is constantly in danger,[A]
yet I do not forget your instruction.
110 The wicked have set a trap for me,
but I have not wandered from your precepts.
111 I have your decrees as a heritage forever;
indeed, they are the joy of my heart.
112 I am resolved to obey your statutes
to the very end.[B]

ס Samek

113 I hate those who are double-minded,
but I love your instruction.
114 You are my shelter and my shield;
I put my hope in your word.
115 Depart from me, you evil ones,
so that I may obey my God's commands.
116 Sustain me as you promised, and I will live;
do not let me be ashamed of my hope.
117 Sustain me so that I can be safe
and always be concerned about
your statutes.
118 You reject all who stray from your statutes,
for their deceit is a lie.
119 You remove all the wicked on earth
as if they were[C] dross from metal;
therefore, I love your decrees.
120 I tremble[D] in awe of you;
I fear your judgments.

ע Ayin

121 I have done what is just and right;
do not leave me to my oppressors.
122 Guarantee your servant's well-being;
do not let the arrogant oppress me.
123 My eyes grow weary looking for
your salvation
and for your righteous promise.
124 Deal with your servant based on
your faithful love;
teach me your statutes.
125 I am your servant; give me understanding
so that I may know your decrees.
126 It is time for the LORD to act,
for they have violated your instruction.
127 Since I love your commands
more than gold, even the purest gold,
128 I carefully follow all your precepts
and hate every false way.

[A]119:109 Lit *in my hand* [B]119:112 Or *statutes; the reward is eternal* [C]119:119 Some Hb mss, DSS, LXX, Aq, Sym, Jer read *All the wicked of the earth you count as* [D]119:120 Lit *My flesh shudders*

פ Pe

129 Your decrees are wondrous;
therefore I obey them.
130 The revelation of your words brings light
and gives understanding to the inexperienced.
131 I open my mouth and pant
because I long for your commands.
132 Turn to me and be gracious to me,
as is your practice toward those who love
your name.
133 Make my steps steady through your promise;
don't let any sin dominate me.
134 Redeem me from human oppression,
and I will keep your precepts.
135 Make your face shine on your servant,
and teach me your statutes.
136 My eyes pour out streams of tears
because people do not follow your instruction.

צ Tsade

137 You are righteous, LORD,
and your judgments are just.
138 The decrees you issue are righteous
and altogether trustworthy.
139 My anger overwhelms me
because my foes forget your words.
140 Your word is completely pure,
and your servant loves it.
141 I am insignificant and despised,
but I do not forget your precepts.
142 Your righteousness is
an everlasting righteousness,
and your instruction is true.
143 Trouble and distress have overtaken me,
but your commands are my delight.
144 Your decrees are righteous forever.
Give me understanding, and I will live.

ק Qoph

145 I call with all my heart; answer me, LORD.
I will obey your statutes.
146 I call to you; save me,
and I will keep your decrees.
147 I rise before dawn and cry out for help;
I put my hope in your word.
148 I am awake through each watch of the night
to meditate on your promise.
149 In keeping with your faithful love, hear my voice.
LORD, give me life in keeping with your justice.
150 Those who pursue evil plans[A] come near;
they are far from your instruction.
151 You are near, LORD,
and all your commands are true.
152 Long ago I learned from your decrees
that you have established them forever.

ר Resh

153 Consider my affliction and rescue me,
for I have not forgotten your instruction.
154 Champion my cause and redeem me;
give me life as you promised.
155 Salvation is far from the wicked
because they do not study your statutes.
156 Your compassions are many, LORD;
give me life according to your judgments.
157 My persecutors and foes are many.
I have not turned from your decrees.
158 I have seen the disloyal and feel disgust
because they do not keep your word.
159 Consider how I love your precepts;
LORD, give me life according to
your faithful love.
160 The entirety of your word is truth,
each of your righteous judgments
endures forever.

שׂ Sin / שׁ Shin

161 Princes have persecuted me without cause,
but my heart fears only your word.
162 I rejoice over your promise
like one who finds vast treasure.
163 I hate and abhor falsehood,
but I love your instruction.
164 I praise you seven times a day
for your righteous judgments.
165 Abundant peace belongs to those
who love your instruction;
nothing makes them stumble.
166 LORD, I hope for your salvation
and carry out your commands.
167 I obey your decrees
and love them greatly.
168 I obey your precepts and decrees,
for all my ways are before you.

ת Taw

169 Let my cry reach you, LORD;
give me understanding according to your word.
170 Let my plea reach you;
rescue me according to your promise.
171 My lips pour out praise,
for you teach me your statutes.
172 My tongue sings about your promise,
for all your commands are righteous.
173 May your hand be ready to help me,
for I have chosen your precepts.
174 I long for your salvation, LORD,
and your instruction is my delight.

[A] **119:150** Some Hb mss, LXX, Sym, Jer read *who maliciously persecute me*

175 Let me live, and I will praise you;
may your judgments help me.
176 I wander like a lost sheep;
seek your servant,
for I do not forget your commands.

A CRY FOR TRUTH AND PEACE

120 *A song of ascents.*
In my distress I called to the LORD,
and he answered me.
2 "LORD, rescue me from lying lips
and a deceitful tongue."

3 What will he give you,
and what will he do to you,
you deceitful tongue?
4 A warrior's sharp arrows
with burning charcoal![A]

5 What misery that I have stayed in Meshech,[B]
that I have lived among the tents of Kedar![C]
6 I have dwelt too long
with those who hate peace.
7 I am for peace; but when I speak,
they are for war.

THE LORD OUR PROTECTOR

121 *A song of ascents.*
I lift my eyes toward the mountains.
Where will my help come from?
2 My help comes from the LORD,
the Maker of heaven and earth.

3 He will not allow your foot to slip;
your Protector will not slumber.
4 Indeed, the Protector of Israel
does not slumber or sleep.

5 The LORD protects you;
the LORD is a shelter right by your side.[D]
6 The sun will not strike you by day
or the moon by night.

7 The LORD will protect you from all harm;
he will protect your life.
8 The LORD will protect your coming
and going
both now and forever.

A PRAYER FOR JERUSALEM

122 *A song of ascents. Of David.*
I rejoiced with those who said to me,
"Let's go to the house of the LORD."
2 Our feet were standing
within your gates, Jerusalem —
3 Jerusalem, built as a city should be,
solidly united,
4 where the tribes, the LORD's tribes, go up
to give thanks to the name of the LORD.
(This is an ordinance for Israel.)
5 There, thrones for judgment are placed,
thrones of the house of David.

6 Pray for the well-being[E] of Jerusalem:
"May those who love you be secure;
7 may there be peace within your walls,
security within your fortresses."
8 Because of my brothers and friends,
I will say, "May peace be in you."[F]
9 Because of the house of the LORD our God,
I will pursue your prosperity.

LOOKING FOR GOD'S FAVOR

123 *A song of ascents.*
I lift my eyes to you,
the one enthroned in heaven.
2 Like a servant's eyes on his master's hand,
like a servant girl's eyes on her mistress's hand,
so our eyes are on the LORD our God
until he shows us favor.

3 Show us favor, LORD, show us favor,
for we've had more than enough contempt.
4 We've had more than enough
scorn from the arrogant
and contempt from the proud.

THE LORD IS ON OUR SIDE

124 *A song of ascents. Of David.*
If the LORD had not been on our side —
let Israel say —
2 if the LORD had not been on our side
when people attacked us,
3 then they would have swallowed us alive
in their burning anger against us.
4 Then the water would have engulfed us;
the torrent would have swept over us;
5 the raging water would have swept over us.

6 Blessed be the LORD,
who has not let us be ripped apart by their teeth.
7 We have escaped like a bird
from the hunter's net;
the net is torn, and we have escaped.
8 Our help is in the name of the LORD,
the Maker of heaven and earth.

[A] **120:4** Lit *with coals of the broom bush* [B] **120:5** = a people far to the north of Palestine [C] **120:5** = a nomadic people of the desert to the southeast [D] **121:5** Lit *is your shelter at your right hand* [E] **122:6** Or *peace* [F] **122:8** = Jerusalem

ISRAEL'S STABILITY

125 *A song of ascents.*
Those who trust in the LORD are
like Mount Zion.
It cannot be shaken; it remains forever.
2 The mountains surround Jerusalem
and the LORD surrounds his people,
both now and forever.

3 The scepter of the wicked will not remain
over the land allotted to the righteous,
so that the righteous will not apply
their hands to injustice.
4 Do what is good, LORD, to the good,
to those whose hearts are upright.
5 But as for those who turn aside to crooked ways,
the LORD will banish them with the evildoers.

Peace be with Israel.

ZION'S RESTORATION

126 *A song of ascents.*
When the LORD restored the fortunes
of Zion,[A]
we were like those who dream.
2 Our mouths were filled with laughter then,
and our tongues with shouts of joy.
Then they said among the nations,
"The LORD has done great things for them."
3 The LORD had done great things for us;
we were joyful.

4 Restore our fortunes,[B] LORD,
like watercourses in the Negev.
5 Those who sow in tears
will reap with shouts of joy.
6 Though one goes along weeping,
carrying the bag of seed,
he will surely come back with shouts of joy,
carrying his sheaves.

THE BLESSING OF THE LORD

127 *A song of ascents. Of Solomon.*
Unless the LORD builds a house,
its builders labor over it in vain;
unless the LORD watches over a city,
the watchman stays alert in vain.
2 In vain you get up early and stay up late,
working hard to have enough food —
yes, he gives sleep to the one he loves.[C]

3 Sons are indeed a heritage from the LORD,
offspring, a reward.
4 Like arrows in the hand of a warrior
are the sons born in one's youth.
5 Happy is the man who has filled his quiver
with them.
They will never be put to shame
when they speak with their enemies
at the city gate.

BLESSINGS FOR THOSE WHO FEAR GOD

128 *A song of ascents.*
How happy is everyone who fears
the LORD,
who walks in his ways!
2 You will surely eat
what your hands have worked for.
You will be happy,
and it will go well for you.
3 Your wife will be like a fruitful vine
within your house,
your children, like young olive trees
around your table.
4 In this very way
the man who fears the LORD
will be blessed.

5 May the LORD bless you from Zion,
so that you will see the prosperity of Jerusalem
all the days of your life
6 and will see your children's children!

Peace be with Israel.

PROTECTION OF THE OPPRESSED

129 *A song of ascents.*
Since my youth they have often
attacked me —
let Israel say —
2 since my youth they have often attacked me,
but they have not prevailed against me.
3 Plowmen plowed over my back;
they made their furrows long.
4 The LORD is righteous;
he has cut the ropes of the wicked.

5 Let all who hate Zion
be driven back in disgrace.
6 Let them be like grass on the rooftops,
which withers before it grows up[D]
7 and can't even fill the hands of the reaper
or the arms of the one who binds sheaves.
8 Then none who pass by will say,
"May the LORD's blessing be on you.
We bless you in the name of the LORD."

[A] **126:1** Or *LORD returned those of Zion who had been captives*
[B] **126:4** Or *Return our captives* [C] **127:2** Or *yes, he gives such things to his loved ones while they sleep* [D] **129:6** Or *it can be pulled out*

AWAITING REDEMPTION

130 *A song of ascents.*
Out of the depths I call to you, LORD!
2 Lord, listen to my voice;
let your ears be attentive
to my cry for help.

3 LORD, if you kept an account of iniquities,
Lord, who could stand?
4 But with you there is forgiveness,
so that you may be revered.

5 I wait for the LORD; I wait
and put my hope in his word.
6 I wait for the Lord
more than watchmen for the morning —
more than watchmen for the morning.

7 Israel, put your hope in the LORD.
For there is faithful love with the LORD,
and with him is redemption in abundance.
8 And he will redeem Israel
from all its iniquities.

A CHILDLIKE SPIRIT

131 *A song of ascents. Of David.*
LORD, my heart is not proud;
my eyes are not haughty.
I do not get involved with things
too great or too wondrous for me.
2 Instead, I have calmed and quieted my soul
like a weaned child with its mother;
my soul is like a weaned child.

3 Israel, put your hope in the LORD,
both now and forever.

DAVID AND ZION CHOSEN

132 *A song of ascents.*
LORD, remember David
and all the hardships he endured,
2 and how he swore an oath to the LORD,
making a vow to the Mighty One
of Jacob:
3 "I will not enter my house
or get into my bed,
4 I will not allow my eyes to sleep
or my eyelids to slumber
5 until I find a place for the LORD,
a dwelling for the Mighty One of Jacob."

6 We heard of the ark in Ephrathah;[A]
we found it in the fields of Jaar.[B]
7 Let's go to his dwelling place;
let's worship at his footstool.
8 Rise up, LORD, come to your resting place,
you and your powerful ark.
9 May your priests be clothed
with righteousness,
and may your faithful people shout for joy.
10 For the sake of your servant David,
do not reject your anointed one.[C]

11 The LORD swore an oath to David,
a promise he will not abandon:
"I will set one of your offspring[D]
on your throne.
12 If your sons keep my covenant
and my decrees that I will teach them,
their sons will also sit on your throne forever."

13 For the LORD has chosen Zion;
he has desired it for his home:
14 "This is my resting place forever;
I will make my home here
because I have desired it.
15 I will abundantly bless its food;
I will satisfy its needy with bread.
16 I will clothe its priests with salvation,
and its faithful people will shout for joy.
17 There I will make a horn grow for David;
I have prepared a lamp[E] for my anointed one.
18 I will clothe his enemies with shame,
but the crown he wears[F] will be glorious."

LIVING IN HARMONY

133 *A song of ascents. Of David.*
How delightfully good
when brothers live together in harmony!
2 It is like fine oil on the head,
running down on the beard,
running down Aaron's beard
onto his robes.
3 It is like the dew of Hermon[G]
falling on the mountains of Zion.
For there the LORD has appointed
the blessing —
life forevermore.

CALL TO EVENING WORSHIP

134 *A song of ascents.*
Now bless the LORD,
all you servants of the LORD
who stand in the LORD's house at night!
2 Lift up your hands in the holy place
and bless the LORD!

[A]**132:6** = Bethlehem [B]**132:6** = Kiriath-jearim [C]**132:10** = the king [D]**132:11** Lit *set the fruit of your belly* [E]**132:17** Or *dominion* [F]**132:18** Lit *but on him his crown* [G]**133:3** The tallest mountain in the region, noted for its abundant precipitation

3 May the LORD,
Maker of heaven and earth,
bless you from Zion.

THE LORD IS GREAT

135 Hallelujah!
Praise the name of the LORD.
Give praise, you servants of the LORD
2 who stand in the house of the LORD,
in the courts of the house of our God.
3 Praise the LORD, for the LORD is good;
sing praise to his name, for it is delightful.
4 For the LORD has chosen Jacob
for himself,
Israel as his treasured possession.

5 For I know that the LORD is great;
our Lord is greater than all gods.
6 The LORD does whatever he pleases
in heaven and on earth,
in the seas and all the depths.
7 He causes the clouds to rise from the ends
of the earth.
He makes lightning for the rain
and brings the wind from his storehouses.
8 He struck down the firstborn of Egypt,
both people and animals.
9 He sent signs and wonders against you, Egypt,
against Pharaoh and all his officials.
10 He struck down many nations
and slaughtered mighty kings:
11 Sihon king of the Amorites,
Og king of Bashan,
and all the kings of Canaan.
12 He gave their land as an inheritance,
an inheritance to his people Israel.

13 LORD, your name endures forever,
your reputation, LORD,
through all generations.
14 For the LORD will vindicate his people
and have compassion on his servants.

15 The idols of the nations are of silver and gold,
made by human hands.
16 They have mouths but cannot speak,
eyes, but cannot see.
17 They have ears but cannot hear;
indeed, there is no breath in their mouths.
18 Those who make them are just like them,
as are all who trust in them.

19 House of Israel, bless the LORD!
House of Aaron, bless the LORD!
20 House of Levi, bless the LORD!
You who revere the LORD,
bless the LORD!
21 Blessed be the LORD from Zion;
he dwells in Jerusalem.
Hallelujah!

GOD'S LOVE IS ETERNAL

136 Give thanks to the LORD, for he is good.
His faithful love endures forever.
2 Give thanks to the God of gods.
His faithful love endures forever.
3 Give thanks to the Lord of lords.
His faithful love endures forever.
4 He alone does great wonders.
His faithful love endures forever.
5 He made the heavens skillfully.
His faithful love endures forever.
6 He spread the land on the waters.
His faithful love endures forever.
7 He made the great lights:
His faithful love endures forever.
8 the sun to rule by day,
His faithful love endures forever.
9 the moon and stars to rule by night.
His faithful love endures forever.
10 He struck the firstborn of the Egyptians
His faithful love endures forever.
11 and brought Israel out from among them
His faithful love endures forever.
12 with a strong hand and outstretched arm.
His faithful love endures forever.
13 He divided the Red Sea
His faithful love endures forever.
14 and led Israel through,
His faithful love endures forever.
15 but hurled Pharaoh
and his army into the Red Sea.
His faithful love endures forever.
16 He led his people in the wilderness.
His faithful love endures forever.
17 He struck down great kings
His faithful love endures forever.
18 and slaughtered famous kings —
His faithful love endures forever.
19 Sihon king of the Amorites
His faithful love endures forever.
20 and Og king of Bashan —
His faithful love endures forever.
21 and gave their land as an inheritance,
His faithful love endures forever.
22 an inheritance to Israel his servant.
His faithful love endures forever.
23 He remembered us in our humiliation
His faithful love endures forever.

24 and rescued us from our foes.
His faithful love endures forever.
25 He gives food to every creature.
His faithful love endures forever.
26 Give thanks to the God of heaven!
His faithful love endures forever.

LAMENT OF THE EXILES

137 By the rivers of Babylon —
there we sat down and wept
when we remembered Zion.
2 There we hung up our lyres
on the poplar trees,
3 for our captors there asked us for songs,
and our tormentors, for rejoicing:
"Sing us one of the songs of Zion."

4 How can we sing the LORD's song
on foreign soil?
5 If I forget you, Jerusalem,
may my right hand forget its skill.
6 May my tongue stick to the roof of my mouth
if I do not remember you,
if I do not exalt Jerusalem as my greatest joy!

7 Remember, LORD, what the Edomites said
that day[A] at Jerusalem:
"Destroy it! Destroy it
down to its foundations!"
8 Daughter Babylon, doomed to destruction,
happy is the one who pays you back
what you have done to us.
9 Happy is he who takes your little ones
and dashes them against the rocks.

A THANKFUL HEART

138 *Of David.*
I will give you thanks with all my heart;
I will sing your praise
before the heavenly beings.[B]
2 I will bow down toward your holy temple
and give thanks to your name
for your constant love and truth.
You have exalted your name
and your promise above everything else.[C]
3 On the day I called, you answered me;
you increased strength within me.[D]

4 All the kings on earth will give you thanks, LORD,
when they hear what you have promised.[E]
5 They will sing of the LORD's ways,
for the LORD's glory is great.
6 Though the LORD is exalted,
he takes note of the humble;
but he knows the haughty from a distance.

7 If I walk into the thick of danger,
you will preserve my life
from the anger of my enemies.
You will extend your hand;
your right hand will save me.
8 The LORD will fulfill his purpose for me.
LORD, your faithful love endures forever;
do not abandon the work of your hands.

THE ALL-KNOWING, EVER-PRESENT GOD

139 *For the choir director. A psalm of David.*
LORD, you have searched me
and known me.
2 You know when I sit down and when
I stand up;
you understand my thoughts from far away.
3 You observe my travels and my rest;
you are aware of all my ways.
4 Before a word is on my tongue,
you know all about it, LORD.
5 You have encircled me;
you have placed your hand on me.
6 This wondrous knowledge is beyond me.
It is lofty; I am unable to reach it.

7 Where can I go to escape your Spirit?
Where can I flee from your presence?
8 If I go up to heaven, you are there;
if I make my bed in Sheol, you are there.
9 If I fly on the wings of the dawn
and settle down on the western horizon,[F]
10 even there your hand will lead me;
your right hand will hold on to me.
11 If I say, "Surely the darkness will hide me,
and the light around me will be night" —
12 even the darkness is not dark to you.
The night shines like the day;
darkness and light are alike to you.

13 For it was you who created my inward parts;[G]
you knit me together in my mother's womb.
14 I will praise you
because I have been remarkably
and wondrously made.[H,D]
Your works are wondrous,
and I know this very well.
15 My bones were not hidden from you
when I was made in secret,
when I was formed in the depths of the earth.

[A]**137:7** The day Jerusalem fell to the Babylonians in 586 BC
[B]**138:1** Or *before the gods*, or *before judges*, or *before kings*; Hb *elohim*
[C]**138:2** Or *You have exalted your promise above all your name*
[D]**138:3; 139:14** Hb obscure [E]**138:4** Lit *hear the words of your mouth*
[F]**139:9** Lit *the end of the sea* [G]**139:13** Lit *my kidneys* [H]**139:14** DSS, some LXX mss, Syr, Jer read *because you are remarkable and wonderful*

The Temple Treasury: Its History and Function

by Harold R. Mosley

The most prominent storehouse was the treasury associated with the tabernacle early in Israel's history and, later, with the temple. The custom of temples having treasuries associated with them was not unique to Israel. Evidence from Egypt, Mesopotamia, and Greece indicates the practice was widespread.[1]

Joshua demanded that the people dedicate the spoils of Jericho to God rather than take them for personal use. All of the city's silver, gold, and other goods were "holy" to the Lord. They were to be brought to "the LORD's treasury" (Jos 6:19). The treasures dedicated to the Lord had a specific place for storage within the tabernacle compound.

Later in Israel's history, the temple became the location for this storehouse. Although the Lord would not allow him to construct the temple, David did develop plans for the structure (1Ch 28:1–12). Mentioned specifically within the plans were the treasuries of the porch or vestibule (v. 11), as well as the treasuries of the house of God and the treasuries of dedicated or holy things (v. 12). Included among "what is dedicated" were items that David and others had taken as the spoils of battle. They were gifts designated specifically for the maintenance of the temple (26:26–27).

The kings also had treasuries to store their precious items (2Kg 12:18; 14:14; 18:15). The contents of these were both the king's personal treasury and the nation's treasury. The sources of the goods included loot from battles, gifts from other kingdoms and individuals, and tribute from foreign enemies. Judah's kings occasionally raided both the royal and the temple treasuries as other kingdoms demanded tribute. King Rehoboam of Judah gave the contents of the treasuries to Pharaoh Shishak to avert a conflict with Egypt. By the end of Judah's existence (586 BC), apparently little remained of the treasures that David, Solomon, and other early kings dedicated. Much of the grandeur of Solomon's temple had been plundered as foreign conquerors demanded tribute.

The people's tithes constituted a major element of the contents of the Lord's treasury. The command in Malachi 3:10 to bring the tithes into the "storehouse" refers to the temple treasury. The treasury thus contained not only durable goods, such as gold and silver vessels, but also the produce of fields, vineyards, flocks, and herds. The tithes were then used for various purposes, such as the maintenance of the temple and the priesthood, as well as provision for the Levites, orphans, widows, and foreigners.[2]

The storehouse from the Israelite period at Hazor. The structure was relocated to this site from its original location south of the Solomonic gate.

In the New Testament, mention of the "treasury" always referred to the treasury in Herod's temple. Herod had expanded greatly the temple complex from the much smaller version built by the returning exiles from Babylon. The temple's ornate and beautiful furnishings as well as the sheer magnitude of the structure were intended to impress the spectator. Jewish tradition refers to the splendor of Herod's temple as "a mass of snowy marble and of gold."[3] Every element of the temple reflected grandeur, and the treasury was no exception.

Within the temple compound were thirteen receptacles that received offerings. These were trumpet-shaped shofars (Hb *shofar*, "trumpet"). Each receptacle had an Aramaic inscription describing the offering's purpose. For example, one was for buying wood for sacrifices, another for frankincense, another for gold, and others for sacrificial birds. Six vessels were for freewill offerings the people would use to buy the burnt offerings used for sacrifice.[4]

A major source of income into the treasury of the New Testament temple was the annual half-shekel temple tax. Exodus 30:14–15 forms the background of this tax. Originally all adults from age twenty and upward paid one half shekel whenever a census was taken. By the time of the New Testament, this payment had become an annual tax dedicated to defraying the cost of the sacrifices.[5]

Scripture occasionally refers to the "storehouses" or "treasuries" of God. These references constitute a figurative use of treasuries. Just as physical treasures are stored in physical treasuries, God stores instruments for his use in storehouses available only to him. The wind resides in the storehouse until used for God's purpose (Ps 135:7). Similarly, the hail and the snow have their place for safe keeping (Jb 38:22).

Obelisk displaying the victories of Assyria's King Shalmaneser III (reigned 858–824 BC).

The familiar passage in Malachi 3:10–12 refers to both the physical treasury of the temple and the metaphorical storehouse of God's blessing. As the people gave the tithe at the temple, God opened the "floodgates of heaven" to pour out a blessing. These "floodgates" here form the sense of God's blessing sent following the obedience of his people. God's blessings come from God's abundant resources stored in his limitless treasury. ❖

---

[1] See, e.g., James Whitley, *The Archaeology of Ancient Greece* (Cambridge: Cambridge University Press, 2001), 228; Norman Bancroft Hunt, *Historical Atlas of Ancient Mesopotamia* (New York: Checkmark, 2004), 30–31. [2] See "Tithe" in *HIBD*, 1600–1601. [3] Alfred Edersheim, *The Temple: Its Ministry and Services as They Were at the Time of Jesus Christ* (New York: Revell, 1908), 5. [4] Mishnah Sheqalim 6:5. [5] Shmuel Safrai, "Temple: Second Temple Ritual" in *Encyclopaedia Judaica* (Jerusalem: Keter, 1971), 15:980.

16 Your eyes saw me when I was formless;
all my days were written in your book
and planned
before a single one of them began.

17 God, how precious[A] your thoughts are to me;
how vast their sum is!
18 If I counted them,
they would outnumber the grains of sand;
when I wake up,[B] I am still with you.

19 God, if only you would kill the wicked —
you bloodthirsty men, stay away
from me —
20 who invoke you deceitfully.
Your enemies swear by you falsely.
21 LORD, don't I hate those who hate you,
and detest those who rebel against you?
22 I hate them with extreme hatred;
I consider them my enemies.

23 Search me, God, and know my heart;
test me and know my concerns.
24 See if there is any offensive[C] way in me;
lead me in the everlasting way.

PRAYER FOR RESCUE

140 *For the choir director. A psalm of David.*
Rescue me, LORD, from evil men.
Keep me safe from violent men
2 who plan evil in their hearts.
They stir up wars all day long.
3 They make their tongues
as sharp as a snake's bite;
viper's venom is under their lips. *Selah*

4 Protect me, LORD,
from the power of the wicked.
Keep me safe from violent men
who plan to make me stumble.[D]
5 The proud hide a trap with ropes for me;
they spread a net along the path
and set snares for me. *Selah*

6 I say to the LORD, "You are my God."
Listen, LORD, to my cry for help.
7 LORD, my Lord, my strong Savior,
you shield my head on the day of battle.
8 LORD, do not grant the desires of the wicked;
do not let them achieve their goals.
Otherwise, they will become proud. *Selah*

9 When those who surround me rise up,[E]
may the trouble their lips cause
overwhelm them.
10 Let hot coals fall on them.
Let them be thrown into the fire,
into the abyss, never again to rise.
11 Do not let a slanderer stay in the land.
Let evil relentlessly[F] hunt down a violent man.

12 I[G] know that the LORD upholds
the just cause of the poor,
justice for the needy.
13 Surely the righteous will praise your name;
the upright will live in your presence.

PROTECTION FROM SIN AND SINNERS

141 *A psalm of David.*
LORD, I call on you; hurry to help me.
Listen to my voice when I call on you.
2 May my prayer be set before you as incense,
the raising of my hands
as the evening offering.

3 LORD, set up a guard for my mouth;
keep watch at the door of my lips.
4 Do not let my heart turn to any evil thing
or perform wicked acts with evildoers.
Do not let me feast on their delicacies.
5 Let the righteous one strike me —
it is an act of faithful love;
let him rebuke me —
it is oil for my head;
let me[H] not refuse it.
Even now my prayer is against
the evil acts of the wicked.[I]
6 When their rulers[J] will be thrown off
the sides of a cliff,
the people[K] will listen to my words,
for they are pleasing.

7 As when one plows and breaks up the soil,
turning up rocks,
so our[L] bones have been scattered
at the mouth of Sheol.

8 But my eyes look to you, LORD, my Lord.
I seek refuge in you; do not let me die.[M]
9 Protect me from the trap
they have set for me,
and from the snares of evildoers.
10 Let the wicked fall into their own nets,
while I pass by safely.

[A] **139:17** Or *difficult* [B] **139:18** Some Hb mss read *I come to an end* [C] **139:24** Or *idolatrous* [D] **140:4** Lit *to trip up my steps* [E] **140:9** Lit *Head of those who surround me* [F] **140:11** Hb obscure [G] **140:12** Alt Hb tradition reads *You* [H] **141:5** Lit *my head* [I] **141:5** Lit *of them* [J] **141:6** Or *judges* [K] **141:6** Lit *cliff, and they* [L] **141:7** DSS reads *my*; some LXX mss, Syr read *their* [M] **141:8** Or *not pour out my life*

A CRY OF DISTRESS

142 *A Maskil of David. When he was in the cave. A prayer.*

1 I cry aloud to the LORD;
I plead aloud to the LORD for mercy.
2 I pour out my complaint before him;
I reveal my trouble to him.
3 Although my spirit is weak within me,
you know my way.

Along this path I travel
they have hidden a trap for me.
4 Look to the right and see:[A]
no one stands up for me;
there is no refuge for me;
no one cares about me.

5 I cry to you, LORD;
I say, "You are my shelter,
my portion in the land of the living."
6 Listen to my cry,
for I am very weak.
Rescue me from those who pursue me,
for they are too strong for me.
7 Free me from prison
so that I can praise your name.
The righteous will gather around me
because you deal generously with me.

A CRY FOR HELP

143 *A psalm of David.*

LORD, hear my prayer.
In your faithfulness listen to my plea,
and in your righteousness answer me.
2 Do not bring your servant into judgment,
for no one alive is righteous in your sight.

3 For the enemy has pursued me,
crushing me to the ground,
making me live in darkness
like those long dead.
4 My spirit is weak within me;
my heart is overcome with dismay.

5 I remember the days of old;
I meditate on all you have done;
I reflect on the work of your hands.
6 I spread out my hands to you;
I am like parched land before you. *Selah*

7 Answer me quickly, LORD;
my spirit fails.
Don't hide your face from me,
or I will be like those
going down to the Pit.
8 Let me experience
your faithful love in the morning,
for I trust in you.
Reveal to me the way I should go
because I appeal to you.
9 Rescue me from my enemies, LORD;
I come to you for protection.[B]
10 Teach me to do your will,
for you are my God.
May your gracious Spirit
lead me on level ground.

11 For your name's sake, LORD,
let me live.
In your righteousness deliver me
from trouble,
12 and in your faithful love destroy my enemies.
Wipe out all those who attack me,
for I am your servant.

A KING'S PRAYER

144 *Of David.*

Blessed be the LORD, my rock
who trains my hands for battle
and my fingers for warfare.
2 He is my faithful love and my fortress,
my stronghold and my deliverer.
He is my shield, and I take refuge in him;
he subdues my people[C] under me.

3 LORD, what is a human that you care for him,
a son of man[D] that you think of him?
4 A human is like a breath;
his days are like a passing shadow.

5 LORD, part your heavens and come down.
Touch the mountains, and they will smoke.
6 Flash your lightning and scatter the foe;[E]
shoot your arrows and rout them.
7 Reach down[F] from on high;
rescue me from deep water, and set me free
from the grasp of foreigners
8 whose mouths speak lies,
whose right hands are deceptive.

9 God, I will sing a new song to you;
I will play on a ten-stringed harp for you —
10 the one who gives victory to kings,
who frees his servant David
from the deadly sword.

[A] **142:4** DSS, LXX, Syr, Vg, Tg read *I look to the right and I see*
[B] **143:9** One Hb ms, LXX; some Hb mss read *I cover myself to you*
[C] **144:2** Some Hb mss, DSS, Aq, Syr, Tg, Jer read *subdues peoples*; 2Sm 22:48; Ps 18:47 [D] **144:3** Or *a mere mortal* [E] **144:6** Lit *scatter them*
[F] **144:7** Lit *down your hands*

by Becky Lombard

Early Hebrew worship patterns developed through the liturgy and practice of worship in the temple, tabernacle, and synagogue, and in yearly festivals. Temple and tabernacle worship was more formal, following a developed liturgy led by appointed priests, and celebrated the presence of God among his people. Synagogue worship was centered in prayer and the reading and preaching of the Torah. Festivals celebrated the cycle of passing time, illuminating God's work in Israel's history and his continuing presence among them. Passover, a major religious festival, was especially important for God's people. It celebrated the deliverance of the Hebrews from Egyptian bondage—a message of redemption and testimony of God's work in their lives. The Hallel psalms were an important part of this celebration.

Hallel, the Hebrew term for "praise," appears often in psalms and primarily in songs of praise. *Hallel* was used to praise God's work in creation, the deliverance of Israel from Egypt, and his power to bless his people. Although most often it was used in worship at religious festivals, it was also part of private devotion and more formal temple worship. Certain celebrative portions of the Psalter came to be known as Hallel psalms. Psalm 136 came to be known as the Great Hallel, but the term *Hallel* was used more generally for other groupings of psalms that were given the title as a description of their use in worship. The Hallel psalms are typically grouped as:

Psalms 113–118;
Psalms 120–136;
Psalms 135–136;
Psalms 145–150.

People sang the first group as part of the Passover seder meal, the second and last group at daily morning worship in the synagogue and temple. They also sang Psalms 135–136 in the Sabbath corporate worship experience.[1]

The setting apart of Psalm 136 as the Great Hallel is likely due to its style and structure. While many Hallel psalms use this same subject matter and call to praise, Psalm 136 is the only psalm where each verse is a couplet, always ending with repeated acclamation: "His faithful love endures forever." The first line was spoken or sung by a worship leader or choir; the second was voiced as a response by a choir or

Ruins at Heshbon, which is about ten miles northeast of Mount Nebo in Jordan. Psalm 136 celebrates the Lord's victory over both Sihon, king of the Amorites, and Og, the king of Bashan (Ps 136:19–20). Sihon was the first king of Heshbon.

Illuminated manuscript of Psalm 136 from the Psalter produced by the St. Albans Abbey in Albans, England; printed on vellum; dated about AD 1125–1140.

the entire congregation. Scholars believe this antiphonal/responsorial pattern was common in Jewish congregational worship. The recurring litany in Psalm 136 is included in the language and practice of biblical worship (Jr 33:11; Ps 106:1; 107:1; 118:29).

Antiphonal response from the entire gathering of people was part of the Hebrew experience at Mount Sinai (Ex 24:1–8), an important spiritual marker in their worship history. It reveals the early structure of worship—God meeting with his people. First, God called them to that place, and they were strategically arranged according to levels of responsibility. Moses, Aaron, Nadab, Abihu, and the seventy elders were given places of leadership, but all of the people in the assembly were to participate in worship, engaging in the dialogue and commitment. The Word of God was proclaimed. God spoke and revealed his will for their future. They proclaimed their assent to God's commandments through the corporate acclamation, "We will do and obey all that the LORD has commanded" (v. 7). Finally, the commitment was sealed with a blood sacrifice, which the priest sprinkled on the worshipers.[2]

The Psalter continued to be important in worship in the Christian era. It became required text for liturgical readings throughout the church year. Some traditions used all 150 psalms in the course of a month, others in the course of a week. All Christian traditions read and sing psalms in worship.

The Reformers had much to say concerning congregational song, especially the Psalms. Martin Luther wrote chorales for the people to sing in their own language. He based his hymn "A Mighty Fortress Is Our God" on Psalm 46. Believing that only Scripture should be sung in worship, John Calvin worked with Louis Bourgeois to create metrical versions of the psalms so they could be sung to measured rhythms with published tunes. He published these in his *Genevan Psalter*.

The poet John Milton wrote a setting of Psalm 136 in 1623: "Let Us with a Gladsome Mind." His arrangement had twenty-four stanzas and addressed the complete psalm. The refrain for each stanza echoes the verses of Psalm 136.

For his mercies aye endure,
Ever faithful, ever sure. ✣

---

[1] R. K. Harrison, "Hallelujah" in *Evangelical Dictionary of Theology*, ed. Walter A. Elwell, 2nd ed. (Grand Rapids: Baker, 2001), 533.
[2] Robert E. Webber, *Worship Old and New* (Grand Rapids: Zondervan, 1982), 24–25.

11 Set me free and rescue me
from foreigners
whose mouths speak lies,
whose right hands are deceptive.

12 Then our sons will be like plants
nurtured in their youth,
our daughters, like corner pillars
that are carved in the palace style.
13 Our storehouses will be full,
supplying all kinds of produce;
our flocks will increase by thousands
and tens of thousands in our open fields.
14 Our cattle will be well fed.[A]
There will be no breach in the walls,
no going into captivity,[B]
and no cry of lament in our public squares.
15 Happy are the people with such blessings.
Happy are the people whose God is the LORD.

PRAISING GOD'S GREATNESS

145 *A hymn of David.*
I[C] exalt you, my God the King,
and bless your name forever and ever.
2 I will bless you every day;
I will praise your name forever and ever.

3 The LORD is great and is highly praised;
his greatness is unsearchable.
4 One generation will declare your works
to the next
and will proclaim your mighty acts.
5 I[D] will speak of your splendor and
glorious majesty
and[E] your wondrous works.
6 They will proclaim the power
of your awe-inspiring acts,
and I will declare your greatness.[F]
7 They will give a testimony
of your great goodness
and will joyfully sing of your righteousness.

8 The LORD is gracious and compassionate,
slow to anger and great in faithful love.
9 The LORD is good to everyone;
his compassion rests on all he has made.
10 All you have made will thank you, LORD;
the[G] faithful will bless you.
11 They will speak of the glory of your kingdom
and will declare your might,
12 informing all people of your mighty acts
and of the glorious splendor
of your[H] kingdom.
13 Your kingdom is an everlasting kingdom;
your rule is for all generations.
The LORD is faithful in all his words
and gracious in all his actions.[I]

14 The LORD helps all who fall;
he raises up all who are oppressed.[J]
15 All eyes look to you,
and you give them their food at the proper time.
16 You open your hand
and satisfy the desire of every living thing.

17 The LORD is righteous in all his ways
and faithful in all his acts.
18 The LORD is near all who call out to him,
all who call out to him with integrity.
19 He fulfills the desires of those who fear him;
he hears their cry for help and saves them.
20 The LORD guards all those who love him,
but he destroys all the wicked.
21 My mouth will declare the LORD's praise;
let every living thing
bless his holy name forever and ever.

THE GOD OF COMPASSION

146 Hallelujah!
My soul, praise the LORD.
2 I will praise the LORD all my life;
I will sing to my God as long as I live.

3 Do not trust in nobles,
in a son of man,[K] who cannot save.
4 When his breath[L] leaves him,
he returns to the ground;
on that day his plans die.

5 Happy is the one whose help is the God of Jacob,
whose hope is in the LORD his God,
6 the Maker of heaven and earth,
the sea and everything in them.
He remains faithful forever,
7 executing justice for the exploited
and giving food to the hungry.
The LORD frees prisoners.
8 The LORD opens the eyes of the blind.
The LORD raises up those who are oppressed.[J]
The LORD loves the righteous.
9 The LORD protects resident aliens
and helps the fatherless and the widow,
but he frustrates the ways of the wicked.

[A] **144:14** Or *will bear heavy loads*, or *will be pregnant* [B] **144:14** Or *be no plague, no miscarriage* [C] **145:1** The lines of this poem form an acrostic. [D] **145:5** LXX, Syr read *They* [E] **145:5** LXX, Syr read *and they will tell of* [F] **145:6** Alt Hb tradition, Jer read *great deeds* [G] **145:10** Lit *your* [H] **145:12** LXX, Syr, Jer; MT reads *his* [I] **145:13** One Hb ms, DSS, LXX, Syr; other Hb mss omit *The LORD is faithful in all his words and gracious in all his actions.* [J] **145:14; 146:8** Lit *bowed down* [K] **146:3** Or *a mere mortal* [L] **146:4** Or *spirit*

The Acrostic Psalms: Praising God from A to Z

by Thomas H. Goodman

The word *scuba* is an acrostic, a word that comes from the initials of other words. *Scuba* refers to a self-contained underwater breathing apparatus. An acrostic can form a word or phrase, or it can go through a sequence of letters in the alphabet.

This literary device is not new. It appeared in ancient Scripture. In each case, Old Testament writers formed poetic lines using in order the letters of the Hebrew alphabet: *aleph, beth, gimel, daleth, he, waw, zayin*, and so forth. A word starting with *Aleph* would begin the first line; a word starting with *Beth*, the second; and so on. Although it gets lost in translation, this poetic technique appears fourteen times in the Bible. Eight poems in the book of Psalms employ the acrostic device: 9–10 (which belong together as one composition); 25; 34; 37; 111; 112; 119; and 145.

ORIGIN OF THE ACROSTIC TECHNIQUE

Some Bible scholars once claimed that the use of acrostics indicated a poem's late development. They based this argument on the assumption that Hebrew poets borrowed the device from Hellenistic writing, where alphabetic acrostic poetry was common. Old Testament theologian Peter C. Craigie, however, regarded this argument as "highly unlikely."[1] History shows that Babylonian literature used acrostics long before the Greek and Roman civilizations came into existence. Instead of alphabetic acrostics, Babylonians used the initial letters or characters of each line to spell out a personal name or sentence. For example, in *Prayer to Marduk and Nabu*, the opening syllables of the lines of both prayers when read top to bottom compose a sentence naming the author of the poem; the ends of the lines read from top to bottom also produce descriptive sentences about the poet.[2]

The existence of acrostic poetry in the cultures surrounding Israel does not lead to the conclusion that Israelites borrowed the device from surrounding cultures, however. It simply proves the popularity of the literary technique from antiquity. ✣

[1] Peter C. Craigie, *Psalms 1–50*, vol. 19 in *WBC* (1983), 129–30. [2] Klaus Seybold, *Introducing the Psalms*, trans. R. Graeme Dunphy (Edinburgh: T&T Clark, 1990), 45, 199–201.

Female figurine musicians of this sort probably formed part of a toy band; from Tell es-Saidiyeh; dated to the ninth century BC (Iron Age II). The acrostic device used in the psalms may have served to highlight the lyrical message in the mind of the hearers.

Abecedary (a portion of the alphabet) on a pottery jar from Lachish; early sixth century BC.

10 The LORD reigns forever;
Zion, your God reigns for all generations.
Hallelujah!

GOD RESTORES JERUSALEM

147 Hallelujah!
How good it is to sing to our God,
for praise is pleasant and lovely.

2 The LORD rebuilds Jerusalem;
he gathers Israel's exiled people.
3 He heals the brokenhearted
and bandages their wounds.
4 He counts the number of the stars;
he gives names to all of them.
5 Our Lord is great, vast in power;
his understanding is infinite.[A]
6 The LORD helps the oppressed
but brings the wicked to the ground.

7 Sing to the LORD with thanksgiving;
play the lyre to our God,
8 who covers the sky with clouds,
prepares rain for the earth,
and causes grass to grow on the hills.
9 He provides the animals with their food,
and the young ravens what they cry for.

10 He is not impressed by the strength
of a horse;
he does not value the power of a warrior.[B]
11 The LORD values those who fear him,
those who put their hope in his faithful love.

12 Exalt the LORD, Jerusalem;
praise your God, Zion!
13 For he strengthens the bars of your city gates
and blesses your children within you.
14 He endows your territory with prosperity;[C]
he satisfies you with the finest wheat.

15 He sends his command throughout the earth;
his word runs swiftly.
16 He spreads snow like wool;
he scatters frost like ashes;
17 he throws his hailstones like crumbs.
Who can withstand his cold?
18 He sends his word and melts them;
he unleashes his winds,[D] and the water flows.

19 He declares his word to Jacob,
his statutes and judgments to Israel.
20 He has not done this for every nation;
they do not know his judgments.
Hallelujah!

CREATION'S PRAISE OF THE LORD

148 Hallelujah!
Praise the LORD from the heavens;
praise him in the heights.
2 Praise him, all his angels;
praise him, all his heavenly armies.
3 Praise him, sun and moon;
praise him, all you shining stars.
4 Praise him, highest heavens,
and you waters above the heavens.
5 Let them praise the name of the LORD,
for he commanded, and they were created.
6 He set them in position forever and ever;
he gave an order that will never pass away.

7 Praise the LORD from the earth,
all sea monsters and ocean depths,
8 lightning[E] and hail, snow and cloud,
stormy wind that executes his command,
9 mountains and all hills,
fruit trees and all cedars,
10 wild animals and all cattle,
creatures that crawl and flying birds,
11 kings of the earth and all peoples,
princes and all judges of the earth,
12 young men as well as young women,
old and young together.
13 Let them praise the name of the LORD,
for his name alone is exalted.
His majesty covers heaven and earth.
14 He has raised up a horn for his people,
resulting in praise to all his faithful ones,
to the Israelites, the people close to him.
Hallelujah!

PRAISE FOR GOD'S TRIUMPH

149 Hallelujah!
Sing to the LORD a new song,
his praise in the assembly of the faithful.
2 Let Israel celebrate its Maker;
let the children of Zion rejoice in their King.
3 Let them praise his name with dancing
and make music to him with tambourine
and lyre.
4 For the LORD takes pleasure in his people;
he adorns the humble with salvation.
5 Let the faithful celebrate in triumphal glory;
let them shout for joy on their beds.

6 Let the exaltation of God be in their mouths[F]
and a double-edged sword in their hands,

[A] **147:5** Lit *understanding has no number* [B] **147:10** Lit *the legs of the man* [C] **147:14** Or *peace* [D] **147:18** Or *breath* [E] **148:8** Or *fire* [F] **149:6** Lit *throat*

7 inflicting vengeance on the nations
and punishment on the peoples,
8 binding their kings with chains
and their dignitaries with iron shackles,
9 carrying out the judgment
decreed against them.
This honor is for all his faithful people.
Hallelujah!

PRAISE THE LORD

150 Hallelujah!
Praise God in his sanctuary.
Praise him in his mighty expanse.
2 Praise him for his powerful acts;
praise him for his abundant greatness.

3 Praise him with the blast of a ram's horn;
praise him with harp and lyre.
4 Praise him with tambourine and dance;
praise him with strings and flute.
5 Praise him with resounding cymbals;
praise him with clashing cymbals.

6 Let everything that breathes
praise the LORD.
Hallelujah!

PROVERBS

Bronze pair of scales from the Roman era. Graduating marks are punched on one arm of the scales, which are equipped with a hook for suspension and a weight in the form of an acorn. The weight gives the scales a steelyard action.

INTRODUCTION TO

PROVERBS

Circumstances of Writing

Solomon is credited with the proverbs in chapters 1–29 of the book of Proverbs (1:1; 10:1). There is biblical evidence that Solomon was wise and a collector of wise sayings (1Kg 3:5–14; 4:29–34; 5:7,12; 10:2–3,23–24; 11:41). Chapters 1–24 may have been written down during his reign (970–931 BC). The proverbs in chapters 25–29 were Solomon's proverbs collected by King Hezekiah, who reigned from 716 to 687 BC (25:1). The last two chapters are credited to Agur and Lemuel (30:1; 31:1), about whom nothing else is known. An editor was inspired to collect the proverbs of Solomon, Agur, and Lemuel into the book we now have.

The reign of Solomon represented the peak of prosperity for the nation of Israel. The period saw the greatest extent of the territory, and there was peace and international trade (1Kg 4:20–25; 10:21–29). It is likely Solomon knew about the ancient tradition of wisdom in Egypt (1Kg 3:1), but through inspiration and God's gift he composed even better sayings (1Kg 3:12; 10:6–7,23). Solomon addressed his teaching to his son or sons, but these inspired wise sayings are applicable to all people. The book of Proverbs, like the rest of the Bible, contains stories, teaching, and examples. People should make appropriate application of these truths to their own situations (1Co 10:11).

Contribution to the Bible

The Law and the Prophets teach how to live in spiritual community. Wisdom teaches how to live practically and courteously with one another. The book of Job addresses one main idea: the sovereignty of God with regard to suffering. Ecclesiastes contemplates the meaning of this ephemeral life. Solomon's Song demonstrates romantic love. Proverbs covers the rest of wisdom's topics, from how to conduct business astutely yet fairly, to how to live happily within marriage.

Structure

The book of Proverbs is in the wisdom genre. Wisdom books consist of the intelligent author's observations on the world and the people in it. However, without an inspired godly perspective, the world would be depressing and hopeless, as parts of Job and Ecclesiastes show. Ultimately, biblical wisdom is informed by and founded on faith in God.

The process of observation, contemplation, and inspiration can be seen in Proverbs 24:30–34. After observing the deteriorated condition of "the field of a slacker" and "the vineyard of one lacking sense," Solomon contemplated what he was seeing and was inspired: "I saw, and took it to heart; I looked, and received instruction" (v. 32). He either composed a new proverb or applied a familiar proverb to the situation: "a little sleep, a little slumber, a little folding of the arms to rest, and your poverty will come like a robber, and your need, like a bandit" (vv. 33–34).

Proverbs is written as Hebrew poetry. Hebrew poetry is terse and concise; it uses a lot of imagery, and generally the second line complements or contrasts the thought of the first. Contemplating how the second line relates to the first is a profitable way to meditate on a proverb.

In chapters 1–9, Solomon used imagery and sustained arguments to teach about the value of wisdom and the seduction of evil. In 22:17–24:34, there are "sayings" made up of several verses each; in chapters 30–31, there are more sayings, including numerical sayings and an alphabetic acrostic in praise of a capable wife. In the rest of the book, each proverb is generally one verse. Some scholars argue that these individual proverbs are carefully arranged in groups and each should be interpreted in the context of its group. Other scholars view the collection as unsystematic and argue that the immediate context seldom has any bearing on interpretation.

In either case, it is important to interpret any single proverb in the context of the book of Proverbs and the Bible as a whole. For example, while 21:14 may seem to encourage bribery, the rest of the book of Proverbs is clearly against it (15:27)—as is the rest of Scripture (Ex 23:8; Ec 7:7).

THE PURPOSE OF PROVERBS

1 The proverbs of Solomon son of David,
king of Israel:
2 For learning wisdom and discipline;
for understanding insightful sayings;
3 for receiving prudent instruction
in righteousness, justice, and integrity;
4 for teaching shrewdness
to the inexperienced,[A]
knowledge and discretion to a young man —
5 let a wise person listen and increase learning,
and let a discerning person obtain guidance —
6 for understanding a proverb or a parable,[B]
the words of the wise, and their riddles.

7 The fear of the LORD
is the beginning of knowledge;
fools despise wisdom and discipline.

AVOID THE PATH OF THE VIOLENT

8 Listen, my son, to your father's instruction,
and don't reject your mother's teaching,
9 for they will be a garland of favor
on your head
and pendants[C] around your neck.
10 My son, if sinners entice you,
don't be persuaded.
11 If they say — "Come with us!
Let's set an ambush and kill someone.[D]
Let's attack some innocent person
just for fun![E]
12 Let's swallow them alive, like Sheol,
whole, like those who go down to the Pit.
13 We'll find all kinds of valuable property
and fill our houses with plunder.
14 Throw in your lot with us,
and we'll all share the loot"[F] —
15 my son, don't travel that road with them
or set foot on their path,
16 because their feet run toward evil
and they hurry to shed blood.
17 It is useless to spread a net
where any bird can see it,
18 but they set an ambush to kill themselves;[G]
they attack their own lives.
19 Such are the paths of all who make
profit dishonestly;
it takes the lives of those who receive it.[H]

WISDOM'S PLEA

20 Wisdom calls out in the street;
she makes her voice heard
in the public squares.
21 She cries out above[I] the commotion;
she speaks at the entrance of the city gates:
22 "How long, inexperienced ones, will you
love ignorance?
How long will you mockers enjoy mocking
and you fools hate knowledge?
23 If you respond to my warning,[J]
then I will pour out my spirit on you
and teach you my words.
24 Since I called out and you refused,
extended my hand and no one paid attention,
25 since you neglected all my counsel
and did not accept my correction,
26 I, in turn, will laugh at your calamity.
I will mock when terror strikes you,
27 when terror strikes you like a storm
and your calamity comes like a whirlwind,
when trouble and stress overcome you.
28 Then they will call me, but I won't answer;
they will search for me, but won't find me.
29 Because they hated knowledge,
didn't choose to fear the LORD,
30 were not interested in my counsel,
and rejected all my correction,
31 they will eat the fruit of their way
and be glutted with their own schemes.
32 For the apostasy of the inexperienced
will kill them,
and the complacency of fools
will destroy them.
33 But whoever listens to me will live securely
and be undisturbed by the dread of danger."

WISDOM'S WORTH

2 My son, if you accept my words
and store up my commands within you,
2 listening closely[K] to wisdom
and directing your heart to understanding;
3 furthermore, if you call out to insight
and lift your voice to understanding,
4 if you seek it like silver
and search for it like hidden treasure,
5 then you will understand the fear of the LORD
and discover the knowledge of God.
6 For the LORD gives wisdom;
from his mouth come knowledge
and understanding.
7 He stores up success[L] for the upright;
He is a shield for those who live with integrity
8 so that he may guard the paths of justice
and protect the way of his faithful followers.

[A] **1:4** Or *simple, or gullible* [B] **1:6** Or *an enigma* [C] **1:9** Lit *chains* [D] **1:11** Lit *Let's ambush for blood* [E] **1:11** Lit *person for no reason* [F] **1:14** Lit *us; one bag will be for all of us* [G] **1:18** Lit *they ambush for their blood* [H] **1:19** Lit *takes the life of its masters* [I] **1:21** Lit *at the head of* [J] **1:23** Lit *you turn back to my reprimand* [K] **2:2** Lit *you, stretching out your ear* [L] **2:7** Or *resourcefulness*

9 Then you will understand righteousness,
justice,
and integrity — every good path.
10 For wisdom will enter your heart,
and knowledge will delight you.
11 Discretion will watch over you,
and understanding will guard you.
12 It will rescue you from the way of evil —
from anyone who says perverse things,
13 from those who abandon the right paths
to walk in ways of darkness,
14 from those who enjoy doing evil
and celebrate perversion,
15 whose paths are crooked,
and whose ways are devious.
16 It will rescue you from a forbidden woman,
from a wayward woman
with her flattering talk,
17 who abandons the companion of her youth
and forgets the covenant of her God;
18 for her house sinks down to death
and her ways to the land of the departed spirits.
19 None return who go to her;
none reach the paths of life.
20 So follow the way of the good,
and keep to the paths of the righteous.
21 For the upright will inhabit the land,
and those of integrity will remain in it;
22 but the wicked will be cut off from the land,
and the treacherous ripped out of it.

TRUST THE LORD

3 My son, don't forget my teaching,
but let your heart keep my commands;
2 for they will bring you
many days, a full life,[A] and well-being.
3 Never let loyalty and faithfulness leave you.
Tie them around your neck;
write them on the tablet of your heart.
4 Then you will find favor and high regard
with God and people.

5 Trust in the LORD with all your heart,
and do not rely on your own understanding;
6 in all your ways know him,
and he will make your paths straight.
7 Don't be wise in your own eyes;
fear the LORD and turn away from evil.
8 This will be healing for your body[B]
and strengthening for your bones.
9 Honor the LORD with your possessions
and with the first produce
of your entire harvest;
10 then your barns will be completely filled,
and your vats will overflow with new wine.
11 Do not despise the LORD's instruction, my son,
and do not loathe his discipline;
12 for the LORD disciplines the one he loves,
just as a father disciplines the son in whom
he delights.

WISDOM BRINGS HAPPINESS

13 Happy is a man who finds wisdom
and who acquires understanding,
14 for she is more profitable than silver,
and her revenue is better than gold.
15 She is more precious than jewels;
nothing you desire can equal her.
16 Long life[C] is in her right hand;
in her left, riches and honor.
17 Her ways are pleasant,
and all her paths, peaceful.
18 She is a tree of life to those who embrace her,
and those who hold on to her are happy.

19 The LORD founded the earth by wisdom
and established the heavens
by understanding.
20 By his knowledge the watery depths
broke open,
and the clouds dripped with dew.

21 Maintain sound wisdom and discretion.
My son, don't lose sight of them.
22 They will be life for you[D]
and adornment[E] for your neck.
23 Then you will go safely on your way;
your foot will not stumble.
24 When you lie[F] down, you will not be afraid;
you will lie down, and your sleep
will be pleasant.
25 Don't fear sudden danger
or the ruin of the wicked when it comes,
26 for the LORD will be your confidence[G]
and will keep your foot from a snare.

TREAT OTHERS FAIRLY

27 When it is in your power,[H]
don't withhold good from the one to whom
it belongs.
28 Don't say to your neighbor, "Go away!
Come back later.
I'll give it tomorrow" — when it is there
with you.
29 Don't plan any harm against your neighbor,
for he trusts you and lives near you.

A 3:2 Lit *days, years of life* B 3:8 Lit *navel* C 3:16 Lit *Length of days* D 3:22 Or *be your throat* E 3:22 Or *grace* F 3:24 LXX reads *sit* G 3:26 Or *be at your side* H 3:27 Lit *in the power of your hands*

30 Don't accuse anyone without cause,
when he has done you no harm.
31 Don't envy a violent man
or choose any of his ways;
32 for the devious are detestable to the LORD,
but he is a friend[A] to the upright.
33 The LORD's curse is on the household
of the wicked,
but he blesses the home of the righteous;
34 He mocks those who mock
but gives grace to the humble.
35 The wise will inherit honor,
but he holds up fools to dishonor.[B]

A FATHER'S EXAMPLE

4 Listen, sons, to a father's discipline,
and pay attention so that
you may gain understanding,
2 for I am giving you good instruction.
Don't abandon my teaching.
3 When I was a son with my father,
tender and precious to my mother,
4 he taught me and said,
"Your heart must hold on to my words.
Keep my commands and live.
5 Get wisdom, get understanding;
don't forget or turn away from the words
from my mouth.
6 Don't abandon wisdom, and she will
watch over you;
love her, and she will guard you.
7 Wisdom is supreme — so get wisdom.
And whatever else you get, get understanding.
8 Cherish her, and she will exalt you;
if you embrace her, she will honor you.
9 She will place a garland of favor on your head;
she will give you a crown of beauty."

TWO WAYS OF LIFE

10 Listen, my son. Accept my words,
and you will live many years.
11 I am teaching you the way of wisdom;
I am guiding you on straight paths.
12 When you walk, your steps will not be hindered;
when you run, you will not stumble.
13 Hold on to instruction; don't let go.
Guard it, for it is your life.
14 Keep off the path of the wicked;
don't proceed on the way of evil ones.
15 Avoid it; don't travel on it.
Turn away from it, and pass it by.
16 For they can't sleep
unless they have done what is evil;
they are robbed of sleep
unless they make someone stumble.
17 They eat the bread of wickedness
and drink the wine of violence.
18 The path of the righteous is like the light
of dawn,
shining brighter and brighter until midday.
19 But the way of the wicked is
like the darkest gloom;
they don't know what makes them stumble.

THE STRAIGHT PATH

20 My son, pay attention to my words;
listen closely to my sayings.
21 Don't lose sight of them;
keep them within your heart.
22 For they are life to those
who find them,
and health to one's whole body.
23 Guard your heart above all else,[C]
for it is the source of life.
24 Don't let your mouth speak dishonestly,
and don't let your lips talk deviously.
25 Let your eyes look forward;
fix your gaze[D] straight ahead.
26 Carefully consider the path[E]
for your feet,
and all your ways will be established.
27 Don't turn to the right or to the left;
keep your feet away from evil.

AVOID SEDUCTION

5 My son, pay attention to my wisdom;
listen closely[F] to my understanding
2 so that you may maintain discretion
and your lips safeguard knowledge.
3 Though the lips of the forbidden woman
drip honey
and her words are[G] smoother than oil,
4 in the end she's as bitter as wormwood
and as sharp as a double-edged sword.
5 Her feet go down to death;
her steps head straight for Sheol.
6 She doesn't consider the path of life;
she doesn't know that her ways
are unstable.

7 So now, sons, listen to me,
and don't turn away from the words
from my mouth.
8 Keep your way far from her.
Don't go near the door of her house.

[A]**3:32** Or *confidential counsel* [B]**3:35** Or *but haughty fools dishonor*, or *but fools exalt dishonor* [C]**4:23** Or *heart with all diligence* [D]**4:25** Lit *eyelids* [E]**4:26** Or *Clear a path* [F]**5:1** Lit *wisdom; stretch out your ear* [G]**5:3** Lit *her palate is*

9 Otherwise, you will give up your vitality
to others
and your years to someone cruel;
10 strangers will drain your resources,
and your hard-earned pay will end up
in a foreigner's house.
11 At the end of your life, you will lament
when your physical body has been consumed,
12 and you will say, "How I hated discipline,
and how my heart despised correction.
13 I didn't obey my teachers
or listen closely[A] to my instructors.
14 I am on the verge of complete ruin
before the entire community."

ENJOY MARRIAGE

15 Drink water from your own cistern,
water flowing from your own well.
16 Should your springs flow in the streets,
streams in the public squares?
17 They should be for you alone
and not for you to share with strangers.
18 Let your fountain be blessed,
and take pleasure in the wife of your youth.
19 A loving deer, a graceful doe[B] —
let her breasts always satisfy you;
be lost in her love forever.
20 Why, my son, would you lose yourself
with a forbidden woman
or embrace a wayward woman?
21 For a man's ways are before the LORD's eyes,
and he considers all his paths.
22 A wicked man's iniquities will trap him;
he will become tangled in the ropes
of his own sin.
23 He will die because there is no discipline,
and be lost because of his great stupidity.

FINANCIAL ENTANGLEMENTS

6 My son, if you have put up security
for your neighbor[C]
or entered into an agreement
with[D] a stranger,
2 you have been snared by the words
of your mouth —
trapped by the words from your mouth.
3 Do this, then, my son, and free yourself,
for you have put yourself
in your neighbor's power:
Go, humble yourself, and plead
with your neighbor.
4 Don't give sleep to your eyes
or slumber to your eyelids.
5 Escape like a gazelle from a hunter,[E]
like a bird from a hunter's trap.[E]

LAZINESS

6 Go to the ant, you slacker!
Observe its ways and become wise.
7 Without leader, administrator, or ruler,
8 it prepares its provisions in summer;
it gathers its food during harvest.
9 How long will you stay in bed, you slacker?
When will you get up from your sleep?
10 A little sleep, a little slumber,
a little folding of the arms to rest,
11 and your poverty will come like a robber,
your need, like a bandit.

THE MALICIOUS MAN

12 A worthless person, a wicked man
goes around speaking dishonestly,
13 winking his eyes, signaling with his feet,
and gesturing with his fingers.
14 He always plots evil with perversity
in his heart;
he stirs up trouble.
15 Therefore calamity will strike him suddenly;
he will be shattered instantly,
beyond recovery.

WHAT THE LORD HATES

16 The LORD hates six things;
in fact, seven are detestable to him:
17 arrogant eyes, a lying tongue,
hands that shed innocent blood,
18 a heart that plots wicked schemes,
feet eager to run to evil,
19 a lying witness who gives false testimony,
and one who stirs up trouble among brothers.

WARNING AGAINST ADULTERY

20 My son, keep your father's command,
and don't reject your mother's teaching.
21 Always bind them to your heart;
tie them around your neck.
22 When you walk here and there, they will
guide you;
when you lie down, they will watch over you;
when you wake up, they will talk to you.
23 For a command is a lamp, teaching is a light,
and corrective discipline is the way to life.
24 They will protect you from an evil woman,[F]
from the flattering tongue of
a wayward woman.
25 Don't lust in your heart for her beauty
or let her captivate you with her eyelashes.

[A] **5:13** Lit *or turn my ear* [B] **5:19** Or *graceful mountain goat*
[C] **6:1** Or *friend* [D] **6:1** Lit *or slapped hands for* [E] **6:5** Lit *hand*
[F] **6:24** LXX reads *from a married woman*

Ancient Near Eastern Lending Practices

by George H. Shaddix

Lending and borrowing predate Israel being established as a nation. Lending and borrowing arose from the basic situation of one individual needing an item and another person having the item and being willing to lend it. Through a bartering system, people would lend to each other. Every known society used this system. In this system, people gave little thought to receiving gain. The action was simply a kind, considerate way of helping one's neighbor. Most lending in this system consisted of materials, tools, and even livestock. In the case of lending livestock for breeding to increase someone else's herd or flock, often the lender would receive a portion of the increase. This was perhaps the first interest payment.

People quickly learned they could profit from lending. The Israelites came out of Egypt where they had been slaves; therefore, they were not a prosperous people. Yet God gave them specific instructions concerning living as a new nation and living in relationship to people of other nations. These included instructions concerning lending to both a "brother" (fellow Israelite) and a foreigner. In Exodus 22:25, God says, "If you lend silver to my people, to the poor person among you, you must not be like a creditor to him; you must not charge him interest." Hebrew law "is noted for its fairness and social responsibility toward the poor."[1] Throughout the Bible, God instructs his people to treat the poor with fairness. In other nations, creditors often charged excessive interest rates in order to gain a good income on their loans. God told his people, though, that they were not to be "creditors" who charged interest to their fellow Israelites.

According to Leviticus 25:35–38, rather than profiting by charging interest, the Israelite was to help his brother, so the brother could work himself out of his destitute situation. Often a borrower could satisfy his loan by working for the lender. An Israelite was not to take as collateral anything the borrower needed for his livelihood (Dt 24:6). Exodus 22:26 says the lender who takes a person's outer coat as a pledge for a loan must return it to the owner before the sun goes down. This garment was a large square of cloth with a place cut for the head to go through and was worn as an outer garment. This garment was used for double duty, a garment by day and a covering by night. Israelites considered willingness to lend to a needy brother to be an honorable characteristic.

Israel was not to borrow from other nations. God said instead they would become a lender to many nations. Borrowing placed an individual or a nation in a position of being indebted to the lender. The lender could set the required actions and responsibilities of the borrower. God intended Israel not to be indebted to any other nation.

A unique instruction in the law concerned the release of the debt between an Israelite lender and an Israelite borrower. Deuteronomy 15:1–3 spells out this instruction:

> At the end of every seven years you must cancel debts. This is how to cancel debt: Every creditor is to cancel what he has lent his neighbor. He is not to collect anything from his neighbor or brother, because

Ancient cultures used cuneiform when writing on clay tablets, which they often sealed in a clay envelope. The tablet (above) indicates that the creditor, debtor, and witnesses sealed a contract for the loan of one mina and 6 ½ shekels of silver that was repayable at the time of harvest. The envelope is to the left. Anatolian; dated 1920–1740 BC.

In Mesopotamian cities, temples were probably both the guardians of official weights and the storehouses of wealth—which they would lend out plus interest. This tablet is an Old Babylonian record of a loan from the Shamash temple at Sippar. The agreement shown right (with the envelope, left) states that Puzurum, son of Ili-kadri, has received from the god Shamash 38 ⅙ shekels of silver. At harvest, he will repay the silver plus interest, which will be at a rate that Shamash sets; dated 1823 BC.

the LORD's release of debts has been proclaimed. You may collect something from a foreigner, but you must forgive whatever your brother owes you.

This was not a deferment but a cancellation of the debt. Also, every fifty years all property that had been mortgaged or otherwise put into someone else's possession was to revert to its original owner (see Lv 25:8–31).

Proverbs 6:1–5 refers to putting up security for a neighbor, which would be equivalent to cosigning a loan today. Solomon explained that this traps the cosignatory and puts him "in [his] neighbor's power"—meaning he was at his neighbor's mercy (v. 3). In this verse, "neighbor" probably refers to both the borrower and the lender. The cosigner would be at the mercy of the borrower since he could leave the cosigner to pay the debt. The cosigner would also be at the mercy of the lender, because the lender would have power to expect payment if the borrower failed to pay. Solomon advised the cosigner to go to the lender and plead to be released from the responsibility of the debt. ✣

[1] Notes on Exodus 22:22–27, *Life Application Study Bible* Notes, WORDsearch Electronic Version, 1991.

26 For a prostitute's fee is only a loaf of bread,[A]
but the wife of another man[B] goes after
a precious life.
27 Can a man embrace fire
and his clothes not be burned?
28 Can a man walk on burning coals
without scorching his feet?
29 So it is with the one who sleeps with
another man's wife;
no one who touches her will go unpunished.
30 People don't despise the thief if he steals
to satisfy himself when he is hungry.
31 Still, if caught, he must pay seven times as much;
he must give up all the wealth in his house.
32 The one who commits adultery[C] lacks sense;
whoever does so destroys himself.
33 He will get a beating[D] and dishonor,
and his disgrace will never be removed.
34 For jealousy enrages a husband,
and he will show no mercy
when he takes revenge.
35 He will not be appeased by anything
or be persuaded by lavish bribes.

7 My son, obey my words,
and treasure my commands.
2 Keep my commands and live,
and guard my instructions
as you would the pupil of your eye.
3 Tie them to your fingers;
write them on the tablet of your heart.
4 Say to wisdom, "You are my sister,"
and call understanding your relative.
5 She will keep you from a forbidden woman,
a wayward woman with her flattering talk.

A STORY OF SEDUCTION

6 At the window of my house
I looked through my lattice.
7 I saw among the inexperienced,[E]
I noticed among the youths,
a young man lacking sense.
8 Crossing the street near her corner,
he strolled down the road to her house
9 at twilight, in the evening,
in the dark of the night.
10 A woman came to meet him
dressed like a prostitute,
having a hidden agenda.[F]
11 She is loud and defiant;
her feet do not stay at home.
12 Now in the street, now in the squares,
she lurks at every corner.
13 She grabs him and kisses him;
she brazenly says[G] to him,
14 "I've made fellowship offerings;
today I've fulfilled my vows.
15 So I came out to meet you,
to search for you, and I've found you.
16 I've spread coverings on my bed —
richly colored linen from Egypt.
17 I've perfumed my bed
with myrrh, aloes, and cinnamon.
18 Come, let's drink deeply of lovemaking
until morning.
Let's feast on each other's love!
19 My husband isn't home;
he went on a long journey.
20 He took a bag of silver with him
and will come home at the time
of the full moon."
21 She seduces him with her persistent pleading;
she lures with her flattering talk.
22 He follows her impulsively
like an ox going to the slaughter,
like a deer bounding toward a trap[H]
23 until an arrow pierces its[I] liver,
like a bird darting into a snare —
he doesn't know it will cost him his life.

24 Now, sons, listen to me,
and pay attention to the words
from my mouth.
25 Don't let your heart turn aside to her ways;
don't stray onto her paths.
26 For she has brought many down to death;
her victims are countless.[J]
27 Her house is the road to Sheol,
descending to the chambers of death.

WISDOM'S APPEAL

8 Doesn't wisdom call out?
Doesn't understanding make her voice heard?
2 At the heights overlooking the road,
at the crossroads, she takes her stand.
3 Beside the gates leading into the city,
at the main entrance, she cries out:
4 "People, I call out to you;
my cry is to the children of Adam.
5 Learn to be shrewd,
you who are inexperienced;
develop common sense, you who are foolish.
6 Listen, for I speak of noble things,
and what my lips say is right.

[A] **6:26** Or *On account of a prostitute, one is left with only a loaf of bread* [B] **6:26** Lit *but a wife of a man* [C] **6:32** Lit *commits adultery with a woman* [D] **6:33** Or *plague* [E] **7:7** Or *simple*, or *gullible*, or *naive* [F] **7:10** Or *prostitute with a guarded heart* [G] **7:13** Lit *she makes her face strong and says* [H] **7:22** Text emended; MT reads *like a shackle to the discipline of a fool*; Hb obscure [I] **7:23** Or *his* [J] **7:26** Or *and powerful men are all her victims*

7 For my mouth tells the truth,
and wickedness is detestable to my lips.
8 All the words from my mouth are righteous;
none of them are deceptive or perverse.
9 All of them are clear to the perceptive,
and right to those who discover knowledge.
10 Accept my instruction instead of silver,
and knowledge rather than pure gold.
11 For wisdom is better than jewels,
and nothing desirable can equal it.
12 I, wisdom, share a home with shrewdness
and have knowledge and discretion.
13 To fear the LORD is to hate evil.
I hate arrogant pride, evil conduct,
and perverse speech.
14 I possess good advice and sound wisdom;[A]
I have understanding and strength.
15 It is by me that kings reign
and rulers enact just law;
16 by me, princes lead,
as do nobles and all righteous judges.[B]
17 I love those who love me,
and those who search for me find me.
18 With me are riches and honor,
lasting wealth and righteousness.
19 My fruit is better than solid gold,
and my harvest than pure silver.
20 I walk in the ways of righteousness,
along the paths of justice,
21 giving wealth as an inheritance to those
who love me,
and filling their treasuries.

22 "The LORD acquired[C] me
at the beginning of his creation,[D]
before his works of long ago.
23 I was formed[E] before ancient times,
from the beginning, before the earth began.
24 I was born
when there were no watery depths
and no springs filled with water.
25 Before the mountains were established,
prior to the hills, I was given birth —
26 before he made the land, the fields,
or the first soil on earth.
27 I was there when he established
the heavens,
when he laid out the horizon on the surface
of the ocean,
28 when he placed the skies above,
when the fountains of the ocean gushed out,
29 when he set a limit for the sea
so that the waters would not violate
his command,
when he laid out the foundations of the earth.
30 I was a skilled craftsman[F] beside him.
I was his[G] delight every day,
always rejoicing before him.
31 I was rejoicing in his inhabited world,
delighting in the children of Adam.

32 "And now, sons, listen to me;
those who keep my ways are happy.
33 Listen to instruction and be wise;
don't ignore it.
34 Anyone who listens to me is happy,
watching at my doors every day,
waiting by the posts of my doorway.
35 For the one who finds me finds life
and obtains favor from the LORD,
36 but the one who misses me[H] harms himself;
all who hate me love death."

WISDOM VERSUS FOOLISHNESS

9 Wisdom has built her house;
she has carved out her seven pillars.
2 She has prepared her meat; she has mixed
her wine;
she has also set her table.
3 She has sent out her female servants;
she calls out from the highest points of the city:
4 "Whoever is inexperienced, enter here!"
To the one who lacks sense, she says,
5 "Come, eat my bread,
and drink the wine I have mixed.
6 Leave inexperience behind, and you will live;
pursue the way of understanding.
7 The one who corrects a mocker
will bring abuse on himself;
the one who rebukes the wicked will get hurt.[I]
8 Don't rebuke a mocker, or he will hate you;
rebuke the wise, and he will love you.
9 Instruct the wise, and he will be wiser still;
teach the righteous, and he will learn more.

10 "The fear of the LORD is the beginning
of wisdom,
and the knowledge of the Holy One
is understanding.
11 For by me your days will be many,
and years will be added to your life.
12 If you are wise, you are wise
for your own benefit;
if you mock, you alone will bear
the consequences."

[A]**8:14** Or *resourcefulness* [B]**8:16** Some Hb mss, LXX read *nobles who judge the earth* [C]**8:22** Or *possessed*, or *made* [D]**8:22** Lit *way* [E]**8:23** Or *consecrated* [F]**8:30** Or *a confidant*, or *a child*, or *was constantly* [G]**8:30** LXX; MT omits *his* [H]**8:36** Or *who sins against me* [I]**9:7** Lit *man: his blemish*

13 Folly is a rowdy woman;
she is gullible and knows nothing.
14 She sits by the doorway of her house,
on a seat at the highest point of the city,
15 calling to those who pass by,
who go straight ahead on their paths:
16 "Whoever is inexperienced, enter here!"
To the one who lacks sense, she says,
17 "Stolen water is sweet,
and bread eaten secretly is tasty!"
18 But he doesn't know that the departed spirits
are there,
that her guests are in the depths of Sheol.

A COLLECTION OF SOLOMON'S PROVERBS

10 Solomon's proverbs:
A wise son brings joy to his father,
but a foolish son, heartache to his mother.

2 Ill-gotten gains do not profit anyone,
but righteousness rescues from death.

3 The LORD will not let the righteous go hungry,
but he denies the wicked what they crave.

4 Idle hands make one poor,
but diligent hands bring riches.

5 The son who gathers during summer
is prudent;
the son who sleeps during harvest
is disgraceful.

6 Blessings are on the head of the righteous,
but the mouth of the wicked
conceals violence.

7 The remembrance of the righteous is
a blessing,
but the name of the wicked will rot.

8 A wise heart accepts commands,
but foolish lips will be destroyed.

9 The one who lives with integrity
lives securely,
but whoever perverts his ways will be
found out.

10 A sly wink of the eye causes grief,
and foolish lips will be destroyed.

11 The mouth of the righteous is a fountain of life,
but the mouth of the wicked
conceals violence.

12 Hatred stirs up conflicts,
but love covers all offenses.

13 Wisdom is found on the lips of the discerning,
but a rod is for the back of the one
who lacks sense.

14 The wise store up knowledge,
but the mouth of the fool
hastens destruction.

15 The wealth of the rich is his fortified city;
the poverty of the poor is their destruction.

16 The reward of the righteous is life;
the wages of the wicked is punishment.

17 The one who follows instruction is on the path
to life,
but the one who rejects correction
goes astray.

18 The one who conceals hatred has lying lips,
and whoever spreads slander is a fool.

19 When there are many words,
sin is unavoidable,
but the one who controls his lips is prudent.

20 The tongue of the righteous is pure silver;
the heart of the wicked is of little value.

21 The lips of the righteous feed many,
but fools die for lack of sense.

22 The LORD's blessing enriches,
and he adds no painful effort to it.[A]

23 As shameful conduct is pleasure for a fool,
so wisdom is for a person of understanding.

24 What the wicked dreads will come to him,
but what the righteous desire will be given
to them.

25 When the whirlwind passes,
the wicked are no more,
but the righteous are secure forever.

26 Like vinegar to the teeth and smoke
to the eyes,
so the slacker is to the one who sends him
on an errand.

[A] **10:22** Or *and painful effort adds nothing to it*

A Lady Named Wisdom

by John Traylor

Lady wisdom is the title interpreters use to personify wisdom in Proverbs 1–9. Through the literary device of personification, writers and speakers give personalities to concepts to make those concepts more attractive and understandable to their readers and hearers. Inspired by God, Solomon introduced lady wisdom and woman folly to give fitting personalities to wisdom and folly, the two major themes of Proverbs 1–9.

Why is wisdom personified as a woman? I do not believe, as some do, that God gave wisdom the personality of a woman to designate a female deity who consorted with him to create the world. Nor do I concur with those who label lady wisdom a female Christ. The Hebrew noun *hokmah*, translated "wisdom," is feminine (as is the Greek noun *sophia*). "Folly" in 9:13 (Hb *kesiyluth*) is also feminine (as are Gk *aphrōn* in the Septuagint and *mōria* in the New Testament). So when giving personality to wisdom and folly, one would naturally choose the feminine gender. ✜

Statue of Sophia Kelsou at the Library of Celsus in Ephesus.

Replica of the mithraeum from Dura-Europos Sanctuary. Mithra was the Persian god of all earthly wisdom, the god who supposedly conquered the demons of darkness and light. Because Mithra was born from the rocks, worshipers gathered in caves called mithraea. Believers claimed that the cave signified the world into which the human soul must descend to be purified by trials before death. Rituals symbolic of these trials were part of the worship in the mithraeum.

27 The fear of the LORD prolongs life,[A]
but the years of the wicked are cut short.

28 The hope of the righteous is joy,
but the expectation of the wicked will perish.

29 The way of the LORD is a stronghold
for the honorable,
but destruction awaits evildoers.

30 The righteous will never be shaken,
but the wicked will not remain on the earth.

31 The mouth of the righteous produces wisdom,
but a perverse tongue will be cut out.

32 The lips of the righteous know
what is appropriate,
but the mouth of the wicked,
only what is perverse.

11 Dishonest scales are detestable to the LORD,
but an accurate weight is his delight.

2 When arrogance comes, disgrace follows,
but with humility comes wisdom.

3 The integrity of the upright guides them,
but the perversity of the treacherous
destroys them.

4 Wealth is not profitable on a day of wrath,
but righteousness rescues from death.

5 The righteousness of the blameless
clears his path,
but the wicked person will fall because of
his wickedness.

6 The righteousness of the upright
rescues them,
but the treacherous are trapped
by their own desires.

7 When the wicked person dies,
his expectation comes to nothing,
and hope placed in wealth[B,C] vanishes.

8 The righteous one is rescued from trouble;
in his place, the wicked one goes in.

9 With his mouth the ungodly
destroys his neighbor,
but through knowledge the righteous
are rescued.

10 When the righteous thrive, a city rejoices;
when the wicked die, there is joyful shouting.

11 A city is built up by the blessing of the upright,
but it is torn down by the mouth of the wicked.

12 Whoever shows contempt for his neighbor
lacks sense,
but a person with understanding keeps silent.

13 A gossip goes around revealing a secret,
but a trustworthy person keeps a confidence.

14 Without guidance, a people will fall,
but with many counselors there is deliverance.

15 If someone puts up security for a stranger,
he will suffer for it,
but the one who hates such agreements
is protected.

16 A gracious woman gains honor,
but violent[D] people gain only riches.

17 A kind man benefits himself,
but a cruel person brings ruin on himself.

18 The wicked person earns an empty wage,
but the one who sows righteousness,
a true reward.

19 Genuine righteousness leads to life,
but pursuing evil leads to death.

20 Those with twisted minds are detestable
to the LORD,
but those with blameless conduct are his delight.

21 Be assured[E] that a wicked person
will not go unpunished,
but the offspring of the righteous will escape.

22 A beautiful woman who rejects good sense
is like a gold ring in a pig's snout.

23 The desire of the righteous turns out well,
but the hope of the wicked leads to wrath.

24 One person gives freely,
yet gains more;
another withholds what is right,
only to become poor.

[A] **10:27** Lit *LORD adds to days* [B] **11:7** LXX reads *hope of the ungodly* [C] **11:7** Or *strength* [D] **11:16** Or *ruthless* [E] **11:21** Lit *Hand to hand*

25 A generous person will be enriched,
and the one who gives a drink of water
will receive water.

26 People will curse anyone who hoards grain,
but a blessing will come to the one
who sells it.

27 The one who searches for what is good
seeks favor,
but if someone looks for trouble, it will come
to him.

28 Anyone trusting in his riches will fall,
but the righteous will flourish like foliage.

29 The one who brings ruin on his household
will inherit the wind,
and a fool will be a slave
to someone whose heart is wise.

30 The fruit of the righteous is a tree of life,
but a cunning person takes lives.

31 If the righteous will be repaid on earth,
how much more the wicked and sinful.

12 Whoever loves discipline loves knowledge,
but one who hates correction is stupid.

2 One who is good obtains favor from the LORD,
but he condemns a person who schemes.

3 No one can be made secure by wickedness,
but the root of the righteous is immovable.

4 A wife of noble character[A] is
her husband's crown,
but a wife who causes shame
is like rottenness in his bones.

5 The thoughts of the righteous are just,
but guidance from the wicked is deceitful.

6 The words of the wicked are a deadly ambush,
but the speech of the upright rescues them.

7 The wicked are overthrown and perish,
but the house of the righteous will stand.

8 A man is praised for his insight,
but a twisted mind is despised.

9 Better to be disregarded, yet have a servant,
than to act important but have no food.

10 The righteous cares about his animal's health,
but even the merciful acts of the wicked
are cruel.

11 The one who works his land will have plenty
of food,
but whoever chases fantasies lacks sense.

12 The wicked desire what evil people
have caught,[B]
but the root of the righteous is productive.

13 By rebellious speech an evil person
is trapped,
but a righteous person escapes from trouble.

14 A person will be satisfied with good
by the fruit of his mouth,
and the work of a person's hands
will reward him.

15 A fool's way is right in his own eyes,
but whoever listens to counsel is wise.

16 A fool's displeasure is known at once,
but whoever ignores an insult is sensible.

17 Whoever speaks the truth declares
what is right,
but a false witness speaks deceit.

18 There is one who speaks rashly,
like a piercing sword;
but the tongue of the wise brings healing.

19 Truthful lips endure forever,
but a lying tongue, only a moment.

20 Deceit is in the hearts of those who plot evil,
but those who promote peace have joy.

21 No disaster overcomes the righteous,
but the wicked are full of misery.

22 Lying lips are detestable to the LORD,
but faithful people are his delight.

23 A shrewd person conceals knowledge,
but a foolish heart publicizes stupidity.

24 The diligent hand will rule,
but laziness will lead to forced labor.

[A] **12:4** Or *A wife of quality*, or *A wife of good character*
[B] **12:12** Or *desire a stronghold of evil*

25 Anxiety in a person's heart weighs it down,
but a good word cheers it up.

26 A righteous person is careful in dealing
with his neighbor,[A]
but the ways of the wicked lead them astray.

27 A lazy hunter doesn't roast his game,
but to a diligent person, his wealth is precious.

28 There is life in the path of righteousness,
and in its path there is no death.[B]

13

A wise son responds to his father's discipline,
but a mocker doesn't listen to rebuke.

2 From the fruit of his mouth,
a person will enjoy good things,
but treacherous people have an appetite
for violence.

3 The one who guards his mouth protects
his life;
the one who opens his lips invites his own ruin.

4 The slacker craves, yet has nothing,
but the diligent is fully satisfied.

5 The righteous hate lying,
but the wicked bring disgust and shame.

6 Righteousness guards people of integrity,[C]
but wickedness undermines the sinner.

7 One person pretends to be rich
but has nothing;
another pretends to be poor but has
abundant wealth.

8 Riches are a ransom for a person's life,
but a poor person hears no threat.

9 The light of the righteous shines brightly,
but the lamp of the wicked is put out.

10 Arrogance leads to nothing but strife,
but wisdom is gained by those
who take advice.

11 Wealth obtained by fraud will dwindle,
but whoever earns it through labor[D]
will multiply it.

12 Hope delayed makes the heart sick,
but desire fulfilled is a tree of life.

13 The one who has contempt for instruction
will pay the penalty,
but the one who respects a command
will be rewarded.

14 A wise person's instruction is a fountain
of life,
turning people away from the snares
of death.

15 Good sense wins favor,
but the way of the treacherous
never changes.[E]

16 Every sensible person acts knowledgeably,
but a fool displays his stupidity.

17 A wicked envoy falls into trouble,
but a trustworthy courier brings healing.

18 Poverty and disgrace come to those
who ignore discipline,
but the one who accepts correction
will be honored.

19 Desire fulfilled is sweet to the taste,
but to turn from evil is detestable to fools.

20 The one who walks with the wise
will become wise,
but a companion of fools will suffer harm.

21 Disaster pursues sinners,
but good rewards the righteous.

22 A good man leaves an inheritance
to his[F] grandchildren,
but the sinner's wealth is stored up
for the righteous.

23 The uncultivated field of the poor yields
abundant food,
but without justice, it is swept away.

24 The one who will not use the rod hates
his son,
but the one who loves him disciplines
him diligently.

25 A righteous person eats until he is satisfied,
but the stomach of the wicked is empty.

[A] **12:26** Or *person guides his neighbor* [B] **12:28** Or *righteousness, but the crooked way leads to death* [C] **13:6** Lit *guards integrity of way* [D] **13:11** Lit *whoever gathers upon his hand* [E] **13:15** LXX, Syr, Tg read *treacherous will perish* [F] **13:22** Or *inheritance: his*

14 Every wise woman builds her house,
but a foolish one tears it down
with her own hands.

2 Whoever lives with integrity fears the LORD,
but the one who is devious in his ways
despises him.

3 The proud speech of a fool brings a rod
of discipline,[A]
but the lips of the wise protect them.

4 Where there are no oxen, the feeding trough
is empty,[B]
but an abundant harvest comes through
the strength of an ox.

5 An honest witness does not deceive,
but a dishonest witness utters lies.

6 A mocker seeks wisdom and doesn't find it,
but knowledge comes easily
to the perceptive.

7 Stay away from a foolish person;
you will gain no knowledge from his speech.

8 The sensible person's wisdom is to consider
his way,
but the stupidity of fools deceives them.

9 Fools mock at making reparation,[C]
but there is goodwill among the upright.

10 The heart knows its own bitterness,
and no outsider shares in its joy.

11 The house of the wicked will be destroyed,
but the tent of the upright will flourish.

12 There is a way that seems right to a person,
but its end is the way to death.

13 Even in laughter a heart may be sad,
and joy may end in grief.

14 The disloyal one will get
what his conduct deserves,
and a good one, what his deeds deserve.

15 The inexperienced one believes anything,
but the sensible one watches[D] his steps.

16 A wise person is cautious and turns from evil,
but a fool is easily angered and is careless.[E]

17 A quick-tempered person acts foolishly,
and one who schemes is hated.

18 The inexperienced inherit foolishness,
but the sensible are crowned with knowledge.

19 The evil bow before those who are good,
and the wicked, at the gates of the righteous.

20 A poor person is hated even by his neighbor,
but there are many who love the rich.

21 The one who despises his neighbor sins,
but whoever shows kindness to the poor
will be happy.

22 Don't those who plan evil go astray?
But those who plan good find loyalty
and faithfulness.

23 There is profit in all hard work,
but endless talk[F] leads only to poverty.

24 The crown of the wise is their wealth,
but the foolishness of fools
produces foolishness.

25 A truthful witness rescues lives,
but one who utters lies is deceitful.

26 In the fear of the LORD one has
strong confidence
and his children have a refuge.

27 The fear of the LORD is a fountain of life,
turning people away from the snares of death.

28 A large population is a king's splendor,
but a shortage of people is
a ruler's devastation.

29 A patient person shows great understanding,
but a quick-tempered one
promotes foolishness.

30 A tranquil heart is life to the body,
but jealousy is rottenness to the bones.

31 The one who oppresses the poor person
insults his Maker,
but one who is kind to the needy honors him.

[A] **14:3** Some emend to *In the mouth of a fool is a rod for his back* [B] **14:4** Or *clean* [C] **14:9** Or *at guilt offerings* [D] **14:15** Lit *the prudent understands* [E] **14:16** Or *and falls* [F] **14:23** Lit *but word of lips*

32 The wicked one is thrown down
by his own sin,
but the righteous one has a refuge
in his death.

33 Wisdom resides in the heart of the discerning;
she is known[A] even among fools.

34 Righteousness exalts a nation,
but sin is a disgrace to any people.

35 A king favors a prudent servant,
but his anger falls on a disgraceful one.

15 A gentle answer turns away anger,
but a harsh word stirs up wrath.

2 The tongue of the wise
makes knowledge attractive,
but the mouth of fools blurts out foolishness.

3 The eyes of the LORD are everywhere,
observing the wicked and the good.

4 The tongue that heals is a tree of life,
but a devious tongue[B] breaks the spirit.

5 A fool despises his father's discipline,
but a person who accepts correction
is sensible.

6 The house of the righteous has great wealth,
but trouble accompanies the income
of the wicked.

7 The lips of the wise broadcast knowledge,
but not so the heart of fools.

8 The sacrifice of the wicked is detestable
to the LORD,
but the prayer of the upright is his delight.

9 The LORD detests the way of the wicked,
but he loves the one
who pursues righteousness.

10 Discipline is harsh for the one who leaves
the path;
the one who hates correction will die.

11 Sheol and Abaddon lie open before the LORD —
how much more, human hearts.

12 A mocker doesn't love one who corrects him;
he will not consult the wise.

13 A joyful heart makes a face cheerful,
but a sad heart produces a broken spirit.

14 A discerning mind seeks knowledge,
but the mouth of fools feeds on foolishness.

15 All the days of the oppressed are miserable,
but a cheerful heart has a continual feast.

16 Better a little with the fear of the LORD
than great treasure with turmoil.

17 Better a meal of vegetables where there is love
than a fattened ox with hatred.

18 A hot-tempered person stirs up conflict,
but one slow to anger calms strife.

19 A slacker's way is like a thorny hedge,
but the path of the upright is a highway.

20 A wise son brings joy to his father,
but a foolish man despises his mother.

21 Foolishness brings joy to one without sense,
but a person with understanding walks
a straight path.

22 Plans fail when there is no counsel,
but with many advisers they succeed.

23 A person takes joy in giving an answer;[C]
and a timely word — how good that is!

24 For the prudent the path of life leads upward,
so that he may avoid going down to Sheol.

25 The LORD tears apart the house of the proud,
but he protects the widow's territory.

26 The LORD detests the plans of the one who
is evil,
but pleasant words are pure.

27 The one who profits dishonestly troubles
his household,
but the one who hates bribes will live.

28 The mind of the righteous person thinks
before answering,
but the mouth of the wicked blurts out
evil things.

[A] **14:33** LXX reads *unknown* [B] **15:4** Lit *but crookedness in it*
[C] **15:23** Lit *in an answer of his mouth*

Wealth, Trade, Money, and Coinage in the Biblical World

by Joel F. Drinkard Jr.

Some persons from civilization's earliest periods in the ancient Near East were wealthy. The wonders of the ancient world spotlight the wealth of some of the ancients. Whether one considers the pyramids of Egypt or the ziggurats of Mesopotamia, these massive structures themselves indicate their builders' wealth. Certainly the rulers of these highly developed societies had to control vast wealth in order to undertake such building projects. Additionally, huge herds and flocks and numerous servants, as in the example of Abraham, were indicators of substantial wealth. Mesha, king of Moab, exhibited his wealth by his annual tribute to the king of Israel: "one hundred thousand lambs and the wool of one hundred thousand rams" (2Kg 3:4). Other indicators of wealth included imported goods, luxury items, gems, and often silver and gold. These imported and luxury goods gave evidence of trade. Neither the empire of Egypt nor Mesopotamia had great stocks of natural resources. Therefore, most metals and luxury goods for these empires came through trade or tribute. Wealth and trade thus usually went hand in hand. Silver and gold were the favorite materials for use in commercial transactions. Other goods such as copper and tin, the ingredients of bronze, were also very valuable commodities. All these metals were relatively easy to refine and were easily transportable.

Trade, including long-distance trade, was part of life for even the early inhabitants in the ancient Near East. At Pre-Pottery Neolithic Jericho, excavators have found obsidian tools. Obsidian, a black or banded volcanic glasslike stone, came from Anatolia, about five hundred miles away. Its presence at Jericho clearly indicates trade, even international trade. The mechanism of trade from that early time is unknown, but the speculation is that those who lived near the natural resources would trade surplus amounts of their natural resources with nearby communities, who in turn traded with more distant communities, and so forth. One would not have to posit full-blown trade routes and caravans at this early period. Other items indicating trade at Pre-Pottery Neolithic Jericho include turquoise from the Sinai Peninsula and cowrie shells from the Mediterranean coast.

One of the clearest evidences of international trade is a fourteenth-century BC shipwreck off the coast of Uluburun, Turkey.[1] This Late Bronze Canaanite merchant vessel carried a cargo of more than ten tons of copper and a ton of tin, much of this metal in large ingots each weighing about sixty pounds. The vessel also carried glass ingots, ivory, ebony wood, cedar wood, and terebinth/pistachio resin. In all, the materials and cargo reflect goods from much of the Mediterranean world: Canaan, Egypt, Cyprus, Anatolia, and the Aegean areas. The ship apparently made a circuit to ports in each of these regions, buying and selling goods.

The Beni Hasan tomb paintings from Egypt, dating to about 1890 BC, depict a Canaanite merchant caravan bringing goods to Egypt. The travelers have with them animals, weapons, and perhaps metal ingots. The item often described as a bellows carried on several of the donkeys is more likely ingots of copper similar to those found in the Uluburun shipwreck. Also

Sheep in the field. The size of one's flock was an indicator of wealth.

such a caravan is reminiscent of the Midianites/Ishmaelites who, while traveling to Egypt, bought Joseph from his brothers (Gn 37:25–28).

Trade would require some means of assessing value. Commodities were not of equal value. How would one compare the value of a goat and a donkey? Or, more to the point, the value of a donkey in terms of silver? Obviously some equivalences were needed and even essential. Since precious metals, especially silver and gold, were the favored means of exchange for trade transactions, a system of weights and measures became essential for buying and selling.

The need for weights and measures also produced the need for standards of weights and measure. We do not know the precise equivalent of all the ancient weights and measures, but we can approximate many of them. Several of the measures came from human anatomy. The *cubit* was a standard of length; it was the distance from the elbow to the tip of the middle finger. Similarly, the *span* was the width from the outstretched thumb to the little finger. The *palm* was the width of the hand across the base of the four fingers, and the *finger* was the width of one finger. Four fingers made a palm, three palms made a span, and two spans made a cubit. Some of the weights and measures were originally descriptive: the measure *homer* was the same as the word for "donkey." The homer measure was probably equivalent to a donkey load. Perhaps a *talent* was the measure of a human load. In terms of surface area, a *yoke* was the amount of land a yoke of oxen could plow in a day. Seed was also used as a form of measure: one would describe a field in terms of the amount of seed it would require for planting. Leviticus 27:16 speaks of a field's size in terms of sowing a homer of barley.

The Uluburun shipwreck mentioned above provides evidence of such standards, with several sets of weights and scales included in the wreckage.

The Old Testament shekel was the primary measure for weight, though both larger and smaller weights existed. When Abraham purchased the burial cave for Sarah, at Machpelah, he negotiated the sale with the owner, Ephron the Hethite, in the presence of Hebron's elders. "Abraham agreed with Ephron, and Abraham weighed out to Ephron the silver that he had agreed to in the hearing of the Hethites: four hundred standard shekels of silver" (lit "four hundred shekels passing to the merchant"; Gn 23:16).

Clearly coinage was not known at this time; the silver was weighed. Abraham also used a set standard; the shekel was in current use among the merchants. The mention of merchants gives further evidence of trade being common in Abraham's time. Because coins were then undeveloped, pieces of jewelry, metal, and ingots served as the money. Though the exact weight of the shekel from Abraham's era is not known, shekel weights from the monarchy's later period and the weight of shekel coins of the New Testament era show that a shekel weighed about 11.4 grams or two-fifths of an ounce.

The narrative of Jeremiah purchasing the field from his cousin Hanamel shows the continued use of metal weights rather than coins. He purchased the field in Anathoth for seventeen shekels, weighing out the money on scales (Jr 32:8–9). The low price in comparison to Abraham's price for a field and burial cave may indicate a much smaller field or the reality that the field was virtually worthless, being in land occupied by the Babylonian army.

The mina and the talent were larger weights used for monetary exchange. Fifty shekels made a mina, and sixty minas made a talent. A talent weighed the same as three thousand shekels. A mina was about 1 1/4 pounds, and a talent was about 75 1/3 pounds. But most often even large weights were in shekels. Thus Goliath's body armor weighed five thousand shekels (ca 125 pounds) of bronze and his spear head weighed six hundred shekels (just over 15 pounds; 1Sm 17:4–7).

By the end of the seventh century BC, coinage had developed. Coins were a means of establishing a guaranteed standard for a weight of metals. Kings began to produce standardized weights of silver and gold to guarantee their weight. The earliest coins come from Asia Minor with the kingdom of Lydia certainly being among the first to produce coins. One notable ruler of Lydia was Croesus, known from the proverbial statement "rich as Croesus." Lydia was especially rich in metal ores, silver and gold, in the mid-500s BC and used these metals for coins. But even early coins could be forged. It was quite possible to make a coin of base metal and plate it with silver or gold. To the casual observer, the coin might well look authentic. So ancients often tested coins, making deep incisions across them; the cut was not to deface the coin but to determine if the coin was pure metal or base metal.

The few Old Testament references to coins are in the latest eras—reflecting the Persian period when coins first appeared. One such coin, the first mentioned in Scripture, the daric (KJV "dram"), was a gold coin about the size of a dime (1Ch 29:7; Ezr 2:69; Neh 7:69–71).

The New Testament mentioned several common coins. The denarius was the most common Roman coin. It weighed about three grams and was about the size of a dime. The denarius was the coin called the tribute "penny" in the KJV. The thirty pieces of silver mentioned as payment to Judas were probably denarii. The Greek drachma was approximately the same weight and value as the denarius.

The tetradrachma (four drachmas) was another common Greek coin. It was basically equivalent to the Jewish shekel in size, weight and value.

The lepton was the smallest Jewish coin. It is most likely the coin called the widow's mite in the KJV. The prutah was the most common bronze coin in Judea in the New Testament era; it was equivalent to the Greek kodrantes. It was the equivalent of two leptons and in the KJV was called a farthing.

One real problem is trying to determine comparable value today for coins mentioned in the Bible. What was the value of a denarius or talent or lepton mentioned by Jesus? For a talent, the ASV has a footnote on Matthew 18 giving the value as £200 or $1,000. Likewise the NIV notes in Matthew 25 that a talent was worth more than $1,000. These translations agree remarkably on the value of the talent. But these amounts do not communicate the value of a talent well.

Another way to compare the relative value of a talent is to determine its weight and then determine the value of that weight of silver today. The talent was equivalent to three thousand shekels of silver, each of which weighed approximately 11.4 grams or two-fifths of an ounce. So the talent of silver would weigh 75 ⅓ pounds. Silver currently (2019-04-02) is worth about $15 per ounce. On that basis, 75 ⅓ pounds of silver would be worth $18,072. But I don't think even that communicates best the meaning or value of the talent in Jesus's day.

A better way to determine the equivalent value of a talent today is to look at the relative earning power or buying power of the talent in that day and consider a comparable earning power or buying power today. The talent was equivalent to a weight of three thousand shekels, and that would be equivalent to twelve thousand denarii. The denarius was a day's wage or salary for the common laborer. In Matthew 20, the owner of the vineyard agreed with the day laborers to the pay of a denarius for a day's work. A denarius was also probably the wage for a soldier. In today's earning power or buying power, a day's wage for a laborer is based on the minimum wage of $7.25 per hour. Typically, unskilled workers earn more than the minimum wage, perhaps $8 or $8.50 per hour. If we take $8 per hour as a typical wage for a laborer, then an eight-hour day would earn $64—that's what a denarius would have meant in Jesus's day translated into a day's wage for us today. The master of the household in the parable of talents gave one servant five talents, another two talents, and another one talent. Remember that a talent was twelve thousand denarii, so it was twelve thousand days' wages. Again, based on the equivalence of value today, a talent would be $768,000! The master of the household was putting a fortune in the hands of each servant. Following our buying equivalent using today's funds:

5 talents = $3,840,000;
2 talents = $1,536,000;
1 talent = $768,000.

Moving from a massive fortune to the minuscule, Jesus pointed out to his disciples a poor widow who put into the treasury "two tiny coins worth very little" (Mk 12:41–44). The Greek text says the poor widow put in 2 lepta, which make a kodrantes. It took 336 lepta to equal a denarius. This widow put into the treasury $^{1}/_{168}$ of a day's wage. Using the same buying power equivalence as above, two lepta would be 38 cents; in terms of two coins, it would be less than two quarters. ✣

[1] Cemal Pulak, "Shipwreck: Recovering 3,000-Year-Old Cargo," *Archaeology Odyssey* 2.4 (1999): 18–29, 59.

Drachma from Parthia: Phraates IV (38–2 BC); shows a bust on the left and an eagle with a wreath.

Owl stands right with head facing over left shoulder, crook and flail; cable border. From Tyre, about 450–400 BC.

This bronze coin from the time of Herod I (40–4 BC) shows a double cornucopia with a caduceus between.

This Tyre shekel (reverse), minted in Jerusalem, shows an eagle.

29 The LORD is far from the wicked,
but he hears the prayer of the righteous.

30 Bright eyes cheer the heart;
good news strengthens[A] the bones.

31 One who[B] listens to life-giving rebukes
will be at home among the wise.

32 Anyone who ignores discipline
despises himself,
but whoever listens to correction acquires
good sense.[C]

33 The fear of the LORD is what wisdom teaches,
and humility comes before honor.

16 The reflections of the heart
belong to mankind,
but the answer of the tongue is from the LORD.

2 All a person's ways seem right to him,
but the LORD weighs motives.[D]

3 Commit your activities to the LORD,
and your plans will be established.

4 The LORD has prepared everything
for his purpose —
even the wicked for the day of disaster.

5 Everyone with a proud heart is detestable
to the LORD;
be assured,[E] he will not go unpunished.

6 Iniquity is atoned for by loyalty
and faithfulness,
and one turns from evil by the fear
of the LORD.

7 When a person's ways please the LORD,
he makes even his enemies to be at peace
with him.

8 Better a little with righteousness
than great income with injustice.

9 A person's heart plans his way,
but the LORD determines his steps.

10 God's verdict is on the lips of a king;[F]
his mouth should not give an unfair judgment.

11 Honest balances and scales are the LORD's;
all the weights in the bag are his concern.

12 Wicked behavior is detestable to kings,
since a throne is established
through righteousness.

13 Righteous lips are a king's delight,
and he loves one who speaks honestly.

14 A king's fury is a messenger of death,
but a wise person appeases it.

15 When a king's face lights up, there is life;
his favor is like a cloud with spring rain.

16 Get wisdom —
how much better it is than gold!
And get understanding —
it is preferable to silver.

17 The highway of the upright avoids evil;
the one who guards his way protects his life.

18 Pride comes before destruction,
and an arrogant spirit before a fall.

19 Better to be lowly of spirit with the humble[G]
than to divide plunder with the proud.

20 The one who understands a matter
finds success,
and the one who trusts in the LORD
will be happy.

21 Anyone with a wise heart is called discerning,
and pleasant speech[H] increases learning.

22 Insight is a fountain of life for its possessor,
but the discipline of fools is folly.

23 The heart of a wise person instructs
his mouth;
it adds learning to his speech.[I]

24 Pleasant words are a honeycomb:
sweet to the taste[J] and health to the body.[K]

25 There is a way that seems right to a person,
but its end is the way to death.

26 A worker's appetite works for him
because his hunger[L] urges him on.

[A]**15:30** Lit *makes fat* [B]**15:31** Lit *An ear that* [C]**15:32** Lit *acquires a heart* [D]**16:2** Lit *spirits* [E]**16:5** Lit *hand to hand* [F]**16:10** Or *A divination is on the lips of a king* [G]**16:19** Alt Hb tradition reads *afflicted* [H]**16:21** Lit *and sweetness of lips* [I]**16:23** Lit *learning upon his lips* [J]**16:24** Lit *throat* [K]**16:24** Lit *bones* [L]**16:26** Lit *mouth*

27 A worthless person digs up evil,
and his speech is like a scorching fire.

28 A contrary person spreads conflict,
and a gossip separates close friends.

29 A violent person lures his neighbor,
leading him on a path that is not good.

30 The one who narrows his eyes
is planning deceptions;
the one who compresses his lips
brings about evil.

31 Gray hair is a glorious crown;
it is found in the ways of righteousness.

32 Patience is better than power,
and controlling one's emotions,[A]
than capturing a city.

33 The lot is cast into the lap,
but its every decision is from the LORD.

17 Better a dry crust with peace
than a house full of feasting with strife.

2 A prudent servant will rule over
a disgraceful son
and share an inheritance among brothers.

3 A crucible for silver, and a smelter for gold,
and the LORD is the tester of hearts.

4 A wicked person listens to malicious talk;[B]
a liar pays attention to a destructive tongue.

5 The one who mocks the poor insults
his Maker,
and one who rejoices over calamity
will not go unpunished.

6 Grandchildren are the crown of the elderly,
and the pride of children is their fathers.

7 Eloquent words are not appropriate
on a fool's lips;
how much worse are lies for a ruler.

8 A bribe seems like a magic stone to its owner;
wherever he turns, he succeeds.

9 Whoever conceals an offense promotes love,
but whoever gossips about it
separates friends.

10 A rebuke cuts into a perceptive person
more than a hundred lashes into a fool.

11 An evil person desires only rebellion;
a cruel messenger[C] will be sent against him.

12 Better for a person to meet a bear robbed
of her cubs
than a fool in his foolishness.

13 If anyone returns evil for good,
evil will never depart from his house.

14 To start a conflict is to release a flood;
stop the dispute before it breaks out.

15 Acquitting the guilty and condemning
the just —
both are detestable to the LORD.

16 Why does a fool have money in his hand
with no intention of buying wisdom?

17 A friend loves at all times,
and a brother is born for a difficult time.

18 One without sense enters an agreement[D]
and puts up security for his friend.

19 One who loves to offend loves strife;
one who builds a high threshold
invites injury.

20 One with a twisted mind will not succeed,
and one with deceitful speech will fall
into ruin.

21 A man fathers a fool to his own sorrow;
the father of a fool has no joy.

22 A joyful heart is good medicine,
but a broken spirit dries up the bones.

23 A wicked person secretly takes a bribe
to subvert the course of justice.

24 Wisdom is the focus of the perceptive,
but a fool's eyes roam to the ends
of the earth.

25 A foolish son is grief to his father
and bitterness to the one who bore him.

[A] **16:32** Lit *and ruling over one's spirit* [B] **17:4** Lit *to lips of iniquity* [C] **17:11** Or *a merciless angel* [D] **17:18** Lit *sense slaps hands*

26 It is certainly not good to fine
an innocent person
or to beat a noble for his honesty.[A]

27 The one who has knowledge restrains
his words,
and one who keeps a cool head[B]
is a person of understanding.

28 Even a fool is considered wise
when he keeps silent —
discerning, when he seals his lips.

18 One who isolates himself pursues
selfish desires;
he rebels against all sound wisdom.

2 A fool does not delight in understanding,
but only wants to show off his opinions.[C]

3 When a wicked person comes,
contempt also comes,
and along with dishonor, derision.

4 The words of a person's mouth
are deep waters,
a flowing river, a fountain of wisdom.[D]

5 It is not good to show partiality to the guilty,
denying an innocent person justice.

6 A fool's lips lead to strife,
and his mouth provokes a beating.

7 A fool's mouth is his devastation,
and his lips are a trap for his life.

8 A gossip's words are like choice food
that goes down to one's innermost being.[E]

9 The one who is lazy in his work
is brother to a vandal.[F]

10 The name of the LORD is a strong tower;
the righteous run to it and are protected.[G]

11 The wealth of the rich is his fortified city;
in his imagination it is like a high wall.

12 Before his downfall a person's heart is proud,
but humility comes before honor.

13 The one who gives an answer
before he listens —
this is foolishness and disgrace for him.

14 A person's spirit can endure sickness,
but who can survive a broken spirit?

15 The mind of the discerning
acquires knowledge,
and the ear of the wise seeks it.

16 A person's gift opens doors[H] for him
and brings him before the great.

17 The first to state his case seems right
until another comes and cross-examines him.

18 Casting the lot ends quarrels
and separates powerful opponents.

19 An offended brother is harder to reach[I]
than a fortified city,
and quarrels are like the bars of a fortress.

20 From the fruit of a person's mouth
his stomach is satisfied;
he is filled with the product of his lips.

21 Death and life are in the power of the tongue,
and those who love it will eat its fruit.

22 A man who finds a wife finds a good thing
and obtains favor from the LORD.

23 The poor person pleads,
but the rich one answers roughly.

24 One with many friends may be harmed,[J]
but there is a friend who stays closer
than a brother.

19 Better a poor person who lives with integrity
than someone who has deceitful lips and is
a fool.

2 Even zeal is not good without knowledge,
and the one who acts hastily[K] sins.

3 A person's own foolishness leads him astray,
yet his heart rages against the LORD.

4 Wealth attracts many friends,
but a poor person is separated from his friend.

[A]**17:26** Or *noble unfairly* [B]**17:27** Lit *spirit* [C]**18:2** Lit *to uncover his heart* [D]**18:4** Or *waters; a fountain of wisdom is a flowing river* [E]**18:8** Lit *to the chambers of the belly* [F]**18:9** Lit *master of destruction* [G]**18:10** Lit *raised high* [H]**18:16** Lit *gift makes room* [I]**18:19** LXX, Syr, Tg, Vg read *is stronger* [J]**18:24** Some LXX mss, Syr, Tg, Vg read *friends must be friendly* [K]**19:2** Lit *who is hasty with feet*

5 A false witness will not go unpunished,
and one who utters lies will not escape.

6 Many seek a ruler's favor,
and everyone is a friend of one
who gives gifts.

7 All the brothers of a poor person hate him;
how much more do his friends
keep their distance from him!
He may pursue them with words,
but they are not there.[A]

8 The one who acquires good sense[B]
loves himself;
one who safeguards understanding
finds success.

9 A false witness will not go unpunished,
and one who utters lies perishes.

10 Luxury is not appropriate for a fool —
how much less for a slave to rule
over princes!

11 A person's insight gives him patience,
and his virtue is to overlook an offense.

12 A king's rage is like the roaring of a lion,
but his favor is like dew on the grass.

13 A foolish son is his father's ruin,
and a wife's nagging is an endless dripping.

14 A house and wealth are inherited
from fathers,
but a prudent wife is from the LORD.

15 Laziness induces deep sleep,
and a lazy person will go hungry.

16 The one who keeps commands
preserves himself;
one who disregards[C] his ways will die.

17 Kindness to the poor is a loan to the LORD,
and he will give a reward to the lender.[D]

18 Discipline your son while there is hope;
don't set your heart on being the cause
of his death.[E]

19 A person with intense anger bears
the penalty;
if you rescue him, you'll have to do it again.

20 Listen to counsel and receive instruction
so that you may be wise later in life.[F]

21 Many plans are in a person's heart,
but the LORD's decree will prevail.

22 What is desirable in a person is his fidelity;
better to be a poor person than a liar.

23 The fear of the LORD leads to life;
one will sleep at night[G] without danger.

24 The slacker buries his hand in the bowl;
he doesn't even bring it back to his mouth!

25 Strike a mocker, and the inexperienced learn
a lesson;
rebuke the discerning,
and he gains knowledge.

26 The one who plunders his father and evicts
his mother
is a disgraceful and shameful son.

27 If you stop listening to correction, my son,
you will stray from the words of knowledge.

28 A worthless witness mocks justice,
and a wicked mouth swallows iniquity.

29 Judgments are prepared for mockers,
and beatings for the backs of fools.

20 Wine is a mocker, beer is a brawler;
whoever goes astray[H] because of them
is not wise.

2 A king's terrible wrath is like the roaring
of a lion;
anyone who provokes him endangers himself.

3 Honor belongs to the person who ends
a dispute,
but any fool can get himself into a quarrel.

4 The slacker does not plow
during planting season;[I]
at harvest time he looks,[J] and there is nothing.

5 Counsel in a person's heart is deep water;
but a person of understanding draws it out.

[A]**19:7** Hb uncertain [B]**19:8** Lit *acquires a heart* [C]**19:16** Or *despises*, or *treats lightly* [D]**19:17** Lit *to him* [E]**19:18** Lit *don't lift up your soul to his death* [F]**19:20** Lit *in your end* [G]**19:23** Lit *will spend the night satisfied* [H]**20:1** Or *whoever staggers* [I]**20:4** Lit *plow in winter* [J]**20:4** Lit *inquires*

6 Many a person proclaims his own loyalty,
but who can find a trustworthy person?

7 A righteous person acts with integrity;
his children who come after him
will be happy.

8 A king sitting on a throne to judge
separates out all evil with his eyes.

9 Who can say, "I have kept my heart pure;
I am cleansed from my sin"?

10 Differing weights and varying measures[A] —
both are detestable to the LORD.

11 Even a young man is known by his actions —
by whether his behavior is pure and upright.

12 The hearing ear and the seeing eye —
the LORD made them both.

13 Don't love sleep, or you will become poor;
open your eyes, and you'll have enough to eat.

14 "It's worthless, it's worthless!" the buyer says,
but after he is on his way, he gloats.

15 There is gold and a multitude of jewels,
but knowledgeable lips are a rare treasure.

16 Take his garment,
for he has put up security for a stranger;
get collateral if it is for foreigners.

17 Food gained by fraud is sweet to a person,
but afterward his mouth is full of gravel.

18 Finalize plans with counsel,
and wage war with sound guidance.

19 The one who reveals secrets is a constant gossip;
avoid someone with a big mouth.

20 Whoever curses his father or mother —
his lamp will go out in deep darkness.

21 An inheritance gained prematurely
will not be blessed ultimately.

22 Don't say, "I will avenge this evil!"
Wait on the LORD, and he will rescue you.

23 Differing weights[B] are detestable to the LORD,
and dishonest scales are unfair.

24 Even a courageous person's steps
are determined by the LORD,
so how can anyone understand his own way?

25 It is a trap for anyone to dedicate
something rashly
and later to reconsider his vows.

26 A wise king separates out the wicked
and drives the threshing wheel over them.

27 The LORD's lamp sheds light on a person's life,[C]
searching the innermost parts.[D]

28 Loyalty and faithfulness guard a king;
through loyalty he maintains his throne.

29 The glory of young men is their strength,
and the splendor of old men is gray hair.

30 Lashes and wounds purge away evil,
and beatings cleanse the innermost parts.[E]

21 A king's heart is like channeled water
in the LORD's hand:
He directs it wherever he chooses.

2 All a person's ways seem right to him,
but the LORD weighs hearts.

3 Doing what is righteous and just
is more acceptable to the LORD
than sacrifice.

4 The lamp that guides the wicked —
haughty eyes and an arrogant heart — is sin.

5 The plans of the diligent certainly lead
to profit,
but anyone who is reckless
certainly becomes poor.

6 Making a fortune through a lying tongue
is a vanishing mist,[F] a pursuit of death.[G,H]

7 The violence of the wicked sweeps them away
because they refuse to act justly.

8 A guilty one's conduct is crooked,
but the behavior of the innocent is upright.

[A] **20:10** Lit *Stone and stone, measure and measure* [B] **20:23** Lit *A stone and a stone* [C] **20:27** Lit *breath* [D] **20:27** Lit *the chambers of the belly* [E] **20:30** Lit *beatings the chambers of the belly* [F] **21:6** Or *a breath blown away* [G] **21:6** Some Hb mss, LXX, Vg read *a snare of death* [H] **21:6** Lit *is vanity, ones seeking death*

9 Better to live on the corner of a roof
than to share a house with a nagging wife.

10 A wicked person desires evil;
he has no consideration[A] for his neighbor.

11 When a mocker is punished,
the inexperienced become wiser;
when one teaches a wise man,
he acquires knowledge.

12 The Righteous One[B] considers the house
of the wicked;
he brings the wicked to ruin.

13 The one who shuts his ears to the cry
of the poor
will himself also call out and not be answered.

14 A secret gift soothes anger,
and a covert bribe, fierce rage.

15 Justice executed is a joy to the righteous
but a terror to evildoers.

16 The person who strays from the way
of prudence
will come to rest in the assembly of
the departed spirits.

17 The one who loves pleasure
will become poor;
whoever loves wine and oil will not
get rich.

18 The wicked are a ransom for the righteous,
and the treacherous, for[C] the upright.

19 Better to live in a wilderness
than with a nagging and hot-tempered wife.

20 Precious treasure and oil are in the dwelling
of a wise person,
but a fool consumes them.[D]

21 The one who pursues righteousness
and faithful love
will find life, righteousness, and honor.

22 A wise person went up against a city
of warriors
and brought down its secure fortress.

23 The one who guards his mouth and tongue
keeps himself out of trouble.

24 The arrogant and proud person,
named "Mocker,"
acts with excessive arrogance.

25 A slacker's craving will kill him
because his hands refuse to work.
26 He is filled with craving[E] all day long,
but the righteous give and don't hold back.

27 The sacrifice of a wicked person
is detestable —
how much more so
when he brings it with ulterior motives!

28 A lying witness will perish,
but the one who listens
will speak successfully.

29 A wicked person puts on a bold face,
but the upright one considers his way.

30 No wisdom, no understanding, and no counsel
will prevail against the LORD.

31 A horse is prepared for the day of battle,
but victory comes from the LORD.

22

A good name is to be chosen
over great wealth;
favor is better than silver and gold.

2 Rich and poor have this in common:[F]
the LORD makes them all.

3 A sensible person sees danger and takes cover,
but the inexperienced keep going
and are punished.

4 Humility, the fear of the LORD,
results in wealth, honor, and life.

5 There are thorns and snares on the way
of the crooked;
the one who guards himself stays
far from them.

6 Start a youth out on his way;
even when he grows old he will not depart
from it.

7 The rich rule over the poor,
and the borrower is a slave to the lender.

[A]21:10 Or *favor* [B]21:12 Or *righteous one* [C]21:18 Or *in place of* [D]21:20 Lit *it* [E]21:26 Lit *He craves a craving* [F]22:2 Lit *poor meet*

8 The one who sows injustice will reap disaster,
and the rod of his fury will be destroyed.

9 A generous person[A] will be blessed,
for he shares his food with the poor.

10 Drive out a mocker, and conflict goes too;
then quarreling and dishonor will cease.

11 The one who loves a pure heart
and gracious lips — the king is his friend.

12 The LORD's eyes keep watch over knowledge,
but he overthrows the words
of the treacherous.

13 The slacker says, "There's a lion outside!
I'll be killed in the public square!"

14 The mouth of the forbidden woman is
a deep pit;
a man cursed by the LORD will fall into it.

15 Foolishness is bound to the heart of a youth;
a rod of discipline will separate it from him.

16 Oppressing the poor to enrich oneself,
and giving to the rich — both lead
only to poverty.

WORDS OF THE WISE

17 Listen closely,[B] pay attention to the words
of the wise,
and apply your mind to my knowledge.
18 For it is pleasing if you keep them
within you
and if they are[C] constantly on your lips.
19 I have instructed you today — even you —
so that your confidence may be in the LORD.
20 Haven't I written for you thirty sayings[D]
about counsel and knowledge,
21 in order to teach you true and reliable words,
so that you may give a dependable report[E]
to those who sent you?

22 Don't rob a poor person because he is poor,
and don't crush the oppressed at the city gate,
23 for the LORD will champion their cause
and will plunder those who plunder them.

24 Don't make friends with an angry person,[F]
and don't be a companion
of a hot-tempered one,
25 or you will learn his ways
and entangle yourself in a snare.

26 Don't be one of those who enter agreements,[G]
who put up security for loans.
27 If you have nothing with which to pay,
even your bed will be taken from under you.

28 Don't move an ancient boundary marker
that your ancestors set up.

29 Do you see a person skilled in his work?
He will stand in the presence of kings.
He will not stand in the presence
of the unknown.

23 When you sit down to dine with a ruler,
consider carefully what[H] is before you,
2 and put a knife to your throat
if you have a big[I] appetite;
3 don't desire his choice food,
for that food is deceptive.

4 Don't wear yourself out to get rich;
because you know better, stop!
5 As soon as your eyes fly to it, it disappears,
for it makes wings for itself
and flies like an eagle to the sky.

6 Don't eat a stingy person's bread,[J]
and don't desire his choice food,
7 for it's like someone calculating inwardly.[K]
"Eat and drink," he says to you,
but his heart is not with you.
8 You will vomit the little you've eaten
and waste your pleasant words.

9 Don't speak to[L] a fool,
for he will despise the insight of your words.

10 Don't move an ancient boundary marker,
and don't encroach on the fields
of the fatherless,
11 for their Redeemer is strong,
and he will champion their cause against you.

12 Apply yourself to discipline
and listen to words of knowledge.

13 Don't withhold discipline from a youth;
if you punish him with a rod, he will not die.

[A] **22:9** Lit *Good of eye* [B] **22:17** Lit *Stretch out your ear* [C] **22:18** Or *you; let them be*, or *you, so that they are* [D] **22:20** Text emended; one Hb tradition reads *you previously*; alt Hb tradition reads *you excellent things*; LXX, Syr, Vg read *you three times* [E] **22:21** Lit *give dependable words* [F] **22:24** Lit *with a master of anger* [G] **22:26** Lit *Don't be among hand slappers* [H] **23:1** Or *who* [I] **23:2** Lit *you are the master of an* [J] **23:6** Lit *eat bread of an evil eye* [K] **23:7** LXX reads *it is like someone swallowing a hair in the throat* [L] **23:9** Lit *in the ears of*

14 Punish him with a rod,
and you will rescue his life from Sheol.

15 My son, if your heart is wise,
my heart will indeed rejoice.
16 My innermost being will celebrate
when your lips say what is right.

17 Don't let your heart envy sinners;
instead, always fear the LORD.
18 For then you will have a future,
and your hope will not be dashed.

19 Listen, my son, and be wise;
keep your mind on the right course.
20 Don't associate with those who drink
too much wine
or with those who gorge themselves on meat.
21 For the drunkard and the glutton
will become poor,
and grogginess will clothe them in rags.

22 Listen to your father who gave you life,
and don't despise your mother
when[A] she is old.
23 Buy — and do not sell — truth,
wisdom, instruction, and understanding.
24 The father of a righteous son
will rejoice greatly,
and one who fathers a wise son will delight
in him.
25 Let your father and mother have joy,
and let her who gave birth to you rejoice.

26 My son, give me your heart,
and let your eyes observe my ways.
27 For a prostitute is a deep pit,
and a wayward woman is a narrow well;
28 indeed, she sets an ambush like a robber
and increases the number
of unfaithful people.

29 Who has woe? Who has sorrow?
Who has conflicts? Who has complaints?
Who has wounds for no reason?
Who has red eyes?
30 Those who linger over wine;
those who go looking for mixed wine.
31 Don't gaze at wine because it is red,
because it gleams in the cup
and goes down smoothly.
32 In the end it bites like a snake
and stings like a viper.
33 Your eyes will see strange things,
and you will say absurd things.[B]
34 You'll be like someone sleeping out at sea
or lying down on the top of a ship's mast.
35 "They struck me, but[C] I feel no pain!
They beat me, but I didn't know it!
When will I wake up?
I'll look for another drink."

24 Don't envy the evil
or desire to be with them,
2 for their hearts plan violence,
and their words stir up trouble.

3 A house is built by wisdom,
and it is established by understanding;
4 by knowledge the rooms are filled
with every precious and beautiful treasure.

5 A wise warrior is better than a strong one,[D]
and a man of knowledge than one
of strength;[E]
6 for you should wage war
with sound guidance —
victory comes with many counselors.

7 Wisdom is inaccessible to[F] a fool;
he does not open his mouth at the city gate.

8 The one who plots evil
will be called a schemer.
9 A foolish scheme is sin,
and a mocker is detestable to people.

10 If you do nothing in a difficult time,
your strength is limited.
11 Rescue those being taken off to death,
and save those stumbling toward slaughter.
12 If you say, "But we didn't know about this,"
won't he who weighs hearts consider it?
Won't he who protects your life know?
Won't he repay a person according to
his work?

13 Eat honey, my son, for it is good,
and the honeycomb is sweet to your palate;
14 realize that wisdom is the same for you.
If you find it, you will have a future,
and your hope will never fade.

15 Don't set an ambush, you wicked one,
at the camp of the righteous man;
don't destroy his dwelling.

[A]**23:22** Or *because* [B]**23:33** Or *will speak perversities*, or *inverted things* [C]**23:35** LXX, Syr, Tg, Vg read *me," you will say, "but* [D]**24:5** LXX, Syr; MT reads *is in strength* [E]**24:5** LXX, Syr, Tg; MT reads *knowledge exerts strength* [F]**24:7** Lit *is too high for*

Boundary Markers

by Joel F. Drinkard Jr.

Boundary markers were common in the ancient Near East. Inscribed stone slabs that stood upright (stelae) marking boundaries are known from Egypt. When Pharaoh Akhenaten (reigned ca 1353–1336 BC) built his new capital city of Akhetaten, he set up boundary stelae marking the boundaries and fields of the city. Fifteen of these stelae have been found. They are inscribed with texts describing the reason the site was chosen, the planning for the city, and the dedication to the god Aten. Boundary stones were also set up along Egypt's border with Nubia to the south.[1] These boundary markers regularly included symbols representing the deities.

In Babylon during the Kassite period (sixteenth–twelfth centuries BC), *kudurru*, which were inscribed stones placed in a temple, recorded land the king granted to vassals. "The size of properties donated to private individuals ranges between 80 and 1,000 hectares (200–2,500 acres), though a surface area of about 250 hectares (625 acres) is most common and appears to have been some kind of standard measure. . . . [The] 250 hectares could provide the nutritional basis for at least two hundred people and hence assure the economic independence and prosperity of a sizable extended family, including service personnel, slaves, and so forth."[2] The *kudurru* stone in the temple was the original document; clay copies were given to the vassal to prove his entitlement to the land grant. In addition to the text describing the land grant, the *kudurru* often bore the symbols of the deities called upon to witness the grant and protect the land.

In 1871, Charles Clermont-Ganneau, a French archaeologist and biblical scholar, was shown stones near Gezer bearing both the Hebrew inscription "the boundary of Gezer" and the Greek inscription *Alkiou*, meaning "belonging to Alkios." Clermont-Ganneau identified the nearby site as ancient Gezer, now a universally accepted identification. Archaeologist R. A. S. Macalister, who had led excavations at the site (1902–1909), published information about six of these boundary markers in his excavation reports on Gezer. A seventh boundary marker was discovered in 1964. These boundary markers all date to the Roman period. Six of the markers bear the same inscription;

Kudurru is the Akkadian word for "frontier" or "boundary." *Kudurru* stones, which were used by the Kassites of ancient Mesopotamia, recorded the granting and transferring of land from the king to one of his subjects. The *kudurru* stones were inscribed with text that recorded the transfer of property and depictions of gods who were responsible for protecting the agreement.

the seventh has not yet been deciphered. Famed archaeologist G. Ernest Wright proposed that the Greek name indicates the owner of the estate in the Roman era. The town had ceased to exist, but workers for the estate may have lived on the site of the town. The boundary markers indicated the extent of the estate.[3] These are the only inscribed boundary markers known thus far from the land of ancient Israel.

In addition to such inscribed boundary markers, many times a large stone, or even a pile of stones—a cairn—served as a boundary marker. The Old Testament references to boundary markers or landmarks are apparently to this latter type that is not inscribed. The Old Testament contains six references to boundary markers or landmarks. In each instance, the reference deals with the moving of a boundary marker or the encroachment upon the property of others.

In both Egypt and Mesopotamia, inscribed boundary markers included references to the deities to serve as witnesses and protectors of the land. The Old Testament gives no indication that boundary markers had any representation of God. However, in Hebrew understanding, the land ultimately belonged to God. He was the one who gave the land to the Hebrews and oversaw the allotment to the tribes, clans, and families. Since the land belonged to God, the prohibitions in the Old Testament served as God's way of guaranteeing property rights. God protected the property within the boundary markers; no one was to remove or move them.

A boundary stone at Gezer. As one entered Gezer, the Hebrew inscription read, "Boundary of Gezer." Leaving, the Greek inscription read, "Belonging to Alkios," probably a reference to a land owner in the Roman era.

The boundary marker set the extent of a person's or city's or nation's property. To move the boundary marker, or to remove it, was to jeopardize the individual's or the community's property. And since the land was ultimately God's, to move or remove a boundary marker was an affront to God. Such action amounted to theft of God's property, and God would punish the offender appropriately. ✣

---

[1] Randy L. Jordan, "The Stelae of Ancient Egypt," cited 13 August 2007, www.touregypt.net/featurestories/stela.htm.

[2] Walter Sommerfeld, "The Kassites of Ancient Mesopotamia: Origins, Politics, and Culture" in *CANE* (2000), 922.

[3] H. Darrell Lance, "Gezer in the Land and in History," *BA* 30.2 (May 1967): 34–47 (esp. 47).

16 Though a righteous person falls seven times,
he will get up,
but the wicked will stumble into ruin.

17 Don't gloat when your enemy falls,
and don't let your heart rejoice
when he stumbles,
18 or the LORD will see, be displeased,
and turn his wrath away from him.

19 Don't be agitated by evildoers,
and don't envy the wicked.
20 For the evil have no future;
the lamp of the wicked will be put out.

21 My son, fear the LORD, as well as the king,
and don't associate with rebels,[A]
22 for destruction will come suddenly
from them;
who knows what distress these two
can bring?

23 These sayings also belong to the wise:

It is not good to show partiality in judgment.
24 Whoever says to the guilty,
"You are innocent" —
peoples will curse him, and nations
will denounce him;
25 but it will go well with those who convict
the guilty,
and a generous blessing will come to them.

26 He who gives an honest answer
gives a kiss on the lips.

27 Complete your outdoor work, and prepare
your field;
afterward, build your house.

28 Don't testify against your neighbor
without cause.
Don't deceive with your lips.
29 Don't say, "I'll do to him what he did to me;
I'll repay the man for what he has done."

30 I went by the field of a slacker
and by the vineyard of one lacking sense.
31 Thistles had come up everywhere,
weeds covered the ground,
and the stone wall was ruined.
32 I saw, and took it to heart;
I looked, and received instruction:
33 a little sleep, a little slumber,
a little folding of the arms to rest,
34 and your poverty will come like a robber,
and your need, like a bandit.

HEZEKIAH'S COLLECTION

25 These too are proverbs of Solomon,
which the men of King Hezekiah of Judah
copied.

2 It is the glory of God to conceal a matter
and the glory of kings to investigate a matter.
3 As the heavens are high and the earth is deep,
so the hearts of kings cannot be investigated.

4 Remove impurities from silver,
and material will be produced[B]
for a silversmith.[C]
5 Remove the wicked from the king's presence,
and his throne will be established
in righteousness.

6 Don't boast about yourself before the king,
and don't stand in the place of the great;
7 for it is better for him to say to you,
"Come up here!"
than to demote you in plain view of a noble.[D]

8 Don't take a matter to court hastily.
Otherwise, what will you do afterward
if your opponent[E] humiliates you?
9 Make your case with your opponent
without revealing another's secret;
10 otherwise, the one who hears
will disgrace you,
and you'll never live it down.[F]

11 A word spoken at the right time
is like gold apples in silver settings.
12 A wise correction to a receptive ear
is like a gold ring or an ornament of gold.

13 To those who send him, a trustworthy envoy
is like the coolness of snow on a harvest day;
he refreshes the life of his masters.

14 The one who boasts about a gift
that does not exist
is like clouds and wind without rain.
15 A ruler can be persuaded through patience,
and a gentle tongue can break a bone.
16 If you find honey, eat only what you need;
otherwise, you'll get sick from it and vomit.

[A] **24:21** Or *those given to change* [B] **25:4** Lit *will come out*; Ex 32:24
[C] **25:4** Or *and a vessel will be produced by a silversmith* [D] **25:7** Lit *you before a noble whom your eyes see* [E] **25:8** Or *neighbor*, also in v. 9
[F] **25:10** Lit *and your evil report will not turn back*

17 Seldom set foot in your neighbor's house;
otherwise, he'll get sick of you and hate you.
18 A person giving false testimony
against his neighbor
is like a club, a sword, or a sharp arrow.
19 Trusting an unreliable person in a difficult time
is like a rotten tooth or a faltering foot.

20 Singing songs to a troubled heart
is like taking off clothing on a cold day
or like pouring vinegar on soda.[A]

21 If your enemy is hungry, give him food to eat,
and if he is thirsty, give him water to drink,
22 for you will heap burning coals on his head,
and the LORD will reward you.

23 The north wind produces rain,
and a backbiting tongue, angry looks.

24 Better to live on the corner of a roof
than to share a house with a nagging wife.

25 Good news from a distant land
is like cold water to a parched throat.[B]

26 A righteous person who yields to the wicked
is like a muddied spring or a polluted well.

27 It is not good to eat too much honey
or to seek glory after glory.[C]

28 A person who does not control his temper
is like a city whose wall is broken down.

26

Like snow in summer and rain at harvest,
honor is inappropriate for a fool.

2 Like a flitting sparrow or a fluttering swallow,
an undeserved curse goes nowhere.

3 A whip for the horse, a bridle for the donkey,
and a rod for the backs of fools.
4 Don't answer a fool according to
his foolishness
or you'll be like him yourself.
5 Answer a fool according to his foolishness
or he'll become wise in his own eyes.
6 The one who sends a message by a fool's hand
cuts off his own feet and drinks violence.
7 A proverb in the mouth of a fool
is like lame legs that hang limp.
8 Giving honor to a fool
is like binding a stone in a sling.
9 A proverb in the mouth of a fool
is like a stick with thorns,
brandished by[D] the hand of a drunkard.
10 The one who hires a fool or who hires
those passing by
is like an archer who wounds everyone
indiscriminately.
11 As a dog returns to its vomit,
so also a fool repeats his foolishness.
12 Do you see a person who is wise
in his own eyes?
There is more hope for a fool than for him.

13 The slacker says, "There's a lion in the road —
a lion in the public square!"
14 A door turns on its hinges,
and a slacker, on his bed.
15 The slacker buries his hand in the bowl;
he is too weary to bring it to his mouth!
16 In his own eyes, a slacker is wiser
than seven who can answer sensibly.

17 A person who is passing by and meddles
in a quarrel that's not his
is like one who grabs a dog by the ears.
18 Like a madman who throws flaming darts
and deadly arrows,
19 so is the person who deceives his neighbor
and says, "I was only joking!"

20 Without wood, fire goes out;
without a gossip, conflict dies down.
21 As charcoal for embers and wood for fire,
so is a quarrelsome person for kindling strife.
22 A gossip's words are like choice food
that goes down to one's innermost being.[E]

23 Smooth[F] lips with an evil heart
are like glaze on an earthen vessel.
24 A hateful person disguises himself
with his speech
and harbors deceit within.
25 When he speaks graciously, don't believe him,
for there are seven detestable things
in his heart.
26 Though his hatred is concealed by deception,
his evil will be revealed in the assembly.
27 The one who digs a pit will fall into it,
and whoever rolls a stone —
it will come back on him.
28 A lying tongue hates those it crushes,
and a flattering mouth causes ruin.

[A] **25:20** Lit *natron*, or *sodium carbonate* [B] **25:25** Or *a weary person* [C] **25:27** Lit *seek their glory, glory* [D] **26:9** Lit *thorn that goes up into* [E] **26:22** Lit *to the chambers of the belly* [F] **26:23** LXX; MT reads *Burning*

27 Don't boast about tomorrow,
for you don't know what a day
might bring.

2 Let another praise you, and not
your own mouth —
a stranger, and not your own lips.

3 A stone is heavy, and sand a burden,
but aggravation from a fool
outweighs them both.

4 Fury is cruel, and anger a flood,
but who can withstand jealousy?

5 Better an open reprimand
than concealed love.

6 The wounds of a friend are trustworthy,
but the kisses of an enemy are excessive.

7 A person who is full tramples
on a honeycomb,
but to a hungry person, any bitter thing
is sweet.

8 Anyone wandering from his home
is like a bird wandering from its nest.

9 Oil and incense bring joy to the heart,
and the sweetness of a friend is better
than self-counsel.[A]

10 Don't abandon your friend
or your father's friend,
and don't go to your brother's house
in your time of calamity;
better a neighbor nearby than a brother
far away.

11 Be wise, my son, and bring my heart joy,
so that I can answer anyone who taunts me.

12 A sensible person sees danger
and takes cover;
the inexperienced keep going
and are punished.

13 Take his garment,
for he has put up security for a stranger;
get collateral if it is for foreigners.[B]

14 If one blesses his neighbor
with a loud voice early in the morning,
it will be counted as a curse to him.

15 An endless dripping on a rainy day
and a nagging wife are alike;
16 the one who controls her controls the wind
and grasps oil with his right hand.

17 Iron sharpens iron,
and one person sharpens another.[C]

18 Whoever tends a fig tree will eat its fruit,
and whoever looks after his master
will be honored.

19 As water reflects the face,
so the heart reflects the person.

20 Sheol and Abaddon are never satisfied,
and people's eyes are never satisfied.

21 As a crucible refines silver,
and a smelter refines gold,
so a person should refine his praise.

22 Though you grind a fool
in a mortar with a pestle along with grain,
you will not separate his foolishness
from him.

23 Know well the condition of your flock,
and pay attention to your herds,
24 for wealth is not forever;
not even a crown lasts for all time.
25 When hay is removed
and new growth appears
and the grain from the hills is gathered in,
26 lambs will provide your clothing,
and goats, the price of a field;
27 there will be enough goat's milk
for your food —
food for your household
and nourishment for your female servants.

28 The wicked flee when no one
is pursuing them,
but the righteous are as bold as a lion.

2 When a land is in rebellion, it has many rulers,
but with a discerning
and knowledgeable person, it endures.

3 A destitute leader[D] who oppresses the poor
is like a driving rain that leaves no food.

[A] **27:9** LXX reads *heart, but the soul is torn up by affliction*
[B] **27:13** Lit *a foreign woman* [C] **27:17** Lit *and a man sharpens his friend's face* [D] **28:3** LXX reads *A wicked man*

4 Those who reject the law praise the wicked,
but those who keep the law pit themselves
against them.

5 The evil do not understand justice,
but those who seek the LORD
understand everything.

6 Better the poor person who lives with integrity
than the rich one who distorts right and wrong.[A]

7 A discerning son keeps the law,
but a companion of gluttons humiliates
his father.

8 Whoever increases his wealth
through excessive interest
collects it for one who is kind to the poor.

9 Anyone who turns his ear away from hearing
the law —
even his prayer is detestable.

10 The one who leads the upright into an evil way
will fall into his own pit,
but the blameless will inherit what is good.

11 A rich person is wise in his own eyes,
but a poor one who has discernment
sees through him.

12 When the righteous triumph,
there is great rejoicing,[B]
but when the wicked come to power,
people hide.

13 The one who conceals his sins
will not prosper,
but whoever confesses and renounces them
will find mercy.

14 Happy is the one who is always reverent,
but one who hardens his heart falls into trouble.

15 A wicked ruler over a helpless people
is like a roaring lion or a charging bear.

16 A leader who lacks understanding
is very oppressive,
but one who hates dishonest profit
prolongs his life.

17 Someone burdened by bloodguilt[C]
will be a fugitive until death.
Let no one help him.

18 The one who lives with integrity
will be helped,
but one who distorts right and wrong[D]
will suddenly fall.

19 The one who works his land
will have plenty of food,
but whoever chases fantasies
will have his fill of poverty.

20 A faithful person will have many blessings,
but one in a hurry to get rich
will not go unpunished.

21 It is not good to show partiality —
yet even a courageous person may sin
for a piece of bread.

22 A greedy one[E] is in a hurry for wealth;
he doesn't know that poverty will come
to him.

23 One who rebukes a person will later find
more favor
than one who flatters with his tongue.

24 The one who robs his father or mother
and says, "That's no sin,"
is a companion to a person who destroys.

25 A greedy person stirs up conflict,
but whoever trusts in the LORD will prosper.

26 The one who trusts in himself[F] is a fool,
but one who walks in wisdom will be safe.

27 The one who gives to the poor
will not be in need,
but one who turns his eyes away[G]
will receive many curses.

28 When the wicked come to power,
people hide,
but when they are destroyed,
the righteous flourish.

29 One who becomes stiff-necked,
after many reprimands
will be shattered instantly —
beyond recovery.

[A]**28:6** Lit *who twists two ways* [B]**28:12** Lit *glory* [C]**28:17** Lit *the blood of a person* [D]**28:18** Lit *who is twisted regarding two ways* [E]**28:22** Lit *A man with an evil eye* [F]**28:26** Lit *his heart* [G]**28:27** Lit *who shuts his eyes*

2 When the righteous flourish,
the people rejoice,
but when the wicked rule, people groan.

3 A man who loves wisdom brings joy
to his father,
but one who consorts with prostitutes
destroys his wealth.

4 By justice a king brings stability to a land,
but a person who demands "contributions"[A]
demolishes it.

5 A person who flatters his neighbor
spreads a net for his feet.

6 An evil person is caught by sin,
but the righteous one sings and rejoices.

7 The righteous person knows the rights[B]
of the poor,
but the wicked one does not understand
these concerns.

8 Mockers inflame a city,
but the wise turn away anger.

9 If a wise person goes to court with a fool,
there will be ranting and raving
but no resolution.[C]

10 Bloodthirsty men hate an honest person,
but the upright care about him.[D]

11 A fool gives full vent to his anger,[E]
but a wise person holds it in check.

12 If a ruler listens to lies,
all his officials will be wicked.

13 The poor and the oppressor have this
in common:[F]
the LORD gives light to the eyes of both.

14 A king who judges the poor
with fairness —
his throne will be established forever.

15 A rod of correction imparts wisdom,
but a youth left to himself[G]
is a disgrace to his mother.

16 When the wicked increase,
rebellion increases,
but the righteous will see their downfall.

17 Discipline your child, and it will bring you
peace of mind
and give you delight.

18 Without revelation[H] people run wild,
but one who follows divine instruction
will be happy.

19 A servant cannot be disciplined by words;
though he understands, he doesn't respond.

20 Do you see someone who speaks too soon?
There is more hope for a fool than for him.

21 A servant pampered from his youth
will become arrogant[I] later on.

22 An angry person stirs up conflict,
and a hot-tempered one[J] increases rebellion.

23 A person's pride will humble him,
but a humble spirit will gain honor.

24 To be a thief's partner is to hate oneself;
he hears the curse but will not testify.

25 The fear of mankind is a snare,
but the one who trusts in the LORD
is protected.[K]

26 Many desire a ruler's favor,
but a person receives justice from the LORD.

27 An unjust person is detestable
to the righteous,
and one whose way is upright
is detestable to the wicked.

THE WORDS OF AGUR

30 The words of Agur son of Jakeh.
The pronouncement.[L]

The man's oration to Ithiel, to Ithiel and Ucal:[M]

2 I am more stupid than any other person,[N]
and I lack a human's ability to understand.

[A]**29:4** The Hb word for *contributions* usually refers to offerings in worship. [B]**29:7** Lit *justice* [C]**29:9** Lit *rest* [D]**29:10** Or *person, and seek the life of the upright* [E]**29:11** Lit *spirit* [F]**29:13** Lit *oppressor meet* [G]**29:15** Lit *youth sent away* [H]**29:18** Lit *vision* [I]**29:21** Hb obscure [J]**29:22** Lit *a master of rage* [K]**29:25** Lit *raised high* [L]**30:1** Or *son of Jakeh from Massa*; Pr 31:1 [M]**30:1** Hb uncertain. Sometimes read with different word division as *oration: I am weary, God, I am weary, God, and I am exhausted*, or *oration: I am not God, I am not God, that I should prevail.* LXX reads *My son, fear my words and when you have received them repent. The man says these things to the believers in God, and I pause.* [N]**30:2** Lit *I am more stupid than a man*

“Sister, Can You Spare a Shekel?” Women in the Ancient Economic World

by Sharon H. Gritz

The early Israelites lived in a preindustrial, agrarian, pastoral society. Their economy centered on the household unit—several closely related families living near one another. Survival and complete self-sufficiency represented the main economic goals. The family owned, maintained, and kept the means of production, such as animals, agricultural tools, and everyday utensils. Households initially produced only for their own use. The Israelites grew, herded, and made everything needed for daily life. They did not sell their goods to others—even in their own village. They did not purchase what others had grown or made. They remained economically independent.[1]

After crossing the Jordan River into Canaan, the Israelites ate the land's produce (Jos 5:12). As their farming methods improved, they produced more crops and by-products than the family required. This excess led to limited trading using the barter system. People swapped animals, food products, or metal for goods, services, and slaves. At first, the Israelites exchanged items locally among themselves. As they seized Canaanite cities in their prolonged conquest of the promised land, their trade expanded. Farmers discovered markets for their surplus in the cities.

Dated about 550 BC; terra-cotta *lekythos* (oil flask) from Attica, Greece; image depicts two women weaving, using a standing loom. The woman to the right is weighing wool.

ECONOMIC CONTRIBUTIONS

Women's labor made the family-centered economy possible. They helped transform raw supplies into consumables—items quickly used and needing to be replaced regularly. Then they distributed these resources. For instance, adult women had the time-consuming task of feeding the household. They had to convert crude materials into edible food, a physically demanding task requiring strength and stamina. Harvesting required every available worker, so women worked in the fields, helping to gather and thresh the grain (Ru 2:2–17). They sorted, cleaned, parched, and ground the grain. They mixed and baked bread. They milked farm animals and used the milk to churn butter and make cheese and yogurt. They drew water and gathered the fuel necessary for food preparation. They butchered, cleaned, and prepared small animals for meals, as well as preserved some meat for storage. Women helped plant and weed vegetable gardens. They gathered and cooked vegetables. They tended orchards and vineyards, then picked the fruit and preserved it for future use.

Women also had to clothe their household members. They started with the raw materials, such as sheep's wool or flax, a plant whose woven fibers make linen. They carded, spun, wove, dyed, and sewed the resulting products into garments. Women usually washed the family's clothing.[2] Further, they made the domestic pottery families used for carrying out their day-to-day tasks.

Wives performed one important contribution to the economy that only women could do—bearing children. This role secured the nation's survival and involved aspects people often overlooked as belonging to the economy. This included the nurture, discipline, and education of children. In addition, women took care of everyone—the men, the older generation, and the sick.[3]

WORK OUTSIDE THE HOUSEHOLD

With the demands of meeting the family's daily needs, as well as the motherly cycle of pregnancy, childbirth, nursing, and care giving, women of the Old Testament era had little time and energy to pursue a "career" outside of the home or even to develop the skills necessary for that kind of venture. Exceptions might include daughters of royalty, the upper class, or professional families who had access to training and slaves to fulfill household tasks.

Women did have some "professional" roles. Midwives fulfilled a vital function for expectant mothers. This involved offering prenatal care, helping with the delivery, presenting the child to the father, and helping the mother to care for the infant immediately after the birth. The Old Testament mentions these health-care workers (Gn 35:17; 38:28; Ex 1:15–21). In other Near Eastern cultures, a midwife served as "a religious specialist as well as a medical technician."[4]

Women served as professional mourners (Jr 9:17) and nurses/caregivers (Gn 24:59; 35:8; Ex 2:7; Ru 4:16; 2Sm 4:4; 2Kg 11:2). Because of the duties to their own families, most women worked at these "professions" part time—unless they were slaves.

When Samuel warned the Israelites what a king would demand of them, he mentioned various specialties women would perform, probably as slaves for the benefit of the royal court: perfumers, bakers, and cooks (1Sm 8:13). Female musicians provided entertainment (2Sm 19:35; Ec 2:8).

The Old Testament mentions another "professional," the prostitute (Lv 21:7,9; 1Kg 3:16). Prostitution occurred primarily in urban centers. Both single and married women worked as prostitutes. Some married women might have turned to prostitution out of economic need—to support their families.

BUSINESSES AND PROPERTY

Evidence dating from the eighth to sixth centuries BC reveals that Hebrew women engaged in business and administrative activities. Archaeologists have uncovered personal stamp seals recorded in Hebrew script bearing women's names, including *Hannah*. Businesses used these seals to stamp goods, such as jars of oil or wine.[5]

Documents from the eastern Mediterranean area during the time of Israel's judges and early kings indicate that some women possessed wealth, including land, slaves, livestock, and precious metals. Legal documents from the ancient Near Eastern city of Ugarit (in present-day Syria) indicate that a man could will his property to his wife.[6] Biblical examples also show women as being wealthy or owning property: the five daughters of Zelophehad (Nm 27:5–8), Rahab (Jos 2), Micah's mother (Jdg 17:1–4), Naomi (Ru 4:1–6), and Job's daughters (Jb 42:13–15).

Some women took the management skills learned at home into the village or city by running alehouses, where men went for music and drinks and could meet prostitutes. These taverns also served as guesthouses. Women who owned these alehouses could trade for supplies and provide loans; they could also serve as a source of information. Rahab provided Joshua's spies with such intelligence (Jos 2:8–11). Law codes of Mesopotamia regulated alewives.[7]

Dated 4500–3150 BC; butter churn excavated at Beer-sheba. The user would suspend the churn using a rope and shake it until the butter separated.

Other women profited from a "cottage industry," a small-scale business developed from the textiles and pottery they made for their own households. The growth of cities made this type of business possible.

EXAMPLE OF ECONOMIC ACTIVITY

Proverbs 31:10–31 depicts a wealthy woman probably in the time of the monarchy fully involved in economic activities both inside and outside the home. Perhaps this woman acted on her own initiative due to her husband's absence. Men conscripted for military service were away from home for extended periods.[8] At any rate, this strong woman managed her prosperous agrarian household effectively and productively. She engaged in business transactions—buying land and planting a vineyard with her own earnings. She produced enough clothing both to clothe her own household and to provide for the poor. She sold her surplus linen garments—a textile cottage industry. This wife of noble character represents an economic planner, manager, and distributor of goods and services.

SISTER, CAN YOU SPARE A SHEKEL?

Women made many economic contributions in the Old Testament era. Their families and nation depended on their efforts. Yet, since coins did not appear until about the seventh century BC,[9] women did not have a shekel to spare before that time. They could, however, spare or make loans of grain, livestock, textiles, metals, and even slaves. They were indeed a vital part of the economy of the ancient Near East. ❖

Wall painting fragment depicts women mourning; from the tomb of Neb-Amon at Thebes; dated about 1400 BC. The women in the front are putting ashes on their heads.

[1] Carol Fontaine, *Smooth Words: Women, Proverbs and Performance in Biblical Wisdom*, Journal for the Study of the Old Testament Supplement Series (JSOTSup) 356 (New York: Sheffield Academic, 2002), 29–30; Carol Meyers, *Discovering Eve: Ancient Israelite Women in Context* (New York: Oxford University Press, 1988), 142–3, 145. [2] Phyllis A. Bird, *Missing Persons and Mistaken Identities: Women and Gender in Ancient Israel* (Minneapolis: Fortress, 1997), 59; Carol Meyers, "The Family in Early Israel" in *Families in Ancient Israel*, ed. Leo G. Perdue et al. (Louisville: Westminster John Knox, 1997), 25. [3] Mercedes L. Garcia Bachmann, *Women at Work in the Deuteronomistic History*, International Voices in Biblical Studies (IVBS) 4 (Atlanta: Society of Biblical Literature, 2013), 161. [4] Bird, *Missing Persons*, 62. [5] Mayer I. Gruber, "Women in Ancient Levant," in *Women's Roles in Ancient Civilizations: A Reference Guide*, ed. Bella Vivante (Westport, CT: Greenwood, 1999), 147. [6] Gruber, "Women," 146. [7] Fontaine, *Smooth Words*, 85–86; Karen Rhea Nemet-Nejat, "Women in Ancient Mesopotamia," in *Women's Roles*, 107. [8] Ellen F. Davis, *Scripture, Culture, and Agriculture: An Agrarian Reading of the Bible* (New York: Cambridge University Press, 2009), 150. [9] Robert D. Bergen, "Trade and Wealth in the Ancient World," *BI* 42.2 (Winter 2014–2015): 68.

3 I have not gained wisdom,
and I have no knowledge of the Holy One.
4 Who has gone up to heaven
and come down?
Who has gathered the wind in his hands?
Who has bound up the waters in a cloak?
Who has established all the ends
of the earth?
What is his name,
and what is the name of his son —
if you know?
5 Every word of God is pure;[A]
he is a shield to those who take refuge in him.
6 Don't add to his words,
or he will rebuke you, and you will be proved
a liar.

7 Two things I ask of you;
don't deny them to me before I die:
8 Keep falsehood and deceitful words
far from me.
Give me neither poverty nor wealth;
feed me with the food I need.
9 Otherwise, I might have too much
and deny you, saying, "Who is the LORD?"
or I might have nothing and steal,
profaning[B] the name of my God.

10 Don't slander a servant to his master
or he will curse you, and you will
become guilty.

11 There is a generation that curses its father
and does not bless its mother.
12 There is a generation that is pure
in its own eyes,
yet is not washed from its filth.
13 There is a generation — how haughty its eyes
and pretentious its looks.[C]
14 There is a generation whose teeth are swords,
whose fangs are knives,
devouring the oppressed from the land
and the needy from among mankind.

15 The leech has two daughters: "Give, Give!"
Three things are never satisfied;
four never say, "Enough!":
16 Sheol; a childless womb;
earth, which is never satisfied with water;
and fire, which never says, "Enough!"

17 As for the eye that ridicules a father
and despises obedience to a mother,
may ravens of the valley pluck it out
and young vultures eat it.

18 Three things are too wondrous for me;
four I can't understand:
19 the way of an eagle in the sky,
the way of a snake on a rock,
the way of a ship at sea,
and the way of a man with a young woman.

20 This is the way of an adulteress:
she eats and wipes her mouth
and says, "I've done nothing wrong."

21 The earth trembles under three things;
it cannot bear up under four:
22 a servant when he becomes king,
a fool when he is stuffed with food,
23 an unloved woman when she marries,
and a servant girl when she ousts her queen.

24 Four things on earth are small,
yet they are extremely wise:
25 ants are not a strong people,
yet they store up their food in the summer;
26 hyraxes are not a mighty people,
yet they make their homes in the cliffs;
27 locusts have no king,
yet all of them march in ranks;
28 a lizard[D] can be caught in your hands,
yet it lives in kings' palaces.

29 Three things are stately in their stride;
four are stately in their walk:
30 a lion, which is mightiest among beasts
and doesn't retreat before anything;
31 a strutting rooster;[E] a goat;
and a king at the head of his army.[F]

32 If you have been foolish by exalting yourself
or if you've been scheming,
put your hand over your mouth.
33 For the churning of milk produces butter,
and twisting a nose draws blood,
and stirring up anger produces strife.

THE WORDS OF LEMUEL

31 The words of King Lemuel,
a pronouncement[G] that his mother
taught him:

2 What should I say, my son?
What, son of my womb?
What, son of my vows?

[A]30:5 Lit *refined* [B]30:9 Lit *grabbing* [C]30:13 Lit *and its eyelids lifted up* [D]30:28 Or *spider* [E]30:31 Or *a greyhound* [F]30:31 LXX reads *king addressing his people* [G]31:1 Or *of Lemuel, king of Massa*, or *of King Lemuel, a burden*

3 Don't spend your energy on women
or your efforts on those who destroy kings.
4 It is not for kings, Lemuel,
it is not for kings to drink wine
or for rulers to desire beer.
5 Otherwise, he will drink,
forget what is decreed,
and pervert justice for all the oppressed.[A]
6 Give beer to one who is dying
and wine to one whose life is bitter.
7 Let him drink so that he can forget his poverty
and remember his trouble no more.
8 Speak up[B] for those who have no voice,[C]
for the justice of all who are dispossessed.[D]
9 Speak up, judge righteously,
and defend the cause of the oppressed
and needy.

IN PRAISE OF A WIFE OF NOBLE CHARACTER

10 Who can find a wife of noble character?[E]
She is far more precious than jewels.[F]
11 The heart of her husband trusts in her,
and he will not lack anything good.
12 She rewards him with good, not evil,
all the days of her life.
13 She selects wool and flax
and works with willing hands.
14 She is like the merchant ships,
bringing her food from far away.
15 She rises while it is still night
and provides food for her household
and portions[G] for her female servants.
16 She evaluates a field and buys it;
she plants a vineyard with her earnings.[H]
17 She draws on her strength[I]
and reveals that her arms are strong.
18 She sees that her profits are good,
and her lamp never goes out at night.
19 She extends her hands to the spinning staff,
and her hands hold the spindle.
20 Her hands reach[J] out to the poor,
and she extends her hands to the needy.
21 She is not afraid for her household
when it snows,
for all in her household are doubly clothed.[K]
22 She makes her own bed coverings;
her clothing is fine linen and purple.
23 Her husband is known at the city gates,
where he sits among the elders of the land.
24 She makes and sells linen garments;
she delivers belts[L] to the merchants.
25 Strength and honor are her clothing,
and she can laugh at the time to come.
26 Her mouth speaks wisdom,
and loving instruction[M] is on her tongue.
27 She watches over the activities
of her household
and is never idle.[N]
28 Her children rise up and call her blessed;
her husband also praises her:
29 "Many women[O] have done noble deeds,
but you surpass them all!"
30 Charm is deceptive and beauty is fleeting,
but a woman who fears the LORD
will be praised.
31 Give her the reward of her labor,[P]
and let her works praise her
at the city gates.

[A] **31:5** Lit *sons of affliction* [B] **31:8** Lit *Open your mouth*, also in v. 9 [C] **31:8** Lit *who are mute* [D] **31:8** Lit *all the sons of passing away* [E] **31:10** Or *a wife of quality*, or *a capable wife* [F] **31:10** Vv. 10–31 form an acrostic. [G] **31:15** Or *tasks* [H] **31:16** Or *vineyard by her own labors* [I] **31:17** Lit *She wraps strength around her like a belt* [J] **31:20** Lit *Her hand reaches* [K] **31:21** LXX, Vg; MT reads *are dressed in scarlet* [L] **31:24** Or *sashes* [M] **31:26** Or *and the teaching of kindness* [N] **31:27** Lit *and does not eat the bread of idleness* [O] **31:29** Lit *daughters* [P] **31:31** Lit *the fruit of her hands*

ECCLESIASTES

Tombs on the side of the Mount of Olives, with the Kidron Valley below and the Dome of the Rock in the distance.

INTRODUCTION TO

ECCLESIASTES

Circumstances of Writing

According to Ecclesiastes 1:1 and 1:12, the author of this book was David's son and a king over Israel from Jerusalem. Also, 12:9 speaks of the author as a writer of proverbs, so Solomon appears to be the author. Many scholars believe that Ecclesiastes was written too late in Israel's history for this to be true, and they want to date the book at least five hundred years after Solomon's time (later than 450 BC). However, strong evidence attests that the book does come from the age of Solomon. For instance, it displays a great knowledge of literature from early Mesopotamia and Egypt.

One example is that the book shows an awareness of the "Harper Songs," poetry from Egypt that is much older than the age of Solomon. Ecclesiastes 9:7–9 is similar to that poetry, and it also resembles a portion of the famous *Epic of Gilgamesh* from Mesopotamia. It makes sense that Solomon, who had close contacts with Egypt and whose empire stretched up to the Euphrates River, would know and reflect on such texts. It is doubtful that an anonymous Jew writing five hundred or more years later, when Egyptian and Mesopotamian glory was finished and when Judah was a backwater nation, would have had access to these texts or could have understood them. By contrast, Ecclesiastes shows no similarities to the Greek philosophy that flourished in the fifth century BC and later. All of these conditions point to the traditional view that Solomon authored this book.

Ecclesiastes is Wisdom literature, meaning that it is in the part of the Bible especially concerned with helping readers cope with the practical and philosophical issues of life. It has roots in the Wisdom literature of Egypt and Babylon. Books like Proverbs and Ecclesiastes are the biblical answer to the search for truth. Proverbs is basic wisdom, giving the reader fundamental principles to live by. Ecclesiastes, by contrast, is for a more mature reader. It engages the question of whether death nullifies all purpose and meaning in life.

Contribution to the Bible

Ecclesiastes must be read with care because some of its verses, if read in isolation, seem to contradict other biblical teachings. It seems to deny the afterlife (3:18–22), to warn us against being too righteous (7:16), and to recommend a life of pleasure (10:19). But the real purpose of Ecclesiastes is to force us to take our mortality seriously and thus to consider carefully how we should live. Ecclesiastes knocks away all the façades by which we disguise the fact that life is short and we deny that all our accomplishments will pass away. In this sense, Ecclesiastes anticipates the New Testament teaching that only God's grace, and not excessive zeal, saves us.

Structure

Ecclesiastes does not have the kind of structure we usually look for in a book of the Bible. At first glance it seems to move to and fro among various topics in a way that seems almost incoherent. It has no simple hierarchical outline, and it often jumps rapidly from one topic to the next. But a closer look reveals a structure that alternates between two perspectives: that of human existence apart from God and that of existence lived before God. If Ecclesiastes were music, it would be seen as antiphonal. The resolution of the tensions that permeate Ecclesiastes is found in the affirmation that the most important thing in life is to "fear God and keep his commands" (12:13).

EVERYTHING IS FUTILE

1 The words of the Teacher,[A] son of David, king in
Jerusalem.

2 "Absolute futility," says the Teacher.
"Absolute futility. Everything is futile."
3 What does a person gain for all his efforts
that he labors at under the sun?
4 A generation goes and a generation comes,
but the earth remains forever.
5 The sun rises and the sun sets;
panting, it hurries back to the place
where it rises.
6 Gusting to the south,
turning to the north,
turning, turning, goes the wind,
and the wind returns in its cycles.
7 All the streams flow to the sea,
yet the sea is never full;
to the place where the streams flow,
there they flow again.
8 All things[B] are wearisome,
more than anyone can say.
The eye is not satisfied by seeing
or the ear filled with hearing.
9 What has been is what will be,
and what has been done is what will be done;
there is nothing new under the sun.
10 Can one say about anything,
"Look, this is new"?
It has already existed in the ages before us.
11 There is no remembrance of those
who[C] came before;
and of those who will come after
there will also be no remembrance
by those who follow them.

THE LIMITATIONS OF WISDOM

12 I, the Teacher, have been[D] king over Israel in Jerusalem. 13 I applied my mind to examine and explore
through wisdom all that is done under heaven. God
has given people[E] this miserable task to keep them
occupied. 14 I have seen all the things that are done
under the sun and have found everything to be futile,
a pursuit of the wind.[F]

15 What is crooked cannot be straightened;
what is lacking cannot be counted.

16 I said to myself, "See, I have amassed wisdom far
beyond all those who were over Jerusalem before me,
and my mind has thoroughly grasped[G] wisdom and
knowledge." 17 I applied my mind to know wisdom and
knowledge, madness and folly; I learned that this too
is a pursuit of the wind.

18 For with much wisdom is much sorrow;
as knowledge increases, grief increases.

THE EMPTINESS OF PLEASURE

2 I said to myself, "Go ahead, I will test you with
pleasure; enjoy what is good." But it turned out
to be futile. 2 I said about laughter, "It is madness,"
and about pleasure, "What does this accomplish?" 3 I
explored with my mind the pull of wine on my body
— my mind still guiding me with wisdom — and how
to grasp folly, until I could see what is good for people
to do under heaven[H] during the few days of their lives.

THE EMPTINESS OF POSSESSIONS

4 I increased my achievements. I built houses and
planted vineyards for myself. 5 I made gardens and
parks for myself and planted every kind of fruit tree
in them. 6 I constructed reservoirs for myself from
which to irrigate a grove of flourishing trees. 7 I acquired male and female servants and had slaves
who were born in my house. I also owned livestock
— large herds and flocks — more than all who were
before me in Jerusalem. 8 I also amassed silver and
gold for myself, and the treasure of kings and provinces. I gathered male and female singers for myself,
and many concubines, the delights of men.[I,J] 9 So I became great and surpassed all who were before me in
Jerusalem; my wisdom also remained with me. 10 All
that my eyes desired, I did not deny them. I did not
refuse myself any pleasure, for I took pleasure in all
my struggles. This was my reward for all my struggles.
11 When I considered all that I had accomplished[K] and
what I had labored to achieve, I found everything to
be futile and a pursuit of the wind.[L] There was nothing to be gained under the sun.

THE RELATIVE VALUE OF WISDOM

12 Then I turned to consider wisdom, madness, and
folly, for what will the king's successor[M] be like? He[N]
will do what has already been done. 13 And I realized
that there is an advantage to wisdom over folly, like
the advantage of light over darkness.

14 The wise person has eyes in his head,
but the fool walks in darkness.

Yet I also knew that one fate comes to them both.
15 So I said to myself, "What happens to the fool
will also happen to me. Why then have I been
overly wise?" And I said to myself that this is also
futile. 16 For, just like the fool, there is no lasting

[A] 1:1 Or *of Qoheleth*, or *of the Leader of the Assembly* [B] 1:8 Or *words* [C] 1:11 Or *of the things that* [D] 1:12 Or *Teacher, was* [E] 1:13 Or *given the descendants of Adam* [F] 1:14 Or *a feeding on wind*, or *an affliction of spirit*; also in v. 17 [G] 1:16 Or *discerned* [H] 2:3 Two Hb mss, LXX, Syr read *the sun* [I] 2:8 LXX, Theod, Syr read *and male cupbearers and female cupbearers*; Aq, Tg, Vg read *a cup and cups*; Hb obscure [J] 2:8 Or *many treasures that people delight in* [K] 2:11 Lit *all my works that my hands had done* [L] 2:11 Or *a feeding on wind*, or *an affliction of spirit*; also in vv. 17,26 [M] 2:12 Lit *the man who comes after the king* [N] 2:12 Some Hb mss read *They*

It's About Time

by Warren McWilliams

Calendars have been used by many civilizations, ancient and contemporary, to mark the passage of time.

Jews and Christians in ancient times were convinced that God created time, God is Lord over time, and God acted in time. Some other ancient cultures understood time as cyclical or essentially repetitive in nature, but God's people knew God was directing time toward an ultimate goal. Today we are familiar with a time line, a design that reflects a biblical view of time. We are not meandering through time; we are going somewhere.

The Bible mentions basic units of time measurement. For instance, Revelation 9:15 notes "hour, day, month, and year." Like other ancient peoples, God's people noticed the movement of the sun, moon, and stars in the heavens and the changes in the seasons.

Sundial at the catacombs at Kom-El-Shoqafa in Alexandria, Egypt. The sundial likely dates to the second–fourth centuries AD.

THE YEAR

From observing the sun's movement, ancient cultures came to understand the concept of a year. They usually dated the beginning of the year from the vernal or autumnal equinoxes, the day in the spring or fall that the length of the days and nights was equal. Many cultures used the spring as the new year because of the new agricultural life evident then.

The Hebrews apparently described the year in several ways.[1] For example, an archaeological discovery known as the Gezer calendar (dated to the tenth century BC) connects the months of a typical year to agricultural activities such as planting and harvesting, beginning in the fall.[2] The Hebrews generally followed a lunar-solar calendar. The sun's movement marked the length of the year, and the new moon determined the beginning of a new month. Since the moon's circuit is about 29 ½ days, calculating a year became complicated. A totally lunar calendar, consisting of twenty-nine- and thirty-day months, would be short of a solar year. The Hebrews apparently borrowed from other cultures the idea of adding an extra time period, known as an intercalary month. The Babylonians, Assyrians, and Persians used the intercalary month system to adjust the calendar.[3]

Not all Jews marked the calendar in the same way. The Essenes, a group that eventually moved to Qumran near the Dead Sea, used a solar calendar. For them, all months had 30 days, but they added an extra day each quarter, creating a year of 364 days. Also, the Jewish book of Jubilees, written about 150 BC, advocated a solar calendar.[4]

Eventually the Jews had two calendars, civil and religious. The new year might start on Nisan 1 (spring) or Tishri 1 (fall).[5] The fall new year was the Festival of Trumpets (Lv 23:24), later known as Rosh Hashanah.[6]

MONTHS

The Hebrews ordinarily noted the months by numbers, such as the second month. Sometimes the Hebrews adopted the names of months from neighboring cultures. For example, four Canaanite names appear in the Old Testament: Abib for March–April (Ex 13:4), Ziv for April–May (1Kg 6:1), Ethanim for September–October (1Kg 8:2), and Bul for October–November (1Kg 6:38). The Jews later adopted Babylonian names for the months.

The New Testament does not indicate that the early Christians adopted the Roman calendar. Some Jewish literature, such as the apocryphal book of 1 Maccabees and Josephus's histories used Hellenistic names for months. In 46 BC, Julius Caesar reformed the Roman calendar, creating a year of 365 days. An extra day, a bissextile day, was added every four years. Our current practice of leap year follows a similar pattern. The so-called Julian calendar was used for centuries, until Pope Gregory XIII reformed the calendar in 1582, creating what is now called the Gregorian calendar.[7]

SEASONS

Religious festivals and agricultural cycles guided much of the biblical calendar.[8] Often the religious festival coincided with a key event, such as a harvest, in the agricultural cycle. For example, the short calendar in Exodus 23:14–17 mentions three festivals: the Festival of Unleavened Bread, the Festival of Harvest (or the Feast of Weeks), and the Festival of Ingathering (or the Feast of Tabernacles). The Festival of Harvest was later known as Pentecost, since it came fifty days after the Festival of Unleavened Bread; it was also a grain harvest festival. Later the Jews added Purim as a celebration of the deliverance by Esther (Est 9:20–29). Hanukkah was added to celebrate the liberation recounted in 1 and 2 Maccabees. This event was also called the Festival of Dedication (Jn 10:22). The New Testament writers often used these religious and agricultural celebrations to set biblical events in their context (e.g., Jn 6:4; 7:2).

CHRONOLOGY

The biblical writers reported the sequence of events in several ways. A common way, called relative chronology, is to mention an event in relation to another event. For instance, the Hebrews arrived at the wilderness of Sinai three months after leaving Egypt (Ex 19:1). Or God appeared to Isaiah in the year that King Uzziah died (Is 6:1). Amos received his messages from God two years before the earthquake (Am 1:1). People living at those times would have understood what date the writer meant.

More useful for readers today would be an absolute chronology. An absolute calendar would match a biblical event with our contemporary calendar. Archaeological discovery of the records of Assyrian kings has helped Bible scholars determine dates with some precision, at least when the biblical kings of Judah and Israel interface with these other rulers. In the New Testament, Luke noted the relation of Jesus's birth to political rulers (Lk 2:1–2) and the relation of early disciples to Roman leaders (Ac 18:12).

A Scythian monk in the sixth century developed the distinction between BC and AD. He took the birth of Jesus to be the decisive event in human history and matched that event with the Roman calendar. Although he miscalculated by a few years, the scheme "before Christ" and "anno Domini," meaning "in the year of the Lord," became popular.[9] ✜

---

[1] Simon J. De Vries, "Calendars" in *HolBD*, 221–22. [2] Jack Finegan, *Handbook of Biblical Chronology* (Princeton: Princeton University Press, 1964), 33. [3] E. Ray Clendenen, "Biblical Chronology" in *Holman Bible Handbook* (*HBH*), ed. David S. Dockery (Nashville: Holman, 1992), 51. [4] James C. Vanderkam, "Calendars; Ancient Israelite and Early Jewish" in *ABD*, 1:818. [5] Finegan, *Handbook*, 92. [6] Larry Walker, "Festivals," in *HolBD*, 489. [7] Clendenen, "Biblical Chronology," 51. [8] John Lilley, "Times and Seasons" in *Eerdmans' Handbook to the Bible*, ed. David Alexander and Pat Alexander (Grand Rapids: Eerdmans, 1983), 111. [9] Finegan, *Handbook*, 132.

A water watch was one of the first timekeepers not related to the movement of stars and planets. These stone vessels had a small hole near the bottom that allowed water to drip at a consistent rate. Though not extremely accurate, the hour was marked as the water level reached markings on the inside. Archaeologists discovered one of the oldest water watches in the tomb of Amenhotep I.

remembrance of the wise, since in the days to come
both will be forgotten. How is it that the wise person dies just like the fool? 17 Therefore, I hated life
because the work that was done under the sun was
distressing to me. For everything is futile and a
pursuit of the wind.

THE EMPTINESS OF WORK

18 I hated all my work that I labored at under the sun
because I must leave it to the one who comes after
me. 19 And who knows whether he will be wise or a
fool? Yet he will take over all my work that I labored
at skillfully under the sun. This too is futile. 20 So I
began to give myself over[A] to despair concerning all
my work that I had labored at under the sun. 21 When
there is a person whose work was done with wisdom,
knowledge, and skill, and he must give his portion to
a person who has not worked for it, this too is futile
and a great wrong. 22 For what does a person get with
all his work and all his efforts that he labors at under
the sun? 23 For all his days are filled with grief, and
his occupation is sorrowful; even at night, his mind
does not rest. This too is futile.

24 There is nothing better for a person than to eat,
drink, and enjoy[B,C] his work. I have seen that even this
is from God's hand, 25 because who can eat and who
can enjoy life[D] apart from him?[E] 26 For to the person
who is pleasing in his sight, he gives wisdom, knowledge, and joy; but to the sinner he gives the task of
gathering and accumulating in order to give to the
one who is pleasing in God's sight. This too is futile
and a pursuit of the wind.

THE MYSTERY OF TIME

3 There is an occasion for everything,
and a time for every activity under heaven:
2 a time to give birth and a time to die;
a time to plant and a time to uproot;[F]
3 a time to kill and a time to heal;
a time to tear down and a time to build;
4 a time to weep and a time to laugh;
a time to mourn and a time to dance;
5 a time to throw stones and a time
to gather stones;
a time to embrace and a time
to avoid embracing;
6 a time to search and a time to count as lost;
a time to keep and a time to throw away;
7 a time to tear and a time to sew;
a time to be silent and a time to speak;
8 a time to love and a time to hate;
a time for war and a time for peace.

9 What does the worker gain from his struggles? 10 I
have seen the task that God has given the children of
Adam to keep them occupied. 11 He has made everything appropriate[G] in its time. He has also put eternity
in their hearts,[H] but no one can discover the work
God has done from beginning to end. 12 I know that
there is nothing better for them than to rejoice and
enjoy the[I] good life. 13 It is also the gift of God whenever anyone eats, drinks, and enjoys all his efforts.
14 I know that everything God does will last forever;
there is no adding to it or taking from it. God works
so that people will be in awe of him. 15 Whatever is,
has already been, and whatever will be, already is.
However, God seeks justice for the persecuted.[J]

THE MYSTERY OF INJUSTICE AND DEATH

16 I also observed under the sun: there is wickedness
at the place of judgment and there is wickedness at
the place of righteousness. 17 I said to myself, "God
will judge the righteous and the wicked, since there
is a time for every activity and every work." 18 I said to
myself, "This happens so that God may test the children of Adam and they may see for themselves that
they are like animals." 19 For the fate of the children of
Adam and the fate of animals is the same. As one dies,
so dies the other; they all have the same breath. People
have no advantage over animals since everything is
futile. 20 All are going to the same place; all come from
dust, and all return to dust. 21 Who knows if the spirits
of the children of Adam go upward and the spirits
of animals go downward to the earth? 22 I have seen
that there is nothing better than for a person to enjoy
his activities because that is his reward. For who can
enable him to see what will happen after he dies?[K]

4 Again, I observed all the acts of oppression being
done under the sun. Look at the tears of those
who are oppressed; they have no one to comfort
them. Power is with those who oppress them; they
have no one to comfort them. 2 So I commended the
dead, who have already died, more than the living,
who are still alive. 3 But better than either of them is
the one who has not yet existed, who has not seen
the evil activity that is done under the sun.

THE LONELINESS OF WEALTH

4 I saw that all labor and all skillful work is due to one
person's jealousy of another. This too is futile and a
pursuit of the wind.[L]
5 The fool folds his arms
and consumes his own flesh.

[A] **2:20** Lit *And I turned to cause my heart* [B] **2:24** Syr, Tg; MT reads *There is no good in a person who eats and drinks and enjoys* [C] **2:24** Lit *and his soul sees good* [D] **2:25** LXX, Theod, Syr read *can drink* [E] **2:25** Some Hb mss, LXX, Syr read *me* [F] **3:2** Lit *uproot what is planted* [G] **3:11** Or *beautiful* [H] **3:11** Or *has put a sense of past and future into their minds*, or *has placed ignorance in their hearts* [I] **3:12** Lit *his* [J] **3:15** Lit *God seeks what is pursued* [K] **3:22** Lit *after him* [L] **4:4** Or *a feeding on wind*, or *an affliction of spirit*; also in vv. 6,16

6 Better one handful with rest
than two handfuls with effort and a pursuit
of the wind.

7 Again, I saw futility under the sun: 8 There is a person without a companion,[A] without even a son or brother, and though there is no end to all his struggles, his eyes are still not content with riches. "Who am I struggling for," he asks, "and depriving myself of good things?" This too is futile and a miserable task.

9 Two are better than one because they have a good reward for their efforts. 10 For if either falls, his companion can lift him up; but pity the one who falls without another to lift him up. 11 Also, if two lie down together, they can keep warm; but how can one person alone keep warm? 12 And if someone overpowers one person, two can resist him. A cord of three strands is not easily broken.

13 Better is a poor but wise youth than an old but foolish king who no longer pays attention to warnings. 14 For he came from prison to be king, even though he was born poor in his kingdom. 15 I saw all the living, who move about under the sun, follow[B] a second youth who succeeds him. 16 There is no limit to all the people who were before them, yet those who come later will not rejoice in him. This too is futile and a pursuit of the wind.

CAUTION IN GOD'S PRESENCE

5 Guard your steps when you go to the house of God. Better to approach in obedience than to offer the sacrifice as fools do, for they ignorantly do wrong. 2 Do not be hasty to speak, and do not be impulsive to make a speech before God. God is in heaven and you are on earth, so let your words be few. 3 Just as dreams accompany much labor, so also a fool's voice comes with many words. 4 When you make a vow to God, don't delay fulfilling it, because he does not delight in fools. Fulfill what you vow. 5 Better that you do not vow than that you vow and not fulfill it. 6 Do not let your mouth bring guilt on you, and do not say in the presence of the messenger that it was a mistake. Why should God be angry with your words and destroy the work of your hands? 7 For many dreams bring futility; so do many words. Therefore, fear God.

THE REALITIES OF WEALTH

8 If you see oppression of the poor and perversion of justice and righteousness in the province, don't be astonished at the situation, because one official protects another official, and higher officials protect them. 9 The profit from the land is taken by all; the king is served by the field.[C]

10 The one who loves silver is never satisfied with silver, and whoever loves wealth is never satisfied with income. This too is futile. 11 When good things increase, the ones who consume them multiply; what, then, is the profit to the owner, except to gaze at them with his eyes? 12 The sleep of the worker is sweet, whether he eats little or much, but the abundance of the rich permits him no sleep.

13 There is a sickening tragedy I have seen under the sun: wealth kept by its owner to his harm. 14 That wealth was lost in a bad venture, so when he fathered a son, he was empty-handed. 15 As he came from his mother's womb, so he will go again, naked as he came; he will take nothing for his efforts that he can carry in his hands. 16 This too is a sickening tragedy: exactly as he comes, so he will go. What does the one gain who struggles for the wind? 17 What is more, he eats in darkness all his days, with much frustration, sickness, and anger.

18 Here is what I have seen to be good: It is appropriate to eat, drink, and experience good in all the labor one does under the sun during the few days of his life God has given him, because that is his reward. 19 Furthermore, everyone to whom God has given riches and wealth, he has also allowed him to enjoy them, take his reward, and rejoice in his labor. This is a gift of God, 20 for he does not often consider the days of his life because God keeps him occupied with the joy of his heart.

6 Here is a tragedy I have observed under the sun, and it weighs heavily on humanity:[D] 2 God gives a person riches, wealth, and honor so that he lacks nothing of all he desires for himself, but God does not allow him to enjoy them. Instead, a stranger will enjoy them. This is futile and a sickening tragedy. 3 A man may father a hundred children and live many years. No matter how long he lives,[E] if he is not satisfied by good things and does not even have a proper burial, I say that a stillborn child is better off than he. 4 For he comes in futility and he goes in darkness, and his name is shrouded in darkness. 5 Though a stillborn child does not see the sun and is not conscious, it has more rest than he. 6 And if a person lives a thousand years twice, but does not experience happiness, do not both go to the same place?

7 All of a person's labor is for his stomach,[F]
yet the appetite is never satisfied.

8 What advantage then does the wise person have over the fool? What advantage is there for the poor person who knows how to conduct himself before others? 9 Better what the eyes see than wandering desire. This too is futile and a pursuit of the wind.[G]

[A] **4:8** Lit *person, but there is not a second,* [B] **4:15** Lit *with* [C] **5:9** Hb obscure [D] **6:1** Or *it is common among men* [E] **6:3** Lit *how many years* [F] **6:7** Lit *mouth* [G] **6:9** Or *a feeding on wind*, or *an affliction of spirit*

Trade and Wealth in the Ancient World

by Robert D. Bergen

Israel and its neighbors in the ancient Near East measured material wealth with a different yardstick than most any American would use today. At no time in the Old Testament era did Israel mint coins or make use of paper currency; in fact, throughout most of the Old Testament period, coinage was not present in any culture. Greeks and Lydians, in about 650 BC, were the first to mint coins,[1] about two hundred years before the last events of the Old Testament. Besides lacking coins and currency, stocks and bonds were also absent from the ancient financial landscape.

In the absence of coinage or financial instruments, people often purchased items using a barter system. People traded quantities of food products, animals, or metal for what they wanted—be it goods, services, and even slaves.

In a barter economy, the nature, quantity, and desirability of items someone owned determined the person's material wealth. Ancient Near Eastern societies calculated a person's material wealth on the basis of several easily measurable classes of items: food grown in the field, vineyard, or orchard; domesticated livestock; metals; useful, pretty, or culturally important objects; and slaves.

Among the food items that people used as measures of wealth were wheat and barley, olive oil, and wine. Individuals as well as nations used food as payment in commercial transactions. Hosea, for example, used five bushels of barley as partial payment for his wife (Hs 3:2); while King Solomon purchased cedar, cypress, and algum (or almug) timber from King Hiram of Tyre with one hundred thousand bushels each of wheat and barley, and one hundred ten thousand gallons each of wine and olive oil (2Ch 2:10).

In the Old Testament world, especially among the seminomadic populations, domesticated animals constituted a major measure of personal wealth. When Scripture described the patriarch Abram's wealth, livestock was the first asset mentioned (Gn 13:2); the same was true for Isaac and Jacob (26:14; 30:43). Sheep were particularly valuable, since they were a source of meat, milk products, and fiber for clothing. Goats were prized for their food value. Oxen were especially important because of their ability to pull carts and plows, though they also had food value. Donkeys were useful for hauling people and moderate loads over moderate distances. Conquered nations could expect to hand over large numbers of livestock to the victor (2Kg 3:4; 2Ch 17:11).

Refined metals were a prized form of wealth in the ancient Near East. Throughout the Old Testament

Three children riding on a donkey outside of Jericho. In ancient cultures, livestock was an indicator of wealth.

Ceremonial ceramic rhyton in the shape of a cluster of grapes; from the ancient Near Eastern city of Alishar, which became part of the Hittite Empire. Alishar thrived during the Middle and Late Bronze Ages, 2200–1200 BC.

world, people expressed the monetary worth of almost anything—for example, real estate (Gn 23:16), livestock (2Sm 24:24), or servants (Lv 27:3–6)—in terms of a particular weight of silver. That is why many versions translate the Hebrew word for silver, *kesephs*, as "money." Even so, the metals that cultures generally counted as forms of wealth included gold, silver, bronze, iron, tin, and lead (Nm 31:22). Gold was the ultimate prestige metal; people used it primarily in jewelry (Gn 24:22), royal adornments (Jdg 8:26; 1Kg 10:16), and sacred objects (Ex 25:17,29,39; 1Kg 6:21). Bronze was much more common than silver or gold and was valuable, especially for weapons (1Sm 17:5–6) and defensive fortifications (Ps 107:16; Is 45:2). Conquering nations took the defeated nation's metals as a prize of war (2Kg 24:13–15; 2Ch 36:3).

Ownership of prestigious manufactured goods and natural products was a fourth expression of wealth in the Old Testament world. Ezekiel's list of items sea traders imported provides a good sampling of things that ancient Near Eastern cultures considered highly desirable. These items included bronze utensils, wrought iron, embroidered and purple-dyed cloth, ivory, ebony, turquoise, fine linen, coral, rubies, honey, cassia, and aromatic cane (Ezk 27:12–21).

Slaves (often termed "servants" in English translations) were also a prestigious indicator of wealth. Possessing them meant the household had an abundance of resources that enabled them to supply food and clothing to nonfamily members. Evidence that the Lord had blessed Abraham included the fact that he possessed "male and female slaves" (Gn 24:35). Among King Solomon's many acquisitions were "male and female servants," in addition to "slaves who were born in [his] house" (Ec 2:7). Job, a non-Israelite, also counted slaves as part of his wealth (Jb 1:3). Victorious armies would sometimes capture and sell people acquired in the lands they defeated (Jl 3:3,6; Am 1:6,9).

MEASURES OF WEALTH

Determining the value of an item—and therefore a person's wealth—has always been a subjective process, and people have used different methods to calculate it. Certainly a major factor in determining a product's worth has been the amount of effort needed to obtain or produce it. Since ancient societies did not have internal combustion engines, electrical power grids, or assembly-line factories, worker productivity remained essentially unchanged for thousands of years. Thus measures of wealth that took labor into account during the entire biblical era would have been pretty much the same across the cultures.

But other factors that had nothing to do with human effort also played a role in determining how wealthy a person was. The value of a person's possessions depended in part on the number of people who wanted them, the general availability of the items, their usefulness, quality, beauty, religious significance, and social prestige. When any of these factors changed, a person's wealth would change accordingly. For example, a carved image of a deity—an object considered extremely valuable within Canaanite culture—was considered to be valueless in orthodox Israelite culture and was to be burned (Dt 7:5).

If wealth was measured according to purchasing power instead of quantity of items owned,[2] it could virtually disappear during times of war or drought. In times of peace and prosperity, food was quite affordable; but it became outrageously expensive during times of national crisis. For example, during a time of famine in Samaria, a cup of dove's dung—probably counted as a form of food because of seeds present in it—was 67 percent more valuable than a sanctuary assessment of a five-year-old female child (see Lv 27:6; 2Kg 6:25)!

In an economic system that relied heavily on bartering, people's purchasing power—and therefore wealth—depended in part on their negotiating skills (Gn 23:7–18; Pr 20:14). Good bargainers were likely richer. In a few instances, the Torah established some economic valuations (see Lv 27:16); these could have been used as guidelines to minimize over- or underpricing within the bartering system. ✣

---

[1] William J. Fallis, "Coins" in *HIBD*, 315.
[2] See the prologue to William W. Lewis, *The Power of Productivity* (Chicago: University of Chicago Press, 2004).

10 Whatever exists was given its name long ago,[A]
and it is known what mankind is. But he is not able
to contend with the one stronger than he. 11 For when
there are many words, they increase futility. What is
the advantage for mankind? 12 For who knows what
is good for anyone in life, in the few days of his futile life that he spends like a shadow? Who can tell
anyone what will happen after him under the sun?

WISE SAYINGS

7 A good name is better than fine perfume,
and the day of one's death is better than
the day of one's birth.
2 It is better to go to a house of mourning
than to go to a house of feasting,
since that is the end of all mankind,
and the living should take it to heart.
3 Grief is better than laughter,
for when a face is sad, a heart may be glad.
4 The heart of the wise is in a house
of mourning,
but the heart of fools is in a house of pleasure.
5 It is better to listen to rebuke
from a wise person
than to listen to the song of fools,
6 for like the crackling of burning thorns
under the pot,
so is the laughter of the fool.
This too is futile.
7 Surely, the practice of extortion turns
a wise person into a fool,
and a bribe corrupts the mind.
8 The end of a matter is better
than its beginning;
a patient spirit is better than a proud spirit.
9 Don't let your spirit rush to be angry,
for anger abides in the heart of fools.
10 Don't say, "Why were the former days better
than these?"
since it is not wise of you to ask this.
11 Wisdom is as good as an inheritance
and an advantage to those who see the sun,
12 because wisdom is protection as silver
is protection;
but the advantage of knowledge
is that wisdom preserves the life
of its owner.
13 Consider the work of God,
for who can straighten out
what he has made crooked?

14 In the day of prosperity be joyful, but in the day
of adversity, consider: God has made the one as well
as the other, so that no one can discover anything
that will come after him.

AVOIDING EXTREMES

15 In my futile life[B] I have seen everything: someone
righteous perishes in spite of his righteousness, and
someone wicked lives long in spite of his evil. 16 Don't
be excessively righteous, and don't be overly wise.
Why should you destroy yourself? 17 Don't be excessively wicked, and don't be foolish. Why should you
die before your time? 18 It is good that you grasp the
one and do not let the other slip from your hand. For
the one who fears God will end up with both of them.
19 Wisdom makes the wise person stronger
than ten rulers of a city.
20 There is certainly no one
righteous on the earth
who does good and never sins.

21 Don't pay attention[C] to everything people say,
or you may hear your servant cursing you, 22 for in
your heart you know that many times you yourself
have cursed others.

WHAT THE TEACHER FOUND

23 I have tested all this by wisdom. I resolved, "I will
be wise," but it was beyond me. 24 What exists is beyond reach and very deep. Who can discover it? 25 I
turned my thoughts to know, explore, and examine
wisdom and an explanation for things, and to know
that wickedness is stupidity and folly is madness.
26 And I find more bitter than death the woman who
is a trap: her heart a net and her hands chains. The
one who pleases God will escape her, but the sinner
will be captured by her. 27 "Look," says the Teacher, "I
have discovered this by adding one thing to another
to find out the explanation, 28 which my soul continually searches for but does not find: I found one person
in a thousand, but none of those was a woman. 29 Only
see this: I have discovered that God made people upright, but they pursued many schemes."

WISDOM, AUTHORITIES, AND INEQUITIES

8 Who is like the wise person, and who knows the
interpretation of a matter? A person's wisdom
brightens his face, and the sternness of his face is
changed.
2 Keep[D] the king's command because of your oath
made before God. 3 Do not be in a hurry; leave his
presence, and don't persist in a bad cause, since he
will do whatever he wants. 4 For the king's word is
authoritative, and who can say to him, "What are you
doing?" 5 The one who keeps a command will not experience anything harmful, and a wise heart knows
the right time and procedure. 6 For every activity

[A] **6:10** Lit *name already* [B] **7:15** Lit *days* [C] **7:21** Lit *Don't give your heart* [D] **8:2** Some Hb mss, LXX, Vg, Tg, Syr; other Hb mss read *As for me, keep*

The Gezer Calendar *from* "It's About Time"

by Warren McWilliams

The Gezer calendar was discovered by R. A. S. Macalister at Tel Gezer (Arabic Tell Jezer) in Palestine. This limestone plaque probably dates from about 925 BC, approximately the time of King Solomon. The calendar may have been a practice exercise for a schoolboy. The seven lines report a twelve-month calendar composed of agricultural activities.[1] It reads as follows:

His two months [mid-September–mid-November]: Ingathering (olives)

His two months [mid-November–mid-January]: Sowing (grain)

His two months [mid-January–mid-March]: Late sowing

His month [mid-March–mid-April]: Chopping flax (or, grass)

His month [mid-April–mid-May]: Barley harvest

His month [mid-May–mid-June]: (Wheat) harvest and measuring (grain)

His two months [mid-June–mid-August]: Vine harvest

His month [mid-August–mid-September]: Summer fruit. ✣

The Gezer calendar.

[1] Jack Finegan, *Handbook of Biblical Chronology* (Princeton: Princeton University, 1964), 33; Philip J. King and Lawrence E. Stager, *Life in Biblical Israel* (Louisville: Westminster John Knox, 2001), 87–88.

there is a right time and procedure, even though a person's troubles are heavy on him. 7 Yet no one knows what will happen because who can tell him what will happen? 8 No one has authority over the wind[A] to restrain it, and there is no authority over the day of death; no one is discharged during battle, and wickedness will not allow those who practice it to escape. 9 All this I have seen, applying my mind to all the work that is done under the sun, at a time when one person has authority over another to his harm.

10 In such circumstances, I saw the wicked buried. They came and went from the holy place, and they were praised[B] in the city where they did those things. This too is futile. 11 Because the sentence against an evil act is not carried out quickly, the heart of people is filled with the desire to commit evil. 12 Although a sinner does evil a hundred times and prolongs his life, I also know that it will go well with God-fearing people, for they are reverent before him. 13 However, it will not go well with the wicked, and they will not lengthen their days like a shadow, for they are not reverent before God.

14 There is a futility that is done on the earth: there are righteous people who get what the actions of the wicked deserve, and there are wicked people who get what the actions of the righteous deserve. I say that this too is futile. 15 So I commended enjoyment because there is nothing better for a person under the sun than to eat, drink, and enjoy himself, for this will accompany him in his labor during the days of his life that God gives him under the sun.

16 When I applied my mind to know wisdom and to observe the activity that is done on the earth (even though one's eyes do not close in sleep day or night), 17 I observed all the work of God and concluded that a person is unable to discover the work that is done under the sun. Even though a person labors hard to explore it, he cannot find it; even if a wise person claims to know it, he is unable to discover it.

ENJOY LIFE DESPITE DEATH

9 Indeed, I took all this to heart and explained it all: The righteous, the wise, and their works are in God's hands. People don't know whether to expect love or hate. Everything lies ahead of them. 2 Everything is the same for everyone: There is one fate for the righteous and the wicked, for the good and the bad,[C] for the clean and the unclean, for the one who sacrifices and the one who does not sacrifice. As it is for the good, so also it is for the sinner; as it is for the one who takes an oath, so also for the one who fears an oath. 3 This is an evil in all that is done under the sun: there is one fate for everyone. In addition, the hearts of people are full of evil, and madness is in their hearts while they live; after that they go to the dead. 4 But there is hope for whoever is joined[D] with all the living, since a live dog is better than a dead lion. 5 For the living know that they will die, but the dead don't know anything. There is no longer a reward for them because the memory of them is forgotten. 6 Their love, their hate, and their envy have already disappeared, and there is no longer a portion for them in all that is done under the sun.

7 Go, eat your bread with pleasure, and drink your wine with a cheerful heart, for God has already accepted your works. 8 Let your clothes be white all the time, and never let oil be lacking on your head. 9 Enjoy life with the wife you love all the days of your fleeting[E] life, which has been given to you under the sun, all your fleeting days. For that is your portion in life and in your struggle under the sun. 10 Whatever your hands find to do, do with all your strength, because there is no work, planning, knowledge, or wisdom in Sheol where you are going.

THE LIMITATIONS OF WISDOM

11 Again I saw under the sun that the race is not to the swift, or the battle to the strong, or bread to the wise, or riches to the discerning, or favor to the skillful; rather, time and chance happen to all of them. 12 For certainly no one knows his time: like fish caught in a cruel net or like birds caught in a trap, so people are trapped in an evil time as it suddenly falls on them.

13 I have observed that this also is wisdom under the sun, and it is significant to me: 14 There was a small city with few men in it. A great king came against it, surrounded it, and built large siege works against it. 15 Now a poor wise man was found in the city, and he delivered the city by his wisdom. Yet no one remembered that poor man. 16 And I said, "Wisdom is better than strength, but the wisdom of the poor man is despised, and his words are not heeded."

17 The calm words of the wise are heeded
more than the shouts of a ruler over fools.
18 Wisdom is better than weapons of war,
but one sinner can destroy much good.

THE BURDEN OF FOLLY

10 Dead flies make a perfumer's oil ferment
and stink;
so a little folly outweighs wisdom and honor.
2 A wise person's heart goes to the[F] right,
but a fool's heart to the left.
3 Even when the fool walks along the road,
his heart lacks sense,
and he shows everyone he is a fool.

[A] **8:8** Or *life-breath* [B] **8:10** Some Hb mss, LXX, Aq, Theod, Sym; other Hb mss read *forgotten* [C] **9:2** LXX, Aq, Syr, Vg; MT omits *and the bad* [D] **9:4** Alt Hb tradition reads *chosen* [E] **9:9** Or *futile* [F] **10:2** Lit *his*

Ecclesiastes and Conventional Wisdom

by Stephen J. Andrews

In the book of Ecclesiastes, Qoheleth ("the Teacher," CSB) struggled with the conventional wisdom and secular thinking of his day. What appear at times to be a wise man's random observations about life are in reality thoughtful reflections on the validity of conventional wisdom. By focusing on studying and applying wisdom, Qoheleth's contemporaries believed they could manipulate life. Qoheleth, or the "Preacher" or "Teacher" (1:1) presented a sharp contrast and a corrective to the wisdom schools of his time. Wisdom has value but alone cannot provide meaningful existence (2:13–15). Qoheleth rejected a simplistic view of wisdom in favor of a deeper and more profound contemplation of God's ways in the mystery of life.

Some biblical scholars have argued that conventional wisdom to Qoheleth "was not only inadequate, but close to blasphemous."[1] Like Job, Qoheleth protested against the easy generalizations with which his fellow teachers taught their pupils to be successful. They had oversimplified life and its rules so as to mislead and frustrate their followers. Their observations seemed superficial and their counsel thin in a world beset by toil, injustice, and death.[2]

The wise men of Qoheleth's day had missed the point when they minimized God's sovereignty in attempting to predict the inevitable outcome of the wise and the foolish. Qoheleth affirmed that God is sovereign over persons both wise and foolish and will judge according to his mercy, justice, and righteousness.

Qoheleth drove this point home in a number of unique ways. The "x of x" pattern of the phrase "vanity of vanities" (KJV) is a typical Hebrew superlative and occurs several times in the book for emphasis.[3] The writer used the expression "everything is futile" numerous times. Such thoughts were not new. The meaninglessness of existence was debated "as early as Sumerian literature and throughout the [wisdom] traditions of the ancient Near East."[4]

The book's structure also highlights Qoheleth's stand against the traditional wisdom of his day, as does his use of personal reflections, proverbs, rhetorical questions, and picturesque descriptive language. Scholars also believe "that Qoheleth often quoted [conventional wisdom] material in order to refute it" (see 4:5).[5] ✣

---

[1] William Sanford LaSor, David Allan Hubbard, and Frederic Wm. Bush, *Old Testament Survey*, 2nd ed. (Grand Rapids: Eerdmans, 1996), 500. [2] LaSor, Hubbard, and Bush, *Survey*. [3] See 1:2 in the KJV. CSB translates the superlative as "absolute futility." See LaSor, Hubbard, and Bush (501) for a list of some of the ways *hebel* has been translated. [4] John H. Walton, Victor H. Matthews, and Mark W. Chavalas, *IVP Bible Background Commentary: Old Testament* (Downers Grove, IL: InterVarsity, 2000), 571. [5] LaSor, Hubbard, and Bush, 503–4. For more on the use of quotations in Ecclesiastes, see Robert Gordis, *Koheleth—The Man and His World*, 3rd ed. (New York: Schocken, 1968), 95–108.

In eastern Turkey, workers and animals in a field. Qoheleth determined that much work is futile as work's rewards are often left to the one who follows.

4 If the ruler's anger rises against you,
don't leave your post,
for calmness puts great offenses to rest.

5 There is an evil I have seen under the sun, an error
proceeding from the presence of the ruler:
6 The fool is appointed to great heights,
but the rich remain in lowly positions.
7 I have seen slaves on horses,
but princes walking on the ground
like slaves.

8 The one who digs a pit may fall into it,
and the one who breaks through a wall
may be bitten by a snake.
9 The one who quarries stones may be hurt
by them;
the one who splits logs may be endangered
by them.
10 If the ax is dull, and one does not sharpen
its edge,
then one must exert more strength;
however, the advantage of wisdom is that
it brings success.
11 If the snake bites before it is charmed,
then there is no advantage for the charmer.[A]
12 The words from the mouth of a wise person
are gracious,
but the lips of a fool consume him.
13 The beginning of the words from his mouth
is folly,
but the end of his speaking is evil madness;
14 yet the fool multiplies words.
No one knows what will happen,
and who can tell anyone what will happen
after him?
15 The struggles of fools weary them,
for they don't know how to go to the city.
16 Woe to you, land, when your king is a youth
and your princes feast in the morning.
17 Blessed are you, land, when your king is a son
of nobles
and your princes feast at the proper time —
for strength and not for drunkenness.
18 Because of laziness the roof caves in,
and because of negligent hands
the house leaks.
19 A feast is prepared for laughter,
and wine makes life happy,
and money[B] is the answer for everything.
20 Do not curse the king even in your thoughts,
and do not curse a rich person
even in your bedroom,
for a bird of the sky may carry the message,
and a winged creature may report the matter.

INVEST IN LIFE

11 Send your bread on the surface of the water,
for after many days you may find it.
2 Give a portion to seven or even to eight,
for you don't know what disaster may happen
on earth.
3 If the clouds are full, they will pour out rain
on the earth;
whether a tree falls to the south
or the north,
the place where the tree falls,
there it will lie.
4 One who watches the wind will not sow,
and the one who looks at the clouds
will not reap.
5 Just as you don't know the path of the wind,
or how bones develop in[C] the womb
of a pregnant woman,
so also you don't know the work of God
who makes everything.
6 In the morning sow your seed,
and at evening do not let your hand rest,
because you don't know which will succeed,
whether one or the other,
or if both of them will be equally good.
7 Light is sweet,
and it is pleasing for the eyes
to see the sun.
8 Indeed, if someone lives many years,
let him rejoice in them all,
and let him remember the days of darkness,
since they will be many.
All that comes is futile.
9 Rejoice, young person,
while you are young,
and let your heart be glad in the days
of your youth.
And walk in the ways of your heart
and in the desire of your eyes;
but know that for all of these things
God will bring you to judgment.
10 Remove sorrow from your heart,
and put away pain from your flesh,
because youth and the prime of life
are fleeting.

THE TWILIGHT OF LIFE

12 So remember your Creator in the days of your
youth:
Before the days of adversity come,
and the years approach when you will say,
"I have no delight in them";

[A] **10:11** Lit *master of the tongue* [B] **10:19** Lit *silver* [C] **11:5** Or *know how the life-breath comes to the bones in*

2 before the sun and the light are darkened,
and the moon and the stars,
and the clouds return after[A] the rain;
3 on the day when the guardians of the house
tremble,
and the strong men stoop,
the women who grind grain cease because
they are few,
and the ones who watch through the windows
see dimly,
4 the doors at the street are shut
while the sound of the mill fades;
when one rises at the sound of a bird,
and all the daughters of song grow faint.
5 Also, they are afraid of heights and dangers
on the road;
the almond tree blossoms,
the grasshopper loses its spring,[B]
and the caper berry has no effect;
for the mere mortal is headed
to his eternal home,
and mourners will walk around in the street;
6 before the silver cord is snapped,[C]
and the gold bowl is broken,
and the jar is shattered at the spring,
and the wheel is broken into the well;
7 and the dust returns to the earth
as it once was,
and the spirit returns to God who gave it.
8 "Absolute futility," says the Teacher. "Everything is
futile."

THE TEACHER'S OBJECTIVES AND CONCLUSION

9 In addition to the Teacher being a wise man, he constantly taught the people knowledge; he weighed, explored, and arranged many proverbs. 10 The Teacher
sought to find delightful sayings and write words of
truth accurately. 11 The sayings of the wise are like
cattle prods, and those from masters of collections
are like firmly embedded nails. The sayings are given
by one Shepherd.[D]
12 But beyond these, my son, be warned: there is no
end to the making of many books, and much study
wearies the body. 13 When all has been heard, the conclusion of the matter is this: fear God and keep his
commands, because this is for all[E] humanity. 14 For
God will bring every act to judgment, including every
hidden thing, whether good or evil.

[A] **12:2** Or *with* [B] **12:5** Or *grasshopper is weighed down*, or *grasshopper drags itself along* [C] **12:6** Alt Hb tradition reads *removed* [D] **12:11** Or *by a shepherd* [E] **12:13** Or *is the whole duty of*

SONG OF SONGS

Gold necklace with oval plaques set with garnets and turquoise. From Uruk ("Erech" in Gn 10:10), which was one of the capitals of the country of Shinar, that is, of Mesopotamia. Built beside the Euphrates, the site was one of the largest enclosed cities in ancient Mesopotamia. The man in the Song of Songs offered to drape his beloved with necklaces of gold and silver (1:10–11).

INTRODUCTION TO

SONG OF SONGS

Circumstances of Writing

The Song claims authorship by Solomon in its title, "The Song of Songs, which is Solomon's." The church has long accepted this at face value, but modern critics raise objections to Solomon as author.

First, critics claim that the title did not originate with the Song but was added later by someone who wanted to attribute the work to the famous Solomon. However, no evidence supports this claim. Moreover, the structure of the book suggests that the title is integral to the book's composition and is thus original. Like other biblical writers, the writer often structured content with attention to certain numbers—three, seven, and ten being some of the most common. Within the Song, for example, the author designed seven sections (see below), a sevenfold praise (4:1–5), twice a tenfold praise (5:10–16; 7:1–5), and a tenfold occurrence of the abstract word for love (2:4–5,7; 3:5; 5:8; 7:6; 8:4,6–7). Apart from the title (1:1), he wove Solomon's name into six other places (1:5; 3:7,9,11; 8:11–12): two in the last section, three in the central, and one in the first. With the inclusion of "Solomon" in the title, the name appears a perfect seven times and is symmetrically balanced within the Song: twice in the first section balanced by twice in the last one, with three in the central. The title is thus as cleverly integrated with the lyrics as possible. It not only conforms to their melodic alliteration and meter, but it completes the sevenfold occurrence of "Solomon" and in a manner that artistically balances it throughout the Song. In fact, the tenfold occurrence of "love" joins the sevenfold appearance of "Solomon" to show the Song's subject and author. Hardly a later addition, the title seems to have been original, constituting its first verse.

Another common objection to Solomon's authorship is the king's well-known possession of seven hundred wives and three hundred concubines (1Kg 11:3). How could a man who lived like that write a song about devotion to one woman? It appears he could do so only because grace touched his heart. In this respect, he foreshadowed other biblical writers who, except for God's grace and calling, were the least qualified to write Scripture. For example, Paul, the great apostle, wrote most eloquently of grace and his unworthiness (see 1Tm 1:12–16). Solomon was a man immersed in power and pleasure, but God opened his eyes to true love. Solomon also authored much of the book of Proverbs. Just as he did not always follow the precepts he recorded there, so too he evidently composed a great love song despite his failure to live in accordance with its ideals.

A compelling historical reason to date the Song as coming from the time of Solomon is its nearest literary parallel—the Egyptian love songs. No one doubts their origin prior to or contemporaneous with the time of Solomon, and the Egyptian love songs are indisputably the Song's closest literary parallels.

Contribution to the Bible

A beautiful love song inspires us like grace, creating within us a desire for its beauty. Like such an enchanting love song, Solomon's Song inspires a pursuit of the love it portrays. This romantic delight is not a modern fairytale or fantasy from the past, but reflects God's desire to form within us a pure and devoted love. We discover that there is a bliss in married love that is reflective of the greater love believers experience as the bride of Christ. As this book's imagery informs us of romantic love, it also helps us anticipate the full consummation of our relationship with Christ when he returns for his bride.

Structure

The Song of Songs is a poem whose components form a chiastic structure. A chiasm takes the form:

A
    B
        C
    B´
A´

where A and A´ mirror each other and where the central element, C, conveys the main point of the poem. The author intended to emphasize the central elements of the structure, which are the day and night of the wedding (3:6–5:1). When God inspired Solomon to write this song, he gave divine approval to romantic love.

The Hebrew text makes a distinction between the various speakers through a change in gender and number. The Christian Standard Bible text has added subheadings to clarify when the speakers change.

1 The Song of Songs, which is Solomon's.

Woman

2 Oh, that he would kiss me with the kisses
of his mouth!
For your caresses[A] are more delightful
than wine.
3 The fragrance of your perfume is intoxicating;
your name is perfume poured out.
No wonder young women[B] adore you.
4 Take me with you — let's hurry.
Oh, that the king would bring[C] me
to his chambers.

Young Women

We will rejoice and be glad in you;
we will celebrate your caresses more than wine.

Woman

It is only right that they adore you.

5 Daughters of Jerusalem,
I am dark like the tents of Kedar,
yet lovely like the curtains of Solomon.
6 Do not stare at me because I am dark,
for the sun has gazed on me.
My mother's sons were angry with me;
they made me take care of the vineyards.
I have not taken care of my own vineyard.

7 Tell me, you whom I love:
Where do you pasture your sheep?
Where do you let them rest at noon?
Why should I be like one who veils herself[D]
beside the flocks of your companions?

Man[E]

8 If you do not know,
most beautiful of women,
follow[F] the tracks of the flock,
and pasture your young goats
near the shepherds' tents.

9 I compare you, my darling,
to a[G] mare among Pharaoh's chariots.
10 Your cheeks are beautiful with jewelry,
your neck with its necklace.
11 We will make gold jewelry for you,
accented with silver.

Woman

12 While the king is on his couch,[H]
my perfume[I] releases its fragrance.
13 The one I love is a sachet of myrrh to me,
spending the night between my breasts.
14 The one I love is a cluster of henna blossoms
to me,
in the vineyards of En-gedi.

Man

15 How beautiful you are, my darling.
How very beautiful!
Your eyes are doves.

Woman

16 How handsome you are, my love.
How delightful!
Our bed is verdant;
17 the beams of our house are cedars,
and our rafters are cypresses.[J]

2 I am a wildflower[K] of Sharon,
a lily[L] of the valleys.

Man

2 Like a lily among thorns,
so is my darling among the young women.

Woman

3 Like an apricot[M] tree among the trees
of the forest,
so is my love among the young men.
I delight to sit in his shade,
and his fruit is sweet to my taste.
4 He brought me to the banquet hall,[N]
and he looked on me with love.[O]
5 Sustain me with raisins;
refresh me with apricots,[P]
for I am lovesick.
6 May his left hand be under my head,
and his right arm embrace me.
7 Young women of Jerusalem, I charge you
by the gazelles and the wild does
of the field,
do not stir up or awaken love
until the appropriate time.[Q]

8 Listen! My love is approaching.
Look! Here he comes,
leaping over the mountains,
bounding over the hills.
9 My love is like a gazelle
or a young stag.
See, he is standing behind our wall,
gazing through the windows,

[A] **1:2** Or *acts of love* [B] **1:3** Or *wonder virgins* [C] **1:4** Or *The king has brought* [D] **1:7** Or *who wanders* [E] **1:8** Some understand the young women to be the speakers in this verse. [F] **1:8** Lit *go out for yourself into* [G] **1:9** Lit *my* [H] **1:12** Or *is at his table* [I] **1:12** Lit *nard* [J] **1:17** Or *firs, or pines* [K] **2:1** Traditionally *rose* [L] **2:1** Or *lotus* [M] **2:3** Or *apple* [N] **2:4** Lit *the house of wine* [O] **2:4** Or *and his banner over me is love* [P] **2:5** Or *apples* [Q] **2:7** Lit *until it pleases*

peering through the lattice.
10 My love calls to me:

Man

Arise, my darling.
Come away, my beautiful one.
11 For now the winter is past;
the rain has ended and gone away.
12 The blossoms appear in the countryside.
The time of singing[A] has come,
and the turtledove's cooing is heard
in our land.
13 The fig tree ripens its figs;
the blossoming vines give off their fragrance.
Arise, my darling.
Come away, my beautiful one.

14 My dove, in the clefts of the rock,
in the crevices of the cliff,
let me see your face,[B]
let me hear your voice;
for your voice is sweet,
and your face is lovely.

Woman[C]

15 Catch the foxes for us —
the little foxes that ruin the vineyards —
for our vineyards are in bloom.

Woman

16 My love is mine and I am his;
he feeds among the lilies.
17 Until the day breaks[D]
and the shadows flee,
turn around, my love, and be like a gazelle
or a young stag on the divided mountains.[E]

3 In my bed at night[F]
I sought the one I love;
I sought him, but did not find him.[G]
2 I will arise now and go about the city,
through the streets and the plazas.
I will seek the one I love.
I sought him, but did not find him.
3 The guards who go about the city found me.
I asked them, "Have you seen the one I love?"
4 I had just passed them
when I found the one I love.
I held on to him and would not let him go
until I brought him to my mother's house —
to the chamber of the one who conceived me.
5 Young women of Jerusalem, I charge you
by the gazelles and the wild does of the field,
do not stir up or awaken love
until the appropriate time.[H]

Narrator

6 Who is this coming up from the wilderness
like columns of smoke,
scented with myrrh and frankincense
from every fragrant powder
of the merchant?

7 Look! Solomon's bed
surrounded by sixty warriors
from the mighty men of Israel.
8 All of them are skilled with swords
and trained in warfare.
Each has his sword at his side
to guard against the terror of the night.

9 King Solomon made a carriage for himself
with wood from Lebanon.
10 He made its posts of silver,
its back[I] of gold,
and its seat of purple.
Its interior is inlaid with love[J]
by the young women of Jerusalem.
11 Go out, young women of Zion,
and gaze at King Solomon,
wearing the crown his mother placed
on him
on the day of his wedding —
the day of his heart's rejoicing.

Man

4 How beautiful you are, my darling.
How very beautiful!
Behind your veil,
your eyes are doves.
Your hair is like a flock of goats
streaming down Mount Gilead.
2 Your teeth are like a flock
of newly shorn sheep
coming up from washing,
each one bearing twins,
and none has lost its young.[K]
3 Your lips are like a scarlet cord,
and your mouth[L] is lovely.
Behind your veil,
your brow[M] is like a slice of pomegranate.
4 Your neck is like the tower of David,
constructed in layers.
A thousand shields are hung on it —
all of them shields of warriors.

[A] **2:12** Or *pruning* [B] **2:14** Or *form* [C] **2:15** The speaker could be the woman, the man, or both. [D] **2:17** Lit *breathes* [E] **2:17** Or *the Bether mountains*, or *the mountains of spices*; Hb obscure [F] **3:1** Or *bed night after night* [G] **3:1** LXX adds *I called him, but he did not answer me* [H] **3:5** Lit *until it pleases* [I] **3:10** Or *base*, or *canopy* [J] **3:10** Or *leather* [K] **4:2** Lit *and no one bereaved among them* [L] **4:3** Or *speech* [M] **4:3** Or *temple*, or *cheek*, or *lips*

Oils, Perfumes, and Cosmetics of the Ancient Near East

by George H. Shaddix

The word translated as "perfume" in Song of Songs 1:3 literally means "fat." The word describes the "fat" or oil of the fruit that people used in cosmetics. In Israel, this fruit was for the most part olive oil. The oil of the olive was typically mixed with fragrances to produce perfumes and other cosmetics in the ancient Near East.

Tree owners allowed olives to ripen on the tree and fall to the ground. If needed, people would beat the trees with long poles to make the remaining fruit fall (Dt 24:20). Once the olives were gathered, those to be pressed for oil were piled up and allowed to ferment. This allowed "a more abundant flow of oil" when pressed.[1] Olive oil was obtained by pressing the olives and straining out the liquid part of the olive. Some of these presses are still used today. At one time, people trampled the olives underfoot as they did grapes (Mc 6:15).

Cosmetic box made of ebony and inlaid with faience plaques and ivory (some ivory inlays have been tinted pink); dated to Egypt's Eighteenth Dynasty, about 1550–1295 BC.

Once the oil was pressed from the fruit, the oil would be mixed with water. The solid matter would sink to the bottom and the oil would float on the water. People would skim the oil from the top and store it in earthenware jars or, for larger quantities, in cisterns.

In addition to olive oil, people used oils from other sources to make the base for cosmetics and perfumes in the ancient Near East. For instance, to make skin creams, people used oils from "almonds, gourds, other trees and plants, and animal and fish fats."[2] Olives were in abundance in Galilee, and "only olive oil seems to have been used among the Hebrews."[3] Both men and women used the oil-based cosmetics and perfumes. Men rubbed oil into the hair of the head and beard.[4] This made the hair both stronger and softer (Pss 23:5; 133:2). Women used cosmetics for personal care and to beautify themselves. These "included eye paint, powders, rouge, ointments for the body, and perfumes."[5]

People have been making and using cosmetics since ancient days. The Bible mentions painting one's eyes (2Kg 9:30; Jr 4:30; Ezk 23:40). These eye cosmetics "were minerally based: black often being made from lead sulfate, greens and blues from copper oxide, and reds from iron oxide."[6] People crushed these materials and mixed them with olive oil or some other oil. Fragrances were often mixed as well. Individuals applied eye paint with a finger, stick, or spatula.

People highlighted their cheeks with powder and rouge in reds, yellow, and white. The Egyptians used powder puffs.[7] Mesopotamians colored the palms of their hands and the soles of their feet with red henna. Fingernail and toenail polish was a mixture of henna paint and beeswax.

Marble cosmetic container, with inscription marking it as the property of Marduk, god of Babylon; dated about 625–550 BC.

Craftsmen made these cosmetics. Some ingredients were imported while others were local. "Fragrances came from seeds, plant leaves, fruits, and flowers, especially roses, jasmines, mints, balsams, and cinnamon."[8]

Some cosmetics were used, not only for beauty, but also for medical purposes. Eye makeup made the eyes look larger. "There may also have been some medicinal value by preventing dryness of the eyelid or discouraging disease-carrying flies."[9]

Perfume was used in ancient times. "The first recorded mention is on the fifteenth century BC tomb of [Egypt's] Queen Hatshepsut who had sent an expedition to the land of Punt to fetch frankincense."[10] In fact, ancient Egyptians especially favored strong scents. During the intertestamental period, Alexandria, Egypt, served as a hub for perfume trade.[11] The Bible mentions several plants that people used when making cosmetics and perfumes. Song of Songs 4:13-14 says, "Your branches are a paradise of pomegranates with choicest fruits; henna with nard, nard and saffron, calamus and cinnamon, with all the trees of frankincense, myrrh and aloes, with all the best spices." All of these "choicest fruits" can produce sweet-smelling fragrances. Proverbs 7:17 also mentions the use of some of these. Scriptures also mention several fragrances people used as perfumes. These "include aloes (Nm 24:6); balm (Ezk 27:17); cinnamon (Pr 7:17); frankincense (Is 43:23; Mt 2:11); myrrh (Sg 5:5; Mt 2:11); and spikenard (Jn 12:3)."[12] Skilled workers (called "perfumer," see Ex 30:25; Ec 10:1) chopped and pressed these raw materials before mixing them with an oil base. "The Israelites mainly used olive oil; in Mesopotamia it was sesame oil; in Ancient Greece it was linseed oil; while the Egyptians used mostly animal fats."[13]

Cosmetics and perfumes were kept in containers made of metal, stone, or glass, or in ceramic jars or boxes (Is 3:20; Jn 12:3). They were sold in the marketplace.

The women of ancient Israel and other countries took pride in their appearance. Living in a hot climate, bathing and adorning the body with oils and perfumes was important. Through the centuries, many traditions have changed. Others, however, are still much the same. ❖

[1] James A. Patch, "Oil" in *ISBE*(1952), 2181. [2] Darlene R. Gautsch, "Cosmetics" in *HIBD*, 351. [3] "Oil" in M. G. Easton, *Illustrated Bible Dictionary*, 3rd ed. (N.P.: Thomas Nelson, 1897). [4] Gautsch, "Cosmetics," 350. [5] Gautsch, "Cosmetics," 350. [6] Norman A. Rubin, "Perfumes and Cosmetics in the Biblical World," *Anistoriton* 9, March 2005, www.anistor.gr/english/enback/v051.htm. [7] Martin H. Heicksen, "Cosmetics" in *The Zondervan Encyclopedia of the Bible*, ed. Merrill C. Tenney, rev. ed. (Grand Rapids: Zondervan, 2009), 1:1034–35. [8] Gautsch, "Cosmetics," 351. [9] Gautsch, "Cosmetics." [10] Gautsch, "Cosmetics." [11] Madeleine S. Miller and J. Lane Miller, *Harper's Encyclopedia of Bible Life*, 3rd ed. (San Francisco: Harper & Row, 1978), 84. [12] Gautsch, "Cosmetics," 351. [13] Rubin, "Perfumes and Cosmetics."

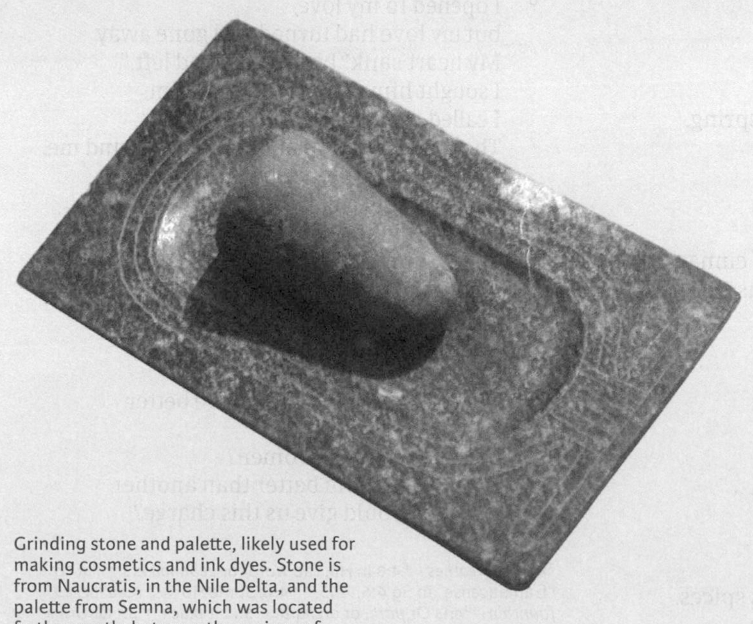

Grinding stone and palette, likely used for making cosmetics and ink dyes. Stone is from Naucratis, in the Nile Delta, and the palette from Semna, which was located farther south, between the regions of Nubia and Cush.

Two-handled glass perfume flask from Rhodes, Greece; dated late sixth century BC.

5 Your breasts are like two fawns,
twins of a gazelle, that feed
among the lilies.
6 Until the day breaks[A]
and the shadows flee,
I will make my way to the mountain
of myrrh
and the hill of frankincense.
7 You are absolutely beautiful, my darling;
there is no imperfection in you.

8 Come with me from Lebanon,[B] my bride;
come with me from Lebanon!
Descend from the peak of Amana,
from the summit of Senir and Hermon,
from the dens of the lions,
from the mountains of the leopards.
9 You have captured my heart, my sister,
my bride.
You have captured my heart with one glance
of your eyes,
with one jewel of your necklace.
10 How delightful your caresses are, my sister,
my bride.
Your caresses are much better than wine,
and the fragrance of your perfume
than any balsam.
11 Your lips drip sweetness like the honeycomb,
my bride.
Honey and milk are under your tongue.
The fragrance of your garments is like
the fragrance of Lebanon.

12 My sister, my bride, you are
a locked garden —
a locked garden[C] and a sealed spring.
13 Your branches are a paradise[D]
of pomegranates
with choicest fruits;
henna with nard,
14 nard and saffron, calamus and cinnamon,
with all the trees of frankincense,
myrrh and aloes,
with all the best spices.
15 You are a garden spring,
a well of flowing water
streaming from Lebanon.

Woman

16 Awaken, north wind;
come, south wind.
Blow on my garden,
and spread the fragrance of its spices.
Let my love come to his garden
and eat its choicest fruits.

Man

5 I have come to my garden — my sister, my bride.
I gather[E] my myrrh with my spices.
I eat my honeycomb with my honey.
I drink my wine with my milk.

Narrator

Eat, friends!
Drink, be intoxicated with caresses![F]

Woman

2 I was sleeping, but my heart was awake.
A sound! My love was knocking!

Man

Open to me, my sister, my darling,
my dove, my perfect one.
For my head is drenched with dew,
my hair with droplets of the night.

Woman

3 I have taken off my clothing.
How can I put it back on?
I have washed my feet.
How can I get them dirty?
4 My love thrust his hand through the opening,
and my feelings were stirred for him.
5 I rose to open for my love.
My hands dripped with myrrh,
my fingers with flowing myrrh
on the handles of the bolt.
6 I opened to my love,
but my love had turned and gone away.
My heart sank[G] because he had left.[H]
I sought him, but did not find him.
I called him, but he did not answer.
7 The guards who go about the city found me.
They beat and wounded me;
they took my cloak[I] from me —
the guardians of the walls.
8 Young women of Jerusalem, I charge you,
if you find my love,
tell him that I am lovesick.

Young Women

9 What makes the one you love better
than another,
most beautiful of women?
What makes him better than another,
that you would give us this charge?

[A] **4:6** Lit *breathes* [B] **4:8** In Hb, the word for *Lebanon* is similar to "frankincense" in Sg 4:6,14,15. [C] **4:12** Some Hb mss read *locked fountain* [D] **4:13** Or *park*, or *orchard* [E] **5:1** Lit *pluck* [F] **5:1** Or *Drink your fill, lovers* [G] **5:6** Lit *My soul went out* [H] **5:6** Or *spoken* [I] **5:7** Or *veil*, or *shawl*

Woman

10 My love is fit and strong,[A]
notable among ten thousand.
11 His head is purest gold.
His hair is wavy[B]
and black as a raven.
12 His eyes are like doves
beside flowing streams,
washed in milk
and set like jewels.[C]
13 His cheeks are like beds of spice,
mounds of[D] perfume.
His lips are lilies,
dripping with flowing myrrh.
14 His arms[E] are rods of gold
set[F] with beryl.
His body[G] is an ivory panel
covered with lapis lazuli.
15 His legs are alabaster pillars
set on pedestals of pure gold.
His presence is like Lebanon,
as majestic as the cedars.
16 His mouth is sweetness.
He is absolutely desirable.
This is my love, and this is my friend,
young women of Jerusalem.

Young Women

6 Where has your love gone,
most beautiful of women?
Which way has he[H] turned?
We will seek him with you.

Woman

2 My love has gone down to his garden,
to beds of spice,
to feed in the gardens
and gather lilies.
3 I am my love's and my love is mine;
he feeds among the lilies.

Man

4 You are as beautiful as Tirzah, my darling,
lovely as Jerusalem,
awe-inspiring as an army with banners.
5 Turn your eyes away from me,
for they captivate me.
Your hair is like a flock of goats
streaming down from Gilead.
6 Your teeth are like a flock of ewes
coming up from washing,
each one having a twin,
and not one missing.[I]
7 Behind your veil,
your brow[J] is like a slice of pomegranate.
8 There are sixty queens
and eighty concubines
and young women[K] without number.
9 But my dove, my virtuous one, is unique;
she is the favorite of her mother,
perfect to the one who gave her birth.
Women see her and declare her fortunate;
queens and concubines also, and they sing
her praises:

10 Who is this who shines like the dawn,
as beautiful as the moon,
bright as the sun,
awe-inspiring as an army with banners?

Woman

11 I came down to the walnut grove
to see the blossoms of the valley,
to see if the vines were budding
and the pomegranates blooming.
12 I didn't know what was happening to me.
I felt like I was
in a chariot with a nobleman.[L]

Young Women

13 Come back, come back, Shulammite![M]
Come back, come back, that we may look
at you!

Man

How you gaze at the Shulammite,
as you look at the dance of the two camps![N]

7 How beautiful are your sandaled feet,
princess![O]
The curves of your thighs are like jewelry,
the handiwork of a master.
2 Your navel is a rounded bowl;
it never lacks mixed wine.
Your belly is a mound of wheat
surrounded by lilies.
3 Your breasts are like two fawns,
twins of a gazelle.
4 Your neck is like a tower of ivory,
your eyes like pools in Heshbon
by Bath-rabbim's gate.
Your nose is like the tower of Lebanon
looking toward Damascus.

[A] **5:10** Or *is radiant and ruddy* [B] **5:11** Or *is like palm leaves*; Hb obscure [C] **5:12** Lit *milk sitting in fullness* [D] **5:13** LXX, Vg read *spice, yielding* [E] **5:14** Lit *hands* [F] **5:14** Lit *filled*; Sg 5:2,12 [G] **5:14** Lit *abdomen* [H] **6:1** Lit *your love* [I] **6:6** Lit *and no one bereaved among them* [J] **6:7** Or *temple*, or *cheek*, or *lips* [K] **6:8** Or *and virgins*; Sg 1:3 [L] **6:12** Hb obscure [M] **6:13** Or *the perfect one*, or *the peaceable one* [N] **6:13** Or *dance of Mahanaim* [O] **7:1** Lit *daughter of a nobleman*, or *prince*

Cedars of Lebanon

by W. Murray Severance

The large cedar of Lebanon was dangerously near extinction; attempts have been made to save the tree.

Cedar was a highly prized wood even before the pyramids of Egypt were built. Today only patches remain of the once formidable forests in Lebanon. At one time, Israel contained vast forests, but never to be compared with Phoenicia.

King Solomon contracted with Hiram, king of Tyre, to provide beams and paneling for building the temple. From the Lebanon mountains, timbers were pushed down to the seacoast of Tyre and Sidon along an artificial path, called a *vovtou,* made of rounded trunks. Once at the seacoast, the timbers were tied together into large rafts and floated the one hundred miles in the Mediterranean Sea to Joppa; at other times, to Egypt and other ports. From Joppa they were dragged with infinite care thirty-five miles up steep and rocky roads to Jerusalem.

Why was cedar such a valuable commodity? The cedar chest of today demonstrates its value;

Hiram's monument near Tyre; he was the Phoenician king who supplied cedar to Solomon.

One of the few clusters of cedars of Lebanon gives but a glimpse of what the forests may have been.

closets in larger homes often are paneled in cedar for the same reasons. Other than the rich reddish-brown color, the most noticeable aspect of cedar is its aroma. The odor is not offensive to humans, but insects resist it. The smell may remain in clothes for a period of time, but that fact is a small inconvenience when compared to losing the garments to moths.

Most conifers, cedars included, prefer moist habitats in hilly or mountainous areas. The Lebanon and Anti-Lebanon mountains provide an ideal locale. They stretch for about a hundred miles just inland and parallel to the Mediterranean Sea where they catch the moisture-laden clouds from the sea. The average height of these mountains is six to seven thousand feet, but several peaks tower to more than ten thousand feet. In Solomon's time, the upper slopes were covered with those marvelous trees.

Some of the trees grow to heights of 120 feet, but most are 60 to 80 feet in height. The girth of some trees is thirty to forty feet. Like those other ancient olive trees in the garden of Gethsemane, some cedars of Lebanon are thought to be about two thousand years old. Their branches spread out, as witnessed in Numbers 24:6, Psalm 92:12, and Hosea 14:5. These horizontal branches begin some ten feet above the ground and grow outward for a considerable distance, sometimes wider than the height of the tree. Numerous branchlets give cedars their distinctive tiered appearance. Old trees are gnarled and majestic, a truly awe-inspiring sight.

The cedars of Lebanon not only furnished timbers and paneling for building purposes, but they also furnished a symbol of strength, splendor, longevity, and glory. Ezekiel compared the king of Assyria to a great cedar of Lebanon (Ezk 31). The Shulammite compared her lover to the cedars of Lebanon, calling him "majestic" (Sg 5:15). ✣

Joppa, where cedars of Lebanon were unloaded to be transported to Jerusalem.

5 Your head crowns you[A] like Mount Carmel,
the hair of your head like purple cloth —
a king could be held captive in your tresses.
6 How beautiful you are and how pleasant,
my love, with such delights!
7 Your stature is like a palm tree;
your breasts are clusters of fruit.
8 I said, "I will climb the palm tree
and take hold of its fruit."
May your breasts be like clusters of grapes,
and the fragrance of your breath
like apricots.
9 Your mouth[B] is like fine wine —

Woman

flowing smoothly for my love,
gliding past my lips and teeth![C]
10 I am my love's,
and his desire is for me.

11 Come, my love,
let's go to the field;
let's spend the night
among the henna blossoms.[D]
12 Let's go early to the vineyards;
let's see if the vine has budded,
if the blossom has opened,
if the pomegranates are in bloom.
There I will give you my caresses.
13 The mandrakes give off a fragrance,
and at our doors is every delicacy,
both new and old.
I have treasured them up for you, my love.

8 If only I could treat you like my brother,[E]
one who nursed at my mother's breasts,
I would find you in public and kiss you,
and no one would scorn me.
2 I would lead you, I would take you,
to the house of my mother who taught me.[F]
I would give you spiced wine to drink
from the juice of my pomegranate.
3 May his left hand be under my head,
and his right arm embrace me.
4 Young women of Jerusalem, I charge you,
do not stir up or awaken love
until the appropriate time.

Young Women

5 Who is this coming up from the wilderness,
leaning on the one she loves?

Woman

I awakened you under the apricot tree.
There your mother conceived you;
there she conceived and gave you birth.
6 Set me as a seal on your heart,
as a seal on your arm.
For love is as strong as death;
jealousy is as unrelenting as Sheol.
Love's flames are fiery flames —
an almighty flame![G]
7 A huge torrent cannot extinguish love;
rivers cannot sweep it away.
If a man were to give all his wealth[H]
for love,
it would be utterly scorned.

Brothers

8 Our sister is young;
she has no breasts.
What will we do for our sister
on the day she is spoken for?
9 If she is a wall,
we will build a silver barricade on her.
If she is a door,
we will enclose her with cedar planks.

Woman

10 I am[I] a wall
and my breasts like towers.
So to him I have become
like one who finds[J] peace.[K]

11 Solomon owned a vineyard in Baal-hamon.
He leased the vineyard to tenants.
Each was to bring for his fruit
one thousand pieces of silver.
12 I have my own vineyard.[L]
The one thousand are for you, Solomon,
but two hundred for those who take care of
its fruits.

Man

13 You[M] who dwell in the gardens,
companions are listening for your voice;
let me hear you!

Woman

14 Run away with me,[N] my love,
and be like a gazelle
or a young stag
on the mountains of spices.

[A] **7:5** Lit *head upon you is* [B] **7:9** Lit *palate* [C] **7:9** LXX, Syr, Vg; MT reads *past lips of sleepers* [D] **7:11** Or *the villages* [E] **8:1** Lit *Would that you were like a brother to me* [F] **8:2** LXX adds *and into the chamber of the one who bore me* [G] **8:6** Or *the blaze of the LORD* [H] **8:7** Lit *all the wealth of his house* [I] **8:10** Or *was* [J] **8:10** Or *brings* [K] **8:10** In Hb, the word for *peace* sounds similar to Solomon and Shulammite. [L] **8:12** Lit *My vineyard, which is mine, is before me*; Sg 1:6 [M] **8:13** In Hb, the word for *You* is feminine. [N] **8:14** Lit *Flee*

ISAIAH

Ruins at Haran. This last Assyrian stronghold was lost to the Babylonians in 609 BC.

INTRODUCTION TO

ISAIAH

Circumstances of Writing

The book presents itself as the writing of one man, Isaiah son of Amoz. The superscription to the book dates his prophetic activity as spanning the reigns of four kings of Judah: Uzziah (783–742 BC, Isaiah's call is dated to this king's last year; 6:1); Jotham (742–735 BC); Ahaz (735–716 BC); and Hezekiah (716–686 BC). On Uzziah (Azariah), see 2 Kings 15:1–7 and 2 Chronicles 26:1–23. On Jotham, see 2 Kings 15:32–38 and 2 Chronicles 27:1–9. On Ahaz, see 2 Kings 16:1–20 and 2 Chronicles 28:1–27. On Hezekiah, see 2 Kings 18:1–20:21 and 2 Chronicles 29:1–32:33. Not much is known about Isaiah apart from his prophecy.

Isaiah's authorship of the whole book has been vehemently contested in the modern period. Many scholars have argued that the historical Isaiah could not have written chapters 40–66. For those who believe that God knows the future and can reveal it to his servants, it is not problematic that God through Isaiah predicted the rise of Babylon, its victory against Judah, the exile, and the return.

Isaiah 6:1 records that Isaiah received his prophetic call in the last year of Uzziah's reign over Judah (ca 742 BC). Uzziah's reign was a particularly prosperous time in the history of Judah, but storm clouds were on the horizon. Assyria was on the rise again in the person of Tiglath-pileser III (745–727 BC). The Assyrian king threatened to engulf Syria and the northern kingdom of Israel. After the death of Tiglath-pileser, his successors, Shalmaneser and Sargon, defeated the northern kingdom in 722 BC and deported its citizens. This event brought Judah even more under the shadow of that great empire. Isaiah 37:38 suggests that the prophet lived until the death of Sennacherib in 681 BC.

Isaiah's vision extended beyond the eighth century, through the rest of the Old Testament period and beyond. The New Testament authors cited Isaiah as finding fulfillment in the great events surrounding Jesus Christ, the Messiah and Suffering Servant.

Contribution to the Bible

It might be argued that without Isaiah, the New Testament could not have been written. There, as nowhere else in the Old Testament, the message is declared and the stage is set for the Davidic King to bring about a new exodus and establish God's kingdom on earth by means of the sin-bearing Servant.

Structure

The book of Isaiah is a combination of both prose and poetry. The prose is found primarily in chapters 36–39, a section that forms a bridge between the two sections of the book. Isaiah's poetry is rich and varied. He wrote hymns, wisdom poetry, and even poetry that resembles a love song (5:1–7). The richness is seen in Isaiah's vocabulary. He used more than twenty-two hundred different Hebrew words, far more variety than is found in any other Old Testament book.

1 The vision concerning Judah and Jerusalem that Isaiah son of Amoz saw during the reigns[A] of Kings Uzziah, Jotham, Ahaz, and Hezekiah of Judah.

JUDAH ON TRIAL

2 Listen, heavens, and pay attention, earth,
for the LORD has spoken:
"I have raised children[B] and brought them up,
but they have rebelled against me.
3 The ox knows its owner,
and the donkey its master's feeding trough,
but Israel does not know;
my people do not understand."

4 Oh sinful nation,
people weighed down with iniquity,
brood of evildoers,
depraved children!
They have abandoned the LORD;
they have despised the Holy One of Israel;
they have turned their backs on him.

5 Why do you want more beatings?
Why do you keep on rebelling?
The whole head is hurt,
and the whole heart is sick.
6 From the sole of the foot even to the head,
no spot is uninjured —
wounds, welts, and festering sores
not cleansed, bandaged,
or soothed with oil.

7 Your land is desolate,
your cities burned down;
foreigners devour your fields
right in front of you —
a desolation, like a place demolished
by foreigners.
8 Daughter Zion is abandoned
like a shelter in a vineyard,
like a shack in a cucumber field,
like a besieged city.
9 If the LORD of Armies
had not left us a few survivors,
we would be like Sodom,
we would resemble Gomorrah.

10 Hear the word of the LORD,
you rulers of Sodom!
Listen to the instruction of our God,
you people of Gomorrah!
11 "What are all your sacrifices to me?"
asks the LORD.
"I have had enough of burnt offerings and rams
and the fat of well-fed cattle;
I have no desire for the blood of bulls,
lambs, or male goats.
12 When you come to appear before me,
who requires this from you —
this trampling of my courts?
13 Stop bringing useless offerings.
Your incense is detestable to me.
New Moons and Sabbaths,
and the calling of solemn assemblies —
I cannot stand iniquity with a festival.
14 I hate your New Moons and prescribed festivals.
They have become a burden to me;
I am tired of putting up with them.
15 When you spread out your hands in prayer,
I will refuse to look at you;
even if you offer countless prayers,
I will not listen.
Your hands are covered with blood.

PURIFICATION OF JERUSALEM

16 "Wash yourselves. Cleanse yourselves.
Remove your evil deeds from my sight.
Stop doing evil.
17 Learn to do what is good.
Pursue justice.
Correct the oppressor.[C]
Defend the rights of the fatherless.
Plead the widow's cause.

18 "Come, let's settle this,"
says the LORD.
"Though your sins are scarlet,
they will be as white as snow;
though they are crimson red,
they will be like wool.
19 If you are willing and obedient,
you will eat the good things of the land.
20 But if you refuse and rebel,
you will be devoured by the sword."
For the mouth of the LORD has spoken.

21 The faithful town —
what an adulteress[D] she has become!
She was once full of justice.
Righteousness once dwelt in her,
but now, murderers!
22 Your silver has become dross to be discarded,
your beer[E] is diluted with water.
23 Your rulers are rebels,
friends of thieves.
They all love graft
and chase after bribes.

[A]1:1 ca 792–686 BC [B]1:2 Or *sons*, also in v. 4 [C]1:17 Or *Aid the oppressed* [D]1:21 Or *prostitute* [E]1:22 Or *wine*

DIGGING DEEPER *Dead Sea Scrolls*

The Dead Sea Scrolls are a cache of approximately eleven hundred ancient texts written in Hebrew, Aramaic, and Greek. Among these are more than 220 biblical manuscripts dating from the second century BC to the first century AD, representing every book of the Old Testament except Esther. Muhammad Ed-Dhib, a young goat herder from the Ta'amirah Bedouin tribe, discovered the first DSS in 1947 when he was searching for his lost goat among the arid limestone caves at Qumran overlooking the shores of the Dead Sea. Subsequent excavations of eleven nearby caves by Father Roland de Vaux from 1951 through 1956 yielded a variety of Jewish literature, yet nothing compared to the initial discovery of a complete copy of the book of Isaiah dating to 125 BC. The importance of the finds cannot be overstated. The scrolls are nearly one thousand years earlier than the previously known oldest Hebrew manuscripts (the Masoretic Text), which was used to translate the Old Testament into English. By studying the scrolls and comparing them to other Old Testament manuscripts, scholars discovered that the scribal copying process was conducted with great care and accuracy. For instance, the Isaiah text from the Dead Sea Scrolls is nearly identical with the later Masoretic Text.

They do not defend the rights of the fatherless,
and the widow's case never comes
before them.

24 Therefore the Lord God of Armies,
the Mighty One of Israel, declares:
"Ah, I will get even with my foes;
I will take revenge against my enemies.
25 I will turn my hand against you
and will burn away your dross completely;[A]
I will remove all your impurities.
26 I will restore your judges to what they
were at first,
and your advisers to what they were at the
start.
Afterward you will be called the Righteous City,
a Faithful Town."

27 Zion will be redeemed by justice,
those who repent, by righteousness.
28 At the same time both rebels and sinners
will be broken,
and those who abandon the LORD will perish.
29 Indeed, they[B] will be ashamed
of the sacred trees
you desired,
and you will be embarrassed because of
the garden shrines
you have chosen.
30 For you will become like an oak
whose leaves are withered,
and like a garden without water.
31 The strong one will become tinder,
and his work a spark;
both will burn together,
with no one to extinguish the flames.

THE CITY OF PEACE

2 The vision that Isaiah son of Amoz saw concerning Judah and Jerusalem:
2 In the last days
the mountain of the LORD's house
will be established
at the top of the mountains
and will be raised above the hills.
All nations will stream to it,
3 and many peoples will come and say,
"Come, let's go up to the mountain of the LORD,
to the house of the God of Jacob.
He will teach us about his ways
so that we may walk in his paths."
For instruction will go out of Zion
and the word of the LORD from Jerusalem.
4 He will settle disputes among the nations
and provide arbitration for many peoples.
They will beat their swords into plows
and their spears into pruning knives.
Nation will not take up the sword
against nation,
and they will never again train for war.

THE DAY OF THE LORD

5 House of Jacob,
come and let's walk in the LORD's light.
6 For you have abandoned your people,
the house of Jacob,
because they are full of divination
from the East
and of fortune-tellers like the Philistines.
They are in league[C] with foreigners.
7 Their[D,E] land is full of silver and gold,
and there is no limit to their treasures;
their land is full of horses,
and there is no limit to their chariots.

[A]1:25 Lit *dross as with lye* [B]1:29 Some Hb mss; other Hb mss, Tg read *you* [C]2:6 Or *They teem*, or *They partner*; Hb obscure [D]2:7 Lit *Its* [E]2:7 = the house of Jacob

8 Their land is full of worthless idols;
they worship the work of their hands,
what their fingers have made.
9 So humanity is brought low,
and each person is humbled.
Do not forgive them!
10 Go into the rocks
and hide in the dust
from the terror of the LORD
and from his majestic splendor.
11 The pride of mankind[A] will be humbled,
and human loftiness will be brought low;
the LORD alone will be exalted on that day.

12 For a day belonging to the LORD of Armies
is coming
against all that is proud and lofty,
against all that is lifted up — it will
be humbled —
13 against all the cedars of Lebanon,
lofty and lifted up,
against all the oaks of Bashan,
14 against all the high mountains,
against all the lofty hills,
15 against every high tower,
against every fortified wall,
16 against every ship of Tarshish,
and against every splendid sea vessel.
17 The pride of mankind will be brought low,
and human loftiness will be humbled;
the LORD alone will be exalted on that day.
18 The worthless idols will vanish completely.

19 People will go into caves in the rocks
and holes in the ground,
away from the terror of the LORD
and from his majestic splendor,
when he rises to terrify the earth.
20 On that day people will throw
their worthless idols of silver and gold,
which they made to worship,
to the moles and the bats.
21 They will go into the caves of the rocks
and the crevices in the cliffs,
away from the terror of the LORD
and from his majestic splendor,
when he rises to terrify the earth.
22 Put no more trust in a mere human,
who has only the breath in his nostrils.
What is he really worth?

JUDAH'S LEADERS JUDGED

3 Note this: The Lord GOD of Armies
is about to remove from Jerusalem
and from Judah
every kind of security:
the entire supply of bread and water,
2 heroes and warriors,
judges and prophets,
fortune-tellers and elders,
3 commanders of fifty and dignitaries,
counselors, cunning magicians,[B]
and necromancers.[C]
4 "I will make youths their leaders,
and unstable rulers[D] will govern them."
5 The people will oppress one another,
man against man, neighbor against neighbor;
the young will act arrogantly toward the old,
and the worthless toward the honorable.
6 A man will even seize his brother
in his father's house, saying,
"You have a cloak — you be our leader!
This heap of rubble will be
under your control."
7 On that day he will cry out, saying,
"I'm not a healer.
I don't even have food or clothing in my house.
Don't make me the leader of the people!"
8 For Jerusalem has stumbled
and Judah has fallen
because they have spoken and acted
against the LORD,
defying his glorious presence.
9 The look on their faces testifies against them,
and like Sodom, they flaunt their sin;
they do not conceal it.
Woe to them,
for they have brought disaster on themselves.
10 Tell the righteous that it will go well for them,
for they will eat the fruit of their labor.
11 Woe to the wicked — it will go badly for them,
for what they have done will be done to them.
12 Youths oppress my people,
and women rule over them.
My people, your leaders mislead you;
they confuse the direction of your paths.

13 The LORD rises to argue the case
and stands to judge the people.
14 The LORD brings this charge
against the elders and leaders of his people:
"You have devastated the vineyard.
The plunder from the poor is in your houses.
15 Why do you crush my people
and grind the faces of the poor?"
This is the declaration
of the Lord GOD of Armies.

[A] 2:11 Lit *Mankind's proud eyes* [B] 3:3 Or *skilled craftsmen* [C] 3:3 Or *mediums* [D] 3:4 Or *mischief-makers*

JERUSALEM'S WOMEN JUDGED

16 The LORD also says:
Because the daughters of Zion are haughty,
walking with heads held high
and seductive eyes,
prancing along,
jingling their ankle bracelets,
17 the Lord will put scabs on the heads
of the daughters of Zion,
and the LORD will shave their foreheads bare.

18 On that day the Lord will strip their finery: ankle
bracelets, headbands, crescents, 19 pendants, bracelets, veils, 20 headdresses, ankle jewelry, sashes,
perfume bottles, amulets, 21 signet rings, nose rings,
22 festive robes, capes, cloaks, purses, 23 garments,
linen clothes, turbans, and shawls.
24 Instead of perfume there will be a stench;
instead of a belt, a rope;
instead of beautifully styled hair, baldness;
instead of fine clothes, sackcloth;
instead of beauty, branding.[A]
25 Your men will fall by the sword,
your warriors in battle.
26 Then her gates will lament and mourn;
deserted, she will sit on the ground.
4 On that day seven women
will seize one man, saying,
"We will eat our own bread
and provide our own clothing.
Just let us bear your name.
Take away our disgrace."

ZION'S FUTURE GLORY

2 On that day the Branch[B] of the LORD will be beautiful and glorious, and the fruit of the land will be
the pride and glory of Israel's survivors. 3 Whoever
remains in Zion and whoever is left in Jerusalem
will be called holy — all in Jerusalem written in the
book of life[C] — 4 when the Lord has washed away
the filth of the daughters of Zion and cleansed the
bloodguilt from the heart of Jerusalem by a spirit
of judgment and a spirit of burning. 5 Then the LORD
will create a cloud of smoke by day and a glowing
flame of fire by night over the entire site of Mount
Zion and over its assemblies. For there will be a canopy over all the glory,[D] 6 and there will be a shelter
for shade from heat by day and a refuge and shelter
from storm and rain.

SONG OF THE VINEYARD

5 I will sing about the one I love,
a song about my loved one's vineyard:
The one I love had a vineyard
on a very fertile hill.
2 He broke up the soil, cleared it of stones,
and planted it with the finest vines.
He built a tower in the middle of it
and even dug out a winepress there.
He expected it to yield good grapes,
but it yielded worthless grapes.

3 So now, residents of Jerusalem
and men of Judah,
please judge between me
and my vineyard.
4 What more could I have done
for my vineyard
than I did?
Why, when I expected a yield
of good grapes,
did it yield worthless grapes?
5 Now I will tell you
what I am about to do to my vineyard:
I will remove its hedge,
and it will be consumed;
I will tear down its wall,
and it will be trampled.
6 I will make it a wasteland.
It will not be pruned or weeded;
thorns and briers will grow up.
I will also give orders to the clouds
that rain should not fall on it.
7 For the vineyard of the LORD of Armies
is the house of Israel,
and the men[E] of Judah,
the plant he delighted in.
He expected justice
but saw injustice;
he expected righteousness
but heard cries of despair.

JUDAH'S SINS DENOUNCED

8 Woe to those who add house to house
and join field to field
until there is no more room
and you alone are left in the land.

9 I heard the LORD of Armies say:
Indeed, many houses will become desolate,
grand and lovely ones
without inhabitants.
10 For a ten-acre[F] vineyard will yield
only six gallons of wine,[G]
and ten bushels[H] of seed will yield
only one bushel of grain.[I]

[A] **3:24** DSS read *shame* [B] **4:2** Or *plant* [C] **4:3** Lit *Jerusalem recorded for life* [D] **4:5** Or *For glory will be a canopy over all* [E] **5:7** Lit *man* [F] **5:10** Lit *ten-yoke* [G] **5:10** Lit *one bath* [H] **5:10** Lit *one homer* [I] **5:10** Lit *yield an ephah*

11 Woe to those who rise early in the morning
in pursuit of beer,
who linger into the evening,
inflamed by wine.
12 At their feasts they have lyre, harp,
tambourine, flute, and wine.
They do not perceive the LORD's actions,
and they do not see the work of his hands.

13 Therefore my people will go into exile
because they lack knowledge;
her[A] dignitaries are starving,
and her masses are parched with thirst.
14 Therefore Sheol enlarges its throat
and opens wide its enormous jaws,
and down go Zion's dignitaries, her masses,
her crowds, and those who celebrate in her!
15 Humanity is brought low, each
person is humbled,
and haughty eyes are humbled.
16 But the LORD of Armies is exalted by his justice,
and the holy God demonstrates his holiness
through his righteousness.
17 Lambs will graze
as if in[B] their own pastures,
and resident aliens[C] will eat
among the ruins of the rich.

18 Woe to those who drag iniquity
with cords of deceit
and pull sin along with cart ropes,
19 to those who say,
"Let him hurry up and do his work quickly
so that we can see it!
Let the plan of the Holy One of Israel take place
so that we can know it!"
20 Woe to those who call evil good
and good evil,
who substitute darkness for light
and light for darkness,
who substitute bitter for sweet
and sweet for bitter.
21 Woe to those who consider themselves wise
and judge themselves clever.[D]
22 Woe to those who are heroes at drinking wine,
who are champions at pouring beer,
23 who acquit the guilty for a bribe
and deprive the innocent of justice.

24 Therefore, as a tongue of fire consumes straw
and as dry grass shrivels in the flame,
so their roots will become like something rotten
and their blossoms will blow away like dust,
for they have rejected
the instruction of the LORD of Armies,
and they have despised
the word of the Holy One of Israel.
25 Therefore the LORD's anger burned
against his people.
He raised his hand against them
and struck them;
the mountains quaked,
and their corpses were like garbage
in the streets.
In all this, his anger has not turned away,
and his hand is still raised to strike.

26 He raises a signal flag for the distant nations
and whistles for them from the ends
of the earth.
Look — how quickly and swiftly they come!
27 None of them grows weary or stumbles;
no one slumbers or sleeps.
No belt is loose
and no sandal strap broken.
28 Their arrows are sharpened,
and all their bows strung.
Their horses' hooves are like flint;
their chariot wheels are like a whirlwind.
29 Their roaring is like a lion's;
they roar like young lions;
they growl and seize their prey
and carry it off,
and no one can rescue it.
30 On that day they will roar over it,
like the roaring of the sea.
When one looks at the land,
there will be darkness and distress;
light will be obscured by clouds.[E]

ISAIAH'S CALL AND MISSION

6 In the year that King Uzziah died, I saw the Lord
seated on a high and lofty throne, and the hem of
his robe filled the temple. 2 Seraphim[F] were standing
above him; they each had six wings: with two they
covered their faces, with two they covered their feet,
and with two they flew. 3 And one called to another:

Holy, holy, holy is the LORD of Armies;
his glory fills the whole earth.

4 The foundations of the doorways shook at the sound
of their voices, and the temple was filled with smoke.
5 Then I said:

Woe is me for I am ruined[G]
because I am a man of unclean lips
and live among a people of unclean lips,
and because my eyes have seen the King,
the LORD of Armies.

[A]5:13 Lit *its* [B]5:17 Syr reads *graze in* [C]5:17 LXX reads *sheep*
[D]5:21 Lit *and clever before their face* [E]5:30 Lit *its clouds*
[F]6:2 = heavenly beings [G]6:5 Or *I must be silent*

6 Then one of the seraphim flew to me, and in his
hand was a glowing coal that he had taken from the altar with tongs. 7 He touched my mouth with it and said:
Now that this has touched your lips,
your iniquity is removed
and your sin is atoned for.

8 Then I heard the voice of the Lord asking:
Who will I send?
Who will go for us?

I said:
Here I am. Send me.

9 And he replied:
Go! Say to these people:
Keep listening, but do not understand;
keep looking, but do not perceive.
10 Make the minds[A] of these people dull;
deafen their ears and blind their eyes;
otherwise they might see with their eyes
and hear with their ears,
understand with their minds,
turn back, and be healed.

11 Then I said, "Until when, Lord?" And he replied:
Until cities lie in ruins without inhabitants,
houses are without people,
the land is ruined and desolate,
12 and the LORD drives the people far away,
leaving great emptiness in the land.
13 Though a tenth will remain in the land,
it will be burned again.
Like the terebinth or the oak
that leaves a stump when felled,
the holy seed is the stump.

THE MESSAGE TO AHAZ

7 This took place during the reign of Ahaz, son
of Jotham, son of Uzziah king of Judah: Aram's
King Rezin and Israel's King Pekah son of Remaliah
went to fight against Jerusalem, but they were not
able to conquer it.
2 When it became known to the house of David that
Aram had occupied Ephraim, the heart of Ahaz[B] and
the hearts of his people trembled like trees of a forest
shaking in the wind.
3 The LORD said to Isaiah, "Go out with your son
Shear-jashub[C] to meet Ahaz at the end of the conduit
of the upper pool, by the road to the Launderer's
Field. 4 Say to him: Calm down and be quiet. Don't be
afraid or cowardly because of these two smoldering
sticks, the fierce anger of Rezin and Aram, and the
son of Remaliah. 5 For Aram, along with Ephraim
and the son of Remaliah, has plotted harm against
you. They say, 6 'Let's go up against Judah, terrorize
it, and conquer it for ourselves. Then we can install
Tabeel's son as king in it.' "
7 This is what the Lord GOD says:
It will not happen; it will not occur.
8 The chief city of Aram is Damascus,
the chief of Damascus is Rezin
(within sixty-five years
Ephraim will be too shattered to be a people),
9 the chief city of Ephraim is Samaria,
and the chief of Samaria is the son of Remaliah.
If you do not stand firm in your faith,
then you will not stand at all.

THE IMMANUEL PROPHECY

10 Then the LORD spoke again to Ahaz: 11 "Ask for a sign
from the LORD your God — it can be as deep as Sheol
or as high as heaven."
12 But Ahaz replied, "I will not ask. I will not test
the LORD."
13 Isaiah said, "Listen, house of David! Is it not
enough for you to try the patience of men? Will you
also try the patience of my God? 14 Therefore, the Lord
himself will give you[D] a sign: See, the virgin will conceive,[E] have a son, and name him Immanuel.[F] 15 By the
time he learns to reject what is bad and choose what
is good, he will be eating curds[G] and honey. 16 For before the boy knows to reject what is bad and choose
what is good, the land of the two kings you dread will
be abandoned. 17 The LORD will bring on you, your
people, and your father's house such a time as has
never been since Ephraim separated from Judah: He
will bring the king of Assyria."
18 On that day
the LORD will whistle to flies
at the farthest streams of the Nile
and to bees in the land of Assyria.
19 All of them will come and settle
in the steep ravines, in the clefts of the rocks,
in all the thornbushes, and in all the water holes.

20 On that day the Lord will use a razor hired from
beyond the Euphrates River — the king of Assyria
— to shave the hair on your heads, the hair on your
legs, and even your beards.
21 On that day
a man will raise a young cow and two sheep,
22 and from the abundant milk they give
he will eat curds,
for every survivor in the land will eat curds
and honey.

[A] **6:10** Lit *heart* [B] **7:2** Lit *Aram has rested upon Ephraim, his heart* [C] **7:3** = A Remnant Will Return [D] **7:14** In Hb, the word *you* is pl [E] **7:14** Or *virgin is pregnant, will* [F] **7:14** = God With Us [G] **7:15** Or *sour milk*

Evil: The Meaning

by Bryan E. Beyer

Genesis 3:1–6 describes evil's introduction to the human race. Satan, in the form of a serpent, approached Adam and Eve in the garden of Eden and began a conversation with Eve. Displaying the evil tendency that already controlled him, the serpent challenged God's earlier command not to eat from the tree of the knowledge of good and evil (2:16–17). In fact, he boldly declared that if Adam and Eve would eat of the fruit God had prohibited, they would become like God, knowing good and evil. Eve took it and shared it with Adam; indeed, their eyes were opened—to their newly gained sinfulness. Instantly sin corrupted them. They did know good and evil (3:22), but they had destroyed their innocence in the process. The Bible describes evil as continuing to corrupt this present age until the Lord Jesus Christ returns to usher in his everlasting kingdom. At that time, he will forever separate his people from evil and every kind of evil practice (Rv 22:14–15). But what is evil?

The English word *evil* usually translates the Hebrew word *ra'* in the Old Testament. The term appears as both a noun and an adjective, and it has a wider range of meaning than our word *evil*. First, *ra'* may describe calamity, misery, or difficult circumstances. In the Joseph accounts, Judah did not wish to see the *ra'* that would overtake his father Jacob if Judah returned to Canaan without Benjamin (Gn 44:34, "grief"). Later, Jacob described his own life to Pharaoh as *ra'* (47:9, "hard"). The book of Proverbs describes all the days of the oppressed as *ra'* (Pr 15:15, "miserable"), and *ra'* also denotes a "troubled" heart (25:20). God brings *ra'* on those who oppose him (Is 31:2; 45:7, "disaster"; Am 9:4, "harm").

Second, *ra'* may denote something of inferior quality. Pharaoh so described the ugly, sickly looking cows he had seen in his dream (Gn 41:19, "sickly"). The law of Moses commanded worshipers to bring good animals to sacrifice, never "bad" or "low" quality animals (Lv 27:10,12). Those who bargained in the marketplace sometimes tried to purchase goods for less by claiming the items were of low quality (Pr 20:14, "worthless"). Jeremiah used the term to describe a basket of "bad" figs (Jr 24:2,3), which symbolized the condition of the people's hearts before God.

Third, *ra'* may depict opposition to God and his ways, the moral perversion of the sinful heart. After evil's introduction into the world in the garden of Eden, its power and effects soon corrupted all humanity and led to the great flood (Gn 6:5, "wickedness"). As the Israelites traveled through the wilderness, the Lord expressed his frustration to Moses that they were an "evil community" that continually grumbled against him (Nm 14:27). In the period of the judges, the high priest Eli admonished his sons Hophni and Phinehas for their wickedness and condemned their "evil actions" against the people of Israel (1Sm 2:23). Those who violate God's law are often said to "do what is evil" in the Lord's sight (Dt 4:25; Jdg 3:12; 2Sm 12:9; Is 65:12; 66:4; and about twenty-five times in the books of Kings). Jeremiah lamented that the people had committed "a double evil": they had forsaken the one true God, their source of life, to worship other gods who were useless (Jr 2:13). In the days of the prophet Malachi, the people even claimed the Lord had lost his sense of justice and was "delighted with" everyone who practiced evil (Mal 2:17). They were bitter because they felt God was treating them unjustly. Malachi assured his audience that God had not forgotten the righteous (3:1–6).

In Isaiah 5:8–30, the prophet Isaiah pronounced six woes against his rebellious generation. In verse 20, he denounced the morally twisted, who "call evil good and good evil, who substitute darkness for light and light for darkness, who substitute bitter for sweet and sweet for bitter." God's people had totally reversed God's moral law to justify their sin. They rebelled against his righteous, holy commands and showed by their behavior that they held evil in high regard.

Ultimately the blood of the Lamb will bring an end to all these things—grief, misery, pain, disaster, badness, and evil, along with sin, guilt, and death (Jr 3:17; Zph 3:13–17; Col 2:15; Rv 12:11). ✜

23 And on that day
every place where there were a thousand vines,
worth a thousand pieces of silver,
will become thorns and briers.
24 A man will go there with bow and arrows
because the whole land will be thorns
and briers.
25 You will not go to all the hills
that were once tilled with a hoe,
for fear of the thorns and briers.
Those hills will be places for oxen to graze
and for sheep to trample.

THE COMING ASSYRIAN INVASION

8 Then the LORD said to me, "Take a large piece of
parchment[A] and write on it with an ordinary
pen:[B] Maher-shalal-hash-baz.[C] 2 I have appointed[D]
trustworthy witnesses — the priest Uriah and Zechariah son of Jeberechiah."
3 I was then intimate with the prophetess, and she
conceived and gave birth to a son. The LORD said to
me, "Name him Maher-shalal-hash-baz, 4 for before
the boy knows how to call 'Father,' or 'Mother,' the
wealth of Damascus and the spoils of Samaria will
be carried off to the king of Assyria."
5 The LORD spoke to me again:
6 Because these people rejected
the slowly flowing water of Shiloah
and rejoiced with[E] Rezin
and the son of Remaliah,
7 the Lord will certainly bring against them
the mighty rushing water
of the Euphrates River —
the king of Assyria and all his glory.
It will overflow its channels
and spill over all its banks.
8 It will pour into Judah,
flood over it, and sweep through,
reaching up to the neck;
and its flooded banks[F]
will fill your entire land, Immanuel!

9 Band together,[G] peoples, and be broken;
pay attention, all you distant lands;
prepare for war, and be broken;
prepare for war, and be broken.
10 Devise a plan; it will fail.
Make a prediction; it will not happen.
For God is with us.[H]

THE LORD OF ARMIES, THE ONLY REFUGE

11 For this is what the LORD said to me with great power, to keep[I] me from going the way of this people:
12 Do not call everything a conspiracy
that these people say is a conspiracy.
Do not fear what they fear;
do not be terrified.
13 You are to regard only the LORD of Armies
as holy.
Only he should be feared;
only he should be held in awe.
14 He will be a sanctuary;
but for the two houses of Israel,
he will be a stone to stumble over
and a rock to trip over,
and a trap and a snare to the inhabitants
of Jerusalem.
15 Many will stumble over these;
they will fall and be broken;
they will be snared and captured.

16 Bind up the testimony.
Seal up the instruction among my disciples.
17 I will wait for the LORD,
who is hiding his face from the house of Jacob.
I will wait for him.

18 Here I am with the children the LORD has given
me to be signs and wonders in Israel from the LORD
of Armies who dwells on Mount Zion. 19 When they
say to you, "Inquire of the mediums and the spiritists
who chirp and mutter," shouldn't a people inquire of
their God?[J] Should they inquire of the dead on behalf
of the living? 20 Go to God's instruction and testimony!
If they do not speak according to this word, there will
be no dawn for them.
21 They will wander through the land, dejected and
hungry. When they are famished, they will become
enraged, and, looking upward, will curse their king
and their God. 22 They will look toward the earth and
see only distress, darkness, and the gloom of affliction, and they will be driven into thick darkness.

BIRTH OF THE PRINCE OF PEACE

9 Nevertheless, the gloom of the distressed land
will not be like that of the former times when he
humbled the land of Zebulun and the land of Naphtali. But in the future he will bring honor to the way of
the sea, to the land east of the Jordan, and to Galilee
of the nations.
2 The people walking in darkness
have seen a great light;
a light has dawned
on those living in the land of darkness.

[A] **8:1** Hb obscure [B] **8:1** Lit *with the pen of a man* [C] **8:1** = Speeding to the Plunder, Hurrying to the Spoil [D] **8:2** Vg; MT, one DSS ms read *I will appoint*; one DSS ms, LXX, Syr, Tg read *Appoint* [E] **8:6** Or *and rejoiced over* [F] **8:8** Lit *its outspread wings* [G] **8:9** Or *Raise the war cry*, or *Be shattered* [H] **8:10** Hb *Immanuel* [I] **8:11** DSS; MT reads *instruct* [J] **8:19** Or *gods*

The Syro-Ephraimitic War

by Harry A. Lane

Solomon's death was followed by the division of Israel into two kingdoms, north and south, each with its own king and capital. Although the northern kingdom (referred to as Israel, Ephraim, or Samaria, after the capital) and the southern kingdom (called Judah or sometimes Jerusalem) occasionally united to form an alliance against a common threat, significant tension still existed between the two. A time of open hostilities erupted during the years of Isaiah's and Micah's ministries to Judah.

Aram was a grandson of Noah and son of Shem (Gn 10:22). The Bible indicates he was an ancestor to the people who would later be known as Arameans. As a people, the Arameans date to the Late Bronze Age (1550–1200 BC). Originally they lived in the regions surrounding Syria and parts of Babylon. They later moved predominantly into Syria and came to control the region.[1] Writings during Assyria's King Tiglath-pileser I (1116–1076 BC) offer the earliest-known extrabiblical mention of the Arameans.[2]

Deuteronomy 26:5 describes Jacob as an "Aramean." By implication, the text seems to call attention to Abraham's stop in Haran and family members who remained there (Gn 11:28–32). In Abraham's time, Haran would have been within the territory of Aram.

Aram was never a nation with a strong centralized government but consisted of a confederation of individual tribes. These loosely knit tribes would band together when other nations were posing a threat, as Assyria posed in the eighth century BC.

Aram's relationship with Israel from the beginning of the monarchy under Saul until the death of Solomon in 931 BC was contentious. Saul fought against the Arameans (1Sm 14:47, Zobah was one of the early capital cities) as did David (2Sm 8:5–12) and Solomon (2Ch 8:3–4). Tensions continued after the division into the northern and southern kingdoms.

In the eighth century BC, however, an imminent threat of an Assyrian attack under Tiglath-pileser III (744–727 BC) caused the two former enemies to create an alliance under Rezin, king of Aram, and Pekah, king of Israel.[3] When Judah's King Ahaz refused to join them, they attacked Judah and besieged Jerusalem (Is 7:1–2). Their goal likely was to replace Ahaz with a king who would be sympathetic to their fear

Monumental stairs located at the top of ancient Samaria, a city whose name was later changed to Sebaste. The steps, which may be located near the site of Ahab's palace, were actually part of a temple built during the reign of Septimus Severus (AD 193–211). Samaria served as capital of the northern kingdom of Israel.

Bronze and iron mace heads topped with lions' heads. These weapons are each inscribed in Aramaic with its owner's name; dated ninth–eighth centuries BC. From Nimrud.

of Assyria and who thus would join their coalition. Ahaz, though, had determined to put his confidence in Assyria—an evidence of his unwillingness to trust God.

The results of Ahaz's decision were disastrous. When Aram and Israel attacked, Judah lost one hundred twenty thousand men in battle in one day, and two hundred thousand Judeans were taken captive to Samaria (2Ch 28:6,8). Despite these horrific losses, Judah survived the attacks (2Kg 16:5), and the prophet Oded convinced Israel to allow the captives to return to Judah (2Ch 28:9–15).

Isaiah's prophetic ministry occurred "during the reigns of Kings Uzziah, Jotham, Ahaz, and Hezekiah of Judah" (Is 1:1). Ahaz (reigned 735–715 BC) was the son of Jotham and the father of Hezekiah. Ahaz lacked the faith and commitment to God of his father and his grandfather, Uzziah, before him. He practiced Baal worship and even sacrificed some of his own children in the Ben Hinnom Valley (2Ch 28:1–4).

In the context of the Syro-Ephraimite War and during this period of national crisis for Judah, Isaiah offered a prophecy with both immediate and messianic significance (Is 7:14). God gave a prediction and a sign through Isaiah to Ahaz. He told him not to fear Rezin of Aram and Pekah of Israel, referring to them as "these two smoldering sticks" (7:4). The imagery indicated the short time they had left before God's judgment overtook them. Isaiah then presented a second image of how short the alliance between Aram and Israel would last. This image came in the form of a promised sign—a virgin would conceive, give birth to a son, and call him "Immanuel." Isaiah's listeners would have understood the interpretation of a child being born to a virgin as the promise of a young maiden, yet to be married, who would soon marry, conceive, and give birth to a son. Before her child was old enough to distinguish right from wrong, that is, in just a short period of time, the Aram-Israel alliance would dissolve. Further, Isaiah predicted Assyria would be the agent of God's deliverance.

In 732 BC, Assyria under Tiglath-pileser III destroyed Damascus (the capital of Aram), which ended the alliance with Israel. Israel's destruction came ten years later during the

Treaty between the king of Arpad, an Aramean city-state in Syria, and Ashur-nirari V, king of Assyria (754–745 BC).

reign of Hoshea, who assassinated Pekah (2Kg 15:30). Shalmaneser V, son of Tiglath-pileser III, attacked Israel when they refused to pay tribute. After a three-year siege, Samaria fell and with it the nation of Israel in 722 BC. Israel would no longer be able to threaten Judah, just as the Lord had promised through Isaiah.

Ahaz's refusal to ask for a sign from God indicated he would seek help from Assyria rather than the Lord (2Ch 28:16). This decision proved to be foolish and costly. Assyria attacked Judah. Although divine intervention spared Judah, the nation still paid a heavy price in loss of life and wealth (Is 7:17–19). Under Ahaz, Judah became a servant to Assyria and had to pay tribute. ❖

---

[1] Niels Peter Lemche, "The History of Ancient Syria and Palestine: An Overview" in *CANE* (2000), 1209. [2] Tim Turnham, "Aramean" in *HIBD* rev. ed. (2015), 96. [3] Daniel C. Browning Jr., "Assyria," *HIBD*, 136–40.

3 You have enlarged the nation
and increased its joy.[A]
The people have rejoiced before you
as they rejoice at harvest time
and as they rejoice when dividing spoils.
4 For you have shattered their oppressive yoke
and the rod on their shoulders,
the staff of their oppressor,
just as you did on the day of Midian.
5 For every trampling boot of battle
and the bloodied garments of war
will be burned as fuel for the fire.
6 For a child will be born for us,
a son will be given to us,
and the government will be on his shoulders.
He will be named
Wonderful Counselor, Mighty God,
Eternal Father, Prince of Peace.
7 The dominion will be vast,
and its prosperity will never end.
He will reign on the throne of David
and over his kingdom,
to establish and sustain it
with justice and righteousness from now on
and forever.
The zeal of the LORD of Armies
will accomplish this.

THE HAND RAISED AGAINST ISRAEL

8 The Lord sent a message against Jacob;
it came against Israel.
9 All the people —
Ephraim and the inhabitants of Samaria —
will know it.
They will say with pride and arrogance,
10 "The bricks have fallen,
but we will rebuild with cut stones;
the sycamores have been cut down,
but we will replace them with cedars."
11 The LORD has raised up Rezin's adversaries
against him
and stirred up his enemies.
12 Aram from the east and Philistia
from the west
have consumed Israel with open mouths.
In all this, his anger has not turned away,
and his hand is still raised to strike.

13 The people did not turn to him
who struck them;
they did not seek the LORD of Armies.
14 So the LORD cut off Israel's head and tail,
palm branch and reed in a single day.
15 The head is the elder, the honored one;
the tail is the prophet, the one teaching lies.
16 The leaders of the people mislead them,
and those they mislead
are swallowed up.[B]
17 Therefore the Lord does not rejoice
over[C] Israel's young men
and has no compassion
on its fatherless and widows,
for everyone is a godless evildoer,
and every mouth speaks folly.
In all this, his anger has not turned away,
and his hand is still raised to strike.

18 For wickedness burns like a fire
that consumes thorns and briers
and kindles the forest thickets
so that they go up in a column of smoke.
19 The land is scorched
by the wrath of the LORD of Armies,
and the people are like fuel for the fire.
No one has compassion on his brother.
20 They carve meat on the right,
but they are still hungry;
they have eaten on the left,
but they are still not satisfied.
Each one eats the flesh of his arm.
21 Manasseh eats Ephraim,
and Ephraim, Manasseh;
together, both are against Judah.
In all this, his anger has not turned away,
and his hand is still raised to strike.

10 Woe to those enacting crooked statutes
and writing oppressive laws
2 to keep the poor from getting a fair trial
and to deprive the needy among my people
of justice,
so that widows can be their spoil
and they can plunder the fatherless.
3 What will you do on the day
of punishment
when devastation comes from far away?
Who will you run to for help?
Where will you leave your wealth?
4 There will be nothing to do
except crouch among the prisoners
or fall among the slain.
In all this, his anger has not turned away,
and his hand is still raised to strike.

ASSYRIA, THE INSTRUMENT OF WRATH

5 Woe to Assyria, the rod of my anger —
the staff in their hands is my wrath.

[A] **9:3** Alt Hb tradition reads *have not increased joy* [B] **9:16** Or *are confused* [C] **9:17** DSS read *not spare*

6 I will send him against a godless nation;
I will command him to go
against a people destined for my rage,
to take spoils, to plunder,
and to trample them down like clay
in the streets.
7 But this is not what he intends;
this is not what he plans.
It is his intent to destroy
and to cut off many nations.
8 For he says,
"Aren't all my commanders kings?
9 Isn't Calno like Carchemish?
Isn't Hamath like Arpad?
Isn't Samaria like Damascus?[A]
10 As my hand seized the kingdoms of
worthless images,
kingdoms whose idols exceeded
those of Jerusalem and Samaria,
11 and as I did to Samaria and its worthless
images
will I not also do to Jerusalem
and its idols?"

JUDGMENT ON ASSYRIA

12 But when the Lord finishes all his work against
Mount Zion and Jerusalem, he will say, "I[B] will punish the king of Assyria for his arrogant acts and the
proud look in his eyes." 13 For he said:
I have done this by my own strength
and wisdom, for I am clever.
I abolished the borders of nations
and plundered their treasures;
like a mighty warrior, I subjugated
the inhabitants.[C]
14 My hand has reached out, as if into a nest,
to seize the wealth of the nations.
Like one gathering abandoned eggs,
I gathered the whole earth.
No wing fluttered;
no beak opened or chirped.

15 Does an ax exalt itself
above the one who chops with it?
Does a saw magnify itself
above the one who saws with it?
It would be like a rod waving the ones
who lift[D] it!
It would be like a staff lifting the one
who isn't wood!
16 Therefore the Lord GOD of Armies
will inflict an emaciating disease
on the well-fed of Assyria,
and he will kindle a burning fire
under its glory.
17 Israel's Light will become a fire,
and its Holy One, a flame.
In one day it will burn and consume
Assyria's thorns and thistles.
18 He will completely destroy
the glory of its forests and orchards
as a sickness consumes a person.
19 The remaining trees of its forest
will be so few in number
that a child could count them.

THE REMNANT WILL RETURN

20 On that day the remnant of Israel and the survivors
of the house of Jacob will no longer depend on the
one who struck them, but they will faithfully depend
on the LORD, the Holy One of Israel.
21 The remnant will return, the remnant
of Jacob,
to the Mighty God.
22 Israel, even if your people were as numerous
as the sand of the sea,
only a remnant of them will return.
Destruction has been decreed;
justice overflows.
23 For throughout the land
the Lord GOD of Armies
is carrying out a destruction that was decreed.

24 Therefore, the Lord GOD of Armies says this: "My
people who dwell in Zion, do not fear Assyria, though
they strike you with a rod and raise their staff over
you as the Egyptians did. 25 In just a little while my
wrath will be spent and my anger will turn to their
destruction." 26 And the LORD of Armies will brandish
a whip against him as he did when he struck Midian
at the rock of Oreb; and he will raise his staff over the
sea as he did in Egypt.

GOD WILL JUDGE ASSYRIA

27 On that day
his burden will fall from your shoulders,
and his yoke from your neck.
The yoke will be broken because your neck
will be too large.[E]
28 Assyria has come to Aiath
and has gone through Migron,
storing their equipment at Michmash.
29 They crossed over at the ford, saying,
"We will spend the night at Geba."
The people of Ramah are trembling;
those at Gibeah of Saul have fled.

[A] **10:9** Cities conquered by Assyria [B] **10:12** LXX reads *Jerusalem, he* [C] **10:13** Or *I brought down their kings* [D] **10:15** Some Hb mss; other Hb mss, Syr, Vg read *the one who lifts* [E] **10:27** Lit *because of fatness*; Hb obscure

30 Cry aloud, daughter of Gallim!
Listen, Laishah!
Anathoth is miserable.
31 Madmenah has fled.
The inhabitants of Gebim have sought refuge.
32 Today the Assyrians will stand at Nob,
shaking their fists at the mountain
of Daughter Zion,
the hill of Jerusalem.
33 Look, the Lord God of Armies
will chop off the branches with terrifying power,
and the tall trees will be cut down,
the high trees felled.
34 He is clearing the thickets of the forest
with an ax,
and Lebanon with its majesty will fall.

REIGN OF THE DAVIDIC KING

11 Then a shoot will grow from the stump of Jesse,
and a branch from his roots will bear fruit.
2 The Spirit of the Lord will rest on him —
a Spirit of wisdom and understanding,
a Spirit of counsel and strength,
a Spirit of knowledge and of the fear
of the Lord.
3 His delight will be in the fear of the Lord.
He will not judge
by what he sees with his eyes,
he will not execute justice
by what he hears with his ears,
4 but he will judge the poor righteously
and execute justice for the oppressed
of the land.
He will strike the land
with a scepter[A] from his mouth,
and he will kill the wicked
with a command[B] from his lips.
5 Righteousness will be a belt around his hips;
faithfulness will be a belt around his waist.
6 The wolf will dwell with the lamb,
and the leopard will lie down with the goat.
The calf, the young lion, and the fattened calf
will be together,
and a child will lead them.
7 The cow and the bear will graze,
their young ones will lie down together,
and the lion will eat straw like cattle.
8 An infant will play beside the cobra's pit,
and a toddler will put his hand
into a snake's den.
9 They will not harm or destroy each other
on my entire holy mountain,
for the land will be as full
of the knowledge of the Lord
as the sea is filled with water.

ISRAEL REGATHERED

10 On that day the root of Jesse
will stand as a banner for the peoples.
The nations will look to him for guidance,
and his resting place will be glorious.

11 On that day the Lord will extend his hand a second
time to recover the remnant of his people who survive
— from Assyria, Egypt, Pathros, Cush, Elam, Shinar,
Hamath, and the coasts and islands of the west.
12 He will lift up a banner for the nations
and gather the dispersed of Israel;
he will collect the scattered of Judah
from the four corners of the earth.
13 Ephraim's envy will cease;
Judah's harassing will end.
Ephraim will no longer be envious of Judah,
and Judah will not harass Ephraim.
14 But they will swoop down
on the Philistine flank to the west.
Together they will plunder the people of the east.
They will extend their power over Edom
and Moab,
and the Ammonites will be their subjects.
15 The Lord will divide[C,D] the Gulf of Suez.[E]
He will wave his hand over the Euphrates
with his mighty wind
and will split it into seven streams,
letting people walk through on foot.
16 There will be a highway for the remnant
of his people
who will survive from Assyria,
as there was for Israel
when they came up from the land of Egypt.

A SONG OF PRAISE

12 On that day you will say:
"I will give thanks to you, Lord,
although you were angry with me.
Your anger has turned away,
and you have comforted me.
2 Indeed, God is my salvation;
I will trust him and not be afraid,
for the Lord, the Lord himself,
is my strength and my song.
He has become my salvation."
3 You will joyfully draw water
from the springs of salvation,
4 and on that day you will say,
"Give thanks to the Lord; proclaim his name!
Make his works known among the peoples.
Declare that his name is exalted.

[A] **11:4** Lit *the rod* [B] **11:4** Lit *with the breath* [C] **11:15** Text emended; MT reads *destroy* [D] **11:15** Or *dry up* [E] **11:15** Lit *the Sea of Egypt*

5 Sing to the LORD, for he has done
glorious things.
Let this be known throughout the earth.
6 Cry out and sing, citizen of Zion,
for the Holy One of Israel is among you
in his greatness."

A PRONOUNCEMENT AGAINST BABYLON

13 A pronouncement concerning Babylon that
Isaiah son of Amoz saw:
2 Lift up a banner on a barren mountain.
Call out to them.
Signal with your hand, and they will go
through the gates of the nobles.
3 I have commanded my consecrated ones;
yes, I have called my warriors,
who celebrate my triumph,
to execute my wrath.
4 Listen, a commotion on the mountains,
like that of a mighty people!
Listen, an uproar among the kingdoms,
like nations being gathered together!
The LORD of Armies is mobilizing an army
for war.
5 They are coming from a distant land,
from the farthest horizon —
the LORD and the weapons of his wrath —
to destroy the whole country.[A]

6 Wail! For the day of the LORD is near.
It will come as destruction from the Almighty.
7 Therefore everyone's hands
will become weak,
and every man will lose heart.
8 They will be horrified;
pain and agony will seize them;
they will be in anguish like a woman in labor.
They will look at each other,
their faces flushed with fear.
9 Look, the day of the LORD is coming —
cruel, with fury and burning anger —
to make the earth a desolation
and to destroy its sinners.
10 Indeed, the stars of the sky
and its constellations[B]
will not give their light.
The sun will be dark when it rises,
and the moon will not shine.
11 I will punish the world for its evil,
and wicked people for their iniquities.
I will put an end to the pride of the arrogant
and humiliate the insolence of tyrants.
12 I will make a human more scarce
than fine gold,
and mankind more rare than the gold of Ophir.
13 Therefore I will make the heavens tremble,
and the earth will shake from its foundations
at the wrath of the LORD of Armies,
on the day of his burning anger.
14 Like wandering gazelles
and like sheep without a shepherd,
each one will turn to his own people,
each one will flee to his own land.
15 Whoever is found will be stabbed,
and whoever is caught will die by the sword.
16 Their children will be dashed to pieces
before their eyes;
their houses will be looted,
and their wives raped.
17 Look! I am stirring up the Medes against them,
who cannot be bought off with[C] silver
and who have no desire for gold.
18 Their bows will cut young men to pieces.
They will have no compassion on offspring;
they will not look with pity on children.

19 And Babylon, the jewel of the kingdoms,
the glory of the pride of the Chaldeans,
will be like Sodom and Gomorrah
when God overthrew them.
20 It will never be inhabited
or lived in from generation to generation;
a nomad will not pitch his tent there,
and shepherds will not let their flocks
rest there.
21 But desert creatures will lie down there,
and owls will fill the houses.
Ostriches will dwell there,
and wild goats will leap about.
22 Hyenas will howl in the fortresses,
and jackals, in the luxurious palaces.
Babylon's time is almost up;
her days are almost over.

ISRAEL'S RETURN

14 For the LORD will have compassion on Jacob
and will choose Israel again. He will settle
them on their own land. The resident alien will join
them and be united with the house of Jacob. 2 The
nations will escort Israel and bring it to its homeland. Then the house of Israel will possess them as
male and female slaves in the LORD's land. They will
make captives of their captors and will rule over their
oppressors.

DOWNFALL OF THE KING OF BABYLON

3 When the LORD gives you rest from your pain, torment, and the hard labor you were forced to do, 4 you

[A] 13:5 Or *earth* [B] 13:10 Or *Orions* [C] 13:17 Lit *who have no regard for*

will sing this song of contempt about the king of
Babylon and say:
How the oppressor has quieted down,
and how the raging[A] has become quiet!
5 The LORD has broken the staff of the wicked,
the scepter of the rulers.
6 It struck the peoples in anger
with unceasing blows.
It subdued the nations in rage
with relentless persecution.
7 The whole earth is calm and at rest;
people shout with a ringing cry.
8 Even the cypresses and the cedars of Lebanon
rejoice over you:
"Since you have been laid low,
no lumberjack has come against us."

9 Sheol below is eager to greet your coming,
stirring up the spirits of the departed
for you —
all the rulers[B] of the earth —
making all the kings of the nations
rise from their thrones.
10 They all respond to you, saying,
"You too have become as weak as we are;
you have become like us!
11 Your splendor has been brought down to Sheol,
along with the music of your harps.
Maggots are spread out under you,
and worms cover you."

12 Shining morning star,[C]
how you have fallen from the heavens!
You destroyer of nations,
you have been cut down to the ground.
13 You said to yourself,
"I will ascend to the heavens;
I will set up my throne
above the stars of God.
I will sit on the mount of the gods' assembly,
in the remotest parts of the North.[D]
14 I will ascend above the highest clouds;
I will make myself like the Most High."
15 But you will be brought down to Sheol
into the deepest regions of the Pit.

16 Those who see you will stare at you;
they will look closely at you:
"Is this the man who caused the earth
to tremble,
who shook the kingdoms,
17 who turned the world into a wilderness,
who destroyed its cities
and would not release the prisoners
to return home?"

18 All the kings of the nations
lie in splendor, each in his own tomb.
19 But you are thrown out without a grave,
like a worthless branch,
covered by those slain with the sword
and dumped into a rocky pit
like a trampled corpse.
20 You will not join them in burial,
because you destroyed your land
and slaughtered your own people.
The offspring of evildoers
will never be mentioned again.
21 Prepare a place of slaughter for his sons,
because of the iniquity of their ancestors.
They will never rise up to possess a land
or fill the surface of the earth with cities.

22 "I will rise up against them" — this is the declaration of the LORD of Armies — "and I will cut off
from Babylon her reputation, remnant, offspring, and
posterity" — this is the LORD's declaration. 23 "I will
make her a swampland and a region for herons,[E] and
I will sweep her away with the broom of destruction."
This is the declaration of the LORD of Armies.

ASSYRIA WILL BE DESTROYED

24 The LORD of Armies has sworn:
As I have purposed, so it will be;
as I have planned it, so it will happen.
25 I will break Assyria in my land;
I will tread him down on my mountain.
Then his yoke will be taken from them,
and his burden will be removed
from their shoulders.
26 This is the plan prepared
for the whole earth,
and this is the hand stretched out
against all the nations.
27 The LORD of Armies himself has planned it;
therefore, who can stand in its way?
It is his hand that is outstretched,
so who can turn it back?

A PRONOUNCEMENT AGAINST PHILISTIA

28 In the year that King Ahaz died, this pronouncement came:
29 Don't rejoice, all of you in Philistia,
because the rod of the one who struck you
is broken.
For a viper will come from the root[F]
of a snake,
and from its egg comes a flying serpent.

[A] **14:4** DSS; Hb uncertain [B] **14:9** Lit *rams* [C] **14:12** Or *Day Star, son of the dawn* [D] **14:13** Or *of Zaphon* [E] **14:23** Or *hedgehogs*; Hb obscure [F] **14:29** Or *stock*

30 Then the firstborn of the poor will be
well fed,
and the impoverished will lie down in safety,
but I will kill your root with hunger,
and your remnant will be slain.
31 Wail, you gates! Cry out, city!
Tremble with fear, all Philistia!
For a cloud of dust is coming
from the north,
and there is no one missing from
the invader's ranks.
32 What answer will be given to the messengers
from that nation?
The LORD has founded Zion,
and his oppressed people find refuge in her.

A PRONOUNCEMENT AGAINST MOAB

15 A pronouncement concerning Moab:
Ar in Moab is devastated,
destroyed in a night.
Kir in Moab is devastated,
destroyed in a night.
2 Dibon went up to its temple
to weep at its high places.
Moab wails on Nebo and at[A] Medeba.
Every head is shaved;
every beard is chopped short.
3 In its streets they wear sackcloth;
on its rooftops and in its public squares
everyone wails,
falling down and weeping.
4 Heshbon and Elealeh cry out;
their voices are heard as far away as Jahaz.
Therefore the soldiers of Moab cry out,
and they tremble.
5 My heart cries out over Moab,
whose fugitives flee as far as Zoar,
to Eglath-shelishiyah;
they go up the Ascent of Luhith weeping;
they raise a cry of destruction
on the road to Horonaim.
6 The Waters of Nimrim are desolate;
the grass is withered, the foliage is gone,
and the vegetation has vanished.
7 So they carry their wealth and belongings
over the Wadi of the Willows.
8 For their cry echoes
throughout the territory of Moab.
Their wailing reaches Eglaim;
their wailing reaches Beer-elim.
9 The Waters of Dibon[B] are full of blood,
but I will bring on Dibon even more
than this —
a lion for those who escape from Moab,
and for the survivors in the land.

16 Send lambs to the ruler of the land,
from Sela in the desert
to the mountain of Daughter Zion.
2 Like a bird fleeing,
forced from the nest,
the daughters of Moab
will be at the fords of the Arnon.

3 Give us counsel and make a decision.
Shelter us at noonday
with shade that is as dark as night.
Hide the refugees;
do not betray the one who flees.
4 Let my refugees stay with you;
be a refuge for Moab[C] from the aggressor.

When the oppressor has gone,
destruction has ended,
and marauders have vanished from the land,
5 a throne will be established in love,
and one will sit on it faithfully[D]
in the tent of David,
judging and pursuing what is right,
quick to execute justice.

6 We have heard of Moab's pride —
how very proud he is —
his haughtiness, his pride, his arrogance,
and his empty boasting.
7 Therefore let Moab wail;
let every one of them wail for Moab.
You who are completely devastated, mourn
for the raisin cakes of Kir-hareseth.
8 For Heshbon's terraced vineyards
and the grapevines of Sibmah have withered.
The rulers of the nations
have trampled its choice vines
that reached as far as Jazer
and spread to the desert.
Their shoots spread out
and reached the sea.
9 So I join with Jazer
to weep for the vines of Sibmah;
I drench Heshbon and Elealeh with my tears.
Triumphant shouts have fallen silent[E]
over your summer fruit and your harvest.
10 Joy and rejoicing have been removed
from the orchard;
no one is singing or shouting for joy
in the vineyards.
No one tramples grapes[F] in the winepresses.
I have put an end to the shouting.

[A] **15:2** Or *wails over Nebo and over* [B] **15:9** DSS, some LXX mss, Vg; MT reads *Dimon*, twice in this v. [C] **16:4** Or *you; Moab — be a refuge for him* [D] **16:5** Or *continually* [E] **16:9** Or *Battle cries have fallen* [F] **16:10** Lit *wine*

Moab

by Robert D. Bergen

Mentioned in twenty-two of the thirty-nine Old Testament books, Moab is remembered in accounts of biblical history from the days of Abraham through the time of Nehemiah. It is the subject of prophecies uttered by Moses and seven of Israel's writing prophets and is mentioned in three different psalms. All but a handful of the references portrayed Moab and the Moabites in a negative light, as Israel's troubler.

THE LAND AND CITIES OF MOAB

The region known as Moab during biblical times is located in what is today modern Jordan. We generally think of ancient Moab as the hilly plain directly east of the Dead Sea. The heart of traditional Moabite territory was situated between the Wadi Arnon (modern Wadi el Mujib) in the north (see Jdg 11:18) and the Wadi Zered (modern Wadi el-Hesa) in the south, which descended westward into the Dead Sea. They served as natural barriers and provided a measure of protection and isolation for Moab.

A second region associated with Moabite culture is the territory just north of the Arnon gorge. Though this area was known as the plains of Moab in biblical times (Nm 22:1), it was not always under Moabite control (33:48).

On its western border along the shore of the Dead Sea, the Moabite heartland lies some thirteen hundred feet below sea level. However, as one moves eastward, the terrain ascends rapidly. A mere ten miles away from the Dead Sea, the elevation is about three thousand feet above sea level, a net rise of about forty-three hundred feet.

This great variation in elevation meant that Moab contained several distinct climatic zones. Nearest the Dead Sea is a desert region that receives fewer than five inches of rain annually. Atop the plateau is a region that normally receives ten to twenty inches of rain per year and is more conducive to farming.[1] Biblical evidence for the relative productivity of Moabite land is seen in Ruth 1:2, which states that the Israelite Elimelech moved his family there to escape a famine.

Archaeological evidence suggests that Moab had established a series of fortresses along its border near the Zered gorge, overlooking the caravan route known as the King's Highway.[2] Other less conspicuous border defenses were discovered in the Arnon gorge. The Bible seldom mentions major cities in Moabite territory. Moses mentioned a city named Ar (Dt 2:18); David left his family with a Moabite king in Mizpah (1Sm 22:3–4); the prophet Amos pronounced judgment on the palaces of Kerioth (Am 2:2); and Isaiah (Is 15:2; 16:7–9) spoke of Dibon, Kir-hareseth, Heshbon, Sibmah, Jazer, and Elealeh.

THE PEOPLE, HISTORY, AND INFLUENCE OF MOAB

Genesis 19:30–37 provides an account of the Moabite nation's origins from the offspring of an incestuous relationship between Lot and his older daughter. The Moabites were thus understood to be a Semitic people group indirectly related to the Israelites. Knowing that Lot and his sons were with Abram in the promised land (chap. 13) and that the Moabite territory eventually came to be located east of the Dead Sea, we can assume that sometime before the days of Moses the descendants of Moab migrated from the western side of the Dead Sea to its eastern highlands. There they displaced the Emim, a people group that had been living there in the days of Abraham (Dt 2:10–11). However, the Bible lacks further details regarding the early stages of Moabite history; so far archaeological sites in the Near East have failed to uncover any documents that shed light on this period of their history.

By the time of the Israelite wanderings in the desert, Moabite culture had adopted a monarchical form of government, with a king that governed with the support and assistance of clan leaders known as elders (Nm 22:4,7,10). At that time, Moab had a smaller population than the Israelites and evidently lacked sufficient military resources to defend their territory from an Israelite invasion. Consequently, they sought the assistance of a Mesopotamian shaman, Balaam son of Beor, to eliminate Israel by means of powerful curses (vv. 2–11).

Prior to the rise of the Israelite monarchy, the Moabites consolidated their territorial holdings and at times even dominated their neighbors (1Sm 12:9). During the days of the judges, Moabite King Eglon forced the Israelites to bring him annual tribute payments for a period of eighteen years (Jdg 3:14). The best-known Moabite king is Mesha, who mounted a revolt against Israel and ruled from Dibon during the mid-ninth century BC. He is known from an inscribed stone found in Dibon in 1868.

On the other hand, many nations, including Israel, sought on occasion to gain control over Moab and its resources. Israelite leaders whom the Bible mentions as winning wars against the Moabites include the judge Ehud (Jdg 3:15–30) and the kings Saul (1Sm 14:47), David (2Sm 8:2), Jehoram (also known as Joram) of Israel, and Jehoshaphat of Judah (2Kg 3:6–27). But Moab's primary troublers were not the Israelites or their southern neighbors the Edomites, but rather, the nations from Mesopotamia—Assyria and Babylon. "The Assyrian texts imply that Moab fell under Assyrian domination during the eighth century BC."[3] Josephus indicated that the Babylonians conquered Moab five years after the destruction of Jerusalem, thus in 581 BC.[4] The Bible mentions no Moabite activities after that time.

Moabite religion exerted an influence—a decidedly negative one—on its neighbors as well. At various points in Israelite history, the Israelites became involved in the worship of at least two different Moabite deities. During the days of Moses, a number of Israelite men took part in religious rites associated with Baal of Peor. As part of their worship of Baal, they participated in sexual rituals (Nm 25:1–8) and ate sacrificial meals presented to the dead (Ps 106:28). Out of respect for a Moabite wife he had taken into his harem, King Solomon built a high place for Chemosh, the national god of Moab, just east of Jerusalem (1Kg 11:7–8). The Israelites maintained this high place of worship for more than three hundred years, up until the time of its desecration by King Josiah in the reforms of 626 BC (2Kg 23:13).

AN ATYPICAL MOABITE

The name Moab may have evoked a negative emotional reaction from the ancient Israelites. Ruth presents, however, a totally different image of those who had been the enemies of the people of God. From her lineage came the One who was and is the Redeemer of humankind (Mt 1:5). Our reaction, rather than fear and dread, is worship and celebration. ✣

Moabite Stone, discovered at Dibon in 1868, with an inscription by Moab's King Mesha, circa 840 BC.

---

[1] J. H. Paterson, "Palestine" in *ZPEB*, 4:578.
[2] R. K. Harrison, "Moab" in ZPEB, 4:262.
[4] J. Maxwell Miller, "Moab" in *ABD*, 4:890.
[5] Josephus, Jewish *Antiquities* 10.9.7.

11 Therefore I moan like the sound of a lyre
for Moab,
as does my innermost being for Kir-heres.
12 When Moab appears
and tires himself out on the high place
and comes to his sanctuary to pray,
it will do him no good.

13 This is the message that the LORD previously announced about Moab. 14 And now the LORD says, "In
three years, as a hired worker counts years, Moab's
splendor will become an object of contempt, in spite
of a very large population. And those who are left will
be few and weak."

A PRONOUNCEMENT AGAINST DAMASCUS

17 A pronouncement concerning Damascus:
Look, Damascus is no longer a city.
It has become a ruined heap.
2 The cities of Aroer are abandoned;
they will be places for flocks.
They will lie down without fear.
3 The fortress disappears from Ephraim,
and a kingdom from Damascus.
The remnant of Aram will be
like the splendor of the Israelites.
This is the declaration of the LORD of Armies.

JUDGMENT AGAINST ISRAEL

4 On that day
the splendor of Jacob will fade,
and his healthy body[A] will become emaciated.
5 It will be as if a reaper had gathered
standing grain —
his arm harvesting the heads of grain —
and as if one had gleaned heads of grain
in Rephaim Valley.
6 Only gleanings will be left in Israel,
as if an olive tree had been beaten —
two or three olives at the very top of the tree,
four or five on its fruitful branches.
This is the declaration of the LORD,
the God of Israel.

7 On that day people will look to their Maker and
will turn their eyes to the Holy One of Israel. 8 They
will not look to the altars they made with their hands
or to the Asherahs and shrines[B] they made with their
fingers.
9 On that day their strong cities will be
like the abandoned woods and mountaintops
that were abandoned because of the Israelites;
there will be desolation.
10 For you have forgotten the God
of your salvation,
and you have failed to remember
the rock of your strength;
therefore you will plant beautiful plants
and set out cuttings from exotic vines.
11 On the day that you plant,
you will help them to grow,
and in the morning
you will help your seed to sprout,
but the harvest will vanish
on the day of disease and incurable pain.

JUDGMENT AGAINST THE NATIONS

12 Ah! The roar of many peoples —
they roar like the roaring of the seas.
The raging of the nations —
they rage like the rumble of rushing water.
13 The nations rage like the rumble of a
huge torrent.
He rebukes them, and they flee far away,
driven before the wind like chaff on the hills
and like tumbleweeds before a gale.
14 In the evening — sudden terror!
Before morning — it is gone!
This is the fate of those who plunder us
and the lot of those who ravage us.

THE LORD'S MESSAGE TO CUSH

18 Woe to the land of buzzing insect wings[C]
beyond the rivers of Cush,
2 which sends envoys by sea,
in reed vessels over the water.

Go, swift messengers,
to a nation tall and smooth-skinned,
to a people feared far and near,
a powerful nation with a strange language,[D]
whose land is divided by rivers.
3 All you inhabitants of the world
and you who live on the earth,
when a banner is raised
on the mountains, look!
When a ram's horn sounds, listen!

4 For the LORD said to me:
I will quietly look out from my place,
like shimmering heat in sunshine,
like a rain cloud in harvest heat.
5 For before the harvest, when the blossoming
is over
and the blossom becomes a ripening grape,
he will cut off the shoots with a pruning knife,
and tear away and remove the branches.

[A] **17:4** Lit *and the fat of his flesh* [B] **17:8** Or *incense altars* [C] **18:1** Or *of sailing ships* [D] **18:2** Hb obscure

6 They will all be left for the birds of prey
on the hills
and for the wild animals of the land.
The birds of prey will spend the summer
feeding on them,
and all the wild animals the winter.

7 At that time a gift will be brought to the LORD of
Armies from[A] a people tall and smooth-skinned, a
people feared far and near, a powerful nation with
a strange language, whose land is divided by rivers
— to Mount Zion, the place of the name of the LORD
of Armies.

A PRONOUNCEMENT AGAINST EGYPT

19 A pronouncement concerning Egypt:
Look, the LORD rides on a swift cloud
and is coming to Egypt.
Egypt's worthless idols will tremble before him,
and Egypt will lose heart.
2 I will provoke Egyptians against Egyptians;
each will fight against his brother
and each against his friend,
city against city, kingdom against kingdom.
3 Egypt's spirit will be disturbed within it,
and I will frustrate its plans.
Then they will inquire of worthless idols, ghosts,
mediums, and spiritists.
4 I will hand over Egypt to harsh masters,
and a strong king will rule it.
This is the declaration of the Lord GOD
of Armies.

5 The water of the sea will dry up,
and the river will be parched and dry.
6 The channels will stink;
they will dwindle, and Egypt's canals
will be parched.
Reed and rush will wilt.
7 The reeds by the Nile, by the mouth of the river,
and all the cultivated areas of the Nile
will wither, blow away, and vanish.
8 Then the fishermen will mourn.
All those who cast hooks into the Nile
will lament,
and those who spread nets on the water
will give up.
9 Those who work with flax will be dismayed;
those combing it and weaving linen
will turn pale.[B]
10 Egypt's weavers[C] will be dejected;
all her wage earners will be demoralized.

11 The princes of Zoan are complete fools;
Pharaoh's wisest advisers give stupid advice!
How can you say to Pharaoh,
"I am one[D] of the wise,
a student of eastern[E] kings"?
12 Where then are your wise men?
Let them tell you and reveal
what the LORD of Armies has planned
against Egypt.
13 The princes of Zoan have been fools;
the princes of Memphis are deceived.
Her tribal chieftains have led Egypt astray.
14 The LORD has mixed within her a spirit
of confusion.
The leaders have made Egypt stagger
in all she does,
as a drunkard staggers in his vomit.
15 No head or tail, palm or reed,
will be able to do anything for Egypt.

EGYPT WILL KNOW THE LORD

16 On that day Egypt will be like women and will tremble with fear because of the threatening hand of the
LORD of Armies when he raises it against them. 17 The
land of Judah will terrify Egypt; whenever Judah is
mentioned, Egypt will tremble because of what the
LORD of Armies has planned against it.
18 On that day five cities in the land of Egypt will
speak the language of Canaan and swear loyalty to
the LORD of Armies. One of the cities will be called
the City of the Sun.[F,G]
19 On that day there will be an altar to the LORD in
the center of the land of Egypt and a pillar to the LORD
near her border. 20 It will be a sign and witness to the
LORD of Armies in the land of Egypt. When they cry
out to the LORD because of their oppressors, he will
send them a savior and leader, and he will rescue
them. 21 The LORD will make himself known to Egypt,
and Egypt will know the LORD on that day. They will
offer sacrifices and offerings; they will make vows
to the LORD and fulfill them. 22 The LORD will strike
Egypt, striking and healing. Then they will turn to
the LORD, and he will be receptive to their prayers
and heal them.
23 On that day there will be a highway from Egypt
to Assyria. Assyria will go to Egypt, Egypt to Assyria,
and Egypt will worship with Assyria.
24 On that day Israel will form a triple alliance with
Egypt and Assyria — a blessing within the land. 25 The
LORD of Armies will bless them, saying, "Egypt my
people, Assyria my handiwork, and Israel my inheritance are blessed."

[A] **18:7** DSS, LXX, Vg; MT omits *from* [B] **19:9** DSS, Tg; MT reads *weavers of white cloth* [C] **19:10** Or *foundations* [D] **19:11** Lit *a son* [E] **19:11** Lit *a son of ancient* [F] **19:18** Some Hb mss, DSS, Sym, Tg, Vg, Arabic; other Hb mss read *of Destruction*; LXX reads *of Righteousness* [G] **19:18** = the ancient Egyptian city Heliopolis

NO HELP FROM CUSH OR EGYPT

20 In the year that the chief commander, sent by
King Sargon of Assyria, came to Ashdod and
attacked and captured it — 2 during that time the
LORD had spoken through Isaiah son of Amoz, saying, "Go, take off your sackcloth from your waist and
remove the sandals from your feet," and he did that,
going stripped and barefoot — 3 the LORD said, "As my
servant Isaiah has gone stripped and barefoot three
years as a sign and omen against Egypt and Cush, 4 so
the king of Assyria will lead the captives of Egypt and
the exiles of Cush, young and old alike, stripped and
barefoot, with bared buttocks — to Egypt's shame.
5 Those who made Cush their hope and Egypt their
boast will be dismayed and ashamed. 6 And the inhabitants of this coastland will say on that day, 'Look,
this is what has happened to those we relied on and
fled to for help to rescue us from the king of Assyria!
Now, how will we escape?' "

A JUDGMENT ON BABYLON

21 A pronouncement concerning the desert by
the sea:

Like storms that pass over the Negev,
it comes from the desert, from the land
of terror.
2 A troubling vision is declared to me:
"The treacherous one acts treacherously,
and the destroyer destroys.
Advance, Elam! Lay siege, you Medes!
I will put an end to all the groaning."

3 Therefore I am[A] filled with anguish.
Pain grips me, like the pain of a woman in labor.
I am too perplexed to hear,
too dismayed to see.
4 My heart staggers;
horror terrifies me.
He has turned my last glimmer of hope[B]
into sheer terror.
5 Prepare a table, and spread out a carpet!
Eat and drink!
Rise up, you princes, and oil the shields!

6 For the Lord has said to me,
"Go, post a lookout;
let him report what he sees.
7 When he sees riders —
pairs of horsemen,
riders on donkeys,
riders on camels —
he must pay close attention."
8 Then the lookout[C] reported,
"Lord, I stand on the watchtower all day,
and I stay at my post all night.
9 Look, riders come —
horsemen in pairs."
And he answered, saying,
"Babylon has fallen, has fallen.
All the images of her gods
have been shattered on the ground."

10 My people who have been crushed
on the threshing floor,
I have declared to you
what I have heard from the LORD of Armies,
the God of Israel.

A PRONOUNCEMENT AGAINST DUMAH

11 A pronouncement concerning Dumah:[D]
One calls to me from Seir,
"Watchman, what is left of the night?
Watchman, what is left of the night?"
12 The watchman said,
"Morning has come, and also night.
If you want to ask, ask!
Come back again."

A PRONOUNCEMENT AGAINST ARABIA

13 A pronouncement concerning Arabia:
In the desert[E] brush
you will camp for the night,
you caravans of Dedanites.
14 Bring water for the thirsty.
The inhabitants of the land of Tema
meet[F] the refugees with food.
15 For they have fled from swords,
from the drawn sword,
from the bow that is strung,
and from the stress of battle.

16 For the Lord said this to me: "Within one year, as
a hired worker counts years, all the glory of Kedar
will be gone. 17 The remaining Kedarite archers will
be few in number." For the LORD, the God of Israel,
has spoken.

A PRONOUNCEMENT AGAINST JERUSALEM

22 A pronouncement concerning the Valley of
Vision:

What's the matter with you?
Why have all of you gone up to the rooftops?
2 The noisy city, the jubilant town,
is filled with celebration.
Your dead did not die by the sword;
they were not killed in battle.

[A] **21:3** Lit *my waist is*, or *my insides are* [B] **21:4** Lit *my twilight* [C] **21:8** DSS, Syr; MT reads *Then a lion* [D] **21:11** Some Hb mss, LXX read *Edom* [E] **21:13** LXX, Syr, Tg, Vg read *desert at evening* [F] **21:14** LXX, Syr, Tg, Vg read *meet* as a command

3 All your rulers have fled together,
captured without a bow.
All your fugitives were captured together;
they had fled far away.
4 Therefore I said,
"Look away from me! Let me weep bitterly!
Do not try to comfort me
about the destruction of my dear[A] people."
5 For the Lord God of Armies
had a day of tumult, trampling, and confusion
in the Valley of Vision —
people shouting[B] and crying to the mountains;
6 Elam took up a quiver
with chariots and horsemen,[C]
and Kir uncovered the shield.
7 Your best valleys were full of chariots,
and horsemen were positioned at the city
gates.
8 He removed the defenses of Judah.

On that day you looked to the weapons in the House
of the Forest. 9 You saw that there were many breaches in the walls of the city of David. You collected water from the lower pool. 10 You counted the houses
of Jerusalem so that you could tear them down to
fortify the wall. 11 You made a reservoir between the
walls for the water of the ancient pool, but you did
not look to the one who made it, or consider the one
who created it long ago.

12 On that day the Lord God of Armies
called for weeping, for wailing,
for shaven heads,
and for the wearing of sackcloth.
13 But look: joy and gladness,
butchering of cattle, slaughtering of sheep
and goats,
eating of meat, and drinking of wine —
"Let's eat and drink, for tomorrow we die!"
14 The LORD of Armies has directly revealed
to me:
"This iniquity will not be wiped out for you
people as long as you live."[D]
The Lord God of Armies has spoken.

A PRONOUNCEMENT AGAINST SHEBNA

15 The Lord God of Armies said, "Go to Shebna, that
steward who is in charge of the palace, and say to
him: 16 What are you doing here? Who authorized
you to carve out a tomb for yourself here, carving
your tomb on the height and cutting a resting place
for yourself out of rock? 17 Look, you strong man!
The LORD is about to shake you violently. He will take
hold of you, 18 wind you up into a ball, and sling you
into a wide land.[E] There you will die, and there your
glorious chariots will be — a disgrace to the house of
your lord. 19 I will remove you from your office; you
will be ousted from your position.

20 "On that day I will call for my servant, Eliakim son
of Hilkiah. 21 I will clothe him with your robe and tie
your sash around him. I will hand your authority over
to him, and he will be like a father to the inhabitants
of Jerusalem and to the house of Judah. 22 I will place
the key of the house of David on his shoulder; what he
opens, no one can close; what he closes, no one can
open. 23 I will drive him, like a peg, into a firm place.
He will be a throne of honor for his father's family.
24 They will hang on him all the glory of his father's
family: the descendants and the offshoots — all the
small vessels, from bowls to every kind of jar. 25 On
that day" — the declaration of the LORD of Armies
— "the peg that was driven into a firm place will
give way, be cut off, and fall, and the load on it will be
destroyed." Indeed, the LORD has spoken.

A PRONOUNCEMENT AGAINST TYRE

23 A pronouncement concerning Tyre:
Wail, ships of Tarshish,
for your haven has been destroyed.
Word has reached them from the land
of Cyprus.[F]
2 Mourn, inhabitants of the coastland,
you merchants of Sidon;
your agents have crossed the sea[G]
3 over deep water.
Tyre's revenue was the grain from Shihor —
the harvest of the Nile.
She was the merchant among the nations.
4 Be ashamed, Sidon, the stronghold of the sea,
for the sea has spoken:
"I have not been in labor or given birth.
I have not raised young men
or brought up young women."
5 When the news reaches Egypt,
they will be in anguish over the news
about Tyre.
6 Cross over to Tarshish;
wail, inhabitants of the coastland!
7 Is this your jubilant city,
whose origin was in ancient times,
whose feet have taken her
to reside far away?
8 Who planned this against Tyre,
the bestower of crowns,
whose traders are princes,
whose merchants are the honored ones
of the earth?

[A] 22:4 Lit *of the daughter of my* [B] 22:5 Or *Vision — a tearing down of a wall*, or *Vision — Kir raged*; Hb obscure [C] 22:6 Lit *chariots of man* [D] 22:14 Lit *for you until you die* [E] 22:17–18 Hb obscure [F] 23:1 Hb *Kittim* [G] 23:2 DSS; MT reads *Sidon, whom the seafarers have filled*

9 The LORD of Armies planned it,
to desecrate all its glorious beauty,
to disgrace all the honored ones of the earth.
10 Overflow[A] your land like the Nile,
daughter of Tarshish;
there is no longer anything to restrain you.[B]
11 He stretched out his hand over the sea;
he made kingdoms tremble.
The LORD has commanded
that the Canaanite fortresses be destroyed.
12 He said,
"You will not celebrate anymore,
ravished young woman, daughter of Sidon.
Get up and cross over to Cyprus —
even there you will have no rest!"
13 Look at the land of the Chaldeans —
a people who no longer exist.
Assyria destined it for desert creatures.
They set up their siege towers
and stripped its palaces.
They made it a ruin.
14 Wail, ships of Tarshish,
because your fortress is destroyed!

15 On that day Tyre will be forgotten for seventy
years — the life span of one king. At the end of seventy years, what the song says about the prostitute
will happen to Tyre:

16 Pick up your lyre,
stroll through the city,
you forgotten prostitute.
Play skillfully,
sing many a song
so that you will be remembered.

17 And at the end of the seventy years, the LORD will
restore Tyre and she will go back into business, prostituting herself with all the kingdoms of the world
throughout the earth. 18 But her profits and wages will
be dedicated to the LORD. They will not be stored or
saved, for her profit will go to those who live in the
LORD's presence, to provide them with ample food
and sacred clothing.

THE EARTH JUDGED

24 Look, the LORD is stripping the earth bare
and making it desolate.
He will twist its surface and scatter
its inhabitants:
2 people and priest alike,
servant and master,
female servant and mistress,
buyer and seller,
lender and borrower,
creditor and debtor.
3 The earth will be stripped completely bare
and will be totally plundered,
for the LORD has spoken this message.

4 The earth mourns and withers;
the world wastes away and withers;
the exalted people of the earth waste away.
5 The earth is polluted by its inhabitants,
for they have transgressed teachings,
overstepped decrees,
and broken the permanent covenant.
6 Therefore a curse has consumed the earth,
and its inhabitants have become guilty;
the earth's inhabitants have been burned,
and only a few survive.
7 The new wine mourns;
the vine withers.
All the carousers now groan.
8 The joyful tambourines have ceased.
The noise of the jubilant has stopped.
The joyful lyre has ceased.
9 They no longer sing and drink wine;
beer is bitter to those who drink it.
10 The city of chaos is shattered;
every house is closed to entry.
11 In the streets they cry[C] for wine.
All joy grows dark;
earth's rejoicing goes into exile.
12 Only desolation remains in the city;
its gate has collapsed in ruins.
13 For this is how it will be on earth
among the nations:
like a harvested olive tree,
like a gleaning after a grape harvest.

14 They raise their voices, they sing out;
they proclaim in the west
the majesty of the LORD.
15 Therefore, in the east honor the LORD!
In the coasts and islands of the west
honor the name of the LORD,
the God of Israel.
16 From the ends of the earth we hear songs:
The Splendor of the Righteous One.

But I said, "I waste away! I waste away![D]
Woe is me."
The treacherous act treacherously;
the treacherous deal very treacherously.
17 Panic, pit, and trap await you
who dwell on the earth.

[A] **23:10** DSS, LXX read *Work* [B] **23:10** Or *longer any harbor* [C] **24:11** Lit *streets she cries* [D] **24:16** Hb obscure

18 Whoever flees at the sound of panic
will fall into a pit,
and whoever escapes from the pit
will be caught in a trap.
For the floodgates on high are opened,
and the foundations of the earth
are shaken.
19 The earth is completely devastated;
the earth is split open;
the earth is violently shaken.
20 The earth staggers like a drunkard
and sways like a hut.
Earth's rebellion weighs it down,
and it falls, never to rise again.

21 On that day the LORD will punish
the army of the heights in the heights
and the kings of the ground on the ground.
22 They will be gathered together
like prisoners in a pit.
They will be confined to a dungeon;
after many days they will be punished.
23 The moon will be put to shame
and the sun disgraced,
because the LORD of Armies will reign
as king
on Mount Zion in Jerusalem,
and he will display his glory
in the presence of his elders.

SALVATION AND JUDGMENT ON THAT DAY

25 LORD, you are my God;
I will exalt you. I will praise your name,
for you have accomplished wonders,
plans formed long ago,
with perfect faithfulness.
2 For you have turned the city into a pile
of rocks,
a fortified city, into ruins;
the fortress of barbarians is no longer a city;
it will never be rebuilt.
3 Therefore, a strong people will honor you.
The cities of violent nations will fear you.
4 For you have been a stronghold for the poor
person,
a stronghold for the needy in his distress,
a refuge from storms and a shade
from heat.
When the breath of the violent
is like a storm against a wall,
5 like heat in a dry land,
you will subdue the uproar of barbarians.
As the shade of a cloud cools the heat
of the day,
so he will silence the song of the violent.

6 On this mountain,[A]
the LORD of Armies will prepare for all the
peoples a feast of choice meat,
a feast with aged wine, prime cuts of choice
meat,[B] fine vintage wine.
7 On this mountain
he will swallow up the burial shroud,
the shroud over all the peoples,
the sheet covering all the nations.
8 When he has swallowed up death
once and for all,
the Lord GOD will wipe away the tears
from every face
and remove his people's disgrace
from the whole earth,
for the LORD has spoken.

9 On that day it will be said,
"Look, this is our God;
we have waited for him, and he has saved us.
This is the LORD; we have waited for him.
Let's rejoice and be glad in his salvation."
10 For the LORD's power will rest
on this mountain.

But Moab will be trampled in his place[C]
as straw is trampled in a dung pile.
11 He will spread out his arms in the middle of it,
as a swimmer spreads out his arms to swim.
His pride will be brought low,
along with the trickery of his hands.
12 The high-walled fortress will be brought down,
thrown to the ground, to the dust.

THE SONG OF JUDAH

26 On that day this song will be sung in the land
of Judah:
We have a strong city.
Salvation is established as walls and ramparts.
2 Open the gates
so a righteous nation can come in —
one that remains faithful.
3 You will keep the mind that is dependent
on you
in perfect peace,
for it is trusting in you.
4 Trust in the LORD forever,
because in the LORD, the LORD himself, is
an everlasting rock!
5 For he has humbled those who live
in lofty places —
an inaccessible city.

[A]**25:6** = Mount Zion [B]**25:6** Lit *wine, fat full of marrow* [C]**25:10** Or *trampled under him*

He brings it down; he brings it down
to the ground;
he throws it to the dust.
6 Feet trample it,
the feet of the humble,
the steps of the poor.

GOD'S PEOPLE VINDICATED

7 The path of the righteous is level;
you clear a straight path for the righteous.
8 Yes, LORD, we wait for you
in the path of your judgments.
Our desire is for your name and renown.
9 I long for you in the night;
yes, my spirit within me diligently seeks you,
for when your judgments are in the land,
the inhabitants of the world
will learn righteousness.
10 But if the wicked man is shown favor,
he does not learn righteousness.
In a righteous land he acts unjustly
and does not see the majesty of the LORD.

11 LORD, your hand is lifted up to take action,
but they do not see it.
Let them see your zeal for your people
and be put to shame.
Let fire consume your adversaries.
12 LORD, you will establish peace for us,
for you have also done all our work for us.
13 LORD our God, lords other than you
have owned[A] us,
but we remember your name alone.

14 The dead do not live;
departed spirits do not rise up.
Indeed, you have punished
and destroyed them;
you have wiped out all memory of them.
15 You have added to the nation, LORD.
You have added to the nation; you are honored.
You have expanded all the borders of the land.
16 LORD, they went to you in their distress;
they poured out whispered prayers
because your discipline fell on them.[B]
17 As a pregnant woman about to give birth
writhes and cries out in her pains,
so we were before you, LORD.
18 We became pregnant, we writhed in pain;
we gave birth to wind.
We have won no victories on earth,
and the earth's inhabitants have not fallen.

19 Your dead will live; their bodies[C] will rise.
Awake and sing, you who dwell in the dust!
For you will be covered with the morning dew,[D]
and the earth will bring out the departed spirits.

20 Go, my people, enter your rooms
and close your doors behind you.
Hide for a little while until the wrath
has passed.
21 For look, the LORD is coming from his place
to punish the inhabitants of the earth
for their iniquity.
The earth will reveal the blood shed on it
and will no longer conceal her slain.

LEVIATHAN SLAIN

27 On that day the LORD with his relentless, large,
strong sword will bring judgment on Leviathan, the fleeing serpent — Leviathan, the twisting
serpent. He will slay the monster that is in the sea.

THE LORD'S VINEYARD

2 On that day
sing about a desirable vineyard:
3 I am the LORD, who watches over it
to water it regularly.
So that no one disturbs it,
I watch over it night and day.
4 I am not angry.
If only there were thorns and briers for me to
battle,
I would trample them
and burn them to the ground.
5 Or let it take hold of my strength;
let it make peace with me —
make peace with me.
6 In days to come, Jacob will take root.
Israel will blossom and bloom
and fill the whole world with fruit.

7 Did the LORD strike Israel
as he struck the one who struck Israel?
Was Israel killed like those killed by the LORD?
8 You disputed with Israel
by banishing and driving her away.[B]
He removed her with his severe storm
on the day of the east wind.
9 Therefore Jacob's iniquity will be atoned for
in this way,
and the result of the removal of his sin
will be this:
when he makes all the altar stones
like crushed bits of chalk,
no Asherah poles or incense altars
will remain standing.

[A]**26:13** Or *married* [B]**26:16; 27:8** Hb obscure [C]**26:19** Lit *live; my body they* [D]**26:19** Lit *For your dew is a dew of lights*

10 For the fortified city will be desolate,
pastures deserted and abandoned
like a wilderness.
Calves will graze there,
and there they will spread out and strip
its branches.
11 When its branches dry out, they will be
broken off.
Women will come and make fires with them,
for they are not a people with understanding.
Therefore their Maker will not
have compassion on them,
and their Creator will not be gracious to them.

12 On that day
the LORD will thresh grain
from the Euphrates River
as far as the Wadi of Egypt,
and you Israelites will be gathered one by one.
13 On that day
a great ram's horn will be blown,
and those lost in the land of Assyria will come,
as well as those dispersed in the land of Egypt;
and they will worship the LORD
at Jerusalem on the holy mountain.

WOE TO SAMARIA

28 Woe to the majestic crown
of Ephraim's drunkards,
and to the fading flower
of its beautiful splendor,
which is on the summit above the rich valley.
Woe to those overcome with wine.
2 Look, the Lord has a strong and mighty one —
like a devastating hail storm,
like a storm with strong flooding water.
He will bring it across the land
with his hand.
3 The majestic crown of Ephraim's drunkards
will be trampled underfoot.
4 The fading flower of his beautiful splendor,
which is on the summit above the rich valley,
will be like a ripe fig
before the summer harvest.
Whoever sees it will swallow it
while it is still in his hand.
5 On that day
the LORD of Armies will become a crown
of beauty
and a diadem of splendor
to the remnant of his people,
6 a spirit of justice
to the one who sits in judgment,
and strength
to those who repel attacks at the city gate.
7 Even these stagger because of wine
and stumble under the influence of beer:
Priest and prophet stagger because of beer.
They are confused by wine.
They stumble because of beer.
They are muddled in their visions.
They stumble in their judgments.
8 Indeed, all their tables are covered
with vomit;
there is no place without a stench.
9 Who is he trying to teach?
Who is he trying to instruct?
Infants[A] just weaned from milk?
Babies[A] removed from the breast?
10 "Law after law, law after law,
line after line, line after line,
a little here, a little there."[B]
11 For he will speak to this people
with stammering speech
and in a foreign language.
12 He had said to them,
"This is the place of rest;
let the weary rest;
this is the place of repose."
But they would not listen.

13 The word of the LORD will come to them:
"Law after law, law after law,
line after line, line after line,
a little here, a little there,"
so they go stumbling backward,
to be broken, trapped, and captured.

A DEAL WITH DEATH

14 Therefore hear the word of the LORD,
you scoffers
who rule this people in Jerusalem.
15 For you said, "We have made a covenant
with Death,
and we have an agreement with Sheol;
when the overwhelming catastrophe[C]
passes through,
it will not touch us,
because we have made falsehood
our refuge
and have hidden behind treachery."
16 Therefore the Lord GOD said:
"Look, I have laid a stone in Zion,
a tested stone,
a precious cornerstone,
a sure foundation;
the one who believes will be unshakable.[D]

[A] 28:9 Lit *Those* [B] 28:10 Hb obscure, also in v. 13 [C] 28:15 Or *whip*; Hb obscure, also in v. 18 [D] 28:16 Lit *will not hurry*

17 And I will make justice the measuring line
and righteousness the mason's level."
Hail will sweep away the false refuge,
and water will flood your hiding place.
18 Your covenant with Death will be dissolved,
and your agreement with Sheol will not last.
When the overwhelming catastrophe
passes through,
you will be trampled.
19 Every time it passes through,
it will carry you away;
it will pass through every morning —
every day and every night.
Only terror will cause you
to understand the message.[A]
20 Indeed, the bed is too short to stretch out on,
and its cover too small to wrap up in.
21 For the LORD will rise up as he did
at Mount Perazim.
He will rise in wrath, as at the Valley of Gibeon,
to do his work, his unexpected work,
and to perform his task, his unfamiliar task.
22 So now, do not scoff,
or your shackles will become stronger.
Indeed, I have heard from the Lord GOD
of Armies
a decree of destruction for the whole land.

GOD'S WONDERFUL ADVICE

23 Listen and hear my voice.
Pay attention and hear what I say.
24 Does the plowman plow every day
to plant seed?
Does he continuously break up and cultivate
the soil?
25 When he has leveled its surface,
does he not then scatter black cumin
and sow cumin?
He plants wheat in rows and barley in plots,
with spelt as their border.
26 His God teaches him order;
he instructs him.
27 Certainly black cumin is not threshed
with a threshing board,
and a cart wheel is not rolled over the cumin.
But black cumin is beaten out with a stick,
and cumin with a rod.
28 Bread grain is crushed,
but is not threshed endlessly.
Though the wheel
of the farmer's cart rumbles,
his horses do not crush it.
29 This also comes from the LORD of Armies.
He gives wondrous advice;
he gives great wisdom.

WOE TO JERUSALEM

29 Woe to Ariel,[B] Ariel,
the city where David camped!
Continue year after year;
let the festivals recur.
2 I will oppress Ariel,
and there will be mourning and crying,
and she will be to me like an Ariel.
3 I will camp in a circle around you;
I will besiege you with earth ramps,
and I will set up my siege towers against you.
4 You will be brought down;
you will speak from the ground,
and your words will come from low
in the dust.
Your voice will be like that of a spirit
from the ground;
your speech will whisper from the dust.
5 Your many foes[C] will be like fine dust,
and many of the ruthless, like blowing chaff.
Then suddenly, in an instant,
6 you will be punished by the LORD of Armies
with thunder, earthquake, and loud noise,
storm, tempest, and a flame
of consuming fire.
7 All the many nations
going out to battle against Ariel —
all the attackers, the siege works against her,
and those who oppress her —
will then be like a dream, a vision in the night.
8 It will be like a hungry one who dreams
he is eating,
then wakes and is still hungry;
and like a thirsty one who dreams
he is drinking,
then wakes and is still thirsty,
longing for water.
So it will be for all the many nations
who go to battle against Mount Zion.

9 Stop and be astonished;
blind yourselves and be blind!
They are drunk,[D] but not with wine;
they stagger,[E] but not with beer.
10 For the LORD has poured out on you
an overwhelming urge to[F] sleep;
he has shut your eyes (the prophets)
and covered your heads (the seers).
11 For you the entire vision will be like the words of a
sealed document. If it is given to one who can read

[A]**28:19** Or *The understanding of the message will cause sheer terror* [B]**29:1** Or *Altar Hearth*, or *Lion of God*; Hb obscure, also in v. 2 [C]**29:5** Lit *foreigners* [D]**29:9** LXX, Tg, Vg read *Be drunk* [E]**29:9** Tg, Vg read *wine; stagger* [F]**29:10** Lit *you a spirit of*

and he is asked to read it,[A] he will say, "I can't read it,
because it is sealed." 12 And if the document is given
to one who cannot read and he is asked to read it,[B]
he will say, "I can't read."

13 The Lord said:
These people approach me
with their speeches
to honor me with lip-service,[C]
yet their hearts are far from me,
and human rules direct their worship of me.[D]
14 Therefore, I will again confound
these people
with wonder after wonder.
The wisdom of their wise will vanish,
and the perception of their perceptive
will be hidden.

15 Woe to those who go to great lengths
to hide their plans from the LORD.
They do their works in the dark,
and say, "Who sees us? Who knows us?"
16 You have turned things around,
as if the potter were the same as the clay.
How can what is made say about its maker,
"He didn't make me"?
How can what is formed
say about the one who formed it,
"He doesn't understand what he's doing"?

17 Isn't it true that in just a little while
Lebanon will become an orchard,
and the orchard will seem like a forest?
18 On that day the deaf will hear
the words of a document,
and out of a deep darkness
the eyes of the blind will see.
19 The humble will have joy
after joy in the LORD,
and the poor people will rejoice
in the Holy One of Israel.
20 For the ruthless one will vanish,
the scorner will disappear,
and all those who lie in wait with evil intent
will be killed —
21 those who, with their speech,
accuse a person of wrongdoing,
who set a trap for the one mediating at
the city gate
and without cause deprive the righteous
of justice.

22 Therefore, the LORD who redeemed Abraham
says this about the house of Jacob:
Jacob will no longer be ashamed,
and his face will no longer be pale.
23 For when he sees his children,
the work of my hands within his nation,
they will honor my name,
they will honor the Holy One of Jacob
and stand in awe of the God of Israel.
24 Those who are confused
will gain understanding,
and those who grumble
will accept instruction.

CONDEMNATION OF THE EGYPTIAN ALLIANCE

30 Woe to the rebellious children!
This is the LORD's declaration.
They carry out a plan, but not mine;
they make an alliance,
but against my will,
piling sin on top of sin.
2 Without asking my advice
they set out to go down to Egypt
in order to seek shelter
under Pharaoh's protection
and take refuge in Egypt's shadow.
3 But Pharaoh's protection will become
your shame,
and refuge in Egypt's shadow your humiliation.
4 For though his[E] princes are at Zoan
and his messengers reach as far as Hanes,
5 everyone will be ashamed
because of a people who can't help.
They are of no benefit, they are no help;
they are good for nothing but shame
and disgrace.

6 A pronouncement concerning the animals of the
Negev:[F]
Through a land of trouble and distress,
of lioness and lion,
of viper and flying serpent,
they carry their wealth on the backs
of donkeys
and their treasures on the humps of camels,
to a people who will not help them.
7 Egypt's help is completely worthless;
therefore, I call her:
Rahab Who Just Sits.

8 Go now, write it on a tablet in their presence
and inscribe it on a scroll;
it will be for the future,
forever and ever.

[A] **29:11** Lit *If one gives it to one who knows the document, saying, "Read this, please"* [B] **29:12** Lit *who does not know the document, saying, "Read this, please"* [C] **29:13** Lit *their mouth and honor me with its lips* [D] **29:13** Lit *their fearing of me is a taught command of men* [E] **30:4** Or *Judah's* [F] **30:6** Or *Southland*

Earthenware Vessels: Pottery and Pottery Production in Ancient Israel *by Joel F. Drinkard Jr.*

Clay may have been first used in mud bricks, as mortar in stone structures, and as a sealant for baskets. The earliest pottery was probably accidentally produced when such clay was burned in a fire. This "accidental" pottery was extremely hard and did not deteriorate in heat, wind, or water. Soon people began deliberately making objects and vessels out of pottery. The first objects were crude and entirely made by hand. The potter's wheel was apparently developed in Egypt during the Old Kingdom (2700–2200 BC). The wheel allowed the production of more symmetrical vessels.

By the time of the Israelite monarchy (1050 BC), the potter's wheel was well developed, and firing was more controlled, producing more consistency in vessels.[1] The ancient Israelite potter began his work by gathering clay. Years of experience would teach him the best sources of clay for his vessels, often from a perennial streambed. After gathering clay, the potter would remove

Potter's wheel with pair of stones for pivoting. The potter's wheel was apparently developed in Egypt during the Old Kingdom (2700–2160 BC).

Drinking bowl and supports for firing in kiln, 275–250 BC.

all the large impurities—such as sticks, roots, and stones. Then it was washed to remove smaller impurities and allowed to settle so that heavier clays would sink to the bottom of the container, and finer clay would rise to the top. The finest clays could be mixed with more water to form a slurry. This served as a slip to finely decorate a vessel. The clay was now ready to be formed into a vessel. Potters would shape coarser clay into the larger, heavier utilitarian vessels of everyday use, such as store jars or mixing bowls. They would form the finer clay into smaller thin-walled vessels such as small bowls and pitchers.[2]

When he was ready to make his vessel, the potter sat at his wheel (Jr 18:3), which was actually two wheels. Two large circular stones were connected by a wooden shaft. The potter would kick the lower wheel with his feet, which turned the upper wheel. This left both his hands free to work the vessel. He would place a ball of clay in the center of the upper wheel and then use his hands and tools to form the vessel. Jeremiah 18 describes the prophet's visit to a potter's shop where he watched the potter making a vessel. But the vessel was not what the potter intended. We are not told why the potter was not satisfied. In any case, the potter reworked the clay back into a ball and began to manipulate the clay to make another vessel.

After the vessel was shaped, the potter would add handles, spouts, and other extra features. He then applied slips, burnishing, and painted designs. The vessel would then air dry for several days. After the vessel had dried sufficiently, it was fired in a kiln to create the final pottery piece.

The process of making handmade vessels has changed little since the time of ancient Israel. Today's wheels are powered by electric motors rather than foot power, and the pottery is fired in an electric or gas-powered kiln rather than in a pit or crude kiln using wood or charcoal as in Jeremiah's day. But the forming of handmade vessels remains virtually the same. People in some remote regions continue to use foot-powered wheels still today.

While every potter might have his own distinct forms, the basic design of most pieces was quite similar: store jars from different potters and regions were similar and are recognizable as store jars, but distinct from jugs or cooking pots or chalices. Differences in design and decoration marked regional or ethnic differences. More important, over time the pottery shapes and designs evolved. These changes can be traced from excavations and serve as a means of dating the strata (or levels) of excavations. Although not an exact analogy, we can date US coins relatively by the change of design on the front and back.

Iron Age pottery from Lachish, dated before tenth–sixth centuries BC.

Pottery from Amarneh in middle Euphrates region, 2650-2000 BC.

Of course, our coins also have dates, but some coins so worn that the date is not visible can still be dated just by the design. The quarter with a standing Liberty face is older than a quarter with Washington's face. The Washington quarters had the same reverse, an eagle, until the Bicentennial quarters of 1975–76, which had a colonial drummer. From 1999 to 2008, quarters featured one of the fifty states on the reverse, five being produced each year. These changes allow an easy relative dating of the coins.

More than a hundred years ago, archaeologists working in the Middle East from Egypt through Israel, Jordan, and Syria were able to develop a typology of pottery forms that could provide a relative chronology.[3] Archaeologists found they could use the shape, decoration, and texture of pottery to identify the region where it was produced and its relative age. Since pottery is ubiquitous and nearly indestructible (although what are found today are usually pieces or "potsherds"), pottery is abundant in virtually every site.[4] Also, since pottery is typically discarded when broken, most of the pottery in a specific stratum will belong to the time frame of that stratum. Archaeologists carefully catalogue where the sherds are found. Then a pottery specialist can "read" the pottery from a specific stratum to date the site relatively. In my home, we have a few pieces of antique china that belonged to my parents and grandparents. But all our everyday china dates to the past forty years or so. If our house were destroyed by some catastrophe today and excavated in a hundred years, archaeologists could use the everyday china to date the house to the approximate period of 1970 to the present.

The focal text in Isaiah poses an absurd situation: "How can what is made say about its maker, 'He didn't make me'? How can what is formed say about the one who formed it, 'He doesn't understand what he's doing'?" (Is 29:16). The answer to the questions posed is: Impossible! How absurd! Clay vessels cannot claim that the potter did not make them or that he has no sense. Clay vessels do not speak, nor do they have a mind. Again, Isaiah says: "Woe to the one who argues with his Maker—one clay pot among many. Does clay say to the one

Cornet-shaped vessels from Ghassul in the Jordan Valley, Chalcolithic era, 4500–3150 BC.

Early pinch-pot chalice from Kerak, circa 2500 BC.

forming it, 'What are you making?' Or does your work say, 'He has no hands'?" (45:9). Isaiah used similar examples a number of times, usually in satires about idols and their makers (see 2:8,20; 17:8; 31:7; 44:10–19; 46:6; 48:5). The absurdity is that humans make idols of wood, stone, metal, or pottery. The idols cannot speak, hear, or move by themselves—yet the worshipers turn to them for help. How absurd!

Then Isaiah reversed the metaphor and made the point that we are metaphorically all clay vessels made by the master Potter, God himself (Is 64:8). The difference in the two metaphors is radical; we do not make gods (idols), but God makes us! Jeremiah used that same metaphor to describe God's dealings with nations and peoples: God is the Potter, the nations are the clay (Jr 18:6–11). The potter-clay imagery is first found in Genesis 2. The word used to depict God "form[ing]" (Hb *yatsar*, Gn 2:7–8,19) his creatures is related to the word used for clay vessels (*yetser*, Is 29:16). The word for "potter" *(yotser)* is the participle of the same verb *(yatsar)*. The same metaphor continues in the New Testament as Paul refers to humans as clay vessels (2Co 4:7). ❖

[1] Ruth Amiran, *Ancient Pottery of the Holy Land* (Jerusalem: Massada Press, 1969), 192; Nancy L. Lapp, "Pottery Chronology of Palestine" in *ABD*, 5:442. [2] Robert H. Johnston, "The Biblical Potter," *BA* 37.4 (1974): 89. [3] Amiran, Ancient Pottery, 13; Lapp, 433; Johnston, "Biblical Potter," 86. [4] Johnston, "Biblical Potter," 87.

9 They are a rebellious people,
deceptive children,
children who do not want to listen to
the LORD's instruction.
10 They say to the seers, "Do not see,"
and to the prophets,
"Do not prophesy the truth to us.
Tell us flattering things.
Prophesy illusions.
11 Get out of the way!
Leave the pathway.
Rid us of the Holy One of Israel."
12 Therefore the Holy One of Israel says:
"Because you have rejected this message
and have trusted in oppression and deceit,
and have depended on them,
13 this iniquity of yours will be
like a crumbling gap,
a bulge in a high wall
whose collapse will come in an instant —
suddenly!
14 Its collapse will be like the shattering
of a potter's jar, crushed to pieces,
so that not even a fragment of pottery
will be found among its shattered remains —
no fragment large enough to take fire
from a hearth
or scoop water from a cistern."
15 For the Lord GOD, the Holy One of Israel,
has said:
"You will be delivered by returning and resting;
your strength will lie in quiet confidence.
But you are not willing."
16 You say, "No!
We will escape on horses" —
therefore you will escape! —
and, "We will ride on fast horses" —
but those who pursue you will be faster.
17 One thousand will flee at the threat of one,
at the threat of five you will flee,
until you remain
like a solitary pole on a mountaintop
or a banner on a hill.

THE LORD'S MERCY TO ISRAEL

18 Therefore the LORD is waiting
to show you mercy,
and is rising up to show you compassion,
for the LORD is a just God.
All who wait patiently for him are happy.

19 For people will live on Zion in Jerusalem. You
will never weep again; he will show favor to you at
the sound of your outcry; as soon as he hears, he will
answer you. 20 The Lord will give you meager bread
and water during oppression, but your Teacher[A] will
not hide any longer. Your eyes will see your Teacher,
21 and whenever you turn to the right or to the left,
your ears will hear this command behind you: "This
is the way. Walk in it." 22 Then you will defile your
silver-plated idols and your gold-plated images. You
will throw them away like menstrual cloths, and call
them filth.

23 Then he will send rain for your seed that you
have sown in the ground, and the food, the produce
of the ground, will be rich and plentiful. On that day
your cattle will graze in open pastures. 24 The oxen
and donkeys that work the ground will eat salted
fodder scattered with winnowing shovel and fork.
25 Streams flowing with water will be on every high
mountain and every raised hill on the day of great
slaughter when the towers fall. 26 The moonlight will
be as bright as the sunlight, and the sunlight will be
seven times brighter — like the light of seven days
— on the day that the LORD bandages his people's
injuries and heals the wounds he inflicted.

ANNIHILATION OF THE ASSYRIANS

27 Look! The name of the LORD is coming
from far away,
his anger burning and heavy with smoke.[B]
His lips are full of fury,
and his tongue is like a consuming fire.
28 His breath is like an overflowing torrent
that rises to the neck.
He comes to sift the nations in a sieve
of destruction
and to put a bridle on the jaws of the peoples
to lead them astray.
29 Your singing will be like that
on the night of a holy festival,
and your heart will rejoice
like one who walks to the music of a flute,
going up to the mountain of the LORD,
to the Rock of Israel.
30 And the LORD will make the splendor
of his voice heard
and reveal his arm striking in angry wrath
and a flame of consuming fire,
in driving rain, a torrent, and hailstones.
31 Assyria will be shattered by the voice
of the LORD.
He will strike with a rod.
32 And every stroke of the appointed[C] staff
that the LORD brings down on him
will be to the sound of tambourines and lyres;
he will fight against him
with brandished weapons.

[A]**30:20** Or *teachers* [B]**30:27** Hb obscure [C]**30:32** Some Hb mss read *punishing*

33 Indeed! Topheth has been ready
for the king for a long time.
Its funeral pyre is deep and wide,
with plenty of fire and wood.
The breath of the LORD, like a torrent
of burning sulfur,
kindles it.

THE LORD, THE ONLY HELP

31 Woe to those who go down to Egypt for help
and who depend on horses!
They trust in the abundance of chariots
and in the large number of horsemen.
They do not look to the Holy One of Israel,
and they do not seek the LORD.
2 But he also is wise and brings disaster.
He does not go back on what he says;
he will rise up against the house
of the wicked
and against the allies of evildoers.
3 Egyptians are men, not God;
their horses are flesh, not spirit.
When the LORD raises his hand to strike,
the helper will stumble
and the one who is helped will fall;
both will perish together.

4 For this is what the LORD said to me:
As a lion or young lion growls over its prey
when a band of shepherds is called out
against it,
and it is not terrified by their shouting
or subdued by their noise,
so the LORD of Armies will come down
to fight on Mount Zion
and on its hill.

5 Like hovering birds,
so the LORD of Armies will protect Jerusalem;
by protecting it, he will rescue it;
by passing over it, he will deliver it.

6 Return to the one the Israelites have greatly rebelled against. 7 For on that day, every one of you will
reject the worthless idols of silver and gold that your
own hands have sinfully made.
8 Then Assyria will fall,
but not by human sword;
a sword will devour him,
but not one made by man.
He will flee from the sword;
his young men will be put to forced labor.
9 His rock[A] will pass away because of fear,
and his officers will be afraid because of
the signal flag.
This is the LORD's declaration — whose fire is in Zion
and whose furnace is in Jerusalem.

THE RIGHTEOUS KINGDOM ANNOUNCED

32 Indeed, a king will reign righteously,
and rulers will rule justly.
2 Each will be like a shelter from the wind,
a refuge from the rain,
like flowing streams in a dry land
and the shade of a massive rock
in an arid land.
3 Then the eyes of those who see will not
be closed,
and the ears of those who hear will listen.
4 The reckless mind will gain knowledge,
and the stammering tongue will speak clearly
and fluently.
5 A fool will no longer be called a noble,
nor a scoundrel said to be important.
6 For a fool speaks foolishness
and his mind plots iniquity.
He lives in a godless way
and speaks falsely about the LORD.
He leaves the hungry empty
and deprives the thirsty of drink.
7 The scoundrel's weapons are destructive;
he hatches plots to destroy the needy
with lies,
even when the poor person says
what is right.
8 But a noble person plans noble things;
he stands up for noble causes.

9 Stand up, you complacent women;
listen to me.
Pay attention to what I say,
you overconfident daughters.
10 In a little more than a year
you overconfident ones will shudder,
for the grapes will fail
and the harvest will not come.
11 Shudder, you complacent ones;
tremble, you overconfident ones!
Strip yourselves bare
and put sackcloth around your waists.
12 Beat your breasts in mourning
for the delightful fields and the fruitful vines,
13 for the ground of my people
growing thorns and briers,
indeed, for every joyous house
in the jubilant city.
14 For the palace will be deserted,
the busy city abandoned.

[A] 31:9 Perhaps the Assyrian king

The hill and the watchtower will become
barren places forever,
the joy of wild donkeys,
and a pasture for flocks,
15 until the Spirit[A] from on high is poured out
on us.
Then the desert will become an orchard,
and the orchard will seem like a forest.
16 Then justice will inhabit the wilderness,
and righteousness will dwell in the orchard.
17 The result of righteousness will be peace;
the effect of righteousness
will be quiet confidence forever.
18 Then my people will dwell
in a peaceful place,
in safe and secure dwellings.
19 But hail will level the forest,[B]
and the city will sink into the depths.
20 You will be happy as you sow seed
beside abundant water,
and as you let oxen and donkeys range freely.

THE LORD RISES UP

33 Woe, you destroyer never destroyed,
you traitor never betrayed!
When you have finished destroying,
you will be destroyed.
When you have finished betraying,
they will betray you.

2 LORD, be gracious to us! We wait for you.
Be our strength every morning
and our salvation in time of trouble.
3 The peoples flee at the thunderous noise;
the nations scatter when you rise
in your majesty.
4 Your spoil will be gathered as locusts
are gathered;
people will swarm over it like an infestation
of locusts.
5 The LORD is exalted, for he dwells on high;
he has filled Zion with justice
and righteousness.
6 There will be times of security for you —
a storehouse of salvation, wisdom,
and knowledge.
The fear of the LORD is Zion's treasure.

7 Listen! Their warriors cry loudly in the streets;
the messengers of peace weep bitterly.
8 The highways are deserted;
travel has ceased.
An agreement has been broken,
cities[C] despised,
and human life disregarded.
9 The land mourns and withers;
Lebanon is ashamed and wilted.
Sharon is like a desert;
Bashan and Carmel shake off their leaves.
10 "Now I will rise up," says the LORD.
"Now I will lift myself up.
Now I will be exalted.
11 You will conceive chaff;
you will give birth to stubble.
Your breath is fire that will consume you.
12 The peoples will be burned to ashes,
like thorns cut down and burned in a fire.
13 You who are far off, hear what I have done;
you who are near, know my strength."

14 The sinners in Zion are afraid;
trembling seizes the ungodly:
"Who among us can dwell
with a consuming fire?
Who among us can dwell with
ever-burning flames?"
15 The one who lives righteously
and speaks rightly,
who refuses profit from extortion,
whose hand never takes a bribe,
who stops his ears from listening
to murderous plots
and shuts his eyes against evil schemes —
16 he will dwell on the heights;
his refuge will be the rocky fortresses,
his food provided, his water assured.

17 Your eyes will see the King in his beauty;
you will see a vast land.
18 Your mind will meditate on the past terror:
"Where is the accountant?[D]
Where is the tribute collector?[E]
Where is the one who spied out our defenses?"[F]
19 You will no longer see the barbarians,
a people whose speech is difficult
to comprehend —
who stammer in a language that is
not understood.
20 Look at Zion, the city of our festival times.
Your eyes will see Jerusalem,
a peaceful pasture, a tent that does not wander;
its tent pegs will not be pulled up
nor will any of its cords be loosened.
21 For the majestic one, our LORD, will be there,
a place of rivers and broad streams
where ships that are rowed will not go,
and majestic vessels will not pass.

[A]**32:15** Or *a wind* [B]**32:19** Hb obscure [C]**33:8** DSS read *witnesses*
[D]**33:18** Lit *counter* [E]**33:18** Lit *weigher* [F]**33:18** Lit *who counts towers*

22 For the LORD is our Judge,
the LORD is our Lawgiver,
the LORD is our King.
He will save us.
23 Your ropes are slack;
they cannot hold the base of the mast
or spread out the flag.
Then abundant spoil will be divided,
the lame will plunder it,
24 and none there will say, "I am sick."
The people who dwell there
will be forgiven their iniquity.

THE JUDGMENT OF THE NATIONS

34 You nations, come here and listen;
you peoples, pay attention!
Let the earth and all that fills it hear,
the world and all that comes from it.
2 The LORD is angry with all the nations,
furious with all their armies.
He will set them apart for destruction,
giving them over to slaughter.
3 Their slain will be thrown out,
and the stench of their corpses will rise;
the mountains will flow[A] with their blood.
4 All[B] the stars in the sky will dissolve.
The sky will roll up like a scroll,
and its stars will all wither
as leaves wither on the vine,
and foliage on the fig tree.

THE JUDGMENT OF EDOM

5 When my sword has drunk its fill[C]
in the heavens,
it will then come down on Edom
and on the people I have set apart
for destruction.
6 The LORD's sword is covered with blood.
It drips with fat,
with the blood of lambs and goats,
with the fat of the kidneys of rams.
For the LORD has a sacrifice in Bozrah,
a great slaughter in the land of Edom.
7 The wild oxen will be struck[D] down
with them,
and young bulls with the mighty bulls.
Their land will be soaked with[E] blood,
and their soil will be saturated with fat.

8 For the LORD has a day of vengeance,
a time of paying back Edom
for its hostility against Zion.
9 Edom's streams will be turned into pitch,
her soil into sulfur;
her land will become burning pitch.
10 It will never go out — day or night.
Its smoke will go up forever.
It will be desolate, from generation
to generation;
no one will pass through it forever and ever.
11 Eagle owls[F] and herons[G] will possess it,
and long-eared owls and ravens
will dwell there.
The LORD will stretch out a measuring line
and a plumb line over her
for her destruction and chaos.
12 No nobles will be left to proclaim a king,
and all her princes will come to nothing.
13 Her palaces will be overgrown with thorns;
her fortified cities, with thistles and briers.
She will become a dwelling for jackals,
an abode[H] for ostriches.
14 The desert creatures will meet hyenas,
and one wild goat will call to another.
Indeed, the night birds will stay there
and will find a resting place.
15 Sand partridges[I] will make their nests there;
they will lay and hatch their eggs
and will gather their broods
under their shadows.
Indeed, the birds of prey will gather there,
each with its mate.
16 Search and read the scroll of the LORD:
Not one of them will be missing,
none will be lacking its mate,
because he has ordered it by my[J] mouth,
and he will gather them by his Spirit.
17 He has cast the lot for them;
his hand allotted their portion
with a measuring line.
They will possess it forever;
they will dwell in it from generation
to generation.

THE RANSOMED RETURN TO ZION

35 The wilderness and the dry land will be glad;
the desert will rejoice and blossom
like a wildflower.[K]
2 It will blossom abundantly
and will also rejoice with joy and singing.
The glory of Lebanon will be given to it,
the splendor of Carmel and Sharon.
They will see the glory of the LORD,
the splendor of our God.

[A] **34:3** Or *melt*, or *dissolve* [B] **34:4** DSS read *And the valleys will be split, and all* [C] **34:5** DSS read *sword will appear* [D] **34:7** Or *will go* [E] **34:7** Or *will drink its fill of* [F] **34:11** Or *Pelicans* [G] **34:11** Or *hedgehogs* [H] **34:13** DSS, LXX, Syr, Tg; MT reads *jackals, grass* [I] **34:15** Or *Arrow snakes*, or *Owls* [J] **34:16** Some Hb mss; other Hb mss, DSS, Syr, Tg read *his* [K] **35:1** Or *meadow saffron*; traditionally *rose*

3 Strengthen the weak hands,
steady the shaking knees!
4 Say to the cowardly:
"Be strong; do not fear!
Here is your God; vengeance is coming.
God's retribution is coming; he will save you."
5 Then the eyes of the blind will be opened,
and the ears of the deaf unstopped.
6 Then the lame will leap like a deer,
and the tongue of the mute will sing for joy,
for water will gush in the wilderness,
and streams in the desert;
7 the parched ground will become a pool,
and the thirsty land, springs.
In the haunt of jackals, in their lairs,
there will be grass, reeds, and papyrus.
8 A road will be there and a way;
it will be called the Holy Way.
The unclean will not travel on it,
but it will be for the one who walks the path.
Fools will not wander on it.
9 There will be no lion there,
and no vicious beast will go up on it;
they will not be found there.
But the redeemed will walk on it,
10 and the ransomed of the LORD will return
and come to Zion with singing,
crowned with unending joy.
Joy and gladness will overtake them,
and sorrow and sighing will flee.

SENNACHERIB'S INVASION

36 In the fourteenth year of King Hezekiah, King
Sennacherib of Assyria attacked all the fortified cities of Judah and captured them. 2 Then the
king of Assyria sent his royal spokesman, along with
a massive army, from Lachish to King Hezekiah at Jerusalem. The Assyrian stood near the conduit of the
upper pool, by the road to Launderer's Field. 3 Eliakim son of Hilkiah, who was in charge of the palace,
Shebna the court secretary, and Joah son of Asaph,
the court historian, came out to him.
4 The royal spokesman said to them, "Tell Hezekiah:
The great king, the king of Assyria, says this:
What are you relying on? 5 You[A] think mere words
are strategy and strength for war. Who are you
now relying on that you have rebelled against
me? 6 Look, you are relying on Egypt, that splintered reed of a staff that will pierce the hand of
anyone who grabs it and leans on it. This is how
Pharaoh king of Egypt is to all who rely on him.
7 Suppose you say to me, 'We rely on the LORD our
God.' Isn't he the one whose high places and altars Hezekiah has removed, saying to Judah and
Jerusalem, 'You are to worship at this altar'?
8 "Now make a deal with my master, the king
of Assyria. I'll give you two thousand horses if
you're able to supply riders for them! 9 How then
can you drive back a single officer among the
least of my master's servants? How can you rely
on Egypt for chariots and horsemen? 10 Have I attacked this land to destroy it without the LORD's
approval? The LORD said to me, 'Attack this land
and destroy it.' "

11 Then Eliakim, Shebna, and Joah said to the royal
spokesman, "Please speak to your servants in Aramaic, since we understand it. Don't speak to us in
Hebrew[B] within earshot of the people who are on
the wall."
12 But the royal spokesman replied, "Has my master
sent me to speak these words to your master and to
you, and not to the men who are sitting on the wall,
who are destined with you to eat their own excrement
and drink their own urine?"
13 Then the royal spokesman stood and called out
loudly in Hebrew:
Listen to the words of the great king, the king of
Assyria! 14 This is what the king says: "Don't let
Hezekiah deceive you, for he cannot rescue you.
15 Don't let Hezekiah persuade you to rely on the
LORD, saying, 'The LORD will certainly rescue us!
This city will not be handed over to the king of
Assyria.' "

16 Don't listen to Hezekiah, for this is what the
king of Assyria says: "Make peace[C] with me and
surrender to me. Then every one of you may
eat from his own vine and his own fig tree and
drink water from his own cistern 17 until I come
and take you away to a land like your own land
— a land of grain and new wine, a land of bread
and vineyards. 18 Beware that Hezekiah does not
mislead you by saying, 'The LORD will rescue us.'
Has any one of the gods of the nations rescued
his land from the power of the king of Assyria?
19 Where are the gods of Hamath and Arpad?
Where are the gods of Sepharvaim? Have they
rescued Samaria from my power? 20 Who among
all the gods of these lands ever rescued his land
from my power? So will the LORD rescue Jerusalem from my power?"

21 But they kept silent; they didn't say anything,
for the king's command was, "Don't answer him."
22 Then Eliakim son of Hilkiah, who was in charge of
the palace, Shebna the court secretary, and Joah son

[A] **36:5** Many Hb mss, DSS, 2Kg 18:20; MT reads *I* [B] **36:11** Lit *Judahite*, also in v. 13 [C] **36:16** Lit *a blessing*

of Asaph, the court historian, came to Hezekiah with
their clothes torn and reported to him the words of
the royal spokesman.

HEZEKIAH SEEKS ISAIAH'S COUNSEL

37 When King Hezekiah heard their report, he
tore his clothes, covered himself with sackcloth, and went to the LORD's temple. 2 He sent Eliakim, who was in charge of the palace, Shebna the
court secretary, and the leading priests, who were
covered with sackcloth, to the prophet Isaiah son
of Amoz. 3 They said to him, "This is what Hezekiah
says: 'Today is a day of distress, rebuke, and disgrace.
It is as if children have come to the point of birth, and
there is no strength to deliver them. 4 Perhaps the
LORD your God will hear all the words of the royal
spokesman, whom his master the king of Assyria sent
to mock the living God, and will rebuke him for the
words that the LORD your God has heard. Therefore
offer a prayer for the surviving remnant.'"

5 So the servants of King Hezekiah went to Isaiah,
6 who said to them, "Tell your master, 'The LORD says
this: Don't be afraid because of the words you have
heard, with which the king of Assyria's attendants
have blasphemed me. 7 I am about to put a spirit in
him and he will hear a rumor and return to his own
land, where I will cause him to fall by the sword.'"

SENNACHERIB'S LETTER

8 When the royal spokesman heard that the king of
Assyria had pulled out of Lachish, he left and found
him fighting against Libnah. 9 The king had heard
concerning King Tirhakah of Cush, "He has set out
to fight against you." So when he heard this, he sent
messengers to Hezekiah, saying, 10 "Say this to King
Hezekiah of Judah: 'Don't let your God, on whom you
rely, deceive you by promising that Jerusalem won't
be handed over to the king of Assyria. 11 Look, you
have heard what the kings of Assyria have done to all
the countries: they completely destroyed them. Will
you be rescued? 12 Did the gods of the nations that
my predecessors destroyed rescue them — Gozan,
Haran, Rezeph, and the Edenites in Telassar? 13 Where
is the king of Hamath, the king of Arpad, the king of
the city of[A] Sepharvaim, Hena, or Ivvah?'"

HEZEKIAH'S PRAYER

14 Hezekiah took the letter from the messengers'
hands, read it, then went up to the LORD's temple
and spread it out before the LORD. 15 Then Hezekiah
prayed to the LORD:

16 LORD of Armies, God of Israel, enthroned between the cherubim, you are God — you alone
— of all the kingdoms of the earth. You made
the heavens and the earth. 17 Listen closely, LORD,
and hear; open your eyes, LORD, and see. Hear
all the words that Sennacherib has sent to mock
the living God. 18 LORD, it is true that the kings of
Assyria have devastated all these countries and
their lands. 19 They have thrown their gods into
the fire, for they were not gods but made from
wood and stone by human hands. So they have
destroyed them. 20 Now LORD our God, save us
from his power so that all the kingdoms of the
earth may know that you, LORD, are God[B] — you
alone.

DIGGING DEEPER *The Annals of Sennacherib*

Ancient kings often recorded their military achievements in stone. *The Annals of Sennacherib* (the Taylor Prism) document Assyrian King Sennacherib's conquest of Israel and siege of Jerusalem during King Hezekiah's reign in 701 BC (2Kg 18–19; 2Ch 32). The *Annals* chronicle Assyria's destruction of forty-six Israelite and Judahite cities (2Kg 18:30; Is 36:1) and the capture of 200,150 people (2Kg 18:11). By the time Sennacherib reached Jerusalem, the prophet Isaiah had declared that Sennacherib's siege would fail (Is 37:1–7,21–35). The *Annals* confirm that Hezekiah sent tribute to Sennacherib (2Kg 18:14–16). The Bible says God delivered Jerusalem from Sennacherib (Is 37:36–37), but the *Annals* report that Sennacherib cornered Hezekiah "in Jerusalem, his royal city, like a bird in a cage." Is this a contradiction? Keep in mind that the Bible agrees that Sennacherib's forces surrounded Jerusalem (Is 36:2). Although the *Annals* say nothing about Sennacherib being turned away at Jerusalem, neither do they say that the siege resulted in the overthrow of the city. Since the purpose of the prism was to brag on Sennacherib's accomplishments, the silence about the outcome most likely indicates that the siege failed. Thus the Bible and the *Annals* agree on details surrounding Sennacherib's campaign.

GOD'S ANSWER THROUGH ISAIAH

21 Then Isaiah son of Amoz sent a message to Hezekiah: "The LORD, the God of Israel, says, 'Because you
prayed to me about King Sennacherib of Assyria,
22 this is the word the LORD has spoken against him:

Virgin Daughter Zion
despises you and scorns you;
Daughter Jerusalem shakes her head
behind your back.

[A] **37:13** Or *king of Lair*, [B] **37:20** *are God* supplied for clarity; see v. 16

23 Who is it you have mocked and blasphemed?
Against whom have you raised your voice
and lifted your eyes in pride?
Against the Holy One of Israel!
24 You have mocked the Lord
through your servants.
You have said, "With my many chariots
I have gone up to the heights of the mountains,
to the far recesses of Lebanon.
I cut down its tallest cedars,
its choice cypress trees.
I came to its distant heights,
its densest forest.
25 I dug wells and drank water in foreign lands.[A]
I dried up all the streams of Egypt
with the soles of my feet."

26 Have you not heard?
I designed it long ago;
I planned it in days gone by.
I have now brought it to pass,
and you have crushed fortified cities
into piles of rubble.
27 Their inhabitants have become powerless,
dismayed, and ashamed.
They are plants of the field,
tender grass,
grass on the rooftops,
blasted by the east wind.[B]

28 But I know your sitting down,
your going out and your coming in,
and your raging against me.
29 Because your raging against me
and your arrogance have reached my ears,
I will put my hook in your nose
and my bit in your mouth;
I will make you go back
the way you came.

30 " 'This will be the sign for you: This year you
will eat what grows on its own, and in the second
year what grows from that. But in the third year sow
and reap, plant vineyards and eat their fruit. 31 The
surviving remnant of the house of Judah will again
take root downward and bear fruit upward. 32 For a
remnant will go out from Jerusalem, and survivors
from Mount Zion. The zeal of the LORD of Armies will
accomplish this.'
33 "Therefore, this is what the LORD says about the
king of Assyria:
He will not enter this city,
shoot an arrow here,
come before it with a shield,
or build up a siege ramp against it.
34 He will go back
the way he came,
and he will not enter this city.
This is the LORD's declaration.
35 I will defend this city and rescue it
for my sake
and for the sake of my servant David."

DEFEAT AND DEATH OF SENNACHERIB

36 Then the angel of the LORD went out and struck
down one hundred eighty-five thousand in the camp
of the Assyrians. When the people got up the next
morning, there were all the dead bodies! 37 So King
Sennacherib of Assyria broke camp and left. He returned home and lived in Nineveh.
38 One day, while he was worshiping in the temple
of his god Nisroch, his sons Adrammelech and Sharezer struck him down with the sword and escaped to
the land of Ararat. Then his son Esar-haddon became
king in his place.

HEZEKIAH'S ILLNESS AND RECOVERY

38 In those days Hezekiah became terminally ill.
The prophet Isaiah son of Amoz came and said
to him, "This is what the LORD says: 'Set your house in
order, for you are about to die; you will not recover.' "[C]
2 Then Hezekiah turned his face to the wall and
prayed to the LORD. 3 He said, "Please, LORD, remember
how I have walked before you faithfully and wholeheartedly, and have done what pleases you." And Hezekiah wept bitterly.
4 Then the word of the LORD came to Isaiah: 5 "Go
and tell Hezekiah, 'This is what the LORD God of your
ancestor David says: I have heard your prayer; I have
seen your tears. Look, I am going to add fifteen years
to your life.[D] 6 And I will rescue you and this city from
the grasp of the king of Assyria; I will defend this city.
7 This is the sign to you from the LORD that he will do
what he has promised: 8 I am going to make the sun's
shadow that goes down on the stairway of Ahaz go
back by ten steps.' " So the sun's shadow[E] went back
the ten steps it had descended.
9 A poem by King Hezekiah of Judah after he had
been sick and had recovered from his illness:
10 I said: In the prime[F] of my life
I must go to the gates of Sheol;
I am deprived of the rest of my years.
11 I said: I will never see the LORD,
the LORD in the land of the living;
I will not look on humanity any longer
with the inhabitants of what is passing away.[G]

[A] **37:25** DSS, 2Kg 19:24; MT omits *in foreign lands* [B] **37:27** DSS; MT reads *rooftops, field before standing grain* [C] **38:1** Lit *live* [D] **38:5** Lit *days*, also in v. 10 [E] **38:8** Lit *And the sun* [F] **38:10** Lit *quiet* [G] **38:11** Some Hb mss, Tg read *of the world*

12 My dwelling is plucked up and removed
from me
like a shepherd's tent.
I have rolled up my life like a weaver;
he cuts me off from the loom.
By nightfall[A] you make an end of me.
13 I thought until the morning:
He will break all my bones like a lion.
By nightfall you make an end of me.
14 I chirp like a swallow or a crane;
I moan like a dove.
My eyes grow weak looking upward.
Lord, I am oppressed; support me.

15 What can I say?
He has spoken to me,
and he himself has done it.
I walk along slowly all my years
because of the bitterness of my soul.
16 Lord, by such things people live,
and in every one of them my spirit finds life;
you have restored me to health
and let me live.
17 Indeed, it was for my own well-being
that I had such intense bitterness;
but your love has delivered me
from the Pit of destruction,
for you have thrown all my sins
behind your back.
18 For Sheol cannot thank you;
Death cannot praise you.
Those who go down to the Pit
cannot hope for your faithfulness.
19 The living, only the living can thank you,
as I do today;
a father will make your faithfulness known
to children.
20 The LORD is ready to save me;
we will play stringed instruments
all the days of our lives
at the house of the LORD.

21 Now Isaiah had said, "Let them take a lump of
pressed figs and apply it to his infected skin, so that
he may recover." 22 And Hezekiah had asked, "What
is the sign that I will go up to the LORD's temple?"

HEZEKIAH'S FOLLY

39 At that time Merodach-baladan son of Baladan, king of Babylon, sent letters and a gift to
Hezekiah since he heard that he had been sick and
had recovered. 2 Hezekiah was pleased with the letters, and he showed the envoys his treasure house
— the silver, the gold, the spices, and the precious oil
— and all his armory, and everything that was found
in his treasuries. There was nothing in his palace and
in all his realm that Hezekiah did not show them.
3 Then the prophet Isaiah came to King Hezekiah
and asked him, "What did these men say, and where
did they come to you from?"

Hezekiah replied, "They came to me from a distant
country, from Babylon."
4 Isaiah asked, "What have they seen in your palace?"

Hezekiah answered, "They have seen everything
in my palace. There isn't anything in my treasuries
that I didn't show them."
5 Then Isaiah said to Hezekiah, "Hear the word
of the LORD of Armies: 6 'Look, the days are coming
when everything in your palace and all that your predecessors have stored up until today will be carried
off to Babylon; nothing will be left,' says the LORD.
7 'Some of your descendants — who come from you,
whom you father — will be taken away, and they
will become eunuchs in the palace of the king of
Babylon.'"
8 Then Hezekiah said to Isaiah, "The word of the
LORD that you have spoken is good," for he thought:
There will be peace and security during my lifetime.

GOD'S PEOPLE COMFORTED

40 "Comfort, comfort my people,"
says your God.
2 "Speak tenderly to[B] Jerusalem,
and announce to her
that her time of hard service is over,
her iniquity has been pardoned,
and she has received from the LORD's hand
double for all her sins."

3 A voice of one crying out:
Prepare the way of the LORD in the wilderness;
make a straight highway for our God
in the desert.
4 Every valley will be lifted up,
and every mountain and hill will be leveled;
the uneven ground will become smooth
and the rough places, a plain.
5 And the glory of the LORD will appear,
and all humanity[C] together will see it,
for the mouth of the LORD has spoken.

6 A voice was saying, "Cry out!"
Another said,[D] "What should I cry out?"
"All humanity is grass,
and all its goodness is like the flower
of the field.

[A] **38:12** Lit *From day until night*, also in v. 13 [B] **40:2** Lit *Speak to the heart of* [C] **40:5** Lit *flesh* [D] **40:6** DSS, LXX, Vg read *I said*

7 The grass withers, the flowers fade
when the breath[A] of the LORD blows on them;[B]
indeed, the people are grass.
8 The grass withers, the flowers fade,
but the word of our God remains forever."

9 Zion, herald of good news,
go up on a high mountain.
Jerusalem, herald of good news,
raise your voice loudly.
Raise it, do not be afraid!
Say to the cities of Judah,
"Here is your God!"
10 See, the Lord GOD comes with strength,
and his power establishes his rule.
His wages are with him,
and his reward accompanies him.
11 He protects his flock like a shepherd;
he gathers the lambs in his arms
and carries them in the fold of his garment.
He gently leads those that are nursing.

12 Who has measured the waters in the hollow
of his hand
or marked off the heavens with the span
of his hand?
Who has gathered the dust of the earth
in a measure
or weighed the mountains on a balance
and the hills on the scales?
13 Who has directed[C] the Spirit of the LORD,
or who gave him counsel?
14 Who did he consult?
Who gave him understanding
and taught him the paths of justice?
Who taught him knowledge
and showed him the way of understanding?
15 Look, the nations are like a drop in a bucket;
they are considered as a speck of dust on
the scales;
he lifts up the islands like fine dust.
16 Lebanon's cedars are not enough for fuel,
or its animals enough for a burnt offering.
17 All the nations are as nothing before him;
they are considered by him
as empty nothingness.

18 With whom will you compare God?
What likeness will you set up for comparison
with him?
19 An idol? — something that a smelter casts
and a metalworker plates with gold
and makes silver chains for?
20 A poor person contributes wood for a pedestal
that will not rot.[D]
He looks for a skilled craftsman
to set up an idol that will not fall over.

21 Do you not know?
Have you not heard?
Has it not been declared to you
from the beginning?
Have you not considered
the foundations of the earth?
22 God is enthroned above the circle
of the earth;
its inhabitants are like grasshoppers.
He stretches out the heavens like thin cloth
and spreads them out like a tent to live in.
23 He reduces princes to nothing
and makes judges of the earth like a
wasteland.
24 They are barely planted, barely sown,
their stem hardly takes root in the ground
when he blows on them and they wither,
and a whirlwind carries them away
like stubble.

25 "To whom will you compare me,
or who is my equal?" asks the Holy One.
26 Look up and see!
Who created these?
He brings out the stars by number;
he calls all of them by name.
Because of his great power and strength,
not one of them is missing.

27 Jacob, why do you say,
and Israel, why do you assert,
"My way is hidden from the LORD,
and my claim is ignored by my God"?
28 Do you not know?
Have you not heard?
The LORD is the everlasting God,
the Creator of the whole earth.
He never becomes faint or weary;
there is no limit to his understanding.
29 He gives strength to the faint
and strengthens the powerless.
30 Youths may become faint and weary,
and young men stumble and fall,
31 but those who trust in the LORD
will renew their strength;
they will soar on wings like eagles;
they will run and not become weary,
they will walk and not faint.

[A] **40:7** Or *wind*, or *Spirit* [B] **40:7** Lit *it* [C] **40:13** Or *measured*, or *comprehended* [D] **40:20** Or *who is too poor for such an offering*, or *who chooses mulberry wood as a votive gift*; Hb obscure

THE LORD VERSUS THE NATIONS' GODS

41 "Be silent before me, coasts and islands!
And let peoples renew their strength.
Let them approach; let them testify;
let's come together for the trial.
2 Who has stirred up someone from the east?
In righteousness he calls him to serve.[A,B]
The LORD hands nations over to him,
and he subdues kings.
He makes them like dust with his sword,
like wind-driven stubble with his bow.
3 He pursues them, going on safely,
hardly touching the path with his feet.
4 Who has performed and done this,
calling the generations from the beginning?
I am the LORD, the first
and with the last — I am he."

5 The coasts and islands see and are afraid,
the whole earth trembles.
They approach and arrive.
6 Each one helps the other,
and says to another, "Take courage!"
7 The craftsman encourages the metalworker;
the one who flattens with the hammer
encourages the one who strikes the anvil,
saying of the soldering, "It is good."
He fastens it with nails so that it will not
fall over.

8 But you, Israel, my servant,
Jacob, whom I have chosen,
descendant of Abraham, my friend —
9 I brought[C] you from the ends of the earth
and called you from its farthest corners.
I said to you: You are my servant;
I have chosen you; I haven't rejected you.
10 Do not fear, for I am with you;
do not be afraid, for I am your God.
I will strengthen you; I will help you;
I will hold on to you with my righteous
right hand.

11 Be sure that all who are enraged against you
will be ashamed and disgraced;
those who contend with you
will become as nothing and will perish.
12 You will look for those who contend with you,
but you will not find them.
Those who war against you
will become absolutely nothing.
13 For I am the LORD your God,
who holds your right hand,
who says to you, "Do not fear,
I will help you.
14 Do not fear, you worm Jacob,
you men[D] of Israel.
I will help you" —
this is the LORD's declaration.
Your Redeemer is the Holy One of Israel.
15 See, I will make you
into a sharp threshing board,
new, with many teeth.
You will thresh mountains and pulverize them
and make hills into chaff.
16 You will winnow them
and a wind will carry them away,
a whirlwind will scatter them.
But you will rejoice in the LORD;
you will boast in the Holy One of Israel.

17 The poor and the needy seek water,
but there is none;
their tongues are parched with thirst.
I will answer them.
I am the LORD, the God of Israel. I will not
abandon them.
18 I will open rivers on the barren heights,
and springs in the middle of the plains.
I will turn the desert into a pool
and dry land into springs.
19 I will plant cedar, acacia, myrtle, and olive trees
in the wilderness.
I will put juniper, elm, and cypress trees
together
in the desert,
20 so that all may see and know,
consider and understand,
that the hand of the LORD has done this,
the Holy One of Israel has created it.

21 "Submit your case," says the LORD.
"Present your arguments," says Jacob's King.
22 "Let them come and tell us
what will happen.
Tell us the past events,
so that we may reflect on them
and know the outcome,
or tell us the future.
23 Tell us the coming events,
then we will know that you are gods.
Indeed, do something good or bad,
then we will be in awe[E] when we see it.
24 Look, you are nothing
and your work is worthless.
Anyone who chooses you is detestable.

[A] **41:2** Or *Righteousness calls him to serve* [B] **41:2** Lit *to his foot*
[C] **41:9** Or *seized* [D] **41:14** LXX reads *small number*; DSS read *dead ones*
[E] **41:23** DSS read *we may hear*

25 "I have stirred up one from the north,
and he has come,
one from the east who invokes my[A] name.
He will march over rulers as if they were mud,
like a potter who treads the clay.
26 Who told about this from the beginning,
so that we might know,
and from times past,
so that we might say, 'He is right'?
No one announced it,
no one told it,
no one heard your words.
27 I was the first to say to Zion,[B]
'Look! Here they are!'
And I gave Jerusalem a herald
with good news.
28 When I look, there is no one;
there is no counselor among them;
when I ask them, they have nothing to say.
29 Look, all of them are a delusion;[C]
their works are nonexistent;
their images are wind and emptiness.

THE SERVANT'S MISSION

42 "This is my servant; I strengthen him,
this is my chosen one; I delight in him.
I have put my Spirit on him;
he will bring justice[D] to the nations.
2 He will not cry out or shout
or make his voice heard in the streets.
3 He will not break a bruised reed,
and he will not put out a smoldering wick;
he will faithfully bring justice.
4 He will not grow weak or be discouraged
until he has established justice on earth.
The coasts and islands will wait
for his instruction."

5 This is what God, the LORD, says —
who created the heavens and stretched
them out,
who spread out the earth and what comes
from it,
who gives breath to the people on it
and spirit to those who walk on it —
6 "I am the LORD. I have called you
for a righteous purpose,[E]
and I will hold you by your hand.
I will watch over you, and I will appoint you
to be a covenant for the people
and a light to the nations,
7 in order to open blind eyes,
to bring out prisoners from the dungeon,
and those sitting in darkness
from the prison house.
8 I am the LORD. That is my name,
and I will not give my glory to another
or my praise to idols.
9 The past events have indeed happened.
Now I declare new events;
I announce them to you before they occur."

A SONG OF PRAISE

10 Sing a new song to the LORD;
sing his praise from the ends of the earth,
you who go down to the sea with all
that fills it,
you coasts and islands with your[F] inhabitants.
11 Let the desert and its cities shout,
the settlements where Kedar dwells cry aloud.
Let the inhabitants of Sela sing for joy;
let them cry out from the mountaintops.
12 Let them give glory to the LORD
and declare his praise in the coasts
and islands.
13 The LORD advances like a warrior;
he stirs up his zeal like a soldier.
He shouts, he roars aloud,
he prevails over his enemies.

14 "I have kept silent from ages past;
I have been quiet and restrained myself.
But now, I will groan like a woman in labor,
gasping breathlessly.
15 I will lay waste mountains and hills
and dry up all their vegetation.
I will turn rivers into islands
and dry up marshes.
16 I will lead the blind by a way
they did not know;
I will guide them on paths they have not known.
I will turn darkness to light in front of them
and rough places into level ground.
This is what I will do for them,
and I will not abandon them.
17 They will be turned back
and utterly ashamed —
those who trust in an idol
and say to a cast image,
'You are our gods!'

ISRAEL'S BLINDNESS AND DEAFNESS

18 "Listen, you deaf!
Look, you blind, so that you may see.
19 Who is blind but my servant,
or deaf like my messenger I am sending?

[A] **41:25** DSS read *his* [B] **41:27** Lit *First to Zion* [C] **41:29** DSS, Syr read *are nothing* [D] **42:1** DSS read *his justice* [E] **42:6** Or *you by my righteousness*; lit *you in righteousness* [F] **42:10** Lit *their*

Who is blind like my dedicated one,[A]
or blind like the servant of the LORD?
20 Though seeing many things,[B]
you pay no attention.
Though his ears are open, he does not listen."

21 Because of his righteousness, the LORD was pleased
to magnify his instruction
and make it glorious.
22 But this is a people plundered and looted,
all of them trapped in holes
or imprisoned in dungeons.
They have become plunder
with no one to rescue them
and loot, with no one saying, "Give it back!"
23 Who among you will hear this?
Let him listen and obey in the future.
24 Who gave Jacob to the robber,[C]
and Israel to the plunderers?
Was it not the LORD?
Have we not sinned against him?
They were not willing to walk in his ways,
and they would not listen to his instruction.
25 So he poured out his furious anger
and the power of war on Jacob.
It surrounded him with fire, but he did not know it;
it burned him, but he didn't take it to heart.

RESTORATION OF ISRAEL

43 Now this is what the LORD says —
the one who created you, Jacob,
and the one who formed you, Israel —
"Do not fear, for I have redeemed you;
I have called you by your name; you are mine.
2 When you pass through the waters,
I will be with you,
and the rivers will not overwhelm you.
When you walk through the fire,
you will not be scorched,
and the flame will not burn you.
3 For I am the LORD your God,
the Holy One of Israel, and your Savior.
I have given Egypt as a ransom for you,
Cush and Seba in your place.
4 Because you are precious in my sight
and honored, and I love you,
I will give people in exchange for you
and nations instead of your life.
5 Do not fear, for I am with you;
I will bring your descendants from the east,
and gather you from the west.
6 I will say to the north, 'Give them up!'
and to the south, 'Do not hold them back!'
Bring my sons from far away,
and my daughters from the ends of the earth —
7 everyone who bears my name
and is created for my glory.
I have formed them;
indeed, I have made them."

8 Bring out a people who are blind, yet have eyes,
and are deaf, yet have ears.
9 All the nations are gathered together,
and the peoples are assembled.
Who among them can declare this,
and tell us the former things?
Let them present their witnesses
to vindicate themselves,
so that people may hear and say, "It is true."
10 "You are my witnesses" —
this is the LORD's declaration —
"and my servant whom I have chosen,
so that you may know and believe me
and understand that I am he.
No god was formed before me,
and there will be none after me.
11 I — I am the LORD.
Besides me, there is no Savior.
12 I alone declared, saved, and proclaimed —
and not some foreign god[D] among you.
So you are my witnesses" —
this is the LORD's declaration —
"and[E] I am God.
13 Also, from today on I am he alone,
and none can rescue from my power.
I act, and who can reverse it?"

GOD'S DELIVERANCE OF REBELLIOUS ISRAEL

14 This is what the LORD, your Redeemer, the Holy One of Israel says:
Because of you, I will send an army[F] to Babylon
and bring all of them as fugitives,[G]
even the Chaldeans in the ships in which
they rejoice.[A]
15 I am the LORD, your Holy One,
the Creator of Israel, your King.

16 This is what the LORD says —
who makes a way in the sea,
and a path through raging water,
17 who brings out the chariot and horse,
the army and the mighty one together
(they lie down, they do not rise again;
they are extinguished, put out like a wick) —

[A] **42:19; 43:14** Hb obscure [B] **42:20** Alt Hb tradition reads *You see many things;* [C] **42:24** Lit *to loot* [D] **43:12** Lit *not a foreigner* [E] **43:12** Or *that* [F] **43:14** *an army* supplied for clarity [G] **43:14** Or *will break down all their bars*

18 "Do not remember the past events;
pay no attention to things of old.
19 Look, I am about to do something new;
even now it is coming. Do you not see it?
Indeed, I will make a way in the wilderness,
rivers[A] in the desert.
20 Wild animals —
jackals and ostriches — will honor me,
because I provide water in the wilderness,
and rivers in the desert,
to give drink to my chosen people.
21 The people I formed for myself
will declare my praise.

22 "But, Jacob, you have not called on me,
because, Israel, you have become weary of me.
23 You have not brought me your sheep
for burnt offerings
or honored me with your sacrifices.
I have not burdened you with offerings
or wearied you with incense.[B]
24 You have not bought me aromatic cane
with silver,
or satisfied me with the fat of your sacrifices.
But you have burdened me with your sins;
you have wearied me with your iniquities.

25 "I am the one, I sweep away
your transgressions
for my own sake
and remember your sins no more.
26 Remind me. Let's argue the case together.
Recount the facts, so that you may
be vindicated.
27 Your first father sinned,
and your mediators have rebelled against me.
28 So I defiled the officers of the sanctuary,
and set Jacob apart for destruction
and Israel for scorn.

SPIRITUAL BLESSING

44 "And now listen, Jacob my servant,
Israel whom I have chosen.
2 This is the word of the LORD
your Maker, the one who formed you
from the womb:
He will help you.
Do not fear, Jacob my servant,
Jeshurun[C] whom I have chosen.
3 For I will pour water on the thirsty land
and streams on the dry ground;
I will pour out my Spirit on your descendants
and my blessing on your offspring.
4 They will sprout among[D] the grass
like poplars by flowing streams.
5 This one will say, 'I am the LORD's';
another will use the name of Jacob;
still another will write on his hand,
'The LORD's,'
and take on the name of Israel."

NO GOD OTHER THAN THE LORD

6 This is what the LORD, the King of Israel and its Re-
deemer, the LORD of Armies, says:
I am the first and I am the last.
There is no God but me.
7 Who, like me, can announce the future?
Let him say so and make a case before me,
since I have established an ancient people.
Let these gods declare[E] the coming things,
and what will take place.
8 Do not be startled or afraid.
Have I not told you and declared it long ago?
You are my witnesses!
Is there any God but me?
There is no other Rock; I do not know any.

9 All who make idols are nothing,
and what they treasure benefits no one.
Their witnesses do not see or know anything,
so they will be put to shame.
10 Who makes a god or casts a metal image
that benefits no one?
11 Look, all its worshipers will be put to shame,
and the craftsmen are humans.
They all will assemble and stand;
they all will be startled and put to shame.

12 The ironworker labors over the coals,
shapes the idol with hammers,
and works it with his strong arm.
Also he grows hungry and his strength fails;
he doesn't drink water and is faint.
13 The woodworker stretches out
a measuring line,
he outlines it with a stylus;
he shapes it with chisels
and outlines it with a compass.
He makes it according to a human form,
like a beautiful person,
to dwell in a temple.
14 He cuts down[F] cedars for his use,
or he takes a cypress or an oak.
He lets it grow strong among the trees
of the forest.
He plants a laurel, and the rain makes it grow.

[A] **43:19** DSS read *paths* [B] **43:23** I.e., with demands for offerings and incense [C] **44:2** = Upright One [D] **44:4** Some Hb mss, DSS, LXX read *as among* [E] **44:7** Lit *declare them* — [F] **44:14** Lit *To cut down for himself*

15 A person can use it for fuel.
He takes some of it and warms himself;
also he kindles a fire and bakes bread;
he even makes it into a god and worships it;
he makes an idol from it
and bows down to it.
16 He burns half of it in a fire,
and he roasts meat on that half.
He eats the roast and is satisfied.
He warms himself and says, "Ah!
I am warm, I see the blaze."
17 He makes a god or his idol with the rest of it.
He bows down to it and worships;
he prays to it, "Save me, for you are
my god."
18 Such people[A] do not comprehend
and cannot understand,
for he has shut their eyes[B]
so they cannot see,
and their minds so they cannot understand.
19 No one comes to his senses;[C]
no one has the perception or insight to say,
"I burned half of it in the fire,
I also baked bread on its coals,
I roasted meat and ate.
Should I make something detestable
with the rest of it?
Should I bow down to a block of wood?"
20 He feeds on[D] ashes.
His deceived mind has led him astray,
and he cannot rescue himself,
or say, "Isn't there a lie in my right hand?"

21 Remember these things, Jacob,
and Israel, for you are my servant;
I formed you, you are my servant;
Israel, you will never be forgotten by me.[E]
22 I have swept away your transgressions
like a cloud,
and your sins like a mist.
Return to me,
for I have redeemed you.
23 Rejoice, heavens, for the LORD has acted;
shout, depths of the earth.
Break out into singing, mountains,
forest, and every tree in it.
For the LORD has redeemed Jacob,
and glorifies himself through Israel.

RESTORATION OF ISRAEL THROUGH CYRUS

24 This is what the LORD, your Redeemer who formed
you from the womb, says:
I am the LORD, who made everything;
who stretched out the heavens by myself;
who alone spread out the earth;
25 who destroys the omens of the false prophets
and makes fools of diviners;
who confounds the wise
and makes their knowledge foolishness;
26 who confirms the message of his servant
and fulfills the counsel of his messengers;
who says to Jerusalem, "She will
be inhabited,"
and to the cities of Judah, "They will
be rebuilt,"
and I will restore her ruins;
27 who says to the depths of the sea, "Be dry,"
and I will dry up your rivers;
28 who says to Cyrus, "My shepherd,
he will fulfill all my pleasure"
and says to Jerusalem,
"She will be rebuilt,"
and of the temple, "Its foundation
will be laid."

45 The LORD says this to Cyrus, his anointed,
whose right hand I have grasped
to subdue nations before him
and disarm[F] kings,
to open doors before him,
and even city gates will not be shut:
2 "I will go before you
and level the uneven places;[G]
I will shatter the bronze doors
and cut the iron bars in two.
3 I will give you the treasures of darkness
and riches from secret places,
so that you may know that I am the LORD.
I am the God of Israel, who calls you
by your name.
4 I call you by your name,
for the sake of my servant Jacob
and Israel my chosen one.
I give a name to you,
though you do not know me.
5 I am the LORD, and there is no other;
there is no God but me.
I will strengthen[H] you,
though you do not know me,
6 so that all may know from the rising
of the sun to its setting
that there is no one but me.
I am the LORD, and there is no other.
7 I form light and create darkness,
I make success and create disaster;
I am the LORD, who does all these things.

[A] **44:18** Lit *They* [B] **44:18** Or *for their eyes are shut* [C] **44:19** Lit *No one returns to his heart* [D] **44:20** Or *He shepherds* [E] **44:21** DSS, LXX, Tg read *Israel, do not forget me* [F] **45:1** Lit *unloosen the waist of* [G] **45:2** DSS, LXX read *the mountains* [H] **45:5** Lit *gird*

DIGGING DEEPER *Cyrus Cylinder*

This Persian clay cylinder dating to the sixth century BC was written in Babylonian cuneiform. It describes King Cyrus's victory in 536 BC over Babylon, which fulfilled prophecies uttered by Isaiah (Is 45:1–13) and Daniel (Dn 2:36–39; 7:4–5,15–28). The cylinder, considered by some to be the first "charter of human rights," declares that Cyrus allowed freedom of worship, the return of foreign gods to their own land, and the rebuilding of destroyed cities and religious buildings (2Ch 36:22–23). The Persian king writes, "I returned to [the] sacred cities on the other side of the Tigris, the sanctuaries of which have been in ruins for a long time, the images which [used] to live therein and established for them permanent sanctuaries. I gathered all their inhabitants and returned them to their habitations." Remarkably, these royal Persian decrees conform to the prophecies enumerated in Isaiah 40–55, Daniel 8:15–27, and the historical accounts mentioned in Ezra 1:1–4; 6:1–5. Additionally, the fall of Babylon in 538 BC as recorded by Cyrus marks an end to Israel's seventy years of Babylonian captivity as prophesied in Jeremiah 25:9–13 and recognized in Daniel 9:2.

8 "Heavens, sprinkle from above,
and let the skies shower righteousness.
Let the earth open up
so that salvation will sprout
and righteousness will spring up with it.
I, the LORD, have created it.

9 "Woe to the one who argues with his Maker —
one clay pot among many.[A]
Does clay say to the one forming it,
'What are you making?'
Or does your work say,
'He has no hands'?[B]
10 Woe to the one who says to his father,
'What are you fathering?'
or to his mother,[C]
'What are you giving birth to?'"
11 This is what the LORD,
the Holy One of Israel and its Maker, says:
"Ask me what is to happen to[D] my sons,
and instruct me about the work of my hands.
12 I made the earth,
and created humans on it.
It was my hands that stretched out
the heavens,
and I commanded everything in them.
13 I have stirred him up in righteousness,
and will level all roads for him.
He will rebuild my city,
and set my exiles free,
not for a price or a bribe,"
says the LORD of Armies.

GOD ALONE IS THE SAVIOR

14 This is what the LORD says:
"The products of Egypt and the merchandise
of Cush
and the Sabeans, men of stature,
will come over to you
and will be yours;
they will follow you,
they will come over in chains
and bow down to you.
They will confess[E] to you,
'God is indeed with you, and there is no other;
there is no other God.'"

15 Yes, you are a God who hides,
God of Israel, Savior.
16 All of them are put to shame, even humiliated;
the makers of idols go in humiliation together.
17 Israel will be saved by the LORD
with an everlasting salvation;
you will not be put to shame or humiliated
for all eternity.

18 For this is what the LORD says —
the Creator of the heavens,
the God who formed the earth and made it,
the one who established it
(he did not create it to be a wasteland,
but formed it to be inhabited) —
he says, "I am the LORD,
and there is no other.
19 I have not spoken in secret,
somewhere in a land of darkness.
I did not say to the descendants of Jacob:
Seek me in a wasteland.
I am the LORD, who speaks righteously,
who declares what is right.

20 "Come, gather together,
and approach, you fugitives of the nations.
Those who carry their wooden idols
and pray to a god who cannot save
have no knowledge.
21 Speak up and present your case[F] —
yes, let them consult each other.

[A] **45:9** Lit *a clay pot with clay pots of the ground* [B] **45:9** Or *making? Your work has no hands.* [C] **45:10** Lit *to a woman* [D] **45:11** Or *me the coming things about* [E] **45:14** Lit *pray* [F] **45:21** Lit *and approach*

Cyrus the Great

by W. Wayne VanHorn

When Alexander the Great found the tomb of Persian King Cyrus II, known as Cyrus the Great, in ancient Pasargadae, an inscription was supposedly on the tomb that has since disappeared, although the tomb remains. It is reported to have said, "O man, I am Cyrus son of Cambyses, who founded the empire of Persia and ruled over Asia. Do not grudge me my monument."[1]

RISING TO POWER

Cyrus's meteoric rise to power began near the site where his tomb now stands. With his defeat of Astyages, king of the Medes, in 559 BC at Pasargadae, Cyrus became the leader of both the Mede and Persian kingdoms. Then in the winter of 546 BC, his additional victory over Croesus, king of Lydia (560–546 BC), strengthened his control, swelled his armies, and presented Cyrus as a legitimate rival to the dominant world power of the day, Babylon.

Three years before Cyrus's victory over Astyages at Pasargadae, Nebuchadnezzar, the great king of Babylon, had died. Following his death in 562 BC, Babylon was ruled by a quick succession of incompetent leaders before Nabonidus ascended to the throne in 556 BC. Nabonidus brought a measure of stability to Babylon, but his ineffectual policies and practices spelled the certain doom of the Babylonian Empire at precisely the same time that Cyrus was on the rise. On October 29, 539 BC, Cyrus entered the city of Babylon unopposed. The great Babylonian Empire that had conquered the world, destroyed Jerusalem, devastated the temple, and deported the Jews was now itself the victim of a conquering king. With the acquisition of Babylon, Cyrus became the undisputed king of the earth.[2]

RECORDING HISTORY

The current phenomenon of "spin doctors" seeking to gain popular consent for their political candidate's view is hardly new. Cyrus published many propaganda pieces to put a positive spin on his accomplishments and to solidify his rule over conquered peoples. One such propaganda piece is a nine-inch-long, baked clay cylinder discovered in 1879, known as the Cyrus Cylinder. On it, Cyrus recounted his conquest of the city of Babylon. Rather than writing of military prowess, the overwhelming might of his armies, or the superiority of his battle strategies, Cyrus depicted himself as a liberating, benevolent hero to the people of Babylon. He accredited his success to Marduk, a chief god of the Babylonians. He even boasted that Bel and Nebo, also Babylonian gods, loved his rule.

Nabonidus had taken a ten-year leave from Babylon and relocated to the oasis of Tema in the Arabian Desert, leaving his son, Belshazzar, in charge of the capital city. Nabonidus had also forsaken the traditional gods of Babylon, including Marduk, Bel, and Nebo. He worshiped a moon-god called Sin. The priests of Marduk in Babylon detested this religious move and thus ensured they would throw their support behind Cyrus, viewing him as an agent of their great god, Marduk. Cyrus

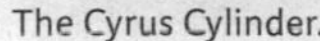

The Cyrus Cylinder.

Tomb of Cyrus the Great, located near Shiraz, Iran. It is about 45 feet by 40 feet at its base and 36 feet high.

seized the opportunity to propagandize his victory, couching it in terms of Marduk's will.

AFFECTING GOD'S PEOPLE

The Hebrews knew that Yahweh, not Marduk, was the one true God and Lord of history. Yahweh, not Marduk, empowered Cyrus to overthrow Babylon and become the dominant leader of the world (2Ch 36:22–23; Ezr 1:1–4; 5:13–15; 6:3–5). Under Yahweh's direction, Cyrus freed the Hebrews exiled in Babylon, permitting them to return to Judah and to rebuild the temple. The ascendancy of Cyrus was a fulfillment of prophecy uttered by Isaiah almost two centuries earlier (Is 44:24–28). Yahweh referred to Cyrus as "my shepherd," calling forth the image of the Hebrews as God's flock. God would tend his sheep through his shepherd Cyrus. The prophecy clearly indicated the Lord would make all these things happen, but he would do so through Cyrus.

Inscribed brick: "Cyrus king of the world, king of Anshan, son of Cambyses, king of Anshan. The great gods delivered all the lands into my hand, and I made this land to dwell in peace."

In Isaiah 45:1–19, the prophet no doubt astounded his audience by declaring Yahweh's designation of Cyrus as "his anointed." This title is the Hebrew word *mashiyach* and was never used elsewhere of a non-Hebrew. But the anointing concept referred to God's empowerment of people to serve him as he chose. The term was applied to kings, prophets, and priests. The ultimate application of the title, of course, is to Jesus of Nazareth, the one true Messiah of all humankind.

Nabonidus Chronicle describing his withdrawal from Babylon for Tema, and also Cyrus's founding of the Achaemenid Empire.

The name Cyrus appears twenty-three times in the Old Testament. In addition to his name in Isaiah (three times), he appears in Ezra, 2 Chronicles, and Daniel. His activity was also a fulfillment of Yahweh's prophecy to Jeremiah (Jr 29:10–14) that the Lord would remember his people and bring them home from captivity. The language of Cyrus's decree in the Bible parallels the language of the decree inscribed on the Cyrus Cylinder. These parallels indicate that Cyrus used similar language for all captive peoples, cited the name of their gods, granted captives permission to return to their native lands, and reestablished each group's unique worship forms. None of this diminishes the biblical record that the Lord enabled Cyrus. In Isaiah 45:4, the prophet declared, "I call you [Cyrus] by your name, for the sake of my servant Jacob and Israel my chosen one. I give a name to you, though you do not know me." This last phrase candidly admits that Cyrus himself did not acknowledge the Lord in any way other than in the language of political expediency.

The book of Ezra begins with an expanded form of the decree of Cyrus found in 2 Chronicles 36:22–23. The context of the decree underscored that the Lord had put it on Cyrus's heart to free the captive Jews, send them home, and enable the rebuilding of the temple. The Ezra passage added that Cyrus encouraged those Jews who were not returning to contribute to the financial success of the temple rebuilding project (Ezr 1:4). We learn from Ezra 4:3–5 that all the days of Cyrus the people of the land of Israel frustrated the Jews' attempts to rebuild the temple. References to Cyrus in Ezra 5:13–17 are part of a letter the local governor sent to Cyrus's successor, Darius, to ascertain the validity of the rebuilding project. Darius responded in the affirmative that the temple was indeed to be rebuilt at the decree of Cyrus, adding his own authorization (6:3,14).

Three additional references to Cyrus in the book of Daniel are useful for date referencing but carry no real interpretive significance.[3] The story of how Cyrus advanced the cause of God's people serves as a historical example of the Lord's sovereignty over all nations. The God whom we know through Christ Jesus, the good Shepherd, is truly an awesome God.

---

[1] Arrian, *Anabasis* 6.29. [2] Michael D. Coogan, ed., *The Oxford History of the Biblical World* (New York: Oxford University Press, 1998), 361–65, 375. [3] See Dn 1:21 (depicts Daniel as still serving in Cyrus's first year, 539 BC, which was Cyrus's first year of control over Babylon. This would make Dn 1:21 consistent with 2Ch 36:22–23 and Ezr 1:1–4 where the reference to Cyrus's first year is to his first year of rule over Babylon, not to his first year as king of the Medio-Persian Empire, twenty years earlier); Dn 6:28 (a passing reference to Cyrus); and Dn 10:1 (useful for dating Daniel's vision to about 537 BC).

Who predicted this long ago?
Who announced it from ancient times?
Was it not I, the LORD?
There is no other God but me,
a righteous God and Savior;
there is no one except me.
22 Turn to me and be saved,
all the ends of the earth.
For I am God,
and there is no other.
23 By myself I have sworn;
truth has gone from my mouth,
a word that will not be revoked:
Every knee will bow to me,
every tongue will swear allegiance.
24 It will be said about me, 'Righteousness
and strength
are found only in the LORD.'"
All who are enraged against him
will come to him and be put to shame.
25 All the descendants of Israel
will be justified and boast in the LORD.

THERE IS NO ONE LIKE GOD

46 Bel crouches; Nebo cowers.
Idols depicting them are consigned
to beasts and cattle.
The images you carry are loaded,
as a burden for the weary animal.
2 The gods cower; they crouch together;
they are not able to rescue the burden,
but they themselves go into captivity.

3 "Listen to me, house of Jacob,
all the remnant of the house of Israel,
who have been sustained from the womb,
carried along since birth.
4 I will be the same until your old age,
and I will bear you up when you turn gray.
I have made you, and I will carry you;
I will bear and rescue you.

5 "To whom will you compare me or make me
equal?
Who will you measure me with,
so that we should be like each other?
6 Those who pour out their bags of gold
and weigh out silver on scales —
they hire a goldsmith and he makes it into a god.
Then they kneel and bow down to it.
7 They lift it to their shoulder and bear it along;
they set it in its place, and there it stands;
it does not budge from its place.
They cry out to it but it doesn't answer;
it saves no one from his trouble.

8 "Remember this and be brave;[A]
take it to heart, you transgressors!
9 Remember what happened long ago,
for I am God, and there is no other;
I am God, and no one is like me.
10 I declare the end from the beginning,
and from long ago what is not yet done,
saying: my plan will take place,
and I will do all my will.
11 I call a bird of prey[B] from the east,
a man for my purpose from a far country.
Yes, I have spoken; so I will also
bring it about.
I have planned it; I will also do it.
12 Listen to me, you hardhearted,
far removed from justice:
13 I am bringing my justice near;
it is not far away,
and my salvation will not delay.
I will put salvation in Zion,
my splendor in Israel.

THE FALL OF BABYLON

47 "Go down and sit in the dust,
Virgin Daughter Babylon.
Sit on the ground without a throne,
Daughter Chaldea!
For you will no longer be called pampered
and spoiled.
2 Take millstones and grind flour;
remove your veil,
strip off your skirt, bare your thigh,
wade through the streams.
3 Your nakedness will be uncovered,
and your disgrace will be exposed.
I will take vengeance;
I will spare no one."[A]
4 The Holy One of Israel is our Redeemer;
The LORD of Armies is his name.

5 "Daughter Chaldea,
sit in silence and go into darkness.
For you will no longer be called mistress
of kingdoms.
6 I was angry with my people;
I profaned my possession,
and I handed them over to you.
You showed them no mercy;
you made your yoke very heavy
on the elderly.
7 You said, 'I will be the queen forever.'
You did not take these things to heart
or think about their outcome.

[A] **46:8; 47:3** Hb obscure [B] **46:11** = Cyrus

8 "So now hear this, lover of luxury,
who sits securely,
who says to herself,
'I am, and there is no one else.
I will never be a widow
or know the loss of children.'
9 These two things will happen to you
suddenly, in one day:
loss of children and widowhood.
They will happen to you in their entirety,
in spite of your many sorceries
and the potency of your spells.
10 You were secure in your wickedness;
you said, 'No one sees me.'
Your wisdom and knowledge
led you astray.
You said to yourself,
'I am, and there is no one else.'
11 But disaster will happen to you;
you will not know how to avert it.
And it will fall on you,
but you will be unable to ward it off.[A]
Devastation will happen to you suddenly
and unexpectedly.
12 So take your stand with your spells
and your many sorceries,
which you have wearied yourself with
from your youth.
Perhaps you will be able to succeed;
perhaps you will inspire terror!
13 You are worn out
with your many consultations.
So let the astrologers stand and save you —
those who observe the stars,
those who predict monthly
what will happen to you.
14 Look, they are like stubble;
fire burns them.
They cannot rescue themselves
from the power of the flame.
This is not a coal for warming themselves,
or a fire to sit beside!
15 This is what they are to you —
those who have wearied you
and have traded with you from your youth —
each wanders on his own way;
no one can save you.

ISRAEL MUST LEAVE BABYLON

48 "Listen to this, house of Jacob —
those who are called by the name Israel
and have descended from[B] Judah,
who swear by the name of the LORD
and declare the God of Israel,
but not in truth or righteousness.
2 For they are named after the holy city,
and lean on the God of Israel;
his name is the LORD of Armies.
3 I declared the past events long ago;
they came out of my mouth;
I proclaimed them.
Suddenly I acted, and they occurred.
4 Because I know that you are stubborn,
and your neck is iron[C]
and your forehead bronze,
5 therefore I declared to you long ago.
I announced it to you before it occurred,
so you could not claim, 'My idol caused them;
my carved image and cast idol control them.'
6 You have heard it. Observe it all.
Will you not acknowledge it?
From now on I will announce new things
to you,
hidden things that you have not known.
7 They have been created now, and not long ago;
you have not heard of them before today,
so you could not claim, 'I already knew them!'
8 You have never heard; you have
never known;
for a long time your ears have not been open.
For I knew that you were very treacherous,
and were known as a rebel from birth.
9 I will delay my anger for the sake of my name,
and I will restrain myself for your benefit
and for my praise,
so that you will not be destroyed.
10 Look, I have refined you, but not as silver;
I have tested[D] you in the furnace of affliction.
11 I will act for my own sake, indeed, my own,
for how can I[E] be defiled?
I will not give my glory to another.

12 "Listen to me, Jacob,
and Israel, the one called by me:
I am he; I am the first,
I am also the last.
13 My own hand founded the earth,
and my right hand spread out the heavens;
when I summoned them,
they stood up together.
14 All of you, assemble and listen!
Who among the idols[F] has declared
these things?
The LORD loves him;[G]
he will accomplish his will against Babylon,
and his arm will be against the Chaldeans.

[A] 47:11 Or *to atone for it* [B] 48:1 Lit *have come from the waters of* [C] 48:4 Lit *is an iron sinew* [D] 48:10 DSS; MT reads *chosen* [E] 48:11 DSS, Syr; MT reads *it* [F] 48:14 Lit *among them* [G] 48:14 = Cyrus

15 I — I have spoken;
yes, I have called him;
I have brought him,
and he will succeed in his mission.
16 Approach me and listen to this.
From the beginning I have not spoken in secret;
from the time anything existed, I was there."
And now the Lord GOD
has sent me and his Spirit.

17 This is what the LORD, your Redeemer, the Holy
One of Israel says:
I am the LORD your God,
who teaches you for your benefit,
who leads you in the way you should go.
18 If only you had paid attention to my commands.
Then your peace would have been like a river,
and your righteousness like the waves
of the sea.
19 Your descendants would have been
as countless as the sand,
and the offspring of your body like its grains;
their name would not be cut off
or eliminated from my presence.

20 Leave Babylon,
flee from the Chaldeans!
Declare with a shout of joy,
proclaim this,
let it go out to the end of the earth;
announce,
"The LORD has redeemed his servant Jacob!"
21 They did not thirst
when he led them through the deserts;
he made water flow from the rock for them;
he split the rock, and water gushed out.
22 "There is no peace for the wicked,"
says the LORD.

THE SERVANT BRINGS SALVATION

49 Coasts and islands,[A] listen to me;
distant peoples, pay attention.
The LORD called me before I was born.
He named me while I was
in my mother's womb.
2 He made my words like a sharp sword;
he hid me in the shadow of his hand.
He made me like a sharpened arrow;
he hid me in his quiver.
3 He said to me, "You are my servant,
Israel, in whom I will be glorified."
4 But I myself said: I have labored in vain,
I have spent my strength for nothing and futility;
yet my vindication is with the LORD,
and my reward is with my God.

5 And now, says the LORD,
who formed me from the womb to be
his servant,
to bring Jacob back to him
so that Israel might be gathered to him;
for I am honored in the sight of the LORD,
and my God is my strength —
6 he says,
"It is not enough for you to be my servant
raising up the tribes of Jacob
and restoring the protected ones of Israel.
I will also make you a light for the nations,
to be my salvation to the ends of the earth."
7 This is what the LORD,
the Redeemer of Israel, his Holy One, says
to one who is despised,
to one abhorred by people,[B]
to a servant of rulers:
"Kings will see, princes will stand up,
and they[C] will all bow down
because of the LORD, who is faithful,
the Holy One of Israel —
and he has chosen you."

8 This is what the LORD says:
I will answer you in a time of favor,
and I will help you in the day of salvation.
I will keep you, and I will appoint you
to be a covenant for the people,
to restore the land,
to make them possess
the desolate inheritances,
9 saying to the prisoners, "Come out,"
and to those who are in darkness,
"Show yourselves."
They will feed along the pathways,
and their pastures will be on all
the barren heights.
10 They will not hunger or thirst,
the scorching heat or sun will not strike them;
for their compassionate one will guide them,
and lead them to springs.
11 I will make all my mountains into a road,
and my highways will be raised up.
12 See, these will come from far away,
from the north and from the west,[D]
and from the land of Sinim.[E,F]

13 Shout for joy, you heavens!
Earth, rejoice!
Mountains break into joyful shouts!

[A] **49:1** Or *Islands* [B] **49:7** Or *by the nation* [C] **49:7** Lit *princes and they* [D] **49:12** Lit *sea* [E] **49:12** DSS read *of the Syenites* [F] **49:12** Perhaps modern Aswan in southern Egypt

For the LORD has comforted his people,
and will have compassion on his afflicted ones.

ZION REMEMBERED

14 Zion says, "The LORD has abandoned me;
the Lord has forgotten me!"
15 "Can a woman forget her nursing child,
or lack compassion for the child of her womb?
Even if these forget,
yet I will not forget you.
16 Look, I have inscribed you on the palms
of my hands;
your walls are continually before me.
17 Your builders[A] hurry;
those who destroy and devastate you
will leave you.
18 Look up, and look around.
They all gather together; they come to you.
As I live" —
this is the LORD's declaration —
"you will wear all your children[B] as jewelry,
and put them on as a bride does.
19 For your waste and desolate places
and your land marked by ruins
will now be indeed too small
for the inhabitants,
and those who swallowed you up will be
far away.
20 Yet as you listen, the children
that you have been deprived of will say,
'This place is too small for me;
make room for me so that I may settle.'
21 Then you will say within yourself,
'Who fathered these for me?
I was deprived of my children and unable
to conceive,
exiled and wandering —
but who brought them up?
See, I was left by myself —
but these, where did they come from?'"[C]

22 This is what the Lord GOD says:
Look, I will lift up my hand to the nations,
and raise my banner to the peoples.
They will bring your sons in their arms,
and your daughters will be carried
on their shoulders.
23 Kings will be your guardians
and their queens[D] your nursing mothers.
They will bow down to you
with their faces to the ground
and lick the dust at your feet.
Then you will know that I am the LORD;
those who put their hope in me
will not be put to shame.
24 Can the prey be taken from a mighty man,
or the captives of a tyrant[E] be delivered?
25 For this is what the LORD says:
"Even the captives of a mighty man
will be taken,
and the prey of a tyrant will be delivered;
I will contend with the one who contends
with you,
and I will save your children.
26 I will make your oppressors eat
their own flesh,
and they will be drunk with their own blood
as with sweet wine.
Then all humanity will know
that I, the LORD, am your Savior,
and your Redeemer, the Mighty One of Jacob."

50 This is what the LORD says:
Where is your mother's divorce certificate
that I used to send her away?
Or to which of my creditors did I sell you?
Look, you were sold for your iniquities,
and your mother was sent away
because of your transgressions.
2 Why was no one there when I came?
Why was there no one to answer
when I called?
Is my arm too weak to redeem?
Or do I have no power to rescue?
Look, I dry up the sea by my rebuke;
I turn the rivers into a wilderness;
their fish rot because of lack of water
and die of thirst.
3 I dress the heavens in black
and make sackcloth their covering.

THE OBEDIENT SERVANT

4 The Lord GOD has given me
the tongue of those who are instructed
to know how to sustain the weary
with a word.
He awakens me each morning;
he awakens my ear to listen like those
being instructed.
5 The Lord GOD has opened my ear,
and I was not rebellious;
I did not turn back.
6 I gave my back to those who beat me,
and my cheeks to those who tore out
my beard.
I did not hide my face from scorn and spitting.

[A] **49:17** DSS, Aq, Theod, Vg; MT, Syr, Sym read *sons* [B] **49:18** Lit *all of them* [C] **49:21** Lit *where are they* [D] **49:23** Lit *princesses* [E] **49:24** DSS, Syr, Vg; MT reads *a righteous man*

7 The Lord God will help me;
therefore I have not been humiliated;
therefore I have set my face like flint,
and I know I will not be put to shame.
8 The one who vindicates me is near;
who will contend with me?
Let us confront each other.[A]
Who has a case against me?[B]
Let him come near me!
9 In truth, the Lord God will help me;
who will condemn me?
Indeed, all of them will wear out
like a garment;
a moth will devour them.
10 Who among you fears the LORD
and listens to his servant?
Who among you walks in darkness,
and has no light?
Let him trust in the name of the LORD;
let him lean on his God.
11 Look, all you who kindle a fire,
who encircle yourselves with[C] torches;
walk in the light of your fire
and of the torches you have lit!
This is what you'll get from my hand:
you will lie down in a place of torment.

SALVATION FOR ZION

51 Listen to me, you who pursue righteousness,
you who seek the LORD:
Look to the rock from which you were cut,
and to the quarry from which you were dug.
2 Look to Abraham your father,
and to Sarah who gave birth to you.
When I called him, he was only one;
I blessed him and made him many.
3 For the LORD will comfort Zion;
he will comfort all her waste places,
and he will make her wilderness like Eden,
and her desert like the garden of the LORD.
Joy and gladness will be found in her,
thanksgiving and melodious song.

4 Pay attention to me, my people,
and listen to me, my nation;
for instruction will come from me,
and my justice for a light to the nations.
I will bring it about quickly.
5 My righteousness is near,
my salvation appears,
and my arms will bring justice
to the nations.
The coasts and islands will put their hope
in me,
and they will look to my strength.[D]
6 Look up to the heavens,
and look at the earth beneath;
for the heavens will vanish like smoke,
the earth will wear out like a garment,
and its inhabitants will die like gnats.[E]
But my salvation will last forever,
and my righteousness will never be shattered.

7 Listen to me, you who know righteousness,
the people in whose heart is my instruction:
do not fear disgrace by men,
and do not be shattered by their taunts.
8 For moths will devour them like a garment,
and worms will eat them like wool.
But my righteousness will last forever,
and my salvation for all generations.

9 Wake up, wake up!
Arm of the LORD, clothe yourself with
strength.
Wake up as in days past,
as in generations long ago.
Wasn't it you who hacked Rahab to pieces,
who pierced the sea monster?
10 Wasn't it you who dried up the sea,
the waters of the great deep,
who made the sea-bed into a road
for the redeemed to pass over?
11 And the ransomed of the LORD will return
and come to Zion with singing,
crowned with unending joy.
Joy and gladness will overtake them,
and sorrow and sighing will flee.

12 I — I am the one who comforts you.
Who are you that you should fear humans
who die,
or a son of man who is given up like grass?
13 But you have forgotten the LORD, your Maker,
who stretched out the heavens
and laid the foundations of the earth.
You are in constant dread all day long
because of the fury of the oppressor,
who has set himself to destroy.
But where is the fury of the oppressor?
14 The prisoner[F] is soon to be set free;
he will not die and go to the Pit,
and his food will not be lacking.
15 For I am the LORD your God
who stirs up the sea so that its waves roar —
his name is the LORD of Armies.

[A] **50:8** Lit *us stand* [B] **50:8** Lit *Who is lord of my judgment* [C] **50:11** Syr reads *who set ablaze* [D] **51:5** Lit *arm* [E] **51:6** Or *die in like manner* [F] **51:14** Hb obscure

16 I have put my words in your mouth,
and covered you in the shadow of my hand,
in order to plant[A] the heavens,
to found the earth,
and to say to Zion, "You are my people."

17 Wake yourself, wake yourself up!
Stand up, Jerusalem,
you who have drunk the cup of his fury
from the LORD's hand;
you who have drunk the goblet to the dregs —
the cup that causes people to stagger.
18 There is no one to guide her
among all the children she has raised;
there is no one to take hold of her hand
among all the offspring she has brought up.
19 These two things have happened to you:
devastation and destruction,
famine and sword.
Who will grieve for you?
How can I[B] comfort you?
20 Your children have fainted;
they lie at the head of every street
like an antelope in a net.
They are full of the LORD's fury,
the rebuke of your God.

21 So listen to this, suffering
and drunken one — but not with wine.
22 This is what your Lord says —
the LORD, even your God,
who defends his people —
"Look, I have removed from your hand
the cup that causes staggering;
that goblet, the cup of my fury.
You will never drink it again.
23 I will put it into the hands of your tormentors,
who said to you,
'Lie down, so we can walk over you.'
You made your back like the ground,
and like a street for those who walk on it.

52 "Wake up, wake up;
put on your strength, Zion!
Put on your beautiful garments,
Jerusalem, the holy city!
For the uncircumcised and the unclean
will no longer enter you.
2 Stand up, shake the dust off yourself!
Take your seat, Jerusalem.
Remove the bonds[C] from your neck,
captive Daughter Zion."
3 For this is what the LORD says:
"You were sold for nothing,
and you will be redeemed without silver."
4 For this is what the Lord GOD says:
"At first my people went down to Egypt
to reside there,
then Assyria oppressed them
without cause.[D]
5 So now what have I here" —
this is the LORD's declaration —
"that my people are taken away
for nothing?
Its rulers wail" —
this is the LORD's declaration —
"and my name is continually blasphemed
all day long.
6 Therefore my people will know my name;
therefore they will know on that day
that I am he who says,
'Here I am.'"

7 How beautiful on the mountains
are the feet of the herald,
who proclaims peace,
who brings news of good things,
who proclaims salvation,
who says to Zion, "Your God reigns!"
8 The voices of your watchmen —
they lift up their voices,
shouting for joy together;
for every eye will see
when the LORD returns to Zion.
9 Be joyful, rejoice together,
you ruins of Jerusalem!
For the LORD has comforted his people;
he has redeemed Jerusalem.
10 The LORD has displayed his holy arm
in the sight of all the nations;
all the ends of the earth will see
the salvation of our God.

11 Leave, leave, go out from there!
Do not touch anything unclean;
go out from her, purify yourselves,
you who carry the vessels of the LORD.
12 For you will not leave in a hurry,
and you will not have to take flight;
because the LORD is going before you,
and the God of Israel is your rear guard.

THE SERVANT'S SUFFERING AND EXALTATION

13 See, my servant[E] will be successful;[F]
he will be raised and lifted up
and greatly exalted.

[A] **51:16** Syr reads *to stretch out* [B] **51:19** DSS, LXX, Syr, Vg read *you? Who can* [C] **52:2** Alt Hb tradition reads *The bonds are removed* [D] **52:4** Or *them at last*, or *them for nothing* [E] **52:13** Tg adds *the Messiah* [F] **52:13** Or *will act wisely*

14 Just as many were appalled at you[A] —
his appearance was so disfigured
that he did not look like a man,
and his form did not resemble
a human being —
15 so he will sprinkle many nations.[B]
Kings will shut their mouths
because of him,
for they will see what had not been told them,
and they will understand
what they had not heard.

53 Who has believed what we have heard?[C]
And to whom has the arm of the LORD
been revealed?
2 He grew up before him like a young plant
and like a root out of dry ground.
He didn't have an impressive form
or majesty that we should look at him,
no appearance that we should desire him.
3 He was despised and rejected by men,
a man of suffering who knew
what sickness was.
He was like someone
people turned away from;[D]
he was despised, and we didn't value him.

4 Yet he himself bore our sicknesses,
and he carried our pains;
but we in turn regarded him stricken,
struck down by God, and afflicted.
5 But he was pierced because of our rebellion,
crushed because of our iniquities;
punishment for our peace was on him,
and we are healed by his wounds.
6 We all went astray like sheep;
we all have turned to our own way;
and the LORD has punished him
for[E] the iniquity of us all.

7 He was oppressed and afflicted,
yet he did not open his mouth.
Like a lamb led to the slaughter
and like a sheep silent before her shearers,
he did not open his mouth.
8 He was taken away because of oppression
and judgment,
and who considered his fate?[F]
For he was cut off from the land of the living;
he was struck because of
my people's rebellion.
9 He was assigned a grave with the wicked,
but he was with a rich man at his death,
because he had done no violence
and had not spoken deceitfully.

10 Yet the LORD was pleased to crush him
severely.[G]
When[H] you make him a guilt offering,
he will see his seed, he will prolong his days,
and by his hand, the LORD's pleasure
will be accomplished.
11 After his anguish,
he will see light[I] and be satisfied.
By his knowledge,
my righteous servant will justify many,
and he will carry their iniquities.
12 Therefore I will give him[J] the many
as a portion,
and he will receive[K] the mighty as spoil,
because he willingly submitted to death,
and was counted among the rebels;
yet he bore the sin of many
and interceded for the rebels.

FUTURE GLORY FOR ISRAEL

54 "Rejoice, childless one, who did not
give birth;
burst into song and shout,
you who have not been in labor!
For the children of the desolate one
will be more
than the children of the married woman,"
says the LORD.
2 "Enlarge the site of your tent,
and let your tent curtains be stretched out;
do not hold back;
lengthen your ropes,
and drive your pegs deep.
3 For you will spread out to the right
and to the left,
and your descendants will dispossess nations
and inhabit the desolate cities.

4 "Do not be afraid, for you will not
be put to shame;
don't be humiliated, for you will not
be disgraced.
For you will forget the shame of your youth,
and you will no longer remember
the disgrace of your widowhood.
5 Indeed, your husband is your Maker —
his name is the LORD of Armies —
and the Holy One of Israel is your Redeemer;
he is called the God of the whole earth.

[A] **52:14** Some Hb mss, Syr, Tg read *him* [B] **52:15** LXX reads *so many nations will marvel at him* [C] **53:1** Or *believed our report* [D] **53:3** Lit *And like a hiding of faces from him* [E] **53:6** Or *has placed on him*; lit *with* [F] **53:8** Or *and as for his generation, who considered him?* [G] **53:10** Or *him; he made him sick.* [H] **53:10** Or *If* [I] **53:11** DSS, LXX; MT omits *light* [J] **53:12** Or *him with* [K] **53:12** Or *receive with*

Old Testament Burial Practices

by Daniel P. Caldwell

Burial cave carved in bedrock on the south slope of the Hinnom Valley in Jerusalem.

In the last of the Servant Song passages, Isaiah mentioned the burial of the servant: "He was assigned a grave with the wicked, but he was with a rich man at his death" (53:9). Old Testament texts offer numerous references to burials. In fact, when someone's death is recorded, the burial is usually also mentioned.[1] The passages are more descriptive in nature than prescriptive. The burial practices for the rich and for the poor were different, as were the burials for the righteous and those who were noted as sinners. Burial practices changed over the course of time.

At the time of death, the eldest son or, in his absence, the nearest next of kin closed the eyes of the deceased.[2] Reflecting this custom, God, speaking in a vision, told Jacob to go to Egypt and there "Joseph will close your eyes when you die" (Gn 46:4).

While burial for kings and other political officials may have involved longer periods of mourning before the actual interment (Gn 50:3), burial for the commoner generally occurred within twenty-four hours. At times, the interment may have taken place on the same day as the death. This was partly because of the climate in Israel and partly because people considered the body to be ceremonially unclean. People thus prepared a body for burial as soon as possible. Even the bodies of executed criminals were not to be left overnight but were to be buried on the same day (Dt 21:23). In Leviticus 10:4–5, the lifeless bodies of Nadab and Abihu were removed immediately from the Israelite camp. To allow a body to decay or to be defiled above ground was highly shameful (2Kg 9:34–37; Ec 6:3). For example, David commanded the burial of the bones of Saul and Jonathan (2Sm 21:10–14).

Archaeological evidence from the early Canaanite period (3150–2200 BC) revealed the use of family burial caves. These caves were generally outside of towns and villages among the hills or cliffs. Some of these caves were natural formations that people expanded to include space for additional family members. In the absence of a natural cave, families hewed caves for the purpose of creating a place for interment. The skeletons in such caves indicate a careful positioning of bodies and thus the great care that people took in burying the dead.[3]

Ostrich egg shell jar from royal tomb at Ur, circa 2600 BC.

Burying funerary gifts with the deceased was not uncommon. Typically, the gifts were small and refined pieces of pottery—bowls, platters, jugs (for liquids), and smaller jugs for oil and perfumes. Some burials included weapons such as knives and daggers. Further, the presence of pins (or fibula) for fastening clothing and other jewelry indicates that people gave attention to dressing and adorning a body for burial.[4]

During the patriarchal period (ca 2200–1950 BC), all patriarchs and matriarchs (Sarah, Abraham, Isaac, Rebekah, Leah, and Jacob) were buried in the Cave of Machpelah, which Abraham purchased as a place of interment (Gn 49:29–32). The only matriarch not buried in the Cave of Machpelah was Rachel. She died after giving birth to Benjamin and was buried outside Bethlehem. To mark the site of Rachel's burial, Jacob set up a pillar (35:19–20).

At times, burial took place at the location of death and near a tree. In Genesis 35:8, Deborah, Rebekah's nurse, died near Bethel and was buried beneath an oak tree. The people of Jabesh-gilead buried the bodies of Saul and his sons under a tamarisk tree (1Sm 31:11–13). Burial by a tree may have expressed a desire to perpetuate the memory of the deceased just as the establishment of a pillar, monument, or the piling up of stones.[5] In one passage, the burial site was marked with a pile of stones. After the stoning of Achan for his sin, the people "raised over him a large pile of rocks" (Jos 7:26).

Although the Old Testament commonly mentions burying a person in a cave or in the ground, it also mentions a few other burial methods. Only in connection with the burials of Jacob and Joseph do we find the Egyptian ritual of embalming being used for Israelites (Gn 50:2–3,26). Their situations were unique because of their presence in Egypt at the time of their deaths. A few texts mention cremation, but evidently this was not a common burial practice. Cremation occurred only in exceptional circumstances such as trying to prevent the threat of plague or following the mutilation of a body at death (1Sm 31:11–13; Am 6:8–10). According to the Mosaic law, bodies were burned for those who had been found guilty of unnatural sins (Lv 21:9) or those who died under a curse, such as Achan and his family, who were burned with fire (Jos 7:25). Toward the end of the monarchy, common people were often buried in public cemeteries.[6]

When the body had been prepared for burial, the deceased would be placed on a funeral bier and transported to the place of interment. Coffins were relatively unknown in the Old Testament world. The bier was a portable litter or a bed. The same Hebrew term designated both an actual bed for sleeping and the funeral bier.[7] The context of the passage was the only means of determining the correct designation (cf. 2Sm 3:31; 2Kg 1:4). The typical bier was a simple set of wooden boards. Sometimes the bier would have a pole at each corner to assist in carrying the deceased. King Asa's body was placed on a bier and laid in a tomb he had made for himself. His seems to be more elaborate than the common bier, being covered with various kinds of spices prepared by the perfumer's art (2Ch 16:13–14).

In Israel's central highlands, archaeologists have found abundant evidence of multiple cave interments from the Late Bronze and Iron Ages. "At each new interment, the skeletal remains of previous burials were simply swept into a corner, and the bones of the dead were not accorded any special reverence."[8]

People carried the body to the place of burial in a procession of family members, friends, and servants. The procession was accompanied by a group of professional mourners, usually women, who cried aloud and wailed in shrieks and lamentation. Jeremiah alluded to this activity: "This is what the LORD of Armies says: Consider, and summon the women who mourn; send for the skillful women. Let them come quickly to raise a lament over us so that our eyes may overflow with tears, our eyelids be soaked with weeping" (Jr 9:17–18). In addition to the professional mourner's loud weeping, other rituals were part of the mourning and grief process. They include tearing one's garments (2Sm 1:11–12), wearing the traditional mourning garment known as sackcloth (2Sm 14:2; Is 3:24), cutting one's hair or beard (Is 22:12; Jr 7:29; Ezk 7:18), and placing dirt on the head and sitting in ashes. The Bible offers no greater lamentation than that of Job. After being told of his loss of his beloved children from a great wind, Job performed the rituals of mourning. He "stood up, tore his robe, and shaved his head. He fell to the ground and worshiped" (Jb 1:20). ✜

---

[1] Philip S. Johnston, *Shades of Sheol* (Downers Grove, IL: InterVarsity, 2002), 51. [2] J. B. Payne, "Burial" in *ISBE*, 1:556–57. [3] Yohanan Aharoni, *The Archaeology of the Land of Israel: From the Prehistoric Beginnings to the End of the First Temple Period* (Philadelphia: Westminster, 1982), 51. [4] Elizabeth Bloch-Smith, "Burials" in *ABD*, 1:785. [5] Bloch-Smith, "Burials." [6] Johnston, *Shades of Sheol*, 53. [7] Marvin R. Wilson, "*mittah*" (bed or bier), *TWOT*, 2:573–75. [8] Johnston, *Shades of Sheol*, 65.

6 For the LORD has called you,
like a wife deserted and wounded in spirit,
a wife of one's youth when she is rejected,"
says your God.
7 "I deserted you for a brief moment,
but I will take you back
with abundant compassion.
8 In a surge of anger
I hid my face from you for a moment,
but I will have compassion on you
with everlasting love,"
says the LORD your Redeemer.
9 "For this is like the days[A] of Noah to me:
when I swore that the water of Noah
would never flood the earth again,
so I have sworn that I will not be angry
with you
or rebuke you.
10 Though the mountains move
and the hills shake,
my love will not be removed from you
and my covenant of peace will not be shaken,"
says your compassionate LORD.

11 "Poor Jerusalem, storm-tossed,
and not comforted,
I will set your stones in black mortar,[B]
and lay your foundations in lapis lazuli.
12 I will make your fortifications[C] out of rubies,
your gates out of sparkling stones,
and all your walls out of precious stones.
13 Then all your children will be taught
by the LORD,
their prosperity will be great,
14 and you will be established
on a foundation of righteousness.
You will be far from oppression,
you will certainly not be afraid;
you will be far from terror,
it will certainly not come near you.
15 If anyone attacks you,
it is not from me;
whoever attacks you
will fall before you.
16 Look, I have created the craftsman
who blows on the charcoal fire
and produces a weapon suitable for its task;
and I have created the destroyer
to cause havoc.
17 No weapon formed against you will succeed,
and you will refute any accusation[D]
raised against you in court.
This is the heritage of the LORD's servants,
and their vindication is from me."
This is the LORD's declaration.

COME TO THE LORD

55 "Come, everyone who is thirsty,
come to the water;
and you without silver,
come, buy, and eat!
Come, buy wine and milk
without silver and without cost!
2 Why do you spend silver on what is not food,
and your wages on what does not satisfy?
Listen carefully to me, and eat what is good,
and you will enjoy the choicest of foods.[E]
3 Pay attention and come to me;
listen, so that you will live.
I will make a permanent covenant with you
on the basis of the faithful kindnesses
of David.[F]
4 Since I have made him a witness
to the peoples,
a leader and commander for the peoples,
5 so you will summon a nation
you do not know,
and nations who do not know you will run
to you.
For the LORD your God,
even the Holy One of Israel,
has glorified you."

6 Seek the LORD while he may be found;
call to him while he is near.
7 Let the wicked one abandon his way
and the sinful one his thoughts;
let him return to the LORD,
so he may have compassion on him,
and to our God, for he will freely forgive.

8 "For my thoughts are not your thoughts,
and your ways are not my ways."
This is the LORD's declaration.
9 "For as heaven is higher than earth,
so my ways are higher than your ways,
and my thoughts than your thoughts.
10 For just as rain and snow fall from heaven
and do not return there
without saturating the earth
and making it germinate and sprout,
and providing seed to sow
and food to eat,
11 so my word that comes from my mouth
will not return to me empty,
but it will accomplish what I please
and will prosper in what I send it to do."

[A]**54:9** DSS, Cairo Geniza; MT, LXX read *waters* [B]**54:11** Lit *in antimony* [C]**54:12** Lit *suns*; perhaps *shields*; Ps 84:11 [D]**54:17** Lit *refute every tongue* [E]**55:2** Lit *enjoy fatness* [F]**55:3** Or *with you, the faithful acts of kindness shown to David*

12 You will indeed go out with joy
and be peacefully guided;
the mountains and the hills will break
into singing before you,
and all the trees of the field will clap
their hands.
13 Instead of the thornbush, a cypress
will come up,
and instead of the brier, a myrtle will come up;
this will stand as a monument for the LORD,
an everlasting sign that will not be destroyed.

A HOUSE OF PRAYER FOR ALL

56 This is what the LORD says:
Preserve justice and do what is right,
for my salvation is coming soon,
and my righteousness will be revealed.
2 Happy is the person who does this,
the son of man who holds it fast,
who keeps the Sabbath without desecrating it,
and keeps his hand from doing any evil.

3 No foreigner who has joined himself
to the LORD
should say,
"The LORD will exclude me from his people,"
and the eunuch should not say,
"Look, I am a dried-up tree."
4 For the LORD says this:
"For the eunuchs who keep my Sabbaths,
and choose what pleases me,
and hold firmly to my covenant,
5 I will give them, in my house and within
my walls,
a memorial and a name
better than sons and daughters.
I will give each of them an everlasting name
that will never be cut off.
6 As for the foreigners who join themselves
to the LORD
to minister to him, to love the name of the LORD,
and to become his servants —
all who keep the Sabbath
without desecrating it
and who hold firmly to my covenant —
7 I will bring them to my holy mountain
and let them rejoice in my house of prayer.
Their burnt offerings and sacrifices
will be acceptable on my altar,
for my house will be called a house of prayer
for all nations."
8 This is the declaration of the Lord GOD,
who gathers the dispersed of Israel:
"I will gather to them still others
besides those already gathered."

UNRIGHTEOUS LEADERS CONDEMNED

9 All you animals of the field and forest,
come and eat!
10 Israel's[A] watchmen are blind,
all of them,
they know nothing;
all of them are mute dogs,
they cannot bark;
they dream, lie down,
and love to sleep.
11 These dogs have fierce appetites;
they never have enough.
And they are shepherds
who have no discernment;
all of them turn to their own way,
every last one for his own profit.
12 "Come, let me get some wine,
let's guzzle some beer;
and tomorrow will be like today,
only far better!"

57 The righteous person perishes,
and no one takes it to heart;
the faithful are taken away,
with no one realizing
that the righteous person is taken away
because of[B] evil.
2 He will enter into peace —
they will rest on their beds[C] —
everyone who lives uprightly.

PAGAN RELIGION DENOUNCED

3 But come here,
you witch's sons,
offspring of an adulterer and a prostitute![D]
4 Who are you mocking?
Who are you opening your mouth
and sticking out your tongue at?
Isn't it you, you rebellious children,
you offspring of liars,
5 who burn with lust among the oaks,
under every green tree,
who slaughter children in the wadis
below the clefts of the rocks?
6 Your portion is among the smooth stones
of the wadi;
indeed, they are your lot.
You have even poured out a drink offering
to them;
you have offered a grain offering;
should I be satisfied with these?

[A] **56:10** Or *His*, or *Its* [B] **57:1** Or *taken away from the presence of* [C] **57:2** Either their deathbeds or their graves [D] **57:3** Lit *and she acted as a prostitute*

7 You have placed your bed
on a high and lofty mountain;
you also went up there to offer sacrifice.
8 You have set up your memorial
behind the door and doorpost.
For away from me, you stripped,
went up, and made your bed wide,
and you have made a bargain[A] for yourself
with them.
You have loved their bed;
you have gazed on their genitals.[B,C]
9 You went to the king with oil
and multiplied your perfumes;
you sent your envoys far away
and sent them down even to Sheol.
10 You became weary on your many journeys,
but you did not say, "It's hopeless!"
You found a renewal of your strength;[D]
therefore you did not grow weak.
11 Who was it you dreaded and feared,
so that you lied and didn't remember me
or take it to heart?
I have kept silent for a long time, haven't I?[E]
So you do not fear me.
12 I will announce your righteousness,
and your works — they will not profit you.
13 When you cry out,
let your collection of idols rescue you!
The wind will carry all of them off,
a breath will take them away.
But whoever takes refuge in me
will inherit the land
and possess my holy mountain.

HEALING AND PEACE

14 He said,
"Build it up, build it up, prepare the way,
remove every obstacle from my people's way."
15 For the High and Exalted One,
who lives forever, whose name is holy, says this:
"I live in a high and holy place,
and with the oppressed and lowly of spirit,
to revive the spirit of the lowly
and revive the heart of the oppressed.
16 For I will not accuse you forever,
and I will not always be angry;
for then the spirit would grow weak before me,
even the breath, which I have made.
17 Because of his sinful greed I was angry,
so I struck him; I was angry and hid;
but he went on turning back to the desires
of his heart.
18 I have seen his ways, but I will heal him;
I will lead him and restore comfort
to him and his mourners,
19 creating words of praise."[F]
The LORD says,
"Peace, peace to the one who is far or near,
and I will heal him.
20 But the wicked are like the storm-tossed sea,
for it cannot be still,
and its water churns up mire and muck.
21 There is no peace for the wicked,"
says my God.

TRUE FASTING

58 "Cry out loudly, don't hold back!
Raise your voice like a ram's horn.
Tell my people their transgression
and the house of Jacob their sins.
2 They seek me day after day
and delight to know my ways,
like a nation that does what is right
and does not abandon the justice
of their God.
They ask me for righteous judgments;
they delight in the nearness of God."

3 "Why have we fasted, but you have not seen?
We have denied ourselves,
but you haven't noticed!"[G]

"Look, you do as you please on the day
of your fast,
and oppress all your workers.
4 You fast with contention and strife
to strike viciously with your fist.
You cannot fast as you do today,
hoping to make your voice heard on high.
5 Will the fast I choose be like this:
A day for a person to deny himself,
to bow his head like a reed,
and to spread out sackcloth and ashes?
Will you call this a fast
and a day acceptable to the LORD?
6 Isn't this the fast I choose:
To break the chains of wickedness,
to untie the ropes of the yoke,
to set the oppressed free,
and to tear off every yoke?
7 Is it not to share your bread with the hungry,
to bring the poor and homeless
into your house,
to clothe the naked when you see him,
and not to ignore your own flesh and blood?[H]

[A]**57:8** Lit *you cut* [B]**57:8** Lit *hand* [C]**57:8** In Hb, the word "hand" is probably a euphemism for *genitals*. [D]**57:10** Lit *found life of your hand* [E]**57:11** LXX reads *And I, when I see you, I pass by* [F]**57:19** Lit *creating fruit of the lips* [G]**58:3** These are Israel's words to God. [H]**58:7** Lit *not hide yourself from your flesh*

8 Then your light will appear like the dawn,
and your recovery will come quickly.
Your righteousness will go before you,
and the LORD's glory will be your rear guard.
9 At that time, when you call, the LORD
will answer;
when you cry out, he will say, 'Here I am.'
If you get rid of the yoke among you,
the finger-pointing and malicious speaking,
10 and if you offer yourself[A] to the hungry,
and satisfy the afflicted one,
then your light will shine in the darkness,
and your night will be like noonday.
11 The LORD will always lead you,
satisfy you in a parched land,
and strengthen your bones.
You will be like a watered garden
and like a spring whose water never runs dry.
12 Some of you will rebuild the ancient ruins;
you will restore the foundations laid long ago;
you will be called the repairer of broken walls,
the restorer of streets where people live.

13 "If you keep from desecrating the Sabbath,
from doing whatever you want
on my holy day;
if you call the Sabbath a delight,
and the holy day of the LORD honorable;
if you honor it, not going your own ways,
seeking your own pleasure,
or talking business;[B,C]
14 then you will delight in the LORD,
and I will make you ride over the heights
of the land,
and let you enjoy the heritage
of your father Jacob."
For the mouth of the LORD has spoken.

SIN AND REDEMPTION

59 Indeed, the LORD's arm is not too weak
to save,
and his ear is not too deaf to hear.
2 But your iniquities are separating you
from your God,
and your sins have hidden his face from you
so that he does not listen.
3 For your hands are defiled with blood
and your fingers, with iniquity;
your lips have spoken lies,
and your tongues mutter injustice.
4 No one makes claims justly;
no one pleads honestly.
They trust in empty and worthless words;
they conceive trouble and give birth
to iniquity.
5 They hatch viper's eggs
and weave spider's webs.
Whoever eats their eggs will die;
crack one open, and a viper is hatched.
6 Their webs cannot become clothing,
and they cannot cover themselves
with their works.
Their works are sinful works,
and violent acts are in their hands.
7 Their feet run after evil,
and they rush to shed innocent blood.
Their thoughts are sinful thoughts;
ruin and wretchedness are in their paths.
8 They have not known the path of peace,
and there is no justice in their ways.
They have made their roads crooked;
no one who walks on them will know peace.

9 Therefore justice is far from us,
and righteousness does not reach us.
We hope for light, but there is darkness;
for brightness, but we live in the night.
10 We grope along a wall like the blind;
we grope like those without eyes.
We stumble at noon as though
it were twilight;
we are like the dead among those
who are healthy.
11 We all growl like bears
and moan like doves.
We hope for justice, but there is none;
for salvation, but it is far from us.
12 For our transgressions have multiplied
before you,
and our sins testify against us.
For our transgressions are with us,
and we know our iniquities:
13 transgression and deception
against the LORD,
turning away from following our God,
speaking oppression and revolt,
conceiving and uttering lying words
from the heart.
14 Justice is turned back,
and righteousness stands far off.
For truth has stumbled in the public square,
and honesty cannot enter.
15 Truth is missing,
and whoever turns from evil is plundered.

The LORD saw that there was no justice,
and he was offended.

[A] **58:10** Some Hb mss, LXX, Syr read *offer your bread* [B] **58:13** Or *idly*
[C] **58:13** Lit *or speak a word*

The Jewish Tradition of Fasting

by Lynn O. Traylor

Fasting for religious reasons preceded its use for health reasons. Some ancient cultures fasted out of a desire to show a penitent spirit, to prepare for a community rite or special occasions, for personal purification, or to establish an altered physical state inducing a hoped-for dream or "vision."[1] Because it involved both personal and community dimensions, some form or practice of fasting was part of every major religion. In fact, in some cultures, fasting predated the development of a formal religion.[2]

Biblical examples of fasting appear in two main forms. Individual fasting was usually prompted by extreme desire or distress; community or national fasting marked significant events or crises.

INDIVIDUAL FASTS

From the viewpoint of pagan cultures, individual fasting referred to a person's refusal to eat or drink, motivated by a desire to earn a special merit. Biblical examples of individual fasting, however, almost always involve an encounter with the divine; such fasting "is a person's whole-body, natural response to life's sacred moments."[3] Such a fast first appears in Moses's experience at Mount Sinai. While receiving the Ten Commandments, "Moses was there with the Lord forty days and forty nights; he did not eat food or drink water" (Ex 34:28). Although neither the Hebrew noun for "fast/fasting" *(tsom)* nor the verb (*tsum*) is used here, the passage nonetheless describes a "fast." Moses later recounted the experience as he pleaded on Israel's behalf: "I did not eat food or drink water because of all the sin you committed" (Dt 9:18). A synonym for the terms *tsom/tsum* is the expression *'innah nephesh,* meaning to "afflict the body" or simply "practice self-denial" (CSB). It occurs in the instructions for the Day of Atonement (Lv 16:29,31; 23:27,29,32; Nm 29:7), the only Torah-sanctioned fast day. It also occurs parallel to *tsom/tsum* in Isaiah 58:3,5.

Individuals also fasted during times of anguish and hurt too deep for words alone to express.[4] Individual fasting also can show humility, as when King Ahab of Israel humbled himself before God (1Kg 21:27); reflect a deep grief, as when Nehemiah mourned Jerusalem's condition (Neh 1:4); or accompany a desire for divine direction, as when Daniel sought understanding (Dn 9:3). This type of fasting hardly ever occurs apart from prayer.[5] The individual feels so "overwhelmed" and thus gives up food in order to seek God, as when King David "pleaded with God" over the life of his son (2Sm 12:16–23).[6] Intense individual fasts could leave a person weak and "emaciated" (Ps 109:24).

COMMUNAL FASTS

As was the case with individual fasting, communal (or national) fasts could mark significant moments or times of crisis, as when the people of Nineveh heeded Jonah's warnings and entered into a national fast (Jnh 3:5–8). The Talmud (a record of rabbinic teachings) shows communal fasts were not always nationwide; elders of any local community could call for a fast when the locals faced dire circumstances such as pestilence, a lack of rainfall, or other calamities.[7]

Nationwide communal fasts followed a set calendar of "fast days," which either the Torah decreed (the Day of Atonement on the tenth day of the month of Tishri) or that became part of the calendar of ritual fasting commemorating significant, historical events. For instance, the Ninth of Av marked the destruction of the Jerusalem temple (Jr 52:12–13), the Seventeenth of Tammuz mourned the Babylonian invasion of Jerusalem (39:2), the Tenth of Tevet marked the Babylonian siege of Jerusalem (2Kg 25:1–2; Ezk 24:1–2), the Third of Tishri commemorated the death of Gedaliah (2Kg 25:25; Jr 41:1–2), and the Fast of Esther recalled the queen fasting before she entered King Ahasuerus's presence and intervened for the Jews (Est 4:16). Of these ancient communal fasts, the ones related to the Day of Atonement and the temple's destruction (the Ninth of Av) remain the most observed; the others have little following in modern Judaism.[8]

Communal fasts could also be spontaneous in nature, as when mourning for a fallen leader as in the death of Saul (1Sm 31:13; 2Sm 1:12; 1Ch 10:12) or celebrating deliverance from catastrophe (Est 9:31). Israel's fast prior to doing battle with the tribe of Benjamin (Jdg 20:26) suggests communal fasting was well established as early as the twelfth century BC.[9]

The method of communal fasts changed little throughout the observances recorded in the Bible. The main features of the communal fast ritual included praying openly, confessing one's sins, publicly reading the Torah, and displaying humility by tearing one's clothes and wearing sackcloth and ashes (1Kg 21:27; Neh 9:1; Ps 35:13; Is 58:5; Jl 2:13). Ordinary "fast days" were from dusk to dawn, but important fasts (such as the Day of Atonement) lasted for twenty-four hours.

Given the number of "fast days" and the practice of calling for fasts in response to localized crises, the practice of communal fasts evidently grew to an overwhelming number. The Babylonian Talmud specifies when "public fasts must not be ordered to commence."[10] As the frequency of such fasts increased, the sincerity of those participating in them evidently waned. Old Testament passages such as Isaiah 58:6–7 and Joel 2:12–13 voice this concern. The rabbis acknowledged the sincerity underlying the practice of fasting as being crucial,

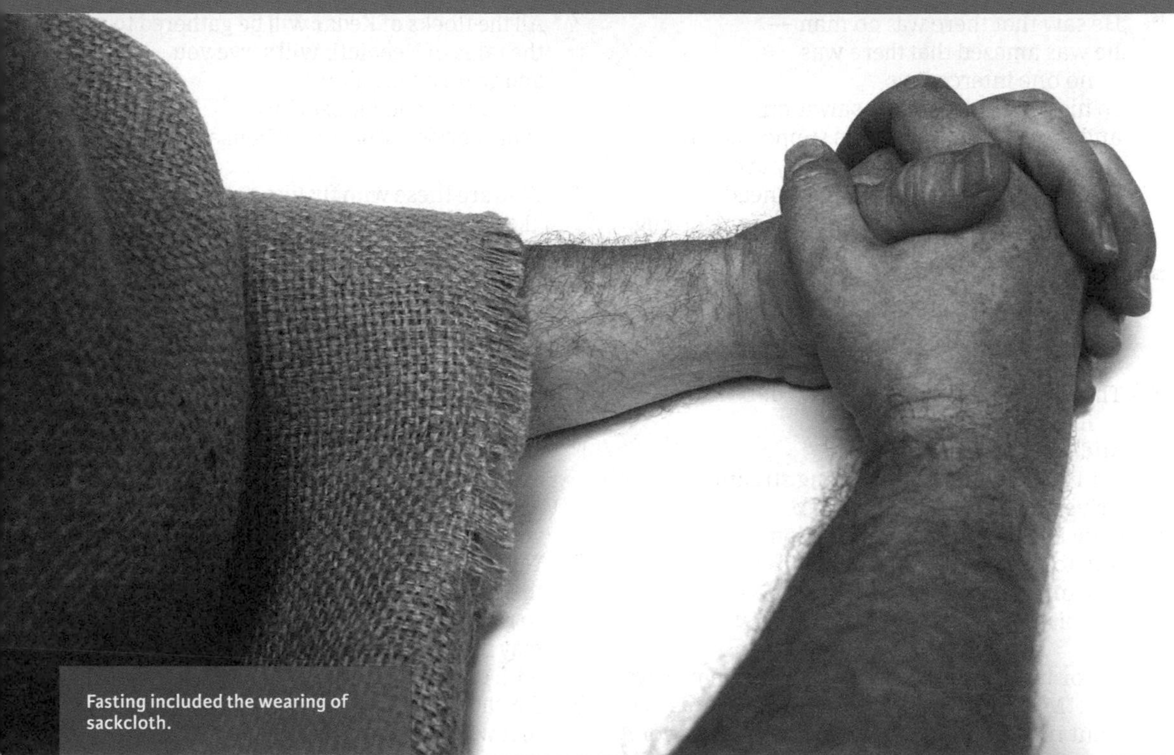
Fasting included the wearing of sackcloth.

explaining that God did not see the "sackcloth and fasting" of the people of Nineveh, but saw "they were turning away from their evil path."[11] Similarly, Jesus's teaching on fasting did not prohibit fasting; instead, he required that fasting be rooted in a sincere desire to draw closer to God, apart from selfish motivations (Mt 6:16–18). ✣

---

[1] David Lambert, "Fasting as a Penitential Rite: A Biblical Phenomenon?" *Harvard Theological Review* (*HTR*) 96.4 (October 2003): 477. [2] Eric N. Rogers, *Fasting: The Phenomenon of Self-Denial* (Nashville: Thomas Nelson, 1976), 27. [3] Scot McKnight, *Fasting* (Nashville: Thomas Nelson, 2009), xiv. [4] Lambert, "Fasting," 480. [5] Lambert, "Fasting," 479. [6] McKnight, *Fasting*, 60. The Old Testament describes two others as not eating during times of personal distress. Upset at her barren condition, Hannah did not eat while at the tabernacle, which was in Shiloh (1Sm 1:1–8). And centuries later, Ahab could not eat after Naboth refused to sell his vineyard to the king (1Kg 21:1–4). Hannah's not eating may have been a genuinely religious fast, whereas Ahab's actions seem to be merely a display of royal pouting over not having gotten his way. [7] Mishnah *Ta'anit* 3. [8] "Jewish Holidays: Fasting & Fast Days," Jewish Virtual Library, accessed 16 July 2014, www.jewishvirtuallibrary.org/fasting-and-fast-days. [9] Josiah Derby, "Fasting and Atonement," *Jewish Bible Quarterly* (*JBQ*) 23.4 (1995): 240. [10] Mishnah *Ta'anit* 2:8. [11] Lambert, "Fasting," 502.

16 He saw that there was no man —
he was amazed that there was
no one interceding;
so his own arm brought salvation,
and his own righteousness supported him.
17 He put on righteousness as body armor,
and a helmet of salvation on his head;
he put on garments of vengeance for clothing,
and he wrapped himself in zeal as in a cloak.
18 So he will repay according to their deeds:
fury to his enemies,
retribution to his foes,
and he will repay the coasts and islands.
19 They will fear the name of the LORD
in the west
and his glory in the east;[A]
for he will come like a rushing stream
driven by the wind of the LORD.
20 "The Redeemer will come to Zion,
and to those in Jacob who turn
from transgression."
This is the LORD's declaration.

21 "As for me, this is my covenant with them," says
the LORD: "My Spirit who is on you, and my words that
I have put in your mouth, will not depart from your
mouth, or from the mouths of your children, or from
the mouths of your children's children, from now on
and forever," says the LORD.

THE LORD'S GLORY IN ZION

60 Arise, shine, for your light has come,
and the glory of the LORD shines over you.[B]
2 For look, darkness will cover the earth,
and total darkness the peoples;
but the LORD will shine over you,
and his glory will appear over you.
3 Nations will come to your light,
and kings to your shining brightness.
4 Raise your eyes and look around:
they all gather and come to you;
your sons will come from far away,
and your daughters on the hips
of nursing mothers.
5 Then you will see and be radiant,
and your heart will tremble and rejoice,[C]
because the riches of the sea
will become yours
and the wealth of the nations will come
to you.
6 Caravans of camels will cover your land[D] —
young camels of Midian and Ephah —
all of them will come from Sheba.
They will carry gold and frankincense
and proclaim the praises of the LORD.
7 All the flocks of Kedar will be gathered to you;
the rams of Nebaioth will serve you
and go up on my altar
as an acceptable sacrifice.
I will glorify my beautiful house.

8 Who are these who fly like a cloud,
like doves to their shelters?
9 Yes, the coasts and islands will wait for me
with the ships of Tarshish in the lead,
to bring your children from far away,
their silver and gold with them,
for the honor of the LORD your God,
the Holy One of Israel,
who has glorified you.
10 Foreigners will rebuild your walls,
and their kings will serve you.
Although I struck you in my wrath,
yet I will show mercy to you with my favor.
11 Your city gates will always be open;
they will never be shut day or night
so that the wealth of the nations
may be brought into you,
with their kings being led in procession.
12 For the nation and the kingdom
that will not serve you will perish;
those nations will be annihilated.
13 The glory of Lebanon will come to you —
its pine, elm, and cypress together —
to beautify the place of my sanctuary,
and I will glorify my dwelling place.[E]
14 The sons of your oppressors
will come and bow down to you;
all who reviled you
will fall facedown at your feet.
They will call you the City of the LORD,
Zion of the Holy One of Israel.
15 Instead of your being deserted and hated,
with no one passing through,
I will make you an object of eternal pride,
a joy from age to age.
16 You will nurse on the milk of nations,
and nurse at the breast of kings;
you will know that I, the LORD, am your Savior
and Redeemer, the Mighty One of Jacob.

17 I will bring gold instead of bronze;
I will bring silver instead of iron,
bronze instead of wood,
and iron instead of stones.
I will appoint peace as your government
and righteousness as your overseers.

[A] **59:19** Lit *sunrise* [B] **60:1** = Jerusalem [C] **60:5** Lit *expand* [D] **60:6** Lit *cover you* [E] **60:13** Lit *glorify the place of my feet*

18 Violence will never again be heard of
in your land;
devastation and destruction
will be gone from your borders.
You will call your walls Salvation
and your city gates Praise.
19 The sun will no longer be your light by day,
and the brightness of the moon will not shine
on you.
The LORD will be your everlasting light,
and your God will be your splendor.
20 Your sun will no longer set,
and your moon will not fade;
for the LORD will be your everlasting light,
and the days of your sorrow will be over.
21 All your people will be righteous;
they will possess the land forever;
they are the branch I planted,
the work of my[A] hands,
so that I may be glorified.
22 The least will become a thousand,
the smallest a mighty nation.
I am the LORD;
I will accomplish it quickly in its time.

MESSIAH'S JUBILEE

61 The Spirit of the Lord GOD is on me,
because the LORD has anointed me
to bring good news to the poor.
He has sent me to heal[B] the brokenhearted,
to proclaim liberty to the captives
and freedom to the prisoners;
2 to proclaim the year of the LORD's favor,
and the day of our God's vengeance;
to comfort all who mourn,
3 to provide for those who mourn in Zion;
to give them a crown of beauty
instead of ashes,
festive oil instead of mourning,
and splendid clothes instead of despair.[C]
And they will be called righteous trees,
planted by the LORD
to glorify him.

4 They will rebuild the ancient ruins;
they will restore the former devastations;
they will renew the ruined cities,
the devastations of many generations.
5 Strangers will stand and feed your flocks,
and foreigners will be your plowmen
and vinedressers.
6 But you will be called the LORD's priests;
they will speak of you as ministers of our God;
you will eat the wealth of the nations,
and you will boast in their riches.
7 In place of your shame, you will have a double
portion;
in place of disgrace, they will rejoice over
their share.
So they will possess double in their land,
and eternal joy will be theirs.

8 For I the LORD love justice;
I hate robbery and injustice;[D]
I will faithfully reward my people
and make a permanent covenant with them.
9 Their descendants will be known
among the nations,
and their posterity among the peoples.
All who see them will recognize
that they are a people the LORD has blessed.

10 I rejoice greatly in the LORD,
I exult in my God;
for he has clothed me with the garments
of salvation
and wrapped me in a robe of righteousness,
as a groom wears a turban
and as a bride adorns herself with her jewels.
11 For as the earth produces its growth,
and as a garden enables what is sown
to spring up,
so the Lord GOD will cause righteousness
and praise
to spring up before all the nations.

ZION'S RESTORATION

62 I will not keep silent because of Zion,
and I will not keep still because of Jerusalem,
until her righteousness shines
like a bright light
and her salvation, like a flaming torch.
2 Nations will see your righteousness
and all kings, your glory.
You will be given a new name
that the LORD's mouth will announce.
3 You will be a glorious crown
in the LORD's hand,
and a royal diadem in the palm of your God's
hand.
4 You will no longer be called Deserted,
and your land will not be called Desolate;
instead, you will be called My Delight
Is in Her,[E]
and your land Married;[F]
for the LORD delights in you,
and your land will be married.

[A] **60:21** LXX, DSS read *his* [B] **61:1** Lit *bind up* [C] **61:3** Lit *a dim spirit* [D] **61:8** Some Hb mss, DSS, LXX, Syr, Tg, Vg; other Hb mss read *robbery with a burnt offering* [E] **62:4** Or *Hephzibah* [F] **62:4** Or *Beulah*

5 For as a young man marries a young woman,
so your sons will marry you;
and as a groom rejoices over his bride,
so your God will rejoice over you.

6 Jerusalem,
I have appointed watchmen on your walls;
they will never be silent, day or night.
There is no rest for you,
who remind the LORD.
7 Do not give him rest
until he establishes and makes Jerusalem
the praise of the earth.

8 The LORD has sworn with his right hand
and his strong arm:
I will no longer give your grain
to your enemies for food,
and foreigners will not drink the new wine
for which you have labored.
9 For those who gather grain will eat it
and praise the LORD,
and those who harvest the grapes will drink
the wine
in my holy courts.

10 Go out, go out through the city gates;
prepare a way for the people!
Build it up, build up the highway;
clear away the stones!
Raise a banner for the peoples.
11 Look, the LORD has proclaimed
to the ends of the earth,
"Say to Daughter Zion:
Look, your salvation is coming,
his wages are with him,
and his reward accompanies him."
12 And they will be called[A] the Holy People,
the LORD's Redeemed;
and you will be called Cared For,
A City Not Deserted.

THE LORD'S DAY OF VENGEANCE

63 Who is this coming from Edom
in crimson-stained garments
from Bozrah —
this one who is splendid in his apparel,
striding in his formidable[B] might?

It is I, proclaiming vindication,[C]
powerful to save.

2 Why are your clothes red,
and your garments like one who treads
a winepress?

3 I trampled the winepress alone,
and no one from the nations was with me.
I trampled them in my anger
and ground them underfoot in my fury;
their blood spattered my garments,
and all my clothes were stained.
4 For I planned the day of vengeance,
and the year of my redemption[D] came.
5 I looked, but there was no one to help,
and I was amazed that no one assisted;
so my arm accomplished victory for me,
and my wrath assisted me.
6 I crushed nations in my anger;
I made them drunk with my wrath
and poured out their blood on the ground.

REMEMBRANCE OF GRACE

7 I will make known the LORD's faithful love
and the LORD's praiseworthy acts,
because of all the LORD has done for us —
even the many good things
he has done for the house of Israel,
which he did for them based on
his compassion
and the abundance of his faithful love.
8 He said, "They are indeed my people,
children who will not be disloyal,"
and he became their Savior.
9 In all their suffering, he suffered,[E]
and the angel of his presence saved them.
He redeemed them
because of his love and compassion;
he lifted them up and carried them
all the days of the past.
10 But they rebelled
and grieved his Holy Spirit.
So he became their enemy
and fought against them.
11 Then he[F] remembered the days of the past,
the days of Moses and his people.
Where is he who brought them out of the sea
with the shepherds[G] of his flock?
Where is he who put his Holy Spirit
among the flock?
12 He made his glorious strength
available at the right hand of Moses,
divided the water before them
to make an eternal name for himself,
13 and led them through the depths
like a horse in the wilderness,
so that they did not stumble.

[A]**62:12** Lit *will call them* [B]**63:1** Syr, Vg read *apparel, striding forward in* [C]**63:1** Or *righteousness* [D]**63:4** Or *blood retribution* [E]**63:9** Alt Hb tradition reads *did not suffer* [F]**63:11** Or *they* [G]**63:11** LXX, Tg, Syr read *shepherd*

14 Like cattle that go down into the valley,
the Spirit of the LORD gave them[A] rest.
You led your people this way
to make a glorious name for yourself.

ISRAEL'S PRAYER

15 Look down from heaven and see
from your lofty home — holy and beautiful.
Where is your zeal and your might?
Your yearning[B] and your compassion
are withheld from me.
16 Yet you are our Father,
even though Abraham does not know us
and Israel doesn't recognize us.
You, LORD, are our Father;
your name is Our Redeemer
from Ancient Times.
17 Why, LORD, do you make us stray
from your ways?
You harden our hearts so we do not fear[C] you.
Return, because of your servants,
the tribes of your heritage.
18 Your holy people had a possession[D]
for a little while,
but our enemies have trampled down
your sanctuary.
19 We have become like those you never ruled,
like those who did not bear your name.
64 If only you would tear the heavens open
and come down,
so that mountains would quake
at your presence —
2 just as fire kindles brushwood,
and fire boils water —
to make your name known to your enemies,
so that nations would tremble at your presence!
3 When you did awesome works
that we did not expect,
you came down,
and the mountains quaked at your presence.
4 From ancient times no one has heard,
no one has listened to,
no eye has seen any God except you
who acts on behalf of the one who waits
for him.
5 You welcome the one who joyfully does
what is right;
they remember you in your ways.
But we have sinned, and you were angry.
How can we be saved if we remain in our sins?[E]
6 All of us have become like something unclean,
and all our righteous acts are
like a polluted[F] garment;
all of us wither like a leaf,
and our iniquities carry us away like the wind.
7 No one calls on your name,
striving to take hold of you.
For you have hidden your face from us
and made us melt because of[G,H] our iniquity.

8 Yet LORD, you are our Father;
we are the clay, and you are our potter;
we all are the work of your hands.
9 LORD, do not be terribly angry
or remember our iniquity forever.
Please look — all of us are your people!
10 Your holy cities have become a wilderness;
Zion has become a wilderness,
Jerusalem a desolation.
11 Our holy and beautiful[I] temple,
where our ancestors praised you,
has been burned down,
and all that was dear to us lies in ruins.
12 LORD, after all this, will you
restrain yourself?
Will you keep silent and afflict us severely?

THE LORD'S RESPONSE

65 "I was sought by those who did not ask;
I was found by those
who did not seek me.
I said, 'Here I am, here I am,'
to a nation that did not call on[J] my name.
2 I spread out my hands all day long
to a rebellious people
who walk in the path that is not good,
following their own thoughts.
3 These people continually anger me
to my face,
sacrificing in gardens,
burning incense on bricks,
4 sitting among the graves,
spending nights in secret places,
eating the meat of pigs,
and putting polluted broth in their bowls.[K]
5 They say, 'Keep to yourself,
don't come near me,
for I am too holy for you!'
These practices are smoke in my nostrils,
a fire that burns all day long.
6 Look, it is written in front of me:
I will not keep silent, but I will repay;
I will repay them fully[L]

[A] **63:14** Lit *him* [B] **63:15** Lit *The agitation of your inward parts* [C] **63:17** Lit *our heart from fearing* [D] **63:18** Or *Your people possessed your holy place* [E] **64:5** Lit *angry; in them continually and we will be saved*; Hb obscure [F] **64:6** Lit *menstrual* [G] **64:7** LXX, Syr, Vg, Tg read *and delivered us into the hand of* [H] **64:7** Lit *melt by the hand of* [I] **64:11** Or *glorious*; Is 60:7 [J] **65:1** Or *that was not called by* [K] **65:3–4** These vv. describe pagan worship. [L] **65:6** Lit *repay into their lap*

7 for your iniquities and the iniquities
of your[A] ancestors together,"
says the LORD.
"Because they burned incense
on the mountains
and reproached me on the hills,
I will reward them fully[B]
for their former deeds."

8 The LORD says this:
"As the new wine is found in a bunch of grapes,
and one says, 'Don't destroy it,
for there's some good[C] in it,'
so I will act because of my servants
and not destroy them all.
9 I will produce descendants from Jacob,
and heirs to my mountains from Judah;
my chosen ones will possess it,
and my servants will dwell there.
10 Sharon will be a pasture for flocks,
and the Valley of Achor a place for herds
to lie down,
for my people who have sought me.
11 But you who abandon the LORD,
who forget my holy mountain,
who prepare a table for Fortune
and fill bowls of mixed wine for Destiny,[D]
12 I will destine you for the sword,
and all of you will kneel down to be slaughtered,
because I called and you did not answer,
I spoke and you did not hear;
you did what was evil in my sight
and chose what I did not delight in."

13 Therefore, this is what the Lord GOD says:
"Look! My servants will eat,
but you will be hungry.
Look! My servants will drink,
but you will be thirsty.
Look! My servants will rejoice,
but you will be put to shame.
14 Look! My servants will shout for joy
from a glad heart,
but you will cry out from an anguished heart,
and you will lament out of a broken spirit.
15 You will leave your name behind
as a curse for my chosen ones,
and the Lord GOD will kill you;
but he will give his servants another name.
16 Whoever asks for a blessing in the land
will ask for a blessing by the God of truth,
and whoever swears in the land
will swear by the God of truth.
For the former troubles will be forgotten
and hidden from my sight.

A NEW CREATION

17 "For I will create new heavens
and a new earth;
the past events will not be remembered
or come to mind.
18 Then be glad and rejoice forever
in what I am creating;
for I will create Jerusalem to be a joy
and its people to be a delight.
19 I will rejoice in Jerusalem
and be glad in my people.
The sound of weeping and crying
will no longer be heard in her.
20 In her, a nursing infant will no longer live
only a few days,[E]
or an old man not live out his days.
Indeed, the one who dies at a hundred
years old
will be mourned as a young man,[F]
and the one who misses a hundred years
will be considered cursed.
21 People will build houses and live in them;
they will plant vineyards and eat
their fruit.
22 They will not build and others live in them;
they will not plant and others eat.
For my people's lives will be
like the lifetime of a tree.
My chosen ones will fully enjoy
the work of their hands.
23 They will not labor without success
or bear children destined for disaster,
for they will be a people blessed
by the LORD
along with their descendants.
24 Even before they call, I will answer;
while they are still speaking, I will hear.
25 The wolf and the lamb will feed together,[G]
and the lion will eat straw like cattle,
but the serpent's food will be dust!
They will not do what is evil or destroy
on my entire holy mountain,"
says the LORD.

FINAL JUDGMENT AND JOYOUS RESTORATION

66 This is what the LORD says:
Heaven is my throne,
and earth is my footstool.
Where could you possibly build a house
for me?
And where would my resting place be?

[A] 65:7 LXX, Syr read *for their iniquities and the iniquities of their* [B] 65:7 Lit *reward into their lap* [C] 65:8 Or *there's a blessing* [D] 65:11 Pagan gods [E] 65:20 Lit *her, no longer infant of days* [F] 65:20 Lit *the youth of a hundred years will die* [G] 65:25 Lit *as one*

2 My hand made all these things,
and so they all came into being.
This is the LORD's declaration.
I will look favorably on this kind of person:
one who is humble, submissive[A] in spirit,
and trembles at my word.
3 One person slaughters an ox, another kills
a person;
one person sacrifices a lamb, another breaks
a dog's neck;
one person offers a grain offering,
another offers pig's blood;
one person offers incense, another praises
an idol —
all these have chosen their ways
and delight in their abhorrent practices.
4 So I will choose their punishment,
and I will bring on them what they dread
because I called and no one answered;
I spoke and they did not listen;
they did what was evil in my sight
and chose what I did not delight in.

5 You who tremble at his word,
hear the word of the LORD:
"Your brothers who hate and exclude you
for my name's sake have said,
'Let the LORD be glorified
so that we can see your joy!'
But they will be put to shame."

6 A sound of uproar from the city!
A voice from the temple —
the voice of the LORD,
paying back his enemies what they deserve!

7 Before Zion was in labor, she gave birth;
before she was in pain, she delivered a boy.
8 Who has heard of such a thing?
Who has seen such things?
Can a land be born in one day
or a nation be delivered in an instant?
Yet as soon as Zion was in labor,
she gave birth to her sons.
9 "Will I bring a baby to the point of birth
and not deliver it?"
says the LORD;
"or will I who deliver, close the womb?"
says your God.
10 Be glad for Jerusalem and rejoice over her,
all who love her.
Rejoice greatly with her,
all who mourn over her —
11 so that you may nurse and be satisfied
from her comforting breast
and drink deeply and delight yourselves
from her glorious breasts.

12 For this is what the LORD says:
I will make peace flow to her like a river,
and the wealth[B] of nations like a flood;
you will nurse and be carried on her hip
and bounced on her lap.
13 As a mother comforts her son,
so I will comfort you,
and you will be comforted in Jerusalem.

14 You will see, you will rejoice,
and you[C] will flourish like grass;
then the LORD's power will be revealed
to his servants,
but he will show his wrath
against his enemies.
15 Look, the LORD will come with fire —
his chariots are like the whirlwind —
to execute his anger with fury
and his rebuke with flames of fire.
16 For the LORD will execute judgment
on all humanity with his fiery sword,
and many will be slain by the LORD.

17 "Those who dedicate and purify themselves to
enter the groves following their leader,[D] eating meat
from pigs, vermin,[E] and rats, will perish together."
This is the LORD's declaration.
18 "Knowing[F] their works and their thoughts, I have
come to gather all nations and languages; they will
come and see my glory. 19 I will establish a sign among
them, and I will send survivors from them to the nations — to Tarshish, Put,[G] Lud (who are archers), Tubal, Javan, and the coasts and islands far away — who
have not heard about me or seen my glory. And they
will proclaim my glory among the nations. 20 They
will bring all your brothers from all the nations as
a gift to the LORD on horses and chariots, in litters,
and on mules and camels, to my holy mountain Jerusalem," says the LORD, "just as the Israelites bring
an offering in a clean vessel to the house of the LORD.
21 I will also take some of them as priests and Levites,"
says the LORD.
22 "For just as the new heavens
and the new earth,
which I will make,
will remain before me" —
this is the LORD's declaration —
"so your offspring and your name
will remain.

[A] **66:2** Lit *broken* [B] **66:12** Or *glory* [C] **66:14** Lit *your bones* [D] **66:17** Hb obscure [E] **66:17** Lit *abhorrent things* [F] **66:18** LXX, Syr; MT omits *Knowing* [G] **66:19** LXX; MT reads *Pul*

23 All humanity will come to worship me
from one New Moon to another
and from one Sabbath to another,"
says the LORD.

24 "As they leave, they will see the dead bodies of
those who have rebelled against me; for their worm
will never die, their fire will never go out, and they
will be a horror to all humanity."

JEREMIAH

Modern Anathoth, northeast of Jerusalem. Jeremiah's hometown.

INTRODUCTION TO

JEREMIAH

Circumstances of Writing

Jeremiah was a priest from the town of Anathoth (Jr 1:1). At the Lord's command, he neither married nor had children because of the impending judgment that would come upon the next generation. His ministry as a prophet began in 626 BC and ended after 586 BC. He was a contemporary of Habakkuk and possibly Obadiah.

The book of Jeremiah discusses the last days of Judah. King Hezekiah reigned for forty-two years (729–686 BC) and began to reverse Judah's spiritual bankruptcy. But when Hezekiah's son, Manasseh, came to the throne, idolatrous and superstitious cultic practices and rites came back like a flood. Manasseh's son Amon ruled for only two years (642–640 BC). He also reinstated idol worship as the official religion of Judah (2Ch 33:22–23).

Amon's eight-year-old son, Josiah, succeeded him on the throne. This lad walked in the ways of the former King David. When he was eighteen years old (622 BC), he called for long-delayed repairs to be made to the temple. During this work, a copy of the law of Moses was found. On the basis of hearing this word, the young king and all his people renewed the covenant with the Lord. However, this reformation failed to overcome the effects of the wickedness Manasseh and Amon had instituted.

Contribution to the Bible

The best-known passage in Jeremiah is the new covenant text in 31:31–34. Not only is it the largest Old Testament text quoted in the New Testament (Heb 8:8–12; 10:16–17), but arguably better than any other passage it links God's ancient promises to Eve (Gn 3:15), Abraham (Gn 12:1–3), and David (2Sm 7:16–19) with New Testament assurances that God in Christ grants believers new hearts, salvation, and fellowship with him.

Structure

One date rings throughout the entire book of Jeremiah: "the fourth year of Jehoiakim son of Josiah, king of Judah." That year, 605 BC, brought major change to the political situation of the ancient Near East. Both Egypt and Assyria were defeated at the battle of Carchemish (2Kg 24:7; 2Ch 35:20; Jr 46:2–12). Nebuchadnezzar ascended the throne of Babylon. In that same year God instructed Jeremiah to put his prophecies into writing as a final test of King Jehoiakim's responsiveness to the word of God.

This significant dateline, "the fourth year of Jehoiakim," was placed at Jeremiah 25:1; 36:1; and 45:1, thereby dividing the prophet's book into three main sections: the prophet's faithfulness in carrying out God's commission (chaps. 2–24), the fierce opposition to his ministry (chaps. 25–35), and the collapse of Judah (chaps. 36–45).

The book of Jeremiah includes poetic sections (especially in chaps. 2–25) and prose accounts as well. Critical scholars generally say that the poetry is Jeremiah's and the prose is either the work of his friends or a person who is labeled a Deuteronomic writer (so designated because the prose sections are said to reflect the book of Deuteronomy). But we may ask, could not Jeremiah have written in both poetic and prose form? There is no reason to suppose he was incapable of writing in both forms.

1 The words of Jeremiah, the son of Hilkiah, one
of the priests living in Anathoth in the territory
of Benjamin. 2 The word of the LORD came to him
in the thirteenth year of the reign of Josiah son of
Amon, king of Judah. 3 It also came throughout the
days of Jehoiakim son of Josiah, king of Judah, until
the fifth month of the eleventh year of Zedekiah son
of Josiah, king of Judah, when the people of Jerusalem went into exile.

THE CALL OF JEREMIAH

4 The word of the LORD came to me:

5 I chose you before I formed you in the womb;
I set you apart before you were born.
I appointed you a prophet to the nations.

6 But I protested, "Oh no, Lord GOD! Look, I don't
know how to speak since I am only a youth."
7 Then the LORD said to me:

Do not say, "I am only a youth,"
for you will go to everyone I send you to
and speak whatever I tell you.
8 Do not be afraid of anyone,
for I will be with you to rescue you.
This is the LORD's declaration.

9 Then the LORD reached out his hand, touched my
mouth, and told me:

I have now filled your mouth with my words.
10 See, I have appointed you today
over nations and kingdoms
to uproot and tear down,
to destroy and demolish,
to build and plant.

TWO VISIONS

11 Then the word of the LORD came to me, asking,
"What do you see, Jeremiah?"
I replied, "I see a branch of an almond tree."
12 The LORD said to me, "You have seen correctly,
for I watch over[A] my word to accomplish it." 13 Again
the word of the LORD came to me asking, "What do
you see?"
And I replied, "I see a boiling pot, its lip tilted from
the north to the south."
14 Then the LORD said to me, "Disaster will be
poured out[B] from the north on all who live in the
land. 15 Indeed, I am about to summon all the clans
and kingdoms of the north."

This is the LORD's declaration.
They will come, and each king will set up
his throne
at the entrance to Jerusalem's gates.
They will attack all her surrounding walls
and all the other cities of Judah.

16 "I will pronounce my judgments against them for
all the evil they did when they abandoned me to burn
incense to other gods and to worship the works of
their own hands.
17 "Now, get ready. Stand up and tell them everything
that I command you. Do not be intimidated by them or
I will cause you to cower before them. 18 Today, I am the
one who has made you a fortified city, an iron pillar,
and bronze walls against the whole land — against
the kings of Judah, its officials, its priests, and the
population. 19 They will fight against you but never
prevail over you, since I am with you to rescue you."
This is the LORD's declaration.

ISRAEL ACCUSED OF APOSTASY

2 The word of the LORD came to me: 2 "Go and announce directly to Jerusalem that this is what
the LORD says:

I remember the loyalty of your youth,
your love as a bride —
how you followed me in the wilderness,
in a land not sown.
3 Israel was holy to the LORD,
the firstfruits of his harvest.
All who ate of it found themselves guilty;
disaster came on them."
This is the LORD's declaration.

4 Hear the word of the LORD, house of Jacob
and all families of the house of Israel.
5 This is what the LORD says:

What fault did your ancestors find in me
that they went so far from me,
followed worthless idols,
and became worthless themselves?
6 They stopped asking, "Where is the LORD
who brought us from the land of Egypt,
who led us through the wilderness,
through a land of deserts and ravines,
through a land of drought and darkness,[C]
a land no one traveled through
and where no one lived?"
7 I brought you to a fertile land
to eat its fruit and bounty,
but after you entered, you defiled my land;
you made my inheritance detestable.
8 The priests quit asking, "Where is the LORD?"
The experts in the law no longer knew me,
and the rulers rebelled against me.
The prophets prophesied by[D] Baal
and followed useless idols.

[A] **1:12** In Hb, the word for *almond tree* sounds like the word for *watch over* [B] **1:14** LXX reads *will boil* [C] **2:6** Or *shadow of death* [D] **2:8** = in the name of

Jeremiah in Its Historical Setting

by Robert D. Bergen

If the 463 years of Israel's monarchy (from King Saul through the fall of Jerusalem) were a regulation football game, Jeremiah's life and ministry would take place in the final five minutes. From about 627 BC,[1] when Jeremiah received his divine call to the prophetic ministry, until 586 BC, when he was forcibly taken off the stage of history, political changes on the grandest scale took place that would forever alter the national and cultural landscape of two continents.

EARLY IN JEREMIAH'S MINISTRY

Jeremiah received his call from God in the thirteenth year of King Josiah's reign (Jr 1:2) and reluctantly entered the prophetic ministry at that time (vv. 1–7). Approximately three years earlier (630 BC), the prophets Habakkuk and Zephaniah had warned of catastrophic divine judgment on Jerusalem for its many sins (Hab 1:2–11; Zph 1:1–18). Then two years later in 628 BC, Judah's twenty-year-old King Josiah had kicked off the greatest spiritual reformation since the days of Samuel (2Ch 34:3–35:18). As part of that religious revival, Josiah had ordered the destruction of every shrine, cult object, and priest not associated with the worship of the Lord (2Kg 23:4–20). Jeremiah's arrival on the scene, marked by his warning of a devastating invasion from the north (Jr 1:13–16), heightened the nation's awareness of the need for spiritual reform.

Interestingly, King Josiah chose to extend the spiritual reforms beyond his own nation's borders. Though he was king only of Judah, he went north to purge the tribal regions of Manasseh, Ephraim, and Naphtali of their pagan cult objects (2Ch 34:6). In so doing, he was reclaiming Assyrian-held territories for the Lord. Josiah's bold action, perhaps justified by the death of Assyria's King Ashurbanipal, provided early evidence that the once-mighty nation of Assyria, which had conquered Israel in 722 BC, was now in decline.

Assyria's weakness became more evident in 625 BC when Nabopolassar ascended the throne in Babylon. Recognized by historians as the founder of the Neo-Babylonian Empire, Nabopolassar aggressively initiated military efforts to free his nation from Assyrian shackles. At the same time, a Scythian tribe (from what is now the steppes of southern Russia) advanced against Assyria. In addition, Cyaxares, king of the land of Media east of Assyria, also moved against the land.[2]

The efforts of these three enemies against Assyria, and especially those of the Babylonians and the Medes, persisted for the next twenty years, during which the Assyrians' losses mounted. In 614 BC, Cyaxares attacked and destroyed Assyria's religious center, the city of Asshur. Two years later, the capital city of Nineveh was overrun and occupied by the combined armies of Media and Babylon and the Assyrian King Sin-shar-ishkun was killed. Nineveh's destruction fulfilled Isaiah's prophecy of Assyria's downfall in Isaiah 10:12 and the vivid prophecies of the Israelite prophet Nahum.

Following Assyria's loss of both its capital city and king, the nation attempted to regroup with a new king (Ashur-uballit II) and a new capital (Haran) and an alliance with Egypt. But in 609 BC, Nabopolassar and the Babylonians, assisted by the Scythians, attacked and defeated the coalition of Assyrian and Egyptian forces and ended the Neo-Assyrian Empire.

The events of 609 BC touched Judah in a particularly tragic way when King Josiah, apparently acting as an ally of the Babylonians, attempted to stop the Egyptians as they marched northward to join the Assyrians. Though God, speaking through Pharaoh Neco II, had warned Josiah not to interfere with the Egyptians, he did so anyway and was mortally wounded in battle (2Ch 35:20–24). As a result, Egypt took control of Judah's government, deposing Josiah's son and successor Jehoahaz (also known as Shallum) and taking him to Egypt, where he died (2Kg 23:34; Jr 22:11–12). Pharaoh Neco II then installed another of Josiah's sons, Eliakim (whom he renamed Jehoiakim), as Judah's next king and forced Judah to pay taxes to Egypt (2Kg 23:34–35).

In 605 BC, Nabopolassar's son Nebuchadnezzar, who had served as Babylon's commanding general, ascended the throne. Also, Judah's loyalties were forcibly switched from Egypt to Babylon when Nebuchadnezzar looted Jerusalem and took many hostages with him, including Daniel and his three friends (Dn 1:1–4).

LATER IN JEREMIAH'S MINISTRY

After 605 BC, Nebuchadnezzar worked to gain more control over former Assyrian holdings. In 602 BC, Jehoiakim rebelled against Babylon, probably by withholding required annual payments. In response, Nebuchadnezzar made the Arameans, Moabites, and Ammonites (Judah's neighbors under Babylonian control) conduct raids against Judah (2Kg 24:2).

Following the death of Jehoiakim, his eighteen-year-old son Jehoiachin ascended Judah's throne. Sensing that a regional threat might be brewing, Nebuchadnezzar had his army besiege Jerusalem in 597 BC, arrest Jehoiachin, and deport him and thousands of the kingdom's most capable citizens to Babylon. Then Nebuchadnezzar made Jehoiachin's uncle Mattaniah king instead, changing his name to Zedekiah as an expression of Babylonian authority over him (2Kg 24:10–17).

For the next few years, Zedekiah acted as an obedient servant of the Babylonians. But in 593 BC, he

Achaemenid seal with Median archer and soldier in crested helmet.

sponsored a meeting of top negotiators from five other neighboring nations in an effort to craft a plan to break free of Babylonian domination. Jeremiah, however, declared God's opposition to any such plan (Jr 27:6–15), and the coordinated revolt against Babylon never occurred.

But Zedekiah never gave up hope of breaking away from Babylon. Encouraged by optimistic oracles from false prophets in Jerusalem (Jr 37:19) and a recent Egyptian military victory in Africa,[3] Zedekiah forged an anti-Babylonian alliance with the Egyptians. The prophet Ezekiel warned Zedekiah that Egypt would fail to help Judah (Ezk 17:11–18), but Zedekiah was undeterred.

Consequently, in 589 BC, Zedekiah rebelled against Babylon (2Kg 24:20). Predictably, the Babylonians responded aggressively to Judah's insurrection. In January 588 BC, Nebuchadnezzar brought his army to Jerusalem and attacked it for a final time (25:1). The Egyptians under the leadership of Pharaoh Hophra (also known as Apries) then mustered their army to fight against Nebuchadnezzar's troops, forcing the Babylonians to temporarily abandon Jerusalem. For a time, Zedekiah's plan seemed to have succeeded; but unhappily for Judah, the Babylonians quickly defeated the Egyptians and then resumed their attack on Jerusalem. Jerusalem was sealed off until its food supply was depleted, a period of about two and a half years. In July 586 BC, the Babylonians entered the beleaguered city, holding a triumphant celebration in its midst (Jr 39:2–4). Many of the city's survivors, including Zedekiah, were deported to Babylon; Zedekiah's sons and top officials were rounded up and executed before Nebuchadnezzar in Riblah (52:8–11,24–30). In August 586 BC, Jerusalem's buildings were ransacked and burned, and its walls broken down (vv. 12–23).

As a final act in this period of Judahite history, the Babylonians established a regional authority to oversee their interests in the area. Stationing a garrison of troops in the makeshift capital city of Mizpah, they installed Gedaliah there as an overseer of the territory. Their efforts were only minimally successful; in October 586 BC, Gedaliah was murdered by a band of Judahite zealots. Many of the remaining citizens fled to Egypt, taking Jeremiah and his friend Baruch with them (2Kg 25:22–26; Jr 40:5–43:7). ✣

---

[1] Dates in this article correspond to the chronologies presented in Edwin R. Thiele, *The Mysterious Numbers of the Hebrew Kings*, rev. ed. (Grand Rapids: Kregel, 1983); and John H. Walton, *Chronological and Background Charts of the Old Testament*, rev. ed. (Grand Rapids: Zondervan, 1994).
[2] Siegfried Herrmann, *A History of Israel in Old Testament Times*, trans. John Bowden (Philadelphia: Fortress, 1975), 264.
[3] J. Maxwell Miller and John H. Hayes, *A History of Ancient Israel and Judah* (Philadelphia: Westminster, 1986), 412.

9 Therefore, I will bring a case against you again.
This is the LORD's declaration.
I will bring a case
against your children's children.
10 Cross over to the coasts of Cyprus[A] and take
a look.
Send someone to Kedar and consider carefully;
see if there has ever been anything like this:
11 Has a nation ever exchanged its gods?
(But they were not gods!)
Yet my people have exchanged their[B] Glory
for useless idols.
12 Be appalled at this, heavens;
be shocked and utterly desolated!
This is the LORD's declaration.

13 For my people have committed a double evil:
They have abandoned me,
the fountain of living water,
and dug cisterns for themselves —
cracked cisterns that cannot hold water.

CONSEQUENCES OF APOSTASY

14 Is Israel a slave?
Was he born into slavery?[C]
Why else has he become a prey?
15 The young lions have roared at him;
they have roared loudly.
They have laid waste his land.
His cities are in ruins, without inhabitants.
16 The men of Memphis and Tahpanhes
have also broken your skull.
17 Have you not brought this on yourself
by abandoning the LORD your God
while he was leading you along the way?
18 Now what will you gain
by traveling along the way to Egypt
to drink the water of the Nile?[D]
What will you gain
by traveling along the way to Assyria
to drink the water of the Euphrates?
19 Your own evil will discipline you;
your own apostasies will reprimand you.
Recognize[E] how evil and bitter it is
for you to abandon the LORD your God
and to have no fear of me.
This is the declaration
of the Lord GOD of Armies.

20 For long ago I[F] broke your yoke;
I[F] tore off your chains.
You insisted, "I will not serve!"
On every high hill
and under every green tree
you lay down like a prostitute.
21 I planted you, a choice vine
from the very best seed.
How then could you turn into
a degenerate, foreign vine?

22 Even if you wash with lye
and use a great amount of bleach,[G]
the stain of your iniquity is still in front of me.
This is the Lord GOD's declaration.
23 How can you protest, "I am not defiled;
I have not followed the Baals"?
Look at your behavior in the valley;
acknowledge what you have done.
You are a swift young camel
twisting and turning on her way,
24 a wild donkey at home[H] in the wilderness.
She sniffs the wind in the heat of her desire.
Who can control her passion?
All who look for her will not become weary;
they will find her in her mating season.[I]
25 Keep your feet from going bare
and your throat from thirst.
But you say, "It's hopeless;
I love strangers,
and I will continue to follow them."

26 Like the shame of a thief when he is caught,
so the house of Israel has been put to shame.
They, their kings, their officials,
their priests, and their prophets
27 say to a tree, "You are my father,"
and to a stone, "You gave birth to me."
For they have turned their back to me
and not their face,
yet in their time of disaster they beg,
"Rise up and save us!"
28 But where are your gods you made
for yourself?
Let them rise up and save you
in your time of disaster if they can,
for your gods are as numerous
as your cities, Judah.

JUDGMENT DESERVED

29 Why do you bring a case against me?
All of you have rebelled against me.
This is the LORD's declaration.
30 I have struck down your children in vain;
they would not accept discipline.
Your own sword has devoured your prophets
like a ravaging lion.

[A]**2:10** Lit *to the islands of Kittim* [B]**2:11** Alt Hb tradition reads *my* [C]**2:14** Lit *born of a house* [D]**2:18** Lit *of Shihor* [E]**2:19** Lit *Know and see* [F]**2:20** LXX reads *you* [G]**2:22** Lit *cleansing agent* [H]**2:24** Lit *donkey taught* [I]**2:24** Lit *her month*

Jeremiah's call to prophetic ministry was a call to the daunting task of announcing God's word of judgment to an unrepentant generation. The failed leadership of kings, priests, and prophets in this era had led to the announcement of God's final invoking of the curses of the covenant. Jeremiah announced that these curses would lead to the destruction of Judah and Jerusalem at the hand of Nebuchadnezzar's army. Infuriated at the prophet's words, the people even of his own hometown of Anathoth, just six miles north of Jerusalem, would seek Jeremiah's life (Jr 11:18–23).

The Lord revealed to Jeremiah that Jerusalem's leaders would oppose him from every side. He was to stand immovably and resolutely like "a fortified city"—against all opposition. The fortifications are portrayed in metaphorical terms, using symbolic language of iron pillars and bronze walls (1:18–19), language not uncommon in the biblical world. For example, in excavating Balawat, archaeologists uncovered an example of Assyrian bronze-reinforced doors.[1] Pharaoh Thutmose III described himself as a rampart of iron, suggesting he was invincible.[2] Likewise, Jeremiah was to brace himself against his adversaries more firmly than the strongest walls of stone and wood. And though kings such as Jehoiakim and Zedekiah would wage war against Jeremiah as if he were a fortified city, placing him in prison and abusing him more than once, God's promised presence would provide the strength to endure the battles. Jeremiah's historical context would have made him thoroughly acquainted with fortified cities.

INTERNATIONAL POLITICS OF REBELLION

The thirteenth year of the reign of Judah's King Josiah, about 626 BC, saw the beginning of the end of the great kingdom of Assyria. The Babylonian insurgents under Nabopolassar threw off the bondage of Assyrian domination. This allowed other kingdoms such as Judah to consider similar tactics to bring relief from the harsh burdens their ruthless captors had imposed on them.

One of the typical responses of rebel states was to fortify strategic cities on the borders of their traditional homeland along with other key cities of the territorial infrastructure. Under Hezekiah, some seventy-five years before Jeremiah's call to ministry (ca 705 BC), numerous cities on the western and southern borders of Judah were fortified to solidify Judah's defenses against an Assyrian attack. Strategically located cities such as Timnah, Ekron, Libnah, and Lachish saw extensive building projects designed to strengthen walls to prevent the boring and undermining techniques

City gate at Gezer.

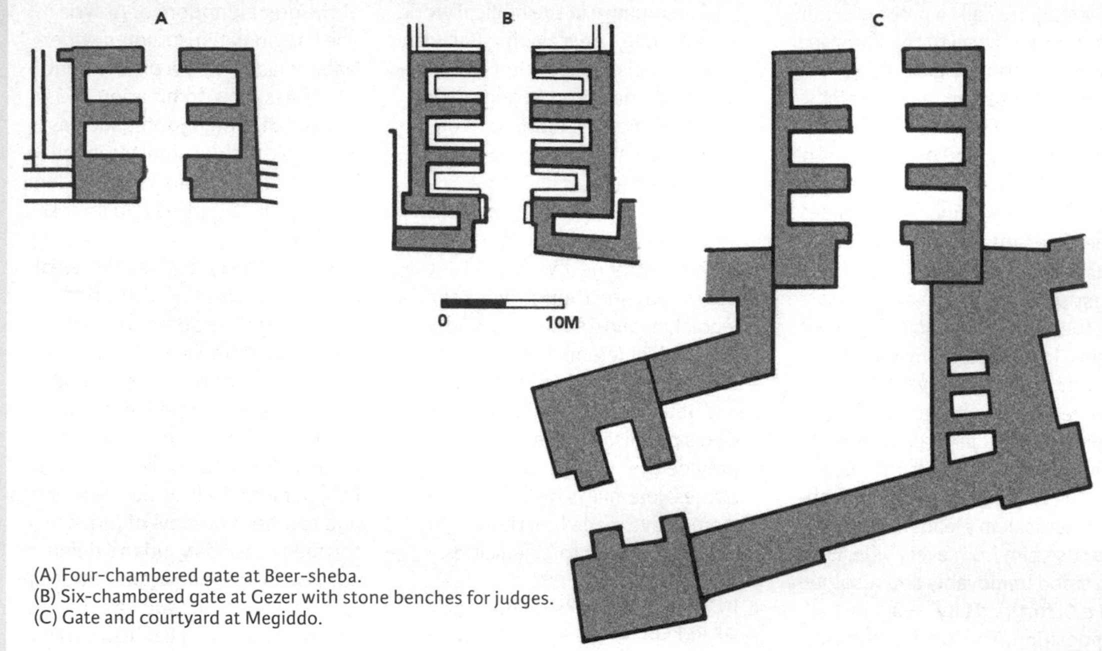

(A) Four-chambered gate at Beer-sheba.
(B) Six-chambered gate at Gezer with stone benches for judges.
(C) Gate and courtyard at Megiddo.

of siege engines. These cities would provide a network of forward battle lines designed to protect Jerusalem against attack.

Similarly, when Zedekiah rebelled against Nebuchadnezzar of Babylon in 589 BC, he reinforced the defenses at Lachish and expanded the fortifications at Beth-shemesh, Hebron, and elsewhere. In the end, these fortifications were no match for the powerful war machines of Assyria and Babylon. The defense of Israel and Judah was ultimately in God himself, as when Jerusalem was delivered from Sennacherib's army in 701 BC (2Kg 19:8–36).

CITY PROTECTION

Fortified cities, whether small such as the four-acre enclosure at Timnah in the Sorek Valley west of Jerusalem, or larger cities such as the thirty-one-acre site of Lachish in southwest Judah, were surrounded by stone-based walls with mud-brick superstructure. In some cities such as Lachish, a double wall would serve to defend the city against attack. Massive stone buildups called revetments were added at more vulnerable points such as the city gate.

Wall and gate architecture went through several stages of development from the Bronze Age to the Iron Age, the latter representing much of Israel's kingdom history. Smaller villages, such as those that provided the early Israelites of the period of the judges their architectural base, were unfortified. These "ring settlements" consisted of small houses strung together in a circular arrangement, with a small opening where the circle overlapped serving as a gate. As Israelite city fortifications emerged during the kingdom period, the outlying villages, where a majority of the population lived, received less attention. Protection for the inhabitants of the villages depended on the fortified cities as a place for retreat during siege or attack.

WALLS

Two basic types of walls were used in the protection of the Israelite town: the solid wall and the casemate. The solid wall consisted of a foundation of cut and uncut stones, first layered into a subterranean trench about eighteen to forty inches in depth. This foundation was then built up to a height of six to ten feet. On the stone, workers would then add layers of large mud bricks until the wall reached a height of roughly ten to fifteen feet or more above the normal ground layer. These walls ranged from six feet in thickness in smaller towns to more than twenty-three feet in places such as Jerusalem.[3] As the wall approached the gate area, they were more heavily fortified by having deeper foundation trenches and larger stones weighing hundreds of pounds—some of which were laid to greater heights.

Casemate wall construction consisted of two parallel walls, each about a yard thick, with a vacant space between them of about six to ten feet. This inner area was subdivided by small lateral perpendicular walls that subdivided the casemate into rooms. People used these rooms for storage or small shops during times of peace and prosperity. In times of war or siege, these compartments could be filled with dirt and stone rubble making a solid wall twelve to twenty feet thick. Casemate walls were more common in the ninth and early eighth centuries BC, but they gave way to the more durable solid walls from the late eighth century (time of Hezekiah) to the end of Judah in 586 BC. Archaeologists have excavated excellent examples of tenth to ninth-century-BC casemate-construction fortifications at Hazor, Megiddo, and Gezer, all key cities in the network of kingdom construction during the reign of Solomon (1Kg 9:15).[4] Occasionally walls were reinforced with long lateral wooden timbers between each of two or three layers of stone, adding further support in case of earthquakes, which were not uncommon in ancient Israel and Judah (Is 13:13; Am 1:1; Zch 14:5).

GATES

Access points to a city were vital to commerce and religious activity, yet they presented challenges to the city's defensibility. The gate structure was a multistoried building with defensive towers on both sides of the outer section of the entryway. From the days of Solomon to the end of the Israelite kingdom of Judah, the most common gate forms were those with four- or six-chambered gates.[5] Some of the chambers, such as those at Gezer, had stone benches on the perimeter of the room where the local judges sat as they carried out their judicial activities. Many gate areas had accompanying large outer courtyards where people from nearby villages and farmlands would bring their agricultural and manufactured goods for sale to the local public. Others like Beer-sheba contained small inner courtyards.

As the threat of an Assyrian siege loomed greater and greater in the latter part of the eighth century BC, Israelite architects began to construct outer revetment walls for added protection. Rather than have the gate directly accessible by the ramp that common people normally used moving in and out of the city, builders erected L-shaped walls on deep foundations. The new design provided only indirect access to the inner gate building itself. The bulky siege machines were less maneuverable in the close quarters of the indirect gate systems. Even small advanced fortified sites such as Timnah came to use this form of defense bulwark. ❖

---

[1] Grant Frame, "Balawat" in *OEANE*, 1:268. Balawat was a fortified station on the road from Nineveh to Arrapha (modern Kirkuk, Iraq). [2] J. Hoffmeier, "The Gebel Barkal Stela of Thutmose III (2.2B)," in *The Context of Scripture*, ed. William W. Hallo (Leiden: Koninklijke Brill NV, 2003), 2:15. This phraseology is used numerous times by Thutmose III and is also used in other historical and poetic contexts. [3] Hezekiah's western wall in the fortification of Jerusalem was about twenty-three feet thick. [4] For detailed discussion of city fortifications, see Philip J. King and Larry Stager, *Life in Biblical Israel, Library of Ancient Israel (LAI)* (Louisville: Westminster John Knox, 2001), 231–36; Z. Herzog, "Fortifications (Levant)" in *ABD*, 1:844–52. [5] Examples of four-chambered gates are at Beer-sheba, Ashdod, and Mizpah. Archaeologists have uncovered six-chamber gates at Hazor, Megiddo, Gezer, and Lachish.

Ruined wall from ancient Lachish.

31 Evil generation,
pay attention to the word of the LORD!
Have I been a wilderness to Israel
or a land of dense darkness?
Why do my people claim,
"We will go where we want;[A]
we will no longer come to you"?
32 Can a young woman forget her jewelry
or a bride her wedding sash?
Yet my people have forgotten me
for countless days.
33 How skillfully you pursue love;
you also teach evil women your ways.
34 Moreover, your skirts are stained
with the blood of the innocent poor.
You did not catch them breaking and entering.
But in spite of all these things
35 you claim, "I am innocent.
His anger is sure to turn away from me."
But I will certainly judge you
because you have said, "I have not sinned."
36 How unstable you are,
constantly changing your ways!
You will be put to shame by Egypt
just as you were put to shame by Assyria.
37 Moreover, you will be led out from here
with your hands on your head
since the LORD has rejected those you trust;
you will not succeed even with their help.[B]

WAGES OF APOSTASY

3 If[C] a man divorces his wife
and she leaves him to marry another,
can he ever return to her?
Wouldn't such a land[D] become totally defiled?
But you!
You have prostituted yourself
with many partners —
can you return to me?
This is the LORD's declaration.
2 Look to the barren heights and see.
Where have you not been immoral?
You sat waiting for them beside the highways
like a nomad in the desert.
You have defiled the land
with your prostitution and wickedness.
3 This is why the showers haven't come —
why there has been no spring rain.
You have the brazen look of a prostitute[E]
and refuse to be ashamed.
4 Haven't you recently called to me,
"My Father!
You were my friend in my youth.
5 Will he bear a grudge forever?
Will he be endlessly infuriated?"
This is what you have said,
but you have done the evil things
you are capable of.

UNFAITHFUL ISRAEL, TREACHEROUS JUDAH

6 In the days of King Josiah the LORD asked me, "Have
you seen what unfaithful Israel has done? She has
ascended every high hill and gone under every
green tree to prostitute herself there. 7 I thought,
'After she has done all these things, she will return
to me.' But she didn't return, and her treacherous
sister Judah saw it. 8 I[F] observed that it was because
unfaithful Israel had committed adultery that I had
sent her away and had given her a certificate of
divorce. Nevertheless, her treacherous sister Judah was not afraid but also went and prostituted
herself. 9 Indifferent to[G] her prostitution, she defiled the land and committed adultery with stones
and trees. 10 Yet in spite of all this, her treacherous
sister Judah didn't return to me with all her heart
— only in pretense."
This is the LORD's declaration.
11 The LORD announced to me, "Unfaithful Israel has
shown herself more righteous than treacherous Judah. 12 Go, proclaim these words to the north, and say,
'Return, unfaithful Israel.
This is the LORD's declaration.
I will not look on you with anger,[H]
for I am unfailing in my love.
This is the LORD's declaration.
I will not be angry forever.
13 Only acknowledge your guilt —
you have rebelled against the LORD your God.
You have scattered your favors to strangers
under every green tree
and have not obeyed me.
This is the LORD's declaration.
14 " 'Return, you faithless children — this is the
LORD's declaration — for I am your master,[I] and I
will take you, one from a city and two from a family,
and I will bring you to Zion. 15 I will give you shepherds who are loyal to me,[J] and they will shepherd
you with knowledge and skill. 16 When you multiply
and increase in the land, in those days — this is the
LORD's declaration — no one will say again, "The ark
of the LORD's covenant." It will never come to mind,
and no one will remember or miss it. Another one
will not be made.[K] 17 At that time Jerusalem will be
called The LORD's Throne, and all the nations will be

[A] **2:31** Or *"We have taken control*, or *"We can roam* [B] **2:37** Lit *with them* [C] **3:1** One Hb ms, LXX, Syr; other Hb mss read *Saying: If* [D] **3:1** LXX reads *woman* [E] **3:3** Lit *have a prostitute's forehead* [F] **3:8** One Hb ms, Syr read *She* [G] **3:9** Lit *From the lightness of* [H] **3:12** Lit *not cause my face to fall on you* [I] **3:14** Or *husband* [J] **3:15** Lit *shepherds according to my heart* [K] **3:16** Or *It will no longer be done*

gathered to it, to the name of the LORD in Jerusalem. They will cease to follow the stubbornness of their evil hearts. 18 In those days the house of Judah will join with the house of Israel, and they will come together from the land of the north to the land I have given your ancestors to inherit.' "

TRUE REPENTANCE

19 I thought, "How I long to make you my sons
and give you a desirable land,
the most beautiful inheritance of all
the nations."
I thought, "You will call me 'My Father'
and never turn away from me."
20 However, as a woman may betray her lover,[A]
so you have betrayed me, house of Israel.
This is the LORD's declaration.

21 A sound is heard on the barren heights:
the children of Israel weeping and begging
for mercy,
for they have perverted their way;
they have forgotten the LORD their God.
22 Return, you faithless children.
I will heal your unfaithfulness.
"Here we are, coming to you,
for you are the LORD our God.
23 Surely, falsehood comes from the hills,
commotion from the mountains,
but the salvation of Israel
is only in the LORD our God.
24 From the time of our youth
the shameful one[B] has consumed
what our ancestors have worked for —
their flocks and their herds,
their sons and their daughters.
25 Let us lie down in our shame;
let our disgrace cover us.
We have sinned against the LORD our God,
both we and our ancestors,
from the time of our youth
even to this day.
We have not obeyed the LORD our God."

BLESSING OR CURSE

4 If you return,[C] Israel —
this is the LORD's declaration —
you will return to me,
if you remove your abhorrent idols
from my presence
and do not waver,
2 then you can swear, "As the LORD lives,"
in truth, justice, and righteousness,
and then the nations will be blessed[D] by him
and will boast in him.

3 For this is what the LORD says to the men of Judah
and Jerusalem:
Break up the unplowed ground;
do not sow among the thorns.
4 Circumcise yourselves to the LORD;
remove the foreskin of your hearts,
men of Judah and residents of Jerusalem.
Otherwise, my wrath will break out like fire
and burn with no one to extinguish it
because of your evil deeds.

JUDGMENT FROM THE NORTH

5 Declare in Judah, proclaim in Jerusalem, and say,
Blow the ram's horn throughout the land.
Cry out loudly and say,
"Assemble yourselves,
and let's flee to the fortified cities."
6 Lift up a signal flag toward Zion.
Run for cover! Don't stand still!
For I am bringing disaster from the north —
a crushing blow.
7 A lion has gone up from his thicket;
a destroyer of nations has set out.
He has left his lair
to make your land a waste.
Your cities will be reduced to uninhabited ruins.
8 Because of this, put on sackcloth;
mourn and wail,
for the LORD's burning anger
has not turned away from us.

9 "On that day" — this is the LORD's declaration
— "the king and the officials will lose their courage.
The priests will tremble in fear, and the prophets will
be scared speechless."
10 I said, "Oh no, Lord GOD, you have certainly deceived this people and Jerusalem, by announcing,
'You will have peace,' while a sword is at[E] our throats."
11 "At that time it will be said to this people and to
Jerusalem, 'A searing wind blows from the barren
heights in the wilderness on the way to my dear[F]
people. It comes not to winnow or to sift; 12 a wind
too strong for this comes at my call.[G] Now I will also
pronounce judgments against them.' "
13 Look, he advances like clouds;
his chariots are like a storm.
His horses are swifter than eagles.
Woe to us, for we are ruined!
14 Wash the evil from your heart, Jerusalem,
so that you will be delivered.
How long will you harbor
malicious thoughts?

[A] 3:20 Lit *friend* [B] 3:24 = Baal [C] 4:1 Or *Repent* [D] 4:2 Or *will bless one another* [E] 4:10 Lit *sword touches* [F] 4:11 Lit *to the daughter of my* [G] 4:12 Lit *comes for me*

15 For a voice announces from Dan,
proclaiming malice from Mount Ephraim.
16 Warn the nations: Look!
Proclaim to Jerusalem:
Those who besiege are coming
from a distant land;
they raise their voices
against the cities of Judah.
17 They have her surrounded
like those who guard a field,
because she has rebelled against me.
This is the LORD's declaration.
18 Your way and your actions
have brought this on you.
This is your punishment. It is very bitter,
because it has reached your heart!

JEREMIAH'S LAMENT

19 My anguish, my anguish![A] I writhe
in agony!
Oh, the pain in[B] my heart!
My heart pounds;
I cannot be silent.
For you, my soul,
have heard the sound of the ram's horn —
the shout of battle.
20 Disaster after disaster is reported
because the whole land is destroyed.
Suddenly my tents are destroyed,
my tent curtains, in a moment.
21 How long must I see the signal flag
and hear the sound of the ram's horn?

22 "For my people are fools;
they do not know me.
They are foolish children,
without understanding.
They are skilled in doing what is evil,
but they do not know how to do
what is good."

23 I looked at the earth,
and it was formless and empty.
I looked to the heavens,
and their light was gone.
24 I looked at the mountains,
and they were quaking;
all the hills shook.
25 I looked, and there was no human being,
and all the birds of the sky had fled.
26 I looked, and the fertile field was
a wilderness.
All its cities were torn down
because of the LORD
and his burning anger.

27 For this is what the LORD says:
"The whole land will be a desolation,
but I will not finish it off.
28 Because of this, the earth will mourn;
the skies above will grow dark.
I have spoken; I have planned,
and I will not relent or turn back from it."

29 Every city flees
at the sound of the horseman and the archer.
They enter the thickets
and climb among the rocks.
Every city is abandoned;
no inhabitant is left.
30 And you, devastated one, what are you doing
that you dress yourself in scarlet,
that you adorn yourself with gold jewelry,
that you enhance your eyes with makeup?
You beautify yourself for nothing.
Your lovers reject you;
they intend to take your life.
31 I hear a cry like a woman in labor,
a cry of anguish like one bearing
her first child.
The cry of Daughter Zion gasping for breath,
stretching out her hands:
"Woe is me, for my life is weary
because of the murderers!"

THE DEPRAVITY OF JERUSALEM

5 Roam through the streets of Jerusalem.
Investigate;[C]
search in her squares.
If you find one person,
any who acts justly,
who pursues faithfulness,
then I will forgive her.
2 When they say, "As the LORD lives,"
they are swearing falsely.
3 LORD, don't your eyes look for faithfulness?
You have struck them, but they felt no pain.
You finished them off,
but they refused to accept discipline.
They made their faces harder than rock,
and they refused to return.

4 Then I thought:
They are just the poor;
they have been foolish.
For they don't understand the way
of the LORD,
the justice of their God.

[A] **4:19** Lit *My inner parts, my inner parts* [B] **4:19** Lit *the walls of* [C] **5:1** Lit *See and know*

5 I will go to the powerful
and speak to them.
Surely they know the way of the LORD,
the justice of their God.
However, these also had broken the yoke
and torn off the chains.
6 Therefore, a lion from the forest
will strike them down.
A wolf from arid plains will ravage them.
A leopard stalks their cities.
Anyone who leaves them will be torn to pieces
because their rebellious acts are many,
their unfaithful deeds numerous.

7 Why should I forgive you?
Your children have abandoned me
and sworn by those who are not gods.
I satisfied their needs, yet they
committed adultery;
they gashed themselves
at the[A] prostitute's house.
8 They are well-fed,[B] eager[C] stallions,
each neighing after someone else's wife.
9 Should I not punish them for these things?
This is the LORD's declaration.
Should I not avenge myself
on such a nation as this?

10 Go up among her vineyard terraces
and destroy them,
but do not finish them off.
Prune away her shoots,
for they do not belong to the LORD.
11 They, the house of Israel and the house of Judah,
have dealt very treacherously with me.
This is the LORD's declaration.
12 They have contradicted the LORD
and insisted, "It won't happen.[D]
Harm won't come to us;
we won't see sword or famine."
13 The prophets become only wind,
for the LORD's word is not in them.
This will in fact happen to them.

COMING JUDGMENT

14 Therefore, this is what the Lord GOD of Armies says:
Because you have spoken this word,
I am going to make my words
become fire in your mouth.
These people are the wood,
and the fire will consume them.
15 I am about to bring a nation
from far away against you,
house of Israel.
This is the LORD's declaration.
It is an established nation,
an ancient nation,
a nation whose language you do not know
and whose speech you do not understand.
16 Their quiver is like an open grave;
they are all warriors.
17 They will consume your harvest and your food.
They will consume your sons
and your daughters.
They will consume your flocks and your herds.
They will consume your vines and your fig trees.
With the sword they will destroy
your fortified cities in which you trust.

18 "But even in those days" — this is the LORD's declaration — "I will not finish you off. 19 When people
ask, 'For what offense has the LORD our God done all
these things to us?' You will respond to them, 'Just
as you abandoned me and served foreign gods in
your land, so will you serve strangers in a land that
is not yours.'

20 "Declare this in the house of Jacob; proclaim it
in Judah, saying:
21 Hear this,
you foolish and senseless[E] people.
They have eyes, but they don't see.
They have ears, but they don't hear.
22 Do you not fear me?
This is the LORD's declaration.
Do you not tremble before me,
the one who set the sand as the boundary
of the sea,
an enduring barrier that it cannot cross?
The waves surge, but they cannot prevail.
They roar but cannot pass over it.
23 But these people have stubborn
and rebellious hearts.
They have turned aside and have gone away.
24 They have not said to themselves,
'Let's fear the LORD our God,
who gives the seasonal rains, both autumn
and spring,
who guarantees to us the fixed weeks
of the harvest.'
25 Your guilty acts have diverted these things
from you.
Your sins have withheld my bounty from you,
26 for wicked men live among my people.
They watch like hunters[F] lying in wait.[G]
They set a trap;
they catch men.

[A] **5:7** Or *adultery and trooped to the*, or *adultery and lodged at the*; Hb obscure [B] **5:8** Lit *well-equipped*; Hb obscure [C] **5:8** Lit *early-rising*; Hb obscure [D] **5:12** Lit *"He does not exist* [E] **5:21** Lit *without heart* [F] **5:26** Lit *hunters of birds* [G] **5:26** Hb obscure

27 Like a cage full of birds,
so their houses are full of deceit.
Therefore they have grown powerful
and rich.
28 They have become fat and sleek.
They have also excelled in evil matters.
They have not taken up cases,
such as the case of the fatherless,
so they might prosper,
and they have not defended the rights
of the needy.
29 Should I not punish them for these things?
This is the LORD's declaration.
Should I not avenge myself
on such a nation as this?

30 "An appalling, horrible thing
has taken place in the land.
31 The prophets prophesy falsely,
and the priests rule by their own authority.
My people love it like this.
But what will you do at the end of it?

THREATENED SIEGE OF JERUSALEM

6 "Run for cover
out of Jerusalem, Benjaminites.
Sound the ram's horn in Tekoa;
raise a smoke signal
over Beth-haccherem,[A]
for disaster threatens from the north,
even a crushing blow.
2 Though she is beautiful and delicate,
I will destroy[B] Daughter Zion.
3 Shepherds and their flocks will come
against her;
they will pitch their tents all around her.
Each will pasture his own portion.
4 Set them apart for war against her;
rise up, let's attack at noon.
Woe to us, for the day is passing;
the evening shadows grow long.
5 Rise up, let's attack by night.
Let's destroy her fortresses."

6 For this is what the LORD of Armies says:
Cut down the trees;
raise a siege ramp against Jerusalem.
This city must be punished.
There is nothing but oppression
within her.
7 As a well gushes out its water,
so she pours out her evil.[C]
Violence and destruction resound in her.
Sickness and wounds keep coming
to my attention.
8 Be warned, Jerusalem,
or I will turn away from you;
I will make you a desolation,
a land without inhabitants.

WRATH ON ISRAEL

9 This is what the LORD of Armies says:
Glean the remnant of Israel
as thoroughly as a vine.
Pass your hand once more like a grape gatherer
over the branches.

10 Who can I speak to and give such a warning[D]
that they will listen?
Look, their ear is uncircumcised,[E]
so they cannot pay attention.
See, the word of the LORD
has become contemptible to them —
they find no pleasure in it.
11 But I am full of the LORD's wrath;
I am tired of holding it back.
Pour it out on the children in the street,
on the gathering of young men as well.
For both husband and wife will be captured,
the old with the very old.[F]
12 Their houses will be turned over to others,
their fields and wives as well,
for I will stretch out my hand
against the inhabitants of the land.
This is the LORD's declaration.

13 For from the least to the greatest of them,
everyone is making profit dishonestly.
From prophet to priest,
everyone deals falsely.
14 They have treated
my people's brokenness superficially,
claiming, "Peace, peace,"
when there is no peace.
15 Were they ashamed when they acted
so detestably?
They weren't at all ashamed.
They can no longer feel humiliation.
Therefore, they will fall among the fallen.
When I punish them, they will collapse,
says the LORD.

DISASTER BECAUSE OF DISOBEDIENCE

16 This is what the LORD says:
Stand by the roadways and look.
Ask about the ancient paths,
"Which is the way to what is good?"

[A] **6:1** = House of the Vineyard [B] **6:2** Or *silence* [C] **6:7** Or *well keeps its water fresh, so she keeps her evil fresh* [D] **6:10** Or *and bear witness* [E] **6:10** They are unresponsive to God. [F] **6:11** Lit *with fullness of days*

Then take it
and find rest for yourselves.
But they protested, "We won't!"
17 I appointed watchmen over you
and said, "Listen for the sound
of the ram's horn."
But they protested, "We won't listen!"

18 Therefore listen, you nations
and you witnesses,
learn what the charge is against them.
19 Listen, earth!
I am about to bring disaster on these people,
the fruit of their own plotting,
for they have paid no attention to my words.
They have rejected my instruction.
20 What use to me is frankincense from Sheba
or sweet cane from a distant land?
Your burnt offerings are not acceptable;
your sacrifices do not please me.
21 Therefore, this is what the LORD says:
I am going to place stumbling blocks
before these people;
fathers and sons together will stumble
over them;
friends and neighbors will also perish.

A CRUEL NATION FROM THE NORTH

22 This is what the LORD says:
Look, an army is coming
from a northern land;
a great nation will be stirred up
from the remote regions of the earth.
23 They grasp bow and javelin.
They are cruel and show no mercy.
Their voice roars like the sea,
and they ride on horses,
lined up like men in battle formation
against you, Daughter Zion.

24 We have heard about it,
and our hands have become weak.
Distress has seized us —
pain, like a woman in labor.
25 Don't go out to the fields;
don't walk on the road.
For the enemy has a sword;
terror is on every side.

26 My dear[A] people, dress yourselves
in sackcloth
and roll in the dust.
Mourn as you would for an only son,
a bitter lament,
for suddenly the destroyer will come on us.

JEREMIAH APPOINTED AS AN EXAMINER

27 I have appointed you to be an assayer
among my people —
a refiner[B] —
so you may know and assay their way of life.
28 All are stubborn rebels
spreading slander.
They are bronze and iron;
all of them are corrupt.
29 The bellows blow,
blasting the lead with fire.
The refining is completely in vain;
the evil ones are not separated out.
30 They are called rejected silver,
for the LORD has rejected them.

FALSE TRUST IN THE TEMPLE

7 This is the word that came to Jeremiah from the
LORD: 2 "Stand in the gate of the house of the LORD
and there call out this word: 'Hear the word of the
LORD, all you people of Judah who enter through
these gates to worship the LORD.
3 "'This is what the LORD of Armies, the God of Israel, says: Correct your ways and your actions, and
I will allow you to live in this place. 4 Do not trust
deceitful words, chanting, "This is the temple of the
LORD, the temple of the LORD, the temple of the LORD."
5 Instead, if you really correct your ways and your
actions, if you act justly toward one another,[C] 6 if you
no longer oppress the resident alien, the fatherless,
and the widow and no longer shed innocent blood
in this place or follow other gods, bringing harm on
yourselves, 7 I will allow you to live in this place, the
land I gave to your ancestors long ago and forever.
8 But look, you keep trusting in deceitful words that
cannot help.
9 "'Do you steal, murder, commit adultery, swear
falsely, burn incense to Baal, and follow other gods
that you have not known? 10 Then do you come and
stand before me in this house that bears my name
and say, "We are rescued, so we can continue doing all
these detestable acts"? 11 Has this house, which bears
my name, become a den of robbers in your view? Yes,
I too have seen it.
This is the LORD's declaration.

SHILOH AS A WARNING

12 "'But return to my place that was at Shiloh, where
I made my name dwell at first. See what I did to it because of the evil of my people Israel. 13 Now, because
you have done all these things — this is the LORD's
declaration — and because I have spoken to you time

[A] 6:26 Lit *Daughter of my* [B] 6:27 Text emended; MT reads *fortress*
[C] 7:5 Lit *justly between a man and his neighbor*

and time again[A] but you wouldn't listen, and I have
called to you, but you wouldn't answer, 14 what I did
to Shiloh I will do to the house that bears my name,
the house in which you trust, the place that I gave
you and your ancestors. 15 I will banish you from my
presence, just as I banished all of your brothers, all
the descendants of Ephraim.'

DO NOT PRAY FOR JUDAH

16 "As for you, do not pray for these people. Do not
offer a cry or a prayer on their behalf, and do not beg
me, for I will not listen to you. 17 Don't you see how
they behave in the cities of Judah and in the streets of
Jerusalem? 18 The sons gather wood, the fathers light
the fire, and the women knead dough to make cakes
for the queen of heaven,[B] and they pour out drink
offerings to other gods so that they provoke me to
anger. 19 But are they really provoking me?" This is
the LORD's declaration. "Isn't it they themselves being
provoked to disgrace?"

20 Therefore, this is what the Lord GOD says: "Look,
my anger — my burning wrath — is about to be
poured out on this place, on people and animals, on
the tree of the field, and on the produce of the land.
My wrath will burn and not be quenched."

OBEDIENCE OVER SACRIFICE

21 This is what the LORD of Armies, the God of Israel, says: "Add your burnt offerings to your other
sacrifices, and eat the meat yourselves, 22 for when
I brought your ancestors out of the land of Egypt,
I did not speak with them or command them concerning burnt offering and sacrifice. 23 However, I
did give them this command: 'Obey me, and then I
will be your God, and you will be my people. Follow every way I command you so that it may go
well with you.' 24 Yet they didn't listen or pay attention but followed their own advice and their own
stubborn, evil heart. They went backward and not
forward. 25 Since the day your ancestors came out
of the land of Egypt until today, I have sent all my
servants the prophets to you time and time again.[C]
26 However, my people wouldn't listen to me or pay
attention but became obstinate; they did more evil
than their ancestors.

A LAMENT FOR DISOBEDIENT JUDAH

27 "When you speak all these things to them, they
will not listen to you. When you call to them, they
will not answer you. 28 Therefore, declare to them,
'This is the nation that would not listen to the LORD
their God and would not accept discipline. Truth[D] has
perished — it has disappeared from their mouths.
29 Cut off the hair of your sacred vow[E] and throw it
away. Raise up a dirge on the barren heights, for the
LORD has rejected and abandoned the generation
under his wrath.'

30 "For the Judeans have done what is evil in my
sight." This is the LORD's declaration. "They have set
up their abhorrent things in the house that bears my
name in order to defile it. 31 They have built the high
places of Topheth[F] in Ben Hinnom Valley[G] in order
to burn their sons and daughters in the fire, a thing
I did not command; I never entertained the thought.

32 "Therefore, look, the days are coming" — the
LORD's declaration — "when this place will no longer be called Topheth and Ben Hinnom Valley, but
Slaughter Valley. Topheth will become a cemetery,[H]
because there will be no other burial place. 33 The
corpses of these people will become food for the
birds of the sky and for the wild animals of the land,
with no one to scare them away. 34 I will remove
from the cities of Judah and the streets of Jerusalem the sound of joy and gladness and the voices of
the groom and the bride, for the land will become
a desolate waste.

DEATH OVER LIFE

8 "At that time" — this is the LORD's declaration
— "the bones of the kings of Judah, the bones
of her officials, the bones of the priests, the bones
of the prophets, and the bones of the residents of
Jerusalem will be brought out of their graves. 2 They
will be exposed to the sun, the moon, and all the stars
in the sky, which they have loved, served, followed,
consulted, and worshiped. Their bones will not be
collected and buried but will become like manure on
the soil's surface. 3 Death will be chosen over life by
all the survivors of this evil family, those who remain
wherever I have banished them." This is the declaration of the LORD of Armies.

4 "You are to say to them: This is what the LORD says:
Do people fall and not get up again?
If they turn away, do they not return?
5 Why have these people turned away?
Why is Jerusalem always turning away?
They take hold of deceit;
they refuse to return.
6 I have paid careful attention.
They do not speak what is right.
No one regrets his evil,
asking, 'What have I done?'
Everyone has stayed his course
like a horse rushing into battle.
7 Even storks in the sky
know their seasons.

[A] 7:13 Lit *you rising early and speaking* [B] 7:18 = a pagan goddess
[C] 7:25 Lit *you, each day rising early and sending* [D] 7:28 Or *Faithfulness*
[E] 7:29 Lit *off your consecration* [F] 7:31 Lit *of the fireplace*
[G] 7:31 A valley south of Jerusalem [H] 7:32 Lit *They will bury in Topheth*

Turtledoves, swallows, and cranes[A]
are aware of their migration,
but my people do not know
the requirements of the LORD.

PUNISHMENT FOR JUDAH'S LEADERS

8 "How can you claim, 'We are wise;
the law of the LORD is with us'?
In fact, the lying pen of scribes
has produced falsehood.
9 The wise will be put to shame;
they will be dismayed and snared.
They have rejected the word of the LORD,
so what wisdom do they really have?
10 Therefore, I will give their wives to other men,
their fields to new occupants,
for from the least to the greatest,
everyone is making profit dishonestly.
From prophet to priest,
everyone deals falsely.
11 They have treated the brokenness
of my dear[B] people superficially,
claiming, 'Peace, peace,'
when there is no peace.
12 Were they ashamed when they acted
so detestably?
They weren't at all ashamed.
They can no longer feel humiliation.
Therefore, they will fall among the fallen.
When I punish them, they will collapse,"
says the LORD.

13 "I will gather them and bring them to an end."[C]
This is the LORD's declaration.
"There will be no grapes on the vine,
no figs on the fig tree,
and even the leaf will wither.
Whatever I have given them will be lost
to them."

GOD'S PEOPLE UNREPENTANT

14 Why are we just sitting here?
Gather together; let's enter the fortified cities
and perish there,[D]
for the LORD our God has destroyed[E] us.
He has given us poisoned water to drink,
because we have sinned against the LORD.
15 We hoped for peace, but there was
nothing good;
for a time of healing, but there was
only terror.

16 From Dan, the snorting of horses is heard.
At the sound of the neighing of mighty steeds,
the whole land quakes.
They come to devour the land and everything
in it,
the city and all its residents.
17 Indeed, I am about to send snakes among you,
poisonous vipers that cannot be charmed.
They will bite you.
This is the LORD's declaration.

LAMENT OVER JUDAH

18 My joy has flown away;
grief has settled on me.
My heart is sick.
19 Listen — the cry of my dear people
from a faraway land,
"Is the LORD no longer in Zion,
her King not within her?"
Why have they angered me
with their carved images,
with their worthless foreign idols?
20 Harvest has passed, summer has ended,
but we have not been saved.
21 I am broken by the brokenness
of my dear people.
I mourn; horror has taken hold of me.
22 Is there no balm in Gilead?
Is there no physician there?
So why has the healing of my dear people
not come about?

9 If my head were a flowing spring,
my eyes a fountain of tears,
I would weep day and night
over the slain of my dear[F] people.
2 If only I had a traveler's lodging place
in the wilderness,
I would abandon my people
and depart from them,
for they are all adulterers,
a solemn assembly of treacherous people.

3 They bent their tongues like their bows;
lies and not faithfulness prevail in the land,
for they proceed from one evil to another,
and they do not take me into account.
This is the LORD's declaration.

IMMINENT RUIN AND EXILE

4 Everyone has to be on guard
against his friend.
Don't trust any brother,
for every brother will certainly deceive,
and every friend spread slander.

[A] **8:7** Hb obscure [B] **8:11** Lit *of the daughter of my*, also in vv. 19,21,22
[C] **8:13** Lit *Gathering I will end them* [D] **8:14** Or *there be silenced*
[E] **8:14** Or *silenced* [F] **9:1** Lit *slain among the daughter of my*

Drink Offerings in the Ancient Near East

by Byron Longino

Assyrian King Ashurnasirpal returning from hunting, pouring libation over a slain bull, circa 865 BC.

About sixty times in the Old Testament reference is made to a "drink offering," probably involving wine (Ex 29:40; Lv 23:13; Nm 15:5–10; 28:14), although it could also be beer (Nm 28:7), and in one case it was water (2Sm 23:16). The most common word for this offering is *nesek*, related to the verb *nasak*, "to pour out," with which it occurs thirteen times in the Old Testament. Since worshipers never "drink" the offering but rather pour it out before God (or gods), the term *drink offering* is a misnomer when applied to the worship of Yahweh. The gods of Mesopotamia, Egypt, Canaan, and other places, as represented by their images, were thought to need food and drink (see Dt 32:38). But that was not the case with the God of Israel. Therefore, "libation" might be preferable in such passages.[1] In one passage referring to "drink offerings" to other gods, the substance offered is blood (Ps 16:4).

The term *nesek* is found eight times in Jeremiah, which is more than any other book except Numbers, where it occurs thirty-four times. Another word referring to a drink offering is *menaqqit*, meaning "drink offering bowl," used in Jeremiah 52:19 and only three times elsewhere in the Old Testament.

Many ancient Near Eastern cultures and religions incorporated drink offerings into their ceremonies. Canaanite literature documents the Canaanites giving drink offerings to their gods prior to the Israelite settlement of the promised land. Other ancient Near Eastern writings mention people giving drink offerings plus other offerings and sacrifices. The theologies each held that offerings and sacrifices provided the primary way to contact and worship the gods. Among most religions, the significant aspect apparently was not the contents as much as the act of pouring. Worshipers poured their liquid offering on the ground, into holes, upon altars, into a bowl, or over a sacrificial object.[2]

The differences in the Israelite and non-Israelite practices, though, were significant. Theology was the basis of those differences. Non-Israelites offered rams, bulls, birds, bread, beer, milk, and wine on a daily basis to "feed" their gods. The Lord clearly stated that he needed nothing from the people to survive (Is 1:11–15). Although the poured offering practices predate by centuries the Israelites entering the promised land, God gave them new and unique meanings. The message was new in that the Israelites were symbolizing their trust, worship, and obedience of the one true God, Yahweh—rather than feeding and nourishing him.[3] One thing that angered the Lord was when his people poured out drink offerings to other gods. In Jeremiah 7:18,20 the Lord declared, "They pour out drink offerings to other gods so that they

Wall plaque from Ur (ca 2500 BC) showing a priest pouring an offering before a seated god.

Terra-cotta jar from Greece showing Apollo and his sister Artemis pouring a libation on an altar, fifth century BC.

provoke me to anger. . . . Therefore, this is what the Lord God says: 'Look, my anger—my burning wrath—is about to be poured out on this place, on people and animals, on the tree of the field, and on the produce of the land. My wrath will burn and not be quenched'" (also 2Kg 22:17; Is 57:6; Jr 19:13; 32:29; 44:17–19,25).

The thought of pouring out an offering to God seems foreign to believers today. We cannot imagine such an action as an act of worship. The Old Testament worship practices, though, have a strong implication for New Testament believers. Although Jesus never mentioned a drink offering, the apostle Paul mentioned it twice—once as an instruction and the other as a testimony. Using himself as an example, he encouraged believers at Philippi to give of themselves selflessly in ministry to others: "But even if I am poured out as a drink offering on the sacrificial service of your faith, I am glad and rejoice with all of you" (Php 2:17). Later, near the end of his life, Paul wrote Timothy, "For I am already being poured out as a drink offering, and the time for my departure is close" (2Tm 4:6). Looking back over his life, Paul could affirm he had given his life to God. What a powerful witness—and example—for believers still today. May we too give our lives to God as a sweet-smelling sacrifice. ✜

[1] Scott Langston and E. Ray Clendenen, "Sacrifice and Offering" in *HIBD rev. ed.* (2015), 1399. [2] Kevin D. Hall, "Libation" in *EDB*, 807. [3] Allen P. Ross, *Holiness to the Lord: A Guide to the Exposition of the Book of Leviticus* (Grand Rapids: Baker Academic, 2002), 21.

Ceramic libation bowl from western Italy, circa 330–310 BC.

5 Each one betrays his friend;
no one tells the truth.
They have taught their tongues
to speak lies;
they wear themselves out doing wrong.
6 You live in a world of deception.[A]
In their deception they refuse
to know me.
This is the LORD's declaration.

7 Therefore, this is what the LORD of Armies says:
I am about to refine them and test them,
for what else can I do
because of my dear[B] people?[C]
8 Their tongues are deadly arrows —
they speak deception.
With his mouth
one speaks peaceably with his friend,
but inwardly he sets up an ambush.
9 Should I not punish them
for these things?
This is the LORD's declaration.
Should I not avenge myself
on such a nation as this?

10 I will raise weeping and a lament
over the mountains,
a dirge over the wilderness grazing land,
for they have been so scorched
that no one passes through.
The sound of cattle is no longer heard.
From the birds of the sky to the animals,
everything has fled — they have
gone away.
11 I will make Jerusalem a heap of rubble,
a jackals' den.
I will make the cities of Judah
a desolation,
an uninhabited place.

12 Who is the person wise enough to understand
this? Who has the LORD spoken to, that he may explain it? Why is the land destroyed and scorched like
a wilderness, so no one can pass through?
13 The LORD said, "It is because they abandoned my
instruction, which I set before them, and did not obey
my voice or walk according to it. 14 Instead, they followed the stubbornness of their hearts and followed
the Baals as their ancestors taught them." 15 Therefore, this is what the LORD of Armies, the God of Israel,
says: "I am about to feed this people wormwood and
give them poisonous water to drink. 16 I will scatter
them among the nations that they and their ancestors
have not known. I will send a sword after them until
I have finished them off."

MOURNING OVER JUDAH

17 This is what the LORD of Armies says:
Consider, and summon the women
who mourn;
send for the skillful women.
18 Let them come quickly to raise a lament
over us
so that our eyes may overflow with tears,
our eyelids be soaked with weeping.
19 For a sound of lamentation is heard
from Zion:
How devastated we are.
We are greatly ashamed,
for we have abandoned the land;
our dwellings have been torn down.

20 Now hear the word of the LORD,
you women.
Pay attention to[D] the words
from his mouth.
Teach your daughters a lament
and one another a dirge,
21 for Death has climbed through our windows;
it has entered our fortresses,
cutting off children from the streets,
young men from the squares.

22 "Speak as follows: 'This is what the LORD declares:
Human corpses will fall like manure on the surface
of the field, like newly cut grain after the reaper with
no one to gather it.

BOAST IN THE LORD

23 " 'This is what the LORD says:
The wise person should not boast
in his wisdom;
the strong should not boast in his strength;
the wealthy should not boast in his wealth.
24 But the one who boasts should boast in this:
that he understands and knows me —
that I am the LORD, showing faithful love,
justice, and righteousness on the earth,
for I delight in these things.
This is the LORD's declaration.

25 " 'Look, the days are coming — this is the LORD's
declaration — when I will punish all the circumcised
yet uncircumcised: 26 Egypt, Judah, Edom, the Ammonites, Moab, and all the inhabitants of the desert
who clip the hair on their temples.[E] All these nations
are uncircumcised, and the whole house of Israel is
uncircumcised in heart.' "

[A] **9:6** LXX reads *Oppression on oppression, deceit on deceit* [B] **9:7** Lit *of the daughter of my* [C] **9:7** LXX, Tg read *because of their evils* [D] **9:20** Lit *Your ears must receive* [E] **9:26** Or *who live in distant places*

FALSE GODS CONTRASTED WITH THE CREATOR

10 Hear the word that the LORD has spoken to[A] you,
house of Israel. 2 This is what the LORD says:
Do not learn the way of the nations
or be terrified by signs in the heavens,
although the nations are terrified by them,
3 for the customs of the peoples are worthless.
Someone cuts down a tree from the forest;
it is worked by the hands of a craftsman
with a chisel.
4 He decorates it with silver and gold.
It is fastened with hammer and nails,
so it won't totter.
5 Like scarecrows in a cucumber patch,
their idols cannot speak.
They must be carried because
they cannot walk.
Do not fear them for they can do no harm —
and they cannot do any good.

6 LORD, there is no one like you.
You are great;
your name is great in power.
7 Who should not fear you,
King of the nations?
It is what you deserve.
For among all the wise people of the nations
and among all their kingdoms,
there is no one like you.
8 They are both stupid and foolish,
instructed by worthless idols
made of wood!
9 Beaten silver is brought from Tarshish
and gold from Uphaz.[B]
The work of a craftsman
and of a goldsmith's hands
is clothed in blue and purple,
all the work of skilled artisans.
10 But the LORD is the true God;
he is the living God and eternal King.
The earth quakes at his wrath,
and the nations cannot endure his fury.
11 You are to say this to them: "The gods that did not
make the heavens and the earth will perish from the
earth and from under these heavens."[C]
12 He made the earth by his power,
established the world by his wisdom,
and spread out the heavens
by his understanding.
13 When he thunders,[D]
the waters in the heavens are in turmoil,
and he causes the clouds to rise
from the ends of the earth.
He makes lightning for the rain
and brings the wind from his storehouses.
14 Everyone is stupid and ignorant.
Every goldsmith is put to shame
by his carved image,
for his cast images are a lie;
there is no breath in them.
15 They are worthless, a work to be mocked.
At the time of their punishment
they will be destroyed.
16 Jacob's Portion[E] is not like these
because he is the one who formed all things.
Israel is the tribe of his inheritance;
the LORD of Armies is his name.

EXILE AFTER THE SIEGE

17 Gather up your belongings[F]
from the ground,
you who live under siege.

18 For this is what the LORD says:
Look, I am flinging away
the land's residents at this time
and bringing them such distress
that they will feel it.

JEREMIAH GRIEVES

19 Woe to me because of my brokenness —
I am severely wounded!
I exclaimed, "This is my intense suffering,
but I must bear it."
20 My tent is destroyed;
all my tent cords are snapped.
My sons have departed from me and are
no more.
I have no one to pitch my tent again
or to hang up my curtains.
21 For the shepherds are stupid:
They don't seek the LORD.
Therefore they have not prospered,
and their whole flock is scattered.
22 Listen! A noise — it is coming —
a great commotion from the land
to the north.
The cities of Judah will be made desolate,
a jackals' den.

23 I know, LORD,
that a person's way of life is not his own;
no one who walks determines his own steps.
24 Discipline me, LORD, but with justice —
not in your anger,
or you will reduce me to nothing.

[A] **10:1** Or *against* [B] **10:9** Or *Ophir* [C] **10:11** This is the only Aramaic v. in Jr. [D] **10:13** Lit *At his giving of the voice* [E] **10:16** = the LORD [F] **10:17** Lit *bundle*

25 Pour out your wrath on the nations
that don't recognize you
and on the families
that don't call on your name,
for they have consumed Jacob;
they have consumed him and finished
him off
and made his homeland desolate.

REMINDER OF THE COVENANT

11 This is the word that came to Jeremiah from
the LORD: 2 "Listen to the words of this covenant
and tell them to the men of Judah and the residents
of Jerusalem. 3 Tell them, 'This is what the LORD, the
God of Israel, says: "Let a curse be on the man who
does not obey the words of this covenant, 4 which I
commanded your ancestors when I brought them
out of the land of Egypt, out of the iron furnace." I
declared, "Obey me, and do everything that I command you, and you will be my people, and I will be
your God," 5 in order to establish the oath I swore to
your ancestors, to give them a land flowing with milk
and honey, as it is today.' "
I answered, "Amen, LORD."
6 The LORD said to me, "Proclaim all these words
in the cities of Judah and in the streets of Jerusalem:
'Obey the words of this covenant and carry them
out.' 7 For I strongly warned your ancestors when
I brought them out of the land of Egypt until today,
warning them time and time again,[A] 'Obey me.' 8 Yet
they would not obey or pay attention; each one followed the stubbornness of his evil heart. So I brought
on them all the curses of this covenant, because they
had not done what I commanded them to do."
9 The LORD said to me, "A conspiracy has been discovered among the men of Judah and the residents
of Jerusalem. 10 They have returned to the iniquities
of their ancestors who refused to obey my words and
have followed other gods to worship them. The house
of Israel and the house of Judah broke my covenant
I made with their ancestors.
11 "Therefore, this is what the LORD says: I am about
to bring on them disaster that they cannot escape.
They will cry out to me, but I will not hear them.
12 Then the cities of Judah and the residents of Jerusalem will go and cry out to the gods they have been
burning incense to, but they certainly will not save
them in their time of disaster. 13 Your gods are indeed
as numerous as your cities, Judah, and the altars you
have set up to Shame[B] — altars to burn incense to
Baal — as numerous as the streets of Jerusalem.
14 "As for you, do not pray for these people. Do not
raise up a cry or a prayer on their behalf, for I will
not be listening when they call out to me at the time
of their disaster.

15 What right does my beloved have
to be in my house,
having carried out so many evil schemes?
Can holy meat[C] prevent your disaster[D]
so you can celebrate?
16 The LORD named you
a flourishing olive tree,
beautiful with well-formed fruit.
He has set fire to it,
and its branches are consumed[E]
with the sound of a mighty tumult.

17 "The LORD of Armies who planted you has decreed disaster against you, because of the disaster[F]
the house of Israel and the house of Judah brought
on themselves when they angered me by burning
incense to Baal."

18 The LORD informed me, so I knew.
Then you helped me to see their deeds,
19 for I was like a docile[G] lamb led to slaughter.
I didn't know that they had devised plots
against me:
"Let's destroy the tree with its fruit;[H]
let's cut him off from the land of the living
so that his name will no longer
be remembered."
20 But, LORD of Armies, who judges righteously,
who tests heart[I] and mind,
let me see your vengeance on them,
for I have presented my case to you.

21 Therefore, here is what the LORD says concerning
the people of Anathoth who intend to take your life.
They warn, "Do not prophesy in the name of the LORD,
or you will certainly die at our hand." 22 Therefore,
this is what the LORD of Armies says: "I am about to
punish them. The young men will die by the sword;
their sons and daughters will die by famine. 23 They
will have no remnant, for I will bring disaster on the
people of Anathoth in the year of their punishment."

JEREMIAH'S COMPLAINT

12 You will be righteous, LORD,
even if I bring a case against you.
Yet, I wish to contend with you:
Why does the way of the wicked prosper?
Why do all the treacherous live at ease?
2 You planted them, and they have taken root.
They have grown and produced fruit.
You are ever on their lips,[J]
but far from their conscience.[I]

[A] **11:7** Lit *today, rising early and warning* [B] **11:13** = Baal
[C] **11:15** = sacrificial meat [D] **11:15** LXX; MT reads *meat pass from you*
[E] **11:16** Vg; MT reads *broken* [F] **11:17** Or *evil* [G] **11:19** Or *pet* [H] **11:19** Lit
bread [I] **11:20; 12:2** Lit *kidneys* [J] **12:2** Lit *are near in their mouth*

3 As for you, LORD, you know me; you see me.
You test whether my heart is with you.
Drag the wicked away like sheep
to slaughter
and set them apart for the day of killing.
4 How long will the land mourn
and the grass of every field wither?
Because of the evil of its residents,
animals and birds have been swept away,
for the people have said,
"He cannot see what our end will be."[A]

THE LORD'S RESPONSE

5 If you have raced with runners
and they have worn you out,
how can you compete with horses?
If you stumble[B] in a peaceful land,
what will you do in the thickets of the Jordan?
6 Even your brothers —
your own father's family —
even they were treacherous to you;
even they have cried out loudly after you.
Do not have confidence in them,
though they speak well of you.

7 I have abandoned my house;
I have deserted my inheritance.
I have handed the love of my life
over to her enemies.
8 My inheritance has behaved toward me
like a lion in the forest.
She has roared against me.
Therefore, I hate her.
9 Is my inheritance like a hyena[C] to me?
Are birds of prey circling her?
Go, gather all the wild animals;
bring them to devour her.
10 Many shepherds have destroyed my vineyard;
they have trampled my plot of land.
They have turned my desirable plot
into a desolate wasteland.
11 They have made it a desolation.
It mourns, desolate, before me.
All the land is desolate,
but no one takes it to heart.
12 Over all the barren heights in the wilderness
the destroyers have come,
for the LORD has a sword that devours
from one end of the earth to the other.
No one has peace.
13 They have sown wheat but harvested thorns.
They have exhausted themselves but have
no profit.
Be put to shame by your harvests
because of the LORD's burning anger.

14 This is what the LORD says: "Concerning all my
evil neighbors who attack the inheritance that I bequeathed to my people, Israel, I am about to uproot
them from their land, and I will uproot the house of
Judah from them. 15 After I have uprooted them, I will
once again have compassion on them and return each
one to his inheritance and to his land. 16 If they will
diligently learn the ways of my people — to swear
by my name, 'As the LORD lives,' just as they taught
my people to swear by Baal — they will be built up
among my people. 17 However, if they will not obey,
then I will uproot and destroy that nation."
This is the LORD's declaration.

LINEN UNDERWEAR

13 This is what the LORD said to me: "Go and buy
yourself a linen undergarment and put it on.[D]
But do not put it in water." 2 So I bought underwear
as the LORD instructed me and put it on.
3 Then the word of the LORD came to me a second
time: 4 "Take the underwear that you bought and are
wearing,[E] and go at once to the Euphrates[F] and hide
it in a rocky crevice." 5 So I went and hid it by the Euphrates, as the LORD commanded me.
6 A long time later the LORD said to me, "Go at once
to the Euphrates and get the underwear that I commanded you to hide there." 7 So I went to the Euphrates and dug up the underwear and got it from the
place where I had hidden it, but it was ruined — of
no use at all.
8 Then the word of the LORD came to me: 9 "This is
what the LORD says: Just like this I will ruin the great
pride of both Judah and Jerusalem. 10 These evil people, who refuse to listen to me, who follow the stubbornness of their own hearts, and who have followed
other gods to serve and bow in worship — they will
be like this underwear, of no use at all. 11 Just as underwear clings to one's waist, so I fastened the whole
house of Israel and of Judah to me" — this is the LORD's
declaration — "so that they might be my people for
my fame, praise, and glory, but they would not obey.

THE WINE JARS

12 "Say this to them: 'This is what the LORD, the God
of Israel, says: Every jar should be filled with wine.'
Then they will respond to you, 'Don't we know that
every jar should be filled with wine?' 13 And you will
say to them, 'This is what the LORD says: I am about
to fill all who live in this land — the kings who reign
for David on his throne, the priests, the prophets, and
all the residents of Jerusalem — with drunkenness.

[A] **12:4** LXX reads *see our ways* [B] **12:5** Or *you are secure* [C] **12:9** Hb obscure [D] **13:1** Lit *around your waist* [E] **13:4** Lit *wearing around your waist* [F] **13:4–7** Perhaps a place near Anathoth with the same spelling as the river

14 I will smash them against each other, fathers and
sons alike — this is the LORD's declaration. I will allow no mercy, pity, or compassion to keep me from
destroying them.'"

THE LORD'S WARNING

15 Listen and pay attention.
Do not be proud,
for the LORD has spoken.
16 Give glory to the LORD your God
before he brings darkness,
before your feet stumble
on the mountains at dusk.
You wait for light,
but he brings darkest gloom[A]
and makes total darkness.
17 But if you will not listen,
my innermost being will weep in secret
because of your pride.
My eyes will overflow with tears,
for the LORD's flock has been
taken captive.

18 Say to the king and the queen mother:
Take a humble seat,
for your glorious crowns
have fallen from your heads.
19 The cities of the Negev are under siege;
no one can help them.
All of Judah has been taken into exile,
taken completely into exile.
20 Look up and see
those coming from the north.
Where is the flock entrusted to you,
the sheep that were your pride?

THE DESTINY OF JERUSALEM

21 What will you say when he appoints
close friends as leaders over you,
ones you yourself trained?
Won't labor pains seize you,
as they do a woman in labor?
22 And when you ask yourself,
"Why have these things
happened to me?"
it is because of your great guilt
that your skirts have been stripped off,
your body exposed.[B]
23 Can the Cushite change his skin,
or a leopard his spots?
If so, you might be able to do
what is good,
you who are instructed in evil.
24 I will scatter you[C] like drifting chaff
before the desert wind.
25 This is your lot,
what I have decreed for you —
this is the LORD's declaration —
because you have forgotten me
and trusted in lies.
26 I will pull your skirts up over your face
so that your shame might be seen.
27 Your adulteries and your lustful neighing,
your depraved prostitution
on the hills, in the fields —
I have seen your abhorrent acts.
Woe to you, Jerusalem!
You are unclean —
for how long yet?

THE DROUGHT

14 This is the word of the LORD that came to Jeremiah concerning the drought:
2 Judah mourns;
her city gates languish.
Her people are on the ground in mourning;
Jerusalem's cry rises up.
3 Their nobles send their servants[D] for water.
They go to the cisterns;
they find no water;
their containers return empty.
They are ashamed and humiliated;
they cover their heads.
4 The ground is cracked
since no rain has fallen on the land.
The farmers are ashamed;
they cover their heads.
5 Even the doe in the field
gives birth and abandons her fawn
since there is no grass.
6 Wild donkeys stand on the barren heights
panting for air like jackals.
Their eyes fail
because there are no green plants.

7 Though our iniquities testify against us,
LORD, act for your name's sake.
Indeed, our rebellions are many;
we have sinned against you.
8 Hope of Israel,
its Savior in time of distress,
why are you like a resident alien in the land,
like a traveler stopping only for the night?
9 Why are you like a helpless man,
like a warrior unable to save?
Yet you are among us, LORD,
and we bear your name.
Don't leave us!

[A] **13:16** Or *brings a shadow of death* [B] **13:22** Lit *your heels have suffered violence* [C] **13:24** Lit *them* [D] **14:3** Lit *little ones*

[10] This is what the LORD says concerning these people:

Truly they love to wander;
they never rest their feet.
So the LORD does not accept them.
Now he will remember their iniquity
and punish their sins.

FALSE PROPHETS TO BE PUNISHED

[11] Then the LORD said to me, "Do not pray for the
well-being of these people. [12] If they fast, I will not
hear their cry of despair. If they offer burnt offering
and grain offering, I will not accept them. Rather, I
will finish them off by sword, famine, and plague."

[13] And I replied, "Oh no, Lord GOD! The prophets are
telling them, 'You won't see sword or suffer famine.
I will certainly give you lasting peace in this place.' "

[14] But the LORD said to me, "These prophets are
prophesying a lie in my name. I did not send them,
nor did I command them or speak to them. They are
prophesying to you a false vision, worthless divination, the deceit of their own minds.

[15] "Therefore, this is what the LORD says concerning the prophets who prophesy in my name, though
I did not send them, and who say, 'There will never be
sword or famine in this land.' By sword and famine
these prophets will meet their end. [16] The people they
are prophesying to will be thrown into the streets
of Jerusalem because of the famine and the sword.
There will be no one to bury them — they, their wives,
their sons, and their daughters. I will pour out their
own evil on them."

JEREMIAH'S REQUEST

17 You are to speak this word to them:
Let my eyes overflow with tears;
day and night may they not stop,
for my dearest people[A]
have been destroyed by a crushing blow,
an extremely severe wound.
18 If I go out to the field,
look — those slain by the sword!
If I enter the city,
look — those ill from famine!
For both prophet and priest
travel to a land they do not know.

19 Have you completely rejected Judah?
Do you detest Zion?
Why do you strike us
with no hope of healing for us?
We hoped for peace,
but there was nothing good;
for a time of healing,
but there was only terror.
20 We acknowledge our wickedness, LORD,
the iniquity of our ancestors;
indeed, we have sinned against you.
21 For your name's sake, don't despise us.
Don't disdain your glorious throne.
Remember your covenant with us;
do not break it.
22 Can any of the worthless idols of the nations
bring rain?
Or can the skies alone give showers?
Are you not the LORD our God?
We therefore put our hope in you,
for you have done all these things.

THE LORD'S NEGATIVE RESPONSE

15 Then the LORD said to me, "Even if Moses and
Samuel should stand before me, my compassions would not reach out to these people. Send them
from my presence, and let them go. [2] If they ask you,
'Where will we go?' tell them: This is what the LORD
says:

Those destined for death, to death;
those destined for the sword, to the sword.
Those destined for famine, to famine;
those destined for captivity, to captivity.

[3] "I will ordain four kinds[B] of judgment for them"
— this is the LORD's declaration — "the sword to kill,
the dogs to drag away, and the birds of the sky and
the wild animals of the land to devour and destroy.
[4] I will make them a horror to all the kingdoms of the
earth because of Manasseh son of Hezekiah, the king
of Judah, for what he did in Jerusalem.

5 Who will have pity on you, Jerusalem?
Who will show sympathy toward you?
Who will turn aside
to ask about your well-being?
6 You have left me."
This is the LORD's declaration.
"You have turned your back,
so I have stretched out my hand against you
and destroyed you.
I am tired of showing compassion.
7 I scattered them with a winnowing fork
at the city gates of the land.
I made them childless; I destroyed my people.
They would not turn from their ways.
8 I made their widows more numerous
than the sand of the seas.
I brought a destroyer at noon
against the mother of young men.
I suddenly released on her
agitation and terrors.

[A] **14:17** Lit *for the virgin daughter of my people* [B] **15:3** Lit *families*

9 The mother of seven grew faint;
she breathed her last breath.
Her sun set while it was still day;
she was ashamed and humiliated.
The rest of them I will give over
to the sword
in the presence of their enemies."
This is the LORD's declaration.

JEREMIAH'S COMPLAINT

10 Woe is me, my mother,
that you gave birth to me,
a man who incites dispute and conflict
in all the land.
I did not lend or borrow,
yet everyone curses me.

THE LORD'S RESPONSE

11 The LORD said:
Haven't I set you loose for your good?
Haven't I punished you
in a time of trouble,
in a time of distress with the enemy?[A]
12 Can anyone smash iron,
iron from the north, or bronze?
13 I will give up your wealth
and your treasures as plunder,
without cost, for all your sins
in all your borders.
14 Then I will make you serve your enemies[B]
in a land you do not know,
for my anger will kindle a fire
that will burn against you.

JEREMIAH'S PRAYER FOR VENGEANCE

15 You know, LORD;
remember me and take note of me.
Avenge me against my persecutors.
In your patience,[C] don't take me away.
Know that I suffer disgrace for your honor.
16 Your words were found, and I ate them.
Your words became a delight to me
and the joy of my heart,
for I bear your name,
LORD God of Armies.
17 I never sat with the band of revelers,
and I did not celebrate with them.
Because your hand was on me,
I sat alone,
for you filled me with indignation.
18 Why has my pain become unending,
my wound incurable,
refusing to be healed?
You truly have become like a mirage to me —
water that is not reliable.

JEREMIAH TOLD TO REPENT

19 Therefore, this is what the LORD says:
If you return, I will take you back;
you will stand in my presence.
And if you speak noble words,
rather than worthless ones,
you will be my spokesman.
It is they who must return to you;
you must not return to them.
20 Then I will make you
a fortified wall of bronze
to this people.
They will fight against you
but will not overcome you,
for I am with you
to save you and rescue you.
This is the LORD's declaration.
21 I will rescue you from the power
of evil people
and redeem you from the grasp
of the ruthless.

NO MARRIAGE FOR JEREMIAH

16 The word of the LORD came to me: 2 "Do not
marry or have sons or daughters in this place.
3 For this is what the LORD says concerning sons and
daughters born in this place as well as concerning
the mothers who bear them and the fathers who
father them in this land: 4 They will die from deadly
diseases. They will not be mourned or buried but
will be like manure on the soil's surface. They will
be finished off by sword and famine. Their corpses
will become food for the birds of the sky and for the
wild animals of the land.
5 "For this is what the LORD says: Don't enter a
house where a mourning feast is taking place.[D] Don't
go to lament or sympathize with them, for I have
removed my peace from these people as well as my
faithful love and compassion." This is the LORD's declaration. 6 "Both great and small will die in this land
without burial. No lament will be made for them, nor
will anyone cut himself or shave his head for them.[E]
7 Food won't be provided for the mourner to comfort
him because of the dead. A consoling drink won't be
given him for the loss of his father or mother. 8 Do
not enter the house where feasting is taking place to
sit with them to eat and drink. 9 For this is what the
LORD of Armies, the God of Israel, says: I am about to
eliminate from this place, before your very eyes and
in your time, the sound of joy and gladness, the voice
of the groom and the bride.

[A] **15:11** Hb obscure [B] **15:14** Some Hb mss, LXX, Syr, Tg; other Hb mss read *you pass through* [C] **15:15** Lit *In the slowness of your anger* [D] **16:5** Lit *house of mourning* [E] **16:6** This custom demonstrated pagan mourning rituals.

ABANDONING THE LORD AND HIS LAW

[10] "When you tell these people all these things, they
will say to you, 'Why has the LORD declared all this terrible disaster against us? What is our iniquity? What
is our sin that we have committed against the LORD
our God?' [11] Then you will answer them, 'Because your
ancestors abandoned me — this is the LORD's declaration — and followed other gods, served them, and
bowed in worship to them. Indeed, they abandoned
me and did not keep my instruction. [12] You did more
evil than your ancestors. Look, each one of you was
following the stubbornness of his evil heart, not obeying me. [13] So I will hurl you from this land into a land
that you and your ancestors have not known. There
you will worship other gods both day and night, for
I will not grant you grace.'[A]

[14] "However, look, the days are coming" — the LORD's
declaration — "when it will no longer be said, 'As the
LORD lives who brought the Israelites from the land of
Egypt,' [15] but rather, 'As the LORD lives who brought the
Israelites from the land of the north and from all the
other lands where he had banished them.' For I will
return them to their land that I gave to their ancestors.

PUNISHMENT OF EXILE

[16] "I am about to send for many fishermen" — this
is the LORD's declaration — "and they will fish for
them. Then I will send for many hunters, and they
will hunt them down on every mountain and hill and
out of the clefts of the rocks, [17] for my gaze takes in
all their ways. They are not concealed from me, and
their iniquity is not hidden from my sight. [18] I will first
repay them double for their iniquity and sin because
they have polluted my land. They have filled my inheritance with the carcasses of their abhorrent and
detestable idols."

19 LORD, my strength and my stronghold,
my refuge in a time of distress,
the nations will come to you
from the ends of the earth, and they will say,
"Our ancestors inherited only lies,
worthless idols of no benefit at all."
20 Can one make gods for himself?
But they are not gods.
21 "Therefore, I am about to inform them,
and this time I will make them know
my power and my might;
then they will know that my name is the LORD."

THE PERSISTENT SIN OF JUDAH

17 The sin of Judah is inscribed
with an iron stylus.
With a diamond point
it is engraved on the tablet of their hearts
and on the horns of their[B] altars,
2 while their children remember their altars
and their Asherah poles, by the green trees
on the high hills —
3 my mountains in the countryside.
I will give up your wealth
and all your treasures as plunder
because of the sin of your high places[C]
in all your borders.
4 You will, on your own, relinquish
your inheritance
that I gave you.
I will make you serve your enemies
in a land you do not know,
for you have set my anger on fire;
it will burn forever.

CURSE AND BLESSING

[5] This is what the LORD says:

Cursed is the person who trusts in mankind.
He makes human flesh his strength,
and his heart turns from the LORD.
6 He will be like a juniper in the Arabah;
he cannot see when good comes
but dwells in the parched places
in the wilderness,
in a salt land where no one lives.
7 The person who trusts in the LORD,
whose confidence indeed is the LORD,
is blessed.
8 He will be like a tree planted by water:
it sends its roots out toward a stream,
it doesn't fear when heat comes,
and its foliage remains green.
It will not worry in a year of drought
or cease producing fruit.

THE DECEITFUL HEART

9 The heart is more deceitful than anything else,
and incurable — who can understand it?
10 I, the LORD, examine the mind,
I test the heart[D]
to give to each according to his way,
according to what his actions deserve.
11 He who makes a fortune unjustly
is like a partridge that hatches eggs it didn't lay.
In the middle of his life
his riches will abandon him,
so in the end he will be a fool.
12 A glorious throne
on high from the beginning
is the place of our sanctuary.

[A] 16:13 Or *compassion* [B] 17:1 Some Hb mss, Syr, Vg; other Hb mss read *your* [C] 17:3 Lit *plunder, your high places because of sin* [D] 17:10 Lit *kidneys*

13 LORD, the hope of Israel,
all who abandon you
will be put to shame.
All who turn away from me
will be written in the dirt,
for they have abandoned
the LORD, the fountain of living water.

JEREMIAH'S PLEA

14 Heal me, LORD, and I will be healed;
save me, and I will be saved,
for you are my praise.
15 Hear how they keep challenging me,
"Where is the word of the LORD?
Let it come!"
16 But I have not run away from being
your shepherd,
and I have not longed for the fatal day.
You know my words were spoken
in your presence.
17 Don't become a terror to me.
You are my refuge in the day of disaster.
18 Let my persecutors be put to shame,
but don't let me be put to shame.
Let them be terrified, but don't let me
be terrified.
Bring on them the day of disaster;
shatter them with total[A] destruction.

OBSERVING THE SABBATH

19 This is what the LORD said to me, "Go and stand at
the People's Gate, through which the kings of Judah
enter and leave, as well as at all the gates of Jerusalem. 20 Announce to them, 'Hear the word of the
LORD, kings of Judah, all Judah, and all the residents
of Jerusalem who enter through these gates. 21 This is
what the LORD says: Watch yourselves; do not pick up
a load and bring it in through Jerusalem's gates on the
Sabbath day. 22 Do not carry a load out of your houses
on the Sabbath day or do any work, but keep the Sabbath day holy, just as I commanded your ancestors.
23 They wouldn't listen or pay attention but became
obstinate, not listening or accepting discipline.
24 " 'However, if you listen to me — this is the LORD's
declaration — and do not bring loads through the
gates of this city on the Sabbath day, but keep the
Sabbath day holy and do no work on it, 25 kings and
princes will enter through the gates of this city. They
will sit on the throne of David; they will ride in chariots and on horses with their officials, the men of
Judah, and the residents of Jerusalem. This city will
be inhabited forever. 26 Then people will come from
the cities of Judah and from the area around Jerusalem, from the land of Benjamin and from the Judean
foothills, from the hill country and from the Negev
bringing burnt offerings and sacrifices, grain offerings and frankincense, and thanksgiving sacrifices to
the house of the LORD. 27 But if you do not listen to me
to keep the Sabbath day holy by not carrying a load
while entering the gates of Jerusalem on the Sabbath
day, I will set fire to its gates, and it will consume the
citadels of Jerusalem and not be extinguished.' "

PARABLE OF THE POTTER

18 This is the word that came to Jeremiah from the
LORD: 2 "Go down at once to the potter's house;
there I will reveal my words to you." 3 So I went down
to the potter's house, and there he was, working away
at the wheel.[B] 4 But the jar that he was making from the
clay became flawed in the potter's hand, so he made
it into another jar, as it seemed right for him to do.
5 The word of the LORD came to me: 6 "House of Israel, can I not treat you as this potter treats his clay?"
— this is the LORD's declaration. "Just like clay in the
potter's hand, so are you in my hand, house of Israel. 7 At one moment I might announce concerning a
nation or a kingdom that I will uproot, tear down,
and destroy it. 8 However, if that nation about which
I have made the announcement turns from its evil, I
will relent concerning the disaster I had planned to do
to it. 9 At another time I might announce concerning
a nation or a kingdom that I will build and plant it.
10 However, if it does what is evil in my sight by not
listening to me, I will relent concerning the good I
had said I would do to it. 11 So now, say to the men of
Judah and to the residents of Jerusalem, 'This is what
the LORD says: Look, I am about to bring harm to you
and make plans against you. Turn now, each from
your evil way, and correct your ways and your deeds.'
12 But they will say, 'It's hopeless. We will continue to
follow our plans, and each of us will continue to act
according to the stubbornness of his evil heart.' "

DELUDED ISRAEL

13 Therefore, this is what the LORD says:
Ask among the nations,
who has heard things like these?
Virgin Israel has done a most horrible thing.
14 Does the snow of Lebanon ever leave
the highland crags?
Or does cold water flowing from a distance
ever fail?
15 Yet my people have forgotten me.
They burn incense to worthless idols
that make them stumble in their ways
on the ancient roads,
and make them walk on new paths,
not the highway.

[A] **17:18** Lit *double* [B] **18:3** Lit *pair of stones*

16 They have made their land a horror,
a perpetual object of scorn;[A]
all who pass by it will be appalled
and shake their heads.
17 I will scatter them before the enemy
like the east wind.
I will show them[B] my back and not my face
on the day of their calamity.

PLOT AGAINST JEREMIAH

18 Then certain ones said, "Come, let's make plans
against Jeremiah, for instruction will never be lost
from the priest, or counsel from the wise, or a word
from the prophet. Come, let's denounce him[C] and pay
no attention to all his words."

19 Pay attention to me, LORD.
Hear what my opponents are saying!
20 Should good be repaid with evil?
Yet they have dug a pit for me.
Remember how I stood before you
to speak good on their behalf,
to turn your anger from them.
21 Therefore, hand their children over to famine,
and give them over to the power of the sword.
Let their wives become childless
and widowed,
their husbands slain by deadly disease,[D]
their young men struck down by the sword
in battle.
22 Let a cry be heard from their houses
when you suddenly bring raiders
against them,
for they have dug a pit to capture me
and have hidden snares for my feet.
23 But you, LORD, know
all their deadly plots against me.
Do not wipe out their iniquity;
do not blot out their sin before you.
Let them be forced to stumble before you;
deal with them in the time of your anger.

THE CLAY JAR

19 This is what the LORD says: "Go, buy a potter's
clay jar. Take[E] some of the elders of the people
and some of the leading priests 2 and go out to Ben
Hinnom Valley near the entrance of the Potsherd
Gate. Proclaim there the words I speak to you. 3 Say,
'Hear the word of the LORD, kings of Judah and residents of Jerusalem. This is what the LORD of Armies,
the God of Israel, says: I am going to bring such a disaster on this place that everyone who hears about
it will shudder[F] 4 because they have abandoned me
and made this a foreign place. They have burned incense in it to other gods that they, their ancestors,
and the kings of Judah have never known. They have
filled this place with the blood of the innocent. 5 They
have built high places to Baal on which to burn their
children in the fire as burnt offerings to Baal, something I have never commanded or mentioned; I never
entertained the thought.[G]

6 " 'Therefore, look, the days are coming — this
is the LORD's declaration — when this place will no
longer be called Topheth and Ben Hinnom Valley, but
Slaughter Valley. 7 I will spoil the plans of Judah and
Jerusalem in this place. I will make them fall by the
sword before their enemies, by the hand of those who
intend to take their life. I will provide their corpses as
food for the birds of the sky and for the wild animals
of the land. 8 I will make this city desolate, an object
of scorn. Everyone who passes by it will be appalled
and scoff because of all its wounds. 9 I will make them
eat the flesh of their sons and their daughters, and
they will eat each other's flesh in the distressing siege
inflicted on them by their enemies who intend to
take their life.'

10 "Then you are to shatter the jar in the presence of
the people going with you, 11 and you are to proclaim
to them, 'This is what the LORD of Armies says: I will
shatter these people and this city, like one shatters a
potter's jar that can never again be mended. They will
bury the dead in Topheth because there is no other
place for burials. 12 That is what I will do to this place
— this is the declaration of the LORD — and to its
residents, making this city like Topheth. 13 The houses of Jerusalem and the houses of the kings of Judah
will become impure like that place Topheth — all the
houses on whose rooftops they have burned incense
to all the stars in the sky and poured out drink offerings to other gods.' "

14 Jeremiah returned from Topheth, where the
LORD had sent him to prophesy, stood in the courtyard of the LORD's temple, and proclaimed to all the
people, 15 "This is what the LORD of Armies, the God
of Israel, says: 'I am about to bring on this city — and
on all its cities — every disaster that I spoke against
it, for they have become obstinate, not obeying my
words.' "

JEREMIAH BEATEN BY PASHHUR

20 Pashhur the priest, the son of Immer and chief
official in the temple of the LORD, heard Jeremiah prophesying these things. 2 So Pashhur had the
prophet Jeremiah beaten and put him in the stocks at
the Upper Benjamin Gate in the LORD's temple. 3 The
next day, when Pashhur released Jeremiah from the
stocks, Jeremiah said to him, "The LORD does not call

[A] **18:16** Lit *hissing* [B] **18:17** LXX, Lat, Syr, Tg; MT reads *will look at them* [C] **18:18** Lit *let's strike him with the tongue* [D] **18:21** Lit *by death* [E] **19:1** Syr, Tg; MT omits *Take* [F] **19:3** Lit *about it, his ears will tingle*; Hb obscure [G] **19:5** Lit *mentioned, and it did not arise on my heart*

DIGGING DEEPER *The Immer Bulla*

Though identifying inscriptions that refer to major individuals mentioned in the Old Testament are rare, it is even rarer when one finds an inscription identifying a minor figure that the Bible describes as having dealt with a biblical prophet. However, this is exactly what surfaced when Jerusalem archaeologists Gabriel Barkay and Zachi Zweig were sifting rubble taken from the archaeologically rich Temple Mount area. As they sifted, they discovered a small charred stamp seal (a bulla) with a Hebrew inscription mentioning "Ga'alyahu son of Immer." This individual belonged to the priestly Immer family that opposed Jeremiah's message (Jr 20:1–6) during the reign of King Zedekiah (21:1). The Bible mentions this family that lived during the final days of the First Temple period and apparently had an administrative function overseeing the Temple Mount during Jeremiah's ministry (1Ch 9:12; 24:14; Ezr 2:37,59; 10:20; Neh 3:29; 7:40,61; 11:13).

you Pashhur, but Terror Is on Every Side,[A] 4 for this is
what the LORD says, 'I am about to make you a terror
to both yourself and those you love. They will fall by
the sword of their enemies before your very eyes.
I will hand Judah over to the king of Babylon, and
he will deport them to Babylon and put them to the
sword. 5 I will give away all the wealth of this city,
all its products and valuables. Indeed, I will hand
all the treasures of the kings of Judah over to their
enemies. They will plunder them, seize them, and
carry them off to Babylon. 6 As for you, Pashhur, and
all who live in your house, you will go into captivity.
You will go to Babylon. There you will die, and there
you will be buried, you and all your friends to whom
you prophesied lies.'"

JEREMIAH COMPELLED TO PREACH

7 You deceived me, LORD, and I was deceived.
You seized me and prevailed.
I am a laughingstock all the time;
everyone ridicules me.
8 For whenever I speak, I cry out,
I proclaim, "Violence and destruction!"
so the word of the LORD has become my
constant disgrace and derision.
9 I say, "I won't mention him
or speak any longer in his name."
But his message becomes a fire burning
in my heart,
shut up in my bones.
I become tired of holding it in,
and I cannot prevail.
10 For I have heard the gossip of many people,
"Terror is on every side!
Report him; let's report him!"
Everyone I trusted[B] watches for my fall.
"Perhaps he will be deceived
so that we might prevail against him
and take our vengeance on him."
11 But the LORD is with me like a violent warrior.
Therefore, my persecutors will stumble
and not prevail.
Since they have not succeeded, they will be
utterly shamed,
an everlasting humiliation that will
never be forgotten.
12 LORD of Armies, testing the righteous
and seeing the heart[C] and mind,
let me see your vengeance on them,
for I have presented my case to you.
13 Sing to the LORD!
Praise the LORD,
for he rescues the life of the needy
from evil people.

JEREMIAH'S LAMENT

14 May the day I was born
be cursed.
May the day my mother bore me
never be blessed.
15 May the man be cursed
who brought the news to my father, saying,
"A male child is born to you,"
bringing him great joy.
16 Let that man be like the cities
the LORD demolished without compassion.
Let him hear an outcry in the morning
and a war cry at noontime
17 because he didn't kill me in the womb
so that my mother might have been
my grave,
her womb eternally pregnant.
18 Why did I come out of the womb
to see only struggle and sorrow,
to end my life in shame?

ZEDEKIAH'S REQUEST DENIED

21 This is the word that came to Jeremiah from
the LORD when King Zedekiah sent Pashhur
son of Malchijah and the priest Zephaniah son of Maaseiah to Jeremiah, asking, 2 "Inquire of the LORD on
our behalf, since King Nebuchadnezzar[D] of Babylon

[A] **20:3** = *Magor-missabib* [B] **20:10** Lit *Every man of my peace* [C] **20:12** Lit *kidneys* [D] **21:2** Lit *Nebuchadrezzar*

Nebuchadnezzar: King of Babylon

by Claude F. Mariottini

Nebuchadnezzar II, the Neo-Babylonian Empire's second king, was the most famous king of the Chaldeans, a people whom Jeremiah called "an established nation, an ancient nation" (Jr 5:15). As king, Nebuchadnezzar brought fame and prosperity to the empire. Of all the foreign kings the Old Testament mentions, this Nebuchadnezzar is the most prominent and the one with whom Bible students are most familiar. Nebuchadnezzar reigned from 605 to 562 BC.

THE KINGSHIP OF NEBUCHADNEZZAR

Nebuchadnezzar had a reputation as a great builder. He boasted in "Babylon the Great that I have built to be a royal residence by my vast power and for my majestic glory" (Dn 4:30). The city spanned the Euphrates River by means of a twelve-hundred-foot bridge (the longest in the ancient world). There were eight gates, each named for a god, the most prominent being the Ishtar Gate, opening onto the "Processional Way" that led through the city. The Ishtar Gate was attached to his palace, whose outer walls were made of baked brick, and each brick was stamped with Nebuchadnezzar's name. Also there was the so-called Hanging Gardens, which he built for his wife, Amytis, the daughter of the king of Media. The most prominent building was the stepped tower or ziggurat called Etemenanki, which was three hundred feet on each side and perhaps three hundred feet high and is often called the tower of Babel. Near it was Esagila, the temple of Marduk, their chief god, but cuneiform documents speak of more than fifty temples and chapels in the city, and more than six thousand figurines were found there (see Jr 50:38).[1]

According to Babylonian texts, Nebuchadnezzar received praise as a lawgiver, a judge, and a king who was devoted to justice and who opposed injustice and corruption. His motivation for fairness was to please his god, Marduk, and to thus enjoy a long life: "O Marduk, my lord, do remember my deeds favorably as good [deeds], may (these) my good deeds be always before your mind (so that) my walking in Esagila and Ezida—which I love—may last to old age."[2]

Nebuchadnezzar's name appears in two different forms in the Hebrew Bible, which could be rendered Nebuchadnezzar (fifty-eight times) and Nebuchadrezzar (thirty-four times), although most English translations render them both Nebuchadnezzar for consistency (contrast KJV, NRSV, JPS). Since Babylonian documents use *Nabu-kudurri-utsur,* meaning "Nabu has protected the son who will inherit,"[3] Nebuchadrezzar was probably closer to the original form.

Lion relief from the throne room of Nebuchadnezzar's palace in Babylon.

Reconstruction of Nebuchadnezzar's hanging gardens in Babylon, built for his wife Amytis.

Nebuchadnezzar's father, Nabopolassar, led a Chaldean revolt against the Assyrians and in 626 BC founded the Neo-Babylonian Empire. After establishing an alliance with the Medes, he and his allies took Nineveh, the Assyrian capital, then proceeded to defeat the Assyrian army at Haran and finally at Carchemish in 605 BC. They were then confronted by the Egyptian army led by Pharaoh Neco, which had been detained by King Josiah of Judah, who had been defeated and killed at Megiddo (2Kg 23:29; 2Ch 35:20–24).

Nabopolassar, unable to fight because of an illness that eventually killed him, sent his oldest son, Nebuchadnezzar, to confront the Egyptians. Nebuchadnezzar soundly defeated Neco at Carchemish and subjugated Sidon, Tyre, Philistia, and other countries in Syro-Palestine (see Jr 46:2; 47:2–7). At this time, Nebuchadnezzar learned of his father's death and returned to Babylon, where he was crowned king of Babylon in 605 BC.

NEBUCHADNEZZAR IN THE BOOK OF KINGS

The Old Testament presents more than one view of Nebuchadnezzar. The book of Kings presents him as Jerusalem's conqueror. After his victory against Egypt at Carchemish, Nebuchadnezzar made Jehoiakim his vassal-king of Judah. Jehoiakim submitted to Nebuchadnezzar for three years (604–601 BC). In 601, Egypt and Babylon met again with heavy losses on both sides. Nebuchadnezzar returned home to reorganize his army, and Jehoiakim, counting on Egyptian help, revolted against the Babylonians (2Kg 24:1).

Nebuchadnezzar did not campaign against Israel from 600 to 598 BC, but he sent mercenary soldiers to fight against Jehoiakim (2Kg 24:2–3). Then in 598 BC, Babylon advanced against Judah. Egypt promised to help Jehoiakim, but Egypt's military help did not materialize (v. 7). Jehoiakim died sometime in 598 BC, although the circumstances are unclear,[4] and his son, Jehoiachin, was made the new king of Judah (597 BC). Three months later, Nebuchadnezzar took Jerusalem and deported to Babylon Jehoiachin the king of Judah, his mother, the royal family, the palace officials, the army officers, fighting men, craftsmen, and smiths. He also took all the men of substance and those who were capable of war. According to 2 Kings 24:12–16, ten thousand people were taken into exile. Nebuchadnezzar also took all the temple and palace treasures and broke all the golden vessels used in temple worship. Jehoiachin remained a prisoner in Babylon for thirty-seven years, until Evil-merodach, Nebuchadnezzar's son, freed him (2Kg 25:27–30; Jr 52:31–34).

In 596 BC, Nebuchadnezzar placed Zedekiah on Judah's throne as the new king, but Zedekiah

Royal building inscription cylinder of Nebuchadnezzar from Lugal-Marada temple at ancient Marad.

rebelled in his ninth year. In 588 BC, Nebuchadnezzar came back to Jerusalem and once again besieged the city. Archaeology has confirmed that many of Judah's fortified cities were destroyed at that time.[5] In March 586 BC, Babylon conquered Jerusalem and burned the temple as well as the great houses of the city. At this time, a second deportation took place; only the poorest were left behind.

Full scale model of Ishtar Gate of Babylon at Berlin State Museum.

NEBUCHADNEZZAR IN THE BOOK OF JEREMIAH

The book of Jeremiah offers an expanded interpretation that affirms the sovereignty of God and his guidance in Judah's destruction. Jeremiah proclaimed that God would "hand . . . over" Judah and their treasures to the king of Babylon, who would "plunder them, seize them, and carry them off to Babylon," along with Pashhur, the temple official who had the prophet beaten (Jr 20:4–6). Then when Nebuchadnezzar had Jerusalem under siege, Zedekiah sent Pashhur to ask Jeremiah to beg God for help. But the Lord answered that he himself would fight against the people of Jerusalem "with an outstretched hand and a strong arm, with anger, rage, and intense wrath," with "the sword, famine, and plague." Only those who surrendered would live (21:4–10). God had already handed over Jehoiachin (called Coniah) to be carried away by Nebuchadnezzar (22:24–30; 24:1), all because the people refused to listen to God's prophet who had been begging them to repent since Josiah's thirteenth year (25:3–7). Ever since 605 BC, Jeremiah had been warning Judah that "my [God's] servant Nebuchadnezzar" was coming, who would "completely destroy them and make them an example of horror and scorn, and ruins forever" (25:1–9).

God calls Nebuchadnezzar his "servant" three times in Jeremiah (25:9; 27:6; 43:10). Old Testament writers generally used the title "servant of Yahweh" to designate persons who had a special relationship with God and who were obedient to God's will in the life of his people. Jeremiah uses it to indicate Nebuchadnezzar was the one God appointed to have dominion over the nations and to act as the instrument of God's justice. Therefore, rebellion against Nebuchadnezzar was rebellion against God. The Lord commanded Jeremiah to write his oracles on a scroll as a warning to Judah (36:1–4). According to Jeremiah, Nebuchadnezzar's conquest and subjugation of the nations would happen with God's approval (27:6–7). ✣

---

[1] Edwin Yamauchi, "Nebuchadnezzar," in *NIDBA*, 333; Daniel C. Browning Jr. and Randall Breland, "Babylon," in *HIBD* rev. ed. (2015), 160–64; H. W. F. Saggs, "Babylon," in *Archaeology and Old Testament Study*, ed. D. W. Thomas (Oxford: Oxford University Press, 1967), 44. [2] James B. Pritchard, ed., *ANET*, 307. [3] Ludwig Koehler and Walter Baumgartner, *HALOT* (2000), 660. [4] Eugene H. Merrill, *Kingdom of Priests: A History of Old Testament Israel* (Grand Rapids: Baker, 1987), 451. [5] Kathleen M. Kenyon, *Archaeology in the Holy Land* (Nashville: Thomas Nelson, 1960), 304–5.

is making war against us. Perhaps the LORD will
perform for us something like all his past wondrous
works so that Nebuchadnezzar will withdraw from
us."
3 But Jeremiah answered, "This is what you are to
say to Zedekiah: 4 'This is what the LORD, the God of
Israel, says: I am about to repel the weapons of war
in your hands, those you are using to fight the king
of Babylon and the Chaldeans[A] who are besieging
you outside the wall, and I will bring them into the
center of this city. 5 I myself will fight against you with
an outstretched hand and a strong arm, with anger,
fury, and intense wrath. 6 I will strike the residents
of this city, both people and animals. They will die
in a severe plague. 7 Afterward — this is the LORD's
declaration — King Zedekiah of Judah, his officers,
and the people — those in this city who survive the
plague, the sword, and the famine — I will hand over
to King Nebuchadnezzar of Babylon, to their enemies,
yes, to those who intend to take their lives. He will
put them to the sword; he won't spare them or show
pity or compassion.'

A WARNING FOR THE PEOPLE

8 "But tell this people, 'This is what the LORD says:
Look, I am setting before you the way of life and the
way of death. 9 Whoever stays in this city will die by
the sword, famine, and plague, but whoever goes out
and surrenders to the Chaldeans who are besieging
you will live and will retain his life like the spoils of
war. 10 For I have set my face against this city to bring
disaster and not good — this is the LORD's declaration. It will be handed over to the king of Babylon,
who will burn it.'
11 "And to the house of the king of Judah say this:
'Hear the word of the LORD! 12 House of David, this is
what the LORD says:

Administer justice every morning,
and rescue the victim of robbery
from his oppressor,
or my anger will flare up like fire
and burn unquenchably
because of your evil deeds.
13 Beware! I am against you,
you who sit above the valley,
you atop the rocky plateau —
this is the LORD's declaration —
you who say, "Who can come down
against us?
Who can enter our hiding places?"
14 I will punish you according to
what you have done —
this is the LORD's declaration.
I will kindle a fire in your forest
that will consume everything around it.'"

JUDGMENT AGAINST SINFUL KINGS

22 This is what the LORD says: "Go down to the
palace of the king of Judah and announce this
word there. 2 You are to say, 'Hear the word of the
LORD, king of Judah, you who sit on the throne of David — you, your officers, and your people who enter
these gates. 3 This is what the LORD says: Administer
justice and righteousness. Rescue the victim of robbery from his oppressor. Don't exploit or brutalize
the resident alien, the fatherless, or the widow. Don't
shed innocent blood in this place. 4 For if you conscientiously carry out this word, then kings sitting on
David's throne will enter through the gates of this
palace riding on chariots and horses — they, their officers, and their people. 5 But if you do not obey these
words, then I swear by myself — this is the LORD's
declaration — that this house will become a ruin.'"
6 For this is what the LORD says concerning the
house of the king of Judah:

"You are like Gilead to me,
or the summit of Lebanon,
but I will certainly turn you
into a wilderness,
uninhabited cities.
7 I will set apart destroyers against you,
each with his weapons.
They will cut down the choicest of your cedars
and throw them into the fire.

8 "Many nations will pass by this city and ask one
another, 'Why did the LORD do such a thing to this
great city?' 9 They will answer, 'Because they abandoned the covenant of the LORD their God and bowed
in worship to other gods and served them.'"

A MESSAGE CONCERNING SHALLUM

10 Do not weep for the dead;
do not mourn for him.
Weep bitterly for the one who has gone away,
for he will never return again
and see his native land.

11 For this is what the LORD says concerning Shallum son of Josiah, king of Judah, who became king in
place of his father Josiah, and who has left this place:
"He will never return here again, 12 but he will die in
the place where they deported him, never seeing
this land again."

A MESSAGE CONCERNING JEHOIAKIM

13 Woe for the one who builds his palace
through unrighteousness,
his upstairs rooms through injustice,

[A] 21:4 = Babylonians

who makes his neighbor serve without pay
and will not give him his wages,
14 who says, "I will build myself
a massive palace,
with spacious upstairs rooms."
He will cut windows[A] in it,
and it will be paneled with cedar
and painted bright red.
15 Are you a king because you excel in cedar?
Didn't your father eat and drink
and administer justice and righteousness?
Then it went well with him.
16 He took up the case of the poor and needy;
then it went well.
Is this not what it means to know me?
This is the LORD's declaration.
17 But you have eyes and a heart for nothing
except your own dishonest profit,
shedding innocent blood
and committing extortion and oppression.

18 Therefore, this is what the LORD says concerning
Jehoiakim son of Josiah, king of Judah:
They will not mourn for him, saying,
"Woe, my brother!" or "Woe, my sister!"
They will not mourn for him, saying,
"Woe, lord! Woe, his majesty!"
19 He will be buried like a donkey,
dragged off and thrown
outside Jerusalem's gates.
20 Go up to Lebanon and cry out;
raise your voice in Bashan;
cry out from Abarim,
for all your lovers[B] have been crushed.
21 I spoke to you when you were secure.
You said, "I will not listen."
This has been your way since youth;
indeed, you have never listened to me.
22 The wind will take charge of[C] all
your shepherds,
and your lovers will go into captivity.
Then you will be ashamed and humiliated
because of all your evil.
23 You residents of Lebanon,
nestled among the cedars,
how you will groan[D] when pains come on you,
agony like a woman in labor.

A MESSAGE CONCERNING CONIAH

24 "As I live" — this is the LORD's declaration —
"though you, Coniah[E] son of Jehoiakim, the king of
Judah, were a signet ring on my right hand, I would
tear you from it. 25 In fact, I will hand you over to
those you dread, who intend to take your life, to Nebuchadnezzar king of Babylon and the Chaldeans. 26 I
will hurl you and the mother who gave birth to you
into another land, where neither of you were born,
and there you will both die. 27 They will never return
to the land they long to return to."
28 Is this man Coniah a despised, shattered pot,
a jar no one wants?
Why are he and his descendants hurled out
and cast into a land they have not known?
29 Earth, earth, earth,
hear the word of the LORD!

30 This is what the LORD says:
Record this man as childless,
a man who will not be successful in his lifetime.
None of his descendants will succeed
in sitting on the throne of David
or ruling again in Judah.

THE LORD AND HIS SHEEP

23 "Woe to the shepherds who destroy and scatter
the sheep of my pasture!" This is the LORD's
declaration. 2 "Therefore, this is what the LORD, the
God of Israel, says about the shepherds who tend
my people: You have scattered my flock, banished
them, and have not attended to them. I am about to
attend to you because of your evil acts" — this is the
LORD's declaration. 3 "I will gather the remnant of my
flock from all the lands where I have banished them,
and I will return them to their grazing land. They
will become fruitful and numerous. 4 I will raise up
shepherds over them who will tend them. They will
no longer be afraid or discouraged, nor will any be
missing." This is the LORD's declaration.

THE RIGHTEOUS BRANCH OF DAVID

5 "Look, the days are coming" — this is
the LORD's declaration —
"when I will raise up a Righteous
Branch for David.
He will reign wisely as king
and administer justice and righteousness
in the land.
6 In his days Judah will be saved,
and Israel will dwell securely.
This is the name he will be called:
The LORD Is Our Righteousness.[F]

7 "Look, the days are coming" — the LORD's declaration — "when it will no longer be said, 'As the
LORD lives who brought the Israelites from the land
of Egypt,' 8 but, 'As the LORD lives, who brought and
led the descendants of the house of Israel from the

[A] 22:14 Lit *my windows* [B] 22:20 Or *friends*, or *allies*, also in v. 22
[C] 22:22 Lit *will shepherd* [D] 22:23 LXX, Syr, Vg; MT reads *will be pitied*
[E] 22:24 = Jehoiachin [F] 23:6 = *Yahweh-zidkenu*

land of the north and from all the other countries where I[A] had banished them.' They will dwell once more in their own land."

FALSE PROPHETS CONDEMNED

9 Concerning the prophets:
My heart is broken within me,
and all my bones tremble.
I have become like a drunkard,
like a man overcome by wine,
because of the LORD,
because of his holy words.
10 For the land is full of adulterers;
the land mourns because of the curse,
and the grazing lands in the wilderness
have dried up.
Their way of life[B] has become evil,
and their power is not rightly used
11 because both prophet and priest are ungodly,
even in my house I have found their evil.
This is the LORD's declaration.
12 Therefore, their way will seem
like slippery paths in the gloom.
They will be driven away and fall down there,
for I will bring disaster on them,
the year of their punishment.
This is the LORD's declaration.

13 Among the prophets of Samaria
I saw something disgusting:
They prophesied by Baal
and led my people Israel astray.
14 Among the prophets of Jerusalem also
I saw a horrible thing:
They commit adultery and walk in lies.
They strengthen the hands of evildoers,
and none turns his back on evil.
They are all like Sodom to me;
Jerusalem's residents are like Gomorrah.

15 Therefore, this is what the LORD of Armies says concerning the prophets:
I am about to feed them wormwood
and give them poisoned water to drink,
for from the prophets of Jerusalem
ungodliness[C] has spread throughout the land.

16 This is what the LORD of Armies says: "Do not listen to the words of the prophets who prophesy to you. They are deluding you. They speak visions from their own minds, not from the LORD's mouth. 17 They keep on saying to those who despise me, 'The LORD has spoken: You will have peace.' They have said to everyone who follows the stubbornness of his heart, 'No harm will come to you.'"

18 For who has stood in the council of the LORD
to see and hear his word?
Who has paid attention to his word
and obeyed?
19 Look, a storm from the LORD!
Wrath has gone out,
a whirling storm.
It will whirl about the heads of the wicked.
20 The LORD's anger will not turn away
until he has completely fulfilled the purposes
of his heart.
In time to come you will understand it clearly.

21 I did not send out these prophets,
yet they ran.
I did not speak to them,
yet they prophesied.
22 If they had really stood in my council,
they would have enabled my people to hear
my words
and would have turned them
from their evil ways
and their evil deeds.

23 "Am I a God who is only near" — this is the LORD's
declaration — "and not a God who is far away? 24 Can
a person hide in secret places where I cannot see
him?" — the LORD's declaration. "Do I not fill the
heavens and the earth?" — the LORD's declaration.
25 "I have heard what the prophets who prophesy
a lie in my name have said: 'I had a dream! I had a
dream!' 26 How long will this continue in the minds
of the prophets prophesying lies, prophets of the
deceit of their own minds? 27 Through their dreams
that they tell one another, they plan to cause my people to forget my name as their ancestors forgot my
name through Baal worship. 28 The prophet who has
only a dream should recount the dream, but the one
who has my word should speak my word truthfully,
for what is straw compared to grain?" — this is the
LORD's declaration. 29 "Is not my word like fire" — this
is the LORD's declaration — "and like a hammer that
pulverizes rock? 30 Therefore, take note! I am against
the prophets" — the LORD's declaration — "who steal
my words from each other. 31 I am against the prophets" — the LORD's declaration — "who use their own
tongues to make a declaration. 32 I am against those
who prophesy false dreams" — the LORD's declaration — "telling them and leading my people astray
with their reckless lies. It was not I who sent or commanded them, and they are of no benefit at all to these
people" — this is the LORD's declaration.

[A]**23:8** LXX reads *he* [B]**23:10** Lit *Their manner of running*
[C]**23:15** Or *pollution*

THE BURDEN OF THE LORD

33 “Now when these people or a prophet or a priest asks you, ‘What is the burden[A] of the LORD?’ you will respond to them, ‘What is the burden? I will throw you away! This is the LORD’s declaration.’ 34 As for the prophet, priest, or people who say, ‘The burden of the LORD,’ I will punish that man and his household. 35 This is what each man is to say to his friend and to his brother: ‘What has the LORD answered?’ or ‘What has the LORD spoken?’ 36 But no longer refer to[B] the burden of the LORD, for each man’s word becomes his burden and you pervert the words of the living God, the LORD of Armies, our God. 37 Say to the prophet, ‘What has the LORD answered you?’ or ‘What has the LORD spoken?’ 38 But if you say, ‘The burden of the LORD,’ then this is what the LORD says: Because you have said, ‘The burden of the LORD,’ and I specifically told you not to say, ‘The burden of the LORD,’ 39 I will surely forget you.[C] I will throw you away from my presence — both you and the city that I gave you and your ancestors. 40 I will bring on you everlasting disgrace and humiliation that will never be forgotten.”

THE GOOD AND THE BAD FIGS

24 After King Nebuchadnezzar of Babylon had deported Jeconiah[D] son of Jehoiakim king of Judah, the officials of Judah, and the craftsmen and metalsmiths from Jerusalem and had brought them to Babylon, the LORD showed me two baskets of figs placed in front of the temple of the LORD. 2 One basket contained very good figs, like early figs, but the other basket contained very bad figs, so bad they were inedible. 3 The LORD said to me, “What do you see, Jeremiah?”

I said, “Figs! The good figs are very good, but the bad figs are extremely bad, so bad they are inedible.”

4 The word of the LORD came to me: 5 “This is what the LORD, the God of Israel, says: Like these good figs, so I regard as good the exiles from Judah I sent away from this place to the land of the Chaldeans. 6 I will keep my eyes on them for their good and will return them to this land. I will build them up and not demolish them; I will plant them and not uproot them. 7 I will give them a heart to know me, that I am the LORD. They will be my people, and I will be their God because they will return to me with all their heart.

8 “But as for the bad figs, so bad they are inedible, this is what the LORD says: In this way I will deal with King Zedekiah of Judah, his officials, and the remnant of Jerusalem — those remaining in this land or living in the land of Egypt. 9 I will make them an object of horror and a disaster to all the kingdoms of the earth, an example for disgrace, scorn, ridicule, and cursing, wherever I have banished them. 10 I will send the sword, famine, and plague against them until they have perished from the land I gave to them and their ancestors.”

THE SEVENTY-YEAR EXILE

25 This is the word that came to Jeremiah concerning all the people of Judah in the fourth year of Jehoiakim son of Josiah, king of Judah (which was the first year of King Nebuchadnezzar of Babylon). 2 The prophet Jeremiah spoke concerning all the people of Judah and all the residents of Jerusalem as follows: 3 “From the thirteenth year of Josiah son of Amon, king of Judah, until this very day — twenty-three years — the word of the LORD has come to me, and I have spoken to you time and time again,[E] but you have not obeyed. 4 The LORD sent all his servants the prophets to you time and time again,[F] but you have not obeyed or even paid attention.[G] 5 He announced, ‘Turn, each of you, from your evil way of life and from your evil deeds. Live in the land the LORD gave to you and your ancestors long ago and forever. 6 Do not follow other gods to serve them and to bow in worship to them, and do not anger me by the work of your hands. Then I will do you no harm.

7 “ ‘But you have not obeyed me’ — this is the LORD’s declaration — ‘with the result that you have angered me by the work of your hands and brought disaster on yourselves.’

8 “Therefore, this is what the LORD of Armies says: ‘Because you have not obeyed my words, 9 I am going to send for all the families of the north’ — this is the LORD’s declaration — ‘and send for my servant Nebuchadnezzar king of Babylon, and I will bring them against this land, against its residents, and against all these surrounding nations, and I will completely destroy them and make them an example of horror and scorn, and ruins forever. 10 I will eliminate the sound of joy and gladness from them — the voice of the groom and the bride, the sound of the millstones and the light of the lamp. 11 This whole land will become a desolate ruin, and these nations will serve the king of Babylon for seventy years. 12 When the seventy years are completed, I will punish the king of Babylon and that nation’ — this is the LORD’s declaration — ‘the land of the Chaldeans, for their iniquity, and I will make it a ruin forever. 13 I will bring on that land all my words I have spoken against it, all that is written in this book that Jeremiah prophesied against all the nations. 14 For many nations and great kings will enslave them, and I will repay them according to their deeds and the work of their hands.’ ”

[A] **23:33** The Hb word for *burden* (Ex 23:5; 2Sm 15:33) can also mean “oracle” (Is 13:1; Nah 1:10). [B] **23:36** Or *longer remember* [C] **23:39** Some Hb mss; other Hb mss, LXX, Syr, Vg read *surely lift you up* [D] **24:1** = Jehoiachin [E] **25:3** Lit *you; rising early and speaking* [F] **25:4** Lit *to you, rising early and sending* [G] **25:4** Lit *even inclined your ear to hear*

Zedekiah: Judah's Last King

by Rick W. Byargeon

The demise of the Davidic kingdom happened during Zedekiah's reign. From start to finish, he reigned under the heavy hand of Babylonian domination. The power that placed him on the throne eventually took away his kingship, his family, and his life. Zedekiah appears as a weak and indecisive leader. He simply did not have the leadership and spiritual qualities to help Judah survive.

THE RISE OF AN INEFFECTUAL LEADER

Zedekiah was not chosen by the people of Judah but by Nebuchadnezzar. According to 2 Kings 24:17–18, Nebuchadnezzar placed Zedekiah on the throne of Judah in 596 BC because of his loyalty to Babylon.

The Babylonians reappeared in Israel in December 598 BC, to punish Jerusalem. King Jehoiakim died before Jerusalem fell, and Jehoiachin, his eighteen-year-old son, ascended to the throne only to surrender the city to Babylon on March 16, 597 BC.[1] The Babylonians deported Jehoiachin, along with the upper crust of Judean society, to Babylon. This crushing blow set the stage for Zedekiah's rise to power.

According to 2 Kings 24:17, "The king of Babylon made Mattaniah, Jehoiachin's uncle, king in his place and changed his name to Zedekiah." Though Zedekiah was part of the Davidic royal family, the people evidently did not accept him as king. Hananiah's false prophecy undoubtedly reflects a hope in Jehoiachin's return (Jr 28:4). Other texts also support the notion that Zedekiah did not have full support of his people. For example, Ezekiel dated his prophetic visions on the basis of "King Jehoiachin's exile" (Ezk 1:2).

ZEDEKIAH'S STORMY REIGN

If Zedekiah lacked the full support of his people, then his decisions and the tumultuous times between 597 and 586 BC did nothing to enhance his credibility. Within three years of taking the reins of government (ca 594 BC), Zedekiah, at the urging of Egypt—along with Edom, Moab, Ammon, Tyre, and Sidon—gathered to plot a rebellion against Babylon. The plot failed perhaps due in part to Jeremiah, who picketed the event and proclaimed its folly (Jr 27:1–11). Soon after this foiled plan, Zedekiah traveled to Babylon and swore renewed allegiance to the Babylonian king (29:3; 51:59).

Zedekiah's renewed allegiance did not last. Eventually he led Judah into open revolt against Babylon about 590–588 BC (cf. 2Kg 24:20; 2Ch 36:13). Three factors may have contributed to Zedekiah's decision. First, Nebuchadnezzar had been absent from Syria-Palestine since 594 BC. Second, the Egyptian Pharaoh Psammetichus II had defeated Nubia to his south and toured Syria-Palestine as a way of flexing his military might.[2] Perhaps these two factors led Zedekiah to trust in Egypt's power (Ezk 17:15) and to doubt Babylon's resolve. Finally, a segment of Zedekiah's court, as well as some prophets, claimed that rebellion was God's will (Jr 28–29). The anti-Babylonian group maintained that God would not allow his city to fall into Babylonian hands (5:12; 14:13).

Jeremiah, however, consistently maintained that God's will was for Judah to submit to the Babylonians. This viewpoint, as you might imagine, was not popular. Jeremiah's fellow citizens considered him a traitor (37:11–21). Large blocks of Jeremiah's prophecy recount the rejection of God's perspective by both priests and prophets (chaps. 26–29) and the royal court (chaps. 34–36). Jeremiah's consistent call to submit to Babylon garnered the prophet multiple arrests and death threats (37:15; 38:1–16).

Zedekiah's failure to listen to Jeremiah eventually led to Jerusalem's destruction. The Babylonians reacted to Zedekiah's revolt by laying siege to the city of Jerusalem for about two years (588–586 BC). Help from Egypt never materialized. Neither did help from God. Numerous times Zedekiah attempted to

Urartian Bronze Age chain. Zedekiah was led off in chains (39:7).

Cistern at Lachish. Jeremiah was thrown into a cistern, and Zedekiah ordered his release (38:1–13).

bargain with God to spare the city. Three times Zedekiah sought a reprieve from God through Jeremiah (37:3,17; 38:14), but to no avail. The answer was the same each time. The city will fall. Possibly even the slave release in Jeremiah 34 was linked to a hope that obeying the law in Exodus 21:2 would cause God to protect the city. Unfortunately, the obedience of the slave owners lasted only a short time. When the siege lifted momentarily, the slave owners reneged on their promises. This led to a stinging pronouncement of judgment: "You have not obeyed me by proclaiming freedom, each for his fellow Hebrew and for his neighbor. I hereby proclaim freedom for you—this is the LORD's declaration—to the sword, to plague, and to famine!" (Jr 34:17).[3]

THE END OF ZEDEKIAH'S REIGN

God's prediction proved true. Jeremiah 52:1–7 tells us that the city finally ran out of food and out of time. The Babylonian army tore down the walls, destroyed the temple, and set fire to the city. Many of the citizens began the long march as captives to Babylon (vv. 28–30). Only the poorest people remained in the land (39:9–10). Zedekiah attempted to escape, but the Babylonians captured him at Jericho. He appeared before Nebuchadnezzar at Riblah and watched his sons die before his eyes. It was the last thing that Zedekiah saw. The Babylonians blinded him and led him away in chains to prison where he later died (52:9–11). ✣

[1] This date is based on correlating our Julian calendar with the Babylonian Chronicle, a source for Nabopolassar and Nebuchadnezzar's activities in the land of Israel. See James B. Pritchard, ed., *ANET*, 564; John Bright, *A History of Israel*, 4th ed. (Louisville: Westminster John Knox, 2000), 327. [2] J. Maxwell Miller and John H. Hayes, *A History of Ancient Israel and Judah* (Philadelphia: Westminster, 1986), 412–13. Daniel I. Block, *The Book of Ezekiel: Chapters 1–24*, NICOT (Grand Rapids: Eerdmans, 1997), 544: "A papyrus from El Hibeh refers to a visit by the pharaoh to Syria-Palestine in his fourth year, ostensibly as a religious pilgrimage to Byblos. But such royal visits usually also have political undertones, especially since these states had revolted against Babylon as recently as three years previously." [3] William S. LaSor, David A. Hubbard, and Frederic William Bush, *Old Testament Survey: The Message, Form, and Background of the Old Testament*, 2nd ed. (Grand Rapids: Eerdmans, 1996), 346.

THE CUP OF GOD'S WRATH

15 This is what the LORD, the God of Israel, said to me:
"Take this cup of the wine of wrath from my hand
and make all the nations to whom I am sending you
drink from it. 16 They will drink, stagger,[A] and go out
of their minds because of the sword I am sending
among them."

17 So I took the cup from the LORD's hand and made
all the nations to whom the LORD sent me drink
from it.

18 Jerusalem and the other cities of Judah, its
kings and its officials, to make them a desolate
ruin, an example for scorn and cursing — as it
is today;
19 Pharaoh king of Egypt, his officers, his leaders,
all his people,
20 and all the mixed peoples;
all the kings of the land of Uz;
all the kings of the land of the Philistines
— Ashkelon, Gaza, Ekron, and the remnant of
Ashdod;
21 Edom, Moab, and the Ammonites;
22 all the kings of Tyre,
all the kings of Sidon,
and the kings of the coasts and islands;
23 Dedan, Tema, Buz, and all those who clip the
hair on their temples;[B]
24 all the kings of Arabia,
and all the kings of the mixed peoples who have
settled in the desert;
25 all the kings of Zimri,
all the kings of Elam,
and all the kings of Media;
26 all the kings of the north, both near and far
from one another;
that is, all the kingdoms of the world throughout
the earth.
Finally, the king of Sheshak[C] will drink after them.

27 "Then you are to say to them, 'This is what the
LORD of Armies, the God of Israel, says: Drink, get
drunk, and vomit. Fall down and never get up again,
as a result of the sword I am sending among you.' 28 If[D]
they refuse to accept the cup from your hand and
drink, you are to say to them, 'This is what the LORD
of Armies says: You must drink! 29 For I am already
bringing disaster on the city that bears my name, so
how could you possibly go unpunished? You will not
go unpunished, for I am summoning a sword against
all the inhabitants of the earth. This is the declaration
of the LORD of Armies.'

JUDGMENT ON THE WHOLE WORLD

30 "As for you, you are to prophesy all these things to
them, and say to them:

The LORD roars from on high;
he makes his voice heard
from his holy dwelling.
He roars loudly over his grazing land;
he calls out with a shout, like those
who tread grapes,
against all the inhabitants of the earth.
31 The tumult reaches to the ends of the earth
because the LORD brings a case
against the nations.
He enters into judgment with all humanity.
As for the wicked, he hands them over
to the sword —
this is the LORD's declaration.

32 "This is what the LORD of Armies says:
Pay attention! Disaster spreads
from nation to nation.
A huge storm is stirred up
from the ends of the earth."

33 Those slain by the LORD on that day will be scattered from one end of the earth to the other. They
will not be mourned, gathered, or buried. They will
be like manure on the soil's surface.

34 Wail, you shepherds, and cry out.
Roll in the dust, you leaders of the flock.
Because the days of your slaughter
have come,
you will fall and become shattered
like a precious vase.
35 Flight will be impossible for the shepherds,
and escape, for the leaders of the flock.
36 Hear the sound of the shepherds' cry,
the wail of the leaders of the flock,
for the LORD is destroying their pasture.
37 Peaceful grazing land will become lifeless
because of the LORD's burning anger.
38 He has left his den like a lion,
for their land has become a desolation
because of the sword[E] of the oppressor,
because of his burning anger.

JEREMIAH'S SPEECH IN THE TEMPLE

26 At the beginning of the reign of Jehoiakim
son of Josiah, king of Judah, this word came
from the LORD: 2 "This is what the LORD says: Stand
in the courtyard of the LORD's temple and speak all
the words I have commanded you to speak to all Judah's cities that are coming to worship there. Do not
hold back a word. 3 Perhaps they will listen and turn
— each from his evil way of life — so that I might

[A] **25:16** Or *vomit* [B] **25:23** Or *who live in distant places* [C] **25:26** = Babylon
[D] **25:28** Or *When* [E] **25:38** Some Hb mss, LXX, Tg; other Hb mss read *burning*

relent concerning the disaster that I plan to do to them because of the evil of their deeds. 4 You are to say to them, 'This is what the LORD says: If you do not listen to me by living according to my instruction that I set before you 5 and by listening to the words of my servants the prophets — whom I have been sending to you time and time again,[A] though you did not listen — 6 I will make this temple like Shiloh. I will make this city an example for cursing for all the nations of the earth.' "

JEREMIAH SEIZED

7 The priests, the prophets, and all the people heard Jeremiah speaking these words in the temple of the LORD. 8 When he finished the address the LORD had commanded him to deliver to all the people, immediately the priests, the prophets, and all the people took hold of him, yelling, "You must surely die! 9 How dare you prophesy in the name of the LORD, 'This temple will become like Shiloh and this city will become an uninhabited ruin'!" Then all the people crowded around Jeremiah at the LORD's temple.

10 When the officials of Judah heard about these things, they went from the king's palace to the LORD's temple and sat at the entrance of the New Gate of the LORD's temple.[B] 11 Then the priests and prophets said to the officials and all the people, "This man deserves the death sentence because he has prophesied against this city, as you have heard with your own ears."

JEREMIAH'S DEFENSE

12 Then Jeremiah said to all the officials and all the people, "The LORD sent me to prophesy all the words that you have heard against this temple and city. 13 So now, correct your ways and deeds, and obey the LORD your God so that he might relent concerning the disaster he had pronounced against you. 14 As for me, here I am in your hands; do to me what you think is good and right. 15 But know for certain that if you put me to death, you will bring innocent blood on yourselves, on this city, and on its residents, for it is certain the LORD has sent me to speak all these things directly to you."

JEREMIAH RELEASED

16 Then the officials and all the people told the priests and prophets, "This man doesn't deserve the death sentence, for he has spoken to us in the name of the LORD our God!"

17 Some of the elders of the land stood up and said to all the assembled people, 18 "Micah the Moreshite prophesied in the days of King Hezekiah of Judah and said to all the people of Judah, 'This is what the LORD of Armies says:

Zion will be plowed like a field,
Jerusalem will become ruins,
and the temple's mountain will be
a high thicket.'

19 Did King Hezekiah of Judah and all the people of Judah put him to death? Did not the king fear the LORD and plead for the LORD's favor,[C] and did not the LORD relent concerning the disaster he had pronounced against them? We are about to bring a terrible disaster on ourselves!"

THE PROPHET URIAH

20 Another man was also prophesying in the name of the LORD — Uriah son of Shemaiah from Kiriath-jearim. He prophesied against this city and against this land in words like all those of Jeremiah. 21 King Jehoiakim, all his warriors, and all the officials heard his words, and the king tried to put him to death. When Uriah heard, he fled in fear and went to Egypt. 22 But King Jehoiakim sent men to Egypt: Elnathan son of Achbor and certain other men with him went to Egypt. 23 They brought Uriah out of Egypt and took him to King Jehoiakim, who executed him with the sword and threw his corpse into the burial place of the common people.[D]

24 But Ahikam son of Shaphan supported Jeremiah, so he was not handed over to the people to be put to death.

THE YOKE OF BABYLON

27 At the beginning of the reign of Zedekiah[E] son of Josiah, king of Judah, this word came to Jeremiah from the LORD:[F] 2 This is what the LORD said to me: "Make chains and yoke bars for yourself and put them on your neck. 3 Send word to the king of Edom, the king of Moab, the king of the Ammonites, the king of Tyre, and the king of Sidon through messengers who are coming to King Zedekiah of Judah in Jerusalem. 4 Command them to go to their masters, saying, 'This is what the LORD of Armies, the God of Israel, says: Tell this to your masters: 5 "By my great strength and outstretched arm, I made the earth, and the people, and animals on the face of the earth. I give it to anyone I please.[G] 6 So now I have placed all these lands under the authority of my servant Nebuchadnezzar, king of Babylon. I have even given him the wild animals to serve him. 7 All nations will serve him, his son, and his grandson until the time for his own land comes, and then many nations and great kings will enslave him.

[A] **26:5** Lit *you, rising early and sending* [B] **26:10** Many Hb mss, Syr, Tg, Vg; other Hb mss read *the New Gate of the LORD* [C] **26:19** Or *and appease the LORD* [D] **26:23** Lit *the sons of the people* [E] **27:1** Some Hb mss, Syr, Arabic; other Hb mss, DSS read *Jehoiakim* [F] **27:1** LXX omits this v. [G] **27:5** Lit *to whomever is upright in my eyes*

8 " ' "As for the nation or kingdom that does not serve King Nebuchadnezzar of Babylon and does not place its neck under the yoke of the king of Babylon, that nation I will punish by sword, famine, and plague — this is the LORD's declaration — until through him I have destroyed it. 9 So you should not listen to your prophets, diviners, dreamers, fortune-tellers, or sorcerers who say to you, 'Don't serve the king of Babylon!' 10 They are prophesying a lie to you so that you will be removed from your land. I will banish you, and you will perish. 11 But as for the nation that will put its neck under the yoke of the king of Babylon and serve him, I will leave it in its own land, and that nation will cultivate[A] it and reside in it. This is the LORD's declaration." ' "

WARNING TO ZEDEKIAH

12 I spoke to King Zedekiah of Judah in the same way: "Put your necks under the yoke of the king of Babylon, serve him and his people, and live! 13 Why should you and your people die by the sword, famine, and plague as the LORD has threatened against any nation that does not serve the king of Babylon? 14 Do not listen to the words of the prophets who are telling you, 'Don't serve the king of Babylon,' for they are prophesying a lie to you. 15 'I have not sent them' — this is the LORD's declaration — 'and they are prophesying falsely in my name; therefore, I will banish you, and you will perish — you and the prophets who are prophesying to you.' "

16 Then I spoke to the priests and all these people, saying, "This is what the LORD says: 'Do not listen to the words of your prophets. They are prophesying to you, claiming, "Look, very soon now the articles of the LORD's temple will be brought back from Babylon." They are prophesying a lie to you. 17 Do not listen to them. Serve the king of Babylon and live! Why should this city become a ruin? 18 If they are indeed prophets and if the word of the LORD is with them, let them intercede with the LORD of Armies not to let the articles that remain in the LORD's temple, in the palace of the king of Judah, and in Jerusalem go to Babylon.' 19 For this is what the LORD of Armies says about the pillars, the basin,[B] the water carts, and the rest of the articles that still remain in this city, 20 those King Nebuchadnezzar of Babylon did not take when he deported Jeconiah[C] son of Jehoiakim, king of Judah, from Jerusalem to Babylon along with all the nobles of Judah and Jerusalem. 21 Yes, this is what the LORD of Armies, the God of Israel, says about the articles that remain in the temple of the LORD, in the palace of the king of Judah, and in Jerusalem: 22 'They will be taken to Babylon and will remain there until I attend to them again.' This is the LORD's declaration. 'Then I will bring them up and restore them to this place.' "

HANANIAH'S FALSE PROPHECY

28 In that same year, at the beginning of the reign of King Zedekiah of Judah, in the fifth month of the fourth year, the prophet Hananiah son of Azzur from Gibeon said to me in the temple of the LORD in the presence of the priests and all the people, 2 "This is what the LORD of Armies, the God of Israel, says: 'I have broken the yoke of the king of Babylon. 3 Within two years I will restore to this place all the articles of the LORD's temple that King Nebuchadnezzar of Babylon took from here and transported to Babylon. 4 And I will restore to this place Jeconiah[C] son of Jehoiakim, king of Judah, and all the exiles from Judah who went to Babylon' — this is the LORD's declaration — 'for I will break the yoke of the king of Babylon.' "

JEREMIAH'S RESPONSE TO HANANIAH

5 The prophet Jeremiah replied to the prophet Hananiah in the presence of the priests and all the people who were standing in the temple of the LORD. 6 The prophet Jeremiah said, "Amen! May the LORD do that. May the LORD make the words you have prophesied come true and may he restore the articles of the LORD's temple and all the exiles from Babylon to this place! 7 Only listen to this message I am speaking in your hearing and in the hearing of all the people. 8 The prophets who preceded you and me from ancient times prophesied war, disaster,[D] and plague against many lands and great kingdoms. 9 As for the prophet who prophesies peace — only when the word of the prophet comes true will the prophet be recognized as one the LORD has truly sent."

HANANIAH BREAKS JEREMIAH'S YOKE

10 The prophet Hananiah then took the yoke bar from the neck of the prophet Jeremiah and broke it. 11 In the presence of all the people Hananiah proclaimed, "This is what the LORD says: 'In this way, within two years I will break the yoke of King Nebuchadnezzar of Babylon from the neck of all the nations.' " The prophet Jeremiah then went on his way.

THE LORD'S WORD AGAINST HANANIAH

12 After the prophet Hananiah had broken the yoke bar from the neck of the prophet Jeremiah, the word of the LORD came to Jeremiah: 13 "Go say to Hananiah, 'This is what the LORD says: You broke a wooden yoke bar, but in its place you will make an iron yoke bar. 14 For this is what the LORD of Armies, the God of Israel, says: I have put an iron yoke on the neck of all these nations that they might serve King Nebuchadnezzar of Babylon, and they will serve him. I have even put the wild animals under him.' "

[A] **27:11** Lit *work* [B] **27:19** Lit *sea* [C] **27:20; 28:4** = Jehoiachin
[D] **28:8** Some Hb mss, Vg read *famine*

15 The prophet Jeremiah said to the prophet Hananiah, "Listen, Hananiah! The LORD did not send
you, but you have led these people to trust in a lie.
16 Therefore, this is what the LORD says: 'I am about
to send you off the face of the earth. You will die this
year because you have preached rebellion against
the LORD.'" 17 And the prophet Hananiah died that
year in the seventh month.

JEREMIAH'S LETTER TO THE EXILES

29 This is the text of the letter that the prophet
Jeremiah sent from Jerusalem to the remaining exiled elders, the priests, the prophets, and all
the people Nebuchadnezzar had deported from Jerusalem to Babylon. 2 This was after King Jeconiah,[A]
the queen mother, the court officials, the officials of
Judah and Jerusalem, the craftsmen, and the metalsmiths had left Jerusalem. 3 He sent the letter with
Elasah son of Shaphan and Gemariah son of Hilkiah,
whom Zedekiah king of Judah sent to Babylon to King
Nebuchadnezzar of Babylon. The letter stated:

4 This is what the LORD of Armies, the God of
Israel, says to all the exiles I deported from
Jerusalem to Babylon: 5 "Build houses and live
in them. Plant gardens and eat their produce.
6 Find wives for yourselves, and have sons and
daughters. Find wives for your sons and give
your daughters to men in marriage so that they
may bear sons and daughters. Multiply there; do
not decrease. 7 Pursue the well-being[B] of the city
I have deported you to. Pray to the LORD on its
behalf, for when it thrives, you will thrive."

8 For this is what the LORD of Armies, the God
of Israel, says: "Don't let your prophets who are
among you and your diviners deceive you, and
don't listen to the dreams you elicit from them,
9 for they are prophesying falsely to you in my
name. I have not sent them." This is the LORD's
declaration.

10 For this is what the LORD says: "When seventy
years for Babylon are complete, I will attend to
you and will confirm my promise concerning
you to restore you to this place. 11 For I know the
plans I have for you" — this is the LORD's declaration — "plans for your well-being, not for
disaster, to give you a future and a hope. 12 You
will call to me and come and pray to me, and I
will listen to you. 13 You will seek me and find
me when you search for me with all your heart.
14 I will be found by you" — this is the LORD's
declaration — "and I will restore your fortunes[C]
and gather you from all the nations and places where I banished you" — this is the LORD's
declaration. "I will restore you to the place from
which I deported you."

15 You have said, "The LORD has raised up prophets for us in Babylon!" 16 But this is what the
LORD says concerning the king sitting on David's
throne and concerning all the people living in
this city — that is, concerning your brothers
who did not go with you into exile. 17 This is what
the LORD of Armies says: "I am about to send
sword, famine, and plague against them, and I
will make them like rotten figs that are inedible
because they are so bad. 18 I will pursue them
with sword, famine, and plague. I will make
them a horror to all the kingdoms of the earth
— a curse and a desolation, an object of scorn
and a disgrace among all the nations where I
have banished them. 19 I will do this because
they have not listened to my words" — this is
the LORD's declaration — "the words that I sent
to them with my servants the prophets time and
time again.[D] And you too have not listened." This
is the LORD's declaration.

20 Hear the word of the LORD, all you exiles I have
sent from Jerusalem to Babylon. 21 This is what
the LORD of Armies, the God of Israel, says about
Ahab son of Kolaiah and concerning Zedekiah
son of Maaseiah, the ones prophesying a lie to
you in my name: "I am about to hand them over
to King Nebuchadnezzar of Babylon, and he will
kill them before your very eyes. 22 Based on what
happens to them, all the exiles of Judah who are
in Babylon will create a curse that says, 'May the
LORD make you like Zedekiah and Ahab, whom
the king of Babylon roasted in the fire!' 23 because they have committed an outrage in Israel
by committing adultery with their neighbors'
wives and have spoken in my name a lie, which I
did not command them. I am he who knows, and
I am a witness." This is the LORD's declaration.

24 To Shemaiah the Nehelamite you are to say,
25 "This is what the LORD of Armies, the God of
Israel, says: You[E] in your own name have sent
out letters to all the people of Jerusalem, to the
priest Zephaniah son of Maaseiah, and to all the
priests, saying, 26 'The LORD has appointed you
priest in place of the priest Jehoiada to be the
chief officer in the temple of the LORD, responsible for every madman who acts like a prophet.

[A] **29:2** = Jehoiachin [B] **29:7** Or *peace* [C] **29:14** Or *will end your captivity* [D] **29:19** Lit *prophets, rising up early and sending* [E] **29:25** Lit *Because you*

You must confine him in the stocks and an iron
collar. 27 So now, why have you not rebuked Jeremiah of Anathoth who has been acting like a
prophet among you? 28 For he has sent word to
us in Babylon, claiming, "The exile will be long.
Build houses and settle down. Plant gardens and
eat their produce."'"
29 The priest Zephaniah read this letter in the hearing
of the prophet Jeremiah.

A MESSAGE ABOUT SHEMAIAH

30 Then the word of the LORD came to Jeremiah:
31 "Send a message to all the exiles, saying, 'This is
what the LORD says concerning Shemaiah the Nehelamite. Because Shemaiah prophesied to you,
though I did not send him, and made you trust a
lie, 32 this is what the LORD says: I am about to punish Shemaiah the Nehelamite and his descendants.
There will not be even one of his descendants living
among these people, nor will any ever see the good
that I will bring to my people — this is the LORD's
declaration — for he has preached rebellion against
the LORD.'"

RESTORATION FROM CAPTIVITY

30 This is the word that came to Jeremiah from
the LORD. 2 "This is what the LORD, the God of
Israel, says: Write on a scroll all the words that I have
spoken to you, 3 for look, the days are coming" — this
is the LORD's declaration — "when I will restore the
fortunes[A] of my people Israel and Judah," says the
LORD. "I will restore them to the land I gave to their
ancestors and they will possess it."
4 These are the words the LORD spoke to Israel and
Judah. 5 This is what the LORD says:

We have heard a cry of terror,
of dread — there is no peace.
6 Ask and see
whether a male can give birth.
Why then do I see every man
with his hands on his stomach like a woman
in labor
and every face turned pale?
7 How awful that day will be!
There will be no other like it!
It will be a time of trouble for Jacob,
but he will be saved out of it.

8 On that day —
this is the declaration of the LORD
of Armies —
I will break his yoke from your neck
and tear off your chains,
and strangers will never again
enslave him.
9 They will serve the LORD their God
and David their king,
whom I will raise up for them.

10 As for you, my servant Jacob,
do not be afraid —
this is the LORD's declaration —
and do not be discouraged, Israel,
for without fail I will save you out of a distant
place,
your descendants, from the land
of their captivity!
Jacob will return and have calm and quiet
with no one to frighten him.
11 For I will be with you —
this is the LORD's declaration —
to save you!
I will bring destruction on all the nations
where I have scattered you;
however, I will not bring destruction on you.
I will discipline you justly,
and I will by no means leave you unpunished.

HEALING ZION'S WOUNDS

12 For this is what the LORD says:

Your injury is incurable;
your wound most severe.
13 You have no defender for your case.
There is no remedy for your sores,
and no healing for you.[B]
14 All your lovers have forgotten you;
they no longer look for you,
for I have struck you as an enemy would,
with the discipline of someone cruel,
because of your enormous guilt
and your innumerable sins.
15 Why do you cry out about your injury?
Your pain has no cure!
I have done these things to you
because of your enormous guilt
and your innumerable sins.
16 Nevertheless, all who devoured you
will be devoured,
and all your adversaries — all of them —
will go off into exile.
Those who plunder you will be plundered,
and all who raid you will be raided.
17 But I will bring you health
and will heal you of your wounds —
this is the LORD's declaration —
for they call you Outcast,
Zion whom no one cares about.

[A] **30:3** Or *will end the captivity* [B] **30:13** Or *No one pleads that your sores should be healed. There is no remedy for you.*

RESTORATION OF THE LAND

[18] This is what the LORD says:
I will certainly restore the fortunes[A]
of Jacob's tents
and show compassion on his dwellings.
Every city will be rebuilt on its mound;
every citadel will stand on its proper site.
19 Thanksgiving will come out of them,
a sound of rejoicing.
I will multiply them,
and they will not decrease;
I will honor them, and they will not
be insignificant.
20 His children will be as in past days;
his congregation will be established
in my presence.
I will punish all his oppressors.
21 Jacob's leader will be one of them;
his ruler will issue from him.
I will invite him to me, and he will
approach me,
for who would otherwise risk his life
to approach me?
This is the LORD's declaration.
22 You will be my people,
and I will be your God.

THE WRATH OF GOD

23 Look, a storm from the LORD!
Wrath has gone out,
a churning storm.
It will whirl about the heads of the wicked.
24 The LORD's burning anger will not
turn back
until he has completely fulfilled the purposes
of his heart.
In time to come you will understand it.

GOD'S RELATIONSHIP WITH HIS PEOPLE

31 "At that time" — this is the LORD's declaration
— "I will be the God of all the families of Israel,
and they will be my people."
[2] This is what the LORD says:
The people who survived the sword
found favor in the wilderness.
When Israel went to find rest,
3 the LORD appeared to him[B] from far away.
I have loved you with an everlasting love;
therefore, I have continued to extend
faithful love to you.
4 Again I will build you so that you will
be rebuilt,
Virgin Israel.
You will take up your tambourines again
and go out in joyful dancing.
5 You will plant vineyards again
on the mountains of Samaria;
the planters will plant and will enjoy the fruit.
6 For there will be a day when watchmen
will call out
in the hill country of Ephraim,
"Come, let's go up to Zion,
to the LORD our God!"

GOD'S PEOPLE BROUGHT HOME

[7] For this is what the LORD says:
Sing with joy for Jacob;
shout for the foremost of the nations!
Proclaim, praise, and say,
"LORD, save your people,
the remnant of Israel!"
8 Watch! I am going to bring them
from the northern land.
I will gather them from remote regions
of the earth —
the blind and the lame will be with them,
along with those who are pregnant and those
about to give birth.
They will return here as a great assembly!
9 They will come weeping,
but I will bring them back with consolation.[C]
I will lead them to wadis filled with water,
by a smooth way where
they will not stumble,
for I am Israel's Father,
and Ephraim is my firstborn.
10 Nations, hear the word of the LORD,
and tell it among the far off coasts and
islands!
Say, "The one who scattered Israel
will gather him.
He will watch over him as a shepherd
guards his flock,
11 for the LORD has ransomed Jacob
and redeemed him from the power of one
stronger than he."
12 They will come and shout for joy
on the heights of Zion;
they will be radiant with joy
because of the LORD's goodness,
because of the grain, the new wine,
the fresh oil,
and because of the young of the flocks
and herds.
Their life will be like an irrigated garden,
and they will no longer grow weak
from hunger.

[A] **30:18** Or *certainly end the captivity* [B] **31:3** LXX; MT reads *me*
[C] **31:9** LXX; MT reads *supplications*

13 Then the young women will rejoice
with dancing,
while young and old men rejoice together.
I will turn their mourning into joy,
give them consolation,
and bring happiness out of grief.
14 I will refresh the priests
with an abundance,[A]
and my people will be satisfied
with my goodness.
This is the LORD's declaration.

LAMENT TURNED TO JOY

15 This is what the LORD says:
A voice was heard in Ramah,
a lament with bitter weeping —
Rachel weeping for her children,
refusing to be comforted for her children
because they are no more.

16 This is what the LORD says:
Keep your voice from weeping
and your eyes from tears,
for the reward for your work will come —
this is the LORD's declaration —
and your children will return
from the enemy's land.
17 There is hope for your future —
this is the LORD's declaration —
and your children will return
to their own territory.
18 I have surely heard Ephraim moaning,
"You disciplined me,
and I have been disciplined
like an untrained calf.
Take me back, so that I can return,
for you, LORD, are my God.
19 After my return, I felt regret;
After I was instructed, I struck my thigh
in grief.
I was ashamed and humiliated
because I bore the disgrace of my youth."
20 Isn't Ephraim a precious son to me,
a delightful child?
Whenever I speak against him,
I certainly still think about him.
Therefore, my inner being yearns for him;
I will truly have compassion on him.
This is the LORD's declaration.

REPENTANCE AND RESTORATION

21 Set up road markers for yourself;
establish signposts!
Keep the highway in mind,
the way you have traveled.
Return, Virgin Israel!
Return to these cities of yours.
22 How long will you turn here and there,
faithless daughter?
For the LORD creates something new
in the land[B] —
a female[C] will shelter[D] a man.

23 This is what the LORD of Armies, the God of Israel,
says: "When I restore their fortunes,[E] they will once
again speak this word in the land of Judah and in its
cities: 'May the LORD bless you, righteous settlement,
holy mountain.' 24 Judah and all its cities will live in it
together — also farmers and those who move[F] with
the flocks — 25 for I satisfy the thirsty person and
feed all those who are weak."
26 At this I awoke and looked around. My sleep had
been most pleasant to me.
27 "Look, the days are coming" — this is the LORD's
declaration — "when I will sow the house of Israel
and the house of Judah with the seed of people and
the seed of animals. 28 Just as I watched over them to
uproot and to tear them down, to demolish and to destroy, and to cause disaster, so will I watch over them
to build and to plant them" — this is the LORD's declaration. 29 "In those days, it will never again be said,
'The fathers have eaten sour grapes,
and the children's teeth are set
on edge.'
30 Rather, each will die for his own iniquity. Anyone
who eats sour grapes — his own teeth will be set
on edge.

THE NEW COVENANT

31 "Look, the days are coming" — this is the LORD's
declaration — "when I will make a new covenant
with the house of Israel and with the house of Judah. 32 This one will not be like the covenant I made
with their ancestors on the day I took them by the
hand to lead them out of the land of Egypt — my
covenant that they broke even though I am their master"[G] — the LORD's declaration. 33 "Instead, this is the
covenant I will make with the house of Israel after
those days" — the LORD's declaration. "I will put my
teaching within them and write it on their hearts. I
will be their God, and they will be my people. 34 No
longer will one teach his neighbor or his brother,
saying, 'Know the LORD,' for they will all know me,
from the least to the greatest of them" — this is the
LORD's declaration. "For I will forgive their iniquity
and never again remember their sin.

[A] **31:14** Lit *fatness* [B] **31:22** Or *new on earth* [C] **31:22** Or *woman* [D] **31:22** Or *female surrounds*, or *female courts*; Hb obscure [E] **31:23** Or *I end their captivity* [F] **31:24** Tg, Vg, Aq, Sym; MT reads *and they will move* [G] **31:32** Or *husband*

35 "This is what the LORD says:
The one who gives the sun for light by day,
the fixed order of moon and stars for light
by night,
who stirs up the sea and makes
its waves roar —
the LORD of Armies is his name:
36 If this fixed order departs from before me —
this is the LORD's declaration —
only then will Israel's descendants cease
to be a nation before me forever.

37 "This is what the LORD says:
Only if the heavens above can be measured
and the foundations
of the earth below explored,
will I reject all of Israel's descendants
because of all they have done —
this is the LORD's declaration.

38 "Look, the days are coming" — the LORD's declaration — "when the city[A] from the Tower of Hananel
to the Corner Gate will be rebuilt for the LORD. 39 A
measuring line will once again stretch out straight
to the hill of Gareb and then turn toward Goah. 40 The
whole valley — the corpses, the ashes, and all the
fields as far as the Kidron Valley to the corner of the
Horse Gate to the east — will be holy to the LORD. It
will never be uprooted or demolished again."

JEREMIAH'S LAND PURCHASE

32 This is the word that came to Jeremiah from
the LORD in the tenth year of King Zedekiah of
Judah, which was the eighteenth year of Nebuchadnezzar. 2 At that time, the army of the king of Babylon
was besieging Jerusalem, and the prophet Jeremiah
was imprisoned in the guard's courtyard in the palace of the king of Judah. 3 King Zedekiah of Judah had
imprisoned him, saying, "Why are you prophesying
as you do? You say, 'This is what the LORD says: Look, I
am about to hand this city over to Babylon's king, and
he will capture it. 4 King Zedekiah of Judah will not
escape from the Chaldeans; indeed, he will certainly
be handed over to Babylon's king. They will speak face
to face[B] and meet eye to eye. 5 He will take Zedekiah
to Babylon, where he will stay until I attend to him
— this is the LORD's declaration. For you will fight
the Chaldeans, but you will not succeed.' "
6 Jeremiah replied, "The word of the LORD came to
me: 7 Watch! Hanamel, the son of your uncle Shallum,
is coming to you to say, 'Buy my field in Anathoth
for yourself, for you own the right of redemption
to buy it.'
8 "Then, as the LORD had said, my cousin Hanamel
came to the guard's courtyard and urged me, 'Please
buy my field in Anathoth in the land of Benjamin, for
you own the right of inheritance and redemption. Buy
it for yourself.' Then I knew that this was the word of
the LORD. 9 So I bought the field in Anathoth from my
cousin Hanamel, and I weighed out the silver to him
— seventeen shekels[C] of silver. 10 I recorded it on a
scroll, sealed it, called in witnesses, and weighed out
the silver on the scales. 11 I took the purchase agreement — the sealed copy with its terms and conditions
and the open copy — 12 and gave the purchase agreement to Baruch son of Neriah, son of Mahseiah. I did
this in the sight of my cousin[D] Hanamel, the witnesses
who had signed the purchase agreement, and all the
Judeans sitting in the guard's courtyard.
13 "I charged Baruch in their sight, 14 'This is what
the LORD of Armies, the God of Israel, says: Take these
scrolls — this purchase agreement with the sealed
copy and this open copy — and put them in an earth-
en storage jar so they will last a long time. 15 For this
is what the LORD of Armies, the God of Israel, says:
Houses, fields, and vineyards will again be bought
in this land.'
16 "After I had given the purchase agreement to
Baruch, son of Neriah, I prayed to the LORD: 17 Oh,
Lord GOD! You yourself made the heavens and earth
by your great power and with your outstretched arm.
Nothing is too difficult for you! 18 You show faithful
love to thousands but lay the fathers' iniquity on their
sons' laps after them, great and mighty God whose
name is the LORD of Armies, 19 the one great in counsel
and powerful in action. Your eyes are on all the ways
of the children of men[E] in order to reward each person
according to his ways and as the result of his actions.
20 You performed signs and wonders in the land of
Egypt and still do today, both in Israel and among all
mankind. You made a name for yourself, as is the case
today. 21 You brought your people Israel out of Egypt
with signs and wonders, with a strong hand and an
outstretched arm, and with great terror. 22 You gave
them this land you swore to give to their ancestors, a
land flowing with milk and honey. 23 They entered and
possessed it, but they did not obey you or live according to your instructions. They failed to perform all you
commanded them to do, and so you have brought all
this disaster on them. 24 Look! Siege ramps have come
against the city to capture it, and the city, as a result
of the sword, famine, and plague, has been handed
over to the Chaldeans who are fighting against it.
What you have spoken has happened. Look, you can
see it! 25 Yet you, Lord GOD, have said to me, 'Purchase
the field and call in witnesses' — even though the city
has been handed over to the Chaldeans!' "

[A] **31:38** = Jerusalem [B] **32:4** Lit *His mouth will speak with his mouth*
[C] **32:9** About seven ounces [D] **32:12** Some Hb mss, LXX, Syr; other Hb mss read *uncle* [E] **32:19** Or *Adam*

26 The word of the LORD came to Jeremiah: 27 "Look, I am the LORD, the God over every creature. Is anything too difficult for me? 28 Therefore, this is what the LORD says: I am about to hand this city over to the Chaldeans, to Babylon's king Nebuchadnezzar, and he will capture it. 29 The Chaldeans who are fighting against this city will come and set this city on fire. They will burn it, including the houses where incense has been burned to Baal on their rooftops and where drink offerings have been poured out to other gods to anger me. 30 From their youth, the Israelites and Judeans have done nothing but what is evil in my sight! They have done nothing but anger me by the work of their hands" — this is the LORD's declaration — 31 "for this city has caused my wrath and fury from the day it was built until now. I will therefore remove it from my presence 32 because of all the evil the Israelites and Judeans have done to anger me — they, their kings, their officials, their priests, and their prophets, the men of Judah, and the residents of Jerusalem. 33 They have turned their backs to me and not their faces. Though I taught them time and time again,[A] they do not listen and receive discipline. 34 They have placed their abhorrent things in the house that bears my name and have defiled it. 35 They have built the high places of Baal in Ben Hinnom Valley to sacrifice their sons and daughters in the fire[B] to Molech — something I had not commanded them. I had never entertained the thought[C] that they do this detestable act causing Judah to sin!

36 "Now therefore, this is what the LORD, the God of Israel, says to this city about which you said, 'It has been handed over to Babylon's king through sword, famine, and plague': 37 I will certainly gather them from all the lands where I have banished them in my anger, fury, and intense wrath, and I will return them to this place and make them live in safety. 38 They will be my people, and I will be their God. 39 I will give them integrity of heart and action[D] so that they will fear me always, for their good and for the good of their descendants after them.

40 "I will make a permanent covenant with them: I will never turn away from doing good to them, and I will put fear of me in their hearts so they will never again turn away from me. 41 I will take delight in them to do what is good for them, and with all my heart and mind I will faithfully plant them in this land.

42 "For this is what the LORD says: Just as I have brought all this terrible disaster on these people, so am I about to bring on them all the good I am promising them. 43 Fields will be bought in this land about which you are saying, 'It's a desolation without people or animals; it has been handed over to the Chaldeans!' 44 Fields will be purchased, the transaction written on a scroll and sealed, and witnesses will be called on in the land of Benjamin, in the areas surrounding Jerusalem, and in Judah's cities — the cities of the hill country, the cities of the Judean foothills, and the cities of the Negev — because I will restore their fortunes."[E]

This is the LORD's declaration.

ISRAEL'S RESTORATION

33 While he was still confined in the guard's courtyard, the word of the LORD came to Jeremiah a second time: 2 "The LORD who made the earth,[F] the LORD who forms it to establish it, the LORD is his name, says this: 3 Call to me and I will answer you and tell you great and incomprehensible things you do not know. 4 For this is what the LORD, the God of Israel, says concerning the houses of this city and the palaces of Judah's kings, the ones torn down for defense against the assault ramps and the sword: 5 The people coming to fight the Chaldeans will fill the houses with the corpses of their own men that I strike down in my wrath and fury. I have hidden my face from this city because of all their evil. 6 Yet I will certainly bring health and healing to it and will indeed heal them. I will let them experience the abundance[G] of true peace. 7 I will restore the fortunes[H] of Judah and of Israel and will rebuild them as in former times. 8 I will purify them from all the iniquity they have committed against me, and I will forgive all the iniquities they have committed against me, rebelling against me. 9 This city will bear on my behalf a name of joy, praise, and glory before all the nations of the earth, who will hear of all the prosperity I will give them. They will tremble with awe because of all the good and all the peace I will bring about for them.

10 "This is what the LORD says: In this place, which you say is a ruin, without people or animals — that is, in Judah's cities and Jerusalem's streets that are a desolation without people, without inhabitants, and without animals — there will be heard again 11 a sound of joy and gladness, the voice of the groom and the bride, and the voice of those saying,

Give thanks to the LORD of Armies,
for the LORD is good;
his faithful love endures forever

as they bring thanksgiving sacrifices to the temple of the LORD. For I will restore the fortunes of the land as in former times, says the LORD.

[A] **32:33** Lit *them, rising up early and teaching* [B] **32:35** Lit *to make their sons and daughters pass through the fire* [C] **32:35** Lit *them, and it did not arise on my heart* [D] **32:39** Lit *give them one heart and one way* [E] **32:44** Or *will end their captivity* [F] **33:2** LXX; MT reads *made it* [G] **33:6** Or *fragrance*; Hb obscure [H] **33:7** Or *will end the captivity*, also in v. 11

Deeds and Seals in Jeremiah

by Conn Davis

Jeremiah proclaimed and passionately experienced God's message of judgment during the last years of Judah, 627–586 BC. Of all the Old Testament prophets, he uniquely shared his ministry with his secretary-scribe, Baruch. Jeremiah dictated God's message directly to Baruch who wrote it down with ink and scroll (Jr 36:4,18,32). When time came to purchase a piece of family property, Baruch was there to draw up the deed, making sure it was signed, sealed, and secured. What did this sealed contract look like?

BACKGROUND INFORMATION

Jeremiah 32 is "the clearest description that we have of the way in which transfers of property were handled in pre-Exilic Judah."[1] One of Jeremiah's cousins, Hanamel, offered for sale family land in Anathoth, only three miles north of Jerusalem. At the time, Jeremiah was a prisoner in King Zedekiah's courtyard. The transaction occurred during the perilous time of the Babylonian siege and invasion of Jerusalem in 588–586 BC.

Jeremiah and Hanamel were from a family of priests who resided in Anathoth, which was one of the thirteen cities or areas that Aaron's descendants received in the promised land (Jos 21:13–19). The basic social units within Israel were the tribe, clan, and family. Under Levitical law, Jeremiah had a responsibility to redeem the ancestral land for his family and clan. God said in Leviticus 25:23–25, "The land is not to be permanently sold because it is mine, and you are only aliens and temporary residents on my land. You are to allow the redemption of any land you occupy. If your brother becomes destitute and sells part of his property, his nearest relative may come and redeem what his brother has sold" (see Jr 32:7–8).

In Egypt, the land belonged to the temple or religious establishment and to the pharaoh on behalf of the community. In Mesopotamia, the king, along with families and individuals, owned property.[2] God's ownership of the land of Canaan or the promised land, however, was a theological principle for ancient Israel. God gave instructions to Aaron that his tribe, the Levites, were to have the responsibility to care for and to maintain the tabernacle with its services, sacrifices, and contents. Thus God provided them with their own "holy land" inheritance of one-tenth of the land (Nm 18:20–24).

With the approaching threat of Babylonian domination, Jeremiah purchased the field from his cousin, Hanamel (Jr 32:9). Then he "recorded it on a scroll, sealed it, called in witnesses, and weighed out the silver on the scales" (v. 10). Finally, in front of witnesses in the prison

Iron Age Hebrew seals from the Israel Museum in Jerusalem.

Fifteenth-century-BC deed from Kirkuk granting rights to a field for three years in return for three measures of barley and a mule.

courtyard, he "took the purchase agreement—the sealed copy with its terms and conditions and the open copy—and gave the purchase agreement to Baruch son of Neriah, son of Mahseiah" (vv. 11–12). But what did the sealing of the purchase agreement involve?

SEALS

As early as the fifth millennium BC, peoples of the ancient Near East used seals to identify ownership of property and to secure documents. Seals were made of metal, shells, bone, stone, or baked clay and were either stamps or cylinders that were rolled.[3] Seals were also used for decoration on food items and pottery.

From 3000 BC on, Egypt and Mesopotamia had highly developed literary cultures that used cylinder seals and stamp seals to secure their legal and social transactions. The seals usually were decorative and had the name or title of officials such as the king or his servants engaged in administrative duties.

By 900 BC, ancient Israel used stamp seals to represent authority and to make legal transactions. One of the earliest examples is when Queen Jezebel used the seal of King Ahab (874–853 BC) to validate her forged letters when she attempted a land-grab of Naboth's vineyard (1Kg 21:7–10).

Archaeologists have discovered hundreds of Israelite stamp seals; most were oval or scarab in shape with a raised surface.[4] One of the oldest stamp seals from Israel's excavations is a jasper seal with a roaring lion found at Megiddo, inscribed "[belonging] to Shema, servant of Jeroboam." It dates from the eighth century BC. Archaeologists found Israelite seals in their original rings; other seals formed part of a necklace. When Pharaoh promoted Joseph to the second-most powerful position in Egypt, he gave Joseph his personal ring and a golden necklace to symbolize his authority. Likely the ring and even the necklace may have contained a seal, the design of which would have been unique to Joseph.

ANCIENT DEEDS

The term *purchase agreement* in Jeremiah 32:11–12 is literally "scroll of purchase." Typically, the Hebrew word *sepher,* "scroll," referred to anything that someone would write, whether a book (Dt 29:21); a letter (Jr 29:1); or a document (Gn 5:1; Est 8:5), including legal documents, such as a bill or "divorce certificate" (Dt 24:1) or a purchase contract, as in Jeremiah 32.

Although Jeremiah 32 speaks of a singular "scroll of purchase," verses 11 and 14 make it clear that besides the sealed "original," there was also an open, unsealed copy. When Jeremiah purchased the field at Anathoth, Baruch wrote and recorded the details of the sale on a single sheet of papyrus. Using what is called a "double deed" or "tied deed," Baruch recorded the transaction twice—one copy of the deed on the upper part of the sheet and one copy with the exact same wording on the lower. The upper copy was rolled up and sealed (usually by sewing) to preserve the original from fraudulent alteration. The lower copy remained open for public inspection.[5]

Remarkably, noted archaeologist Yigael Yadin found intact examples of tied deeds in his 1960–61 excavations in a canyon near the Dead Sea. Yadin and his team excavated caves that contained artifacts (including letters) belonging to Bar Kokhba and some of his followers. Bar Kokhba was the leader of the AD 132–135 Jewish revolt against Rome. Among the letters were tied deeds. The deeds were in two halves, the upper part sealed and the lower open. The writing style on the sealed part of the Bar Kokhba documents was smaller and more decorative than the larger, more block-style writing in the lower part. The deeds had signatures affixed beside the tying strings. This sheds light on why Jeremiah had the deed sealed and then witnessed (v. 10) rather than witnessed and then sealed. Says Yadin, "The use of 'tied deeds' is a very old and known practice of the ancient world; . . . This system was used, of course, for the more important documents."[6] Though Yadin's find dated centuries after Jeremiah's time, this particular method of sealing deeds evidently had not changed for generations.

Archaeology thus sheds light on the Jeremiah account and on our understanding of some types of seals used in preexilic Judah. We are likely familiar with ancient seals and how they secured letters, contracts, and important documents. Not all seals, though, were stamped or rolled through a soft clay or wax. Some, like the deed for the Anathoth field, were evidently sewn and then signed to secure them for a later date. The archaeological find from Bar Kokhba helps us better understand the Jeremiah text and helps us better visualize the use of seals with deeds and other ancient documents. ✜

---

[1] John Bright, *Jeremiah, vol. 21 of Anchor Bible (AB)* (New York: Doubleday, 1964), 239. [2] Roland de Vaux, *Ancient Israel* (New York: McGraw-Hill, 1961), 164. [3] Bonnie S. Magness-Gardener, "Seals, Mesopotamian" in *ABD*, 5:1062–63; O. Tufnell, "Seals and Scarabs," *IDB*, 4:254–59. [4] N. Avigad, "The Contribution of Hebrew Seals to an Understanding of Israelite Religion and Society," in *Ancient Israelite Religion*, ed. Patrick D. Miller Jr. et al. (Philadelphia: Fortress, 1987), 195–208. Avigad counted 328 published Hebrew seals, mostly from the eighth to sixth centuries BC. Many more have been found and published since. [5] "Examples of such documents in two copies are known from Elephantine in Egypt." Bright, *Jeremiah*, 238. [6] Yigael Yadin, *Bar-Kokhba* (London: Weidenfeld & Nicolson, 1978), 229.

12 "This is what the LORD of Armies says: In this desolate place — without people or animals — and in all its cities there will once more be a grazing land where shepherds may rest flocks. 13 The flocks will again pass under the hands of the one who counts them in the cities of the hill country, the cities of the Judean foothills, the cities of the Negev, the land of Benjamin — the areas around Jerusalem and in Judah's cities, says the LORD.

GOD'S COVENANT WITH DAVID

14 "Look, the days are coming" —
this is the LORD's declaration —
"when I will fulfill the good promise
that I have spoken
concerning the house of Israel
and the house of Judah.
15 In those days and at that time
I will cause a Righteous Branch
to sprout up for David,
and he will administer justice
and righteousness in the land.
16 In those days Judah will be saved,
and Jerusalem will dwell securely,
and this is what she will be named:
The LORD Is Our Righteousness.[A]

17 "For this is what the LORD says: David will never fail to have a man sitting on the throne of the house of Israel. 18 The Levitical priests will never fail to have a man always before me to offer burnt offerings, to burn grain offerings, and to make sacrifices."

19 The word of the LORD came to Jeremiah: 20 "This is what the LORD says: If you can break my covenant with the day and my covenant with the night so that day and night cease to come at their regular time, 21 then also my covenant with my servant David may be broken. If that could happen, then he would not have a son reigning on his throne and the Levitical priests would not be my ministers. 22 Even as the stars of heaven cannot be counted, and the sand of the sea cannot be measured, so too I will make innumerable the descendants of my servant David and the Levites who minister to me."

23 The word of the LORD came to Jeremiah: 24 "Have you not noticed what these people have said? They say, 'The LORD has rejected the two families he had chosen.' My people are treated with contempt and no longer regarded as a nation among them. 25 This is what the LORD says: If I do not keep my covenant with the day and with the night, and if I fail to establish the fixed order of heaven and earth, 26 then I might also reject the descendants of Jacob and of my servant David. That is, I would not take rulers from his descendants to rule over the descendants of Abraham, Isaac, and Jacob. But in fact, I will restore their fortunes[B] and have compassion on them."

JEREMIAH'S WORD TO KING ZEDEKIAH

34 This is the word that came to Jeremiah from the LORD when King Nebuchadnezzar of Babylon, his whole army, all the kingdoms of the lands under his control, and all other peoples were fighting against Jerusalem and all its surrounding cities: 2 "This is what the LORD, the God of Israel, says: Go, speak to King Zedekiah of Judah, and tell him, 'This is what the LORD says: I am about to hand this city over to the king of Babylon, and he will burn it. 3 As for you, you will not escape from him but are certain to be captured and handed over to him. You will meet the king of Babylon eye to eye and speak face to face;[C] you will go to Babylon.

4 " 'Yet hear the LORD's word, King Zedekiah of Judah. This is what the LORD says concerning you: You will not die by the sword; 5 you will die peacefully. There will be a burning ceremony for you just like the burning ceremonies for your ancestors, the kings of old who came before you. "Oh, master!" will be the lament for you, for I have spoken this word. This is the LORD's declaration.' "

6 So the prophet Jeremiah related all these words to King Zedekiah of Judah in Jerusalem 7 while the king of Babylon's army was attacking Jerusalem and all of Judah's remaining cities — that is, Lachish and Azekah, for they were the only ones left of Judah's fortified cities.

THE PEOPLE AND THEIR SLAVES

8 This is the word that came to Jeremiah from the LORD after King Zedekiah made a covenant with all the people who were in Jerusalem to proclaim freedom to them. 9 As a result, each was to let his male and female Hebrew slaves go free, and no one was to enslave his fellow Judean. 10 All the officials and people who entered into covenant to let their male and female slaves go free — in order not to enslave them any longer — obeyed and let them go free. 11 Afterward, however, they changed their minds and took back their male and female slaves they had let go free and forced them to become slaves again.

12 Then the word of the LORD came to Jeremiah from the LORD: 13 "This is what the LORD, the God of Israel, says: I made a covenant with your ancestors when I brought them out of the land of Egypt, out of the place of slavery, saying, 14 'At the end of seven years, each of you must let his fellow Hebrew who sold himself[D] to you go. He may serve you six years,

[A] **33:16** = *Yahweh-zidkenu* [B] **33:26** Or *I will end their captivity*
[C] **34:3** Lit *and his mouth will speak to your mouth* [D] **34:14** Or *who was sold*

but then you must let him go free from your service.'
But your ancestors did not obey me or pay any attention. 15 Today you repented and did what pleased me,
each of you proclaiming freedom for his neighbor.
You made a covenant before me at the house that
bears my name. 16 But you have changed your minds
and profaned my name. Each has taken back his male
and female slaves who had been set free to go wherever they wanted, and you have again forced them
to be your slaves.
17 "Therefore, this is what the LORD says: You have
not obeyed me by proclaiming freedom, each for his
fellow Hebrew and for his neighbor. I hereby proclaim freedom for you — this is the LORD's declaration — to the sword, to plague, and to famine! I will
make you a horror to all the earth's kingdoms. 18 As
for those who disobeyed my covenant, not keeping
the terms of the covenant they made before me, I
will treat them like the calf they cut in two in order
to pass between its pieces. 19 The officials of Judah
and Jerusalem, the court officials, the priests, and
all the people of the land who passed between the
pieces of the calf — 20 all these I will hand over to
their enemies, to those who intend to take their life.
Their corpses will become food for the birds of the
sky and for the wild animals of the land. 21 I will hand
King Zedekiah of Judah and his officials over to their
enemies, to those who intend to take their lives, to
the king of Babylon's army that is withdrawing. 22 I
am about to give the command — this is the LORD's
declaration — and I will bring them back to this city.
They will fight against it, capture it, and burn it. I will
make Judah's cities a desolation, without inhabitant."

THE RECHABITES' EXAMPLE

35 This is the word that came to Jeremiah from
the LORD in the days of Jehoiakim son of Josiah, king of Judah: 2 "Go to the house of the Rechabites,
speak to them, and bring them to one of the chambers
of the temple of the LORD to offer them a drink of wine."
3 So I took Jaazaniah son of Jeremiah, son of Habaz-
ziniah, and his brothers and all his sons — the entire
house of the Rechabites — 4 and I brought them into
the temple of the LORD to a chamber occupied by the
sons of Hanan son of Igdaliah, a man of God, who
had a chamber near the officials' chamber, which
was above the chamber of Maaseiah son of Shallum
the doorkeeper. 5 I set jars filled with wine and some
cups before the sons of the house of the Rechabites
and said to them, "Drink wine!"
6 But they replied, "We do not drink wine, for Jonadab, son of our ancestor Rechab, commanded, 'You
and your descendants must never drink wine. 7 You
must not build a house or sow seed or plant a vineyard. Those things are not for you. Rather, you must
live in tents your whole life, so you may live a long
time on the soil where you stay as a resident alien.'
8 We have obeyed Jonadab, son of our ancestor Rechab, in all he commanded us. So we haven't drunk
wine our whole life — we, our wives, our sons, and
our daughters. 9 We also have not built houses to live
in and do not have vineyard, field, or seed. 10 But we
have lived in tents and have obeyed and done everything our ancestor Jonadab commanded us. 11 However, when King Nebuchadnezzar of Babylon marched
into the land, we said, 'Come, let's go into Jerusalem
to get away from the Chaldean and Aramean armies.'
So we have been living in Jerusalem."
12 Then the word of the LORD came to Jeremiah:
13 "This is what the LORD of Armies, the God of Israel,
says: Go, say to the men of Judah and the residents of
Jerusalem, 'Will you not accept discipline by listening
to my words? — this is the LORD's declaration. 14 The
words of Jonadab, son of Rechab, have been carried
out. He commanded his descendants not to drink
wine, and they have not drunk to this day because
they have obeyed their ancestor's command. But I
have spoken to you time and time again,[A] and you
have not obeyed me! 15 Time and time again[B] I have
sent you all my servants the prophets, proclaiming,
"Turn, each one from his evil way, and correct your
actions. Stop following other gods to serve them. Live
in the land that I gave you and your ancestors." But
you did not pay attention or obey me. 16 Yes, the sons
of Jonadab son of Rechab carried out their ancestor's
command he gave them, but these people have not
obeyed me. 17 Therefore, this is what the LORD, the God
of Armies, the God of Israel, says: I will certainly bring
on Judah and on all the residents of Jerusalem all the
disaster I have pronounced against them because I
have spoken to them, but they have not obeyed, and
I have called to them, but they did not answer.'"
18 But to the house of the Rechabites Jeremiah said,
"This is what the LORD of Armies, the God of Israel,
says: 'Because you have obeyed the command of your
ancestor Jonadab and have kept all his commands
and have done everything he commanded you, 19 this
is what the LORD of Armies, the God of Israel, says:
Jonadab son of Rechab will never fail to have a man
to stand before me always.'"

JEREMIAH DICTATES A SCROLL

36 In the fourth year of Jehoiakim son of Josiah,
king of Judah, this word came to Jeremiah
from the LORD: 2 "Take a scroll, and write on it all the
words I have spoken to you concerning Israel, Judah,
and all the nations from the time I first spoke to you

[A] **35:14** Lit *you, rising up early and speaking* [B] **35:15** Lit *Rising up early and sending*

DIGGING DEEPER *The Baruch Seal*

Kings and other authorities often sealed their official letters by pressing their seal into a moist lump of clay and affixing it to a document, thus sealing it and declaring it official (1Kg 21:6–10). Archaeologists call the clay impression a bulla (pl. bullae). Hundreds of bullae have been identified and catalogued, and a number of them are linked to people mentioned in the Bible. Many of the bullae were discovered among the ruins at the city of David in Jerusalem (2Sm 5:6–7). The Baruch seal is one of two bullae containing a Hebrew script that reads "Belonging to Barekyahu, son of Neriyahu, the scribe." Bulla specialist Nahman Avigad deciphered this late seventh-century BC inscription and determined that "Barekyahu, son of Neriyahu" is Jeremiah's scribe, Baruch son of Neriah (Jr 36:1–32). Several other bullae have links to persons mentioned in the book of Jeremiah, including Jehucal (Jr 37:3; 38:1), Gedaliah (38:1), and "Ga'alyahu son of Immer" which is inscribed incompletely on a bulla Gabriel Barkay discovered while sifting rubble from the Temple Mount, thus confirming the existence of the priestly family that opposed Jeremiah (20:1–6) during the reign of King Zedekiah (21:1).

during Josiah's reign until today. 3 Perhaps when the
house of Judah hears about all the disaster I am planning to bring on them, each one of them will turn
from his evil way. Then I will forgive their iniquity
and their sin."
4 So Jeremiah summoned Baruch son of Neriah. At
Jeremiah's dictation,[A] Baruch wrote on a scroll all the
words the LORD had spoken to Jeremiah. 5 Then Jeremiah commanded Baruch, "I am restricted; I cannot
enter the temple of the LORD, 6 so you must go and
read from the scroll — which you wrote at my dictation[B] — the words of the LORD in the hearing of the
people at the temple of the LORD on a day of fasting.
Read his words in the hearing of all the Judeans who
are coming from their cities. 7 Perhaps their petition
will come before the LORD, and each one will turn
from his evil way, for the anger and fury that the LORD
has pronounced against this people are intense." 8 So
Baruch son of Neriah did everything the prophet Jeremiah had commanded him. At the LORD's temple he
read the LORD's words from the scroll.

BARUCH READS THE SCROLL

9 In the fifth year of Jehoiakim son of Josiah, king of
Judah, in the ninth month, all the people of Jerusalem and all those coming in from Judah's cities into
Jerusalem proclaimed a fast before the LORD. 10 Then
at the LORD's temple, in the chamber of Gemariah
son of Shaphan the scribe, in the upper courtyard at
the opening of the New Gate of the LORD's temple, in
the hearing of all the people, Baruch read Jeremiah's
words from the scroll.
11 When Micaiah son of Gemariah, son of Shaphan,
heard all the words of the LORD from the scroll, 12 he
went down to the scribe's chamber in the king's palace. All the officials were sitting there — Elishama
the scribe, Delaiah son of Shemaiah, Elnathan son
of Achbor, Gemariah son of Shaphan, Zedekiah son
of Hananiah, and all the other officials. 13 Micaiah
reported to them all the words he had heard when
Baruch read from the scroll in the hearing of the
people. 14 Then all the officials sent word to Baruch
through Jehudi son of Nethaniah, son of Shelemiah,
son of Cushi, saying, "Bring the scroll that you read in
the hearing of the people, and come." So Baruch son
of Neriah took the scroll and went to them. 15 They
said to him, "Sit down and read it in our hearing." So
Baruch read it in their hearing.
16 When they had heard all the words, they turned
to each other in fear and said to Baruch, "We must
surely tell the king all these things." 17 Then they asked
Baruch, "Tell us, how did you write all these words?
At his dictation?"[C]
18 Baruch said to them, "At his dictation. He recited all these words to me while I was writing on the
scroll in ink."

JEHOIAKIM BURNS THE SCROLL

19 The officials said to Baruch, "You and Jeremiah must
hide and tell no one where you are." 20 Then, after
depositing the scroll in the chamber of Elishama the
scribe, the officials came to the king at the courtyard
and reported everything in the hearing of the king.
21 The king sent Jehudi to get the scroll, and he took it
from the chamber of Elishama the scribe. Jehudi then
read it in the hearing of the king and all the officials
who were standing by the king. 22 Since it was the
ninth month, the king was sitting in his winter quarters with a fire burning in front of him. 23 As soon as
Jehudi would read three or four columns, Jehoiakim
would cut the scroll[D] with a scribe's knife and throw
the columns into the fire in the hearth until the entire
scroll was consumed by the fire in the hearth. 24 As
they heard all these words, the king and all his servants did not become terrified or tear their clothes.
25 Even though Elnathan, Delaiah, and Gemariah had
urged the king not to burn the scroll, he did not listen

[A] **36:4** Lit *From Jeremiah's mouth* [B] **36:6** Lit *wrote from my mouth* [C] **36:17** Lit *From his mouth*, also in v. 18 [D] **36:23** Lit *columns, he would tear it*

to them. 26 Then the king commanded Jerahmeel the king's son, Seraiah son of Azriel, and Shelemiah son of Abdeel to seize the scribe Baruch and the prophet Jeremiah, but the LORD hid them.

JEREMIAH DICTATES ANOTHER SCROLL

27 After the king had burned the scroll and the words Baruch had written at Jeremiah's dictation,[A] the word of the LORD came to Jeremiah: 28 "Take another scroll, and once again write on it the original words that were on the original scroll that King Jehoiakim of Judah burned. 29 You are to proclaim concerning King Jehoiakim of Judah, 'This is what the LORD says: You have burned the scroll, asking, "Why have you written on it that the king of Babylon will certainly come and destroy this land and cause it to be without people or animals?" 30 Therefore, this is what the LORD says concerning King Jehoiakim of Judah: He will have no one to sit on David's throne, and his corpse will be thrown out to be exposed to the heat of day and the frost of night. 31 I will punish him, his descendants, and his officers for their iniquity. I will bring on them, on the residents of Jerusalem, and on the people of Judah all the disaster, which I warned them about but they did not listen.'"

32 Then Jeremiah took another scroll and gave it to Baruch son of Neriah, the scribe, and he wrote on it at Jeremiah's dictation[B] all the words of the scroll that Jehoiakim, Judah's king, had burned in the fire. And many other words like them were added.

JERUSALEM'S LAST DAYS

37 Zedekiah son of Josiah reigned as king in the land of Judah in place of Coniah[C] son of Jehoiakim, for King Nebuchadnezzar of Babylon made him king. 2 He and his officers and the people of the land did not obey the words of the LORD that he spoke through the prophet Jeremiah.

3 Nevertheless, King Zedekiah sent Jehucal son of Shelemiah and Zephaniah son of Maaseiah, the priest, to the prophet Jeremiah, requesting, "Please pray to the LORD our God on our behalf!" 4 Jeremiah was going about his daily tasks[D] among the people, for he had not yet been put into the prison. 5 Pharaoh's army had left Egypt, and when the Chaldeans, who were besieging Jerusalem, heard the report, they withdrew from Jerusalem.

6 The word of the LORD came to the prophet Jeremiah: 7 "This is what the LORD, the God of Israel, says: This is what you will say to Judah's king, who is sending you to inquire of me: 'Watch: Pharaoh's army, which has come out to help you, is going to return to its own land of Egypt. 8 The Chaldeans will then return and fight against this city. They will capture it and burn it. 9 This is what the LORD says: Don't deceive yourselves by saying, "The Chaldeans will leave us for good," for they will not leave. 10 Indeed, if you were to strike down the entire Chaldean army that is fighting with you, and there remained among them only the badly wounded[E] men, each in his tent, they would get up and burn this city.'"

JEREMIAH'S IMPRISONMENT

11 When the Chaldean army withdrew from Jerusalem because of Pharaoh's army, 12 Jeremiah started to leave Jerusalem to go to the land of Benjamin to claim his portion there among the people. 13 But when he was at the Benjamin Gate, an officer of the guard was there, whose name was Irijah son of Shelemiah, son of Hananiah, and he apprehended the prophet Jeremiah, saying, "You are defecting to the Chaldeans."

14 "That's a lie," Jeremiah replied. "I am not defecting to the Chaldeans!" Irijah would not listen to him but apprehended Jeremiah and took him to the officials. 15 The officials were angry at Jeremiah and beat him and placed him in jail in the house of Jonathan the scribe, for it had been made into a prison. 16 So Jeremiah went into a cell in the dungeon and stayed there many days.

JEREMIAH SUMMONED BY ZEDEKIAH

17 King Zedekiah later sent for him and received him, and in his house privately asked him, "Is there a word from the LORD?"

"There is," Jeremiah responded. He continued, "You will be handed over to the king of Babylon." 18 Then Jeremiah said to King Zedekiah, "How have I sinned against you or your servants or these people that you have put me in prison? 19 Where are your prophets who prophesied to you, claiming, 'The king of Babylon will not come against you and this land'? 20 So now please listen, my lord the king. May my petition come before you. Don't send me back to the house of Jonathan the scribe, or I will die there."

21 So King Zedekiah gave orders, and Jeremiah was placed in the guard's courtyard. He was given a loaf of bread each day from the bakers' street until all the bread was gone from the city. So Jeremiah remained in the guard's courtyard.

JEREMIAH THROWN INTO A CISTERN

38 Now Shephatiah son of Mattan, Gedaliah son of Pashhur, Jucal[F] son of Shelemiah, and Pashhur son of Malchijah heard the words Jeremiah was speaking to all the people: 2 "This is what the LORD says: 'Whoever stays in this city will die by the sword, famine, and plague, but whoever surrenders to the

[A] **36:27** Lit *written from Jeremiah's mouth* [B] **36:32** Lit *it from Jeremiah's mouth* [C] **37:1** = Jehoiachin [D] **37:4** Lit *was coming in and going out* [E] **37:10** Lit *the pierced* [F] **38:1** = Jehucal in Jr 37:3

DIGGING DEEPER *Sarsechim Tablet*

In 2007, the British Museum brought to light a forgotten piece of history from its warehouse when Assyriologist Michael Jursa noticed the Babylonian name Sarsechim (lit *Nabu-sharrussu-ukin*) written on a tiny cuneiform tablet dating to the sixth century BC. The artifact was soon recognized as mentioning the minor biblical figure identified as Babylonian King Nebuchadnezzar's chief military officer (*rab-saris*) and eunuch in Jeremiah 39:3. The tablet describes a generous gold donation given by Sarsechim to the temple of Esagila in the tenth year of Nebuchadnezzar's reign (ca 595 BC). Josephus also mentions Sarsechim as being one of Nebuchadnezzar's officers in 586 BC (*Jewish Antiquities* 8). If these minor figures of the Bible have been confirmed, it seems reasonable to trust in the existence of major figures mentioned in Scripture.

Chaldeans will live. He will retain his life like the
spoils of war and will live.' 3 This is what the LORD
says: 'This city will most certainly be handed over to
the king of Babylon's army, and he will capture it.' "
4 The officials then said to the king, "This man ought
to die, because he is weakening the morale[A] of the
warriors who remain in this city and of all the people by speaking to them in this way. This man is not
pursuing the welfare of this people, but their harm."
5 King Zedekiah said, "Here he is; he's in your hands
since the king can't do anything against you." 6 So they
took Jeremiah and dropped him into the cistern of
Malchiah the king's son, which was in the guard's
courtyard, lowering Jeremiah with ropes. There was
no water in the cistern, only mud, and Jeremiah sank
in the mud.
7 But Ebed-melech, a Cushite court official in the
king's palace, heard Jeremiah had been put into the
cistern. While the king was sitting at the Benjamin
Gate, 8 Ebed-melech went from the king's palace and
spoke to the king: 9 "My lord the king, these men have
been evil in all they have done to the prophet Jeremiah. They have dropped him into the cistern where
he will die from hunger, because there is no more
bread in the city."
10 So the king commanded Ebed-melech, the Cushite, "Take from here thirty men under your authority[B]
and pull the prophet Jeremiah up from the cistern
before he dies."
11 So Ebed-melech took the men under his authority[C] and went to the king's palace to a place below the
storehouse.[D] From there he took old rags and worn-
out clothes and lowered them by ropes to Jeremiah in
the cistern. 12 Ebed-melech the Cushite called down to
Jeremiah, "Place these old rags and clothes between
your armpits and the ropes." Jeremiah did this. 13 They
pulled him up with the ropes and lifted him out of the
cistern, but he remained in the guard's courtyard.

ZEDEKIAH'S FINAL MEETING WITH JEREMIAH

14 King Zedekiah sent for the prophet Jeremiah and
received him at the third entrance of the LORD's temple. The king said to Jeremiah, "I am going to ask you
something; don't hide anything from me."
15 Jeremiah replied to Zedekiah, "If I tell you, you
will kill me, won't you? Besides, if I give you advice,
you won't listen to me anyway."
16 King Zedekiah swore to Jeremiah in private, "As
the LORD lives, who has given us this life, I will not
kill you or hand you over to these men who intend
to take your life."
17 Jeremiah therefore said to Zedekiah, "This is
what the LORD, the God of Armies, the God of Israel,
says: 'If indeed you surrender to the officials of the
king of Babylon, then you will live, this city will not
be burned, and you and your household will survive.
18 But if you do not surrender to the officials of the
king of Babylon, then this city will be handed over
to the Chaldeans. They will burn it, and you yourself
will not escape from them.' "
19 But King Zedekiah said to Jeremiah, "I am worried
about the Judeans who have defected to the Chaldeans. They may hand me over to the Judeans to abuse
me."
20 "They will not hand you over," Jeremiah replied.
"Obey the LORD in what I am telling you, so it may go
well for you and you can live. 21 But if you refuse to
surrender, this is the verdict[E] that the LORD has shown
me: 22 'All the women[F] who remain in the palace of
Judah's king will be brought out to the officials of
the king of Babylon and will say to you,[G]

> "Your trusted friends[H] misled[I] you
> and overcame you.
> Your feet sank into the mire,
> and they deserted you."

23 All your wives and children will be brought out
to the Chaldeans. You yourself will not escape from
them, for you will be seized by the king of Babylon
and this city will burn.' "
24 Then Zedekiah warned Jeremiah, "Don't let anyone know about this conversation[J] or you will die.
25 The officials may hear that I have spoken with you
and come and demand of you, 'Tell us what you said

[A] **38:4** Lit *hands* [B] **38:10** Lit *men in your hand* [C] **38:11** Lit *men in his hand* [D] **38:11** Or *treasury* [E] **38:21** Or *promise*; lit *word* [F] **38:22** Or *wives* [G] **38:22** *to you* supplied for clarity [H] **38:22** Lit *"The men of your peace* [I] **38:22** Or *incited* [J] **38:24** Lit *about these words*

to the king; don't hide anything from us and we won't kill you. Also, what did the king say to you?' 26 If they do, tell them, 'I was bringing before the king my petition that he not return me to the house of Jonathan to die there.'" 27 All the officials did come to Jeremiah, and they questioned him. He reported the exact words to them the king had commanded, and they quit speaking with him because the conversation[A] had not been overheard. 28 Jeremiah remained in the guard's courtyard until the day Jerusalem was captured, and he was there when it happened.[B]

THE FALL OF JERUSALEM TO BABYLON

39 In the ninth year of King Zedekiah of Judah, in the tenth month, King Nebuchadnezzar of Babylon advanced against Jerusalem with his entire army and laid siege to it. 2 In the fourth month of Zedekiah's eleventh year, on the ninth day of the month, the city was broken into. 3 All the officials of the king of Babylon entered and sat at the Middle Gate: Nergal-sharezer, Samgar, Nebusarsechim[C] the chief of staff, Nergal-sharezer the chief soothsayer, and all the rest of the officials of Babylon's king.

4 When King Zedekiah of Judah and all the fighting men saw them, they fled. They left the city at night by way of the king's garden through the city gate between the two walls. They left along the route to the Arabah. 5 However, the Chaldean army pursued them and overtook Zedekiah in the plains of Jericho. They arrested him and brought him up to Nebuchadnezzar, Babylon's king, at Riblah in the land of Hamath. The king passed sentence on him there.

6 At Riblah the king of Babylon slaughtered Zedekiah's sons before his eyes, and he also slaughtered all Judah's nobles. 7 Then he blinded Zedekiah and put him in bronze chains to take him to Babylon. 8 The Chaldeans next burned down the king's palace and the people's houses and tore down the walls of Jerusalem. 9 Nebuzaradan, the captain of the guards, deported the rest of the people to Babylon — those who had remained in the city and those deserters who had defected to him along with the rest of the people who remained. 10 However, Nebuzaradan, the captain of the guards, left in the land of Judah some of the poor people who owned nothing, and he gave them vineyards and fields at that time.

JEREMIAH FREED BY NEBUCHADNEZZAR

11 Speaking through Nebuzaradan, captain of the guards, King Nebuchadnezzar of Babylon gave orders concerning Jeremiah: 12 "Take him and look after him. Don't do him any harm, but do for him whatever he says." 13 Nebuzaradan, captain of the guards, Nebushazban the chief of staff, Nergal-sharezer the chief soothsayer, and all the captains of Babylon's king 14 had Jeremiah brought from the guard's courtyard and turned him over to Gedaliah son of Ahikam, son of Shaphan, to take him home. So he settled among his own people.

15 Now the word of the LORD had come to Jeremiah when he was confined in the guard's courtyard: 16 "Go tell Ebed-melech the Cushite, 'This is what the LORD of Armies, the God of Israel, says: I am about to fulfill my words for disaster and not for good against this city. They will take place before your eyes on that day. 17 But I will rescue you on that day — this is the LORD's declaration — and you will not be handed over to the men you dread. 18 Indeed, I will certainly deliver you so that you do not fall by the sword. Because you have trusted in me, you will retain your life like the spoils of war. This is the LORD's declaration.'"

JEREMIAH STAYS IN JUDAH

40 This is the word that came to Jeremiah from the LORD after Nebuzaradan, captain of the guards, released him at Ramah. When he found him, he was bound in chains with all the exiles of Jerusalem and Judah who were being exiled to Babylon. 2 The captain of the guards took Jeremiah and said to him, "The LORD your God decreed this disaster on this place, 3 and the LORD has fulfilled it. He has done just what he decreed. Because you people have sinned against the LORD and have not obeyed him, this thing has happened. 4 Now pay attention: Today I am setting you free from the chains that were on your hands. If it pleases you to come with me to Babylon, come, and I will take care of you. But if it seems wrong to you to come with me to Babylon, go no farther.[D] Look — the whole land is in front of you. Wherever it seems good and right for you to go, go there." 5 When Jeremiah had not yet turned to go, Nebuzaradan said to him,[E] "Return[F] to Gedaliah son of Ahikam, son of Shaphan, whom the king of Babylon has appointed over the cities of Judah, and stay with him among the people or go wherever it seems right for you to go." So the captain of the guards gave him a ration and a gift and released him. 6 Jeremiah therefore went to Gedaliah son of Ahikam at Mizpah, and he stayed with him among the people who remained in the land.

GEDALIAH ADVISES PEACE

7 All the commanders of the armies that were in the countryside — they and their men — heard that the king of Babylon had appointed Gedaliah son of Ahikam over the land. He had been put in charge of the

[A] **38:27** Lit *word* [B] **38:28** Or *captured. This is what happened when Jerusalem was captured:* [C] **39:3** LXX; MT reads *Samgar-nebu, Sarsechim* [D] **40:4** Lit *Babylon, stop* [E] **40:5** *Nebuzaradan said to him* supplied for clarity [F] **40:5** LXX reads *"But if not, run, return*; Hb obscure

men, women, and children from among the poorest
of the land, who had not been deported to Babylon.
8 So they came to Gedaliah at Mizpah. The commanders included Ishmael son of Nethaniah, Johanan and
Jonathan the sons of Kareah, Seraiah son of Tanhumeth, the sons of Ephai the Netophathite, and Jezaniah son of the Maacathite — they and their men.
9 Gedaliah son of Ahikam, son of Shaphan, swore
an oath to them and their men, assuring them, "Don't
be afraid to serve the Chaldeans. Live in the land and
serve the king of Babylon, and it will go well for you.
10 As for me, I am going to live in Mizpah to represent
you[A] before the Chaldeans who come to us. As for
you, gather wine, summer fruit, and oil, place them
in your storage jars, and live in the cities you have
captured."

11 When all the Judeans in Moab and among the
Ammonites and in Edom and in all the other lands
also heard that the king of Babylon had left a remnant in Judah and had appointed Gedaliah son of
Ahikam, son of Shaphan, over them, 12 they all returned from all the places where they had been banished and came to the land of Judah, to Gedaliah at
Mizpah, and harvested a great amount of wine and
summer fruit.

13 Meanwhile, Johanan son of Kareah and all the
commanders of the armies in the countryside came
to Gedaliah at Mizpah 14 and warned him, "Don't you
realize that Baalis, king of the Ammonites, has sent
Ishmael son of Nethaniah to kill you?" But Gedaliah
son of Ahikam would not believe them. 15 Then Johanan son of Kareah suggested to Gedaliah in private
at Mizpah, "Let me go kill Ishmael son of Nethaniah.
No one will know it. Why should he kill you and allow
all of Judah that has gathered around you to scatter
and the remnant of Judah to perish?"

16 But Gedaliah son of Ahikam responded to Johanan son of Kareah, "Don't do that! What you're saying
about Ishmael is a lie."

GEDALIAH ASSASSINATED BY ISHMAEL

41 In the seventh month, Ishmael son of Nethaniah, son of Elishama, of the royal family and
one of the king's chief officers, came with ten men to
Gedaliah son of Ahikam at Mizpah. They ate a meal
together there in Mizpah, 2 but then Ishmael son of
Nethaniah and the ten men who were with him got
up and struck down Gedaliah son of Ahikam, son of
Shaphan, with the sword; he killed the one the king
of Babylon had appointed in the land. 3 Ishmael also
struck down all the Judeans who were with Gedaliah at Mizpah, as well as the Chaldean soldiers who
were there.

4 On the day after he had killed Gedaliah, when
no one knew yet, 5 eighty men came from Shechem,
Shiloh, and Samaria who had shaved their beards,
torn their clothes, and gashed themselves, and who
were carrying grain and incense offerings to bring
to the temple of the LORD. 6 Ishmael son of Nethaniah came out of Mizpah to meet them, weeping as he
came. When he encountered them, he said, "Come to
Gedaliah son of Ahikam!" 7 But when they came into
the city, Ishmael son of Nethaniah and the men with
him slaughtered them and threw them into[B] a cistern.

8 However, there were ten men among them who
said to Ishmael, "Don't kill us, for we have hidden
treasure in the field — wheat, barley, oil, and honey!" So he stopped and did not kill them along with
their companions. 9 Now the cistern where Ishmael
had thrown all the corpses of the men he had struck
down was a large one[C] that King Asa had made in the
encounter with King Baasha of Israel. Ishmael son of
Nethaniah filled it with the slain.

10 Then Ishmael took captive all the rest of the people of Mizpah including the daughters of the king
— all those who remained in Mizpah over whom
Nebuzaradan, captain of the guards, had appointed
Gedaliah son of Ahikam. Ishmael son of Nethaniah
took them captive and set off to cross over to the
Ammonites.

THE CAPTIVES RESCUED BY JOHANAN

11 When Johanan son of Kareah and all the commanders of the armies with him heard of all the
evil that Ishmael son of Nethaniah had done, 12 they
took all their men and went to fight with Ishmael
son of Nethaniah. They found him by the great pool
in Gibeon. 13 When all the people held by Ishmael
saw Johanan son of Kareah and all the commanders
of the army with him, they rejoiced. 14 All the people whom Ishmael had taken captive from Mizpah
turned around and rejoined Johanan son of Kareah.
15 But Ishmael son of Nethaniah escaped from Johanan with eight men and went to the Ammonites.
16 Johanan son of Kareah and all the commanders
of the armies with him then took from Mizpah all
the remnant of the people whom he had recovered
from Ishmael son of Nethaniah after Ishmael had
killed Gedaliah son of Ahikam — men, soldiers,
women, children, and court officials whom he
brought back from Gibeon. 17 They left, stopping in
Geruth Chimham, which is near Bethlehem, in order to make their way into Egypt, 18 away from the
Chaldeans. For they feared them because Ishmael
son of Nethaniah had struck down Gedaliah son of
Ahikam, whom the king of Babylon had appointed
over the land.

[A] **40:10** Lit *to stand* [B] **41:7** Syr; MT reads *slaughtered them in*
[C] **41:9** LXX; MT reads *down by the hand of Gedaliah*

THE PEOPLE SEEK JEREMIAH'S COUNSEL

42 Then all the commanders of the armies, along with Johanan son of Kareah, Jezaniah son of Hoshaiah, and all the people from the least to the greatest, approached 2 the prophet Jeremiah and said, "May our petition come before you; pray to the LORD your God on our behalf, on behalf of this entire remnant (for few of us remain out of the many, as you can see with your own eyes), 3 that the LORD your God may tell us the way we should go and the thing we should do."

4 So the prophet Jeremiah said to them, "I have heard. I will now pray to the LORD your God according to your words, and I will tell you every word that the LORD answers you; I won't withhold a word from you."

5 And they said to Jeremiah, "May the LORD be a true and faithful witness against us if we don't act according to every word the LORD your God sends you to tell us. 6 Whether it is pleasant or unpleasant, we will obey the LORD our God to whom we are sending you so that it may go well with us. We will certainly obey the LORD our God!"

JEREMIAH'S ADVICE TO STAY

7 At the end of ten days, the word of the LORD came to Jeremiah, 8 and he summoned Johanan son of Kareah, all the commanders of the armies who were with him, and all the people from the least to the greatest.

9 He said to them, "This is what the LORD says, the God of Israel to whom you sent me to bring your petition before him: 10 'If you will indeed stay in this land, then I will rebuild and not demolish you, and I will plant and not uproot you, because I relent concerning the disaster that I have brought on you. 11 Don't be afraid of the king of Babylon whom you now fear; don't be afraid of him' — this is the LORD's declaration — 'because I am with you to save you and rescue you from him. 12 I will grant you compassion, and he[A] will have compassion on you and allow you to return to your own soil.'

13 "But if you say, 'We will not stay in this land,' in order to disobey the LORD your God, 14 and if you say, 'No, instead we'll go to the land of Egypt where we will not see war or hear the sound of the ram's horn or hunger for food, and we'll live there,' 15 then hear the word of the LORD, remnant of Judah! This is what the LORD of Armies, the God of Israel, says: 'If you are firmly resolved to go to Egypt and stay there for a while, 16 then the sword you fear will overtake you there in the land of Egypt, and the famine you are worried about will follow on your heels[B] there to Egypt, and you will die there. 17 All who resolve to go to Egypt to stay there for a while will die by the sword, famine, and plague. They will have no survivor or fugitive from the disaster I will bring on them.'

18 "For this is what the LORD of Armies, the God of Israel, says: 'Just as my anger and fury were poured out on Jerusalem's residents, so will my fury pour out on you if you go to Egypt. You will become an example for cursing, scorn, execration, and disgrace, and you will never see this place again.' 19 The LORD has spoken concerning you, remnant of Judah: 'Don't go to Egypt.' Know for certain that I have warned you today! 20 You have gone astray at the cost of your lives[C] because you are the ones who sent me to the LORD your God, saying, 'Pray to the LORD our God on our behalf, and as for all that the LORD our God says, tell it to us, and we'll act accordingly.' 21 For I have told you today, but you have not obeyed the LORD your God in everything he has sent me to tell you. 22 Now therefore, know for certain that by the sword, famine, and plague you will die in the place where you desired to go to stay for a while."

JEREMIAH'S COUNSEL REJECTED

43 When Jeremiah had finished speaking to all the people all the words of the LORD their God — all these words the LORD their God had sent him to give them — 2 then Azariah[D] son of Hoshaiah, Johanan son of Kareah, and all the other arrogant men responded to Jeremiah, "You are speaking a lie! The LORD our God has not sent you to say, 'You must not go to Egypt to stay there for a while!' 3 Rather, Baruch son of Neriah is inciting you against us to hand us over to the Chaldeans to put us to death or to deport us to Babylon!"

4 So Johanan son of Kareah, all the commanders of the armies, and all the people failed to obey the LORD's command to stay in the land of Judah. 5 Instead, Johanan son of Kareah and all the commanders of the armies led away the whole remnant of Judah, those who had returned to stay in the land of Judah from all the nations where they had been banished. 6 They led away the men, women, children, king's daughters, and everyone whom Nebuzaradan, captain of the guards, had allowed to remain with Gedaliah son of Ahikam son of Shaphan. They also led the prophet Jeremiah and Baruch son of Neriah away. 7 They went to the land of Egypt because they did not obey the LORD. They went as far as Tahpanhes.

GOD'S SIGN TO THE PEOPLE IN EGYPT

8 Then the word of the LORD came to Jeremiah at Tahpanhes: 9 "Pick up some large stones and set them in the mortar of the brick pavement that is at the opening of Pharaoh's palace at Tahpanhes. Do this in the sight of the Judean men 10 and tell them, 'This is what the LORD of Armies, the God of Israel, says:

[A] **42:12** LXX reads *I* [B] **42:16** Lit *will cling after you* [C] **42:20** Or *You have led your own selves astray* [D] **43:2** = Jezaniah

Don't Go to Egypt

by Dorman Laird

Jeremiah 46–51 has messages for several nations, but three in particular loomed large in the background of his times and messages—Assyria, Egypt, and Babylon. As the Assyrian Empire began to collapse, Josiah became entangled in the power struggle between Egypt and Babylon. Egypt, under Pharaoh Neco II, allied itself with the remnant of Assyria and sent an army to support them in a battle against Babylon at Haran. Although Judah's King Josiah tried to stop him at Megiddo, Josiah was killed there in 609 BC, and Egypt gained control of Judah.

Jehoahaz (Shallum in Jr 22:11), a son of Josiah, became Judah's next king, but Neco replaced him after only three months with Eliakim, another son of Josiah, changing his name to Jehoiakim. Jehoahaz was imprisoned in Egypt. After Babylon defeated Egypt at Carchemish in 605 BC, Jehoiakim switched his allegiance to Babylon. Seemingly Egypt had occupied Carchemish after the battle at Megiddo. Even so, a few years later, Jehoiakim was encouraged by the promise of Egyptian military help (cf. 2:36–37) and rebelled against Babylon (2Kg 24:1). In 598 BC, Nebuchadnezzar marched against Judah. Second Kings 24:7 tells us, "Now the king of Egypt did not march out of his land again, for the king of Babylon took everything that had belonged to the king of Egypt, from the Brook of Egypt to the Euphrates River."

After the short reign of Jehoiakim and the even shorter reign of his son, Jehoiachin, Nebuchadnezzar destroyed Jerusalem in 587/586 BC. To Jeremiah, who had advised submission to Babylon, he granted liberty either to go to Babylon in peace or to stay in the land of Judah. He also allowed other survivors to remain in the land, including some daughters of the royal family, and he appointed Gedaliah to be governor. Jeremiah decided to stay in Judah and joined Gedaliah at Mizpah, the new seat of government, which was about six miles from Jerusalem (Jr 40:1–6).

But a man named Ishmael, evidently wanting to resist Babylon, assassinated Gedaliah and also killed other Jews who had gathered to him at Mizpah, together with some Babylonian soldiers who were stationed at Mizpah (41:1–3). Johanan and the other commanders drove Ishmael from Judah and determined to lead the rest to Egypt, fearing reprisals from the Babylonians. The people with Johanan asked Jeremiah to pray and seek God's will about whether they should go to Egypt. Jeremiah inquired of Yahweh for ten days (42:7). God's word to the people was, don't go to Egypt (42:13). The

Ramesses II making an offering to Amun-Re, a combination of the god Amun with the sun god Re from Heliopolis, whose temple Jeremiah prophesied would be destroyed (43:13).

Gulf of Suez and Suez Canal where Tahpanhes (Jer 44:1) is now located.

war was over in Judah, and Babylon would do them no more harm (vv. 7–17). Jeremiah warned the survivors that if they went to Egypt they wouldn't resist the temptation to worship the gods of Egypt (44:7–19). Perhaps most compelling of all, Jeremiah warned that Babylon would invade Egypt, kill, take captives, and burn the land (43:8–13). Resistance against Babylon's invasion of Egypt was futile.

In a second poem about Egypt's destruction, Jeremiah described how the invading enemy from the north (Babylon) would put Egypt to shame (46:13–24). The Judeans who survived Jerusalem's destruction would throw themselves once more in the path of Babylon's armies if they were to go to Egypt. Unfortunately, the Judeans refused to heed the word of God and distrusted Jeremiah. Johanan and his company forsook sound advice, went to Egypt anyway (43:4–7), and suffered the consequences. ❖

I will send for my servant Nebuchadnezzar king of
Babylon, and I will place his throne on these stones
that I have embedded, and he will pitch his pavilion
over them. 11 He will come and strike down the land
of Egypt — those destined for death, to death; those
destined for captivity, to captivity; and those destined
for the sword, to the sword. 12 I[A] will kindle a fire in
the temples of Egypt's gods, and he will burn them
and take them captive. He will clean the land of Egypt
as a shepherd picks lice off[B] his clothes, and he will
leave there unscathed. 13 He will smash the sacred
pillars of the sun temple[C,D] in the land of Egypt and
burn the temples of the Egyptian gods.' "

GOD'S JUDGMENT AGAINST HIS PEOPLE IN EGYPT

44 This is the word that came to Jeremiah for all
the Jews living in the land of Egypt — at Migdol, Tahpanhes, Memphis, and in the land of Pathros:
2 "This is what the LORD of Armies, the God of Israel,
says: You have seen all the disaster I brought against
Jerusalem and all Judah's cities. Look, they are a ruin
today without an inhabitant in them 3 because of
the evil they committed to anger me, by going and
burning incense to serve other gods that they, you,
and your ancestors did not know. 4 So I sent you all
my servants the prophets time and time again,[E] saying, 'Don't commit this detestable action that I hate.'
5 But they did not listen or pay attention; they did not
turn from their evil or stop burning incense to other
gods. 6 So my fierce wrath poured out and burned in
Judah's cities and Jerusalem's streets so that they
became the desolate ruin they are today.

7 "So now, this is what the LORD, the God of Armies,
the God of Israel, says: Why are you doing such terrible harm to yourselves? You are cutting off man and
woman, infant and nursing baby from Judah, leaving
yourselves without a remnant. 8 You are angering me
by the work of your hands. You are burning incense
to other gods in the land of Egypt where you have
gone to stay for a while. As a result, you will be cut
off and become an example for cursing and insult
among all the nations of earth. 9 Have you forgotten
the evils of your ancestors, the evils of Judah's kings,
the evils of their wives, your own evils, and the evils
of your wives that were committed in the land of
Judah and in the streets of Jerusalem? 10 They have
not become humble to this day, and they have not
feared or followed my instruction or my statutes
that I set before you and your ancestors.

11 "Therefore, this is what the LORD of Armies, the
God of Israel, says: I am about to set my face against
you to bring disaster, to cut off all Judah. 12 And I will
take away the remnant of Judah, those who have set
their face to go to the land of Egypt to stay there. All
of them will meet their end in the land of Egypt. They
will fall by the sword; they will meet their end by
famine. From the least to the greatest, they will die by
the sword and by famine. Then they will become an
example for cursing, scorn, execration, and disgrace.
13 I will punish those living in the land of Egypt just as
I punished Jerusalem by sword, famine, and plague.
14 Then the remnant of Judah — those going to live
for a while there in the land of Egypt — will have no
fugitive or survivor to return to the land of Judah
where they are longing[F] to return to stay, for they
will not return except for a few fugitives."

THE PEOPLE'S STUBBORN RESPONSE

15 However, all the men who knew that their wives
were burning incense to other gods, all the women
standing by — a great assembly — and all the people
who were living in the land of Egypt at Pathros answered Jeremiah, 16 "As for the word you spoke to us
in the name of the LORD, we are not going to listen to
you! 17 Instead, we will do everything we promised:[G]
we will burn incense to the queen of heaven[H] and
offer drink offerings to her just as we, our ancestors,
our kings, and our officials did in Judah's cities and
in Jerusalem's streets. Then we had enough food, we
were well off, and we saw no disaster, 18 but from the
time we ceased to burn incense to the queen of heav-
en and to offer her drink offerings, we have lacked
everything, and through sword and famine we have
met our end."

19 And the women said,[I] "When we burned incense
to the queen of heaven and poured out drink offerings to her, was it apart from our husbands' knowledge that we made sacrificial cakes in her image and
poured out drink offerings to her?"

20 But Jeremiah responded to all the people — the
men, women, and all the people who were answering him: 21 "As for the incense you burned in Judah's
cities and in Jerusalem's streets — you, your ancestors, your kings, your officials, and the people
of the land — did the LORD not remember them?
He brought this to mind. 22 The LORD can no longer
bear your evil deeds and the detestable acts you
have committed, so your land has become a waste,
a desolation, and an example for cursing, without
inhabitant, as you see today. 23 Because you burned
incense and sinned against the LORD and didn't obey
the LORD and didn't follow his instruction, his statutes, and his testimonies, this disaster has come to
you, as you see today."

[A] **43:12** LXX, Syr, Vg read *He* [B] **43:12** Or *will wrap himself in the land of Egypt as a shepherd wraps himself in* [C] **43:13** Or *Beth-shemesh* [D] **43:13** = of Heliopolis [E] **44:4** Lit *prophets, rising up early and sending* [F] **44:14** Lit *lifting up their soul* [G] **44:17** Lit *do every word that came from our mouth* [H] **44:17** = Ashtoreth, or Astarte [I] **44:19** LXX, Syr; MT omits *And the women said*

24 Then Jeremiah said to all the people, including
all the women, "Hear the word of the LORD, all you
people of Judah who are in the land of Egypt. 25 This
is what the LORD of Armies, the God of Israel, says:
'As for you and your wives, you women have spoken
with your mouths, and you men fulfilled it by your
deeds, saying, "We will keep our vows that we have
made to burn incense to the queen of heaven and to
pour out drink offerings for her." Go ahead, confirm
your vows! Keep your vows!'
26 "Therefore, hear the word of the LORD, all you
Judeans who live in the land of Egypt: 'I have sworn
by my great name, says the LORD, that my name will
never again be invoked by anyone of Judah in all
the land of Egypt, saying, "As the Lord GOD lives."
27 I am watching over them for disaster and not for
good, and everyone from Judah who is in the land
of Egypt will meet his end by sword or famine until
they are finished off. 28 Those who escape the sword
will return from the land of Egypt to the land of Judah only few in number, and the whole remnant of
Judah, the ones going to the land of Egypt to stay
there for a while, will know whose word stands, mine
or theirs! 29 This will be a sign to you' — this is the
LORD's declaration — 'that I will punish you in this
place, so you may know that my words of disaster
concerning you will certainly come to pass. 30 This is
what the LORD says: I am about to hand over Pharaoh
Hophra, Egypt's king, to his enemies, to those who
intend to take his life, just as I handed over Judah's
King Zedekiah to Babylon's King Nebuchadnezzar,
who was his enemy, the one who intended to take
his life.'"

THE LORD'S MESSAGE TO BARUCH

45 This is the word that the prophet Jeremiah
spoke to Baruch son of Neriah when he wrote
these words on a scroll at Jeremiah's dictation[A] in
the fourth year of Jehoiakim son of Josiah, king of
Judah: 2 "This is what the LORD, the God of Israel, says
to you, Baruch: 3 'You have said, "Woe is me, because
the LORD has added misery to my pain! I am worn out
with[B] groaning and have found no rest."'
4 "This is what you are to say to him: 'This is what
the LORD says: "What I have built I am about to demolish, and what I have planted I am about to uproot
— the whole land! 5 But as for you, do you pursue
great things for yourself? Stop pursuing! For I am
about to bring disaster on all humanity" — this is the
LORD's declaration — "but I will grant you your life
like the spoils of war wherever you go."'"

PROPHECIES AGAINST THE NATIONS

46 This is the word of the LORD that came to the
prophet Jeremiah about the nations:

PROPHECIES AGAINST EGYPT

2 About Egypt and the army of Pharaoh Neco, Egypt's
king, which was defeated at Carchemish on the Euphrates River by King Nebuchadnezzar of Babylon
in the fourth year of Judah's King Jehoiakim son of
Josiah:

3 Deploy small shields and large;
approach for battle!
4 Harness the horses;
mount the steeds;[C]
take your positions with helmets on!
Polish the lances;
put on armor!
5 Why have I seen this?
They are terrified,
they are retreating,
their warriors are crushed,
they flee headlong,
they never look back,
terror is on every side!
This is the LORD's declaration.
6 The swift cannot flee,
and the warrior cannot escape!
In the north by the bank of the Euphrates River,
they stumble and fall.

7 Who is this, rising like the Nile,
with waters that churn like rivers?
8 Egypt rises like the Nile,
and its waters churn like rivers.
He boasts, "I will go up, I will cover the earth;
I will destroy cities with their residents."
9 Rise up, you cavalry!
Race furiously, you chariots!
Let the warriors march out —
Cush and Put,
who are able to handle shields,
and the men of Lud,
who are able to handle and string the bow.
10 That day belongs to the Lord, the GOD of Armies,
a day of vengeance to avenge himself
against his adversaries.
The sword will devour and be satisfied;
it will drink its fill of their blood,
because it will be a sacrifice to the Lord,
the GOD of Armies,
in the northern land by the Euphrates River.

11 Go up to Gilead and get balm,
Virgin Daughter Egypt!
You have multiplied remedies in vain;
there is no healing for you.

[A] **45:1** Lit *scroll from Jeremiah's mouth* [B] **45:3** Lit *I labored in my* [C] **46:4** Or *mount up, riders*

12 The nations have heard of your dishonor,
and your cries fill the earth,
because warrior stumbles against warrior
and together both of them have fallen.

[13] This is the word the LORD spoke to the prophet
Jeremiah about the coming of King Nebuchadnezzar
of Babylon to defeat the land of Egypt:
14 Announce it in Egypt, and proclaim it in Migdol!
Proclaim it in Memphis and in Tahpanhes!
Say, "Take positions! Prepare yourself,
for the sword devours all around you."
15 Why have your strong ones been swept away?
Each has not stood,
for the LORD has thrust him down.
16 He continues to stumble.
Indeed, each falls over the other.
They say, "Get up! Let's return to our people
and to our native land,
away from the oppressor's sword."
17 There they will cry out,
"Pharaoh king of Egypt was all noise;
he let the opportune moment pass."

18 As I live —
this is the King's declaration;
the LORD of Armies is his name —
the king of Babylon[A] will come like Tabor
among the mountains
and like Carmel by the sea.
19 Get your bags ready for exile,
inhabitant of Daughter Egypt!
For Memphis will become a desolation,
uninhabited ruins.

20 Egypt is a beautiful young cow,
but a horsefly from the north is coming
against her.[B]
21 Even her mercenaries among her
are like stall-fed calves.
They too will turn back;
together they will flee;
they will not take their stand,
for the day of their calamity is coming
on them,
the time of their punishment.
22 Egypt will hiss like a slithering snake,[C]
for the enemy will come with an army;
with axes they will come against her
like those who cut trees.
23 They will cut down her forest —
this is the LORD's declaration —
though it is dense,
for they are more numerous than locusts;
they cannot be counted.
24 Daughter Egypt will be put to shame,
handed over to a northern people.

[25] The LORD of Armies, the God of Israel, says, "I
am about to punish Amon, god of Thebes, along with
Pharaoh, Egypt, her gods, and her kings — Pharaoh
and those trusting in him. [26] I will hand them over to
those who intend to take their lives — to King Nebuchadnezzar of Babylon and his officers. But after this,
Egypt[D] will be inhabited again as in ancient times."
This is the LORD's declaration.

REASSURANCE FOR ISRAEL

27 But you, my servant Jacob, do not be afraid,
and do not be discouraged, Israel,
for without fail I will save you
from far away,
and your descendants from the land
of their captivity!
Jacob will return and have calm and quiet
with no one to frighten him.
28 And you, my servant Jacob,
do not be afraid —
this is the LORD's declaration —
for I will be with you.
I will bring destruction on all the nations
where I have banished you,
but I will not bring destruction on you.
I will discipline you with justice,
and I will by no means leave you unpunished.

PROPHECIES AGAINST THE PHILISTINES

47 This is the word of the LORD that came to the
prophet Jeremiah about the Philistines before
Pharaoh defeated Gaza. [2] This is what the LORD says:
Look, water is rising from the north
and becoming an overflowing wadi.
It will overflow the land
and everything in it,
the cities and their inhabitants.
The people will cry out,
and every inhabitant of the land will wail.
3 At the sound of the stomping hooves
of his stallions,
the rumbling of his chariots,
and the clatter of their wheels,
fathers will not turn back for their sons.
They will be utterly helpless[E]
4 on account of the day that is coming
to destroy all the Philistines,
to cut off from Tyre and Sidon
every remaining ally.

[A] **46:18** Lit *He* [B] **46:20** Some Hb mss, LXX, Syr; other Hb mss read *is coming, coming* [C] **46:22** Lit *Her sound is like a snake as it goes* [D] **46:26** Lit *it* [E] **47:3** Lit *Because of weakened hands*

Indeed, the LORD is about to destroy
the Philistines,
the remnant of the coastland of Caphtor.[A]
5 Baldness is coming to Gaza;
Ashkelon will become silent.
Remnant of their valley,
how long will you gash yourself?

6 Oh, sword of the LORD!
How long will you be restless?
Go back to your sheath;
be still; be silent!
7 How can it[B] rest
when the LORD has given it a command?
He has assigned it
against Ashkelon and the shore of the sea.

PROPHECIES AGAINST MOAB

48 About Moab, this is what the LORD of Armies,
the God of Israel, says:
Woe to Nebo, because it is
about to be destroyed;
Kiriathaim will be put to shame; it will be
taken captive.
The fortress will be put to shame
and dismayed!
2 There is no longer praise for Moab;
they plan harm against her in Heshbon:
Come, let's cut her off from nationhood.
Also, Madmen, you will be silenced;
the sword will follow you.
3 A voice cries out from Horonaim,
"devastation and a crushing blow!"
4 Moab will be shattered;
her little ones will cry out.
5 For on the Ascent to Luhith
they will be weeping continually,[C]
and on the descent to Horonaim
will be heard cries of distress
over the destruction:
6 Flee! Save your lives!
Be like a juniper bush[D] in the wilderness.
7 Because you trust in your works and treasures,
you will be captured also.
Chemosh will go into exile
with his priests and officials.
8 The destroyer will move against every town;
not one town will escape.
The valley will perish,
and the plain will be annihilated,
as the LORD has said.
9 Make Moab a salt marsh,[E]
for she will run away;[F]
her towns will become a desolation,
without inhabitant.
10 The one who does
the LORD's business deceitfully[G] is cursed,
and the one who withholds
his sword from bloodshed is cursed.

11 Moab has been left quiet since his youth,
settled like wine on its dregs.
He hasn't been poured from one container
to another
or gone into exile.
So his taste has remained the same,
and his aroma hasn't changed.
12 Therefore look, the days are coming —
this is the LORD's declaration —
when I will send pourers to him,
who will pour him out.
They will empty his containers
and smash his jars.
13 Moab will be put to shame because of Chemosh,
just as the house of Israel was put to shame
because of Bethel that they trusted in.

14 How can you say, "We are warriors —
valiant men for battle"?
15 The destroyer of Moab and its towns
has come up,[H]
and the best of its young men
have gone down to slaughter.
This is the King's declaration;
the LORD of Armies is his name.
16 Moab's calamity is near at hand;
his disaster is rushing swiftly.
17 Mourn for him, all you surrounding nations,
everyone who knows his name.
Say, "How the mighty scepter is shattered,
the glorious staff!"

18 Come down from glory; sit on parched ground,
resident of the daughter of Dibon,
for the destroyer of Moab has come
against you;
he has destroyed your fortresses.
19 Stand by the highway and watch,
resident of Aroer!
Ask him who is fleeing or her who is escaping,
"What happened?"
20 Moab is put to shame, indeed dismayed.
Wail and cry out!
Declare by the Arnon
that Moab is destroyed.

[A] **47:4** Probably Crete [B] **47:7** LXX, Vg; MT reads *you* [C] **48:5** Lit *Luhith, weeping goes up with weeping* [D] **48:6** Or *like Aroer*; Is 17:2; Jr 48:19 [E] **48:9** LXX reads *a sign*; Vg reads *a flower*; Syr, Tg read *a crown* [F] **48:9** Hb obscure [G] **48:10** Or *negligently* [H] **48:15** Or *Moab is destroyed; he has come up against its cities*

[21] "Judgment has come to the land of the plateau
— to Holon, Jahzah, Mephaath, [22] Dibon, Nebo, Beth-
diblathaim, [23] Kiriathaim, Beth-gamul, Beth-meon,
[24] Kerioth, Bozrah, and all the towns of the land of
Moab, those far and near. [25] Moab's horn is chopped
off; his arm is shattered."
This is the LORD's declaration.
[26] "Make him drunk, because he has exalted himself against the LORD. Moab will wallow in his own
vomit, and he will also become a laughingstock.
[27] Wasn't Israel a laughingstock to you? Was he ever
found among thieves? For whenever you speak of
him you shake your head."

28 Abandon the towns! Live in the cliffs,
residents of Moab!
Be like a dove
that nests inside the mouth of a cave.

29 We have heard of Moab's pride,
great pride, indeed —
his insolence, arrogance, pride,
and haughty heart.
30 I know his outburst.
This is the LORD's declaration.
It is empty.
His boast is empty.
31 Therefore, I will wail over Moab.
I will cry out for Moab, all of it;
he will moan for the men of Kir-heres.
32 I will weep for you, vine of Sibmah,
with more than the weeping for Jazer.
Your tendrils have extended to the sea;
they have reached to the sea and to Jazer.[A]
The destroyer has fallen on your summer fruit
and grape harvest.
33 Gladness and celebration are taken
from the fertile field
and from the land of Moab.
I have stopped the flow of wine
from the winepresses;
no one will tread with shouts of joy.
The shouting is not a shout of joy.

[34] "There is a cry from Heshbon to Elealeh; they
make their voices heard as far as Jahaz — from Zoar
to Horonaim and Eglath-shelishiyah — because
even the Waters of Nimrim have become desolate.
[35] In Moab, I will stop" — this is the LORD's declaration — "the one who offers sacrifices on the high
place and burns incense to his gods. [36] Therefore,
my heart moans like flutes for Moab, and my heart
moans like flutes for the people of Kir-heres. And
therefore, the wealth he has gained has perished.
[37] Indeed, every head is bald and every beard is
chopped short. On every hand is a gash and sackcloth around the waist. [38] On all the rooftops of Moab
and in her public squares, everyone is mourning because I have shattered Moab like a jar no one wants."
This is the LORD's declaration. [39] "How broken it is!
They wail! How Moab has turned his back! He is
ashamed. Moab will become a laughingstock and a
shock to all those around him."
[40] For this is what the LORD says:

Look! He will swoop down like an eagle
and spread his wings against Moab.
41 The towns have[B] been captured,
and the strongholds seized.
In that day the heart of Moab's warriors
will be like the heart of a woman
with contractions.
42 Moab will be destroyed as a people
because he has exalted himself
against the LORD.
43 Panic, pit, and trap
await you, resident of Moab.
This is the LORD's declaration.
44 He who flees from the panic
will fall in the pit,
and he who climbs from the pit
will be captured in the trap,
for I will bring against Moab
the year of their punishment.
This is the LORD's declaration.

45 Those who flee will stand exhausted
in Heshbon's shadow
because fire has come out from Heshbon
and a flame from within Sihon.
It will devour Moab's forehead
and the skull of the noisemakers.
46 Woe to you, Moab!
The people of Chemosh have perished
because your sons have been taken captive
and your daughters have gone
into captivity.
47 Yet, I will restore the fortunes[C] of Moab
in the last days.
This is the LORD's declaration.
The judgment on Moab ends here.

PROPHECIES AGAINST AMMON

49 About the Ammonites, this is what the LORD says:

Does Israel have no sons?
Is he without an heir?
Why then has Milcom[D,E] dispossessed Gad
and his people settled in their cities?

[A] **48:32** Some Hb mss read *reached as far as Jazer* [B] **48:41** Or *Kerioth has* [C] **48:47** Or *will end the captivity* [D] **49:1** LXX, Syr, Vg; MT reads *Mulkam* [E] **49:1** = Molech

2 Therefore look, the days are coming —
this is the LORD's declaration —
when I will make the shout of battle heard
against Rabbah of the Ammonites.
It will become a desolate mound,
and its surrounding villages will be set on fire.
Israel will dispossess their dispossessors,
says the LORD.
3 Wail, Heshbon, for Ai is devastated;
cry out, daughters of Rabbah!
Clothe yourselves with sackcloth, and lament;
run back and forth within your walls,[A]
because Milcom will go into exile
together with his priests and officials.
4 Why do you boast about your valleys,
your flowing valley,[B]
you faithless daughter —
you who trust in your treasures
and say, "Who can attack me?"
5 Look, I am about to bring terror on you —
this is the declaration of the Lord GOD
of Armies —
from all those around you.
You will be banished, each person headlong,
with no one to gather up the fugitives.
6 But after that, I will restore the fortunes[C]
of the Ammonites.
This is the LORD's declaration.

PROPHECIES AGAINST EDOM

7 About Edom, this is what the LORD of Armies says:
Is there no longer wisdom in Teman?
Has counsel perished from the prudent?
Has their wisdom rotted away?
8 Run! Turn back! Lie low,
residents of Dedan,
for I will bring Esau's calamity on him
at the time I punish him.
9 If grape harvesters came to you,
wouldn't they leave a few grapes?
Were thieves to come in the night,
they would destroy only what they wanted.
10 But I will strip Esau bare;
I will uncover his secret places.
He will try to hide, but he will be unable.
His descendants will be destroyed
along with his relatives and neighbors.
He will exist no longer.
11 Abandon your fatherless; I will preserve them;
let your widows trust in me.

12 For this is what the LORD says: "If those who do
not deserve to drink the cup must drink it, can you
possibly remain unpunished? You will not remain unpunished, for you must drink it too. 13 For by myself I
have sworn" — this is the LORD's declaration — "Bozrah[D] will become a desolation, a disgrace, a ruin, and
an example for cursing, and all its surrounding cities
will become ruins forever."
14 I have heard an envoy from the LORD;
a messenger has been sent
among the nations:
Assemble yourselves to come against her.
Rise up for war!

15 I will certainly make you insignificant
among the nations,
despised among humanity.
16 As to the terror you cause,[E]
your arrogant heart has deceived you.
You who live in the clefts of the rock,[F]
you who occupy the mountain summit,
though you elevate your nest like the eagles,
even from there I will bring you down.
This is the LORD's declaration.

17 "Edom will become a desolation. Everyone who
passes by her will be appalled and scoff because of
all her wounds. 18 As when Sodom and Gomorrah
were overthrown along with their neighbors," says
the LORD, "no one will live there; no human being will
stay in it even temporarily.
19 "Look, it will be like a lion coming from the thickets[G] of the Jordan to the watered grazing land. I will
chase Edom away from her land in a flash. I will appoint whoever is chosen for her. For who is like me?
Who will issue me a summons? Who is the shepherd
who can stand against me?"
20 Therefore, hear the plans that the LORD has
drawn up against Edom and the strategies he has
devised against the people of Teman: The flock's little lambs will certainly be dragged away, and their
grazing land will be made desolate because of them.
21 At the sound of their fall the earth will quake; the
sound of her cry will be heard at the Red Sea. 22 Look!
It will be like an eagle soaring upward, then swooping
down and spreading its wings over Bozrah. In that
day the hearts of Edom's warriors will be like the
heart of a woman with contractions.

PROPHECIES AGAINST DAMASCUS

23 About Damascus:
Hamath and Arpad are put to shame,
for they have heard a bad report
and are agitated,
like[H] the anxious sea that cannot be calmed.

[A] **49:3** Or *sheep pens* [B] **49:4** Or *about your strength, your ebbing strength* [C] **49:6** Or *will end the captivity*, also in v. 39
[D] **49:13** = Edom's capital [E] **49:16** Lit *Your horror* [F] **49:16** = Petra
[G] **49:19** Lit *pride* [H] **49:23** Lit *in*

24 Damascus has become weak;
she has turned to run;
panic has gripped her.
Distress and labor pains have seized her
like a woman in labor.
25 How can the city of praise
not be abandoned,
the town that brings me joy?
26 Therefore, her young men will fall
in her public squares;
all the warriors will perish in that day.
This is the declaration of the LORD
of Armies.
27 I will set fire to the wall of Damascus;
it will consume Ben-hadad's citadels.

PROPHECIES AGAINST KEDAR AND HAZOR

28 About Kedar and the kingdoms of Hazor, which King Nebuchadnezzar of Babylon defeated, this is what the LORD says:
Rise up, attack Kedar,
and destroy the people of the east!
29 They will take their tents and their flocks
along with their tent curtains
and all their equipment.
They will take their camels
for themselves.
They will call out to them,
"Terror is on every side!"
30 Run! Escape quickly! Lie low,
residents of Hazor —
this is the LORD's declaration —
for King Nebuchadnezzar of Babylon
has drawn up a plan against you;
he has devised a strategy against you.

31 Rise up, attack a nation at ease,
one living in security.
This is the LORD's declaration.
They have no doors, not even a gate bar;
they live alone.
32 Their camels will become plunder,
and their massive herds of cattle will
become spoil.
I will scatter them to the wind
in every direction,
those who clip the hair on their temples;
I will bring calamity on them
across all their borders.
This is the LORD's declaration.
33 Hazor will become a jackals' den,
a desolation forever.
No one will live there;
no human being will stay in it even
temporarily.

PROPHECIES AGAINST ELAM

34 This is the word of the LORD that came to the prophet Jeremiah about Elam[A] at the beginning of the reign
of King Zedekiah of Judah. 35 This is what the LORD
of Armies says:
I am about to shatter Elam's bow,
the source[B] of their might.
36 I will bring the four winds against Elam
from the four corners of the heavens,
and I will scatter them to all these winds.
There will not be a nation
to which Elam's banished ones will not go.
37 I will devastate Elam before their enemies,
before those who intend to take their lives.
I will bring disaster on them,
my burning anger.
This is the LORD's declaration.
I will send the sword after them
until I finish them off.
38 I will set my throne in Elam,
and I will destroy the king and officials
from there.
This is the LORD's declaration.

39 Yet, in the last days,
I will restore the fortunes of Elam.
This is the LORD's declaration.

PROPHECIES AGAINST BABYLON

50 This is the word the LORD spoke about Babylon, the land of the Chaldeans, through the
prophet Jeremiah:
2 Announce to the nations;
proclaim and raise up a signal flag;
proclaim, and hide nothing.
Say, "Babylon is captured;
Bel is put to shame;
Marduk is terrified."
Her idols are put to shame;
her false gods, devastated.
3 For a nation from the north will attack her;
it will make her land desolate.
No one will be living in it —
both people and animals will escape.[C]
4 In those days and at that time —
this is the LORD's declaration —
the Israelites and Judeans
will come together,
weeping as they come,
and will seek the LORD their God.
5 They will ask about Zion,
turning their faces to this road.

[A] **49:34** = modern Iran [B] **49:35** Lit *first* [C] **50:3** Lit *escape; they will walk*

They will come and join themselves[A]
to the LORD
in a permanent covenant that will never
be forgotten.

6 My people were lost sheep;
their shepherds led them astray,
guiding them the wrong way in the mountains.
They wandered from mountain to hill;
they forgot their resting place.
7 Whoever found them devoured them.
Their adversaries said, "We're not guilty;
instead, they have sinned against the LORD,
their righteous grazing land,
the hope of their ancestors, the LORD."

8 Escape from Babylon;
depart from the Chaldeans' land.
Be like the rams that lead the flock.
9 For I will soon stir up and bring
against Babylon
an assembly of great nations
from the north country.
They will line up in battle formation
against her;
from there she will be captured.
Their arrows will be like a skilled[B] warrior
who does not return empty-handed.
10 The Chaldeans will become plunder;
all Babylon's plunderers will be fully satisfied.
This is the LORD's declaration.
11 Because you rejoice,
because you celebrate —
you who plundered my inheritance —
because you frolic like a young cow
treading grain
and neigh like stallions,
12 your mother will be utterly humiliated;
she who bore you will be put to shame.
Look! She will lag behind all[C] the nations —
an arid wilderness, a desert.
13 Because of the LORD's wrath,
she will not be inhabited;
she will become a desolation, every bit of her.
Everyone who passes through Babylon
will be appalled
and scoff because of all her wounds.
14 Line up in battle formation around Babylon,
all you archers!
Shoot at her! Do not spare an arrow,
for she has sinned against the LORD.
15 Raise a war cry against her on every side!
She has thrown up her hands in surrender;
her defense towers have fallen;
her walls are demolished.
Since this is the LORD's vengeance,
take your vengeance on her;
as she has done, do the same to her.
16 Cut off the sower from Babylon
as well as him who wields the sickle
at harvest time.
Because of the oppressor's sword,
each will turn to his own people,
each will flee to his own land.

THE RETURN OF GOD'S PEOPLE

17 Israel is a stray lamb, chased by lions.
The first who devoured him was the king
of Assyria;
the last who crushed his bones
was King Nebuchadnezzar of Babylon.

18 Therefore, this is what the LORD of Armies, the
God of Israel, says: I am about to punish the king of
Babylon and his land just as I punished the king of
Assyria.

19 I will return Israel to his grazing land,
and he will feed on Carmel and Bashan;
he will be satisfied
in the hill country of Ephraim and of Gilead.
20 In those days and at that time —
this is the LORD's declaration —
one will search for Israel's iniquity,
but there will be none,
and for Judah's sins,
but they will not be found,
for I will forgive those I leave as a remnant.

THE INVASION OF BABYLON

21 Attack the land of Merathaim,
and those living in Pekod.
Put them to the sword;
completely destroy them —
this is the LORD's declaration —
do everything I have commanded you.
22 The sound of war is in the land —
a crushing blow!
23 How the hammer of the whole earth
is cut down and smashed!
What a horror Babylon has become
among the nations!
24 Babylon, I laid a trap for you, and you
were caught,
but you did not even know it.
You were found and captured
because you pitted yourself
against the LORD.

[A] **50:5** LXX; MT reads *Come and join yourselves* [B] **50:9** Some Hb mss, LXX, Syr; other Hb mss read *bereaving* [C] **50:12** Lit *Look! The last of*

25 The LORD opened his armory
and brought out his weapons of wrath,
because it is a task of the Lord GOD
of Armies
in the land of the Chaldeans.
26 Come against her
from the most distant places.[A]
Open her granaries;
pile her up like mounds of grain
and completely destroy her.
Leave her no survivors.
27 Put all her young bulls to the sword;
let them go down to the slaughter.
Woe to them because their day has come,
the time of their punishment.

THE HUMILIATION OF BABYLON

28 There is a voice of fugitives and refugees
from the land of Babylon.
The voice announces in Zion the vengeance
of the LORD our God,
the vengeance for his temple.
29 Summon the archers to Babylon,
all who string the bow;
camp all around her; let none escape.
Repay her according to her deeds;
just as she has done, do the same to her,
for she has acted arrogantly
against the LORD,
against the Holy One of Israel.
30 Therefore, her young men will fall
in her public squares;
all the warriors will perish in that day.
This is the LORD's declaration.
31 Look, I am against you, you arrogant one —
this is the declaration of
the Lord GOD of Armies —
for your day has come,
the time when I will punish you.
32 The arrogant will stumble and fall
with no one to pick him up.
I will set fire to his cities,
and it will consume everything around him.

THE DESOLATION OF BABYLON

33 This is what the LORD of Armies says:
Israelites and Judeans alike
have been oppressed.
All their captors hold them fast;
they refuse to release them.
34 Their Redeemer is strong;
the LORD of Armies is his name.
He will fervently champion their cause
so that he might bring rest to the earth
but turmoil to those who live in Babylon.
35 A sword is over the Chaldeans —
this is the LORD's declaration —
against those who live in Babylon,
against her officials, and against her sages.
36 A sword is against the diviners,
and they will act foolishly.
A sword is against her heroic warriors,
and they will be terrified.
37 A sword is against his horses and chariots
and against all the foreigners among them,
and they will be like women.
A sword is against her treasuries,
and they will be plundered.
38 A drought will come on her waters,
and they will be dried up.
For it is a land of carved images,
and they go mad because of terrifying things.[B]

39 Therefore, desert creatures[C] will live
with hyenas,
and ostriches will also live in her.
It will never again be inhabited
or lived in through all generations.
40 Just as God demolished Sodom and Gomorrah
and their neighboring towns —
this is the LORD's declaration —
so no one will live there;
no human being will stay in it even temporarily
as a temporary resident.

THE CONQUEST OF BABYLON

41 Look! A people comes from the north.
A great nation and many kings will be
stirred up
from the remote regions of the earth.
42 They grasp bow and javelin.
They are cruel and show no mercy.
Their voice roars like the sea,
and they ride on horses,
lined up like men in battle formation
against you, Daughter Babylon.
43 The king of Babylon has heard about them;
his hands have become weak.
Distress has seized him —
pain, like a woman in labor.

44 "Look, it will be like a lion coming from the thickets[D] of the Jordan to the watered grazing land. I will
chase Babylon[E] away from her land in a flash. I will
appoint whoever is chosen for her. For who is like
me? Who will issue me a summons? Who is the shepherd who can stand against me?"

[A] **50:26** Lit *from the end* [B] **50:38** Or *of dreaded gods* [C] **50:39** Or *desert demons* [D] **50:44** Lit *pride* [E] **50:44** Lit *them*

[45] Therefore, hear the plans that the LORD has
drawn up against Babylon and the strategies he has
devised against the land of the Chaldeans: Certainly
the flock's little lambs will be dragged away; certainly the grazing land will be made desolate because of
them. [46] At the sound of Babylon's conquest the earth
will quake; a cry will be heard among the nations.

GOD'S JUDGMENT ON BABYLON

51 This is what the LORD says:
I am about to rouse the spirit of a destroyer[A]
against Babylon
and against the population of Leb-qamai.[B,C]
2 I will send strangers to Babylon
who will scatter her and strip
her land bare,
for they will come against her
from every side in the day of disaster.
3 Don't let the archer string his bow;
don't let him put on[D] his armor.
Don't spare her young men;
completely destroy her entire army!
4 Those who were slain will fall in the land
of the Chaldeans,
those who were pierced through,
in her streets.
5 For Israel and Judah are not left widowed
by their God, the LORD of Armies,
though their land is full of guilt
against the Holy One of Israel.

6 Leave Babylon;
save your lives, each of you!
Don't perish because of her guilt.
For this is the time of the LORD's vengeance —
he will pay her what she deserves.
7 Babylon was a gold cup in the LORD's hand,
making the whole earth drunk.
The nations drank her wine;
therefore, the nations go mad.
8 Suddenly Babylon fell and was shattered.
Wail for her;
get balm for her wound —
perhaps she can be healed.

9 We tried to heal Babylon,
but she could not be healed.
Abandon her!
Let each of us go to his own land,
for her judgment extends to the sky
and reaches as far as the clouds.

10 The LORD has brought about our vindication;
come, let's tell in Zion
what the LORD our God has accomplished.

11 Sharpen the arrows!
Fill the quivers![E]
The LORD has roused the spirit
of the kings of the Medes
because his plan is aimed at Babylon
to destroy her,
for it is the LORD's vengeance,
vengeance for his temple.
12 Raise up a signal flag
against the walls of Babylon;
fortify the watch post;
set the watchmen in place;
prepare the ambush.
For the LORD has both planned
and accomplished
what he has threatened
against those who live in Babylon.
13 You who reside by abundant water,
rich in treasures,
your end has come,
your life thread is cut.

[14] The LORD of Armies has sworn by himself:
I will fill you up with men as with locusts,
and they will sing the victory song
over you.

15 He made the earth by his power,
established the world by his wisdom,
and spread out the heavens
by his understanding.
16 When he thunders,[F]
the waters in the heavens are tumultuous,
and he causes the clouds
to rise from the ends of the earth.
He makes lightning for the rain
and brings the wind from his storehouses.

17 Everyone is stupid and ignorant.
Every goldsmith is put to shame
by his carved image,
for his cast images are a lie;
there is no breath in them.
18 They are worthless, a work to be mocked.
At the time of their punishment they will
be destroyed.
19 Jacob's Portion[G] is not like these
because he is the one who formed
all things.
Israel is the tribe of his inheritance;
the LORD of Armies is his name.

[A] **51:1** Or *to stir up a destructive wind* [B] **51:1** Lit *heart of my adversaries* [C] **51:1** = Chaldeans [D] **51:3** Hb obscure [E] **51:11** Or *Grasp the shields!* [F] **51:16** Lit *At his giving of the voice* [G] **51:19** = The LORD

20 You are my war club,
my weapons of war.
With you I will smash nations;
with you I will bring kingdoms to ruin.
21 With you I will smash the horse and its rider;
with you I will smash the chariot
and its rider.
22 With you I will smash man and woman;
with you I will smash the old man
and the youth;
with you I will smash the young man
and the young woman.
23 With you I will smash the shepherd
and his flock;
with you I will smash the farmer
and his ox-team.[A]
With you I will smash governors and officials.

24 "Before your very eyes, I will repay Babylon and
all the residents of Chaldea for all their evil they have
done in Zion."
This is the LORD's declaration.
25 Look, I am against you, devastating mountain.
This is the LORD's declaration.
You devastate the whole earth.
I will stretch out my hand against you,
roll you down from the cliffs,
and turn you into a charred mountain.
26 No one will be able to retrieve a cornerstone
or a foundation stone from you,
because you will become desolate forever.
This is the LORD's declaration.

27 Raise a signal flag in the land;
blow a ram's horn among the nations;
set apart the nations against her.
Summon kingdoms against her —
Ararat, Minni, and Ashkenaz.
Appoint a marshal against her;
bring up horses like a swarm[B] of locusts.
28 Set apart the nations for battle against her —
the kings of Media,
her governors and all her officials,
and all the lands they rule.
29 The earth quakes and trembles
because the LORD's intentions against Babylon
stand:
to make the land of Babylon a desolation,
without inhabitant.
30 Babylon's warriors have stopped fighting;
they sit in their strongholds.
Their might is exhausted;
they have become like women.
Babylon's homes have been set ablaze,
her gate bars are shattered.
31 Messenger races to meet messenger,
and herald to meet herald,
to announce to the king of Babylon
that his city has been captured
from end to end.
32 The fords have been seized,
the marshes set on fire,
and the fighting men are terrified.

33 For this is what the LORD of Armies, the God of
Israel, says:
Daughter Babylon is like a threshing floor
at the time it is trampled.
In just a little while her harvest time
will come.

34 "King Nebuchadnezzar of Babylon
has devoured me;
he has crushed me.
He has set me aside like an empty dish;
he has swallowed me
like a sea monster;
he filled his belly with my delicacies;
he has vomited me out.[C]
35 Let the violence done to me and my family
be done to Babylon,"
says the inhabitant of Zion.
"Let my blood be on the inhabitants
of Chaldea,"
says Jerusalem.

36 Therefore, this is what the LORD says:
I am about to champion your cause
and take vengeance on your behalf;
I will dry up her sea
and make her fountain run dry.
37 Babylon will become a heap of rubble,
a jackals' den,
a desolation and an object of scorn,
without inhabitant.
38 They will roar together like young lions;
they will growl like lion cubs.
39 While they are flushed with heat,
I will serve them a feast,
and I will make them drunk so that
they celebrate.[D]
Then they will fall asleep forever
and never wake up.
This is the LORD's declaration.
40 I will bring them down like lambs
to the slaughter,
like rams together with male goats.

[A] **51:23** Lit *yoke* [B] **51:27** Hb obscure [C] **51:34** Lit *has rinsed me off*
[D] **51:39** LXX reads *pass out*

41 How Sheshak[A] has been captured,
the praise of the whole earth seized.
What a horror Babylon has become
among the nations!
42 The sea has risen over Babylon;
she is covered with its tumultuous waves.
43 Her cities have become a desolation,
an arid desert,
a land where no one lives,
where no human being even passes through.
44 I will punish Bel in Babylon.
I will make him vomit what he swallowed.
The nations will no longer stream to him;
even Babylon's wall will fall.

45 Come out from among her, my people!
Save your lives, each of you,
from the LORD's burning anger.
46 May you not become cowardly and fearful
when the report is proclaimed
in the land,
for the report will come one year,
and then another the next year.
There will be violence in the land
with ruler against ruler.
47 Therefore, look, the days are coming
when I will punish Babylon's carved images.
Her entire land will suffer shame,
and all her slain will lie fallen within her.
48 Heaven and earth and everything in them
will shout for joy over Babylon
because the destroyers from the north
will come against her.
This is the LORD's declaration.

49 Babylon must fall because of the slain
of Israel,
even as the slain of the whole earth fell
because of Babylon.
50 You who have escaped the sword,
go and do not stand still!
Remember the LORD from far away,
and let Jerusalem come to your mind.

51 We are ashamed
because we have heard insults.
Humiliation covers our faces
because foreigners have entered
the holy places of the LORD's temple.

52 Therefore, look, the days are coming —
this is the LORD's declaration —
when I will punish her carved images,
and the wounded will groan
throughout her land.
53 Even if Babylon should ascend
to the heavens
and fortify her tall fortresses,
destroyers will come against her from me.
This is the LORD's declaration.

54 The sound of a cry from Babylon!
The sound of terrible destruction
from the land of the Chaldeans!
55 For the LORD is going to devastate Babylon;
he will silence her mighty voice.
Their waves roar like a huge torrent;
the tumult of their voice resounds,
56 for a destroyer is coming against her,
against Babylon.
Her warriors will be captured,
their bows shattered,
for the LORD is a God of retribution;
he will certainly repay.
57 I will make her princes and sages drunk,
along with her governors, officials,
and warriors.
Then they will fall asleep forever
and never wake up.
This is the King's declaration;
the LORD of Armies is his name.

58 This is what the LORD of Armies says:
Babylon's thick walls will be
totally demolished,
and her high gates set ablaze.
The peoples will have labored for nothing;
the nations will weary themselves only to feed
the fire.

59 This is what the prophet Jeremiah commanded
Seraiah son of Neriah son of Mahseiah, the quartermaster, when he went to Babylon with King Zedekiah
of Judah in the fourth year of Zedekiah's reign. 60 Jeremiah wrote on one scroll about all the disaster that
would come to Babylon; all these words were written
against Babylon.
61 Jeremiah told Seraiah, "When you get to Babylon,
see that you read all these words aloud. 62 Say, 'LORD,
you have threatened to cut off this place so that no
one will live in it — people or animals. Indeed, it will
remain desolate forever.' 63 When you have finished
reading this scroll, tie a stone to it and throw it into
the middle of the Euphrates River. 64 Then say, 'In the
same way, Babylon will sink and never rise again
because of the disaster I am bringing on her. They
will grow weary.' "
The words of Jeremiah end here.

[A] **51:41** = Babylon

THE FALL OF JERUSALEM

52 Zedekiah was twenty-one years old when he became king, and he reigned eleven years in Jerusalem. His mother's name was Hamutal daughter of Jeremiah; she was from Libnah. 2 Zedekiah did what was evil in the LORD's sight just as Jehoiakim had done. 3 Because of the LORD's anger, it came to the point in Jerusalem and Judah that he finally banished them from his presence. Then Zedekiah rebelled against the king of Babylon.

4 In the ninth year of Zedekiah's reign, on the tenth day of the tenth month, King Nebuchadnezzar of Babylon advanced against Jerusalem with his entire army. They laid siege to the city and built a siege wall against it all around. 5 The city was under siege until King Zedekiah's eleventh year.

6 By the ninth day of the fourth month the famine was so severe in the city that the common people had no food. 7 Then the city was broken into, and all the warriors fled. They left the city at night by way of the city gate between the two walls near the king's garden, though the Chaldeans surrounded the city. They made their way along the route to the Arabah. 8 The Chaldean army pursued the king and overtook Zedekiah in the plains of Jericho. Zedekiah's entire army left him and scattered. 9 The Chaldeans seized the king and brought him to the king of Babylon at Riblah in the land of Hamath, and he passed sentence on him.

10 At Riblah the king of Babylon slaughtered Zedekiah's sons before his eyes, and he also slaughtered the Judean commanders. 11 Then he blinded Zedekiah and bound him with bronze chains. The king of Babylon brought Zedekiah to Babylon, where he kept him in custody[A] until his dying day.

12 On the tenth day of the fifth month — which was the nineteenth year of King Nebuchadnezzar, king of Babylon — Nebuzaradan, the captain of the guards, entered Jerusalem as the representative of[B] the king of Babylon. 13 He burned the LORD's temple, the king's palace, all the houses of Jerusalem; he burned down all the great houses. 14 The whole Chaldean army with the captain of the guards tore down all the walls surrounding Jerusalem. 15 Nebuzaradan, the captain of the guards, deported some of the poorest of the people, as well as the rest of the people who remained in the city, the deserters who had defected to the king of Babylon, and the rest of the craftsmen. 16 But Nebuzaradan, the captain of the guards, left some of the poorest of the land to be vinedressers and farmers.

17 Now the Chaldeans broke into pieces the bronze pillars for the LORD's temple and the water carts and the bronze basin[C] that were in the LORD's temple, and they carried all the bronze to Babylon. 18 They also took the pots, shovels, wick trimmers, sprinkling basins, dishes, and all the bronze articles used in the temple service. 19 The captain of the guards took away the bowls, firepans, sprinkling basins, pots, lampstands, pans, and drink offering bowls — whatever was gold or silver.

20 As for the two pillars, the one basin, with the twelve bronze oxen under it, and the water carts[D] that King Solomon had made for the LORD's temple, the weight of the bronze of all these articles was beyond measure. 21 One pillar was 27 feet[E] tall, had a circumference of 18 feet,[F] was hollow — four fingers thick — 22 and had a bronze capital on top of it. One capital, encircled by bronze grating and pomegranates, stood 7 1/2 feet[G] high. The second pillar was the same, with pomegranates. 23 Each capital had ninety-six pomegranates all around it. All the pomegranates around the grating numbered one hundred.

24 The captain of the guards also took away Seraiah the chief priest, Zephaniah the priest of the second rank, and the three doorkeepers. 25 From the city he took a court official[H] who had been appointed over the warriors; seven trusted royal aides[I] found in the city; the secretary of the commander of the army, who enlisted the people of the land for military duty; and sixty men from the common people[J] who were found within the city. 26 Nebuzaradan, the captain of the guards, took them and brought them to the king of Babylon at Riblah. 27 The king of Babylon put them to death at Riblah in the land of Hamath. So Judah went into exile from its land.

28 These are the people Nebuchadnezzar deported: in the seventh year, 3,023 Jews; 29 in his eighteenth year,[K] 832 people from Jerusalem; 30 in Nebuchadnezzar's twenty-third year, Nebuzaradan, the captain of the guards, deported 745 Jews. Altogether, 4,600 people were deported.

JEHOIACHIN PARDONED

31 On the twenty-fifth day of the twelfth month of the thirty-seventh year of the exile of Judah's King Jehoiachin, King Evil-merodach of Babylon, in the first year of his reign, pardoned King Jehoiachin of Judah and released him from prison. 32 He spoke kindly to him and set his throne above the thrones of the kings who were with him in Babylon. 33 So Jehoiachin changed his prison clothes, and he dined regularly in the presence of the king of Babylon for the rest of his life. 34 As for his allowance, a regular allowance was given to him by the king of Babylon, a portion for each day until the day of his death, for the rest of his life.

[A] **52:11** Lit *in a house of guards* [B] **52:12** Lit *Jerusalem; he stood before* [C] **52:17** Lit *sea* [D] **52:20** LXX, Syr; MT reads *oxen under the water carts* [E] **52:21** Lit *18 cubits* [F] **52:21** Lit *12 cubits* [G] **52:22** Lit *five cubits* [H] **52:25** Or *a eunuch* [I] **52:25** Lit *seven men who look on the king's face* [J] **52:25** Lit *the people of the land* [K] **52:29** Some Hb mss, Syr add *he deported*

LAMENTATIONS

Reconstruction of the Coptic Hall at the Monastery of Jeremiah in Saqqara, Egypt, dating sixth century AD.

INTRODUCTION TO

LAMENTATIONS

Circumstances of Writing

Jeremiah's name has long been associated with this book. The Alexandrian form of the Greek Septuagint has these words preceding Jeremiah 1:1: "And it came to pass, after Israel had been carried away captive, and Jerusalem became desolate, that Jeremiah sat weeping, and lamented with this lamentation over Jerusalem." The Latin Vulgate adds this phrase: "and with a sorrowful mind, sighing and moaning, he said." The Talmud observes that "Jeremiah wrote his own book and the book of Kings and Lamentations." Given this rich tradition linking Jeremiah to Lamentations, it seems safe to conclude he did indeed write this book.

The sad background for these five poems of lament was the sacking of Jerusalem and the burning of the temple in 587 BC by the Babylonian army. Even though the book lists only one proper name ("Edom"; 4:21–22), the allusions and the historical connections to the events listed so dramatically in 2 Kings 25; 2 Chronicles 36:11–21; and the book of Jeremiah are unmistakable.

Contribution to the Bible

Few things contrast religious and humanistic traditions more than their respective responses to suffering. The humanist sees suffering as a bare, impersonal event without ultimate meaning or purpose. For believers, suffering is a personal problem because they believe that all events of history are under the hand of a personal God. And if that is true, then how can God's love and justice be reconciled with our pain?

Lamentations gives no easy answers to this question, but it helps us meet God in the midst of our suffering and teaches us the language of prayer. Instead of offering a set of techniques, easy answers, or inspiring slogans for facing pain and grief, Lamentations supplies: (1) an orientation, (2) a voice for working through grief from "A" to "Z," (3) instruction on how and what to pray, and (4) a focal point on the faithfulness of God and the affirmation that he alone is our portion.

Structure

The book of Lamentations exhibits a remarkably fine artistic structure. Each of its five chapters (five poems) is a structurally unified text. The fact that there is an uneven number of poems allows the middle poem (chap. 3) to be the midpoint of the book. Thus, there is an ascent (or crescendo) up to a fixed climax for the entire book, thereby making chapter 3 central in its form and the message it imparts. Accordingly, the first two chapters form the steps leading up to the climax of 3:22–24, and from here there is a descent in chapters 4 and 5.

The poems or songs of this book also exhibit the so-called acrostic form (a crisscross inversion such as a-b, b-a). As such, chapters 1 and 5 are overall summaries of the disaster, 2 and 4 are more detailed descriptions of what took place, and chapter 3 occupies the central position.

Lamentations also uses the form of the alphabetic acrostic with the twenty-two-letter Hebrew alphabet. In chapter 5, each of its twenty-two stanzas consists of a single line, but this is the only chapter that is not in an alphabetic acrostic. Chapter 3 is the most structured of the five poems.

LAMENT OVER JERUSALEM

א Aleph

1 How[A] she sits alone,
the city once crowded with people!
She who was great among the nations
has become like a widow.
The princess among the provinces
has been put to forced labor.

ב Beth

2 She weeps bitterly during the night,
with tears on her cheeks.
There is no one to offer her comfort,
not one from all her lovers.[B]
All her friends have betrayed her;
they have become her enemies.

ג Gimel

3 Judah has gone into exile
following[C] affliction and harsh slavery;
she lives among the nations
but finds no place to rest.
All her pursuers have overtaken her
in narrow places.

ד Daleth

4 The roads to Zion mourn,
for no one comes to the appointed festivals.
All her gates are deserted;
her priests groan,
her young women grieve,
and she herself is bitter.

ה He

5 Her adversaries have become her masters;
her enemies are at ease,
for the LORD has made her suffer
because of her many transgressions.
Her children have gone away
as captives before the adversary.

ו Waw

6 All the splendor has vanished
from Daughter Zion.
Her leaders are like stags
that find no pasture;
they stumble away exhausted
before the hunter.

ז Zayin

7 During the days of her affliction
and homelessness
Jerusalem remembers all
her precious belongings
that were hers in days of old.
When her people fell into the adversary's hand,
she had no one to help.
The adversaries looked at her,
laughing over her downfall.

ח Cheth

8 Jerusalem has sinned grievously;
therefore, she has become an object of scorn.[D]
All who honored her now despise her,
for they have seen her nakedness.
She herself groans and turns away.

ט Teth

9 Her uncleanness stains her skirts.
She never considered her end.
Her downfall was astonishing;
there was no one to comfort her.
LORD, look on my affliction,
for the enemy boasts.

י Yod

10 The adversary has seized
all her precious belongings.
She has even seen the nations
enter her sanctuary —
those you had forbidden
to enter your assembly.

כ Kaph

11 All her people groan
while they search for bread.
They have traded their precious belongings
for food
in order to stay alive.
LORD, look and see
how I have become despised.

ל Lamed

12 Is this nothing to you, all you who pass by?
Look and see!
Is there any pain like mine,
which was dealt out to me,
which the LORD made me suffer
on the day of his burning anger?

מ Mem

13 He sent fire from on high into my bones;
he made it descend.[E]
He spread a net for my feet
and turned me back.
He made me desolate,
sick all day long.

[A]**1:1** The stanzas in Lm 1–4 form an acrostic. [B]**1:2** = Jerusalem's political allies [C]**1:3** Or *because of* [D]**1:8** Or *become impure*
[E]**1:13** DSS, LXX; MT reads *bones, and it prevailed against them*

Lamentations: Its Historical and Literary Context

by E. Ray Clendenen

Control of Judah had changed from Assyria to Egypt in 609 BC, then to Babylon in 605 BC. Made bold by the near defeat of the Babylonians by Pharaoh Neco II in 601, the vassal Judean king rebelled and suffered the punitive actions of King Nebuchadnezzar in 597 BC. Besides looting the city, the Babylonians deported the king, his family, and thousands of officials and leading citizens to Babylon, and installed a puppet king (2Kg 23:28–24:17). Encouraged, perhaps, by news of a Jewish rebellion (unsuccessful) in Babylon in 595/594 BC (Jr 29) and by anti-Babylonian sentiment in surrounding provinces, rebellion broke out again in Judah in 589, supported by Egypt. A Babylonian army was quickly dispatched, which captured and burned the surviving towns in Judah, and, after a lengthy and severe siege, captured Jerusalem in July of 587 or 586 BC.[1] The puppet king Zedekiah was deported to Babylon where he soon died. His sons and many of the Jewish officials were executed, Jerusalem and the Jewish temple were looted and destroyed, and several hundred more citizens were deported (2Kg 24:18–25:21; 2Ch 36:3–21; Jr 37:1–39:10; 52:1–30).

No longer a monarchy, Judah became a province of the Babylonian Empire, administered from a new capital at Mizpah by a Jewish governor, Gedaliah, who had served under Zedekiah. After an unspecified time, however, Gedaliah was assassinated along with some Babylonian soldiers by a surviving member of the royal family. As a result, there was another deportation of several hundred in 582 BC, a number of Jews fled to Egypt, and Judah may have become part of the province of Samaria (Jr 39:11–44:30).

Both literary and archaeological evidence points to severe devastation and depopulation in the sixth century BC (cf. Lm 2:2,5,11–12,20–22; 4:9–20; 5:1–18). The texts indicate that thousands of men had been deported. Though the total according to Jeremiah 52:28–30 is given as forty-six hundred, Edwin Yamauchi suggests that this may have counted only nobles, since Kings gives the figure of eighteen thousand men (excluding their families) for 597 BC alone.[2] Jews are known to have settled in various towns in Egypt (Tahpanhes/Tell Defenneh, Migdol/Tell Kedua, Noph/Memphis, Patros, and the island of Elephantine, called Sinim/Syene in Is 49:12; Ezk 29:10; 30:6) and throughout the eastern Mediterranean.[3]

Scholars debate how extensively the population of Judah was reduced before and after 586 BC. According to Ezra-Nehemiah,

Black granite block from a foundation deposit of a temple of Neco II (610–595 BC), with Neco's names and titles inscribed on four sides.

the number returning over some period of time was 42,360 (Ezr 2:64; Neh 7:66), yet we know that many remained in Babylon. In addition to those deported, thousands had certainly died in battle or of starvation and disease; many were executed, and many had fled. According to John Bright, "Nebuchadnezzar's army left Judah a shambles," with archaeological evidence that "all, or virtually all, of the fortified towns in the heartland of Judah were razed to the ground." His estimated population of 250,000 in Judah in the eighth century was reduced to "scarcely above 20,000 even after the first exiles had returned."[4] Ephraim Stern essentially confirms Bright's evaluation of the situation in Judah, with a decrease in population due to slaughter, deportation, pestilence, flight, and resultant total economic collapse. . . . So rudimentary must this existence have been that it has proved extremely difficult to find traces in the material remains. Of the destroyed cities and towns, many ceased to exist entirely; others were inhabited by poorer elements, who must have salvaged material for their shelters from the rubble.[5]

Oded Lipschits estimates a population decrease from about 108,000 before 586 BC to about 30,125 in the fifth century.[6] B. E. Kelle summarizes that "the Judean experience of exile was a severe and traumatic personal, social and psychological event."[7]

The extent of the physical destruction helps us understand why the Jews mourned Jerusalem's demise. "The city once crowded with people" that was "great among the nations," now sat alone weeping bitterly "like a widow." Once a "princess," she had been "put to forced labor" with "no one to offer her comfort" (Lm 1:1–2). The author of Lamentations, whom Jewish tradition identifies as Jeremiah, uses a genre at least as old as the second millennium BC Sumerian laments over the cities of Ur, Nippur, Eridu, and Uruk. The theology of the book, however, is vastly different. Contrary to the polytheistic context of Sumerian laments, our author makes it clear that Yahweh is the ultimate agent of Jerusalem's fall, which was made necessary by his own righteousness and Israel's sinful violation of its covenant with him.[8] God had "thrown down Israel's glory" (2:1), had "swallowed up" their dwellings and "demolished" their cities (2:2). It was ultimately not the Babylonians but the Lord who had "destroyed and shattered" her gates (2:9) and even "wrecked his temple as if it were merely a shack in a field" (2:6). Also unlike the Sumerian laments, there is no plea here for God to return and bless his city. What brings hope to his personally devastated people is the knowledge of the Lord's faithful love and mercy, which never end (3:22). When everything else is taken away, like Job, the Lord's people can say, "The Lord is my portion, therefore I will put my hope in him" (3:24). ✣

---

[1] The precise date depends upon whether Judah was following at the time a calendar beginning in the spring or fall. [2] Edwin M. Yamauchi, "The Archaeological Background of Ezra," *Bibliotheca Sacra* (*BSac*) 137 (1980): 196. [3] Peter van der Veen, "Sixth-Century Issues," in *Ancient Israel's History: An Introduction to Issues and Sources*, ed. Bill T. Arnold and Richard S. Hess (Grand Rapids: Baker, 2014), 385. [4] John Bright, *A History of Israel*, 3rd ed. (Philadelphia: Westminster, 1981), 344. [5] Ephraim Stern, *Archaeology of the Land of the Bible, vol. 2: The Assyrian, Babylonian, and Persian Periods (732–332 BCE)* (New York: Doubleday, 2001), 323. [6] Oded Lipschits, "Demographic Changes in Judah between the Seventh and the Fifth Centuries BCE," in *Judah and the Judeans in the Neo-Babylonian Period*, ed. O. Lipschits and J. Blenkinsopp (Winona Lake, IN: Eisenbrauns, 2003), 363–66. [7] B. E. Kelle, "Israelite History" in *Dictionary of Old Testament Prophets*, ed. Mark J. Boda and J. Gordon McConville (Downers Grove, IL: InterVarsity, 2012), 413. [8] See John H. Walton, *Ancient Israelite Literature in Its Cultural Context* (Grand Rapids: Zondervan, 1989), 160–63.

נ Nun

14 My transgressions have been formed
into a yoke,[A,B]
fastened together by his hand;
they have been placed on my neck,
and the Lord has broken my strength.
He has handed me over
to those I cannot withstand.

ס Samek

15 The Lord has rejected
all the mighty men within me.
He has summoned an army[C] against me
to crush my young warriors.
The Lord has trampled
Virgin Daughter Judah
like grapes in a winepress.

ע Ayin

16 I weep because of these things;
my eyes flow[D] with tears.
For there is no one nearby to comfort me,
no one to keep me alive.
My children are desolate
because the enemy has prevailed.

פ Pe

17 Zion stretches out her hands;
there is no one to comfort her.
The LORD has issued a decree against Jacob
that his neighbors should be his adversaries.
Jerusalem has become
something impure among them.

צ Tsade

18 The LORD is just,
for I have rebelled against his command.
Listen, all you people;
look at my pain.
My young women and young men
have gone into captivity.

ק Qoph

19 I called to my lovers,
but they betrayed me.
My priests and elders
perished in the city
while searching for food
to keep themselves alive.

ר Resh

20 LORD, see how I am in distress.
I am churning within;
my heart is broken,[E]
for I have been very rebellious.
Outside, the sword takes the children;
inside, there is death.

שׁ Shin

21 People have heard me groaning,
but there is no one to comfort me.
All my enemies have heard of my misfortune;
they are glad that you have caused it.
Bring on the day you have announced,
so that they may become like me.

ת Taw

22 Let all their wickedness come before you,
and deal with them
as you have dealt with me
because of all my transgressions.
For my groans are many,
and I am sick at heart.

JUDGMENT ON JERUSALEM

א Aleph

2 How the Lord has overshadowed
Daughter Zion with his anger!
He has thrown down Israel's glory
from heaven to earth.
He did not acknowledge his footstool
in the day of his anger.

ב Beth

2 Without compassion the Lord has swallowed up
all the dwellings of Jacob.
In his wrath he has demolished
the fortified cities of Daughter Judah.
He brought them to the ground
and defiled the kingdom and its leaders.

ג Gimel

3 He has cut off every horn of Israel
in his burning anger
and withdrawn his right hand
in the presence of the enemy.
He has blazed against Jacob like a flaming fire
that consumes everything.

ד Daleth

4 He has strung his bow like an enemy;
his right hand is positioned like an adversary.
He has killed everyone who was the delight to
the eye,
pouring out his wrath like fire
on the tent of Daughter Zion.

[A] **1:14** Some Hb mss, LXX read *He kept watch over my transgressions*
[B] **1:14** Or *The yoke of my transgressions is bound*; Hb obscure
[C] **1:15** Or *has announced an appointed time* [D] **1:16** Lit *my eye, my eye flows* [E] **1:20** Lit *is turned within me*

ה He

5 The Lord is like an enemy;
he has swallowed up Israel.
He swallowed up all its palaces
and destroyed its fortified cities.
He has multiplied mourning and lamentation
within Daughter Judah.

ו Waw

6 He has wrecked his temple[A]
as if it were merely a shack in a field,[B]
destroying his place of meeting.
The LORD has abolished
appointed festivals and Sabbaths in Zion.
He has despised king and priest
in his fierce anger.

ז Zayin

7 The Lord has rejected his altar,
repudiated his sanctuary;
he has handed the walls of her palaces
over to the enemy.
They have raised a shout in the house
of the LORD
as on the day of an appointed festival.

ח Cheth

8 The LORD determined to destroy
the wall of Daughter Zion.
He stretched out a measuring line
and did not restrain himself from destroying.
He made the ramparts and walls grieve;
together they waste away.

ט Teth

9 Zion's gates have fallen to the ground;
he has destroyed and shattered the bars
on her gates.
Her king and her leaders live
among the nations,
instruction[C] is no more,
and even her prophets receive
no vision from the LORD.

י Yod

10 The elders of Daughter Zion
sit on the ground in silence.
They have thrown dust on their heads
and put on sackcloth.
The young women of Jerusalem
have bowed their heads to the ground.

כ Kaph

11 My eyes are worn out from weeping;
I am churning within.
My heart is poured out in grief[D]
because of the destruction of my dear people,
because infants and nursing babies faint
in the streets of the city.

ל Lamed

12 They cry out to their mothers,
"Where is the grain and wine?"
as they faint like the wounded
in the streets of the city,
as their life pours out
in the arms of their mothers.

מ Mem

13 What can I say on your behalf?
What can I compare you to,
Daughter Jerusalem?
What can I liken you to,
so that I may console you,
Virgin Daughter Zion?
For your ruin is as vast as the sea.
Who can heal you?

נ Nun

14 Your prophets saw visions for you
that were empty and deceptive;[E]
they did not reveal your iniquity
and so restore your fortunes.
They saw pronouncements for you
that were empty and misleading.

ס Samek

15 All who pass by
scornfully clap their hands at you.
They hiss and shake their heads
at Daughter Jerusalem:
Is this the city that was called
the perfection of beauty,
the joy of the whole earth?

פ Pe

16 All your enemies
open their mouths against you.
They hiss and gnash their teeth,
saying, "We have swallowed her up.
This is the day we have waited for!
We have lived to see it."

ע Ayin

17 The LORD has done what he planned;
he has accomplished his decree,
which he ordained in days of old.

[A]2:6 Lit *booth* [B]2:6 Lit *it were a garden* [C]2:9 Or *the law*
[D]2:11 Lit *My liver is poured out on the ground* [E]2:14 Or *insipid*

He has demolished without compassion,
letting the enemy gloat over you
and exalting the horn of your adversaries.

צ Tsade

18 The hearts of the people cry out to the Lord.
Wall of Daughter Zion,
let your tears run down like a river
day and night.
Give yourself no relief
and your[A] eyes no rest.

ק Qoph

19 Arise, cry out in the night
from the first watch of the night.
Pour out your heart like water
before the Lord's presence.
Lift up your hands to him
for the lives of your children
who are fainting from hunger
at the head of every street.

ר Resh

20 LORD, look and consider
to whom you have done this.
Should women eat their own children,
the infants they have nurtured?[B]
Should priests and prophets
be killed in the Lord's sanctuary?

ש Shin

21 Both young and old
are lying on the ground in the streets.
My young women and young men
have fallen by the sword.
You have killed them in the day of your anger,
slaughtering without compassion.

ת Taw

22 You summon those who terrorize me[C]
on every side,
as if for an appointed festival day;
on the day of the LORD's anger
no one escaped or survived.
My enemy has destroyed
those I nurtured[D] and reared.

HOPE THROUGH GOD'S MERCY

א Aleph

3 I am the man who has seen affliction
under the rod of God's wrath.
2 He has driven me away and forced me to walk
in darkness instead of light.
3 Yes, he repeatedly turns his hand
against me all day long.

ב Beth

4 He has worn away my flesh and skin;
he has broken my bones.
5 He has laid siege against me,
encircling me with bitterness and hardship.
6 He has made me dwell in darkness
like those who have been dead for ages.

ג Gimel

7 He has walled me in so I cannot get out;
he has weighed me down with chains.
8 Even when I cry out and plead for help,
he blocks out my prayer.
9 He has walled in my ways with blocks of stone;
he has made my paths crooked.

ד Daleth

10 He is[E] a bear waiting in ambush,
a lion in hiding.
11 He forced me off my way and tore me
to pieces;
he left me desolate.
12 He strung his bow
and set me as the target for his arrow.

ה He

13 He pierced my kidneys
with shafts from his quiver.
14 I am a laughingstock to all my people,[F]
mocked by their songs all day long.
15 He filled me with bitterness,
satiated me with wormwood.

ו Waw

16 He ground my teeth with gravel
and made me cower[G] in the dust.
17 I have been deprived[H] of peace;
I have forgotten what prosperity is.
18 Then I thought, "My future[I] is lost,
as well as my hope from the LORD."

ז Zayin

19 Remember[J] my affliction
and my homelessness,
the wormwood and the poison.
20 I continually remember them
and have become depressed.[K]
21 Yet I call this to mind,
and therefore I have hope:

[A]**2:18** Lit *and the daughter of your* [B]**2:20** Or *infants in a healthy condition*; Hb obscure [C]**2:22** Or *terrors* [D]**2:22** Or *I bore healthy*; Hb obscure [E]**3:10** Lit *is to me* [F]**3:14** Some Hb mss, LXX, Vg; other Hb mss, Syr read *all peoples* [G]**3:16** Or *and trampled me* [H]**3:17** Syr, Vg; MT reads *You deprived my soul* [I]**3:18** Or *splendor* [J]**3:19** Or *I remember* [K]**3:20** Alt Hb tradition reads *and you cause me to collapse*

ח Cheth

22 Because of the LORD's faithful love
we do not perish,[A]
for his mercies never end.
23 They are new every morning;
great is your faithfulness!
24 I say, "The LORD is my portion,
therefore I will put my hope in him."

ט Teth

25 The LORD is good to those who wait for him,
to the person who seeks him.
26 It is good to wait quietly
for salvation from the LORD.
27 It is good for a man to bear the yoke
while he is still young.

י Yod

28 Let him sit alone and be silent,
for God has disciplined[B] him.
29 Let him put his mouth in the dust —
perhaps there is still hope.
30 Let him offer his cheek
to the one who would strike him;
let him be filled with disgrace.

כ Kaph

31 For the Lord
will not reject us forever.
32 Even if he causes suffering,
he will show compassion
according to the abundance of his faithful love.
33 For he does not enjoy bringing affliction
or suffering on mankind.

ל Lamed

34 Crushing all the prisoners of the land[C]
beneath one's feet,
35 denying justice to a man
in the presence of the Most High,
36 or subverting a person in his lawsuit —
the Lord does not approve of these things.

מ Mem

37 Who is there who speaks and it happens,
unless the Lord has ordained it?
38 Do not both adversity and good
come from the mouth of the Most High?
39 Why should any living person complain,
any man, because of the punishment
for his sins?

נ Nun

40 Let's examine and probe our ways,
and turn back to the LORD.
41 Let's lift up our hearts and our hands
to God in heaven:
42 "We have sinned and rebelled;
you have not forgiven.

ס Samek

43 "You have covered yourself in anger
and pursued us;
you have killed without compassion.
44 You have covered yourself with a cloud
so that no prayer can get through.
45 You have made us disgusting filth
among the peoples.

פ Pe

46 "All our enemies
open their mouths against us.
47 We have experienced panic and pitfall,
devastation and destruction."
48 My eyes flow with streams of tears
because of the destruction of my dear people.

ע Ayin

49 My eyes overflow unceasingly,
without end,
50 until the LORD looks down
from heaven and sees.
51 My eyes bring me grief
because of the fate of all the women in my city.

צ Tsade

52 For no reason, my enemies[D]
hunted me like a bird.
53 They smothered my life in[E] a pit
and threw stones on me.
54 Water flooded over my head,
and I thought, "I'm going to die!"

ק Qoph

55 I called on your name, LORD,
from the depths of the pit.
56 You heard my plea:
Do not ignore my cry for relief.
57 You came near whenever I called you;
you said, "Do not be afraid."

ר Resh

58 You championed my cause, Lord;
you redeemed my life.
59 LORD, you saw the wrong done to me;
judge my case.

[A] **3:22** One Hb mss, Syr, Tg read *The LORD's faithful love, indeed, does not perish* [B] **3:28** Lit *has laid a burden on* [C] **3:34** Or *earth* [D] **3:52** Or *Those who were my enemies for no reason* [E] **3:53** Or *They ended my life in*; Hb obscure

60 You saw all their vengefulness,
all their plots against me.

ש Sin / ש Shin

61 LORD, you heard their insults,
all their plots against me.
62 The slander[A] and murmuring of my opponents
attack me all day long.
63 When they sit and when they rise, look,
I am mocked by their songs.

ת Taw

64 You will pay them back what they deserve, LORD,
according to the work of their hands.
65 You will give them a heart filled with anguish.[B]
May your curse be on them!
66 You will pursue them in anger and destroy them
under your heavens.[C]

TERRORS OF THE BESIEGED CITY

א Aleph

4 How the gold has become tarnished,
the fine gold become dull!
The stones of the temple[D] lie scattered
at the head of every street.

ב Beth

2 Zion's precious children —
once worth their weight in pure gold —
how they are regarded as clay jars,
the work of a potter's hands!

ג Gimel

3 Even jackals offer their breasts
to nurse their young,
but my dear people have become cruel
like ostriches in the wilderness.

ד Daleth

4 The nursing baby's tongue
clings to the roof of his mouth from thirst.
Infants beg for food,
but no one gives them any.

ה He

5 Those who used to eat delicacies
are destitute in the streets;
those who were reared in purple garments
huddle in trash heaps.

ו Waw

6 The punishment of my dear people
is greater than that of Sodom,
which was overthrown in an instant
without a hand laid on it.

ז Zayin

7 Her dignitaries were brighter than snow,
whiter than milk;
their bodies[E] were more ruddy than coral,
their appearance like lapis lazuli.

ח Cheth

8 Now they appear darker than soot;
they are not recognized in the streets.
Their skin has shriveled on their bones;
it has become dry like wood.

ט Teth

9 Those slain by the sword are better off
than those slain by hunger,
who waste away, pierced with pain
because the fields lack produce.

י Yod

10 The hands of compassionate women
have cooked their own children;
they became their food
during the destruction of my dear people.

כ Kaph

11 The LORD has exhausted his wrath,
poured out his burning anger;
he has ignited a fire in Zion,
and it has consumed her foundations.

ל Lamed

12 The kings of the earth
and all the world's inhabitants did not believe
that an enemy or adversary
could enter Jerusalem's gates.

מ Mem

13 Yet it happened because of the sins
of her prophets
and the iniquities of her priests,
who shed the blood of the righteous
within her.

נ Nun

14 Blind, they stumbled in the streets,
defiled by this blood,
so that no one dared
to touch their garments.

ס Samek

15 "Stay away! Unclean!" people shouted at them.
"Away, away! Don't touch us!"

[A] **3:62** Lit *lips* [B] **3:65** Or *them an obstinate heart*; Hb obscure
[C] **3:66** Lit *under the LORD's heavens* [D] **4:1** Or *The sacred gems*
[E] **4:7** Lit *bones*

So they wandered aimlessly.
It was said among the nations,
"They can stay here no longer."

פ Pe

16 The LORD himself has scattered them;
he no longer watches over them.
The priests are not respected;
the elders find no favor.

ע Ayin

17 All the while our eyes were failing
as we looked in vain for help;
we watched from our towers
for a nation that would not save us.

צ Tsade

18 Our steps were closely followed
so that we could not walk
in our streets.
Our end approached; our time ran out.
Our end had come!

ק Qoph

19 Those who chased us were swifter
than eagles in the sky;
they relentlessly pursued us
over the mountains
and ambushed us in the wilderness.

ר Resh

20 The LORD's anointed, the breath
of our life,[A]
was captured in their traps.
We had said about him,
"We will live under his protection
among the nations."

שׂ Sin

21 So rejoice and be glad, Daughter Edom,
you resident of the land of Uz!
Yet the cup will pass to you as well;
you will get drunk and expose yourself.

ת Taw

22 Daughter Zion, your punishment
is complete;
he will not lengthen your exile.[B]
But he will punish your iniquity,
Daughter Edom,
and will expose your sins.

PRAYER FOR RESTORATION

5 LORD, remember what has happened to us.
Look, and see our disgrace!
2 Our inheritance has been turned over
to strangers,
our houses to foreigners.
3 We have become orphans, fatherless;
our mothers are widows.
4 We must pay for the water we drink;
our wood comes at a price.
5 We are closely pursued;
we are tired, and no one offers us rest.
6 We made a treaty with[C] Egypt
and with Assyria, to get enough food.
7 Our ancestors sinned; they no longer exist,
but we bear their punishment.
8 Slaves rule over us;
no one rescues us from them.
9 We secure our food at the risk of our lives
because of the sword in the wilderness.
10 Our skin is as hot[D] as an oven
from the ravages of hunger.
11 Women have been raped in Zion,
virgins in the cities of Judah.
12 Princes have been hung up by their hands;
elders are shown no respect.
13 Young men labor at millstones;
boys stumble under loads of wood.
14 The elders have left the city gate,
the young men, their music.
15 Joy has left our hearts;
our dancing has turned to mourning.
16 The crown has fallen from our head.
Woe to us, for we have sinned.
17 Because of this, our heart is sick;
because of these, our eyes grow dim:
18 because of Mount Zion, which lies desolate
and has jackals prowling in it.
19 You, LORD, are enthroned forever;
your throne endures from generation
to generation.
20 Why do you continually forget us,
abandon us for our entire lives?
21 LORD, bring us back to yourself, so we
may return;
renew our days as in former times,
22 unless you have completely rejected us
and are intensely angry with us.

[A] **4:20** Lit *nostrils* [B] **4:22** Or *not deport you again* [C] **5:6** Lit *We gave the hand to* [D] **5:10** Or *black*; Hb obscure

EZEKIEL

In the foreground is the watchtower at Gamla. Ezekiel, like a watchman, was to warn the people of God of pending danger.

INTRODUCTION TO

EZEKIEL

Circumstances of Writing

There is sufficient reason for maintaining that the prophet Ezekiel composed the book of Ezekiel in Babylon. The work demonstrates such homogeneity and literary coherence that it is reasonable to conclude that all editorial work was done by the prophet himself.

The inclusion of historical dates at the beginning of many of the oracles and prophecies in Ezekiel is another important unifying factor. The book is one of the most chronologically ordered books of the Bible. Thirteen times a passage is introduced by an indication of time. The common point of orientation for the dates given in Ezekiel is the exile of King Jehoiachin of Judah in 598/597 BC. The occurrence of visions throughout the book (chaps. 1; 8–11; 40–48) is another strong argument in favor of its overall unity. Finally, stylistic features throughout the book strengthen the unity argument.

Ezekiel, son of Buzi, was among the approximately ten thousand citizens of Judah deported to Babylon when King Nebuchadnezzar invaded Jerusalem in 598/597 BC (2Kg 24:10–17). His prophetic call came to him five years later (the fifth year of King Jehoiachin's exile), in 593 BC. He received his call at the age of thirty (Ezk 1:1), the year he should have begun his duties as a priest (Nm 4:3). The last dated oracle in the book occurs in the twenty-seventh year of King Jehoiachin (Ezk 29:17), thus indicating that Ezekiel's ministry lasted twenty-two or twenty-three years. The prophet lived during the greatest crisis in Israel's history—the destruction of Jerusalem and its temple, plus the exile of Judah's leading citizens to Babylon.

Contribution to the Bible

There are few quotations of the book of Ezekiel in the New Testament, but there are some notable correlations. For instance, the structure of the book of Revelation, which begins with a vision of Christ, corresponds to the appearances of God in Ezekiel's visions. The end of the book of Revelation also reflects the end of Ezekiel, where the river flows from the presence of God (Ezk 47:1–12; Rv 21:1–22:6). Finally, the depiction of the return of the exiles as resurrected from the dead is analogous to Paul's concept of regeneration (Eph 2:5).

Structure

The prophet Ezekiel displayed a distinct style throughout his prophetic work. The phrase "son of man" occurs ninety-three times as a title for Ezekiel, focusing on the prophet's human nature. The expression "the hand of the Lord was on me," which is said elsewhere only of Elijah (1Kg 18:46) and Elisha (2Kg 3:15), occurs in the various major sections of Ezekiel (1:3; 3:22; 33:22; 37:1). The so-called recognition formula, that "you (or they) may know that I am the Lord," a characteristic phrase of the exodus narrative (Ex 6:6–8; 7:5; 10:1–2; 14:4,18), occurs about sixty times in Ezekiel. The introductory oracle phrase "the word of the Lord came to me" occurs forty-six times in the book and alerts the reader to the beginning of a separate section. The phrase "I, the Lord, have spoken" also occurs frequently in Ezekiel. Another feature for which Ezekiel is well known is his performance of symbolic, dramatic actions. He also used the literary technique of allegory to communicate his prophecies. His allegories include Jerusalem as a vine (chap. 15) and majestic eagles (17:1–21), the Davidic dynasty as a lioness (19:1–9) and a vineyard (19:10–14), a sword as judgment (21:1–17), and Samaria and Jerusalem as Oholah and Oholibah, the corrupt sisters (23:1–35).

A final characteristic of the book is the citation of previously written Scripture in Ezekiel's prophecies. This is evident in the judgment oracles of chapters 4–5 that depend heavily on the curses listed in Leviticus 26.

Ezekiel and Jeremiah: A Comparison

by Kevin C. Peacock

Jeremiah was about twenty years Ezekiel's senior. But as contemporaries, each with a life-changing call from God to be a prophet to his people and to the foreign nations, their messages had great harmony. They preached on many of the same subjects, though often with different emphases. They both wrote on individual responsibility (Jr 31:27–30; Ezk 18:1–32; 33:7–20), the destruction of the Jerusalem temple (Jr 7:1–15; 26:1–24; Ezk 1–24), and a new covenant resulting in a new heart and new spirit (though the term *new covenant* is only in Jr 31:31, and the terms *new heart* and *new spirit* are only in Ezk 18:31; 36:26; see Jr 24:7; 31:31–34; 32:38–40; Ezk 11:19–20; 36:26–27). These similarities do not mean, however, that God simply called the same type of person to deliver these messages. Each prophet had a unique background, personality, and giftedness with which to deliver God's message.

BACKGROUND

Jeremiah's ministry began "in the thirteenth year" of Josiah's reign (627 BC) and extended into the exile to about 580 BC, a ministry of about forty-seven years (Jr 1:1–3; 40–44).[1] He was "a youth" at the time of his call (1:6), probably about eighteen to twenty years of age.[2] He ministered in and around Jerusalem, while apparently continuing to live in Anathoth, his hometown, located about three miles northeast of Jerusalem (11:21; 12:6; 32:7). He was, therefore, an eyewitness to the fall of Jerusalem.

The Babylonians took Ezekiel from Jerusalem into exile in 597 BC along with Judah's King Jehoiachin and ten thousand captives (2Kg 24:10–14). He began his ministry "in the thirtieth year," which probably refers to his age, which was when priests normally began their ministry (Ezk 1:1; see Nm 4:30). His visionary call came in "the fifth year of King Jehoiachin's exile" (Ezk 1:1–2), which was about 593 BC (assuming a spring new year).[3] So Ezekiel would have been born around 623 BC and taken into captivity at age twenty-five or twenty-six, four or five years before his call from God. In his early years, Ezekiel may have heard Jeremiah's preaching, because Jeremiah had caused quite a stir in the city.

The two prophets could have known each other, since they both had priestly backgrounds, though from different families. Jeremiah

Incantation bowl from Nippur, Iraq, with quotations from Ezekiel 21 and Jeremiah 2 in Hebrew. People wrote spells on the inside and outside of such bowls to ward off evil spirits or to imprison those who came near.

Torah scroll from a sixteenth-century-AD Spanish synagogue in the city of Zafed. When God called Ezekiel, he instructed the prophet to eat the scroll, which had writing on both front and back.

was "the son of Hilkiah, one of the priests living in Anathoth in the territory of Benjamin" (Jr 1:1). His priestly lineage probably came from Abiathar, David's priest whom Solomon banished to Anathoth (1Kg 1:7; 2:26–27), thus descended through Eli back to Aaron's son Ithamar.[4] Ezekiel was a priest, son of Buzi (Ezk 1:3). His familiarity with the Jerusalem temple's layout, correct and aberrant worship forms, Israel's spiritual heritage, and Levitical and priestly issues indicates that even as a young man before the exile, Ezekiel was at least a priest in training, preparing to serve in the Jerusalem temple. Ezekiel's interest in the Zadokite priests (44:15–31) may indicate that his descent was from Zadok back to Aaron's son Eleazar (1Ch 6:3–15; 24:3).[5]

Although expecting to be installed as a priest in his thirtieth year, Ezekiel received a call from God to be a prophet. The family life of both prophets became a vital part of their messages. The Lord never allowed Jeremiah to marry (Jr 16:1–4). His life was to display the loneliness and lack of joy his people would soon experience. Although Ezekiel, on the other hand, was happily married, the death of his beloved wife coincided with the fall of Jerusalem (Ezk 24:15–27). God did not allow Ezekiel to express his grief publicly, emulating the inconsolable sorrow the people would soon experience as their beloved city fell and their loved ones died.

PERSONALITY AND STYLE

Jeremiah's messages of God's judgment filled him with agony and grief (Jr 8:18–22). A series of prayers known as his "confessions" displays his personal struggles with God about his lot in life and the messages he was to preach.[6]

Ironically, even though almost all of Ezekiel's prophetic oracles are written in first person, seldom do they display his personal thoughts and reactions.[7] For the most part, he accepted his divine assignments without any protest, even though they took their physical and emotional toll.[8] Unlike Jeremiah, Ezekiel's response was not to complain, but instead to see these difficult assignments as God's call to make himself totally available to him, "to place himself and all that he [had and was] at the service of God's cause."[9]

Visions from God were not uncommon for prophets, and Jeremiah had a few (Jr 1:11–14); Ezekiel's visions were numerous, long, and expanded.[10] Ezekiel did not just see the vision; he became part of it. He personally ate the scroll offered to him (Ezk 3:2–3); God personally transported Ezekiel from one place to another (3:12–15; 8:3–4; 37:1;

40:1–3); he walked through the old temple (chap. 8) and also the new (chaps. 40–42); he also walked through the valley of dry bones (37:2), and there he delivered God's word (11:4; 37:4,9). His powerful prophecy brought death (11:13) and caused life (37:7–10).

Both prophets accompanied their messages with symbolic actions, but dramatic actions and visual aids were far more frequent in Ezekiel's ministry. He would face the recipients of his message,[11] clap his hands, and stomp his feet to heighten the impact (6:11; 21:14). Other prophets used images and figures of speech; Ezekiel had actual experiences. Jeremiah said of God's words, "Your words were found, and I ate them. Your words became a delight to me and the joy of my heart" (Jr 15:16), but, for Ezekiel, God's words became a meal (Ezk 3:2–3). Isaiah pictured God's judgment like a razor that would shave the head, body, and beard of his people (Is 7:20), but Ezekiel got a literal haircut (Ezk 5:1–2).

MINISTRY AND MESSAGE

Jeremiah faced open hostility throughout much of his ministry. Although Ezekiel's audience was stubborn (3:4–11), he did not face hatred and open resistance. The elders of the community consulted with him (8:1; 14:1; 20:1), and the people flocked to hear him after his prophecies about the fall of Jerusalem came true (33:30–33).

Generally speaking, the two major influences on Jeremiah's preaching were the life and ministry of Hosea[12] and the newly discovered law scroll of Deuteronomy.[13] Ezekiel's messages were also infused with two major influences: the messages of Jeremiah and the book of Leviticus. For thirty years, Jeremiah had been preaching in Jerusalem, causing quite a stir, including the first twenty-five years of Ezekiel's life. Many of Jeremiah's prophecies had circulated in writing before and during the exile (Jr 29:1–20), and communication seemed to have flowed freely, which kept the exiles informed of happenings back in Judah. But Ezekiel was also greatly influenced by his priestly heritage and by the book of Leviticus. He was intensely interested in Levitical and priestly concerns, such as sacrifices, the Israelite worship system, regulations concerning ceremonial purity, and the temple.

Jeremiah denounced the corrupt worship practices and defiled temple and announced God's plan to destroy the temple (7:1–15; 26:1–24). Ezekiel saw God's intention to destroy the corrupted and polluted temple, but, beyond the destruction, Ezekiel envisioned the Jerusalem temple rebuilt and worship restored in purity and holiness (Ezk 40–48). ✜

---

[1] Leon J. Wood, *The Prophets of Israel* (Grand Rapids: Baker, 1979), 329–30. [2] See Douglas R. Jones, *Jeremiah*, New Century Bible Commentary (Grand Rapids: Eerdmans, 1992), 70. [3] Daniel I. Block, *The Book of Ezekiel Chapters 1–24*, NICOT (1997), 83. [4] See 1Sm 14:3; 22:20; 1Kg 2:27; 1Ch 24:6. See John Bright, *Jeremiah*, AB, lxxxvii–lxxxviii, for a fuller explanation. [5] Block, *Ezekiel 1–24*, 88. See R. Laird Harris, "Zadok, Zadokites" in *HIBD*, 1698–99, for Zadok's lineage. [6] Jeremiah 11:18–12:6; 15:10–21; 17:14–18; 18:18–23; 20:7–13,14–18. [7] Ezekiel 4:14; 9:8; 11:13; 20:49; 24:20; 37:3. See Block, *Ezekiel 1–24*, 27–30 for a fuller discussion. [8] Ezekiel 1:28; 3:14–15; 12:17–20; 21:6; 24:16,27. Ezekiel was struck speechless several times (3:15; 24:25–27; 33:21–22). [9] Walther Eichrodt, *Ezekiel: A Commentary*, OTL (1970), 25–26. [10] Ezekiel 1–3; 8–11; 37; 40–48. [11] Toward the false prophets (Ezk 13:17), Jerusalem (21:2), Ammon (25:2), Sidon (28:21), Pharaoh in Egypt (29:2), the mountains of Seir (35:2), and Gog (38:2). [12] J. A. Thompson, *The Book of Jeremiah*, NICOT (1980), 81–85. [13] R. K. Harrison, *Jeremiah & Lamentations*, TOTC (1973), 38.

number of days you lie on your side, 390 days. 10 The food you eat each day will weigh eight ounces;[A] you will eat it at set times.[B] 11 You will also drink a ration of water, a sixth of a gallon,[C] which you will drink at set times. 12 You will eat it as you would a barley cake and bake it over dried human excrement in their sight." 13 The LORD said, "This is how the Israelites will eat their bread — ceremonially unclean — among the nations where I will banish them."

14 But I said, "Oh, Lord GOD, I have never been defiled. From my youth until now I have not eaten anything that died naturally or was mauled by wild beasts. And impure meat has never entered my mouth."

15 He replied to me, "Look, I will let you use cow dung instead of human excrement, and you can make your bread over that." 16 He said to me, "Son of man, I am going to cut off the supply of bread in Jerusalem. They will anxiously eat food they have weighed out and in dread drink rationed water 17 for lack of bread and water. Everyone will be devastated and waste away because of their iniquity.

EZEKIEL DRAMATIZES JERUSALEM'S FALL

5 "Now you, son of man, take a sharp sword, use it as you would a barber's razor, and shave your head and beard. Then take a set of scales and divide the hair. 2 You are to burn a third of it in the city when the days of the siege have ended; you are to take a third and slash it with the sword all around the city; and you are to scatter a third to the wind, for I will draw a sword to chase after them. 3 But you are to take a few strands from the hair and secure them in the folds of your robe. 4 Take some more of them, throw them into the fire, and burn them in it. A fire will spread from it to the whole house of Israel.

5 "This is what the Lord GOD says: I have set this Jerusalem in the center of the nations, with countries all around her. 6 She has rebelled against my ordinances with more wickedness than the nations, and against my statutes more than the countries that surround her. For her people have rejected my ordinances and have not walked in my statutes.

7 "Therefore, this is what the Lord GOD says: Because you have been more insubordinate than the nations around you — you have not walked in my statutes or kept my ordinances; you have not even kept the ordinances of the nations around you — 8 therefore, this is what the Lord GOD says: See, I myself am against you, Jerusalem, and I will execute judgments within you in the sight of the nations. 9 Because of all your detestable practices, I will do to you what I have never done before and what I will never do again. 10 As a result, fathers will eat their sons within Jerusalem,[D] and sons will eat their fathers. I will execute judgments against you and scatter all your survivors to every direction of the wind.

11 "Therefore, as I live" — this is the declaration of the Lord GOD — "I will withdraw and show you no pity, because you have defiled my sanctuary with all your abhorrent acts and detestable practices. Yes, I will not spare you. 12 A third of your people will die by plague and be consumed by famine within you; a third will fall by the sword all around you; and I will scatter a third to every direction of the wind, and I will draw a sword to chase after them. 13 When my anger is spent and I have vented my wrath on them, I will be appeased. Then after I have spent my wrath on them, they will know that I, the LORD, have spoken in my jealousy.

14 "I will make you a ruin and a disgrace among the nations around you, in the sight of everyone who passes by. 15 So you[E] will be a disgrace and a taunt, a warning and a horror, to the nations around you when I execute judgments against you in anger, wrath, and furious rebukes. I, the LORD, have spoken. 16 When I shoot deadly arrows of famine at them, arrows for destruction that I will send to destroy you, inhabitants of Jerusalem, I will intensify the famine against you and cut off your supply of bread. 17 I will send famine and dangerous animals against you. They will leave you childless. Plague and bloodshed will sweep through you, and I will bring a sword against you. I, the LORD, have spoken."

PROPHECY AGAINST ISRAEL'S IDOLATRY

6 The word of the LORD came to me: 2 "Son of man, face the mountains of Israel and prophesy against them. 3 You are to say: Mountains of Israel, hear the word of the Lord GOD! This is what the Lord GOD says to the mountains and the hills, to the ravines and the valleys: I am about to bring a sword against you, and I will destroy your high places. 4 Your altars will be desolated and your shrines[F] smashed. I will throw down your slain in front of your idols. 5 I will lay the corpses of the Israelites in front of their idols and scatter your bones around your altars. 6 Wherever you live the cities will be in ruins and the high places will be desolate, so that your altars will lie in ruins and be desecrated,[G] your idols smashed and obliterated, your shrines cut down, and what you have made wiped out. 7 The slain will fall among you, and you will know that I am the LORD.

8 "Yet I will leave a remnant when you are scattered among the nations, for throughout the countries there will be some of you who will escape the sword. 9 Then your survivors will remember me

[A] **4:10** Lit *20 shekels* [B] **4:10** Lit *from time to time*, also in v. 11 [C] **4:11** Lit *hin* [D] **5:10** Lit *you* [E] **5:15** DSS, LXX, Syr, Tg, Vg; MT reads *she* [F] **6:4** Or *incense altars*, also in v. 6 [G] **6:6** Hb obscure

among the nations where they are taken captive,
how I was crushed by their promiscuous hearts that
turned away from me and by their eyes that lusted
after their idols. They will loathe themselves because
of the evil things they did, their detestable actions of
every kind. 10 And they will know that I am the LORD;
I did not threaten to bring this disaster on them without a reason.

LAMENT OVER THE FALL OF JERUSALEM

11 "This is what the Lord GOD says: Clap your hands,
stamp your feet, and cry out over all the evil and
detestable practices of the house of Israel, who will
fall by the sword, famine, and plague. 12 The one who
is far off will die by plague; the one who is near will
fall by the sword; and the one who remains and is
spared[A] will die of famine. In this way I will exhaust
my wrath on them. 13 You will all know that I am the
LORD when their slain lie among their idols around
their altars, on every high hill, on all the mountaintops, and under every green tree and every leafy oak
— the places where they offered pleasing aromas
to all their idols. 14 I will stretch out my hand against
them, and wherever they live I will make the land a
desolate waste, from the wilderness to Riblah.[B] Then
they will know that I am the LORD."

ANNOUNCEMENT OF THE END

7 The word of the LORD came to me: 2 "Son of man,
this is what the Lord GOD says to the land of Israel:
An end! The end has come
on the four corners of the earth.
3 The end is now upon you;
I will send my anger against you
and judge you according to your ways.
I will punish you for all your detestable practices.
4 I will not look on you with pity or spare you,
but I will punish you for your ways
and for your detestable practices within you.
Then you will know that I am the LORD."

5 This is what the Lord GOD says:
Look, one disaster after another is coming!
6 An end has come; the end has come!
It has awakened against you.
Look, it is coming!
7 Doom[C] has come on you,
inhabitants of the land.
The time has come; the day is near.
There will be panic on the mountains
and not celebration.

8 I will pour out my wrath on you very soon;
I will exhaust my anger against you
and judge you according to your ways.
I will punish you for all your
detestable practices.
9 I will not look on you with pity or spare you.
I will punish you for your ways
and for your detestable practices within you.
Then you will know
that it is I, the LORD, who strikes.

10 Here is the day! Here it comes!
Doom is on its way.
The rod has blossomed;
arrogance has bloomed.
11 Violence has grown into a rod of wickedness.
None of them will remain:
none of that crowd,
none of their wealth,
and none of the eminent[D] among them.

12 The time has come; the day has arrived.
Let the buyer not rejoice
and the seller not mourn,
for wrath is on her whole crowd.
13 The seller will certainly not return
to what was sold
as long as he and the buyer remain alive.[E]
For the vision concerning her whole crowd
will not be revoked,
and because of the iniquity of each one,
none will preserve his life.

14 They have blown the trumpet
and prepared everything,
but no one goes to war,
for my wrath is on her whole crowd.
15 The sword is on the outside;
plague and famine are on the inside.
Whoever is in the field will die by the sword,
and famine and plague will devour
whoever is in the city.

16 The survivors among them will escape
and live on the mountains.
Like doves of the valley,
all of them will moan,
each over his own iniquity.
17 All their hands will become weak,
and all their knees will run with urine.[F]
18 They will put on sackcloth,
and horror will overwhelm them.
Shame will cover all their faces,
and all their heads will be bald.

[A] **6:12** Or *besieged* [B] **6:14** Some Hb mss, some LXX mss; other Hb mss read *Diblah*; 2Kg 23:33; Jr 39:5 [C] **7:7** Or *A leash*; Hb obscure, also in v. 10 [D] **7:11** Some Hb mss, Syr, Vg read *and no rest* [E] **7:13** Lit *sold, while still in life is their life* [F] **7:17** Lit *knees will go water*

19 They will throw their silver into the streets,
and their gold will seem like something filthy.
Their silver and gold will be unable
to save them
in the day of the LORD's wrath.
They will not satisfy their appetites
or fill their stomachs,
for these were the stumbling blocks
that brought about their iniquity.

20 He appointed his beautiful ornaments
for majesty,
but[A] they made their detestable images
from them,
their abhorrent things.
Therefore, I have made these
into something filthy to them.
21 I will hand these things over
to foreigners as plunder
and to the wicked of the earth as spoil,
and they will profane them.
22 I will turn my face from them
as they profane my treasured place.
Violent men will enter it and profane it.

23 Forge the chain,
for the land is filled with crimes of bloodshed,
and the city is filled with violence.
24 So I will bring the most evil of nations
to take possession of their houses.
I will put an end to the pride of the strong,
and their sacred places will be profaned.
25 Anguish is coming!
They will look for peace,
but there will be none.
26 Disaster after disaster will come,
and there will be rumor after rumor.
Then they will look for a vision
from a prophet,
but instruction will perish from the priests
and counsel from the elders.
27 The king will mourn;
the prince will be clothed in grief;
and the hands of the people of the land
will tremble.
I will deal with them according to
their own conduct,
and I will judge them by their own standards.
Then they will know that I am the LORD.

VISIONARY JOURNEY TO JERUSALEM

8 In the sixth year, in the sixth month, on the fifth
day of the month, I was sitting in my house and
the elders of Judah were sitting in front of me, and
there the hand of the Lord GOD came down on me.
2 I looked, and there was someone who looked like a
man.[B] From what seemed to be his waist down was
fire, and from his waist up was something that looked
bright, like the gleam of amber. 3 He stretched out
what appeared to be a hand and took me by the hair
of my head. Then the Spirit lifted me up between
earth and heaven and carried me in visions of God
to Jerusalem, to the entrance of the inner gate that
faces north, where the offensive statue that provokes
jealousy was located. 4 I saw the glory of the God of
Israel there, like the vision I had seen in the plain.

PAGAN PRACTICES IN THE TEMPLE

5 The LORD said to me, "Son of man, look toward the
north." I looked to the north, and there was this offensive statue north of the Altar Gate, at the entrance.
6 He said to me, "Son of man, do you see what they are
doing here — more detestable acts that the house of
Israel is committing — so that I must depart from my
sanctuary? You will see even more detestable acts."
7 Then he brought me to the entrance of the court,
and when I looked there was a hole in the wall. 8 He
said to me, "Son of man, dig through the wall." So I
dug through the wall and discovered a doorway. 9 He
said to me, "Go in and see the detestable, wicked acts
they are committing here."
10 I went in and looked, and there engraved all
around the wall was every kind of abhorrent thing
— crawling creatures and beasts — as well as all the
idols of the house of Israel. 11 Seventy elders from the
house of Israel were standing before them, with Jaazaniah son of Shaphan standing among them. Each
had a firepan in his hand, and a fragrant cloud of
incense was rising up. 12 He said to me, "Son of man,
do you see what the elders of the house of Israel are
doing in the darkness, each at the shrine of his idol?
For they are saying, 'The LORD does not see us. The
LORD has abandoned the land.' " 13 Again he said to
me, "You will see even more detestable acts that they
are committing."
14 Then he brought me to the entrance of the north
gate of the LORD's house, and I saw women sitting
there weeping for Tammuz. 15 And he said to me, "Do
you see this, son of man? You will see even more detestable acts than these."
16 So he brought me to the inner court of the LORD's
house, and there were about twenty-five men at the
entrance of the LORD's temple, between the portico
and the altar, with their backs to the LORD's temple
and their faces turned to the east. They were bowing
to the east in worship of the sun. 17 And he said to me,
"Do you see this, son of man? Is it not enough for the

[A] **7:20** Or *They turned their beautiful ornaments into objects of pride, and* [B] **8:2** LXX; MT, Vg read *like fire*

house of Judah to commit the detestable acts they are doing here, that they must also fill the land with violence and repeatedly anger me, even putting the branch to their nose?[A] 18 Therefore I will respond with wrath. I will not show pity or spare them. Though they call loudly in my hearing, I will not listen to them."

VISION OF SLAUGHTER IN JERUSALEM

9 Then he called loudly in my hearing, "Come near, executioners of the city, each of you with a destructive weapon in his hand." 2 And I saw six men coming from the direction of the Upper Gate, which faces north, each with a war club in his hand. There was another man among them, clothed in linen, carrying writing equipment. They came and stood beside the bronze altar.

3 Then the glory of the God of Israel rose from above the cherub where it had been, to the threshold of the temple. He called to the man clothed in linen and carrying writing equipment. 4 "Pass throughout the city of Jerusalem," the LORD said to him, "and put a mark on the foreheads of the men who sigh and groan over all the detestable practices committed in it."

5 He spoke to the others in my hearing: "Pass through the city after him and start killing; do not show pity or spare them! 6 Slaughter the old men, the young men and women, as well as the children and older women, but do not come near anyone who has the mark. Begin at my sanctuary." So they began with the elders who were in front of the temple. 7 Then he said to them, "Defile the temple and fill the courts with the slain. Go!" So they went out killing people in the city.

8 While they were killing, I was left alone. And I fell facedown and cried out, "Oh, Lord GOD! Are you going to destroy the entire remnant of Israel when you pour out your wrath on Jerusalem?"

9 He answered me, "The iniquity of the house of Israel and Judah is extremely great; the land is full of bloodshed, and the city full of perversity. For they say, 'The LORD has abandoned the land; he does not see.' 10 But as for me, I will not show pity or spare them. I will bring their conduct down on their own heads."

11 Then the man clothed in linen and carrying writing equipment reported back, "I have done all that you commanded me."

GOD'S GLORY LEAVES THE TEMPLE

10 Then I looked, and there above the expanse over the heads of the cherubim was something like a throne with the appearance of lapis lazuli. 2 The LORD spoke to the man clothed in linen and said, "Go inside the wheelwork beneath the cherubim. Fill your hands with blazing coals from among the cherubim and scatter them over the city." So he went in as I watched.

3 Now the cherubim were standing to the south of the temple when the man went in, and the cloud filled the inner court. 4 Then the glory of the LORD rose from above the cherub to the threshold of the temple. The temple was filled with the cloud, and the court was filled with the brightness of the LORD's glory. 5 The sound of the cherubim's wings could be heard as far as the outer court; it was like the voice of God Almighty when he speaks.

6 After the LORD commanded the man clothed in linen, saying, "Take fire from inside the wheelwork, from among the cherubim," the man went in and stood beside a wheel. 7 Then the cherub reached out his hand to the fire that was among them. He took some and put it into the hands of the man clothed in linen, who took it and went out. 8 The cherubim appeared to have the form of human hands under their wings.

9 I looked, and there were four wheels beside the cherubim, one wheel beside each cherub. The luster of the wheels was like the gleam of beryl. 10 In appearance, all four looked alike, like a wheel within a wheel. 11 When they moved, they would go in any of the four directions, without pivoting as they moved. But wherever the head faced, they would go in that direction, without pivoting as they went. 12 Their entire bodies, including their backs, hands, wings, and the wheels that the four of them had, were full of eyes all around. 13 As I listened the wheels were called "the wheelwork." 14 Each one had four faces: one was the face of a cherub, the second the face of a human, the third the face of a lion, and the fourth the face of an eagle.

15 The cherubim ascended; these were the living creatures I had seen by the Chebar Canal. 16 When the cherubim moved, the wheels moved beside them, and when they lifted their wings to rise from the earth, even then the wheels did not veer away from them. 17 When the cherubim stopped, the wheels stood still, and when they ascended, the wheels ascended with them, for the spirit of the living creatures was in them.

18 Then the glory of the LORD moved away from the threshold of the temple and stopped above the cherubim. 19 The cherubim lifted their wings and ascended from the earth right before my eyes; the wheels were beside them as they went. The glory of the God of Israel was above them, and it stopped at the entrance to the eastern gate of the LORD's house.

20 These were the living creatures I had seen beneath the God of Israel by the Chebar Canal, and I

[A] **8:17** Alt Hb tradition reads *my nose*

Ezekiel: His Call and Message

by Harold R. Mosley

Few Christians can recount anything about the man Ezekiel or his book. Why is Ezekiel so often overlooked? Part of the reason may lie in the unusual forms in the book. Ezekiel's visions, actions, and seemingly his personality were not the "normal" variety found among the prophets. Practically nothing about the man or his book seems "ordinary." Rather, the book of Ezekiel leans toward the extraordinary. The unusual nature of the prophecy causes some interpreters to avoid the book altogether, while other interpreters engage in endless speculation about its meaning. Even early Jewish interpreters, aware of the difficulties of the book, warned against reading some sections outside the presence of one skilled in its explanation.[1]

The first thing the reader of Ezekiel is faced with is the

Replica of a winged human-headed bull. The original was part of the palace courtyard of Assyria's King Sargon II, in Khorsabad. Sargon II (see Is 20:1) ruled 722–705 BC and likely resettled many of the Israelite captives in Assyria.

extraordinary language of Ezekiel's inaugural vision, which echoes Isaiah's temple vision in Isaiah 6. Both portray God seated on his throne. Isaiah's account of what he saw, however, is much clearer than is Ezekiel's, who related his vision in mysterious language difficult to understand. What he saw almost defied the ability of language to describe, much as we would be challenged to describe in words a beautiful sunset, with its variations of colors and the array of the clouds. Such was Ezekiel's vision. The prophet could not describe fully the impact of what he saw. Thus, scattered throughout the chapter, we find the repetition of "something like," "appearance," "form," "shape," and "seemed." He tried to describe a vision that was indescribable.

But the difficulty facing the reader of Ezekiel's visions in chapters 1 and 10 is only partly due to the prophet's inability to describe God's glory in human terms. Another problem lies in the particular imagery of the visions. Ezekiel saw four "living creatures" in the first vision, each beside "a wheel within a wheel" (Ezk 1:5–16). The wheels were "full of eyes" (1:18; 10:12). The creatures are identified in the second vision with four cherubim (10:1–22). The creatures were hybrid or composite beings, each with four faces: a man, a lion, an ox, and an eagle (1:10) and a cherub, a man, a lion, and an eagle (10:14). Each creature also had human hands and wings and feet like a calf. Are the creatures symbolic of something beyond the vision itself? Are they actual beings from the heavenly realm? What is the point of the vision?

Understanding Ezekiel's Babylonian context can help in interpreting the vision. Ezekiel was a captive in Babylon (1:3). As such, he knew Mesopotamian culture. God used imagery (somewhat) familiar to Ezekiel and his immediate audience. God condescends to our level of understanding by employing elements from our experience. Statues of composite beasts had long been a feature of Mesopotamian history. In Babylonian lore, part-beast/part-human creatures signified divine presence.[2] These statues often consisted of the head of the king, the body of a lion or bull, and the wings of an eagle. The statues were intended to denote the power and authority of the kingdom as well as the supposed gods' protection of the kingdom.

The living creatures of Ezekiel's vision gave the impression of mystery and power, but that was not the point of the vision. As powerful and awe-inspiring as they were, the living creatures were still creatures. Human kingdoms may appear to be powerful because of military or economic dominance, but they are still human entities. Ezekiel's vision emphasized the frailty of creation, for separated from and high above the creatures was God's throne (1:26; 10:1). The essential focus of the vision is not the creatures but the God who is above everything. God's power is never threatened by human kingdoms. Even though Ezekiel lived among an exiled people, God was still in control. This was important for Ezekiel to know since God called him to minister to a defeated and discouraged people. Isaiah, Jeremiah, and Daniel also emphasized God's control of human history. Isaiah 10:5–19 depicts the militarily powerful Assyria as nothing more than a rod in the hand of God to discipline his people. Jeremiah 29:4 has God reminding the nation that "I deported [them] from Jerusalem to Babylon." In Daniel 2, the interpretation of Nebuchadnezzar's dream revealed God's kingdom will crush all human kingdoms. Each of these prophecies was originally spoken when human kingdoms dominated Israel. ✜

---

[1] Mishnah Hagigah 2:1. The call vision of Ezekiel 1 was of specific concern for the rabbis. [2] See Bruce Vawter and Leslie J. Hoppe, *A New Heart: A Commentary on the Book of Ezekiel* (Grand Rapids: Eerdmans, 1991), 26–27.

recognized that they were cherubim. 21 Each had four faces and each had four wings, with what looked something like human hands under their wings. 22 Their faces looked like the same faces I had seen by the Chebar Canal. Each creature went straight ahead.

VISION OF ISRAEL'S CORRUPT LEADERS

11 The Spirit then lifted me up and brought me to the eastern gate of the LORD's house, which faces east, and at the gate's entrance were twenty-five men. Among them I saw Jaazaniah son of Azzur, and Pelatiah son of Benaiah, leaders of the people. 2 The LORD[A] said to me, "Son of man, these are the men who plot evil and give wicked advice in this city. 3 They are saying, 'Isn't the time near to build houses?[B] The city is the pot, and we are the meat.' 4 Therefore, prophesy against them. Prophesy, son of man!"

5 Then the Spirit of the LORD came on me, and he told me, "You are to say, 'This is what the LORD says: That is what you are thinking, house of Israel; and I know the thoughts that arise in your mind. 6 You have multiplied your slain in this city, filling its streets with them.

7 " 'Therefore, this is what the Lord GOD says: The slain you have put within it are the meat, and the city is the pot, but I[C] will take you out of it. 8 You fear the sword, so I will bring the sword against you. This is the declaration of the Lord GOD. 9 I will take you out of the city and hand you over to foreigners; I will execute judgments against you. 10 You will fall by the sword, and I will judge you at the border of Israel. Then you will know that I am the LORD. 11 The city will not be a pot for you, and you will not be the meat within it. I will judge you at the border of Israel, 12 so you will know that I am the LORD, whose statutes you have not followed and whose ordinances you have not practiced. Instead, you have acted according to the ordinances of the nations around you.' "

13 Now while I was prophesying, Pelatiah son of Benaiah died. Then I fell facedown and cried out loudly, "Oh, Lord GOD! You are bringing the remnant of Israel to an end!"

PROMISE OF ISRAEL'S RESTORATION

14 The word of the LORD came to me again: 15 "Son of man, your own relatives, those who have the right to redeem your property,[D,E] along with the entire house of Israel — all of them — are those to whom the residents of Jerusalem have said, 'You are far from the LORD; this land has been given to us as a possession.'

16 "Therefore say, 'This is what the Lord GOD says: Though I sent them far away among the nations and scattered them among the countries, yet for a little while I have been a sanctuary for them in the countries where they have gone.'

17 "Therefore say, 'This is what the Lord GOD says: I will gather you from the peoples and assemble you from the countries where you have been scattered, and I will give you the land of Israel.'

18 "When they arrive there, they will remove all its abhorrent acts and detestable practices from it. 19 I will give them integrity of[F] heart and put a new spirit within them; I will remove their heart of stone from their bodies[G] and give them a heart of flesh, 20 so that they will follow my statutes, keep my ordinances, and practice them. They will be my people, and I will be their God. 21 But as for those whose hearts pursue their desire for abhorrent acts and detestable practices, I will bring their conduct down on their own heads." This is the declaration of the Lord GOD.

GOD'S GLORY LEAVES JERUSALEM

22 Then the cherubim, with the wheels beside them, lifted their wings, and the glory of the God of Israel was above them. 23 The glory of the LORD rose up from within the city and stopped on the mountain east of the city.[H] 24 The Spirit lifted me up and brought me to Chaldea and to the exiles in a vision from the Spirit of God. After the vision I had seen left me, 25 I spoke to the exiles about all the things the LORD had shown me.

EZEKIEL DRAMATIZES THE EXILE

12 The word of the LORD came to me: 2 "Son of man, you are living among a rebellious house. They have eyes to see but do not see, and ears to hear but do not hear, for they are a rebellious house.

3 "Now you, son of man, get your bags ready for exile and go into exile in their sight during the day. You will go into exile from your place to another place while they watch; perhaps they will understand, though they are a rebellious house. 4 During the day, bring out your bags like an exile's bags while they look on. Then in the evening go out in their sight like those going into exile. 5 As they watch, dig through the wall and take the bags out through it. 6 And while they look on, lift the bags to your shoulder and take them out in the dark; cover your face so that you cannot see the land. For I have made you a sign to the house of Israel."

7 So I did just as I was commanded. In the daytime I brought out my bags like an exile's bags. In the evening I dug through the wall by hand; I took them out in the dark, carrying them on my shoulder in their sight.

[A] **11:2** Lit *He* [B] **11:3** Or *"The time is not near to build houses.*
[C] **11:7** Some Hb mss, LXX, Syr, Tg, Vg; other Hb mss read *he*
[D] **11:15** LXX, Syr read *your relatives, your fellow exiles* [E] **11:15** Or *own brothers, your relatives* [F] **11:19** Lit *give them one* [G] **11:19** Lit *flesh*
[H] **11:23** = the Mount of Olives

8 In the morning the word of the LORD came to me: 9 "Son of man, hasn't the house of Israel, that rebellious house, asked you, 'What are you doing?' 10 Say to them, 'This is what the Lord GOD says: This pronouncement concerns the prince[A] in Jerusalem and the whole house of Israel living there.'[B] 11 You are to say, 'I am a sign for you. Just as I have done, it will be done to them; they will go into exile, into captivity.' 12 The prince who is among them will lift his bags to his shoulder in the dark and go out. They[C] will dig through the wall to bring him out through it. He will cover his face so he cannot see the land with his eyes. 13 But I will spread my net over him, and he will be caught in my snare. I will bring him to Babylon, the land of the Chaldeans, yet he will not see it, and he will die there. 14 I will also scatter all the attendants who surround him and all his troops to every direction of the wind, and I will draw a sword to chase after them. 15 They will know that I am the LORD when I disperse them among the nations and scatter them among the countries. 16 But I will spare a few of them from the sword, famine, and plague, so that among the nations where they go they can tell about all their detestable practices. Then they will know that I am the LORD."

EZEKIEL DRAMATIZES ISRAEL'S ANXIETY

17 The word of the LORD came to me: 18 "Son of man, eat your bread with trembling and drink your water with anxious shaking. 19 Then say to the people of the land, 'This is what the Lord GOD says about the residents of Jerusalem in the land of Israel: They will eat their bread with anxiety and drink their water in dread, for their[D,E] land will be stripped of everything in it because of the violence of all who live there. 20 The inhabited cities will be destroyed, and the land will become dreadful. Then you will know that I am the LORD.'"

A DECEPTIVE PROVERB STOPPED

21 Again the word of the LORD came to me: 22 "Son of man, what is this proverb you people have about the land of Israel, which goes, 'The days keep passing by, and every vision fails'? 23 Therefore say to them, 'This is what the Lord GOD says: I will put a stop to this proverb, and they will not use it again in Israel.' But say to them, 'The days have arrived, as well as the fulfillment of every vision. 24 For there will no longer be any false vision or flattering divination within the house of Israel. 25 But I, the LORD, will speak whatever message I will speak, and it will be done. It will no longer be delayed. For in your days, rebellious house, I will speak a message and bring it to pass. This is the declaration of the Lord GOD.'"

26 The word of the LORD came to me: 27 "Son of man, notice that the house of Israel is saying, 'The vision that he sees concerns many years from now; he prophesies about distant times.' 28 Therefore say to them, 'This is what the Lord GOD says: None of my words will be delayed any longer. The message I speak will be fulfilled. This is the declaration of the Lord GOD.'"

ISRAEL'S FALSE PROPHETS CONDEMNED

13 The word of the LORD came to me: 2 "Son of man, prophesy against the prophets of Israel who are prophesying. Say to those who prophesy out of their own imagination, 'Hear the word of the LORD! 3 This is what the Lord GOD says: Woe to the foolish prophets who follow their own spirit and have seen nothing. 4 Your prophets, Israel, are like jackals among ruins. 5 You did not go up to the gaps or restore the wall around the house of Israel so that it might stand in battle on the day of the LORD. 6 They saw false visions and their divinations were a lie. They claimed, "This is the LORD's declaration," when the LORD did not send them, yet they wait for the fulfillment of their message. 7 Didn't you see a false vision and speak a lying divination when you proclaimed, "This is the LORD's declaration," even though I had not spoken?

8 "'Therefore, this is what the Lord GOD says: You have spoken falsely and had lying visions; that's why you discover that I am against you. This is the declaration of the Lord GOD. 9 My hand will be against the prophets who see false visions and speak lying divinations. They will not be present in the council of my people or be recorded in the register of the house of Israel, and they will not enter the land of Israel. Then you will know that I am the Lord GOD.

10 "'Since they have led my people astray by saying, "Peace," when there is no peace, and since when a flimsy wall is being built, they plaster it with whitewash, 11 therefore, tell those plastering it with whitewash that it will fall. Torrential rain will come, and I will send hailstones plunging[F] down, and a whirlwind will be released. 12 When the wall has fallen, will you not be asked, "Where's the whitewash you plastered on it?"

13 "'So this is what the Lord GOD says: I will release a whirlwind in my wrath. Torrential rain will come in my anger, and hailstones will fall in destructive fury. 14 I will demolish the wall you plastered with whitewash and knock it to the ground so that its foundation is exposed. The city will fall, and you will

[A] **12:10** = King Zedekiah [B] **12:10** Lit *Israel among them* [C] **12:12** LXX, Syr read *He* [D] **12:19** Lit *its* [E] **12:19** = Jerusalem's [F] **13:11** One Hb ms, LXX, Vg; other Hb mss read *and you, hailstones, will plunge*

be destroyed within it. Then you will know that I am the LORD. 15 After I exhaust my wrath against the wall and against those who plaster it with whitewash, I will say to you, "The wall is no more and neither are those who plastered it — 16 those prophets of Israel who prophesied to Jerusalem and saw a vision of peace for her when there was no peace." This is the declaration of the Lord GOD.'

17 "Now you, son of man, face[A] the women among your people who prophesy out of their own imagination, and prophesy against them. 18 Say, 'This is what the Lord GOD says: Woe to the women who sew magic bands on the wrist of every hand and who make veils for the heads of people of every size in order to ensnare lives. Will you ensnare the lives of my people but preserve your own? 19 You profane me among my people for handfuls of barley and scraps of bread; you put those to death who should not die and spare those who should not live, when you lie to my people, who listen to lies.

20 " 'Therefore, this is what the Lord GOD says: I am against your magic bands with which you ensnare people like birds, and I will tear them from your arms. I will free the people you have ensnared like birds. 21 I will also tear off your veils and rescue my people from your hands, so that they will no longer be prey in your hands. Then you will know that I am the LORD. 22 Because you have disheartened the righteous person with lies (when I intended no distress), and because you have supported[B] the wicked person so that he does not turn from his evil way to save his life, 23 therefore you will no longer see false visions or practice divination. I will rescue my people from your hands. Then you will know that I am the LORD.' "

IDOLATROUS ELDERS PUNISHED

14 Some of the elders of Israel came to me and sat down in front of me. 2 Then the word of the LORD came to me: 3 "Son of man, these men have set up idols in their hearts and have put their sinful stumbling blocks in front of themselves. Should I actually let them inquire of me?

4 "Therefore, speak to them and tell them, 'This is what the Lord GOD says: When anyone from the house of Israel sets up idols in his heart and puts his sinful stumbling block in front of himself, and then comes to the prophet, I, the LORD, will answer him appropriately.[C] I will answer him according to his many idols, 5 so that I may take hold of the house of Israel by their hearts. They are all estranged from me because of their idols.'

6 "Therefore, say to the house of Israel, 'This is what the Lord GOD says: Repent and turn away from your idols; turn your faces away from all your detestable things. 7 For when anyone from the house of Israel or from the aliens who reside in Israel separates himself from me, setting up idols in his heart and putting his sinful stumbling block in front of himself, and then comes to the prophet to inquire of me, I, the LORD, will answer him myself. 8 I will turn against that one and make him a sign and a proverb; I will cut him off from among my people. Then you will know that I am the LORD.

9 " 'But if the prophet is deceived and speaks a message, it was I, the LORD, who deceived that prophet. I will stretch out my hand against him and destroy him from among my people Israel. 10 They will bear their punishment — the punishment of the one who inquires will be the same as that of the prophet — 11 in order that the house of Israel may no longer stray from following me and no longer defile themselves with all their transgressions. Then they will be my people and I will be their God. This is the declaration of the Lord GOD.' "

FOUR DEVASTATING JUDGMENTS

12 The word of the LORD came to me: 13 "Son of man, suppose a land sins against me by acting faithlessly, and I stretch out my hand against it to cut off its supply of bread, to send famine through it, and to wipe out both people and animals from it. 14 Even if these three men — Noah, Daniel, and Job — were in it, they would rescue only themselves by their righteousness." This is the declaration of the Lord GOD.

15 "Suppose I allow dangerous animals to pass through the land and depopulate it so that it becomes desolate, with no one passing through it for fear of the animals. 16 Even if these three men were in it, as I live" — the declaration of the Lord GOD — "they could not rescue their sons or daughters. They alone would be rescued, but the land would be desolate.

17 "Or suppose I bring a sword against that land and say, 'Let a sword pass through it,' so that I wipe out both people and animals from it. 18 Even if these three men were in it, as I live" — the declaration of the Lord GOD — "they could not rescue their sons or daughters, but they alone would be rescued.

19 "Or suppose I send a plague into that land and pour out my wrath on it with bloodshed to wipe out both people and animals from it. 20 Even if Noah, Daniel, and Job were in it, as I live" — the declaration of the Lord GOD — "they could not rescue their son or daughter. They would rescue only themselves by their righteousness.

21 "For this is what the Lord GOD says: How much worse will it be when I send my four devastating

[A] **13:17** Lit *set your face* [B] **13:22** Lit *strengthened the hand of* [C] **14:4** Alt Hb tradition reads *him who comes*

judgments against Jerusalem — sword, famine, dangerous animals, and plague — in order to wipe out
both people and animals from it! 22 Even so, there will
be survivors left in it, sons and daughters who will be
brought out. Indeed, they will come out to you, and
you will observe their conduct and actions. Then you
will be consoled about the devastation I have brought
on Jerusalem, about all I have brought on it. 23 They
will bring you consolation when you see their conduct and actions, and you will know that it was not
without cause that I have done what I did to it." This
is the declaration of the Lord God.

PARABLE OF THE USELESS VINE

15 Then the word of the Lord came to me: 2 "Son
of man, how does the wood of the vine, that
branch among the trees of the forest, compare to any
other wood? 3 Can wood be taken from it to make
something useful? Or can anyone make a peg from
it to hang things on? 4 In fact, it is put into the fire as
fuel. The fire devours both of its ends, and the middle is charred. Can it be useful for anything? 5 Even
when it was whole it could not be made into a useful object. How much less can it ever be made into
anything useful when the fire has devoured it and
it is charred!"

6 Therefore, this is what the Lord God says, "Like
the wood of the vine among the trees of the forest,
which I have given to the fire as fuel, so I will give up
the residents of Jerusalem. 7 I will turn against them.
They may have escaped from the fire, but it will still
consume them. And you will know that I am the Lord
when I turn against them. 8 I will make the land desolate because they have acted unfaithfully." This is the
declaration of the Lord God.

PARABLE OF GOD'S ADULTEROUS WIFE

16 The word of the Lord came to me again: 2 "Son
of man, confront Jerusalem with her detestable practices. 3 You are to say, 'This is what the Lord
God says to Jerusalem: Your origin and your birth
were in the land of the Canaanites. Your father was
an Amorite and your mother a Hethite. 4 As for your
birth, your umbilical cord wasn't cut on the day you
were born, and you weren't washed clean[A] with water. You were not rubbed with salt or wrapped in
cloths. 5 No one cared enough about you to do even
one of these things out of compassion for you. But
you were thrown out into the open field because you
were despised on the day you were born.

6 " 'I passed by you and saw you thrashing around
in your blood, and I said to you as you lay in your
blood, "Live!" Yes, I said to you as you lay in your
blood, "Live!"[B] 7 I made you thrive[C] like plants of the
field. You grew up and matured and became very
beautiful.[D] Your breasts were formed and your hair
grew, but you were stark naked.

8 " 'Then I passed by you and saw you, and you were
indeed at the age for love. So I spread the edge of my
garment over you and covered your nakedness. I
pledged myself to you, entered into a covenant with
you — this is the declaration of the Lord God — and
you became mine. 9 I washed you with water, rinsed
off your blood, and anointed you with oil. 10 I clothed
you in embroidered cloth and provided you with fine
leather[A] sandals. I also wrapped you in fine linen and
covered you with silk. 11 I adorned you with jewelry, putting bracelets on your wrists and a necklace
around your neck. 12 I put a ring in your nose, earrings on your ears, and a beautiful crown on your
head. 13 So you were adorned with gold and silver,
and your clothing was made of fine linen, silk, and
embroidered cloth. You ate fine flour, honey, and oil.
You became extremely beautiful and attained royalty.
14 Your fame spread among the nations because of
your beauty, for it was perfect through my splendor,
which I had bestowed on you. This is the declaration
of the Lord God.

15 " 'But you trusted in your beauty and acted like
a prostitute because of your fame. You lavished your
sexual favors on everyone who passed by. Your beauty
became his.[A] 16 You took some of your clothing and
made colorful high places for yourself, and you engaged in prostitution on them. These places should
not have been built, and this should never have happened![A] 17 You also took your beautiful jewelry made
from the gold and silver I had given you, and you
made male images so that you could engage in prostitution with them. 18 Then you took your embroidered
clothing to cover them and set my oil and incense
before them. 19 The food that I gave you — the fine
flour, oil, and honey that I fed you — you set it before
them as a pleasing aroma. That is what happened.
This is the declaration of the Lord God.

20 " 'You even took your sons and daughters you
bore to me and sacrificed them to these images as
food. Wasn't your prostitution enough? 21 You slaughtered my children and gave them up when you passed
them through the fire to the images. 22 In all your
detestable practices and acts of prostitution, you did
not remember the days of your youth when you were
stark naked and thrashing around in your blood.

23 " 'Then after all your evil — Woe, woe to you!
— the declaration of the Lord God — 24 you built
yourself a mound and made yourself an elevated
place in every square. 25 You built your elevated place

[A] **16:4,10,15,16** Hb obscure [B] **16:6** Some Hb mss, LXX, Syr omit *Yes, I said to you as you lay in your blood, "Live!"* [C] **16:7** LXX reads *Thrive; I made you* [D] **16:7** Or *matured and developed the loveliest of ornaments*

at the head of every street and turned your beauty into a detestable thing. You spread your legs to everyone who passed by and increased your prostitution. 26 You engaged in promiscuous acts with Egyptian men, your well-endowed neighbors, and increased your prostitution to anger me.

27 " 'Therefore, I stretched out my hand against you and reduced your provisions. I gave you over to the desire of those who hate you, the Philistine women, who were embarrassed by your indecent conduct. 28 Then you engaged in prostitution with the Assyrian men because you were not satisfied. Even though you did this with them, you were still not satisfied. 29 So you extended your prostitution to Chaldea, the land of merchants, but you were not even satisfied with this!

30 " 'How your heart was inflamed with lust[A] — the declaration of the Lord GOD — when you did all these things, the acts of a brazen prostitute, 31 building your mound at the head of every street and making your elevated place in every square. But you were unlike a prostitute because you scorned payment. 32 You adulterous wife, who receives strangers instead of her husband! 33 Men give gifts to all prostitutes, but you gave gifts to all your lovers. You bribed them to come to you from all around for your sexual favors. 34 So you were the opposite of other women in your acts of prostitution; no one solicited you. When you paid a fee instead of one being paid to you, you were the opposite.

35 " 'Therefore, you prostitute, hear the word of the LORD! 36 This is what the Lord GOD says: Because your lust was poured out and your nakedness exposed by your acts of prostitution with your lovers, and because of all your detestable idols and the blood of your children that you gave to them, 37 I am therefore going to gather all the lovers you pleased — all those you loved as well as all those you hated. I will gather them against you from all around and expose your nakedness to them so they see you completely naked. 38 I will judge you the way adulteresses and those who shed blood are judged. Then I will bring about the shedding of your blood in jealous wrath. 39 I will hand you over to them, and they will demolish your mounds and tear down your elevated places. They will strip off your clothes, take your beautiful jewelry, and leave you stark naked. 40 They will bring a mob against you to stone you and to cut you to pieces with their swords. 41 They will burn your houses and execute judgments against you in the sight of many women. I will stop you from being a prostitute, and you will never again pay fees for lovers. 42 So I will satisfy my wrath against you, and my jealousy will turn away from you. Then I will be calm and no longer angry. 43 Because you did not remember the days of your youth but enraged me with all these things, I will also bring your conduct down on your own head. This is the declaration of the Lord GOD. Haven't you committed depravity in addition to all your detestable practices?

44 " 'Look, everyone who uses proverbs will quote this proverb about you: "Like mother, like daughter." 45 You are the daughter of your mother, who despised her husband and children. You are the sister of your sisters, who despised their husbands and children. Your mother was a Hethite and your father an Amorite. 46 Your older sister was Samaria, who lived with her daughters to the north of you, and your younger sister was Sodom, who lived with her daughters to the south of you. 47 Didn't you walk in their ways and do their detestable practices? It was only a short time before all your ways were more corrupt than theirs.

48 " 'As I live — the declaration of the Lord GOD — your sister Sodom and her daughters have not behaved as you and your daughters have. 49 Now this was the iniquity of your sister Sodom: She and her daughters had pride, plenty of food, and comfortable security, but didn't support[B] the poor and needy. 50 They were haughty and did detestable acts before me, so I removed them when I saw this.[C] 51 But Samaria did not commit even half your sins. You have multiplied your detestable practices beyond theirs and made your sisters appear righteous by all the detestable acts you have committed. 52 You must also bear your disgrace, since you have helped your sisters out.[D] For they appear more righteous than you because of your sins, which you committed more detestably than they did. So you also, be ashamed and bear your disgrace, since you have made your sisters appear righteous.

53 " 'I will restore their fortunes, the fortunes of Sodom and her daughters and those of Samaria and her daughters. I will also restore[E] your fortunes among them, 54 so you will bear your disgrace and be ashamed of all you did when you comforted them. 55 As for your sisters, Sodom and her daughters and Samaria and her daughters will return to their former state. You and your daughters will also return to your former state. 56 Didn't you treat your sister Sodom as an object of scorn when you were proud, 57 before your wickedness was exposed? It was like the time you were scorned by the daughters of Aram[F] and all those around her, and by the daughters of the Philistines — those who treated you with contempt from every side. 58 You yourself must bear the consequences of your depravity and detestable practices — this is the LORD's declaration.

[A] **16:30** Or *was sick* [B] **16:49** Lit *strengthen the hand of* [C] **16:50** Or *them as you have seen* [D] **16:52** Lit *you have been the advocate for your sisters* [E] **16:53** LXX, Vg; MT reads *Samaria and her daughters and the fortunes of* [F] **16:57** Some Hb mss, Syr read *Edom*

59 " 'For this is what the Lord GOD says: I will deal with you according to what you have done, since you have despised the oath by breaking the covenant. 60 But I will remember the covenant I made with you in the days of your youth, and I will establish a permanent covenant with you. 61 Then you will remember your ways and be ashamed when you[A] receive your older and younger sisters. I will give them to you as daughters, but not because of your covenant. 62 I will establish my covenant with you, and you will know that I am the LORD, 63 so that when I make atonement for all you have done, you will remember and be ashamed, and never open your mouth again because of your disgrace. This is the declaration of the Lord GOD.' "

PARABLE OF THE EAGLES

17 The word of the LORD came to me: 2 "Son of man, pose a riddle and speak a parable to the house of Israel. 3 You are to say, 'This is what the Lord GOD says: A huge eagle with powerful wings, long feathers, and full plumage of many colors came to Lebanon and took the top of the cedar. 4 He plucked off its topmost shoot, brought it to the land of merchants, and set it in a city of traders. 5 Then he took some of the land's seed and put it in a fertile field; he set it like a willow, a plant[B] by abundant water. 6 It sprouted and became a spreading vine, low in height with its branches turned toward him, yet its roots stayed under it. So it became a vine, produced branches, and sent out shoots.

7 " 'But there was another huge eagle with powerful wings and thick plumage. And this vine bent its roots toward him! It stretched out its branches to him from the plot where it was planted, so that he might water it. 8 It had been planted in a good field by abundant water in order to produce branches, bear fruit, and become a splendid vine.'

9 "You are to say, 'This is what the Lord GOD says: Will it flourish? Will he not tear out its roots and strip off its fruit so that it shrivels? All its fresh leaves will wither! Great strength and many people will not be needed to pull it from its roots. 10 Even though it is planted, will it flourish? Won't it wither completely when the east wind strikes it? It will wither on the plot where it sprouted.' "

11 The word of the LORD came to me: 12 "Now say to that rebellious house, 'Don't you know what these things mean?' Tell them, 'The king of Babylon came to Jerusalem, took its king and officials, and brought them back with him to Babylon. 13 He took one of the royal family and made a covenant with him, putting him under oath. Then he took away the leading men of the land, 14 so that the kingdom would be humble and not exalt itself but would keep his covenant in order to endure. 15 However, this king revolted against him by sending his ambassadors to Egypt so they might give him horses and a large army. Will he flourish? Will the one who does such things escape? Can he break a covenant and still escape?

16 " 'As I live — this is the declaration of the Lord GOD — he will die in Babylon, in the land of the king who put him on the throne, whose oath he despised and whose covenant he broke. 17 Pharaoh with his mighty army and vast company will not help him in battle, when ramps are built and siege walls constructed to destroy many lives. 18 He despised the oath by breaking the covenant. He did all these things even though he gave his hand in pledge. He will not escape!

19 " 'Therefore, this is what the Lord GOD says: As I live, I will bring down on his head my oath that he despised and my covenant that he broke. 20 I will spread my net over him, and he will be caught in my snare. I will bring him to Babylon and execute judgment on him there for the treachery he committed against me. 21 All the fugitives[C] among his troops will fall by the sword, and those who survive will be scattered to every direction of the wind. Then you will know that I, the LORD, have spoken.

22 " 'This is what the Lord GOD says:

I will take a sprig
from the lofty top of the cedar and plant it.
I will pluck a tender sprig
from its topmost shoots,
and I will plant it
on a high towering mountain.
23 I will plant it on Israel's high mountain
so that it may bear branches, produce fruit,
and become a majestic cedar.
Birds of every kind will nest under it,
taking shelter in the shade of its branches.
24 Then all the trees of the field will know
that I am the LORD.
I bring down the tall tree,
and make the low tree tall.
I cause the green tree to wither
and make the withered tree thrive.
I, the LORD, have spoken
and I will do it.' "

PERSONAL RESPONSIBILITY FOR SIN

18 The word of the LORD came to me: 2 "What do you mean by using this proverb concerning the land of Israel:

'The fathers eat sour grapes,
and the children's teeth are set on edge'?

[A] **16:61** Some LXX mss, Syr read *I* [B] **17:5** Hb obscure [C] **17:21** Some Hb mss, LXX, Syr, Tg read *choice men*

Proverbs: True or False?

by Randall L. Adkisson and E. Ray Clendenen

A proverb is a popular saying, based on experience, that many people accept as generally true and tend to apply to various situations. David, for example, said to King Saul, who was chasing him to harm him, "As the old proverb says, 'Wickedness comes from wicked people'" (1Sm 24:13). Archaeologists have found many collections of proverbs from all over the ancient Near East, especially from Egypt and Sumer and Babylonia, that date from before the second millennium BC and throughout the first millennium and later. This helps us better appreciate the author of Kings, who praises Solomon's wisdom as "greater than the wisdom of all the people of the East, greater than all the wisdom of Egypt." Emissaries from "all peoples" were even "sent by every king on earth who had heard of his wisdom" (1Kg 4:30,34).

Many of the Near Eastern proverbs are even similar to Solomon's, such as "Withhold not thy son from the rod, else thou wilt not be able to save [him from wickedness]. If I smite thee, my son, thou wilt not die, but if I leave thee to thine own heart [thou wilt not live]."[1] Another is "Their plan is one thing, and that of the Lord of Life is another."[2] One even reminds us of the words of Jesus: "He makes the humble surpass the great, and the last is the first."[3] Another proverb, quite offensive to a modern audience, is "A woman without a husband is like a field without cultivation."[4] More encouraging is "Do right and you will live long on earth."[5] One more satisfying to the poor is "The rich man of last year is a vagabond this year."[6]

The prophecy of Ezekiel also contains several proverbs. In Ezekiel 16:44, God says to people of Jerusalem through his prophet, "Look, everyone who uses proverbs will quote this proverb about you: 'Like mother, like daughter.'" Not all proverbs, however, are true. In 12:22–23, God called to Ezekiel's attention a popular saying that expressed the people's cynical attitude toward prophets of doom like Ezekiel: "Son of man, what is this proverb you people have about the land of Israel, which goes, 'The days keep passing by, and every vision fails'? Therefore say to them, 'This is what the Lord God says: I will put a stop to this proverb, and they will not use it again in Israel.' But say to them, 'The days have arrived, as well as the fulfillment of every vision." Judgment would come according to God's timetable, and it would be soon.

God confronted another false proverb in Ezekiel 18. Sin had always had a communal nature. Not only did a ruler's sinful behavior affect the nation, but each person's iniquity also brought consequences to others, directly or indirectly, as in the case of Adam and Eve, and later of David. God declared that parents' sinful behavior had an especially devastating effect on their children and grandchildren for successive generations. Thus, in Exodus, God declared: "I, the Lord your God, am a jealous God, bringing the consequences of the fathers' iniquity on the children to the third and fourth generations of those who hate me, but showing faithful love to a thousand generations of those who love me and keep my commands" (Ex 20:5–6; see 34:6–7; Nm 14:18; Dt 5:8–10). God's Word warns consistently by statement and example that a parent's sin would bring suffering to children. Sometimes the consequences were direct; often the consequences were influential, a legacy of unfaithfulness. The chronicles of Israel's kings are replete with judgment borne by sons who were influenced to rebellion by the sinful practices of their fathers, in-laws, or grandfathers.

Insights, however, must not become excuses. What God intended as a sober warning to parents had, by the time of Ezekiel and Jeremiah, become an excuse for their children. Generations of Israelites had learned to deflect their own culpability for rebellion. A proverb of blame had become pervasive by the period of the exile. Its repudiation by Ezekiel, who was part of the exile, and Jeremiah, a resident in Judah, clearly shows that the proverb had become a universal excuse for irresponsible behavior. "The fathers eat sour grapes, and the children's teeth are set on edge" (Ezk 18:2; see Jr 31:29). Their point was that "God is unjustly causing us to suffer for something our ancestors did."

Seven hundred years earlier, the Hittite King Mursilis II had blamed his woes on his father and by extension an unjust god: "My father sinned and transgressed against the word of the Hattian storm-god, my lord. But I have not sinned in any respect. It is only too true, however, that the father's sin falls upon the son."[7] Similarly, the Israelites would blame their plight on their fathers' rebellion, declaring God unjust. The people had taken what the Lord had given as a dire warning of the familial consequences of sin and perverted it into an excuse for avoiding personal responsibility.

God spoke through both Ezekiel and Jeremiah to demand that the proverb be stricken from use. Each person must take responsibility for his or her own spiritual and religious condition. Ezekiel 18 employs a story of three generations (a righteous father, his violent son, and the violent son's reflective son) to clarify that each person bears his own responsibility. The father was not judged because of his son's actions, nor would a son gain righteous status or suffer judgment based upon his father's behavior. The Torah had stated the same long before: "Fathers are not to be put to death for their children, and children are not to be put to death for their fathers; each person will be put to death for his own sin" (Dt 24:16).

Ezekiel makes clear that repentance changes a sinful individual's destiny. Likewise, the positive influence of a righteous person may be lost through rebellion. Old Testament scholar William Brownlee explains:

> Ezekiel's disputation was not intended as a purely moral or intellectual discourse on divine justice, but as a means of getting individuals to accept responsibility for their own lives, to dare to venture forth in righteous living, in reversal of the behavior of wicked parents, and even in complete reversal of what they had themselves been. One's future is not to be held hostage to the character of previous generations, nor even to one's own personal depravity. If one dares, if one wills, one can break the shackles of sin and become a new person.[8]

One may think of the emotional pain Adam and Eve suffered at the murder of Abel or of the tragic effects of David's adultery upon the behavior of his children as examples of sin's collateral damage. ✣

[1] J. B. Pritchard, ed. *ANET*, 3rd ed. with sup, 428. [2] Walter Beyerlin, ed. *Near Eastern Religious Texts Relating to the Old Testament*, OTL (1978), 49. [3] Beyerlin, *Near Eastern Religious Texts*, 47. [4] Pritchard, *ANET*, 426. [5] Beyerlin, *Near Eastern Religious Texts*, 45. [6] Beyerlin, *Near Eastern Religious Texts*, 49. [7] Pritchard, *ANET*, 395. [8] William H. Brownlee, *Ezekiel 1–19*, WBC (1986), 292.

Bronze figurine; likely Teshub, the Hittite storm god, whose symbol was the bull. He was typically portrayed as a man with a beard, sometimes standing on two mountains, and having a club in his hand. From Anatolia, sixteenth–thirteenth centuries BC. Complaining to the storm god, the Hittites King Mursilis II said his personal difficulties came because of his father's transgressions.

3 As I live" — this is the declaration of the Lord GOD —
"you will no longer use this proverb in Israel. 4 Look,
every life belongs to me. The life of the father is like
the life of the son — both belong to me. The person
who sins is the one who will die.

5 "Suppose a man is righteous and does what is
just and right: 6 He does not eat at the mountain
shrines[A] or look to the idols of the house of Israel.
He does not defile his neighbor's wife or approach a
woman during her menstrual impurity. 7 He doesn't
oppress anyone but returns his collateral to the debt-
or. He does not commit robbery, but gives his bread
to the hungry and covers the naked with clothing.
8 He doesn't lend at interest or for profit but keeps
his hand from injustice and carries out true justice
between men. 9 He follows my statutes and keeps my
ordinances, acting faithfully. Such a person is righteous; he will certainly live." This is the declaration
of the Lord GOD.

10 "But suppose the man has a violent son, who
sheds blood and does any of these things, 11 though
the father has done none of them. Indeed, when the
son eats at the mountain shrines and defiles his
neighbor's wife, 12 and when he oppresses the poor
and needy, commits robbery, and does not return
collateral, and when he looks to the idols, commits
detestable acts, 13 and lends at interest or for profit,
will he live? He will not live! Since he has committed
all these detestable acts, he will certainly die. His
death will be his own fault.[B]

14 "Now suppose he has a son who sees all the sins
his father has committed, and though he sees them,
he does not do likewise. 15 He does not eat at the
mountain shrines or look to the idols of the house
of Israel. He does not defile his neighbor's wife. 16 He
doesn't oppress anyone, hold collateral, or commit
robbery. He gives his bread to the hungry and covers
the naked with clothing. 17 He keeps his hand from
harming the poor, not taking interest or profit on a
loan. He practices my ordinances and follows my
statutes. Such a person will not die for his father's
iniquity. He will certainly live.

18 "As for his father, he will die for his own iniquity because he practiced fraud, robbed his brother,
and did among his people what was not good. 19 But
you may ask, 'Why doesn't the son suffer punishment for the father's iniquity?' Since the son has
done what is just and right, carefully observing
all my statutes, he will certainly live. 20 The person
who sins is the one who will die. A son won't suffer
punishment for the father's iniquity, and a father
won't suffer punishment for the son's iniquity. The
righteousness of the righteous person will be on
him, and the wickedness of the wicked person will
be on him.

21 "But if the wicked person turns from all the sins
he has committed, keeps all my statutes, and does
what is just and right, he will certainly live; he will
not die. 22 None of the transgressions he has committed will be held against him. He will live because
of the righteousness he has practiced. 23 Do I take
any pleasure in the death of the wicked?" This is the
declaration of the Lord GOD. "Instead, don't I take
pleasure when he turns from his ways and lives?
24 But when a righteous person turns from his righteousness and acts unjustly, committing the same
detestable acts that the wicked do, will he live? None
of the righteous acts he did will be remembered. He
will die because of the treachery he has engaged in
and the sin he has committed.

25 "But you say, 'The Lord's way isn't fair.' Now listen,
house of Israel: Is it my way that is unfair? Instead,
isn't it your ways that are unfair? 26 When a righteous
person turns from his righteousness and acts unjustly,
he will die for this. He will die because of the injustice
he has committed. 27 But if a wicked person turns from
the wickedness he has committed and does what is
just and right, he will preserve his life. 28 He will certainly live because he thought it over and turned from
all the transgressions he had committed; he will not
die. 29 But the house of Israel says, 'The Lord's way
isn't fair.' Is it my ways that are unfair, house of Israel?
Instead, isn't it your ways that are unfair?

30 "Therefore, house of Israel, I will judge each one
of you according to his ways." This is the declaration
of the Lord GOD. "Repent and turn from all your rebellious acts, so they will not become a sinful stumbling
block to you. 31 Throw off all the transgressions you
have committed, and get yourselves a new heart and
a new spirit. Why should you die, house of Israel?
32 For I take no pleasure in anyone's death." This is
the declaration of the Lord GOD. "So repent and live!

A LAMENT FOR ISRAEL'S PRINCES

19 "As for you, take up a lament for the princes of
Israel, 2 and say:

What was your mother? A lioness!
She lay down among the lions;
she reared her cubs among the young lions.
3 She brought up one of her cubs,
and he became a young lion.
After he learned to tear prey,
he devoured people.
4 When the nations heard about him,
he was caught in their pit.
Then they led him away with hooks
to the land of Egypt.

[A] **18:6** Lit *the mountains*, also in vv. 11,15 [B] **18:13** Lit *His blood will be on him*

5 When she saw that she waited in vain,
that her hope was lost,
she took another of her cubs
and made him a young lion.
6 He prowled among the lions,
and he became a young lion.
After he learned to tear prey,
he devoured people.
7 He devastated their strongholds[A]
and destroyed their cities.
The land and everything in it shuddered
at the sound of his roaring.
8 Then the nations from
the surrounding provinces
set out against him.
They spread their net over him;
he was caught in their pit.
9 They put a wooden yoke on him[B] with hooks
and led him away to the king of Babylon.
They brought him into the fortresses
so his roar could no longer be heard
on the mountains of Israel.

10 Your mother was like a vine in your vineyard,[C]
planted by the water;
it was fruitful and full of branches
because of abundant water.
11 It had strong branches, fit for the scepters
of rulers;
its height towered among the clouds.[D]
So it was conspicuous for its height
as well as its many branches.
12 But it was uprooted in fury,
thrown to the ground,
and the east wind dried up its fruit.
Its strong branches were torn off
and dried up;
fire consumed them.
13 Now it is planted in the wilderness,
in a dry and thirsty land.
14 Fire has gone out from its main branch[E]
and has devoured its fruit,
so that it no longer has a strong branch,
a scepter for ruling.

This is a lament and should be used as a lament."

ISRAEL'S REBELLION

20 In the seventh year, in the fifth month, on the
tenth day of the month, some of Israel's elders
came to inquire of the LORD, and they sat down in
front of me. 2 Then the word of the LORD came to me:
3 "Son of man, speak with the elders of Israel and tell
them, 'This is what the Lord GOD says: Are you coming
to inquire of me? As I live, I will not let you inquire of
me. This is the declaration of the Lord GOD.'

4 "Will you pass judgment against them, will you
pass judgment, son of man? Explain the detestable
practices of their ancestors to them. 5 Say to them,
'This is what the Lord GOD says: On the day I chose
Israel, I swore an oath[F] to the descendants of Jacob's
house and made myself known to them in the land of
Egypt. I swore to them, saying, "I am the LORD your
God." 6 On that day I swore[G] to them that I would
bring them out of the land of Egypt into a land I had
searched out for them, a land flowing with milk and
honey, the most beautiful of all lands. 7 I also said to
them, "Throw away, each of you, the abhorrent things
that you prize,[H] and do not defile yourselves with the
idols of Egypt. I am the LORD your God."

8 " 'But they rebelled against me and were unwilling to listen to me. None of them threw away the
abhorrent things that they prized,[I] and they did not
abandon the idols of Egypt. So I considered pouring
out my wrath on them, exhausting my anger against
them within the land of Egypt. 9 But I acted for the
sake of my name, so that it would not be profaned
in the eyes of the nations they were living among, in
whose sight I had made myself known to Israel by
bringing them out of Egypt.

10 " 'So I brought them out of the land of Egypt and
led them into the wilderness. 11 Then I gave them my
statutes and explained my ordinances to them — the
person who does them will live by them. 12 I also gave
them my Sabbaths to serve as a sign between me and
them, so that they would know that I am the LORD
who consecrates them.

13 " 'But the house of Israel rebelled against me in
the wilderness. They did not follow my statutes and
they rejected my ordinances — the person who does
them will live by them. They also completely profaned
my Sabbaths. So I considered pouring out my wrath
on them in the wilderness to put an end to them. 14 But
I acted for the sake of my name, so that it would not
be profaned in the eyes of the nations in whose sight
I had brought them out. 15 However, I swore to them
in the wilderness that I would not bring them into
the land I had given them — the most beautiful of
all lands, flowing with milk and honey — 16 because
they rejected my ordinances, profaned my Sabbaths,
and did not follow my statutes. For their hearts went
after their idols. 17 Yet I spared them from destruction
and did not bring them to an end in the wilderness.

18 " 'Then I said to their children in the wilderness,
"Don't follow the statutes of your fathers, defile yourselves with their idols, or keep their ordinances.

[A] **19:7** Tg, Aq; MT reads *knew their widows* [B] **19:9** Or *put him in a cage* [C] **19:10** Some Hb mss; other Hb mss read *blood* [D] **19:11** Or *thick foliage* [E] **19:14** Lit *from the branch of its parts* [F] **20:5** Lit *I lifted my hand* [G] **20:6** Lit *lifted my hand*, also in vv. 15,23,28,42 [H] **20:7** Lit *things of your eyes* [I] **20:8** Lit *things of their eyes*

The Old Testament writers frequently used lion imagery because the readers and hearers would have readily identified with it. Lions were common in ancient Israel and Judah and remained in the area until early in the fourteenth century AD. Mesopotamia also had lions throughout the Old Testament era and even until the late 1800s AD.[1]

"LIONS" IN THE OLD TESTAMENT

At least seven Hebrew words in the Old Testament refer to a lion: (1) *'ari* or *'aryeh,* a general word; (2) *kephir,* a young lion, but covered with a mane; (3) *lebe', lib'ah, labi', lebiyya',* or *libyah,* an older lion or lioness; (4) *layish,* a strong lion; (5) *shachal,* a fierce lion or an old lion; and (6) *gur,* a lion cub. These words occur approximately 150 times in 112 verses.[2] Ezekiel used the words the most (16 times), and Nahum has the highest proportional usage by far (10 times in three chapters).

The Pentateuch uses "lions" illustratively and in the context of blessing. For instance, Jacob blessed Judah and spoke of him as a lion cub (*gur*), a lion (*'ari*), and an older lion (*labi'*, see Gn 49:9). Other examples in the Pentateuch include Moses's blessing of Gad and Dan (Dt 33:20,22) and Balaam's blessing of Israel/Jacob (Nm 23:24; 24:9).

In the Historical Books (Joshua–Esther), the words often described a lion literally attacking a person (e.g., Samson in Jdg 14). Because of such encounters, people associated lions with fierceness and courage. Saul and Jonathan were reportedly "stronger than lions" (2Sm 1:23), and David's mightiest soldiers had "the heart of a lion" (2Sm 17:10). Further, artisans even used lions as decorations in the temple and in Solomon's palace (1Kg 10:20; 2Ch 9:18–19).

Because a lion could attack suddenly and ferociously, lions became symbolic of judgment, destruction, and punishment. One writer recorded that God sent lions against the people in Samaria (2Kg 17:25). Later the prophets spoke of God roaring in judgment against his people Israel.

In the Prophets, the writers used lions to picture the wicked who ate the poor as prey (Zph 3:3); God's punishment, which comes swiftly and forcefully (Is 15:9; Hs 5:14); impending danger of any kind (Is 21:8, see CSB note; Jr 4:7); and God's deliverance in the messianic age when he will roar and enable the lion to live with the lamb (Is 11:6; Hs 11:10).

Limestone lion standing over a bull's head, from Damascus, Syria.

ARCHAEOLOGY AND LIONS

Archaeologists have excavated very few lion remains because animal remains are limited primarily to domesticated animals, to animals used as food, or to animals used in sacrifices. Lions would not normally fit into any of these categories.

Images of lions appear regularly in artifacts, however. Mesopotamian, Assyrian, and Egyptian reliefs depict lion hunting.[3] A basalt orthostat in a Canaanite temple at Beth-shean illustrates a fight between a lion and a dog.[4] The ivories found in a royal palace in Samaria included lions.[5] A Canaanite shrine at Hazor contained a small figure of a lion.[6] Probably the most famous example, though for its reference to a king rather than for its lion image, is the Shema seal, an eighth-century BC seal from Megiddo with a picture of a roaring lion and an inscription of its owner ("Shema, the servant of Jeroboam").[7]

At Jaffa and Dan, archaeologists have even found evidence of lion sacrifice. At Jaffa, a Canaanite temple contained a lion's skull with an Egyptian scarab in its eye. At Dan, lion bones were found near an altar; the Canaanite name of Dan was Laish ("lion").[8] In 2001, French archaeologists discovered the first mummified lion in an Egyptian tomb; the Egyptians worshiped the lion goddess Sekhmet.[9]

LIONS IN EZEKIEL 19

Ezekiel refers to lions ten times in chapter 19 and only six times elsewhere (1:10; 10:14; 22:25; 32:2; 38:13; 41:19). Chapter 19 is a lament for the princes of Israel, using two separate images: lions (vv. 2–9) and a vine (vv. 10–14). In the lion passage, the mother of the princes is a lioness (*lebiyya'*). She would lie down among the lions (*'ari*) and the young lions (*kephir*). She raised many cubs (*gur*). One cub (*gur*) grew up and became a young lion (*kephir*). He learned to eat prey and even men, but he was trapped and led to Egypt.

With her hope dashed, the lioness took another cub (*gur*) and raised him until he also became a young lion (*kephir*). He then walked about as a young lion (*kephir*) among the other lions (*'ari*). He also learned to eat prey and men. As he roared, the land was made desolate before him, but he was trapped and led to Babylon.

Ezekiel used the two cubs to symbolize the activities of the Israelite princes—the wicked. The two have attacked and killed; they have lived wickedly and have consumed the helpless. Ironically, the lions were objects of God's punishment; the hunters were the hunted and the trapped.

God used Egypt and Babylon as the vehicles of his punishment. Because of these references and because of the date of the prophecies (1:2–3), this lament seems to refer to the historical events of Ezekiel's day. The young lions are the young kings Jehoahaz and Jehoiachin. Jehoahaz was taken to Egypt by Pharaoh Neco, and Jehoiachin was taken to Babylon by Nebuchadnezzar.

Ezekiel used lion imagery to depict God's judgment on these two wicked kings in the occurring political tragedies of his day. The kings who had hunted prey were eventually hunted by God through foreign, conquering kings. In the end, all faced destruction. ✣

---

[1] W. S. McCullough and F. S. Bodenheimer, "Lions" in *IDB*, 3:136. [2] Twenty-seven of the thirty-nine books in the Old Testament have one of these words; therefore, only twelve books do not have any occurrence (Exodus, Leviticus, Joshua, Ruth, Ezra, Nehemiah, Esther, Obadiah, Jonah, Habakkuk, Haggai, and Malachi). The words are used more than ten times in eight books (1 Kings, Job, Psalms, Isaiah, Jeremiah, Ezekiel, Daniel, and Nahum). Abraham Even-Shoshan, *A New Concordance of the Bible* (Jerusalem: Kiryath Sepher, 1989). [3] Oded Borowski, *Every Living Thing: Daily Use of Animals in Ancient Israel* (Walnut Creek, CA: AltaMira Press, 1998), 197–98. [4] Basalt is a black volcanic stone commonly found in northern Israel. An orthostat is a rectangular stone placed vertically at the base of a wall. "Beth Shean (Tel); Husn (Tell El-)" in *Archaeological Encyclopedia of the Holy Land* ed. Avraham Negev and Shimon Gibson (New York: Continuum, 2001), 83. [5] "Samaria; Shomron; Sebaste" in *Archaeological Encyclopedia*, 447–48. [6] "Hazor (a) (Tel)" in *Archaeological Encyclopedia*, 221. [7] "Seals" in *Archaeological Encyclopedia*, 452; see "Megiddo," 327. [8] Borowski, *Every Living Thing*, 226–27. [9] Stefan Lovgren, "Egyptian Lion Mummy Found in Ancient Tomb," *National Geographic News* (14 January 2004), www.news.nationalgeographic.com.

19 I am the LORD your God. Follow my statutes, keep my ordinances, and practice them. 20 Keep my Sabbaths holy, and they will be a sign between me and you, so you may know that I am the LORD your God."

21 " 'But the children rebelled against me. They did not follow my statutes or carefully keep my ordinances — the person who does them will live by them. They also profaned my Sabbaths. So I considered pouring out my wrath on them and exhausting my anger against them in the wilderness. 22 But I withheld my hand and acted for the sake of my name, so that it would not be profaned in the eyes of the nations in whose sight I brought them out. 23 However, I swore to them in the wilderness that I would disperse them among the nations and scatter them among the countries. 24 For they did not practice my ordinances but rejected my statutes and profaned my Sabbaths, and their eyes were fixed on their fathers' idols. 25 I also gave them statutes that were not good and ordinances they could not live by. 26 When they sacrificed every firstborn in the fire,[A] I defiled them through their gifts in order to devastate them so they would know that I am the LORD.'

27 "Therefore, son of man, speak to the house of Israel, and tell them, 'This is what the Lord GOD says: In this way also your ancestors blasphemed me by committing treachery against me: 28 When I brought them into the land that I swore to give them and they saw any high hill or leafy tree, they offered their sacrifices and presented their offensive offerings there. They also sent up their pleasing aromas and poured out their drink offerings there. 29 So I asked them, "What is this high place you are going to?" And it is still called Bamah[B] today.'

30 "Therefore say to the house of Israel, 'This is what the Lord GOD says: Are you defiling yourselves the way your ancestors did, and prostituting yourselves with their abhorrent things? 31 When you offer your gifts, sacrificing your children in the fire,[C] you still continue to defile yourselves with all your idols today. So should I let you inquire of me, house of Israel? As I live — this is the declaration of the Lord GOD — I will not let you inquire of me!

ISRAEL'S RESTORATION

32 " 'When you say, "Let's be like the nations, like the clans of other countries, serving wood and stone," what you have in mind will never happen. 33 As I live — the declaration of the Lord GOD — I will reign over you with a strong hand, an outstretched arm, and outpoured wrath. 34 I will bring you from the peoples and gather you from the countries where you were scattered, with a strong hand, an outstretched arm, and outpoured wrath. 35 I will lead you into the wilderness of the peoples and enter into judgment with you there face to face. 36 Just as I entered into judgment with your ancestors in the wilderness of the land of Egypt, so I will enter into judgment with you. This is the declaration of the Lord GOD. 37 I will make you pass under the rod and will bring you into the bond of the covenant. 38 I will purge you of those who rebel and transgress against me. I will bring them out of the land where they live as foreign residents, but they will not enter the land of Israel. Then you will know that I am the LORD.

39 " 'As for you, house of Israel, this is what the Lord GOD says: Go and serve your idols, each of you. But afterward you will surely listen to me, and you will no longer defile my holy name with your gifts and idols. 40 For on my holy mountain, Israel's high mountain — the declaration of the Lord GOD — there the entire house of Israel, all of them, will serve me in the land. There I will accept them and will require your contributions and choicest gifts, all your holy offerings. 41 When I bring you from the peoples and gather you from the countries where you have been scattered, I will accept you as a pleasing aroma. And I will demonstrate my holiness through you in the sight of the nations. 42 When I lead you into the land of Israel, the land I swore to give your ancestors, you will know that I am the LORD. 43 There you will remember your ways and all your deeds by which you have defiled yourself, and you will loathe yourselves for all the evil things you have done. 44 You will know that I am the LORD, house of Israel, when I have dealt with you for the sake of my name rather than according to your evil ways and corrupt acts. This is the declaration of the Lord GOD.' "

FIRE IN THE SOUTH

45 The word of the LORD came to me: 46 "Son of man, face the south and preach against it. Prophesy against the forest land in the Negev, 47 and say to the forest there, 'Hear the word of the LORD! This is what the Lord GOD says: I am about to ignite a fire in you, and it will devour every green tree and every dry tree in you. The blazing flame will not be extinguished, and every face from the south to the north will be scorched by it. 48 Then all humanity will see that I, the LORD, have kindled it. It will not be extinguished.' "

49 Then I said, "Oh, Lord GOD, they are saying of me, 'Isn't he just composing parables?' "

GOD'S SWORD OF JUDGMENT

21 The word of the LORD came to me again: 2 "Son of man, face Jerusalem and preach against the sanctuaries. Prophesy against the land of Israel, 3 and

[A] **20:26** Lit *they made every firstborn pass through the fire*
[B] **20:29** = High Place [C] **20:31** Lit *gifts, making your children pass through the fire*

say to it, 'This is what the LORD says: I am against you.
I will draw my sword from its sheath and cut off from
you both the righteous and the wicked. 4 Since I will
cut off[A] both the righteous and the wicked, my sword
will therefore come out of its sheath against all humanity from the south to the north. 5 So all humanity
will know that I, the LORD, have taken my sword from
its sheath — it will not be sheathed again.'

6 "But you, son of man, groan! Groan bitterly with a
broken heart[B] right before their eyes. 7 And when they
ask you, 'Why are you groaning?' then say, 'Because
of the news that is coming. Every heart will melt, and
every hand will become weak. Every spirit will be
discouraged, and all knees will run with urine.[C] Yes,
it is coming and it will happen. This is the declaration
of the Lord GOD.'"

8 The word of the LORD came to me: 9 "Son of man,
prophesy, 'This is what the Lord says!' You are to proclaim,

'A sword! A sword is sharpened
and also polished.
10 It is sharpened for slaughter,
polished to flash like lightning!
Should we rejoice?
The scepter of my son,
the sword despises every tree.[D]
11 The sword is given to be polished,
to be grasped in the hand.
It is sharpened, and it is polished,
to be put in the hand of the slayer.'

12 "Cry out and wail, son of man, for it is against my
people. It is against all the princes of Israel! They are
given over to the sword with my people. Therefore
strike your thigh in grief. 13 Surely it will be a trial!
And what if the sword despises even the scepter? The
scepter will not continue."[D] This is the declaration of
the Lord GOD.

14 "So you, son of man, prophesy and clap your
hands together:

Let the sword strike two times, even three.
It is a sword for massacre,
a sword for great massacre —
it surrounds[E] them!
15 I have appointed a sword for slaughter[D]
at all their gates,
so that their hearts may melt
and many may stumble.
Yes! It is ready to flash like lightning;
it is drawn[D] for slaughter.
16 Slash to the right;
turn to the left —
wherever your blade is directed.

17 I also will clap my hands together, and I will satisfy
my wrath. I, the LORD, have spoken."

18 The word of the LORD came to me: 19 "Now you,
son of man, mark out two roads that the sword of
Babylon's king can take. Both of them should originate from the same land. And make a signpost at
the fork in the road to each city. 20 Mark out a road
that the sword can take to Rabbah of the Ammonites
and to Judah into fortified Jerusalem. 21 For the king
of Babylon stands at the split in the road, at the fork
of the two roads, to practice divination: he shakes
the arrows, consults the idols, and observes the liver. 22 The answer marked[F] Jerusalem appears in his
right hand, indicating that he should set up battering
rams, give the order to[G] slaughter, raise a battle cry,
set battering rams against the gates, build a ramp,
and construct a siege wall. 23 It will seem like false
divination to those who have sworn an oath to the
Babylonians,[H] but it will draw attention to their guilt
so that they will be captured.

24 "Therefore, this is what the Lord GOD says: Because you have drawn attention to your guilt, exposing your transgressions, so that your sins are revealed
in all your actions — since you have done this, you
will be captured by them. 25 And you, profane and
wicked prince of Israel,[I] the day has come for your
punishment.[J]

26 "This is what the Lord GOD says:

Remove the turban, and take off
the crown.
Things will not remain as they are;[K]
exalt the lowly and bring down
the exalted.
27 A ruin, a ruin,
I will make it a ruin!
Yet this will not happen
until he comes;
I have given the judgment to him.[L]

28 "Now you, son of man, prophesy, and say, 'This is
what the Lord GOD says concerning the Ammonites
and their contempt.' You are to proclaim,

'A sword! A sword
is drawn for slaughter,
polished to consume, to flash like lightning.
29 While they offer false visions
and lying divinations about you,
the time has come to put you
to the necks of the profane wicked ones;
the day has come
for final punishment.

[A] **21:4** Lit *off from you* [B] **21:6** Lit *insides*, or *waist* [C] **21:7** Lit *knees will go water* [D] **21:10,13,15** Hb obscure [E] **21:14** Or *penetrates* [F] **21:22** Lit *The divination for* [G] **21:22** Lit *rams, open the mouth in* [H] **21:23** Lit *them* [I] **21:25** = King Zedekiah [J] **21:25** Lit *come in the time of the punishment of the end*, also in v. 29 [K] **21:26** Lit *This not this* [L] **21:27** Or *comes to whom it rightfully belongs, and I will give it to him*

30 " 'Return it to its sheath!

" 'I will judge you[A]
in the place where you were created,
in the land of your origin.
31 I will pour out my indignation on you;
I will blow the fire of my fury on you.
I will hand you over to brutal men,
skilled at destruction.
32 You will be fuel for the fire.
Your blood will be spilled
within the land.
You will not be remembered,
for I, the LORD, have spoken.' "

INDICTMENT OF SINFUL JERUSALEM

22 The word of the LORD came to me: 2 "As for
you, son of man, will you pass judgment? Will
you pass judgment against the city of blood? Then
explain all her detestable practices to her. 3 You are
to say, 'This is what the Lord GOD says: A city that
sheds blood within her walls so that her time of judgment has come and who makes idols for herself so
that she is defiled! 4 You are guilty of the blood you
have shed, and you are defiled from the idols you
have made. You have brought your judgment[B] days
near and have come to your years of punishment.[C]
Therefore, I have made you a disgrace to the nations
and a mockery to all the lands. 5 Those who are near
and those far away from you will mock you, you infamous one full of turmoil.

6 " 'Look, every prince of Israel within you has
used his strength to shed blood. 7 Father and mother
are treated with contempt, and the resident alien is
exploited within you. The fatherless and widow are
oppressed in you. 8 You despise my holy things and
profane my Sabbaths. 9 There are men within you
who slander in order to shed blood. People who live
in you eat at the mountain shrines;[D] they commit
depraved acts within you. 10 Men within you have
sexual intercourse with their father's wife and violate women during their menstrual impurity. 11 One
man within you commits a detestable act with his
neighbor's wife; another defiles his daughter-in-law
with depravity; and yet another violates his sister,
his father's daughter. 12 People who live in you accept
bribes in order to shed blood. You take interest and
profit on a loan and brutally extort your neighbors.
You have forgotten me. This is the declaration of
the Lord GOD.

13 " 'Now look, I clap my hands together against
the dishonest profit you have made and against the
blood shed among you. 14 Will your courage endure
or your hands be strong in the days when I deal with
you? I, the LORD, have spoken, and I will act. 15 I will
disperse you among the nations and scatter you
among the countries; I will purge your uncleanness.
16 You[E] will be profaned in the sight of the nations.
Then you will know that I am the LORD.' "

JERUSALEM AS GOD'S FURNACE

17 The word of the LORD came to me: 18 "Son of man,
the house of Israel has become merely dross to me.
All of them are copper, tin, iron, and lead inside the
furnace; they are just dross from silver. 19 Therefore,
this is what the Lord GOD says: Because all of you
have become dross, I am about to gather you into
Jerusalem. 20 Just as one gathers silver, copper, iron,
lead, and tin into the furnace to blow fire on them and
melt them, so I will gather you in my anger and wrath,
put you inside, and melt you. 21 Yes, I will gather you
together and blow on you with the fire of my fury,
and you will be melted within the city. 22 As silver is
melted inside a furnace, so you will be melted inside
the city. Then you will know that I, the LORD, have
poured out my wrath on you."

INDICTMENT OF A SINFUL LAND

23 The word of the LORD came to me: 24 "Son of man,
say to her, 'You are a land that has not been cleansed,
that has not received rain in the day of indignation.' 25 The conspiracy of her prophets within her
is[F] like a roaring lion tearing its prey: they devour
people, seize wealth and valuables, and multiply the
widows within her. 26 Her priests do violence to my
instruction and profane my holy things. They make
no distinction between the holy and the common,
and they do not explain the difference between the
clean and the unclean. They close their eyes to my
Sabbaths, and I am profaned among them.

27 "Her officials within her are like wolves tearing
their prey, shedding blood, and destroying lives in
order to make profit dishonestly. 28 Her prophets
plaster for them with whitewash by seeing false
visions and lying divinations, saying, 'This is what
the Lord GOD says,' when the LORD has not spoken.
29 The people of the land have practiced extortion
and committed robbery. They have oppressed the
poor and needy and unlawfully exploited the resident alien. 30 I searched for a man among them who
would repair the wall and stand in the gap before me
on behalf of the land so that I might not destroy it,
but I found no one. 31 So I have poured out my indignation on them and consumed them with the fire of
my fury. I have brought their conduct down on their
own heads." This is the declaration of the Lord GOD.

[A] **21:30** = the Ammonites [B] **22:4** *judgment* supplied for clarity
[C] **22:4** *punishment* supplied for clarity [D] **22:9** Lit *the mountains*
[E] **22:16** One Hb ms, LXX, Syr, Vg read *I* [F] **22:24–25** LXX reads
indignation, [25]whose princes within her are

THE TWO IMMORAL SISTERS

23 The word of the LORD came to me again: 2 "Son
of man, there were two women, daughters
of the same mother, 3 who acted like prostitutes in
Egypt, behaving promiscuously in their youth. Their
breasts were fondled there, and their virgin nipples
caressed. 4 The older one was named Oholah,[A] and
her sister was Oholibah.[B] They became mine and
gave birth to sons and daughters. As for their names,
Oholah represents Samaria and Oholibah represents
Jerusalem.

5 "Oholah acted like a prostitute even though she
was mine. She lusted after her lovers, the Assyrians:
warriors 6 dressed in blue, governors and prefects,
all of them desirable young men, horsemen riding
on steeds. 7 She offered her sexual favors to them;
all of them were the elite of Assyria. She defiled herself with all those she lusted after and with all their
idols. 8 She didn't give up her promiscuity that began
in Egypt, when men slept with her in her youth, caressed her virgin nipples, and poured out their lust
on her. 9 Therefore, I handed her over to her lovers,
the Assyrians she lusted for. 10 They exposed her nakedness, seized her sons and daughters, and killed
her with the sword. Since they executed judgment
against her, she became notorious among women.

11 "Now her sister Oholibah saw this, but she was
even more depraved in her lust than Oholah, and
made her promiscuous acts worse than those of her
sister. 12 She lusted after the Assyrians: governors
and prefects, warriors splendidly dressed, horsemen riding on steeds, all of them desirable young
men. 13 And I saw that she had defiled herself; both
of them had taken the same path. 14 But she increased
her promiscuity when she saw male figures carved
on the wall, images of the Chaldeans, engraved in
bright red, 15 wearing belts on their waists and flowing turbans on their heads; all of them looked like
officers, a depiction of the Babylonians in Chaldea,
their native land. 16 At the sight of them[C] she lusted
after them and sent messengers to them in Chaldea.
17 Then the Babylonians came to her, to the bed of
love, and defiled her with their lust. But after she
was defiled by them, she turned away from them in
disgust. 18 When she flaunted her promiscuity and
exposed her nakedness, I turned away from her in
disgust just as I turned away from her sister. 19 Yet she
multiplied her acts of promiscuity, remembering the
days of her youth when she acted like a prostitute
in the land of Egypt 20 and lusted after their lovers,
whose sexual members[D] were like those of donkeys
and whose emission was like that of stallions. 21 So
you revisited the depravity of your youth, when the
Egyptians caressed your nipples to enjoy your youthful breasts.

22 "Therefore, Oholibah, this is what the Lord GOD
says: I am going to incite your lovers against you,
those you turned away from in disgust. I will bring
them against you from every side: 23 the Babylonians
and all the Chaldeans; Pekod, Shoa, and Koa; and all
the Assyrians with them — desirable young men,
all of them governors and prefects, officers and administrators, all of them riding on steeds. 24 They
will come against you with an assembly of peoples
and with weapons, chariots, and[E] wagons. They will
set themselves against you on every side with large
and small shields and helmets. I will delegate judgment to them, and they will judge you by their own
standards. 25 When I vent my jealous fury on you,
they will deal with you in wrath. They will cut off
your nose and ears, and the rest of you[F] will fall by
the sword. They will seize your sons and daughters,
and the rest of you will be consumed by fire. 26 They
will strip off your clothes and take your beautiful
jewelry. 27 So I will put an end to your depravity and
sexual immorality, which began in the land of Egypt,
and you will not look longingly at them or remember
Egypt anymore.

28 "For this is what the Lord GOD says: I am going to
hand you over to those you hate, to those you turned
away from in disgust. 29 They will treat you with hatred, take all you have worked for, and leave you stark
naked, so that the shame of your debauchery will
be exposed, both your depravity and promiscuity.
30 These things will be done to you because you acted
like a prostitute with the nations, defiling yourself
with their idols. 31 You have followed the path of your
sister, so I will put her cup in your hand."

32 This is what the Lord GOD says:

"You will drink your sister's cup,
which is deep and wide.
You will be an object of[G] ridicule and scorn,
for it holds so much.
33 You will be filled with drunkenness and grief,
with a cup of devastation and desolation,
the cup of your sister Samaria.
34 You will drink it and drain it;
then you will gnaw its broken pieces,
and tear your breasts.
For I have spoken."
This is the declaration of the Lord GOD.

35 Therefore, this is what the Lord GOD says: "Because you have forgotten me and cast me behind
your back, you must bear the consequences of your
indecency and promiscuity."

[A] **23:4** = Her Tent [B] **23:4** = My Tent Is in Her [C] **23:16** Lit *of her eyes* [D] **23:20** Lit *whose flesh* [E] **23:24** LXX reads *peoples, from the north, chariots and*; Hb obscure [F] **23:25** Or *and your descendants* [G] **23:32** Or *It will bring*

Smelting and Metallurgy in Ancient Judah

by W. Wayne VanHorn

Archaeologists measure human civilization in terms of eras named after the materials with which people made their tools and weapons. We speak of the Stone Age (10,000–4500 BC), the Bronze Age (4500–1200 BC), and the Iron Age (1200–332 BC). These eras are broken down into smaller periods labeled Early, Middle, and Late.

Ezekiel prophesied between 592 and 561 BC, during the period of Babylonian exile. From an archaeological perspective, Ezekiel lived in the Middle to Late Iron Age. Metallurgy and smelting were relatively advanced by this time, and Ezekiel employed imagery from the smelting process of his day as an illustration of the judgment and refinement God would bring on his people.

METALWORKING: THE PROCESS

As early as Genesis 4:22, the Scriptures mention metallurgy, the process of mining and refining metal ores for the production of tools and weapons. Cain's descendant, Tubal-cain, "made all kinds of bronze and iron tools."[1] The development of metallurgic techniques corresponded with the progress of civilization. Techniques became gradually more sophisticated over time.

The smelting process involved heating metals in crucibles to temperatures sufficient to bring them to a molten state. Crucibles initially were made of earthenware and later various metals. Gold, which melted at low temperatures, was found in a purer state than most other metals.

Artisans would pour the liquefied metal into prefabricated molds where it cooled into the desired shape. This process caused impurities to rise to the top of the molten metal, where they were skimmed from the top.[2] Thus the smelting process purified the metal ore and rendered it pliable for the formation of tools and weapons. Artisans also discovered ways to combine metals to form hybrid materials or alloys that were stronger or more pliable. Around 3200 BC, before the time of Abraham, craftsmen discovered that they could form a stronger metal with a decreased melting point by mixing up to 10 percent of tin to their copper to form bronze.[3] These alloys generated additional possibilities for use. For example, bronze plow tips outlasted wooden or stone implements and made farming more productive. Alloys also became emblematic of impure mixtures, because they represented a departure from the original purity of the primary metal.

By Ezekiel's day, iron had become the preferred metal for making weapons and fittings for war chariots. Its relatively late usage is due to the fact that iron had a much higher melting point, which required more developed forms of smelting to liquefy it. Such technology did not develop until after 1300 BC when the disruption of copper and tin supplies forced people of the ancient Near East to turn to iron as an alternative to bronze. Iron

Bronze brazier; held coals for heating.

Egyptian figurine of a metal worker with furnace and blow pipe (ca 2460–2350 BC).

deposits were closer to the surface, were easier to mine, and thus were widely used by King David's time, about 1000 BC. Another contributor to iron's popularity was improved bellows. These newer bellows allowed the smelting temperature to be increased to that required by iron (four hundred degrees higher than copper).[4]

METALWORK IMAGERY IN EZEKIEL 18–24

According to Daniel Block, the book of Ezekiel has two major sections: judgment on Judah and Jerusalem (chaps. 1–24) and oracles of hope (chaps. 25–48).[5]

In Ezekiel 18–24, the Lord inspired Ezekiel to use the smelting process and images from metallurgy to prophesy concerning the approaching judgment against the sins of Judah (see 22:17–22). First, the Lord described sinful Judah as "dross" (v. 18). The Hebrew term *sug* or *sig* refers to the waste materials in metals that are brought to the surface and skimmed off through the application of extreme heat. The verb *sug* can mean "to turn away, be disloyal" (see Ps 80:13; Pr 14:14) or "to remove." Just as dross is the waste to be removed from the pure metal in smelting, God was going to remove sinful Judah through the fires of judgment.

Ezekiel mentioned five different metals in 22:18: brass/copper, tin, iron, lead, and silver. All of these were in use during the Late Iron Age of Ezekiel's day. Once metals were liquefied, they were removed from the furnace to be molded and cooled. Inevitably, some small residue of metal was left in the furnace and thus wasted. God's people had become like this wasted metal. They had potential for godly use, but due to sin they had become no more useful than dross.

Smelting involved using a furnace with sufficient capacity to handle the volume of metal being purged. The furnace also had temperatures required to liquefy the ores. The prophetic application of the smelting process involved Jerusalem as the furnace. More than any other place in Judah, Jerusalem represented the heart of the promised land, the place where God chose to put his name (Dt 12:11). The idea of putting metals in the furnace "to blow fire on them and melt them" (Ezk 22:20) clearly reflects the use of bellows to achieve the extreme heat required to smelt iron and other metals. Ezekiel used the image as a reference to the burning wrath of God (vv. 20b–22a). Unbridled sin and unheeded prophetic warnings had brought God's people to the point of unmitigated judgment.

The Lord declared, "As silver is melted inside a furnace, so you will be melted inside the city. Then you will know that I, the Lord, have poured out my wrath on you" (v. 22). The word *wrath* is the Hebrew *chemah*, referring to heat, rage, and burning anger. Judah's sin had kindled divine wrath hotter than a smelter's furnace. In the end, Judah would fare no better than the dross the smelters threw away as refuse. Judah had mixed, like alloyed metals and dross, themselves and their religion with that of the inhabitants of the land. They had become useless.

A reference to smelting is also found in Ezekiel 24:11, where Jerusalem, "the city of bloodshed" (v. 9), is depicted as a rusted cooking pot: "Set the empty pot on its coals so that it becomes hot and its copper glows. Then its impurity will melt inside it; its corrosion will be consumed." The intent of the reference is not to reclaim usable metal, but rather to utterly destroy the metal due to its impurities. In this way, metallurgy and smelting provided a suitable metaphor for God's judgment on both sinful Judah and Jerusalem. ✣

---

[1] We don't know, however, how widespread this technology was at this time or whether it survived the flood. [2] Ralph Gower, *The New Manners and Customs of Bible Times* (Chicago: Moody, 1987), 157. [3] David C. Maltsberger, "Mines and Mining" in *HIBD, rev. ed.* (2015), 1108. See also Gower, *New Manners*, 158. [4] Maltsberger, "Mines and Mining," 1108. [5] Daniel I. Block, "Ezekiel, Book of" in *HIBD*, 539.

36 Then the LORD said to me, "Son of man, will you
pass judgment against Oholah and Oholibah? Then
declare their detestable practices to them. 37 For they
have committed adultery, and blood is on their hands;
they have committed adultery with their idols. And
the children they bore to me they have sacrificed in
the fire[A] as food for the idols. 38 They also did this
to me: they defiled my sanctuary on that same day
and profaned my Sabbaths. 39 On the same day they
slaughtered their children for their idols, they entered my sanctuary to profane it. Yes, that is what
they did inside my house.

40 "In addition, they sent for men who came from
far away when a messenger was dispatched to them.
And look how they came! You bathed, painted your
eyes, and adorned yourself with jewelry for them.
41 You sat on a luxurious couch with a table spread
before it, on which you had set my incense and oil.
42 The sound of a carefree crowd was there. Drunkards[B] from the desert were brought in, along with
common men. They put bracelets on the women's
hands and beautiful tiaras on their heads. 43 Then
I said concerning this woman worn out by adultery: Will they[C] now have illicit sex with her, even
her? 44 Yet they had sex with her as one does with a
prostitute. This is how they had sex with Oholah and
Oholibah, those depraved women. 45 But righteous
men will judge them the way adulteresses and those
who shed blood are judged, for they are adulteresses
and blood is on their hands.

46 "This is what the Lord GOD says: Summon[D] an
assembly against them and consign them to terror
and plunder. 47 The assembly will stone them and cut
them down with their swords. They will kill their
sons and daughters and burn their houses. 48 So I will
put an end to depravity in the land, and all the wom-
en will be admonished not to imitate your depraved
behavior. 49 They will punish you for your depravity,
and you will bear the consequences for your sins of
idolatry. Then you will know that I am the Lord GOD."

PARABLE OF THE BOILING POT

24 The word of the LORD came to me in the ninth
year, in the tenth month, on the tenth day of
the month: 2 "Son of man, write down today's date,
this very day. The king of Babylon has laid siege to
Jerusalem this very day. 3 Now speak a parable to
the rebellious house. Tell them, 'This is what the Lord
GOD says:

Put the pot on the fire —
put it on,
and then pour water into it!
4 Place the pieces of meat in it,
every good piece —
thigh and shoulder.
Fill it with choice bones.
5 Take the choicest of the flock
and also pile up the fuel[E] under it.
Bring it to a boil
and cook the bones in it.

6 " 'Therefore, this is what the Lord GOD says:
Woe to the city of bloodshed,
the pot that has corrosion inside it,
and its corrosion has not come out of it!
Empty it piece by piece;
lots should not be cast for its contents.
7 For the blood she shed[F] is still within her.
She put it out on the bare rock;
she didn't pour it on the ground
to cover it with dust.
8 In order to stir up wrath
and take vengeance,
I have put her blood on the bare rock,
so that it would not be covered.

9 " 'Therefore, this is what the Lord GOD says:
Woe to the city of bloodshed!
I myself will make the pile of kindling large.
10 Pile on the logs and kindle the fire!
Cook the meat well
and mix in the spices![G,H]
Let the bones be burned!
11 Set the empty pot on its coals
so that it becomes hot and its copper glows.
Then its impurity will melt inside it;
its corrosion will be consumed.
12 It has frustrated every effort;[I]
its thick corrosion will not come off.
Into the fire with its corrosion!
13 Because of the depravity
of your uncleanness —
since I tried to purify you,
but you would not be purified
from your uncleanness —
you will not be pure again
until I have satisfied my wrath on you.
14 I, the LORD, have spoken.
It is coming, and I will do it!
I will not refrain, I will not show pity,
and I will not relent.
I[J] will judge you
according to your ways and deeds.
This is the declaration of the Lord GOD.' "

[A] **23:37** Lit *have made pass through the fire* [B] **23:42** Or *Sabeans* [C] **23:43** Or *They will* [D] **23:46** Or *I will summon* [E] **24:5** Lit *bones* [F] **24:7** Lit *For her blood* [G] **24:10** Some Hb mss read *well; remove the broth*; LXX reads *fire so that the meat may be cooked and the broth may be reduced* [H] **24:10** Or *and stir the broth* [I] **24:12** Hb obscure [J] **24:14** Some Hb mss, LXX, Syr, Tg, Vg; other Hb mss read *They*

THE DEATH OF EZEKIEL'S WIFE: A SIGN

15 Then the word of the LORD came to me: 16 "Son of man, I am about to take the delight of your eyes away from you with a fatal blow. But you must not lament or weep or let your tears flow. 17 Groan quietly; do not observe mourning rites for the dead. Put on your turban and strap your sandals on your feet; do not cover your mustache or eat the bread of mourners."[A]

18 I spoke to the people in the morning, and my wife died in the evening. The next morning I did just as I was commanded. 19 Then the people asked me, "Won't you tell us what these things you are doing mean for us?"

20 So I answered them, "The word of the LORD came to me: 21 Say to the house of Israel, 'This is what the Lord GOD says: I am about to desecrate my sanctuary, the pride of your power, the delight of your eyes, and the desire of your heart. Also, the sons and daughters you left behind will fall by the sword. 22 Then you will do just as I have done: You will not cover your mustache or eat the bread of mourners. 23 Your turbans will remain on your heads and your sandals on your feet. You will not lament or weep but will waste away because of your iniquities and will groan to one another. 24 Now Ezekiel will be a sign for you. You will do everything that he has done. When this happens, you will know that I am the Lord GOD.'

25 "As for you, son of man, know that on that day I will take from them their stronghold — their pride and joy, the delight of their eyes, and the longing of their hearts — as well as their sons and daughters. 26 On that day a fugitive will come to you and report the news. 27 On that day your mouth will be opened to talk with him; you will speak and no longer be mute. So you will be a sign for them, and they will know that I am the LORD."

PROPHECIES AGAINST THE NATIONS

JUDGMENT AGAINST AMMON

25 Then the word of the LORD came to me: 2 "Son of man, face the Ammonites and prophesy against them. 3 Say to the Ammonites, 'Hear the word of the Lord GOD: This is what the Lord GOD says: Because you said, "Aha!" about my sanctuary when it was desecrated, about the land of Israel when it was laid waste, and about the house of Judah when they went into exile, 4 therefore I am about to give you to the people of the east as a possession. They will set up their encampments and pitch their tents among you. They will eat your fruit and drink your milk. 5 I will make Rabbah a pasture for camels and Ammon a resting place for sheep. Then you will know that I am the LORD.

6 " 'For this is what the Lord GOD says: Because you clapped your hands, stamped your feet, and rejoiced over the land of Israel with wholehearted contempt, 7 therefore I am about to stretch out my hand against you and give you as plunder to the nations. I will cut you off from the peoples and eliminate you from the countries. I will destroy you, and you will know that I am the LORD.

JUDGMENT AGAINST MOAB

8 " 'This is what the Lord GOD says: Because Moab and Seir said, "Look, the house of Judah is like all the other nations." 9 Therefore I am about to expose Moab's flank beginning with its[B] frontier cities, the splendor of the land: Beth-jeshimoth, Baal-meon, and Kiriathaim. 10 I will give it along with Ammon to the people of the east as a possession, so that Ammon will not be remembered among the nations. 11 So I will execute judgments against Moab, and they will know that I am the LORD.

JUDGMENT AGAINST EDOM

12 " 'This is what the Lord GOD says: Because Edom acted vengefully against the house of Judah and incurred grievous guilt by taking revenge on them, 13 therefore this is what the Lord GOD says: I will stretch out my hand against Edom and cut off both people and animals from it. I will make it a wasteland; they will fall by the sword from Teman to Dedan. 14 I will take my vengeance on Edom through my people Israel, and they will deal with Edom according to my anger and wrath. So they will know my vengeance. This is the declaration of the Lord GOD.

JUDGMENT AGAINST PHILISTIA

15 " 'This is what the Lord GOD says: Because the Philistines acted in vengeance and took revenge with deep contempt, destroying because of their perpetual hatred, 16 therefore this is what the Lord GOD says: I am about to stretch out my hand against the Philistines, cutting off the Cherethites and wiping out what remains of the coastal peoples.[C] 17 I will execute severe vengeance against them with furious rebukes. They will know that I am the LORD when I take my vengeance on them.' "

THE DOWNFALL OF TYRE

26 In the eleventh year, on the first day of the month, the word of the LORD came to me: 2 "Son of man, because Tyre said about Jerusalem, 'Aha! The gateway to the peoples is shattered. She has been turned over to me.[D] I will be filled now that she lies in ruins,' 3 therefore this is what the Lord GOD says: See, I am against you, Tyre! I will raise up many nations

[A] 24:17 Lit *men*, also in v. 22 [B] 25:9 Lit *with the cities, with its* [C] 25:16 Lit *the seacoast* [D] 26:2 Or *It has swung open for me*

against you, just as the sea raises its waves. 4 They will
destroy the walls of Tyre and demolish her towers. I
will scrape the soil from her and turn her into a bare
rock. 5 She will become a place in the sea to spread
nets, for I have spoken." This is the declaration of the
Lord GOD. "She will become plunder for the nations,
6 and her villages on the mainland will be slaughtered
by the sword. Then they will know that I am the LORD."

7 For this is what the Lord GOD says: "See, I am about
to bring King Nebuchadnezzar[A] of Babylon, king of
kings, against Tyre from the north with horses, chariots, cavalry, and a huge assembly of troops. 8 He will
slaughter your villages on the mainland with the
sword. He will set up siege works, build a ramp, and
raise a wall of shields against you. 9 He will direct
the blows of his battering rams against your walls
and tear down your towers with his iron tools. 10 His
horses will be so numerous that their dust will cover
you. When he enters your gates as an army entering
a breached city, your walls will shake from the noise
of cavalry, wagons, and chariots. 11 He will trample
all your streets with the hooves of his horses. He
will slaughter your people with the sword, and your
mighty pillars will fall to the ground. 12 They will take
your wealth as spoil and plunder your merchandise.
They will also demolish your walls and tear down
your beautiful homes. Then they will throw your
stones, timber, and soil into the water. 13 I will put an
end to the noise of your songs, and the sound of your
lyres will no longer be heard. 14 I will turn you into a
bare rock, and you will be a place to spread nets. You
will never be rebuilt, for I, the LORD, have spoken."
This is the declaration of the Lord GOD.

15 This is what the Lord GOD says to Tyre: "Won't the
coasts and islands quake at the sound of your downfall, when the wounded groan and slaughter occurs
within you? 16 All the princes of the sea will descend
from their thrones, remove their robes, and strip off
their embroidered garments. They will clothe themselves with trembling; they will sit on the ground,
tremble continually, and be appalled at you. 17 Then
they will lament for you and say of you,

'How you have perished, city of renown,
you who were populated from the seas![B]
She who was powerful on the sea,
she and all of her inhabitants
inflicted their terror.[C]
18 Now the coastlands tremble
on the day of your downfall;
the islands in the sea
are alarmed by your demise.' "

19 For this is what the Lord GOD says: "When I make
you a ruined city like other deserted cities, when
I raise up the deep against you so that the mighty
waters cover you, 20 then I will bring you down to be
with those who descend to the Pit, to the people of
antiquity. I will make you dwell in the underworld[D]
like[E] the ancient ruins, with those who descend to the
Pit, so that you will no longer be inhabited or display
your splendor[F] in the land of the living. 21 I will make
you an object of horror, and you will no longer exist.
You will be sought but will never be found again." This
is the declaration of the Lord GOD.

THE SINKING OF TYRE

27 The word of the LORD came to me: 2 "Now, son
of man, lament for Tyre. 3 Say to Tyre, who is
situated at the entrance of the sea, merchant of the
peoples to many coasts and islands, 'This is what the
Lord GOD says:

Tyre, you declared,
"I am perfect in beauty."
4 Your realm was in the heart of the sea;
your builders perfected your beauty.
5 They constructed all your planking
with pine trees from Senir.
They took a cedar from Lebanon
to make a mast for you.
6 They made your oars of oaks from Bashan.
They made your deck of cypress wood
from the coasts of Cyprus,
inlaid with ivory.
7 Your sail was made of
fine embroidered linen from Egypt,
and served as your banner.
Your awning was of blue and purple fabric
from the coasts of Elishah.
8 The inhabitants of Sidon and Arvad
were your rowers.
Your wise men were within you, Tyre;
they were your captains.
9 The elders of Gebal and its wise men
were within you, repairing your leaks.

" 'All the ships of the sea and their sailors
came to you to barter for your goods.
10 Men of Persia, Lud, and Put
were in your army, serving
as your warriors.
They hung shields and helmets in you;
they gave you splendor.
11 Men of Arvad and Helech
were stationed on your walls all around,
and Gammadites were in your towers.

[A] **26:7** Lit *Nebuchadrezzar* [B] **26:17** Some LXX mss read *'How you were destroyed from the seas, city of renown!* [C] **26:17** Lit *and all her inhabitants who put their terror on all her inhabitants*; Hb obscure [D] **26:20** Lit *the lower parts of the earth* [E] **26:20** Some Hb mss, LXX; other Hb mss, Syr read *in* [F] **26:20** LXX reads *or appear*

Ancient Tyre

by Phillip J. Swanson

A FAVORABLE LOCATION

Tyre (*Tsor* in the Phoenician language) means "rock" and aptly names and describes the ancient city. Tyre was situated on a rocky island about one-half mile off the eastern coast of the Mediterranean Sea. It owed its long history, in part, to its location and the fortifications various kings erected on the island. The expanse of water between Tyre and the mainland afforded the city a measure of security. Although the straits between Tyre and the coast did not span a great distance, any attacker would have to be proficient on the seas. The construction of a wall encircling the island, estimated to have been 150 feet high in some places, added to the city's security.[1] The city boasted two harbors, the earliest being a natural cove toward the northern end of the island, called the Sidonian port. This port provided adequate protection to Tyre's growing fleet. King Ithobaal I (887–856 BC) later built another harbor at the southern end of the island, referred to as the Egyptian port.[2]

As secure as Tyre may have been, living on an island has its disadvantages. All necessities not already on the island had to be brought in by boat. Tyre lacked sufficient drinkable water and food, as well as building supplies. To acquire these resources, they depended on a supply from the mainland. The town of Ushur, part of Tyre, on the mainland, probably provided that service to the island inhabitants.[3]

AN ENTERPRISING CITY

As with many ancient cities and towns, knowledge of Tyre's origin and earliest inhabitants has faded with time. Its emergence as a significant force in the ancient Near East appears to have begun in the tenth century with the ascension of King Hiram (970–936 BC) to the throne. For two centuries before that time, Tyre's sister city, Sidon, was the dominant force. Hiram enlarged the island by joining it with a second island.[4] He also rebuilt and reestablished worship at the temples of Melkart and Ashtart.[5] This same King Hiram assisted Kings David and Solomon with the building of David's palace and Solomon's temple. In fact, during Israel's golden age, treaties were in force between the two nations. Although ties existed between Tyre and Israel, when King Ahab married Jezebel, the daughter of the king of the Sidon—which was under Tyrian dominance—he further cemented the relationship between the two nations.

Tyre's prosperity, especially during Hiram's time, was proverbial. During this time, Tyre became one of the most significant

Roman columns in ancient Tyre.

Main arch in Roman-era Tyre.

city-states in the known world. Industry flourished. Fishing was primary to the economy. Going beyond the simple catching of fish for sustenance, the Tyrians developed fisheries as large industrial plants.[6] Additionally, Tyre gained a reputation for its highly effective red dye.[7] Expanding its economic base even further, Tyre developed artists and craftsmen. Hiram's association with the construction of David's palace and the Jerusalem temple is well known and well documented in 2 Samuel 5:11 and 1 Kings 5:18, respectively. Second Chronicles 2:13–14 reports the skill and activity of Huram-abi, a Tyrian who worked on the temple. The text describes him as one who was proficient with all kinds of metals, wood, stone, yarns, and linen.

Tyre's greatest importance centered on its capacity for seamanship and overseas trade. Ezekiel 27 provides a list of the cargo Tyre's sailors carried: lumber, linen, various metals, ivory, emeralds, wines, wool, and many other commodities. Tyrian ships carried goods to every part of the known world.[8] Isaiah 23:3 proclaims that Tyre "was the merchant among the nations." Beginning with King Hiram, Tyre was not content to simply exist as merchants and seamen in their travels to foreign ports. From the tenth to ninth centuries BC, Tyre engaged in colonizing efforts around their world—efforts that possibly reached as far as Spain.[9] The most important of these colonies were Carthage and Utica in northern Africa.

A PENDING JUDGMENT

The picture that emerges of Tyre is of a city of great importance to its neighbors around the world. So what caused Israel's prophets such dismay that profound judgment against Tyre was the only answer?[10]

Most likely, the cause was not related to any single factor. The alliance made between Ahab and his Phoenician wife, Jezebel, introduced idolatry into the land, but that was a common enough occurrence throughout Israel's history.

Ezekiel reported that Tyre took advantage of Israel's misfortune (especially Jerusalem) when it found itself decimated by the Babylonians (Ezk 26:2–7). Quite possibly, even more disgusting to the prophet, the ruler of Tyre proclaimed himself to be a god (28:2–5). In the mind of the prophet, these two events would be more than sufficient to warrant God's judgment. Amos explained the matter further by saying that Tyre turned its back on the treaty between Israel and Tyre, a "treaty of brotherhood" (Am 1:9). Tyre had sold the inhabitants of Jerusalem into slavery to the Edomites.

Judgment was going to come to Tyre according to the testimony of the prophets. The only question was *when*.

A DISASTROUS END

For all its economic prosperity, Tyre's history was going to change for the worse with the rise of the Assyrian Empire. Through the ninth and eighth centuries BC, Assyria forced Tyre to pay tribute to them and also attacked Tyre on several occasions.[11] Although the Assyrian kings did subjugate Tyre, their actions did not approach the devastation the prophets pronounced.

The city did not fare any better under the Babylonians. Babylon's King Nebuchadnezzar attacked Tyre in 585 BC and laid siege to the city for thirteen years. Tyre finally relented and became a Babylonian province.[12] Nonetheless, the city-state remained intact.

The lot fell to Alexander the Great (332 BC) to carry out the sentence of the prophets. As he moved against Tyre, the city dug in once again to withstand the onslaught of another enemy. They held out for seven months, to no avail. As one historian put it, Tyre was "obliterated."[13]

Block with inscription mentioning "Tyrdos."

---

[1] Glenn E. Markoe, *Phoenicia* (Berkeley: University of California Press, 2000), 197. [2] Markoe, *Phoenicia*, 198. [3] LaMoine F. DeVries, *Cities of the Biblical World* (Peabody, MA: Hendrickson, 1997), 78–79. [4] Michael Grant, *The Ancient Mediterranean* (New York: Meridian Pocket, 1969), 121–22. [5] Avraham Negev, ed., *The Archaeological Encyclopedia of the Holy Land*, rev. ed. (Nashville: Thomas Nelson, 1986), 388. [6] Markoe, *Phoenicia*, 197. [7] Grant, *Ancient Mediterranean*, 122. [8] Negev, *Archaeological Encyclopedia*, 387. [9] Negev, *Archaeological Encyclopedia*, 388. [10] See Is 23; Jr 25; Ezk 26–28; Jl 3; Am 1 and Zch 9. [11] DeVries, *Cities*, 81. [12] DeVries, *Cities*. [13] Grant, *Ancient Mediterranean*, 213.

They hung their shields[A] all around
your walls;
they perfected your beauty.

12 " 'Tarshish was your trading partner because
of your abundant wealth of every kind. They exchanged silver, iron, tin, and lead for your merchandise. 13 Javan, Tubal, and Meshech were your
merchants. They exchanged slaves[B] and bronze utensils for your goods. 14 Those from Beth-togarmah
exchanged horses, war horses, and mules for your
merchandise. 15 Men of Dedan[C] were also your merchants; many coasts and islands were your regular
markets. They brought back ivory tusks and ebony
as your payment. 16 Aram[D] was your trading partner because of your numerous products. They exchanged turquoise,[E] purple and embroidered cloth,
fine linen, coral,[E] and rubies[E] for your merchandise.
17 Judah and the land of Israel were your merchants.
They exchanged wheat from Minnith, meal,[F] honey, oil, and balm, for your goods. 18 Damascus was
also your trading partner because of your numerous products and your abundant wealth of every
kind, trading in wine from Helbon and white wool.[G]
19 Vedan[H] and Javan from Uzal[E] dealt in your merchandise; wrought iron, cassia, and aromatic cane
were exchanged for your goods. 20 Dedan was your
merchant in saddlecloths for riding. 21 Arabia and all
the princes of Kedar were your business partners,
trading with you in lambs, rams, and goats. 22 The
merchants of Sheba and Raamah traded with you.
For your merchandise they exchanged the best of
all spices and all kinds of precious stones as well
as gold. 23 Haran, Canneh, Eden, the merchants of
Sheba, Asshur, and Chilmad traded with you. 24 They
were your merchants in choice garments, cloaks of
blue and embroidered materials, and multicolored
carpets,[E] which were bound and secured with cords
in your marketplace. 25 Ships of Tarshish were the
carriers for your goods.

" 'So you became full and heavily loaded[I]
in the heart of the sea.
26 Your rowers have brought you
onto the high seas,
but the east wind has wrecked you
in the heart of the sea.
27 Your wealth, merchandise,
and goods,
your sailors and captains,
those who repair your leaks,
those who barter for your goods,
and all the warriors on board,
with all the other people within you,
sink into the heart of the sea
on the day of your downfall.
28 " 'The countryside shakes
at the sound of your sailors' cries.
29 All the oarsmen
disembark from their ships.
The sailors and all the captains of the sea
stand on the shore.
30 Because of you, they raise their voices
and cry out bitterly.
They throw dust on their heads;
they roll in ashes.
31 They shave their heads because of you
and wrap themselves in sackcloth.
They weep over you
with deep anguish and bitter mourning.

32 " 'In their wailing they lament for you,
mourning over you:
"Who was like Tyre,
silenced[E] in the middle of the sea?
33 When your merchandise was unloaded
from the seas,
you satisfied many peoples.
You enriched the kings of the earth
with your abundant wealth and goods.
34 Now you are wrecked by the sea
in the depths of the waters;
your goods and the people within you
have gone down.
35 All the inhabitants of the coasts and islands
are appalled at you.
Their kings shudder with fear;
their faces are contorted.
36 Those who trade among the peoples
scoff[J] at you;
you have become an object of horror
and will never exist again." ' "

THE FALL OF TYRE'S RULER

28 The word of the LORD came to me: 2 "Son of man,
say to the ruler of Tyre, 'This is what the Lord
GOD says: Your[K] heart is proud, and you have said, "I
am a god; I sit in the seat of gods in the heart of the
sea." Yet you are a man and not a god, though you have
regarded your heart as that of a god. 3 Yes, you are
wiser than Daniel; no secret is hidden from you! 4 By
your wisdom and understanding you have acquired
wealth for yourself. You have acquired gold and silver for your treasuries. 5 By your great skill in trading
you have increased your wealth, but your heart has
become proud because of your wealth.

[A] **27:11** Or *quivers*; Hb obscure [B] **27:13** Lit *souls of men*
[C] **27:15** LXX reads *Rhodes* [D] **27:16** Some Hb mss, Aq, Syr read *Edom*
[E] **27:16,19,24,32** Hb obscure [F] **27:17** Or *resin*; Hb obscure [G] **27:18** Or *and wool from Zahar* [H] **27:19** Or *Dan* [I] **27:25** Or *and very glorious*
[J] **27:36** Lit *hiss* [K] **28:2** Lit *Because your*

6 "'Therefore, this is what the Lord GOD says:
Because you regard your heart as that
of a god,
7 I am about to bring strangers against you,
ruthless men from the nations.
They will draw their swords
against your magnificent wisdom
and will pierce your splendor.
8 They will bring you down to the Pit,
and you will die a violent death
in the heart of the sea.
9 Will you still say, "I am a god,"
in the presence of those who slay[A] you?
Yet you will be only a man, not a god,
in the hands of those who kill you.
10 You will die the death of the uncircumcised
at the hands of strangers.
For I have spoken.
This is the declaration of the Lord GOD.'"

A LAMENT FOR TYRE'S KING

11 The word of the LORD came to me: 12 "Son of man,
lament for the king of Tyre and say to him, 'This is
what the Lord GOD says:
You were the seal[B] of perfection,[C]
full of wisdom and perfect in beauty.
13 You were in Eden, the garden of God.
Every kind of precious stone covered you:
carnelian, topaz, and diamond,[C]
beryl, onyx, and jasper,
lapis lazuli, turquoise[D] and emerald.[E]
Your mountings and settings were crafted
in gold;
they were prepared on the day
you were created.
14 You were an anointed guardian cherub,
for[F] I had appointed you.
You were on the holy mountain of God;
you walked among the fiery stones.
15 From the day you were created
you were blameless in your ways
until wickedness was found in you.
16 Through the abundance of your trade,
you were filled with violence,
and you sinned.
So I expelled you in disgrace
from the mountain of God,
and banished you, guardian cherub,[G]
from among the fiery stones.
17 Your heart became proud because of
your beauty;
For the sake of your splendor
you corrupted your wisdom.
So I threw you down to the ground;[H]
I made you a spectacle before kings.
18 You profaned your sanctuaries
by the magnitude of your iniquities
in your dishonest trade.
So I made fire come from within you,
and it consumed you.
I reduced you to ashes on the ground
in the sight of everyone watching you.
19 All those who know you among the peoples
are appalled at you.
You have become an object of horror
and will never exist again.'"

A PROPHECY AGAINST SIDON

20 The word of the LORD came to me: 21 "Son of man,
face Sidon and prophesy against it. 22 You are to say,
'This is what the Lord GOD says:
Look! I am against you, Sidon,
and I will display my glory within you.
They will know that I am the LORD
when I execute judgments against her
and demonstrate my holiness through her.
23 I will send a plague against her
and bloodshed in her streets;
the slain will fall within her,
while the sword is against her[I]
on every side.
Then they will know that I am the LORD.

24 "'The house of Israel will no longer be hurt by[J]
prickly briers or painful thorns from all their neighbors who treat them with contempt. Then they will
know that I am the Lord GOD.

25 "'This is what the Lord GOD says: When I gather
the house of Israel from the peoples where they are
scattered, I will demonstrate my holiness through
them in the sight of the nations, and they will live
in their own land, which I gave to my servant Jacob.
26 They will live there securely, build houses, and plant
vineyards. They will live securely when I execute
judgments against all their neighbors who treat them
with contempt. Then they will know that I am the
LORD their God.'"

A PROPHECY OF EGYPT'S RUIN

29 In the tenth year, in the tenth month on the
twelfth day of the month, the word of the
LORD came to me: 2 "Son of man, face Pharaoh king
of Egypt and prophesy against him and against all
of Egypt. 3 Speak to him and say, 'This is what the
Lord GOD says:

[A] **28:9** Some Hb mss, LXX, Syr, Vg; other Hb mss read *of the one who kills* [B] **28:12** Or *sealer* [C] **28:12,13** Hb obscure [D] **28:13** Or *malachite*, or *garnet* [E] **28:13** Or *beryl* [F] **28:14** Or *With an anointed guardian cherub* [G] **28:16** Or *and the guardian cherub banished you* [H] **28:17** Or *earth* [I] **28:23** Or *within her by the sword* [J] **28:24** Lit *longer have*

Look, I am against you, Pharaoh king of Egypt,
the great monster[A] lying in the middle
of his Nile,
who says, "My Nile is my own;
I made it for myself."
4 I will put hooks in your jaws
and make the fish of your streams
cling to your scales.
I will haul you up
from the middle of your Nile,
and all the fish of your streams
will cling to your scales.
5 I will leave you in the desert,
you and all the fish of your streams.
You will fall on the open ground
and will not be taken away
or gathered for burial.
I have given you
to the wild creatures of the earth
and the birds of the sky as food.

6 " 'Then all the inhabitants of Egypt
will know that I am the LORD,
for they[B] have been a staff made of reed
to the house of Israel.
7 When Israel grasped you by the hand,
you splintered, tearing all their shoulders;
when they leaned on you,
you shattered and made all their hips unsteady.[C]

8 " 'Therefore, this is what the Lord GOD says: I am
going to bring a sword against you and cut off both
people and animals from you. 9 The land of Egypt will
be a desolate ruin. Then they will know that I am the
LORD. Because you[D] said, "The Nile is my own; I made
it," 10 therefore, I am against you and your Nile. I will
turn the land of Egypt into ruins, a desolate waste
from Migdol to Syene, as far as the border of Cush.
11 No human foot will pass through it, and no animal
foot will pass through it. It will be uninhabited for
forty years. 12 I will make the land of Egypt a desolation among[E] desolate lands, and its cities will be
a desolation among[F] ruined cities for forty years. I
will disperse the Egyptians among the nations and
scatter them throughout the lands.

13 " 'For this is what the Lord GOD says: At the end
of forty years I will gather the Egyptians from the
peoples where they were dispersed. 14 I will restore
the fortunes of Egypt and bring them back to the
land of Pathros, the land of their origin. There they
will be a lowly kingdom. 15 Egypt will be the lowliest
of kingdoms and will never again exalt itself over the
nations. I will make them so small they cannot rule
over the nations. 16 It will never again be an object
of trust for the house of Israel, drawing attention to
their iniquity of turning to the Egyptians. Then they
will know that I am the Lord GOD.' "

BABYLON RECEIVES EGYPT AS COMPENSATION

17 In the twenty-seventh year, in the first month,
on the first day of the month, the word of the LORD
came to me: 18 "Son of man, King Nebuchadnezzar of
Babylon made his army labor strenuously against
Tyre. Every head was made bald and every shoulder
chafed, but he and his army received no compensation from Tyre for the labor he expended against it.
19 Therefore, this is what the Lord GOD says: I am going
to give the land of Egypt to King Nebuchadnezzar of
Babylon, and he will carry off its wealth, seizing its
spoil and taking its plunder. This will be his army's
compensation. 20 I have given him the land of Egypt
as the pay he labored for, since they worked for me."
This is the declaration of the Lord GOD. 21 "In that day
I will cause a horn to sprout for the house of Israel,
and I will enable you to speak out among them. Then
they will know that I am the LORD."

EGYPT'S DOOM

30 The word of the LORD came to me: 2 "Son of
man, prophesy and say, 'This is what the Lord
GOD says:
Wail, "Woe because of that day!"
3 For a day is near;
a day belonging to the LORD is near.
It will be a day of clouds,
a time of doom[G] for the nations.
4 A sword will come against Egypt,
and there will be anguish in Cush
when the slain fall in Egypt,
and its wealth is taken away,
and its foundations are demolished.
5 Cush, Put, and Lud,
and all the various foreign troops,[H]
plus Libya[I] and the men of the covenant land
will fall by the sword along with them.
6 This is what the LORD says:
Those who support Egypt will fall,
and its proud strength will collapse.
From Migdol to Syene
they will fall within it by the sword.
This is the declaration of the Lord GOD.
7 They will be desolate
among[F] desolate lands,
and their cities will lie
among ruined[J] cities.

[A] **29:3** Or *crocodile* [B] **29:6** LXX, Syr, Vg read *you* [C] **29:7** LXX, Syr, Vg; MT reads *and you caused their hips to stand* [D] **29:9** LXX, Syr, Vg; MT reads *he* [E] **29:12** Or *Egypt the most desolate of* [F] **29:12; 30:7** Or *be the most desolate of* [G] **30:3** *of doom* supplied for clarity [H] **30:5** Or *all Arabia* [I] **30:5** Lit *Cub*; Hb obscure [J] **30:7** Or *will be the most ruined of*

8 They will know that I am the LORD
when I set fire to Egypt
and all its allies are shattered.
9 On that day, messengers will go out from me in ships
to terrify confident Cush. Anguish will come over
them on the day of Egypt's doom.[A] For indeed it is
coming.

10 "'This is what the Lord GOD says:
I will put an end to the hordes[B] of Egypt
by the hand of King Nebuchadnezzar
of Babylon.
11 He along with his people,
ruthless men from the nations,
will be brought in to destroy the land.
They will draw their swords against Egypt
and fill the land with the slain.
12 I will make the streams dry
and sell the land to evil men.
I will bring desolation
on the land and everything in it
by the hands of foreigners.
I, the LORD, have spoken.

13 "'This is what the Lord GOD says:
I will destroy the worthless idols
and put an end to the false gods in Memphis.
There will no longer be
a prince from the land of Egypt.
And I will instill fear in that land.
14 I will make Pathros desolate,
set fire to Zoan,
and execute judgments on Thebes.
15 I will pour out my wrath on Pelusium,
the stronghold of Egypt,
and will wipe out the hordes of Thebes.
16 I will set fire to Egypt;
Pelusium will writhe in anguish,
Thebes will be breached,
and Memphis will face foes in broad daylight.[C]
17 The young men of On[D] and Pi-beseth
will fall by the sword,
and those cities[E] will go into captivity.
18 The day will be dark[F] in Tehaphnehes,
when I break the yoke of Egypt there
and its proud strength
comes to an end in the city.
A cloud will cover Tehaphnehes,[G]
and its surrounding villages will go
into captivity.
19 So I will execute judgments against Egypt,
and they will know that I am the LORD.'"

PHARAOH'S POWER BROKEN

20 In the eleventh year, in the first month, on the seventh day of the month, the word of the LORD came
to me: 21 "Son of man, I have broken the arm of Pharaoh king of Egypt. Look, it has not been bandaged
— no medicine has been applied and no splint put
on to bandage it so that it can grow strong enough
to handle a sword. 22 Therefore, this is what the Lord
GOD says: Look! I am against Pharaoh king of Egypt. I
will break his arms, both the strong one and the one
already broken, and will make the sword fall from
his hand. 23 I will disperse the Egyptians among the
nations and scatter them among the countries. 24 I
will strengthen the arms of Babylon's king and place
my sword in his hand. But I will break the arms of
Pharaoh, and he will groan before him as a mortally
wounded man. 25 I will strengthen the arms of Babylon's king, but Pharaoh's arms will fall. They will
know that I am the LORD when I place my sword in
the hand of Babylon's king and he wields it against
the land of Egypt. 26 When I disperse the Egyptians
among the nations and scatter them among the countries, they will know that I am the LORD."

DOWNFALL OF EGYPT AND ASSYRIA

31 In the eleventh year, in the third month, on the
first day of the month, the word of the LORD
came to me: 2 "Son of man, say to Pharaoh king of
Egypt and to his hordes,
'Who are you like in your greatness?
3 Think of Assyria, a cedar in Lebanon,
with beautiful branches
and shady foliage
and of lofty height.
Its top was among the clouds.[H]
4 The waters caused it to grow;
the underground springs made it tall,
directing their rivers all around
the place where the tree was planted
and sending their channels
to all the trees of the field.
5 Therefore the cedar became greater
in height
than all the trees of the field.
Its branches multiplied,
and its boughs grew long
as it spread them out
because of the abundant water.
6 All the birds of the sky
nested in its branches,
and all the animals of the field
gave birth beneath its boughs;
all the great nations lived in its shade.

[A]**30:9** Lit *of Egypt* [B]**30:10** Or *pomp*, or *wealth*, also in v. 15 [C]**30:16** Or *foes daily* [D]**30:17** LXX, Vg; MT reads *iniquity* [E]**30:17** Or *and the women*; lit *and they* [F]**30:18** Some Hb mss, LXX, Syr, Tg, Vg; other Hb mss read *will withhold* [G]**30:18** Or *Egypt* [H]**31:3** Or *thick foliage*, also in vv. 10,14

7 It was beautiful in its size,
in the length of its limbs,
for its roots extended
to abundant water.
8 The cedars in God's garden could not
eclipse it;
the pine trees couldn't compare
with its branches,
nor could the plane trees match
its boughs.
No tree in the garden of God
could compare with it in beauty.
9 I made it beautiful with its many limbs,
and all the trees of Eden,
which were in God's garden, envied it.

10 " 'Therefore, this is what the Lord GOD says:
Since it[A] towered high in stature and set its top
among the clouds, and it[B] grew proud on account
of its height, 11 I determined to hand it over to a
ruler of nations; he would surely deal with it. I banished it because of its wickedness. 12 Foreigners,
ruthless men from the nations, cut it down and
left it lying. Its limbs fell on the mountains and in
every valley; its boughs lay broken in all the earth's
ravines. All the peoples of the earth left its shade
and abandoned it. 13 All the birds of the sky nested
on its fallen trunk, and all the animals of the field
were among its boughs. 14 This happened so that
no trees planted beside water would become great
in height and set their tops among the clouds, and
so that no other well-watered trees would reach
them in height. For they have all been consigned to
death, to the underworld, among the people[C] who
descend to the Pit.
15 " 'This is what the Lord GOD says: I caused grieving on the day the cedar went down to Sheol. I closed
off the underground deep because of it:[D] I held back
the rivers of the deep, and its abundant water was
restrained. I made Lebanon mourn on account of it,
and all the trees of the field fainted because of it. 16 I
made the nations quake at the sound of its downfall,
when I threw it down to Sheol to be with those who
descend to the Pit. Then all the trees of Eden, the
choice and best of Lebanon, all the well-watered
trees, were comforted in the underworld. 17 They
too descended with it to Sheol, to those slain by
the sword. As its allies[E,F] they had lived in its shade
among the nations.
18 " 'Who then are you like in glory and greatness
among Eden's trees? You also will be brought down
to the underworld to be with the trees of Eden. You
will lie among the uncircumcised with those slain by
the sword. This is Pharaoh and all his hordes. This is
the declaration of the Lord GOD.' "

A LAMENT FOR PHARAOH

32 In the twelfth year, in the twelfth month, on the
first day of the month, the word of the LORD
came to me: 2 "Son of man, lament for Pharaoh king
of Egypt and say to him,

'You compare yourself to a lion of the nations,
but[G] you are like a monster[H] in the seas.
You thrash about in your rivers,
churn up the waters with your feet,
and muddy the[I] rivers.

3 " 'This is what the Lord GOD says:
I will spread my net over you
with an assembly of many peoples,
and they[J] will haul you up in my net.
4 I will abandon you on the land
and throw you onto the open field.
I will cause all the birds of the sky
to settle on you
and let the wild creatures of the entire earth
eat their fill of you.
5 I will put your flesh on the mountains
and fill the valleys with your carcass.
6 I will drench the land
with the flow of your blood,
even to the mountains;
the ravines will be filled with your gore.

7 " 'When I snuff you out,
I will cover the heavens
and darken their stars.
I will cover the sun with a cloud,
and the moon will not give its light.
8 I will darken all the shining lights
in the heavens over you,
and will bring darkness on your land.
This is the declaration of the Lord GOD.

9 " 'I will trouble the hearts of many peoples,
when I bring about your destruction
among the nations,
in countries you have not known.
10 I will cause many peoples to be appalled
at you,
and their kings will shudder with fear
because of you
when I brandish my sword in front of them.
On the day of your downfall
each of them will tremble
every moment for his life.

[A] **31:10** Syr, Vg; MT, LXX read *you* [B] **31:10** Lit *its heart* [C] **31:14** Or *the descendants of Adam* [D] **31:15** Or *I covered it with the underground deep* [E] **31:17** LXX, Syr read *offspring* [F] **31:17** Lit *arm* [G] **32:2** Or *'Lion of the nations, you are destroyed;* [H] **32:2** Or *crocodile* [I] **32:2** Lit *their* [J] **32:3** LXX, Vg read *I*

Battle of Carchemish

by Kevin C. Peacock

Carchemish is not mentioned in Ezekiel (but see 2Ch 35:20; Is 10:9; Jr 46:2). Nevertheless, chapters 29–32 speak of divine judgment on Egypt and its pharaoh. The battle of Carchemish played a crucial role in that judgment, after which the nation was no longer a power to be reckoned with. Ezekiel's judgment was ultimately fulfilled when the Persian King Cambyses conquered it in 525 BC.

Our knowledge of the ancient Near East is due in large part to cuneiform texts from Assyria and Babylonia. Many of these are chronographic texts that comprise seventeen king lists and twenty-five chronicles. The chronicles offer a yearly (with gaps) account of the king's military actions and other significant events. Chronicles 1–13b are known as the Babylonian Chronicle Series, which covers the period from Nabopolassar's founding of the Babylonian/Chaldean Empire in 626 BC to the Seleucid Empire in the third century BC.[1] Though often referred to as the Babylonian Chronicle, as if it were a unified text, it is actually a collection of tablets from many places, which mostly ended up in the British Museum in London. They are sometimes referred to not as a text but as a genre.[2]

Babylonian Chronicle for 605–595 BC.

Chronicle 5 covers the early years of Nebuchadnezzar II, from 604 to 595 BC, which includes his capture of Jerusalem in 597. It also describes Pharaoh Neco II's campaign to support the Assyrians at Haran in northern Syria in 610 or 609 BC. The Egyptians retreated from the Babylonians under King Nabonidus (625–605 BC), however, to Judah, where Neco II deposed King Jehoahaz II and installed Jehoiakim as king in 609 BC. Babylon campaigned in the north until they encountered the Assyrians at Carchemish, about fifty miles west of Haran. The Babylonian army under the command of crown-prince Nebuchadnezzar was victorious and drove the Egyptians southwest about 150 miles and defeated them again at Hamath. "The battle of Carchemish . . . was, for the kingdom of Judah, one of the most consequential battles in ancient times."[3]

THE IMPORTANCE OF CARCHEMISH

Carchemish/Karkemish (modern-day Jerablus) held a strategic location on a major bend of the Euphrates River. Just west of the river, the city of Carchemish controlled an important river crossing in northern Syria. Controlling Carchemish meant controlling the international east-west trade route. The Babylonians desired to control Carchemish, the Phoenician coast, and the territory inland, because most Babylonian trade was with the west, and much wealth lay in Syria-Palestine. Carchemish was Babylon's gateway to the Mediterranean, and they could ill afford to have the Egyptians block it. Egypt controlled the Way of the Sea (Via Maris, see Is 9:1; Mt 4:15) through central Syria as far as Carchemish. The Via Maris was the major trade route that followed the Mediterranean coast and linked Egypt with Mesopotamia.

The Neo-Babylonian Empire's brief history thus was marked with numerous campaigns into "the land of Hatti" (i.e., Syria-Palestine), campaigns vital for securing a life-line of prosperity.[4] With the Medes being gone and the collapse of the Assyrian Empire, the main struggle for the control of Syria-Palestine in the last few years of the seventh century BC was between Egypt and Babylon. Carchemish was the key.

THE BATTLE OF CARCHEMISH

The Egyptians put up a strong resistance at Carchemish against the Babylonians, but in June–July 605 BC they finally withdrew, fleeing for their lives.[5] The Babylonian Chronicle, referring to Nebuchadnezzar, reports,

> He defeated them (smashing) them out of existence. As for the remnant of the Egyptian army which had escaped from the defeat so (hastily) that no weapon had touched them, the Babylonian army overtook and defeated them in the district of Hamath, so that not a single man [escaped] to his own country. At that time Nebuchadrezzar conquered the whole of the land of Ha[math].[6]

Nebuchadnezzar likely pursued the fleeing Egyptian forces down the Mediterranean coast (see Jr 46:2–12). The city of Riblah in southern Syria became the main Babylonian garrison center in southern Syria. Immediately after hearing of his father's death in Babylon, Nebuchadnezzar hurried home to secure his throne.[7]

Nebuchadnezzar then marched back to Hatti-land, secured his dominance there, and "took the heavy tribute of Hatti-land back to Babylon." He exerted control over Judah probably at this time. Daniel 1:1 states, "In the third year of the reign of King Jehoiakim of Judah, King Nebuchadnezzar of Babylon came to Jerusalem and laid siege to it." Then he took some of the temple vessels to Babylon (v. 2).[8] The Hebrew term translated "laid siege" may simply mean "showed hostility" or "treated as an enemy" and not an actual siege.[9] Nebuchadnezzar bound Jehoiakim in chains "to take him to Babylon" (2Ch 36:6), but could simply have been exerting dominance. This probably happened late in 605 BC.[10] The "heavy tribute of Hatti-land" thus included temple articles (v. 7) and Daniel and his three friends, who were taken into exile (Dn 1:1–7).[11] For four successive years, Nebuchadnezzar campaigned in Hatti, securing his control over Syria-Palestine (Jr 47:4–5; Hab 1–2).

THE SIGNIFICANCE OF THE BATTLE

Biblical reflection on the battle of Carchemish and its immediate aftermath reveals several emphases:

Step pyramid and temple at Saqqara, Egypt.

God's Final Judgment on Assyria—For all practical purposes, the Assyrian Empire ceased to exist in 609 BC at the battle of Haran when its last king disappeared from history. But a few Assyrians probably joined the Egyptian forces at Carchemish. Nebuchadnezzar was the ax, but Yahweh's hand wielded it. Yahweh had promised that Assyria would be defeated (Is 10:5–34; 14:24–27; 31:8–9; Zph 2:13; Zch 10:11; see Nahum), and Ezekiel used Assyria's defeat as a warning for Egypt (Ezk 31:2–18).

Judah's New Boss—Immediately after Carchemish, Jeremiah began prophesying of Babylon's seventy-year rule over Judah and the entire land (Jr 25:1–14; 29:10; 36:1–3). If Judah would voluntarily submit to Babylon, then destruction might not come (21:8–9; 38:2–3). Jeremiah sent his message on a scroll to Jehoiakim (36:1–19), but Jehoiakim refused to heed Jeremiah's warning and chose instead to rebel (v. 29).

Punishment for Egypt—Carchemish was a humiliating loss for the Egyptian army (Jr 46:2–26), which fled slithering like a serpent seeking refuge (v. 22). "The king of Egypt did not march out of his land again, for the king of Babylon took everything that had belonged to the king of Egypt, from the Brook of Egypt to the Euphrates River" (2Kg 24:7). Egypt's pride and aggression against its neighbors brought Yahweh's judgment (Jr 46:7–8,26). The Egyptians trusted their own might, their own king, and their own gods (v. 25); therefore, Yahweh punished them, thrust them down, and put them to shame (vv. 15,21,24).

Judgment for God's People—Shortly after the battle of Carchemish, Nebuchadnezzar approached Jerusalem, and "the Lord handed King Jehoiakim of Judah over to him, along with some of the vessels from the house of God" (Dn 1:2a). God caused Nebuchadnezzar's dominance over Judah. Why? Because King Jehoiakim "did what was evil in the sight of the LORD his God" (2Ch 36:5b; cf. 2Kg 23:36–24:4). The subsequent exile was God's judgment on his people's sin (Dn 9:5–14; cf. Dt 28:32–64; 1Kg 8:33–34,46–51). Because Israel refused to heed Yahweh's repeated warnings through his prophets (Dn 9:6), the people suffered the consequences for their sin. ✣

---

[1] See D. B. Weisberg, "Non-Israelite Written Sources: Babylonian" in *Dictionary of the Old Testament Historical Books*, ed. Bill T. Arnold and H. G. M. Williamson (Downers Grove, IL: IVP Academic, 2005), 731–33. [2] British Museum tablet 21901, lines 38–50, in D. J. Wiseman, *Chronicles of Chaldean Kings (626–556 BC) in the British Museum* (London: Trustees of the British Museum, 1956), 58–61. See also D. J. Wiseman, "Historical Records of Assyria and Babylonia" in *Documents from Old Testament Times*, ed. D. Winton Thomas (New York: Harper & Row, 1961), 77–79, from which the translation of the tablet here is taken. [3] LeMoine F. DeVries, *Cities of the Biblical World* (Peabody, MA: Hendrickson, 1997), 53. [4] Georges Roux, *Ancient Iraq* (New York: Penguin Books, 1977), 343. [5] D. J. Wiseman, *Nebuchadrezzar and Babylon*, The Schweich Lectures of the British Academy (Oxford: Oxford University Press, 1985), 16. Excavations of the town and citadel in 1912–14 reveal that the city was burned about this time. The site is on the Turkish-Syrian border and is covered by a Turkish military base. Access is greatly restricted, and future excavations are highly unlikely. [6] Wiseman earlier translated the final phrase "the whole of the land of Hatti," meaning Syria-Palestine. In 1985, he retranslated the phrase "the whole region of Hamath," referring to northern Syria. See Wiseman, *Nebuchadrezzar and Babylon*, 17. [7] Wiseman, *Nebuchadrezzar and Babylon*, 17–18. [8] On the chronological discrepancy between Dn 1:1 and Jr 25:1, see Tremper Longman III, *Daniel*, NIV Application Commentary (Grand Rapids: Zondervan, 1999), 43–44. [9] See Dt 20:12; 2Kg 16:5; 24:10–11; Sg 8:9. See Wiseman, *Nebuchadrezzar and Babylon*, 23. The Babylonian Chronicle mentions no siege of Jerusalem at this time. [10] Wiseman, *Nebuchadrezzar and Babylon*, 23. See Jack Finegan, *Handbook of Biblical Chronology*, rev. ed. (Peabody, MA: Hendrickson, 1998), 254. The text does not state that Jehoiakim was actually taken into exile; it could mean that he was threatened with the possibility. [11] Ezekiel was probably taken into exile with King Jehoiachin and a group of ten thousand captives in the so-called "first deportation" in 597 BC. See Christopher J. H. Wright, *The Message of Ezekiel* (Downers Grove, IL: InterVarsity, 2001), 19–20.

11 " 'For this is what the Lord GOD says:
The sword of Babylon's king
will come against you!
12 I will make your hordes fall
by the swords of warriors,
all of them ruthless men from the nations.
They will ravage Egypt's pride,
and all its hordes will be destroyed.
13 I will slaughter all its cattle
that are beside many waters.
No human foot will churn them again,
and no cattle hooves will disturb them.
14 Then I will let their waters settle
and will make their rivers flow like oil.
This is the declaration of the Lord GOD.
15 When I make the land of Egypt
a desolation,
so that it is emptied of everything in it,
when I strike down all who live there,
then they will know that I am the LORD.

16 " 'The daughters of the nations will chant that lament. They will chant it over Egypt and all its hordes.
This is the declaration of the Lord GOD.' "

EGYPT IN SHEOL

17 In the twelfth year,[A] on the fifteenth day of the
month, the word of the LORD came to me: 18 "Son of
man, wail over the hordes of Egypt and bring Egypt
and the daughters of mighty nations down to the
underworld,[B] to be with those who descend to the Pit:
19 Who do you surpass in loveliness?
Go down and be laid to rest
with the uncircumcised!
20 They will fall among those slain
by the sword.
A sword is appointed!
They drag her and all her hordes away.
21 Warrior leaders will speak
from the middle of Sheol
about him[C] and his allies:
'They have come down;
the uncircumcised lie
slain by the sword.'

22 "Assyria is there with her whole assembly;
her graves are all around her.
All of them are slain, fallen by the sword.
23 Her graves are set in the deepest regions
of the Pit,
and her assembly is all around
her burial place.
All of them are slain, fallen by the sword —
those who once spread terror
in the land of the living.

24 "Elam is there
with all her hordes around her grave.
All of them are slain, fallen by the sword —
those who went down
to the underworld uncircumcised,
who once spread their terror
in the land of the living.
They bear their disgrace
with those who descend to the Pit.
25 Among the slain
they prepare a bed for Elam
with all her hordes.
Her graves are all around her.
All of them are uncircumcised,
slain by the sword,
although their terror was once spread
in the land of the living.
They bear their disgrace
with those who descend to the Pit.
They are placed among the slain.

26 "Meshech and Tubal[D] are there,
with all their hordes.
Their graves are all around them.
All of them are uncircumcised,
slain by the sword,
although their terror was once spread
in the land of the living.
27 They do not lie down
with the fallen warriors
of the uncircumcised,[E]
who went down to Sheol
with their weapons of war,
whose swords were placed under their heads[F]
and their shields[G]
rested on their bones,
although the terror of these warriors
was once in the land of the living.
28 But you will be shattered
and will lie down among the uncircumcised,
with those slain by the sword.

29 "Edom is there, her kings and all her princes,
who, despite their strength, have been placed
among those slain by the sword.
They lie down with the uncircumcised,
with those who descend to the Pit.
30 All the leaders of the north
and all the Sidonians are there.
They went down in shame with the slain,
despite the terror their strength inspired.

[A] **32:17** LXX reads *year, in the first month,* [B] **32:18** Lit *the lower parts of the earth*, also in v. 24 [C] **32:21** Either Pharaoh or Egypt [D] **32:26** Lit *Meshech-tubal* [E] **32:27** LXX reads *of antiquity* [F] **32:27** Or *Do they not . . . heads?* [G] **32:27** Emended; MT reads *iniquities*

They lie down uncircumcised
with those slain by the sword.
They bear their disgrace
with those who descend to the Pit.

31 "Pharaoh will see them
and be comforted over all his hordes —
Pharaoh and his whole army,
slain by the sword."
This is the declaration of the Lord GOD.
32 "For I will spread my[A] terror
in the land of the living,
so Pharaoh and all his hordes
will be laid to rest among the uncircumcised,
with those slain by the sword."
This is the declaration of the Lord GOD.

EZEKIEL AS ISRAEL'S WATCHMAN

33 The word of the LORD came to me: [2] "Son of
man, speak to your people and tell them, 'Suppose I bring the sword against a land, and the people
of that land select a man from among them, appointing him as their watchman. [3] And suppose he sees the
sword coming against the land and blows his ram's
horn to warn the people. [4] Then, if anyone hears the
sound of the ram's horn but ignores the warning, and
the sword comes and takes him away, his death will
be his own fault.[B] [5] Since he heard the sound of the
ram's horn but ignored the warning, his death is his
own fault.[C] If he had taken warning, he would have
saved his life. [6] However, suppose the watchman sees
the sword coming but doesn't blow the ram's horn, so
that the people aren't warned, and the sword comes
and takes away their lives. Then they have been tak-
en away because of their iniquity, but I will hold the
watchman accountable for their blood.'

[7] "As for you, son of man, I have made you a watchman for the house of Israel. When you hear a word
from my mouth, give them a warning from me. [8] If I
say to the wicked, 'Wicked one, you will surely die,'
but you do not speak out to warn him about his way,
that wicked person will die for his iniquity, yet I will
hold you responsible for his blood. [9] But if you warn
a wicked person to turn from his way and he doesn't
turn from it, he will die for his iniquity, but you will
have rescued yourself.

[10] "Now as for you, son of man, say to the house of
Israel, 'You have said this: "Our transgressions and
our sins are heavy on us, and we are wasting away
because of them! How then can we survive?" ' [11] Tell
them, 'As I live — this is the declaration of the Lord
GOD — I take no pleasure in the death of the wicked,
but rather that the wicked person should turn from
his way and live. Repent, repent of your evil ways!
Why will you die, house of Israel?'

[12] "Now, son of man, say to your people, 'The righteousness of the righteous person will not save him
on the day of his transgression; neither will the wickedness of the wicked person cause him to stumble on
the day he turns from his wickedness. The righteous
person won't be able to survive by his righteousness on the day he sins. [13] When I tell the righteous
person that he will surely live, but he trusts in his
righteousness and acts unjustly, then none of his
righteousness will be remembered, and he will die
because of the injustice he has committed.

[14] " 'So when I tell the wicked person, "You will
surely die," but he repents of his sin and does what
is just and right — [15] he returns collateral, makes
restitution for what he has stolen, and walks in the
statutes of life without committing injustice — he
will certainly live; he will not die. [16] None of the sins
he committed will be held[D] against him. He has done
what is just and right; he will certainly live.

[17] " 'But your people say, "The Lord's way isn't fair,"
even though it is their own way that isn't fair. [18] When
a righteous person turns from his righteousness and
commits injustice, he will die for it. [19] But if a wicked
person turns from his wickedness and does what is
just and right, he will live because of it. [20] Yet you say,
"The Lord's way isn't fair." I will judge each of you
according to his ways, house of Israel.' "

THE NEWS OF JERUSALEM'S FALL

[21] In the twelfth year of our exile, in the tenth month,
on the fifth day of the month, a fugitive from Jerusalem came to me and reported, "The city has been
taken!" [22] Now the hand of the LORD had been on
me the evening before the fugitive arrived, and he
opened my mouth before the man came to me in
the morning. So my mouth was opened and I was
no longer mute.

ISRAEL'S CONTINUED REBELLION

[23] Then the word of the LORD came to me: [24] "Son of
man, those who live in the[E] ruins in the land of Israel
are saying, 'Abraham was only one person, yet he
received possession of the land. But we are many;
surely the land has been given to us as a possession.'
[25] Therefore say to them, 'This is what the Lord GOD
says: You eat meat with blood in it, you look to your
idols, and you shed blood. Should you then receive
possession of the land? [26] You have relied on your
swords, you have committed detestable acts, and
each of you has defiled his neighbor's wife. Should
you then receive possession of the land?'

[A] **32:32** Alt Hb tradition, LXX, Syr read *his* [B] **33:4** Lit *his blood will be on his head* [C] **33:5** Lit *his blood will be on him* [D] **33:16** Lit *remembered* [E] **33:24** Lit *these*

27 "Tell them this: 'This is what the Lord GOD says: As surely as I live, those who are in the ruins will fall by the sword, those in the open field I have given to wild animals to be devoured, and those in the strongholds and caves will die by plague. 28 I will make the land a desolate waste, and its proud strength will come to an end. The mountains of Israel will become desolate, with no one passing through. 29 They will know that I am the LORD when I make the land a desolate waste because of all the detestable acts they have committed.'

30 "As for you, son of man, your people are talking about you near the city walls and in the doorways of their houses. One person speaks to another, each saying to his brother, 'Come and hear what the message is that comes from the LORD!' 31 So my people come to you in crowds,[A] sit in front of you, and hear your words, but they don't obey them. Their mouths go on passionately, but their hearts pursue dishonest profit. 32 Yes, to them you are like a singer of passionate songs who has a beautiful voice and plays skillfully on an instrument. They hear your words, but they don't obey them. 33 Yet when all this comes true — and it definitely will — then they will know that a prophet has been among them."

THE SHEPHERDS AND GOD'S FLOCK

34 The word of the LORD came to me: 2 "Son of man, prophesy against the shepherds of Israel. Prophesy, and say to them, 'This is what the Lord GOD says to the shepherds: Woe to the shepherds of Israel, who have been feeding themselves! Shouldn't the shepherds feed their flock? 3 You eat the fat, wear the wool, and butcher the fattened animals, but you do not tend the flock. 4 You have not strengthened the weak, healed the sick, bandaged the injured, brought back the strays, or sought the lost. Instead, you have ruled them with violence and cruelty. 5 They were scattered for lack of a shepherd; they became food for all the wild animals when they were scattered. 6 My flock went astray on all the mountains and every high hill. My flock was scattered over the whole face of the earth, and there was no one searching or seeking for them.

7 " 'Therefore, you shepherds, hear the word of the LORD. 8 As I live — this is the declaration of the Lord GOD — because my flock, lacking a shepherd, has become prey and food for every wild animal, and because my shepherds do not search for my flock, and because the shepherds feed themselves rather than my flock, 9 therefore, you shepherds, hear the word of the LORD!

10 " 'This is what the Lord GOD says: Look, I am against the shepherds. I will demand my flock from them[B] and prevent them from shepherding the flock. The shepherds will no longer feed themselves, for I will rescue my flock from their mouths so that they will not be food for them.

11 " 'For this is what the Lord GOD says: See, I myself will search for my flock and look for them. 12 As a shepherd looks for his sheep on the day he is among his scattered flock, so I will look for my flock. I will rescue them from all the places where they have been scattered on a day of clouds and total darkness. 13 I will bring them out from the peoples, gather them from the countries, and bring them to their own soil. I will shepherd them on the mountains of Israel, in the ravines, and in all the inhabited places of the land. 14 I will tend them in good pasture, and their grazing place will be on Israel's lofty mountains. There they will lie down in a good grazing place; they will feed in rich pasture on the mountains of Israel. 15 I will tend my flock and let them lie down. This is the declaration of the Lord GOD. 16 I will seek the lost, bring back the strays, bandage the injured, and strengthen the weak, but I will destroy[C] the fat and the strong. I will shepherd them with justice.

17 " 'As for you, my flock, the Lord GOD says this: Look, I am going to judge between one sheep and another, between the rams and goats. 18 Isn't it enough for you to feed on the good pasture? Must you also trample the rest of the pasture with your feet? Or isn't it enough that you drink the clear water? Must you also muddy the rest with your feet? 19 Yet my flock has to feed on what your feet have trampled, and drink what your feet have muddied.

20 " 'Therefore, this is what the Lord GOD says to them: See, I myself will judge between the fat sheep and the lean sheep. 21 Since you have pushed with flank and shoulder and butted all the weak ones with your horns until you scattered them all over, 22 I will save my flock. They will no longer be prey, and I will judge between one sheep and another. 23 I will establish over them one shepherd, my servant David, and he will shepherd them. He will tend them himself and will be their shepherd. 24 I, the LORD, will be their God, and my servant David will be a prince among them. I, the LORD, have spoken.

25 " 'I will make a covenant of peace with them and eliminate dangerous creatures from the land, so that they may live securely in the wilderness and sleep in the forest. 26 I will make them and the area around my hill a blessing: I will send down showers in their season; they will be showers of blessing. 27 The trees of the field will yield their fruit, and the land will yield its produce; my flock will be secure in their land. They will know that I am the LORD when I break the bars of

[A] **33:31** Lit *you like the coming of a people* [B] **34:10** Lit *their hand*
[C] **34:16** Some Hb mss, LXX, Syr, Vg read *watch over*

their yoke and rescue them from the power of those who enslave them. 28 They will no longer be prey for the nations, and the wild creatures of the earth will not consume them. They will live securely, and no one will frighten them. 29 I will establish for them a place renowned for its agriculture,[A] and they will no longer be victims of famine in the land. They will no longer endure the insults of the nations. 30 Then they will know that I, the LORD their God, am with them, and that they, the house of Israel, are my people. This is the declaration of the Lord GOD. 31 You are my flock, the human flock of my pasture, and I am your God. This is the declaration of the Lord GOD.' "

A PROPHECY AGAINST EDOM

35 The word of the LORD came to me: 2 "Son of man, face Mount Seir and prophesy against it. 3 Say to it, 'This is what the Lord GOD says:

Look! I am against you, Mount Seir.
I will stretch out my hand against you
and make you a desolate waste.
4 I will turn your cities into ruins,
and you will become a desolation.
Then you will know that I am the LORD.

5 " 'Because you maintained a perpetual hatred and gave the Israelites over to the power of the sword in the time of their disaster, the time of final punishment, 6 therefore, as I live — this is the declaration of the Lord GOD — I will destine you for bloodshed, and it will pursue you. Since you did not hate bloodshed, it will pursue you. 7 I will make Mount Seir a desolate waste and will cut off from it those who come and go. 8 I will fill its mountains with the slain; those slain by the sword will fall on your hills, in your valleys, and in all your ravines. 9 I will make you a perpetual desolation; your cities will not be inhabited. Then you will know that I am the LORD.

10 " 'Because you said, "These two nations and two lands will be mine, and we will possess them" — though the LORD was there — 11 therefore, as I live — this is the declaration of the Lord GOD — I will treat you according to the anger and jealousy you showed in your hatred of them. I will make myself known among them[B] when I judge you. 12 Then you will know that I, the LORD, have heard all the blasphemies you uttered against the mountains of Israel, saying, "They are desolate. They have been given to us to devour!" 13 You boasted against me with your mouth, and spoke many words against me. I heard it myself!

14 " 'This is what the Lord GOD says: While the whole world rejoices, I will make you a desolation. 15 Just as you rejoiced over the inheritance of the house of Israel because it became a desolation, I will deal the same way with you: you will become a desolation, Mount Seir, and so will all Edom in its entirety. Then they will know that I am the LORD.'

RESTORATION OF ISRAEL'S MOUNTAINS

36 "Son of man, prophesy to the mountains of Israel and say, 'Mountains of Israel, hear the word of the LORD. 2 This is what the Lord GOD says: Because the enemy has said about you, "Aha! The ancient heights have become our possession," ' 3 therefore, prophesy and say, 'This is what the Lord GOD says: Because they have made you desolate and have trampled you from every side, so that you became a possession for the rest of the nations and an object of people's gossip and slander, 4 therefore, mountains of Israel, hear the word of the Lord GOD. This is what the Lord GOD says to the mountains and hills, to the ravines and valleys, to the desolate ruins and abandoned cities, which have become plunder and a mockery to the rest of the nations all around.

5 " 'This is what the Lord GOD says: Certainly in my burning zeal I speak against the rest of the nations and all of Edom, who took[C] my land as their own possession with wholehearted rejoicing and utter contempt so that its pastureland became[D] plunder. 6 Therefore, prophesy concerning Israel's land, and say to the mountains and hills, to the ravines and valleys: This is what the Lord GOD says: Look, I speak in my burning zeal because you have endured the insults of the nations. 7 Therefore, this is what the Lord GOD says: I swear[E] that the nations all around you will endure their own insults.

8 " 'You, mountains of Israel, will produce your branches and bear your fruit for my people Israel, since their arrival is near. 9 Look! I am on your side; I will turn toward you, and you will be tilled and sown. 10 I will fill you with people, with the whole house of Israel in its entirety. The cities will be inhabited and the ruins rebuilt. 11 I will fill you with people and animals, and they will increase and be fruitful. I will make you inhabited as you once were and make you better off than you were before. Then you will know that I am the LORD. 12 I will cause people, my people Israel, to walk on you; they will possess you, and you will be their inheritance. You will no longer deprive them of their children.

13 " 'This is what the Lord GOD says: Because some are saying to you, "You devour people and deprive your nation of children," 14 therefore, you will no longer devour people and deprive your nation of children.[F] This is the declaration of the Lord GOD.

[A] **34:29** LXX, Syr read *a plant of peace* [B] **35:11** LXX reads *you* [C] **36:5** Lit *gave* [D] **36:5** Or *contempt, to empty it of*; Hb obscure [E] **36:7** Lit *lift up my hand* [F] **36:14** Alt Hb tradition reads *and cause your nation to stumble*

15 I will no longer allow the insults of the nations to
be heard against you, and you will not have to endure the reproach of the peoples anymore; you will
no longer cause your nation to stumble.[A] This is the
declaration of the Lord GOD.' "

RESTORATION OF ISRAEL'S PEOPLE

16 The word of the LORD came to me: 17 "Son of man,
while the house of Israel lived in their land, they
defiled it with their conduct and actions. Their
behavior before me was like menstrual impurity.
18 So I poured out my wrath on them because of
the blood they had shed on the land, and because
they had defiled it with their idols. 19 I dispersed
them among the nations, and they were scattered
among the countries. I judged them according to
their conduct and actions. 20 When they came to
the nations where they went, they profaned my
holy name, because it was said about them, 'These
are the people of the LORD, yet they had to leave
his land in exile.' 21 Then I had concern for my holy
name, which the house of Israel profaned among
the nations where they went.

22 "Therefore, say to the house of Israel, 'This is
what the Lord GOD says: It is not for your sake that I
will act, house of Israel, but for my holy name, which
you profaned among the nations where you went.
23 I will honor the holiness of my great name, which
has been profaned among the nations — the name
you have profaned among them. The nations will
know that I am the LORD — this is the declaration
of the Lord GOD — when I demonstrate my holiness
through you in their sight.

24 " 'For I will take you from the nations and gather
you from all the countries, and will bring you into your
own land. 25 I will also sprinkle clean water on you,
and you will be clean. I will cleanse you from all
your impurities and all your idols. 26 I will give you
a new heart and put a new spirit within you; I will
remove your heart of stone[B] and give you a heart of
flesh. 27 I will place my Spirit within you and cause
you to follow my statutes and carefully observe my
ordinances. 28 You will live in the land that I gave your
ancestors; you will be my people, and I will be your
God. 29 I will save you from all your uncleanness. I will
summon the grain and make it plentiful, and I will
not bring famine on you. 30 I will also make the fruit
of the trees and the produce of the field plentiful, so
that you will no longer experience reproach among
the nations on account of famine.

31 " 'You will remember your evil ways and your
deeds that were not good, and you will loathe yourselves for your iniquities and detestable practices.
32 It is not for your sake that I will act — this is the
declaration of the Lord GOD — let this be known to
you. Be ashamed and humiliated because of your
ways, house of Israel!

33 " 'This is what the Lord GOD says: On the day I
cleanse you from all your iniquities, I will cause the
cities to be inhabited, and the ruins will be rebuilt.
34 The desolate land will be cultivated instead of lying desolate in the sight of everyone who passes by.
35 They will say, "This land that was desolate has become like the garden of Eden. The cities that were
once ruined, desolate, and demolished are now fortified and inhabited." 36 Then the nations that remain
around you will know that I, the LORD, have rebuilt
what was demolished and have replanted what was
desolate. I, the LORD, have spoken and I will do it.

37 " 'This is what the Lord GOD says: I will respond to
the house of Israel and do this for them: I will multiply
them in number like a flock.[C] 38 So the ruined cities
will be filled with a flock of people, just as Jerusalem
is filled with a flock of sheep for sacrifice[D] during
its appointed festivals. Then they will know that I
am the LORD.' "

THE VALLEY OF DRY BONES

37 The hand of the LORD was on me, and he
brought me out by his Spirit and set me down
in the middle of the valley; it was full of bones. 2 He
led me all around them. There were a great many
of them on the surface of the valley, and they were
very dry. 3 Then he said to me, "Son of man, can these
bones live?"

I replied, "Lord GOD, only you know."

4 He said to me, "Prophesy concerning these bones
and say to them: Dry bones, hear the word of the
LORD! 5 This is what the Lord GOD says to these bones:
I will cause breath to enter you, and you will live. 6 I
will put tendons on you, make flesh grow on you,
and cover you with skin. I will put breath in you so
that you come to life. Then you will know that I am
the LORD."

7 So I prophesied as I had been commanded. While
I was prophesying, there was a noise, a rattling
sound, and the bones came together, bone to bone.
8 As I looked, tendons appeared on them, flesh grew,
and skin covered them, but there was no breath
in them. 9 He said to me, "Prophesy to the breath,[E]
prophesy, son of man. Say to it: This is what the Lord
GOD says: Breath, come from the four winds and
breathe into these slain so that they may live!" 10 So
I prophesied as he commanded me; the breath entered them, and they came to life and stood on their
feet, a vast army.

[A] **36:15** Some Hb mss, Tg read *no longer bereave your nation of children* [B] **36:26** Lit *stone from your flesh* [C] **36:37** Lit *flock of people*
[D] **36:38** Lit *as the consecrated flock, as the flock of Jerusalem*
[E] **37:9** Or *wind*, or *spirit*, also in v. 10

[11] Then he said to me, "Son of man, these bones are the whole house of Israel. Look how they say, 'Our bones are dried up, and our hope has perished; we are cut off.' [12] Therefore, prophesy and say to them, 'This is what the Lord GOD says: I am going to open your graves and bring you up from them, my people, and lead you into the land of Israel. [13] You will know that I am the LORD, my people, when I open your graves and bring you up from them. [14] I will put my Spirit in you, and you will live, and I will settle you in your own land. Then you will know that I am the LORD. I have spoken, and I will do it. This is the declaration of the LORD.' "

THE REUNIFICATION OF ISRAEL

[15] The word of the LORD came to me: [16] "Son of man, take a single stick and write on it: Belonging to Judah and the Israelites associated with him. Then take another stick and write on it: Belonging to Joseph — the stick of Ephraim — and all the house of Israel associated with him. [17] Then join them together into a single stick so that they become one in your hand. [18] When your people ask you, 'Won't you explain to us what you mean by these things?' — [19] tell them, 'This is what the Lord GOD says: I am going to take the stick of Joseph, which is in the hand of Ephraim, and the tribes of Israel associated with him, and put them together with the stick of Judah. I will make them into a single stick so that they become one in my hand.'

[20] "When the sticks you have written on are in your hand and in full view of the people, [21] tell them, 'This is what the Lord GOD says: I am going to take the Israelites out of the nations where they have gone. I will gather them from all around and bring them into their own land. [22] I will make them one nation in the land, on the mountains of Israel, and one king will rule over all of them. They will no longer be two nations and will no longer be divided into two kingdoms. [23] They will not defile themselves anymore with their idols, their abhorrent things, and all their transgressions. I will save them from all their apostasies by which[A] they sinned, and I will cleanse them. Then they will be my people, and I will be their God. [24] My servant David will be king over them, and there will be one shepherd for all of them. They will follow my ordinances, and keep my statutes and obey them.

[25] " 'They will live in the land that I gave to my servant Jacob, where your ancestors lived. They will live in it forever with their children and grandchildren, and my servant David will be their prince forever. [26] I will make a covenant of peace with them; it will be a permanent covenant with them. I will establish and multiply them and will set my sanctuary among them forever. [27] My dwelling place will be with them; I will be their God, and they will be my people. [28] When my sanctuary is among them forever, the nations will know that I, the LORD, sanctify Israel.' "

THE DEFEAT OF GOG

38 The word of the LORD came to me: [2] "Son of man, face Gog, of the land of Magog, the chief prince of[B] Meshech and Tubal. Prophesy against him [3] and say, 'This is what the Lord GOD says: Look, I am against you, Gog, chief prince of Meshech and Tubal. [4] I will turn you around, put hooks in your jaws, and bring you out with all your army, including horses and riders, who are all splendidly dressed, a huge assembly armed with large and small shields, all of them brandishing swords. [5] Persia, Cush, and Put are with them, all of them with shields and helmets; [6] Gomer with all its troops; and Beth-togarmah from the remotest parts of the north along with all its troops — many peoples are with you.

[7] " 'Be prepared and get yourself ready, you and your whole assembly that has been mobilized around you; you will be their guard. [8] After a long time you will be summoned. In the last years you will enter a land that has been restored from war[C] and regathered from many peoples to the mountains of Israel, which had long been a ruin. They were brought out from the peoples, and all of them now live securely. [9] You, all of your troops, and many peoples with you will advance, coming like a thunderstorm; you will be like a cloud covering the land.

[10] " 'This is what the Lord GOD says: On that day, thoughts will arise in your mind, and you will devise an evil plan. [11] You will say, "I will advance against a land of open villages; I will come against a tranquil people who are living securely, all of them living without walls and without bars or gates" — [12] in order to seize spoil and carry off plunder, to turn your hand against ruins now inhabited and against a people gathered from the nations, who have been acquiring cattle and possessions and who live at the center of the world. [13] Sheba and Dedan and the merchants of Tarshish with all its rulers[D] will ask you, "Have you come to seize spoil? Have you mobilized your assembly to carry off plunder, to make off with silver and gold, to take cattle and possessions, to seize plenty of spoil?" '

[14] "Therefore prophesy, son of man, and say to Gog, 'This is what the Lord GOD says: On that day when my people Israel are dwelling securely, will you not know this [15] and come from your place in the remotest parts of the north — you and many peoples with you, who

[A] **37:23** Some Hb mss, LXX, Sym; other Hb mss read *their settlements where* [B] **38:2** Or *the prince of Rosh,* [C] **38:8** Lit *from the sword* [D] **38:13** Lit *young lions,* or *villages*

are all riding horses — a huge assembly, a powerful army? 16 You will advance against my people Israel like a cloud covering the land. It will happen in the last days, Gog, that I will bring you against my land so that the nations may know me, when I demonstrate my holiness through you in their sight.

17 " 'This is what the Lord God says: Are you the one I spoke about in former times through my servants, the prophets of Israel, who for years prophesied in those times that I would bring you against them? 18 Now on that day, the day when Gog comes against the land of Israel — this is the declaration of the Lord God — my wrath will flare up.[A] 19 I swear in my zeal and fiery wrath: On that day there will be a great earthquake in the land of Israel. 20 The fish of the sea, the birds of the sky, the animals of the field, every creature that crawls on the ground, and every human being on the face of the earth will tremble before me. The mountains will be demolished, the cliffs will collapse, and every wall will fall to the ground. 21 I will call for a sword against him on all my mountains — this is the declaration of the Lord God — and every man's sword will be against his brother. 22 I will execute judgment on him with plague and bloodshed. I will pour out torrential rain, hailstones, fire, and burning sulfur on him, as well as his troops and the many peoples who are with him. 23 I will display my greatness and holiness, and I will reveal myself in the sight of many nations. Then they will know that I am the Lord.'

THE DISPOSAL OF GOG

39 "As for you, son of man, prophesy against Gog and say, 'This is what the Lord God says: Look, I am against you, Gog, chief prince of[B] Meshech and Tubal. 2 I will turn you around, drive you on, and lead you up from the remotest parts of the north. I will bring you against the mountains of Israel. 3 Then I will knock your bow from your left hand and make your arrows drop from your right hand. 4 You, all your troops, and the peoples who are with you will fall on the mountains of Israel. I will give you as food to every kind of predatory bird and to the wild animals. 5 You will fall on the open field, for I have spoken. This is the declaration of the Lord God.

6 " 'I will send fire against Magog and those who live securely on the coasts and islands. Then they will know that I am the Lord. 7 So I will make my holy name known among my people Israel and will no longer allow it to be profaned. Then the nations will know that I am the Lord, the Holy One in Israel. 8 Yes, it is coming, and it will happen. This is the declaration of the Lord God. This is the day I have spoken about.

9 " 'Then the inhabitants of Israel's cities will go out, kindle fires, and burn the weapons — the small and large shields, the bows and arrows, the clubs and spears. For seven years they will use them to make fires. 10 They will not gather wood from the countryside or cut it down from the forests, for they will use the weapons to make fires. They will take the loot from those who looted them and plunder those who plundered them. This is the declaration of the Lord God.

11 " 'Now on that day I will give Gog a burial place there in Israel — the Travelers' Valley[C] east of the Sea. It will block those who travel through, for Gog and all his hordes will be buried there. So it will be called Hordes of Gog[D] Valley. 12 The house of Israel will spend seven months burying them in order to cleanse the land. 13 All the people of the land will bury them and their fame will spread on the day I display my glory. This is the declaration of the Lord God.

14 " 'They will appoint men on a full-time basis to pass through the land and bury the invaders[E] who remain on the surface of the ground, in order to cleanse it. They will make their search at the end of the seven months. 15 When they pass through the land and one of them sees a human bone, he will set up a marker next to it until the buriers have buried it in Hordes of Gog Valley. 16 There will even be a city named Hamonah[F] there. So they will cleanse the land.'

17 "Son of man, this is what the Lord God says: Tell every kind of bird and all the wild animals, 'Assemble and come! Gather from all around to my sacrificial feast that I am slaughtering for you, a great feast on the mountains of Israel; you will eat flesh and drink blood. 18 You will eat the flesh of mighty men and drink the blood of the earth's princes: rams, lambs, male goats, and all the fattened bulls of Bashan. 19 You will eat fat until you are satisfied and drink blood until you are drunk, at my sacrificial feast that I have prepared for you. 20 At my table you will eat your fill of horses and riders, of mighty men and all the warriors. This is the declaration of the Lord God.'

ISRAEL'S RESTORATION TO GOD

21 "I will display my glory among the nations, and all the nations will see the judgment I have executed and the hand I have laid on them. 22 From that day forward the house of Israel will know that I am the Lord their God. 23 And the nations will know that the house of Israel went into exile on account of their iniquity, because they dealt unfaithfully with me. Therefore, I hid my face from them and handed them over to their enemies, so that they all fell by the sword. 24 I dealt with them according to their uncleanness and transgressions, and I hid my face from them.

[A] **38:18** Lit *up in my anger* [B] **39:1** Or *Gog, prince of Rosh,* [C] **39:11** Hb obscure [D] **39:11** = Hamon-gog, also in v. 15 [E] **39:14** Or *basis, some to pass through the land, and with them some to bury those* [F] **39:16** In Hb, *Hamonah* is related to the word "horde."

25 "So this is what the Lord GOD says: Now I will restore the fortunes of Jacob and have compassion on the whole house of Israel, and I will be jealous for my holy name. 26 They will feel remorse for[A,B] their disgrace and all the unfaithfulness they committed against me, when they live securely in their land with no one to frighten them. 27 When I bring them back from the peoples and gather them from the countries of their enemies, I will demonstrate my holiness through them in the sight of many nations. 28 They will know that I am the LORD their God when I regather them to their own land after having exiled them among the nations. I will leave none of them behind.[C] 29 I will no longer hide my face from them, for I will pour out my Spirit on the house of Israel." This is the declaration of the Lord GOD.

THE NEW TEMPLE

40 In the twenty-fifth year of our exile, at the beginning of the year, on the tenth day of the month in the fourteenth year after Jerusalem had been captured, on that very day the LORD's hand was on me, and he brought me there. 2 In visions of God he took me to the land of Israel and set me down on a very high mountain. On its southern slope was a structure resembling a city. 3 He brought me there, and I saw a man whose appearance was like bronze, with a linen cord and a measuring rod in his hand. He was standing by the city gate. 4 He spoke to me: "Son of man, look with your eyes, listen with your ears, and pay attention to everything I am going to show you, for you have been brought here so that I might show it to you. Report everything you see to the house of Israel."

THE WALL AND OUTER GATES

5 Now there was a wall surrounding the outside of the temple. The measuring rod in the man's hand was six units of twenty-one inches;[D] each unit was the standard length plus three inches.[E] He measured the thickness of the wall structure; it was 10½ feet,[F] and its height was the same. 6 Then he came to the gate that faced east and climbed its steps. He measured the threshold of the gate; it was 10½ feet deep — one threshold was 10½ feet deep. 7 Each recess was 10½ feet long and 10½ feet deep, and there was a space of 8¾ feet[G] between the recesses. The inner threshold of the gate on the temple side next to the gate's portico was 10½ feet. 8 Next he measured the gate's portico; 9 it[H] was 14 feet,[I] and its jambs were 3½ feet.[J] The gate's portico was on the temple side.

10 There were three recesses on each side of the east gate, each with the same measurements, and the jambs on either side also had the same measurements. 11 Then he measured the width of the gate's entrance; it was 17½ feet,[K] while the width[L] of the gate was 22¾ feet.[M] 12 There was a barrier of 21 inches[N] in front of the recesses on both sides, and the recesses on each side were 10½ feet[O] square. 13 Then he measured the gate from the roof of one recess to the roof of the opposite one; the distance was 43¾ feet.[P] The openings of the recesses faced each other. 14 Next, he measured the porch — 105 feet.[Q,R] 15 The distance from the front of the gate at the entrance to the front of the gate's portico on the inside was 87½ feet.[S] 16 The recesses and their jambs had beveled windows all around the inside of the gate. The porticoes also had windows all around on the inside. Each jamb was decorated with palm trees.

17 Then he brought me into the outer court, and there were chambers and a paved surface laid out all around the court. Thirty chambers faced the pavement, 18 which flanked the courtyard's gates and corresponded to the length of the gates; this was the lower pavement. 19 Then he measured the distance from the front of the lower gate to the exterior front of the inner court; it was 175 feet.[T] This was the east; next the north is described.

20 He measured the gate of the outer court facing north, both its length and width. 21 Its three recesses on each side, its jambs, and its portico had the same measurements as the first gate: 87½ feet long and 43¾ feet wide. 22 Its windows, portico, and palm trees had the same measurements as those of the gate that faced east. Seven steps led up to the gate, and its portico was ahead of them. 23 The inner court had a gate facing the north gate, like the one on the east. He measured the distance from gate to gate; it was 175 feet.

24 He brought me to the south side, and there was also a gate on the south. He measured its jambs and portico; they had the same measurements as the others. 25 Both the gate and its portico had windows all around, like the other windows. It was 87½ feet long and 43¾ feet wide. 26 Its stairway had seven steps, and its portico was ahead of them. It had palm trees on its jambs, one on each side. 27 The inner court had a gate on the south. He measured from gate to gate on the south; it was 175 feet.

[A] **39:26** Some emend to *will forget* [B] **39:26** Lit *will bear* [C] **39:28** Lit *behind there any longer* [D] **40:5** = a long cubit [E] **40:5** Lit *six cubits by the cubit and a handbreadth* [F] **40:5** Lit *was one rod*, also in v. 7 [G] **40:7** Lit *five cubits*, also in v. 30 [H] **40:8–9** Some Hb mss, Syr, Vg; other Hb mss read *gate facing the temple side; it was one rod.* [9] *Then he measured the gate's portico; it* [I] **40:9** Lit *eight cubits* [J] **40:9** Lit *two cubits* [K] **40:11** Lit *10 cubits* [L] **40:11** Lit *length* [M] **40:11** Lit *13 cubits* [N] **40:12** Lit *one cubit*, also in v. 42 [O] **40:12** Lit *six cubits* [P] **40:13** Lit *25 cubits*, also in vv. 21,25,29,33,36 [Q] **40:14** MT adds *To the jamb of the court, the gate was all around*; Hb obscure [R] **40:14** Lit *60 cubits* [S] **40:15** Lit *50 cubits*, also in vv. 21,25,29,33,36 [T] **40:19** Lit *100 cubits*, also in vv. 23,27,47

THE INNER GATES

28 Then he brought me to the inner court through the
south gate. When he measured the south gate, it had
the same measurements as the others. 29 Its recesses, jambs, and portico had the same measurements
as the others. Both it and its portico had windows
all around. It was 87 ½ feet long and 43 ¾ feet wide.
30 (There were porticoes all around, 43 ¾ feet long and
8 ¾ feet wide.[A]) 31 Its portico faced the outer court,
and its jambs were decorated with palm trees. Its
stairway had eight steps.

32 Then he brought me to the inner court on the
east side. When he measured the gate, it had the same
measurements as the others. 33 Its recesses, jambs,
and portico had the same measurements as the others. Both it and its portico had windows all around.
It was 87 ½ feet long and 43 ¾ feet wide. 34 Its portico
faced the outer court, and its jambs were decorated
with palm trees on each side. Its stairway had eight
steps.

35 Then he brought me to the north gate. When he
measured it, it had the same measurements as the
others, 36 as did its recesses, jambs, and portico. It also
had windows all around. It was 87 ½ feet long and
43 ¾ feet wide. 37 Its portico[B] faced the outer court,
and its jambs were decorated with palm trees on
each side. Its stairway had eight steps.

ROOMS FOR PREPARING SACRIFICES

38 There was a chamber whose door opened into the
gate's portico.[C] The burnt offering was to be washed
there. 39 Inside the gate's portico there were two tables on each side, on which to slaughter the burnt
offering, sin offering, and guilt offering. 40 Outside,
as one approaches the entrance of the north gate,
there were two tables on one side and two more
tables on the other side of the gate's portico. 41 So
there were four tables inside the gate and four outside, eight tables in all on which the slaughtering
was to be done. 42 There were also four tables of
cut stone for the burnt offering, each 31 ½ inches[D] long, 31 ½ inches wide, and 21 inches high. The
utensils used to slaughter the burnt offerings and
other sacrifices were placed on them. 43 There were
three-inch[E] hooks[F] fastened all around the inside
of the room, and the flesh of the offering was to be
laid on the tables.

ROOMS FOR SINGERS AND PRIESTS

44 Outside the inner gate, within the inner court, there
were chambers for the singers:[G] one[H] beside the north
gate, facing south, and another beside the south[I] gate,
facing north. 45 Then the man said to me, "This chamber that faces south is for the priests who keep charge
of the temple. 46 The chamber that faces north is for
the priests who keep charge of the altar. These are
the sons of Zadok, the ones from the sons of Levi
who may approach the LORD to serve him." 47 Next
he measured the court. It was square, 175 feet long
and 175 feet wide. The altar was in front of the temple.

48 Then he brought me to the portico of the temple
and measured the jambs of the portico; they were 8 ¾
feet thick on each side. The width of the gate was 24 ½
feet,[J] and the side walls of the gate were[K] 5 ¼ feet[L]
wide on each side. 49 The portico was 35 feet[M] across
and 21[N] feet[O] deep, and 10 steps led[P] up to it. There
were pillars by the jambs, one on each side.

INSIDE THE TEMPLE

41 Next he brought me into the great hall and
measured the jambs; on each side the width of
the jamb was 10 ½ feet.[Q,R] 2 The width of the entrance
was 17 ½ feet,[S] and the side walls of the entrance were
8 ¾ feet[T] wide on each side. He also measured the
length of the great hall, 70 feet,[U] and the width, 35
feet.[V] 3 He went inside the next room and measured
the jambs at the entrance; they were 3 ½ feet[W] wide.
The entrance was 10 ½ feet wide, and the width of
the entrance's side walls on each side[X] was 12 ¼ feet.[Y]
4 He then measured the length of the room adjacent
to the great hall, 35 feet, and the width, 35 feet. And
he said to me, "This is the most holy place."

OUTSIDE THE TEMPLE

5 Then he measured the wall of the temple; it was 10 ½
feet thick. The width of the side rooms all around the
temple was 7 feet.[Z] 6 The side rooms were arranged
one above another in three stories of thirty rooms
each.[AA] There were ledges on the wall of the temple all
around to serve as supports for the side rooms, so that
the supports would not be in the temple wall itself.
7 The side rooms surrounding the temple widened at
each successive story, for the structure surrounding
the temple went up by stages. This was the reason for
the temple's broadness as it rose. And so, one would
go up from the lowest story to the highest by means
of the middle one.[AB]

[A] **40:30** Some Hb mss, LXX omit v. 30 [B] **40:37** LXX; MT reads *jambs* [C] **40:38** Text emended; MT reads *door was by the jambs, at the gates* [D] **40:42** Lit *one and a half cubits* [E] **40:43** Lit *one handbreadth* [F] **40:43** Or *ledges* [G] **40:44** LXX reads *were two chambers* [H] **40:44** LXX; MT reads *singers, which was* [I] **40:44** LXX; MT reads *east* [J] **40:48** Lit *14 cubits* [K] **40:48** LXX; MT omits *24 ½ feet, and the side walls of the gate were* [L] **40:48** Lit *three cubits* [M] **40:49** Lit *20 cubits* [N] **40:49** LXX; MT reads *19 ¼* [O] **40:49** Lit *12 cubits* [P] **40:49** MT reads *and it was on steps that they would go* [Q] **41:1** LXX; MT reads *jambs; they were 10 ½ feet wide on each side — the width of the tabernacle* [R] **41:1** Lit *six cubits*, also in vv. 3,5 [S] **41:2** Lit *10 cubits* [T] **41:2** Lit *five cubits*, also in vv. 9,11,12 [U] **41:2** Lit *40 cubits* [V] **41:2** Lit *20 cubits*, also in vv. 4,10 [W] **41:3** Lit *two cubits*, also in v. 22 [X] **41:3** LXX; MT reads *width of the entrance* [Y] **41:3** Lit *seven cubits* [Z] **41:5** Lit *four cubits* [AA] **41:6** Lit *another three and thirty times* [AB] **41:7** Hb obscure

8 I saw that the temple had a raised platform surrounding it; this foundation for the side rooms was 10 ½ feet high.[A] 9 The thickness of the outer wall of the side rooms was 8 ¾ feet. The free space between the side rooms of the temple 10 and the outer chambers was 35 feet wide all around the temple. 11 The side rooms opened into the free space, one entrance toward the north and another to the south. The area of free space was 8 ¾ feet wide all around.

12 Now the building that faced the temple yard toward the west was 122 ½ feet[B] wide. The wall of the building was 8 ¾ feet thick on all sides, and the building's length was 157 ½ feet.[C]

13 Then the man measured the temple; it was 175 feet[D] long. In addition, the temple yard and the building, including its walls, were 175 feet long. 14 The width of the front of the temple along with the temple yard to the east was 175 feet. 15 Next he measured the length of the building facing the temple yard to the west, with its galleries[E] on each side; it was 175 feet.

INTERIOR WOODEN STRUCTURES

The interior of the great hall and the porticoes of the court — 16 the thresholds, the beveled windows, and the balconies all around with their three levels opposite the threshold — were overlaid with wood on all sides. They were paneled from the ground to the windows (but the windows were covered), 17 reaching to the top of the entrance, and as far as the inner temple and on the outside. On every wall all around, on the inside and outside, was a pattern 18 carved with cherubim and palm trees. There was a palm tree between each pair of cherubim. Each cherub had two faces: 19 a human face turned toward the palm tree on one side, and a lion's face turned toward it on the other. They were carved throughout the temple on all sides. 20 Cherubim and palm trees were carved from the ground to the top of the entrance and on the wall of the great hall.

21 The doorposts of the great hall were square, and the front of the sanctuary had the same appearance. 22 The altar was[F] made of wood, 5 ¼ feet[G] high and 3 ½ feet long.[H] It had corners, and its length[I] and sides were of wood. The man told me, "This is the table that stands before the LORD."

23 The great hall and the sanctuary each had a double door, 24 and each of the doors had two swinging panels. There were two panels for one door and two for the other. 25 Cherubim and palm trees were carved on the doors of the great hall like those carved on the walls. There was a wooden canopy[J] outside, in front of the portico. 26 There were beveled windows and palm trees on both sides, on the side walls of the portico, the side rooms of the temple, and the canopies.[J]

THE PRIESTS' CHAMBERS

42 Then the man led me out by way of the north gate into the outer court. He brought me to the group of chambers opposite the temple yard and opposite the building to the north. 2 Along the length of the chambers, which was 175 feet,[K] there was an entrance on the north; the width was 87 ½ feet.[L] 3 Opposite the 35 foot space[M] belonging to the inner court and opposite the paved surface belonging to the outer court, the structure rose gallery by gallery in three tiers. 4 In front of the chambers was a walkway toward the inside, 17 ½ feet[N] wide and 175 feet long,[O] and their entrances were on the north. 5 The upper chambers were narrower because the galleries took away more space from them than from the lower and middle stories of the building. 6 For they were arranged in three stories and had no pillars like the pillars of the courts; therefore the upper chambers were set back from the ground more than the lower and middle stories. 7 A wall on the outside ran in front of the chambers, parallel to them, toward the outer court; it was 87 ½ feet long. 8 For the chambers on the outer court were 87 ½ feet long, while those facing the great hall were 175 feet long. 9 At the base of these chambers there was an entryway on the east side as one enters them from the outer court.

10 In the thickness of the wall of the court toward the south,[P] there were chambers facing the temple yard and the western building, 11 with a passageway in front of them, just like the chambers that faced north. Their length and width, as well as all their exits, measurements, and entrances, were identical. 12 The entrance at the beginning of the passageway, the way in front of the corresponding[Q] wall as one enters on the east side, was similar to the entrances of the chambers that were on the south side.

13 Then the man said to me, "The northern and southern chambers that face the courtyard are the holy chambers where the priests who approach the LORD will eat the most holy offerings. There they will deposit the most holy offerings — the grain offerings, sin offerings, and guilt offerings — for the place is holy. 14 Once the priests have entered, they are not to go out from the holy area to the outer court until they have removed the clothes they minister in, for these are holy. They are to put on other clothes before they approach the public area."

[A] **41:8** Lit *a full rod of six cubits of a joint*; Hb obscure [B] **41:12** Lit *70 cubits* [C] **41:12** Lit *90 cubits* [D] **41:13** Lit *100 cubits* [E] **41:15** Or *ledges* [F] **41:21–22** Or *and in front of the sanctuary was something that looked like* [22]*an altar* [G] **41:22** Lit *three cubits* [H] **41:22** LXX reads *long and 3 ½ feet wide* [I] **41:22** LXX reads *base* [J] **41:25,26** Hb obscure [K] **42:2** Lit *100 cubits*, also in vv. 4,8 [L] **42:2** Lit *50 cubits*, also in v. 7 [M] **42:3** Lit *20 cubits* [N] **42:4** Lit *10 cubits* [O] **42:4** LXX, Syr; MT reads *wide, a way of one cubit* [P] **42:10** LXX; MT reads *east* [Q] **42:12** Or *protective*; Hb obscure

OUTSIDE DIMENSIONS OF THE TEMPLE COMPLEX

15 When he finished measuring inside the temple complex, he led me out by way of the gate that faced east and measured all around the complex.

16 He measured the east side with a measuring rod;
it was 875 feet[A] by the measuring rod.[B]
17 He[C] measured the north side;
it was 875 feet by the measuring rod.
18 He[D] measured the south side;
it was 875 feet by the measuring rod.
19 Then he turned to the west side
and measured 875 feet by the measuring rod.

20 He measured the temple complex on all four sides. It had a wall all around it, 875 feet long and 875 feet wide, to separate the holy from the common.

RETURN OF THE LORD'S GLORY

43 He led me to the gate, the one that faces east, 2 and I saw the glory of the God of Israel coming from the east. His voice sounded like the roar of a huge torrent, and the earth shone with his glory. 3 The vision I saw was like the one I had seen when he[E] came to destroy the city, and like the ones I had seen by the Chebar Canal. I fell facedown. 4 The glory of the LORD entered the temple by way of the gate that faced east. 5 Then the Spirit lifted me up and brought me to the inner court, and the glory of the LORD filled the temple.

6 While the man was standing beside me, I heard someone speaking to me from the temple. 7 He said to me, "Son of man, this is the place of my throne and the place for the soles of my feet, where I will dwell among the Israelites forever. The house of Israel and their kings will no longer defile my holy name by their religious prostitution and by the corpses[F] of their kings at their high places.[G] 8 Whenever they placed their threshold next to my threshold and their doorposts beside my doorposts, with only a wall between me and them, they were defiling my holy name by the detestable acts they committed. So I destroyed them in my anger. 9 Now let them remove their prostitution and the corpses of their kings far from me, and I will dwell among them forever.

10 "As for you, son of man, describe the temple to the house of Israel, so that they may be ashamed of their iniquities. Let them measure its pattern, 11 and they will be ashamed of all that they have done. Reveal[H] the design of the temple to them — its layout with its exits and entrances — its complete design along with all its statutes, design specifications, and laws. Write it down in their sight so that they may observe its complete design and all its statutes and may carry them out. 12 This is the law of the temple: All its surrounding territory on top of the mountain will be especially holy. Yes, this is the law of the temple.

THE ALTAR

13 "These are the measurements of the altar in units of length (each unit being the standard length plus three inches):[I] The gutter is 21 inches[J] deep and 21 inches wide, with a rim of nine inches[K] around its edge. This is the base[L] of the altar. 14 The distance from the gutter on the ground to the lower ledge is 3 1/2 feet,[M] and the width of the ledge is 21 inches. There are 7 feet[N] from the small ledge to the large ledge, whose width is also 21 inches. 15 The altar hearth[O] is 7 feet high, and four horns project upward from the hearth. 16 The hearth is square, 21 feet[P] long by 21 feet wide. 17 The ledge is 24 1/2 feet[Q] long by 24 1/2 feet wide, with four equal sides. The rim all around it is 10 1/2 inches,[R] and its gutter is 21 inches all around it. The altar's steps face east."

18 Then he said to me, "Son of man, this is what the Lord GOD says: These are the statutes for the altar on the day it is constructed, so that burnt offerings may be sacrificed on it and blood may be splattered on it: 19 You are to give a bull from the herd as a sin offering to the Levitical priests who are from the offspring of Zadok, who approach me in order to serve me." This is the declaration of the Lord GOD. 20 "You are to take some of its blood and apply it to the four horns of the altar, the four corners of the ledge, and all around the rim. In this way you will purify the altar and make atonement for it. 21 Then you are to take away the bull for the sin offering, and it must be burned outside the sanctuary in the place appointed for the temple.

22 "On the second day you are to present an unblemished male goat as a sin offering. They will purify the altar just as they did with the bull. 23 When you have finished the purification, you are to present a young, unblemished bull and an unblemished ram from the flock. 24 You are to present them before the LORD; the priests will throw salt on them and sacrifice them as a burnt offering to the LORD. 25 You will offer a goat for a sin offering each day for seven days. A young bull and a ram from the flock, both unblemished, are also to be offered. 26 For seven days the priests are to make atonement for the altar and cleanse it. In this way they will consecrate it[S] 27 and complete the days of purification. Then on the eighth day and afterward, the priests will offer your burnt offerings and fellowship offerings on the altar, and I will accept you." This is the declaration of the Lord GOD.

[A] **42:16** Lit *500 in rods*, also in vv. 17,18,19 [B] **42:16** Lit *rod all around*, also in vv. 17,18,19 [C] **42:17** LXX reads *Then he turned to the north and* [D] **42:18** LXX reads *Then he turned to the south and* [E] **43:3** Some Hb mss, Theod, Vg; other Hb mss, LXX, Syr read *I* [F] **43:7** Or *monuments*, also in v. 9 [G] **43:7** Some Hb mss, Theod, Tg read *their death* [H] **43:10–11** LXX, Vg; MT reads *pattern.* [11] *And if they are ashamed . . . done, reveal* [I] **43:13** Lit *in cubits (a cubit being a cubit plus a handbreadth)* [J] **43:13** Lit *one cubit*, also in vv. 14,17 [K] **43:13** Lit *one span* [L] **43:13** LXX reads *height* [M] **43:14** Lit *two cubits* [N] **43:14** Lit *four cubits*, also in v. 15 [O] **43:15** Hb obscure [P] **43:16** Lit *12 cubits* [Q] **43:17** Lit *14 cubits* [R] **43:17** Lit *one-half cubit* [S] **43:26** Lit *will fill its hands*

THE PRINCE'S PRIVILEGE

44 The man then brought me back toward the sanctuary's outer gate that faced east, and it was closed. 2 The LORD said to me, "This gate will remain closed. It will not be opened, and no one will enter through it, because the LORD, the God of Israel, has entered through it. Therefore it will remain closed. 3 The prince himself will sit in the gate to eat a meal before the LORD. He is to enter by way of the portico of the gate and go out the same way."

4 Then the man brought me by way of the north gate to the front of the temple. I looked, and the glory of the LORD filled his temple. And I fell facedown. 5 The LORD said to me, "Son of man, pay attention; look with your eyes and listen with your ears to everything I tell you about all the statutes and laws of the LORD's temple. Take careful note of the entrance of the temple along with all the exits of the sanctuary.

THE LEVITES' DUTIES AND PRIVILEGES

6 "Say to the rebellious people, the house of Israel, 'This is what the Lord GOD says: I have had enough of all your detestable practices, house of Israel. 7 When you brought in foreigners, uncircumcised in both heart and flesh, to occupy my sanctuary, you defiled my temple while you offered my food — the fat and the blood. You[A] broke my covenant by all your detestable practices. 8 You have not kept charge of my holy things but have appointed others to keep charge of my sanctuary for you.'

9 "This is what the Lord GOD says: No foreigner, uncircumcised in heart and flesh, may enter my sanctuary, not even a foreigner who is among the Israelites. 10 Surely the Levites who wandered away from me when Israel went astray, and who strayed from me after their idols, will bear the consequences of their iniquity. 11 Yet they will occupy my sanctuary, serving as guards at the temple gates and ministering at the temple. They will slaughter the burnt offerings and other sacrifices for the people and will stand before them to serve them. 12 Because they ministered to the house of Israel before their idols and became a sinful stumbling block to them, therefore I swore an oath[B] against them" — this is the declaration of the Lord GOD — "that they would bear the consequences of their iniquity. 13 They must not approach me to serve me as priests or come near any of my holy things or the most holy things. They will bear their disgrace and the consequences of the detestable acts they committed. 14 Yet I will make them responsible for the duties of the temple — for all its work and everything done in it.

THE PRIESTS' DUTIES AND PRIVILEGES

15 "But the Levitical priests descended from Zadok, who kept charge of my sanctuary when the Israelites went astray from me, will approach me to serve me. They will stand before me to offer me fat and blood." This is the declaration of the Lord GOD. 16 "They are the ones who may enter my sanctuary and approach my table to serve me. They will keep my mandate. 17 When they enter the gates of the inner court they are to wear linen garments; they must not have on them anything made of wool when they minister at the gates of the inner court and within it. 18 They are to wear linen turbans on their heads and linen undergarments around their waists. They are not to put on anything that makes them sweat. 19 Before they go out to the outer court,[C] to the people, they must take off the clothes they have been ministering in, leave them in the holy chambers, and dress in other clothes so that they do not transmit holiness to the people through their clothes.

20 "They may not shave their heads or let their hair grow long, but are to carefully trim their hair. 21 No priest may drink wine before he enters the inner court. 22 He is not to marry a widow or a divorced woman, but may marry only a virgin from the offspring of the house of Israel, or a widow who is the widow of a priest. 23 They are to teach my people the difference between the holy and the common, and explain to them the difference between the clean and the unclean.

24 "In a dispute, they will officiate as judges and decide the case according to my ordinances. They are to observe my laws and statutes regarding all my appointed festivals, and keep my Sabbaths holy. 25 A priest may not come near a dead person so that he becomes defiled. However, he may defile himself for a father, a mother, a son, a daughter, a brother, or an unmarried sister. 26 After he is cleansed, he is to count off seven days for himself. 27 On the day he goes into the sanctuary, into the inner court to minister in the sanctuary, he is to present his sin offering." This is the declaration of the Lord GOD.

28 "This will be their inheritance: I am their inheritance. You are to give them no possession in Israel: I am their possession. 29 They will eat the grain offering, the sin offering, and the guilt offering. Everything in Israel that is permanently dedicated to the LORD will belong to them. 30 The best of all the firstfruits of every kind and contribution of every kind from all your gifts will belong to the priests. You are to give your first batch of dough to the priest so that a blessing may rest on your homes. 31 The priests may not eat any bird or animal that died naturally or was mauled by wild beasts.

[A] **44:7** LXX, Syr, Vg; MT reads *They* [B] **44:12** Lit *I lifted my hand*
[C] **44:19** Some Hb mss, LXX, Syr, Vg; other Hb mss read *court, to the outer court*

THE SACRED PORTION OF THE LAND

45 "When you divide the land by lot as an inheritance, set aside a donation to the LORD, a holy portion of the land, 8 1/3 miles[A] long and 6 2/3 miles[B] wide. This entire region will be holy. 2 In this area there will be a square section[C] for the sanctuary, 875 by 875 feet,[D] with 87 1/2 feet[E] of open space all around it. 3 From this holy portion,[F] you will measure off an area 8 1/3 miles long and 3 1/3 miles[G] wide, in which the sanctuary, the most holy place, will stand.[H] 4 It will be a holy area of the land to be used by the priests who minister in the sanctuary, who approach to serve the LORD. It will be a place for their houses, as well as a holy area for the sanctuary. 5 There will be another area 8 1/3 miles long and 3 1/3 miles wide for the Levites who minister in the temple; it will be their possession for towns to live in.[I]

6 "As the property of the city, set aside an area 1 2/3 miles[J] wide and 8 1/3 miles long, adjacent to the holy donation of land. It will be for the whole house of Israel. 7 And the prince will have the area on each side of the holy donation of land and the city's property, adjacent to the holy donation and the city's property, stretching to the west on the west side and to the east on the east side. Its length will correspond to one of the tribal portions from the western boundary to the eastern boundary. 8 This will be his land as a possession in Israel. My princes will no longer oppress my people but give the rest of the land to the house of Israel according to their tribes.

9 "This is what the Lord GOD says: You have gone too far,[K] princes of Israel! Put away violence and oppression and do what is just and right. Put an end to your evictions of my people." This is the declaration of the Lord GOD. 10 "You are to have honest scales, an honest dry measure,[L] and an honest liquid measure.[M] 11 The dry measure[N] and the liquid measure[O] will be uniform, with the liquid measure containing 5 1/2 gallons[P] and the dry measure holding half a bushel.[P] Their measurement will be a tenth of the standard larger capacity measure.[Q] 12 The shekel[R] will weigh twenty gerahs. Your mina will equal sixty shekels.

THE PEOPLE'S CONTRIBUTION TO THE SACRIFICES

13 "This is the contribution you are to offer: Three quarts[S] from six bushels[T] of wheat and[U] three quarts from six bushels of barley. 14 The quota of oil in liquid measures[V] will be one percent of every[W] cor. The cor equals ten liquid measures or one standard larger capacity measure,[X] since ten liquid measures equal one standard larger capacity measure. 15 And the quota from the flock is one animal out of every two hundred from the well-watered pastures of Israel. These are for the grain offerings, burnt offerings, and fellowship offerings, to make atonement for the people." This is the declaration of the Lord GOD. 16 "All the people of the land must take part in this contribution for the prince in Israel. 17 Then the burnt offerings, grain offerings, and drink offerings for the festivals, New Moons, and Sabbaths — for all the appointed times of the house of Israel — will be the prince's responsibility. He will provide the sin offerings, grain offerings, burnt offerings, and fellowship offerings to make atonement on behalf of the house of Israel.

18 "This is what the Lord GOD says: In the first month, on the first day of the month, you are to take a young, unblemished bull and purify the sanctuary. 19 The priest is to take some of the blood from the sin offering and apply it to the temple doorposts, the four corners of the altar's ledge, and the doorposts of the gate of the inner court. 20 You are to do the same thing on the seventh day of the month for everyone who sins unintentionally or through ignorance. In this way you will make atonement for the temple.

21 "In the first month, on the fourteenth day of the month, you are to celebrate the Passover, a festival of seven days during which unleavened bread will be eaten. 22 On that day the prince will provide a bull as a sin offering on behalf of himself and all the people of the land. 23 During the seven days of the festival, he will provide seven bulls and seven rams without blemish as a burnt offering to the LORD on each of the seven days, along with a male goat each day for a sin offering. 24 He will also provide a grain offering of half a bushel[Y] per bull and half a bushel per ram, along with a gallon[Z] of oil for every half bushel. 25 At the festival that begins on the fifteenth day of the seventh month,[AA] he will provide the same things for seven days — the same sin offerings, burnt offerings, grain offerings, and oil.

SACRIFICES AT APPOINTED TIMES

46 "This is what the Lord GOD says: The gate of the inner court that faces east is to be closed during the six days of work, but it will be opened on the Sabbath day and opened on the day of the New Moon. 2 The prince should enter from the outside

[A] **45:1** Lit *25,000 cubits*, also in vv. 3,5,6 [B] **45:1** LXX reads *20,000 cubits*; MT reads *10,000 cubits* [C] **45:2** Lit *square all around* [D] **45:2** Lit *500 by 500 cubits* [E] **45:2** Lit *50 cubits* [F] **45:3** Lit *this measured portion* [G] **45:3** Lit *10,000 cubits*, also in v. 5 [H] **45:3** Lit *be* [I] **45:5** LXX; MT, Syr, Tg, Vg read *possession — 20 chambers* [J] **45:6** Lit *5,000 cubits* [K] **45:9** Lit *Enough of you* [L] **45:10** Lit *an honest ephah* [M] **45:10** Lit *and an honest bath* [N] **45:11** Lit *The ephah* [O] **45:11** Lit *the bath* [P] **45:11** Lit *one-tenth of a homer* [Q] **45:11** Lit *be based on the homer* [R] **45:12** A shekel is about two-fifths of an ounce of silver [S] **45:13** Lit *One-sixth of an ephah* [T] **45:13** Lit *a homer* [U] **45:13** LXX, Vg; MT reads *and you are to give* [V] **45:14** Lit *oil, the bath, the oil* [W] **45:14** Lit *be a tenth of the bath from the* [X] **45:14** Lit *10 baths, a homer* [Y] **45:24** Lit *an ephah* [Z] **45:24** Lit *a hin* [AA] **45:25** = the Festival of Shelters

by way of the gate's portico and stand at the gate's doorpost while the priests sacrifice his burnt offerings and fellowship offerings. He will bow in worship at the gate's threshold and then depart, but the gate is not to be closed until evening. 3 The people of the land will also bow in worship before the LORD at the entrance of that gate on the Sabbaths and New Moons.

4 "The burnt offering that the prince presents to the LORD on the Sabbath day is to be six unblemished lambs and an unblemished ram. 5 The grain offering will be half a bushel[A] with the ram, and the grain offering with the lambs will be whatever he wants to give, as well as a gallon[B] of oil for every half bushel. 6 On the day of the New Moon, the burnt offering is to be a young, unblemished bull, as well as six lambs and a ram without blemish. 7 He will provide a grain offering of half a bushel with the bull, half a bushel with the ram, and whatever he can afford with the lambs, together with a gallon of oil for every half bushel. 8 When the prince enters, he is to go in by way of the gate's portico and go out the same way.

9 "When the people of the land come before the LORD at the appointed times,[C] whoever enters by way of the north gate to worship is to go out by way of the south gate, and whoever enters by way of the south gate is to go out by way of the north gate. No one may return through the gate by which he entered, but is to go out by the opposite gate. 10 When the people enter, the prince will enter with them, and when they leave, he will leave. 11 At the festivals and appointed times, the grain offering will be half a bushel with the bull, half a bushel with the ram, and whatever he wants to give with the lambs, along with a gallon of oil for every half bushel.

12 "When the prince makes a freewill offering, whether a burnt offering or a fellowship offering as a freewill offering to the LORD, the gate that faces east is to be opened for him. He is to offer his burnt offering or fellowship offering just as he does on the Sabbath day. Then he will go out, and the gate is to be closed after he leaves.

13 "You are to offer an unblemished year-old male lamb as a daily burnt offering to the LORD; you will offer it every morning. 14 You are also to prepare a grain offering every morning along with it: three quarts,[D] with one-third of a gallon[E] of oil to moisten the fine flour — a grain offering to the LORD. This is a permanent statute to be observed regularly. 15 They will offer the lamb, the grain offering, and the oil every morning as a regular burnt offering.

TRANSFER OF ROYAL LANDS

16 "This is what the Lord GOD says: If the prince gives a gift to each of his sons as their inheritance, it will belong to his sons. It will become their property by inheritance. 17 But if he gives a gift from his inheritance to one of his servants, it will belong to that servant until the year of freedom, when it will revert to the prince. His inheritance belongs only to his sons; it is theirs. 18 The prince must not take any of the people's inheritance, evicting them from their property. He is to provide an inheritance for his sons from his own property, so that none of my people will be displaced from his own property."

THE TEMPLE KITCHENS

19 Then he brought me through the entrance that was at the side of the gate, into the priests' holy chambers, which faced north. I saw a place there at the far western end. 20 He said to me, "This is the place where the priests will boil the guilt offering and the sin offering, and where they will bake the grain offering, so that they do not bring them into the outer court and transmit holiness to the people." 21 Next he brought me into the outer court and led me past its four corners. There was a separate court in each of its corners. 22 In the four corners of the outer court there were enclosed[F] courts, 70 feet[G] long by 52 1/2 feet[H] wide. All four corner areas had the same dimensions. 23 There was a stone wall[I] around the inside of them, around the four of them, with ovens built at the base of the walls on all sides. 24 He said to me, "These are the kitchens where those who minister at the temple will cook the people's sacrifices."

THE LIFE-GIVING RIVER

47 Then he brought me back to the entrance of the temple and there was water flowing from under the threshold of the temple toward the east, for the temple faced east. The water was coming down from under the south side of the threshold of the temple, south of the altar. 2 Next he brought me out by way of the north gate and led me around the outside to the outer gate that faced east; there the water was trickling from the south side. 3 As the man went out east with a measuring line in his hand, he measured off a third of a mile[J] and led me through the water. It came up to my ankles. 4 Then he measured off a third of a mile and led me through the water. It came up to my knees. He measured off another third of a mile and led me through the water. It came up to my waist. 5 Again he measured off a third of a mile, and it was a river that I could not cross on foot. For the water had risen; it was deep enough to swim in, a river that could not be crossed on foot.

[A] **46:5** Lit *an ephah*, also in vv. 7,11 [B] **46:5** Lit *a hin*, also in vv. 7,11 [C] **46:9** Or *the festivals* [D] **46:14** Lit *one-sixth of an ephah* [E] **46:14** Lit *one-third of a hin* [F] **46:22** Hb obscure [G] **46:22** Lit *40 cubits* [H] **46:22** Lit *30 cubits* [I] **46:23** Or *a row* [J] **47:3** Lit *1,000 cubits*, also in vv. 4,5

6 He asked me, "Do you see this, son of man?" Then he led me back to the bank of the river. 7 When I had returned, I saw a very large number of trees along both sides of the riverbank. 8 He said to me, "This water flows out to the eastern region and goes down to the Arabah. When it enters the sea, the sea of foul water,[A,B] the water of the sea becomes fresh. 9 Every kind of living creature that swarms will live wherever the river flows,[C] and there will be a huge number of fish because this water goes there. Since the water will become fresh, there will be life everywhere the river goes. 10 Fishermen will stand beside it from En-gedi to En-eglaim.[D] These will become places where nets are spread out to dry. Their fish will consist of many different kinds, like the fish of the Mediterranean Sea. 11 Yet its swamps and marshes will not be healed; they will be left for salt. 12 All kinds of trees providing food will grow along both banks of the river. Their leaves will not wither, and their fruit will not fail. Each month they will bear fresh fruit because the water comes from the sanctuary. Their fruit will be used for eating and their leaves for healing."

THE BORDERS OF THE LAND

13 This is what the Lord God says: "This is[E] the border you will use to divide the land as an inheritance for the twelve tribes of Israel. Joseph will receive two shares. 14 You will inherit it in equal portions, since I swore[F] to give it to your ancestors. So this land will fall to you as an inheritance.

15 This is to be the border of the land:

On the north side it will extend from the Mediterranean Sea by way of Hethlon and Lebo-hamath to Zedad,[G] 16 Berothah, and Sibraim (which is between the border of Damascus and the border of Hamath), as far as Hazer-hatticon, which is on the border of Hauran. 17 So the border will run from the sea to Hazar-enon at the border of Damascus, with the territory of Hamath to the north. This will be the northern side.

18 On the east side it will run between Hauran and Damascus, along the Jordan between Gilead and the land of Israel; you will measure from the northern border to the eastern sea.[B] This will be the eastern side.

19 On the south side it will run from Tamar to the Waters of Meribath-kadesh,[H] and on to the Brook of Egypt as far as the Mediterranean Sea. This will be the southern side.

20 On the west side the Mediterranean Sea will be the border, from the southern border up to a point opposite Lebo-hamath. This will be the western side.

21 "You are to divide this land among yourselves according to the tribes of Israel. 22 You will allot it as an inheritance for yourselves and for the aliens residing among you, who have fathered children among you. You will treat them[I] like native-born Israelites; along with you, they will be allotted an inheritance among the tribes of Israel. 23 In whatever tribe the alien resides, you will assign his inheritance there." This is the declaration of the Lord God.

THE TRIBAL ALLOTMENTS

48 "Now these are the names of the tribes:

From the northern end, along the road of Hethlon, to Lebo-hamath as far as Hazar-enon, at the northern border of Damascus, alongside Hamath and extending from the eastern side to the sea, will be Dan — one portion.

2 Next to the territory of Dan, from the east side to the west, will be Asher — one portion.

3 Next to the territory of Asher, from the east side to the west, will be Naphtali — one portion.

4 Next to the territory of Naphtali, from the east side to the west, will be Manasseh — one portion.

5 Next to the territory of Manasseh, from the east side to the west, will be Ephraim — one portion.

6 Next to the territory of Ephraim, from the east side to the west, will be Reuben — one portion.

7 Next to the territory of Reuben, from the east side to the west, will be Judah — one portion.

8 "Next to the territory of Judah, from the east side to the west, will be the portion you donate to the Lord, 8 1/3 miles[J] wide, and as long as one of the tribal portions from the east side to the west. The sanctuary will be in the middle of it.

9 "The special portion you donate to the Lord will be 8 1/3 miles long and 3 1/3 miles[K] wide. 10 This holy donation will be set apart for the priests alone. It will be 8 1/3 miles long on the northern side, 3 1/3 miles wide on the western side, 3 1/3 miles wide on the eastern side, and 8 1/3 miles long on the southern side. The Lord's sanctuary will be in the middle of it. 11 It is for the consecrated priests, the sons of Zadok, who kept my charge and did not go astray as the Levites did when the Israelites went astray. 12 It will be a special donation for them out of the holy donation

[A] **47:8** Or *enters the sea, being brought out to the sea*; Hb obscure [B] **47:8,18** = the Dead Sea [C] **47:9** LXX, Vg; MT reads *the two rivers flow* [D] **47:10** Two springs near the Dead Sea [E] **47:13** Tg, Vg; Syr reads *The valley of* [F] **47:14** Lit *lifted my hand* [G] **47:15** LXX; MT reads *and Lebo to Zedad, Hamath*; Ezk 48:1 [H] **47:19** = Kadesh-barnea [I] **47:22** Lit *They will be to you* [J] **48:8** Lit *25,000 cubits*, also in vv. 9,10,13,15,20, 21 [K] **48:9** Lit *10,000 cubits*, also in vv. 10,13,18

of the land, a most holy place adjacent to the territory of the Levites.

13 "Next to the territory of the priests, the Levites will have an area 8 1/3 miles long and 3 1/3 miles wide. The total length will be 8 1/3 miles and the width 3 1/3 miles. 14 They must not sell or exchange any of it, and they must not transfer this choice part of the land, for it is holy to the LORD.

15 "The remaining area, 1 2/3 miles[A] wide and 8 1/3 miles long, will be for common use by the city, for both residential and open space. The city will be in the middle of it. 16 These are the city's measurements:

1 1/2 miles[B] on the north side;
1 1/2 miles on the south side;
1 1/2 miles on the east side;
and 1 1/2 miles on the west side.

17 The city's open space will extend:

425 feet[C] to the north,
425 feet to the south,
425 feet to the east,
and 425 feet to the west.

18 "The remainder of the length alongside the holy donation will be 3 1/3 miles to the east and 3 1/3 miles to the west. It will run alongside the holy donation. Its produce will be food for the workers of the city. 19 The city's workers from all the tribes of Israel will cultivate it. 20 The entire donation will be 8 1/3 miles by 8 1/3 miles; you are to set apart the holy donation along with the city property as a square area.

21 "The remaining area on both sides of the holy donation and the city property will belong to the prince. He will own the land adjacent to the tribal portions, next to the 8 1/3 miles of the donation as far as the eastern border and[D] next to the 8 1/3 miles of the donation as far as the western border. The holy donation and the sanctuary of the temple will be in the middle of it. 22 Except for the Levitical property and the city property in the middle of the area belonging to the prince, the area between the territory of Judah and that of Benjamin will belong to the prince.

23 "As for the rest of the tribes:

From the east side to the west, will be Benjamin — one portion.
24 Next to the territory of Benjamin, from the east side to the west, will be Simeon — one portion.
25 Next to the territory of Simeon, from the east side to the west, will be Issachar — one portion.
26 Next to the territory of Issachar, from the east side to the west, will be Zebulun — one portion.
27 Next to the territory of Zebulun, from the east side to the west, will be Gad — one portion.

28 Next to the territory of Gad toward the south side, the border will run from Tamar to the Waters of Meribath-kadesh, to the Brook of Egypt, and out to the Mediterranean Sea. 29 This is the land you are to allot as an inheritance to Israel's tribes, and these will be their portions." This is the declaration of the Lord GOD.

THE NEW CITY

30 "These are the exits of the city:

On the north side, which measures 1 1/2 miles,
31 there will be three gates facing north, the gates of the city being named for the tribes of Israel: one, the gate of Reuben; one, the gate of Judah; and one, the gate of Levi.
32 On the east side, which is 1 1/2 miles, there will be three gates: one, the gate of Joseph; one, the gate of Benjamin; and one, the gate of Dan.
33 On the south side, which measures 1 1/2 miles, there will be three gates: one, the gate of Simeon; one, the gate of Issachar; and one, the gate of Zebulun.
34 On the west side, which is 1 1/2 miles, there will be three gates: one, the gate of Gad; one, the gate of Asher; and one, the gate of Naphtali.

35 The perimeter of the city will be six miles,[E] and the name of the city from that day on will be The LORD Is There."

[A] **48:15** Lit *5,000 cubits* [B] **48:16** Lit *4,500 cubits*, also in vv. 30,32,33,34 [C] **48:17** Lit *250 cubits* [D] **48:21** Lit *border, and to the west,* [E] **48:35** Lit *18,000 cubits*

DANIEL

Ivory-carved pyxis (cosmetic or jewelry bowl) with a scene of Daniel standing in prayer under a canopy, flanked by two lions. From North Africa or Syria; fifth–sixth centuries AD.

INTRODUCTION TO

DANIEL

Circumstances of Writing

The critical view of the book of Daniel suggests it was written by a second-century-BC Jewish author, not the historical Daniel. This view is largely based on a naturalistic perspective that denies the possibility of the authentic foretelling found in Daniel. On the other hand, the traditional view maintains that Daniel the prophet did indeed write this book sometime shortly after the end of the Babylonian captivity (sixth century BC). Internal testimony supports this claim. In the text itself, Daniel claimed to have written down visions given by God (Dn 8:2; 9:2,20; 12:5). Passages which contain third-person references to Daniel do not disprove his authorship. The prophet Ezekiel referred to Daniel several times (Ezk 14:14,20; 28:3), a prominence that would befit the writing prophet. Finally, Jesus Christ attributed the book of Daniel to Daniel himself (Mt 24:15; Mk 13:14).

The historical setting of the book of Daniel is the Babylonian captivity. The book opens after King Nebuchadnezzar's first siege of Judah (605 BC) when he brought Daniel and his friends to Babylon along with other captives among the Judean nobility. Nebuchadnezzar assaulted Judah again in 597 BC and brought ten thousand captives back to Babylon. In 586, he once again besieged Jerusalem, this time destroying the city, the holy temple, and exiling the people of Judah to Babylon. Daniel's ministry began in 605 when he arrived at Babylon with the first Jewish captives, extended throughout the Babylonian captivity (which ended in 539), and concluded sometime after the third year of Cyrus the Great, the Medo-Persian king who overthrew Babylonia (see Dn 1:21; 10:1).

When was the book written? While the critical view maintains a date of 165 BC in the Maccabean period primarily because of the precise prophecies related to that time, the traditional view asserts that it was written just after the end of the Babylonian captivity in the late sixth century BC. The book contains a factual recounting of events from the life of Daniel, supernatural prediction of events that took place during the intertestamental period, and prophecies that are yet to be fulfilled.

Manuscript evidence supports the early date. Fragments from Daniel were found among the Dead Sea Scrolls, a collection that included other books of the Bible that were written well before the second century. Historical evidence also supports the early date. For example, Daniel accurately described Belshazzar as coregent with another king (Nabonidus), a fact that was not known elsewhere until modern times. In summary, the late-date view is driven by a presuppositional rejection of supernatural prophecy and not objective evidence.

Contribution to the Bible

Daniel's book establishes the validity of predictive prophecy and lays the foundation for understanding end-times prophecy, especially the book of Revelation in the New Testament. Most important, it emphasizes that the Lord has dominion over all the kingdoms of the earth, even in evil days when wicked empires reign. Two key words in the book are *king* (used more than 150 times) and *kingdom* (used more than 50 times). Above all, Daniel teaches that the God of Israel is the Sovereign of the universe, "for his dominion is an everlasting dominion, and his kingdom is from generation to generation" (4:34).

Structure

The genre of the book of Daniel is narrative, recounting historical events for the purpose of present and future instruction. The narrative contains history, prophecy, and apocalyptic visions. Apocalyptic literature refers to revelation by God given through visions and symbols with a message of eschatological (end-time) triumph.

Noting that the book of Daniel contains both history (chaps. 1–6) and prophecy (chaps. 7–12), some divide the book into two sections. A better way to view the book's structure is based on the two languages it uses: 1:1–2:3 (Hebrew); 2:4–7:28 (Aramaic); and 8:1–12:13 (Hebrew). The Hebrew sections pertain primarily to the people of Israel, which is fitting since Hebrew was Israel's national language. Aramaic was the international language of that time. The Aramaic section of Daniel demonstrates God's dominion over the international Gentile nations.

DANIEL'S CAPTIVITY IN BABYLON

1 In the third year of the reign of King Jehoiakim of Judah, King Nebuchadnezzar[A] of Babylon came to Jerusalem and laid siege to it. 2 The Lord handed King Jehoiakim of Judah over to him, along with some of the vessels from the house of God. Nebuchadnezzar carried them to the land of Babylon,[B] to the house of his god,[C] and put the vessels in the treasury of his god.

3 The king ordered Ashpenaz, his chief eunuch, to bring some of the Israelites from the royal family and from the nobility — 4 young men without any physical defect, good-looking, suitable for instruction in all wisdom, knowledgeable, perceptive, and capable of serving in the king's palace. He was to teach them the Chaldean language and literature. 5 The king assigned them daily provisions from the royal food and from the wine that he drank. They were to be trained for three years, and at the end of that time they were to attend the king.[D] 6 Among them, from the Judahites, were Daniel, Hananiah, Mishael, and Azariah. 7 The chief eunuch gave them names; he gave the name Belteshazzar to Daniel, Shadrach to Hananiah, Meshach to Mishael, and Abednego to Azariah.

FAITHFULNESS IN BABYLON

8 Daniel determined that he would not defile himself with the king's food or with the wine he drank. So he asked permission from the chief eunuch not to defile himself. 9 God had granted Daniel kindness and compassion from the chief eunuch, 10 yet he said to Daniel, "I fear my lord the king, who assigned your food and drink. What if he sees your faces looking thinner than the other young men your age? You would endanger my life[E] with the king."

11 So Daniel said to the guard whom the chief eunuch had assigned to Daniel, Hananiah, Mishael, and Azariah, 12 "Please test your servants for ten days. Let us be given vegetables to eat and water to drink. 13 Then examine our appearance and the appearance of the young men who are eating the king's food, and deal with your servants based on what you see." 14 He agreed with them about this and tested them for ten days. 15 At the end of ten days they looked better and healthier[F] than all the young men who were eating the king's food. 16 So the guard continued to remove their food and the wine they were to drink and gave them vegetables.

FAITHFULNESS REWARDED

17 God gave these four young men knowledge and understanding in every kind of literature and wisdom. Daniel also understood visions and dreams of every kind. 18 At the end of the time that the king had said to present them, the chief eunuch presented them to Nebuchadnezzar. 19 The king interviewed them, and among all of them, no one was found equal to Daniel, Hananiah, Mishael, and Azariah. So they began to attend the king. 20 In every matter of wisdom and understanding that the king consulted them about, he found them ten times[G] better than all the magicians and mediums in his entire kingdom. 21 Daniel remained there until the first year of King Cyrus.

NEBUCHADNEZZAR'S DREAM

2 In the second year of his reign, Nebuchadnezzar had dreams that troubled him, and sleep deserted him. 2 So the king gave orders to summon the magicians, mediums, sorcerers, and Chaldeans[H] to tell the king his dreams. When they came and stood before the king, 3 he said to them, "I have had a dream and am anxious to understand it."

4 The Chaldeans spoke to the king (Aramaic[I] begins here): "May the king live forever. Tell your servants the dream, and we will give the interpretation."

5 The king replied to the Chaldeans, "My word is final: If you don't tell me the dream and its interpretation, you will be torn limb from limb,[J] and your houses will be made a garbage dump. 6 But if you make the dream and its interpretation known to me, you'll receive gifts, a reward, and great honor from me. So make the dream and its interpretation known to me."

7 They answered a second time, "May the king tell the dream to his servants, and we will make known the interpretation."

8 The king replied, "I know for certain you are trying to gain some time, because you see that my word is final. 9 If you don't tell me the dream, there is one decree for you. You have conspired to tell me something false or fraudulent until the situation changes. So tell me the dream and I will know you can give me its interpretation."

10 The Chaldeans answered the king, "No one on earth can make known what the king requests. Consequently, no king, however great and powerful, has ever asked anything like this of any magician, medium, or Chaldean. 11 What the king is asking is so difficult that no one can make it known to him except the gods, whose dwelling is not with mortals." 12 Because of this, the king became violently angry and gave orders to destroy all the wise men of Babylon. 13 The decree was issued that the wise men were to be executed, and they searched for Daniel and his friends, to execute them.

[A] **1:1** Or *Nebuchadrezzar* [B] **1:2** Lit *Shinar* [C] **1:2** Or *gods* [D] **1:5** Lit *to stand before the king* [E] **1:10** Lit *would make my head guilty* [F] **1:15** Lit *fatter of flesh* [G] **1:20** Lit *hands* [H] **2:2** In this chap. Chaldeans are influential Babylonian wise men. [I] **2:4** Dn 2:4–7:28 is written in Aramaic. [J] **2:5** Lit *be made into limbs*

DIGGING DEEPER ***The Babylon of Nebuchadnezzar II***

The book of Daniel describes King Nebuchadnezzar II (605–562 BC) of Babylon as a powerful ruler (Dn 2:32,37–38) who built his royal city into a magnificent spectacle that was unparalleled in the ancient Near East (4:30). After the overthrow of the Assyrian Empire in 612 BC, Nebuchadnezzar began an ambitious building campaign that transformed the city of Babylon from an average metropolis into a superpower. The inner city covered approximately five hundred acres while the entire city spread over more than three thousand acres. Archaeologists have uncovered evidence near modern Baghdad that confirms Nebuchadnezzar II as a real person who inaugurated the unprecedented building campaign described in Daniel 4:30. For example, Nebuchadnezzar ordered the construction of the Ishtar Gate, which was dedicated to the goddess Ishtar. The gate contains a dedication inscription that confirms Nebuchadnezzar's title as king and Babylon as his place of reign. Additionally, several of the nearly fifteen million baked bricks used in the construction of the royal administrative buildings bear an inscription reading "Nebuchadnezzar, King of Babylon . . . eldest son of Nabopolassar, king of Babylon."

14 Then Daniel responded with tact and discretion
to Arioch, the captain of the king's guard,[A] who had
gone out to execute the wise men of Babylon. 15 He
asked Arioch, the king's officer, "Why is the decree
from the king so harsh?"[B] Then Arioch explained the
situation to Daniel. 16 So Daniel went and asked
the king to give him some time, so that he could give
the king the interpretation.
17 Then Daniel went to his house and told his
friends Hananiah, Mishael, and Azariah about the
matter, 18 urging them to ask the God of the heavens
for mercy concerning this mystery, so Daniel and
his friends would not be destroyed with the rest of
Babylon's wise men. 19 The mystery was then revealed
to Daniel in a vision at night, and Daniel praised the
God of the heavens 20 and declared:

May the name of God
be praised forever and ever,
for wisdom and power belong to him.
21 He changes the times and seasons;
he removes kings and establishes kings.
He gives wisdom to the wise
and knowledge to those
who have understanding.
22 He reveals the deep and hidden things;
he knows what is in the darkness,
and light dwells with him.
23 I offer thanks and praise to you,
God of my ancestors,
because you have given me
wisdom and power.
And now you have let me know
what we asked of you,
for you have let us know
the king's mystery.[C]

24 Therefore Daniel went to Arioch, whom the king
had assigned to destroy the wise men of Babylon. He
came and said to him, "Don't destroy the wise men
of Babylon! Bring me before the king, and I will give
him the interpretation."
25 Then Arioch quickly brought Daniel before the
king and said to him, "I have found a man among
the Judean exiles who can let the king know the interpretation."
26 The king said in reply to Daniel, whose name was
Belteshazzar, "Are you able to tell me the dream I had
and its interpretation?"
27 Daniel answered the king, "No wise man, medium, magician, or diviner is able to make known to
the king the mystery he asked about. 28 But there is
a God in heaven who reveals mysteries, and he has
let King Nebuchadnezzar know what will happen in
the last days. Your dream and the visions that came
into your mind as you lay in bed were these: 29 Your
Majesty, while you were in your bed, thoughts came
to your mind about what will happen in the future.[D]
The revealer of mysteries has let you know what will
happen. 30 As for me, this mystery has been revealed
to me, not because I have more wisdom than anyone
living, but in order that the interpretation might be
made known to the king, and that you may understand the thoughts of your mind.

THE DREAM'S INTERPRETATION

31 "Your Majesty, as you were watching, suddenly a
colossal statue appeared. That statue, tall and dazzling, was standing in front of you, and its appearance
was terrifying. 32 The head of the statue was pure
gold, its chest and arms were silver, its stomach and
thighs were bronze, 33 its legs were iron, and its feet
were partly iron and partly fired clay. 34 As you were
watching, a stone broke off without a hand touching
it,[E] struck the statue on its feet of iron and fired clay,
and crushed them. 35 Then the iron, the fired clay, the
bronze, the silver, and the gold were shattered and

[A] **2:14** Or *executioners* [B] **2:15** Or *urgent* [C] **2:23** Lit *matter* [D] **2:29** Lit *happen after this*, also in v. 45 [E] **2:34** Lit *off not by hands*

Jehoiakim: Racing toward Disaster

by Leon Hyatt Jr.

The story of Daniel begins "in the third year of the reign of King Jehoiakim of Judah" (Dn 1:1). When Jehoiakim came to the throne of Judah, the Assyrian Empire was embroiled in its final desperate struggles with the rising power of Babylon. Jehoiakim's own nation of Judah was in its death throes because of its rebellions against God. Jehoiakim's reign (608–598 BC) only made matters worse.

ASCENSION TO THE THRONE

Jehoiakim's father was the good king Josiah (640–609 BC), but Josiah made a serious mistake when he attempted to prevent Egypt's Pharaoh Neco (Jr 46:2) from taking his army past Judah. Neco's purpose was to assist the Assyrians against the armies of Babylon's King Nabopolassar. Josiah personally led his army against Neco at Megiddo and was killed, so the people of Judah chose Josiah's son Jehoahaz to succeed him (2Kg 23:29–30; 2Ch 35:20–25). Before facing the Babylonians, Pharaoh Neco sent for Jehoahaz and deposed him. He later took him to Egypt as a prisoner, where he died (2Kg 23:33–34; 2Ch 36:14).

Neco replaced Jehoahaz with another of Josiah's sons, twenty-five-year-old Eliakim, renamed Jehoiakim, who ruled for eleven years (2Kg 23:36; 2Ch 36:5). Neco also made Judah pay an enormous amount of tribute (2Kg 23:34–35; 2Ch 36:3), forcing Jehoiakim to begin his reign under heavy oppression and a crushing financial burden.

SOCIAL AND POLITICAL CONDITIONS

Domestically the nation of Judah was in serious disarray because of its peoples' deeply ingrained rebellion against God. Josiah had made a determined effort to call the people of Judah back to God (2Kg 22:1–23:25), but his efforts failed. The priests and the people responded only with passive submission (23:3,9), and God promised to destroy them (vv. 26–27). Jehoiakim added to God's wrath by joining the people in their rebellion.

Internationally Judah was faced with oppression from every aggressive nation in the ancient Near East. After placing Jehoiakim under his authority, Neco battled with Babylon's armies for three years. Then Babylon's King Nabopolassar sent his son Nebuchadnezzar with a massive army to attack the Egyptians at Carchemish, where Nebuchadnezzar won a resounding victory.

Nebuchadnezzar chased the bedraggled Egyptian army all the way back to Egypt. As Nebuchadnezzar passed through Judah, he placed Jehoiakim under his control. Judah then became a nation subject to Babylon instead of Egypt (2Kg 24:1). At that time, Nebuchadnezzar made captives of some of the most promising young men from Judah's leading families and sent them to Babylon so his wise men could train them. His plan was to use these captives later to control the Israelite people. Among the young men were Daniel, Hananiah, Mishael, and Azariah—whose names the Babylonians changed to Belteshazzar, Shadrach, Meshach, and Abednego (Dn 1:17).

While in Egypt, Nebuchadnezzar received word his father had died, and he hastened home to be installed as king of the Neo-Babylonian Empire. He ruled as an absolute monarch from 605 to 562 BC, though with a divinely orchestrated interlude to humble his pride (4:1–37).

Jehoiakim was consistent. No matter whether Egypt or Assyria or Babylon was in ascendancy, he managed to be oppressed by each one.

JEHOIAKIM'S FOOLISH POLICIES

King Jehoiakim could not have been more wrong in the way he dealt with his problems. To pay the tribute money Neco demanded of him, he placed a heavy property tax on all of his people (2Kg 23:35). At the same time, he came under heavy attack from Jeremiah for building an elaborate palace and failing to pay wages to those who worked to build it (Jr 22:13–17).

Wanting to free himself of Nebuchadnezzar's heavy oppression, Jehoiakim decided to take advantage of a time when Nebuchadnezzar was occupied with other problems, so he rebelled against him. Nebuchadnezzar's response was to encourage Chaldean, Syrian, Moabite, and Ammonite raiders to attack Judah (2Kg 24:12). Those nations, also under oppression by Nebuchadnezzar, could have joined with Jehoiakim to seek better conditions for all of them; but Jehoiakim's misjudgment caused them all to turn against him. Judah was left standing alone, surrounded by enemy nations.

Jehoiakim dealt with prophetic criticism by persecuting the prophets. Jeremiah preached during Jehoiakim's entire reign and directed many of his sermons toward the king. Jehoiakim rejected Jeremiah's every warning. When Jeremiah had his scribe Baruch read the entire scroll of his sermons in the temple, Baruch was brought before Judah's officials in the king's palace to read the scroll to them. The officials in turn took the scroll to the king and read it to him. Each time a few columns were read to the king, Jehoiakim cut them off from the scroll and threw them into the fire. He continued until nothing was left. Jeremiah was able to reproduce the whole scroll, however, and add much more besides (Jr 36:1–32). Because of Jehoiakim's rebellions, Jeremiah prophesied that the people would not mourn the king's death and his body would be cast into an open field like a donkey's corpse (22:18–19; 36:30).

Carchemish rises on the horizon, just left of center; this city was under Hittite and then Neo-Assyrian rule. Nebuchadnezzar overthrew Carchemish in 605 BC and made it part of the Babylonian Empire. After Carchemish fell, Nebuchadnezzar's father Nabopolassar died, an event that brought Nebuchadnezzar back to Babylon to rule.

Probably because of a second rebellion, Nebuchadnezzar finally placed Jehoiakim in shackles to take him to Babylon as a prisoner (2Ch 36:6). Neither Scripture nor Babylonian records tell how Jehoiakim actually died or how Jeremiah's prophecy about the abandonment and exposure of Jehoiakim's body was fulfilled, but they must have been painful and humiliating.

Eleven years and three months after Jehoiakim's captivity, Nebuchadnezzar overran Judah, killed many of its people, and took most of the remainder into captivity (2Kg 24:8,18–25:21). Jehoiakim bore his share of the blame for that awful disaster. ✣

became like chaff from the summer threshing floors.
The wind carried them away, and not a trace of them
could be found. But the stone that struck the statue
became a great mountain and filled the whole earth.
36 "This was the dream; now we will tell the king
its interpretation. 37 Your Majesty, you are king of
kings. The God of the heavens has given you sovereignty, power, strength, and glory. 38 Wherever people
live — or wild animals, or birds of the sky — he has
handed them over to you and made you ruler over
them all. You are the head of gold.
39 "After you, there will arise another kingdom, inferior to yours, and then another, a third kingdom, of
bronze, which will rule the whole earth. 40 A fourth
kingdom will be as strong as iron; for iron crushes
and shatters everything, and like iron that smashes,
it will crush and smash all the others.[A] 41 You saw the
feet and toes, partly of a potter's fired clay and partly
of iron — it will be a divided kingdom, though some
of the strength of iron will be in it. You saw the iron
mixed with clay, 42 and that the toes of the feet were
partly iron and partly fired clay — part of the kingdom will be strong, and part will be brittle. 43 You saw
the iron mixed with clay — the peoples will mix with
one another[B] but will not hold together, just as iron
does not mix with fired clay.
44 "In the days of those kings, the God of the heavens will set up a kingdom that will never be destroyed,
and this kingdom will not be left to another people.
It will crush all these kingdoms and bring them to an
end, but will itself endure forever. 45 You saw a stone
break off from the mountain without a hand touching
it,[C] and it crushed the iron, bronze, fired clay, silver,
and gold. The great God has told the king what will
happen in the future. The dream is certain, and its
interpretation reliable."

NEBUCHADNEZZAR'S RESPONSE

46 Then King Nebuchadnezzar fell facedown, worshiped Daniel, and gave orders to present an offering
and incense to him. 47 The king said to Daniel, "Your
God is indeed God of gods, Lord of kings, and a revealer of mysteries, since you were able to reveal this
mystery." 48 Then the king promoted Daniel and gave
him many generous gifts. He made him ruler over the
entire province of Babylon and chief governor over
all the wise men of Babylon. 49 At Daniel's request,
the king appointed Shadrach, Meshach, and Abednego to manage the province of Babylon. But Daniel
remained at the king's court.

NEBUCHADNEZZAR'S GOLD STATUE

3 King Nebuchadnezzar made a gold statue, ninety feet high and nine feet wide.[D] He set it up on
the plain of Dura in the province of Babylon. 2 King
Nebuchadnezzar sent word to assemble the satraps,
prefects, governors, advisers, treasurers, judges,
magistrates, and all the rulers of the provinces to attend the dedication of the statue King Nebuchadnezzar had set up. 3 So the satraps, prefects, governors,
advisers, treasurers, judges, magistrates, and all the
rulers of the provinces assembled for the dedication
of the statue the king had set up. Then they stood
before the statue Nebuchadnezzar had set up.
4 A herald loudly proclaimed, "People of every nation and language, you are commanded: 5 When you
hear the sound of the horn, flute, zither,[E] lyre,[F] harp,
drum,[G] and every kind of music, you are to fall facedown and worship the gold statue that King Nebuchadnezzar has set up. 6 But whoever does not fall
down and worship will immediately be thrown into
a furnace of blazing fire."
7 Therefore, when all the people heard the sound
of the horn, flute, zither, lyre, harp, and every kind of
music, people of every nation and language fell down
and worshiped the gold statue that King Nebuchadnezzar had set up.

THE FURNACE OF BLAZING FIRE

8 Some Chaldeans took this occasion to come forward
and maliciously accuse[H] the Jews. 9 They said to King
Nebuchadnezzar, "May the king live forever. 10 You as
king have issued a decree that everyone who hears
the sound of the horn, flute, zither, lyre, harp, drum,
and every kind of music must fall down and worship
the gold statue. 11 Whoever does not fall down and
worship will be thrown into a furnace of blazing fire.
12 There are some Jews you have appointed to manage
the province of Babylon: Shadrach, Meshach, and
Abednego. These men have ignored you, the king;
they do not serve your gods or worship the gold statue you have set up."
13 Then in a furious rage Nebuchadnezzar gave orders to bring in Shadrach, Meshach, and Abednego.
So these men were brought before the king. 14 Nebuchadnezzar asked them, "Shadrach, Meshach, and
Abednego, is it true that you don't serve my gods or
worship the gold statue I have set up? 15 Now if you're
ready, when you hear the sound of the horn, flute,
zither, lyre, harp, drum, and every kind of music, fall
down and worship the statue I made. But if you don't
worship it, you will immediately be thrown into a
furnace of blazing fire — and who is the god who
can rescue you from my power?"
16 Shadrach, Meshach, and Abednego replied to the
king, "Nebuchadnezzar, we don't need to give you an

[A] **2:40** Lit *all these* [B] **2:43** Lit *another in the seed of men* [C] **2:45** Lit *mountain, not by hands* [D] **3:1** Lit *statue, its height sixty cubits, its width six cubits* [E] **3:5** Or *lyre* [F] **3:5** Or *sambuke* [G] **3:5** Or *pipe* [H] **3:8** Lit *and eat the pieces of*

answer to this question. 17 If the God we serve exists, then he can rescue us from the furnace of blazing fire, and he can[A] rescue us from the power of you, the king. 18 But even if he does not rescue us,[B] we want you as king to know that we will not serve your gods or worship the gold statue you set up."

19 Then Nebuchadnezzar was filled with rage, and the expression on his face changed toward Shadrach, Meshach, and Abednego. He gave orders to heat the furnace seven times more than was customary, 20 and he commanded some of the best soldiers in his army to tie up Shadrach, Meshach, and Abednego and throw them into the furnace of blazing fire. 21 So these men, in their trousers, robes, head coverings,[C] and other clothes, were tied up and thrown into the furnace of blazing fire. 22 Since the king's command was so urgent[D] and the furnace extremely hot, the raging flames[E] killed those men who carried up Shadrach, Meshach, and Abednego. 23 And these three men, Shadrach, Meshach, and Abednego fell, bound, into the furnace of blazing fire.

DELIVERED FROM THE FIRE

24 Then King Nebuchadnezzar jumped up in alarm. He said to his advisers, "Didn't we throw three men, bound, into the fire?"

"Yes, of course, Your Majesty," they replied to the king.

25 He exclaimed, "Look! I see four men, not tied, walking around in the fire unharmed; and the fourth looks like a son of the gods."[F]

26 Nebuchadnezzar then approached the door of the furnace of blazing fire and called, "Shadrach, Meshach, and Abednego, you servants of the Most High God — come out!" So Shadrach, Meshach, and Abednego came out of the fire. 27 When the satraps, prefects, governors, and the king's advisers gathered around, they saw that the fire had no effect on[G] the bodies of these men: not a hair of their heads was singed, their robes were unaffected, and there was no smell of fire on them. 28 Nebuchadnezzar exclaimed, "Praise to the God of Shadrach, Meshach, and Abednego! He sent his angel[H] and rescued his servants who trusted in him. They violated the king's command and risked their lives rather than serve or worship any god except their own God. 29 Therefore I issue a decree that anyone of any people, nation, or language who says anything offensive against the God of Shadrach, Meshach, and Abednego will be torn limb from limb and his house made a garbage dump. For there is no other god who is able to deliver like this." 30 Then the king rewarded Shadrach, Meshach, and Abednego in the province of Babylon.

NEBUCHADNEZZAR'S PROCLAMATION

4 King Nebuchadnezzar,

To those of every people, nation, and language, who live on the whole earth:

May your prosperity increase. 2 I am pleased to tell you about the miracles and wonders the Most High God has done for me.

3 How great are his miracles,
and how mighty his wonders!
His kingdom is an eternal kingdom,
and his dominion is from generation
to generation.

THE DREAM

4 I, Nebuchadnezzar, was at ease in my house and flourishing in my palace. 5 I had a dream, and it frightened me; while in my bed, the images and visions in my mind alarmed me. 6 So I issued a decree to bring all the wise men of Babylon to me in order that they might make the dream's interpretation known to me. 7 When the magicians, mediums, Chaldeans, and diviners came in, I told them the dream, but they could not make its interpretation known to me.

8 Finally Daniel, named Belteshazzar after the name of my god — and a spirit of the holy gods is in him — came before me. I told him the dream: 9 "Belteshazzar, head of the magicians, because I know that you have the spirit of the holy gods and that no mystery puzzles you, explain to me the visions of my dream that I saw, and its interpretation. 10 In the visions of my mind as I was lying in bed, I saw this:

There was a tree in the middle of the earth,
and it was very tall.
11 The tree grew large and strong;
its top reached to the sky,
and it was visible to the ends of the[I] earth.
12 Its leaves were beautiful, its fruit
was abundant,
and on it was food for all.
Wild animals found shelter under it,
the birds of the sky lived in its branches,
and every creature was fed from it.

13 "As I was lying in my bed, I also saw in the visions of my mind a watcher, a holy one,[J] coming down from heaven. 14 He called out loudly:

[A] **3:17** Or *If the God whom we serve is willing to save us from the furnace of blazing fire, then he will* [B] **3:18** Lit *But if not* [C] **3:21** The identity of these articles of clothing is uncertain. [D] **3:22** Or *harsh* [E] **3:22** Lit *the flame of the fire* [F] **3:25** Or *of a divine being* [G] **3:27** Lit *fire had not overcome* [H] **3:28** Or *messenger* [I] **4:11** Lit *of all the* [J] **4:13** = an angel

Life in the Royal Court of Babylon

by Daniel P. Caldwell

Relief from the palace of Sargon II showing eunuchs in the king's service.

Under King Nebuchadnezzar, the Babylonians attacked and conquered the city of Jerusalem in 605 BC. As a result, Daniel and his friends, as well as others "from the royal family and from the nobility" (Dn 1:3) were seized from their homes, taken to a strange land, given new names, and introduced to new customs and a new language. Even in the midst of Judah's darkest hours, Daniel would see the sovereign hand of God at work.

Daniel and his friends were *yeladim*, Hebrew for "young men." They and others residing in the palace were to be trained to serve as functionaries in the royal court (1:4,17). Once they completed their three years of instruction (v. 5), no longer were they *yeladim*. Instead, they were "wise men" of Babylon (2:12).

Nebuchadnezzar had a policy of taking the intelligentsia and artisans from conquered territories for service in his kingdom (1:3–7). Being members of the royal family and nobility, these Jewish captives also would deter rebellion against Babylon lest they be harmed. Nebuchadnezzar ordered his chief eunuch, Ashpenaz, to teach and train some of the "young men."

Ashpenaz was the "chief eunuch" (Hb *rab saris*; 1:3). The term *eunuch* (*saris*) could be literal (Is 56:3–4) or a technical term for a court official. The other uses of the title (2Kg 18:17; Jr 39:3,13) are translated "chief of staff." Most of the forty-five uses of *saris* in the Old Testament are translated "officer" or "official." It is only translated "eunuch" in its seven uses in Daniel, its twelve uses in Esther, and in 2 Kings 9:32; 20:18; 23:11; Isaiah 39:7; 56:3–4. In Genesis 37:36, it is used to describe Potiphar, who was married. Eunuchs were widely used at the Persian court because they had a reputation for being trustworthy.[1]

The trainees had to be a certain age, probably about fourteen or fifteen years old as based on common Persian practice.[2] Daniel and his friends were required to be handsome and free of physical defects, as well as intelligent and with good social skills so that they would be "capable of serving in the king's palace" (Dn 1:4).They would eventually serve as the king's advisers.

Clearly intended for more than menial service, Daniel and his friends learned "Chaldean language and literature" (v. 4b). The language was a form of Akkadian known as Neo-Babylonian. Like earlier Assyrian, it was written in cuneiform, which was made up of wedge-shaped characters pressed in clay. In addition to their languages of origin (Aramaic and Hebrew) and Akkadian, Daniel and his cohorts would later learn Persian and serve as "administrators" in the court of Darius (6:2).

They also received a privileged diet, being given "daily provisions from the royal food and from the

Golden bowl inscribed with the words "Darius the Great King" in three languages: Old Persian, Elamite, and Babylonian.

wine that he drank" (1:5). This would have been the best quality food available. Due to a fear of defilement, however, Daniel and his friends refused and instead asked for water and vegetables (1:8). Numerous factors could have led them to this decision, and Bible interpreters through the centuries have offered many suggestions. The food and drink could have come from a temple, having been offered to a pagan deity, but this would also be true of the vegetables.

Whatever their reasoning, Daniel and his friends determined to avoid defilement if at all possible. Ezekiel (Ezk 4:13) and Hosea (Hs 9:3–4) spoke of the situation of exile as having to eat unclean food. Certain animals the Babylonians consumed (pig and horse) were unclean for the Hebrews (Lv 11; Dt 12; 14), and meat would not be properly prepared (Lv 17:13–14). The wine was avoided, perhaps simply because it came from the king's table. Daniel is later said to partake of meat and wine under other circumstances: "I didn't eat any rich food, no meat or wine entered my mouth, and I didn't put any oil on my body until the three weeks were over" (Dn 10:3).

Even though Daniel and his friends were in the king's service, they did not take part in the pagan practices of the magicians, enchanters, sorcerers, astrologers, or soothsayers. Daniel readily acknowledged his desire to serve God when he refused the king's food (1:8). Indicating his continued loyalty to God, Daniel thanked the Lord for revealing the meaning of the king's dream to him (2:18–19). ✣

[1] John J. Collins, *Daniel, in Hermeneia* (Minneapolis: Fortress, 1993), 134.
[2] Edward J. Young, *The Prophecy of Daniel: A Commentary* (Grand Rapids: Eerdmans, 1949), 40; Stephen R. Miller, *Daniel*, NAC (1994), 60.

Clay covers that originally provided protection for a tablet honoring the Babylonian sun god.

Pottery box where Nabopolassar stored the sun god tablet; from Sippar; dated about 620–610 BC.

Cut down the tree and chop off its branches;
strip off its leaves and scatter its fruit.
Let the animals flee from under it,
and the birds from its branches.
15 But leave the stump with its roots
in the ground
and with a band of iron and bronze around it
in the tender grass of the field.
Let him be drenched with dew from the sky
and share the plants of the earth
with the animals.
16 Let his mind be changed from that
of a human,
and let him be given the mind of an animal
for seven periods of time.[A,B]
17 This word is by decree of the watchers,
and the decision is by command
from the holy ones.
This is so that the living will know
that the Most High is ruler
over human kingdoms.
He gives them to anyone he wants
and sets the lowliest of people over them.

18 This is the dream that I, King Nebuchadnezzar, had.
Now, Belteshazzar, tell me the interpretation, because
none of the wise men of my kingdom can make the
interpretation known to me. But you can, because
you have a spirit of the holy gods."

THE DREAM INTERPRETED

19 Then Daniel, whose name is Belteshazzar, was
stunned for a moment, and his thoughts alarmed
him. The king said, "Belteshazzar, don't let the dream
or its interpretation alarm you."

Belteshazzar answered, "My lord, may the dream
apply to those who hate you, and its interpretation
to your enemies! 20 The tree you saw, which grew
large and strong, whose top reached to the sky and
was visible to the whole earth, 21 and whose leaves
were beautiful and its fruit abundant — and on it
was food for all, under it the wild animals lived, and
in its branches the birds of the sky lived — 22 that tree
is you, Your Majesty. For you have become great and
strong: your greatness has grown and even reaches
the sky, and your dominion extends to the ends of
the earth.

23 "The king saw a watcher, a holy one, coming
down from heaven and saying, 'Cut down the tree
and destroy it, but leave the stump with its roots in the
ground and with a band of iron and bronze around it
in the tender grass of the field. Let him be drenched
with dew from the sky and share food with the wild
animals for seven periods of time.' 24 This is the interpretation, Your Majesty, and this is the decree of the
Most High that has been issued against my lord the
king: 25 You will be driven away from people to live
with the wild animals. You will feed on grass like cattle and be drenched with dew from the sky for seven
periods of time, until you acknowledge that the Most
High is ruler over human kingdoms, and he gives
them to anyone he wants. 26 As for the command to
leave the tree's stump with its roots, your kingdom
will be restored[C] to you as soon as you acknowledge
that Heaven[D] rules. 27 Therefore, may my advice seem
good to you my king. Separate yourself from your
sins by doing what is right, and from your injustices
by showing mercy to the needy. Perhaps there will
be an extension of your prosperity."

THE SENTENCE EXECUTED

28 All this happened to King Nebuchadnezzar. 29 At the
end of twelve months, as he was walking on the roof
of the royal palace in Babylon, 30 the king exclaimed,
"Is this not Babylon the Great that I have built to be
a royal residence by my vast power and for my majestic glory?"

31 While the words were still in the king's mouth,
a voice came from heaven: "King Nebuchadnezzar,
to you it is declared that the kingdom has departed
from you. 32 You will be driven away from people
to live with the wild animals, and you will feed on
grass like cattle for seven periods of time, until you
acknowledge that the Most High is ruler over human
kingdoms, and he gives them to anyone he wants."

33 At that moment the message against Nebuchadnezzar was fulfilled. He was driven away from people.
He ate grass like cattle, and his body was drenched
with dew from the sky, until his hair grew like eagles'
feathers and his nails like birds' claws.

NEBUCHADNEZZAR'S PRAISE

34 But at the end of those days, I, Nebuchadnezzar,
looked up to heaven, and my sanity returned to me.
Then I praised the Most High and honored and glorified him who lives forever:

For his dominion is an everlasting dominion,
and his kingdom is from generation
to generation.
35 All the inhabitants of the earth are counted
as nothing,
and he does what he wants with the army
of heaven
and the inhabitants of the earth.
There is no one who can block his hand
or say to him, "What have you done?"

36 At that time my sanity returned to me, and my majesty and splendor returned to me for the glory of

[A] **4:16** Lit *animal as seven times pass over him* [B] **4:16** Perhaps seven years [C] **4:26** Lit *enduring* [D] **4:26** = God

Wise Men from the East

by E. Ray Clendenen

Having had a dream that disturbed him, Babylon's King Nebuchadnezzar summoned his wise men. Six different terms are used for these servants of the king in the book of Daniel. They are collectively referred to as "wise men" (Hb *chakkim*) in 2:12–14,18,24,48; 4:6,18; 5:7–8. But they are called Chaldeans (*kasdim*) in 2:4–5,10. And in 4:9, the general term "magicians" (*chartom*) is used. On the other hand, sometimes they are referred to as comprising two or more presumably specialized groups: "magicians and mediums [*'ashaph*]" in 1:20; "wise men and mediums" in 5:15; "magician, medium, [and] Chaldean" in 2:10; "mediums, Chaldeans, and diviners [*gazerin*]" in 5:7; "magicians, mediums, sorcerers [*mekashephim*], and Chaldeans" in 2:2; "wise man, medium, magician, [and] diviner" in 2:27; and "magicians, mediums, Chaldeans, and diviners" in 4:7 and 5:11. It is difficult to know what to make of this terminology. Clearly "wise men" is the most common general designation, although others are also used.

Perhaps only an insider was equipped to distinguish the various types of "wise men." That term itself described someone who was skillful in technical work, wise in administration, and had considerable expertise in certain intellectual disciplines. The disciplines of these various functionaries probably overlapped. The ability to interpret dreams was evidently shared by several, although the term for "medium" (*chartom*) was derived from an Akkadian word that referred to an interpreter of dreams. Perhaps the factor that unified all these disciplines was the ability to foresee the future by the observation of various signs or omens, including dreams, astronomic phenomena, animal behavior, and the entrails of sacrificial animals. This was called divination.

Practitioners of these arts were used to advise the king on the timing of certain ventures based on such signs. However, casting spells, exorcism, and communication with the dead were also supposedly their forte. Although often said to practice astrology, the ancient Babylonians only observed correlations between certain astronomic phenomena and certain earthly events. The zodiac and the use of horoscopes first appeared in the Hellenistic period. The term for "magicians" is also applied to the Egyptian magicians in Genesis 41:8,24 and Exodus 7–9. Magic was "the exploitation of miraculous or occult powers by carefully specified methods."[1] In ancient Babylon, it was mainly used for deliverance from affliction such as illness or demon possession and could therefore involve exorcism through the use of rites and spells.[2]

Although Daniel is called "chief governor over all the wise men of Babylon" (Dn 2:48), "head of the magicians" (4:9), and "chief of the magicians, mediums, Chaldeans, and diviners" (5:11), this does not mean Daniel dabbled in the occult or attempted to read the future via the stars. As Stephen Miller explains,

> Although Daniel and his friends "entered the king's service" [1:19 NIV], we can rest assured that they did not engage in occult practices. These young men who risked their positions and probably their lives to please God in the matter of the king's food certainly would not have become involved in paganism and witchcraft. Moses grew up in Pharaoh's court and was taught the wisdom of the Egyptians (cf. Exod 2:10; Acts 7:22), but he recorded the regulations condemning the magic arts (Lev 19:26,31; 20:6,27; Deut 18:10–11).[3] ✜

---

[1] Kenneth A. Kitchen, "Magic and Sorcery: Egyptian and Assyro-Babylonian" in *The Illustrated Bible Dictionary*, ed. J. D. Douglas and N. Hillyer (Leicester: Inter-Varsity, 1980), 2:934. [2] Kitchen, "Magic and Sorcery." [3] Stephen R. Miller, *Daniel*, NAC (1994), 73.

my kingdom. My advisers and my nobles sought me out, I was reestablished over my kingdom, and even more greatness came to me. 37 Now I, Nebuchadnezzar, praise, exalt, and glorify the King of the heavens, because all his works are true and his ways are just. He is able to humble those who walk in pride.

BELSHAZZAR'S FEAST

5 King Belshazzar held a great feast for a thousand of his nobles and drank wine in their presence. 2 Under the influence of[A] the wine, Belshazzar gave orders to bring in the gold and silver vessels that his predecessor[B] Nebuchadnezzar had taken from the temple in Jerusalem, so that the king and his nobles, wives, and concubines could drink from them. 3 So they brought in the gold[C] vessels that had been taken from the temple, the house of God in Jerusalem, and the king and his nobles, wives, and concubines drank from them. 4 They drank the wine and praised their gods made of gold and silver, bronze, iron, wood, and stone.

THE HANDWRITING ON THE WALL

5 At that moment the fingers of a man's hand appeared and began writing on the plaster of the king's palace wall next to the lampstand. As the king watched the hand[D] that was writing, 6 his face turned pale,[E] and his thoughts so terrified him that he soiled himself[F] and his knees knocked together. 7 The king shouted to bring in the mediums, Chaldeans, and diviners. He said to these wise men of Babylon, "Whoever reads this inscription and gives me its interpretation will be clothed in purple, have a gold chain around his neck, and have the third highest position in the kingdom." 8 So all the king's wise men came in, but none could read the inscription or make its interpretation known to him. 9 Then King Belshazzar became even more terrified, his face turned pale,[G] and his nobles were bewildered.

10 Because of the outcry of the king and his nobles, the queen[H] came to the banquet hall. "May the king live forever," she said. "Don't let your thoughts terrify you or your face be pale.[I] 11 There is a man in your kingdom who has a spirit of the holy gods in him. In the days of your predecessor he was found to have insight, intelligence, and wisdom like the wisdom of the gods. Your predecessor, King Nebuchadnezzar, appointed him chief of the magicians, mediums, Chaldeans, and diviners. Your own predecessor, the king, 12 did this because Daniel, the one the king named Belteshazzar, was found to have an extraordinary spirit, knowledge and intelligence, and the ability to interpret dreams, explain riddles, and solve problems.[J] Therefore, summon Daniel, and he will give the interpretation."

DANIEL BEFORE THE KING

13 Then Daniel was brought before the king. The king said to him, "Are you Daniel, one of the Judean exiles that my predecessor the king brought from Judah? 14 I've heard that you have a spirit of the gods in you, and that insight, intelligence, and extraordinary wisdom are found in you. 15 Now the wise men and mediums were brought before me to read this inscription and make its interpretation known to me, but they could not give its interpretation. 16 However, I have heard about you that you can give interpretations and solve problems. Therefore, if you can read this inscription and give me its interpretation, you will be clothed in purple, have a gold chain around your neck, and have the third highest position in the kingdom."

17 Then Daniel answered the king, "You may keep your gifts and give your rewards to someone else; however, I will read the inscription for the king and make the interpretation known to him. 18 Your Majesty, the Most High God gave sovereignty, greatness, glory, and majesty to your predecessor Nebuchadnezzar. 19 Because of the greatness he gave him, all peoples, nations, and languages were terrified and fearful of him. He killed anyone he wanted and kept alive anyone he wanted; he exalted anyone he wanted and humbled anyone he wanted. 20 But when his heart was exalted and his spirit became arrogant, he was deposed from his royal throne and his glory was taken from him. 21 He was driven away from people, his mind was like an animal's, he lived with the wild donkeys, he was fed grass like cattle, and his body was drenched with dew from the sky until he acknowledged that the Most High God is ruler over human kingdoms and sets anyone he wants over them.

22 "But you his successor, Belshazzar, have not humbled your heart, even though you knew all this. 23 Instead, you have exalted yourself against the Lord of the heavens. The vessels from his house were brought to you, and as you and your nobles, wives, and concubines drank wine from them, you praised the gods made of silver and gold, bronze, iron, wood, and stone, which do not see or hear or understand. But you have not glorified the God who holds your life-breath in his hand and who controls the whole course of your life.[K] 24 Therefore, he sent the hand, and this writing was inscribed.

[A] **5:2** Or *When he tasted* [B] **5:2** Or *father*, or *grandfather* [C] **5:3** Theod, Vg add *and silver* [D] **5:5** Lit *part of the hand* [E] **5:5–6** Lit *writing, 6the king's brightness changed* [F] **5:6** Or *that the joints of his hips gave way*; lit *that the knots of his loins were untied* [G] **5:9** Lit *his brightness changed on him* [H] **5:10** Perhaps the queen mother [I] **5:10** Lit *your brightness change* [J] **5:12** Lit *and untie knots*; also in v. 16 [K] **5:23** Lit *and all your ways belong to him*

THE INSCRIPTION'S INTERPRETATION

25 "This is the writing that was inscribed: MENE, MENE,
TEKEL, and PARSIN. 26 This is the interpretation of the
message:

'Mene'[A] means that God has numbered[B] the days
of your kingdom and brought it to an end.
27 'Tekel'[C] means that you have been weighed[D] on
the balance and found deficient.
28 'Peres'[E,F] means that your kingdom has been
divided and given to the Medes and Persians."[G]

29 Then Belshazzar gave an order, and they clothed
Daniel in purple, placed a gold chain around his neck,
and issued a proclamation concerning him that he
should be the third ruler in the kingdom.
30 That very night Belshazzar the king of the Chaldeans was killed, 31 and Darius the Mede received the
kingdom at the age of sixty-two.

THE PLOT AGAINST DANIEL

6 Darius decided[H] to appoint 120 satraps over the
kingdom, stationed throughout the realm, 2 and
over them three administrators, including Daniel.
These satraps would be accountable to them so that
the king would not be defrauded. 3 Daniel[I] distinguished himself above the administrators and satraps because he had an extraordinary spirit, so the
king planned to set him over the whole realm. 4 The
administrators and satraps, therefore, kept trying to
find a charge against Daniel regarding the kingdom.
But they could find no charge or corruption, for he
was trustworthy, and no negligence or corruption
was found in him. 5 Then these men said, "We will
never find any charge against this Daniel unless we
find something against him concerning the law of
his God."
6 So the administrators and satraps went together
to the king and said to him, "May King Darius live forever. 7 All the administrators of the kingdom — the
prefects, satraps, advisers, and governors — have
agreed that the king should establish an ordinance
and enforce an edict that, for thirty days, anyone who
petitions any god or man except you, the king, will be
thrown into the lions' den. 8 Therefore, Your Majesty,
establish the edict and sign the document so that,
as a law of the Medes and Persians, it is irrevocable
and cannot be changed." 9 So King Darius signed the
written edict.

DANIEL IN THE LIONS' DEN

10 When Daniel learned that the document had been
signed, he went into his house. The windows in its
upstairs room opened toward Jerusalem, and three
times a day he got down on his knees, prayed, and
gave thanks to his God, just as he had done before.

DIGGING DEEPER *Cylinder of Nabonidus*

While excavating at the temple of Shamash in Sippar (southern Iraq), archaeologists discovered the clay cuneiform Cylinder of Nabonidus, which chronicles the exploits of Babylonian King Nabonidus (555–539 BC) undertook prior to the Persian overthrow of Babylon in 539 BC (Dn 5:22–30). The cylinder tells of King Nabonidus's construction of pagan temples and the discovery of ancient inscriptions of former Babylonian kings. More important, however, the cylinder confirms the existence of the biblical figure named Belshazzar (5:1). Earlier critics considered Belshazzar to be legendary since he was absent from the official Babylonian king lists they knew about outside the Bible. Discovery of the Babylonian Chronicles and Cylinder of Nabonidus provided scholars with extrabiblical proof that King Belshazzar (Bel-shar-usur) was real. He was the firstborn son of King Nabonidus, who often traveled throughout the Near East. Nabonidus left Belshazzar as king and coregent while he was away on his journeys. Belshazzar's position as second (rather than first) most powerful in the kingdom also explains why Daniel could rise no higher than *third* most powerful (5:29).

11 Then these men went as a group and found Daniel petitioning and imploring his God. 12 So they approached the king and asked about his edict: "Didn't
you sign an edict that for thirty days any person who
petitions any god or man except you, the king, will
be thrown into the lions' den?"
The king answered, "As a law of the Medes and
Persians, the order stands[J] and is irrevocable."
13 Then they replied to the king, "Daniel, one of the
Judean exiles, has ignored you, the king, and the edict
you signed, for he prays three times a day." 14 As soon
as the king heard this, he was very displeased; he set
his mind on rescuing Daniel and made every effort
until sundown to deliver him.
15 Then these men went together to the king and
said to him, "You know, Your Majesty, that it is a law
of the Medes and Persians that no edict or ordinance
the king establishes can be changed."

[A] **5:26** Or *a mina* [B] **5:26** The Aramaic word for *numbered* sounds like *mene.* [C] **5:27** Or *a shekel* [D] **5:27** The Aramaic word for *weighed* sounds like *tekel.* [E] **5:28** Or *half a shekel* [F] **5:28** In Aramaic, the word *peres* is the sg form of "parsin" in v. 25. [G] **5:28** The Aramaic word for *divided* and *Persians* sounds like *peres.* [H] **6:1** Lit *It was pleasing before Darius* [I] **6:3** Lit *Now this Daniel* [J] **6:12** Lit *the word is certain*

Just Who Was Belshazzar?

by Robert C. Dunston

Daniel 5:1–31 records events that occurred at and just after the great feast Belshazzar hosted for a thousand of his nobles. During the meal, they drank their wine from the gold vessels that Babylon's King Nebuchadnezzar had taken from the Jerusalem temple. As they drank and celebrated, they praised their gods and, in the process, desecrated the holy vessels that the Hebrews consecrated for the worship of God.

Suddenly a finger appeared in the air and began to write on the plaster wall of the king's palace. Belshazzar was terrified and offered wealth and position to anyone who could interpret the words. The queen informed them that Daniel could interpret the meaning. When he arrived, he refused the wealth and position but gave Belshazzar a lesson in God's previous dealings with Nebuchadnezzar. Whereas Nebuchadnezzar had eventually repented, Belshazzar had continued to sin. Daniel then read the inscription—*Mene, Mene, Tekel,* and *Parsin*—and explained that it meant Belshazzar's days, as well as those of Babylon's kingdom, were numbered. After awarding Daniel what he had promised, Belshazzar was killed that same night.

Only the book of Daniel mentions Belshazzar. Chapter 5 refers to him as "king" and indicates that Nebuchadnezzar was his "predecessor" (lit "father"; vv. 2,11,13,18). Until the latter part of the nineteenth century, Bible students knew little about Belshazzar. Since that time, a variety of sources have been discovered that provide additional information about him.[1]

Nabonidus, who ruled Babylonia from 555 to 539 BC, was Belshazzar's biological father rather than Nebuchadnezzar; and Nabonidus was not a biological descendant of Nebuchadnezzar. Some Bible students believe that following Nebuchadnezzar's death, Nabonidus inherited his harem, perhaps married one of his wives, and adopted one of Nebuchadnezzar's sons as his own in an effort to solidify his hold on the empire.

A simpler explanation is more likely. The word *father* in Semitic languages can refer to a biological father, grandfather, ancestor, or a king's predecessor. *Son* can refer to a biological son, grandson, descendant, or king's successor. As Stephen Miller points out, on the Assyrian black obelisk of Shalmaneser III, "Jehu is called the 'son of Omri,' although Jehu was not a descendant of Omri. He was of another lineage altogether."[2]

Rather than Marduk the high god in Babylon, Nabonidus worshiped the moon-god Sin, like his mother, who was high priestess of the moon-god in Haran.[3] The priests of Marduk wielded great power economically and spiritually, and Nabonidus and others resented them. To break the priests' power, Nabonidus encouraged the people to worship Sin rather than Marduk and revived many long-abandoned rites that honored Sin. His actions infuriated the priests of Marduk and sparked an uprising among the people. In response, Nabonidus moved

Terra-cotta cylinder describing work on the temple of the moon god Sin at Ur by Nabonidus (555–539 BC). The cylinder also includes Nabonidus's prayer for himself and his son Belshazzar.

his residence from Babylon to Teima, an oasis southeast of Edom in the Arabian desert.[4] Worship of Sin was prominent in Teima, and Nabonidus probably felt far more comfortable there.

During Nabonidus's long absences from Babylon, his son Belshazzar ruled in his place. The name *Belshazzar* means "Bel protect the king." Bel served as another name for Marduk. Thus Belshazzar's name linked him to the worship of Marduk and would have made him far more acceptable to the citizens of Babylon than his father.

Although Belshazzar performed the basic duties of king, he was never officially crowned king and never had the authority to participate as king in the Akitu festival. This celebration of the Babylonian new year was the most important festival of the year and was considered necessary to secure Marduk's blessing on the kingdom. Nabonidus's absence required the cancellation of the ceremonies, which no doubt angered the people.[5]

After being gone for about ten years, Nabonidus returned to Babylon. As he did, Cyrus of Persia moved his army closer to the city. Nabonidus fled Babylon but was later taken prisoner. The city of Babylon fell to the Persians in 539 BC. Some Bible scholars suggest Belshazzar knew Babylon would soon fall to the Persian army and decided to hold a banquet anyway, enjoying his last days as king even as the city was on the verge of defeat. Others suggest that Daniel 5:1–31 does not hint at the imminent fall of Babylon. The fact that Belshazzar is terrified by the ominous sign of the finger writing on the wall indicates he had no reason at that time to fear an invasion. In addition, his promoting Daniel to third highest in the empire suggests Belshazzar expected to rule for a long time to come and expected Daniel to hold his new office for many years. The threatening words seem to have been not so much a judgment on Babylon, but a judgment on Belshazzar for his disregard for God and the holy objects used in his worship.[6]

Ruins of a castle at Haran; Roman period; later occupied as a Crusader castle in the Byzantine Era. Haran had been the chief home of the moon god Sin, whose temple was rebuilt by several kings, among them Ashurbanipal and Nabonidus.

Daniel 5:30 states that Belshazzar was killed on the same night the finger wrote on the wall. Some believe he was killed as part of a coup rather than as a result of an invading army. After his death, the Persians conquered Babylon and created their own great empire. "Darius" (5:31) might have been a throne name for Cyrus the Great or for Cambyses, the son of Cyrus, who for part of his life had the title "king of Babylon."

---

[1] Stephen R. Miller, *Daniel*, NAC (1994), 147. [2] Miller, *Daniel*, 149. [3] D. Winton Thomas, *Documents from Old Testament Times* (New York: Harper & Row, 1958), 89. [4] John Bright, *A History of Israel*, 4th ed. (Louisville: Westminster John Knox, 2000), 353. [5] John J. Collins, "Belshazzar" in *Harper's Bible Dictionary*, ed. Paul J. Achtemeier (San Francisco: Harper & Row, 1985), 102. [6] John E. Goldingay, *Daniel*, vol. 30 in WBC (1987), 107–8.

16 So the king gave the order, and they brought Daniel and threw him into the lions' den. The king said to
Daniel, "May your God, whom you continually serve,
rescue you!" 17 A stone was brought and placed over
the mouth of the den. The king sealed it with his own
signet ring and with the signet rings of his nobles, so
that nothing in regard to Daniel could be changed.
18 Then the king went to his palace and spent the night
fasting. No diversions[A] were brought to him, and he
could not sleep.

DANIEL RELEASED

19 At the first light of dawn the king got up and hurried
to the lions' den. 20 When he reached the den, he cried
out in anguish to Daniel. "Daniel, servant of the living
God," the king said,[B] "has your God, whom you continually serve, been able to rescue you from the lions?"
21 Then Daniel spoke with the king: "May the king
live forever. 22 My God sent his angel and shut the lions' mouths; and they haven't harmed me, for I was
found innocent before him. And also before you, Your
Majesty, I have not done harm."
23 The king was overjoyed and gave orders to take
Daniel out of the den. When Daniel was brought up
from the den, he was found to be unharmed, for he
trusted in his God. 24 The king then gave the command, and those men who had maliciously accused
Daniel[C] were brought and thrown into the lions' den
— they, their children, and their wives. They had not
reached the bottom of the den before the lions overpowered them and crushed all their bones.

DARIUS HONORS GOD

25 Then King Darius wrote to those of every people,
nation, and language who live on the whole earth:
"May your prosperity abound. 26 I issue a decree that
in all my royal dominion, people must tremble in fear
before the God of Daniel:

For he is the living God,
and he endures forever;
his kingdom will never be destroyed,
and his dominion has no end.
27 He rescues and delivers;
he performs signs and wonders
in the heavens and on the earth,
for he has rescued Daniel
from the power of the lions."

28 So Daniel prospered during the reign of Darius
and[D] the reign of Cyrus the Persian.

DANIEL'S VISION OF THE FOUR BEASTS

7 In the first year of King Belshazzar of Babylon,
Daniel had a dream with visions in his mind as
he was lying in his bed. He wrote down the dream,
and here is the summary[E] of his account. 2 Daniel
said, "In my vision at night I was watching, and suddenly the four winds of heaven stirred up the great
sea. 3 Four huge beasts came up from the sea, each
different from the other.
4 "The first was like a lion but had eagle's wings. I
continued watching until its wings were torn off. It
was lifted up from the ground, set on its feet like a
man, and given a human mind.
5 "Suddenly, another beast appeared, a second one,
that looked like a bear. It was raised up on one side,
with three ribs in its mouth between its teeth. It was
told, 'Get up! Gorge yourself on flesh.'
6 "After this, while I was watching, suddenly another beast appeared. It was like a leopard with four
wings of a bird on its back. It had four heads, and it
was given dominion.
7 "After this, while I was watching in the night visions, suddenly a fourth beast appeared, frightening
and dreadful, and incredibly strong, with large iron
teeth. It devoured and crushed, and it trampled with
its feet whatever was left. It was different from all the
beasts before it, and it had ten horns.
8 "While I was considering the horns, suddenly
another horn, a little one, came up among them, and
three of the first horns were uprooted before it. And
suddenly in this horn there were eyes like the eyes of
a human and a mouth that was speaking arrogantly.

THE ANCIENT OF DAYS AND THE SON OF MAN

9 "As I kept watching,
thrones were set in place,
and the Ancient of Days took his seat.
His clothing was white like snow,
and the hair of his head like whitest wool.
His throne was flaming fire;
its wheels were blazing fire.
10 A river of fire was flowing,
coming out from his presence.
Thousands upon thousands served him;
ten thousand times ten thousand
stood before him.
The court was convened,
and the books were opened.

11 "I watched, then, because of the sound of the arrogant words the horn was speaking. As I continued
watching, the beast was killed and its body destroyed
and given over to the burning fire. 12 As for the rest of
the beasts, their dominion was removed, but an extension of life was granted to them for a certain period
of time. 13 I continued watching in the night visions,

A 6:18 Aramaic obscure B 6:20 Lit *said to Daniel* C 6:24 Lit *had eaten his pieces* D 6:28 Or *Darius, even* E 7:1 Lit *beginning*

Babylonian and Persian Kings

by Daniel P. Caldwell

Kingdoms rise, and kingdoms fall. With the rise of each new kingdom, changes take place that affect not only the kingdom but also the surrounding territories. These changes can be positive or negative. The rise of the Neo-Babylonian Empire (625–539 BC) and the Persian Empire (539–331 BC) had a tremendous impact on the kingdom of Judah in both positive and negative ways.

Babylon didn't exist long after conquering Judah. Following two short and unstable reigns, Nabonidus was placed on the throne. Though in some ways he was an able leader, the kingdom was weak and conflict was rampant. Making matters worse, Nabonidus brought to Babylon several pagan gods from surrounding cities. Instead of honoring the Babylonian god, Marduk, he gave special devotion to the moon-god, Sin, at the centers of worship at Haran, Ur, and Tema (or Teima). As a result of his religious focus, he alienated the priesthood, the military leaders, and the people of the kingdom. His reign marked the end of the Neo-Babylonian Empire.

JUDAH AND THE PERSIAN EMPIRE

While the Babylonian Empire had a negative impact on the Judean people, the Persian Empire would impact them in a positive manner. When Cyrus the Great, ruler of Persia, entered the territory of Babylonia, he had little difficulty defeating the people in 539 BC. The prophet Isaiah two hundred years earlier had prophesied that the great city of Babylon would be overthrown the same way God overthrew Sodom and Gomorrah (Is 13:17–22).

Because of the tremendous responsibilities the new empire placed on him, Cyrus initially delegated the

Black marble record of Marduk-apla-iddina II, known in the Bible as Merodach-baladan (2Kg 20:12). He seized the throne of Babylon from the Assyrians in 722 BC.

Panels at Persepolis in Iran showing homage brought to King Darius (522–486 BC).

Tomb of Artaxerxes I, who died in 424 BC.

rule of Babylon to Darius. Scholars differ on the exact role of Darius. Since his name doesn't appear anywhere but in the book of Daniel, Darius may have been a lesser leader under Cyrus.[1] When Darius was over the kingdom, Daniel was placed in the lions' den (Dn 6:1–28) and also received the prophecy of the seventy weeks (9:1–20).

Cyrus demonstrated unprecedented toleration toward the captives in Babylon. In the first year of his rule, Cyrus decreed that the Jews could return to the Judean territory. His decree also included the opportunity to rebuild the temple. Cyrus graciously returned many of the temple items that were taken when Jerusalem had been destroyed (Ezr 1:7–11).

Many of the Hebrews had become so successful in Babylon that they did not desire to return to Judah. Perhaps they followed Jeremiah's encouragement for them to build homes and to carry on with their lives (Jr 29:4–10). Daniel remained in Babylon with the exiles who chose to stay behind. However, a large group did return to begin the task of reconstruction.

In the years following the Hebrews' return from exile in 539 BC, the Persian Empire generally maintained peace throughout the ancient Near East. For almost two hundred years, the Persians reigned without any significant challenge.

Cyrus died in 530 BC and was followed by his son, Cambyses, who conquered Egypt in 525. His continued success drove him deep into the Ethiopian territory. Yet Cambyses was unsuccessful in subduing Ethiopia. On his return journey to Persia, Cambyses may have committed suicide in 522.

When Darius I ("the Great") succeeded Cambyses, he faced pockets of rebellion and disharmony in the recently conquered territories. Judah was no exception. The Israelites faced opposition to their rebuilding efforts. During Darius's reign, Haggai and Zechariah encouraged the people to complete the rebuilding of the temple. In 516–515 BC, the temple was completed.

Darius was succeeded by Xerxes (486–464 BC), who was the King Ahasuerus of the book of Esther. He received a letter from unidentified inhabitants of Israel stating that Jerusalem was being rebuilt (Ezr 4:6). Xerxes suppressed a revolt in Egypt and abolished the kingdom of Babylon. Xerxes was murdered in 465 and succeeded by Artaxerxes I (465–424 BC).

Artaxerxes I faced no political revolt but was a weak ruler. Under his reign, Ezra obtained the needed treasure for the temple of God in Jerusalem (Ezr 7:11–26). In the twentieth year of Artaxerxes I's reign, Nehemiah, the king's cupbearer, was sent to Judah and appointed as governor over the region (Neh 1:1–2:11; 5:14).

Artaxerxes I died in 424 BC and was followed by his son, Xerxes II. Not yet two months into his rule, Xerxes II was murdered by his half brother. Following his death, the Persian Empire entered into a period

Persian horse and rider from the late Persian period.

of continuous rebellions. When Artaxerxes II became ruler, his younger brother rebelled against him. The rebellion was put down but the damage lingered.

Artaxerxes II was succeeded by his son Artaxerxes III. This spirited but cruel ruler was murdered in 338 BC. The last three kings to rule the Persian Empire were either murdered or killed in battle. The Persian Empire, once splendid and powerful, was waning in its ability to dominate the surrounding nations. This opened the door for a new world power. In its weakened state, Alexander the Great entered into the territory in 334. This sounded the death knell. In less than three years, the Persian Empire fell. A new empire arose as the Greeks began a long period of domination.

FALLEN EMPIRES

Both the Neo-Babylonian and Persian Empires were dominating forces. Individuals and nations marveled and feared the empires' power. Each kingdom would attempt to leave its mark on the successive generations. Yet both empires met the same fate; each rose and ultimately fell.

History has witnessed many great empires rise, dominate for a time, and eventually fall. Earthly kingdoms come with no guarantees. This makes the words of Daniel 2:44 ring truer: "In the days of those kings, the God of the heavens will set up a kingdom that will never be destroyed, and this kingdom will not be left to another people. It will crush all these kingdoms and bring them to an end, but will itself endure forever." ✣

---

[1] Edward J. Young, *The Prophecy of Daniel* (Grand Rapids: Eerdmans, 1980), 299–300.

and suddenly one like a son of man
was coming with the clouds of heaven.
He approached the Ancient of Days
and was escorted before him.
14 He was given dominion
and glory and a kingdom,
so that those of every people,
nation, and language
should serve him.
His dominion is an everlasting dominion
that will not pass away,
and his kingdom is one
that will not be destroyed.

INTERPRETATION OF THE VISION

15 "As for me, Daniel, my spirit was deeply distressed within me,[A] and the visions in my mind terrified me. 16 I approached one of those who were standing by and asked him to clarify all this. So he let me know the interpretation of these things: 17 'These huge beasts, four in number, are four kings who will rise from the earth. 18 But the holy ones of the Most High will receive the kingdom and possess it forever, yes, forever and ever.'

19 "Then I wanted to be clear about the fourth beast, the one different from all the others, extremely terrifying, with iron teeth and bronze claws, devouring, crushing, and trampling with its feet whatever was left. 20 I also wanted to know about the ten horns on its head and about the other horn that came up, before which three fell — the horn that had eyes, and a mouth that spoke arrogantly, and that looked bigger than the others. 21 As I was watching, this horn waged war against the holy ones and was prevailing over them 22 until the Ancient of Days arrived and a judgment was given in favor of the holy ones of the Most High, for the time had come, and the holy ones took possession of the kingdom.

23 "This is what he said: 'The fourth beast will be a fourth kingdom on the earth, different from all the other kingdoms. It will devour the whole earth, trample it down, and crush it. 24 The ten horns are ten kings who will rise from this kingdom. Another king, different from the previous ones, will rise after them and subdue three kings. 25 He will speak words against the Most High and oppress[B] the holy ones of the Most High. He will intend to change religious festivals[C] and laws, and the holy ones will be handed over to him for a time, times, and half a time.[D] 26 But the court will convene, and his dominion will be taken away, to be completely destroyed forever. 27 The kingdom, dominion, and greatness of the kingdoms under all of heaven will be given to the people, the holy ones of the Most High. His kingdom will be an everlasting kingdom, and all rulers will serve and obey him.'

28 "This is the end of the account. As for me, Daniel, my thoughts terrified me greatly, and my face turned pale,[E] but I kept the matter to myself."

THE VISION OF A RAM AND A GOAT

8 In the third year of King Belshazzar's reign, a vision appeared to me, Daniel, after the one that had appeared to me earlier. 2 I saw the vision, and as I watched, I was in the fortress city of Susa, in the province of Elam. I saw in the vision that I was beside the Ulai Canal. 3 I looked up,[F] and there was a ram standing beside the canal. He had two horns. The two horns were long, but one was longer than the other, and the longer one came up last. 4 I saw the ram charging to the west, the north, and the south. No animal could stand against him, and there was no rescue from his power. He did whatever he wanted and became great.

5 As I was observing, a male goat appeared, coming from the west across the surface of the entire earth without touching the ground. The goat had a conspicuous horn[G] between his eyes. 6 He came toward the two-horned ram I had seen standing beside the canal and rushed at him with savage fury. 7 I saw him approaching the ram, and infuriated with him, he struck the ram, breaking his two horns, and the ram was not strong enough to stand against him. The goat threw him to the ground and trampled him, and there was no one to rescue the ram from his power. 8 Then the male goat acted even more arrogantly, but when he became powerful, the large horn was broken. Four conspicuous horns came up in its place, pointing toward the four winds of heaven.

THE LITTLE HORN

9 From one of them a little horn emerged and grew extensively toward the south and the east and toward the beautiful land.[H] 10 It grew as high as the heavenly army, made some of the army and some of the stars[I] fall to the earth, and trampled them. 11 It acted arrogantly even against the Prince of the heavenly army; it revoked his regular sacrifice and overthrew the place of his sanctuary. 12 In the rebellion, the army was given up, together with the regular sacrifice. The horn threw truth to the ground and was successful in what it did.

13 Then I heard a holy one speaking, and another holy one said to the speaker, "How long will the events of this vision last — the regular sacrifice, the rebellion that makes desolate, and the giving over of the sanctuary and of the army to be trampled?"

[A] **7:15** Lit *was distressed in the middle of its sheath* [B] **7:25** Lit *wear out* [C] **7:25** Lit *change times* [D] **7:25** Or *for three and a half years* [E] **7:28** Lit *my brightness changed on me* [F] **8:3** Lit *I lifted my eyes and looked* [G] **8:5** Lit *a horn of a vision* [H] **8:9** = Israel [I] **8:10** Or *some of the army, that is, some of the stars*

14 He said to me,[A] "For 2,300 evenings and mornings; then the sanctuary will be restored."

INTERPRETATION OF THE VISION

15 While I, Daniel, was watching the vision and trying to understand it, there stood before me someone who appeared to be a man. 16 I heard a human voice calling from the middle of the Ulai: "Gabriel, explain the vision to this man."

17 So he approached where I was standing; when he came near, I was terrified and fell facedown. "Son of man," he said to me, "understand that the vision refers to the time of the end." 18 While he was speaking to me, I fell into a deep sleep, with my face to the ground. Then he touched me, made me stand up, 19 and said, "I am here to tell you what will happen at the conclusion of the time of wrath, because it refers to the appointed time of the end. 20 The two-horned ram that you saw represents the kings of Media and Persia. 21 The shaggy goat represents the king of Greece, and the large horn between his eyes represents the first king.[B] 22 The four horns that took the place of the broken horn represent four kingdoms. They will rise from that nation, but without its power.

23 Near the end of their kingdoms,
when the rebels have reached
the full measure of their sin,[C]
a ruthless[D] king, skilled in intrigue,[E]
will come to the throne.
24 His power will be great,
but it will not be his own.
He will cause outrageous destruction
and succeed in whatever he does.
He will destroy the powerful
along with the holy people.
25 He will cause deceit to prosper
through his cunning and by his influence,
and in his own mind he will
exalt himself.
He will destroy many in a time of peace;
he will even stand against the Prince
of princes.
Yet he will be broken — not by human hands.
26 The vision of the evenings
and the mornings
that has been told is true.
Now you are to seal up the vision
because it refers to many days
in the future."

27 I, Daniel, was overcome and lay sick for days. Then I got up and went about the king's business. I was greatly disturbed by the vision and could not understand it.

DANIEL'S PRAYER

9 In the first year of Darius, the son of Ahasuerus, a Mede by birth, who was made king over the Chaldean kingdom — 2 in the first year of his reign, I, Daniel, understood from the books according to the word of the LORD to the prophet Jeremiah that the number of years for the desolation of Jerusalem would be seventy. 3 So I turned my attention to the Lord God to seek him by prayer and petitions, with fasting, sackcloth, and ashes.

4 I prayed to the LORD my God and confessed:
Ah, Lord — the great and awe-inspiring God who keeps his gracious covenant with those who love him and keep his commands — 5 we have sinned, done wrong, acted wickedly, rebelled, and turned away from your commands and ordinances. 6 We have not listened to your servants the prophets, who spoke in your name to our kings, leaders, ancestors, and all the people of the land.

7 Lord, righteousness belongs to you, but this day public shame belongs to us: the men of Judah, the residents of Jerusalem, and all Israel — those who are near and those who are far, in all the countries where you have banished them because of the disloyalty they have shown toward you. 8 LORD, public shame belongs to us, our kings, our leaders, and our ancestors, because we have sinned against you. 9 Compassion and forgiveness belong to the Lord our God, though we have rebelled against him 10 and have not obeyed the LORD our God by following his instructions that he set before us through his servants the prophets.

11 All Israel has broken your law and turned away, refusing to obey you. The promised curse[F] written in the law of Moses, the servant of God, has been poured out on us because we have sinned against him. 12 He has carried out his words that he spoke against us and against our rulers[G] by bringing on us a disaster that is so great that nothing like what has been done to Jerusalem has ever been done under all of heaven. 13 Just as it is written in the law of Moses, all this disaster has come on us, yet we have not sought the favor of the LORD our God by turning from our iniquities and paying attention to your truth. 14 So the LORD kept the disaster in mind and brought it on us, for the LORD our God is righteous in all he has done. But we have not obeyed him.

[A] **8:14** LXX, Theod, Syr, Vg read *him* [B] **8:21** = Alexander the Great [C] **8:23** Lit *have become complete* [D] **8:23** Lit *strong of face* [E] **8:23** Lit *king, and understanding riddles* [F] **9:11** Lit *The curse and the oath* [G] **9:12** Lit *against rulers who ruled us*

15 Now, Lord our God — who brought your people out of the land of Egypt with a strong hand
and made your name renowned as it is this day
— we have sinned, we have acted wickedly.
16 Lord, in keeping with all your righteous acts,
may your anger and wrath turn away from your
city Jerusalem, your holy mountain; for because
of our sins and the iniquities of our ancestors,
Jerusalem and your people have become an object of ridicule to all those around us.

17 Therefore, our God, hear the prayer and the
petitions of your servant. Make your face shine
on your desolate sanctuary for the Lord's sake.
18 Listen closely,[A] my God, and hear. Open your
eyes and see our desolations and the city that
bears your name. For we are not presenting our
petitions before you based on our righteous acts,
but based on your abundant compassion. 19 Lord,
hear! Lord, forgive! Lord, listen and act! My God,
for your own sake, do not delay, because your
city and your people bear your name.

THE SEVENTY WEEKS OF YEARS

20 While I was speaking, praying, confessing my sin
and the sin of my people Israel, and presenting my
petition before the LORD my God concerning the holy
mountain of my God — 21 while I was praying, Gabriel, the man I had seen in the first vision, reached me in
my extreme weariness, about the time of the evening
offering. 22 He gave me this explanation: "Daniel, I've
come now to give you understanding. 23 At the beginning of your petitions an answer went out, and I
have come to give it, for you are treasured by God.[B]
So consider the message and understand the vision:

24 Seventy weeks are decreed
about your people and your holy city —
to bring the rebellion to an end,
to put a stop to sin,
to atone for iniquity,
to bring in everlasting righteousness,
to seal up vision and prophecy,
and to anoint the most holy place.
25 Know and understand this:
From the issuing of the decree
to restore and rebuild Jerusalem
until an Anointed One, the ruler,[C]
will be seven weeks and sixty-two weeks.
It will be rebuilt with a plaza and a moat,
but in difficult times.
26 After those sixty-two weeks
the Anointed One will be cut off
and will have nothing.
The people of the coming ruler
will destroy the city and the sanctuary.[D]
The[E] end will come with a flood,
and until the end there will be[F] war;
desolations are decreed.
27 He will make a firm covenant[G]
with many for one week,
but in the middle of the week
he will put a stop to sacrifice
and offering.
And the abomination of desolation
will be on a wing of the temple[H,I]
until the decreed destruction
is poured out on the desolator."

VISION OF A GLORIOUS ONE

10 In the third year of King Cyrus of Persia, a message was revealed to Daniel, who was named
Belteshazzar. The message was true and was about
a great conflict. He understood the message and had
understanding of the vision.
2 In those days I, Daniel, was mourning for three
full weeks. 3 I didn't eat any rich food, no meat or
wine entered my mouth, and I didn't put any oil on
my body until the three weeks were over. 4 On the
twenty-fourth day of the first month,[J] as I was standing on the bank of the great river, the Tigris, 5 I looked
up, and there was a man dressed in linen, with a belt
of gold from Uphaz[K] around his waist. 6 His body was
like beryl,[L] his face like the brilliance of lightning, his
eyes like flaming torches, his arms and feet like the
gleam of polished bronze, and the sound of his words
like the sound of a multitude.
7 Only I, Daniel, saw the vision. The men who were
with me did not see it, but a great terror fell on them,
and they ran and hid. 8 I was left alone, looking at
this great vision. No strength was left in me; my face
grew deathly pale,[M] and I was powerless. 9 I heard
the words he said, and when I heard them I fell into
a deep sleep,[N] with my face to the ground.

ANGELIC CONFLICT

10 Suddenly, a hand touched me and set me shaking
on my hands and knees. 11 He said to me, "Daniel, you
are a man treasured by God.[O] Understand the words
that I'm saying to you. Stand on your feet, for I have
now been sent to you." After he said this to me, I stood
trembling.

[A] **9:18** Lit *Stretch out your ear* [B] **9:23** *by God* added for clarity [C] **9:25** Or *until an anointed one, a prince* [D] **9:26** MT; Theod, some mss read *The city and the sanctuary will be destroyed when the ruler comes.* [E] **9:26** Lit *Its*, or *His* [F] **9:26** Or *end of a* [G] **9:27** Or *will enforce a covenant* [H] **9:27** LXX; MT reads *of abominations* [I] **9:27** Or *And the desolator will be on the wing of abominations*, or *And the desolator will come on the wings of monsters* (or *of horror*); Hb obscure [J] **10:4** = Nisan (March–April) [K] **10:5** Some Hb mss read *Ophir* [L] **10:6** The identity of this stone is uncertain. [M] **10:8** Lit *my splendor was turned on me to ruin* [N] **10:9** Lit *a sleep on my face* [O] **10:11** *by God* added for clarity, also in v. 19

12 "Don't be afraid, Daniel," he said to me, "for from
the first day that you purposed to understand and
to humble yourself before your God, your prayers
were heard. I have come because of your prayers.
13 But the prince of the kingdom of Persia opposed
me for twenty-one days. Then Michael, one of the
chief princes, came to help me after I had been left
there with the kings of Persia. 14 Now I have come to
help you understand what will happen to your people
in the last days, for the vision refers to those days."

15 While he was saying these words to me, I turned
my face toward the ground and was speechless.
16 Suddenly one with human likeness touched my
lips. I opened my mouth and said to the one standing
in front of me, "My lord, because of the vision, anguish overwhelms me and I am powerless. 17 How can
someone like me, your servant,[A] speak with someone
like you, my lord? Now I have no strength, and there
is no breath in me."

18 Then the one with a human appearance touched
me again and strengthened me. 19 He said, "Don't be
afraid, you who are[B] treasured by God. Peace to you;
be very strong!"

As he spoke to me, I was strengthened and said,
"Let my lord speak, for you have strengthened me."

20 He said, "Do you know why I've come to you? I
must return at once to fight against the prince of Persia, and when I leave, the prince of Greece will come.
21 However, I will tell you what is recorded in the
book of truth. (No one has the courage to support me
against those princes except Michael, your prince.

11 1 In the first year of Darius the Mede, I stood up
to strengthen and protect him.) 2 Now I will tell
you the truth.

PROPHECIES ABOUT PERSIA AND GREECE

"Three more kings will arise in Persia, and the fourth
will be far richer than the others. By the power he
gains through his riches, he will stir up everyone
against the kingdom of Greece. 3 Then a warrior king
will arise; he will rule a vast realm and do whatever he
wants. 4 But as soon as he is established, his kingdom
will be broken up and divided to the four winds of
heaven, but not to his descendants; it will not be the
same kingdom that he ruled, because his kingdom
will be uprooted and will go to others besides them.

KINGS OF THE SOUTH AND THE NORTH

5 "The king of the South will grow powerful, but one
of his commanders will grow more powerful and will
rule a kingdom greater than his. 6 After some years
they will form an alliance, and the daughter of the
king of the South will go to the king of the North to
seal the agreement. She will not retain power, and his
strength will not endure. She will be given up, together with her entourage, her father,[C] and the one who
supported her during those times. 7 In the place of the
king of the South, one from her family[D] will rise up,
come against the army, and enter the fortress of the
king of the North. He will take action against them
and triumph. 8 He will take even their gods captive
to Egypt, with their metal images and their precious
articles of silver and gold. For some years he will stay
away from the king of the North, 9 who will enter the
kingdom of the king of the South and then return to
his own land.

10 "His sons will mobilize for war and assemble a
large number of armed forces. They will advance,
sweeping through like a flood,[E] and will again wage
war as far as his fortress. 11 Infuriated, the king of
the South will march out to fight with the king of
the North, who will raise a large army, but they will
be handed over to his enemy. 12 When the army is
carried off, he will become arrogant and cause tens
of thousands to fall, but he will not triumph. 13 The
king of the North will again raise a multitude larger
than the first. After some years[F] he will advance with
a great army and many supplies.

14 "In those times many will rise up against the king
of the South. Violent ones among your own people
will assert themselves to fulfill a vision, but they will
fail. 15 Then the king of the North will come, build up
a siege ramp, and capture a well-fortified city. The
forces of the South will not stand; even their select
troops will not be able to resist. 16 The king of the
North who comes against him will do whatever he
wants, and no one can oppose him. He will establish
himself in the beautiful land[G] with total destruction
in his hand. 17 He will resolve to come with the force
of his whole kingdom and will reach an agreement
with him.[H] He will give him a daughter in marriage[I] to
destroy it,[J] but she will not stand with him or support
him. 18 Then he will turn his attention to the coasts
and islands[K] and capture many. But a commander
will put an end to his taunting; instead, he will turn
his taunts against him. 19 He will turn his attention
back to the fortresses of his own land, but he will
stumble, fall, and be no more.

20 "In his place one will arise who will send out a
tax collector for the glory of the kingdom; but within
a few days he will be broken, though not in anger[L]
or in battle.

21 "In his place a despised person will arise; royal
honors will not be given to him, but he will come

[A] **10:17** Lit *Can I, a servant of my lord* [B] **10:19** Lit *afraid, man*
[C] **11:6** Some Hb mss, Theod read *the child*; Syr, Vg read *her children*
[D] **11:7** Lit *from the shoot of her roots* [E] **11:10** Lit *advance and overflow and pass through* [F] **11:13** Lit *At the end of the times* [G] **11:16** = Israel
[H] **11:17** = the king of the South [I] **11:17** Lit *him the daughter of women*
[J] **11:17** Perhaps the kingdom [K] **11:18** of the Mediterranean
[L] **11:20** Or *not openly*

during a time of peace[A] and seize the kingdom by
intrigue. 22 A flood of forces will be swept away before him; they will be broken, as well as the covenant
prince. 23 After an alliance is made with him, he will
act deceitfully. He will rise to power with a small nation.[B] 24 During a time of peace,[C] he will come into the
richest parts of the province and do what his fathers
and predecessors never did. He will lavish plunder,
loot, and wealth on his followers, and he will make
plans against fortified cities, but only for a time.
25 "With a large army he will stir up his power and
his courage against the king of the South. The king of
the South will prepare for battle with an extremely
large and powerful army, but he will not succeed,
because plots will be made against him. 26 Those who
eat his provisions will destroy him; his army will be
swept away, and many will fall slain. 27 The two kings,
whose hearts are bent on evil, will speak lies at the
same table but to no avail, for still the end will come
at the appointed time. 28 The king of the North will
return to his land with great wealth, but his heart
will be set against the holy covenant;[D] he will take
action, then return to his own land.
29 "At the appointed time he will come again to the
South, but this time[E] will not be like the first. 30 Ships
of Kittim[F] will come against him, and being intimidated, he will withdraw. Then he will rage against
the holy covenant and take action. On his return, he
will favor those who abandon the holy covenant.
31 His forces will rise up and desecrate the temple
fortress. They will abolish the regular sacrifice and
set up the abomination of desolation. 32 With flattery
he will corrupt those who act wickedly toward the
covenant, but the people who know their God will
be strong and take action. 33 Those who have insight
among the people will give understanding to many,
yet they will fall by the sword and flame, and they will
be captured and plundered for a time. 34 When they
fall, they will be helped by some, but many others
will join them insincerely. 35 Some of those who have
insight will fall so that they may be refined, purified,
and cleansed until the time of the end, for it will still
come at the appointed time.
36 "Then the king will do whatever he wants. He will
exalt and magnify himself above every god, and he
will say outrageous things against the God of gods.
He will be successful until the time of wrath is completed, because what has been decreed will be accomplished. 37 He will not show regard for the gods[G] of
his ancestors, the god desired by women, or for any
other god, because he will magnify himself above
all. 38 Instead, he will honor a god of fortresses — a
god his ancestors did not know — with gold, silver,
precious stones, and riches. 39 He will deal with the
strongest fortresses with the help of a foreign god.
He will greatly honor those who acknowledge him,[H]
making them rulers over many and distributing land
as a reward.
40 "At the time of the end, the king of the South
will engage him in battle, but the king of the North
will storm against him with chariots, horsemen,
and many ships. He will invade countries and sweep
through them like a flood. 41 He will also invade the
beautiful land, and many will fall. But these will escape from his power: Edom, Moab, and the prominent people[I] of the Ammonites. 42 He will extend his
power against the countries, and not even the land
of Egypt will escape. 43 He will get control over the
hidden treasures of gold and silver and over all the
riches of Egypt. The Libyans and Cushites will also be
in submission.[J] 44 But reports from the east and the
north will terrify him, and he will go out with great
fury to annihilate and completely destroy many. 45 He
will pitch his royal tents between the sea and[K] the
beautiful holy mountain, but he will meet his end
with no one to help him.

12 At that time
Michael, the great prince
who stands watch over your people,
will rise up.
There will be a time of distress
such as never has occurred
since nations came into being until that time.
But at that time all your people
who are found written in the book
will escape.
2 Many who sleep in the dust
of the earth will awake,
some to eternal life,
and some to disgrace and eternal contempt.
3 Those who have insight will shine
like the bright expanse of the heavens,
and those who lead many to righteousness,
like the stars forever and ever.

4 "But you, Daniel, keep these words secret and seal
the book until the time of the end. Many will roam
about, and knowledge will increase."[L]
5 Then I, Daniel, looked, and two others were
standing there, one on this bank of the river and one
on the other. 6 One of them said to the man dressed
in linen, who was above the water of the river, "How
long until the end of these wondrous things?" 7 Then
I heard the man dressed in linen, who was above the

[A] **11:21** Or *come without warning* [B] **11:23** Or *a few people* [C] **11:24** Or *Without warning* [D] **11:28** Or *the Jewish people and religion* [E] **11:29** Lit *but the last* [F] **11:30** = the Romans [G] **11:37** Or *God* [H] **11:39** Or *those he acknowledges* [I] **11:41** Lit *the first* [J] **11:43** Lit *Cushites at his steps* [K] **11:45** Or *the seas at* [L] **12:4** LXX reads *and the earth will be filled with unrighteousness*

water of the river. He raised both his hands[A] toward
heaven and swore by him who lives eternally that
it would be for a time, times, and half a time. When
the power of the holy people is shattered, all these
things will be completed.
8 I heard but did not understand. So I asked, "My
lord, what will be the outcome of these things?"
9 He said, "Go on your way, Daniel, for the words
are secret and sealed until the time of the end.
10 Many will be purified, cleansed, and refined, but
the wicked will act wickedly; none of the wicked
will understand, but those who have insight will
understand. 11 From the time the daily sacrifice is
abolished and the abomination of desolation is set
up, there will be 1,290 days. 12 Happy is the one who
waits for and reaches 1,335 days. 13 But as for you, go
on your way to the end;[B] you will rest, and then you
will rise[C] to receive your allotted inheritance at the
end of the days."

[A] **12:7** Lit *raised his right and his left* [B] **12:13** LXX omits *to the end*
[C] **12:13** Or *stand*

HOSEA

From Ur, a terra-cotta plaque depicting an affectionate couple; Old Babylonian, 2000–1750 BC.

INTRODUCTION TO

HOSEA

Circumstances of Writing

According to the first verse, Hosea's prophetic career spanned at least forty years. It began sometime during the reign of Jeroboam II, who ruled Israel, the northern kingdom, as coregent with his father Jehoash from 793 to 782 BC, then independently until 753 BC. Hosea's ministry ended sometime during the reign of Hezekiah, who ruled Judah from 716 to 686 BC.

Although the southern kingdom of Judah was not neglected in Hosea's prophecy (e.g., Hs 1:7,11; 6:11; 12:2), his messages were directed primarily to the northern kingdom of Israel, often referred to as "Ephraim" (5:3,12–14; 6:4; 7:1) and represented by the royal city Samaria (7:1; 8:5–6; 10:5,7; 13:16). Hosea apparently lived and worked in or around Samaria, probably moving to Jerusalem at least by the time Samaria fell to the Assyrians in 722 BC.

The reign of Jeroboam II, the northern kingdom's greatest ruler by worldly standards, was a time of general affluence, military might, and national stability. The economy was strong, the future looked bright, and the mood of the country was optimistic—at least for the upper class (Hs 12:8; Am 3:15; 6:4–6). Syria was a constant problem to Israel, but Adad-nirari III of Assyria had brought Israel relief with an expedition against Damascus, the Syrian capital, in 805 BC.

After Adad-nirari's death in 783 BC, Israel and Judah expanded during a time of Assyrian weakness (the time of Jonah). But after Jeroboam's death in 753 BC, Israel sank into near anarchy, going through six kings in about thirty years, four of whom were assassinated (Zechariah, Shallum, Pekahiah, and Pekah). Since Assyria also regained power during this time, Israel was doomed. Of course the real reason Israel crumbled was God's determination to judge the people for their sins, as Hosea and Amos made clear. Most of Hosea's messages were probably delivered during these last thirty years of Israel's nationhood.

Structure

The first three chapters of the book establish a parallel between the Lord and Hosea. Both were loving husbands of unfaithful wives. Hosea's three children, whose names served as messages to Israel, represent an overture to the second main division of the book, which presents its accusations and the calls to repentance in groups of three. Just as chapter 1—a third-person account of Hosea's family—is balanced by chapter 3—a first-person account—so the final main division of the book alternates between first-person announcements of God's message and third-person reports from the prophet.

Contribution to the Bible

Hosea compared the relationship between God and his people to that of a husband and his wife, drawing a parallel between spiritual and marital unfaithfulness. "The Bible is very clear in its moral code that the sexual act can only legitimately take place within the context of the marriage relationship. Thus the image of marriage and sex, a relationship that is purely exclusive and allows no rivals, is an ideal image of the relationship between God and his people."[1] Yet nothing can quench God's love for his covenant people. Like a marriage partner, God is deeply involved in our lives and is pained when we go our own way. God demands love and loyalty from

---

[1] Leland Ryken, James C. Wilhoit, and Tremper Longman III, eds., *Dictionary of Biblical Imagery* (Downers Grove, IL: InterVarsity, 1988), 778.

his own. Often God's people have failed to demonstrate whole-hearted love for him, but he stands ready to forgive and restore those who turn to him in repentance. In buying Gomer's freedom, Hosea pointed ahead to God's love perfectly expressed In Christ, who bought the freedom of his bride, the church, with his own life.

1 The word of the LORD that came to Hosea son of Beeri during the reigns of Uzziah, Jotham, Ahaz, and Hezekiah, kings of Judah, and of Jeroboam son of Jehoash, king of Israel.

HOSEA'S MARRIAGE AND CHILDREN

2 When the LORD first spoke to Hosea, he said this to him:

Go and marry a woman of promiscuity,
and have children of promiscuity,
for the land is committing
blatant acts of promiscuity
by abandoning the LORD.

3 So he went and married Gomer daughter of Diblaim, and she conceived and bore him a son. 4 Then
the LORD said to him:

Name him Jezreel,[A] for in a little while
I will bring the bloodshed of Jezreel
on the house of Jehu
and put an end to the kingdom of the house
of Israel.
5 On that day I will break the bow of Israel
in Jezreel Valley.

6 She conceived again and gave birth to a daughter, and the LORD said to him:

Name her Lo-ruhamah,[B]
for I will no longer have compassion
on the house of Israel.
I will certainly take them away.
7 But I will have compassion on the house
of Judah,
and I will deliver them by the LORD their God.
I will not deliver them by bow, sword, or war,
or by horses and cavalry.

8 After Gomer had weaned Lo-ruhamah, she conceived and gave birth to a son. 9 Then the LORD said:

Name him Lo-ammi,[C]
for you are not my people,
and I will not be your God.[D]
10 Yet the number of the Israelites
will be like the sand of the sea,
which cannot be measured or counted.
And in the place where they were told:
You are not my people,
they will be called: Sons of the living God.
11 And the Judeans and the Israelites
will be gathered together.
They will appoint for themselves a single ruler
and go up from[E] the land.
For the day of Jezreel will be great.

2 Call[F] your brothers: My People
and your sisters: Compassion.

ISRAEL'S ADULTERY REBUKED

2 Rebuke your mother; rebuke her.
For she is not my wife and I am not
her husband.
Let her remove the promiscuous look
from her face
and her adultery from between her breasts.
3 Otherwise, I will strip her naked
and expose her as she was on the day
of her birth.
I will make her like a desert
and like a parched land,
and I will let her die of thirst.
4 I will have no compassion on her children
because they are the children of promiscuity.
5 Yes, their mother is promiscuous;
she conceived them and acted shamefully.
For she thought, "I will follow my lovers,
the men who give me my food and water,
my wool and flax, my oil and drink."
6 Therefore, this is what I will do:
I will block her[G] way with thorns;
I will enclose her with a wall,
so that she cannot find her paths.
7 She will pursue her lovers but not catch them;
she will look for them but not find them.
Then she will think,
"I will go back to my former husband,
for then it was better for me than now."
8 She does not recognize
that it is I who gave her the grain,
the new wine, and the fresh oil.
I lavished silver and gold on her,
which they used for Baal.
9 Therefore, I will take back my grain in its time
and my new wine in its season;
I will take away my wool and linen,
which were to cover her nakedness.
10 Now I will expose her shame
in the sight of her lovers,
and no one will rescue her from my power.
11 I will put an end to all her celebrations:
her feasts, New Moons, and Sabbaths —
all her festivals.
12 I will devastate her vines and fig trees.
She thinks that these are her wages
that her lovers have given her.
I will turn them into a thicket,
and the wild animals will eat them.
13 And I will punish her for the days of the Baals,
to which she burned incense.

[A]**1:4** = God Sows [B]**1:6** = No Compassion [C]**1:9** = Not My People
[D]**1:9** Lit *not be yours* [E]**1:11** Or *and flourish in*; Hb obscure
[F]**2:1** Lit *Say to* [G]**2:6** LXX, Syr; MT reads *your*

Hosea the Prophet

By Leon Hyatt

Reconstructed Canaanite high place and altar established by Jeroboam I (930–909 BC) at Tel Dan in northern Israel.

Hosea was one of four writing prophets who lived and preached during the eighth century BC. Isaiah and Micah served God in Judah, while Amos and Hosea ministered in Israel. The only information we have about Hosea's life is what is in his book. Concerning his background, Hosea revealed only his father's name, which was Beeri. Concerning his experiences in life, he told only of his marriage. He told that story, not for its own sake, but as an illustration of God's feelings toward Israel. The first message God gave to Hosea was a command to marry, but the kind of woman God told him to marry likely seemed startling and puzzling. Jehovah told Hosea to take to himself "a woman of promiscuity, and have children of promiscuity" (Hs 1:2). Hosea obeyed God and married a woman named Gomer, daughter of Diblaim. The description of the children God told Hosea to take was exactly the same as the description of the woman, literally "a woman of fornication and children of fornication." The meaning of these strange instructions has had various interpretations. Some suggest that the woman and the marriage were only symbolic. This view seeks to relieve the shame of a prophet's marrying a fallen woman. Turning the story into a symbol does not relieve the moral dilemma, and it ignores the fact that Hosea told the story as a real experience. Others suggest that Gomer was stained by immorality, perhaps even prostitution, before Hosea married her. This view conflicts with God's holiness and the moral standards he expects of his servants. Still others suggest that God described the woman not in terms of what she already was but in terms of what she was going to become. This explanation relieves the moral dilemma somewhat, but it does not deal with the fact that the children were described with the same words as the woman. The words should have the same meaning in each case. Nothing in the story suggests that the children were guilty of adultery or prostitution. A fourth suggestion is that "of promiscuity" described the society and atmosphere in which everyone in Israel lived at that time. The reason God gave for his instruction to Hosea supports this view. God told Hosea to take the woman and the children "for the land is committing blatant acts of promiscuity by abandoning the Lord" (1:2). This view also explains best how both the woman and her children could be described with the same words, "of promiscuity." The description certainly fits the times in which Hosea lived. The whole land was unfaithful to its God. Hosea may have wondered if any woman and children could live in and come out of such a corrupt society and devote themselves to the sacrificial life needed in a preacher's family. God told Hosea to go ahead and marry. He intended to use the marriage for his own purposes. In time, Gomer clearly fell into the corruptions of the times and became unfaithful to Hosea. The first hint is in 1:3, which says Gomer bore Hosea a son, while verses 6 and 8 say only that Gomer gave birth to a daughter and then to a second son. The text makes no definite statement that the daughter and the second son were Hosea's. Hosea 2:2–13 begins by seeming to describe Hosea's anguish because his wife had become a prostitute openly. However, starting with verse 6, the wording describes not Hosea's anguish but God's anguish over Israel's unfaithfulness to him. In chapter 3, Hosea said God told him to go love an adulteress. In response, Hosea bought a woman out of slavery for the price of the least valuable of slaves. The chapter implies she had fallen into degradation and slavery because of her sins. Hosea took her into his home and proposed that both of them live without physical intimacy with each other or with others for many days. Apparently, his purpose was to give them time to adjust to each other and see if they wanted to try their marriage again. Some hold that this woman is someone other than Gomer. This explanation is unnatural and strained. What prophet would take a woman to live with him who was not his wife? We do not need to soften the full impact of Hosea's experience with Gomer. His experience powerfully shows the amazing love and forgiveness of a man truly in love. It also shows how this woman had to learn how to love her husband enough to be faithful to him. ✣

She put on her rings and her jewelry
and followed her lovers,
but she forgot me.
This is the LORD's declaration.

ISRAEL'S ADULTERY FORGIVEN

14 Therefore, I am going to persuade her,
lead her to the wilderness,
and speak tenderly to her.[A]
15 There I will give her vineyards back to her
and make the Valley of Achor[B]
into a gateway of hope.
There she will respond as she did
in the days of her youth,
as in the day she came out of the land
of Egypt.
16 In that day —
this is the LORD's declaration —
you will call me "my husband"
and no longer call me "my Baal."[C]
17 For I will remove the names of the Baals
from her mouth;
they will no longer be remembered
by their names.
18 On that day I will make a covenant for them
with the wild animals, the birds of the sky,
and the creatures that crawl on the ground.
I will shatter bow, sword,
and weapons of war in the land[D]
and will enable the people to rest securely.
19 I will take you to be my wife forever.
I will take you to be my wife
in righteousness,
justice, love, and compassion.
20 I will take you to be my wife in faithfulness,
and you will know the LORD.
21 On that day I will respond —
this is the LORD's declaration.
I will respond to the sky,
and it will respond to the earth.
22 The earth will respond to the grain,
the new wine, and the fresh oil,
and they will respond to Jezreel.
23 I will sow her[E] in the land for myself,
and I will have compassion
on Lo-ruhamah;
I will say to Lo-ammi:
You are my people,
and he will say, "You are my God."

WAITING FOR RESTORATION

3 Then the LORD said to me, "Go again; show love
to a woman who is loved by another man and
is an adulteress, just as the LORD loves the Israelites
though they turn to other gods and love raisin cakes."
2 So I bought her for fifteen shekels of silver and
nine bushels of barley.[F,G] 3 I said to her, "You are to live
with me many days. You must not be promiscuous
or belong to any man, and I will act the same way
toward you."
4 For the Israelites must live many days without
king or prince, without sacrifice or sacred pillar, and
without ephod or household idols. 5 Afterward, the
people of Israel will return and seek the LORD their
God and David their king. They will come with awe to
the LORD and to his goodness in the last days.

GOD'S CASE AGAINST ISRAEL

4 Hear the word of the LORD, people of Israel,
for the LORD has a case
against the inhabitants of the land:
There is no truth, no faithful love,
and no knowledge of God in the land!
2 Cursing, lying, murder, stealing,
and adultery are rampant;
one act of bloodshed follows another.
3 For this reason the land mourns,
and everyone who lives in it languishes,
along with the wild animals and the birds
of the sky;
even the fish of the sea disappear.
4 But let no one dispute; let no one argue,
for my case is against you priests.[H,I]
5 You will stumble by day;
the prophet will also stumble with you
by night.
And I will destroy your mother.
6 My people are destroyed for lack
of knowledge.
Because you have rejected knowledge,
I will reject you from serving as my priest.
Since you have forgotten the law of your God,
I will also forget your sons.
7 The more they multiplied,
the more they sinned against me.
I[J] will change their[K] honor into disgrace.
8 They feed on the sin[L] of my people;
they have an appetite for their iniquity.
9 The same judgment will happen
to both people and priests.
I will punish them for their ways
and repay them for their deeds.

[A] 2:14 Lit *speak to her heart* [B] 2:15 = Trouble [C] 2:16 Or *my master* [D] 2:18 Or *war on the earth* [E] 2:23 = Israel [F] 3:2 LXX reads *barley and a measure of wine* [G] 3:2 Lit *silver, a homer of barley, and a lethek of barley* [H] 4:4 Text emended; MT reads *argue, and your people are like those contending with a priest* [I] 4:4 Hb obscure [J] 4:7 Alt Hb tradition, Syr, Tg read *They* [K] 4:7 Alt Hb tradition reads *my* [L] 4:8 Or *sin offerings*

10 They will eat but not be satisfied;
they will be promiscuous but not multiply.
For they have abandoned their devotion
to the LORD.
11 Promiscuity, wine, and new wine
take away one's understanding.

12 My people consult their wooden idols,
and their divining rods inform them.
For a spirit of promiscuity
leads them astray;
they act promiscuously
in disobedience to[A] their God.
13 They sacrifice on the mountaintops,
and they burn offerings on the hills,
and under oaks, poplars, and terebinths,
because their shade is pleasant.
And so your daughters act promiscuously
and your daughters-in-law commit adultery.
14 I will not punish your daughters
when they act promiscuously
or your daughters-in-law
when they commit adultery,
for the men themselves go off
with prostitutes
and make sacrifices with cult prostitutes.
People without discernment are doomed.

WARNINGS FOR ISRAEL AND JUDAH

15 Israel, if you act promiscuously,
don't let Judah become guilty!
Do not go to Gilgal
or make a pilgrimage to Beth-aven,[B]
and do not swear an oath: As the LORD lives!
16 For Israel is as obstinate as a stubborn cow.
Can the LORD now shepherd them
like a lamb in an open meadow?
17 Ephraim is attached to idols;
leave him alone!
18 When their drinking is over,
they turn to promiscuity.
Israel's leaders[C] fervently love disgrace.[D]
19 A wind with its wings will carry them off,[E]
and they will be ashamed of their sacrifices.

5 Hear this, priests!
Pay attention, house of Israel!
Listen, royal house!
For the judgment applies to you
because you have been a snare at Mizpah
and a net spread out on Tabor.
2 Rebels are deeply involved in slaughter;
I will be a punishment for all of them.[D]
3 I know Ephraim,
and Israel is not hidden from me.
For now, Ephraim,
you have acted promiscuously;
Israel is defiled.
4 Their actions do not allow them
to return to their God,
for a spirit of promiscuity is among them,
and they do not know the LORD.
5 Israel's arrogance testifies against them.[F]
Both Israel and Ephraim stumble
because of their iniquity;
even Judah will stumble with them.
6 They go with their flocks and herds
to seek the LORD
but do not find him;
he has withdrawn from them.
7 They betrayed the LORD;
indeed, they gave birth to illegitimate children.
Now the New Moon will devour them
along with their fields.

8 Blow the ram's horn in Gibeah,
the trumpet in Ramah;
raise the war cry in Beth-aven:
Look behind you,[G] Benjamin!
9 Ephraim will become a desolation
on the day of punishment;
I announce what is certain
among the tribes of Israel.
10 The princes of Judah are like those
who move boundary markers;
I will pour out my fury on them like water.
11 Ephraim is oppressed, crushed in judgment,
for he is determined to follow
what is worthless.[H]
12 So I am like rot to Ephraim
and like decay to the house of Judah.
13 When Ephraim saw his sickness
and Judah his wound,
Ephraim went to Assyria
and sent a delegation to the great king.[I]
But he cannot cure you or heal your wound.
14 For I am like a lion to Ephraim
and like a young lion to the house of Judah.
Yes, I will tear them to pieces and depart.
I will carry them off,
and no one can rescue them.
15 I will depart and return to my place
until they recognize their guilt and seek
my face;
they will search for me in their distress.

[A] **4:12** Lit *promiscuously from under* [B] **4:15** = House of Wickedness
[C] **4:18** Lit *Her shields*; Ps 47:9; 89:18 [D] **4:18; 5:2** Hb obscure
[E] **4:19** Lit *wind will bind it in its wings* [F] **5:5** Lit *against his face*
[G] **5:8** Or *We will follow you* [H] **5:11** Or *follow a command*; Hb obscure
[I] **5:13** Or *to King Yareb*

The Significance of a Name

by Scott Hummel

As would be expected, parents were primarily responsible for naming their children, a couple of exceptions being Adam naming Eve (Gn 3:20) and Naomi's friends naming Ruth's son Obed (Ru 4:17). Parents often chose a name from a stock of generally well-known names because the name sounded like or related to a characteristic of the child or circumstance surrounding the birth.[1] For example, Moses named his son Gershom because he had been an alien in the land (Ex 2:22; Hb *Ger*, "sojourner"). When Esau was born, he was hairy, so he was named Esau (meaning "hairy"; Gn 25:25). The majority of the time mothers named their children, but fathers did so as well. For example, Leah and Rachel named all of Jacob's sons, each with a name reflecting his personal circumstances (29:31–30:24). On Rachel's deathbed, she named her son Ben-oni, which means "Son of My Sorrow." Jacob, though, changed the son's name to Benjamin, which means "Son of the Right Hand" (35:18; CSB footnote). Most children received positive names; Jacob changed the negative name into a positive one. Parents typically named a child immediately after birth.[2] "The custom of postponing the naming until circumcision, eight days later, is not recorded until New Testament times" (Lk 1:59; 2:21).[3]

Because names meant more in the biblical period than today, people chose them with great care. For example, Abigail said concerning her husband Nabal, "His name means 'stupid,' and stupidity is all he knows" (1Sm 25:25). The name Moses, which means "to draw out," pertains to his birth, since the infant Moses was drawn out of the Nile River (Ex 2:1–10) and foreshadows his destiny to draw Israel out of Egypt. "Jesus," which is a form of "Joshua" (meaning "Yahweh saves"), is appropriate because it points to his destiny and purpose (Mt 1:21).

Since people so closely identified a name with a person, the word "name" could represent one's reputation, authority, and life (Gn 11:4; 48:16). Expressions such as "wipe out our name from the earth" meant to be killed (Jos 7:9). To speak or act in the name of another was to speak or act as that person or with that person's authority (Ex 5:23; 1Sm 17:45). For example, Jesus spoke of those who prophesied, performed miracles, and cast out demons in his name (Mt 7:22).

Hebrew names were usually structured as single-element names, phrase names, or sentence names. Single-element names referred to common concepts, objects, animals, or less frequently plants. Several examples are Barak ("lightning"), Hannah ("grace"), Deborah ("bee"), Caleb ("dog"), Jonah ("dove"), Nahash ("serpent"), and Tamar ("palm tree").[4] Phrase names and sentence names combined different elements, such as Obadiah ("Yahweh's servant"), Melchizedek ("king of righteousness"), Jehoshaphat ("Yahweh has given justice"), and Jonathan ("Yahweh has given"). Isaiah named one son Shear-jashub ("A Remnant Will Return," Is 7:3; CSB footnote) and another Maher-shal-al-hash-baz ("One Who Hastens to the Plunder or the Loot," Is 8:3; CSB footnote) to foreshadow the coming Assyrian destruction. Many Hebrew names embedded the two most common names for God (El and Yahweh) within the names. For example, Elijah means "Yahweh is God." However, many Israelite names included the names of Baal. Saul named a son Esh-baal (Man of Baal," 1Ch 8:33; CSB footnote). To avoid the name Baal, some biblical passages change the name from Baal to Bosheth, which means "shame." Therefore, Esh-baal was changed to Ish-bosheth ("Man of Shame," 2Sm 2:8; CSB footnote). Many eighth-century ostraca (broken pottery with writing) from

A silver drachma dated 500–480 BC, honoring the priestesses at the Artemis temple in Ephesus, who were called "Melissai," which meant "bees."

Samaria have names containing "Baal," suggesting that a large number of people in the northern kingdom participated in Canaanite religious practices.[5]

Hosea gave his children names full of meaning that symbolized his prophetic message. Jezreel means "God sows, plants" and emphasized Hosea's message of God sowing judgment. This name recalled the town of Jezreel where Jehu killed the king of Israel and mortally wounded the king of Judah (2Kg 9:14–10:17). The name also foreshadowed Israel's coming slaughter and destruction. Hosea named his daughter Lo-ruhamah, which means "No Compassion" (Hs 1:6; CSB footnote), to signify that God would no longer have compassion for Israel because of its sins. The name Ruhamah is related to a word meaning "womb," suggesting motherly love and compassion. The third child was named Lo-ammi ("not my people"). The name was frightening; it suggested the people had broken their covenant with God. He was no longer their God and they were no longer his people (Lv 26:14–33). Fortunately, God demonstrated his mercy by changing the names of Hosea's children. Jezreel would no longer signify judgment, instead it would point to a day of hope when God would "sow or plant" Israel back in the land (Hs 1:11; 2:23). Lo-ruhamah would become Ruhamah ("Compassion"), because God would once again have compassion on Israel, and Lo-ammi would become Ammi ("My People") because, after they faced God's judgment and even deportation, God would reestablish his covenant and embrace Israel once again as his people (2:1,23). The change in the names of Hosea's children signified God's change of heart toward his children, Israel. Hosea's naming his children reflected God's pending judgment. God's renaming them reflected his enduring mercy. ✤

---

[1] Douglas Stuart, "Names, Proper," in *ISBE* (1986), 3:485. [2] Douglas Stuart, *Hosea–Jonah, WBC* (1987), 34. [3] Roland de Vaux, *Ancient Israel* (Grand Rapids: Eerdmans, 1997), 43. [4] De Vaux, *Ancient Israel*, 43–44. [5] E. W. Heaton, *Everyday Life in Old Testament Times* (New York: Scribner's Sons, 1956), 231; De Vaux, *Ancient Israel*, 45.

Terra-cotta figurine depicting a pregnant woman, common throughout the ancient world. People believed such figurines affected both fertility and abundance.

A CALL TO REPENTANCE

6 Come, let's return to the LORD.
For he has torn us,
and he will heal us;
he has wounded us,
and he will bind up our wounds.
2 He will revive us after two days,
and on the third day he will raise us up
so we can live in his presence.
3 Let's strive to know the LORD.
His appearance is as sure as the dawn.
He will come to us like the rain,
like the spring showers that water the land.

THE LORD'S FIRST LAMENT

4 What am I going to do with you, Ephraim?
What am I going to do with you, Judah?
Your love is like the morning mist
and like the early dew that vanishes.
5 This is why I have used the prophets
to cut them down;[A]
I have killed them with the words
from my mouth.
My judgment strikes like lightning.[B]
6 For I desire faithful love and not sacrifice,
the knowledge of God rather than
burnt offerings.

7 But they, like Adam,[C] have violated
the covenant;
there they have betrayed me.
8 Gilead is a city of evildoers,
tracked with bloody footprints.
9 Like raiders who wait in ambush for someone,
a band of priests murders on the road
to Shechem.
They commit atrocities.
10 I have seen something horrible in the house
of Israel:
Ephraim's promiscuity is there;
Israel is defiled.
11 A harvest is also appointed for you, Judah.

When I restore the fortunes of my people,
7 1 when I heal Israel,
the iniquity of Ephraim and the crimes
of Samaria
will be exposed.
For they practice fraud;
a thief breaks in;
a raiding party pillages outside.
2 But they never consider that I remember
all their evil.
Now their actions are all around them;
they are right in front of my face.

ISRAEL'S CORRUPTION

3 They please the king with their evil,
the princes with their lies.
4 All of them commit adultery;
they are like an oven heated by a baker
who stops stirring the fire
from the kneading of the dough
until it is leavened.
5 On the day of our king,
the princes are sick with the heat of wine —
there is a conspiracy with traitors.[D]
6 For they — their hearts like an oven —
draw him into their oven.
Their anger smolders all night;
in the morning it blazes like a flaming fire.
7 All of them are as hot as an oven,
and they consume their rulers.
All their kings fall;
not one of them calls on me.[E]

8 Ephraim has allowed himself to get mixed up
with the nations.
Ephraim is unturned bread
baked on a griddle.
9 Foreigners consume his strength,
but he does not notice.
Even his hair is streaked with gray,
but he does not notice.
10 Israel's arrogance testifies against them,[F]
yet they do not return to the LORD
their God,
and for all this, they do not seek him.

11 So Ephraim has become like a silly,
senseless dove;
they call to Egypt, and they go to Assyria.
12 As they are going, I will spread my net
over them;
I will bring them down like birds of the sky.
I will discipline them in accordance
with the news that reaches[G] their assembly.

THE LORD'S SECOND LAMENT

13 Woe to them, for they fled from me;
destruction to them, for they rebelled
against me!
Though I want to redeem them,
they speak lies against me.
14 They do not cry to me from their hearts;
rather, they wail on their beds.

[A] **6:5** Or *have cut down the prophets* [B] **6:5** LXX, Syr, Tg; MT reads *Your judgments go out as light* [C] **6:7** Or *they, as at Adam*, or *they, like men,* [D] **7:5** Lit *wine — he stretches out his hand to scorners*; Hb obscure [E] **7:3–7** These vv. may refer to a king's assassination; Hb obscure. [F] **7:10** Lit *against his face* [G] **7:12** Lit *news to*

They slash themselves[A] for grain
and new wine;
they turn away from me.
15 I trained and strengthened their arms,
but they plot evil against me.
16 They turn, but not to what is above;[B]
they are like a faulty bow.
Their leaders will fall by the sword
because of their insolent tongue.
They will be ridiculed for this in the land
of Egypt.

ISRAEL'S FALSE HOPES

8 Put the ram's horn to your mouth!
One like an eagle comes
against the house of the LORD,
because they transgress my covenant
and rebel against my law.
2 Israel cries out to me,
"My God, we know you!"
3 Israel has rejected what is good;
an enemy will pursue him.

4 They have installed kings,
but not through me.
They have appointed leaders,
but without my approval.
They make their silver and gold
into idols for themselves
for their own destruction.[C]
5 Your calf-idol[D] is rejected, Samaria.
My anger burns against them.
How long will they be incapable
of innocence?
6 For this thing is from Israel —
a craftsman made it, and it is not God.
The calf of Samaria will be smashed to bits!

7 Indeed, they sow the wind
and reap the whirlwind.
There is no standing grain;
what sprouts fails to yield flour.
Even if they did,
foreigners would swallow it up.
8 Israel is swallowed up!
Now they are among the nations
like discarded pottery.
9 For they have gone up to Assyria
like a wild donkey going off on its own.
Ephraim has paid for love.
10 Even though they hire lovers
among the nations,
I will now round them up,
and they will begin to decrease in number
under the burden of the king and leaders.
11 When Ephraim multiplied his altars for sin,
they became his altars for sinning.
12 Though I were to write out for him
ten thousand points of my instruction,
they would be[E] regarded
as something strange.
13 Though they offer sacrificial gifts[F]
and eat the flesh,
the LORD does not accept them.
Now he will remember their guilt
and punish their sins;
they will return to Egypt.
14 Israel has forgotten his Maker
and built palaces;
Judah has also multiplied fortified cities.
I will send fire on their cities,
and it will consume their citadels.

THE COMING EXILE

9 Israel, do not rejoice jubilantly
as the nations do,
for you have acted promiscuously,
leaving your God.
You love the wages of a prostitute
on every grain-threshing floor.
2 Threshing floor and wine vat will not
sustain them,
and the new wine will fail them.
3 They will not stay in the land of the LORD.
Instead, Ephraim will return to Egypt,
and they will eat unclean food in Assyria.

4 They will not pour out
their wine offerings to the LORD,
and their sacrifices will not please him.
Their food will be like the bread of mourners;
all who eat it become defiled.
For their bread will be for their appetites alone;
it will not enter the house of the LORD.
5 What will you do on a festival day,
on the day of the LORD's feast?
6 For even if they flee from devastation,
Egypt will gather them, and Memphis
will bury them.
Thistles will take possession
of their precious silver;
thorns will invade their tents.

7 The days of punishment have come;
the days of retribution have come.
Let Israel recognize it!

[A] **7:14** Some Hb mss, LXX; other Hb mss read *They stay* [B] **7:16** Some emend to *turn to what is useless* [C] **8:4** Lit *themselves that it might be cut off* [D] **8:5** Lit *calf* [E] **8:12** Or *Though I wrote out . . . instruction, they are* [F] **8:13** Hb obscure

Assyria in the Eighth Century

by Daniel C. Browning Jr.

Assyria, which first emerged as an important power in northern Mesopotamia during the time of Abraham, Isaac, and Jacob, waxed and waned for centuries until Israel's divided monarchy period (late ninth–seventh centuries BC). This era of Assyria's renewed dominance, known as the Neo-Assyrian Empire, is well known from cuneiform documents, bas-reliefs (sculptured panels) from Assyrian royal palaces, and other archaeological evidence.

Almost annually, the Assyrian king gathered his troops and set out in predatory campaigns. He invaded smaller nations and gave them an ultimatum demanding "presents" and allegiance. From these now-subservient nations, the Assyrian king demanded annual tribute payments—typically gold, silver, or other products of value. Those who resisted were subjected to violent military action. The Assyrian army dominated in the field because of its cavalry; thus, many foes took refuge within fortified citadels. The Assyrians, however, having become experts at siege warfare, invariably breached the walls and took resistant cities. Survivors of the assault were subjected to extreme cruelties. Rulers' heads were severed and set on pikes. Supporters of the resistant ruler were flayed alive or impaled, while prisoners were hauled away as slaves.

Artists duly recorded all these actions. Assyrian rulers, beginning with Ashurnasirpal II (883–859 BC), built huge palaces decorated throughout with bas-reliefs showing these atrocities. Back in the conquered area, the Assyrian king would set up a puppet ruler and impose heavy tribute on the already-devastated nation. Those delivering tribute to the royal palace passed through halls and rooms decorated with the macabre scenes as reminders of what awaited those who would resist or rebel.

After the reign of Assyrian king Shalmaneser III (858–824 BC), Assyria entered an eighty-year decline. The eighth century BC began with brighter prospects for the Hebrew kingdoms. Indeed, the first half of the century saw a period of peace and growth unknown since the united monarchy. Prosperity did not equal righteousness, however. Israel in particular was consumed with social, economic, and religious decay. By midcentury, judgment was due, and the golden age ended suddenly at the hands of Assyrian resurgence.

Assyrian power restarted with Tiglath-pileser III's accession to the throne in 745 BC. He reestablished Assyria's aggressive expansionist ways, reorganized the government, and transformed the nation into a true empire. He reformed the military, making it even more fearsome; his policy of mass deportation meant tens of thousands of persons were forcibly displaced from conquered nations. Tiglath-pileser revived the practice of building palaces decorated with depictions

Scene on the black obelisk of Shalmaneser III depicting Shalmaneser accepting tribute from Israel's King Jehu. This is the only discovered image of a Hebrew king.

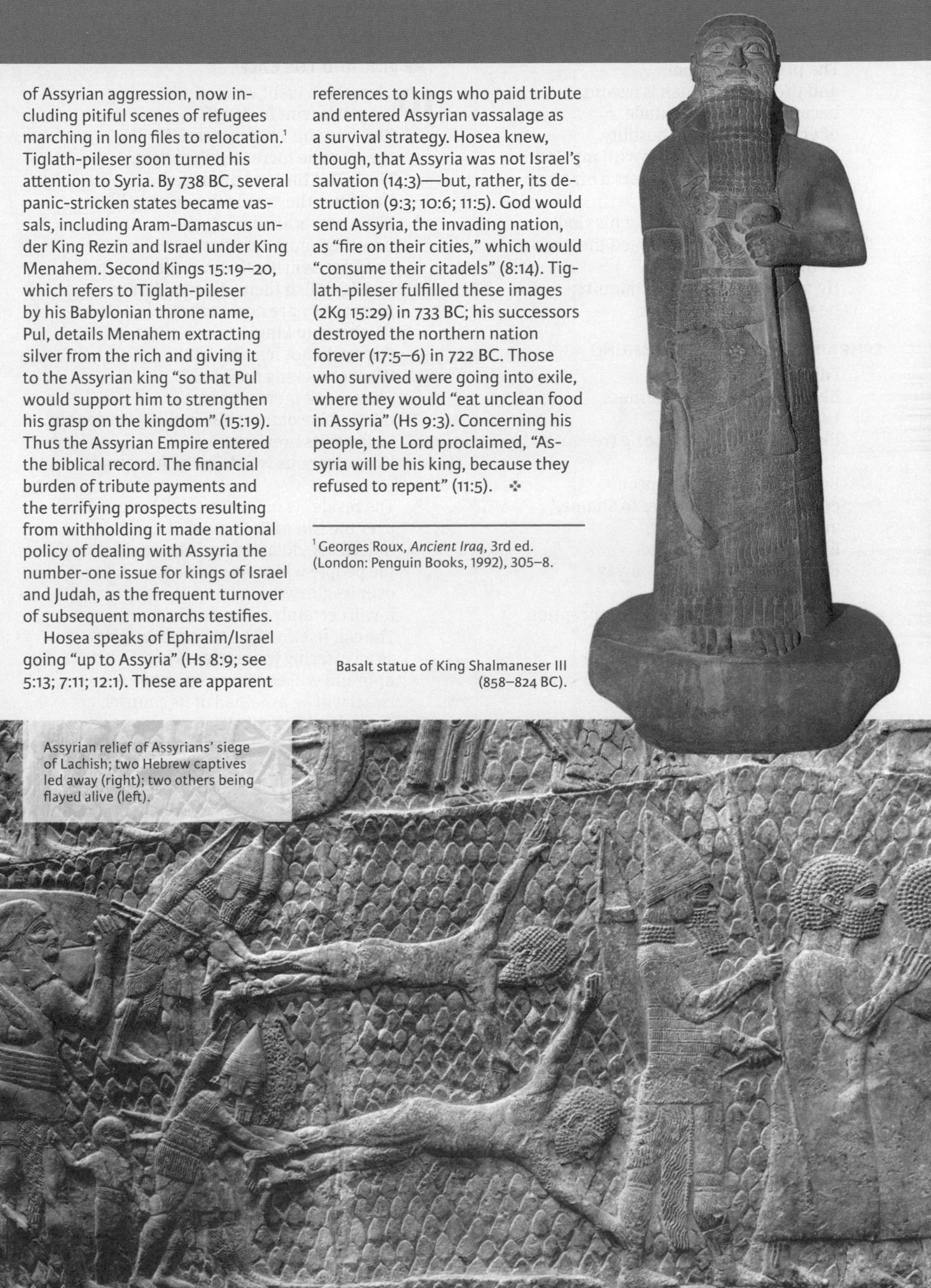

of Assyrian aggression, now including pitiful scenes of refugees marching in long files to relocation.[1] Tiglath-pileser soon turned his attention to Syria. By 738 BC, several panic-stricken states became vassals, including Aram-Damascus under King Rezin and Israel under King Menahem. Second Kings 15:19–20, which refers to Tiglath-pileser by his Babylonian throne name, Pul, details Menahem extracting silver from the rich and giving it to the Assyrian king "so that Pul would support him to strengthen his grasp on the kingdom" (15:19). Thus the Assyrian Empire entered the biblical record. The financial burden of tribute payments and the terrifying prospects resulting from withholding it made national policy of dealing with Assyria the number-one issue for kings of Israel and Judah, as the frequent turnover of subsequent monarchs testifies.

Hosea speaks of Ephraim/Israel going "up to Assyria" (Hs 8:9; see 5:13; 7:11; 12:1). These are apparent references to kings who paid tribute and entered Assyrian vassalage as a survival strategy. Hosea knew, though, that Assyria was not Israel's salvation (14:3)—but, rather, its destruction (9:3; 10:6; 11:5). God would send Assyria, the invading nation, as "fire on their cities," which would "consume their citadels" (8:14). Tiglath-pileser fulfilled these images (2Kg 15:29) in 733 BC; his successors destroyed the northern nation forever (17:5–6) in 722 BC. Those who survived were going into exile, where they would "eat unclean food in Assyria" (Hs 9:3). Concerning his people, the Lord proclaimed, "Assyria will be his king, because they refused to repent" (11:5). ✣

[1] Georges Roux, *Ancient Iraq*, 3rd ed. (London: Penguin Books, 1992), 305–8.

Basalt statue of King Shalmaneser III (858–824 BC).

Assyrian relief of Assyrians' siege of Lachish; two Hebrew captives led away (right); two others being flayed alive (left).

The prophet is a fool,
and the inspired man is insane,
because of the magnitude
of your iniquity and hostility.
8 Ephraim's watchman is with my God.
Yet the prophet encounters a bird trap
on all his pathways.
Hostility is in the house of his God!
9 They have deeply corrupted themselves
as in the days of Gibeah.
He will remember their iniquity;
he will punish their sins.

EPHRAIM BEREAVED OF OFFSPRING

10 I discovered Israel
like grapes in the wilderness.
I saw your ancestors
like the first fruit of the fig tree
in its first season.
But they went to Baal-peor,
consecrated themselves to Shame,[A]
and became abhorrent,
like the thing they loved.
11 Ephraim's glory will fly away
like a bird:
no birth, no pregnancy, no conception.
12 Even if they raise children,
I will bereave them of each one.
Yes, woe to them when I depart
from them!
13 I have seen Ephraim like Tyre,
planted in a meadow,
so Ephraim will bring out his children
to the executioner.
14 Give them, LORD —
What should you give?
Give them a womb that miscarries
and breasts that are dry!

15 All their evil appears at Gilgal,
for there I began to hate them.
I will drive them from my house
because of their evil, wicked actions.
I will no longer love them;
all their leaders are rebellious.
16 Ephraim is struck down;
their roots are withered;
they cannot bear fruit.
Even if they bear children,
I will kill the precious offspring
of their wombs.
17 My God will reject them
because they have not listened to him;
they will become wanderers
among the nations.

THE VINE AND THE CALF

10 Israel is a lush[B] vine;
it yields fruit for itself.
The more his fruit increased,
the more he increased the altars.
The better his land produced,
the better they made the sacred pillars.
2 Their hearts are devious;[C]
now they must bear their guilt.
The LORD will break down their altars
and demolish their sacred pillars.
3 In fact, they are now saying,
"We have no king!
For we do not fear the LORD.
What can a king do for us?"
4 They speak mere words,
taking false oaths while making covenants.
So lawsuits break out
like poisonous weeds in the furrows of a field.
5 The residents of Samaria will have anxiety
over the calf of Beth-aven.
Indeed, its idolatrous priests rejoiced over it;
the people will mourn over it,
over its glory.
It will certainly go into exile.
6 The calf itself will be taken to Assyria
as an offering to the great king.[D]
Ephraim will experience shame;
Israel will be ashamed of its counsel.
7 Samaria's king will disappear[E]
like foam[F] on the surface of the water.
8 The high places of Aven, the sin of Israel,
will be destroyed;
thorns and thistles will grow over their altars.
They will say to the mountains, "Cover us!"
and to the hills, "Fall on us!"

ISRAEL'S DEFEAT BECAUSE OF SIN

9 Israel, you have sinned
since the days of Gibeah;
they have taken their stand there.
Will not war against the unjust
overtake them in Gibeah?
10 I will discipline them at my discretion;
nations will be gathered against them
to put them in bondage[G]
for their double iniquity.

11 Ephraim is a well-trained calf
that loves to thresh,
but I will place a yoke on[H] her fine neck.

[A] **9:10** = Baal [B] **10:1** Or *ravaged* [C] **10:2** Or *divided* [D] **10:6** Or *to King Yareb* [E] **10:7** Or *will be cut off* [F] **10:7** Or *a stick* [G] **10:10** LXX, Syr, Vg read *against them when they are disciplined* [H] **10:11** Lit *will pass over*

Eagle: Symbol of Strength

by Rick W. Byargeon

The Hebrew word for "eagle" (*nesher*) can refer to either an eagle or a vulture. It occurs twenty-six times in the Old Testament. Two Hebrew words meaning "to lacerate or to tear to pieces" and "to fall, or drop down" may be related to *nesher*.[1] An eagle both tears its prey and dives to capture it.

From Babylon to Rome, the eagle (not the vulture) was a common military and royal symbol in the ancient world.[2] Assyria's King Sennacherib referred to the eagle as the "king of birds."[3] The eagle also appears as a help to the king of Kish, Etana, in his quest for an heir.[4] Elsewhere in the ancient Near East, we find the double-headed eagle as the Hittites' royal insignia. Esar-haddon, another Assyrian king, boasted of his military might, "Like a furious eagle I spread my pinions to destroy my enemies."[5] Often the writers of the Old Testament applied the imagery of the eagle to the conquering armies of Babylon (Jr 48:40; Lm 4:19; Hab 1:8) and Persia (Is 46:11) that came against God's own people (Dt 28:49–50).

In the various contexts of *nesher*, the various qualities of the eagle captured the imagination of the writers of Scripture. The most common characteristic of the eagle is soaring (Ex 19:4; Jb 39:27; Pr 23:5; 30:19; Is 40:31; Jr 49:22). The eagle's ability to stay aloft was a thing of mystery to sages (Pr 30:19), and the eagle was also a picture of divine protection (Ex 19:4). Another major characteristic of the eagle is its ability to strike a killing blow (Dt 28:49; Jb 9:26; Jr 48:40; 49:22; Hab 1:8). Coupled with its striking ability is the quality of speed (2Sm 1:23; Jr 4:13; Lm 4:19). Yet the most enduring picture of the eagle is its seeming ability to stay aloft forever. This captured the imagination of both the prophet (Is 40:31) and the psalmist (Ps 103:5). ✣

A relief depicting an eagle-headed protective spirit that guarded Assyria's King Ashurnasirpal II (ruled 883–859 BC).

---

[1] Tryggve Kronholm, "nešer [or nesher]" (eagle) in *TDOT*, 10:77. [2] Daniel I. Block, *The Book of Ezekiel, Chapters 1–24* (Grand Rapids: Eerdmans, 1997), 540. [3] Daniel David Luckenbill, *The Annals of Sennacherib* (Chicago: University of Chicago Press, 1924), 36. [4] "Etana" in ANET with sup., 117. [5] Block, *Ezekiel*, 540.

I will harness Ephraim;
Judah will plow;
Jacob will do the final plowing.
12 Sow righteousness for yourselves
and reap faithful love;
break up your unplowed ground.
It is time to seek the LORD
until he comes and sends righteousness
on you like the rain.

13 You have plowed wickedness
and reaped injustice;
you have eaten the fruit of lies.
Because you have trusted in your own way[A]
and in your large number of soldiers,
14 the roar of battle will rise against your people,
and all your fortifications will be demolished
in a day of war,
like Shalman's destruction of Beth-arbel.
Mothers will be dashed to pieces
along with their children.
15 So it will be done to you, Bethel,
because of your extreme evil.
At dawn the king of Israel will be
totally destroyed.

THE LORD'S LOVE FOR ISRAEL

11 When Israel was a child, I loved him,
and out of Egypt I called my son.
2 Israel called to the Egyptians
even as Israel was leaving them.[B]
They kept sacrificing to the Baals
and burning offerings to idols.
3 It was I who taught Ephraim to walk,
taking them[C] by the hand,[D]
but they never knew that I healed them.
4 I led them with human cords,
with ropes of love.
To them I was like one
who eases the yoke from their jaws;
I bent down to give them food.
5 Israel will not return to the land of Egypt
and Assyria will be his king,
because they refused to repent.
6 A sword will whirl through his cities;
it will destroy and devour the bars of his gates,[E]
because of their schemes.
7 My people are bent on turning from me.
Though they call to him on high,
he will not exalt them at all.

8 How can I give you up, Ephraim?
How can I surrender you, Israel?
How can I make you like Admah?
How can I treat you like Zeboiim?
I have had a change of heart;
my compassion is stirred!
9 I will not vent the full fury of my anger;
I will not turn back to destroy Ephraim.
For I am God and not man,
the Holy One among you;
I will not come in rage.[F]
10 They will follow the LORD;
he will roar like a lion.
When he roars,
his children will come trembling
from the west.
11 They will be roused like birds from Egypt
and like doves from the land of Assyria.
Then I will settle them in their homes.
This is the LORD's declaration.
12 Ephraim surrounds me with lies,
the house of Israel, with deceit.
Judah still wanders with God
and is faithful to the holy ones.[G]

GOD'S CASE AGAINST JACOB'S HEIRS

12 Ephraim chases[H] the wind
and pursues the east wind.
He continually multiplies lies and violence.
He makes a covenant with Assyria,
and olive oil is carried to Egypt.

2 The LORD also has a dispute with Judah.
He is about to punish Jacob
according to his conduct;
he will repay him based on his actions.
3 In the womb he grasped his brother's heel,
and as an adult he wrestled with God.
4 Jacob struggled with the angel and prevailed;
he wept and sought his favor.
He found him at Bethel,
and there he spoke with him.[I]
5 The LORD is the God of Armies;
the LORD is his name.
6 But you must return to your God.
Maintain love and justice,
and always put your hope in God.

7 A merchant loves to extort
with dishonest scales in his hands.
8 But Ephraim thinks,
"How rich I have become;
I made it all myself.

[A] **10:13** LXX reads *your chariots* [B] **11:2** Lit *They called to them; thus they went from before them* [C] **11:3** LXX, Syr, Vg; MT reads *him* [D] **11:3** Lit *them on his arms* [E] **11:6** Or *devour his empty talkers*, or *devour his limbs*; Hb obscure [F] **11:9** Or *come into any city*; Hb obscure [G] **11:12** Hb obscure [H] **12:1** Or *grazes on*, or *tends* [I] **12:4** LXX, Syr; MT reads *us*

In all my earnings,
no one can find any iniquity in me
that I can be punished for!"[A]

JUDGMENT ON APOSTATE ISRAEL

9 I have been the LORD your God
ever since[B] the land of Egypt.
I will make you live in tents again,
as in the festival days.
10 I will speak through the prophets
and grant many visions;
I will give parables through the prophets.
11 Since Gilead is full of evil,
they will certainly come to nothing.
They sacrifice bulls in Gilgal;
even their altars will be like piles of rocks
on the furrows of a field.

FURTHER INDICTMENT OF JACOB'S HEIRS

12 Jacob fled to the territory of Aram.
Israel worked to earn a wife;
he tended flocks for a wife.
13 The LORD brought Israel from Egypt
by a prophet,
and Israel was tended by a prophet.

14 Ephraim has provoked bitter anger,
so his Lord will leave his bloodguilt on him
and repay him for his contempt.

13 When Ephraim spoke, there was trembling;
he was exalted in Israel.
But he incurred guilt through Baal and died.

2 Now they continue to sin
and make themselves a cast image,
idols skillfully made from their silver,
all of them the work of craftsmen.
People say about them,
"Let the men who sacrifice[C] kiss the calves."
3 Therefore, they will be like the morning mist,
like the early dew that vanishes,
like chaff blown from a threshing floor,
or like smoke from a window.

DEATH AND RESURRECTION

4 I have been the LORD your God
ever since[D] the land of Egypt;
you know no God but me,
and no Savior exists besides me.
5 I knew[E] you in the wilderness,
in the land of drought.
6 When they had pasture,
they became satisfied;
they were satisfied,
and their hearts became proud.
Therefore they forgot me.
7 So I will be like a lion to them;
I will lurk like a leopard on the path.
8 I will attack them
like a bear robbed of her cubs
and tear open the rib cage
over their hearts.
I will devour them there like a lioness,
like a wild beast that would rip them open.
9 I will destroy you, Israel;
you have no help but me.[F]

10 Where now is your king,[G]
that he may save you in all your cities,
and the[H] rulers[I] you demanded, saying,
"Give me a king and leaders"?
11 I give you a king in my anger
and take away a king in my wrath.
12 Ephraim's guilt is preserved;
his sin is stored up.
13 Labor pains come on him.
He is not a wise son;
when the time comes,
he will not be born.[J]

14 I will ransom them from the power of Sheol.
I will redeem[K] them from death.
Death, where are your barbs?
Sheol, where is your sting?
Compassion is hidden from my eyes.

THE COMING JUDGMENT

15 Although he flourishes among his brothers,[L]
an east wind will come,
a wind from the LORD rising up
from the desert.
His water source will fail,
and his spring will run dry.
The wind[M] will plunder the treasury
of every precious item.

16 Samaria will bear her guilt
because she has rebelled against her God.
They will fall by the sword;
their children will be dashed to pieces,
and their pregnant women ripped open.

[A] **12:8** Lit *iniquity which is sin* [B] **12:9** LXX reads *God who brought you out of* [C] **13:2** Or *"Those who make human sacrifices* [D] **13:4** DSS, LXX read *God who brought you out of* [E] **13:5** LXX, Syr read *fed* [F] **13:9** LXX reads *At your destruction, Israel, who will help you?* [G] **13:10** LXX, Syr, Vg; MT reads *I will be your king* [H] **13:10** Lit *your* [I] **13:10** Or *judges* [J] **13:13** Lit *he will not present himself at the opening of the womb for sons* [K] **13:14** Or *Should I ransom . . . ? Should I redeem . . . ?* [L] **13:15** Or *among reeds* [M] **13:15** Probably the Assyrian king

A PLEA TO REPENT

14 Israel, return to the LORD your God,
for you have stumbled in your iniquity.
2 Take words of repentance with you
and return to the LORD.
Say to him, "Forgive all our iniquity
and accept what is good,
so that we may repay you
with praise[A] from our[B] lips.
3 Assyria will not save us,
we will not ride on horses,
and we will no longer proclaim, 'Our gods!'
to the work of our hands.
For the fatherless receives compassion
in you."

A PROMISE OF RESTORATION

4 I will heal their apostasy;
I will freely love them,
for my anger will have turned from him.
5 I will be like the dew to Israel;
he will blossom like the lily
and take root like the cedars of Lebanon.
6 His new branches will spread,
and his splendor will be like the olive tree,
his fragrance, like the forest of Lebanon.
7 The people will return and live
beneath his shade.
They will grow grain
and blossom like the vine.
His renown will be like the wine of Lebanon.

8 Ephraim, why should I[C] have anything more
to do with idols?
It is I who answer and watch over him.
I am like a flourishing pine tree;
your fruit comes from me.

9 Let whoever is wise understand these things,
and whoever is insightful recognize them.
For the ways of the LORD are right,
and the righteous walk in them,
but the rebellious stumble in them.

[A] **14:2** LXX reads *with the fruit* [B] **14:2** Lit *repay the bulls of our*
[C] **14:8** LXX reads *he*

JOEL

Scene that decorated the wall of Nineveh's South-West Palace shows Assyria's King Sennacherib as he watches the capture of Lachish. Sennacherib's face has been deliberately slashed, perhaps by an enemy soldier at the fall of Nineveh in 612 BC. Bishop Theodore of Mopsuestia guessed that the locusts mentioned in the book of Joel represented Assyrian conquerors—one of whom may have been Sennacherib.

INTRODUCTION TO

JOEL

Circumstances of Writing

Joel ("Yahweh is God") is identified as the son of Pethuel. He is not easily identified with the other Joels of Scripture (1Sm 8:2; 1Ch 4:35; 6:33; 11:38; 15:7; Ezr 10:43; Neh 11:9), leaving us only his book to know him, his calling from God, and his work. The book itself gives no biographical information other than his father's name.

Dating the book of Joel has always been difficult and mainly conjecture, with suggestions ranging as widely as premonarchial Israel to the postexilic period, sometimes well into the Hellenistic period.

Contribution to the Bible

The book of Joel shows us the Creator and Redeemer God of all the universe in complete control of nature. Joel made it clear that the God of judgment also is a God of mercy who stands ready to redeem and restore when his people come before him in repentance. Joel points to a time when the Spirit of God would be present upon all people. On the day of Pentecost, Peter proclaimed that the new day of Spirit-filled discipleship, foretold by Joel, had arrived (Ac 2:17–21).

Structure

Joel's use of repetition gives the book the appearance of a series of folding doors, in some cases doors within doors. The overall structure balances the section on God's judgment through the locust plague (Jl 1:1–20) with a section on the land's physical restoration (2:21–27). The prophecy of an invading army (2:1–11) is balanced by a prophecy on the destruction of this army (2:20). In the center is the highly prominent call to repent and the promise of renewal (2:12–19). But this balanced structure overlaps with another. The prophecy of the destruction of the invading army (2:20) is also balanced with the final prophecy of the Lord's vengeance against all the nations (3:1–21). Finally, the assurance of the land's physical restoration through rain (2:21–27) is balanced by the promise of the people's spiritual restoration through the outpouring of God's Spirit (2:28–32).

1 The word of the LORD that came to Joel son of Pethuel:

A PLAGUE OF LOCUSTS

2 Hear this, you elders;
listen, all you inhabitants of the land.
Has anything like this ever happened
in your days
or in the days of your ancestors?
3 Tell your children about it,
and let your children tell their children,
and their children the next generation.
4 What the devouring locust has left,
the swarming locust has eaten;
what the swarming locust has left,
the young locust has eaten;
and what the young locust has left,
the destroying locust has eaten.

5 Wake up, you drunkards, and weep;
wail, all you wine drinkers,
because of the sweet wine,
for it has been taken from your mouth.
6 For a nation has invaded my land,
powerful and without number;
its teeth are the teeth of a lion,
and it has the fangs of a lioness.
7 It has devastated my grapevine
and splintered my fig tree.
It has stripped off its bark
and thrown it away;
its branches have turned white.
8 Grieve like a young woman dressed
in sackcloth,
mourning for the husband of her youth.
9 Grain and drink offerings have been cut off
from the house of the LORD;
the priests, who are ministers
of the LORD, mourn.
10 The fields are destroyed;
the land grieves;
indeed, the grain is destroyed;
the new wine is dried up;
and the fresh oil fails.
11 Be ashamed, you farmers,
wail, you vinedressers,[A]
over the wheat and the barley,
because the harvest of the field
has perished.
12 The grapevine is dried up,
and the fig tree is withered;
the pomegranate, the date palm,
and the apple —
all the trees of the orchard — have withered.
Indeed, human joy has dried up.
13 Dress in sackcloth and lament, you priests;
wail, you ministers of the altar.
Come and spend the night in sackcloth,
you ministers of my God,
because grain and drink offerings
are withheld from the house of your God.
14 Announce a sacred fast;
proclaim a solemn assembly!
Gather the elders
and all the residents of the land
at the house of the LORD your God,
and cry out to the LORD.

THE DAY OF THE LORD

15 Woe because of that day!
For the day of the LORD is near
and will come as devastation from the Almighty.
16 Hasn't the food been cut off
before our eyes,
joy and gladness
from the house of our God?
17 The seeds lie shriveled in their casings.[B]
The storehouses are in ruin,
and the granaries are broken down,
because the grain has withered away.
18 How the animals groan!
The herds of cattle wander in confusion
since they have no pasture.
Even the flocks of sheep and goats
suffer punishment.
19 I call to you, LORD,
for fire has consumed
the pastures of the wilderness,
and flames have devoured
all the trees of the orchard.
20 Even the wild animals cry out to[C] you,
for the river beds are dried up,
and fire has consumed
the pastures of the wilderness.

2 Blow the ram's horn in Zion;
sound the alarm on my holy mountain!
Let all the residents of the land tremble,
for the day of the LORD is coming;
in fact, it is near —
2 a day of darkness and gloom,
a day of clouds and total darkness,
like the dawn spreading over the mountains;
a great and strong people appears,
such as never existed in ages past
and never will again
in all the generations to come.

[A]**1:11** Or *The farmers are dismayed, the vinedressers wail* [B]**1:17** Or *clods*; Hb obscure [C]**1:20** Or *animals pant for*; Hb obscure

Joel: The Man and His Ministry

by Allan Moseley

Nothing is known about the prophet Joel outside his book. The Old Testament mentions several other men named Joel, but none of those could be the prophet. Joel's father, Pethuel (1:1), is also unknown. Perhaps Joel did not provide more information about himself because he was well known to his contemporaries and further introduction was not needed. The book reveals nothing about Joel's hometown and occupation. Since Joel seems to have had sympathies with the temple and priesthood (1:9,13,16; 2:14,17), some have suggested that he was a priest or a temple prophet. This, however, is speculation; any Israelite faithful to the Lord would have thought often of temple worship. Others have speculated that Joel's frequent references to Jerusalem (2:1,15,23,32; 3:1,16,17,20) indicate that he must have lived in or near Jerusalem. This too is not known; all orthodox Israelites viewed Jerusalem as central to the Lord's activity and plan.

Ostracon found at the seventh-century-AD monastery of Epiphanius near Luxor, Egypt. It contains a text from the book of Joel.

What then can we know about Joel? First, he knew the Lord's law. In 2:13, he quoted Exodus 34:6. He declared that the locust plague in his day was the Lord's judgment. Joel likely knew that the law stated that one of the Lord's judgments for Israel's sin would be a locust plague. According to Deuteronomy 28:38, one result of Israel's sin would be that the people would "sow much seed in the field but harvest little, because locusts will devour it."

Second, Joel believed the Lord rules over everything. The Lord's management of the locust plague proved that he rules over nature. The swarm of locusts was "his army" and "his camp" (2:11). The Lord called them "my great army that I sent against you" (2:25). Joel also believed that the Lord rules over nations and their histories. Specifically, the book of Joel mentions the Phoenicians (Tyre and Sidon, in 3:4), the Philistines (v. 4), the Greeks (v. 6), the Sabeans (v. 8) who dominated the trade routes in Arabia, the Egyptians (v. 19), and the Edomites (v. 19). Joel heard God summon these nations and all others to hear the pronouncement of his judgment on them (2:2,11,12). He, the Lord, would determine their futures, as he determines the entire course of human history.

Third, Joel cared deeply about the spiritual condition of the people of Israel. He passionately called them to mourn over their sin and its results, and he implored them to repent (2:12–14). Superficial repentance, or the observance of repentance rituals, would not suffice. The mere tearing of clothes as a sign of repentance was insufficient. Joel saw that the Lord required the people to tear their hearts with mourning over sin, turn from their sin, and return to the Lord (vv. 12–13). Joel urgently called all the people to gather together to seek the Lord (vv. 15–17).

Fourth, Joel cared about the Lord's glory, or his reputation. He urged the people to pray for the Lord to spare them so that other peoples would not question the Lord's presence or power (v. 17). Israel's glory was not what motivated Joel; it was the Lord's glory. Joel wanted the Lord's glory to be manifested so that people would know him. He saw that a purpose of

Plaque from Fosse temple at Lachish depicting a woman looking out of a balustraded window, a popular Phoenician theme, possibly connected with the goddess Astarte and ritual prostitution.

the Lord's activity in history was to show himself so people would know him (2:26–27; 3:17).

Fifth, Joel evidently knew the preaching of other prophets. The words Joel used often reflect intimate awareness of other prophets' messages. The best-known example is Joel's reference to the "day of the Lord" (1:15; 2:1,11,31; 3:14). Other prophets used the same phrase to refer to the Lord's coming judgment (Is 13:6,9; Jr 46:10; Ezk 30:3; Am 5:18; Ob 15; Zph 1:14). Unless Joel coined the phrase, he had likely heard it from other prophets, and he used it in the same way. When Joel called the nations to a confrontation with the Lord's judgment, he invited them to beat their plowshares into swords and their pruning hooks into spears (3:10). Both Isaiah and Micah used those same words (Is 2:4; Mc 4:3), but Joel used them in reverse. Joel's reference to the Lord roaring from Zion (3:16) is also in Amos 1:2. The image of a fountain flowing from the temple (Jl 3:18) is in Ezekiel's vision of a future temple (Ezk 47:1). Clearly Joel knew what other prophets had preached. Though the Lord inspired him uniquely to write a distinct message through his own personality, Joel's use of common prophetic language indicates he highly valued the work of other biblical prophets.

Sixth, God gave Joel visions of the future. Some prophecies seem to refer to the near future (2:18–27), some to the more distant future (3:1–8), and some to the far distant future (2:28–32; 3:9–21). Some of Joel's prophecies predict judgment, and some predict blessing. In the short term, God would restore what had been lost in the locust plague (2:19–27). Joel 3:1–8 seems to refer to a time further in the future when God would judge Israel's enemies. Still further in the future, God promised he would pour out his Spirit "on all humanity" (2:28–29). The apostle Peter quoted that prophecy when he preached on the day of Pentecost after Jesus's ascension, so those words of Joel refer to the church age in which we live. Two of Joel's prophecies seem to reach into a time yet to come. Joel described ominous cosmic events (2:30–32) that resemble the apocalyptic images in the book of Revelation. And in 3:9–21, Joel prophesied that one day God will judge all nations and restore all creation. At some point in the future, God will gather the nations to hear his judgments against them and to see the exaltation of God's people and God's city Jerusalem (3:16,17,21). ✣

3 A fire devours in front of them,
and behind them a flame blazes.
The land in front of them
is like the garden of Eden,
but behind them,
it is like a desert wasteland;
there is no escape from them.
4 Their appearance is like that of horses,
and they gallop like war horses.
5 They bound on the tops of the mountains.
Their sound is like the sound
of chariots,
like the sound of fiery flames
consuming stubble,
like a mighty army deployed for war.

6 Nations writhe in horror before them;
all faces turn pale.
7 They attack as warriors attack;
they scale walls as men of war do.
Each goes on his own path,
and they do not change their course.
8 They do not push each other;
each proceeds on his own path.
They dodge the arrows, never stopping.
9 They storm the city;
they run on the wall;
they climb into the houses;
they enter through the windows
like thieves.

10 The earth quakes before them;
the sky shakes.
The sun and moon grow dark,
and the stars cease their shining.
11 The LORD makes his voice heard
in the presence of his army.
His camp is very large;
those who carry out his command
are powerful.
Indeed, the day of the LORD is terrible
and dreadful —
who can endure it?

GOD'S CALL FOR REPENTANCE

12 Even now —
this is the LORD's declaration —
turn to me with all your heart,
with fasting, weeping, and mourning.
13 Tear your hearts,
not just your clothes,
and return to the LORD your God.
For he is gracious and compassionate,
slow to anger, abounding in faithful love,
and he relents from sending disaster.
14 Who knows? He may turn and relent
and leave a blessing behind him,
so you can offer a grain offering and
a drink offering
to the LORD your God.

15 Blow the ram's horn in Zion!
Announce a sacred fast;
proclaim a solemn assembly.
16 Gather the people;
sanctify the congregation;
assemble the aged;[A]
gather the infants,
even babies nursing at the breast.
Let the groom leave his bedroom,
and the bride her honeymoon chamber.
17 Let the priests, the LORD's ministers,
weep between the portico and the altar.
Let them say,
"Have pity on your people, LORD,
and do not make your inheritance
a disgrace,
an object of scorn among the nations.
Why should it be said among the peoples,
'Where is their God?'"

GOD'S RESPONSE TO HIS PEOPLE

18 Then the LORD became jealous for his land and
spared his people. 19 The LORD answered his people:
Look, I am about to send you
grain, new wine, and fresh oil.
You will be satiated with them,
and I will no longer make you
a disgrace among the nations.

20 I will drive the northerner far from you
and banish him to a dry and desolate land,
his front ranks into the Dead Sea,
and his rear guard
into the Mediterranean Sea.
His stench will rise;
yes, his rotten smell will rise,
for he has done astonishing things.

21 Don't be afraid, land;
rejoice and be glad,
for the LORD has done astonishing things.
22 Don't be afraid, wild animals,
for the wilderness pastures
have turned green,
the trees bear their fruit,
and the fig tree and grapevine yield
their riches.

[A] **2:16** Or *elders*

23 Children of Zion, rejoice and be glad
in the LORD your God,
because he gives you the autumn rain[A]
for your vindication.[B]
He sends showers for you,
both autumn and spring rain as before.
24 The threshing floors will be full of grain,
and the vats will overflow
with new wine and fresh oil.

25 I will repay you for the years
that the swarming locust ate,
the young locust, the destroying locust,
and the devouring locust —
my great army that I sent against you.
26 You will have plenty to eat and be satisfied.
You will praise the name of the LORD your God,
who has dealt wondrously with you.
My people will never again be put to shame.
27 You will know that I am present in Israel
and that I am the LORD your God,
and there is no other.
My people will never again be put to shame.

GOD'S PROMISE OF HIS SPIRIT

28 After this
I will pour out my Spirit on all humanity;
then your sons and your daughters
will prophesy,
your old men will have dreams,
and your young men will see visions.
29 I will even pour out my Spirit
on the male and female slaves in those days.
30 I will display wonders
in the heavens and on the earth:
blood, fire, and columns of smoke.
31 The sun will be turned to darkness
and the moon to blood
before the great and terrible day
of the LORD comes.
32 Then everyone who calls
on the name of the LORD will be saved,
for there will be an escape
for those on Mount Zion and in Jerusalem,
as the LORD promised,
among the survivors the LORD calls.

JUDGMENT OF THE NATIONS

3 Yes, in those days and at that time,
when I restore the fortunes of Judah
and Jerusalem,
2 I will gather all the nations
and take them to the Valley of Jehoshaphat.[C]
I will enter into judgment with them there
because of my people, my inheritance Israel.
The nations have scattered
the Israelites
in foreign countries
and divided up my land.
3 They cast lots for my people;
they bartered a boy for a prostitute
and sold a girl for wine to drink.

4 And also: Tyre, Sidon, and all the territories of
Philistia — what are you to me? Are you paying me
back or trying to get even with me? I will quickly
bring retribution on your heads. 5 For you took my
silver and gold and carried my finest treasures to your
temples. 6 You sold the people of Judah and Jerusalem
to the Greeks to remove them far from their own territory. 7 Look, I am about to rouse them up from the
place where you sold them; I will bring retribution
on your heads. 8 I will sell your sons and daughters
to the people of Judah, and they will sell them to the
Sabeans,[D] to a distant nation, for the LORD has spoken.
9 Proclaim this among the nations:
Prepare for holy war;
rouse the warriors;
let all the men of war advance
and attack!
10 Beat your plows into swords
and your pruning knives into spears.
Let even the weakling say,
"I am a warrior."
11 Come quickly,[E] all you surrounding nations;
gather yourselves.
Bring down your warriors there, LORD.

12 Let the nations be roused
and come to the Valley of Jehoshaphat,
for there I will sit down
to judge all the surrounding nations.
13 Swing the sickle
because the harvest is ripe.
Come and trample the grapes
because the winepress is full;
the wine vats overflow
because the wickedness of the nations
is extreme.

14 Multitudes, multitudes
in the valley of decision!
For the day of the LORD is near
in the valley of decision.
15 The sun and moon will grow dark,
and the stars will cease their shining.

[A] **2:23** Or *the teacher of righteousness* [B] **2:23** Or *righteousness* [C] **3:2** = The LORD Will Judge [D] **3:8** Probably the south Arabian kingdom of Sheba (modern Yemen) [E] **3:11** LXX, Syr, Tg read *Gather yourselves and come*; Hb obscure

ISRAEL'S CLIMATE

Israel's geography affects its climate. The moisture in the air comes from the Mediterranean Sea. This is the only source of moisture because to the east lies the Arabian Desert and to the south the Sinai. The breeze off the Mediterranean carries rain clouds eastward across Israel. As the moisture-laden clouds encounter the tall hills that bisect the land, the clouds rise and cool and drop their rain on the western slopes. For this reason, the western part of Israel receives more rain, and the western slopes are always greener than the eastern.

Israel does not have four distinct seasons as does most of North America. Instead, it has two main seasons: the rainy season, which lasts from mid-October through April, and the dry season, which lasts from mid-June through mid-September. The so-called transitional months divide these two seasons. During the months of the dry season, rain never falls, and most days are cloudless. Israel's weather is generally sunny, and the daytime temperatures are quite warm, averaging eighty-six degrees Fahrenheit. The breezes off the Mediterranean provide welcome cooling to the coastal plain and hills.

During the warm, dry summer the farmers grow fruit crops. These include grapes, figs, pomegranates, and melons. The dew of the summer brings some moisture to these crops, which are harvested mainly in August and September. In Bible times, the dry season proved a good time to travel. Both armies and caravans took advantage of the dry ground to move through the region.

In the rainy season, rain storms blow in from the Mediterranean. Typically, rains will fall for about three days, and then several fair days follow.

Jerusalem is cooler than much of Israel because its elevation is about twenty-two hundred feet above sea level. Sometimes Jerusalem gets a brief snowfall in January. Jerusalem's average temperature in January is fifty degrees Fahrenheit.

Natural waterfall at En-gedi, just west of the Dead Sea, where annual rainfall is less than eight inches.

RAINFALL IN ISRAEL

After the autumn or "early" rains come in October, the farmers plow their fields and plant their grain. The wheat and barley grow quickly from December until February, when most of the rain comes. The grain ripens during March and April as the rain gradually diminishes. The spring or latter rains of April help to produce a good harvest. God says in Deuteronomy 11:14, "I will provide rain for your land in the proper time, the autumn and spring rains, and you will harvest your grain, new wine, and fresh oil."

Israel's rainfall varies considerably from region to region and from year to year. The rainfall is greater in the north than in the south, and the coastal plain receives more than the Jordan Valley. The hills receive more rain than the plains and valleys. For example, Beer-sheba in the south receives an average of eight inches of rain each year, while Jerusalem receives twenty-two inches. Joppa on the sea coast receives twenty inches per year, but Jericho in the Jordan River (or Jordan Rift) Valley averages only five inches.

Modern farmers use irrigation to ensure an adequate harvest, but this was not so in ancient times. The farmers of biblical times depended on the rain to make a good crop. Even a small difference in rainfall could mean famine for the people of Israel. With rainfall amounts so low, five or six inches less could bring disaster. Israel frequently experiences these climatic variations. Sometimes the rainy season begins in December instead of October, delaying the grain planting. In some years, the latter rains do not fall, resulting in a meager harvest. Even if the rains arrive on time, the amount of rain can vary. Beyond that, the early rains are usually thundershowers, and one area may experience torrential rains, while another district remains dry.

RAIN AS GOD'S BLESSING

Many farmers today are really agro-business persons; they farm for profit. This was not the case in ancient Israel. The farmers of ancient time farmed for food; their families ate the food they grew. Any surplus they would sell or store for the future. The Israelites understood that rainfall was totally under God's control. He gave it or withheld it according to his will (Am 4:6–8). In fact, Moses warned the Israelites that God would send or withhold the rain according to their obedience (Dt 11:13–17).

The variations in rainfall, however, tempted some farmers to make sacrifices to Baal, the god of rain and thunder, and to engage in ritual orgies. Wanting to ensure a favorable harvest, Israelites were enticed to join in the worship practices. Voicing their alarm, the prophets of Israel vehemently condemned Baal worship. They knew that dishonoring Yahweh could result in his withholding rain from the land (see Jr 3:1–3).

Joel reminded the people that the opposite was also true—rains also came as a blessing from God: "Children of Zion, rejoice and be glad in the LORD your God, because he gives you the autumn rain for your vindication. He sends showers for you, both autumn and spring rain as before" (Jl 2:23). ✣

16 The LORD will roar from Zion
and make his voice heard from Jerusalem;
heaven and earth will shake.
But the LORD will be a refuge for his people,
a stronghold for the Israelites.

ISRAEL BLESSED

17 Then you will know
that I am the LORD your God,
who dwells in Zion, my holy mountain.
Jerusalem will be holy,
and foreigners will never overrun it again.
18 In that day
the mountains will drip with sweet wine,
and the hills will flow with milk.
All the streams of Judah will flow with water,
and a spring will issue from the LORD's house,
watering the Valley of Acacias.[A]
19 Egypt will become desolate,
and Edom a desert wasteland,
because of the violence done to the people
of Judah
in whose land they shed innocent blood.
20 But Judah will be inhabited forever,
and Jerusalem from generation to generation.
21 I will pardon their bloodguilt,[B]
which I have not pardoned,
for the LORD dwells in Zion.

[A] **3:18** Or *Shittim* [B] **3:21** LXX, Syr read *I will avenge their blood*

AMOS

Amos saw the Lord "standing there by a vertical wall with a plumb line in his hand" (7:7).

INTRODUCTION TO

AMOS

Circumstances of Writing

Amos was a shepherd from Tekoa, a village about ten miles south of Jerusalem. He received a call from God to go north and prophesy against Samaria and the kingdom of Israel around 760 BC. We do not know how long he actually was in the north; it appears to have been a fairly short time. He provoked a great deal of opposition and anger, as illustrated by his encounter with Amaziah, the priest of Bethel (Am 7:10-17). He wrote his book, a summary of his prophecies, after his return to Judah. He probably wrote it with the aid of a scribe.

Amos prophesied during the reigns of Uzziah of Judah (792–740 BC) and Jeroboam II of Israel (793–753 BC). This was a time of great prosperity and military success for both nations, as all their traditional enemies were in a weakened condition. Samaria, the capital city of Israel, enjoyed enormous wealth, and luxuries flowed into the city.

At the same time, decades of struggle with Damascus had left the population exhausted. Many farmers were reduced to poverty. Their more affluent neighbors, and especially the aristocracy, swooped in with loans that the poor could not repay and then reduced the debtors to slavery and seized their lands. The leaders of society believed they had no reason to fear for the future. Their city had high walls and fortified citadels, and their army was everywhere victorious. They were the chosen people of God, and they considered themselves immune from judgment.

Contribution to the Bible

Amos reminds us of the sovereignty of God in his involvement with his people. God will bring his judgment, a reality that certainly came to pass. Amos's emphasis on "the day of the Lord" had implications for his contemporaries, but it also reminds the modern reader of a coming day referred to repeatedly in the New Testament—the day of Christ's return.

Structure

After the superscription (1:1), the book of Amos is divided into seven parts. The first part, the introduction, is a single verse (1:2). This is followed by six major divisions: 1:3–2:16; 3:1–15; 4:1–13; 5:1–6:14; 7:1–8:3; 8:4–9:15. Remarkably, formulas of divine speech (statements such as "the LORD says," "the LORD has spoken," and "the LORD's declaration") are evenly distributed in these sections. Amos 1:3–2:16 has fourteen such formulas, and each of the following sections have seven each, for a total of forty-nine.

1 The words of Amos, who was one of the sheep
breeders[A] from Tekoa — what he saw regarding
Israel in the days of King Uzziah of Judah and Jeroboam son of Jehoash, king of Israel, two years before
the earthquake.
2 He said:
The LORD roars from Zion
and makes his voice heard from Jerusalem;
the pastures of the shepherds mourn,[B]
and the summit of Carmel withers.

JUDGMENT ON ISRAEL'S NEIGHBORS

3 The LORD says:
I will not relent from punishing Damascus
for three crimes, even four,
because they threshed Gilead with iron sledges.
4 Therefore, I will send fire
against Hazael's palace,
and it will consume Ben-hadad's citadels.
5 I will break down the gates[C] of Damascus.
I will cut off the ruler from the Valley of Aven,
and the one who wields the scepter
from Beth-eden.
The people of Aram will be exiled to Kir.
The LORD has spoken.

6 The LORD says:
I will not relent from punishing Gaza
for three crimes, even four,
because they exiled a whole community,
handing them over to Edom.
7 Therefore, I will send fire against the walls
of Gaza,
and it will consume its citadels.
8 I will cut off the ruler from Ashdod,
and the one who wields the scepter
from Ashkelon.
I will also turn my hand against Ekron,
and the remainder of the Philistines will perish.
The Lord GOD has spoken.

9 The LORD says:
I will not relent from punishing Tyre
for three crimes, even four,
because they handed over
a whole community of exiles to Edom
and broke[D] a treaty of brotherhood.
10 Therefore, I will send fire against the walls
of Tyre,
and it will consume its citadels.

11 The LORD says:
I will not relent from punishing Edom
for three crimes, even four,
because he pursued his brother with the sword.
He stifled his compassion,
his anger tore at him continually,
and he harbored his rage incessantly.
12 Therefore, I will send fire against Teman,
and it will consume the citadels of Bozrah.

13 The LORD says:
I will not relent from punishing
the Ammonites
for three crimes, even four,
because they ripped open
the pregnant women of Gilead
in order to enlarge their territory.
14 Therefore, I will set fire to the walls of Rabbah,
and it will consume its citadels.
There will be shouting on the day of battle
and a violent wind on the day of the storm.
15 Their king and his princes
will go into exile together.
The LORD has spoken.

2 The LORD says:
I will not relent from punishing Moab
for three crimes, even four,
because he burned the bones
of the king of Edom to lime.
2 Therefore, I will send fire against Moab,
and it will consume the citadels of Kerioth.
Moab will die with a tumult,
with shouting and the sound of the ram's horn.
3 I will cut off the judge from the land
and kill all its officials with him.
The LORD has spoken.

JUDGMENT ON JUDAH

4 The LORD says:
I will not relent from punishing Judah
for three crimes, even four,
because they have rejected the instruction
of the LORD
and have not kept his statutes.
The lies that their ancestors followed
have led them astray.
5 Therefore, I will send fire against Judah,
and it will consume the citadels of Jerusalem.

JUDGMENT ON ISRAEL

6 The LORD says:
I will not relent from punishing Israel
for three crimes, even four,
because they sell a righteous person for silver
and a needy person for a pair of sandals.

[A] **1:1** Or *the shepherds* [B] **1:2** Or *dry up* [C] **1:5** Lit *gate bars*
[D] **1:9** Lit *and did not remember*

Amos: His Life and Call

by Scott Langston

Base of the altar established by Jeroboam I at Dan.

Amos 1:1 places Amos in the early- to mid-eighth century BC. A more precise date for the beginning of Amos's ministry would be possible if the date of the earthquake mentioned in 1:1 could be ascertained. It must have been severe, because the verse refers to it simply as "the earthquake." Evidence of an earthquake dated to the mid-eighth century has been found, according to some archaeologists, at the city of Hazor. On the basis of this and other evidence, some scholars date the beginning of Amos's ministry to about 760 BC.[1] Others prefer a slightly later date, but Amos probably began his work sometime between 760 and 750. Israel and Judah had yet to experience Assyria's renewed power and wrath. Times were peaceful, and many people prospered.

Many of Amos's messages concentrated on the relationship between prosperity and religion. The religion of the day in essence supported the oppression of people. The worship centers were filled with people bringing their sacrifices, but they felt no remorse as they commonly engaged in unethical business practices, perversion of justice, and oppression of the people. The religious leadership did not denounce these actions and, therefore, lent their approval to this kind of religion. The people and the religious leadership failed to connect their actions in the worship service with their everyday actions. They believed that God only wanted ritual acts of worship and that the peace and prosperity of the times signaled God's approval of this religion. The book of Amos denounces and warns against religious leadership that concerns itself only with matters of worship or doctrine and neglects the just treatment of all people. To Amos, true religion expressed itself in social justice and did not limit itself to ritual acts and doctrine.

Amos's willingness to denounce Israel's religious and political leadership indicates that he possessed courage, integrity, and commitment to God. Israel's leaders had great power, but Amos did not allow himself to be intimidated by them. His integrity helped him not to modify his message to conform to that typically advocated by the religious leaders. This kind of courage and integrity stemmed from his commitment to God.

According to Amos 1:1 and 7:14, he was a shepherd. Scholars, however, disagree over whether he was a poor shepherd who watched others' flocks or a wealthy owner of herds. The words used to describe

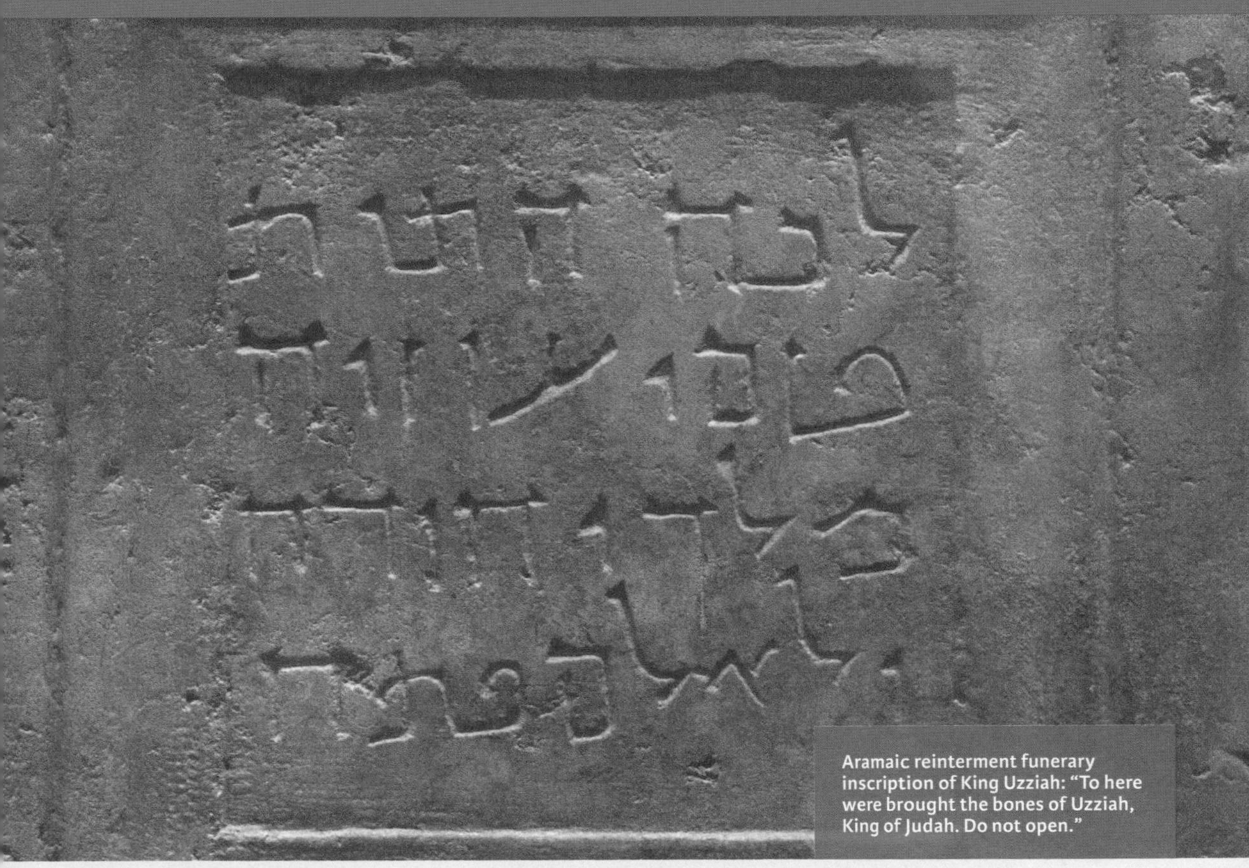

Aramaic reinterment funerary inscription of King Uzziah: "To here were brought the bones of Uzziah, King of Judah. Do not open."

Amos as a shepherd occur only a few times in the Old Testament, making it difficult to know their exact meaning. One word is used in 2 Kings 3:4 to describe Mesha, king of Moab. This usage suggests it refers to a wealthy owner of herds rather than a simple shepherd, thus indicating that Amos owned herds rather than watched them. He also is described in Amos 7:14 as taking care of sycamore figs. While the poor often ate these figs, they also were commonly fed to cattle. Amos, therefore, may have owned sycamore orchards from which he fed his herds. Amos may have been an influential and somewhat wealthy individual.[2]

Amos also described himself in 7:14 as one who was not part of the religious leadership. Scholars debate whether Amos's words should be understood as "I am not a prophet" or "I was not a prophet." The first rendering suggests Amos never claimed to be a professional prophet; the second indicates that he originally was not one, but now claimed authority as one. What is clear, however, is that while Amos was engaged in his original occupation, God chose him to deliver his message. In other words, Amos was a layperson. As one who had no formal religious training, he challenged the priests and prophets. As one from Judah (Tekoa was located near Bethlehem), he addressed his messages to Israel. As a member of the wealthy, he confronted the rich and powerful on behalf of the oppressed. Courage, integrity, and commitment to God seem to be apt descriptions of Amos. ✣

[1] Philip J. King, *Amos, Hosea, Micah: An Archaeological Commentary* (Philadelphia: Westminster, 1988), 21, 38; Bruce H. Willoughby, "Amos, Book of," *ABD*, 1:203–4; James Limburg, *Hosea–Micah*, Interpretation: A Bible Commentary (IBC) (Atlanta: John Knox, 1988), 84.
[2] Willoughby, "Amos."

7 They trample the heads of the poor
on the dust of the ground
and obstruct the path of the needy.
A man and his father have sexual relations
with the same girl,
profaning my holy name.
8 They stretch out beside every altar
on garments taken as collateral,
and in the house of their God
they drink wine obtained through fines.

9 Yet I destroyed the Amorite
as Israel advanced;
his height was like the cedars,
and he was as sturdy as the oaks;
I destroyed his fruit above
and his roots beneath.
10 And I brought you from the land of Egypt
and led you forty years in the wilderness
in order to possess the land of the Amorite.
11 I raised up some of your sons as prophets
and some of your young men as Nazirites.
Is this not the case, Israelites?
This is the LORD's declaration.
12 But you made the Nazirites drink wine
and commanded the prophets,
"Do not prophesy."
13 Look, I am about to crush[A] you in your place
as a wagon crushes when full of grain.
14 Escape will fail the swift,
the strong one will not maintain his strength,
and the warrior will not save his life.
15 The archer will not stand his ground,
the one who is swift of foot
will not save himself,
and the one riding a horse will not save
his life.
16 Even the most courageous of the warriors
will flee naked on that day —
this is the LORD's declaration.

GOD'S REASONS FOR PUNISHING ISRAEL

3 Listen to this message that the LORD has spoken
against you, Israelites, against the entire clan
that I brought from the land of Egypt:
2 I have known only you
out of all the clans of the earth;
therefore, I will punish you for all
your iniquities.
3 Can two walk together
without agreeing to meet?
4 Does a lion roar in the forest
when it has no prey?
Does a young lion growl from its lair
unless it has captured something?
5 Does a bird land in a trap on the ground
if there is no bait for it?
Does a trap spring from the ground
when it has caught nothing?
6 If a ram's horn is blown in a city,
aren't people afraid?
If a disaster occurs in a city,
hasn't the LORD done it?
7 Indeed, the Lord GOD does nothing
without revealing his counsel
to his servants the prophets.
8 A lion has roared;
who will not fear?
The Lord GOD has spoken;
who will not prophesy?

9 Proclaim on the citadels in Ashdod
and on the citadels in the land of Egypt:
Assemble on the mountains of Samaria,
and see the great turmoil in the city
and the acts of oppression within it.
10 The people are incapable of doing right —
this is the LORD's declaration —
those who store up violence and destruction
in their citadels.
11 Therefore, the Lord GOD says:
An enemy will surround the land;
he will destroy your strongholds
and plunder your citadels.

12 The LORD says:
As the shepherd snatches two legs
or a piece of an ear
from the lion's mouth,
so the Israelites who live in Samaria
will be rescued
with only the corner of a bed
or the[B] cushion[C] of a couch.[D]
13 Listen and testify against the house
of Jacob —
this is the declaration of the Lord GOD,
the God of Armies.
14 I will punish the altars of Bethel
on the day I punish Israel for its crimes;
the horns of the altar will be cut off
and fall to the ground.
15 I will demolish the winter house
and the summer house;
the houses inlaid with ivory will be destroyed,
and the great houses will come to an end.
This is the LORD's declaration.

[A] **2:13** Or *hinder*; Hb obscure [B] **3:12** Or *Israelites will be rescued, those who sit in Samaria on a corner of a bed or a* [C] **3:12** Hb obscure [D] **3:12** LXX, Aq, Sym, Theod, Syr, Tg, Vg read *or in Damascus*

SOCIAL AND SPIRITUAL CORRUPTION

4 Listen to this message, you cows
of Bashan
who are on the hill of Samaria,
women who oppress the poor
and crush the needy,
who say to their husbands,
"Bring us something to drink."

2 The Lord God has sworn by his holiness:
Look, the days are coming[A]
when you will be taken away with hooks,
every last one of you with fishhooks.
3 You will go through breaches in the wall,
each woman straight ahead,
and you will be driven along
toward Harmon.
This is the LORD's declaration.

4 Come to Bethel and rebel;
rebel even more at Gilgal!
Bring your sacrifices every morning,
your tenths every three days.
5 Offer leavened bread as
a thanksgiving sacrifice,
and loudly proclaim your freewill offerings,
for that is what you Israelites love to do!
This is the declaration of the Lord God.

GOD'S DISCIPLINE AND ISRAEL'S APOSTASY

6 I gave you absolutely nothing to eat[B] in all
your cities,
a shortage of food in all your communities,
yet you did not return to me.
This is the LORD's declaration.

7 I also withheld the rain from you
while there were still three months
until harvest.
I sent rain on one city
but no rain on another.
One field received rain
while a field with no rain withered.
8 Two or three cities staggered
to another city to drink water
but were not satisfied,
yet you did not return to me.
This is the LORD's declaration.

9 I struck you with blight and mildew;
the locust devoured
your many gardens and vineyards,
your fig trees and olive trees,
yet you did not return to me.
This is the LORD's declaration.

10 I sent plagues like those of Egypt;
I killed your young men with the sword,
along with your captured horses.
I caused the stench of your camp
to fill your nostrils,
yet you did not return to me.
This is the LORD's declaration.

11 I overthrew some of you
as I[C] overthrew Sodom and Gomorrah,
and you were like a burning stick
snatched from a fire,
yet you did not return to me —
This is the LORD's declaration.

12 Therefore, Israel, that is what I will do to you,
and since I will do that to you,
Israel, prepare to meet your God!
13 He is here:
the one who forms the mountains,
creates the wind,
and reveals his thoughts to man,
the one who makes the dawn out of darkness
and strides on the heights of the earth.
The LORD, the God of Armies, is his name.

LAMENTATION FOR ISRAEL

5 Listen to this message that I am singing for you,
a lament, house of Israel:
2 She has fallen;
Virgin Israel will never rise again.
She lies abandoned on her land
with no one to raise her up.
3 For the Lord God says:
The city that marches out a thousand strong
will have only a hundred left,
and the one that marches out
a hundred strong
will have only ten left in the house of Israel.

SEEK GOD AND LIVE

4 For the LORD says to the house of Israel:
Seek me and live!
5 Do not seek Bethel
or go to Gilgal
or journey to Beer-sheba,
for Gilgal will certainly go into exile,
and Bethel will come to nothing.
6 Seek the LORD and live,
or he will spread like fire
throughout the house of Joseph;
it will consume everything
with no one at Bethel to extinguish it.

[A] 4:2 Lit *coming on you* [B] 4:6 Lit *you cleanness of teeth* [C] 4:11 Lit *God*

7 Those who turn justice into wormwood
also throw righteousness to the ground.
8 The one who made the Pleiades and Orion,
who turns darkness[A] into dawn
and darkens day into night,
who summons the water of the sea
and pours it out over the surface
of the earth —
the LORD is his name.
9 He brings destruction[B] on the strong,[C]
and it falls on the fortress.

10 They hate the one who convicts the guilty
at the city gate,
and they despise the one who speaks
with integrity.
11 Therefore, because you trample on the poor
and exact a grain tax from him,
you will never live in the houses of cut stone
you have built;
you will never drink the wine
from the lush vineyards
you have planted.
12 For I know your crimes are many
and your sins innumerable.
They oppress the righteous, take a bribe,
and deprive the poor of justice at the city
gates.
13 Therefore, those who have insight
will keep silent[D]
at such a time,
for the days are evil.

14 Pursue good and not evil
so that you may live,
and the LORD, the God of Armies,
will be with you
as you have claimed.
15 Hate evil and love good;
establish justice at the city gate.
Perhaps the LORD, the God of Armies,
will be gracious
to the remnant of Joseph.

16 Therefore the LORD, the God of Armies, the Lord,
says:
There will be wailing in all
the public squares;
they will cry out in anguish[E] in all the streets.
The farmer will be called on to mourn,
and professional mourners[F] to wail.
17 There will be wailing in all the vineyards,
for I will pass among you.
The LORD has spoken.

THE DAY OF THE LORD

18 Woe to you who long for the day
of the LORD!
What will the day of the LORD be for you?
It will be darkness and not light.
19 It will be like a man who flees from a lion
only to have a bear confront him.
He goes home and rests his hand
against the wall
only to have a snake bite him.
20 Won't the day of the LORD
be darkness rather than light,
even gloom without any brightness in it?
21 I hate, I despise, your feasts!
I can't stand the stench
of your solemn assemblies.
22 Even if you offer me
your burnt offerings and grain offerings,
I will not accept them;
I will have no regard
for your fellowship offerings
of fattened cattle.
23 Take away from me the noise
of your songs!
I will not listen to the music of your harps.
24 But let justice flow like water,
and righteousness, like an unfailing stream.

25 "House of Israel, was it sacrifices and grain offerings that you presented to me during the forty
years in the wilderness? 26 But you have taken up[G]
Sakkuth your king and Kaiwan your star god,[H] images you have made for yourselves. 27 So I will send
you into exile beyond Damascus." The LORD, the God
of Armies, is his name. He has spoken.

WOE TO THE COMPLACENT

6 Woe to those who are at ease in Zion
and to those who feel secure on the hill
of Samaria —
the notable people in this first
of the nations,
those the house of Israel comes to.
2 Cross over to Calneh and see;
go from there to great Hamath;
then go down to Gath of the Philistines.
Are you better than these kingdoms?
Is their territory larger than yours?
3 You dismiss any thought of the evil day
and bring in a reign of violence.

[A] **5:8** Or *turns the shadow of death* [B] **5:9** Hb obscure [C] **5:9** Or *stronghold* [D] **5:13** Or *who are prudent will perish* [E] **5:16** Lit *will say, "Alas! Alas!"* [F] **5:16** Lit *and those skilled in lamentation* [G] **5:26** Or *you will lift up* [H] **5:26** LXX reads *taken up the tent of Molech and the star of your god Rephan*; Ac 7:43

Economic Conditions in the Eighth Century BC

by R. Raymond Lloyd

By the second quarter of the eighth century, the great power of Assyria was about to be broken. Syria, having been greatly weakened by Assyria, was being challenged by another bitter rival from the north, the city-state of Hamath, and was no longer a threat to Israel.

THE RICH BECAME RICHER

With the major powers of the ancient Near East focused elsewhere, Israel—during the reign of Jeroboam II (793–753 BC)—expanded its territory in the north as far as Hamath and Syria (2Kg 14:25,28); in the south as far as the northern end of the Dead Sea (2Kg 14:25; Am 6:14), possibly even including Moab; and as far south as the Brook Zered.[1] At the same time—during the reign of Uzziah (or Azariah; 792–740 BC)—Judah rebuilt the port of Ezion-geber (also called Elath; 2Kg 14:22) and brought both the Negev and the Philistine territory firmly under control (2Ch 26:6–8). The expanse of Israel and Judah had reached its greatest extent since the days of Solomon's empire. Furthermore, a general aura of peace existed between Israel and Judah during the reigns of Jeroboam II and Uzziah.

After military successes during the reigns of Jeroboam II and Uzziah, Israel (and perhaps to a lesser extent Judah) experienced a period of considerable economic prosperity. This prosperity and the correlative class distinctions of the rich and the poor did not develop overnight. Earlier, throughout the ninth-century Omride Dynasty, which lasted from the reigns of Omri to Jehu, Israel had a period of considerable prosperity (1Kg 16:24; 22:39). The injustice Ahab and Jezebel inflicted on Naboth and his family vineyard (1Kg 21) and the impoverished widow who was ready to mortgage her two sons, unable to pay her debt (2Kg 4:1–7), probably not isolated instances, are evidences of the poor being at the mercy of the rich.

By the early years of the eighth century, the pattern, already well established, expanded. Now in control of all territory from Hamath in the north to Ezion-geber on the Gulf of Aqaba in the south, Judah and Israel experienced a great revival of trade, controlling the great caravan routes on each side of the Jordan Valley (the Kings Highway, the Via Maris, and the Ridge Route) that connected the ancient Near Eastern merchants and entrepreneurs with those of Egypt and the world beyond. Great trade moved inland from the Phoenician seaport cities of Tyre and Sidon. The toll for use and security of the trade routes and the unlimited profits that issued from the exchange of goods and services brought great wealth to both Israel and Judah.[2]

An economic boom of Solomonic proportions was taking place. When territory is increased, "to the victor goes the spoils of war." Vast supplies of all sorts of goods were no doubt seized with the plundering of captured cities. A wealthy merchant class developed. The monarchy had its chosen officials upon whom it heaped favor. Prosperity was evident. "But Ephraim thinks, 'How rich I have become; I made it all myself'" (Hs 12:8). "Their land is full of silver and gold, and there is no limit to their treasures" (Is 2:7). Luxurious building activity flourished. Palaces made of sun-baked brick were replaced by ones

Cattle grazing on the hillside in Bashan, northeast of the Sea of Galilee. Amos spoke against the wealthy of his day, who were taking advantage of the poor: "Listen to this message, you cows of Bashan who are on the hill of Samaria, women who oppress the poor and crush the needy" (Am 4:1).

Columns at Tyre along a street leading to the sea.

of hewn stone (Am 3:15; 5:11; 6:8; Hs 8:14). Houses were furnished elaborately (Am 3:12,15; 6:4). Excavations at Samaria have revealed "splendid buildings and costly ivory inlays of Phoenician or Damascene [i.e., from Damascus] origin."[3] Elegant couches on which to recline replaced the ancient custom of sitting on the floor (6:4). Sycamore trees were replaced by far more valuable cedar, like those of Lebanon (Is 9:10). The rich had extravagant, sumptuous feasts and rollicking drinking parties (Am 4:1; 6:4,6; Is 5:11–12).

THE POOR BECAME POORER

Not all, though, became richer. One Old Testament scholar summarized, "But the price for this prosperity was high, for an oppressive social pyramid grew up with the royal courtiers and the merchant class at the top and the great mass of people ground into poverty at the bottom."[4] The old tradition of land ownership—with its well-defined and protected boundaries—passing from one generation to the next and often containing the family tomb (Dt 19:14; 27:17; Jos 24:30–32; 1Sm 25:1; 1Kg 2:34; 21:1–29) had collapsed because of the power brokers' greed. A massive and unjust social and economic upheaval was taking place.

The prophets spoke against social and economic abuses. They charged that the rich lay awake at night to plot and then engage in wholesale cheating to build their estates (Hs 12:8; Am 8:4–5; Mc 2:1). They were coveting and seizing houses and fields and stealing the peasants' inheritance, leaving them with virtually nothing from which they could make a living (Is 5:8; Mc 2:2). They were exacting exorbitant rent and a heavy tribute from the produce of the land. When the tenant could no longer pay, he forfeited his land and became a slave (Am 2:6; 8:6). Further, the rich corrupted the courts, legislated evil statutes, and robbed the poor and destitute of their dignity (Is 10:1–2). Justice was dashed to the ground (Am 2:6; 4:1; 5:7,11-12; 6:12; 8:4–6).

Eighth-century-BC Basalt altar or relief, likely Hittite, of a man or a god seated on a couch.

This massive redistribution of land benefiting the monarchy and the merchant class left the poor destitute and powerless. To be sure, the Hebrew laws were meant to protect the poor. For instance, it required people to help the needy (Dt 15:7–11). God's people were to cancel other people's debts in the seventh year (vv. 1–3) so that "there will be no poor among you" (15:4). Those who had been enslaved for failure to pay their debts were to be set free. Furthermore, in the Year of Jubilee, property inherited from one's ancestors that had been acquired by someone else was to be returned to the family of the original owner (Lv 25:8–17,23–28). God's people, however, apparently never carried out these laws. The economic chasm progressively widened. The oppressed and neglected had no recourse.

Into this scene stepped Amos, the prophet from Tekoa, as well as his eighth-century counterparts in both Israel and Judah. They championed the cause of the poor and condemned the high-handedness of the elite (Am 4:1–3; 5:10–12). In Israel, Amos delivered one devastating attack after another on those who perpetrated injustice, who exploited the poor. ✣

---

[1] John Bright, *A History of Israel*, 3rd ed. (Philadelphia: Westminster, 1981), 257–58; Otto Kaiser, *Isaiah 13–39, OTL* (1974), 69. [2] Bright, *History of Israel*, 258–59. [3] Bright, *History of Israel*, 259. [4] Bernhard Anderson, *Understanding the Old Testament* (Englewood Cliffs, NJ: Prentice-Hall, 1957), 224.

4 They lie on beds inlaid with ivory,
sprawled out on their couches,
and dine on lambs from the flock
and calves from the stall.
5 They improvise songs[A] to the sound
of the harp
and invent[B] their own musical instruments
like David.
6 They drink wine by the bowlful
and anoint themselves with the finest oils
but do not grieve over the ruin of Joseph.
7 Therefore, they will now go into exile
as the first of the captives,
and the feasting of those who sprawl out
will come to an end.

ISRAEL'S PRIDE JUDGED

8 The Lord God has sworn by himself — this is the
declaration of the LORD, the God of Armies:

I loathe Jacob's pride
and hate his citadels,
so I will hand over the city and everything
in it.

9 And if there are ten men left in one house, they
will die. 10 A close relative[C] and burner[D] will remove
his corpse[E] from the house. He will call to someone in
the inner recesses of the house, "Any more with you?"
That person will reply, "None."
Then he will say, "Silence, because the LORD's name
must not be invoked."
11 For the LORD commands:

The large house will be smashed to pieces,
and the small house to rubble.

12 Do horses gallop on the cliffs?
Does anyone plow there with oxen?[F]
Yet you have turned justice into poison
and the fruit of righteousness
into wormwood —
13 you who rejoice over Lo-debar
and say, "Didn't we capture Karnaim
for ourselves by our own strength?"
14 But look, I am raising up a nation
against you, house of Israel —
this is the declaration of the Lord,
the God of Armies —
and they will oppress you
from the entrance of Hamath[G]
to the Brook of the Arabah.[H]

FIRST VISION: LOCUSTS

7 The Lord God showed me this: He was forming a
swarm of locusts at the time the spring crop first
began to sprout — after the cutting of the king's hay.
2 When the locusts finished eating the vegetation of
the land, I said, "Lord God, please forgive! How will
Jacob survive since he is so small?"
3 The LORD relented concerning this. "It will not
happen," he said.

SECOND VISION: FIRE

4 The Lord God showed me this: The Lord God was
calling for a judgment by fire. It consumed the great
deep and devoured the land. 5 Then I said, "Lord God,
please stop! How will Jacob survive since he is so
small?"
6 The LORD relented concerning this. "This will not
happen either," said the Lord God.

THIRD VISION: A PLUMB LINE

7 He showed me this: The Lord was standing there by
a vertical wall with a plumb line in his hand. 8 The
LORD asked me, "What do you see, Amos?"
I replied, "A plumb line."
Then the Lord said, "I am setting a plumb line
among my people Israel; I will no longer spare them:

9 Isaac's high places will be deserted,
and Israel's sanctuaries
will be in ruins;
I will rise up against the house of Jeroboam
with a sword."

AMAZIAH'S OPPOSITION

10 Amaziah the priest of Bethel sent word to King Jeroboam of Israel, saying, "Amos has conspired against
you right here in the house of Israel. The land cannot
endure all his words, 11 for Amos has said this: 'Jeroboam will die by the sword, and Israel will certainly
go into exile from its homeland.'"
12 Then Amaziah said to Amos, "Go away, you seer!
Flee to the land of Judah. Earn your living[I] and give
your prophecies there, 13 but don't ever prophesy
at Bethel again, for it is the king's sanctuary and a
royal temple."
14 So Amos answered Amaziah, "I was[J] not a prophet or the son of a prophet;[K] rather, I was[J] a herds-
man, and I took care of sycamore figs. 15 But the LORD
took me from following the flock and said to me, 'Go,
prophesy to my people Israel.'"
16 Now hear the word of the LORD. You say:

Do not prophesy against Israel;
do not preach against the house
of Isaac.

[A] **6:5** Hb obscure [B] **6:5** Or *compose on* [C] **6:10** Lit *His uncle*
[D] **6:10** A burner of incense, a memorial fire, or a body; Hb obscure
[E] **6:10** Lit *remove bones* [F] **6:12** Some emend to *plow the sea*
[G] **6:14** Or *from Lebo-hamath* [H] **6:14** Probably the Valley of Zared at the southeast end of the Dead Sea [I] **7:12** Lit *Eat bread* [J] **7:14** Or *am*
[K] **7:14** = a prophet's disciple or a member of a prophetic guild

[17] Therefore, this is what the LORD says:
Your wife will be a prostitute in the city,
your sons and daughters will fall
by the sword,
and your land will be divided up
with a measuring line.
You yourself will die on pagan[A] soil,
and Israel will certainly go into exile
from its homeland.

FOURTH VISION: A BASKET OF SUMMER FRUIT

8 The Lord GOD showed me this: a basket of summer
fruit. [2] He asked me, "What do you see, Amos?"
I replied, "A basket of summer fruit."[B]
The LORD said to me, "The end has come for my
people Israel; I will no longer spare them. [3] In that day
the temple[C] songs will become wailing" — this is the
Lord GOD's declaration. "Many dead bodies, thrown
everywhere! Silence!"

4 Hear this, you who trample on the needy
and do away with the poor of the land,
5 asking, "When will the New Moon be over
so we may sell grain,
and the Sabbath,
so we may market wheat?
We can reduce the measure
while increasing the price[D]
and cheat with dishonest scales.
6 We can buy the poor with silver
and the needy for a pair of sandals
and even sell the chaff!"

[7] The LORD has sworn by the Pride of Jacob:[E]
I will never forget all their deeds.
8 Because of this, won't the land quake
and all who dwell in it mourn?
All of it will rise like the Nile;
it will surge and then subside
like the Nile in Egypt.

9 And in that day —
this is the declaration of the Lord GOD —
I will make the sun go down at noon;
I will darken the land in the daytime.
10 I will turn your feasts into mourning
and all your songs into lamentation;
I will cause everyone[F] to wear sackcloth
and every head to be shaved.
I will make that grief
like mourning for an only son
and its outcome like a bitter day.

11 Look, the days are coming —
this is the declaration of the Lord GOD —
when I will send a famine through the land:
not a famine of bread or a thirst for water,
but of hearing the words of the LORD.
12 People will stagger from sea to sea
and roam from north to east
seeking the word of the LORD,
but they will not find it.
13 In that day the beautiful young women,
the young men also, will faint from thirst.
14 Those who swear by the guilt of Samaria
and say, "As your god lives, Dan,"
or, "As the way[G,H] of Beer-sheba lives" —
they will fall, never to rise again.

FIFTH VISION: THE LORD BESIDE THE ALTAR

9 I saw the Lord standing beside the altar, and he
said:
Strike the capitals of the pillars
so that the thresholds shake;
knock them down on the heads of all
the people.
Then I will kill the rest of them with the sword.
None of those who flee will get away;
none of the fugitives will escape.
2 If they dig down to Sheol,
from there my hand will take them;
if they climb up to heaven,
from there I will bring them down.
3 If they hide
on the top of Carmel,
from there I will track them down
and seize them;
if they conceal themselves
from my sight on the sea floor,
from there I will command
the sea serpent to bite them.
4 And if they are driven
by their enemies into captivity,
from there I will command
the sword to kill them.
I will keep my eye on them
for harm and not for good.

5 The Lord, the GOD of Armies —
he touches the earth;
it melts, and all who dwell in it mourn;
all of it rises like the Nile
and subsides like the Nile of Egypt.
6 He builds his upper chambers
in the heavens
and lays the foundation of his vault
on the earth.

[A] **7:17** Lit *unclean* [B] **8:2** In Hb the word for *summer fruit* sounds like the word for *end.* [C] **8:3** Or *palace* [D] **8:5** Lit *reduce the ephah and make the shekel great* [E] **8:7** = the LORD or the promised land [F] **8:10** Lit *every waist* [G] **8:14** LXX reads *god* [H] **8:14** Or *power*

He summons the water of the sea
and pours it out over the surface of the earth.
The LORD is his name.

ANNOUNCEMENT OF JUDGMENT

7 Israelites, are you not like the Cushites to me?
This is the LORD's declaration.
Didn't I bring Israel from the land of Egypt,
the Philistines from Caphtor,[A]
and the Arameans from Kir?
8 Look, the eyes of the Lord GOD
are on the sinful kingdom,
and I will obliterate it
from the face of the earth.
However, I will not totally destroy
the house of Jacob —
this is the LORD's declaration —
9 for I am about to give the command,
and I will shake the house of Israel
among all the nations,
as one shakes a sieve,
but not a pebble will fall to the ground.
10 All the sinners among my people
who say, "Disaster will never overtake[B]
or confront us,"
will die by the sword.

ANNOUNCEMENT OF RESTORATION

11 In that day
I will restore the fallen shelter of David:
I will repair its gaps,
restore its ruins,
and rebuild it as in the days of old,
12 so that they may possess
the remnant of Edom
and all the nations
that bear my name[C] —
this is the declaration of the LORD; he will do this.

13 Look, the days are coming —
this is the LORD's declaration —
when the plowman will overtake the reaper
and the one who treads grapes,
the sower of seed.
The mountains will drip with sweet wine,
and all the hills will flow with it.
14 I will restore the fortunes
of my people Israel.[D]
They will rebuild and occupy ruined cities,
plant vineyards and drink their wine,
make gardens and eat their produce.
15 I will plant them on their land,
and they will never again be uprooted
from the land I have given them.
The LORD your God has spoken.

[A] **9:7** Probably Crete [B] **9:10** Or *"You will not let disaster come near* [C] **9:12** LXX reads *so that the remnant of man and all the nations . . . may seek me*; Ac 15:17 [D] **9:14** Or *restore my people Israel from captivity*

OBADIAH

Sheep near the Wadi Hasa (Brook Zered), the border between Edom and Moab.

INTRODUCTION TO

OBADIAH

Circumstances of Writing

Presumably Obadiah (v. 1) was the author of this book, but nothing else is known about him. His common Hebrew name, denoting "servant of the Lord," is shared by at least a dozen men in the Old Testament.

The time of writing of Obadiah is disputed, with a wide variety of proposed dates from the tenth to the fifth centuries BC, depending on when the invasion and plunder of Jerusalem (vv. 11–14) occurred. The two most popular views are during the reign of King Jehoram of Judah (ca 848–841 BC) and shortly after the final destruction of Jerusalem by the Babylonians (587/586 BC).

The former date (ca 845 BC) was when the Philistines and Arabs plundered Judah (2Ch 21:16–17) and the Edomites revolted (2Kg 8:20), presumably then becoming allies of the invaders. Since the text does not explicitly indicate the cooperation of the Edomites with the Philistines and Arabs, the latter date (mid-sixth or even fifth century BC) fits the biblical data better, including Obadiah 20 (the dispersed exiles of the Israelites and of Jerusalem to be restored), as opposed to dates before the dispersion of Israel (by 722 BC) or of Judah (605–586 BC). This postexilic view is also supported by the mention of Edomite involvement in Jerusalem's downfall (vv. 10–14, gloating over the fall of Jerusalem, as in other sixth-century BC texts—Lm 4:21; Ezk 35:15; see Lm 2:15–17—and participating in the plunder) which would result in the Lord's promised justice ("As you have done, it will be done to you"; Ob 15) on their heads.

Contribution

Like the book of Revelation, which proclaims the downfall of the persecuting Roman Empire, the book of Obadiah sustains faith in God's moral government and hope in the eventual triumph of his just will. It brings a pastoral message to aching hearts that God is on his throne and he cares for his own.

Structure

The text declares the book of Obadiah is a prophetic "vision" from the Lord (v. 1) that also appears to be a war oracle (v. 1) communicating the Lord's imminent judgment upon Edom (vv. 2–9). As a subtype of the prophetic "oracle against foreign nations" (Is 13–23; Jr 46–51; Ezk 25–32; Am 1–2; Zph 2:4–15), it is typical in announcing judgment on a foreign power (specifically Edom; see also Lm 4:21–22) to bring deliverance for Judah (Ob 17–20; see Jr 46:25–28; Nah 1:1–15; Zph 3:14–20). Yet it, like Nahum and Jonah, is atypical in focusing solely on judgment for a foreign nation, rather than specifying judgment for Israel as well.

This shortest Old Testament book consists of several parts. A war oracle from the Lord announces certain judgment on Edom for their arrogant presumption and self-deception (Ob 3) that they were immune from divine intervention (vv. 1–9). Next is an explanation of the further cause for coming judgment on Edom (vv. 10–14), a lack of brotherly commitment (vv. 10–11) in gloating over the day of disaster for God's people Judah (vv. 12–13) and cooperating with Judah's enemies in her destruction (vv. 10–11,13–14). Then the text focuses on the day of the Lord (vv. 15–21), on which imminent judgment falls on the historical nation of Edom (vv. 15–16), followed by ultimate judgment on "Edom" as representative of Israel's end-time enemies (v. 16), that would result in the deliverance of both Judah and Israel (vv. 17–21).

1 The vision of Obadiah.

EDOM'S CERTAIN JUDGMENT

This is what the Lord God has said about Edom:
We have heard a message from the LORD;
an envoy has been sent among the nations:
"Rise up, and let's go to war against her."[A]
2 Look, I will make you insignificant
among the nations;
you will be deeply despised.
3 Your arrogant heart has deceived you,
you who live in clefts of the rock[B,C]
in your home on the heights,
who say to yourself,
"Who can bring me down to the ground?"
4 Though you seem to soar[D] like an eagle
and make your nest among the stars,
even from there I will bring you down.
This is the LORD's declaration.

5 If thieves came to you,
if marauders by night —
how ravaged you would be! —
wouldn't they steal only
what they wanted?
If grape harvesters came to you,
wouldn't they leave a few grapes?
6 How Esau will be pillaged,
his hidden treasures searched out!
7 Everyone who has a treaty with you
will drive you to the border;
everyone at peace with you
will deceive and conquer you.
Those who eat your bread
will set[E] a trap for you.
He will be unaware of it.
8 In that day —
this is the LORD's declaration —
will I not eliminate the wise ones of Edom
and those who understand
from the hill country of Esau?
9 Teman,[F] your warriors will be terrified
so that everyone from the hill country of Esau
will be destroyed by slaughter.

EDOM'S SINS AGAINST JUDAH

10 You will be covered with shame
and destroyed forever
because of violence done
to your brother Jacob.
11 On the day you stood aloof,
on the day strangers captured his wealth,[G]
while foreigners entered his city gate
and cast lots for Jerusalem,
you were just like one of them.
12 Do not[H] gloat over your brother
in the day of his calamity;
do not rejoice over the people of Judah
in the day of their destruction;
do not boastfully mock[I]
in the day of distress.
13 Do not enter my people's city gate
in the day of their disaster.
Yes, you — do not gloat over their misery
in the day of their disaster,
and do not appropriate their possessions
in the day of their disaster.
14 Do not stand at the crossroads[J]
to cut off their fugitives,
and do not hand over their survivors
in the day of distress.

JUDGMENT OF THE NATIONS

15 For the day of the LORD is near,
against all the nations.
As you have done, it will be done to you;
what you deserve will return
on your own head.
16 As you have drunk on my holy mountain,
so all the nations will drink continually.
They will drink and gulp down
and be as though they had never been.
17 But there will be a deliverance on Mount Zion,
and it will be holy;
the house of Jacob will dispossess
those who dispossessed them.[K]
18 Then the house of Jacob will be a blazing fire,
and the house of Joseph, a burning flame,
but the house of Esau will be stubble;
Jacob[L] will set them on fire
and consume Edom.[M]
Therefore no survivor will remain
of the house of Esau,
for the LORD has spoken.

FUTURE BLESSING FOR ISRAEL

19 People from the Negev will possess
the hill country of Esau;
those from the Judean foothills will possess
the land of the Philistines.
They[N] will possess
the territories of Ephraim and Samaria,
while Benjamin will possess Gilead.

[A] **1** = Edom [B] **3** Or *in Sela*; probably = Petra [C] **3** Probably Petra [D] **4** Or *to build high* [E] **7** Some LXX mss, Sym, Tg, Vg; MT reads *They will set your bread as* [F] **9** = a region or city in Edom [G] **11** Or *forces* [H] **12–14** Or *You should not* throughout vv. 12–14 [I] **12** Lit *not make your mouth big* [J] **14** Hb obscure [K] **17** DSS, LXX, Syr, Vg, Tg; MT reads *Jacob will possess its inheritance* [L] **18** Lit *they* [M] **18** Lit *them* [N] **19** = The house of Jacob

Obadiah: The Man and His Message

by Kevin C. Peacock

About the only thing we know for certain about Obadiah the prophet is that he was a prophet. His name was a common one that means "servant of the LORD." (At least twelve people in the Old Testament had the name.) Obadiah, however, could have been his title rather than his name. Scholars date Obadiah anywhere from the ninth century to the fifth century BC,[1] but the most traditional dating of Obadiah's prophecy would be during the exile, shortly after the fall of Jerusalem in 586 BC. He spoke of the attack on Jerusalem in the past (Ob 11); but Edom's fall (ca 533 BC) was still in the future, making Obadiah likely a contemporary with Jeremiah and Ezekiel.[2]

Foreigners (i.e., the Babylonians) invaded Jerusalem and divided the spoils of the city (v. 11). The Edomites, distant relatives and near neighbors to the Judeans, could have assisted Judah; instead, they sided with the invaders, gloated over Jerusalem's fall, and took advantage of their brothers' plight (vv. 10–14). They then fled to their mountain fortresses, feeling smugly secure after their mistreatment of God's chosen people (vv. 3–4). Obadiah's message was directed against such wickedness and pride. Their actions proved the Edomites to be God's enemies, and they would soon face his justice. The Lord's purpose for his people was not finished, and God's reign would become universal and eternal.

Israel's contentious history with the Edomites originated with Jacob and Esau (or Edom; see Gn 25:30). Settled in Seir on the southeastern edge of the Dead Sea (Gn 36:1–9), the Edomites denied the Israelites passage through their territory after the exodus, threatening them with force (Nm 20:14–21; 21:4). Centuries of struggle between the two peoples followed (see 1Sm 14:47–48; 2Sm 8:13–14; 1Kg 9:26–28; 11:14–22; 2Kg 8:20–22; 14:7; 2Ch 21:8–10; 25:11–12; 28:17). When the Babylonians destroyed Jerusalem in 586 BC, the Edomites sided with the attackers to take advantage of Israel's plight (Ps 137:7; Ezk 25:12–14; 35:10–11). Later, a strong Arab presence appeared in Edomite territory during the Persian Empire (late sixth to fourth centuries BC; see Neh 2:19; 4:7; 6:1). "By late in the fourth century BC, the Arab kingdom of Nabatea was centered around Petra [the Edomite capital]. Pressure from the Nabateans displaced many Edomites into the Negev of Judah. This region then came to be called 'Idumea,' preserving [a form of] the ancient name of Edom."[3] ✜

---

[1] See J. LeCureux, "Obadiah, Book of" in *Dictionary of the Old Testament Prophets*, ed. Mark J. Boda and J. Gordon McConville (Downers Grove, IL: IVP Academic, 2012), 570, for the proposed dating options.
[2] See John Barton, *Joel and Obadiah*, OTL (2001), 120–21, for details and comparisons.
[3] See 1 Macc 4:29; Raymond B. Dillard and Tremper Longman III, *An Introduction to the Old Testament* (Grand Rapids: Zondervan, 1995), 387–88.

Ruins of Triple Arched Gate at Petra.

Sheep near the Wadi Hasa (Brook Zered), the border between Edom and Moab.

The Rock of Edom in the Wilderness of Zin.

Edom: Its Land and People

by George H. Shaddix

The nation of Edom originated with Esau, the older son of Isaac and Rebekah (Gn 25:21–24). Esau and Jacob were twins, but Esau was the firstborn. These two brothers grew into men with different interests. Jacob enjoyed staying around the house. Esau, who had a ruddy and rough appearance, enjoyed the outdoors. Genesis 25:25 describes Esau at his birth: "The first one came out red-looking, covered with hair like a fur coat, and they named him Esau." As these twin boys grew up, Esau became a skilled hunter (v. 27). These two, Esau and Jacob, struggled with each other even before birth (v. 22), and this struggle extended beyond the two individuals to the two nations, Edom and Israel, that would be their descendants.

Two major events marked Esau's life. First, he sold his birthright to Jacob for some red stew (vv. 29–34); according to verse 30, "that is why he was also named Edom," which is related to the verb *ādam,* meaning "be red," as well as the noun *dām,* meaning "blood." Second, Jacob, with the help of his mother, Rebekah, got the blessing of his father, Isaac. This blessing usually went to the firstborn. Once Isaac had given Jacob Esau's birthright, though, he could not take it back and give it to Esau. These events set the stage for longstanding hostility between these twins and their descendants.

This narrow and natural crag called the Siq is the only access route to the ancient Nabatean city of Petra.

In marrying two Hittite women (26:35), Esau disregarded God's covenant with his father, Isaac, and his grandfather, Abraham. Later he married the daughter of Ishmael, who was Abraham's son by Sarah's handmaid. Again, these factors built tension between Esau and his parents, Esau and his brother, and ultimately the nations of Israel and Edom.

THE LAND

Esau settled in the mountain region south and east of the Dead Sea, where red sandstone is prevalent. This area extended south to Elath and Ezion-geber on the north shore of the Gulf of Aqaba (Dt 2:8).[1] Moab's southern border was the northern border of Edom. Sometimes Edom was called Seir (see Gn 32:3).

This mountainous area is forty miles wide and one hundred miles long. The sides of the area "rise steeply from the valley."[2] The northern part of the plateau forms a spacious grazing ground. Mountains in the north rise fifteen hundred to two thousand feet; some in the south reach twenty-six hundred feet. Many areas are inaccessible peaks and gorges. These features help us understand why Genesis 36:8 says that Esau lived in the mountains of Seir. In the days of Obadiah, the capital of Edom was Sela, which means "rock." It is usually identified with the Nabatean rock-city known as Petra.

ITS PEOPLE

The descendants of Esau conquered the Horites who lived in this area before them (cf. Gn 14:6; Dt 2:22). After leaving Egypt, the Israelites approached Edom. Moses sent messengers to ask the king of Edom for permission to go through their land (Nm 20:14–21). Moses sent the messengers from Kadesh telling them to refer to the Israelites as "your brother Israel" (v. 14). No doubt this was an effort to encourage the Edomites to be generous and allow them to go through the land. The animosity between Jacob and Esau evidently continued; the Edomites would not allow the Israelites to go through their land.

This refusal was in spite of Moses's promises that they would go along the King's Highway and not through the fields or vineyards, nor would they drink water from a well in the land. The king's response was, "You will not travel through our land, or we will come out and confront you with the sword" (v. 18). To be sure that Israel did not come through their land, the Edomites came against them with a large army. The Israelites turned away and did not attempt to go through the land of Edom.

DISPOSSESSED AND DESTROYED

Balaam, in his final oracle (Nm 23–24), declared, "Edom will become a possession; Seir will become a possession of its enemies, but Israel will be triumphant" (24:18). When Saul was king of Israel, "he fought against all his enemies in every direction," including Moab, the Ammonites, Edom, Zobah, and the Philistines. "Wherever he turned, he caused havoc" (1Sm 14:47).

Then when David became king, he struck down eighteen thousand Edomites and put garrisons of soldiers throughout Edom. The Edomites became subjects of David (2Sm 8:13–14). Solomon assembled a fleet of ships at Ezion-geber on the Red Sea in the land of Edom—an indicator that Edom was under Solomon's rule. These ships sailed to Ophir and brought back to Solomon 420 talents of gold (sixteen tons; see 1Kg 9:26–28). During the reign of Judah's King Jehoram (850–843 BC), Edom revolted and appointed its own king (2Kg 8:20).

Edom is mentioned many times in the Prophets and is "noted in the Bible for its pride, treachery, greed, and violence" (see 2Ch 20:10–11; 25:14,20; Jr 49:16; Am 1:9,11; Ob 3). Its treatment of the people of Israel when the Babylonians invaded is a particular sore spot (see Ps 137:7; Ezk 25:12; 35:15; 36:5; Jl 3:19; Ob 10–14). God's judgment on Edom is declared several times (see Is 34:5–17; Jr 49:7–22; Lm 4:21; Ezk 25:12–14; 35:1–15; Am 1:11–12; Ob).[3] Devastation probably came in the sixth century. Kyle McCarter concluded his discussion of the dating of the destruction of Edom, "The precise date of the final expulsion of the Edomites is undetermined, but is placed late in the sixth century by general agreement. The archaeological evidence, still regrettably meager, shows the last part of that century to have been a period of general collapse in Edomite culture."[4] ⁘

---

[1] Burton MacDonald, "Archaeology of Edom," *Anchor Yale Bible Dictionary*, 2:295. [2] W. Ewing, "Edom; Edomites" in *ISBE* (1952), 2:899. [3] E. Ray Clendenen, "Malachi," in *Haggai, Malachi*, NAC (2004), 250–51. [4] P. Kyle McCarter Jr., "Obadiah 7 and the Fall of Edom," *BASOR* 221 (1976): 89.

20 The exiles of the Israelites who are in Halah[A]
and who are among the Canaanites
as far as Zarephath
as well as the exiles of Jerusalem who are
in Sepharad
will possess the cities of the Negev.

21 Saviors[B] will ascend Mount Zion
to rule over the hill country of Esau,
and the kingdom will be the LORD's.

[A] **20** Or *of this host of the Israelites*; Hb obscure [B] **21** Or *Those who have been delivered*

JONAH

Scene on the Santa Maria Antiqua Sarcophagus discovered at Rome is decorated with stories of Jonah, including this one as the prophet has just been thrown out of the boat.

INTRODUCTION TO

JONAH

Circumstances of Writing

Jonah appears in 2 Kings 14:25 as a prophet from Gath-hepher in the territory of Zebulun in northern Israel. He was active around the first half of the eighth century BC. Jonah predicted the restoration of the northern kingdom's boundaries. This occurred during the reign of Jeroboam II (ca 793–753 BC). This book about Jonah could have been composed at any time from the eighth century to the end of the Old Testament period.

Jonah preached to the city of Nineveh. Nineveh was a major city of the Assyrians, a cruel and warlike people who were longtime enemies of Israel. Assyrian artwork emphasizes war, including scenes of execution, impalement, flaying the skin off prisoners, and beheadings. This explains Jonah's reluctance to preach to the infamous city of Nineveh.

The key debate about the book of Jonah is the question of its genre. Is Jonah history or parable? The parable view argues that Jonah is a fictional story or fable made up to convey a theological point about God's attitude toward Gentiles. Proponents of the parable view argue that the ironic and fantastic events described by the book (e.g., Jonah living and praying in the stomach of a fish) is the author's way of tipping the reader off that this is not literal history. There are also historical difficulties that the fictional view would resolve: the exaggerated size of Nineveh (Jnh 3:3) and the lack of extrabiblical, Assyrian evidence to confirm that the city ever repented.

Five considerations suggest taking the book of Jonah as genuine history. First, Jonah was a real historical figure, said to be a prophet in 2 Kings 14:25. The book of Jonah portrays Jonah as a flawed character. Were the book of Jonah a piece of fiction, it would be guilty of slander, saying something derogatory and untrue about a real person who is elsewhere presented positively.

Second, Jonah is part of the collection of twelve Minor Prophets. All the other books of this collection convey prophecies by genuine, historical prophets.

Third, the miracles in Jonah are not impossible for the God of the Bible. Presuming otherwise, some interpreters allow their antisupernaturalism to drive them to the parable view of Jonah.

Fourth, Jesus in Matthew 12:39–41 and Luke 11:29–32 spoke of Jonah being in the fish and preaching in Nineveh as if these were real events. In particular, Jesus's statement that "the men of Nineveh will stand up at the judgment with this generation and condemn it, because they repented at Jonah's preaching" (Mt 12:41; Lk 11:32) makes little sense if the people of Nineveh never actually repented due to Jonah's preaching. Unless one is willing to affirm that Jesus was wrong, it is best to say that the book of Jonah is historical.

Contribution to the Bible

The book of Jonah shows God's gracious concern for the whole world, his power over nature, and the futility of running from him. In addition, it foreshadows Jesus's burial and resurrection. Matthew 12:38–45 and Luke 11:24–32 compare the ministry of Jesus with that of Jonah, Jesus being the greater. Both texts see Jonah's great fish as a foreshadowing of Jesus's burial in the tomb, making Jonah a "type" of Christ.

Structure

The book of Jonah exhibits a high degree of Hebrew literary excellence. Its style is rich and varied. It is considered by many as a masterpiece of rhetoric. There is symmetry and balance in the book, and it can be divided into two sections of two chapters each. The peak of the first discourse is marked by its poetic form, which has a higher prominence in narrative than prose. The peak in the second discourse is marked by the dialogue between Jonah and God. The Lord and Jonah are indicated as the two main characters of the story by being the only ones who are named; the other characters are anonymous.

Phenomena of nature also serve in each half as props: wind, storm, sea, dry land, and fish in the first half; herd and flock, plant, worm, sun, and wind in the second half. When placed side by side, chapters 1 and 3 and chapters 2 and 4 can be seen as parallel. Finally, both chapters 1 and 3 begin with Jonah receiving a word from the Lord consisting of a call to go to Nineveh.

JONAH'S FLIGHT

1 The word of the LORD came to Jonah son of Amittai: 2 “Get up! Go to the great city of Nineveh and
preach against it because their evil has come up before
me.” 3 Jonah got up to flee to Tarshish from the LORD's
presence. He went down to Joppa and found a ship going to Tarshish. He paid the fare and went down into it
to go with them to Tarshish from the LORD's presence.
4 But the LORD threw a great wind onto the sea,
and such a great storm arose on the sea that the ship
threatened to break apart. 5 The sailors were afraid,
and each cried out to his god. They threw the ship's
cargo into the sea to lighten the load. Meanwhile,
Jonah had gone down to the lowest part of the vessel
and had stretched out and fallen into a deep sleep.
6 The captain approached him and said, “What are
you doing sound asleep? Get up! Call to your god.[A]
Maybe this god will consider us, and we won't perish.”
7 “Come on!” the sailors said to each other. “Let's
cast lots. Then we'll know who is to blame for this
trouble we're in.” So they cast lots, and the lot singled
out Jonah. 8 Then they said to him, “Tell us who is to
blame for this trouble we're in. What is your business,
and where are you from? What is your country, and
what people are you from?”
9 He answered them, “I'm a Hebrew. I worship[B] the
LORD, the God of the heavens, who made the sea and
the dry land.”
10 Then the men were seized by a great fear and
said to him, “What have you done?” The men knew
he was fleeing from the LORD's presence because he
had told them. 11 So they said to him, “What should
we do to you so that the sea will calm down for us?”
For the sea was getting worse and worse.
12 He answered them, “Pick me up and throw me
into the sea so that it will calm down for you, for I
know that I'm to blame for this great storm that is
against you.” 13 Nevertheless, the men rowed hard to
get back to dry land, but they couldn't because the sea
was raging against them more and more.
14 So they called out to the LORD, “Please, LORD, don't
let us perish because of this man's life, and don't charge
us with innocent blood! For you, LORD, have done just
as you pleased.” 15 Then they picked up Jonah and
threw him into the sea, and the sea stopped its raging.
16 The men were seized by great fear of the LORD, and
they offered a sacrifice to the LORD and made vows.
17 The LORD appointed a great fish to swallow Jonah, and Jonah was in the belly of the fish three days
and three nights.

JONAH'S PRAYER

2 Jonah prayed to the LORD his God from the belly
of the fish:

2 I called to the LORD in my distress,
and he answered me.
I cried out for help from deep inside[C] Sheol;
you heard my voice.
3 When you threw me into the depths,
into the heart of the seas,
the current[D] overcame me.
All your breakers and your billows
swept over me.
4 And I said, “I have been banished
from your sight,
yet I will look[E] once more
toward your holy temple.”
5 The water engulfed me up to the neck;[F]
the watery depths overcame me;
seaweed was wrapped around my head.
6 I sank to the foundations of the mountains,
the earth's gates shut behind me forever!
Then you raised my life from the Pit,
LORD my God!
7 As my life was fading away,
I remembered the LORD,
and my prayer came to you,
to your holy temple.
8 Those who cherish worthless idols
abandon their faithful love,
9 but as for me, I will sacrifice to you
with a voice of thanksgiving.
I will fulfill what I have vowed.
Salvation[G] belongs to the LORD.

10 Then the LORD commanded the fish, and it vomited Jonah onto dry land.

JONAH'S PREACHING

3 The word of the LORD came to Jonah a second
time: 2 “Get up! Go to the great city of Nineveh and
preach the message that I tell you.” 3 Jonah got up and
went to Nineveh according to the LORD's command.
Now Nineveh was an extremely great city,[H] a three-
day walk. 4 Jonah set out on the first day of his walk
in the city and proclaimed, “In forty days Nineveh
will be demolished!” 5 Then the people of Nineveh
believed God. They proclaimed a fast and dressed in
sackcloth — from the greatest of them to the least.
6 When word reached the king of Nineveh, he got
up from his throne, took off his royal robe, covered
himself with sackcloth, and sat in ashes. 7 Then he
issued a decree in Nineveh:

By order of the king and his nobles: No person or
animal, herd or flock, is to taste anything at all.
They must not eat or drink water. 8 Furthermore,
both people and animals must be covered with

[A] 1:6 Or *God* [B] 1:9 Or *fear* [C] 2:2 Lit *from the stomach of* [D] 2:3 Lit *river*
[E] 2:4 LXX reads *sight. Will I look . . . ?* [F] 2:5 Or *me, threatening my life*
[G] 2:9 Or *Deliverance* [H] 3:3 Or *was a great city to God*

Jonah's Historical Setting

by John L. Harris

God spoke to Jonah in the first half of the eighth century when Jeroboam II (793–753 BC) ruled Israel and the Assyrian Empire was experiencing a period of decline. The Assyrian weakness allowed Jeroboam II to regain large amounts of territory that had previously been lost (2Kg 14:25).

NINEVEH AND THE ASSYRIAN EMPIRE

Ancient Nineveh was located in Mesopotamia on the Tigris River. It was one of the oldest and most important cities in ancient Assyria. In the third millennium BC, Nineveh was part of the Akkadian Empire and served as a major religious and cultural center. During this time, the temple of Ishtar was built. The city did not become prominent, however, until about 1500 BC, when the Assyrian kings constructed several new palaces and renovated the temple of Ishtar. Late in the eighth century, Assyria's King Sennacherib (704–681 BC) made Nineveh the capital city.

For most of the ninth century, Assyria experienced one of the golden ages of its history. However, in 827 BC, a major rebellion broke out because King Shalmaneser III (858–824 BC) was unable to contain the power of the provincial governors who usurped his authority. Although the rebels were defeated in 820, the years of internal strife had weakened the nation and marked the beginning of a century of internal discord and significant deterioration for Assyria.[1]

When Adad-nirari III (810–783 BC) succeeded to Assyria's throne, he inherited a weak and declining kingdom. Then matters only worsened, for after Adad-nirari III died, a series of weak kings followed: Shalmaneser IV (782–773 BC), Ashur-dan III (772–755 BC), and Ashur-nirari V (754–745 BC). This time period was the weakest period of the Neo-Assyrian Empire. Less powerful, the Assyrian kings decreased their foreign campaigns and had to deal with internal rebellions in the cities of Ashur, Arrapkha, and Calah.

In addition to the political and militaristic struggles during this period, the Assyrians experienced several natural phenomena, including a famine, a total solar eclipse, and an earthquake, all of which many Assyrians attributed to divine anger.[2] According to the Assyrian Eponym Chronicle, during the reign of Ashur-dan III, the nation's woes were exacerbated by a famine that occurred in 765 BC and either returned in 759 or continued for the entire seven-year period.[3] On June 15, 763 BC, Assyria experienced a total eclipse, an event the people would have considered an ominous sign. Even though it would not have directly damaged the empire, an eclipse certainly would have created considerable anxiety

Portion of an epic poem about the military exploits of the Assyrian King Tukulti-Ninurta I, dated about 1230–1210 BC.

Black limestone obelisk of Assyrian King Shalmaneser III (858–824 BC). Erected in the center of Nimrud, it depicts his military campaigns and tribute received.

and trepidation. Being a rarity, the eclipse gave rise to prophetic utterances regarding public disasters. Predictions included statements such as "a deity will strike the king and fire consume the land" and "the city-walls will be destroyed."[4] Another natural omen, an earthquake (Am 1:1), occurred during the reign of Jeroboam II. In the Assyrian texts, an earthquake was taken as a menacing sign for both king and nation.

NINEVEH AND THE BOOK OF JONAH

During the eighth century, an Assyrian king, nobles, and the general public would have given a visiting prophet respect and proper consideration. According to the Mari texts, men from one city-state would commonly enter another for political, medical, and religious purposes; prophets were often included among the delegations sent from one country to another

Terra-cotta model of sheep's lung used to teach divination.

to negotiate terms of treaties.[5] The use of the phrase "king of Nineveh," instead of "king of Assyria," and the mention of the "nobles" (Jnh 3:6–7) have caused some confusion. The Hebrew Bible commonly designates a king by only one city within the region he ruled. Perhaps the closest parallel to the "king of Nineveh" is in 1 Kings 21:1, where Ahab is called "King Ahab of Samaria" in contrast to the "king of Israel."[6]

Clearly a king could be associated either with the capital or a main city within the empire. In light of the weakness of the Assyrian monarchy and the power of the provincial governors, the mentioning of the "nobles" probably indicates that the position of the Assyrian king was so unstable that any action or proclamation required the approval of the provincial governors.[7]

Clearly, life was difficult for the Ninevites at the time of Jonah's visit. With all the political struggles and natural calamities still fresh on their minds, the Ninevites might have had a sense of urgency and possibly were sensitive to signs and omens. The Assyrian belief system that maintained the existence of a link between celestial and terrestrial events no doubt lay at the foundation for accepting Jonah's presence and preaching as a divine warning.[8] Assyrian tradition dictated that when an eclipse did happen, the king would declare a solemn fast and hand his position of authority over to a substitute monarch until the anticipated danger to the throne due to divine anger passed.[9] According to Jonah 3:5–9, after hearing Jonah's message, the people of Nineveh proclaimed a fast and adorned themselves with sackcloth, and the "king of Nineveh" stepped down from his throne, took off his robe, put on sackcloth, and sat in ashes. These actions were in keeping with the designated proceedings described in ancient texts that detail an Assyrian king's actions during a solar eclipse. So although the Assyrian cuneiform records make no reference to the Ninevites' penitence, it is plausible for the type of contrition to avert divine wrath described in the book of Jonah to have taken place.

When Jonah visited Nineveh, the Assyrian Empire was in the midst of political turmoil and constant religious paganism. God decided that annihilation was the best course of action and sent his prophet to communicate this message. The Ninevites, however, did the unexpected; they turned from their evil ways. Unlike the nation of Israel, they considered God's message and did what was required to avert destruction. Ironically it was the Assyrians, the people who did what God's own people would not do, who were responsible for the total destruction of Israel. The readers of the book of Jonah could hardly have failed to notice the paradox. ✣

Votive image of Assyrian goddess of war and fertility, Ishtar.

[1] A. Kirk Grayson, "Assyria: Ashur-dan II to Ashur-Nirari V (934–745 BC)" in *The Prehistory of the Balkans; and the Middle East and the Aegean World, Tenth to Eighth Centuries BC*, CAH (1982), 268–69; T. Desmond Alexander, "Jonah" in vol. 23a TOTC (Downers Grove, IL: InterVarsity, 1988), 77–78. [2] D. J. Wiseman, "Jonah's Nineveh," *Tyndale Bulletin* (*TynBul*) 30 (1979): 47. [3] Billy K. Smith and Frank S. Page, *Amos, Obadiah, Jonah*, NAC (1995), 204–5; Alexander, "Jonah," 80. [4] Wiseman, "Jonah's Nineveh," 45–46. [5] Wiseman, "Jonah's Nineveh," 42–43. [6] Edward J. Young, *An Introduction to the Old Testament* (Grand Rapids: Eerdmans, 1964), 263. Designating a king by only one city he ruled was not uncommon. See Douglas Stuart, *Hosea-Jonah*, WBC (1987), 441. [7] Smith and Page, *Amos, Obadiah, Jonah*, 205; P. J. N. Lawrence, "Assyrian Nobles and the Book of Jonah," *TynBul* 37 (1986): 131. [8] A. Kirk Grayson, "Mesopotamia" in *ABD*, 4:754. [9] Wiseman, "Jonah's Nineveh," 47.

Fasting in Sackcloth

by Stephen J. Andrews

THE REPENTANCE OF THE NINEVITES

When Jonah finally preached the message God had given him concerning Nineveh, the people of that great city believed God and proclaimed a fast and put on sackcloth. The king of Nineveh also heard what had happened, and he too responded by rising from his throne, removing his royal robe, covering himself with sackcloth, and then sitting in ashes (Jnh 3:5–6). Both of these acts—fasting and wearing sackcloth—were designed to express a serious attitude and a sincere change of heart.

SACKCLOTH AND FASTING IN THE OLD TESTAMENT

Fasting may involve absolute (no food or drink), normal (no food), or partial (restricted diet) dietary restriction for a specific period of time.[1] The act of fasting in the Old Testament is associated with various religious circumstances, such as private acts of prayer (2Sm 12:16; Ps 35:13), mourning (2Sm 1:12; 12:21; Is 32:13), national emergency or distress (Jdg 20:26; 2Ch 20:3), repentance of sin (1Sm 7:6; 1Kg 21:27; Neh 9:1), and official fast days (Lv 16:29; Zch 7:5; 8:19). Fasting is a time of seeking to know God and his will in a deeper experience (Is 58:3–7; Zch 7:5). It is a time of confession (Ps 69:10) and prevailing prayer (Ezr 8:23; Jl 2:12–13). Fasting became necessary when circumstances required that an individual or a whole country seek a humble relationship with God. In such circumstances, physical needs were of no concern.

Sackcloth is a coarse, woven cloth probably black in color (Is 50:3) and usually made from goat hair. It was worn as a sign of mourning and anguish.[2] Sackcloth was employed together with fasting on many occasions (Ps 69:10–11; Is 58:3–6; Jl 1:13–14). Consequently, it was worn as a sign of mourning (Gn 37:34; 2Sm 3:31; Jl 1:8), for fear of personal or national disaster (Jb 16:15; Lm 2:10; Est 4:1), for penitence for sin (1Kg 21:27; Neh 9:1,3), and for times of prayer for deliverance (2Kg 19:1–2; Dn 9:3). Also associated with wearing sackcloth were the acts of sitting/lying in ashes (Is 58:5; Est 4:1–3) and throwing dust on the head (Lm 2:10). Prophets often wore sackcloth as a symbol of repentance when they preached (Is 20:2). The use of sackcloth indicated humbleness before God.

SACKCLOTH AND FASTING IN THE ANCIENT NEAR EAST

The use of sackcloth and fasting is not attested frequently outside the Bible. The Old Testament indicates that several of Israel's neighbors did practice the same kind of ritual. Besides the reference to Nineveh in Jonah, wearing sackcloth for mourning and penitence was practiced in Syria (1Kg 20:31), Moab (Is 15:3), Ammon (Jr 49:3), and Tyre (Ezk 27:31). In addition, Darius spent the night fasting while Daniel was shut up in the lions' den (Dn 6:18).

Also, cognate terms for fasting and sackcloth are found in other Semitic literatures. A similar word for *fasting* is found in Aramaic, Syriac, Arabic, Ethiopic, and possibly Ugaritic.[3] A corresponding term for *sackcloth* is also found in Aramaic, Syriac, Ethiopic, and once in Akkadian.[4]

The ritual use of sackcloth and fasting attested in these texts appears to be consistent with Old Testament practice. For example, the Elephantine papyri[5] contain a petition to the governor of Judea from the Jewish mercenaries stationed on an island in the Nile just below the first cataract at Aswan. When faced with the destruction of their temple to Yahweh, Yedoniah and the priests covered themselves with sackcloth and fasted.[6]

Although the exact terms are not used, similar rituals may be seen in three texts involving mourning. In one Amarna letter, Tushratta, king of Mittani, told Pharaoh Akhenaten that when he grieved over the death of his brother, he did not take food or drink.[7] Also in the epic of Baal and Mot, the Canaanite god El responded to the news of Baal's death by leaving his throne and covering himself with sackcloth.[8] Sackcloth is also mentioned in a Neo-Babylonian text from the time of Nabonidus.[9]

Occasionally a Mesopotamian might vow not to eat or drink until a certain act or task was accomplished.[10] One Babylonian text does indicate a religious reason for fasting. For the seventh day of the month of Tashritu (September–October), the following injunction is recorded: "One may not eat anything at all; it is an abomination to the god Urasha and the goddess Ningal."[11] Finally, two Assyrian texts from the times of Esar-haddon and Ashurbanipal speak about donning sackcloth "as befitting a penitent sinner."[12]

SACKCLOTH AND FASTING IN JONAH

To most readers it seems strange that the response of the Ninevites to Jonah's preaching mentions the inclusion of animals. However, livestock also wore sackcloth in a national act of supplication in the apocryphal book of Judith (4:10–14). Also a number of Assyrian omens show a marked concern on the effects of solar eclipses as a means of divine wrath on the king, the land, and the animals, as does Jonah (3:7–8).[13]

What is more unusual, however, is the atypical reaction of the Ninevites; there seems to be little evidence for fasting as a religious response in the practice of the Assyrians. Their usual approach would be to try to appease the deity, or deities, by means of sacrifices, libations, or incantations.[14] If this is so, where did the Ninevites come up with the idea of fasting? That Jonah told them is uncertain.[15] The religious specialists of Nineveh

Elephantine Island from the Nile River.

most likely figured out that Jonah was an Israelite and that the Israelite God was interested in justice. Repentance for injustice meant fasting and wearing sackcloth. That the Ninevites chose to follow the Israelite custom indicates that they took Jonah seriously. The Ninevites were not sure that such a plan of action would work (3:6,9).

Israel's God saw their actions and decided not to bring their punishment to pass (3:10). But this was not because they were so good at fasting or wearing sackcloth or because they possessed any righteousness. Because they humbled themselves before God and because of God's grace, he had compassion on them. ⁘

[1] See R. K. Harrison, "Fast" in *ISBE*, 11:284; C. Robert Marsh, "Fasting" in *HIBD*, 478–79; H. A. Brangers, "Fasting in Israel in Biblical and Post-Biblical Times," in *Instruction and Interpretation: Studies in Hebrew Language, Palestinian Archaeology and Biblical Exegesis*, ed. H. A. Brangers et al. (Leiden: Brill, 1977), 1–21. The Hebrew verb and noun for *fasting* occur forty-seven times in the Old Testament. [2] G. Herr, "Sackcloth" in *ISBE*, 4:256. A picture of modern-day sackcloth may be seen in J. D. Douglas et al., eds., *The Illustrated Bible Dictionary* (Leicester: Inter-Varsity, 1980), 3:1357. The English word *sack* is a transliteration of the Hebrew term and not a translation. When referring to the ritual use of "sackcloth," the Hebrew word occurs forty times in the Old Testament. [3] See Ludwig Koehler and Walter Baumgartner, *HALOT* (1996), 101–2. [4] See Koehler and Baumgartner, *HALOT*, 1349. [5] For details on the contents of the Elephantine papyri, see R. K. Harrison, "Elephantine Papyri" in *ISBE*, 2:58–59. [6] A. Cowley, *Aramaic Papyri of the Fifth Century BC* (Osnabruck: Otto Zeller, 1997), 113–14. [7] A fair English translation may be found in Samuel A. B. Mercer, *The Tell El-Amarna Tablets* (New York: AMS Press, 1983), 171. [8] Although the Ugaritic text uses the word *loincloth*, it is clear that a garment of mourning like sackcloth is intended. See J. C. L. Gibson, *Canaanite Myths and Legends* (Edinburgh: T&T Clark, 1977), 73. [9] See Koehler and Baumgartner, *HALOT*, 1349. This text reflects West Semitic mourning rites. [10] John Walton, *Jonah*, Bible Study Commentary (Grand Rapids: Zondervan, 1982), 49. Compare Ac 23:12. [11] Walton, *Jonah*, 49. [12] A. Leo Oppenheim et al., *The Assyrian Dictionary of the Oriental Institute of the University of Chicago (CAD)*, vol. 1, part 2 (Chicago: Oriental Institute), 299. [13] D. J. Wiseman, "Jonah's Nineveh," *TynBul* 301 (1979): 47. [14] John H. Walton, Victor H. Matthews, and Mark W. Chavalas, *The IVP Bible Background Commentary: Old Testament* (Downers Grove, IL: InterVarsity, 2000), 780. [15] Walton, *Jonah*, 52.

sackcloth, and everyone must call out earnestly
to God. Each must turn from his evil ways and
from his wrongdoing.[A] 9 Who knows? God may
turn and relent; he may turn from his burning
anger so that we will not perish.

10 God saw their actions — that they had turned
from their evil ways — so God relented from the disaster he had threatened them with. And he did not
do it.

JONAH'S ANGER

4 Jonah was greatly displeased and became furious. 2 He prayed to the LORD, "Please, LORD, isn't
this what I said while I was still in my own country?
That's why I fled toward Tarshish in the first place.
I knew that you are a gracious and compassionate
God, slow to anger, abounding in faithful love, and
one who relents from sending disaster. 3 And now,
LORD, take my life from me, for it is better for me to
die than to live."
4 The LORD asked, "Is it right for you to be angry?"
5 Jonah left the city and found a place east of it. He
made himself a shelter there and sat in its shade to
see what would happen to the city. 6 Then the LORD
God appointed a plant, and it grew over Jonah to
provide shade for his head to rescue him from his
trouble.[B] Jonah was greatly pleased with the plant.
7 When dawn came the next day, God appointed a
worm that attacked the plant, and it withered.
8 As the sun was rising, God appointed a scorching east wind. The sun beat down on Jonah's head so
much that he almost fainted, and he wanted to die. He
said, "It's better for me to die than to live."
9 Then God asked Jonah, "Is it right for you to be
angry about the plant?"
"Yes, it's right!" he replied. "I'm angry enough to
die!"
10 And the LORD said, "You cared about the plant,
which you did not labor over and did not grow. It appeared in a night and perished in a night. 11 So may I
not care about the great city of Nineveh, which has
more than a hundred twenty thousand people who
cannot distinguish between their right and their left,
as well as many animals?"

[A] **3:8** Or *injustice*, or *violence* [B] **4:6** Or *disaster*, or *evil*

MICAH

Late Bronze-Age necklace reconstructed from beads recovered from Lachish.

INTRODUCTION TO

MICAH

Circumstances of Writing

Micah's hometown of Moresheth-gath (Mc 1:1,14) in the lowlands of Judah was about twenty-five miles southwest of Jerusalem. The fact that his hometown is mentioned probably means that Micah ministered elsewhere, including Jerusalem, and since no genealogy is given we can probably assume that his family was not prominent. Micah was a skilled orator, a master of metaphors with a genius for wordplay and blunt, vivid imagery. Few prophets saw the future more clearly. Micah prophesied the fall of Samaria (1:5–9), Jerusalem's destruction (1:1–16; 3:12), the Babylonian captivity and return from exile (4:6–10), as well as the birth of God's future Davidic ruler in Bethlehem (5:2).

Micah's ministry probably began late in Jotham's reign and ended early in Hezekiah's, dating between 730 and 690 BC. His reference to the future judgment of Samaria (1:6) shows that his ministry began sometime before 722 BC. As such, Micah's ministry overlapped Isaiah's. The elders in Jeremiah's day remembered Micah's prophecy as having spurred Hezekiah's religious reform (Jr 26:17–19).

Both Israel and Judah experienced affluence and material prosperity in the late eighth century BC. In the south, King Uzziah's military victories brought wealth for some. A wealthy merchant class developed, and many poorer farmers found themselves at the mercy of government-supported businessmen. As business dealings became more corrupt, God's prophets spoke to the nation, confronting the ill-gotten wealth and accompanying godlessness. Amos and Hosea prophesied in the northern kingdom of Israel, and Isaiah and Micah prophesied in Judah to the south.

Judah's commercial and secular culture replaced God's covenant ideal. The rich became wealthy at the expense of the poor. The growing affluence in Micah's day led to increasing callousness toward the weak (Mc 2:1–2) and a blatant disregard for God's foundational laws (6:10–12). Judges and lawmakers became involved in conspiracy, bribery, and other corruption (3:1–3,9–11; 7:3). Religious leaders were concerned more about making money than teaching God's Word (3:11). The wealthy learned to separate their worship from everyday practice.

At this time, the ancient Near East experienced an international power shift. Assyria was ascending, becoming one of the most evil, bloodthirsty, manipulative, and arrogant empires of the ancient world. Four Assyrian kings made military inroads into Israel during Micah's ministry, taking Samaria in 722 BC and making Israel an Assyrian province. In 701 BC, Sennacherib took forty-six Judean towns and villages and besieged Jerusalem. King Hezekiah had allied with Egypt and Babylon against Assyria, for which both Micah and Isaiah urged him to repent. God miraculously spared Jerusalem (2Kg 19:35–36; 2Ch 32:22–23; Is 37:36–37); according to Micah, the Jerusalem siege was both an act of God's judgment and an occasion for God's deliverance.

Judah never learned its lesson. The people wavered between faith and apostasy and suffered many crises. As the rulers proved increasingly unfaithful, Micah prophesied Judah's destruction and exile by the Babylonians (586 BC). Beyond that, however, he saw a future restoration for a remnant of the people (539 BC).

Contribution to the Bible

Micah's holy and just God demands holiness and justice from all people. This is the "good" he requires (Mc 6:8). The people had grown content with going through the religious motions while practicing very little genuine spiritual devotion. Even the religious leaders chose to speak popular messages in order to support their standard of living. Micah preached that true religion comes from a heart tuned to God, resulting in godly living. As such, religion and ethics are inseparable. People who refuse to repent will face his judgment, but the faithful will find his salvation and be led by God's King, who would usher in his peace and prosperity.

Structure

Structured thematically as a balanced chiasm, the book highlights the central and final sections. Each matching section reflects on the other. This literary structure emphasizes Micah's main themes of Judah's social sins, the moral failure of its leadership, and the establishment of God's kingship over the land.

1 The word of the LORD that came to Micah the Moreshite — what he saw regarding Samaria and Jerusalem in the days of Jotham, Ahaz, and Hezekiah, kings of Judah.

COMING JUDGMENT ON ISRAEL

2 Listen, all you peoples;
pay attention, earth[A] and everyone in it!
The Lord GOD will be a witness against you,
the Lord, from his holy temple.
3 Look, the LORD is leaving his place
and coming down to trample
the heights[B] of the earth.
4 The mountains will melt beneath him,
and the valleys will split apart,
like wax near a fire,
like water cascading down a mountainside.
5 All this will happen because of
Jacob's rebellion
and the sins of the house of Israel.
What is the rebellion of Jacob?
Isn't it Samaria?
And what is the high place of Judah?
Isn't it Jerusalem?
6 Therefore, I will make Samaria
a heap of ruins in the countryside,
a planting area for a vineyard.
I will roll her stones into the valley
and expose her foundations.
7 All her carved images will be smashed
to pieces;
all her wages will be burned in the fire,
and I will destroy all her idols.
Since she collected the wages
of a prostitute,
they will be used again for a prostitute.

MICAH'S LAMENT

8 Because of this I will lament and wail;
I will walk barefoot and naked.
I will howl like the jackals
and mourn like ostriches.[C]
9 For her wound is incurable
and has reached even Judah;
it has approached my people's city gate,
as far as Jerusalem.

10 Don't announce it in Gath,
don't weep at all.
Roll in the dust in Beth-leaphrah.
11 Depart in shameful nakedness,
you residents of Shaphir;
the residents of Zaanan will not come out.
Beth-ezel is lamenting;
its support[D] is taken from you.
12 Though the residents of Maroth
anxiously wait for something good,
disaster has come from the LORD
to the gate of Jerusalem.
13 Harness the horses to the chariot,
you residents of Lachish.
This was the beginning of sin
for Daughter Zion
because Israel's acts of rebellion can be traced
to you.
14 Therefore, send farewell gifts
to Moresheth-gath;
the houses of Achzib are a deception
to the kings of Israel.
15 I will again bring a conqueror
against you who live in Mareshah.
The nobility[E] of Israel will come
to Adullam.
16 Shave yourselves bald and cut off your hair
in sorrow for your precious children;
make yourselves as bald as an eagle,
for they have been taken from you
into exile.

OPPRESSORS JUDGED

2 Woe to those who dream up wickedness
and prepare evil plans on their beds!
At morning light they accomplish it
because the power is in their hands.
2 They covet fields and seize them;
they also take houses.
They deprive a man of his home,
a person of his inheritance.

3 Therefore, the LORD says:
I am now planning a disaster
against this nation;
you cannot free your necks from it.
Then you will not walk so proudly
because it will be an evil time.
4 In that day one will take up a taunt
against you
and lament mournfully, saying,
"We are totally ruined!
He measures out the allotted land
of my people.
How he removes it from me!
He allots our fields to traitors."
5 Therefore, there will be no one
in the assembly of the LORD
to divide the land by casting lots.[F]

[A] **1:2** Or *land* [B] **1:3** Or *high places* [C] **1:8** Or *eagle owls*; lit *daughters of the desert* [D] **1:11** Lit *its standing place*; Hb obscure [E] **1:15** Lit *glory* [F] **2:5** Lit *LORD stretching the measuring line by lot*

Lachish

by Joel F. Drinkard Jr.

Partial remains of the palace-fortress atop Lachish, which fell to the Babylonians in 586 BC. King Sennacherib had earlier laid siege to and conquered Lachish in 701 BC. Warning of the coming Assyrian invasion, Micah said the residents of Lachish would need riding steeds to power chariots for a fast getaway (Mc 1:13).

Lachish (Tel Lachish, Tell ed-Duweir) was one of the major cities in Judah, located about thirty miles southwest of Jerusalem in the Shephelah, the foothills of the Judean mountains. Lachish is located along the Via Maris, the primary international roadway leading from Egypt through Canaan/Israel up to Syria and Mesopotamia. At more than thirty acres in size, the site is the largest tell in the region. The tell is surrounded on three sides by the Nahal Lachish, providing significant natural defense. Both its size and location made Lachish the logical choice to guard that portion of the Via Maris as well as access up into Judah. It also served to guard the border between Philistia and Judah.

A GROWING CITY

The Canaanites built the first major city on the site in the Middle Bronze Age (ca 2000–1550 BC). That Canaanite city had a strong defensive wall, a palace, and a temple/sanctuary. A supportive embankment, known as a *glacis*, surrounded the walls (and largely gave the site the slope it currently has). A rock-hewn *fosse*, which is a ditch or moat used in fortifications, was found on the west side of the tell at the bottom of the glacis. The large palace was probably the ruler's residence. Since most of this palace lies under the Judean palace-fortress, excavations are incomplete. Artifacts dating to the Middle Bronze Age that were found at the site give evidence of a strong Egyptian influence in Lachish during this era. The city was destroyed, however, at the end of the Middle Bronze Age. The Late Bronze city of Lachish may have been the largest in Canaan after Hazor was destroyed in the thirteenth century BC. The presence of buildings on the edge of the mound as well as a temple in the fosse/moat indicate that the Late Bronze city was unfortified.

The Israelites captured and destroyed the Late Bronze city at the time of Joshua (Jos 10:31–32). It was part of Judah's tribal territory (15:39). According to 2 Chronicles 11:9, Lachish was one of the fortified cities Rehoboam rebuilt. Lachish had on its acropolis a large palace that probably served as the residence of the governor. It was one of the most important fortified cities of Judah during the monarchy, second in size and importance only to Jerusalem itself. The city is mentioned again in connection with the plot against Amaziah, king of Judah, in 2 Kings 14:19 and 2 Chronicles 25:27. Some unnamed people in Jerusalem plotted the assassination of Amaziah. He learned of the plot and fled to Lachish, perhaps because it was such a strongly fortified city. Nevertheless, the ones plotting against him had allies in Lachish, and Amaziah was assassinated there.

Lachish had a striking feature of a double-wall system protecting it. Whereas other fortified cities in Israel and Judah were protected by a single wall system with a glacis or dry moat adding further protection, Lachish had a nineteen-foot-thick inner wall along with a revetment wall about halfway down the slope of the tell. This second wall prevented erosion. A sloping glacis ran from the inner wall down to the revetment wall. Both wall structures had stone foundations and mud-brick superstructures. In times of enemy attack, defenders could be stationed along both the inner and outer walls. The city also had a double-gate structure. The road to the city followed along the city's outer wall, exposing anyone attacking the city to defenders on the wall. Massive towers protected the outer gate. From the outer gate, persons entering the city came into a courtyard, made a right angle turn and came to the inner gate, a six-chamber gate that was among the largest found in Syria-Palestine (eighty-two feet by eighty-two feet). The reliefs recovered from Sennacherib's throne room that depict the siege of Lachish clearly show the double-wall structure.

The major building complex inside the city itself was the palace-fortress. This structure was built on a raised platform producing a kind of acropolis. A massive wall connected the palace with the city wall. The palace-fortress complex was in effect an inner fortress. The palace-fortress at the time of the Assyrian invasion was approximately 120 feet by 250 feet in size. It included a large courtyard, two building complexes that have been described either as stables or warehouses, and the palace complex proper. Probably the city served as a military and administrative center and perhaps housed a chariot unit at the time. Micah 1:13 refers to the horses and chariots of Lachish, supporting this possibility. As such, both warehouse and stable complexes likely would have been present in the inner structure.

The city played an important role during the Assyrian campaign against Judah in 701 BC. Apparently, in 701 BC Assyria's King Sennacherib set up his headquarters near Lachish. The city became the focal point in a series of reliefs that later decorated Sennacherib's throne

Amarna letter from Shipti-Ba'al of Lachish to the Egyptian pharaoh.

room in his capital city of Nineveh. Remains of the massive siege ramp built against the wall have been excavated on the southwest of the mound. The Assyrian ramp was more than 230 feet wide and 165 feet long. This siege ramp reached the outer revetment wall and allowed the Assyrians to bring their battering rams and siege instruments directly against the wall. The archaeological evidence shows that the defenders in the city built a counter ramp inside the wall as the Assyrians built the ramp outside the wall. The counter ramp was actually several yards taller than the main city wall and provided a higher defensive line inside the main city wall. This counter ramp also kept the Assyrians from scaling the wall. Nevertheless, the efforts proved futile, and Lachish fell to Sennacherib's forces. Numerous arrowheads and other weapons and armor were recovered from the ruins surrounding the area of the ramps. Second Kings 18–19 describes the Assyrian invasion of 701 BC. Although Lachish fell to Sennacherib, 2 Kings 19 records that Jerusalem was not taken at that time. Sennacherib's accounts of the campaign also agree that Lachish fell, but Jerusalem was not taken. He reported concerning Hezekiah, "He himself I locked up within Jerusalem, his royal city, like a bird in a cage." The Old Testament records that Hezekiah paid a tribute of thirty talents of gold and three hundred talents of silver to Sennacherib (2Kg 18:14). Sennacherib bragged, however, of Hezekiah paying a larger tribute to end the invasion: thirty talents of gold, eight hundred talents of silver, precious stones,

Two ostraca letters found at Lachish describing the situation just before Nebuchadnezzar's destruction of Jerusalem.

furniture, musicians, concubines, and much more.

POSTINVASION LACHISH

Lachish was rebuilt after it fell to the Assyrians, but as a much less well-fortified city. The palace-fortress remained in ruins. Based on the archaeological remains, Lachish never regained the power or wealth it had previously. Nevertheless, it remained a major fortified city of Judah along Judah's southwestern flank.

Slightly more than one hundred years later, Lachish was again the site of a major siege by a Mesopotamian power, this time the Babylonians under Nebuchadnezzar. The prophet Jeremiah recorded an oracle against Zedekiah dated to the last stages of the Babylonian siege against Lachish. Nebuchadnezzar had laid siege against Jerusalem. The Egyptian army approached Jerusalem, hoping to offer the city its aid. Nebuchadnezzar moved his army, which was besieging Jerusalem, to face off the Egyptians—who quickly returned to Egypt. The Babylonians' siege of Jerusalem resumed immediately (Jr 37:5–11). Jeremiah mentioned that at that time only Lachish and Azekah remained of the fortified cities of Judah (in addition to Jerusalem, see 34:7). An ostracon excavated in the gate area of Lachish gives a poignant glimpse of the final days: "And he knows that concerning the fire signals of Lachish, we are watching them according to all the signs which my lord gave. Indeed, we do not see Azekah." This report sent to Lachish probably from an outpost between Lachish and Azekah may well record the situation just after Jeremiah's oracle. If so, the report indicates that Azekah had fallen, and only Lachish and Jerusalem remained. And within just days or weeks Lachish fell and lastly Jerusalem.

Lachish is mentioned again only in Nehemiah 11:30 as one of the cities of Judah inhabited by those returning from exile in Babylon. It had a palace and a sanctuary, the Solar Shrine, during the Persian period and into the Hellenistic period. The site was abandoned after the Hellenistic period and was never rebuilt. ✣

GOD'S WORD REJECTED

6 "Quit your preaching," they[A] preach.
"They should not preach these things;
shame will not overtake us."[B]
7 House of Jacob, should it be asked,
"Is the Spirit of the LORD impatient?
Are these the things he does?"
Don't my words bring good
to the one who walks uprightly?
8 But recently my people have risen up
like an enemy:
You strip off the splendid robe
from those who are
passing through confidently,
like those returning from war.
9 You force the women of my people
out of their comfortable homes,
and you take my blessing[C]
from their children forever.
10 Get up and leave,
for this is not your place of rest
because defilement brings destruction —
a grievous destruction!
11 If a man comes
and utters empty lies —
"I will preach to you about wine and beer" —
he would be just the preacher for this people!

THE REMNANT REGATHERED

12 I will indeed gather all of you, Jacob;
I will collect the remnant of Israel.
I will bring them together like sheep
in a pen,
like a flock in the middle of its pasture.
It will be noisy with people.
13 One who breaks open the way
will advance before them;
they will break out, pass through the city gate,
and leave by it.
Their King will pass through before them,
the LORD as their leader.

UNJUST LEADERS JUDGED

3 Then I said, "Now listen, leaders of Jacob,
you rulers of the house of Israel.
Aren't you supposed to know what is just?
2 You hate good and love evil.
You tear off people's skin
and strip their flesh from their bones.
3 You eat the flesh of my people
after you strip their skin from them
and break their bones.
You chop them up
like flesh for the cooking pot,
like meat in a cauldron."
4 Then they will cry out to the LORD,
but he will not answer them.
He will hide his face from them at that time
because of the crimes they have committed.

FALSE PROPHETS JUDGED

5 This is what the LORD says
concerning the prophets
who lead my people astray,
who proclaim peace
when they have food to sink
their teeth into
but declare war against the one
who puts nothing in their mouths.
6 Therefore, it will be night for you —
without visions;
it will grow dark for you —
without divination.
The sun will set on these prophets,
and the daylight will turn black over them.
7 Then the seers will be ashamed
and the diviners disappointed.
They will all cover their mouths[D]
because there will be no answer
from God.

8 As for me, however, I am filled with power
by the Spirit of the LORD,
with justice and courage,
to proclaim to Jacob his rebellion
and to Israel his sin.

ZION'S DESTRUCTION

9 Listen to this, leaders of the house
of Jacob,
you rulers of the house of Israel,
who abhor justice
and pervert everything that is right,
10 who build Zion with bloodshed
and Jerusalem with injustice.
11 Her leaders issue rulings for a bribe,
her priests teach for payment,
and her prophets practice divination
for silver.
Yet they lean on the LORD, saying,
"Isn't the LORD among us?
No disaster will overtake us."
12 Therefore, because of you,
Zion will be plowed like a field,
Jerusalem will become ruins,
and the temple's mountain
will be a high thicket.

[A]**2:6** = the prophets [B]**2:6** Text emended; MT reads *things. Shame will not depart* [C]**2:9** Perhaps the land [D]**3:7** Lit *mustache*

THE LORD'S RULE FROM RESTORED ZION

4 In the last days
the mountain of the LORD's house
will be established
at the top of the mountains
and will be raised above the hills.
Peoples will stream to it,
2 and many nations will come and say,
"Come, let's go up to the mountain
of the LORD,
to the house of the God of Jacob.
He will teach us about his ways
so we may walk in his paths."
For instruction will go out of Zion
and the word of the LORD from Jerusalem.
3 He will settle disputes among many peoples
and provide arbitration for strong nations
that are far away.
They will beat their swords into plows
and their spears into pruning knives.
Nation will not take up the sword
against nation,
and they will never again train for war.
4 But each person will sit under his grapevine
and under his fig tree
with no one to frighten him.
For the mouth of the LORD of Armies
has spoken.
5 Though all the peoples walk
in the name of their own gods,
we will walk in the name of the
LORD our God
forever and ever.

6 On that day —
this is the LORD's declaration —
I will assemble the lame
and gather the scattered,
those I have injured.
7 I will make the lame into a remnant,
those far removed into a strong nation.
Then the LORD will reign over them
in Mount Zion
from this time on and forever.
8 And you, watchtower for the flock,
fortified hill[A] of Daughter Zion,
the former rule will come to you;
sovereignty will come to Daughter Jerusalem.

FROM EXILE TO VICTORY

9 Now, why are you shouting loudly?
Is there no king with you?
Has your counselor perished
so that anguish grips you like a woman
in labor?
10 Writhe and cry out,[B] Daughter Zion,
like a woman in labor,
for now you will leave the city
and camp in the open fields.
You will go to Babylon;
there you will be rescued;
there the LORD will redeem you
from the grasp of your enemies!
11 Many nations have now assembled
against you;
they say, "Let her be defiled,
and let us feast our eyes on Zion."
12 But they do not know the LORD's intentions
or understand his plan,
that he has gathered them
like sheaves to the threshing floor.
13 Rise and thresh, Daughter Zion,
for I will make your horns iron
and your hooves bronze
so you can crush many peoples.
Then you[C] will set apart their plunder
for the LORD,
their wealth for the Lord of the whole earth.

FROM DEFEATED RULER TO CONQUERING KING

5 Now, daughter who is under attack,
you slash yourself in grief;
a siege is set against us!
They are striking the judge of Israel
on the cheek with a rod.
2 Bethlehem Ephrathah,
you are small among the clans of Judah;
one will come from you
to be ruler over Israel for me.
His origin[D] is from antiquity,
from ancient times.
3 Therefore, Israel will be abandoned
until the time
when she who is in labor has given birth;
then the rest of the ruler's brothers will return
to the people of Israel.
4 He will stand and shepherd them
in the strength of the LORD,
in the majestic name of the LORD his God.
They will live securely,
for then his greatness will extend
to the ends of the earth.
5 He will be their peace.
When Assyria invades our land,
when it marches against our fortresses,
we will raise against it seven shepherds,
even eight leaders of men.

[A] **4:8** Or *flock, Ophel* [B] **4:10** Hb obscure [C] **4:13** LXX, Syr, Tg; MT reads *I* [D] **5:2** Lit *His going out*

"Zion" as a Place and a Symbol

by Robert C. Dunston

LOCATION AND IMPORTANCE

Between the Kidron Valley and the Tyropoean Valley in Jerusalem lies a plateau shaped like an elongated triangle. The Gihon spring lies on the plateau's eastern side. The plateau's steep slope and the close supply of fresh water provided a good location for a settlement and a fortress. Realizing the good location, the Jebusites constructed on the plateau a fortress they called Zion.[1]

Bible scholars have offered several suggestions for the derivation of the name Zion. Some believe the name comes from a Hebrew word meaning "to be dry." Zion would then refer to the relative dryness of the area despite its proximity to the Gihon spring. Others, noting the closeness of the Gihon spring, suggest Zion derives from a Hurrian word meaning "brook" or "river." Still others posit a derivation from an Arabic word meaning "hillcrest" or "ridge." Any of these root words could have provided the name.[2]

The first biblical mention of Zion occurs in 2 Samuel 5:6–9. As David and his private army prepared to attack the Jebusite city of Jerusalem, the inhabitants mocked them, believing their fortress was impregnable. By a clever strategy, David and his troops conquered the city and the stronghold of Zion.

Bronze coin from Jerusalelm, AD 66–70, with Hebrew inscription "to the redemption of Zion."

The 2 Samuel text seems to use the terms *Jerusalem* and *Zion* interchangeably.[3] David moved into the fortress and strengthened its fortifications. Thereafter, the city was called the city of David.

After capturing Jerusalem, David moved the ark of the covenant into the city (6:17), making Jerusalem his religious and political capital. David's military victories brought neighboring nations under his control. As part of recognizing David's sovereignty over them, he forced the conquered nations to recognize God's sovereignty and bring God tribute (8:1–12). David's rule over all Israel gave credibility to Israel's belief that God ruled all people. Israel's belief and teachings regarding God's sovereignty in turn provided David's empire with legitimacy and made Zion/Jerusalem the seat of David's and God's rule.[4]

Following David's death, his son Solomon extended the city northward and constructed a temple for God and a palace for himself. Solomon brought the ark of the covenant from Zion into the new temple (1Kg 8:1–6) and in a beautiful prayer dedicated the temple to God (vv. 23–53). Although Solomon acknowledged the temple could not contain God, he asked God to be present in the temple, and Zion became known as the place where God dwelled (Is 8:18).[5]

Following the building of the temple, Israel's worship centered in Jerusalem. The name Zion or Mount Zion came to refer to the temple (Ps 20:2) and to the entire city (2Kg 19:31; Ps 51:18). Although a specific place, Zion also became a symbol of God's presence and rule.[6] God had chosen Zion (Ps 132:13) and chosen to dwell there (74:2). From Zion the king ruled (2:6; 110:2) as God's representative—dispensing his justice and righteousness. From Zion God blessed his people (134:3).

SYMBOLIC MEANINGS

As Israel's capital city, Jerusalem came to represent the inhabitants of the city (Is 3:8; 51:17) and, by extension, the people of the entire nation. As a synonym for Jerusalem, Zion or "Daughter Zion" also referred to the inhabitants of the capital city (Ps 147:12; Is 52:2) and the nation as a whole (1:27).[7]

Following the division of Israel into the northern kingdom of Israel and the southern kingdom of Judah after Solomon's death, the prophets often spoke of Jerusalem's and Zion's rebellion as representative of the nation's sin. Isaiah said that sin caused both Jerusalem and Judah to stumble (3:8). Micah singled out the inhabitants of Jerusalem as the greatest example of Judah's sin (Mc 1:5). Amos, another eighth-century prophet, compared the sin of the people of Zion with the sin of the citizens of Samaria (Am 6:1).

The word *Zion* occurs forty-seven times in Isaiah and nine times in Micah. The only other Old Testament book that uses *Zion* so frequently is Psalms (thirty-eight times). Thus Isaiah and Micah provide excellent examples of Zion as both a place and an important symbol in Judah's theological tradition.

Like other prophets, Isaiah and Micah prophesied God's judgment on Zion and Judah as a result of their sin (Mc 1:13; 3:9–12). Although Zion would not fall to Assyria (Is 10:24–26), the city would eventually experience conquest and destruction. Many nations would come against Zion (29:8). Eventually Babylon would carry some of the people into exile (Mc 4:10). Conquest would turn Zion into a wilderness resembling plowed fields, ruins, and thickets rather than a once-great city (Is 64:10; Mc 3:12). Zion would be abandoned (Is 1:8) and feel abandoned by God (49:14).

Yet God's final word would not be judgment. Despite the destruction, God would preserve a

Village of Silwan (ancient Siloam) near the old city of David.

remnant from Zion (Is 37:32). God would comfort his people (51:3) and restore them through his justice and righteousness (1:27). He would bring justice and salvation to Zion (46:13) and cleanse and sanctify his city (4:3–6). From Babylon exiles would return with joy (35:10; 51:11) and then God would return to Zion, his dwelling, and once again embrace his people (51:16; 52:8). The inhabitants of Zion would join together praising God's renewed presence with them (12:6).

God's promise to restore his people came true when King Cyrus of Persia conquered Babylon and allowed exiles in Babylon from every nation to return home and rebuild their nations and temples. Many Judean exiles returned to Zion, but the conditions they found hardly matched the prophets' words. The people began to understand that many of the words Isaiah, Micah, and others had spoken regarding Zion's future did not refer to the rebuilding and restoration of an earthly Zion but to the creation of a heavenly Zion.

Someday God would lay a foundation stone in a new Zion (Is 28:16) and prepare a new, miraculous birth of his city and people (66:7–11). In the new Zion, mourning and tears would be distant memories and new life would replace despair (30:19; 61:3). God would reign from Zion (Is 24:23; Mc 4:7–8); Judah's enemies would come to Zion, recognizing the place as God's city and seeking to learn of and follow God (4:2). In this new heavenly Zion, God's kingdom would finally be realized in all its glory and righteousness.

Zion does not figure prominently in the New Testament, although writers connect Jesus to Zion and mention the heavenly Zion. Paul and Peter understood the cornerstone Isaiah had prophesied (Is 28:16) to be Jesus (1Pt 2:6), who would come from Zion to liberate his people (Rm 11:26). John and the author of Hebrews pointed toward the heavenly Zion as a place that, although hidden from physical sight, existed and from which God ruled (Heb 12:22; Rv 14:1).

As early as the fourth century AD, Christians referred to the southwest hill of Jerusalem as Zion rather than to Zion's original location. It was believed that the house in which the disciples gathered on Pentecost and from which the gospel first began to be preached lay on the southwest hill; this probably provides the best explanation for the transfer of Zion to the new location. For the early Christians, Zion was less a place than a symbol. God had sent his Messiah, Jesus Christ, who was building his kingdom, and would one day consummate the kingdom in a heavenly Zion.[8] ✣

[1] Lamontte M. Luker, "Zion" in *MDB*, 985. [2] W. Harold Mare, "Zion" in *ABD*, 6:1096; James Newell, "Zion" in *HIBD*, 1711. [3] Georg Fohrer, "Zion and Jerusalem in the OT" in *TDNT abridged ed.* (1985), 295. [4] J. J. M. Roberts, "Zion Tradition" in *IDBSup* (1976), 986. [5] G. A. Barrois, "Zion" in *IDB*, 4:959; Luker, "Zion," 985. [6] Luker, "Zion," 985–86; Mare, "Zion," 1096. [7] Elaine R. Follis, "Zion, Daughter of" in *ABD*, 6:1103. [8] Barrois, "Zion," 960; Luker, "Zion," 986.

6 They will shepherd the land of Assyria
with the sword,
the land of Nimrod with a drawn blade.[A]
So he will rescue us from Assyria
when it invades our land,
when it marches against our territory.

THE GLORIOUS AND PURIFIED REMNANT

7 Then the remnant of Jacob
will be among many peoples
like dew from the LORD,
like showers on the grass,
which do not wait for anyone
or linger for mankind.
8 Then the remnant of Jacob
will be among the nations,
among many peoples,
like a lion among animals of the forest,
like a young lion among flocks of sheep,
which tramples and tears as it passes through,
and there is no one to rescue them.
9 Your hand will be lifted up
against your adversaries,
and all your enemies will be destroyed.

10 In that day —
this is the LORD's declaration —
I will remove your horses from you
and wreck your chariots.
11 I will remove the cities of your land
and tear down all your fortresses.
12 I will remove sorceries from your hands,
and you will not have any more fortune-tellers.
13 I will remove your carved images
and sacred pillars from you
so that you will no longer worship
the work of your hands.
14 I will pull up the Asherah poles
from among you
and demolish your cities.[B]
15 I will take vengeance in anger and wrath
against the nations that have not obeyed me.

GOD'S LAWSUIT AGAINST JUDAH

6 Now listen to what the LORD is saying:
Rise, plead your case before the mountains,
and let the hills hear your complaint.[C]
2 Listen to the LORD's lawsuit,
you mountains and enduring foundations
of the earth,
because the LORD has a case against his people,
and he will argue it against Israel.
3 My people, what have I done to you,
or how have I wearied you?
Testify against me!
4 Indeed, I brought you up from the land
of Egypt
and redeemed you from that place of slavery.
I sent Moses, Aaron, and Miriam ahead of you.
5 My people,
remember what King
Balak of Moab proposed,
what Balaam son of Beor answered him,
and what happened from the Acacia Grove[D]
to Gilgal
so that you may acknowledge
the LORD's righteous acts.

6 What should I bring before the LORD
when I come to bow before God on high?
Should I come before him
with burnt offerings,
with year-old calves?
7 Would the LORD be pleased with thousands
of rams
or with ten thousand streams of oil?
Should I give my firstborn
for my transgression,
the offspring of my body for my own sin?

8 Mankind, he has told each of you what is good
and what it is the LORD requires of you:
to act justly,
to love faithfulness,
and to walk humbly with your God.

VERDICT OF JUDGMENT

9 The voice of the LORD calls out to the city[E]
(and it is wise to fear your name):
"Pay attention to the rod
and the one who ordained it.[F]
10 Are there still[G] the treasures of wickedness
and the accursed short measure
in the house of the wicked?
11 Can I excuse wicked scales
or bags of deceptive weights?
12 For the wealthy of the city are full of violence,
and its residents speak lies;
the tongues in their mouths are deceitful.

13 "As a result, I have begun to strike
you severely,[H]
bringing desolation because of your sins.
14 You will eat but not be satisfied,
for there will be hunger within you.

[A] **5:6** Aq, Vg; MT, Sym read *Nimrod at its gateways* [B] **5:14** Or *shrines*
[C] **6:1** Lit *voice* [D] **6:5** Or *from Shittim* [E] **6:9** = Jerusalem
[F] **6:9** Or *attention, you tribe. Who has ordained it?*; Hb obscure
[G] **6:10** Hb obscure [H] **6:13** LXX, Aq, Theod, Syr, Vg; MT reads *I have made you sick by striking you down*

Grapevines and Fig Trees

by Robert A. Street

The Old Testament mentions the grapevine (Hb *gephen*) fifty-five times. Isaiah 5 uses the analogy of a vineyard to refer to Israel. This vineyard was properly planted, cultivated, and protected but yielded sour grapes rather than good ones. As a result, the intent of the vineyard owner (the Lord) was to destroy the vineyard and start over. Knowing how much work and time was involved in establishing a vineyard, Micah's listeners were probably astonished at the prophet's words.

Getting an acceptable harvest from a vineyard could take years. Vines take "at least three years to become productive."[1] People ate the fruit fresh or dried as raisins or used its juice to make grape juice or wine. To keep the grapes from rotting, growers raised the vines from the ground on sticks or allowed them to grow along rock walls. The use of the trellis to support the vine did not occur until the Roman era.[2] The frequent mention of the vine with the fig tree suggests the vines were also allowed to climb on the tree for support.

Thirty-nine times the Old Testament mentions the fig and fig tree (Hb *tәʾēnâ*). Though fig trees come in numerous varieties, the most common is the *Ficus carica*. Growing to a height of ten to fifteen feet, the domesticated tree produces at least two crops per year—the winter figs maturing in May and June and the summer figs ripening in August and September.[3] Occasionally, in sheltered areas, a third crop of figs appears during the spring. An unusual feature of the fig tree is that the fruit appears before the leaves, which gives some understanding of Jesus's cursing the fig tree in Mark 11:12–14.[4]

The wild fig tree seldom produces many figs. To have a tree bear sufficient fruit required many years of annual efforts including pruning. People would eat the figs fresh or dried; they would press them into cakes for later use; they would crush the figs and use them as a spread for bread.

First Kings 4:25 referred to the reign of Solomon and described those days when "Judah and Israel lived in safety from Dan to Beer-sheba, each person under his own vine and his own fig tree." The importance of having a vine and a fig tree was known outside Israel as well. Rab-shakeh, an emissary of Assyria's King Sennacherib, used similar terminology when he spoke to warn the people of Jerusalem not to listen to Hezekiah but to submit to the Assyrian monarch (2Kg 18:31; Is 36:16). Rab-shakeh spoke of each person eating from his own vine and own fig tree and drinking from his own cistern.

Micah told of a time when the people would not be afraid, and each man would be able to sit under his own fig tree or under his own grapevine. Interestingly, during the same time of invasion and war with Assyria, the prophet Micah gave the message that peace and prosperity were to come—provided the people would trust God to deliver them from the oppressor. When Micah delivered God's message in the eighth century BC, he used the symbolism the people knew and understood and Rab-shakeh had used. The difference between Micah and the emissary of Sennacherib of Assyria was that Micah said to trust God, and Rab-shakeh said to trust Sennacherib.

Ancient Israel's economy was based on the land. Families depended on the produce of the earth for their livelihood. Working the fields and harvesting crops were vital to having the "good life." Only in times of peace was this possible. The only time that prosperity and security could exist was when the people were faithful to the Lord. Spiritual and economic richness went hand in hand. We have support that the peace and security of Micah's day lasted a long time, since neither the vine nor the fig tree produce much in a short time. The economic prosperity and peace of which Micah spoke were not limited to the rich but were for everyone, for each man would be sitting under his own fig tree or his own grapevine.

Other occurrences of the vine and fig tree are in Zechariah 3:10 and Habakkuk 3:17. Zechariah, like Micah, told of a time of expected peace in the future. Habakkuk 3:17–18 stands in contrast with the prosperity and peace imagery. Habakkuk indicated that in times when the fig tree does not blossom and the vine does not yield fruit, he would rejoice in the Lord. Whether the times are prosperous or not, surely Habakkuk and Micah would agree that God's people are to rejoice in the Lord and find joy in the God of salvation. ✣

---

[1] Delbert R. Hillers, *Micah*, in Hermeneia (Philadelphia: Fortress Press, (1984), 51. [2] Joseph F. Green, "Vines and Vineyards of the First Century," *The Sunday School Lesson Illustrator*, Winter 1978, 68. [3] Glenn McCoy, "The Fig Tree," *BI*, Summer 1985, 32. [4] See "Fig" in *Easton's Illustrated Dictionary*, https://www.wordsearchbible.com/products/12552-easton-s-illustrated-bible-dictionary

Roman drinking cup (AD 50–100) decorated with vine leaves and grapes.

What you acquire, you cannot save,
and what you do save,
I will give to the sword.[A]
15 You will sow but not reap;
you will press olives
but not anoint yourself with oil;
and you will tread grapes
but not drink the wine.
16 The statutes of Omri
and all the practices of Ahab's house
have been observed;
you have followed their policies.
Therefore, I will make you a desolate place
and the city's[B] residents an object
of contempt;[C]
you will bear the scorn of my people."[D]

ISRAEL'S MORAL DECLINE

7 How sad for me!
For I am like one who —
when the summer fruit has been gathered
after the gleaning of the grape harvest —
finds no grape cluster to eat,
no early fig, which I crave.
2 Faithful people have vanished
from the land;
there is no one upright among the people.
All of them wait in ambush
to shed blood;
they hunt each other with a net.
3 Both hands are good
at accomplishing evil:
the official and the judge demand a bribe;
when the powerful man communicates
his evil desire,
they plot it together.
4 The best of them is like a brier;
the most upright is worse than a hedge
of thorns.
The day of your watchmen,
the day of your punishment, is coming;
at this time their panic is here.
5 Do not rely on a friend;
don't trust in a close companion.
Seal your mouth
from the woman who lies in your arms.
6 Surely a son considers his father a fool,
a daughter opposes her mother,
and a daughter-in-law is
against her mother-in-law;
a man's enemies are the men
of his own household.
7 But I will look to the LORD;
I will wait for the God of my salvation.
My God will hear me.

ZION'S VINDICATION

8 Do not rejoice over me, my enemy!
Though I have fallen, I will stand up;
though I sit in darkness,
the LORD will be my light.
9 Because I have sinned against him,
I must endure the LORD's fury
until he champions my cause
and establishes justice for me.
He will bring me into the light;
I will see his salvation.[E]
10 Then my enemy will see,
and she will be covered with shame,
the one who said to me,
"Where is the LORD your God?"
My eyes will look at her in triumph;
at that time she will be trampled
like mud in the streets.

11 A day will come for rebuilding your walls;
on that day your boundary will be extended.
12 On that day people will come to you
from Assyria and the cities of Egypt,
even from Egypt to the Euphrates River
and from sea to sea
and mountain to mountain.
13 Then the earth will become a wasteland
because of its inhabitants
and as a result of their actions.

MICAH'S PRAYER ANSWERED

14 Shepherd your people with your staff,
the flock that is your possession.
They live alone in a woodland
surrounded by pastures.
Let them graze in Bashan and Gilead
as in ancient times.

15 I will perform miracles for them[F]
as in the days of your exodus
from the land of Egypt.
16 Nations will see and be ashamed
of[G] all their power.
They will put their hands over their mouths,
and their ears will become deaf.
17 They will lick the dust like a snake;
they will come trembling out of
their hiding places
like reptiles slithering on the ground.
They will tremble in the presence of the LORD
our God;
they will stand in awe of you.

[A] **6:14** Hb obscure [B] **6:16** Lit *and its* [C] **6:16** Lit *residents a hissing* [D] **6:16** LXX reads *of the peoples* [E] **7:9** Or *righteousness* [F] **7:15** = Israel [G] **7:16** Or *ashamed in spite of*

Political Climate for Micah

by R. Kelvin Moore

Micah dated his ministry during the reigns of Kings Jotham, Ahaz, and Hezekiah (Mc 1:1), who ruled from about 740 to 686 BC. Between 740 and 700 BC, the Assyrians (mentioned in 5:6; 7:12) invaded Israel repeatedly. Much of Micah's ministry dates before the destruction of Samaria (1:6) or 722 BC. Isaiah and Micah, contemporaries, both preached to the southern kingdom of Judah.

The rise and fall of the Assyrian Empire played a major role in Judah's economic prosperity and political stability in the eighth century BC. The death of King Shalmaneser III in 824 BC led to a period of decline for Assyria that lasted almost one hundred years. Judah benefited from the decline economically and politically. But the political climate changed during the reign of the Assyrian King Tiglath-pileser III (745–727 BC, called Pul in 2Kg 15:19), whose military and administrative policies led to the rise and dominance of the Assyrian Empire.[1] Tiglath-pileser had conquered all of northern Syria by 740 BC. His policies of aggression threatened other nations, including Judah and Israel.

Judah's political health in the time of Isaiah and Micah can be summarized in one word: crisis. Within an approximate thirty-five-year period, Isaiah and Micah ministered during three national crises, any of which could have led to Judah's destruction. Scholars refer to these as the Syro-Ephraimitic crisis (734 BC), when Israel and Judah lost their independence; the Ashdod Rebellion (711 BC), when Hezekiah was forced to pay Assyria a heavy fine; and the Sennacherib crisis (701 BC), resulting in deliverance but another heavy fine.

The Syro-Ephraimitic crisis[2] (Is 7:1ff) began as Israel's King Pekah and Syria's King Rezin recognized the danger posed by the rise of Assyria. Pekah and Rezin formed a military alliance against Assyria. Pekah and Rezin knew if they could coax Judah's King Ahaz to join the alliance, they would strengthen their armies. King Ahaz, though, refused to join. Pekah and Rezin invaded Judah. Simplicity marked Pekah and Rezin's plan: they intended to dethrone Ahaz and place a puppet king on the throne. Isaiah encouraged Ahaz to trust the Lord. Ahaz's response must have disappointed Isaiah and Micah. Instead of trusting God for protection, Ahaz requested assistance from Assyria! Tiglath-pileser III eagerly assisted Ahaz, but the aid did not come cheaply. To pay tribute, Ahaz depleted his treasuries and stripped the temple (2Kg 16:5–9,17–20). Additionally, Judah became an Assyrian vassal (2Ch 28:20–21).

Underground water system at Hazor built in the ninth century BC and in use until the Assyrians conquered Hazor in 732 BC.

Relief from Nimrud showing women prisoners leading camels captured by Tiglath-pileser III (744–727 BC).

Taylor Prism, a terra-cotta foundation document describing Sennacherib's campaigns, including his siege of Jerusalem in 701 BC.

Encouraged by the surging Egyptian Empire, several nations that had become vassals of Assyria organized a rebellion against Assyria's King Sargon II (722–705 BC). Bible scholars refer to this as the Ashdod Rebellion because the inhabitants of Ashdod spearheaded the insurrection. Sargon II, at the pinnacle of power, reacted with swift and lethal force that shattered the rebels. Little doubt exists that without another intervention of the Lord, had Judah chosen to participate in the Ashdod Rebellion the nation would have suffered the same disastrous fate.

In 704 BC, Sennacherib succeeded Sargon II. Evidently Judah's King Hezekiah believed that a new king on the Assyrian throne offered the best opportunity for rebellion. In what has become known as the Sennacherib crisis, Hezekiah led Judah to rebel against Assyria (2Kg 18:13–19:37; Is 36:1–37:38). Sennacherib marched toward Judah. Isaiah encouraged Hezekiah that, because

Bone arrowheads used at Lachish during Sennacherib's siege when iron became scarce.

the Assyrians had taunted God, Sennacherib would never capture Jerusalem (37:5–7). As Isaiah prophesied, 185,000 Assyrian soldiers perished in a single night. Sennacherib retreated. Although Sennacherib reigned for an additional twenty years, he never returned to Jerusalem.

Considering the political stability and economic prosperity of the latter half of the eighth century BC, one might expect spiritual conditions resembling a revival. Nothing could be further from the truth. Judah was in a state of spiritual decay. Worship was ritualistic, devoid of repentance and genuineness. The Hebrews severed their Sabbath worship from their weekly living. In essence, many of the Hebrews said, "I have sacrificed on the Sabbath and can live any way I choose during the week." The Hebrews evidently were "long on religion and short on morality."[3] Micah prophesied the destruction of Judah: "Zion will be plowed like a field, Jerusalem will become ruins, and the temple's mountain will be a high thicket" (Mc 3:12). With such religious insensitivity, little wonder that Judah, a little more than a hundred years after the prophets Isaiah and Micah, experienced God's displeasure. The Babylonians destroyed much of Judah and Jerusalem in 586 BC. ✣

---

[1] Daniel C. Browning Jr. and Brian Stachowski, "Assyria" in HIBD, rev. ed. (2015), 138–39. [2] Scholars so name this crisis because of Is 7:2: "And it was told the house of David [nation of Judah], saying, Syria is confederate with Ephraim" (KJV). "Syro" symbolized Syria and "Ephraim" symbolized Israel. Thus "Syro-Ephraimitic" symbolizes the combined forces of Syria and Israel. [3] Alec Motyer, *Isaiah: An Introduction and Commentary* (Downers Grove, IL: InterVarsity, 1999), 45. Motyer wrote that we can "pray on Sunday and prey on our neighbours for the rest of the week," 46.

18 Who is a God like you,
forgiving iniquity and passing
over rebellion
for the remnant of his inheritance?
He does not hold on to his anger forever
because he delights in faithful love.
19 He will again have compassion on us;
he will vanquish our iniquities.
You will cast all our[A] sins
into the depths of the sea.
20 You will show loyalty to Jacob
and faithful love to Abraham,
as you swore to our ancestors
from days long ago.

[A] **7:19** Some Hb mss, LXX, Syr, Vg; other Hb mss read *their*

NAHUM

Hypostyle Hall of Ramesses in Thebes, Egypt, conquered by Ashurbanipal in 663 BC.

INTRODUCTION TO

NAHUM

Circumstances of Writing

The presumed author, Nahum (Nah 1:1), is the only person with that name in the Old Testament. Like Jonah in the previous century, Nahum prophesied judgment upon Nineveh. The Ninevites in Jonah's time had repented (Jnh 3). But now that Nineveh's leaders had resumed their wicked actions, the Lord called Nahum to reaffirm his coming judgment. Ironically Nahum's Hebrew name means "comfort"—comfort for Judah (Nah 1:12–15) because its cruel overlord Assyria would be punished without any comforters (3:7). Except for the name of his hometown Elkosh (1:1), nothing certain is known about Nahum.

Two events circumscribe the earliest and latest possible dates for the composition of the book of Nahum: the capture and downfall of Thebes in about 663 BC and the announcements of Nineveh's certain destruction (1:1; 2:8; 3:7) which would happen in 612 BC. The book's emphasis on the fall of Thebes, seemingly a recent event, would favor a date shortly after 663 BC, during the reign of the notoriously wicked King Manasseh (ca 686–642 BC) and/or his evil son Amon (642–640 BC). Certainly Nahum 1:12 (Assyria was still "strong [at full strength] and numerous") suggests a time before the decline of that empire. This fits the reign of cruel Ashurbanipal (ca 668–627 BC) when Assyria was at the pinnacle of its power.

Contribution to the Bible

The book of Nahum provides a great view of a powerful, just God who maintains his absolute moral standards and offers hope to those who are despised and downtrodden. Nahum teaches us to trust God. Even when we despair of any help, we can know that God will stand with those who belong to him.

Structure

Nahum interweaved typical prophetic strands such as judgment songs against God's enemies (1:9–11,14; cf. 2:13; 3:5–7), a woe oracle or mock lament (3:1–7), salvation oracles for his people Judah (1:12–15), a victory hymn to Yahweh the divine warrior (1:2–8; see Ex 15; Ps 98), and a sarcastic "word vision" of imminent enemy invasion (Nah 2:1–10; see 3:2–3). He colored this literary tapestry with satirical "taunt songs" mocking Nineveh's soon-coming role reversal (2:11–12; 3:8–19; see 2:1–2; 3:4–5). He ridiculed Nineveh's practice of scattering of peoples to other nations by announcing that God's "scatterer" (2:1–2; 3:18–19) would pay her back in like manner. He taunted that her lion's lair of military booty would soon be looted (2:11–13). He also mocked her as a witch-prostitute condemned to appropriate punishment: nakedness exposed with shame (3:4–7).

Using psychological warfare (as the Assyrians had used against Judah), Nahum taunted Nineveh's dependence on allies and other supposed defenses (Nah 3:8–10; see Is 36:4–20). Esar-haddon, father of Ashurbanipal, had threatened King Manasseh of Judah in 672 BC with treaty curses from the gods if they rebelled. The Lord converted borrowed treaty terminology to reverse this curse on Judah. It would not be Judah but Assyria's military men who would become defenseless like women (Nah 3:13). The Assyrians' ravaging of the land like a swarming army of locusts (see Jl 1:4–12; 2:4–9) was evoked and modified to mock Nineveh's merchants and military personnel, comparing them to harmless locusts on a wall, easily frightened and scattered (Nah 3:15–18). The incurable disease threatened from their gods would boomerang and inflict Assyria instead (3:19).

Yahweh as the caring warrior who would bring vengeance on his enemies, especially Nineveh, to save Judah, forms the backbone of Nahum's purpose statement and also of the book's literary structure.

1 The pronouncement concerning Nineveh. The book of the vision of Nahum the Elkoshite.

GOD'S VENGEANCE

2 The LORD is a jealous and avenging God;
the LORD takes vengeance
and is fierce in[A] wrath.
The LORD takes vengeance against his foes;
he is furious with his enemies.
3 The LORD is slow to anger but great in power;
the LORD will never leave
the guilty unpunished.
His path is in the whirlwind and storm,
and clouds are the dust beneath his feet.
4 He rebukes the sea and dries it up,
and he makes all the rivers run dry.
Bashan and Carmel wither;
even the flower of Lebanon withers.
5 The mountains quake before him,
and the hills melt;
the earth trembles[B,C] at his presence —
the world and all who live in it.
6 Who can withstand his indignation?
Who can endure his burning anger?
His wrath is poured out like fire;
even rocks are shattered before him.

DESTRUCTION OF NINEVEH

7 The LORD is good,
a stronghold in a day of distress;
he cares for those who take refuge in him.
8 But he will completely destroy Nineveh[D]
with an overwhelming flood,
and he will chase his enemies into darkness.

9 Whatever you[E] plot against the LORD,
he will bring it to complete destruction;
oppression will not rise up a second time.
10 For they will be consumed
like entangled thorns,
like the drink of a drunkard
and like straw that is fully dry.[F]
11 One has gone out from you,[G]
who plots evil against the LORD,
and is a wicked counselor.

PROMISE OF JUDAH'S DELIVERANCE

12 This is what the LORD says:
Though they are strong[H] and numerous,
they will still be mowed down,
and he[I] will pass away.
Though I have punished you,[J]
I will punish you no longer.
13 For I will now break off his yoke from you
and tear off your shackles.

THE ASSYRIAN KING'S DEMISE

14 The LORD has issued an order concerning you:
There will be no offspring
to carry on your name.[K]
I will eliminate the carved idol
and cast image
from the house of your gods;
I will prepare your grave,
for you are contemptible.

15 Look to the mountains —
the feet of the herald,
who proclaims peace.
Celebrate your festivals, Judah;
fulfill your vows.
For the wicked one will never again
march through you;
he will be entirely wiped out.

ATTACK AGAINST NINEVEH

2 One who scatters is coming up against you.
Man the fortifications!
Watch the road!
Brace[L] yourself!
Summon all your strength!

2 For the LORD will restore the majesty
of Jacob,
yes,[M] the majesty of Israel,
though ravagers have ravaged them
and ruined their vine branches.

3 The shields of his[N] warriors
are dyed red;
the valiant men are dressed in scarlet.
The fittings of the chariot flash like fire
on the day of its battle preparations,
and the spears are brandished.
4 The chariots dash madly
through the streets;
they rush around in the plazas.
They look like torches;
they dart back and forth like lightning.
5 He gives orders to his officers;
they stumble as they advance.
They race to its wall;
the protective shield is set in place.
6 The river gates are opened,
and the palace erodes away.

[A] **1:2** Lit *is a master of* [B] **1:5** Some emend to *earth is laid waste* [C] **1:5** Lit *lifts* [D] **1:8** Lit *her place* [E] **1:9** = Nineveh [F] **1:10** Hb obscure [G] **1:11** Possibly Nineveh [H] **1:12** Lit *intact* [I] **1:12** Either the king of Assyria or his army [J] **1:12** = Judah [K] **1:14** Lit *It will not be sown from your name any longer* [L] **2:1** Lit *Strengthen* [M] **2:2** Or *like* [N] **2:3** = the army commander attacking Nineveh

7 Beauty[A] is stripped;[B]
she is carried away;
her ladies-in-waiting moan
like the sound of doves
and beat their breasts.
8 Nineveh has been like a pool of water
from her first days,[B]
but they are fleeing.
"Stop! Stop!" they cry,
but no one turns back.
9 "Plunder the silver! Plunder the gold!"
There is no end to the treasure,
an abundance of every precious thing.
10 Desolation, decimation, devastation!
Hearts melt,
knees tremble,
insides churn,
every face grows pale!

11 Where is the lions' lair,
or the feeding ground of the young lions,
where the lion and lioness prowled,
and the lion's cub,
with nothing to frighten them away?
12 The lion mauled whatever its cubs needed
and strangled prey for its lionesses.
It filled up its dens with the kill,
and its lairs with mauled prey.
13 Beware, I am against you.
This is the declaration of the LORD
of Armies.
I will make your chariots go up
in smoke,[C]
and the sword will devour
your young lions.
I will cut off your prey from the earth,
and the sound of your messengers
will never be heard again.

NINEVEH'S DOWNFALL

3 Woe to the city of blood,
totally deceitful,
full of plunder,
never without prey.
2 The crack of the whip
and rumble of the wheel,
galloping horse
and jolting chariot!
3 Charging horseman,
flashing sword,
shining spear;
heaps of slain,
mounds of corpses,
dead bodies without end —
they stumble over their dead.
4 Because of the continual prostitution
of the prostitute,
the attractive mistress of sorcery,
who treats nations and clans like merchandise
by her prostitution and sorcery,
5 I am against you.
This is the declaration of the LORD of Armies.
I will lift your skirts over your face
and display your nakedness to nations,
your shame to kingdoms.
6 I will throw filth on you
and treat you with contempt;
I will make a spectacle of you.
7 Then all who see you will recoil
from you, saying,
"Nineveh is devastated;
who will show sympathy to her?"
Where can I find anyone to comfort you?

8 Are you better than Thebes[D]
that sat along the Nile
with water surrounding her,
whose rampart was the sea,
the river[E,F] her wall?
9 Cush and Egypt were her endless source
of strength;
Put and Libya were among her[G] allies.
10 Yet she became an exile;
she went into captivity.
Her children were also dashed to pieces
at the head of every street.
They cast lots for her dignitaries,
and all her nobles were bound in chains.
11 You[H] also will become drunk;
you will hide.[I]
You also will seek refuge from the enemy.

12 All your fortresses are fig trees
with figs that ripened first;
when shaken, they fall —
right into the mouth of the eater!

13 Look, your troops are like women among you;
your land's city gates
are wide open to your enemies.
Fire will devour the bars of your gates.

14 Draw water for the siege;
strengthen your fortresses.
Step into the clay and tread the mortar;
take hold of the brick-mold!

[A]**2:7** Text emended; MT reads *Huzzab* [B]**2:7,8** Hb obscure [C]**2:13** Lit *will burn her chariots in smoke* [D]**3:8** Hb *No-amon* [E]**3:8** LXX, Syr, Vg read *water* [F]**3:8** Lit *sea from sea* [G]**3:9** Lit *your* [H]**3:11** = Nineveh [I]**3:11** Or *will be overcome*

Nahum's Historical Setting

by Robert A. Street

Unlike most of the prophetic books, Nahum does not mention any king of any country to help identify his historical context. Nahum says only he was an Elkoshite. Even the location of Elkosh is uncertain.[1]

Nahum's message is identified in Hebrew in 1:1 as *massa' Nineveh,* variously translated as "the pronouncement concerning Nineveh" (CSB), "an oracle concerning Nineveh" (ESV), "the burden of Nineveh" (KJV), among others. The reference to Nineveh is an excellent place to begin as we set Nahum in history. Nineveh, however, had a long history (see Gn 10:11). Nahum also refers to the fall of the Egyptian city of No-Amon, also known as Thebes (Nah 3:8).

Using this historical background, dating the book is not extremely difficult. The fall of Nineveh sets the latest date for the book, its *terminus ad quem*, which was 612 BC. The earliest date for the book, its *terminus a quo*, is the fall of Thebes to Ashurbanipal in 663 BC. Thus, the historical setting is between 663 and 612 BC. Gordon Johnston believes that Nahum can be dated after Ashurbanipal's last campaign in the west in 640 BC when he reasserted sovereignty over Judah and other Syro-Palestinian vassals, since 1:12,15 says that Assyria would not invade Judah again.[2]

ASSYRIAN DOMINANCE

The historical setting and background for Nahum was one of Assyrian (Ninevite) oppression, which actually began in the eighth century with Tiglath-pileser III (reigned 744–727 BC), who captured and controlled the Fertile Crescent from the Persian Gulf to Gaza. He actually aided Ahaz (735–715 BC) in defending Judah against the Syro-Ephraimitic alliance. A later Assyrian monarch, Esar-haddon (681–669 BC), invaded and conquered Upper Egypt in 671 BC. A few years later, Assyria's King Ashurbanipal (668–627 BC), son of Esar-haddon, destroyed Thebes in 663 BC. After conquering Thebes, Ashurbanipal, who was "the last strong king of Assyria,"[3] placed Psammetichus I (Psamtik) on the throne of Egypt. This was the same Psamtik who revolted against Assyrian control and gained independence in 654 BC. Perhaps the rebellion at home made it impossible for Ashurbanipal to deal harshly with Psammetichus. Shamash-shum-ukin, who was Ashurbanipal's brother and the king of Babylon (a subkingdom of Assyria at this time), formed an alliance with Elam and Arabia that sought to overthrow Ashurbanipal. The alliance did not accomplish its goal, even though it continued to fight

Ancient site of Nineveh, first excavated in the mid-1800s by the Englishman A. H. Layard. He unearthed Sennacherib's palace, and later excavations unearthed massive palaces belonging to Ashurbanipal and Esar-haddon.

Jezreel Valley as seen from Megiddo, where armies of Pharaoh Neco II defeated King Josiah and his soldiers at the Battle of Megiddo in 609 BC.

until about 648 BC and the death of Shamash-shum-ukin.

When the eight-year-old Josiah (2Kg 22:1) became Judah's king in 640 BC, Ashurbanipal had subdued the entire ancient Near East. During the latter years of Ashurbanipal's reign, the Assyrian Empire suffered from decay. Ashurbanipal became more interested in art and scholarship than in running his empire.

At Ashurbanipal's death in 627 BC, his son Ashur-etel-ilani (627–623 BC) ascended the throne. Coinciding with Ashurbanipal's death were rebellions by both the Babylonians under Nabopolassar in 626 BC and the Judean vassals. Furthermore, the Median Empire began its rise, as did the threat of the Scythians, from the area now known as the Steppes of Russia. All of these forces were more than the Assyrian Empire could bear. The Assyrian monarch Sin-shar-ishkun (reigned 623–612 BC) lost two chief Assyrian cities, Ashur in 614 and Nineveh in 612 BC.

This conflict impacted tiny Judah. Going back to 722 BC and the destruction of Samaria, Judah was really all that was left of the once proud Hebrew nation. The Judean kingdom existed mainly as a vassal state under Assyria's control until the death of Ashurbanipal.

KINGS OF JUDAH

A cursory examination of three kings of Judah during the years between the fall of Thebes and the fall of Nineveh can help us better understand Nahum's historical setting. The Judean monarch at the fall of Thebes was Manasseh, who was an idolatrous and evil ruler. He "shed so much innocent blood that he filled Jerusalem with it from one end to another" (2Kg 21:16). Second Chronicles adds that Manasseh repented in his later years, although 2 Kings does not mention this. Amon, Manasseh's son, reigned only two years before his servants assassinated him (2Kg 21:19–23). Following Amon's assassination, his eight-year-old son Josiah became king.

Josiah asserted political independence while the rebellion was taking place in the other countries following Ashurbanipal's death. Josiah's assertion of political and religious freedom was spurred on when workers discovered the book of law (probably parts of Deuteronomy) in 622 BC while rebuilding the temple.

Clay tablet, the Annals of Tiglath-pileser III (ruled 744–727 BC), recording details of building operations and military campaigns of Tiglath-pileser III. It mentions the kings of Ammon, Ashkelon, Edom, Gaza, Judah, Moab, and Tyre.

ASSYRIA'S DEMISE

The death throes of Assyria occurred under Ashur-uballit II. After Nineveh fell to the Medes and Babylonians in 612 BC, Assyria's King Ashur-uballit II retreated to Haran. The resistance continued; in 610, the Babylonians captured Haran. In 609 BC, Pharaoh Neco II marched to join forces with the Assyrians. At Megiddo, King Josiah met the Egyptian monarch, who was on his way to Haran. In the ensuing battle, Josiah died; his forces were defeated (2Ch 35:20–24). Josiah seems to have been supporting the rebels against Assyria. Jehoahaz, Josiah's son, was Judah's next king.

Jehoahaz served only three months before Neco replaced him with Jehoiakim (Eliakim), another of Josiah's sons. Neco took Jehoahaz captive to Riblah in Hamath and demanded tribute money, which Jehoiakim paid. Jehoahaz was later sent from Riblah to Egypt, where he died.

After Megiddo, Neco continued to Haran to help the Assyrians as they fought the Babylonians. His help, though, was of no avail; the Babylonians were victorious. Undeterred, Neco continued his campaigning on behalf of Assyria. In 605 BC, Neco and the Egyptians, along with the remnants of Assyria's army, suffered a crushing defeat at Carchemish at the hands of the Babylonians. With Assyria's defeat and Babylon's victory at Carchemish, Judah became subject (vassal) to Babylon's King Nebuchadnezzar.

The historical period of Nahum was evil both inside and outside of Judah. Not only did the Assyrians worship a multitude of gods, but also the people of Judah did not remain faithful to the Lord. Nahum offered hope to Judah and Jerusalem that the oppression would end and God would comfort his people. The enemy, symbolized by the city of Nineveh, would be utterly and totally destroyed. It was. ✣

---

[1] According to Pseudo-Epiphanius, the location was in southwest Judah near Begabar, modern Beit Jibrin. Jerome placed Elkosh at Hilkesi of Galilee (modern El-Kauzeh). The city of Capernaum ("village of Nahum") has been proposed but is unlikely. A location on the Tigris River at Alkush (Al-Qush, Alqosh) opposite of Nineveh was proposed in the sixteenth century. The tomb of Nahum is said to be at Alkush. [2] G. H. Johnston, "Nahum's Rhetorical Allusions to the Neo-Assyrian Lion Motif," *BSac* 158 (2001): 302. [3] Burlan A. Sizemore Jr., *The Centuries of Decline* (Nashville: Convention Press, 1970), 73.

Horses in Ancient Warfare

by Daniel P. Caldwell

Of all the domestic animals, the horse was one of the last to be tamed. This may be due to its size or perhaps its high-strung temperament, which would make it difficult to catch and tame. Nonetheless, the horse has a long and distinguished history. The advent of its use by people changed humankind forever.

EARLY USE AND DOMESTICATION

The people responsible for domesticating the horse were probably nomadic Aryan tribes. The animals grazed about the grasslands bordering the Caspian and Black Seas. The Aryan nomads possibly began as herders of a breed of partially wild but docile reindeer. Out of practical considerations, they later switched to horses. Unlike the reindeer, horses are not migratory animals. The reindeer's movement was dictated by the location of special foods on which they fed.[1]

Initially horses were herded for a variety of uses. Their flesh provided food, and their hides were used to make hut coverings and clothes. Since there were few trees in the grasslands, the manure could be dried to fuel their fires. Eventually the mares were even used to supply their herders with milk. In time, the herders used the less-spirited breeds to transport their personal property. The natural consequence thereafter was for the men to transport themselves by riding the horses, which made the task of herding, hunting, and migrating much simpler. It was only the beginning of people's use of the horse as a domestic animal.

Early horsemen generally rode the horses bareback and without bits (mouthpieces) and reins. Riders guided the horses by applying pressure with their knees and by leaning their bodies in the desired direction. To advance their means of transporting and riding the horse, later generations developed special items (called tack) to better control the animals. These included bridles made of bone and antlers and crude saddles without stirrups. Eventually horses were employed to pull small four-wheeled and two-wheeled carts. These devices served as the forerunners of early forms of military equipment.[2]

Aside from hunting, the single greatest use of the horse in ancient history was for combat. The introduction of the horse into battle changed warfare. It provided a swiftness and strength not seen before. The impact of its use was devastating for any foe.

Reconstruction of the bands from the Balawat Gates of the palace of Shalmaneser III (858–824 BC) outside Nineveh.

HORSES AND CHARIOTS IN BATTLE

The horse in war is seen in two different contexts. The first is driven in pairs or in a group of three to four while pulling a chariot. The chariot was the earliest means of transportation in combat. The earliest known chariots date to about 2500 BC. These early chariots were not the advanced two-wheeled devices seen in early art. They were actually four-wheeled carts with wheels made of solid wood. These simple chariots were both heavy and awkward to drive. Since they had no pivoting front axle, the cart would require a wide, skidding turn. Even though originally a team of oxen, donkeys, or wild asses pulled the chariot, the horse eventually became the animal of choice for speed and strength.

Basalt relief from Carchemish, dated 950–850 BC.

Around 1600 BC, a two-wheeled chariot was developed. This vehicle was lighter than its predecessor and much easier to maneuver. Because of its lighter weight, it also was faster and more versatile on the battlefield. This chariot was pulled by two or sometimes three horses.[3] Two men worked the typical chariot: one would be a bowman to fire at enemy forces, while the other would control the vehicle. Over time, chariots were developed that could carry up to five warriors. Some of these warriors were archers, and the others protected the archers and directed the chariots into battle. The greatest contribution of the horse-drawn chariot was the tactical mobility it provided to the archer. Tightly packed foot soldiers were the formation of choice in early battle. Offering the military commanders both control during the battle and mutual protection, a force of chariots could stand off at long range and rain arrows down on the enemies' heads. Because of the chariots' speed, any attempts for the enemies to attack head-on could be easily evaded. If, on the other hand, the foot soldiers spread out to minimize the damage from the enemy's arrows, they would lose the benefit of strength in numbers and the charioteers could easily overrun them. The power of the chariot as a device both of transportation and of battle became the central weapon of the peoples of the ancient Near East in the second millennium BC.[4]

HORSES AND THE CAVALRY

The second historical context in which we see horses is in a primitive form of cavalry. From as early as the second and third millennia BC, men rode horses into battle. Some of the earliest groups to fight effectively on horseback were the Hittites, Assyrians, Babylonians, and Hyksos. The latter group may have been responsible for introducing horses to Egypt. Egypt in turn would ultimately introduce the horse to Canaan.

The ancient rider warriors used two common weapons, spears and bows. While both were effective in dealing with the enemy, the more lethal method was the bow. The horse-archers could advance quickly on enemy foot soldiers but keep their distance while shooting the arrow. Many of these riders rode without reins to keep their hands free to shoot their bows. They later developed an attack and retreat method of combat. While maintaining a full gallop, they would ride within range of the enemy, release a volley of arrows, and then retreat. However, the retreat was simply a disguised means of continuing the attack on the unsuspecting enemy. One group of horse-archers, the Parthians, were so skilled that they were able to shoot as skillfully backward in retreat as they did forward in their attack.[5]

Horses ridden or driven in war not only gave a speed and strength advantage to the individual soldier but also served as a mobile command post. A commander of the army would not have this advantage at ground level. The height advantage enabled the rider or driver to view the battle more clearly and effectively lead his army in battle.

HORSES IN SCRIPTURE

Most biblical references to the horse are associated with military use. The most common Hebrew term for *horse* was *sus*. Depending on the context, the term could be interpreted to mean horse in general or a type of war horse.[6] Although the Scriptures offer a few references to horses prior to the monarchy period, the common use of the horse in Israel did not begin until the time of David and Solomon. Solomon was the first to use horses for military purposes in Israel.

The Old Testament portrays horses typically as the property of kings, not the common man. They were used for a variety of purposes. The horse provided an excellent means of transportation (horseback and by chariot) for royalty, aristocrats, and the wealthy. When Joseph interpreted Pharaoh's dream, Pharaoh honored Joseph by allowing him to ride in a chariot drawn by horses (Gn 41:43).[7]

A few passages mention the use of horses for other tasks. For instance, in the judgment oracle against Jerusalem, Isaiah 28:28 mentions horses being used for threshing grain. Many agree horses were far too valuable to use in such menial work. Thus the passage would be understood in a poetic fashion as Isaiah's attempt to describe the destructive action of an enemy.[8]

The Mosaic law also warned against possessing many horses for excessive pleasure and war (Dt 17:16), as did Samuel (1Sm 8). However, the supremacy of the horse in warfare caused the Israelites to ignore this law. This could be the reason why Solomon imported horses from Egypt (2Ch 1:16) and had thousands of stalls built to house them (1Kg 4:26; 2Ch 9:25). In the Assyrian writings of Sennacherib's conquests, horses are listed

Terra-cotta model of a mounted warrior with Assyrian shield. Seventh century BC; from Cyprus.

Bronze bit, likely produced by the Medes about 1800 BC.

among the spoils taken from the defeated nation of Judah.[9]

The domestication of the horse and its eventual use in combat has left a mark on civilization. However, in spite of how majestic and noble the horse is and in spite of how effective it may be in warfare, God reminds us that our ultimate trust is to be in him. The psalms and the prophets warned against trusting in horses rather than the Lord for victory:[10] "Some take pride in chariots, and others in horses, but we take pride in the name of the LORD our God" (Ps 20:7). ✣

---

[1] Elwyn Hartley Edwards, *The Encyclopedia of the Horse* (New York: DK Publishing, 1994), 28–29. [2] C. E. Crawford, "Horses and Horsemanship" in *The New Encyclopedia Britannica* (Chicago: Encyclopedia Britannica, 2002), 20:651. [3] G. R. Taylor, "Technology of War" in *The New Encyclopedia Britannica*, 29:535. [3] Taylor, "Technology of War." [4] Edwards, *Encyclopedia of the Horse*, 35. [5] F. J. Stendebach, "סוס" in *TDOT* (1999), 10:180. [6] For other references to horses being used for means of transportation, see 2Sm 15:1; 2Kg 5:9; 14:20. [7] John N. Oswalt, *The Book of Isaiah Chapters 1–39*, NICOT (1986), 523–24. For other passages supporting this poetic understanding, see Is 17:4–6; 27:12; 41:15–16. [8] James B. Pritchard, ed., *The Ancient Near East: An Anthology of Texts and Pictures* (Princeton: Princeton University Press, 1973), 1:200. [9] See Is 31:1; 36:8–10; Ezk 17:15.

15 The fire will devour you there;
the sword will cut you down.
It will devour you like the young locust.
Multiply yourselves like the young locust;
multiply like the swarming locust!
16 You have made your merchants
more numerous than the stars of the sky.
The young locust strips[A] the land
and flies away.
17 Your court officials are
like the swarming locust,
and your scribes like clouds of locusts,
which settle on the walls on a cold day;
when the sun rises, they take off,
and no one knows where they are.
18 King of Assyria,
your shepherds slumber;
your officers sleep.
Your people are scattered
across the mountains
with no one to gather
them together.
19 There is no remedy for your injury;
your wound is severe.
All who hear the news about you
will clap their hands because of you,
for who has not experienced
your constant cruelty?

[A]**3:16** Or *sheds its skin*

HABAKKUK

Mosaic scene from ancient Damascus depicts deer. The book of Habakkuk closes with the prophet affirming his confidence in God, "The LORD my Lord is my strength; he makes my feet like those of a deer and enables me to walk on mountain heights!" (Hab 3:19).

INTRODUCTION TO

HABAKKUK

Circumstances of Writing

Habakkuk is not mentioned anywhere else in the Bible. His name is thought to derive from the Hebrew word *chabaq*, "to embrace," but its form appears non-Hebraic. More likely, the name is related to *habbaququ*, a word found in the related Semitic language of Akkadian. It denotes a species of garden plant or fruit tree.

Habakkuk predicted the invasion of Judah by the Chaldeans (Hab 1:6). The term *Chaldean* (Hb *kasdim*; Akk *kaldu*) was originally used of an ethnic group that appeared in southern Babylonia in the ninth century BC. In the eighth century BC, Chaldeans began to rise to power in Babylon. By the time of Habakkuk, *Chaldean* had come to be a synonym for "Babylonian."

These world events came to affect Judah. Pharaoh Neco of Egypt passed through Israel in an attempt to support the remnant of the Assyrians in northern Syria against Babylon. The godly King Josiah confronted him at Megiddo but was killed by Neco in 609 BC. Judah then fell into the hands of Egypt from 609 to 605 BC.

Judah's fortunes changed again when Nebuchadnezzar II defeated Neco at the battle of Carchemish (May/June 605 BC) and succeeded his father on the throne of Babylon in September of that year. The Babylonian army pursued Neco back to Egypt. This led to Judah falling under control of the Babylonians by 604 BC.

Habakkuk predicted the Chaldean devastation of Judah (1:5–11), but that does not seem to have been fulfilled by the relatively bloodless Babylonian occupation in 604 BC. But when Jehoiakim, whom Neco had placed on Judah's throne in 609 BC, rebelled against Babylon in roughly 600 BC, Nebuchadnezzar eventually invaded the land and besieged Jerusalem from 598 to 597 BC. This led to Jehoiakim being deposed and killed in 598 and his son Jehoiachin going into Babylonian exile in 597. The last king of Judah, Zedekiah, brought even more devastation upon Judah by rebelling against Babylon in 588 BC. When Judah fell to the Babylonians in August of 587 or 586 BC, Nebuchadnezzar devastated Jerusalem and destroyed the temple. And yet as Habakkuk predicted (2:6–20), Babylon had its own day of reckoning in 539 BC when Cyrus of Persia conquered it.

These historical events help us to attach a date to the book of Habakkuk. Habakkuk probably wrote his prophecy during the time of trouble after the death of King Josiah of Judah in 609 BC but before the devastations of Judah in 598/597 BC and 587/586 BC by the Chaldeans. That places the prophecy during the reign of Jehoiakim (ca 609–599 BC), probably in the period of Egyptian domination before Babylon invaded Judah (609–605 BC).

Contribution to the Bible

The book of Habakkuk looks at an issue that often confronts people: trying to discern God's purposes in the midst of this world. There is a realization of the will of God for this world. This truth is seen throughout the Scripture: God's promises to Abraham; God's desire for us to have life abundantly; and God's will for a human community of joy, security, and righteousness. We ultimately triumph in the world and live abundantly only through faith. Habakkuk's message that the righteous will live by faith prepared the way for the greater understanding of this truth in the New Testament, which emphasizes salvation through faith in Christ (Rm 1:17; Gl 3:11; Heb 10:38–39).

Structure

The first two chapters consist of a dialogue between the prophet and God. Habakkuk first complained of injustice in Judah (Hab 1:2–4). God responded by announcing that he was sending the Chaldeans to punish Judah (1:5–11). Habakkuk then complained about God's answer, arguing that it seemed unfair for God to use the more wicked Babylonians to punish the less wicked Judeans (1:12–2:1). God responded that the Babylonians were indeed arrogant and would ultimately be punished; nonetheless, God would use the Babylonians just as he had determined (2:2–20). The final chapter consists of a psalm in which Habakkuk reflected on this dialogue with God.

1 The pronouncement that the prophet Habakkuk saw.

HABAKKUK'S FIRST PRAYER

2 How long, LORD, must I call for help
and you do not listen
or cry out to you about violence
and you do not save?
3 Why do you force me to look at injustice?
Why do you tolerate[A] wrongdoing?
Oppression and violence are right
in front of me.
Strife is ongoing, and conflict escalates.
4 This is why the law is ineffective
and justice never emerges.
For the wicked restrict the righteous;
therefore, justice comes out perverted.

GOD'S FIRST ANSWER

5 Look at the nations[B] and observe —
be utterly astounded!
For I am doing something in your days
that you will not believe
when you hear about it.
6 Look! I am raising up the Chaldeans,[C]
that bitter, impetuous nation
that marches across the earth's open spaces
to seize territories not its own.
7 They are fierce and terrifying;
their views of justice and sovereignty
stem from themselves.
8 Their horses are swifter than leopards
and more fierce[D] than wolves of the night.
Their horsemen charge ahead;
their horsemen come from distant lands.
They fly like eagles, swooping to devour.
9 All of them come to do violence;
their faces are set in determination.[E]
They gather prisoners like sand.
10 They mock kings,
and rulers are a joke to them.
They laugh at every fortress
and build siege ramps to capture it.
11 Then they sweep by like the wind
and pass through.
They are guilty;[F] their strength
is their god.

HABAKKUK'S SECOND PRAYER

12 Are you not from eternity,
LORD my God?
My Holy One, you[G] will not die.
LORD, you appointed them
to execute judgment;
my Rock, you destined them to punish us.
13 Your eyes are too pure to look on evil,
and you cannot tolerate wrongdoing.
So why do you tolerate those
who are treacherous?
Why are you silent
while one[H] who is wicked swallows up
one[I] who is more righteous than himself?
14 You have made mankind
like the fish of the sea,
like marine creatures that have no ruler.
15 The Chaldeans pull them all up
with a hook,
catch them in their dragnet,
and gather them in their fishing net;
that is why they are glad and rejoice.
16 That is why they sacrifice to their dragnet
and burn incense to their fishing net,
for by these things their portion is rich
and their food plentiful.
17 Will they therefore empty their net
and continually slaughter nations
without mercy?

HABAKKUK WAITS FOR GOD'S RESPONSE

2 I will stand at my guard post
and station myself on the lookout tower.
I will watch to see what he will say to me
and what I should[J] reply about my complaint.

GOD'S SECOND ANSWER

2 The LORD answered me:
Write down this vision;
clearly inscribe it on tablets
so one may easily read it.[K]
3 For the vision is yet for the appointed time;
it testifies about the end and will not lie.
Though it delays, wait for it,
since it will certainly come
and not be late.
4 Look, his ego is inflated;[E]
he is without integrity.
But the righteous one will live
by his faith.[L]
5 Moreover, wine[M] betrays;
an arrogant man is never at rest.[N]
He enlarges his appetite like Sheol,
and like Death he is never satisfied.
He gathers all the nations to himself;
he collects all the peoples for himself.

[A] **1:3** Lit *observe*, also in v. 13 [B] **1:5** DSS, LXX, Syr read *Look, you treacherous people* [C] **1:6** = the Babylonians [D] **1:8** Or *and quicker* [E] **1:9; 2:4** Hb obscure [F] **1:11** Or *wind, and transgress and incur guilt* [G] **1:12** Alt Hb tradition reads *we* [H] **1:13** = Babylon [I] **1:13** = Judah [J] **2:1** Syr reads *what he will* [K] **2:2** Lit *one who reads in it may run* [L] **2:4** Or *faithfulness* [M] **2:5** DSS read *wealth* [N] **2:5** Or *man does not endure*; Hb obscure

The Historical Setting of Habakkuk

by J. Daniel Hays

Unlike several of the other Old Testament prophetic books, Habakkuk does not present an opening historical superscription identifying the time (e.g., "in the fifth year of king so-and-so"). As we read through the book, however, we can deduce the setting from statements in the text. Habakkuk lived in the southern kingdom of Judah. His dialogue with God took place just prior to one of the Babylonian invasions of Judah (597 or 586 BC). The prophet Jeremiah also lived and prophesied at this time. The lengthy book of Jeremiah, along with the corresponding chapters in 2 Kings from this same period (2Kg 22–25), painted a clear picture of the tumultuous times in which Habakkuk lived. A series of weak, unfaithful kings, in collusion with corrupt priests and false prophets, had led Judah away from the true God of Abraham and Moses and into idolatry. Not surprisingly, as the people turned away from serving God, they abandoned the moral code embedded in God's law, especially as expressed in Deuteronomy. Further, they allowed serious social and economic injustices to flourish. The dialogue in the book of Habakkuk took place in this context. ✣

Site of ancient Lachish, which was one of the last cities to fall to Nebuchadnezzar and his army. After taking Lachish, the Babylonians continued their military campaign and conquered Jerusalem in 586 BC.

THE FIVE WOE ORACLES

6 Won't all of these take up a taunt against him,
with mockery and riddles about him?
They will say,

"Woe to him who amasses what is not his —
how much longer? —
and loads himself with goods taken in pledge."
7 Won't your creditors suddenly arise,
and those who disturb you wake up?
Then you will become spoil for them.
8 Since you have plundered many nations,
all the peoples who remain
will plunder you —
because of human bloodshed
and violence against lands, cities,
and all who live in them.

9 Woe to him who dishonestly makes
wealth for his house[A]
to place his nest on high,
to escape the grasp of disaster!
10 You have planned shame for your house
by wiping out many peoples
and sinning against your own self.
11 For the stones will cry out from the wall,
and the rafters will answer them
from the woodwork.

12 Woe to him who builds a city with bloodshed
and founds a town with injustice!
13 Is it not from the LORD of Armies
that the peoples labor only to fuel the fire
and countries exhaust themselves for nothing?
14 For the earth will be filled
with the knowledge of the LORD's glory,
as the water covers the sea.

15 Woe to him who gives his neighbors drink,
pouring out your wrath[B]
and even making them drunk,
in order to look at their nakedness!
16 You will be filled with disgrace
instead of glory.
You also — drink,
and expose your uncircumcision![C]
The cup in the LORD's right hand
will come around to you,
and utter disgrace will cover your glory.
17 For your violence against Lebanon
will overwhelm you;
the destruction of animals will terrify you[D]
because of your human bloodshed
and violence
against lands, cities, and all who live in them.

18 What use is a carved idol
after its craftsman carves it?
It is only a cast image, a teacher of lies.
For the one who crafts its shape trusts in it
and makes worthless idols that cannot speak.
19 Woe to him who says to wood: Wake up!
or to mute stone: Come alive!
Can it teach?
Look! It may be plated with gold and silver,
yet there is no breath in it at all.

20 But the LORD is in his holy temple;
let the whole earth
be silent in his presence.

HABAKKUK'S THIRD PRAYER

3 A prayer of the prophet Habakkuk. According
to *Shigionoth*.[E]
2 LORD, I have heard the report about you;
LORD, I stand in awe of your deeds.
Revive your work in these years;
make it known in these years.
In your wrath remember mercy!

3 God comes from Teman,
the Holy One from Mount Paran. *Selah*
His splendor covers the heavens,
and the earth is full of his praise.
4 His brilliance is like light;
rays are flashing from his hand.
This is where his power is hidden.
5 Plague goes before him,
and pestilence follows in his steps.
6 He stands and shakes[F] the earth;
he looks and startles the nations.
The age-old mountains break apart;
the ancient hills sink down.
His pathways are ancient.
7 I see the tents of Cushan[G] in distress;
the tent curtains of the land
of Midian tremble.
8 Are you angry at the rivers, LORD?
Is your wrath against the rivers?
Or is your fury against the sea
when you ride on your horses,
your victorious chariot?
9 You took the sheath from your bow;
the arrows are ready[H] to be used
with an oath.[I] *Selah*
You split the earth with rivers.

[A] **2:9** Or *dynasty* [B] **2:15** Or *venom* [C] **2:16** DSS, LXX, Aq, Syr, Vg read *and stagger* [D] **2:17** DSS, LXX, Aq, Syr, Tg, Vg; MT reads *them*
[E] **3:1** Perhaps a passionate song with rapid changes of rhythm, or a dirge [F] **3:6** Or *surveys* [G] **3:7** = Midian [H] **3:9** Or *set*
[I] **3:9** Hb obscure

Though mention of the Chaldeans in the Old Testament is limited, their historical significance was substantial over a long period of ancient history. The term *Chaldeans* was not always applied with consistency in ancient records. Sometimes it referred to tribes of western Semites known collectively as Chaldeans and other times to peoples in the locale who were not Chaldeans ethnically. In the Hellenistic era, the term referred often to astrologers from Babylonia.[1]

HOME OF THE CHALDEANS

Chaldea, the homeland of the Chaldeans, was in southern Babylonia just northwest of the Persian Gulf. The land was primarily marshes and coastal plains. The area was once under control of the Sumerian kingdom and is associated with Ur, the home city of Abraham, referred to in Genesis 11:31 as "Ur of the Chaldeans." As early as the ninth century BC, the archives of Assyria's King Shalmaneser II refer to the area and its people. The term *Chaldeans* referred to a number of tribes that migrated into this region. Although history does not indicate their locale prior to this migration or the exact time of their entry into the region, it does teach that they settled along the Tigris and Euphrates Rivers and became townspeople and farmers.[2] This era of migration involved many other tribal groups and confederations that settled in various regions throughout the Fertile Crescent.

Babylon was a city-state in southern Mesopotamia in Old Testament times. Babylon dominated the ancient Near Eastern political scene at several points between 3000 and 539 BC. The city was located about fifty miles south of modern Baghdad, Iraq. "Babylon may have been an important cultural center during the early period of the Sumerian city-states (before 2000 BC), but the corresponding archaeological levels of the site are below the present water table and remain unexplored."[3]

CHALDEANS AND ANCIENT HISTORY

Shortly after 2000 BC, about the time of Abraham, Babylon's history became available for modern study. Amorite kings, such as Hammurabi (ca 1792–1750 BC), brought the city to international prominence and ultimately built an impressive empire by conquering other nations, establishing national treaties, and imposing a vassal status on conquered peoples. Because of its expanding empire, Babylon became the political seat for southern Mesopotamia.

The Hittites conquered Babylon about 1595 BC but soon withdrew, leaving a political vacuum. History offers little information about the period that followed. It teaches, though, that the Kassite tribe seized Babylon's throne and held it for more than four centuries. The long Kassite Dynasty was relatively peaceful and helped Babylon's culture to reach new heights of international prestige. Seeking some relief, though, from Assyria's growing power and influence, around 1350 BC, Babylon's kings began to work with Egypt. An Elamite invasion brought an end to the Kassite Dynasty about 1160 BC.

As the Elamites withdrew, Babylonian princes came to power and

Foundation deposit left by Nabopolassar, the last Chaldean king (625–605 BC) in the temple of Shamash the sun god in ancient Sippar, about 35 miles north of Babylon.

Lyre decoration from Ur. Panel of shell and lapis lazuli representing a banquet scene.

founded Babylon's Fourth Dynasty. During this era, Nebuchadnezzar I (ca 1124–1103 BC) brought political victory to Babylon by invading the Elamites, recapturing the Marduk statue the Edomites had taken from the Kassites, and returning the statue to Babylon. Afterward, though, Babylon became anemic and remained so for almost two centuries. Several factors afflicted Babylon during this time, such as floods, famine, widespread settlement of nomadic tribes, and the arrival of the Chaldeans in the south.

A number of times Chaldean tribal leaders ruled Babylonia. While Babylon was autonomous, rule changed hands among several Semitic tribal peoples. Later, Babylon often came under Assyrian control. The Assyrians repeatedly gained and lost control of the region. Assyrian kings ruled Babylon directly through their own families or as a vassal kingdom with a local titular head subservient to the Assyrians. During much of the seventh and sixth centuries BC, the Chaldeans competed with the Assyrians for control of northern Babylonia, sometimes prevailing.[4] But the cycle continued as Assyrian fortunes improved and declined repeatedly.

Assyria's greatest time of weakness occurred during the impressive expansion of Israel under Jeroboam II (793–753 BC) and a similar period of Judah's prosperity under King Uzziah (792–740 BC). Jeroboam II, encouraged by professional court prophets, mistakenly believed that God was pleased with his syncretistic and pagan worship practices. In reality, the idolatrous period sealed the fate of both Israel and Judah. Because Hoshea, king of Israel, failed to pay tribute to Assyria, Shalmaneser V (727–722 BC) besieged Samaria for 3 years (2Kg 17:3–5). The city finally fell to Shalmaneser in 722 BC (17:6; 18:9–12), and the northern kingdom of Israel passed off the scene permanently. But Judah

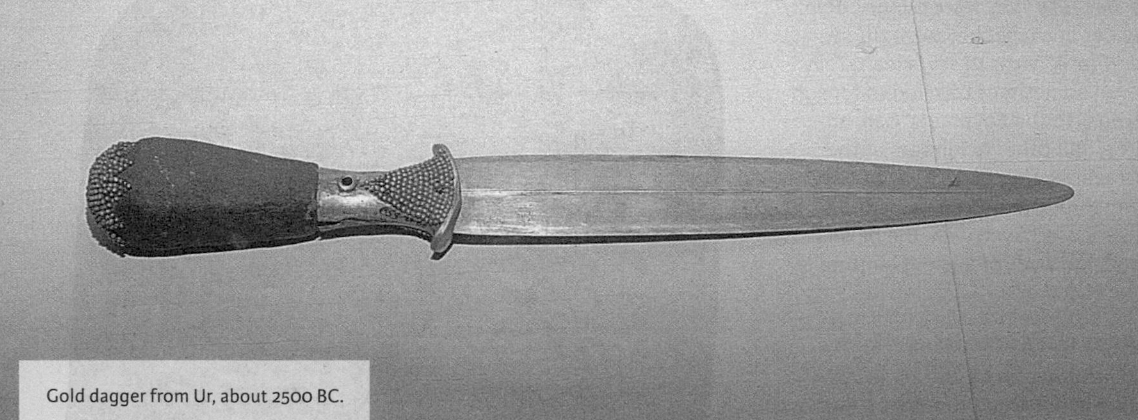
Gold dagger from Ur, about 2500 BC.

survived for another 135 years before the new world power, Babylon, lay her waste and took her survivors into exile.

Ironically, the Assyrian Empire's success led to its own collapse. Having maintained a substantial empire for centuries, Assyria reached its maximum size in the middle of the seventh century BC. The entire Fertile Crescent was under Assyrian domination, from Egypt and the shores of the Mediterranean in the west to the Persian Gulf in the east and almost to the coast of the Black Sea and the Caspian Sea in the north.

Chaldean power and influence reached its height during the era known as the Neo-Babylonian Empire (ca 609–539 BC). This empire was instrumental in the downfall of Assyria. The brief era of Babylon's international power was centuries in the making. Babylon had proven troublesome to the Assyrians over a long period, often in conjunction with Elam, a kingdom bordering Babylonia on the east. Elam, though often attacked by Assyria, continued to support and encourage Chaldean resistance to Assyria.

COLLAPSING KINGDOMS

Even after the fall of Samaria, Judah continued to presume on the Lord's pleasure. Its kings were unmindful of impending doom, despite the faithful ministry of the prophets sent to each generation. Ahaz (735–715 BC) did not test Assyrian resolve, remaining compliant. Hezekiah, Ahaz's son (715–687 BC), instituted substantial religious reforms but unwisely rebelled against Assyria. During his reign, an emissary of Merodach-baladan visited Hezekiah, who naively revealed the wealth of the temple to him, leading to the ultimate devastation of Jerusalem by the Babylonians (2Kg 20:12–18).

Manasseh, Judah's most wicked and longest-reigning king (687–642 BC), sacrificed his sons in a pagan ritual (2Ch 33:6). Then Josiah (640–609 BC) reinstituted the observance of Passover and sought to restore faithfulness and integrity to the religious life of God's people. Believing the collapse of Assyria offered an opportunity, Josiah tried to block the army of Pharaoh Neco II in their belated support of the Assyrians. Tragically, Josiah died in battle (2Kg 23) and the decline of Judah accelerated.

Babylon installed Zedekiah, a puppet king, to follow two weak kings: Jehoiakim and Jehoiachin. Remarkably, Zedekiah also decided to rebel against Babylonian rule. Finally, after twenty years of headaches, Babylon's King Nebuchadnezzar resolved the question of Judah decisively by destroying Jerusalem in 586 BC, relocating many survivors to Babylon.

CHALDEAN VICTORY

Though they were latecomers to the region, the Chaldeans' success ultimately resulted in the term *Chaldean* becoming virtually synonymous with the term *Babylonian*. Chaldean ascendancy was short-lived. Yet the Chaldeans served as God's instrument in fulfilling his promise to the Israelites through Moses: abandoning covenantal obligations would result in both loss of the land and the people being scattered to the four winds. Second Kings 24–25 documents the tragedy that Habakkuk had vividly described in his prophecy (Hab 1:5–11). Though shaken to his core by what the Lord revealed to him, Habakkuk clung to hope, as God's promise of judgment was tempered by his grace. ✣

[1] Alfred J. Hoerth et al., *Peoples of the Old Testament World* (Grand Rapids: Baker, 1994), 57–58. [2] James Orr, ed., *The International Standard Bible Encyclopedia* (Peabody, MA: Hendrickson, 1956), 1:589–90. [3] Daniel C. Browning Jr. and Randall Breland, "Babylon," *HIBD*, rev. ed. (2015), 160. [4] Hoerth et al., *Peoples*, 57.

Idols in Production and Rituals

by David M. Wallace

Idols ate two meals every day because they were hungry, drank water because they were thirsty, and took baths to stay clean. They even sometimes traveled to foreign lands. To the Egyptians, Canaanites, and other neighbors of the Israelites, they were gods fit to be worshiped and to be cared for in every way.[1] Such were the beliefs and practices of ancient cultures in the Near East.

Stone mold for casting Assyrian idols; dated 1920–1740 BC.

WHAT DOES IDOL MEAN?

An idol was an object made by human hands that presented a likeness or image of the god to be worshiped. The Hebrew word translated as "idol" or "graven image" is *pesel*, related to the verb *pasal*, meaning to "hew" or "cut."[2] We learn from both language and archaeology that idols were hewn or carved out of wood or stone.

God instructed the Israelites in Exodus 20:5, "Do not bow in worship to them, and do not serve them; for I, the LORD your God, am a jealous God." Several times the Old Testament repeated this prohibition of idols (Ex 20:23; 34:17; Lv 19:4; 26:1; Dt 4:15–19,25; 5:8). The Hebrews were directed not to worship anything that looked like or represented any type of deity. Isaiah told the people that God was unique, unlike anyone or anything else (Js 40:18–19). No idol made by a craftsman could compare to him.

God instructed the Israelites to make no form or image of any kind with which to worship him (Dt 4:15–18). Though Israel struggled to remain loyal to God alone, monotheism made Israel's faith unique among the nations, especially among those who lived nearby and against whom they fought. Thus, obeying God's commands against idol worship throughout Old Testament times proved to be a constant challenge for the people of Israel.

HOW WERE IDOLS MADE?

Israel and its neighbors typically made their idols of wood, stone, silver, or gold. The gold and silver made idols more expensive as well as attractive. The more attractive the idol god or goddess, the more that people wanted the blessing available to them from that particular idol. Some idols could be held in the palm of the hand; others might be several feet tall. Most idols that were originally sheathed in gold or silver eventually lost their beautiful dazzling covers.

Whenever foreign armies overran a city or nation, they naturally took every possible item made of gold or silver. Houses of worship and temples were among the first places soldiers would search for treasures. Often metals would be melted down to reuse the gold or silver.

When heated to the melting point, both silver and gold are soft and easily formed into objects. Both are capable of being shaped by beating them with a hammer or by the pressure of rollers. Hammers can shape the precious metals into extremely thin sheets that can then be overlaid—one on top of the other—onto most objects, including ancient idols.

When exposed to air, silver oxidizes, so it must be polished. Gold, on the other hand, does not oxidize, even if buried underground or left in a cave or burial vault for hundreds of years.

Bronze dragon, sacred animal of Babylonian god Marduk, 700–550 BC.

In the Old Testament era, if not made of wood or stone, idols were first shaped and cast of metal, typically iron or bronze. After cooling, the cast was removed and gold was applied by hand one layer at a time, or the object was dipped into liquid gold. The final product was an idol covered with a gold veneer. This gilding process is still in use today.

HOW IDOLS WERE CARED FOR

The neighbors of Israel believed their images and statues were alive. Their idols had thoughts and feelings. The god was living in their image or statue. The people cared for their idol because they believed it needed care and attention just like any other living being.

The idols at Uruk temple, for example, received two meals daily. A table was carried in with a bowl of water for cleaning. The idol received a variety of foods. Musicians played at mealtime while the idol ate in private. Afterward, the items were removed and the idol was again provided water with which to clean itself.

In Egypt, idols usually reposed in a dark corner inside the temple where only the priest had access to the idol. The priest was responsible for caring for the shrine that contained the idol. The priest cleaned and perfumed the idol with incense and applied cosmetics. The priest also placed a crown on the idol, identifying it as a deity.[3] ✣

[1] Edward M. Curtis, "Idol, Idolatry" in *ABD*, 3:377–78. [2] Francis Brown, S. R. Driver, and Charles A Briggs, *A Hebrew and English Lexicon of the Old Testament* (Oxford: Clarendon Press, 1980), 820. [3] Curtis, "Idol, Idolatry," 377–78.

Votive statue of food being offered to the Sumerian god Anu at Uruk.

Pestilence and Plague in the Ancient World

by Francis X. Kimmitt

Habakkuk 3:3–15 describes God's terrible judgment on the earth. The judgment's weapons included pestilence and plague.

Figurine and document from a Hurrian temple that honored Nergal; dated to the end of the third millennium BC.

IN THE ANCIENT NEAR EAST

People of the ancient Near East, including the nations of Israel and Judah, viewed pestilence (Hb *resheph*) and plague (Hb *deber*) as agents of divine judgment. Habakkuk and his hearers understood pestilence and plague to be personified members of the Lord's army. They marched alongside God into battle. Pestilence led the way in judgment, and plague formed his rear guard.[1] Throughout the ancient Near East, people understood plagues and pestilence as "the visible manifestation of unseen weapons wielded by the country's deity (or deities) to enforce the moral and social code."[2]

Pestilence—The Judahites would have recognized *resheph* as the name of the Canaanite god of the plague (the deity so designated in Ugaritic, Phoenician, and Aramaic inscriptions). Habakkuk's Babylonian audience would have recognized this as their god, Nergal, also connected with disease and plague.[3] Through Moses's final speeches, God promised he would punish any of Israel's acts of apostasy by consuming his people by *resheph* (Dt 32:24). *Resheph* carries the meaning of a fire, of objects being consumed by flames. In that passage's context, God's other agents of judgment parallel the other possible meanings of *resheph*: flame, glow, and arrow.[4] Together, "flame" and "arrow" convey the idea of lightning flashes and bolts from God's bow, bringing death and destruction.[5]

Plague—Deber likely described bubonic plague, one of history's most deadly diseases. Modern medicine and science explain the rat-flea's bite as the cause. Not knowing the cause of such a terrible calamity, ancient peoples believed the disease originated in the spiritual realm. The Hebrews understood the plague as God pouring out his wrath and going to war against his enemies. Leviticus 26:25 and Numbers 14:12 reveal the threat of bubonic plague as one of Yahweh's most serious judgments on Israel and its enemies.[6]

In 1 Samuel 5, the Philistines in Ashdod and Gath were stricken with tumors—probably the characteristic buboes of bubonic plague—when the Lord punished them to show that he, and not their god Dagon, was God over all the earth. Related cognates in other Semitic languages reveal that Israel's neighbors had similar dread for this punishment; the Ugaritic word *dbr* meant "death," and the Akkadian *dibiru*, "disaster."[7]

Habakkuk's audience believed plague and pestilence would accompany Yahweh when he went to war against Israel's enemies. God promised to protect his people and to punish those who disobeyed his commandments. The God who created the world surely controlled its natural forces. All who heard Habakkuk's words understood that God could, and would, use pestilence and plague to punish those who stood against him. All peoples of the ancient Near East recognized and feared the inherent destruction God's twin agents, plague and pestilence, caused.

IN HABAKKUK

Habakkuk 3 shows that the prophet understood the inevitability of destruction at God's hand. Where can one hide when the Creator unleashes his wrath on the earth? His radiance is like the sunlight; rays flash from his hand (v. 4). When he surveys the earth, the mountains shatter and the hills collapse (v. 6). He splits the earth with rivers, and the sight of him makes the mountains quake (vv. 9–10). The light of his arrows (not *resheph* but, in context, a synonym) and the radiance of his spear cause the sun and moon to stand in their established places (v. 11). He marches through the earth and in righteous anger, tramples the nations (v. 12). He tramples on the sea with his horses and halts the advance of ocean waves upon the shore (v. 15).

The prophet made full use of imagery to convey God's actions on behalf of his honor and his people (vv. 8–15). The mountains and hills portray strength and stability. God's presence in judgment on the nations shakes these immovable objects. The sun standing still would remind Judah that Yahweh fought for his people, causing the sun to stand still and thus allowing Israel to defeat her enemies (Jos 10:12–14). All these images display the Lord's power and might—for the purpose of defeating his enemies and delivering his people.

When the Lord pronounces judgment, no precautions or safety measures can provide protection. Plague and pestilence are God's weapons; they will bring certain destruction and devastation. In Habakkuk's prophecy, plague and pestilence struck terror in the hearts of Judah and its enemies. Yahweh had seen the rampant violence and wickedness of his people, and he announced impending judgment. Additionally, he had seen the gross wickedness of his chosen agents of that judgment, the Babylonians. They too would suffer the consequence of their sin and rebellion. When the Lord entered the battle fray against Babylon, his foreguard, pestilence, would go before him, and his rearguard, plague, would follow. The forces of nature obey their Maker and rain justice down on all who choose to stand against the Lord. ✠

Syrian deity, thought to be Resheph; dated to the second millennium BC.

---

[1] F. F. Bruce, "Habakkuk" in *The Minor Prophets*, ed. Thomas Edward McComiskey (Grand Rapids: Baker, 1993), 2:883. [2] "Plague" in *Dictionary of Biblical Imagery*, ed. Leland Ryken et al. (Downers Grove, IL: IVP Academic, 1998), 648. [3] John H. Walton, Victor H. Matthews, and Mark W. Chavalas, *The IVP Bible Background Commentary: Old Testament* (Downers Grove, IL: InterVarsity, 2000), 793. [4] Jackie A. Naud and R. K. Harrison, "רֶשֶׁף [*resheph*]" in *NIDOTTE*, 3:1205. See Ludwig Koehler and Walter Baumgartner, "רֶשֶׁף" in *HALOT*, 3:1298. [5] *HALOT*, 3:1298. [6] R. K. Harrison, "דָּבָר [*dabar* I]" in *NIDOTTE*, 1:915. [7] *HALOT*, 1:212.

10 The mountains see you and shudder;
a downpour of water sweeps by.
The deep roars with its voice
and lifts its waves[A] high.
11 Sun and moon stand still
in their lofty residence,
at the flash of your flying arrows,
at the brightness of your shining spear.
12 You march across the earth with indignation;
you trample down the nations in wrath.
13 You come out to save your people,
to save your anointed.[B]
You crush the leader of the house
of the wicked
and strip him from foot[C] to neck. *Selah*
14 You pierce his head
with his own spears;
his warriors storm out to scatter us,
gloating as if ready to secretly devour
the weak.
15 You tread the sea with your horses,
stirring up the vast water.

HABAKKUK'S CONFIDENCE IN GOD EXPRESSED

16 I heard, and I trembled within;
my lips quivered at the sound.
Rottenness entered my bones;
I trembled where I stood.
Now I must quietly wait for the day of distress
to come against the people invading us.
17 Though the fig tree does not bud
and there is no fruit on the vines,
though the olive crop fails
and the fields produce no food,
though the flocks disappear from the pen
and there are no herds in the stalls,
18 yet I will celebrate in the LORD;
I will rejoice in the God of my salvation!
19 The LORD my Lord is my strength;
he makes my feet like those of a deer
and enables me to walk on mountain heights!
For the choir director: on[D] stringed instruments.

[A] **3:10** Lit *hands* [B] **3:13** The Davidic king or the nation of Israel
[C] **3:13** Lit *foundation* [D] **3:19** Lit *on my*

ZEPHANIAH

Bronze arrowheads used when Babylon defeated Assyria at Carchemish, 605 BC.

INTRODUCTION TO

ZEPHANIAH

Circumstances of Writing

Zephaniah's lengthy genealogy (Zph 1:1, four generations back to Hezekiah) suggests he was of royal lineage. Why list four generations (other prophets, at most, listed two generations; see Zch 1:1) unless this final name was significant? Perhaps because his father's name was Cushi, people tended to suspect that Zephaniah was of mixed ancestry, including Cushite bloodlines. In fact, Zephaniah twice mentions the Cushites/Cush (Ethiopians) in his short prophecy (Zph 2:12; 3:10), possibly suggesting his Cushite roots.

Internal evidence indicates the book of Zephaniah was written sometime between 640 and 612 BC. Zephaniah 1:1 refers to King Josiah's reign (ca 640–609 BC), and 2:13–15 prophesies Nineveh's fall. Since Nineveh fell in 612 BC, Zephaniah's prophecy would have been given prior to that time. Furthermore, existing idolatrous practices in Judah (1:4–6) imply Zephaniah's ministry began before Josiah's reforms in roughly 621 BC (2Kg 23).

King Josiah's father, King Amon (Zph 1:1), was a wicked man, as was his father before him, King Manasseh (2Kg 21:1–7,11,16,20–22). This heritage of wickedness helps explain the rampant idolatry in the land when Josiah inherited the throne in 640 BC. Josiah struggled to squelch idolatry in Judah (Zph 1:4–9). Together pagan and "orthodox priests" led worship of the Lord while also bowing before Baal, Molech, and other pagan gods (1:4–6). The public reading of the book of the law (ca 621 BC) helped spawn the reforms of Josiah as people repented and tore down the numerous altars (cf. Jr 11:13) and other idolatrous paraphernalia of Baal and Molech (2Kg 23:1–14; see Zph 1:3–4). This included abolishing the false priests (2Kg 23:5).

Contribution to the Bible

The promise of a remnant illustrates God's amazing grace counterbalancing his jealous wrath and blazing fury against the wicked (Nah 1:2–8). He would judge the proud nations (Zph 2:8–11,13–15) and purge the haughty braggarts from his people (3:11) to preserve the humble. Thus Zephaniah invited everyone who humbly obeyed the Lord to seek him for possible deliverance (2:2–3). The New Testament highlights the wonderful truth that all of us can find salvation through faith in Christ. Paul underscored the idea of the Jewish remnant and reminded us that the remnant is "chosen by grace," not by works (Rm 11:5–6).

Structure

"The word of the Lord [Yahweh]" (Zph 1:1a) and "the Lord [Yahweh] has spoken" (3:20b) frame the whole book of Zephaniah to emphasize crucial complementary messages: imminent, universal judgment (1:1–3:8) but eventual blessing for the remnant (3:9–20). The chiastic first section, interlaced by the reinforcing refrain "this is the Lord's declaration" (see 1:2–3,10a; 2:9a; 3:8a; cf. 2:5, "word of the Lord"), highlights an all-inclusive judgment.

Zephaniah 3:8 is a transitional exhortation that looks both backward ("therefore"; v. 8a) and forward (wait patiently for God to consummate judgment which will yield salvation for the remnant; vv. 9–13, introduced by Hb *ki*, "for/because" in vv. 9,11). To offer hope during judgment in 3:8–13 may synthesize two exhortations: 1:7 (hush/wait for the day of the Lord's "cutting off" the wicked) and 2:1–3 (pivotal invitation to seek him for possible salvation).

1 The word of the LORD that came to Zephaniah son of Cushi, son of Gedaliah, son of Amariah, son of Hezekiah, in the days of Josiah son of Amon, king of Judah.

THE GREAT DAY OF THE LORD

2 I will completely sweep away everything
from the face of the earth —
this is the LORD's declaration.
3 I will sweep away people and animals;
I will sweep away the birds of the sky
and the fish of the sea,
and the ruins[A] along with the wicked.
I will cut off mankind
from the face of the earth.
This is the LORD's declaration.

4 I will stretch out my hand against Judah
and against all the residents of Jerusalem.
I will cut off every vestige of Baal
from this place,
the names of the pagan priests
along with the priests;
5 those who bow in worship
on the rooftops
to the stars in the sky;
those who bow and pledge loyalty
to the LORD
but also pledge loyalty to Milcom;[B]
6 and those who turn back from following
the LORD,
who do not seek the LORD or inquire
of him.
7 Be silent in the presence of the Lord GOD,
for the day of the LORD is near.
Indeed, the LORD has prepared a sacrifice;
he has consecrated his guests.

8 On the day of the LORD's sacrifice
I will punish the officials, the king's sons,
and all who are dressed
in foreign clothing.
9 On that day I will punish
all who skip over the threshold,[C]
who fill their master's house
with violence and deceit.

10 On that day —
this is the LORD's declaration —
there will be an outcry from the Fish Gate,
a wailing from the Second District,
and a loud crashing from the hills.
11 Wail, you residents of the Hollow,[D]
for all the merchants[E] will be silenced;
all those loaded with silver will be cut off.
12 And at that time I will search Jerusalem
with lamps
and punish
those who settle down comfortably,[F]
who say to themselves:
The LORD will do nothing — good or bad.
13 Their wealth will become plunder
and their houses a ruin.
They will build houses but never live in them,
plant vineyards but never drink their wine.

14 The great day of the LORD is near,
near and rapidly approaching.
Listen, the day of the LORD —
then the warrior's cry is bitter.
15 That day is a day of wrath,
a day of trouble and distress,
a day of destruction and desolation,
a day of darkness and gloom,
a day of clouds and total darkness,
16 a day of ram's horn and battle cry
against the fortified cities,
and against the high corner towers.
17 I will bring distress on mankind,
and they will walk like the blind
because they have sinned against the LORD.
Their blood will be poured out like dust
and their flesh like dung.
18 Their silver and their gold
will be unable to rescue them
on the day of the LORD's wrath.
The whole earth will be consumed
by the fire of his jealousy,
for he will make a complete,
yes, a horrifying end
of all the inhabitants of the earth.

A CALL TO REPENTANCE

2 Gather yourselves together;
gather together, undesirable[G] nation,
2 before the decree takes effect
and the day passes like chaff,
before the burning of the LORD's anger
overtakes you,
before the day of the LORD's anger
overtakes you.
3 Seek the LORD, all you humble of the earth,
who carry out what he commands.
Seek righteousness, seek humility;
perhaps you will be concealed
on the day of the LORD's anger.

[A] **1:3** Perhaps objects connected with idolatry [B] **1:5** Some LXX mss, Syr, Vg; MT, other LXX mss read *their king* [C] **1:9** Hb obscure [D] **1:11** Or *the market district* [E] **1:11** Or *Canaanites* [F] **1:12** Lit *who thicken on their dregs* [G] **2:1** Or *shameless*

JUDGMENT AGAINST THE NATIONS

4 For Gaza will be abandoned,
and Ashkelon will become a ruin.
Ashdod will be driven out at noon,
and Ekron will be uprooted.
5 Woe, inhabitants of the seacoast,
nation of the Cherethites![A]
The word of the LORD is against you,
Canaan, land of the Philistines:
I will destroy you until there is no one left.
6 The seacoast will become pasturelands
with caves for shepherds and pens for sheep.
7 The coastland will belong
to the remnant of the house of Judah;
they will find pasture there.
They will lie down in the evening
among the houses of Ashkelon,
for the LORD their God will return to them
and restore their fortunes.

8 I have heard the taunting of Moab
and the insults of the Ammonites,
who have taunted my people
and threatened their territory.
9 Therefore, as I live —
this is the declaration of the LORD
of Armies,
the God of Israel —
Moab will be like Sodom
and the Ammonites like Gomorrah:
a place overgrown with weeds,
a salt pit, and a perpetual wasteland.
The remnant of my people will plunder them;
the remainder of my nation
will dispossess them.
10 This is what they get for their pride,
because they have taunted
and acted arrogantly
against the people of the LORD of Armies.
11 The LORD will be terrifying to them
when he starves all the gods of the earth.
Then all the distant coasts and islands
of the nations
will bow in worship to him,
each in its own place.

12 You Cushites will also be slain by my sword.

13 He will also stretch out his hand
against the north
and destroy Assyria;
he will make Nineveh a desolate ruin,
dry as the desert.
14 Herds will lie down in the middle of it,
every kind of wild animal.[B]
Both eagle owls[C] and herons[D]
will roost in the capitals of its pillars.
Their calls will sound[E] from the window,
but devastation[F] will be
on the threshold,
for he will expose the cedar work.[G]
15 This is the jubilant city
that lives in security,
that says to herself:
I exist, and there is no one else.
What a desolation she has become,
a place for wild animals to lie down!
Everyone who passes by her
scoffs[H] and shakes his fist.

WOE TO OPPRESSIVE JERUSALEM

3 Woe to the city that is rebellious[I]
and defiled,
the oppressive city!
2 She has not obeyed;
she has not accepted discipline.
She has not trusted in the LORD;
she has not drawn near to her God.
3 The[J] princes within her are roaring lions;
her judges are wolves of the night,
which leave nothing for[K] the morning.
4 Her prophets are reckless —
treacherous men.
Her priests profane the sanctuary;
they do violence to instruction.
5 The righteous LORD is in her;
he does no wrong.
He applies his justice morning by morning;
he does not fail at dawn,
yet the one who does wrong
knows no shame.

6 I have cut off nations;
their corner towers are destroyed.
I have laid waste their streets,
with no one to pass through.
Their cities lie devastated,
without a person, without an inhabitant.
7 I said: You will certainly fear me
and accept correction.
Then her dwelling place[L]
would not be cut off
based on all that I had allocated to her.
However, they became more corrupt
in all their actions.

[A] **2:5** = Sea Peoples [B] **2:14** Lit *every wild animal of a nation* [C] **2:14** Or *the pelicans* [D] **2:14** Or *the hedgehogs* [E] **2:14** Lit *sing* [F] **2:14** LXX, Vg read *ravens* [G] **2:14** Hb obscure [H] **2:15** Or *hisses* [I] **3:1** Or *filthy* [J] **3:3** Lit *Her* [K] **3:3** Or *that had nothing to gnaw in* [L] **3:7** LXX, Syr read *her eyes*

As the eighth century BC drew to a close, King Hezekiah of Judah found his capital city, Jerusalem, confronted by 185,000 Assyrian soldiers and a demand for unconditional surrender. A hundred years later, toward the close of the seventh century, Jerusalem faced threats again, this time from the Babylonians. During the intervening century, Judah was ruled by two world powers, governed by six different kings, and confronted by at least five different prophets.

Cuneiform clay tablet describing Assyrian King Ashurbanipal's (668–627 BC) Egyptian campaigns.

THE CHANGING POLITICAL SCENE

The siege of Jerusalem by 185,000 troops occurred in 701 BC and is known as the Sennacherib crisis, named after the Assyrian king. This event placed the dominant world power, Assyria, against a weak vassal nation, Judah, in a showdown where only one side would win. Assyria had an overpowering army and a record of military success. Judah had a faithful king, Hezekiah, who entrusted the situation to the Lord. Hezekiah had a prophet of the Lord named Isaiah. At the peak of the crisis, when it appeared that Judah would capitulate, the Assyrian troops died by the hands of "the angel of the LORD" (2Kgs 19:35). Josephus, a Jewish historian in the first century AD, indicated that Sennacherib's troops died because "God had sent a pestilential distemper upon his army."[1] After the failed siege of Jerusalem in 701 BC, the Assyrians withdrew for a while. Yet under Sennacherib's successors, Esarhaddon (680–669 BC) and Ashurbanipal (668–627 BC), the Assyrians marched again. The Assyrian Empire reached the zenith of its power in 663 BC with the overthrow of Thebes, deep in Egyptian territory. Later, about 612 BC, the prophet Nahum ironically used this historic event to address Assyria's own vulnerability (Nah 3:8).

Some scholars believe Assyria besieged Jerusalem twice, once in 701 BC and again around 688 BC According to this view, Hezekiah paid tribute to Sennacherib to end the siege in 701 BC. Then thirteen years later during a second siege, he entrusted the fate of Jerusalem to the Lord, who wiped out 185,000 troops and sent Sennacherib fleeing back to Assyria. Scholars who favor this view see a telescoping of both invasions into one account in 2 Kings 18. The result was the same whether Sennacherib invaded once or twice.

When Jerusalem was miraculously spared, the people developed a theology of Jerusalem's inviolability, the belief that Jerusalem could

Stone record of Esarhaddon's restoration of Babylon, circa 670 BC.

not be conquered due to divine protection. The major Assyrian king of the seventh century was Ashurbanipal. He was an able king, a good administrator, and an efficient consolidator of power. During the four decades of his leadership, Assyria remained the dominant world power. His death in 627 BC coupled with the weakness of his successors and the emergence of Babylon as a dominant power resulted in the fall of Nineveh, the Assyrian capital, in 612 BC. The prophet Nahum had predicted this result, concluding his prophecy by writing, "All who hear the news about you will clap their hands because of you, for who has not experienced your constant cruelty?" (Nah 3:19).

A last-ditch effort to ally with the Egyptians and to defeat the Babylonians failed in the battle of Carchemish in 605 BC. Assyria was defeated and became a second-rate power subservient to the Babylonian Empire. How did the international powers affect Judah during the seventh century BC? Judah was a vassal of the Assyrians until the death of Ashurbanipal in 627 BC. Vassal nations were required to pay tribute money to their overlords in the form of gold, silver, and other treasures. The degree of compliance fluctuated with the relative strength of the current international power's ability to enforce the policy. Hezekiah's refusal to pay tribute may have triggered Sennacherib's second invasion in 688 BC (2Kgs 18:7). Manasseh might have refused tribute money around 652 BC when Ashurbanipal was busy quelling rebellions elsewhere. During the two decades of Assyria's decline and Babylon's ascendancy (627–608 BC), Judah enjoyed a measure of freedom from paying tribute money. This period of relative freedom coincided with the time of Josiah's reforms initiated in 622 BC. In 608 BC, the Egyptians reinstituted heavy tribute, and the Babylonians continued the practice after 605 BC.[3] Such was the fate of Judah.

During Hezekiah's reign, Judah moved toward the exclusive worship of Yahweh. However, his son Manasseh moved the nation toward syncretistic religion, mixing Yahweh worship with the worship of other gods such as Baal and Asherah. The priests of the land seemed to equate correct religious ritual with meaningful worship, thus eliminating ethical demands as an expression of genuine religion. The result was the abuse of the poor and helpless members of society.

Bronze arrowheads used when Babylon defeated Assyria at Carchemish, 605 BC.

THE PROPHETS

God's prophets denounced the sins of the people and declared impending judgment. Interestingly, they pointed to the movements of the world powers, such as Assyria, Babylon, and Persia as evidence of divine wrath. Only repentance from sin and reliance on the Lord could avert the onslaught of the pagan powers.

Zephaniah is dated to the reign of King Josiah, who began his rule of Judah in 640 BC at the age of eight. The prophet's preaching probably inspired the king's advocacy of a spiritual reformation that began in 628 BC (2Ch 34:3). Zephaniah announced coming devastation and called for Judah to cease their empty and adulterous affirmations of faith (Zph 1:5) and to submit to the Lord in silent humility and fear (1:7). He also motivated them with the promise that a purified remnant would remain to celebrate (3:9–20).

Jeremiah the prophet was called to prophesy in Josiah's thirteenth year, or 627 BC (Jr 1:2). Part of Jeremiah's call experience included a vision of a boiling pot facing Judah from the north (vv. 13–16). The vision meant that political turmoil brewing in the north would spill over and affect Judah. Jeremiah's vision came to pass in historical terms when Ashurbanipal, the great king, died in 627 BC. In 612 BC, Babylon conquered Nineveh, the capital of Assyria; the Babylonians subsequently entered Jerusalem in 605 BC.

Habakkuk, another prophet of the seventh century, prophesied between 609 and 605 BC, during Jehoiakim's early years. Habakkuk disparaged Jerusalem's unbridled sin and lack of repentance. He cried out to the Lord, questioning God's silence during such a time of relentless evil (Hab 1:2–4). God's answer surprised and confused Habakkuk. The Lord indicated that he was about to judge Judah's sins by using the Babylonians. Thus God's word to Habakkuk harmonized with his word to Jeremiah. The Babylonians would be the instrument the Lord used to judge the sins of his people.

SEVEN LESSONS FROM THE SEVENTH CENTURY

What can we learn from the seventh century BC? First, God's people usually are subjected to the powers of this world and must find ways to be loyal to the Lord within the context of subservience to others. Second, the Lord is sovereign over all nations and kings. He uses them for his purposes. Third, no place on earth is inviolable. If Jerusalem could fall, every city is vulnerable. Fourth, divine protection issues out of a faithful relationship with God. Fifth, God utilizes prophets to confront his people's sins and to warn them of judgment. Sixth, God's word cannot be destroyed or stopped. His word is truth and the truth shall come to pass. Seventh, we should never give up on the Lord, even when those around us seemingly get ahead by sinning. The Lord will make things right in his time and in his way. ✣

---

[1] Josephus, *Antiquities*, 10.1.5.

The Philistines

by Claude F. Mariottini

Ruins of a collapsed tower at Ashkelon.

A few years after the Israelites conquered their land, a group of people invaded Canaan and settled along the coastal plain between Joppa and the desert area south of Gaza. These people became known as the Philistines. They became the rulers of five cities, Gaza, Ashdod, Ashkelon, Ekron, and Gath, known collectively as the Philistine pentapolis.

EARLY HISTORY

The words *Philistines* and *Philistia* appear more than 250 times in the Old Testament. Archaeological evidence and what the Bible says about the culture and social organization of the Philistines provide evidence of their foreign origin. Archaeologists believe the Philistines came from the eastern Mediterranean area, but their original homeland and migration route are unclear. The Philistines came to Canaan with the migration of the Sea Peoples. According to Amos 9:7 and Jeremiah 47:4, the Philistines came from Caphtor, that is, Crete. Some of the Philistines may have come from Asia Minor. [illegible] had a large Cana[illegible] Anatolia) element. The Che[illegible] and the Pelethites of 2 Samuel 8:18 were mercenaries who served as David's bodyguards. Scholars believe the Cherethites were Cretan mercenaries and that the Pelethites referred to the Philistines.

The Philistines appear in Egyptian documents as the Pelasata. In one of these documents dated to the reign of Ramesses III (ca 1183–1152 BC), Ramesses mentioned a naval battle that took place at the mouth of the Nile in which the Egyptians fought a coalition of Sea Peoples. Among the Sea Peoples who invaded Egypt, Ramesses III mentions the Shakarusha, the Pelasata, the Danuna, and others.[1]

In describing his struggle against the Sea Peoples, Ramesses said the Sea Peoples came from isles in the midst of the sea and that they advanced against Egypt, relying on their iron weapons. Images on the walls of Ramesses's temple at Medinet Habu depict the Philistines as armed with swords and round shields. A few soldiers wore what looked like

Silver coin from Aradus (on the Phoenician coast) depicting the Philistine god Dagon and a ship.

laminated corselets. The Philistine soldiers' headgear was topped with feathers.[2]

In his account of the battle, Ramesses declared he was victorious in his struggle against the invaders and took many prisoners. Although Ramesses claimed victory over the Sea Peoples, the attack weakened Egypt. Unable to defeat the invaders completely, Ramesses had to make an alliance with the Philistines.

Ramesses allowed the Philistines to settle in the eastern Mediterranean coast. He made them his vassals and employed many of the conquered soldiers as mercenaries and placed them in the garrisons on the borders of the empire. The Philistine territory went from the northwestern Negev north to the city of Ekron and from the Mediterranean Sea to the western slopes of Judah.[3] As the Philistines began settling into Canaan, they were still under Egyptian control. After Ramesses's death, Egypt's power in Canaan waned and Ramesses's successors were unable to regain control of Canaan. Exploiting Egypt's political weakness, the Philistines eventually gained their independence. From the end of the twelfth and through the eleventh centuries, the Philistines expanded their presence in Canaan and consolidated their power by assimilating the culture and language of Canaan's indigenous people.[4]

Ruins at Gaza.

IN SCRIPTURE

The Philistines appear in the Bible as Israel's enemy. During the period of the judges, the Philistines were already a menace to the Israelites. In the days of Shamgar, who was one of Israel's minor judges, the Israelites were already fighting the Philistines. Shamgar delivered Israel by killing six hundred Philistines with a cattle prod (Jdg 3:31). Samson judged Israel for twenty years at the time the Philistines were expanding their power in Canaan, but he was unable to defeat them (15:20). The Philistines defeated the Israelites and captured the ark of the covenant at Ebenezer and took it to Ashdod, where the temple of Dagon, the primary Philistine god, was located (1Sm 5:1–2). After this battle, the Philistines extended their presence in Canaan, moving into the central mountain range.

After Samson died, the Danites, under pressure from the Philistines, had to migrate from the territory Joshua had allotted to them. One of the cities allotted to the tribe of Dan was Ekron (Jos 19:43), a city that eventually became one of the five cities in the Philistine pentapolis (13:3). The Danites moved from the Shephelah to the northernmost part of Canaan where they conquered Laish, a Canaanite city, and renamed it Dan (18:27–29).

The book of 1 Samuel indicates the Philistines increased the number of settlements they controlled. They influenced and controlled the northern Negev and

Anthropoid coffin from ancient Gaza, thirteenth century BC.

were present in much of the territory that belonged to the tribes of Simeon, Judah, and Dan (prior to the Danites' relocation). Israel established the monarchy in order to deal with the threat the Philistines posed as they expanded into the central mountain range. Years later in a battle on Mount Gilboa, the Philistines defeated Israel's army and killed Israel's King Saul and his sons Jonathan, Abinadab, and Malchishua (1Sm 31:2). The Philistines desecrated Saul's body by cutting off his head and hanging his body on the walls of Beth-shean (vv. 9–10).

PHILISTINES IN ZEPHANIAH

Zephaniah used the seventh-century political situation and couched his words in the language of the conquest of Canaan. He saw Judah's enemies as Canaanites. Philistia was to receive the same fate as the Canaanites and lose its inhabitation by conquest and complete annihilation. The Philistines were in the land God promised to Israel, but they did not belong there; so, like the Canaanites of old, the Philistines would be eradicated. The Philistine cities would be depleted of their residents, and Judean shepherds would live there instead (Zph 2:6–7). Zephaniah's words found fulfillment when the Babylonians invaded Canaan.[5] In 604 BC, Nebuchadnezzar conquered the four Philistine cities and deported their kings to Babylon. As Zephaniah had predicted, the conquest of the four Philistine cities was the end of Philistia as a political entity.

---

[1] John Bright, *A History of Israel* (Philadelphia: Westminster, 1981), 174. [2] R. K. Harrison, "Philistines" in *NIDBA*, 362–63. [3] G. Ernest Wright, "Fresh Evidence for the Philistine Story," *BA* 29 (September 1966): 69–86. [4] Bright, *History of Israel*, 176. [5] Kenneth A. Kitchen, "The Philistines" in *People of Old Testament Times*, ed. D. J. Wiseman (Oxford: Clarendon, 1973), 67.

8 Therefore, wait for me —
this is the LORD's declaration —
until the day I rise up for plunder.[A]
For my decision is to gather nations,
to assemble kingdoms,
in order to pour out my indignation on them,
all my burning anger;
for the whole earth will be consumed
by the fire of my jealousy.

FINAL RESTORATION PROMISED

9 For I will then restore
pure speech to the peoples
so that all of them may call
on the name of the LORD
and serve him with a single purpose.[B]
10 From beyond the rivers of Cush
my supplicants, my dispersed people,
will bring an offering to me.
11 On that day you[C] will not be put to shame
because of everything you have done
in rebelling against me.
For then I will remove
from among you your jubilant,
arrogant people,
and you will never again be haughty
on my holy mountain.
12 I will leave
a meek and humble people among you,
and they will take refuge in the name of the
LORD.
13 The remnant of Israel will no longer
do wrong or tell lies;
a deceitful tongue will not be found
in their mouths.
They will pasture and lie down,
with nothing to make them afraid.

14 Sing for joy, Daughter Zion;
shout loudly, Israel!
Be glad and celebrate with all your heart,
Daughter Jerusalem!
15 The LORD has removed your punishment;
he has turned back your enemy.
The King of Israel, the LORD, is among you;
you need no longer fear harm.
16 On that day it will be said to Jerusalem:
"Do not fear;
Zion, do not let your hands grow weak.
17 The LORD your God is among you,
a warrior who saves.
He will rejoice over you with gladness.
He will be quiet[D] in his love.
He will delight in you with singing."

18 I will gather those who have been driven
from the appointed festivals;
they will be a tribute from you[E]
and a reproach on her.[F]
19 Yes, at that time
I will deal with all who oppress you.
I will save the lame and gather the outcasts;
I will make those who were disgraced
throughout the earth
receive praise and fame.
20 At that time I will bring you[G] back,
yes, at the time I will gather you.
I will give you fame and praise
among all the peoples of the earth,
when I restore your fortunes before your eyes.
The LORD has spoken.

[A] **3:8** LXX, Syr read *for a witness*; Vg reads *up forever* [B] **3:9** Lit *with one shoulder* [C] **3:11** = Israel [D] **3:17** LXX, Syr read *He will renew you* [E] **3:18** = Jerusalem [F] **3:18** Hb obscure [G] **3:20** = people of Israel

8 Therefore, wait for me —
this is the LORD's declaration —
until the day I rise up for plunder.
For my decision is to gather nations,
to assemble kingdoms,
in order to pour out my indignation on them,
all my burning anger;
for the whole earth will be consumed
by the fire of my jealousy.

FINAL RESTORATION PROMISED

9 For I will then restore
pure speech to the peoples
so that all of them may call
on the name of the LORD
and serve him with a single purpose.
10 From beyond the rivers of Cush
my supplicants, my dispersed people,
will bring an offering to me.
11 On that day you will not be put to shame
because of all your acts by which you have done
in rebelling against me.
For then I will remove
from among you your jubilant,
arrogant people,
and you will never again be haughty
on my holy mountain.
12 I will leave
a meek and humble people among you,
and they will take refuge in the name of the
LORD.
13 The remnant of Israel will no longer
do wrong or tell lies;
a deceitful tongue will not be found
in their mouths.
They will pasture and lie down
with nothing to make them afraid.

14 Sing for joy, Daughter Zion;
shout loudly, Israel!
Be glad and celebrate with all your heart,
Daughter Jerusalem!
15 The LORD has removed your punishment;
he has turned back your enemy.
The King of Israel, the LORD, is among you;
you need no longer fear harm.
16 On that day it will be said to Jerusalem:
"Do not fear;
Zion, do not let your hands grow weak.
17 The LORD your God is among you,
a warrior who saves.
He will rejoice over you with gladness.
He will be quiet in his love.
He will delight in you with singing."

18 I will gather those who have been grieving
from the appointed festivals;
they will be a tribute from you
and reproach on her.
19 Yes, at that time
I will deal with all who oppress you.
I will save the lame and gather the outcasts;
I will make those who were disgraced
throughout the earth
receive praise and fame.
20 At that time I will bring you back,
yes, at the time I will gather you.
I will give you fame and praise
among all the peoples of the earth,
when I restore your fortunes before your eyes.
The LORD has spoken.

[illegible]

HAGGAI

Relief at Persepolis showing Persian King Darius (probably) receiving visiting dignitaries.

INTRODUCTION TO

HAGGAI

Circumstances of Writing

There is no statement that strictly identifies who wrote this book, but the words recorded are repeatedly connected to what God spoke to the prophet Haggai (Hg 1:1,3,13; 2:1,10,14,20).

In 587 BC, Nebuchadnezzar came to Jerusalem for the third time, this time destroying the walls, the temple, and the city (2Kg 25:8–21; Jr 39–40). Most of the people were taken into Babylonian captivity for seventy years (Jr 25:11–12; 29:10), although Jeremiah and a few survivors stayed in Jerusalem (Jr 41–43). God predicted through Isaiah that the strong king named Cyrus (Is 44:24–45:2) would defeat Babylon and her gods (Is 46–47). After the Persian King Cyrus defeated Babylon, he issued a decree in 538 BC that allowed the exiled nations in Babylon to return to their homelands (Ezr 1:1–4; Cyrus Cylinder). Sheshbazzar (Ezr 1:8–11) led about forty-three thousand Jewish pilgrims back to the state of Yehud (Judah) to rebuild the temple in Jerusalem (2:64–65). In the seventh month, the governor Zerubbabel and the high priest Joshua led the people in building an altar to worship God (3:1–7); in their second year, the people laid the foundation of the new temple (3:8–10). But this effort was stopped for the next sixteen years because the Samaritan people who lived north of Jerusalem frustrated these rebuilding efforts, plus they hired lawyers to cause the Persian authorities to stop supporting the work on this temple (4:1–5). This led to a period of great discouragement. Apathy set in because many of the hopes of the Jewish people were unfulfilled. The walls of the city were not repaired, the temple was not rebuilt, there was a famine in the land (Hg 2:9–11), and the people were still under Persian control. They could do nothing without the approval of Tattenai, the governor of the "region west of the Euphrates River," and his officials (Ezr 5:3–5). There seemed to be no way to move forward and rebuild the temple.

After the death of Cyrus, his son Cambyses became king (530–522 BC). He marched through Judah and conquered most of Egypt, but on his way home he died (possibly an assassination). A high army official named Darius took control of the Persian army, marched back to Babylon, defeated a rebel force led by Gaumata, and became king in 522 BC. Darius put down several revolts and then reformed the satrapy administrative system, with the result that by 520 BC the Persian Empire was at peace.

In the second year of Darius (520 BC; Hg 1:1; see Ezr 4:24–5:2) when the conflict over political control of the empire was over, God directed Haggai to encourage the leaders in Jerusalem to rebuild the temple. When governor Tattenai heard about this rebuilding, he questioned the plan's legitimacy and wrote to Darius to find out whether the government was sanctioning this project (Ezr 5:3–17). Darius approved the rebuilding campaign and even supported it through the royal treasury, as was confirmed by the discovery of Cyrus's original decree in a palace at Ecbatana (6:1–12). Consequently, the temple rebuilding was completed in four years (6:15).

Contribution to the Bible

Throughout the Bible, there is a call and a reminder to place God first. The period following the return from exile was no exception. Haggai's challenge was to call the postexilic community of Jews living in Jerusalem not simply to focus on their own creature comforts but to honor God. This commitment would be reflected in their work on the temple. Haggai's call was later reflected in the words of Jesus: "Seek first the kingdom of God and his righteousness, and all these things will be provided for you" (Mt 6:33).

Haggai's call for the people to get their priorities in order and place God first by rebuilding his temple was of great importance. For the people to return to this task was a sign of their priorities. It also showed that God was with the remnant and that his promises of restoration had begun to be fulfilled. Their obedience in this matter declared God's glory and thus brought him pleasure. It served to vindicate the Lord since the temple's destruction had disgraced the Lord's name. Finally, their obedience to Haggai's words served as a pledge of the new covenant and the messianic age. The restoration of the temple was a sign that God had not revoked his covenant with Levi or his covenant with David. He would provide cleansing and restoration through a glorious temple and a messianic ruler.

Structure

The book of Haggai contains four short confrontational speeches in chronological order that identify ways the leaders and people in Jerusalem should change their theological thinking and behavior. There is a logical progression in the structure. People must glorify God (1:1–15), stay committed to God's plans (2:1–9), please God by living holy lives (2:10–19), and serve him faithfully (2:20–23).

Haggai the Prophet and His Ministry

by Stephen R. Miller

THE PROPHET

Haggai's name means "festal" or "my festival." The significance of the name is not certain. Likely his parents named him Haggai because he was born on Passover, Pentecost, the Festival of Shelters, or another of Israel's great feast days.

This prophet is the only person named Haggai in the Old Testament, but extrabiblical evidence indicates this was a popular Jewish name in the postexilic era. Eleven persons are named Haggai at Elephantine Island (a Jewish colony in Egypt) and four in texts from Babylonia.[1]

Like seven other prophetic books, Haggai provides no information about the prophet's parents or ancestry. Other than his name, we know nothing of his personal life.

Haggai gave no details about his call to ministry, but he referred to himself as a prophet five times (Hg 1:1,3,12; 2:1,10). Ezra twice called him a "prophet" (Ezr 5:1; 6:14). Haggai affirmed the divine authority of his prophetic messages with phrases such as "the word of the LORD came," "the LORD of Armies says this," and "this is the declaration of the LORD of Armies" at least twenty-five times in his two short chapters. Jews recognized the book's canonicity from the outset; Hebrews also cites the book (Heb 12:26; cf. Hg 2:6,21). The Dead Sea Scrolls also contain portions of the book of Haggai.

HIS MINISTRY

According to the biblical record, Haggai was the first prophet to preach in Jerusalem after the Babylonian captivity—the postexilic period. Presumably he returned to Jerusalem from Babylon with Zerubbabel in 538 BC. Haggai carefully dated each of his messages. His first prophecy was "in the second year of King Darius, on the first day of the sixth month" (1:1). "Darius" is the Medo-Persian king, Darius I (reigned 522–486 BC). On the Hebrew calendar, "the sixth month" was Elul; this included portions of our August and September. The first day of Elul in 520 BC (Darius's second year) was August 29, about two months before Haggai's contemporary, Zechariah, began his prophetic work (Zch 1:1–6). Haggai's last message came less than four months after the first. Ezra records the historical

Ruins at Elephantine Island in the Nile River at Aswan, Egypt. Legal documents found here indicate many Jews settled here, especially in the sixth century BC. They erected a Jewish temple here.

MESSAGE	HAGGAI TEXT	DATE
Rebuke and repentance	1:1–15	Sixth month, first day (August 29, 520 BC)
Call to courage	2:1–9	Seventh month, twenty-first day (October 17, 520 BC)
Call to holiness and a reminder of sin's consequences	2:10–19	Ninth month, twenty-fourth day (December 18, 520 BC)
A glorious future for God's people	2:20–23	Ninth month, twenty-fourth day (December 18, 520 BC)

background for Haggai's ministry and mentions Haggai and Zechariah by name (Ezr 5:1; 6:14).

Haggai's prophecy consists of an introduction and four brief messages, each beginning with "the word of the LORD came" (1:3; 2:1,10,20).[2] The chart below summarizes these messages with their dates.[3]

Haggai's writing has been labeled "elevated prose."[4] His style was generally simple and direct but quite effective and powerful. The prophet's use of repetition and other rhetorical devices gives evidence of his literary skill. For example, the threefold exhortation to "be strong" in Haggai 2:4 is stirring. ✣

[1] Edwin Yamauchi, "Ezra–Nehemiah" in *The Expositor's Bible Commentary*, ed. Frank E. Gaebelein (Grand Rapids: Zondervan, 1988), 4:635; Richard A. Taylor, "Haggai" in *Haggai, Malachi*, NAC (2004), 43. [2] For a brief introduction and survey of Haggai, see Stephen R. Miller, *Nahum, Habakkuk, Zephaniah, Haggai, Zechariah, Malachi*, Holman Old Testament Commentary (Nashville: Broadman & Holman, 2004), 114–32. [3] For these dates, see Joyce G. Baldwin, *Haggai, Zechariah, Malachi*, TOTC (1972), 29. [4] Taylor, "Haggai," 73.

Part of the Temple Mount called Zerubbabel's Marking. Change in style of stonework shows Herod's extension on the southwest corner. The rougher stones to the north probably date to Solomon, which Zerubbabel reset after the exile. The lower four courses appear to be undisturbed and may be in their original positions.

COMMAND TO REBUILD THE TEMPLE

1 In the second year of King Darius,[A] on the first day
of the sixth month, the word of the LORD came
through the prophet Haggai to Zerubbabel son of
Shealtiel, the governor of Judah, and to Joshua son
of Jehozadak, the high priest:
2 "The LORD of Armies says this: These people say:
The time has not come for the house of the LORD to
be rebuilt."
3 The word of the LORD came through the prophet Haggai: 4 "Is it a time for you yourselves to live in
your paneled houses, while this house[B] lies in ruins?"
5 Now, the LORD of Armies says this: "Think carefully
about[C] your ways:

6 You have planted much
but harvested little.
You eat
but never have enough to be satisfied.
You drink
but never have enough to be happy.
You put on clothes
but never have enough to get warm.
The wage earner puts his wages
into a bag with a hole in it."

7 The LORD of Armies says this: "Think carefully
about your ways. 8 Go up into the hills, bring down
lumber, and build the house; and I will be pleased
with it and be glorified," says the LORD. 9 "You expected much, but then it amounted to little. When
you brought the harvest to your house, I ruined[D] it.
Why?" This is the declaration of the LORD of Armies.
"Because my house still lies in ruins, while each of
you is busy with his own house.

10 So on your account,[E]
the skies have withheld the dew
and the land its crops.
11 I have summoned a drought
on the fields and the hills,
on the grain, new wine, fresh oil,
and whatever the ground yields,
on people and animals,
and on all that your hands produce."

THE PEOPLE'S RESPONSE

12 Then Zerubbabel son of Shealtiel, the high priest
Joshua son of Jehozadak, and the entire remnant of
the people obeyed the LORD their God and the words
of the prophet Haggai, because the LORD their God
had sent him. So the people feared the LORD.
13 Then Haggai, the LORD's messenger, delivered the
LORD's message to the people: "I am with you — this
is the LORD's declaration."
14 The LORD roused the spirit of Zerubbabel son of
Shealtiel, governor of Judah, the spirit of the high
priest Joshua son of Jehozadak, and the spirit of all
the remnant of the people. They began work on the
house of the LORD of Armies, their God, 15 on the twenty-fourth day of the sixth month, in the second year
of King Darius.

ENCOURAGEMENT AND PROMISE

2 On the twenty-first day of the seventh month, the
word of the LORD came through the prophet Haggai: 2 "Speak to Zerubbabel son of Shealtiel, governor
of Judah, to the high priest Joshua son of Jehozadak,
and to the remnant of the people: 3 'Who is left among
you who saw this house in its former glory? How does
it look to you now? Doesn't it seem to you like nothing by comparison? 4 Even so, be strong, Zerubbabel
— this is the LORD's declaration. Be strong, Joshua son
of Jehozadak, high priest. Be strong, all you people
of the land — this is the LORD's declaration. Work!
For I am with you — the declaration of the LORD of
Armies. 5 This is the promise I made to you when you
came out of Egypt, and my Spirit is present among
you; don't be afraid.'"
6 For the LORD of Armies says this: "Once more, in
a little while, I am going to shake the heavens and
the earth, the sea and the dry land. 7 I will shake all
the nations so that the treasures of all the nations
will come, and I will fill this house with glory," says
the LORD of Armies. 8 "The silver and gold belong to
me" — this is the declaration of the LORD of Armies.
9 "The final glory of this house[F] will be greater than
the first," says the LORD of Armies. "I will provide
peace in this place" — this is the declaration of the
LORD of Armies.

FROM DEPRIVATION TO BLESSING

10 On the twenty-fourth day of the ninth month, in the
second year of Darius, the word of the LORD came to
the prophet Haggai: 11 "This is what the LORD of Armies says: Ask the priests for a ruling. 12 If a man is
carrying consecrated meat in the fold of his garment,
and it touches bread, stew, wine, oil, or any other food,
does it become holy?"
The priests answered, "No."
13 Then Haggai asked, "If someone defiled by contact with a corpse touches any of these, does it become defiled?"
The priests answered, "It becomes defiled."
14 Then Haggai replied, "So is this people, and so is
this nation before me — this is the LORD's declaration.
And so is every work of their hands; even what they
offer there is defiled.

[A] **1:1** King of Persia reigned 522–486 BC [B] **1:4** = the temple [C] **1:5** Lit *Place your heart on*, also in v. 7 [D] **1:9** Lit *blew on* [E] **1:10** Or *So above you* [F] **2:9** Or *The glory of this latter house*

What Did the Governor Do?

by Janice Meier

Relief at Persepolis showing Persian King Darius (probably) receiving visiting dignitaries.

What did the governor do during the time of Haggai, whose prophetic ministry occurred around 520 BC, approximately twenty years after Persia's King Cyrus allowed the Jews to return to their homeland? Who bore the title *governor*?

The basic form of the Hebrew term rendered "governor" in Haggai 1:1,14 can be transliterated or written in English as *pechah*. The Hebrew term may have derived from an ancient Persian or an Akkadian word signifying a high governmental official.[1] Some view the title as an abbreviated loan word from the Assyrians that originally meant "lord of a district."[2]

The title refers to an appointed office, not an inherited one. The term generally designated the leader of the Jewish people following the exile (Neh 12:26; Hg 1:1,14; 2:2,21; Mal 1:8). In other contexts, the noun could denote a deputy bureaucrat (Est 8:9; Jr 51:23) or a military leader (1Kg 20:24, "captains"). Other Old Testament passages use an Aramaic noun with the same transliterated spelling as the Hebrew *pechah* to refer to "a provincial governor in the Persian Empire (Ezra 5:6); the postexilic leader of the Jewish nation (Ezra 6:7); and various similar officers involved in the political structure (Dan 6:7 [v. 8 in Hebrew])."[3]

The fact that the term was applied to appointed officials who held differing governmental status and responsibilities suggests that what it meant to function as a governor in the Persian Empire probably varied from one area of the empire to another. This fact may have resulted in part from the Persians' desire to keep their subjects as content as possible without undermining the expected allegiance to Persia.

The Hebrew term *pechah* occurs in 2 Kings 18:24 ("officer") to denote a Neo-Assyrian provincial governor who had been appointed over the conquered territory of Judah at the end of the eighth century BC. In this reference, the royal spokesman boasted that King Hezekiah's army lacked the power to stand against even one *pechah* ("officer"). Thus the inspired writer of 2 Kings 18:24 depicted an Assyrian provincial governor as commanding the district's military unit. This depiction accurately harmonizes with the Assyrian policy of putting a regional army under the provincial governor's command.[4]

The title also occurs in Ezekiel 23:23, where it is translated "governors," as part of the Lord's announcement to the sixth-century-BC prophet Ezekiel that God would bring judgment on Judah's inhabitants. That judgment came at the hands of the Babylonians during Ezekiel's ministry. Thus the title could refer to various kinds of leaders in varying countries or empires over a period of several centuries.

When Cyrus of Persia conquered Babylon and its territories in 539 BC, he retained the existing provincial system of administration. Thus the title *pechah* continued to designate provincial governors as it did under the Assyrians and Babylonians. Cyrus allowed Jews to return to their homeland under Sheshbazzar, who bore the title *pechah* (Ezr 5:13–15). Apparently Sheshbazzar served as governor only briefly because Zerubbabel already had been identified as leader (3:2).[5] Some Bible scholars contend that the meaning of *pechah* in postexilic times is vague and may denote simply a special commissioner whose appointment was limited in scope as well as in length of time. These scholars argue that the first governor of Judah was Nehemiah, not Sheshbazzar. A good case can be made, however, in support of Sheshbazzar as the first governor of Judah.[6] In fact, one scholar commenting on Ezra 5:6–17 concluded that when King Cyrus of Persia released the articles from the temple to Sheshbazzar early in the king's reign, Sheshbazzar probably was viewed as the official governor and Zerubbabel as the popular leader.[7]

During the reign of Persia's King Darius I (522–486 BC), the title *pechah* was somewhat ambiguous. Upon taking the throne, Darius I reorganized the empire into twenty satrapies or territories. He divided the empire in this manner to create a more efficient system of control and taxation.[8] Darius appointed an administrator over the whole Fertile Crescent. He also put a subordinate satrap or governor over the area sometimes designated "Beyond the River" or Trans-Euphrates. This satrap has been identified with Tattenai, "governor of the region west of the Euphrates River" (5:3,6; 6:6,13).[9] These references in Ezra use *pechah*, the corresponding Aramaic word for *governor*. The title *governor*, however, was not used only of Tattenai; it also referred to the governor of Judah (Ezr 6:7), a provincial area that was part of the Trans-Euphrates or Beyond the River satrapy. This overlapping of the term likely occurred when Darius I applied his new satrapy system in an area that already had an existing provincial system. This caused confusion and eventually tension. Darius had appointed Tattenai as governor or satrap of the Trans-Euphrates region, an area where Cyrus had previously appointed Sheshbazzar to serve as governor of Judah (5:1–17). How could both rule the same area? Darius resolved the conflict by declaring that "Judah could function as a semi-autonomous province under their own governor, free from interference from the satrap of Trans-Euphrates

Cyrus Cylinder, late sixth century BC, recounting the Babylonian god Marduk giving Babylon to Cyrus, and Cyrus allowing captives to return home and rebuild their temples.

(6:1–12)."[10] Zerubbabel bore the title *pechah* (Hg 1:1,14). Since the brief book of Haggai mentions the high priest Joshua along with Zerubbabel five times (1:1,12,14; 2:2,4), these two men apparently shared local leadership. Both functioned, though, under Persian authority. This arrangement suggests the merging of political and religious leadership. The fact that Zerubbabel's name consistently appears first indicates his supremacy.

As governor of Judah, Zerubbabel ruled a tiny district that was part of the huge Persian Empire. That small area was commonly known as Yehud, an Aramaic name. Yehud, also called Judah, constituted a small part of the much larger Trans-Euphrates region. The province was probably so small that an individual could have walked from one end of it to the other in a couple of days.

During this period, Judah's size and population posed no threat to the distant Persian king. He thus granted the people of Judah freedom to govern themselves, including the right to appoint both their own ruler from the line of David and someone to serve as priest. The arrangement helped stabilize the region politically, which in turn ensured that trade could continue through Judah and that Persia could focus its attention elsewhere.[11] All involved benefited.

In conclusion, while the evidence regarding the governor's role during Haggai's time (ca 520 BC) remains sketchy, the term definitely was fluid in meaning. What it meant to function as a governor in the Persian Empire apparently varied from one part of the empire to another. Reasons for these differences included the Persians' desire to keep their subjects as satisfied as possible and also Darius's appointing satrapies in areas with already-existing governmental systems.

In general, these governors functioned in ways similar to governors in the United States today, in that they possessed a limited amount of military power and were responsible for maintaining law and order within their jurisdictions. In contrast to US governors, these leaders were appointed officials, not elected. Furthermore, the governor of Yehud or Judah apparently retained more freedom than governors in other parts of the empire. He also shared leadership with the high priest. ✣

[1] Ralph L. Smith, *Micah–Malachi*, WBC (1984), 152. [2] Francis Brown, S. R. Driver, and Charles A. Briggs, *A Hebrew and English Lexicon of the Old Testament* (Oxford: Clarendon, 1980), 808. [3] Warren Baker and Eugene Carpenter, *The Complete Word Study Dictionary: Old Testament* (Chattanooga: AMG, 2003), 895. [4] Gordon H. Johnston, "*Pechah*," *NIDOTTE*, 3:603. [5] Mervin Breneman, *Ezra, Nehemiah, Esther*, NAC (1993), 112. [6] Johnston, "*Pechah*," 604. [7] Edwin M. Yamauchi, *Persia and the Bible* (Grand Rapids: Baker, 1990), 157, n. 141. [8] Herodotus, *Histories* 3.89. [9] Johnston, "*Pechah*," 605. [10] Johnston, "*Pechah*." [11] Richard A. Taylor, "Haggai," in *Haggai, Malachi*, NAC (2004), 110–11.

Statue of Khema, governor of Elephantine, Egypt.

by Martha S. Bergen

SETTING

God raised up two prophets, Haggai and Zechariah, who were contemporaries, to encourage the nation to complete the unfinished task of rebuilding the temple. Their task was made necessary because the Babylonians under King Nebuchadnezzar in 586 BC had captured Jerusalem and destroyed the earlier temple. Many of the Israelites were also taken captive to Babylon. The great Babylonian Empire, however, soon fell.

Cyrus the Great, founder of the Persian Empire, conquered Babylon in 538 BC. He gave the Israelites freedom to return to Israel for the express purpose of rebuilding their temple (2Ch 36:22–23). Those returning to Israel started the project, but the rebuilding work soon came to a halt.

Part of the reason for the delay in the temple's reconstruction was the opposition raised from those who were left behind during the exile, as well as non-Jews who were brought to Samaria by the Assyrians after their devastation of Israel in 722 BC. These were enemies of the Jews who felt threatened by the returnees and the religious and political implications associated with the temple. Under the pretense of wanting to help the Jews, they sought to discourage and frustrate the work, with the ultimate intent of undermining their success.[1]

Additionally, the adjustments the Israelites faced when they returned from exile overwhelmed them and strained their resources as they built their own homes and also worked on the temple. The Israelites became discouraged and lost hope of ever seeing the temple restored.[2] When Persia's King Darius came to power in 522 BC, he gave the Jews permission once again to work on the temple. Darius appointed Zerubbabel governor over Judah and charged him with the responsibility of overseeing the temple project. Zerubbabel's leadership, along with the preaching of Zechariah and Haggai, prompted the Jews to finish what they had started approximately sixteen years earlier.

THE MEN AND THEIR MISSION

Zechariah and Haggai were best known as prophets, although Zechariah likewise was a priest. This probably strengthened his personal interest in the temple's completion. Some have suggested that Haggai also descended from priestly origin, but this is mere speculation;

Griffin that sat atop the columns of the palace of Darius the Great (522–486 BC) in Persepolis (modern Iran). These highly stylized column capitals supported the roof's massive beams.

early Jewish tradition never made such a claim.[3]

Typically, the prophet's message was twofold: to proclaim God's judgment and to offer God's forgiveness and impart hope. Though God revealed his messages to individual prophets, he did so in ways congruent with each prophet's unique personality and permitted the prophet his own distinct style for conveying these messages. Zechariah and Haggai used similar methods (rebuke and encouragement) as they followed the twofold message pattern stated above. But their styles varied according to their personalities, abilities, and experiences.

The prophet Haggai is mentioned only in the book bearing his name and in Ezra 5:1; 6:14. His messages were delivered over a period of four months in 520 BC. Haggai, like Zechariah, employed both rebuke and encouragement to motivate the Jews to finish the temple. In chapter 1, he called for the Jews to renounce their complacency regarding the temple. "The Lord of Armies says this: 'Think carefully about your ways. Go . . . and build the house [temple]. . . . When you brought the harvest to your house, I ruined it. Why? . . . Because my house still lies in ruins, while each of you is busy with his own house'" (Hg 1:7–9). Yet Haggai assured the people with God's message of "I am with you" (1:13) so their spirits were stirred and "They began work on the house of the Lord of Armies, their God" (1:14).

Haggai also predicted the Messiah's association with the temple (2:7). Regarding the second temple he stated: "the final glory of this house will be greater than the first" (2:9). The earlier temple King Solomon built had been far more glorious in its material structure and elaborate gold ornamentation than the temple Zerubbabel built. However, the glory associated with the ornateness of Solomon's temple would pale in comparison to the glory of the second temple because the incarnate Christ would walk among the Jews there, showing the fullness of God's glory as he taught them.

A GOAL ACCOMPLISHED

The temple was completed in 516 BC. Without the encouragement of Zechariah and Haggai, however, the temple likely would have remained a partially constructed edifice, symbolic of Israel's lost hope for that generation. Israel was faithful to the divinely mandated task of rebuilding, mainly because of the messages of these unwavering prophets. As a result, the people of Israel achieved their goal of a finished temple. Ezra recorded it as follows: "So the Jewish elders continued successfully with the building under the prophesying of Haggai the prophet and Zechariah son of Iddo. They finished the building according to the command of the God of Israel . . . in the sixth year of the reign of King Darius" (Ezr 6:14–15).

Due to the preaching of Zechariah and Haggai, Israel persisted, giving evidence of what can be done when people are motivated and rally together to accomplish a significant task. More important, their achievement is a testimony to a faithful God who kept his promise to Israel. The Lord restored his people and magnified his own name through the completion of the temple. The temple not only helped Israel in its unique relationship with God but also served as a witness to the nations of the world that Yahweh is indeed the one true God. This temple connected Israel's present with their past but would also relate to God's plan for the nation's future, as Christ himself would become a temple destroyed, yet raised again (Jn 2:19).[4] Zechariah and Haggai rose to the challenge of inspiring Israel to complete the new temple. As a result, they not only helped establish a building, but they also became instruments that shaped a nation for God's divine purpose. ✣

---

[1] Martha S. Bergen, *Ezra/Nehemiah*, Shepherd's Notes (Nashville: Broadman & Holman, 1999), 24–25. [2] Paul L. Redditt, "Zerubbabel" and E. Ray Clendenen, "Haggai" in *HIBD* rev. ed. (2015), 1698–99, 691–93, respectively. [3] Richard A. Taylor, "Haggai," in *Haggai, Malachi,* NAC (2004), 38–39. [4] Joyce G. Baldwin, *Haggai, Zechariah, Malachi: An Introduction and Commentary* (Downers Grove, IL: InterVarsity, 1972), 19, 21.

15 "Now from this day on, think carefully: Before
one stone was placed on another in the LORD's temple,
16 what state were you in?[A] When someone came to
a grain heap of twenty measures, it only amounted
to ten; when one came to the winepress to dip fifty
measures from the vat, it only amounted to twenty.
17 I struck you — all the work of your hands — with
blight, mildew, and hail, but you didn't turn to me
— this is the LORD's declaration. 18 From this day on,
think carefully; from the twenty-fourth day of the
ninth month, from the day the foundation of the
LORD's temple was laid; think carefully. 19 Is there
still seed left in the granary? The vine, the fig, the
pomegranate, and the olive tree have not yet produced. But from this day on I will bless you."

PROMISE TO ZERUBBABEL

20 The word of the LORD came to Haggai a second time
on the twenty-fourth day of the month: 21 "Speak to
Zerubbabel, governor of Judah: I am going to shake
the heavens and the earth. 22 I will overturn royal
thrones and destroy the power of the Gentile kingdoms. I will overturn chariots and their riders. Horses
and their riders will fall, each by his brother's sword.
23 On that day" — this is the declaration of the LORD
of Armies — "I will take you, Zerubbabel son of Shealtiel, my servant" — this is the LORD's declaration
— "and make you like my signet ring, for I have chosen you." This is the declaration of the LORD of Armies.

[A] **2:16** Hb obscure

ZECHARIAH

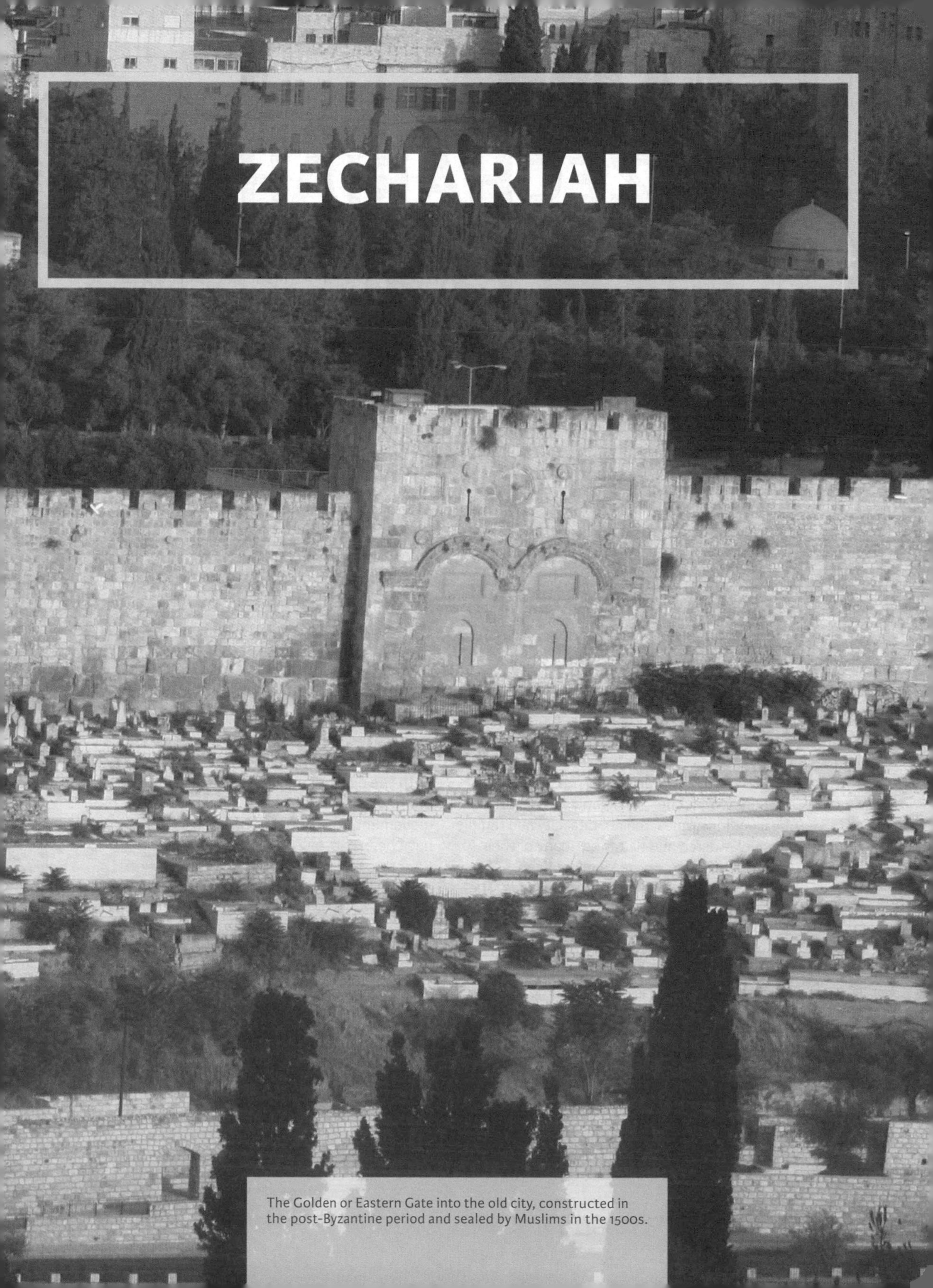

The Golden or Eastern Gate into the old city, constructed in the post-Byzantine period and sealed by Muslims in the 1500s.

INTRODUCTION TO

ZECHARIAH

Circumstances of Writing

Zechariah returned to Judah with the former exiles and was apparently a priest (Neh 12:16). He was a contemporary of Haggai. Though nothing is known of cooperation between the two prophets, they had similar missions and are credited with the successful reconstruction of the temple (Ezr 5:1–2; 6:14). Zechariah gave dates for two periods of his prophetic ministry (520 and 518 BC; Zch 1:1,7; 7:1). Whether he was the author of the entire book is debated. Many scholars, impressed with the differences between chapters 1–8 and 9–14, conclude that Zechariah did not write the last six chapters. The concept of authorship at the time of the Bible, however, was different from modern standards. In the Old Testament, there is evidence of portions of books under a single author's name that were not written by that author (Nm 12:3; Dt 34:5–12; Jr 51:64c).

A key moment in the history of the Israelites came after King Cyrus of Persia granted the captives permission to return to Israel (538 BC). The chosen people had just come through one of the worst experiences possible in the ancient world. Their homeland was devastated by invading armies, their capital city and temple were plundered and flattened, many of their people and leaders were killed, and most of the rest were carried off into pagan lands. The returnees who made the long trek back to Judah were faced with the challenge of reestablishing Jerusalem and the temple. Based on the account in the book of Ezra, work began immediately. But after the altar was rebuilt and the foundation stones were laid, problems arose and the work stopped (Ezr 3:1–4:24). Though sacrifices were offered on the altar, the temple continued to lie in ruins for almost two more decades.

Contribution to the Bible

The book of Zechariah is full of the language of judgment, but it is also full of God's promises. The Lord challenged his people to undertake an overwhelmingly difficult task, and he assured them of their success through his power. But the nature of these promises extended beyond rebuilding the temple. From beginning to end, the Bible tells the story of God's redemptive plan, culminating in God's triumph over evil and salvation for sinners. Zechariah's prophecies anticipate this grand culmination of history, describing a coming glorious king, a God who triumphs over all, and a world with all wrongs corrected. These promises set the stage for God's future kingdom, as evidenced by the quotes and allusions to Zechariah in the New Testament.

Structure

The book of Zechariah is complex, sometimes with seemingly disjointed units, like a series of snapshots that need to be put in order. The apparent lack of organization may reflect the oral origin of the book, a collection of sermons that were patched together in written form. But it may also have been intentional. With the goal of shocking the hearers and bringing them to their senses, rapid-fire movement from one thought to another may have been part of Zechariah's technique. Chapters 1–8 contain carefully dated visions and sermons, while chapters 9–14 consist of undated poetic oracles and narrative descriptions of judgment and blessing.

Zechariah used a mix of genres. His sermons, poetry, and oracles of judgment and salvation were typical of the prophetic genre. But his visions had similarities with apocalyptic literature, best represented in the Old Testament by the book of Daniel. The content of some of his oracles, describing divine intervention and a radically different world, are also typical of apocalyptic literature. Thus Zechariah may represent a stage of development between a prophetic form and an apocalyptic form.

A PLEA FOR REPENTANCE

1 In the eighth month, in the second year of Darius, the word of the LORD came to the prophet Zechariah son of Berechiah, son of Iddo: 2 "The LORD was extremely angry with your ancestors. 3 So tell the people, 'This is what the LORD of Armies says: Return to me — this is the declaration of the LORD of Armies — and I will return to you, says the LORD of Armies. 4 Do not be like your ancestors; the earlier prophets proclaimed to them: This is what the LORD of Armies says: Turn from your evil ways and your evil deeds. But they did not listen or pay attention to me — this is the LORD's declaration. 5 Where are your ancestors now? And do the prophets live forever? 6 But didn't my words and my statutes that I commanded my servants the prophets overtake your ancestors?' "

So the people repented and said, "As the LORD of Armies decided to deal with us for our ways and our deeds, so he has dealt with us."

THE NIGHT VISIONS

7 On the twenty-fourth day of the eleventh month, which is the month of Shebat, in the second year of Darius, the word of the LORD came to the prophet Zechariah son of Berechiah, son of Iddo:

FIRST VISION: HORSEMEN

8 I looked out in the night and saw a man riding on a chestnut[A] horse. He was standing among the myrtle trees in the valley.[B] Behind him were chestnut, brown, and white horses. 9 I asked, "What are these, my lord?"

The angel who was talking to me replied, "I will show you what they are."

10 Then the man standing among the myrtle trees explained, "They are the ones the LORD has sent to patrol the earth."

11 They reported to the angel of the LORD standing among the myrtle trees, "We have patrolled the earth, and right now the whole earth is calm and quiet."

12 Then the angel of the LORD responded, "How long, LORD of Armies, will you withhold mercy from Jerusalem and the cities of Judah that you have been angry with these seventy years?" 13 The LORD replied with kind and comforting words to the angel who was speaking with me.

14 So the angel who was speaking with me said, "Proclaim: The LORD of Armies says: I am extremely jealous for Jerusalem and Zion. 15 I am fiercely angry with the nations that are at ease, for I was a little angry, but they made the destruction worse.[C] 16 Therefore, this is what the LORD says: In mercy, I have returned to Jerusalem; my house will be rebuilt within it — this is the declaration of the LORD of Armies — and a measuring line will be stretched out over Jerusalem.

17 "Proclaim further: This is what the LORD of Armies says: My cities will again overflow with prosperity; the LORD will once more comfort Zion and again choose Jerusalem."

SECOND VISION: FOUR HORNS AND CRAFTSMEN

18 Then I looked up and saw four horns. 19 So I asked the angel who was speaking with me, "What are these?"

And he said to me, "These are the horns that scattered Judah, Israel, and Jerusalem."

20 Then the LORD showed me four craftsmen. 21 I asked, "What are they coming to do?"

He replied, "These are the horns that scattered Judah so no one could raise his head. These craftsmen have come to terrify them, to cut off[D] the horns of the nations that raised a horn against the land of Judah to scatter it."

THIRD VISION: SURVEYOR

2 I looked up and saw a man with a measuring line in his hand. 2 I asked, "Where are you going?"

He answered me, "To measure Jerusalem to determine its width and length."

3 Then the angel who was speaking with me went out, and another angel went out to meet him. 4 He said to him, "Run and tell this young man: Jerusalem will be inhabited without walls because of the number of people and animals in it." 5 The declaration of the LORD: "I myself will be a wall of fire around it, and I will be the glory within it."

6 "Listen! Listen! Flee from the land of the north" — this is the LORD's declaration — "for I have scattered you like the four winds of heaven" — this is the LORD's declaration. 7 "Listen, Zion! Escape, you who are living with Daughter Babylon." 8 For the LORD of Armies says this: "In pursuit of his glory, he sent me against the nations plundering you, for whoever touches you touches the pupil[E] of my[F] eye. 9 For look, I am raising my hand against them, and they will become plunder for their own servants. Then you will know that the LORD of Armies has sent me.

10 "Daughter Zion, shout for joy and be glad, for I am coming to dwell among you" — this is the LORD's declaration. 11 "Many nations will join themselves to the LORD on that day and become my[G] people. I will dwell among you, and you will know that the LORD of Armies has sent me to you. 12 The LORD will take possession of Judah as his portion in the Holy Land, and he will once again choose Jerusalem. 13 Let all humanity be silent before the LORD, for from his holy dwelling he has roused himself."

[A] **1:8** Lit *red* [B] **1:8** Lit *depths* [C] **1:15** Lit *they helped for evil* [D] **1:21** Lit *throw down* [E] **2:8** Or *apple* [F] **2:8** Alt Hb tradition; MT reads *his* [G] **2:11** LXX, Syr read *his*

Zechariah: Temple Builder

by Martha S. Bergen

The Church of St. Peter in Gallicantu, which serves as the traditional site where Peter denied knowing Jesus. Zechariah foretold that the Messiah would be abandoned: "Strike the shepherd, and the sheep will be scattered" (Zch 13:7).

As seen in the article found in Haggai, "The Temple-Building Prophets," God used Zechariah and Haggai to motivate the postexilic people of Judah to finish rebuilding the temple destroyed by the Babylonian King Nebuchadnezzar in 586 BC. Under the leadership of Jerusalem's governor, Zerubbabel, the temple was completed in 516 BC.

Zechariah's name, which in Hebrew is *Zechar-Yah,* means "Yahweh remembers/remembered." The verb *zachar* means to "remember." Yahweh (God's personal name) was fully aware of Israel's circumstances. He knew the nation's past and future. The temple's current condition did not escape his knowledge. Furthermore, he was concerned about its disrepair. Just as the first temple's success was linked to the Lord's concern for Israel, so would be the success of this second temple.

Zechariah was born in Babylonia and came to Judah under Zerubbabel's leadership. His prophetic role began in 520 BC, two years into the reign of Persia's King Darius and approximately eighteen years after the first group of Jews returned from Babylonian exile. The book of Zechariah opens with reference to the prophet's call from God and cites his genealogical association (Zch 1:1). His grandfather Iddo is mentioned not only here but also in Nehemiah 12:4,16 as being among the Levitical priests who returned with Zerubbabel. Nehemiah's list gives evidence of Zechariah's priestly heritage. According to verse 16, Zechariah was the head of his priestly family.

The prophetic content of Zechariah was conveyed especially through a series of eight night visions (see chaps. 1–6), intended to incite the Jews by rebuking them for not already having completed the temple. Appropriately, one vision emphasized the high priest and the role he played in Israel's restoration process (see chap. 3). The night visions were also a means of assuring God's people that he would help them because the temple was part of his plan for their new beginning after the exile experience. In essence, God's message through Zechariah was a call for Israel to return to him, a call for repentance and a new start.[1] "So tell the people, 'This is what the Lord of Armies says: Return to me—this is the declaration of the Lord of Armies—and I will return to you, says the Lord of Armies" (Zch 1:3). Completing the temple structure would be a way for the Israelites to demonstrate their loyal obedience to the Lord. God in turn stood ever ready to show his love and faithfulness to Israel.

Zechariah also laced his prophecies with messianic predictions. Evangelical scholars have suggested that the whole of Christ's life and work is predicted within this book, from Christ's coming to earth in lowliness (3:8) to his ultimate rule beyond time into eternity (14:9). Other key messianic elements are Zechariah's prophecies of Christ's triumphal entry into Jerusalem (9:9), his betrayal for thirty pieces of silver (11:12–13), the scattering of his disciples when he was arrested (13:7), and his crucifixion (12:10–14).[2] ✣

---

[1] Bill T. Arnold and Bryan E. Beyer, *Encountering the Old Testament* (Grand Rapids: Baker, 1999), 466. [2] Kenneth L. Barker and Larry L. Walker, "Introduction: Zechariah" in *The NIV Study Bible* (Grand Rapids: Zondervan, 1995), 1399.

Silver coins from the first century AD. Found in Jericho, they are the type Judas would have received.

FOURTH VISION: HIGH PRIEST AND BRANCH

3 Then he showed me the high priest Joshua standing before the angel of the LORD, with Satan[A] standing at his right side to accuse him. 2 The LORD[B] said to Satan, "The LORD rebuke you, Satan! May the LORD who has chosen Jerusalem rebuke you! Isn't this man a burning stick snatched from the fire?"

3 Now Joshua was dressed with filthy[C] clothes as he stood before the angel. 4 So the angel of the LORD[D] spoke to those[E] standing before him, "Take off his filthy clothes!" Then he said to him, "See, I have removed your iniquity from you, and I will clothe you with festive robes."

5 Then I said, "Let them put a clean turban on his head." So a clean turban was placed on his head, and they clothed him in garments while the angel of the LORD was standing nearby.

6 Then the angel of the LORD charged Joshua, 7 "This is what the LORD of Armies says: If you walk in my ways and keep my mandates, you will both rule my house and take care of my courts; I will also grant you access among these who are standing here.

8 "Listen, High Priest Joshua, you and your colleagues sitting before you; indeed, these men are a sign that I am about to bring my servant, the Branch. 9 Notice the stone I have set before Joshua; on that one stone are seven eyes. I will engrave an inscription on it" — this is the declaration of the LORD of Armies — "and I will take away the iniquity of this land in a single day. 10 On that day, each of you will invite his neighbor to sit under his vine and fig tree." This is the declaration of the LORD of Armies.

FIFTH VISION: GOLD LAMPSTAND

4 The angel who was speaking with me then returned and roused me as one awakened out of sleep. 2 He asked me, "What do you see?"

I replied, "I see a solid gold lampstand with a bowl at the top. The lampstand also has seven lamps at the top with seven spouts for each of[F] the lamps. 3 There are also two olive trees beside it, one on the right of the bowl and the other on its left."

4 Then I asked the angel who was speaking with me, "What are these, my lord?"

5 "Don't you know what they are?" replied the angel who was speaking with me.

I said, "No, my lord."

6 So he answered me, "This is the word of the LORD to Zerubbabel: 'Not by strength or by might, but by my Spirit,' says the LORD of Armies. 7 'What are you, great mountain? Before Zerubbabel you will become a plain. And he will bring out the capstone accompanied by shouts of: Grace, grace to it!'"

8 Then the word of the LORD came to me: 9 "Zerubbabel's hands have laid the foundation of this house, and his hands will complete it. Then you will know that the LORD of Armies has sent me to you. 10 For who despises the day of small things? These seven eyes of the LORD, which scan throughout the whole earth, will rejoice when they see the ceremonial stone[G] in Zerubbabel's hand."

11 I asked him, "What are the two olive trees on the right and left of the lampstand?" 12 And I questioned him further, "What are the two streams[H] of the olive trees, from which the golden oil is pouring through the two golden conduits?"

13 Then he inquired of me, "Don't you know what these are?"

"No, my lord," I replied.

14 "These are the two anointed ones,"[I] he said, "who stand by the Lord of the whole earth."

SIXTH VISION: FLYING SCROLL

5 I looked up again and saw a flying scroll. 2 "What do you see?" he asked me.

"I see a flying scroll," I replied, "thirty feet[J] long and fifteen feet[K] wide."

3 Then he said to me, "This is the curse that is going out over the whole land, for everyone who is a thief, contrary to what is written on one side, has gone unpunished,[L] and everyone who swears falsely, contrary to what is written on the other side, has gone unpunished. 4 I will send it out," — this is the declaration of the LORD of Armies — "and it will enter the house of the thief and the house of the one who swears falsely by my name. It will stay inside his house and destroy it along with its timbers and stones."

SEVENTH VISION: WOMAN IN THE BASKET

5 Then the angel who was speaking with me came forward and told me, "Look up and see what this is that is approaching."

6 So I asked, "What is it?"

He responded, "It's a measuring basket[M] that is approaching." And he continued, "This is their iniquity[N] in all the land." 7 Then a lead cover was lifted, and there was a woman sitting inside the basket. 8 "This is Wickedness," he said. He shoved her down into the basket and pushed the lead weight over its opening. 9 Then I looked up and saw two women approaching with the wind in their wings. Their wings were like those of a stork, and they lifted up the basket between earth and sky.

[A] **3:1** Or *the accuser* [B] **3:2** Syr reads *The Angel of the LORD*
[C] **3:3** Probably stained with human excrement [D] **3:4** Lit *he*
[E] **3:4** = the angels [F] **4:2** Or *seven lips to* [G] **4:10** Lit *the tin stone*
[H] **4:12** Or *branches* [I] **4:14** = Joshua and Zerubbabel [J] **5:2** Lit *20 cubits*
[K] **5:2** Lit *10 cubits* [L] **5:3** Or *side, will be removed* [M] **5:6** Lit *It's an ephah*
[N] **5:6** One Hb ms, LXX, Syr; other Hb mss read *eye*

10 So I asked the angel who was speaking with me, "Where are they taking the basket?"

11 "To build a shrine for it in the land of Shinar," he told me. "When that is ready, the basket will be placed there on its pedestal."

EIGHTH VISION: FOUR CHARIOTS

6 Then I looked up again and saw four chariots coming from between two mountains. The mountains were made of bronze. 2 The first chariot had chestnut[A] horses, the second chariot black horses, 3 the third chariot white horses, and the fourth chariot dappled horses — all strong horses. 4 So I inquired of the angel who was speaking with me, "What are these, my lord?"

5 The angel told me, "These are the four spirits[B] of heaven going out after presenting themselves to the Lord of the whole earth. 6 The one with the black horses is going to the land of the north, the white horses are going after them, but the dappled horses are going to the land of the south." 7 As the strong horses went out, they wanted to go patrol the earth, and the LORD said, "Go, patrol the earth." So they patrolled the earth. 8 Then he summoned me saying, "See, those going to the land of the north have pacified my Spirit in the northern land."

CROWNING OF THE BRANCH

9 The word of the LORD came to me: 10 "Take an offering from the exiles, from Heldai, Tobijah, and Jedaiah, who have arrived from Babylon, and go that same day to the house of Josiah son of Zephaniah. 11 Take silver and gold, make a crown,[C] and place it on the head of Joshua son of Jehozadak, the high priest. 12 You are to tell him: This is what the LORD of Armies says: Here is a man whose name is Branch; he will branch out from his place and build the LORD's temple. 13 Yes, he will build the LORD's temple; he will bear royal splendor and will sit on his throne and rule. There will be a priest on his throne, and there will be peaceful counsel between the two of them. 14 The crown will reside in the LORD's temple as a memorial to Heldai, Tobijah, Jedaiah, and Hen[D] son of Zephaniah. 15 People who are far off will come and build the LORD's temple, and you will know that the LORD of Armies has sent me to you. This will happen when you fully obey the LORD your God."

DISOBEDIENCE AND FASTING

7 In the fourth year of King Darius, the word of the LORD came to Zechariah on the fourth day of the ninth month, which is Chislev. 2 Now the people of Bethel had sent Sharezer, Regem-melech, and their men to plead for the LORD's favor 3 by asking the priests who were at the house of the LORD of Armies as well as the prophets, "Should we mourn and fast in the fifth month as we have done these many years?"

4 Then the word of the LORD of Armies came to me: 5 "Ask all the people of the land and the priests: When you fasted and lamented in the fifth and in the seventh months for these seventy years, did you really fast for me? 6 When you eat and drink, don't you eat and drink simply for yourselves? 7 Aren't these the words that the LORD proclaimed through the earlier prophets when Jerusalem was inhabited and secure,[E] along with its surrounding cities, and when the southern region and the Judean foothills were inhabited?"

8 The word of the LORD came to Zechariah: 9 "The LORD of Armies says this: 'Make fair decisions. Show faithful love and compassion to one another. 10 Do not oppress the widow or the fatherless, the resident alien or the poor, and do not plot evil in your hearts against one another.' 11 But they refused to pay attention and turned a stubborn shoulder; they closed their ears so they could not hear. 12 They made their hearts like a rock so as not to obey the law or the words that the LORD of Armies had sent by his Spirit through the earlier prophets. Therefore intense anger came from the LORD of Armies. 13 Just as he had called, and they would not listen, so when they called, I would not listen, says the LORD of Armies. 14 I scattered them with a windstorm over all the nations that had not known them, and the land was left desolate behind them, with no one coming or going. They turned a pleasant land into a desolation."

OBEDIENCE AND FEASTING

8 The word of the LORD of Armies came: 2 The LORD of Armies says this: "I am extremely jealous for Zion; I am jealous for her with great wrath." 3 The LORD says this: "I will return to Zion and live in Jerusalem. Then Jerusalem will be called the Faithful City; the mountain of the LORD of Armies will be called the Holy Mountain." 4 The LORD of Armies says this: "Old men and women will again sit along the streets of Jerusalem, each with a staff in hand because of advanced age. 5 The streets of the city will be filled with boys and girls playing in them." 6 The LORD of Armies says this: "Though it may seem impossible to the remnant of this people in those days, should it also seem impossible to me?" — this is the declaration of the LORD of Armies. 7 The LORD of Armies says this: "I will save my people from the land of the east and the land of the west.[F] 8 I will bring them back to live in Jerusalem. They will be my people, and I will be their faithful and righteous God."

[A] **6:2** Lit *red* [B] **6:5** Or *winds* [C] **6:11** Lit *crowns* [D] **6:14** Probably Josiah [E] **7:7** Or *prosperous* [F] **8:7** Lit *sunset*

Zechariah's Visions

by Robert A. Street

Like the prophets before him, Zechariah used literary forms and imagery to convey his inspired message. The first eight chapters contain visions accompanied with their interpretations, oracles from the prophet, question-and-answer dialogue, and even a decalogue of words from the Lord.

Zechariah was not unique in employing visions to convey God's message. Amos, Isaiah, Jeremiah, and Ezekiel had used them. In Amos's visions, the Lord spoke directly to Amos, as he did in the visions of Isaiah and Jeremiah. In Ezekiel, the Lord was often the interpreter of the visions, but sometimes the angel of the Lord provided the explanations.

Though the angel of the Lord appeared in Zechariah's visions, the book consistently provides an interpretation of the visions through another angel who spoke to Zechariah. Zechariah's visions also include other angels (twice), men (twice), horses, chariots, olive trees, lampstands, a flying scroll, a basket, a woman, and winged women.

Zechariah's visions "are somewhat like parables in that each one carries a central truth. This should caution us against giving undue attention to the minor details of the visions, many of which are obscure and have defied interpretation."[1] Therefore the reader should not look for a hidden meaning in every detail in the visions. The book actually offers the visions' meanings and the accompanying messages. The reader should allow the scriptural explanations to guide the visions' interpretation. This approach leads to discovering the theology of the visions.

After an opening section (Zch 1:1–6) calling for the people to return to God, Zechariah commenced with a series of visions. The prophet's visions (1:7–6:8) have received the moniker "Visions in the Night." The visions follow a basic pattern of Zechariah seeing something, which is followed by an angel giving a brief explanation of the vision.

Traditional (not actual) tomb of Zechariah in the Kidron Valley east of Jerusalem. Carved circa 200 BC into the limestone of the Mount of Olives.

The first vision (1:8–17) is of four equestrians who patrol the earth and report its conditions to God. They report that the earth remains at peace. Under the rule of Darius, a "pony express" was established for communication in the Persian Empire. "Zechariah's visions of patrols riding on horses was probably influenced by this Persian innovation."[2] Within the vision, the angel asks God when the exile will end. God's response is simply that he has returned to Jerusalem, and he will restore and comfort Zion again.

The second vision (1:18–21) describes four horns that will be cast down or destroyed by four craftsmen or smiths. The horns represent the powers that oppressed Judah, Israel, and Jerusalem. The message is that God will deal with them.

The third vision (2:1–13), which portrays a man trying to measure Jerusalem, conveys the idea Jerusalem will not need a wall as the city will be protected by a wall of fire coming

Basalt gate orthostat with a scene showing an eighth-century-BC Assyrian chariot.

from God himself. This vision is followed by a call for the exiles in Babylon to return to the city where God will protect them.

The fourth vision (3:1–10) depicts the high priest Joshua standing before the angel of the Lord along with the accuser ("Satan"). Even before the accuser has a chance to bring charges, God silences him. The filthy garments of Joshua the high priest that represent the iniquity of the land are removed and replaced with clean ones. The vision continues with Joshua being told that peace and prosperity would come with his high priesthood and that the messianic age would begin.

The fifth vision (4:1–14) is of a golden lampstand and two olive trees. This vision continues the fourth vision in that it identifies not only Joshua but also Zerubbabel as the Lord's anointed who are to usher in the messianic age. The reader is faced with a problem since neither Zerubbabel nor Joshua ruled in a glorious restored Jerusalem. The facts are that these chosen and anointed rulers simply disappear from the scene and that a glorious, prosperous, and peaceful restoration of Jerusalem did not occur during their lifetime.

The sixth vision (5:1–4) has a flying scroll of enormous proportions that moves to remove impurity from the land. This vision is closely related to the following one.

The seventh vision (5:5–11) speaks of a woman called "Wickedness" sealed in a basket. This basket is carried away by two women with wings of storks to Shinar, an ancient name for Babylon. The meaning is that the wickedness will be removed from the land.

The last vision (6:1–8) parallels the first since both describe a patrolling of the earth. This vision has chariots, not just horsemen, going out to the four corners of the earth to establish the Spirit of God there. ✣

---

[1] Page H. Kelley, *Micah, Nahum, Habakkuk, Zephaniah, Haggai, Zechariah, Malachi*, in Layman's Bible Book Commentary (Nashville: Broadman, 1984), 116. [2] Kelley, *Micah*, 119; Herodotus, *Histories* 8.98.

9 The LORD of Armies says this: "Let your hands
be strong, you who now hear these words that the
prophets spoke when the foundations were laid for
the rebuilding of the temple, the house of the LORD
of Armies. 10 For prior to those days neither people
nor animals had wages. There was no safety from the
enemy for anyone who came or went, for I turned
everyone against his neighbor. 11 But now, I will not
treat the remnant of this people as in the former days"
— this is the declaration of the LORD of Armies. 12 "For
they will sow in peace: the vine will yield its fruit, the
land will yield its produce, and the skies will yield
their dew. I will give the remnant of this people all
these things as an inheritance. 13 As you have been a
curse among the nations, house of Judah and house
of Israel, so I will save you, and you will be a blessing.
Don't be afraid; let your hands be strong." 14 For the
LORD of Armies says this: "As I resolved to treat you
badly when your ancestors provoked me to anger,
and I did not relent," says the LORD of Armies, 15 "so I
have resolved again in these days to do what is good
to Jerusalem and the house of Judah. Don't be afraid.
16 These are the things you must do: Speak truth to one
another; make true and sound decisions within your
city gates. 17 Do not plot evil in your hearts against
your neighbor, and do not love perjury, for I hate all
this" — this is the LORD's declaration.

18 Then the word of the LORD of Armies came to
me: 19 The LORD of Armies says this: "The fast of the
fourth month, the fast of the fifth, the fast of the seventh, and the fast of the tenth will become times of
joy, gladness, and cheerful festivals for the house of
Judah. Therefore, love truth and peace." 20 The LORD
of Armies says this: "Peoples will yet come, the residents of many cities; 21 the residents of one city will
go to another, saying: Let's go at once to plead for the
LORD's favor and to seek the LORD of Armies. I am also
going. 22 Many peoples and strong nations will come to
seek the LORD of Armies in Jerusalem and to plead for
the LORD's favor." 23 The LORD of Armies says this: "In
those days, ten men from nations of every language
will grab the robe of a Jewish man tightly, urging: Let
us go with you, for we have heard that God is with you."

JUDGMENT OF ZION'S ENEMIES

9 A pronouncement:
The word of the LORD
is against the land of Hadrach,
and Damascus is its resting place —
for the eyes of humanity
and all the tribes of Israel
are on the LORD[A] —
2 and also against Hamath, which borders it,
as well as Tyre and Sidon,
though they are very shrewd.
3 Tyre has built herself a fortress;
she has heaped up silver like dust
and gold like the dirt of the streets.
4 Listen! The Lord will impoverish her
and cast her wealth into the sea;
she herself will be consumed by fire.
5 Ashkelon will see it and be afraid;
Gaza too, and will writhe in great pain,
as will Ekron, for her hope will fail.
There will cease to be a king in Gaza,
and Ashkelon will become uninhabited.
6 A mongrel people will live in Ashdod,
and I will destroy the pride of the Philistines.
7 I will remove the blood from their mouths
and the abhorrent things
from between their teeth.
Then they too will become a remnant
for our God;
they will become like a clan in Judah
and Ekron like the Jebusites.
8 I will encamp at my house as a guard,
against those who march back and forth,
and no oppressor will march
against them again,
for now I have seen with my own eyes.

THE COMING OF ZION'S KING

9 Rejoice greatly, Daughter Zion!
Shout in triumph, Daughter Jerusalem!
Look, your King is coming to you;
he is righteous and victorious,[B]
humble and riding on a donkey,
on a colt, the foal of a donkey.
10 I will cut off the chariot from Ephraim
and the horse from Jerusalem.
The bow of war will be removed,
and he will proclaim peace to the nations.
His dominion will extend from sea to sea,
from the Euphrates River
to the ends of the earth.
11 As for you,
because of the blood of your covenant,
I will release your prisoners
from the waterless cistern.
12 Return to a stronghold,
you prisoners who have hope;
today I declare that I will restore double to you.
13 For I will bend Judah as my bow;
I will fill that bow with Ephraim.
I will rouse your sons, Zion,
against your sons, Greece.[C]
I will make you like a warrior's sword.

[A] **9:1** Or *eyes of the LORD are on mankind* — [B] **9:9** Or *and has salvation* [C] **9:13** Lit *Javan*

The Remnant in the Old Testament

by R. Raymond Lloyd

The concept of "remnant" (Hb *she'erit*) occurs throughout the Old Testament and played a major developing role in the national consciousness of the Hebrew people. The Hebrew word carries the idea of what is left over or remains from a larger quantity. So it could relate to things such as sacrificial blood or to people. Moses spoke to Aaron and Aaron's "remaining sons," after Nadab and Abihu were struck down by the Lord. He instructed them to eat the grain offering that was "left over," for it was holy (Lv 10:12). David was the subject of his father's response to Samuel: "there is still the youngest" (1Sm 16:11). Nebuchadnezzar carried captive "the rest of the people" of Jerusalem (Jr 39:9).

Most of the biblical pictures of the remnant idea develop in the context of God judging wickedness through catastrophe, defeat, or exile. Sometimes no one was left, especially of God's/Israel's enemies (see Dt 3:3; Jos 10:30,37; Ob 18). Yet a remnant of God's people would always survive because of Yahweh's grace. The remnant would be the core for a renewed spiritual community that would inherit Yahweh's promises. Some of the earliest Old Testament stories lay the foundation for a remnant. Because he was a "righteous man," only Noah and his family were "left" following the flood (Gn 6:9; 7:23). Joseph's message to his brothers was "God sent me ahead of you to establish you as a remnant within the land" (Gn 45:7). God delivered the Hebrews at the Red Sea; yet not one of Pharaoh's army survived (Ex 14:28). During the wicked rule of Ahab, Yahweh, in a regal theophany, reminded Elijah, "I will leave seven thousand in Israel—every knee that has not bowed to Baal" (1Kg 19:18). This is the first picture of a remnant from Israel, that is, of persons who had been loyal to their covenant faith.

The eighth-century prophets clearly articulated the remnant theme. They referred to the remnant as those the Assyrians left in the land of Israel. Amos, mostly in threatening terms, addressed a self-confident yet wicked Israel, proclaiming that only a few would be spared from a horrible and overwhelming loss at the hands of the Assyrians.

Isaiah vividly referred to a remnant; he spoke of a threat from which few would survive. When Yahweh called Isaiah, God spoke of the "ruined and desolate" land and people being driven "far away"—yet a "holy seed" would survive (Is 6:11–13). Years later, Isaiah appeared with his son Shear-jashub (meaning "A Remnant Will Return") before Ahaz (7:3). The name conveys the same idea that only a few would survive. At the conclusion of Hezekiah's plea for deliverance from the Assyrian invasion, Isaiah promised a remnant would be spared by Yahweh's grace and for his purposes: "The surviving remnant of the house of Judah will again take root downward and bear fruit upward. For a remnant will go out from Jerusalem, and survivors from Mount Zion. The zeal of the Lord of Armies will accomplish this" (37:31–32).

The postexilic community viewed themselves as the surviving remnant. Zechariah described this small group as those who returned to the ruins of Jerusalem and who were living in peace and prosperity (Zch 8:12). Yahweh's promises portray a completed action, the assurance of his blessings upon the "remnant of this people" (8:6,11,12). Certainly the remnant saw their return as an incredible miracle. The Lord made clear that the return was the result of his mercy: "So I have resolved again in these days to do what is good to Jerusalem and the house of Judah" (8:15). Further, Zechariah envisioned other peoples beyond Israel being "a remnant for our God" (9:7). ✣

Scene on bronze bands of the Balawat Gates shows Assyrian soldiers bringing spoils of war; found at Balawat, southeast of Nineveh.

14 Then the LORD will appear over them,
and his arrow will fly like lightning.
The Lord GOD will sound the ram's horn
and advance with the southern storms.
15 The LORD of Armies will defend them.
They will consume and conquer
with slingstones;
they will drink and be rowdy as if with wine.
They will be as full as the sprinkling basin,
like those at the corners of the altar.
16 The LORD their God will save them on that day
as the flock of his people;
for they are like jewels in a crown,
sparkling over his land.
17 How lovely and beautiful!
Grain will make the young men flourish,
and new wine, the young women.

THE LORD RESTORES HIS PEOPLE

10 Ask the LORD for rain
in the season of spring rain.
The LORD makes the rain clouds,
and he will give them showers of rain
and crops in the field for everyone.
2 For the idols speak falsehood,
and the diviners see illusions;
they relate empty dreams
and offer empty comfort.
Therefore the people wander like sheep;
they suffer affliction because there is
no shepherd.
3 My anger burns against the shepherds,
so I will punish the leaders.[A]
For the LORD of Armies has tended his flock,
the house of Judah;
he will make them like his majestic steed
in battle.
4 The cornerstone, the tent peg,
the battle bow, and every ruler —
all will go out from him together.
5 They will be like warriors in battle
trampling down the mud of the streets.
They will fight because the LORD is
with them,
and they will put horsemen to shame.
6 I will strengthen the house of Judah
and deliver the house of Joseph.[B]
I will restore[C] them
because I have compassion on them,
and they will be
as though I had never rejected them.
For I am the LORD their God,
and I will answer them.
7 Ephraim will be like a warrior,
and their hearts will be glad as if with wine.
Their children will see it and be glad;
their hearts will rejoice in the LORD.
8 I will whistle and gather them
because I have redeemed them;
they will be as numerous as they once were.
9 Though I sow them among the nations,
they will remember me in the distant lands;
they and their children will live and return.
10 I will bring them back from the land of Egypt
and gather them from Assyria.
I will bring them to the land of Gilead
and to Lebanon,
but it will not be enough for them.
11 The LORD[D] will pass through the sea
of distress
and strike the waves of the sea;
all the depths of the Nile will dry up.
The pride of Assyria will be brought down,
and the scepter of Egypt will come to an end.
12 I will strengthen them in the LORD,
and they will march in his name —
this is the LORD's declaration.

ISRAEL'S SHEPHERDS: GOOD AND BAD

11 Open your gates, Lebanon,
and fire will consume your cedars.
2 Wail, cypress, for the cedar has fallen;
the glorious trees are destroyed!
Wail, oaks of Bashan,
for the stately forest has fallen!
3 Listen to the wail of the shepherds,
for their glory is destroyed.
Listen to the roar of young lions,
for the thickets of the Jordan are[E] destroyed.

4 The LORD my God says this: "Shepherd the flock
intended for slaughter. 5 Those who buy them slaughter them but are not punished. Those who sell them
say, 'Blessed be the LORD because I have become rich!'
Even their own shepherds have no compassion for
them. 6 Indeed, I will no longer have compassion on
the inhabitants of the land" — this is the LORD's declaration. "Instead, I will turn everyone over to his
neighbor and his king. They will devastate the land,
and I will not rescue it from their hand."
7 So I shepherded the flock intended for slaughter,
the oppressed of the flock.[F] I took two staffs, calling
one Favor and the other Union, and I shepherded the
flock. 8 In one month I got rid of three shepherds. I became impatient with them, and they also detested me.

[A] **10:3** Lit *male goats* [B] **10:6** = the northern kingdom [C] **10:6** Other Hb mss, LXX read *settle* [D] **10:11** Lit *He* [E] **11:3** Lit *for the majesty of the Jordan is* [F] **11:7** LXX reads *slaughter that belonged to the sheep merchants*

9 Then I said, "I will no longer shepherd you. Let what
is dying die, and let what is perishing perish; let the
rest devour each other's flesh." 10 Next I took my staff
called Favor and cut it in two, annulling the covenant
I had made with all the peoples. 11 It was annulled on
that day, and so the oppressed of the flock[A] who were
watching me knew that it was the word of the LORD.
12 Then I said to them, "If it seems right to you, give
me my wages; but if not, keep them." So they weighed
my wages, thirty pieces of silver.
13 "Throw it to the potter,"[B] the LORD said to me
— this magnificent price I was valued by them. So I
took the thirty pieces of silver and threw it into the
house of the LORD, to the potter.[C] 14 Then I cut in two
my second staff, Union, annulling the brotherhood
between Judah and Israel.
15 The LORD also said to me, "Take the equipment of
a foolish shepherd. 16 I am about to raise up a shepherd in the land who will not care for those who are
perishing, and he will not seek the lost[D] or heal the
broken. He will not sustain the healthy,[E] but he will
devour the flesh of the fat sheep and tear off their
hooves.

17 Woe to the worthless shepherd
who deserts the flock!
May a sword strike[F] his arm
and his right eye!
May his arm wither away
and his right eye go completely blind!"

JUDAH'S SECURITY

12 A pronouncement:
The word of the LORD concerning Israel.
A declaration of the LORD,
who stretched out the heavens,
laid the foundation of the earth,
and formed the spirit of man within him.

2 "Look, I will make Jerusalem a cup that causes
staggering for the peoples who surround the city.
The siege against Jerusalem will also involve Judah.
3 On that day I will make Jerusalem a heavy stone
for all the peoples; all who try to lift it will injure
themselves severely when all the nations of the earth
gather against her. 4 On that day" — this is the LORD's
declaration — "I will strike every horse with panic
and its rider with madness. I will keep a watchful eye
on the house of Judah but strike all the horses of the
nations with blindness. 5 Then each of the leaders of
Judah will think to himself: The residents of Jerusalem are my strength through the LORD of Armies,
their God. 6 On that day I will make the leaders of Judah like a firepot in a woodpile, like a flaming torch
among sheaves; they will consume all the peoples
around them on the right and the left, while Jerusalem continues to be inhabited on its site, in Jerusalem.
7 The LORD will save the tents of Judah first, so that the
glory of David's house and the glory of Jerusalem's
residents may not be greater than that of Judah. 8 On
that day the LORD will defend the inhabitants of Jerusalem, so that on that day the one who is weakest
among them will be like David on that day, and the
house of David will be like God, like the angel of the
LORD, before them. 9 On that day I will set out to destroy all the nations that come against Jerusalem.

MOURNING FOR THE PIERCED ONE

10 "Then I will pour out a spirit[G] of grace and prayer
on the house of David and the residents of Jerusalem, and they will look at[H] me whom they pierced.
They will mourn for him as one mourns for an only
child and weep bitterly for him as one weeps for a
firstborn. 11 On that day the mourning in Jerusalem
will be as great as the mourning of Hadad-rimmon
in the plain of Megiddo. 12 The land will mourn, every family by itself: the family of David's house by
itself and their women by themselves; the family of
Nathan's[I] house by itself and their women by themselves; 13 the family of Levi's house by itself and their
women by themselves; the family of Shimei[J] by itself
and their women by themselves; 14 all the remaining
families, every family by itself, and their women by
themselves.

GOD'S PEOPLE CLEANSED

13 "On that day a fountain will be opened for the
house of David and for the residents of Jerusalem, to wash away sin and impurity. 2 On that day"
— this is the declaration of the LORD of Armies — "I
will remove the names of the idols from the land, and
they will no longer be remembered. I will banish the
prophets[K] and the unclean spirit from the land. 3 If a
man still prophesies, his father and his mother who
bore him will say to him, 'You cannot remain alive
because you have spoken a lie in the name of the
LORD.' When he prophesies, his father and his mother
who bore him will pierce him through. 4 On that day
every prophet will be ashamed of his vision when he
prophesies; they will not put on a hairy cloak in order
to deceive. 5 He will say, 'I am not a prophet; I work the
land, for a man purchased[L] me as a servant since my
youth.' 6 If someone asks him, 'What are these wounds
on your chest?'[M] — then he will answer, 'I received
the wounds in the house of my friends.'

[A] **11:11** LXX reads *and the sheep merchants* [B] **11:13** Syr reads *treasury* [C] **11:13** One Hb ms, Syr read *treasury* [D] **11:16** Or *young* [E] **11:16** Or *exhausted* [F] **11:17** Lit *be against* [G] **12:10** Or *out the Spirit* [H] **12:10** Or *to* [I] **12:12** = a son of David [J] **12:13** = a descendant of Levi [K] **13:2** = false prophets [L] **13:5** Or *sold* [M] **13:6** Lit *wounds between your hands*

7 Sword, awake against my shepherd,
against the man who is my associate —
this is the declaration of the LORD
of Armies.
Strike the shepherd, and the sheep
will be scattered;
I will turn my hand against the little ones.
8 In the whole land —
this is the LORD's declaration —
two-thirds[A] will be cut off and die,
but a third will be left in it.
9 I will put this third through the fire;
I will refine them as silver is refined
and test them as gold is tested.
They will call on my name,
and I will answer them.
I will say, 'They are my people,'
and they will say, 'The LORD is our God.'"

THE LORD'S TRIUMPH AND REIGN

14 Look, a day belonging to the LORD is coming
when the plunder taken from you will be divided in your presence. 2 I will gather all the nations
against Jerusalem for battle. The city will be captured,
the houses looted, and the women raped. Half the city
will go into exile, but the rest of the people will not
be removed from the city.
3 Then the LORD will go out to fight against those
nations as he fights on a day of battle. 4 On that day
his feet will stand on the Mount of Olives, which faces Jerusalem on the east. The Mount of Olives will be
split in half from east to west, forming a huge valley,
so that half the mountain will move to the north and
half to the south. 5 You will flee by my mountain valley,[B] for the valley of the mountains will extend to
Azal. You will flee as you fled[C] from the earthquake
in the days of King Uzziah of Judah. Then the LORD
my God will come and all the holy ones with him.[D]
6 On that day there will be no light; the sunlight
and moonlight will diminish.[E,F] 7 It will be a unique
day known only to the LORD, without day or night,
but there will be light at evening.
8 On that day living water will flow out from Jerusalem, half of it toward the eastern sea[G] and the
other half toward the western sea,[H] in summer and
winter alike. 9 On that day the LORD will become
King over the whole earth — the LORD alone, and
his name alone. 10 All the land from Geba to Rimmon
south of Jerusalem will be changed into a plain. But
Jerusalem will be raised up and will remain[I] on its
site from the Benjamin Gate to the place of the First
Gate,[J] to the Corner Gate, and from the Tower of
Hananel to the royal winepresses. 11 People will live
there, and never again will there be a curse of complete destruction. So Jerusalem will dwell in security.
12 This will be the plague with which the LORD
strikes all the people who have warred against Jerusalem: their flesh will rot while they stand on their
feet, their eyes will rot in their sockets, and their
tongues will rot in their mouths. 13 On that day a great
panic from the LORD will be among them, so that
each will seize the hand of another, and the hand of
one will rise against the other. 14 Judah will also fight
at Jerusalem, and the wealth of all the surrounding
nations will be collected: gold, silver, and clothing in
great abundance. 15 The same plague as the previous
one will strike[K] the horses, mules, camels, donkeys,
and all the animals that are in those camps.
16 Then all the survivors from the nations that came
against Jerusalem will go up year after year to worship the King, the LORD of Armies, and to celebrate
the Festival of Shelters. 17 Should any of the families
of the earth not go up to Jerusalem to worship the
King, the LORD of Armies, rain will not fall on them.
18 And if the people[L] of Egypt will not go up and enter,
then rain will not fall on them; this will be the plague
the LORD inflicts on the nations who do not go up to
celebrate the Festival of Shelters. 19 This will be the
punishment of Egypt and all the nations that do not
go up to celebrate the Festival of Shelters.
20 On that day, the words HOLY TO THE LORD will
be on the bells of the horses. The pots in the house
of the LORD will be like the sprinkling basins before
the altar. 21 Every pot in Jerusalem and in Judah will
be holy to the LORD of Armies. All who sacrifice will
come and use the pots to cook in. And on that day
there will no longer be a Canaanite[M] in the house of
the LORD of Armies.

[A] **13:8** Lit *two-thirds in it* [B] **14:5** Some Hb mss, LXX, Sym, Tg read *The valley of my mountains will be blocked* [C] **14:5** LXX reads *It will be blocked as it was blocked* [D] **14:5** Some Hb mss, LXX, Vg, Tg, Syr; other Hb mss read *you* [E] **14:6** LXX, Sym, Syr, Tg, Vg read *no light or cold or ice* [F] **14:6** Lit *no light; the precious ones will congeal* [G] **14:8** = the Dead Sea [H] **14:8** = the Mediterranean Sea [I] **14:10** Or *will be inhabited* [J] **14:10** Or *the former gate* [K] **14:15** Lit *be on* [L] **14:18** Lit *family* [M] **14:21** Or *merchant*

MALACHI

Alabaster statue of John the Baptist, from Spain circa AD 1550.

INTRODUCTION TO

MALACHI

Circumstances of Writing

Nothing is known about the author except his name. The book emphasizes the message rather than the messenger; God is the speaker in about forty-seven of the fifty-five verses. The one prophesied in Malachi 3:1 to "clear the way" for God to come to his temple is identified as *malakiy*, "my messenger," a Hebrew word identical to the name of the book's author.

Although the book is not dated by a reference to a ruler or a specific event, internal evidence, as well as its position in the canon, favors a postexilic date. Reference to a governor in 1:8 favors the Persian period when Judah was a province or subprovince of the Persian satrapy Abar Nahara, which included Israel, Syria, Phoenicia, Cyprus, and, until 485 BC, Babylon. The temple had been rebuilt (515 BC) and worship reestablished there (1:6–11; 2:1–3; 3:1,10). But the excitement and enthusiasm for which the prophets Haggai and Zechariah were the catalysts had waned. The social and religious problems that Malachi addressed reflect the situation portrayed in Ezra 9 and 10 and Nehemiah 5 and 13, suggesting dates not long before Ezra's return to Judah (ca 460 BC) or Nehemiah's second term as governor of Judah (Neh 13:6–7; ca 435 BC). Linguistic data favors the earlier date.

Contribution to the Bible

Malachi was the last prophetic message from God before the close of the Old Testament period. This book is a fitting conclusion to the Old Testament and a transition for understanding the kingdom proclamation in the New Testament. Malachi spoke to the hearts of a troubled people whose circumstances of financial insecurity, religious skepticism, and personal disappointments were similar to those often experienced by God's people today. The book contains a message that must not be overlooked by those who wish to encounter God and his kingdom and to lead others to a similar encounter. We have a great, loving, and holy God, who has unchanging and glorious purposes for his people. Our God calls us to genuine worship, fidelity to himself and to one another, and to expectant faith in what he is doing and says he will do in this world and for his people.

God's love is paramount. It is expressed in Malachi in terms of God's election and protection of Israel above all the nations of the world. Since God had served the interests of Judah out of his unchanging love, he required Judah to live up to its obligations by obedience, loyalty, and sincere worship. This love relationship between God and Judah is the model for how people were expected to treat other members of the redeemed community. They were required to be faithful in all their dealings with one another.

As a community devoted to God, his people enjoy his protection and provision. But failure to live right before God and one another will bring God's judgment. Thus God's people could not expect the joy of his blessings if they continued to fail in their duties to him and to one another. Before God would hold Judah in the balance of judgment, he would grant one last call for repentance. A forerunner would precede the fearsome day of the Lord and herald the coming of God's kingdom on earth.

Structure

Malachi's message is communicated in three interrelated addresses. Each address contains five sections arranged in a mirrorlike repetitive structure surrounding a central section (a-b-c-b-a). The first two addresses begin with positive motivation or hope (1:2–5; 2:10a) and end with negative motivation or judgment (2:1–9; 3:1–6). In between is God's indictment (1:6–9,11–14; 2:10b–15a,17) surrounding his commands (1:10; 2:15b–16). The final climactic address begins and ends with commands to repent (3:7–10a; 4:4–6). In between are sections of motivation (3:10b–12; 3:16–4:3) surrounding the indictment (3:13–15).

THE LORD'S LOVE FOR ISRAEL

1 A pronouncement:

The word of the LORD to Israel through Malachi.[A]

2 "I have loved you," says the LORD.

Yet you ask, "How have you loved us?"

"Wasn't Esau Jacob's brother?" This is the LORD's declaration. "Even so, I loved Jacob, 3 but I hated Esau. I turned his mountains into a wasteland, and gave his inheritance to the desert jackals."

4 Though Edom says, "We have been devastated, but we will rebuild[B] the ruins," the LORD of Armies says this: "They may build, but I will demolish. They will be called a wicked country and the people the LORD has cursed[C] forever. 5 Your own eyes will see this, and you yourselves will say, 'The LORD is great, even beyond[D] the borders of Israel.'

DISOBEDIENCE OF THE PRIESTS

6 "A son honors his father, and a servant his master. But if I am a father, where is my honor? And if I am a master, where is your fear of me? says the LORD of Armies to you priests, who despise my name."

Yet you ask, "How have we despised your name?"

7 "By presenting defiled food on my altar."

"How have we defiled you?" you ask.

When you say, "The LORD's table is contemptible."

8 "When you present a blind animal for sacrifice, is it not wrong? And when you present a lame or sick animal, is it not wrong? Bring it to your governor! Would he be pleased with you or show you favor?" asks the LORD of Armies. 9 "And now plead for God's favor. Will he be gracious to us? Since this has come from your hands, will he show any of you favor?" asks the LORD of Armies. 10 "I wish one of you would shut the temple doors, so that you would no longer kindle a useless fire on my altar! I am not pleased with you," says the LORD of Armies, "and I will accept no offering from your hands.

11 "My name will be great among the nations, from the rising of the sun to its setting. Incense[E] and pure offerings will be presented in my name in every place because my name will be great among the nations,"[F] says the LORD of Armies.

12 "But you are profaning it when you say, 'The Lord's table is defiled, and its product, its food, is contemptible.' 13 You also say, 'Look, what a nuisance!' And you scorn[G] it,"[H] says the LORD of Armies. "You bring stolen,[I] lame, or sick animals. You bring this as an offering! Am I to accept that from your hands?" asks the LORD.

14 "The deceiver is cursed who has an acceptable male in his flock and makes a vow but sacrifices a defective animal to the Lord. For I am a great King," says the LORD of Armies, "and my name will be feared among the nations.

WARNING TO THE PRIESTS

2 "Therefore, this decree is for you priests: 2 If you don't listen, and if you don't take it to heart to honor my name," says the LORD of Armies, "I will send a curse among you, and I will curse your blessings. In fact, I have already begun to curse them because you are not taking it to heart.

3 "Look, I am going to rebuke your descendants, and I will spread animal waste[J] over your faces, the waste from your festival sacrifices, and you will be taken away with it. 4 Then you will know that I sent you this decree, so that my covenant with Levi may continue," says the LORD of Armies. 5 "My covenant with him was one of life and peace, and I gave these to him; it called for reverence, and he revered me and stood in awe of my name. 6 True instruction was in his mouth, and nothing wrong was found on his lips. He walked with me in peace and integrity and turned many from iniquity. 7 For the lips of a priest should guard knowledge, and people should desire instruction from his mouth, because he is the messenger of the LORD of Armies.

8 "You, on the other hand, have turned from the way. You have caused many to stumble by your instruction. You have violated[K] the covenant of Levi," says the LORD of Armies. 9 "So I in turn have made you despised and humiliated before all the people because you are not keeping my ways but are showing partiality in your instruction."

JUDAH'S MARITAL UNFAITHFULNESS

10 Don't all of us have one Father? Didn't one God create us? Why then do we act treacherously against one another, profaning the covenant of our ancestors? 11 Judah has acted treacherously, and a detestable act has been done in Israel and in Jerusalem. For Judah has profaned the LORD's sanctuary,[L] which he loves, and has married the daughter of a foreign god.[M] 12 May the LORD cut off from the tents of Jacob the man who does this, whoever he may be,[N] even if he presents an offering to the LORD of Armies.

13 This is another thing you do. You are covering the LORD's altar with tears, with weeping and groaning, because he no longer respects your offerings or receives them gladly from your hands.

14 And you ask, "Why?" Because even though the LORD has been a witness between you and the wife of your youth, you have acted treacherously against her. She was your marriage partner and your wife

[A] **1:1** = My Messenger [B] **1:4** Or *will return and build* [C] **1:4** Or *LORD is angry with* [D] **1:5** Or *great over* [E] **1:11** Or *Burnt offerings* [F] **1:11** Or *is great . . . are presented . . . is great* [G] **1:13** Lit *blow at* [H] **1:13** Alt Hb tradition reads *me* [I] **1:13** Or *injured* [J] **2:3** Dung or entrails [K] **2:8** Lit *corrupted* [L] **2:11** Or *profaned what is holy to the LORD* [M] **2:11** = a woman who worshiped a foreign god [N] **2:12** Hb obscure

Spiritual Climate in the Time of Malachi

by Jeff S. Anderson

The optimism of the Jews returning to Jerusalem in the time of Cyrus (reigned 559–530 BC) faded under the reign of the Persian monarch Xerxes (486–465 BC). The empire now stretched from Persia to Egypt, so Xerxes set his eyes on Greece. Xerxes attacked and burned the city of Athens, enraging the Greeks and escalating a conflict that would last for nearly two centuries. Distracted by Egypt and Greece, Persia needed revenue to fund its armies engaged on multiple fronts. Revenues that had originally been routed to assist in the support of religious practices of their captive peoples were replaced by a sudden shortfall of cash.[1]

The temple administration and priesthood, which had grown accustomed to and even dependent on the assistance of the empire, now suffered. Much of the priesthood's livelihood was lost as outside economic support collapsed. Although the second temple had stood complete for decades, life seemed no better than before. Judah had no monarchy, no messianic age, and certainly no age of prosperity.

Stone weight with inscription in three languages; from Persepolis and dated to the reign of Darius I.

Artaxerxes I (465-24 BC), who followed Xerxes, was more supportive of religious reforms than his predecessor, but the troubles with Greece did not allow him to make any substantive changes. These circumstances led to what some have called "the low ebb of the spiritual life of the nation."[2] Pervasive apathy and dark disillusionment ruled the day, not excitement, promise, or hopeful expectation. Malachi's message almost certainly arose from this period of malaise. His method of startling the people into realizing how far they had fallen was forceful, point-blank, and controversial. Using a question-and-answer disputation format, he targeted the fatal flaws threatening the nation, including disrespect for temple service by priests and laity, cessation of tithing, questionable marriages accompanied by heightened divorce rates, and the oppression of the poor. ✣

Hebrew half shekel with chalice and pomegranate stem.

---

[1] Jon L. Berquist, *Judaism in Persia's Shadow: A Social and Historical Approach* (Minneapolis: Fortress, 1995), 91–102.

[2] Henry Flanders, Robert Crapps, and David Smith, *People of the Covenant*, 2nd ed. (New York: Oxford University Press, 1973), 428.

by E. Ray Clendenen

God's people had returned to their homeland of Judah, which, after the Persian conquest of Babylon, was a Persian province. The date of Malachi's prophetic activity is disputed. But the view is virtually unanimous that it occurred during the reigns of the Persian Kings Darius I (521–486 BC), Xerxes I (486–465 BC), or Artaxerxes I (465–424 BC). The people had rebuilt the temple (515 BC) and reestablished worship. But the excitement and enthusiasm engendered by the prophets Haggai and Zechariah had waned. As Malachi addressed God's people, he faced cynicism, hypocrisy, and spiritual apathy. Times were hard. He also faced a failure of leadership.

With three interrelated addresses, Malachi confronted three problems. First, the priests no longer served God wholeheartedly or the people conscientiously. They were insulting God with indifferent and careless worship and had contributed to Judah's indifference toward God (Mal 1:2–2:9).

Four-horned altar from Megiddo, circa 975–925 BC.

Wilderness beside the Jordan River at Bethany, where, according to tradition, John baptized Jesus.

Akkadian seal depicting offerings being brought to a goddess, circa 2350–2200 BC.

Second, blaming their economic and social troubles on the Lord's supposed unfaithfulness, the people were living selfish lives. Watching out only for themselves, they gave little more than a nod to their responsibilities to God or to one another (2:10–3:6).

Third, the people also had a self-protective sense of ownership of their personal property. This caused them not only to bring God their worst animals as sacrifices, but also to refuse to pay the tithes, which would have supported the temple personnel and the landless poor (3:7–4:6). Priests and people were interested only in self and in "what's in it for me?"

To address the situation, the prophet Malachi weaves together vivid portrayals of the people's sinful attitudes and behaviors, instruction about what must be done, and motivation in both positive and negative terms. For example, speaking through the prophet, the Lord begins by directing Judah's attention to his past demonstrations of loyal love and contrasts his treatment of them with his judgment on Edom. The book concludes with the Lord's threat if they fail to respond properly: "Otherwise, I will come and strike the land with a curse" (4:6). ✣

Egyptian funerary statue showing a calf being sacrificed, circa 2477 BC.

Cleaning Clothes in the Ancient Near East

by Harry D. Champy III

Wool garments were commonly soiled with perspiration, dirt, or food. They were notoriously difficult to clean. People would clean their clothes by beating them with a stick or more typically by treading them under foot. To communicate God's coming judgment, this was the imagery Malachi used (Mal 3:2). His audience would have been familiar with both the task and the terminology. Levitical law used the same verb that Malachi used to describe cleansing priestly vestments or clothing that had been contaminated by coming in contact with something unclean (Lv 6:27). David used the verb when he asked God, "Completely wash away my guilt. . . . wash me, and I will be whiter than snow" (Ps 51:2a,7b).

Some people would treat dirty clothes chemically with an alkaline detergent solution of soda and potash, which came from the ashes of burned wood. "They likewise used, for cleansing their cloth, urine and chalk, and bean meal mixed with water."[1] The smell of the cleaning solutions was offensive, so fullers often worked on the outskirts of a town.[2] Jeremiah mentioned that the cleaning solution was incapable of removing the stain of guilt (Jr 2:22). Cleaning clothes was a regular domestic activity. Thus the prophet Malachi used images everyone could understand. God was a cleansing soap. The process would be forceful and offensive. Yet God's intent was not to destroy his people; he was going to judge and purify them through the process. ✣

Terra-cotta oil flask from Greece, 550 BC, showing women dyeing and weaving wool.

---

[1] James M. Freeman, *Manners and Customs of the Bible* (Plainfield, NJ: Logos, 1972), 329.
[2] "Fuller" in *HIBD rev. ed.* (2015), 598.

by covenant. 15 Didn't God make them one and give them a portion of spirit? What is the one seeking?[A] Godly offspring. So watch yourselves carefully,[B] so that no one acts treacherously against the wife of his[C] youth.

16 "If he hates and divorces his wife," says the LORD God of Israel, "he[D] covers his garment with injustice," says the LORD of Armies. Therefore, watch yourselves carefully,[E] and do not act treacherously.

JUDGMENT AT THE LORD'S COMING

17 You have wearied the LORD with your words.

Yet you ask, "How have we wearied him?"

When you say, "Everyone who does what is evil is good in the LORD's sight, and he is delighted with them, or else where is the God of justice?"

3 "See, I am going to send my messenger, and he will clear the way before me. Then the Lord you seek will suddenly come to his temple, the Messenger of the covenant you delight in — see, he is coming," says the LORD of Armies. 2 But who can endure the day of his coming? And who will be able to stand when he appears? For he will be like a refiner's fire and like launderer's bleach.[F] 3 He will be like a refiner and purifier of silver; he will purify the sons of Levi and refine them like gold and silver. Then they will present offerings to the LORD in righteousness. 4 And the offerings of Judah and Jerusalem will please the LORD as in days of old and years gone by.

5 "I will come to you in judgment, and I will be ready to witness against sorcerers and adulterers; against those who swear falsely; against those who oppress the hired worker, the widow, and the fatherless; and against those who deny justice to the resident alien. They do not fear me," says the LORD of Armies. 6 "Because I, the LORD, have not changed, you descendants of Jacob have not been destroyed.[G]

ROBBING GOD

7 "Since the days of your ancestors, you have turned from my statutes; you have not kept them. Return to me, and I will return to you," says the LORD of Armies.

Yet you ask, "How can we return?"

8 "Will a man rob God? Yet you are robbing me!"

"How do we rob you?" you ask.

"By not making the payments of the tenth and the contributions. 9 You are suffering under a curse, yet[H] you — the whole nation — are still robbing me. 10 Bring the full tenth into the storehouse so that there may be food in my house. Test me in this way," says the LORD of Armies. "See if I will not open the floodgates of heaven and pour out a blessing for you without measure. 11 I will rebuke the devourer[I] for you, so that it will not ruin the produce of your land and your vine in your field will not fail to produce fruit," says the LORD of Armies. 12 "Then all the nations will consider you fortunate, for you will be a delightful land," says the LORD of Armies.

THE RIGHTEOUS AND THE WICKED

13 "Your words against me are harsh," says the LORD.

Yet you ask, "What have we spoken against you?"

14 You have said, "It is useless to serve God. What have we gained by keeping his requirements and walking mournfully before the LORD of Armies? 15 So now we consider the arrogant to be fortunate. Not only do those who commit wickedness prosper, they even test God and escape."

16 At that time those who feared the LORD spoke to one another. The LORD took notice and listened. So a book of remembrance was written before him for those who feared the LORD and had high regard for his name. 17 "They will be mine," says the LORD of Armies, "my own possession on the day I am preparing. I will have compassion on them as a man has compassion on his son who serves him. 18 So you will again see the difference between the righteous and the wicked, between one who serves God and one who does not serve him.

THE DAY OF THE LORD

4 "For look, the day is coming, burning like a furnace, when all the arrogant and everyone who commits wickedness will become stubble. The coming day will consume them," says the LORD of Armies, "not leaving them root or branches. 2 But for you who fear my name, the sun of righteousness will rise with healing in its wings, and you will go out and playfully jump like calves from the stall.[J] 3 You will trample the wicked, for they will be ashes under the soles of your feet on the day I am preparing," says the LORD of Armies.

A FINAL WARNING

4 "Remember the instruction of Moses my servant, the statutes and ordinances I commanded him at Horeb for all Israel. 5 Look, I am going to send you the prophet Elijah before the great and terrible day of the LORD comes. 6 And he will turn the hearts of fathers to their children and the hearts of children to their fathers. Otherwise, I will come and strike the land[K] with a curse."

[A] **2:15** Hb obscure [B] **2:15** Lit *So guard yourselves in your spirit* [C] **2:15** Lit *your* [D] **2:16** Or *The LORD God of Israel says that he hates divorce and the one who* [E] **2:16** Lit *Therefore, guard yourselves in your spirit* [F] **3:2** Lit *cleansing agent* [G] **3:6** Or *Because I, the LORD, do not change, you descendants of Jacob are not destroyed* [H] **3:9** Or *because* [I] **3:11** Perhaps locusts [J] **4:2** Or *like stall-fed calves* [K] **4:6** Or *earth*

THE
NEW TESTAMENT

MATTHEW

View of Bethlehem in Israel from atop the Herodium.

INTRODUCTION TO

MATTHEW

Circumstances of Writing

The author did not identify himself in the text. However, the title that ascribes this Gospel to Matthew appears in the earliest manuscripts and is possibly original. Titles became necessary to distinguish one Gospel from another when the four Gospels began to circulate as a single collection. Many early church fathers (Papias, Irenaeus, Pantaenus, and Origen) acknowledged Matthew as the author. Papias also contended that Matthew first wrote in Hebrew, implying that this Gospel was later translated into Greek.

Many modern scholars dispute these traditional claims. For instance, against Papias they argue that this Gospel was not originally written in Hebrew, because the Greek of Matthew does not appear to be translation Greek. They further argue that if the early church, following Papias's opinion, was wrong about the original language, they were likely incorrect about the author as well. However, the excellent Greek of Matthew could have been produced by a skilled translator of an original Hebrew text.

Even if Papias was wrong about the original language of the Gospel of Matthew, this does not imply that he and other early church leaders were wrong to identify Matthew as the author of this Gospel. In fact, the early church unanimously affirmed that the Gospel of Matthew was authored by the apostle Matthew. It would require impressive evidence to overturn this early consensus.

Clues from the Gospel itself support its ascription to Matthew. First, both Mark 2:14 and Luke 5:27 identify the tax collector whom Jesus called to be his disciple as Levi. This Gospel, however, identifies Levi as Matthew. Matthew, a Hebrew name meaning "gift of God," appears to be the apostolic name that Jesus gave to Levi after he chose to follow Christ, much as Simon was named Peter by Jesus after his confession of faith (Mt 16:18). The use of *Matthew* in this Gospel may be Matthew's personal touch, a self-reference that gives us a clue about authorship.

Determining the date of composition of Matthew's Gospel depends largely on the relationship of the Gospels to one another. Most scholars believe that Matthew used Mark's Gospel in writing his own Gospel. If this is correct, Matthew's Gospel must postdate Mark's. However, the date of Mark's Gospel is also shrouded in mystery. Irenaeus (ca AD 180) seems to claim that Mark wrote his Gospel after Peter's death in the mid-60s. However, Clement of Alexandria, who wrote only twenty years after Irenaeus, claimed that Mark wrote his Gospel while Peter was still alive. Given the ambiguity of the historical evidence, a decision must be based on other factors.

The date of composition for Mark is best inferred from the date of Luke and Acts. The abrupt ending of Acts, which left Paul under house arrest in Rome, implies that Acts was written before Paul's release. Since one of the major themes of Acts is the legality of Christianity in the Roman Empire, one would have expected Luke to mention Paul's release by the emperor if it had already occurred. This evidence dates Acts to the early 60s. Luke and Acts were two volumes of a single work, as the prologues to these books demonstrate. Luke was written before Acts. Given the amount of research that Luke invested in the book and the travel that eyewitness interviews probably required, a date in the late 50s is reasonable. If Luke used Mark in writing his own Gospel, as seems likely, by implication Mark was written some time before the late 50s, perhaps the early to mid-50s. Thus, despite Matthew's dependence on Mark, Matthew may have been written any time beginning in the mid-50s once Mark was completed.

Contribution to the Bible

As the first book in the New Testament, the Gospel of Matthew serves as a gateway between the two testaments. Of the New Testament books, and certainly of the four Gospels, Matthew has the strongest connections to the Old Testament. Matthew gave us God's entire plan from Genesis to Revelation. Matthew looked back and referred to Hebrew prophecies some sixty times ("was fulfilled" and "so that what was spoken . . . might be fulfilled"). He also looked forward by dealing not only with the Messiah's coming and his ministry, but also his future plan for his church and kingdom.

Structure

Matthew divided his Gospel into three major sections. He introduced new major sections with "from then on Jesus began to" (4:17; 16:21). These transitional statements divide the Gospel into the introduction (1:1–4:16), body (4:17–16:20), and conclusion (16:21–28:20). Matthew also divided his Gospel into five major blocks of teaching, each of which concludes with a summary statement (8:1; 11:1; 13:53; 19:1; 26:1). Some scholars believe these five major discourses were meant to correspond to the five books of Moses and to confirm Jesus's identity as the new Moses.

THE GENEALOGY OF JESUS CHRIST

1 An account of the genealogy of Jesus Christ, the
Son of David, the Son of Abraham:

FROM ABRAHAM TO DAVID

2 Abraham fathered[A] Isaac,
Isaac fathered Jacob,
Jacob fathered Judah and his brothers,
3 Judah fathered Perez and Zerah by Tamar,
Perez fathered Hezron,
Hezron fathered Aram,
4 Aram fathered Amminadab,
Amminadab fathered Nahshon,
Nahshon fathered Salmon,
5 Salmon fathered Boaz by Rahab,
Boaz fathered Obed by Ruth,
Obed fathered Jesse,
6 and Jesse fathered King David.

FROM DAVID TO THE BABYLONIAN EXILE

David fathered Solomon[B] by Uriah's wife,
7 Solomon fathered Rehoboam,
Rehoboam fathered Abijah,
Abijah fathered Asa,[C]
8 Asa[C] fathered Jehoshaphat,
Jehoshaphat fathered Joram,[D]
Joram fathered Uzziah,
9 Uzziah fathered Jotham,
Jotham fathered Ahaz,
Ahaz fathered Hezekiah,
10 Hezekiah fathered Manasseh,
Manasseh fathered Amon,[E]
Amon fathered Josiah,
11 and Josiah fathered Jeconiah and his brothers
at the time of the exile to Babylon.

FROM THE EXILE TO THE MESSIAH

12 After the exile to Babylon
Jeconiah fathered Shealtiel,
Shealtiel fathered Zerubbabel,
13 Zerubbabel fathered Abiud,
Abiud fathered Eliakim,
Eliakim fathered Azor,
14 Azor fathered Zadok,
Zadok fathered Achim,
Achim fathered Eliud,
15 Eliud fathered Eleazar,
Eleazar fathered Matthan,
Matthan fathered Jacob,
16 and Jacob fathered Joseph the husband of Mary,
who gave birth to Jesus who is called
the Messiah.

17 So all the generations from Abraham to David
were fourteen generations; and from David until the
exile to Babylon, fourteen generations; and from the
exile to Babylon until the Messiah, fourteen generations.

THE NATIVITY OF THE MESSIAH

18 The birth of Jesus Christ came about this way: After his mother Mary had been engaged[F] to Joseph, it
was discovered before they came together that she
was pregnant from the Holy Spirit. 19 So her husband,
Joseph, being a righteous man, and not wanting to
disgrace her publicly, decided to divorce her secretly.
20 But after he had considered these things, an angel of the Lord appeared to him in a dream, saying,
"Joseph, son of David, don't be afraid to take Mary as
your wife, because what has been conceived in her
is from the Holy Spirit. 21 She will give birth to a son,
and you are to name him Jesus, because he will save
his people from their sins."
22 Now all this took place to fulfill what was spoken
by the Lord through the prophet:

23 **See, the virgin will become pregnant**
and give birth to a son,
and they will name him Immanuel,[G]

which is translated "God is with us."
24 When Joseph woke up, he did as the Lord's angel
had commanded him. He married her 25 but did not
have sexual relations with her until she gave birth to
a son.[H] And he named him Jesus.

WISE MEN VISIT THE KING

2 After Jesus was born in Bethlehem of Judea in
the days of King Herod, wise men from the east
arrived in Jerusalem, 2 saying, "Where is he who has
been born king of the Jews? For we saw his star at its
rising and have come to worship him."[I]
3 When King Herod heard this, he was deeply disturbed, and all Jerusalem with him. 4 So he assembled
all the chief priests and scribes of the people and
asked them where the Messiah would be born.
5 "In Bethlehem of Judea," they told him, "because
this is what was written by the prophet:

6 **And you, Bethlehem**, in the land of Judah,
are by no means **least among the rulers**
of Judah:
Because out of you will come a ruler
who will shepherd my people Israel."[J]

7 Then Herod secretly summoned the wise men and
asked them the exact time the star appeared. 8 He sent
them to Bethlehem and said, "Go and search carefully

[A] **1:2** In vv. 2–16 either a son, as here, or a later descendant, as in v. 8
[B] **1:6** Other mss add *King* [C] **1:7,8** Other mss read *Asaph*
[D] **1:8** = Jehoram [E] **1:10** Other mss read *Amos* [F] **1:18** Or *betrothed*
[G] **1:23** Is 7:14 [H] **1:25** Other mss read *to her firstborn son* [I] **2:2** Or *to pay him homage* [J] **2:6** Mc 5:2

for the child. When you find him, report back to me
so that I too can go and worship him."[A]
9 After hearing the king, they went on their way.
And there it was — the star they had seen at its rising.
It led them until it came and stopped above the place
where the child was. 10 When they saw the star, they
were overwhelmed with joy. 11 Entering the house,
they saw the child with Mary his mother, and falling to their knees, they worshiped him.[B] Then they
opened their treasures and presented him with gifts:
gold, frankincense, and myrrh. 12 And being warned
in a dream not to go back to Herod, they returned to
their own country by another route.

THE FLIGHT INTO EGYPT

13 After they were gone, an angel of the Lord appeared
to Joseph in a dream, saying, "Get up! Take the child
and his mother, flee to Egypt, and stay there until I
tell you. For Herod is about to search for the child to
kill him." 14 So he got up, took the child and his mother
during the night, and escaped to Egypt. 15 He stayed
there until Herod's death, so that what was spoken
by the Lord through the prophet might be fulfilled:
Out of Egypt I called my Son.[C]

THE MASSACRE OF THE INNOCENTS

16 Then Herod, when he realized that he had been
outwitted by the wise men, flew into a rage. He
gave orders to massacre all the boys in and around
Bethlehem who were two years old and under, in
keeping with the time he had learned from the wise
men. 17 Then what was spoken through Jeremiah the
prophet was fulfilled:

18 **A voice was heard in Ramah,**
weeping,[D] **and great mourning,**
Rachel weeping for her children;
and she refused to be consoled,
because they are no more.[E]

THE RETURN TO NAZARETH

19 After Herod died, an angel of the Lord appeared in a
dream to Joseph in Egypt, 20 saying, "Get up, take the
child and his mother, and go to the land of Israel, because those who intended to kill the child are dead."
21 So he got up, took the child and his mother, and
entered the land of Israel. 22 But when he heard that
Archelaus was ruling over Judea in place of his father
Herod, he was afraid to go there. And being warned in
a dream, he withdrew to the region of Galilee. 23 Then
he went and settled in a town called Nazareth to fulfill what was spoken through the prophets, that he
would be called a Nazarene.

THE HERALD OF THE MESSIAH

3 In those days John the Baptist came, preaching
in the wilderness of Judea 2 and saying, "Repent,
because the kingdom of heaven has come near!" 3 For
he is the one spoken of through the prophet Isaiah,
who said:

A voice of one crying out in the wilderness:
Prepare the way for the Lord;
make his paths straight![F]

[A] **2:8** Or *and pay him homage* [B] **2:11** Or *they paid him homage* [C] **2:15** Hs 11:1 [D] **2:18** Other mss read *Ramah, lamentation, and weeping,* [E] **2:18** Jr 31:15 [F] **3:3** Is 40:3

The Wilderness of Judea southeast of Bethlehem and west of the Dead Sea. John the Baptist preached in this area.

Of Marrying Age

by Roberta Jones

A mosaic of the wedding festival of Ariadne and Dionysus found at Philippopolis. The mosaic is Roman and dates to the first century AD.

Jewish parents often arranged a betrothal for their son or daughter. In the betrothal period, which was a legal and binding engagement, the man and woman lived separately. They waited until after marriage for intimate relations. Yet, as with a legal husband and wife, only death or divorce broke a betrothal. During their betrothal, Joseph discovered Mary's pregnancy. Even though disappointed, Joseph chose kindness. He planned to spare Mary any public humiliation (Mt 1:18–20). Joseph seemingly considered his predicament in light of Old Testament Scriptures. Deuteronomy 22:20–21 suggested stoning women guilty of adultery; however, another choice allowed the man to write a divorce certificate if he found his wife to be "displeasing" (Dt 24:1).

Marriage scene etched in gold glass, likely from Rome, inscribed "Live in God." Dated to the fourth–fifth centuries AD.

Marriage customs in other countries influenced Israel. Two factors in Greece contributed to a higher ratio of men to women. Many women died in childbirth. Further, Grecian parents often abandoned baby girls. This female shortage likely encouraged men to marry increasingly younger wives. Sadly, Grecian cemetery inscriptions indicate many extremely young girls died in childbirth. If women survived childbirth, they expected to live about thirty-seven years.[1]

Rome ruled Israel at the time of Jesus's birth. Emperor Caesar Augustus strongly favored marriage. Ten-year-old girls could be engaged and marry two years later. Upper-class women, however, usually waited until their late teens to marry. They would not tarry too long, for twenty-year-old unmarried women might be penalized. Roman men usually married in their twenties or possibly older. A male who married younger was to show physical signs of maturity or be age fourteen before he wed.[2]

Jewish brides between ages thirteen and sixteen were especially common. But unlike other cultures, some women married past twenty. Many Jewish men married at eighteen to twenty. By the second century AD, many rabbis declared that men who were still unmarried at the age of twenty or older were sinning against God. Jewish culture urged early marriage for two reasons. First, an early marriage would likely produce offspring to continue the family name. Second, matrimony was considered a means by which young men could control their sexual passions.[3]

Terra-cotta *lekythos* (oil flask) dated to about 550–530 BC from Attica, Greece. The best man rides with the wedding couple in a cart that is being drawn by two donkeys.

Although we cannot verify the ages at which Mary and Joseph married, Israelite customs suggest they were young. Consider, also, Jesus had at least six younger half-siblings (Mk 6:3).

Josephus, a Jewish historian writing in the first century AD, explained typical customs of those times. As a betrothed couple, both Mary and Joseph likely expected that Joseph would oversee their family. For, Josephus declared, a woman was "inferior to her husband in all things." He also warned abusive husbands and encouraged obedient, dutiful wives.[4] Josephus suggested a woman could be stoned if convicted of not preserving her virginity. Men should marry, "at the age fit for it, virgins that are free, and born of good parents."[5] ✣

---

[1] C. C. Kroeger, "Women in Greco-Roman World and Judaism" in *Dictionary of New Testament Background*, ed. Craig A. Evans and Stanley E. Porter (Downers Grove, IL: InterVarsity, 2000), 1278. [2] C. S. Keener, "Marriage" in *Dictionary of New Testament Background*, 683–84. [3] Keener, "Marriage," 684. [4] Josephus, *Against Apion* 2.25. [5] Josephus, *Jewish Antiquities* 4.8.23.

4 Now John had a camel-hair garment with a leather belt around his waist, and his food was locusts and
wild honey. 5 Then people from Jerusalem, all Judea,
and all the vicinity of the Jordan were going out to
him, 6 and they were baptized by him in the Jordan
River, confessing their sins.
7 When he saw many of the Pharisees and Sadducees coming to his baptism, he said to them, "Brood
of vipers! Who warned you to flee from the coming
wrath? 8 Therefore produce fruit consistent with[A]
repentance. 9 And don't presume to say to yourselves,
'We have Abraham as our father.' For I tell you that
God is able to raise up children for Abraham from
these stones. 10 The ax is already at the root of the
trees. Therefore, every tree that doesn't produce good
fruit will be cut down and thrown into the fire.
11 "I baptize you with[B] water for repentance, but the
one who is coming after me is more powerful than I.
I am not worthy to remove[C] his sandals. He himself
will baptize you with the Holy Spirit and fire. 12 His
winnowing shovel is in his hand, and he will clear
his threshing floor and gather his wheat into the
barn. But the chaff he will burn with fire that never
goes out."

THE BAPTISM OF JESUS

13 Then Jesus came from Galilee to John at the Jordan,
to be baptized by him. 14 But John tried to stop him,
saying, "I need to be baptized by you, and yet you
come to me?"
15 Jesus answered him, "Allow it for now, because
this is the way for us to fulfill all righteousness." Then
John allowed him to be baptized.
16 When Jesus was baptized, he went up immediately from the water. The heavens suddenly opened
for him,[D] and he saw the Spirit of God descending like
a dove and coming down on him. 17 And a voice from
heaven said, "This is my beloved Son, with whom I
am well-pleased."

THE TEMPTATION OF JESUS

4 Then Jesus was led up by the Spirit into the wilderness to be tempted by the devil. 2 After he had
fasted forty days and forty nights, he was hungry.
3 Then the tempter approached him and said, "If you
are the Son of God, tell these stones to become bread."

[A] **3:8** Lit *fruit worthy of* [B] **3:11** Or *in* [C] **3:11** Or *to carry* [D] **3:16** Other mss omit *for him*

Man winnowing wheat in Jordan.

4 He answered, "It is written: **Man must not live on
bread alone but on every word that comes from
the mouth of God.**"[A]
5 Then the devil took him to the holy city, had him
stand on the pinnacle of the temple, 6 and said to him,
"If you are the Son of God, throw yourself down. For
it is written:

He will give his angels orders
concerning you,
and **they will support you with their hands**
so that you will not strike
your foot against a stone."[B]

7 Jesus told him, "It is also written: **Do not test the
Lord your God.**"[C]
8 Again, the devil took him to a very high mountain
and showed him all the kingdoms of the world and
their splendor. 9 And he said to him, "I will give you all
these things if you will fall down and worship me."[D]
10 Then Jesus told him, "Go away,[E] Satan! For it is
written: **Worship the Lord your God, and serve
only him.**"[F]
11 Then the devil left him, and angels came and began to serve him.

MINISTRY IN GALILEE

12 When he heard that John had been arrested, he
withdrew into Galilee. 13 He left Nazareth and went to
live in Capernaum by the sea, in the region of Zebulun
and Naphtali. 14 This was to fulfill what was spoken
through the prophet Isaiah:

15 **Land of Zebulun and land of Naphtali,**
along the road by the sea,
beyond the Jordan,
Galilee of the Gentiles.
16 **The people who live in darkness**
have seen a great light,
and for those living in the land of the
shadow of death,
a light has dawned.[G,H]

17 From then on Jesus began to preach, "Repent, because the kingdom of heaven has come near."

THE FIRST DISCIPLES

18 As he was walking along the Sea of Galilee, he saw
two brothers, Simon (who is called Peter), and his
brother Andrew. They were casting a net into the sea
— for they were fishermen. 19 "Follow me," he told
them, "and I will make you fish for[I] people." 20 Immediately they left their nets and followed him.
21 Going on from there, he saw two other brothers,
James the son of Zebedee, and his brother John. They
were in a boat with Zebedee their father, preparing
their nets, and he called them. 22 Immediately they left
the boat and their father and followed him.

TEACHING, PREACHING, AND HEALING

23 Now Jesus began to go all over Galilee, teaching in
their synagogues, preaching the good news of the
kingdom, and healing every[J] disease and sickness[K]
among the people. 24 Then the news about him spread
throughout Syria. So they brought to him all those
who were afflicted, those suffering from various
diseases and intense pains, the demon-possessed,
the epileptics, and the paralytics. And he healed them.
25 Large crowds followed him from Galilee, the Decapolis, Jerusalem, Judea, and beyond the Jordan.

THE SERMON ON THE MOUNT

5 When he saw the crowds, he went up on the
mountain, and after he sat down, his disciples
came to him. 2 Then[L] he began to teach them, saying:

THE BEATITUDES

3 "Blessed are the poor in spirit,
for the kingdom of heaven is theirs.
4 Blessed are those who mourn,
for they will be comforted.
5 Blessed are the humble,
for they will inherit the earth.
6 Blessed are those who hunger and thirst
for righteousness,
for they will be filled.
7 Blessed are the merciful,
for they will be shown mercy.
8 Blessed are the pure in heart,
for they will see God.
9 Blessed are the peacemakers,
for they will be called sons of God.
10 Blessed are those who are persecuted because
of righteousness,
for the kingdom of heaven is theirs.

11 "You are blessed when they insult you and persecute you and falsely say every kind of evil against
you because of me. 12 Be glad and rejoice, because
your reward is great in heaven. For that is how they
persecuted the prophets who were before you.

BELIEVERS ARE SALT AND LIGHT

13 "You are the salt of the earth. But if the salt should
lose its taste, how can it be made salty?[M] It's no longer
good for anything but to be thrown out and trampled
under people's feet.
14 "You are the light of the world. A city situated on
a hill cannot be hidden. 15 No one lights a lamp and

[A] **4:4** Dt 8:3 [B] **4:6** Ps 91:11–12 [C] **4:7** Dt 6:16 [D] **4:9** Or *and pay me homage* [E] **4:10** Other mss read *"Get behind me* [F] **4:10** Dt 6:13 [G] **4:16** Lit *dawned on them* [H] **4:15–16** Is 9:1–2 [I] **4:19** Or *you fishers of* [J] **4:23** Or *every kind of* [K] **4:23** Or *physical ailment* [L] **5:2** Lit *Then opening his mouth* [M] **5:13** Or *how can the earth be salted?*

Nazareth in the First Century

by Roy E. Lucas Jr.

Overview of the modern city of Nazareth. The conical structure in the center is the Church of the Annunciation.

Eliminate Gabriel's announcement to Mary, and Nazareth's visibility wanes. Subtract Nathaniel's comment about nothing good coming from Nazareth, and the city fades. But remove its foremost citizen, Jesus, and Nazareth vanishes.

The Jewish Talmud, which refers to sixty-three Galilean villages, disregards Nazareth, as does the Apocrypha. The first-century Jewish historian Josephus never mentions the town. Archaeological investigation substantiates Nazareth's lack of significance.

LOCATION AND RESOURCES

Nazareth lies in an "elevated and steeped plateau-land"[1] at about 1,150 feet above sea level. It is fifteen miles southwest of the Sea of Galilee and twenty from the Mediterranean. Six miles east of Nazareth runs the Via Maris, the road that connected Egypt and Israel with Damascus.

Nazareth has wet winters. Winter temperatures vacillate between forty and fifty degrees Fahrenheit with occasional freezing temperatures. Annually, Nazareth receives twenty to thirty inches of rain. Dew forms on about two hundred nights. Summer temperatures vary between sixty-five and eighty-five degrees. Nazareth's altitude, adequate rainfall, and hilly surroundings on all sides but the south help produce abundant vegetation. Nazareth's single water source, a spring, may have both hindered its growth and served as its social center.

CULTURE

Rome appointed Herod the Great as king of Judea (37–4 BC). Herod Antipas, Herod's youngest son, ruled as tetrarch in Galilee and Perea from 4 BC to AD 39 (Lk 3:1). This means Nazareth was under the rule of Herod Antipas throughout Jesus's earthly ministry.

Galileans were reportedly "generous, impulsive, simple in manners, full of intense nationalism, free, and independent of the traditionalism of Judea,"[2] the region that included Jerusalem. The reason the rabbis in Jerusalem despised the Galileans, "was likely due to the unpolished dialect, lack of culture, and the hamlet-size of the Nazareth community."[3]

Nazareth covered approximately ten acres. Lower population estimates range from four hundred to five hundred citizens; higher estimates reach sixteen hundred to two thousand.[4] Nazareth's occupants owned land, were tenant farmers, or provided craft services for those needing their skills. "The remains of olive and wine presses, water cisterns, grinding stones, and other materials found scattered about, all indicate the poor, peasant nature of Nazareth during the time of Jesus."[5] Local artisans made eating and

Mary's Well, located inside the Greek Orthodox Church in Nazareth, was likely the only water source of Nazareth for centuries.

cooking utensils. Regionally grown foods included wheat, barley, beans, peas, lentils, onions, cucumbers, olives, grapes, and figs.

Houses in Nazareth typically had two to four rooms with mud-packed floors. Homes were constructed of native stone. Roofs consisted of mud packed on flat thatch. Larger houses had second stories. Joseph and Jesus were *tektons*—a Greek term that may refer to carpenters or stonemasons.

The number of family members and a household's income dictated house size. Many homes were small and built close together. Three or four of these close-built homes formed an open courtyard; a stone wall encircled and secured the compound. These multihouse units shared a kitchen area with an outside oven, cistern, and millstone. Families often kept animals in a ground-floor room of the house.

The religious background in first-century Nazareth is not easily discerned. Evidently the Roman provincial (Gentile) cultures of nearby Sepphoris and Tiberias had little effect on the surrounding region, including Nazareth, which seems to have had a significant Jewish population. The contents of two rock tombs near Nazareth indicate the presence of a Jewish settlement there during the Roman period. Rabbinic tradition also indicates priests at one time lived in Nazareth. Although no first-century synagogue buildings have been excavated in Nazareth, the New Testament states that one existed (Mt 13:54; Mk 6:1–2; Lk 4:16). ✣

---

[1] Paul Barnett, *Behind the Scenes of the New Testament* (Downers Grove, IL: InterVarsity, 1990), 38. [2] J. Dwight Pentecost, *The Words and Works of Jesus Christ* (Grand Rapids: Zondervan, 1981), 520. [3] Jerry W. Batson and Lucas P. Grimsley, "Nazareth, Nazarene" in the *HIBD*, rev. ed. (2015), 1148. [4] Donald L. Blake Sr., *Jesus, A Visual History: The Dramatic Story of the Messiah in the Holy Land* (Grand Rapids: Zondervan, 2014), 42; Bernard J. Lee, *The Galilean Jewishness of Jesus: Retrieving the Jewish Origins of Christianity* (New York: Paulist, 1988), 65. [5] John C. H. Laughlin, *Fifty Major Cities of the Bible* (New York: Routledge, 2006), 194.

puts it under a basket, but rather on a lampstand,
and it gives light for all who are in the house. 16 In
the same way, let your light shine before others, so
that they may see your good works and give glory to
your Father in heaven.

CHRIST FULFILLS THE LAW

17 "Don't think that I came to abolish the Law or the
Prophets. I did not come to abolish but to fulfill. 18 For
truly I tell you, until heaven and earth pass away, not
the smallest letter[A] or one stroke of a letter will pass
away from the law until all things are accomplished.
19 Therefore, whoever breaks one of the least of these
commands and teaches others to do the same will be
called least in the kingdom of heaven. But whoever
does and teaches these commands will be called great
in the kingdom of heaven. 20 For I tell you, unless your
righteousness surpasses that of the scribes and Pharisees, you will never get into the kingdom of heaven.

MURDER BEGINS IN THE HEART

21 "You have heard that it was said to our ancestors, **Do
not murder**,[B] and whoever murders will be subject
to judgment. 22 But I tell you, everyone who is angry
with his brother or sister[C] will be subject to judgment.
Whoever insults[D] his brother or sister will be subject
to the court.[E] Whoever says, 'You fool!' will be subject
to hellfire.[F] 23 So if you are offering your gift on the
altar, and there you remember that your brother or
sister has something against you, 24 leave your gift
there in front of the altar. First go and be reconciled
with your brother or sister, and then come and offer
your gift. 25 Reach a settlement quickly with your
adversary while you're on the way with him to the
court, or your adversary will hand you over to the
judge, and the judge to[G] the officer, and you will be
thrown into prison. 26 Truly I tell you, you will never
get out of there until you have paid the last penny.[H]

ADULTERY BEGINS IN THE HEART

27 "You have heard that it was said, **Do not commit
adultery.**[I] 28 But I tell you, everyone who looks at a
woman lustfully has already committed adultery with
her in his heart. 29 If your right eye causes you to sin,
gouge it out and throw it away. For it is better that you
lose one of the parts of your body than for your whole
body to be thrown into hell. 30 And if your right hand
causes you to sin, cut it off and throw it away. For it

[A]**5:18** Or *not one iota*; *iota* is the smallest letter of the Gk alphabet.
[B]**5:21** Ex 20:13; Dt 5:17 [C]**5:22** Other mss add *without a cause*
[D]**5:22** Lit *Whoever says 'Raca'*; an Aramaic term of abuse that puts someone down, insulting one's intelligence [E]**5:22** Lit *Sanhedrin*
[F]**5:22** Lit *the gehenna of fire* [G]**5:25** Other mss read *judge will hand you over to* [H]**5:26** Lit *quadrans*, the smallest and least valuable Roman coin, worth 1⁄64 of a daily wage [I]**5:27** Ex 20:14; Dt 5:18

The Plain of Gennesaret overlooking the northwest corner of the Sea of Galilee is where many believe Jesus preached his Sermon on the Mount. The geography formed a natural amphitheater where Jesus's voice could be heard by the crowds.

is better that you lose one of the parts of your body than for your whole body to go into hell.

DIVORCE PRACTICES CENSURED

31 "It was also said, **Whoever divorces his wife must give her a written notice of divorce.**[A] 32 But I tell you, everyone who divorces his wife, except in a case of sexual immorality, causes her to commit adultery. And whoever marries a divorced woman commits adultery.

TELL THE TRUTH

33 "Again, you have heard that it was said to our ancestors, **You must not break your oath, but you must keep your oaths to the Lord.**[B] 34 But I tell you, don't take an oath at all: either by heaven, because it is God's throne; 35 or by the earth, because it is his footstool; or by Jerusalem, because it is the city of the great King. 36 Do not swear by your head, because you cannot make a single hair white or black. 37 But let your 'yes' mean 'yes,' and your 'no' mean 'no.' Anything more than this is from the evil one.

GO THE SECOND MILE

38 "You have heard that it was said, **An eye for an eye** and **a tooth for a tooth.**[C] 39 But I tell you, don't resist[D] an evildoer. On the contrary, if anyone slaps you on your right cheek, turn the other to him also. 40 As for the one who wants to sue you and take away your shirt, let him have your coat as well. 41 And if anyone forces you to go one mile, go with him two. 42 Give to the one who asks you, and don't turn away from the one who wants to borrow from you.

LOVE YOUR ENEMIES

43 "You have heard that it was said, **Love your neighbor**[E] and hate your enemy. 44 But I tell you, love your enemies[F] and pray for those who[G] persecute you, 45 so that you may be[H] children of your Father in heaven. For he causes his sun to rise on the evil and the good, and sends rain on the righteous and the unrighteous. 46 For if you love those who love you, what reward will you have? Don't even the tax collectors do the same? 47 And if you greet only your brothers and sisters, what are you doing out of the ordinary?[I] Don't even the Gentiles[J] do the same? 48 Be perfect, therefore, as your heavenly Father is perfect.

HOW TO GIVE

6 "Be careful not to practice your righteousness[K] in front of others to be seen by them. Otherwise, you have no reward with your Father in heaven. 2 So whenever you give to the poor, don't sound a trumpet before you, as the hypocrites do in the synagogues and on the streets, to be applauded by people. Truly I tell you, they have their reward. 3 But when you give to the poor, don't let your left hand know what your right hand is doing, 4 so that your giving may be in secret. And your Father who sees in secret will reward you.[L]

HOW TO PRAY

5 "Whenever you pray, you must not be like the hypocrites, because they love to pray standing in the synagogues and on the street corners to be seen by people. Truly I tell you, they have their reward. 6 But when you pray, go into your private room, shut your door, and pray to your Father who is in secret. And your Father who sees in secret will reward you.[M] 7 When you pray, don't babble like the Gentiles, since they imagine they'll be heard for their many words. 8 Don't be like them, because your Father knows the things you need before you ask him.

THE LORD'S PRAYER

9 "Therefore, you should pray like this:

Our Father in heaven,
your name be honored as holy.
10 Your kingdom come.
Your will be done
on earth as it is in heaven.
11 Give us today our daily bread.[N]
12 And forgive us our debts,
as we also have forgiven our debtors.
13 And do not bring us into[O] temptation,
but deliver us from the evil one.[P]

14 "For if you forgive others their offenses, your heavenly Father will forgive you as well. 15 But if you don't forgive others,[Q] your Father will not forgive your offenses.

HOW TO FAST

16 "Whenever you fast, don't be gloomy like the hypocrites. For they disfigure their faces so that their fasting is obvious to people. Truly I tell you, they have their reward. 17 But when you fast, put oil on your head and wash your face, 18 so that your fasting isn't obvious to others but to your Father who is in secret. And your Father who sees in secret will reward you.[M]

[A] **5:31** Dt 24:1 [B] **5:33** Lv 19:12; Nm 30:2; Dt 23:21 [C] **5:38** Ex 21:24; Lv 24:20; Dt 19:21 [D] **5:39** Or *don't set yourself against*, or *don't retaliate against* [E] **5:43** Lv 19:18 [F] **5:44** Other mss add *bless those who curse you, do good to those who hate you,* [G] **5:44** Other mss add *mistreat you and* [H] **5:45** Or *may become*, or *may show yourselves to be* [I] **5:47** Or *doing that is superior*; lit *doing more* [J] **5:47** Other mss read *tax collectors* [K] **6:1** Other mss read *charitable giving* [L] **6:4** Other mss read *will himself reward you openly* [M] **6:6,18** Other mss add *openly* [N] **6:11** Or *our necessary bread*, or *our bread for tomorrow* [O] **6:13** Or *do not cause us to come into* [P] **6:13** Or *from evil*; some later mss add *For yours is the kingdom and the power and the glory forever. Amen.* [Q] **6:15** Other mss add *their wrongdoing*

Fishermen in the First Century

by Argile A. Smith Jr.

Located on Mount Nebo in the Church of Saint Lot and Saint Procopius (early Christian martyrs); a mosaic dating to the mid-sixth century AD depicts a man pole fishing.

In Jesus's day, most people living in Israel depended on farming and fishing for food. Fishing thus became an important industry, one that was quite profitable. Fishermen generally made more money than farmers.[1]

While fishing was a good way to make a living, it was not easy. It involved back-breaking work that required fishermen to stay busy for long hours every day. The fishing industry involved a predictable but grueling routine. Fishermen would go out in their boats at night and bring in their catch early in the morning. Then they would separate the fish they caught, salt them down to preserve them, and deliver them to the market. They sold some fish in Jerusalem at the designated entrance to the city that everyone referred to as the Fish Gate.[2]

WHERE DID THEY FISH?

All kinds of fish flourished in the Mediterranean Sea, but the fishermen in Israel did not seem to be drawn there. They gave their attention to the fresh-water inland lake commonly known as the Sea of Galilee.

The prominence of the fishing industry was evident in the growth of towns and villages surrounding the Sea of Galilee. Jesus chose Capernaum, a town on the northern shore of the lake, to be the center of his Galilean ministry. Capernaum also happened to be a center of business for the Galilean fishing industry. Fishing influenced the names of towns and villages in the area. For example, not far from Capernaum was the predominantly Gentile seashore town of Bethsaida; its name meant "the fishing place."[3]

Fishermen in Israel favored the Sea of Galilee because they could harvest different kinds of fish there. Three varieties were particularly plentiful: a small fish that resembled a sardine, tilapia (or musht, otherwise known as St. Peter's fish), and carp. Although fishermen on the Sea of Galilee caught catfish and eels, they normally discarded them because Jewish people did not eat them.[4]

Fishermen focused their work on the Sea of Galilee for another reason. No other significant body of fresh water suitable for fishing existed in Israel. Even the Jordan River held little promise for productive fishing. The Jordan flowed from the Sea of Galilee to the Dead Sea. Fish that made their way from the lake and down the Jordan were not as

Limestone decorative fragment from Egypt, which dates about 2700–2200 BC and shows three flathead mullets.

plentiful or very large. If they got to the mouth of the Dead Sea, they died in the salt water.[5]

WHAT EQUIPMENT DID THEY USE?

The New Testament has an account involving the use of hooks to catch a fish (Mt 17:27). Hooks were made of bone or iron and attached to a line that the fisherman held by hand.[6] However, the vast majority of fishing references in the New Testament involve nets. Fishermen in the first century used three different kinds of nets, each indicated by a different Greek word. Matthew mentions each.

Fishermen sometimes used a simple cast net (Gk *amphiblēstron*, 4:18), typically round and about thirteen feet in diameter. Fishermen placed heavy objects like stones around the edge so the net would sink quickly. Whether in a boat, on shore, or in shallow water, fishermen would keep this type of net close at hand so they could cast it over a school of fish. Even though this simple net was useful, fishermen could use it only during the day.[7]

Another kind of net was something like a dragnet or a seine (Gk *sagēnē*, 13:47–48). About sixteen feet high and up to eight hundred feet long, this net had rocks tied to the bottom and floaters attached to the top. Fishermen in one boat could use it, or they could suspend it between two boats that were guided close to shore. From there, they would pull the dragnet on to shore with ropes. That was why fishermen favored a sandy shore with a gentle slope.

Still another kind of net was a little more complex and resembled a modern-day trammel net (Gk *diktuon*, 4:20). It consisted of a series of parallel nets that fishermen suspended between two boats. Fishermen in a third boat would drive the fish into the nets. This kind of complex net worked particularly well for catching big fish in deep water. ✣

---

1 Craig S. Keener, *The IVP Bible Background Commentary: New Testament* (Downers Grove, IL: InterVarsity, 1993), 55. 2 Roland K. Harrison, "Fish" in *ISBE* (1989), 2:309. 3 Roger Crook, "Galilee, Sea of" in *HIBD*, 618. 4 "Fish" in *Eerdmans Bible Dictionary*, ed. Allen C. Myers (Grand Rapids: Eerdmans, 1987), 384; Harrison, "Fish," 309. 5 "Fish," in *Eerdmans Bible Dictionary*, 384. 6 Roland K. Harrison, "Fishhook" in *ISBE*, 2:309. 7 Information on nets in this and the following paragraphs is drawn mainly from "Fishing" in *Eerdmans Bible Dictionary*, 385.

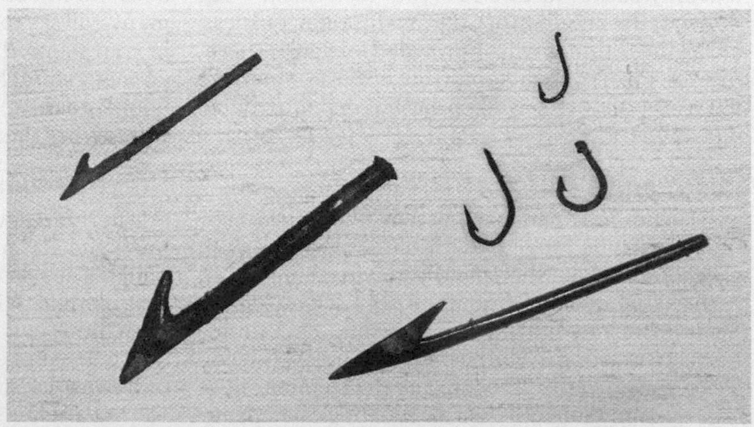

Bronze harpoons and hooks, Egyptian, dated about 1300 BC. Harpoon use was typically for sport fishing. Single fishermen used rods, lines, and hooks. Those who made their living off of fishing, though, typically used nets.

GOD AND POSSESSIONS

19 "Don't store up for yourselves treasures[A] on earth,
where moth and rust destroy and where thieves break
in and steal. 20 But store up for yourselves treasures
in heaven, where neither moth nor rust destroys, and
where thieves don't break in and steal. 21 For where
your treasure is, there your heart will be also.

22 "The eye is the lamp of the body. If your eye is
healthy, your whole body will be full of light. 23 But
if your eye is bad, your whole body will be full of
darkness. So if the light within you is darkness, how
deep is that darkness!

24 "No one can serve two masters, since either he
will hate one and love the other, or he will be devoted
to one and despise the other. You cannot serve both
God and money.

THE CURE FOR ANXIETY

25 "Therefore I tell you: Don't worry about your life,
what you will eat or what you will drink; or about
your body, what you will wear. Isn't life more than
food and the body more than clothing? 26 Consider
the birds of the sky: They don't sow or reap or gather into barns, yet your heavenly Father feeds them.
Aren't you worth more than they? 27 Can any of you
add one moment to his life span[B] by worrying? 28 And
why do you worry about clothes? Observe how the
wildflowers of the field grow: They don't labor or
spin thread. 29 Yet I tell you that not even Solomon in
all his splendor was adorned like one of these. 30 If
that's how God clothes the grass of the field, which
is here today and thrown into the furnace tomorrow, won't he do much more for you — you of little
faith? 31 So don't worry, saying, 'What will we eat?' or
'What will we drink?' or 'What will we wear?' 32 For
the Gentiles eagerly seek all these things, and your
heavenly Father knows that you need them. 33 But
seek first the kingdom of God[C] and his righteousness,
and all these things will be provided for you. 34 Therefore don't worry about tomorrow, because tomorrow
will worry about itself. Each day has enough trouble
of its own.

DO NOT JUDGE

7 "Do not judge, so that you won't be judged. 2 For
you will be judged by the same standard with
which you judge others, and you will be measured
by the same measure you use. 3 Why do you look at
the splinter in your brother's eye but don't notice
the beam of wood in your own eye? 4 Or how can you
say to your brother, 'Let me take the splinter out of
your eye,' and look, there's a beam of wood in your
own eye? 5 Hypocrite! First take the beam of wood
out of your eye, and then you will see clearly to take
the splinter out of your brother's eye. 6 Don't give
what is holy to dogs or toss your pearls before pigs,
or they will trample them under their feet, turn, and
tear you to pieces.

ASK, SEARCH, KNOCK

7 "Ask, and it will be given to you. Seek, and you will
find. Knock, and the door[D] will be opened to you.
8 For everyone who asks receives, and the one who
seeks finds, and to the one who knocks, the door
will be opened. 9 Who among you, if his son asks him
for bread, will give him a stone? 10 Or if he asks for
a fish, will give him a snake? 11 If you then, who are
evil, know how to give good gifts to your children,
how much more will your Father in heaven give good
things to those who ask him. 12 Therefore, whatever
you want others to do for you, do also the same for
them, for this is the Law and the Prophets.

ENTERING THE KINGDOM

13 "Enter through the narrow gate. For the gate is wide
and the road broad that leads to destruction, and
there are many who go through it. 14 How narrow is
the gate and difficult the road that leads to life, and
few find it.

15 "Be on your guard against false prophets who
come to you in sheep's clothing but inwardly are ravaging wolves. 16 You'll recognize them by their fruit.
Are grapes gathered from thornbushes or figs from
thistles? 17 In the same way, every good tree produces
good fruit, but a bad tree produces bad fruit. 18 A good
tree can't produce bad fruit; neither can a bad tree
produce good fruit. 19 Every tree that doesn't produce
good fruit is cut down and thrown into the fire. 20 So
you'll recognize them by their fruit.

21 "Not everyone who says to me, 'Lord, Lord,' will
enter the kingdom of heaven, but only the one who
does the will of my Father in heaven. 22 On that day
many will say to me, 'Lord, Lord, didn't we prophesy
in your name, drive out demons in your name, and
do many miracles in your name?' 23 Then I will announce to them, 'I never knew you. **Depart from me,
you lawbreakers!**'[E,F]

THE TWO FOUNDATIONS

24 "Therefore, everyone who hears these words of
mine and acts on them will be like a wise man who
built his house on the rock. 25 The rain fell, the rivers
rose, and the winds blew and pounded that house.
Yet it didn't collapse, because its foundation was on
the rock. 26 But everyone who hears these words of
mine and doesn't act on them will be like a foolish

[A] **6:19** Or *valuables* [B] **6:27** Or *add a single cubit to his height*
[C] **6:33** Other mss omit *of God* [D] **7:7** Lit *and it* [E] **7:23** Lit *you who work lawlessness* [F] **7:23** Ps 6:8

man who built his house on the sand. 27 The rain fell, the rivers rose, the winds blew and pounded that house, and it collapsed. It collapsed with a great crash."

28 When Jesus had finished saying these things, the crowds were astonished at his teaching, 29 because he was teaching them like one who had authority, and not like their scribes.

A MAN CLEANSED

8 When he came down from the mountain, large crowds followed him. 2 Right away a man with leprosy[A] came up and knelt before him, saying, "Lord, if you are willing, you can make me clean."

3 Reaching out his hand, Jesus touched him, saying, "I am willing; be made clean." Immediately his leprosy was cleansed. 4 Then Jesus told him, "See that you don't tell anyone; but go, show yourself to the priest, and offer the gift that Moses commanded, as a testimony to them."

A CENTURION'S FAITH

5 When he entered Capernaum, a centurion came to him, pleading with him, 6 "Lord, my servant is lying at home paralyzed, in terrible agony."

7 He said to him, "Am I to come and heal him?"[B]

8 "Lord," the centurion replied, "I am not worthy to have you come under my roof. But just say the word, and my servant will be healed. 9 For I too am a man under authority, having soldiers under my command.[C] I say to this one, 'Go,' and he goes; and to another, 'Come,' and he comes; and to my servant, 'Do this!' and he does it."

10 Hearing this, Jesus was amazed and said to those following him, "Truly I tell you, I have not found anyone in Israel with so great a faith. 11 I tell you that many will come from east and west to share the banquet[D] with Abraham, Isaac, and Jacob in the kingdom of heaven. 12 But the sons of the kingdom will be thrown into the outer darkness where there will be weeping and gnashing of teeth." 13 Then Jesus told the centurion, "Go. As you have believed, let it be done for you." And his servant was healed that very moment.[E]

HEALINGS AT CAPERNAUM

14 Jesus went into Peter's house and saw his mother-in-law lying in bed with a fever. 15 So he touched her hand, and the fever left her. Then she got up and began to serve him. 16 When evening came, they brought to him many who were demon-possessed. He drove out the spirits with a word and healed all who were sick, 17 so that what was spoken through the prophet Isaiah might be fulfilled:

> **He himself took our weaknesses**
> **and carried our diseases.**[F]

THE COST OF FOLLOWING JESUS

18 When Jesus saw a large crowd[G] around him, he gave the order to go to the other side of the sea. 19 A scribe approached him and said, "Teacher, I will follow you wherever you go."

20 Jesus told him, "Foxes have dens, and birds of the sky have nests, but the Son of Man has no place to lay his head."

21 "Lord," another of his disciples said, "first let me go bury my father."

22 But Jesus told him, "Follow me, and let the dead bury their own dead."

WIND AND WAVES OBEY JESUS

23 As he got into the boat, his disciples followed him. 24 Suddenly, a violent storm arose on the sea, so that the boat was being swamped by the waves — but Jesus kept sleeping. 25 So the disciples came and woke him up, saying, "Lord, save us! We're going to die!"

26 He said to them, "Why are you afraid, you of little faith?" Then he got up and rebuked the winds and the sea, and there was a great calm.

27 The men were amazed and asked, "What kind of man is this? Even the winds and the sea obey him!"

DEMONS DRIVEN OUT BY JESUS

28 When he had come to the other side, to the region of the Gadarenes,[H] two demon-possessed men met him as they came out of the tombs. They were so violent that no one could pass that way. 29 Suddenly they shouted, "What do you have to do with us,[I] Son of God? Have you come here to torment us before the time?"

30 A long way off from them, a large herd of pigs was feeding. 31 "If you drive us out," the demons begged him, "send us into the herd of pigs."

32 "Go!" he told them. So when they had come out, they entered the pigs, and the whole herd rushed down the steep bank into the sea and perished in the water. 33 Then the men who tended them fled. They went into the city and reported everything, especially what had happened to those who were demon-possessed. 34 At that, the whole town went out to meet Jesus. When they saw him, they begged him to leave their region.

THE SON OF MAN FORGIVES AND HEALS

9 So he got into a boat, crossed over, and came to his own town. 2 Just then some men[J] brought to him a paralytic lying on a stretcher. Seeing their faith, Jesus told the paralytic, "Have courage, son, your sins are forgiven."

[A] **8:2** Gk *lepros*; a term for various skin diseases, also in v. 3; see Lv 13–14 [B] **8:7** Or *"I will come and heal him."* [C] **8:9** Lit *under me* [D] **8:11** Lit *recline at the table* [E] **8:13** Or *that hour*; lit *very hour* [F] **8:17** Is 53:4 [G] **8:18** Other mss read *saw large crowds* [H] **8:28** Other mss read *Gergesenes* [I] **8:29** Other mss add *Jesus* [J] **9:2** Lit *then they*

Banking in the First Century

By C. Mack Roark

Treasury of the Athenians at Delphi. Such treasuries were built in honor of a city's patron god. Athenians visiting Delphi would bring an offering to their treasury in hopes of winning the approval of their favored deity.

From the New Testament itself we learn very little about banking in Judea and Galilee. The Greek word translated as "bank" (*trapeza*) occurs fifteen times in the New Testament, but only in one instance does it refer to a place where money was kept and circulated, for the word also means "table" in daily household use. Three times it refers to the money changers' tables (Mt 21:12; Mk 11:15; Jn 2:15). Only in Luke 19:23 does it signify a bank,[1] and that would not have been a bank in any modern sense. Under Roman rule in the first century AD, banking was still quite primitive, in spite of the fact that in various forms banking had been around for centuries.[2]

Banking was the result of a process that began with the barter system, wherein people exchanged goods or services for other goods or services. Although barter continued throughout the ancient world, the development of coinage and the exchange of money for goods and services introduced a new era in commerce. Throughout the Roman world, a unified system of coinage slowly developed.[3] The system was more common in urban areas and less so in the rural villages where Jesus primarily ministered. There bartering remained common practice and, with bartering, the old methods of storing treasures. People of Judea began using coins in the fourth century BC; Roman coins came into use there in the first century BC. Herod the Great, as well as his sons and successors, produced and put into use coins that were serviceable but were in fact of lesser value than imperial coinage.[4] Individuals often carried coins in a purse or pocket.

The minting of coins marked a step forward in commerce but at the same time presented new problems. No one had established a uniform standard for the value of coins, plus numerous nations and city-states were minting their own. Coins could be gold, silver, bronze, or copper; many were stamped with images and icons of the various states.[5] The resulting diversity of

The banker's ticket, called a *tasserae*, was adhered to a sealed sack of coins. The mark, which was inscribed with the name of the coin authenticator, or assayer, would serve to verify that the sealed money sack contained genuine coins and an expected amount of money. Bankers exchanged sacks of coins, often without even opening them for verification beyond the banker's mark. This system, which the general population never used, relied on trustworthy slaves for money transport.

coinage gave rise to the money changers, who were in effect small-time bankers. Stationing themselves where traffic passed—at the gates of the city or of the temple—they performed the necessary but often corrupt service of exchanging coins for local use.[6] Their desk was called a *trapeza*, the same word used for a bank in Luke 19:23.

When transactions based on money replaced transactions based on barter, money changers became essential. Also essential, people had to have a repository to hold the cash and provide methods of payment, not unlike today's system of checking accounts and lines of credit.[7]

Banks and banking originated in temples or kingdom treasuries. Especially in Athens, but also throughout the Mediterranean world, temple treasuries were banking facilities.[8] These temple banks were not so much commercial banks designed for transactions, but deposit banks for the safekeeping of wealth. The assumption that temples were sacred and their contents inviolate was likely behind their use. Also the fact that the temple was a central institution for public life may have been a major reason banks were often attached to them.[9] In addition to temple banks, some cities had royal or state banks, which were tied to the king's treasury. In contrast, private banks served the public.

For the private citizen, perhaps especially in Galilee, banks were not the most important financial institution. The wealthier citizens were more likely to provide loans for the average person than were banks.[10] Even in Rome, where bank accounts had existed for decades, most families relied on a personal strong box, which would contain cash and have a list of due dates for loans and bills.[11] Many people, perhaps most, would have had no need for a bank. Jesus knew his listeners and knew he was addressing people whose meager treasure was not in a bank. ✣

Dated to the fourth century AD, this relief shows a money changer working at his bench, which doubles as his bank.

[1] The parallel text at Matthew 25:27 has "with the bankers" instead of "in the bank." [2] Steven E. Sidebotham, "Trade and Commerce (Roman)," in *ABD*, 6:630. [3] Sidebotham, "Trade," 629. [4] John W. Betlyon, "Coinage" in *ABD*, 1:1085–86. [5] Helmut Koester, *Introduction to the New Testament*, vol. 1, *History, Culture, and Religion of the Hellenistic Age* (Philadelphia: Fortress, 1980), 88. [6] Betlyon, "Coinage," 1086–87. [7] Michael Grant, *From Alexander to Cleopatra* (New York: Scribner's Sons, 1982), 124. [8] Koester, *Introduction*, 90. [9] Grant, *From Alexander to Cleopatra*, 45. [10] Bruce W. Frier, "Interest and Usury in the Greco-Roman Period" in *ABD*, 3:424. [11] Paul Veyne, ed., *A History of Private Life I: From Pagan Rome to Byzantium* (Cambridge, MA: Harvard University Press, 1987), 149.

3 At this, some of the scribes said to themselves, "He's blaspheming!"

4 Perceiving their thoughts, Jesus said, "Why are you thinking evil things in your hearts?[A] 5 For which is easier: to say, 'Your sins are forgiven,' or to say, 'Get up and walk'? 6 But so that you may know that the Son of Man has authority on earth to forgive sins" — then he told the paralytic, "Get up, take your stretcher, and go home." 7 So he got up and went home. 8 When the crowds saw this, they were awestruck[B,C] and gave glory to God, who had given such authority to men.

THE CALL OF MATTHEW

9 As Jesus went on from there, he saw a man named Matthew sitting at the tax office, and he said to him, "Follow me," and he got up and followed him.

10 While he was reclining at the table in the house, many tax collectors and sinners came to eat with Jesus and his disciples. 11 When the Pharisees saw this, they asked his disciples, "Why does your teacher eat with tax collectors and sinners?"

12 Now when he heard this, he said, "It is not those who are well who need a doctor, but those who are sick. 13 Go and learn what this means: **I desire mercy and not sacrifice.**[D] For I didn't come to call the righteous, but sinners."[E]

This stone plaque depicts the Mesopotamian demon Pazuzu, who was king of the evil wind demons. Pazuzu was a composite creature with a lion or dog-like face, the horns of a goat, a human torso, the front paws of a lion, a scaly lower body, a scorpion's tail, and the talons and wings of a bird. Pazuzu emerged from the mountains of the underworld. Dated eighth–seventh centuries BC.

A QUESTION ABOUT FASTING

14 Then John's disciples came to him, saying, "Why do we and the Pharisees fast often, but your disciples do not fast?"

15 Jesus said to them, "Can the wedding guests[F] be sad while the groom is with them? The time[G] will come when the groom will be taken away from them, and then they will fast. 16 No one patches an old garment with unshrunk cloth, because the patch pulls away from the garment and makes the tear worse. 17 And no one puts[H] new wine into old wineskins. Otherwise, the skins burst, the wine spills out, and the skins are ruined. No, they put new wine into fresh wineskins, and both are preserved."

A GIRL RESTORED AND A WOMAN HEALED

18 As he was telling them these things, suddenly one of the leaders came and knelt down before him, saying, "My daughter just died,[I] but come and lay your hand on her, and she will live." 19 So Jesus and his disciples got up and followed him.

20 Just then, a woman who had suffered from bleeding for twelve years approached from behind and touched the end of his robe, 21 for she said to herself, "If I can just touch his robe, I'll be made well."[J]

22 Jesus turned and saw her. "Have courage, daughter," he said. "Your faith has saved you."[K] And the woman was made well from that moment.[L]

23 When Jesus came to the leader's house, he saw the flute players and a crowd lamenting loudly. 24 "Leave," he said, "because the girl is not dead but asleep." And they laughed at him. 25 After the crowd had been put outside, he went in and took her by the hand, and the girl got up. 26 Then news of this spread throughout that whole area.

HEALING THE BLIND

27 As Jesus went on from there, two blind men followed him, calling out, "Have mercy on us, Son of David!"

28 When he entered the house, the blind men approached him, and Jesus said to them, "Do you believe that I can do this?"

They said to him, "Yes, Lord."

29 Then he touched their eyes, saying, "Let it be done for you according to your faith." 30 And their eyes were opened. Then Jesus warned them sternly, "Be sure that no one finds out." 31 But they went out and spread the news about him throughout that whole area.

[A] **9:4** Or *minds* [B] **9:8** Other mss read *amazed* [C] **9:8** Lit *afraid* [D] **9:13** Hs 6:6 [E] **9:13** Other mss add *to repentance* [F] **9:15** Lit *the sons of the bridal chamber* [G] **9:15** Lit *days* [H] **9:17** Lit *And they do not put* [I] **9:18** Lit *daughter has now come to the end* [J] **9:21** Or *be saved* [K] **9:22** Or *has made you well* [L] **9:22** Lit *hour*

Capernaum in Jesus's Day

by David M. Wallace

Interior of the rebuilt synagogue at Capernaum; worshipers would sit on the benches along the wall. Although the visible structure dates from the fourth century AD, the foundation below was part of the synagogue that existed in Jesus's day.

GEOGRAPHY

Located in Lower Galilee along the Sea of Galilee, Capernaum stretched west to east along the lakefront. The lake was on the southern edge of the city, and mountains rose steeply to the north. Lower Galilee was a beautiful, fruitful, fertile region dominated by the Sea of Galilee.

Lying at the northern end of the Jordan Rift Valley, the Sea of Galilee is a freshwater lake at 696 feet below sea level with a depth of about 150 feet. The Jordan River, which enters the lake just to the east within walking distance of Capernaum, is the primary water source for the Sea of Galilee. The lake is heart-shaped, about thirteen miles long and eight miles wide at most. Because of the steep surrounding hills, sudden storms sometimes occur. The hills and mountains surrounding the lake rise from 1,500 to more than 3,000 feet above sea level. Snow-capped Mount Hermon overlooks the region.

Summers are hot and humid, and winters are warm and wet. The rainy season is between October and the end of April. Rainfall is sufficient for farming, and permanent streams flow through the area. The year-round warm weather encourages growth wherever there is water. A flood plain, ideal for growing crops, lies along the north end of the lake near Capernaum, where the locals grow many foods mentioned in the Bible.

LOCAL RESOURCES

Located on the international trade route from Egypt to Syria and beyond, Capernaum saw caravans from around the world pass by, since it was one of the major cities of Galilee in Jesus's time. While much of Galilee was covered with forests in Jesus's day, lower Galilee was also blessed with fertile soil, plenty of rain, and a near-tropical climate, excellent for agriculture. Farmers terraced the hills and used the fertile valley for growing their crops, such as olives, figs, date palms, citrus fruit,[1] walnut trees, grapes, wheat, and even wildflowers.[2] Black basalt stones found near the water and in the surrounding fields were typically used for buildings.

The fish in the Sea of Galilee were the staple of the local economy. Today the lake holds about forty species of fish.[3] Fishing boats departed Capernaum before dawn and returned at dusk.[4] Fishermen used hooks and lines, spears, and nets.[5] Businesses made and repaired these tools, and some built and repaired fishing boats. Located at the water's edge was a jetty for boats. The local fish was both salted and pickled to store for later use or to export to other towns. Much of this work appears to have been done at nearby Magdala, about two miles away. A first-century AD fishing boat was discovered in 1986 at nearby Kibbutz Ginosar. It is now on display at the Yigal Allon Museum at the kibbutz.[6] Jesus and his disciples may have used boats similar to the one discovered.

Others in Capernaum earned their living by transporting the local produce and fish to other markets. Basalt implements, such as grain grinders and olive presses, may have been made at Capernaum.[7] Common glass and ceramic ware were also produced there for local use. Market days were probably held in tents or booths near the shoreline.[8] Aramaic and Hebrew, as well as Greek and Latin, were the languages of Capernaum.[9]

SIZE AND POPULATION

The Bible mentions Capernaum sixteen times, all in the Gospels. The city appears to have been founded after Old Testament times. Capernaum was small and had no defensive walls or civic buildings.[10] The synagogue may have been the only public building. Some believe the population was as few as six hundred to fifteen hundred.[11] Others estimate it between five thousand and sixty-five hundred.[12]

The Romans assigned a government and military presence in Capernaum. This included a garrison, commanded by a centurion who had built the Jewish synagogue (Lk 7:1–10). The Romans also collected taxes there. Capernaum is where Matthew, a tax collector, worked when Jesus called him to be his disciple (Mt 9:9).

Archaeology indicates the population of Capernaum was lower class. Exploration has unveiled no large houses or other finds that would indicate wealth, such as imported or decorative objects. The almost entirely Jewish population made their living from farming and fishing. Any extra income had to go to the tax collectors.[13]

Church built over the ruins of what is believed to be the home of Simon Peter at Capernaum. Archaeological evidence indicates early believers met for worship on the site. Inside the modern church, the floor is made of thick glass, which allows visitors to look into the structure below. Ruins of basalt-stone houses are in the foreground.

Model of an ancient boat at Nof Ginosar on the Sea of Galilee. Often called the "Jesus boat," the ancient vessel was discovered stuck in the mud when the sea had receded during an unusually dry season.

Visitors today will see remains of a limestone synagogue built some one hundred to four hundred years after Jesus lived in Capernaum. But black basalt walls, four feet thick, have been discovered under all four corners of the synagogue. Many believe these walls are the remains of the synagogue in which Jesus preached. Visitors today will also see the remains of what many believe was the house of Simon Peter, where Jesus may have lived and performed miracles (8:14–17). ✜

[1] LeMoine F. DeVries, *Cities of the Biblical World* (Peabody, MA: Hendrickson, 1997), 269. [2] Harry Thomas Frank, *Discovering the Biblical World* (New York: Harper & Row, 1975), 20. [3] William H. Stephens, "The Sea of Galilee" in *Where Jesus Walked*, ed. William H. Stephens (Nashville: Broadman, 1981), 73. [4] Frank, *Discovering the Biblical World*, 206. [5] Phillip J. Swanson, "Occupations and Professions in the Bible" in *HolBD*, 1038. [6] DeVries, *Cities of the Biblical World*, 269. [7] Henry H. Halley, *Halley's Bible Handbook* (Grand Rapids: Zondervan, 2007), 568. [8] Jonathan L. Reed, *Archaeology and the Galilean Jesus* (Harrisburg, PA: Trinity Press, 2000), 155. [9] J. E. Sanderson, "Capernaum" in *Major Cities of the Biblical World*, ed. R. K. Harrison (Nashville: Thomas Nelson, 1985), 77. [10] Reed, *Archaeology*, 153–54. [11] Reed, *Archaeology*, 152. [12] Sanderson, "Capernaum," 75. [13] Reed, *Archaeology*, 164–65.

DRIVING OUT A DEMON

32 Just as they were going out, a demon-possessed man who was unable to speak was brought to him. 33 When the demon had been driven out, the man who had been mute spoke, and the crowds were amazed, saying, "Nothing like this has ever been seen in Israel!"

34 But the Pharisees said, "He drives out demons by the ruler of the demons."

THE LORD OF THE HARVEST

35 Jesus continued going around to all the towns and villages, teaching in their synagogues, preaching the good news of the kingdom, and healing every[A] disease and every sickness.[B,C] 36 When he saw the crowds, he felt compassion for them, because they were distressed and dejected, like sheep without a shepherd. 37 Then he said to his disciples, "The harvest is abundant, but the workers are few. 38 Therefore, pray to the Lord of the harvest to send out workers into his harvest."

COMMISSIONING THE TWELVE

10 Summoning his twelve disciples, he gave them authority over unclean spirits, to drive them out and to heal every[A] disease and sickness.[C] 2 These are the names of the twelve apostles: First, Simon, who is called Peter, and Andrew his brother; James the son of Zebedee, and John his brother; 3 Philip and Bartholomew; Thomas and Matthew the tax collector; James the son of Alphaeus, and Thaddaeus;[D] 4 Simon the Zealot,[E] and Judas Iscariot, who also betrayed him.

5 Jesus sent out these twelve after giving them instructions: "Don't take the road that leads to the Gentiles, and don't enter any Samaritan town. 6 Instead, go to the lost sheep of the house of Israel. 7 As you go, proclaim, 'The kingdom of heaven has come near.' 8 Heal the sick, raise the dead, cleanse those with leprosy,[F] drive out demons. Freely you received, freely give. 9 Don't acquire gold, silver, or copper for your money-belts. 10 Don't take a traveling bag for the road, or an extra shirt, sandals, or a staff, for the worker is worthy of his food. 11 When you enter any town or village, find out who is worthy, and stay there until you leave. 12 Greet a household when you enter it, 13 and if the household is worthy, let your peace be on it; but if it is unworthy, let your peace return to you. 14 If anyone does not welcome you or listen to your words, shake the dust off your feet when you leave that house or town. 15 Truly I tell you, it will be more tolerable on the day of judgment for the land of Sodom and Gomorrah than for that town.

PERSECUTIONS PREDICTED

16 "Look, I'm sending you out like sheep among wolves. Therefore be as shrewd as serpents and as

Pair of Egyptian basketry-woven papyrus sandals; dated 1570–1070 BC.

innocent as doves. 17 Beware of them, because they will hand you over to local courts[G] and flog you in their synagogues. 18 You will even be brought before governors and kings because of me, to bear witness to them and to the Gentiles. 19 But when they hand you over, don't worry about how or what you are to speak. For you will be given what to say at that hour, 20 because it isn't you speaking, but the Spirit of your Father is speaking through you.

21 "Brother will betray brother to death, and a father his child. Children will rise up against parents and have them put to death. 22 You will be hated by everyone because of my name. But the one who endures to the end will be saved. 23 When they persecute you in one town, flee to another. For truly I tell you, you will not have gone through the towns of Israel before the Son of Man comes. 24 A disciple[H] is not above his teacher, or a slave above his master. 25 It is enough for a disciple to become like his teacher and a slave like his master. If they called the head of the house 'Beelzebul,' how much more the members of his household!

FEAR GOD

26 "Therefore, don't be afraid of them, since there is nothing covered that won't be uncovered and nothing hidden that won't be made known. 27 What I tell you

[A] **9:35; 10:1** Or *every kind of* [B] **9:35** Other mss add *among the people* [C] **9:35; 10:1** Or *physical ailment* [D] **10:3** Other mss read *and Lebbaeus, whose surname was Thaddaeus* [E] **10:4** Lit *the Cananaean* [F] **10:8** Gk *lepros*; a term for various skin diseases; see Lv 13–14 [G] **10:17** Or *sanhedrins* [H] **10:24** Or *student*

in the dark, speak in the light. What you hear in a whisper,[A] proclaim on the housetops. 28 Don't fear those who kill the body but are not able to kill the soul; rather, fear him who is able to destroy both soul and body in hell. 29 Aren't two sparrows sold for a penny?[B] Yet not one of them falls to the ground without your Father's consent.[C] 30 But even the hairs of your head have all been counted. 31 So don't be afraid; you are worth more than many sparrows.

ACKNOWLEDGING CHRIST

32 "Therefore, everyone who will acknowledge me before others, I will also acknowledge him before my Father in heaven. 33 But whoever denies me before others, I will also deny him before my Father in heaven. 34 Don't assume that I came to bring peace on the earth. I did not come to bring peace, but a sword. 35 For I came to turn

a man against his father,
a daughter against her mother,
a daughter-in-law against her mother-in-law;
36 **and a man's enemies will be**
the members of his household.[D]

37 The one who loves a father or mother more than me is not worthy of me; the one who loves a son or daughter more than me is not worthy of me. 38 And whoever doesn't take up his cross and follow me is not worthy of me. 39 Anyone who finds his life will lose it, and anyone who loses his life because of me will find it.

A CUP OF COLD WATER

40 "The one who welcomes you welcomes me, and the one who welcomes me welcomes him who sent me. 41 Anyone who welcomes a prophet because he is a prophet[E] will receive a prophet's reward. And anyone who welcomes a righteous person because he's righteous[F] will receive a righteous person's reward. 42 And whoever gives even a cup of cold water to one of these little ones because he is a disciple,[G] truly I tell you, he will never lose his reward."

JOHN THE BAPTIST DOUBTS

11 When Jesus had finished giving instructions to his twelve disciples, he moved on from there to teach and preach in their towns. 2 Now when John heard in prison what the Christ was doing, he sent a message through his disciples 3 and asked him, "Are you the one who is to come, or should we expect someone else?"

4 Jesus replied to them, "Go and report to John what you hear and see: 5 The blind receive their sight, the lame walk, those with leprosy[H] are cleansed, the deaf hear, the dead are raised, and the poor are told the good news, 6 and blessed is the one who isn't offended by me."

7 As these men were leaving, Jesus began to speak to the crowds about John: "What did you go out into the wilderness to see? A reed swaying in the wind? 8 What then did you go out to see? A man dressed in soft clothes? See, those who wear soft clothes are in royal palaces. 9 What then did you go out to see? A prophet? Yes, I tell you, and more than a prophet. 10 This is the one about whom it is written:

See, I am sending my messenger
ahead of you;
he will prepare your way before you.[I]

11 "Truly I tell you, among those born of women no one greater than John the Baptist has appeared,[J] but the least in the kingdom of heaven is greater than he. 12 From the days of John the Baptist until now, the kingdom of heaven has been suffering violence,[K] and the violent have been seizing it by force. 13 For all the prophets and the law prophesied until John. 14 And if you're willing to accept it, he is the Elijah who is to come. 15 Let anyone who has ears[L] listen.

AN UNRESPONSIVE GENERATION

16 "To what should I compare this generation? It's like children sitting in the marketplaces who call out to other children:

17 We played the flute for you,
but you didn't dance;
we sang a lament,
but you didn't mourn![M]

18 For John came neither eating nor drinking, and they say, 'He has a demon!' 19 The Son of Man came eating and drinking, and they say, 'Look, a glutton and a drunkard, a friend of tax collectors and sinners!' Yet wisdom is vindicated[N] by her deeds."[O]

20 Then he proceeded to denounce the towns where most of his miracles were done, because they did not repent: 21 "Woe to you, Chorazin! Woe to you, Bethsaida! For if the miracles that were done in you had been done in Tyre and Sidon, they would have repented in sackcloth and ashes long ago. 22 But I tell you, it will be more tolerable for Tyre and Sidon on the day of judgment than for you. 23 And you, Capernaum, will you be exalted to heaven? No, you will go down to Hades. For if the miracles that were done in you had been done in Sodom, it would have remained until today. 24 But I tell you, it will be more tolerable for the land of Sodom on the day of judgment than for you."

[A] **10:27** Lit *in the ear* [B] **10:29** Gk *assarion*, a small copper coin [C] **10:29** Lit *ground apart from your Father* [D] **10:35–36** Mc 7:6 [E] **10:41** Lit *prophet in the name of a prophet* [F] **10:41** Lit *person in the name of a righteous person* [G] **10:42** Lit *little ones in the name of a disciple* [H] **11:5** Gk *lepros*; a term for various skin diseases; see Lv 13–14 [I] **11:10** Mal 3:1 [J] **11:11** Lit *arisen* [K] **11:12** Or *has been forcefully advancing* [L] **11:15** Other mss add *to hear* [M] **11:17** Or *beat your chests in grief* [N] **11:19** Or *declared right* [O] **11:19** Other mss read *children*

Shore of the Sea of Galilee at Capernaum.

THE SON GIVES KNOWLEDGE AND REST

25 At that time Jesus said, "I praise you, Father, Lord
of heaven and earth, because you have hidden these
things from the wise and intelligent and revealed
them to infants. 26 Yes, Father, because this was your
good pleasure.[A] 27 All things have been entrusted to
me by my Father. No one knows the Son except the
Father, and no one knows the Father except the Son
and anyone to whom the Son desires[B] to reveal him.
28 "Come to me, all of you who are weary and burdened, and I will give you rest. 29 Take up my yoke
and learn from me, because I am lowly and humble
in heart, and you will find rest for your souls. 30 For
my yoke is easy and my burden is light."

LORD OF THE SABBATH

12 At that time Jesus passed through the grainfields on the Sabbath. His disciples were hungry and began to pick and eat some heads of grain.
2 When the Pharisees saw this, they said to him, "See,
your disciples are doing what is not lawful to do on
the Sabbath."
3 He said to them, "Haven't you read what David did
when he and those who were with him were hungry:
4 how he entered the house of God, and they ate[C] the
bread of the Presence — which is not lawful for him
or for those with him to eat, but only for the priests?
5 Or haven't you read in the law that on Sabbath days
the priests in the temple violate the Sabbath and are
innocent? 6 I tell you that something greater than the
temple is here. 7 If you had known what this means,
I desire mercy and not sacrifice,[D] you would not
have condemned the innocent. 8 For the Son of Man
is Lord of the Sabbath."

THE MAN WITH THE SHRIVELED HAND

9 Moving on from there, he entered their synagogue.
10 There he saw a man who had a shriveled hand, and
in order to accuse him they asked him, "Is it lawful
to heal on the Sabbath?"
11 He replied to them, "Who among you, if he had
a sheep that fell into a pit on the Sabbath, wouldn't
take hold of it and lift it out? 12 A person is worth far
more than a sheep; so it is lawful to do what is good
on the Sabbath."
13 Then he told the man, "Stretch out your hand."
So he stretched it out, and it was restored, as good as
the other. 14 But the Pharisees went out and plotted
against him, how they might kill him.

THE SERVANT OF THE LORD

15 Jesus was aware of this and withdrew. Large crowds[E]
followed him, and he healed them all. 16 He warned
them not to make him known, 17 so that what was
spoken through the prophet Isaiah might be fulfilled:

18 **Here is my servant whom I have chosen,**
my beloved in whom I delight;
I will put my Spirit on him,
and he will proclaim justice to the nations.
19 **He will not argue or shout,**
and no one will hear his voice
in the streets.
20 **He will not break a bruised reed,**
and he will not put out a smoldering wick,
until he has led justice to victory.[F]
21 **The nations will put their hope in his name.**[G]

A HOUSE DIVIDED

22 Then a demon-possessed man who was blind and
unable to speak was brought to him. He healed him,
so that the man[H] could both speak and see. 23 All the
crowds were astounded and said, "Could this be the
Son of David?"

[A] **11:26** Lit *was well-pleasing in your sight* [B] **11:27** Or *wills,* or *chooses* [C] **12:4** Other mss read *he ate* [D] **12:7** Hs 6:6 [E] **12:15** Other mss read *Many* [F] **12:20** Or *until he has successfully put forth justice* [G] **12:18–21** Is 42:1–4 [H] **12:22** Lit *mute*

24 When the Pharisees heard this, they said, "This man drives out demons only by Beelzebul, the ruler of the demons."

25 Knowing their thoughts, he told them, "Every kingdom divided against itself is headed for destruction, and no city or house divided against itself will stand. 26 If Satan drives out Satan, he is divided against himself. How then will his kingdom stand? 27 And if I drive out demons by Beelzebul, by whom do your sons drive them out? For this reason they will be your judges. 28 If I drive out demons by the Spirit of God, then the kingdom of God has come upon you. 29 How can someone enter a strong man's house and steal his possessions unless he first ties up the strong man? Then he can plunder his house. 30 Anyone who is not with me is against me, and anyone who does not gather with me scatters. 31 Therefore, I tell you, people will be forgiven every sin and blasphemy, but the blasphemy against[A] the Spirit will not be forgiven.[B] 32 Whoever speaks a word against the Son of Man, it will be forgiven him; but whoever speaks against the Holy Spirit, it will not be forgiven him, either in this age or in the one to come.

A TREE AND ITS FRUIT

33 "Either make the tree good and its fruit will be good, or make the tree bad[C] and its fruit will be bad; for a tree is known by its fruit. 34 Brood of vipers! How can you speak good things when you are evil? For the mouth speaks from the overflow of the heart. 35 A good person produces good things from his storeroom of good, and an evil person produces evil things from his storeroom of evil. 36 I tell you that on the day of judgment people will have to account for every careless[D] word they speak.[E] 37 For by your words you will be acquitted, and by your words you will be condemned."

THE SIGN OF JONAH

38 Then some of the scribes and Pharisees said to him, "Teacher, we want to see a sign from you."

39 He answered them, "An evil and adulterous generation demands a sign, but no sign will be given to it except the sign of the prophet Jonah. 40 For as Jonah was in the belly of the huge fish[F] three days and three nights, so the Son of Man will be in the heart of the earth three days and three nights. 41 The men of Nineveh will stand up at the judgment with this generation and condemn it, because they repented at Jonah's preaching; and look — something greater than Jonah is here. 42 The queen of the south will rise up at the judgment with this generation and condemn it, because she came from the ends of the earth to hear the wisdom of Solomon; and look — something greater than Solomon is here.

AN UNCLEAN SPIRIT'S RETURN

43 "When an unclean spirit comes out of a person, it roams through waterless places looking for rest but doesn't find any. 44 Then it says, 'I'll go back to my house that I came from.' Returning, it finds the house vacant, swept, and put in order. 45 Then it goes and brings with it seven other spirits more evil than itself, and they enter and settle down there. As a result, that person's last condition is worse than the first. That's how it will also be with this evil generation."

TRUE RELATIONSHIPS

46 While he was still speaking with the crowds, his mother and brothers were standing outside wanting to speak to him. 47 Someone told him, "Look, your mother and your brothers are standing outside, wanting to speak to you."[G]

48 He replied to the one who was speaking to him, "Who is my mother and who are my brothers?" 49 Stretching out his hand toward his disciples, he said, "Here are my mother and my brothers! 50 For whoever does the will of my Father in heaven is my brother and sister and mother."

THE PARABLE OF THE SOWER

13 On that day Jesus went out of the house and was sitting by the sea. 2 Such large crowds gathered around him that he got into a boat and sat down, while the whole crowd stood on the shore.

3 Then he told them many things in parables, saying, "Consider the sower who went out to sow. 4 As he sowed, some seed fell along the path, and the birds came and devoured them. 5 Other seed fell on rocky ground where it didn't have much soil, and it grew up quickly since the soil wasn't deep. 6 But when the sun came up, it was scorched, and since it had no root, it withered away. 7 Other seed fell among thorns, and the thorns came up and choked it. 8 Still other seed fell on good ground and produced fruit: some a hundred, some sixty, and some thirty times what was sown. 9 Let anyone who has ears[H] listen."

WHY JESUS USED PARABLES

10 Then the disciples came up and asked him, "Why are you speaking to them in parables?"

11 He answered, "Because the secrets of the kingdom of heaven have been given for you to know, but it has not been given to them. 12 For whoever has, more will be given to him, and he will have more than enough; but whoever does not have, even what he has will be taken away from him. 13 That is why I

[A] **12:31** Or *of* [B] **12:31** Other mss add *people* [C] **12:33** Or *decayed*; lit *rotten* [D] **12:36** Lit *worthless* [E] **12:36** Lit *will speak* [F] **12:40** Or *sea creature*; Jnh 1:17 [G] **12:47** Other mss omit this v. [H] **13:9** Other mss add *to hear*

Agriculture and Farming in Ancient Israel

by Mark R. Dunn

Israel had an agriculture-based economy throughout biblical times.[1] Consequently, such references saturate the Bible. An understanding of ancient Israel's agricultural life helps highlight the significance of Jesus's frequent use of agrarian imagery in his teaching.

The geography of the land greatly influenced the development of agriculture.

Israel had flatland along the Mediterranean coast, in the plain of Esdraelon, and in the Jordan plain. Those living there grew grains and various vegetables. The highlands were less productive; farmers first had to clear forests and then build terraces, which held the soil and moisture.

The agricultural calendar opened with the ingathering of olives from August to October, followed by the sowing of grain from October to December. Next came the late sowing of legumes and vegetables from December to February, followed by a month of hoeing weeds. The barley harvest came in March to April. Wheat was harvested in April and May. Grapes were harvested from May to July. Finally, the summer fruit arrived from July to August.[2]

Though common crops included grapes and olives, the following discussion will focus on Israelite grain agriculture. The soil was generally fertile but also famously rocky and at times shallow. Plowing was necessary to break up the ground and loosen stones embedded in the soil, so that water could penetrate and young plants could take root.[3] Israelites used a variety of farm tools, such as plows to prepare the soil. The earliest plows were forked sticks. Centuries later, farmers developed iron-tipped plows that could penetrate the soil about five inches. Harrows broke up clods after plowing. Hoes and mattocks turned up the ground for seeding and weeding.

Arab farmer sowing seed, a task typically done sometime from mid-October to early-December.

Farmer's seed bag from Egypt's New Kingdom (1550–1069 BC).

Three tools used for farming: a pick (top), a hoe or mattock, and a hoe (each from Beth-shemesh; dated 701–586 BC).

Farmers commonly sowed grains using the broadcast method,[4] though some used a sack with a hole in it to drop seeds as the plow turned the soil.[5] Workers then used sickles to cut grain. Next the grain had to be winnowed. This required the use of wooden or stone rollers or oxen to break the heads of grain and release the kernels. Workers then used pitchforks, shovels, or fans to toss the grain into the air so the chaff could blow away. Sieves sifted the grain from the remaining unwanted material. Finally, the grain was milled into flour. ✜

---

[1] See "Agriculture" in *Nelson's New Illustrated Bible Dictionary*, ed. Ronald F. Youngblood (Nashville: Thomas Nelson, 1995), 27–31. [2] Oded Borowski, "Agriculture" in *EDB*, 28–30. [3] See "Agriculture" in *Nelson's Illustrated Manners and Customs of the Bible*, ed. James I. Packer, Merrill C. Tenney, and William White Jr. (Nashville: Thomas Nelson, 1997). [4] J. L. Kelso and F. N. Hepper, "Agriculture" in *New Bible Dictionary*, ed. D. R. W. Wood, 3rd ed. (Downers Grove, IL: InterVarsity, 1996). [5] Craig S. Keener, *The IVP Bible Background Commentary: New Testament* (Downers Grove, IL: InterVarsity, 1993), 82.

speak to them in parables, because looking they do
not see, and hearing they do not listen or understand.
14 Isaiah's prophecy is fulfilled in them, which says:

> **You will listen and listen,**
> **but never understand;**
> **you will look and look,**
> **but never perceive.**
> 15 **For this people's heart has grown callous;**
> **their ears are hard of hearing,**
> **and they have shut their eyes;**
> **otherwise they might see with their eyes,**
> **and hear with their ears, and**
> **understand with their hearts,**
> **and turn back —**
> **and I would heal them.**[A]

16 "Blessed are your eyes because they do see, and
your ears because they do hear. 17 For truly I tell you,
many prophets and righteous people longed to see
the things you see but didn't see them, to hear the
things you hear but didn't hear them.

THE PARABLE OF THE SOWER EXPLAINED

18 "So listen to the parable of the sower: 19 When anyone hears the word about the kingdom and doesn't
understand it, the evil one comes and snatches away
what was sown in his heart. This is the one sown
along the path. 20 And the one sown on rocky ground
— this is one who hears the word and immediately
receives it with joy. 21 But he has no root and is short-
lived. When distress or persecution comes because
of the word, immediately he falls away. 22 Now the
one sown among the thorns — this is one who hears
the word, but the worries of this age and the deceitfulness[B] of wealth choke the word, and it becomes
unfruitful. 23 But the one sown on the good ground
— this is one who hears and understands the word,
who does produce fruit and yields: some a hundred,
some sixty, some thirty times what was sown."

THE PARABLE OF THE WHEAT AND THE WEEDS

24 He presented another parable to them: "The kingdom of heaven may be compared to a man who
sowed good seed in his field. 25 But while people were
sleeping, his enemy came, sowed weeds among the
wheat, and left. 26 When the plants sprouted and produced grain, then the weeds also appeared. 27 The
landowner's servants came to him and said, 'Master,
didn't you sow good seed in your field? Then where
did the weeds come from?'

28 " 'An enemy did this,' he told them.

" 'So, do you want us to go and pull them up?' the
servants asked him.

29 " 'No,' he said. 'When you pull up the weeds, you
might also uproot the wheat with them. 30 Let both
grow together until the harvest. At harvest time I'll tell
the reapers: Gather the weeds first and tie them in bundles to burn them, but collect the wheat in my barn.' "

THE PARABLES OF THE MUSTARD SEED AND OF THE LEAVEN

31 He presented another parable to them: "The kingdom of heaven is like a mustard seed that a man took
and sowed in his field. 32 It's the smallest of all the
seeds, but when grown, it's taller than the garden
plants and becomes a tree, so that the birds of the
sky come and nest in its branches."

33 He told them another parable: "The kingdom of
heaven is like leaven[C] that a woman took and mixed
into fifty pounds[D] of flour until all of it was leavened."

USING PARABLES FULFILLS PROPHECY

34 Jesus told the crowds all these things in parables,
and he did not tell them anything without a parable, 35 so that what was spoken through the prophet
might be fulfilled:

> **I will open my mouth in parables;**
> **I will declare things kept secret**
> **from the foundation** of the world.[E,F]

JESUS INTERPRETS THE PARABLE OF THE WHEAT AND THE WEEDS

36 Then he left the crowds and went into the house.
His disciples approached him and said, "Explain to
us the parable of the weeds in the field."

37 He replied, "The one who sows the good seed is
the Son of Man; 38 the field is the world; and the good
seed — these are the children of the kingdom. The
weeds are the children of the evil one, 39 and the enemy who sowed them is the devil. The harvest is the
end of the age, and the harvesters are angels. 40 Therefore, just as the weeds are gathered and burned in
the fire, so it will be at the end of the age. 41 The Son
of Man will send out his angels, and they will gather from his kingdom all who cause sin[G] and those
guilty of lawlessness.[H] 42 They will throw them into
the blazing furnace where there will be weeping and
gnashing of teeth. 43 Then the righteous will shine
like the sun in their Father's kingdom. Let anyone
who has ears[I] listen.

THE PARABLES OF THE HIDDEN TREASURE AND OF THE PRICELESS PEARL

44 "The kingdom of heaven is like treasure, buried
in a field, that a man found and reburied. Then in
his joy he goes and sells everything he has and buys
that field.

[A] **13:14–15** Is 6:9–10 [B] **13:22** Or *pleasure* [C] **13:33** Or *yeast* [D] **13:33** Lit *three sata*; about forty liters [E] **13:35** Some mss omit *of the world* [F] **13:35** Ps 78:2 [G] **13:41** Or *stumbling* [H] **13:41** Or *those who do lawlessness* [I] **13:43** Other mss add *to hear*

45 “Again, the kingdom of heaven is like a merchant in search of fine pearls. 46 When he found one priceless[A] pearl, he went and sold everything he had and bought it.

THE PARABLE OF THE NET

47 “Again, the kingdom of heaven is like a large net thrown into the sea. It collected every kind of fish, 48 and when it was full, they dragged it ashore, sat down, and gathered the good fish into containers, but threw out the worthless ones. 49 So it will be at the end of the age. The angels will go out, separate the evil people from the righteous, 50 and throw them into the blazing furnace, where there will be weeping and gnashing of teeth.

THE STOREHOUSE OF TRUTH

51 “Have you understood all these things?”[B]

They answered him, “Yes.”

52 “Therefore,” he said to them, “every teacher of the law[C] who has become a disciple in the kingdom of heaven is like the owner of a house who brings out of his storeroom treasures new and old.”

REJECTION AT NAZARETH

53 When Jesus had finished these parables, he left there. 54 He went to his hometown and began to teach them in their synagogue, so that they were astonished and said, “Where did this man get this wisdom and these miraculous powers? 55 Isn’t this the carpenter’s son? Isn’t his mother called Mary, and his brothers James, Joseph,[D] Simon, and Judas? 56 And his sisters, aren’t they all with us? So where does he get all these things?” 57 And they were offended by him.

Jesus said to them, “A prophet is not without honor except in his hometown and in his household.” 58 And he did not do many miracles there because of their unbelief.

JOHN THE BAPTIST BEHEADED

14 At that time Herod the tetrarch heard the report about Jesus. 2 “This is John the Baptist,” he told his servants. “He has been raised from the dead, and that’s why miraculous powers are at work in him.”

3 For Herod had arrested John, chained[E] him, and put him in prison on account of Herodias, his brother Philip’s wife, 4 since John had been telling him, “It’s not lawful for you to have her.” 5 Though Herod wanted to kill John, he feared the crowd since they regarded John as a prophet.

6 When Herod’s birthday celebration came, Herodias’s daughter danced before them[F] and pleased Herod. 7 So he promised with an oath to give her whatever she asked. 8 Prompted by her mother, she answered, “Give me John the Baptist’s head here on a platter.”

Bronze coin of Herod Antipas. Obverse shows a palm tree with the Greek inscription reading, “Herod the Tetrarch, Year 43.”

9 Although the king regretted it, he commanded that it be granted because of his oaths and his guests. 10 So he sent orders and had John beheaded in the prison. 11 His head was brought on a platter and given to the girl, who carried it to her mother. 12 Then his disciples came, removed the corpse,[G] buried it, and went and reported to Jesus.

FEEDING OF THE FIVE THOUSAND

13 When Jesus heard about it, he withdrew from there by boat to a remote place to be alone. When the crowds heard this, they followed him on foot from the towns. 14 When he went ashore,[H] he saw a large crowd, had compassion on them, and healed their sick.

15 When evening came, the disciples approached him and said, “This place is deserted, and it is already late.[I] Send the crowds away so that they can go into the villages and buy food for themselves.”

16 “They don’t need to go away,” Jesus told them. “You give them something to eat.”

17 “But we only have five loaves and two fish here,” they said to him.

18 “Bring them here to me,” he said. 19 Then he commanded the crowds to sit down on the grass. He took the five loaves and the two fish, and looking up to heaven, he blessed them. He broke the loaves and

[A] **13:46** Or *very precious* [B] **13:51** Other mss add *Jesus asked them* [C] **13:52** Or *every scribe* [D] **13:55** Other mss read *Joses*; Mk 6:3 [E] **14:3** Or *bound* [F] **14:6** Lit *danced in the middle* [G] **14:12** Other mss read *body* [H] **14:14** Lit *Coming out* (of the boat) [I] **14:15** Lit *and the time* (for the evening meal) *has already passed*

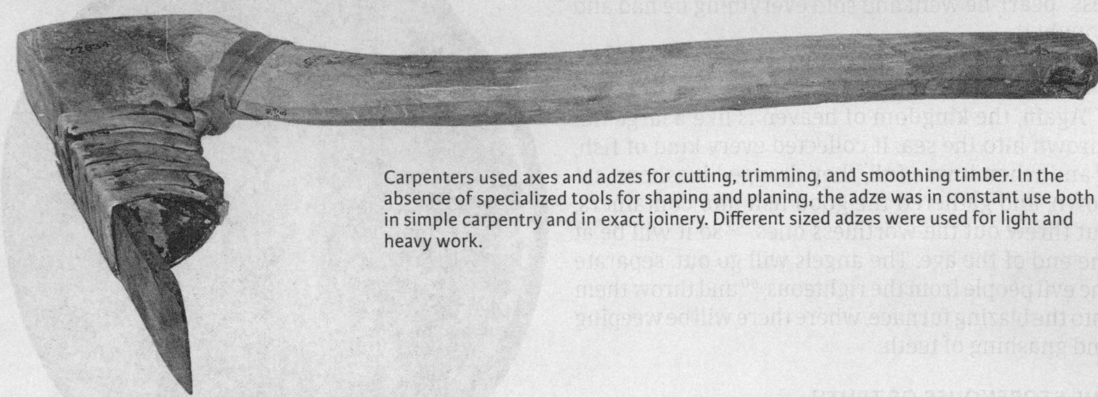

Carpenters used axes and adzes for cutting, trimming, and smoothing timber. In the absence of specialized tools for shaping and planing, the adze was in constant use both in simple carpentry and in exact joinery. Different sized adzes were used for light and heavy work.

The Scriptures refer to both Joseph (Mt 13:55) and Jesus (Mk 6:3) as carpenters. In Bible times, sons customarily learned trades from their fathers. Perhaps Joseph learned this trade from his father and in turn passed it on to Jesus. Most likely, Joseph and Jesus worked side by side at a carpenter's shop in Nazareth. A. T. Robertson suggested that the description of Joseph as the carpenter in Matthew 13:55 indicates he was "the leading, or even for a time the only carpenter in Nazareth till Jesus took the place of Joseph as the carpenter."[1]

The Greek term for "carpenter" (*tektōn*) originally applied to a worker in wood or builder with wood. Later the term referred to any artisan or craftsman who worked in metal, stone, or wood.[2] In all likelihood, the carpenter did not limit his work to woodworking but did metalworking and masonry when the job required these skills.

The carpenter's skills were needed to build any and all kinds of structures. Certainly in the first century, these objects would have included yokes, plows, threshing boards, benches, beds, boxes, coffins, boats, and houses.[3] Some more enterprising carpenters may have helped in building local synagogues or even larger structures such as markets, food shops, theaters, or aqueducts.

Most carpenters likely spent a majority of their time building and repairing houses. A majority of houses in Israel were built of

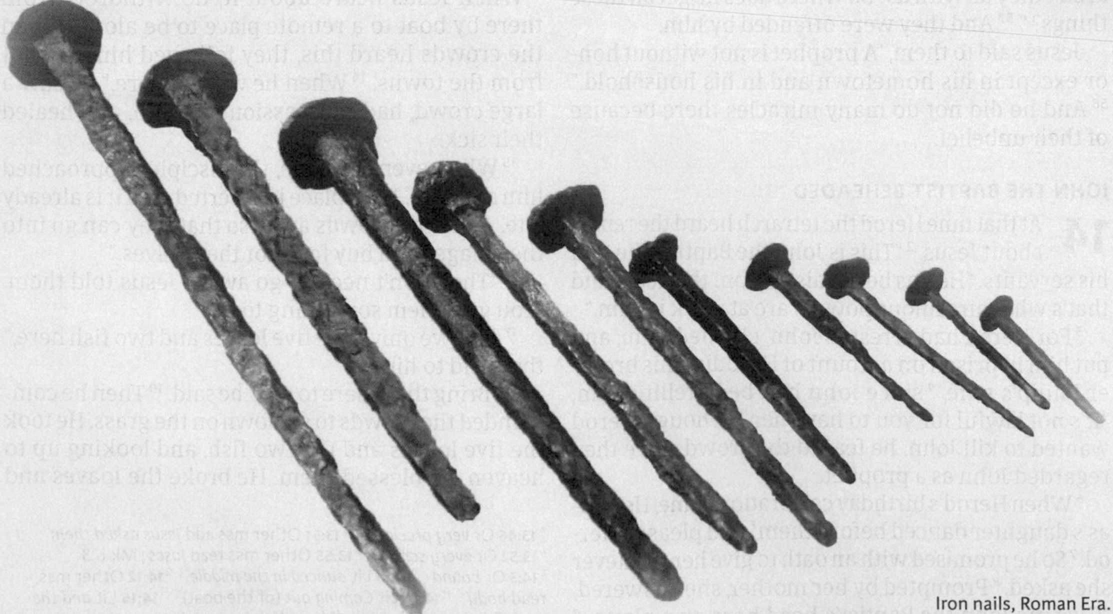

Iron nails, Roman Era.

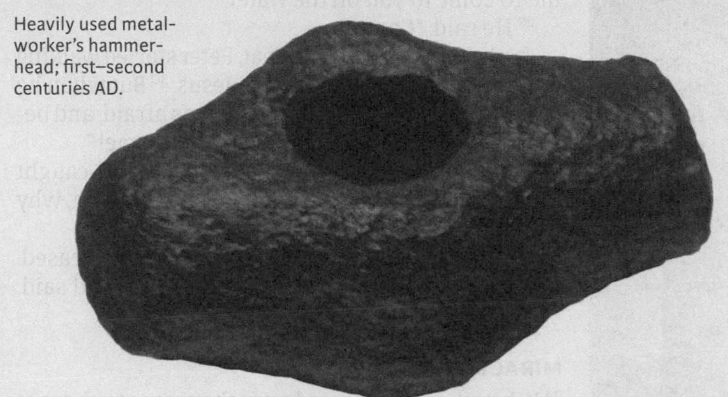

Heavily used metal-worker's hammer-head; first–second centuries AD.

stone. Still, the upper story, roof, and doors were made of wood. Larger homes even had wooden floors and wall panels. "Roofs were constructed by laying timber beams from wall to wall and filling the gaps with matting that was plastered down with mud."[4] Trees were cut down and squared up for the beams. Wooden beams were held together by nails or wooden/metal pegs, or beams were cut so they would fit together naturally by themselves.[5]

In Joseph's day, enough timber grew in the region to meet local building demands. The carpenter could choose from cypress or cedar trees in the northern part of the country, sycamore (a fig-like tree), acacia, oak, and ash. Most of these trees did not grow tall enough and straight enough to provide long timbers. Hence, David and Solomon, in an earlier day, imported cypress and cedar from Lebanon when they built their palaces and the temple (2Sm 5:11; 1Kg 5:8).

The ancient carpenter had essentially the same basic tools used by today's carpenters, though the ancient tools were crude and simple. Tools the first-century carpenter used include the adze (an ax-like tool used to shape wood), a mallet (an oversized hammer, usually made of wood), a hammer (normally made of stone), and an ax (made of iron and bound to a shaft with a cord). Other tools at a carpenter's disposal included handsaws (made of metal blades with teeth that cut into the wood), a larger saw for bigger timbers or trees, a bow drill used to bore holes in wood, chisels of various sizes, awls (pointed for boring wood), wood planes, spokeshaves, and files. ❖

---

[1] Archibald Thomas Robertson, Word Pictures in the New Testament (Nashville: Broadman, 1930), 1:111. [2] Robertson, Word Pictures, 306. [3] C. U. Wolf, "Carpenter" in IDB, 1:539. [4] Ralph Gower, The New Manners and Customs of Bible Times (Chicago: Moody, 1987), 153. [5] Gower, New Manners.

Columns of Herod the Great's palace at Machaerus. Herod turned Machaerus into one of his fortress cities. The palace, which covered almost a full acre, was the site of Herod Antipas's birthday celebration. Antipas had John the Baptist executed at Machaerus.

gave them to the disciples, and the disciples gave
them to the crowds. 20 Everyone ate and was satisfied.
They picked up twelve baskets full of leftover pieces.
21 Now those who ate were about five thousand men,
besides women and children.

WALKING ON THE WATER

22 Immediately he[A] made the disciples get into the
boat and go ahead of him to the other side, while he
dismissed the crowds. 23 After dismissing the crowds,
he went up on the mountain by himself to pray. Well
into the night, he was there alone. 24 Meanwhile, the
boat was already some distance[B] from land,[C] battered
by the waves, because the wind was against them.
25 Jesus came toward them walking on the sea very
early in the morning.[D] 26 When the disciples saw him
walking on the sea, they were terrified. "It's a ghost!"
they said, and they cried out in fear.

27 Immediately Jesus spoke to them. "Have courage!
It is I. Don't be afraid."

28 "Lord, if it's you," Peter answered him, "command
me to come to you on the water."

29 He said, "Come."

And climbing out of the boat, Peter started walking
on the water and came toward Jesus. 30 But when he
saw the strength of the wind,[E] he was afraid, and beginning to sink he cried out, "Lord, save me!"

31 Immediately Jesus reached out his hand, caught
hold of him, and said to him, "You of little faith, why
did you doubt?"

32 When they got into the boat, the wind ceased.
33 Then those in the boat worshiped him and said,
"Truly you are the Son of God."

MIRACULOUS HEALINGS

34 When they had crossed over, they came to shore at
Gennesaret. 35 When the men of that place recognized
him, they alerted the whole vicinity and brought to
him all who were sick. 36 They begged him that they
might only touch the end of his robe, and as many as
touched it were healed.

THE TRADITION OF THE ELDERS

15 Then Jesus was approached by Pharisees and
scribes from Jerusalem, who asked, 2 "Why do
your disciples break the tradition of the elders? For
they don't wash their hands when they eat."[F]

3 He answered them, "Why do you break God's
commandment because of your tradition? 4 For God
said:[G] **Honor your father and your mother;**[H] and,
**Whoever speaks evil of father or mother must
be put to death.**[I] 5 But you say, 'Whoever tells his
father or mother, "Whatever benefit you might have
received from me is a gift committed to the temple,"
6 he does not have to honor his father.'[J] In this way,
you have nullified the word of God[K] because of your
tradition. 7 Hypocrites! Isaiah prophesied correctly
about you when he said:

8 **This people[L] honors me with their lips,**
but their heart is far from me.
9 **They worship me in vain,**
teaching as doctrines
human commands."[M]

DEFILEMENT IS FROM WITHIN

10 Summoning the crowd, he told them, "Listen and
understand: 11 It's not what goes into the mouth that

[A] **14:22** Other mss read *Jesus* [B] **14:24** Lit *already many stadia*; one *stadion* = 600 feet [C] **14:24** Other mss read *already in the middle of the sea* [D] **14:25** Lit *fourth watch of the night* = 3 to 6 a.m.
[E] **14:30** Other mss read *saw the wind* [F] **15:2** Lit *eat bread* = eat a meal
[G] **15:4** Other mss read *commanded, saying* [H] **15:4** Ex 20:12; Dt 5:16
[I] **15:4** Ex 21:17; Lv 20:9 [J] **15:6** Other mss read *then he does not have to honor his father or mother* [K] **15:6** Other mss read *commandment*
[L] **15:8** Other mss add *draw near to me with their mouths, and*
[M] **15:8–9** Is 29:13 LXX

defiles a person, but what comes out of the mouth — this defiles a person."

12 Then the disciples came up and told him, "Do you know that the Pharisees took offense when they heard what you said?"

13 He replied, "Every plant that my heavenly Father didn't plant will be uprooted. 14 Leave them alone! They are blind guides.[A] And if the blind guide the blind, both will fall into a pit."

15 Then Peter said, "Explain this parable to us."

16 "Do you still lack understanding?" he[B] asked. 17 "Don't you realize[C] that whatever goes into the mouth passes into the stomach and is eliminated?[D] 18 But what comes out of the mouth comes from the heart, and this defiles a person. 19 For from the heart come evil thoughts, murders, adulteries, sexual immoralities, thefts, false testimonies, slander. 20 These are the things that defile a person; but eating with unwashed hands does not defile a person."

A GENTILE MOTHER'S FAITH

21 When Jesus left there, he withdrew to the area of Tyre and Sidon. 22 Just then a Canaanite woman from that region came and kept crying out,[E] "Have mercy on me, Lord, Son of David! My daughter is severely tormented by a demon."

23 Jesus did not say a word to her. His disciples approached him and urged him, "Send her away because she's crying out after us."

24 He replied, "I was sent only to the lost sheep of the house of Israel."

25 But she came, knelt before him, and said, "Lord, help me!"

26 He answered, "It isn't right to take the children's bread and throw it to the dogs."

27 "Yes, Lord," she said, "yet even the dogs eat the crumbs that fall from their masters' table."

28 Then Jesus replied to her, "Woman, your faith is great. Let it be done for you as you want." And from that moment[F] her daughter was healed.

HEALING MANY PEOPLE

29 Moving on from there, Jesus passed along the Sea of Galilee. He went up on a mountain and sat there, 30 and large crowds came to him, including the lame, the blind, the crippled, those unable to speak, and many others. They put them at his feet, and he healed them. 31 So the crowd was amazed when they saw

[A] **15:14** Other mss add *for the blind* [B] **15:16** Other mss read *Jesus* [C] **15:17** Other mss add *yet* [D] **15:17** Lit *and goes out into the toilet* [E] **15:22** Other mss read *and cried out to him* [F] **15:28** Lit *hour*

Sea of Galilee as seen from Nof Ginosar.

those unable to speak talking, the crippled restored,
the lame walking, and the blind seeing, and they gave
glory to the God of Israel.

FEEDING OF THE FOUR THOUSAND

32 Jesus called his disciples and said, "I have compassion on the crowd, because they've already stayed
with me three days and have nothing to eat. I don't
want to send them away hungry, otherwise they
might collapse on the way."
33 The disciples said to him, "Where could we get
enough bread in this desolate place to feed such a
crowd?"
34 "How many loaves do you have?" Jesus asked
them.

"Seven," they said, "and a few small fish."
35 After commanding the crowd to sit down on the
ground, 36 he took the seven loaves and the fish, gave
thanks, broke them, and gave them to the disciples,
and the disciples gave them to the crowds. 37 They
all ate and were satisfied. They collected the leftover
pieces — seven large baskets full. 38 Now there were
four thousand men who had eaten, besides women
and children. 39 After dismissing the crowds, he got
into the boat and went to the region of Magadan.[A]

THE LEAVEN OF THE PHARISEES AND THE SADDUCEES

16 The Pharisees and Sadducees approached, and
tested him, asking him to show them a sign
from heaven. 2 He replied, "When evening comes you
say, 'It will be good weather because the sky is red.'
3 And in the morning, 'Today will be stormy because
the sky is red and threatening.' You[B] know how to
read the appearance of the sky, but you can't read
the signs of the times.[C] 4 An evil and adulterous generation demands a sign, but no sign will be given to
it except the sign of[D] Jonah." Then he left them and
went away.
5 The disciples reached the other shore,[E] and they
had forgotten to take bread. 6 Then Jesus told them,
"Watch out and beware of the leaven[F] of the Pharisees
and Sadducees."
7 They were discussing among themselves, "We
didn't bring any bread."
8 Aware of this, Jesus said, "You of little faith, why
are you discussing among yourselves that you do
not have bread? 9 Don't you understand yet? Don't
you remember the five loaves for the five thousand
and how many baskets you collected? 10 Or the seven
loaves for the four thousand and how many large
baskets you collected? 11 Why is it you don't understand that when I told you, 'Beware of the leaven of
the Pharisees and Sadducees,' it wasn't about bread?"
12 Then they understood that he had not told them to

DIGGING DEEPER *Caesarea Philippi*

Caesarea Philippi was originally named Paneas during the Greek period in the late fourth century BC because of its importance as a center for pagan worship, especially worship of the god Pan. Herod the Great later constructed a temple for Caesar worship. After Herod's death his son Herod Philip was given jurisdiction of the area. He began a construction and renovation campaign that transformed Paneas into Caesarea Philippi. The city is located nearly twenty-five miles north of the Sea of Galilee and is actually composed of several small towns linked together (Mk 8:27). Jesus and his disciples visited these during their travels. The towns were built in honor of Caesar Augustus; to avoid confusion with another city known as Caesarea, Philip added his own name: Caesarea Philippi. Several decades after Jesus's death and resurrection, Herod Agrippa II (AD 28–100) remodeled the city and called it Neronias in honor of Emperor Nero. Today the city is uninhabited.

beware of the leaven in bread, but of the teaching of
the Pharisees and Sadducees.

PETER'S CONFESSION OF THE MESSIAH

13 When Jesus came to the region of Caesarea Philippi,[G] he asked his disciples, "Who do people say that
the Son of Man is?"[H]
14 They replied, "Some say John the Baptist; others,
Elijah; still others, Jeremiah or one of the prophets."
15 "But you," he asked them, "who do you say that
I am?"
16 Simon Peter answered, "You are the Messiah, the
Son of the living God."
17 Jesus responded, "Blessed are you, Simon son of
Jonah,[I] because flesh and blood did not reveal this to
you, but my Father in heaven. 18 And I also say to you
that you are Peter, and on this rock I will build my
church, and the gates of Hades will not overpower it.
19 I will give you the keys of the kingdom of heaven,
and whatever you bind on earth will have been bound[J]
in heaven, and whatever you loose on earth will have
been loosed[K] in heaven." 20 Then he gave the disciples
orders to tell no one that he was[L] the Messiah.

[A] **15:39** Other mss read *Magdala* [B] **16:3** Other mss read *Hypocrites! You* [C] **16:2-3** Other mss omit *When* (v. 2) through end of v. 3 [D] **16:4** Other mss add *the prophet* [E] **16:5** Lit *disciples went to the other side* [F] **16:6** Or *yeast*, also in vv. 11,12 [G] **16:13** A town north of Galilee at the base of Mount Hermon [H] **16:13** Other mss read *that I, the Son of Man, am* [I] **16:17** Or *son of John* [J] **16:19** Or *earth will be bound* [K] **16:19** Or *earth will be loosed* [L] **16:20** Other mss add *Jesus*

Hades: A First-Century Understanding

by Steve W. Lemke

When Jesus told Simon Peter and his fellow disciples that God would build his church so securely that the gates of Hades would not prevail against it (Mt 16:18), what exactly did he mean by *Hades*? How did New Testament Christians understand the concept? Is Hades distinguishable from similar concepts such as Sheol, Gehenna, or hell?

THE ABODE OF THE DEAD

More than sixty times, the Old Testament refers to the place of the dead as *Sheol*. This was the shadowy dwelling place of the dead in the underworld, virtually synonymous with the grave or death itself (Gn 37:35; Ps 16:10; Pr 5:5; Is 14:9). When scholars translated the Old Testament from Hebrew into Greek in the Septuagint during the intertestamental period, translators rendered the Old Testament Hebrew word *Sheol* with the Greek word *Hades*.[1] Thus when Peter referenced Psalm 16:10 in his Pentecost sermon (Ac 2:27), the text used *Hades* to translate the Hebrew word *Sheol*. When the New Testament uses it this way, *Hades* simply refers to the abode of the dead, following the Old Testament pattern.

In Greek mythology, Hades (also called Pluto) was the brother of Zeus and king of the underworld. Mythology claimed that Hades abducted Persephone, daughter of Zeus, and forced her to live in his underworld realm. This domain over which Hades ruled came to be called by his name or by Tartarus. The New Testament uses both terms but pours new meaning into them.

In Matthew 16:18, the primary sense of the word *Hades* probably refers to death. Death has no power over the church. Jesus told the disciples he would be crucified in Jerusalem, and then raised on the third day (Mt 16:21). When he was resurrected, he became the "firstfruits" of the resurrection; his resurrection paved the way for all believers to be raised to life, for he will abolish death (1Co 15:24–26). Believers may experience death, but death is not their final destination. Death and Hades have no more power over believers than they did over Christ himself. Jesus spoke of giving the church the "keys of

Part of the Ben Hinnom Valley, which is on the southern end of the city of Jerusalem. The valley was the site where people gave their children as burnt offerings to the Canaanite god Molech (2Ch 28:3; 33:6).

Greek mythology taught that Hades ruled the underworld. The priest Hadaios dedicated this votive relief to the god Hades who is depicted climbing into a chariot. The relief was uncovered west of Corinth, in the Derveni region; dated to the second century AD.

the kingdom of heaven" (Mt 16:19). But Jesus has another set of keys. Because of his victory over death, he has the keys to death and Hades (Rv 1:18). Jesus has gone to prepare a place for believers—a place in which death, grief, crying, and pain have been abolished (Jn 14:1–3; Rv 21:1–4). Many interpreters understand the "gates" or "forces" of Hades in Matthew 16:18 to represent Satan's constant opposition to the church. So Jesus was assuring the disciples that Satan will never overpower the church.

HADES AS HELL

Even in the Old Testament, however, Sheol does not always refer to the final resting place for all persons. Although all people go to Sheol, only ungodly or foolish persons remain in Sheol. The Old Testament teaches that God will raise godly and wise persons to a new life with him (Jb 19:23–27; Ps 49:1–19; Is 26:4–19; Dn 12:2–3). Dating to the intertestamental period, noncanonical books portray Hades as the place of torment for the wicked, while the righteous enter paradise (Pss Sol 14:1–7; Wis 2:1; 3:1). These two senses of the word *Sheol* led to a theological disagreement between the Sadducees and Pharisees. Sadducees believed that all the dead continued in Sheol, whereas Pharisees affirmed that God would resurrect the just to eternal life. Some believed Hades was the lower region of Sheol and paradise was the top level of Sheol.

This distinction between Hades as a hellish place of torment rather than the abode of all the dead emerges more clearly in the New Testament. Several New Testament texts draw a clear distinction between "death" and "Hades" (Rv 1:18; 20:13–14). Jesus's account of Lazarus and the rich man (Lk 16:19–31) draws one of the clearest distinctions between the two abodes. Jesus described the righteous man Lazarus as being beside Abraham (a Jewish euphemism for being with God in paradise), while the unrighteous rich man was in a fiery torment (vv. 23–25,28). An enormous chasm or gulf separated these two places (vv. 23,26). Jesus painted a similar picture in his depiction of the eternal destiny of the people of Capernaum who were unrepentant even after seeing miracles performed. Jesus said they would not "be exalted to heaven" but would "go down to Hades" (Mt 11:23–24; Lk 10:15). Again, Hades here is the abode of the unrighteous dead, while the righteous dead are lifted upward. In Revelation 20:13, Hades is essentially a holding place for the unrighteous dead until judgment, after which they will be cast into the lake of fire.

The New Testament often uses words such as *Gehenna* or *Tartarus*, or descriptions such as "the bottomless pit" or "the abyss" to describe hell. Gehenna was originally a valley or ravine just south of the walls of Jerusalem. *Gehenna* is a Greek transliteration of "valley of Hinnom" in Hebrew. In the Hinnom Valley, idolaters burned children as an offering to the heathen god Molech (2Ch 28:3; 33:6). By the time of King Josiah's reign, people regarded the Hinnom Valley as a place of abomination (2Kg 23:10–14). In Gehenna, God imposed judgment on idolaters and those who rejected him (Jr 7:31–34; 32:35). Gehenna thus came to symbolize hell's unending fires where the unclean and ungodly dead are continually tormented.

Bronze head of Hades; dated first–second centuries AD. The Greeks believed Hades was grim and merciless, but not evil.

In the New Testament, *Gehenna* always refers to hell, a place of fiery torment, not simply death (Mt 5:22, 29–30; Mk 9:43–47; Lk 12:5; Jms 3:6). Jesus warned that sinful disobedience could lead to a fiery Gehenna (Mt 5:22,29–30). In Gehenna, both the soul and body are destroyed (Mt 10:28). James described uncontrolled speech as being set on fire by Gehenna (Jms 3:6).

Another Greek word used to describe hell is *Tartarus*, a term Greeks used to describe a place of eternal torment. In his second epistle, Peter described Tartarus as a place where rebellious angels were imprisoned pending final judgment (2Pt 2:4). Another biblical synonym for Hades is the "abyss." Romans 10:6–7 (citing Dt 30:12–14) contrasts the ascent into heaven with descending "down into the abyss" of death. In Luke 8:31 and Revelation 9:1–3; 20:1–3, however, the abyss is the abode of demons, similar to Tartarus in 2 Peter 2:4. In Revelation 9:1–11, the abyss is opened, releasing a horde of demons. The "angel of the abyss" named Apollyon (meaning "destruction," Rv 9:11), also called the beast or antichrist, will be thrown into the lake of fire (19:20). Satan, too, is chained in the abyss for a thousand years (20:1–3), until he also is thrown into the lake of fire (v. 10).

Believers need not fear death or the forces of Satan. Christ has already defeated these threats and has won the victory (Rm 8:36–39; 1Co 15:55–57; Rv 1:18). ✣

---

[1] E. Ray Clendenen, "Hades" in *HIBD*, rev. ed. (2015), 689.

HIS DEATH AND RESURRECTION PREDICTED

21 From then on Jesus began to point out to his disciples that it was necessary for him to go to Jerusalem and suffer many things from the elders, chief priests, and scribes, be killed, and be raised the third day. 22 Peter took him aside and began to rebuke him, "Oh no,[A] Lord! This will never happen to you!"

23 Jesus turned and told Peter, "Get behind me, Satan! You are a hindrance to me because you're not thinking about God's concerns[B] but human concerns."

TAKE UP YOUR CROSS

24 Then Jesus said to his disciples, "If anyone wants to follow after me, let him deny himself, take up his cross, and follow me. 25 For whoever wants to save his life will lose it, but whoever loses his life because of me will find it. 26 For what will it benefit someone if he gains the whole world yet loses his life? Or what will anyone give in exchange for his life? 27 For the Son of Man is going to come with his angels in the glory of his Father, and then he will reward each according to what he has done. 28 Truly I tell you, there are some standing here who will not taste death until they see the Son of Man coming in his kingdom."

Church of the Transfiguration atop Mount Tabor. According to tradition, the church marks the spot where Jesus appeared in his glory before three of his disciples. A church has been on the site since the sixth century; the present Franciscan church was built in 1924. Rising to 1,843 feet above sea level, Mount Tabor overlooks the Jezreel Valley.

THE TRANSFIGURATION

17 After six days Jesus took Peter, James, and his brother John and led them up on a high mountain by themselves. 2 He was transfigured in front of them, and his face shone like the sun; his clothes became as white as the light. 3 Suddenly, Moses and Elijah appeared to them, talking with him. 4 Then Peter said to Jesus, "Lord, it's good for us to be here. If you want, I will set up[C] three shelters here: one for you, one for Moses, and one for Elijah."

5 While he was still speaking, suddenly a bright cloud covered[D] them, and a voice from the cloud said, "This is my beloved Son, with whom I am well-pleased. Listen to him!" 6 When the disciples heard this, they fell facedown and were terrified.

7 Jesus came up, touched them, and said, "Get up; don't be afraid." 8 When they looked up they saw no one except Jesus alone.

9 As they were coming down the mountain, Jesus commanded them, "Don't tell anyone about the vision until the Son of Man is raised[E] from the dead."

10 So the disciples asked him, "Why then do the scribes say that Elijah must come first?"

11 "Elijah is coming[F] and will restore everything," he replied.[G] 12 "But I tell you: Elijah has already come, and they didn't recognize him. On the contrary, they did whatever they pleased to him. In the same way the Son of Man is going to suffer at their hands." 13 Then the disciples understood that he had spoken to them about John the Baptist.

THE POWER OF JESUS OVER A DEMON

14 When they reached the crowd, a man approached and knelt down before him. 15 "Lord," he said, "have mercy on my son, because he has seizures[H] and suffers terribly. He often falls into the fire and often into the water. 16 I brought him to your disciples, but they couldn't heal him."

17 Jesus replied, "You unbelieving and perverse generation, how long will I be with you? How long must I put up with you? Bring him here to me." 18 Then Jesus rebuked the demon,[I] and it[J] came out of him, and from that moment[K] the boy was healed.

[A] **16:22** Lit *"Mercy to you* = *"May God have mercy on you* [B] **16:23** Lit *about the things of God* [C] **17:4** Other mss read *Let's make* [D] **17:5** Or *enveloped*; Ex 40:34–35 [E] **17:9** Other mss read *Man has risen* [F] **17:11** Other mss add *first* [G] **17:11** Other mss read *Jesus said to them* [H] **17:15** Lit *he is moonstruck*; thought to be a form of epilepsy [I] **17:18** Lit *rebuked him*, or *it* [J] **17:18** Lit *the demon* [K] **17:18** Lit *hour*

19 Then the disciples approached Jesus privately and said, "Why couldn't we drive it out?"

20 "Because of your little faith," he[A] told them. "For truly I tell you, if you have faith the size of[B] a mustard seed, you will tell this mountain, 'Move from here to there,' and it will move. Nothing will be impossible for you."[C]

THE SECOND PREDICTION OF HIS DEATH

22 As they were gathering together[D] in Galilee, Jesus told them, "The Son of Man is about to be betrayed into the hands of men. 23 They will kill him, and on the third day he will be raised up." And they were deeply distressed.

PAYING THE TEMPLE TAX

24 When they came to Capernaum, those who collected the temple tax approached Peter and said, "Doesn't your teacher pay the temple tax?"

25 "Yes," he said.

When he went into the house, Jesus spoke to him first,[E] "What do you think, Simon? From whom do earthly kings collect tariffs or taxes? From their sons or from strangers?"[F]

26 "From strangers," he said.[G]

"Then the sons are free," Jesus told him. 27 "But, so we won't offend them, go to the sea, cast in a fishhook, and take the first fish that you catch. When you open its mouth you'll find a coin.[H] Take it and give it to them for me and you."

WHO IS THE GREATEST?

18 At that time[I] the disciples came to Jesus and asked, "So who is greatest in the kingdom of heaven?" 2 He called a small child and had him stand among them. 3 "Truly I tell you," he said, "unless you turn and become like little children, you will never enter the kingdom of heaven. 4 Therefore, whoever humbles himself like this child — this one is the greatest in the kingdom of heaven. 5 And whoever welcomes[J] one child like this in my name welcomes me.

6 "But whoever causes one of these little ones who believe in me to fall away — it would be better for him if a heavy millstone were hung around his neck and he were drowned in the depths of the sea. 7 Woe to the world because of offenses. For offenses will inevitably come, but woe to that person by whom the offense comes. 8 If your hand or your foot causes you to fall away, cut it off and throw it away. It is better for you to enter life maimed or lame than to have two hands or two feet and be thrown into the eternal fire. 9 And if your eye causes you to fall away, gouge it out and throw it away. It is better for you to enter life with one eye than to have two eyes and be thrown into hellfire.[K]

THE PARABLE OF THE LOST SHEEP

10 "See to it that you don't despise one of these little ones, because I tell you that in heaven their angels continually view the face of my Father in heaven.[L] 12 What do you think? If someone has a hundred sheep, and one of them goes astray, won't he leave the ninety-nine on the hillside and go and search for the stray? 13 And if he finds it, truly I tell you, he rejoices over that sheep[M] more than over the ninety-nine that did not go astray. 14 In the same way, it is not the will of your Father in heaven that one of these little ones perish.

RESTORING A BROTHER

15 "If your brother sins against you,[N] go tell him his fault, between you and him alone. If he listens to you, you have won your brother. 16 But if he won't listen, take one or two others with you, so that **by the testimony**[O] **of two or three witnesses every fact may be established.**[P] 17 If he doesn't pay attention to them, tell the church.[Q] If he doesn't pay attention even to the church, let him be like a Gentile and a tax collector to you. 18 Truly I tell you, whatever you bind on earth will have been bound[R] in heaven, and whatever you loose on earth will have been loosed[S] in heaven. 19 Again, truly I tell you, if two of you on earth agree about any matter that you[T] pray for, it will be done for you[U] by my Father in heaven. 20 For where two or three are gathered together in my name, I am there among them."

THE PARABLE OF THE UNFORGIVING SERVANT

21 Then Peter approached him and asked, "Lord, how many times must I forgive my brother or sister who sins against me? As many as seven times?"

22 "I tell you, not as many as seven," Jesus replied, "but seventy times seven.[V]

23 "For this reason, the kingdom of heaven can be compared to a king who wanted to settle accounts with his servants. 24 When he began to settle accounts, one who owed ten thousand talents[W] was brought before him. 25 Since he did not have the money to pay it back, his master commanded that he, his wife, his children, and everything he had be sold to pay the debt.

[A] **17:20** Other mss read *your unbelief, Jesus* [B] **17:20** Lit *faith like* [C] **17:20** Some mss include v. 21: *"However, this kind does not come out except by prayer and fasting."* [D] **17:22** Other mss read *were staying* [E] **17:25** Lit *Jesus anticipated him by saying* [F] **17:25** Or *foreigners* [G] **17:26** Other mss read *Peter said to him* [H] **17:27** Gk *stater*, worth 2 double-drachmas [I] **18:1** Lit *hour* [J] **18:5** Or *receives* [K] **18:9** Lit *gehenna of fire* [L] **18:10** Some mss include v. 11: *For the Son of Man has come to save the lost.* [M] **18:13** Lit *over it* [N] **18:15** Other mss omit *against you* [O] **18:16** Lit *mouth* [P] **18:16** Dt 19:15 [Q] **18:17** Or *congregation* [R] **18:18** Or *earth will be bound* [S] **18:18** Or *earth will be loosed* [T] **18:19** Lit *they* [U] **18:19** Lit *for them* [V] **18:22** Or *but seventy-seven times* [W] **18:24** A talent is worth about 6,000 denarii, or twenty years' wages for a laborer

26 “At this, the servant fell facedown before him and said, ‘Be patient with me, and I will pay you everything.’ 27 Then the master of that servant had compassion, released him, and forgave him the loan.

28 “That servant went out and found one of his fellow servants who owed him a hundred denarii.[A] He grabbed him, started choking him, and said, ‘Pay what you owe!’

29 “At this, his fellow servant fell down[B] and began begging him, ‘Be patient with me, and I will pay you back.’ 30 But he wasn’t willing. Instead, he went and threw him into prison until he could pay what was owed. 31 When the other servants saw what had taken place, they were deeply distressed and went and reported to their master everything that had happened. 32 Then, after he had summoned him, his master said to him, ‘You wicked servant! I forgave you all that debt because you begged me. 33 Shouldn’t you also have had mercy on your fellow servant, as I had mercy on you?’ 34 And because he was angry, his master handed him over to the jailers to be tortured until he could pay everything that was owed. 35 So also my heavenly Father will do to you unless every one of you forgives his brother or sister[C] from your[D] heart.”

THE QUESTION OF DIVORCE

19 When Jesus had finished saying these things, he departed from Galilee and went to the region of Judea across the Jordan. 2 Large crowds followed him, and he healed them there. 3 Some Pharisees approached him to test him. They asked, “Is it lawful for a man to divorce his wife on any grounds?”

4 “Haven’t you read,” he replied, “that he who created[E] them in the beginning **made them male and female**,[F] 5 and he also said, ‘**For this reason a man will leave his father and mother and be joined to his wife, and the two will become one flesh**’?[G] 6 So they are no longer two, but one flesh. Therefore, what God has joined together, let no one separate.”

7 “Why then,” they asked him, “did Moses command us to give divorce papers and to send her away?”

8 He told them, “Moses permitted you to divorce your wives because of the hardness of your hearts, but it was not like that from the beginning. 9 I tell you, whoever divorces his wife, except for sexual immorality, and marries another commits adultery.”[H]

10 His disciples said to him, “If the relationship of a man with his wife is like this, it’s better not to marry.”

11 He responded, “Not everyone can accept this saying, but only those to whom it has been given. 12 For there are eunuchs who were born that way from their mother’s womb, there are eunuchs who were made by men, and there are eunuchs who have made themselves that way because of the kingdom of heaven. The one who is able to accept it should accept it.”

BLESSING THE CHILDREN

13 Then little children were brought to Jesus for him to place his hands on them and pray, but the disciples rebuked them. 14 Jesus said, “Leave the little children alone, and don’t try to keep them from coming to me, because the kingdom of heaven belongs to such as these.”[I] 15 After placing his hands on them, he went on from there.

THE RICH YOUNG RULER

16 Just then someone came up and asked him, “Teacher, what good must I do to have eternal life?”

17 “Why do you ask me about what is good?”[J] he said to him. “There is only one who is good.[K] If you want to enter into life, keep the commandments.”

18 “Which ones?” he asked him.

Jesus answered: **Do not murder; do not commit adultery; do not steal; do not bear false witness;** 19 **honor your father and your mother; and love your neighbor as yourself.**[L]

20 “I have kept all these,”[M] the young man told him. “What do I still lack?”

21 “If you want to be perfect,”[N] Jesus said to him, “go, sell your belongings and give to the poor, and you will have treasure in heaven. Then come, follow me.”

22 When the young man heard that, he went away grieving, because he had many possessions.

POSSESSIONS AND THE KINGDOM

23 Jesus said to his disciples, “Truly I tell you, it will be hard for a rich person to enter the kingdom of heaven. 24 Again I tell you, it is easier for a camel to go through the eye of a needle than for a rich person to enter the kingdom of God.”

25 When the disciples heard this, they were utterly astonished and asked, “Then who can be saved?”

26 Jesus looked at them and said, “With man this is impossible, but with God all things are possible.”

27 Then Peter responded to him, “See, we have left everything and followed you. So what will there be for us?”

28 Jesus said to them, “Truly I tell you, in the renewal of all things, when the Son of Man sits on his glorious throne, you who have followed me will also sit on twelve thrones, judging the twelve tribes of Israel. 29 And everyone who has left houses or brothers or sisters or father or mother[O] or children or fields

[A] **18:28** A denarius = one day’s wage [B] **18:29** Other mss add *at his feet* [C] **18:35** Other mss add *their trespasses* [D] **18:35** Lit *his* [E] **19:4** Other mss read *made* [F] **19:4** Gn 1:27; 5:2 [G] **19:5** Gn 2:24 [H] **19:9** Other mss add *Also whoever marries a divorced woman commits adultery*; Mt 5:32 [I] **19:14** Lit *heaven is of such ones* [J] **19:17** Other mss read *“Why do you call me good?”* [K] **19:17** Other mss read *“No one is good but one — God* [L] **19:18–19** Ex 20:12–16; Lv 19:18; Dt 5:16–20 [M] **19:20** Other mss add *from my youth* [N] **19:21** Or *complete* [O] **19:29** Other mss add *or wife*

because of my name will receive a hundred times more and will inherit eternal life. 30 But many who are first will be last, and the last first.

THE PARABLE OF THE VINEYARD WORKERS

20 "For the kingdom of heaven is like a landowner who went out early in the morning to hire workers for his vineyard. 2 After agreeing with the workers on one denarius,[A] he sent them into his vineyard for the day. 3 When he went out about nine in the morning,[B] he saw others standing in the marketplace doing nothing. 4 He said to them, 'You also go into my vineyard, and I'll give you whatever is right.' So off they went. 5 About noon and about three,[C] he went out again and did the same thing. 6 Then about five[D] he went and found others standing around[E] and said to them, 'Why have you been standing here all day doing nothing?'

7 "'Because no one hired us,' they said to him.

"'You also go into my vineyard,' he told them.[F] 8 When evening came, the owner of the vineyard told his foreman, 'Call the workers and give them their pay, starting with the last and ending with the first.'

9 "When those who were hired about five came, they each received one denarius. 10 So when the first ones came, they assumed they would get more, but they also received a denarius each. 11 When they received it, they began to complain to the landowner: 12 'These last men put in one hour, and you made them equal to us who bore the burden of the day's work and the burning heat.'

13 "He replied to one of them, 'Friend, I'm doing you no wrong. Didn't you agree with me on a denarius? 14 Take what's yours and go. I want to give this last man the same as I gave you. 15 Don't I have the right to do what I want with what is mine? Are you jealous[G] because I'm generous?'[H]

16 "So the last will be first, and the first last."[I]

THE THIRD PREDICTION OF HIS DEATH

17 While going up to Jerusalem, Jesus took the twelve disciples aside privately and said to them on the way, 18 "See, we are going up to Jerusalem. The Son of Man will be handed over to the chief priests and scribes, and they will condemn him to death. 19 They will hand him over to the Gentiles to be mocked, flogged,[J] and crucified, and on the third day he will be raised."[K]

SUFFERING AND SERVICE

20 Then the mother of Zebedee's sons approached him with her sons. She knelt down to ask him for something. 21 "What do you want?" he asked her.

"Promise,"[L] she said to him, "that these two sons of mine may sit, one on your right and the other on your left, in your kingdom."

22 Jesus answered, "You don't know what you're asking. Are you able to drink the cup that I am about to drink?"[M]

"We are able," they said to him.

23 He told them, "You will indeed drink my cup,[N] but to sit at my right and left is not mine to give; instead, it is for those for whom it has been prepared by my Father."

24 When the ten disciples heard this, they became indignant with the two brothers. 25 Jesus called them over and said, "You know that the rulers of the Gentiles lord it over them, and those in high positions act as tyrants over them. 26 It must not be like that among you. On the contrary, whoever wants to become great among you must be your servant, 27 and whoever wants to be first among you must be your slave; 28 just as the Son of Man did not come to be served, but to serve, and to give his life as a ransom for many."

TWO BLIND MEN HEALED

29 As they were leaving Jericho, a large crowd followed him. 30 There were two blind men sitting by the road. When they heard that Jesus was passing by, they cried out, "Lord, have mercy on us, Son of David!" 31 The crowd demanded that they keep quiet, but they cried out all the more, "Lord, have mercy on us, Son of David!"

32 Jesus stopped, called them, and said, "What do you want me to do for you?"

33 "Lord," they said to him, "open our eyes." 34 Moved with compassion, Jesus touched their eyes. Immediately they could see, and they followed him.

THE TRIUMPHAL ENTRY

21 When they approached Jerusalem and came to Bethphage at the Mount of Olives, Jesus then sent two disciples, 2 telling them, "Go into the village ahead of you. At once you will find a donkey tied there with her colt. Untie them and bring them to me. 3 If anyone says anything to you, say that the Lord needs them, and he will send them at once."

4 This took place so that what was spoken through the prophet might be fulfilled:

[A] **20:2** A denarius = one day's wage, also in vv. 9,10,13 [B] **20:3** Lit *about the third hour* [C] **20:5** Lit *about the sixth hour and the ninth hour* [D] **20:6** Lit *about the eleventh hour*, also in v. 9 [E] **20:6** Other mss add *doing nothing* [F] **20:7** Other mss add *'and you'll get whatever is right.'* [G] **20:15** Lit *Is your eye evil*; an idiom for jealousy or stinginess [H] **20:15** Lit *good* [I] **20:16** Other mss add *"For many are called, but few are chosen."* [J] **20:19** Or *scourged* [K] **20:19** Other mss read *will rise again* [L] **20:21** Lit *Say* [M] **20:22** Other mss add *and (or) to be baptized with the baptism which I am baptized?"* [N] **20:23** Other mss add *and be baptized with the baptism with which I am baptized.*

5 **Tell Daughter Zion,**
"See, your King is coming to you,
gentle, and mounted on a donkey,
and on a colt,
the foal of a donkey."[A]

6 The disciples went and did just as Jesus directed them. 7 They brought the donkey and the colt;
then they laid their clothes on them, and he sat on
them. 8 A very large crowd spread their clothes on
the road; others were cutting branches from the
trees and spreading them on the road. 9 Then the
crowds who went ahead of him and those who followed shouted:

Hosanna to the Son of David!
Blessed is he who comes in the name
of the Lord![B]
Hosanna in the highest heaven!

10 When he entered Jerusalem, the whole city was in
an uproar, saying, "Who is this?" 11 The crowds were
saying, "This is the prophet Jesus from Nazareth in
Galilee."

CLEANSING THE TEMPLE

12 Jesus went into the temple[C] and threw out all those
buying and selling. He overturned the tables of the
money changers and the chairs of those selling doves.
13 He said to them, "It is written, **my house will be
called a house of prayer,**[D] but you are making it a
den of thieves!"[E]

CHILDREN PRAISE JESUS

14 The blind and the lame came to him in the temple,
and he healed them. 15 When the chief priests and the
scribes saw the wonders that he did and the children
shouting in the temple, "*Hosanna* to the Son of David!" they were indignant 16 and said to him, "Do you
hear what these children are saying?"

Jesus replied, "Yes, have you never read:

You have prepared[F] **praise**
from the mouths of infants
and nursing babies?"[G]

17 Then he left them, went out of the city to Bethany,
and spent the night there.

THE BARREN FIG TREE

18 Early in the morning, as he was returning to the city,
he was hungry. 19 Seeing a lone fig tree by the road, he
went up to it and found nothing on it except leaves.
And he said to it, "May no fruit ever come from you
again!" At once the fig tree withered.

[A] **21:5** Is 62:11; Zch 9:9 [B] **21:9** Ps 118:25–26 [C] **21:12** Other mss add *of God* [D] **21:13** Is 56:7 [E] **21:13** Jr 7:11 [F] **21:16** Or *restored* [G] **21:16** Ps 8:2

Close-up of a fig tree, growing in Bethphage, a Greek term meaning "house of unripe figs."

20 When the disciples saw it, they were amazed
and said, "How did the fig tree wither so quickly?"
21 Jesus answered them, "Truly I tell you, if you have
faith and do not doubt, you will not only do what was
done to the fig tree, but even if you tell this mountain,
'Be lifted up and thrown into the sea,' it will be done.
22 And if you believe, you will receive whatever you
ask for in prayer."

THE AUTHORITY OF JESUS CHALLENGED

23 When he entered the temple, the chief priests and
the elders of the people came to him as he was teaching and said, "By what authority are you doing these
things? Who gave you this authority?"
24 Jesus answered them, "I will also ask you one
question, and if you answer it for me, then I will
tell you by what authority I do these things. 25 Did
John's baptism come from heaven, or was it of human
origin?"

They discussed it among themselves, "If we say,
'From heaven,' he will say to us, 'Then why didn't
you believe him?' 26 But if we say, 'Of human origin,'
we're afraid of the crowd, because everyone considers John to be a prophet." 27 So they answered Jesus,
"We don't know."

And he said to them, "Neither will I tell you by what
authority I do these things.

THE PARABLE OF THE TWO SONS

28 "What do you think? A man had two sons. He went
to the first and said, 'My son, go work in the vineyard
today.'
29 "He answered, 'I don't want to,' but later he
changed his mind and went. 30 Then the man went to
the other and said the same thing. 'I will, sir,' he answered, but he didn't go. 31 Which of the two did his
father's will?"

They said, "The first."

Jesus said to them, "Truly I tell you, tax collectors
and prostitutes are entering the kingdom of God before you. 32 For John came to you in the way of righteousness, and you didn't believe him. Tax collectors
and prostitutes did believe him; but you, when you
saw it, didn't even change your minds then and believe him.

THE PARABLE OF THE VINEYARD OWNER

33 "Listen to another parable: There was a landowner,
who planted a vineyard, put a fence around it, dug a
winepress in it, and built a watchtower. He leased it to
tenant farmers and went away. 34 When the time came
to harvest fruit, he sent his servants to the farmers
to collect his fruit. 35 The farmers took his servants,
beat one, killed another, and stoned a third. 36 Again,
he sent other servants, more than the first group, and
they did the same to them. 37 Finally, he sent his son
to them. 'They will respect my son,' he said.
38 "But when the tenant farmers saw the son, they
said to each other, 'This is the heir. Come, let's kill him
and take his inheritance.' 39 So they seized him, threw
him out of the vineyard, and killed him. 40 Therefore,
when the owner of the vineyard comes, what will he
do to those farmers?"
41 "He will completely destroy those terrible men,"
they told him, "and lease his vineyard to other farmers who will give him his fruit at the harvest."
42 Jesus said to them, "Have you never read in the
Scriptures:

> **The stone that the builders rejected**
> **has become the cornerstone.**[A]
> **This is what the Lord has done**
> **and it is wonderful in our eyes?**[B]

43 Therefore I tell you, the kingdom of God will be tak-
en away from you and given to a people producing its
fruit. 44 Whoever falls on this stone will be broken to
pieces; but on whomever it falls, it will shatter him."[C]
45 When the chief priests and the Pharisees heard
his parables, they knew he was speaking about them.
46 Although they were looking for a way to arrest him,
they feared the crowds, because the people regarded
him as a prophet.

THE PARABLE OF THE WEDDING BANQUET

22 Once more Jesus spoke to them in parables:
2 "The kingdom of heaven is like a king who
gave a wedding banquet for his son. 3 He sent his servants to summon those invited to the banquet, but
they didn't want to come. 4 Again, he sent out other
servants and said, 'Tell those who are invited: See,
I've prepared my dinner; my oxen and fattened cattle have been slaughtered, and everything is ready.
Come to the wedding banquet.'
5 "But they paid no attention and went away, one
to his own farm, another to his business, 6 while
the rest seized his servants, mistreated them, and
killed them. 7 The king[D] was enraged, and he sent
out his troops, killed those murderers, and burned
down their city.
8 "Then he told his servants, 'The banquet is ready,
but those who were invited were not worthy. 9 Go
then to where the roads exit the city and invite everyone you find to the banquet.' 10 So those servants
went out on the roads and gathered everyone they
found, both evil and good. The wedding banquet was
filled with guests.[E] 11 When the king came in to see
the guests, he saw a man there who was not dressed

[A] **21:42** Lit *the head of the corner* [B] **21:42** Ps 118:22–23 [C] **21:44** Some mss omit this verse [D] **22:7** Other mss read *But when the (that) king heard about it he* [E] **22:10** Lit *those reclining* (to eat)

Denarius of the Roman emperor Tiberius (reigned AD 14–37); known today as the Tribute Penny.

for a wedding. 12 So he said to him, 'Friend, how did
you get in here without wedding clothes?' The man
was speechless.

13 "Then the king told the attendants, 'Tie him up
hand and foot,[A] and throw him into the outer darkness, where there will be weeping and gnashing of
teeth.'

14 "For many are invited, but few are chosen."

GOD AND CAESAR

15 Then the Pharisees went and plotted how to trap
him by what he said.[B] 16 So they sent their disciples to
him, along with the Herodians. "Teacher," they said,
"we know that you are truthful and teach truthfully
the way of God. You don't care what anyone thinks
nor do you show partiality.[C] 17 Tell us, then, what you
think. Is it lawful to pay taxes to Caesar or not?"

18 Perceiving their malicious intent, Jesus said,
"Why are you testing me, hypocrites? 19 Show me
the coin used for the tax." They brought him a denarius.[D] 20 "Whose image and inscription is this?"
he asked them.

21 "Caesar's," they said to him.

Then he said to them, "Give, then, to Caesar the
things that are Caesar's, and to God the things that
are God's." 22 When they heard this, they were amazed.
So they left him and went away.

THE SADDUCEES AND THE RESURRECTION

23 That same day some Sadducees, who say there is
no resurrection, came up to him and questioned
him: 24 "Teacher, Moses said, **if a man dies, having
no children, his brother is to marry his wife and
raise up offspring for his brother.**[E] 25 Now there
were seven brothers among us. The first got married and died. Having no offspring, he left his wife
to his brother. 26 The same thing happened to the
second also, and the third, and so on to all seven.
27 Last of all, the woman died. 28 In the resurrection,
then, whose wife will she be of the seven? For they
all had married her."[F]

29 Jesus answered them, "You are mistaken, because you don't know the Scriptures or the power
of God. 30 For in the resurrection they neither marry
nor are given in marriage but are like[G] angels in heav-
en. 31 Now concerning the resurrection of the dead,
haven't you read what was spoken to you by God: 32 **I
am the God of Abraham and the God of Isaac and
the God of Jacob**?[H] He[I] is not the God of the dead,
but of the living."

33 And when the crowds heard this, they were astonished at his teaching.

THE PRIMARY COMMANDS

34 When the Pharisees heard that he had silenced the
Sadducees, they came together. 35 And one of them,
an expert in the law, asked a question to test him:
36 "Teacher, which command in the law is the greatest?"

37 He said to him, "**Love the Lord your God with
all your heart, with all your soul, and with all your
mind.**[J] 38 This is the greatest and most important[K]
command. 39 The second is like it: **Love your neighbor as yourself.**[L] 40 All the Law and the Prophets
depend[M] on these two commands."

[A] **22:13** Other mss add *take him away* [B] **22:15** Lit *trap him in a word* [C] **22:16** Lit *don't look on the face of men* [D] **22:19** A denarius = one day's wage [E] **22:24** Dt 25:5 [F] **22:28** Lit *all had her* [G] **22:30** Other mss add *God's* [H] **22:32** Ex 3:6,15–16 [I] **22:32** Other mss read *God* [J] **22:37** Dt 6:5 [K] **22:38** Lit *and first* [L] **22:39** Lv 19:18 [M] **22:40** Or *hang*

THE QUESTION ABOUT THE MESSIAH

41 While the Pharisees were together, Jesus questioned them, 42 "What do you think about the Messiah? Whose son is he?"

They replied, "David's."

43 He asked them, "How is it then that David, inspired by the Spirit,[A] calls him 'Lord':

44 **The Lord declared to my Lord,**
'Sit at my right hand
until I put your enemies
under your feet'?[B,C]

45 "If David calls him 'Lord,' how, then, can he be his son?" 46 No one was able to answer him at all,[D] and from that day no one dared to question him anymore.

RELIGIOUS HYPOCRITES DENOUNCED

23 Then Jesus spoke to the crowds and to his disciples: 2 "The scribes and the Pharisees are seated in the chair of Moses. 3 Therefore do whatever they tell you, and observe it. But don't do what they do, because they don't practice what they teach. 4 They tie up heavy loads that are hard to carry[E] and put them on people's shoulders, but they themselves aren't willing to lift a finger to move them. 5 They do everything[F] to be seen by others: They enlarge their phylacteries and lengthen their tassels.[G] 6 They love the place of honor at banquets, the front seats in the synagogues, 7 greetings in the marketplaces, and to be called 'Rabbi' by people.

8 "But you are not to be called 'Rabbi,' because you have one Teacher,[H] and you are all brothers and sisters. 9 Do not call anyone on earth your father, because you have one Father, who is in heaven. 10 You are not to be called instructors either, because you have one Instructor, the Messiah. 11 The greatest among you will be your servant. 12 Whoever exalts himself will be humbled, and whoever humbles himself will be exalted.

13 "Woe to you, scribes and Pharisees, hypocrites! You shut the door of the kingdom of heaven in people's faces. For you don't go in, and you don't allow those entering to go in.[I]

15 "Woe to you, scribes and Pharisees, hypocrites! You travel over land and sea to make one convert, and when he becomes one, you make him twice as much a child of hell as you are!

16 "Woe to you, blind guides, who say, 'Whoever takes an oath by the temple, it means nothing. But whoever takes an oath by the gold of the temple is bound by his oath.'[J] 17 Blind fools! For which is greater, the gold or the temple that sanctified the gold? 18 Also, 'Whoever takes an oath by the altar, it means nothing; but whoever takes an oath by the gift that is on it is bound by his oath.' 19 Blind people![K] For which is greater, the gift or the altar that sanctifies the gift? 20 Therefore, the one who takes an oath by the altar takes an oath by it and by everything on it. 21 The one who takes an oath by the temple takes an oath by it and by him who dwells in it. 22 And the one who takes an oath by heaven takes an oath by God's throne and by him who sits on it.

23 "Woe to you, scribes and Pharisees, hypocrites! You pay a tenth of[L] mint, dill, and cumin, and yet you have neglected the more important matters of the law — justice, mercy, and faithfulness.[M] These things should have been done without neglecting the others. 24 Blind guides! You strain out a gnat, but gulp down a camel!

25 "Woe to you, scribes and Pharisees, hypocrites! You clean the outside of the cup and dish, but inside they are full of greed[N] and self-indulgence. 26 Blind Pharisee! First clean the inside of the cup,[O] so that the outside of it[P] may also become clean.

27 "Woe to you, scribes and Pharisees, hypocrites! You are like whitewashed tombs, which appear beautiful on the outside, but inside are full of the bones of the dead and every kind of impurity. 28 In the same way, on the outside you seem righteous to people, but inside you are full of hypocrisy and lawlessness.

29 "Woe to you, scribes and Pharisees, hypocrites! You build the tombs of the prophets and decorate the graves of the righteous, 30 and you say, 'If we had lived in the days of our ancestors, we wouldn't have taken part with them in shedding the prophets' blood.' 31 So you testify against yourselves that you are descendants of those who murdered the prophets. 32 Fill up, then, the measure of your ancestors' sins!

33 "Snakes! Brood of vipers! How can you escape being condemned to hell?[Q] 34 This is why I am sending you prophets, sages, and scribes. Some of them you will kill and crucify, and some of them you will flog in your synagogues and pursue from town to town. 35 So all the righteous blood shed on the earth will be charged to you,[R] from the blood of righteous Abel to the blood of Zechariah, son of Berechiah, whom you murdered between the sanctuary and the altar. 36 Truly I tell you, all these things will come on this generation.

[A] **22:43** Lit *David in Spirit* [B] **22:44** Other mss read *until I make your enemies your footstool'* [C] **22:44** Ps 110:1 [D] **22:46** Lit *answer him a word* [E] **23:4** Other mss omit *that are hard to carry* [F] **23:5** Lit *do all their works* [G] **23:5** Other mss add *on their robes* [H] **23:8** Other mss add *the Christ* [I] **23:13** Some mss include v. 14: *"Woe to you, scribes and Pharisees, hypocrites! You devour widows' houses and make long prayers just for show. This is why you will receive a harsher punishment.* [J] **23:16** Lit *is obligated*, also in v. 18 [K] **23:19** Other mss read *Fools and blind* [L] **23:23** Or *You tithe* [M] **23:23** Or *faith* [N] **23:25** Or *full of violence* [O] **23:26** Other mss add *and dish* [P] **23:26** Other mss read *of them* [Q] **23:33** Lit *escape from the judgment of gehenna* [R] **23:35** Lit *will come on you*

JESUS'S LAMENTING OVER JERUSALEM

37 "Jerusalem, Jerusalem, who kills the prophets and
stones those who are sent to her. How often I wanted
to gather your children together, as a hen gathers her
chicks[A] under her wings, but you were not willing!
38 See, your house is left to you desolate. 39 For I tell
you, you will not see me again until you say, **'Blessed
is he who comes in the name of the Lord'**!"[B]

DESTRUCTION OF THE TEMPLE PREDICTED

24 As Jesus left and was going out of the temple,
his disciples came up and called his attention
to its buildings. 2 He replied to them, "Do you see all
these things? Truly I tell you, not one stone will be
left here on another that will not be thrown down."

SIGNS OF THE END OF THE AGE

3 While he was sitting on the Mount of Olives, the
disciples approached him privately and said, "Tell us,
when will these things happen? And what is the sign
of your coming and of the end of the age?"
4 Jesus replied to them, "Watch out that no one deceives you. 5 For many will come in my name, saying,
'I am the Messiah,' and they will deceive many. 6 You
are going to hear of wars and rumors of wars. See that
you are not alarmed, because these things must take
place, but the end is not yet. 7 For nation will rise up
against nation, and kingdom against kingdom. There
will be famines[C] and earthquakes in various places.
8 All these events are the beginning of labor pains.

PERSECUTIONS PREDICTED

9 "Then they will hand you over to be persecuted,
and they will kill you. You will be hated by all nations
because of my name. 10 Then many will fall away, betray one another, and hate one another. 11 Many false
prophets will rise up and deceive many. 12 Because
lawlessness will multiply, the love of many will grow
cold. 13 But the one who endures to the end will be
saved. 14 This good news of the kingdom will be proclaimed in all the world[D] as a testimony to all nations,
and then the end will come.

THE GREAT TRIBULATION

15 "So when you see **the abomination of desolation**,[E]
spoken of by the prophet Daniel, standing in the holy
place" (let the reader understand), 16 "then those in
Judea must flee to the mountains. 17 A man on the
housetop[F] must not come down to get things out of
his house, 18 and a man in the field must not go back
to get his coat. 19 Woe to pregnant women and nursing
mothers in those days! 20 Pray that your escape may
not be in winter or on a Sabbath. 21 For at that time
there will be great distress,[G] the kind that hasn't taken
place from the beginning of the world until now and
never will again. 22 Unless those days were cut short,
no one would[H] be saved. But those days will be cut
short because of the elect.
23 "If anyone tells you then, 'See, here is the Messiah!' or, 'Over here!' do not believe it. 24 For false
messiahs and false prophets will arise and perform
great signs and wonders to lead astray, if possible,
even the elect. 25 Take note: I have told you in advance.
26 So if they tell you, 'See, he's in the wilderness!' don't
go out; or, 'See, he's in the storerooms!' do not believe
it. 27 For as the lightning comes from the east and
flashes as far as the west, so will be the coming of
the Son of Man. 28 Wherever the carcass is, there the
vultures[I] will gather.

THE COMING OF THE SON OF MAN

29 "Immediately after the distress of those days, the
sun will be darkened, and the moon will not shed its
light; the stars will fall from the sky, and the powers of
the heavens will be shaken. 30 Then the sign of the Son
of Man will appear in the sky, and then all the peoples
of the earth[J] will mourn;[K] and they will see the Son of
Man coming on the clouds of heaven with power and
great glory. 31 He will send out his angels with a loud
trumpet, and they will gather his elect from the four
winds, from one end of the sky to the other.

THE PARABLE OF THE FIG TREE

32 "Learn this lesson from the fig tree: As soon as its
branch becomes tender and sprouts leaves, you know
that summer is near. 33 In the same way, when you
see all these things, recognize[L] that he[M] is near—at
the door. 34 Truly I tell you, this generation will certainly not pass away until all these things take place.
35 Heaven and earth will pass away, but my words will
never pass away.

NO ONE KNOWS THE DAY OR HOUR

36 "Now concerning that day and hour no one knows
—neither the angels of heaven nor the Son[N]—except the Father alone. 37 As the days of Noah were, so
the coming of the Son of Man will be. 38 For in those
days before the flood they were eating and drinking,
marrying and giving in marriage, until the day Noah
boarded the ark. 39 They didn't know until the flood
came and swept them all away. This is the way the
coming of the Son of Man will be. 40 Then two men
will be in the field; one will be taken and one left.

[A] **23:37** Or *as a mother bird gathers her young* [B] **23:39** Ps 118:26
[C] **24:7** Other mss add *epidemics* [D] **24:14** Or *in all the inhabited earth*
[E] **24:15** Dn 9:27 [F] **24:17** Or *roof* [G] **24:21** Or *tribulation*, also in v. 29
[H] **24:22** Lit *short, all flesh would not* [I] **24:28** Or *eagles* [J] **24:30** Or *all the tribes of the land* [K] **24:30** Lit *will beat*; that is, beat their chests
[L] **24:33** Or *things, you know* [M] **24:33** Or *it*; that is, summer
[N] **24:36** Other mss omit *nor the Son*

Herod's Temple

by Timothy Trammell

During Jesus's earthly ministry and the first Christian century, the temple in Jerusalem, Herod's temple, was the heart of Jewish worship.

SOLOMON'S TEMPLE

Bible students refer to Herod's temple as the "second temple." The first temple was the magnificent structure Solomon built. The biblical description of Solomon's temple suggests that the inside ceiling was 180 feet long, 90 feet wide, and 50 feet high. The highest point of the structure soared to about 207 feet or approximately ten stories. Nebuchadnezzar and the Babylonians destroyed the temple in 586 BC.

When the Jewish people returned from the Babylonian captivity, Zerubbabel led the people to build a new temple. But those who had seen Solomon's temple considered this structure disappointingly inferior (see Ezr 3:12–13). Zerubbabel's temple was the one that Herod the Great determined to rebuild and enlarge. Since Herod was really an Idumean rather than a Jew, he thought doing this would "please the Jews as well as win recognition for himself"—particularly in the eyes of his Roman overlords.[1]

THE TEMPLE PLATFORM

Reconstruction began between 20 and 19 BC, and the majority of the work was completed in eighteen months. But to provide a foundation for the massive structure that Herod and his workmen envisioned, an enlarged platform was essential. Laborers built massive retaining walls on the slopes of Mount Moriah to hold the platform in place. The completed structure, with its arches and vaults, was 1,575 feet long and 919 feet wide, yielding almost 1.5 million square feet in area.[2] Portions of these retaining walls are still visible today, especially on the eastern, southern, and western sides. The western exposure is the best known, called the Western Wall. Today this wall is a center of Jewish worship and the site of national celebration.

The huge limestone blocks used to build the structure came from quarries within the city of Jerusalem. The smallest of the quarried and dressed stones, known as ashlars, weigh two to five tons each; many larger ashlars weigh about fifty tons each. The largest ashlar, at forty feet long, ten feet high, and thirteen feet thick, weighs an astonishing four hundred tons.[3] Two Muslim structures occupy the Temple Mount today, the Dome of the Rock and the Al-Aqsa Mosque.

At Herod's temple, one could enter the Court of the Gentiles, the dominant area of the Temple Mount, through eight gates: two on the south, four on the west, one on the north, and one on the east. The court was surrounded on all four sides by columned porticoes. On the south was the Royal Porch, with a total of 162 columns aligned in four rows. The last row was attached to the south wall. Josephus recorded that the thickness of each column

Protruding from the southern end of the western side of the Temple Mount are the springer courses of an arch that supported a monumental stairway leading up to the Temple Mount Plaza. The arch, named Robinson's Arch after the American who first identified it, was part of Herod's expansion of the temple.

Men's plaza at the Western Wall in Jerusalem. The exposed rock face here at the prayer plaza rises to a height of about sixty feet; originally, the wall stood almost two-hundred feet tall.

was such "that three men might, with their arms extended, fathom it round, and join their hands again."[4] The columns were more than thirty-five feet tall.

On the east, north, and west sides of the court, the porches had two rows of columns. They were roofed, and they opened to the court. The porch along the east was named Solomon's Porch or Colonnade. John recorded that Jesus walked in this area during the Festival of Dedication (Jn 10:22–23).

The southeast corner of the court was the "pinnacle of the temple" mentioned in Matthew 4:5 in connection with Jesus's temptation. This point overlooked the Kidron Valley some one hundred yards below. Early church history states that James, the half brother of Jesus, was thrown down from this point and killed in AD 66.

THE TEMPLE PROPER

The Greek New Testament has two terms that can be translated as "temple." The first, *hieron*, designates the entire temple complex. The other, *naos*, referred to the temple proper, the sanctuary.[5] The *naos* was set on a small terrace and was surrounded by a stone balustrade that was just over three feet high. On the balustrade was a sign written in both Greek and Latin, which warned non-Jews: "No Gentile may enter within the railing around the Sanctuary and within the enclosure. Whosoever should be caught will render himself liable to the death penalty which will inevitably follow."[6]

Within the balustrade were three distinct areas. The first section was called the women's court because women could go no farther. Around it were small storage rooms. Between these rooms were thirteen coffers, each in the form of an inverted trumpet, into which people placed offerings. These offerings covered the expenses of the temple.

The next section was the court of the men of Israel. It was elevated above the court of the women; men entered by ascending fifteen semicircular steps. Access was gained through six gates, three on the north and three on the south, and by an opening, the Nicanor Gate, from the women's court.

Moving into and through the court of the priests, one came to the

Model of the sanctuary of Herod's temple.

inner recesses of the sanctuary. This structure measured 172 feet long, broad, and high, and it had two stories. It consisted of a porch, the holy place, and the most holy place.

Twelve steps led up about 10 feet from the court of the priests to the porch, which featured a façade measuring about 172 feet wide and high. Beyond the porch was the holy place, an area that measured 68.8 feet long by 34.4 feet wide, with walls 68.8 feet high. In this room stood the golden lampstand, the table of showbread (Bread of the Presence), and the altar of incense. A thick veil served as the west wall.

Beyond the veil was the most holy place. It measured 34.4 feet square with walls 68.8 feet tall. At the time of the second temple, this area was empty.[7] The high priest entered this sacred area annually on the Day of Atonement to repent, sprinkle sacrificial goat's blood, and obtain forgiveness for his sins and those of the people.

By any standard, Herod's temple was magnificent. One would surmise that this edifice would stand throughout the centuries. Tragically, however, during the Roman invasion in AD 70, the temple was destroyed, as Jesus predicted (Mt 24:2). ✣

[1] Floyd Filson, "The Significance of the Temple in the Ancient Near East. Part 4: Temple, Synagogue and Church," *BA* 7.44 (1944): 79. [2] Leslie J. Hoppe, "Herod's Quarries," *The Bible Today* (*TBT*) 48.1 (2010): 35. [3] Simon Goldhill, *The Temple of Jerusalem* (London: Profile Books, 2004), 60–61. [4] Josephus, *Jewish Antiquities* 15.11.4. [5] "Temple" in *The New International Dictionary of New Testament Theology* (*NIDNTT*), ed. Colin Brown, 4 vols. (Grand Rapids: Zondervan, 1978), 3:781. [6] Leen Ritmeyer, *The Quest: Revealing the Temple Mount in Jerusalem* (Jerusalem: Carta Jerusalem and the LAMB Foundation, 2006), 346. [7] For full details of Herod's temple, see Ritmeyer, *The Quest*.

41 Two women will be grinding grain with a hand mill;
one will be taken and one left. 42 Therefore be alert,
since you don't know what day[A] your Lord is coming.
43 But know this: If the homeowner had known what
time[B] the thief was coming, he would have stayed
alert and not let his house be broken into. 44 This is
why you are also to be ready, because the Son of Man
is coming at an hour you do not expect.

FAITHFUL SERVICE TO CHRIST

45 "Who then is a faithful and wise servant, whom his
master has put in charge of his household, to give
them food at the proper time? 46 Blessed is that servant whom the master finds doing his job when he
comes. 47 Truly I tell you, he will put him in charge of
all his possessions. 48 But if that wicked servant says
in his heart, 'My master is delayed,' 49 and starts to
beat his fellow servants, and eats and drinks with
drunkards, 50 that servant's master will come on a
day he does not expect him and at an hour he does
not know. 51 He will cut him to pieces and assign him a
place with the hypocrites, where there will be weeping and gnashing of teeth.

THE PARABLE OF THE TEN VIRGINS

25 "At that time the kingdom of heaven will be like
ten virgins[C] who took their lamps[D] and went
out to meet the groom. 2 Five of them were foolish and
five were wise. 3 When the foolish took their lamps,
they didn't take oil with them; 4 but the wise ones took
oil in their flasks with their lamps. 5 When the groom
was delayed, they all became drowsy and fell asleep.
6 "In the middle of the night there was a shout:
'Here's the groom! Come out to meet him.'
7 "Then all the virgins got up and trimmed their
lamps. 8 The foolish ones said to the wise ones, 'Give
us some of your oil, because our lamps are going out.'
9 "The wise ones answered, 'No, there won't be
enough for us and for you. Go instead to those who
sell oil, and buy some for yourselves.'
10 "When they had gone to buy some, the groom
arrived, and those who were ready went in with him
to the wedding banquet, and the door was shut. 11 Later the rest of the virgins also came and said, 'Master,
master, open up for us!'
12 "He replied, 'Truly I tell you, I don't know you!'
13 "Therefore be alert, because you don't know either the day or the hour.[E]

THE PARABLE OF THE TALENTS

14 "For it is just like a man about to go on a journey.
He called his own servants and entrusted his possessions to them. 15 To one he gave five talents,[F] to another two talents, and to another one talent, depending
on each one's ability. Then he went on a journey. Immediately 16 the man who had received five talents
went, put them to work, and earned five more. 17 In
the same way the man with two earned two more.
18 But the man who had received one talent went off,
dug a hole in the ground, and hid his master's money.
19 "After a long time the master of those servants
came and settled accounts with them. 20 The man
who had received five talents approached, presented
five more talents, and said, 'Master, you gave me five
talents. See, I've earned five more talents.'
21 "His master said to him, 'Well done, good and
faithful servant! You were faithful over a few things;
I will put you in charge of many things. Share your
master's joy.'
22 "The man with two talents also approached. He
said, 'Master, you gave me two talents. See, I've earned
two more talents.'
23 "His master said to him, 'Well done, good and
faithful servant! You were faithful over a few things;
I will put you in charge of many things. Share your
master's joy.'
24 "The man who had received one talent also approached and said, 'Master, I know you. You're a harsh
man, reaping where you haven't sown and gathering
where you haven't scattered seed. 25 So I was afraid
and went off and hid your talent in the ground. See,
you have what is yours.'
26 "His master replied to him, 'You evil, lazy servant! If you knew that I reap where I haven't sown
and gather where I haven't scattered, 27 then[G] you
should have deposited my money with the bankers,
and I would have received my money[H] back with interest when I returned.
28 " 'So take the talent from him and give it to the
one who has ten talents. 29 For to everyone who
has, more will be given, and he will have more than
enough. But from the one who does not have, even
what he has will be taken away from him. 30 And
throw this good-for-nothing servant into the outer
darkness, where there will be weeping and gnashing of teeth.'

THE SHEEP AND THE GOATS

31 "When the Son of Man comes in his glory, and all
the angels[I] with him, then he will sit on his glorious
throne. 32 All the nations[J] will be gathered before him,
and he will separate them one from another, just
as a shepherd separates the sheep from the goats.

[A] **24:42** Other mss read *hour*; = time [B] **24:43** Lit *watch*; a division of the night in ancient times [C] **25:1** Or *bridesmaids* [D] **25:1** Or *torches*, also in vv. 3,4,7,8 [E] **25:13** Other mss add *in which the Son of Man is coming.* [F] **25:15** A talent is worth about 6,000 denarii, or twenty years' wages for a laborer [G] **25:26–27** Or *So you knew . . . scattered? Then* (as a question) [H] **25:27** Lit *received what is mine* [I] **25:31** Other mss read *holy angels* [J] **25:32** Or *the Gentiles*

Coins Used in Banking

by Mona Stewart

Used in making trades, the shekel started out as a standardized weight in ancient Mesopotamia before the advent of money or coins (see Gn 23:15–16). After the Lydians developed coinage, the term *shekel* still referred to a coin used to make trades. These shekels originally tended to be heavy, crude, and often without a uniform shape. Since shekels had varying amounts of metal in their makeup, people would still weigh the shekel to ascertain its worth. The earliest coins were not stamped with their value. This fact precipitated the need for weighing.

The talent was actually a weight and not a coin and was made from gold, silver, or copper. Its value depended upon the metal from which it was made. Silver was the most common.[1] Three thousand shekels equaled one talent. A talent usually weighed between sixty and ninety pounds and thus represented a large sum of money.

The silver denarius was a Roman coin that usually represented a day's pay. The drachma was its equivalent and the basic Greek coin. The mina was equal to one hundred drachmas. The widow's mite is the New Testament's only mention of a Jewish coin. This small copper or bronze coin was worth a fraction of our modern penny.[2] ❖

[1] William Barclay, *The Gospel of Matthew*, rev. ed. (Philadelphia: Westminster, 1975), 2:322. [2] "Money of the Bible" in *Nelson's New Illustrated Bible Dictionary*, ed. Ronald F. Youngblood (Nashville: Thomas Nelson, 1995), 856.

Jerusalem "Tyrian" shekel; minted in Jerusalem (reverse side, eagle); dated AD 47 or 48. The Tyrian shekel was commonly used for the temple tax of Jerusalem.

A Roman denarius. People were commonly anxious about their money. Many ancient coins had cuts in them, indicating a person had checked that the silver or gold was solid.

A Jewish widow's mite from the time of Tiberius. The obverse side shows a *simpulum*, which was a vessel for pouring out libations. The Greek inscription reads: *TIBERION KAICAROS LIS*, which means "of Tiberius, year 16." This coin was found at Herodium, near Bethlehem.

33 He will put the sheep on his right and the goats on the left. 34 Then the King will say to those on his right, 'Come, you who are blessed by my Father; inherit the kingdom prepared for you from the foundation of the world.

35 " 'For I was hungry and you gave me something to eat; I was thirsty and you gave me something to drink; I was a stranger and you took me in; 36 I was naked and you clothed me; I was sick and you took care of me; I was in prison and you visited me.'

37 "Then the righteous will answer him, 'Lord, when did we see you hungry and feed you, or thirsty and give you something to drink? 38 When did we see you a stranger and take you in, or without clothes and clothe you? 39 When did we see you sick, or in prison, and visit you?'

40 "And the King will answer them, 'Truly I tell you, whatever you did for one of the least of these brothers and sisters of mine, you did for me.'

41 "Then he will also say to those on the left, 'Depart from me, you who are cursed, into the eternal fire prepared for the devil and his angels! 42 For I was hungry and you gave me nothing to eat; I was thirsty and you gave me nothing to drink; 43 I was a stranger and you didn't take me in; I was naked and you didn't clothe me, sick and in prison and you didn't take care of me.'

44 "Then they too will answer, 'Lord, when did we see you hungry, or thirsty, or a stranger, or without clothes, or sick, or in prison, and not help you?'

45 "Then he will answer them, 'Truly I tell you, whatever you did not do for one of the least of these, you did not do for me.'

46 "And they will go away into eternal punishment, but the righteous into eternal life."

THE PLOT TO KILL JESUS

26 When Jesus had finished saying all these things, he told his disciples, 2 "You know[A] that the Passover takes place after two days, and the Son of Man will be handed over to be crucified."

3 Then the chief priests[B] and the elders of the people assembled in the courtyard of the high priest, who was named Caiaphas, 4 and they conspired to arrest Jesus in a treacherous way and kill him. 5 "Not during the festival," they said, "so there won't be rioting among the people."

THE ANOINTING AT BETHANY

6 While Jesus was in Bethany at the house of Simon the leper,[C] 7 a woman approached him with an alabaster jar of very expensive perfume. She poured it on his head as he was reclining at the table. 8 When the disciples saw it, they were indignant. "Why this waste?" they asked. 9 "This might have been sold for a great deal and given to the poor."

10 Aware of this, Jesus said to them, "Why are you bothering this woman? She has done a noble thing for me. 11 You always have the poor with you, but you do not always have me. 12 By pouring this perfume on my body, she has prepared me for burial. 13 Truly I tell you, wherever this gospel is proclaimed in the whole world, what she has done will also be told in memory of her."

14 Then one of the Twelve, the man called Judas Iscariot, went to the chief priests 15 and said, "What are you willing to give me if I hand him over to you?" So they weighed out thirty pieces of silver for him. 16 And from that time he started looking for a good opportunity to betray him.

BETRAYAL AT THE PASSOVER

17 On the first day of Unleavened Bread the disciples came to Jesus and asked, "Where do you want us to make preparations for you to eat the Passover?"

18 "Go into the city to a certain man," he said, "and tell him, 'The Teacher says: My time is near; I am celebrating the Passover at your place[D] with my disciples.' " 19 So the disciples did as Jesus had directed them and prepared the Passover. 20 When evening came, he was reclining at the table with the Twelve. 21 While they were eating, he said, "Truly I tell you, one of you will betray me."

22 Deeply distressed, each one began to say to him, "Surely not I, Lord?"

23 He replied, "The one who dipped his hand with me in the bowl — he will betray me. 24 The Son of Man will go just as it is written about him, but woe to that man by whom the Son of Man is betrayed! It would have been better for him if he had not been born."

25 Judas, his betrayer, replied, "Surely not I, Rabbi?"

"You have said it," he told him.

THE FIRST LORD'S SUPPER

26 As they were eating, Jesus took bread, blessed and broke it, gave it to the disciples, and said, "Take and eat it; this is my body." 27 Then he took a cup, and after giving thanks, he gave it to them and said, "Drink from it, all of you. 28 For this is my blood of the covenant,[E] which is poured out for many for the forgiveness of sins. 29 But I tell you, I will not drink from this fruit of the vine from now on until that day when I drink it new with you in my Father's kingdom." 30 After singing a hymn, they went out to the Mount of Olives.

[A] **26:2** Or *"Know* (as a command) [B] **26:3** Other mss add *and the scribes* [C] **26:6** Gk *lepros*; a term for various skin diseases; see Lv 13–14 [D] **26:18** Lit *Passover with you* [E] **26:28** Other mss read *new covenant*

PETER'S DENIAL PREDICTED

31 Then Jesus said to them, "Tonight all of you will fall
away because of me, for it is written:

I will strike the shepherd,
and the sheep of the flock
will be scattered.[A]

32 But after I have risen, I will go ahead of you to Galilee."
33 Peter told him, "Even if everyone falls away because of you, I will never fall away."
34 "Truly I tell you," Jesus said to him, "tonight, before the rooster crows, you will deny me three times."
35 "Even if I have to die with you," Peter told him,
"I will never deny you," and all the disciples said the
same thing.

THE PRAYER IN THE GARDEN

36 Then Jesus came with them to a place called Gethsemane, and he told the disciples, "Sit here while I go
over there and pray." 37 Taking along Peter and the
two sons of Zebedee, he began to be sorrowful and
troubled. 38 He said to them, "I am deeply grieved[B] to
the point of death. Remain here and stay awake with
me." 39 Going a little farther,[C] he fell facedown and
prayed, "My Father, if it is possible, let this cup pass
from me. Yet not as I will, but as you will."
40 Then he came to the disciples and found them
sleeping. He asked Peter, "So, couldn't you stay awake
with me one hour? 41 Stay awake and pray, so that you
won't enter into temptation. The spirit is willing, but
the flesh is weak."
42 Again, a second time, he went away and prayed,
"My Father, if this[D] cannot pass[E] unless I drink it, your
will be done." 43 And he came again and found them
sleeping, because they could not keep their eyes open.
44 After leaving them, he went away again and
prayed a third time, saying the same thing once more.
45 Then he came to the disciples and said to them, "Are
you still sleeping and resting? See, the time is near.
The Son of Man is betrayed into the hands of sinners.
46 Get up; let's go. See, my betrayer is near."

JUDAS'S BETRAYAL OF JESUS

47 While he was still speaking, Judas, one of the
Twelve, suddenly arrived. A large mob with swords
and clubs was with him from the chief priests and
elders of the people. 48 His betrayer had given them
a sign: "The one I kiss, he's the one; arrest him." 49 So
immediately he went up to Jesus and said, "Greetings,
Rabbi!" and kissed him.
50 "Friend," Jesus asked him, "why have you come?"[F]
Then they came up, took hold of Jesus, and arrested him. 51 At that moment one of those with Jesus
reached out his hand and drew his sword. He struck
the high priest's servant and cut off his ear.

An alabaster perfume jar from Jericho.

52 Then Jesus told him, "Put your sword back in its
place because all who take up the sword will perish
by the sword. 53 Or do you think that I cannot call on
my Father, and he will provide me here and now with
more than twelve legions of angels? 54 How, then,
would the Scriptures be fulfilled that say it must happen this way?"
55 At that time Jesus said to the crowds, "Have you
come out with swords and clubs, as if I were a criminal,[G] to capture me? Every day I used to sit, teaching
in the temple, and you didn't arrest me. 56 But all this
has happened so that the writings of the prophets
would be fulfilled." Then all the disciples deserted
him and ran away.

JESUS FACES THE SANHEDRIN

57 Those who had arrested Jesus led him away to Caiaphas the high priest, where the scribes and the elders
had convened. 58 Peter was following him at a distance right to the high priest's courtyard. He went in
and was sitting with the servants to see the outcome.

[A] **26:31** Zch 13:7 [B] **26:38** Lit *"My soul is swallowed up in sorrow* [C] **26:39** Other mss read *Drawing nearer* [D] **26:42** Other mss add *cup* [E] **26:42** Other mss add *from me* [F] **26:50** Or *Jesus told him, "do what you have come for."* [G] **26:55** Lit *as against a criminal*

First-Century Dining Practices

by Martha S. Bergen

Triclinium with carved couches at Petra.

Several times the Gospels speak of Jesus and others "reclining at table." This was not, however, the usual posture for ordinary day-to-day meals. Families typically sat on the floor or squatted around a rug or low tables on which sat a communal pot of lentil or vegetable stew along with bread. Sometimes, though, seating was available for special ceremonies or events associated with royalty or the wealthy. By the first century AD, some among the Jews had adopted the Roman practice of using the triclinium for meals. The triclinium was an arrangement of tables in a U-shaped format with couches or cushions extending in a perpendicular angle from the outer sides. This left the inner part of the "U" open, which allowed servants

Banqueters shown reclining on draped and cushioned couches. They are accompanied by servants and other attendants; dated to the fourth century BC; from the Nereid Monument at the Arbinas tomb, from Xanthos, Lycia.

easy access for placing or removing food as needed. Guests, along with their host, would recline or lean on their left arm, leaving their right arm free. Thus persons would use the right hand for eating, since the left hand was relegated for unclean tasks. The right hand was the main utensil, although people did use spoons with some foods. People used bread for scooping stew from the communal pot or soaking up gravies, soups, or sauces.[1]

When Jesus directed the disciples to make preparations for the Last Supper, he was perhaps asking them, in part, to find a place with a triclinium. The intimate arrangement of the triclinium setup, along with what Jesus wanted to share with the Twelve, would have made this setting most appropriate, including his act of servanthood in washing the disciples' feet. Furthermore, associated with the triclinium arrangement were cultural dictates for guest placement. Next to the host were the two most-honored guests; the highest-honored was on the host's right, the next, on his left. The mother of James and John, fathered by Zebedee, no doubt had this cultural norm in mind when she asked Jesus that her sons be allowed these privileged positions in his kingdom (Mt 20:20–21). Scripture lends support that on the night of the Passover meal preceding Jesus's arrest, the apostle John was seated to Jesus's right, while, ironically, Judas was likely the one to his left (Jn 13:22–27). The fact that Jesus could hand Judas the piece of bread dipped into the dish would necessitate close physical proximity between the two, especially considering their reclining position. ✜

---

[1] Ralph Gower, "Food" in *HIBD*, 589–90; Fred H. Wight, *Manners and Customs of Bible Lands* (Chicago: Moody, 1953), 59, 63.

Olive trees growing in the Garden of Gethsemane on the Mount of Olives, east of Jerusalem.

59 The chief priests and the whole Sanhedrin were
looking for false testimony against Jesus so that they
could put him to death, 60 but they could not find any,
even though many false witnesses came forward.[A]
Finally, two[B] who came forward 61 stated, "This man
said, 'I can destroy the temple of God and rebuild it
in three days.' "
62 The high priest stood up and said to him, "Don't
you have an answer to what these men are testifying
against you?" 63 But Jesus kept silent. The high priest
said to him, "I charge you under oath by the living
God: Tell us if you are the Messiah, the Son of God."
64 "You have said it," Jesus told him. "But I tell you,
in the future[C] you will see **the Son of Man seated at
the right hand** of Power and **coming on the clouds
of heaven.**"[D]
65 Then the high priest tore his robes and said, "He
has blasphemed! Why do we still need witnesses?
See, now you've heard the blasphemy. 66 What is your
decision?"
They answered, "He deserves death!" 67 Then they
spat in his face and beat him; others slapped him
68 and said, "Prophesy to us, Messiah! Who was it
that hit you?"

PETER DENIES HIS LORD

69 Now Peter was sitting outside in the courtyard. A
servant girl approached him and said, "You were with
Jesus the Galilean too."
70 But he denied it in front of everyone: "I don't
know what you're talking about."
71 When he had gone out to the gateway, another
woman saw him and told those who were there, "This
man was with Jesus the Nazarene!"
72 And again he denied it with an oath: "I don't
know the man!"
73 After a little while those standing there approached and said to Peter, "You really are one of
them, since even your accent[E] gives you away."
74 Then he started to curse and to swear with an
oath, "I don't know the man!" Immediately a rooster

[A] **26:60** Other mss add *they found none* [B] **26:60** Other mss add *false witnesses* [C] **26:64** Lit *you, from now* [D] **26:64** Ps 110:1; Dn 7:13 [E] **26:73** Or *speech*

crowed, 75 and Peter remembered the words Jesus had
spoken, "Before the rooster crows, you will deny me
three times." And he went outside and wept bitterly.

JESUS HANDED OVER TO PILATE

27 When daybreak came, all the chief priests and
the elders of the people plotted against Jesus
to put him to death. 2 After tying him up, they led him
away and handed him over to Pilate,[A] the governor.

JUDAS HANGS HIMSELF

3 Then Judas, his betrayer, seeing that Jesus had been
condemned, was full of remorse and returned the
thirty pieces of silver to the chief priests and elders.
4 "I have sinned by betraying innocent blood," he said.
"What's that to us?" they said. "See to it yourself!"
5 So he threw the silver into the temple and departed.
Then he went and hanged himself.
6 The chief priests took the silver and said, "It's not
permitted to put it into the temple treasury, since it is
blood money." 7 They conferred together and bought
the potter's field with it as a burial place for foreigners. 8 Therefore that field has been called "Field of
Blood" to this day. 9 Then what was spoken through
the prophet Jeremiah was fulfilled: **They took[B] the
thirty pieces of silver, the price of him whose price
was set by the Israelites, 10 and they gave[C] them for
the potter's field, as the Lord directed me.**[D]

JESUS FACES THE GOVERNOR

11 Now Jesus stood before the governor. "Are you the
king of the Jews?" the governor asked him.
Jesus answered, "You say so." 12 While he was being accused by the chief priests and elders, he didn't
answer.
13 Then Pilate said to him, "Don't you hear how
much they are testifying against you?" 14 But he didn't
answer him on even one charge, so that the governor
was quite amazed.

JESUS OR BARABBAS

15 At the festival the governor's custom was to release to the crowd a prisoner they wanted. 16 At that
time they had a notorious prisoner called Barabbas.[E]
17 So when they had gathered together, Pilate said
to them, "Who is it you want me to release for you
— Barabbas, or Jesus who is called Christ?" 18 For he
knew it was because of envy that they had handed
him over.
19 While he was sitting on the judge's bench, his
wife sent word to him, "Have nothing to do with that
righteous man, for today I've suffered terribly in a
dream because of him."
20 The chief priests and the elders, however, persuaded the crowds to ask for Barabbas and to execute
Jesus. 21 The governor asked them, "Which of the two
do you want me to release for you?"
"Barabbas!" they answered.
22 Pilate asked them, "What should I do then with
Jesus, who is called Christ?"
They all answered, "Crucify him!"
23 Then he said, "Why? What has he done wrong?"
But they kept shouting all the more, "Crucify him!"
24 When Pilate saw that he was getting nowhere,
but that a riot was starting instead, he took some
water, washed his hands in front of the crowd, and
said, "I am innocent of this man's blood.[F] See to it
yourselves!"
25 All the people answered, "His blood be on us
and on our children!" 26 Then he released Barabbas
to them and, after having Jesus flogged, handed him
over to be crucified.

MOCKED BY THE MILITARY

27 Then the governor's soldiers took Jesus into the
governor's residence and gathered the whole company[G] around him. 28 They stripped him and dressed
him in a scarlet robe. 29 They twisted together a crown
of thorns, put it on his head, and placed a staff in
his right hand. And they knelt down before him and
mocked him: "Hail, king of the Jews!" 30 Then they
spat on him, took the staff, and kept hitting him on
the head. 31 After they had mocked him, they stripped
him of the robe, put his own clothes on him, and led
him away to crucify him.

CRUCIFIED BETWEEN TWO CRIMINALS

32 As they were going out, they found a Cyrenian
man named Simon. They forced him to carry his
cross. 33 When they came to a place called *Golgotha*
(which means Place of the Skull), 34 they gave him
wine[H] mixed with gall to drink. But when he tasted
it, he refused to drink it. 35 After crucifying him, they
divided his clothes by casting lots.[I] 36 Then they sat
down and were guarding him there. 37 Above his head
they put up the charge against him in writing: THIS
IS JESUS, THE KING OF THE JEWS.
38 Then two criminals[J] were crucified with him, one
on the right and one on the left. 39 Those who passed
by were yelling insults at[K] him, shaking their heads
40 and saying, "You who would destroy the temple
and rebuild it in three days, save yourself! If you are
the Son of God, come down from the cross!" 41 In the

[A] **27:2** Other mss read *Pontius Pilate* [B] **27:9** Or *I took* [C] **27:10** Some mss read *I gave* [D] **27:9–10** Jr 32:6–9; Zch 11:12–13 [E] **27:16** Other mss read *Jesus Barabbas*, also in v. 17 [F] **27:24** Other mss read *this righteous man's blood* [G] **27:27** Lit *cohort* [H] **27:34** Other mss read *sour wine* [I] **27:35** Other mss add *that what was spoken by the prophet might be fulfilled: "They divided my clothes among them, and for my clothing they cast lots."* [J] **27:38** Or *revolutionaries* [K] **27:39** Lit *passed by blasphemed*, or *were blaspheming*

same way the chief priests, with the scribes and elders,[A] mocked him and said, 42 "He saved others, but he cannot save himself! He is the King of Israel! Let him[B] come down now from the cross, and we will believe in him. 43 He trusts in God; let God rescue him now — if he takes pleasure in him![C] For he said, 'I am the Son of God.'" 44 In the same way even the criminals who were crucified with him taunted him.

THE DEATH OF JESUS

45 From noon until three in the afternoon,[D] darkness came over the whole land.[E] 46 About three in the afternoon Jesus cried out with a loud voice, *"Elí, Elí, lemá*[F] *sabachtháni?"* that is, **"My God, my God, why have you abandoned me?"**[G]

47 When some of those standing there heard this, they said, "He's calling for Elijah."

48 Immediately one of them ran and got a sponge, filled it with sour wine, put it on a stick, and offered him a drink. 49 But the rest said, "Let's see if Elijah comes to save him."

50 But Jesus cried out again with a loud voice and gave up his spirit. 51 Suddenly, the curtain of the sanctuary was torn in two from top to bottom, the earth quaked, and the rocks were split. 52 The tombs were also opened and many bodies of the saints who had fallen asleep were raised. 53 And they came out of the tombs after his resurrection, entered the holy city, and appeared to many.

54 When the centurion and those with him, who were keeping watch over Jesus, saw the earthquake and the things that had happened, they were terrified and said, "Truly this man was the Son of God!"

55 Many women who had followed Jesus from Galilee and looked after him were there, watching from a distance. 56 Among them were Mary Magdalene, Mary the mother of James and Joseph, and the mother of Zebedee's sons.

[A] **27:41** Other mss add *and Pharisees* [B] **27:42** Other mss read *If he . . . Israel, let him* [C] **27:43** Or *if he wants him* [D] **27:45** Lit *From the sixth hour to the ninth hour* [E] **27:45** Or *whole earth* [F] **27:46** Some mss read *lama*; other mss read *lima* [G] **27:46** Ps 22:1

Artist's rendering of the interior of Royal Stoa, which ran the length of the southern side of the Temple Mount. The Sanhedrin held court in the apse at the far end.

The Practice of Roman Crucifixion

by R. D. Fowler

HISTORY

The precursor to crucifixion was impalement. The Greek word translated as "cross" in the New Testament originally referred to a pointed wooden stake or pole firmly fixed in the ground. Walls of these stakes formed protective palisade fortifications around settlements. Eastern countries, particularly Assyria, developed the practice of publicly displaying the corpses or heads of criminals, traitors, and enemies on these walls as a means of humiliation and intimidation. This practice led to people using the stakes themselves as a means of torture and execution—by impaling offenders on the stake and leaving them to die.[1]

History does not indicate when impalement ceased and crucifixion began, but historians generally agree that crucifixion began among the Persians.[2] The Romans likely adopted it from the Carthaginians.[3] Many ancient texts refer to both impalement and crucifixion but often fail to distinguish between the two and provide little descriptive detail of crucifixion. The Greeks and Romans used crucifixion well before the time of Christ. Alexander the Great used it in the fourth century BC. As early as 250 BC, the Romans were crucifying those they considered deserving. The ancient Romans generally thought of crucifixion as "the slave's punishment." Over time, however, the Romans used it for slaves, thieves, insurgents, and enemies of the empire in general.

Assyrian relief from Nineveh's South-West Palace shows captives being impaled. The Assyrians impaled either under a person's rib cage or between his legs. The bodies were put on display as a deterrent to others and to emphasize the brutality of the Assyrian army.

People never considered crucifixion to be a Jewish form of punishment, yet Alexander Jannaeus, a Jewish high priest and king who crucified eight hundred Pharisees in one day, used it in the first century BC as an act of revenge for the Pharisees' rebellion against him. By the first century AD, Rome used crucifixion extensively in the pacification of Judea. Romans also used it throughout the empire as a means of maintaining order and suppressing insurrection. While crucifixion was primarily limited to noncitizens, Roman citizens were not totally free from its terrible shadow. In certain cases, particularly treason, Caesar would issue an edict allowing authorities to crucify even Roman citizens.

Crucifixion took place in public areas outside the city walls—where the bodies were clearly visible. Crucifixion thus punished offenders and intimidated one's enemies. Bodies on crosses were a common sight in the first century AD. The number of people crucified reached into the thousands. This excessive use, along with its barbaric nature and the religious idea of being cursed, made crucifixion particularly offensive to the Jews (see Dt 21:22–23).

Artist's renderings of first-century crucifixions. A Saint Anthony's cross is on the left and a Latin Cross on the right. The Saint Anthony's has a small wooden block seat.

METHOD

"Crucifixion was a punishment in which the caprice and sadism of the executioners was given full rein."[4] Scourging was the first brutal act related to crucifixion. Roman citizens, though, were exempt from this part of the punishment. The condemned person was stripped of clothing, tied to a post, and beaten with the dreaded Roman flagellum, a whip consisting of leather straps embedded with metal, bone, or rock. Scourging was designed to shred flesh, in some cases exposing both bones and internal organs. Roman law, unlike Jewish law, set no limits on the number of lashes a person could receive. The severity of the scourging was completely at the discretion of the person administering it. In some cases, the scourging caused death; in others, it expedited death. In most cases, though, the scourging merely increased the agony the condemned person experienced on the cross.

Following scourging, the condemned person was clothed and then forced to carry the horizontal beam to the crucifixion site.[5] Typically the Romans hung a sign around the criminal's neck, specifying his offense. Scripture does not mention Jesus wearing the sign Pilate made, though custom dictated that he likely did. At the crucifixion site, the person was again stripped of his clothing and placed on the cross. The sign was also placed on the cross.

Upon arrival at the site, the authorities would secure the person to the cross using ropes, nails—or both. We know Jesus was nailed to his cross; not discounting the theological significance, nothing suggests otherwise. At this point in the process, details vary about how the actual crucifixion took place. Some believe the person was secured to the cross as it lay on the ground; the entire cross was then lifted up and dropped into a hole prepared for it. Others suggest the vertical beam was already in the ground; soldiers attached the person to the horizontal beam and hoisted both up the vertical beam.

Although the Romans had no standard form for the crosses they used, at least four variations were prominent. The Latin cross, likely the form on which Jesus died, had a crossbeam that attached a little below the top of the vertical beam. The second form, a St. Anthony's cross, looked like a capital T. The third design, the Greek cross, had equal beams and looked like a plus sign. The fourth configuration, the St. Andrew's cross, looked like the letter X. The variation in crosses, the possibility that crosses could be reused, and the absence of specific details mean that the method of crucifixion could vary—depending on the circumstances and the type of cross. The Latin cross, the St. Anthony's cross, and the Greek cross each had a small wooden block or seat. This supported the body and prolonged death. Later, after the first century, a footrest was added. After death, bodies were, as a rule, left on the cross to be exposed to the elements and to decay. We know from Scripture this was not the case with Jesus.

This barbaric punishment method continued until the fourth century. Emperor Constantine abolished crucifixion during the later years of his reign. While many details are unclear, one detail is indisputable; crucifixion brought extreme suffering. The tremendous loss of blood, the excruciating pain from the nails, the stretched position, and the exposure to the elements all contributed to extreme suffering prior to death. ✜

Bust of Rome's Emperor Titus, who ruled AD 79–81. Before he became emperor of Rome, Titus distinguished himself as a military commander. One of his campaigns included sacking Jerusalem and crucifying thousands.

---

[1] See D. G. Burke, "Cross" in *ISBE* (1979), 825–26. [2] Burke, "Cross," 828. [3] Martin Hengel, *Crucifixion*, trans. John Bowden (Philadelphia: Fortress, 1977), 23. [4] Hengel, *Crucifixion*, 25. [5] Images often depict Jesus carrying the entire cross; however, the weight of both beams would have been close to three hundred pounds, making this highly unlikely. The cross beam itself was quite heavy; carrying it would have been difficult, especially for someone who had been scourged (see Mt 27:32).

THE BURIAL OF JESUS

57 When it was evening, a rich man from Arimathea named Joseph came, who himself had also become a disciple of Jesus. 58 He approached Pilate and asked for Jesus's body. Then Pilate ordered that it[A] be released. 59 So Joseph took the body, wrapped it in clean, fine linen, 60 and placed it in his new tomb, which he had cut into the rock. He left after rolling a great stone against the entrance of the tomb. 61 Mary Magdalene and the other Mary were seated there, facing the tomb.

THE CLOSELY GUARDED TOMB

62 The next day, which followed the preparation day, the chief priests and the Pharisees gathered before Pilate 63 and said, "Sir, we remember that while this deceiver was still alive he said, 'After three days I will rise again.' 64 So give orders that the tomb be made secure until the third day. Otherwise, his disciples may come, steal him, and tell the people, 'He has been raised from the dead,' and the last deception will be worse than the first."

65 "Take[B] guards," Pilate told them. "Go and make it as secure as you know how." 66 They went and secured the tomb by setting a seal on the stone and placing the guards.

RESURRECTION MORNING

28 After the Sabbath, as the first day of the week was dawning, Mary Magdalene and the other Mary went to view the tomb. 2 There was a violent earthquake, because an angel of the Lord descended from heaven and approached the tomb. He rolled back the stone and was sitting on it. 3 His appearance was like lightning, and his clothing was as white as snow. 4 The guards were so shaken by fear of him that they became like dead men.

5 The angel told the women, "Don't be afraid, because I know you are looking for Jesus who was crucified. 6 He is not here. For he has risen, just as he said. Come and see the place where he lay. 7 Then go quickly and tell his disciples, 'He has risen from the dead and indeed he is going ahead of you to Galilee; you will see him there.' Listen, I have told you."

8 So, departing quickly from the tomb with fear and great joy, they ran to tell his disciples the news. 9 Just then[C] Jesus met them and said, "Greetings!" They came up, took hold of his feet, and worshiped him. 10 Then Jesus told them, "Do not be afraid. Go and tell my brothers to leave for Galilee, and they will see me there."

THE SOLDIERS BRIBED TO LIE

11 As they were on their way, some of the guards came into the city and reported to the chief priests everything that had happened. 12 After the priests[D] had assembled with the elders and agreed on a plan, they gave the soldiers a large sum of money 13 and told them, "Say this, 'His disciples came during the night and stole him while we were sleeping.' 14 If this reaches the governor's ears, we will deal with[E] him and keep you out of trouble." 15 They took the money and did as they were instructed, and this story has been spread among Jewish people to this day.

THE GREAT COMMISSION

16 The eleven disciples traveled to Galilee, to the mountain where Jesus had directed them. 17 When they saw him, they worshiped,[F] but some doubted. 18 Jesus came near and said to them, "All authority has been given to me in heaven and on earth. 19 Go, therefore, and make disciples of[G] all nations, baptizing them in the name of the Father and of the Son and of the Holy Spirit, 20 teaching them to observe everything I have commanded you. And remember,[H] I am with you always,[I] to the end of the age."

[A] **27:58** Other mss read *that the body* [B] **27:65** Or *"You have* [C] **28:9** Other mss add *as they were on their way to tell the news to his disciples* [D] **28:12** Lit *After they* [E] **28:14** Lit *will persuade* [F] **28:17** Other mss add *him* [G] **28:19** Or *and disciple* [H] **28:20** Lit *see* [I] **28:20** Lit *all the days*

MARK

On the far side of the ravine, this part of the winding path that ran through Israel's Western Mountains was the old Jericho Road.

INTRODUCTION TO

MARK

Circumstances of Writing

The Gospel of Mark is anonymous. Eusebius, the early church historian, writing in AD 326, preserved the words of Papias, an early church father. Papias quoted "the elder," probably John, as saying that Mark recorded Peter's preaching about the things Jesus said and did, but not in order. Thus Mark was considered the author of this Gospel even in the first century.

The Mark who wrote this Gospel was John Mark, the son of a widow named Mary, in whose house the church in Jerusalem sometimes gathered (Ac 12:12–17) and where Jesus possibly ate the Last Supper with his disciples. Mark was the cousin of Barnabas (Col 4:10), and he accompanied Barnabas and Paul back to Antioch after their famine relief mission to Jerusalem (Ac 12:25). Mark next went with Barnabas and Paul on part of the first missionary journey as an assistant (13:5), but at Perga, Mark turned back (13:13).

When the apostle Peter wrote to the churches in Asia Minor shortly before his martyrdom, he sent greetings from Mark, whom he called "my son" (1Pt 5:13). Then shortly before his execution, Paul asked Timothy to "bring Mark with you, for he is useful to me in the ministry" (2Tm 4:11). After Paul's execution, Mark is said to have moved to Egypt, established churches, and served them in Alexandria (Eusebius, *Ecclesiastical History* 2:16). Some have suggested the young man in Mark 14:51–52 was Mark himself.

Background

According to the early church fathers, Mark wrote his Gospel in Rome just before or just after Peter's martyrdom. Further confirmation of the Roman origin of Mark's Gospel is found in Mark 15:21 where Mark noted that Simon, a Cyrenian who carried Jesus's cross, was the father of Alexander and Rufus, men apparently known to the believers in Rome.

Because Mark wrote primarily for Roman Gentiles, he explained Jewish customs, translated Aramaic words and phrases into Greek, used Latin terms rather than their Greek equivalents, and rarely quoted from the Old Testament. Most Bible scholars are convinced that Mark was the earliest Gospel and served as one of the sources for Matthew and Luke.

Contribution to the Bible

Many concepts of the Messiah existed in Jesus's day, and several individuals laid claim to the title. What Mark contributes is a clarification of the concept of Messiah and a redefining of the term. Peter's insightful confession at Caesarea Philippi in 8:29 became the turning point at which Jesus began to explain that the divine conception of the Messiah involved rejection, suffering, death, and then resurrection (8:31). Mark also shows us the human side of Jesus. In fact, more than the other Gospel writers, Mark emphasizes Jesus's human side and his emotions. Thus Mark gives us a strong picture of both the humanity and the divinity of Jesus.

Structure

Mark's Gospel begins with a prologue (1:1–13), which is then followed by three major sections. The first (1:14–8:21) tells of Jesus's Galilean ministry. There Jesus healed and cast out demons and worked miracles. The second section (8:22–10:52) is transitional. Jesus began his journey that would take him to Jerusalem. The final section (11:1–16:8) involves a week in Jerusalem. From the time Jesus entered the city, he was at odds with the religious leaders, who quickly brought about his execution. A brief appendix (16:9–20), recording some of Jesus's appearances, his commissioning of his disciples, and his ascension, is attached to the Gospel.

THE MESSIAH'S HERALD

1 The beginning of the gospel of Jesus Christ, the Son
of God.[A] 2 As it is written in Isaiah the prophet:[B]

See, I am sending my messenger ahead
of you;
he will prepare your way.[C,D]
3 **A voice of one crying out**
in the wilderness:
Prepare the way for the Lord;
make his paths straight![E]

4 John came baptizing[F] in the wilderness and proclaiming a baptism of repentance for the forgiveness of sins. 5 The whole Judean countryside and all
the people of Jerusalem were going out to him, and
they were baptized by him in the Jordan River, confessing their sins. 6 John wore a camel-hair garment
with a leather belt around his waist and ate locusts
and wild honey.

7 He proclaimed, "One who is more powerful than I
am is coming after me. I am not worthy to stoop down
and untie the strap of his sandals. 8 I baptize you with[G]
water, but he will baptize you with the Holy Spirit."

THE BAPTISM OF JESUS

9 In those days Jesus came from Nazareth in Galilee
and was baptized in the Jordan by John. 10 As soon
as he came up out of the water, he saw the heavens
being torn open and the Spirit descending on him
like a dove. 11 And a voice came from heaven: "You are
my beloved Son; with you I am well-pleased."

THE TEMPTATION OF JESUS

12 Immediately the Spirit drove him into the wilderness. 13 He was in the wilderness forty days, being
tempted by Satan. He was with the wild animals, and
the angels were serving him.

MINISTRY IN GALILEE

14 After John was arrested, Jesus went to Galilee, proclaiming the good news[H,I] of God: 15 "The time is fulfilled, and the kingdom of God has come near. Repent
and believe the good news!"

THE FIRST DISCIPLES

16 As he passed alongside the Sea of Galilee, he saw
Simon and Andrew, Simon's brother, casting a net
into the sea — for they were fishermen. 17 "Follow
me," Jesus told them, "and I will make you fish for[J]

[A] **1:1** Some mss omit *the Son of God* [B] **1:2** Other mss read *in the prophets* [C] **1:2** Other mss add *before you* [D] **1:2** Mal 3:1 [E] **1:3** Is 40:3 [F] **1:4** Or *John the Baptist came* [G] **1:8** Or *in* [H] **1:14** Other mss add *of the kingdom* [I] **1:14** Or *gospel* [J] **1:17** Or *you to become fishers of*

Marking the location where, according to tradition, Jesus was baptized, the Greek Orthodox Church of John the Baptist is located at Bethany Beyond the Jordan. Excavations in the area have unearthed the ruins of over twenty churches and baptismal pools dating from the Roman and Byzantine eras.

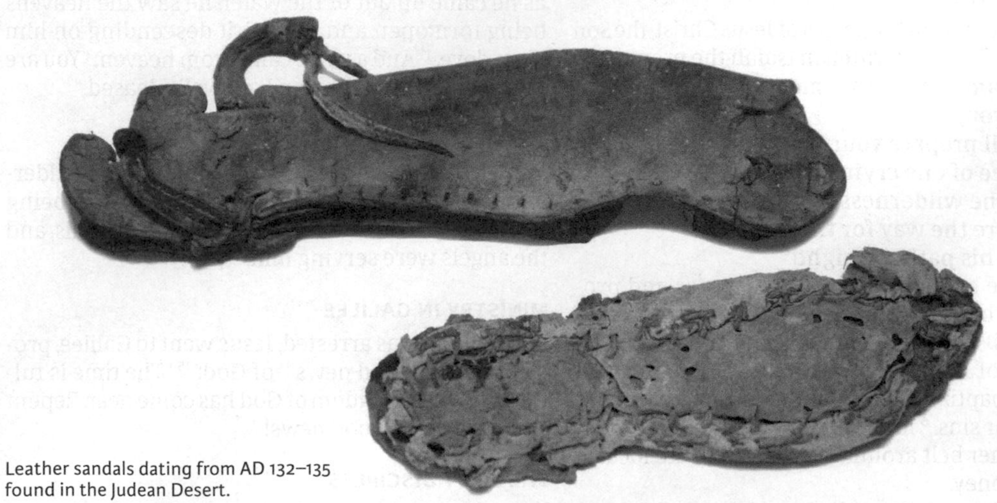

Leather sandals dating from AD 132–135 found in the Judean Desert.

people." [18] Immediately they left their nets and followed him. [19] Going on a little farther, he saw James the son of Zebedee and his brother John in a boat putting their nets in order. [20] Immediately he called them, and they left their father Zebedee in the boat with the hired men and followed him.

DRIVING OUT AN UNCLEAN SPIRIT

[21] They went into Capernaum, and right away he entered the synagogue on the Sabbath and began to teach. [22] They were astonished at his teaching because he was teaching them as one who had authority, and not like the scribes.

[23] Just then a man with an unclean spirit was in their synagogue. He cried out, [24] "What do you have to do with us, Jesus of Nazareth? Have you come to destroy us? I know who you are — the Holy One of God!"

[25] Jesus rebuked him saying, "Be silent, and come out of him!" [26] And the unclean spirit threw him into convulsions, shouted with a loud voice, and came out of him.

[27] They were all amazed, and so they began to ask each other, "What is this? A new teaching with authority![A] He commands even the unclean spirits, and they obey him." [28] At once the news about him spread throughout the entire vicinity of Galilee.

HEALINGS AT CAPERNAUM

[29] As soon as they left the synagogue, they went into Simon and Andrew's house with James and John. [30] Simon's mother-in-law was lying in bed with a fever, and they told him about her at once. [31] So he went to her, took her by the hand, and raised her up. The fever left her,[B] and she began to serve them.

[32] When evening came, after the sun had set, they brought to him all those who were sick and demon-possessed. [33] The whole town was assembled at the door, [34] and he healed many who were sick with various diseases and drove out many demons. And he would not permit the demons to speak, because they knew him.

PREACHING IN GALILEE

[35] Very early in the morning, while it was still dark, he got up, went out, and made his way to a deserted place; and there he was praying. [36] Simon and his companions searched for him, [37] and when they found him they said, "Everyone is looking for you."

[38] And he said to them, "Let's go on to the neighboring villages so that I may preach there too. This is why I have come."

A MAN CLEANSED

[39] He went into all of Galilee, preaching in their synagogues and driving out demons. [40] Then a man with leprosy[C] came to him and, on his knees,[D] begged him, "If you are willing, you can make me clean." [41] Moved with compassion,[E] Jesus reached out his hand and touched him. "I am willing," he told him. "Be made clean." [42] Immediately the leprosy left him, and he was made clean. [43] Then he sternly warned him and sent him away at once, [44] telling him, "See that you say nothing to anyone; but go and show yourself to the

[A] **1:27** Other mss read *"What is this? What is this new teaching? For with authority* [B] **1:31** Other mss add *at once* [C] **1:40** Gk *lepros*; a term for various skin diseases, also in v. 42; see Lv 13–14 [D] **1:40** Other mss omit *on his knees* [E] **1:41** Other mss *Moved with indignation*

priest, and offer what Moses commanded for your
cleansing, as a testimony to them."[A] 45 Yet he went
out and began to proclaim it widely and to spread
the news, with the result that Jesus could no longer
enter a town openly. But he was out in deserted places, and they came to him from everywhere.

THE SON OF MAN FORGIVES AND HEALS

2 When he entered Capernaum again after some
days, it was reported that he was at home. 2 So
many people gathered together that there was no
more room, not even in the doorway, and he was
speaking the word to them. 3 They came to him
bringing a paralytic, carried by four of them. 4 Since
they were not able to bring him to[B] Jesus because of
the crowd, they removed the roof above him, and
after digging through it, they lowered the mat on
which the paralytic was lying. 5 Seeing their faith,
Jesus told the paralytic, "Son, your sins are forgiven."

6 But some of the scribes were sitting there, questioning in their hearts: 7 "Why does he speak like
this? He's blaspheming! Who can forgive sins but
God alone?"

8 Right away Jesus perceived in his spirit that they
were thinking like this within themselves and said
to them, "Why are you thinking these things in your
hearts? 9 Which is easier: to say to the paralytic, 'Your
sins are forgiven,' or to say, 'Get up, take your mat,
and walk'? 10 But so that you may know that the Son
of Man has authority on earth to forgive sins" — he
told the paralytic — 11 "I tell you: get up, take your
mat, and go home."

12 Immediately he got up, took the mat, and went
out in front of everyone. As a result, they were all
astounded and gave glory to God, saying, "We have
never seen anything like this!"

THE CALL OF LEVI

13 Jesus went out again beside the sea. The whole
crowd was coming to him, and he was teaching them.
14 Then, passing by, he saw Levi the son of Alphaeus
sitting at the tax office, and he said to him, "Follow
me," and he got up and followed him.

15 While he was reclining at the table in Levi's
house, many tax collectors and sinners were eating[C]
with Jesus and his disciples, for there were many who
were following him. 16 When the scribes who were
Pharisees[D] saw that he was eating with sinners and
tax collectors, they asked his disciples, "Why does he
eat[E] with tax collectors and sinners?"

17 When Jesus heard this, he told them, "It is not
those who are well who need a doctor, but those
who are sick. I didn't come to call the righteous, but
sinners."

A QUESTION ABOUT FASTING

18 Now John's disciples and the Pharisees[F] were fasting. People came and asked him, "Why do John's
disciples and the Pharisees' disciples fast, but your
disciples do not fast?"

19 Jesus said to them, "The wedding guests cannot
fast while the groom is with them, can they? As long
as they have the groom with them, they cannot fast.
20 But the time[G] will come when the groom will be
taken away from them, and then they will fast on
that day. 21 No one sews a patch of unshrunk cloth
on an old garment. Otherwise, the new patch pulls
away from the old cloth, and a worse tear is made.
22 And no one puts new wine into old wineskins. Otherwise, the wine will burst the skins, and the wine
is lost as well as the skins. No, new wine is put into
fresh wineskins."

LORD OF THE SABBATH

23 On the Sabbath he was going through the grainfields, and his disciples began to make their way,
picking some heads of grain. 24 The Pharisees said
to him, "Look, why are they doing what is not lawful
on the Sabbath?"

25 He said to them, "Have you never read what David and those who were with him did when he was in
need and hungry — 26 how he entered the house of
God in the time of Abiathar the high priest and ate the
bread of the Presence — which is not lawful for anyone to eat except the priests — and also gave some to
his companions?" 27 Then he told them, "The Sabbath
was made for[H] man and not man for the Sabbath. 28 So
then, the Son of Man is Lord even of the Sabbath."

3 Jesus entered the synagogue again, and a man
was there who had a shriveled hand. 2 In order
to accuse him, they were watching him closely to see
whether he would heal him on the Sabbath. 3 He told
the man with the shriveled hand, "Stand before us."
4 Then he said to them, "Is it lawful to do good on the
Sabbath or to do evil, to save life or to kill?" But they
were silent. 5 After looking around at them with anger, he was grieved at the hardness of their hearts and
told the man, "Stretch out your hand." So he stretched
it out, and his hand was restored. 6 Immediately the
Pharisees went out and started plotting with the Herodians against him, how they might kill him.

MINISTERING TO THE MULTITUDE

7 Jesus departed with his disciples to the sea, and a
large crowd followed from Galilee, and a large crowd

[A] **1:44** Or *against them* [B] **2:4** Other mss read *able to get near* [C] **2:15** Lit *reclining together* [D] **2:16** Other mss read *scribes and Pharisees* [E] **2:16** Other mss add *and drink* [F] **2:18** Other mss read *The disciples of John and of the Pharisees* [G] **2:20** Or *the days* [H] **2:27** Or *because of*

Using a method that dates back centuries, this Iraqi stone house has a roof constructed of wooden poles that have been covered over with thatch and compacted mud.

DESIGN

Houses in the first century were designed and built with the most simple of details. Workers used tools such as the handsaw, adze (stone chisel), bow drill, hammer, and mallet. Many homes today are still built with similar construction methods in rural locations in Third World nations where the poor have few options. First-century house design used the basic square or rectangular shape with a short span across the narrowest width. This span was accomplished using wood beams set upon load-bearing dried mud-brick walls or locally mined and cut stone.

The roof composition was constructed with dried wood poles, thatch, or tiles that spanned perpendicular to the thicker, wood-beam supports. The same wood beams served as lintels above some of the wall features, such as doors. The roof surface was a layered composition of dried, compacted mud covered with brick paver or flat stone, which was typically a durable and impervious surface. Most ancient houses had an outside stairway that led to a flat roof area, which people used for various domestic activities, such as drying fruit or sleeping on hot nights or when the owner needed an outside work space or simply an area of repose. The roof area would sometimes adjoin other houses, depending on the spatial density of the building layout area and whether this was a rural or urban house. This enabled neighbors to share a common wall, which meant less labor and expense than building four walls, as was required in a freestanding house. Interestingly, each Israelite house typically had a parapet to keep a nonowner from falling off and creating a "blood guiltiness" condition (Dt 22:8). This practical safety feature is still used on modern flat roofs and balconies as required by local building codes.

A prodigious amount of archaeological excavations have exposed many stonewall foundations. The foundations reveal that most small, common houses were approximately fifteen by fifteen feet, although some may have been about thirty by thirty.[1] The floor plan consisted of two to four rooms with at least one larger area for sleeping and another

After the third Jewish revolt against the Romans, known as the Bar Kokhba revolt (AD 132–136), the Jews were not allowed to live in Jerusalem. Many of them thus settled in the region north of the Sea of Galilee. One such community was at Yehudiya, which dates to about AD 200–400. During the Ottoman period, many Arabs, using stones and materials they found on the site, resettled here and built these structures on top of the centuries-old foundations and footprints of the earlier structures. These remains thus give a good impression of what an early Jewish village would have looked like.

to accommodate cooking. Some houses had livestock stabling inside the house, for use during the cold winter months. The door would be the only entrance; small windows helped with air circulation or smoke exhaust. The floors were compacted dirt covered with straw or loose gravel. More affluent houses had marble floors or at least a plaster surface.

Most houses were modestly furnished, usually with a table and chairs. People slept on pallets on the floor. Essential supplies included cooking pots, an oven, plates, lamps, and storage jars known as amphora. Of course, the more affluent owners' homes had vases, beds, and furniture for reclining. Excavations reveal that many houses depended on cisterns for water.

TYPES OF HOUSES

In the New Testament era, house construction reflected the owner's financial resources. Small houses were more numerous and built of austere means. Many times, these smaller houses were clustered around a shared courtyard, especially in areas where a city's population density restricted expansion. The courtyard served as an entertainment and outdoor cooking center that neighbors shared.

Meanwhile, the wealthy would build large, spacious, and palatial houses that usually occupied the hillside areas of cities. In Jerusalem, the affluent neighborhood was known as the upper city in contrast with the lower city (or the Tyropoeon Valley) separated by the Herodian Wall.[2] These affluent houses would be multilevel structures with large and open spaces, many of which were used for sleeping. The larger homes also had additional living areas designated for entertaining. Some rooms were designated as work areas for the servants, who had their own separate sleeping quarters. Interior finishes include exposed cedar beams from Lebanon and marble from Greece or Italy. The wealthy were not only Jewish aristocracy but also foreign ambassadors and, of course, the Romans—both government and military. ✣

---

[1] John S. Holladay Jr., "House, Israelite" in *ABD*, 3:314–16. [2] Marsha A. Ellis Smith, ed., *Holman Book of Biblical Charts, Maps, and Reconstructions* (Nashville: Broadman & Holman, 1993), 158–59.

followed from Judea, 8 Jerusalem, Idumea, beyond the
Jordan, and around Tyre and Sidon. The large crowd
came to him because they heard about everything
he was doing. 9 Then he told his disciples to have a
small boat ready for him, so that the crowd wouldn't
crush him. 10 Since he had healed many, all who had
diseases were pressing toward him to touch him.
11 Whenever the unclean spirits saw him, they fell
down before him and cried out, "You are the Son of
God!" 12 And he would strongly warn them not to
make him known.

THE TWELVE APOSTLES

13 Jesus went up the mountain and summoned those
he wanted, and they came to him. 14 He appointed
twelve, whom he also named apostles,[A] to be with
him, to send them out to preach, 15 and to have authority to[B] drive out demons. 16 He appointed the
Twelve:[C] To Simon, he gave the name Peter; 17 and to
James the son of Zebedee, and to his brother John,
he gave the name "Boanerges" (that is, "Sons of Thunder"); 18 Andrew; Philip and Bartholomew; Matthew
and Thomas; James the son of Alphaeus, and Thaddaeus; Simon the Zealot, 19 and Judas Iscariot, who
also betrayed him.

A HOUSE DIVIDED

20 Jesus entered a house, and the crowd gathered
again so that they were not even able to eat.[D] 21 When
his family heard this, they set out to restrain him,
because they said, "He's out of his mind."

22 The scribes who had come down from Jerusalem
said, "He is possessed by Beelzebul," and, "He drives
out demons by the ruler of the demons."

23 So he summoned them and spoke to them in
parables: "How can Satan drive out Satan? 24 If a
kingdom is divided against itself, that kingdom cannot stand. 25 If a house is divided against itself, that
house cannot stand. 26 And if Satan opposes himself
and is divided, he cannot stand but is finished. 27 But
no one can enter a strong man's house and plunder
his possessions unless he first ties up the strong
man. Then he can plunder his house.

28 "Truly I tell you, people will be forgiven for all
sins and whatever blasphemies they utter. 29 But
whoever blasphemes against the Holy Spirit never
has forgiveness, but is guilty of an eternal sin"[E] —

[A] **3:14** Other mss omit *he also named them apostles* [B] **3:15** Other mss add *heal diseases, and to* [C] **3:16** Other mss omit *He appointed the Twelve* [D] **3:20** Or *eat a meal*; lit *eat bread* [E] **3:29** Other mss read *is subject to eternal judgment*

Remains of one of the oldest ancient synagogues in Israel, located in Shiloh.

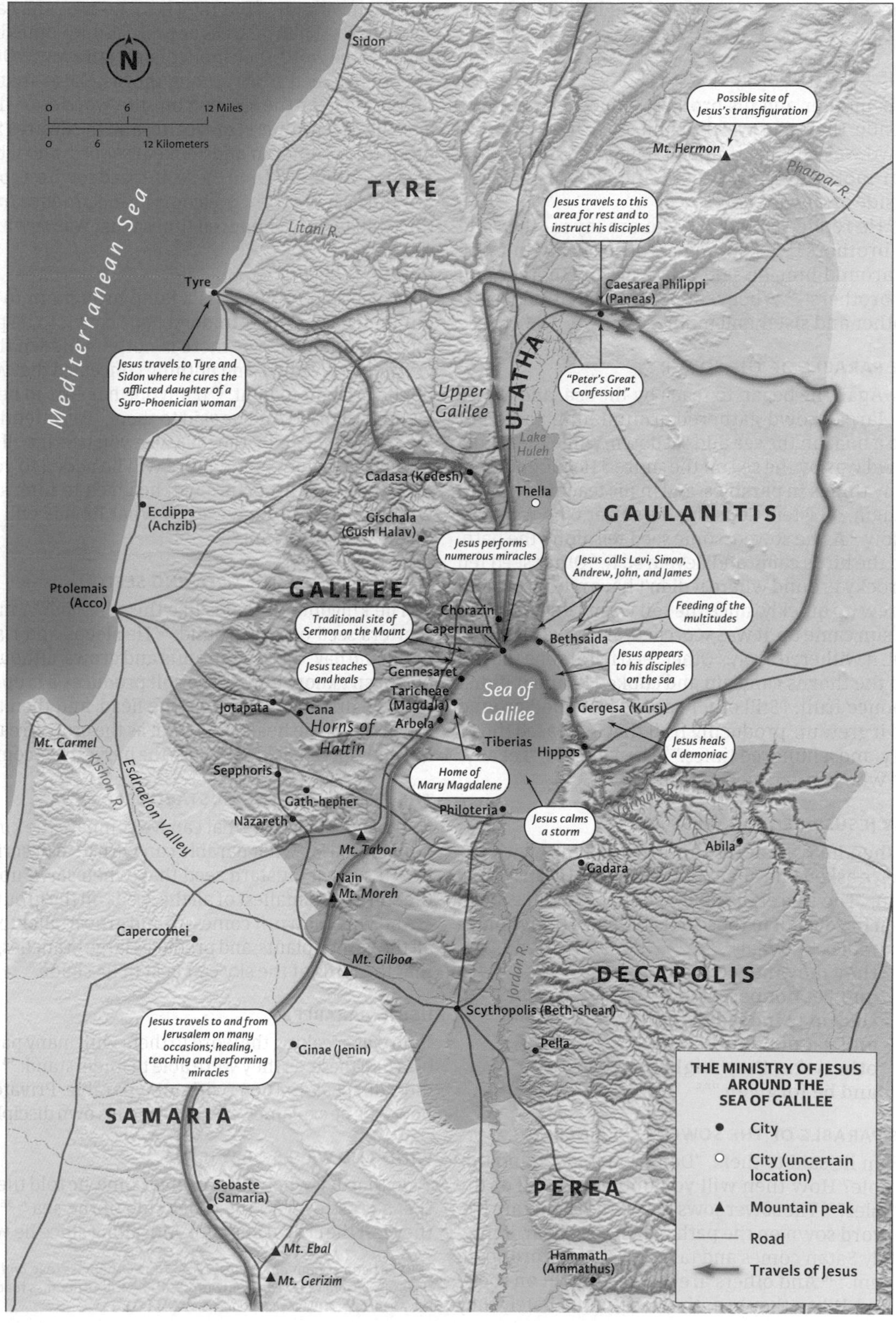
THE MINISTRY OF JESUS AROUND THE SEA OF GALILEE
City
City (uncertain location)
Mountain peak
Road
Travels of Jesus
0 6 12 Miles
0 6 12 Kilometers
Mediterranean Sea
Sidon
TYRE
Litani R.
Tyre
Possible site of Jesus's transfiguration
Mt. Hermon
Pharpar R.
Jesus travels to this area for rest and to instruct his disciples
Caesarea Philippi (Paneas)
Jesus travels to Tyre and Sidon where he cures the afflicted daughter of a Syro-Phoenician woman
"Peter's Great Confession"
Upper Galilee
ULATHA
Lake Huleh
Cadasa (Kedesh)
Thella
GAULANITIS
Ecdippa (Achzib)
Gischala (Gush Halav)
Jesus performs numerous miracles
Jesus calls Levi, Simon, Andrew, John, and James
Ptolemais (Acco)
GALILEE
Chorazin
Feeding of the multitudes
Traditional site of Sermon on the Mount
Capernaum
Bethsaida
Jesus appears to his disciples on the sea
Jesus teaches and heals
Gennesaret
Taricheae (Magdala)
Sea of Galilee
Jotapata
Cana
Gergesa (Kursi)
Horns of Hattin
Arbela
Mt. Carmel
Tiberias
Hippos
Jesus heals a demoniac
Kishon R.
Esdraelon Valley
Sepphoris
Home of Mary Magdalene
Gath-hepher
Yarmuk R.
Nazareth
Philoteria
Jesus calms a storm
Mt. Tabor
Abila
Gadara
Nain
Mt. Moreh
Capercotnei
Mt. Gilboa
Jordan R.
DECAPOLIS
Scythopolis (Beth-shean)
Jesus travels to and from Jerusalem on many occasions; healing, teaching and performing miracles
Ginae (Jenin)
Pella
SAMARIA
Sebaste (Samaria)
PEREA
Mt. Ebal
Hammath (Ammathus)
Mt. Gerizim

30 because they were saying, "He has an unclean spirit."

TRUE RELATIONSHIPS

31 His mother and his brothers came, and standing outside, they sent word to him and called him. 32 A crowd was sitting around him and told him, "Look, your mother, your brothers, and your sisters[A] are outside asking for you."

33 He replied to them, "Who are my mother and my brothers?" 34 Looking at those sitting in a circle around him, he said, "Here are my mother and my brothers! 35 Whoever does the will of God is my brother and sister and mother."

THE PARABLE OF THE SOWER

4 Again he began to teach by the sea, and a very large crowd gathered around him. So he got into a boat on the sea and sat down, while the whole crowd was by the sea on the shore. 2 He taught them many things in parables, and in his teaching he said to them, 3 "Listen! Consider the sower who went out to sow. 4 As he sowed, some seed fell along the path, and the birds came and devoured it. 5 Other seed fell on rocky ground where it didn't have much soil, and it grew up quickly, since the soil wasn't deep. 6 When the sun came up, it was scorched, and since it had no root, it withered away. 7 Other seed fell among thorns, and the thorns came up and choked it, and it didn't produce fruit. 8 Still other seed fell on good ground and it grew up, producing fruit that increased thirty, sixty, and a hundred times." 9 Then he said, "Let anyone who has ears to hear listen."

WHY JESUS USED PARABLES

10 When he was alone, those around him with the Twelve asked him about the parables. 11 He answered them, "The secret of the kingdom of God has been given to you, but to those outside, everything comes in parables 12 so that

they may indeed look,
and yet not perceive;
they may indeed listen,
and yet not understand;
otherwise, they might turn back
and be forgiven."[B,C]

THE PARABLE OF THE SOWER EXPLAINED

13 Then he said to them, "Don't you understand this parable? How then will you understand all of the parables? 14 The sower sows the word. 15 Some are like the word sown on the path. When they hear, immediately Satan comes and takes away the word sown in them.[D] 16 And others are like seed sown on rocky ground. When they hear the word, immediately they receive it with joy. 17 But they have no root; they are short-lived. When distress or persecution comes because of the word, they immediately fall away. 18 Others are like seed sown among thorns; these are the ones who hear the word, 19 but the worries of this age, the deceitfulness[E] of wealth, and the desires for other things enter in and choke the word, and it becomes unfruitful. 20 And those like seed sown on good ground hear the word, welcome it, and produce fruit thirty, sixty, and a hundred times what was sown."

USING YOUR LIGHT

21 He also said to them, "Is a lamp brought in to be put under a basket or under a bed? Isn't it to be put on a lampstand? 22 For there is nothing hidden that will not be revealed, and nothing concealed that will not be brought to light. 23 If anyone has ears to hear, let him listen." 24 And he said to them, "Pay attention to what you hear. By the measure you use, it will be measured to you — and more will be added to you. 25 For whoever has, more will be given to him, and whoever does not have, even what he has will be taken away from him."

THE PARABLE OF THE GROWING SEED

26 "The kingdom of God is like this," he said. "A man scatters seed on the ground. 27 He sleeps and rises night and day; the seed sprouts and grows, although he doesn't know how. 28 The soil produces a crop by itself — first the blade, then the head, and then the full grain on the head. 29 As soon as the crop is ready, he sends for the sickle, because the harvest has come."

THE PARABLE OF THE MUSTARD SEED

30 And he said, "With what can we compare the kingdom of God, or what parable can we use to describe it? 31 It's like a mustard seed that, when sown upon the soil, is the smallest of all the seeds on the ground. 32 And when sown, it comes up and grows taller than all the garden plants, and produces large branches, so that the birds of the sky can nest in its shade."

USING PARABLES

33 He was speaking the word to them with many parables like these, as they were able to understand. 34 He did not speak to them without a parable. Privately, however, he explained everything to his own disciples.

WIND AND WAVES OBEY JESUS

35 On that day, when evening had come, he told them, "Let's cross over to the other side of the sea." 36 So they left the crowd and took him along since he was

[A] **3:32** Other mss omit *and your sisters* [B] **4:12** Other mss read *and their sins be forgiven them* [C] **4:12** Is 6:9–10 [D] **4:15** Other mss read *in their hearts* [E] **4:19** Or *seduction*

in the boat. And other boats were with him. 37 A great
windstorm arose, and the waves were breaking over
the boat, so that the boat was already being swamped.
38 He was in the stern, sleeping on the cushion. So
they woke him up and said to him, "Teacher! Don't
you care that we're going to die?"

39 He got up, rebuked the wind, and said to the sea,
"Silence! Be still!" The wind ceased, and there was a
great calm. 40 Then he said to them, "Why are you
afraid? Do you still have no faith?"

41 And they were terrified[A] and asked one another,
"Who then is this? Even the wind and the sea obey
him!"

DEMONS DRIVEN OUT BY JESUS

5 They came to the other side of the sea, to the
region of the Gerasenes.[B] 2 As soon as he got out
of the boat, a man with an unclean spirit came out of
the tombs and met him. 3 He lived in the tombs, and
no one was able to restrain him anymore — not even
with a chain — 4 because he often had been bound
with shackles and chains, but had torn the chains
apart and smashed the shackles. No one was strong
enough to subdue him. 5 Night and day among the
tombs and on the mountains, he was always crying
out and cutting himself with stones.

6 When he saw Jesus from a distance, he ran and
knelt down before him. 7 And he cried out with a loud
voice, "What do you have to do with me, Jesus, Son
of the Most High God? I beg you before God, don't
torment me!" 8 For he had told him, "Come out of the
man, you unclean spirit!"

9 "What is your name?" he asked him.

"My name is Legion," he answered him, "because
we are many." 10 And he begged him earnestly not to
send them out of the region.

11 A large herd of pigs was there, feeding on the
hillside. 12 The demons[C] begged him, "Send us to the
pigs, so that we may enter them." 13 So he gave them
permission, and the unclean spirits came out and entered the pigs. The herd of about two thousand rushed
down the steep bank into the sea and drowned there.

14 The men who tended them ran off and reported
it in the town and the countryside, and people went
to see what had happened. 15 They came to Jesus and
saw the man who had been demon-possessed, sitting
there, dressed and in his right mind; and they were
afraid. 16 Those who had seen it described to them
what had happened to the demon-possessed man

[A] **4:41** Or *were filled with awe* [B] **5:1** Some mss read *Gadarenes*; other mss read *Gergesenes* [C] **5:12** Other mss read *All the demons*

The slope of the hill from Gergesa into the Sea of Galilee; many believe this is where Jesus cast the demons into the pigs.

and told about the pigs. 17 Then they began to beg him to leave their region.

18 As he was getting into the boat, the man who had been demon-possessed begged him earnestly that he might remain with him. 19 Jesus did not let him but told him, "Go home to your own people, and report to them how much the Lord has done for you and how he has had mercy on you." 20 So he went out and began to proclaim in the Decapolis how much Jesus had done for him, and they were all amazed.

A GIRL RESTORED AND A WOMAN HEALED

21 When Jesus had crossed over again by boat[A] to the other side, a large crowd gathered around him while he was by the sea. 22 One of the synagogue leaders, named Jairus, came, and when he saw Jesus, he fell at his feet 23 and begged him earnestly, "My little daughter is dying. Come and lay your hands on her so that she can get well[B] and live." 24 So Jesus went with him, and a large crowd was following and pressing against him.

25 Now a woman suffering from bleeding for twelve years 26 had endured much under many doctors. She had spent everything she had and was not helped at all. On the contrary, she became worse. 27 Having heard about Jesus, she came up behind him in the crowd and touched his clothing. 28 For she said, "If I just touch his clothes, I'll be made well." 29 Instantly her flow of blood ceased, and she sensed in her body that she was healed of her affliction.

30 Immediately Jesus realized that power had gone out from him. He turned around in the crowd and said, "Who touched my clothes?"

31 His disciples said to him, "You see the crowd pressing against you, and yet you say, 'Who touched me?'"

32 But he was looking around to see who had done this. 33 The woman, with fear and trembling, knowing what had happened to her, came and fell down before him, and told him the whole truth. 34 "Daughter," he said to her, "your faith has saved you. Go in peace and be healed from your affliction."

35 While he was still speaking, people came from the synagogue leader's house and said, "Your daughter is dead. Why bother the teacher anymore?"

36 When Jesus overheard[C] what was said, he told the synagogue leader, "Don't be afraid. Only believe." 37 He did not let anyone accompany him except Peter, James, and John, James's brother. 38 They came to the leader's house, and he saw a commotion — people weeping and wailing loudly. 39 He went in and said to them, "Why are you making a commotion and weeping? The child is not dead but asleep." 40 They laughed at him, but he put them all outside. He took the child's father, mother, and those who were with him, and entered the place where the child was. 41 Then he took the child by the hand and said to her, "*Talitha koum*"[D] (which is translated, "Little girl, I say to you, get up"). 42 Immediately the girl got up and began to walk. (She was twelve years old.) At this they were utterly astounded. 43 Then he gave them strict orders that no one should know about this and told them to give her something to eat.

REJECTION AT NAZARETH

6 He left there and came to his hometown, and his disciples followed him. 2 When the Sabbath came, he began to teach in the synagogue, and many who heard him were astonished. "Where did this man get these things?" they said. "What is this wisdom that has been given to him, and how are these miracles performed by his hands? 3 Isn't this the carpenter, the son of Mary, and the brother of James, Joses, Judas, and Simon? And aren't his sisters here with us?" So they were offended by him.

4 Jesus said to them, "A prophet is not without honor except in his hometown, among his relatives, and in his household." 5 He was not able to do a miracle there, except that he laid his hands on a few sick people and healed them. 6 And he was amazed at their unbelief. He was going around the villages teaching.

COMMISSIONING THE TWELVE

7 He summoned the Twelve and began to send them out in pairs and gave them authority over unclean spirits. 8 He instructed them to take nothing for the road except a staff — no bread, no traveling bag, no money in their belts, 9 but to wear sandals and not put on an extra shirt. 10 He said to them, "Whenever you enter a house, stay there until you leave that place. 11 If any place does not welcome you or listen to you, when you leave there, shake the dust off your feet as a testimony against them."[E] 12 So they went out and preached that people should repent. 13 They drove out many demons, anointed many sick people with oil and healed them.

JOHN THE BAPTIST BEHEADED

14 King Herod heard about it, because Jesus's name had become well known. Some[F] said, "John the Baptist has been raised from the dead, and that's why miraculous powers are at work in him." 15 But others said, "He's Elijah." Still others said, "He's a prophet, like one of the prophets from long ago."

16 When Herod heard of it, he said, "John, the one I beheaded, has been raised!"

[A] **5:21** Other mss omit *by boat* [B] **5:23** Or *she might be saved* [C] **5:36** Or *ignored* [D] **5:41** An Aramaic expression [E] **6:11** Other mss add *Truly I tell you, it will be more tolerable for Sodom or Gomorrah on judgment day than for that town.* [F] **6:14** Other mss read *He*

[17] For Herod himself had given orders to arrest John
and to chain him in prison on account of Herodias,
his brother Philip's wife, because he had married
her. [18] John had been telling Herod, "It is not lawful
for you to have your brother's wife." [19] So Herodias
held a grudge against him and wanted to kill him.
But she could not, [20] because Herod feared John and
protected him, knowing he was a righteous and holy
man. When Herod heard him he would be very perplexed,[A] and yet he liked to listen to him.

[21] An opportune time came on his birthday, when
Herod gave a banquet for his nobles, military commanders, and the leading men of Galilee. [22] When
Herodias's own daughter[B] came in and danced, she
pleased Herod and his guests. The king said to the girl,
"Ask me whatever you want, and I'll give it to you."
[23] He promised her with an oath: "Whatever you ask
me I will give you, up to half my kingdom."

[24] She went out and said to her mother, "What
should I ask for?"

"John the Baptist's head," she said.

[25] At once she hurried to the king and said, "I want
you to give me John the Baptist's head on a platter
immediately." [26] Although the king was deeply distressed, because of his oaths and the guests[C] he did
not want to refuse her. [27] The king immediately sent
for an executioner and commanded him to bring
John's head. So he went and beheaded him in prison,
[28] brought his head on a platter, and gave it to the girl.
Then the girl gave it to her mother. [29] When John's
disciples heard about it, they came and removed his
corpse and placed it in a tomb.

FEEDING OF THE FIVE THOUSAND

[30] The apostles gathered around Jesus and reported
to him all that they had done and taught. [31] He said to
them, "Come away by yourselves to a remote place
and rest for a while." For many people were coming
and going, and they did not even have time to eat.

[32] So they went away in the boat by themselves to
a remote place, [33] but many saw them leaving and
recognized them, and they ran on foot from all the
towns and arrived ahead of them.[D]

[34] When he went ashore, he saw a large crowd and
had compassion on them, because they were like
sheep without a shepherd. Then he began to teach
them many things.

[A] **6:20** Other mss read *When he heard him, he did many things*
[B] **6:22** Other mss read *When his daughter Herodias*
[C] **6:26** Lit *and those reclining at the table*
[D] **6:33** Other mss add *and gathered around him*

Sheep and shepherd at Carmel.

Machaerus, Herod, and John the Baptist

by David E. Lanier

Herod built his fortress palace at Machaerus, overlooking the Dead Sea (in background). Covering 43,000 square feet, the palace sat atop the hill to the left and was detailed with colonnades, courtyards, and mosaics.

The name Machaerus ("black fortress," today preserved in the locally used name *Mukawir*) does not appear in Scripture. Alexander Jannaeus, the Maccabean king (103–76 BC), originally built the fortress, which was destroyed by Roman forces in 57 BC. It lay in waste until Herod the Great, a friend of the Romans, rebuilt and fortified the site. Machaerus stood at the southern frontier of the region of Perea and was Herod's first line of defense against attacks from Arabia. The fortress overlooked the gorge of Callirrhoe, east of the Dead Sea. Standing 3,860 feet above the Dead Sea and 2,546 feet above the Mediterranean, the site was extremely defensible. At a mere eighteen miles southeast of the mouth of the Jordan, it was accessible to Herod and his friends.[1] When Herod died (4 BC), his son Herod Antipas inherited the fortress. The ancient Jewish historian Josephus identifies Machaerus as the place where Herod had John the Baptist brought in order to behead him.[2]

At the death of Herod Agrippa I in AD 44, the fortress reverted to Roman control until the First Jewish Revolt in AD 66. The Romans abandoned it to the rebels, who held out until AD 72, when Rome's General Lucilius Bassus besieged and destroyed it. Josephus describes the site at the time of its siege and destruction by the Tenth Legion: "The nature of the place was very capable of affording the surest hopes of safety to those that possessed it, as well as delay and fear to those that should attack it."[3]

According to Josephus, even inside the walls was a rocky hill that was so high it could be taken only with the utmost difficulty. The fortress was surrounded with ditches that were frighteningly deep and could not be filled with dirt. The western valley extended to the Dead Sea. Machaerus occupied the commanding position on the other side of this natural defile. On the east, the valley was about 150 feet deep and extended to the foot of a mountain. To the north were defensive valleys also, not as deep, but still impracticable to cross.[4]

Josephus relates that when Herod the Great rebuilt the site, he surrounded a large area with walls and towers. He constructed a city for the convenience of the defenders, with a road that led to the top of the highest mountain. He added a second defensive wall around the top of the mountain with towers at the corners, about 240 feet high. In the middle of that enclosed area stood a magnificent palace. The site had many reservoirs for the collection of water to enable the fortress to withstand a protracted siege, and the citadel was stocked with large quantities of darts and instruments of war.[5] In addition to the military strength of the site, the springs at Callirrhoe were known for their medicinal properties. Hot and

Reconstructed Roman ballista. Each legion of the Roman army was equipped with ten ballistae, used to propel stone missiles into enemy territory. The ballista could hurl stones weighing up to fifty pounds over one thousand feet, which were extremely effective in breaking through stone fortification walls.

cold mineral springs were considered beneficial for strengthening the nerves, and a plant called rue grew there in abundance, thought to counteract the negative effects of demons.[6]

Archaeological excavations have confirmed many of Josephus's descriptions of both the upper and the lower cities, including protective walls and towers at the base of Machaerus and at the rim of the citadel at the top.[7] ✣

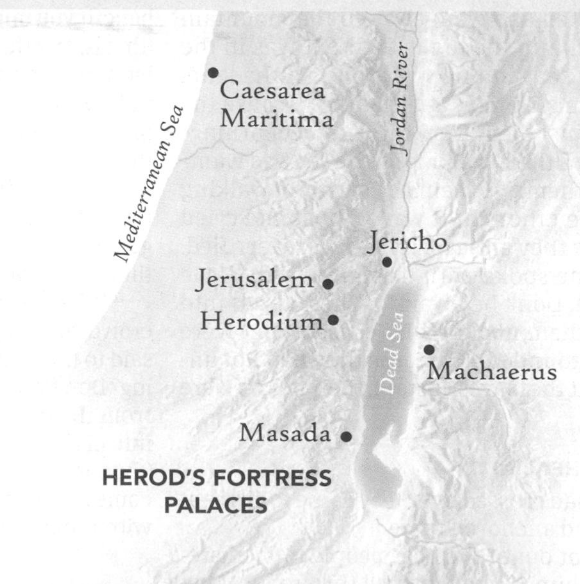

---

[1] Merrill Unger, "Machae'rus" in *The New Unger's Bible Dictionary*, ed. R. K. Harrison, rev. ed. (Chicago: Moody, 1988), 796. [2] Josephus, *Jewish Antiquities* 18.5.2. See Mt 4:12; 14:6–12; Mk 6:16–29; Lk 3:19–20. [3] Josephus, *Jewish War* 7.6.1. [4] Josephus, *Jewish War* 7.6.1. [5] Josephus, *Jewish War* 7.6.2. This may have been the site of Antipas's birthday banquet (Mk 6). Or it may have been held in Galilee, as many nobles from that area were invited. If that were the case, it would have taken some time to retrieve John's head and bring it back. Either way, the head would have been delivered after the banquet had ended. If the nobles were enjoying an extended stay at the palace, it would have taken little time (see Mk 6). See Harold W. Hoehner, *Herod Antipas* (Cambridge: Cambridge University Press, 1972), 146–49. [6] Josephus, *Jewish War* 7.6.3. [7] Stanislao Loffreda, "Machaerus" in *ABD*, 4:457; Josephus, *Jewish War* 7.6.2. Shimon Gibson, *The Cave of John the Baptist* (New York: Doubleday, 2004), 246.

35 When it grew late, his disciples approached him
and said, "This place is deserted, and it is already late.
36 Send them away so that they can go into the surrounding countryside and villages to buy themselves
something to eat."

37 "You give them something to eat," he responded.

They said to him, "Should we go and buy two hundred denarii[A] worth of bread and give them something to eat?"

38 He asked them, "How many loaves do you have?
Go and see."

When they found out they said, "Five, and two
fish." 39 Then he instructed them to have all the people sit down in groups on the green grass. 40 So they
sat down in groups of hundreds and fifties. 41 He
took the five loaves and the two fish, and looking
up to heaven, he blessed and broke the loaves. He
kept giving them to his disciples to set before the
people. He also divided the two fish among them
all. 42 Everyone ate and was satisfied. 43 They picked
up twelve baskets full of pieces of bread and fish.
44 Now those who had eaten the loaves were five
thousand men.

WALKING ON THE WATER

45 Immediately he made his disciples get into the
boat and go ahead of him to the other side, to Bethsaida, while he dismissed the crowd. 46 After he said
good-bye to them, he went away to the mountain
to pray. 47 Well into the night, the boat was in the
middle of the sea, and he was alone on the land.
48 He saw them straining at the oars,[B] because the
wind was against them. Very early in the morning[C]
he came toward them walking on the sea and wanted to pass by them. 49 When they saw him walking
on the sea, they thought it was a ghost and cried
out, 50 because they all saw him and were terrified.
Immediately he spoke with them and said, "Have
courage! It is I. Don't be afraid." 51 Then he got into
the boat with them, and the wind ceased. They were
completely astounded, 52 because they had not understood about the loaves. Instead, their hearts were
hardened.

MIRACULOUS HEALINGS

53 When they had crossed over, they came to shore at
Gennesaret and anchored there.

54 As they got out of the boat, people immediately recognized him. 55 They hurried throughout that
region and began to carry the sick on mats to wherever they heard he was. 56 Wherever he went, into
villages, towns, or the country, they laid the sick in
the marketplaces and begged him that they might
touch just the end of his robe. And everyone who
touched it was healed.

THE TRADITIONS OF THE ELDERS

7 The Pharisees and some of the scribes who had
come from Jerusalem gathered around him.
2 They observed that some of his disciples were eating
bread with unclean — that is, unwashed — hands.
3 (For the Pharisees and all the Jews do not eat unless
they give their hands a ceremonial washing, keeping
the tradition of the elders. 4 When they come from
the marketplace, they do not eat unless they have
washed. And there are many other customs they have
received and keep, like the washing of cups, pitchers,
kettles, and dining couches.[D]) 5 So the Pharisees and
the scribes asked him, "Why don't your disciples live[E]
according to the tradition of the elders, instead of
eating bread with ceremonially unclean[F] hands?"

6 He answered them, "Isaiah prophesied correctly
about you hypocrites, as it is written:

This people honors me with their lips,
but their heart is far from me.
7 **They worship me in vain,**
teaching as doctrines human commands.[G]

8 Abandoning the command of God, you hold on to
human tradition."[H] 9 He also said to them, "You have
a fine way of invalidating God's command in order to
set up[I] your tradition! 10 For Moses said: **Honor your
father and your mother;**[J] and **Whoever speaks evil
of father or mother must be put to death.**[K] 11 But you
say, 'If anyone tells his father or mother: Whatever
benefit you might have received from me is *corban*'"
(that is, an offering devoted to God), 12 "you no longer
let him do anything for his father or mother. 13 You
nullify the word of God by your tradition that you
have handed down. And you do many other similar
things."

14 Summoning the crowd again, he told them, "Listen to me, all of you, and understand: 15 Nothing that
goes into a person from outside can defile him but the
things that come out of a person are what defile him."[L]

17 When he went into the house away from the
crowd, his disciples asked him about the parable. 18 He
said to them, "Are you also as lacking in understanding? Don't you realize that nothing going into a person
from the outside can defile him? 19 For it doesn't go
into his heart but into the stomach and is eliminated"
(thus he declared all foods clean). 20 And he said, "What
comes out of a person is what defiles him. 21 For from
within, out of people's hearts, come evil thoughts, sex-

[A] **6:37** A denarius = one day's wage [B] **6:48** Or *them being battered as they rowed* [C] **6:48** Lit *Around the fourth watch of the night* = 3 to 6 a.m. [D] **7:4** Other mss omit *and dining couches* [E] **7:5** Lit *walk* [F] **7:5** Other mss read *with unwashed* [G] **7:6–7** Is 29:13 [H] **7:8** Other mss add *The washing of jugs, and cups, and many other similar things you practice.* [I] **7:9** Or *to maintain* [J] **7:10** Ex 20:12; Dt 5:16 [K] **7:10** Ex 21:17; Lv 20:9 [L] **7:15** Some mss include v. 16: *"If anyone has ears to hear, let him listen."*

ual immoralities, thefts, murders, 22 adulteries, greed,
evil actions, deceit, self-indulgence, envy,[A] slander,
pride, and foolishness. 23 All these evil things come
from within and defile a person."

A GENTILE MOTHER'S FAITH

24 He got up and departed from there to the region of
Tyre.[B] He entered a house and did not want anyone
to know it, but he could not escape notice. 25 Instead,
immediately after hearing about him, a woman whose
little daughter had an unclean spirit came and fell at
his feet. 26 The woman was a Gentile,[C] a Syrophoenician
by birth, and she was asking him to cast the demon
out of her daughter. 27 He said to her, "Let the children
be fed first, because it isn't right to take the children's
bread and throw it to the dogs."

28 But she replied to him, "Lord, even the dogs under
the table eat the children's crumbs."

29 Then he told her, "Because of this reply, you may
go. The demon has left your daughter." 30 When she
went back to her home, she found her child lying on
the bed, and the demon was gone.

JESUS DOES EVERYTHING WELL

31 Again, leaving the region of Tyre, he went by way
of Sidon to the Sea of Galilee, through[D] the region of
the Decapolis. 32 They brought to him a deaf man who
had difficulty speaking and begged Jesus to lay his
hand on him. 33 So he took him away from the crowd
in private. After putting his fingers in the man's ears
and spitting, he touched his tongue. 34 Looking up
to heaven, he sighed deeply and said to him, "*Eph-
phatha!*"[E] (that is, "Be opened!"). 35 Immediately his
ears were opened, his tongue was loosened, and he
began to speak clearly. 36 He ordered them to tell no
one, but the more he ordered them, the more they
proclaimed it.

37 They were extremely astonished and said, "He
has done everything well. He even makes the deaf
hear and the mute speak."

FEEDING FOUR THOUSAND

8 In those days there was again a large crowd, and
they had nothing to eat. He called the disciples
and said to them, 2 "I have compassion on the crowd,
because they've already stayed with me three days
and have nothing to eat. 3 If I send them home hungry,
they will collapse on the way, and some of them have
come a long distance."

[A]**7:22** Or *evil eye* [B]**7:24** Many early mss add *and Sidon* [C]**7:26** Or *a Greek (speaker)* [D]**7:31** Or *into* [E]**7:34** An Aramaic expression

Ruins of a Byzantine church in Amman, Jordan (first-century-AD Philadelphia, a Decapolis city).

Hippos; some believe Jesus was in Hippos when He healed the deaf man.

[4] His disciples answered him, "Where can anyone
get enough bread here in this desolate place to feed
these people?"
[5] "How many loaves do you have?" he asked them.
"Seven," they said. [6] He commanded the crowd to
sit down on the ground. Taking the seven loaves, he
gave thanks, broke them, and gave them to his disciples to set before the people. So they served them
to the crowd. [7] They also had a few small fish, and
after he had blessed them, he said these were to be
served as well. [8] They ate and were satisfied. Then
they collected seven large baskets of leftover pieces.
[9] About four thousand were there. He dismissed
them. [10] And he immediately got into the boat with
his disciples and went to the district of Dalmanutha.

THE LEAVEN OF THE PHARISEES AND HEROD

[11] The Pharisees came and began to argue with him,
demanding of him a sign from heaven to test him.
[12] Sighing deeply in his spirit, he said, "Why does
this generation demand a sign? Truly I tell you, no
sign will be given to this generation." [13] Then he
left them, got back into the boat, and went to the
other side.
[14] The disciples had forgotten to take bread and
had only one loaf with them in the boat. [15] Then he
gave them strict orders: "Watch out! Beware of the
leaven[A] of the Pharisees and the leaven of Herod."
[16] They were discussing among themselves that they
did not have any bread. [17] Aware of this, he said to
them, "Why are you discussing the fact you have no
bread? Don't you understand or comprehend? Do
you have hardened hearts? [18] **Do you have eyes and
not see; do you have ears and not hear?**[B] And do
you not remember? [19] When I broke the five loaves
for the five thousand, how many baskets full of leftovers did you collect?"
"Twelve," they told him.
[20] "When I broke the seven loaves for the four thousand, how many baskets full of pieces did you collect?"
"Seven," they said.
[21] And he said to them, "Don't you understand yet?"

[A] **8:15** Or *yeast* [B] **8:18** Jr 5:21; Ezk 12:2

HEALING A BLIND MAN

22 They came to Bethsaida. They brought a blind man to him and begged him to touch him. 23 He took the blind man by the hand and brought him out of the village. Spitting on his eyes and laying his hands on him, he asked him, "Do you see anything?"

24 He looked up and said, "I see people — they look like trees walking."

25 Again Jesus placed his hands on the man's eyes. The man looked intently and his sight was restored and he saw everything clearly. 26 Then he sent him home, saying, "Don't even go into the village."[A]

PETER'S CONFESSION OF THE MESSIAH

27 Jesus went out with his disciples to the villages of Caesarea Philippi. And on the road he asked his disciples, "Who do people say that I am?"

28 They answered him, "John the Baptist; others, Elijah; still others, one of the prophets."

29 "But you," he asked them, "who do you say that I am?"

Peter answered him, "You are the Messiah." 30 And he strictly warned them to tell no one about him.

HIS DEATH AND RESURRECTION PREDICTED

31 Then he began to teach them that it was necessary for the Son of Man to suffer many things and be rejected by the elders, chief priests, and scribes, be killed, and rise after three days. 32 He spoke openly about this. Peter took him aside and began to rebuke him. 33 But turning around and looking at his disciples, he rebuked Peter and said, "Get behind me, Satan! You are not thinking about God's concerns[B] but human concerns."

TAKE UP YOUR CROSS

34 Calling the crowd along with his disciples, he said to them, "If anyone wants to follow after me, let him deny himself, take up his cross, and follow me. 35 For whoever wants to save his life will lose it, but whoever loses his life because of me and the gospel will save it. 36 For what does it benefit someone to gain the whole world and yet lose his life? 37 What can anyone give in exchange for his life? 38 For whoever is ashamed of me and my words in this adulterous and sinful generation, the Son of Man will also be ashamed of him when he comes in the glory of his Father with the holy angels."

9 Then he said to them, "Truly I tell you, there are some standing here who will not taste death until they see the kingdom of God come in power."

THE TRANSFIGURATION

2 After six days Jesus took Peter, James, and John and led them up a high mountain by themselves to be alone. He was transfigured in front of them, 3 and his clothes became dazzling — extremely white as no launderer on earth could whiten them. 4 Elijah appeared to them with Moses, and they were talking with Jesus. 5 Peter said to Jesus, "Rabbi, it's good for us to be here. Let's set up three shelters: one for you, one for Moses, and one for Elijah" — 6 because he did not know what to say, since they were terrified.

7 A cloud appeared, overshadowing them, and a voice came from the cloud: "This is my beloved Son; listen to him!"

8 Suddenly, looking around, they no longer saw anyone with them except Jesus.

9 As they were coming down the mountain, he ordered them to tell no one what they had seen until the Son of Man had risen from the dead. 10 They kept this word to themselves, questioning what "rising from the dead" meant.

11 Then they asked him, "Why do the scribes say that Elijah must come first?"

12 "Elijah does come first and restores all things," he replied. "Why then is it written that the Son of Man must suffer many things and be treated with contempt? 13 But I tell you that Elijah has come, and they did whatever they pleased to him, just as it is written about him."

THE POWER OF FAITH OVER A DEMON

14 When they came to the disciples, they saw a large crowd around them and scribes disputing with them. 15 When the whole crowd saw him, they were amazed and ran to greet him. 16 He asked them, "What are you arguing with them about?"

17 Someone from the crowd answered him, "Teacher, I brought my son to you. He has a spirit that makes him unable to speak. 18 Whenever it seizes him, it throws him down, and he foams at the mouth, grinds his teeth, and becomes rigid. I asked your disciples to drive it out, but they couldn't."

19 He replied to them, "You unbelieving generation, how long will I be with you? How long must I put up with you? Bring him to me." 20 So they brought the boy to him. When the spirit saw him, it immediately threw the boy into convulsions. He fell to the ground and rolled around, foaming at the mouth. 21 "How long has this been happening to him?" Jesus asked his father.

"From childhood," he said. 22 "And many times it has thrown him into fire or water to destroy him. But if you can do anything, have compassion on us and help us."

[A] **8:26** Other mss add *or tell anyone in the village* [B] **8:33** Or *about the things of God*

23 Jesus said to him, "'If you can'?[A] Everything is
possible for the one who believes."
24 Immediately the father of the boy cried out, "I do
believe; help my unbelief!"
25 When Jesus saw that a crowd was quickly gathering, he rebuked the unclean spirit, saying to it, "You
mute and deaf spirit, I command you: Come out of
him and never enter him again."
26 Then it came out, shrieking and throwing him
into terrible convulsions. The boy became like a
corpse, so that many said, "He's dead." 27 But Jesus,
taking him by the hand, raised him, and he stood up.
28 After he had gone into the house, his disciples
asked him privately, "Why couldn't we drive it out?"
29 And he told them, "This kind can come out by
nothing but prayer."[B]

THE SECOND PREDICTION OF HIS DEATH

30 Then they left that place and made their way
through Galilee, but he did not want anyone to
know it. 31 For he was teaching his disciples and telling them, "The Son of Man is going to be betrayed[C]
into the hands of men. They will kill him, and after
he is killed, he will rise three days later." 32 But they
did not understand this statement, and they were
afraid to ask him.

WHO IS THE GREATEST?

33 They came to Capernaum. When he was in the
house, he asked them, "What were you arguing about
on the way?" 34 But they were silent, because on the
way they had been arguing with one another about
who was the greatest. 35 Sitting down, he called the
Twelve and said to them, "If anyone wants to be first,
he must be last and servant of all." 36 He took a child,
had him stand among them, and taking him in his
arms, he said to them, 37 "Whoever welcomes[D] one
little child such as this in my name welcomes me.
And whoever welcomes me does not welcome me,
but him who sent me."

IN HIS NAME

38 John said to him, "Teacher, we saw someone[E] driving out demons in your name, and we tried to stop
him because he wasn't following us."
39 "Don't stop him," said Jesus, "because there is no
one who will perform a miracle in my name who can
soon afterward speak evil of me. 40 For whoever is not
against us is for us. 41 And whoever gives you a cup
of water to drink in my name, because you belong to
Christ — truly I tell you, he will never lose his reward.

WARNINGS FROM JESUS

42 "But whoever causes one of these little ones who
believe in me to fall away — it would be better for
him if a heavy millstone were hung around his neck
and he were thrown into the sea.
43 "And if your hand causes you to fall away, cut
it off. It is better for you to enter life maimed than
to have two hands and go to hell, the unquenchable
fire.[F] 45 And if your foot causes you to fall away, cut it
off. It is better for you to enter life lame than to have
two feet and be thrown into hell.[G] 47 And if your eye
causes you to fall away, gouge it out. It is better for
you to enter the kingdom of God with one eye than to
have two eyes and be thrown into hell, 48 where **their
worm does not die, and the fire is not quenched.**[H]
49 For everyone will be salted with fire.[I,J] 50 Salt is good,
but if the salt should lose its flavor, how can you season it? Have salt among yourselves, and be at peace
with one another."

THE QUESTION OF DIVORCE

10 He set out from there and went to the region
of Judea and across the Jordan. Then crowds
converged on him again, and as was his custom he
taught them again.
2 Some Pharisees came to test him, asking, "Is it
lawful for a man to divorce his wife?"
3 He replied to them, "What did Moses command
you?"
4 They said, "Moses permitted us to write divorce
papers and send her away."
5 But Jesus told them, "He wrote this command for
you because of the hardness of your hearts. 6 But from
the beginning of creation God[K] **made them male
and female.**[L] 7 **For this reason a man will leave
his father and mother**[M] 8 **and the two will become
one flesh.**[N] So they are no longer two, but one flesh.
9 Therefore what God has joined together, let no one
separate."
10 When they were in the house again, the disciples
questioned him about this matter. 11 He said to them,
"Whoever divorces his wife and marries another
commits adultery against her. 12 Also, if she divorces her husband and marries another, she commits
adultery."

BLESSING THE CHILDREN

13 People were bringing little children to him in order
that he might touch them, but the disciples rebuked
them. 14 When Jesus saw it, he was indignant and said

[A] **9:23** Other mss add *believe* [B] **9:29** Other mss add *and fasting* [C] **9:31** Or *handed over* [D] **9:37** Or *"Whoever receives* [E] **9:38** Other mss add *who didn't go along with us* [F] **9:43** Some mss include v. 44: *Where their worm does not die, and the fire is not quenched.* [G] **9:45** Some mss include v. 46: *Where their worm does not die, and the fire is not quenched.* [H] **9:48** Is 66:24 [I] **9:49** Other mss add *and every sacrifice will be salted with salt* [J] **9:49** Lv 2:13; Ezk 43:24 [K] **10:6** Other mss omit *God* [L] **10:6** Gn 1:27; 5:2 [M] **10:7** Some mss add *and be joined to his wife* [N] **10:7–8** Gn 2:24

to them, "Let the little children come to me. Don't stop them, because the kingdom of God belongs to such as these. 15 Truly I tell you, whoever does not receive[A] the kingdom of God like a little child will never enter it." 16 After taking them in his arms, he laid his hands on them and blessed them.

THE RICH YOUNG RULER

17 As he was setting out on a journey, a man ran up, knelt down before him, and asked him, "Good teacher, what must I do to inherit eternal life?"

18 "Why do you call me good?" Jesus asked him. "No one is good except God alone. 19 You know the commandments: **Do not murder; do not commit adultery; do not steal; do not bear false witness; do not defraud; honor your father and mother.**"[B]

20 He said to him, "Teacher, I have kept all these from my youth."

21 Looking at him, Jesus loved him and said to him, "You lack one thing: Go, sell all you have and give to the poor, and you will have treasure in heaven. Then come,[C] follow me." 22 But he was dismayed by this demand, and he went away grieving, because he had many possessions.

POSSESSIONS AND THE KINGDOM

23 Jesus looked around and said to his disciples, "How hard it is for those who have wealth to enter the kingdom of God!"

24 The disciples were astonished at his words. Again Jesus said to them, "Children, how hard it is[D] to enter the kingdom of God! 25 It is easier for a camel to go through the eye of a needle than for a rich person to enter the kingdom of God."

26 They were even more astonished, saying to one another, "Then who can be saved?"

27 Looking at them, Jesus said, "With man it is impossible, but not with God, because all things are possible with God."

28 Peter began to tell him, "Look, we have left everything and followed you."

29 "Truly I tell you," Jesus said, "there is no one who has left house or brothers or sisters or mother or father[E] or children or fields for my sake and for the sake of the gospel, 30 who will not receive a hundred times more, now at this time — houses, brothers and

[A] **10:15** Or *not welcome* [B] **10:19** Ex 20:12–16; Dt 5:16–20
[C] **10:21** Other mss add *taking up the cross, and* [D] **10:24** Other mss add *for those trusting in wealth* [E] **10:29** Other mss add *or wife*

The springs at Dan serve as headwaters to the Jordan River.

sisters, mothers and children, and fields, with persecutions — and eternal life in the age to come. 31 But many who are first will be last, and the last first."

THE THIRD PREDICTION OF HIS DEATH

32 They were on the road, going up to Jerusalem, and Jesus was walking ahead of them. The disciples were astonished, but those who followed him were afraid. Taking the Twelve aside again, he began to tell them the things that would happen to him. 33 "See, we are going up to Jerusalem. The Son of Man will be handed over to the chief priests and the scribes, and they will condemn him to death. Then they will hand him over to the Gentiles, 34 and they will mock him, spit on him, flog[A] him, and kill him, and he will rise after three days."

SUFFERING AND SERVICE

35 James and John, the sons of Zebedee, approached him and said, "Teacher, we want you to do whatever we ask you."

36 "What do you want me to do for you?" he asked them.

37 They answered him, "Allow us to sit at your right and at your left in your glory."

38 Jesus said to them, "You don't know what you're asking. Are you able to drink the cup I drink or to be baptized with the baptism I am baptized with?"

39 "We are able," they told him.

Jesus said to them, "You will drink the cup I drink, and you will be baptized with the baptism I am baptized with. 40 But to sit at my right or left is not mine to give; instead, it is for those for whom it has been prepared."

41 When the ten disciples heard this, they began to be indignant with James and John. 42 Jesus called them over and said to them, "You know that those who are regarded as rulers of the Gentiles lord it over them, and those in high positions act as tyrants over them. 43 But it is not so among you. On the contrary, whoever wants to become great among you will be your servant, 44 and whoever wants to be first among you will be a slave to all. 45 For even the Son of Man did not come to be served, but to serve, and to give his life as a ransom for many."[B]

A BLIND MAN HEALED

46 They came to Jericho. And as he was leaving Jericho with his disciples and a large crowd, Bartimaeus (the son of Timaeus), a blind beggar, was sitting by the road. 47 When he heard that it was Jesus of Nazareth, he began to cry out, "Jesus, Son of David, have mercy on me!" 48 Many warned him to keep quiet, but he was crying out all the more, "Have mercy on me, Son of David!"

49 Jesus stopped and said, "Call him."

So they called the blind man and said to him, "Have courage! Get up; he's calling for you." 50 He threw off his coat, jumped up, and came to Jesus.

51 Then Jesus answered him, "What do you want me to do for you?"

"*Rabboni*,"[C] the blind man said to him, "I want to see."

52 Jesus said to him, "Go, your faith has saved you." Immediately he could see and began to follow Jesus on the road.

THE TRIUMPHAL ENTRY

11 When they approached Jerusalem, at Bethphage and Bethany near the Mount of Olives, he sent two of his disciples 2 and told them, "Go into the village ahead of you. As soon as you enter it, you will find a colt tied there, on which no one has ever sat. Untie it and bring it. 3 If anyone says to you, 'Why are you doing this?' say, 'The Lord needs it and will send it back here right away.'"

4 So they went and found a colt outside in the street, tied by a door. They untied it, 5 and some of those standing there said to them, "What are you doing, untying the colt?" 6 They answered them just as Jesus had said; so they let them go.

7 They brought the colt to Jesus and threw their clothes on it, and he sat on it. 8 Many people spread their clothes on the road, and others spread leafy branches cut from the fields.[D] 9 Those who went ahead and those who followed shouted:

Hosanna!
Blessed is he who comes
in the name of the Lord![E]
10 Blessed is the coming kingdom
of our father David!
Hosanna in the highest heaven!

11 He went into Jerusalem and into the temple. After looking around at everything, since it was already late, he went out to Bethany with the Twelve.

THE BARREN FIG TREE IS CURSED

12 The next day when they went out from Bethany, he was hungry. 13 Seeing in the distance a fig tree with leaves, he went to find out if there was anything on it. When he came to it, he found nothing but leaves; for it was not the season for figs. 14 He said to it, "May no one ever eat fruit from you again!" And his disciples heard it.

CLEANSING THE TEMPLE

15 They came to Jerusalem, and he went into the temple and began to throw out those buying and selling.

[A] **10:34** Or *scourge* [B] **10:45** Or *in the place of many*; Is 53:10–12
[C] **10:51** Hb word for *my lord* [D] **11:8** Other mss read *others were cutting leafy branches from the trees and spreading them on the road*
[E] **11:9** Ps 118:26

Interior and exterior of the nineteenth-century Franciscan Church built at Bethphage to commemorate the place where Jesus began his donkey ride into Jerusalem. Ruins of an earlier church were found here in 1876.

He overturned the tables of the money changers and
the chairs of those selling doves, 16 and would not
permit anyone to carry goods through the temple.
17 He was teaching them: "Is it not written, **My house
will be called a house of prayer for all nations**?[A]
But you have made it **a den of thieves**!"[B]
18 The chief priests and the scribes heard it and
started looking for a way to kill him. For they were
afraid of him, because the whole crowd was astonished by his teaching.
19 Whenever evening came, they would go out of
the city.

THE BARREN FIG TREE IS WITHERED

20 Early in the morning, as they were passing by, they
saw the fig tree withered from the roots up. 21 Then
Peter remembered and said to him, "Rabbi, look! The
fig tree that you cursed has withered."
22 Jesus replied to them, "Have faith in God. 23 Truly
I tell you, if anyone says to this mountain, 'Be lifted
up and thrown into the sea,' and does not doubt in
his heart, but believes that what he says will happen,
it will be done for him. 24 Therefore I tell you, everything you pray and ask for — believe that you have
received[C] it and it will be yours. 25 And whenever you
stand praying, if you have anything against anyone,
forgive him, so that your Father in heaven will also
forgive you your wrongdoing."[D]

THE AUTHORITY OF JESUS CHALLENGED

27 They came again to Jerusalem. As he was walking
in the temple, the chief priests, the scribes, and the
elders came 28 and asked him, "By what authority are
you doing these things? Who gave you this authority
to do these things?"
29 Jesus said to them, "I will ask you one question;
then answer me, and I will tell you by what authority
I do these things. 30 Was John's baptism from heaven
or of human origin? Answer me."

[A] **11:17** Is 56:7 [B] **11:17** Jr 7:11 [C] **11:24** Some mss read *you receive*; other mss read *you will receive* [D] **11:25** Some mss include v. 26: *"But if you don't forgive, neither will your Father in heaven forgive your wrongdoing."*

31 They discussed it among themselves: "If we say, 'From heaven,' he will say, 'Then why didn't you believe him?' 32 But if we say, 'Of human origin' " — they were afraid of the crowd, because everyone thought that John was truly a prophet. 33 So they answered Jesus, "We don't know."

And Jesus said to them, "Neither will I tell you by what authority I do these things."

THE PARABLE OF THE VINEYARD OWNER

12 He began to speak to them in parables: "A man planted a vineyard, put a fence around it, dug out a pit for a winepress, and built a watchtower. Then he leased it to tenant farmers and went away. 2 At harvest time he sent a servant to the farmers to collect some of the fruit of the vineyard from them. 3 But they took him, beat him, and sent him away empty-handed. 4 Again he sent another servant to them, and they[A] hit him on the head and treated him shamefully.[B] 5 Then he sent another, and they killed that one. He also sent many others; some they beat, and others they killed. 6 He still had one to send, a beloved son. Finally he sent him to them, saying, 'They will respect my son.' 7 But those tenant farmers said to one another, 'This is the heir. Come, let's kill him, and the inheritance will be ours.' 8 So they seized him, killed him, and threw him out of the vineyard. 9 What then will the owner[C] of the vineyard do? He will come and kill the farmers and give the vineyard to others. 10 Haven't you read this Scripture:

> **The stone that**
> **the builders rejected**
> **has become the cornerstone.**
> 11 **This came about from the Lord**
> **and is wonderful in our eyes?"**[D]

12 They were looking for a way to arrest him but feared the crowd because they knew he had spoken this parable against them. So they left him and went away.

GOD AND CAESAR

13 Then they sent some of the Pharisees and the Herodians to Jesus to trap him in his words. 14 When they came, they said to him, "Teacher, we know you are truthful and don't care what anyone thinks, nor do you show partiality but teach the way of God truthfully. Is it lawful to pay taxes to Caesar or not? Should we pay or shouldn't we?"

15 But knowing their hypocrisy, he said to them, "Why are you testing me? Bring me a denarius[E] to look at." 16 They brought a coin. "Whose image and inscription is this?" he asked them.

"Caesar's," they replied.

17 Jesus told them, "Give to Caesar the things that are Caesar's, and to God the things that are God's." And they were utterly amazed at him.

THE SADDUCEES AND THE RESURRECTION

18 Sadducees, who say there is no resurrection, came to him and questioned him: 19 "Teacher, Moses wrote for us that **if a man's brother dies**, leaving a wife behind but **no child, that man should take the wife and raise up offspring for his brother.**[F] 20 There were seven brothers. The first married a woman, and dying, left no offspring. 21 The second also took her, and he died, leaving no offspring. And the third likewise. 22 None of the seven[G] left offspring. Last of all, the woman died too. 23 In the resurrection, when they rise,[H] whose wife will she be, since the seven had married her?"

24 Jesus spoke to them, "Isn't this the reason why you're mistaken: you don't know the Scriptures or the power of God? 25 For when they rise from the dead, they neither marry nor are given in marriage but are like angels in heaven. 26 And as for the dead being raised — haven't you read in the book of Moses, in the passage about the burning bush, how God said to him: **I am the God of Abraham and the God of Isaac and the God of Jacob?**[I] 27 He is not the God of the dead but of the living. You are badly mistaken."

THE PRIMARY COMMANDS

28 One of the scribes approached. When he heard them debating and saw that Jesus answered them well, he asked him, "Which command is the most important of all?"

29 Jesus answered, "The most important[J] is **Listen, Israel! The Lord our God, the Lord is one.**[K] 30 **Love the Lord your God with all your heart, with all your soul, with all your mind, and with all your strength.**[L,M] 31 The second is, **Love your neighbor as yourself.**[N] There is no other command greater than these."

32 Then the scribe said to him, "You are right, teacher. You have correctly said that he is one, and there is no one else except him. 33 And to love him with all your heart, with all your understanding,[O] and with all your strength, and to love your neighbor as yourself, is far more important than all the burnt offerings and sacrifices."

[A] **12:4** Other mss add *threw stones and* [B] **12:4** Other mss add *and sent him off* [C] **12:9** Or *lord* [D] **12:10–11** Ps 118:22–23 [E] **12:15** A denarius = one day's wage [F] **12:19** Gn 38:8; Dt 25:5 [G] **12:22** Other mss add *had taken her and* [H] **12:23** Other mss omit *when they rise* [I] **12:26** Ex 3:6,15–16 [J] **12:29** Other mss add *of all the commands* [K] **12:29** Or *the Lord our God is Lord alone.* [L] **12:30** Other mss add *This is the first commandment.* [M] **12:30** Dt 6:4–5; Jos 22:5 [N] **12:31** Lv 19:18 [O] **12:33** Other mss add *with all your soul*

Bust of Emperor Tiberius, who ruled AD 14–37, which included the years of Jesus's ministry.

34 When Jesus saw that he answered wisely, he said to him, "You are not far from the kingdom of God." And no one dared to question him any longer.

THE QUESTION ABOUT THE MESSIAH

35 While Jesus was teaching in the temple, he asked, "How can the scribes say that the Messiah is the son of David? 36 David himself says by the Holy Spirit:

> **The Lord declared to my Lord,**
> **'Sit at my right hand**
> **until I put your enemies under your feet.'**[A]

37 David himself calls him 'Lord.' How, then, can he be his son?" And the large crowd was listening to him with delight.

WARNING AGAINST THE SCRIBES

38 He also said in his teaching, "Beware of the scribes, who want to go around in long robes and who want greetings in the marketplaces, 39 the best seats in the synagogues, and the places of honor at banquets. 40 They devour widows' houses and say long prayers just for show. These will receive harsher judgment."

THE WIDOW'S GIFT

41 Sitting across from the temple treasury, he watched how the crowd dropped money into the treasury. Many rich people were putting in large sums. 42 Then a poor widow came and dropped in two tiny coins worth very little. 43 Summoning his disciples, he said to them, "Truly I tell you, this poor widow has put more into the treasury than all the others. 44 For they all gave out of their surplus, but she out of her poverty has put in everything she had — all she had to live on."

DESTRUCTION OF THE TEMPLE PREDICTED

13 As he was going out of the temple, one of his disciples said to him, "Teacher, look! What massive stones! What impressive buildings!"

2 Jesus said to him, "Do you see these great buildings? Not one stone will be left upon another — all will be thrown down."

SIGNS OF THE END OF THE AGE

3 While he was sitting on the Mount of Olives across from the temple, Peter, James, John, and Andrew asked him privately, 4 "Tell us, when will these things happen? And what will be the sign when all these things are about to be accomplished?"

5 Jesus told them, "Watch out that no one deceives you. 6 Many will come in my name, saying, 'I am he,' and they will deceive many. 7 When you hear of wars and rumors of wars, don't be alarmed; these things must take place, but it is not yet the end. 8 For nation will rise up against nation, and kingdom against kingdom. There will be earthquakes in various places, and famines.[B] These are the beginning of birth pains.

PERSECUTIONS PREDICTED

9 "But you, be on your guard! They will hand you over to local courts,[C] and you will be flogged in the synagogues. You will stand before governors and kings because of me, as a witness to them. 10 And it is necessary that the gospel be preached to all nations. 11 So when they arrest you and hand you over, don't worry beforehand what you will say, but say whatever is given to you at that time, for it isn't you speaking, but the Holy Spirit.

12 "Brother will betray brother to death, and a father his child. Children will rise up against parents and have them put to death. 13 You will be hated by everyone because of my name, but the one who endures to the end will be saved.

[A] **12:36** Ps 110:1 [B] **13:8** Other mss add *and disturbances* [C] **13:9** Or *sanhedrins*

THE GREAT TRIBULATION

14 "When you see **the abomination of desolation**[A]
standing where it should not be" (let the reader understand), "then those in Judea must flee to the mountains. 15 A man on the housetop must not come down
or go in to get anything out of his house, 16 and a man
in the field must not go back to get his coat. 17 Woe to
pregnant women and nursing mothers in those days!
18 "Pray it[B] won't happen in winter. 19 For those will
be days of tribulation, the kind that hasn't been from
the beginning of creation until now and never will
be again. 20 If the Lord had not cut those days short,
no one would be saved. But he cut those days short
for the sake of the elect, whom he chose.
21 "Then if anyone tells you, 'See, here is the Messiah! See, there!' do not believe it. 22 For false messiahs
and false prophets will arise and will perform signs
and wonders to lead astray, if possible, the elect.
23 And you must watch! I have told you everything
in advance.

THE COMING OF THE SON OF MAN

24 "But in those days, after that tribulation: The sun
will be darkened, and the moon will not shed its light;
25 the stars will be falling from the sky, and the powers
in the heavens will be shaken. 26 Then they will see
the Son of Man coming in clouds with great power
and glory. 27 He will send out the angels and gather
his elect from the four winds, from the ends of the
earth to the ends of heaven.

THE PARABLE OF THE FIG TREE

28 "Learn this lesson from the fig tree: As soon as its
branch becomes tender and sprouts leaves, you know
that summer is near. 29 In the same way, when you see
these things happening, recognize[C] that he[D] is near
— at the door.
30 "Truly I tell you, this generation will certainly not
pass away until all these things take place. 31 Heaven
and earth will pass away, but my words will never
pass away.

NO ONE KNOWS THE DAY OR HOUR

32 "Now concerning that day or hour no one knows
— neither the angels in heaven nor the Son — but
only the Father.
33 "Watch! Be alert![E] For you don't know when the
time is coming.
34 "It is like a man on a journey, who left his house,
gave authority to his servants, gave each one his

[A] **13:14** Dn 9:27 [B] **13:18** Other mss read *"Pray that your escape*
[C] **13:29** Or *you know* [D] **13:29** Or *it* [E] **13:33** Other mss add *and pray*

Ruins at Pella in Jordan. After the fall of Jerusalem in AD 70, many Jerusalem Christians resettled in Pella. In the foreground is the temple and community center complex; excavations on the hills (right) have revealed a tenth-century-BC Philistine settlement and a first-century Jewish community. The Jordan River is in the distance.

work, and commanded the doorkeeper to be alert. 35 Therefore be alert, since you don't know when the master of the house is coming — whether in the evening or at midnight or at the crowing of the rooster or early in the morning. 36 Otherwise, when he comes suddenly he might find you sleeping. 37 And what I say to you, I say to everyone: Be alert! "

THE PLOT TO KILL JESUS

14 It was two days before the Passover and the Festival of Unleavened Bread. The chief priests and the scribes were looking for a cunning way to arrest Jesus and kill him. 2 "Not during the festival," they said, "so that there won't be a riot among the people."

THE ANOINTING AT BETHANY

3 While he was in Bethany at the house of Simon the leper,[A] as he was reclining at the table, a woman came with an alabaster jar of very expensive perfume of pure nard. She broke the jar and poured it on his head. 4 But some were expressing indignation to one another: "Why has this perfume been wasted? 5 For this perfume might have been sold for more than three hundred denarii[B] and given to the poor." And they began to scold her.

6 Jesus replied, "Leave her alone. Why are you bothering her? She has done a noble thing for me. 7 You always have the poor with you, and you can do what is good for them whenever you want, but you do not always have me. 8 She has done what she could; she has anointed my body in advance for burial. 9 Truly I tell you, wherever the gospel is proclaimed in the whole world, what she has done will also be told in memory of her."

10 Then Judas Iscariot, one of the Twelve, went to the chief priests to betray Jesus to them. 11 And when they heard this, they were glad and promised to give him money. So he started looking for a good opportunity to betray him.

PREPARATION FOR PASSOVER

12 On the first day of Unleavened Bread, when they sacrifice the Passover lamb, his disciples asked him, "Where do you want us to go and prepare the Passover so that you may eat it? "

13 So he sent two of his disciples and told them, "Go into the city, and a man carrying a jar of water will meet you. Follow him. 14 Wherever he enters, tell the owner of the house, 'The Teacher says, "Where is my guest room where I may eat the Passover with my disciples? " ' 15 He will show you a large room upstairs, furnished and ready. Make the preparations for us there." 16 So the disciples went out, entered the city, and found it just as he had told them, and they prepared the Passover.

BETRAYAL AT THE PASSOVER

17 When evening came, he arrived with the Twelve. 18 While they were reclining and eating, Jesus said, "Truly I tell you, one of you will betray me — one who is eating with me."

19 They began to be distressed and to say to him one by one, "Surely not I? "

20 He said to them, "It is one of the Twelve — the one who is dipping bread in the bowl with me. 21 For the Son of Man will go just as it is written about him, but woe to that man by whom the Son of Man is betrayed! It would have been better for him if he had not been born."

THE FIRST LORD'S SUPPER

22 As they were eating, he took bread, blessed and broke it, gave it to them, and said, "Take it; this is my body." 23 Then he took a cup, and after giving thanks, he gave it to them, and they all drank from it. 24 He said to them, "This is my blood of the covenant,[C] which is poured out for many. 25 Truly I tell you, I will no longer drink of the fruit of the vine until that day when I drink it new[D] in the kingdom of God."

26 After singing a hymn, they went out to the Mount of Olives.

PETER'S DENIAL PREDICTED

27 Then Jesus said to them, "All of you will fall away,[E] because it is written:

> **I will strike the shepherd,**
> **and the sheep will be scattered.**[F]

28 But after I have risen, I will go ahead of you to Galilee."

29 Peter told him, "Even if everyone falls away, I will not."

30 "Truly I tell you," Jesus said to him, "today, this very night, before the rooster crows twice, you will deny me three times."

31 But he kept insisting, "If I have to die with you, I will never deny you." And they all said the same thing.

THE PRAYER IN THE GARDEN

32 Then they came to a place named Gethsemane, and he told his disciples, "Sit here while I pray." 33 He took Peter, James, and John with him, and he began to be deeply distressed and troubled. 34 He said to them, "I am deeply grieved[G] to the point of death. Remain here and stay awake." 35 He went a little farther, fell to the ground, and prayed that if it were possible, the hour might pass from him. 36 And he said, "*Abba*,[H] Father! All things are possible for you. Take this cup away

[A] **14:3** Gk *lepros*; a term for various skin diseases; see Lv 13–14
[B] **14:5** A denarius = one day's wage [C] **14:24** Other mss read *the new covenant* [D] **14:25** Or *drink new wine*; lit *drink it new* [E] **14:27** Other mss add *because of me this night* [F] **14:27** Zch 13:7 [G] **14:34** Or *"My soul is swallowed up in sorrow* [H] **14:36** Aramaic for *father*

Gethsemane

by Darryl Wood

The word *gethsemane* derives from two Hebrew words and translates literally as "press of oils." Production of olive oil was prevalent in ancient Near Eastern cultures. It made sense to place a press or presses at the location where the product was grown. So the Gethsemane of the Gospels seems to have been at a place where people grew olive trees and manufactured olive oil. In the siege of Jerusalem by Titus in AD 70, the Roman army cut down all trees in and around the city; any olive trees in the area during Jesus's time do not remain.

Jesus and the disciples left the Passover supper to go to the Mount of Olives (Mt 26:30; Mk 14:26; Lk 22:39). Matthew and Mark indicate that they went to a specific place named Gethsemane (Mt 26:36; Mk 14:32). John specified the location as being "across the Kidron Valley, where there was a garden" (Jn 18:1). The Kidron Valley runs just to the east of Jerusalem's walls, with the Mount of Olives lying immediately across the valley. The Mount of Olives rises three hundred feet higher than the Temple Mount. Quite possibly Gethsemane existed on the slopes of the Kidron Valley, between the valley floor and the peak of the Mount of Olives, facing the Temple Mount.

Identification of the exact place where Jesus crossed the Kidron and his destination on the Mount of Olives eludes Bible scholars. Throughout church history, however, writers have speculated about the specific locale.[1] A large cave on the lower slopes might have been a quiet place for contemplation if it was indeed there in the first century. Evidence indicates this cave held an oil press for olive production or was a storage cistern. A building now sits over this cave.[2] A more traditional site on the hillside is at a large rock inside the Church of All Nations. Regardless of the exact location, in the first century, olive trees dominated the area and provided a garden-like atmosphere.[3] ✣

---

[1] For an extensive summary of the opinions of ancient writers related to the location of Gethsemane, see Clemens Kopp, The Holy Places of the Gospels (New York: Herder & Herder, 1963), 337–50. [2] Joan E. Taylor, "The Garden of Gethsemane: Not the Place of Jesus' Arrest," BAR 21.4 (1995): 26, 28, 35. [3] W. Harold Mare, The Archaeology of the Jerusalem Area (Grand Rapids: Baker, 1987), 247–48.

Small chapel located in what is known as the Cave at Gethsemane. Archaeological evidence indicates the cave was used for producing olive oil. The olive presses would have been used in the fall and winter of the year, after the olive harvest. Jesus and his disciples would have been in Jerusalem at Passover, which was in the springtime.

The Tomb of Zechariah (with the pyramid roof) and the Tomb of Absalom (conical roof), both in the Kidron Valley. Although neither is the burial site of its Old Testament namesake, both of the burial monuments would have been in place when Jesus walked through the valley to and from Gethsemane.

from me. Nevertheless, not what I will, but what you will." 37 Then he came and found them sleeping. He said to Peter, "Simon, are you sleeping? Couldn't you stay awake one hour? 38 Stay awake and pray so that you won't enter into temptation.[A] The spirit is willing, but the flesh is weak." 39 Once again he went away and prayed, saying the same thing. 40 And again he came and found them sleeping, because they could not keep their eyes open. They did not know what to say to him. 41 Then he came a third time and said to them, "Are you still sleeping and resting? Enough! The time has come. See, the Son of Man is betrayed into the hands of sinners. 42 Get up; let's go. See, my betrayer is near."

JUDAS'S BETRAYAL OF JESUS

43 While he was still speaking, Judas, one of the Twelve, suddenly arrived. With him was a mob, with swords and clubs, from the chief priests, the scribes, and the elders. 44 His betrayer had given them a signal. "The one I kiss," he said, "he's the one; arrest him and take him away under guard." 45 So when he came, immediately he went up to Jesus and said, "Rabbi!" and kissed him. 46 They took hold of him and arrested him. 47 One of those who stood by drew his sword, struck the high priest's servant, and cut off his ear.

48 Jesus said to them, "Have you come out with swords and clubs, as if I were a criminal,[B] to capture me? 49 Every day I was among you, teaching in the temple, and you didn't arrest me. But the Scriptures must be fulfilled."

50 Then they all deserted him and ran away. 51 Now a certain young man, wearing nothing but a linen cloth, was following him. They caught hold of him, 52 but he left the linen cloth behind and ran away naked.

JESUS FACES THE SANHEDRIN

53 They led Jesus away to the high priest, and all the chief priests, the elders, and the scribes assembled. 54 Peter followed him at a distance, right into the high priest's courtyard. He was sitting with the servants,[C] warming himself by the fire.

55 The chief priests and the whole Sanhedrin were looking for testimony against Jesus to put him to death, but they could not find any. 56 For many were giving false testimony against him, and the testimonies did not agree. 57 Some stood up and gave false testimony against him, stating, 58 "We heard him say, 'I will destroy this temple made with human hands, and in three days I will build another not made by hands.'" 59 Yet their testimony did not agree even on this.

60 Then the high priest stood up before them all and questioned Jesus, "Don't you have an answer to what these men are testifying against you?" 61 But he kept silent and did not answer. Again the high priest questioned him, "Are you the Messiah, the Son of the Blessed One?"

62 "I am," said Jesus, "and you will see **the Son of Man seated at the right hand** of Power and **coming with the clouds of heaven.**"[D]

63 Then the high priest tore his robes and said, "Why do we still need witnesses? 64 You have heard the blasphemy. What is your decision?" They all condemned him as deserving death.

65 Then some began to spit on him, to blindfold him, and to beat him, saying, "Prophesy!" The temple servants also took him and slapped him.

PETER DENIES HIS LORD

66 While Peter was in the courtyard below, one of the high priest's maidservants came. 67 When she saw Peter warming himself, she looked at him and said, "You also were with Jesus, the man from Nazareth."

68 But he denied it: "I don't know or understand what you're talking about." Then he went out to the entryway,[E] and a rooster crowed.[F]

69 When the maidservant saw him again, she began to tell those standing nearby, "This man is one of them."

70 But again he denied it. After a little while those standing there said to Peter again, "You certainly are one of them, since you're also a Galilean."[G]

71 Then he started to curse and swear, "I don't know this man you're talking about!"

72 Immediately a rooster crowed a second time, and Peter remembered when Jesus had spoken the word to him, "Before the rooster crows twice, you will deny me three times." And he broke down and wept.

JESUS FACES PILATE

15 As soon as it was morning, having held a meeting with the elders, scribes, and the whole Sanhedrin, the chief priests tied Jesus up, led him away, and handed him over to Pilate.

2 So Pilate asked him, "Are you the king of the Jews?"

He answered him, "You say so."

3 And the chief priests accused him of many things. 4 Pilate questioned him again, "Aren't you going to answer? Look how many things they are accusing you of!" 5 But Jesus still did not answer, and so Pilate was amazed.

JESUS OR BARABBAS

6 At the festival Pilate used to release for the people a prisoner whom they requested. 7 There was one named Barabbas, who was in prison with rebels who

[A] **14:38** Or *won't be put to the test* [B] **14:48** Or *insurrectionist* [C] **14:54** Or *temple police*, or *officers*, also in v. 65 [D] **14:62** Ps 110:1; Dn 7:13 [E] **14:68** Or *forecourt* [F] **14:68** Other mss omit *and a rooster crowed* [G] **14:70** Other mss add *and your speech shows it*

had committed murder during the rebellion. 8 The crowd came up and began to ask Pilate to do for them as was his custom. 9 Pilate answered them, "Do you want me to release the king of the Jews for you?" 10 For he knew it was because of envy that the chief priests had handed him over. 11 But the chief priests stirred up the crowd so that he would release Barabbas to them instead. 12 Pilate asked them again, "Then what do you want me to do with the one you call the king of the Jews?"

13 Again they shouted, "Crucify him!"

14 Pilate said to them, "Why? What has he done wrong?"

But they shouted all the more, "Crucify him!"

15 Wanting to satisfy the crowd, Pilate released Barabbas to them; and after having Jesus flogged, he handed him over to be crucified.

MOCKED BY THE MILITARY

16 The soldiers led him away into the palace (that is, the governor's residence) and called the whole company together. 17 They dressed him in a purple robe, twisted together a crown of thorns, and put it on him. 18 And they began to salute him, "Hail, king of the Jews!" 19 They were hitting him on the head with a stick and spitting on him. Getting down on their knees, they were paying him homage. 20 After they had mocked him, they stripped him of the purple robe and put his clothes on him.

CRUCIFIED BETWEEN TWO CRIMINALS

They led him out to crucify him. 21 They forced a man coming in from the country, who was passing by, to carry Jesus's cross. He was Simon of Cyrene, the father of Alexander and Rufus.

22 They brought Jesus to the place called *Golgotha* (which means Place of the Skull). 23 They tried to give him wine mixed with myrrh, but he did not take it.

24 Then they crucified him and divided his clothes, casting lots for them to decide what each would get. 25 Now it was nine in the morning[A] when they crucified him. 26 The inscription of the charge written against him was: THE KING OF THE JEWS. 27 They crucified two criminals[B] with him, one on his right and one on his left.[C]

29 Those who passed by were yelling insults at[D] him, shaking their heads, and saying, "Ha! The one who would destroy the temple and rebuild it in three days, 30 save yourself by coming down from the cross!" 31 In the same way, the chief priests with the scribes were mocking him among themselves and saying, "He saved others, but he cannot save himself! 32 Let the Messiah, the King of Israel, come down now from the cross, so that we may see and believe." Even those who were crucified with him taunted him.

DIGGING DEEPER *Crucifixion and Burial of Jesus*

Two locations in Jerusalem are named as possible sites for Jesus's crucifixion and burial. One location, known as the Garden Tomb, was discovered by British army officer Charles Gordon in the 1880s. It is located outside the northeastern end of the Old City walls, adjacent to the Damascus Gate. The tomb is nestled within an enclosed garden that may be in the same location as the garden John mentioned (Jn 19:41). Gordon also identified what he believed to be the place of Christ's crucifixion. The Gospels say Christ was crucified at Golgotha, a name meaning "Place of the Skull" (Mt 27:33; Mk 15:22; Lk 23:33; Jn 19:17). The more likely candidate for Jesus's tomb is located within the Church of the Holy Sepulchre. This too is located outside the original city walls. Gardens flourished here in Jesus's day, and tombs were hewn out of the rock until the first century AD. Fourth-century historian Eusebius said locals identified this site with Emperor Constantine's mother, Helena. She and the church father Jerome revered it as the location of Christ's crucifixion and resurrection. Both tomb locations are good candidates and closely match various descriptions offered in the Bible.

THE DEATH OF JESUS

33 When it was noon,[E] darkness came over the whole land until three in the afternoon.[F] 34 And at three Jesus cried out with a loud voice, *"Eloi, Eloi, lemá sabachtháni?"* which is translated, **"My God, my God, why have you abandoned me?"**[G]

35 When some of those standing there heard this, they said, "See, he's calling for Elijah."

36 Someone ran and filled a sponge with sour wine, fixed it on a stick, offered him a drink, and said, "Let's see if Elijah comes to take him down."

37 Jesus let out a loud cry and breathed his last. 38 Then the curtain of the temple was torn in two from top to bottom. 39 When the centurion, who was standing opposite him, saw the way he[H] breathed his last, he said, "Truly this man was the Son of God!"[I]

40 There were also women watching from a distance. Among them were Mary Magdalene, Mary

[A] **15:25** Lit *was the third hour* [B] **15:27** Or *revolutionaries* [C] **15:27** Some mss include v. 28: *So the Scripture was fulfilled that says: And he was counted among criminals.* [D] **15:29** Or *passed by blasphemed* [E] **15:33** Lit *the sixth hour* [F] **15:33** Lit *the ninth hour*, also in v. 34 [G] **15:34** Ps 22:1 [H] **15:39** Other mss read *saw that he cried out like this and* [I] **15:39** Or *a son of God*

Pilate's Role in Jesus's Death

by Thomas H. Goodman

The harbor at Caesarea Maritima. Herod the Great acquired this region from Augustus Caesar in 30 BC and constructed a massive harbor and accompanying modern city, replete with opulent Hellenistic architecture. In AD 6, Caesarea became the capital of the province of Judea and the official home for those serving as governors.

Pilate's encounter with Jewish leadership at Jesus's trial was not the Roman governor's first experience navigating the complexities of Judean politics. Extrabiblical references to Pilate reveal a leader who became vulnerable to the emperor's criticism as Pilate proved himself increasingly incapable of providing regional stability. This vulnerability was a factor in how he handled Jesus's trial. Pilate should have upheld Roman justice and released Jesus. In the end, however, Pilate did what was best for Pilate.

In Jesus's day, Judea was under the governance of Roman procurators, a role in which Pilate served from AD 26 to 36. A procurator was a governor whom the emperor appointed directly; he was to manage the military, financial, and judicial operations of strategically sensitive regions of the Roman Empire.[1] The Roman government established a procurator's residence at the harbor city of Caesarea Maritima, located on the Mediterranean coast.

FIVE INCIDENTS

Five incidents reported in biblical and extrabiblical sources set the context for the accounts of Pilate's involvement with Jesus's crucifixion.[2] The first incident took place immediately after his being appointed governor. The Jewish historian Josephus reports that Pilate's soldiers posted standards bearing the emperor's image within sight of the temple in Jerusalem. Regarding the act as idolatrous, the Jews demanded the standards be removed. When Pilate threatened them with execution, the protestors bared their necks in defiant willingness to die rather than back down. Pilate was the one to back down. He removed the standards to Caesarea Maritima.

In the second incident, Pilate killed some Galileans who were offering sacrifices (Lk 13:1). We have no explanation about what provoked the killing, but the incident illustrates the occasionally tumultuous relationship between Pilate and his subjects.

Third, Pilate used money from the temple treasury to construct an aqueduct. The Jews objected to what they regarded as sacrilege of the temple offerings, and Pilate had the protestors beaten into subjection.

Fourth, according to the Jewish philosopher Philo, Pilate had votive shields hung in Herod's Jerusalem palace. Some believe the shields bore the name of the emperor as a deity. Regardless, the Jews found the shields to be offensive and appealed directly to Tiberius Caesar when Pilate refused to respond to their objections. Tiberius ordered that Pilate remove the shields to Caesarea Maritima and reprimanded his procurator for the unnecessary controversy.

Fifth, Josephus reports that Pilate ordered the execution of a number of Samaritan villagers who had followed a rebellious leader to Mount Gerizim. Hearing of this, Tiberius recalled Pilate to Rome in AD 36 and replaced him with Marcellus.

These five incidents provide a helpful context for understanding

Pilate's role in Jesus's death. Three leadership patterns that Pilate displayed in these historical records also show up in the records of Jesus's trial: general incompetence, vacillation, and vulnerability to imperial criticism.

THREE LEADERSHIP PATTERNS

First, Pilate was out of his depth trying to introduce Roman rule into the politically volatile province of Judea. He "displayed a general lack of sensitivity, tact, and knowledge" with the strange subjects he ruled.[3] In Jesus's trial, Pilate sought to maintain standards of Roman jurisprudence, yet he could not understand why his efforts to release the innocent man ended up raising the threat of revolt in Jerusalem. After his attempt to shift the decision to Herod (Lk 23:5–15), to satisfy the bloodlust by a flogging (Lk 23:16), and then to offer the crowd Jesus for Barabbas (Mt 27:15–21), he still faced an unruly mob. Unable to uphold Roman judicial standards and maintain order at the same time, he yielded to the easiest course to stability and gave Jesus up.

Second, Pilate tended toward vacillation. He posted the military standards and later the votive shields in an apparent declaration of his intent to exert Roman rule, only to waver quickly when things got complicated. This vacillating too showed up in Jesus's trial. Seven times in John 18:28–19:16, Pilate alternately went out to speak with the crowd and went in to speak with Jesus. That physical back and forth parallels what must have been his mental back and forth. On the one hand, after investigating Jesus, he knew that to kill him would be an abdication of the justice he was responsible to uphold. On the other hand, he knew that to release Jesus would so upset the turbulent crowd that the region could erupt in revolt.

The "Ecce Homo" arch spans the Via Dolorosa in Jerusalem. It marks the traditional spot where Pilate presented Jesus to the crowds and said, "Here is the man!" (*Ecce homo* in Latin; Jn 19:5).

Third, the extrabiblical and biblical sources display a procurator who was vulnerable to the waning favor of the emperor. In the incident with the votive shields, Philo reports that when the Jews complained to Tiberius, the emperor wrote Pilate, "reproaching and reviling him in the most bitter manner for his act of unprecedented audacity and wickedness, and commanding him immediately to take down the shields." In Jesus's trial, the Jewish leadership played on this vulnerability, saying, "If you release this man, you are not Caesar's friend" (Jn 19:12). After receiving previous imperial reprimands, Pilate had no motivation for defending Jesus if doing so meant losing the peace—and his job. Pilate's motivation for his decision was simple: he wanted "to satisfy the crowd" (Mk 15:15). ✣

[1] David S. Dockery, ed., *Holman Bible Handbook* (Nashville: Holman, 1992), 628. [2] The ancient Jewish writers Josephus and Philo are the sources for the extrabiblical stories about Pilate. The first account is found in Josephus, *Jewish Antiquities* 18.3.1, and Josephus, *Jewish War* 2.9.2–4. The third appears in Josephus, *Jewish Antiquities* 18.3.2. The fourth in Philo, *On the Embassy to Gaius* 38.299–305. The fifth, Josephus, *Jewish Antiquities* 18.4.1–2. [3] Brian C. McGing, "Pontius Pilate and the Sources," *Catholic Biblical Quarterly* (*CBQ*) 53.3 (1991): 438.

the mother of James the younger and of Joses, and Salome. 41 In Galilee these women followed him and took care of him. Many other women had come up with him to Jerusalem.

THE BURIAL OF JESUS

42 When it was already evening, because it was the day of preparation (that is, the day before the Sabbath), 43 Joseph of Arimathea, a prominent member of the Sanhedrin who was himself looking forward to the kingdom of God, came and boldly went to Pilate and asked for Jesus's body. 44 Pilate was surprised that he was already dead. Summoning the centurion, he asked him whether he had already died. 45 When he found out from the centurion, he gave the corpse to Joseph. 46 After he bought some linen cloth, Joseph took him down and wrapped him in the linen. Then he laid him in a tomb cut out of the rock and rolled a stone against the entrance to the tomb. 47 Mary Magdalene and Mary the mother of Joses were watching where he was laid.

RESURRECTION MORNING

16 When the Sabbath was over, Mary Magdalene, Mary the mother of James, and Salome bought spices, so that they could go and anoint him. 2 Very early in the morning, on the first day of the week, they went to the tomb at sunrise. 3 They were saying to one another, "Who will roll away the stone from the entrance to the tomb for us?" 4 Looking up, they noticed that the stone — which was very large — had been rolled away.

5 When they entered the tomb, they saw a young man dressed in a white robe sitting on the right side; they were alarmed. 6 "Don't be alarmed," he told them. "You are looking for Jesus of Nazareth, who was crucified. He has risen! He is not here. See the place where they put him. 7 But go, tell his disciples and Peter, 'He is going ahead of you to Galilee; you will see him there just as he told you.' "

8 They went out and ran from the tomb, because trembling and astonishment overwhelmed them. And they said nothing to anyone, since they were afraid.

[Some of the earliest mss conclude with 16:8.][A]

THE LONGER ENDING OF MARK: APPEARANCES OF THE RISEN LORD

[9 Early on the first day of the week, after he had risen, he appeared first to Mary Magdalene, out of whom he had driven seven demons. 10 She went and reported to those who had been with him, as they were mourning and weeping. 11 Yet, when they heard that he was alive and had been seen by her, they did not believe it.

12 After this, he appeared in a different form to two of them walking on their way into the country. 13 And they went and reported it to the rest, who did not believe them either.

THE GREAT COMMISSION

14 Later he appeared to the Eleven themselves as they were reclining at the table. He rebuked their unbelief and hardness of heart, because they did not believe those who saw him after he had risen. 15 Then he said to them, "Go into all the world and preach the gospel to all creation. 16 Whoever believes and is baptized will be saved, but whoever does not believe will be condemned. 17 And these signs will accompany those who believe: In my name they will drive out demons; they will speak in new tongues;[B] 18 they will pick up snakes;[C] if they should drink anything deadly, it will not harm them; they will lay hands on the sick, and they will get well."

THE ASCENSION

19 So the Lord Jesus, after speaking to them, was taken up into heaven and sat down at the right hand of God. 20 And they went out and preached everywhere, while the Lord worked with them and confirmed the word by the accompanying signs.]

[A] **16:8** Other mss include vv. 9-20 as a longer ending. The following shorter ending is found in some mss between v. 8 and v. 9 and in one ms after v. 8 (each of which omits vv. 9-20): *And all that had been commanded to them they quickly reported to those around Peter. After these things, Jesus himself sent out through them from east to west, the holy and imperishable proclamation of eternal salvation. Amen.* [B] **16:17** = languages [C] **16:18** Other mss add *with their hands*

LUKE

Located about four miles from Jerusalem is the village of Ein Karem, which tradition holds to be the hometown of Elizabeth and Zechariah. Shown is the Church of the Visitation, which commemorates Mary's visit to Elizabeth.

INTRODUCTION TO

LUKE

Circumstances of Writing

The author of the Third Gospel is not named. Considerable evidence points to Luke as its author. Much of that proof is found in the book of Acts, which identifies itself as a sequel to Luke (Ac 1:1–3). A major line of evidence has to do with the so-called "we" sections of the book (Ac 16:10–17; 20:5–15; 21:1–18; 27:1–37; 28:1–16). Most of Acts is narrated in third-person plural ("they," "them"), but some later sections having to do with the ministry of the apostle Paul unexpectedly shift to first-person plural ("we," "us"). This indicates that the author had joined the apostle Paul for the events recorded in those passages. Since there are no "we" passages in the Gospel of Luke, that fits with the author stating that he used eyewitness testimony to the life of Jesus (Lk 1:2), indicating he was not such an eyewitness himself.

Among Paul's well-known coworkers, the most likely candidate is Luke, the doctor (see Col 4:14; Phm 24). That is also the unanimous testimony of the earliest Christian writers (e.g., Justin Martyr, the Muratorian Canon, and Tertullian). Since Luke is not named among the workers who were "of the circumcised" (i.e., a Jew; Col 4:11), he was almost certainly a Gentile. That explains the healthy emphasis on Gentiles in Luke (Lk 6:17; 7:1–10). Luke also reflects an interest in medical matters (e.g., 4:38; 14:2).

Traditionally, the Gospel of Luke is believed to have been written after both Matthew and Mark. Those who date Matthew and Mark in the AD 60s or 70s have tended to push the dating of Luke back to the AD 70s or 80s.

Since Luke wrote both the Third Gospel and the book of Acts (Ac 1:1–3), it is relevant to consider the dating of both books together. The events at the end of Acts occurred around AD 62–63. That is the earliest point at which Acts could have been written. If Acts was written in the early AD 60s from Rome, where Paul was imprisoned for two years (28:30), the Third Gospel could date from an earlier stage of that period of imprisonment. The other reasonable possibility is during Paul's earlier two-year imprisonment in Caesarea (24:27). From that location, Luke would have been able to travel and interview the eyewitnesses to Jesus's life and ministry who were still alive.

The Third Gospel is addressed to "most honorable Theophilus" (Lk 1:3), about whom nothing else is known other than that he is also the recipient of the book of Acts (Ac 1:1). The Greek name Theophilus means "lover of God" or "friend of God" and implies that he was a Gentile, probably Greek. He seems to have been a relatively new believer, recently instructed about Jesus and the Christian faith (Lk 1:4). The title "most honorable" indicates that, at the least, he was a person of high standing and financial substance. It may also reflect that he was an official with some governmental authority and power.

Contribution to the Bible

Nearly 60 percent of the material in the Gospel of Luke is unique. Thus there is a great deal that readers of Scripture would not know if the Third Gospel were not in the Bible. The following are notable among the larger distinctive portions: (1) much of the material in Luke 1–2 about the births of John the Baptist and Jesus, (2) the only biblical material on Jesus's childhood and preministry adult life (2:40–52), (3) a genealogy for Jesus (3:23–38) that is significantly different from the one in Matthew 1:1–17, (4) most of the "travelogue" section about Jesus's journey to Jerusalem (Lk 9:51–19:44), (5) a considerably different slant on the destruction of the temple (21:5–38) from the Olivet Discourse in Matthew 24–25 and Mark 13, and (6) quite a bit of fresh material in the postresurrection appearances, including the Emmaus Road, a distinctive statement of the Great Commission, and the only description in the Gospels of Jesus's ascension into heaven (Lk 24:13–53).

Structure

Luke's distinctive "narrative about the events" (1:1) of the life of Jesus is written in "orderly sequence" (1:3), though not strict chronological sequence in many cases. Generally, after the key events leading up to the beginning of Christ's public ministry (1:5–4:13), the flow of the book is from his early ministry in and around Galilee (4:14–9:50), through an extended description of ministry related to his journey to Jerusalem (9:51–19:44), climaxing in the events of Passion Week and postresurrection appearances in and around Jerusalem (19:45–24:53).

THE DEDICATION TO THEOPHILUS

1 Many have undertaken to compile a narrative about the events that have been fulfilled[A] among us, 2 just as the original eyewitnesses and servants of the word handed them down to us. 3 So it also seemed good to me, since I have carefully investigated everything from the very first, to write to you in an orderly sequence, most honorable Theophilus, 4 so that you may know the certainty of the things about which you have been instructed.[B]

GABRIEL PREDICTS JOHN'S BIRTH

5 In the days of King Herod of Judea, there was a priest of Abijah's division named Zechariah. His wife was from the daughters of Aaron, and her name was Elizabeth. 6 Both were righteous in God's sight, living without blame according to all the commands and requirements of the Lord. 7 But they had no children because Elizabeth could not conceive, and both of them were well along in years.

8 When his division was on duty and he was serving as priest before God, 9 it happened that he was chosen by lot, according to the custom of the priesthood, to enter the sanctuary of the Lord and burn incense. 10 At the hour of incense the whole assembly of the people was praying outside. 11 An angel of the Lord appeared to him, standing to the right of the altar of incense. 12 When Zechariah saw him, he was terrified and overcome with fear. 13 But the angel said to him, "Do not be afraid, Zechariah, because your prayer has been heard. Your wife Elizabeth will bear you a son, and you will name him John. 14 There will be joy and delight for you, and many will rejoice at his birth. 15 For he will be great in the sight of the Lord and will never drink wine or beer. He will be filled with the Holy Spirit while still in his mother's womb. 16 He will turn many of the children of Israel to the Lord their God. 17 And he will go before him in the spirit and power of Elijah, to turn the hearts of fathers to their children, and the disobedient to the understanding of the righteous, to make ready for the Lord a prepared people."

18 "How can I know this?" Zechariah asked the angel. "For I am an old man, and my wife is well along in years."

19 The angel answered him, "I am Gabriel, who stands in the presence of God, and I was sent to speak to you and tell you this good news. 20 Now listen. You will become silent and unable to speak until the day these things take place, because you did not believe my words, which will be fulfilled in their proper time."

21 Meanwhile, the people were waiting for Zechariah, amazed that he stayed so long in the sanctuary. 22 When he did come out, he could not speak to them. Then they realized that he had seen a vision in the sanctuary. He was making signs to them and remained speechless. 23 When the days of his ministry were completed, he went back home.

24 After these days his wife Elizabeth conceived and kept herself in seclusion for five months. She said, 25 "The Lord has done this for me. He has looked with favor in these days to take away my disgrace among the people."

GABRIEL PREDICTS JESUS'S BIRTH

26 In the sixth month, the angel Gabriel was sent by God to a town in Galilee called Nazareth, 27 to a virgin engaged[C] to a man named Joseph, of the house of David. The virgin's name was Mary. 28 And the angel came to her and said, "Greetings, favored woman! The Lord is with you."[D] 29 But she was deeply troubled by this statement, wondering what kind of greeting this could be. 30 Then the angel told her, "Do not be afraid, Mary, for you have found favor with God. 31 Now listen: You will conceive and give birth to a son, and you will name him Jesus. 32 He will be great and will be called the Son of the Most High, and the Lord God will give him the throne of his father David. 33 He will reign over the house of Jacob forever, and his kingdom will have no end."

34 Mary asked the angel, "How can this be, since I have not had sexual relations with a man?"[E]

35 The angel replied to her, "The Holy Spirit will come upon you, and the power of the Most High will overshadow you. Therefore, the holy one to be born will be called the Son of God. 36 And consider your relative Elizabeth — even she has conceived a son in her old age, and this is the sixth month for her who was called childless. 37 For nothing will be impossible with God."

38 "See, I am the Lord's servant," said Mary. "May it happen to me as you have said." Then the angel left her.

MARY'S VISIT TO ELIZABETH

39 In those days Mary set out and hurried to a town in the hill country of Judah 40 where she entered Zechariah's house and greeted Elizabeth. 41 When Elizabeth heard Mary's greeting, the baby leaped inside her, and Elizabeth was filled with the Holy Spirit. 42 Then she exclaimed with a loud cry, "Blessed are you among women, and your child will be blessed![F] 43 How could this happen to me, that the mother of my Lord should come to me? 44 For you see, when the sound of your greeting reached my ears, the baby leaped for joy inside me. 45 Blessed is she who has believed that the Lord would fulfill what he has spoken to her!"

[A] **1:1** Or *events that have been accomplished*, or *events most surely believed* [B] **1:4** Or *informed* [C] **1:27** Lit *betrothed* [D] **1:28** Other mss add *Blessed are you among women.* [E] **1:34** Lit *since I do not know a man* [F] **1:42** Lit *and the fruit of your abdomen* (or *womb*) *is blessed*

MARY'S PRAISE

46 And Mary said:
My soul magnifies the Lord,
47 and my spirit rejoices in God my Savior,
48 because he has looked with favor
on the humble condition of his servant.
Surely, from now on all generations
will call me blessed,
49 because the Mighty One
has done great things for me,
and his name is holy.
50 His mercy is from generation to generation
on those who fear him.
51 He has done a mighty deed with his arm;
he has scattered the proud
because of the thoughts of their hearts;
52 he has toppled the mighty
from their thrones
and exalted the lowly.
53 He has satisfied the hungry
with good things
and sent the rich away empty.
54 He has helped his servant Israel,
remembering his mercy
55 to Abraham and his descendants[A] forever,
just as he spoke to our ancestors.

56 And Mary stayed with her about three months;
then she returned to her home.

THE BIRTH AND NAMING OF JOHN

57 Now the time had come for Elizabeth to give birth,
and she had a son. 58 Then her neighbors and relatives
heard that the Lord had shown her his great mercy,
and they rejoiced with her.
59 When they came to circumcise the child on the
eighth day, they were going to name him Zechariah,
after his father. 60 But his mother responded, "No. He
will be called John."
61 Then they said to her, "None of your relatives
has that name." 62 So they motioned to his father to
find out what he wanted him to be called. 63 He asked
for a writing tablet and wrote, "His name is John."
And they were all amazed. 64 Immediately his mouth
was opened and his tongue set free, and he began to
speak, praising God. 65 Fear came on all those who
lived around them, and all these things were being
talked about throughout the hill country of Judea.
66 All who heard about him took it to heart, saying,
"What then will this child become?" For, indeed, the
Lord's hand was with him.

[A] **1:55** Or *offspring*; lit *seed*

The interior of the Church of Annunciation in Nazareth. The cave ("grotto") under the arch at the bottom of the image is the traditional site where the angel appeared to Mary.

A Mother's Role in the First Century

by Sharon H. Gritz

Motherhood represented an important role for first-century Jewish women. This responsibility began for many as early as age sixteen, if not younger. Bearing a child ensured the continuity of the family name, thus fulfilling a vital function in the family. In a broader sense, providing children meant the stability and growth of the Jewish people or nation. Consequently, the Jews valued mothers and viewed children as a blessing, a gift and reward from the Lord (Ps 127:3–5).

Arab woman blows air into a sealed goatskin, which contains milk. She will seal the opening; afterward she and her family will take turns rocking the filled skin on the frame in order to make butter.

GIVING BIRTH AND INFANT CARE

Most women gave birth at home with the help of a midwife. A woman's mother and perhaps other female family members would have aided as well. Even if they offered no medical help, these family figures provided emotional support. Childbirth in the first-century Greco-Roman world was risky. Medical knowledge and practices were limited, vague, or wrong. Consequently infant mortality was high. Some estimate that 30 percent of babies did not survive their first year.[1] Mothers also died giving birth. These deaths occurred across all socioeconomic levels.

Immediately after birth, the midwife or another female assistant washed the baby and rubbed the infant's skin with salt (Ezk 16:4; the purpose of the salt is unclear). Both boys and girls received this treatment.[2] After this, babies were swaddled by being wrapped with a square of fabric and tied with strips or bands of cloth. Believing it kept the baby's limbs straight, mothers would swaddle their infants for several months; swaddling also kept the children warm. Salting the infant's skin and wrapping the baby in swaddling clothes was part of the midwife's care. Mary likely had none of the customary female support system when she gave birth far from home. Supporting this possibility is Luke's indication that Mary herself wrapped Jesus and placed him in the manger.

Mothers breast-fed their infants for two to three years. Jewish law even required women to do this for twenty-four months.[3] Certain rituals or cultural practices accompanied the child's birth, including naming the infant. Both fathers and mothers could name the newborn, whether it was a girl or boy. They often used family names or names with special meaning. Circumcision initiated male babies into Jewish society; this took place eight days after birth. Mothers also observed the rite of purification following childbirth.

EDUCATING CHILDREN

Mothers served as the main parental influence on all their children until their sons reached the age of five to seven. From their mothers, boys and girls learned many basics of their Jewish faith—hearing the stories of Israel's heroes, being instructed in morals, memorizing certain passages of the law.

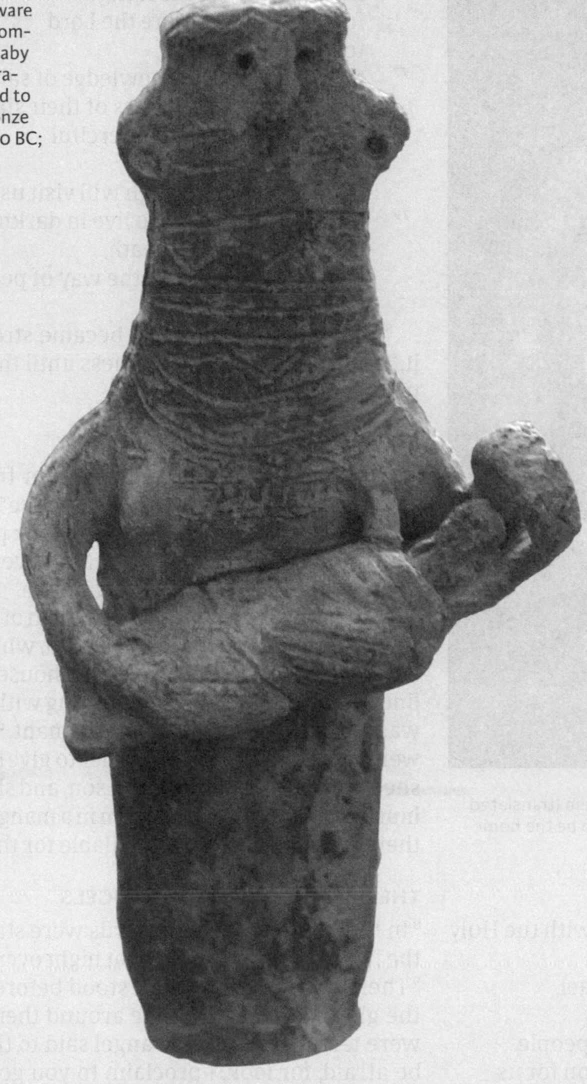

Red-polished ware figurine of a woman carrying a baby on a hooped cradleboard; dated to the Middle Bronze Age, 2200–1550 BC; Cypriot.

While his son was still young, the father assumed responsibility for his education by teaching him a trade, usually his own vocation, such as carpentry, metalworking, or fishing. Fathers also taught their sons religious laws and life duties. Mothers continued the training of their daughters by instructing them in all the domestic skills expected of women. Additionally, girls had to learn the law's regulations concerning purity issues and the responsibilities of women. A girl remained under her mother's influence until she married.

DAILY TASKS

Mothers (and wives) worked hard to maintain their households and meet their families' needs. Each helped to hold together and preserve the all-important family unit. Their activities demanded time-consuming manual labor. A woman's tasks included cooking and cleaning. Beyond this, she had to perform those duties that related to her husband, duties that included washing her husband's face, hands, and feet. Women could delegate many of their domestic chores to any bondservants or hired help if they had them.[4]

Food preparation consumed much of a mother's day. She sifted grain to remove any impurities and would then grind the grain into flour for baking bread. Preparing food also included gardening and butchering. The mother often milked the family's goat. Some even worked in the fields. Some women made trips to the local market for food and supplies, although some scholars suggest only the men could perform this domestic chore since society did not expect women to visit a public area where nonfamily men might be present.[5]

Mothers were responsible for making and keeping clean the family's clothing. This included spinning the thread, weaving the fabric, sewing, mending, and washing. Women made the trip to the local well many times a day, especially in the morning and evening, to secure fresh water to meet the family's daily needs. Women also kept the small lamps burning in the house by filling them with oil. Mothers or young daughters also gathered small twigs to provide fuel for fire in clay ovens. Mothers kept their homes clean, often assigning floor sweeping to a young daughter. They also met the needs of any guests or visitors to the home. ✣

---

[1] Carolyn Osiek and Margaret Y. MacDonald with Janet H. Tulloch, *A Woman's Place: House Churches in Earliest Christianity* (Minneapolis: Fortress, 2006), 65. [2] Larry G. Herr, "Salt" in *ISBE* (1988), 4:286. [3] Leonie J. Archer, *Her Price Is beyond Rubies: The Jewish Woman in Graeco-Roman Palestine* (Sheffield: Sheffield Academic, 1990), 227. [4] Ben Witherington III, *Women in the Ministry of Jesus* (Cambridge: Cambridge University Press, 1984), 4. [5] Archer, *Her Price*, 227.

Well inside the Church of the Visitation at Ein Karem (translated "Spring of the Vineyard"), which tradition holds to be the hometown of Elizabeth and Zechariah.

ZECHARIAH'S PROPHECY

67 Then his father Zechariah was filled with the Holy
Spirit and prophesied:

68 Blessed is the Lord, the God of Israel,
because he has visited
and provided redemption for his people.
69 He has raised up a horn of salvation for us
in the house of his servant David,
70 just as he spoke by the mouth
of his holy prophets in ancient times;
71 salvation from our enemies
and from the hand of those who hate us.
72 He has dealt mercifully
with our ancestors
and remembered his holy covenant —
73 the oath that he swore to our father Abraham,
to grant that we,
74 having been rescued
from the hand of our enemies,
would serve him without fear
75 in holiness and righteousness
in his presence all our days.
76 And you, child, will be called
a prophet of the Most High,
for you will go before the Lord
to prepare his ways,
77 to give his people knowledge of salvation
through the forgiveness of their sins.
78 Because of our God's merciful
compassion,
the dawn from on high will visit us
79 to shine on those who live in darkness
and the shadow of death,
to guide our feet into the way of peace.

80 The child grew up and became strong in spirit,[A] and he was in the wilderness until the day of his
public appearance to Israel.

THE BIRTH OF JESUS

2 In those days a decree went out from Caesar
Augustus that the whole empire[B] should be
registered. 2 This first registration took place while[C]
Quirinius was governing Syria. 3 So everyone went
to be registered, each to his own town.
4 Joseph also went up from the town of Nazareth in
Galilee, to Judea, to the city of David, which is called
Bethlehem, because he was of the house and family
line of David, 5 to be registered along with Mary, who
was engaged to him[D] and was pregnant. 6 While they
were there, the time came for her to give birth. 7 Then
she gave birth to her firstborn son, and she wrapped
him tightly in cloth and laid him in a manger,[E] because
there was no guest room available for them.

THE SHEPHERDS AND THE ANGELS

8 In the same region, shepherds were staying out in
the fields and keeping watch at night over their flock.
9 Then an angel of the Lord stood before them, and
the glory of the Lord shone around them, and they
were terrified.[F] 10 But the angel said to them, "Don't
be afraid, for look, I proclaim to you good news of
great joy that will be for all the people:[G] 11 Today in
the city of David a Savior was born for you, who is
the Messiah, the Lord. 12 This will be the sign for you:
You will find a baby wrapped tightly in cloth and
lying in a manger."
13 Suddenly there was a multitude of the heavenly
host[H] with the angel, praising God and saying:

14 Glory to God in the highest heaven,
and peace on earth to people he favors![I,J]

[A] **1:80** Or *strong in the Spirit* [B] **2:1** Or *the whole inhabited world*
[C] **2:2** Or *This registration was the first while*, or *This registration was before* [D] **2:5** Lit *betrothed* [E] **2:7** Or *feeding trough*, also in vv. 12,16
[F] **2:9** Lit *they feared a great fear* [G] **2:10** Or *the whole nation*
[H] **2:13** Lit *heavenly army* [I] **2:14** Other mss read *earth good will to people* [J] **2:14** Or *earth to men of good will*

15 When the angels had left them and returned to
heaven, the shepherds said to one another, "Let's go
straight to Bethlehem and see what has happened,
which the Lord has made known to us."
16 They hurried off and found both Mary and Joseph, and the baby who was lying in the manger.
17 After seeing them, they reported the message they
were told about this child, 18 and all who heard it were
amazed at what the shepherds said to them. 19 But
Mary was treasuring up all these things in her heart
and meditating on them. 20 The shepherds returned,
glorifying and praising God for all the things they
had seen and heard, which were just as they had
been told.

THE CIRCUMCISION AND PRESENTATION OF JESUS

21 When the eight days were completed for his circumcision, he was named Jesus — the name given
by the angel before he was conceived. 22 And when
the days of their purification according to the law of
Moses were finished, they brought him up to Jerusalem to present him to the Lord 23 (just as it is written
in the law of the Lord, **Every firstborn male will be
dedicated**[A] **to the Lord**[B]) 24 and to offer a sacrifice
(according to what is stated in the law of the Lord, **a
pair of turtledoves or two young pigeons**[C]).

SIMEON'S PROPHETIC PRAISE

25 There was a man in Jerusalem whose name was
Simeon. This man was righteous and devout, looking
forward to Israel's consolation, and the Holy Spirit
was on him. 26 It had been revealed to him by the Holy
Spirit that he would not see death before he saw the
Lord's Messiah. 27 Guided by the Spirit, he entered
the temple. When the parents brought in the child
Jesus to perform for him what was customary under
the law, 28 Simeon took him up in his arms, praised
God, and said,

29 Now, Master,
you can dismiss your servant in peace,
as you promised.
30 For my eyes have seen your salvation.
31 You have prepared it
in the presence of all peoples —
32 a light for revelation to the Gentiles[D]
and glory to your people Israel.

33 His father and mother[E] were amazed at what was
being said about him. 34 Then Simeon blessed them
and told his mother Mary, "Indeed, this child is destined to cause the fall and rise of many in Israel and
to be a sign that will be opposed[F] — 35 and a sword
will pierce your own soul — that the thoughts[G] of
many hearts may be revealed."

DIGGING DEEPER *Bethlehem*

Though the exact origin of the name Bethlehem is not fully understood, the Hebrew word is generally thought to mean "house of bread." Bethlehem is located in what is now Palestinian territory among the Judean hills six miles south of Jerusalem. Its ruins lie about twenty feet below the modern streets of Bethlehem, making excavation difficult. In fact, conditions have allowed only minor work over the years. Bethlehem is one of the oldest cities in the biblical world, dating to prehistoric times. Many biblically significant events occurred in Bethlehem. Rachel was buried here (Gn 35:19); Elimelech and his wife, Naomi, originated at Bethlehem and then moved to Moab (Ru 1:1–2); David was raised and anointed as king in Bethlehem (1Sm 16:4,13; 17:12); Micah describes it as "Ephrathah" in his prophecy of the birthplace of the Messiah (Mc 5:2); and, most important, Jesus was born in Bethlehem (Mt 2:1; Lk 2:4). In the fourth century AD, Emperor Constantine built a church over the alleged site of Jesus's birth. Bethlehem is also the place where Jerome translated the Bible into Latin, thus producing what became the standard Bible in the Catholic Church for one thousand years.

ANNA'S TESTIMONY

36 There was also a prophetess, Anna, a daughter of
Phanuel, of the tribe of Asher. She was well along in
years, having lived with her husband seven years
after her marriage,[H] 37 and was a widow for eighty-
four years.[I] She did not leave the temple, serving God
night and day with fasting and prayers. 38 At that very
moment,[J] she came up and began to thank God and
to speak about him to all who were looking forward
to the redemption of Jerusalem.[K]

THE FAMILY'S RETURN TO NAZARETH

39 When they had completed everything according
to the law of the Lord, they returned to Galilee, to
their own town of Nazareth. 40 The boy grew up and
became strong, filled with wisdom, and God's grace
was on him.

IN HIS FATHER'S HOUSE

41 Every year his parents traveled to Jerusalem for
the Passover Festival. 42 When he was twelve years

[A] **2:23** Lit *be called holy* [B] **2:23** Ex 13:2,12 [C] **2:24** Lv 5:11; 12:8
[D] **2:32** Or *the nations* [E] **2:33** Other mss read *But Joseph and his mother*
[F] **2:34** Or *spoken against* [G] **2:35** Or *schemes* [H] **2:36** Lit *years from her virginity* [I] **2:37** Or *she was a widow until the age of eighty-four*
[J] **2:38** Lit *very hour* [K] **2:38** Other mss read *in Jerusalem*

Caesar Augustus: his mother was Julius Caesar's niece; his grandmother, who raised him, was Julius Caesar's sister. Although born a plebian, he gained patrician status by Julius Caesar's adoption in early 44 BC, just before Caesar's murder by senatorial conspirators. He was destined to turn his adoptive family's name into a powerful dynastic institution with implications that would have ripple effects for millennia. His given name was Octavian/ Octavius. His granted name was Augustus. He was the first and greatest emperor of the Roman Empire, as well as its supreme architect.

The veiled bust represents Caesar Augustus at a mature age as Pontifex Maximus.

CONQUEST AND CONFLICT

Rome's rapid Mediterranean conquest in the second century before Christ brought increasing power and wealth to Romans back in Italy. Aristocratic families garnished huge supplies of slaves to operate their landed estates. Equestrians took advantage of newly opened trade routes for even more lucrative commercial enterprises.

But Rome's internal class conflicts stifled territorial expansion. Powerful aristocratic families based on kinship were pitted against a newer equestrian class based on wealth. The aristocrats had their power base in the Senate. The businessmen had their power base in their money and connections.[1]

Class conflict became class warfare with competing armies.[2] Each involving a coalition of three powerful leaders, two triumvirate experiments were desperate moves to end the incessant fighting. Each attempt at power distribution was doomed. The First Triumvirate (60–53 BC) set up among three generals—Pompey, Crassus, and (Julius) Caesar—fell apart, and Caesar gained sole control of Rome as dictator. Republican senators fearing Caesar's monarchial aspirations formed a conspiracy and murdered him in 44 BC. Out of the political chaos following this assassination came a Second Triumvirate (43–36 BC) among Lepidus, Antony, and Octavian.[3] This attempt also fell apart, producing the famous showdown between Antony's forces in the East and Octavian's forces in the West. Antony lost the decisive naval battle of Actium in 31 BC, committed suicide, and left Octavian sole ruler of all Roman territories. After centuries of conflict, Rome finally had peace.

These years of class warfare and desperate triumvirate experiments simply meant the old political system known as the Roman Republic was falling apart. Anarchy loomed on Rome's horizon. Octavian's victory at Actium was only the beginning of a greater war to stabilize and reconstruct Roman government. This reconstruction had to keep at bay the lurking tensions and power struggles of Roman classes and their institutions.

FROM REPUBLIC TO EMPIRE

Of all the leaders born of Roman blood, history has declared no one more suited for this monumental task than Octavian. He was politically astute, militarily successful, financially wealthy, and an artful negotiator. He brought a calculated public humility to the task of abetting senatorial suspicions of aspirations to kingship. He gained public admiration by his absence of pretense and emphasis on traditional Roman morals and values. He commanded his armies' allegiance

Altar of Peace dedicated by the Senate to honor Augustus. Built on Rome's Campus Martius between 13 and 9 BC, this monument commemorates Augustus's victories in Spain and Gaul, resulting in a sustained era of peace for the Roman Empire. Reliefs of three sides show the emperor, senators, and their families in procession to the altar's dedication.

with good pay, generous retirement, and strong leadership. Octavian skillfully dodged all the phobias real or imagined genetic to the Roman political psyche, whether tyrannical monarchy, oppressive oligarchy, or the self-destructive class conflicts of the waning Republican years.

Octavian created a *princeps* system ("first man"; "principle man"). This system depended not on a specific public office, but on the consolidation of authority into one person through accumulation of titles and responsibilities. Some titles were simply symbolic, but others held significant religious, political, or military connotations. One of these titles, *augustus* ("highly honored"; "most revered"), became the name by which Octavian would be known to history.[4] Another important title was imperator, supreme commander of all Roman legions.

In 27 BC, Octavian began reorganizing the Roman government. His greatest contributions were political and military. He devised a provincial system administrating territories that were conquered, bequeathed, or annexed. The system worked successfully for centuries. The genius of the design was a simple division into two basic types of provinces. The first type of Roman province was senatorial. Senatorial provinces were the stable, older, prosperous territories that were politically more reliable and had traditional civil administration. Senatorial provinces were delegated to the control of the Roman Senate. The apex of a senator's career was for him to be named by the emperor and formally ratified by the Senate, as proconsul (governor) of one of these senatorial provinces. Paul met the proconsul Sergius Paulus on Cyprus on his first missionary journey (Ac 13:7) and appeared before Gallio, the proconsul of Achaia, in Corinth on his second (18:12). Besides Cyprus and Achaia (Greece), other New Testament examples of senatorial provinces are Asia (see Ephesus) and Macedonia (see Philippi, Thessalonica).

The other type of Roman province was imperial. Imperial provinces were unstable, newer territories prone to insurrection or violence. Such provinces required constant military supervision and were under the direct control of the emperor as imperator, commander of the armies. Thus these provinces had military governments and permanently stationed Roman legions under the command of a legate, a military officer who answered directly to the emperor. Subdistricts within imperial provinces would be delegated to local governors. Governors responsible for tax collection were called procurators.

Procurators were military officers drawn from equestrian ranks. In the New Testament, we meet three governors: Pontius Pilate (AD 26–36), Marcus Antonius Felix (AD 52–58), and Porcius Festus (AD 58–62). Since the territory of Judea was part of the Syrian province, Judean governors were answerable to the legate stationed in Syria. Luke mentioned Quirinius as the legate of Syria when Jesus was born (Lk 2:2).

Octavian also reorganized the Roman army. He divided troops into two main categories, legions and auxiliaries. Roman legions had five thousand to six thousand professional soldiers who served for a lifetime. Because Judea was always prone to disturbance and instability, several legions were always stationed in the region. The premier boots-on-the-ground officer, loved and respected for leadership and standing shoulder to shoulder in the heat of battle, was the centurion, the officer over a century (a hundred) men.

Auxiliaries were local recruits from the provinces. Logically, recruits could not serve in their own country. Service usually was for twenty years. Non-Romans desired military service because highly valued Roman citizenship came with honorable discharge. Octavian's reorganized Roman military established itself as the supreme fighting force in the ancient world. Their strict disciplinary codes and brilliant engineering feats drove them to overcome even the most daunting of enemy defenses. One of these extraordinary feats was building a great siege ramp to scale Masada, where Jewish Zealots who had escaped Jerusalem's final hours held out for three years at the end of the First Jewish War. Remains of this Roman ramp survive to this day.

CONTRIBUTIONS TO CHRISTIANITY

Augustus had a tremendous impact on the world of Jesus, the apostles, and later Christian history. His contributions include the following:

Governmental stability—the end of political chaos. Stability facilitated political and military consolidation of power, contributing to the rapid expansion of the empire. A traveler dealt with the same government even in far-flung regions; this included the same laws, officials, currency, and regulations.

Pax Romana—the "peace of Rome." Centuries of conflict were ended. A time of peace and prosperity followed. Travel and

communication became easier and safer. Missionaries could travel, safe from foreign armies and conflicts. In the East, Syria and Galatia no longer had to face the feared Parthian threat, paving the way for Paul's first missionary journey. His second missionary journey was made more feasible because the barbarian tribes of Illyria no longer menaced Macedonia and Achaia. The Roman poet Virgil hailed Augustus as savior of the world because of this peace.[5]

Roman roads—built to move troops. Roman engineers built military roads still standing today as testimony to their extraordinary skills. Along these same roads commercial and private traffic moved swiftly and easily. Communication became regular and much more dependable. Traveling evangelists moved down the same roads as Roman legions. Missionary pastors could send letters to newly established congregations. Paul traveled the Via Egnatia while in Macedonia moving from Philippi through Amphipolis and Apollonia on to Thessalonica (see Ac 16–17).

Religious toleration—a general Roman piety. Traditional Roman values encouraged by Augustus included piety toward all gods. The Roman Pantheon ("all gods") in the heart of the city expressed this traditional piety. A new sect could develop within an established religion, such as Judaism, without arousing Roman suspicion. Thus Gallio immediately dismissed as irrelevant the Jewish charges trumped up against Paul by synagogue leaders in Corinth (Ac 18:16). ✣

---

[1] Both of these wealthy and powerful classes also had to manage a third class, the huge mass of the underprivileged and poor, ready to riot at the first sign of food shortages. [2] On behalf of the businessmen's party, Pompey engaged his armies in an eastern campaign that brought him to the doorstep of the Jerusalem temple in 63 BC. From that point on, Judea was under the shadow of Rome. [3] During this Second Triumvirate, the Roman Senate declared Herod king of Judea in 40 BC. [4] The Romans renamed the eighth month of the year in Augustus's honor because so many important events of his career happened in that month. Thus two months in our calendar bear the names of Roman rulers: July for Julius Caesar and August for Augustus. [5] Vergil, *Eclogae* 4.4–52.

Vestibule of the Church of the Nativity in Bethlehem, the traditional site of Jesus's birth.

old, they went up according to the custom of the
festival. 43 After those days were over, as they were
returning, the boy Jesus stayed behind in Jerusalem,
but his parents[A] did not know it. 44 Assuming he was
in the traveling party, they went a day's journey. Then
they began looking for him among their relatives and
friends. 45 When they did not find him, they returned
to Jerusalem to search for him. 46 After three days,
they found him in the temple sitting among the teachers, listening to them and asking them questions.
47 And all those who heard him were astounded at his
understanding and his answers. 48 When his parents
saw him, they were astonished, and his mother said
to him, "Son, why have you treated us like this? Your
father and I have been anxiously searching for you."
49 "Why were you searching for me?" he asked
them. "Didn't you know that it was necessary for
me to be in my Father's house?"[B] 50 But they did not
understand what he said to them.

IN FAVOR WITH GOD AND WITH PEOPLE

51 Then he went down with them and came to Nazareth and was obedient to them. His mother kept
all these things in her heart. 52 And Jesus increased
in wisdom and stature, and in favor with God and
with people.

THE MESSIAH'S HERALD

3 In the fifteenth year of the reign of Tiberius Caesar, while Pontius Pilate was governor of Judea,
Herod was tetrarch[C] of Galilee, his brother Philip
tetrarch of the region of Iturea and Trachonitis, and
Lysanias tetrarch of Abilene, 2 during the high priesthood of Annas and Caiaphas, God's word came to
John the son of Zechariah in the wilderness. 3 He went
into all the vicinity of the Jordan, proclaiming a baptism of repentance for the forgiveness of sins, 4 as it is
written in the book of the words of the prophet Isaiah:

A voice of one crying out in the wilderness:
Prepare the way for the Lord;
make his paths straight!
5 **Every valley will be filled,**
and every mountain and hill will be
made low;[D]
the crooked will become straight,
the rough ways smooth,
6 **and everyone will see the salvation of God.**[E]

7 He then said to the crowds who came out to be
baptized by him, "Brood of vipers! Who warned you to
flee from the coming wrath? 8 Therefore produce fruit
consistent with repentance. And don't start saying to
yourselves, 'We have Abraham as our father,' for I tell
you that God is able to raise up children for Abraham
from these stones. 9 The ax is already at the root of
the trees. Therefore, every tree that doesn't produce
good fruit will be cut down and thrown into the fire."
10 "What then should we do?" the crowds were
asking him.
11 He replied to them, "The one who has two shirts
must share with someone who has none, and the one
who has food must do the same."
12 Tax collectors also came to be baptized, and they
asked him, "Teacher, what should we do?"
13 He told them, "Don't collect any more than what
you have been authorized."
14 Some soldiers also questioned him, "What should
we do?"
He said to them, "Don't take money from anyone
by force or false accusation, and be satisfied with
your wages."
15 Now the people were waiting expectantly, and
all of them were questioning in their hearts whether
John might be the Messiah. 16 John answered them all,

[A] **2:43** Other mss read *but Joseph and his mother* [B] **2:49** Or *be involved in my Father's interests* (or *things*), or *be among my Father's people* [C] **3:1** Or *ruler* [D] **3:5** Lit *be humbled* [E] **3:4–6** Is 40:3–5

"I baptize you with water, but one who is more powerful than I am is coming. I am not worthy to untie the strap of his sandals. He will baptize you with[A] the Holy Spirit and fire. 17 His winnowing shovel is in his hand to clear his threshing floor and gather the wheat into his barn, but the chaff he will burn with fire that never goes out." 18 Then, along with many other exhortations, he proclaimed good news to the people. 19 But when John rebuked Herod the tetrarch because of Herodias, his brother's wife, and all the evil things he had done, 20 Herod added this to everything else — he locked up John in prison.

THE BAPTISM OF JESUS

21 When all the people were baptized, Jesus also was baptized. As he was praying, heaven opened, 22 and the Holy Spirit descended on him in a physical appearance like a dove. And a voice came from heaven: "You are my beloved Son; with you I am well-pleased."

THE GENEALOGY OF JESUS CHRIST

23 As he began his ministry, Jesus was about thirty years old and was thought to be the

son of Joseph, son of Heli,
24 son of Matthat, son of Levi,
son of Melchi, son of Jannai,
son of Joseph, 25 son of Mattathias,
son of Amos, son of Nahum,
son of Esli, son of Naggai,
26 son of Maath, son of Mattathias,
son of Semein, son of Josech,
son of Joda, 27 son of Joanan,
son of Rhesa, son of Zerubbabel,
son of Shealtiel, son of Neri,
28 son of Melchi, son of Addi,
son of Cosam, son of Elmadam,
son of Er, 29 son of Joshua,
son of Eliezer, son of Jorim,
son of Matthat, son of Levi,
30 son of Simeon, son of Judah,
son of Joseph, son of Jonam,
son of Eliakim, 31 son of Melea,
son of Menna, son of Mattatha,
son of Nathan, son of David,
32 son of Jesse, son of Obed,
son of Boaz, son of Salmon,[B]
son of Nahshon, 33 son of Amminadab,
son of Ram,[C] son of Hezron,
son of Perez, son of Judah,

[A] **3:16** Or *in* [B] **3:32** Other mss read *Sala* [C] **3:33** Other mss read *Amminadab, son of Aram, son of Joram*; other mss read *Amminadab, son of Admin, son of Arni*

The Jordan River.

When Jesus was born in Bethlehem, the Roman Empire had undisputed control of the Mediterranean world. The Roman governor was a crucial element in Rome's ability to control its provinces efficiently.

THE GOVERNOR AND THE PROVINCES

The Latin word *provincia* is a military expression indicating a particular region that was a general's responsibility. By the close of the First Punic War (241 BC), the Romans had conquered Sicily, which became Rome's first province. By the first Christian century, however, the empire consisted of more than thirty provinces. At first the provinces were ill defined geographically, but by the New Testament era they had come to have rather clearly defined boundaries.

Rome had two types of provinces, senatorial and imperial, designations Augustus Caesar introduced. A senatorial province was more peaceful, did not have legions stationed within its borders, and was governed by a proconsul—which the Senate appointed. The Greek term in the New Testament for a proconsul is *anthupatos.* Luke employed this designation for Sergius Paulus, governor of Cyprus (Ac 13:7), and Gallio, governor of Achaia (18:12). The town clerk of Ephesus used this noun when he quelled the riot during Paul's ministry there (19:38).

An imperial province was under the direct jurisdiction of the emperor and typically had a significant military force stationed within its borders. Technically the emperor himself would be the governor of such a province, but he delegated his authority to a personally appointed legate. Such a governor's official title was a *legatus propraetore Augusti,* "imperial legate of praetorian rank," or a *legatus Caesaris,* "legate of Caesar."[1] He would command the legion in addition to his other duties.

Occasionally the emperor had smaller provinces—yet nonetheless difficult ones—under his control. A procurator, sometimes called a prefect, governed such a province. Judea was one of these. The Synoptic Gospels use the Greek word *hegemon,* "governor," to designate Pontius Pilate as procurator of Judea.

THE GOVERNOR'S RESPONSIBILITIES

Although the primary task of the Roman governor was to maintain the peace, his powers were normally exercised in three areas—military, administrative, and judicial.

Military—The governor commanded the military forces in his province. In some provinces that was his sole responsibility. Controlling bands of robbers and conquered peoples was a necessary function, but how much attention this task required varied from place to place.

Administrative—The amount of time invested in administrative duties also varied in different provinces, with the personality of the governor serving as the determining factor. As one writer phrased it, "Its quantity depended on his view as to how far self-government was a symptom of health or of disease."[2] When Rome saw fit, they entrusted

Roman soldier figurine from the Greco-Roman period. Roman governors had both civil and military forces at their disposal.

petty sovereigns with the day-to-day affairs of the region.

An important member of the governor's staff, a financial official called a *quaestor,* functioned as a sort of second in command. On behalf of the governor, he received credit or money from Rome for meeting the expenses of the province and supervised the collection of taxes. Since keeping records of financial matters was his responsibility, he gave an accounting annually in both his and the governor's name.

Judicial—In time of peace, most of the governors focused most of their energies on jurisdiction, both civil and criminal. The governor had access to a corpus called the Twelve Tables, a significant segment of Roman law that detailed all-important or disputed points and contained private, public, and criminal statutes.[3]

The governor could be as harsh and arbitrary in dealing with the ordinary person as he desired, just so he did not take money or property for himself. He consulted with a group of advisers before taking harsh action, but their counsel did not bind him.

Following a publicized schedule, the governor visited the cities in the province and held court in each one. Although he had the authority to hear any case, routine cases normally fell to the local judicial processes. The governor might choose to send major litigation—especially those involving treason and revolt—to Rome for trial. The governor had the sole right to inflict the death penalty, so he tried capital cases. ✣

---

[1] William Smith, *Smith's Bible Dictionary* (Old Tappan, NJ: Revell, 1967), 579. [2] A. H. J. Greenidge, *Roman Public Life* (New York: Cooper Square, 1970), 324. [3] Greenidge, *Roman Public Life,* 105. See the extensive discussion of forensic topics on 325–30.

Roman coin honoring Caesar Augustus.

34 son of Jacob, son of Isaac,
son of Abraham, son of Terah,
son of Nahor, 35 son of Serug,
son of Reu, son of Peleg,
son of Eber, son of Shelah,
36 son of Cainan,[A] son of Arphaxad,
son of Shem, son of Noah,
son of Lamech, 37 son of Methuselah,
son of Enoch, son of Jared,
son of Mahalalel, son of Cainan,
38 son of Enos, son of Seth,
son of Adam, son of God.

THE TEMPTATION OF JESUS

4 Then Jesus left the Jordan, full of the Holy Spirit,
and was led by the Spirit in the wilderness 2 for
forty days to be tempted by the devil. He ate nothing
during those days, and when they were over, he was
hungry. 3 The devil said to him, "If you are the Son of
God, tell this stone to become bread."
4 But Jesus answered him, "It is written: **Man must
not live on bread alone.**"[B,C]
5 So he took him up[D] and showed him all the kingdoms of the world in a moment of time. 6 The devil
said to him, "I will give you their splendor and all
this authority, because it has been given over to me,
and I can give it to anyone I want. 7 If you, then, will
worship me,[E] all will be yours."
8 And Jesus answered him,[F] "It is written: **Worship
the Lord your God, and serve him only.**"[G]
9 So he took him to Jerusalem, had him stand on
the pinnacle of the temple, and said to him, "If you
are the Son of God, throw yourself down from here.
10 For it is written:

He will give his angels orders
concerning you,
to protect you,[H] 11 and
they will support you with their hands,
so that you will not strike
your foot against a stone."[I]

12 And Jesus answered him, "It is said: **Do not test
the Lord your God.**"[J]
13 After the devil had finished every temptation,
he departed from him for a time.

[A] **3:36** Some mss omit *son of Cainan* [B] **4:4** Other mss add *but on every word of God* [C] **4:4** Dt 8:3 [D] **4:5** Other mss read *So the devil took him up on a high mountain* [E] **4:7** Lit *will fall down before me* [F] **4:8** Other mss add *"Get behind me, Satan!* [G] **4:8** Dt 6:13 [H] **4:10** Ps 91:11 [I] **4:11** Ps 91:12 [J] **4:12** Dt 6:16

West of Jericho is the Mount of Temptation, where, according to tradition, Satan tempted Jesus in the wilderness.

MINISTRY IN GALILEE

[14] Then Jesus returned to Galilee in the power of the
Spirit, and news about him spread throughout the
entire vicinity. [15] He was teaching in their synagogues,
being praised[A] by everyone.

REJECTION AT NAZARETH

[16] He came to Nazareth, where he had been brought
up. As usual, he entered the synagogue on the Sabbath
day and stood up to read. [17] The scroll of the prophet
Isaiah was given to him, and unrolling the scroll, he
found the place where it was written:

[18] **The Spirit of the Lord is on me,**
because he has anointed me
to preach good news to the poor.
He has sent me[B]
to proclaim release[C] **to the captives**
and recovery of sight to the blind,
to set free the oppressed,
[19] **to proclaim the year of the Lord's favor.**[D]

[20] He then rolled up the scroll, gave it back to the
attendant, and sat down. And the eyes of everyone
in the synagogue were fixed on him. [21] He began by
saying to them, "Today as you listen, this Scripture
has been fulfilled."

[22] They were all speaking well of him[E] and were
amazed by the gracious words that came from his
mouth; yet they said, "Isn't this Joseph's son?"

[23] Then he said to them, "No doubt you will quote
this proverb[F] to me: 'Doctor, heal yourself. What we've
heard that took place in Capernaum, do here in your
hometown also.' "

[24] He also said, "Truly I tell you, no prophet is accepted in his hometown. [25] But I say to you, there were
certainly many widows in Israel in Elijah's days, when
the sky was shut up for three years and six months
while a great famine came over all the land. [26] Yet
Elijah was not sent to any of them except a widow
at Zarephath in Sidon. [27] And in the prophet Elisha's
time, there were many in Israel who had leprosy,[G]
and yet not one of them was cleansed except Naaman the Syrian."

[28] When they heard this, everyone in the synagogue was enraged. [29] They got up, drove him out
of town, and brought him to the edge of the hill that
their town was built on, intending to hurl him over

[A] **4:15** Or *glorified* [B] **4:18** Other mss add *to heal the brokenhearted,* [C] **4:18** Or *freedom,* or *forgiveness* [D] **4:18–19** Is 61:1–2 [E] **4:22** Or *They were testifying against him* [F] **4:23** Or *parable* [G] **4:27** Gk *lepros*; a term for various skin diseases; see Lv 13–14

Interior of a synagogue in Nazareth believed to have been the one Mary, Joseph, and Jesus would have attended.

the cliff. 30 But he passed right through the crowd
and went on his way.

DRIVING OUT AN UNCLEAN SPIRIT

31 Then he went down to Capernaum, a town in Galilee, and was teaching them on the Sabbath. 32 They
were astonished at his teaching because his message
had authority. 33 In the synagogue there was a man
with an unclean demonic spirit who cried out with a
loud voice, 34 "Leave us alone! What do you have to do
with us, Jesus of Nazareth? Have you come to destroy
us? I know who you are — the Holy One of God!"

35 But Jesus rebuked him and said, "Be silent and
come out of him!" And throwing him down before
them, the demon came out of him without hurting
him at all.

36 Amazement came over them all, and they were
saying to one another, "What is this message? For he
commands the unclean spirits with authority and
power, and they come out!" 37 And news about him
began to go out to every place in the vicinity.

HEALINGS AT CAPERNAUM

38 After he left the synagogue, he entered Simon's
house. Simon's mother-in-law was suffering from
a high fever, and they asked him about her. 39 So he
stood over her and rebuked the fever, and it left her.
She got up immediately and began to serve them.

40 When the sun was setting, all those who had
anyone sick with various diseases brought them to
him. As he laid his hands on each one of them, he
healed them. 41 Also, demons were coming out of
many, shouting and saying, "You are the Son of God!"
But he rebuked them and would not allow them to
speak, because they knew he was the Messiah.

42 When it was day, he went out and made his way
to a deserted place. But the crowds were searching
for him. They came to him and tried to keep him
from leaving them. 43 But he said to them, "It is necessary for me to proclaim the good news about the
kingdom of God to the other towns also, because I
was sent for this purpose." 44 And he was preaching
in the synagogues of Judea.[A]

THE FIRST DISCIPLES

5 As the crowd was pressing in on Jesus to hear
God's word, he was standing by Lake Gennesaret.[B]
2 He saw two boats at the edge of the lake; the fishermen had left them and were washing their nets. 3 He
got into one of the boats, which belonged to Simon,
and asked him to put out a little from the land. Then he
sat down and was teaching the crowds from the boat.

4 When he had finished speaking, he said to Simon,
"Put out into deep water and let down your nets for
a catch."

5 "Master," Simon replied, "we've worked hard all
night long and caught nothing. But if you say so, I'll
let down the nets."[C]

6 When they did this, they caught a great number of
fish, and their nets[C] began to tear. 7 So they signaled
to their partners in the other boat to come and help
them; they came and filled both boats so full that
they began to sink.

8 When Simon Peter saw this, he fell at Jesus's
knees and said, "Go away from me, because I'm a
sinful man, Lord!" 9 For he and all those with him
were amazed at the catch of fish they had taken, 10 and
so were James and John, Zebedee's sons, who were
Simon's partners.

"Don't be afraid," Jesus told Simon. "From now on
you will be catching people." 11 Then they brought
the boats to land, left everything, and followed him.

A MAN CLEANSED

12 While he was in one of the towns, a man was there
who had leprosy[D] all over him. He saw Jesus, fell facedown, and begged him, "Lord, if you are willing, you
can make me clean."

13 Reaching out his hand, Jesus touched him, saying, "I am willing; be made clean," and immediately
the leprosy left him. 14 Then he ordered him to tell
no one: "But go and show yourself to the priest, and
offer what Moses commanded for your cleansing as
a testimony to them."

15 But the news[E] about him spread even more, and
large crowds would come together to hear him and
to be healed of their sicknesses. 16 Yet he often withdrew to deserted places and prayed.

THE SON OF MAN FORGIVES AND HEALS

17 On one of those days while he was teaching, Pharisees and teachers of the law were sitting there who
had come from every village of Galilee and Judea, and
also from Jerusalem. And the Lord's power to heal
was in him. 18 Just then some men came, carrying on
a stretcher a man who was paralyzed. They tried to
bring him in and set him down before him. 19 Since
they could not find a way to bring him in because
of the crowd, they went up on the roof and lowered
him on the stretcher through the roof tiles into the
middle of the crowd before Jesus.

20 Seeing their faith he said, "Friend,[F] your sins
are forgiven."

21 Then the scribes and the Pharisees began to
think to themselves, "Who is this man who speaks
blasphemies? Who can forgive sins but God alone?"

[A] **4:44** Other mss read *Galilee* [B] **5:1** Another name for the Sea of Galilee [C] **5:5,6** Other mss read *net* (Gk sg) [D] **5:12** Gk *lepros*; a term for various skin diseases, also in v. 13; see Lv 13–14 [E] **5:15** Lit *the word* [F] **5:20** Lit *"Man*

22 But perceiving their thoughts, Jesus replied to them, "Why are you thinking this in your hearts?[A] 23 Which is easier: to say, 'Your sins are forgiven,' or to say, 'Get up and walk'? 24 But so that you may know that the Son of Man has authority on earth to forgive sins" — he told the paralyzed man, "I tell you: Get up, take your stretcher, and go home."

25 Immediately he got up before them, picked up what he had been lying on, and went home glorifying God. 26 Then everyone was astounded, and they were giving glory to God. And they were filled with awe and said, "We have seen incredible things today."

THE CALL OF LEVI

27 After this, Jesus went out and saw a tax collector named Levi sitting at the tax office, and he said to him, "Follow me." 28 So, leaving everything behind, he got up and began to follow him.

29 Then Levi hosted a grand banquet for him at his house. Now there was a large crowd of tax collectors and others who were reclining at the table with them. 30 But the Pharisees and their scribes were complaining to his disciples, "Why do you eat and drink with tax collectors and sinners?"

31 Jesus replied to them, "It is not those who are healthy who need a doctor, but those who are sick. 32 I have not come to call the righteous, but sinners to repentance."

A QUESTION ABOUT FASTING

33 Then they said to him, "John's disciples fast often and say prayers, and those of the Pharisees do the same, but yours eat and drink."

34 Jesus said to them, "You can't make the wedding guests fast while the groom is with them, can you? 35 But the time[B] will come when the groom will be taken away from them — then they will fast in those days."

36 He also told them a parable: "No one tears a patch from a new garment and puts it on an old garment. Otherwise, not only will he tear the new, but also the piece from the new garment will not match the old. 37 And no one puts new wine into old wineskins. Otherwise, the new wine will burst the skins, it will spill, and the skins will be ruined. 38 No, new wine is put into fresh wineskins.[C] 39 And no one, after drinking old wine, wants new, because he says, 'The old is better.'"[D]

LORD OF THE SABBATH

6 On a Sabbath, he passed through the grainfields. His disciples were picking heads of grain, rubbing them in their hands, and eating them. 2 But some of the Pharisees said, "Why are you doing what is not lawful on the Sabbath?"

3 Jesus answered them, "Haven't you read what David and those who were with him did when he was hungry — 4 how he entered the house of God and took and ate the bread of the Presence, which is not lawful for any but the priests to eat? He even gave some to those who were with him." 5 Then he told them, "The Son of Man is Lord of the Sabbath."

6 On another Sabbath he entered the synagogue and was teaching. A man was there whose right hand was shriveled. 7 The scribes and Pharisees were watching him closely, to see if he would heal on the Sabbath, so that they could find a charge against him. 8 But he knew their thoughts and told the man with the shriveled hand, "Get up and stand here."[E] So he got up and stood there. 9 Then Jesus said to them, "I ask you: Is it lawful to do good on the Sabbath or to do evil, to save life or to destroy it?" 10 After looking around at them all, he told him, "Stretch out your hand." He did, and his hand was restored.[F] 11 They, however, were filled with rage and started discussing with one another what they might do to Jesus.

THE TWELVE APOSTLES

12 During those days he went out to the mountain to pray and spent all night in prayer to God. 13 When daylight came, he summoned his disciples, and he chose twelve of them, whom he also named apostles: 14 Simon, whom he also named Peter, and Andrew his brother; James and John; Philip and Bartholomew; 15 Matthew and Thomas; James the son of Alphaeus, and Simon called the Zealot; 16 Judas the son of James, and Judas Iscariot, who became a traitor.

TEACHING AND HEALING

17 After coming down with them, he stood on a level place with a large crowd of his disciples and a great number of people from all Judea and Jerusalem and from the seacoast of Tyre and Sidon. 18 They came to hear him and to be healed of their diseases; and those tormented by unclean spirits were made well. 19 The whole crowd was trying to touch him, because power was coming out from him and healing them all.

THE BEATITUDES

20 Then looking up at his disciples, he said:

Blessed are you who are poor,
because the kingdom of God is yours.
21 Blessed are you who are hungry now,
because you will be filled.
Blessed are you who weep now,
because you will laugh.

[A] **5:22** Or *minds* [B] **5:35** Lit *days* [C] **5:38** Other mss add *And so both are preserved.* [D] **5:39** Or *good* [E] **6:8** Lit *stand in the middle* [F] **6:10** Other mss add *as sound as the other*

22 Blessed are you when people hate you,
when they exclude you, insult you,
and slander your name as evil
because of the Son of Man.
23 "Rejoice in that day and leap for joy. Take note —
your reward is great in heaven, for this is the way
their ancestors used to treat the prophets.

WOE TO THE SELF-SATISFIED

24 But woe to you who are rich,
for you have received your comfort.
25 Woe to you who are now full,
for you will be hungry.
Woe to you[A] who are now laughing,
for you will mourn and weep.
26 Woe to you[A]
when all people speak well of you,
for this is the way their ancestors
used to treat the false prophets.

LOVE YOUR ENEMIES

27 "But I say to you who listen: Love your enemies, do
what is good to those who hate you, 28 bless those
who curse you, pray for those who mistreat you. 29 If
anyone hits you on the cheek, offer the other also.
And if anyone takes away your coat, don't hold back
your shirt either. 30 Give to everyone who asks you,
and from someone who takes your things, don't ask
for them back. 31 Just as you want others to do for
you, do the same for them. 32 If you love those who
love you, what credit is that to you? Even sinners love
those who love them. 33 If you do what is good to those
who are good to you, what credit is that to you? Even
sinners do that. 34 And if you lend to those from whom
you expect to receive, what credit is that to you? Even
sinners lend to sinners to be repaid in full. 35 But love
your enemies, do what is good, and lend, expecting
nothing in return. Then your reward will be great,
and you will be children of the Most High. For he is
gracious to the ungrateful and evil. 36 Be merciful,
just as your Father also is merciful.

DO NOT JUDGE

37 "Do not judge, and you will not be judged. Do not
condemn, and you will not be condemned. Forgive,
and you will be forgiven. 38 Give, and it will be given
to you; a good measure — pressed down, shaken
together, and running over — will be poured into

[A]**6:25,26** Other mss omit *to you*

Ruins found at the house of Kathros in Jerusalem. Kathros was a priestly family that served in the Jerusalem temple before the temple and city were destroyed in AD 70. The house was located in the Upper City of Jerusalem and overlooked the Temple Mount.

your lap. For with the measure you use, it will be measured back to you."

39 He also told them a parable: "Can the blind guide the blind? Won't they both fall into a pit? 40 A disciple is not above his teacher, but everyone who is fully trained will be like his teacher.

41 "Why do you look at the splinter in your brother's eye, but don't notice the beam of wood in your own eye? 42 Or how can you say to your brother, 'Brother, let me take out the splinter that is in your eye,' when you yourself don't see the beam of wood in your eye? Hypocrite! First take the beam of wood out of your eye, and then you will see clearly to take out the splinter in your brother's eye.

A TREE AND ITS FRUIT

43 "A good tree doesn't produce bad fruit; on the other hand, a bad tree doesn't produce good fruit.[A] 44 For each tree is known by its own fruit. Figs aren't gathered from thornbushes, or grapes picked from a bramble bush. 45 A good person produces good out of the good stored up in his heart. An evil person produces evil out of the evil stored up in his heart, for his mouth speaks from the overflow of the heart.

THE TWO FOUNDATIONS

46 "Why do you call me 'Lord, Lord,' and don't do the things I say? 47 I will show you what someone is like who comes to me, hears my words, and acts on them: 48 He is like a man building a house, who dug deep and laid the foundation on the rock. When the flood came, the river crashed against that house and couldn't shake it, because it was well built. 49 But the one who hears and does not act is like a man who built a house on the ground without a foundation. The river crashed against it, and immediately it collapsed. And the destruction of that house was great."

A CENTURION'S FAITH

7 When he had concluded saying all this to the people who were listening, he entered Capernaum. 2 A centurion's servant, who was highly valued by him, was sick and about to die. 3 When the centurion heard about Jesus, he sent some Jewish elders to him, requesting him to come and save the life of his servant. 4 When they reached Jesus, they pleaded with him earnestly, saying, "He is worthy for you to grant this, 5 because he loves our nation and has built us a synagogue."

6 Jesus went with them, and when he was not far from the house, the centurion sent friends to tell him, "Lord, don't trouble yourself, since I am not worthy to have you come under my roof. 7 That is why I didn't even consider myself worthy to come to you. But say the word, and my servant will be healed.[B] 8 For I too am a man placed under authority, having soldiers under my command. I say to this one, 'Go,' and he goes; and to another, 'Come,' and he comes; and to my servant, 'Do this,' and he does it."

9 Jesus heard this and was amazed at him, and turning to the crowd following him, he said, "I tell you, I have not found so great a faith even in Israel." 10 When those who had been sent returned to the house, they found the servant in good health.

A WIDOW'S SON RAISED TO LIFE

11 Afterward he was on his way to a town called Nain. His disciples and a large crowd were traveling with him. 12 Just as he neared the gate of the town, a dead man was being carried out. He was his mother's only son, and she was a widow. A large crowd from the town was also with her. 13 When the Lord saw her, he had compassion on her and said, "Don't weep." 14 Then he came up and touched the open coffin, and the pallbearers stopped. And he said, "Young man, I tell you, get up!"

15 The dead man sat up and began to speak, and Jesus gave him to his mother. 16 Then fear[C] came over everyone, and they glorified God, saying, "A great prophet has risen among us," and "God has visited[D] his people." 17 This report about him went throughout Judea and all the vicinity.

IN PRAISE OF JOHN THE BAPTIST

18 Then John's disciples told him about all these things. So John summoned two of his disciples 19 and sent them to the Lord, asking, "Are you the one who is to come, or should we expect someone else?"

20 When the men reached him, they said, "John the Baptist sent us to ask you, 'Are you the one who is to come, or should we expect someone else?'"

21 At that time Jesus healed many people of diseases, afflictions, and evil spirits, and he granted sight to many blind people. 22 He replied to them, "Go and report to John what you have seen and heard: The blind receive their sight, the lame walk, those with leprosy[E] are cleansed, the deaf hear, the dead are raised, and the poor are told the good news, 23 and blessed is the one who isn't offended by me."

24 After John's messengers left, he began to speak to the crowds about John: "What did you go out into the wilderness to see? A reed swaying in the wind? 25 What then did you go out to see? A man dressed in soft clothes? See, those who are splendidly dressed and live in luxury are in royal palaces. 26 What then

[A] **6:43** Lit *on the other hand, again, a bad tree doesn't produce good fruit* [B] **7:7** Other mss read *and let my servant be healed* [C] **7:16** Or *awe* [D] **7:16** Or *come to help* [E] **7:22** Gk *lepros*; a term for various skin diseases; see Lv 13–14

Alabaster bottle dated to Egypt's Twenty-Sixth Dynasty (664–525 BC). Bottles like this were common during the period when the Greeks were first becoming familiar with Egyptian culture. From such an alabaster cruse of ointment Jesus's feet were anointed.

did you go out to see? A prophet? Yes, I tell you, and
more than a prophet. 27 This is the one about whom
it is written:

> **See, I am sending my messenger**
> **ahead of you;**
> **he will prepare your way**
> **before you.**[A]

28 I tell you, among those born of women no one is
greater than John,[B] but the least in the kingdom of
God is greater than he."

29 (And when all the people, including the tax collectors, heard this, they acknowledged God's way of
righteousness, because they had been baptized with
John's baptism. 30 But since the Pharisees and experts
in the law had not been baptized by him, they rejected
the plan of God for themselves.)

AN UNRESPONSIVE GENERATION

31 "To what then should I compare the people of this
generation, and what are they like? 32 They are like
children sitting in the marketplace and calling to
each other:

> We played the flute for you,
> but you didn't dance;
> we sang a lament,
> but you didn't weep!

33 For John the Baptist did not come eating bread or
drinking wine, and you say, 'He has a demon!' 34 The
Son of Man has come eating and drinking, and you
say, 'Look, a glutton and a drunkard, a friend of tax
collectors and sinners!' 35 Yet wisdom is vindicated
by all her children."

MUCH FORGIVENESS, MUCH LOVE

36 Then one of the Pharisees invited him to eat with
him. He entered the Pharisee's house and reclined at
the table. 37 And a woman in the town who was a sinner found out that Jesus was reclining at the table in
the Pharisee's house. She brought an alabaster jar of
perfume 38 and stood behind him at his feet, weeping,
and began to wash his feet with her tears. She wiped
his feet with her hair, kissing them and anointing
them with the perfume.

39 When the Pharisee who had invited him saw
this, he said to himself, "This man, if he were a prophet, would know who and what kind of woman this is
who is touching him — she's a sinner!"

40 Jesus replied to him, "Simon, I have something
to say to you."

He said, "Say it, teacher."

41 "A creditor had two debtors. One owed five hundred denarii,[C] and the other fifty. 42 Since they could
not pay it back, he graciously forgave them both. So,
which of them will love him more?"

43 Simon answered, "I suppose the one he forgave
more."

"You have judged correctly," he told him. 44 Turning
to the woman, he said to Simon, "Do you see this woman? I entered your house; you gave me no water for
my feet, but she, with her tears, has washed my feet
and wiped them with her hair. 45 You gave me no kiss,
but she hasn't stopped kissing my feet since I came
in. 46 You didn't anoint my head with olive oil, but she
has anointed my feet with perfume. 47 Therefore I tell
you, her many sins have been forgiven; that's why she
loved much. But the one who is forgiven little, loves
little." 48 Then he said to her, "Your sins are forgiven."

49 Those who were at the table with him began to
say among themselves, "Who is this man who even
forgives sins?"

[A] **7:27** Mal 3:1 [B] **7:28** Other mss read *women is not a greater prophet than John the Baptist* [C] **7:41** A denarius = one day's wage

50 And he said to the woman, "Your faith has saved you. Go in peace."

MANY WOMEN SUPPORT CHRIST'S WORK

8 Afterward he was traveling from one town and village to another, preaching and telling the good news of the kingdom of God. The Twelve were with him, 2 and also some women who had been healed of evil spirits and sicknesses: Mary, called Magdalene (seven demons had come out of her); 3 Joanna the wife of Chuza, Herod's steward; Susanna; and many others who were supporting them from their possessions.

THE PARABLE OF THE SOWER

4 As a large crowd was gathering, and people were coming to Jesus from every town, he said in a parable, 5 "A sower went out to sow his seed. As he sowed, some seed fell along the path; it was trampled on, and the birds of the sky devoured it. 6 Other seed fell on the rock; when it grew up, it withered away, since it lacked moisture. 7 Other seed fell among thorns; the thorns grew up with it and choked it. 8 Still other seed fell on good ground; when it grew up, it produced fruit: a hundred times what was sown." As he said this, he called out, "Let anyone who has ears to hear listen."

WHY JESUS USED PARABLES

9 Then his disciples asked him, "What does this parable mean?" 10 So he said, "The secrets of the kingdom of God have been given for you to know, but to the rest it is in parables, so that

> **Looking they may not see,**
> **and hearing they may not understand.**[A]

THE PARABLE OF THE SOWER EXPLAINED

11 "This is the meaning of the parable: The seed is the word of God. 12 The seed along the path are those who have heard and then the devil comes and takes away the word from their hearts, so that they may not believe and be saved. 13 And the seed on the rock are those who, when they hear, receive the word with joy. Having no root, these believe for a while and fall away in a time of testing. 14 As for the seed that fell among thorns, these are the ones who, when they have heard, go on their way and are choked with worries, riches, and pleasures of life, and produce no mature fruit. 15 But the seed in the good ground — these are the ones who, having heard the word with an honest and good heart, hold on to it and by enduring, produce fruit.

USING YOUR LIGHT

16 "No one, after lighting a lamp, covers it with a basket or puts it under a bed, but puts it on a lampstand so that those who come in may see its light. 17 For nothing is concealed that won't be revealed, and nothing hidden that won't be made known and brought to light. 18 Therefore take care how you listen. For whoever has, more will be given to him; and whoever does not have, even what he thinks he has will be taken away from him."

TRUE RELATIONSHIPS

19 Then his mother and brothers came to him, but they could not meet with him because of the crowd. 20 He was told, "Your mother and your brothers are standing outside, wanting to see you."

21 But he replied to them, "My mother and my brothers are those who hear and do the word of God."

WIND AND WAVES OBEY JESUS

22 One day he and his disciples got into a boat, and he told them, "Let's cross over to the other side of the lake." So they set out, 23 and as they were sailing he fell asleep. Then a fierce windstorm came down on the lake; they were being swamped and were in danger. 24 They came and woke him up, saying, "Master, Master, we're going to die!"

Then he got up and rebuked the wind and the raging waves. So they ceased, and there was a calm. 25 He said to them, "Where is your faith?"

They were fearful and amazed, asking one another, "Who then is this? He commands even the winds and the waves, and they obey him!"

DEMONS DRIVEN OUT BY JESUS

26 Then they sailed to the region of the Gerasenes,[B] which is opposite Galilee. 27 When he got out on land, a demon-possessed man from the town met him. For a long time he had worn no clothes and did not stay in a house but in the tombs. 28 When he saw Jesus, he cried out, fell down before him, and said in a loud voice, "What do you have to do with me, Jesus, Son of the Most High God? I beg you, don't torment me!" 29 For he had commanded the unclean spirit to come out of the man. Many times it had seized him, and though he was guarded, bound by chains and shackles, he would snap the restraints and be driven by the demon into deserted places.

30 "What is your name?" Jesus asked him.

"Legion," he said, because many demons had entered him. 31 And they begged him not to banish them to the abyss.

32 A large herd of pigs was there, feeding on the hillside. The demons begged him to permit them to enter the pigs, and he gave them permission. 33 The demons came out of the man and entered the pigs,

[A] **8:10** Is 6:9 [B] **8:26** Other mss read *the Gadarenes*

DIGGING DEEPER *Jesus in Ancient Non-Christian Sources*

Extrabiblical literature and archaeological sources support the historical reality of Jesus. In fact, so numerous are these sources—some more reliable than others—that scholars can now reconstruct the salient features of the life of Christ without appealing to the Bible.

- Jesus lived during the reign of Tiberius Caesar (Cornelius Tacitus, Roman historian).
- He lived a virtuous life (Flavius Josephus, Jewish historian).
- He was a wonder worker (Josephus).
- He was acclaimed to be the Messiah (Josephus, Mara bar-Serapion).
- He was executed (Mara bar-Serapion, Alexamenos Graffito).
- He was crucified under Pontius Pilate (Tacitus, Josephus, Yehohanan Ossuary).
- He was crucified on the eve of Passover (Babylonian Talmud).
- Darkness and an earthquake occurred when he died (Thallus, Phlegon, Lucian of Samosata, Julius Africanus).
- His disciples believed he rose from the dead (Josephus).
- Conspiracy surrounding the disciples' alleged attempt to steal the body of Jesus circulated early (Teledoth Jesu).
- Jesus's disciples were willing to die for their beliefs (Tacitus, Suetonius).
- Christianity spread rapidly, even as far as Rome (Tacitus).
- Jesus was seen as the center of civil disobedience in Rome (Gaius Suetonius Tranquillas).
- His disciples denied the Roman gods and worshiped Jesus as God (Pliny the Younger, Lucian, Megiddo church mosaic floor inscription).

In all, there are a dozen non-Christian documentary sources extant from within 150 years of Jesus that offer support for his life, death, and ministry. This stands in stark contrast to the secondhand histories that document the life of Alexander the Great, the basics of which are generally accepted as accurate; they are 300 to 500 years removed from the events they describe.

and the herd rushed down the steep bank into the
lake and drowned.
34 When the men who tended them saw what had
happened, they ran off and reported it in the town
and in the countryside. 35 Then people went out to see
what had happened. They came to Jesus and found
the man the demons had departed from, sitting at
Jesus's feet, dressed and in his right mind. And they
were afraid. 36 Meanwhile, the eyewitnesses reported
to them how the demon-possessed man was delivered.
37 Then all the people of the Gerasene region[A]
asked him to leave them, because they were gripped
by great fear. So getting into the boat, he returned.
38 The man from whom the demons had departed
begged him earnestly to be with him. But he sent
him away and said, 39 "Go back to your home, and
tell all that God has done for you." And off he went,
proclaiming throughout the town how much Jesus
had done for him.

A GIRL RESTORED AND A WOMAN HEALED

40 When Jesus returned, the crowd welcomed him, for
they were all expecting him. 41 Just then, a man named
Jairus came. He was a leader of the synagogue. He fell
down at Jesus's feet and pleaded with him to come to
his house, 42 because he had an only daughter about
twelve years old, and she was dying.
While he was going, the crowds were nearly crushing him.
43 A woman suffering from bleeding for
twelve years, who had spent all she had on doctors[B]
and yet could not be healed by any, 44 approached
from behind and touched the end of his robe. Instantly her bleeding stopped.
45 "Who touched me?" Jesus asked.
When they all denied it, Peter[C] said, "Master, the
crowds are hemming you in and pressing against
you."[D]
46 "Someone did touch me," said Jesus. "I know that
power has gone out from me." 47 When the woman
saw that she was discovered, she came trembling
and fell down before him. In the presence of all the
people, she declared the reason she had touched him
and how she was instantly healed. 48 "Daughter," he
said to her, "your faith has saved you.[E] Go in peace."
49 While he was still speaking, someone came from
the synagogue leader's house and said, "Your daughter is dead. Don't bother the teacher anymore."
50 When Jesus heard it, he answered him, "Don't be
afraid. Only believe, and she will be saved."[F] 51 After he
came to the house, he let no one enter with him except
Peter, John, James, and the child's father and mother.

[A] **8:37** Other mss read *the Gadarenes* [B] **8:43** Other mss omit *who had spent all she had on doctors* [C] **8:45** Other mss add *and those with him* [D] **8:45** Other mss add *and you say, 'Who touched me?'* [E] **8:48** Or *has made you well* [F] **8:50** Or *she will be made well*

52 Everyone was crying and mourning for her. But he
said, "Stop crying, because she is not dead but asleep."
53 They laughed at him, because they knew she was
dead. 54 So he[A] took her by the hand and called out,
"Child, get up!" 55 Her spirit returned, and she got up
at once. Then he gave orders that she be given something to eat. 56 Her parents were astounded, but he
instructed them to tell no one what had happened.

COMMISSIONING THE TWELVE

9 Summoning the Twelve, he gave them power and
authority over all the demons and to heal diseases. 2 Then he sent them to proclaim the kingdom of
God and to heal the sick.
3 "Take nothing for the road," he told them, "no
staff, no traveling bag, no bread, no money; and don't
take an extra shirt. 4 Whatever house you enter, stay
there and leave from there. 5 If they do not welcome
you, when you leave that town, shake off the dust
from your feet as a testimony against them." 6 So they
went out and traveled from village to village, proclaiming the good news and healing everywhere.

HEROD'S DESIRE TO SEE JESUS

7 Herod the tetrarch heard about everything that was
going on. He was perplexed, because some said that
John had been raised from the dead, 8 some that Elijah had appeared, and others that one of the ancient
prophets had risen. 9 "I beheaded John," Herod said,
"but who is this I hear such things about?" And he
wanted to see him.

FEEDING OF THE FIVE THOUSAND

10 When the apostles returned, they reported to Jesus
all that they had done. He took them along and withdrew privately to a[B] town called Bethsaida. 11 When
the crowds found out, they followed him. He welcomed them, spoke to them about the kingdom of
God, and healed those who needed healing.
12 Late in the day, the Twelve approached and said
to him, "Send the crowd away, so that they can go into
the surrounding villages and countryside to find food
and lodging, because we are in a deserted place here."
13 "You give them something to eat," he told them.
"We have no more than five loaves and two fish,"
they said, "unless we go and buy food for all these
people." 14 (For about five thousand men were there.)
Then he told his disciples, "Have them sit down[C]
in groups of about fifty each." 15 They did what he
said, and had them all sit down. 16 Then he took the
five loaves and the two fish, and looking up to heav-
en, he blessed and broke them. He kept giving them
to the disciples to set before the crowd. 17 Everyone
ate and was filled. They picked up twelve baskets of
leftover pieces.

PETER'S CONFESSION OF THE MESSIAH

18 While he was praying in private and his disciples
were with him, he asked them, "Who do the crowds
say that I am?"
19 They answered, "John the Baptist; others, Elijah; still others, that one of the ancient prophets has
come back."[D]
20 "But you," he asked them, "who do you say that
I am?"
Peter answered, "God's Messiah."

HIS DEATH AND RESURRECTION PREDICTED

21 But he strictly warned and instructed them to tell
this to no one, 22 saying, "It is necessary that the Son
of Man suffer many things and be rejected by the
elders, chief priests, and scribes, be killed, and be
raised the third day."

TAKE UP YOUR CROSS

23 Then he said to them all, "If anyone wants to follow
after[E] me, let him deny himself, take up his cross daily,[F] and follow me. 24 For whoever wants to save his
life will lose it, but whoever loses his life because of
me will save it. 25 For what does it benefit someone
if he gains the whole world, and yet loses or forfeits
himself? 26 For whoever is ashamed of me and my
words, the Son of Man will be ashamed of him when
he comes in his glory and that of the Father and the
holy angels. 27 Truly I tell you, there are some standing here who will not taste death until they see the
kingdom of God."

THE TRANSFIGURATION

28 About eight days after this conversation, he took
along Peter, John, and James and went up on the
mountain to pray. 29 As he was praying, the appearance of his face changed, and his clothes became
dazzling white. 30 Suddenly, two men were talking
with him — Moses and Elijah. 31 They appeared in
glory and were speaking of his departure, which he
was about to accomplish in Jerusalem.
32 Peter and those with him were in a deep sleep,[G]
and when they became fully awake, they saw his
glory and the two men who were standing with him.
33 As the two men were departing from him, Peter
said to Jesus, "Master, it's good for us to be here. Let's
set up three shelters: one for you, one for Moses, and
one for Elijah" — not knowing what he was saying.
34 While he was saying this, a cloud appeared and
overshadowed them. They became afraid as they entered the cloud. 35 Then a voice came from the cloud,

[A] **8:54** Other mss add *having put them all outside* [B] **9:10** Other mss add *deserted place near a* [C] **9:14** Lit *them recline* [D] **9:19** Lit *has risen* [E] **9:23** Lit *come after* [F] **9:23** Other mss omit *daily* [G] **9:32** Lit *were weighed down with sleep*

saying, "This is my Son, the Chosen One;[A] listen to him!"

36 After the voice had spoken, Jesus was found alone. They kept silent, and at that time told no one what they had seen.

THE POWER OF JESUS OVER A DEMON

37 The next day, when they came down from the mountain, a large crowd met him. 38 Just then a man from the crowd cried out, "Teacher, I beg you to look at my son, because he's my only child. 39 A spirit seizes him; suddenly he shrieks, and it throws him into convulsions until he foams at the mouth; severely bruising him, it scarcely ever leaves him. 40 I begged your disciples to drive it out, but they couldn't."

41 Jesus replied, "You unbelieving and perverse[B] generation, how long will I be with you and put up with you? Bring your son here."

42 As the boy was still approaching, the demon knocked him down and threw him into severe convulsions. But Jesus rebuked the unclean spirit, healed the boy, and gave him back to his father. 43 And they were all astonished at the greatness of God.

THE SECOND PREDICTION OF HIS DEATH

While everyone was amazed at all the things he was doing, he told his disciples, 44 "Let these words sink in:[C] The Son of Man is about to be betrayed into the hands of men."

45 But they did not understand this statement; it was concealed from them so that they could not grasp it, and they were afraid to ask him about it.

WHO IS THE GREATEST?

46 An argument started among them about who was the greatest of them. 47 But Jesus, knowing their inner thoughts,[D] took a little child and had him stand next to him. 48 He told them, "Whoever welcomes[E] this little child in my name welcomes me. And whoever welcomes me welcomes him who sent me. For whoever is least among you — this one is great."

IN HIS NAME

49 John responded, "Master, we saw someone driving out demons in your name, and we tried to stop him because he does not follow us."

50 "Don't stop him," Jesus told him, "because whoever is not against you is for you."[F]

THE JOURNEY TO JERUSALEM

51 When the days were coming to a close for him to be taken up, he determined[G] to journey to Jerusalem. 52 He sent messengers ahead of himself, and on the way they entered a village of the Samaritans to make preparations for him. 53 But they did not welcome him, because he determined to journey to Jerusalem. 54 When the disciples James and John saw this, they said, "Lord, do you want us to call down fire from heaven to consume them?"[H]

55 But he turned and rebuked them,[I] 56 and they went to another village.

FOLLOWING JESUS

57 As they were traveling on the road someone said to him, "I will follow you wherever you go."

58 Jesus told him, "Foxes have dens, and birds of the sky have nests, but the Son of Man has no place to lay his head." 59 Then he said to another, "Follow me."

"Lord," he said, "first let me go bury my father."

60 But he told him, "Let the dead bury their own dead, but you go and spread the news of the kingdom of God."

61 Another said, "I will follow you, Lord, but first let me go and say good-bye to those at my house."

62 But Jesus said to him, "No one who puts his hand to the plow and looks back is fit for the kingdom of God."

SENDING OUT THE SEVENTY-TWO

10 After this, the Lord appointed seventy-two[J] others, and he sent them ahead of him in pairs to every town and place where he himself was about to go. 2 He told them, "The harvest is abundant, but the workers are few. Therefore, pray to the Lord of the harvest to send out workers into his harvest. 3 Now go; I'm sending you out like lambs among wolves. 4 Don't carry a money-bag, traveling bag, or sandals; don't greet anyone along the road. 5 Whatever house you enter, first say, 'Peace to this household.' 6 If a person of peace is there, your peace will rest on him; but if not, it will return to you. 7 Remain in the same house, eating and drinking what they offer, for the worker is worthy of his wages. Don't move from house to house. 8 When you enter any town, and they welcome you, eat the things set before you. 9 Heal the sick who are there, and tell them, 'The kingdom of God has come near you.' 10 When you enter any town, and they don't welcome you, go out into its streets and say, 11 'We are wiping off even the dust of your town that clings to our feet as a witness against you. Know this for certain: The kingdom of God has come near.' 12 I tell you, on that day it will be more tolerable for Sodom than for that town.

[A] **9:35** Other mss read *the Beloved* [B] **9:41** Or *corrupt*, or *perverted*, or *twisted*; Dt 32:5 [C] **9:44** Lit *"Put these words in your ears* [D] **9:47** Lit *the thoughts of their hearts* [E] **9:48** Or *receives*, throughout the verse [F] **9:50** Other mss read *against us is for us* [G] **9:51** Lit *he stiffened his face to go*; Is 50:7 [H] **9:54** Other mss add *as Elijah also did* [I] **9:55–56** Other mss add *and said, "You don't know what kind of spirit you belong to. 56 For the Son of Man did not come to destroy people's lives but to save them,"* [J] **10:1** Other mss read *seventy*

UNREPENTANT TOWNS

13 "Woe to you, Chorazin! Woe to you, Bethsaida! For if the miracles that were done in you had been done in Tyre and Sidon, they would have repented long ago, sitting in sackcloth and ashes. 14 But it will be more tolerable for Tyre and Sidon at the judgment than for you. 15 And you, Capernaum, will you be exalted to heaven? No, you will go down to Hades. 16 Whoever listens to you listens to me. Whoever rejects you rejects me. And whoever rejects me rejects the one who sent me."

THE RETURN OF THE SEVENTY-TWO

17 The seventy-two[A] returned with joy, saying, "Lord, even the demons submit to us in your name."

18 He said to them, "I watched Satan fall from heaven like lightning. 19 Look, I have given you the authority to trample on snakes and scorpions and over all the power of the enemy; nothing at all will harm you. 20 However, don't rejoice that[B] the spirits submit to you, but rejoice that your names are written in heaven."

THE SON REVEALS THE FATHER

21 At that time he[C] rejoiced in the Holy[D] Spirit and said, "I praise[E] you, Father, Lord of heaven and earth, because you have hidden these things from the wise and intelligent and revealed them to infants. Yes, Father, because this was your good pleasure.[F] 22 All things have[G] been entrusted to me by my Father. No one knows who the Son is except the Father, and who the Father is except the Son, and anyone to whom the Son desires[H] to reveal him."

23 Then turning to his disciples he said privately, "Blessed are the eyes that see the things you see! 24 For I tell you that many prophets and kings wanted to see the things you see but didn't see them; to hear the things you hear but didn't hear them."

THE PARABLE OF THE GOOD SAMARITAN

25 Then an expert in the law stood up to test him, saying, "Teacher, what must I do to inherit eternal life?"

26 "What is written in the law?" he asked him. "How do you read it?"

27 He answered, **"Love the Lord your God with all your heart, with all your soul, with all your strength, and with all your mind,"** and **"your neighbor as yourself."**[I]

28 "You've answered correctly," he told him. "Do this and you will live."

[A] **10:17** Other mss read *The seventy* [B] **10:20** Lit *don't rejoice in this, that* [C] **10:21** Other mss read *Jesus* [D] **10:21** Other mss omit *Holy* [E] **10:21** Or *thank*, or *confess* [F] **10:21** Lit *was well-pleasing in your sight* [G] **10:22** Other mss read *And turning to the disciples, he said, "Everything has* [H] **10:22** Or *wills*, or *chooses* [I] **10:27** Lv 19:18; Dt 6:5

Road from Jerusalem to Jericho.

Who Were the Samaritans?

by Robert A. Weathers

City gate on top of Mount Gerizim.

At the time of Jesus, the Samaritans "were regarded by the Jews as despised half-breeds."[1] The Samaritans likewise detested the Jews. Their mutual contempt arose from a long and checkered history.

In 922 BC, King Solomon died, and his son Rehoboam inherited the throne (1Kg 12). Rehoboam was a foolish leader who listened to unwise advisers and initiated a series of events that so angered the people that the kingdom disintegrated. The ten northern tribes rebelled and formed their own kingdom. The capital of the northern kingdom of Israel became its best-known city, Samaria.

Samaria's location made it vulnerable to hostile nations. In 722 BC, the Assyrians swept in, conquered Samaria, carrying leaders and prime citizens into exile. Then, to weaken the morale of the citizens and prevent a future uprising, the Assyrians carted non-Israelite people into Samaria and interspersed them among the remaining Israelites. Over time, these groups intermarried, creating a mixed race known as the Samaritans, impure in the minds of their Judean neighbors.[2]

In addition to the intense racial prejudice, a religious dispute that left enduring scars aggravated the animosity between the Jews and Samaritans. In the sixth century BC, the Jews in the southern kingdom suffered their own exile at the hands of the Babylonians, who invaded Judah and destroyed the temple in Jerusalem (2Kg 25). In turn, the Persians conquered the Babylonians and (in 538 BC) allowed the Jews to return to their homeland. When they arrived, the Samaritans offered to help them rebuild the temple. The Jews rebuffed their despised neighbors. Snubbed, the Samaritans applied their energy to hindering the Jews' efforts to build (Ezr 4–5; Neh 2–4). An action that further deepened the chasm between

Ruins at Aphek. Located on the *Via Maris* between Caesarea Maritima and Jerusalem, Aphek (later called "Antipatris") was on the Yarkon River and served as a southern border city for the region of Samaria.

Jacob's well at Sychar— between Mounts Ebal and Gerizim. Measurements in the 1930s indicated the well is about 135 feet deep.

the two peoples, the Jews, under the leadership of Ezra, enacted strict segregation policies against anyone of mixed backgrounds, including Samaritans.[3]

The Samaritans eventually built their own temple on Mount Gerizim, and they accepted only the Torah as Scripture. Clearly, when Jesus arrived on the scene, the hostility between Samaritans and Jews was deeply ingrained in their cultures.[4] ✣

---

[1] Gerald L. Borchert, *John 1–11*, NAC (1996), 199. [2] Borchert, *John 1–11*, 200; Robert H. Stein, *Luke*, NAC (1992), 318; Thomas D. Lea and David Alan Black, *The New Testament: Its Background and Message*, 2nd ed. (Nashville: B&H Academic, 2003), 87. [3] Borchert, *John 1–11*, 200. [4] Stein, *Luke*, 318.

29 But wanting to justify himself, he asked Jesus, "And who is my neighbor?"

30 Jesus took up the question and said, "A man was going down from Jerusalem to Jericho and fell into the hands of robbers. They stripped him, beat him up, and fled, leaving him half dead. 31 A priest happened to be going down that road. When he saw him, he passed by on the other side. 32 In the same way, a Levite, when he arrived at the place and saw him, passed by on the other side. 33 But a Samaritan on his journey came up to him, and when he saw the man, he had compassion. 34 He went over to him and bandaged his wounds, pouring on olive oil and wine. Then he put him on his own animal, brought him to an inn, and took care of him. 35 The next day[A] he took out two denarii,[B] gave them to the innkeeper, and said, 'Take care of him. When I come back I'll reimburse you for whatever extra you spend.'

36 "Which of these three do you think proved to be a neighbor to the man who fell into the hands of the robbers?"

37 "The one who showed mercy to him," he said.

Then Jesus told him, "Go and do the same."

MARTHA AND MARY

38 While they were traveling, he entered a village, and a woman named Martha welcomed him into her home.[C] 39 She had a sister named Mary, who also sat at the Lord's[D] feet and was listening to what he said.[E] 40 But Martha was distracted by her many tasks, and she came up and asked, "Lord, don't you care that my sister has left me to serve alone? So tell her to give me a hand."[F]

41 The Lord[G] answered her, "Martha, Martha, you are worried and upset about many things, 42 but one thing is necessary.[H] Mary has made the right choice,[I] and it will not be taken away from her."

THE LORD'S PRAYER

11 He was praying in a certain place, and when he finished, one of his disciples said to him, "Lord, teach us to pray, just as John also taught his disciples."

2 He said to them, "Whenever you pray, say,

Father,[J]
your name be honored as holy.
Your kingdom come.[K]
3 Give us each day our daily bread.[L]
4 And forgive us our sins,
for we ourselves also forgive everyone
in debt to us.[M]
And do not bring us into temptation."[N]

ASK, SEARCH, KNOCK

5 He also said to them, "Suppose one of you[O] has a friend and goes to him at midnight and says to him, 'Friend, lend me three loaves of bread, 6 because a friend of mine on a journey has come to me, and I don't have anything to offer him.' 7 Then he will answer from inside and say, 'Don't bother me! The door is already locked, and my children and I have gone to bed. I can't get up to give you anything.' 8 I tell you, even though he won't get up and give him anything because he is his friend, yet because of his friend's shameless boldness,[P] he will get up and give him as much as he needs.

9 "So I say to you, ask, and it will be given to you. Seek, and you will find. Knock, and the door will be opened to you. 10 For everyone who asks receives, and the one who seeks finds, and to the one who knocks, the door will be opened. 11 What father among you, if his son[Q] asks for a fish, will give him a snake instead of a fish? 12 Or if he asks for an egg, will give him a scorpion? 13 If you then, who are evil, know how to give good gifts to your children, how much more will the heavenly Father give the Holy Spirit to those who ask him?"

A HOUSE DIVIDED

14 Now he was driving out a demon that was mute. When the demon came out, the man who had been mute spoke, and the crowds were amazed. 15 But some of them said, "He drives out demons by Beelzebul, the ruler of the demons." 16 And others, as a test, were demanding of him a sign from heaven.

17 Knowing their thoughts, he told them, "Every kingdom divided against itself is headed for destruction, and a house divided against itself falls. 18 If Satan also is divided against himself, how will his kingdom stand? For you say I drive out demons by Beelzebul. 19 And if I drive out demons by Beelzebul, by whom do your sons drive them out? For this reason they will be your judges. 20 If I drive out demons by the finger of God, then the kingdom of God has come upon you. 21 When a strong man, fully armed, guards his estate, his possessions are secure. 22 But when one stronger than he attacks and overpowers him, he takes from him all his weapons[R] he trusted in, and divides up his plunder. 23 Anyone who is not with me is against me, and anyone who does not gather with me scatters.

[A] **10:35** Other mss add *as he was leaving* [B] **10:35** A denarius = one day's wage. [C] **10:38** Other mss omit *into her home* [D] **10:39** Other mss read *at Jesus's* [E] **10:39** Lit *to his word* or *message* [F] **10:40** Or *tell her to help me* [G] **10:41** Other mss read *Jesus* [H] **10:42** Some mss read *few things are necessary*, or *only one* [I] **10:42** Lit *has chosen the good part*, or *has chosen the better portion*; = the right meal
[J] **11:2** Other mss read *Our Father in heaven* [K] **11:2** Other mss add *Your will be done on earth as it is in heaven* [L] **11:3** Or *our bread for tomorrow* [M] **11:4** Or *everyone who wrongs us* [N] **11:4** Other mss add *But deliver us from the evil one* [O] **11:5** Lit *Who of you*
[P] **11:8** Or *persistence* [Q] **11:11** Other mss read *son asks for bread, would give him a stone? Or if he* [R] **11:22** Gk *panoplia*, the armor and weapons of a foot soldier; Eph 6:11,13

AN UNCLEAN SPIRIT'S RETURN

24 "When an unclean spirit comes out of a person,
it roams through waterless places looking for rest,
and not finding rest, it then[A] says, 'I'll go back to my
house that I came from.' 25 Returning, it finds the
house swept and put in order. 26 Then it goes and
brings seven other spirits more evil than itself, and
they enter and settle down there. As a result, that
person's last condition is worse than the first."

TRUE BLESSEDNESS

27 As he was saying these things, a woman from the
crowd raised her voice and said to him, "Blessed is the
womb that bore you and the one who nursed you!"
28 He said, "Rather, blessed are those who hear the
word of God and keep it."

THE SIGN OF JONAH

29 As the crowds were increasing, he began saying,
"This generation is an evil generation. It demands
a sign, but no sign will be given to it except the sign
of Jonah.[B] 30 For just as Jonah became a sign to the
people of Nineveh, so also the Son of Man will be to
this generation. 31 The queen of the south will rise up
at the judgment with the men of this generation and
condemn them, because she came from the ends of
the earth to hear the wisdom of Solomon, and look
— something greater than Solomon is here. 32 The
men of Nineveh will stand up at the judgment with
this generation and condemn it, because they repented at Jonah's preaching, and look — something
greater than Jonah is here.

THE LAMP OF THE BODY

33 "No one lights a lamp and puts it in the cellar or under a basket,[C] but on a lampstand, so that those who
come in may see its light. 34 Your eye is the lamp of the
body. When your eye is healthy, your whole body is
also full of light. But when it is bad, your body is also
full of darkness. 35 Take care, then, that the light in you
is not darkness. 36 If, therefore, your whole body is full
of light, with no part of it in darkness, it will be entirely
illuminated, as when a lamp shines its light on you."

RELIGIOUS HYPOCRISY DENOUNCED

37 As he was speaking, a Pharisee asked him to dine
with him. So he went in and reclined at the table.
38 When the Pharisee saw this, he was amazed that
he did not first perform the ritual washing[D] before
dinner. 39 But the Lord said to him, "Now you Pharisees clean the outside of the cup and dish, but inside
you are full of greed and evil. 40 Fools! Didn't he who
made the outside make the inside too? 41 But give
from what is within to the poor,[E] and then everything
is clean for you.
42 "But woe to you Pharisees! You give a tenth[F] of
mint, rue, and every kind of herb, and you bypass[G]
justice and love for God.[H] These things you should
have done without neglecting the others.
43 "Woe to you Pharisees! You love the front seat in
the synagogues and greetings in the marketplaces.
44 "Woe to you![I] You are like unmarked graves; the
people who walk over them don't know it."
45 One of the experts in the law answered him,
"Teacher, when you say these things you insult us too."
46 Then he said, "Woe also to you experts in the law!
You load people with burdens that are hard to carry,
and yet you yourselves don't touch these burdens
with one of your fingers.
47 "Woe to you! You build tombs[J] for the prophets,
and your fathers killed them. 48 Therefore, you are
witnesses that you approve[K] the deeds of your fathers,
for they killed them, and you build their monuments.[L]
49 Because of this, the wisdom of God said, 'I will send
them prophets and apostles, and some of them they
will kill and persecute,' 50 so that this generation may
be held responsible for the blood of all the prophets
shed since the foundation of the world[M] — 51 from the
blood of Abel to the blood of Zechariah, who perished
between the altar and the sanctuary.
"Yes, I tell you, this generation will be held responsible.[N]
52 "Woe to you experts in the law! You have taken
away the key to knowledge. You didn't go in yourselves,
and you hindered those who were trying to go in."
53 When he left there,[O] the scribes and the Pharisees
began to oppose him fiercely and to cross-examine
him about many things; 54 they were lying in wait for
him to trap him in something he said.[P]

BEWARE OF RELIGIOUS HYPOCRISY

12 Meanwhile, a crowd of many thousands came
together, so that they were trampling on one
another. He began to say to his disciples first, "Be
on your guard against the leaven[Q] of the Pharisees,
which is hypocrisy. 2 There is nothing covered that
won't be uncovered, nothing hidden that won't be
made known. 3 Therefore, whatever you have said
in the dark will be heard in the light, and what you
have whispered in an ear in private rooms will be
proclaimed on the housetops.

[A] **11:24** Other mss omit *then* [B] **11:29** Other mss add *the prophet* [C] **11:33** Other mss omit *or under a basket* [D] **11:38** Lit *he did not first wash* [E] **11:41** Or *But donate from the heart as charity* [F] **11:42** Or *a tithe* [G] **11:42** Or *neglect* [H] **11:42** Lit *the justice and the love of God* [I] **11:44** Other mss add *scribes and Pharisees, hypocrites!* [J] **11:47** Or *graves* [K] **11:48** Lit *witnesses and approve* [L] **11:48** Other mss omit *their monuments* [M] **11:50** Lit *so that the blood of all . . . world may be required of this generation,* [N] **11:51** Lit *you, it will be required of this generation* [O] **11:53** Other mss read *And as he was saying these things to them* [P] **11:54** Other mss add *so that they might bring charges against him* [Q] **12:1** Or *yeast*

FEAR GOD

4 "I say to you, my friends, don't fear those who kill the body, and after that can do nothing more. 5 But I will show you the one to fear: Fear him who has authority to throw people into hell after death. Yes, I say to you, this is the one to fear! 6 Aren't five sparrows sold for two pennies?[A] Yet not one of them is forgotten in God's sight. 7 Indeed, the hairs of your head are all counted. Don't be afraid; you are worth more than many sparrows.

ACKNOWLEDGING CHRIST

8 "And I say to you, anyone who acknowledges me before others, the Son of Man will also acknowledge him before the angels of God, 9 but whoever denies me before others will be denied before the angels of God. 10 Anyone who speaks a word against the Son of Man will be forgiven, but the one who blasphemes against the Holy Spirit will not be forgiven. 11 Whenever they bring you before synagogues and rulers and authorities, don't worry about how you should defend yourselves or what you should say. 12 For the Holy Spirit will teach you at that very hour what must be said."

THE PARABLE OF THE RICH FOOL

13 Someone from the crowd said to him, "Teacher, tell my brother to divide the inheritance with me."

14 "Friend,"[B] he said to him, "who appointed me a judge or arbitrator over you?" 15 He then told them, "Watch out and be on guard against all greed, because one's life is not in the abundance of his possessions."

16 Then he told them a parable: "A rich man's land was very productive. 17 He thought to himself, 'What should I do, since I don't have anywhere to store my crops? 18 I will do this,' he said. 'I'll tear down my barns and build bigger ones and store all my grain and my goods there. 19 Then I'll say to myself, "You have many goods stored up for many years. Take it easy; eat, drink, and enjoy yourself." '

20 "But God said to him, 'You fool! This very night your life is demanded of you. And the things you have prepared — whose will they be?'

21 "That's how it is with the one who stores up treasure for himself and is not rich toward God."

THE CURE FOR ANXIETY

22 Then he said to his disciples, "Therefore I tell you, don't worry about your life, what you will eat; or about the body, what you will wear. 23 For life is more than food and the body more than clothing. 24 Consider the ravens: They don't sow or reap; they don't have a storeroom or a barn; yet God feeds them. Aren't you worth much more than the birds? 25 Can any of you add one moment to his life span[C] by worrying?

Document from ancient Sippar, detailing an arrangement concerning an inheritance; from the time of Awil-Sin, about 1766–1749 BC.

26 If then you're not able to do even a little thing, why worry about the rest?

27 "Consider how the wildflowers grow: They don't labor or spin thread. Yet I tell you, not even Solomon in all his splendor was adorned like one of these. 28 If that's how God clothes the grass, which is in the field today and is thrown into the furnace tomorrow, how much more will he do for you — you of little faith? 29 Don't strive for what you should eat and what you should drink, and don't be anxious. 30 For the Gentile world eagerly seeks all these things, and your Father knows that you need them.

31 "But seek his kingdom, and these things will be provided for you. 32 Don't be afraid, little flock, because your Father delights to give you the kingdom. 33 Sell your possessions and give to the poor. Make money-bags for yourselves that won't grow old, an inexhaustible treasure in heaven, where no thief comes near and no moth destroys. 34 For where your treasure is, there your heart will be also.

[A] **12:6** Lit *two assaria*; a small copper coin [B] **12:14** Lit *Man* [C] **12:25** Or *add a cubit to his height*

READY FOR THE MASTER'S RETURN

35 "Be ready for service[A] and have your lamps lit. 36 You
are to be like people waiting for their master to return
from the wedding banquet so that when he comes
and knocks, they can open the door for him at once.
37 Blessed will be those servants the master finds alert
when he comes. Truly I tell you, he will get ready,[B]
have them recline at the table, then come and serve
them. 38 If he comes in the middle of the night, or even
near dawn,[C] and finds them alert, blessed are those
servants. 39 But know this: If the homeowner had
known at what hour the thief was coming, he would
not have let his house be broken into. 40 You also be
ready, because the Son of Man is coming at an hour
you do not expect."

REWARDS AND PUNISHMENT

41 "Lord," Peter asked, "are you telling this parable to
us or to everyone?"

42 The Lord said, "Who then is the faithful and sensible manager his master will put in charge of his
household servants to give them their allotted food
at the proper time? 43 Blessed is that servant whom
the master finds doing his job when he comes. 44 Truly
I tell you, he will put him in charge of all his possessions. 45 But if that servant says in his heart, 'My
master is delaying his coming,' and starts to beat
the male and female servants, and to eat and drink
and get drunk, 46 that servant's master will come on
a day he does not expect him and at an hour he does
not know. He will cut him to pieces[D] and assign him
a place with the unfaithful.[E] 47 And that servant who
knew his master's will and didn't prepare himself
or do it[F] will be severely beaten. 48 But the one who
did not know and did what deserved punishment
will receive a light beating. From everyone who has
been given much, much will be required; and from
the one who has been entrusted with much, even
more will be expected.[G]

NOT PEACE BUT DIVISION

49 "I came to bring fire on the earth, and how I wish
it were already set ablaze! 50 But I have a baptism to
undergo, and how it consumes me until it is finished!
51 Do you think that I came here to bring peace on
the earth? No, I tell you, but rather division. 52 From
now on, five in one household will be divided: three
against two, and two against three.

53 **They will be divided, father against son,**
son against father,
mother against daughter,
daughter against mother,
mother-in-law against her daughter-in-law,
and daughter-in-law
against mother-in-law."[H]

INTERPRETING THE TIME

54 He also said to the crowds, "When you see a cloud
rising in the west, right away you say, 'A storm is coming,' and so it does. 55 And when the south wind is
blowing, you say, 'It's going to be hot,' and it is. 56 Hypocrites! You know how to interpret the appearance of
the earth and the sky, but why don't you know how
to interpret this present time?

SETTLING ACCOUNTS

57 "Why don't you judge for yourselves what is right?
58 As you are going with your adversary to the ruler,
make an effort to settle with him on the way. Then
he won't drag you before the judge, the judge hand
you over to the bailiff, and the bailiff throw you into
prison. 59 I tell you, you will never get out of there
until you have paid the last penny."[I]

REPENT OR PERISH

13 At that time, some people came and reported
to him about the Galileans whose blood Pilate
had mixed with their sacrifices. 2 And he[J] responded to them, "Do you think that these Galileans were
more sinful than all the other Galileans because they
suffered these things? 3 No, I tell you; but unless you
repent, you will all perish as well. 4 Or those eighteen
that the tower in Siloam fell on and killed — do you
think they were more sinful than all the other people
who live in Jerusalem? 5 No, I tell you; but unless you
repent, you will all perish as well."

THE PARABLE OF THE BARREN FIG TREE

6 And he told this parable: "A man had a fig tree that
was planted in his vineyard. He came looking for fruit
on it and found none. 7 He told the vineyard worker,
'Listen, for three years I have come looking for fruit
on this fig tree and haven't found any. Cut it down!
Why should it even waste the soil?'

8 "But he replied to him, 'Sir,[K] leave it this year also,
until I dig around it and fertilize it. 9 Perhaps it will produce fruit next year, but if not, you can cut it down.'"

HEALING A DAUGHTER OF ABRAHAM

10 As he was teaching in one of the synagogues on the
Sabbath, 11 a woman was there who had been disabled
by a spirit[L] for over eighteen years. She was bent over
and could not straighten up at all.[M] 12 When Jesus saw
her, he called out to her,[N] "Woman, you are free of

[A] **12:35** Lit *"Let your loins be girded"*; an idiom for tying up loose outer clothing in preparation for action; Ex 12:11 [B] **12:37** Lit *will gird himself* [C] **12:38** Lit *even in the second or third watch* [D] **12:46** Lit *him in two* [E] **12:46** Or *unbelievers* [F] **12:47** Lit *or do toward his will,* [G] **12:48** Or *much* [H] **12:53** Mc 7:6 [I] **12:59** Gk *lepton*, the smallest and least valuable copper coin in use [J] **13:2** Other mss read *Jesus* [K] **13:8** Or *Lord* [L] **13:11** Lit *had a spirit of disability* [M] **13:11** Or *straighten up completely* [N] **13:12** Or *he summoned her*

your disability." 13 Then he laid his hands on her, and instantly she was restored and began to glorify God.

14 But the leader of the synagogue, indignant because Jesus had healed on the Sabbath, responded by telling the crowd, "There are six days when work should be done; therefore come on those days and be healed and not on the Sabbath day."

15 But the Lord answered him and said, "Hypocrites! Doesn't each one of you untie his ox or donkey from the feeding trough on the Sabbath and lead it to water? 16 Satan has bound this woman, a daughter of Abraham, for eighteen years — shouldn't she be untied from this bondage[A] on the Sabbath day?"

17 When he had said these things, all his adversaries were humiliated, but the whole crowd was rejoicing over all the glorious things he was doing.

THE PARABLES OF THE MUSTARD SEED AND OF THE LEAVEN

18 He said, therefore, "What is the kingdom of God like, and what can I compare it to? 19 It's like a mustard seed that a man took and sowed in his garden. It grew and became a tree, and the birds of the sky nested in its branches."

20 Again he said, "What can I compare the kingdom of God to? 21 It's like leaven[B] that a woman took and mixed into fifty pounds[C] of flour until all of it was leavened."

THE NARROW WAY

22 He went through one town and village after another, teaching and making his way to Jerusalem. 23 "Lord," someone asked him, "are only a few people going to be saved?"

He said to them, 24 "Make every effort to enter through the narrow door, because I tell you, many will try to enter and won't be able 25 once the homeowner gets up and shuts the door. Then you will stand outside and knock on the door, saying, 'Lord, open up for us!' He will answer you, 'I don't know you or where you're from.' 26 Then you will say, 'We ate and drank in your presence, and you taught in our streets.' 27 But he will say, 'I tell you, I don't know you or where you're from. Get away from me, all you evildoers!' 28 There will be weeping and gnashing of teeth in that place, when you see Abraham, Isaac, Jacob, and all the prophets in the kingdom of God, but yourselves thrown out. 29 They will come from east and west, from north and south, to share the banquet[D] in the kingdom of God. 30 Note this: Some who are last will be first, and some who are first will be last."

JESUS AND HEROD ANTIPAS

31 At that time some Pharisees came and told him, "Go, get out of here. Herod wants to kill you."

32 He said to them, "Go tell that fox, 'Look, I'm driving out demons and performing healings today and tomorrow, and on the third day I will complete my work.'[E] 33 Yet it is necessary that I travel today, tomorrow, and the next day, because it is not possible for a prophet to perish outside of Jerusalem.

JESUS'S LAMENTATION OVER JERUSALEM

34 "Jerusalem, Jerusalem, who kills the prophets and stones those who are sent to her. How often I wanted to gather your children together, as a hen gathers her chicks under her wings, but you were not willing! 35 See, your house is abandoned to you. I tell you, you will not see me until the time comes when[F] you say, '**Blessed is he who comes in the name of the Lord**'!"[G]

A SABBATH CONTROVERSY

14 One Sabbath, when he went in to eat[H] at the house of one of the leading Pharisees, they were watching him closely. 2 There in front of him was a man whose body was swollen with fluid. 3 In response, Jesus asked the law experts and the Pharisees, "Is it lawful to heal on the Sabbath or not?" 4 But they kept silent. He took the man, healed him, and sent him away. 5 And to them, he said, "Which of you whose son or ox falls into a well, will not immediately pull him out on the Sabbath day?" 6 They could find no answer to these things.

TEACHINGS ON HUMILITY

7 He told a parable to those who were invited, when he noticed how they would choose the best places for themselves: 8 "When you are invited by someone to a wedding banquet, don't sit in the place of honor, because a more distinguished person than you may have been invited by your host. 9 The one who invited both of you may come and say to you, 'Give your place to this man,' and then in humiliation, you will proceed to take the lowest place.

10 "But when you are invited, go and sit in the lowest place, so that when the one who invited you comes, he will say to you, 'Friend, move up higher.' You will then be honored in the presence of all the other guests. 11 For everyone who exalts himself will be humbled, and the one who humbles himself will be exalted."

12 He also said to the one who had invited him, "When you give a lunch or a dinner, don't invite your friends, your brothers or sisters, your relatives, or your rich neighbors, because they might invite you back, and you would be repaid. 13 On the contrary,

[A] **13:16** Or *isn't it necessary that she be untied from this bondage* [B] **13:21** Or *yeast* [C] **13:21** Lit *three sata*; about forty liters [D] **13:29** Lit *recline at the table* [E] **13:32** Lit *I will be finished* [F] **13:35** Other mss omit *the time comes when* [G] **13:35** Ps 118:26 [H] **14:1** Lit *eat bread*

when you host a banquet, invite those who are poor, maimed, lame, or blind. 14 And you will be blessed, because they cannot repay you; for you will be repaid at the resurrection of the righteous."

THE PARABLE OF THE LARGE BANQUET

15 When one of those who reclined at the table with him heard these things, he said to him, "Blessed is the one who will eat bread in the kingdom of God!"

16 Then he told him, "A man was giving a large banquet and invited many. 17 At the time of the banquet, he sent his servant to tell those who were invited, 'Come, because everything is now ready.'

18 "But without exception[A] they all began to make excuses. The first one said to him, 'I have bought a field, and I must go out and see it. I ask you to excuse me.'

19 "Another said, 'I have bought five yoke of oxen, and I'm going to try them out. I ask you to excuse me.'

20 "And another said, 'I just got married, and therefore I'm unable to come.'

21 "So the servant came back and reported these things to his master. Then in anger, the master of the house told his servant, 'Go out quickly into the streets and alleys of the city, and bring in here the poor, maimed, blind, and lame.'

22 " 'Master,' the servant said, 'what you ordered has been done, and there's still room.'

23 "Then the master told the servant, 'Go out into the highways and hedges and make them come in, so that my house may be filled. 24 For I tell you, not one of those people who were invited will enjoy my banquet.' "

THE COST OF FOLLOWING JESUS

25 Now great crowds were traveling with him. So he turned and said to them, 26 "If anyone comes to me and does not hate his own father and mother, wife and children, brothers and sisters — yes, and even his own life — he cannot be my disciple. 27 Whoever does not bear his own cross and come after me cannot be my disciple.

28 "For which of you, wanting to build a tower, doesn't first sit down and calculate the cost to see if he has enough to complete it? 29 Otherwise, after he has laid the foundation and cannot finish it, all the onlookers will begin to ridicule him, 30 saying, 'This man started to build and wasn't able to finish.'

31 "Or what king, going to war against another king, will not first sit down and decide if he is able with ten thousand to oppose the one who comes against him with twenty thousand? 32 If not, while the other is still far off, he sends a delegation and asks for terms of peace. 33 In the same way, therefore, every one of you who does not renounce[B] all his possessions cannot be my disciple.

34 "Now, salt is good, but if salt should lose its taste, how will it be made salty? 35 It isn't fit for the soil or for the manure pile; they throw it out. Let anyone who has ears to hear listen."

THE PARABLE OF THE LOST SHEEP

15 All the tax collectors and sinners were approaching to listen to him. 2 And the Pharisees and scribes were complaining, "This man welcomes sinners and eats with them."

3 So he told them this parable: 4 "What man among you, who has a hundred sheep and loses one of them, does not leave the ninety-nine in the open field[C] and go after the lost one until he finds it? 5 When he has found it, he joyfully puts it on his shoulders, 6 and coming home, he calls his friends and neighbors together, saying to them, 'Rejoice with me, because I have found my lost sheep!' 7 I tell you, in the same way, there will be more joy in heaven over one sinner who repents than over ninety-nine righteous people who don't need repentance.

THE PARABLE OF THE LOST COIN

8 "Or what woman who has ten silver coins,[D,E] if she loses one coin, does not light a lamp, sweep the house, and search carefully until she finds it? 9 When she finds it, she calls her friends and neighbors together, saying, 'Rejoice with me, because I have found the silver coin I lost!' 10 I tell you, in the same way, there is joy in the presence of God's angels over one sinner who repents."

THE PARABLE OF THE LOST SON

11 He also said, "A man had two sons. 12 The younger of them said to his father, 'Father, give me the share of the estate I have coming to me.' So he distributed the assets[F] to them. 13 Not many days later, the younger son gathered together all he had and traveled to a distant country, where he squandered his estate in foolish living. 14 After he had spent everything, a severe famine struck that country, and he had nothing.[G] 15 Then he went to work for one of the citizens of that country, who sent him into his fields to feed pigs. 16 He longed to eat his fill from[H] the pods that the pigs were eating, but no one would give him anything. 17 When he came to his senses,[I] he said, 'How many of my father's hired workers have more than enough food, and here I am dying of hunger![J] 18 I'll get up, go to my father, and say to him, "Father, I have sinned

[A] **14:18** Lit *"And from one* (voice) [B] **14:33** Or *leave* [C] **15:4** Or *the wilderness* [D] **15:8** Gk *ten drachmas* [E] **15:8** A Gk drachma was equivalent to a Roman denarius = one day's wage [F] **15:12** Or *life*, or *livelihood*, also in v. 30 [G] **15:14** Lit *and he began to be in need* [H] **15:16** Other mss read *to fill his stomach with* [I] **15:17** Lit *to himself* [J] **15:17** Or *dying in the famine*; v. 14

Growing in Maresha, Israel, the carob tree produces the fruit the prodigal son would have fed to swine.

against heaven and in your sight. 19 I'm no longer worthy to be called your son. Make me like one of your hired workers." ' 20 So he got up and went to his father. But while the son was still a long way off, his father saw him and was filled with compassion. He ran, threw his arms around his neck, and kissed him. 21 The son said to him, 'Father, I have sinned against heaven and in your sight. I'm no longer worthy to be called your son.'

22 "But the father told his servants, 'Quick! Bring out the best robe and put it on him; put a ring on his finger and sandals on his feet. 23 Then bring the fattened calf and slaughter it, and let's celebrate with a feast, 24 because this son of mine was dead and is alive again; he was lost and is found!' So they began to celebrate.

25 "Now his older son was in the field; as he came near the house, he heard music and dancing. 26 So he summoned one of the servants, questioning what these things meant. 27 'Your brother is here,' he told him, 'and your father has slaughtered the fattened calf because he has him back safe and sound.'[A]

28 "Then he became angry and didn't want to go in. So his father came out and pleaded with him. 29 But he replied to his father, 'Look, I have been slaving many years for you, and I have never disobeyed your orders, yet you never gave me a goat so that I could celebrate with my friends. 30 But when this son of yours came, who has devoured your assets[B] with prostitutes, you slaughtered the fattened calf for him.'

31 " 'Son,'[C] he said to him, 'you are always with me, and everything I have is yours. 32 But we had to celebrate and rejoice, because this brother of yours was dead and is alive again; he was lost and is found.' "

THE PARABLE OF THE DISHONEST MANAGER

16 Now he said to the disciples, "There was a rich man who received an accusation that his manager was squandering his possessions. 2 So he called the manager in and asked, 'What is this I hear about you? Give an account of your management, because you can no longer be my manager.'

3 "Then the manager said to himself, 'What will I do since my master is taking the management away from me? I'm not strong enough to dig; I'm ashamed to beg. 4 I know what I'll do so that when I'm removed from management, people will welcome me into their homes.'

5 "So he summoned each one of his master's debtors. 'How much do you owe my master?' he asked the first one.

6 " 'A hundred measures of olive oil,' he said.

" 'Take your invoice,' he told him, 'sit down quickly, and write fifty.'

7 "Next he asked another, 'How much do you owe?'

" 'A hundred measures of wheat,' he said.

" 'Take your invoice,' he told him, 'and write eighty.'

8 "The master praised the unrighteous manager because he had acted shrewdly. For the children of this age are more shrewd than the children of light in dealing with their own people.[D] 9 And I tell you, make friends for yourselves by means of worldly wealth[E] so that when it fails, they may welcome you into eternal dwellings. 10 Whoever is faithful in very little is also faithful in much, and whoever is unrighteous in very little is also unrighteous in much. 11 So if you have not been faithful with worldly wealth, who will trust you with what is genuine? 12 And if you have not been faithful with what belongs to someone else, who will give you what is your own? 13 No servant can serve two masters, since either he will hate one and love the other, or he will be devoted to one and despise the other. You cannot serve both God and money."

[A] **15:27** Lit *him back healthy* [B] **15:30** Or *life*, or *livelihood* [C] **15:31** Lit *Child* [D] **16:8** Lit *own generation* [E] **16:9** Lit *unrighteous money*, also in v. 11

Signet ring from the time of Jesus; a son or daughter would have worn the ring as a sign of special affection from a father. The seal on top is carved in reverse so it could be used as a signature stamp.

KINGDOM VALUES

14 The Pharisees, who were lovers of money, were listening to all these things and scoffing at him. 15 And
he told them, "You are the ones who justify yourselves
in the sight of others, but God knows your hearts.
For what is highly admired by people is revolting in
God's sight.
16 "The Law and the Prophets were until John; since
then, the good news of the kingdom of God has been
proclaimed, and everyone is urgently invited to enter
it.[A] 17 But it is easier for heaven and earth to pass away
than for one stroke of a letter in the law to drop out.
18 "Everyone who divorces his wife and marries
another woman commits adultery, and everyone
who marries a woman divorced from her husband
commits adultery.

THE RICH MAN AND LAZARUS

19 "There was a rich man who would dress in purple
and fine linen, feasting lavishly every day. 20 But a
poor man named Lazarus, covered with sores, was
lying at his gate. 21 He longed to be filled with what
fell from the rich man's table, but instead the dogs
would come and lick his sores. 22 One day the poor
man died and was carried away by the angels to Abraham's side.[B] The rich man also died and was buried.
23 And being in torment in Hades, he looked up and
saw Abraham a long way off, with Lazarus at his
side. 24 'Father Abraham!' he called out, 'Have mercy
on me and send Lazarus to dip the tip of his finger
in water and cool my tongue, because I am in agony
in this flame!'
25 " 'Son,'[C] Abraham said, 'remember that during
your life you received your good things, just as Lazarus received bad things, but now he is comforted
here, while you are in agony. 26 Besides all this, a great
chasm has been fixed between us and you, so that
those who want to pass over from here to you cannot; neither can those from there cross over to us.'
27 " 'Father,' he said, 'then I beg you to send him to
my father's house — 28 because I have five brothers
— to warn them, so that they won't also come to this
place of torment.'
29 "But Abraham said, 'They have Moses and the
prophets; they should listen to them.'
30 " 'No, father Abraham,' he said. 'But if someone
from the dead goes to them, they will repent.'
31 "But he told him, 'If they don't listen to Moses and
the prophets, they will not be persuaded if someone
rises from the dead.' "

WARNINGS FROM JESUS

17 He said to his disciples, "Offenses will certainly
come,[D] but woe to the one through whom they
come! 2 It would be better for him if a millstone were
hung around his neck and he were thrown into the
sea than for him to cause one of these little ones to
stumble. 3 Be on your guard. If your brother sins,[E]
rebuke him, and if he repents, forgive him. 4 And if
he sins against you seven times in a day, and comes
back to you seven times, saying, 'I repent,' you must
forgive him."

FAITH AND DUTY

5 The apostles said to the Lord, "Increase our faith."
6 "If you have faith the size of[F] a mustard seed,"
the Lord said, "you can say to this mulberry tree, 'Be
uprooted and planted in the sea,' and it will obey you.
7 "Which one of you having a servant tending sheep
or plowing will say to him when he comes in from

[A] **16:16** Or *everyone is forcing his way into it* [B] **16:22** Or *to Abraham's bosom*; lit *to the fold of Abraham's robe*; Jn 13:23 [C] **16:25** Lit *Child* [D] **17:1** Lit *"It is impossible for offenses not to come* [E] **17:3** Other mss add *against you* [F] **17:6** Lit *faith like*

Wearing Purple

by Darryl Wood

Fondness for the color purple existed for centuries. As a clothing color, it was available primarily to the wealthy. Let's consider the background and significance of wearing purple in the first century AD.

PURPLE DYE

Purple dye has a long history of coming from the sea.[1] The ancients extracted purple from a mollusk (*Murex trunculus* or *Murex brandaris*) found along the Mediterranean coast. The Phoenician coast, especially, contained large quantities of these mussels. Tyre and Sidon ranked among the central cities for processing this dye. Manufacture of the mussels produced varying shades of purple. Violet, crimson, or blue might result. The shade of the dyed fabric depended on the mussels' species, the strength of the dye, and other factors in the process. Pliny, the first-century Roman historian, described the manufacturing method.[2] After entrapment and extraction from the sea, workers broke the shells. They removed slimy glands and heated them in salt water. This routine required many laborers and proved to be difficult work. A sickening smell resulted from the process. Modern excavations at Sidon revealed large heaps of discarded shells from these factories.

EARLY USE OF PURPLE

The earliest evidence for the use of purple dye dates to the second millennium BC. Murex shells discovered near Ugarit in northern Syria support that date. Trade relationships between Ugarit and the Phoenician cities suggest that purple dye existed that early in Phoenicia as well.

Purple products proved to be of great value to the Phoenician economy, as illustrated on coins from Tyre dated to the fifth century BC. Some coins from that period carried an image of the *Murex*. Apparently the Phoenicians dominated trade in purple. They extracted *Murex* in such great quantities that it is rarely found in the area today. A location

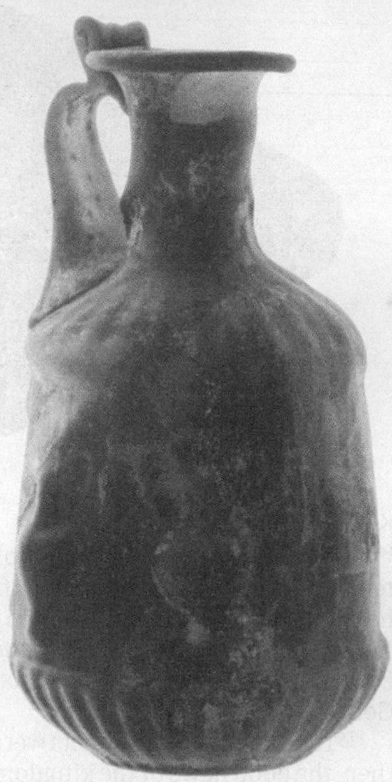

Mold-blown purple vessel from Sidon with relief decorations; approximately 3 ½ inches tall.

Ruins overlooking the Mediterranean at Tyre.

near the sea enhanced the ability of those who manufactured purple to trade those products in places far from their homeland. Dyed fabrics, enhanced by embroidery, found their way to distant parts of the world. The Greek poet Homer wrote about the beauty of robes the Sidonian women made.[3]

In the Hellenistic culture of the first millennium BC, some vassal kings wore purple.[4] Pliny records that Romulus, one of the mythological founders of Rome, dressed in a purple cloak. Further, Rome's third king, Tullus Hostilius (seventh century BC), wore a purple striped robe after he defeated the Etruscans.[5] References to purple cloth appear frequently in the Old Testament (Ex 26:1,31; 28:6; Jdg 8:26; 2Ch 2:14; Est 8:15; 3:14; Sg 3:10; Ezk 27:16; Dn 5:7).

Limited sources, difficulty of production, and the requirement that it be shipped likely restricted availability of purple fabric. These factors drove up the price. Access to purple cloth, then, remained with the religious elite, royals, and wealthy in ancient times.

FIRST-CENTURY USE

Knowing first-century-AD uses of purple fabrics enhances our understanding of their significance in Jesus's time. The societal elite dressed in purple clothing in first-century Roman culture. Roman historians noted its costliness. Pliny comments on the high price of "double-dyed Tyrian purple."[6] The Roman Senate practiced a tradition in which a victorious general might be proclaimed *imperator*. He paraded into the city riding a chariot and was received by the public with great fanfare. The general wore the triumphal dress of the day, which included a purple robe embroidered in gold.[7] Although this practice originated earlier, it remained a staple of first-century Roman culture.

Purple clothing highlighted the influential status of the wearer. Roman senators wore it to distinguish themselves from other nobility. Priests, who offered religious sacrifices, donned purple garments to gain approval from the gods.[8] Men and women alike believed purple clothing complemented their appearance and made them beautiful. Many associated the color purple with luxury.[9] The cost of purple clothes probably confined access to the wealthy or privileged.

References to purple clothing in the New Testament reflect its prominence and value. Lydia, a leader in the formation of the church at Philippi, dealt in purple fabrics (Ac 16:14). The book of Revelation states that merchants would mourn the fall of Babylon and the loss of a market for their fine products, including purple (18:12,16). In the parable of the rich man and Lazarus, the rich man's purple clothing (Lk 16:19) and sumptuous living pointed to his elevated status in life. ✣

---

[1] See 1Macc 4:23 and Josephus, *Jewish War* 5.5.4. [2] Pliny, *Natural History* 9.60.124–64.141 [3] Homer, *The Iliad* 6.285–95. [4] 1 Maccabees 10:20,62; 11:58; 14:43–44. [5] Pliny, *Natural History* 9.63.136–37. [6] Pliny, *Natural History* 9.63.137. [7] Dio Cassius, *Roman History* 6; Livy, *Livy* 10.7.9–10; T. E. Schmidt, "Mark 15.16-32: The Crucifixion Narrative and the Roman Triumphal Procession," *New Testament Studies* (*NTS*) 41.1 (1995): 2–3. [8] Pliny, *Natural History* 9.60.127. [9] Pliny, *Natural History* 9.65.139–41.

Scene on the Arch of Titus at the Roman Forum shows General Titus riding victoriously in a chariot.

the field, 'Come at once and sit down to eat'? 8 Instead, will he not tell him, 'Prepare something for me to eat, get ready, and serve me while I eat and drink; later you can eat and drink'? 9 Does he thank that servant because he did what was commanded?[A] 10 In the same way, when you have done all that you were commanded, you should say, 'We are unworthy servants; we've only done our duty.' "

TEN MEN HEALED

11 While traveling to Jerusalem, he passed between[B] Samaria and Galilee. 12 As he entered a village, ten men with leprosy[C] met him. They stood at a distance 13 and raised their voices, saying, "Jesus, Master, have mercy on us!"

14 When he saw them, he told them, "Go and show yourselves to the priests." And while they were going, they were cleansed.

15 But one of them, seeing that he was healed, returned and, with a loud voice, gave glory to God. 16 He fell facedown at his feet, thanking him. And he was a Samaritan.

17 Then Jesus said, "Were not ten cleansed? Where are the nine? 18 Didn't any return to give glory to God except this foreigner?" 19 And he told him, "Get up and go on your way. Your faith has saved you."[D]

THE COMING OF THE KINGDOM

20 When he was asked by the Pharisees when the kingdom of God would come, he answered them, "The kingdom of God is not coming with something observable; 21 no one will say,[E] 'See here!' or 'There!' For you see, the kingdom of God is in your midst."[F]

22 Then he told the disciples, "The days are coming when you will long to see one of the days of the Son of Man, but you won't see it. 23 They will say to you, 'See there!' or 'See here!' Don't follow or run after them. 24 For as the lightning flashes from horizon to horizon and lights up the sky, so the Son of Man will be in his day. 25 But first it is necessary that he suffer many things and be rejected by this generation.

26 "Just as it was in the days of Noah, so it will be in the days of the Son of Man: 27 People went on eating, drinking, marrying and being given in marriage until the day Noah boarded the ark, and the flood came and destroyed them all. 28 It will be the same as it was in the days of Lot: People went on eating, drinking, buying, selling, planting, building. 29 But on the day Lot left Sodom, fire and sulfur rained from heaven and destroyed them all. 30 It will be like that on the day the Son of Man is revealed. 31 On that day, a man on the housetop, whose belongings are in the house, must not come down to get them. Likewise the man who is in the field must not turn back. 32 Remember Lot's wife! 33 Whoever tries to make his life secure[G,H] will lose it, and whoever loses his life will preserve it. 34 I tell you, on that night two will be in one bed; one will be taken and the other will be left. 35 Two women will be grinding grain together; one will be taken and the other left."[I]

37 "Where, Lord?" they asked him.

He said to them, "Where the corpse is, there also the vultures will be gathered."

THE PARABLE OF THE PERSISTENT WIDOW

18 Now he told them a parable on the need for them to pray always and not give up. 2 "There was a judge in a certain town who didn't fear God or respect people. 3 And a widow in that town kept coming to him, saying, 'Give me justice against my adversary.'

4 "For a while he was unwilling, but later he said to himself, 'Even though I don't fear God or respect people, 5 yet because this widow keeps pestering me,[J] I will give her justice, so that she doesn't wear me out[K] by her persistent coming.' "

6 Then the Lord said, "Listen to what the unjust judge says. 7 Will not God grant justice to his elect who cry out to him day and night? Will he delay helping them?[L] 8 I tell you that he will swiftly grant them justice. Nevertheless, when the Son of Man comes, will he find faith on earth?"

THE PARABLE OF THE PHARISEE AND THE TAX COLLECTOR

9 He also told this parable to some who trusted in themselves that they were righteous and looked down on everyone else: 10 "Two men went up to the temple to pray, one a Pharisee and the other a tax collector. 11 The Pharisee was standing and praying like this about himself:[M] 'God, I thank you that I'm not like other people — greedy, unrighteous, adulterers, or even like this tax collector. 12 I fast twice a week; I give a tenth[N] of everything I get.'

13 "But the tax collector, standing far off, would not even raise his eyes to heaven but kept striking his chest and saying, 'God, have mercy on me,[O] a sinner!' 14 I tell you, this one went down to his house justified rather than the other, because everyone who exalts himself will be humbled, but the one who humbles himself will be exalted."

[A] **17:9** Other mss add *I don't think so* [B] **17:11** Or *through the middle of* [C] **17:12** Gk *lepros*; a term for various skin diseases; see Lv 13–14 [D] **17:19** Or *faith has made you well* [E] **17:21** Lit *they will not say* [F] **17:21** Or *within you* [G] **17:33** Other mss read *to save his life* [H] **17:33** Or *tries to retain his life* [I] **17:35** Some mss include v. 36: *"Two will be in a field: One will be taken, and the other will be left."* [J] **18:5** Lit *widow causes me trouble* [K] **18:5** Or *doesn't ruin my reputation* [L] **18:7** Or *Will he put up with them?* [M] **18:11** Or *by himself* [N] **18:12** Or *give tithes* [O] **18:13** Or *God, turn your wrath from me*

BLESSING THE CHILDREN

15 People were bringing infants to him so that he might touch them, but when the disciples saw it, they rebuked them. 16 Jesus, however, invited them: "Let the little children come to me, and don't stop them, because the kingdom of God belongs to such as these. 17 Truly I tell you, whoever does not receive the kingdom of God like a little child will never enter it."

THE RICH YOUNG RULER

18 A ruler asked him, "Good teacher, what must I do to inherit eternal life?"

19 "Why do you call me good?" Jesus asked him. "No one is good except God alone. 20 You know the commandments: **Do not commit adultery; do not murder; do not steal; do not bear false witness; honor your father and mother.**"[A]

21 "I have kept all these from my youth," he said.

22 When Jesus heard this, he told him, "You still lack one thing: Sell all you have and distribute it to the poor, and you will have treasure in heaven. Then come, follow me."

23 After he heard this, he became extremely sad, because he was very rich.

POSSESSIONS AND THE KINGDOM

24 Seeing that he became sad,[B] Jesus said, "How hard it is for those who have wealth to enter the kingdom of God! 25 For it is easier for a camel to go through the eye of a needle than for a rich person to enter the kingdom of God."

26 Those who heard this asked, "Then who can be saved?"

27 He replied, "What is impossible with man is possible with God."

28 Then Peter said, "Look, we have left what we had and followed you."

29 So he said to them, "Truly I tell you, there is no one who has left a house, wife or brothers or sisters, parents or children because of the kingdom of God, 30 who will not receive many times more at this time, and eternal life in the age to come."

THE THIRD PREDICTION OF HIS DEATH

31 Then he took the Twelve aside and told them, "See, we are going up to Jerusalem. Everything that is written through the prophets about the Son of Man will be accomplished. 32 For he will be handed over to the Gentiles, and he will be mocked, insulted, spit on; 33 and after they flog him, they will kill him, and he will rise on the third day."

34 They understood none of these things. The meaning of the saying[C] was hidden from them, and they did not grasp what was said.

A BLIND MAN RECEIVES HIS SIGHT

35 As he approached Jericho, a blind man was sitting by the road begging. 36 Hearing a crowd passing by, he inquired what was happening. 37 "Jesus of Nazareth is passing by," they told him.

38 So he called out, "Jesus, Son of David, have mercy on me!" 39 Then those in front told him to keep quiet,[D] but he kept crying out all the more, "Son of David, have mercy on me!"

40 Jesus stopped and commanded that he be brought to him. When he came closer, he asked him, 41 "What do you want me to do for you?"

"Lord," he said, "I want to see."

42 "Receive your sight," Jesus told him. "Your faith has saved you." 43 Instantly he could see, and he began to follow him, glorifying God. All the people, when they saw it, gave praise to God.

JESUS VISITS ZACCHAEUS

19 He entered Jericho and was passing through. 2 There was a man named Zacchaeus who was a chief tax collector, and he was rich. 3 He was trying to see who Jesus was, but he was not able because of the crowd, since he was a short man. 4 So running ahead, he climbed up a sycamore tree to see Jesus, since he was about to pass that way. 5 When Jesus came to the place, he looked up and said to him, "Zacchaeus, hurry and come down because today it is necessary for me to stay at your house."

6 So he quickly came down and welcomed him joyfully. 7 All who saw it began to complain, "He's gone to stay with a sinful man."

8 But Zacchaeus stood there and said to the Lord, "Look, I'll give half of my possessions to the poor, Lord. And if I have extorted anything from anyone, I'll pay back four times as much."

9 "Today salvation has come to this house," Jesus told him, "because he too is a son of Abraham. 10 For the Son of Man has come to seek and to save the lost."

THE PARABLE OF THE TEN MINAS

11 As they were listening to this, he went on to tell a parable because he was near Jerusalem, and they thought the kingdom of God was going to appear right away.

12 Therefore he said, "A nobleman traveled to a far country to receive for himself authority to be king[E] and then to return. 13 He called ten of his servants, gave them ten minas,[F] and told them, 'Engage in business until I come back.'

[A] **18:20** Ex 20:12–16; Dt 5:16–20 [B] **18:24** Other mss omit *he became sad* [C] **18:34** Lit *This saying* [D] **18:39** Or *those in front rebuked him* [E] **19:12** Lit *to receive for himself a kingdom*, or *sovereignty*, also in v. 15 [F] **19:13** = Gk coin worth a hundred drachmas or about a hundred days' wages

Jericho in Jesus's Day

by William F. Cook III

At Jericho, part of the bath complex at Herod's palace, likely the frigidarium.

Jericho is in the southern Jordan Valley. The city is 740 feet below sea level, the lowest inhabited city in the world. The lowest point on the face of the earth, the Dead Sea (1,300 feet below sea level), is about eight miles south of the city. To the west of Jericho rises Mount Quarantania, the traditional site of Jesus's forty-day fast and temptation. Five miles east is the Jordan River and the traditional site of Jesus's baptism. Qumran, where the Dead Sea Scrolls were discovered, is located about eight miles south of the city on the northwest shore of the Dead Sea. Jerusalem is approximately thirteen miles southwest of Jericho. Old Testament Jericho (Tel es-Sultan) is located two miles north of New Testament Jericho. The Old Testament site was not inhabited in Jesus's day.

Although less than seven inches of rain falls annually, mostly between November and February, Jericho in Jesus's day was an oasis in a barren land. God provided the city with water, good soil, a moderate winter climate, and a strategic location. Springs near the foot of the western hills provide the city its fresh water. The major spring is known as Elijah's fountain. Flowing eastward, the stream waters the heart of the oasis. Water from other nearby springs brought in by an aqueduct enlarged the oasis. The combination of water availability and the rich alluvial soil made Jericho an attractive place for settlement.

These conditions made Jericho suitable for farming. Grapes, pomegranates, wheat, and vegetables thrived here. The area was also famous for its sycamore and balsam trees. The Jewish historian Josephus and the Roman geographer Strabo both commented on Jericho's famous groves.[1] The Jericho balsam was renowned for its medicinal qualities and for its use in perfume. These factors, along with the mild winter climate, made Jericho an attractive location for the winter capital city during the reigns of the Hasmoneans and Herod the Great. That it was culturally and politically aloof from Jerusalem added to its attractiveness.

New Testament Jericho, also called Herodian Jericho, had its beginnings in the period following the Jews' returning from Babylonian exile. When the Ptolemies and Seleucids controlled the Jewish homeland, they considered Jericho to be royal property.[2] This royal setting continued in the first century BC. Excavators have unearthed extensive remains at New Testament Jericho. Today two large mounds distinguish the site. The earliest building project was a Hasmonean complex. The palace covered more than six acres and became the pleasure resort of the reigning kings.[3]

Herod was especially fond of Jericho. The city gave him a place of repose from Jerusalem's demands.

The area surrounding Jericho is lush with vegetation. The Old Testament referred to Jericho as the City of Palms (Dt 34:3; Jdg 1:16; 3:13).

He captured Jericho in 37 BC from Antigonus, a Hasmonean descendant. Josephus describes how Herod had his brother-in-law, the high priest Aristobulus, drowned in the swimming pool at the site of the Hasmonean palace.[4]

Herod built extensively at Jericho, transforming the city into something of a garden. Further, he constructed a number of public buildings: an amphitheater, hippodrome, a gymnasium, parks, gardens, pools, villas, a fortress, and most impressive—a large palace complex. His magnificent winter palace was built in three stages and may be considered three separate palaces. Herod's most extensive project was the third palace, which covered more than seven acres. This palace was planned and built following exceptional architectural standards. Because the palace extended to both sides of the Wadi Qelt, its residents could enjoy the seasonal flow of water. Another of Herod's building projects was a complex accommodating horse races, athletics, boxing, theater, and musical shows. It was unique in the entire Greco-Roman world.[5]

Jericho in Jesus's day was probably spread over the irrigated areas of the plain like a garden city; homes were side by side with royal villas. Many members of the Jerusalem aristocracy used the city as a winter resort. Excavations of a nearby cemetery give evidence of extensive habitation in this period.[6]

Following Herod's death at Jericho in 4 BC, his palaces began to decline. After the removal of Herod the Great's son, Archelaus, Roman prefects ruled Judea (with the exception of AD 41–44). The prefects ruled from Caesarea on the coast rather than Jerusalem and vacationed elsewhere. Although the palaces may not have been as well maintained, the city remained impressive and important. Under Roman rule, Jericho remained an important town for travelers coming from Galilee (around Samaria) and the Transjordan to Jerusalem.

When Jesus entered Jericho, he would have seen a beautiful city, the magnificent hippodrome, a large palace complex, winter villas, large plantations, and a bustling community. The presence of a chief tax collector in Jericho (Zacchaeus) is understandable since the city was on the main road from the Transjordan to Judea. After the Jewish revolts of AD 66–70 and 132–135, Jericho's importance greatly diminished. ✣

---

[1] Josephus, *Jewish War* 4.8.3; Strabo, *Geography* 16.41. [2] Gideon Foerster, "Jericho: Hellenistic to Early Arab Periods: History" in *NEAEHL*, 2:681. [3] Ehud Netzer, "Jericho: Exploration since 1973" in *NEAEHL*, 2:683. [4] Josephus, *Jewish Antiquities* 15.3.2–3. [5] Ehud Netzer, "Roman Jericho (Tulul Abu el-`Alayiq)" in *ABD*, 3:739. [6] Netzer, "Roman Jericho."

14 "But his subjects hated him and sent a delegation after him, saying, 'We don't want this man to rule over us.'

15 "At his return, having received the authority to be king, he summoned those servants he had given the money to, so that he could find out how much they had made in business. 16 The first came forward and said, 'Master, your mina has earned ten more minas.'

17 " 'Well done, good[A] servant!' he told him. 'Because you have been faithful in a very small matter, have authority over ten towns.'

18 "The second came and said, 'Master, your mina has made five minas.'

19 "So he said to him, 'You will be over five towns.'

20 "And another came and said, 'Master, here is your mina. I have kept it safe in a cloth 21 because I was afraid of you since you're a harsh man: you collect what you didn't deposit and reap what you didn't sow.'

22 "He told him, 'I will condemn you by what you have said, you evil servant! If you knew I was a harsh man, collecting what I didn't deposit and reaping what I didn't sow, 23 why, then, didn't you put my money in the bank? And when I returned, I would have collected it with interest.' 24 So he said to those standing there, 'Take the mina away from him and give it to the one who has ten minas.'

25 "But they said to him, 'Master, he has ten minas.'

26 " 'I tell you, that to everyone who has, more will be given; and from the one who does not have, even what he does have will be taken away. 27 But bring here these enemies of mine, who did not want me to rule over them, and slaughter[B] them in my presence.' "

THE TRIUMPHAL ENTRY

28 When he had said these things, he went on ahead, going up to Jerusalem. 29 As he approached Bethphage and Bethany, at the place called the Mount of Olives, he sent two of the disciples 30 and said, "Go into the village ahead of you. As you enter it, you will find a colt tied there, on which no one has ever sat. Untie it and bring it. 31 If anyone asks you, 'Why are you untying it?' say this: 'The Lord needs it.' "

32 So those who were sent left and found it just as he had told them. 33 As they were untying the colt, its owners said to them, "Why are you untying the colt?"

34 "The Lord needs it," they said. 35 Then they brought it to Jesus, and after throwing their clothes on the colt, they helped Jesus get on it. 36 As he was going along, they were spreading their clothes on the road. 37 Now he came near the path down the Mount of Olives, and the whole crowd of the disciples began to praise God joyfully with a loud voice for all the miracles they had seen:

38 **Blessed is the King who comes**
in the name of the Lord.[C]
Peace in heaven
and glory in the highest heaven!

39 Some of the Pharisees from the crowd told him, "Teacher, rebuke your disciples."

40 He answered, "I tell you, if they were to keep silent, the stones would cry out."

JESUS'S LOVE FOR JERUSALEM

41 As he approached and saw the city, he wept for it, 42 saying, "If you knew this day what would bring peace — but now it is hidden from your eyes. 43 For the days will come on you when your enemies will build a barricade around you, surround you, and hem you in on every side. 44 They will crush you and your children among you to the ground, and they will not leave one stone on another in your midst, because you did not recognize the time when God visited you."

CLEANSING THE TEMPLE

45 He went into the temple and began to throw out those who were selling,[D] 46 and he said, "It is written, **my house will be a house of prayer**, but you have made it **a den of thieves!**"[E]

47 Every day he was teaching in the temple. The chief priests, the scribes, and the leaders of the people were looking for a way to kill him, 48 but they could not find a way to do it, because all the people were captivated by what they heard.

THE AUTHORITY OF JESUS CHALLENGED

20 One day as he was teaching the people in the temple and proclaiming the good news, the chief priests and the scribes, with the elders, came 2 and said to him, "Tell us, by what authority are you doing these things? Who is it who gave you this authority?"

3 He answered them, "I will also ask you a question. Tell me, 4 was the baptism of John from heaven or of human origin?"

5 They discussed it among themselves: "If we say, 'From heaven,' he will say, 'Why didn't you believe him?' 6 But if we say, 'Of human origin,' all the people will stone us, because they are convinced that John was a prophet." 7 So they answered that they did not know its origin.

8 And Jesus said to them, "Neither will I tell you by what authority I do these things."

THE PARABLE OF THE VINEYARD OWNER

9 Now he began to tell the people this parable: "A man planted a vineyard, leased it to tenant farmers, and

[A] **19:17** Or *capable* [B] **19:27** Or *execute* [C] **19:38** Ps 118:26 [D] **19:45** Other mss add *and buying in it* [E] **19:46** Is 56:7; Jr 7:11

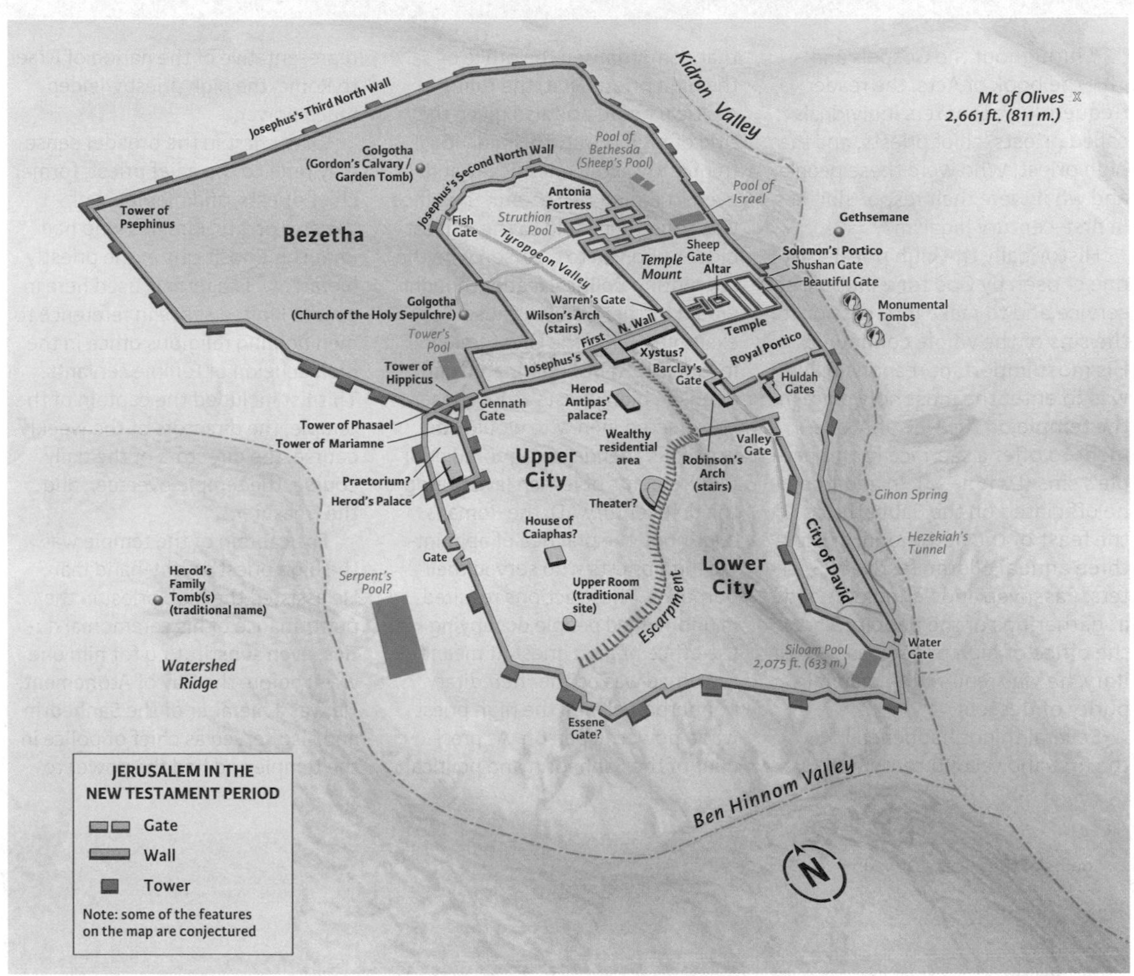

went away for a long time. 10 At harvest time he sent
a servant to the farmers so that they might give him
some fruit from the vineyard. But the farmers beat
him and sent him away empty-handed. 11 He sent yet
another servant, but they beat that one too, treated
him shamefully, and sent him away empty-handed.
12 And he sent yet a third, but they wounded this one
too and threw him out.

13 "Then the owner of the vineyard said, 'What
should I do? I will send my beloved son. Perhaps[A]
they will respect him.'

14 "But when the tenant farmers saw him, they discussed it among themselves and said, 'This is the heir.
Let's kill him, so that the inheritance will be ours.' 15 So
they threw him out of the vineyard and killed him.

"What then will the owner of the vineyard do to
them? 16 He will come and kill those farmers and give
the vineyard to others."

But when they heard this they said, "That must
never happen!"

17 But he looked at them and said, "Then what is the
meaning of this Scripture:[B]

The stone that the builders rejected
has become the cornerstone?[C]

18 Everyone who falls on that stone will be broken to
pieces, but on whomever it falls, it will shatter him."

19 Then the scribes and the chief priests looked
for a way to get their hands on him that very hour,
because they knew he had told this parable against
them, but they feared the people.

GOD AND CAESAR

20 They watched closely and sent spies who pretended
to be righteous,[D] so that they could catch him in what
he said, to hand him over to the governor's rule and
authority. 21 They questioned him, "Teacher, we know
that you speak and teach correctly, and you don't

[A] **20:13** Other mss add *when they see him* [B] **20:17** Lit *"What then is this that is written* [C] **20:17** Ps 118:22 [D] **20:20** Or *upright*

First-Century Priesthood

by Glenn McCoy

Throughout the Gospels and the book of Acts, the reader frequently encounters individuals called priests, chief priests, and the high priest. Who were these people, and what were their responsibilities in first-century Judaism?

Historically the high priest was one chosen by God for a lifetime of service and to make intercession for the sins of the whole community. His most important responsibility was to enter the most holy place in the temple on the Day of Atonement to offer a sacrifice for his people's sins (Lv 16:1–34). In addition, he officiated on the Sabbaths, at the feast of the new moon, at the three annual pilgrim festivals (Shelters, Passover, and Pentecost), and at gatherings of the people. Since the office of high priest was hereditary, he was required to maintain a purity of descent.

Several things happened in the first and second centuries BC that compromised the office of the high priest. First, the ruling political figure was also given the title of high priest. This individual frequently acted unethically and even irreligiously. Second, the office was sometimes sold to the highest bidder or given to a person who the appointing political leader thought would further his own cause. For example, Herod the Great (reigned in Judea 37–4 BC) nominated and deposed high priests as he chose. He selected men who would advance his agenda and ignored prior requirements of Jewish law. During the first century AD, the Romans continued the practice of appointing high priests who served their purposes. These actions resulted in unqualified people occupying the office of high priest. It meant the office was neither hereditary nor perpetual. Still the high priest was a powerful person. As president of the Sanhedrin and political representative of the nation of Israel to Rome, the high priest wielded much power.

Chief priest in the broader sense may refer to the chief priest, former chief priests, and members of the aristocratic families who had important positions in the priestly hierarchy.[1] The term is used here in a more limited sense in reference to men holding religious office in the high echelon of temple servants. This list included the captain of the temple, the directors of the weekly course, the directors of the daily course, the temple overseer, and the treasurer.[2]

The captain of the temple was the high priest's right-hand man. He assisted the high priest in the performance of his ceremonial duties, even substituting for him one week before the Day of Atonement. He was a member of the Sanhedrin and also served as chief of police in the temple and had the power to

Tombs of the Jewish Sanhedrin.

arrest (see Ac 4:1–3; 5:24,26). He was usually next in line for the office of high priest.[3]

The directors of the weekly courses (twenty-four in number) resided wherever they chose and came to the Jerusalem temple for only two weeks of service during the year (in addition to the three pilgrim festivals). The director performed the rites of purification for lepers and women after childbirth (Mt 8:4; Lk 2:22–24). The directors of the daily courses (some 156 priests were required each week) came to Jerusalem with the same frequency as the directors of the weekly courses. During his day on duty, the director of daily courses had to be present at the offering of sacrifice.

The temple overseer apparently had the power of supervision over the temple (Lk 22:4,52). The treasurers handled the financial affairs of the temple. Lots of money came into the temple coffers in the form of sacrifices and offerings. At the same time, expenses were necessary for the upkeep of the temple, the provision of sacrifices, and the support of the priesthood.

The common priest made up the major part of the priesthood in Jesus's time. There were perhaps more than seven thousand priests (estimates of the number vary) who were divided into twenty-four courses and did service for two weeks (from Sabbath to Sabbath) out of the year (plus major festivals). Each weekly course was divided into four to nine daily courses carrying out their specific responsibilities during the week.

When the priest was on duty, he was extremely busy. There were both public and private sacrifices to offer each day. The public sacrifices seem to have been paid for from temple funds while private sacrifices had to be paid for by the individual. Among the sacrifices that the individual could offer were burnt offerings, sin offerings, guilt offerings, and meal offerings. The priests had a choice as to which of these sacrifices they would make. Lots were cast to determine which priest on duty would prepare and offer the daily morning sacrifice (Lk 1:9). This seems to be the ritual Zechariah was performing when the angel appeared announcing that his wife Elizabeth would bear a son (1:13).

When the priest was not on duty, he was free to live where he pleased. Most lived outside Jerusalem. During the remainder of the year, when he did not have temple duty, the priest was trying to make a living. He did receive some support from temple tithes and taxes, but this was not adequate to support an individual, let alone a family. Consequently, the priest had to engage in some sort of trade such as carpentry, masonry, selling merchandise, serving as a scribe, or any number of other professions.

The Levite held a lower rank than the priest and thus could not offer sacrifices. There were some ten thousand Levites (the exact number is uncertain) in the first century. They, like the priests, were divided into twenty-four courses, serving only two weeks out of the year. The singers and musicians were the higher order of Levites, furnishing music for temple services and festivals. The temple servants (also Levites) helped with the function and maintenance of the temple. Specific duties included helping the priest with his priestly garments, preparing the Scripture for reading, and cleaning the temple. In addition, the Levites furnished the temple guards. The guards acted as doorkeepers at the temple, patrolled the court of the Gentiles and closed the doors of the temple when the day was over. The Sanhedrin could call on these guards when needed.[4] Most likely the temple guards were a part of the contingent sent to arrest Jesus on the Mount of Olives. ✜

Roman period relief of a priest making sacrifice. Bells can be seen around the bottom of the skirt.

---

[1] James A Brooks, *Mark*, NAC (1991), 136.
[2] Joachim Jeremias, *Jerusalem in the Time of Jesus* (Philadelphia: Fortress, 1969), 160.
[3] Merrill C. Tenney, ed., *ZPEB* (1980), 4:849.
[4] Jeremias, *Jerusalem*, 209–10.

show partiality[A] but teach truthfully the way of God. 22 Is it lawful for us to pay taxes to Caesar or not?"

23 But detecting their craftiness, he said to them,[B] 24 "Show me a denarius.[C] Whose image and inscription does it have?"

"Caesar's," they said.

25 "Well then," he told them, "give to Caesar the things that are Caesar's, and to God the things that are God's."

26 They were not able to catch him in what he said in public, and being amazed at his answer, they became silent.

THE SADDUCEES AND THE RESURRECTION

27 Some of the Sadducees, who say there is no resurrection, came up and questioned him: 28 "Teacher, Moses wrote for us that **if a man's brother** has a wife, and **dies childless, his brother should take the wife and produce offspring for his brother.**[D] 29 Now there were seven brothers. The first took a wife and died without children. 30 Also the second[E] 31 and the third took her. In the same way, all seven died and left no children. 32 Finally, the woman died too. 33 In the resurrection, therefore, whose wife will the woman be? For all seven had married her."

34 Jesus told them, "The children of this age marry and are given in marriage. 35 But those who are counted worthy to take part in that age and in the resurrection from the dead neither marry nor are given in marriage. 36 For they can no longer die, because they are like angels and are children of God, since they are children of the resurrection. 37 Moses even indicated in the passage about the burning bush that the dead are raised, where he calls the Lord **the God of Abraham and the God of Isaac and the God of Jacob.**[F] 38 He is not the God of the dead but of the living, because all are living to[G] him."

39 Some of the scribes answered, "Teacher, you have spoken well." 40 And they no longer dared to ask him anything.

THE QUESTION ABOUT THE MESSIAH

41 Then he said to them, "How can they say that the Messiah is the son of David? 42 For David himself says in the Book of Psalms:

> **The Lord declared to my Lord,**
> **'Sit at my right hand**
> 43 **until I make your enemies your footstool.'**[H]

44 David calls him 'Lord.' How, then, can he be his son?"

WARNING AGAINST THE SCRIBES

45 While all the people were listening, he said to his disciples, 46 "Beware of the scribes, who want to go around in long robes and who love greetings in the marketplaces, the best seats in the synagogues, and the places of honor at banquets. 47 They devour widows' houses and say long prayers just for show. These will receive harsher judgment."

THE WIDOW'S GIFT

21 He looked up and saw the rich dropping their offerings into the temple treasury. 2 He also saw a poor widow dropping in two tiny coins.[I] 3 "Truly I tell you," he said, "this poor widow has put in more than all of them. 4 For all these people have put in gifts out of their surplus, but she out of her poverty has put in all she had to live on."

DESTRUCTION OF THE TEMPLE PREDICTED

5 As some were talking about the temple, how it was adorned with beautiful stones and gifts dedicated to God, he said, 6 "These things that you see — the days will come when not one stone will be left on another that will not be thrown down."

SIGNS OF THE END OF THE AGE

7 "Teacher," they asked him, "so when will these things happen? And what will be the sign when these things are about to take place?"

8 Then he said, "Watch out that you are not deceived. For many will come in my name, saying, 'I am he,' and, 'The time is near.' Don't follow them. 9 When you hear of wars and rebellions,[J] don't be alarmed. Indeed, it is necessary that these things take place first, but the end won't come right away."

10 Then he told them, "Nation will be raised up against nation, and kingdom against kingdom. 11 There will be violent earthquakes, and famines and plagues in various places, and there will be terrifying sights and great signs from heaven. 12 But before all these things, they will lay their hands on you and persecute you. They will hand you over to the synagogues and prisons, and you will be brought before kings and governors because of my name. 13 This will give you an opportunity to bear witness. 14 Therefore make up your minds[K] not to prepare your defense ahead of time, 15 for I will give you such words and a wisdom that none of your adversaries will be able to resist or contradict. 16 You will even be betrayed by parents, brothers, relatives, and friends. They will kill some of you. 17 You will be hated by everyone because of my name, 18 but not a hair of your head will be lost. 19 By your endurance, gain[L] your lives.

[A] **20:21** Lit *you don't receive a face* [B] **20:23** Other mss add *"Why are you testing me?* [C] **20:24** A denarius = one day's wage [D] **20:28** Dt 25:5 [E] **20:30** Other mss add *took her as wife, and he died without children* [F] **20:37** Ex 3:6,15 [G] **20:38** Or *with* [H] **20:42–43** Ps 110:1 [I] **21:2** Lit *two lepta*; the *lepton* was the smallest and least valuable Gk coin in use. [J] **21:9** Or *insurrections*, or *revolutions*, or *chaos* [K] **21:14** Lit *Therefore place* (determine) *in your hearts* [L] **21:19** Other mss read *endurance, you will gain*

A Jewish widow's mite from the time of Tiberius (AD 14–37). This coin was found at the Herodium, near Bethlehem.

THE DESTRUCTION OF JERUSALEM

20 "When you see Jerusalem surrounded by armies,
then recognize that its desolation has come near.
21 Then those in Judea must flee to the mountains.
Those inside the city must leave it, and those who
are in the country must not enter it, 22 because
these are days of vengeance to fulfill all the things
that are written. 23 Woe to pregnant women and
nursing mothers in those days, for there will be
great distress in the land[A] and wrath against this
people. 24 They will be killed by the sword[B] and be
led captive into all the nations, and Jerusalem will
be trampled by the Gentiles[C] until the times of the
Gentiles are fulfilled.

THE COMING OF THE SON OF MAN

25 "Then there will be signs in the sun, moon, and
stars; and there will be anguish on the earth among
nations bewildered by the roaring of the sea and the
waves. 26 People will faint from fear and expectation
of the things that are coming on the world, because
the powers of the heavens will be shaken. 27 Then
they will see the Son of Man coming in a cloud with
power and great glory. 28 But when these things begin
to take place, stand up and lift your heads, because
your redemption is near."

THE PARABLE OF THE FIG TREE

29 Then he told them a parable: "Look at the fig tree,
and all the trees. 30 As soon as they put out leaves you
can see for yourselves and recognize that summer is
already near. 31 In the same way, when you see these
things happening, recognize[D] that the kingdom of
God is near. 32 Truly I tell you, this generation will
certainly not pass away until all things take place.
33 Heaven and earth will pass away, but my words
will never pass away.

THE NEED FOR WATCHFULNESS

34 "Be on your guard, so that your minds are not
dulled[E] from carousing,[F] drunkenness, and worries
of life, or that day will come on you unexpectedly
35 like a trap. For it will come on all who live on the
face of the whole earth. 36 But be alert at all times,
praying that you may have strength[G] to escape all
these things that are going to take place and to stand
before the Son of Man."

37 During the day, he was teaching in the temple,
but in the evening he would go out and spend the
night on what is called the Mount of Olives. 38 Then
all the people would come early in the morning to
hear him in the temple.

THE PLOT TO KILL JESUS

22 The Festival of Unleavened Bread, which is
called Passover, was approaching. 2 The chief
priests and the scribes were looking for a way to
put him to death, because they were afraid of the
people.

3 Then Satan entered Judas, called Iscariot, who
was numbered among the Twelve. 4 He went away
and discussed with the chief priests and temple police how he could hand him over to them. 5 They were
glad and agreed to give him silver.[H] 6 So he accepted
the offer and started looking for a good opportunity to betray him to them when the crowd was not
present.

PREPARATION FOR PASSOVER

7 Then the Day of Unleavened Bread came when the
Passover lamb had to be sacrificed. 8 Jesus sent Peter
and John, saying, "Go and make preparations for us
to eat the Passover."

9 "Where do you want us to prepare it?" they asked
him.

10 "Listen," he said to them, "when you've entered
the city, a man carrying a water jug will meet you.
Follow him into the house he enters. 11 Tell the owner of the house, 'The Teacher asks you, "Where is the
guest room where I can eat the Passover with my disciples?" ' 12 Then he will show you a large, furnished
room upstairs. Make the preparations there."

13 So they went and found it just as he had told
them, and they prepared the Passover.

[A] **21:23** Or *the earth* [B] **21:24** Lit *will fall by the edge of the sword* [C] **21:24** Or *nations* [D] **21:31** Or *you know* [E] **21:34** Lit *your hearts are not weighed down* [F] **21:34** Or *hangovers* [G] **21:36** Other mss read *you may be counted worthy* [H] **22:5** Or *money*

Passover in Jesus's Day[1]

by G. B. Howell Jr.

Passover, commemorating the Israelites' deliverance from slavery in Egypt, was the most important of three festivals Jewish men were required to attend each year. Some have guessed that Jerusalem's population doubled for Passover. Merchants and worshipers alike made their way to the city.

Passover officially began on the eve of the fourteenth day of the Jewish month of Nisan (March–April), which was always a full moon (Ps 81). On the thirteenth, the family would completely clean the house and meticulously inspect it for leaven or any leavened product. This inspection would last into the night hours; the family would use oil lamps to complete their work.

On the morning of the fourteenth, the family could still eat products with leaven. When the priest signaled from the temple, the people could eat no more *chametz* (leaven and leavened bread). The priest would offer a second signal, and the families would burn their *chametz*. In the temple, thousands of priests would take their places in the temple before midday.

At midday, the head of each household would bring his sacrificial sheep or goat to the temple. When worshipers arrived at the temple, its doors would be shut. In three waves, the doors of the temple were opened and subsequently shut, allowing worshipers entrance. Once inside, each man would slay his own sacrificial animal. Rather than a clamoring crowd, however, people offered their temple sacrifices in relative quiet. With the sacrificial meat in hand, worshipers would return to their homes.

Houses were filled to capacity. Rich and poor, friend and relative, bond and free assembled freely together. No Jew was to be excluded. Following tradition, the families would cook the sacrificial meat in clay ovens reserved for this particular celebration.

Once the food was cooked, all would recline on sofas, propped up on their left elbows. The head of the house offered a *Kiddush*, which was a blessing said over the first cup. The right hand was ceremonially cleansed and was left free for eating. Worshipers dipped lettuce or celery into a bitter liquid and ate. They broke unleavened bread (called *matzah*), and they ate the Passover lamb (called *Pesach*) with bitter herbs, which they would dip. They also ate *charoset*, a nutty fruit mixture that represented the mortar used by the Hebrew slaves in Egypt.

At the second cup, the son would ask three questions:[2] "Why on all other nights do we dip only once, on this night twice? Why on all other nights do we eat *chametz* and *matzah*, on this night only *matzah*? Why on all other nights do we eat roast or boiled meat, on this night only roast?" The father explained the two dippings; the first referred to the hyssop, used to paint the doorposts; the second emphasized the bitter herbs that made this night different. The *matzah* emphasized the haste with which the Hebrews left Egypt, and roasting

A Nabatean terra-cotta cup from about the first centuries BC or AD.

In this early 1900s photo, a man applies blood to the lintel of his home as part of a Passover celebration.

was the fastest way to cook an animal. The father would weave details of the Hebrews' enslavement in and exodus from Egypt into his responses.

Afterward, they took the third cup, and the father would sing Hallel psalms (Pss 113–118). Others joined in, loudly. The father would conclude with a benediction. Participants would consume the fourth cup as they relaxed after the meal.

Children were expected to remain quiet and the overall mood, reverent. Highlighting the solemnity, no dessert was served. Feasters would eventually parade back toward the temple, with its doors wide open, and join in a night of singing and prayer. ✣

---

[1] The details of Passover in the first century come from Hayyim Schauss, *The Jewish Festivals: From Their Beginnings to Our Own Day* (Cincinnati: Union of American Hebrew Congregations, 1938), 52–55. [2] Abraham P. Bloch, *The Biblical and Historical Background of the Jewish Holy Days* (New York: Ktav, 1978), 130.

THE FIRST LORD'S SUPPER

14 When the hour came, he reclined at the table, and the apostles with him. 15 Then he said to them, "I have fervently desired to eat this Passover with you before I suffer. 16 For I tell you, I will not eat it again[A] until it is fulfilled in the kingdom of God." 17 Then he took a cup, and after giving thanks, he said, "Take this and share it among yourselves. 18 For I tell you, from now on I will not drink of the fruit of the vine until the kingdom of God comes."

19 And he took bread, gave thanks, broke it, gave it to them, and said, "This is my body, which is given for you. Do this in remembrance of me."

20 In the same way he also took the cup after supper and said, "This cup is the new covenant in my blood, which is poured out for you.[B] 21 But look, the hand of the one betraying me is at the table with me. 22 For the Son of Man will go away as it has been determined, but woe to that man by whom he is betrayed!"

23 So they began to argue among themselves which of them it could be who was going to do it.

THE DISPUTE OVER GREATNESS

24 Then a dispute also arose among them about who should be considered the greatest. 25 But he said to them, "The kings of the Gentiles lord it over them, and those who have authority over them have themselves called[C] 'Benefactors.' 26 It is not to be like that among you. On the contrary, whoever is greatest among you should become like the youngest, and whoever leads, like the one serving. 27 For who is greater, the one at the table or the one serving? Isn't it the one at the table? But I am among you as the one who serves. 28 You are those who stood by me in my trials. 29 I bestow on you a kingdom, just as my Father bestowed one on me, 30 so that you may eat and drink at my table in my kingdom. And you will sit on thrones judging the twelve tribes of Israel.

PETER'S DENIAL PREDICTED

31 "Simon, Simon,[D] look out. Satan has asked to sift you[E] like wheat. 32 But I have prayed for you[F] that your faith may not fail. And you, when you have turned back, strengthen your brothers."

33 "Lord," he told him, "I'm ready to go with you both to prison and to death."

34 "I tell you, Peter," he said, "the rooster will not crow today until[G] you deny three times that you know me."

BE READY FOR TROUBLE

35 He also said to them, "When I sent you out without money-bag, traveling bag, or sandals, did you lack anything?"

"Not a thing," they said.

36 Then he said to them, "But now, whoever has a money-bag should take it, and also a traveling bag. And whoever doesn't have a sword should sell his robe and buy one. 37 For I tell you, what is written must be fulfilled in me:[H] **And he was counted among the lawless.**[I] Yes, what is written about me is coming to its fulfillment."

38 "Lord," they said, "look, here are two swords."

"That is enough!" he told them.

THE PRAYER IN THE GARDEN

39 He went out and made his way as usual to the Mount of Olives, and the disciples followed him. 40 When he reached the place, he told them, "Pray that you may not fall into temptation." 41 Then he withdrew from them about a stone's throw, knelt down, and began to pray, 42 "Father, if you are willing, take this cup away from me — nevertheless, not my will, but yours, be done."

43 Then an angel from heaven appeared to him, strengthening him. 44 Being in anguish, he prayed more fervently, and his sweat became like drops of blood falling to the ground.[J] 45 When he got up from prayer and came to the disciples, he found them sleeping, exhausted from their grief. 46 "Why are you sleeping?" he asked them. "Get up and pray, so that you won't fall into temptation."

JUDAS'S BETRAYAL OF JESUS

47 While he was still speaking, suddenly a mob came, and one of the Twelve named Judas was leading them. He came near Jesus to kiss him, 48 but Jesus said to him, "Judas, are you betraying the Son of Man with a kiss?"

49 When those around him saw what was going to happen, they asked, "Lord, should we strike with the sword?" 50 Then one of them struck the high priest's servant and cut off his right ear.

51 But Jesus responded, "No more of this!" And touching his ear, he healed him. 52 Then Jesus said to the chief priests, temple police, and the elders who had come for him, "Have you come out with swords and clubs as if I were a criminal?[K] 53 Every day while I was with you in the temple, you never laid a hand on me. But this is your hour — and the dominion of darkness."

PETER DENIES HIS LORD

54 They seized him, led him away, and brought him into the high priest's house. Meanwhile Peter was

[A] **22:16** Other mss omit *again* [B] **22:19–20** Other mss omit *which is given for you* (v. 19) through the end of v. 20 [C] **22:25** Or *them call themselves* [D] **22:31** Other mss read *Then the Lord said, "Simon, Simon* [E] **22:31** *you* is plural in Gk [F] **22:32** *you* is singular in Gk [G] **22:34** Other mss read *before* [H] **22:37** Or *it is necessary that what is written be fulfilled in me* [I] **22:37** Is 53:12 [J] **22:43–44** Other mss omit vv. 43–44 [K] **22:52** Lit *as against a thief*, or *a bandit*

following at a distance. 55 They lit a fire in the middle
of the courtyard and sat down together, and Peter sat
among them. 56 When a servant saw him sitting in the
light, and looked closely at him, she said, "This man
was with him too."
57 But he denied it: "Woman, I don't know him."
58 After a little while, someone else saw him and
said, "You're one of them too."
"Man, I am not!" Peter said.
59 About an hour later, another kept insisting, "This
man was certainly with him, since he's also a Galilean."
60 But Peter said, "Man, I don't know what you're
talking about!" Immediately, while he was still speaking, a rooster crowed. 61 Then the Lord turned and
looked at Peter. So Peter remembered the word of
the Lord, how he had said to him, "Before the rooster
crows today, you will deny me three times." 62 And he
went outside and wept bitterly.

JESUS MOCKED AND BEATEN

63 The men who were holding Jesus started mocking and beating him. 64 After blindfolding him, they
kept[A] asking, "Prophesy! Who was it that hit you?"
65 And they were saying many other blasphemous
things to him.

JESUS FACES THE SANHEDRIN

66 When daylight came, the elders[B] of the people,
both the chief priests and the scribes, convened and
brought him before their Sanhedrin. 67 They said, "If
you are the Messiah, tell us."
But he said to them, "If I do tell you, you will not
believe. 68 And if I ask you, you will not answer. 69 But
from now on, the Son of Man will be seated at the
right hand of the power of God."
70 They all asked, "Are you, then, the Son of God?"
And he said to them, "You say that I am."
71 "Why do we need any more testimony," they said,
"since we've heard it ourselves from his mouth?"

JESUS FACES PILATE

23 Then their whole assembly rose up and brought
him before Pilate. 2 They began to accuse him,
saying, "We found this man misleading our nation,
opposing payment of taxes to Caesar, and saying that
he himself is the Messiah, a king."
3 So Pilate asked him, "Are you the king of the
Jews?"
He answered him, "You say so."[C]
4 Pilate then told the chief priests and the crowds,
"I find no grounds for charging this man."
5 But they kept insisting, "He stirs up the people,
teaching throughout all Judea, from Galilee where
he started even to here."

DIGGING DEEPER *Pontius Pilate*

Pontius Pilate is identified in all four Gospels (Mt 27:1–2; Mk 15:1–5; Lk 23:1–5; Jn 18:28–38) as the Roman governor of Judea (AD 26–36) who condemned Christ to crucifixion during the reign of Emperor Tiberius (AD 14–37). Critical scholars questioned his role in Jesus's life and even his very existence until 1962 when Italian archaeologist Antonio Frova led an expedition at Caesarea Maritima. There he discovered a stone slab with a Latin inscription that reads "Tiberium Pontius Pilate Prefect of Judea." Though reasonable scholars never doubted Pilate's existence or part in Jesus's death, as first-century historians Josephus (AD 37–100) and Tacitus (AD 56–117) declare that Pilate was the one who condemned Christ to death, the slab is the first piece of archaeological evidence confirming Pilate's existence, title, years in power, and area of rule. Caesarea had a long history, becoming the center of Roman rule over Israel. It is also interesting to note the significance of the city in which this slab was found. It was the site of Paul's trial before Festus (Ac 24:27; 25:1–6) and the death of Herod Agrippa I (see Josephus, *Antiquities* 19.344–350; Ac 12:21–23).

JESUS FACES HEROD ANTIPAS

6 When Pilate heard this,[D] he asked if the man was a
Galilean. 7 Finding that he was under Herod's jurisdiction, he sent him to Herod, who was also in Jerusalem
during those days. 8 Herod was very glad to see Jesus;
for a long time he had wanted to see him because he
had heard about him and was hoping to see some
miracle[E] performed by him. 9 So he kept asking him
questions, but Jesus did not answer him. 10 The chief
priests and the scribes stood by, vehemently accusing him. 11 Then Herod, with his soldiers, treated him
with contempt, mocked him, dressed him in bright
clothing, and sent him back to Pilate. 12 That very day
Herod and Pilate became friends.[F] Previously, they
had been enemies.

JESUS OR BARABBAS

13 Pilate called together the chief priests, the leaders, and the people, 14 and said to them, "You have
brought me this man as one who misleads the people.
But in fact, after examining him in your presence,
I have found no grounds to charge this man with
those things you accuse him of. 15 Neither has Herod,

[A] **22:64** Other mss add *striking him on the face and* [B] **22:66** Or *council of elders* [C] **23:3** Or *"That is true."* [D] **23:6** Other mss read *heard "Galilee"* [E] **23:8** Or *sign* [F] **23:12** Lit *friends with one another*

because he sent him back to us. Clearly, he has done
nothing to deserve death. 16 Therefore, I will have him
whipped[A] and then release him."[B]

18 Then they all cried out together, "Take this man
away! Release Barabbas to us!" 19 (He had been thrown
into prison for a rebellion that had taken place in the
city, and for murder.)

20 Wanting to release Jesus, Pilate addressed them
again, 21 but they kept shouting, "Crucify! Crucify him!"

22 A third time he said to them, "Why? What has this
man done wrong? I have found in him no grounds for
the death penalty. Therefore, I will have him whipped
and then release him."

23 But they kept up the pressure, demanding with
loud voices that he be crucified, and their voices[C] won
out. 24 So Pilate decided to grant their demand 25 and
released the one they were asking for, who had been
thrown into prison for rebellion and murder. But he
handed Jesus over to their will.

THE WAY TO THE CROSS

26 As they led him away, they seized Simon, a Cyrenian,
who was coming in from the country, and laid the
cross on him to carry behind Jesus. 27 A large crowd
of people followed him, including women who were
mourning and lamenting him. 28 But turning to them,
Jesus said, "Daughters of Jerusalem, do not weep
for me, but weep for yourselves and your children.
29 Look, the days are coming when they will say,
'Blessed are the women without children, the wombs
that never bore, and the breasts that never nursed!'
30 Then they will begin **to say to the mountains, 'Fall
on us!' and to the hills, 'Cover us!'**[D] 31 For if they do
these things when the wood is green, what will happen when it is dry?"

CRUCIFIED BETWEEN TWO CRIMINALS

32 Two others — criminals — were also led away to be
executed with him. 33 When they arrived at the place
called The Skull, they crucified him there, along with
the criminals, one on the right and one on the left.
34 Then Jesus said, "Father, forgive them, because they
do not know what they are doing."[E] And they divided
his clothes and cast lots.

35 The people stood watching, and even the leaders
were scoffing: "He saved others; let him save himself if this is God's Messiah, the Chosen One!" 36 The
soldiers also mocked him. They came offering him
sour wine 37 and said, "If you are the king of the Jews,
save yourself!"

38 An inscription was above him:[F] THIS IS THE KING
OF THE JEWS.

39 Then one of the criminals hanging there began
to yell insults at[G] him: "Aren't you the Messiah? Save
yourself and us!"

40 But the other answered, rebuking him: "Don't
you even fear God, since you are undergoing the same
punishment? 41 We are punished justly, because we're
getting back what we deserve for the things we did,
but this man has done nothing wrong." 42 Then he
said, "Jesus, remember me[H] when you come into your
kingdom."

43 And he said to him, "Truly I tell you, today you
will be with me in paradise."

THE DEATH OF JESUS

44 It was now about noon,[I] and darkness came over
the whole land[J] until three,[K] 45 because the sun's light
failed.[L] The curtain of the sanctuary was split down
the middle. 46 And Jesus called out with a loud voice,
"Father, **into your hands I entrust my spirit.**"[M] Saying this, he breathed his last.

47 When the centurion saw what happened, he began to glorify God, saying, "This man really was righteous!"[N] 48 All the crowds that had gathered for this
spectacle, when they saw what had taken place, went
home, striking their chests. 49 But all who knew him,
including the women who had followed him from
Galilee, stood at a distance, watching these things.

THE BURIAL OF JESUS

50 There was a good and righteous man named Joseph, a member of the Sanhedrin, 51 who had not
agreed with their plan and action. He was from Arimathea, a Judean town, and was looking forward
to the kingdom of God. 52 He approached Pilate and
asked for Jesus's body. 53 Taking it down, he wrapped
it in fine linen and placed it in a tomb cut into the
rock, where no one had ever been placed.[O] 54 It was
the preparation day, and the Sabbath was about to
begin.[P] 55 The women who had come with him from
Galilee followed along and observed the tomb and
how his body was placed. 56 Then they returned and
prepared spices and perfumes. And they rested on
the Sabbath according to the commandment.

RESURRECTION MORNING

24 On the first day of the week, very early in the
morning, they[Q] came to the tomb, bringing
the spices they had prepared. 2 They found the stone

[A] **23:16** Gk *paideuo*; to discipline or "teach a lesson" [B] **23:16** Some mss include v. 17: *For according to the festival he had to release someone to them.* [C] **23:23** Other mss add *and those of the chief priests* [D] **23:30** Hs 10:8 [E] **23:34** Other mss omit *Then Jesus said, "Father, forgive them, because they do not know what they are doing."* [F] **23:38** Other mss add *written in Greek, Latin, and Hebrew letters* [G] **23:39** Or *began to blaspheme* [H] **23:42** Other mss add *Lord* [I] **23:44** Lit *about the sixth hour* [J] **23:44** Or *whole earth* [K] **23:44** Lit *the ninth hour* [L] **23:45** Other mss read *three, and the sun was darkened* [M] **23:46** Ps 31:5 [N] **23:47** Or *innocent* [O] **23:53** Or *interred*, or *laid* [P] **23:54** Lit *was dawning* [Q] **24:1** Other mss add *and other women with them*

rolled away from the tomb. 3 They went in but did not
find the body of the Lord Jesus. 4 While they were perplexed about this, suddenly two men stood by them
in dazzling clothes. 5 So the women were terrified and
bowed down to the ground.
"Why are you looking for the living among the
dead?" asked the men. 6 "He is not here, but he has
risen! Remember how he spoke to you when he was
still in Galilee, 7 saying, 'It is necessary that the Son
of Man be betrayed into the hands of sinful men, be
crucified, and rise on the third day'?" 8 And they remembered his words.

9 Returning from the tomb, they reported all these
things to the Eleven and to all the rest. 10 Mary Magdalene, Joanna, Mary the mother of James, and the
other women with them were telling the apostles
these things. 11 But these words seemed like nonsense
to them, and they did not believe the women. 12 Peter, however, got up and ran to the tomb. When he
stooped to look in, he saw only the linen cloths.[A] So
he went away, amazed at what had happened.

THE EMMAUS DISCIPLES

13 Now that same day two of them were on their way
to a village called Emmaus, which was about seven
miles[B] from Jerusalem. 14 Together they were discussing everything that had taken place. 15 And while they
were discussing and arguing, Jesus himself came
near and began to walk along with them. 16 But they[C]
were prevented from recognizing him. 17 Then he
asked them, "What is this dispute that you're having[D] with each other as you are walking?" And they
stopped walking and looked discouraged.

18 The one named Cleopas answered him, "Are you
the only visitor in Jerusalem who doesn't know the
things that happened there in these days?"

19 "What things?" he asked them.

So they said to him, "The things concerning Jesus
of Nazareth, who was a prophet powerful in action
and speech before God and all the people, 20 and how
our chief priests and leaders handed him over to be
sentenced to death, and they crucified him. 21 But we
were hoping that he was the one who was about to
redeem Israel. Besides all this, it's the third day since
these things happened. 22 Moreover, some women
from our group astounded us. They arrived early at
the tomb, 23 and when they didn't find his body, they
came and reported that they had seen a vision of
angels who said he was alive. 24 Some of those who
were with us went to the tomb and found it just as
the women had said, but they didn't see him."

25 He said to them, "How foolish you are, and how
slow[E] to believe all that the prophets have spoken!
26 Wasn't it necessary for the Messiah to suffer these
things and enter into his glory?" 27 Then beginning

The arch-windowed bell-tower (right) and the two domes of the Church of the Holy Sepulchre in Jerusalem. Constantine erected the original church in AD 335.

with Moses and all the Prophets, he interpreted for
them the things concerning himself in all the Scriptures.

28 They came near the village where they were going, and he gave the impression that he was going
farther. 29 But they urged him, "Stay with us, because
it's almost evening, and now the day is almost over."
So he went in to stay with them.

30 It was as he reclined at the table with them that
he took the bread, blessed and broke it, and gave it
to them. 31 Then their eyes were opened, and they
recognized him, but he disappeared from their sight.
32 They said to each other, "Weren't our hearts burning
within us while he was talking with us on the road
and explaining the Scriptures to us?" 33 That very hour
they got up and returned to Jerusalem. They found
the Eleven and those with them gathered together,
34 who said, "The Lord has truly been raised and has
appeared to Simon!" 35 Then they began to describe
what had happened on the road and how he was
made known to them in the breaking of the bread.

[A] **24:12** Other mss add *lying there* [B] **24:13** Lit *about sixty stadia*; one *stadion* = 600 feet [C] **24:16** Lit *their eyes* [D] **24:17** Lit *"What are these words that you are exchanging* [E] **24:25** Lit *slow of heart*

Funeral practices in the first-century world varied. Romans, Egyptians, Parthians, Jews, and Christians each had their own convictions on what constituted proper handling of a body.

ROMAN

When the dying person took his final breath, his eyes would be closed by a close family member. The others gathered would begin to call out the name of the now-deceased person as a sign of grief. Persons would then wash and anoint the body before dressing it. If available and especially if earned in life, a crown was placed on the deceased person's head. A family member would then place a coin in the person's mouth so the deceased could pay the mythological ferryman Charon to row him across the river Styx to the land of the dead. The body would lie in state for about seven days, with the feet toward the door of the house. Next came the funeral procession and disposal of the body. Financial resources dictated how elaborate these services would be.[1]

From the early days of Rome's history, both burial and cremation were practiced widely. By the first century AD, cremation had become "almost universal among the Romans."[2] At the end of the funerary procession, the body was placed upon a funeral pyre and burned. Families kept the ash remains in carved chests, ceramic containers, or glass cinerary urns. Some ash containers were kept in homes. Others were placed in columbaria, tombs that allowed many to be interred in a small space.

During Hadrian's reign (AD 117–138), craftsmen began making increasingly decorative sarcophagi.[3] Cremation's popularity decreased as more people used sarcophagi. Often, but not always, after a body had decomposed, family members would gather the bones into smaller boxes called ossuaries (see more detail below). Except for the highest-ranking dignitaries, burials always occurred outside the city.[4]

EGYPTIAN

Though many Romans who occupied their land practiced cremation, Egyptians regarded the

Roman burial stones described or depicted the deceased person's past achievements, common elements from his daily life, or anticipated details of the next life. Many (like the one shown) had an epitaph for the deceased. The stones were usually attached to the tomb wall or under the niche that held the person's ash urn.

The Book of the Dead was a collection of funerary texts used in Egypt for about 1,500 years.

practice with "extreme horror, for it deprived the dead man once and for all of any chance of enjoying the offerings made by the living."[5] Many Egyptians continued to practice embalming, in keeping with their ancient conviction that the process of mummification and the rituals associated with it ensured the person's transition to, and full participation in, the next life.[6]

PARTHIAN

The Parthian Empire (238 BC–AD 224) was located mostly in what we know today as Iran (the region of the former Persian Empire). In the first century, the carry-over religion of the region was Zoroastrianism (began ca 1200 BC). Although burial was the traditional practice of the region, the Zoroastrians practiced neither burial nor cremation, convinced that a dead body would compromise the purity of the elements of earth and fire. Zoroastrians left bodies on an open raised structure called a *dakhma* or "tower of silence," to be eaten by birds. "Outside of some Jews and the Christians, the only people of the ancient world to believe in a resurrection of the flesh were the Zoroastrians."[7]

JEWISH

Burial in caves or rock sepulchers, rather than cremation, was the universal Jewish practice. After a person died, Jews washed the body and then wrapped it with cloth strips rather than repose it within a sarcophagus; they also used heavy spices to help cover the smell of decay. Jews always tried to bury an individual before dark on the day of death.

Accompanied by family members, professional mourners, pipers, and even strangers, pallbearers would carry the coffin or funerary bier to a well-marked grave in a field (see Lk 11:44) or to the burial cave. A large stone covered the cave opening.

Typically, a year after the burial, a family member would visit the burial site to collect the remaining bones and place them in an ossuary (lit "bone box"). Jews may have considered this a joyous occasion that marked the end of the time of mourning.[8] Ossuaries were stacked together in extended family sepulchers.[9] A father's wishes in a rabbinic teaching on mourning illustrate this practice: "My son, bury me at first. . . . In the course of time, collect my bones and put them in an ossuary."[10] Indeed, the Jews regarded such secondary burial among the most important of family duties.

CHRISTIAN

Jewish and Roman Christians followed the body-preparation steps that were common in the day: washing the body, wrapping it in cloth, and covering it in spices. They also continued the Jewish practice of burial (on the day of death) rather than cremation. Why the preference for burial? Writings of the early Christian apologist and theologian Tertullian (ca 160–225 AD) offer a hint. He wrote of a Christian who intended to join the army, which would, upon a soldier's death, cremate the body. Because of the practice, Tertullian objected, saying: "And shall the Christian be burned according to camp rule, when he was not permitted to burn incense to an idol, when to him Christ remitted the punishment of fire?"[11]

Christians also shared funerary meals by providing food for the family, especially in the case of martyrdom. Afterward, "Christians met on the anniversary of the person's death, not of his birth (death was for the Christians the 'birthday of immortality'); and the meal became a eucharist or love-feast."[12] ✣

---

[1] J. M. C. Toynbee, *Death and Burial in the Roman World* (Ithaca, NY: Cornell University Press, 1971), 43–44. [2] C. J. Hemer, "Bury, Grave, Tomb" in *NIDNTT*, 264. [3] Toynbee, *Death and Burial*, 40. [4] Toynbee, *Death and Burial*, 48. [5] Arthur Darby Nock, "Cremation and Burial in the Roman Empire," *HTR* 25.4 (1932): 341. [6] "Funerary Art, Roman Egypt," Louvre, accessed 21 February 2013, *www.louvre.fr/en/routes/funerary-art*. [7] Everett Ferguson, *Backgrounds of Early Christianity*, 3rd ed. (Grand Rapids: Eerdmans, 2003), 250. [8] Ferguson, *Backgrounds*, 246 [9] Craig A. Evans, *Jesus and the Ossuaries: What Jewish Burial Practices Reveal about the Beginning of Christianity* (Waco, TX: Baylor University Press, 2003), 12; see Hemer "Bury, Grave, Tomb," 264. [10] Evans, *Jesus and the Ossuaries*, 11. [11] Tertullian, *The Chaplet*, or *De Cornoa* 11 in Ante-Nicene Fathers, ed. Alexander Roberts and James Donaldson, vol 3 (Peabody, MA: Hendrickson, 1994), 100. [2] Ferguson, *Backgrounds*, 244.

Emmaus (Imwas). According to the Sinai manuscript, Emmaus is thought to be the site of the house of Cleopas. Shown are ruins of a Byzantine church that stands on the site of the house.

THE REALITY OF THE RISEN JESUS

36 As they were saying these things, he himself stood
in their midst. He said to them, "Peace to you!" 37 But
they were startled and terrified and thought they
were seeing a ghost. 38 "Why are you troubled?" he
asked them. "And why do doubts arise in your hearts?
39 Look at my hands and my feet, that it is I myself!
Touch me and see, because a ghost does not have flesh
and bones as you can see I have." 40 Having said this,
he showed them his hands and feet. 41 But while they
still were amazed and in disbelief because of their joy,
he asked them, "Do you have anything here to eat?"
42 So they gave him a piece of a broiled fish,[A] 43 and
he took it and ate in their presence.

44 He told them, "These are my words that I spoke
to you while I was still with you — that everything
written about me in the Law of Moses, the Prophets,
and the Psalms must be fulfilled." 45 Then he opened
their minds to understand the Scriptures. 46 He also
said to them, "This is what is written:[B] The Messiah
will suffer and rise from the dead the third day, 47 and
repentance for[C] forgiveness of sins will be proclaimed
in his name to all the nations, beginning at Jerusalem.
48 You are witnesses of these things. 49 And look, I
am sending you[D] what my Father promised. As for
you, stay in the city[E] until you are empowered[F] from
on high."

THE ASCENSION OF JESUS

50 Then he led them out to the vicinity of Bethany, and
lifting up his hands he blessed them. 51 And while he
was blessing them, he left them and was carried up
into heaven. 52 After worshiping him, they returned
to Jerusalem with great joy. 53 And they were continually in the temple praising God.[G]

[A]**24:42** Other mss add *and some honeycomb* [B]**24:46** Other mss add *and thus it was necessary that* [C]**24:47** Many mss read *repentance and* [D]**24:49** Lit *upon you* [E]**24:49** Other mss add *of Jerusalem* [F]**24:49** Lit *clothed with power* [G]**24:53** Other mss read *praising and blessing God. Amen.*

JOHN

Empty tomb with rolling stone near Megiddo.

INTRODUCTION TO

JOHN

Circumstances of Writing

A close reading of the Gospel of John suggests that the author was an apostle (Jn 1:14; cf. 2:11; 19:35), one of the Twelve ("the disciple Jesus loved"; see 13:23; 19:26; 20:2; 21:20; cf. 21:24–25), and, still more specifically, John, the son of Zebedee. The church fathers, too, attested to this identification (e.g., Irenaeus). Because the apostolic office was foundational in the history of the church (Ac 2:42; Eph 2:20), the apostolic authorship of John's Gospel invests it with special authority as a firsthand eyewitness (Jn 15:27; 1Jn 1:1–4).

The most plausible date of writing is the period between AD 70 (the date of the destruction of the temple) and 100 (the end of John's lifetime), with a date in the 80s most likely. A date after 70 is suggested by the references to the Sea of Tiberias in John 6:1 and 21:1 (a name widely used for the Sea of Galilee only toward the end of the first century); Thomas's confession of Jesus as "my Lord and my God" in 20:28 (possibly a statement against emperor worship in the time of Domitian); the reference to Peter's martyrdom, which occurred in 65 or 66 (21:19); the lack of reference to the Sadducees, who ceased to be a Jewish religious party after 70; and the comparative ease with which John equated Jesus with God (1:1,14,18; 10:30; 20:28).

The testimony of the early church also favors a date after AD 70. Clement of Alexandria stated, "Last of all, John, perceiving that the external facts had been made plain [in the other canonical Gospels] . . . composed a spiritual gospel" (Eusebius, *Ecclesiastical History* 6.14.7). The most likely place of writing is Ephesus (Irenaeus, *Against Heresies* 3.1.2; see Eusebius, *Ecclesiastical History* 3.1.1), one of the most important urban centers of the Roman Empire at the time, though the envisioned readership of John's Gospel transcends any one historical setting.

John's original audience was probably composed of people in the larger Greco-Roman world in Ephesus and beyond toward the close of the first century AD. Hence John frequently explained Jewish customs and Palestinian geography and translated Aramaic terms into Greek.

Contribution to the Bible

Of all the Gospels and any of the New Testament books, the Gospel of John most clearly teaches the deity and preexistence of Christ (1:1–2,18; 8:58; 17:5,24; 20:28). Together with the Gospel of Matthew, it provides the most striking proofs of Jesus's messiahship. It does so by narrating seven messianic signs, by seven "I am" statements of Jesus, by specific fulfillment quotations, especially at Jesus's passion, and by showing how Jesus fulfilled the symbolism inherent in a variety of Jewish festivals and institutions. Jesus's messianic mission is shown to originate with God the Father, "the one who sent" Jesus (7:16,18,28,33; 8:26,29; 15:21), and to culminate in his commissioning of his new messianic community in the power of his Spirit (20:21–22). John's Trinitarian teaching is among the most overt presentations of the tri-unity of the Godhead—Father, Son, and Spirit—in the entire New Testament and has provided much of the material for early Trinitarian and Christological formulations in the history of the church.

Structure

John is divided into two main parts. In the first section (chaps. 2–11) the focus is on both Jesus's ministry to "the world" and the signs he performed. Jesus performed seven signs that met with varying responses. The second major section (chaps. 12–21) reveals Jesus's teaching to his disciples and the triumphant "hour" of his passion. John's record of the passion focuses on Jesus's control of the events.

He had to instruct his adversaries on how to arrest him (18:4–8). Pilate struggled with his decision, but Jesus knew what would happen.

Jesus died as the Lamb and was sacrificed at the very time lambs were being sacrificed for Passover (19:14).

PROLOGUE

1 In the beginning was the Word, and the Word was with God, and the Word was God. 2 He was with God in the beginning. 3 All things were created through him, and apart from him not one thing was created that has been created. 4 In him was life,[A] and that life was the light of men. 5 That light shines in the darkness, and yet the darkness did not overcome[B] it.

6 There was a man sent from God whose name was John. 7 He came as a witness to testify about the light, so that all might believe through him.[C] 8 He was not the light, but he came to testify about the light. 9 The true light that gives light to everyone was coming into the world.[D]

10 He was in the world, and the world was created through him, and yet the world did not recognize him. 11 He came to his own, and his own people did not receive him. 12 But to all who did receive him, he gave them the right to be[E] children of God, to those who believe in his name, 13 who were born, not of natural descent,[F] or of the will of the flesh, or of the will of man,[G] but of God.

14 The Word became flesh and dwelt[H] among us. We observed his glory, the glory as the one and only Son[I] from the Father, full of grace and truth. 15 (John testified concerning him and exclaimed, "This was the one of whom I said, 'The one coming after me ranks ahead of me, because he existed before me.' ") 16 Indeed, we have all received grace upon[J] grace from his fullness, 17 for the law was given through Moses; grace and truth came through Jesus Christ. 18 No one has ever seen God. The one and only Son, who is himself God and is at the Father's side[K]—he has revealed him.

JOHN THE BAPTIST'S TESTIMONY

19 This was John's testimony when the Jews from Jerusalem sent priests and Levites to ask him, "Who are you?"

20 He didn't deny it but confessed, "I am not the Messiah."

21 "What then?" they asked him. "Are you Elijah?"

"I am not," he said.

"Are you the Prophet?"

"No," he answered.

22 "Who are you, then?" they asked. "We need to give an answer to those who sent us. What can you tell us about yourself?"

23 He said, "I am a **voice of one crying out in the wilderness: Make straight the way of the Lord**[L]—just as Isaiah the prophet said."

24 Now they had been sent from the Pharisees. 25 So they asked him, "Why then do you baptize if you aren't the Messiah, or Elijah, or the Prophet?"

26 "I baptize with[M] water," John answered them. "Someone stands among you, but you don't know him. 27 He is the one coming after me,[N] whose sandal strap I'm not worthy to untie." 28 All this happened in Bethany[O] across the Jordan, where John was baptizing.

THE LAMB OF GOD

29 The next day John saw Jesus coming toward him and said, "Look, the Lamb of God, who takes away the sin of the world! 30 This is the one I told you about: 'After me comes a man who ranks ahead of me, because he existed before me.' 31 I didn't know him, but I came baptizing with water so that he might be revealed to Israel." 32 And John testified, "I saw the Spirit descending from heaven like a dove, and he rested on him.

> **DIGGING DEEPER** *Biblical Archaeology*
>
> Until the late eighteenth century, the pursuit of biblical relics in the Near East was the work of amateur treasure hunters whose methods included grave robbing. The discovery of the Rosetta Stone in Egypt by Napoleon's army in 1799 changed everything. Biblical archaeology became the domain of respected archaeologists. The discovery of ancient ruins all across the Near East has shed new light on peoples and events mentioned in Scripture. We can now better understand the customs and lifestyles that are foreign to the modern mind. Archaeology has also established the historicity of the people and events described in the Bible, yielding more than twenty-five thousand finds that either directly or indirectly relate to Scripture. Moreover, the historical existence of some thirty individuals named in the New Testament and nearly sixty in the Old Testament has been confirmed through archaeological and historical research. Only a small fraction of possible biblical sites have been excavated in the Holy Land and much more could be published on existing excavations. Even so, the archaeological data we possess clearly indicates that the Bible is historically reliable and is not the product of myth, superstition, or embellishment.

[A] **1:3–4** Other punctuation is possible: . . . *not one thing was created. What was created in him was life* [B] **1:5** Or *grasp*, or *comprehend*, or *overtake*; Jn 12:35 [C] **1:7** Or *it (the light)* [D] **1:9** Or *The true light who comes into the world gives light to everyone*, or *The true light enlightens everyone coming into the world.* [E] **1:12** Or *become* [F] **1:13** Lit *blood* [G] **1:13** Or *not of human lineage, or of human capacity, or of human volition* [H] **1:14** Or *and dwelt in a tent*; lit *and tabernacled* [I] **1:14** *Son* is implied from the reference to the Father and from Gk usage. [J] **1:16** Or *in place of* [K] **1:18** Other mss read *The one and only Son, who is at the Father's side* [L] **1:23** Is 40:3 [M] **1:26** Or *in*, also in vv. 31,33 [N] **1:27** Other mss add *who came before me* [O] **1:28** Other mss read *in Bethabara*

33 I didn't know him, but he who sent me to baptize with water told me, 'The one you see the Spirit descending and resting on — he is the one who baptizes with the Holy Spirit.' 34 I have seen and testified that this is the Son of God."[A]

35 The next day, John was standing with two of his disciples. 36 When he saw Jesus passing by, he said, "Look, the Lamb of God!"

37 The two disciples heard him say this and followed Jesus. 38 When Jesus turned and noticed them following him, he asked them, "What are you looking for?"

They said to him, "Rabbi" (which means "Teacher"), "where are you staying?"

39 "Come and you'll see," he replied. So they went and saw where he was staying, and they stayed with him that day. It was about four in the afternoon.[B]

40 Andrew, Simon Peter's brother, was one of the two who heard John and followed him. 41 He first found his own brother Simon and told him, "We have found the Messiah"[C] (which is translated "the Christ"), 42 and he brought Simon to Jesus.

When Jesus saw him, he said, "You are Simon, son of John.[D] You will be called Cephas" (which is translated "Peter"[E]).

PHILIP AND NATHANAEL

43 The next day Jesus[F] decided to leave for Galilee. He found Philip and told him, "Follow me."

44 Now Philip was from Bethsaida, the hometown of Andrew and Peter. 45 Philip found Nathanael and told him, "We have found the one Moses wrote about in the law (and so did the prophets): Jesus the son of Joseph, from Nazareth."

46 "Can anything good come out of Nazareth?" Nathanael asked him.

"Come and see," Philip answered.

47 Then Jesus saw Nathanael coming toward him and said about him, "Here truly is an Israelite in whom there is no deceit."

48 "How do you know me?" Nathanael asked.

"Before Philip called you, when you were under the fig tree, I saw you," Jesus answered.

49 "Rabbi," Nathanael replied, "You are the Son of God; you are the King of Israel!"

50 Jesus responded to him, "Do you believe because I told you I saw you under the fig tree? You will see greater things than this." 51 Then he said, "Truly I tell you, you will see heaven opened and the angels of God ascending and descending on the Son of Man."

THE FIRST SIGN: TURNING WATER INTO WINE

2 On the third day a wedding took place in Cana of Galilee. Jesus's mother was there, 2 and Jesus and his disciples were invited to the wedding as well. 3 When the wine ran out, Jesus's mother told him, "They don't have any wine."

4 "What has this concern of yours to do with me,[G] woman?" Jesus asked. "My hour has not yet come."

5 "Do whatever he tells you," his mother told the servants.

6 Now six stone water jars had been set there for Jewish purification. Each contained twenty or thirty gallons.[H]

7 "Fill the jars with water," Jesus told them. So they filled them to the brim. 8 Then he said to them, "Now draw some out and take it to the headwaiter."[I] And they did.

9 When the headwaiter tasted the water (after it had become wine), he did not know where it came from — though the servants who had drawn the water knew. He called the groom 10 and told him, "Everyone sets out the fine wine first, then, after people are drunk, the inferior. But you have kept the fine wine until now."

11 Jesus did this, the first of his signs, in Cana of Galilee. He revealed his glory, and his disciples believed in him.

12 After this, he went down to Capernaum, together with his mother, his brothers, and his disciples, and they stayed there only a few days.

CLEANSING THE TEMPLE

13 The Jewish Passover was near, and so Jesus went up to Jerusalem. 14 In the temple he found people selling oxen, sheep, and doves, and he also found the money changers sitting there. 15 After making a whip out of cords, he drove everyone out of the temple with their sheep and oxen. He also poured out the money changers' coins and overturned the tables. 16 He told those who were selling doves, "Get these things out of here! Stop turning my Father's house into a marketplace!"[J]

17 And his disciples remembered that it is written: **Zeal for your house will consume me.**[K]

18 So the Jews replied to him, "What sign will you show us for doing these things?"

19 Jesus answered, "Destroy this temple,[L] and I will raise it up in three days."

20 Therefore the Jews said, "This temple took forty-six years to build,[M] and will you raise it up in three days?"

[A] **1:34** Other mss read *is the Chosen One of God* [B] **1:39** Lit *about the tenth hour* [C] **1:41** Both Hb *Messiah* and Gk *Christos* mean "anointed one" [D] **1:42** Other mss read *"Simon, son of Jonah* [E] **1:42** Both Aramaic *Cephas* and Gk *Petros* mean "rock" [F] **1:43** Lit *he* [G] **2:4** Or *"What does that have to do with you and me*; lit *"What to me and to you*; Mt 8:29; Mk 1:24; 5:7; Lk 8:28 [H] **2:6** Lit *two or three measures* [I] **2:8** Lit *ruler of the table* [J] **2:16** Lit *a house of business* [K] **2:17** Ps 69:9 [L] **2:19** Or *sanctuary*, also in vv. 20,21 [M] **2:20** Or *was built forty-six years ago*

Cana of Galilee

by Roy E. Lucas Jr.

Cana of Galilee, locally called "Kafr Kenna," is located about four miles northeast of Nazareth. Two churches, one Roman Catholic and the other one Greek, claim to preserve ruins related to Jesus's miracle at Cana. This is a popular destination for visitors. Others believe, though, Jesus's first miracle was in a different location–a small and barren hill called "Khirbet Kana," which is about eight miles north of Nazareth.

THE LOCATION OF CANA

Bible scholars have located three sites in Galilee that are possible locations for the ancient city of Cana: Kafr Kenna, Kerem al-Ras, and Khirbet Qana. One other site, though less viable as a candidate for ancient Cana and much to the north, is Qana of Lebanon.

The traditional site, Kafr Kenna ("village/city of Cana"), shown to visitors since the Middle Ages, lies about four miles northeast of Nazareth on the road to Tiberias. At Kafr Kenna, a Roman Catholic church and a Greek Orthodox church each assert that they preserve the traditions related to the miracle of water turned to wine. The lack of archaeological evidence from the Roman period, however, has caused some to doubt Kafr Kenna is the site of the biblical Cana.[1] Additionally, the Semitic name should have come across in Greek as *Qana*, not *Kanna*—with only one "n" and not two.

In recent years, the Israeli Antiquities Authority sponsored excavations on the edge of Kafr Kenna. The locally used name of this site is Kerem al-Ras. Excavators located a large Jewish village dating to the time of Jesus. Unlike the excavations at Khirbet Qana, those at Kerem al-Ras revealed several large stone pots.[2]

Some scholars believe Qana of Lebanon meets the requirements of the Cana mentioned in John's Gospel. Lebanese archaeologist Youssef Hourani has excavated several items there including six stone wine pots. His proposed site is southeast of the city of Tyre and fifteen miles west of the Israeli border.[3]

Khirbet Qana (also spelled Khirbet Kana; "ruins of Cana") holds the position of being the site archaeologists favor most strongly. Recent excavations unearthed various kinds of artifacts from the first century AD, including fragments of small stone pots.[4] (The stone water pots mentioned in John 2:6, though, would have held about twenty to thirty gallons each.)

Khirbet Qana is about eight miles north of Nazareth. Several roads led down the northern side of Nazareth into the Beth Netofa Valley where the city of Sepphoris was located. A road went north and then east down the Beth Netofa Valley before coming to the Wadi Arbel pass, which led down into the area north of the Sea of Galilee to Capernaum. The trip covered twelve miles from Cana to the Sea of Galilee, and it would take about six hours to walk.[5]

This site fits the geographical location more than Kafr Kenna. Khirbet Qana "overlooks a marshy plain featuring plenty of reeds. To date, that site has not been excavated, but cisterns and the remains of buildings are visible, and nearby tombs are cut into the rocks. Some first-century coins also have been found on the site."[6]

LOCAL LIVELIHOOD

The region where Cana was located contained small villages (like Capernaum) with populations varying from one hundred to four hundred residents. Larger towns (Bethsaida) had populations of two thousand to three thousand. Yet even larger, Tiberias and Sepphoris had populations that grew to about eight

In the Asochis Valley; the otherwise nondescript hill in the middle of the image is thought to be the actual site of Cana of Galilee.

thousand to twelve thousand.[7] In general, Galileans had the opportunity to be involved in light industry and agricultural activities.

The Beth Netofa Valley below Cana had fertile soil. When adequate rains fell in winter, the valley produced abundant crops. In first-century Israel, the most important crops were wheat, olives, and grapes—with grapes yielding the most profit. The local farmer tried to grow more produce than his family could consume and the surplus, if any, he sold.[8]

Alongside the agricultural endeavors, a citizen of Cana could serve the community in a number of ways. He might be a leather worker, shoemaker, ditch digger, carpenter, blacksmith, baker, or even a quarry worker. In the first century AD, every town had a local store; some towns had more than one. Normally residents could buy everyday necessities like eggs, fruits, and vegetables. Some stores specialized, offering perfumes and breads; others employed blacksmiths and dyers. Perhaps most surprising is the fact that some stores even served as local restaurants.[9] ✤

---

[1] John McRay, "Cana of Galilee" in *Archaeology and the New Testament* (Grand Rapids: Baker, 1991), 173–74; Jonathan L. Reed, *The HarperCollins Visual Guide to the New Testament: What Archaeology Reveals about the First Christians* (New York: HarperCollins, 2007), 5. [2] Reed, *HarperCollins Visual Guide*, 5. [3] Rima Salameh, "Lebanese Town Says It's Wine Miracle Site," *Free Lance-Star* (Fredericksburg, VA), 12 February 1994. [4] Reed, *HarperCollins Visual Guide*, 5. [5] Anson F. Rainey and R. Steven Notley, *The Sacred Bridge: Carta's Atlas of the Biblical World* (Jerusalem: Carta, 2006), 352. [6] Andreas J. Kostenberger, *John* (Grand Rapids: Baker, 2004), 92. [7] Reed, *HarperCollins Visual Guide*, 66–67. [8] Ze'ev Safrai, *The Economy of Roman Palestine* (New York: Routledge, 1994), 72–73, 126. [9] Safrai, 121, 126.

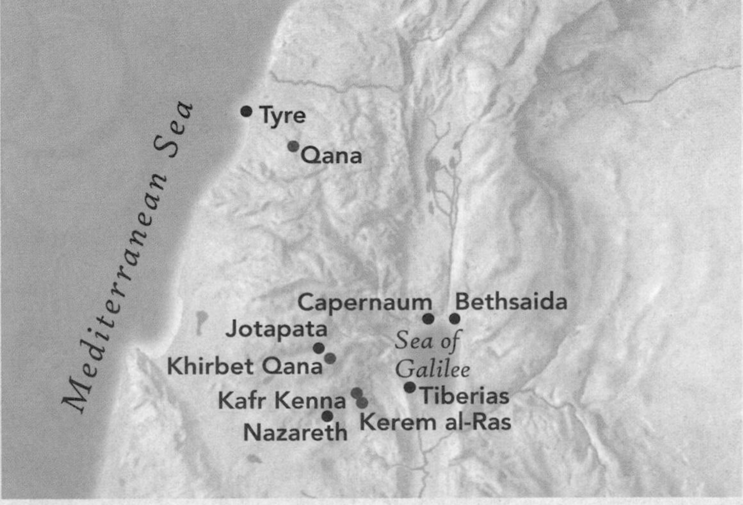

21 But he was speaking about the temple of his body.
22 So when he was raised from the dead, his disciples
remembered that he had said this, and they believed
the Scripture and the statement Jesus had made.
23 While he was in Jerusalem during the Passover
Festival, many believed in his name when they saw
the signs he was doing. 24 Jesus, however, would not
entrust himself to them, since he knew them all 25 and
because he did not need anyone to testify about man;
for he himself knew what was in man.

JESUS AND NICODEMUS

3 There was a man from the Pharisees named Nicodemus, a ruler of the Jews. 2 This man came to
him at night and said, "Rabbi, we know that you are a
teacher who has come from God, for no one could perform these signs you do unless God were with him."
3 Jesus replied, "Truly I tell you, unless someone
is born again,[A] he cannot see the kingdom of God."
4 "How can anyone be born when he is old?" Nicodemus asked him. "Can he enter his mother's womb
a second time and be born?"
5 Jesus answered, "Truly I tell you, unless someone
is born of water and the Spirit, he cannot enter the
kingdom of God. 6 Whatever is born of the flesh is
flesh, and whatever is born of the Spirit is spirit. 7 Do
not be amazed that I told you that you must be born
again. 8 The wind blows where it pleases, and you
hear its sound, but you don't know where it comes
from or where it is going. So it is with everyone born
of the Spirit."
9 "How can these things be?" asked Nicodemus.
10 "Are you a teacher[B] of Israel and don't know these
things?" Jesus replied. 11 "Truly I tell you, we speak
what we know and we testify to what we have seen,
but you do not accept our testimony. 12 If I have told
you about earthly things and you don't believe, how
will you believe if I tell you about heavenly things?
13 No one has ascended into heaven except the one
who descended from heaven — the Son of Man.[C]
14 "Just as Moses lifted up the snake in the wilderness, so the Son of Man must be lifted up, 15 so that
everyone who believes in him may[D] have eternal life.
16 For God loved the world in this way:[E] He gave[F] his
one and only Son, so that everyone who believes in
him will not perish but have eternal life. 17 For God
did not send his Son into the world to condemn the
world, but to save the world through him. 18 Anyone

[A] **3:3** Or *from above*, also in v. 7 [B] **3:10** Or *the teacher* [C] **3:13** Other mss add *who is in heaven* [D] **3:15** Other mss add *not perish, but* [E] **3:16** Or *this much* [F] **3:16** Or *For in this way God loved the world, and so he gave*, or *For God so loved the world that he gave*

Silver coins found near Pella.

who believes in him is not condemned, but anyone
who does not believe is already condemned, because
he has not believed in the name of the one and only
Son of God. 19 This is the judgment: The light has come
into the world, and people loved darkness rather
than the light because their deeds were evil. 20 For
everyone who does evil hates the light and avoids it,[A]
so that his deeds may not be exposed. 21 But anyone
who lives by[B] the truth comes to the light, so that his
works may be shown to be accomplished by God."

JESUS AND JOHN THE BAPTIST

22 After this, Jesus and his disciples went to the Judean countryside, where he spent time with them
and baptized.

23 John also was baptizing in Aenon near Salim,
because there was plenty of water there. People were
coming and being baptized, 24 since John had not yet
been thrown into prison.

25 Then a dispute arose between John's disciples
and a Jew[C] about purification. 26 So they came to John
and told him, "Rabbi, the one you testified about, and
who was with you across the Jordan, is baptizing
— and everyone is going to him."

27 John responded, "No one can receive anything
unless it has been given to him from heaven. 28 You
yourselves can testify that I said, 'I am not the Messiah, but I've been sent ahead of him.' 29 He who has
the bride is the groom. But the groom's friend, who
stands by and listens for him, rejoices greatly[D] at the
groom's voice. So this joy of mine is complete. 30 He
must increase, but I must decrease."

THE ONE FROM HEAVEN

31 The one who comes from above is above all. The
one who is from the earth is earthly and speaks in
earthly terms.[E] The one who comes from heaven is
above all. 32 He testifies to what he has seen and heard,
and yet no one accepts his testimony. 33 The one who
has accepted his testimony has affirmed that God
is true. 34 For the one whom God sent speaks God's
words, since he[F] gives the Spirit without measure.
35 The Father loves the Son and has given all things
into his hands. 36 The one who believes in the Son has
eternal life, but the one who rejects the Son[G] will not
see life; instead, the wrath of God remains on him.

JESUS AND THE SAMARITAN WOMAN

4 When Jesus[H] learned that the Pharisees had
heard he was making and baptizing more disciples than John 2 (though Jesus himself was not baptizing, but his disciples were), 3 he left Judea and went
again to Galilee. 4 He had to travel through Samaria;
5 so he came to a town of Samaria called Sychar near
the property[I] that Jacob had given his son Joseph.

[A] **3:20** Lit *and does not come to the light* [B] **3:21** Lit *who does*
[C] **3:25** Other mss read *and the Jews* [D] **3:29** Lit *with joy rejoices*
[E] **3:31** Or *of earthly things* [F] **3:34** Other mss read *since God*
[G] **3:36** Or *refuses to believe in the Son*, or *disobeys the Son* [H] **4:1** Other
mss read *the Lord* [I] **4:5** Lit *piece of land*

Courtyard of the Greek Orthodox Church at Jacob's well at Sychar.

6 Jacob's well was there, and Jesus, worn out from
his journey, sat down at the well. It was about noon.[A]
7 A woman of Samaria came to draw water.

"Give me a drink," Jesus said to her, 8 because his
disciples had gone into town to buy food.
9 "How is it that you, a Jew, ask for a drink from
me, a Samaritan woman?" she asked him. For Jews
do not associate with[B] Samaritans.[C]
10 Jesus answered, "If you knew the gift of God, and
who is saying to you, 'Give me a drink,' you would ask
him, and he would give you living water."
11 "Sir," said the woman, "you don't even have a
bucket, and the well is deep. So where do you get this
'living water'? 12 You aren't greater than our father
Jacob, are you? He gave us the well and drank from
it himself, as did his sons and livestock."
13 Jesus said, "Everyone who drinks from this water
will get thirsty again. 14 But whoever drinks from the
water that I will give him will never get thirsty again.
In fact, the water I will give him will become a well[D]
of water springing up in him for eternal life."
15 "Sir," the woman said to him, "give me this water so that I won't get thirsty and come here to draw
water."
16 "Go call your husband," he told her, "and come
back here."
17 "I don't have a husband," she answered.

"You have correctly said, 'I don't have a husband,'"
Jesus said. 18 "For you've had five husbands, and the
man you now have is not your husband. What you
have said is true."
19 "Sir," the woman replied, "I see that you are a
prophet. 20 Our ancestors worshiped on this mountain, but you Jews say that the place to worship is in
Jerusalem."
21 Jesus told her, "Believe me, woman, an hour is
coming when you will worship the Father neither
on this mountain nor in Jerusalem. 22 You Samaritans
worship what you do not know. We worship what we
do know, because salvation is from the Jews. 23 But
an hour is coming, and is now here, when the true
worshipers will worship the Father in Spirit and in
truth.[E] Yes, the Father wants such people to worship
him. 24 God is spirit, and those who worship him must
worship in Spirit and in truth."

[A] **4:6** Lit *about the sixth hour* [B] **4:9** Or *do not share vessels with*
[C] **4:9** Other mss omit *For Jews do not associate with Samaritans.*
[D] **4:14** Or *spring* [E] **4:23** Or *in spirit and truth*, also in v. 24

Ruins of the Samaritan temple on Mount Gerizim.

25 The woman said to him, "I know that the Messiah is coming" (who is called Christ). "When he comes, he will explain everything to us."

26 Jesus told her, "I, the one speaking to you, am he."

THE RIPENED HARVEST

27 Just then his disciples arrived, and they were amazed that he was talking with a woman. Yet no one said, "What do you want?" or "Why are you talking with her?"

28 Then the woman left her water jar, went into town, and told the people, 29 "Come, see a man who told me everything I ever did. Could this be the Messiah?" 30 They left the town and made their way to him.

31 In the meantime the disciples kept urging him, "Rabbi, eat something."

32 But he said, "I have food to eat that you don't know about."

33 The disciples said to one another, "Could someone have brought him something to eat?"

34 "My food is to do the will of him who sent me and to finish his work," Jesus told them. 35 "Don't you say, 'There are still four more months, and then comes the harvest'? Listen to what I'm telling you: Open[A] your eyes and look at the fields, because they are ready[B] for harvest. 36 The reaper is already receiving pay and gathering fruit for eternal life, so that the sower and reaper can rejoice together. 37 For in this case the saying is true: 'One sows and another reaps.' 38 I sent you to reap what you didn't labor for; others have labored, and you have benefited from[C] their labor."

THE SAVIOR OF THE WORLD

39 Now many Samaritans from that town believed in him because of what the woman said[D] when she testified, "He told me everything I ever did." 40 So when the Samaritans came to him, they asked him to stay with them, and he stayed there two days. 41 Many more believed because of what he said.[E] 42 And they told the woman, "We no longer believe because of what you said, since we have heard for ourselves and know that this really is the Savior of the world."[F]

A GALILEAN WELCOME

43 After two days he left there for Galilee. 44 (Jesus himself had testified that a prophet has no honor in his own country.) 45 When they entered Galilee, the Galileans welcomed him because they had seen everything he did in Jerusalem during the festival. For they also had gone to the festival.

THE SECOND SIGN: HEALING AN OFFICIAL'S SON

46 He went again to Cana of Galilee, where he had turned the water into wine. There was a certain royal official whose son was ill at Capernaum. 47 When this man heard that Jesus had come from Judea into Galilee, he went to him and pleaded with him to come down and heal his son, since he was about to die.

48 Jesus told him, "Unless you people see signs and wonders, you will not believe."

49 "Sir," the official said to him, "come down before my boy dies."

50 "Go," Jesus told him, "your son will live." The man believed what[G] Jesus said to him and departed.

51 While he was still going down, his servants met him saying that his boy was alive. 52 He asked them at what time he got better. "Yesterday at one in the afternoon[H] the fever left him," they answered. 53 The father realized this was the very hour at which Jesus had told him, "Your son will live." So he himself believed, along with his whole household.

54 Now this was also the second sign Jesus performed after he came from Judea to Galilee.

THE THIRD SIGN: HEALING THE SICK

5 After this, a Jewish festival took place, and Jesus went up to Jerusalem. 2 By the Sheep Gate in Jerusalem there is a pool, called Bethesda[I] in Aramaic, which has five colonnades. 3 Within these lay a large number of the disabled — blind, lame, and paralyzed.[J]

5 One man was there who had been disabled for thirty-eight years. 6 When Jesus saw him lying there and realized he had already been there a long time, he said to him, "Do you want to get well?"

7 "Sir," the disabled man answered, "I have no one to put me into the pool when the water is stirred up, but while I'm coming, someone goes down ahead of me."

8 "Get up," Jesus told him, "pick up your mat and walk." 9 Instantly the man got well, picked up his mat, and started to walk.

Now that day was the Sabbath, 10 and so the Jews said to the man who had been healed, "This is the Sabbath. The law prohibits you from picking up your mat."

11 He replied, "The man who made me well told me, 'Pick up your mat and walk.'"

12 "Who is this man who told you, 'Pick up your mat and walk'?" they asked. 13 But the man who was healed did not know who it was, because Jesus had slipped away into the crowd that was there.[K]

14 After this, Jesus found him in the temple and said to him, "See, you are well. Do not sin anymore, so that something worse doesn't happen to you."

[A] **4:35** Lit *Raise* [B] **4:35** Lit *white* [C] **4:38** Lit *you have entered into* [D] **4:39** Lit *because of the woman's word* [E] **4:41** Lit *because of his word* [F] **4:42** Other mss add , *the Messiah* [G] **4:50** Lit *the word* [H] **4:52** Lit *at the seventh hour* [I] **5:2** Some mss read *Bethzatha* ; other mss read *Bethsaida* [J] **5:3** Some mss include vv. 3b-4: — *waiting for the moving of the water,* [4] *because an angel would go down into the pool from time to time and stir up the water. Then the first one who got in after the water was stirred up recovered from whatever ailment he had.* [K] **5:13** Lit *slipped away, there being a crowd in that place*

DIGGING DEEPER *Pool of Bethesda*

The pool of Bethesda (meaning "house of mercy/grace") was originally constructed in the eighth century BC. John mentions it in his Gospel (Jn 5:1–15); in the Old Testament it is known as the upper pool (2Kg 18:17; Is 7:3; 36:2). It is located north of the Temple Mount a short distance from the Sheep Gate (Neh 3:1,32; 12:39; Jn 5:2). Archaeologists unearthed the site in the late nineteenth century and recognized that the ruins are consistent with the descriptions of the pool mentioned in the Gospel of John. For instance, the pool was said to be a retaining pool with five colonnades (5:2). A narrow set of stairs led into the water (5:7). Archaeologists also found remains of columns and bases that formed the first-century porches and colonnades as well as later Byzantine architecture that may indicate that later Christians worked to preserve this historically significant site. Written records from fourth-century church historian Eusebius and the Pilgrim of Bordeaux support the site's biblical authenticity.

15 The man went and reported to the Jews that it was
Jesus who had made him well. 16 Therefore, the Jews
began persecuting Jesus[A] because he was doing these
things on the Sabbath.

HONORING THE FATHER AND THE SON

17 Jesus responded to them, "My Father is still working, and I am working also." 18 This is why the Jews
began trying all the more to kill him: Not only was he
breaking the Sabbath, but he was even calling God his
own Father, making himself equal to God.
19 Jesus replied, "Truly I tell you, the Son is not able
to do anything on his own, but only what he sees the
Father doing. For whatever the Father[B] does, the Son
likewise does these things. 20 For the Father loves the
Son and shows him everything he is doing, and he
will show him greater works than these so that you
will be amazed. 21 And just as the Father raises the
dead and gives them life, so the Son also gives life
to whom he wants. 22 The Father, in fact, judges no
one but has given all judgment to the Son, 23 so that
all people may honor the Son just as they honor the
Father. Anyone who does not honor the Son does not
honor the Father who sent him.

LIFE AND JUDGMENT

24 "Truly I tell you, anyone who hears my word and
believes him who sent me has eternal life and will not
come under judgment but has passed from death to life.
25 "Truly I tell you, an hour is coming, and is now
here, when the dead will hear the voice of the Son of
God, and those who hear will live. 26 For just as the Father has life in himself, so also he has granted to the
Son to have life in himself. 27 And he has granted him
the right to pass judgment, because he is the Son of
Man. 28 Do not be amazed at this, because a time is coming when all who are in the graves will hear his voice
29 and come out — those who have done good things,
to the resurrection of life, but those who have done
wicked things, to the resurrection of condemnation.
30 "I can do nothing on my own. I judge only as I
hear, and my judgment is just, because I do not seek
my own will, but the will of him who sent me.

WITNESSES TO JESUS

31 "If I testify about myself, my testimony is not true.
32 There is another who testifies about me, and I know
that the testimony he gives about me is true. 33 You
sent messengers to John, and he testified to the truth.
34 I don't receive human testimony, but I say these
things so that you may be saved. 35 John[C] was a burning and shining lamp, and you were willing to rejoice
for a while in his light.
36 "But I have a greater testimony than John's because of the works that the Father has given me to accomplish. These very works I am doing testify about
me that the Father has sent me. 37 The Father who sent
me has himself testified about me. You have not heard
his voice at any time, and you haven't seen his form.
38 You don't have his word residing in you, because
you don't believe the one he sent. 39 You pore over the
Scriptures because you think you have eternal life in
them, and yet they testify about me. 40 But you are
not willing to come to me so that you may have life.
41 "I do not accept glory from people, 42 but I know
you — that you have no love for God within you. 43 I
have come in my Father's name, and yet you don't
accept me. If someone else comes in his own name,
you will accept him. 44 How can you believe, since
you accept glory from one another but don't seek the
glory that comes from the only God? 45 Do not think
that I will accuse you to the Father. Your accuser is
Moses, on whom you have set your hope. 46 For if you
believed Moses, you would believe me, because he
wrote about me. 47 But if you don't believe what he
wrote, how will you believe my words?"

THE FOURTH SIGN: FEEDING OF THE FIVE THOUSAND

6 After this, Jesus crossed the Sea of Galilee (or
Tiberias). 2 A huge crowd was following him because they saw the signs that he was performing by

[A] **5:16** Other mss add *and trying to kill him* [B] **5:19** Lit *whatever that one* [C] **5:35** Lit *That man*

Sabbath Law

by Robert E. Jones

Orthodox Jews at the Western Wall in Jerusalem.

To enforce Sabbath law, Jewish rabbis set forth thirty-nine classifications of work. Their action resulted in the developing and systematizing of numerous rules and regulations the rabbis deduced from the Sabbath commandment. The rabbis worked out these Sabbath-day requirements in an increasingly complicated manner with the goal of applying them to every conceivable situation. For example, Jewish Sabbath law prohibited kindling a fire, carrying on trade, treading the winepress, placing a load on an animal, or holding markets. No business activity of any kind or any other activity could occur that might desecrate the Sabbath.[1] Jews, therefore, had to make all necessary arrangements for the Sabbath on the day of preparation so that the day of rest might remain free of all work. Only an urgent obligation or mortal danger could overrule these laws. ✣

A rabbi in the Jewish Quarter of Jerusalem.

---

[1] Eduard Lohse, "*sabbaton*, Sabbath" in *TDNT* (1971), 7:5.

Partial ruins of the Pool of Bethesda, which was near the
Sheep Gate in Jerusalem.

healing the sick. 3 Jesus went up a mountain and sat
down there with his disciples.
4 Now the Passover, a Jewish festival, was near.
5 So when Jesus looked up and noticed a huge crowd
coming toward him, he asked Philip, "Where will we
buy bread so that these people can eat?" 6 He asked
this to test him, for he himself knew what he was
going to do.
7 Philip answered him, "Two hundred denarii[A]
worth of bread wouldn't be enough for each of them
to have a little."
8 One of his disciples, Andrew, Simon Peter's brother,
said to him, 9 "There's a boy here who has five barley
loaves and two fish — but what are they for so many?"
10 Jesus said, "Have the people sit down."
There was plenty of grass in that place; so they
sat down. The men numbered about five thousand.
11 Then Jesus took the loaves, and after giving thanks
he distributed them to those who were seated — so
also with the fish, as much as they wanted.
12 When they were full, he told his disciples, "Collect the leftovers so that nothing is wasted." 13 So they
collected them and filled twelve baskets with the
pieces from the five barley loaves that were left over
by those who had eaten.
14 When the people saw the sign[B] he had done, they
said, "This truly is the Prophet who is to come into the
world."
15 Therefore, when Jesus realized that they were
about to come and take him by force to make him
king, he withdrew again to the mountain by himself.

THE FIFTH SIGN: WALKING ON WATER

16 When evening came, his disciples went down to the
sea, 17 got into a boat, and started across the sea to Capernaum. Darkness had already set in, but Jesus had
not yet come to them. 18 A high wind arose, and the sea
began to churn. 19 After they had rowed about three
or four miles,[C] they saw Jesus walking on the sea.
He was coming near the boat, and they were afraid.
20 But he said to them, "It is I.[D] Don't be afraid." 21 Then
they were willing to take him on board, and at once
the boat was at the shore where they were heading.

THE BREAD OF LIFE

22 The next day, the crowd that had stayed on the other side of the sea saw there had been only one boat.[E]
They also saw that Jesus had not boarded the boat
with his disciples, but that his disciples had gone
off alone. 23 Some boats from Tiberias came near the
place where they had eaten the bread after the Lord
had given thanks. 24 When the crowd saw that neither Jesus nor his disciples were there, they got into
the boats and went to Capernaum looking for Jesus.
25 When they found him on the other side of the sea,
they said to him, "Rabbi, when did you get here?"
26 Jesus answered, "Truly I tell you, you are looking
for me, not because you saw[F] the signs, but because
you ate the loaves and were filled. 27 Don't work for the
food that perishes but for the food that lasts for eternal life, which the Son of Man will give you, because
God the Father has set his seal of approval on him."
28 "What can we do to perform the works of God?"
they asked.
29 Jesus replied, "This is the work of God — that
you believe in the one he has sent."
30 "What sign, then, are you going to do so that we
may see and believe you?" they asked. "What are you
going to perform? 31 Our ancestors ate the manna in
the wilderness, just as it is written: **He gave them
bread from heaven to eat.**"[G]
32 Jesus said to them, "Truly I tell you, Moses didn't
give you the bread from heaven, but my Father gives
you the true bread from heaven. 33 For the bread of
God is the one who comes down from heaven and
gives life to the world."

[A] **6:7** A denarius = one day's wage [B] **6:14** Other mss read *signs*
[C] **6:19** Lit *twenty-five or thirty stadia*; one *stadion* = 600 feet
[D] **6:20** Lit *"I am* [E] **6:22** Other mss add *into which his disciples had entered* [F] **6:26** Or *perceived* [G] **6:31** Ex 16:4; Ps 78:24

34 Then they said, "Sir, give us this bread always."

35 "I am the bread of life," Jesus told them. "No one who comes to me will ever be hungry, and no one who believes in me will ever be thirsty again. 36 But as I told you, you've seen me,[A] and yet you do not believe. 37 Everyone the Father gives me will come to me, and the one who comes to me I will never cast out. 38 For I have come down from heaven, not to do my own will, but the will of him who sent me. 39 This is the will of him who sent me: that I should lose none of those he has given me but should raise them up on the last day. 40 For this is the will of my Father: that everyone who sees the Son and believes in him will have eternal life, and I will raise him up on the last day."

41 Therefore the Jews started grumbling about him because he said, "I am the bread that came down from heaven." 42 They were saying, "Isn't this Jesus the son of Joseph, whose father and mother we know? How can he now say, 'I have come down from heaven'?"

43 Jesus answered them, "Stop grumbling among yourselves. 44 No one can come to me unless the Father who sent me draws[B] him, and I will raise him up on the last day. 45 It is written in the Prophets: **And they will all be taught by God.**[C] Everyone who has listened to and learned from the Father comes to me — 46 not that anyone has seen the Father except the one who is from God. He has seen the Father.

47 "Truly I tell you, anyone who believes[D] has eternal life. 48 I am the bread of life. 49 Your ancestors ate the manna in the wilderness, and they died. 50 This is the bread that comes down from heaven so that anyone may eat of it and not die. 51 I am the living bread that came down from heaven. If anyone eats of this bread he will live forever. The bread that I will give for the life of the world is my flesh."

52 At that, the Jews argued among themselves, "How can this man give us his flesh to eat?"

53 So Jesus said to them, "Truly I tell you, unless you eat the flesh of the Son of Man and drink his blood, you do not have life in yourselves. 54 The one who eats my flesh and drinks my blood has eternal life, and I will raise him up on the last day, 55 because my flesh is true food and my blood is true drink. 56 The one who eats my flesh and drinks my blood remains in me, and I in him. 57 Just as the living Father sent me and I live because of the Father, so the one who feeds on me will live because of me. 58 This is the bread that came down from heaven; it is not like the manna[E] your ancestors ate — and they died. The one who eats this bread will live forever."

59 He said these things while teaching in the synagogue in Capernaum.

Exterior of the Church of the Multiplication in Galilee, which is the traditional location where Jesus fed the five thousand.

MANY DISCIPLES DESERT JESUS

60 Therefore, when many of his disciples heard this, they said, "This teaching is hard. Who can accept[F] it?"

61 Jesus, knowing in himself that his disciples were grumbling about this, asked them, "Does this offend you? 62 Then what if you were to observe the Son of Man ascending to where he was before? 63 The Spirit is the one who gives life. The flesh doesn't help at all. The words that I have spoken to you are spirit and are life. 64 But there are some among you who don't believe." (For Jesus knew from the beginning those who did not[G] believe and the one who would betray him.) 65 He said, "This is why I told you that no one can come to me unless it is granted to him by the Father."

66 From that moment[H] many of his disciples turned back and no longer accompanied him. 67 So Jesus said to the Twelve, "You don't want to go away too, do you?"

68 Simon Peter answered, "Lord, to whom will we go? You have the words of eternal life. 69 We have come to believe and know that you are the Holy One of God."[I]

[A] **6:36** Other mss omit *me* [B] **6:44** Or *brings*, or *leads* [C] **6:45** Is 54:13
[D] **6:47** Other mss add *in me* [E] **6:58** Gk text lacks *the manna*
[F] **6:60** Lit *hear* [G] **6:64** Other mss omit *not* [H] **6:66** Or *Because of this*
[I] **6:69** Other mss read *you are the Messiah, the Son of the Living God*

Bread Making in the Ancient World

by Mona Stewart

Bread is the oldest of all manufactured foods. It was the basic food in the ancient world and is still the staple in most countries except in East Asia where rice is the staple.

KINDS OF BREAD

Barley meal has husks and is coarser than wheat flour.[1] It is also less appetizing and less expensive. It was the first grain, however, ready for harvest (Ex 9:31,32). The poor could not afford wheat bread, so barley bread became their staple. The boy in John 6:9 had five barley loaves, which were probably flat disks much like small tortillas. Having barley rather than wheat indicated his family's economic condition. The rich preferred wheat bread.

Bread is as varied as there are countries. The thick, light loaf popular in the West is unfamiliar in the East.[2] Multigrain breads are popular everywhere and often made with as many as nine different grains.

GRINDING THE GRAIN

People used different methods for grinding grain. Women who were either the wives, daughters, or slaves of the wealthy did this work. The poor used hand mills made of two stones. The upper stone was of a lighter material than the lower, which was firmly anchored in the ground. People inserted handles into holes in the upper stone and turned them by hand.[3] Animals turned the larger millstones.

Sowing, gathering, winnowing, grinding, kneading, and cooking were part of daily life in each Old and New Testament home. Community bakeries became available in urban areas where people took the loaves to be baked. Only later did bakeries make bread available for purchase.

BAKING THE BREAD

The earliest breads, which were flat and circular, were cooked on heated stones. Fermenting yeast leavened the dough, causing it to rise. Saving a small part of dough from the previous day also served as a sourdough leavening. The leaven made the texture of the loaf bread much lighter than the previous hard flat cakes.[4]

One of three methods of baking the small, thin cakes was to use a heated stone rather than a permanent oven.[5] Another method of baking was to place the dough in a pan or on a griddle made of clay or iron. This disk-shaped bread looked much like a pancake, about one-half inch thick and up to twelve inches in diameter.[6] Sometimes smaller disks were perforated or carried on a stick by means of a hole in the middle. The third baking method was in an oven of clay or iron (Lv 2:4). Those preparing the bread would form their dough into different shapes and sizes. ❖

Using a technique that has been in use for centuries, this gentleman is separating wheat on a threshing floor in Gadara, Jordan.

[1] William H. Stephens, *The New Testament World in Pictures* (Nashville: Broadman, 1987), 182–85. [2] George B. Eager, "Bread" in *ISBE* (1939), 516. [3] Eager, "Bread," 515; Stephens, *New Testament World*, 182–83. [4] Arthur B. Fowler, "Bread" in *The Zondervan Pictorial Bible Dictionary*, ed. Merrill C. Tenney (Grand Rapids: Zondervan, 1963), 132. [5] Victor H. Matthews, *Manners and Customs in the Bible* (Peabody, MA: Hendrickson, 1988), 20. [6] Matthews, *Manners*.

Ovens similar to this would have been typical in Old Testament era dwellings or houses. A cooking pot is on top of the oven.

Mosaic inside the Church of the Multiplication in Galilee.

[70] Jesus replied to them, "Didn't I choose you, the Twelve? Yet one of you is a devil." [71] He was referring to Judas, Simon Iscariot's son,[A] one of the Twelve, because he was going to betray him.

THE UNBELIEF OF JESUS'S BROTHERS

7 After this, Jesus traveled in Galilee, since he did not want to travel in Judea because the Jews were trying to kill him. [2] The Jewish Festival of Shelters[B] was near. [3] So his brothers said to him, "Leave here and go to Judea so that your disciples can see your works that you are doing. [4] For no one does anything in secret while he's seeking public recognition. If you do these things, show yourself to the world." [5] (For not even his brothers believed in him.)

[6] Jesus told them, "My time has not yet arrived, but your time is always at hand. [7] The world cannot hate you, but it does hate me because I testify about it — that its works are evil. [8] Go up to the festival yourselves. I'm not going up to this festival,[C] because my time has not yet fully come." [9] After he had said these things, he stayed in Galilee.

JESUS AT THE FESTIVAL OF SHELTERS

[10] After his brothers had gone up to the festival, then he also went up, not openly but secretly. [11] The Jews were looking for him at the festival and saying, "Where is he?" [12] And there was a lot of murmuring about him among the crowds. Some were saying, "He's a good man." Others were saying, "No, on the contrary, he's deceiving the people." [13] Still, nobody was talking publicly about him for fear of the Jews.

[14] When the festival was already half over, Jesus went up into the temple and began to teach. [15] Then the Jews were amazed and said, "How is this man so learned, since he hasn't been trained?"

[16] Jesus answered them, "My teaching isn't mine but is from the one who sent me. [17] If anyone wants to do his will, he will know whether the teaching is from God or whether I am speaking on my own. [18] The one who speaks on his own seeks his own glory; but he who seeks the glory of the one who sent him is true, and there is no unrighteousness in him. [19] Didn't Moses give you the law? Yet none of you keeps the law. Why are you trying to kill me?"

[20] "You have a demon!" the crowd responded. "Who is trying to kill you?"

[21] "I performed one work, and you are all amazed," Jesus answered. [22] "This is why Moses has given you circumcision — not that it comes from Moses but from the fathers — and you circumcise a man on

[A] **6:71** Or *Judas Iscariot, Simon's son* [B] **7:2** Or *Tabernacles*, or *Booths*
[C] **7:8** Other mss add *yet*

the Sabbath. 23 If a man receives circumcision on the Sabbath so that the law of Moses won't be broken, are you angry at me because I made a man entirely well on the Sabbath? 24 Stop judging according to outward appearances; rather judge according to righteous judgment."

THE IDENTITY OF THE MESSIAH

25 Some of the people of Jerusalem were saying, "Isn't this the man they are trying to kill? 26 Yet, look, he's speaking publicly and they're saying nothing to him. Can it be true that the authorities know he is the Messiah? 27 But we know where this man is from. When the Messiah comes, nobody will know where he is from."

28 As he was teaching in the temple, Jesus cried out, "You know me and you know where I am from. Yet I have not come on my own, but the one who sent me is true. You don't know him; 29 I know him because I am from him, and he sent me."

30 Then they tried to seize him. Yet no one laid a hand on him because his hour had not yet come. 31 However, many from the crowd believed in him and said, "When the Messiah comes, he won't perform more signs than this man has done, will he?" 32 The Pharisees heard the crowd murmuring these things about him, and so the chief priests and the Pharisees sent servants[A] to arrest him.

33 Then Jesus said, "I am only with you for a short time. Then I'm going to the one who sent me. 34 You will look for me, but you will not find me; and where I am, you cannot come."

35 Then the Jews said to one another, "Where does he intend to go that we won't find him? He doesn't intend to go to the Jewish people dispersed[B] among the Greeks and teach the Greeks, does he? 36 What is this remark he made: 'You will look for me, and you will not find me; and where I am, you cannot come'?"

THE PROMISE OF THE SPIRIT

37 On the last and most important day of the festival, Jesus stood up and cried out, "If anyone is thirsty, let him come to me[C] and drink. 38 The one who believes in me, as the Scripture has said, will have streams of living water flow from deep within him." 39 He said this about the Spirit. Those who believed in Jesus were going to receive the Spirit, for the Spirit[D] had not yet been given[E] because Jesus had not yet been glorified.

THE PEOPLE ARE DIVIDED OVER JESUS

40 When some from the crowd heard these words, they said, "This truly is the Prophet." 41 Others said, "This is the Messiah." But some said, "Surely the Messiah doesn't come from Galilee, does he? 42 Doesn't the Scripture say that the Messiah comes from David's offspring[F] and from the town of Bethlehem, where David lived?" 43 So the crowd was divided because of him. 44 Some of them wanted to seize him, but no one laid hands on him.

DEBATE OVER JESUS'S CLAIMS

45 Then the servants came to the chief priests and Pharisees, who asked them, "Why didn't you bring him?"

46 The servants answered, "No man ever spoke like this!"[G]

47 Then the Pharisees responded to them, "Are you fooled too? 48 Have any of the rulers or Pharisees believed in him? 49 But this crowd, which doesn't know the law, is accursed."

50 Nicodemus — the one who came to him previously and who was one of them — said to them, 51 "Our law doesn't judge a man before it hears from him and knows what he's doing, does it?"

52 "You aren't from Galilee too, are you?" they replied. "Investigate and you will see that no prophet arises from Galilee."

[The earliest mss do not include 7:53–8:11.][H]

8

[53 Then each one went to his house. 1 But Jesus went to the Mount of Olives.

AN ADULTERESS FORGIVEN

2 At dawn he went to the temple again, and all the people were coming to him. He sat down and began to teach them.

3 Then the scribes and the Pharisees brought a woman caught in adultery, making her stand in the center. 4 "Teacher," they said to him, "this woman was caught in the act of committing adultery. 5 In the law Moses commanded us to stone such women. So what do you say?" 6 They asked this to trap him, in order that they might have evidence to accuse him.

Jesus stooped down and started writing on the ground with his finger. 7 When they persisted in questioning him, he stood up and said to them, "The one without sin among you should be the first to throw a stone at her." 8 Then he stooped down again and continued writing on the ground. 9 When they heard this, they left one by one, starting with the older men. Only he was left, with the woman in the center. 10 When Jesus stood up, he said to her, "Woman, where are they? Has no one condemned you?"

[A] **7:32** Or *temple police*, or *officers*, also in vv. 45,46 [B] **7:35** Gk *diaspora*; Jewish people scattered throughout Gentile lands [C] **7:37** Other mss omit *to me* [D] **7:39** Other mss read *Holy Spirit* [E] **7:39** Lit *the Spirit was not yet* [F] **7:42** Lit *seed* [G] **7:46** Other mss read *like this man* [H] **7:53–8:11** Other mss include all or some of the passage after Jn 7:36,44,52; 21:25; or Lk 21:38.

11 "No one, Lord,"[A] she answered.

"Neither do I condemn you," said Jesus. "Go, and from now on do not sin anymore."]

THE LIGHT OF THE WORLD

12 Jesus spoke to them again: "I am the light of the world. Anyone who follows me will never walk in the darkness but will have the light of life."

13 So the Pharisees said to him, "You are testifying about yourself. Your testimony is not valid."

14 "Even if I testify about myself," Jesus replied, "My testimony is true, because I know where I came from and where I'm going. But you don't know where I come from or where I'm going. 15 You judge by human standards.[B] I judge no one. 16 And if I do judge, my judgment is true, because it is not I alone who judge, but I and the Father who sent me. 17 Even in your law it is written that the testimony of two witnesses is true. 18 I am the one who testifies about myself, and the Father who sent me testifies about me."

19 Then they asked him, "Where is your Father?"

"You know neither me nor my Father," Jesus answered. "If you knew me, you would also know my Father." 20 He spoke these words by the treasury, while teaching in the temple. But no one seized him, because his hour had not yet come.

JESUS PREDICTS HIS DEPARTURE

21 Then he said to them again, "I'm going away; you will look for me, and you will die in your sin. Where I'm going, you cannot come."

22 So the Jews said again, "He won't kill himself, will he, since he says, 'Where I'm going, you cannot come'?"

23 "You are from below," he told them, "I am from above. You are of this world; I am not of this world. 24 Therefore I told you that you will die in your sins. For if you do not believe that I am he, you will die in your sins."

25 "Who are you?" they questioned.

"Exactly what I've been telling you from the very beginning," Jesus told them. 26 "I have many things to say and to judge about you, but the one who sent me is true, and what I have heard from him — these things I tell the world."

27 They did not know he was speaking to them about the Father. 28 So Jesus said to them, "When you lift up the Son of Man, then you will know that I am he, and that I do nothing on my own. But just as the Father taught me, I say these things. 29 The one who sent me is with me. He has not left me alone, because I always do what pleases him."

TRUTH AND FREEDOM

30 As he was saying these things, many believed in him.

31 Then Jesus said to the Jews who had believed him, "If you continue in my word,[C] you really are my disciples. 32 You will know the truth, and the truth will set you free."

33 "We are descendants[D] of Abraham," they answered him, "and we have never been enslaved to anyone. How can you say, 'You will become free'?"

34 Jesus responded, "Truly I tell you, everyone who commits sin is a slave of sin. 35 A slave does not remain in the household forever, but a son does remain forever. 36 So if the Son sets you free, you really will be free. 37 I know you are descendants of Abraham, but you are trying to kill me because my word has no place among you. 38 I speak what I have seen in the presence of the Father;[E] so then, you do what you have heard from your father."

39 "Our father is Abraham," they replied.

"If you were Abraham's children," Jesus told them, "you would do what Abraham did. 40 But now you are trying to kill me, a man who has told you the truth that I heard from God. Abraham did not do this. 41 You're doing what your father does."

"We weren't born of sexual immorality," they said. "We have one Father — God."

42 Jesus said to them, "If God were your Father, you would love me, because I came from God and I am here. For I didn't come on my own, but he sent me. 43 Why don't you understand what I say? Because you cannot listen to[F] my word. 44 You are of your father the devil, and you want to carry out your father's desires. He was a murderer from the beginning and does not stand in the truth, because there is no truth in him. When he tells a lie, he speaks from his own nature,[G] because he is a liar and the father of lies. 45 Yet because I tell the truth, you do not believe me. 46 Who among you can convict me of sin? If I am telling the truth, why don't you believe me? 47 The one who is from God listens to God's words. This is why you don't listen, because you are not from God."

JESUS AND ABRAHAM

48 The Jews responded to him, "Aren't we right in saying that you're a Samaritan and have a demon?"

49 "I do not have a demon," Jesus answered. "On the contrary, I honor my Father and you dishonor me. 50 I do not seek my own glory; there is one who seeks it and judges. 51 Truly I tell you, if anyone keeps my word, he will never see death."

[A] **8:11** Or *Sir*; Jn 4:15,49; 5:7; 6:34; 9:36 [B] **8:15** Lit *You judge according to the flesh* [C] **8:31** Or *my teaching*, or *my message*, also in v. 37 [D] **8:33** Or *offspring*; lit *seed*, also in v. 37; Jn 7:42 [E] **8:38** Other mss read *of my Father* [F] **8:43** Or *cannot hear* [G] **8:44** Lit *from his own things*

52 Then the Jews said, "Now we know you have a demon. Abraham died and so did the prophets. You say, 'If anyone keeps my word, he will never taste death.' 53 Are you greater than our father Abraham who died? And the prophets died. Who do you claim to be?"

54 "If I glorify myself," Jesus answered, "my glory is nothing. My Father — about whom you say, 'He is our God' — he is the one who glorifies me. 55 You do not know him, but I know him. If I were to say I don't know him, I would be a liar like you. But I do know him, and I keep his word. 56 Your father Abraham rejoiced to see my day; he saw it and was glad."

57 The Jews replied, "You aren't fifty years old yet, and you've seen Abraham?"[A]

58 Jesus said to them, "Truly I tell you, before Abraham was, I am."

59 So they picked up stones to throw at him. But Jesus was hidden[B] and went out of the temple.[C]

THE SIXTH SIGN: HEALING A MAN BORN BLIND

9 As he was passing by, he saw a man blind from birth. 2 His disciples asked him, "Rabbi, who sinned, this man or his parents, that he was born blind?"

3 "Neither this man nor his parents sinned," Jesus answered. "This came about so that God's works might be displayed in him. 4 We[D] must do the works of him who sent me[E] while it is day. Night is coming when no one can work. 5 As long as I am in the world, I am the light of the world."

6 After he said these things he spit on the ground, made some mud from the saliva, and spread the mud on his eyes. 7 "Go," he told him, "wash in the pool of Siloam" (which means "Sent"). So he left, washed, and came back seeing.

8 His neighbors and those who had seen him before as a beggar said, "Isn't this the one who used to sit begging?" 9 Some said, "He's the one." Others were saying, "No, but he looks like him."

He kept saying, "I'm the one."

10 So they asked him, "Then how were your eyes opened?"

11 He answered, "The man called Jesus made mud, spread it on my eyes, and told me, 'Go to Siloam and wash.' So when I went and washed I received my sight."

12 "Where is he?" they asked.

"I don't know," he said.

THE HEALED MAN'S TESTIMONY

13 They brought the man who used to be blind to the Pharisees. 14 The day that Jesus made the mud and opened his eyes was a Sabbath. 15 Then the Pharisees asked him again how he received his sight.

"He put mud on my eyes," he told them. "I washed and I can see."

16 Some of the Pharisees said, "This man is not from God, because he doesn't keep the Sabbath." But others were saying, "How can a sinful man perform such signs?" And there was a division among them.

17 Again they asked the blind man, "What do you say about him, since he opened your eyes?"

"He's a prophet," he said.

18 The Jews did not believe this about him — that he was blind and received sight — until they summoned the parents of the one who had received his sight.

19 They asked them, "Is this your son, the one you say was born blind? How then does he now see?"

20 "We know this is our son and that he was born blind," his parents answered. 21 "But we don't know how he now sees, and we don't know who opened his eyes. Ask him; he's of age. He will speak for himself." 22 His parents said these things because they were afraid of the Jews, since the Jews had already agreed that if anyone confessed him as the Messiah, he would be banned from the synagogue. 23 This is why his parents said, "He's of age; ask him."

24 So a second time they summoned the man who had been blind and told him, "Give glory to God. We know that this man is a sinner."

DIGGING DEEPER *Pool of Siloam*

The pool of Siloam (Jn 9:1–12) was discovered by accident in 2004 as workers in Jerusalem dug to repair a sewer pipe that was located only a few feet above the buried ruins. Subsequent excavations by Ronny Reich and Eli Shukrun revealed that the pool was surrounded on all four sides by three tiers of steps that led down into the water. The pool was fed by the Gihon spring and most likely was used as a ritual purification bath (*mikveh*) for those on their way to the temple. Ancient coinage and pottery found at the site date from the time of Christ, placing the pool well within the context of the story of Jesus healing a blind man here. The Old Testament mentions an earlier pool that was in existence during the eighth century BC (Is 8:6). Like the pool of Jesus's day, the earlier pool was fed by the Gihon spring and served as a retaining pool for water channeled through King Hezekiah's seventeen-hundred-foot tunnel. The pool's discovery leaves little doubt among both liberal and conservative archaeologists that the pool mentioned in John 9:7 is the pool of Siloam.

[A] **8:57** Other mss read *and Abraham has seen you?* [B] **8:59** Or *Jesus hid himself* [C] **8:59** Other mss add *and having gone through their midst, he passed by* [D] **9:4** Other mss read *I* [E] **9:4** Other mss read *us*

A Woman's Status

by Martha S. Bergen

Dated to about 500 BC, a terra-cotta figurine from central Greece depicts a woman seated in front of an oven.

IN ISRAELITE CULTURE

Within ancient Hebrew society, Torah laws were binding for both men and women. Women, just as men, were obligated to follow the Ten Commandments and other moral laws, along with laws governing civil and ceremonial matters. Yet laws differed in relation to the sexes. For example, laws regarding the priesthood, circumcision, and appearance before the Lord three times a year applied only to males. Old Testament laws maintained a distinction between the roles men and women played in Hebrew society. Thus all Old Testament laws directed exclusively toward women dealt with the unique concerns associated with their bodies, such as purification after menstruating (Lv 15:19; 2Sm 11:2–4). To the Jews, the symbolic significance of washing resembled holiness; thus a clean body reflected a clean soul. Though early Jewish literature gave no explicit details on ritual washings related to the menstrual cycle, it assumed a natural connection.[1]

Jewish laws were implemented during Moses's time, but generally they were still applicable to Jews approximately fourteen hundred years later as evidenced in the New Testament. Israelite law, for example, required a woman to present a purification offering to the priest to become ceremonially clean after childbirth. We know that Mary, Jesus's mother, observed this Levitical law. Because she was unable to afford the accompanying sacrificial lamb, she offered the substitute pair of turtledoves or young pigeons (Lv 12; Lk 2:22–24).

SOCIAL AND FINANCIAL OPPORTUNITIES

The center of social opportunities for first-century women of both Judaism and Christianity was the home (e.g., Ti 2:4–5). Among a woman's greatest privileges and influence is that of shaping her children for God. A woman in the first century had authority over her children. She nurtured and taught them in the early years of life when foundational values were established. She partnered with her husband to raise them in the Lord's instruction.

Various New Testament passages give evidence of acceptable public social contact between the genders within certain settings. For example, Martha welcomed Jesus to her home in Bethany where she prepared him a meal (Lk 10:38,40). Her role of extending hospitality to guests in her home was normative of Jewish women in this time period.

Some social contacts would have been inappropriate for Jewish women; reactions of the Pharisees and teachers of the law confirm this. Mary, a woman with a past, publicly anointed Jesus's feet (Lk 7:37–39). Any woman who touched a man in public almost certainly would have dishonored herself and the man. The woman with the blood issue touched Jesus's garment (Mt 9:20), thereby making him ceremonially unclean according to Levitical law (Lv 15:25).

Women were economically dependent upon their husbands or male family members. They did not hold jobs during the first century. However, upper-class women had at least partial control of the family's wealth. The Scriptures speak of such women who supported Jesus and his disciples, namely Joanna, Susanna, and others (Lk 8:3). Lydia, the first known European convert to Christianity, was a seller of purple—perhaps reflective of freedoms people had in areas that were under Roman control but were also outside ancient Israel (Ac 16:14). Purple cloth was an expensive commodity, suggesting Lydia was wealthy. Priscilla and her husband, Aquila, helped Paul in his missionary endeavors (Ac 18:18; Rm 16:3), hosted a house church (1Co 16:19), and instructed Apollos (Ac 18:26). Priscilla also assisted Aquila in his tent-making activities (18:2–3).

Terra-cotta figurine of a woman in Greek dress carrying a pitcher; from the Shrine of Demeter at Kourion on Cyprus.

NON-JEWISH WOMEN

During the New Testament era and for hundreds of years prior to that time, Roman women could own property, appear in court, and compose a will. Among the most significant tasks for a woman was making clothes, especially in larger households. Spinning wool showed a family was self-sufficient. Although some wealthy women had their slaves spin wool for the family, many did it themselves.[2] Women were primarily involved with family concerns and rearing children. Other tasks included assisting with the family business, field labor, or midwifery. Educational opportunities were available for wealthy women.[3] ✣

[1] "Baths, Bathing" in *JE* (1906), *http://www.jewishencyclopedia.com/articles/2661-baths-bathing.* [2] Mary Ann Bevis, *The Lost Coin: Parables of Women, Work, and Wisdom* (New York: Sheffield, 2002), 139. [3] Lynn H. Cohick, *Women in the World of the Earliest Christians: Illuminating Ancient Ways of Life* (Grand Rapids: Baker Academic, 2009), 225.

[25] He answered, "Whether or not he's a sinner, I don't know. One thing I do know: I was blind, and now I can see!"

[26] Then they asked him, "What did he do to you? How did he open your eyes?"

[27] "I already told you," he said, "and you didn't listen. Why do you want to hear it again? You don't want to become his disciples too, do you?"

[28] They ridiculed him: "You're that man's disciple, but we're Moses's disciples. [29] We know that God has spoken to Moses. But this man — we don't know where he's from."

[30] "This is an amazing thing!" the man told them. "You don't know where he is from, and yet he opened my eyes. [31] We know that God doesn't listen to sinners, but if anyone is God-fearing and does his will, he listens to him. [32] Throughout history[A] no one has ever heard of someone opening the eyes of a person born blind. [33] If this man were not from God, he wouldn't be able to do anything."

[34] "You were born entirely in sin," they replied, "and are you trying to teach us?" Then they threw him out.

SPIRITUAL BLINDNESS

[35] Jesus heard that they had thrown the man out, and when he found him, he asked, "Do you believe in the Son of Man?"[B]

[36] "Who is he, Sir, that I may believe in him?" he asked.

[37] Jesus answered, "You have seen him; in fact, he is the one speaking with you."

[38] "I believe, Lord!" he said, and he worshiped him.

[39] Jesus said, "I came into this world for judgment, in order that those who do not see will see and those who do see will become blind."

[40] Some of the Pharisees who were with him heard these things and asked him, "We aren't blind too, are we?"

[41] "If you were blind," Jesus told them, "you wouldn't have sin. But now that you say, 'We see,' your sin remains.

THE GOOD SHEPHERD

10 "Truly I tell you, anyone who doesn't enter the sheep pen by the gate but climbs in some other way is a thief and a robber. [2] The one who enters by the gate is the shepherd of the sheep. [3] The gatekeeper opens it for him, and the sheep hear his voice. He calls his own sheep by name and leads them out. [4] When he has brought all his own outside, he goes ahead of them. The sheep follow him because they know his voice. [5] They will never follow a stranger; instead they will run away from him, because they don't know the voice of strangers." [6] Jesus gave them this figure of speech, but they did not understand what he was telling them.

[A] **9:32** Lit *From the age* [B] **9:35** Other mss read *the Son of God*

Discovered in 2004 are steps leading into the Pool of Siloam on the southern tip of Jerusalem. Pottery found in the excavation indicates the pool was in use in Jesus's day.

[7] Jesus said again, "Truly I tell you, I am the gate for
the sheep. [8] All who came before me[A] are thieves and
robbers, but the sheep didn't listen to them. [9] I am the
gate. If anyone enters by me, he will be saved and will
come in and go out and find pasture. [10] A thief comes
only to steal and kill and destroy. I have come so that
they may have life and have it in abundance.
[11] "I am the good shepherd. The good shepherd lays
down his life for the sheep. [12] The hired hand, since
he is not the shepherd and doesn't own the sheep,
leaves them[B] and runs away when he sees a wolf
coming. The wolf then snatches and scatters them.
[13] This happens because he is a hired hand and doesn't
care about the sheep.
[14] "I am the good shepherd. I know my own, and my
own know me, [15] just as the Father knows me, and I
know the Father. I lay down my life for the sheep. [16] But
I have other sheep that are not from this sheep pen; I
must bring them also, and they will listen to my voice.
Then there will be one flock, one shepherd. [17] This is
why the Father loves me, because I lay down my life
so that I may take it up again. [18] No one takes it from
me, but I lay it down on my own. I have the right to
lay it down, and I have the right to take it up again. I
have received this command from my Father."
[19] Again the Jews were divided because of these
words. [20] Many of them were saying, "He has a demon
and he's crazy. Why do you listen to him?" [21] Others
were saying, "These aren't the words of someone who
is demon-possessed. Can a demon open the eyes of
the blind?"

JESUS AT THE FESTIVAL OF DEDICATION

[22] Then the Festival of Dedication took place in Jerusalem, and it was winter. [23] Jesus was walking in
the temple in Solomon's Colonnade. [24] The Jews surrounded him and asked, "How long are you going
to keep us in suspense?[C] If you are the Messiah, tell
us plainly."[D]
[25] "I did tell you and you don't believe," Jesus answered them. "The works that I do in my Father's
name testify about me. [26] But you don't believe because you are not of my sheep.[E] [27] My sheep hear my
voice, I know them, and they follow me. [28] I give them
eternal life, and they will never perish. No one will
snatch them out of my hand. [29] My Father, who has
given them to me, is greater than all. No one is able
to snatch them out of the Father's hand. [30] I and the
Father are one."

RENEWED EFFORTS TO STONE JESUS

[31] Again the Jews picked up rocks to stone him.
[32] Jesus replied, "I have shown you many good
works from the Father. For which of these works
are you stoning me?"

Depictions of a shepherd carrying a sheep across his shoulders became a popular Christian figure, especially in the Byzantine era. This one is on a wall in Sousse, Tunisia, in northern Africa.

[33] "We aren't stoning you for a good work," the Jews
answered, "but for blasphemy, because you — being
a man — make yourself God."
[34] Jesus answered them, "Isn't it written in your
law,[F] **I said, you are gods**?[G] [35] If he called those to
whom the word of God came 'gods' — and the Scripture cannot be broken — [36] do you say, 'You are blaspheming' to the one the Father set apart and sent into
the world, because I said: I am the Son of God? [37] If I am
not doing my Father's works, don't believe me. [38] But
if I am doing them and you don't believe me, believe
the works. This way you will know and understand[H]
that the Father is in me and I in the Father." [39] Then
they were trying again to seize him, but he escaped
their grasp.

MANY BEYOND THE JORDAN BELIEVE IN JESUS

[40] So he departed again across the Jordan to the
place where John had been baptizing earlier, and
he remained there. [41] Many came to him and said,
"John never did a sign, but everything John said about
this man was true." [42] And many believed in him there.

[A] **10:8** Other mss omit *before me* [B] **10:12** Lit *leaves the sheep*
[C] **10:24** Lit *"How long are you taking away our life?* [D] **10:24** Or *openly, or publicly* [E] **10:26** Other mss add *just as I told you* [F] **10:34** Other mss read *in the scripture* [G] **10:34** Ps 82:6 [H] **10:38** Other mss read *know and believe*

Robbers

by Timothy Trammell

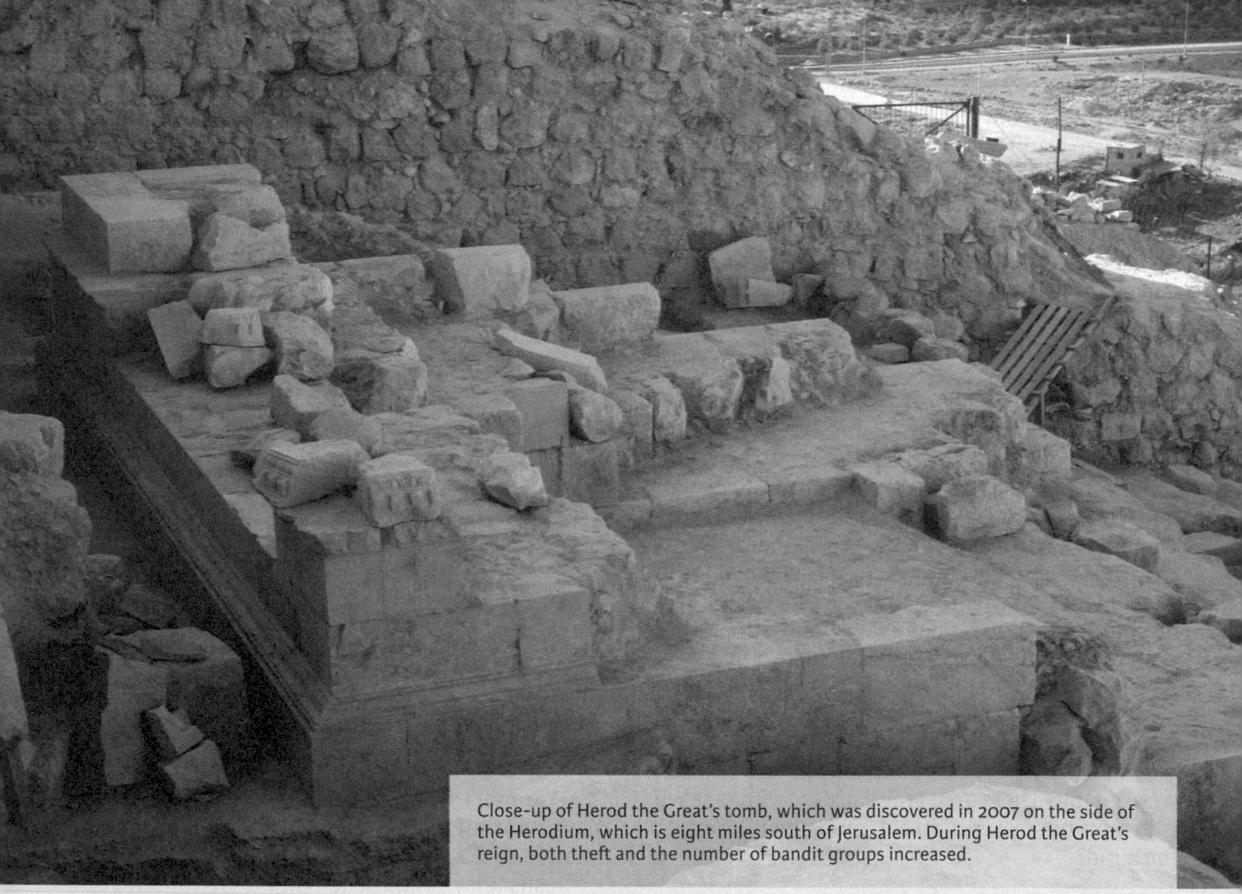

Close-up of Herod the Great's tomb, which was discovered in 2007 on the side of the Herodium, which is eight miles south of Jerusalem. During Herod the Great's reign, both theft and the number of bandit groups increased.

The Greek word for *robber* primarily describes the armed bands of brigands who were intentionally brutal in carrying out their activities. These were marauders who usually operated outdoors, attacking caravans and individual travelers. Jesus set the scene of his parable of the good Samaritan east of Jerusalem in the rugged Judean hills. The robbers, usually in sizable bands, would often use such terrain as their hunting ground. Consequently the wise traveler would seek safety in numbers, especially if he was carrying goods or valuables, for the violent nature of these bands was well known.

Another aspect of these robber bands is also significant. The Jewish people were under the domination of the Roman Empire in the first century. Both the Roman overlords and the Jewish landowning elite exploited the peasants. Economic crises caused by famine, high taxation, and social injustice fostered the development of groups seeking to right these wrongs.[1] When foreign conquest was accompanied by the exactions of an unsympathetic ruling class, the rural people saw the bandits as their protectors.

To be more specific, the regressive policies of Herod the Great contributed to the rise of such groups. Although his reign brought an end to much of the political turmoil, his ambitious building projects, with Rome's excessive taxation, made the people's poverty more severe. Payments to the Romans were a continuing burden, as were tithes for the priesthood and the temple in Jerusalem. Josephus records that upon Herod's death, the Jewish aristocracy pleaded with Caesar for a change from "kingly government." They told of the multitudes that had perished during his reign, of the estates he had stolen, and that he had "filled the nation with the utmost degree of poverty."[2] The nobility suffered at the hands of Herod—and the poor even more so. Such injustice had forced some people to look to robber bands for redress.

The first half of the first century was marked by famine, inflation, high taxation, and theft of the people's land. Consequently banditry escalated to epidemic proportions. This growth had its beginning in approximately AD 6 with the

Dated to Egypt's Nineteenth–Twentieth Dynasties (1295–1069 BC); a limestone ostracon from Thebes inscribed with a letter. In it, the writer denies stealing precious objects that had belonged to the pharaoh and begs to be released from the imposed penalty of forced labor.

activities of Judas of Galilee. In discussing the various parties in Judaism, Josephus recorded that Judas founded "the fourth sect of Jewish philosophy"; also known as the "Fourth Philosophy,"[3] this was foundational to what followed, namely the Jewish rebellion or revolt against Rome.

The Jewish rebellion brought with it an explosion of banditry. Many of these bands operated for only a brief time, for banditry was a lonely profession, away from family and society at large. In addition, most procurators made an intense effort to capture and punish these lawbreakers. ✣

[1] Richard A. Horsley and John S. Hanson, *Bandits, Prophets, and Messiahs* (San Francisco: Harper & Row, 1985), 49–50.
[2] Josephus, *Jewish Antiquities* 17.11.2.
[3] Josephus, *Jewish Antiquities* 18.1.6.

Sheep at the edge of the northern Negev Desert where it meets the central plains of Israel. The hill country rises in the background.

LAZARUS DIES AT BETHANY

11 Now a man was sick, Lazarus from Bethany, the
village of Mary and her sister Martha. 2 Mary
was the one who anointed the Lord with perfume and
wiped his feet with her hair, and it was her brother
Lazarus who was sick. 3 So the sisters sent a message
to him: "Lord, the one you love is sick."
4 When Jesus heard it, he said, "This sickness will
not end in death but is for the glory of God, so that the
Son of God may be glorified through it." 5 Now Jesus
loved Martha, her sister, and Lazarus. 6 So when he
heard that he was sick, he stayed two more days in
the place where he was. 7 Then after that, he said to
the disciples, "Let's go to Judea again."
8 "Rabbi," the disciples told him, "just now the Jews
tried to stone you, and you're going there again?"
9 "Aren't there twelve hours in a day?" Jesus answered. "If anyone walks during the day, he doesn't
stumble, because he sees the light of this world. 10 But
if anyone walks during the night, he does stumble,
because the light is not in him."
11 He said this, and then he told them, "Our friend
Lazarus has fallen asleep, but I'm on my way to wake
him up."
12 Then the disciples said to him, "Lord, if he has
fallen asleep, he will get well."
13 Jesus, however, was speaking about his death, but
they thought he was speaking about natural sleep.
14 So Jesus then told them plainly, "Lazarus has died.
15 I'm glad for you that I wasn't there so that you may
believe. But let's go to him."
16 Then Thomas (called "Twin"[A]) said to his fellow
disciples, "Let's go too so that we may die with him."

THE RESURRECTION AND THE LIFE

17 When Jesus arrived, he found that Lazarus had already been in the tomb four days. 18 Bethany was near
Jerusalem (less than two miles[B] away). 19 Many of the
Jews had come to Martha and Mary to comfort them
about their brother.
20 As soon as Martha heard that Jesus was coming,
she went to meet him, but Mary remained seated in
the house. 21 Then Martha said to Jesus, "Lord, if you
had been here, my brother wouldn't have died. 22 Yet
even now I know that whatever you ask from God,
God will give you."
23 "Your brother will rise again," Jesus told her.
24 Martha said to him, "I know that he will rise
again in the resurrection at the last day."
25 Jesus said to her, "I am the resurrection and the
life. The one who believes in me, even if he dies, will
live. 26 Everyone who lives and believes in me will
never die. Do you believe this?"
27 "Yes, Lord," she told him, "I believe you are the
Messiah, the Son of God, who comes into the world."

JESUS SHARES THE SORROW OF DEATH

28 Having said this, she went back and called her sister Mary, saying in private, "The Teacher is here and
is calling for you."
29 As soon as Mary heard this, she got up quickly
and went to him. 30 Jesus had not yet come into the
village but was still in the place where Martha had
met him. 31 The Jews who were with her in the house
consoling her saw that Mary got up quickly and went
out. They followed her, supposing that she was going
to the tomb to cry there.
32 As soon as Mary came to where Jesus was and
saw him, she fell at his feet and told him, "Lord, if
you had been here, my brother wouldn't have died!"

[A] **11:16** Gk *Didymus* [B] **11:18** Lit *fifteen stadia*; one *stadion* = 600 feet

33 When Jesus saw her crying, and the Jews who
had come with her crying, he was deeply moved[A]
in his spirit and troubled. 34 "Where have you put
him?" he asked.
"Lord," they told him, "come and see."
35 Jesus wept.
36 So the Jews said, "See how he loved him!" 37 But
some of them said, "Couldn't he who opened the blind
man's eyes also have kept this man from dying?"

THE SEVENTH SIGN: RAISING LAZARUS FROM THE DEAD

38 Then Jesus, deeply moved again, came to the tomb.
It was a cave, and a stone was lying against it. 39 "Remove the stone," Jesus said.
Martha, the dead man's sister, told him, "Lord,
there is already a stench because he has been dead
four days."
40 Jesus said to her, "Didn't I tell you that if you believed you would see the glory of God?"
41 So they removed the stone. Then Jesus raised
his eyes and said, "Father, I thank you that you heard
me. 42 I know that you always hear me, but because of
the crowd standing here I said this, so that they may
believe you sent me." 43 After he said this, he shouted
with a loud voice, "Lazarus, come out!" 44 The dead
man came out bound hand and foot with linen strips
and with his face wrapped in a cloth. Jesus said to
them, "Unwrap him and let him go."

THE PLOT TO KILL JESUS

45 Therefore, many of the Jews who came to Mary
and saw what he did believed in him. 46 But some
of them went to the Pharisees and told them what
Jesus had done.
47 So the chief priests and the Pharisees convened
the Sanhedrin and were saying, "What are we going
to do since this man is doing many signs? 48 If we let
him go on like this, everyone will believe in him, and
the Romans will come and take away both our place
and our nation."
49 One of them, Caiaphas, who was high priest
that year, said to them, "You know nothing at all!
50 You're not considering that it is to your[B] advantage that one man should die for the people rather than the whole nation perish." 51 He did not say
this on his own, but being high priest that year he
prophesied that Jesus was going to die for the nation, 52 and not for the nation only, but also to unite
the scattered children of God. 53 So from that day
on they plotted to kill him.
54 Jesus therefore no longer walked openly among
the Jews but departed from there to the countryside
near the wilderness, to a town called Ephraim, and
he stayed there with the disciples.

DIGGING DEEPER — *Tomb of Lazarus*

Ancient Bethany was the hometown of biblical figures such as Mary, Martha, and Lazarus (Jn 11:1). It is located approximately two miles from Jerusalem on the eastern side of the Mount of Olives. Today it is primarily occupied by Arabs and Palestinians and is known by its modern Arabic name *el-Azariyeh*, which means "the place of Lazarus." From as early as the second century AD, local tradition has identified a specific tomb as being the one in which Lazarus lay until Jesus raised him from the dead four days after his death (11:38–44; 12:1). Beginning in the fourth century AD, churches were built and rebuilt at the site, demonstrating that the location was viewed as having spiritual and historical value for Christian worshipers. The long-standing identification of this site is strong evidence for its authenticity. Today visitors can enter the tomb by descending a series of stairs that land in the forward vestibule of two chambers.

55 Now the Jewish Passover was near, and many
went up to Jerusalem from the country to purify
themselves before the Passover. 56 They were looking for Jesus and asking one another as they stood
in the temple, "What do you think? He won't come
to the festival, will he?" 57 The chief priests and the
Pharisees had given orders that if anyone knew
where he was, he should report it so that they could
arrest him.

THE ANOINTING AT BETHANY

12 Six days before the Passover, Jesus came to
Bethany where Lazarus[C] was, the one Jesus had
raised from the dead. 2 So they gave a dinner for him
there; Martha was serving them, and Lazarus was
one of those reclining at the table with him. 3 Then
Mary took a pound of perfume, pure and expensive
nard, anointed Jesus's feet, and wiped his feet with
her hair. So the house was filled with the fragrance
of the perfume.
4 Then one of his disciples, Judas Iscariot (who
was about to betray him), said, 5 "Why wasn't this
perfume sold for three hundred denarii[D] and given
to the poor?" 6 He didn't say this because he cared
about the poor but because he was a thief. He was
in charge of the money-bag and would steal part of
what was put in it.

[A] **11:33** Or *angry*, also in v. 38 [B] **11:50** Other mss read *to our*
[C] **12:1** Other mss read *Lazarus who died* [D] **12:5** A denarius = one day's wage

[7] Jesus answered, "Leave her alone; she has kept
it for the day of my burial. [8] For you always have the
poor with you, but you do not always have me."

THE DECISION TO KILL LAZARUS

[9] Then a large crowd of the Jews learned he was there.
They came not only because of Jesus but also to see
Lazarus, the one he had raised from the dead. [10] But
the chief priests had decided to kill Lazarus also,
[11] because he was the reason many of the Jews were
deserting them[A] and believing in Jesus.

THE TRIUMPHAL ENTRY

[12] The next day, when the large crowd that had come
to the festival heard that Jesus was coming to Jerusalem, [13] they took palm branches and went out to
meet him. They kept shouting:

> **"*Hosanna!***
> **Blessed is he who comes in the name of**
> **the Lord**[B] **— the King of Israel!"**

[14] Jesus found a young donkey and sat on it, just as
it is written:

> 15 **Do not be afraid,**
> **Daughter Zion. Look, your King**
> **is coming,**
> **sitting on a donkey's colt.**[C]

[16] His disciples did not understand these things at
first. However, when Jesus was glorified, then they remembered that these things had been written about
him and that they had done these things to him.

[17] Meanwhile, the crowd, which had been with him
when he called Lazarus out of the tomb and raised
him from the dead, continued to testify.[D] [18] This is also
why the crowd met him, because they heard he had
done this sign. [19] Then the Pharisees said to one another, "You see? You've accomplished nothing. Look,
the world has gone after him!"

JESUS PREDICTS HIS CRUCIFIXION

[20] Now some Greeks were among those who went up
to worship at the festival. [21] So they came to Philip,
who was from Bethsaida in Galilee, and requested
of him, "Sir, we want to see Jesus." [22] Philip went
and told Andrew; then Andrew and Philip went and
told Jesus.

[23] Jesus replied to them, "The hour has come for the
Son of Man to be glorified. [24] Truly I tell you, unless a
grain of wheat falls to the ground and dies, it remains

[A] **12:11** Lit *going away* [B] **12:13** Ps 118:25–26 [C] **12:15** Zch 9:9
[D] **12:17** Other mss read *Meanwhile the crowd, which had been with him, continued to testify that he had called Lazarus out of the tomb and raised him from the dead.*

Exterior of the Church of Lazarus in Bethany. The church is built adjacent to the tomb of Lazarus.

The small door opening in the stone wall is the entrance to the tomb of Lazarus at Bethany.

by itself. But if it dies, it produces much fruit. 25 The
one who loves his life will lose it, and the one who
hates his life in this world will keep it for eternal life.
26 If anyone serves me, he must follow me. Where I
am, there my servant also will be. If anyone serves
me, the Father will honor him.
27 "Now my soul is troubled. What should I say —
Father, save me from this hour? But that is why I came
to this hour. 28 Father, glorify your name."[A]
Then a voice came from heaven: "I have glorified
it, and I will glorify it again."
29 The crowd standing there heard it and said it was
thunder. Others said, "An angel has spoken to him."
30 Jesus responded, "This voice came, not for me,
but for you. 31 Now is the judgment of this world. Now
the ruler of this world will be cast out. 32 As for me, if
I am lifted up[B] from the earth I will draw all people to
myself." 33 He said this to indicate what kind of death
he was about to die.
34 Then the crowd replied to him, "We have heard
from the law that the Messiah will remain forever.
So how can you say, 'The Son of Man must be lifted
up'? Who is this Son of Man?"
35 Jesus answered, "The light will be with you only
a little longer. Walk while you have the light so that
darkness doesn't overtake you. The one who walks
in darkness doesn't know where he's going. 36 While
you have the light, believe in the light so that you may
become children of light." Jesus said this, then went
away and hid from them.

ISAIAH'S PROPHECIES FULFILLED

37 Even though he had performed so many signs in
their presence, they did not believe in him. 38 This was
to fulfill the word of Isaiah the prophet, who said:[C]

Lord, who has believed our message?
And to whom has the arm of the Lord been
revealed?[D]

39 This is why they were unable to believe, because
Isaiah also said:

40 **He has blinded their eyes**
and hardened their hearts,
so that they would not see
with their eyes
or understand with their hearts,
and turn,
and I would heal them.[E]

41 Isaiah said these things because[F] he saw his glory
and spoke about him.
42 Nevertheless, many did believe in him even
among the rulers, but because of the Pharisees they
did not confess him, so that they would not be banned
from the synagogue. 43 For they loved human praise
more than praise from God.

A SUMMARY OF JESUS'S MISSION

44 Jesus cried out, "The one who believes in me believes not in me, but in him who sent me. 45 And the
one who sees me sees him who sent me. 46 I have
come as light into the world, so that everyone who
believes in me would not remain in darkness. 47 If
anyone hears my words and doesn't keep them, I do
not judge him; for I did not come to judge the world
but to save the world. 48 The one who rejects me and
doesn't receive my sayings has this as his judge:[G] The
word I have spoken will judge him on the last day.
49 For I have not spoken on my own, but the Father
himself who sent me has given me a command to say
everything I have said. 50 I know that his command
is eternal life. So the things that I speak, I speak just
as the Father has told me."

JESUS WASHES HIS DISCIPLES' FEET

13 Before the Passover Festival, Jesus knew that
his hour had come to depart from this world
to the Father. Having loved his own who were in the
world, he loved them to the end.

[A] **12:28** Other mss read *your Son* [B] **12:32** Or *exalted*, also in v. 34
[C] **12:38** Lit *which he said* [D] **12:38** Is 53:1 [E] **12:40** Is 6:10 [F] **12:41** Other
mss read *when* [G] **12:48** Lit *has the one judging him*

PRODUCTION

Almost all of the spices and perfumes used in Israel came from plants, although a few came from animal products. Most of the aroma-producing plants did not grow in Israel. They came to Israel as imports from places such as India, Asia Minor, Arabia, Egypt, and Africa.[1]

Some plants produced leaves or seeds that people used in making fragrant spices. Cumin, for example, was a spice sometimes used in bread. It came from a soft seed that was pulverized before being used in baking. Aloe and mint came from leaves; dill came from seeds as well as leaves. Coriander, which was included in many perfumes, also came from seeds.

Other fragrances were rendered from plant resins. Two of the most popular resins were frankincense and myrrh. Frankincense came from a tree by that name. It produced a resinous gum that was collected by removing the bark of the tree and cutting into the trunk. Similarly, myrrh was gum—collected from a shrub in Africa and Arabia.

Still other spices and perfumes were produced as oils. For instance, nard was a very expensive fragrant oil produced from a plant native to India. Once the oil was extracted from the plant, it was preserved in sealed alabaster jars before being exported to Israel.[2]

ACQUISITION

People in Israel often acquired perfumes and spices by means of one of the busy trade routes that traversed through Israel. One of the better-known biblical references to such a route is in Genesis 37; Joseph's brothers sold him to Ishmaelite traders coming from Gilead, their camels loaded with an assortment of "gum, balsam, and resin" (v. 25) from distant places and were on their way to Egypt.

The road that took the Ishmaelites through Dothan was one of several major land routes spice traders commonly used. Another route started in Asia Minor (in modern Turkey) and ended in Israel. Yet another route that ended in Israel began in what is now Iraq and Iran. All of the land routes went through Israel, making the purchase of spices and perfumes possible—albeit expensive.

Another major trade route, this one along the Mediterranean coast, likewise brought spices and perfumes to the country. The Phoenicians controlled the sea route until the Roman era. Ships departed from the ports of Lebanon, made stops at some of the key coastal ports in Israel, and ended in Egypt.[3]

USE

Because of their wide variety of possible uses, spices and perfumes were popular with people in the

Faience *aryballos* (perfume flask); probably from Rhodes; dates from 600–550 BC. Greek men used these bottles, which they hung from their wrists, to carry oil for cleaning their bodies after exercise.

Alabastron (perfume flask) decorated with griffins below a lotus and palmette chain; made in Corinth; dates from 680–650 BC.

ancient Near East. The fragrances of the spices and perfumes made them appealing as cosmetics. People would mix spices with oils and rub the ointment on their skin. They would also sprinkle them on garments, couches, and beds to give them a pleasant scent (see Ps 45:8; Pr 7:17).

Not only were spices and perfumes enjoyed for their appealing fragrance but also for the social status implied by having them. Since they were imported from so far away, they were typically expensive.[4] When Hezekiah gave a tour of his treasure house to the Babylonians who visited him, he showed them his spices along with his other precious possessions (2Kg 20:13). The wise men presented to Jesus not only gold, but also frankincense and myrrh (Mt 2:11), providing evidence of their value. The nard with which Mary anointed Jesus was valued at the lavish price of three hundred denarii (Jn 12:3–5), indicating the sacrificial nature of her act.

The liturgical role of spices and perfumes was linked to the use of incense in temple worship. Incense was the perfumed smoke that emanated from burning spices blended with other materials.

Burial practices in Israel also demanded a constant supply of spices. Spices were used in burial preparation to provide a pleasant aroma in the otherwise unpleasant environment associated with the decomposition of a corpse.[5] ✣

This small glass vessel from Rhodes probably contained scented oil. Rhodes was a center for glass manufacturing; dates from 460–440 BC.

---

[1] Claude Mariottini, "Spices" in *HolBD*, 1297. [2] "Plants of the Bible" in *The Lion Encyclopedia of the Bible* (Herts, UK: Lion), 15. [3] "Trade and Commerce" in *The Lion Encyclopedia of the Bible*, 237–38. [4] Victor H. Matthews, "Perfumes and Spices" in *ABD*, 5:227. [5] Gerald L. Borchert, *John 12–21*, NAC (2002), 282.

2 Now when it was time for supper, the devil had already put it into the heart of Judas, Simon Iscariot's son,[A] to betray him. 3 Jesus knew that the Father had given everything into his hands, that he had come from God, and that he was going back to God. 4 So he got up from supper, laid aside his outer clothing, took a towel, and tied it around himself. 5 Next, he poured water into a basin and began to wash his disciples' feet and to dry them with the towel tied around him.

6 He came to Simon Peter, who asked him, "Lord, are you going to wash my feet?"

7 Jesus answered him, "What I'm doing you don't realize now, but afterward you will understand."

8 "You will never wash my feet," Peter said.

Jesus replied, "If I don't wash you, you have no part with me."

9 Simon Peter said to him, "Lord, not only my feet, but also my hands and my head."

10 "One who has bathed," Jesus told him, "doesn't need to wash anything except his feet, but he is completely clean. You are clean, but not all of you." 11 For he knew who would betray him. This is why he said, "Not all of you are clean."

THE MEANING OF FOOT WASHING

12 When Jesus had washed their feet and put on his outer clothing, he reclined again and said to them, "Do you know what I have done for you? 13 You call me Teacher and Lord — and you are speaking rightly, since that is what I am. 14 So if I, your Lord and Teacher, have washed your feet, you also ought to wash one another's feet. 15 For I have given you an example, that you also should do just as I have done for you.

16 "Truly I tell you, a servant is not greater than his master,[B] and a messenger is not greater than the one who sent him. 17 If you know these things, you are blessed if you do them.

18 "I'm not speaking about all of you; I know those I have chosen. But the Scripture must be fulfilled: **The one who eats my bread**[C] **has raised his heel against me.**[D] 19 I am telling you now before it happens, so that when it does happen you will believe that I am he. 20 Truly I tell you, whoever receives anyone I send receives me, and the one who receives me receives him who sent me."

JUDAS'S BETRAYAL PREDICTED

21 When Jesus had said this, he was troubled in his spirit and testified, "Truly I tell you, one of you will betray me."

22 The disciples started looking at one another — uncertain which one he was speaking about. 23 One of his disciples, the one Jesus loved, was reclining close beside Jesus.[E] 24 Simon Peter motioned to him to find out who it was he was talking about. 25 So he leaned back against Jesus and asked him, "Lord, who is it?"

26 Jesus replied, "He's the one I give the piece of bread to after I have dipped it." When he had dipped the bread, he gave it to Judas, Simon Iscariot's son.[A] 27 After Judas ate the piece of bread, Satan entered him. So Jesus told him, "What you're doing, do quickly."

28 None of those reclining at the table knew why he said this to him. 29 Since Judas kept the money-bag, some thought that Jesus was telling him, "Buy what we need for the festival," or that he should give something to the poor. 30 After receiving the piece of bread, he immediately left. And it was night.

THE NEW COMMAND

31 When he had left, Jesus said, "Now the Son of Man is glorified, and God is glorified in him. 32 If God is glorified in him,[F] God will also glorify him in himself and will glorify him at once. 33 Little children, I am with you a little while longer. You will look for me, and just as I told the Jews, so now I tell you, 'Where I am going, you cannot come.'

34 "I give you a new command: Love one another. Just as I have loved you, you are also to love one another. 35 By this everyone will know that you are my disciples, if you love one another."

PETER'S DENIALS PREDICTED

36 "Lord," Simon Peter said to him, "where are you going?"

Jesus answered, "Where I am going you cannot follow me now, but you will follow later."

37 "Lord," Peter asked, "why can't I follow you now? I will lay down my life for you."

38 Jesus replied, "Will you lay down your life for me? Truly I tell you, a rooster will not crow until you have denied me three times.

THE WAY TO THE FATHER

14 "Don't let your heart be troubled. Believe[G] in God; believe also in me. 2 In my Father's house are many rooms. If it were not so, would I have told you that I am going to prepare a place for you? 3 If I go away and prepare a place for you, I will come again and take you to myself, so that where I am you may be also. 4 You know the way to where I am going."[H]

5 "Lord," Thomas said, "we don't know where you're going. How can we know the way?"

6 Jesus told him, "I am the way, the truth, and the life. No one comes to the Father except through me.

[A] **13:2,26** Or *Judas Iscariot, Simon's son* [B] **13:16** Or *lord* [C] **13:18** Other mss read *eats bread with me* [D] **13:18** Ps 41:9 [E] **13:23** Lit *reclining at Jesus's breast*; that is, on his right; Jn 1:18 [F] **13:32** Other mss omit *If God is glorified in him* [G] **14:1** Or *You believe* [H] **14:4** Other mss read this verse: *And you know where I am going, and you know the way*

7 If you know me, you will also know[A] my Father. From
now on you do know him and have seen him."

JESUS REVEALS THE FATHER

8 "Lord," said Philip, "show us the Father, and that's
enough for us."

9 Jesus said to him, "Have I been among you all
this time and you do not know me, Philip? The one
who has seen me has seen the Father. How can you
say, 'Show us the Father'? 10 Don't you believe that I
am in the Father and the Father is in me? The words
I speak to you I do not speak on my own. The Father
who lives in me does his works. 11 Believe me that I
am in the Father and the Father is in me. Otherwise,
believe[B] because of the works themselves.

PRAYING IN JESUS'S NAME

12 "Truly I tell you, the one who believes in me will also
do the works that I do. And he will do even greater
works than these, because I am going to the Father.
13 Whatever you ask in my name, I will do it so that
the Father may be glorified in the Son. 14 If you ask
me[C] anything in my name, I will do it.[D]

ANOTHER COUNSELOR PROMISED

15 "If you love me, you will keep[E] my commands. 16 And
I will ask the Father, and he will give you another
Counselor[F] to be with you forever. 17 He is the Spirit
of truth. The world is unable to receive him because
it doesn't see him or know him. But you do know him,
because he remains with you and will be[G] in you.

THE FATHER, THE SON, AND THE HOLY SPIRIT

18 "I will not leave you as orphans; I am coming to
you. 19 In a little while the world will no longer see
me, but you will see me. Because I live, you will live
too. 20 On that day you will know that I am in my Father, you are in me, and I am in you. 21 The one who
has my commands and keeps them is the one who
loves me. And the one who loves me will be loved
by my Father. I also will love him and will reveal
myself to him."

22 Judas (not Iscariot) said to him, "Lord, how is it
you're going to reveal yourself to us and not to the
world?"

23 Jesus answered, "If anyone loves me, he will keep
my word. My Father will love him, and we will come
to him and make our home with him. 24 The one who
doesn't love me will not keep my words. The word
that you hear is not mine but is from the Father who
sent me.

25 "I have spoken these things to you while I remain
with you. 26 But the Counselor, the Holy Spirit, whom
the Father will send in my name, will teach you all
things and remind you of everything I have told you.

Roman-era frieze depicting a banquet scene. Some persons recline. A three-legged table with food is in the center. Two servants, shown in smaller scale, attend the banqueters.

JESUS'S GIFT OF PEACE

27 "Peace I leave with you. My peace I give to you. I
do not give to you as the world gives. Don't let your
heart be troubled or fearful. 28 You have heard me tell
you, 'I am going away and I am coming to you.' If you
loved me, you would rejoice that I am going to the
Father, because the Father is greater than I. 29 I have
told you now before it happens so that when it does
happen you may believe. 30 I will not talk with you
much longer, because the ruler of the world is coming. He has no power over me.[H] 31 On the contrary, so
that the world may know that I love the Father, I do
as the Father commanded me.

"Get up; let's leave this place.

THE VINE AND THE BRANCHES

15 "I am the true vine, and my Father is the gardener. 2 Every branch in me that does not produce fruit he removes, and he prunes every branch
that produces fruit so that it will produce more fruit.
3 You are already clean because of the word I have
spoken to you. 4 Remain in me, and I in you. Just as
a branch is unable to produce fruit by itself unless
it remains on the vine, neither can you unless you
remain in me. 5 I am the vine; you are the branches.
The one who remains in me and I in him produces
much fruit, because you can do nothing without
me. 6 If anyone does not remain in me, he is thrown
aside like a branch and he withers. They gather them,

[A] **14:7** Other mss read *If you had known me, you would have known*
[B] **14:11** Other mss read *believe me* [C] **14:14** Other mss omit *me*
[D] **14:14** Other mss omit all of v. 14 [E] **14:15** Other mss read *"If you love me, keep* (as a command) [F] **14:16** Or *advocate*, or *comforter*, also in v. 26 [G] **14:17** Other mss read *and is* [H] **14:30** Lit *He has nothing in me*

Foot Washing in Ancient Practice

by Don H. Stewart

Dated from the eighth–seventh centuries BC; a basin for washing a person's foot. Once the basin was filled with water, a person would rest his or her foot on the raised platform in the center.

By the first century AD, hospitable foot washing for one's guests was a standard cultural practice of Near Eastern peoples. In fact, to fail to offer such a gesture was an insult. Thus, at minimum, hosts provided a bowl of water and a towel by the door for guests to wash their own feet. On occasion, the host would provide one or more household servants to wash and dry the feet of the arriving guests. Sometimes a wife might wash the feet of special guests.

What happened to Jesus when he was a dinner guest at the home of Simon (a Pharisee) highlights the social importance of washing a guest's feet in the first century (Lk 7:36–50). Jesus knew Simon had not followed the common and expected hospitable courtesies of the day. Failing to wash his guest's feet indicated Simon was rejecting Jesus and was trying to publicly humiliate him.[1] Jesus wanted Simon to understand that Jesus recognized that his host had slighted and insulted him.

Paul also addressed the importance of washing someone's feet as an expression of hospitality. Paul addressed how Timothy was to determine which widows qualified for church benevolence. Those who qualified had "brought up children, shown hospitality, washed the saints' feet, helped the afflicted, and devoted herself to every good work" (1Tm 5:10). ✣

[1] Kenneth E. Bailey, *Jesus through Middle Eastern Eyes: Cultural Studies in the Gospels* (Downers Grove, IL: IVP Academic, 2008), 247.

Gothic-style archway near the Gate of the Chain at Jerusalem. It has been filled in for secondary use as a Muslim public basin; the pipe near the ground brings in water for the washing of feet.

throw them into the fire, and they are burned. 7 If you remain in me and my words remain in you, ask whatever you want and it will be done for you. 8 My Father is glorified by this: that you produce much fruit and prove to be[A] my disciples.

CHRISTLIKE LOVE

9 "As the Father has loved me, I have also loved you. Remain in my love. 10 If you keep my commands you will remain in my love, just as I have kept my Father's commands and remain in his love.

11 "I have told you these things so that my joy may be in you and your joy may be complete.

12 "This is my command: Love one another as I have loved you. 13 No one has greater love than this: to lay down his life for his friends. 14 You are my friends if you do what I command you. 15 I do not call you servants anymore, because a servant doesn't know what his master[B] is doing. I have called you friends, because I have made known to you everything I have heard from my Father. 16 You did not choose me, but I chose you. I appointed you to go and produce fruit and that your fruit should remain, so that whatever you ask the Father in my name, he will give you.

17 "This is what I command you: Love one another.

PERSECUTIONS PREDICTED

18 "If the world hates you, understand that it hated me before it hated you. 19 If you were of the world, the world would love you as its own. However, because you are not of the world, but I have chosen you out of it, the world hates you. 20 Remember the word I spoke to you: 'A servant is not greater than his master.' If they persecuted me, they will also persecute you. If they kept my word, they will also keep yours. 21 But they will do all these things to you on account of my name, because they don't know the one who sent me. 22 If I had not come and spoken to them, they would not be guilty of sin. Now they have no excuse for their sin. 23 The one who hates me also hates my Father. 24 If I had not done the works among them that no one else has done, they would not be guilty of sin. Now they have seen and hated both me and my Father. 25 But this happened so that the statement written in their law might be fulfilled: **They hated me for no reason.**[C]

THE COUNSELOR'S MINISTRY

26 "When the Counselor comes, the one I will send to you from the Father — the Spirit of truth who proceeds from the Father — he will testify about me. 27 You also will testify, because you have been with me from the beginning.

16 "I have told you these things to keep you from stumbling. 2 They will ban you from the synagogues. In fact, a time is coming when anyone who kills you will think he is offering service to God. 3 They will do these things because they haven't known the Father or me. 4 But I have told you these things so that when their time[D] comes you will remember I told them to you. I didn't tell you these things from the beginning, because I was with you. 5 But now I am going away to him who sent me, and not one of you asks me, 'Where are you going?' 6 Yet, because I have spoken these things to you, sorrow has filled your heart. 7 Nevertheless, I am telling you the truth. It is for your benefit that I go away, because if I don't go away the Counselor will not come to you. If I go, I will send him to you. 8 When he comes, he will convict the world about sin, righteousness, and judgment: 9 About sin, because they do not believe in me; 10 about righteousness, because I am going to the Father and you will no longer see me; 11 and about judgment, because the ruler of this world has been judged.

12 "I still have many things to tell you, but you can't bear them now. 13 When the Spirit of truth comes, he will guide you into all the truth. For he will not speak on his own, but he will speak whatever he hears. He will also declare to you what is to come. 14 He will glorify me, because he will take from what is mine and declare it to you. 15 Everything the Father has is mine. This is why I told you that he takes from what is mine and will declare it to you.

SORROW TURNED TO JOY

16 "In a little while, you will no longer see me; again in a little while, you will see me."[E]

17 Then some of his disciples said to one another, "What is this he's telling us: 'In a little while, you will not see me; again in a little while, you will see me,' and, 'Because I am going to the Father'?" 18 They said, "What is this he is saying,[F] 'In a little while'? We don't know what he's talking about."

19 Jesus knew they wanted to ask him, and so he said to them, "Are you asking one another about what I said, 'In a little while, you will not see me; again in a little while, you will see me'? 20 Truly I tell you, you will weep and mourn, but the world will rejoice. You will become sorrowful, but your sorrow will turn to joy. 21 When a woman is in labor, she has pain because her time has come. But when she has given birth to a child, she no longer remembers the suffering because of the joy that a person has been born into the world. 22 So you also have sorrow[G] now. But I will see you again. Your hearts will rejoice, and no one will take away your joy from you.

[A] **15:8** Or *and become* [B] **15:15** Or *lord* [C] **15:25** Ps 69:4 [D] **16:4** Other mss read *when the time* [E] **16:16** Other mss add *because I am going to the Father* [F] **16:18** Other mss omit *he is saying* [G] **16:22** Other mss read *will have sorrow*

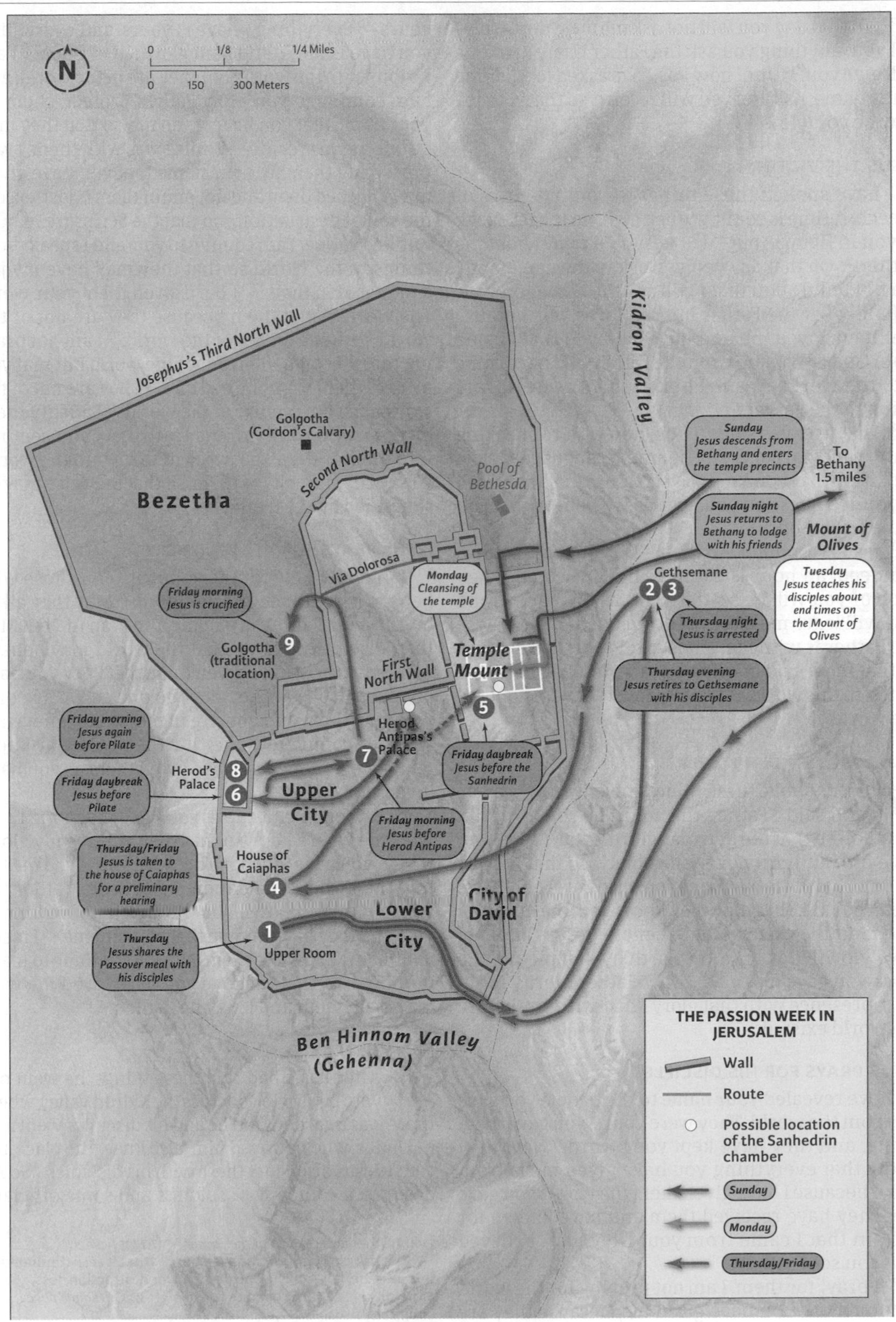
N
0 1/8 1/4 Miles
0 150 300 Meters
Josephus's Third North Wall
Golgotha
(Gordon's Calvary)
Second North Wall
Bezetha
Pool of
Bethesda
Kidron Valley
Sunday
Jesus descends from
Bethany and enters
the temple precincts
To
Bethany
1.5 miles
Sunday night
Jesus returns to
Bethany to lodge
with his friends
Mount of
Olives
Via Dolorosa
Monday
Cleansing of
the temple
Gethsemane
Tuesday
Jesus teaches his
disciples about
end times on
the Mount of
Olives
Friday morning
Jesus is crucified
Thursday night
Jesus is arrested
Golgotha
(traditional
location)
Temple
Mount
First
North Wall
Thursday evening
Jesus retires to Gethsemane
with his disciples
Friday morning
Jesus again
before Pilate
Herod
Antipas's
Palace
Herod's
Palace
Friday daybreak
Jesus before the
Sanhedrin
Friday daybreak
Jesus before
Pilate
Upper
City
Friday morning
Jesus before
Herod Antipas
Thursday/Friday
Jesus is taken to
the house of Caiaphas
for a preliminary
hearing
House of
Caiaphas
City of
David
Lower
City
Thursday
Jesus shares the
Passover meal with
his disciples
Upper Room
Ben Hinnom Valley
(Gehenna)
THE PASSION WEEK IN
JERUSALEM
Wall
Route
Possible location
of the Sanhedrin
chamber
Sunday
Monday
Thursday/Friday

23 "In that day you will not ask me anything. Truly I tell you, anything you ask the Father in my name, he will give you. 24 Until now you have asked for nothing in my name. Ask and you will receive, so that your joy may be complete.

JESUS THE VICTOR

25 "I have spoken these things to you in figures of speech. A time is coming when I will no longer speak to you in figures, but I will tell you plainly about the Father. 26 On that day you will ask in my name, and I am not telling you that I will ask the Father on your behalf. 27 For the Father himself loves you, because you have loved me and have believed that I came from God.[A] 28 I came from the Father and have come into the world. Again, I am leaving the world and going to the Father."

29 His disciples said, "Look, now you're speaking plainly and not using any figurative language. 30 Now we know that you know everything and don't need anyone to question you. By this we believe that you came from God."

31 Jesus responded to them, "Do you now believe? 32 Indeed, an hour is coming, and has come, when each of you will be scattered to his own home, and you will leave me alone. Yet I am not alone, because the Father is with me. 33 I have told you these things so that in me you may have peace. You will have suffering in this world. Be courageous! I have conquered the world."

JESUS PRAYS FOR HIMSELF

17 Jesus spoke these things, looked up to heaven, and said, "Father, the hour has come. Glorify your Son so that the Son may glorify you, 2 since you gave him authority over all people,[B] so that he may give eternal life to everyone you have given him. 3 This is eternal life: that they may know you, the only true God, and the one you have sent — Jesus Christ. 4 I have glorified you on the earth by completing the work you gave me to do. 5 Now, Father, glorify me in your presence with that glory I had with you before the world existed.

JESUS PRAYS FOR HIS DISCIPLES

6 "I have revealed your name to the people you gave me from the world. They were yours, you gave them to me, and they have kept your word. 7 Now they know that everything you have given me is from you, 8 because I have given them the words you gave me. They have received them and have known for certain that I came from you. They have believed that you sent me.

9 "I pray[C] for them. I am not praying for the world but for those you have given me, because they are yours. 10 Everything I have is yours, and everything you have is mine, and I am glorified in them. 11 I am no longer in the world, but they are in the world, and I am coming to you. Holy Father, protect[D] them by your name that you have given me, so that they may be one as we are one. 12 While I was with them, I was protecting them by your name that you have given me. I guarded them and not one of them is lost, except the son of destruction,[E] so that the Scripture may be fulfilled. 13 Now I am coming to you, and I speak these things in the world so that they may have my joy completed in them. 14 I have given them your word. The world hated them because they are not of the world, just as I am not of the world. 15 I am not praying that you take them out of the world but that you protect them from the evil one. 16 They are not of the world, just as I am not of the world. 17 Sanctify them by the truth; your word is truth. 18 As you sent me into the world, I also have sent them into the world. 19 I sanctify myself for them, so that they also may be sanctified by the truth.

JESUS PRAYS FOR ALL BELIEVERS

20 "I pray not only for these, but also for those who believe in me through their word. 21 May they all be one, as you, Father, are in me and I am in you. May they also be[F] in us, so that the world may believe you sent me. 22 I have given them the glory you have given me, so that they may be one as we are one. 23 I am in them and you are in me, so that they may be made completely one, that the world may know you have sent me and have loved them as you have loved me.

24 "Father, I want those you have given me to be with me where I am, so that they will see my glory, which you have given me because you loved me before the world's foundation. 25 Righteous Father, the world has not known you. However, I have known you, and they have known that you sent me. 26 I made your name known to them and will continue to make it known, so that the love you have loved me with may be in them and I may be in them."

JESUS BETRAYED

18 After Jesus had said these things, he went out with his disciples across the Kidron Valley, where there was a garden, and he and his disciples went into it. 2 Judas, who betrayed him, also knew the place, because Jesus often met there with his disciples. 3 So Judas took a company of soldiers and some officials[G]

[A] **16:27** Other mss read *from the Father* [B] **17:2** Or *flesh* [C] **17:9** Lit *ask* (throughout this passage) [D] **17:11** Lit *keep* (throughout this passage) [E] **17:12** The one destined for destruction, loss, or perdition [F] **17:21** Other mss add *one* [G] **18:3** Or *temple police*, or *officers*, also in vv. 12,18,22

from the chief priests and the Pharisees and came
there with lanterns, torches, and weapons.
4 Then Jesus, knowing everything that was about
to happen to him, went out and said to them, "Who
is it that you're seeking?"
5 "Jesus of Nazareth," they answered.
"I am he," Jesus told them.
Judas, who betrayed him, was also standing with
them. 6 When Jesus told them, "I am he," they stepped
back and fell to the ground.
7 Then he asked them again, "Who is it that you're
seeking?"
"Jesus of Nazareth," they said.
8 "I told you I am he," Jesus replied. "So if you're
looking for me, let these men go." 9 This was to fulfill
the words he had said: "I have not lost one of those
you have given me."
10 Then Simon Peter, who had a sword, drew it,
struck the high priest's servant, and cut off his right
ear. (The servant's name was Malchus.)
11 At that, Jesus said to Peter, "Put your sword away!
Am I not to drink the cup the Father has given me?"

JESUS ARRESTED AND TAKEN TO ANNAS

12 Then the company of soldiers, the commander,
and the Jewish officials arrested Jesus and tied him
up. 13 First they led him to Annas, since he was the
father-in-law of Caiaphas, who was high priest that
year. 14 Caiaphas was the one who had advised the
Jews that it would be better for one man to die for
the people.

PETER DENIES JESUS

15 Simon Peter was following Jesus, as was another disciple. That disciple was an acquaintance of
the high priest; so he went with Jesus into the high
priest's courtyard. 16 But Peter remained standing
outside by the door. So the other disciple, the one
known to the high priest, went out and spoke to the
girl who was the doorkeeper and brought Peter in.
17 Then the servant girl who was the doorkeeper
said to Peter, "You aren't one of this man's disciples
too, are you?"
"I am not," he said. 18 Now the servants and the
officials had made a charcoal fire, because it was
cold. They were standing there warming themselves,
and Peter was standing with them, warming himself.

JESUS BEFORE ANNAS

19 The high priest questioned Jesus about his disciples
and about his teaching.
20 "I have spoken openly to the world," Jesus answered him. "I have always taught in the synagogue
and in the temple, where all the Jews gather, and
I haven't spoken anything in secret. 21 Why do you
question me? Question those who heard what I told
them. Look, they know what I said."
22 When he had said these things, one of the officials standing by slapped Jesus, saying, "Is this the
way you answer the high priest?"
23 "If I have spoken wrongly," Jesus answered him,
"give evidence[A] about the wrong; but if rightly, why
do you hit me?" 24 Then Annas sent him bound to
Caiaphas the high priest.

PETER DENIES JESUS TWICE MORE

25 Now Simon Peter was standing and warming himself. They said to him, "You aren't one of his disciples
too, are you?"
He denied it and said, "I am not."
26 One of the high priest's servants, a relative of the
man whose ear Peter had cut off, said, "Didn't I see
you with him in the garden?" 27 Peter denied it again.
Immediately a rooster crowed.

JESUS BEFORE PILATE

28 Then they led Jesus from Caiaphas to the governor's headquarters. It was early morning. They did
not enter the headquarters themselves; otherwise
they would be defiled and unable to eat the Passover.
29 So Pilate came out to them and said, "What charge
do you bring against this man?"
30 They answered him, "If this man weren't a criminal,[B] we wouldn't have handed him over to you."
31 Pilate told them, "You take him and judge him
according to your law."
"It's not legal for us to put anyone to death," the
Jews declared. 32 They said this so that Jesus's words
might be fulfilled indicating what kind of death he
was going to die.
33 Then Pilate went back into the headquarters,
summoned Jesus, and said to him, "Are you the king
of the Jews?"
34 Jesus answered, "Are you asking this on your
own, or have others told you about me?"
35 "I'm not a Jew, am I?" Pilate replied. "Your own
nation and the chief priests handed you over to me.
What have you done?"
36 "My kingdom is not of this world," said Jesus. "If
my kingdom were of this world, my servants would
fight, so that I wouldn't be handed over to the Jews.
But as it is,[C] my kingdom is not from here."
37 "You are a king then?" Pilate asked.
"You say that I'm a king," Jesus replied. "I was born
for this, and I have come into the world for this: to
testify to the truth. Everyone who is of the truth listens to my voice."
38 "What is truth?" said Pilate.

[A] **18:23** Or *him, "testify* [B] **18:30** Lit *an evil doer* [C] **18:36** Or *But now*

The Kidron Valley

by Jeff S. Anderson

Just east of the Old City of Jerusalem lies a deep valley called the Kidron. This important valley runs north to south and separates the ancient city of David and the Temple Mount from the Mount of Olives to the east. The highest point on the Mount of Olives is 2,636 feet above sea level, some 400 feet above the valley floor, which lies below. The ravine of the Kidron is precipitous as it drops 4,000 feet in just twenty miles, where it ultimately empties into the Dead Sea, almost 1,300 feet below sea level. The slope of the Kidron immediately adjacent to the city of David is equally abrupt. Near the bottom of the valley floor lies a perennial spring called the Gihon, which produces up to four hundred thousand gallons of fresh water a day, enough for a small city like ancient Jerusalem. Two other peaks on the same ridge join the Mount of Olives; the one to the north is Mount Scopus. To the south is the Mount of Corruption, which is, according to tradition, where Solomon abandoned his promise to God and built numerous high places for Chemosh and Molech, gods of the Moabites and the Ammonites (1Kg 11:78).

A PHYSICAL BOUNDARY

Kidron is a place of ambiguity. In the Old Testament, Kidron is a consistent geographical marker of Jerusalem's eastern boundary. The word *Kidron* means "dark" or "unclear." To cross the Kidron was to cross a geographical boundary, to leave the city of David. The expression, "from the LORD's temple to the Kidron Valley" in 2 Kings 23:6 denotes such geographical limitations.

Both slopes of the Kidron Valley were also infamous burial places with a long history of association with ancient tombs, particularly the slope on the eastern side of the ravine. Many tombs from the time of the kings of Judah were excavated there, shortly after the 1967 Six-Day War.[1] Adjacent and among these tombs today is the village of Silwan, with forty thousand Palestinian and four hundred Jewish residents.[2] Significant evidence also indicates that in ancient times the slopes were terraced and used partially for agriculture (2Kg 23:4).[3]

A THEOLOGICAL BOUNDARY

The spatial framework of the Kidron denoted a geographical boundary—and a theological boundary as well. To cross the Kidron also meant to cross a metaphorical line. Let's take a few examples. Solomon established a vibrant center of foreign cult worship on the eastern slope of the Kidron, associating the site with idolatry and apostasy. The Old Testament conveys the

View of the Kidron Valley, as seen from the north. The cone-topped Tomb of Absalom rises from the valley floor; the Temple Mount is to the right.

accounts of three good kings, Asa, Hezekiah, and Josiah, who carried the unclean vessels from the temple to the Kidron Valley, a metaphorical boundary line, and burned the pagan altars and Asherah idols there. Josiah unceremoniously cast the dust of these idols on the graves of the common people (1Kg 15:13; 2Kg 23:4–12; 2Ch 15:16; 29:16; 30:14). Later in Jewish, Christian, and Muslim tradition, the upper northern end of the Kidron became known as the Valley of Jehoshaphat, the place of the final judgment (Jl 3:12).[4] The intertestamental book of 1 Enoch (26:1–27:5) graphically depicts the Kidron and surrounding area as a cursed valley, a place where the cursed would gather at the last judgment.

The Kidron thus served as a boundary line, across which existed a spiritual wilderness, a burial ground and a dump of illicit cult objects—a literal and metaphorical graveyard. Today more than one hundred fifty thousand Jewish, Christian, and Muslim graves cover the western slopes of the Mount of Olives, the valley floor, and the slopes of the Kidron all the way up to the eastern wall of the Old City of Jerusalem. ✣

The Stepped Stone Structure is one of the largest Iron Age structures in Israel. Located in the City of David, its exact purpose has been debated; some believe it supported a royal building, maybe David's palace.

[1] David Ussishkin, *The Village of Silwan: The Necropolis from the Period of the Judean Kingdom* (Jerusalem: Israel Exploration Society, 1993). [2] Raphael Greenberg and Yonathan Mizrachi, *From Shiloah to Silwan* (Jerusalem: Keter, 2011), 34. [3] Lawrence E. Stager, "The Archaeology of the East Slope of Jerusalem and the Terraces of the Kidron," *JNES* 41.2 (1982): 111–21 (esp. 113). [4] John Briggs Curtis, "An Investigation of the Mount of Olives in Judeo-Christian Tradition," *Hebrew Union College Annual* (*HUCA*) 23 (1957): 137–80.

JESUS OR BARABBAS

After he had said this, he went out to the Jews again and told them, "I find no grounds for charging him. 39 You have a custom that I release one prisoner to you at the Passover. So, do you want me to release to you the king of the Jews?"

40 They shouted back, "Not this man, but Barabbas!" Now Barabbas was a revolutionary.[A]

JESUS FLOGGED AND MOCKED

19 Then Pilate took Jesus and had him flogged. 2 The soldiers also twisted together a crown of thorns, put it on his head, and clothed him in a purple robe. 3 And they kept coming up to him and saying, "Hail, king of the Jews!" and were slapping his face.

4 Pilate went outside again and said to them, "Look, I'm bringing him out to you to let you know I find no grounds for charging him." 5 Then Jesus came out wearing the crown of thorns and the purple robe. Pilate said to them, "Here is the man!"

PILATE SENTENCES JESUS TO DEATH

6 When the chief priests and the temple servants[B] saw him, they shouted, "Crucify! Crucify!"

Pilate responded, "Take him and crucify him yourselves, since I find no grounds for charging him."

Dungeon where, according to fourth-century tradition, Jesus would have been scourged not only by Pilate but by Caiaphas, and where Peter and John would have been held and scourged for preaching in the temple area.

7 "We have a law," the Jews replied to him, "and according to that law he ought to die, because he made himself the Son of God."

8 When Pilate heard this statement, he was more afraid than ever. 9 He went back into the headquarters and asked Jesus, "Where are you from?" But Jesus did not give him an answer. 10 So Pilate said to him, "Do you refuse to speak to me? Don't you know that I have the authority to release you and the authority to crucify you?"

11 "You would have no authority over me at all," Jesus answered him, "if it hadn't been given you from above. This is why the one who handed me over to you has the greater sin."

12 From that moment Pilate kept trying[C] to release him. But the Jews shouted, "If you release this man, you are not Caesar's friend. Anyone who makes himself a king opposes Caesar!"

13 When Pilate heard these words, he brought Jesus outside. He sat down on the judge's seat in a place called the Stone Pavement (but in Aramaic,[D] *Gabbatha*). 14 It was the preparation day for the Passover, and it was about noon.[E] Then he told the Jews, "Here is your king!"

15 They shouted, "Take him away! Take him away! Crucify him!"

Pilate said to them, "Should I crucify your king?"

"We have no king but Caesar!" the chief priests answered.

16 Then he handed him over to be crucified.

THE CRUCIFIXION

Then they took Jesus away.[F] 17 Carrying the cross by himself, he went out to what is called Place of the Skull, which in Aramaic is called *Golgotha*. 18 There they crucified him and two others with him, one on either side, with Jesus in the middle. 19 Pilate also had a sign made and put on the cross. It said: JESUS OF NAZARETH, THE KING OF THE JEWS. 20 Many of the Jews read this sign, because the place where Jesus was crucified was near the city, and it was written in Aramaic, Latin, and Greek. 21 So the chief priests of the Jews said to Pilate, "Don't write, 'The king of the Jews,' but that he said, 'I am the king of the Jews.'"

22 Pilate replied, "What I have written, I have written."

23 When the soldiers crucified Jesus, they took his clothes and divided them into four parts, a part for each soldier. They also took the tunic, which was seamless, woven in one piece from the top. 24 So they said to one another, "Let's not tear it, but cast lots for it, to see who gets it." This happened that the Scripture

[A] **18:40** Or *robber*; see Jn 10:1,8 for the same Gk word used here
[B] **19:6** Or *temple police*, or *officers* [C] **19:12** Lit *Pilate was trying*
[D] **19:13** Or *Hebrew*, also in vv. 17,20 [E] **19:14** Lit *about the sixth hour*
[F] **19:16** Other mss add *and led him out*

might be fulfilled that says: **They divided my clothes among themselves, and they cast lots for my clothing.**[A] This is what the soldiers did.

JESUS'S PROVISION FOR HIS MOTHER

25 Standing by the cross of Jesus were his mother, his mother's sister, Mary the wife of Clopas, and Mary Magdalene. 26 When Jesus saw his mother and the disciple he loved standing there, he said to his mother, "Woman, here is your son." 27 Then he said to the disciple, "Here is your mother." And from that hour the disciple took her into his home.

THE FINISHED WORK OF JESUS

28 After this, when Jesus knew that everything was now finished that the Scripture might be fulfilled, he said, "I'm thirsty." 29 A jar full of sour wine was sitting there; so they fixed a sponge full of sour wine on a hyssop branch and held it up to his mouth.

30 When Jesus had received the sour wine, he said, "It is finished." Then bowing his head, he gave up his spirit.

JESUS'S SIDE PIERCED

31 Since it was the preparation day, the Jews did not want the bodies to remain on the cross on the Sabbath (for that Sabbath was a special[B] day). They requested that Pilate have the men's legs broken and that their bodies be taken away. 32 So the soldiers came and broke the legs of the first man and of the other one who had been crucified with him. 33 When they came to Jesus, they did not break his legs since they saw that he was already dead. 34 But one of the soldiers pierced his side with a spear, and at once blood and water came out. 35 He who saw this has testified so that you also may believe. His testimony is true, and he knows he is telling the truth. 36 For these things happened so that the Scripture would be fulfilled: **Not one of his bones will be broken.**[C] 37 Also, another Scripture says: **They will look at the one they pierced.**[D]

JESUS'S BURIAL

38 After this, Joseph of Arimathea, who was a disciple of Jesus — but secretly because of his fear of the Jews — asked Pilate that he might remove Jesus's body. Pilate gave him permission; so he came and took his body away. 39 Nicodemus (who had previously come to him at night) also came, bringing a mixture of about seventy-five pounds[E] of myrrh and aloes. 40 They took Jesus's body and wrapped it in linen cloths with the fragrant spices, according to the burial custom of the Jews. 41 There was a garden in the place where he was crucified. A new tomb was in the garden; no one had yet been placed in it. 42 They placed Jesus there because of the Jewish day of preparation and since the tomb was nearby.

THE EMPTY TOMB

20 On the first day of the week Mary Magdalene came to the tomb early, while it was still dark. She saw that the stone had been removed from the tomb. 2 So she went running to Simon Peter and to the other disciple, the one Jesus loved, and said to them, "They've taken the Lord out of the tomb, and we don't know where they've put him!"

3 At that, Peter and the other disciple went out, heading for the tomb. 4 The two were running together, but the other disciple outran Peter and got to the tomb first. 5 Stooping down, he saw the linen cloths lying there, but he did not go in. 6 Then, following him, Simon Peter also came. He entered the tomb and saw the linen cloths lying there. 7 The wrapping that had been on his head was not lying with the linen cloths but was folded up in a separate place by itself. 8 The other disciple, who had reached the tomb first, then also went in, saw, and believed. 9 For they did not yet understand the Scripture that he must rise from the dead. 10 Then the disciples returned to the place where they were staying.

MARY MAGDALENE SEES THE RISEN LORD

11 But Mary stood outside the tomb, crying. As she was crying, she stooped to look into the tomb. 12 She saw two angels in white sitting where Jesus's body had been lying, one at the head and the other at the feet. 13 They said to her, "Woman, why are you crying?"

"Because they've taken away my Lord," she told them, "and I don't know where they've put him."

14 Having said this, she turned around and saw Jesus standing there, but she did not know it was Jesus. 15 "Woman," Jesus said to her, "why are you crying? Who is it that you're seeking?"

Supposing he was the gardener, she replied, "Sir, if you've carried him away, tell me where you've put him, and I will take him away."

16 Jesus said to her, "Mary."

Turning around, she said to him in Aramaic,[F] "*Rabboni!*" — which means "Teacher."

17 "Don't cling to me," Jesus told her, "since I have not yet ascended to the Father. But go to my brothers and tell them that I am ascending to my Father and your Father, to my God and your God."

18 Mary Magdalene went and announced to the disciples, "I have seen the Lord!" And she told them what[G] he had said to her.

[A] **19:24** Ps 22:18 [B] **19:31** Lit *great* [C] **19:36** Ex 12:46; Nm 9:12; Ps 34:20 [D] **19:37** Zch 12:10 [E] **19:39** Lit *a hundred litrai*; a Roman *litrai* = 12 ounces [F] **20:16** Or *Hebrew* [G] **20:18** Lit *these things*

THE DISCIPLES COMMISSIONED

19 When it was evening on that first day of the week,
the disciples were gathered together with the doors
locked because they feared the Jews. Jesus came, stood
among them, and said to them, "Peace be with you."
20 Having said this, he showed them his hands and
his side. So the disciples rejoiced when they saw the
Lord.
21 Jesus said to them again, "Peace be with you.
As the Father has sent me, I also send you." 22 After
saying this, he breathed on them and said,[A] "Receive
the Holy Spirit. 23 If you forgive the sins of any, they
are forgiven them; if you retain the sins of any, they
are retained."

THOMAS SEES AND BELIEVES

24 But Thomas (called "Twin"[B]), one of the Twelve, was
not with them when Jesus came. 25 So the other disciples were telling him, "We've seen the Lord!"
But he said to them, "If I don't see the mark of the nails in his hands, put my finger into the mark of the nails, and put my hand into his side, I will never believe."
26 A week later his disciples were indoors again,
and Thomas was with them. Even though the doors were locked, Jesus came and stood among them and said, "Peace be with you."
27 Then he said to Thomas, "Put your finger here
and look at my hands. Reach out your hand and put it into my side. Don't be faithless, but believe."
28 Thomas responded to him, "My Lord and my
God!"
29 Jesus said, "Because you have seen me, you have
believed.[C] Blessed are those who have not seen and yet believe."

THE PURPOSE OF THIS GOSPEL

30 Jesus performed many other signs in the presence
of his disciples that are not written in this book. 31 But
these are written so that you may believe that Jesus is the Messiah, the Son of God,[D] and that by believing you may have life in his name.

JESUS'S THIRD APPEARANCE TO THE DISCIPLES

21 After this, Jesus revealed himself again to his disciples by the Sea of Tiberias.[E] He revealed himself in this way:
2 Simon Peter, Thomas (called "Twin"[B]), Nathanael
from Cana of Galilee, Zebedee's sons, and two others of his disciples were together.

[A]20:22 Lit *he breathed and said to them* [B]20:24; 21:2 Gk *Didymus* [C]20:29 Or *have you believed?* [D]20:31 Or *that the Messiah, the Son of God, is Jesus* [E]21:1 Another name for the Sea of Galilee

A tomb from the Second Temple Period in the area of Jerusalem. Slabs can be seen on either side of the tomb. Bodies of the deceased were laid on these slabs, prepared with spices and wraps, and allowed to decompose.

[3] "I'm going fishing," Simon Peter said to them.
"We're coming with you," they told him. They went
out and got into the boat, but that night they caught
nothing.
[4] When daybreak came, Jesus stood on the
shore, but the disciples did not know it was Jesus.
[5] "Friends,"[A] Jesus called to them, "you don't have
any fish, do you?"
"No," they answered.
[6] "Cast the net on the right side of the boat," he told
them, "and you'll find some." So they did,[B] and they
were unable to haul it in because of the large number of fish. [7] The disciple, the one Jesus loved, said to
Peter, "It is the Lord!"
When Simon Peter heard that it was the Lord, he
tied his outer clothing around him (for he had tak-
en it off) and plunged into the sea. [8] Since they were
not far from land (about a hundred yards[C] away),
the other disciples came in the boat, dragging the
net full of fish.
[9] When they got out on land, they saw a charcoal
fire there, with fish lying on it, and bread. [10] "Bring
some of the fish you've just caught," Jesus told them.
[11] So Simon Peter climbed up and hauled the net
ashore, full of large fish — 153 of them. Even though
there were so many, the net was not torn.
[12] "Come and have breakfast," Jesus told them.
None of the disciples dared ask him, "Who are you?"
because they knew it was the Lord. [13] Jesus came,
took the bread, and gave it to them. He did the same
with the fish. [14] This was now the third time Jesus
appeared[D] to the disciples after he was raised from
the dead.

JESUS'S THREEFOLD RESTORATION OF PETER

[15] When they had eaten breakfast, Jesus asked Simon
Peter, "Simon, son of John,[E] do you love me more than
these?"
"Yes, Lord," he said to him, "you know that I love
you."
"Feed my lambs," he told him. [16] A second time he
asked him, "Simon, son of John, do you love me?"
"Yes, Lord," he said to him, "you know that I love
you."
"Shepherd my sheep," he told him.
[17] He asked him the third time, "Simon, son of John,
do you love me?"
Peter was grieved that he asked him the third time,
"Do you love me?" He said, "Lord, you know everything; you know that I love you."
"Feed my sheep," Jesus said. [18] "Truly I tell you,
when you were younger, you would tie your belt and
walk wherever you wanted. But when you grow old,
you will stretch out your hands and someone else
will tie you and carry you where you don't want to
go." [19] He said this to indicate by what kind of death
Peter would glorify God. After saying this, he told
him, "Follow me."

CORRECTING A FALSE REPORT

[20] So Peter turned around and saw the disciple Jesus
loved following them, the one who had leaned back
against Jesus at the supper and asked, "Lord, who is
the one that's going to betray you?" [21] When Peter
saw him, he said to Jesus, "Lord, what about him?"
[22] "If I want him to remain until I come," Jesus answered, "what is that to you? As for you, follow me."
[23] So this rumor[F] spread to the brothers and sisters
that this disciple would not die. Yet Jesus did not tell
him that he would not die, but, "If I want him to remain until I come, what is that to you?"

EPILOGUE

[24] This is the disciple who testifies to these things
and who wrote them down. We know that his testimony is true.
[25] And there are also many other things that Jesus
did, which, if every one of them were written down,
I suppose not even the world itself could contain the
books[G] that would be written.

[A] **21:5** Lit *"Children"* [B] **21:6** Lit *they cast* [C] **21:8** Lit *about two hundred cubits* [D] **21:14** Lit *was revealed* (v. 1) [E] **21:15–17** Other mss read *"Simon, son of Jonah*; Mt 16:17; Jn 1:42 [F] **21:23** Lit *this word* [G] **21:25** Lit *scroll*

ACTS

Located on the northwest corner of the agora in Athens, the temple of Hephaestus is one of the finest surviving examples of an ancient Greek temple.

INTRODUCTION TO

ACTS

Circumstances of Writing

The book of Acts is formally anonymous. The traditional view is that the author was the same person who wrote the Gospel of Luke—Luke the physician and traveling companion of Paul (Col 4:14; 2Tm 4:11; Phm 24). As early as the second century AD, church leaders such as Irenaeus wrote that Luke was the author of Acts. Irenaeus based his view on the "we" passages in Acts, five sections where the author changed from the third person ("he/she," "they") to first-person plural ("we") as he narrated the action (Ac 16:10–17; 20:5–15; 21:1–18; 27:1–29; 28:1–16). Irenaeus and many scholars since his time have interpreted these passages to mean that the author of Acts was one of the eyewitness companions of Paul. Luke fits this description better than any other candidate, especially given the similar themes between the Gospel of Luke and the book of Acts.

The date of composition of the book of Acts is to a large extent directly tied to the issue of authorship. A number of scholars have argued that Acts should be dated to the early 60s (at the time of Paul's imprisonment). Acts closes with Paul still in prison in Rome (28:30–31). Although it is possible that Luke wrote at a later date, a time when Paul had been released, it is more plausible to think that he completed this book while Paul was still in prison. Otherwise he would have ended the book by telling about Paul's release.

Contribution to the Bible

The book of Acts ties together the other books of the New Testament. It does so by first providing "the rest of the story" to the Gospels. The gospel and the message of the kingdom of God did not end with Jesus's ascension to heaven forty days after his resurrection but continued on in the lives of his followers. Acts shows us how the words and promises of Jesus were carried out by the apostles and other believers through the power of the Holy Spirit. Second, the book of Acts gives us the context for much of the rest of the New Testament, especially the letters Paul wrote to the churches he had helped establish during his missionary journeys.

Structure

So far as literary form is concerned, the book of Acts is an ancient biography that focuses on several central characters, especially Peter and Paul. Ancient biography was not concerned simply with narrating events but with displaying the character of the people involved, especially their ethical behavior. Other features included genealogies and rhetorical elements such as speeches. Ancient biographies also commonly drew from both written and oral sources for information.

Acts 1:8 provides the introduction and outline for the book. Once empowered by the Holy Spirit, the disciples proclaimed the gospel boldly in Jerusalem. As the book progresses, the gospel spread farther into Judea and Samaria and then finally into the outer reaches of the known world through the missionary work of Paul.

PROLOGUE

1 I wrote the first narrative, Theophilus, about all that Jesus began to do and teach 2 until the day he was taken up, after he had given instructions through the Holy Spirit to the apostles he had chosen. 3 After he had suffered, he also presented himself alive to them by many convincing proofs, appearing to them over a period of forty days and speaking about the kingdom of God.

THE HOLY SPIRIT PROMISED

4 While he was[A] with them, he commanded them not to leave Jerusalem, but to wait for the Father's promise. "Which," he said, "you have heard me speak about; 5 for John baptized with water, but you will be baptized with the Holy Spirit in a few days."

6 So when they had come together, they asked him, "Lord, are you restoring the kingdom to Israel at this time?"

7 He said to them, "It is not for you to know times or periods that the Father has set by his own authority. 8 But you will receive power when the Holy Spirit has come on you, and you will be my witnesses in Jerusalem, in all Judea and Samaria, and to the ends of the earth."

THE ASCENSION

9 After he had said this, he was taken up as they were watching, and a cloud took him out of their sight. 10 While he was going, they were gazing into heaven, and suddenly two men in white clothes stood by them. 11 They said, "Men of Galilee, why do you stand looking up into heaven? This same Jesus, who has been taken from you into heaven, will come in the same way that you have seen him going into heaven."

UNITED IN PRAYER

12 Then they returned to Jerusalem from the Mount of Olives, which is near Jerusalem — a Sabbath day's journey away. 13 When they arrived, they went to the room upstairs where they were staying: Peter, John, James, Andrew, Philip, Thomas, Bartholomew, Matthew, James the son of Alphaeus, Simon the Zealot, and Judas the son of James. 14 They all were continually united in prayer,[B] along with the women, including Mary the mother of Jesus, and his brothers.

MATTHIAS CHOSEN

15 In those days Peter stood up among the brothers and sisters[C] — the number of people who were together was about a hundred twenty — and said, 16 "Brothers and sisters, it was necessary that the Scripture be fulfilled that the Holy Spirit through the mouth of David foretold about Judas, who became a guide to those who arrested Jesus. 17 For he was one of our number and shared in this ministry." 18 Now this man acquired a field with his unrighteous wages. He fell headfirst, his body burst open and his intestines spilled out. 19 This became known to all the residents of Jerusalem, so that in their own language that field is called *Hakeldama* (that is, "Field of Blood"). 20 "For it is written in the Book of Psalms:

> **Let his dwelling become desolate;**
> **let no one live in it;**[D] and
> **Let someone else take his position.**[E]

21 "Therefore, from among the men who have accompanied us during the whole time the Lord Jesus went in and out among us — 22 beginning from the baptism of John until the day he was taken up from us — from among these, it is necessary that one become a witness with us of his resurrection."

23 So they proposed two: Joseph, called Barsabbas, who was also known as Justus, and Matthias. 24 Then they prayed, "You, Lord, know everyone's hearts; show which of these two you have chosen 25 to take the place[F] in this apostolic ministry that Judas left to go where he belongs." 26 Then they cast lots for them, and the lot fell to Matthias and he was added to the eleven apostles.

PENTECOST

2 When the day of Pentecost had arrived, they were all together in one place. 2 Suddenly a sound like that of a violent rushing wind came from heaven, and it filled the whole house where they were staying. 3 They saw tongues like flames of fire that separated and rested on each one of them. 4 Then they were all filled with the Holy Spirit and began to speak in different tongues,[G] as the Spirit enabled them.

5 Now there were Jews staying in Jerusalem, devout people from every nation under heaven. 6 When this sound occurred, a crowd came together and was confused because each one heard them speaking in his own language. 7 They were astounded and amazed, saying,[H] "Look, aren't all these who are speaking Galileans? 8 How is it that each of us can hear them in our own native language? 9 Parthians, Medes, Elamites; those who live in Mesopotamia, in Judea and Cappadocia, Pontus and Asia, 10 Phrygia and Pamphylia, Egypt and the parts of Libya near Cyrene; visitors from Rome (both Jews and converts), 11 Cretans and Arabs — we hear them declaring the magnificent acts of God in our own tongues." 12 They were all astounded and perplexed, saying to one another, "What does this mean?" 13 But some sneered and said, "They're drunk on new wine."

[A] **1:4** Or *he was eating*, or *he was lodging* [B] **1:14** Other mss add *and petition* [C] **1:15** Other mss read *disciples* [D] **1:20** Ps 69:25 [E] **1:20** Ps 109:8 [F] **1:25** Other mss read *to share* [G] **2:4** languages, also in v. 11 [H] **2:7** Other mss add *to one another*

PETER'S SERMON

14 Peter stood up with the Eleven, raised his voice,
and proclaimed to them, "Fellow Jews and all you
residents of Jerusalem, let this be known to you, and
pay attention to my words. 15 For these people are
not drunk, as you suppose, since it's only nine in the
morning.[A] 16 On the contrary, this is what was spoken
through the prophet Joel:

17 **And it will be** in the last days, says God,
that **I will pour out my Spirit on all people;**
then your sons and your daughters
will prophesy,
your young men will see visions,
and your old men will dream dreams.
18 **I will even pour out my Spirit**
on my servants in those days, both men and
women
and they will prophesy.
19 **I will display wonders in the heaven** above
and signs on the earth below:
blood and fire and a cloud of smoke.
20 **The sun will be turned to darkness**
and the moon to blood
before the great and glorious day of the
Lord comes.
21 **Then everyone who calls**
on the name of the Lord will be saved.[B]

22 "Fellow Israelites, listen to these words: This
Jesus of Nazareth was a man attested to you by
God with miracles, wonders, and signs that God did
among you through him, just as you yourselves know.
23 Though he was delivered up according to God's
determined plan and foreknowledge, you used[C] lawless people to nail him to a cross and kill him. 24 God
raised him up, ending the pains of death, because it
was not possible for him to be held by death. 25 For
David says of him:

I saw the Lord ever before me;
because he is at my right hand,
I will not be shaken.
26 **Therefore my heart is glad**
and my tongue rejoices.
Moreover, my flesh will rest in hope,
27 **because you will not abandon me**
in Hades
or allow your holy one to see decay.
28 **You have revealed the paths of life to me;**
you will fill me with gladness
in your presence.[D]

29 "Brothers and sisters, I can confidently speak to
you about the patriarch David: He is both dead and
buried, and his tomb is with us to this day. 30 Since
he was a prophet, he knew that God had sworn an
oath to him to seat one of his descendants[E] on his
throne. 31 Seeing what was to come, he spoke concerning the resurrection of the Messiah: **He**[F] **was**
not abandoned in Hades, and his flesh **did not ex-**
perience decay.[G]

32 "God has raised this Jesus; we are all witnesses
of this. 33 Therefore, since he has been exalted to the
right hand of God and has received from the Father
the promised Holy Spirit, he has poured out what
you both see and hear. 34 For it was not David who
ascended into the heavens, but he himself says:

The Lord declared to my Lord,
'Sit at my right hand
35 **until I make your enemies**
your footstool.'[H]

36 "Therefore let all the house of Israel know with
certainty that God has made this Jesus, whom you
crucified, both Lord and Messiah."

CALL TO REPENTANCE

37 When they heard this, they were pierced to the
heart and said to Peter and the rest of the apostles,
"Brothers, what should we do?"

38 Peter replied, "Repent and be baptized, each of
you, in the name of Jesus Christ for the forgiveness
of your sins, and you will receive the gift of the Holy
Spirit. 39 For the promise is for you and for your children, and for all who are far off, as many as the Lord
our God will call." 40 With many other words he testified and strongly urged them, saying, "Be saved from
this corrupt[I] generation!" 41 So those who accepted
his message were baptized, and that day about three
thousand people were added to them.

A GENEROUS AND GROWING CHURCH

42 They devoted themselves to the apostles' teaching, to the fellowship, to the breaking of bread, and
to prayer.

43 Everyone was filled with awe, and many wonders and signs were being performed through the
apostles. 44 Now all the believers were together and
held all things in common. 45 They sold their possessions and property and distributed the proceeds to
all, as any had need. 46 Every day they devoted themselves to meeting together in the temple, and broke
bread from house to house. They ate their food with
joyful and sincere hearts, 47 praising God and enjoying the favor of all the people. Every day the Lord
added to their number[J] those who were being saved.

[A] **2:15** Lit *it's the third hour of the day* [B] **2:17–21** Jl 2:28–32
[C] **2:23** Other mss read *you have taken* [D] **2:25–28** Ps 16:8–11
[E] **2:30** Other mss add *according to the flesh to raise up the Messiah*
[F] **2:31** Other mss read *His soul* [G] **2:31** Ps 16:10 [H] **2:34–35** Ps 110:1
[I] **2:40** Or *crooked*, or *twisted* [J] **2:47** Other mss read *to the church*

First-Century Roads and Travel

by Paul E. Kullman

Ruins of a Roman aqueduct along the Appian Way, outside of Puteoli.

TRAVEL THROUGHOUT THE EMPIRE

Before Rome built its vast array of roads, travel was a burdensome hardship and often dangerous. Caravans used the roads as established trade routes that brought economic vitality to cities, towns, and villages. The same roads, however, brought travelers many dangers such as bandits and occasional interactions with military troop movements. First-century travelers journeyed primarily by walking, but other modes of travel included wagon, chariot, or donkey. Road construction methods allowed heavy wagons, war chariots, and military siege engines to travel throughout the empire without the burdensome mud they encountered on ordinary dirt pathways. Roman engineering, famous for its architecture, aqueducts, bridges, and road construction, eventually made travel to various locations throughout the empire possible.

The superiorly designed road system allowed governmental patrons the advantage both to defeat nations and spread Roman influence and culture. A good roadway system also gave Rome the benefit of new business opportunities such as overnight lodging, mercantile shops, and commercial services. Christianity would benefit greatly as believers used this same network to spread the gospel.

TYPES OF ROADS AND STREETS

Several factors affected first-century road design and construction. One was the road's setting, either rural or urban. In urban settings, the Romans followed the Greeks' meticulous city-planning habits, strategically building each city with its center at the agora (marketplace). Jewish cities had the most important places of activity at the city gate and temple (Jerusalem). Walled cities typically had a grid of major streets with alleyways branching off to provide pedestrian access to smaller neighborhoods and shops. In rural settings, being able to move military troops across expansive terrain was the primary reason for constructing good roads. However, once built, the road system benefited civilian traffic and the transportation of commerce.

Another more technical factor was the different approach the Romans and Jews took in rural road construction. Rome used its military soldiers and engineers—and its immense vassal labor—for achieving the best-constructed roads. When not actively engaged in military assignments, soldiers provided the important maintenance labor needed. Well-constructed and maintained roads helped troops and governmental couriers to perform business rapidly on behalf of the empire.

The Cardo Maximus, a main north/south street at Gerasa (modern Jerash).

The Jewish approach to constructing a roadway system was quite different. Prior to New Testament times, roads in Israel were ordinary trade routes across nothing more than centuries-old, well-worn paths where people had removed rocks and boulders and had leveled the dirt. Roads the Jews built were less durable; the people lacked the means and methods of both construction and maintenance. Many established roads ran along dry riverbeds or other natural landmarks; these tended to lengthen a journey rather than facilitate travel in a straight line.[1] Roman design changed all of that by the first century AD.

MATERIALS AND CONSTRUCTION

Transportation via good roadways is a high priority for any government, whether local or national. Governments invest large capital to ensure that people can travel quickly and without delay. Proper planning is essential to meet the various geographical challenges across a diverse empire. The Romans did not invent the road design, but they did enhance its constructability from its first use during the Bronze Age. Since the road system ran like arteries throughout the empire, they physically tied hundreds of villages, cities, and provinces together. Therefore, this civil engineering endeavor had to be well designed and built to last.

Romans designed their city-street pattern with one major roadway running north-south and the other east-west. This served as an axis for a grid that allowed street construction to be built in straight lines. Street widths ranged from 6 ½ feet to 26 feet.[2] Workers used the site work method of "cut and fill" to move dirt they excavated from higher ground to fill in the low areas, resulting in straight roads. The Romans' road engineering was successful and durable because of the multilayer system they used. They began with a subbase layer where they first excavated soil and refilled the area with compacted soil and rubble. This supported layers of foundational material. They then set a surface topping of flat stones or bricks in a mixture of lime, sand, pozzalana (volcanic ash where available), and water. These, the basic ingredients in concrete, are still in use throughout the world today. The roads crowned in the center and sloped downward toward the outer edges, which had a continuous curbstone for drainage.

Most first-century roads used stone milestone markers to measure distance to specific destinations such as from a town to a city. Across Israel, the discovery of about five hundred milestone markers bearing ancient inscriptions as early as AD 56 provide tangible evidence that ancient cities and towns were linked together by providing navigational information to the first-century traveler. In AD 69, the Roman Legion X recorded on a milestone marker the construction of a new road from Scythopolis (Beth-shean) to Legio (Megiddo).[3]

Rome took pride in its engineering achievements, and roadways were its crown jewel. Concerning the Jewish roads already in existence, the Romans redeveloped and absorbed them into a capital improvement master plan. They paid for these with vassal contributions, giving further testimony to the Romans' power, influence, and success. Local governmental overseers provided the funds for routine road maintenance once a road was built. ✣

[1] Max Schwartz, *The Biblical Engineer: How the Temple in Jerusalem Was Built* (Hoboken, NJ: Ktav, 2002), 48. [2] J. Julius Scott Jr., *Customs and Controversies: Intertestamental Jewish Backgrounds of the New Testament* (Grand Rapids: Baker, 1995), 240. [3] David F. Graf, Benjamin Isaac, and Israel Roll, "Roads and Highways (Roman)" in *ABD*, 5:782–87.

The oldest and most famous road of the Roman Empire, the Appian Way served as the main route between Rome and Greece. More than 350 miles long, the road was constructed in the fourth century BC by the Roman magistrate (or censor), Appius Claudius Caecus.

HEALING OF A LAME MAN

3 Now Peter and John were going up to the temple for the time of prayer at three in the afternoon.[A] 2 A man who was lame from birth was being carried there. He was placed each day at the temple gate called Beautiful, so that he could beg from those entering the temple. 3 When he saw Peter and John about to enter the temple, he asked for money. 4 Peter, along with John, looked straight at him and said, "Look at us." 5 So he turned to them, expecting to get something from them. 6 But Peter said, "I don't have silver or gold, but what I do have, I give you: In the name of Jesus Christ of Nazareth, get up and walk!" 7 Then, taking him by the right hand he raised him up, and at once his feet and ankles became strong. 8 So he jumped up and started to walk, and he entered the temple with them — walking, leaping, and praising God. 9 All the people saw him walking and praising God, 10 and they recognized that he was the one who used to sit and beg at the Beautiful Gate of the temple. So they were filled with awe and astonishment at what had happened to him.

PREACHING IN SOLOMON'S COLONNADE

11 While he[B] was holding on to Peter and John, all the people, utterly astonished, ran toward them in what is called Solomon's Colonnade. 12 When Peter saw this, he addressed the people: "Fellow Israelites, why are you amazed at this? Why do you stare at us, as though we had made him walk by our own power or godliness? 13 The God of Abraham, Isaac, and Jacob, the God of our ancestors, has glorified his servant Jesus, whom you handed over and denied before Pilate, though he had decided to release him. 14 You denied the Holy and Righteous One and asked to have a murderer released to you. 15 You killed the source[C] of life, whom God raised from the dead; we are witnesses of this. 16 By faith in his name, his name has made this man strong, whom you see and know. So the faith that comes through Jesus has given him this perfect health in front of all of you.

17 "And now, brothers and sisters, I know that you acted in ignorance, just as your leaders also did. 18 In this way God fulfilled what he had predicted through all the prophets — that his Messiah would suffer. 19 Therefore repent and turn back, so that your sins may be wiped out, 20 that seasons of refreshing may come from the presence of the Lord, and that he may send Jesus, who has been appointed for you as the Messiah. 21 Heaven must receive him until the time of the restoration of all things, which God spoke about through his holy prophets from the beginning. 22 Moses said:[D] **The Lord your God will raise up for you a prophet like me from among your brothers. You must listen to everything he tells you.** 23 **And everyone who does not listen to that prophet will be completely cut off from the people.**[E]

Beggar at the Damascus Gate in Jerusalem.

24 "In addition, all the prophets who have spoken, from Samuel and those after him, have also foretold these days. 25 You are the sons[F] of the prophets and of the covenant that God made with your ancestors, saying to Abraham, **And all the families of the earth will be blessed through your offspring.**[G] 26 God raised up his servant[H] and sent him first to you to bless you by turning each of you from your evil ways."

PETER AND JOHN ARRESTED

4 While they were speaking to the people, the priests, the captain of the temple police, and the Sadducees confronted them, 2 because they were annoyed that they were teaching the people and proclaiming in Jesus the resurrection of the dead. 3 So they seized them and took them into custody until the next day since it was already evening. 4 But many of those who heard the message believed, and the number of the men[I] came to about five thousand.

[A] **3:1** Lit *at the ninth hour* [B] **3:11** Other mss read *the lame man who was healed* [C] **3:15** Or *the Prince*, or *the Ruler* [D] **3:22** Other mss add *to the fathers* [E] **3:22–23** Dt 18:15–19 [F] **3:25** = heirs [G] **3:25** Gn 12:3; 18:18; 22:18; 26:4 [H] **3:26** Other mss add *Jesus* [I] **4:4** Or *people*

PETER AND JOHN FACE THE JEWISH LEADERSHIP

5 The next day, their rulers, elders, and scribes assembled in Jerusalem 6 with Annas the high priest,
Caiaphas, John, Alexander, and all the members of the
high-priestly family. 7 After they had Peter and John
stand before them, they began to question them: "By
what power or in what name have you done this?"
8 Then Peter was filled with the Holy Spirit and
said to them, "Rulers of the people and elders:[A] 9 If we
are being examined today about a good deed done
to a disabled man, by what means he was healed,
10 let it be known to all of you and to all the people of
Israel, that by the name of Jesus Christ of Nazareth,
whom you crucified and whom God raised from the
dead — by him this man is standing here before you
healthy. 11 This Jesus is

> **the stone rejected by you builders,**
> **which has become the cornerstone.**[B]

12 There is salvation in no one else, for there is no
other name under heaven given to people by which
we must be saved."

THE BOLDNESS OF THE DISCIPLES

13 When they observed the boldness of Peter and
John and realized that they were uneducated and
untrained men, they were amazed and recognized
that they had been with Jesus. 14 And since they saw
the man who had been healed standing with them,
they had nothing to say in opposition. 15 After they
ordered them to leave the Sanhedrin, they conferred
among themselves, 16 saying, "What should we do
with these men? For an obvious sign has been done
through them, clear to everyone living in Jerusalem,
and we cannot deny it. 17 But so that this does not
spread any further among the people, let's threat-
en them against speaking to anyone in this name
again." 18 So they called for them and ordered them
not to speak or teach at all in the name of Jesus.
19 Peter and John answered them, "Whether it's
right in the sight of God for us to listen to you rather
than to God, you decide; 20 for we are unable to stop
speaking about what we have seen and heard."
21 After threatening them further, they released
them. They found no way to punish them because
the people were all giving glory to God over what
had been done. 22 For this sign of healing had been
performed on a man over forty years old.

PRAYER FOR BOLDNESS

23 After they were released, they went to their own
people and reported everything the chief priests and
the elders had said to them. 24 When they heard this,
they raised their voices together to God and said,
"Master, you are the one who made the heaven, the
earth, and the sea, and everything in them. 25 You said

A bas-relief of a Roman imperial eagle found in Jerusalem. The eagle was the symbol of Rome and its power over the empire.

through the Holy Spirit, by the mouth of our father
David your servant:[C]

> **Why do the Gentiles rage**
> **and the peoples plot futile things?**
> 26 **The kings of the earth take their stand**
> **and the rulers assemble together**
> **against the Lord and**
> **against his Messiah.**[D]

27 "For, in fact, in this city both Herod and Pontius
Pilate, with the Gentiles and the people of Israel, assembled together against your holy servant Jesus,
whom you anointed, 28 to do whatever your hand and
your will had predestined to take place. 29 And now,
Lord, consider their threats, and grant that your servants may speak your word with all boldness, 30 while
you stretch out your hand for healing, and signs and
wonders are performed through the name of your
holy servant Jesus." 31 When they had prayed, the
place where they were assembled was shaken, and
they were all filled with the Holy Spirit and began to
speak the word of God boldly.

[A] **4:8** Other mss add *of Israel* [B] **4:11** Ps 118:22 [C] **4:25** Other mss read *through the mouth of David your servant* [D] **4:25–26** Ps 2:1–2

ALL THINGS IN COMMON

32 Now the entire group of those who believed were
of one heart and mind, and no one claimed that any
of his possessions was his own, but instead they held
everything in common. 33 With great power the apostles were giving testimony to the resurrection of the
Lord Jesus, and great grace was on all of them. 34 For
there was not a needy person among them because all
those who owned lands or houses sold them, brought
the proceeds of what was sold, 35 and laid them at
the apostles' feet. This was then distributed to each
person as any had need.
36 Joseph, a Levite from Cyprus by birth, the one
the apostles called Barnabas (which is translated Son
of Encouragement), 37 sold a field he owned, brought
the money, and laid it at the apostles' feet.

LYING TO THE HOLY SPIRIT

5 But a man named Ananias, with his wife Sapphira,
sold a piece of property. 2 However, he kept back
part of the proceeds with his wife's knowledge, and
brought a portion of it and laid it at the apostles' feet.
3 "Ananias," Peter asked, "why has Satan filled your
heart to lie to the Holy Spirit and keep back part of
the proceeds of the land? 4 Wasn't it yours while you
possessed it? And after it was sold, wasn't it at your
disposal? Why is it that you planned this thing in
your heart? You have not lied to people but to God."
5 When he heard these words, Ananias dropped dead,
and a great fear came on all who heard. 6 The young
men got up, wrapped his body, carried him out, and
buried him.
7 About three hours later, his wife came in, not
knowing what had happened. 8 "Tell me," Peter asked
her, "did you sell the land for this price?"
"Yes," she said, "for that price."
9 Then Peter said to her, "Why did you agree to test
the Spirit of the Lord? Look, the feet of those who
have buried your husband are at the door, and they
will carry you out."
10 Instantly she dropped dead at his feet. When the
young men came in, they found her dead, carried
her out, and buried her beside her husband. 11 Then
great fear came on the whole church and on all who
heard these things.

APOSTOLIC SIGNS AND WONDERS

12 Many signs and wonders were being done among
the people through the hands of the apostles. They
were all together in Solomon's Colonnade. 13 No one
else dared to join them, but the people spoke well of
them. 14 Believers were added to the Lord in increasing numbers — multitudes of both men and women.
15 As a result, they would carry the sick out into the
streets and lay them on cots and mats so that when
Peter came by, at least his shadow might fall on some
of them. 16 In addition, a multitude came together
from the towns surrounding Jerusalem, bringing
the sick and those who were tormented by unclean
spirits, and they were all healed.

IN AND OUT OF PRISON

17 Then the high priest rose up. He and all who were
with him, who belonged to the party of the Sadducees, were filled with jealousy. 18 So they arrested the
apostles and put them in the public jail. 19 But an angel
of the Lord opened the doors of the jail during the
night, brought them out, and said, 20 "Go and stand
in the temple, and tell the people all about this life."
21 Hearing this, they entered the temple at daybreak
and began to teach.

THE APOSTLES ON TRIAL AGAIN

When the high priest and those who were with him
arrived, they convened the Sanhedrin — the full
council of the Israelites — and sent orders to the
jail to have them brought. 22 But when the servants[A]
got there, they did not find them in the jail; so they
returned and reported, 23 "We found the jail securely
locked, with the guards standing in front of the doors,
but when we opened them, we found no one inside."
24 As[B] the captain of the temple police and the chief
priests heard these things, they were baffled about
them, wondering what would come of this.
25 Someone came and reported to them, "Look! The
men you put in jail are standing in the temple and
teaching the people." 26 Then the commander went
with the servants and brought them in without force,
because they were afraid the people might stone them.
27 After they brought them in, they had them stand before the Sanhedrin, and the high priest asked, 28 "Didn't
we strictly order you not to teach in this name? Look,
you have filled Jerusalem with your teaching and are
determined to make us guilty of this man's blood."
29 Peter and the apostles replied, "We must obey
God rather than people. 30 The God of our ancestors
raised up Jesus, whom you had murdered by hanging him on a tree. 31 God exalted this man to his right
hand as ruler and Savior, to give repentance to Israel
and forgiveness of sins. 32 We are witnesses of these
things, and so is the Holy Spirit whom God has given
to those who obey him."

GAMALIEL'S ADVICE

33 When they heard this, they were enraged and wanted to kill them. 34 But a Pharisee named Gamaliel, a
teacher of the law who was respected by all the people,

[A] **5:22** Or *temple police*, or *officers*, also in v. 26 [B] **5:24** Other mss add *the high priest and*

stood up in the Sanhedrin and ordered the men[A] to be taken outside for a little while. 35 He said to them, "Men of Israel, be careful about what you're about to do to these men. 36 Some time ago Theudas rose up, claiming to be somebody, and a group of about four hundred men rallied to him. He was killed, and all his followers were dispersed and came to nothing. 37 After this man, Judas the Galilean rose up in the days of the census and attracted a following. He also perished, and all his followers were scattered. 38 So in the present case, I tell you, stay away from these men and leave them alone. For if this plan or this work is of human origin, it will fail; 39 but if it is of God, you will not be able to overthrow them. You may even be found fighting against God." They were persuaded by him. 40 After they called in the apostles and had them flogged, they ordered them not to speak in the name of Jesus and released them. 41 Then they went out from the presence of the Sanhedrin, rejoicing that they were counted worthy to be treated shamefully on behalf of the Name.[B] 42 Every day in the temple, and in various homes, they continued teaching and proclaiming the good news that Jesus is the Messiah.

SEVEN CHOSEN TO SERVE

6 In those days, as the disciples were increasing in number, there arose a complaint by the Hellenistic Jews against the Hebraic Jews that their widows were being overlooked in the daily distribution. 2 The Twelve summoned the whole company of the disciples and said, "It would not be right for us to give up preaching the word of God to wait on tables. 3 Brothers and sisters, select from among you seven men of good reputation, full of the Spirit and wisdom, whom we can appoint to this duty. 4 But we will devote ourselves to prayer and to the ministry of the word." 5 This proposal pleased the whole company. So they chose Stephen, a man full of faith and the Holy Spirit, and Philip, Prochorus, Nicanor, Timon, Parmenas, and Nicolaus, a convert from Antioch. 6 They had them stand before the apostles, who prayed and laid their hands on them.

7 So the word of God spread, the disciples in Jerusalem increased greatly in number, and a large group of priests became obedient to the faith.

STEPHEN ACCUSED OF BLASPHEMY

8 Now Stephen, full of grace and power, was performing great wonders and signs among the people. 9 Opposition arose, however, from some members of the Freedmen's Synagogue, composed of both Cyrenians and Alexandrians, and some from Cilicia and Asia, and they began to argue with Stephen. 10 But they were unable to stand up against his wisdom and the Spirit by whom he was speaking.

Bust of Alexander the Great, the son of Philip II of Macedon.

11 Then they secretly persuaded some men to say, "We heard him speaking blasphemous words against Moses and God." 12 They stirred up the people, the elders, and the scribes; so they came, seized him, and took him to the Sanhedrin. 13 They also presented false witnesses who said, "This man never stops speaking against this holy place and the law. 14 For we heard him say that this Jesus of Nazareth will destroy this place and change the customs that Moses handed down to us." 15 And all who were sitting in the Sanhedrin looked intently at him and saw that his face was like the face of an angel.

STEPHEN'S SERMON

7 "Are these things true?" the high priest asked.

2 "Brothers and fathers," he replied, "listen: The God of glory appeared to our father Abraham when he was in Mesopotamia, before he settled in Haran, 3 and said to him: **Leave your country and relatives, and come to the land that I will show you.**[C]

[A] **5:34** Other mss read *apostles* [B] **5:41** Other mss add *of Jesus*, or *of Christ* [C] **7:3** Gn 12:1

An amphora from Athens; dated to around 520 BC. Most Greek pottery was designed to hold either olive oil, water, or wine. Such vessels were made by a potter and decorated separately by a painter. The scene depicts Apollo, the Greek god of music, flanked by two female attendants.

4 "Then he left the land of the Chaldeans and settled
in Haran. From there, after his father died, God had
him move to this land in which you are now living.
5 He didn't give him an inheritance in it — not even a
foot of ground — but he promised to give it to him as
a possession, and to his descendants after him, even
though he was childless. 6 God spoke in this way: His
descendants would **be strangers in a foreign coun-**
try, and they would **enslave and oppress them for**
four hundred years. 7 I will judge the nation that
they will serve as slaves, God said. **After this, they**
will come out and worship me in this place.[A] 8 And
so he gave Abraham the covenant of circumcision.
After this, he fathered Isaac and circumcised him on
the eighth day. Isaac became the father of Jacob, and
Jacob became the father of the twelve patriarchs.

THE PATRIARCHS IN EGYPT

9 "The patriarchs became jealous of Joseph and sold
him into Egypt, but God was with him 10 and rescued
him out of all his troubles. He gave him favor and
wisdom in the sight of Pharaoh, king of Egypt, who
appointed him ruler over Egypt and over his whole
household. 11 Now a famine and great suffering came
over all of Egypt and Canaan, and our ancestors could
find no food. 12 When Jacob heard there was grain in
Egypt, he sent our ancestors there the first time. 13 The
second time, Joseph revealed himself to his brothers, and Joseph's family became known to Pharaoh.
14 Joseph invited his father Jacob and all his relatives,
seventy-five people in all, 15 and Jacob went down to
Egypt. He and our ancestors died there, 16 were carried back to Shechem, and were placed in the tomb
that Abraham had bought for a sum of silver from
the sons of Hamor in Shechem.

MOSES, A REJECTED SAVIOR

17 "As the time was approaching to fulfill the promise
that God had made to Abraham, the people flourished
and multiplied in Egypt 18 until a different king who
did not know Joseph ruled over Egypt.[B] 19 He dealt deceitfully with our race and oppressed our ancestors
by making them abandon their infants outside so that
they wouldn't survive. 20 At this time Moses was born,
and he was beautiful in God's sight. He was cared for
in his father's home for three months. 21 When he was
put outside, Pharaoh's daughter adopted and raised
him as her own son. 22 So Moses was educated in all
the wisdom of the Egyptians and was powerful in his
speech and actions.

23 "When he was forty years old, he decided to visit
his own people, the Israelites. 24 When he saw one of
them being mistreated, he came to his rescue and
avenged the oppressed man by striking down the
Egyptian. 25 He assumed his people would understand that God would give them deliverance through
him, but they did not understand. 26 The next day he
showed up while they were fighting and tried to reconcile them peacefully, saying, 'Men, you are brothers. Why are you mistreating each other?'

27 "But the one who was mistreating his neighbor
pushed Moses aside, saying: **Who appointed you a**
ruler and a judge over us? 28 Do you want to kill me,
the same way you killed the Egyptian yesterday?[C]

29 "When he heard this, Moses fled and became
an exile in the land of Midian, where he became the
father of two sons. 30 After forty years had passed, an
angel[D] appeared to him in the wilderness of Mount
Sinai, in the flame of a burning bush. 31 When Moses
saw it, he was amazed at the sight. As he was approaching to look at it, the voice of the Lord came:
32 I am the God of your ancestors — the God of
Abraham, of Isaac, and of Jacob.[E] Moses began to
tremble and did not dare to look.

[A] **7:6–7** Gn 15:13–14 [B] **7:18** Other mss omit *over Egypt*
[C] **7:27–28** Ex 2:14 [D] **7:30** Other mss add *of the Lord* [E] **7:32** Ex 3:6,15

33 "The Lord said to him: **Take off the sandals from
your feet, because the place where you are standing is holy ground.** 34 **I have certainly seen the oppression of my people in Egypt; I have heard their
groaning and have come down to set them free.
And now, come, I will send you to Egypt.**[A]
35 "This Moses, whom they rejected when they said,
Who appointed you a ruler and a judge?[B] — this
one God sent as a ruler and a deliverer through the
angel who appeared to him in the bush. 36 This man
led them out and performed wonders and signs in the
land of Egypt, at the Red Sea, and in the wilderness
for forty years.

ISRAEL'S REBELLION AGAINST GOD

37 "This is the Moses who said to the Israelites: **God**[C]
**will raise up for you a prophet like me from among
your brothers.**[D] 38 He is the one who was in the assembly in the wilderness, with the angel who spoke
to him on Mount Sinai, and with our ancestors. He
received living oracles to give to us. 39 Our ancestors
were unwilling to obey him. Instead, they pushed
him aside, and in their hearts turned back to Egypt.
40 They told Aaron: **Make us gods who will go before
us. As for this Moses who brought us out of the
land of Egypt, we don't know what's happened to
him.**[E] 41 They even made a calf in those days, offered
sacrifice to the idol, and were celebrating what their
hands had made. 42 God turned away and gave them
up to worship the stars of heaven, as it is written in
the book of the prophets:

House of Israel, did you bring me offerings
and sacrifices
for forty years in the wilderness?
43 **You took up the tent of Moloch**
and the star of your god Rephan,
the images that you made to worship.
So I will send you into exile
beyond Babylon.[F]

GOD'S REAL TABERNACLE

44 "Our ancestors had the tabernacle of the testimony in the wilderness, just as he who spoke to Moses
commanded him to make it according to the pattern
he had seen. 45 Our ancestors in turn received it and
with Joshua brought it in when they dispossessed
the nations that God drove out before them, until the
days of David. 46 He found favor in God's sight and
asked that he might provide a dwelling place for the
God[G] of Jacob. 47 It was Solomon, rather, who built
him a house, 48 but the Most High does not dwell in
sanctuaries made with hands, as the prophet says:

49 **Heaven is my throne,**
and the earth my footstool.
What sort of house will you build for me?
says the Lord,
or what will be my resting place?
50 **Did not my hand make all these things?**[H]

RESISTING THE HOLY SPIRIT

51 "You stiff-necked people with uncircumcised hearts
and ears! You are always resisting the Holy Spirit.
As your ancestors did, you do also. 52 Which of the
prophets did your ancestors not persecute? They
even killed those who foretold the coming of the
Righteous One, whose betrayers and murderers you
have now become. 53 You received the law under the
direction of angels and yet have not kept it."

THE FIRST CHRISTIAN MARTYR

54 When they heard these things, they were enraged[I]
and gnashed their teeth at him. 55 Stephen, full of the
Holy Spirit, gazed into heaven. He saw the glory of
God, and Jesus standing at the right hand of God. 56 He
said, "Look, I see the heavens opened and the Son of
Man standing at the right hand of God!"
57 They yelled at the top of their voices, covered
their ears, and together rushed against him. 58 They
dragged him out of the city and began to stone him.
And the witnesses laid their garments at the feet of
a young man named Saul. 59 While they were stoning
Stephen, he called out, "Lord Jesus, receive my spirit!" 60 He knelt down and cried out with a loud voice,
"Lord, do not hold this sin against them!" And after
saying this, he fell asleep.

SAUL THE PERSECUTOR

8 Saul agreed with putting him to death.
On that day a severe persecution broke out
against the church in Jerusalem, and all except the
apostles were scattered throughout the land of Judea and Samaria. 2 Devout men buried Stephen and
mourned deeply over him. 3 Saul, however, was ravaging the church. He would enter house after house,
drag off men and women, and put them in prison.

PHILIP IN SAMARIA

4 So those who were scattered went on their way
preaching the word. 5 Philip went down to a[J] city in
Samaria and proclaimed the Messiah to them. 6 The
crowds were all paying attention to what Philip said,
as they listened and saw the signs he was performing.
7 For unclean spirits, crying out with a loud voice,
came out of many who were possessed, and many
who were paralyzed and lame were healed. 8 So there
was great joy in that city.

[A] **7:33–34** Ex 3:5,7–8,10 [B] **7:35** Ex 2:14 [C] **7:37** Other mss read *The Lord your God* [D] **7:37** Dt 18:15 [E] **7:40** Ex 32:1,23 [F] **7:42–43** Am 5:25–27 [G] **7:46** Other mss read *house* [H] **7:49–50** Is 66:1–2 [I] **7:54** Or *were cut to the quick* [J] **8:5** Other mss read *the*

Mosaic at Antioch depicting three male magicians.

THE RESPONSE OF SIMON

9 A man named Simon had previously practiced sorcery in that city and amazed the Samaritan people, while claiming to be somebody great. 10 They all paid attention to him, from the least of them to the greatest, and they said, "This man is called the Great Power of God."[A] 11 They were attentive to him because he had amazed them with his sorceries for a long time. 12 But when they believed Philip, as he proclaimed the good news about the kingdom of God and the name of Jesus Christ, both men and women were baptized. 13 Even Simon himself believed. And after he was baptized, he followed Philip everywhere and was amazed as he observed the signs and great miracles that were being performed.

SIMON'S SIN

14 When the apostles who were at Jerusalem heard that Samaria had received the word of God, they sent Peter and John to them. 15 After they went down there, they prayed for them so that the Samaritans might receive the Holy Spirit because he had not yet come down on any of them. 16 (They had only been baptized in the name of the Lord Jesus.) 17 Then Peter and John laid their hands on them, and they received the Holy Spirit.

18 When Simon saw that the Spirit[B] was given through the laying on of the apostles' hands, he offered them money, 19 saying, "Give me this power also so that anyone I lay hands on may receive the Holy Spirit."

20 But Peter told him, "May your silver be destroyed with you, because you thought you could obtain the gift of God with money! 21 You have no part or share in this matter, because your heart is not right before God. 22 Therefore repent of this wickedness of yours, and pray to the Lord that, if possible, your heart's intent may be forgiven. 23 For I see you are poisoned by bitterness and bound by wickedness."

24 "Pray to the Lord for me," Simon replied, "so that nothing you have said may happen to me."

25 So, after they had testified and spoken the word of the Lord, they traveled back to Jerusalem, preaching the gospel in many villages of the Samaritans.

THE CONVERSION OF THE ETHIOPIAN OFFICIAL

26 An angel of the Lord spoke to Philip: "Get up and go south to the road that goes down from Jerusalem to Gaza." (This is the desert road.[C]) 27 So he got up and went. There was an Ethiopian man, a eunuch and high official of Candace, queen of the Ethiopians, who was in charge of her entire treasury. He had come to worship in Jerusalem 28 and was sitting in his chariot on his way home, reading the prophet Isaiah aloud.

29 The Spirit told Philip, "Go and join that chariot."

30 When Philip ran up to it, he heard him reading the prophet Isaiah, and said, "Do you understand what you're reading?"

[A] **8:10** Or *"This is the power of God called Great* [B] **8:18** Other mss add *Holy* [C] **8:26** Or *is a desert place*

Limestone relief, thought to be from Rome, depicts Philip and the Ethiopian eunuch.

31 "How can I," he said, "unless someone guides
me?" So he invited Philip to come up and sit with him.
32 Now the Scripture passage he was reading was this:

He was led like a sheep to the slaughter,
and as a lamb is silent before its shearer,
so he does not open his mouth.
33 **In his humiliation justice**
was denied him.
Who will describe his generation?
For his life is taken from the earth.[A]

34 The eunuch said to Philip, "I ask you, who is the
prophet saying this about — himself or someone
else?" 35 Philip proceeded to tell him the good news
about Jesus, beginning with that Scripture.
36 As they were traveling down the road, they came
to some water. The eunuch said, "Look, there's water.
What would keep me from being baptized?"[B] 38 So he
ordered the chariot to stop, and both Philip and the
eunuch went down into the water, and he baptized
him. 39 When they came up out of the water, the Spirit
of the Lord carried Philip away, and the eunuch did
not see him any longer but went on his way rejoicing.
40 Philip appeared in[C] Azotus,[D] and he was traveling
and preaching the gospel in all the towns until he
came to Caesarea.

[A] **8:32–33** Is 53:7–8 [B] **8:36** Some mss include v. 37: *Philip said, "If you believe with all your heart you may." And he replied, "I believe that Jesus Christ is the Son of God."* [C] **8:40** Or *Philip was found at*, or *Philip found himself in* [D] **8:40** Or *Ashdod*

Road in the wadi that leads to Gaza.

THE DAMASCUS ROAD

9 Now Saul was still breathing threats and murder
against the disciples of the Lord. He went to the
high priest 2 and requested letters from him to the
synagogues in Damascus, so that if he found any men
or women who belonged to the Way, he might bring
them as prisoners to Jerusalem. 3 As he traveled and
was nearing Damascus, a light from heaven suddenly
flashed around him. 4 Falling to the ground, he heard
a voice saying to him, "Saul, Saul, why are you persecuting me?"
5 "Who are you, Lord?" Saul said.
"I am Jesus, the one you are persecuting," he replied. 6 "But get up and go into the city, and you will
be told what you must do."
7 The men who were traveling with him stood
speechless, hearing the sound but seeing no one.
8 Saul got up from the ground, and though his eyes
were open, he could see nothing. So they took him
by the hand and led him into Damascus. 9 He was
unable to see for three days and did not eat or drink.

SAUL'S BAPTISM

10 There was a disciple in Damascus named Ananias,
and the Lord said to him in a vision, "Ananias."
"Here I am, Lord," he replied.
11 "Get up and go to the street called Straight," the
Lord said to him, "to the house of Judas, and ask for
a man from Tarsus named Saul, since he is praying
there. 12 In a vision[A] he has seen a man named Ananias coming in and placing his hands on him so that
he may regain his sight."
13 "Lord," Ananias answered, "I have heard from
many people about this man, how much harm he
has done to your saints in Jerusalem. 14 And he has
authority here from the chief priests to arrest all who
call on your name."
15 But the Lord said to him, "Go, for this man is
my chosen instrument to take my name to Gentiles,
kings, and Israelites. 16 I will show him how much he
must suffer for my name."
17 Ananias went and entered the house. He placed
his hands on him and said, "Brother Saul, the Lord
Jesus, who appeared to you on the road you were
traveling, has sent me so that you may regain your
sight and be filled with the Holy Spirit."
18 At once something like scales fell from his eyes,
and he regained his sight. Then he got up and was
baptized. 19 And after taking some food, he regained
his strength.

SAUL PROCLAIMING THE MESSIAH

Saul was with the disciples in Damascus for some
time. 20 Immediately he began proclaiming Jesus in
the synagogues: "He is the Son of God."

[A] **9:12** Other mss omit *In a vision*

Damascus, the capital and largest city in Syria, is one of the oldest continually inhabited cities in the world.

[21] All who heard him were astounded and said,
"Isn't this the man in Jerusalem who was causing
havoc for those who called on this name and came
here for the purpose of taking them as prisoners to
the chief priests?"
[22] But Saul grew stronger and kept confounding the
Jews who lived in Damascus by proving that Jesus is
the Messiah.
[23] After many days had passed, the Jews conspired
to kill him, [24] but Saul learned of their plot. So they
were watching the gates day and night intending to
kill him, [25] but his disciples took him by night and
lowered him in a large basket through an opening
in the wall.

SAUL IN JERUSALEM

[26] When he arrived in Jerusalem, he tried to join the
disciples, but they were all afraid of him, since they
did not believe he was a disciple. [27] Barnabas, however, took him and brought him to the apostles and
explained to them how Saul had seen the Lord on
the road and that the Lord had talked to him, and
how in Damascus he had spoken boldly in the name
of Jesus. [28] Saul was coming and going with them in
Jerusalem, speaking boldly in the name of the Lord.
[29] He conversed and debated with the Hellenistic Jews,
but they tried to kill him. [30] When the brothers found
out, they took him down to Caesarea and sent him
off to Tarsus.

THE CHURCH'S GROWTH

[31] So the church throughout all Judea, Galilee, and
Samaria had peace and was strengthened. Living
in the fear of the Lord and encouraged by the Holy
Spirit, it increased in numbers.

THE HEALING OF AENEAS

[32] As Peter was traveling from place to place, he also
came down to the saints who lived in Lydda. [33] There
he found a man named Aeneas, who was paralyzed
and had been bedridden for eight years. [34] Peter said
to him, "Aeneas, Jesus Christ heals you. Get up and
make your bed,"[A] and immediately he got up. [35] So all
who lived in Lydda and Sharon saw him and turned
to the Lord.

DORCAS RESTORED TO LIFE

[36] In Joppa there was a disciple named Tabitha (which
is translated Dorcas). She was always doing good
works and acts of charity. [37] About that time she became sick and died. After washing her, they placed
her in a room upstairs. [38] Since Lydda was near Joppa,
the disciples heard that Peter was there and sent two
men to him who urged him, "Don't delay in coming
with us." [39] Peter got up and went with them. When he
arrived, they led him to the room upstairs. And all the
widows approached him, weeping and showing him

[A] **9:34** Or *and get ready to eat*

Interior of the Church of Ananias in Damascus.

Traditional site where Paul was lowered out of the window and over the wall at Damascus.

the robes and clothes that Dorcas had made while she
was with them. 40 Peter sent them all out of the room.
He knelt down, prayed, and turning toward the body
said, "Tabitha, get up." She opened her eyes, saw Peter,
and sat up. 41 He gave her his hand and helped her
stand up. He called the saints and widows and presented her alive. 42 This became known throughout
Joppa, and many believed in the Lord. 43 Peter stayed
for some time in Joppa with Simon, a leather tanner.

CORNELIUS'S VISION

10 There was a man in Caesarea named Cornelius,
a centurion of what was called the Italian Regiment. 2 He was a devout man and feared God along
with his whole household. He did many charitable
deeds for the Jewish people and always prayed to
God. 3 About three in the afternoon[A] he distinctly saw
in a vision an angel of God who came in and said to
him, "Cornelius."

4 Staring at him in awe, he said, "What is it, Lord?"

The angel told him, "Your prayers and your acts of
charity have ascended as a memorial offering before
God. 5 Now send men to Joppa and call for Simon,
who is also named Peter. 6 He is lodging with Simon,
a tanner, whose house is by the sea."

7 When the angel who spoke to him had gone, he
called two of his household servants and a devout soldier, who was one of those who attended him. 8 After
explaining everything to them, he sent them to Joppa.

PETER'S VISION

9 The next day, as they were traveling and nearing
the city, Peter went up to pray on the roof about
noon.[B] 10 He became hungry and wanted to eat, but
while they were preparing something, he fell into a
trance. 11 He saw heaven opened and an object that
resembled a large sheet coming down, being lowered
by its four corners to the earth. 12 In it were all the
four-footed animals and reptiles of the earth, and
the birds of the sky. 13 A voice said to him, "Get up,
Peter; kill and eat."

14 "No, Lord!" Peter said. "For I have never eaten
anything impure and ritually unclean."

15 Again, a second time, the voice said to him, "What
God has made clean, do not call impure." 16 This happened three times, and suddenly the object was taken
up into heaven.

PETER VISITS CORNELIUS

17 While Peter was deeply perplexed about what the
vision he had seen might mean, right away the men
who had been sent by Cornelius, having asked directions to Simon's house, stood at the gate. 18 They called
out, asking if Simon, who was also named Peter, was
lodging there.

19 While Peter was thinking about the vision, the
Spirit told him, "Three men are here looking for you.

[A] **10:3** Lit *About the ninth hour* [B] **10:9** Lit *about the sixth hour*

Breakwater wall at Joppa; modern Tel Aviv is in the distance.

[20] Get up, go downstairs, and go with them with no
doubts at all, because I have sent them."
[21] Then Peter went down to the men and said, "Here
I am, the one you're looking for. What is the reason
you're here?"
[22] They said, "Cornelius, a centurion, an upright
and God-fearing man, who has a good reputation
with the whole Jewish nation, was divinely directed
by a holy angel to call you to his house and to hear a
message from you." [23] Peter then invited them in and
gave them lodging.

The next day he got up and set out with them, and
some of the brothers from Joppa went with him.
[24] The following day he entered Caesarea. Now Cornelius was expecting them and had called together
his relatives and close friends. [25] When Peter entered,
Cornelius met him, fell at his feet, and worshiped him.
[26] But Peter lifted him up and said, "Stand up. I myself am also a man." [27] While talking with him, he went
in and found a large gathering of people. [28] Peter said
to them, "You know it's forbidden for a Jewish man to
associate with or visit a foreigner, but God has shown
me that I must not call any person impure or unclean.
[29] That's why I came without any objection when I was
sent for. So may I ask why you sent for me?"
[30] Cornelius replied, "Four days ago at this hour, at
three in the afternoon,[A] I was[B] praying in my house.
Just then a man in dazzling clothing stood before me
[31] and said, 'Cornelius, your prayer has been heard,
and your acts of charity have been remembered in
God's sight. [32] Therefore send someone to Joppa and
invite Simon here, who is also named Peter. He is
lodging in Simon the tanner's house by the sea.'[C] [33] So
I immediately sent for you, and it was good of you to
come. So now we are all in the presence of God to hear
everything you have been commanded by the Lord."

GOOD NEWS FOR GENTILES

[34] Peter began to speak: "Now I truly understand that
God doesn't show favoritism, [35] but in every nation
the person who fears him and does what is right is
acceptable to him. [36] He sent the message to the Israelites, proclaiming the good news of peace through
Jesus Christ — he is Lord of all. [37] You know the events
that took place throughout all Judea, beginning from
Galilee after the baptism that John preached: [38] how
God anointed Jesus of Nazareth with the Holy Spirit
and with power, and how he went about doing good
and healing all who were under the tyranny of the
devil, because God was with him. [39] We ourselves are
witnesses of everything he did in both the Judean
country and in Jerusalem, and yet they killed him
by hanging him on a tree. [40] God raised up this man
on the third day and caused him to be seen, [41] not
by all the people, but by us whom God appointed as

[A] **10:30** Lit *at the ninth hour* [B] **10:30** Other mss add *fasting and*
[C] **10:32** Other mss add *When he arrives, he will speak to you.*

The house of Simon the tanner at Joppa.

witnesses, who ate and drank with him after he rose
from the dead. 42 He commanded us to preach to the
people and to testify that he is the one appointed by
God to be the judge of the living and the dead. 43 All
the prophets testify about him that through his name
everyone who believes in him receives forgiveness
of sins."

GENTILE CONVERSION AND BAPTISM

44 While Peter was still speaking these words, the
Holy Spirit came down on all those who heard the
message. 45 The circumcised believers who had come
with Peter were amazed because the gift of the Holy
Spirit had been poured out even on the Gentiles. 46 For
they heard them speaking in tongues[A] and declaring
the greatness of God.

Then Peter responded, 47 "Can anyone withhold
water and prevent these people from being baptized,
who have received the Holy Spirit just as we have?"
48 He commanded them to be baptized in the name
of Jesus Christ. Then they asked him to stay for a
few days.

GENTILE SALVATION DEFENDED

11 The apostles and the brothers and sisters who
were throughout Judea heard that the Gentiles
had also received the word of God. 2 When Peter went
up to Jerusalem, the circumcision party criticized
him, 3 saying, "You went to uncircumcised men and
ate with them."

4 Peter began to explain to them step by step, 5 "I
was in the town of Joppa praying, and I saw, in a
trance, an object that resembled a large sheet coming down, being lowered by its four corners from
heaven, and it came to me. 6 When I looked closely
and considered it, I saw the four-footed animals of
the earth, the wild beasts, the reptiles, and the birds
of the sky. 7 I also heard a voice telling me, 'Get up,
Peter; kill and eat.'

8 " 'No, Lord!' I said. 'For nothing impure or ritually
unclean has ever entered my mouth.' 9 But a voice
answered from heaven a second time, 'What God has
made clean, you must not call impure.'

10 "Now this happened three times, and everything
was drawn up again into heaven. 11 At that very moment, three men who had been sent to me from Caesarea arrived at the house where we were. 12 The Spirit
told me to accompany them with no doubts at all.
These six brothers also accompanied me, and we
went into the man's house. 13 He reported to us how he
had seen the angel standing in his house and saying,
'Send to Joppa, and call for Simon, who is also named
Peter. 14 He will speak a message to you by which you
and all your household will be saved.'

15 "As I began to speak, the Holy Spirit came down
on them, just as on us at the beginning. 16 I remembered the word of the Lord, how he said, 'John baptized with water, but you will be baptized with the
Holy Spirit.' 17 If, then, God gave them the same gift
that he also gave to us when we believed in the Lord
Jesus Christ, how could I possibly hinder God?"

18 When they heard this they became silent. And
they glorified God, saying, "So then, God has given
repentance resulting in life even to the Gentiles."

THE CHURCH IN ANTIOCH

19 Now those who had been scattered as a result of
the persecution that started because of Stephen
made their way as far as Phoenicia, Cyprus, and
Antioch, speaking the word to no one except Jews.
20 But there were some of them, men from Cyprus
and Cyrene, who came to Antioch and began speaking to the Greeks[B] also, proclaiming the good news
about the Lord Jesus. 21 The Lord's hand was with
them, and a large number who believed turned to

[A] **10:46** Or *other languages* [B] **11:20** Lit *Hellenists*

the Lord. 22 News about them reached[A] the church in Jerusalem, and they sent out Barnabas to travel[B] as far as Antioch. 23 When he arrived and saw the grace of God, he was glad and encouraged all of them to remain true to the Lord with devoted hearts, 24 for he was a good man, full of the Holy Spirit and of faith. And large numbers of people were added to the Lord.

25 Then he went to Tarsus to search for Saul, 26 and when he found him he brought him to Antioch. For a whole year they met with the church and taught large numbers. The disciples were first called Christians at Antioch.

FAMINE RELIEF

27 In those days some prophets came down from Jerusalem to Antioch. 28 One of them, named Agabus, stood up and predicted by the Spirit that there would be a severe famine throughout the Roman world.[C] This took place during the reign of Claudius. 29 Each of the disciples, according to his ability, determined to send relief to the brothers and sisters who lived in Judea. 30 They did this, sending it to the elders by means of Barnabas and Saul.

JAMES MARTYRED AND PETER JAILED

12 About that time King Herod violently attacked some who belonged to the church, 2 and he executed James, John's brother, with the sword. 3 When he saw that it pleased the Jews, he proceeded to arrest Peter too, during the Festival of Unleavened Bread. 4 After the arrest, he put him in prison and assigned four squads of four soldiers each to guard him, intending to bring him out to the people after the Passover. 5 So Peter was kept in prison, but the church was praying fervently to God for him.

PETER RESCUED

6 When Herod was about to bring him out for trial, that very night Peter, bound with two chains, was sleeping between two soldiers, while the sentries in front of the door guarded the prison. 7 Suddenly an angel of the Lord appeared, and a light shone in the cell. Striking Peter on the side, he woke him up and said, "Quick, get up! " And the chains fell off his wrists. 8 "Get dressed," the angel told him, "and put on your sandals." And he did. "Wrap your cloak around you," he told him, "and follow me." 9 So he went out and followed, and he did not know that what the angel did was really happening, but he thought he was seeing a vision. 10 After they passed the first and second guards, they came to the iron gate that leads into the city, which opened to them by itself. They went outside and passed one street, and suddenly the angel left him.

11 When Peter came to himself, he said, "Now I know for certain that the Lord has sent his angel and rescued me from Herod's grasp and from all that the Jewish people expected." 12 As soon as he realized this, he went to the house of Mary, the mother of John who was called Mark, where many had assembled and were praying. 13 He knocked at the door of the outer gate, and a servant named Rhoda came to answer. 14 She recognized Peter's voice, and because of her joy, she did not open the gate but ran in and announced that Peter was standing at the outer gate.

15 "You're out of your mind! " they told her. But she kept insisting that it was true, and they said, "It's his angel." 16 Peter, however, kept on knocking, and when they opened the door and saw him, they were amazed.

17 Motioning to them with his hand to be silent, he described to them how the Lord had brought him out of the prison. "Tell these things to James and the brothers," he said, and he left and went to another place.

18 At daylight, there was a great commotion among the soldiers as to what had become of Peter. 19 After Herod had searched and did not find him, he interrogated the guards and ordered their execution. Then Herod went down from Judea to Caesarea and stayed there.

HEROD'S DEATH

20 Herod had been very angry with the people of Tyre and Sidon. Together they presented themselves before him. After winning over Blastus, who was in charge of the king's bedroom, they asked for peace, because their country was supplied with food from the king's country. 21 On an appointed day, dressed in royal robes and seated on the throne, Herod delivered a speech to them. 22 The assembled people began to shout, "It's the voice of a god and not of a man! " 23 At once an angel of the Lord struck him because he did not give the glory to God, and he was eaten by worms and died.

24 But the word of God spread and multiplied. 25 After they had completed their relief mission, Barnabas and Saul returned to[D] Jerusalem, taking along John who was called Mark.

PREPARING FOR THE MISSION FIELD

13 Now in the church at Antioch there were prophets and teachers: Barnabas, Simeon who was called Niger, Lucius of Cyrene, Manaen, a close friend of Herod the tetrarch, and Saul.

[A] **11:22** Lit *reached the ears of* [B] **11:22** Other mss omit *to travel*
[C] **11:28** Or *the whole world* [D] **12:25** Other mss read *from*

Antioch of Syria

by Robert E. Jones

ANTIOCH'S PRE-CHRISTIAN HISTORY

Around 300 BC, Seleucus I (Nicator) founded Antioch as his capital city, one of sixteen cities Seleucus named in honor of his father Antiochus. Seleucus located the city on the bank of the Orontes River about fifteen miles from the Mediterranean Sea, giving the city access to a nearby port. Following Seleucus's death, successive kings enlarged and fortified the city. In 83 BC, the city fell into the control of Armenia for nineteen years.

Then in 64 BC, the Roman general Pompey defeated Syria, and Antioch came under the control of the Roman Empire, becoming both the capital and the military center of the Roman province of Syria. During the Roman period, Antioch grew and became increasingly impressive. Officials improved the roads leading to the city and further developed the nearby seaport. As a result, communication with the entire Mediterranean world became more rapid and secure. These improvements later would prove helpful for the spreading of the gospel westward in the Roman world.

Antioch became a prosperous city during the Roman period, in part from its political position but also because of commerce. Examples of goods one could purchase in Antioch were fine leather, shoes, perfume, spices, textiles, and jewelry, as well as locally produced gold and silver products. Also Antioch had schools of rhetoric and teachers of Greek wisdom that attracted students from all across the Mediterranean world. All of these combined factors have led some historians to consider Antioch the third-greatest city in the Roman world behind only Rome and Alexandria.

Prosperity, luxury, and ease led to an emphasis on "luxurious immorality."[1] The pleasure garden of Daphne, about five miles out of Antioch, became a virtual "hotbed of every kind of vice and depravity"[2] that made the city infamous. In the pleasure garden, which was about ten miles in circumference, stood the temple of Daphne, amidst a beautiful grove of laurels, old cypresses, and flowing, gushing waters. Nightly the temple prostitutes would practice sensual rights in the name of religion. These activities led to the so-called Daphnic morals, a phrase that referred to immoral living.[3]

In 20 BC, Augustus established local games that later came to be known as the Olympic Games of Antioch and one of the most famous festivals in the Roman world. Every four years during July and August, people traveled to Antioch from all over the Greco-Roman world to attend these games, which included boxing, wrestling, chariot racing, and other forms of competition. The games ceased briefly from AD 41 to 54, but later Claudius reinstated them.

ANTIOCH IN THE FIRST CENTURY

From its beginning, Antioch had a mixed population that eventually numbered approximately five hundred thousand people by the first century AD and possibly double that number by the third century. By the beginning of the Christian era, about twenty-five thousand Jews may have lived in

Antakya today (ancient Antioch of Syria) is part of the Republic of Turkey, although Syrian maps still show it as part of Syria.

Tetradrachma of Seleucus I (Nicator), who founded Antioch as his capital.

Dating to the third century BC, a colossal Charonian carving in the mountainside overlooking Antioch. Ancient records indicate the figure was carved in an attempt to save the city below from a plague afflicting persons in the area.

Antioch. Such a large and influential Jewish community would have offered a fertile field for Christian teaching. In addition Antioch was also a cosmopolitan city where many Greek-thinking Gentiles lived. In a sense, then, Antioch was a place where two worlds, those of the Jews and the Greeks, came together. In such a setting as this, Christianity flourished.

Acts 11:19 records the scattering of believers from Jerusalem because of persecution surrounding Stephen's death. Some believers made their way north to Antioch, initially preaching the gospel to Jews only. Once in Antioch, these Christian missionaries apparently discovered they did not have to fear attacks from the Jews as they had in Jerusalem. One reason may have been the cosmopolitan atmosphere in Antioch that allowed for both classical and Asian cults. Therefore, new religions were no novelty in Antioch. A second reason may have been that the Jews successfully attracted a large number of Gentiles to their synagogues, and many of these Gentiles actually became proselytes to Judaism. This group of Gentiles may have been a target for the Christian preachers. In addition, according to Acts 11:21, many Gentiles, probably from the God-fearers who had been attracted to the Jewish synagogues, became believers; thus the composition of the church in Antioch would have been largely Gentile. We might say, then, that Antioch became a cradle of Gentile Christianity and the Christian missionary effort.

We could hardly overstate the importance Antioch had in the early history of Christianity. "Antioch of Syria was second only to Jerusalem as a center of early Christianity. Antioch was a commercial center in the Roman Empire. It was a citadel of the Greco-Roman culture, and it became the primary home of Christianity when it moved beyond its Jewish beginnings to the Gentile world."[4]

Due to Antioch's strong economy, the Antioch believers were able to provide the financial resources necessary for the growth of the missionary enterprise. Moreover, Antioch's geographical location served well for the city to be a focal point for the expansion of Christianity toward the west. Indeed, from this city Paul and Barnabas, and later Silas, left for their missionary journeys. To the Antioch church they would return from time to time to report on their successes. ❖

---

[1] William Barclay, *The Acts of the Apostles* (Philadelphia: Westminster, 1976), 89. [2] Charles F. Pfeiffer and Howard F. Vos, *The Wycliffe Historical Geography of Bible Lands* (Chicago: Moody, 1967), 247. [3] William Ewing and Howard F. Vos, "Daphne" in *ISBE* (1979), 1:866. [4] LaMoine F. DeVries, *Cities of the Biblical World* (Peabody, MA: Hendrickson, 1997), 345.

Marble statue depicting the nymph Cyrene overcoming a lion. According to the myth, Cyrene killed a lion that had terrorized Libya. She was given part of the kingdom as a reward. Found in the temple of Apollo at Cyrene; dated AD 125–150.

2 As they were worshiping[A] the Lord and fasting,
the Holy Spirit said, "Set apart for me Barnabas and
Saul for the work to which I have called them." 3 Then
after they had fasted, prayed, and laid hands on them,
they sent them off.

THE MISSION TO CYPRUS

4 So being sent out by the Holy Spirit, they went down
to Seleucia, and from there they sailed to Cyprus.
5 Arriving in Salamis, they proclaimed the word of
God in the Jewish synagogues. They also had John as
their assistant. 6 When they had traveled the whole
island as far as Paphos, they came across a sorcerer, a
Jewish false prophet named Bar-Jesus. 7 He was with
the proconsul, Sergius Paulus, an intelligent man. This
man summoned Barnabas and Saul and wanted to
hear the word of God. 8 But Elymas the sorcerer (that
is the meaning of his name) opposed them and tried
to turn the proconsul away from the faith.

9 But Saul — also called Paul — filled with the Holy
Spirit, stared straight at Elymas 10 and said, "You are
full of all kinds of deceit and trickery, you son of the
devil and enemy of all that is right. Won't you ever
stop perverting the straight paths of the Lord? 11 Now,
look, the Lord's hand is against you. You are going to
be blind, and will not see the sun for a time." Immediately a mist and darkness fell on him, and he went
around seeking someone to lead him by the hand.

12 Then, when he saw what happened, the proconsul believed, because he was astonished at the teaching of the Lord.

PAUL'S SERMON IN ANTIOCH OF PISIDIA

13 Paul and his companions set sail from Paphos and
came to Perga in Pamphylia, but John left them and
went back to Jerusalem. 14 They continued their journey from Perga and reached Pisidian Antioch. On the
Sabbath day they went into the synagogue and sat
down. 15 After the reading of the Law and the Prophets, the leaders of the synagogue sent word to them,
saying, "Brothers, if you have any word of encouragement for the people, you can speak."

16 Paul stood up and motioned with his hand and
said, "Fellow Israelites, and you who fear God, listen!
17 The God of this people Israel chose our ancestors,
made the people prosper during their stay in the land
of Egypt, and led them out of it with a mighty[B] arm.
18 And for about forty years he put up with them[C] in
the wilderness; 19 and after destroying seven nations
in the land of Canaan, he gave them their land as an
inheritance. 20 This all took about 450 years. After
this, he gave them judges until Samuel the prophet. 21 Then they asked for a king, and God gave them
Saul the son of Kish, a man of the tribe of Benjamin,
for forty years. 22 After removing him, he raised up
David as their king and testified about him, '**I have
found David** the son of Jesse to be **a man after my
own heart**,[D] who will carry out all my will.'

23 "From this man's descendants, as he promised,
God brought to Israel the Savior, Jesus.[E] 24 Before
his coming to public attention, John had previously

[A] **13:2** Or *were ministering to* [B] **13:17** Lit *with an uplifted* [C] **13:18** Other mss read *he cared for them* [D] **13:22** 1Sm 13:14; Ps 89:20
[E] **13:23** Other mss read *brought salvation*

Caesarea: Herod's Port City

by Timothy Trammell

Ruins show Herod spared no expense in building his palace at Caesarea Maritima. He used only imported materials and covered many of the walls with marble.

From an insignificant Phoenician fishing village to a major Mediterranean port and the capital of a Roman province is quite a transformation, but that is the story of Caesarea. This dramatic metamorphosis took place because of the vision and vanity of Herod the Great, ruler of the Jewish people from 37 BC to his death in 4 BC. Herod is remembered for his monumental building projects, and none was more impressive and remarkable than Caesarea Maritima, "Caesarea-on-the-Sea."

CAESAREA BEFORE HEROD

Called Straton or Strato's Tower, the original fishing village apparently had been built in the fourth century BC by Strato I, king of Sidon. Located on the coastal plain, it was a minor settlement on the caravan route between Tyre and Egypt. Pompey, the Roman military leader, claimed the village for Rome in 63 BC and elevated its status to that of autonomous city. Under Roman rule, Caesarea first became a part of Syria. Later Mark Antony gave it to Cleopatra of Egypt. Finally Augustus Caesar ceded the city to Herod, who named it after his patron.

CAESAREA UNDER HEROD

In 40 BC, the Roman rulers Antony and Octavian (Augustus Caesar) bestowed on Herod the title "king of the Jews." When the Roman senate confirmed the title, Herod sailed from Italy. With the help of Rome, he raised an army and in 37 BC conquered Jerusalem. He began a decade-long consolidation of his power and then initiated his building projects about 25 BC. Herod first began translating his architectural visions into stone in Jerusalem, erecting a theater with an amphitheater nearby, following these projects with a gigantic royal palace.

But Herod's dream was to construct a completely new city on the Mediterranean coast where no city had previously stood. This would be an international city that would rival the opulence and magnificence of the capital of the empire, with port facilities that would outstrip the size and significance of Alexandria, Egypt. He stipulated that the city would be laid out on the Roman grid plan, with a forum, baths, temples, tenements inside the walls, and villas outside.[1]

But why this location? Why not at Joppa, the city that had for centuries served Israel as a port? Herod's reasons were both political and religious. Joppa was Jewish and national, while Caesarea was cosmopolitan and Roman.[2] Building temples in Judea where Greek gods and Roman emperors were to be worshiped would have been unthinkable. So Herod, always the cunning diplomat, chose Caesarea and explained to Jewish religious leaders that he was merely seeking to please Caesar and the Romans, not at all following his own inclinations.[3]

Josephus recorded that Herod built the city of "white stone" and of "materials from other places, and at very great expense."[4] The stone was chiefly limestone and was likely quarried in the mountains approximately ten miles away across the plain of Sharon. These local materials were supplemented by marble and statuary brought from Rome.

The Temple—A central feature of the city was a temple dedicated to Augustus Caesar, Herod's patron. Built on an elevated platform and noted for its beauty and grand proportions, the temple was visible to sailors from a great distance. Two statues, "the one of Rome, the other of Caesar,"[5] adorned the temple.

The Amphitheater—South of the city and built on a promontory that jutted into the Mediterranean, the amphitheater was situated so that those seated in it had a magnificent view of the sea. This structure was discovered in 1961. During the excavation, the workmen found an

Surrounded by the sea, this rock-cut, freshwater swimming pool at Herod's Palace in Caesarea Maritima was seemingly built in defiance of nature. The entire pool complex (including dining halls, baths, and porticos) measured about 200 by 360 feet.

important dedication tablet. The inscription on the tablet mentioned Tiberius Caesar and Pontius Pilate. "This is the first archaeological evidence of the famed procurator of Judaea under whose rule . . . Jesus' crucifixion took place."[6]

The Hippodrome—In the eastern section of the city, Herod built a hippodrome, called by the Romans a circus—measuring 1,056 by 264 feet and seating twenty thousand spectators. A square granite pillar stood in the center, with three conical blocks erected nearby. Highly polished, these three blocks reflected sunlight and thus excited the horses during the races. The Romans called the pillars Taraxippos, meaning "horse-frightener."[7]

The Aqueduct—Determined to build a world-class city, Herod made sure Caesarea had an abundance of fountains, reflecting pools, and public baths. The challenge with this ambitious plan, though, was the lack of clean and drinkable water. To resolve this issue, Herod had workers construct an aqueduct to bring water from the closest springs, which were "nine miles distant, in the foothills of Mount Carmel. To reach them, thousands of laborers armed with picks, hammers, and chisels tunneled more than four miles through rock."[8] Archaeological remains visible to this day give evidence of this extraordinary accomplishment.

The Harbor—As impressive as his other structures were in Caesarea, Herod put his most vigorous efforts and innovative planning into the harbor. The sandy, unstable coastline lacked coastal islands or bays that could be incorporated into a harbor. So Herod had to design and construct a totally artificial harbor. "To bar undertrenching of breakwaters by currents and heavy seas, [Herod's workmen] first laid a foundation of rubble on the ocean floor wider than the breakwater that would rest on it."[9] Then using enormous stone blocks, the workmen built a breakwater two hundred feet wide in twenty fathoms of water. The southern breakwater stretched west from the coastline, then turned north—about six hundred yards in total length. The northern breakwater extended three hundred yards due west from the shore, leaving an entrance from the north for ships. Archaeological evidence seems to indicate that on either side of the harbor's entrance were three huge statues that helped guide the ships. Along the landward side of the harbor was the quay where workers unloaded the cargo and stored the goods in nearby vaults.

This massive harbor project challenged the creativeness of Rome's most skilled engineers. Hydraulic concrete that hardens underwater was used extensively. An ingenious sluice system periodically flushed the harbor to reduce silting. The finished harbor encompassed approximately two hundred thousand square yards. Indeed, as the largest anchorage constructed to that time, the harbor of Caesarea "could be called the world's first modern harbor."[10] Although these harbor structures have fallen prey to twenty centuries of waves and to a sinking coastline, the shadowy underwater remains can still be seen quite clearly from the air.

CAESAREA IN THE NEW TESTAMENT

Herod the Great died in 4 BC. With his death, his son Archelaus became ruler of Judea and Samaria, bringing Caesarea under his control. But even the Romans could not condone Archelaus's viciousness, so they exiled him to Gaul in AD 6, and Caesarea became the capital of the Roman province of Judea. This set the stage for a number of events recorded in the New Testament. ❖

An aqueduct carried water into Caesarea Maritima from Mount Carmel, which was nearly ten miles away.

[1] Robert L. Hohlfelder, "Caesarea Maritima," *National Geographic* 171.2 (1987): 270. [2] George Adam Smith, *The Historical Geography of the Holy Land* (New York: A. C. Armstrong, 1895), 139. [3] Josephus, *Jewish Antiquities* 15.9.5. [4] Josephus, *Jewish Antiquities* 15.9.6. [5] Josephus, *Jewish Antiquities* 15.9.6. [6] Zev Vilnay, *The Guide to Israel*, 22nd rev. ed. (Jerusalem: Daf-Chen, 1982), 368. [7] Vilnay, *Guide*, 369. [8] Hohlfelder, "Caesarea Maritima," 270–71. [9] Hohlfelder, "Caesarea Maritima," 275. [10] Hohlfelder, "Caesarea Maritima," 271–77.

DIGGING DEEPER *Sergius Paulus*

Sergius Paulus was the proconsul of Cyprus during Paul's first missionary journey (Ac 13:6–7). He became a Christian as a result of seeing God perform miracles through Paul and from hearing the message of the gospel (13:11–12). By the late nineteenth century, several inscriptions had been located confirming Paulus as a legitimate biblical figure. The first of these was found near Paphos, Cyprus. It bears his name and title. Another stone inscription was erected by Emperor Claudius as a memorial stone in Rome, and it bears Paulus's name and says he was an overseer of the banks of the Tiber River. These discoveries allow us to date Paul's visit to Cyprus to the early AD 40s and assign Sergius Paulus's Roman appointment as an overseer of the Tiber to around AD 47. An additional find in Pisidian Antioch (modern Turkey) lists the name of "L. Sergius Paulus" on a stone marker. This is likely a reference to Sergius Paulus himself or to his son Lucius, since it is believed that the Paulus family owned an estate in the area.

Coin from Cyrene, reverse showing the silphium (also "silphion") plant. Silphium was native to Cyrene and grew only in a thirty-mile strip of land along the Mediterranean. In the seventh century BC, silphium, which was commonly used as a spice, was discovered to have contraceptive value. Its value as a birth control agent caused it to be harvested and exported to extinction. It proved to be so important to the local economy that Cyrene regularly depicted the plant on its coins.

proclaimed a baptism of repentance to all the people
of Israel. 25 Now as John was completing his mission,
he said, 'Who do you think I am? I am not the one. But
one is coming after me, and I am not worthy to untie
the sandals on his feet.'

26 "Brothers and sisters, children of Abraham's
race, and those among you who fear God, it is to us
that the word of this salvation has been sent. 27 Since
the residents of Jerusalem and their rulers did not
recognize him or the sayings of the prophets that
are read every Sabbath, they have fulfilled their
words by condemning him. 28 Though they found
no grounds for the death sentence, they asked Pilate to have him killed. 29 When they had carried out
all that had been written about him, they took him
down from the tree and put him in a tomb. 30 But
God raised him from the dead, 31 and he appeared
for many days to those who came up with him from
Galilee to Jerusalem, who are now his witnesses
to the people. 32 And we ourselves proclaim to you
the good news of the promise that was made to
our ancestors. 33 God has fulfilled this for us, their
children, by raising up Jesus, as it is written in the
second Psalm:

> **You are my Son;**
> **today I have become your Father.**[A,B]

34 As to his raising him from the dead, never to
return to decay, he has spoken in this way, **I will
give you the holy and sure promises of David.**[C]
35 Therefore he also says in another passage, **You
will not let your Holy One see decay.**[D] 36 For David,
after serving God's purpose in his own generation,
fell asleep, was buried with his fathers, and decayed,
37 but the one God raised up did not decay. 38 Therefore, let it be known to you, brothers and sisters,
that through this man forgiveness of sins is being
proclaimed to you. 39 Everyone who believes is justified[E] through him from everything that you could
not be justified from through the law of Moses. 40 So
beware that what is said in the prophets does not
happen to you:

> 41 **Look, you scoffers,**
> **marvel and vanish away,**
> **because I am doing a work**
> **in your days,**
> **a work that you will never believe,**
> **even if someone were to explain it**
> **to you."**[F]

PAUL AND BARNABAS IN ANTIOCH

42 As they were leaving, the people[G] urged them to
speak about these matters the following Sabbath.
43 After the synagogue had been dismissed, many of
the Jews and devout converts to Judaism followed

[A] **13:33** Or *I have begotten you* [B] **13:33** Ps 2:7 [C] **13:34** Is 55:3 [D] **13:35** Ps 16:10 [E] **13:39** Or *freed*, also later in this verse [F] **13:41** Hab 1:5 [G] **13:42** Other mss read *they were leaving the synagogue of the Jews, the Gentiles*

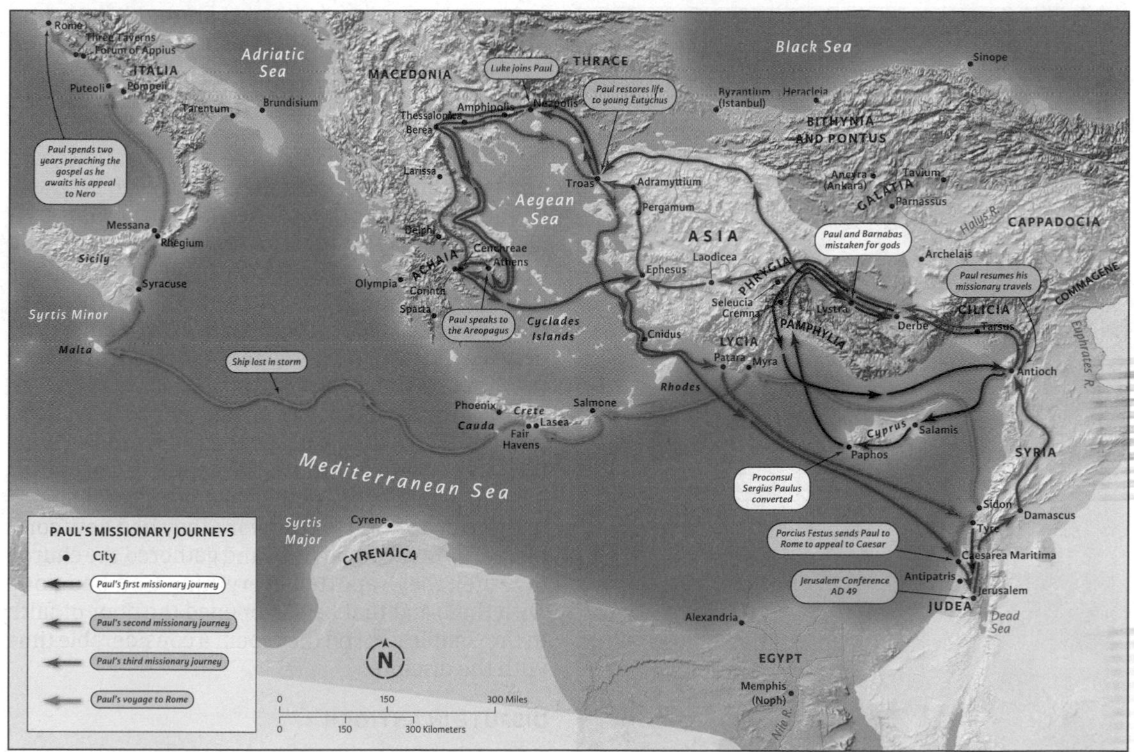

Paul and Barnabas, who were speaking with them
and urging them to continue in the grace of God.
44 The following Sabbath almost the whole town
assembled to hear the word of the Lord.[A] 45 But when
the Jews saw the crowds, they were filled with jealousy and began to contradict what Paul was saying,
insulting him.
46 Paul and Barnabas boldly replied, "It was necessary that the word of God be spoken to you first.
Since you reject it and judge yourselves unworthy of
eternal life, we are turning to the Gentiles. 47 For this
is what the Lord has commanded us:

I have made you
a light for the Gentiles
to bring salvation
to the ends of the earth."[B]

48 When the Gentiles heard this, they rejoiced and
honored the word of the Lord, and all who had been
appointed to eternal life believed. 49 The word of the
Lord spread through the whole region. 50 But the Jews
incited the prominent God-fearing women and the
leading men of the city. They stirred up persecution
against Paul and Barnabas and expelled them from
their district. 51 But Paul and Barnabas shook the
dust off their feet against them and went to Iconium. 52 And the disciples were filled with joy and the
Holy Spirit.

GROWTH AND PERSECUTION IN ICONIUM

14 In Iconium they entered the Jewish synagogue,
as usual, and spoke in such a way that a great
number of both Jews and Greeks believed. 2 But the
unbelieving Jews stirred up the Gentiles and poisoned their minds against the brothers. 3 So they
stayed there a long time and spoke boldly for the
Lord, who testified to the message of his grace by
enabling them to do signs and wonders. 4 But the
people of the city were divided, some siding with the
Jews and others with the apostles. 5 When an attempt
was made by both the Gentiles and Jews, with their
rulers, to mistreat and stone them, 6 they found out
about it and fled to the Lycaonian towns of Lystra and
Derbe and to the surrounding countryside. 7 There
they continued preaching the gospel.

MISTAKEN FOR GODS IN LYSTRA

8 In Lystra a man was sitting who was without
strength in his feet, had never walked, and had been
lame from birth. 9 He listened as Paul spoke. After
looking directly at him and seeing that he had faith
to be healed, 10 Paul said in a loud voice, "Stand up
on your feet!" And he jumped up and began to walk
around.

[A] **13:44** Other mss read *of God* [B] **13:47** Is 49:6

Inside the Church of St. Peter's at Antioch; many believe this to be one of the oldest Christian churches; it may have been in use in the first century AD.

11 When the crowds saw what Paul had done, they
shouted, saying in the Lycaonian language, "The gods
have come down to us in human form!" 12 Barnabas
they called Zeus, and Paul, Hermes, because he was
the chief speaker. 13 The priest of Zeus, whose temple
was just outside the town, brought bulls and wreaths
to the gates because he intended, with the crowds, to
offer sacrifice.
14 The apostles Barnabas and Paul tore their robes
when they heard this and rushed into the crowd,
shouting, 15 "People! Why are you doing these things?
We are people also, just like you, and we are proclaiming good news to you, that you turn from these worthless things to the living God, **who made the heaven,
the earth, the sea, and everything in them.**[A] 16 In
past generations he allowed all the nations to go their
own way, 17 although he did not leave himself without
a witness, since he did what is good by giving you rain
from heaven and fruitful seasons and filling you with
food and your hearts with joy." 18 Even though they
said these things, they barely stopped the crowds
from sacrificing to them.
19 Some Jews came from Antioch and Iconium, and
when they won over the crowds, they stoned Paul and
dragged him out of the city, thinking he was dead.
20 After the disciples gathered around him, he got
up and went into the town. The next day he left with
Barnabas for Derbe.

CHURCH PLANTING

21 After they had preached the gospel in that town
and made many disciples, they returned to Lystra, to
Iconium, and to Antioch, 22 strengthening the[B] disciples by encouraging them to continue in the faith and
by telling them, "It is necessary to go through many
hardships to enter the kingdom of God." 23 When they
had appointed elders for them in every church and
prayed with fasting, they committed them to the Lord
in whom they had believed.
24 They passed through Pisidia and came to Pamphylia. 25 After they had spoken the word in Perga,
they went down to Attalia. 26 From there they sailed
back to Antioch where they had been commended
to the grace of God for the work they had now completed. 27 After they arrived and gathered the church
together, they reported everything God had done
with them and that he had opened the door of faith
to the Gentiles. 28 And they spent a considerable time
with the disciples.

DISPUTE IN ANTIOCH

15 Some men came down from Judea and began to
teach the brothers, "Unless you are circumcised
according to the custom prescribed by Moses, you
cannot be saved." 2 After Paul and Barnabas had engaged them in serious argument and debate, Paul and
Barnabas and some others were appointed to go up to
the apostles and elders in Jerusalem about this issue.
3 When they had been sent on their way by the church,
they passed through both Phoenicia and Samaria, describing in detail the conversion of the Gentiles, and
they brought great joy to all the brothers and sisters.
4 When they arrived at Jerusalem, they were welcomed by the church, the apostles, and the elders,
and they reported all that God had done with them.
5 But some of the believers who belonged to the party
of the Pharisees stood up and said, "It is necessary to
circumcise them and to command them to keep the
law of Moses."

THE JERUSALEM COUNCIL

6 The apostles and the elders gathered to consider
this matter. 7 After there had been much debate, Peter
stood up and said to them, "Brothers, you are aware
that in the early days God made a choice among you,[C]
that by my mouth the Gentiles would hear the gospel
message and believe. 8 And God, who knows the heart,

[A] **14:15** Ex 20:11; Ps 146:6 [B] **14:22** Lit *the souls of the* [C] **15:7** Other mss read *us*

bore witness to them by giving them the Holy Spirit,
just as he also did to us. [9] He made no distinction between us and them, cleansing their hearts by faith.
[10] Now then, why are you testing God by putting a
yoke on the disciples' necks that neither our ancestors nor we have been able to bear? [11] On the contrary,
we believe that we are saved through the grace of the
Lord Jesus in the same way they are."
[12] The whole assembly became silent and listened
to Barnabas and Paul describe all the signs and wonders God had done through them among the Gentiles.
[13] After they stopped speaking, James responded,
"Brothers, listen to me. [14] Simeon[A] has reported how
God first intervened to take from the Gentiles a people for his name. [15] And the words of the prophets
agree with this, as it is written:

16 **After these things I will return**
and rebuild David's fallen tent.
I will rebuild its ruins
and set it up again,
17 **so that the rest of humanity**
may seek the Lord —
even all the Gentiles
who are called by my name —
declares the Lord
who makes these things [18] known
from long ago.[B,C]

[19] Therefore, in my judgment, we should not cause
difficulties for those among the Gentiles who turn to
God, [20] but instead we should write to them to abstain
from things polluted by idols, from sexual immorality, from eating anything that has been strangled, and
from blood. [21] For since ancient times, Moses has had
those who proclaim him in every city, and every Sabbath day he is read aloud in the synagogues."

THE LETTER TO THE GENTILE BELIEVERS

[22] Then the apostles and the elders, with the whole
church, decided to select men who were among them
and to send them to Antioch with Paul and Barnabas:
Judas, called Barsabbas, and Silas, both leading men
among the brothers. [23] They wrote:

"From the apostles and the elders, your brothers,
To the brothers and sisters among the Gentiles
in Antioch, Syria, and Cilicia:
Greetings.
[24] Since we have heard that some without our
authorization went out from us and troubled
you with their words and unsettled your hearts,[D]
[25] we have unanimously decided to select men
and send them to you along with our dearly
loved Barnabas and Paul, [26] who have risked
their lives for the name of our Lord Jesus Christ.
[27] Therefore we have sent Judas and Silas, who
will personally report the same things by word
of mouth. [28] For it was the Holy Spirit's decision
— and ours — not to place further burdens
on you beyond these requirements: [29] that you
abstain from food offered to idols, from blood,
from eating anything that has been strangled,
and from sexual immorality. You will do well if
you keep yourselves from these things.
Farewell."

Alabaster *aryballos*, which is a small Greek vessel that held perfumed oil. From Syrian Antioch; fourth century BC.

THE OUTCOME OF THE JERUSALEM LETTER

[30] So they were sent off and went down to Antioch,
and after gathering the assembly, they delivered the
letter. [31] When they read it, they rejoiced because of
its encouragement. [32] Both Judas and Silas, who were
also prophets themselves, encouraged the brothers
and sisters and strengthened them with a long message. [33] After spending some time there, they were
sent back in peace by the brothers and sisters to those
who had sent them.[E,F] [35] But Paul and Barnabas, along
with many others, remained in Antioch, teaching and
proclaiming the word of the Lord.

PAUL AND BARNABAS PART COMPANY

[36] After some time had passed, Paul said to Barnabas,
"Let's go back and visit the brothers and sisters in
every town where we have preached the word of the
Lord and see how they're doing." [37] Barnabas wanted
to take along John who was called Mark. [38] But Paul
insisted that they should not take along this man
who had deserted them in Pamphylia and had not
gone on with them to the work. [39] They had such a
sharp disagreement that they parted company, and
Barnabas took Mark with him and sailed off to Cyprus. [40] But Paul chose Silas and departed, after being
commended by the brothers and sisters to the grace
of the Lord. [41] He traveled through Syria and Cilicia,
strengthening the churches.

[A] **15:14** Simon (Peter) [B] **15:17–18** Other mss read *says the Lord who does all these things. Known to God from long ago are all his works.* [C] **15:16–18** Am 9:11–12; Is 45:21 [D] **15:24** Other mss add *by saying, 'Be circumcised and keep the law,'* [E] **15:33** Other mss read *the brothers to the apostles* [F] **15:33** Other mss add v. 34: *But Silas decided to stay there.*

PAUL SELECTS TIMOTHY

16 Paul went on to Derbe and Lystra, where
there was a disciple named Timothy, the son
of a believing Jewish woman, but his father was a
Greek. 2 The brothers and sisters at Lystra and Iconium spoke highly of him. 3 Paul wanted Timothy to
go with him; so he took him and circumcised him
because of the Jews who were in those places, since
they all knew that his father was a Greek. 4 As they
traveled through the towns, they delivered the decisions reached by the apostles and elders at Jerusalem
for the people to observe. 5 So the churches were
strengthened in the faith and grew daily in numbers.

EVANGELIZATION OF EUROPE

6 They went through the region of Phrygia and Galatia; they had been forbidden by the Holy Spirit to
speak the word in Asia. 7 When they came to Mysia,
they tried to go into Bithynia, but the Spirit of Jesus
did not allow them. 8 Passing by Mysia they went
down to Troas. 9 During the night Paul had a vision in
which a Macedonian man was standing and pleading with him, "Cross over to Macedonia and help
us!" 10 After he had seen the vision, we immediately
made efforts to set out for Macedonia, concluding
that God had called us to preach the gospel to them.

LYDIA'S CONVERSION

11 From Troas we put out to sea and sailed straight
for Samothrace, the next day to Neapolis, 12 and
from there to Philippi, a Roman colony and a leading city of the district of Macedonia. We stayed in
that city for several days. 13 On the Sabbath day we
went outside the city gate by the river, where we
expected to find a place of prayer. We sat down and
spoke to the women gathered there. 14 A God-fearing woman named Lydia, a dealer in purple cloth
from the city of Thyatira, was listening. The Lord
opened her heart to respond to what Paul was saying. 15 After she and her household were baptized,
she urged us, "If you consider me a believer in the
Lord, come and stay at my house." And she persuaded us.

PAUL AND SILAS IN PRISON

16 Once, as we were on our way to prayer, a slave girl
met us who had a spirit by which she predicted the
future. She made a large profit for her owners by
fortune-telling. 17 As she followed Paul and us she
cried out, "These men, who are proclaiming to you[A]
a way of salvation, are the servants of the Most High
God." 18 She did this for many days.

Paul was greatly annoyed. Turning to the spirit, he
said, "I command you in the name of Jesus Christ to
come out of her!" And it came out right away.

19 When her owners realized that their hope of profit was gone, they seized Paul and Silas and dragged
them into the marketplace to the authorities. 20 Bringing them before the chief magistrates, they said,
"These men are seriously disturbing our city. They
are Jews 21 and are promoting customs that are not
legal for us as Romans to adopt or practice." 22 The
crowd joined in the attack against them, and the chief
magistrates stripped off their clothes and ordered
them to be beaten with rods. 23 After they had severely
flogged them, they threw them in jail, ordering the
jailer to guard them carefully. 24 Receiving such an
order, he put them into the inner prison and secured
their feet in the stocks.

A MIDNIGHT DELIVERANCE

25 About midnight Paul and Silas were praying and
singing hymns to God, and the prisoners were listening to them. 26 Suddenly there was such a violent earthquake that the foundations of the jail were
shaken, and immediately all the doors were opened,
and everyone's chains came loose. 27 When the jailer
woke up and saw the doors of the prison standing
open, he drew his sword and was going to kill himself, since he thought the prisoners had escaped.

28 But Paul called out in a loud voice, "Don't harm
yourself, because we're all here!"

29 The jailer called for lights, rushed in, and fell
down trembling before Paul and Silas. 30 He escorted
them out and said, "Sirs, what must I do to be saved?"

31 They said, "Believe in the Lord Jesus, and you will
be saved — you and your household." 32 And they
spoke the word of the Lord to him along with everyone in his house. 33 He took them the same hour of
the night and washed their wounds. Right away he
and all his family were baptized. 34 He brought them
into his house, set a meal before them, and rejoiced
because he had come to believe in God with his entire household.

AN OFFICIAL APOLOGY

35 When daylight came, the chief magistrates sent the
police to say, "Release those men."

36 The jailer reported these words to Paul: "The
magistrates have sent orders for you to be released.
So come out now and go in peace."

37 But Paul said to them, "They beat us in public
without a trial, although we are Roman citizens, and
threw us in jail. And now are they going to send us
away secretly? Certainly not! On the contrary, let them
come themselves and escort us out."

38 The police reported these words to the magistrates. They were afraid when they heard that Paul

[A] **16:17** Other mss read *us*

The Rise of Macedonia

by Mark R. Dunn

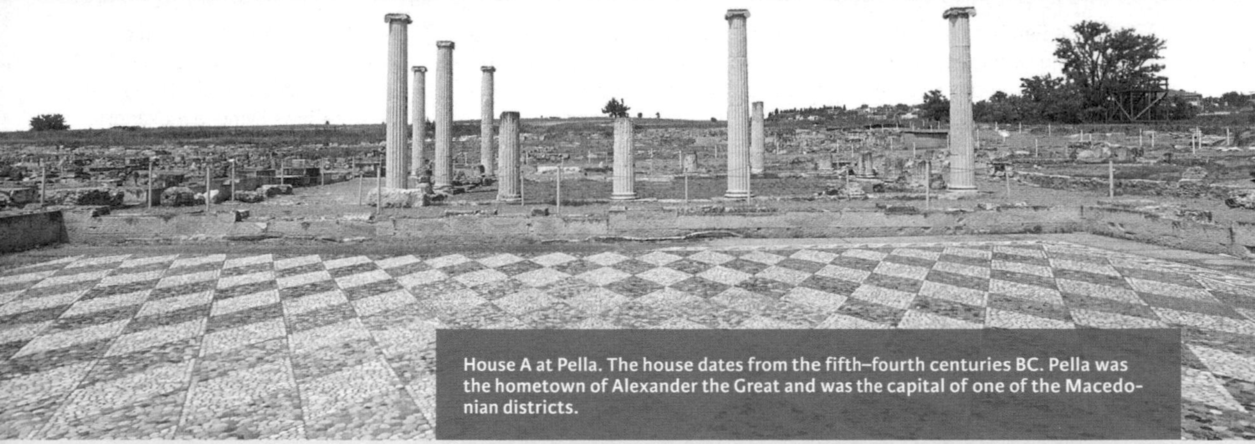

House A at Pella. The house dates from the fifth–fourth centuries BC. Pella was the hometown of Alexander the Great and was the capital of one of the Macedonian districts.

The Macedonian Empire, Europe's first world superpower, shaped world history in a way that not only dominated life during the New Testament era but still resonates in our world today. Macedonia burst upon the consciousness of the world through the exploits of its favorite son, Alexander the Great (356–323 BC). Three hundred and fifty years after Macedonia exposed the world to Greek culture, the world of the New Testament era was still gripped by Greek influence. Hellenistic Greek dominated as the international common language of the eastern Mediterranean provinces. The New Testament authors, desiring the widest exposure for the good news, wrote in Greek. Hence, Macedonia indirectly influenced the language of the sacred texts that have proclaimed the message of Jesus Christ across the ages.

What led to the Macedonians' rise to supremacy in both Greece and the world? Their struggle for national unity eventually led to world dominance and achievements that changed the course of history. For hundreds of years before its meteoric rise to fame, Macedonia was an isolated region on the northern periphery of the Greek world. Saturated with rugged mountains and timberland to the north and west, and watered by numerous rivers winding through the coastal plains to the south and east, Macedonia was untamed and undeveloped. Its northern limits stretched into the Balkan regions, at times reaching to the banks of the Danube. Mount Olympus sat on its southeastern coastal border. Macedonia also faced challenges from her neighbors, bounded by Thrace on the east, Illyria to the northwest, Epirus to the southwest, and Thessaly to the south.[1]

Originally populated by non-Greeks, Macedonia in its early history saw many people seeking to obtain control of the region. Sensing the instability, the Dorian-speaking Greeks moved in the twelfth century BC into south-central Macedonia and eventually dominated the region. The Argead Dynasty emerged and ruled Macedonia from the ninth century BC until the death of its last king, Alexander IV, in 309 BC.[2]

The Argeads first ruled from the city of Aegae and later from Pella.[3] By the fifth century BC, the mixed population of Macedonia had adopted the Greek language. Because Athens dominated the coastal regions, Macedonian rulers focused on extending their power over the highlands and plains—a lofty goal rarely accomplished.[4]

Macedonia had abundant natural resources in timber, livestock, grain, and minerals, which Greece and other peoples desired. Eventually Macedonia became the foremost supplier of such items to the Greeks. The abundant resources attracted Greek expansionist schemes. Macedonian leaders responded resolutely and led Macedonia to dominate Greece by the mid-fourth century BC.

The beginning of the fifth century BC witnessed the arrival of the armies of Persia to campaign against the Greeks. Unable to resist the Persian might, the Macedonians avoided conflict by supplying the Persians with timber for shipbuilding. However, Alexander I, king of Macedonia during the period of the Persian occupation, also secretly provided aid to the Greeks in their fight against the Persians. An admirer of Greek culture, Alexander I sought to bring Greek influence to Macedonia. The efforts of Alexander I and his successors to import Greek culture led to the Hellenization of Macedonia.[5]

The Persian invasion gave the Macedonians the opportunity to observe both Persian tactics and the Greeks' response. In spite of their long history of fighting among themselves, they were forced to unite against the threat of a superior common enemy. The strength and success of the Greeks against the Persians and the future possibilities for a united Greece did not go unnoticed by the Macedonians.

When the Persian War ended in 448 BC, the Greek city-states resumed their previous rivalries and often ranged into Macedonia.[6] The Argead struggle to consolidate Macedonian holdings now faced an added challenge. Nevertheless, the Macedonians made progress in the coastal plains. Having gained strength, the Macedonians established Pella as their new capital city in about 410 BC.[7] Pella came to be the birthplace of Macedonia's most famous rulers: Philip II and his son Alexander the Great.

In 365 BC, Perdiccas III ascended the Macedonian throne. By now, gold had been discovered in eastern Macedonia and was exported through the port city of Amphipolis. Athens desired control of Amphipolis and forced Perdiccas to conquer it in their behalf. With Athenian aid, he did so, but kept the city for himself. Instantly wealthy with Macedonian gold, he hired an army and set about consolidating the holdings of the Macedonian crown.[8] This stroke of leadership set the stage for Macedonia to gain Greek and world dominance.

In 360 BC, Perdiccas died and his brother Philip II seized the throne. Philip first focused on securing Macedonia. In 356 BC, he captured Macedonia's gold mines and named the adjacent city for himself: Philippi. Then Philip moved southward. Successful in his expansion efforts, by 338 BC Philip had gained control of Greece. A year later, as he mobilized his army to invade Asia Minor, Philip was assassinated.

Philip of Macedon gold coin.

The road to Macedonian greatness had many difficult steps, but the last one was the most challenging. Alexander seamlessly continued his father's plans. Philip had trained Alexander for the throne, securing the famous Macedonian philosopher Aristotle as his tutor. Aristotle cultivated in Alexander a love for Greek culture and possibly the sense that Alexander was destined for greatness and that he was the one who would bring about a world dominated by Greek culture.[9]

Alexander ably served as Macedonia's regent during Philip's Greek campaigns. He was also a spirited warrior; at the battle of Chaeronea, he led the decisive cavalry charge that brought victory over Athens and Thebes, and completed Philip's bid to control Greece. Then at age twenty, Alexander III became Macedonia's king and heir of his father's expansionist vision. With inspired leadership, he quickly subdued uprisings that had sprung up in Greece after Philip's death. Alexander first secured Macedonia, pressing its northern frontier to the Danube. He then turned south. Thebes revolted, and Alexander responded by razing Thebes and enslaving its inhabitants. Athens and the rest of Greece readily acceded to Alexander.[10]

With lightning speed that staggered his opponents, Alexander accomplished in less than two years what more than five hundred years of Greek strife had not: the unification of Greece under a visionary leader. Now Alexander pursued his father's dream of liberating Greek lands in Asia Minor. His vigorous leadership yielded unimagined results by conquering the fragile Persian Empire with all its old-world holdings, including Egypt and Babylon.

While in Egypt, Alexander established on the Nile Delta a city in his own name. Alexandria would become a leading city of learning. The city library actively collected world literature. Jews living in Alexandria secured copies of the Hebrew Scriptures and began translating them into Greek. The Greek Old Testament, called the Septuagint, was influential even in Israel and became the "Bible" of the early church while the New Testament books were being produced and collected. The Septuagint also influenced translations of the Hebrew Scriptures into European languages such as Latin and English. Unforeseen by the Macedonians, their indirect influence on propagating the Bible was enormous.

Greek culture (Hellenism) breathed fresh air into the old world. Hellenism emphasized varied pursuits such as commerce, communication, construction, travel, education, the sciences, sports, the arts, and philosophy. These elements were then drawn into cultural civic centers served by democratic governments. Above all, Hellenism encouraged freedom and the love of life.[11] Macedonian military prowess cleared the way for Greek culture to liberate the dispirited masses. The response was so positive that Greek culture was popular for centuries after Macedonia's demise and well beyond the New Testament era. Macedonia's lasting legacy was not merely in its astounding military gains but in the cultural changes it unleashed.

In twelve short years, Alexander conquered the eastern world—and just as quickly he was gone, dead in Babylon in 323 BC at age thirty-three. His generals reverted to the old Greek legacy, splitting the Macedonian Empire into four sections to be used as bases to campaign for the whole. Two divisions of the Macedonian Empire directly influenced the Holy Land. Seleucus seized Babylon, Mesopotamia, Persia, and India and established his government in Syria, Israel's old nemesis. Ptolemy grabbed the

Holy Land, Egypt, and parts of Asia Minor. Naturally the two regimes fought over the promised land and Jewish residents suffered. One hundred and twenty-five years of relatively peaceful Ptolemaic rule were followed by thirty much harsher years under the Seleucids, culminating in terror under the rule of Antiochus IV. To strengthen their hold on the Holy Land, the Seleucid regime forced Hellenism upon the Jews, aspects of which conflicted with Jewish religious practice.[12]

Macedonia's glory did not last long. Having lost its king and empire, Macedonia struggled to control its Greek holdings. Finally, in confident control of its coast, Macedonia founded the harbor city of Thessalonica in 315 BC. By the New Testament era, Thessalonica would be Macedonia's leading city.

Macedonia's power and influence steadily waned. In 215 BC, the first of three wars with Rome began. In 146 BC, the Romans annexed Macedonia as a senatorial province, implying military occupation was unnecessary. Soon afterward, the Roman governor in Macedonia ordered construction of the Egnatian Way, a Roman highway. The road connected Thrace and Macedonia with the Adriatic coast and to Rome. A century later, Mark Antony and Octavian marched east along the Egnatian Way to Philippi to battle Julius Caesar's assassins. A century later, Paul traveled west along the Egnatian Way preaching the gospel in Macedonia, visiting Neapolis (now Kavala), Philippi, Amphipolis, Apollonia, Thessalonica, and Berea (see Ac 16–17). ✣

---

[1] While the exact borders are uncertain, what was once ancient Macedonia probably lies within the boundaries of southeastern Albania, Macedonia, and northern Greece. See Helmut Koester, "Macedonia," in *HIBD*, 1063. [2] F. F. Bruce, "Macedonia" in *ABD*, 4:454; James F. Strange, "Macedonia" in *ISBE* (1986), 3:206. [3] Aegae is located near modern Vergina, roughly forty-eight miles southwest of Thessaloniki. Even after Pella became the Macedonian capital, the Macedonians continued to bury all their kings at Aegae except for Alexander the Great. See Strange, "Macedonia," 206. [4] "Macedonia" in *Encyclopedia Britannica* (Chicago: Encyclopedia Britannica, 2005), 7:620. [5] Strange, "Macedonia," 206; Duane F. Watson, "Greece and Macedon" in *Dictionary of New Testament Background* (*DNTB*), ed. Craig A. Evans and Stanley E. Porter (Downers Grove, IL: InterVarsity, 2000), 424–25. [6] See "Historical Review of Macedonia," www.macedonia.com/english/history/review/ www.macedonia.com. [7] Jona Lendering, "Macedonia 4," *Livius*, www.livius.org/articles/place/macedonia/macedonia-4/. [8] Lendering, "Macedonia 4." [9] Timothy Boatswain and Colin Nicolson, *A Traveller's History of Greece*, 3rd ed. (New York: Interlink, 2001), 84. [10] R. D. Milns, "Alexander the Great" in *ABD*, 1:146. [11] "Hellenism" in *The Columbia Encyclopedia*, 6th ed., www.bartleby.com. [12] Arthur A. Rupprecht, "Macedonia" in *ZPEB*, 4:24.

DIGGING DEEPER *Politarch Inscription*

Thessalonica (known today as Thessaloniki or Salonica) is the second-largest city in Greece. Located on the western shores of the Aegean Sea in the area of Macedonia, the city came under Roman control in the second century BC. By the time Paul and Luke visited, Jewish settlements and synagogues had sprung up (Ac 17:1). Many scholars doubted Luke's assertion that the "city officials" of Thessalonica were known by the Greek designation *politarch* (v. 6) due to the absence of extrabiblical literature mentioning the term. However, recent excavations throughout Greece have yielded thirty-two *politarch* inscriptions; nineteen were found at Thessalonica and three of these have been dated to the first century AD, the very time when Paul and Luke visited. Elsewhere in Acts, Luke correctly identifies the rulers in Philippi as *praetors* (16:20), members of the court in Athens as *areopagites* (17:34), uses the correct Roman title *neokoros* for honor (19:35), identifies the city clerk in Ephesus as *Grammateus* (19:35), and the leading magistrate of Malta as "the leading man of the island" (28:7).

and Silas were Roman citizens. 39 So they came to appease them, and escorting them from prison, they urged them to leave town. 40 After leaving the jail, they came to Lydia's house, where they saw and encouraged the brothers and sisters, and departed.

A SHORT MINISTRY IN THESSALONICA

17 After they passed through Amphipolis and Apollonia, they came to Thessalonica, where there was a Jewish synagogue. 2 As usual, Paul went into the synagogue, and on three Sabbath days reasoned with them from the Scriptures, 3 explaining and proving that it was necessary for the Messiah to suffer and rise from the dead: "This Jesus I am proclaiming to you is the Messiah." 4 Some of them were persuaded and joined Paul and Silas, including a large number of God-fearing Greeks, as well as a number of the leading women.

RIOT IN THE CITY

5 But the Jews became jealous, and they brought together some wicked men from the marketplace, formed a mob, and started a riot in the city. Attacking Jason's house, they searched for them to bring them out to the public assembly. 6 When they did not find them, they dragged Jason and some of the brothers before the city officials, shouting, "These men who have turned the world upside down have come here too, 7 and Jason has welcomed them. They are all acting contrary to Caesar's decrees, saying that there is another king — Jesus." 8 The crowd and city officials who heard these things were upset. 9 After taking a security bond from Jason and the others, they released them.

THE BEREANS SEARCH THE SCRIPTURES

10 As soon as it was night, the brothers and sisters sent Paul and Silas away to Berea. Upon arrival, they went into the synagogue of the Jews. 11 The people here were of more noble character than those in Thessalonica, since they received the word with eagerness and examined[A] the Scriptures daily to see if these things were so. 12 Consequently, many of them believed, including a number of the prominent Greek women as well as men. 13 But when the Jews from Thessalonica found out that the word of God had been proclaimed by Paul at Berea, they came there too, agitating and upsetting[B] the crowds. 14 Then the brothers and sisters immediately sent Paul away to go to the coast, but Silas and Timothy stayed on there. 15 Those who escorted Paul brought him as far as Athens, and after receiving instructions for Silas and Timothy to come to him as quickly as possible, they departed.

PAUL IN ATHENS

16 While Paul was waiting for them in Athens, he was deeply distressed when he saw that the city was full of idols. 17 So he reasoned in the synagogue with the Jews and with those who worshiped God, as well as in the marketplace every day with those who happened to be there. 18 Some of the Epicurean and Stoic philosophers also debated with him. Some said, "What is this ignorant show-off[C] trying to say?"

Others replied, "He seems to be a preacher of foreign deities" — because he was telling the good news about Jesus and the resurrection.

19 They took him and brought him to the Areopagus,[D] and said, "May we learn about this new teaching you are presenting? 20 Because what you say sounds strange to us, and we want to know what these things mean." 21 Now all the Athenians and the foreigners residing there spent their time on nothing else but telling or hearing something new.

THE AREOPAGUS ADDRESS

22 Paul stood in the middle of the Areopagus and said, "People of Athens! I see that you are extremely religious in every respect. 23 For as I was passing through and observing the objects of your worship,

[A] **17:11** Or *asked about* [B] **17:13** Other mss omit *and upsetting*
[C] **17:18** Lit *this seed picker* [D] **17:19** Or *Mars Hill*

First-Century Athens

by David M. Wallace

GEOGRAPHY AND TRADE

Athens is located on the small Attica Peninsula near the eastern edge of Achaia, where the Mediterranean and Aegean Seas meet. The region around Athens is extremely hot and dry in summer, with short rainy seasons in winter. In spite of an average of only sixteen inches of rain annually, this area was rich in olive trees and vineyards. Olive oil and wine were chief exports. Timber was scarce; most resources in Achaia were agricultural.

Athens became famous for manufacturing pottery due to the excellent clay beds nearby. Both silver and lead mines were located at Laurium, on the southern tip of Attica. Nearby Mount Pentelicus provided the famous marble, which artisans throughout Athens and beyond used. Access to water and excellent harbors near Athens and throughout Achaia made exporting products easy.

HISTORY AND CULTURE

According to tradition, Cecrops, who had come to Athens from Egypt about 1556 BC, founded the city. Yet archaeological evidence indicates settlement during the fourth millennium BC. The city was built around a steep, easily defended hill known as the Acropolis. Athens grew in ancient times to a population of about two hundred and fifty thousand people.[1]

Athens reached its zenith during the fifth century BC but lost much of its political influence as a result of the Peloponnesian War with the Spartans near the end of that century. After the Romans conquered Greece, they made Athens a Roman territory (146 BC). Rome ruled first-century Athens. "In deference to her glorious past, they granted Athens the status of a free and federated city."[2]

Rome's General Sulla destroyed much of the city in 86 BC after Athens rebelled and allied itself with Mithridates of Pontus. However, when Paul arrived on his way to nearby Corinth, Athens continued to enjoy fame as a center for the arts, architecture, history, culture, philosophy, learning, and sports. The university there was perhaps the most important in the Roman world at that time.[3] Many great classical structures remained standing and intact. Athens was a city of magnificent stone, ivory, and marble buildings that celebrated its history, culture, and the worship of its gods and goddesses. It was still a beautiful city in the first century AD, in spite of some of its former glory having faded.

Parthenon and Acropolis in Athens, Greece.

Close-up of the Propylaeum (Acropolis entrance) shows the building to the north of the Propylaeum (left) and temple of Nike (right). Nike was the goddess of victory.

When Paul visited, a wall encircled Athens, protecting it from any potential siege. Two parallel walls, some 250 feet apart, running from the sea to the city about five miles inland, kept the city connected to the sea.[4]

Near the Ilissus River, outside the city wall, stood the horseshoe-shaped stadium where athletes and spectators honored Athena. Foot races, boxing, javelin, and wrestling were some of the events. The stadium opened to the north; its racetrack was about two hundred yards long and thirty-six yards wide.[5]

To find lodging and get oriented to the city, Paul and his traveling companions would have entered Athens through the Dipylon (double) Gate and continued along the Panathenaic Way to the agora or marketplace. The agora was the city's social, commercial, and political center. The city itself was comprised of three areas—the Acropolis, the agora, and the Areopagus.

THE ACROPOLIS

Although the Bible does not say, Paul likely ascended the marble staircase to the top of the Acropolis and toured the buildings, which glorified pagan gods. The Acropolis was a spectacular outcropping of stone rising some five hundred feet above the surrounding plain and city. During the golden age of Athens when Pericles reigned (443–429 BC), the Parthenon was built on top of the Acropolis and dedicated to Athena, the goddess of wisdom for whom the city was named. Construction had taken about fifteen years. Other structures on top of the hill included the temple of Wingless Victory (the temple of Athena Nike), the Erechtheum (a temple dedicated to Athena and Poseidon), and the Propylaeum. The temples, shrines, monuments, and public buildings gave Athens its unique character. It was a showplace for art and architecture.

THE AGORA

Below the Acropolis to the north-northwest was the agora. This marketplace or business center was the city's social and political hub. During New Testament days, Athens had both a Greek agora and a newer Roman forum.

"By Paul's time the Greek agora had become more of a museum for monuments recalling Athens's former glory."[6] The new Roman forum had become the modern center of city business and activity. This is probably where Paul talked and debated with philosophers and the religious and civic leaders. While Paul held discussions with the Jews in the local synagogue, he also made direct appeals to the local people in the agora (Ac 17:17).

THE AREOPAGUS

As Paul debated the Epicureans and Stoics, his preaching about Jesus sounded to the Greeks like he was

Tower of the Winds, in the Roman forum in Athens. Built in the first century BC, the originally-domed tower was equipped with a bronze weather vane, a water clock, an astronomical clock, and sundials.

introducing them to a new god. Those who heard Paul sent him, therefore, to the Areopagus. Both the council and a marble hill immediately northwest of the Acropolis were called the Areopagus. The group was "a civic body responsible for the religious and moral life of Athens. As such it had to approve any new deity."[7] The site was named for Ares, the god of war. The hill was also one of the locations where the city council met and possibly the site where Paul appeared before the council.[8] ✣

---

[1] J. D. Douglas and Merrill C. Tenney, "Athens" in *The New International Dictionary of the Bible* (Grand Rapids: Zondervan, 1987), 108. [2] Frank Stagg, *The Book of Acts: The Early Struggle for an Unhindered Gospel* (Nashville: Broadman, 1955), 179. [3] Douglas and Tenney, "Athens," 108. [4] Arthur A. Rupprecht, "Athens" in *ZPEB*, 403. [5] Charles F. Pfeiffer, ed., "Athens" in *The Biblical World: A Dictionary of Biblical Archaeology* (Nashville: Broadman, 1976), 118. [6] Thomas V. Brisco, *Holman Bible Atlas* (Nashville: Broadman & Holman, 1998), 251. [7] Walter A. Elwell, ed., "Athens" in *Baker Encyclopedia of the Bible* (*BEB*) (Grand Rapids: Baker, 1989), 230. [8] Merrill F. Unger, *Archaeology and the New Testament* (Grand Rapids: Zondervan, 1964), 237.

I even found an altar on which was inscribed, 'To an
Unknown God.' Therefore, what you worship in ignorance, this I proclaim to you. 24 The God who made
the world and everything in it — he is Lord of heaven
and earth — does not live in shrines made by hands.
25 Neither is he served by human hands, as though he
needed anything, since he himself gives everyone life
and breath and all things. 26 From one man[A] he has
made every nationality to live over the whole earth
and has determined their appointed times and the
boundaries of where they live. 27 He did this so that
they might seek God, and perhaps they might reach
out and find him, though he is not far from each one
of us. 28 For in him we live and move and have our being, as even some of your own poets have said, 'For
we are also his offspring.' 29 Since, then, we are God's
offspring, we shouldn't think that the divine nature
is like gold or silver or stone, an image fashioned by
human art and imagination.
30 "Therefore, having overlooked the times of ignorance, God now commands all people everywhere to
repent, 31 because he has set a day when he is going to
judge the world in righteousness by the man he has
appointed. He has provided proof of this to everyone
by raising him from the dead."
32 When they heard about the resurrection of the
dead, some began to ridicule him, but others said,
"We'd like to hear from you again about this." 33 So Paul
left their presence. 34 However, some people joined
him and believed, including Dionysius the Areopa-
gite, a woman named Damaris, and others with them.

FOUNDING THE CORINTHIAN CHURCH

18 After this, he[B] left Athens and went to Corinth,
2 where he found a Jew named Aquila, a native
of Pontus, who had recently come from Italy with his
wife Priscilla because Claudius had ordered all the
Jews to leave Rome. Paul came to them, 3 and since
they were of the same occupation, tentmakers by
trade, he stayed with them and worked. 4 He reasoned
in the synagogue every Sabbath and tried to persuade
both Jews and Greeks.
5 When Silas and Timothy arrived from Macedonia, Paul devoted himself to preaching the word[C]
and testified to the Jews that Jesus is the Messiah.
6 When they resisted and blasphemed, he shook out
his clothes and told them, "Your blood is on your own
heads! I am innocent.[D] From now on I will go to the

[A] **17:26** Other mss read *blood* [B] **18:1** Other mss read *Paul*
[C] **18:5** Other mss read *was urged by the Spirit* [D] **18:6** Lit *clean*

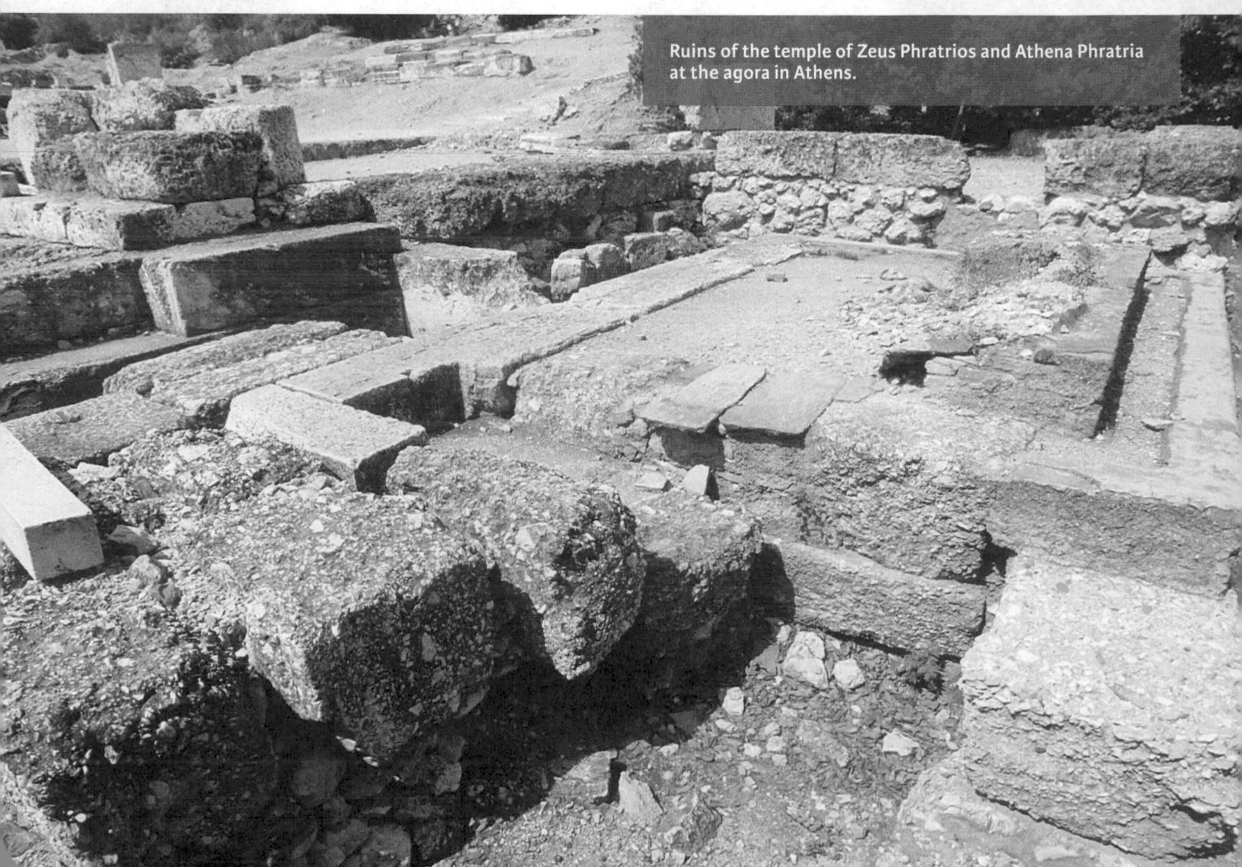
Ruins of the temple of Zeus Phratrios and Athena Phratria at the agora in Athens.

DIGGING DEEPER ***Gallio Inscription***

Paul ministered in Corinth for eighteen months (Ac 18:11) and wrote letters to the church there. While in Corinth, he appeared before Gallio the proconsul on charges of breaking Jewish law (18:12–13). Gallio dismissed the complaint. As a result, the synagogue leader who charged Paul was beaten by an angry mob. The dismissal also enabled Paul to remain in Corinth (18:14–18). Confirmation of Gallio's existence surfaced in 1908 when a proclamation issued by Emperor Claudius (AD 41–54) was unearthed. It names Gallio as the appointed proconsul of the region. From this inscription, we can date Gallio's rule and Paul's stay in Corinth to between AD 51 and 53. Sir William Ramsay (1852–1916) was once skeptical of Luke's accuracy, but his studies led him to conclude that Luke correctly documented thirty-two countries, fifty-four cities, and nine islands.

Gentiles." 7 So he left there and went to the house of a
man named Titius Justus, a worshiper of God, whose
house was next door to the synagogue. 8 Crispus, the
leader of the synagogue, believed in the Lord, along
with his whole household. Many of the Corinthians,
when they heard, believed and were baptized.
9 The Lord said to Paul in a night vision, "Don't be
afraid, but keep on speaking and don't be silent. 10 For
I am with you, and no one will lay a hand on you to
hurt you, because I have many people in this city."
11 He stayed there a year and a half, teaching the word
of God among them.
12 While Gallio was proconsul of Achaia, the Jews
made a united attack against Paul and brought him to
the tribunal. 13 "This man," they said, " is persuading
people to worship God in ways contrary to the law."
14 As Paul was about to open his mouth, Gallio said
to the Jews, "If it were a matter of wrongdoing or of
a serious crime, it would be reasonable for me to put
up with you Jews. 15 But if these are questions about
words, names, and your own law, see to it yourselves.
I refuse to be a judge of such things." 16 So he drove
them from the tribunal. 17 And they all[A] seized Sosthenes, the leader of the synagogue, and beat him in
front of the tribunal, but none of these things mattered to Gallio.

THE RETURN TRIP TO ANTIOCH

18 After staying for some time, Paul said farewell to
the brothers and sisters and sailed away to Syria,
accompanied by Priscilla and Aquila. He shaved his
head at Cenchreae because of a vow he had taken.
19 When they reached Ephesus he left them there, but
he himself entered the synagogue and debated with
the Jews. 20 When they asked him to stay for a longer
time, he declined, 21 but he said farewell and added,[B]
"I'll come back to you again, if God wills." Then he set
sail from Ephesus.
22 On landing at Caesarea, he went up to Jerusalem
and greeted the church, then went down to Antioch.
23 After spending some time there, he set out, traveling through one place after another in the region of
Galatia and Phrygia, strengthening all the disciples.

THE ELOQUENT APOLLOS

24 Now a Jew named Apollos, a native Alexandrian,
an eloquent man who was competent in the use of
the Scriptures, arrived in Ephesus. 25 He had been
instructed in the way of the Lord; and being fervent
in spirit,[C] he was speaking and teaching accurately
about Jesus, although he knew only John's baptism.
26 He began to speak boldly in the synagogue. After
Priscilla and Aquila heard him, they took him aside[D]
and explained the way of God to him more accurately.
27 When he wanted to cross over to Achaia, the brothers and sisters wrote to the disciples to welcome him.
After he arrived, he was a great help to those who by
grace had believed. 28 For he vigorously refuted the
Jews in public, demonstrating through the Scriptures
that Jesus is the Messiah.

TWELVE DISCIPLES OF JOHN THE BAPTIST

19 While Apollos was in Corinth, Paul traveled
through the interior regions and came to Ephesus. He found some disciples 2 and asked them, "Did
you receive the Holy Spirit when you believed? "
"No," they told him, "we haven't even heard that
there is a Holy Spirit."
3 "Into what then were you baptized? " he asked
them.
"Into John's baptism," they replied.
4 Paul said, "John baptized with a baptism of repentance, telling the people that they should believe in
the one who would come after him, that is, in Jesus."
5 When they heard this, they were baptized into
the name of the Lord Jesus. 6 And when Paul had laid
his hands on them, the Holy Spirit came on them, and
they began to speak in tongues[E] and to prophesy.
7 Now there were about twelve men in all.

IN THE LECTURE HALL OF TYRANNUS

8 Paul entered the synagogue and spoke boldly over a
period of three months, arguing and persuading them

[A] **18:17** Other mss read *Then all the Greeks* [B] **18:21** Other mss add *"By all means it is necessary to keep the coming festival in Jerusalem. But* [C] **18:25** Or *in the Spirit* [D] **18:26** Lit *they received him* [E] **19:6** Or *other languages*

The Parthenon, a temple dedicated to the goddess Athena, at the Acropolis.

Statuette of Artemis, dated to the second century AD.

about the kingdom of God. 9 But when some became
hardened and would not believe, slandering the Way
in front of the crowd, he withdrew from them, taking
the disciples, and conducted discussions every day in
the lecture hall of Tyrannus. 10 This went on for two
years, so that all the residents of Asia, both Jews and
Greeks, heard the word of the Lord.

DEMONISM DEFEATED AT EPHESUS

11 God was performing extraordinary miracles by
Paul's hands, 12 so that even facecloths or aprons[A]
that had touched his skin were brought to the sick,
and the diseases left them, and the evil spirits came
out of them.
13 Now some of the itinerant Jewish exorcists also
attempted to pronounce the name of the Lord Jesus
over those who had evil spirits, saying, "I command
you by the Jesus that Paul preaches!" 14 Seven sons of
Sceva, a Jewish high priest, were doing this. 15 The evil
spirit answered them, "I know Jesus, and I recognize
Paul — but who are you?" 16 Then the man who had
the evil spirit jumped on them, overpowered them all,
and prevailed against them, so that they ran out of
that house naked and wounded. 17 When this became
known to everyone who lived in Ephesus, both Jews
and Greeks, they became afraid, and the name of the
Lord Jesus was held in high esteem.
18 And many who had become believers came confessing and disclosing their practices, 19 while many
of those who had practiced magic collected their
books and burned them in front of everyone. So they
calculated their value and found it to be fifty thousand pieces of silver. 20 In this way the word of the
Lord spread and prevailed.

THE RIOT IN EPHESUS

21 After these events, Paul resolved by the Spirit[B] to
pass through Macedonia and Achaia and go to Jerusalem. "After I've been there," he said, "It is necessary for me to see Rome as well." 22 After sending to
Macedonia two of those who assisted him, Timothy
and Erastus, he himself stayed in Asia for a while.
23 About that time there was a major disturbance
about the Way. 24 For a person named Demetrius,
a silversmith who made silver shrines of Artemis,
provided a great deal of business for the craftsmen.

[A] **19:12** Or *sweat cloths* [B] **19:21** Or *in his spirit*

The theater at Ephesus. Originally a smaller structure, the theater was first built as early as the second century BC. Later additions and renovations in the first–third centuries AD brought seating capacity up to about 25,000 persons.

25 When he had assembled them, as well as the workers engaged in this type of business, he said, "Men,
you know that our prosperity is derived from this
business. 26 You see and hear that not only in Ephesus,
but in almost all of Asia, this man Paul has persuaded and misled a considerable number of people by
saying that gods made by hand are not gods. 27 Not
only do we run a risk that our business may be dis-
credited, but also that the temple of the great goddess
Artemis may be despised and her magnificence come
to the verge of ruin — the very one all of Asia and the
world worship."
28 When they had heard this, they were filled with
rage and began to cry out, "Great is Artemis of the
Ephesians!" 29 So the city was filled with confusion,
and they rushed all together into the amphitheater,
dragging along Gaius and Aristarchus, Macedonians
who were Paul's traveling companions. 30 Although
Paul wanted to go in before the people, the disciples did not let him. 31 Even some of the provincial
officials of Asia, who were his friends, sent word
to him, pleading with him not to venture[A] into the
amphitheater. 32 Some were shouting one thing and
some another, because the assembly was in confusion, and most of them did not know why they had
come together. 33 Some Jews in the crowd gave instructions to Alexander[B] after they pushed him to the
front. Motioning with his hand, Alexander wanted
to make his defense to the people. 34 But when they
recognized that he was a Jew, they all shouted in
unison for about two hours, "Great is Artemis of the
Ephesians!"
35 When the city clerk had calmed the crowd down,
he said, "People of Ephesus! What person is there
who doesn't know that the city of the Ephesians is
the temple guardian of the great[C] Artemis, and of the
image that fell from heaven? 36 Therefore, since these
things are undeniable, you must keep calm and not
do anything rash. 37 For you have brought these men
here who are not temple robbers or blasphemers of
our[D] goddess. 38 So if Demetrius and the craftsmen
who are with him have a case against anyone, the
courts are in session, and there are proconsuls. Let
them bring charges against one another. 39 But if you
seek anything further, it must be decided in a legal
assembly. 40 In fact, we run a risk of being charged
with rioting for what happened today, since there
is no justification that we can give as a reason for
this disturbance." 41 After saying this, he dismissed
the assembly.

[A] **19:31** Lit *not to give himself* [B] **19:33** Or *thought it was about Alexander* [C] **19:35** Other mss add *goddess* [D] **19:37** Other mss read *your*

PAUL IN MACEDONIA

20 After the uproar was over, Paul sent for the disciples, encouraged them, and after saying farewell, departed to go to Macedonia. 2 And when he had passed through those areas and offered them many words of encouragement, he came to Greece 3 and stayed three months. The Jews plotted against him when he was about to set sail for Syria, and so he decided to go back through Macedonia. 4 He was accompanied[A] by Sopater son of Pyrrhus[B] from Berea, Aristarchus and Secundus from Thessalonica, Gaius from Derbe, Timothy, and Tychicus and Trophimus from the province of Asia. 5 These men went on ahead and waited for us in Troas, 6 but we sailed away from Philippi after the Festival of Unleavened Bread. In five days we reached them at Troas, where we spent seven days.

EUTYCHUS REVIVED AT TROAS

7 On the first day of the week, we assembled to break bread. Paul spoke to them, and since he was about to depart the next day, he kept on talking until midnight. 8 There were many lamps in the room upstairs where we were assembled, 9 and a young man named Eutychus was sitting on a window sill and sank into a deep sleep as Paul kept on talking. When he was overcome by sleep, he fell down from the third story and was picked up dead. 10 But Paul went down, bent over him, embraced him, and said, "Don't be alarmed, because he's alive." 11 After going upstairs, breaking the bread, and eating, Paul talked a long time until dawn. Then he left. 12 They brought the boy home alive and were greatly comforted.

FROM TROAS TO MILETUS

13 We went on ahead to the ship and sailed for Assos, where we were going to take Paul on board, because these were his instructions, since he himself was going by land. 14 When he met us at Assos, we took him on board and went on to Mitylene. 15 Sailing from there, the next day we arrived off Chios. The following day we crossed over to Samos, and[C] the day after, we came to Miletus. 16 For Paul had decided to sail past Ephesus to avoid spending time in the province of Asia, because he was hurrying to be in Jerusalem, if possible, for the day of Pentecost.

FAREWELL ADDRESS TO THE EPHESIAN ELDERS

17 Now from Miletus, he sent to Ephesus and summoned the elders of the church. 18 When they came

[A] **20:4** Other mss add *to Asia* [B] **20:4** Other mss omit *son of Pyrrhus*
[C] **20:15** Other mss add *after staying at Trogyllium*

Rising in the distance, Mount Olympus, which many considered to be home of the gods.

to him, he said to them, "You know, from the first day I set foot in Asia, how I was with you the whole time, 19 serving the Lord with all humility, with tears, and during the trials that came to me through the plots of the Jews. 20 You know that I did not avoid proclaiming to you anything that was profitable or from teaching you publicly and from house to house. 21 I testified to both Jews and Greeks about repentance toward God and faith in our Lord Jesus.

22 "And now I am on my way to Jerusalem, compelled by the Spirit,[A] not knowing what I will encounter there, 23 except that in every town the Holy Spirit warns me that chains and afflictions are waiting for me. 24 But I consider my life of no value to myself; my purpose is to finish my course[B] and the ministry I received from the Lord Jesus, to testify to the gospel of God's grace.

25 "And now I know that none of you, among whom I went about preaching the kingdom, will ever see me again. 26 Therefore I declare to you this day that I am innocent[C] of the blood of all of you, 27 because I did not avoid declaring to you the whole plan of God. 28 Be on guard for yourselves and for all the flock of which the Holy Spirit has appointed you as overseers, to shepherd the church of God,[D] which he purchased with his own blood. 29 I know that after my departure savage wolves will come in among you, not sparing the flock. 30 Men will rise up even from your own number and distort the truth to lure the disciples into following them. 31 Therefore be on the alert, remembering that night and day for three years I never stopped warning each one of you with tears.

32 "And now I commit you to God and to the word of his grace, which is able to build you up and to give you an inheritance among all who are sanctified. 33 I have not coveted anyone's silver or gold or clothing. 34 You yourselves know that I worked with my own hands to support myself and those who are with me. 35 In every way I've shown you that it is necessary to help the weak by laboring like this and to remember the words of the Lord Jesus, because he said, 'It is more blessed to give than to receive.' "

36 After he said this, he knelt down and prayed with all of them. 37 There were many tears shed by everyone. They embraced Paul and kissed him, 38 grieving most of all over his statement that they would never see his face again. And they accompanied him to the ship.

[A] **20:22** Or *in my spirit* [B] **20:24** Other mss add *with joy* [C] **20:26** Lit *clean* [D] **20:28** Some mss read *church of the Lord*; other mss read *church of the Lord and God*

Overlooking Philippi, which was named after Philip II, king of Macedon. Established after 400 BC as a center for mining gold in this region of Macedonia, Philippi's wealth and location along the Via Egnatia caused it to become a prosperous and popular city.

WARNINGS ON THE JOURNEY TO JERUSALEM

21 After we tore ourselves away from them,
we set sail straight for Cos, the next day to
Rhodes, and from there to Patara. 2 Finding a ship
crossing over to Phoenicia, we boarded and set sail.
3 After we sighted Cyprus, passing to the south of it,[A]
we sailed on to Syria and arrived at Tyre, since the
ship was to unload its cargo there. 4 We sought out
the disciples and stayed there seven days. Through
the Spirit they told Paul not to go to Jerusalem.
5 When our time had come to an end, we left to
continue our journey, while all of them, with their
wives and children, accompanied us out of the city.
After kneeling down on the beach to pray, 6 we said
farewell to one another and boarded the ship, and
they returned home.
7 When we completed our voyage[B] from Tyre, we
reached Ptolemais, where we greeted the brothers
and sisters and stayed with them for a day. 8 The next
day we left and came to Caesarea, where we entered
the house of Philip the evangelist, who was one of
the Seven, and stayed with him. 9 This man had four
virgin daughters who prophesied.
10 After we had been there for several days, a
prophet named Agabus came down from Judea. 11 He
came to us, took Paul's belt, tied his own feet and
hands, and said, "This is what the Holy Spirit says: 'In
this way the Jews in Jerusalem will bind the man who
owns this belt and deliver him over to the Gentiles.' "
12 When we heard this, both we and the local people
pleaded with him not to go up to Jerusalem.
13 Then Paul replied, "What are you doing, weeping
and breaking my heart? For I am ready not only to be
bound but also to die in Jerusalem for the name of
the Lord Jesus."
14 Since he would not be persuaded, we said no
more except, "The Lord's will be done."

CONFLICT OVER THE GENTILE MISSION

15 After this we got ready and went up to Jerusalem.
16 Some of the disciples from Caesarea also went with
us and brought us to Mnason of Cyprus, an early disciple, with whom we were to stay.
17 When we reached Jerusalem, the brothers and
sisters welcomed us warmly. 18 The following day
Paul went in with us to James, and all the elders
were present. 19 After greeting them, he reported
in detail what God had done among the Gentiles
through his ministry.
20 When they heard it, they glorified God and said,
"You see, brother, how many thousands of Jews there
are who have believed, and they are all zealous for

[A] **21:3** Lit *leaving it on the left* [B] **21:7** Or *As we continued our voyage*

Exterior walls and seating area at the theater at Caesarea Maritima.

the law. 21 But they have been informed about you
— that you are teaching all the Jews who are among
the Gentiles to abandon Moses, telling them not to
circumcise their children or to live according to our
customs. 22 So what is to be done?[A] They will certainly hear that you've come. 23 Therefore do what we
tell you: We have four men who have made a vow.
24 Take these men, purify yourself along with them,
and pay for them to get their heads shaved. Then
everyone will know that what they were told about
you amounts to nothing, but that you yourself are
also careful about observing the law. 25 With regard
to the Gentiles who have believed, we have written
a letter containing our decision that[B] they should
keep themselves from food sacrificed to idols, from
blood, from what is strangled, and from sexual immorality."

THE RIOT IN THE TEMPLE

26 So the next day, Paul took the men, having purified himself along with them, and entered the temple, announcing the completion of the purification
days when the offering would be made for each
of them. 27 When the seven days were nearly over,
some Jews from the province of Asia saw him in
the temple, stirred up the whole crowd, and seized
him, 28 shouting, "Fellow Israelites, help! This is the
man who teaches everyone everywhere against our
people, our law, and this place. What's more, he also
brought Greeks into the temple and has defiled this
holy place." 29 For they had previously seen Trophimus the Ephesian in the city with him, and they
supposed that Paul had brought him into the temple.
30 The whole city was stirred up, and the people
rushed together. They seized Paul, dragged him out
of the temple, and at once the gates were shut.
31 As they were trying to kill him, word went up to
the commander of the regiment that all Jerusalem
was in chaos. 32 Taking along soldiers and centurions, he immediately ran down to them. Seeing the
commander and the soldiers, they stopped beating
Paul. 33 Then the commander approached, took him
into custody, and ordered him to be bound with two
chains. He asked who he was and what he had done.
34 Some in the crowd were shouting one thing and
some another. Since he was not able to get reliable
information because of the uproar, he ordered him
to be taken into the barracks. 35 When Paul got to the
steps, he had to be carried by the soldiers because of
the violence of the crowd, 36 for the mass of people
followed, yelling, "Get rid of him!"

[A] **21:22** Other mss add *A multitude has to come together, since*
[B] **21:25** Other mss add *they should observe no such thing, except that*

The Cilician Pass through the Taurus Mountains.

PAUL'S DEFENSE BEFORE THE JERUSALEM MOB

37 As he was about to be brought into the barracks,
Paul said to the commander, "Am I allowed to say
something to you?"
He replied, "You know how to speak Greek?
38 Aren't you the Egyptian who started a revolt some
time ago and led four thousand men of the Assassins
into the wilderness?"
39 Paul said, "I am a Jewish man from Tarsus of
Cilicia, a citizen of an important city. Now I ask you,
let me speak to the people."
40 After he had given permission, Paul stood on
the steps and motioned with his hand to the people.
When there was a great hush, he addressed them in
22 Aramaic:[A] 1 "Brothers and fathers, listen now
to my defense before you." 2 When they heard
that he was addressing them in Aramaic,[A] they became even quieter. 3 He continued, "I am a Jew, born in
Tarsus of Cilicia but brought up in this city, educated
at the feet of Gamaliel according to the strictness of
our ancestral law. I was zealous for God, just as all of
you are today. 4 I persecuted this Way to the death,
arresting and putting both men and women in jail,
5 as both the high priest and the whole council of
elders can testify about me. After I received letters
from them to the brothers, I traveled to Damascus
to arrest those who were there and bring them to
Jerusalem to be punished.

PAUL'S TESTIMONY

6 "As I was traveling and approaching Damascus,
about noon an intense light from heaven suddenly
flashed around me. 7 I fell to the ground and heard
a voice saying to me, 'Saul, Saul, why are you persecuting me?'
8 "I answered, 'Who are you, Lord?'
"He said to me, 'I am Jesus of Nazareth, the one you
are persecuting.' 9 Now those who were with me saw
the light,[B] but they did not hear the voice of the one
who was speaking to me.
10 "I said, 'What should I do, Lord?'
"The Lord told me, 'Get up and go into Damascus,
and there you will be told everything that you have
been assigned to do.'
11 "Since I couldn't see because of the brightness of
the light,[C] I was led by the hand by those who were
with me, and went into Damascus. 12 Someone named

[A] **21:40; 22:2** Or *Hebrew* [B] **22:9** Other mss add *and were afraid*
[C] **22:11** Lit *the glory of that light*

Partially excavated at Tarsus, ruins dating to the first century AD. Shown are a Roman-Era basalt stone road, columns, and drainage system. The remains in the distance are probably the site of the agora.

Ananias, a devout man according to the law, who
had a good reputation with all the Jews living there,
13 came and stood by me and said, 'Brother Saul, regain your sight.' And in that very hour I looked up and
saw him. 14 And he said, 'The God of our ancestors has
appointed you to know his will, to see the Righteous
One, and to hear the words from his mouth, 15 since
you will be a witness for him to all people of what
you have seen and heard. 16 And now, why are you
delaying? Get up and be baptized, and wash away
your sins, calling on his name.'

17 "After I returned to Jerusalem and was praying in
the temple, I fell into a trance 18 and saw him telling
me, 'Hurry and get out of Jerusalem quickly, because
they will not accept your testimony about me.'

19 "But I said, 'Lord, they know that in synagogue
after synagogue I had those who believed in you imprisoned and beaten. 20 And when the blood of your
witness Stephen was being shed, I stood there giving
approval[A] and guarding the clothes of those who
killed him.'

21 "He said to me, 'Go, because I will send you far
away to the Gentiles.' "

PAUL'S ROMAN PROTECTION

22 They listened to him up to this point. Then they
raised their voices, shouting, "Wipe this man off the
face of the earth! He should not be allowed to live!"

23 As they were yelling and flinging aside their garments and throwing dust into the air, 24 the commander
ordered him to be brought into the barracks, directing
that he be interrogated with the scourge to discover
the reason they were shouting against him like this.
25 As they stretched him out for the lash, Paul said to
the centurion standing by, "Is it legal for you to scourge
a man who is a Roman citizen and is uncondemned?"

26 When the centurion heard this, he went and
reported to the commander, saying, "What are you
going to do? For this man is a Roman citizen."

27 The commander came and said to him, "Tell me,
are you a Roman citizen?"

"Yes," he said.

28 The commander replied, "I bought this citizenship for a large amount of money."

"But I was born a citizen," Paul said.

29 So those who were about to examine him withdrew from him immediately. The commander too was
alarmed when he realized Paul was a Roman citizen
and he had bound him.

PAUL BEFORE THE SANHEDRIN

30 The next day, since he wanted to find out exactly why Paul was being accused by the Jews, he released him[B] and instructed the chief priests and all
the Sanhedrin to convene. He brought Paul down and
23 placed him before them. 1 Paul looked straight
at the Sanhedrin and said, "Brothers, I have
lived my life before God in all good conscience to this
day." 2 The high priest Ananias ordered those who
were standing next to him to strike him on the mouth.
3 Then Paul said to him, "God is going to strike you,
you whitewashed wall! You are sitting there judging
me according to the law, and yet in violation of the
law are you ordering me to be struck?"

4 Those standing nearby said, "Do you dare revile
God's high priest?"

5 "I did not know, brothers, that he was the high
priest," replied Paul. "For it is written, **You must not
speak evil of a ruler of your people.**"[C] 6 When Paul
realized that one part of them were Sadducees and
the other part were Pharisees, he cried out in the Sanhedrin, "Brothers, I am a Pharisee, a son of Pharisees.
I am being judged because of the hope of the resurrection of the dead!" 7 When he said this, a dispute
broke out between the Pharisees and the Sadducees,
and the assembly was divided. 8 For the Sadducees
say there is no resurrection, and neither angel nor
spirit, but the Pharisees affirm them all.

9 The shouting grew loud, and some of the scribes
of the Pharisees' party got up and argued vehemently,
"We find nothing evil in this man. What if a spirit or
an angel has spoken to him?"[D]

10 When the dispute became violent, the commander feared that Paul might be torn apart by them and
ordered the troops to go down, take him away from
them, and bring him into the barracks. 11 The following night, the Lord stood by him and said, "Have courage! For as you have testified about me in Jerusalem,
so it is necessary for you to testify in Rome."

THE PLOT AGAINST PAUL

12 When it was morning, the Jews formed a conspiracy and bound themselves under a curse not to eat or
drink until they had killed Paul. 13 There were more
than forty who had formed this plot. 14 These men
went to the chief priests and elders and said, "We
have bound ourselves under a solemn curse that we
won't eat anything until we have killed Paul. 15 So now
you, along with the Sanhedrin, make a request to the
commander that he bring him down to you[E] as if you
were going to investigate his case more thoroughly.
But, before he gets near, we are ready to kill him."

16 But the son of Paul's sister, hearing about their
ambush, came and entered the barracks and reported
it to Paul. 17 Paul called one of the centurions and said,
"Take this young man to the commander, because he
has something to report to him."

[A] **22:20** Other mss add *of his murder* [B] **22:30** Other mss add *from his chains* [C] **23:5** Ex 22:28 [D] **23:9** Other mss add *Let us not fight God.* [E] **23:15** Other mss add *tomorrow*

18 So he took him, brought him to the commander, and said, "The prisoner Paul called me and asked me to bring this young man to you, because he has something to tell you."

19 The commander took him by the hand, led him aside, and inquired privately, "What is it you have to report to me?"

20 "The Jews," he said, "have agreed to ask you to bring Paul down to the Sanhedrin tomorrow, as though they are going to hold a somewhat more careful inquiry about him. 21 Don't let them persuade you, because there are more than forty of them lying in ambush — men who have bound themselves under a curse not to eat or drink until they have killed him. Now they are ready, waiting for your consent."

22 So the commander dismissed the young man and instructed him, "Don't tell anyone that you have informed me about this."

TO CAESAREA BY NIGHT

23 He summoned two of his centurions and said, "Get two hundred soldiers ready with seventy cavalry and two hundred spearmen to go to Caesarea at nine tonight.[A] 24 Also provide mounts to ride so that Paul may be brought safely to Felix the governor."

25 He wrote the following letter:[B]

26 Claudius Lysias,
To the most excellent governor Felix:
Greetings.

27 When this man had been seized by the Jews and was about to be killed by them, I arrived with my troops and rescued him because I learned that he is a Roman citizen. 28 Wanting to know the charge they were accusing him of, I brought him down before their Sanhedrin. 29 I found out that the accusations were concerning questions of their law, and that there was no charge that merited death or imprisonment. 30 When I was informed that there was a plot against the man,[C] I sent him to you right away. I also ordered his accusers to state their case against him in your presence.[D]

31 So the soldiers took Paul during the night and brought him to Antipatris as they were ordered. 32 The next day, they returned to the barracks, allowing the cavalry to go on with him. 33 When these men entered Caesarea and delivered the letter to the governor, they also presented Paul to him. 34 After he[E] read it, he asked what province he was from. When he learned he was from Cilicia, 35 he said, "I will give you a hearing whenever your accusers also get here." He ordered that he be kept under guard in Herod's palace.[F]

THE ACCUSATION AGAINST PAUL

24 Five days later Ananias the high priest came down with some elders and a lawyer named Tertullus. These men presented their case against Paul to the governor. 2 When Paul was called in, Tertullus began to accuse him and said, "We enjoy great peace because of you, and reforms are taking place for the benefit of this nation because of your foresight. 3 We acknowledge this in every way and everywhere, most excellent Felix, with utmost gratitude. 4 But, so that I will not burden you any further, I request that you would be kind enough to give us a brief hearing. 5 For we have found this man to be a plague, an agitator among all the Jews throughout the Roman world, and a ringleader of the sect of the Nazarenes. 6 He even tried to desecrate the temple, and so we apprehended him.[G] By examining him yourself you will be able to discern the truth about these charges we are bringing against him." 9 The Jews also joined in the attack, alleging that these things were true.

PAUL'S DEFENSE BEFORE FELIX

10 When the governor motioned for him to speak, Paul replied, "Because I know you have been a judge of this nation for many years, I am glad to offer my defense in what concerns me. 11 You can verify for yourself that it is no more than twelve days since I went up to worship in Jerusalem. 12 They didn't find me arguing with anyone or causing a disturbance among the crowd, either in the temple or in the synagogues or anywhere in the city. 13 Neither can they prove the charges they are now making against me. 14 But I admit this to you: I worship the God of my ancestors according to the Way, which they call a sect, believing everything that is in accordance with the law and written in the prophets. 15 I have a hope in God, which these men themselves also accept, that there will be a resurrection,[H] both of the righteous and the unrighteous. 16 I always strive to have a clear conscience toward God and men. 17 After many years, I came to bring charitable gifts and offerings to my people. 18 While I was doing this, some Jews from Asia found me ritually purified in the temple, without a crowd and without any uproar. 19 It is they who ought to be here before you to bring charges, if they have anything against me. 20 Or let these men here state what wrongdoing they found in me when I stood before the Sanhedrin, 21 other than this one statement

[A] **23:23** Lit *at the third hour tonight* [B] **23:25** Or *He wrote a letter to this effect:* [C] **23:30** Other mss add *by the Jews* [D] **23:30** Other mss add *Farewell* [E] **23:34** Other mss read *the governor* [F] **23:35** Or *headquarters* [G] **24:6** Some mss include vv. 6b–8a: *and wanted to judge him according to our law.* ***7*** *But Lysias the commander came and took him from our hands with great force,* ***8*** *commanding his accusers to come to you.* [H] **24:15** Other mss add *of the dead*

I shouted while standing among them, 'Today I am
on trial before you concerning the resurrection of
the dead.' "

THE VERDICT POSTPONED

22 Since Felix was well informed about the Way, he
adjourned the hearing, saying, "When Lysias the commander comes down, I will decide your case." 23 He
ordered that the centurion keep Paul under guard,
though he could have some freedom, and that he
should not prevent any of his friends from meeting[A]
his needs.
24 Several days later, when Felix came with his wife
Drusilla, who was Jewish, he sent for Paul and listened to him on the subject of faith in Christ Jesus.
25 Now as he spoke about righteousness, self-control,
and the judgment to come, Felix became afraid and
replied, "Leave for now, but when I have an opportunity I'll call for you." 26 At the same time he was also
hoping that Paul would offer him money.[B] So he sent
for him quite often and conversed with him.
27 After two years had passed, Porcius Festus succeeded Felix, and because Felix wanted to do the Jews
a favor, he left Paul in prison.

APPEAL TO CAESAR

25 Three days after Festus arrived in the province,
he went up to Jerusalem from Caesarea. 2 The
chief priests and the leaders of the Jews presented
their case against Paul to him; and they appealed,
3 asking for a favor against Paul, that Festus summon
him to Jerusalem. They were, in fact, preparing an
ambush along the road to kill him. 4 Festus, however, answered that Paul should be kept at Caesarea,
and that he himself was about to go there shortly.
5 "Therefore," he said, "let those of you who have authority go down with me and accuse him, if he has
done anything wrong."
6 When he had spent not more than eight or ten
days among them, he went down to Caesarea. The
next day, seated at the tribunal, he commanded Paul
to be brought in. 7 When he arrived, the Jews who had
come down from Jerusalem stood around him and
brought many serious charges that they were not
able to prove. 8 Then Paul made his defense: "Neither
against the Jewish law, nor against the temple, nor
against Caesar have I sinned in any way."
9 But Festus, wanting to do the Jews a favor, replied
to Paul, "Are you willing to go up to Jerusalem to be
tried before me there on these charges?"
10 Paul replied, "I am standing at Caesar's tribunal,
where I ought to be tried. I have done no wrong to the
Jews, as even you yourself know very well. 11 If then I
did anything wrong and am deserving of death, I am
not trying to escape death; but if there is nothing to
what these men accuse me of, no one can give me up
to them. I appeal to Caesar!"
12 Then after Festus conferred with his council,
he replied, "You have appealed to Caesar; to Caesar
you will go."

[A] **24:23** Other mss add *or visiting* [B] **24:26** Other mss add *so that he might release him*

At Caesarea Maritima, traditional site where Paul appeared before Festus. Because Paul was a Roman citizen, he had the right to make the appeal that the emperor hear his case.

Felix and Festus: Roman Governors

by William B. Tolar

Rome ruled the land of ancient Israel from 37 to 4 BC through a client-king, Herod the Great. Upon Herod's death in 4 BC, his son Archelaus ruled Judea (and Samaria) for ten years but was removed by Augustus Caesar in AD 6 because of complaints by disgruntled Jewish leaders. Rome then governed Judea from AD 6 to 66 with fourteen "governors" or "procurators" except for a three-year kingly reign (41–44) by one of Herod the Great's grandsons. Antonius Felix and Porcius Festus were numbers ten and eleven in this list and ruled AD 52–60 and 60–62 respectively.[1]

There were two kinds of provinces—imperial and senatorial—and thus, two kinds of procuratorial appointments: by the emperor and by the Senate.[2] The procurator of Judea was administratively under the emperor's "legate" who governed the province of Syria. Procurators appointed by the emperor were regimental commanders and, thus, the highest military tribunal. They exercised power as a superior court because of their military position but could also pass the death sentence on civilians. They could at times intervene in local civilian administrative matters. But the Jews preserved a large measure of autonomy, especially in religious matters.

ANTONIUS FELIX (52–60 AD)

Judea was a highly volatile place in AD 52 when Claudius appointed Felix as the procurator of procurator. The emperor had just banished the previous procurator, publicly executed a Roman army commander, and put to death three of the Samaritan leaders who were involved in atrocities against Jewish civilians. Josephus recorded a series of violent events that escalated tensions, ill will, and animosity during the rule of the earlier procurators.

Usually, procurators were drawn from the equestrian class (persons of dignity and high rank), but Felix was a freedman—a freed slave! He was the "first slave in history ever to become the governor of a Roman province."[3] Historians agree that he was appointed originally because of family influences and personal wealth—not because of personal qualifications. Tacitus said of Felix, "with all manner of cruelty and lust he exercised the functions of a prince with the disposition of a slave."[4] Felix was "totally lacking in understanding of or sympathy for the Jews."[5]

According to Josephus, Felix inherited a chaotic situation when he became procurator. He said the land had become filled with "robbers" and "fanatics." Felix was determined to eliminate the terrorism that had plagued Judea for many years, so he bribed informers, used torture, and relentlessly pursued troublemakers. He crucified many of them (including leaders of the Zealots and other religious groups).

The Zealots became more fanatical and desperate. In Jerusalem they organized themselves into a group of assassins called *sicarii*, a name derived from the short, curved daggers they hid under their clothes and with which they killed anyone who sympathized with the Romans. According to Josephus, they committed numerous murders every day in broad daylight, causing everybody to live in terror.

The final event that brought Felix's downfall was his sending Roman troops to put down a serious outbreak of hostilities between Jews and Gentiles in Caesarea. Thousands of Jews were killed; Roman troops, with the consent of Felix, sacked and looted the houses of the wealthiest Jews in the city. Outraged Jewish leaders sent a

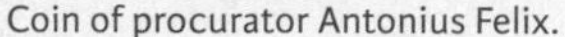
Coin of procurator Antonius Felix.

Coin of procurator Porcius Festus.

delegation to Nero who removed Felix from office.

PORCIUS FESTUS (60–62 AD)

Nero appointed Porcius Festus to succeed Felix. Unlike Felix, Festus was of a higher social status, an equestrian. We know much less about him than we do Felix, because he is mentioned only in Acts and in Josephus—the latter giving him little attention. Most scholars write about Festus in positive tones, stating that he was fair minded, tough, and incorruptible.

Festus inherited problems of many years' standing. He faced a virtually impossible situation. One modern scholar says of Festus, "It appears he was a prudent and honorable man, and in happier circumstances might have proved a successful ruler. But he was charged with an impossible task; after Felix's maladministration the province was a hotbed of bigotry, faction, and intrigue."[6]

Among the many problems Festus inherited upon becoming procurator was the deep, continual, bitter strife between Jews and Gentiles in Caesarea. Eventually blood was shed between the two groups. When Festus arrived in Caesarea, the situation was very tense, and the matter was referred to Rome for Nero to decide. The decision did not come until AD 62—long after Paul had been sent to Rome. When Nero decided in favor of the Gentiles, the Jews were infuriated by the decision; bands of assassins spread out once again over the land. More false messiahs arose, and the army had to be called out. Order broke down, and Festus died in office at this critical time. His sudden death in 62 brought renewed vigor to the extremists.

Four years later, in AD 66, the tension between the Jews and Gentiles in Caesarea burst into bloodshed again. This time it turned into a war that spread all over the country, eventually resulting in the destruction of the temple and Jerusalem in AD 70. ✣

---

[1] Along with Luke's account in the book of Acts, three important extrabiblical historians provide essential information in our study of Felix and Festus. One is the Jewish historian Josephus (born in Jerusalem ca AD 38) who wrote *Jewish War* and *Jewish Antiquities*. The other two are Roman historians: Tacitus (ca AD 55–120) wrote *The Annals* and *The Histories*; Suetonius (ca AD 69–121) wrote *The Lives of the Twelve Caesars*. [2] "Roman Provinces," *HBH*, 654. [3] William Barclay, *The Acts of the Apostles* (Philadelphia: Westminster, 1976), 167. [4] Tacitus, *Histories* 5.9. [5] John B. Polhill, *Acts* in NAC (1992), 176. [6] G. H. C. MacGregor, "Acts" in *The Interpreter's Bible* (*IB*) (Nashville: Abingdon, 1954), 9:316.

KING AGRIPPA AND BERNICE VISIT FESTUS

13 Several days later, King Agrippa and Bernice arrived in Caesarea and paid a courtesy call on Festus. 14 Since they were staying there several days, Festus presented Paul's case to the king, saying, "There's a man who was left as a prisoner by Felix. 15 When I was in Jerusalem, the chief priests and the elders of the Jews presented their case and asked that he be condemned. 16 I answered them that it is not the Roman custom to give someone up[A] before the accused faces the accusers and has an opportunity for a defense against the charges. 17 So when they had assembled here, I did not delay. The next day I took my seat at the tribunal and ordered the man to be brought in. 18 The accusers stood up but brought no charge against him of the evils I was expecting. 19 Instead they had some disagreements with him about their own religion and about a certain Jesus, a dead man Paul claimed to be alive. 20 Since I was at a loss in a dispute over such things, I asked him if he wanted to go to Jerusalem and be tried there regarding these matters. 21 But when Paul appealed to be held for trial by the Emperor,[B] I ordered him to be kept in custody until I could send him to Caesar."

22 Agrippa said to Festus, "I would like to hear the man myself."

"Tomorrow you will hear him," he replied.

PAUL BEFORE AGRIPPA

23 So the next day, Agrippa and Bernice came with great pomp and entered the auditorium with the military commanders and prominent men of the city. When Festus gave the command, Paul was brought in. 24 Then Festus said, "King Agrippa and all men present with us, you see this man. The whole Jewish community has appealed to me concerning him both in Jerusalem and here, shouting that he should not live any longer. 25 I found that he had not done anything deserving of death, but when he himself appealed to the Emperor, I decided to send him. 26 I have nothing definite to write to my lord about him. Therefore, I have brought him before all of you, and especially before you, King Agrippa, so that after this examination is over, I may have something to write. 27 For it seems unreasonable to me to send a prisoner without indicating the charges against him."

PAUL'S DEFENSE BEFORE AGRIPPA

26 Agrippa said to Paul, "You have permission to speak for yourself."

Then Paul stretched out his hand and began his defense: 2 "I consider myself fortunate that it is before you, King Agrippa, I am to make my defense today against all the accusations of the Jews, 3 especially since you are very knowledgeable about all the Jewish customs and controversies. Therefore I beg you to listen to me patiently.

4 "All the Jews know my way of life from my youth, which was spent from the beginning among my own people and in Jerusalem. 5 They have known me for a long time, if they are willing to testify, that according to the strictest sect of our religion I lived as a Pharisee. 6 And now I stand on trial because of the hope in what God promised to our ancestors, 7 the promise our twelve tribes hope to reach as they earnestly serve him night and day. King Agrippa, I am being accused by the Jews because of this hope. 8 Why do any of you consider it incredible that God raises the dead? 9 In fact, I myself was convinced that it was necessary to do many things in opposition to the name of Jesus of Nazareth. 10 I actually did this in Jerusalem, and I locked up many of the saints in prison, since I had received authority for that from the chief priests. When they were put to death, I was in agreement against them. 11 In all the synagogues I often punished them and tried to make them blaspheme. Since I was terribly enraged at them, I pursued them even to foreign cities.

PAUL'S ACCOUNT OF HIS CONVERSION AND COMMISSION

12 "I was traveling to Damascus under these circumstances with authority and a commission from the chief priests. 13 King Agrippa, while on the road at midday, I saw a light from heaven brighter than the sun, shining around me and those traveling with me. 14 We all fell to the ground, and I heard a voice speaking to me in Aramaic,[C] 'Saul, Saul, why are you persecuting me? It is hard for you to kick against the goads.'

15 "I asked, 'Who are you, Lord?'

"And the Lord replied, 'I am Jesus, the one you are persecuting. 16 But get up and stand on your feet. For I have appeared to you for this purpose, to appoint you as a servant and a witness of what you have seen and will see of me. 17 I will rescue you from your people and from the Gentiles. I am sending you to them 18 to open their eyes so that they may turn[D] from darkness to light and from the power of Satan to God, that they may receive forgiveness of sins and a share among those who are sanctified by faith in me.'

19 "So then, King Agrippa, I was not disobedient to the heavenly vision. 20 Instead, I preached to those in Damascus first, and to those in Jerusalem and in all the region of Judea, and to the Gentiles, that they should repent and turn to God, and do works worthy of repentance. 21 For this reason the Jews seized me

[A] **25:16** Other mss add *to destruction* [B] **25:21** Lit *his majesty*, also in v. 25 [C] **26:14** Or *Hebrew* [D] **26:18** Or *to turn them*

in the temple and were trying to kill me. 22 To this very day, I have had help from God, and I stand and testify to both small and great, saying nothing other than what the prophets and Moses said would take place — 23 that the Messiah would suffer, and that, as the first to rise from the dead, he would proclaim light to our people and to the Gentiles."

AGRIPPA NOT QUITE PERSUADED

24 As he was saying these things in his defense, Festus exclaimed in a loud voice, "You're out of your mind, Paul! Too much study is driving you mad."

25 But Paul replied, "I'm not out of my mind, most excellent Festus. On the contrary, I'm speaking words of truth and good judgment. 26 For the king knows about these matters, and I can speak boldly to him. For I am convinced that none of these things has escaped his notice, since this was not done in a corner. 27 King Agrippa, do you believe the prophets? I know you believe."

28 Agrippa said to Paul, "Are you going to persuade me to become a Christian so easily?"[A]

29 "I wish before God," replied Paul, "that whether easily or with difficulty,[B] not only you but all who listen to me today might become as I am — except for these chains."

30 The king, the governor, Bernice, and those sitting with them got up, 31 and when they had left they talked with each other and said, "This man is not doing anything to deserve death or imprisonment."

32 Agrippa said to Festus, "This man could have been released if he had not appealed to Caesar."

SAILING FOR ROME

27 When it was decided that we were to sail to Italy, they handed over Paul and some other prisoners to a centurion named Julius, of the Imperial Regiment.[C] 2 When we had boarded a ship of Adramyttium, we put to sea, intending to sail to ports along the coast of Asia. Aristarchus, a Macedonian of Thessalonica, was with us. 3 The next day we put in at Sidon, and Julius treated Paul kindly and allowed him to go to his friends to receive their care. 4 When we had put out to sea from there, we sailed along the northern coast[D] of Cyprus because the winds were against us. 5 After sailing through the open sea off Cilicia and Pamphylia, we reached Myra in Lycia. 6 There the centurion found an Alexandrian ship sailing for Italy and put us on board. 7 Sailing slowly for many days, with difficulty we arrived off Cnidus. Since the wind did not allow us to approach it, we sailed along the south side of Crete off Salmone. 8 With still more difficulty we sailed along the coast and came to a place called Fair Havens near the city of Lasea.

PAUL'S ADVICE IGNORED

9 By now much time had passed, and the voyage was already dangerous. Since the Day of Atonement[E] was already over, Paul gave his advice 10 and told them, "Men, I can see that this voyage is headed toward disaster and heavy loss, not only of the cargo and the ship but also of our lives." 11 But the centurion paid attention to the captain and the owner of the ship rather than to what Paul said. 12 Since the harbor was unsuitable to winter in, the majority decided to set sail from there, hoping somehow to reach Phoenix, a harbor on Crete facing the southwest and northwest, and to winter there.

STORM-TOSSED SHIP

13 When a gentle south wind sprang up, they thought they had achieved their purpose. They weighed anchor and sailed along the shore of Crete. 14 But before long, a fierce wind called the "northeaster" rushed down from the island. 15 Since the ship was caught and unable to head into the wind, we gave way to it and were driven along. 16 After running under the shelter of a little island called Cauda,[F] we were barely able to get control of the skiff. 17 After hoisting it up, they used ropes and tackle and girded the ship. Fearing they would run aground on the Syrtis, they lowered the drift-anchor, and in this way they were driven along. 18 Because we were being severely battered by the storm, they began to jettison the cargo the next day. 19 On the third day, they threw the ship's tackle overboard with their own hands. 20 For many days neither sun nor stars appeared, and the severe storm kept raging. Finally all hope was fading that we would be saved.

21 Since they had been without food for a long time, Paul then stood up among them and said, "You men should have followed my advice not to sail from Crete and sustain this damage and loss. 22 Now I urge you to take courage, because there will be no loss of any of your lives, but only of the ship. 23 For last night an angel of the God I belong to and serve stood by me 24 and said, 'Don't be afraid, Paul. It is necessary for you to appear before Caesar. And indeed, God has graciously given you all those who are sailing with you.' 25 So take courage, men, because I believe God that it will be just the way it was told to me. 26 But we have to run aground on some island."

27 When the fourteenth night came, we were drifting in the Adriatic Sea, and about midnight the sailors thought they were approaching land.

[A] **26:28** Or *so quickly* [B] **26:29** Or *whether a short time or long*
[C] **27:1** Or *Augustan Cohort* [D] **27:4** Lit *sailed under the lee*, also in v. 7
[E] **27:9** Lit *the Fast* [F] **27:16** Or *Clauda*

Agrippa II: Last of the Herodians

by Timothy N. Boyd

Herod Agrippa II (also known by his Roman name, Julius Marcus Agrippa) is the last of the family of Herod the Great that readers encounter in the pages of the New Testament. He was born in AD 27 in Rome, the son of Herod Agrippa I and great grandson of Herod the Great. His father had a rather checkered career. At one point, he was completely bankrupt; at another point, he was ruler over a kingdom as large as that of Herod the Great. Because of his father's changing situation, Agrippa was shuttled around as a child. He visited the land of Israel for the first time when he was about five years old because his father was fleeing creditors.

When his father's fortunes were finally restored, Agrippa returned to Rome at the age of fourteen to be educated in the royal palace. This allowed him access to the entire Roman ruling family. His father died approximately two years later in AD 44 when Agrippa was about seventeen. The Roman emperor, Claudius, had grown to like Agrippa and was inclined to give him his father's territory. However, members of the court persuaded Claudius that Agrippa was too young. Because the territory was large and volatile, even an experienced administrator would have been challenged. Therefore, Claudius placed the territory under the authority of Roman governors.

In AD 48, Agrippa's uncle, also a Herod, died. He had ruled over the independent city of Chalcis from AD 41 to 48. After Herod of Chalcis died, the emperor decided to give Agrippa this much more manageable position. In his new position, Agrippa also gained control over the temple in Jerusalem. This gave him the power to depose and nominate the high priest. This authority brought Agrippa into conflict with the religious leaders of the Jews. The Jews felt that Agrippa abused this power by appointing men with no real consideration of the qualifications of the office. For this reason, throughout Agrippa's reign, he and the Jewish leaders were in constant conflict.

In AD 53, Claudius gave Agrippa the territory ruled by his father's uncle, Philip, in exchange for the city of Chalcis. This territory included Abilene (or Abila), Trachonitis, and Acra. When Emperor Nero came to power, he added the city of Tiberias and parts of Perea. Agrippa retained

Overview of the eastern side of the Banias palace complex. When Agrippa rebuilt Banias (Caesarea Philippi) in honor of Nero, he renamed it "Neronias."

his control over the temple and the high priesthood.

Agrippa established residences in both Jerusalem and Caesarea Philippi. These two cities also held the residence of the Roman governors of Judea. Strong cooperation existed between Agrippa and these governors. The Romans consulted Agrippa on religious matters in Judea because of his knowledge of the Jewish faith.[1]

The way the emperors treated Agrippa shows the friendship that existed between them. Prior to Agrippa, other members of the Herodian family had strong ties to the Roman throne. Agrippa, however, maintained closer ties with the Roman emperors than had the previous Herods. His friendship with the throne extended through multiple emperors, and he was always in good favor with them, reigning longer than any other Herod.

As with most of the other Herodians, Agrippa was a builder. Under his direction, his palace in Jerusalem was extended. Part of this extension was a watchtower built high enough to allow Agrippa to peer into the temple area and observe what was happening. This offended the priests, and they extended the height of a temple wall to block his view. Both Agrippa and Festus, the Roman governor, were displeased with this, and Festus ordered the wall lowered. The priests, however, sent petitioners to Rome to seek an audience with Nero. Through the influence of the emperor's wife, they were granted the right to retain the higher wall.[2]

Even though he did not have a positive relationship with the Jewish religious leaders, Agrippa did fund and direct a remodeling of the temple. He also was known as an advocate for the Jewish religion. For example, the Roman procurator Fadus had taken control over the garments of the high priest. He wanted to keep the garments in the fortress Antonia under the control of the Roman army to demonstrate Roman domination over the Jews. Agrippa persuaded Claudius, the emperor at that time, to allow the Jews to retain control over the garments.[3]

In his private life, Agrippa scandalized the Jewish community as well as other groups by his supposed incestuous relationship with his sister, Bernice. This relationship began when she came to live with Agrippa after the death of her second husband, Herod of Chalcis. The relationship created so much gossip that Agrippa betrothed her to Polemo, the king of Cilicia. Polemo was so enamored with her that he agreed to her request that he be circumcised. This marriage, however, did not last, and she soon returned to Agrippa. Her relationship with Agrippa was finally disrupted when she began a long-term affair with Titus, the future emperor.[4]

Even though Agrippa had been a friend to the Jews, he was firmly committed to the Romans. When the Jews revolted against Rome in AD 66, Agrippa tried to convince the Jews not to revolt. In a speech to the Jewish leaders, Agrippa reminded the leaders of how they could not successfully resist when General Pompey had brought a small Roman army into the region. Agrippa asked the Jews how they hoped to defeat an even more powerful Roman presence; the idea of revolt would lead to defeat and ruin for the nation. The Romans would kill all the people or take them into slavery. The Jews refused to listen to Agrippa and pursued their revolt.[5]

Agrippa and his sister, Bernice, fled to Galilee and allied themselves with the Romans. Agrippa furnished

Referring to Agrippa II, bronze inscription in Greek reads "King Agrippa Nero"; dated AD 67/68.

two thousand soldiers to Vespasian, the general who was sent to put down the revolt. Agrippa personally participated in the battle for Gamala, a town near Capernaum. In that battle, he was wounded by a sling stone. Agrippa later entertained the Roman commanders and troops at his palace in Caesarea Philippi after they had defeated the rebels in that region.[6]

After the final defeat of the Jews and the destruction of Jerusalem, the Roman government gave Agrippa territories in Syria to rule for his consistent loyalty to Rome. He continued to rule for at least twenty-five more years. When he died, Agrippa left no heirs. With his death, the line of the Herodian rulers ended.[7] ✣

---

[1] See Harold W. Hoehner, "Herod" in *ISBE* (1982), 2:688–98. [2] Josephus, *Jewish Antiquities* 20.8.11. [3] Josephus, *Jewish Antiquities* 20.1–2. [4] Josephus, *Jewish Antiquities* 20.7.3; Richard Gottheil and Heinrich Bloch, "Berenice" in *JE* (1906), www.jewishencyclopedia.com/articles/3050-berenice. [5] Josephus, *Jewish War* 2.16.3–4. [6] Josephus, *Jewish War* 3.4.2; 4.1.3; M. Brann, "Agrippa II" in *JE* (1906), www.jewishencyclopedia.com/articles/913-agrippa-ii. [7] Hoehner, "Herod," 698; Josephus, *The Life* 65.364–67.

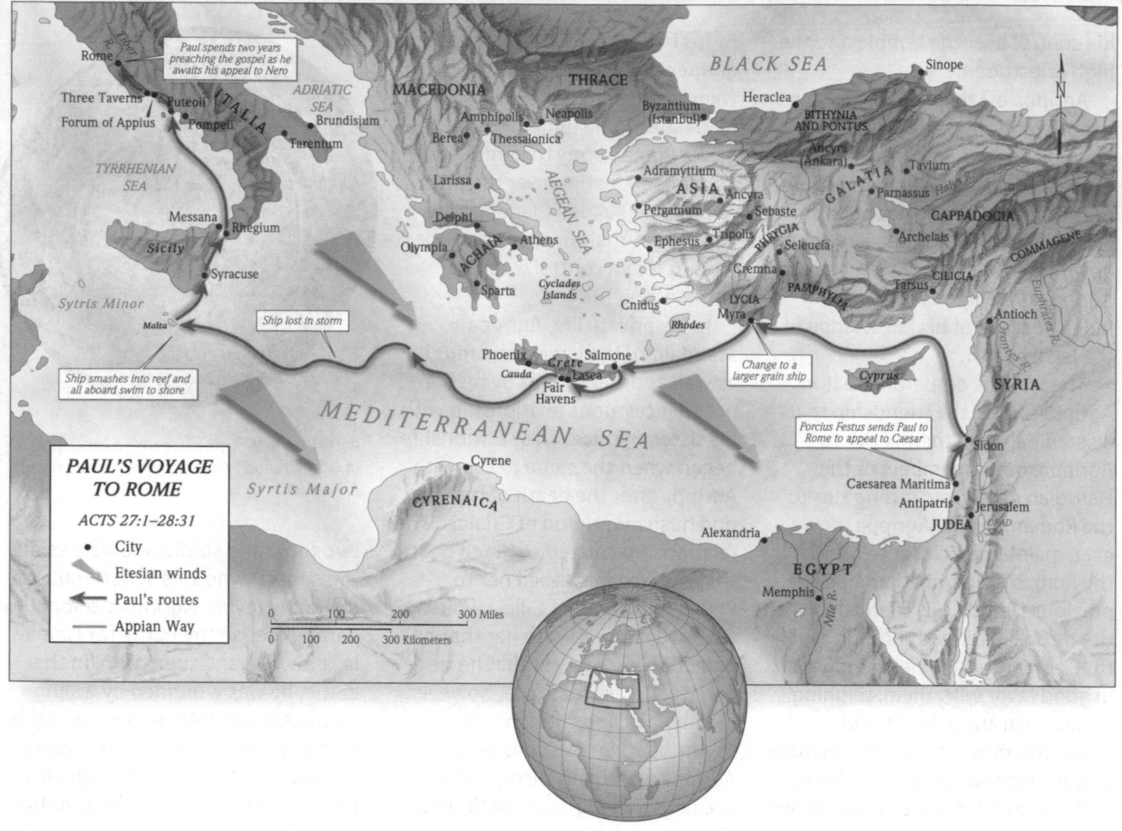

[28]They took soundings and found it to be a hundred
twenty feet[A] deep; when they had sailed a little farther and sounded again, they found it to be ninety
feet[B] deep. [29]Then, fearing we might run aground
on the rocks, they dropped four anchors from the
stern and prayed for daylight to come. [30]Some sailors tried to escape from the ship; they had let down
the skiff into the sea, pretending that they were
going to put out anchors from the bow. [31]Paul said
to the centurion and the soldiers, "Unless these
men stay in the ship, you cannot be saved." [32]Then
the soldiers cut the ropes holding the skiff and let
it drop away.

[33]When it was about daylight, Paul urged them
all to take food, saying, "Today is the fourteenth day
that you have been waiting and going without food,
having eaten nothing. [34]So I urge you to take some
food. For this is for your survival, since none of you
will lose a hair from your head." [35]After he said these
things and had taken some bread, he gave thanks to
God in the presence of all of them, and after he broke
it, he began to eat. [36]They all were encouraged and
took food themselves. [37]In all there were 276 of us on
the ship. [38]When they had eaten enough, they began
to lighten the ship by throwing the grain overboard
into the sea.

SHIPWRECK

[39]When daylight came, they did not recognize the
land but sighted a bay with a beach. They planned
to run the ship ashore if they could. [40]After cutting loose the anchors, they left them in the sea,
at the same time loosening the ropes that held the
rudders. Then they hoisted the foresail to the wind
and headed for the beach. [41]But they struck a sand-
bar and ran the ship aground. The bow jammed fast
and remained immovable, while the stern began to
break up by the pounding of the waves. [42]The soldiers' plan was to kill the prisoners so that no one
could swim away and escape. [43]But the centurion
kept them from carrying out their plan because he
wanted to save Paul, and so he ordered those who
could swim to jump overboard first and get to land.
[44]The rest were to follow, some on planks and some
on debris from the ship. In this way, everyone safely
reached the shore.

[A] **27:28** Lit *twenty fathoms* [B] **27:28** Lit *fifteen fathoms*

MALTA'S HOSPITALITY

28 Once safely ashore, we then learned that the island was called Malta. 2 The local people showed us extraordinary kindness. They lit a fire and took us all in, since it was raining and cold. 3 As Paul gathered a bundle of brushwood and put it on the fire, a viper came out because of the heat and fastened itself on his hand. 4 When the local people saw the snake hanging from his hand, they said to one another, "This man, no doubt, is a murderer. Even though he has escaped the sea, Justice has not allowed him to live." 5 But he shook the snake off into the fire and suffered no harm. 6 They expected that he would begin to swell up or suddenly drop dead. After they waited a long time and saw nothing unusual happen to him, they changed their minds and said he was a god.

MINISTRY IN MALTA

7 Now in the area around that place was an estate belonging to the leading man of the island, named Publius, who welcomed us and entertained us hospitably for three days. 8 Publius's father was in bed suffering from fever and dysentery. Paul went to him, and praying and laying his hands on him, he healed him. 9 After this, the rest of those on the island who had diseases also came and were healed. 10 So they heaped many honors on us, and when we sailed, they gave us what we needed.

ROME AT LAST

11 After three months we set sail in an Alexandrian ship that had wintered at the island, with the Twin Gods[A] as its figurehead. 12 Putting in at Syracuse, we stayed three days. 13 From there, after making a circuit along the coast,[B] we reached Rhegium. After one day a south wind sprang up, and the second day we came to Puteoli. 14 There we found brothers and sisters and were invited to stay a week with them. And so we came to Rome. 15 Now the brothers and sisters from there had heard the news about us and had come to meet us as far as the Forum of Appius and the Three Taverns. When Paul saw them, he thanked God and took courage. 16 When we entered Rome,[C] Paul was allowed to live by himself with the soldier who guarded him.

PAUL'S FIRST INTERVIEW WITH ROMAN JEWS

17 After three days he called together the leaders of the Jews. When they had gathered he said to them, "Brothers, although I have done nothing against our people or the customs of our ancestors, I was delivered as a prisoner from Jerusalem into the hands of the Romans. 18 After they examined me, they wanted to release me, since there was no reason for the death penalty in my case. 19 Because the Jews objected, I was compelled to appeal to Caesar; even though I had no charge to bring against my people. 20 For this reason I've asked to see you and speak to you. In fact, it is for the hope of Israel that I'm wearing this chain."

21 Then they said to him, "We haven't received any letters about you from Judea. None of the brothers has come and reported or spoken anything evil about you. 22 But we want to hear what your views are, since we know that people everywhere are speaking against this sect."

THE RESPONSE TO PAUL'S MESSAGE

23 After arranging a day with him, many came to him at his lodging. From dawn to dusk he expounded and testified about the kingdom of God. He tried to persuade them about Jesus from both the Law of Moses and the Prophets. 24 Some were persuaded by what he said, but others did not believe.

25 Disagreeing among themselves, they began to leave after Paul made one statement:[D] "The Holy Spirit was right in saying to your[E] ancestors through the prophet Isaiah 26 when he said,

Go to these people and say:
You will always be listening,
but never understanding;
and you will always be looking,
but never perceiving.
27 **For the hearts of these people**
have grown callous,
their ears are hard of hearing,
and they have shut their eyes;
otherwise they might see
with their eyes
and hear with their ears,
understand with their heart
and turn,
and I would heal them.[F]

28 Therefore, let it be known to you that this salvation of God has been sent to the Gentiles; they will listen." [G]

PAUL'S MINISTRY UNHINDERED

30 Paul stayed two whole years in his own rented house. And he welcomed all who visited him, 31 proclaiming the kingdom of God and teaching about the Lord Jesus Christ with all boldness and without hindrance.

[A] **28:11** Gk *Dioscuri*, twin sons of Zeus, Castor and Pollux [B] **28:13** Other mss read *From there, casting off,* [C] **28:16** Other mss add *the centurion turned the prisoners over to the military commander; but* [D] **28:25** Or *after they began to leave, Paul made one statement* [E] **28:25** Other mss read *our* [F] **28:26–27** Is 6:9–10 [G] **28:28** Some mss include v. 29: *After he said these things, the Jews departed, while engaging in a vigorous debate among themselves.*

Ships and Shipping in the New Testament World

by Gerald L. Stevens

Scene on the first spiral of Trajan's Column in Rome depicts Roman boats being loaded with supplies along the Danube River; a fort and small town are located riverside.

Judea had no deep harbor on its Mediterranean coastline, and Israelite desert nomads who settled in the hill country were not a seafaring people. Philistine Sea Peoples settled the coastal plain. Israelites did not conduct maritime commerce, with the exception of King Solomon, who used alliances with King Hiram of Tyre and harboring facilities at Ezion-geber on the Red Sea, but his sailors were Phoenician (1Kg 9:26–27). Solomon traded gold, silver, and other rare merchandise (10:22). Jehoshaphat constructed a fleet for gold from Ophir, but an east wind in the Ezion-geber harbor wrecked the entire fleet (22:48–49).

Joppa was one of the few Judean ports. Farther north, Herod the Great built a harbor at Caesarea, capitalizing on Roman engineering to harden submerged cement for his breakwaters. Other cities along the Mediterranean coastline such as Tyre, however, were far more legendary for their commercial maritime prowess (Is 23:1; Ezk 27:32–35).

By Roman times, seafaring had become normal for international travel. The main arrangement was by cabotage, the business of sailing near the shoreline and putting in each night, which allowed ancient commercial ship captains to offer individuals short transportation arrangements for hire on the spur of the moment. Other contracts facilitated extended distances. Commercial ports were integral to Paul's journeys, such as Seleucia (Ac 13:4), Troas (16:8), Thessalonica (17:1), Corinth (18:1), Ephesus (19:1), Miletus (20:15), Tyre (21:3), Syracuse (28:12), Puteoli (v. 13), and others with less well-known names, but no less famous in their day.

Shipping was dependent entirely on the seasons. Summer was the best (for steady and dependable trade winds), winter the worst (for ferocious and unpredictable winter northeasters), and spring and fall marginal. The dangerous fall season ran from mid-September to mid-November, and the impossible winter season ran from late November through February. Thus Paul naturally urges Timothy to "come before winter" (2Ti 4:21). Sailing in late fall universally was risky and undertaken with caution.

Delivering crucial goods late in the sailing season could garner significant bonuses. The grain route between Alexandria and Rome of a thousand nautical miles took ten to twelve days eastward, but westward about two to three months, and often required hugging the coastlines of Phoenicia, Asia Minor, and Greece.[1] Accommodations for these voyages were minimal, even for the privileged, who at best could hope for a crowded spot in the cargo hold or a small cabin in the stern. Otherwise, one staked a spot on the open deck, exposed to the weather, but perhaps with a tent enclosure.[2]

Roman grain ships were built with flat hulls for maximum cargo, which meant minimum structural integrity. Cross-lateral movements, such as in stormy weather with assaults of wind and wave, could be devastating. Further, grain cargo was a tremendous liability in storms. Wet grain would swell, adding further stress to watertight seams. A Roman grain ship was the worst ship to be on in a storm at sea.[3]

One of the most detailed accounts of sailing, storm, and shipwreck from the ancient world actually is Luke's account of Paul's voyage and shipwreck in Acts 27–28. Luke's attention to detail, while expressed in layman and not technical terms, is a treasure trove of nautical information, including tackle, winds, topography, and strategies. ✣

Block showing inscription that mentions "Tyrdos." The old harbor of Tyre is in the background.

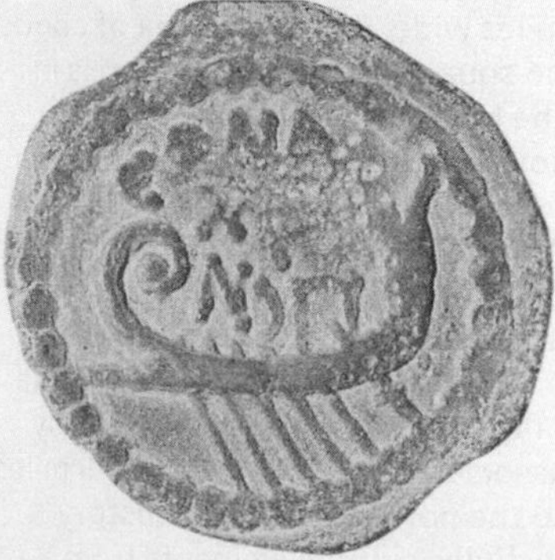

Roman coin; obverse: two cornucopia, Greek inscription: Herod, meaning Herod Archelaus; reverse: galley ship, Greek inscription: Ethnarch.

---

[1] These estimates follow Lionel Casson's work using references from Pliny, *Natural History* 19.3–4. Casson compiled charts of Mediterranean distance, time, and speed; see Casson, *Ships and Seamanship in the Ancient World* (Princeton, NJ: Princeton University Press, 1971). [2] Earle Hilgert, "Ships; Boats" in *ISBE* (1988), 4:486. [3] One of the best resources for understanding the structure of an Alexandrian grain ship is Nicolle Hirschfeld, "The Ship of Saint Paul, Part 1: Historical Background," *BA* 53.1 (1990): 25–30.

The Island of Malta

by George W. Knight

St. Paul's Bay, Malta.

Malta is the largest of a group of five islands collectively known today as the nation of Malta.[1] It is approximately 18 miles long and 8 miles wide, making an area of about 96 square miles. The location is in the Mediterranean Sea 60 miles south of Sicily and about 220 miles north of the Libyan coast in North Africa. On the north and west coasts of the island are located many bays and inlets that provide natural harbors. The largest is near the middle of the island; the one traditionally associated with Paul is about 8 miles to the northeast. Malta's history includes cultural elements from Sicily, Italy, Phoenicia, Carthage, and Rome.

The largest influence on first-century Malta began with the coming of the Phoenicians about 1000 BC. They established a settlement on the island as part of the expansion of their trade empire to the west. The abundance of natural harbors and location near their shipping lanes made this an ideal location for protection, rest, and resupply. Their occupation grew, and, in addition to the shipping installations along the coast, a city, Malta, was built near the modern Citta Vecchia. Excavations have shown it to have been a city of importance and wealth. Large Phoenician tombs are found there. By the sixth century BC, Carthage came to power, and that culture also left its mark. But the Roman Empire ultimately shaped the Malta of Paul's day.

The island's history that is reflected in the land of Paul's shipwreck began with Roman control in 218 BC when the island became part of the province of Sicily. Augustus Caesar granted the island nation its own procurator; although civil war crippled the small country during those days, when Paul arrived the island was thriving.

Leading into the first century AD, the island was often visited by pirates who, according to Cicero, spent their winters there.[2] These outlaws were usually controlled by Rome's power, but when Paul landed there, their influences were surely a part of the local inhabitants' culture.

Archaeological excavations on the island have identified early Christian tombs. Additionally an excavation of a Roman villa at "San Pawl Milqi . . . is traditionally the site of Publius' villa where the shipwrecked St. Paul was received." Also of significance was a Punic sanctuary that fell into disuse toward the end of the first century and later was converted into a Christian church.[3] ✣

---

[1] This discussion relies on the following: A. Claridge, "Melita" in *The Princeton Encyclopedia of Classical Sites*, ed. Richard Stillwell (Princeton, NJ: Princeton University Press, 1976), 568–69; Ernst Haenchen, *The Acts of the Apostles*, trans. Bernard Noble and Gerald Shinn (Philadelphia: Westminster, 1971); Dennis R. Macdonald, "The Shipwrecks of Odysseus and Paul," *NTS* 45 (1999): 88–107; John Polhill, *Acts*, NAC (1992). [2] Cicero, *Against Verres* 11.4.103–4. [3] Claridge, "Melita," 569.

Aerial view of Malta.

ROMANS

Flavian Amphitheater, also known as the Roman Colosseum.

INTRODUCTION TO

ROMANS

Circumstances of Writing

Paul the apostle is the stated and indisputable author of the book of Romans. From the book of Acts and statements in Romans, we learn that Paul wrote this letter while he was in Corinth and on his way to Jerusalem in the spring of AD 57, to deliver an offering from the Gentile churches to poor Jewish Christians (Ac 20:3; Rm 15:25–29).

All of Paul's writings grew out of his missionary/pastoral work and were about the problems and needs of local churches. The book of Romans is also of this genre, but it is the least "local" in the sense that Paul had not yet been to Rome. This letter was his opportunity to expound the good news message (the gospel). He could discuss the essence of sin, the salvation accomplished on the cross, the union of the believer with Christ, how the Spirit works in the Christian to promote holiness, the place of the Jewish people in God's plan, future things, and Christian living or ethics. Though Paul did not write Romans as a systematic theology, his somewhat orderly exposition has been the fountain for the development of that discipline.

The origin of the Roman house churches is unknown. The founding of the Roman church likely goes back to the "visitors from Rome (both Jews and converts)" who came to Jerusalem at Pentecost (Ac 2:10). Many of these visitors converted to Christianity (2:41). In Acts 18:2, Luke mentioned Aquila and Priscilla, who left Rome because Emperor Claudius had ordered all Jews to leave the city (AD 49). This exodus was caused by strife among Jews over "Chrestus" (Christ). The remaining Christians in Rome would be from a Gentile background. The Jewish-Gentile tensions in Rome had a long history. These tensions are somewhat reflected throughout the letter, most specifically in chapters 2, 11, and 14–15.

Rome was the primary destination of this letter. Yet some manuscripts lack the phrase "in Rome" (1:7), giving some support to the conclusion that Paul intended a wider audience for the book of Romans and sent copies to other churches.

Contribution to the Bible

What is the gospel? The word *gospel* means "good news." The good news is about Jesus and what he did for us. Most Bible students would say that the gospel is outlined in 1 Corinthians 15:3–5. Romans fills in that outline and clarifies the gospel in relation to the Old Testament promises and the Mosaic law, the role of good works, and the gift of God's righteousness. Paul emphasized righteousness and justification in this letter to a depth and detail not found elsewhere in the Bible. Sin is traced to its core in our union with Adam and the imputation of original sin. Paul also mapped out the spread of human sin and its results in both believers and nonbelievers.

There are three passages in the New Testament (each one long sentence in the Greek text) that contain the most important theology of the New Testament: John 1:14 on the incarnation; Ephesians 1:3–14 about the triune purpose and glory of God; and Romans 3:21–26 on justification, redemption, and propitiation. If a Christian understands these three sentences, he has a solid foundation for faith.

Paul, in Romans 6–8, gave the most comprehensive development of our union with Christ and the Spirit's work in us. Romans 9–11 (on the role of Israel in God's plan) has been called the key to understanding the Bible. Romans 13 is the classic New Testament passage on the Christian's relation to and duties to the state. Romans 14–15 covers how Christians can relate to one another yet have different opinions and convictions on nonessential religious matters.

Structure

Paul wrote thirteen of the twenty-one letters (or "epistles") contained in the New Testament. The four Gospels, the book of Acts, and the book of Revelation are not classified as letters.

Romans is the longest of Paul's letters, and it contains the elements found in a standard letter at that time: salutation (1:1–7); thanksgiving (1:8–17); the main body (1:18–16:18); and a farewell (16:19–24). Some scholars refer to Romans as a tractate (a formal treatise). But it bears all the marks of a real letter, although it is a finely tuned literary composition.

THE GOSPEL OF GOD FOR ROME

1 Paul, a servant of Christ Jesus, called as an apostle[A] and set apart for the gospel of God — [2] which he promised beforehand through his prophets in the Holy Scriptures — [3] concerning his Son, Jesus Christ our Lord, who was a descendant of David[B] according to the flesh [4] and was appointed to be the powerful Son of God according to the Spirit of holiness[C] by the resurrection of the dead. [5] Through him we have received grace and apostleship to bring about[D] the obedience of faith for the sake of his name among all the Gentiles,[E] [6] including you who are also called by Jesus Christ.

[7] To all who are in Rome, loved by God, called as saints.

Grace to you and peace from God our Father and the Lord Jesus Christ.

PAUL'S DESIRE TO VISIT ROME

[8] First, I thank my God through Jesus Christ for all of you because the news of your faith[F] is being reported in all the world. [9] God is my witness, whom I serve with my spirit in telling the good news about his Son — that I constantly mention you, [10] always asking in my prayers that if it is somehow in God's will, I may now at last succeed in coming to you. [11] For I want very much to see you, so that I may impart to you some spiritual gift to strengthen you, [12] that is, to be mutually encouraged by each other's faith, both yours and mine.

[13] Now I don't want you to be unaware, brothers and sisters, that I often planned to come to you (but was prevented until now) in order that I might have a fruitful ministry[G] among you, just as I have had among the rest of the Gentiles. [14] I am obligated both to Greeks and barbarians,[H] both to the wise and the foolish. [15] So I am eager to preach the gospel to you also who are in Rome.

THE RIGHTEOUS WILL LIVE BY FAITH

[16] For I am not ashamed of the gospel,[I] because it is the power of God for salvation to everyone who believes, first to the Jew, and also to the Greek. [17] For in it the righteousness of God is revealed from faith to faith,[J] just as it is written: **The righteous will live by faith.**[K,L]

THE GUILT OF THE GENTILE WORLD

[18] For God's wrath is revealed from heaven against all godlessness and unrighteousness of people who by their unrighteousness suppress the truth, [19] since what can be known[M] about God is evident among them, because God has shown it to them. [20] For his invisible attributes, that is, his eternal power and divine nature, have been clearly seen since the creation of the world, being understood through what he has made. As a result, people are without excuse. [21] For though they knew God, they did not glorify him as God or show gratitude. Instead, their thinking became worthless, and their senseless hearts were darkened. [22] Claiming to be wise, they became fools [23] and exchanged the glory of the immortal God for images resembling mortal man, birds, four-footed animals, and reptiles.

[24] Therefore God delivered them over in the desires of their hearts to sexual impurity, so that their bodies were degraded among themselves. [25] They exchanged the truth of God for a lie, and worshiped and served what has been created instead of the Creator, who is praised forever. Amen.

FROM IDOLATRY TO DEPRAVITY

[26] For this reason God delivered them over to disgraceful passions. Their women[N] exchanged natural sexual relations[O] for unnatural ones. [27] The men[P] in the same way also left natural relations with women and were inflamed in their lust for one another. Men committed shameless acts with men and received in their own persons[Q] the appropriate penalty of their error.

[28] And because they did not think it worthwhile to acknowledge God, God delivered them over to a corrupt mind so that they do what is not right. [29] They are filled with all unrighteousness,[R] evil, greed, and wickedness. They are full of envy, murder, quarrels, deceit, and malice. They are gossips, [30] slanderers, God-haters, arrogant, proud, boastful, inventors of evil, disobedient to parents, [31] senseless, untrustworthy, unloving,[S] and unmerciful. [32] Although they know God's just sentence — that those who practice such things deserve to die[T] — they not only do them, but even applaud[U] others who practice them.

GOD'S RIGHTEOUS JUDGMENT

2 Therefore, every one of you[V] who judges is without excuse. For when you judge another, you condemn yourself, since you, the judge, do the same things. [2] Now we know that God's judgment on those who do such things is based on the truth. [3] Do you think — anyone of you who judges those

[A] **1:1** Or *Jesus, a called apostle* [B] **1:3** Lit *was of the seed of David* [C] **1:4** Or *the spirit of holiness*, or *the Holy Spirit* [D] **1:5** Or *him for*; lit *him into* [E] **1:5** Or *nations*, also in v. 13 [F] **1:8** Or *because your faith* [G] **1:13** Lit *have some fruit* [H] **1:14** Or *non-Greeks* [I] **1:16** Other mss add *of Christ* [J] **1:17** Or *revealed out of faith into faith* [K] **1:17** Or *The one who is righteous by faith will live* [L] **1:17** Hab 2:4 [M] **1:19** Or *what is known* [N] **1:26** Lit *females*, also in v. 27 [O] **1:26** Lit *natural use*, also in v. 27 [P] **1:27** Lit *males*, also later in v. [Q] **1:27** Or *in themselves* [R] **1:29** Other mss add *sexual immorality* [S] **1:31** Other mss add *unforgiving* [T] **1:32** Lit *things are worthy of death* [U] **1:32** Lit *even take pleasure in* [V] **2:1** Lit *Therefore, O man, every one*

Rome: The Growth of the Eternal City

by Martha S. Bergen

The city of Rome, nicknamed the Eternal City, stands as one of the most influential cities in the course of human history. Some of the most famous personalities, architectural features, and events in all of Western culture came under the influence of ancient Rome. Julius Caesar, Augustus, Nero, the Colosseum, the Forum, gladiator fights, and Christian martyrdoms are all inseparably linked to this city. Rome's rule shaped the destinies of nations and individuals as well as the course of Christendom. In light of Rome's wide-ranging significance, knowing something of its history and development is helpful.

THE BIRTH OF ROME

An ancient myth credits the founding of Rome in 753 BC to Romulus and Remus, descendants of the Trojan hero Aeneas. According to the story, these two individuals were initially nursed on the banks of the Tiber River by a she-wolf and then raised by a shepherd. Romulus later executed his brother for breaking one of the city's laws. Named for its first king, the city was called Roma.

Archaeological studies suggest that the earliest period of the region's history can be traced to the second millennium BC, when the Italian Peninsula attracted Indo-European tribes seeking a new home. Settlers were drawn to the region in part by the warm and hospitable climate. Located in the Mediterranean basin, the central region of the Italian Peninsula received abundant sunshine and favorable amounts of rain. They were also drawn by the region's geographical advantages—fertile soil, defensible hills, and the presence of the Tiberis (modern English, "Tiber") River, the third-longest river in the Italian Peninsula. The location that became Rome was considered especially desirable because it provided the best place to cross the Tiber River. Thus the site was a natural crossroads for people and goods traveling any direction throughout the Italian Peninsula.

The Umbrians, Sabines, and Samnites (or Oscans) in the area north of the Tiber River, and Latins to the south, moved into the region and displaced central Italy's original inhabitants.[1] Also immigrating into this region late in the eighth century BC were non-Indo-European tribes from Asia Minor known as the Etruscans. They were more culturally advanced than the Indo-European settlers and thus dominated central Italy during its earliest phase of development.[2]

The Latins receive credit for establishing a settlement on Palatine Hill close to the mouth of the Tiber River, about twenty miles from the Tyrrhenian Sea. Though precise

Ruins of the amphitheater that stood on the outskirts of Carthage in North Africa, which was part of the Roman Empire. The amphitheater was often the scene of violent and bloody entertainment—combat to the death between armed men, between men and animals, or fighting between animals.

According to writers of the time, the opening celebration at the Roman Colosseum lasted one hundred days; nine thousand wild beasts were slaughtered, and two thousand gladiators fought and died. The facility was designed so the fifty thousand spectators could evacuate in five minutes.

details are lost in antiquity, historians have shown that the Latins established a series of additional settlements on the hilltops in the area of Palatine Hill. To protect themselves from the Etruscans, the Latins also established a fortress known as Roma on a nearby island in the Tiber River.[3] These separate settlements would later unite to form a single entity known as Rome. Because of their favorable location, the island fortress and the nearby hilltop villages became an important center for trade, even containing some paved roads. For a number of years, Latin kings ruled the region.

The Etruscans apparently conquered the city in the sixth century BC, resulting in the last three kings of Rome being from that civilization.[4] During the Etruscan period, Rome had many major construction projects, including the building of the great temple of Jupiter on Capitoline Hill and a temple dedicated to the goddess Diana on the Aventine Hill.[5]

Somewhere between 510 and 506 BC, an alliance of Latin settlements fought against and defeated the Etruscans.[6] Abolishing the monarchy, they established the Roman Republic. In the new system, government consisted of magistrates, called consuls, who were elected annually, and a Senate that played an advisory role to the consuls. Members of the Senate had been leading citizens from the aristocratic families in the old republic.

Over the next two hundred years, the city of Rome fought an extended series of battles against various invaders and people groups within the Italian Peninsula. Following a war against the Gauls in the early fourth century BC, the Romans constructed a twenty-four-foot-high, twelve-foot-thick wall of volcanic rock around the seven hills of their city—an area of more than one thousand acres.[7] This helped ensure that Rome would be not only the largest and most favorably situated city in the peninsula, but also the best protected. The whole of Italy fell under Rome's control by 275 BC. Over time, the acquisition of provinces outside the Italian Peninsula occurred (i.e., Sicily, Macedonia), leading to an increase in the city's size and wealth.

The port city of Ostia, located downstream from Rome on the

Terra-cotta figurine of a gladiator from the first century AD.

coast of the Tyrrhenian Sea at the mouth of the Tiber River, served as Rome's primary commercial port. Founded in the fourth century BC, the city also became the home of Rome's navy. As water traffic increased, Claudius (41–54 AD) built Portus, an artificial harbor about two miles north of Ostia, to handle Rome's growing maritime enterprises.[8]

ROME IN THE NEW TESTAMENT ERA

By the first century AD, Rome had become the most important city in the world. Its empire stretched from Spain to Syria and from Egypt to Germany. The wealth gained from her conquests allowed Rome to become the center of architectural magnificence. It was said of Caesar Augustus (reigned 27 BC–AD 14) that he "found Rome built of brick, and left it a city of marble."[9] Its citizens received their water via the Aqua Claudia, a forty-two-mile-long aqueduct built between AD 38 and 52, that brought water from a source near Subiaco.[10] By the first century AD, Rome had a sophisticated sewer system with several components to it, the largest of which was the Cloaca Maxima. Originally started as a drainage ditch in the sixth century BC, improvements through the centuries meant that by 33 BC the system had become an underground canal with a vaulted roof.[11]

At the beginning of the New Testament era, a series of paved roads, some of which are still used today, linked Rome to other parts of the Italian Peninsula. The most famous of these is the Appian Way, a coastal road leading to Capua, initially constructed in 312 BC. A second major artery was the Via Valeria, a military road built in 306 BC that ran eastward through the Apennine Mountains and connected Rome with the Adriatic region.[12] With these and other lesser roads, Rome had excellent land routes that permitted trade and travel in every direction.

In the first century, Rome had a number of truly remarkable and unique architectural features. The most impressive of these in Paul's day was the Circus Maximus, the greatest chariot racetrack in the empire. Though its first construction probably dates to the sixth century BC, it was modified through the centuries, especially by Julius Caesar (100–44 BC), who enlarged it to accommodate one hundred fifty thousand spectators and extended the track, making it 1,800 feet long and 600 feet wide. Smaller in scale but more famous was the Colosseum, a massive structure that stood 187 feet high and could hold about fifty thousand people. The Colosseum was built between AD 71 and 80, a few years after the apostle Paul's death, and served as the site for gruesome gladiatorial fights that resulted in the slaughter of large numbers of people and exotic animals. Theaters—the largest of which was at Pompey and seated twenty-seven thousand spectators—were used to put on plays depicting acts of rape, cannibalism, and murder.[13]

Along with its wealth, impressive architectural features, and immorality, imperial Rome was also a center of urban filth and degradation. By the end of the first century, the city's population was estimated to be more than one million.[14] Many of these were unemployed or underemployed and had to live in dirty, poorly maintained tenement housing. Because its sewers emptied raw sewage into the Tiber, the river was heavily polluted.

Thus in many ways, Rome in the first century was a city ready for the good news of Jesus Christ. ✣

---

[1] W. Warde Fowler, *Rome*, rev. M. P. Charlesworth, 2nd ed. (London: Oxford University Press, 1947), 14–15. [2] E. M. Blaiklock, "Rome" in *ZPEB*, 5:162. [3] Fowler, *Rome*, 18. [4] Fowler, *Rome*, 20. [5] Christopher Hibbert, *Rome: The Biography of a City* (New York: Norton, 1985), 315–16, 320. [6] Michael Grant, *History of Rome* (New York: Scribner's Sons, 1978), 36. [7] Grant, *History of Rome*, 54–55. [8] Tim Cornell and John Matthews, *Atlas of the Roman World* (New York: Facts on File, 1982), 92. [9] Blaiklock, "Rome," 164. [10] Cornell and Matthews, *Atlas*, 91. [11] Hibbert, *Rome*, 316. [12] Cornell and Matthews, *Atlas*, 37. [13] Hibbert, *Rome*, 45, 49, 50–51. [14] Cornell and Matthews, *Atlas*, 90.

who do such things yet do the same — that you
will escape God's judgment? 4 Or do you despise
the riches of his kindness, restraint, and patience,
not recognizing[A] that God's kindness is intended to
lead you to repentance? 5 Because of your hardened
and unrepentant heart you are storing up wrath for
yourself in the day of wrath, when God's righteous
judgment is revealed. 6 **He will repay each one according to his works**:[B] 7 eternal life to those who
by persistence in doing good seek glory, honor, and
immortality; 8 but wrath and anger to those who
are self-seeking and disobey the truth while obeying unrighteousness. 9 There will be affliction and
distress for every human being who does evil, first
to the Jew, and also to the Greek; 10 but glory, honor,
and peace for everyone who does what is good, first
to the Jew, and also to the Greek. 11 For there is no
favoritism with God.

12 For all who sin without the law will also perish
without the law, and all who sin under[C] the law will
be judged by the law. 13 For the hearers of the law are
not righteous before God, but the doers of the law
will be justified.[D] 14 So, when Gentiles, who do not
by nature have the law, do[E] what the law demands,
they are a law to themselves even though they do
not have the law. 15 They show that the work of the
law[F] is written on their hearts. Their consciences
confirm this. Their competing thoughts either accuse or even excuse them[G] 16 on the day when God
judges what people have kept secret, according to
my gospel through Christ Jesus.

JEWISH VIOLATION OF THE LAW

17 Now if[H] you call yourself a Jew, and rely on the law,
and boast in God, 18 and know his will, and approve
the things that are superior, being instructed from
the law, 19 and if you are convinced that you are a
guide for the blind, a light to those in darkness, 20 an
instructor of the ignorant, a teacher of the immature,
having the embodiment of knowledge and truth in
the law — 21 you then, who teach another, don't you
teach yourself? You who preach, "You must not steal"
— do you steal? 22 You who say, "You must not commit
adultery" — do you commit adultery? You who detest
idols, do you rob temples? 23 You who boast in the law,
do you dishonor God by breaking the law?[I] 24 For, as it
is written: **The name of God is blasphemed among
the Gentiles because of you.**[J]

CIRCUMCISION OF THE HEART

25 Circumcision benefits you if you observe the law,
but if you are a lawbreaker, your circumcision has
become uncircumcision. 26 So if an uncircumcised
man keeps the law's requirements, will not his uncircumcision be counted as circumcision? 27 A man
who is physically uncircumcised, but who keeps the
law, will judge you who are a lawbreaker in spite
of having the letter of the law and circumcision.

[A] **2:4** Or *patience, because you do not recognize* [B] **2:6** Ps 62:12; Pr 24:12 [C] **2:12** Lit *in* [D] **2:13** Or *acquitted* [E] **2:14** Or *who do not have the law, instinctively do* [F] **2:15** The code of conduct required by the law [G] **2:15** Internal debate, either in a person or among the pagan moralists [H] **2:17** Other mss read *Look —* [I] **2:23** Or *you dishonor God by breaking the law.* [J] **2:24** Is 52:5

Interior of the Church of San Clementi in Rome, which was built over a Mithraeum. Mithraism, a mystery religion, was part of the astral religion of the Hellenistic and Roman periods. Mithraeum sanctuaries were designed to resemble caves; ceilings were commonly decorated with stars.

[28] For a person is not a Jew who is one outwardly, and true circumcision is not something visible in the flesh. [29] On the contrary, a person is a Jew who is one inwardly, and circumcision is of the heart — by the Spirit, not the letter.[A] That person's praise is not from people but from God.

PAUL ANSWERS AN OBJECTION

3 So what advantage does the Jew have? Or what is the benefit of circumcision? [2] Considerable in every way. First, they were entrusted with the very words of God. [3] What then? If some were unfaithful, will their unfaithfulness nullify God's faithfulness? [4] Absolutely not! Let God be true, even though everyone is a liar, as it is written:

That you may be justified in your words
and triumph when you judge.[B]

[5] But if our unrighteousness highlights[C] God's righteousness, what are we to say? I am using a human argument:[D] Is God unrighteous to inflict wrath? [6] Absolutely not! Otherwise, how will God judge the world? [7] But if by my lie God's truth abounds to his glory, why am I also still being judged as a sinner? [8] And why not say, just as some people slanderously claim we say, "Let us do what is evil so that good may come"? Their condemnation is deserved!

THE WHOLE WORLD GUILTY BEFORE GOD

[9] What then? Are we any better off?[E] Not at all! For we have already charged that both Jews and Greeks are all under sin,[F] [10] as it is written:

There is no one righteous, not even one.
11 **There is no one who understands;**
there is no one who seeks God.
12 **All have turned away;**
all alike have become worthless.
There is no one who does what is good,
not even one.[G]
13 **Their throat is an open grave;**
they deceive with their tongues.[H]
Vipers' venom is under their lips.[I]

[A] **2:29** Or *heart — spiritually, not literally* [B] **3:4** Ps 51:4 [C] **3:5** Or *shows*, or *demonstrates* [D] **3:5** Lit *I speak as a man* [E] **3:9** Are we Jews any better than the Gentiles? [F] **3:9** Under sin's power or dominion [G] **3:10–12** Ps 14:1–3; 53:1–3; Ec 7:20 [H] **3:13** Ps 5:9 [I] **3:13** Ps 140:3

Statue depicting the god Mithras slaying the bull. Such a feat showed he had the power to control the cosmos. Adherents to Mithraism understood Mithras to protect souls after death as they traveled through the planetary spheres.

Scene on the lid of this Roman sarcophagus shows the last judgment as Jesus separates the sheep from the goats; from the Byzantine Era.

14 **Their mouth is full of cursing**
and bitterness.[A]
15 **Their feet are swift to shed blood;**
16 **ruin and wretchedness are**
in their paths,
17 **and the path of peace**
they have not known.[B]
18 **There is no fear of God**
before their eyes.[C]

19 Now we know that whatever the law says, it
speaks to those who are subject to the law,[D] so that
every mouth may be shut and the whole world may
become subject to God's judgment.[E] 20 For no one
will be justified[F] in his sight by the works of the
law, because the knowledge of sin comes through
the law.

THE RIGHTEOUSNESS OF GOD THROUGH FAITH

21 But now, apart from the law, the righteousness of
God has been revealed, attested by the Law and the
Prophets.[G] 22 The righteousness of God is through
faith in Jesus Christ[H] to all who believe, since there
is no distinction. 23 For all have sinned and fall short
of the[I] glory of God; 24 they are justified freely by
his grace through the redemption that is in Christ
Jesus. 25 God presented him as the mercy seat[J] by his
blood, through faith, to demonstrate his righteousness, because in his restraint God passed over the
sins previously committed. 26 God presented him to
demonstrate his righteousness at the present time,
so that he would be just and justify the one who has
faith in Jesus.

BOASTING EXCLUDED

27 Where, then, is boasting? It is excluded. By what
kind of law?[K] By one of works? No, on the contrary,
by a law[L] of faith. 28 For we conclude that a person
is justified by faith apart from the works of the law.
29 Or is God the God of Jews only? Is he not the God
of Gentiles too? Yes, of Gentiles too, 30 since there is
one God who will justify the circumcised by faith
and the uncircumcised through faith. 31 Do we then
nullify the law through faith? Absolutely not! On the
contrary, we uphold the law.

ABRAHAM JUSTIFIED BY FAITH

4 What then will we say that Abraham, our forefather according to the flesh, has found?[M] 2 If
Abraham was justified[N] by works, he has something
to boast about — but not before God. 3 For what does
the Scripture say? **Abraham believed God, and it
was credited to him for righteousness.**[O] 4 Now to
the one who works, pay is not credited as a gift, but
as something owed. 5 But to the one who does not
work, but believes on him who justifies the ungodly,
his faith is credited for righteousness.

DAVID CELEBRATING THE SAME TRUTH

6 Likewise, David also speaks of the blessing of the
person to whom God credits righteousness apart
from works:

7 **Blessed are those whose lawless acts**
are forgiven
and whose sins are covered.
8 **Blessed is the person**
the Lord will never charge with sin.[P]

ABRAHAM JUSTIFIED BEFORE CIRCUMCISION

9 Is this blessing only for the circumcised, then? Or
is it also for the uncircumcised? For we say, **Faith
was credited to Abraham for righteousness.**[O] 10 In
what way, then, was it credited — while he was circumcised, or uncircumcised? It was not while he was
circumcised, but uncircumcised. 11 And he received
the sign of circumcision as a seal of the righteousness that he had by faith[Q] while still uncircumcised.
This was to make him the father of all who believe
but are not circumcised, so that righteousness may
be credited to them also. 12 And he became the father
of the circumcised, who are not only circumcised but

[A] **3:14** Ps 10:7 [B] **3:15–17** Is 59:7–8 [C] **3:18** Ps 36:1 [D] **3:19** Lit *those in the law* [E] **3:19** Or *become guilty before God*, or *may be accountable to God* [F] **3:20** Or *will be declared righteous*, or *will be acquitted* [G] **3:21** When capitalized, *the Law and the Prophets* = OT [H] **3:22** Or *through the faithfulness of Jesus Christ* [I] **3:23** Or *and lack the* [J] **3:25** Or *propitiation*, or *place of atonement* [K] **3:27** Or *what principle?* [L] **3:27** Or *a principle* [M] **4:1** Or *What then shall we say? Have we found Abraham to be our forefather according to the flesh?* or *What, then, shall we say that Abraham our forefather found according to the flesh?* [N] **4:2** Or *was declared righteous*, or *was acquitted* [O] **4:3,9** Gn 15:6 [P] **4:7–8** Ps 32:1–2 [Q] **4:11** Lit *righteousness of faith*, also in v. 13

who also follow in the footsteps of the faith our father Abraham had while he was still uncircumcised.

THE PROMISE GRANTED THROUGH FAITH

13 For the promise to Abraham or to his descendants that he would inherit the world was not through the law, but through the righteousness that comes by faith. 14 If those who are of the law are heirs, faith is made empty and the promise nullified, 15 because the law produces wrath. And where there is no law, there is no transgression.

16 This is why the promise is by faith, so that it may be according to grace, to guarantee it to all the descendants — not only to the one who is of the law[A] but also to the one who is of Abraham's faith. He is the father of us all. 17 As it is written: **I have made you the father of many nations** —[B] in the presence of the God in whom he believed, the one who gives life to the dead and calls things into existence that do not exist. 18 He believed, hoping against hope, so that he became **the father of many nations**[B] according to what had been spoken: **So will your descendants be.**[C] 19 He did not weaken in faith when he considered[D] his own body to be already dead (since he was about a hundred years old) and also the deadness of Sarah's womb. 20 He did not waver in unbelief at God's promise but was strengthened in his faith and gave glory to God, 21 because he was fully convinced that what God had promised, he was also able to do. 22 Therefore, **it was credited to him for righteousness.**[E] 23 Now **it was credited to him**[E] was not written for Abraham alone, 24 but also for us. It will be credited to us who believe in him who raised Jesus our Lord from the dead. 25 He was delivered up for[F] our trespasses and raised for our justification.

FAITH TRIUMPHS

5 Therefore, since we have been justified by faith, we have peace[G] with God through our Lord Jesus Christ. 2 We have also obtained access through him by faith[H] into this grace in which we stand, and we boast[I] in the hope of the glory of God. 3 And not only that, but we also boast in our afflictions, because we know that affliction produces endurance, 4 endurance produces proven character, and proven character produces hope. 5 This hope will not disappoint us, because God's love has been poured out in our hearts through the Holy Spirit who was given to us.

THE JUSTIFIED ARE RECONCILED

6 For while we were still helpless, at the right time, Christ died for the ungodly. 7 For rarely will someone die for a just person — though for a good person perhaps someone might even dare to die. 8 But God proves his own love for us in that while we were still sinners, Christ died for us. 9 How much more then, since we have now been justified by his blood, will we be saved through him from wrath. 10 For if, while we were enemies, we were reconciled to God through the death of his Son, then how much more, having been reconciled, will we be saved by his life. 11 And not only that, but we also boast in God through our Lord Jesus Christ, through whom we have now received this reconciliation.

DEATH THROUGH ADAM AND LIFE THROUGH CHRIST

12 Therefore, just as sin entered the world through one man, and death through sin, in this way death spread to all people, because all sinned.[J] 13 In fact, sin was in the world before the law, but sin is not charged to a person's account when there is no law. 14 Nevertheless, death reigned from Adam to Moses, even over those who did not sin in the likeness of Adam's transgression. He is a type of the Coming One.

15 But the gift is not like the trespass. For if by the one man's trespass the many died, how much more have the grace of God and the gift which comes through the grace of the one man Jesus Christ overflowed to the many. 16 And the gift is not like the one man's sin, because from one sin came the judgment, resulting in condemnation, but from many trespasses came the gift, resulting in justification.[K] 17 If by the one man's trespass, death reigned through that one man, how much more will those who receive the overflow of grace and the gift of righteousness reign in life through the one man, Jesus Christ.

18 So then, as through one trespass there is condemnation for everyone, so also through one righteous act there is justification leading to life for everyone. 19 For just as through one man's disobedience the many were made sinners, so also through the one man's obedience the many will be made righteous. 20 The law came along to multiply the trespass. But where sin multiplied, grace multiplied even more 21 so that, just as sin reigned in death, so also grace will reign through righteousness, resulting in eternal life through Jesus Christ our Lord.

THE NEW LIFE IN CHRIST

6 What should we say then? Should we continue in sin so that grace may multiply? 2 Absolutely not! How can we who died to sin still live in it? 3 Or are you unaware that all of us who were baptized into Christ

[A] **4:16** Or *not to the one who is of the law only* [B] **4:17,18** Gn 17:5 [C] **4:18** Gn 15:5 [D] **4:19** Other mss read *He did not consider* [E] **4:22,23** Gn 15:6 [F] **4:25** Or *because of* [G] **5:1** Other mss read *faith, let us have peace,* which can also be translated *faith, let us grasp the fact that we have peace* [H] **5:2** Other mss omit *by faith* [I] **5:2** Or *rejoice,* also in vv. 3,11 [J] **5:12** Or *have sinned* [K] **5:16** Or *acquittal*

The Roman Forum

by Scott Hummel

At the heart of the city of Rome was the Forum with its monuments, government buildings, and ancient temples. The Roman Forum was in a valley that ran among the hills on which Rome was built. The Forum was more than six hundred yards long, two hundred fifty yards wide, and ran in a northwest-southeast direction. The Via Sacra, the oldest and most famous street in Rome, ran down the spine of the Forum.

According to tradition, when Rome was founded in 753 BC, the area of the Forum stood outside the small community built on the Palatine hill. Only after the marshy valley was drained could the area be incorporated into the city.[1] The transformed valley became Rome's marketplace and civic center where leaders conducted the city's most important commercial, legal, political, and religious business.[2]

The political and religious importance of the Forum grew when the Roman kings built there the palace known as the Regia and the temple of Vesta. The round temple of Vesta had a conical roof like an ancient hut with an opening in the center to allow the sacred fire's smoke to exit. The worship of Vesta, the goddess of the sacred fire and guardian of Rome, was performed by the Vestal Virgins who were chosen as young girls to serve for thirty years during which time they were required to maintain their chastity.[3] If they did not, they were buried alive. Because the fire ensured Rome's protection, any Vestal Virgin who let the sacred fire go out was flogged.[4] During their service, they lived next to the temple in the Vestal house under the care of the pontifex maximus or high priest. As the only priestesses in Roman religion and as guardians of the sacred fire, the Vestal Virgins were shown great respect by the public and given privileges no other women enjoyed.[5]

The Republican Period (510–27 BC) witnessed dramatic changes. Many of the shops lining the Forum were forced out to make room for several temples and basilicas, and the Comitium or assembly area became the Forum's focal point. The Basilica Aemilia was a large rectangular hall, lined with columns and ending with a large semicircular recess.[6] The hall housed court proceedings and other governmental functions. The basilica was beautifully decorated and considered one of the most beautiful buildings in the world.[7]

Roman temples were usually rectangular and built on a high platform. The front steps led through a columned porch to the main room where the statue of the god stood. Religious ceremonies were conducted outside at the altar instead of inside, which was the home of the god.[8] The temple of Saturn also served as the state treasury and housed the standards of the Legions and the decrees of the Senate. Sacred treasures were held in its underground chamber. The Romans worshiped Saturn as a god-king who ruled over a golden age of prosperity, peace, and equality.[9]

With the rise of the republic, the Regia became the official headquarters of the Pontifex Maximus, who carried out the sacred duties

Overview of the Roman Forum. Pictured left is the columned porch of the temple of Saturn. The three white columns in the distance are from the temple of Castor. To its left is the temple of Antonius and Faustina. On the horizon is the Roman Colosseum.

of the state and cared for the Vestal Virgins.[10] The Comitium was an open area where assemblies gathered. It became the epicenter of the government because it included the Rostra or speakers' platform, and the Curia or Senate House. Some of the most famous speeches in Roman history were delivered from the Rostra, such as those given by Cicero and Mark Antony. It was a large platform adorned with the beaks (rostra) of ships captured from the naval battle of Antium in 338 BC.[11] The Senate deliberated in the Curia, which held three hundred senators on three tiers of steps.[12]

The fall of the Roman Republic and the rise of the Roman Empire were reflected in Julius Caesar's massive renovation of the Forum. Augustus completed Caesar's reconstructions and added the temple of Divus Julius where Caesar's body had been cremated in the Forum.[13] The buildings of the Forum demonstrated the subordination of the Senate and the elevation of the emperors to the status of gods. The emperors themselves were now worshiped in the Forum. Emperors further diminished the political importance of the Forum by building several other forums known as the Imperial Fora. They also assumed the office of the Pontifex Maximus (who had traditionally lived in the Forum), but they built their palaces elsewhere.

By the time Paul arrived in Rome (ca AD 60), the Forum was less the seat of power and more a seat of monuments, temples, and triumphal arches. A massive fire ravaged most of Rome in AD 64 and destroyed many of the Forum's buildings. Nero blamed the Christians for the fire and martyred many of them, possibly including Paul.

The Forum had recovered from previous fires and earthquakes. It fell into permanent decline, however, with the transfer of the imperial residence to Constantinople and with subsequent invasions. When Constantine established Christianity as the official religion of the empire, the temples fell into ruin or were converted into churches. The Forum's state of ruin became so complete that for centuries it was known only as Campo Vaccino, "the cow field."[14] ✣

Temple of the Vestal Virgins in the Roman Forum.

[1] The Romans built the Cloaca Maxima to drain the valley. At first it was an open canal, but circa 200 BC it was arched over. Luca Mozzati, *Rome*, trans. Felicity Lutz and Susan White (Milan: Mondadovi Electa, 2003), 15; see Ernest Nash, *Pictorial Dictionary of Ancient Rome* (London: Zwemmer, 1961), 1:442. [2] D. B. Saddington, "Rome," in *Major Cities of the Biblical World*, ed. R. K. Harrison (Nashville: Thomas Nelson, 1985), 210. [3] Stewart Perowne, *Roman Mythology* (London: Paul Hamlyn, 1969), 32; Samuel Ball Platner, *A Topographical Dictionary of Ancient Rome* (London: Oxford University Press, 1929), 557. [4] See Herbert Rose, "Vesta, Vestals" in *The Oxford Classical Dictionary* (Oxford: Clarendon, 1970), 1116; and Perowne, *Roman Mythology*, 32. [5] Perowne, *Roman Mythology*, 32. [6] Platner, *Topographical Dictionary*, 71. This basilica floor plan was later adopted by many churches. [7] Mozzati, *Rome*, 15; Platner, *Topographical Dictionary*, 74. [8] Saddington, "Rome," 215. [9] H. J. Rose, *Religion in Greece and Rome* (New York: Harper, 1959), 225; John Ferguson, *The Religions of the Roman Empire* (Ithaca, NY: Cornell University Press, 1970), 215; H. H. Scullard, *Festivals and Ceremonies of the Roman Republic* (Ithaca, NY: Cornell University Press, 1981), 206. [10] Saddington, "Rome," 211, 218. [11] Ian Richmond and Donald Strong, "Rostra" in *Oxford Classical Dictionary*, 937; Nash, *Pictorial Dictionary*, 2:272. [12] Mozzati, *Rome*, 15. [13] Richard Stillwell, ed., *The Princeton Encyclopedia of Classical Sites* (Princeton, NJ: Princeton University Press, 1976), 764. [14] Nash, *Pictorial Dictionary*, 1:446.

Exterior of Etruscan tombs at Caere, which is about thirty-five miles northwest of Rome. During the sixth century BC, the wealthy Etruscans at Caere offered elaborate funerals and stately resting places for the deceased.

Jesus were baptized into his death? 4 Therefore we were buried with him by baptism into death, in order that, just as Christ was raised from the dead by the glory of the Father, so we too may walk in newness[A] of life. 5 For if we have been united with him in the likeness of his death, we will certainly also be[B] in the likeness of his resurrection. 6 For we know that our old self[C] was crucified with him so that the body ruled by sin[D] might be rendered powerless so that we may no longer be enslaved to sin, 7 since a person who has died is freed[E] from sin. 8 Now if we died with Christ, we believe that we will also live with him, 9 because we know that Christ, having been raised from the dead, will not die again. Death no longer rules over him. 10 For the death he died, he died to sin once for all time; but the life he lives, he lives to God. 11 So, you too consider yourselves dead to sin and alive to God in Christ Jesus.[F]

12 Therefore do not let sin reign in your mortal body, so that you obey[G] its desires. 13 And do not offer any parts[H] of it to sin as weapons for unrighteousness. But as those who are alive from the dead, offer yourselves to God, and all the parts of yourselves to God as weapons for righteousness. 14 For sin will not rule over you, because you are not under the law but under grace.

FROM SLAVES OF SIN TO SLAVES OF GOD

15 What then? Should we sin because we are not under the law but under grace? Absolutely not! 16 Don't you know that if you offer yourselves to someone[I] as obedient slaves, you are slaves of that one you obey — either of sin leading to death or of obedience leading to righteousness? 17 But thank God that, although you used to be slaves of sin, you obeyed from the heart that pattern of teaching to which you were handed[J] over, 18 and having been set free from sin, you became enslaved to righteousness. 19 I am using a human analogy because of the weakness of your flesh.[K] For just as you offered the parts of yourselves as slaves to impurity, and to greater and greater lawlessness, so now offer them as slaves to righteousness, which results in sanctification. 20 For when you were slaves of sin, you were free with regard to righteousness.[L] 21 So what fruit was produced[M] then from the things you are now ashamed of? The outcome of those things is death. 22 But now, since you have been set free from sin and have become enslaved to God, you have your fruit, which results in sanctification — and the outcome is eternal life! 23 For the wages of sin is death, but the gift of God is eternal life in Christ Jesus our Lord.

AN ILLUSTRATION FROM MARRIAGE

7 Since I am speaking to those who know the law, brothers and sisters, don't you know that the law rules over someone as long as he lives? 2 For example, a married woman is legally bound to her husband while he lives. But if her husband dies, she is released from the law regarding the husband. 3 So then, if she is married to another man while her husband is living, she will be called an adulteress. But if her husband dies, she is free from that law. Then, if she is married to another man, she is not an adulteress.

4 Therefore, my brothers and sisters, you also were put to death in relation to the law through the body of Christ so that you may belong to another. You belong to him who was raised from the dead in order that we may bear fruit for God. 5 For when we were in the flesh, the sinful passions aroused through the law were working in us[N] to bear fruit for death. 6 But now we have been released from the law, since we have died to what held us, so that we may serve in the newness of the Spirit and not in the old letter of the law.

[A] **6:4** Or *a new way* [B] **6:5** Be joined with him [C] **6:6** Lit *man* [D] **6:6** Lit *that the body of sin* [E] **6:7** Or *justified*; lit *acquitted* [F] **6:11** Other mss add *our Lord* [G] **6:12** Other mss add *sin* (lit *it*) *in* [H] **6:13** Or *members*, also in v. 19 [I] **6:16** Lit *that to whom you offer yourselves* [J] **6:17** Or *entrusted* [K] **6:19** Or *your human nature* [L] **6:20** Lit *free to righteousness* [M] **6:21** Lit *what fruit do you have* [N] **7:5** Lit *in our members*

SIN'S USE OF THE LAW

7 What should we say then? Is the law sin? Absolutely
not! But I would not have known sin if it were not for
the law. For example, I would not have known what
it is to covet if the law had not said, **Do not covet.**[A]
8 And sin, seizing an opportunity through the commandment, produced in me coveting of every kind.
For apart from the law sin is dead. 9 Once I was alive
apart from the law, but when the commandment
came, sin sprang to life again 10 and I died. The commandment that was meant for life resulted in death
for me. 11 For sin, seizing an opportunity through the
commandment, deceived me, and through it killed
me. 12 So then, the law is holy, and the commandment
is holy and just and good. 13 Therefore, did what is
good become death to me? Absolutely not! But sin, in
order to be recognized as sin, was producing death in
me through what is good, so that through the commandment, sin might become sinful beyond measure.

THE PROBLEM OF SIN IN US

14 For we know that the law is spiritual, but I am of
the flesh,[B] sold as a slave under sin. 15 For I do not understand what I am doing, because I do not practice
what I want to do, but I do what I hate. 16 Now if I do
what I do not want to do, I agree with the law that it
is good. 17 So now I am no longer the one doing it, but
it is sin living in me. 18 For I know that nothing good
lives in me, that is, in my flesh. For the desire to do
what is good is with me, but there is no ability to do
it. 19 For I do not do the good that I want to do, but I
practice the evil that I do not want to do. 20 Now if I
do what I do not want, I am no longer the one that
does it, but it is the sin that lives in me. 21 So I discover this law:[C] When I want to do what is good,[D] evil is
present with me. 22 For in my inner self[E] I delight in
God's law, 23 but I see a different law in the parts of
my body,[F] waging war against the law of my mind
and taking me prisoner to the law of sin in the parts
of my body. 24 What a wretched man I am! Who will
rescue me from this body of death? 25 Thanks be to
God through Jesus Christ our Lord! So then, with my
mind I myself am serving the law of God, but with my
flesh, the law of sin.

THE LIFE-GIVING SPIRIT

8 Therefore, there is now no condemnation for
those in Christ Jesus,[G] 2 because the law[C] of the
Spirit of life in Christ Jesus has set you[H] free from the
law[C] of sin and death. 3 For what the law could not
do since it was weakened by the flesh, God did. He
condemned sin in the flesh by sending his own Son
in the likeness of sinful flesh as a sin offering,[I] 4 in
order that the law's requirement would be fulfilled
in us who do not walk according to the flesh but according to the Spirit. 5 For those who live according
to the flesh have their minds set on the things of the
flesh, but those who live according to the Spirit have
their minds set on the things of the Spirit. 6 Now the
mindset of the flesh is death, but the mindset of the
Spirit is life and peace. 7 The mindset of the flesh is
hostile to God because it does not submit to God's
law. Indeed, it is unable to do so. 8 Those who are in
the flesh cannot please God. 9 You, however, are not
in the flesh, but in the Spirit, if indeed the Spirit of
God lives in you. If anyone does not have the Spirit of
Christ, he does not belong to him. 10 Now if Christ is
in you, the body is dead because of sin, but the Spirit[J]
gives life[K] because of righteousness. 11 And if the Spirit
of him who raised Jesus from the dead lives in you,
then he who raised Christ from the dead will also
bring your mortal bodies to life through[L] his Spirit
who lives in you.

THE HOLY SPIRIT'S MINISTRIES

12 So then, brothers and sisters, we are not obligated
to the flesh to live according to the flesh, 13 because if
you live according to the flesh, you are going to die.
But if by the Spirit you put to death the deeds of the
body, you will live. 14 For all those led by God's Spirit
are God's sons. 15 For you did not receive a spirit of
slavery to fall back into fear. Instead, you received
the Spirit of adoption, by whom we cry out, "*Abba*,[M]
Father!" 16 The Spirit himself testifies together with
our spirit that we are God's children, 17 and if children,
also heirs — heirs of God and coheirs with Christ
— if indeed we suffer with him so that we may also
be glorified with him.

FROM GROANS TO GLORY

18 For I consider that the sufferings of this present
time are not worth comparing with the glory that is
going to be revealed to us. 19 For the creation eagerly
waits with anticipation for God's sons to be revealed.
20 For the creation was subjected to futility — not
willingly, but because of him who subjected it — in
the hope 21 that the creation itself will also be set free
from the bondage to decay into the glorious freedom
of God's children. 22 For we know that the whole creation has been groaning together with labor pains
until now. 23 Not only that, but we ourselves who have
the Spirit as the firstfruits — we also groan within
ourselves, eagerly waiting for adoption, the redemption of our bodies. 24 Now in this hope we were saved,

[A] 7:7 Ex 20:17 [B] **7:14** Or *unspiritual* [C] **7:21; 8:2** Or *principle* [D] **7:21** Or *I find with respect to the law that when I want to do good* [E] **7:22** Lit *inner man* [F] **7:23** Lit *my members* [G] **8:1** Other mss add *who do not walk according to the flesh but according to the Spirit* [H] **8:2** Other mss read *me* [I] **8:3** Or *for sin* [J] **8:10** Or *spirit* [K] **8:10** Or *your spirit is alive* [L] **8:11** Other mss read *because of* [M] **8:15** Aramaic for *father*

Jews in First-Century Rome

by William B. Tolar

When his life was in serious danger in Egypt, Julius Caesar was rescued by a Jewish mercenary army. The Romans had earlier chosen an Idumean named Antipater (the father of Herod the Great) to be a military adviser to Jewish national leaders. Antipater led the army that rescued Caesar. As a result, Caesar rewarded the Jews for their help by granting special privileges and rights both on taxation and in their religious practices. He also appointed Antipater to be governor[1] over the Jews, but of course, under Roman authority.

Antipater (and his son Herod) thus made some powerful and influential friends in Rome. Jewish merchants would now be far more welcome in Rome and their business opportunities increased tremendously. Jewish families could move to the great city and live there with the approval of those who followed Julius Caesar's powerful leadership. Even after Caesar's assassination in 44 BC, his supporters and successors Mark Antony and Octavian (later designated as Augustus Caesar) led the Roman Senate in 40 BC to declare Herod to be "king of the Jews" under Roman rule. The special tax and religious privileges Julius Caesar had granted continued. The roads and sea lanes continued to be wide open for the expansions of a Jewish presence in Rome. Monotheistic Jews did not have to worship Rome's national gods and goddesses.

So by the time Jesus was born (during the reign of Augustus, the grandnephew of Julius Caesar), the Jewish people had enjoyed special privileges under the sovereignty of Rome for nearly forty years. Herod the Great (reigned 37–4 BC) was a brilliant businessman and one of history's greatest builders. He led an incredible surge of business activity that brought Roman businessmen, architects, and engineers into the country to help build cities such as Caesarea Maritima. Commerce between this great seaport and Rome was daily and direct. Jewish merchants and their families had direct access to the capital city. Their number probably surged in the years immediately preceding the birth of Christ while Herod and his family members exercised influence with Rome's leaders.

In the latter part of the first century BC and in the first half of the first century AD, Jews in Rome seem to have lived and worshiped generally as they did in other cities of the world at that time. They lived together in close proximity because of racial and religious differences with most of Rome's inhabitants. The daily life of devout Jews centered on family life, work, and local synagogue activities. Their monotheism separated them from their polytheistic pagan neighbors, so they probably spent their time mostly with other Jews, except for business activities. Other racial and religious enclaves were present in Rome, so the Jews were not the only ones who lived segregated lives among their own kind in the big city.

Jewish people, however, had to be especially careful in Rome, which was relatively tolerant of foreign religions if those religions were not politically active and did not advocate rebellion against Rome and its national religions. Polytheists

House of Augustus at Palatine Hill in Rome.

Senate building in the Roman Forum.

could worship Rome's gods, but Jews would not; so they had to be extra careful to show they were loyal, honest, hardworking, and nonthreatening to Rome's customs and manners.

The Romans tolerated most all religious groups on principle as potential invokers of all gods' divine graces upon the state and society. However, only the Jews were excused from supporting the imperial cult because of the special favors Julius Caesar and his successors granted. These special privileges, and the rigorous and aggressive defense of them by the Jews, caused many Romans to have contempt for them. Jews would not worship the deified emperors nor serve in the military legions of Rome, but the Jewish community was not numerous enough to prove a real danger. In Rome itself, the regulations governing the Jews were somewhat stricter than they were in other parts of the empire, and on several occasions the Jews were exiled from the city. In general, however, they were not molested. The privileges granted to the monotheistic Jews, in spite of their refusal to worship the emperors, were possible only because their religion was limited to a single small race.

If a non-Roman religion did not proselytize Roman citizens away from their national religion, refuse obedience to the state by refusing to pay taxes, threaten public morality, or create public strife, then Rome was typically very tolerant of it. Officials could be indifferent to various religions when tolerance served their purposes, and they could be incredibly brutal when it did not.

Jews and proselytes from Rome were in Jerusalem at Pentecost when Peter preached his sermon about Christ (Ac 2:10–11). In all probability, some converted Jews went back to Rome and started the first Christian church in the capital city. The date would have been about AD 28 to 30.

On his second missionary journey, Paul met a Jewish couple named Aquila and Priscilla in Corinth "who had recently come from Italy . . . because Claudius had ordered all the Jews to leave Rome" (Ac 18:2). After many years of tolerance by former emperors of non-Roman religions in Rome, Claudius during his reign (AD 41–54) issued an edict (ca AD 49) banishing the Jews from Rome. According to the Roman historian Suetonius, Claudius did this because "the Jews constantly made disturbances at the instigation of Chrestus."[2] Many scholars believe this was a confused or misspelled reference to "Christus," the Latin spelling for Christ. Unbelieving Jews in Rome had apparently reacted violently to Christian preaching that Jesus was the Christ, as we find them doing in Acts in response to Paul's preaching. The emperor's decree meant many Jews and Jewish Christians were expelled from their homes. Thus the church in Rome was comprised mostly of Gentile Christians until Jews were permitted to return after Claudius's reign. ❖

---

[1] Josephus, *Jewish War* 1.10.3. [2] Suetonius, *Claudius* 25.4.

Coin of Caesar Augustus.

Bust of Aristotle; from Athens; Roman copy of the original, which dated about 325–300 BC.

but hope that is seen is not hope, because who hopes
for what he sees? 25 Now if we hope for what we do
not see, we eagerly wait for it with patience.

26 In the same way the Spirit also helps us in our
weakness, because we do not know what to pray for
as we should, but the Spirit himself intercedes for us[A]
with inexpressible groanings. 27 And he who searches
our hearts knows the mind of the Spirit, because he
intercedes for the saints according to the will of God.

28 We know that all things work together[B] for the
good[C] of those who love God, who are called according to his purpose. 29 For those he foreknew he also
predestined to be conformed to the image of his Son,
so that he would be the firstborn among many brothers and sisters. 30 And those he predestined, he also
called; and those he called, he also justified; and those
he justified, he also glorified.

THE BELIEVER'S TRIUMPH

31 What, then, are we to say about these things? If God
is for us, who is against us? 32 He did not even spare
his own Son but gave him up for us all. How will he
not also with him grant us everything? 33 Who can
bring an accusation against God's elect? God is the
one who justifies. 34 Who is the one who condemns?
Christ Jesus is the one who died, but even more, has
been raised; he also is at the right hand of God and
intercedes for us. 35 Who can separate us from the
love of Christ? Can affliction or distress or persecution or famine or nakedness or danger or sword?
36 As it is written:

> **Because of you**
> **we are being put to death all day long;**
> **we are counted as sheep to be slaughtered.**[D]

37 No, in all these things we are more than conquerors through him who loved us. 38 For I am persuaded
that neither death nor life, nor angels nor rulers, nor
things present nor things to come, nor powers, 39 nor
height nor depth, nor any other created thing will
be able to separate us from the love of God that is in
Christ Jesus our Lord.

ISRAEL'S REJECTION OF CHRIST

9 I speak the truth in Christ — I am not lying; my
conscience testifies to me through the Holy Spirit[E] — 2 that I have great sorrow and unceasing anguish in my heart. 3 For I could wish that I myself were
cursed and cut off[F] from Christ for the benefit of my
brothers and sisters, my own flesh and blood. 4 They
are Israelites, and to them belong the adoption, the
glory, the covenants, the giving of the law, the temple
service, and the promises. 5 The ancestors are theirs,
and from them, by physical descent,[G] came the Christ,
who is God over all, praised forever.[H] Amen.

GOD'S GRACIOUS ELECTION OF ISRAEL

6 Now it is not as though the word of God has failed,
because not all who are descended from Israel are
Israel. 7 Neither is it the case that all of Abraham's
children are his descendants.[I] On the contrary, **your
offspring will be traced**[J] **through Isaac.**[K] 8 That is, it
is not the children by physical descent[L] who are God's
children, but the children of the promise are considered to be the offspring. 9 For this is the statement of
the promise: **At this time I will come, and Sarah will
have a son.**[M] 10 And not only that, but Rebekah conceived children through one man, our father Isaac.
11 For though her sons had not been born yet or done
anything good or bad, so that God's purpose according to election might stand — 12 not from works but
from the one who calls — she was told, **The older
will serve the younger.**[N] 13 As it is written: **I have
loved Jacob, but I have hated Esau.**[O]

[A] **8:26** Some mss omit *for us* [B] **8:28** Other mss read *that God works together in all things* [C] **8:28** The ultimate good [D] **8:36** Ps 44:22 [E] **9:1** Or *testifying with me by the Holy Spirit* [F] **9:3** Lit *to be anathema* [G] **9:5** Lit *them, according to the flesh* [H] **9:5** Or *the Messiah, the one who is over all, the God who is blessed forever*, or *Messiah. God, who is over all, be blessed forever* [I] **9:7** Lit *seed* [J] **9:7** Lit *called* [K] **9:7** Gn 21:12 [L] **9:8** Lit *children of the flesh* [M] **9:9** Gn 18:10,14 [N] **9:12** Gn 25:23 [O] **9:13** Mal 1:2–3

GOD'S SELECTION IS JUST

14 What should we say then? Is there injustice with God? Absolutely not! 15 For he tells Moses, **I will show mercy to whom I will show mercy, and I will have compassion on whom I will have compassion.**[A] 16 So then, it does not depend on human will or effort but on God who shows mercy. 17 For the Scripture tells Pharaoh, **I raised you up for this reason so that I may display my power in you and that my name may be proclaimed in the whole earth.**[B] 18 So then, he has mercy on whom he wants to have mercy and he hardens whom he wants to harden.

19 You will say to me, therefore, "Why then does he still find fault? For who resists his will?" 20 On the contrary, who are you, a human being, to talk back to God? Will what is formed say to the one who formed it, "Why did you make me like this?" 21 Or has the potter no right over the clay, to make from the same lump one piece of pottery for honor and another for dishonor? 22 And what if God, wanting to display his wrath and to make his power known, endured with much patience objects of wrath prepared for destruction? 23 And what if he did this to make known the riches of his glory on objects of mercy that he prepared beforehand for glory — 24 on us, the ones he also called, not only from the Jews but also from the Gentiles? 25 As it[C] also says in Hosea,

I will call Not My People, My People,
and she who is Unloved, Beloved.[D]
26 **And it will be in the place where**
they were told,
you are not my people,
there they will be called sons
of the living God.[E]

27 But Isaiah cries out concerning Israel,

Though the number of Israelites
is like the sand of the sea,
only the remnant will be saved;
28 **since the Lord will execute his sentence**
completely and decisively on the earth.[F,G]

29 And just as Isaiah predicted:

If the Lord of Armies had not left us offspring,
we would have become like Sodom,
and we would have been made
like Gomorrah.[H]

ISRAEL'S PRESENT STATE

30 What should we say then? Gentiles, who did not pursue righteousness, have obtained righteousness — namely the righteousness that comes from faith. 31 But Israel, pursuing the law of righteousness, has not achieved the righteousness of the law.[I] 32 Why is that? Because they did not pursue it by faith, but as if it were by works.[J] They stumbled over the stumbling stone. 33 As it is written,

Look, I am putting a stone in Zion
to stumble over
and a rock to trip over,
and the one who believes on him
will not be put to shame.[K]

RIGHTEOUSNESS BY FAITH ALONE

10 Brothers and sisters, my heart's desire and prayer to God concerning them[L] is for their salvation. 2 I can testify about them that they have zeal for God, but not according to knowledge. 3 Since they are ignorant of the righteousness of God and attempted to establish their own righteousness, they have not submitted to God's righteousness. 4 For Christ is the end[M] of the law for righteousness to everyone who believes, 5 since Moses writes about the righteousness that is from the law: **The one who does these things will live by them.**[N] 6 But the righteousness that comes from faith speaks like this: **Do not say in your heart, "Who will go up to heaven?"**[O] that is, to bring Christ down 7 or, **"Who will go down into the abyss?"**[P] that is, to bring Christ up from the dead. 8 On the contrary, what does it say? **The message is near you, in your mouth and in your heart.**[Q] This is the message of faith that we proclaim: 9 If you confess with your mouth, "Jesus is Lord," and believe in your heart that God raised him from the dead, you will be saved. 10 One believes with the heart, resulting in righteousness, and one confesses with the mouth, resulting in salvation. 11 For the Scripture says, **Everyone who believes on him will not be put to shame,**[R] 12 since there is no distinction between Jew and Greek, because the same Lord of all richly blesses all who call on him. 13 For **everyone who calls on the name of the Lord will be saved.**[S]

ISRAEL'S REJECTION OF THE MESSAGE

14 How, then, can they call on him they have not believed in? And how can they believe without hearing about him? And how can they hear without a preacher? 15 And how can they preach unless they are sent? As it is written: **How beautiful**[T] **are the feet of those who bring good news.**[U] 16 But not all obeyed the gospel. For Isaiah says, **Lord, who has believed our message?**[V] 17 So faith comes from what is heard, and what is heard comes through the message about Christ.[W] 18 But I ask, "Did they not hear?" Yes, they did:

[A] **9:15** Ex 33:19 [B] **9:17** Ex 9:16 [C] **9:25** Or *he* [D] **9:25** Hs 2:23 [E] **9:26** Hs 1:10 [F] **9:28** Or *land* [G] **9:27–28** Is 10:22–23; 28:22; Hs 1:10 [H] **9:29** Is 1:9 [I] **9:31** Other mss read *the law for righteousness* [J] **9:32** Other mss add *of the law* [K] **9:33** Is 8:14; 28:16 [L] **10:1** Other mss read *God for Israel* [M] **10:4** Or *goal* [N] **10:5** Lv 18:5 [O] **10:6** Dt 9:4; 30:12 [P] **10:7** Dt 30:13 [Q] **10:8** Dt 30:14 [R] **10:11** Is 28:16 [S] **10:13** Jl 2:32 [T] **10:15** Or *welcome*, or *timely* [U] **10:15** Is 52:7; Nah 1:15 [V] **10:16** Is 53:1 [W] **10:17** Other mss read *God*

Their voice has gone out to
the whole earth,
and their words to the ends
of the world.[A]
19 But I ask, "Did Israel not understand?" First, Moses said,
I will make you jealous
of those who are not a nation;
I will make you angry by a nation
that lacks understanding.[B]
20 And Isaiah says boldly,
I was found
by those who were not looking for me;
I revealed myself
to those who were not asking for me.[C]
21 But to Israel he says, **All day long I have held out**
my hands to a disobedient and defiant people.[D]

ISRAEL'S REJECTION NOT TOTAL

11 I ask, then, has God rejected his people? Absolutely not! For I too am an Israelite, a descendant of Abraham, from the tribe of Benjamin. 2 God
has not rejected his people whom he foreknew. Or
don't you know what the Scripture says in the passage about Elijah — how he pleads with God against
Israel? 3 **Lord, they have killed your prophets and**
torn down your altars. I am the only one left, and
they are trying to take my life![E] 4 But what was
God's answer to him? **I have left seven thousand**
for myself who have not bowed down to Baal.[F]
5 In the same way, then, there is also at the present
time a remnant chosen by grace. 6 Now if by grace,
then it is not by works; otherwise grace ceases to
be grace.[G]
7 What then? Israel did not find what it was looking
for, but the elect did find it. The rest were hardened,
8 as it is written,
God gave them a spirit of stupor,
eyes that cannot see
and ears that cannot hear,
to this day.[H]
9 And David says,
Let their table become a snare
and a trap,
a pitfall and a retribution to them.
10 **Let their eyes be darkened**
so that they cannot see,
and their backs be bent continually.[I]

[A] **10:18** Ps 19:4 [B] **10:19** Dt 32:21 [C] **10:20** Is 65:1 [D] **10:21** Is 65:2
[E] **11:3** 1Kg 19:10,14 [F] **11:4** 1Kg 19:18 [G] **11:6** Other mss add *But if of works it is no longer grace; otherwise work is no longer work.*
[H] **11:8** Dt 29:4; Is 29:10 [I] **11:9–10** Ps 69:22–23

Stadium of Domitian (AD 81–96) at his palace on the Palatine Hill.

ISRAEL'S REJECTION NOT FINAL

11 I ask, then, have they stumbled so as to fall? Absolutely not! On the contrary, by their transgression, salvation has come to the Gentiles to make Israel jealous. 12 Now if their transgression brings riches for the world, and their failure riches for the Gentiles, how much more will their fullness bring!

13 Now I am speaking to you Gentiles. Insofar as I am an apostle to the Gentiles, I magnify my ministry, 14 if I might somehow make my own people[A] jealous and save some of them. 15 For if their rejection brings reconciliation to the world, what will their acceptance mean but life from the dead? 16 Now if the firstfruits are holy, so is the whole batch. And if the root is holy, so are the branches.

17 Now if some of the branches were broken off, and you, though a wild olive branch, were grafted in among them and have come to share in the rich root[B] of the cultivated olive tree, 18 do not boast that you are better than those branches. But if you do boast —you do not sustain the root, but the root sustains you. 19 Then you will say, "Branches were broken off so that I might be grafted in." 20 True enough; they were broken off because of unbelief, but you stand by faith. Do not be arrogant, but beware,[C] 21 because if God did not spare the natural branches, he will not spare you either. 22 Therefore, consider God's kindness and severity: severity toward those who have fallen but God's kindness toward you — if you remain in his kindness. Otherwise you too will be cut off. 23 And even they, if they do not remain in unbelief, will be grafted in, because God has the power to graft them in again. 24 For if you were cut off from your native wild olive tree and against nature were grafted into a cultivated olive tree, how much more will these — the natural branches — be grafted into their own olive tree?

25 I don't want you to be ignorant of this mystery, brothers and sisters, so that you will not be conceited: A partial hardening has come upon Israel until the fullness of the Gentiles has come in. 26 And in this way all[D] Israel will be saved, as it is written,

The Deliverer will come from Zion;
he will turn godlessness away from Jacob.
27 **And this will be my covenant with them**[E]
when I take away their sins.[F]

28 Regarding the gospel, they are enemies for your advantage, but regarding election, they are loved because of the patriarchs, 29 since God's gracious gifts and calling are irrevocable.[G] 30 As you once disobeyed God but now have received mercy through their disobedience, 31 so they too have now disobeyed, resulting in mercy to you, so that they also may now[H] receive mercy. 32 For God has imprisoned all in disobedience so that he may have mercy on all.

A HYMN OF PRAISE

33 Oh, the depth of the riches
and the wisdom and the knowledge of God!
How unsearchable his judgments
and untraceable his ways!
34 **For who has known the mind of the Lord?**
Or who has been his counselor?
35 **And who has ever given to God,**
that he should be repaid?[I]
36 For from him and through him
and to him are all things.
To him be the glory forever. Amen.

A LIVING SACRIFICE

12 Therefore, brothers and sisters, in view of the mercies of God, I urge you to present your bodies as a living sacrifice, holy and pleasing to God; this is your true worship.[J] 2 Do not be conformed to this age, but be transformed by the renewing of your mind, so that you may discern what is the good, pleasing, and perfect will of God.

MANY GIFTS BUT ONE BODY

3 For by the grace given to me, I tell everyone among you not to think of himself more highly than he should think. Instead, think sensibly, as God has distributed a measure of faith to each one. 4 Now as we have many parts in one body, and all the parts do not have the same function, 5 in the same way we who are many are one body in Christ and individually members of one another. 6 According to the grace given to us, we have different gifts: If prophecy, use it according to the proportion of one's[K] faith; 7 if service, use it in service; if teaching, in teaching; 8 if exhorting, in exhortation; giving, with generosity; leading, with diligence; showing mercy, with cheerfulness.

CHRISTIAN ETHICS

9 Let love be without hypocrisy. Detest evil; cling to what is good. 10 Love one another deeply as brothers and sisters. Take the lead in honoring one another. 11 Do not lack diligence in zeal; be fervent in the Spirit;[L] serve the Lord. 12 Rejoice in hope; be patient in affliction; be persistent in prayer. 13 Share with the saints in their needs; pursue hospitality. 14 Bless those who persecute you; bless and do not curse. 15 Rejoice with those who rejoice; weep with those who weep. 16 Live in harmony with one another. Do not be proud; instead, associate with the humble. Do not be wise in your own estimation. 17 Do not repay anyone evil for

[A] **11:14** Lit *flesh* [B] **11:17** Other mss read *the root and the richness* [C] **11:20** Lit *fear* [D] **11:26** Or *And then all* [E] **11:26-27** Is 59:20-21 [F] **11:27** Jr 31:31-34 [G] **11:29** Or *are not taken back* [H] **11:31** Other mss omit *now* [I] **11:34-35** Jb 41:11; Is 40:13; Jr 23:18 [J] **12:1** Or *your reasonable service* [K] **12:6** Or *the*, also in v. 19 [L] **12:11** Or *in spirit*

evil. Give careful thought to do what is honorable
in everyone's eyes. 18 If possible, as far as it depends
on you, live at peace with everyone. 19 Friends, do
not avenge yourselves; instead, leave room for God's
wrath, because it is written, **Vengeance belongs to**
me; I will repay,[A] says the Lord. 20 But

> **If your enemy is hungry, feed him.**
> **If he is thirsty, give him something**
> **to drink.**
> **For in so doing**
> **you will be heaping fiery coals**
> **on his head.**[B]

21 Do not be conquered by evil, but conquer evil with
good.

A CHRISTIAN'S DUTIES TO THE STATE

13 Let everyone submit to the governing authorities, since there is no authority except from
God, and the authorities that exist are instituted by
God. 2 So then, the one who resists the authority is
opposing God's command, and those who oppose it
will bring judgment on themselves. 3 For rulers are
not a terror to good conduct, but to bad. Do you want
to be unafraid of the one in authority? Do what is
good, and you will have its approval. 4 For it is God's
servant for your good. But if you do wrong, be afraid,
because it does not carry the sword for no reason.
For it is God's servant, an avenger that brings wrath
on the one who does wrong. 5 Therefore, you must
submit, not only because of wrath but also because of
your conscience. 6 And for this reason you pay taxes,
since the authorities are God's servants, continually
attending to these tasks.[C] 7 Pay your obligations to
everyone: taxes to those you owe taxes, tolls to those
you owe tolls, respect to those you owe respect, and
honor to those you owe honor.

Roman era cheese press.

LOVE, OUR PRIMARY DUTY

8 Do not owe anyone anything, except to love one another, for the one who loves another has fulfilled the
law. 9 The commandments, **Do not commit adultery;**
do not murder; do not steal;[D] **do not covet;**[E] and
any other commandment, are summed up by this
commandment: **Love your neighbor as yourself.**[F]
10 Love does no wrong to a neighbor. Love, therefore,
is the fulfillment of the law.

PUT ON CHRIST

11 Besides this, since you know the time, it is already
the hour for you[G] to wake up from sleep, because
now our salvation is nearer than when we first believed. 12 The night is nearly over, and the day is near;
so let us discard the deeds of darkness and put on the
armor of light. 13 Let us walk with decency, as in the
daytime: not in carousing and drunkenness; not in
sexual impurity and promiscuity; not in quarreling
and jealousy. 14 But put on the Lord Jesus Christ, and
make no provision for the flesh to gratify its desires.

THE LAW OF LIBERTY

14 Welcome anyone who is weak in faith, but don't
argue about disputed matters. 2 One person believes he may eat anything, while one who is weak eats
only vegetables. 3 One who eats must not look down on
one who does not eat, and one who does not eat must
not judge one who does, because God has accepted
him. 4 Who are you to judge another's household servant? Before his own Lord he stands or falls. And he
will stand, because the Lord is able[H] to make him stand.
5 One person judges one day to be more important
than another day. Someone else judges every day to
be the same. Let each one be fully convinced in his
own mind. 6 Whoever observes the day, observes it
for the honor of the Lord.[I] Whoever eats, eats for
the Lord, since he gives thanks to God; and whoever
does not eat, it is for the Lord that he does not eat it,
and he gives thanks to God. 7 For none of us lives for
himself, and no one dies for himself. 8 If we live, we
live for the Lord; and if we die, we die for the Lord.
Therefore, whether we live or die, we belong to the
Lord. 9 Christ died and returned to life for this: that
he might be Lord over both the dead and the living.
10 But you, why do you judge your brother or sister?
Or you, why do you despise your brother or sister?
For we will all stand before the judgment seat of God.[J]
11 For it is written,

[A] **12:19** Dt 32:35 [B] **12:20** Pr 25:21–22 [C] **13:6** Lit *to this very thing*
[D] **13:9** Other mss add *do not bear false witness* [E] **13:9** Ex 20:13–17; Dt 5:17–21 [F] **13:9** Lv 19:18 [G] **13:11** Other mss read *for us* [H] **14:4** Other mss read *For God has the power* [I] **14:6** Other mss add *but whoever does not observe the day, it is to the Lord that he does not observe it*
[J] **14:10** Other mss read *of Christ*

by Scott A. Andrew

Olive grove at Tekoa.

Italy is a land blessed by rich soil, a mild climate, and abundant rainfall. This was also true in ancient times. Italy's climate "invited possibilities of agriculture on a scale that no other Mediterranean country had ever before been able to attempt."[1] The diets of those living in pre-Roman Italy featured domestic animals, grain, wine, and olive oil. Each of these items were in ample supply.

Grain, oil, and wine—called the "Mediterranean triad"[2]—were the basic food items for the ancient Mediterranean world. As the empire grew, Romans came into contact with new varieties of food. They developed a taste for walnuts, almonds, pistachios, peaches, apricots, pomegranates, cherries, and lemons. When Romans introduced their culture to other lands, they carried with them the fruits, grains, and vegetables they had known at home.

The demand for food grew within the Roman Empire. Merchants discovered that grain could be grown more economically in areas outside Italy. Soon Italy imported all of its grain. By the time of Cicero (106–43 BC), orchards and vineyards covered the Italian countryside. Grapes and olives were Italy's principal farm products.

Olives became increasingly important in the ancient Mediterranean world. Olive cultivation began in Syria as early as 6000 BC. Earthenware tablets from Crete mention the prominence of olives in that culture as early as 2500 BC. After the fall of Crete around 1200 BC, the Phoenicians became masters of trade in the Mediterranean. By the fifth century BC, the Phoenicians and Greeks had distributed olives throughout the Mediterranean world. The Greeks introduced olives to Italy.

Olives became an important part of Roman culture. Though they were grown throughout the Roman Empire, the best olives came from Italy. Olives were prominent in the Roman diet. The economic value of olives came from its oil. Olive oil was irreplaceable in cooking. People anointed their bodies with olive oil after bathing. Romans used it in making perfumes. It fueled lamps throughout the ancient world. Some olive oil was even used as fertilizer. ✣

[1] Michael Grant, *The Founders of the Western World* (New York: Scribner's Sons, 1991), 142. [2] Kevin Greene, *The Archaeology of the Roman Economy* (Berkeley: University of California Press, 1986), 73.

Almonds became a staple of the Roman diet as the empire expanded.

As I live, says the Lord,
every knee will bow to me,
and every tongue will give praise to God.[A]

12 So then, each of us will give an account of himself to God.

THE LAW OF LOVE

13 Therefore, let us no longer judge one another. Instead decide never to put a stumbling block or pitfall in the way of your brother or sister. 14 I know and am persuaded in the Lord Jesus that nothing is unclean in itself. Still, to someone who considers a thing to be unclean, to that one it is unclean. 15 For if your brother or sister is hurt by what you eat, you are no longer walking according to love. Do not destroy, by what you eat, someone for whom Christ died. 16 Therefore, do not let your good be slandered, 17 for the kingdom of God is not eating and drinking, but righteousness, peace, and joy in the Holy Spirit. 18 Whoever serves Christ in this way is acceptable to God and receives human approval.

19 So then, let us pursue what promotes peace and what builds up one another. 20 Do not tear down God's work because of food. Everything is clean, but it is wrong to make someone fall by what he eats. 21 It is a good thing not to eat meat, or drink wine, or do anything that makes your brother or sister stumble.[B] 22 Whatever you believe about these things, keep between yourself and God. Blessed is the one who does not condemn himself by what he approves. 23 But whoever doubts stands condemned if he eats, because his eating is not from faith,[C] and everything that is not from faith is sin.

PLEASING OTHERS, NOT OURSELVES

15 Now we who are strong have an obligation to bear the weaknesses of those without strength, and not to please ourselves. 2 Each one of us is to please his neighbor for his good, to build him up. 3 For even Christ did not please himself. On the contrary, as it is written, **The insults of those who insult you have fallen on me.**[D] 4 For whatever was written in the past was written for our instruction, so that we may have hope through endurance and through the encouragement from the Scriptures. 5 Now may the God who gives[E] endurance and encouragement grant you to live in harmony with one another, according to Christ Jesus, 6 so that you may glorify the God and Father of our Lord Jesus Christ with one mind and one voice.

GLORIFYING GOD TOGETHER

7 Therefore welcome one another, just as[F] Christ also welcomed you, to the glory of God. 8 For I say that Christ became a servant of the circumcised[G] on behalf of God's truth, to confirm the promises to the fathers, 9 and so that Gentiles may glorify God for his mercy. As it is written,

Therefore I will praise you
among the Gentiles,
and I will sing praise to your name.[H]

10 Again it says, **Rejoice, you Gentiles, with his people!**[I] 11 And again,

Praise the Lord, all you Gentiles;
let all the peoples praise him![J]

12 And again, Isaiah says,

The root of Jesse will appear,
the one who rises to rule the Gentiles;
the Gentiles will hope in him.[K]

13 Now may the God of hope fill you with all joy and peace as you believe so that you may overflow with hope by the power of the Holy Spirit.

FROM JERUSALEM TO ILLYRICUM

14 My brothers and sisters, I myself am convinced about you that you also are full of goodness, filled with all knowledge, and able to instruct one another. 15 Nevertheless, I have written to remind you more boldly on some points[L] because of the grace given me by God 16 to be a minister of Christ Jesus to the Gentiles, serving as a priest of the gospel of God. God's purpose is that the Gentiles may be an acceptable offering, sanctified by the Holy Spirit. 17 Therefore I have reason to boast in Christ Jesus regarding what pertains to God. 18 For I would not dare say anything except what Christ has accomplished through me by word and deed for the obedience of the Gentiles, 19 by the power of miraculous signs and wonders, and by the power of God's Spirit. As a result, I have fully proclaimed the gospel of Christ from Jerusalem all the way around to Illyricum.[M] 20 My aim is to preach the gospel where Christ has not been named, so that I will not build on someone else's foundation, 21 but, as it is written,

Those who were not told about him
will see,
and those who have not heard
will understand.[N]

PAUL'S TRAVEL PLANS

22 That is why I have been prevented many times from coming to you. 23 But now I no longer have any work to do in these regions,[O] and I have strongly desired

[A] **14:11** Is 45:23; 49:18 [B] **14:21** Other mss add *or offended or weakened* [C] **14:23** Or *conviction* [D] **15:3** Ps 69:9 [E] **15:5** Lit *God of* [F] **15:7** Or *because* [G] **15:8** The Jews [H] **15:9** 2Sm 22:50; Ps 18:49 [I] **15:10** Dt 32:43 [J] **15:11** Ps 117:1 [K] **15:12** Is 11:10 [L] **15:15** Other mss add *brothers* [M] **15:19** A Roman province northwest of Greece on the eastern shore of the Adriatic Sea [N] **15:21** Is 52:15 [O] **15:23** Lit *now, having no longer a place in these parts*

Nero: Ruler of Rome

by Charles A. Ray Jr.

Nero was born in AD 37 as Lucius Domitius Ahenobarbus. His father's family could trace an unbroken line of nobility back more than two hundred years. His grandfather on his mother's side was the popular Roman General Germanicus, a descendant of the great Emperor Augustus. Nobility, however, does not guarantee civility. Michael Grant begins his biography of Nero saying, "Nero was born of murderous parents, and brought up in a murderous atmosphere. And he too was murderous. But only when frightened, though unfortunately he got frightened easily."[1]

ASCENT TO POWER

Nero's uncle Gauis Caligula became emperor the year Nero was born. Two years later, Nero's mother, Agrippina, was accused of plotting to kill her brother, Caligula, and was banished from Rome. Nero was placed in the care of his father's sister. Nero's fortunes turned the following year (AD 41), when Caligula was murdered by his own palace guards. Caligula's uncle Claudius was selected as the next emperor, and he allowed his niece, Agrippina, to return from exile.

Upon her return to Rome, Agrippina immediately remarried, this time to a wealthy orator, who died suddenly three years later. In AD 48, Claudius's wife was forced to commit suicide for her alleged involvement in a plot to assassinate Claudius; by the following year, Agrippina was the new wife of the emperor.

Bust of Emperor Gaius Caligula (AD 37–41).

Claudius had one son, Britannicus, by his former wife, but Agrippina set out to undermine his claim to the throne. In her first year of marriage to Claudius, she arranged the engagement of Nero to Claudius's daughter Octavia, and the following year she convinced Claudius to adopt her son. At this time Nero's name was changed to Nero Claudius Drusus Germanicus.

That same year, Agrippina secured the Roman senator, orator, and philosopher Seneca as Nero's personal tutor. Seneca had been exiled to the island of Corsica in AD 41 under the influence of Claudius's first wife, and Agrippina was instrumental in securing his return to Rome. Nero's career accelerated rapidly, soon eclipsing the younger Britannicus. Nero's name appeared first on official inscriptions; his image, not that of Britannicus, appeared on coins; and he was allowed to march in parades at the head of the emperor's palace guard, the praetorian guard.[2]

In February AD 54, Britannicus turned thirteen, the age at which Claudius had allowed Nero to become a legal adult. Claudius gave some indication of giving a similar status to Britannicus, a situation that would have threatened Nero's claim to the throne. Claudius made a new will, but he died in October without having taken any steps to strengthen Britannicus's position. With the aid of Burrus, the commander of the praetorian guard, Agrippina had Nero declared emperor and Claudius's revised will suppressed. Burrus owed his appointment as commander to the political maneuvering of Agrippina, and rumors circulated that she was responsible for Claudius's death, probably through poisoning.

GOLDEN YEARS

Agrippina had assumed significantly more political clout under Claudius than was customary for the wife of

Bronze statuette likely made in Gaul showing Nero in imperial dress.

an emperor. Nero was not yet seventeen when he ascended to the throne (reigned AD 54–68), and for at least the first year of his reign, Agrippina exercised even more power. Her portrait appeared on coins with Nero's, hers occupying the more prominent place. Rumors circulated in the first century that Agrippina controlled Nero in part through an incestuous relationship with him.[3]

Soon, however, the relationship between Nero and his mother deteriorated. She threatened to champion Britannicus over Nero, and early in AD 55 Nero enlisted help in having Britannicus poisoned. He then forced Agrippina to move out of the palace to another residence across town. Working together, Burrus and Seneca used Nero's poor relationship with his mother to channel his energies, at least partially, to the task of governing the empire. The result was a period early in Nero's reign of almost five years during which Rome experienced stability.

Nero appears to have been influenced by Seneca's concepts of generosity and leniency. On one occasion, he attempted to eliminate all forms of indirect taxation from the empire. The move proved to be economically impractical but increased Nero's popularity among the people. Nero was reported to have taken his judicial duties very seriously, studying written briefs overnight before making decisions. He appears to have worked hard at removing some of the abuses common among previous emperors. Paul wrote his letter to the church at Rome sometime during this period of Nero's reign, most likely during the mid-to-late 50s.

YEARS OF GROWING TYRANNY

Nero had shown an early interest in the performing arts and athletic competition. Most Roman nobility believed strongly in the superiority of the Roman practical arts of war and government. While the pursuit of the arts for relaxation and diversion was encouraged, serious pursuit of the arts was left for slaves and other foreigners.

Nero did not share this opinion and had worked privately to excel in music, oratory, and art. His mother had always discouraged these pursuits, and Burrus and Seneca were able to limit Nero's performances to private audiences. A series of events beginning in AD 59 changed things.

Nero became less tolerant of his mother's attempts to control him and finally resolved to have her murdered. Following a bungled attempt to have her drowned in a collapsible boat, Nero had her killed on charges of plotting to assassinate him. In contrast to Agrippina's domineering control, the counsel of Burrus and Seneca must have seemed mild. Without that contrast, the two men had less success controlling Nero's wilder side.

In the following years, Nero became more determined to fulfill his interests, which included singing, acting, chariot racing, and pursuing sexual exploits. When Burrus died in AD 62, Nero replaced him with Tigellinus, who encouraged Nero's licentious self-absorption. Without the aid of Burrus, Seneca asked Nero if he could retire from government. Although Nero refused his request, Seneca became less involved in governmental affairs. That same year, Nero divorced his wife, Octavia, and married Poppaea, who was the wife of a friend and pregnant with Nero's child. Two years later, Nero began to make public appearances on the stage and in athletic events, much to the dismay of the Roman Senate and other nobility.

Nero also was active in remodeling and enlarging his own palace. Eventually his rather large palace became the entrance hall into an immensely larger palace known as the Golden House. Depending on which estimate one accepts, the Golden House and surrounding gardens covered between 125 and 370 acres.[4] The notorious fire of July AD 64 caused destruction, which made possible this massive construction project.

Marble bust of the emperor Claudius, who adopted Nero in AD 50.

The origin of the fire is unknowable, though several aspects of the situation led to finger pointing in Nero's direction. Reports circulated that during the fire gangs of men were seen throwing torches into buildings and threatening anyone who tried to extinguish the flames. After burning for six days, the fire appeared to be stamped out only to reignite on the property of Tigellinus, the new commander of the emperor's palace guard.

Nero's own attitude toward the fire seemed suspect as well. Inspired by the sight of the city burning, he sang in its entirety his original composition, *Fall of Troy*, while he played his lyre. The ancient sources differ as to where the performance took place, either on the roof of his palace or in his private theater.[5] The public outrage was intense and was not abated by the emperor's acts of benevolence. Needing a scapegoat, Nero blamed the fire on the Christians in the city and began an intense time of persecution. Paul and Peter were probably martyred in the aftermath of this event.

The following year, a conspiracy against the emperor erupted. Nero brutally suppressed it. As discontent continued to grow in Rome, Nero went to Greece, where he spent a year competing in various athletic games and other events. To no one's surprise, Nero won every event he entered, even the ten-horse chariot race in which he fell from his chariot and was unable to complete the race.

Nero finally returned to Rome in January 68 to at least three separate uprisings. His feeble attempts at restoring order failed miserably. When the Senate voted to condemn Nero to death by flogging, his palace guard deserted him. On June 9, 68, Nero committed suicide. His famous statement, "What an artist dies with me," was uttered as he gave directions on how to decorate his tomb.[6] ✣

---

[1] Michael Grant, *Nero* (New York: Dorset, 1970), 13. [2] Grant, *Nero*, 26. [3] Grant, *Nero*, 32. [4] Grant, *Nero*, 140. [5] Grant, *Nero*, 126. [6] Miriam T. Griffin, *Nero: The End of a Dynasty* (New Haven, CT: Yale University Press, 1985), 182.

for many years to come to you 24 whenever I travel to Spain.[A] For I hope to see you when I pass through and to be assisted by you for my journey there, once I have first enjoyed your company for a while. 25 Right now I am traveling to Jerusalem to serve the saints, 26 because Macedonia and Achaia were pleased to make a contribution for the poor among the saints in Jerusalem. 27 Yes, they were pleased, and indeed are indebted to them. For if the Gentiles have shared in their spiritual benefits, then they are obligated to minister to them in material needs. 28 So when I have finished this and safely delivered the funds[B] to them,[C] I will visit you on the way to Spain. 29 I know that when I come to you, I will come in the fullness of the blessing[D] of Christ.

30 Now I appeal to you, brothers and sisters, through our Lord Jesus Christ and through the love of the Spirit, to strive together with me in prayers to God on my behalf. 31 Pray that I may be rescued from the unbelievers in Judea, that my ministry to[E] Jerusalem may be acceptable to the saints, 32 and that, by God's will, I may come to you with joy and be refreshed together with you.

33 May the God of peace be with all of you. Amen.

In the latter part of the fourth century BC play production flourished, especially in Athens. Actors wore masks to indicate the gender and status of the person being portrayed. Marble theater masks, such as this one, decorated theaters and funerary monuments.

PAUL'S COMMENDATION OF PHOEBE

16 I commend to you our sister Phoebe, who is a servant[F] of the church in Cenchreae. 2 So you should welcome her in the Lord in a manner worthy of the saints and assist her in whatever matter she may require your help. For indeed she has been a benefactor of many — and of me also.

GREETING TO ROMAN CHRISTIANS

3 Give my greetings to Prisca[G] and Aquila, my coworkers in Christ Jesus, 4 who risked their own necks for my life. Not only do I thank them, but so do all the Gentile churches. 5 Greet also the church that meets in their home. Greet my dear friend Epaenetus, who is the first convert[H] to Christ from Asia.[I] 6 Greet Mary,[J] who has worked very hard for you.[K] 7 Greet Andronicus and Junia, my fellow Jews[L] and fellow prisoners. They are noteworthy in the eyes of the apostles,[M] and they were also in Christ before me. 8 Greet Ampliatus, my dear friend in the Lord. 9 Greet Urbanus, our coworker in Christ, and my dear friend Stachys. 10 Greet Apelles, who is approved in Christ. Greet those who belong to the household of Aristobulus. 11 Greet Herodion, my fellow Jew.[N] Greet those who belong to the household of Narcissus who are in the Lord. 12 Greet Tryphaena and Tryphosa, who have worked hard in the Lord. Greet my dear friend Persis, who has worked very hard in the Lord. 13 Greet Rufus, chosen in the Lord; also his mother — and mine. 14 Greet Asyncritus, Phlegon, Hermes, Patrobas, Hermas, and the brothers and sisters who are with them. 15 Greet Philologus and Julia, Nereus and his sister, and Olympas, and all the saints who are with them. 16 Greet one another with a holy kiss. All the churches of Christ send you greetings.

WARNING AGAINST DIVISIVE PEOPLE

17 Now I urge you, brothers and sisters, to watch out for those who create divisions and obstacles contrary to the teaching that you learned. Avoid them, 18 because such people do not serve our Lord Christ but their own appetites.[O] They deceive the hearts of the unsuspecting with smooth talk and flattering words.

[A] **15:24** Other mss add *I will come to you.* [B] **15:28** Lit *delivered this fruit* [C] **15:28** Or *and placed my seal of approval on this fruit for them* [D] **15:29** Other mss add *of the gospel* [E] **15:31** Lit *that my service for* [F] **16:1** Others interpret this term in a technical sense: *deacon*, or *deaconess*, or *minister*, or *courier* [G] **16:3** Traditionally, *Priscilla*, as in Ac 18:2,18,26 [H] **16:5** Lit *the firstfruits* [I] **16:5** Other mss read *Achaia* [J] **16:6** Or *Maria* [K] **16:6** Other mss read *us* [L] **16:7** Or *family members* [M] **16:7** Or *They are noteworthy among the apostles* [N] **16:11** Or *family member* [O] **16:18** Lit *belly*

PAUL'S GRACIOUS CONCLUSION

[19] The report of your obedience has reached everyone.
Therefore I rejoice over you, but I want you to be wise
about what is good, and yet innocent about what is
evil. [20] The God of peace will soon crush Satan under
your feet. The grace of our Lord Jesus be with you.

[21] Timothy, my coworker, and Lucius, Jason, and
Sosipater, my fellow countrymen, greet you.

[22] I, Tertius, who wrote this letter, greet you in the
Lord.[A]

[23] Gaius, who is host to me and to the whole church,
greets you. Erastus, the city treasurer, and our brother Quartus greet you.[B]

GLORY TO GOD

[25] Now to him who is able to strengthen you according to my gospel and the proclamation about Jesus
Christ, according to the revelation of the mystery
kept silent for long ages [26] but now revealed and
made known through the prophetic Scriptures, according to the command of the eternal God to advance the obedience of faith among all the Gentiles
— [27] to the only wise God, through Jesus Christ — to
him be the glory forever![C] Amen.

[A] **16:22** Or *letter in the Lord, greet you* [B] **16:23** Some mss include v. 24: *The grace of our Lord Jesus Christ be with you all.* [C] **16:25–27** Other mss have these vv. at the end of chap. 14 or 15.

1 CORINTHIANS

Ruins of the temple of Apollo at Corinth in the agora.

INTRODUCTION TO

1 CORINTHIANS

Circumstances of Writing

First Corinthians ascribes Paul as its author (1Co 1:1; 16:21). Biblical scholars are almost unanimous that Paul wrote the letter. He wrote it during the last year of his three-year ministry at Ephesus, probably a few weeks before Pentecost in the spring of AD 56 (15:32; 16:8; Ac 20:31).

During Paul's second missionary journey, he had a vision at Troas; he heard a man call to him, "Cross over to Macedonia and help us!" (Ac 16:9). That change in plans led Paul to Philippi, Thessalonica, Athens, and ultimately to Corinth (18:5). Paul ministered in Corinth for at least eighteen months (18:1–18). He left Corinth accompanied by Aquila and Priscilla (18:18), leaving them at Ephesus where they met and instructed "an eloquent man" named Apollos (18:24–26). Apollos then went to Corinth and had a powerful ministry there (18:27–19:1).

First Corinthians is the second letter that Paul wrote to the Corinthian church. He had written them an earlier letter that included an admonition not to mix with the sexually immoral (1Co 5:9). The writing of this second letter (1 Corinthians) was prompted by oral reports from Chloe's household about factional strife within the church (1:11). Paul had also received reports about an incestuous relationship among the membership (5:1), factions that arose during observance of the Lord's Supper (11:18), and confusion over the resurrection of the dead (15:12). As a result, Paul addressed these issues in 1 Corinthians. Apparently, as he was writing the letter, he received a letter from the Corinthians asking his opinion on various issues (7:1,25; 8:1; 12:1; 16:1). Therefore, he included his replies within this letter to the Corinthian believers.

Contribution to the Bible

First Corinthians contributes greatly to our understanding of the Christian life, ministry, and relationships by showing us how the members of the church—Christ's body—are to function together. Problems can arise in any church because the church is composed of sinful people (redeemed certainly, but still prone to follow the tug of sin). Paul gave specific solutions to specific problems, but the underlying answer to all these problems is for the church and its members to live Christ-centered lives. It all comes down to living under the lordship and authority of Christ, the head of his body (the church).

Structure

Paul's writing is in the form of a letter, using the standard four parts of a first-century letter: salutation (1:1–3), thanksgiving (1:4–9), the main body (1:10–16:18), and a farewell (16:19–21). It is a pastoral letter, driven by the occasion and the present needs of the recipients.

Perhaps the most noteworthy feature of the way Paul structured his letter was his use of the word *about* to introduce a subject. It is apparent that "about" signals that Paul was responding to items on a list of questions that he had received—perhaps by way of a committee of men (16:17). These questions dealt with males and females in marriage (7:1); virgins (7:25); food offered to idols (8:1); spiritual gifts (12:1); the collection for the saints in Jerusalem (16:1); and Apollos (16:12).

GREETING

1 Paul, called as an apostle of Christ Jesus by God's will, and Sosthenes our brother:

2 To the church of God at Corinth, to those sanctified in Christ Jesus, called as saints, with all those in every place who call on the name of Jesus Christ our Lord — both their Lord and ours.

3 Grace to you and peace from God our Father and the Lord Jesus Christ.

THANKSGIVING

4 I always thank my God for you because of the grace of God given to you in Christ Jesus, 5 that you were enriched in him in every way, in all speech and all knowledge. 6 In this way, the testimony about Christ was confirmed among you, 7 so that you do not lack any spiritual gift as you eagerly wait for the revelation of our Lord Jesus Christ. 8 He will also strengthen you to the end, so that you will be blameless in the day of our Lord Jesus Christ. 9 God is faithful; you were called by him into fellowship with his Son, Jesus Christ our Lord.

DIVISIONS AT CORINTH

10 Now I urge you, brothers and sisters, in the name of our Lord Jesus Christ, that all of you agree in what you say, that there be no divisions among you, and that you be united with the same understanding and the same conviction. 11 For it has been reported to me about you, my brothers and sisters, by members of Chloe's people, that there is rivalry among you. 12 What I am saying is this: One of you says, "I belong to Paul," or "I belong to Apollos," or "I belong to Cephas," or "I belong to Christ." 13 Is Christ divided? Was Paul crucified for you? Or were you baptized in Paul's name? 14 I thank God[A,B] that I baptized none of you except Crispus and Gaius, 15 so that no one can say you were baptized in my name. 16 I did, in fact, baptize the household of Stephanas; beyond that, I don't recall if I baptized anyone else. 17 For Christ did not send me to baptize, but to preach the gospel — not with eloquent wisdom, so that the cross of Christ will not be emptied of its effect.

CHRIST THE POWER AND WISDOM OF GOD

18 For the word of the cross is foolishness to those who are perishing, but it is the power of God to us who are being saved. 19 For it is written,

> **I will destroy the wisdom of the wise,**
> **and I will set aside the intelligence**
> **of the intelligent.**[C]

[A] **1:14** Other mss omit *God* [B] **1:14** Or *I am thankful* [C] **1:19** Is 29:14

The ruins of ancient Hippo, in modern Algeria, North Africa, include the ruins of a church. This is a view of a cross-shaped baptistery, which came to be housed in a building separate from the place of corporate worship.

Corinth: A Roman Greek City

by Bob Simmons

GEOGRAPHY AND HISTORY

Corinth was located on the Peloponnesus, that southern part of Greece connected to the mainland by an isthmus. The Isthmus of Corinth was ten miles long and four miles wide. It was so prominent that the famed Isthmian games were named after it. Its name came to describe every such piece of land—a narrow stretch connecting two larger land areas. In Paul's day, a strong wall six miles in circumference surrounded Corinth. Each end stopped at the base of the rock-mountain called the Acrocorinth, which was 1,886 feet high. This long wall and this high rocklike mountain together surrounded the city and provided it with needed protection.[1]

Corinth had both enjoyed and endured a surprising past. For centuries, it was one of the richest and most important Grecian cities. But in 146 BC, the Roman leader Mummius invaded and decimated Corinth, killed its men, and enslaved its women and children.[2] The city remained devastated until 44 BC when Julius Caesar led Rome to rebuild it. Its new population consisted mostly of freedmen.[3]

Once rebuilt, Corinth used its advantageous geographical position to achieve a strong financial status. Workers dragged small ships both ways across its narrow isthmus on a cleverly constructed road to opposite harbors four miles away. The eastern harbor was Cenchreae; Schoenus and Lechaeum (or Lechaion) were on the west.[4] Larger ships had to have their cargos carried across the isthmus to other large ships waiting on the opposite side. This process allowed ships going to or from the Aegean Sea to avoid the two-hundred-mile, dangerous fourteen-day journey around the stormy southern tip of the Peloponnesus. Spending money in Corinth's shops and then taking the city's produce aboard, these sailors made the city famous again—and wealthy. Corinth had quite a reputation for its ceramics and its works in bronze.[5] It was never an agricultural power and never needed to be. Corinth eventually became the leading city of the new senatorial province created there.[6]

POPULATION

Population changes took place during the time of Roman control. Rome sent people from numerous countries into the Corinthian area. Many new settlers were former slaves or discharged Roman soldiers, some indeed from Greece. Rome had brought still others to Corinth from Asia, Syria, Judea, Egypt, and other regions.[7] These strangers came to Corinth bringing

Facing south, the Lechaion Road in Corinth was lined with shops on the right, temples, baths, and fountains on the left. The Acrocorinth (or "upper Corinth") rises almost 1,900 feet in the background.

their own customs, languages, and religious superstitions. Longtime residents of the Achaian region, many Jews probably had chosen to remain in Corinth when possible or to return there when they could.

This "invasion" of foreigners eventually changed or diluted some of Corinth's Greek religious ways and views. Newcomers gave some of the deities their own temples. They even worshiped the Egyptian Isis and Serapis there. Gradually, gods and goddesses new to the Corinthians became prominent. By Paul's day, the formerly strong Greek city gradually had become far less decidedly Greek. Likewise, Corinth's Roman population had lost many of its distinctive Roman ways. The Rome-owned Greek city had changed drastically over the years.[8] ✣

---

[1] R. E. Glaze, "Corinth" in *HolBD*, 299. [2] Glaze, "Corinth," 299. [3] W. J. Woodhouse, "Corinth" in *Encyclopedia Biblia* (London: Adam & Charles Black, 1899), 898. [4] J. E. Harvey, "Corinth" in *International Bible Encyclopedia* (Chicago: Howard Severance, n.d.), 710. [5] J. Murphy-O'Conner, "Corinth" in *ABD*, 1:1136. [6] Murphy-O'Conner, "Corinth," 1138. [7] J. H. Harrop, "Corinth" in *New Bible Dictionary* (London: Inter-Varsity, 1982), 1136. [8] Murphy-O'Conner, "Corinth," 1138.

Canal across the isthmus from Corinth to Cenchreae. The canal was first attempted by Nero but was not completed until 1893. The canal is 3½ miles long, seventy-five feet wide at the top, and sixty-five feet at the bottom.

20 Where is the one who is wise? Where is the teacher of the law?[A] Where is the debater of this age? Hasn't God made the world's wisdom foolish? 21 For since, in God's wisdom, the world did not know God through wisdom, God was pleased to save those who believe through the foolishness of what is preached. 22 For the Jews ask for signs and the Greeks seek wisdom, 23 but we preach Christ crucified, a stumbling block to the Jews and foolishness to the Gentiles.[B] 24 Yet to those who are called, both Jews and Greeks, Christ is the power of God and the wisdom of God, 25 because God's foolishness is wiser than human wisdom, and God's weakness is stronger than human strength.

BOASTING ONLY IN THE LORD

26 Brothers and sisters, consider your calling: Not many were wise from a human perspective,[C] not many powerful, not many of noble birth. 27 Instead, God has chosen what is foolish in the world to shame the wise, and God has chosen what is weak in the world to shame the strong. 28 God has chosen what is insignificant and despised in the world — what is viewed as nothing — to bring to nothing what is viewed as something, 29 so that no one[D] may boast in his presence. 30 It is from him that you are in Christ Jesus, who became wisdom from God for us — our righteousness, sanctification, and redemption — 31 in order that, as it is written: **Let the one who boasts, boast in the Lord.**[E]

PAUL'S PROCLAMATION

2 When I came to you, brothers and sisters, announcing the mystery[F] of God to you, I did not come with brilliance of speech or wisdom. 2 I decided to know nothing among you except Jesus Christ and him crucified. 3 I came to you in weakness, in fear, and in much trembling. 4 My speech and my preaching were not with persuasive words of wisdom[G] but with a demonstration of the Spirit's power, 5 so that your faith might not be based on human wisdom but on God's power.

SPIRITUAL WISDOM

6 We do, however, speak a wisdom among the mature, but not a wisdom of this age, or of the rulers of this age, who are coming to nothing. 7 On the contrary, we speak God's hidden wisdom in a mystery, a wisdom God predestined before the ages for our glory. 8 None of the rulers of this age knew this wisdom, because if they had known it, they would not have crucified the Lord of glory. 9 But as it is written,

> **What no eye has seen, no ear has heard,**
> **and no human heart has conceived —**
> **God has prepared these things for those**
> **who love him.**[H]

10 Now God has revealed these things to us by the Spirit, since the Spirit searches everything, even the depths of God. 11 For who knows a person's thoughts[I] except his spirit within him? In the same way, no one knows the thoughts of God except the Spirit of God. 12 Now we have not received the spirit of the world, but the Spirit who comes from God, so that we may understand what has been freely given to us by God. 13 We also speak these things, not in words taught by human wisdom, but in those taught by the Spirit, explaining spiritual things to spiritual people.[J] 14 But the person without the Spirit[K] does not receive what comes from God's Spirit, because it is foolishness to him; he is not able to understand it since it is evaluated[L] spiritually. 15 The spiritual person, however, can evaluate[M] everything, and yet he himself cannot be evaluated by anyone. 16 For

> **who has known the Lord's mind,**
> **that he may instruct him?**[N]

But we have the mind of Christ.

THE PROBLEM OF IMMATURITY

3 For my part, brothers and sisters, I was not able to speak to you as spiritual people but as people of the flesh, as babies in Christ. 2 I gave you milk to drink, not solid food, since you were not yet ready for it. In fact, you are still not ready, 3 because you are still worldly. For since there is envy and strife[O] among you, are you not worldly and behaving like mere humans? 4 For whenever someone says, "I belong to Paul," and another, "I belong to Apollos," are you not acting like mere humans?

THE ROLE OF GOD'S SERVANTS

5 What then is Apollos? What is Paul? They are servants through whom you believed, and each has the role the Lord has given. 6 I planted, Apollos watered, but God gave the growth. 7 So, then, neither the one who plants nor the one who waters is anything, but only God who gives the growth. 8 Now he who plants and he who waters are one,[P] and each will receive his own reward according to his own labor. 9 For we are God's coworkers.[Q] You are God's field, God's building.

10 According to God's grace that was given to me, I have laid a foundation as a skilled master builder,[R] and another builds on it. But each one is to be careful how he builds on it. 11 For no one can lay any foundation other than what has been laid down.

[A] **1:20** Or *scholar* [B] **1:23** Other mss read *Greeks* [C] **1:26** Lit *wise according to the flesh* [D] **1:29** Lit *that not all flesh* [E] **1:31** Jr 9:24 [F] **2:1** Other mss read *testimony* [G] **2:4** Other mss read *human wisdom* [H] **2:9** Is 52:15; 64:4 [I] **2:11** Or *things* [J] **2:13** Or *things with spiritual words* [K] **2:14** Lit *natural person* [L] **2:14** Or *judged*, or *discerned*, also in v. 15 [M] **2:15** Or *judge*, or *discern* [N] **2:16** Is 40:13 [O] **3:3** Other mss add *and divisions* [P] **3:8** Or *of equal status*, or *united in purpose* [Q] **3:9** Or *are coworkers belonging to God* [R] **3:10** Or *wise master builder*

That foundation is Jesus Christ. 12 If anyone builds on
the foundation with gold, silver, costly stones, wood,
hay, or straw, 13 each one's work will become obvious.
For the day will disclose it, because it will be revealed
by fire; the fire will test the quality of each one's work.
14 If anyone's work that he has built survives, he will
receive a reward. 15 If anyone's work is burned up,
he will experience[A] loss, but he himself will be saved
— but only as through fire.

16 Don't you yourselves know that you are God's
temple and that the Spirit of God lives in you? 17 If
anyone destroys God's temple, God will destroy him;
for God's temple is holy, and that is what you are.

THE FOLLY OF HUMAN WISDOM

18 Let no one deceive himself. If anyone among you
thinks he is wise in this age, let him become a fool
so that he can become wise. 19 For the wisdom of this
world is foolishness with God, since it is written, **He
catches the wise in their craftiness**;[B] 20 and again,
**The Lord knows that the reasonings of the wise
are futile.**[C] 21 So let no one boast in human leaders, for
everything is yours — 22 whether Paul or Apollos or
Cephas or the world or life or death or things present
or things to come — everything is yours, 23 and you
belong to Christ, and Christ belongs to God.

THE FAITHFUL MANAGER

4 A person should think of us in this way: as servants of Christ and managers of the mysteries of
God. 2 In this regard, it is required that managers be
found faithful. 3 It is of little importance to me that I
should be judged by you or by any human court.[D] In
fact, I don't even judge myself. 4 For I am not conscious
of anything against myself, but I am not justified by
this. It is the Lord who judges me. 5 So don't judge
anything prematurely, before the Lord comes, who
will both bring to light what is hidden in darkness
and reveal the intentions of the hearts. And then
praise will come to each one from God.

THE APOSTLES' EXAMPLE OF HUMILITY

6 Now, brothers and sisters, I have applied these things
to myself and Apollos for your benefit, so that you
may learn from us the meaning of the saying: "Nothing beyond what is written." The purpose is that none
of you will be arrogant, favoring one person over
another. 7 For who makes you so superior? What do
you have that you didn't receive? If, in fact, you did receive it, why do you boast as if you hadn't received it?
8 You are already full! You are already rich! You have

[A] **3:15** Or *suffer* [B] **3:19** Jb 5:13 [C] **3:20** Ps 94:11 [D] **4:3** Lit *a human day*

Interior of the Roman theater at Alexandria, Egypt.

Julius Caesar, who restored ancient Corinth; marble portrait
dates to the first quarter of the first century AD.

begun to reign as kings without us — and I wish you
did reign, so that we could also reign with you! 9 For I
think God has displayed us, the apostles, in last place,
like men condemned to die: We have become a spectacle to the world, both to angels and to people. 10 We
are fools for Christ, but you are wise in Christ! We
are weak, but you are strong! You are distinguished,
but we are dishonored! 11 Up to the present hour we
are both hungry and thirsty; we are poorly clothed,
roughly treated, homeless; 12 we labor, working with
our own hands. When we are reviled, we bless; when
we are persecuted, we endure it; 13 when we are slandered, we respond graciously. Even now, we are like
the scum of the earth, like everyone's garbage.

PAUL'S FATHERLY CARE

14 I'm not writing this to shame you, but to warn you
as my dear children. 15 For you may have countless
instructors in Christ, but you don't have many fathers.
For I became your father in Christ Jesus through the
gospel. 16 Therefore I urge you to imitate me. 17 This
is why I have sent Timothy to you. He is my dearly
loved and faithful child in the Lord. He will remind
you about my ways in Christ Jesus, just as I teach
everywhere in every church.

18 Now some are arrogant, as though I were not
coming to you. 19 But I will come to you soon, if the
Lord wills, and I will find out not the talk, but the
power of those who are arrogant. 20 For the kingdom
of God is not a matter of talk but of power. 21 What do
you want? Should I come to you with a rod, or in love
and a spirit of gentleness?

IMMORAL CHURCH MEMBERS

5 It is actually reported that there is sexual immorality among you, and the kind of sexual immorality that is not even tolerated[A] among the Gentiles
— a man is sleeping with his father's wife. 2 And you
are arrogant! Shouldn't you be filled with grief and
remove from your congregation the one who did this?
3 Even though I am absent in the body, I am present in
spirit. As one who is present with you in this way, I
have already pronounced judgment on the one who
has been doing such a thing. 4 When you are assembled in the name of our Lord Jesus, and I am with you
in spirit, with the power of our Lord Jesus, 5 hand that
one over to Satan for the destruction of the flesh, so
that his spirit may be saved in the day of the Lord.
6 Your boasting is not good. Don't you know that
a little leaven[B] leavens the whole batch of dough?
7 Clean out the old leaven so that you may be a new
unleavened batch, as indeed you are. For Christ our
Passover lamb has been sacrificed.[C] 8 Therefore, let
us observe the feast, not with old leaven or with the
leaven of malice and evil, but with the unleavened
bread of sincerity and truth.

CHURCH DISCIPLINE

9 I wrote to you in a letter not to associate with sexually immoral people. 10 I did not mean the immoral
people of this world or the greedy and swindlers
or idolaters; otherwise you would have to leave the
world. 11 But actually, I wrote[D] you not to associate
with anyone who claims to be a brother or sister
and is sexually immoral or greedy, an idolater or verbally abusive, a drunkard or a swindler. Do not even
eat with such a person. 12 For what business is it of
mine to judge outsiders? Don't you judge those who
are inside? 13 God judges outsiders. **Remove the evil
person from among you.**[E]

LAWSUITS AMONG BELIEVERS

6 If any of you has a dispute against another, how
dare you take it to court before the unrighteous,[F]
and not before the saints? 2 Or don't you know that the
saints will judge the world? And if the world is judged
by you, are you unworthy to judge the trivial cases?

[A] **5:1** Other mss read *named* [B] **5:6** Or *yeast*, also in vv. 7,8
[C] **5:7** Other mss add *for us* [D] **5:11** Or *But now I am writing*
[E] **5:13** Dt 17:7 [F] **6:1** Unbelievers; v. 6

3 Don't you know that we will judge angels — how
much more matters of this life? 4 So if you have such
matters, do you appoint as your judges those who
have no standing in the church? 5 I say this to your
shame! Can it be that there is not one wise person
among you who is able to arbitrate between fellow
believers? 6 Instead, brother goes to court against
brother, and that before unbelievers!

7 As it is, to have legal disputes against one another is already a defeat for you. Why not rather be
wronged? Why not rather be cheated? 8 Instead, you
yourselves do wrong and cheat — and you do this
to brothers and sisters! 9 Don't you know that the
unrighteous will not inherit God's kingdom? Do not
be deceived: No sexually immoral people, idolaters,
adulterers, or males who have sex with males,[A] 10 no
thieves, greedy people, drunkards, verbally abusive
people, or swindlers will inherit God's kingdom.
11 And some of you used to be like this. But you were
washed, you were sanctified, you were justified in
the name of the Lord Jesus Christ and by the Spirit
of our God.

GLORIFYING GOD IN BODY AND SPIRIT

12 "Everything is permissible for me," but not everything is beneficial. "Everything is permissible for me,"
but I will not be mastered by anything. 13 "Food is for
the stomach and the stomach for food," and God will
do away with both of them. However, the body is not
for sexual immorality but for the Lord, and the Lord
for the body. 14 God raised up the Lord and will also
raise us up by his power. 15 Don't you know that your
bodies are a part of Christ's body? So should I take a
part of Christ's body and make it part of a prostitute?
Absolutely not! 16 Don't you know that anyone joined
to a prostitute is one body with her? For Scripture
says, **The two will become one flesh.**[B] 17 But anyone
joined to the Lord is one spirit with him.

18 Flee sexual immorality! Every other sin[C] a person
commits is outside the body, but the person who is
sexually immoral sins against his own body. 19 Don't
you know that your body is a temple of the Holy Spirit
who is in you, whom you have from God? You are not
your own, 20 for you were bought at a price. So glorify
God with your body.[D]

PRINCIPLES OF MARRIAGE

7 Now in response to the matters you wrote[E] about:
"It is good for a man not to have sexual relations
with a woman."[F] 2 But because sexual immorality is
so common,[G] each man should have sexual relations
with his own wife, and each woman should have
sexual relations with her own husband. 3 A husband
should fulfill his marital duty to his wife, and likewise a wife to her husband. 4 A wife does not have
the right over her own body, but her husband does.
In the same way, a husband does not have the right
over his own body, but his wife does. 5 Do not deprive
one another — except when you agree for a time, to
devote yourselves to[H] prayer. Then come together
again; otherwise, Satan may tempt you because of
your lack of self-control. 6 I say this as a concession,
not as a command. 7 I wish that all people were as I
am. But each has his own gift from God, one person
has this gift, another has that.

A WORD TO THE UNMARRIED

8 I say to the unmarried[I] and to widows: It is good for
them if they remain as I am. 9 But if they do not have
self-control, they should marry, since it is better to
marry than to burn with desire.

ABOUT MARRIED PEOPLE

10 To the married I give this command — not I, but
the Lord — a wife is not to leave[J] her husband. 11 But
if she does leave, she must remain unmarried or be

[A] **6:9** Both passive and active participants in homosexual acts
[B] **6:16** Gn 2:24 [C] **6:18** Lit *Every sin* [D] **6:20** Other mss add *and in your spirit, which belong to God.* [E] **7:1** Other mss add *to me* [F] **7:1** Or *"It is good for a man not to use a woman for sex"*; lit *"It is good for a man not to touch a woman."* [G] **7:2** Lit *because of immoralities* [H] **7:5** Other mss add *fasting and to* [I] **7:8** Or *widowers* [J] **7:10** Or *separate from, or divorce*

Greek inscription on a lintel stone from the synagogue at Corinth. The synagogue dates from the first century AD. Jews were known to be in Corinth as early as the reign of Caligula (AD 37–41).

Greek and Roman Temples of the First Century

by Don H. Stewart

When Hellenism was at its height, the concept of interaction between people and the gods was prevalent among the intellectuals. Greeks thought of the gods as superhuman, and temple architecture reflected religious systems that encouraged people to negotiate directly with the gods in an effort to buy divine favor. Convenient access to the idols of the gods was important. This was accomplished by providing open architectural designs for the temples and by erecting multiple temples to the same gods and goddesses. These temples were located in population centers stretched across the empire to provide maximum accessibility.

At times, a single temple would house multiple gods or goddesses. For instance, the Parthenon in Athens housed the idol of Athena and a number of other idols. In Rome, the Pantheon was the temple honoring all gods, although it actually housed statues of the seven "deities the Romans associated with the heavens—including Mars, Mercury, Venus, and Jupiter."[1] A statue of each deity was located in its own large niche along the interior wall of the circular Pantheon.

In the environment of the Greco-Roman world, a burgeoning number of beautifully appointed temples served as houses of worship for an almost innumerable number of gods and goddesses. At least one such temple was built on the acropolis (the high place) of nearly every major city, as well as many smaller ones. Most communities had a patron god or goddess. The Romans followed the Greeks' lead, extending the Greek passion for building religious temples, and they did so wherever the gods or goddesses had not been honored before. ✣

[1] Jason McManus, ed., *Empires Ascendant: Time Frame 400 BC–AD 200* (Alexandria, VA: Time-Life Books, 1987), 93.

The Parthenon rises in the distance, atop the Acropolis in Athens, which was a prominent city in the Roman province of Achaia.

Interior of the Pantheon in Rome. The structure was originally constructed to honor the seven gods of the seven planets recognized by the state religion of Rome. Although the building has been revised several times through the centuries, it has been in continual use since its construction was completed in AD 125.

From Corinth, bust of Zeus, dating from the first century AD.

reconciled to her husband — and a husband is not to divorce his wife. 12 But I (not the Lord) say to the rest: If any brother has an unbelieving wife and she is willing to live with him, he must not divorce her. 13 Also, if any woman has an unbelieving husband and he is willing to live with her, she must not divorce her husband. 14 For the unbelieving husband is made holy by the wife, and the unbelieving wife is made holy by the husband.[A] Otherwise your children would be unclean, but as it is they are holy. 15 But if the unbeliever leaves, let him leave. A brother or a sister is not bound in such cases. God has called you[B] to live in peace. 16 Wife, for all you know, you might save your husband. Husband, for all you know, you might save your wife.[C]

VARIOUS SITUATIONS OF LIFE

17 Let each one live his life in the situation the Lord assigned when God called him.[D] This is what I command in all the churches. 18 Was anyone already circumcised when he was called? He should not undo his circumcision. Was anyone called while uncircumcised? He should not get circumcised. 19 Circumcision does not matter and uncircumcision does not matter. Keeping God's commands is what matters. 20 Let each of you remain in the situation[E] in which he was called. 21 Were you called while a slave? Don't let it concern you. But if you can become free, by all means take the opportunity.[F] 22 For he who is called by the Lord as a slave is the Lord's freedman. Likewise he who is called as a free man is Christ's slave. 23 You were bought at a price; do not become slaves of people. 24 Brothers and sisters, each person is to remain with God in the situation in which he was called.

ABOUT THE UNMARRIED AND WIDOWS

25 Now about virgins:[G] I have no command from the Lord, but I do give an opinion as one who by the Lord's mercy is faithful. 26 Because of the present distress, I think that it is good for a man to remain as he is. 27 Are you bound to a wife? Do not seek to be released. Are you released from a wife? Do not seek a wife. 28 However, if you do get married, you have not sinned, and if a virgin[H] marries, she has not sinned. But such people will have trouble in this life,[I] and I am trying to spare you.

29 This is what I mean, brothers and sisters: The time is limited, so from now on those who have wives should be as though they had none, 30 those who weep as though they did not weep, those who rejoice as though they did not rejoice, those who buy as though they didn't own anything, 31 and those who use the world as though they did not make full use of it. For this world in its current form is passing away.

32 I want you to be without concerns. The unmarried man is concerned about the things of the Lord — how he may please the Lord. 33 But the married man is concerned about the things of the world — how he may please his wife — 34 and his interests are divided. The unmarried woman or virgin is concerned about the things of the Lord, so that she may be holy both in body and in spirit. But the married woman is concerned about the things of the world — how she may please her husband. 35 I am saying this for your own benefit, not to put a restraint on you, but to promote what is proper and so that you may be devoted to the Lord without distraction.

36 If any man thinks he is acting improperly toward the virgin he is engaged to, if she is getting beyond the usual age for marriage, and he feels he should marry — he can do what he wants. He is not sinning; they can get married. 37 But he who stands firm in his heart (who is under no compulsion, but has control over his own will) and has decided in his heart to keep her as his fiancée, will do well. 38 So, then, he who marries his fiancée does well, but he who does not marry will do better.[J]

39 A wife is bound[K] as long as her husband is living. But if her husband dies, she is free to be married to anyone she wants — only in the Lord. 40 But she is happier if she remains as she is, in my opinion. And I think that I also have the Spirit of God.

FOOD OFFERED TO IDOLS

8 Now about food sacrificed to idols: We know that "we all have knowledge." Knowledge puffs up, but love builds up. 2 If anyone thinks he knows anything, he does not yet know it as he ought to know it. 3 But if anyone loves God, he is known by him.

4 About eating food sacrificed to idols, then, we know that "an idol is nothing in the world,"[L] and that "there is no God but one." 5 For even if there are so-called gods, whether in heaven or on earth — as there are many "gods" and many "lords" — 6 yet for us there is one God, the Father. All things are from him, and we exist for him. And there is one Lord, Jesus Christ. All things are through him, and we exist through him.

[A] **7:14** Lit *the brother* [B] **7:15** Other mss read *us* [C] **7:16** Or *Wife, how do you know that you will save your husband? Husband, how do you know that you will save your wife?* [D] **7:17** Lit *called each* [E] **7:20** Lit *in the calling* [F] **7:21** Or *But even though you can become free, make the most of your position as a slave* [G] **7:25** Or *betrothed*, or *those not yet married* [H] **7:28** Or *betrothed woman* [I] **7:28** Lit *in the flesh* [J] **7:36–38** Or *36If any man thinks he is acting improperly toward his virgin daughter, if she is getting beyond the usual age for marriage, and he feels she should marry — he can do what he wants. He is not sinning; she can get married. 37But he who stands firm in his heart (who is under no compulsion, but has control over his own will) and has decided in his heart to keep his own virgin daughter will do well. 38So then he who gives his own virgin daughter in marriage does well, but he who does not give his own virgin daughter in marriage will do better.* [K] **7:39** Other mss add *by law* [L] **8:4** Or *an idol has no real existence*

7 However, not everyone has this knowledge. Some have been so used to idolatry up until now that when they eat food sacrificed to an idol, their conscience, being weak, is defiled. 8 Food will not bring us close to God.[A] We are not worse off if we don't eat, and we are not better if we do eat. 9 But be careful that this right of yours in no way becomes a stumbling block to the weak. 10 For if someone sees you, the one who has knowledge, dining in an idol's temple, won't his weak conscience be encouraged[B] to eat food offered to idols? 11 So the weak person, the brother or sister for whom Christ died, is ruined[C] by your knowledge. 12 Now when you sin like this against brothers and sisters and wound their weak conscience, you are sinning against Christ. 13 Therefore, if food causes my brother or sister to fall, I will never again eat meat, so that I won't cause my brother or sister to fall.

PAUL'S EXAMPLE AS AN APOSTLE

9 Am I not free? Am I not an apostle? Have I not seen Jesus our Lord? Are you not my work in the Lord? 2 If I am not an apostle to others, at least I am to you, because you are the seal of my apostleship in the Lord.

3 My defense to those who examine me is this: 4 Don't we have the right to eat and drink? 5 Don't we have the right to be accompanied by a believing wife[D] like the other apostles, the Lord's brothers, and Cephas? 6 Or do only Barnabas and I have no right to refrain from working? 7 Who serves as a soldier at his own expense? Who plants a vineyard and does not eat its fruit? Or who shepherds a flock and does not drink the milk from the flock?

8 Am I saying this from a human perspective? Doesn't the law also say the same thing? 9 For it is written in the law of Moses, **Do not muzzle an ox while it treads out grain.**[E] Is God really concerned about oxen? 10 Isn't he really saying it for our sake? Yes, this is written for our sake, because he who plows ought to plow in hope, and he who threshes should thresh in hope of sharing the crop. 11 If we have sown spiritual things for you, is it too much if we reap material benefits from you? 12 If others have this right to receive benefits from you, don't we even more? Nevertheless, we have not made use of this right; instead, we endure everything so that we will not hinder the gospel of Christ.

13 Don't you know that those who perform the temple services eat the food from the temple, and those who serve at the altar share in the offerings of the altar? 14 In the same way, the Lord has commanded that those who preach the gospel should earn their living by the gospel.

15 For my part I have used none of these rights, nor have I written these things that they may be applied in my case. For it would be better for me to die than for anyone to deprive me of my boast! 16 For if I preach the gospel, I have no reason to boast, because I am compelled to preach[F] — and woe to me if I do not preach the gospel! 17 For if I do this willingly, I have a reward, but if unwillingly, I am entrusted with a commission. 18 What then is my reward? To preach the gospel and offer it free of charge and not make full use of my rights in the gospel.

19 Although I am free from all and not anyone's slave, I have made myself a slave to everyone, in order to win more people. 20 To the Jews I became like a Jew, to win Jews; to those under the law, like one under the law — though I myself am not under the law[G] — to win those under the law. 21 To those who are without the law, like one without the law — though I am not without God's law but under the law of Christ — to win those without the law. 22 To the weak I became weak, in order to win the weak. I have become all things to all people, so that I may by every possible means save some. 23 Now I do all this because of the gospel, so that I may share in the blessings.

24 Don't you know that the runners in a stadium all race, but only one receives the prize? Run in such a way to win the prize. 25 Now everyone who competes exercises self-control in everything. They do it to receive a perishable crown, but we an imperishable crown. 26 So I do not run like one who runs aimlessly or box like one beating the air. 27 Instead, I discipline my body and bring it under strict control, so that after preaching to others, I myself will not be disqualified.

WARNINGS FROM ISRAEL'S PAST

10 Now I do not want you to be unaware, brothers and sisters, that our ancestors were all under the cloud, all passed through the sea, 2 and all were baptized into Moses in the cloud and in the sea. 3 They all ate the same spiritual food, 4 and all drank the same spiritual drink. For they drank from the spiritual rock that followed them, and that rock was Christ. 5 Nevertheless God was not pleased with most of them, since they were struck down in the wilderness.

6 Now these things took place as examples for us, so that we will not desire evil things as they did.[H] 7 Don't become idolaters as some of them were; as it is written, **The people sat down to eat and drink, and got up to party.**[I,J] 8 Let us not commit sexual immorality as some of them did,[K] and in a single day twenty-three thousand people died. 9 Let us not test Christ as some

[A] **8:8** Or *bring us before* (the judgment seat of) *God* [B] **8:10** Or *built up* [C] **8:11** Or *destroyed* [D] **9:5** Lit *a sister as a wife* [E] **9:9** Dt 25:4 [F] **9:16** Lit *because necessity is laid upon me* [G] **9:20** Other mss omit *though I myself am not under the law* [H] **10:6** Lit *they desired* [I] **10:7** Or *to dance* [J] **10:7** Ex 32:6 [K] **10:8** Lit *them committed sexual immorality*

Meat Sacrificed to Idols

by Alan Branch

Corinth in Paul's day was a religiously diverse Roman colony that embraced pluralism. Sacrificing to the gods was central to Greco-Roman religion. Although some sacrifices involved the consumption of the entire animal by fire, a standard sacrifice was one in which a worshiper dedicated a portion of the animal to the god or goddess. The rest of the animal was food for the priests, the temple personnel, and/or the worshiper and his family.[1] If the worshiper received part of the meat, he may have taken it home for a private feast. Some of the meat also may have been sold in the marketplace.[2]

Lavish banquets were closely tied to these sacrifices. The portions of the animal not burned to the god or left in the temple were used at social gatherings central to the Corinthian culture. Dining rooms were a common part of ancient temples; people could rent these for social functions (much like today's community centers). For example, one of the most famous temples in Corinth was dedicated to Asclepios, the god of healing. Excavators have discovered three dining rooms at the ancient temple site. Of many religious sites on the Acrocorinth, the sanctuary of Demeter and Kore had been remodeled in Paul's day and ritual dining was observed outside.[3]

Dated AD 150–200, from Thessalonica; a statue head of Serapis (the Hellenized form of Egypt's god of the dead, Osiris). The head was probably from a statue that someone gave as a worship offering. Devotees worshiped Serapis, Isis, and other gods at Corinth.

Archaeologists have discovered ancient papyri that were invitations to meals dedicated to pagan gods. These meals were held at various temples or private houses. One example is an invitation to a dinner dedicated to the Greek-Egyptian god Serapis; it says, "Chaeremon invites you to dine at the banquet of the Lord Serapis in the Sarapeum tomorrow, the 15th, beginning at the 9th hour."[4] Such feasts in antiquity often included drunkenness and sexual carousing.[5]

People in the twenty-first century have difficulty appreciating the degree to which these "idol banquets" served as a social glue in the Greco-Roman culture. The sacrifices were not just the center of the religious life of a city, but they served as the heart of the social life as well. People associated sacrificial meals with a wedding, a birthday, a funeral, or other important occasions. ⁂

---

[1] Dennis E. Smith, "Greco-Roman Sacred Meals" in *ABD*, 4:653–55. [2] Colin Brown, "θύω" in *NIDNTT* (1986), 3:432. [3] John McRay, *Archaeology and the New Testament* (Grand Rapids: Baker, 1991), 323. [4] H. Lietzmann, *An die Korinther I–II*, 4th ed. (Tübingen: Mohr, 1949), 49, cited in Robert M. Grant, *Paul in the Roman World: The Conflict at Corinth* (Louisville: Westminster John Knox, 2001), 36, n. 51. [5] Gordon D. Fee, "εἰδωλόθυτα Once Again: An Interpretation of 1 Corinthians 8–10," *Biblica* (*Bib*) 61.1 (1980): 186.

Meat market or "Macellum" at Puteoli, which is on the western coast of Italy.

In Corinth, the western shops were adjacent to the temple of the imperial cult, which supplied meat for sale locally.

of them did[A] and were destroyed by snakes. 10 And
don't grumble as some of them did,[B] and were killed
by the destroyer.[C] 11 These things happened to them
as examples, and they were written for our instruction, on whom the ends of the ages[D] have come. 12 So,
whoever thinks he stands must be careful not to fall.
13 No temptation has come upon you except what is
common to humanity. But God is faithful; he will not
allow you to be tempted beyond what you are able,
but with the temptation he will also provide the way
out so that you may be able to bear it.

WARNING AGAINST IDOLATRY

14 So then, my dear friends, flee from idolatry. 15 I am
speaking as to sensible people. Judge for yourselves
what I am saying. 16 The cup of blessing that we bless,
is it not a sharing in the blood of Christ? The bread
that we break, is it not a sharing in the body of Christ?
17 Because there is one bread, we who are many are
one body, since all of us share the one bread. 18 Consider the people of Israel.[E] Do not those who eat the
sacrifices participate in the altar? 19 What am I saying
then? That food sacrificed to idols is anything, or that
an idol is anything? 20 No, but I do say that what they[F]
sacrifice, they sacrifice to demons and not to God.
I do not want you to be participants with demons!
21 You cannot drink the cup of the Lord and the cup
of demons. You cannot share in the Lord's table and
the table of demons. 22 Or are we provoking the Lord
to jealousy? Are we stronger than he?

CHRISTIAN LIBERTY

23 "Everything is permissible,"[G] but not everything is
beneficial. "Everything is permissible,"[G] but not everything builds up. 24 No one is to seek his own good,
but the good of the other person.

25 Eat everything that is sold in the meat market,
without raising questions for the sake of conscience,
26 since **the earth is the Lord's, and all that is in it.**[H]
27 If any of the unbelievers invites you over and you
want to go, eat everything that is set before you, without raising questions for the sake of conscience. 28 But
if someone says to you, "This is food from a sacrifice,"
do not eat it, out of consideration for the one who told
you, and for the sake of conscience.[I] 29 I do not mean
your own conscience, but the other person's. For why
is my freedom judged by another person's conscience?
30 If I partake with thanksgiving, why am I criticized
because of something for which I give thanks?

31 So, whether you eat or drink, or whatever you do,
do everything for the glory of God. 32 Give no offense
to Jews or Greeks or the church of God, 33 just as I
also try to please everyone in everything, not seeking my own benefit, but the benefit of many, so that
they may be saved.

11 1 Imitate me, as I also imitate
Christ.

[A] **10:9** Lit *them tested* [B] **10:10** Lit *them grumbled* [C] **10:10** Or *the destroying angel* [D] **10:11** Or *goals of the ages*, or *culmination of the ages* [E] **10:18** Lit *Look at Israel according to the flesh* [F] **10:20** Other mss read *Gentiles* [G] **10:23** Other mss add *for me* [H] **10:26** Ps 24:1 [I] **10:28** Other mss add *"For the earth is the Lord's and all that is in it."*

The Erastus inscription at Corinth indicates an official named Erastus laid a pavement at his own expense. He may be the man named by Paul (Ac 19:22; Rm 16:23; 2Tm 4:20), who probably held the same office.

INSTRUCTIONS ABOUT HEAD COVERINGS

[2] Now I praise you[A] because you remember me in
everything and hold fast to the traditions just as I
delivered them to you. [3] But I want you to know that
Christ is the head of every man, and the man is the
head of the woman,[B] and God is the head of Christ.
[4] Every man who prays or prophesies with something on his head dishonors his head. [5] Every woman
who prays or prophesies with her head uncovered
dishonors her head, since that is one and the same
as having her head shaved. [6] For if a woman doesn't
cover her head, she should have her hair cut off. But
if it is disgraceful for a woman to have her hair cut
off or her head shaved, let her head be covered.
[7] A man should not cover his head, because he is
the image and glory of God. So too, woman is the glory of man. [8] For man did not come from woman, but
woman came from man. [9] Neither was man created
for the sake of woman, but woman for the sake of
man. [10] This is why a woman should have a symbol
of authority on her head, because of the angels. [11] In
the Lord, however, woman is not independent of man,
and man is not independent of woman. [12] For just
as woman came from man, so man comes through
woman, and all things come from God.
[13] Judge for yourselves: Is it proper for a woman
to pray to God with her head uncovered? [14] Does not
even nature itself teach you that if a man has long hair
it is a disgrace to him, [15] but that if a woman has long
hair, it is her glory? For her hair is given to her[C] as a
covering. [16] If anyone wants to argue about this, we
have no other[D] custom, nor do the churches of God.

A Coptic bread stamp with a representation of a dove. This stamp, which dates from the seventh to ninth centuries AD, would have been used in a Coptic Lord's Supper service.

Wine press at Chorazin.

THE LORD'S SUPPER

[17] Now in giving this instruction I do not praise you,
since you come together not for the better but for the
worse. [18] For to begin with, I hear that when you come
together as a church there are divisions among you,
and in part I believe it. [19] Indeed, it is necessary that
there be factions among you, so that those who are
approved may be recognized among you. [20] When you
come together, then, it is not to eat the Lord's Supper. [21] For at the meal, each one eats his own supper.[E]
So one person is hungry while another gets drunk!
[22] Don't you have homes in which to eat and drink?
Or do you despise the church of God and humiliate
those who have nothing? What should I say to you?
Should I praise you? I do not praise you in this matter!
[23] For I received from the Lord what I also passed on
to you: On the night when he was betrayed, the Lord
Jesus took bread, [24] and when he had given thanks,
broke it, and said,[F] "This is my body, which is[G] for you.
Do this in remembrance of me."
[25] In the same way also he took the cup, after supper, and said, "This cup is the new covenant in my
blood. Do this, as often as you drink it, in remembrance of me." [26] For as often as you eat this bread
and drink the cup, you proclaim the Lord's death
until he comes.

[A] **11:2** Other mss add *brothers,* [B] **11:3** Or *the husband is the head of the wife* [C] **11:15** Other mss omit *to her* [D] **11:16** Or *no such* [E] **11:21** Or *eats his own supper ahead of others* [F] **11:24** Other mss add *"Take, eat.* [G] **11:24** Other mss add *broken*

Isthmian Games

by Cecil R. Taylor

Stadium at Delphi, home to the Pythian Games, which were held in year three of the Panhellenic Games cycle.

The games held at Olympia may be the best-known athletic contests from history, primarily because of their modern rebirth. In the world of the first century, many Greek cities offered their own local versions. A set of four of these games came to be known as the Panhellenic ("all Greek") Games because they were open to competitors from any Greek city in the world. These four games ran in a staggered cycle, so individual athletes could compete in all four and in at least one per year. The Olympic Games were held at Olympia every four years in year one of the cycle. Both the Isthmian Games near Corinth and the Nemean Games near Nemea took place in different months of year two. In year three, the Pythian Games were staged near Delphi. Year four featured the Isthmian and the Nemean Games again. Then the cycle repeated.

Held at the chief religious centers of Greece, these games honored eminent deities. Olympia and Nemea honored Zeus; Delphi honored Apollos; Isthmia honored Poseidon. Far more than sport for participants and spectators alike, these games formed part of the worship of the gods. Each athlete offered his best to the gods both before and during competition. Since Greek society understood that strength, speed, and skill came from the gods, the athletes prayed to them and offered thanks for success.[1]

The festival at Isthmia may have been the most popular of the games for two reasons. First, a visit to Corinth, the wealthy provincial capital of Achaia, was often considered the thrill of a lifetime. Second, held on a site near the eastern coast of the Isthmus of Corinth about eight to ten miles southeast of the city, Isthmia was easily accessible by land and by sea.[2]

BEFORE THE GAMES BEGAN

Rules of the games required every participant to spend at least ten months in strict and regimented training, which involved special diets and serious exercises. Before an athlete could compete, he had to swear a solemn oath that he had obeyed these strict rules. Every major Greek city had training facilities where men could prepare for competition in all events. Many athletes used trainers who coached them in style and technique and also advised them about diet and exercise.[3]

When time came for the Isthmian Games (in the spring of the

designated years), competitors and thousands of spectators gathered from cities and colonies all over the Mediterranean world, from Alexandria to Asia Minor to Spain. Only men could compete. Of the major games, Isthmia alone allowed non-Greeks to compete.[4] The festival had the look and feel of a carnival. Vendors sold everything from refreshments to souvenirs to offerings for the gods. Street performers offered musical, theatrical, artistic, and poetic entertainment.[5]

No one knows for sure how many days were given over to the athletic contests, how sacrifices to the honored deity meshed with the sports events, or precisely when the winners received their prizes. The agenda of events, however, was generally the same for all the games.

THE COMPETITION BEGINS

On opening day, contestants solemnly swore before the festival's judges that they had trained for the past ten months and would follow all the rules of the games. The judges also swore to evaluate contests fairly.[6]

Six events formed the core for all the games: foot racing, wrestling, jumping, boxing, javelin hurling, and discus throwing. Competition at Isthmia also included music, dance, drama, debate, chariot and horse races, and even a regatta.[7]

Heralds called participants to each event, giving out the name and city for each contestant, and announced the names of the victors to the crowds.[8] Only the winners got prizes. No awards were given for second or third place finishers. Often the victors' city-states honored them not only with free room and board and theater seats but also with cash. Those honors and awards, however, were less prized than the victor's wreath. Wreaths at Isthmia were circlets sometimes made of pine but more often of withered wild celery.[9] ✤

Starter's pit at the stadium in Isthmia. The Isthmian Games were begun in the sixth century BC by the Corinthians.

[1] Richard Woff, *The Ancient Greek Olympics* (New York: Oxford University Press, 1999), 9; Judith Swaddling, "Olympics BC," *Natural History* 97.8 (1988): 8. [2] Oscar Broneer, "The Isthmian Games," accessed 15 May 2004, http://www/ioa.leeds.ac.uk/1970s/70094.htm; Oscar Broneer, "The Apostle Paul and the Isthmian Games," *BA* 25 (1962): 7. [3] Woff, *Ancient Greek Olympics*, 6. [4] E. Norman Gardiner, *Greek Athletic Sports and Festivals*, Handbooks of Archaeology and Antiquities (London: Macmillan, 1910), 218. [5] Woff, *Ancient Greek Olympics*, 9; Broneer, "Apostle Paul," 23–24. [6] Woff, *Ancient Greek Olympics*, 10. [7] Gordon D. Fee, *The First Epistle to the Corinthians*, New International Commentary on the New Testament (NICNT) (Grand Rapids: Eerdmans, 1987), 433–34, n. 1; Swaddling, "Olympics BC," 8; Woff, *Ancient Greek Olympics*, 12; Broneer, "Isthmian Games," 2–3. [8] See William Smith, "Games" in *Smith's Bible Dictionary* (1884), http://www.ntslibrary.com/PDF%20Books/Smith%27s%20Bible%20Dictionary.pdf, 224. [9] Judith Swaddling, *The Ancient Olympic Games*, 2nd ed. (Austin: University of Texas Press, 1999), 40; Swaddling, "Olympics BC," 8; Broneer, "Apostle Paul and the Isthmian Games," 16–17.

Laver (wash basin) from the temple of Poseidon at Isthmia, which dates from the seventh century BC. Here a person would swear he had kept the rules for nine months, perhaps as part of their purification rite. Poseidon was the patron deity of the Isthmian Games.

SELF-EXAMINATION

27 So, then, whoever eats the bread or drinks the cup
of the Lord in an unworthy manner will be guilty of
sin against the body[A] and blood of the Lord. 28 Let a
person examine himself; in this way let him eat the
bread and drink from the cup. 29 For whoever eats
and drinks without recognizing the body,[B] eats and
drinks judgment on himself. 30 This is why many are
sick and ill among you, and many have fallen asleep.
31 If we were properly judging ourselves, we would
not be judged, 32 but when we are judged by the Lord,
we are disciplined, so that we may not be condemned
with the world.

33 Therefore, my brothers and sisters, when you
come together to eat, welcome one another.[C] 34 If anyone is hungry, he should eat at home, so that when
you gather together you will not come under judgment. I will give instructions about the other matters
whenever I come.

DIVERSITY OF SPIRITUAL GIFTS

12 Now concerning spiritual gifts:[D] brothers and
sisters, I do not want you to be unaware. 2 You
know that when you were pagans, you used to be enticed and led astray by mute idols. 3 Therefore I want
you to know that no one speaking by the Spirit of God
says, "Jesus is cursed," and no one can say, "Jesus is
Lord," except by the Holy Spirit.

4 Now there are different gifts, but the same Spirit.
5 There are different ministries, but the same Lord.
6 And there are different activities, but the same God
works all of them in each person. 7 A manifestation
of the Spirit is given to each person for the common
good: 8 to one is given a message of wisdom through
the Spirit, to another, a message of knowledge by the
same Spirit, 9 to another, faith by the same Spirit, to
another, gifts of healing by the one Spirit, 10 to another, the performing of miracles, to another, prophecy,
to another, distinguishing between spirits, to another,
different kinds of tongues,[E] to another, interpretation
of tongues. 11 One and the same Spirit is active in all
these, distributing to each person as he wills.

UNITY YET DIVERSITY IN THE BODY

12 For just as the body is one and has many parts, and
all the parts of that body, though many, are one body
— so also is Christ. 13 For we were all baptized by[F]
one Spirit into one body — whether Jews or Greeks,
whether slaves or free — and we were all given one
Spirit to drink. 14 Indeed, the body is not one part but
many. 15 If the foot should say, "Because I'm not a hand,
I don't belong to the body," it is not for that reason
any less a part of the body. 16 And if the ear should
say, "Because I'm not an eye, I don't belong to the
body," it is not for that reason any less a part of the

Statue of Asclepius, the Greek god of health. His father was Apollos.

body. 17 If the whole body were an eye, where would
the hearing be? If the whole body were an ear, where
would the sense of smell be? 18 But as it is, God has
arranged each one of the parts in the body just as he
wanted. 19 And if they were all the same part, where
would the body be? 20 As it is, there are many parts,
but one body. 21 The eye cannot say to the hand, "I don't
need you!" Or again, the head can't say to the feet, "I
don't need you!" 22 On the contrary, those parts of the
body that are weaker are indispensable. 23 And those
parts of the body that we consider less honorable, we
clothe these with greater honor, and our unrespect-
able parts are treated with greater respect, 24 which
our respectable parts do not need.

Instead, God has put the body together, giving
greater honor to the less honorable, 25 so that there

[A] **11:27** Lit *be guilty of the body* [B] **11:29** Other mss read *drinks unworthily, not discerning the Lord's body* [C] **11:33** Or *wait for one another* [D] **12:1** Or *spiritual things*, or *spiritual people* [E] **12:10** languages [F] **12:13** Or *with*, or *in*

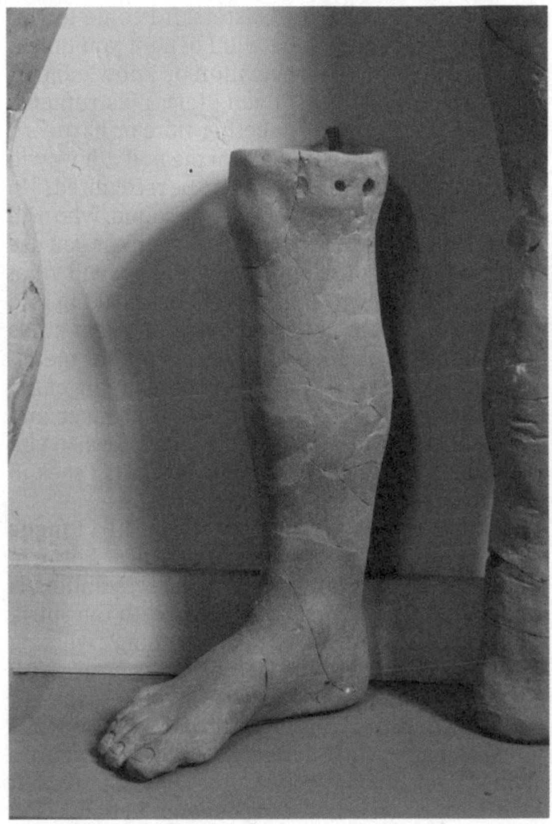

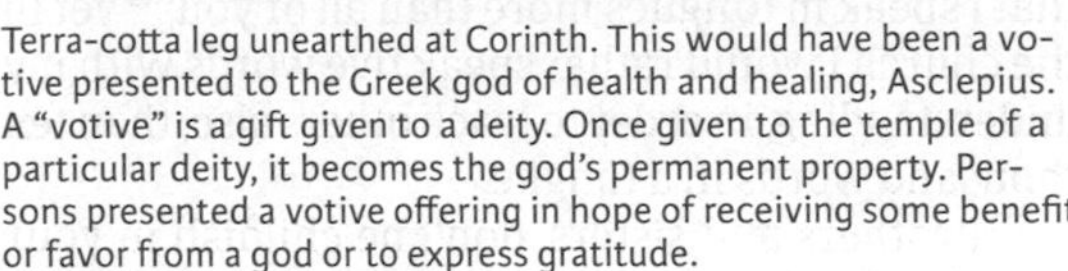

Terra-cotta leg unearthed at Corinth. This would have been a votive presented to the Greek god of health and healing, Asclepius. A "votive" is a gift given to a deity. Once given to the temple of a particular deity, it becomes the god's permanent property. Persons presented a votive offering in hope of receiving some benefit or favor from a god or to express gratitude.

Next to the temple of Asceplius at Pergamum are the ruins of what is thought to be a two-story medical center, likely the first in Europe. The lower level (shown) had a central rotunda and six semi-circular rooms, likely for treating different ailments.

would be no division in the body, but that the members would have the same concern for each other.
26 So if one member suffers, all the members suffer
with it; if one member is honored, all the members
rejoice with it.

27 Now you are the body of Christ, and individual
members of it. 28 And God has appointed these in the
church: first apostles, second prophets, third teachers, next miracles, then gifts of healing, helping, leading, various kinds of tongues.[A] 29 Are all apostles? Are
all prophets? Are all teachers? Do all do miracles?
30 Do all have gifts of healing? Do all speak in tongues?
Do all interpret? 31 But desire the greater gifts. And I
will show you an even better way.

LOVE: THE SUPERIOR WAY

13 If I speak human or angelic tongues[B] but do
not have love, I am a noisy gong or a clanging
cymbal. 2 If I have the gift of prophecy and understand all mysteries and all knowledge, and if I have
all faith so that I can move mountains but do not
have love, I am nothing. 3 And if I give away all my
possessions, and if I give over my body in order to
boast[C] but do not have love, I gain nothing.

4 Love is patient, love is kind. Love does not envy,
is not boastful, is not arrogant, 5 is not rude, is not
self-seeking, is not irritable, and does not keep a record of wrongs. 6 Love finds no joy in unrighteousness
but rejoices in the truth. 7 It bears all things, believes
all things, hopes all things, endures all things.

8 Love never ends. But as for prophecies, they will
come to an end; as for tongues, they will cease; as for
knowledge, it will come to an end. 9 For we know in
part, and we prophesy in part, 10 but when the perfect
comes, the partial will come to an end. 11 When I was a
child, I spoke like a child, I thought like a child, I reasoned like a child. When I became a man, I put aside

[A] **12:28** languages, also in v. 30 [B] **13:1** languages, also in v. 8
[C] **13:3** Other mss read *body to be burned*

Corinth was a center for innovation in pottery decoration and dominated pottery exportation in the seventh and early sixth centuries BC. The Corinthians developed the Black Figure painting technique in which a black silhouetted figure with incised interior details and some added colors stands against the natural color of the clay.

childish things. 12 For now we see only a reflection[A] as in a mirror, but then face to face. Now I know in part, but then I will know fully, as I am fully known. 13 Now these three remain: faith, hope, and love — but the greatest of these is love.

PROPHECY: A SUPERIOR GIFT

14 Pursue love and desire spiritual gifts, and especially that you may prophesy. 2 For the person who speaks in a tongue[B] is not speaking to people but to God, since no one understands him; he speaks mysteries in the Spirit.[C] 3 On the other hand, the person who prophesies speaks to people for their strengthening,[D] encouragement, and consolation. 4 The person who speaks in a tongue builds himself up, but the one who prophesies builds up the church. 5 I wish all of you spoke in tongues,[E] but even more that you prophesied. The person who prophesies is greater than the person who speaks in tongues, unless he interprets so that the church may be built up.

6 So now, brothers and sisters, if I come to you speaking in tongues, how will I benefit you unless I speak to you with a revelation or knowledge or prophecy or teaching? 7 Even lifeless instruments that produce sounds — whether flute or harp — if they don't make a distinction in the notes, how will what is played on the flute or harp be recognized? 8 In fact, if the bugle makes an unclear sound, who will prepare for battle? 9 In the same way, unless you use your tongue for intelligible speech, how will what is spoken be known? For you will be speaking into the air. 10 There are doubtless many different kinds of languages in the world, none is without meaning. 11 Therefore, if I do not know the meaning of the language, I will be a foreigner[F] to the speaker, and the speaker will be a foreigner to me. 12 So also you — since you are zealous for spiritual gifts,[G] seek to excel in building up the church.

13 Therefore the person who speaks in a tongue should pray that he can interpret. 14 For if I pray in a tongue, my spirit prays, but my understanding is unfruitful. 15 What then? I will pray with the spirit, and I will also pray with my understanding. I will sing praise with the spirit, and I will also sing praise with my understanding. 16 Otherwise, if you praise with the spirit,[H] how will the outsider[I] say "Amen" at your giving of thanks, since he does not know what you are saying? 17 For you may very well be giving thanks, but the other person is not being built up. 18 I thank God that I speak in tongues more than all of you; 19 yet in the church I would rather speak five words with my understanding, in order to teach others also, than ten thousand words in a tongue.

20 Brothers and sisters, don't be childish in your thinking, but be infants in regard to evil and adult in your thinking. 21 It is written in the law,

> **I will speak to this people**
> **by people of other tongues**
> **and by the lips of foreigners,**
> **and even then, they will not listen to me,**[J]

says the Lord. 22 Speaking in tongues, then, is intended as a sign, not for believers but for unbelievers, while prophecy is not for unbelievers but for believers. 23 If, therefore, the whole church assembles together and all are speaking in tongues and people who are outsiders or unbelievers come in, will they not say that you are out of your minds? 24 But if all are prophesying and some unbeliever or outsider comes in, he is convicted by all and is called to account by all.

[A] **13:12** Lit *we see indirectly* [B] **14:2** Or *another language*, also in vv. 4, 13,14,19,26,27 [C] **14:2** Or *in spirit*, or *in his spirit* [D] **14:3** Lit *building up* [E] **14:5** Or *other languages*, also in vv. 6,18,21,22,23,39 [F] **14:11** Gk *barbaros*, or *barbarian* [G] **14:12** Lit *zealous of spirits* [H] **14:16** Or *praise by the Spirit* [I] **14:16** Lit *the one filling the place of the uninformed* [J] **14:21** Is 28:11–12

...eart will be revealed, and as a ... fall facedown and worship God, pro-...ing, "God is really among you."

ORDER IN CHURCH MEETINGS

26 What then, brothers and sisters? Whenever you come together, each one[A] has a hymn, a teaching, a revelation, a tongue, or an interpretation. Everything is to be done for building up. 27 If anyone speaks in a tongue, there are to be only two, or at the most three, each in turn, and let someone interpret. 28 But if there is no interpreter, that person is to keep silent in the church and speak to himself and God. 29 Two or three prophets should speak, and the others should evaluate. 30 But if something has been revealed to another person sitting there, the first prophet should be silent. 31 For you can all prophesy one by one, so that everyone may learn and everyone may be encouraged. 32 And the prophets' spirits are subject to the prophets, 33 since God is not a God of disorder but of peace.

As in all the churches of the saints, 34 the women[B] should be silent in the churches, for they are not permitted to speak, but are to submit themselves, as the law also says. 35 If they want to learn something, let them ask their own husbands at home, since it is disgraceful for a woman to speak in the church. 36 Or did the word of God originate from you, or did it come to you only?

37 If anyone thinks he is a prophet or spiritual, he should recognize that what I write to you is the Lord's command. 38 If anyone ignores this, he will be ignored.[C] 39 So then, my brothers and sisters, be eager to prophesy, and do not forbid speaking in tongues. 40 But everything is to be done decently and in order.

RESURRECTION ESSENTIAL TO THE GOSPEL

15 Now I want to make clear for you, brothers and sisters, the gospel I preached to you, which you received, on which you have taken your stand 2 and by which you are being saved, if you hold to the message I preached to you — unless you believed in vain. 3 For I passed on to you as most important what I also received: that Christ died for our sins according to the Scriptures, 4 that he was buried, that he was raised on the third day according to the Scriptures, 5 and that he appeared to Cephas, then to the Twelve. 6 Then he appeared to over five hundred brothers and sisters at one time; most of them are still alive, but some have fallen asleep. 7 Then he appeared to James, then to all the apostles. 8 Last of all, as to one born at the wrong time,[D] he also appeared to me.

9 For I am the least of the apostles, not worthy to be called an apostle, because I persecuted the church of God. 10 But by the grace of God I am what I am, and his grace toward me was not in vain. On the contrary, I worked harder than any of them, yet not I, but th[e] grace of God that was with me. 11 Whether, then, it is I or they, so we proclaim and so you have believed.

RESURRECTION ESSENTIAL TO THE FAITH

12 Now if Christ is proclaimed as raised from the dead, how can some of you say, "There is no resurrection of the dead"? 13 If there is no resurrection of the dead, then not even Christ has been raised; 14 and if Christ has not been raised, then our proclamation is in vain, and so is your faith.[E] 15 Moreover, we are found to be false witnesses about God, because we have testified wrongly about God that he raised up Christ — whom he did not raise up, if in fact the dead are not raised. 16 For if the dead are not raised, not even Christ has been raised. 17 And if Christ has not been raised, your faith is worthless; you are still in your sins. 18 Those, then, who have fallen asleep in Christ have also perished. 19 If we have put our hope in Christ for this life only, we should be pitied more than anyone.

CHRIST'S RESURRECTION GUARANTEES OURS

20 But as it is, Christ has been raised from the dead, the firstfruits of those who have fallen asleep. 21 For since death came through a man, the resurrection of the dead also comes through a man. 22 For just as in Adam all die, so also in Christ all will be made alive.

23 But each in his own order: Christ, the firstfruits; afterward, at his coming, those who belong to Christ. 24 Then comes the end, when he hands over the kingdom to God the Father, when he abolishes all rule and all authority and power. 25 For he must reign until he puts all his enemies under his feet. 26 The last enemy to be abolished is death. 27 For **God has put everything under his feet.**[F] Now when it says "everything" is put under him, it is obvious that he who puts everything under him is the exception. 28 When everything is subject to Christ, then the Son himself will also be subject to the one who subjected everything to him, so that God may be all in all.

RESURRECTION SUPPORTED BY CHRISTIAN EXPERIENCE

29 Otherwise what will they do who are being baptized for the dead?[G] If the dead are not raised at all, then why are people baptized for them?[H] 30 Why are we in danger every hour? 31 I face death every day, as surely as I may boast about you, brothers and sisters, in Christ Jesus our Lord. 32 If I fought wild beasts in

[A] **14:26** Other mss add *of you* [B] **14:34** Other mss read *your women* [C] **14:38** Other mss read *he should be ignored* [D] **15:8** Or *one whose birth was unusual* [E] **15:14** Or *proclamation is useless, and your faith also is useless*, or *proclamation is empty, and your faith also is empty* [F] **15:27** Ps 8:6; 110:1 [G] **15:29** Or *baptized on account of the dead* [H] **15:29** Other mss read *for the dead*

Ephesus as a mere man, what good did that do me?
If the dead are not raised, **Let us eat and drink, for
tomorrow we die.**[A] 33 Do not be deceived: "Bad company corrupts good morals." 34 Come to your senses[B]
and stop sinning; for some people are ignorant about
God. I say this to your shame.

THE NATURE OF THE RESURRECTION BODY

35 But someone will ask, "How are the dead raised?
What kind of body will they have when they come?"
36 You fool! What you sow does not come to life unless it dies. 37 And as for what you sow — you are
not sowing the body that will be, but only a seed,
perhaps of wheat or another grain. 38 But God gives
it a body as he wants, and to each of the seeds its
own body. 39 Not all flesh is the same flesh; there is
one flesh for humans, another for animals, another
for birds, and another for fish. 40 There are heavenly
bodies and earthly bodies, but the splendor of the
heavenly bodies is different from that of the earthly
ones. 41 There is a splendor of the sun, another of the
moon, and another of the stars; in fact, one star differs from another star in splendor. 42 So it is with the
resurrection of the dead: Sown in corruption, raised
in incorruption; 43 sown in dishonor, raised in glory;

sown in we
ral body, raise
body, there is also
The first man Adam
last Adam became a life-giv
spiritual is not first, but the natu
47 The first man was from the ea
the second man is[D] from heaven. 48
dust, so are those who are of the dust; like of
heaven, so are those who are of heaven. 49 An st as
we have borne the image of the man of dust, we will
also bear the image of the man of heaven.

VICTORIOUS RESURRECTION

50 What I am saying, brothers and sisters, is this:
Flesh and blood cannot inherit the kingdom of God,
nor can corruption inherit incorruption. 51 Listen, I
am telling you a mystery: We will not all fall asleep,
but we will all be changed, 52 in a moment, in the
twinkling of an eye, at the last trumpet. For the
trumpet will sound, and the dead will be raised incorruptible, and we will be changed. 53 For this corruptible body must be clothed with incorruptibility,

[A] **15:32** Is 22:13 [B] **15:34** Lit *Sober up* [C] **15:45** Gn 2:7 [D] **15:47** Other mss add *the Lord*

Dating to about 500 BC; interior of Etruscan tombs at Tarquinia. North of Rome, Tarquinia is one of the best places to see Etruscan tombs. The earliest date to the ninth century BC; the majority, though, date to the sixth to fourth centuries. Over 150 tombs have been found at Tarquinia.

and this mortal body must be clothed with immortality. 54 When this corruptible body is clothed with incorruptibility, and this mortal body is clothed with immortality, then the saying that is written will take place:

Death has been swallowed up
in victory.[A]
55 **Where, death, is your victory?**
Where, death, is your sting?[B]

56 The sting of death is sin, and the power of sin is the law. 57 But thanks be to God, who gives us the victory through our Lord Jesus Christ!

58 Therefore, my dear brothers and sisters, be steadfast, immovable, always excelling in the Lord's work, because you know that your labor in the Lord is not in vain.

COLLECTION FOR THE JERUSALEM CHURCH

16 Now about the collection for the saints: Do the same as I instructed the Galatian churches. 2 On the first day of the week, each of you is to set something aside and save in keeping with how he is prospering, so that no collections will need to be made when I come. 3 When I arrive, I will send with letters those you recommend to carry your gift to Jerusalem. 4 If it is suitable for me to go as well, they will travel with me.

PAUL'S TRAVEL PLANS

5 I will come to you after I pass through Macedonia — for I will be traveling through Macedonia — 6 and perhaps I will remain with you or even spend the winter, so that you may send me on my way wherever I go. 7 I don't want to see you now just in passing, since I hope to spend some time with you, if the Lord allows. 8 But I will stay in Ephesus until Pentecost, 9 because a wide door for effective ministry has opened for me[C] — yet many oppose me. 10 If Timothy comes, see that he has nothing to fear while with you, because he is doing the Lord's work, just as I am. 11 So let no one look down on him. Send him on his way in peace so that he can come to me, because I am expecting him with the brothers.

12 Now about our brother Apollos: I strongly urged him to come to you with the brothers, but he was not at all willing to come now. However, he will come when he has an opportunity.

FINAL EXHORTATION

13 Be alert, stand firm in the faith, be courageous,[D] be strong. 14 Do everything in love.

15 Brothers and sisters, you know the household of Stephanas: They are the firstfruits of Achaia and have devoted themselves to serving the saints. I urge you 16 also to submit to such people, and to everyone who works and labors with them. 17 I am delighted to have Stephanas, Fortunatus, and Achaicus present, because these men have made up for your absence. 18 For they have refreshed my spirit and yours. Therefore recognize such people.

CONCLUSION

19 The churches of Asia send you greetings. Aquila and Priscilla send you greetings warmly in the Lord, along with the church that meets in their home. 20 All the brothers and sisters send you greetings. Greet one another with a holy kiss.

21 This greeting is in my own hand — Paul. 22 If anyone does not love the Lord, a curse be on him. Our Lord, come![E] 23 The grace of the Lord Jesus be with you. 24 My love be with all of you in Christ Jesus.

[A] **15:54** Is 25:8 [B] **15:55** Hs 13:14 [C] **16:9** Lit *door has opened to me, great and effective* [D] **16:13** Lit *act like men* [E] **16:22** Aramaic *Marana tha*

2 CORINTHIANS

Columns at Corinth's Temple E. The identity of the deity worshiped at this temple is unknown.

INTRODUCTION TO

2 CORINTHIANS

Circumstances of Writing

All biblical scholars agree that Paul wrote this letter (2Co 1:1; 10:1). It contains more personal information about him than any other letter, and its Greek style is especially like that of Romans and 1 Corinthians. Proposed chronologies of Paul's life and ministry include a number of variations. Yet for 2 Corinthians, the consensus is that the letter was written about AD 56 (from Ephesus during Paul's third missionary journey).

First Corinthians was not well received by the church at Corinth. Timothy had returned to Paul in Ephesus (1Co 4:17; 16:10). He reported that the church was still greatly troubled. This was partly caused by the arrival in Corinth of "false apostles" (2Co 11:13–15). These were perhaps Judaizers, asking Corinthian believers of Gentile heritage to live according to Mosaic regulations (Gl 2:14).

Paul visited Corinth a second time, the first time being his church-planting visit. He described this visit as sorrowful or "painful" (2Co 2:1; 13:2). Apparently the false apostles agitated the Corinthians to disown Paul. This second visit, not mentioned in Acts 19, occurred sometime during the apostle's long ministry in Ephesus.

Paul then wrote a (now lost) severe letter of stinging rebuke to Corinth from Ephesus (2Co 2:3–4,9). He sent this letter by Titus. Titus came to Paul with the news that most of the Corinthian church had repented. They now accepted Paul's authority (7:5–7). Paul decided to write the Corinthians one more time, expressing his relief but still pleading with an unrepentant minority. He promised to come to Corinth a third time (12:14; 13:1). This was fulfilled when Paul stayed in Corinth while on his way to Jerusalem with the financial collection from many churches (Ac 20:2–3).

Contribution to the Bible

Second Corinthians contributes to our understanding of ministry. On this subject, we learn four key truths: (1) God was in Christ reconciling the world to himself and has given to us a ministry of reconciliation; (2) true ministry in Christ's name involves both suffering and victory; (3) serving Christ means ministering in his name to every need of the people; and (4) leaders in ministry need support and trust from those to whom they minister.

Structure

This letter follows the standard format found in the other letters bearing Paul's name. The salutation (2Co 1:1–2) and thanksgiving (1:3–11) at the beginning are followed by the main body of the letter (1:12–13:10). A final greeting (13:11–13) stands as the conclusion.

The body of 2 Corinthians is the most disjointed of Paul's letters. It is hard to miss Paul's change of tone from chapters 1–9 (which are warm and encouraging) to chapters 10–13 (which are harsh and threatening). Whatever one decides about the original unity of the letter, no doubt the major turning point of 2 Corinthians occurs at 10:1.

Largely because of the change in tone between the first part of the letter and the last part, some interpreters have proposed a different understanding of the original form of 2 Corinthians. They propose that two separate letters of Paul have been joined to make up what is now known as 2 Corinthians.

However, it seems much more plausible that the letter originated in the form in which we now have it. All the ancient Christian writers knew the letter only in its present form, which is to say unified as one single letter. Surely within a single letter an author may address two different sets of issues (a majority concern and a minority concern) and use two different tones (encouraging and threatening).

GREETING

1 Paul, an apostle of Christ Jesus by God's will, and
Timothy our[A] brother:
To the church of God at Corinth, with all the saints
who are throughout Achaia.
2 Grace to you and peace from God our Father and
the Lord Jesus Christ.

THE GOD OF COMFORT

3 Blessed be the God and Father of our Lord Jesus
Christ, the Father of mercies and the God of all comfort. 4 He comforts us in all our affliction,[B] so that we
may be able to comfort those who are in any kind
of affliction, through the comfort we ourselves receive from God. 5 For just as the sufferings of Christ
overflow to us, so also through Christ our comfort
overflows. 6 If we are afflicted, it is for your comfort and salvation. If we are comforted, it is for your
comfort, which produces in you patient endurance
of the same sufferings that we suffer. 7 And our hope
for you is firm, because we know that as you share in
the sufferings, so you will also share in the comfort.
8 We don't want you to be unaware, brothers
and sisters, of our affliction that took place in Asia.
We were completely overwhelmed — beyond our
strength — so that we even despaired of life itself.
9 Indeed, we felt that we had received the sentence
of death, so that we would not trust in ourselves but
in God who raises the dead. 10 He has delivered us
from such a terrible death, and he will deliver us. We
have put our hope in him that he will deliver us again
11 while you join in helping us by your prayers. Then
many will give thanks on our[C] behalf for the gift that
came to us through the prayers of many.

A CLEAR CONSCIENCE

12 Indeed, this is our boast: The testimony of our conscience is that we have conducted ourselves in the
world, and especially toward you, with godly sincerity
and purity, not by human wisdom but by God's grace.
13 For we are writing nothing to you other than what
you can read and also understand. I hope you will
understand completely — 14 just as you have partially
understood us — that we are your reason for pride,
just as you also are ours in the day of our[D] Lord Jesus.

A VISIT POSTPONED

15 Because of this confidence, I planned to come to
you first, so that you could have a second benefit,[E]
16 and to visit you on my way to Macedonia, and then
come to you again from Macedonia and be helped by
you on my journey to Judea. 17 Now when I planned
this, was I of two minds? Or what I plan, do I plan in a
purely human[F] way so that I say "Yes, yes" and "No, no"
at the same time? 18 As God is faithful, our message

The Lion of Amphipolis supposedly looked over the spirits of dead sailors at Amphipolis, a town beside the River Strymon in Macedonia. Philip II erected the lion in the fourth century BC.

to you is not "Yes and no." 19 For the Son of God, Jesus
Christ, whom we proclaimed among you — Silvanus,[G]
Timothy, and I — did not become "Yes and no." On the
contrary, in him it is always "Yes." 20 For every one of
God's promises is "Yes" in him. Therefore, through
him we also say "Amen" to the glory of God. 21 Now
it is God who strengthens us together with you in
Christ, and who has anointed us. 22 He has also put
his seal on us and given us the Spirit in our hearts as
a down payment.
23 I call on God as a witness, on my life, that it was
to spare you that I did not come to Corinth. 24 I do not
mean that we lord it over your faith, but we are workers with you for your joy, because you stand firm in
2 your faith. 1 In fact, I made up my mind about
this: I would not come to you on another painful
visit.[H] 2 For if I cause you pain, then who will cheer
me other than the one being hurt by me?[I] 3 I wrote
this very thing so that when I came I wouldn't have
pain from those who ought to give me joy, because

[A] **1:1** Lit *the* [B] **1:4** Or *trouble*, or *tribulation*, or *trials*, or *oppression* [C] **1:11** Other mss read *your* [D] **1:14** Other mss omit *our* [E] **1:15** Other mss read *a second joy* [F] **1:17** Or *a worldly*, or *a fleshly*, or *a selfish* [G] **1:19** Or *Silas*; Ac 15:22–32; 16:19–40; 17:1–16 [H] **2:1** Lit *not again in sorrow to come to you* [I] **2:2** Lit *the one pained*

Roman Triumphal Processions

by M. Dean Register

Created between the Palatine and Aventine Hills in Rome, the Circus Maximus hosted chariot races, gladiatorial contests, and processions. At its largest, the arena was over 2,000 by 500 feet.

Roman military victory parades were a spectacle to behold. Well documented in ancient sources, at least three hundred times the city of Rome staged a triumphal procession as a demonstration of civic pride, conquest, and power.[1]

DEVELOPMENT OF THE PROCESSION

The Roman practice of the triumphal parade developed gradually. Archaeological evidence from stone inscriptions and ancient paintings suggests the Romans borrowed the concept from Etruscan kings of central Italy who had been influenced by similar ceremonies in Asia Minor. The earliest known triumphal pageant outside Rome was in Asia Minor in the fourth century BC.[2] First-century Roman tablets called the *Fasti Triumphales* record triumphs from the time of the mythical Romulus in 753 BC until the triumph of Balbus in 19 BC. Josephus, the Jewish historian, describes the victory parade of Vespasian and Titus as one of "pompous solemnity" in which both were crowned with laurel wreaths and clothed in purple. The parade carried the two generals before an approving Senate, applauding soldiers, jubilant citizens, and humiliated captives. Furthermore, Josephus's account provides extenuating details regarding the religious aspect of the procession, stressing that the culmination of the parade was located at the temple of Jupiter.[3]

ORDER AND PATH OF THE PROCESSION

Triumphal processions in Rome observed a specific sequence. As one historian has emphasized: "Rome celebrated the triumph and the triumph celebrated Rome."[4] A triumphal procession saturated every aspect of Rome's social, political, and religious life. Although a party atmosphere prevailed, decorum and propriety marked the procession. To heighten the festive mood, organizers carefully choreographed the formality, repetition, and position in the pageant.

On the morning of the parade, the general assembled his victorious army along with the humiliated captives outside the city boundaries at the Campus Maritus (Field of Mars).[5] From there, the parade moved through the Porta Triumphalis (Triumphal Arch), the Circus Flaminius (a small racetrack), and the Circus Maximus—the great stadium that could seat up to one hundred fifty thousand spectators. The parade

Triumph scene depicting Rome's Emperor Marcus Aurelius, who ruled AD 161–180. The winged figure above the emperor's head represents his divinity.

Victory scene showing those conquered bowing to Marcus Aurelius. In the background, banners are raised in celebration of the emperor's victory.

Scene showing Marcus Aurelius, at the conclusion of the triumphant procession, offering sacrifices to the gods for his victory over the barbarians.

continued along the Via Sacra and arrived finally at the temple of Jupiter on Capitoline Hill, where a worship ceremony preceded the distribution of the spoils of war to the soldiers and the public.[6]

Essential to the procession was the display of painted banners representing battle scenes, victorious slogans, and models of conquered fortresses. This display magnified the victory and exalted the general whom the people lauded as *triumphator*. Following the banner carriers, priests and attendants marched holding censers of burning incense and escorting white sacrificial oxen.[7] Carrying golden saucers that the priests would use to catch sacrificial blood, children jumped and skipped behind the oxen.[8] Musicians and dancers accentuated the pageantry by adding mockery to the prisoners on display. Typically the captives were positioned in front of the victorious general's chariot. The conclusion of the parade involved leading some of the captives off for execution, selling some as slaves, and making a sacrificial offering at the temple of Jupiter. ✣

---

[1] Mary Beard, *The Roman Triumph* (Cambridge, MA: Harvard University Press, 2007), 4. [2] H. S. Versnel, *Triumphus: An Inquiry into the Origin, Development and Meaning of the Roman Triumph* (Leiden: Brill, 1970), 299. [3] Josephus, *Jewish War* 7.5; Ida Ostenberg, *Staging the World: Spoils, Captives and Representations in the Roman Triumphal Procession* (Oxford: Oxford University Press, 2009), 13. [4] Ostenberg, *Staging the World*, 13. [5] Beard, *Roman Triumph*, 81. [6] David J. Williams, *Paul's Metaphors: Their Context and Character* (Peabody, MA: Hendrickson, 1999), 257. [7] Williams, *Paul's Metaphors*, 258. [8] Nigel Rodgers, *The Rise and Fall of Ancient Rome* (London: Anness, 2004), 170.

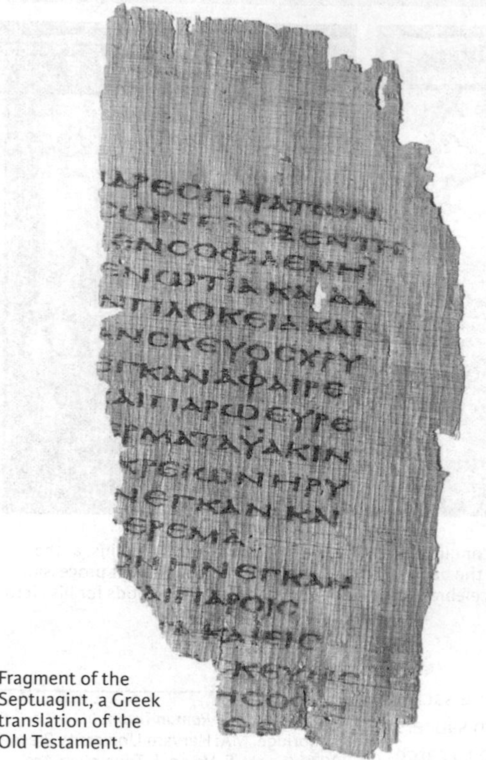

Fragment of the Septuagint, a Greek translation of the Old Testament.

I am confident about all of you that my joy will also
be yours. [4] For I wrote to you with many tears out of
an extremely troubled and anguished heart — not to
cause you pain, but that you should know the abundant love I have for you.

A SINNER FORGIVEN

[5] If anyone has caused pain, he has caused pain not so
much to me but to some degree — not to exaggerate
— to all of you. [6] This punishment by the majority is
sufficient for that person. [7] As a result, you should
instead forgive and comfort him. Otherwise, he may
be overwhelmed by excessive grief. [8] Therefore I urge
you to reaffirm your love to him. [9] I wrote for this
purpose: to test your character to see if you are obedient in everything. [10] Anyone you forgive, I do too.
For what I have forgiven — if I have forgiven anything
— it is for your benefit in the presence of Christ, [11] so
that we may not be taken advantage of by Satan. For
we are not ignorant of his schemes.

A TRIP TO MACEDONIA

[12] When I came to Troas to preach the gospel of Christ,
even though the Lord opened a door for me, [13] I had
no rest in my spirit because I did not find my brother Titus. Instead, I said good-bye to them and left for
Macedonia.

A MINISTRY OF LIFE OR DEATH

[14] But thanks be to God, who always leads us in Christ's
triumphal procession and through us spreads the
aroma of the knowledge of him in every place. [15] For
to God we are the fragrance of Christ among those
who are being saved and among those who are perishing. [16] To some we are an aroma of death leading
to death, but to others, an aroma of life leading to
life. Who is adequate for these things? [17] For we do
not market the word of God for profit like so many.[A]
On the contrary, we speak with sincerity in Christ, as
from God and before God.

LIVING LETTERS

3 Are we beginning to commend ourselves again?
Or do we need, like some, letters of recommendation to you or from you? [2] You yourselves are our
letter, written on our hearts, known and read by everyone. [3] You show that you are Christ's letter, delivered[B] by us, not written with ink but with the Spirit
of the living God — not on tablets of stone but on
tablets of human hearts.[C]

PAUL'S COMPETENCE

[4] Such is the confidence we have through Christ before God. [5] It is not that we are competent in[D] ourselves to claim anything as coming from ourselves,
but our adequacy is from God. [6] He has made us competent to be ministers of a new covenant, not of the
letter, but of the Spirit. For the letter kills, but the
Spirit gives life.

NEW COVENANT MINISTRY

[7] Now if the ministry that brought death, chiseled
in letters on stones, came with glory, so that the Israelites were not able to gaze steadily at Moses's
face because of its glory, which was set aside, [8] how
will the ministry of the Spirit not be more glorious?
[9] For if the ministry that brought condemnation had
glory, the ministry that brings righteousness overflows with even more glory. [10] In fact, what had been
glorious is not glorious now by comparison because
of the glory that surpasses it. [11] For if what was set
aside was glorious, what endures will be even more
glorious.

[12] Since, then, we have such a hope, we act with
great boldness. [13] We are not like Moses, who used
to put a veil over his face to prevent the Israelites
from gazing steadily until the end[E] of the glory of
what was being set aside, [14] but their minds were
hardened. For to this day, at the reading of the old
covenant, the same veil remains; it is not lifted,

[A] **2:17** Other mss read *like the rest* [B] **3:3** Lit *ministered to* [C] **3:3** Lit *fleshly hearts* [D] **3:5** Lit *from* [E] **3:13** Or *at the outcome*

because it is set aside only in Christ. 15 Yet still today,
whenever Moses is read, a veil lies over their hearts,
16 but whenever a person turns to the Lord, the veil
is removed. 17 Now the Lord is the Spirit, and where
the Spirit of the Lord is, there is freedom. 18 We all,
with unveiled faces, are looking as in a mirror at[A]
the glory of the Lord and are being transformed into
the same image from glory to glory; this is from the
Lord who is the Spirit.[B]

THE LIGHT OF THE GOSPEL

4 Therefore, since we have this ministry because
we were shown mercy, we do not give up. 2 Instead, we have renounced secret and shameful things,
not acting deceitfully or distorting the word of God,
but commending ourselves before God to everyone's
conscience by an open display of the truth. 3 But if our
gospel is veiled, it is veiled to those who are perishing. 4 In their case, the god of this age has blinded the
minds of the unbelievers to keep them from seeing
the light of the gospel of the glory of Christ,[C] who is
the image of God. 5 For we are not proclaiming ourselves but Jesus Christ as Lord, and ourselves as your
servants for Jesus's sake. 6 For God who said, "Let
light shine out of darkness," has shone in our hearts
to give the light of the knowledge of God's glory in
the face of Jesus Christ.

TREASURE IN CLAY JARS

7 Now we have this treasure in clay jars, so that this
extraordinary power may be from God and not from
us. 8 We are afflicted in every way but not crushed; we
are perplexed but not in despair; 9 we are persecuted
but not abandoned; we are struck down but not destroyed. 10 We always carry the death of Jesus in our
body, so that the life of Jesus may also be displayed
in our body. 11 For we who live are always being giv-
en over to death for Jesus's sake, so that Jesus's life
may also be displayed in our mortal flesh. 12 So then,
death is at work in us, but life in you. 13 And since we
have the same spirit of faith in keeping with what
is written, **I believed, therefore I spoke,**[D] we also
believe, and therefore speak. 14 For we know that the
one who raised the Lord Jesus will also raise us with
Jesus and present us with you. 15 Indeed, everything
is for your benefit so that, as grace extends through
more and more people, it may cause thanksgiving to
increase to the glory of God.
16 Therefore we do not give up. Even though our
outer person is being destroyed, our inner person is
being renewed day by day. 17 For our momentary light
affliction is producing for us an absolutely incomparable eternal weight of glory. 18 So we do not focus on
what is seen, but on what is unseen. For what is seen
is temporary, but what is unseen is eternal.

Corinthian painted pottery of the fifth century BC was mostly decorated with simple bands and floral patterns, but some workshops were more creative. A lively black-figured frieze of lions, boars, storks, and a goat encircles this richly patterned handleless amphora. From Corinth; dated about 450–410 BC.

OUR FUTURE AFTER DEATH

5 For we know that if our earthly tent we live in
is destroyed, we have a building from God, an
eternal dwelling in the heavens, not made with hands.
2 Indeed, we groan in this tent, desiring to put on our
heavenly dwelling, 3 since, when we are clothed,[E] we
will not be found naked. 4 Indeed, we groan while we
are in this tent, burdened as we are, because we do
not want to be unclothed but clothed, so that mortality may be swallowed up by life. 5 Now the one who
prepared us for this very purpose is God, who gave
us the Spirit as a down payment.
6 So we are always confident and know that while
we are at home in the body we are away from the
Lord. 7 For we walk by faith, not by sight. 8 In fact,
we are confident, and we would prefer to be away
from the body and at home with the Lord. 9 Therefore, whether we are at home or away, we make it our
aim to be pleasing to him. 10 For we must all appear
before the judgment seat of Christ, so that each may
be repaid for what he has done in the body, whether
good or evil.

[A] **3:18** Or *are reflecting* [B] **3:18** Or *from the Spirit of the Lord*, or *from the Lord, the Spirit* [C] **4:4** Or *the gospel of the glorious Christ*, or *the glorious gospel of Christ* [D] **4:13** Ps 116:10 LXX [E] **5:3** Other mss read *when we have taken it off*

11 Therefore, since we know the fear of the Lord,
we try to persuade people. What we are is plain to
God, and I hope it is also plain to your consciences.
12 We are not commending ourselves to you again,
but giving you an opportunity to be proud of us, so
that you may have a reply for those who take pride in
outward appearance rather than in the heart. 13 For
if we are out of our mind, it is for God; if we are in
our right mind, it is for you. 14 For the love of Christ
compels us, since we have reached this conclusion,
that one died for all, and therefore all died. 15 And he
died for all so that those who live should no longer
live for themselves, but for the one who died for them
and was raised.

THE MINISTRY OF RECONCILIATION

16 From now on, then, we do not know anyone from a
worldly perspective.[A] Even if we have known Christ
from a worldly perspective,[B] yet now we no longer
know him in this way. 17 Therefore, if anyone is in
Christ, he is a new creation; the old has passed away,
and see, the new has[C] come! 18 Everything is from God,
who has reconciled us to himself through Christ and
has given us the ministry of reconciliation. 19 That is,
in Christ, God was reconciling the world to himself,
not counting their trespasses against them, and he
has committed the message of reconciliation to us.

20 Therefore, we are ambassadors for Christ, since
God is making his appeal through us. We plead on
Christ's behalf, "Be reconciled to God." 21 He made
the one who did not know sin to be sin[D] for us, so that
in him we might become the righteousness of God.

6 Working together with him, we also appeal to
you, "Don't receive the grace of God in vain."
2 For he says:

> **At an acceptable time I listened to you,**
> **and in the day of salvation I helped you.**[E]

See, now is the acceptable time; now is the day of
salvation!

THE CHARACTER OF PAUL'S MINISTRY

3 We are not giving anyone an occasion for offense,
so that the ministry will not be blamed. 4 Instead, as
God's ministers, we commend ourselves in everything: by great endurance, by afflictions, by hardships, by difficulties, 5 by beatings, by imprisonments,
by riots, by labors, by sleepless nights, by times of
hunger, 6 by purity, by knowledge, by patience, by
kindness, by the Holy Spirit, by sincere love, 7 by the
word of truth,[F] by the power of God; through weapons of righteousness for the right hand and the left,

[A] **5:16** Lit *anyone according to the flesh* [B] **5:16** Lit *Christ according to the flesh* [C] **5:17** Other mss read *look, all new things have* [D] **5:21** Or *be a sin offering* [E] **6:2** Is 49:8 [F] **6:7** Or *by truthful speech*

The bema in the Roman forum at Corinth. This may be the bema (speaker's platform) of Acts 18:16–17. Paul was brought to the bema by the elders of Corinth's synagogue, who accused him of subversive teaching against the Mosaic law. The Acropolis is in the background.

8 through glory and dishonor, through slander and good report; regarded as deceivers, yet true; 9 as unknown, yet recognized; as dying, yet see — we live; as being disciplined, yet not killed; 10 as grieving, yet always rejoicing; as poor, yet enriching many; as having nothing, yet possessing everything. 11 We have spoken openly to you, Corinthians; our heart has been opened wide. 12 We are not withholding our affection from you, but you are withholding yours from us. 13 I speak as to my children; as a proper response, open your heart to us.

SEPARATION TO GOD

14 Do not be yoked together with those who do not believe. For what partnership is there between righteousness and lawlessness? Or what fellowship does light have with darkness? 15 What agreement does Christ have with Belial?[A] Or what does a believer have in common with an unbeliever? 16 And what agreement does the temple of God have with idols? For we[B] are the temple of the living God, as God said:

I will dwell
and walk among them,
and I will be their God,
and they will be my people.[C]
17 Therefore, **come out from among them**
and **be separate, says the Lord;**
do not touch any unclean thing,
and I will welcome you.[D]
18 And **I will be a Father** to you,
and you will be **sons** and daughters **to me,**
says the Lord Almighty.[E]

7 So then, dear friends, since we have these promises, let us cleanse ourselves from every impurity of the flesh and spirit, bringing holiness to completion[F] in the fear of God.

JOY AND REPENTANCE

2 Make room for us in your hearts. We have wronged no one, corrupted no one, taken advantage of no one. 3 I don't say this to condemn you, since I have already said that you are in our hearts, to die together and to live together. 4 I am very frank with you; I have great pride in you. I am filled with encouragement; I am overflowing with joy in all our afflictions.

5 In fact, when we came into Macedonia, we[G] had no rest. Instead, we were troubled in every way: conflicts on the outside, fears within. 6 But God, who comforts the downcast, comforted us by the arrival of Titus, 7 and not only by his arrival but also by the comfort he received from you. He told us about your deep longing, your sorrow, and your zeal for me, so that I rejoiced even more. 8 For even if I grieved you with my letter, I don't regret it. And if I regretted it — since I saw that the letter grieved you, yet only for a while — 9 I now rejoice, not because you were grieved, but because your grief led to repentance. For you were grieved as God willed, so that you didn't experience any loss from us. 10 For godly grief produces a repentance that leads to salvation without regret, but worldly grief produces death. 11 For consider how much diligence this very thing — this grieving as God wills — has produced in you: what a desire to clear yourselves, what indignation, what fear, what deep longing, what zeal, what justice! In every way you showed yourselves to be pure in this matter. 12 So even though I wrote to you, it was not because of the one who did wrong, or because of the one who was wronged, but in order that your devotion to us might be made plain to you in the sight of God. 13 For this reason we have been comforted.

In addition to our own comfort, we rejoiced even more over the joy Titus had, because his spirit was refreshed by all of you. 14 For if I have made any boast to him about you, I have not been disappointed; but as I have spoken everything to you in truth, so our boasting to Titus has also turned out to be the truth. 15 And his affection toward you is even greater as he remembers the obedience of all of you, and how you received him with fear and trembling. 16 I rejoice that I have complete confidence in you.

APPEAL TO COMPLETE THE COLLECTION

8 We want you to know, brothers and sisters, about the grace of God that was given to the churches of Macedonia: 2 During a severe trial brought about by affliction, their abundant joy and their extreme poverty overflowed in a wealth of generosity on their part. 3 I can testify that, according to their ability and even beyond their ability, of their own accord, 4 they begged us earnestly for the privilege of sharing in the ministry to the saints, 5 and not just as we had hoped. Instead, they gave themselves first to the Lord and then to us by God's will. 6 So we urged Titus that just as he had begun, so he should also complete among you this act of grace.

7 Now as you excel in everything — in faith, speech, knowledge, and in all diligence, and in your love for us[H] — excel also in this act of grace. 8 I am not saying this as a command. Rather, by means of the diligence of others, I am testing the genuineness of your love. 9 For you know the grace of our Lord Jesus Christ: Though he was rich, for your sake he became poor, so that by his poverty you might become rich. 10 And in this matter I am giving advice because it is profitable

[A] **6:15** Or *Beliar* [B] **6:16** Other mss read *you* [C] **6:16** Lv 26:12; Jr 31:33; 32:38; Ezk 37:26 [D] **6:17** Is 52:11 [E] **6:18** 2Sm 7:14; Is 43:6; 49:22; 60:4; Hs 1:10 [F] **7:1** Or *spirit, perfecting holiness* [G] **7:5** Lit *our flesh* [H] **8:7** Other mss read *in our love for you*

The Temples at Corinth

by Mark A. Rathel

If Paul entered the city of Corinth on the main road from the north (the graveled Lechaion Road), he would have encountered the temple of Asclepius, the god of healing. Asclepius's origin is unknown. Later Greek religions regarded him as the son of Apollos and the recipient of training in the healing arts by the Centaur Chiron. Inside the temple was a pit for nonpoisonous snakes. Asclepius's symbol, a snake wound around a staff, has been used in modern times as a symbol for the medical profession. The temple of Asclepius functioned like a sanatorium with a dormitory in which patients slept, a well for purification, and a facility for the regimentation of diet and exercise. Often the one looking for healing made a votive terra-cotta offering of the diseased body part. At the Asclepius temple in Corinth, archaeologists have discovered replicas of hands, feet, eyes, and other body parts. The temple also contained three large dining rooms for hosting ritual feasts in the god's honor.

Continuing from the north entrance to the center of the city, Paul would have encountered the impressive edifice of the temple of Apollo. The temple originally contained thirty-eight large columns; the seven surviving columns measure twenty-four feet in height by six feet in diameter. Apollos was associated with music, archery, prophecy, flocks, herds, law, and civilization.

Farther south, Paul would have passed through a Roman arch and entered the Corinthian marketplace. In this business-government district, Paul would have viewed temples dedicated to major and minor pagan deities. The Romans built the majority of the temples in the marketplace during the reigns of the emperors Augustus, Tiberius, and Claudius; thus the temples would have been of recent origin in Paul's day. In the marketplace, Paul would have seen temples to Poseidon, Heracles, Hermes, Aphrodite, and Athena.

The marketplace at Corinth also contained a temple of Octavia, the sister of the first Roman emperor, Augustus. Corinth, like most cities in the empire, contained in the center of town various temples that honored the emperor or his family.

In the distance are the seven standing columns of the temple of Apollo, one of the most prominent landmarks of Corinth. The columns rise about twenty-four feet high and are about six feet in diameter. In the foreground are the ruins of the western shops.

Bust of Aphrodite. Her temple was on the Acrocorinth and overlooked the city.

Head of a cult statue of Isis. The surface of the face is polished; the hair is colored and may have been gilded. Dated after AD 138; from Thessalonica.

The first emperor and his sister were thought to be descendants of Venus, the Roman goddess equivalent to Aphrodite.

From the marketplace, Paul could have followed a winding trail leading up the Acrocorinth, the 1,886-foot-high mountain that formed the base of old Corinth. If Paul continued his journey south toward the Acrocorinth, he passed ten more temples, including temples to Isis, Demeter, and another to Aphrodite.

Isis was the Egyptian goddess of the sea, fertility, agriculture, and the afterlife. Devotees of Isis proclaimed her to be the ruler over all things. The rituals involved a celebration of the resurrection of Isis's husband, Osiris, from death. The immoralities of the rituals of Isis shocked the tolerant Romans who attempted to suppress the religion.[1]

Archaeologists discovered a temple to Demeter, the goddess of grain, on top of the Acrocorinth. Originally the temple contained fifty dining halls. The myth of Demeter explained the agricultural cycle, a type of annual rebirth, in ancient Greek religion. The agricultural religions invariably involved sexual activity.

Corinth gained fame because of its temples of Aphrodite, the goddess of love, beauty, and fertility. The Greeks associated Aphrodite with the Canaanite fertility goddess Astarte, the female consort of Baal, the worship of whom Old Testament prophets such as Elijah strongly condemned. ✣

[1] Everett Ferguson, *Backgrounds of Early Christianity*, 2nd ed. (Grand Rapids: Eerdmans, 1992), 252.

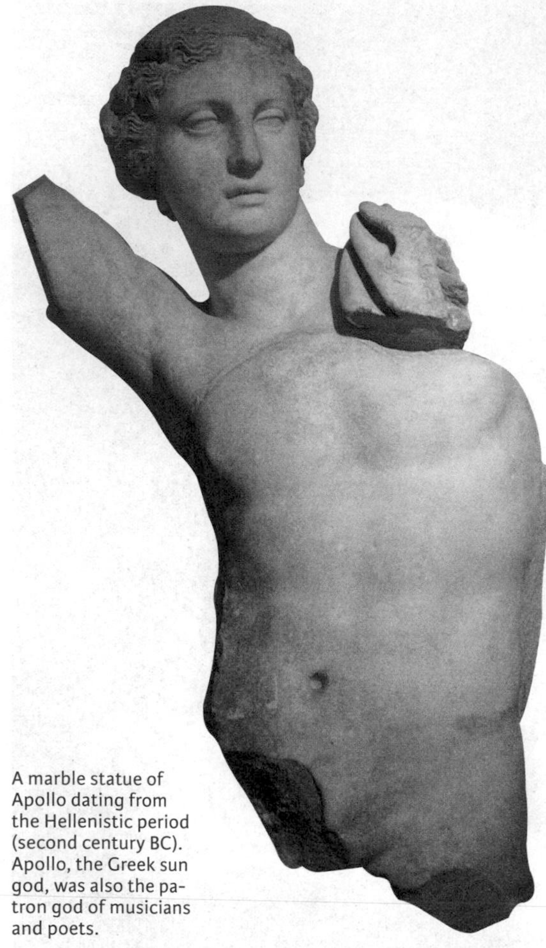

A marble statue of Apollo dating from the Hellenistic period (second century BC). Apollo, the Greek sun god, was also the patron god of musicians and poets.

for you, who began last year not only to do something but also to want to do it. 11 Now also finish the task, so that just as there was an eager desire, there may also be a completion, according to what you have. 12 For if the eagerness is there, the gift is acceptable according to what a person has, not according to what he does not have. 13 It is not that there should be relief for others and hardship for you, but it is a question of equality.[A] 14 At the present time your surplus is available for their need, so that their abundance may in turn meet your need, in order that there may be equality. 15 As it is written: **The person who had much did not have too much, and the person who had little did not have too little.**[B]

ADMINISTRATION OF THE COLLECTION

16 Thanks be to God, who put the same concern for you into the heart of Titus. 17 For he welcomed our appeal and, being very diligent, went out to you by his own choice. 18 We have sent with him the brother who is praised among all the churches for his gospel ministry.[C] 19 And not only that, but he was also appointed by the churches to accompany us with this gracious gift that we are administering for the glory of the Lord himself and to show our eagerness to help. 20 We are taking this precaution so that no one will criticize us about this large sum that we are administering. 21 Indeed, we are giving careful thought to do what is right, not only before the Lord but also before people. 22 We have also sent with them our brother. We have often tested him in many circumstances and found him to be diligent — and now even more diligent because of his great confidence in you. 23 As for Titus, he is my partner and coworker for you; as for our brothers, they are the messengers of the churches, the glory of Christ. 24 Therefore, show them proof before the churches of your love and of our boasting about you.

MOTIVATIONS FOR GIVING

9 Now concerning the ministry to the saints, it is unnecessary for me to write to you. 2 For I know your eagerness, and I boast about you to the Macedonians, "Achaia has been ready since last year," and your zeal has stirred up most of them. 3 But I am sending the brothers so that our boasting about you in this matter would not prove empty, and so that you would be ready just as I said. 4 Otherwise, if any Macedonians come with me and find you unprepared, we, not to mention you, would be put to shame in that situation.[D] 5 Therefore I considered it necessary to urge the brothers to go on ahead to you and arrange in advance the generous gift you promised, so that it will be ready as a gift and not as an extortion.

6 The point is this:[E] The person who sows sparingly will also reap sparingly, and the person who sows generously will also reap generously. 7 Each person should do as he has decided in his heart — not reluctantly or out of compulsion, since God loves a cheerful giver. 8 And God is able to make every grace overflow to you, so that in every way, always having everything you need, you may excel in every good work. 9 As it is written:

> **He distributed freely;**
> **he gave to the poor;**
> **his righteousness endures forever.**[F]

10 Now the one who provides seed for the sower and bread for food will also provide and multiply your seed and increase the harvest of your righteousness. 11 You will be enriched in every way for all generosity, which produces thanksgiving to God through us. 12 For the ministry of this service is not only supplying

[A] **8:13** Lit *but from equality* [B] **8:15** Ex 16:18 [C] **8:18** Lit *churches, in the gospel* [D] **9:4** Or *in this confidence* [E] **9:6** Lit *And this* [F] **9:9** Ps 112:9

the needs of the saints but is also overflowing in many
expressions of thanks to God. 13 Because of the proof
provided by this ministry, they will glorify God for
your obedient confession of the gospel of Christ, and
for your generosity in sharing with them and with
everyone. 14 And as they pray on your behalf, they
will have deep affection for you because of the surpassing grace of God in you. 15 Thanks be to God for
his indescribable gift!

PAUL'S APOSTOLIC AUTHORITY

10 Now I, Paul, myself, appeal to you by the
meekness and gentleness of Christ — I who
am humble among you in person but bold toward
you when absent. 2 I beg you that when I am present I will not need to be bold with the confidence by
which I plan to challenge certain people who think
we are living according to the flesh. 3 For although
we live in the flesh, we do not wage war according
to the flesh, 4 since the weapons of our warfare are
not of the flesh, but are powerful through God for the
demolition of strongholds. We demolish arguments
5 and every proud thing that is raised up against the
knowledge of God, and we take every thought captive to obey Christ. 6 And we are ready to punish any
disobedience, once your obedience is complete.

7 Look at what is obvious.[A] If anyone is confident
that he belongs to Christ, let him remind himself of
this: Just as he belongs to Christ, so do we. 8 For if I
boast a little too much about our authority, which
the Lord gave for building you up and not for tearing
you down, I will not be put to shame. 9 I don't want
to seem as though I am trying to terrify you with
my letters. 10 For it is said, "His letters are weighty
and powerful, but his physical presence is weak and
his public speaking amounts to nothing." 11 Let such
a person consider this: What we are in our letters,
when we are absent, we will also be in our actions
when we are present.

12 For we don't dare classify or compare ourselves
with some who commend themselves. But in measuring themselves by themselves and comparing

[A] **10:7** Or *You are looking at things outwardly*

The western shops at Corinth; the Acrocorinth rises in the background.

Achaia

by David M. Wallace

View of the sea at Delos, which the Greeks considered to be the religious heart of the Cyclades Islands. Greek mythology claimed that both Apollo and his sister Artemis were born at Delos.

LOCATION AND GEOGRAPHY[1]

Achaia in the New Testament refers to a geographic area in the southern portion of Greece, which included the cities of Athens, Corinth, and Sparta, as well as the Cyclades Islands—a group of more than two hundred islands southeast of the mainland. Bounded by the Adriatic Sea on the west and the Aegean Sea to the east, with the Gulf of Corinth largely splitting it in half, Achaia is about the size of Maine.

The region has only two discernible seasons. Winter lasts October to April and is usually mild; it sees about forty inches of rain and some snow. Summer, which lasts May to September, is hot and dry; yet many areas get relief because of coastal breezes.

Mountains cover approximately three-fourths of the land, leaving only a quarter of the land available for farming. Although the mountains of Achaia are not unusually high, they are numerous. Mountain ranges and ridges crisscross the region, creating numerous ravines and valleys. Rain and melting snow produce many streams and even some large rivers in the mountains during the rainy winter season. During New Testament times, the resulting floods in the valleys below kept farmers from tilling the land. The rapidly flowing water was typically muddy, rendering it unusable to humans. Erosion was a problem; silt would fill the harbors.

In general, travel in the region was difficult. Snow often covered the mountain passes in winter. Crossing the swollen rivers was hazardous and, at times, impossible. Silt-filled harbors could halt boat and ship travel. Constructing bridges was impractical because of the sheer number of ravines, valleys, and rivers. Many travelers thus waited until the summertime and would use the then-dry riverbeds as roadways.

Although Achaia was dominated by mountains, it was mostly surrounded by water. No one in Achaia was ever more than forty miles from the sea. Many inlets and harbors dot the coastline. Although Achaia was primarily a rural and agricultural region, Achaians were also active seafaring people.

RESOURCES IN ACHAIA

The resources of Achaia varied greatly. Timber was in short supply. Most resources were agricultural. The region around the city of Argos produced a significant citrus crop. By terracing the hillsides, the people of Achaia were able to grow grapevines and olive trees. Because of the stony terrain, growing wheat was impossible, so the people imported it. Farmers instead raised barley and millet. Pastures, which would not support cattle, were better suited to raising sheep and goats. The area around Laconia produced copper and iron. Workers mined silver and lead from the region of Attica, on the peninsula southeast of Athens. Corinth and Athens produced potters' clay in abundance. These two cities became quite famous for their ceramics. White marble was quarried on the Cyclades Islands.

A plateau at the foot of the mountains near the region of Elis, on the Adriatic Sea to the west, had perhaps the best pastureland in the region. Elis was good for raising horses and cattle and for growing flax.

Corinth saw much activity from the shipping trade. Because the city was only 1 ½ miles from the Isthmus of Corinth, and because traveling around the southern tip of Achaia at Cape Malea was long and dangerous, travelers and merchants customarily pulled cargo and smaller ships across the narrow, 4-mile-wide Isthmus of Corinth on a tramway from Cenchreae to Lechaeum, the western harbor of Corinth, saving about 150 miles in travel distance. ❖

Ruins at Cenchreae, which was the port city for ancient Corinth. The city, which had at one time been bustling with commerce and activity, was hit with catastrophic earthquakes in AD 365 and 375. Some rebuilding occurred beginning around AD 400, but by the sixth century the city was virtually abandoned.

[1] Information in this article comes primarily from Charles F. Pfeiffer and Howard F. Vos, "Greece," in *Wycliffe Historical Geography of Bible Lands* (Chicago: Moody, 1967), 407–16.

Road leading from Corinth toward the port city of Cenchreae.

themselves to themselves, they lack understanding.
13 We, however, will not boast beyond measure but
according to the measure of the area of ministry
that God has assigned to us, which reaches even to
you. 14 For we are not overextending ourselves, as
if we had not reached you, since we have come to
you with the gospel of Christ. 15 We are not boasting
beyond measure about other people's labors. On the
contrary, we have the hope that as your faith increases, our area of ministry will be greatly enlarged, 16 so
that we may preach the gospel to the regions beyond
you without boasting about what has already been
done in someone else's area of ministry. 17 So **let the
one who boasts, boast in the Lord.**[A] 18 For it is not
the one commending himself who is approved, but
the one the Lord commends.

PAUL AND THE FALSE APOSTLES

11 I wish you would put up with a little foolishness from me. Yes, do put up with me![B] 2 For I
am jealous for you with a godly jealousy, because I
have promised you in marriage to one husband — to
present a pure virgin to Christ. 3 But I fear that, as the
serpent deceived Eve by his cunning, your minds
may be seduced from a sincere and pure[C] devotion
to Christ. 4 For if a person comes and preaches another Jesus, whom we did not preach, or you receive
a different spirit, which you had not received, or a
different gospel, which you had not accepted, you
put up with it splendidly!
5 Now I consider myself in no way inferior to those
"super-apostles." 6 Even if I am untrained in public
speaking, I am certainly not untrained in knowledge.
Indeed, we have in every way made that clear to you
in everything. 7 Or did I commit a sin by humbling myself so that you might be exalted, because I preached
the gospel of God to you free of charge? 8 I robbed
other churches by taking pay from them to minister
to you. 9 When I was present with you and in need, I
did not burden anyone, since the brothers who came
from Macedonia supplied my needs. I have kept myself, and will keep myself, from burdening you in any
way. 10 As the truth of Christ is in me, this boasting of
mine will not be stopped[D] in the regions of Achaia.
11 Why? Because I don't love you? God knows I do!
12 But I will continue to do what I am doing, in order
to deny[E] an opportunity to those who want to be regarded as our equals in what they boast about. 13 For
such people are false apostles, deceitful workers,
disguising themselves as apostles of Christ. 14 And
no wonder! For Satan disguises himself as an angel
of light. 15 So it is no great surprise if his servants also
disguise themselves as servants of righteousness.
Their end will be according to their works.

PAUL'S SUFFERINGS FOR CHRIST

16 I repeat: Let no one consider me a fool. But if you
do, at least accept me as a fool so that I can also boast
a little. 17 What I am saying in this matter[F] of boasting, I don't speak as the Lord would, but as it were,
foolishly. 18 Since many boast according to the flesh,
I will also boast. 19 For you, being so wise, gladly put
up with fools! 20 In fact, you put up with it if someone
enslaves you, if someone exploits you, if someone
takes advantage of you, if someone is arrogant toward you, if someone slaps you in the face. 21 I say
this to our shame: We have been too weak for that!
But in whatever anyone dares to boast — I am talking foolishly — I also dare: 22 Are they Hebrews? So
am I. Are they Israelites? So am I. Are they the descendants of Abraham? So am I. 23 Are they servants of
Christ? I'm talking like a madman — I'm a better one:
with far more labors, many more imprisonments, far
worse beatings, many times near death.
24 Five times I received the forty lashes minus one
from the Jews. 25 Three times I was beaten with rods.
Once I received a stoning. Three times I was shipwrecked. I have spent a night and a day in the open sea.

[A] **10:17** Jr 9:24 [B] **11:1** Or *Yes, you are putting up with me* [C] **11:3** Other mss omit *and pure* [D] **11:10** Or *silenced* [E] **11:12** Lit *cut off* [F] **11:17** Or *business*, or *confidence*

From the theater at Corinth; a frieze depicting the battle between Greeks and Amazons.

[26] On frequent journeys, I faced dangers from rivers,
dangers from robbers, dangers from my own people,
dangers from Gentiles, dangers in the city, dangers in
the wilderness, dangers at sea, and dangers among
false brothers; [27] toil and hardship, many sleepless
nights, hunger and thirst, often without food, cold,
and without clothing. [28] Not to mention[A] other things,
there is the daily pressure on me: my concern for all
the churches. [29] Who is weak, and I am not weak? Who
is made to stumble, and I do not burn with indignation?
[30] If boasting is necessary, I will boast about my
weaknesses. [31] The God and Father of the Lord Jesus,
who is blessed forever, knows I am not lying. [32] In
Damascus, a ruler[B] under King Aretas guarded the
city of Damascus in order to arrest me. [33] So I was let
down in a basket through a window in the wall and
escaped from his hands.

SUFFICIENT GRACE

12 Boasting is necessary. It is not profitable, but
I will move on to visions and revelations of
the Lord. [2] I know a man in Christ who was caught
up to the third heaven fourteen years ago. Whether
he was in the body or out of the body, I don't know;
God knows. [3] I know that this man — whether in the
body or out of the body I don't know; God knows —
[4] was caught up into paradise and heard inexpressible words, which a human being is not allowed to
speak. [5] I will boast about this person, but not about
myself, except of my weaknesses.
[6] For if I want to boast, I wouldn't be a fool, because
I would be telling the truth. But I will spare you, so that
no one can credit me with something beyond what
he sees in me or hears from me, [7] especially because
of the extraordinary revelations. Therefore, so that I
would not exalt myself, a thorn in the flesh was given
to me, a messenger of Satan to torment me so that I
would not exalt myself. [8] Concerning this, I pleaded
with the Lord three times that it would leave me. [9] But
he said to me, "My grace is sufficient for you, for my
power is perfected in weakness."
Therefore, I will most gladly boast all the more
about my weaknesses, so that Christ's power may reside in me. [10] So I take pleasure in weaknesses, insults,
hardships, persecutions, and in difficulties, for the
sake of Christ. For when I am weak, then I am strong.

SIGNS OF AN APOSTLE

[11] I have been a fool; you forced it on me. You ought to
have commended me, since I am not in any way inferior to those "super-apostles," even though I am nothing. [12] The signs of an apostle were performed with
unfailing endurance among you, including signs and
wonders and miracles. [13] So in what way are you worse
off than the other churches, except that I personally
did not burden you? Forgive me for this wrong!

PAUL'S CONCERN FOR THE CORINTHIANS

[14] Look, I am ready to come to you this third time. I
will not burden you, since I am not seeking what is
yours, but you. For children ought not save up for

[A] **11:28** Lit *Apart from* [B] **11:32** Gk *ethnarches*; a leader of an ethnic community

In the first century, most writers used black ink, which was made from lamp black or ground charcoal. This ink was cheap and easy to make but not waterproof. Although someone could wash a document off and reuse it, writing could also be lost accidentally if the letter became wet. For the protection of the documents, people often kept valuable scrolls in waxed leather cases. Ancient writers also had a cheap source of pens. Most used a small reed cut about eight to ten inches long, much like our fountain pen today.

Ancients wrote on a variety of materials. For sending a quick note, they often wrote on shards of broken pots. Such notes were called ostraca. For quick notes or receipts to be given to another, people also commonly wrote on the back of an old document. For a temporary note, ancient writers often used wooden tablets, which were thin sheets of wood with a recessed middle. The recessed middle could be written on directly with ink or more commonly was filled with a thin layer of wax. The raised rim protected the wax when the tablets were stacked. The wax was easily smoothed and reused.

Two leaves from a set of hinged writing boards inscribed with astrological omens. Fragments of the original wax showing part of the cuneiform text still survive. Very few such boards, which once were plentiful, have been recovered. These were intended for Sargon's (721–705 BC) palace at Khorsabad.

Nevertheless, for dispatched letters during the time of Paul, the two major options for "paper" were parchment and papyrus. Parchment sheets were made from the hide of a calf, goat, or sheep. These sheets (if properly done) were tough but light and flexible. The sheets were sewn together to make a longer strip that was rolled up—what is today commonly called a scroll. Parchment was tough and long lasting, but it was probably more expensive and more difficult to write on than papyrus. Letter writers in Paul's day probably preferred papyrus.

Papyrus reeds grew in abundance along the banks of the Nile. Reeds were more than five feet tall. The reed is about as thick as a man's wrist. To make papyrus paper, the reeds were cut into sections and sliced lengthwise in thin, tape-like strips. These strips were laid side by side on a pattern board. Another layer of strips was placed on top of these at a right angle. The dried sheet was then smoothed and trimmed to a standard size.

Papyrus was not normally sold in individual sheets. Like parchment, sheets were pasted together to make a scroll. When a secretary finished a letter, he cut off the excess papyrus, to be saved for another patron. If the letter was longer than he anticipated, he could glue on additional sheets. Rolls of either parchment or papyrus could be made any length but a roll of twenty sheets (ca twelve feet) seems to have been the standard in the time of Paul. Theoretically, scrolls could be continuously lengthened, but ancients had discovered that scrolls of more than thirty feet became too cumbersome to handle.

Today, paper and pen are so inexpensive as to be negligible. In antiquity, this was not so. The entire process of writing his letter to the Romans probably cost Paul (in today's dollars) more than $2,000.[1] This did not include the cost of paying someone to carry it to Rome. About two-thirds of the cost was materials. The remaining one-third was labor, the expense of a secretary.

Many students of the New Testament are surprised to learn Paul used a secretary. The evidence in his letters is clear. In one letter, we even know that secretary's name: Tertius (Rm 16:22). Ancients rarely wrote in the letter, "I am using a secretary," because the practice was expected. Etiquette, however, required the writer to finish the letter's final comments in his own handwriting, much as we sign a letter. In an original ancient letter, you can see the shift in handwriting at the end. Writers also commonly made a comment, such as "I am writing this in my own hand."[2] Paul often made such a comment (see 1Co 16:21; Gl 6:11; Col 4:18; 2Th 3:17). ✣

---

[1] I outline how I arrived at this figure in E. Randolph Richards, *Paul and First-Century Letter Writing* (Downers Grove, IL: InterVarsity, 2004), 165–69. [2] For a full explanation with examples, see E. Randolph Richards, *The Secretary in the Letters of Paul* (Tübingen: Mohr Siebeck, 1991), 68–90.

From the Roman Era, stili used to write on wax-surfaced wooden writing tablets.

Scribes commonly used erasers made of sandstone. The erasers shown are from Tell Defenneh (Tahpanhes, Egypt).

their parents, but parents for their children. 15 I will
most gladly spend and be spent for you.[A] If I love you
more, am I to be loved less? 16 Now granted, I did not
burden you; yet sly as I am, I took you in by deceit!
17 Did I take advantage of you by any of those I sent
you? 18 I urged Titus to go, and I sent the brother with
him. Titus didn't take advantage of you, did he? Didn't
we walk in the same spirit and in the same footsteps?

19 Have you been thinking all along that we were
defending ourselves to you? No, in the sight of God we
are speaking in Christ, and everything, dear friends,
is for building you up. 20 For I fear that perhaps when
I come I will not find you to be what I want, and you
may not find me to be what you want. Perhaps there
will be quarreling, jealousy, angry outbursts, selfish
ambitions, slander, gossip, arrogance, and disorder.
21 I fear that when I come my God will again[B] humiliate me in your presence, and I will grieve for many
who sinned before and have not repented of the moral impurity, sexual immorality, and sensuality they
practiced.

FINAL WARNINGS AND EXHORTATIONS

13 This is the third time I am coming to you. **Every
matter must be established by the testimo-
ny of two or three witnesses.**[C] 2 I gave a warning
when I was present the second time, and now I give
a warning while I am absent to those who sinned
before and to all the rest: If I come again, I will not be
lenient, 3 since you seek proof of Christ speaking in
me. He is not weak in dealing with you, but powerful
among you. 4 For he was crucified in weakness, but
he lives by the power of God. For we also are weak
in him, but in dealing with you we will live with him
by God's power.

5 Test yourselves to see if you are in the faith. Examine yourselves. Or do you yourselves not recognize
that Jesus Christ is in you? — unless you fail the test.[D]
6 And I hope you will recognize that we ourselves do
not fail the test. 7 But we pray to God that you do nothing wrong — not that we may appear to pass the test,
but that you may do what is right, even though we
may appear to fail. 8 For we can't do anything against
the truth, but only for the truth. 9 We rejoice when
we are weak and you are strong. We also pray that
you become fully mature.[E] 10 This is why I am writing
these things while absent, so that when I am there I
may not have to deal harshly with you, in keeping
with the authority the Lord gave me for building up
and not for tearing down.

11 Finally, brothers and sisters, rejoice.[F] Become
mature, be encouraged,[G] be of the same mind, be at
peace, and the God of love and peace will be with you.
12 Greet one another with a holy kiss. All the saints
send you greetings.

13 The grace of the Lord Jesus Christ, and the love
of God, and the fellowship of the Holy Spirit be with
you all.[H]

[A] **12:15** Lit *for your souls*, or *for your lives* [B] **12:21** Or *come again my God will* [C] **13:1** Dt 17:6; 19:15 [D] **13:5** Or *you are disqualified*, or *you are counterfeit* [E] **13:9** Or *become complete*, or *be restored* [F] **13:11** Or *farewell* [G] **13:11** Or *listen to my appeal* [H] **13:12–13** Some translations divide these two vv. into three vv. so that v. 13 begins with *All the saints . . .* and v. 14 begins with *The grace of . . .*

GALATIANS

Library in Alexandria, Egypt. Shown are the niches where papyrus scrolls were kept. Dates to about AD 300.

INTRODUCTION TO

GALATIANS

Circumstances of Writing

The author's name is stated as Paul, and he claims to be "an apostle" of Christ (Gl 1:1). The autobiographical information in the letter is consistent with what is known about the apostle Paul from Acts and his other letters. Theologically, everything in Galatians agrees with Paul's views elsewhere, notably in Romans.

It is not certain where the Galatian churches were located or when Paul wrote Galatians. The reason is that during the New Testament era, the term *Galatians* was used both ethnically and politically. If *Galatians* is understood ethnically, the founding of the Galatian churches is only implied in the New Testament. On Paul's second missionary journey, he "went through the region of Phrygia and Galatia" (Ac 16:6) in north-central Asia Minor.

Understood politically, *Galatians* can refer to those living in the southern part of the Roman province of Galatia. That region included the cities of Pisidian Antioch, Iconium, Lystra, and Derbe, where Paul worked to plant churches, as recorded in Acts 13:14–14:23.

The view that Galatians was written to the area where the ethnic Galatians lived is called the North Galatian theory. The possible dates of writing related to this understanding range from AD 52 or 53 (if shortly after the second missionary journey) to AD 56 (if written about the same time as Romans, to which it is similar theologically).

The view that Galatians was sent to churches in the southern portion of the Roman province of Galatia is the South Galatian theory. Some holding this view date Galatians in the early 50s, but others as early as AD 48 or 49, before the Jerusalem Council, which is usually dated to about AD 49.

The key problem addressed in Galatians is that "the works of the law" of Moses (Gl 2:16–17; 3:2; cf. 5:4), notably circumcision (5:2; 6:12–13), were added by some teachers to what was required in being justified before God. This is the same issue that Acts records as the reason why the Jerusalem Council met (Ac 15:1,5), supporting the idea that the existing problem in the Galatian churches was part of the reason for the Jerusalem Council.

If Galatians was written after the Jerusalem Council, it is inconceivable that Paul would not have cited the conclusions of the council, which supported his works-free view of the gospel. This strongly implies that the Jerusalem Council had not yet occurred when Paul wrote Galatians.

Contribution to the Bible

There is much about the life and movements of the apostle Paul that is only known—or filled in significantly—from Galatians 1:13–2:14 (and the personal glimpse in 4:13–14). Among these factors are Paul's sojourn in "Arabia" (1:17) and descriptions of two trips to Jerusalem (1:18–19; 2:1–10). Paul described a confrontation with Peter (2:11–14) that is mentioned nowhere else in the New Testament.

In the middle third of Galatians, certain aspects of the gospel's Old Testament background are explained in unique ways. Notable are (1) the curse related to Jesus being crucified, as cited from Deuteronomy 21:23 (Gl 3:13); (2) Jesus's fulfilling the prophecy of the singular physical "seed" of Abraham (3:16; see Gn 22:18); (3) the roles of the law as prison (Gl 3:22–23) and guardian (3:24–25) until Christ; and (4) the extended allegory of the slave and free sons of Abraham (4:21–31).

Galatians tells us much about the ministry of the Holy Spirit in relation to the Christian life. After the Spirit's role in the ministry of adoption (4:5–6), believers are commanded to "walk by the Spirit" (5:16), be "led by the Spirit" (5:18) and "keep in step with the Spirit" (5:25), as well as "[sow] to the Spirit" and "reap" the related eternal harvest (6:8). The moment-by-moment outcome of that kind of sensitivity to the ministry of the Holy Spirit is what is meant by "the fruit of the Spirit" (5:22–23).

Structure

The book of Galatians follows the typical pattern for a first-century letter but lacks the element of thanksgiving: salutation (1:1–5), the main body (1:6–6:15), and a farewell (6:16–18). Contrasting concepts are prominent in the letter: divine revelation versus human insight, grace versus law, justification versus condemnation, Jerusalem versus Mount Sinai, sonship versus slavery, the fruit of the Spirit versus the works of the flesh, and liberty versus bondage.

GREETING

1 Paul, an apostle — not from men or by man, but
by Jesus Christ and God the Father who raised
him from the dead — 2 and all the brothers who are
with me:
To the churches of Galatia.
3 Grace to you and peace from God the Father and
our Lord[A] Jesus Christ, 4 who gave himself for our sins
to rescue us from this present evil age, according to
the will of our God and Father. 5 To him be the glory
forever and ever. Amen.

NO OTHER GOSPEL

6 I am amazed that you are so quickly turning away
from him who called you by the grace of Christ and
are turning to a different gospel — 7 not that there is
another gospel, but there are some who are troubling
you and want to distort the gospel of Christ. 8 But even
if we or an angel from heaven should preach to you a
gospel contrary to what we have preached to you, a
curse be on him![B] 9 As we have said before, I now say
again: If anyone is preaching to you a gospel contrary
to what you received, a curse be on him!
10 For am I now trying to persuade people,[C] or God?
Or am I striving to please people? If I were still trying
to please people, I would not be a servant of Christ.

THE ORIGIN OF PAUL'S GOSPEL

11 For I want you to know, brothers and sisters, that the
gospel preached by me is not of human origin. 12 For I
did not receive it from a human source and I was not
taught it, but it came by a revelation of Jesus Christ.
13 For you have heard about my former way of life
in Judaism: I intensely persecuted God's church and
tried to destroy it. 14 I advanced in Judaism beyond
many contemporaries among my people, because I
was extremely zealous for the traditions of my ancestors. 15 But when God, who from my mother's womb
set me apart and called me by his grace, was pleased
16 to reveal his Son in me, so that I could preach him
among the Gentiles, I did not immediately consult
with anyone.[D] 17 I did not go up to Jerusalem to those
who had become apostles before me; instead I went
to Arabia and came back to Damascus.
18 Then after three years I did go up to Jerusalem
to get to know Cephas,[E] and I stayed with him fifteen
days. 19 But I didn't see any of the other apostles except
James, the Lord's brother. 20 I declare in the sight of
God: I am not lying in what I write to you.
21 Afterward, I went to the regions of Syria and Cilicia. 22 I remained personally unknown to the Judean
churches that are in Christ. 23 They simply kept hearing, "He who formerly persecuted us now preaches
the faith he once tried to destroy." 24 And they glorified God because of me.[F]

From Ankara, large two-handled terra-cotta vase. Dating to the Roman Era, the vase has a Celtic style.

PAUL DEFENDS HIS GOSPEL AT JERUSALEM

2 Then after fourteen years I went up again to Jerusalem with Barnabas, taking Titus along also.
2 I went up according to a revelation and presented
to them the gospel I preach among the Gentiles, but
privately to those recognized as leaders. I wanted to
be sure I was not running, and had not been running,
in vain. 3 But not even Titus, who was with me, was
compelled to be circumcised, even though he was a
Greek. 4 This matter arose because some false brothers had infiltrated our ranks to spy on the freedom
we have in Christ Jesus in order to enslave us. 5 But we
did not give up and submit to these people for even
a moment, so that the truth of the gospel would be
preserved for you.
6 Now from those recognized as important (what
they[G] once were makes no difference to me; God does
not show favoritism[H]) — they added nothing to me.
7 On the contrary, they saw that I had been entrusted

[A] **1:3** Other mss read *God our Father and the Lord* [B] **1:8** Or *you, let him be condemned*, or *you, let him be condemned to hell*; Gk *anathema* [C] **1:10** Or *win the approval of people* [D] **1:16** Lit *flesh and blood* [E] **1:18** Other mss read *Peter* [F] **1:24** Or *in me* [G] **2:6** Lit *the recognized ones* [H] **2:6** Or *God is not a respecter of persons*; lit *God does not receive the face of man*

with the gospel for the uncircumcised, just as Peter was for the circumcised, 8 since the one at work in Peter for an apostleship to the circumcised was also at work in me for the Gentiles. 9 When James, Cephas,[A] and John — those recognized as pillars — acknowledged the grace that had been given to me, they gave the right hand of fellowship to me and Barnabas, agreeing that we should go to the Gentiles and they to the circumcised. 10 They asked only that we would remember the poor, which I had made every effort to do.

FREEDOM FROM THE LAW

11 But when Cephas[A] came to Antioch, I opposed him to his face because he stood condemned.[B] 12 For he regularly ate with the Gentiles before certain men came from James. However, when they came, he withdrew and separated himself, because he feared those from the circumcision party. 13 Then the rest of the Jews joined his hypocrisy, so that even Barnabas was led astray by their hypocrisy. 14 But when I saw that they were deviating from the truth of the gospel, I told Cephas[A] in front of everyone, "If you, who are a Jew, live like a Gentile and not like a Jew, how can you compel Gentiles to live like Jews?"[C]

15 We are Jews by birth and not "Gentile sinners," 16 and yet because we know that a person is not justified by the works of the law but by faith in Jesus Christ,[D] even we ourselves have believed in Christ Jesus. This was so that we might be justified by faith in Christ[E] and not by the works of the law, because by the works of the law no human being will[F] be justified. 17 But if we ourselves are also found to be "sinners" while seeking to be justified by Christ, is Christ then a promoter[G] of sin? Absolutely not! 18 If I rebuild those things that I tore down, I show myself to be a lawbreaker. 19 For through the law I died to the law, so that I might live for God. 20 I have been crucified with Christ, and I no longer live, but Christ lives in me. The life I now live in the body,[H] I live by faith in the Son of God, who loved me and gave himself for me. 21 I do not set aside the grace of God, for if righteousness comes through the law, then Christ died for nothing.

JUSTIFICATION THROUGH FAITH

3 You foolish Galatians! Who has cast a spell on you,[I] before whose eyes Jesus Christ was publicly portrayed[J] as crucified? 2 I only want to learn this from you: Did you receive the Spirit by the works of the law or by believing what you heard?[K] 3 Are you so foolish? After beginning by the Spirit, are you now finishing by the flesh? 4 Did you experience[L] so much for nothing — if in fact it was for nothing? 5 So then, does God give you the Spirit and work miracles among you by your doing the works of the law? Or is it by believing what you heard — 6 just like Abraham who **believed God, and it was credited to him for righteousness?**[M]

7 You know, then, that those who have faith, these are Abraham's sons. 8 Now the Scripture saw in advance that God would justify the Gentiles by faith and proclaimed the gospel ahead of time to Abraham, saying, **All the nations**[N] **will be blessed through you.**[O] 9 Consequently, those who have faith are blessed with Abraham, who had faith.[P]

LAW AND PROMISE

10 For all who rely on the works of the law are under a curse, because it is written, **Everyone who does not do everything written in the book of the law is cursed.**[Q] 11 Now it is clear that no one is justified before God by the law, because **the righteous will live by faith.**[R] 12 But the law is not based on faith; instead, **the one who does these things will live by them.**[S]

At Iconium, seat of judgment, possibly from a Jewish synagogue.

[A] **2:9,11,14** Other mss read *Peter* [B] **2:11** Or *he was in the wrong* [C] **2:14** Some translations continue the quotation through v. 16 or v. 21. [D] **2:16** Or *by the faithfulness of Jesus Christ* [E] **2:16** Or *by the faithfulness of Christ* [F] **2:16** Lit *law all flesh will not* [G] **2:17** Or *servant* [H] **2:20** Lit *flesh* [I] **3:1** Other mss add *not to obey the truth* [J] **3:1** Other mss add *among you* [K] **3:2** Lit *hearing with faith*, also in v. 5 [L] **3:4** Or *suffer* [M] **3:6** Gn 15:6 [N] **3:8** Or *Gentiles* [O] **3:8** Gn 12:3; 18:18 [P] **3:9** Or *with believing Abraham* [Q] **3:10** Dt 27:26 [R] **3:11** Hab 2:4 [S] **3:12** Lv 18:5

The Galatians' ancestral roots trace back to the better-known Celts of France and England. Originally called Keltoi or Galatai by the Greeks or Gauls by the Romans, a group of Celts migrated from central Europe southward and entered Greece and Macedonia around 280 BC. Galatia as a region came into being in 278 BC when twenty thousand Celts (three tribes: the Trocmi, the Tectosages, and the Tolistobogii) crossed into Asia Minor and took over the region that is currently centered at modern Ankara (Turkey). From the Greek word *Galatai*, the region itself came to be known as Galatia.[1]

Being powerful warriors, the Gauls came across the Strait of Bosporus from Europe at the invitation of Nicomedes, the king of Bithynia, around 278 BC, to help Nicomedes gain a victory in what had been a long-term civil war in Bithynia (a geographical region located on the north-central coast of Asia Minor). Once that task had been accomplished, the Gauls, who had brought their families with them, settled mainly into the rural areas, reaching as far south as the territories of Phrygia and Pamphylia. They continued to be a distinct ethnic group, identifiably different from the tribes of Asia Minor.[2]

Originally brought to Asia Minor to be mercenaries, the Gauls became instead a "loose cannon," fighting on their own and for their own interests as they began raiding western and north-central Asia Minor. The first check on the Gaulish ambitions came in 275 BC, when the Seleucid King Antiochus I defeated the Gauls and contained them.

By the time of their defeat by Antiochus, the Gauls controlled the northern part of the central plateau of Asia Minor. They and their descendants existed in part by continuing to raid neighboring tribal regions in western and north-central Asia Minor for many years. Finally, in 232 BC, Attalus I, king of Pergamum,

Coin of King Mithridates VI from Pontus (120–63 BC). The consummate enemy of Rome, Mithridates expanded his rule northwest into Bithynia and southeast into Cappadocia.

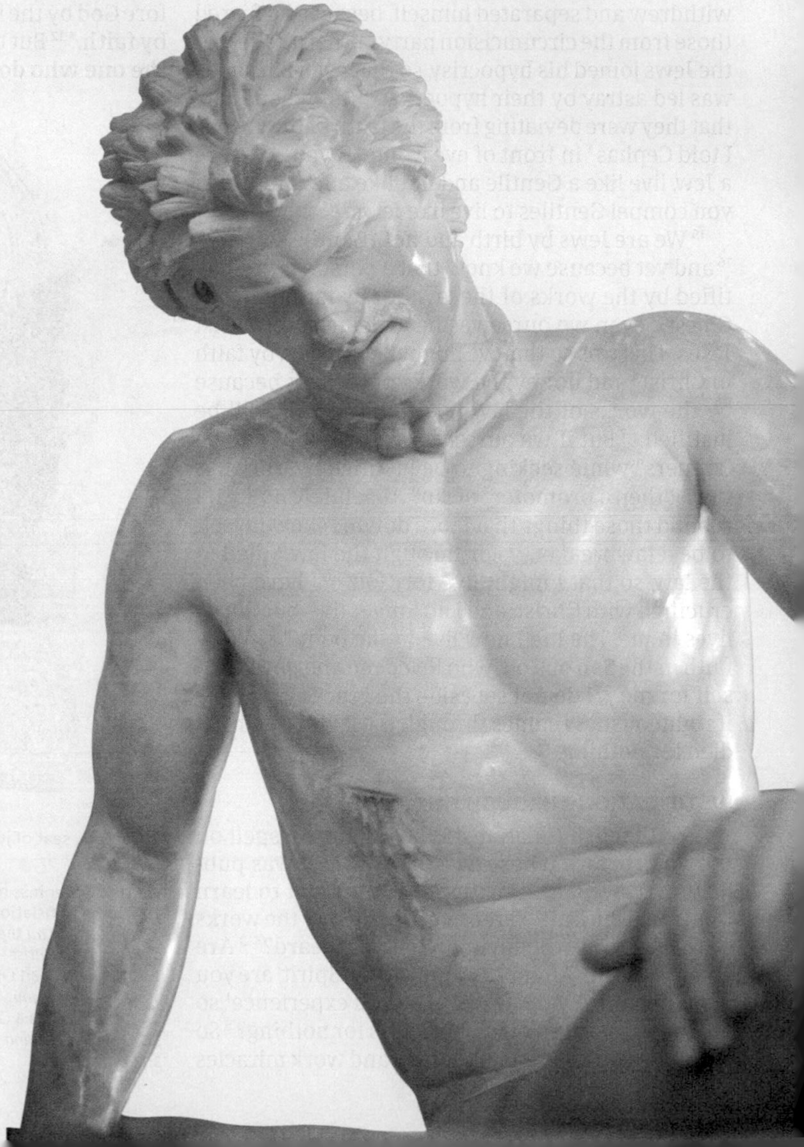

Roman copy of the Greek statue, "The Dying Gaul." Attalus I of Pergamum commissioned the work (230–220 BC) as a recognition of his victory over the Galatians. True to form, the Gallic soldier typically had this style hair, a moustache, and went into battle naked, carrying only a weapon and shield.

The region of Galatia.

was able to defeat the Gauls and restrict the Galatians within the boundaries of their territory. "Their territory was over 200 miles from southwest to northeast, bounded by Lyconia and Pamphylia to the south, by Bithynia, Paphlagonia and Pontus to the north, by Cappadocia to the east and by Phrygia to the west."[3]

Even in defeat, the Galatians retained their independence, keeping their language and Celtic traditions. Ancyra served as their governmental capital. Over the next two centuries, they remained actively involved in the power struggles of the region, finally allying themselves with the Romans against Mithridates VI of Pontus (95–63 BC). In 64 BC, General Pompey rewarded the Galatians for their support by making Galatia a client kingdom of Rome and granting them additional territories.

The last king to rule the entirety of the occupied region of central and northern Asia Minor alone was Amyntas (36–25 BC). At his death, the Romans assumed greater control of the region, reorganizing it into a Roman province. The Romans officially named the region Galatia and expanded the region to the south and east and included the territories of Pisidia, Phrygia, and Pamphylia. ✣

---

[1] Colin J. Hemer, "Gauls" in *ISBE* (1982), 2:415; G. Walter Hansen, "Galatians, Letter to the" in *Dictionary of Paul and His Letters* (*DPL*), ed. Gerald F. Hawthorne and Ralph P. Martin (Downers Grove, IL: InterVarsity, 1993), 323–24; Stephen Mitchell, "Galatia" in *ABD*, 2:870. [2] William M. Ramsay and Colin J. Hemer, "Galatia" in *ISBE*, 2:378. [3] Hansen, "Galatians," 324.

From Ephesus, stone slab with nine inscribed depressions, likely a board game. Roman; dated first to third centuries AD.

13 Christ redeemed us from the curse of the law by becoming a curse for us, because it is written, **Cursed is everyone who is hung on a tree.**[A] 14 The purpose was that the blessing of Abraham would come to the Gentiles by Christ Jesus, so that we could receive the promised Spirit through faith.

15 Brothers and sisters, I'm using a human illustration. No one sets aside or makes additions to a validated human will.[B] 16 Now the promises were spoken to Abraham and to his seed. He does not say "and to seeds," as though referring to many, but referring to one, **and to your seed**,[C] who is Christ. 17 My point is this: The law, which came 430 years later, does not invalidate a covenant previously established by God[D] and thus cancel the promise. 18 For if the inheritance is based on the law, it is no longer based on the promise; but God has graciously given it to Abraham through the promise.

Painted wooden toy horse with wheels; dated to the Roman period.

THE PURPOSE OF THE LAW

19 Why, then, was the law given? It was added for the sake of transgressions[E] until the Seed to whom the promise was made would come. The law was put into effect through angels by means of a mediator. 20 Now a mediator is not just for one person alone, but God is one. 21 Is the law therefore contrary to God's promises? Absolutely not! For if the law had been granted with the ability to give life, then righteousness would certainly be on the basis of the law. 22 But the Scripture imprisoned everything under sin's power,[F] so that the promise might be given on the basis of faith in Jesus Christ to those who believe. 23 Before this faith came, we were confined under the law, imprisoned until the coming faith was revealed. 24 The law, then, was our guardian until Christ, so that we could be justified by faith. 25 But since that faith has come, we are no longer under a guardian, 26 for through faith you are all sons of God in Christ Jesus.

SONS AND HEIRS

27 For those of you who were baptized into Christ have been clothed with Christ. 28 There is no Jew or Greek, slave or free, male and female; since you are all one in Christ Jesus. 29 And if you belong to Christ, then you are Abraham's seed, heirs according to the promise.

4 1 Now I say that as long as the heir is a child, he differs in no way from a slave, though he is the owner of everything. 2 Instead, he is under guardians and trustees until the time set by his father. 3 In the same way we also, when we were children, were in

[A] **3:13** Dt 21:23 [B] **3:15** Or *a human covenant that has been ratified* [C] **3:16** Gn 12:7; 13:15; 17:8; 24:7 [D] **3:17** Other mss add *in Christ* [E] **3:19** Or *because of transgressions* [F] **3:22** Lit *under sin*

A child's terra-cotta rattle shaped like a pig with a child crouching
on its back; dated to the first century BC.

slavery under the elements[A] of the world. 4 When the
time came to completion, God sent his Son, born of a
woman, born under the law, 5 to redeem those under
the law, so that we might receive adoption as sons.
6 And because you are sons, God sent the Spirit of his
Son into our[B] hearts, crying, "*Abba*,[C] Father!" 7 So you
are no longer a slave but a son, and if a son, then God
has made you an heir.

PAUL'S CONCERN FOR THE GALATIANS

8 But in the past, since you didn't know God, you were
enslaved to things[D] that by nature are not gods. 9 But
now, since you know God, or rather have become
known by God, how can you turn back again to the
weak and worthless elements? Do you want to be enslaved to them all over again? 10 You are observing special days, months, seasons, and years. 11 I am fearful for
you, that perhaps my labor for you has been wasted.

12 I beg you, brothers and sisters: Become as I
am, for I also have become as you are. You have not
wronged me; 13 you know[E] that previously I preached
the gospel to you because of a weakness of the flesh.
14 You did not despise or reject me though my physical
condition was a trial for you.[F] On the contrary, you received me as an angel of God, as Christ Jesus himself.

15 Where, then, is your blessing? For I testify to you
that, if possible, you would have torn out your eyes
and given them to me. 16 So then, have I become your
enemy because I told you the truth? 17 They court you
eagerly, but not for good. They want to exclude you
from me, so that you would pursue them. 18 But it is
always good to be pursued[G] in a good manner — and
not just when I am with you. 19 My children, I am again
suffering labor pains for you until Christ is formed
in you. 20 I would like to be with you right now and
change my tone of voice, because I don't know what
to do about you.

SARAH AND HAGAR: TWO COVENANTS

21 Tell me, you who want to be under the law, don't
you hear the law? 22 For it is written that Abraham
had two sons, one by a slave and the other by a free
woman. 23 But the one by the slave was born as a result of the flesh, while the one by the free woman was
born through promise. 24 These things are being taken
figuratively, for the women represent two covenants.
One is from Mount Sinai and bears children into slavery — this is Hagar. 25 Now Hagar represents Mount
Sinai in Arabia and corresponds to the present Jerusalem, for she is in slavery with her children. 26 But
the Jerusalem above is free, and she is our mother.
27 For it is written,

Rejoice, childless woman,
unable to give birth.
Burst into song and shout,
you who are not in labor,
for the children of the desolate woman will
be many,
more numerous than those
of the woman who has a husband.[H]

28 Now you too, brothers and sisters, like Isaac, are
children of promise. 29 But just as then the child born
as a result of the flesh persecuted the one born as a
result of the Spirit, so also now. 30 But what does the
Scripture say? **"Drive out the slave and her son, for**
the son of the slave will never be a coheir with
the son of the free woman."[I] 31 Therefore, brothers
and sisters, we are not children of a slave but of the
free woman.

FREEDOM OF THE CHRISTIAN

5 For freedom, Christ set us free. Stand firm, then,
and don't submit again to a yoke of slavery. 2 Take
note! I, Paul, am telling you that if you get yourselves
circumcised, Christ will not benefit you at all. 3 Again
I testify to every man who gets himself circumcised
that he is obligated to do the entire law. 4 You who are
trying to be justified by the law are alienated from
Christ; you have fallen from grace. 5 For we eagerly
await through the Spirit, by faith, the hope of righteousness. 6 For in Christ Jesus neither circumcision
nor uncircumcision accomplishes anything; what
matters is faith working through love.

[A] **4:3** Or *spirits*, or *principles* [B] **4:6** Other mss read *your*
[C] **4:6** Aramaic for *father* [D] **4:8** Or *beings* [E] **4:12–13** Or 12 *Become like I am, because I — inasmuch as you are brothers and sisters — am not requesting anything of you. You wronged me.* 13 *You know*
[F] **4:14** Other mss read *me* [G] **4:18** Lit *zealously courted* [H] **4:27** Is 54:1
[I] **4:30** Gn 21:10

To Live Like a Jew

by Dale "Geno" Robinson

First-century Jews enjoyed a favored status in the Roman Empire. Julius Caesar granted it to them in 48 BC when the Jewish king, John Hyrcanus, sent reinforcements to assist Caesar in his Egyptian military campaign. As a reward, Caesar exempted Jews from imperial requirements contrary to their faith.[1] This special status proved to be a constant irritant to their Gentile neighbors. It allowed the Jews to refrain from participating in Greco-Roman civic responsibilities and ceremonies.

Jewish monotheism repelled and attracted disillusioned idolaters. Circumcision offended the widely held ideal view of the human body. Jewish lifestyles went against common customs. Yet Jews proudly held to those practices as markers of their faith. The Gentiles considered Jewish practices an affront to society; Jews saw them as obedience to God's commands. The most prominent of these practices were circumcision of male children, the Sabbath day of rest, and food restrictions.

This Torah scroll dates from the sixteenth century AD. It was used in the Spanish Jewish synagogue in the city of Zafed (upper Galilee). Part of the scroll was damaged in an earthquake in 1837. The scroll was then placed in a genizah, a repository for old, damaged, worn, or defective scrolls. The scroll is mounted on wooden rollers, that, though not originally belonging to this scroll, are of approximately the same age.

CIRCUMCISION

Ancient Egypt, Ethiopia, Edom, and Moab circumcised their male children as a rite of passage to manhood. The Jews practiced circumcision as a mark of their covenant with God. Hebrew boys were circumcised eight days after birth as a sign of their entrance into that covenant (Gn 17:9–14). It was the universally required element of Jewish faith, practice, and cultural distinctiveness. It was the sign of their uniqueness.

After 334 BC, the Jews' Greek conquerors attempted to impose Hellenistic cultural values and practices on them. Some Jews resorted to a painful and often unsuccessful plastic surgery called epispasm to "reverse" their circumcision.[2] This was an affront to a pious practicing Jew. Jewish ethics and morality attracted many thoughtful Gentiles. Though many Gentiles were God-fearing, few converted. The strict life-rules were difficult to accept. Circumcision was a barrier to male converts. Jews, however, never abandoned it.

THE SABBATH

Only the Jews observed a weekly day of rest. God commanded them (Ex 20:8–11) to honor the Sabbath or seventh day as a special and holy day with rest and worship. From sunset on Friday to the appearance of three stars on Saturday night, the Jews honored *Shabbat*. Their Gentile neighbors, not seeing its value, criticized them. They saw Jewish Sabbath observance as a sign of slothfulness.

Sabbath was a joyful celebration filled with rest, feasts, and joy. It was also dangerous. During wartime, Jews often refused to fight on the Sabbath to their detriment. When the Romans besieged Jerusalem in 63 BC, the Jews continued temple worship and Sabbath observance. The Romans capitalized on this perceived "weakness" and used siege machines on the Sabbath. Jerusalem fell soon afterward.[3]

FOOD LAWS

The Jews were also unique because of their diet. God had declared some foods clean and others unclean for them. Thus Jews found ways to observe their food restrictions and separate themselves from "unclean" Gentiles. If a Jewish businessman ate with a Gentile friend, he brought his own food. Most Gentiles saw these food rules as disruptive to their concept of a unified culture and state. The Jews saw "keeping kosher" as a means of cultural unity, both the source and occasion of purity before God.

FAITH IN JESUS, NOT WORKS OF THE LAW

Sadly, many Jews paid so much attention to these outward signs of their religion that they believed such practices commended them to God. Moreover, some insisted that Gentiles who believed in Jesus as the Messiah also had to keep these "works of the law" to truly be part of the people of God. But Paul would have none of this. The only way to be justified before God, receive the Spirit, and be true children of Abraham is through faith in Jesus Christ (Gl 3:1–29). ✣

Found at Timrat, a village just west of Nazareth, a stone carved with the Hebrew word "Sabbath." Measuring almost eight by twenty-four inches, the carving indicated to Jews the farthest limit they could travel from their village on the Sabbath. This is the only Sabbath boundary marker ever discovered written in Hebrew. It is located just under a mile between Tel Shimron and Mahalul, two Jewish villages from the Roman Era.

[1] Eduard Lohse, *The New Testament Environment*, trans. John E. Steely (Nashville: Abingdon, 1976), 36. [2] Joel B. Green and Lee Martin McDonald, eds., *The World of the New Testament: Cultural, Social, and Historical Contexts* (Grand Rapids: Baker Academic, 2013), 313; Robert G. Hall, "Epispasm: Circumcision in Reverse," *BRev* (1992): 52–57. [3] Josephus, *Jewish War* 1.7.3–4.

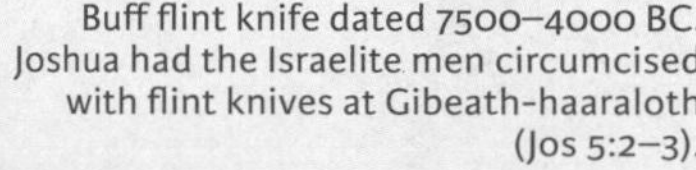

Buff flint knife dated 7500–4000 BC. Joshua had the Israelite men circumcised with flint knives at Gibeath-haaraloth (Jos 5:2–3).

Roman theater in Merida, Spain. The three sections of seating were designed to distinguish social class. The lowest section–the *ima cavea*–has twenty-two rows of seating and was reserved for wealthy families. The *media* and *summa cavea*, the middle and top sections, provided seating for poor people and slaves.

7 You were running well. Who prevented you from
being persuaded regarding the truth?[A] 8 This persua-
sion does not come from the one who calls you. 9 A
little leaven[B] leavens the whole batch of dough. 10 I
myself am persuaded in the Lord you will not accept
any other view. But whoever it is that is confusing you
will pay the penalty. 11 Now brothers and sisters, if I
still preach circumcision, why am I still persecuted?
In that case the offense of the cross has been abolished. 12 I wish those who are disturbing you might
also let themselves be mutilated!
13 For you were called to be free, brothers and sisters; only don't use this freedom as an opportunity[C]
for the flesh, but serve one another through love.
14 For the whole law is fulfilled in one statement: **Love
your neighbor as yourself.**[D] 15 But if you bite and
devour one another, watch out, or you will be consumed by one another.

THE SPIRIT VERSUS THE FLESH

16 I say, then, walk by the Spirit and you will certainly
not carry out the desire of the flesh. 17 For the flesh
desires what is against the Spirit, and the Spirit desires what is against the flesh; these are opposed to
each other, so that you don't do what you want. 18 But
if you are led by the Spirit, you are not under the law.
19 Now the works of the flesh are obvious:[E] sexual
immorality, moral impurity, promiscuity, 20 idolatry,
sorcery, hatreds, strife, jealousy, outbursts of anger,

[A] **5:7** Or *obeying the truth* [B] **5:9** Or *yeast* [C] **5:13** Lit *a pretext*; a military term for abuse of position [D] **5:14** Lv 19:18 [E] **5:19** Other mss add *adultery,*

selfish ambitions, dissensions, factions, 21 envy,[A]
drunkenness, carousing, and anything similar. I am
warning you about these things — as I warned you
before — that those who practice such things will
not inherit the kingdom of God.
22 But the fruit of the Spirit is love, joy, peace, patience, kindness, goodness, faithfulness, 23 gentleness,
and self-control. The law is not against such things.[B]
24 Now those who belong to Christ Jesus have crucified the flesh with its passions and desires. 25 If we
live by the Spirit, let us also keep in step with the
Spirit. 26 Let us not become conceited, provoking one
another, envying one another.

CARRY ONE ANOTHER'S BURDENS

6 Brothers and sisters, if someone is overtaken in
any wrongdoing, you who are spiritual, restore
such a person with a gentle spirit,[C] watching out for
yourselves so that you also won't be tempted. 2 Carry
one another's burdens; in this way you will fulfill the
law of Christ. 3 For if anyone considers himself to be
something when he is nothing, he deceives himself.
4 Let each person examine his own work, and then
he can take pride in himself alone, and not compare
himself with someone else. 5 For each person will
have to carry his own load.
6 Let the one who is taught the word share all his
good things with the teacher. 7 Don't be deceived: God
is not mocked. For whatever a person sows he will
also reap, 8 because the one who sows to his flesh will
reap destruction from the flesh, but the one who sows
to the Spirit will reap eternal life from the Spirit. 9 Let
us not get tired of doing good, for we will reap at the
proper time if we don't give up. 10 Therefore, as we
have opportunity, let us work for the good of all, especially for those who belong to the household of faith.

CONCLUDING EXHORTATION

11 Look at what large letters I use as I write to you in
my own handwriting. 12 Those who want to make a
good impression in the flesh are the ones who would
compel you to be circumcised — but only to avoid
being persecuted for the cross of Christ. 13 For even
the circumcised don't keep the law themselves, and
yet they want you to be circumcised in order to boast
about your flesh. 14 But as for me, I will never boast
about anything except the cross of our Lord Jesus
Christ. The world has been crucified to me through
the cross, and I to the world. 15 For[D] both circumcision
and uncircumcision mean nothing; what matters
instead is a new creation. 16 May peace come to all
those who follow this standard, and mercy even to
the Israel of God![E]
17 From now on, let no one cause me trouble, because I bear on my body the marks of Jesus. 18 Brothers and sisters, the grace of our Lord Jesus Christ be
with your spirit. Amen.

Rome's Emperor Claudius (reigned AD 41–54) ruled that sick slaves were to be set free. This bust was originally part of a life-sized bronze statue of the emperor.

[A] **5:21** Other mss add *murders,* [B] **5:23** Or *Against such things there is no law* [C] **6:1** Or *with the Spirit of gentleness* [D] **6:15** Other mss add *in Christ Jesus* [E] **6:16** Or *And for those who follow this standard, may peace and mercy be upon them, even upon the Israel of God,* or *And as many who will follow this standard, peace be upon them and mercy even upon the Israel of God.*

From Greece, a funerary monument relief depicts the members of the family that constructed the monument. According to the inscriptions, this was a family of freed slaves. Also depicted are the family's slaves. The difference in the figures' size as well as the depth and detail of the carving contrasts the social status of those who were free and those who were slaves. Dated about 50 BC.

[illegible] Emperor Claudius's reign (AD 41–54) ruled that sick slaves were to be set free. This bust was originally part of a life-sized bronze statue of the emperor.

selfish ambitions, dissensions, factions, 21 envy,
drunkenness, carousing, and anything similar. I am
warning you about these things — as I warned you
before — that those who practice such things will
not inherit the kingdom of God.
22 But the fruit of the Spirit is love, joy, peace, patience, kindness, goodness, faithfulness, 23 gentleness,
and self-control. The law is not against such things.
24 Now those who belong to Christ Jesus have crucified the flesh with its passions and desires. 25 If we
live by the Spirit, let us also keep in step with the
Spirit. 26 Let us not become conceited, provoking one
another, envying one another.

CARRY ONE ANOTHER'S BURDENS

6 Brothers and sisters, if someone is overtaken in
any wrongdoing, you who are spiritual, restore
such a person with a gentle spirit, watching out for
yourselves so that you also won't be tempted. 2 Carry
one another's burdens; in this way you will fulfill the
law of Christ. 3 For if anyone considers himself to be
something when he is nothing, he deceives himself.
4 Let each person examine his own work, and then
he can take pride in himself alone, and not compare
himself with someone else. 5 For each person will
have to carry his own load.
6 Let the one who is taught the word share all his
good things with the teacher. 7 Don't be deceived: God
is not mocked. For whatever a person sows he will
also reap, 8 because the one who sows to his flesh will
reap destruction from the flesh, but the one who sows
to the Spirit will reap eternal life from the Spirit. 9 Let
us not get tired of doing good, for we will reap at the
proper time if we don't give up. 10 Therefore, as we
have opportunity, let us work for the good of all, especially for those who belong to the household of faith.

CONCLUDING EXHORTATION

11 Look at what large letters I use as I write to you in
my own handwriting. 12 Those who want to make a
good impression in the flesh are the ones who would
compel you to be circumcised — but only to avoid
being persecuted for the cross of Christ. 13 For even
the circumcised don't keep the law themselves, and
yet they want you to be circumcised in order to boast
about your flesh. 14 But as for me, I will never boast
about anything except the cross of our Lord Jesus

Christ. The world has been crucified to me through
the cross, and I to the world. 15 For both circumcision
and uncircumcision mean nothing; what matters
instead is a new creation. 16 May peace come to all
those who follow this standard, and mercy even to
the Israel of God!
17 From now on, let no one cause me trouble, because I bear on my body the marks of Jesus. 18 Brothers and sisters, the grace of our Lord Jesus Christ be
with your spirit. Amen.

5:22–23 Other [illegible] ... Against such things there is
no law. [illegible] ... gentleness ... Other [illegible]
in Christ Jesus ... and ... for those who follow this standard,
peace and mercy be upon them, even upon the Israel of God, ... those who will follow this standard, peace be upon them and mercy,
[illegible] the Israel of God.

[illegible] ... consecrated [illegible] ...
of the family ... According to the
... it was a family ... slaves. Also ...
... slaves ... the figure ... the
left ... detail of ... social status of these
who were free and those who were slaves. (Dated about 50 BC.)

EPHESIANS

The odium at Ephesus, which originally held about fifteen hundred people, was primarily a concert venue.

INTRODUCTION TO

EPHESIANS

Circumstances of Writing

Paul referred to himself by name as the author of the book of Ephesians in two places (1:1; 3:1). Many regard this book as the crown of all of Paul's writings. Today some scholars think the book contains a writing style, vocabulary, and even some teachings that are not typical of the apostle. If that is the case, then it would mean a disciple of Paul had surpassed him in theological insight and spiritual perception. Of such an erudite disciple the early church has no record. Furthermore, pseudonymity (a writer writing under someone else's name) probably was not practiced by early Christians. We can conclude, in line with the undisputable acceptance of Pauline authorship in the early church, that there is no reason to dispute the Pauline authorship of Ephesians.

Paul penned the letter while in prison (3:1; 4:1; 6:20). Disagreement exists concerning whether Paul wrote this letter when he was imprisoned in Caesarea (Ac 24:22) around AD 57–59 or in Rome (Ac 28:30) around 60–62. Paul most likely wrote Colossians, Philemon, and Philippians during the same imprisonment. Tradition suggests that Paul wrote the letter from Rome around 60–61, which would have transpired while Paul was under house arrest in guarded rental quarters (Ac 28:30).

Relatively little is known about the recipients of the letter called Ephesians. Some important and early manuscripts do not contain the words "at Ephesus" (1:1). The letter was carried to its destination by Tychicus, who in Ephesians 6:21 and Colossians 4:7 is identified as Paul's emissary. The Ephesian and Colossian letters probably were delivered at the same time since in both letters the apostle noted that Tychicus would inform the churches concerning Paul's situation.

We can suggest the following possible scenario: While Paul was imprisoned in Rome, the need arose to respond to new religious philosophies influencing the Asia Minor area. The impetus to write the letters came to Paul from Epaphras, who informed him of the threats to Christianity in the Lycus Valley. In response, Paul wrote a letter to the church at Colossae. About the same time (either shortly before or shortly thereafter), he penned a more expansive and general letter intended for churches in Asia Minor, including Laodicea (see Col 4:16) and Ephesus.

Contribution to the Bible

The letter to the Ephesians was probably a circular letter, with Ephesus being the primary church addressed. Paul stayed at Ephesus, the capital city of the province of Asia, for almost three years (see Ac 20:31). The fact that it was a circular letter helps explain the absence of personal names of Ephesian believers. From its inception Paul intended for the letter to gain a wider audience than that which would be found in Ephesus alone. After the Ephesians read it, the letter would have been routed to Colossae, Laodicea, and other churches in the area. Known to be a letter of the apostle Paul, the letter was readily accepted as Scripture by the recipients.

Structure

The salutation and structure of Ephesians are quite similar to Colossians. Many topics are commonly treated in both letters. The message is strikingly similar. Of the 155 verses in Ephesians, more than half contain identical expressions with those in Colossians. Colossians, however, is abrupt, argumentative, and seemingly compressed. Ephesians presents a bigger, finished picture that is meditative, instructive, and expansive.

Though Ephesians and Colossians contain many similarities, it is important to observe the distinctives of Ephesians. When the content of Ephesians that is common to Colossians is removed, there remain at least seven units of material unique to Ephesians.

GREETING

1 Paul, an apostle of Christ Jesus by God's will:
To the faithful saints in Christ Jesus[A] at Ephesus.[B]
2 Grace to you and peace from God our Father and the Lord Jesus Christ.

GOD'S RICH BLESSINGS

3 Blessed is the God and Father of our Lord Jesus Christ, who has blessed us with every spiritual blessing in the heavens in Christ. 4 For he chose us in him, before the foundation of the world, to be holy and blameless in love before him.[C] 5 He predestined us to be adopted as sons through Jesus Christ for himself, according to the good pleasure of his will, 6 to the praise of his glorious grace that he lavished on us in the Beloved One.

7 In him we have redemption through his blood, the forgiveness of our trespasses, according to the riches of his grace 8 that he richly poured out on us with all wisdom and understanding.[D] 9 He made known to us the mystery of his will, according to his good pleasure that he purposed in Christ 10 as a plan for the right time[E] — to bring everything together in Christ, both things in heaven and things on earth in him.

11 In him we have also received an inheritance,[F] because we were predestined according to the plan of the one who works out everything in agreement with the purpose of his will, 12 so that we who had already put our hope in Christ might bring praise to his glory.

13 In him you also were sealed with the promised Holy Spirit when you heard the word of truth, the gospel of your salvation, and when you believed. 14 The Holy Spirit is the down payment of our inheritance, until the redemption of the possession, to the praise of his glory.

PRAYER FOR SPIRITUAL INSIGHT

15 This is why, since I heard about your faith in the Lord Jesus and your love for all the saints, 16 I never stop giving thanks for you as I remember you in my prayers. 17 I pray that the God of our Lord Jesus Christ, the glorious Father,[G] would give you the Spirit[H] of wisdom and revelation in the knowledge of him. 18 I pray that the eyes of your heart may be enlightened so that you may know what is the hope of his calling, what is the wealth of his glorious inheritance in the saints, 19 and what is the immeasurable greatness of his power toward us who believe, according to the mighty working of his strength.

[A] **1:1** Or *to the saints, the believers in Christ Jesus* [B] **1:1** Other mss omit *at Ephesus* [C] **1:4** Or *in his sight. In love* [D] **1:8** Or *on us. With all wisdom and understanding* [E] **1:10** Or *the fulfillment of times* [F] **1:11** Or *In him we are also an inheritance,* [G] **1:17** Or *the Father of glory* [H] **1:17** Or *a spirit*

The reerected marble two-story facade of the second-century-AD Library of Celsus at Ephesus. Julias Aguila originally constructed the building as a grave-monument in honor of his father Celsus, a consul from Sardis who was the South Asia governor of Rome.

From Ephesus; a terra-cotta base depicting Dioskouroi, who were the Greeks' twin gods of horsemanship. The owner likely would have used this base to hold a statue.

GOD'S POWER IN CHRIST

20 He exercised this power in Christ by raising him
from the dead and seating him at his right hand in
the heavens — 21 far above every ruler and authority, power and dominion, and every title given,[A] not
only in this age but also in the one to come. 22 And **he**
subjected everything under his feet[B] and appointed
him[C] as head over everything for the church, 23 which
is his body, the fullness of the one who fills all things
in every way.

FROM DEATH TO LIFE

2 And you were dead in your trespasses and sins
2 in which you previously walked according to
the ways of this world, according to the ruler of the
power of the air, the spirit now working in the disobedient.[D] 3 We too all previously lived among them in our
fleshly desires, carrying out the inclinations of our
flesh and thoughts, and we were by nature children
under wrath as the others were also. 4 But God, who
is rich in mercy, because of his great love that he had
for us,[E] 5 made us alive with Christ even though we
were dead in trespasses. You are saved by grace! 6 He
also raised us up with him and seated us with him in

[A]**1:21** Lit *every name named* [B]**1:22** Ps 8:6 [C]**1:22** Lit *gave him*
[D]**2:2** Lit *sons of disobedience* [E]**2:4** Lit *love with which he loved us*

Interior of one of the bath houses at Ephesus. The original structure dated to the end of the first century AD. Shown is the structure that was renovated in the fourth century by a wealthy Christian woman named Scholasticia.

Ephesus: A Historical Survey

by Randall L. Adkisson

The grand theater at Ephesus was built in the third century BC. Through the years it was modified until it reached its final form during the reign of the emperor Trajan (AD 98–117). The theater had seating capacity for twenty-four thousand.

Located at the mouth of the Cayster River, Ephesus served as an important access route for trade into and out of the interior of Asia Minor and its profitable land routes. Both the location and imperial favor the city enjoyed through several different eras propelled Ephesus as a cultural and commercial wonder of the ancient world. Estimates place the population during Paul's time at two hundred fifty thousand residents.[1]

The history of Ephesus is long and storied. Evidently established as a free Greek colony for the purpose of opening trade routes into the interior, the city dates at least to the mid-eleventh century BC. Ephesus was one of twelve cities comprising the Ionian Confederacy. The port at Ephesus gave merchants access to the coastal road running north through Smyrna to Troas, as well as an interior route to Colossae, Hierapolis, Laodicea, and farther to the Phygian regions. As nearby ports succumbed to erosion and political intrigue, Ephesus flourished in importance and prestige.

One ancient myth records that Amazons, a culture of mighty female warriors, were the earliest builders of the town, establishing a temple where the "mother goddess of the earth was reputedly born."[2] Ephesus's connection to pagan goddess worship prospered under each successive occupation. The Greeks established a strong cult to Artemis. The Romans accepted the association between the city and goddess worship, equating Artemis with their goddess Diana.

From its position as a free city-state, Ephesus fell into subservience, first to King Croesus of Lydia in 560 BC and then to the Persians. By defeating the Persians, Alexander the Great brought the city back into Greek hands and into his empire in 334 BC. At his death, the city's ownership passed to Lysimachus, one of Alexander's generals. Lysimachus lost the region when defeated by Seleucus I in 281 BC. Ninety-one years later, the Seleucid Empire fell to the Romans. In appreciation to King Eumeness II of Pergamum for his assistance against the Seleucids, Ephesus and the surrounding region were ceded to the Pergamum Empire. The city prospered and was peacefully bequeathed to the Romans by Pergamum's last king, Attalus III, in 133 BC.

From this period through the New Testament era, Ephesus functioned as a strong and vibrant part of the Roman Empire. As a proconsular seat and the capital of the Roman province of Asia, the

South Street at Ephesus. Giving evidence of how heavy traffic was in the city's earlier history, chariot ruts in the pavement stones are still visible.

Relief of the mask of tragedy at the grand theatre; Ephesus.

city enjoyed influence and standing in the region and beyond. The temple complex was a center of commerce and tourism. The city also served as an ancient banking institution. A city of great prominence, ancient Ephesus reflected its wealth and culture in its buildings and landscape. A traveler entering the first-century city was walking on the streets of the fourth-largest city in the world.[3]

As a central feature of the city, the temple of Artemis was listed as one of the seven wonders of the ancient world and stood four times larger than the Athenian Parthenon. At 420 feet long and 240 feet wide, the temple was as tall as a six-story building, its roof being supported by more than one hundred large columns. The impressive temple reflected and compelled an expansive industry of tourism associated with worship of the goddess. Travelers from across the ancient world swelled the ranks of the inhabitants in Ephesus during April for a festival involving a great procession to the temple, as well as various athletic and musical competitions.

The large population and influx of tourists allowed Ephesus to maintain a huge theater, the ruins of which may still be visited today. Seating approximately twenty-four thousand, the theater had sixty-six tiers of seating.[4] From the entrance to the theater, the Arcadian Way, a broad marble paved thoroughfare flanked by ornate columns, buildings, and shops stretched through the city to the port.

Archaeological efforts at Ephesus suggest a city that once swarmed with people and commerce. From the impressive and imposing main thoroughfare—flanked by ancient baths, a smaller theater, government buildings, a music hall, and a multistory library—stretched smaller streets leading to the city's vast area of residences and warehouses. The ruins highlight the ancient city's character. A thriving port city, Ephesus was adorned with both the advantages and vices of its position and commerce.

Ephesus successfully combined the cultures and histories of many different people and periods. The city's original population assumed the flavor of Greek culture and religion. With Roman conquest, the city continued to thrive, synchronizing the various religions and welcoming immigrants from across the region. Records reveal subcultures of Egyptian, Jewish, Greek, and Roman citizenry. ✣

---

[1] Mitchell G. Reddish, "Ephesus" in *HolBD*, 425. [2] Merrill F. Unger, *Archaeology and the New Testament* (Grand Rapids: Zondervan, 1962), 249. [3] Reddish, "Ephesus," 425. [4] Gerald L. Borchert, "Ephesus" in *ISBE* (1982), 2:116.

the heavens in Christ Jesus, 7 so that in the coming
ages he might display the immeasurable riches of his
grace through his kindness to us in Christ Jesus. 8 For
you are saved by grace through faith, and this is not
from yourselves; it is God's gift — 9 not from works,
so that no one can boast. 10 For we are his workmanship, created in Christ Jesus for good works, which
God prepared ahead of time for us to do.

UNITY IN CHRIST

11 So, then, remember that at one time you were Gentiles in the flesh — called "the uncircumcised" by
those called "the circumcised," which is done in the
flesh by human hands. 12 At that time you were without Christ, excluded from the citizenship of Israel,
and foreigners to the covenants of promise, without hope and without God in the world. 13 But now
in Christ Jesus, you who were far away have been
brought near by the blood of Christ. 14 For he is our
peace, who made both groups one and tore down the
dividing wall of hostility. In his flesh, 15 he made of no
effect the law consisting of commands and expressed
in regulations, so that he might create in himself one
new man from the two, resulting in peace. 16 He did
this so that he might reconcile both to God in one
body through the cross by which he put the hostility
to death.[A] 17 He came and proclaimed the good news
of peace to you who were far away and peace to those
who were near. 18 For through him we both have access in one Spirit to the Father. 19 So, then, you are no
longer foreigners and strangers, but fellow citizens
with the saints, and members of God's household,
20 built on the foundation of the apostles and prophets, with Christ Jesus himself as the cornerstone. 21 In
him the whole building, being put together, grows
into a holy temple in the Lord. 22 In him you are also
being built together for God's dwelling in the Spirit.

PAUL'S MINISTRY TO THE GENTILES

3 For this reason, I, Paul, the prisoner of Christ
Jesus on behalf of you Gentiles — 2 assuming you
have heard about the administration of God's grace
that he gave me for you. 3 The mystery was made
known to me by revelation, as I have briefly written
above. 4 By reading this you are able to understand
my insight into the mystery of Christ. 5 This was not
made known to people[B] in other generations as it
is now revealed to his holy apostles and prophets
by the Spirit: 6 The Gentiles are coheirs, members of
the same body, and partners in the promise in Christ

[A] **2:16** Or *death in himself* [B] **3:5** Lit *to the sons of men*

Ruins from the Basilica of St. John at Ephesus. The apostle John, according to an early tradition, died at Ephesus and was buried on this hill. A chapel stood over the grave during the Roman period. Most of these remains are from Justinian, who erected an even larger basilica in the sixth century AD.

Jesus through the gospel. [7] I was made a servant of
this gospel by the gift of God's grace that was given
to me by the working of his power.
[8] This grace was given to me — the least of all the
saints — to proclaim to the Gentiles the incalculable
riches of Christ, [9] and to shed light for all about the
administration of the mystery hidden for ages in
God who created all things. [10] This is so that God's
multi-faceted wisdom may now be made known
through the church to the rulers and authorities in
the heavens. [11] This is according to his eternal purpose
accomplished in Christ Jesus our Lord. [12] In him we
have boldness and confident access through faith in
him.[A] [13] So, then, I ask you not to be discouraged over
my afflictions on your behalf, for they are your glory.

PRAYER FOR SPIRITUAL POWER

[14] For this reason I kneel before the Father[B] [15] from
whom every family in heaven and on earth is named.
[16] I pray that he may grant you, according to the riches
of his glory, to be strengthened with power in your
inner being through his Spirit, [17] and that Christ may
dwell in your hearts through faith. I pray that you,
being rooted and firmly established in love, [18] may
be able to comprehend with all the saints what is
the length and width, height and depth of God's love,
[19] and to know Christ's love that surpasses knowledge,
so that you may be filled with all the fullness of God.
[20] Now to him who is able to do above and beyond
all that we ask or think according to the power that
works in us — [21] to him be glory in the church and
in Christ Jesus to all generations, forever and ever.
Amen.

UNITY AND DIVERSITY IN THE BODY OF CHRIST

4 Therefore I, the prisoner in the Lord, urge you
to walk worthy of the calling you have received,
[2] with all humility and gentleness, with patience,
bearing with one another in love, [3] making every effort to keep the unity of the Spirit through the bond
of peace. [4] There is one body and one Spirit — just as
you were called to one hope[C] at your calling — [5] one
Lord, one faith, one baptism, [6] one God and Father of
all, who is above all and through all and in all.
[7] Now grace was given to each one of us according
to the measure of Christ's gift. [8] For it says:

> **When he ascended on high,**
> **he took the captives captive;**
> **he gave gifts to people.**[D]

[A] **3:12** Or *through his faithfulness* [B] **3:14** Other mss add *of our Lord Jesus Christ* [C] **4:4** Lit *called in one hope* [D] **4:8** Ps 68:18

Partially uncovered inscription at the South Gate of Ephesus, written in Latin and Greek. The full inscription, now fully excavated, says Mithriates and Mazaeus, both freedmen, erected the gate in honor of Emperor Augustus, his wife Livia, his daughter Julia, and his son-in-law, Agrippa.

9 But what does "he ascended" mean except that he[A]
also descended to the lower parts of the earth?[B] 10 The
one who descended is also the one who ascended far
above all the heavens, to fill all things. 11 And he himself gave some to be apostles, some prophets, some
evangelists, some pastors and teachers, 12 to equip the
saints for the work of ministry, to build up the body of
Christ, 13 until we all reach unity in the faith and in the
knowledge of God's Son, growing into maturity with a
stature measured by Christ's fullness. 14 Then we will
no longer be little children, tossed by the waves and
blown around by every wind of teaching, by human
cunning with cleverness in the techniques of deceit.
15 But speaking the truth in love, let us grow in every
way into him who is the head — Christ. 16 From him
the whole body, fitted and knit together by every supporting ligament, promotes the growth of the body
for building itself up in love by the proper working
of each individual part.

LIVING THE NEW LIFE

17 Therefore, I say this and testify in the Lord: You
should no longer walk as the Gentiles do, in the futility of their thoughts. 18 They are darkened in their
understanding, excluded from the life of God, because
of the ignorance that is in them and because[C] of the
hardness of their hearts. 19 They became callous and
gave themselves over to promiscuity for the practice of every kind of impurity with a desire for more
and more.[D]

20 But that is not how you came to know Christ,
21 assuming you heard about him and were taught
by him, as the truth is in Jesus, 22 to take off[E] your
former way of life, the old self that is corrupted by
deceitful desires, 23 to be renewed[F] in the spirit of
your minds, 24 and to put on[G] the new self, the one
created according to God's likeness in righteousness
and purity of the truth.

25 Therefore, putting away lying, **speak the truth,
each one to his neighbor,**[H] because we are members
of one another. 26 **Be angry and do not sin.**[I] Don't let
the sun go down on your anger, 27 and don't give the
devil an opportunity. 28 Let the thief no longer steal.
Instead, he is to do honest work with his own hands,
so that he has something to share with anyone in
need. 29 No foul language should come from your
mouth, but only what is good for building up some-

[A] **4:9** Other mss add *first* [B] **4:9** Or *the lower parts, namely, the earth* [C] **4:18** Or *in them because* [D] **4:19** Lit *with greediness* [E] **4:21–22** Or *Jesus. This means: take off* (as a command) [F] **4:22–23** Or *desires; renew* (as a command) [G] **4:23–24** Or *minds; and put on* (as a command) [H] **4:25** Zch 8:16 [I] **4:26** Ps 4:4

Marketplace at Ephesus.

one in need,[A] so that it gives grace to those who hear.
30 And don't grieve God's Holy Spirit. You were sealed
by him[B] for the day of redemption. 31 Let all bitterness,
anger and wrath, shouting and slander be removed
from you, along with all malice. 32 And be kind and
compassionate to one another, forgiving one another,
just as God also forgave you[C] in Christ.
5 Therefore, be imitators of God, as dearly loved
children, 2 and walk in love, as Christ also loved
us and gave himself for us, a sacrificial and fragrant
offering to God. 3 But sexual immorality and any impurity or greed should not even be heard of[D] among
you, as is proper for saints. 4 Obscene and foolish
talking or crude joking are not suitable, but rather
giving thanks. 5 For know and recognize this: Every
sexually immoral or impure or greedy person, who
is an idolater, does not have an inheritance in the
kingdom of Christ and of God.

LIGHT VERSUS DARKNESS

6 Let no one deceive you with empty arguments, for
God's wrath is coming on the disobedient[E] because
of these things. 7 Therefore, do not become their partners. 8 For you were once darkness, but now you are
light in the Lord. Walk as children of light — 9 for
the fruit of the light[F] consists of all goodness, righteousness, and truth — 10 testing what is pleasing to
the Lord. 11 Don't participate in the fruitless works of
darkness, but instead expose them. 12 For it is shameful even to mention what is done by them in secret.
13 Everything exposed by the light is made visible,
14 for what makes everything visible is light. Therefore it is said:

> Get up, sleeper, and rise up from the dead,
> and Christ will shine on you.

CONSISTENCY IN THE CHRISTIAN LIFE

15 Pay careful attention, then, to how you walk — not
as unwise people but as wise — 16 making the most
of the time,[G] because the days are evil. 17 So don't be
foolish, but understand what the Lord's will is. 18 And
don't get drunk with wine, which leads to reckless
living, but be filled by the Spirit: 19 speaking to one another in psalms, hymns, and spiritual songs, singing
and making music with your heart to the Lord, 20 giving thanks always for everything to God the Father
in the name of our Lord Jesus Christ, 21 submitting to
one another in the fear of Christ.

[A] **4:29** Lit *for the building up of the need* [B] **4:30** Or *Spirit, by whom you were sealed* [C] **4:32** Other mss read *us* [D] **5:3** Or *be named* [E] **5:6** Lit *sons of disobedience* [F] **5:9** Other mss read *fruit of the Spirit* [G] **5:16** Lit *buying back the time*

Exterior of one of the hillside houses at Ephesus.

by Gregory T. Pouncey

Relief depicting Roman soldiers, first century AD.

In Paul's day, the Roman army contained four classes of soldiers.[1] The first class, known as *velites*, included the youngest and poorest of the soldiers. They fought on the front lines and were lightly armored, considering their position on the battlefield. The second class, or *hastati*, fought behind the *velites*. They were the strongest and most heavily armed forces. The *principes* included the most capable soldiers in the prime of their careers. They provided the third line of defense for the army. The final line, the *triarii*, included the oldest soldiers and were considerably smaller in number than the other divisions. They provided a connection to the army's central command.

According to descriptions of the armor of the *hastati*, Paul probably had these soldiers in mind as he referred to a Christian's spiritual armor (Eph 6:10–20). The Greek historian Polybius described the equipment of the *hastati*.[2] His weapon list included a large shield, a sword hanging on the right side, two spears, a brass helmet, a brass breastplate, and greaves (leg protection below the knees). Soldiers who came from the higher classes had a coat of mail underneath the breastplate.

A soldier wore two belts, the first underneath the armor. This belt gathered the tunic so movement was possible without hindrances from the undergarment.[3] The second belt fit over the outside armor and held the sword. Both belts functioned as a piece of armor that held all the others in place. Polybius described the breastplate as the armor that protected the heart.[4] Some soldiers in that day wore segmented armor, while others wore a one-piece breastplate made of brass.[5]

The Jewish historian Josephus described the soldier's shoes as thickly studded leather-soled shoes.[6] Their main purpose was to create a solid foundation for the soldier so he would not slide when fighting on a hillside. They also provided limited protection from the weather. The shield was wooden and covered with calfskin. It was large, 4 by 2½ feet.[7] The shield extinguished burning arrows that embedded themselves between the layers, where the lack of oxygen would snuff out the flames.

A Roman centurion made of basalt, from the early Roman period.

The helmet was a large, one-piece bowl with a front guard, cheek pieces, and neck guard.[8] Most helmets contained a feather or crest piece (up to eighteen inches tall) designed to make the soldier appear taller and thus more intimidating. A soldier's sword was double edged and worn on the outside belt.

Paul envisioned Christians fitting the spiritual armor in place through prayer and then engaging the enemies of God—not in one's own strength but in the power the Lord provides. ✣

[1] H. M. D. Parker, *The Roman Legions* (Oxford: Clarendon, 1928; repr., New York: Barnes & Noble), 14. [2] Polybius, *The Histories* 6.23. [3] Peter T. O'Brien, *The Letter to the Ephesians*, Pillar New Testament Commentary (Grand Rapids: Eerdmans, 1999), 473. [4] Polybius, *The Histories* 6.23. [5] John Warry, *Warfare in the Classical World* (New York: St. Martin's, 1980), 191. [6] Josephus, *Jewish War* 6.1.8. [7] Polybius, *The Histories* 6.23. [8] Michael P. Speidel, *Riding for Caesar* (Cambridge, MA: Harvard University Press, 1994), 106.

Bronze Roman helmet with a peak-like projection at the back of the neck, believed to be Celtic in origin. This type of helmet was popular among the legions. Many of this type have been found at Montefortino in northern Italy.

WIVES AND HUSBANDS

22 Wives, submit[A] to your husbands as to the Lord, 23 because the husband is the head of the wife as Christ is the head of the church. He is the Savior of the body. 24 Now as the church submits to Christ, so also wives are to submit to their husbands in everything. 25 Husbands, love your wives, just as Christ loved the church and gave himself for her 26 to make her holy, cleansing[B] her with the washing of water by the word. 27 He did this to present the church to himself in splendor, without spot or wrinkle or anything like that, but holy and blameless. 28 In the same way, husbands are to love their wives as their own bodies. He who loves his wife loves himself. 29 For no one ever hates his own flesh but provides and cares for it, just as Christ does for the church, 30 since we are members of his body.[C] 31 **For this reason a man will leave his father and mother and be joined to his wife, and the two will become one flesh.**[D] 32 This mystery is profound, but I am talking about Christ and the church. 33 To sum up, each one of you is to love his wife as himself, and the wife is to respect her husband.

A sign of wealth, mosaics were part of the hillside houses in Ephesus.

CHILDREN AND PARENTS

6 Children, obey your parents in the Lord, because this is right. 2 **Honor your father and mother**, which is the first commandment with a promise, 3 **so that it may go well with you and that you may have a long life in the land.**[E,F] 4 Fathers, don't stir up anger in your children, but bring them up in the training and instruction of the Lord.

SLAVES AND MASTERS

5 Slaves, obey your human[G] masters with fear and trembling, in the sincerity of your heart, as you would Christ. 6 Don't work only while being watched, as people-pleasers, but as slaves of Christ, doing God's will from your heart. 7 Serve with a good attitude, as to the Lord and not to people, 8 knowing that whatever good each one does, slave or free, he will receive this back from the Lord. 9 And masters, treat your slaves the same way, without threatening them, because you know that both their Master and yours is in heaven, and there is no favoritism with him.

CHRISTIAN WARFARE

10 Finally, be strengthened by the Lord and by his vast strength. 11 Put on the full armor of God so that you can stand against the schemes of the devil. 12 For our struggle is not against flesh and blood, but against the rulers, against the authorities, against the cosmic powers of this darkness, against evil, spiritual forces in the heavens. 13 For this reason take up the full armor of God, so that you may be able to resist in the evil day, and having prepared everything, to take your stand. 14 Stand, therefore, with truth like a belt around your waist, righteousness like armor on your chest, 15 and your feet sandaled with readiness for the gospel of peace. 16 In every situation take up the shield of faith with which you can extinguish all the flaming arrows of the evil one. 17 Take the helmet of salvation and the sword of the Spirit — which is the word of God. 18 Pray at all times in the Spirit with every prayer and request, and stay alert with all perseverance and intercession for all the saints. 19 Pray also for me, that the message may be given to me when I open my mouth to make known with boldness the mystery of the gospel. 20 For this I am an ambassador in chains. Pray that I might be bold enough to speak about it as I should.

PAUL'S FAREWELL

21 Tychicus, our dearly loved brother and faithful servant[H] in the Lord, will tell you all the news about me so that you may be informed. 22 I am sending him to you for this very reason, to let you know how we are and to encourage your hearts.

23 Peace to the brothers and sisters, and love with faith, from God the Father and the Lord Jesus Christ. 24 Grace be with all who have undying love for our Lord Jesus Christ.[I,J]

[A] **5:22** Other mss omit *submit* [B] **5:26** Or *having cleansed* [C] **5:30** Other mss add *and of his flesh and of his bones* [D] **5:31** Gn 2:24 [E] **6:3** Or *life on the earth* [F] **6:2–3** Ex 20:12 [G] **6:5** Lit *according to the flesh* [H] **6:21** Or *deacon* [I] **6:24** Other mss add *Amen.* [J] **6:24** Lit *all who love our Lord Jesus Christ in incorruption*

PHILIPPIANS

A relief from the south portico of the theater at Philippi.

INTRODUCTION TO

PHILIPPIANS

Circumstances of Writing

Paul the apostle wrote this short letter, a fact that no scholar seriously questions. The traditional date for the writing of Philippians is during Paul's first Roman imprisonment (AD 60–62); few have challenged this conclusion.

Paul planted the church at Philippi during his second missionary journey (AD 51) in response to his "Macedonian vision" (Ac 16:9–10). This was the first church in Europe (Ac 16).

The text of this letter from Paul suggests several characteristics of the church at Philippi. First, Gentiles predominated. Few Jews lived in Philippi, and apparently the church included few. Second, women had a significant role (Ac 16:11–15; Php 4:1–2). Third, the church was generous. Fourth, they remained deeply loyal to Paul.

Philippi, the ancient city of Krenides, had a military significance. It was the capital of Alexander the Great, who renamed it for his father, Philip of Macedon, and it became the capital of the Greek Empire (332 BC). The Romans conquered Greece, and in the civil war after Julius Caesar's death (44 BC), Antony and Octavian repopulated Philippi by allowing the defeated armies (Brutus and Cassius) to settle there (eight hundred miles from Rome). They declared the city a Roman colony. It flourished, proud of its history and entrenched in Roman political and social life. In his epistle to the Philippians, Paul alluded to military and political structures as metaphors for the church.

Paul wanted to thank the church for their financial support (4:10–20). He also addressed disunity and the threat of heresy. Disunity threatened the church, spawned by personal conflicts (4:2) and disagreements over theology (3:1–16). The heresy came from radical Jewish teachers. Paul addressed both issues personally and warmly.

The church at Philippi sent Epaphroditus to help Paul in Rome. While there, he became ill (2:25–28). The church learned of Epaphroditus's illness, and Paul wished to ease their concern for him. Some people possibly blamed Epaphroditus for failing his commission, but Paul commended him and sent him home. Perhaps Epaphroditus carried this letter with him.

Contribution to the Bible

Paul's letter to the Philippians teaches us much about genuine Christianity. Although most of its themes may be found elsewhere in Scripture, it is within this letter that we can see how those themes and messages affect life. Within the New Testament, Philippians contributes to our understanding of Christian commitment and what it means to be Christlike.

Structure

Philippians can be divided into four primary sections. Paul had definite concerns that he wanted to express, and he also wrote to warn about false teachers who threatened the church. Many of Paul's letters can be divided into theological and practical sections, but Philippians does not follow that pattern. Paul's theological instruction is woven throughout the fabric of a highly personal letter.

GREETING

1 Paul and Timothy, servants of Christ Jesus:

To all the saints in Christ Jesus who are in Philippi, including the overseers and deacons.

2 Grace to you and peace from God our Father and the Lord Jesus Christ.

THANKSGIVING AND PRAYER

3 I give thanks to my God for every remembrance of you,[A] 4 always praying with joy for all of you in my every prayer, 5 because of your partnership in the gospel from the first day until now. 6 I am sure of this, that he who started a good work in you[B] will carry it on to completion until the day of Christ Jesus. 7 Indeed, it is right for me to think this way about all of you, because I have you in my heart,[C] and you are all partners with me in grace, both in my imprisonment and in the defense and confirmation of the gospel. 8 For God is my witness, how deeply I miss all of you with the affection of Christ Jesus. 9 And I pray this: that your love will keep on growing in knowledge and every kind of discernment, 10 so that you may approve the things that are superior and may be pure and blameless in the day of Christ, 11 filled with the fruit of righteousness that comes through Jesus Christ to the glory and praise of God.

ADVANCE OF THE GOSPEL

12 Now I want you to know, brothers and sisters, that what has happened to me has actually advanced the gospel, 13 so that it has become known throughout the whole imperial guard, and to everyone else, that my imprisonment is because I am in Christ. 14 Most of the brothers have gained confidence in the Lord from my imprisonment and dare even more to speak the word[D] fearlessly. 15 To be sure, some preach Christ out of envy and rivalry, but others out of good will. 16 These preach out of love, knowing that I am appointed for the defense of the gospel; 17 the others proclaim Christ out of selfish ambition, not sincerely, thinking that they will cause me trouble in my imprisonment. 18 What does it matter? Only that in every way, whether from false motives or true, Christ is proclaimed, and in this I rejoice. Yes, and I will continue to rejoice 19 because I know this will lead to my salvation[E] through your prayers and help from the Spirit of Jesus Christ. 20 My eager expectation and hope is that I will not be ashamed about anything, but that now as always, with all courage, Christ will be highly honored in my body, whether by life or by death.

[A] **1:3** Or *for your every remembrance of me* [B] **1:6** Or *work among you* [C] **1:7** Or *because you have me in your heart* [D] **1:14** Other mss add *of God* [E] **1:19** Or *vindication*

In the bottom right is the bema (speaker's platform) at Philippi.

Philippi: A Historical and Archaeological Study

by Steve Booth

Roman gate to the city of ancient Neapolis.

In contrast to many biblical sites, visitors to the archaeological site of Philippi today are able to visualize the lay of the land in large part as it looked when Paul first visited the city around AD 49 or 50. From the summit of the naturally fortified hill (acropolis) that was a part of ancient Philippi, a large fertile plain stretches westward. This locale in modern-day Greece was ideal for a settlement dating back to 360 BC, originally called Krenides ("springs"). Its natural advantages included an abundant supply of water, rich agricultural land, and a defensible location.[1] In addition, rich gold and silver deposits were in the surrounding area.

LOCATION, LOCATION, LOCATION

Philip II of Macedon, Alexander the Great's father, recognized the strategic value of this town, took it over in 356 BC, and renamed it after himself. He fortified the acropolis and built a wall around the city, some parts of which still remain. "The wealth [he] received here enabled him to enlarge his army and unify his kingdom."[2] In 168–167 BC, Rome conquered Macedon and eventually made this region a province, dividing it into four administrative districts.[3]

Another factor that raised Philippi to a higher level of importance was the construction of the famous Via Egnatia (Egnatian Way), begun approximately 145 BC and completed around 130 BC. This highway connected Rome to the east and ran through the middle of Philippi, serving as its main street. As a major stopping place, Philippi benefited from the movement of Roman troops back and forth as well as from commerce that developed due to the increased ease of transportation. Just ten miles southeast of Philippi on the Via Egnatia, the port city of Neapolis (modern Kavalla) made interaction with the regions beyond even more accessible.

The event that really put this city on the map of the Roman Empire was the battle of Philippi in 42 BC. Just beyond its western wall, Octavian (later known as Caesar Augustus) and Mark Antony squared off against Brutus and Cassius, who had been instrumental in Julius Caesar's assassination two years earlier. Antony and Octavian were victorious, while Brutus and Cassius both committed suicide on the battlefield. The victors enlarged and further fortified the city, establishing it as a Roman colony and naming it Colonia Victrix Philippensium.[4] They also resettled veterans there, granting them generous sections of farmland.

The alliance between Antony and Octavian broke down, and the score was settled in the battle of Actium in 31 BC. As victor, Octavian settled many of Antony's soldiers in Philippi and renamed this strategic city Colonia Iulia Augusta Philippensis after his daughter Julia (Augusta being added in 27 BC after he received the title from the Senate).[5] The status of colony was the highest privilege granted a Roman city and gave its citizens the same civil rights as if they lived in Italy, including freedom from taxation. The official language was Latin, which is verified by many of the inscriptions from the period, although Greek continued to be the language of the marketplace.[6]

Monumental stairway leading to Basilica A in Philippi.

In Paul's day, the city of Philippi was modest in size with a blended population of descendants from the Roman veterans, Greeks that predated the Romans, and native Thracians that predated the Greeks. Also living there were immigrants from Asia Minor that were involved in commerce like Lydia of Thyatira (Ac 16:14) and some Jews.[7] Roman soldiers were stationed in Philippi to protect the Via Egnatia. The inhabitants were "proud of their ties with Rome, proud to observe Roman customs and obey Roman laws, [and were] proud to be Roman citizens."[8]

PAUL'S ARRIVAL

With Paul's landing at Neapolis, Christianity advanced from Asia to Europe. Traveling the Via Egnatia to Philippi, Paul would have entered the Neapolis Gate, part of which archaeologists have uncovered. Traveling west, Paul would have soon passed the impressive theater of Philip II on his right. Although later modified and enlarged in the second and third centuries, its basic form would have looked similar to the one still visible today. The same is true of the Roman forum on the city's main street. Various administrative buildings, shops, monuments, and temples bordered this large public square.[9] This is the marketplace where the slave girl's owners dragged Paul and Silas before the magistrates and where they suffered severe beating before being thrown into prison (Ac 16:19–23).

Evidence of the emperors' cult—including public displays honoring Augustus and his adopted sons Gaius and Lucius Caesar—were also in the forum. A few years prior to Paul's arrival, the then-reigning Caesar Claudius (AD 41–54) had already introduced the cult of Livia (wife of Augustus and Claudius's deceased grandmother).[10] The people generally appreciated and revered the Roman rulers for maintaining peace and providing protection, justice, and relief in times of hardship.

A remarkable mix of other pagan worship practices coexisted in first-century Philippi as well. The traditional Greek gods like Zeus, Apollo, Dionysus, and especially Artemis had their place, though sometimes known by their Latin counterparts, including a shrine to Silvanus. Ancient Thracian religions persisted too, for example, Artemis Bendis and devotion to the Hero-Horseman.[11] Sanctuaries to gods from Egypt included those honoring Isis and Serapis as well as the Phrygian Cybele, the great mother-goddess. ✣

---

[1] Holland L. Hendrix, "Philippi" in *ABD*, 5:313–14; Gordon D. Fee, *Paul's Letter to the Philippians* (Grand Rapids: Eerdmans, 1995), 25. [2] Lee Martin McDonald, "Philippi" in *DNTB*, 787. [3] Peter T. O'Brien, *The Epistle to the Philippians: A Commentary on the Greek Text* (Grand Rapids: Eerdmans, 1991), 3–4. [4] F. F. Bruce, *Paul: Apostle of the Heart Set Free* (Grand Rapids: Eerdmans, 1977), 219. [5] Bruce, *Paul*. [6] McDonald, "Philippi," 788. [7] Hendrix, "Philippi," 315. [8] Gerald F. Hawthorne, *Philippians*, WBC (1983), xxxiii–xxxiv; O'Brien, *Philippians*, 4. [9] Chaido Koukouli-Chrysantaki and Charalambos Bakirtzis, *Philippi* (Athens: Hellenic Ministry of Culture, 2006), 38–41. [10] Chaido Koukouli-Chrysantaki, "Colonia Iulia Augusta Philippensis," in *Philippi at the Time of Paul and after His Death*, ed. Charalambos Bakirtzis and Helmut Koester (Harrisburg, PA: Trinity Press, 1998), 16. [11] Koukouli-Chrysantaki and Bakirtzis, *Philippi*, 25–28.

LIVING IS CHRIST

21 For me, to live is Christ and to die is gain. 22 Now if I
live on in the flesh, this means fruitful work for me;
and I don't know which one I should choose. 23 I am
torn between the two. I long to depart and be with
Christ — which is far better — 24 but to remain in
the flesh is more necessary for your sake. 25 Since I
am persuaded of this, I know that I will remain and
continue with all of you for your progress and joy
in the faith, 26 so that, because of my coming to you
again, your boasting in Christ Jesus may abound.
27 Just one thing: As citizens of heaven, live your life
worthy of the gospel of Christ. Then, whether I come
and see you or am absent, I will hear about you that
you are standing firm in one spirit, in one accord,[A]
contending together for the faith of the gospel, 28 not
being frightened in any way by your opponents. This
is a sign of destruction for them, but of your salvation
— and this is from God. 29 For it has been granted to
you on Christ's behalf not only to believe in him, but
also to suffer for him, 30 since you are engaged in
the same struggle that you saw I had and now hear
that I have.

CHRISTIAN HUMILITY

2 If, then, there is any encouragement in Christ, if
any consolation of love, if any fellowship with
the Spirit, if any affection and mercy, 2 make my joy
complete by thinking the same way, having the same
love, united in spirit, intent on one purpose. 3 Do nothing out of selfish ambition or conceit, but in humility
consider others as more important than yourselves.
4 Everyone should look not to his own interests, but
rather to the interests of others.

CHRIST'S HUMILITY AND EXALTATION

5 Adopt the same attitude as that of Christ Jesus,

6 who, existing in the form of God,
did not consider equality with God
as something to be exploited.[B]
7 Instead he emptied himself
by assuming the form of a servant,
taking on the likeness of humanity.
And when he had come as a man,
8 he humbled himself by becoming obedient
to the point of death —
even to death on a cross.
9 For this reason God highly exalted him
and gave him the name
that is above every name,
10 so that at the name of Jesus
every knee will bow —
in heaven and on earth
and under the earth —

[A] 1:27 Lit *soul* [B] 2:6 Or *to be grasped*, or *to be held on to*

Ruins of a two-room Hellenistic temple (called a "heroon"); thought to have been built to honor Philip II (340–328 BC).

Mount Olympus was revered in ancient times as the home of the Greek gods and goddesses. The mountain is southeast and across the bay from Thessalonica and is part of the entire Olympus range.

11 and every tongue will confess
that Jesus Christ is Lord,
to the glory of God the Father.

LIGHTS IN THE WORLD

12 Therefore, my dear friends, just as you have always
obeyed, so now, not only in my presence but even
more in my absence, work out your own salvation
with fear and trembling. 13 For it is God who is working in you both to will and to work according to his
good purpose. 14 Do everything without grumbling
and arguing, 15 so that you may be blameless and pure,
children of God who are faultless in a crooked and
perverted generation, among whom you shine like
stars in the world, 16 by holding firm to the word of
life. Then I can boast in the day of Christ that I didn't
run or labor for nothing. 17 But even if I am poured out
as a drink offering on the sacrificial service of your
faith, I am glad and rejoice with all of you. 18 In the
same way you should also be glad and rejoice with me.

Bull head at Philippi draped with garland and accompanied by what may be two priests.

TIMOTHY AND EPAPHRODITUS

19 Now I hope in the Lord Jesus to send Timothy to you
soon so that I too may be encouraged by news about
you. 20 For I have no one else like-minded who will
genuinely care about your interests; 21 all seek their
own interests, not those of Jesus Christ. 22 But you
know his proven character, because he has served
with me in the gospel ministry like a son with a father. 23 Therefore, I hope to send him as soon as I see
how things go with me. 24 I am confident in the Lord
that I myself will also come soon.

25 But I considered it necessary to send you Epaphroditus — my brother, coworker, and fellow soldier,
as well as your messenger and minister to my need
— 26 since he has been longing for all of you and
was distressed because you heard that he was sick.
27 Indeed, he was so sick that he nearly died. However,
God had mercy on him, and not only on him but also
on me, so that I would not have sorrow upon sorrow.
28 For this reason, I am very eager to send him so that
you may rejoice again when you see him and I may
be less anxious. 29 Therefore, welcome him in the
Lord with great joy and hold people like him in hon-
or, 30 because he came close to death for the work of
Christ, risking his life to make up what was lacking
in your ministry to me.

KNOWING CHRIST

3 In addition, my brothers and sisters, rejoice in
the Lord. To write to you again about this is no
trouble for me and is a safeguard for you.

2 Watch out for the dogs, watch out for the evil
workers, watch out for those who mutilate the flesh.
3 For we are the circumcision, the ones who worship
by the Spirit of God, boast in Christ Jesus, and do not
put confidence in the flesh — 4 although I have reasons for confidence in the flesh. If anyone else thinks
he has grounds for confidence in the flesh, I have
more: 5 circumcised the eighth day; of the nation of
Israel, of the tribe of Benjamin, a Hebrew born of Hebrews; regarding the law, a Pharisee; 6 regarding zeal,
persecuting the church; regarding the righteousness
that is in the law, blameless.

7 But everything that was a gain to me, I have considered to be a loss because of Christ. 8 More than that,
I also consider everything to be a loss in view of the
surpassing value of knowing Christ Jesus my Lord. Because of him I have suffered the loss of all things and
consider them as dung, so that I may gain Christ 9 and
be found in him, not having a righteousness of my own
from the law, but one that is through faith in Christ[A]

[A] **3:9** Or *through the faithfulness of Christ*

Excavations at Tarsus. The first-century site features a basalt-stone road, columns, drainage system, and cisterns. This was probably the Tarsus agora.

—the righteousness from God based on faith. 10 My goal is to know him and the power of his resurrection and the fellowship of his sufferings, being conformed to his death, 11 assuming that I will somehow reach the resurrection from among the dead.

REACHING FORWARD TO GOD'S GOAL

12 Not that I have already reached the goal or am already perfect, but I make every effort to take hold of it because I also have been taken hold of by Christ Jesus. 13 Brothers and sisters, I do not[A] consider myself to have taken hold of it. But one thing I do: Forgetting what is behind and reaching forward to what is ahead, 14 I pursue as my goal the prize promised by God's heavenly[B] call in Christ Jesus. 15 Therefore, let all of us who are mature think this way. And if you think differently about anything, God will reveal this also to you. 16 In any case, we should live up to whatever truth we have attained. 17 Join in imitating me, brothers and sisters, and pay careful attention to those who live according to the example you have in us. 18 For I have often told you, and now say again with tears, that many live as enemies of the cross of Christ. 19 Their end is destruction; their god is their stomach; their glory is in their shame; and they are focused on earthly things. 20 Our citizenship is in heaven, and we eagerly wait for a Savior from there, the Lord Jesus Christ. 21 He will transform the body of our humble condition into the likeness of his glorious body, by the power that enables him to subject everything to himself.

4 So then, my dearly loved and longed for brothers and sisters, my joy and crown, in this manner stand firm in the Lord, dear friends.

PRACTICAL COUNSEL

2 I urge Euodia and I urge Syntyche to agree in the Lord. 3 Yes, I also ask you, true partner,[C] to help these women who have contended for the gospel at my side, along with Clement and the rest of my coworkers whose names are in the book of life. 4 Rejoice in the Lord always. I will say it again: Rejoice! 5 Let your graciousness[D] be known to everyone. The Lord is near. 6 Don't worry about anything, but in everything, through prayer and petition with thanksgiving, present your requests to God. 7 And the peace of God, which surpasses all understanding, will guard your hearts and minds in Christ Jesus.

[A] **3:13** Other mss read *not yet* [B] **3:14** Or *upward* [C] **4:3** Or *true Syzygus*, possibly a person's name [D] **4:5** Or *gentleness*

Tell of Lystra, which has never been excavated (see Ac 14:1–20).

Roman Citizenship: Privileges and Expectations

by Sharon H. Gritz

The Philippians lived in a city that was officially named both a Roman colony and an Italian city (*ius Italicum*).[1] These distinctions raised the status of this urban center and gave it a Roman flavor despite its being in a Greek province hundreds of miles from Rome. Paul reminded the Philippians that their citizenship was in heaven (Php 1:27; 3:20). Why did Paul choose the concept of citizenship in writing to the Philippians? What significance did Roman citizenship have in the first-century world?

BECOMING A ROMAN CITIZEN

An individual could become a Roman citizen in several ways. A child born to Roman citizens became one automatically. Initially, only freeborn natives of the city of Rome could be citizens. As the empire expanded beyond Italy, others who were not Roman by birth received this honor. A slave whose Roman-citizen owner awarded him his freedom (manumission) gained citizenship status. Rome also granted this honor to people who performed some valuable service benefiting Roman interests.[2] For example, Rome granted citizenship to auxiliary soldiers who served in the Roman army for twenty-five years. Groups of people were declared citizens all at once through the colonization of their town or its promotion to Latin rights.

The ancient historian Dio Cassius (ca AD 150–235) stated that citizenship could be purchased, especially during the reign of Claudius (AD 41–54), who continued the practice begun under Caesar Augustus.[3] Actually, persons could not purchase citizenship—but they could pay bribes to lesser officials to add their names to a list of candidates for citizenship. Evidently, the tribune Claudius Lysias obtained his citizenship in this way (Ac 22:28).

ADVANTAGES AND RESPONSIBILITIES OF CITIZENSHIP

Being a citizen of Rome made a person a member of the ruling power. Wherever they traveled throughout the empire, citizens were allowed all the rights and privileges of Roman law. Citizenship shaped every area of life. Citizens received better treatment than noncitizens in family matters, such as getting married, having children, and making wills, and in business concerns, such as holding property and making contracts.

Citizens had advantages in legal concerns involving courts, custody, and punishments. For instance, citizens accused of any crime had the right to a fair and public trial. They also could appeal to Rome. This exempted a person from having to leave final control of his case in the hands of local authorities. Paul claimed this right when he appealed to Caesar while stating his case before Festus, the local Roman governor (25:10–12).

Authorities could not use shameful forms of punishment against Roman citizens. This included scourging and death by crucifixion. The Philippian magistrates became alarmed when they learned that Paul and Silas were Roman citizens after they had publicly beaten and thrown them into prison without a trial (16:22–39). Rome did punish some cities for such crimes; the most serious penalty was causing them to lose their Roman rights.[4] The early traditions regarding the deaths of Paul and Peter reflect their different citizenship status. Paul, the Roman citizen, was said to have been beheaded. The law considered such a quick death to be merciful and thus proper for a citizen of Rome. In contrast, Peter, the noncitizen, was reportedly crucified upside down.[5]

Generally, authorities used torture when questioning slaves and noncitizens who had been accused of committing some crime; Roman citizens could not receive such treatment. Only the imperial court in Rome could impose the death penalty on a citizen.

Citizens were responsible for all the civic duties Roman law imposed. During the Roman Republic (509–27 BC), citizens had to serve in the army. With the beginning of the Principate or early part of the empire, though, "the onerous military duty of Roman citizens was greatly lessened by the general shift to a volunteer, professional army."[6]

Toga-clad figure shows a man in the formal dress of the Romans in the first–second centuries AD. The toga, a large trapezoid cloth, typically wool, that wrapped around the whole person, was for citizens; they wore them over a tunica. Slaves typically wore only a tunica.

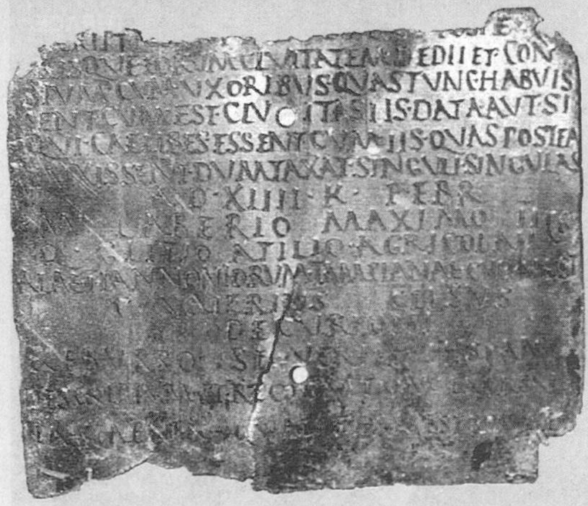

Emperor Trajan (ruled AD 98–117) issued this bronze military diploma to Reburrus, a Spanish junior officer in the First Pannonian Cavalry regiment. It granted him citizenship and the right to marry; dated AD 103.

Citizens enjoyed the right to vote, although they had to be in Rome to exercise this privilege. Some individuals, however, were given citizenship status without voting rights. Under the Principate, the right to vote was an illusion, not a reality.

PROVING CITIZENSHIP

Proving citizenship in one's hometown was easy, because this was part of the public records. Citizen parents had to register their legitimately born child within thirty days of birth. The difficulty of proving citizenship arose when one traveled. Roman citizens could have private copies made of a document, called a *testatio*, confirming their status. Such a testimony consisted of a diptych, two wooden tablets connected with a cord or hinges. The writing was engraved on the interior sides, covered with a bright wax. Seven witnesses had to attest to this certificate of citizenship.[7] Perhaps a citizen who took trips frequently would, by habit, carry such a document with him. Retired auxiliary soldiers received a document in bronze that held up better for travel. In time, Roman law considered making a false claim of citizenship to be a capital offense. The guilty party could be prosecuted and even receive the death penalty.[8]

PHILIPPI AND CITIZENSHIP

After winning the battle of Philippi in 42 BC, Mark Antony and Octavian (later known as Caesar Augustus) made the city a Roman colony. This provided its residents with Roman citizenship. The two victors settled many army veterans in the city. When Octavian overcame Antony in 31 BC, he reestablished Philippi as a Roman colony and settled some of the defeated soldiers there. Octavian also gave the city the status of *ius Italicum*. This gave the colonists the same rights and privileges those who lived in Italy possessed and secured their loyalty to Rome. As a Roman colony, Philippi possessed the right of self-government under Roman laws and freedom from direct taxation of the city's citizens and lands.

Paul knew that the church at Philippi understood the implications of being a colony of Rome. No doubt the Philippians prized their Roman citizenship. The apostle reminded the church that they represented a colony of heaven in Philippi.[9] He wanted them to remain loyal to the Lord Jesus Christ and conduct themselves in Philippi as worthy citizens of their heavenly home. ✣

---

[1] Richard R. Melick Jr., *Philippians, Colossians, Philemon*, NAC (1991), 24; Ralph Martin, *Philippians*, Tyndale New Testament Commentaries (TNTC) (Grand Rapids: Eerdmans, 1987), 18. [2] Everett Ferguson, *Backgrounds of Early Christianity*, 3rd ed. (Grand Rapids: Eerdmans, 2003), 62–63. [3] Dio Cassius, *History* 60.17.4–6. [4] Francis Lyall, "Roman Law in the Writings of Paul—Aliens and Citizens," *Evangelical Quarterly* (EvQ) 48.1 (1976): 10. [5] Ferguson, *Backgrounds of Early Christianity*, 63. [6] Mary T. Boatwright, Daniel J. Gargola, and Richard J. A. Talbert, *The Romans: From Village to Empire* (New York: Oxford University Press, 2004), 421. [7] Eckhard J. Schnabel, *Paul and the Early Church*, vol. 2 in *Early Christian Mission* (Downers Grove, IL: InterVarsity, 2004), 1156; F. F. Bruce, *Paul: Apostle of the Heart Set Free* (Grand Rapids: Eerdmans, 1977), 39. [8] Brian M. Rapske, "Citizenship, Roman" in *DNTD*, 216. [9] Gordon D. Fee, *Paul's Letter to the Philippians* (Grand Rapids: Eerdmans, 1995), 162.

The *Via Egnatia* (Egnatian Way) that runs alongside the Roman forum at Philippi. Chariot ruts are visible in the stone.

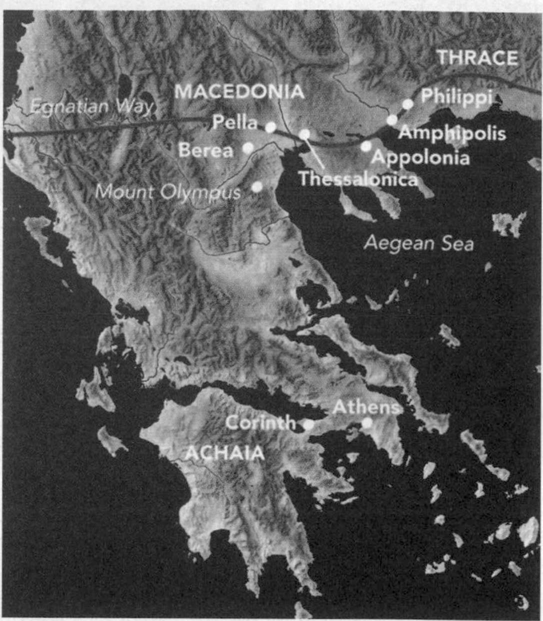

8 Finally[A] brothers and sisters, whatever is true,
whatever is honorable, whatever is just, whatever
is pure, whatever is lovely, whatever is commend-
able — if there is any moral excellence and if there
is anything praiseworthy — dwell on these things.
9 Do what you have learned and received and heard
from me, and seen in me, and the God of peace will
be with you.

APPRECIATION OF SUPPORT

10 I rejoiced in the Lord greatly because once again
you renewed your care for me. You were, in fact, concerned about me but lacked the opportunity to show
it. 11 I don't say this out of need, for I have learned to
be content in whatever circumstances I find myself.
12 I know how to make do with little, and I know how
to make do with a lot. In any and all circumstances I
have learned the secret of being content — whether well fed or hungry, whether in abundance or in
need. 13 I am able to do all things through him[B] who
strengthens me. 14 Still, you did well by partnering
with me in my hardship.

15 And you Philippians know that in the early days
of the gospel, when I left Macedonia, no church
shared with me in the matter of giving and receiving except you alone. 16 For even in Thessalonica you
sent gifts for my need several times. 17 Not that I seek
the gift, but I seek the profit[C] that is increasing to your
account. 18 But I have received everything in full, and
I have an abundance. I am fully supplied,[D] having received from Epaphroditus what you provided — a
fragrant offering, an acceptable sacrifice, pleasing
to God. 19 And my God will supply all your needs according to his riches in glory in Christ Jesus. 20 Now to
our God and Father be glory forever and ever. Amen.

FINAL GREETINGS

21 Greet every saint in Christ Jesus. The brothers who
are with me send you greetings. 22 All the saints send
you greetings, especially those who belong to Caesar's household. 23 The grace of the Lord Jesus Christ
be with your spirit.[E]

[A] **4:8** Or *In addition* [B] **4:13** Other mss read *Christ* [C] **4:17** Lit *fruit* [D] **4:18** Or *Here, then, is my receipt for everything, I have an abundance, for I am fully supplied* [E] **4:23** Other mss add *Amen.*

COLOSSIANS

Mineral deposits from the hot mineral springs at Hierapolis within sight of ancient Colossae across the Lycus Valley, not far from Laodicea. The hot springs were used as a health spa both during and since the Roman period.

INTRODUCTION TO

COLOSSIANS

Circumstances of Writing

Colossians retains its place among the epistles of Paul, who identified himself as the author (Col 1:1; 4:18). The church fathers unreservedly endorsed Pauline authorship (Irenaeus, *Against Heresies* 3.14.1; Tertullian, *Prescription against Heretics* 7; Clement of Alexandria, *Miscellanies* 1.1; see Justin, *Dialogue with Trypho* 85.2; 138.2). A close reading of Colossians reveals a considerable number of lexical, grammatical, and theological similarities with the other Pauline writings (1:9,26; 2:11–14,16,20–21; 3:1,3,5–17). Also favoring the authenticity of Colossians as a letter of Paul is its close connection with Philemon, an epistle widely regarded as Pauline.

During his ministry in Ephesus (Ac 19:10), Paul sent Epaphras to spread the gospel in the Lycus Valley. Epaphras subsequently established the church at Colossae (Col 1:7; 4:12–13). The city's population consisted mostly of Phrygians and Greeks, but it also included a significant number of Jews. The church, likewise, was mostly composed of Gentiles (1:21,27; 2:13), but it also had Jewish members (2:11,16,18,21; 3:11). When Epaphras (Phm 23) informed Paul of certain heretical teachings that had spread there, Paul wrote the letter to the Colossians as a theological antidote.

Paul wrote Colossians during his first Roman imprisonment (Col 4:3,10,18; see Ac 28:30–31; Eusebius, *Ecclesiastical History* 2.22.1) in the early AD 60s. Together with Philemon, Philippians, and Ephesians, Colossians is commonly classified as a Prison Epistle. All four epistles share several personal links that warrant this conclusion (Col 1:7; 4:7–8,17; Eph 6:21–22; Phm 2,12,23).

Contribution to the Bible

Colossians provides one of the Bible's fullest expressions of the deity and supremacy of Christ. This is most evident in the magnificent hymn of praise (Col 1:15–20) that sets forth Christ as the image of the invisible God, the Creator and sustainer of the universe, and the head of his body, the church. In Christ, are all the "treasures of wisdom and knowledge" (2:3), because in him "the entire fullness of God's nature dwells bodily" (2:9). The supremacy of Christ also has implication for believers' salvation (2:10,13,20; 3:1,11–12,17) and conduct (3:5–4:6). Colossians contributes to Scripture a high Christology and a presentation of its implications for the believer's conduct.

Structure

Colossians may be divided into two main parts. The first (1:3–2:23) is a polemic against false teachings. The second (3:1–4:17) is made up of exhortations to proper Christian living. This is typical of Paul's approach, presenting a theology position first, a position on which the practical exhortations are built. The introduction (1:1–2) is in the form of a Hellenistic, personal letter.

Notable in the final section are the mention of Onesimus (4:9), which links this letter with Philemon; the mention of a letter at Laodicea (4:16) that may have been Ephesians; and Paul's concluding signature, which indicates that the letter was prepared by an amanuensis (secretary; see 4:18).

GREETING

1 Paul, an apostle of Christ Jesus by God's will, and
Timothy our brother:
2 To the saints in Christ at Colossae, who are faithful
brothers and sisters.
Grace to you and peace from God our Father.[A]

THANKSGIVING

3 We always thank God, the Father of our Lord Jesus
Christ, when we pray for you, 4 for we have heard of
your faith in Christ Jesus and of the love you have for
all the saints 5 because of the hope reserved for you
in heaven. You have already heard about this hope in
the word of truth, the gospel 6 that has come to you. It
is bearing fruit and growing all over the world, just as
it has among you since the day you heard it and came
to truly appreciate God's grace.[B] 7 You learned this
from Epaphras, our dearly loved fellow servant. He
is a faithful minister of Christ on your[C] behalf, 8 and
he has told us about your love in the Spirit.

PRAYER FOR SPIRITUAL GROWTH

9 For this reason also, since the day we heard this, we
haven't stopped praying for you. We are asking that
you may be filled with the knowledge of his will in
all wisdom and spiritual understanding,[D] 10 so that
you may walk worthy of the Lord, fully pleasing to
him: bearing fruit in every good work and growing
in the knowledge of God, 11 being strengthened with
all power, according to his glorious might, so that
you may have great endurance and patience, joyfully 12 giving thanks to the Father, who has enabled
you[E] to share in the saints' inheritance in the light.
13 He has rescued us from the domain of darkness
and transferred us into the kingdom of the Son he
loves. 14 In him we have redemption,[F] the forgiveness of sins.

THE CENTRALITY OF CHRIST

15 He is the image of the invisible God,
the firstborn over all creation.
16 For everything was created by him,
in heaven and on earth,
the visible and the invisible,
whether thrones or dominions
or rulers or authorities —
all things have been created through him
and for him.

[A] **1:2** Other mss add *and the Lord Jesus Christ* [B] **1:6** Or *and truly recognized God's grace* [C] **1:7** Other mss read *our* [D] **1:9** Or *all spiritual wisdom and understanding* [E] **1:12** Other mss read *us* [F] **1:14** Other mss add *through his blood*

An unexcavated Roman theater, the smaller of the two theaters of Laodicea.

Colossae in the First Century

by Robert A. Weathers

Although the exact time of its founding is shrouded in uncertainty, Colossae emerged as early as 485 BC as a city rooted in the former Phrygian Empire. In 480 BC, Herodotus, a Greek historian, called it a "great city of Phrygia."[1] Another historian, Xenophon, wrote that it was a "large and prosperous city."[2]

This greatness was largely a result of the city's position in the Lycus Valley of Asia Minor, a lush area fed by the Lycus River. The city benefited from travelers who would usually come to Colossae first as they entered the valley on the way to Ephesus, about one hundred miles to the west. In addition, the popular city of Hierapolis was just thirteen miles away, and Laodicea was even closer, a mere twelve miles away (see Col 4:15–16). After enjoying a brief stay in Colossae, then Laodicea, a visitor could journey to Ephesus and then to Rome, roughly an eleven-hundred-mile trip.[3]

In its early history, the area accumulated great wealth. The river provided fertile pastures for grazing and fields for growing produce, so Colossae enjoyed a thriving sheep and cattle industry. Additionally, the city had grown rich from growing and selling figs and olives. Colossae also shared with Laodicea an abundance of chalk deposits, left by the flowing river, which provided merchants with ample resources for dying cloth. As a result, Colossae was famous for its wool manufacturing, especially for its production of a fine, reddish-purple cloth called colossinus.[4]

Colossae began a slow decline when the Roman Empire chose to shift the route through the valley. Asia became a Roman province in 190 BC, and the Romans decided that the best place for a capital city for this district was Laodicea. Therefore, they rerouted the road system to make Laodicea the most important junction in the region. Prosperity was literally diverted from the smaller city of Colossae. The decline of the city was slow but assured. Writing about twenty years prior to Paul, a Greek geographer named Strabo noted that the receding city had become a "small town."[5] In Paul's day, Colossae "had declined in political and financial importance," making it perhaps "the least important city to which Paul ever wrote."[6]

Even so, despite Colossae's political and economic weaknesses, the city was layered with a mixed and colorful population. Phrygian descendants still lived there, and the Roman military and political presence was dominant. Commerce had brought in various ethnic groups and religions. Included in these groups would have been a

Tell Colossae near the modern town of Honaz, Turkey. Nothing more than a small hill, the site of Colossae has never been excavated.

large population of Greek-speaking Jews. Many of these Jews descended from families imported into the Lycus Valley by the Seleucid King Antiochus the Great (223–187 BC).

In AD 60, a devastating earthquake struck the valley. Hierapolis and Laodicea were heavily damaged but managed to recover and remained strong for years. Already weakened from shifting politics and economic blows, Colossae never fully recovered. Most inhabitants moved to nearby stronger cities. In its latter history, Colossae was pummeled by invading armies, until finally, in the twelfth century, "the church was destroyed by the Turks and the city disappeared."[7] Ancient Colossae has never been fully excavated. ✣

A cornice stone at Colossae.

---

[1] Richard R. Melick Jr., *Philippians, Colossians, Philemon*, NAC (1991), 162; See Herodotus, *Persian Wars* 7.30. [2] Gene Lacoste Munn, "Introduction to Colossians," *Southwestern Journal of Theology* (*SwJT*) 16.1 (1973): 9; Xenophon, *Anabasis* 1.2.6. [3] Edgar J. Banks, "Colossae" in *ISBE* (1979), 1:732; Melick, *Philippians, Colossians, Philemon*, 162. [4] Scott Nash, "Colossae" in *EDB*, 269–70; Melick, *Philippians, Colossians, Philemon*, 163; Banks, "Colossae," 732; Munn, "Introduction," 10. [5] Melick, *Philippians, Colossians, Philemon*, 163; see J. B. Lightfoot, *Saint Paul's Epistles to the Colossians and to Philemon*, rev. ed. (Grand Rapids: Zondervan, 1879), 16. [6] Munn, "Introduction," 10. [7] Banks, "Colossae," 732; see Melick, *Philippians, Colossians, Philemon*, 162–63.

Phrygian terra-cotta jug with a cut beaked spout. Dates from the seventh–sixth centuries BC. Descendants of the Phrygians lived in Colossae.

17 He is before all things,
and by him all things hold together.
18 He is also the head of the body, the church;
he is the beginning,
the firstborn from the dead,
so that he might come to have
first place in everything.
19 For God was pleased to have
all his fullness dwell in him,
20 and through him to reconcile
everything to himself,
whether things on earth or things in heaven,
by making peace
through his blood, shed on the cross.[A]

21 Once you were alienated and hostile in your
minds as expressed in your evil actions. 22 But now
he has reconciled you by his physical body through
his death, to present you holy, faultless, and blameless
before him — 23 if indeed you remain grounded and
steadfast in the faith and are not shifted away from
the hope of the gospel that you heard. This gospel has
been proclaimed in all creation under heaven, and I,
Paul, have become a servant of it.

PAUL'S MINISTRY

24 Now I rejoice in my sufferings for you, and I am
completing in my flesh what is lacking in Christ's
afflictions for his body, that is, the church. 25 I have
become its servant, according to God's commission
that was given to me for you, to make the word of
God fully known, 26 the mystery hidden for ages and
generations but now revealed to his saints. 27 God
wanted to make known among the Gentiles the glorious wealth of this mystery, which is Christ in you, the
hope of glory. 28 We proclaim him, warning and teaching everyone with all wisdom, so that we may present
everyone mature in Christ. 29 I labor for this, striving
with his strength that works powerfully in me.

2 For I want you to know how greatly I am struggling for you, for those in Laodicea, and for all
who have not seen me in person. 2 I want their hearts
to be encouraged and joined together in love, so
that they may have all the riches of complete understanding and have the knowledge of God's mystery
— Christ.[B] 3 In him are hidden all the treasures of
wisdom and knowledge.

CHRIST VERSUS THE COLOSSIAN HERESY

4 I am saying this so that no one will deceive you with
arguments that sound reasonable. 5 For I may be absent in body, but I am with you in spirit, rejoicing to
see how well ordered you are and the strength of
your faith in Christ.

6 So then, just as you have received Christ Jesus
as Lord, continue to walk in him, 7 being rooted and
built up in him and established in the faith, just as
you were taught, and overflowing with gratitude.

8 Be careful that no one takes you captive through
philosophy and empty deceit based on human tradition, based on the elements of the world, rather than
Christ. 9 For the entire fullness of God's nature dwells
bodily[C] in Christ, 10 and you have been filled by him,
who is the head over every ruler and authority. 11 You
were also circumcised in him with a circumcision not
done with hands, by putting off the body of flesh, in
the circumcision of Christ, 12 when you were buried
with him in baptism, in which you were also raised
with him through faith in the working of God, who
raised him from the dead. 13 And when you were dead
in trespasses and in the uncircumcision of your flesh,
he made you alive with him and forgave us all our
trespasses. 14 He erased the certificate of debt, with
its obligations, that was against us and opposed to us,
and has taken it away by nailing it to the cross. 15 He
disarmed the rulers and authorities and disgraced
them publicly; he triumphed over them in him.[D]

16 Therefore, don't let anyone judge you in regard to
food and drink or in the matter of a festival or a new
moon or a Sabbath day.[E] 17 These are a shadow of what
was to come; the substance is[F] Christ. 18 Let no one

[A] **1:20** Other mss add *through him* [B] **2:2** Other mss read *mystery of God, both of the Father and of Christ*; other ms variations exist on this v. [C] **2:9** Or *nature lives in a human body* [D] **2:15** Or *them through it* [E] **2:16** Or *or sabbaths* [F] **2:17** Or *substance belongs to*

Funerary relief depicting a family. Reliefs of this type, in which the figures appear as busts within a circular frame, are sometimes freestanding and sometimes integrated into the facades of funerary structures, as here. Late first century AD.

Relief inscribed stele depicting parents and their daughter. To the left is a young slave. The relief dates to the mid-fourth century BC and is from Vergina, a small town west of Thessalonica.

condemn[A] you by delighting in ascetic practices and
the worship of angels, claiming access to a visionary
realm. Such people are inflated by empty notions of
their unspiritual[B] mind. 19 He doesn't hold on to the
head, from whom the whole body, nourished and
held together by its ligaments and tendons, grows
with growth from God.
20 If you died with Christ to the elements of this
world, why do you live as if you still belonged to the
world? Why do you submit to regulations: 21 "Don't
handle, don't taste, don't touch"? 22 All these regulations
refer to what is destined to perish by being
used up; they are human commands and doctrines.
23 Although these have a reputation for wisdom by
promoting self-made religion, false humility, and severe
treatment of the body, they are not of any value
in curbing self-indulgence.[C]

THE LIFE OF THE NEW MAN

3 So if you have been raised with Christ, seek the
things above, where Christ is, seated at the right
hand of God. 2 Set your minds on things above, not on
earthly things. 3 For you died, and your life is hidden
with Christ in God. 4 When Christ, who is your[D] life,
appears, then you also will appear with him in glory.
5 Therefore, put to death what belongs to your
earthly nature: sexual immorality, impurity, lust,
evil desire, and greed, which is idolatry. 6 Because of
these, God's wrath is coming upon the disobedient,[E]
7 and you once walked in these things when you were
living in them. 8 But now, put away all the following:
anger, wrath, malice, slander, and filthy language
from your mouth. 9 Do not lie to one another, since
you have put off the old self with its practices 10 and
have put on the new self. You are being renewed in
knowledge according to the image of your[F] Creator.
11 In Christ there is not Greek and Jew, circumcision
and uncircumcision, barbarian, Scythian, slave and
free; but Christ is all and in all.

THE CHRISTIAN LIFE

12 Therefore, as God's chosen ones, holy and dearly
loved, put on compassion, kindness, humility, gentleness,
and patience, 13 bearing with one another
and forgiving one another if anyone has a grievance
against another. Just as the Lord has forgiven you, so
you are also to forgive. 14 Above all, put on love, which
is the perfect bond of unity. 15 And let the peace of
Christ, to which you were also called in one body, rule
your hearts. And be thankful. 16 Let the word of Christ
dwell richly among you, in all wisdom teaching and
admonishing one another through psalms, hymns,

[A] **2:18** Or *disqualify* [B] **2:18** Lit *fleshly* [C] **2:23** Lit *value against indulgence of the flesh* [D] **3:4** Other mss read *our* [E] **3:6** Other mss omit *upon the disobedient* [F] **3:10** Lit *his*

and spiritual songs,[A] singing to God with gratitude in your hearts. 17 And whatever you do, in word or in deed, do everything in the name of the Lord Jesus, giving thanks to God the Father through him.

CHRIST IN YOUR HOME

18 Wives, submit yourselves to your husbands, as is fitting in the Lord. 19 Husbands, love your wives and don't be bitter toward them. 20 Children, obey your parents in everything, for this pleases the Lord. 21 Fathers, do not exasperate your children, so that they won't become discouraged. 22 Slaves, obey your human masters in everything. Don't work only while being watched, as people-pleasers, but work wholeheartedly, fearing the Lord. 23 Whatever you do, do it from the heart, as something done for the Lord and not for people, 24 knowing that you will receive the reward of an inheritance from the Lord. You serve the Lord Christ. 25 For the wrongdoer will be paid back for whatever wrong he has done, and there is no favoritism.

4 Masters, deal with your slaves justly and fairly, since you know that you too have a Master in heaven.

SPEAKING TO GOD AND OTHERS

2 Devote yourselves to prayer; stay alert in it with thanksgiving. 3 At the same time, pray also for us that God may open a door to us for the word, to speak the mystery of Christ, for which I am in chains, 4 so that I may make it known as I should. 5 Act wisely toward outsiders, making the most of the time. 6 Let your speech always be gracious, seasoned with salt, so that you may know how you should answer each person.

FINAL GREETINGS

7 Tychicus, our dearly loved brother, faithful minister, and fellow servant in the Lord, will tell you all the news about me. 8 I have sent him to you for this very purpose, so that you may know how we are[B] and so that he may encourage your hearts. 9 He is coming with Onesimus, a faithful and dearly loved brother, who is one of you. They will tell you about everything here.

10 Aristarchus, my fellow prisoner, sends you greetings, as does Mark, Barnabas's cousin (concerning whom you have received instructions: if he comes to you, welcome him), 11 and so does Jesus who is called Justus. These alone of the circumcised are my coworkers for the kingdom of God, and they have been a comfort to me. 12 Epaphras, who is one of you, a servant of Christ Jesus, sends you greetings. He is always wrestling for you in his prayers, so that you can stand mature and fully assured[C] in everything God wills. 13 For I testify about him that he works hard[D] for you, for those in Laodicea, and for those in Hierapolis. 14 Luke, the dearly loved physician, and Demas send you greetings. 15 Give my greetings to the brothers and sisters in Laodicea, and to Nympha and the church in her home. 16 After this letter has been read at your gathering, have it read also in the church of the Laodiceans; and see that you also read the letter from Laodicea. 17 And tell Archippus, "Pay attention to the ministry you have received in the Lord, so that you can accomplish it."

18 I, Paul, am writing this greeting with my own hand. Remember my chains. Grace be with you.[E]

[A] **3:16** Or *and songs prompted by the Spirit* [B] **4:8** Other mss read *that he may know how you are* [C] **4:12** Other mss read *and complete* [D] **4:13** Other mss read *he has a great zeal* [E] **4:18** Other mss add *Amen.*

Medical center at ancient Pergamum in western Turkey.

1 THESSALONIANS

Church of St. Paul, Thessaloniki, Greece.

INTRODUCTION TO

1 THESSALONIANS

Circumstances of Writing

No serious objections have been made to dispute that Paul was the author of 1 Thessalonians (1:1). The greeting also mentions Silvanus and Timothy. Sometimes Paul wrote from the team perspective, but he was the primary author (2:18; 3:2).

About AD 50, the missionary team led by Paul and Silas left Philippi and traveled westward on the Roman road known as the *Via Egnatia*. They proceeded toward the strategic capital city of the Roman province of Macedonia—Thessalonica.

Thessalonica was a large port city on the Aegean Sea in modern-day Greece, with a population of about two hundred thousand. The city was filled with pagan worshipers of idols, the full pantheon of Greek and Roman gods, and was well known for its emperor worship. Thessalonica was loyal to Caesar, and he had granted its citizens many privileges.

As was his custom, Paul found the local Jewish synagogue and started teaching there. For three Sabbaths, he reasoned with the Jews from the Scriptures. He explained and demonstrated that the promised Messiah had to suffer and rise from the dead. After explaining the life, death, and resurrection of Jesus, he then stated boldly, "This Jesus I am proclaiming to you is the Messiah" (Ac 17:3). Some of the Jews were persuaded, along with some of the devout Greeks who were worshipers at the synagogue, and some of the prominent women. They joined Paul and Silas, and the church in Thessalonica was born.

There were Jews in the city who were not persuaded, and they became envious of what Paul and Silas had done. They incited the people into an uproar and attacked Jason's house where the missionary team had been staying. Wanting to drag Paul and Silas out before the crowd, they found only Jason and some new believers. They dragged these out before the city authorities. The rulers, not wanting more unrest, forced Jason and the rest of the brothers to make a financial payment of security to ensure that there would not be a repeat of such a disturbance. That very night the Thessalonian believers sent Paul and Silas away to Berea, where they could continue their ministry (17:1–9).

From Berea, Paul went to Athens. He wanted to see the Thessalonians again. When he could endure the separation no longer, he sent Timothy to encourage the Thessalonian believers (1Th 3:2). Timothy came back with an encouraging report about the Thessalonian church (3:6). Paul wrote to them from Corinth in response to Timothy's report. Based on the archaeological evidence of a dated inscription mentioning Gallio, proconsul of Achaia, by name (Ac 18:12) and correlating this with Paul's visit to Corinth when Gallio was there, 1 Thessalonians can be reliably dated to AD 50 or 51. This would make 1 Thessalonians the earliest of Paul's letters with the probable exception of the book of Galatians.

Contribution to the Bible

First Thessalonians contributes to our understanding of the second coming of Christ. Paul wrote to correct some misunderstandings of this doctrine. In doing so, he showed us that Christ's return gives us true hope. First Thessalonians and 1 Corinthians (chap. 15) are the only books that explicitly mention that Christians who are alive at Christ's return will be changed and will meet Christ in the air without dying.

Structure

First Thessalonians follows the standard form for a first-century letter: greeting (1Th1:1), thanksgiving (1:2–4), body (1:5–5:22), and farewell (5:23–28). The body of the letter does not follow Paul's typical structure of presenting doctrine first, followed by practical exhortation based on that doctrine. Instead, 1 Thessalonians moves back and forth between the doctrinal and the practical.

GREETING

1 Paul, Silvanus,[A] and Timothy:
To the church of the Thessalonians in God the Father and the Lord Jesus Christ.
Grace to you and peace.[B]

THANKSGIVING

2 We always thank God for all of you, making mention of you constantly in our prayers. 3 We recall, in the presence of our God and Father, your work produced by faith, your labor motivated by love, and your endurance inspired by hope in our Lord Jesus Christ. 4 For we know, brothers and sisters loved by God, that he has chosen you, 5 because our gospel did not come to you in word only, but also in power, in the Holy Spirit, and with full assurance. You know how we lived among you for your benefit, 6 and you yourselves became imitators of us and of the Lord when, in spite of severe persecution, you welcomed the message with joy from the Holy Spirit. 7 As a result, you became an example to all the believers in Macedonia and Achaia. 8 For the word of the Lord rang out from you, not only in Macedonia and Achaia, but in every place that your faith[C] in God has gone out. Therefore, we don't need to say anything, 9 for they themselves report[D] what kind of reception we had from you: how you turned to God from idols to serve the living and true God 10 and to wait for his Son from heaven, whom he raised from the dead — Jesus, who rescues us from the coming wrath.

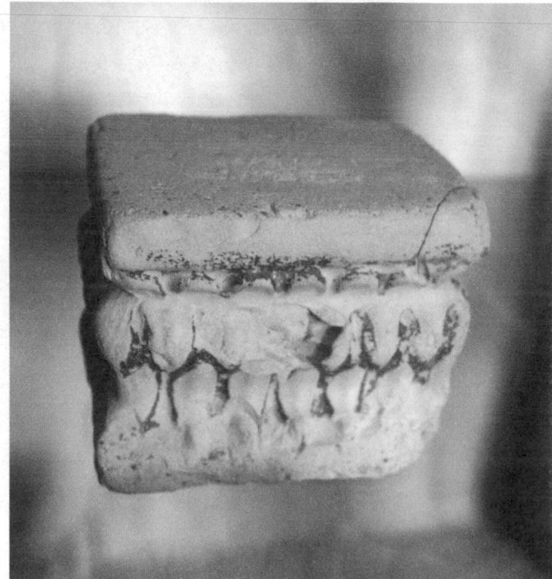

Worship was not only an action for the public arena, but family worship and personal piety were also important in Greek culture. Shown, terra-cotta house altar dated sixth–fourth centuries BC.

Rare wooden relief depicting Hercules. Credited with having the ability to avert evil of all kings and to protect royalty, Hercules received a tithe from the profits of local merchants.

PAUL'S CONDUCT

2 For you yourselves know, brothers and sisters, that our visit with you was not without result. 2 On the contrary, after we had previously suffered and were treated outrageously in Philippi, as you know, we were emboldened by our God to speak the gospel of God to you in spite of great opposition. 3 For our exhortation didn't come from error or impurity or an intent to deceive. 4 Instead, just as we have been approved by God to be entrusted with the gospel, so we speak, not to please people, but rather God, who examines our hearts. 5 For we never used flattering speech, as you know, or had greedy motives — God is our witness — 6 and we didn't seek glory from people, either from you or from others. 7 Although we could have been a burden as Christ's apostles, instead we were gentle[E] among you, as a nurse[F] nurtures her own children. 8 We cared so much for you that we were pleased to share with you not only the gospel of God but also our own lives, because you had become dear to us. 9 For you remember our labor and hardship, brothers and sisters. Working night and day so that we would not burden any of you, we preached God's gospel to you. 10 You are witnesses, and so is God, of how devoutly, righteously, and blamelessly we conducted ourselves with you believers. 11 As you know, like a father with his own children, 12 we encouraged, comforted, and implored each one of you to walk worthy of God, who calls you into his own kingdom and glory.

[A] **1:1** Or *Silas*; Ac 15:22–32; 16:19–40; 17:1–16 [B] **1:1** Other mss add *from God our Father and the Lord Jesus Christ* [C] **1:8** Or *in every place news of your faith* [D] **1:9** Lit *report about us* [E] **2:7** Many mss read *infants* [F] **2:7** Or *nursing mother*

The Gods of Thessalonica

by Scott Hummel

Although predominantly an Egyptian deity, Isis was worshiped throughout the Roman Empire, as evidenced in this temple of Isis at Pompeii.

Thessalonica was located in Macedonia. Even though many Greeks looked down on the Macedonians as semibarbarian, Greek mythology recognized that the Macedonians were related to the Greeks as "cousins."[1] By the time of Alexander the Great, who was himself Macedonian, the Macedonians had largely become "Greek" in culture and religion. The Macedonians told Greek myths and worshiped Greek gods. Mount Olympus itself was located in Macedonia about fifty miles from Thessalonica.

The two main sources of Greek mythology are Homer (who wrote the *Odyssey*) and Hesiod (who wrote *Theogony*).[2] Although many myths dealt with only the gods, the majority of the myths described the interaction between gods and heroes. The myths permeated all of Greek society as expressed through literature, art, drama, temple worship, and stories told to children. Myths helped to define social roles and values as well as describe the character of the gods. While the gods were perceived as immortal and powerful, each had its own sphere of influence. One god was not worshiped to the exclusion of the others, because to neglect one god was to neglect that area of reality.[3]

Among the Greek gods were Titans, Olympians, and lesser gods. The Titans were the earliest gods and represented the basic elements of reality. At Mount Olympus, the twelve Olympian gods led by Zeus overthrew the Titans. All the other Olympian gods were either the siblings or children of Zeus. By the time of Paul, many of the Greek gods were equated with Roman gods. For example, the Roman god Jupiter was equated with Zeus.

Countless myths offer details about Zeus and his numerous affairs with goddesses and women. Many of his children, such as Hercules, became the heroes of old. Heroes were greater than normal men, but less powerful than the gods. After their deaths, the heroes were worshiped with special honors.[4] Hero worship later paved the way for ruler and emperor worship. Following Alexander the Great, the main Greek and Macedonian kings portrayed themselves as descended from the gods. Some kings were honored as divine after their deaths, but others, such as Antiochus IV, were worshiped as gods, even in life.[5]

Since the Greeks believed the gods took pleasure in the quality of their temples and images, Greek artisans produced some of the best architecture and art in the ancient world. The statue of Zeus at Olympia and the temple of Artemis at Ephesus were among the seven Wonders of the Ancient World.

Worshipers offered prayers, incense, and sacrifices to the gods in the temples. In exchange for sacrifices or offerings, the worshipers hoped to receive a blessing or a divine message (oracle) from the gods. The most famous oracle in Greece was located at the temple of Apollo in Delphi. There the priestess inhaled vapors within the temple. In an ecstatic state, she uttered the message of Apollo, which the priest then interpreted for the worshiper.[6]

Not everyone in Greece believed the oracles, priests, or myths. In fact, for centuries a growing number of Greek philosophers grew increasingly skeptical about the very existence of the gods. They sought instead more natural explanations of the world, and they grew increasingly embarrassed by the immorality of the gods as expressed in their myths. They also objected to anthropomorphism (gods in human form) and began to argue for a single disembodied mind, force, or principle.[7]

While walking through Thessalonica, Paul would have passed temples to Zeus and Aphrodite. Thessalonians also worshiped the Egyptian god Serapis and his wife Isis as evidenced by the remains of their temples. The two most prominent traditional gods in Thessalonica were Dionysus and Cabirus. Since Dionysus was the god of wine and joy, his celebrations and worship involved intoxication and orgies. Cabirus was a lesser god elsewhere in Macedonia and Greece but was the chief and most popular god in Thessalonica. During the time of Paul, the mystery religion of Cabirus would have been one of the most important cults in the city. Much remains unknown about the religion, but we know that Cabirus was worshiped as a fertility god. The cult's mythology held that Cabirus had been martyred by his two brothers and had been buried at Mount Olympus, but he would often return from the dead to aid his followers, especially sailors.[8]

One of the primary gods of Thessalonica was Serapis. Adopted into Greek culture, Serapis had been the Egyptian god of the underworld and the Nile River. Devotees understood Serapis to provide fertility and protect seafarers, traits that made Serapis attractive to the culture of Thessalonica.

With the rise of Roman control, the Thessalonians embraced worship of the goddess Roma and Caesar Augustus. Paul probably saw the temple of Augustus in Thessalonica, and he certainly would have seen the divinity of Caesar proclaimed on coins minted in Thessalonica. Many of the coins had even replaced the image of Zeus with that of Augustus. Any challenge to emperor worship or promotion of another kingdom or lord threatened retaliation from Rome.[9]

Religion permeated every aspect of life and society in first-century Thessalonica. Festivals, theater, education, war, government, and athletics were all religious events or institutions. Turning from Greek religion meant more than turning from idol worship; it meant turning from one's traditions, community, and family. Although many Greeks saw Christianity as having "turned the world upside down" (Ac 17:6), Paul knew it meant turning the world to the only true and living God. ✣

At Corinth, mosaic of Dionysus, god of wine; dated first century BC to first century AD.

[1] For the relationship between the Macedonians and Greeks see N. G. L. Hammond, *The Macedonian State: Origins, Institutions, and History* (Oxford: Clarendon, 1989), 12–15. [2] See Jasper Griffin, "Greek Myth and Hesiod," in *Greece and the Hellenistic World*, ed. John Boardman, Jasper Griffin, and Oswyn Murray (Oxford: Oxford University Press, 1988), 73–82; Simon Price, *Religions of the Ancient Greeks* (Cambridge: Cambridge University Press, 1999), 12–14. [3] Robert Parker, "Greek Religion" in *Greece and the Hellenistic World*, 248. [4] Parker, "Greek Religion," 250; Maria Mavromataki, *Greek Mythology and Religion* (Athens, Greece: Haitalis, 1997), 148. [5] Hammond, *Macedonian State*, 21–22; Peter Green, *Alexander to Actium: The Historical Evolution of the Hellenistic Age* (Los Angeles: University of California Press, 1990), 397–99; Bruce K. Waltke, "Antiochus IV Epiphanes" in *ISBE* (1979), 1:146. [6] Price, *Religions of the Ancient Greeks*, 37; Mavromataki, *Greek Mythology and Religion*, 145–46. [7] Antonía Tripolitis, *Religions of the Hellenistic-Roman Age* (Grand Rapids: Eerdmans, 2001), 14–15; Griffin, "Greek Myth and Hesiod," 80; Parker, "Greek Religion," 266. [8] Michael W. Holmes, *1 and 2 Thessalonians*, NIV Application Commentary (Grand Rapids: Zondervan, 1998), 19; Karl P. Donfried, "The Cults of Thessalonica and the Thessalonian Correspondence," *NTS* 31 (1985): 338–39; Charles A. Wanamaker, *The Epistles to the Thessalonians*, New International Greek Testament Commentary (NIGTC) (Grand Rapids: Eerdmans, 1990), 5, 12. [9] Wanamaker, *Thessalonians*, 5–6; David W. J. Gill and Conrad Gempf, eds., *The Book of Acts in Its First Century Setting*, vol. 2., The Book of Acts in Its Graeco-Roman Setting (Eugene, OR: Wipf & Stock, 2000), 408, 415; Ben Witherington III, *The Acts of the Apostles: A Socio-Rhetorical Commentary* (Grand Rapids: Eerdmans, 1998), 503.

Marble bust of Homer; Roman copy made from a Hellenistic original dated to the second century BC. Much of the information we have about Greek mythology comes from Homer's writings.

Relief sculpture at Ashkelon featuring Isis with the child-god, Horus.

RECEPTION AND OPPOSITION TO THE MESSAGE

13 This is why we constantly thank God, because when
you received the word of God that you heard from us,
you welcomed it not as a human message, but as it
truly is, the word of God, which also works effectively
in you who believe. 14 For you, brothers and sisters,
became imitators of God's churches in Christ Jesus
that are in Judea, since you have also suffered the
same things from people of your own country, just
as they did from the Jews 15 who killed the Lord Jesus
and the prophets and persecuted us. They displease
God and are hostile to everyone, 16 by keeping us from
speaking to the Gentiles so that they may be saved.
As a result, they are constantly filling up their sins
to the limit, and wrath has overtaken them at last.[A]

PAUL'S DESIRE TO SEE THEM

17 But as for us, brothers and sisters, after we were
forced to leave you[B] for a short time (in person, not
in heart), we greatly desired and made every effort
to return and see you face to face. 18 So we wanted to
come to you — even I, Paul, time and again — but
Satan hindered us. 19 For who is our hope or joy or
crown of boasting in the presence of our Lord Jesus
at his coming? Is it not you? 20 Indeed you are our
glory and joy!

ANXIETY IN ATHENS

3 Therefore, when we could no longer stand it,
we thought it was better to be left alone in Athens. 2 And we sent Timothy, our brother and God's
coworker[C] in the gospel of Christ, to strengthen and
encourage you concerning your faith, 3 so that no one
will be shaken by these afflictions. For you yourselves
know that we are appointed to this. 4 In fact, when we
were with you, we told you in advance that we were
going to experience affliction, and as you know, it
happened. 5 For this reason, when I could no longer
stand it, I also sent him to find out about your faith,
fearing that the tempter had tempted you and that
our labor might be for nothing.

ENCOURAGED BY TIMOTHY

6 But now Timothy has come to us from you and
brought us good news about your faith and love. He
reported that you always have good memories of
us and that you long to see us, as we also long to see
you. 7 Therefore, brothers and sisters, in all our distress and affliction, we were encouraged about you
through your faith. 8 For now we live, if you stand

[A] **2:16** Or *to the end* [B] **2:17** Lit *orphaned from you* [C] **3:2** Other mss read *servant*

From the theatre frieze at Delphi, panel depicting scenes left-to-right of Centaur, the Lernean Hydra, Antaeus, the girdle of Hippolyte, and the three-bodied giant Geryon.

firm in the Lord. 9 How can we thank God for you in return for all the joy we experience before our God because of you, 10 as we pray very earnestly night and day to see you face to face and to complete what is lacking in your faith?

PRAYER FOR THE CHURCH

11 Now may our God and Father himself, and our Lord Jesus, direct our way to you. 12 And may the Lord cause you to increase and overflow with love for one another and for everyone, just as we do for you. 13 May he make your hearts blameless in holiness before our God and Father at the coming of our Lord Jesus with all his saints. Amen.[A]

THE CALL TO SANCTIFICATION

4 Additionally then, brothers and sisters, we ask and encourage you in the Lord Jesus, that as you have received instruction from us on how you should live and please God — as you are doing[B] — do this even more. 2 For you know what commands we gave you through the Lord Jesus.

3 For this is God's will, your sanctification: that you keep away from sexual immorality, 4 that each of you knows how to control his own body[C] in holiness and honor, 5 not with lustful passions, like the Gentiles, who don't know God. 6 This means one must not transgress against and take advantage of a brother or sister in this manner, because the Lord is an avenger of all these offenses, as we also previously told and warned you. 7 For God has not called us to impurity but to live in holiness. 8 Consequently, anyone who rejects this does not reject man, but God, who gives you his Holy Spirit.

LOVING AND WORKING

9 About brotherly love: You don't need me to write you because you yourselves are taught by God to love one another. 10 In fact, you are doing this toward all the brothers and sisters in the entire region of Macedonia. But we encourage you, brothers and sisters, to do this even more, 11 to seek to lead a quiet life, to mind your own business,[D] and to work with your own hands, as we commanded you, 12 so that you may behave properly in the presence of outsiders and not be dependent on anyone.[E]

THE COMFORT OF CHRIST'S COMING

13 We do not want you to be uninformed, brothers and sisters, concerning those who are asleep, so that you will not grieve like the rest, who have no hope. 14 For if we believe that Jesus died and rose again, in the same way, through Jesus, God will bring with him those who have fallen asleep. 15 For we say this to you by a word from the Lord: We who are still alive at the Lord's coming will certainly not precede those who have fallen asleep. 16 For the Lord himself will descend from heaven with a shout,[F] with the archangel's voice, and with the trumpet of God, and the dead in Christ will rise first. 17 Then we who are still alive, who are left, will be caught up together with them in the clouds to meet the Lord in the air, and so we will always be with the Lord. 18 Therefore encourage[G] one another with these words.

[A] **3:13** Other mss omit *Amen.* [B] **4:1** Lit *walking* [C] **4:4** Or *to acquire his own wife*; lit *to possess his own vessel* [D] **4:11** Lit *to practice one's own things* [E] **4:12** Or *not need anything*, or *not be in need* [F] **4:16** Or *command* [G] **4:18** Or *comfort*

Persons would take on the names of deities as evidenced in this funerary relief from Thessalonica. Hegesandra (pictured seated) commissioned this stele in memory of her husband named Dionysius. The husband is depicted as a hero, as indicated by the snake and the horse's head. Dated about 50 BC to the second century AD.

THE DAY OF THE LORD

5 About the times and the seasons: Brothers and
sisters, you do not need anything to be written
to you. 2 For you yourselves know very well that the
day of the Lord will come just like a thief in the night.
3 When they say, "Peace and security," then sudden destruction will come upon them, like labor pains on a
pregnant woman, and they will not escape. 4 But you,
brothers and sisters, are not in the dark, for this day
to surprise you like a thief. 5 For you are all children of
light and children of the day. We do not belong to the
night or the darkness. 6 So then, let us not sleep, like
the rest, but let us stay awake and be self-controlled.
7 For those who sleep, sleep at night, and those who
get drunk, get drunk at night. 8 But since we belong
to the day, let us be self-controlled and put on the
armor of faith and love, and a helmet of the hope of
salvation. 9 For God did not appoint us to wrath, but
to obtain salvation through our Lord Jesus Christ,
10 who died for us, so that whether we are awake or
asleep, we may live together with him. 11 Therefore
encourage one another and build each other up as
you are already doing.

EXHORTATIONS AND BLESSINGS

12 Now we ask you, brothers and sisters, to give recognition to those who labor among you and lead you[A]
in the Lord and admonish you, 13 and to regard them
very highly in love because of their work. Be at peace
among yourselves. 14 And we exhort you, brothers
and sisters: warn those who are idle,[B] comfort the
discouraged, help the weak, be patient with everyone. 15 See to it that no one repays evil for evil to any-

The goat-footed god Pan wears an animal pelt, from which protrude only his hairy legs; in his left hand is a panpipe. Pan was the Greek god of shepherds, fields, and flocks. This statue is from the first century AD; found in Sparta.

one, but always pursue what is good for one another
and for all. 16 Rejoice always, 17 pray constantly, 18 give
thanks in everything; for this is God's will for you in
Christ Jesus. 19 Don't stifle the Spirit. 20 Don't despise
prophecies, 21 but test all things. Hold on to what is
good. 22 Stay away from every kind of evil.
23 Now may the God of peace himself sanctify you
completely. And may your whole spirit, soul, and
body be kept sound and blameless at the coming of
our Lord Jesus Christ. 24 He who calls you is faithful;
he will do it. 25 Brothers and sisters, pray for us also.
26 Greet all the brothers and sisters with a holy kiss.
27 I charge you by the Lord that this letter be read to
all the brothers and sisters. 28 The grace of our Lord
Jesus Christ be with you.

[A] **5:12** Or *care for you* [B] **5:14** Or *who are disorderly*, or *who are undisciplined*

2 THESSALONIANS

Ruins of the Roman forum at Thessalonica; shops were on the lower level; the stoa was above.

INTRODUCTION TO

2 THESSALONIANS

Circumstances of Writing

Paul is stated to be the author of 2 Thessalonians (1:1). The greeting also mentions Silvanus and Timothy, but Paul was the primary author (3:17).

See discussion under introduction to 1 Thessalonians. Although there are few indicators of the date and place of writing of 2 Thessalonians, it was probably written from Corinth around AD 50–51 shortly after 1 Thessalonians. The mention of Paul, Silvanus, and Timothy together in the salutation, as was the case with 1 Thessalonians 1:1, supports this conclusion. An additional support for this view is the mention of a previous letter, which was probably 1 Thessalonians (2Th 2:15).

Contribution to the Bible

Second Thessalonians continues and further amplifies some of the same themes as 1 Thessalonians: persecution, sanctification, and end-time events associated with the second coming of Christ. One important difference is that 2 Thessalonians describes the "man of lawlessness" who will be revealed in the end times and what restrains him from being revealed (2:1–12). The book also contains a lengthy discourse on the need for believers to have a proper work ethic to provide for their own needs (3:6–15).

Structure

The tone of Paul's second letter to the Thessalonians is markedly "cooler" than his first letter. In his first letter, Paul was enthusiastic about the Thessalonians' progress in the gospel, and he offered calm advice about congregational life (1Th 5:12–22). In this second letter, though, Paul expressed grave concern about the spiritual state of the Thessalonian believers. He gave them a sharp rebuke about congregational life (2Th 3:6–15). His style is typical of his other letters—a doctrinal section followed by practical exhortation.

GREETING

1 Paul, Silvanus,[A] and Timothy:
To the church of the Thessalonians in God our
Father and the Lord Jesus Christ.
2 Grace to you and peace from God our Father and
the Lord Jesus Christ.

GOD'S JUDGMENT AND GLORY

3 We ought to thank God always for you, brothers and
sisters, and rightly so, since your faith is flourishing
and the love each one of you has for one another is
increasing. 4 Therefore, we ourselves boast about
you among God's churches — about your perseverance and faith in all the persecutions and afflictions
that you are enduring. 5 It is clear evidence of God's
righteous judgment that you will be counted worthy
of God's kingdom, for which you also are suffering,
6 since it is just for God to repay with affliction those
who afflict you 7 and to give relief to you who are
afflicted, along with us. This will take place at the
revelation of the Lord Jesus from heaven with his
powerful angels, 8 when he takes vengeance with
flaming fire on those who don't know God and on
those who don't obey the gospel of our Lord Jesus.
9 They will pay the penalty of eternal destruction from
the Lord's presence and from his glorious strength
10 on that day when he comes to be glorified by his
saints and to be marveled at by all those who have
believed, because our testimony among you was believed. 11 In view of this, we always pray for you that
our God will make you worthy of his calling, and by
his power fulfill your every desire to do good[B] and
your work produced by faith, 12 so that the name of
our Lord Jesus will be glorified by you, and you by
him, according to the grace of our God and the Lord
Jesus Christ.

THE MAN OF LAWLESSNESS

2 Now concerning the coming of our Lord Jesus
Christ and our being gathered to him: We ask you,
brothers and sisters, 2 not to be easily upset or troubled, either by a prophecy[C] or by a message or by a
letter supposedly from us, alleging that the day of the
Lord[D] has come. 3 Don't let anyone deceive you in any
way. For that day will not come unless the apostasy[E]
comes first and the man of lawlessness[F] is revealed,
the man doomed to destruction. 4 He opposes and
exalts himself above every so-called god or object of

[A] **1:1** Or *Silas*; Ac 15:22–32; 16:19–40; 17:1–16 [B] **1:11** Or *power bring to fruition your desire to do good* [C] **2:2** Or *spiritual utterance* [D] **2:2** Other mss read *Christ* [E] **2:3** Or *rebellion* [F] **2:3** Other mss read *man of sin*

Closeup of the triumphal arch of the Roman emperor Galerius which sits astride the Egnatian Way in the center of Thessalonica (modern Salonica), Greece.

First-Century Thessalonica

by Timothy Trammell

The Odeum, restored, at the Roman forum in Thessalonica. In the background are current excavations at the forum. The fact that Thessalonica has been continually inhabited has made excavation difficult throughout most parts of the city.

HISTORY

Prehistoric settlements in the area date to 2300 BC. Thessalonica was at first a small village called Alia, but it was subsequently named Therma because of the thermal springs to the east and south of it. Cassander, one of the four key generals who had served under Alexander the Great, enlarged the city in 315 BC, naming it Thessalonica after his wife, Thessalonike, the half sister of Alexander. He formed the city by forcing twenty-six villages to unite; then he designated it his capital.[1]

In 167 BC, the city came under Roman control when Rome defeated Perseus, king of Macedonia. At that time the kingdom was divided into four districts with Thessalonica as capital of the second district. In 146 BC Macedonia was made a Roman province, and Thessalonica became the provincial capital. As the capital of Macedonia it was known as "The Metropolis of Macedonia"—literally, the "mother city" of the province.

The economic strength of the city was solidified in 130 BC when Rome constructed a roadway, the Via Egnatia, linking Thessalonica with the Adriatic Sea on the west and Neapolis on the east.[2] The city supported Antony and Octavian (later Augustus Caesar) in their conflict against the Triumvirs (ca 42 BC) and thus received the status of a free city. As a result, Thessalonica was allowed to administer her own affairs.

However, the city's privileged status was interrupted in AD 15 for a few years. The increasing prosperity of the region caused a protest against what the leadership of the city considered high taxation. This caused Tiberius to change Macedonia from a proconsular province to an imperial province, that is, one under the direct control of Caesar.[3] Yet this ultimately proved to be positive, for this gave the city intimate and immediate access to Rome. Claudius reversed this action in AD 44 by making Macedonia a senatorial province again.[4]

LOCATION

Ancient Thessalonica was located on the eastern coast of the province of Macedonia between the Balkan mountain range and the Greek peninsula. It was near the Axius and the Haliacmon Rivers, both major waterways. Although nearby Pella had been the capital chosen by Philip II, father of Alexander the Great, Cassander selected Thessalonica because of several favorable geographic features. Situated on the Thermaic Gulf, it offered protection from the dangerous southeast winds. In addition, the hills surrounding the city provided shelter from the north winds that blew in from central Europe.[5]

The region surrounding Thessalonica was rich in natural resources. Located on the edge of the great central plain of Macedonia, the area had fertile soil and abundant rainfall. The mountains around the city were covered with timber, providing wood for houses and boats. The mild climate enabled the people to grow grain and fruit, but not Mediterranean crops such as dates and olives. Fish filled the nearby lakes and rivers. Mines producing gold, silver, copper, iron, and lead dotted the surrounding area.[6]

In the first century AD, Thessalonica was the main seaport and naval base of Macedonia. The Via Egnatia, Rome's major road to its eastern provinces, ran along the northern outskirts of the city. In addition, the main route from the Danube down to the Aegean Sea passed through Thessalonica, which means the city was situated at the junction of these two important thoroughfares.

The White Tower is the most famous tower in Greece and is the symbol of Thessalonica. Built in AD 1500, the tower was part of the city's defense system and served as the city jail.

RELIGIOUS CLIMATE

In the first century AD, the worship of Dionysus and the mystery god Cabirus was quite popular in Thessalonica. Devotees of Zeus, Heracles, Apollo, Asclepius, Aphrodite, Demeter, Athene, Serapis, Isis, and the Dioskuri were also part of the religious life of the city.

Further, evidence of Thessalonian involvement with the imperial cult—that is, worship of rulers—is abundant. Even prior to the Roman period, Alexander the Great had been accorded divine honors. These honors came because of supposed revelations received at the oracles at Delphi—oracles that affirmed his divinity. Inscriptions even into the second and third centuries AD ascribe divine status to him and tell of a priesthood that served his cult in Thessalonica. Citizens worshiped Julius Caesar and Augustus Caesar. Titles such as "god" and "son of god" are found on inscriptions and coins from the period.[7] ✣

---

[1] John B. Polhill, *Paul and His Letters* (Nashville: B&H Academic, 1999), 181; Gene L. Green, *The Letters to the Thessalonians*, Pillar New Testament Commentary (Grand Rapids: Eerdmans, 2002), 2. [2] Jerome Murphy-O'Conner, *Paul: A Critical Life* (Oxford: Oxford University Press, 1997), 114. [3] Tacitus, *Annals* 1.76. [4] Dio Cassius, *History* 40.24.1; Suetonius, *Claudius* 25.1. [5] Green, *Thessalonians*, 2. [6] Green, *Thessalonians*, 6. [7] Green, *Thessalonians*, 39–40.

Partial marble statue of Rome's Emperor Nero, who ruled AD 54–68. Because of his actions against Christians, some thought the antichrist would be a reincarnation of Nero.

worship, so that he sits[A] in God's temple, proclaiming
that he himself is God.
5 Don't you remember that when I was still with
you I used to tell you about this? 6 And you know what
currently restrains him, so that he will be revealed in
his time. 7 For the mystery of lawlessness is already
at work, but the one now restraining will do so until
he is out of the way, 8 and then the lawless one will
be revealed. The Lord Jesus will destroy him with the
breath of his mouth and will bring him to nothing at
the appearance of his coming. 9 The coming of the
lawless one is based on Satan's working, with every
kind of miracle, both signs and wonders serving the
lie, 10 and with every wicked deception among those
who are perishing. They perish because they did not
accept the love of the truth and so be saved. 11 For this
reason God sends them a strong delusion so that they
will believe the lie, 12 so that all will be condemned
— those who did not believe the truth but delighted
in unrighteousness.

Awl used for piercing hides and leather; dated to the first to second centuries AD.

STAND FIRM

13 But we ought to thank God always for you, brothers
and sisters loved by the Lord, because from the beginning[B] God has chosen you for salvation through
sanctification by the Spirit and through belief in the
truth. 14 He called you to this through our gospel, so
that you might obtain the glory of our Lord Jesus
Christ. 15 So then, brothers and sisters, stand firm and
hold to the traditions you were taught, whether by
what we said or what we wrote.
16 May our Lord Jesus Christ himself and God our
Father, who has loved us and given us eternal encouragement and good hope by grace, 17 encourage
your hearts and strengthen you in every good work
and word.

PRAY FOR US

3 In addition, brothers and sisters, pray for us that
the word of the Lord may spread rapidly and
be honored, just as it was with you, 2 and that we
may be delivered from wicked and evil people, for
not all have faith.[C] 3 But the Lord is faithful; he will
strengthen you and guard you from the evil one. 4 We
have confidence in the Lord about you, that you are
doing and will continue to do what we command.
5 May the Lord direct your hearts to God's love and
Christ's endurance.

WARNING AGAINST IRRESPONSIBLE BEHAVIOR

6 Now we command you, brothers and sisters, in the
name of our Lord Jesus Christ, to keep away from
every brother or sister who is idle and does not live[D]
according to the tradition received from us. 7 For
you yourselves know how you should imitate us:

[A] **2:4** Other mss add *as God* [B] **2:13** Other mss read *because as a firstfruit* [C] **3:2** Or *for the faith is not in everyone* [D] **3:6** Lit *walk*

Marble relief of freedmen; made about 30–13 BC; from the Villa Muti near Rome. In the pediment is a set of blacksmith's tools: a crosspene hammer, flanged tongs, and an anvil. To the right of the portraits is a set of carpenter's tools: a drill with the bow used to rotate it, a marking knife, an adze, and a short-bladed chisel. To the left are the fasces (bundle of rods), the axe, and the vindicta—a rod used in the ceremony of freeing a slave.

We were not idle among you; 8 we did not eat anyone's
food free of charge; instead, we labored and toiled,
working night and day, so that we would not be a
burden to any of you. 9 It is not that we don't have the
right to support, but we did it to make ourselves an
example to you so that you would imitate us. 10 In fact,
when we were with you, this is what we commanded you: "If anyone isn't willing to work, he should
not eat." 11 For we hear that there are some among
you who are idle. They are not busy but busybodies.
12 Now we command and exhort such people by the
Lord Jesus Christ to work quietly and provide for
themselves.[A] 13 But as for you, brothers and sisters,
do not grow weary in doing good.

14 If anyone does not obey our instruction in this
letter, take note of that person; don't associate with
him, so that he may be ashamed. 15 Yet don't consider
him as an enemy, but warn him as a brother.

FINAL GREETINGS

16 May the Lord of peace himself give you peace always in every way. The Lord be with all of you. 17 I,
Paul, am writing this greeting with my own hand,
which is an authenticating mark in every letter; this
is how I write. 18 The grace of our Lord Jesus Christ
be with you all.

[A] **3:12** Lit *they may eat their own bread*

1 TIMOTHY

Terrace house ruins in historical ancient city Ephesus.

INTRODUCTION TO

1 TIMOTHY

Circumstances of Writing

As stated in the opening of each letter, 1 Timothy, 2 Timothy, and Titus were written by Paul (1Tm 1:1; 2Tm 1:1; Ti 1:1). However, many scholars today assume that Paul did not write them. This opinion is based on the differences from his other letters in vocabulary and style, alleged differences in theology, and uncertainties about where these letters fit chronologically in the life of the apostle. But the differences in style and vocabulary are not troublesome when one considers that authors often use different vocabulary when addressing different groups and situations. Rather than addressing churches in these letters, Paul was writing to coworkers who were in unique ministry settings. Hence we would expect different vocabulary. Also, the traditional view of the historical situation in which Paul wrote these letters is reasonable and defensible. Therefore, in spite of significant opposition by some scholars, there is a solid basis for accepting the Pastoral Epistles as Pauline.

Paul most likely wrote these letters after the time covered in the book of Acts. Acts closes with Paul in prison. Traditionally it has been believed that Paul was released from this imprisonment, then continued his work around the Mediterranean, perhaps even reaching Spain (Rm 15:22–29). During this time, he visited Crete and other places. First Timothy and Titus were written during this period of further mission work. Timothy had been left in Ephesus to handle some problems with false teaching there (1Tm 1:3–4). Titus had been left in Crete after the initial work to set up the church there (Ti 1:5). Eventually Paul was imprisoned again, and this led to his execution. During this final imprisonment, Paul wrote 2 Timothy to request another visit from Timothy and to give final exhortations as he anticipated his martyrdom.

Contribution to the Bible

These letters are rich theologically and ethically. One of their key contributions is the clear way they show the connection between doctrine and ethics, belief and behavior.

Although these letters were not intended to provide a detailed account of church government, they do provide some significant insights on this topic. The lists of characteristics for overseers (1Tm 3:1–7; Ti 1:5–9) and deacons (1Tm 3:8–13) are the only such lists in the New Testament.

Structure

All three letters follow the typical pattern of a Greek epistle. Although there are some lexical differences with many of Paul's other letters, keep in mind that these letters were written to specific individuals. One thing unique to the structure of these letters is the focus on church leadership.

GREETING

1 Paul, an apostle of Christ Jesus by the command
of God our Savior and of Christ Jesus our hope:
2 To Timothy, my true son in the faith.
Grace, mercy, and peace from God the[A] Father and
Christ Jesus our Lord.

FALSE DOCTRINE AND MISUSE OF THE LAW

3 As I urged you when I went to Macedonia, remain
in Ephesus so that you may instruct certain people not to teach false doctrine 4 or to pay attention
to myths and endless genealogies. These promote
empty speculations rather than God's plan, which
operates by faith. 5 Now the goal of our instruction
is love that comes from a pure heart, a good conscience, and a sincere faith. 6 Some have departed
from these and turned aside to fruitless discussion.
7 They want to be teachers of the law, although they
don't understand what they are saying or what they
are insisting on. 8 But we know that the law is good,
provided one uses it legitimately. 9 We know that the
law is not meant for a righteous person, but for the
lawless and rebellious, for the ungodly and sinful, for
the unholy and irreverent, for those who kill their
fathers and mothers, for murderers, 10 for the sexually immoral and males who have sex with males, for
slave traders, liars, perjurers, and for whatever else
is contrary to the sound teaching 11 that conforms to
the gospel concerning the glory of the blessed God,
which was entrusted to me.

PAUL'S TESTIMONY

12 I give thanks to Christ Jesus our Lord who has
strengthened me, because he considered me faithful, appointing me to the ministry — 13 even though
I was formerly a blasphemer, a persecutor, and an
arrogant man. But I received mercy because I acted out of ignorance in unbelief, 14 and the grace of
our Lord overflowed, along with the faith and love
that are in Christ Jesus. 15 This saying is trustworthy and deserving of full acceptance: "Christ Jesus
came into the world to save sinners" — and I am the
worst of them. 16 But I received mercy for this reason, so that in me, the worst of them, Christ Jesus
might demonstrate his extraordinary patience as
an example to those who would believe in him for
eternal life. 17 Now to the King eternal, immortal,
invisible, the only[B] God, be honor and glory forever
and ever. Amen.

ENGAGE IN BATTLE

18 Timothy, my son, I am giving you this instruction in
keeping with the prophecies previously made about
you, so that by recalling them you may fight the good
fight, 19 having faith and a good conscience, which
some have rejected and have shipwrecked the faith.
20 Among them are Hymenaeus and Alexander, whom
I have delivered to Satan, so that they may be taught
not to blaspheme.

Artemis was the Greek goddess of the moon. She watched over both humans and animals and gave fertility to humankind. A similar goddess among the Romans was named Diana. As the Roman and Greek cultures met, Diana was quickly identified with Artemis. The most famous statue of Artemis was located in Ephesus, where she was revered as the city's chief deity. Her temple in Ephesus was considered one of the Seven Wonders of the ancient world.

INSTRUCTIONS ON PRAYER

2 First of all, then, I urge that petitions, prayers,
intercessions, and thanksgivings be made for
everyone, 2 for kings and all those who are in authority, so that we may lead a tranquil and quiet life in all
godliness and dignity. 3 This is good, and it pleases
God our Savior, 4 who wants everyone to be saved
and to come to the knowledge of the truth.
5 For there is one God and one mediator between
God and mankind, the man Christ Jesus, 6 who gave
himself as a ransom for all, a testimony at the proper time.
7 For this I was appointed a herald, an apostle (I am
telling the truth;[C] I am not lying), and a teacher of the
Gentiles in faith and truth.

[A] **1:2** Other mss read *our* [B] **1:17** Other mss add *wise* [C] **2:7** Other mss add *in Christ*

Arched gate leading to the agora in Ephesus.

Roman gold jewelry from the first century AD.

INSTRUCTIONS TO MEN AND WOMEN

[8] Therefore, I want the men in every place to pray, lifting up holy hands without anger or argument. [9] Also,
the women are to dress themselves in modest clothing, with decency and good sense, not with elaborate
hairstyles, gold, pearls, or expensive apparel, [10] but
with good works, as is proper for women who profess
to worship God. [11] A woman is to learn quietly with
full submission. [12] I do not allow a woman to teach
or to have authority over a man; instead, she is to
remain quiet. [13] For Adam was formed first, then Eve.
[14] And Adam was not deceived, but the woman was
deceived and transgressed. [15] But she will be saved
through childbearing, if they continue in faith, love,
and holiness, with good sense.

QUALIFICATIONS FOR OVERSEERS AND DEACONS

3 This saying is trustworthy: "If anyone aspires
to be an overseer,[A] he desires a noble work."
[2] An overseer, therefore, must be above reproach,
the husband of one wife, self-controlled, sensible,
respectable, hospitable, able to teach, [3] not an excessive drinker, not a bully but gentle, not quarrelsome,
not greedy. [4] He must manage his own household
competently and have his children under control
with all dignity. [5] (If anyone does not know how to
manage his own household, how will he take care
of God's church?) [6] He must not be a new convert,
or he might become conceited and incur the same
condemnation as the devil. [7] Furthermore, he must
have a good reputation among outsiders, so that
he does not fall into disgrace and the devil's trap.
[8] Deacons, likewise, should be worthy of respect,
not hypocritical, not drinking a lot of wine, not
greedy for money, [9] holding the mystery of the faith
with a clear conscience. [10] They must also be tested
first; if they prove blameless, then they can serve
as deacons. [11] Wives,[B] likewise, should be worthy
of respect, not slanderers, self-controlled, faithful in everything. [12] Deacons are to be husbands of
one wife, managing their children and their own
households competently. [13] For those who have
served well as deacons acquire a good standing
for themselves and great boldness in the faith that
is in Christ Jesus.

THE MYSTERY OF GODLINESS

[14] I write these things to you, hoping to come to you
soon. [15] But if I should be delayed, I have written so
that you will know how people ought to conduct
themselves in God's household, which is the church

[A] 3:1 Or *bishop, or pastor* [B] 3:11 Or *Women*

of the living God, the pillar and foundation of the
truth. 16 And most certainly, the mystery of godliness
is great:

He[A] was manifested in the flesh,
vindicated in the Spirit,
seen by angels,
preached among the nations,
believed on in the world,
taken up in glory.

DEMONIC INFLUENCE

4 Now the Spirit explicitly says that in later times
some will depart from the faith, paying attention to deceitful spirits and the teachings of demons,
2 through the hypocrisy of liars whose consciences
are seared. 3 They forbid marriage and demand ab-
stinence from foods that God created to be received
with gratitude by those who believe and know the
truth. 4 For everything created by God is good, and
nothing is to be rejected if it is received with thanksgiving, 5 since it is sanctified by the word of God and
by prayer.

A GOOD SERVANT OF JESUS CHRIST

6 If you point these things out to the brothers and
sisters, you will be a good servant of Christ Jesus,
nourished by the words of the faith and the good
teaching that you have followed. 7 But have nothing
to do with pointless and silly myths. Rather, train
yourself in godliness. 8 For the training of the body
has limited benefit, but godliness is beneficial in every way, since it holds promise for the present life and
also for the life to come. 9 This saying is trustworthy
and deserves full acceptance. 10 For this reason we
labor and strive,[B] because we have put our hope in the
living God, who is the Savior of all people, especially
of those who believe.

INSTRUCTIONS FOR MINISTRY

11 Command and teach these things. 12 Don't let anyone despise your youth, but set an example for the
believers in speech, in conduct, in love,[C] in faith, and
in purity. 13 Until I come, give your attention to public
reading, exhortation, and teaching. 14 Don't neglect
the gift that is in you; it was given to you through
prophecy, with the laying on of hands by the council
of elders. 15 Practice these things; be committed to
them, so that your progress may be evident to all.
16 Pay close attention to your life and your teaching;
persevere in these things, for in doing this you will
save both yourself and your hearers.

5 Don't rebuke an older man, but exhort him as a
father, younger men as brothers, 2 older women
as mothers, and the younger women as sisters with
all purity.

Terra-cotta figure showing Zeus driving a four-horse chariot. Zeus, the Greek god of the sky and weather, was the father of Artemis and her twin, Apollo.

THE SUPPORT OF WIDOWS

3 Support[D] widows who are genuinely in need. 4 But
if any widow has children or grandchildren, let them
learn to practice godliness toward their own family
first and to repay their parents, for this pleases God.
5 The widow who is truly in need and left all alone
has put her hope in God and continues night and
day in her petitions and prayers; 6 however, she who
is self-indulgent is dead even while she lives. 7 Command this also, so that they will be above reproach.
8 But if anyone does not provide for his own family,
especially for his own household, he has denied the
faith and is worse than an unbeliever.

9 No widow is to be enrolled on the list for support
unless she is at least sixty years old, has been the wife
of one husband, 10 and is well known for good works
— that is, if she has brought up children, shown hospitality, washed the saints' feet, helped the afflicted,
and devoted herself to every good work. 11 But refuse
to enroll younger widows, for when they are drawn
away from Christ by desire, they want to marry 12 and
will therefore receive condemnation because they

[A] **3:16** Other mss read *God* [B] **4:10** Other mss read *and suffer reproach* [C] **4:12** Other mss add *in spirit,* [D] **5:3** Lit *Honor*

Older Adults in First-Century Culture

by Dorman Laird

GRECO-ROMAN ATTITUDES AND ACTIONS

In the Greco-Roman world of the first century, family members (typically children and grandchildren) were to provide complete and essential care for older relatives. Doing so was a sacred duty. Failure to do so could result in penalties and fines and in Athens even the restriction of a person's citizenship rights.[1] Among the Romans, children likewise had the legal responsibility of taking care of their aged parents.[2] However, because of the high rate of infant and child mortality, life expectancy was only between twenty and thirty years. Only about 6 to 8 percent of the empire's population lived to be more than sixty years old.[3]

Relief depicting Roman men carrying a sick or injured man. Basil, the bishop of Caesarea, founded a hospital in Cappadocia around AD 370. The facility, which came to be called "Basileias," took care of the poor, orphans, the elderly, lepers, the sick, and the infirm.

The Romans expected adults who reached a senior age to remain useful in the society as long as they were in control of their faculties.[4] The oldest living male of a household (the *paterfamilias*) had total rights over his natural descendants (male and female), his wife, his adopted sons, and even the children of his sons in the male line of his descendants. That is, the oldest living male ancestor "controlled his descendants . . . their persons and 'their' property—in law they had no possessions of their own. He held everything."[5] He was responsible for representing the family before the gods, for approving descendants' marriages, and even for deciding whether or not a newborn was legitimate and therefore worth keeping. In principle, the rule of the *paterfamilias* continued over his descendants regardless of how old they were. That meant that a mature man or even an old man could still be regarded legally as the child of his living father and subject to his authority.[6] Only when the paterfamilias died did the members of his household become legally independent.[7]

Cultural records from the era reveal that Romans held ambivalent attitudes toward older individuals. Some art pieces and dramatic presentations disdainfully depicted the elderly as toothless and wrinkled men and women. In contrast, some images respectfully reveal older couples as being supportive and loving of each other in their old age. Additionally, the Romans typically respected and appreciated older senators for their wisdom. As a show of that respect, the law would allow aging senators to be excused from attending all the sessions of the Senate if they so chose. Also, men older than fifty-five could be excused from some public duties.[8]

CHRISTIAN ATTITUDES AND ACTIONS

The differences between Christian attitudes and those of Greeks and Romans toward the aged and the poor were stark. Believers were motivated to care for people out of Christian love because all individuals have inherent value as image bearers of God.[9] Believers' conviction in personal and corporate benevolence led Christians to offer care during times of an epidemic outbreak, something that had been unheard of for a religious group in the classical world.[10]

During the first two centuries, especially in times of epidemics, the systematic care that believers gave to those who were sick—whether Christian or pagan—seemingly had a powerful effect on public attitudes about Christianity. For instance, "during the plague of Cyprian [AD 250], Christian churches, even though they were undergoing their first large-scale persecution, devised in several cities a program for the systematic care of the sick. . . . Their activity contrasted with that of the pagans, who deserted the sick or threw the bodies of the dead out into the streets."[11]

The compassion shown to the aged and the indigent who received nursing care from Christians was met with

Figurine from Tanagra (north of Athens, Greece) depicts an elderly man; dated to early Hellenistic Era (332–152 BC).

gratitude by pagans, resulting in many conversions to Christianity.[12] Strong evidence indicates that the model of care that the church practiced ultimately led to the creation of what some believe to be the earliest hospital open to the public, the Basileias, completed about AD 372. At the time of the construction of the Basileias, a social conscience about the institutional care of the aged had clearly developed. Along with the provision of separate areas for the poor, the homeless, orphans, lepers, and the sick, the facility also included a section for older patients.[13] ✣

---

[1] "Greece" in *The Ancient World*, vol. 1 of *The Greenwood Encyclopedia of Daily Life*, ed. Gregory S. Aldrete (Westport, CT: Greenwood, 2004), 1:25–26. [2] Martin Goodman, *The Roman World 44 BC–AD 180*, 2nd ed. (London: Routledge, 2012), 196. [3] Goodman, *Roman World*, 196. [4] Goodman, *Roman World*, 196–97. [5] Francis Lyall, *Slaves, Citizens, Sons: Legal Metaphors in the Epistles* (Grand Rapids: Zondervan, 1984), 120. [6] Lyall, *Slaves, Citizens, Sons*, 120–21. [7] Karl-J. Holkeskamp, "Under Roman Roofs: Family, House, and Household," in *The Cambridge Companion to the Roman Republic*, ed. Harriet I. Flower (New York: Cambridge University Press, 2004), 122–23. [8] Goodman, *The Roman World*, 196. [9] Gary B. Ferngren, *Medicine & Health Care in Early Christianity* (Baltimore: Johns Hopkins University Press, 2009), 117–18. [10] Ferngren, *Medicine & Health Care*, 117–18. [11] Ferngren, *Medicine & Health Care*, 118. [12] Ferngren, *Medicine & Health Care*, 121. [13] Ferngren, *Medicine & Health Care*, 124–25.

have renounced their original pledge. 13 At the same
time, they also learn to be idle, going from house to
house; they are not only idle, but are also gossips and
busybodies, saying things they shouldn't say. 14 Therefore, I want younger women to marry, have children,
manage their households, and give the adversary no
opportunity to accuse us. 15 For some have already
turned away to follow Satan. 16 If any[A] believing woman has widows in her family, let her help them. Let the
church not be burdened, so that it can help widows
in genuine need.

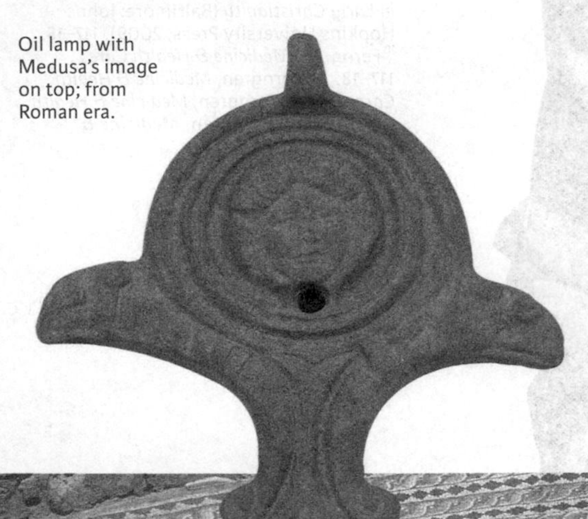
Oil lamp with Medusa's image on top; from Roman era.

HONORING THE ELDERS

17 The elders who are good leaders are to be considered worthy of double honor,[B] especially those
who work hard at preaching and teaching. 18 For
the Scripture says: **Do not muzzle an ox while it is
treading out the grain**,[C] and, "The worker is worthy
of his wages."

19 Don't accept an accusation against an elder
unless it is supported by two or three witnesses.
20 Publicly rebuke those who sin, so that the rest will
be afraid. 21 I solemnly charge you before God and
Christ Jesus and the elect angels to observe these
things without prejudice, doing nothing out of favoritism. 22 Don't be too quick to appoint[D] anyone
as an elder, and don't share in the sins of others.
Keep yourself pure. 23 Don't continue drinking only
water, but use a little wine because of your stomach
and your frequent illnesses. 24 Some people's sins
are obvious, preceding them to judgment, but the
sins of others surface[E] later. 25 Likewise, good works
are obvious, and those that are not obvious cannot
remain hidden.

[A] **5:16** Other mss add *believing man or* [B] **5:17** Or *of respect and remuneration* [C] **5:18** Dt 25:4 [D] **5:22** Lit *to lay hands on* [E] **5:24** Lit *follow*

Circular mosaic in House of Orpheus. The image in the center shows several Greek gods in a scene.

HONORING MASTERS

6 All who are under the yoke as slaves should regard their own masters[A] as worthy of all respect, so that God's name and his teaching will not be blasphemed. 2 Let those who have believing masters not be disrespectful to them because they are brothers, but serve them even better, since those who benefit from their service are believers and dearly loved.[B]

FALSE DOCTRINE AND HUMAN GREED

Teach and encourage these things. 3 If anyone teaches false doctrine and does not agree with the sound teaching of our Lord Jesus Christ and with the teaching that promotes godliness, 4 he is conceited and understands nothing, but has an unhealthy interest in disputes and arguments over words. From these come envy, quarreling, slander, evil suspicions, 5 and constant disagreement among people whose minds are depraved and deprived of the truth, who imagine that godliness is a way to material gain.[C] 6 But godliness with contentment is great gain. 7 For we brought nothing into the world, and[D] we can take nothing out. 8 If we have food and clothing,[E] we will be content with these. 9 But those who want to be rich fall into temptation, a trap, and many foolish and harmful desires, which plunge people into ruin and destruction. 10 For the love of money is a root[F] of all kinds of evil, and by craving it, some have wandered away from the faith and pierced themselves with many griefs.

FIGHT THE GOOD FIGHT

11 But you, man of God, flee from these things, and pursue righteousness, godliness, faith, love, endurance, and gentleness. 12 Fight the good fight of the faith. Take hold of eternal life to which you were called and about which you have made a good confession in the presence of many witnesses. 13 In the presence of God, who gives life to all, and of Christ Jesus, who gave a good confession before Pontius Pilate, I charge you 14 to keep this command without fault or failure until the appearing of our Lord Jesus Christ. 15 God will bring this about in his own time. He is the blessed and only Sovereign, the King of kings, and the Lord of lords, 16 who alone is immortal and who lives in unapproachable light, whom no one has seen or can see, to him be honor and eternal power. Amen.

[A] **6:1** Or *owners* [B] **6:2** Or *because, as believers who are dearly loved, they are devoted to others' welfare* [C] **6:5** Other mss add *From such people withdraw yourself.* [D] **6:7** Other mss add *it is clear that* [E] **6:8** Or *food and shelter* [F] **6:10** Or *is the root*

Heracles Gate at Ephesus, where Curetes Street ends.

Round-mouthed jug found in the foundations of the temple of Artemis at Ephesus, plus a cache of coins.

INSTRUCTIONS TO THE RICH

17 Instruct those who are rich in the present age not to
be arrogant or to set their hope on the uncertainty of
wealth, but on God,[A] who richly provides us with all
things to enjoy. 18 Instruct them to do what is good, to
be rich in good works, to be generous and willing to
share, 19 storing up treasure for themselves as a good
foundation for the coming age, so that they may take
hold of what is truly life.

GUARD THE HERITAGE

20 Timothy, guard what has been entrusted to you,
avoiding irreverent and empty speech and contra-
dictions from what is falsely called knowledge. 21 By
professing it, some people have departed from the
faith.

Grace be with you all.

[A] **6:17** Other mss read *on the living God*

2 TIMOTHY

St. Paul's Outside the Walls in Rome.

INTRODUCTION TO

2 TIMOTHY

Circumstances of Writing

As stated in the opening of each letter, 1 Timothy, 2 Timothy, and Titus were written by Paul (1Tm 1:1; 2Tm 1:1; Ti 1:1). However, many scholars today assume that Paul did not write them. This opinion is based on the differences from his other letters in vocabulary and style, alleged differences in theology, and uncertainties about where these letters fit chronologically in the life of the apostle. But the differences in style and vocabulary are not troublesome when one considers that authors often use different vocabulary when addressing different groups and situations. Rather than addressing churches in these letters, Paul was writing to coworkers in unique ministry settings. Hence we would expect different vocabulary. Also, the traditional view of the historical situation in which Paul wrote these letters is reasonable and defensible. Therefore, in spite of significant opposition by some scholars, there is a solid basis for accepting the Pastoral Epistles as Pauline.

Paul most likely wrote these letters after the time covered in the book of Acts. Acts closes with Paul in prison. Traditionally it has been believed that Paul was released from this imprisonment, then continued his work around the Mediterranean, perhaps even reaching Spain (Rm 15:22–29). During this time, he visited Crete and other places. First Timothy and Titus were written during this period of further mission work. Timothy had been left in Ephesus to handle some problems with false teaching there (1Tm 1:3–4). Titus had been left in Crete after the initial work to set up the church there (Ti 1:5). Eventually Paul was imprisoned again, and this led to his execution. During this final imprisonment, Paul wrote 2 Timothy to request another visit from Timothy and to give final exhortations as he anticipated his martyrdom.

Contribution to the Bible

These letters are rich theologically and ethically. One of their key contributions is the clear way they show the connection between doctrine and ethics, belief and behavior.

While these letters were not intended to provide a detailed account of church government, they do provide some significant insights on this topic. The lists of characteristics for overseers (1Tm 3:1–7; Ti 1:5–9) and deacons (1Tm 3:8–13) are the only such lists in the New Testament.

Structure

All three letters follow the typical pattern of a Greek epistle. While there are some lexical differences with many of Paul's other letters, keep in mind that these letters were written to specific individuals. One thing unique to the structure of these letters is the focus on church leadership.

GREETING

1 Paul, an apostle of Christ Jesus by God's will, for
the sake of the promise of life in Christ Jesus:
2 To Timothy, my dearly loved son.
Grace, mercy, and peace from God the Father and
Christ Jesus our Lord.

THANKSGIVING

3 I thank God, whom I serve with a clear conscience
as my ancestors did, when I constantly remember
you in my prayers night and day. 4 Remembering your
tears, I long to see you so that I may be filled with
joy. 5 I recall your sincere faith that first lived in your
grandmother Lois and in your mother Eunice and
now, I am convinced, is in you also.
6 Therefore, I remind you to rekindle the gift of
God that is in you through the laying on of my hands.
7 For God has not given us a spirit of fear, but one of
power,[A] love, and sound judgment.

NOT ASHAMED OF THE GOSPEL

8 So don't be ashamed of the testimony about our
Lord, or of me his prisoner. Instead, share in suffering for the gospel, relying on the power of God. 9 He
has saved us and called us with a holy calling, not
according to our works, but according to his own
purpose and grace, which was given to us in Christ
Jesus before time began. 10 This has now been made
evident through the appearing of our Savior Christ
Jesus, who has abolished death and has brought life
and immortality to light through the gospel. 11 For this
gospel I was appointed a herald, apostle, and teacher,[B]
12 and that is why I suffer these things. But I am not
ashamed, because I know whom I have believed and
am persuaded that he is able to guard what has been
entrusted to me[C] until that day.

BE LOYAL TO THE FAITH

13 Hold on to the pattern of sound teaching that you
have heard from me, in the faith and love that are in
Christ Jesus. 14 Guard the good deposit through the
Holy Spirit who lives in us. 15 You know that all those
in the province of Asia have deserted me, including
Phygelus and Hermogenes. 16 May the Lord grant mercy to the household of Onesiphorus, because he often
refreshed me and was not ashamed of my chains.
17 On the contrary, when he was in Rome, he diligently
searched for me and found me. 18 May the Lord grant
that he obtain mercy from him on that day. You know
very well how much he ministered at Ephesus.

[A] 1:7 Or *For the Spirit God gave us does not make us fearful, but gives us power* [B] 1:11 Other mss add *of the Gentiles* [C] 1:12 Or *guard what I have entrusted to him*, or *guard my deposit*

Interior of the Mamertine prison where Paul was imprisoned at one time. It is beneath the church of Giuseppe dei Falegnami in modern Rome. This lower chamber was probably initially a cistern and dated to the sixth century BC.

CRIMINALS AND PUNISHMENT

Roman prisons and custody in the first century served at least six purposes: protection, remand, awaiting sentencing, execution, coercion, and punishment.[1] Emperor Vitellius used prisons to protect soldiers who had been threatened by fellow soldiers.[2] The Romans also held many people on remand until trials could occur;[3] both John the Baptist (Mk 6:14–29) and Peter (Ac 12:3–11) were such cases.

Those for whom the Romans pronounced a death sentence often died in prison. The bodies of prisoners who died in Rome could be thrown onto the steps of Capitoline Hill, then be dragged with hooks to the Forum, and finally cast into the Tiber River.[4]

The Romans also used prisons to coerce people to reveal guilty colleagues or to extract confessions. Lastly, Roman officers could leave a person in prison for a variety of reasons as a form of punishment.[5] Emperor Tiberius was inhumane toward prisoners, since he extended the life of several people for the purpose of psychological torture, which included a perpetual experience of fear and oppression.[6]

At least four different levels of imprisonment existed: prison, military custody, entrustment to sureties, and release with conditions. Depending on the severity of the charge and the social status of the individual, a prisoner could have chains or not. Military custody was less severe than imprisonment and could include being held in a barracks or camp anywhere in the empire or in someone's home. Custody also covered those going to a provincial capital or Rome for trial or those under watch prior to being sentenced to exile.

Prisoners who had committed less serious crimes were entrusted to sureties, rather than given military custody. Sometimes the Romans entrusted prisoners who were Roman citizens to family members for safekeeping. On rare occasions, a person under military custody could be released on his own pledge to the Roman magistrate. Though technically not in prison, one in military custody (especially a non-Roman) could encounter harsh treatment, but the magistrates sometimes accorded favor to Roman citizens or those with high social standing.

Offenses punishable by imprisonment concerned both capital crimes and lesser offenses. Capital crimes included enemies of war, murder, rape, or treason against the state; these offenses often resulted in execution. Treason had many facets, including initiating civil disturbances and rioting. High treason—which involved betrayal of Rome, the emperor, or any Roman citizen—was cause for automatic imprisonment and execution. Related to treasonous crimes, the authorities judged philosophers and those practicing occult rituals as betraying the state's interests. Other crimes included theft, piracy,

A model of the Antonia fortress adjacent to the Jerusalem Temple. The Romans would have held Paul here.

mismanagement of money, debt, and desecration of the state's temples. For these crimes, punishments varied from place to place.[7]

CONDITIONS IN THE PRISONS

Custodial situations and the conditions in Roman prisons changed depending on the severity of the crime, the prisoner's social standing, the magistrate's kindness or cruelty, and the location of the imprisonment. Many prisons were underground and dark, accompanied by a shortage of food and sanitary surroundings. One prisoner of Tiberius remarked that prison food gave no satisfaction but also would not permit one to die.[8] Some magistrates allowed prisoners the benefit of care by family or friends (Ac 23:16–17).[9]

Paul's imprisonment at the time of writing 2 Timothy conveys several conditions. He asked Timothy to bring his coat left at Troas, his scrolls, and his parchments (2Tm 4:13). Though lacking warmth, Paul had the freedom to read and write. In the same period as Paul, Tacitus reported a man who wrote poetry while in prison and later was executed for doing so.[10] Paul's chains, however, were more serious (Eph 6:20; Php 1:7,13–14,17; Col 4:3,18), for Roman chains caused wounds, infections, and shame for many prisoners.[11]

A bust of Nero as a child. Nero's persecution of Christians was most likely the cause of Paul's second imprisonment.

On numerous occasions, Roman soldiers raped and abused female prisoners. Suicide rates of men and women in prison were high. Yet irresponsible jailers could be executed for failing in their duty (Ac 12:19).

People greatly feared the prison in Rome, a facility used for serious offenders and those who had no social standing. Later named Mamertine prison, it had a chamber twelve feet underground called the Tullianum. Sallust, the ancient Roman historian and politician, said the Tullianum was an enclosure with walls all around and a chamber above with a stone roof. Its conditions were hideous and fearful because of the neglect of prisoners, the darkness inside, and the putrid smell.[12]

The Romans used the prison in Alba Fucens, a city near Rome, to house enemies of the state. One ancient historian described the prison as an underground dungeon, full of darkness, and noisy because of the large numbers of people condemned on capital charges. The prisoners' food became mixed with the unsanitary conditions of their personal uncleanness. The resulting smell was so offensive that people tried to avoid even going near the prison.[13]

Some prisons were in stone quarries. A person in chains or bonds could be condemned to work in a quarry where walls, functioning as chains, kept one imprisoned. Rome had several such quarry prisons; they were typically reserved for prisoners with higher social status. Despite the grueling work, prisoners preferred the quarry prison over the Tullianum or a dungeon. ✣

---

[1] Brian Rapske, *The Book of Acts and Paul in Roman Custody*, vol. 3 in *The Book of Acts in Its First Century Setting* (Grand Rapids: Eerdmans, 1994), 10–20. [2] Tacitus, *Histories* 1.58. [3] Josephus, *Jewish Antiquities* 18.6.5. [4] Dio Cassius, *History* 58.1.3; 59.18.3; 60.16. [5] Rapske, *Book of Acts and Paul*, 16–20. [6] Dio Cassius, *History* 58.3.3–5. [7] Rapske, *The Book of Acts and Paul*, 20–46. [8] Dio Cassius, *History* 58.3.6. [9] Craig S. Wansink, *Chained in Christ: The Experience and Rhetoric of Paul's Imprisonment* (Sheffield: Sheffield Academic, 1996), 82–84. [10] Tacitus, *Annals* 6.39. [11] Wansink, *Chained in Christ*, 47–48. [12] Sallust, *Conspiracy of Catiline* 55.6. [13] Diodorus of Sicily, *Library of History* 31.9.1–2.

St. Paul's Outside the Walls marks, according to tradition,
Paul's burial place.

BE STRONG IN GRACE

2 You, therefore, my son, be strong in the grace that
is in Christ Jesus. 2 What you have heard from me
in the presence of many witnesses, commit to faithful
men[A] who will be able to teach others also.
3 Share in suffering as a good soldier of Christ Jesus.
4 No one serving as a soldier gets entangled in the concerns of civilian life; he seeks to please the commanding officer. 5 Also, if anyone competes as an athlete, he
is not crowned unless he competes according to the
rules. 6 The hardworking farmer ought to be the first
to get a share of the crops. 7 Consider what I say, for
the Lord will give you understanding in everything.
8 Remember Jesus Christ, risen from the dead and
descended from David, according to my gospel, 9 for
which I suffer to the point of being bound like a criminal. But the word of God is not bound. 10 This is why I
endure all things for the elect: so that they also may
obtain salvation, which is in Christ Jesus, with eternal
glory. 11 This saying is trustworthy:

For if we died with him,
we will also live with him;
12 if we endure, we will also reign with him;
if we deny him, he will also deny us;
13 if we are faithless, he remains faithful,
for he cannot deny himself.

AN APPROVED WORKER

14 Remind them of these things, and charge them before God[B] not to fight about words. This is useless and
leads to the ruin of those who listen. 15 Be diligent to
present yourself to God as one approved, a worker
who doesn't need to be ashamed, correctly teaching the word of truth. 16 Avoid irreverent and empty
speech, since those who engage in it will produce
even more godlessness, 17 and their teaching will
spread like gangrene. Hymenaeus and Philetus are
among them. 18 They have departed from the truth,
saying that the resurrection has already taken place,
and are ruining the faith of some. 19 Nevertheless,
God's solid foundation stands firm, bearing this inscription: **The Lord knows those who are his,**[C] and
let everyone who calls on the name of[D] the Lord turn
away from wickedness.
20 Now in a large house there are not only gold
and silver vessels, but also those of wood and clay;
some for honorable[E] use and some for dishonorable.[F] 21 So if anyone purifies himself from anything
dishonorable,[G] he will be a special[H] instrument, set
apart, useful to the Master, prepared for every good
work.
22 Flee from youthful passions, and pursue righteousness, faith, love, and peace, along with those
who call on the Lord from a pure heart. 23 But reject
foolish and ignorant disputes, because you know
that they breed quarrels. 24 The Lord's servant must
not quarrel, but must be gentle to everyone, able to
teach,[I] and patient, 25 instructing his opponents with
gentleness. Perhaps God will grant them repentance
leading them to the knowledge of the truth. 26 Then
they may come to their senses and escape the trap of
the devil, who has taken them captive to do his will.

DIFFICULT TIMES AHEAD

3 But know this: Hard times will come in the last
days. 2 For people will be lovers of self, lovers of
money, boastful, proud, demeaning, disobedient to
parents, ungrateful, unholy, 3 unloving, irreconcilable,
slanderers, without self-control, brutal, without love
for what is good, 4 traitors, reckless, conceited, lovers
of pleasure rather than lovers of God, 5 holding to
the form of godliness but denying its power. Avoid
these people.
6 For among them are those who worm their way
into households and deceive gullible women overwhelmed by sins and led astray by a variety of passions, 7 always learning and never able to come to a
knowledge of the truth. 8 Just as Jannes and Jambres

[A] **2:2** Or *faithful people* [B] **2:14** Other mss read *before the Lord*
[C] **2:19** Nm 16:5 [D] **2:19** Lit *everyone who names the name of*
[E] **2:20** Or *special* [F] **2:20** Or *ordinary* [G] **2:21** Lit *from these*
[H] **2:21** Or *an honorable* [I] **2:24** Or *everyone, skillful in teaching*

resisted Moses, so these also resist the truth. They
are men who are corrupt in mind and worthless in
regard to the faith. 9 But they will not make further
progress, for their foolishness will be clear to all, as
was the foolishness of Jannes and Jambres.

STRUGGLES IN THE CHRISTIAN LIFE

10 But you have followed my teaching, conduct, purpose, faith, patience, love, and endurance, 11 along
with the persecutions and sufferings that came to
me in Antioch, Iconium, and Lystra. What persecutions I endured — and yet the Lord rescued me from
them all. 12 In fact, all who want to live a godly life
in Christ Jesus will be persecuted. 13 Evil people and
impostors will become worse, deceiving and being
deceived. 14 But as for you, continue in what you
have learned and firmly believed. You know those
who taught you, 15 and you know that from infan-
cy you have known the sacred Scriptures, which
are able to give you wisdom for salvation through
faith in Christ Jesus. 16 All Scripture is inspired by
God[A] and is profitable for teaching, for rebuking,
for correcting, for training in righteousness, 17 so
that the man of God may be complete, equipped for
every good work.

FULFILL YOUR MINISTRY

4 I solemnly charge you before God and Christ
Jesus, who is going to judge the living and the
dead, and because of his appearing and his kingdom: 2 Preach the word; be ready in season and out
of season; correct, rebuke, and encourage with great
patience and teaching. 3 For the time will come when
people will not tolerate sound doctrine, but according to their own desires, will multiply teachers for
themselves because they have an itch to hear what
they want to hear. 4 They will turn away from hearing the truth and will turn aside to myths. 5 But as
for you, exercise self-control in everything, endure
hardship, do the work of an evangelist, fulfill your
ministry.

6 For I am already being poured out as a drink offering, and the time for my departure is close. 7 I have
fought the good fight, I have finished the race, I have
kept the faith. 8 There is reserved for me the crown of
righteousness, which the Lord, the righteous Judge,
will give me on that day, and not only to me, but to all
those who have loved his appearing.[B]

FINAL INSTRUCTIONS

9 Make every effort to come to me soon, 10 because
Demas has deserted me, since he loved this present
world, and has gone to Thessalonica. Crescens has
gone to Galatia, Titus to Dalmatia. 11 Only Luke is with
me. Bring Mark with you, for he is useful to me in the

Roman officer who won Greek athletic games in Neapolis, Corinth, and Aktia.

[A] **3:16** Lit *breathed out by God* [B] **4:8** Or *have longed for his appearing*

ministry. [12] I have sent Tychicus to Ephesus. [13] When
you come, bring the cloak I left in Troas with Carpus,
as well as the scrolls, especially the parchments. [14] Alexander the coppersmith did great harm to me. The
Lord will repay him according to his works. [15] Watch
out for him yourself because he strongly opposed
our words.

[16] At my first defense, no one stood by me, but everyone deserted me. May it not be counted against
them. [17] But the Lord stood with me and strengthened
me, so that I might fully preach the word and all the
Gentiles might hear it. So I was rescued from the
lion's mouth. [18] The Lord will rescue me from every
evil work and will bring me safely into his heavenly
kingdom. To him be the glory forever and ever! Amen.

BENEDICTION

[19] Greet Prisca and Aquila, and the household of Onesiphorus. [20] Erastus has remained at Corinth; I left
Trophimus sick at Miletus. [21] Make every effort to
come before winter. Eubulus greets you, as do Pu-
dens, Linus, Claudia, and all the brothers and sisters.

[22] The Lord be with your spirit. Grace be with you all.

Marble statue of an *ephebe* (young athlete) leaning against a pillar, wrapped in a tunic, recovering from his exertions. Probably dates from the late first century BC to the early first century AD.

TITUS

Greek village of Loutro, Crete

INTRODUCTION TO

TITUS

Circumstances of Writing

As stated in the opening of the letter, Titus was written by Paul (Ti 1:1). However, many scholars today assume that Paul did not write Titus. This opinion is based on the differences from his other letters in vocabulary and style, alleged differences in theology, and uncertainties about where Titus along with 1 and 2 Timothy fit chronologically in the life of the apostle. But the differences in style and vocabulary are not troublesome when one considers that authors often use different vocabulary when addressing different groups and situations. Rather than addressing churches in these Pastoral Epistles, Paul was writing to coworkers who were in unique ministry settings. Hence we would expect different vocabulary. Also, the traditional view of the historical situation in which Paul wrote Titus is reasonable and defensible. Therefore, in spite of significant opposition by some scholars, there is a solid basis for accepting the Pastoral Epistles as Pauline.

Paul most likely wrote Titus after the time covered in the book of Acts. Acts closes with Paul in prison. Traditionally it has been believed that Paul was released from this imprisonment, then continued his work around the Mediterranean, perhaps even reaching Spain (Rm 15:22–29). During this time, he visited Crete and other places. Titus was written during this period of further mission work. Titus had been left in Crete after the initial work to set up the church there (Ti 1:5). Eventually Paul was imprisoned again, and this led to his execution.

Contribution to the Bible

Titus is rich theologically and ethically. One of the key contributions is the clear way it shows the connection between doctrine and ethics, belief and behavior.

While this letter was not intended to provide a detailed account of church government, it does provide some significant insights on this topic.

Structure

Titus follows the typical pattern of a Greek epistle. Although there are some lexical differences with many of Paul's other letters, keep in mind that this letter is written to a specific individual. One thing unique to the structure of this letter is the focus on church leadership.

GREETING

1 Paul, a servant of God and an apostle of Jesus
Christ, for[A] the faith of God's elect and their
knowledge of the truth that leads[B] to godliness, 2 in
the hope of eternal life that God, who cannot lie,
promised before time began. 3 In his own time he
has revealed his word in the preaching with which
I was entrusted by the command of God our Savior:
4 To Titus, my true son in our common faith.
Grace and peace from God the Father and Christ
Jesus our Savior.

TITUS'S MINISTRY IN CRETE

5 The reason I left you in Crete was to set right what
was left undone and, as I directed you, to appoint elders in every town. 6 An elder must be blameless, the
husband of one wife, with faithful[C] children who are
not accused of wildness or rebellion. 7 As an overseer
of God's household, he must be blameless, not arrogant, not hot-tempered, not an excessive drinker, not
a bully, not greedy for money, 8 but hospitable, loving
what is good, sensible, righteous, holy, self-controlled,
9 holding to the faithful message as taught, so that he
will be able both to encourage with sound teaching
and to refute those who contradict it.
10 For there are many rebellious people, full of
empty talk and deception, especially those from the
circumcision party. 11 It is necessary to silence them;
they are ruining entire households by teaching what
they shouldn't in order to get money dishonestly.
12 One of their very own prophets said, "Cretans are
always liars, evil beasts, lazy gluttons." 13 This testimony is true. For this reason, rebuke them sharply,
so that they may be sound in the faith 14 and may not
pay attention to Jewish myths and the commands of
people who reject the truth.
15 To the pure, everything is pure, but to those who
are defiled and unbelieving nothing is pure; in fact,
both their mind and conscience are defiled. 16 They
claim to know God, but they deny him by their works.
They are detestable, disobedient, and unfit for any
good work.

SOUND TEACHING AND CHRISTIAN LIVING

2 But you are to proclaim things consistent with
sound teaching. 2 Older men are to be self-controlled, worthy of respect, sensible, and sound in faith,
love, and endurance. 3 In the same way, older women

[A] **1:1** Or *according to* [B] **1:1** Or *corresponds* [C] **1:6** Or *believing*

Springs of Daphne cascade over the Cave (Grotto) of Daphne at Antioch of Syria (modern Antakya, Turkey), which was once a temple city for a pantheon of pagan gods and goddesses.

First-Century Crete

by Timothy T. Faber

Remains of the Church of St. Titus at Gortyn, Crete; dated to the eighth century AD.

Crete had a reputation, and it was not a good one. In Titus 1:12, Paul quotes the sixth century BC Greek poet Epimenides: "Cretans are always liars, evil beasts, lazy gluttons." Not only did Paul make use of this quotation, but he went on to say, "This testimony is true" (v. 13).

What caused Epimenides to make such a statement about his fellow Cretans? The people of Crete claimed that the tomb of Zeus, the chief Greek god, was located on their island. Epimenides's sentiment was based in the concept that Zeus, being a god, could not be dead—and those who claimed his tomb was on the island had to be lying. Therefore, all Cretans must be liars. By Paul's time, Epimenides's words had become a popular slogan that highlighted the widespread reputation of Cretans as untruthful.[1]

A people known as Minoans inhabited Crete at least as early as 2800 BC. Rather than being isolationists, the Minoans were a seafaring people that influenced the entire Mediterranean world with a "rich culture" of impressive "architecture, pottery, metalwork and painting."[2] Minoan civilization collapsed about 1400 BC, possibly due to a massive earthquake.

Their history made the Cretans a proud people. Centuries later, as different world powers dominated the region, the Cretans were able to maintain a somewhat separate identity—even from the Greeks, Romans, and others who sought to claim the island as their own. Factions did develop among the Cretans, though, based partly on their affinity with various powers seeking to conquer them and also on both nationality and ethnic origins. The centrally located city of Gortyn is an example of the Cretans' changing affinities and affiliations.

Hannibal, born in 247 BC, became a Carthaginian general who led a revolt against Rome—a revolt that became a war. Gortyn temporarily served as a refuge for Hannibal as he was fleeing Rome in 189 BC. Opposition to the Romans unified the Cretans for decades after Hannibal's departure. In fact, they were able to repulse a Roman attempt at conquest in 74 BC.

Just a few years later, though, in 66 BC, the city of Gortyn changed its affiliation and sided with Rome in their eventual conquest of Crete. Rome rewarded this support by making

Ruins of the praetorium (governor's residence) at Gortyn, Crete. Gortyn, centrally located on the island, served for a time as the capital of the Roman province of Crete and Cyrene.

Gortyn the capital of the Roman province of Crete and Cyrene[3]—a province that stretched into North Africa.

The history of Crete during the first and second centuries AD is rather ambiguous. What little exists does not give a definitive snapshot of Christianity on the island. In the city of Gortyn, however, are the remains of the Church of Saint Titus. Tradition claims Titus's ministry was headquartered in Gortyn and that he died there in AD 107.

Mediterranean cultures surrounded and infiltrated Crete, but the Cretan peoples also became an influence upon the entire Mediterranean world. Located in the middle of the Mediterranean Sea, almost equally between Greece, North Africa, and Asia Minor, Crete was a great place for seafaring trade—both legitimate and otherwise. Human trafficking and piracy were a real part of life on Crete. Whether Crete was more the victim or the perpetrator of piracy is unclear; the evidence for both possibilities is staggering.[4] ✣

---

[1] Walter C. Kaiser et al., *Hard Sayings of the Bible* (Downers Grove, IL: InterVarsity, 1996), 675–76. [2] Avraham Negev, ed., *Archaeological Encyclopedia of the Holy Land* (Jerusalem: G. A. Jerusalem Publishing House, 1972), 82. [3] Dana Facaros and Michael Pauls, *Crete* (London: Cadogan Guides, 2010), 216–17. [4] Barry Unsworth, *Crete* (Washington, DC: National Geographic Society, 2004), 27.

This ivory Coptic wine cup, likely used in Lord's Supper services, dates from the seventh–ninth centuries AD.

In the first century AD, Roman soldiers carried both a sword (*gladius*) and dagger (*pugio*), which they strapped on using two crossed belts.

are to be reverent in behavior, not slanderers, not
slaves to excessive drinking. They are to teach what is
good, 4 so that they may encourage the young women
to love their husbands and to love their children, 5 to
be self-controlled, pure, workers at home, kind, and
in submission to their husbands, so that God's word
will not be slandered.

6 In the same way, encourage the young men to
be self-controlled 7 in everything. Make yourself an
example of good works with integrity and dignity[A] in
your teaching. 8 Your message is to be sound beyond
reproach, so that any opponent will be ashamed, because he doesn't have anything bad to say about us.

9 Slaves are to submit to their masters in everything, and to be well-pleasing, not talking back 10 or
stealing, but demonstrating utter faithfulness, so that
they may adorn the teaching of God our Savior in
everything.

11 For the grace of God has appeared, bringing salvation[B] for all people, 12 instructing us to deny godlessness and worldly lusts and to live in a sensible,
righteous, and godly way in the present age, 13 while
we wait for the blessed hope, the appearing of the
glory of our great God and Savior, Jesus Christ. 14 He
gave himself for us to redeem us from all lawlessness
and to cleanse for himself a people for his own possession, eager to do good works.

15 Proclaim these things; encourage and rebuke
with all authority. Let no one disregard[C] you.

CHRISTIAN LIVING AMONG OUTSIDERS

3 Remind them to submit to rulers and authorities, to obey, to be ready for every good work,
2 to slander no one, to avoid fighting, and to be kind,
always showing gentleness to all people. 3 For we too
were once foolish, disobedient, deceived, enslaved by
various passions and pleasures, living in malice and
envy, hateful, detesting one another.

4 But when the kindness of God our Savior and
his love for mankind appeared, 5 he saved us —not
by works of righteousness that we had done, but
according to his mercy — through the washing of
regeneration and renewal by the Holy Spirit. 6 He
poured out his Spirit on us abundantly through Jesus
Christ our Savior 7 so that, having been justified by
his grace, we may become heirs with the hope of
eternal life. 8 This saying is trustworthy. I want you
to insist on these things, so that those who have believed God might be careful to devote themselves
to good works. These are good and profitable for

[A] **2:7** Other mss add *and incorruptibility* [B] **2:11** Or *appeared with saving power* [C] **2:15** Or *despise*

everyone. 9 But avoid foolish debates, genealogies,
quarrels, and disputes about the law, because they
are unprofitable and worthless. 10 Reject a divisive
person after a first and second warning. 11 For you
know that such a person has gone astray and is sinning; he is self-condemned.

FINAL INSTRUCTIONS AND CLOSING

12 When I send Artemas or Tychicus to you, make
every effort to come to me in Nicopolis, because I
have decided to spend the winter there. 13 Diligently
help Zenas the lawyer and Apollos on their journey,
so that they will lack nothing.
14 Let our people learn to devote themselves to
good works for pressing needs, so that they will not
be unfruitful. 15 All those who are with me send you
greetings. Greet those who love us in the faith. Grace
be with all of you.

Bronze gladiatorial helmet; Roman; first–second centuries AD.

PHILEMON

Bakery at Pompeii; an oven is in the back. On left are grinding mills; the one in the rear still has its grinding stone on top. Grain was poured into the tops of the mills; Slaves or donkeys turned the upper portion to grind the grain.

INTRODUCTION TO

PHILEMON

Circumstances of Writing

During Paul's two-year imprisonment in Rome (Ac 28:30), probably during AD 60–61, he wrote four letters called the Prison Epistles, one of which is Philemon (the others are Colossians, Ephesians, and Philippians).

References to Paul's being in prison at the time of writing are found in Philemon 1,9–10,13, and perhaps 23. Paul was kept under house arrest—what the Romans called "free custody"—in his own rented house as he awaited trial (Ac 28:30).

Although Paul addresses the letter to Apphia, Archippus, and the church that met in Philemon's house (Phm 1–2), the main addressee is Philemon himself, for "you" or "your" (vv. 2,4–21,23) is singular and refers to Philemon. Apparently he was a prosperous businessman living in Colossae (implied in Col 4:9) whose household included several slaves and whose house was large enough to accommodate meetings of the young church. He had been converted through Paul's ministry, perhaps by Paul himself (Phm 10,19), and had become Paul's "dear friend and coworker" (v. 1) and "partner" (v. 17) in the gospel service. Although the letter is basically Paul's personal appeal to Philemon, the plural "you" (vv. 3,22) and "your" (Phm 22,25) indicate that the whole church would have listened to its reading and thus been witnesses of Philemon's response to Paul's requests.

Onesimus had apparently run away and taken with him some of his master's money or possessions (vv. 15,18). Perhaps attracted by the anonymity of a large, distant city, he traveled to Rome seeking a life of freedom. His path crossed Paul's, and he became a Christian (vv. 10,16) and a useful helper to Paul (v. 11).

An alternative view denies that Onesimus was a runaway looking for freedom. It instead suggests that he left Philemon and looked for Paul so that Paul could become his advocate regarding some serious loss Philemon had experienced. All along Onesimus had intended to return to his master's household. Paul was therefore not guilty of harboring a fugitive slave. But on this view we would expect Paul to reassure Philemon that Onesimus had always intended to return.

Contribution to the Bible

Although it is the shortest and most personal of Paul's letters, Philemon was included in the New Testament canon for several reasons.

First, it illustrates the breaking down of social and cultural barriers that occurred between Christians (see Gl 3:28). Paul, a highly educated Roman citizen, takes up the cause of a poor runaway slave whose life was in danger because of his theft and flight (Phm 18). Social and cultural barriers are eliminated in Christian fellowship.

Second, it reflects early Christian attitudes toward slavery. Although Paul accepts (but does not endorse) slavery as an existing social condition and as a legal fact (v. 12), he emphasizes Onesimus's higher identity as a Christian brother and sets the master-slave relationship on a new footing (v. 16) and so ultimately undermines the institution of slavery. This contrasts with dominant views of the ancient world. For instance, Aristotle defined a slave as "a living tool, just as a tool is an inanimate slave" (*Nicomachean Ethics* 8.11.6).

Third, it shows a skillful pastor at work: Paul gives up his apostolic right to issue commands (vv. 8–9) and prefers to appeal to Philemon's free choice (vv. 10,14) to follow his Christian conscience in deciding how his love should be expressed (vv. 5,7); he identifies with Onesimus, his spiritual son (v. 10), calling him "my very own heart" (v. 12) and guaranteeing to repay his debts (vv. 18–19); and he gives his requests to Philemon in the hearing of the whole local church (vv. 1–3,22–25).

Fourth, it pictures the heart of the gospel (vv. 16–19). When we come to God in repentance and faith, he gives us a new status and welcomes us as if we were Christ. What we owe God, he has debited to Christ's account. Christ assumed personal responsibility for the full repayment of our debt to God.

Structure

Paul's letter to Philemon follows the form of a standard first-century Greek letter: address and greeting (vv. 1–3), body (vv. 8–20), and closing/farewell (vv. 21–25). Moreover, Paul includes a section of thanksgiving after the greeting (vv. 4–7), a typical feature found in his letters.

Slavery in the Ancient World[1]

by James A. Brooks

At Souk Ahras, Algeria, North Africa, view of the slave market (circular area) in the ruins of ancient Thagaste.

Slavery was prevalent and widely accepted in the ancient world. The economy of Egypt, Greece, and Rome was based on slave labor. In the first Christian century, one out of three persons in Italy and one out of five elsewhere was a slave. Huge gangs toiled in the fields and mines and on building projects. Many were domestic and civil servants. Some were temple slaves and others were craftsmen. Some were forced to become gladiators. Some were highly intelligent and held responsible positions. Legally, a slave had no rights, but, except for the gangs, most were treated humanely and were better off than many free persons. Domestics were considered part of the family, and some were greatly loved by their masters. Canaan, Aram, Assyria, Babylonia, and Persia had fewer slaves because it proved less expensive to hire free persons. Still, the institution of slavery was unquestioned. The Stoics insisted that slaves were humans and should be treated accordingly. Israel's law protected slaves in various ways.

A person could become a slave as a result of capture in war, default on a debt, inability to support and "voluntarily" selling oneself, being sold as a child by destitute parents, birth to slave parents, conviction of a crime, or kidnapping and piracy. Slavery cut across races and nationalities.

Manumission or freeing of slaves was possible and common in Roman times. Masters in their wills often freed their slaves, and sometimes they did so during their lifetimes. Industrious slaves could make and save money and purchase their own freedom. By the first Christian century, a large class of freedmen had developed. There was even a synagogue of the Freedmen in Jerusalem (Ac 6:9). ✣

[1] Excerpted from the *Holman Illustrated Bible Dictionary*, rev. and expanded ed. (Nashville: Holman, 2015).

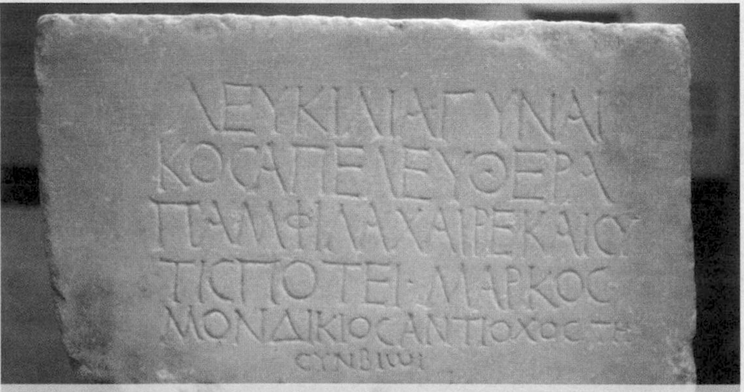

Dated from the first century BC, inscribed relief stele commemorating the freeing of a female slave by her mistress.

GREETING

Paul, a prisoner of Christ Jesus, and Timothy our
brother:
To Philemon our dear friend and coworker, 2 to
Apphia our sister,[A] to Archippus our fellow soldier,
and to the church that meets in your home.
3 Grace to you and peace from God our Father and
the Lord Jesus Christ.

PHILEMON'S LOVE AND FAITH

4 I always thank my God when I mention you in my
prayers, 5 because I hear of your love for all the saints
and the faith that you have in the Lord Jesus. 6 I pray
that your participation in the faith may become effective through knowing every good thing that is
in us[B] for the glory of Christ. 7 For I have great joy
and encouragement from your love, because the
hearts of the saints have been refreshed through
you, brother.

AN APPEAL FOR ONESIMUS

8 For this reason, although I have great boldness in
Christ to command you to do what is right, 9 I appeal
to you, instead, on the basis of love. I, Paul, as an elderly man[C] and now also as a prisoner of Christ Jesus,
10 appeal to you for my son, Onesimus.[D] I became his
father while I was in chains. 11 Once he was useless
to you, but now he is useful both to you and to me.
12 I am sending him back to you — I am sending my
very own heart.[E,F] 13 I wanted to keep him with me,
so that in my imprisonment for the gospel he might
serve me in your place. 14 But I didn't want to do anything without your consent, so that your good deed
might not be out of obligation, but of your own free
will. 15 For perhaps this is why he was separated from
you for a brief time, so that you might get him back
permanently, 16 no longer as a slave, but more than a
slave — as a dearly loved brother. He is especially so
to me, but how much more to you, both in the flesh
and in the Lord.
17 So if you consider me a partner, welcome him as
you would me. 18 And if he has wronged you in any
way, or owes you anything, charge that to my account.
19 I, Paul, write this with my own hand: I will repay it
— not to mention to you that you owe me even your
very self. 20 Yes, brother, may I benefit from you in the
Lord; refresh my heart in Christ. 21 Since I am confident of your obedience, I am writing to you, knowing
that you will do even more than I say. 22 Meanwhile,
also prepare a guest room for me, since I hope that
through your prayers I will be restored to you.

FINAL GREETINGS

23 Epaphras, my fellow prisoner in Christ Jesus, sends
you greetings, and so do 24 Mark, Aristarchus, Demas,
and Luke, my coworkers.
25 The grace of the Lord[G] Jesus Christ be with your
spirit.

[A] **2** Other mss read *our beloved* [B] **6** Other mss read *in you* [C] **9** Or *an ambassador* [D] **10** In Gk, *Onesimus* means "useful" [E] **12** Other mss read *him back. Receive him, my own heart.* [F] **12** Lit *you — that is, my own heart* [G] **25** Other mss read *our Lord*

HEBREWS

Jebel Musa, the traditional location of Mount Sinai.

INTRODUCTION TO

HEBREWS

Circumstances of Writing

The text of Hebrews does not identify its author. What we do know is that the author was a second-generation Christian, for he said he received the confirmed message of Christ from "those who heard" Jesus himself (Heb 2:3). Because Paul claimed his gospel was revealed directly by the Lord (1Co 15:8; Gl 1:12), it is doubtful that he was the author of Hebrews. The author was familiar with Timothy, but he referred to him as "our brother" (Heb 13:23), rather than as "my true son in the faith," as did Paul (1Tm 1:2).

Scholars have also proposed the following people as authors: Luke, Clement of Rome, Barnabas, Apollos, Timothy, Philip, Peter, Silas, Jude, and Aristion. Ultimately it does not matter that the identity of the author is now lost. We should be satisfied with the fact that early Christians received the letter as inspired and authoritative Scripture and that its value for Christian discipleship is unquestioned.

The author of Hebrews knew his recipients well, calling them "brothers and sisters" (Heb 3:12; 7:5; 10:19; 13:22) and "dearly loved friends" (6:9). Like the writer, they were converts who had heard the gospel through the earliest followers of Christ (2:3). Scholars have speculated that those to whom the book was written were a breakaway group, such as a house church that had separated from the main church. Another theory holds that the recipients were former Jewish priests who had converted to Christianity and were considering a return to Judaism (at least in conformity to certain practices) to avoid persecution from fellow Jews. Another theory holds that the group was not necessarily Jewish since Gentile Christians also revered the Old Testament as Scripture.

Regarding when the book was written, it is clear that the fall of Jerusalem (AD 70) had not yet occurred. The destruction of the temple would have been mentioned if it had already occurred, for it would have strengthened the letter's argument about Christ's sacrifice spelling the end of the temple sacrificial system. The public persecution mentioned in 10:32–34 implies one of two possibilities for dating the book. We know that Roman Emperors Nero and Domitian (in AD 64–68 and 81–82 respectively) persecuted Christians. Most likely, Hebrews was written during the persecution under Nero, perhaps just before the destruction of the temple.

Contribution to the Bible

No other book in the New Testament ties together Old Testament history and practices with the life of Jesus Christ as thoroughly as the book of Hebrews. Just as Jesus Christ taught that the Old Testament was fulfilled in himself (Mt 5:17–18; Lk 24:27), so the author of Hebrews taught that the old covenant was brought to completion in the new covenant (Heb 7:20–8:13). Hebrews also shows that because the old covenant has been fulfilled in the new covenant, the new covenant is "better" (7:22). The new covenant was made superior by the ministry of Jesus Christ.

Structure

In concluding the book of Hebrews, the author wrote, "I urge you to receive this message of exhortation, for I have written to you briefly" (13:22). If the literary style of Hebrews indicates anything, it is that it is a written theological sermon. It is not so much a letter—although it certainly ends like one—because it has no opening superscription, as was the norm with ancient letters. Hebrews instead begins with an introductory essay about the superiority of Jesus Christ (1:1–4). However, its capacity to encounter the reader's soul indicates it is more than just a literary essay. Indeed, it has a definite sermonic character since it expounds the Scriptures at length in order to challenge the reader to faith and faithfulness. The sustained development of a complex, holistic theology of covenant indicates that Hebrews is a written theological sermon that discloses the broad sweep of God's grand redemptive plan for humanity.

THE NATURE OF THE SON

1 Long ago God spoke to our ancestors by the
prophets at different times and in different ways.
2 In these last days, he has spoken to us by his Son.
God has appointed him heir of all things and made
the universe[A] through him. 3 The Son is the radiance[B]
of God's glory and the exact expression[C] of his nature, sustaining all things by his powerful word. After
making purification for sins,[D] he sat down at the right
hand of the Majesty on high.[E] 4 So he became superior
to the angels, just as the name he inherited is more
excellent than theirs.

THE SON SUPERIOR TO ANGELS

5 For to which of the angels did he ever say,
You are my Son;
today I have become your Father,[F,G]
or again,
I will be his Father,
and he will be my Son?[H]
6 Again, when he[I] brings his firstborn into the world,
he says,
And let all God's angels worship him.[J]
7 And about the angels he says:
He makes his angels winds,[K]
and his servants[L] **a fiery flame,**[M]
8 but to[N] the Son:
Your throne, God,
is forever and ever,
and the scepter of your kingdom
is a scepter of justice.
9 **You have loved righteousness**
and hated lawlessness;
this is why God, your God,
has anointed you
with the oil of joy
beyond your companions.[O,P]
10 And:
In the beginning, Lord,
you established the earth,
and the heavens are the works
of your hands;
11 **they will perish, but you remain.**
They will all wear out like clothing;
12 **you will roll them up like a cloak,**[Q]
and they will be changed
like clothing.
But you are the same,
and your years will never end.[R]
13 Now to which of the angels has he ever said:
Sit at my right hand
until I make your enemies
your footstool?[S]
14 Are they not all ministering spirits sent out to serve
those who are going to inherit salvation?

Throne of King Tutankhamun; carved wood covered with gold leaf. The throne back shows Tutankhamun and his wife Ankhe-senamun in their garden pavilion—basking in the rays of the sun god Re. Lions' heads were common decorations for Egyptian furniture, as were claws for furniture legs.

WARNING AGAINST NEGLECT

2 For this reason, we must pay attention all the
more to what we have heard, so that we will
not drift away. 2 For if the message spoken through
angels was legally binding[T] and every transgression
and disobedience received a just punishment, 3 how
will we escape if we neglect such a great salvation?
This salvation had its beginning when it was spoken
of by the Lord, and it was confirmed to us by those
who heard him. 4 At the same time, God also testified by signs and wonders, various miracles, and
distributions of gifts from the Holy Spirit according
to his will.

[A] **1:2** Lit *ages* [B] **1:3** Or *reflection* [C] **1:3** Or *representation*, or *copy*, or *reproduction* [D] **1:3** Other mss read *for our sins by himself* [E] **1:3** Or *he sat down on high at the right hand of the Majesty* [F] **1:5** Or *have begotten you* [G] **1:5** Ps 2:7 [H] **1:5** 2Sm 7:14; 1Ch 17:13 [I] **1:6** Or *When he again* [J] **1:6** Dt 32:43 LXX; Ps 97:7 [K] **1:7** Or *spirits* [L] **1:7** Or *ministers* [M] **1:7** Ps 104:4 [N] **1:8** Or *about* [O] **1:9** Or *associates* [P] **1:8–9** Ps 45:6–7 [Q] **1:12** Other mss omit *like a cloak* [R] **1:10–12** Ps 102:25–27 [S] **1:13** Ps 110:1 [T] **2:2** Or *valid*, or *reliable*

JESUS AND HUMANITY

[5] For he has not subjected to angels the world to come that we are talking about. [6] But someone somewhere has testified:

What is man that you remember him,
or the son of man that you care for him?
[7] **You made him lower than the angels**
for a short time;
you crowned him with glory and honor[A]
[8] **and subjected everything under his feet.**[B]

For in **subjecting everything** to him, he left nothing that is not subject to him. As it is, we do not yet see **everything subjected** to him. [9] But we do see Jesus — **made lower than the angels for a short time** so that by God's grace he might taste death for everyone — **crowned with glory and honor** because he suffered death.

[10] For in bringing many sons and daughters to glory, it was entirely appropriate that God — for whom and through whom all things exist — should make the pioneer[C] of their salvation perfect through sufferings. [11] For the one who sanctifies and those who are sanctified all have one Father.[D] That is why Jesus is not ashamed to call them brothers and sisters, [12] saying:

I will proclaim your name to my brothers
and sisters;
I will sing hymns to you
in the congregation.[E]

[13] Again, **I will trust in him.**[F] And again, **Here I am with the children God gave me.**[G]

[14] Now since the children have flesh and blood in common, Jesus also shared in these, so that through his death he might destroy the one holding the power of death — that is, the devil — [15] and free those who were held in slavery all their lives by the fear of death. [16] For it is clear that he does not reach out to help angels, but to help Abraham's offspring. [17] Therefore, he had to be like his brothers and sisters in every way, so that he could become a merciful and faithful high priest in matters[H] pertaining to God, to make atonement[I] for the sins of the people. [18] For since he himself has suffered when he was tempted, he is able to help those who are tempted.

OUR APOSTLE AND HIGH PRIEST

3 Therefore, holy brothers and sisters, who share in a heavenly calling, consider Jesus, the apostle and high priest of our confession. [2] He was faithful to the one who appointed him, just as Moses was in all God's household. [3] For Jesus is considered worthy of more glory than Moses, just as the builder has more honor than the house. [4] Now every house is built by someone, but the one who built everything is God. [5] Moses was faithful as a servant in all God's household, as a testimony to what would be said in

Pair of Egyptian basketry-woven papyrus sandals; dated 1570–1070 BC.

the future. [6] But Christ was faithful as a Son over his household. And we are that household if we hold on to our confidence and the hope in which we boast.[J]

WARNING AGAINST UNBELIEF

[7] Therefore, as the Holy Spirit says:

Today, if you hear his voice,
[8] **do not harden your hearts as in the rebellion,**
on the day of testing in the wilderness,
[9] **where your ancestors tested me, tried me,**
and saw my works [10] **for forty years.**
Therefore I was provoked to anger
with that generation
and said, "They always go astray
in their hearts,
and they have not known my ways."
[11] **So I swore in my anger,**
"They will not enter my rest."[K]

[A] **2:7** Other mss add *and set him over the works of your hands* [B] **2:6–8** Ps 8:4–6 LXX [C] **2:10** Or *source*, or *leader* [D] **2:11** Or *father*, or *origin*; lit *all are of one* [E] **2:12** Ps 22:22 [F] **2:13** 2Sm 22:3 LXX; Is 8:17 LXX; 12:2 LXX [G] **2:13** Is 8:18 LXX [H] **2:17** Lit *things* [I] **2:17** Or *propitiation* [J] **3:6** Other mss add *firm to the end* [K] **3:7–11** Ps 95:7–11

12 Watch out, brothers and sisters, so that there won't
be in any of you an evil, unbelieving heart that turns
away from the living God. 13 But encourage each other
daily, while it is still called **today**, so that none of you
is hardened by sin's deception. 14 For we have become
participants in Christ if we hold firmly until the end
the reality[A] that we had at the start. 15 As it is said:

Today, if you hear his voice,
do not harden your hearts
as in the rebellion.[B]

16 For who heard and rebelled? Wasn't it all who came
out of Egypt under Moses? 17 With whom was God angry for forty years? Wasn't it with those who sinned,
whose bodies fell in the wilderness? 18 And to whom
did he swear that they would not enter his rest, if not
to those who disobeyed? 19 So we see that they were
unable to enter because of unbelief.

THE PROMISED REST

4 Therefore, since the promise to enter his rest remains, let us beware[C] that none of you be found
to have fallen short.[D] 2 For we also have received the
good news just as they did. But the message they
heard did not benefit them, since they were not united with those who heard it in faith.[E] 3 For we who
have believed enter the rest, in keeping with what[F]
he has said,

So I swore in my anger,
"They will not enter my rest,"[G]

even though his works have been finished since the
foundation of the world. 4 For somewhere he has spoken about the seventh day in this way: **And on the**
seventh day God rested from all his works.[H] 5 Again,
in that passage he says, **They will never enter my**
rest.[G] 6 Therefore, since it remains for some to enter it,
and those who formerly received the good news did
not enter because of disobedience, 7 he again specifies
a certain day — **today**. He specified this speaking
through David after such a long time:

Today, if you hear his voice,
do not harden your hearts.[B]

8 For if Joshua had given them rest, God would not
have spoken later about another day. 9 Therefore, a
Sabbath rest remains for God's people. 10 For the person who has entered his rest has rested from his own
works, just as God did from his. 11 Let us, then, make

[A] **3:14** Or *confidence* [B] **3:15; 4:7** Ps 95:7–8 [C] **4:1** Lit *fear* [D] **4:1** Or *that any of you might seem to have missed it* [E] **4:2** Other mss read *since it was not united by faith in those who heard* [F] **4:3** Or *rest, just as* [G] **4:3,5** Ps 95:11 [H] **4:4** Gn 2:2

The desert of Paran where the Israelites spent part of the wilderness wanderings.

every effort to enter that rest, so that no one will fall
into the same pattern of disobedience.
12 For the word of God is living and effective and
sharper than any double-edged sword, penetrating
as far as the separation of soul and spirit, joints and
marrow. It is able to judge the thoughts and intentions
of the heart. 13 No creature is hidden from him, but
all things are naked and exposed to the eyes of him
to whom we must give an account.

OUR GREAT HIGH PRIEST

14 Therefore, since we have a great high priest who
has passed through the heavens — Jesus the Son of
God — let us hold fast to our confession. 15 For we do
not have a high priest who is unable to sympathize
with our weaknesses, but one who has been tempted
in every way as we are, yet without sin. 16 Therefore,
let us approach the throne of grace with boldness,
so that we may receive mercy and find grace to help
us in time of need.

CHRIST, A HIGH PRIEST

5 For every high priest taken from among men is
appointed in matters pertaining to God for the
people, to offer both gifts and sacrifices for sins. 2 He
is able to deal gently with those who are ignorant and
are going astray, since he is also clothed with weakness. 3 Because of this, he must make an offering for
his own sins as well as for the people. 4 No one takes
this honor on himself; instead, a person is called by
God, just as Aaron was. 5 In the same way, Christ did
not exalt himself to become a high priest, but God
who said to him,

> **You are my Son;**
> **today I have become your Father,**[A,B]

6 also says in another place,

> **You are a priest forever**
> **according to the order of Melchizedek.**[C]

7 During his earthly life,[D] he offered prayers and
appeals with loud cries and tears to the one who
was able to save him from death, and he was heard
because of his reverence. 8 Although he was the Son,
he learned obedience from what he suffered. 9 After
he was perfected, he became the source of eternal
salvation for all who obey him, 10 and he was declared
by God a high priest according to the order of Melchizedek.

THE PROBLEM OF IMMATURITY

11 We have a great deal to say about this, and it is difficult to explain, since you have become too lazy to
understand. 12 Although by this time you ought to be
teachers, you need someone to teach you the basic
principles of God's revelation again. You need milk,

The Arch of Titus, built AD 81–85, at the Roman Forum commemorates General Titus's destruction of Jerusalem in AD 70.

not solid food. 13 Now everyone who lives on milk is
inexperienced with the message about righteousness,
because he is an infant. 14 But solid food is for the mature — for those whose senses have been trained to
distinguish between good and evil.

WARNING AGAINST FALLING AWAY

6 Therefore, let us leave the elementary teaching
about Christ and go on to maturity, not laying
again a foundation of repentance from dead works,
faith in God, 2 teaching about ritual washings,[E] laying
on of hands, the resurrection of the dead, and eternal
judgment. 3 And we will do this if God permits.
4 For it is impossible to renew to repentance those
who were once enlightened, who tasted the heavenly gift, who shared in the Holy Spirit, 5 who tasted
God's good word and the powers of the coming age,
6 and who have fallen away. This is because,[F] to their
own harm, they are recrucifying the Son of God and

[A] **5:5** Lit *I have begotten you* [B] **5:5** Ps 2:7 [C] **5:6** Gn 14:18–20; Ps 110:4
[D] **5:7** Lit *In the days of his flesh* [E] **6:2** Or *about baptisms* [F] **6:6** Or *while*

DIGGING DEEPER *Arch of Titus*

When Jesus talked with his disciples on the Mount of Olives about the buildings of the temple, he said "Do you see all these things? Truly I tell you, not one stone will be left here on another that will not be thrown down" (Mt 24:1–2). The accuracy of Jesus's prophecy is demonstrated by the Arch of Titus which was constructed as a victory memorial for Roman Emperor Titus (AD 79–81) by his younger brother Emperor Domitian (AD 81–96). Located in Rome between the ancient Forum and the Colosseum, the marble arch depicts the transportation of spoils (the menorah and sacred trumpets) from the ransacked Jerusalem temple. In addition to this important evidence, excavations at the lower street along the southwest corner of the Jerusalem Temple Mount in the 1970s revealed large stones that had been toppled from the heights by the Romans in their military campaign of AD 70. Today, none of the original building structures remain standing on the Temple Mount. The depictions and inscription on the Arch of Titus, as well as the rubble found at the Temple Mount in Jerusalem, provide historical verification for the fulfillment of Jesus's prediction that the Jewish temple would be utterly destroyed.

holding him up to contempt. 7 For the ground that drinks the rain that often falls on it and that produces vegetation useful to those for whom it is cultivated receives a blessing from God. 8 But if it produces thorns and thistles, it is worthless and about to be cursed, and at the end will be burned.

9 Even though we are speaking this way, dearly loved friends, in your case we are confident of things that are better and that pertain to salvation. 10 For God is not unjust; he will not forget your work and the love[A] you demonstrated for his name by serving the saints — and by continuing to serve them. 11 Now we desire each of you to demonstrate the same diligence for the full assurance of your hope until the end, 12 so that you won't become lazy but will be imitators of those who inherit the promises through faith and perseverance.

INHERITING THE PROMISE

13 For when God made a promise to Abraham, since he had no one greater to swear by, he swore by himself: 14 **I will indeed bless you, and I will greatly multiply you.**[B] 15 And so, after waiting patiently, Abraham obtained the promise. 16 For people swear by something greater than themselves, and for them a confirming oath ends every dispute. 17 Because God wanted to show his unchangeable purpose even more clearly to the heirs of the promise, he guaranteed it with an oath, 18 so that through two unchangeable things, in which it is impossible for God to lie, we who have fled for refuge might have strong encouragement to seize the hope set before us. 19 We have this hope as an anchor for the soul, firm and secure. It enters the inner sanctuary behind the curtain. 20 Jesus has entered there on our behalf as a forerunner, because he has become a high priest forever according to the order of Melchizedek.

THE GREATNESS OF MELCHIZEDEK

7 For this Melchizedek, king of Salem, priest of God Most High, met Abraham and blessed him as he returned from defeating the kings, 2 and Abraham gave him a tenth of everything. First, his name means king of righteousness, then also, king of Salem, meaning king of peace. 3 Without father, mother, or genealogy, having neither beginning of days nor end of life, but resembling the Son of God, he remains a priest forever.

4 Now consider how great this man was: even Abraham the patriarch gave a tenth of the plunder to him. 5 The sons of Levi who receive the priestly office have a command according to the law to collect a tenth from the people — that is, from their brothers and sisters — though they have also descended from Abraham. 6 But one without this[C] lineage collected a tenth from Abraham and blessed the one who had the promises. 7 Without a doubt, the inferior is blessed by the superior. 8 In the one case, men who will die receive a tenth, but in the other case, Scripture testifies that he lives. 9 And in a sense Levi himself, who receives a tenth, has paid a tenth through Abraham, 10 for he was still within his ancestor[D] when Melchizedek met him.

A SUPERIOR PRIESTHOOD

11 Now if perfection came through the Levitical priesthood (for on the basis of it the people received the law), what further need was there for another priest to appear, said to be according to the order of Melchizedek and not according to the order of Aaron? 12 For when there is a change of the priesthood, there must be a change of law as well. 13 For the one these things are spoken about belonged to a different tribe. No one from it has served at the altar. 14 Now it is evident that our Lord came from Judah, and Moses said nothing about that tribe concerning priests.

15 And this becomes clearer if another priest like Melchizedek appears, 16 who did not become a priest

[A] **6:10** Other mss read *labor of love* [B] **6:14** Gn 22:17 [C] **7:6** Lit *their* [D] **7:10** Lit *still in his father's loins*

Incense shovel from Ashkelon (second–third centuries AD).

based on a legal regulation about physical[A] descent
but based on the power of an indestructible life. 17 For
it has been testified:

You are a priest forever
according to the order of Melchizedek.[B]

18 So the previous command is annulled because it
was weak and unprofitable 19 (for the law perfected
nothing), but a better hope is introduced, through
which we draw near to God.

20 None of this happened without an oath. For others became priests without an oath, 21 but he became a
priest with an oath made by the one who said to him:

The Lord has sworn
and will not change his mind,
"You are a priest forever."[B]

22 Because of this oath, Jesus has also become the
guarantee of a better covenant.

23 Now many have become Levitical priests, since
they are prevented by death from remaining in office. 24 But because he remains forever, he holds his
priesthood permanently. 25 Therefore, he is able to
save completely those who come to God through him,
since he always lives to intercede for them.

26 For this is the kind of high priest we need: holy,
innocent, undefiled, separated from sinners, and exalted above the heavens. 27 He doesn't need to offer
sacrifices every day, as high priests do — first for
their own sins, then for those of the people. He did
this once for all time when he offered himself. 28 For
the law appoints as high priests men who are weak,
but the promise of the oath, which came after the
law, appoints a Son, who has been perfected forever.

A HEAVENLY PRIESTHOOD

8 Now the main point of what is being said is this:
We have this kind of high priest, who sat down
at the right hand of the throne of the Majesty in the
heavens, 2 a minister of the sanctuary and the true
tabernacle that was set up by the Lord and not man.
3 For every high priest is appointed to offer gifts and
sacrifices; therefore, it was necessary for this priest
also to have something to offer. 4 Now if he were on
earth, he wouldn't be a priest, since there are those[C]
offering the gifts prescribed by the law. 5 These serve
as a copy and shadow of the heavenly things, as Moses was warned when he was about to complete the
tabernacle. For God said, **Be careful that you make
everything according to the pattern that was
shown to you on the mountain.**[D] 6 But Jesus has
now obtained a superior ministry, and to that degree
he is the mediator of a better covenant, which has
been established on better promises.

A SUPERIOR COVENANT

7 For if that first covenant had been faultless, there
would have been no occasion for a second one. 8 But
finding fault with his people,[E] he says:[F]

See, the days are coming, says the Lord,
when I will make a new covenant
with the house of Israel
and with the house of Judah —
9 **not like the covenant**
that I made with their ancestors
on the day I took them by the hand
to lead them out of the land of Egypt.
I showed no concern for them,
says the Lord,
because they did not continue
in my covenant.

[A] **7:16** Or *fleshly* [B] **7:17,21** Ps 110:4 [C] **8:4** Other mss read *priests*
[D] **8:5** Ex 25:40 [E] **8:8** Lit *with them* [F] **8:8** Other mss read *finding fault, he says to them*

What Were Oracles?

by Bennie R. Crockett Jr.

Six restored columns stand at the northeast end of the temple of Apollo at Delphi, situated on Mount Parnassus.

Within their polytheistic cultures, the Greeks and Romans believed that oracles functioned on behalf of their gods. Three basic meanings of *oracle* were prominent in Greek and Roman culture. First, the word referred to the place where a priest or priestess spoke on behalf of a god. Second, the word could refer to the priest or priestess who spoke. Third, the word could refer to the content of divine words spoken.

ORACLE AS A PLACE

Dedicated to Zeus, the oldest and principal oracle from Greece was the city of Dodona in Epirus, northwestern Greece. At this site, ancient travelers worshiped Gaia, mother earth, also known as Diona, the wife of Zeus. The ancients believed these two pagan gods lived in the branches of the oak tree where the priests on the site interpreted Zeus's oracles through the rustling of the oak leaves.[1] In the fourth century BC, worshipers built a temple to Zeus in Epirus,[2] and Octavian (later named Caesar Augustus) enlarged the temple in 31 BC for Apollo.[3]

The most famous oracle in the ancient world was at Delphi in central Greece near Mount Parnassus, north of the Corinth Gulf. All other sacred shrines eventually were secondary to Delphi, and people from the world over consulted the oracle at Delphi.

Possibly the most famous person to interact with the Delphi oracle was Socrates, Plato's mentor. Socrates's friend Chaerephon told him that the oracle declared Socrates to be the world's wisest person. As a result, Socrates moved throughout Athens trying to find a wiser person than himself.[4] Socrates also began to popularize the saying "know yourself," which was inscribed on the wall at Delphi's entrance.[5] Plato later referred to the Delphi oracle as establishing festivals and settling civil law issues.[6]

ORACLE AS A PAGAN GOD OR GODDESS

The ancient Greeks dedicated Delphi to the Greek god Phoebus Apollo. Apollo was the Greek and Roman god of the sun, prophecy, music, poetry, and healing; the name Phoebus described his radiant image. Often Apollo appeared as a beautiful figure playing a golden lyre or as a master archer shooting his bow. By the decree of Zeus, Apollo always told the truth.

Apollo's spokeswoman bore the name Pythia, priestess of the Greek goddess Gaia. In Greek mythology, Pythia was named for Python, the dragon snake that Apollo had slain.[7] At Delphi, Pythia inhaled the underground, sweet-smelling vapors and spoke inspired words from Apollo to Apollo's petitioners (usually for a fee). Usually people came asking for a prophecy related to a spouse or children. Because Pythia spoke (often incorrectly) under the hallucinogenic influence of the vapors, her priest would translate her words into poetic verses and give them to the inquirer.

During the first century AD, Plutarch functioned as a priest in the Delphi shrine, but he recounted the decline of the Delphi oracle.[8] Plutarch blamed demons for the oracles' decline. Undoubtedly, however, the fact that Pythia failed to predict the Greek military victory over the Persians and her willingness to take bribes also contributed to her decline.[9]

A relief in the east pediment of the Siphnian Treasury at Delphi depicts Apollo (left) and Heracles (right) disputing over a tripod. The central figure, thought to be Hermes, tries to separate the two deities. According to tradition, Apollo uttered his oracles while sitting on this tripod. Heracles was enraged because other gods had denied him the ability to pronounce oracles. Thus, he was attempting to take the tripod from Apollo.

Despite the decline of the Delphi oracle, other oracular cults became popular. Asclepius—son of Apollo and Greek god of medicine and healing—spawned an oracular religion in Asia Minor. The cult associated Asclepius with his father, Apollo. A temple of Asclepius was at Pergamum. People came to the site for healings and received the priests' oracular interpretations of dreams or visions of Asclepius. The Asclepius cult was so widespread that by AD 300, more than four hundred sanctuaries dedicated to Asclepius existed throughout the Roman Empire.[10]

ORACLE AS DIVINE WORDS

In the first century, many Christians also were familiar with the Sibylline oracles. These oracles (possibly forgeries) were texts based on practices from a variety of cultures and contained oracles from Sibyl, one of Apollo's prophetic priestesses dating back as early as the sixth century BC. Topics covered in the oracles included the prediction of various worldwide catastrophes and, in later times, even some Christian events.[11]

Because of the prominence of Greek and Roman influences on first-century culture, early believers would have thus been familiar with oracles and the worship practices associated with them. In contrast to Greek and Roman polytheism, however, early Christians understood oracles as referring to the words of the one true God. The New Testament uses the Greek term *logion* (sometimes translated as "oracle") four times to refer to God's self-revelation in words (Ac 7:38; Rm 3:2; Heb 5:12; 1Pt 4:11).

The contrast of "oracle" in Greek and Roman religions and in early Christianity is dramatic. Rather than consulting rustling oak leaves, idols, or hallucinatory priests who could be bribed, the early Christians rested upon the foundation of the one true God who spoke ultimately and definitively in his Son (Heb 1:1–2). ❖

---

[1] Homer, *Odyssey* 14.327. [2] Walter Burkert, *Greek Religion*, trans. John Raffan (Cambridge, MA: Harvard University Press, 1985), 114. [3] Suetonius, *Lives of the Caesars* 27. [4] Plato, *Apology* 21–22. [5] Plato, *Charmides* 164d–65a. [6] Plato, *Laws* 8.828; 9.856; 11.913–14. [7] Thelma Sargent, *The Homeric Hymns: A Verse Translation* (New York: Norton, 1973), 24–25. [8] Plutarch, *The Obsolescence of Oracles in Moralia* 415A; 417E–F. [9] Burkert, *Greek Religion*, 116. [10] Luther H. Martin, *Hellenistic Religions: An Introduction* (New York: Oxford University Press, 1987), 50. [11] See J. J. Collins, "Sibylline Oracles," in *Apocalyptic Literature and Testaments*, vol. 1 of *The Old Testament Pseudepigrapha* (*OTP*), ed. James H. Charlesworth (New York: Doubleday, 1983), 317–25.

10 **For this is the covenant**
that I will make with the house of Israel
after those days, says the Lord:
I will put my laws into their minds
and write them on their hearts.
I will be their God,
and they will be my people.
11 **And each person will not teach**
his fellow citizen,[A]
and each his brother or sister, saying,
"Know the Lord,"
because they will all know me,
from the least to the greatest of them.
12 **For I will forgive their wrongdoing,**
and I will never again remember
their sins.[B,C]

13 By saying **a new covenant**, he has declared that the
first is obsolete. And what is obsolete and growing
old is about to pass away.

OLD COVENANT MINISTRY

9 Now the first covenant also had regulations for
ministry and an earthly sanctuary. 2 For a tabernacle was set up, and in the first room, which is called
the holy place, were the lampstand, the table, and the
presentation loaves. 3 Behind the second curtain was
a tent called the most holy place. 4 It had the gold altar
of incense and the ark of the covenant, covered with
gold on all sides, in which was a gold jar containing
the manna, Aaron's staff that budded, and the tablets
of the covenant. 5 The cherubim of glory were above
the ark overshadowing the mercy seat. It is not possible to speak about these things in detail right now.
6 With these things prepared like this, the priests
enter the first room repeatedly, performing their ministry. 7 But the high priest alone enters the second
room, and he does that only once a year, and never
without blood, which he offers for himself and for
the sins the people had committed in ignorance. 8 The
Holy Spirit was making it clear that the way into the
most holy place had not yet been disclosed while the
first tabernacle was still standing. 9 This is a symbol
for the present time, during which gifts and sacrifices are offered that cannot perfect the worshiper's
conscience. 10 They are physical regulations and only
deal with food, drink, and various washings imposed
until the time of the new order.

[A] **8:11** Other mss read *neighbor* [B] **8:12** Other mss add *and their lawless deeds* [C] **8:8–12** Jr 31:31–34

Overview of the Israelite temple at Arad. The architecture of this temple is similar to the tabernacle and temple at Jerusalem. The holy of holies is along the back wall.

From Rome; dated to the first century AD, a marble relief depicting a procession converging at two altars (the right one is only partially visible). In honor of the god Mars, worshipers are sacrificing a pig, a sheep, and a bull.

NEW COVENANT MINISTRY

11 But Christ has appeared as a high priest of the good things that have come.[A] In the greater and more perfect tabernacle not made with hands (that is, not of this creation), 12 he entered the most holy place once for all time, not by the blood of goats and calves, but by his own blood, having obtained eternal redemption. 13 For if the blood of goats and bulls and the ashes of a young cow, sprinkling those who are defiled, sanctify for the purification of the flesh, 14 how much more will the blood of Christ, who through the eternal Spirit offered himself without blemish to God, cleanse our[B] consciences from dead works so that we can serve the living God?

15 Therefore, he is the mediator of a new covenant,[C] so that those who are called might receive the promise of the eternal inheritance, because a death has taken place for redemption from the transgressions committed under the first covenant. 16 Where a will exists, the death of the one who made it must be established. 17 For a will is valid only when people die, since it is never in effect while the one who made it is living. 18 That is why even the first covenant was inaugurated with blood. 19 For when every command had been proclaimed by Moses to all the people according to the law, he took the blood of calves and goats,[D] along with water, scarlet wool, and hyssop, and sprinkled the scroll itself and all the people, 20 saying, **This is the blood of the covenant that God has ordained for you.**[E] 21 In the same way, he sprinkled the tabernacle and all the articles of worship with blood. 22 According to the law almost everything is purified with blood, and without the shedding of blood there is no forgiveness.

23 Therefore, it was necessary for the copies of the things in the heavens to be purified with these sacrifices, but the heavenly things themselves to be purified with better sacrifices than these. 24 For Christ did not enter a sanctuary made with hands (only a model[F] of the true one) but into heaven itself, so that he might now appear in the presence of God for us. 25 He did not do this to offer himself many times, as the high priest enters the sanctuary yearly with the blood of another. 26 Otherwise, he would have had to suffer many times since the foundation of the world. But now he has appeared one time, at the end of the ages, for the removal of sin by the sacrifice of himself. 27 And just as it is appointed for people to die once — and after this, judgment — 28 so also Christ, having been offered once to bear the sins of many, will appear a second time, not to bear sin, but[G] to bring salvation to those who are waiting for him.

THE PERFECT SACRIFICE

10 Since the law has only a shadow of the good things to come, and not the reality itself of those things, it can never perfect the worshipers by the same sacrifices they continually offer year after year. 2 Otherwise, wouldn't they have stopped being offered, since the worshipers, purified once and for all, would no longer have any consciousness of sins? 3 But in the sacrifices there is a reminder of sins year after year. 4 For it is impossible for the blood of bulls and goats to take away sins.

[A] **9:11** Other mss read *that are to come* [B] **9:14** Other mss read *your* [C] **9:15** The Gk word used here can be translated covenant, will, or testament, also in vv. 16,17,18. [D] **9:19** Some mss omit *and goats* [E] **9:20** Ex 24:8 [F] **9:24** Or *antitype*, or *figure* [G] **9:28** Lit *time, apart from sin,*

5 Therefore, as he was coming into the world, he
said:

You did not desire sacrifice and offering,
but you prepared a body for me.
6 **You did not delight**
in whole burnt offerings and sin offerings.
7 **Then I said, "See —**
it is written about me
in the scroll —
I have come to do your will, God."[A]

8 After he says above, **You did not desire or delight in sacrifices and offerings, whole burnt offerings and sin offerings** (which are offered according to the law), 9 he then says, **See, I have come
to do your will.**[B] He takes away the first to establish
the second. 10 By this will, we have been sanctified
through the offering of the body of Jesus Christ once
for all time.

11 Every priest stands day after day ministering and
offering the same sacrifices time after time, which
can never take away sins. 12 But this man, after offering one sacrifice for sins forever, sat down at the
right hand of God.[C] 13 He is now waiting until his enemies are made his footstool. 14 For by one offering
he has perfected forever those who are sanctified.
15 The Holy Spirit also testifies to us about this. For
after he says:

16 **This is the covenant I will make with them**
after those days,
the Lord says,
I will put my laws on their hearts
and write them on their minds,
17 and **I will never again remember**
their sins and their lawless acts.[D]

18 Now where there is forgiveness of these, there is
no longer an offering for sin.

EXHORTATIONS TO GODLINESS

19 Therefore, brothers and sisters, since we have boldness to enter the sanctuary through the blood of Jesus
— 20 he has inaugurated[E] for us a new and living
way through the curtain (that is, through his flesh)
— 21 and since we have a great high priest over the
house of God, 22 let us draw near with a true heart
in full assurance of faith, with our hearts sprinkled
clean from an evil conscience and our bodies washed
in pure water. 23 Let us hold on to the confession of
our hope without wavering, since he who promised

[A] **10:5–7** Ps 40:6–8 [B] **10:9** Other mss add *God* [C] **10:12** Or *offering one sacrifice for sins, sat down forever at the right hand of God* [D] **10:16–17** Jr 31:33–34 [E] **10:20** Or *opened*

Egyptian temple at Timna in the Arabah, south of the Dead Sea. Timna, which housed copper mines, had a temple to the goddess Hathor, goddess of mining. In its final phase, the temple probably had a cloth canopy, as textile fragments were found across the floor. The Hathor temple was likely similar in design to Solomon's temple.

is faithful. 24 And let us consider one another in order
to provoke love and good works, 25 not neglecting to
gather together, as some are in the habit of doing, but
encouraging each other, and all the more as you see
the day approaching.

WARNING AGAINST DELIBERATE SIN

26 For if we deliberately go on sinning after receiving
the knowledge of the truth, there no longer remains
a sacrifice for sins, 27 but a terrifying expectation of
judgment and the fury of a fire about to consume
the adversaries. 28 Anyone who disregarded the law
of Moses died without mercy, based on the testimony of two or three witnesses. 29 How much worse
punishment do you think one will deserve who has
trampled on the Son of God, who has regarded as
profane[A] the blood of the covenant by which he was
sanctified, and who has insulted the Spirit of grace?
30 For we know the one who has said,

> **Vengeance belongs to me; I will repay,**[B,C]

and again,

> **The Lord will judge his people.**[D]

31 It is a terrifying thing to fall into the hands of the
living God.

32 Remember the earlier days when, after you had
been enlightened, you endured a hard struggle with
sufferings. 33 Sometimes you were publicly exposed
to taunts and afflictions, and at other times you were
companions of those who were treated that way.
34 For you sympathized with the prisoners[E] and accepted with joy the confiscation of your possessions,
because you know that you yourselves have a better
and enduring possession.[F] 35 So don't throw away
your confidence, which has a great reward. 36 For you
need endurance, so that after you have done God's
will, you may receive what was promised.

> 37 For yet in **a very little while,**
> **the Coming One will come and not delay.**
> 38 **But my righteous one**[G] **will live by faith;**
> **and if he draws back,**
> **I have no pleasure**[H] **in him.**[I]

39 But we are not those who draw back and are destroyed, but those who have faith and are saved.

LIVING BY FAITH

11 Now faith is the reality[J] of what is hoped for,
the proof[K] of what is not seen. 2 For by this our
ancestors were approved.

3 By faith we understand that the universe was[L]
created by the word of God, so that what is seen was
made from things that are not visible.[M]

4 By faith Abel offered to God a better sacrifice
than Cain did. By faith he was approved as a righteous man, because God approved his gifts, and even
though he is dead, he still speaks through his faith.

5 By faith Enoch was taken away, and so he did not
experience death. **He was not to be found because
God took him away.**[N] For before he was taken away,
he was approved as one who pleased God. 6 Now without faith it is impossible to please God, since the one
who draws near to him must believe that he exists
and that he rewards those who seek him.

7 By faith Noah, after he was warned about what
was not yet seen and motivated by godly fear, built
an ark to deliver his family. By faith he condemned
the world and became an heir of the righteousness
that comes by faith.

8 By faith Abraham, when he was called, obeyed
and set out for a place that he was going to receive as
an inheritance. He went out, even though he did not
know where he was going. 9 By faith he stayed as a
foreigner in the land of promise, living in tents as did
Isaac and Jacob, coheirs of the same promise. 10 For he
was looking forward to the city that has foundations,
whose architect and builder is God.

11 By faith even Sarah herself, when she was unable to have children, received power to conceive
offspring, even though she was past the age, since
she[O] considered that the one who had promised was
faithful. 12 Therefore, from one man — in fact, from
one as good as dead — came offspring as numerous
as the stars of the sky and as innumerable as the
grains of sand along the seashore.

13 These all died in faith, although they had not received the things that were promised. But they saw
them from a distance, greeted them, and confessed
that they were foreigners and temporary residents on
the earth. 14 Now those who say such things make it
clear that they are seeking a homeland. 15 If they were
thinking about where they came from, they would
have had an opportunity to return. 16 But they now
desire a better place — a heavenly one. Therefore,
God is not ashamed to be called their God, for he has
prepared a city for them.

17 By faith Abraham, when he was tested, offered
up Isaac. He received the promises and yet he was offering his one and only son, 18 the one to whom it had
been said, **Your offspring**[P] **will be traced through
Isaac.**[Q] 19 He considered God to be able even to raise
someone from the dead; therefore, he received him
back, figuratively speaking.[R]

[A] **10:29** Or *ordinary* [B] **10:30** Other mss add *says the Lord* [C] **10:30** Dt 32:35 [D] **10:30** Dt 32:36 [E] **10:34** Other mss read *sympathized with my imprisonment* [F] **10:34** Other mss add *in heaven* [G] **10:38** Other mss read *the righteous one* [H] **10:38** Lit *my soul has no pleasure* [I] **10:37–38** Is 26:20 LXX; Hab 2:3–4 [J] **11:1** Or *assurance* [K] **11:1** Or *conviction* [L] **11:3** Or *the worlds were*, or *the ages were* [M] **11:3** Or *so that what is seen was made out of what was not visible* [N] **11:5** Gn 5:21–24 [O] **11:11** Or *By faith Abraham, even though he was past age — and Sarah herself was barren — received the ability to procreate since he* [P] **11:18** Lit *seed* [Q] **11:18** Gn 21:12 [R] **11:19** Or *back, as a foreshadowing*, or *as a type*

20 By faith Isaac blessed Jacob and Esau concerning
things to come. 21 By faith Jacob, when he was dying,
blessed each of the sons of Joseph, and **he worshiped,**
leaning on the top of his staff.[A] 22 By faith Joseph,
as he was nearing the end of his life, mentioned[B] the
exodus of the Israelites and gave instructions concerning his bones.

23 By faith Moses, after he was born, was hidden
by his parents for three months, because they saw
that the child was beautiful, and they didn't fear the
king's edict. 24 By faith Moses, when he had grown up,
refused to be called the son of Pharaoh's daughter
25 and chose to suffer with the people of God rather than to enjoy the fleeting pleasure of sin. 26 For
he considered reproach for the sake of Christ to be
greater wealth than the treasures of Egypt, since he
was looking ahead to the reward.

27 By faith he left Egypt behind, not being afraid of
the king's anger, for Moses persevered as one who
sees him who is invisible. 28 By faith he instituted the
Passover and the sprinkling of the blood, so that the
destroyer of the firstborn might not touch the Israelites. 29 By faith they crossed the Red Sea as though
they were on dry land. When the Egyptians attempted
to do this, they were drowned.

30 By faith the walls of Jericho fell down after being marched around by the Israelites for seven days.
31 By faith Rahab the prostitute welcomed the spies in
peace and didn't perish with those who disobeyed.

32 And what more can I say? Time is too short for
me to tell about Gideon, Barak, Samson, Jephthah,
David, Samuel, and the prophets, 33 who by faith conquered kingdoms, administered justice, obtained
promises, shut the mouths of lions, 34 quenched the
raging of fire, escaped the edge of the sword, gained
strength in weakness, became mighty in battle, and
put foreign armies to flight. 35 Women received their
dead, raised to life again. Other people were tortured, not accepting release, so that they might gain
a better resurrection. 36 Others experienced mock-
ings and scourgings, as well as bonds and imprisonment. 37 They were stoned,[C] they were sawed in
two, they died by the sword, they wandered about
in sheepskins, in goatskins, destitute, afflicted, and
mistreated. 38 The world was not worthy of them.
They wandered in deserts and on mountains, hiding
in caves and holes in the ground.

[A] **11:21** Gn 47:31 [B] **11:22** Or *remembered* [C] **11:37** Other mss add *they were tempted,*

Mosque at Machpelah, the site near Hebron that Abraham bought to bury Sarah. It is the traditional burial site of not only Abraham and Sarah, but also Isaac, Rebekah, Jacob, and Leah.

Hospitality in the First Century

by C. Mack Roark

Hospitality was a major component of the expected social code of conduct in the first century. It had long been one of the ground rules of ancient societies. Residents had a moral responsibility to protect travelers who could not protect themselves.

From those with a nomadic lifestyle in Egypt to the traveling merchants of Asia Minor, the Mediterranean world was on the move. And the absence, or at least the scarcity, of accommodations made travelers aware of the need for hospitable homes along the way. Without this social protocol, travel was unsafe. Both Paul and Peter commanded believers to show hospitality (Rm 12:13; 1Pt 4:9). Paul also explained that hospitality was required of one who would be an overseer (1Tm 3:2).

What were the antecedents of this custom? The literature of both the Greco-Roman and Jewish worlds makes clear that the custom was as old as their earliest civilizations.

Homer's Odyssey is the oldest, best known, and most cited of ancient Greek literature. In it, scenes of hospitality punctuate the travels of Odysseus. Here are a few examples. When Telemachus and Nestor approached the kingdom of Menelaos, a servant questioned whether to send them on their way. Menelaos responded, "How often have we eaten the food of a stranger, you and I, in other parts of the world, on our long journey home, praying that Zeus might somewhere give us rest and peace at last. Go and take out their horses, and bring the men in to share our feast."[1]

Later, when Odysseus came to the palace of Alcinoos, he humbly sat down in the ashes beside the fire. Seeing this, Echeneos, a wise elder who knew the ancient traditions, said, "It is not right and proper that a stranger should sit on the ground amid the ashes of the hearth." Odysseus was then given food and Alcinoos proclaimed, "We must see to it that he meets no hurt or misfortune until he sets foot in his own country"[2] Peisistratos later reminded his friend Telemachus, who was on his way back to Ithaca, "That's what a guest remembers to his dying day, when a hospitable man has been kind to him."[3]

In Jewish antiquity, the practice goes back to Abraham. In Genesis 18:1–8, Abraham is the consummate host, sharing his finest with these heavenly strangers. The Levitical code commanded hospitality to the alien in the land (Lv 19:33–34). Job defended his ethical code, declaring, "No stranger had to spend the night on the street, for I opened my door to the traveler" (Jb 31:32).

What made showing hospitality so important? Traveling was common; trips were usually days or weeks long, not hours. A forty-mile round trip could take four days. Inns were on main roads; the accommodations, though, were often more dangerous than sleeping on the roadside. And many could not afford the expense. The scarcity of hotel-like accommodations coupled with the uncertainty of the road meant travel was always risky. The inns were spread a day's journey apart, usually about twenty miles. With enough money, one *might* get a private room. More likely, the traveler would sleep on a floor, while trying to hide his money (or, as in Paul's case, a satchel of letters) from nighttime thievery. Finding a safe place to stay was a constant struggle for every traveler.[4]

The rise of Rome and the Pax Romana brought with it a network of roads and a greater facility for travel. Although travel between population centers became easier, the secondary roads saw little improvement.

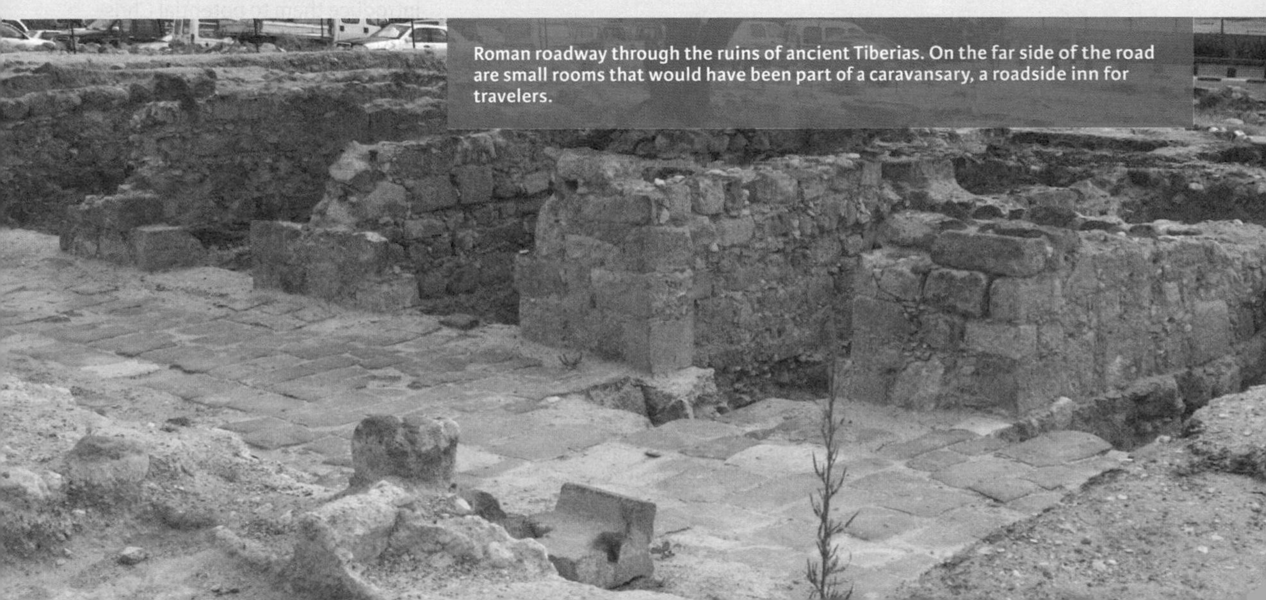

Roman roadway through the ruins of ancient Tiberias. On the far side of the road are small rooms that would have been part of a caravansary, a roadside inn for travelers.

Relief showing a Greek banquet scene. The host reclines and is drinking from a *rhyton*.

Traveling would have been almost impossible, or at least terribly dangerous, without an expectation of hospitality for strangers.

If travelers averaged three miles per hour (a twenty-minute mile), they would walk about fifteen to twenty miles per day. A donkey, which was not much faster than a person walking, traveled about twenty miles per day. Mail carriers on the Roman road system covered twenty-five to thirty miles per day, but they had stations where they could get fresh horses.[5]

The early Christians were no less active in travel than others. Reading the Gospels, Acts, or Paul's letters makes clear that travel from one locale to another was common. Paul traveled as far as ten thousand miles in his missionary journeys.[6] In his travels, he was not exempt from the dangers all travelers faced.

Paul, though, was not the only Christian on the road. These travelers frequently carried letters with them. Without personal contact, letters were the only means of communication between churches and believers. Of the twenty-seven books of the New Testament, twenty-one are letters. Even Acts contains two letters (15:23–29; 23:25–30), and Revelation has seven (chaps. 2–3).

If Philippians was written from Rome, transporting the letter would involve 730 land miles and at least two days at sea—plus almost forty nights on the road. Saul and Barnabas's trip from Antioch to Galatia was about 640 miles. At 15 miles per day, this would require forty-three days and nights on the road.[7] Only a network of believers and believing communities could provide any semblance of safety for these missionaries and letter couriers.

Some took advantage of this hospitality.[8] Thus, as a caution, Christians who traveled were often given letters of recommendation to introduce them to potential Christian hosts. These letters not only continued the practice of hospitality, but also helped the host distinguish the legitimate from the illegitimate. Letters of recommendation demonstrate that Christians traveling could expect to find both welcome and aid, even from complete strangers. ✣

Dated to early in the first century AD, a pair of silver *trullae* or serving pans. One is slightly smaller than the other so that they could be nested together when not in use. These were probably used for serving liquids. This pair, unusually fine and decorated with floral patterns and duck heads, is likely from the region of the Black Sea. Also shown is a silver wine strainer, dated to the mid-first century BC. From the region of Lake Trasimene, this strainer has a deep, pointed bowl perforated with tiny holes. It has two vertical handles, each shaped to fit the grip of the thumb and forefinger, an arrangement usually found on drinking cups.

[1] Homer, *Odyssey* 4.26–36. [2] Homer, *Odyssey* 7.153–66. [3] Homer, *Odyssey* 15.54–55. [4] Jerome Murphy-O'Connor, *Paul: A Critical Life* (Oxford: Oxford University Press, 1996), 99–100. Not all inns were unsafe; see Epictetus, *Discourses* 2.23.36–37. [5] Wayne A. Meeks, *The First Urban Christians* (New Haven, CT: Yale University Press, 1983), 18. [6] Meeks, *First Urban Christians*, 16. [7] Murphy-O'Connor, *Paul*, 27. [8] See 3 John and Didache 11–12.

39 All these were approved through their faith, but
they did not receive what was promised, 40 since God
had provided something better for us, so that they
would not be made perfect without us.

THE CALL TO ENDURANCE

12 Therefore, since we also have such a large cloud
of witnesses surrounding us, let us lay aside
every hindrance and the sin that so easily ensnares
us. Let us run with endurance the race that lies before
us, 2 keeping our eyes on Jesus,[A] the pioneer and perfecter[B] of our faith. For the joy that lay before him,[C]
he endured the cross, despising the shame, and sat
down at the right hand of the throne of God.

FATHERLY DISCIPLINE

3 For consider him who endured such hostility from
sinners against himself, so that you won't grow weary and give up. 4 In struggling against sin, you have
not yet resisted to the point of shedding your blood.
5 And you have forgotten the exhortation that addresses you as sons:

My son, do not take the Lord's
discipline lightly
or lose heart when you are reproved by him,
6 **for the Lord disciplines**
the one he loves
and punishes every son he receives.[D]

7 Endure suffering as discipline: God is dealing with
you as sons. For what son is there that a father does
not discipline? 8 But if you are without discipline
— which all receive[E] — then you are illegitimate
children and not sons. 9 Furthermore, we had human fathers discipline us, and we respected them.
Shouldn't we submit even more to the Father of
spirits and live? 10 For they disciplined us for a short
time based on what seemed good to them, but he
does it for our benefit, so that we can share his holiness. 11 No discipline seems enjoyable at the time,
but painful. Later on, however, it yields the peaceful fruit of righteousness to those who have been
trained by it.

12 Therefore, strengthen your tired hands and
weakened knees, 13 and make straight paths for your
feet, so that what is lame may not be dislocated[F] but
healed instead.

[A] **12:2** Or *us, looking to Jesus* [B] **12:2** Or *the founder and completer*, or *the source and perfecter* [C] **12:2** Or *who instead of the joy lying before him* [D] **12:6** Pr 3:11–12 [E] **12:8** Lit *discipline, of which all have become participants* [F] **12:13** Or *so that the lame will not be turned aside*

Stadium area at Tyre, from the Roman Era.

WARNING AGAINST REJECTING GOD'S GRACE

14 Pursue peace with everyone, and holiness — without it no one will see the Lord. 15 Make sure that no one falls short of the grace of God and that no root of bitterness springs up, causing trouble and defiling many. 16 And make sure that there isn't any immoral[A] or irreverent person like Esau, who sold his birthright in exchange for a single meal. 17 For you know that later, when he wanted to inherit the blessing, he was rejected, even though he sought it with tears, because he didn't find any opportunity for repentance.

18 For you have not come to what could be touched, to a blazing fire, to darkness, gloom, and storm, 19 to the blast of a trumpet, and the sound of words. Those who heard it begged that not another word be spoken to them, 20 for they could not bear what was commanded: **If even an animal touches the mountain, it must be stoned.**[B] 21 The appearance was so terrifying that Moses said, **I am trembling with fear.**[C] 22 Instead, you have come to Mount Zion, to the city of the living God (the heavenly Jerusalem), to myriads of angels, a festive gathering, 23 to the assembly of the firstborn whose names have been written[D] in heaven, to a Judge, who is God of all, to the spirits of righteous people made perfect, 24 and to Jesus, the mediator of a new covenant, and to the sprinkled blood, which says better things than the blood of Abel.

25 See to it that you do not reject the one who speaks. For if they did not escape when they rejected him who warned them on earth, even less will we if we turn away from him who warns us from heaven. 26 His voice shook the earth at that time, but now he has promised, **Yet once more I will shake not only the earth but also the heavens.**[E] 27 This expression, "Yet once more," indicates the removal of what can be shaken — that is, created things — so that what is not shaken might remain. 28 Therefore, since we are receiving a kingdom that cannot be shaken, let us be thankful. By it, we may serve God acceptably, with reverence and awe, 29 for our God is a consuming fire.

FINAL EXHORTATIONS

13 Let brotherly love continue. 2 Don't neglect to show hospitality, for by doing this some have welcomed angels as guests without knowing it. 3 Remember those in prison, as though you were in prison with them, and the mistreated,[F] as though you yourselves were suffering bodily.[G] 4 Marriage is to be honored by all and the marriage bed kept undefiled, because God will judge the sexually immoral and adulterers. 5 Keep your life free from the love of money. Be satisfied with what you have, for he himself has said, **I will never leave you or abandon you.**[H] 6 Therefore, we may boldly say,

The Lord is my helper;
I will not be afraid.
What can man do to me?[I]

7 Remember your leaders who have spoken God's word to you. As you carefully observe the outcome of their lives, imitate their faith. 8 Jesus Christ is the same yesterday, today, and forever. 9 Don't be led astray by various kinds of strange teachings; for it is good for the heart to be established by grace and not by food regulations, since those who observe them have not benefited. 10 We have an altar from which those who worship at the tabernacle do not have a right to eat. 11 For the bodies of those animals whose blood is brought into the most holy place by the high priest as a sin offering are burned outside the camp. 12 Therefore, Jesus also suffered outside the gate, so that he might sanctify[J] the people by his own blood. 13 Let us, then, go to him outside the camp, bearing his disgrace. 14 For we do not have an enduring city here; instead, we seek the one to come. 15 Therefore, through him let us continually offer up to God a sacrifice of praise, that is, the fruit of lips that confess his name. 16 Don't neglect to do what is good and to share, for God is pleased with such sacrifices. 17 Obey your leaders[K] and submit to them, since they keep watch over your souls as those who will give an account, so that they can do this with joy and not with grief, for that would be unprofitable for you. 18 Pray for us, for we are convinced that we have a clear conscience, wanting to conduct ourselves honorably in everything. 19 And I urge you all the more to pray[L] that I may be restored to you very soon.

BENEDICTION AND FAREWELL

20 Now may the God of peace, who brought up from the dead our Lord Jesus — the great Shepherd of the sheep — through the blood of the everlasting covenant, 21 equip[M] you with everything good to do his will, working in us what is pleasing in his sight, through Jesus Christ, to whom be glory forever and ever.[N] Amen.

22 Brothers and sisters, I urge you to receive this message of exhortation, for I have written to you briefly. 23 Be aware that our brother Timothy has been released. If he comes soon enough, he will be with me when I see you. 24 Greet all your leaders and all the saints. Those who are from Italy send you greetings. 25 Grace be with you all.

[A] **12:16** Or *sexually immoral* [B] **12:20** Ex 19:12 [C] **12:21** Dt 9:19 [D] **12:23** Or *registered* [E] **12:26** Hg 2:6 [F] **13:3** Or *tortured* [G] **13:3** Or *mistreated, since you are also in a body* [H] **13:5** Dt 31:6 [I] **13:6** Ps 118:6 [J] **13:12** Or *set apart*, or *consecrate* [K] **13:17** Or *rulers* [L] **13:19** Lit *to do this* [M] **13:21** Or *perfect* [N] **13:21** Other mss omit *and ever*

JAMES

This courtyard of an excavated house in Pompeii demonstrates an ostentatious display of wealth for its day. One of the owners of the house, Aulus Vettius Conviva, made large contributions to Rome's extravagant works projects and was rewarded by having the emperor nominate him to a special order, the Augustales.

INTRODUCTION TO

JAMES

Circumstances of Writing

James is named as the author in James 1:1. A number of New Testament personalities were named James, but only three are candidates for the authorship of this book. James the son of Zebedee died in AD 44, too early to have been the author. No tradition names James the son of Alphaeus (Mk 3:18) as the author. This leaves James the brother of Jesus, also called James the Just (Mk 6:3; Ac 1:14; 12:17; 15:13; 21:18; 1Co 15:7; Gl 2:9,12), as the most likely candidate.

This James is identified as the brother of Jesus in Matthew 13:55; Mark 6:3; and Galatians 1:19. Though he was not a follower of Christ during his earthly ministry (Jn 7:3–5), a postresurrection appearance convinced James that Jesus is indeed the Christ (Ac 1:14; 1Co 15:7). James later led the Jerusalem church (Gl 2:9,12), exercising great influence there (Ac 1:14; 12:17; 15:13; 21:18; 1Co 15:7; Gl 2:9,12).

The book of James was probably written between AD 48 and 52, though nothing in the epistle suggests a more precise date. James's death in AD 62 or 66 means the epistle was written before this time. Similarities to Gospel traditions and Pauline themes are suggestive. If Mark was written around AD 65 and time is allowed for the events of Acts 15 and 21 to have occurred between Paul's first and second missionary journeys, a date between AD 48 and 52 seems most likely.

James led the Jerusalem church. The reference to "the twelve tribes dispersed abroad" (Jms 1:1) suggests the letter was written to Jewish Christians living outside of Israel. The reference to a synagogue (Gk; 2:2) also suggests that his audience was Jewish Christians. References to their circumstances (e.g., oppression by wealthy landowners; 5:1–6) could refer to congregations anywhere in the Roman Empire. However, Semitic word order, quotations from the Septuagint, and the overall dependence of the letter on the Jewish wisdom tradition suggest a specifically Jewish Christian audience.

Contribution to the Bible

James continually called for obedience to the law of God. He never referred to the ceremonial law, but to the moral law. Although some people think James is at odds with Paul about the Christian's relationship to the law, both authors combine to give us a solid understanding of the Old Testament law. Paul showed believers that Christ met the demands of the law and, thus, brings us to salvation. James showed believers that their obedience to God's moral standards is an indication of a living faith, which is a life lived in step with the one who met the demands of the law. Some choose to oversimplify the distinctions between the Old Testament and the New Testament and say the Old Testament is grounded in works and the New Testament is grounded in faith, but James brings both testaments together to show that faith and works are integrally related in both the old and new covenants.

Structure

The book of James is a letter (an epistle), though only the greeting conforms to the ancient Greek form exemplified in Paul's letters, especially Galatians. The greeting identifies the author as James, includes a title demonstrating the source of his authority ("a servant of God and of the Lord Jesus Christ"), names the recipients ("the twelve tribes dispersed abroad"), and conveys "greetings" (1:1). Epistles were often used as a means of spurring the recipients to a change in behavior or belief based on the authoritative word and guidance of the sender.

The book of James has been compared to Old Testament Wisdom literature. Although there are wisdom elements in James, such as comparing the wisdom of the world with the wisdom that comes from God, it also contains exhortations and prophetic elements not common to Wisdom literature.

GREETING

1 James, a servant of God and of the Lord Jesus
Christ:
To the twelve tribes dispersed abroad.[A]
Greetings.

TRIALS AND MATURITY

2 Consider it a great joy, my brothers and sisters,
whenever you experience various trials, 3 because
you know that the testing of your faith produces
endurance. 4 And let endurance have its full effect,
so that you may be mature and complete, lacking
nothing.
5 Now if any of you lacks wisdom, he should ask
God — who gives to all generously and ungrudgingly
— and it will be given to him. 6 But let him ask in faith
without doubting.[B] For the doubter is like the surging sea, driven and tossed by the wind. 7 That person
should not expect to receive anything from the Lord,
8 being double-minded and unstable in all his ways.[C]
9 Let the brother of humble circumstances boast
in his exaltation, 10 but let the rich boast in his humiliation because he will pass away like a flower of
the field. 11 For the sun rises and, together with the
scorching wind, dries up the grass; its flower falls off,
and its beautiful appearance perishes. In the same
way, the rich person will wither away while pursuing his activities.
12 Blessed is the one who endures trials, because
when he has stood the test he will receive the crown
of life that God[D] has promised to those who love him.
13 No one undergoing a trial should say, "I am being
tempted by God," since God is not tempted by evil, and
he himself doesn't tempt anyone. 14 But each person
is tempted when he is drawn away and enticed by his
own evil desire. 15 Then after desire has conceived,
it gives birth to sin, and when sin is fully grown, it
gives birth to death.
16 Don't be deceived, my dear brothers and sisters.
17 Every good and perfect gift is from above, coming
down from the Father of lights, who does not change
like shifting shadows. 18 By his own choice, he gave
us birth by the word of truth so that we would be a
kind of firstfruits of his creatures.

HEARING AND DOING THE WORD

19 My dear brothers and sisters, understand this: Everyone should be quick to listen, slow to speak, and
slow to anger, 20 for human anger does not accomplish
God's righteousness. 21 Therefore, ridding yourselves
of all moral filth and the evil that is so prevalent,[E]
humbly receive the implanted word, which is able
to save your souls.

[A] **1:1** Gk *diaspora*; Jewish people scattered throughout Gentile lands
[B] **1:6** Or *without divided loyalties* [C] **1:8** Or *in all his conduct*
[D] **1:12** Other mss read *that the Lord* [E] **1:21** Or *the abundance of evil*

The Odeum of Herod Atticus at the Acropolis in Athens. Herod Atticus, a wealthy banker and friend of the emperor Hadrian, had the 5,000-seat theater carved into the rock in memory of his wife, Annia Regilla.

22 But be doers of the word and not hearers only, deceiving yourselves. 23 Because if anyone is a hearer of the word and not a doer, he is like someone looking at his own face[A] in a mirror. 24 For he looks at himself, goes away, and immediately forgets what kind of person he was. 25 But the one who looks intently into the perfect law of freedom and perseveres in it, and is not a forgetful hearer but a doer who works — this person will be blessed in what he does.

26 If anyone[B] thinks he is religious without controlling his tongue, his religion is useless and he deceives himself. 27 Pure and undefiled religion before God the Father is this: to look after orphans and widows in their distress and to keep oneself unstained from the world.

Etruscan inscribed bronze mirror; dated about 250–200 BC.

THE SIN OF FAVORITISM

2 My brothers and sisters, do not show favoritism as you hold on to the faith in our glorious Lord Jesus Christ. 2 For if someone comes into your meeting wearing a gold ring and dressed in fine clothes, and a poor person dressed in filthy clothes also comes in, 3 if you look with favor on the one wearing the fine clothes and say, "Sit here in a good place," and yet you say to the poor person, "Stand over there," or "Sit here on the floor by my footstool," 4 haven't you made distinctions among yourselves and become judges with evil thoughts?

5 Listen, my dear brothers and sisters: Didn't God choose the poor in this world to be rich in faith and heirs of the kingdom that he has promised to those who love him? 6 Yet you have dishonored the poor. Don't the rich oppress you and drag you into court? 7 Don't they blaspheme the good name that was invoked over you?

8 Indeed, if you fulfill the royal law prescribed in the Scripture, **Love your neighbor as yourself**,[C] you are doing well. 9 If, however, you show favoritism, you commit sin and are convicted by the law as transgressors. 10 For whoever keeps the entire law, and yet stumbles at one point, is guilty of breaking it all. 11 For he who said, **Do not commit adultery**,[D] also said, **Do not murder.**[E] So if you do not commit adultery, but you murder, you are a lawbreaker.

12 Speak and act as those who are to be judged by the law of freedom. 13 For judgment is without mercy to the one who has not shown mercy. Mercy triumphs over judgment.

FAITH AND WORKS

14 What good is it, my brothers and sisters, if someone claims to have faith but does not have works? Can such faith save him?

15 If a brother or sister is without clothes and lacks daily food 16 and one of you says to them, "Go in peace, stay warm, and be well fed," but you don't give them what the body needs, what good is it? 17 In the same way faith, if it does not have works, is dead by itself.

18 But someone will say, "You have faith, and I have works."[F] Show me your faith without works, and I will show you faith by my works. 19 You believe that God is one. Good! Even the demons believe — and they shudder.

20 Senseless person! Are you willing to learn that faith without works is useless? 21 Wasn't Abraham our father justified by works in offering Isaac his son on the altar? 22 You see that faith was active together with his works, and by works, faith was made complete, 23 and the Scripture was fulfilled that says, **Abraham believed God, and it was credited to him as righteousness**,[G] and he was called God's friend. 24 You see that a person is justified by works and not by faith alone. 25 In the same way, wasn't Rahab the prostitute also justified by works in receiving the messengers and sending them out by a different route? 26 For just as the body without the spirit is dead, so also faith without works is dead.

[A] **1:23** Or *at his natural face* [B] **1:26** Other mss add *among you*
[C] **2:8** Lv 19:18 [D] **2:11** Ex 20:14; Dt 5:18 [E] **2:11** Ex 20:13; Dt 5:17
[F] **2:18** The quotation may end here or after v. 18b or v. 19.
[G] **2:23** Gn 15:6

An incantation bowl; people had superstitious beliefs about these bowls. A protective spell was written on each bowl, and it was buried upside down. This action had two purposes: to ward off evil spirits and to serve as a trap for any demons that came near.

CONTROLLING THE TONGUE

3 Not many should become teachers, my brothers,[A] because you know that we will receive a stricter judgment. 2 For we all stumble in many ways. If anyone does not stumble in what he says, he is mature, able also to control the whole body. 3 Now if we put bits into the mouths of horses so that they obey us, we direct their whole bodies. 4 And consider ships: Though very large and driven by fierce winds, they are guided by a very small rudder wherever the will of the pilot directs. 5 So too, though the tongue is a small part of the body, it boasts great things. Consider how a small fire sets ablaze a large forest. 6 And the tongue is a fire. The tongue, a world of unrighteousness, is placed[B] among our members. It stains the whole body, sets the course of life on fire, and is itself set on fire by hell. 7 Every kind of animal, bird, reptile, and fish is tamed and has been tamed by humankind, 8 but no one can tame the tongue. It is a restless evil, full of deadly poison. 9 With the tongue we bless our Lord and Father, and with it we curse people who are made in God's likeness. 10 Blessing and cursing come out of the same mouth. My brothers and sisters, these things should not be this way. 11 Does a spring pour out sweet and bitter water from the same opening? 12 Can a fig tree produce olives, my brothers and sisters, or a grapevine produce figs? Neither can a saltwater spring yield fresh water.

THE WISDOM FROM ABOVE

13 Who among you is wise and understanding? By his good conduct he should show that his works are done in the gentleness that comes from wisdom. 14 But if you have bitter envy and selfish ambition in your heart, don't boast and deny the truth. 15 Such wisdom does not come down from above but is earthly, unspiritual, demonic. 16 For where there is envy and selfish ambition, there is disorder and every evil practice. 17 But the wisdom from above is first pure, then peace-loving, gentle, compliant, full of mercy and good fruits, unwavering, without pretense. 18 And the fruit of righteousness is sown in peace by those who cultivate peace.

PROUD OR HUMBLE

4 What is the source of wars and fights among you? Don't they come from your passions that wage war within you?[C] 2 You desire and do not have. You murder and covet and cannot obtain. You fight and wage war.[D] You do not have because you do not ask. 3 You ask and don't receive because you ask with wrong motives, so that you may spend it on your pleasures.

4 You adulterous people![E] Don't you know that friendship with the world is hostility toward God? So whoever wants to be the friend of the world becomes the enemy of God. 5 Or do you think it's without reason that the Scripture says: The spirit he made to dwell in us envies intensely?[F]

6 But he gives greater grace. Therefore he says:

God resists the proud
but gives grace to the humble.[G]

7 Therefore, submit to God. Resist the devil, and he will flee from you. 8 Draw near to God, and he will draw near to you. Cleanse your hands, sinners, and purify your hearts, you double-minded. 9 Be miserable and mourn and weep. Let your laughter be turned to mourning and your joy to gloom. 10 Humble yourselves before the Lord, and he will exalt you.

11 Don't criticize one another, brothers and sisters. Anyone who defames or judges a fellow believer[H] defames and judges the law. If you judge the law, you are not a doer of the law but a judge. 12 There is one lawgiver and judge[I] who is able to save and to destroy. But who are you to judge your neighbor?

OUR WILL AND GOD'S WILL

13 Come now, you who say, "Today or tomorrow we will travel to such and such a city and spend a year

[A] **3:1** Or *brothers and sisters* [B] **3:6** Or *places itself*, or *appoints itself* [C] **4:1** Or *war in your members* [D] **4:2** Or *You desire and do not have, so you murder. You covet and cannot obtain, so you fight and wage war.* [E] **4:4** Lit *Adulteresses* [F] **4:5** Or *Scripture says: He jealously yearns for the spirit he made to live in us?*, or *Scripture says: The Spirit he made to dwell in us longs jealously?* [G] **4:6** Pr 3:34 [H] **4:11** Or *his brother or sister* [I] **4:12** Other mss omit *and judge*

there and do business and make a profit." 14 Yet you
do not know what tomorrow will bring — what your
life will be! For you are like vapor that appears for a
little while, then vanishes.
15 Instead, you should say, "If the Lord wills, we will
live and do this or that." 16 But as it is, you boast in your
arrogance. All such boasting is evil. 17 So it is sin to
know the good and yet not do it.

Horse-bit with cheek-pieces in the form of horses; from the Early Iron Age (1200–1000 BC).

WARNING TO THE RICH

5 Come now, you rich people, weep and wail over
the miseries that are coming on you. 2 Your
wealth has rotted and your clothes are moth-eaten.
3 Your gold and silver are corroded, and their corrosion will be a witness against you and will eat your
flesh like fire. You have stored up treasure in the
last days. 4 Look! The pay that you withheld from
the workers who mowed your fields cries out, and the
outcry of the harvesters has reached the ears of
the Lord of Armies. 5 You have lived luxuriously on
the earth and have indulged yourselves. You have
fattened your hearts in a day of slaughter. 6 You have
condemned, you have murdered the righteous, who
does not resist you.

WAITING FOR THE LORD

7 Therefore, brothers and sisters, be patient until the
Lord's coming. See how the farmer waits for the precious fruit of the earth and is patient with it until it
receives the early and the late rains. 8 You also must
be patient. Strengthen your hearts, because the Lord's
coming is near.
9 Brothers and sisters, do not complain about one
another, so that you will not be judged. Look, the judge
stands at the door!

Olive press complex in Mareshah, a town in western Judah. This dual press dates to the third to second centuries BC. Each press operated with a weighted leverage system, one of which has been reconstructed. Olives were placed in a collapsible basket just behind the slitted wall. The beam, one end of which is shown, was drawn down with the system of pulleys and weights to press the olives. The oil was gathered in a catch basin.

The Rich and the Poor in the First Century: A Contrast

by Mona Stewart

In the first century, the orphan and the widow were in the lowest economic class and most in need of aid. The rich and powerful took advantage of those who had no social or economic status. The court system often defrauded the poor. To be poor implied the person was both impoverished and wrongly oppressed.[1]

"In the first Christian century, one out of three persons in Italy and one out of five elsewhere was a slave."[2] Yet not all slaves fit in the same category as the poor. Roman masters provided their household slaves with food, clothing, and shelter. Some even provided them with an education. Most of the free poor, however, existed with meager sustenance and often struggled to find even the barest of essentials.

Often the poor were tenant farmers indebted to absentee rich landowners. Crop failure meant losing everything. Their meager homes, food, and clothing indicated an impoverished lifestyle. The basic diet was bread (made of barley), wine, and olive oil, supplemented with porridge and fish. Providing their families a mere existence was a daily chore.

In contrast, the rich enjoyed large dwellings, excessive and expensive clothing, and the finest food

Overview of ruins at Hamat Gader (meaning "Hot Springs of Gadara"), southeast of the Sea of Galilee on the Yarmuk River. Jews drawn to the area for the springs' medicinal benefits built a synagogue, the floors of which were carpeted with decorative mosaics. One of the mosaics asks God's blessings on a group of wealthy contributors "whose acts of charity are constant everywhere and who have given here five coins of gold. May the King of the Universe bestow the blessing upon their work. Amen. Amen. Selah."

available. They enjoyed three meals daily while the poor were fortunate to have one. The evening meal often consisted of multiple courses. Jewelry was plentiful and ostentatious; both males and females wore rings on many fingers.

Large bathhouses could accommodate thousands at a time. Hot and cold baths were available after which slaves provided massages. Gymnasiums were often located close to the baths and provided another luxury exclusively for the rich. Brothels were plentiful and frequented by the affluent males.

Music, large libraries, and theaters helped fill part of the leisure time of the wealthy. Ruins of theaters built into the side of a hill or mountain stand all over Europe, Asia Minor, and Israel today testifying to the opulent lifestyle. These structures could seat many thousands and had excellent acoustics. The sections down front were reserved for the wealthy while the upper sections were for the common people. This was important because people often used theaters to promote and spread political propaganda. Excavations of towns and villages have yielded large marketplaces with stalls for various crafts—stalls owned predominantly by the rich.

The children and often the slaves of the wealthy received an education. An educated slave would later become the teacher for the next generation of children. "The poor had neither the time, the money, nor the need for an education."[3]

Funerals for the rich and powerful were grand and opulent affairs. Paid musicians and mourners accompanied the family and friends to the burial site. The tombs of the wealthy were elaborate. While alive, the rich would have great monuments built to honor them after death. The funerals of the poor were simple affairs usually held outside the towns and villages. ✣

Greek ostracon (piece of broken pottery with writing) reads, "Give to Tatris in Mesore for her wage one artabas (of wheat)." An artabas is approximately ten gallons.

[1] Gary V. Smith, "Poor, Orphan, Widow" in *HIBD*, 1311. [2] James A. Brooks, "Slave, Servant" in *HIBD*, 1511. [3] John McRay "Rome and the Roman Empire" in *HolBD*, 1212.

Glass bottle, Roman Era; from the eastern Mediterranean region. A bottle of this shape would have likely held perfume, a balm, or sacrificial oil.

[10] Brothers and sisters, take the prophets who
spoke in the Lord's name as an example of suffering
and patience. [11] See, we count as blessed those who
have endured.[A] You have heard of Job's endurance
and have seen the outcome that the Lord brought
about — the Lord is compassionate and merciful.

TRUTHFUL SPEECH

[12] Above all, my brothers and sisters, do not swear, either by heaven or by earth or with any other oath. But let your "yes" mean "yes," and your "no" mean "no," so that you won't fall under judgment.[B]

EFFECTIVE PRAYER

[13] Is anyone among you suffering? He should pray. Is
anyone cheerful? He should sing praises. [14] Is anyone
among you sick? He should call for the elders of the
church, and they are to pray over him, anointing
him with oil in the name of the Lord. [15] The prayer
of faith will save the sick person, and the Lord will
raise him up; if he has committed sins, he will be forgiven. [16] Therefore, confess your sins to one another
and pray for one another, so that you may be healed.
The prayer of a righteous person is very powerful
in its effect. [17] Elijah was a human being as we are,
and he prayed earnestly that it would not rain, and
for three years and six months it did not rain on the
land. [18] Then he prayed again, and the sky gave rain
and the land produced its fruit.
[19] My brothers and sisters, if any among you strays
from the truth, and someone turns him back, [20] let
that person know that whoever turns a sinner from
the error of his way will save his soul from death and
cover a multitude of sins.

[A] **5:11** Or *persevered* [B] **5:12** Other mss read *fall into hypocrisy*

1 PETER

The Monastery of the Nuns, one of the cave-churches in the ancient Roman province of Cappadocia in Asia Minor (modern Turkey). The soft volcanic tufts provided a haven for early Christians fleeing persecution.

INTRODUCTION TO

1 PETER

Circumstances of Writing

The author of 1 Peter identified himself as "Peter, an apostle of Jesus Christ" (1Pt 1:1). He viewed himself as a divinely ordained, directly commissioned, authoritative representative of the Lord Jesus himself. Several statements in the letter indicate that the Peter who plays a prominent role in the Gospels is the author. For example, he called himself an "elder and witness" to Christ's sufferings (5:1). Further, he described Christ's crucifixion with an intimate knowledge that only a disciple would have of that event (2:21–24).

Several expressions in 1 Peter reflect Peter's experiences with Jesus. For example, the exhortation for elders to "shepherd God's flock" (5:2) evokes the charge that Jesus gave Peter in John 21:15–17. Moreover, the command to "clothe yourselves with humility" (5:5) may recall the episode in John 13:2–17 where Jesus washed the disciples' feet.

Objections to the letter's authorship by Peter are inconclusive and cannot be proven. The claim that someone wrote this letter using the apostle's name as a pseudonym cannot be sustained. A number of early church leaders, including Irenaeus, Tertullian, and Clement of Alexandria, accepted the letter as authentic. Further, the early church soundly rejected the practice of writing under an apostolic pseudonym as forgery. In light of the above, the epistle should be accepted as genuinely written by the apostle Peter. Silvanus may have in some fashion helped Peter write the letter while serving as his secretary (amanuensis), but more likely he was merely the letter carrier (5:12).

The recipients of 1 Peter are identified in 1:1. Peter wrote to the "exiles dispersed abroad in Pontus, Galatia, Cappadocia, Asia, and Bithynia." These were Roman provinces located in the northern part of what is now modern Turkey, unless Galatia includes the Galatia in the southern region of Asia Minor. These people were likely persecuted Gentile Christians. They had earlier been involved in idolatry (4:3), were ignorant (1:14) and "empty" (1:18) before they came to Christ, and they formerly were "not a people" but now were "God's people" (2:9–10).

The reference in 1 Peter 5:13—"She who is in Babylon, chosen together with you, sends you greetings"—suggests Rome as the place of the letter's origin. "Babylon" was used cryptically to refer to a place of exile, but specifically for Rome. Other possibilities for Babylon include the cities of Babylon in Mesopotamia and in the Nile Delta in Egypt, but these places are highly unlikely because we have no record of Peter ever being in those places.

First Peter was probably written sometime between AD 62 and 64. While Paul was under house arrest from AD 60 to 62, he did not refer to Peter in Rome. Peter likewise did not mention Paul as being in Rome; only Silvanus and Mark were his companions (5:12–13). These facts suggest that Peter wrote 1 Peter sometime after AD 62 and before the writing of 2 Peter.

The theme of suffering appears throughout 1 Peter. The recipients of the letter are the sufferers in four of its five chapters. Given a composition date of about AD 62 to 64, 1 Peter was written during the persecution of Christians under Nero's reign. The persecution arose in Rome and was spreading into Asia Minor.

Contribution to the Bible

Peter's intent in writing was to strengthen believers in the midst of the suffering and persecution they were facing. His message to them continues to speak to modern believers, reminding us of our heavenly hope and eternal inheritance in the midst of our sufferings. We are called to holiness and a life of love. We are also called to glorify God in our daily lives and to imitate Christ.

Structure

The structure of 1 Peter has been the subject of discussion from the earliest history of the church. The diversity of outlines illustrates that the task of exegesis is not merely a science but also an art. Peter wrote this letter with a typical opening for a letter (1:1–2) and then began the next major section (1:3–2:10) with a blessing (1:3). The two succeeding sections are marked by "dear friends" (2:11; 4:12), and, as noted earlier, the segment from 2:11 to 4:11 concludes with a doxology and "amen." The fourth section of the letter also ends with a doxology and "amen" (5:11) before the closing.

GREETING

1 Peter, an apostle of Jesus Christ:
To those chosen, living as exiles dispersed abroad
in Pontus, Galatia, Cappadocia, Asia, and Bithynia,
chosen 2 according to the foreknowledge of God the
Father, through the sanctifying work of the Spirit,
to be obedient and to be sprinkled with the blood of
Jesus Christ.
May grace and peace be multiplied to you.

A LIVING HOPE

3 Blessed be the God and Father of our Lord Jesus
Christ. Because of his great mercy he has given us
new birth into a living hope through the resurrection
of Jesus Christ from the dead 4 and into an inheritance that is imperishable, undefiled, and unfading, kept in heaven for you. 5 You are being guarded
by God's power through faith for a salvation that is
ready to be revealed in the last time. 6 You rejoice in
this,[A] even though now for a short time, if necessary,
you suffer grief in various trials 7 so that the proven
character of your faith — more valuable than gold
which, though perishable, is refined by fire — may
result in praise, glory, and honor at the revelation of
Jesus Christ. 8 Though you have not seen him, you
love him; though not seeing him now, you believe in
him, and you rejoice with inexpressible and glorious
joy, 9 because you are receiving the goal of your faith,
the salvation of your souls.
10 Concerning this salvation, the prophets, who
prophesied about the grace that would come to you,
searched and carefully investigated. 11 They inquired
into what time or what circumstances the Spirit of
Christ within them was indicating when he testified
in advance to the sufferings of Christ and the glories
that would follow.[B] 12 It was revealed to them that they
were not serving themselves but you. These things
have now been announced to you through those who
preached the gospel to you by the Holy Spirit sent
from heaven — angels long to catch a glimpse of
these things.

A CALL TO HOLY LIVING

13 Therefore, with your minds ready for action, be
sober-minded and set your hope completely on the
grace to be brought to you at the revelation of Jesus
Christ. 14 As obedient children, do not be conformed
to the desires of your former ignorance. 15 But as the
one who called you is holy, you also are to be holy in
all your conduct; 16 for it is written, **Be holy, because
I am holy.**[C] 17 If you appeal to the Father who judges
impartially according to each one's work, you are to
conduct yourselves in reverence during your time
living as strangers. 18 For you know that you were redeemed from your empty way of life inherited from

Dated from the first–second centuries AD, this bird-shaped piece has a hole in the beak tip, which likely functioned like a dropper for feeding a baby.

your ancestors, not with perishable things like silver
or gold, 19 but with the precious blood of Christ, like
that of an unblemished and spotless lamb. 20 He was
foreknown before the foundation of the world but
was revealed in these last times for you. 21 Through
him you believe in God, who raised him from the
dead and gave him glory, so that your faith and hope
are in God.
22 Since you have purified yourselves by your obedience to the truth,[D] so that you show sincere brotherly love for each other, from a pure[E] heart love one
another constantly,[F] 23 because you have been born
again — not of perishable seed but of imperishable
— through the living and enduring word of God.
24 For

> **All flesh is like grass,**
> **and all its glory like a flower of the grass.**
> **The grass withers, and the flower falls,**
> 25 **but the word of the Lord endures forever.**[G]

And this word is the gospel that was proclaimed to
you.

THE LIVING STONE AND A HOLY PEOPLE

2 Therefore, rid yourselves of all malice, all deceit,
hypocrisy, envy, and all slander. 2 Like newborn
infants, desire the pure milk of the word,[H] so that
by it you may grow up into your salvation, 3 if **you
have tasted that the Lord is good.**[I] 4 As you come to
him, a living stone — rejected by people but chosen
and honored by[J] God — 5 you yourselves, as living
stones, a spiritual house, are being built to be a holy

[A] **1:6** Or *In this fact rejoice* [B] **1:11** Or *the glories after that* [C] **1:16** Lv 11:44–45; 19:2; 20:7 [D] **1:22** Other mss add *through the Spirit* [E] **1:22** Other mss omit *pure* [F] **1:22** Or *fervently* [G] **1:24-25** Is 40:6–8 [H] **2:2** Or *desire pure spiritual milk* [I] **2:3** Ps 34:8 [J] **2:4** Or *precious to*

Cappadocia in the First Century

by Alan Ray Buescher

According to 1 Maccabees 15, by at least 139 BC, Jews inhabited Cappadocia, which was part of the Roman Empire at this point. Quite likely, the first Christians in Cappadocia came from such Jewish communities. Though the growth of Christianity was apparently slow there, near the end of the fourth century the Cappadocian fathers—Basil of Caesarea, Gregory of Nyssa, and Gregory of Nazianzus—directed the growth of the church in central and eastern Asia Minor through their writings and ministry. All three of these men helped define the orthodox doctrine of the Trinity at the Council of Constantinople in AD 381.[1] The influence of early Christians in Cappadocia would give direction to Christians and Christian theology through the centuries.

GEOGRAPHY, CLIMATE, AND PEOPLE

The geography and climate of Cappadocia, located in the highlands of central-eastern Asia Minor (in present-day eastern Turkey), may partially explain the slow growth of Christianity in this region. To the south, the Taurus Mountains hampered easy access to the region of Cilicia on the northeastern Mediterranean coast. Traveling west toward Galatia, the elevated steppe seemed never ending. The regions most accessible to Cappadocia existed to the north (Pontus and northeastern Galatia) and east (Armenia).[2]

Brutal Cappadocian winters entertained blizzards—sometimes making roads impassable until spring. Heavy snows could confine people inside their homes for as long as two months. When the snows melted and farming season had begun, swarms of beetles always posed a potential threat to grain crops.[3]

Perhaps their harsh environment and living conditions contributed to their character and reputation. An early adage remarked, "A venomous viper bit a Cappadocian . . . the viper died."[4] No one had many kind words to say about Cappadocians. Worthless, deceitful, selfish, brutish—these describe how many viewed them.[5]

As a result of its geography and climate, throughout ancient history, Cappadocia remained on the outskirts of great civilizations and cultures that thrived along the Mediterranean coast and lowlands. Greek culture and Roman rule struggled to influence this rugged region, and Christianity was no exception.

ROMAN RULE

Cappadocia, while not lacking in natural resources, became significant to the Romans not only as another source of income to fuel its expansion, but also as a frontier border from which to defend its empire from outside attack and to protect its interests in the Near East.

Urgup, about twelve miles east of Nevsehir, is one of the most important centers in Cappadocia. The erosion by water and wind produced these formations, called the "Fairy Chimneys."

At Zelve, volcanic rocks and cones provided comfortable dwelling places for the area's inhabitants. Zelve remains one of the best-preserved examples of a cave dweller community.

Archelaus, appointed by Marcus Antonius as the last king of Cappadocia before Cappadocia became a Roman province, ruled from 36 BC until his death in AD 17. Archelaus understood and sought political alliances. However, approximately three years before his death, the authorities summoned Archelaus to Rome, charging him with treason. The results of this trial remain unknown. Upon Archelaus's death, the Romans immediately incorporated Cappadocia into their empire as a province—with little objection from the Cappadocians. Their agreeing was perhaps largely aided by a reduction in taxes.[6]

Roman procurators of equestrian rank replaced the Cappadocian monarchy from AD 17 until 72. Cappadocia, with only two significant cities (Tyana and Mazaca) at the time of its incorporation into the Roman Empire, posed a unique situation for Rome. Without municipal governments in place, the procurators did little to alter the existing feudal internal organization.

Roman rule provided a catalyst for more urban development, but the growth of cities was slow. The lower classes lived in feudal villages, and many of the Cappadocians in Rome came from the large slave population in Cappadocia.[7] Mazaca served as the capital city for the Cappadocian kings through the reign of Archelaus in AD 17. Archelaus renamed the city Caesarea in honor of Emperor Caesar Augustus. Located on a plateau on the north side of the thirteen-thousand-foot, volcanic, snow-capped Mount Argaeus, Caesarea developed into the leading Roman city of the region. Not until the fourth century AD, however, did it boast several schools, gymnasiums, and temples to the Greek gods Zeus, Apollo, and Fortune.[8]

Although Rome had lowered taxes on the feudal lords, much revenue flowed to the Roman emperor from the lands previously owned by Archelaus. Mines yielded translucent marble, crystal alabaster, onyx, silver, lead, and iron. Varieties of domesticated animals flourished in Cappadocia: sheep, goats, cattle, pigs, mules, camels, and horses. However, most of the revenues generated from the land came from the minerals and precious stones.[9]

Despite the land's rich resources, most of Cappadocia remained

Coin dating AD 81–96 from Caesarea, Cappadocia; reverse has an image of a club.

backward and impoverished. Many people lived in caves carved in the soft volcanic rock formations, often sharing their homes with their animals. The land yielded enough grain for export, but most of the wine and olive oil that locals consumed was imported.[10]

WAR AND PEACE

The Euphrates River provided the region's eastern border, dividing the Roman Empire to the west from Rome's primary adversary to the east, the Parthians, whose empire encompassed a large part of present-day Iran. The country of Armenia, on the east bank of the Euphrates, also provided an additional buffer from the Parthians, making the politics of Armenia of great interest to the Romans and Parthians alike as they vied for control in the Near East.[11]

Peace prevailed between the Roman province of Cappadocia and the Parthians for sixteen years after the Roman procurator took office in AD 17. However, when Armenia's King Artaxias died in AD 34, a hostile three-year struggle began between Rome and the Parthians to determine the next ruler of Armenia. Rome never actually sent forces against the Parthians; rather Pharasamanes, the king of Iberia, took the lead in skirmishes against the Parthians. Rome had chosen Pharasamanes's brother, Mithridates, as their candidate for king of Armenia. History is silent about how this war affected Cappadocia, but the settlement reached between Rome and the Parthians in AD 37 established Mithridates as the new ruler of Armenia.[12]

The greatest struggle for Armenia arose in the reign of Nero, with Cappadocia becoming a strategic military outpost for Rome during the Parthian and Armenian War, which waged from the mid-50s to 66. Rome recruited throughout Cappadocia and Galatia to fill its legions, which normally were composed of Roman citizens. As a result, some Cappadocians gained Roman citizenship through enrolling in the legion. The wives and children of these military recruits also gained citizenship upon their husbands'/fathers' return to civilian life. Rome and Parthia reached a peace settlement in AD 66, and Rome withdrew its legions from Cappadocia.[13]

CHRISTIAN GROWTH

Acts 2:9 indicates that Parthians (Jews or proselytes) witnessed the miracle of Pentecost together with residents of Cappadocia. Cappadocia proved to be a great laboratory for witnessing the efficacy of the gospel of Jesus Christ to penetrate hearts conditioned to resist change by a harsh and relatively isolated environment. The Jewish Diaspora had planted Jewish communities in Cappadocia, and this provided the basis for the expansion of the gospel in the Roman Empire. Perhaps that first seed of God's grace germinated in a Cappadocian heart in Jerusalem on Pentecost and transplanted itself to a people of volcanic crags and feudal lords. The seed grew slowly, with its flowers blossoming and fruit ripening in the fourth century through the ministry and writings of the Cappadocian fathers. ✣

---

[1] Raymond Van Dam, *Becoming Christian: The Conversion of Roman Cappadocia* (Philadelphia: University of Pennsylvania Press, 2003), 1–2. [2] Raymond Van Dam, *Kingdom of Snow: Roman Rule and Greek Culture in Cappadocia* (Philadelphia: University of Pennsylvania Press, 2002), 13. [3] Van Dam, *Kingdom of Snow*, 13–15. [4] Van Dam, *Kingdom of Snow*, 13. [5] Van Dam, *Kingdom of Snow*, 1. [6] William Emmett Gwatkin Jr., "Cappadocia as a Roman Procuratorial Province," *University of Missouri Studies* 5.4 (October 1930): 5–16, 19; William Emmett Gwatkin Jr., "Cappadocia" in *ABD*, 1:870–72. [7] Gwatkin, "Cappadocia as a Roman Procuratorial Province," 17–19; Van Dam, *Kingdom of Snow*, 24–25. [8] Jack Finegan, *The Archeology of the New Testament: The Mediterranean World of the Early Christian Apostles* (Boulder, CO: Westview, 1981), 83; Van Dam, *Kingdom of Snow*, 24–27. [9] Gwatkin, "Cappadocia as a Roman Procuratorial Province," 19; Van Dam, *Kingdom of Snow*, 15. [10] Van Dam, *Kingdom of Snow*, 15–16. [11] Jesse Curtis Pope, "Parthians" in *EDB*, 1010. [12] Gwatkin, "Cappadocia as a Roman Procuratorial Province," 30. [13] Gwatkin, "Cappadocia as a Roman Procuratorial Province," 44–45, 55.

priesthood[A] to offer spiritual sacrifices acceptable to
God through Jesus Christ. 6 For it stands in Scripture:

See, I lay a stone in Zion,
a chosen and honored[B] cornerstone,
and the one who believes in him
will never be put to shame.[C]

7 So honor will come to you who believe; but for the
unbelieving,

The stone that the builders rejected —
this one has become the cornerstone,[D]

8 and

A stone to stumble over,
and a rock to trip over.[E]

They stumble because they disobey the word; they
were destined for this.

9 But you are **a chosen race,**[F,G] **a royal priesthood,**[H]
a holy nation,[I] **a people for his possession,**[J] **so that
you may proclaim the praises**[K,L] of the one who
called you out of darkness into his marvelous light.
10 Once you were not a people, but now you are God's
people; you had not received mercy, but now you have
received mercy.

A CALL TO GOOD WORKS

11 Dear friends, I urge you as strangers and exiles to
abstain from sinful desires that wage war against
the soul. 12 Conduct yourselves honorably among the
Gentiles,[M] so that when they slander you as evildoers,
they will observe your good works and will glorify
God on the day he visits.

13 Submit to every human authority because of
the Lord, whether to the emperor[N] as the supreme
authority 14 or to governors as those sent out by him
to punish those who do what is evil and to praise
those who do what is good. 15 For it is God's will that
you silence the ignorance of foolish people by doing
good. 16 Submit as free people, not using your freedom
as a cover-up for evil, but as God's slaves. 17 Honor
everyone. Love the brothers and sisters. Fear God.
Honor the emperor.

SUBMISSION OF SLAVES TO MASTERS

18 Household slaves, submit to your masters with all
reverence not only to the good and gentle ones but
also to the cruel. 19 For it brings favor if, because of a
consciousness of God, someone endures grief from
suffering unjustly. 20 For what credit is there if when
you do wrong and are beaten, you endure it? But
when you do what is good and suffer, if you endure
it, this brings favor with God.

21 For you were called to this, because Christ also
suffered for you, leaving you an example, that you
should follow in his steps. 22 He did not commit sin,
and no deceit was found in his mouth;[O] 23 when
he was insulted, he did not insult in return; when he

Nero (ruled AD 54–68); coin minted in Rome. After the great fire in Rome in AD 64, Nero placed blame on Christians and began persecuting them.

suffered, he did not threaten but entrusted himself to
the one who judges justly. 24 He himself bore our sins
in his body on the tree; so that, having died to sins,
we might live for righteousness. **By his wounds**[P] **you
have been healed.** 25 For you **were like sheep going
astray,**[Q] but you have now returned to the Shepherd
and Overseer[R] of your souls.

WIVES AND HUSBANDS

3 In the same way, wives, submit yourselves to your
own husbands so that, even if some disobey the
word, they may be won over without a word by the
way their wives live 2 when they observe your pure,
reverent lives. 3 Don't let your beauty consist of outward things like elaborate hairstyles and wearing
gold jewelry or fine clothes, 4 but rather what is inside
the heart[S] — the imperishable quality of a gentle and
quiet spirit, which is of great worth in God's sight.
5 For in the past, the holy women who put their hope
in God also adorned themselves in this way, submitting to their own husbands, 6 just as Sarah obeyed
Abraham, calling him lord. You have become her
children when you do what is good and do not fear
any intimidation.

[A] **2:5** Or *you yourselves, as living stones, are being built into a spiritual house for a holy priesthood* [B] **2:6** Or *precious* [C] **2:6** Is 28:16 LXX [D] **2:7** Ps 118:22 [E] **2:8** Is 8:14 [F] **2:9** Or *generation*, or *nation* [G] **2:9** Dt 7:6; 10:15; Is 43:20 LXX [H] **2:9** Ex 19:6; 23:22 LXX; Is 61:6 [I] **2:9** Ex 19:6; 23:22 LXX [J] **2:9** Ex 19:5; 23:22 LXX; Dt 4:20; 7:6; Is 43:21 LXX [K] **2:9** Or *the mighty deeds* [L] **2:9** Is 42:12; 43:21 [M] **2:12** Or *among the nations*, or *among the pagans* [N] **2:13** Or *king* [O] **2:22** Is 53:9 [P] **2:24** Is 53:5 [Q] **2:25** Is 53:6 [R] **2:25** Or *Guardian* [S] **3:4** Or *rather, the hidden person of the heart*

Entrance to the Karanlik or "Dark" Church at Cappadocia. Many believers fled to the region to escape Rome's persecution of Christians.

Used by early Christians when endangered, an escape tunnel located inside the Church of St. Peter in Antioch (modern Antakya, Turkey). Many believe this to be one of the oldest churches in Christianity, and it may have been in use in the first century AD.

7 Husbands, in the same way, live with your wives
in an understanding way, as with a weaker partner,
showing them honor as coheirs of the grace of life,
so that your prayers will not be hindered.

DO NO EVIL

8 Finally, all of you be like-minded and sympathetic,
love one another, and be compassionate and humble,[A]
9 not paying back evil for evil or insult for insult but,
on the contrary, giving a blessing, since you were
called for this, so that you may inherit a blessing.

10 For **the one who wants**
to love life
and to see good days,
let him keep his tongue from evil
and his lips from speaking deceit,
11 **and let him turn away from evil**
and do what is good.
Let him seek peace and pursue it,
12 **because the eyes of the Lord are**
on the righteous
and his ears are open
to their prayer.
But the face of the Lord is against
those who do what is evil.[B]

UNDESERVED SUFFERING

13 Who then will harm you if you are devoted to what
is good? 14 But even if you should suffer for righteousness, you are blessed. **Do not fear them**[C] **or be intim-**
idated,[D] 15 but in your hearts regard[E] Christ[F] the Lord
as holy, ready at any time to give a defense to anyone
who asks you for a reason for the hope that is in you.
16 Yet do this with gentleness and reverence, keeping
a clear conscience, so that when you are accused,[G]
those who disparage your good conduct in Christ will
be put to shame. 17 For it is better to suffer for doing
good, if that should be God's will, than for doing evil.
18 For Christ also suffered for sins once for all, the
righteous for the unrighteous, that he might bring
you to God. He was put to death in the flesh[H] but
made alive by the Spirit,[I] 19 in which[J] he also went
and made proclamation to the spirits in prison 20 who
in the past were disobedient, when God patiently
waited in the days of Noah while the ark was being

[A] **3:8** Other mss read *courteous* [B] **3:10–12** Ps 34:12–16 [C] **3:14** Or *Do not fear what they fear* [D] **3:14** Is 8:12 [E] **3:15** Or *sanctify*, or *set apart* [F] **3:15** Other mss read *set God* [G] **3:16** Other mss read *when they speak against you as evildoers* [H] **3:18** Or *by the flesh*, or *in the fleshly realm* [I] **3:18** Or *in the spirit*, or *in the Spirit*, or *in the spiritual realm* [J] **3:19** Or *by whom*, or *in whom*, or *at that time*

Dated about 400 BC, a *rhyton* (drinking vessel) fashioned in the form of Dionysus, the Greek god of wine.

prepared. In it a few — that is, eight people[A] — were saved through water. [21] Baptism, which corresponds to this, now saves you (not as the removal of dirt from the body, but the pledge[B] of a good conscience toward God) through the resurrection of Jesus Christ, [22] who has gone into heaven and is at the right hand of God with angels, authorities, and powers subject to him.

FOLLOWING CHRIST

4 Therefore, since Christ suffered[C] in the flesh, arm yourselves also with the same understanding[D] — because the one who suffers in the flesh is finished with sin[E] — [2] in order to live the remaining time in the flesh no longer for human desires, but for God's will. [3] For there has already been enough time spent in doing what the Gentiles choose to do: carrying on in unrestrained behavior, evil desires, drunkenness, orgies, carousing, and lawless idolatry. [4] They are surprised that you don't join them in the same flood of wild living — and they slander[F] you. [5] They will give an account to the one who stands ready to judge the living and the dead. [6] For this reason the gospel was also preached to those who are now dead,[G] so that, although they might be judged in the flesh according to human standards, they might live in the spirit according to God's standards.

END-TIME ETHICS

[7] The end of all things is near; therefore, be alert and sober-minded for prayer. [8] Above all, maintain constant love for one another, since **love covers a multitude of sins.**[H] [9] Be hospitable to one another without complaining. [10] Just as each one has received a gift, use it to serve others, as good stewards of the varied grace of God. [11] If anyone speaks, let it be as one who speaks God's words; if anyone serves, let it be from the strength God provides, so that God may be glorified through Jesus Christ in everything. To him be the glory and the power forever and ever. Amen.

CHRISTIAN SUFFERING

[12] Dear friends, don't be surprised when the fiery ordeal comes among you to test you, as if something unusual were happening to you. [13] Instead, rejoice as you share in the sufferings of Christ, so that you may also rejoice with great joy when his glory is revealed. [14] If you are ridiculed for the name of Christ, you are blessed, because the Spirit of glory and of God[I] rests on you. [15] Let none of you suffer as a murderer, a thief, an evildoer, or a meddler.[J] [16] But if anyone suffers as a Christian, let him not be ashamed but let him glorify God in having that name.[K] [17] For the time has come for judgment to begin with God's household, and if it begins with us, what will the outcome be for those who disobey the gospel of God?

18 And **if a righteous person is saved
with difficulty,
what will become of the ungodly
and the sinner?**[L]

[19] So then, let those who suffer according to God's will entrust themselves to a faithful Creator while doing what is good.

ABOUT THE ELDERS

5 I exhort the elders among you as a fellow elder and witness to the sufferings of Christ, as well as one who shares in the glory about to be revealed: [2] Shepherd God's flock among you, not overseeing[M] out of compulsion but willingly, as God would have you;[N] not out of greed for money but eagerly; [3] not lording it over those entrusted to you, but being examples to the flock. [4] And when the chief Shepherd appears, you will receive the unfading crown of glory. [5] In the same way, you who are younger, be subject to the elders. All of you clothe yourselves with[O] humility toward one another, because

[A] **3:20** Or *souls* [B] **3:21** Or *the appeal* [C] **4:1** Other mss read *suffered for us* [D] **4:1** Or *perspective*, or *attitude* [E] **4:1** Or *the one who suffered in the flesh has finished with sin* [F] **4:4** Or *blaspheme* [G] **4:6** Or *those who are dead* [H] **4:8** Pr 10:12 [I] **4:14** Or *God's glorious Spirit* [J] **4:15** Or *as one who defrauds others* [K] **4:16** Other mss read *in that case* [L] **4:18** Pr 11:31 LXX [M] **5:2** Other mss omit *overseeing* [N] **5:2** Other mss omit *as God would have you* [O] **5:5** Or *you tie around yourselves*

Fragment of a sarcophagus cover; this panel segment shows a youthful shepherd leaning on his staff, clothed in a sleeved tunic; he carries a satchel on his back.

God resists the proud
but gives grace to the humble.[A]

CONCLUSION

6 Humble yourselves, therefore, under the mighty
hand of God, so that he may exalt you at the proper
time, 7 casting all your cares on him, because he cares
about you. 8 Be sober-minded, be alert. Your adversary the devil is prowling around like a roaring lion,
looking for anyone he can devour. 9 Resist him, firm
in the faith, knowing that the same kind of sufferings are being experienced by your fellow believers
throughout the world.

10 The God of all grace, who called you to his eternal glory in Christ,[B] will himself restore, establish,
strengthen, and support you after you have suffered a little while.[C] 11 To him be dominion[D] forever.[E]
Amen.

12 Through Silvanus,[F] a faithful brother (as I consider him), I have written to you briefly in order to
encourage you and to testify that this is the true grace
of God. Stand firm in it! 13 She who is in Babylon, chosen together with you, sends you greetings, as does
Mark, my son. 14 Greet one another with a kiss of love.
Peace to all of you who are in Christ.[G]

[A] **5:5** Pr 3:34 LXX [B] **5:10** Other mss read *in Christ Jesus* [C] **5:10** Or *to a small extent* [D] **5:11** Some mss read *dominion and glory*; other mss read *glory and dominion* [E] **5:11** Other mss read *forever and ever* [F] **5:12** Or *Silas*; Ac 15:22–32; 16:19–40; 17:1–16 [G] **5:14** Other mss read *Christ Jesus. Amen.*

2 PETER

The Basilica of St. Peter at the Vatican in Rome. Tradition holds that the church marks the burial place of Simon Peter. The four-columned dark canopy, which stands over the papal altar, is about ninety feet tall. The canopy, called a *baldacchino*, was constructed in the 1600s, using over nine hundred tons of dark bronze.

INTRODUCTION TO

2 PETER

Circumstances of Writing

The author of 2 Peter plainly identified himself as the apostle Peter (2Pt 1:1). He called himself "Simeon Peter" (1:1), a name not generally used of the apostle (elsewhere only in Ac 15:14). The spelling is Semitic and lends a sense of authenticity to Peter's letter. Moreover, it was natural for Peter, as a Semite, to use the original form of his name. Peter designated himself as "a servant and an apostle of Jesus Christ." He viewed himself as a servant submitted to Christ's lordship and as a divinely ordained, directly commissioned, authoritative representative of the Lord Jesus himself.

The letter contains several personal allusions to Peter's life. He mentioned that his death was close (2Pt 1:14), described himself as an eyewitness of the transfiguration of Jesus (1:16–18), quoted the words of the voice from heaven at this event (1:17), indicated that he had previously written to the letter's recipients (whom he called "dear friends" in 3:1), and also called Paul "our dear brother" (3:15). This suggests that the author was close to Paul. Such references point to Peter as the author.

Many contemporary scholars, however, reject Peter as the author of this letter. They argue, for example, that (1) the personal references to Peter's life are a literary device used by someone who wrote under the apostle's name to create the appearance of authenticity; (2) the style of Greek in 2 Peter is different from that of 1 Peter; (3) the reference to Paul's letters as a collection (3:15–16) points to a date later than Peter's lifetime; and (4) 2 Peter was dependent upon Jude. If this is true, Peter's authorship is problematic.

In response to these objections, one should consider that (1) the early church soundly rejected the practice of writing under an apostolic pseudonym, regarding it as outright forgery; (2) Peter may have had help in writing 1 Peter (1Pt 5:12) and not in writing 2 Peter, which would lead to different styles in his Greek; (3) rather than the whole collection, Peter may have referred only to those Pauline letters that were known at the time of writing; and (4) Peter may have borrowed some from Jude, or both may have used a common source. All of these evidences suggest that 2 Peter should be accepted as authentic.

Unlike 1 Peter, 2 Peter does not mention specific recipients or refer to an exact destination. The apostle referred to his epistle as the "second letter" he had written to his readers (2Pt 3:1). If the letter written prior to 2 Peter is 1 Peter, then he wrote to the same recipients ("exiles dispersed abroad in Pontus, Galatia, Cappadocia, Asia, and Bithynia"; 1Pt 1:1). But if the previous letter is a reference to some other epistle that is now unknown, we cannot determine with certainty to whom or to where 2 Peter was written.

Peter likely wrote 2 Peter from Rome, where church tradition placed the apostle in his latter days. The date of his martyrdom was about AD 67 during Nero's reign (AD 54–68).

Peter wrote this letter shortly before he died (1:14) and, though not mentioned, possibly while in prison. He wrote to Christian friends confronted with the threat of false teachers who were denying Christ's saving work and second coming. As an eyewitness of Jesus's life (1:16–18), Peter sought to affirm for his readers the reality of Christ's return and to remind them of truths they might otherwise forget (3:1).

Contribution to the Bible

Peter made strong connections with the Old Testament and challenged his audience to live authentic Christian lives. Peter had been with Jesus when Jesus first spoke of his return (Mt 24–25), and he gave emphasis to the surety of the second coming.

It is the Word of God that holds the forefront of this short letter. Peter does this in chapter 1 by emphasizing knowledge (vv. 3,5–6,8,12,20–21) and its divine origin; in chapter 2, by showing its historicity (vv. 4–8); in chapter 3, by indicating Paul's letters are equal with "the rest of the Scriptures" (vv. 15–16). Peter insisted on the importance of Scripture for guiding and preserving our faith.

Structure

Second Peter is a general letter with the typical features of a salutation, main body, and farewell. What is missing is an expression of thanksgiving. Its style is that of a pastoral letter, driven by the needs of the recipients, rather than some type of formal treatise.

GREETING

1 Simeon[A] Peter, a servant and an apostle of Jesus
Christ:
To those who have received a faith equal to ours
through the righteousness of our God and Savior
Jesus Christ.
2 May grace and peace be multiplied to you through
the knowledge of God and of Jesus our Lord.

GROWTH IN THE FAITH

3 His[B] divine power has given us everything required
for life and godliness through the knowledge of him
who called us by[C] his own glory and goodness. 4 By
these he has given us very great and precious promises, so that through them you may share in the divine
nature, escaping the corruption that is in the world
because of evil desire. 5 For this very reason, make
every effort to supplement your faith with goodness, goodness with knowledge, 6 knowledge with
self-control, self-control with endurance, endurance
with godliness, 7 godliness with brotherly affection,
and brotherly affection with love. 8 For if you possess
these qualities in increasing measure, they will keep
you from being useless or unfruitful in the knowledge
of our Lord Jesus Christ. 9 The person who lacks these
things is blind and shortsighted and has forgotten the
cleansing from his past sins. 10 Therefore, brothers
and sisters, make every effort to confirm your calling and election, because if you do these things you
will never stumble. 11 For in this way, entry into the
eternal kingdom of our Lord and Savior Jesus Christ
will be richly provided for you.
12 Therefore I will always remind you about these
things, even though you know them and are established in the truth you now have. 13 I think it is right,
as long as I am in this bodily tent, to wake you up
with a reminder, 14 since I know that I will soon lay
aside my tent, as our Lord Jesus Christ has indeed
made clear to me. 15 And I will also make every effort
so that you are able to recall these things at any time
after my departure.[D]

THE TRUSTWORTHY PROPHETIC WORD

16 For we did not follow cleverly contrived myths
when we made known to you the power and coming
of our Lord Jesus Christ; instead, we were eyewitnesses of his majesty. 17 For he received honor and glory
from God the Father when the voice came to him
from the Majestic Glory, saying "This is my beloved
Son,[E] with whom I am well-pleased!" 18 We ourselves

[A] **1:1** Other mss read *Simon* [B] **1:3** Lit *As his* [C] **1:3** Or *to* [D] **1:15** Or *death* [E] **1:17** Or *my Son, my beloved*

Church of the Transfiguration atop Mount Tabor, marking the traditional spot where Jesus appeared in glory before Peter, James, and John.

heard this voice when it came from heaven while we
were with him on the holy mountain. 19 We also have
the prophetic word strongly confirmed, and you will
do well to pay attention to it, as to a lamp shining in a
dark place, until the day dawns and the morning star
rises in your hearts. 20 Above all, you know this: No
prophecy of Scripture comes from the prophet's own
interpretation, 21 because no prophecy ever came by
the will of man; instead, men spoke from God as they
were carried along by the Holy Spirit.

THE JUDGMENT OF FALSE TEACHERS

2 There were indeed false prophets among the
people, just as there will be false teachers among
you. They will bring in destructive heresies, even denying the Master who bought them, and will bring
swift destruction on themselves. 2 Many will follow
their depraved ways, and the way of truth will be
maligned because of them. 3 They will exploit you
in their greed with made-up stories. Their condemnation, pronounced long ago, is not idle, and their
destruction does not sleep.

4 For if God didn't spare the angels who sinned but
cast them into hell[A] and delivered them in chains[B] of
utter darkness to be kept for judgment; 5 and if he
didn't spare the ancient world, but protected Noah, a
preacher of righteousness, and seven others,[C] when he
brought the flood on the world of the ungodly; 6 and if
he reduced the cities of Sodom and Gomorrah to ashes and condemned them to extinction,[D] making them
an example of what is coming to the ungodly; 7 and if
he rescued righteous Lot, distressed by the depraved
behavior of the immoral 8 (for as that righteous man
lived among them day by day, his righteous soul was
tormented by the lawless deeds he saw and heard) —
9 then the Lord knows how to rescue the godly from
trials and to keep the unrighteous under punishment
for the day of judgment, 10 especially those who follow
the polluting desires of the flesh and despise authority.

Bold, arrogant people! They are not afraid to slander the glorious ones; 11 however, angels, who are
greater in might and power, do not bring a slanderous
charge against them before the Lord.[E] 12 But these
people, like irrational animals — creatures of instinct
born to be caught and destroyed — slander what
they do not understand, and in their destruction they
too will be destroyed. 13 They will be paid back with
harm for the harm they have done. They consider it a

[A] **2:4** Gk *Tartarus* [B] **2:4** Other mss read *in pits* [C] **2:5** Lit *Noah, the eighth, a preacher of righteousness* [D] **2:6** Other mss omit *to extinction* [E] **2:11** Other mss read *them from the Lord*

Ruins at Bab edh-Dhra, which is in the Wadi Araba in Jordan. Some believe this to be the site of ancient Sodom.

pleasure to carouse in broad daylight. They are spots
and blemishes, delighting in their deceptions[A] while
they feast with you. 14 They have eyes full of adultery
that never stop looking for sin. They seduce unstable
people and have hearts trained in greed. Children
under a curse! 15 They have gone astray by abandoning the straight path and have followed the path of
Balaam, the son of Bosor,[B] who loved the wages of
wickedness 16 but received a rebuke for his lawlessness: A speechless donkey spoke with a human voice
and restrained the prophet's madness.

17 These people are springs without water, mists
driven by a storm. The gloom of darkness has been
reserved for them. 18 For by uttering boastful, empty
words, they seduce, with fleshly desires and debauchery, people who have barely escaped[C] from those who
live in error. 19 They promise them freedom, but they
themselves are slaves of corruption, since people are
enslaved to whatever defeats them. 20 For if, having
escaped the world's impurity through the knowledge
of the Lord[D] and Savior Jesus Christ, they are again
entangled in these things and defeated, the last state
is worse for them than the first. 21 For it would have
been better for them not to have known the way of
righteousness than, after knowing it, to turn back
from the holy command delivered to them. 22 It has
happened to them according to the true proverb: **A
dog returns to its own vomit,**[E] and, "A washed sow
returns to wallowing in the mud."

THE DAY OF THE LORD

3 Dear friends, this is now the second letter I have
written to you; in both letters, I want to stir up
your sincere understanding by way of reminder, 2 so
that you recall the words previously spoken by the
holy prophets and the command of our Lord and Savior given through your apostles. 3 Above all, be aware
of this: Scoffers will come in the last days scoffing and
following their own evil desires, 4 saying, "Where is
his 'coming' that he promised? Ever since our ancestors fell asleep, all things continue as they have been
since the beginning of creation." 5 They deliberately
overlook this: By the word of God the heavens came
into being long ago and the earth was brought about
from water and through water. 6 Through these the
world of that time perished when it was flooded. 7 By
the same word, the present heavens and earth are
stored up for fire, being kept for the day of judgment
and destruction of the ungodly.

[A] **2:13** Other mss read *delighting in the love feasts* [B] **2:15** Other mss read *Beor* [C] **2:18** Or *people who are actually escaping* [D] **2:20** Other mss read *our Lord* [E] **2:22** Pr 26:11

In Jordan, local tradition claims this to be Lot's cave. The cave overlooks the south end of the Dead Sea. In the sixth century AD, a monastery was built around the cave. The door in the cave faces the plains that some people believe were once part of Sodom and Gomorrah.

[8] Dear friends, don't overlook this one fact: With
the Lord one day is like a thousand years, and a thousand years like one day. [9] The Lord does not delay his
promise, as some understand delay, but is patient
with you, not wanting any to perish but all to come
to repentance.
[10] But the day of the Lord will come like a thief;[A] on
that day the heavens will pass away with a loud noise,
the elements will burn and be dissolved, and the earth
and the works on it will be disclosed.[B,C] [11] Since all
these things are to be dissolved in this way, it is clear
what sort of people you should be in holy conduct
and godliness [12] as you wait for the day of God and
hasten its coming.[D] Because of that day, the heavens
will be dissolved with fire and the elements will melt
with heat. [13] But based on his promise, we wait for
new heavens and a new earth, where righteousness
dwells.

CONCLUSION

[14] Therefore, dear friends, while you wait for these
things, make every effort to be found without spot
or blemish in his sight, at peace. [15] Also, regard the
patience of our Lord as salvation, just as our dear
brother Paul has written to you according to the wisdom given to him. [16] He speaks about these things in

Part of the silverware trove discovered in the House of Menander at Pompeii; decorated with a chariot race. The full collection, which consisted of 118 pieces, would have likely been for a banquet; they were preserved when Mount Vesuvius erupted because they were stored in a basement.

[A] **3:10** Other mss add *in the night* [B] **3:10** Other mss read *will be burned up* [C] **3:10** Some Syriac and Coptic mss read *will not be found* [D] **3:12** Or *and speed the coming*

One of three massive construction stones that were part of the foundation for the temple of Jupiter in Baalbek, Lebanon. The block, which weighs over eight hundred tons, measures about sixty-five feet long and is over seventeen feet wide at the top end. Comparing the stone's height to the gentleman standing at the raised end highlights the stone's massive size.

all his letters. There are some things hard to understand in them. The untaught and unstable will twist them to their own destruction, as they also do with the rest of the Scriptures.

[17] Therefore, dear friends, since you know this in advance, be on your guard, so that you are not led away by the error of lawless people and fall from your own stable position. [18] But grow in the grace and knowledge of our Lord and Savior Jesus Christ. To him be the glory both now and to the day of eternity.[A]

[A] **3:18** Other mss add *Amen.*

1 JOHN

Bells of St. John's Monastery on Patmos.

INTRODUCTION TO

1 JOHN

Circumstances of Writing

Ancient manuscripts are unanimous in naming John as the author of 1 John. This was understood to be John the son of Zebedee, the "disciple Jesus loved" who was also the author of the Fourth Gospel. The style and vocabulary of 1, 2, and 3 John are so close to that of John's Gospel that they beg to be understood as arising from the same person. Some contemporary scholars theorize that an "elder John" (see 2Jn 1; 3Jn 1), not the apostle, may have written the letters. Others speak of a "Johannine school" or "circle" as the originators of the epistles of John (and perhaps Revelation). But the view with the best support is that Jesus's disciple John was the author.

Second-century sources reported that around AD 70, the year the Romans destroyed Jerusalem and the temple, John left Jerusalem where he was a church leader and relocated to Ephesus. He continued his pastoral work in that region and lived until nearly AD 100. Ephesus is probably the place where John wrote the three New Testament letters that bear his name. They could have been composed at any time in the last quarter of the first century.

Contribution to the Bible

First John maps out the three main components of a saving knowledge of God: (1) faith in Jesus Christ, (2) obedient response to God's commands, and (3) love for God and others from the heart. This epistle shows how Jesus expects his followers to honor him in practical church life and wherever God calls his people to go and serve.

Structure

It is widely agreed that 1 John does not logically, methodically, or rigorously set forth and develop its arguments. For this reason scholars are divided on the best way to structurally outline the letter. It is the least letter-like of the three Johannine epistles because of its lack of identification of the sender and the recipient. It is more like an unsystematic treatise. It often makes assertions along thematic lines, moves to related or contrasting themes, and then returns to the earlier topic, or perhaps takes up a different subject altogether.

PROLOGUE: OUR DECLARATION

1 What was from the beginning, what we have
heard, what we have seen with our eyes, what
we have observed and have touched with our hands,
concerning the word of life — 2 that life was revealed,
and we have seen it and we testify and declare to you
the eternal life that was with the Father and was revealed to us — 3 what we have seen and heard we also
declare to you, so that you may also have fellowship
with us; and indeed our fellowship is with the Father
and with his Son, Jesus Christ. 4 We are writing these
things[A] so that our[B] joy may be complete.

FELLOWSHIP WITH GOD

5 This is the message we have heard from him and
declare to you: God is light, and there is absolutely no
darkness in him. 6 If we say, "We have fellowship with
him," and yet we walk in darkness, we are lying and
are not practicing the truth. 7 If we walk in the light
as he himself is in the light, we have fellowship with
one another, and the blood of Jesus his Son cleanses
us from all sin. 8 If we say, "We have no sin," we are
deceiving ourselves, and the truth is not in us. 9 If
we confess our sins, he is faithful and righteous to
forgive us our sins and to cleanse us from all unrighteousness. 10 If we say, "We have not sinned," we make
him a liar, and his word is not in us.

2 My little children, I am writing you these things
so that you may not sin. But if anyone does sin, we
have an advocate with the Father — Jesus Christ the
righteous one. 2 He himself is the atoning sacrifice[C]
for our sins, and not only for ours, but also for those
of the whole world.

GOD'S COMMANDS

3 This is how we know that we know him: if we keep
his commands. 4 The one who says, "I have come
to know him," and yet doesn't keep his commands,
is a liar, and the truth is not in him. 5 But whoever
keeps his word, truly in him the love of God is made
complete. This is how we know we are in him: 6 The
one who says he remains in him should walk just
as he walked.

7 Dear friends, I am not writing you a new command but an old command that you have had from
the beginning. The old command is the word you
have heard. 8 Yet I am writing you a new command,
which is true in him and in you, because the darkness
is passing away and the true light is already shining.
9 The one who says he is in the light but hates his
brother or sister is in the darkness until now. 10 The
one who loves his brother or sister remains in the
light, and there is no cause for stumbling in him.[D]
11 But the one who hates his brother or sister is in
the darkness, walks in the darkness, and doesn't
know where he's going, because the darkness has
blinded his eyes.

Terra-cotta lamp, made and found at Ephesus; about 100 BC–AD 25.

REASONS FOR WRITING

12 I am writing to you, little children,
since your sins have been forgiven
on account of his name.
13 I am writing to you, fathers,
because you have come to know
the one who is from the beginning.
I am writing to you, young men,
because you have conquered the evil one.
14 I have written to you, children,
because you have come to know
the Father.
I have written to you, fathers,
because you have come to know
the one who is from the beginning.
I have written to you, young men,
because you are strong,
God's word remains in you,
and you have conquered the evil one.

[A] 1:4 Other mss add *to you* [B] 1:4 Other mss read *your* [C] 2:2 Or *the propitiation* [D] 2:10 Or *it*

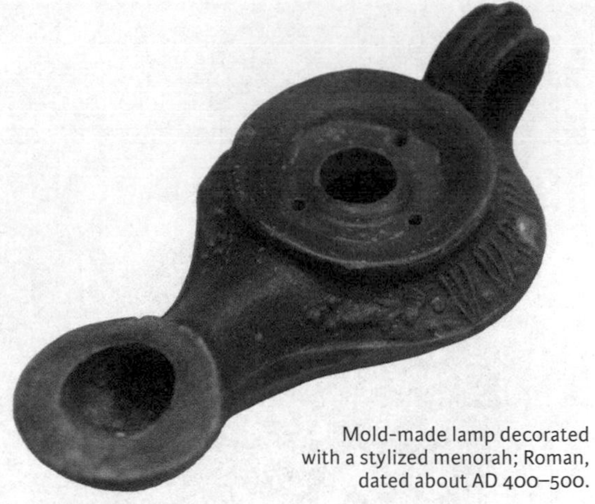

Mold-made lamp decorated with a stylized menorah; Roman, dated about AD 400–500.

A WARNING ABOUT THE WORLD

15 Do not love the world or the things in the world. If anyone loves the world, the love of the Father is not in him. 16 For everything in the world — the lust of the flesh, the lust of the eyes, and the pride in one's possessions — is not from the Father, but is from the world. 17 And the world with its lust is passing away, but the one who does the will of God remains forever.

THE LAST HOUR

18 Children, it is the last hour. And as you have heard that antichrist is coming, even now many antichrists have come. By this we know that it is the last hour. 19 They went out from us, but they did not belong to us; for if they had belonged to us, they would have remained with us. However, they went out so that it might be made clear that none of them belongs to us.

20 But you have an anointing from the Holy One, and all of you know the truth.[A] 21 I have not written to you because you don't know the truth, but because you do know it, and because no lie comes from the truth. 22 Who is the liar, if not the one who denies that Jesus is the Christ? This one is the antichrist: the one who denies the Father and the Son. 23 No one who denies the Son has the Father; he who confesses the Son has the Father as well.

REMAINING WITH GOD

24 What you have heard from the beginning is to remain in you. If what you have heard from the beginning remains in you, then you will remain in the Son and in the Father. 25 And this is the promise that he himself made to us: eternal life.

26 I have written these things to you concerning those who are trying to deceive you. 27 As for you, the anointing you received from him remains in you, and you don't need anyone to teach you. Instead, his anointing teaches you about all things and is true and is not a lie; just as it has taught you,[B] remain in him.

GOD'S CHILDREN

28 So now, little children, remain in him so that when he appears we may have confidence and not be ashamed before him at his coming. 29 If you know that he is righteous, you know this as well: Everyone who does what is right has been born of him.

3 1 See what great love[C] the Father has given us that we should be called God's children — and we are! The reason the world does not know us is that it didn't know him. 2 Dear friends, we are God's children now, and what we will be has not yet been revealed. We know that when he appears,[D] we will be like him because we will see him as he is. 3 And everyone who has this hope in him purifies himself just as he is pure.

4 Everyone who commits sin practices lawlessness; and sin is lawlessness. 5 You know that he was revealed so that he might take away sins,[E] and there is no sin in him. 6 Everyone who remains in him does not sin;[F] everyone who sins[G] has not seen him or known him.

7 Little children, let no one deceive you. The one who does what is right is righteous, just as he is righteous. 8 The one who commits[H] sin is of the devil, for the devil has sinned from the beginning. The Son of God was revealed for this purpose: to destroy the devil's works. 9 Everyone who has been born of God does not sin,[I] because his seed remains in him; he is not able to sin,[J] because he has been born of God. 10 This is how God's children and the devil's children become obvious. Whoever does not do what is right is not of God, especially the one who does not love his brother or sister.

LOVE IN ACTION

11 For this is the message you have heard from the beginning: We should love one another, 12 unlike Cain, who was of the evil one and murdered his brother. And why did he murder him? Because his deeds were evil, and his brother's were righteous.

13 Do not be surprised, brothers and sisters, if the world hates you. 14 We know that we have passed from death to life because we love our brothers and sisters. The one who does not love remains in death. 15 Everyone who hates his brother or sister is a murderer, and you know that no murderer has eternal

[A] **2:20** Other mss read *and you know all things* [B] **2:27** Or *as he has taught you* [C] **3:1** Or *what sort of love* [D] **3:2** Or *when it appears* [E] **3:5** Other mss read *our sins* [F] **3:6** Or *not keep on sinning* [G] **3:6** Or *who keeps on sinning* [H] **3:8** Or *practices* [I] **3:9** Or *not practice sin* [J] **3:9** Or *to keep on sinning*

life residing in him. [16] This is how we have come to
know love: He laid down his life for us. We should
also lay down our lives for our brothers and sisters.
[17] If anyone has this world's goods and sees a fellow
believer[A] in need but withholds compassion from
him — how does God's love reside in him? [18] Little
children, let us not love in word or speech, but in
action and in truth.

[19] This is how we will know that we belong to
the truth and will reassure our hearts before him
[20] whenever our hearts condemn us; for God is greater than our hearts, and he knows all things.

[21] Dear friends, if our hearts don't condemn us, we
have confidence before God [22] and receive whatever
we ask from him because we keep his commands and
do what is pleasing in his sight. [23] Now this is his command: that we believe in the name of his Son, Jesus
Christ, and love one another as he commanded us.
[24] The one who keeps his commands remains in him,
and he in him. And the way we know that he remains
in us is from the Spirit he has given us.

THE SPIRIT OF TRUTH AND THE SPIRIT OF ERROR

4 Dear friends, do not believe every spirit, but test
the spirits to see if they are from God, because
many false prophets have gone out into the world.

[2] This is how you know the Spirit of God: Every
spirit that confesses that Jesus Christ has come in
the flesh is from God, [3] but every spirit that does not
confess Jesus[B] is not from God. This is the spirit of
the antichrist, which you have heard is coming; even
now it is already in the world.

[4] You are from God, little children, and you have
conquered them, because the one who is in you is
greater than the one who is in the world. [5] They are
from the world. Therefore what they say is from the
world, and the world listens to them. [6] We are from
God. Anyone who knows God listens to us; anyone
who is not from God does not listen to us. This is
how we know the Spirit of truth and the spirit of
deception.

[A] **3:17** Lit *sees his brother or sister* [B] **4:3** Other mss read *confess that Jesus has come in the flesh*

Basilica of St. John at Ephesus commemorates the traditional location of John's burial.

Statue of Sophia Kelsou at the Celsus Library in Ephesus.

KNOWING GOD THROUGH LOVE

7 Dear friends, let us love one another, because love is from God, and everyone who loves has been born of God and knows God. 8 The one who does not love does not know God, because God is love. 9 God's love was revealed among us[A] in this way: God sent his one and only Son into the world so that we might live through him. 10 Love consists in this: not that we loved God, but that he loved us and sent his Son to be the atoning sacrifice[B] for our sins. 11 Dear friends, if God loved us in this way, we also must love one another. 12 No one has ever seen God. If we love one another, God remains in[C] us and his love is made complete in us. 13 This is how we know that we remain in him and he in us: He has given us of his Spirit. 14 And we have seen and we testify that the Father has sent his Son as the world's Savior. 15 Whoever confesses that Jesus is the Son of God — God remains in him and he in God. 16 And we have come to know and to believe the love that God has for us.

God is love, and the one who remains in love remains in God, and God remains in him. 17 In this, love is made complete with us so that we may have confidence in the day of judgment, because as he is, so also are we in this world. 18 There is no fear in love; instead, perfect love drives out fear, because fear involves punishment.[D] So the one who fears is not complete in love. 19 We love[E] because he first loved us. 20 If anyone says, "I love God," and yet hates his brother or sister, he is a liar. For the person who does not love his brother or sister whom he has seen cannot love God whom he has not seen.[F] 21 And we have this command from him: The one who loves God must also love his brother and sister.

5 Everyone who believes that Jesus is the Christ has been born of God, and everyone who loves the Father[G] also loves the one born of him. 2 This is how we know that we love God's children: when we love God and obey[H] his commands. 3 For this is what love for God is: to keep his commands. And his commands are not a burden, 4 because everyone who has been born of God conquers the world. This is the victory that has conquered the world: our faith.

THE CERTAINTY OF GOD'S TESTIMONY

5 Who is the one who conquers the world but the one who believes that Jesus is the Son of God? 6 Jesus Christ — he is the one who came by water and blood, not by water only, but by water and by blood. And the Spirit is the one who testifies, because the Spirit is the truth. 7 For there are three that testify:[I] 8 the Spirit, the water, and the blood — and these three are in agreement. 9 If we accept human testimony, God's testimony is greater, because it is God's testimony that he has given about his Son. 10 The one who believes in the Son of God has this testimony within himself. The one who does not believe God has made him a liar, because he has not believed in the testimony God has given about his Son. 11 And this is the testimony: God has given us eternal life, and this life is in his Son. 12 The one who has the Son has life. The one who does not have the Son of God does not have life. 13 I have written these things to you who believe in the name of the Son of God so that you may know that you have eternal life.

EFFECTIVE PRAYER

14 This is the confidence we have before him: If we ask anything according to his will, he hears us. 15 And if we know that he hears whatever we ask, we know that we have what we have asked of him.

16 If anyone sees a fellow believer[J] committing a sin that doesn't lead to death, he should ask, and God will give life to him — to those who commit sin

[A] **4:9** Or *in us* [B] **4:10** Or *the propitiation* [C] **4:12** Or *remains among* [D] **4:18** Or *fear has its own punishment* or *torment* [E] **4:19** Other mss add *him* [F] **4:20** Other mss read *has seen, how is he able to love . . . seen?* (as a question) [G] **5:1** Or *loves the one who has given birth* [H] **5:2** Other mss read *keep* [I] **5:7–8** A few late Gk mss and some late Vg mss add *testify in heaven: the Father, the Word, and the Holy Spirit, and these three are one.* **8** *And there are three who bear witness on earth:* [J] **5:16** Lit *sees his brother or sister*

A well-preserved baptismal in the Baptisterion (baptistery) of the Church of St. John at Ephesus.

that doesn't lead to death. There is sin[A] that leads to
death. I am not saying he should pray about that. 17 All
unrighteousness is sin, and there is sin that doesn't
lead to death.

CONCLUSION

18 We know that everyone who has been born of God
does not sin, but the one who is born of God keeps
him,[B] and the evil one does not touch him. 19 We know
that we are of God, and the whole world is under the
sway of the evil one. 20 And we know that the Son of
God has come and has given us understanding so
that we may know the true one.[C] We are in the true
one — that is, in his Son, Jesus Christ. He is the true
God and eternal life.

21 Little children, guard yourselves from idols.

[A] **5:16** Or *is a sin* [B] **5:18** Other mss read *himself* [C] **5:20** Other mss read *the true God*

2 JOHN

Marble alley with columns leading to the Celsus Library in ancient Ephesus.

INTRODUCTION TO

2 JOHN

Circumstances of Writing

"The elder" (2Jn 1) is a title that the apostle John applied to himself late in life. (The apostle Peter referred to himself the same way; 1Pt 5:1.) No one other than the apostle John was ever suggested by the early church as the writer of 1 John. Since there are so many similarities between 1 and 2 John, it is generally accepted that John also wrote the second letter.

Second John likely was written during the last two decades of the first century. During this era, John gave pastoral leadership to churches in the area of Ephesus. We have no way of precisely dating 2 John, but it is reasonable that it was written around the same time as 1 John or slightly afterward. Its tone reveals it to be a highly personal letter that reflects John's affection for these believers and his deep concern for their welfare.

Contribution to the Bible

It is easy for congregations to get off track. Second John reminds readers of the high priority of the most basic Christian outlook and activity—mutual love. Yet another priority is no less critical—true Christian teaching. This epistle strikes a short but strong blow for steadfastness, assuring that attentive readers would take the right steps to "receive a full reward" (v. 8).

Structure

Second John is an excellent example of hortatory or exhortation discourse, which has the intent of moving readers to action. It follows the normal New Testament pattern for a letter with an opening, main body, and closing. There are only two commands in this short letter: a call to "watch yourselves" (v. 8) and the command, "do not receive" those who plant false teaching (v. 10). There is the reminder to "love one another" in verse 5. This bears the force of an imperative, in part because of the close proximity of the word command, which occurs four times in verses 4–6.

GREETING

The elder:
To the elect lady and her children, whom I love in
the truth — and not only I, but also all who know the
truth — 2 because of the truth that remains in us and
will be with us forever.
3 Grace, mercy, and peace will be with us from God
the Father and from Jesus Christ, the Son of the Father, in truth and love.

TRUTH AND DECEPTION

4 I was very glad to find some of your children walking in truth, in keeping with a command we have
received from the Father. 5 So now I ask you, dear lady
— not as if I were writing you a new command, but
one we have had from the beginning — that we love
one another. 6 This is love: that we walk according
to his commands. This is the command as you have
heard it from the beginning: that you walk in love.[A]
7 Many deceivers have gone out into the world; they
do not confess the coming of Jesus Christ in the flesh.
This is the deceiver and the antichrist. 8 Watch yourselves so that you don't lose what we[B] have worked
for, but that you may receive a full reward. 9 Anyone
who does not remain in Christ's teaching but goes
beyond it does not have God. The one who remains
in that teaching, this one has both the Father and the
Son. 10 If anyone comes to you and does not bring this
teaching, do not receive him into your home, and do
not greet him; 11 for the one who greets him shares
in his evil works.

FAREWELL

12 Though I have many things to write to you, I don't
want to use paper and ink. Instead, I hope to come
to you and talk face to face so that our joy may be
complete.
13 The children of your elect sister send you greetings.

Fresco depicting the apostle John in the apse of the chapel of the Church of St. John at Ephesus; dated to the eleventh or twelfth century AD.

[A] **6** Or *in it* [B] **8** Other mss read *you*

12 [illegible]
[illegible]
[illegible]

3 JOHN

Remains of the Basilica of St. John at Ephesus.

INTRODUCTION TO

3 JOHN

Circumstances of Writing

"The elder" (3Jn 1) is a title that the apostle John applied to himself late in life. (The apostle Peter referred to himself the same way; 1Pt 5:1.) No one other than the apostle John was ever suggested by the early church as the writer of 1 John. Since there are so many similarities between 1 and 3 John, it is generally accepted that John also wrote the third letter.

Third John likely was written during the last two decades of the first century. During this era, John gave pastoral leadership to churches in the area of Ephesus. We have no way of precisely dating 3 John, but it is reasonable that it was written around the same time as 1 and 2 John or slightly afterwards. Its tone reveals it to be a highly personal letter that reflects John's affection for these believers and his deep concern for their welfare.

The two short epistles of 2 and 3 John are often described as "twin epistles," though they should be viewed as fraternal and not identical. There are some significant similarities worth noting. In both epistles, the author described himself as "the elder" (2Jn 1; 3Jn 1), and the recipients were those whom he loved "in the truth" (2Jn 1; 3Jn 1). The recipients were a cause for great rejoicing by John (2Jn 4; 3Jn 3). They were "walking in truth" (2Jn 4; 3Jn 3), and the elder had received good reports about them (2Jn 4; 3Jn 3,5). Both letters contain a warning (2Jn 8; 3Jn 9–11), and the elder desired to see the recipients face to face (2Jn 12; 3Jn 14). Finally, both letters convey greetings from others (2Jn 13; 3Jn 15).

Contribution to the Bible

This brief letter of apostolic instruction underscores certain central Christian convictions: love, truth, faithfulness, the church, and witness. It also testifies to the God-centeredness of apostolic faith (vv. 7,11). Jesus and the Spirit are not mentioned specifically (unless "the truth itself" in v. 12 refers to Jesus; see Jn 14:6; 1Jn 5:20). But in the writer's view, Jesus and the Spirit were undoubtedly included in the reference to "God" whose "truth" this epistle appeals to so frequently (3Jn 1,3,4,8,12).

Structure

The letter follows the basic epistolary pattern with an introduction (vv. 1–4), body (vv. 5–12), and a conclusion (vv. 13–15). Though verses 1–4 clearly function as the salutation, it is also possible to outline the letter around the four personalities of the book. Verses 1–8 contain a multifold commendation of Gaius. Verses 9–10 condemn the highhanded and malicious autocracy of Diotrephes. Verses 11–12, taken as a unit, praise the godly Demetrius. Verses 13–15 close with a glimpse into the heart of the elder. Four men and their reputations (growing out of their behavior) are the sum and substance of 3 John's subject matter. John constructed this letter with the building blocks of key-word repetition: "dear friend" (vv. 1,2,5,11); "truth" or "true" (vv. 1,3,4,8,12). Third John provides insight into a personality conflict that arose at the end of the first century and the strategy adopted by the elder to resolve it.

GREETING

The elder:
To my dear friend Gaius, whom I love in the truth.
[2] Dear friend, I pray that you are prospering in every way and are in good health, just as your whole
life is going well.[A] [3] For I was very glad when fellow
believers came and testified to your fidelity to the
truth — how you are walking in truth. [4] I have no
greater joy than this: to hear that my children are
walking in truth.

GAIUS COMMENDED

[5] Dear friend, you are acting faithfully in whatever
you do for the brothers and sisters, especially when
they are strangers. [6] They have testified to your love
before the church. You will do well to send them on
their journey in a manner worthy of God, [7] since
they set out for the sake of the Name, accepting
nothing from pagans.[B] [8] Therefore, we ought to support such people so that we can be coworkers with
the truth.

DIOTREPHES AND DEMETRIUS

[9] I wrote something to the church, but Diotrephes,
who loves to have first place among them, does not
receive our authority. [10] This is why, if I come, I will
remind him of the works he is doing, slandering us
with malicious words. And he is not satisfied with
that! He not only refuses to welcome fellow believers,
but he even stops those who want to do so and expels
them from the church.
[11] Dear friend, do not imitate what is evil, but what
is good. The one who does good is of God; the one who
does evil has not seen God. [12] Everyone speaks well of
Demetrius — even the truth itself. And we also speak
well of him, and you know that our testimony is true.

FAREWELL

[13] I have many things to write you, but I don't want
to write to you with pen and ink. [14] I hope to see you
soon, and we will talk face to face.
[15] Peace to you. The friends send you greetings.
Greet the friends by name.

[A] **2** Or *as your soul prospers* [B] **7** Or *Gentiles*

JUDE

Front façade details of the Library of Celsus at Ephesus. The library was constructed early in the second century AD (110–135).

INTRODUCTION TO

JUDE

Circumstances of Writing

Jude called himself "a servant of Jesus Christ and a brother of James" (Jd 1). The James to whom Jude referred is not the son of Zebedee. He can be ruled out of consideration because he was martyred at an early date (Ac 12:1–2). The James to whom Jude refers is surely the well-known leader of the Jerusalem church (Ac 15:13–21; Gl 2:9). This is significant, for this James was the brother of Jesus (Mk 6:3). If Jude was a brother of James, then he was also a brother of Jesus. Rather than call himself Jesus's brother outright, Jude chose humbly to designate himself as Christ's servant.

Jude wrote to those who are "the called, loved by God the Father and kept for Jesus Christ" (Jd 1). This designation is general enough to apply to Christian believers anywhere. But Jude clearly had a specific group in mind because he called them "dear friends" (vv. 3,17,20) and addressed a situation that affected them. The readers were probably Jewish Christians because of Jude's several references to Hebrew history. Beyond this information we do not know exactly who the recipients of the letter were.

Jude is difficult to date precisely. If Jude the brother of Jesus was the author, the letter must be dated sometime within his lifetime. Any date for the letter's writing must also allow time for the false teachings to have developed. Jude may be dated reasonably somewhere between AD 65 and 80. Nothing in the letter points to a date of writing beyond this time. A date within Jude's lifetime rules out the viewpoint that the false teaching in question was second-century Gnosticism.

Contribution to the Bible

Jude is often overlooked because of its brevity. The book is also neglected because of unexpected features such as its quotation of *1 Enoch* and its allusion to the *Assumption of Moses*. Some readers wonder how a canonical book could cite noninspired, nonbiblical writings. Furthermore, the message of Jude is alien to many in today's world because Jude emphasized that the Lord will judge evil intruders who are attempting to corrupt the church. The message of judgment strikes many people today as intolerant, unloving, and contrary to the message of love proclaimed elsewhere in the New Testament.

Nevertheless, some of the Bible's most beautiful statements about God's sustaining grace are found in Jude (vv. 1,24–25), and they shine with a greater brilliance when contrasted with the false teachers who had departed from the Christian faith.

The message of judgment is especially relevant to people today. Jude's letter reminds us that errant teaching and promiscuous living have dire consequences. Jude was written so believers would contend for the faith that was transmitted to them (v. 3) and so they would not abandon God's love at a crucial time in the life of the church.

Structure

The epistle of Jude is a vigorous and pointed piece of writing. Scholars have often remarked that its Greek is quite good and that Jude used imagery effectively. The letter bears the marks of a careful and disciplined structure and was directed to specific circumstances in the life of the church. Jude was steeped in the Old Testament and Jewish tradition, and he regularly applied Old Testament types and texts to the false teachers who had invaded the church (vv. 8,12,16).

Pseudepigraphal writings are noncanonical books not written by their purported authors. Jude cited from the pseudepigraphic book of *1 Enoch* (1:9) in verses 14–15. He

likely also referred to an event found in the *Assumption of Moses* (v. 9). But this does not mean that Jude viewed these noncanonical books as authoritative Scripture. Under the inspiration of the Holy Spirit, he used them as illustrations.

GREETING

Jude, a servant of Jesus Christ and a brother of James:
To those who are the called, loved[A] by God the Father and kept for Jesus Christ.
2 May mercy, peace, and love be multiplied to you.

JUDE'S PURPOSE IN WRITING

3 Dear friends, although I was eager to write you
about the salvation we share, I found it necessary to
write, appealing to you to contend for the faith that
was delivered to the saints once for all. 4 For some
people, who were designated for this judgment long
ago,[B] have come in by stealth; they are ungodly, turning the grace of our God into sensuality and denying
Jesus Christ, our only Master and Lord.

APOSTATES: PAST AND PRESENT

5 Now I want to remind you, although you came to
know all these things once and for all, that Jesus[C]
saved a people out of Egypt and later destroyed those
who did not believe; 6 and the angels who did not
keep their own position but abandoned their proper
dwelling, he has kept in eternal chains in deep darkness for the judgment on the great day. 7 Likewise,
Sodom and Gomorrah and the surrounding towns
committed sexual immorality and perversions,[D] and
serve as an example by undergoing the punishment
of eternal fire.
8 In the same way these people — relying on their
dreams — defile their flesh, reject authority, and
slander glorious ones. 9 Yet when Michael the archangel was disputing with the devil in an argument
about Moses's body, he did not dare utter a slanderous condemnation against him but said, "The
Lord rebuke you!" 10 But these people blaspheme
anything they do not understand. And what they
do understand by instinct — like irrational animals
— by these things they are destroyed. 11 Woe to them!
For they have gone the way of Cain, have plunged
into Balaam's error for profit, and have perished in
Korah's rebellion.

THE APOSTATES' DOOM

12 These people are dangerous reefs[E] at your love
feasts as they eat with you without reverence. They

[A] **1** Other mss read *sanctified* [B] **4** Or *whose judgment was written about long ago* [C] **5** Other mss read *the Lord*, or *God* [D] **7** Or *and went after other flesh* [E] **12** Or *are like blemishes*

Three unfired figurines from Bab edh-Dhra, which many scholars believe to be the traditional site of Sodom.

are shepherds who only look after themselves. They
are waterless clouds carried along by winds; trees in
late autumn — fruitless, twice dead and uprooted.
13 They are wild waves of the sea, foaming up their
shameful deeds; wandering stars for whom the blackness of darkness is reserved forever.

14 It was about these that Enoch, in the seventh
generation from Adam, prophesied: "Look! The Lord
comes with tens of thousands of his holy ones 15 to
execute judgment on all and to convict all the ungodly
concerning all the ungodly acts that they have done in
an ungodly way, and concerning all the harsh things
ungodly sinners have said against him." 16 These people are discontented grumblers, living according to
their desires; their mouths utter arrogant words,
flattering people for their own advantage.

17 But you, dear friends, remember what was predicted by the apostles of our Lord Jesus Christ. 18 They
told you, "In the end time there will be scoffers living according to their own ungodly desires." 19 These
people create divisions and are worldly, not having
the Spirit.

EXHORTATION AND BENEDICTION

20 But you, dear friends, as you build yourselves up in
your most holy faith, praying in the Holy Spirit, 21 keep
yourselves in the love of God, waiting expectantly for
the mercy of our Lord Jesus Christ for eternal life.
22 Have mercy on those who waver; 23 save others by
snatching them from the fire; have mercy on others
but with fear, hating even the garment defiled by
the flesh.

24 Now to him who is able to protect you from
stumbling and to make you stand in the presence
of his glory, without blemish and with great joy, 25 to
the only God our Savior, through Jesus Christ our
Lord,[A] be glory, majesty, power, and authority before
all time,[B] now and forever. Amen.

[A]**25** Other mss omit *through Jesus Christ our Lord* [B]**25** Other mss omit *before all time*

Part of the Dead Sea Scrolls discovered at Qumran, this papyrus fragment is from the noncanonical book of Enoch.

are shepherds who only look after themselves. They
are waterless clouds carried along by winds; trees in
late autumn — fruitless, twice dead and uprooted.
[13] They are wild waves of the sea, foaming up their
shameful deeds; wandering stars for whom the blackness of darkness is reserved forever.
[14] It was about these that Enoch, in the seventh
generation from Adam, prophesied: "Look! The Lord
comes with tens of thousands of his holy ones [15] to
execute judgment on all and to convict all the ungodly
concerning all the ungodly acts that they have done in
an ungodly way, and concerning all the harsh things
ungodly sinners have said against him." [16] These people are discontented grumblers, living according to
their desires; their mouths utter arrogant words,
flattering people for their own advantage.
[17] But you, dear friends, remember what was predicted by the apostles of our Lord Jesus Christ. [18] They
told you, "In the end time there will be scoffers living according to their own ungodly desires." [19] These
people create divisions and are worldly, not having
the Spirit.

EXHORTATION AND BENEDICTION

[20] But you, dear friends, as you build yourselves up in
your most holy faith, praying in the Holy Spirit, [21] keep
yourselves in the love of God, waiting expectantly for
the mercy of our Lord Jesus Christ for eternal life.
[22] Have mercy on those who waver; [23] save others by
snatching them from the fire; have mercy on others
but with fear, hating even the garment defiled by
the flesh.
[24] Now to him who is able to protect you from
stumbling and to make you stand in the presence
of his glory, without blemish and with great joy, [25] to
the only God our Savior, through Jesus Christ our
Lord,[a] be glory, majesty, power, and authority before
all time,[b] now and forever. Amen.

a25 Other mss omit through Jesus Christ our Lord b25 Other mss omit before all time

Part of the Dead Sea Scrolls discovered at Qumran, this papyrus fragment is from the noncanonical book of Enoch.

REVELATION

Early Bronze Age temple complex at Megiddo. Partially shown at the deepest level and in the upper left corner of the photo are the remains of a mud-brick altar that was a part of the complex.

INTRODUCTION TO

REVELATION

Circumstances of Writing

The traditional view holds that the author of Revelation is the apostle John, who wrote the Fourth Gospel and the three letters of John. Evidences for this view include the following: (1) the writer referred to himself as John (1:4,9; 22:8); (2) he had personal relationships with the seven churches of Asia Minor (1:4,11; chaps. 2–3); (3) his circumstances at the time of writing (1:9) matched those of John the apostle (who was placed in Asia Minor from ca AD 70 to 100 by reliable historical sources from the second century AD); and (4) the saturation of the book with Old Testament imagery and echoes implies a Jewish writer, like John, operating in overwhelmingly Gentile Asia Minor.

The initial audience that received the book of Revelation was a group of seven local churches in southwest Asia Minor (1:11; chaps. 2–3). Some of these congregations were experiencing persecution (2:9–10,13), probably under the Roman Emperor Domitian (reigned AD 81–96). Others had doctrinal and practical problems (2:6,13–15,20–23). Also behind these surface problems was the backdrop of unseen but powerful spiritual warfare (2:10,14,24; 3:9).

Though some scholars have dated the book later and a few have dated it earlier, commonly held dates of Revelation among evangelical scholars are the mid-90s and the late 60s of the first century AD. The mid-90s view is the stronger view, and it is held by majority opinion. Each view gives a different account of the persecution portrayed in the letters to the churches (2:9–10,13). Substantial historical evidence shows that some of the churches were persecuted intensely by Nero in the late 60s. But the reference in 17:10 to seven kings, five of whom have fallen, supports a date in the mid-90s, during the reign of Domitian.

While a case can be made for a late-60s date based on the Nero-related inferences and a possible reference to the Jerusalem temple in 11:1–2 (which may imply that the temple had not yet been destroyed, as it was by the Romans in AD 70), all other factors favor a date of about AD 95. Most notable among these factors is the tradition that John the apostle was exiled to Patmos during a period of intensifying local persecution of Christians by Emperor Domitian.

Contribution to the Bible

The book of Revelation provides an almost complete overview of theology. There is much in this book about Christ, humankind and sin, the people of God (both the church and Israel), holy angels, and Satan and the demons. There is important material on God's power and tri-unity (i.e., Trinity), plus aspects of the work of the Holy Spirit and the nature of Scripture.

Structure

The book of Revelation previews its sequential structure in 1:19: "Therefore write what you have seen, what is, and what will take place after this." From the apostle John's vantage point in being commanded to "write," he had already seen the vision of the exalted Son of Man (chap. 1). Next, he was told to "write" letters to the seven churches, telling each the state of its spiritual health (chaps. 2–3). Last comes the body of the book (4:1–22:5), which covers all the events that would "take place after this."

PROLOGUE

1 The revelation of[A] Jesus Christ that God gave him
to show his servants what must soon take place.
He made it known by sending his angel to his servant John, 2 who testified to the word of God and
to the testimony[B] of Jesus Christ, whatever he saw.[C]
3 Blessed is the one who reads aloud the words of
this prophecy, and blessed are those who hear the
words of this prophecy and keep[D] what is written in
it, because the time is near.

4 John: To the seven churches in Asia. Grace and
peace to you from[E] the one who is, who was, and
who is to come, and from the seven spirits[F] before
his throne, 5 and from Jesus Christ, the faithful witness, the firstborn from the dead and the ruler of the
kings of the earth.

To him who loves us and has set us free[G] from our
sins by his blood, 6 and made us a kingdom,[H] priests[I]
to his God and Father — to him be glory and dominion forever and ever. Amen.

7 **Look, he is coming with the clouds,**
and every eye will see him,
even those who pierced him.
And all the tribes[J] of the earth[K]
will mourn over him.[L,M]
So it is to be. Amen.

8 "I am the Alpha and the Omega," says the Lord
God, "the one who is, who was, and who is to come,
the Almighty."

JOHN'S VISION OF THE RISEN LORD

9 I, John, your brother and partner in the affliction,
kingdom, and endurance that are in Jesus, was on the
island called Patmos because of the word of God and
the testimony of Jesus. 10 I was in the Spirit[N] on the
Lord's day, and I heard a loud voice behind me like a
trumpet 11 saying, "Write on a scroll[O] what you see and
send it to the seven churches: Ephesus, Smyrna, Pergamum, Thyatira, Sardis, Philadelphia, and Laodicea."

12 Then I turned to see whose voice it was that spoke
to me. When I turned I saw seven golden lampstands,
13 and among the lampstands was one like the Son
of Man,[P] dressed in a robe and with a golden sash
wrapped around his chest. 14 The hair of his head was

[A] **1:1** Or *Revelation of*, or *A revelation of* [B] **1:2** Or *witness* [C] **1:2** Or *as many as he saw* [D] **1:3** Or *follow*, or *obey* [E] **1:4** Other mss add *God* [F] **1:4** Or *the sevenfold Spirit* [G] **1:5** Other mss read *has washed us* [H] **1:6** Other mss read *kings and* [I] **1:6** Or *made us into* (or *to be*) *a kingdom of priests*; Ex 19:6 [J] **1:7** Or *peoples* [K] **1:7** Gn 12:3; 28:14; Zch 14:17 [L] **1:7** Or *will wail because of him* [M] **1:7** Dn 7:13; Zch 12:10 [N] **1:10** Or *in spirit*; lit *I became in the Spirit* [O] **1:11** Or *book* [P] **1:13** Or *like a son of man*

Ruins of ancient Thyatira in modern Akhisar, Turkey.

Patmos

by Gary Hardin

Overlooking part of the shoreline at Patmos.

Patmos, a small rocky island in the Aegean Sea, stretches ten miles long and six miles wide. Its formation resulted from volcanic activity in the Dodecanese, a cluster of islands in the Aegean Sea near Asia Minor. About sixty miles southwest of Ephesus, Patmos provided the last stop on a voyage from Rome to Ephesus. Its crescent shape created a natural harbor for ships.

With its rocky soil and an abundance of flowering plants and shrubs, the island featured low hills, small plateaus, and a large number of coves. Patmos experienced a mostly mild climate. Ancient sources suggest that a large quantity of trees originally covered the island. The trees were cut down, leaving Patmos bare.[1]

The Cariens, ancient inhabitants of Caria in southwest Asia Minor, were likely the original inhabitants of Patmos. The Doriens and Ionians, ancient Greek groups, colonized the island in the eleventh century BC. The island's early inhabitants adored the goddess Diana, considered the patroness of the island. At the time of John's exile, Patmos featured a temple to Diana, who bore a close resemblance to Artemis (Apollo's twin), the goddess whom early Greeks believed protected all living things.

The Romans typically condemned lower-class criminals to work in mines or to die in combat as gladiators. Rome banished some upper-class criminals to a lonely island. The Romans used two groups of Aegean islands—the Cyclades and Sporades—as places of banishment. Emperors Domitian and Diocletian chose Patmos as a place of exile for the better class of offenders. Patmos was a suitable place for exile, because it was desolate, barren, sparsely settled, seldom visited, and infested with snakes and scorpions.

Patmos had no significant historical role until the Christian era. During late Roman and Byzantine times, a religious aura rested on Patmos, due mainly to John's exile. During the Middle Ages, pirates attacked and depopulated Patmos and plundered the island for its resources, including the animals.[2]

Around 1088, a new period began for Patmos, when the Greek monk Christodoulos Latrenos built St. John's Monastery on the site of an earlier temple to Artemis. This monastery resembled a fortress and became Patmos's most famous landmark. The years that followed

Entrance foyer in the Cave of the Apocalypse, on Patmos. According to tradition, John was in this cave when he received his visions.

brought more change. Patmos saw the development of numerous churches and monasteries and became a place of learning for Greek Orthodox monks, who assembled a notable library on the island. Today the library of St. John's Monastery contains one of the most important collections of items from Greek monastic history. The collection includes embroidered stoles from the fifteenth to the eighteenth centuries, rare icons, illuminated manuscripts, and church furniture from the seventeenth century. The monastery chapel features art that dates back to the early 1200s.[3] ✜

[1] R. C. Stone, "Patmos" in *ZPEB* (1976), 5:619. [2] "Patmos," accessed 26 October 2003, www.abrock.com/Greece-Turkey/patmos.html. [3] "Patmos," www.abrock.com.

Overview of ancient Pergamum; this theater seated up to 10,000 spectators. The columns in the background were part of the temple of Trajan.

white as wool — white as snow — and his eyes like
a fiery flame. 15 His feet were like fine bronze as it is
fired in a furnace, and his voice like the sound of cascading[A] waters. 16 He had seven stars in his right hand;
a sharp double-edged sword came from his mouth,
and his face was shining like the sun at full strength.
17 When I saw him, I fell at his feet like a dead man.
He laid his right hand on me and said, "Don't be afraid.
I am the First and the Last, 18 and the Living One. I was
dead, but look — I am alive forever and ever, and I
hold the keys of death and Hades. 19 Therefore write
what you have seen, what is, and what will take place
after this. 20 The mystery of the seven stars you saw
in my right hand and of the seven golden lampstands
is this: The seven stars are the angels[B] of the seven
churches, and the seven lampstands[C] are the seven
churches.

THE LETTERS TO THE SEVEN CHURCHES

THE LETTER TO EPHESUS

2 "Write to the angel[D] of the church in Ephesus:
Thus says the one who holds the seven stars in
his right hand and who walks among the seven gold-
en lampstands: 2 I know your works, your labor, and
your endurance, and that you cannot tolerate evil
people. You have tested those who call themselves
apostles and are not, and you have found them to be
liars. 3 I know that you have persevered and endured
hardships for the sake of my name, and you have not
grown weary. 4 But I have this against you: You have
abandoned the love you had at first. 5 Remember then
how far you have fallen; repent, and do the works
you did at first. Otherwise, I will come to you[E] and
remove your lampstand from its place, unless you
repent. 6 Yet you do have this: You hate the practices
of the Nicolaitans, which I also hate.
7 "Let anyone who has ears to hear listen to what
the Spirit says to the churches. To the one who conquers, I will give the right to eat from the tree of life,
which is in[F] the paradise of God.

THE LETTER TO SMYRNA

8 "Write to the angel of the church in Smyrna: Thus
says the First and the Last, the one who was dead and
came to life: 9 I know your[G] affliction and poverty, but
you are rich. I know the slander of those who say they
are Jews and are not, but are a synagogue of Satan.
10 Don't be afraid of what you are about to suffer.
Look, the devil is about to throw some of you into
prison to test you, and you will experience affliction
for ten days. Be faithful to the point of death, and I
will give you the crown[H] of life.
11 "Let anyone who has ears to hear listen to what
the Spirit says to the churches. The one who conquers
will never be harmed by the second death.

THE LETTER TO PERGAMUM

12 "Write to the angel of the church in Pergamum: Thus
says the one who has the sharp, double-edged sword:
13 I know[I] where you live — where Satan's throne is.
Yet you are holding on to my name and did not deny
your faith in me,[J] even in the days of Antipas, my
faithful witness who was put to death among you,
where Satan lives. 14 But I have a few things against
you. You have some there who hold to the teaching of
Balaam, who taught Balak to place a stumbling block[K]
in front of the Israelites: to eat meat sacrificed to idols
and to commit sexual immorality. 15 In the same way,
you also have those who hold to the teaching of the
Nicolaitans.[L] 16 So repent! Otherwise, I will come to
you quickly and fight against them with the sword
of my mouth.
17 "Let anyone who has ears to hear listen to what the
Spirit says to the churches. To the one who conquers,

[A] **1:15** Lit *many* [B] **1:20** Or *messengers* [C] **1:20** Other mss add *that you saw* [D] **2:1** Or *messenger*, also in vv. 8,12,18 [E] **2:5** Other mss add *quickly* [F] **2:7** Other mss read *in the midst of* [G] **2:9** Other mss add *works and* [H] **2:10** Or *wreath* [I] **2:13** Other mss add *your works and* [J] **2:13** Or *deny my faith* [K] **2:14** Or *to place a trap* [L] **2:15** Other mss add *which I hate*

I will give some of the hidden manna.[A] I will also give
him a white stone, and on the stone a new name is
inscribed that no one knows except the one who receives it.

THE LETTER TO THYATIRA

18 "Write to the angel of the church in Thyatira: Thus
says the Son of God, the one whose eyes are like a
fiery flame and whose feet are like fine bronze: 19 I
know your works — your love, faithfulness,[B] service, and endurance. I know that your last works are
greater than the first. 20 But I have this against you:
You tolerate the woman Jezebel, who calls herself a
prophetess and teaches and deceives my servants to
commit sexual immorality and to eat meat sacrificed
to idols. 21 I gave her time to repent, but she does not
want to repent of her sexual immorality. 22 Look, I
will throw her into a sickbed and those who commit adultery with her into great affliction. Unless
they repent of her[C] works, 23 I will strike her children
dead.[D] Then all the churches will know that I am the
one who examines minds and hearts, and I will give
to each of you according to your works. 24 I say to the
rest of you in Thyatira, who do not hold this teaching,
who haven't known "the so-called secrets[E] of Satan"
— as they say — I am not putting any other burden
on you. 25 Only hold on to what you have until I come.
26 The one who conquers and who keeps my works to
the end: I will give him authority over the nations —

27 **and he will rule[F] them with an iron scepter;**
he will shatter them like pottery[G] —

28 just as I have received this from my Father. I will
also give him the morning star.
29 "Let anyone who has ears to hear listen to what
the Spirit says to the churches.

THE LETTER TO SARDIS

3 "Write to the angel[H] of the church in Sardis: Thus
says the one who has the seven spirits of God
and the seven stars: I know your works; you have a
reputation[I] for being alive, but you are dead. 2 Be alert
and strengthen[J] what remains, which is about to die,[K]
for I have not found your works complete before my
God. 3 Remember, then, what you have received and
heard; keep it, and repent. If you are not alert, I will
come[L] like a thief, and you have no idea at what hour
I will come upon you. 4 But you have a few people[M] in
Sardis who have not defiled[N] their clothes, and they
will walk with me in white, because they are worthy.
5 "In the same way, the one who conquers will be
dressed in white clothes, and I will never erase his
name from the book of life but will acknowledge his
name before my Father and before his angels.
6 "Let anyone who has ears to hear listen to what
the Spirit says to the churches.

The colonnaded forum in Smyrna. It dates from the first centuries BC and AD.

THE LETTER TO PHILADELPHIA

7 "Write to the angel of the church in Philadelphia:
Thus says the Holy One, the true one, the one who has
the key of David, who opens and no one will close, and
who closes and no one opens: 8 I know your works.
Look, I have placed before you an open door that no
one can close because you have but little power; yet
you have kept my word and have not denied my name.
9 Note this: I will make those from the synagogue of
Satan, who claim to be Jews and are not, but are lying
— I will make them come and bow down at your feet,
and they will know that I have loved you. 10 Because
you have kept my command to endure, I will also keep
you from the hour of testing that is going to come on
the whole world to test those who live on the earth.
11 I am coming soon. Hold on to what you have, so that
no one takes your crown.
12 "The one who conquers I will make a pillar in
the temple of my God, and he will never go out again.

[A] **2:17** Other mss add *to eat* [B] **2:19** Or *faith* [C] **2:22** Other mss read *their* [D] **2:23** Or *with a plague* [E] **2:24** Or *the secret things* [F] **2:27** Or *shepherd* [G] **2:27** Ps 2:9 [H] **3:1** Or *messenger*, also in vv. 7,14 [I] **3:1** Or *have a name* [J] **3:2** Other mss read *guard* [K] **3:2** Or *strengthen who remain, who are about to die* [L] **3:3** Other mss add *upon you* [M] **3:4** Lit *few names* [N] **3:4** Or *soiled*

I will write on him the name of my God and the name
of the city of my God — the new Jerusalem, which
comes down out of heaven from my God — and my
new name.
13 "Let anyone who has ears to hear listen to what
the Spirit says to the churches.

THE LETTER TO LAODICEA

14 "Write to the angel of the church in Laodicea: Thus
says the Amen, the faithful and true witness, the orig-
inator[A] of God's creation: 15 I know your works, that
you are neither cold nor hot. I wish that you were
cold or hot. 16 So, because you are lukewarm, and
neither hot nor cold, I am going to vomit[B] you out
of my mouth. 17 For you say, 'I'm rich; I have become
wealthy and need nothing,' and you don't realize that
you are wretched, pitiful, poor, blind, and naked. 18 I
advise you to buy from me gold refined in the fire
so that you may be rich, white clothes so that you
may be dressed and your shameful nakedness not
be exposed, and ointment to spread on your eyes so
that you may see. 19 As many as I love, I rebuke and
discipline. So be zealous and repent. 20 See! I stand at
the door and knock. If anyone hears my voice and
opens the door, I will come in to him and eat with
him, and he with me.
21 "To the one who conquers I will give the right to
sit with me on my throne, just as I also conquered and
sat down with my Father on his throne.
22 "Let anyone who has ears to hear listen to what
the Spirit says to the churches."

THE THRONE ROOM OF HEAVEN

4 After this I looked, and there in heaven was an
open door. The first voice that I had heard speaking to me like a trumpet said, "Come up here, and I
will show you what must take place after this."
2 Immediately I was in the Spirit, and there was a
throne in heaven and someone was seated on it. 3 The
one seated[C] there had the appearance of jasper and
carnelian stone. A rainbow that had the appearance
of an emerald surrounded the throne.
4 Around the throne were twenty-four thrones,
and on the thrones sat twenty-four elders dressed
in white clothes, with golden crowns on their heads.
5 Flashes of lightning and rumblings and peals of
thunder came from the throne. Seven fiery torches
were burning before the throne, which are the seven
spirits of God. 6 Something like a sea of glass, similar
to crystal, was also before the throne.

[A] **3:14** Or *beginning of God's creation*, or *ruler of God's creation*
[B] **3:16** Or *spit* [C] **4:3** Other mss omit *The one seated*

The southern gate of Ephesus. The Ephesian Odeum is in the background.

Four living creatures covered with eyes in front and
in back were around the throne on each side. 7 The
first living creature was like a lion; the second living
creature was like an ox; the third living creature had
a face like a man; and the fourth living creature was
like a flying eagle. 8 Each of the four living creatures
had six wings; they were covered with eyes around
and inside. Day and night they never stop,[A] saying,

Holy, holy, holy,
Lord God, the Almighty,
who was, who is, and who is to come.

9 Whenever the living creatures give glory, honor,
and thanks to the one seated on the throne, the one
who lives forever and ever, 10 the twenty-four elders
fall down before the one seated on the throne and
worship the one who lives forever and ever. They cast
their crowns before the throne and say,

11 Our Lord and God,[B]
you are worthy to receive
glory and honor and power,
because you have created all things,
and by your will
they exist and were created.

[A] **4:8** Or *rest* [B] **4:11** Some mss add *the Holy One*; other mss read *Lord*

The Lycus Valley

by Roy E. Lucas Jr.

Roman ruins at Laodicea, which is about one hundred miles east of Ephesus.

GEOGRAPHY

The Lycus Valley, which is triangular in shape, is formed by four mountain ranges. The Salbakus and Cadmus ranges run across the southern end of the valley. The Messogis Mountains form the northwestern side of the valley and the Mossyna Mountains, the northeastern side. Two major rivers run through the Lycus Valley—the Lycus River, which empties into the Maeander River.

Colossae, Hierapolis, and Laodicea were the most significant cities in the Lycus Valley. Laodicea and Hierapolis sat on opposite sides of the Lycus River, six miles apart. Colossae sat on both sides of the Lycus River, about ten miles to the southeast of Laodicea. A major trade route from the Aegean Coast to the Euphrates River ran through the valley. A second road followed the path from Pergamum to Sardis, on to Perga, and finally to Attalia.

Earthquakes frequently struck the Lycus Valley. The Greek geographer Strabo (ca 63 BC–AD 23) described this valley as "good for earth-quakes."[1] Chalk infused the Lycus River and its streams. The chalk from these riverbeds would bury ancient monuments, cover the fertile land, clog the river flow, redirect streams, and destroy crops. Visible from a distance of twenty miles, these deposits glistened in the sun like glaciers.[2]

Volcanic activity in the region produced rich soil. The resultant abundant vegetation was helpful for those raising livestock. Large herds enriched the producers of wool apparel in all three cities. Due to an abundant water supply, Hierapolis developed a strong textile business. The textile producers used chalk from the rivers in their dyes. The madder root along with the calcareous waters produced a fade-resistant dye. Thermal springs near Hierapolis attracted visitors seeking therapeutic treatments.

HISTORY

Cyrus the Great defeated Lydia's King Croesus in 546 BC, placing the Lycus Valley under Persian control. Alexander the Great conquered the valley in 334 BC. Greek rule continued for about 150 years. The Romans, with the assistance of Pergamum's King Eumenes II (reigned 197–159 BC), defeated the Seleucid King Antiochus III in 189 BC at the battle of Magnesia. Afterward, the Lycus Valley became part of the kingdom of Pergamum. The last king

View of the Lycus River Valley from atop Tel Colossae near the modern town of Honaz, Turkey. Mount Cadmus is in the distance.

of Pergamum, Attilus III (reigned 138–133 BC), bequeathed the kingdom of Pergamum to the Romans in his will in 133 BC. The region was incorporated into the Senatorial Province of Asia and remained under Roman control for hundreds of years.

Colossae stood as the most important town in the valley during the fourth to fifth centuries BC. Like Hierapolis and Laodicea in later history, it supported a strong textile business from fine wool products. During the Roman period, Laodicea and Hierapolis surpassed Colossae in importance; by the ninth century AD, Colossae was a ghost town.

Some scholars believe Hierapolis was founded in the fourth or third century BC. Others claim it began under Eumenes II of Pergamum. Hierapolis's importance peaked in the second and third centuries AD. Rome's Emperor Hadrian (AD 117–138) financially supported major construction projects there, including a theater seating twelve thousand to fifteen thousand people.

Laodicea sat between two small tributaries that flowed into the Lycus River: The Asopus River ran to the western portion of the city while the Caprus River flowed east of the city. Pliny the Elder (ca AD 23–79) wrote that Laodicea stood on top of an earlier city, Diospolis, later called Rhoas.[3] "Antiochus II, the Seleucid king [reigned 261–246 BC], founded the city during the middle of the third century. . . . He named the city in honor of his wife Laodice."[4]

Earthquakes struck the region and destroyed Colossae, Hierapolis, and Laodicea in both AD 17 and AD 60. The cities rebuilt after both earthquakes. ⁂

[1] Strabo, *Geography* 12.8.16. [2] J. B. Lightfoot, *St Paul Epistles to the Colossians and to Philemon* (London: Macmillan, 1880), 3. [3] Pliny the Elder, *Natural History* 5.39. [4] Clyde E. Fant and Mitchell G. Reddish, *A Guide to Biblical Sites in Greece and Turkey* (Oxford: Oxford University Press, 2003), 232.

Silver tetradrachm of Syria's King Antiochus II, who named the city for his wife Laodice in the third century BC.

THE LAMB TAKES THE SCROLL

5 Then I saw in the right hand of the one seated on
the throne a scroll with writing on both sides,
sealed with seven seals. 2 I also saw a mighty angel
proclaiming with a loud voice, "Who is worthy to
open the scroll and break its seals?" 3 But no one in
heaven or on earth or under the earth was able to
open the scroll or even to look in it. 4 I wept and wept
because no one was found worthy to open[A] the scroll
or even to look in it. 5 Then one of the elders said to
me, "Do not weep. Look, the Lion from the tribe of
Judah, the Root of David, has conquered so that he is
able to open the scroll and[B] its seven seals."
6 Then I saw one like a slaughtered lamb standing
in the midst of the throne and the four living creatures and among the elders. He had seven horns and
seven eyes, which are the seven spirits of God sent
into all the earth. 7 He went and took the scroll out of
the right hand of the one seated on the throne.

THE LAMB IS WORTHY

8 When he took the scroll, the four living creatures
and the twenty-four elders fell down before the Lamb.
Each one had a harp and golden bowls filled with
incense, which are the prayers of the saints. 9 And
they sang a new song:

You are worthy to take the scroll
and to open its seals,
because you were slaughtered,
and you purchased[C] people[D]
for God by your blood
from every tribe and language
and people and nation.
10 You made them a kingdom[E]
and priests to our God,
and they will reign on the earth.

11 Then I looked and heard the voice of many angels around the throne, and also of the living creatures and of the elders. Their number was countless
thousands, plus thousands of thousands. 12 They said
with a loud voice,

Worthy is the Lamb who was
slaughtered
to receive power and riches
and wisdom and strength
and honor and glory and blessing!

13 I heard every creature in heaven, on earth, under
the earth, on the sea, and everything in them say,

[A] **5:4** Other mss add *and read* [B] **5:5** Other mss add *loose*
[C] **5:9** Or *redeemed* [D] **5:9** Other mss read *us* [E] **5:10** Other mss read
them kings

Partial ruins of the temple of Artemis at Sardis; the original structure, dated to about 300 BC, measured about 300 by 160 feet.

Blessing and honor and glory and power
be to the one seated on the throne,
and to the Lamb, forever and ever!
14 The four living creatures said, "Amen," and the elders fell down and worshiped.

THE FIRST SEAL ON THE SCROLL

6 Then I saw the Lamb open one of the seven[A] seals,
and I heard one of the four living creatures say
with a voice like thunder, "Come!" 2 I looked, and
there was a white horse. Its rider held a bow; a crown
was given to him, and he went out as a conqueror in
order to conquer.[B]

THE SECOND SEAL

3 When he opened the second seal, I heard the second
living creature say, "Come!" 4 Then another horse
went out, a fiery red one, and its rider was allowed
to take peace from the earth, so that people would
slaughter one another. And a large sword was given
to him.

THE THIRD SEAL

5 When he opened the third seal, I heard the third living creature say, "Come!" And I looked, and there was
a black horse. Its rider held a set of scales in his hand.
6 Then I heard something like a voice among the four
living creatures say, "A quart of wheat for a denarius,[C]
and three quarts of barley for a denarius, but do not
harm the oil and the wine."

THE FOURTH SEAL

7 When he opened the fourth seal, I heard the voice
of the fourth living creature say, "Come!" 8 And I
looked, and there was a pale green[D] horse. Its rider
was named Death, and Hades was following after
him. They were[E] given authority over a fourth of the
earth, to kill by the sword, by famine, by plague, and
by the wild animals of the earth.

THE FIFTH SEAL

9 When he opened the fifth seal, I saw under the altar
the souls of those who had been slaughtered because
of the word of God and the testimony they had given.[F]
10 They cried out with a loud voice, "Lord,[G] the one
who is holy and true, how long until you judge those
who live on the earth and avenge our blood?" 11 So
they were each given a white robe, and they were told

[A] **6:1** Other mss omit *seven* [B] **6:2** Or *went out conquering and in order to conquer* [C] **6:6** A denarius = one day's wage [D] **6:8** Or *a greenish gray* [E] **6:8** Other mss read *He was* [F] **6:9** Other mss add *about the Lamb* [G] **6:10** Or *"Master*

In modern Aksephir, Turkey, excavations of St. John's Church at ancient Philadelphia; the church dates from AD 600.

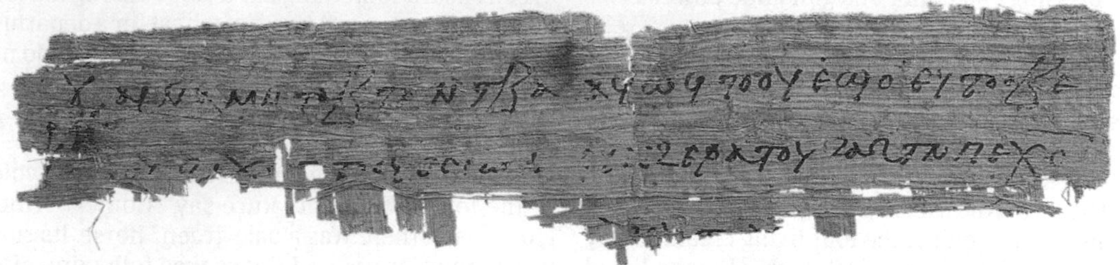

Early Coptic papyrus fragment dating to the fourth–fifth centuries AD; the text refers to the 144,000 in Revelation 7:4.

to rest a little while longer until the number would be completed of their fellow servants and their brothers and sisters, who were going to be killed just as they had been.

THE SIXTH SEAL

12 Then I saw him open[A] the sixth seal. A violent earthquake occurred; the sun turned black like sackcloth
made of hair; the entire moon[B] became like blood;
13 the stars[C] of heaven fell to the earth as a fig tree
drops its unripe figs when shaken by a high wind;
14 the sky was split apart like a scroll being rolled
up; and every mountain and island was moved from
its place.

15 Then the kings of the earth, the nobles, the generals, the rich, the powerful, and every slave and free
person hid in the caves and among the rocks of the
mountains. 16 And they said to the mountains and
to the rocks, "Fall on us and hide us from the face of
the one seated on the throne and from the wrath of
the Lamb, 17 because the great day of their[D] wrath has
come! And who is able to stand?"

THE SEALED OF ISRAEL

7 After this I saw four angels standing at the four
corners of the earth, restraining the four winds of
the earth so that no wind could blow on the earth or
on the sea or on any tree. 2 Then I saw another angel
rising up from the east, who had the seal of the living
God. He cried out in a loud voice to the four angels
who were allowed to harm the earth and the sea,
3 "Don't harm the earth or the sea or the trees until
we seal the servants of our God on their foreheads."
4 And I heard the number of the sealed:

144,000 sealed from every tribe
of the Israelites:
5 12,000 sealed from the tribe of Judah,
12,000 from the tribe of Reuben,
12,000 from the tribe of Gad,
6 12,000 from the tribe of Asher,
12,000 from the tribe of Naphtali,
12,000 from the tribe of Manasseh,
7 12,000 from the tribe of Simeon,
12,000 from the tribe of Levi,
12,000 from the tribe of Issachar,
8 12,000 from the tribe of Zebulun,
12,000 from the tribe of Joseph,
12,000 sealed from the tribe of Benjamin.

A MULTITUDE FROM THE GREAT TRIBULATION

9 After this I looked, and there was a vast multitude
from every nation, tribe, people, and language, which
no one could number, standing before the throne and
before the Lamb. They were clothed in white robes
with palm branches in their hands. 10 And they cried
out in a loud voice:

Salvation belongs to our God,
who is seated on the throne,
and to the Lamb!

11 All the angels stood around the throne, and along
with the elders and the four living creatures they
fell facedown before the throne and worshiped God,
12 saying,

Amen! Blessing and glory and wisdom
and thanksgiving and honor
and power and strength
be to our God forever and ever. Amen.

13 Then one of the elders asked me, "Who are these
people in white robes, and where did they come from?"
14 I said to him, "Sir,[E] you know."

Then he told me: These are the ones coming out of
the great tribulation. They washed their robes and
made them white in the blood of the Lamb.

15 For this reason they are before the throne
of God,
and they serve him day and night
in his temple.
The one seated on the throne
will shelter[F] them:

[A] **6:12** Or *I saw when he opened* [B] **6:12** Or *the full moon* [C] **6:13** Perhaps meteors [D] **6:17** Other mss read *his* [E] **7:14** Or *"My lord* [F] **7:15** Or *will spread his tent over*

16 They will no longer hunger;
they will no longer thirst;
the sun will no longer strike them,
nor will any scorching heat.
17 For the Lamb who is at the center
of the throne
will shepherd them;
he will guide them to springs of the waters
of life,
and God will wipe away every tear
from their eyes.

THE SEVENTH SEAL

8 When he opened the seventh seal, there was silence in heaven for about half an hour. 2 Then I
saw the seven angels who stand in the presence of
God; seven trumpets were given to them. 3 Another
angel, with a golden incense burner, came and stood
at the altar. He was given a large amount of incense to
offer with the prayers of all the saints on the golden
altar in front of the throne. 4 The smoke of the incense,
with the prayers of the saints, went up in the presence
of God from the angel's hand. 5 The angel took the
incense burner, filled it with fire from the altar, and
hurled it to the earth; there were peals of thunder,
rumblings, flashes of lightning, and an earthquake.

THE SEVEN TRUMPETS

6 And the seven angels who had the seven trumpets
prepared to blow them.

THE FIRST TRUMPET

7 The first angel blew his trumpet, and hail and fire,
mixed with blood, were hurled to the earth. So a third
of the earth was burned up, a third of the trees were
burned up, and all the green grass was burned up.

THE SECOND TRUMPET

8 The second angel blew his trumpet, and something
like a great mountain ablaze with fire was hurled into
the sea. So a third of the sea became blood, 9 a third
of the living creatures in the sea died, and a third of
the ships were destroyed.

THE THIRD TRUMPET

10 The third angel blew his trumpet, and a great star,
blazing like a torch, fell from heaven. It fell on a third
of the rivers and springs of water. 11 The name of the
star is Wormwood, and a third of the waters became
wormwood. So, many of the people died from the
waters, because they had been made bitter.

THE FOURTH TRUMPET

12 The fourth angel blew his trumpet, and a third of the
sun was struck, a third of the moon, and a third of the
stars, so that a third of them were darkened. A third of
the day was without light and also a third of the night.
13 I looked and heard an eagle[A] flying high overhead, crying out in a loud voice, "Woe! Woe! Woe to
those who live on the earth, because of the remaining trumpet blasts that the three angels are about
to sound!"

THE FIFTH TRUMPET

9 The fifth angel blew his trumpet, and I saw a star
that had fallen from heaven to earth. The key for
the shaft to the abyss was given to him. 2 He opened
the shaft to the abyss, and smoke came up out of the
shaft like smoke from a great[B] furnace so that the
sun and the air were darkened by the smoke from
the shaft. 3 Then locusts came out of the smoke on
to the earth, and power[C] was given to them like the
power that scorpions have on the earth. 4 They were
told not to harm the grass of the earth, or any green
plant, or any tree, but only those people who do not
have God's seal on their foreheads. 5 They were not
permitted to kill them but were to torment them for
five months; their torment is like the torment caused
by a scorpion when it stings someone. 6 In those days
people will seek death and will not find it; they will
long to die, but death will flee from them.
7 The appearance of the locusts was like horses
prepared for battle. Something like golden crowns
was on their heads; their faces were like human faces;
8 they had hair like women's hair; their teeth were like
lions' teeth; 9 they had chests like iron breastplates;
the sound of their wings was like the sound of many
chariots with horses rushing into battle; 10 and they
had tails with stingers like scorpions, so that with
their tails they had the power to harm people for
five months. 11 They had as their king[D] the angel of
the abyss; his name in Hebrew is Abaddon,[E] and in
Greek he has the name Apollyon.[F]
12 The first woe has passed. There are still two more
woes to come after this.

THE SIXTH TRUMPET

13 The sixth angel blew his trumpet. From the four[G]
horns of the golden altar that is before God, I heard
a voice 14 say to the sixth angel who had the trumpet,
"Release the four angels bound at the great river Euphrates." 15 So the four angels who were prepared
for the hour, day, month, and year were released
to kill a third of the human race. 16 The number of
mounted troops was two hundred million;[H] I heard
their number. 17 This is how I saw the horses and their

[A] **8:13** Other mss read *angel* [B] **9:2** Other mss omit *great*
[C] **9:3** Or *authority*, also in v. 10 [D] **9:11** Or *as king over them*
[E] **9:11** Or *Destruction* [F] **9:11** Or *Destroyer* [G] **9:13** Other mss omit *four*
[H] **9:16** Other mss read *a hundred million*

Bust of Rome's Emperor Domitian, who ruled AD 81–96.

riders in the vision: They had breastplates that were
fiery red, hyacinth blue, and sulfur yellow. The heads
of the horses were like the heads of lions, and from
their mouths came fire, smoke, and sulfur. 18 A third
of the human race was killed by these three plagues
— by the fire, the smoke, and the sulfur that came
from their mouths. 19 For the power of the horses is
in their mouths and in their tails, because their tails,
which resemble snakes, have heads that inflict injury.
20 The rest of the people, who were not killed by
these plagues, did not repent of the works of their
hands to stop worshiping demons and idols of gold,
silver, bronze, stone, and wood, which cannot see, hear,
or walk. 21 And they did not repent of their murders,
their sorceries, their sexual immorality, or their thefts.

THE MIGHTY ANGEL AND THE SMALL SCROLL

10 Then I saw another mighty angel coming down
from heaven, wrapped in a cloud, with a rainbow over his head.[A] His face was like the sun, his
legs[B] were like pillars of fire, 2 and he held a little
scroll opened in his hand. He put his right foot on
the sea, his left on the land, 3 and he called out with
a loud voice like a roaring lion. When he cried out,
the seven thunders raised their voices. 4 And when
the seven thunders spoke, I was about to write, but
I heard a voice from heaven, saying, "Seal up what
the seven thunders said, and do not write it down!"
5 Then the angel that I had seen standing on the sea
and on the land raised his right hand to heaven. 6 He
swore by the one who lives forever and ever, who
created heaven and what is in it, the earth and what
is in it, and the sea and what is in it, "There will no
longer be a delay, 7 but in the days when the seventh
angel will blow his trumpet, then the mystery of God
will be completed, as he announced to his servants
the prophets."
8 Then the voice that I heard from heaven spoke to
me again and said, "Go, take the scroll that lies open
in the hand of the angel who is standing on the sea
and on the land."
9 So I went to the angel and asked him to give me
the little scroll. He said to me, "Take and eat it; it will
be bitter in your stomach, but it will be as sweet as
honey in your mouth."
10 Then I took the little scroll from the angel's hand
and ate it. It was as sweet as honey in my mouth, but
when I ate it, my stomach became bitter. 11 And they
said to me, "You must prophesy again about[C] many
peoples, nations, languages, and kings."

THE TWO WITNESSES

11 Then I was given a measuring reed like a rod,[D]
with these words: "Go[E] and measure the temple
of God and the altar, and count those who worship
there. 2 But exclude the courtyard outside the temple.
Don't measure it, because it is given to the nations,[F]
and they will trample the holy city for forty-two
months. 3 I will grant[G] my two witnesses authority to
prophesy for 1,260 days, dressed in sackcloth." 4 These
are the two olive trees and the two lampstands that
stand before the Lord[H] of the earth. 5 If anyone wants
to harm them, fire comes from their mouths and consumes their enemies; if anyone wants to harm them,
he must be killed in this way. 6 They have authority
to close up the sky so that it does not rain during the
days of their prophecy. They also have power over the
waters to turn them into blood and to strike the earth
with every plague whenever they want.

THE WITNESSES MARTYRED

7 When they finish their testimony, the beast that
comes up out of the abyss will make war on them,

[A] **10:1** Or *a halo on his head* [B] **10:1** Or *feet* [C] **10:11** Or *prophesy again against* [D] **11:1** Other mss add *and the angel stood up* [E] **11:1** Lit *"Arise* [F] **11:2** Or *Gentiles* [G] **11:3** Or *I will give to* [H] **11:4** Other mss read *God*

conquer them, and kill them. 8 Their dead bodies[A]
will lie in the main street[B] of the great city, which
figuratively[C] is called Sodom and Egypt, where also
their Lord was crucified. 9 And some of[D] the peoples,
tribes, languages, and nations will view their bodies
for three and a half days and not permit their bodies
to be put into a tomb. 10 Those who live on the earth
will gloat over them and celebrate and send gifts to
one another because these two prophets had tormented those who live on the earth.

THE WITNESSES RESURRECTED

11 But after three and a half days, the breath[E] of life
from God entered them, and they stood on their feet.
Great fear fell on those who saw them. 12 Then they
heard[F] a loud voice from heaven saying to them,
"Come up here." They went up to heaven in a cloud,
while their enemies watched them. 13 At that moment
a violent earthquake took place, a tenth of the city
fell, and seven thousand people were killed in the
earthquake. The survivors were terrified and gave
glory to the God of heaven.
14 The second woe has passed. Take note: The third
woe is coming soon!

THE SEVENTH TRUMPET

15 The seventh angel blew his trumpet, and there were
loud voices in heaven saying,

The kingdom of the world has become
the kingdom
of our Lord and of his Christ,
and he will reign forever and ever.

16 The twenty-four elders, who were seated before
God on their thrones, fell facedown and worshiped
God, 17 saying,

We give you thanks, Lord God, the Almighty,
who is and who was,[G]
because you have taken your great power
and have begun to reign.
18 The nations were angry,
but your wrath has come.
The time has come
for the dead to be judged
and to give the reward
to your servants the prophets,
to the saints, and to those who fear
your name,
both small and great,
and the time has come to destroy
those who destroy the earth.

19 Then the temple of God in heaven was opened,
and the ark of his covenant[H] appeared in his temple.
There were flashes of lightning, rumblings and peals
of thunder, an earthquake,[I] and severe hail.

Top fragment of a *kudurru* with a *mushhushshu* dragon and divine symbols; limestone; Mesopotamia, Second Dynasty of Isin (1156–1025 BC). *Kudurru* (boundary stones) were irregularly shaped boulders, often made of black limestone or diorite, that people set up in temples as records of land grants. They were carved with divine symbols and inscribed. This fragment shows the supernatural creature and spade-shaped symbol associated with Marduk, the city god of Babylon and chief Babylonian deity.

THE WOMAN, THE CHILD, AND THE DRAGON

12 A great sign[J] appeared in heaven: a woman
clothed with the sun, with the moon under her
feet and a crown of twelve stars on her head. 2 She
was pregnant and cried out in labor and agony as
she was about to give birth. 3 Then another sign[K] appeared in heaven: There was a great fiery red dragon
having seven heads and ten horns, and on its heads
were seven crowns.[L] 4 Its tail swept away a third of
the stars in heaven and hurled them to the earth.
And the dragon stood in front of the woman who
was about to give birth, so that when she did give

[A] **11:8** Or *Their corpse* [B] **11:8** Or *lie on the broad street* [C] **11:8** Or *spiritually* [D] **11:9** Lit *And from* [E] **11:11** Or *spirit* [F] **11:12** Other mss read *Then I heard* [G] **11:17** Other mss add *and who is to come* [H] **11:19** Other mss read *ark of the covenant of the Lord* [I] **11:19** Other mss omit *an earthquake* [J] **12:1** Or *great symbolic display*; see Rv 12:3 [K] **12:3** Or *another symbolic display* [L] **12:3** Or *diadems*

birth it might devour her child. 5 She gave birth to a
Son, a male who is going to rule[A] all nations with an
iron rod. Her child was caught up to God and to his
throne. 6 The woman fled into the wilderness, where
she had a place prepared by God, to be nourished
there[B] for 1,260 days.

THE DRAGON THROWN OUT OF HEAVEN

7 Then war broke out in heaven: Michael and his angels fought against the dragon. The dragon and his
angels also fought, 8 but he could not prevail, and
there was no place for them in heaven any longer.
9 So the great dragon was thrown out — the ancient
serpent, who is called the devil and Satan, the one
who deceives the whole world. He was thrown to
earth, and his angels with him. 10 Then I heard a loud
voice in heaven say,

The salvation and the power
and the kingdom of our God
and the authority of his Christ
have now come,
because the accuser of our brothers and
sisters,
who accuses them
before our God day and night,
has been thrown down.

11 They conquered him
by the blood of the Lamb
and by the word of their testimony;
for they did not love their lives
to the point of death.
12 Therefore rejoice, you heavens,
and you who dwell in them!
Woe to the earth and the sea,
because the devil has come down to you
with great fury,
because he knows his time is short.

THE WOMAN PERSECUTED

13 When the dragon saw that he had been thrown
down to the earth, he persecuted[C] the woman who
had given birth to the male child. 14 The woman was
given two wings of a great eagle, so that she could fly
from the serpent's presence to her place in the wilderness, where she was nourished for a time, times,
and half a time. 15 From his mouth the serpent spewed
water like a river flowing after the woman, to sweep
her away with a flood. 16 But the earth helped the
woman. The earth opened its mouth and swallowed

[A] **12:5** Or *shepherd* [B] **12:6** Or *God, that they might feed her there*
[C] **12:13** Or *pursued*

Bronze dragon dated about 700–550 BC. This represents the sacred animal of Marduk, the primary god of Babylon.

up the river that the dragon had spewed from his mouth. 17 So the dragon was furious with the woman and went off to wage war against the rest of her offspring[A] — those who keep the commands of God and hold firmly to the testimony about Jesus.

THE BEAST FROM THE SEA

18 The dragon[B] stood on the sand of the sea.[C]

13 And I saw a beast coming up out of the sea. It had ten horns and seven heads. On its horns were ten crowns,[D] and on its heads were blasphemous names.[E] 2 The beast I saw was like a leopard, its feet were like a bear's, and its mouth was like a lion's mouth. The dragon gave the beast his power, his throne, and great authority. 3 One of its heads appeared to be fatally wounded, but its fatal wound was healed.

The whole earth was amazed and followed the beast. 4 They worshiped the dragon because he gave authority to the beast. And they worshiped the beast, saying, "Who is like the beast? Who is able to wage war against it?"

5 The beast was given a mouth to utter boasts and blasphemies. It was allowed to exercise authority[F,G] for forty-two months. 6 It began to speak[H] blasphemies against God: to blaspheme his name and his dwelling — those who dwell in heaven. 7 And it was permitted to wage war against the saints and to conquer them. It was also given authority over every tribe, people, language, and nation. 8 All those who live on the earth will worship it, everyone whose name was not written from the foundation of the world in the book[I] of life of the Lamb who was slaughtered.[J]

9 If anyone has ears to hear, let him listen.

10 If anyone is to be taken captive,
into captivity he goes.
If anyone is to be killed[K] with a sword,
with a sword he will be killed.

This calls for endurance[L] and faithfulness from the saints.

THE BEAST FROM THE EARTH

11 Then I saw another beast coming up out of the earth; it had two horns like a lamb,[M] but it spoke like a dragon. 12 It exercises all the authority of the first beast on its behalf and compels the earth and those who live on it to worship the first beast, whose fatal wound was healed. 13 It also performs great signs, even causing fire to come down from heaven to earth in front of people. 14 It deceives those who live on the earth because of the signs that it is permitted to perform in the presence of the beast, telling those who live on the earth to make an image[N] of the beast who was wounded by the sword and yet lived. 15 It was permitted to give breath[O] to the image of the beast, so that the image of the beast could both speak and cause whoever would not worship the image of the beast to be killed. 16 And it makes everyone — small and great, rich and poor, free and slave — to receive a mark on his right hand or on his forehead, 17 so that no one can buy or sell unless he has the mark: the beast's name or the number of its name.

18 This calls for wisdom:[P] Let the one who has understanding calculate[Q] the number of the beast, because it is the number of a person. Its number is 666.[R]

THE LAMB AND THE 144,000

14 Then I looked, and there was the Lamb, standing on Mount Zion, and with him were 144,000 who had his name and his Father's name written on their foreheads. 2 I heard a sound[S] from heaven like the sound of cascading waters and like the rumbling of loud thunder. The sound I heard was like harpists playing on their harps. 3 They sang[T] a new song before the throne and before the four living creatures and the elders, but no one could learn the song except the 144,000 who had been redeemed from the earth. 4 These are the ones who have not defiled themselves with women, since they remained virgins. These are the ones who follow the Lamb wherever he goes. They were redeemed[U] from humanity as the firstfruits for God and the Lamb. 5 No lie was found in their mouths; they are blameless.

THE PROCLAMATION OF THREE ANGELS

6 Then I saw another angel flying high overhead, with the eternal gospel to announce to the inhabitants of the earth — to every nation, tribe, language, and people. 7 He spoke with a loud voice: "Fear God and give him glory, because the hour of his judgment has come. Worship the one who made heaven and earth, the sea and the springs of water."

8 And another, a second angel, followed, saying, "It has fallen, Babylon the Great has fallen.[V] She made all the nations drink the wine of her sexual immorality,[W] which brings wrath."

9 And another, a third angel, followed them and spoke with a loud voice: "If anyone worships the beast

[A] **12:17** Or *seed* [B] **12:18** Or *he*; other mss read *I* [C] **12:18** Some translations put Rv 12:18 either in Rv 12:17 or Rv 13:1. [D] **13:1** Or *diadems* [E] **13:1** Other mss read *heads was a blasphemous name* [F] **13:5** Other mss read *to wage war* [G] **13:5** Or *to rule* [H] **13:6** Or *He opened his mouth in* [I] **13:8** Or *scroll* [J] **13:8** Or *written in the book of life of the Lamb who was slaughtered from the foundation of the world* [K] **13:10** Other mss read *anyone kills* [L] **13:10** Or *Here is the perseverance* [M] **13:11** Or *ram* [N] **13:14** Or *a statue*, or *a likeness* [O] **13:15** Or *a spirit*, or *life* [P] **13:18** Or *Here is wisdom* [Q] **13:18** Or *count*, or *figure out* [R] **13:18** Other Gk mss read *616* [S] **14:2** Or *voice* [T] **14:3** Other mss add *as it were* [U] **14:4** Other mss add *by Jesus* [V] **14:8** Other mss omit the second *has fallen* [W] **14:8** Or *wine of her passionate immorality*

and its image and receives a mark on his forehead
or on his hand, 10 he will also drink the wine of God's
wrath, which is poured full strength into the cup of
his anger. He will be tormented with fire and sulfur
in the sight of the holy angels and in the sight of the
Lamb, 11 and the smoke of their torment will go up
forever and ever. There is no rest[A] day or night for
those who worship the beast and its image, or anyone
who receives the mark of its name. 12 This calls for endurance from the saints, who keep God's commands
and their faith in Jesus."[B]

13 Then I heard a voice from heaven saying, "Write:
Blessed are the dead who die in the Lord from now on."

"Yes," says the Spirit, "so they will rest from their
labors, since their works follow them."

REAPING THE EARTH'S HARVEST

14 Then I looked, and there was a white cloud, and one
like the Son of Man[C] was seated on the cloud, with a
golden crown on his head and a sharp sickle in his
hand. 15 Another angel came out of the temple, crying
out in a loud voice to the one who was seated on the
cloud, "Use your sickle and reap, for the time to reap
has come, since the harvest of the earth is ripe." 16 So
the one seated on the cloud swung his sickle over the
earth, and the earth was harvested.

17 Then another angel who also had a sharp sickle
came out of the temple in heaven. 18 Yet another angel,
who had authority over fire, came from the altar, and
he called with a loud voice to the one who had the
sharp sickle, "Use your sharp sickle and gather the
clusters of grapes from the vineyard of the earth, because its grapes have ripened." 19 So the angel swung
his sickle at the earth and gathered the grapes from
the vineyard of the earth, and he threw them into the
great winepress of God's wrath. 20 Then the press was
trampled outside the city, and blood flowed out of the
press up to the horses' bridles for about 180 miles.[D]

PREPARATION FOR THE BOWL JUDGMENTS

15 Then I saw another great and awe-inspiring
sign[E] in heaven: seven angels with the seven
last plagues; for with them God's wrath will be completed. 2 I also saw something like a sea of glass mixed
with fire, and those who had won the victory over the
beast, its image,[F] and the number of its name, were
standing on the sea of glass with harps from God.
3 They sang the song of God's servant Moses and the
song of the Lamb:

Great and awe-inspiring are your works,
Lord God, the Almighty;
just and true are your ways,
King of the nations.[G]
4 Lord, who will not fear
and glorify your name?
For you alone are holy.
All the nations will come
and worship before you
because your righteous acts
have been revealed.

5 After this I looked, and the heavenly temple —
the tabernacle of testimony — was opened. 6 Out of
the temple came the seven angels with the seven
plagues, dressed in pure, bright linen, with golden
sashes wrapped around their chests. 7 One of the four
living creatures gave the seven angels seven golden
bowls filled with the wrath of God who lives forever and ever. 8 Then the temple was filled with smoke
from the glory of God and from his power, and no
one could enter the temple until the seven plagues
of the seven angels were completed.

THE FIRST BOWL

16 Then I heard a loud voice from the temple saying to the seven angels, "Go and pour out the
seven[H] bowls of God's wrath on the earth." 2 The first
went and poured out his bowl on the earth, and severely painful sores broke out on the people who had
the mark of the beast and who worshiped its image.

THE SECOND BOWL

3 The second[I] poured out his bowl into the sea. It
turned to blood like that of a dead person, and all
life in the sea died.

THE THIRD BOWL

4 The third[I] poured out his bowl into the rivers and
the springs of water, and they became blood. 5 I heard
the angel of the waters say,

You are just,
the Holy One, who is and who was,
because you have passed judgment
on these things.
6 Because they poured out
the blood of the saints and the prophets,
you have given them blood to drink;
they deserve it!

7 I heard the altar say,

Yes, Lord God, the Almighty,
true and just are your judgments.

THE FOURTH BOWL

8 The fourth[I] poured out his bowl on the sun. It was
allowed to scorch people with fire, 9 and people were

[A] **14:11** Or *They have no rest* [B] **14:12** Or *and the faith of Jesus*, or *and faithfulness to Jesus* [C] **14:14** Or *like a son of man* [D] **14:20** Lit *1,600 stadia* [E] **15:1** Or *and awesome symbolic display* [F] **15:2** Other mss add *his mark* [G] **15:3** Other mss read *ages* [H] **16:1** Other mss omit *seven* [I] **16:3,4,8** Other mss add *angel*

Megiddo: A Crucial Locale

by Jeff S. Anderson

Megiddo, the crown jewel of biblical archaeology, is one of the most important sites in Israel, and for that matter, the entire ancient Near East. A World Heritage Site, Megiddo stands watch over the expansive Jezreel Valley. Megiddo had it all: a fertile and well-watered plain nearby, a strategic location on the crossroads of two major trade routes between Asia and Egypt (the Via Maris and Jezreel trade routes), and a defensible location. Ancient letters discovered at el-Amarna, Egypt, indicate Megiddo was one of Canaan's most dominant city-states. Biridiya, king of Megiddo, sent these letters to Egyptian Pharaoh Akhenaten in the fourteenth century BC. Megiddo enjoyed robust periods of occupation from 3500 to 500 BC and was inhabited during every era of Israel's history.

A HISTORICAL BATTLEFIELD

Megiddo preserves a long history of being an international battleground with thirty-four recorded battles in that area.[1] Over successive generations Megiddo witnessed many formidable armies, including the Canaanites, Egyptians, Assyrians, Israelites, Philistines, Persians, and Romans. More than one thousand years after the fall of the Roman Empire, Napoleon fought near the site in 1799. Concerning Megiddo, he is purported to have proclaimed, "There is no place in the whole world more suited for war than this . . . [It is] the most natural battleground of the whole earth."[2] In the twentieth century, Megiddo witnessed the defeat of the armies of the Turks and Germans during World War I as well as the victory of the Israelis in the 1948 War of Independence. Today the Ramat David Airfield of the Israeli Air Force is fewer than twenty miles from Megiddo.

THE GREAT TEMPLE

Four excavations have revealed more than twenty different occupation layers at Megiddo from 3500 to 500 BC. Since 1994, Tel Aviv University has assumed work at Megiddo as well as several other projects in the Jezreel Valley. Discoveries in 2012 included a hoard of gold and silver jewelry dating from 1100 BC, but the primary focus of the Tel Aviv operation has been to clarify chronology at the site.

Archaeologists continue to make exciting discoveries at Megiddo to this day. One noteworthy recent project has been the excavation of a huge temple (ca 11,840 square feet) dating to around 3000 BC, centuries before the arrival of the Israelites. This temple is the most monumental single edifice uncovered in the promised land and one of the largest structures of the Near East.[3]

A Canaanite temple, designed by a professional, highly skilled team of architects, was part of a massive temple complex that was re-envisioned and reconstructed many times over many centuries.

Megiddo was a Canaanite stronghold that overlooked the Jezreel Valley and guarded the main pass through the Carmel Mountains.

With walls more than 3 ½ meters (ca 11 ½ feet) thick, the floor of the building contains massive basalt slabs weighing more than a ton each. These are in two rows flanking the longitudinal axis of the temple. These basalt slabs were clearly not for roof support but for some unknown and highly sophisticated cultic practices. Two rear corridors called favissa were filled with sacrificial bone refuse, mostly young sheep and goats. The site had no evidence of human sacrifice.

Inhabitants of the lower village accessed this hilltop temple from the eastern slope of the mound and the main entry faced a mud-brick and stone altar that stood at the geometric center of the temple.[4] This magnificent shrine was abandoned for a time and later reoccupied. A series of later temples were built one on top of the other, including the shrine that contained the famous Early Bronze Age round altar.

BIBLICAL REFERENCES

The Bible contains about a dozen references to Megiddo. The first is to a certain "king of Megiddo," who is on a list of vanquished monarchs that Joshua conquered (Jos 12:21). Megiddo was then allotted to the tribe of Manasseh (17:11). The book of Judges (1:27), however, indicates that the situation was not quite that simple. Israel was seemingly unable to completely subdue Megiddo after all. Later in the same book, Deborah and Barak overcame Sisera near this site. The Song of Deborah refers to the "Waters of Megiddo" as the place where God delivered Israel (5:19).

During the Israelite monarchy, Solomon made Megiddo a district administrative capital along with two other major fortified sites: Hazor and Gezer. The gate systems at these three sites are nearly identical. The Bible refers to Solomon's robust building activity, which included the addition of palaces, terraces, and city walls (1Kg 9:15). A century later, the Bible records that Jehu killed Israel's King Joram and Judah's King Ahaziah near Megiddo (2Kg 9:27), while the Tel Dan inscription boasts that Syria's King Hazael was the one who murdered these two kings.

A few later references to Megiddo may point toward an emerging popularity of the site in apocalyptic thought. Josiah, the last "good" king from the Davidic dynasty, was fatally wounded at Megiddo in battle against Pharaoh Neco (2Kg 23:29; 2Ch 35:22–24). Even though a few more kings ruled briefly after Josiah, for all practical purposes the death of Josiah brought an abrupt and tragic end to the monarchy.

MEGIDDO AND ARMAGEDDON

Without a doubt, one of the most popular biblical texts pertaining to Megiddo is Revelation 16:16. Some

Dated to about 2500 BC, circular Canaanite altar at Megiddo; the altar measures 25 feet in diameter and about 4 ½ feet high. Four steps lead to the top of the altar. The altar was located behind the actual temple.

interpret that this pivotal location will be where the spiritual forces of the heavens and the kings of the earth gather together for the ultimate battle of good versus evil. The New Testament adopts the term *Armageddon*, a corruption of the Hebrew, *Har-Megiddo*, which translates "Mount Megiddo." This reference in Revelation reveals the context of the sixth and seventh bowls of wrath, which predict the fall of Babylon the Great. Whether the reference in Revelation is to a historical battle or the metaphorical demise of evil, Megiddo retains both a lively past and an intriguing future in the Bible's history and theology. ❖

An ivory game board with fifty-eight holes; inlaid with gold; from Megiddo.

[1] Eric H. Cline, *The Battles of Armageddon: Megiddo and the Jezreel Valley from the Bronze Age to the Nuclear Age* (Ann Arbor: University of Michigan Press, 2000), 1.
[2] Cline, *Battles of Armageddon*, 142.
[3] Matthew J. Adams, Israel Finkelstein, and David Ussishkin, "The Great Temple of Early Bronze I Megiddo," *AJA* 118 (April 2014): 285–305. [4] Matthew J. Adams et al., "The Rise of a Complex Society: New Evidence from Tel Megiddo East in the Late Fourth Millennium," *NEA* 77.1 (2014): 32–43.

scorched by the intense heat. So they blasphemed the name of God, who has the power[A] over these plagues, and they did not repent and give him glory.

THE FIFTH BOWL

10 The fifth[B] poured out his bowl on the throne of the beast, and its kingdom was plunged into darkness. People[C] gnawed their tongues because of their pain 11 and blasphemed the God of heaven because of their pains and their sores, but they did not repent of their works.

THE SIXTH BOWL

12 The sixth[B] poured out his bowl on the great river Euphrates, and its water was dried up to prepare the way for the kings from the east. 13 Then I saw three unclean spirits like frogs coming from the dragon's mouth, from the beast's mouth, and from the mouth of the false prophet. 14 For they are demonic spirits performing signs, who travel to the kings of the whole world to assemble them for the battle on the great day of God, the Almighty. 15 "Look, I am coming like a thief. Blessed is the one who is alert and remains clothed[D] so that he may not go around naked and people see his shame." 16 So they assembled the kings at the place called in Hebrew, Armageddon.[E]

THE SEVENTH BOWL

17 Then the seventh[B] poured out his bowl into the air,[F] and a loud voice came out of the temple[G] from the throne, saying, "It is done!" 18 There were flashes of lightning, rumblings, and peals of thunder. And a severe earthquake occurred like no other since people have been on the earth, so great was the quake. 19 The great city split into three parts, and the cities of the nations[H] fell. Babylon the Great was remembered in God's presence; he gave her the cup filled with the wine of his fierce anger. 20 Every island fled, and the mountains disappeared. 21 Enormous hailstones, each weighing about a hundred pounds,[I] fell from the sky on people, and they blasphemed God for the plague of hail because that plague was extremely severe.

THE WOMAN AND THE SCARLET BEAST

17 Then one of the seven angels who had the seven bowls came and spoke with me: "Come, I will show you the judgment of the notorious prostitute[J] who is seated on many[K] waters. 2 The kings of the earth committed sexual immorality with her, and those who live on the earth became drunk on the wine of her sexual immorality." 3 Then he carried me away in the Spirit[L] to a wilderness.

I saw a woman sitting on a scarlet beast that was covered[M] with blasphemous names and had seven heads and ten horns. 4 The woman was dressed in purple and scarlet, adorned with gold, jewels, and pearls. She had a golden cup in her hand filled with everything detestable and with the impurities of her[N] prostitution. 5 On her forehead was written a name, a mystery: BABYLON THE GREAT, THE MOTHER OF PROSTITUTES AND OF THE DETESTABLE THINGS OF THE EARTH. 6 Then I saw that the woman was drunk with the blood of the saints and with the blood of the witnesses to Jesus. When I saw her, I was greatly astonished.

THE MEANING OF THE WOMAN AND OF THE BEAST

7 Then the angel said to me, "Why are you astonished? I will explain to you the mystery of the woman and of the beast, with the seven heads and the ten horns, that carries her. 8 The beast that you saw was, and is not, and is about to come up from the abyss and go to destruction. Those who live on the earth whose names have not been written in the book of life from the foundation of the world will be astonished when they see the beast that was, and is not, and is to come. 9 This calls for a mind that has wisdom.[O]

"The seven heads are seven mountains on which the woman is seated. They are also seven kings: 10 Five have fallen, one is, the other has not yet come, and when he comes, he must remain for only a little while. 11 The beast that was and is not, is itself an eighth king, but it belongs to the seven and is going to destruction. 12 The ten horns you saw are ten kings who have not yet received a kingdom, but they will receive authority as kings with the beast for one hour. 13 These have one purpose, and they give their power and authority to the beast. 14 These will make war against the Lamb, but the Lamb will conquer them because he is Lord of lords and King of kings. Those with him are called, chosen, and faithful."

15 He also said to me, "The waters you saw, where the prostitute was seated, are peoples, multitudes, nations, and languages. 16 The ten horns you saw, and the beast, will hate the prostitute. They will make her desolate and naked, devour her flesh, and burn her up with fire. 17 For God has put it into their hearts to carry out his plan by having one purpose and to give their kingdom[P] to the beast until the words of God are fulfilled. 18 And the woman you saw is the great city that has royal power over the kings of the earth."

[A] **16:9** Or *authority* [B] **16:10,12,17** Other mss add *angel* [C] **16:10** Lit *They* [D] **16:15** Or *and guards his clothes* [E] **16:16** Some mss read *Armagedon*; other mss read *Harmegedon*; other mss read *Mageddon*; other mss read *Magedon* [F] **16:17** Or *bowl on the air* [G] **16:17** Other mss add *of heaven* [H] **16:19** Or *the Gentile cities* [I] **16:21** Lit *about a talent*; talents varied in weight upwards from 75 pounds [J] **17:1** Traditionally translated *the great whore* [K] **17:1** Or *by many* [L] **17:3** Or *in spirit* [M] **17:3** Or *was filled* [N] **17:4** Other mss read *earth's* [O] **17:9** Or *Here is the mind of wisdom* [P] **17:17** Or *sovereignty*

THE FALL OF BABYLON THE GREAT

18 After this I saw another angel with great authority coming down from heaven, and the
earth was illuminated by his splendor. 2 He called out
in a mighty voice:

It has fallen,[A]
Babylon the Great has fallen!
She has become a home for demons,
a haunt for every unclean spirit,
a haunt for every unclean bird,
and a haunt[B] for every unclean
and despicable beast.[C]
3 For all the nations have drunk[D]
the wine of her sexual immorality,
which brings wrath.
The kings of the earth
have committed sexual immorality with her,
and the merchants of the earth
have grown wealthy from her sensuality
and excess.

4 Then I heard another voice from heaven:

Come out of her, my people,
so that you will not share in her sins
or receive any of her plagues.
5 For her sins are piled up[E] to heaven,
and God has remembered her crimes.
6 Pay her back the way she also paid,
and double it according to her works.
In the cup in which she mixed,
mix a double portion for her.
7 As much as she glorified herself and indulged
her sensual and excessive ways,
give her that much torment and grief.
For she says in her heart,
"I sit as a queen;
I am not a widow,
and I will never see grief."
8 For this reason her plagues will come in just
one day —
death and grief and famine.
She will be burned up with fire,
because the Lord God who judges her
is mighty.

THE WORLD MOURNS BABYLON'S FALL

9 The kings of the earth who have committed sexual
immorality and shared her sensual and excessive

[A] **18:2** Other mss omit *It has fallen* [B] **18:2** Or *prison* [C] **18:2** Other mss omit the words *and a haunt for every unclean beast*. The words *and despicable* then refer to the *bird* of the previous line.
[D] **18:3** Some mss read *collapsed*; other mss read *fallen* [E] **18:5** Or *sins have reached up*

Ruins of the stables at Megiddo, which date to the ninth century BC.

ways will weep and mourn over her when they see
the smoke from her burning. 10 They will stand far
off in fear of her torment, saying,

Woe, woe, the great city,
Babylon, the mighty city!
For in a single hour
your judgment has come.

11 The merchants of the earth will weep and mourn
over her, because no one buys their cargo any longer
— 12 cargo of gold, silver, jewels, and pearls; fine lin-
en, purple, silk, and scarlet; all kinds of fragrant wood
products; objects of ivory; objects of expensive wood,
brass,[A] iron, and marble; 13 cinnamon, spice,[B] incense,
myrrh,[C] and frankincense; wine, olive oil, fine flour,
and grain; cattle and sheep; horses and carriages; and
slaves — human lives.

14 The fruit you craved has left you.
All your splendid and glamorous things
are gone;
they will never find them again.

15 The merchants of these things, who became rich
from her, will stand far off in fear of her torment,
weeping and mourning, 16 saying,

Woe, woe, the great city,
dressed in fine linen, purple, and scarlet,
adorned with gold, jewels, and pearls;
17 for in a single hour
such fabulous wealth was destroyed!

And every shipmaster, seafarer, the sailors, and
all who do business by sea, stood far off 18 as they
watched the smoke from her burning and kept crying out, "Who was like the great city?" 19 They threw
dust on their heads and kept crying out, weeping,
and mourning,

Woe, woe, the great city,
where all those who have ships on the sea
became rich from her wealth;
for in a single hour she was destroyed.
20 Rejoice over her, heaven,
and you saints, apostles, and prophets,
because God has pronounced on her the
judgment she passed on you!

THE FINALITY OF BABYLON'S FALL

21 Then a mighty angel picked up a stone like a large
millstone and threw it into the sea, saying,

In this way, Babylon the great city
will be thrown down violently
and never be found again.
22 The sound of harpists, musicians,
flutists, and trumpeters
will never be heard in you again;
no craftsman of any trade
will ever be found in you again;
the sound of a mill
will never be heard in you again;
23 the light of a lamp
will never shine in you again;
and the voice of a groom and bride
will never be heard in you again.
All this will happen
because your merchants
were the nobility of the earth,
because all the nations were deceived
by your sorcery.
24 In her was found the blood of prophets
and saints,
and of all those slaughtered on the earth.

CELEBRATION IN HEAVEN

19 After this I heard something like the loud voice
of a vast multitude in heaven, saying,

Hallelujah!
Salvation, glory, and power belong to our God,
2 because his judgments are true[D]
and righteous,
because he has judged
the notorious prostitute
who corrupted the earth
with her sexual immorality;
and he has avenged the blood of his servants
that was on her hands.

3 A second time they said,

Hallelujah!
Her smoke ascends forever and ever!

4 Then the twenty-four elders and the four living creatures fell down and worshiped God, who is seated on
the throne, saying,

Amen! Hallelujah!

5 A voice came from the throne, saying,

Praise our God,
all his servants, and the ones who fear him,
both small and great!

6 Then I heard something like the voice of a vast multitude, like the sound of cascading waters, and like
the rumbling of loud thunder, saying,

Hallelujah, because our Lord God,
the Almighty,
reigns!
7 Let us be glad, rejoice, and give him glory,
because the marriage of the Lamb has come,
and his bride has prepared herself.
8 She was given fine linen to wear, bright
and pure.

[A] **18:12** Or *bronze*, or *copper* [B] **18:13** Other mss omit *spice* [C] **18:13** Or *perfume* [D] **19:2** Valid; Jn 8:16; 19:35

For the fine linen represents the righteous acts of the saints.

9 Then he[A] said to me, "Write: Blessed are those invited to the marriage feast of the Lamb!" He also said to me, "These words of God are true." 10 Then I fell at his feet to worship him, but he said to me, "Don't do that! I am a fellow servant with you and your brothers and sisters who hold firmly to the testimony of Jesus. Worship God, because the testimony of Jesus is the spirit[B] of prophecy."

THE RIDER ON A WHITE HORSE

11 Then I saw heaven opened, and there was a white horse. Its rider is called Faithful and True, and with justice he judges and makes war. 12 His eyes were like a fiery flame, and many crowns[C] were on his head. He had a name written that no one knows except himself. 13 He wore a robe dipped in blood, and his name is called the Word of God. 14 The armies that were in heaven followed him on white horses, wearing pure white linen. 15 A sharp[D] sword came from his mouth, so that he might strike the nations with it. He will rule[E] them with an iron rod. He will also trample the winepress of the fierce anger of God, the Almighty. 16 And he has a name written on his robe and on his thigh: KING OF KINGS AND LORD OF LORDS.

THE BEAST AND ITS ARMIES DEFEATED

17 Then I saw an angel standing in the sun, and he called out in a loud voice, saying to all the birds flying high overhead, "Come, gather together for the great supper of God, 18 so that you may eat the flesh of kings, the flesh of military commanders, the flesh of the mighty, the flesh of horses and of their riders, and the flesh of everyone, both free and slave, small and great."

19 Then I saw the beast, the kings of the earth, and their armies gathered together to wage war against the rider on the horse and against his army. 20 But the beast was taken prisoner, and along with it the false prophet, who had performed the signs in its presence. He deceived those who accepted the mark of the beast and those who worshiped its image with these signs. Both of them were thrown alive into the lake of fire that burns with sulfur. 21 The rest were killed with the sword that came from the mouth of the rider on the horse, and all the birds ate their fill of their flesh.

SATAN BOUND

20 Then I saw an angel coming down from heaven holding the key to the abyss and a great chain in his hand. 2 He seized the dragon, that ancient serpent who is the devil and Satan,[F] and bound him for a thousand years. 3 He threw him into the abyss, closed it, and put a seal on it so that he would no longer deceive the nations until the thousand years were completed. After that, he must be released for a short time.

THE SAINTS REIGN WITH CHRIST

4 Then I saw thrones, and people seated on them who were given authority to judge. I also saw the souls of those who had been beheaded because of their testimony about Jesus and because of the word of God, who had not worshiped the beast or his image, and who had not accepted the mark on their foreheads or their hands. They came to life and reigned with Christ for a thousand years. 5 The rest of the dead did not come to life until the thousand years were completed.

This is the first resurrection. 6 Blessed and holy is the one who shares in the first resurrection! The second death has no power[G] over them, but they will be priests of God and of Christ, and they will reign with him for a thousand years.

SATANIC REBELLION CRUSHED

7 When the thousand years are completed, Satan will be released from his prison 8 and will go out to deceive the nations at the four corners of the earth, Gog and Magog, to gather them for battle. Their number is like the sand of the sea. 9 They came up across the breadth of the earth and surrounded the encampment of the saints, the beloved city. Then fire came down from heaven[H] and consumed them. 10 The devil who deceived them was thrown into the lake of fire and sulfur where the beast and the false prophet are, and they will be tormented day and night forever and ever.

THE GREAT WHITE THRONE JUDGMENT

11 Then I saw a great white throne and one seated on it. Earth and heaven fled from his presence, and no place was found for them. 12 I also saw the dead, the great and the small, standing before the throne, and books were opened. Another book was opened, which is the book of life, and the dead were judged according to their works by what was written in the books. 13 Then the sea gave up the dead that were in it, and death and Hades gave up the dead that were in them; each one was judged according to their works. 14 Death and Hades were thrown into the lake of fire. This is the second death, the lake of fire. 15 And anyone whose name was not found written in the book of life was thrown into the lake of fire.

[A] **19:9** Probably an angel; Rv 17:1; 22:8–9 [B] **19:10** Or *the Spirit* [C] **19:12** Or *diadems* [D] **19:15** Other mss add *double-edged* [E] **19:15** Or *shepherd* [F] **20:2** Other mss add *who deceives the whole world* [G] **20:6** Or *authority* [H] **20:9** Other mss add *from God*

THE NEW CREATION

21 Then I saw a new heaven and a new earth; for the first heaven and the first earth had passed away, and the sea was no more. 2 I also saw the holy city, the new Jerusalem, coming down out of heaven from God, prepared like a bride adorned for her husband.

3 Then I heard a loud voice from the throne:[A] Look, God's dwelling[B] is with humanity, and he will live with them. They will be his peoples,[C] and God himself will be with them and will be their God.[D] 4 He will wipe away every tear from their eyes. Death will be no more; grief, crying, and pain will be no more, because the previous things[E] have passed away.

5 Then the one seated on the throne said, "Look, I am making everything new." He also said, "Write, because these words[F] are faithful and true." 6 Then he said to me, "It is done! I am the Alpha and the Omega, the beginning and the end. I will freely give to the thirsty from the spring of the water of life. 7 The one who conquers will inherit these things, and I will be his God, and he will be my son. 8 But the cowards, faithless,[G] detestable, murderers, sexually immoral, sorcerers, idolaters, and all liars — their share will be in the lake that burns with fire and sulfur, which is the second death."

THE NEW JERUSALEM

9 Then one of the seven angels, who had held the seven bowls filled with the seven last plagues, came and spoke with me: "Come, I will show you the bride, the wife of the Lamb." 10 He then carried me away in the Spirit[H] to a great, high mountain and showed me the holy city, Jerusalem, coming down out of heaven from God, 11 arrayed with God's glory. Her radiance was like a precious jewel, like a jasper stone, clear as crystal. 12 The city had a massive high wall, with twelve gates. Twelve angels were at the gates; the names of the twelve tribes of Israel's sons were inscribed on the gates. 13 There were three gates on the east, three gates on the north, three gates on the south, and three gates on the west. 14 The city wall had twelve foundations, and the twelve names of the twelve apostles of the Lamb were on the foundations.

15 The one who spoke with me had a golden measuring rod to measure the city, its gates, and its wall. 16 The city is laid out in a square; its length and width are the same. He measured the city with the rod

[A] **21:3** Other mss read *from heaven* [B] **21:3** Or *tent*, or *tabernacle* [C] **21:3** Other mss read *people* [D] **21:3** Other mss omit *and will be their God* [E] **21:4** Or *the first things* [F] **21:5** Other mss add *of God* [G] **21:8** Other mss add *the sinful,* [H] **21:10** Or *in spirit*

Frescoes decorate the ceiling at the entrance of the Monastery of St. John on Patmos.

at 12,000 *stadia*.[A] Its length, width, and height are equal. 17 Then he measured its wall, 144 cubits according to human measurement, which the angel used. 18 The building material of its wall was jasper, and the city was pure gold clear as glass. 19 The foundations of the city wall were adorned with every kind of jewel: the first foundation is jasper, the second sapphire, the third chalcedony, the fourth emerald, 20 the fifth sardonyx, the sixth carnelian, the seventh chrysolite, the eighth beryl, the ninth topaz, the tenth chrysoprase, the eleventh jacinth, the twelfth amethyst. 21 The twelve gates are twelve pearls; each individual gate was made of a single pearl. The main street[B] of the city was pure gold, transparent as glass.

22 I did not see a temple in it, because the Lord God the Almighty and the Lamb are its temple. 23 The city does not need the sun or the moon to shine on it, because the glory of God illuminates it, and its lamp is the Lamb. 24 The nations will walk by its light, and the kings of the earth will bring their glory into it.[C] 25 Its gates will never close by day because it will never be night there. 26 They will bring the glory and honor of the nations into it.[D] 27 Nothing unclean will ever enter it, nor anyone who does what is detestable or false, but only those written in the Lamb's book of life.

THE SOURCE OF LIFE

22 Then he showed me the river[E] of the water of life, clear as crystal, flowing from the throne of God and of the Lamb 2 down the middle of the city's main street. The tree of life was on each side of the river, bearing twelve kinds of fruit, producing its fruit every month. The leaves of the tree are for healing the nations, 3 and there will no longer be any curse. The throne of God and of the Lamb will be in the city, and his servants will worship him. 4 They will see his face, and his name will be on their foreheads. 5 Night will be no more; people will not need the light of a lamp or the light of the sun, because the Lord God will give them light, and they will reign forever and ever.

THE TIME IS NEAR

6 Then he said to me, "These words are faithful[F] and true. The Lord, the God of the spirits of the prophets,[G] has sent his angel to show his servants what must soon take place."

7 "Look, I am coming soon! Blessed is the one who keeps the words of the prophecy of this book."

8 I, John, am the one who heard and saw these things. When I heard and saw them, I fell down to worship at the feet of the angel who had shown them to me. 9 But he said to me, "Don't do that! I am a fellow servant with you, your brothers the prophets, and those who keep the words of this book. Worship God!"

Founded by Greek Orthodox believers; St. John's Monastery on Patmos. The bell tower's interior (shown) has marble floors, gold-covered furniture and fixtures, and fresco panels above.

10 Then he said to me, "Don't seal up the words of the prophecy of this book, because the time is near. 11 Let the unrighteous go on in unrighteousness; let the filthy still be filthy; let the righteous go on in righteousness; let the holy still be holy."

12 "Look, I am coming soon, and my reward is with me to repay each person according to his work. 13 I am the Alpha and the Omega, the first and the last, the beginning and the end.

14 "Blessed are those who wash their robes,[H] so that they may have the right to the tree of life and may enter the city by the gates. 15 Outside are the dogs, the sorcerers, the sexually immoral, the murderers, the idolaters, and everyone who loves and practices falsehood.

[A] **21:16** A *stadion* (sg) = about 600 feet; 12,000 *stadia* = 1,400 miles. [B] **21:21** Or *The public square* [C] **21:24** Other mss read *will bring to him the nations' glory and honor* [D] **21:26** Other mss add *in order that they might go in* [E] **22:1** Other mss read *pure river* [F] **22:6** Or *trustworthy* [G] **22:6** Other mss read *God of the holy prophets* [H] **22:14** Other mss read *who keep his commands*

[16] "I, Jesus, have sent my angel to attest these things
to you for the churches. I am the Root and descendant
of David, the bright morning star."

[17] Both the Spirit and the bride say, "Come!" Let
anyone who hears, say, "Come!" Let the one who is
thirsty come. Let the one who desires take the water
of life freely.

[18] I testify to everyone who hears the words of the
prophecy of this book: If anyone adds to them, God
will add to him the plagues that are written in this
book. [19] And if anyone takes away from the words
of the book of this prophecy, God will take away his
share of the tree of life and the holy city, which are
written about in this book.

[20] He who testifies about these things says, "Yes, I
am coming soon."

Amen! Come, Lord Jesus!

[21] The grace of the Lord Jesus[A] be with everyone.[B]
Amen.[C]

[A] **22:21** Other mss add *Christ* [B] **22:21** Other mss read *with all the saints* [C] **22:21** Other mss omit *Amen.*

TABLE OF WEIGHTS AND MEASURES

WEIGHTS

Gerah	Hebrew	1/20 shekel	1/50 ounce	.6 gram	gerah; oboli
Bekah	Hebrew	1/2 shekel or 10 gerahs	1/5 ounce	5.7 grams	bekah; half a shekel; quarter ounce; fifty cents
Pim	Hebrew	2/3 shekel	1/3 ounce	7.6 grams	2/3 of a shekel; quarter
Shekel	Hebrew	2 bekahs	2/5 ounce	11.5 grams	shekel; piece; dollar; fifty dollars
Litra (pound)	Greco-Roman	30 shekels	12 ounces	.4 kilogram	pound; pounds
Mina	Hebrew/Greek	50 shekels	1 1/4 pounds	.6 kilogram	mina; pound
Talent	Hebrew/Greek	3,000 shekels or 60 minas	75 pounds/88 pounds	34 kilograms/40 kilograms	talent/talents; 100 pounds

LENGTH

Handbreadth	Hebrew	1/6 cubit or 1/3 span	3 inches	8 centimeters	handbreadth; three inches; four inches
Span	Hebrew	1/2 cubit or 3 handbreadths	9 inches	23 centimeters	span
Cubit/Pechys	Hebrew/Greek	2 spans	18 inches	.5 meter	cubit/cubits; yard; half a yard; foot
Fathom	Greco-Roman	4 cubits	2 yards	2 meters	fathom; six feet
Kalamos	Greco-Roman	6 cubits	3 yards	3 meters	rod; reed; measuring rod
Stadion	Greco-Roman	1/8 milion or 400 cubits	1/8 mile	185 meters	miles; furlongs; race
Milion	Greco-Roman	8 stadia	1,620 yards	1.5 kilometers	mile

DRY MEASURE

Xestes	Greco-Roman	1/2 cab	1 1/6 pints	.5 liter	pots; pitchers; kettles; copper pots; copper bowls; vessels of bronze
Cab	Hebrew	1/18 ephah	1 quart	1 liter	cab; kab
Choinix	Greco-Roman	1/18 ephah	1 quart	1 liter	measure; quart
Omer	Hebrew	1/10 ephah	2 quarts	2 liters	omer; tenth of a deal; tenth of an ephah; six pints
Seah/Saton	Hebrew/Greek	1/3 ephah	7 quarts	7.3 liters	measures; pecks; large amounts
Modios	Greco-Roman	4 omers	1 peck or 1/4 bushel	9 liters	bushel; bowl; peck
Ephah [Bath]	Hebrew	10 omers	3/5 bushel	22 liters	bushel; peck; deal; part; measure; six pints; seven pints
Lethek	Hebrew	5 ephahs	3 bushels	110 liters	half homer; half sack
Kor [Homer]/ Koros	Hebrew/Greek	10 ephahs	6 bushels or 200 quarts	220 liters/525 liters	cor; homer; sack; measures; bushels

LIQUID MEASURE

Log	Hebrew	1/72 bath	1/3 quart	.3 liter	log; pint; cotulus
Xestes	Greco-Roman	1/8 hin	1 1/6 pints	.5 liter	pots; pitchers; kettles; copper bowls; vessels of bronze
Hin	Hebrew	1/6 bath	1 gallon or 4 quarts	4 liters	hin; pints
Bath/Batos	Hebrew/Greek	1 ephah	6 gallons	22 liters	gallon(s); barrels; liquid measures
Metretes	Greco-Roman	10 hins	10 gallons	39 liters	firkins; gallons

CONCORDANCE

A

AARON
Levite, brother of Moses (Ex 4:14; 6:16-20). Spokesman for Moses (4:14-16; 7:1-2). Consecrated (Ex 29) and ordained (Lv 8) as priest (Ex 28:1; 1Ch 6:49; Heb 5:1-4; 7). Made golden calf (Ex 32). Died outside the promised land (Nm 20:1-12,22-29; 33:38-39).

ABADDON
your faithfulness in A? .... Ps 88:11
Sheol and A lie open before the LORD ... Pr 15:11
his name in Hebrew is A, ... Rv 9:11

ABANDON
I will a them and hide my face .... Dt 31:17
I will not leave you or a you .... Jos 1:5
certainly not a the LORD .... Jos 24:16
the LORD has **a-ed** us .... Jdg 6:13
LORD will not a his people, ... 1Sm 12:22
but if you a him, he will a you 2Ch 15:2
For you will not a me to Sheol; .... Ps 16:10
my God, why have you **a-ed** me? .... Ps 22:1
or a his heritage, ... Ps 94:14
Don't a wisdom, ... Pr 4:6
My God, why have you **a-ed** me? .... Mt 27:46
will never leave you or a you. .... Heb 13:5
a-ed the love you had at first. .... Rv 2:4

ABBA
He said, "*A*, Father! .... Mk 14:36
we cry out, "*A*, Father!" .... Rm 8:15
crying, "*A*, Father!" .... Gl 4:6

ABEL
Shepherd, second son of Adam; brought acceptable sacrifice; was murdered (Gn 4:2-8; Mt 23:35; Heb 11:4).

ABIGAIL
Intelligent wife of the fool Nabal; pled for his life; married David after Nabal died (1Sm 25).

ABIJAH
1. Tragic son of King Jeroboam of Israel (1Kg 14:1,13).
2. Son of Rehoboam, King of Judah (2Ch 13). Also known as Abijam (1Kg 15:1-8).

ABILITY
depending on each one's a. .... Mt 25:15
according to their a. 2Co 8:3

ABIMELECH
1. King of Gerar at the time of Abraham (Gn 20:1-18; 21:22-32).
2. King of Gerar at the time of Isaac (Gn 26:1-31).
3. Son of Gideon, tried to become king of Shechem (Jdg 9).

ABLE
count the stars, if you are a. .... Gn 15:5
Moses chose a men .... Ex 18:25
God is a to raise up children .... Mt 3:9
Are you a to drink the cup .... Mt 20:22
the Lord is a to make him stand. .... Rm 14:4
tempted beyond what you are a, ... 1Co 10:13
Now to him who is a to do .... Eph 3:20
to him who is a to protect you .... Jd 24
a to open the scroll .... Rv 5:3

ABNER
Saul's cousin and commander of his army (1Sm 14:50). At first supported Saul's son Ish-bosheth (2Sm 2:8-9) but defected to David (3:6-21). Killed by Joab and mourned by David (3:22-39).

ABOMINATION
and set up the a of desolation. .... Dn 11:31
see the a of desolation, ... Mt 24:15

ABOVE
the LORD is God in heaven a .... Dt 4:39
the name that is a every name, ... Php 2:9
Set your minds on things a, ... Col 3:2

ABRAHAM
Born Abram son of Terah in Ur, Mesopotamia; married Sarai, then lived in Haran (Gn 11:31; Ac 7:2-4). Called to Canaan and given a promise of progeny and prosperity (Gn 12:1-3). Lied to Pharaoh in Egypt about Sarai (12:10-20). Separated from his nephew Lot (Gn 13). Rescued Lot (14:1-16) and was blessed by Melchizedek (14:17-20; Heb 7:1-10). God declared him righteous because of his faith (Gn 15:6; Rm 4:3,20-22; Gl 3:6; Jms 2:23).

Fathered Ishmael by Hagar (Gn 16). Name changed (17:5); circumcised (17:9-27; Rm 4:9-12). Visited by angels (Gn 18); promised a son with Sarah (18:9-14; cp. 17:15-19). Lied to Abimelech in Gerar about Sarah (Gn 20). Fathered Isaac (21:1-7). Sent Hagar away at Sarah's request (21:8-14). Tested by God concerning Isaac (Gn 22; Heb 11:17-19; Jms 2:21-24). Buried Sarah at Machpelah (Gn 23). Sent servant to find wife for Isaac (24:1-9). Died and was buried with Sarah (25:7-11).

God promised a covenant with Abraham, then made it and confirmed it (Gn 12:1-3; 13:14-17; 15; 17; 22:15-18). It was the basis of future blessings for many people (Ex 2:24; Lv 26:42; 2Kg 13:23; Ps 105:6-11; Ac 3:25).

ABSALOM
Son of David by Maacah (2Sm 3:3). Known for his looks and hair (14:25-26). Killed Amnon for raping Tamar and was banished by David (2Sm 13). Reinstated by David at Joab's insistence (2Sm 14). Rebelled, ousted David (2Sm 15–17). Killed by Joab (18:9-15) despite David's warning (18:5). Greatly mourned by David (18:33–19:4).

ABSENT
a in the body, I am present in spirit, ... 1Co 5:3
I may be a in body, but .... Col 2:5

ABSTAIN
he is to a from wine and beer. .... Nm 6:3
a from food offered to idols, ... Ac 15:29
a from sinful desires 1Pt 2:11

ABUNDANCE
Seven years of great a .... Gn 41:29
bearing spices, gold in great a, ... 1Kg 10:2
have life and have it in a. .... Jn 10:10

ABUNDANTLY
He poured out his Spirit on us a .... Ti 3:6

ABUSED
a her all night .... Jdg 19:25

ABYSS
not to banish them to the a. .... Lk 8:31
Who will go down into the a? .... Rm 10:7

ACCEPT
Should we a only good
from God. .... Jb 2:10
the LORD **a-ed** Job's prayer. .... Jb 42:9
My son, if you a my words .... Pr 2:1
A my instruction .... Pr 8:10
Not everyone can a this
saying, ... Mt 19:11

ACCEPTABLE
the meditation of my heart be a .... Ps 19:14
See, now is the a time; 2Co 6:2
spiritual sacrifices a to God 1Pt 2:5

ACCEPTANCE
what will their a mean. .... Rm 11:15
and deserving of full a: 1Tm 1:15

ACCESS
a through him by faith
into ... grace .... Rm 5:2
we both have a in one Spirit .... Eph 2:18

ACCOMPANY
signs will a those who believe: .... Mk 16:17

ACCOMPLISH
it will a what I please .... Is 55:11
I watch over my word to a it." .... Jr 1:12

ACCORDING
be done for you a to your faith! .... Mt 9:29
who do not walk a to the flesh .... Rm 8:4

ask anything a to his will, 1Jn 5:14
were judged a to their works Rv 20:12

ACCOUNT
a for every careless word Mt 12:36

ACCUSATION
Who can bring an a Rm 8:33
an a against an elder 1Tm 5:19

ACCUSE
He will not always a us Ps 103:9
standing at his right side to a Zch 3:1
in order to a him Mt 12:10; Mk 3:2
They began to a him, Lk 23:2
Your **a-r** is Moses, Jn 5:45
so that when you are **a-d**, 1Pt 3:16

ACHAIA
he wanted to cross over to A, Ac 18:27

ACHAN
Sinned at Jericho; stoned (Jos 7; 1Ch 2:7).

ACHISH
King of Gath before whom David feigned madness (1Sm 21:10-15). Later, he favored David (1Sm 27–29).

ACKNOWLEDGE
Then I **a-d** my sin to you Ps 32:5
I will also a him before my Father in heaven Mt 10:32

ACQUIT
I know you will not a me Jb 9:28

ACT (N)
an outstretched arm and great **a-s** Ex 6:6
deeds and mighty **a-s** like yours? Dt 3:24
this woman was caught in the a Jn 8:4

ACT (V)
trust in him, and he will a, Ps 37:5
I **a-ed** for the sake of my name, Ezk 20:9
these words of mine and **a-s** Mt 7:24
a-ed out of ignorance in unbelief. 1Tm 1:13

ACTION
a-s are weighed by him. 1Sm 2:3
with your minds ready for a, 1Pt 1:13
word or speech, but in a 1Jn 3:18

ACTIVE
You see that faith was a Jms 2:22

ADAM
First man. Created by God (Gn 1:26-27; 2:7). Named animals (2:18-20). Given Eve (2:21-25). Failed to obey and was evicted (1:15-17; 3:6-24; Rm 5:14; 1Co 15:22). Died at 930 years (Gn 5:3-5).

ADD
no **a-ing** to it or taking from it Ec 3:14
Can any of you a one moment Mt 6:27
three thousand people were **a-ed** Ac 2:41

ADMINISTRATION
the a of the mystery Eph 3:9

ADMONISHING
teaching and a one another Col 3:16

ADONIJAH
Son of David (2Sm 3:4). Conspired for the throne and was executed by Solomon (1Kg 1–2).

ADOPTION
you received the Spirit of a, Rm 8:15
to them belong the a, Rm 9:4
that we might receive a as sons Gl 4:5

ADORN
A yourself with majesty Jb 40:10
as a bride **a-s** herself Is 61:10
it was **a-ed** with beautiful stones Lk 21:5
a the teaching of God our Savior Ti 2:10
also **a-ed** themselves in this way, 1Pt 3:5
a-ed with gold, jewels, and pearls Rv 17:4
a bride **a-ed** for her husband. Rv 21:2

ADORNMENT
life for you and a for your neck Pr 3:22

ADULTERER
both the a and the adulteress Lv 20:10
a-'s eye watches for twilight, Jb 24:15
you associate with **a-s** Ps 50:18
the land is full of **a-s**; Jr 23:10
idolaters, **a-s**, male who have 1Co 6:9
judge sexually immoral and **a-s**, Heb 13:4

ADULTERESS
both the adulterer and the a Lv 20:10
This is the way of an a: she eats Pr 30:20
they are **a-es** Ezk 23:45

ADULTEROUS
You a wife, Ezk 16:32
An evil and a generation Mt 12:39; 16:4
this a and sinful generation, Mk 8:38
You a people! Don't you know Jms 4:4

ADULTERY
Do not commit a. Ex 20:14; Dt 5:18
If a man commits a Lv 20:10
already committed a with her Mt 5:28
marries another, commits a. Mt 19:9
do not commit a; do not steal; Mt 19:18
brought a woman caught in a, Jn 8:3
who said, Do not commit a, also Jms 2:11

ADVANCE (N)
Scripture saw in a that God Gl 3:8

ADVANCE (V)
has actually **a-d** the gospel, Php 1:12

ADVANTAGE
the a of wisdom Ec 10:10
So what a does the Jew have? Rm 3:1

ADVERSARY
I will take vengeance on my **a-ies** Dt 32:41
You exalt me above my **a-ies**; Ps 18:48
give the a no opportunity 1Tm 5:14
Your a the devil is prowling 1Pt 5:8

ADVERSITY
life and prosperity, death and a Dt 30:15
only good from God and not a? Jb 2:10
both a and good come from Lm 3:38

ADVICE
rejected the elders' a 2Ch 10:13
walk in the a of the wicked Ps 1:1
should have followed my a Ac 27:21

ADVISERS
with many a they succeed Pr 15:22

ADVOCATE
we have an a with the Father 1Jn 2:1

AFFECTION
not withholding our a from you 2Co 6:12
with the a of Christ Jesus. Php 1:8

AFFLICT
the Almighty has **a-ed** me? Ru 1:20
He was oppressed and **a-ed**, Is 53:7
you who are **a-ed**, along with us 2Th 1:7
destitute, **a-ed**, and mistreated. Heb 11:37

AFFLICTION
fruitful in the land of my a Gn 41:52
LORD saw that the a of Israel 2Kg 14:26
Consider my a and trouble, Ps 25:18
He does not enjoy bringing a Lm 3:33
she was healed of her a. Mk 5:29
a-s are waiting for me Ac 20:23
a produces endurance, Rm 5:3
momentary light a is producing 2Co 4:17

AFRAID
I was a because I was naked, Gn 3:10
not be a, Abram. I am your shield Gn 15:1
he was a to look at God Ex 3:6
Do not be a, alarmed, or terrified Dt 20:3
Do not be a or discouraged, Jos 1:9
I will not be a of the thousands Ps 3:6
of whom should I be a? Ps 27:1
When I am a, I will trust in you Ps 56:3
She is not a for her household Pr 31:21
I will trust him and not be a, Is 12:2
Do not be a of anyone, for I will be Jr 1:8
don't be a to take Mary Mt 1:20

Jesus told them, "Do not be a...........Mt 28:10
Don't be a. Only believe..................Mk 5:36
they were a of him,.......................Mk 11:18
they were a of the crowd.........Mk 11:32; 12:12
Do not be a, Mary,.........................Lk 1:30
they were a of the people...............Lk 22:2
It is I. Don't be a!..........................Jn 6:20
they were a of the Jews,.................Jn 9:22
I will not be a. What can man do........Heb 13:6

AGABUS

Early church prophet (Ac 11:28; 21:10).

AGAG

Amalekite king spared by Saul, executed by Samuel (1Sm 15).

AGAINST

who is not with me is a me,.............Mt 12:30
whoever is not a us is for us............Mk 9:40
If God is for us, who is a us?............Rm 8:31

AGE

already existed in the a-s before.........Ec 1:10
the worries of this a...........Mt 13:22; Mk 4:19

AGONY

a like a woman in labor..................Jr 22:23
I am in a in this flame!....................Lk 16:24

AGREE

If two of you on earth a.................Mt 18:19
the testimonies did not a................Mk 14:56
Why did you a to test the Spirit...........Ac 5:9
Saul a-d with putting him to death........Ac 8:1
I a with the law that it is good...........Rm 7:16
does not a with the sound teaching.....1Tm 6:3

AGREEMENT

making a binding a in writing.........Neh 9:38
we have an a with Sheol;..................Is 28:15
a does Christ have with Belial?..........2Co 6:15
these three are in a.........................1Jn 5:8

AGRIPPA

Herodian king who heard Paul's testimony (Ac 25–26).

AHAB

Son of Omri, king of Israel (1Kg 16:28–22:40). Married Jezebel and promoted baalism (16:31-33). Killed Naboth (21:1-14). Condemned by Elijah (18:18; 21:17-24) and other prophets (20:35-43; 22:19-28). Died in disguise in battle (22:29-40).

AHASUERUS

King of Persia, son of Darius and grandson of Cyrus. Greek name is Xerxes. Dismissed Vashti and married Esther (Est 1–2). Signed Haman's decree (Est 3) then was convinced by Esther to reverse it and hang Haman (Est 4–7) and allow the Jews to defend themselves (Est 8–9).

AHAZ

Idolatrous king of Judah (2Kg 16:2-4). Son of Jotham. Attacked by Aram and Israel (16:5-6; 2Ch 28:5-7). Refused Isaiah's advice and turned to Assyria for help (Is 7). Not buried among the kings (2Ch 28:27).

AHAZIAH

1. Son of Ahab; king of Israel (1Kg 22:40). Injured in a fall; condemned by Elijah for seeking Baal (2Kg 1:2-17).
2. Son of Jehoram; king of Judah (2Kg 8:25-27). Mortally wounded by Jehu while visiting King Joram of Israel (9:27).

AHEAD

Each creature went straight a.....Ezk 1:9; 10:22
sending my messenger a of you;.......Mt 11:10
I will go a of you to Galilee............Mt 26:32
which God prepared a of time..........Eph 2:10
reaching forward to what is a,.........Php 3:13

AHIJAH

1. Priest at the time of Saul (1Sm 14:3-4,18).
2. Prophet from Shiloh to Jeroboam (1Kg 4:3; 11:29-39).

AI

Bethel on the west and A on the.........Gn 12:8
they fled from the men of A..............Jos 7:4
Joshua burned A..........................Jos 8:28

AIJALON

moon, over the Valley of A..............Jos 10:12
A with its pasturelands,................Jos 21:24

AIMLESSLY

do not run like one who runs a.........1Co 9:26

AIR

box like one beating the a..............1Co 9:26
meet the Lord in the a...................1Th 4:17
poured out his bowl into the a,..........Rv 16:17

ALABASTER

an a jar..........................Mt 26:7; Mk 14:3

ALARM

sound the a on my holy mountain!.........Jl 2:1

ALARMED

and rumors of wars, don't be a;..........Mk 13:7

ALERT

be a, since you don't know.............Mt 24:42
Be a, stand firm in the faith,...........1Co 16:13
stay a with all perseverance...........Eph 6:18
prayer; stay a in it........................Col 4:2
Be sober-minded! Be a!.....................1Pt 5:8

ALEXANDER

Hymenaeus and A.........................1Tm 1:20
A the coppersmith.......................2Tm 4:14

ALIEN

Your offspring will be resident a.......Gn 15:13
"I have been a resident a"...................Ex 2:22
the land they lived in as a-s...............Ex 6:4
and resident a-s in Canaan,............Ps 105:12
no longer oppress the resident a,.........Jr 7:6

ALIENATED

are a from Christ;............................Gl 5:4
Once you were a and hostile.............Col 1:21

ALIVE

to keep them a with you..................Gn 6:19
when they heard that he was a.........Mk 16:11
he also presented himself a...............Ac 1:3
dead to sin and a to God..................Rm 6:11
in Christ all will be made a.............1Co 15:22
made us a with Christ.....................Eph 2:5
he made you a with him....................Col 2:13
We who are still a..........................1Th 4:17
made a by the Spirit,.......................1Pt 3:18
but look—I am a forever..................Rv 1:18

ALL

with a your heart, with a your soul, and with a your strength......................Dt 6:5
search for me with a your heart.........Jr 29:13
love the Lord ... with a your heart,.....Lk 10:27
a have sinned and fall short............Rm 3:23
He died to sin once for a.................Rm 6:10
We will not a fall asleep, but we will a be changed,.....................................1Co 15:51
the one who fills a things................Eph 1:23
I am able to do a things..................Php 4:13
A Scripture is inspired by God.........2Tm 3:16
but a to come to repentance..............2Pt 3:9

ALLEGIANCE

every tongue will swear a.................Is 45:23

ALLIANCE

Solomon made an a with Pharaoh.......1Kg 3:1
they will form an a,........................Dn 11:6

ALLOTMENT

Israel according to their tribal a-s:......Jos 12:7

ALLOW

will not a your faithful one to see.......Ps 16:10
A it for now,..................................Mt 3:15
a your holy one to see decay.............Ac 2:27
will not a you to be tempted...........1Co 10:13

ALMIGHTY

I am God A.....................................Gn 17:1
Isaac, and Jacob as God A,.................Ex 6:3
discover the limits of the A?..............Jb 11:7
dwells in the shadow of the A.............Ps 91:1
was, and who is coming, the A.............Rv 1:8
Holy, holy, holy, Lord God, the A,..........Rv 4:8
God, the A, reigns!..........................Rv 19:6

ALMOND

the a tree blossoms,.........................Ec 12:5

ALONE

not good for the man to be a............Gn 2:18
man does not live on bread a..............Dt 8:3
I a am left,...................................1Kg 19:10
Against you—you a—.........................Ps 51:4

the LORD a will be exalted ... Is 2:11
Man must not live on bread a ... Mt 4:4
to a remote place to be a. ... Mt 14:13
Who can forgive sins but God a? ... Mk 2:7
by works and not by faith a. ... Jms 2:24

ALPHA

the A and the Omega, ... Rv 1:8; 21:6; 22:13

ALREADY

Whatever is, has a been, and whatever will be, a is. ... Ec 3:15
has a committed adultery ... Mt 5:28
how I wish it were a set ablaze! ... Lk 12:49
does not believe is a judged, ... Jn 3:18
You are a clean. ... Jn 15:3
You are a full! You are a rich! ... 1Co 4:8
Not that I have a reached ... Php 3:12
it is a in the world now. ... 1Jn 4:3

ALTAR

Noah built an a to the LORD. ... Gn 8:20
Isaac and placed him on the a ... Gn 22:9
construct the a of acacia wood. ... Ex 27:1
an a for the burning of incense; ... Ex 30:1
tear down their a-s, ... Ex 34:13
take hold of the horns of the a. ... 1Kg 1:50
I will come to the a of God, ... Ps 43:4
leave your gift ... in front of the a. ... Mt 5:24
takes an oath by the a, ... Mt 23:18
We have an a from which. ... Heb 13:10
in offering Isaac ... on the a? ... Jms 2:21
I saw under the a the souls ... Rv 6:9

ALTOGETHER

reliable and a righteous. ... Ps 19:9
righteous and a trustworthy. ... Ps 119:138

ALWAYS

my sin is a before me. ... Ps 51:3
You a have the poor with you, ... Mt 26:11
I am with you a, ... Mt 28:20
Rejoice in the Lord a. ... Php 4:4
A be ready to give a defense ... 1Pt 3:15

AM *SEE* I AM

AMASA

David's nephew; commander of Absalom's army (2Sm 17:25). Reinstated by David (19:13). Killed by Joab (20:10).

AMAZED

a and asked, "What kind of man ... Mt 8:27
the crowds were a, ... Mt 9:33
he was a at their unbelief. ... Mk 6:6
they were astounded and a, ... Ac 2:7

AMAZIAH

Son of Joash; king of Judah. Defeated Edom but adopted their gods (2Ch 25:11-14). Rejected God's rebuke, challenged King Jehoash of Israel, and was defeated (26:15-24). Killed by a conspiracy (26:27).

AMBASSADOR

we are a-s for Christ, ... 2Co 5:20
For this I am an a in chains. ... Eph 6:20

AMBITION

bitter envy and selfish a ... Jms 3:14

AMBUSH

Set an a behind the city. ... Jos 8:2
set up an a around Gibeah. ... Jdg 20:29
Let's set an a and kill someone. ... Pr 1:11
forty of them lying in a, ... Ac 23:21

AMEN

all the people will reply, 'A!'. ... Dt 27:15
be the LORD forever. A and a. ... Ps 89:52
will the outsider say "A" ... 1Co 14:16
through him we also say "A" ... 2Co 1:20
The A, the faithful and true ... Rv 3:14
A! Come, Lord Jesus! ... Rv 22:20

AMNON

Oldest son of David (2Sm 3:2). Raped his sister Tamar; killed by Absalom (2Sm 13).

AMON

Son of Manasseh; king of Judah; killed by his servants (2Kg 21:18-26).

AMOS

Prophet against moral decay in Israel under Jeroboam II (Am 5:24).

ANANIAS

1. Lied about gift to the church at Jerusalem and died (Ac 5:1-6).
2. Disciple in Damascus who visited Paul (Ac 9:10-19).
3. High priest at Paul's arrest (Ac 23:1-5; 24:1).

ANCESTOR

from the day their a-s came out ... 2Kg 21:15
a clear conscience as my a-s did, ... 2Tm 1:3

ANCHOR

this hope as an a for our lives, ... Heb 6:19

ANCIENT

Will you continue on the a path ... Jb 22:15
Rise up, a doors! ... Ps 24:7,9
Ask about the a paths, ... Jr 6:16
the A of Days took his seat. ... Dn 7:9
since a times, Moses ... Ac 15:21
if he didn't spare the a world, ... 2Pt 2:5
seized the dragon, that a serpent ... Rv 20:2

ANDREW

Apostle; fisherman; Peter's brother (Mt 4:18; 10:2; Mk 1:16,29; 3:18; 13:3; Lk 6:14; Jn 1:35-44; 6:8-9; 12:12; Ac 1:13).

ANGEL

two a-s entered Sodom ... Gn 19:1
a of the LORD called to him ... Gn 22:11
he will send his a before you, ... Gn 24:7
a-s were going up and down ... Gn 28:12
going to send an a before you ... Ex 23:20
a of the LORD took his stand ... Nm 22:22
God sent an a to Jerusalem ... 1Ch 21:15
A of the LORD encamps around. ... Ps 34:7
he will give his a-s orders. ... Ps 91:11
Bless the LORD, all his a-s ... Ps 103:20
the a of the LORD ... struck down. ... Is 37:36
He sent his a and rescued. ... Dn 3:28
My God sent his a and shut ... Dn 6:22
Jacob struggled with the a. ... Hs 12:4
a of the Lord appeared ... Mt 2:13
He will give his a-s orders ... Mt 4:6
is going to come with his a-s ... Mt 16:27
their a-s continually view ... Mt 18:10
are like a-s in heaven. ... Mt 22:30
for the devil and his a-s! ... Mt 25:41
the a-s were serving him. ... Mk 1:13
the a Gabriel was sent ... Lk 1:26
a said to them, "Don't be afraid ... Lk 2:10
the a-s of God ascending ... Jn 1:51
face was like the face of an a. ... Ac 6:15
we will judge a-s ... 1Co 6:3
If I speak human or a-ic tongues ... 1Co 13:1
disguises himself as an a of light. ... 2Co 11:14
even if we or an a from heaven ... Gl 1:8
the worship of a-s, ... Col 2:18
some have welcomed a-s as guests ... Heb 13:2
A-s long to catch a glimpse ... 1Pt 1:12
if God didn't spare the a-s ... 2Pt 2:4
Write to the a of the church in. ... Rv 2–3

ANGER

until your brother's a subsides ... Gn 27:44
alone, so that my a can burn. ... Ex 32:10
gracious God, slow to a ... Ex 34:6
LORD's a burned against Israel ... Jdg 2:14
his a may ignite at any moment. ... Ps 2:12
do not rebuke me in your a; ... Ps 6:1
For his a lasts only a moment, ... Ps 30:5
I swore in my a, "They will not. ... Ps 95:11
A gentle answer turns away a, ... Pr 15:1
A fool gives full vent to his a, ... Pr 29:11
compassionate, slow to a, ... Jl 2:13
slow to a, ... Jnh 4:2
jealousy, outbursts of a, ... Gl 5:20
sun go down on your a, ... Eph 4:26
All bitterness, a and wrath, ... Eph 4:31
a, wrath, malice, slander, ... Col 3:8
So I swore in my a, ... Heb 3:11
slow to speak, and slow to a, ... Jms 1:19
the cup of his a. ... Rv 14:10
winepress of the fierce a of God, ... Rv 19:15

ANGRY

the Son or he will be a ... Ps 2:12
Be a and do not sin; ... Ps 4:4
An a person stirs up conflict, ... Pr 29:22
Is it right for you to be a? ... Jnh 4:4
who is a with his brother ... Mt 5:22
Be a and do not sin. ... Eph 4:26

ANGUISH

After his a, he will see light, ... Is 53:11
in a, he prayed more fervently, ... Lk 22:44
I wrote to you with ... a-ed heart. ... 2Co 2:4

ANIMAL

LORD God formed ... every wild a ... Gn 2:19
with an a must be put to death. ... Ex 22:19
may eat all these ... land a-s. ... Lv 11:2
every a of the forest is mine, ... Ps 50:10
cares about his a-'s health, ... Pr 12:10
and the fate of a-s is the same. ... Ec 3:19
four-footed a-s and reptiles ... Ac 10:12

ANNIHILATE
a all the Jewish people.... Est 3:13

ANNOUNCE
I a them to you before they occur.... Is 42:9

ANOINT
A Aaron and his sons.... Ex 30:30
LORD sent me to a you as king.... 1Sm 15:1
The LORD **a-ed** you king.... 1Sm 15:17
You a my head with oil;.... Ps 23:5
a-ed me to bring good news.... Is 61:1
a-ed my body in advance.... Mk 14:8
a-ed me to preach good news.... Lk 4:18
You didn't a my head with ... oil,.... Lk 7:46
a-ed Jesus's feet,.... Jn 12:3
against ... Jesus, whom you **a-ed**,.... Ac 4:27
pray over him, **a-ing** him.... Jms 5:14

ANOINTED (ADJ)
If the a priest sins,.... Lv 4:3
he will walk before my a one.... 1Sm 2:35
Do not touch my a ones.... 1Ch 16:22
against the LORD and his A One:.... Ps 2:2
Do not touch my a ones,.... Ps 105:15
an a guardian cherub,.... Ezk 28:14
until the A One, the ruler.... Dn 9:25
These are the two a ones,.... Zch 4:14

ANOINTED (N)
lift my hand against ... LORD's a..... 1Sm 24:6

ANOINTING (N)
an a from the Holy One,.... 1Jn 2:20
his a teaches you.... 1Jn 2:27

ANOINTING (ADJ)
spices for the a oil.... Ex 25:6

ANOTHER
Let a praise you, and not your.... Pr 27:2
I will not give my glory to a..... Is 48:11
he will give you a Counselor.... Jn 14:16
not that there is a gospel,.... Gl 1:7

ANSWER (N)
A gentle a turns away anger,.... Pr 15:1
a of the tongue is from the LORD.... Pr 16:1
who gives an a before he listens.... Pr 18:13
money is the a for everything..... Ec 10:19
were astounded at ... his **a-s**.... Lk 2:47

ANSWER (V)
he **a-ed** him with fire.... 1Ch 21:26
but you do not a me;.... Jb 30:20
a me, for I am poor and needy.... Ps 86:1
Don't a a fool according to.... Pr 26:4
A a fool according to.... Pr 26:5
But Jesus still did not a.... Mk 15:5

ANT
Go to the a, you slacker!.... Pr 6:6
a-s are not a strong people,.... Pr 30:25

ANTICHRIST
heard that a is coming, even now many **a-s** have come.... 1Jn 2:18
is the a: the one who denies.... 1Jn 2:22
spirit of the a; which you have.... 1Jn 4:3
This is the deceiver and the a..... 2Jn 7

ANTIOCH
first called Christians at A..... Ac 11:26
reached Pisidian A..... Ac 13:14

ANTIQUITY
origin is from a, from eternity..... Mc 5:2

ANXIETY
A in a person's heart weighs.... Pr 12:25

ANXIOUS
don't be a.... Lk 12:29

ANYTHING
Is a impossible for the LORD?.... Gn 18:14
Is a too difficult for me?.... Jr 32:27
A you ask the Father.... Jn 16:23

APART
Set a for me Barnabas and Saul.... Ac 13:2
a from the law, the righteousness of ... Rm 3:21
my mother's womb set me a and called .. Gl 1:15

APOLLOS
Alexandrian Jew, became a Christian apologist after being instructed in doctrine by Priscilla and Aquila in Ephesus (Ac 18:24-28). Was popular like Paul and Peter (1Co 1:12) but not a rival (3:5-6,22; 4:6; 16:12; Ti 3:13).

APOSTASY
a-ies will reprimand you..... Jr 2:19
save them from all their **a-ies**.... Ezk 37:23
I will heal their a;.... Hs 14:4
unless the a comes first.... 2Th 2:3

APOSTLE
the names of the twelve **a-s**:.... Mt 10:2
twelve, whom he also named **a-s**,.... Mk 3:14
he was added to the eleven **a-s**.... Ac 1:26
laid it at the **a-s'** feet.... Ac 5:2
called as an a and set apart.... Rm 1:1
I am an a to the Gentiles,.... Rm 11:13
first **a-s**, second prophets,.... 1Co 12:28
not worthy to be called an a,.... 1Co 15:9
such people are false **a-s**,.... 2Co 11:13
signs of an a were performed.... 2Co 12:12
on the foundation of the **a-s**.... Eph 2:20
some to be **a-s**, some prophets,.... Eph 4:11
Jesus, the a and high priest.... Heb 3:1
twelve names of twelve **a-s**.... Rv 21:14

APOSTLESHIP
We have received grace and a.... Rm 1:5
you are the seal of my a.... 1Co 9:2
Peter for an a to the circumcised.... Gl 2:8

APPEAL (N)
God is making his a through us.... 2Co 5:20

APPEAL (V)
I a to Caesar!.... Ac 25:11
I a, ... on the basis of love..... Phm 9

APPEAR
the LORD **a-ed** to Abram.... Gn 12:7
sign of the Son of Man will a.... Mt 24:30
and **a-ed** to many..... Mt 27:53
the third time Jesus **a-ed**.... Jn 21:14
he **a-ed** to over five hundred.... 1Co 15:6
all a before the judgment seat.... 2Co 5:10
until the **a-ing** of our Lord.... 1Tm 6:14
those who have loved his **a-ing**.... 2Tm 4:8
blessed hope, the **a-ing** of the glory.... Ti 2:13
will a a second time,.... Heb 9:28

APPEARANCE
Do not look at his a.... 1Sm 16:7
no a that we should desire him..... Is 53:2
judging according to outward **a-s**;.... Jn 7:24

APPETITE
A worker's a works for him.... Pr 16:26
if you have a big a;.... Pr 23:2
yet the a is never satisfied..... Ec 6:7
He enlarges his a like Sheol,.... Hab 2:5
Lord Christ but their own **a-s**..... Rm 16:18

APPLES
is like gold a in silver settings..... Pr 25:11

APPLY
A yourself to discipline.... Pr 23:12
I **a-ied** my mind to seek.... Ec 1:13

APPOINT
These are the LORD's **a-ed** times,.... Lv 23:4
a a king to judge us.... 1Sm 8:5
A a king for them..... 1Sm 8:22
I will a peace as your government.... Is 60:17
A harvest is also **a-ed** for you,.... Hs 6:11
the LORD **a-ed** a great fish.... Jnh 1:17
God **a-ed** a worm.... Jnh 4:7
vision is yet for the **a-ed** time;.... Hab 2:3
He **a-ed** twelve,.... Mk 3:14
been **a-ed** for you as the Messiah..... Ac 3:20
God did not a us to wrath,.... 1Th 5:9
For this I was **a-ed** a herald,.... 1Tm 2:7
Don't be too quick to a anyone.... 1Tm 5:22
a elders in every town:.... Ti 1:5
God has **a-ed** him heir of all things.... Heb 1:2
it is **a-ed** for people to die once.... Heb 9:27

APPROACH
let us a the throne of grace.... Heb 4:16

APPROPRIATE
Luxury is not a for a fool.... Pr 19:10
made everything a in its time..... Ec 3:11

is a of me and of my words .... Mk 8:38
I am not a of the gospel, ... Rm 1:16
don't be a of the testimony 2Tm 1:8
who doesn't need to be a, ... 2Tm 2:15
not a to call them brothers, ... Heb 2:11
is not a to be called their God, ... Heb 11:16
Christian, let him not be a 1Pt 4:16

ASHER

Jacob's eighth son, born of Zilpah (Gn 30:13; 35:26). The tribe's territory was in the northwest on the Phoenician coast (Jos 19:24-31). Also, a town (17:7).

ASHERAH

cut down the A pole beside it. .... Jdg 6:25
and the 400 prophets of A 1Kg 18:19
an obscene image of A. 2Ch 15:16

ASHES

even though I am dust and a .... Gn 18:27
is to gather up the cow's a .... Nm 19:9
Tamar put a on her head. 2Sm 13:19
the a poured from the altar, ... 1Kg 13:5
put on sackcloth and a, ... Est 4:1
he sat among the a. .... Jb 2:8
I am dust and a. .... Jb 42:6
a crown of beauty instead of a, ... Is 61:3
covered himself with sackcloth,
and sat in a. .... Jnh 3:6
in sackcloth and a long ago! .... Mt 11:21
the a of a young cow .... Heb 9:13

ASIA

forbidden ... to speak the word in A. .... Ac 16:6
first convert to Christ from A. .... Rm 16:5
To the seven churches in A. .... Rv 1:4

ASIDE

Do not turn a to the right or .... Dt 28:14
took the twelve disciples a .... Mt 20:17
set something a and save 1Co 16:2
let us lay a every hindrance .... Heb 12:1

ASK

When your children a you, ... Ex 12:26
When your son a-s you .... Dt 6:20
A of me, and I will make .... Ps 2:8
Two things I a of you; .... Pr 30:7
sought by those who did not a; .... Is 65:1
Give to the one who a-s you, ... Mt 5:42
you need before you a him. .... Mt 6:8
A, and it will be given .... Mt 7:7
you pray and a for—believe. .... Mk 11:24
Holy Spirit to those who a .... Lk 11:13
Whatever you a in my name, ... Jn 14:13
a whatever you want .... Jn 15:7
A and you will receive, ... Jn 16:24
the Jews a for signs 1Co 1:22
lacks wisdom, he should a God, ... Jms 1:5
You a and don't receive because you
a with wrong motives, ... Jms 4:3
a anything according to his will, ... 1Jn 5:14

ASLEEP

The child is not dead but a. .... Mk 5:39
as they were sailing he fell a. .... Lk 8:23
Lazarus has fallen a, ... Jn 11:11
We will not all fall a, ... 1Co 15:51
concerning those who are a, ... 1Th 4:13

ASSEMBLE

a the whole community .... Lv 8:3
A on the mountains of Samaria .... Am 3:9
to gather nations, to a kingdoms, ... Zph 3:8
a-d together against your holy
servant Jesus, ... Ac 4:27
to a them for the battle .... Rv 16:14

ASSEMBLY

sacred a on the first day and another
sacred a on the seventh day. .... Ex 12:16
the a in front of the rock, ... Nm 20:10
his praise in the a of the faithful. .... Ps 149:1
the a was divided. .... Ac 23:7
the a of the firstborn. .... Heb 12:23

ASSOCIATE

you a with adulterers. .... Ps 50:18
Don't a with those who drink .... Pr 23:20
don't a with rebels, ... Pr 24:21
a with the humble. .... Rm 12:16
not to a with anyone who claims
to be a believer. 1Co 5:11
don't a with him, ... 2Th 3:14

ASSURANCE

Holy Spirit, and with full a. 1Th 1:5
true heart in full a of faith, ... Heb 10:22

ASSURED

stand mature and fully a. .... Col 4:12

ASSYRIA

From that land he went to A. .... Gn 10:11
The king of A deported the
Israelites to A 2Kg 18:11
Woe to A, the rod of my anger .... Is 10:5

ASTONISHED

crowds were a at his teaching, ... Mt 7:28
were a and said, "Where did this .... Mt 13:54
they were a at his teaching. .... Mt 22:33
were a. "Where did this man get. .... Mk 6:2
disciples were a at his words. .... Mk 10:24
parents saw him, they were a, ... Lk 2:48
all a at the greatness of God. .... Lk 9:43

ASTOUNDED

were a at his understanding. .... Lk 2:47

ASTRAY

led a to bow down ... to other
gods. .... Dt 30:17
who rejects correction goes a. .... Pr 10:17
We all went a like sheep; .... Is 53:6
their shepherds led them a, ... Jr 50:6
and one of them goes a, ... Mt 18:12
lead a, if possible, the elect. .... Mk 13:22
always go a in their hearts, ... Heb 3:10
you were like sheep going a, ... 1Pt 2:25

ATHALIAH

Wife of Jehoram and mother of Ahaziah, kings of Judah; descendant of Omri (2Kg 8:26). Encouraged Baal worship (8:27). Killed heirs and ruled after her son's death (2Kg 11:1-3). Jehoiada the priest executed her and crowned Josiah, the only surviving heir (11:4-20).

ATHENS

City in Greece (Ac 17; 1Th 3:1).

ATHLETE

if anyone competes as an a, ... 2Tm 2:5

ATONE

only you can a for our rebellions .... Ps 65:3
Rescue us and a for our sins, ... Ps 79:9

ATONEMENT

blood of the sin offering for a. .... Ex 30:10
priest will make a on their
behalf, ... Lv 4:20
make a before the LORD. .... Lv 14:31
is the Day of A. .... Lv 23:27
he ... made a for the Israelites. .... Nm 25:13
to make a for the sins of the .... Heb 2:17

ATONING SACRIFICE

himself is the a for our sins, ... 1Jn 2:2
Son to be the a for our sins. 1Jn 4:10

ATTACK

he may come and a me, ... Gn 32:11
I will a him while he is weary 2Sm 17:2
a worm that a-ed the plant, ... Jnh 4:7

ATTEMPTED

a to establish their ...
righteousness, ... Rm 10:3
When the Egyptians a to do this, ... Heb 11:29

ATTENDANT

gave it back to the a, and sat .... Lk 4:20

ATTENTION

to pay a is better than the fat 1Sm 15:22
Pay a to the sound of my cry, ... Ps 5:2
The God of Jacob doesn't pay a. .... Ps 94:7
My son, pay a to my words; .... Pr 4:20
pay a to the words of the wise, ... Pr 22:17
pay a to myths and endless 1Tm 1:4
give your a to public reading, ... 1Tm 4:13
not pay a to Jewish myths .... Ti 1:14
pay a all the more to what we
have heard .... Heb 2:1

ATTIRE

attendants' service and their a, ... 1Kg 10:5

ATTITUDE

Serve with a good a, as to the Lord ...... Eph 6:7
Adopt the same a as that of Christ. ...... Php 2:5

ATTRIBUTES

For his invisible a, ... Rm 1:20

AUTHORITY

Confer some of your a on him .... Nm 27:20
like one who had a, ... Mt 7:29
Son of Man has a on earth .... Mt 9:6
gave them a over unclean spirits .... Mt 10:1
All a has been given to me .... Mt 28:18
you gave him a over all people; .... Jn 17:2

You would have no a over me .... Jn 19:11
submit to the governing **a-ies**, ... Rm 13:1
there is no a except from God, ... Rm 13:1
a symbol of a on her head, ... 1Co 11:10
far above every ruler and a, ... Eph 1:21
rulers, against the **a-ies**, ... Eph 6:12
disarmed the rulers and **a-ies** .... Col 2:15
teach or to have a over a man; 1Tm 2:12
submit to rulers and **a-ies**, ... Ti 3:1
Submit to every human a 1Pt 2:13
a-ies, and powers subject to him. 1Pt 3:22
glory, majesty, power, and a .... Jd 25
I will give him a over the nations .... Rv 2:26
who were given a to judge. .... Rv 20:4

AVENGE

He will a the blood .... Dt 32:43
Should I not a myself .... Jr 5:9
do not a yourselves; .... Rm 12:19
how long until you ... a .... Rv 6:10

AVENGER

cities as a refuge from the a, ... Nm 35:12
hand him over to the a of blood .... Dt 19:12
to silence the enemy and the a .... Ps 8:2
Lord is an a of all these offenses, ... 1Th 4:6

AVOID

a irreverent and empty speech 2Tm 2:16
But a foolish debates, genealogies, ... Ti 3:9

AWAKE

A! A, Deborah! .... Jdg 5:12
when I a, I will be satisfied .... Ps 17:15
or **a-n** love until .... Sg 2:7; 3:5; 8:4
I **a-ned** you under the apricot tree .... Sg 8:5
He **a-ns** me each morning; he **a-ns**
my ear to listen .... Is 50:4
in the dust of the earth will a, ... Dn 12:2
Couldn't you stay a one hour? .... Mk 14:37
let us stay a and be self-controlled 1Th 5:6
whether we are a or asleep, ... 1Th 5:10

AWAY

All have turned a; .... Ps 53:3

AWE

of the world stand in a of him. .... Ps 33:8
I tremble in a of you; .... Ps 119:120
so that people will be in a of him. .... Ec 3:14
stand in a of the God of Israel. .... Is 29:23
I stand in a of your deeds. .... Hab 3:2

AWE-INSPIRING

the great, mighty, and a God, ... Dt 10:17
glorious and a name—the Lord, ... Dt 28:58
looked like the a Angel of God. .... Jdg 13:6
the great and a God who keeps .... Neh 1:5
great, mighty, and a God .... Neh 9:32
right hand show your a acts. .... Ps 45:4
the LORD, the Most High, is a, ... Ps 47:2
You answer us ... with a works, ... Ps 65:5
his acts for humanity are a. .... Ps 66:5
you are a in your sanctuaries. .... Ps 68:35
LORD—the great and a God .... Dn 9:4
Great and a are your works, ... Rv 15:3

AWESOME

What an a place this is! .... Gn 28:17

AX

iron a head fell into the water, ... 2Kg 6:5
Does an a exalt itself .... Is 10:15
the a is already at the root of .... Mt 3:10; Lk 3:9

AZARIAH

1. Prophet (2Ch 15:1-8).
2. King of Judah, also called Uzziah (2Kg 15:1-7).

B

BAAL

Israel aligned itself with
B of Peor, ... Nm 25:3
the 450 prophets of **B** 1Kg 18:19
knee that has not bowed to **B**. 1Kg 19:18
no longer call me "my **B**." .... Hs 2:16
who have not bowed down to **B**. .... Rm 11:4

BAASHA

King of Israel (1Kg 15:16–16:7). Exterminated Jeroboam's family (15:29).

BABY

Give the living **b** to the first 1Kg 3:27
the **b** leaped inside her, ... Lk 1:41
You will find a **b** wrapped .... Lk 2:12
and the **b** who was lying in .... Lk 2:16

BABYLON

Mesopotamian city; place of captivity (2Kg 24; Dn 1:1-6); symbol of wickedness (Rv 17:5).
Therefore it is called **B**, ... Gn 11:9
from a distant country, from **B**. 2Kg 20:14
went up from **B** to Jerusalem. .... Ezr 1:11
By the rivers of **B**— .... Ps 137:1
B has fallen, has fallen. .... Is 21:9
the king of **B** for seventy years. .... Jr 25:11
She who is in **B**, chosen 1Pt 5:13
It has fallen, **B** the Great .... Rv 14:8

BACK (N)

gave my **b** to those who beat me, ... Is 50:6

BACK (ADV)

looked **b** and became a pillar .... Gn 19:26
ahead ten steps or go **b** ten steps? 2Kg 20:9
plow and looks **b** is fit for .... Lk 9:62

BAD

but a **b** tree produces **b** fruit. .... Mt 7:17
B company corrupts good 1Co 15:33

BAG

in each man's sack was his **b** of .... Gn 42:35
different weights in your **b**, ... Dt 25:13
David put his hand in the **b**, ... 1Sm 17:49
weeping, carrying the **b** of seed, ... Ps 126:6
or **b-s** of deceptive weights? .... Mc 6:11
wages into a **b** with a hole in it .... Hg 1:6

BAKE

b-d unleavened bread for them, ... Gn 19:3
b-d the dough they had brought .... Ex 12:39
B what you want to **b**, ... Ex 16:23
a grain offering **b-d** in an oven, ... Lv 2:4

BAKER

king of Egypt's cupbearer and **b**. .... Gn 40:1

BALAAM

Prophet hired by King Balak of Moab to curse Israel (Nm 22). His donkey talked (22:21-30; 2Pt 2:16). He blessed Israel (Nm 23–24; Jos 24:10; Neh 13:2). Executed for practicing divination (Nm 31:8; Jos 13:22; 2Pt 2:15; Jd 11; Rv 2:14).

BALAK

King of Moab who hired Balaam to curse Israel (Nm 22–24).

BALANCE

You are to have honest **b-s**, ... Lv 19:36
b-s and scales are the LORD's; .... Pr 16:11
weighed the mountains on a **b** .... Is 40:12

BALDY

chanting, "Go up, **b**! 2Kg 2:23

BALM

Is there no **b** in Gilead? .... Jr 8:22

BAN

will **b** you from the synagogues. .... Jn 16:2

BANDAGE

For he wounds but also **b-s**; .... Jb 5:18
and **b-s** their wounds. .... Ps 147:3
cleansed, **b-d**, or soothed
with oil. .... Is 1:6
LORD **b-s** his people's injuries .... Is 30:26
Look, it has not been **b-d**. .... Ezk 30:21
healed the sick, **b-d** the injured. .... Ezk 34:4
and **b-d** his wounds, ... Lk 10:34

BANDIT

your need, like a **b**. .... Pr 6:11; 24:34

BANISH

plans so that the one **b-ed** from him
does not remain **b-ed**. 2Sm 14:14
not **b** me from your presence .... Ps 51:11
nations where I will **b** them. .... Ezk 4:13

BANK

put my money in the **b**? .... Lk 19:23

BANNER

The LORD Is My **B**. .... Ex 17:15
lift the **b** in the name of our God .... Ps 20:5
as an army with **b-s** .... Sg 6:4,10

BANQUET

the king held a week-long **b** .... Est 1:5
He brought me to the **b** hall, ... Sg 2:4
love the place of honor at **b-s**, ... Mt 23:6
a **b**, invite those who are poor, ... Lk 14:13

BAPTISM

Sadducees coming to his **b**, ... Mt 3:7
proclaiming a **b** of repentance .... Mk 1:4

with the **b** I am baptized with? .... Mk 10:38
baptized with John's **b**. .... Lk 7:29
I have a **b** to undergo, ... Lk 12:50
he knew only John's **b**. .... Ac 18:25
we were buried with him by **b**. .... Rm 6:4
one Lord, one faith, one **b**, ... Eph 4:5
buried with him in **b**, ... Col 2:12
B . . . now saves you 1Pt 3:21

BAPTIST

In those days John the B came, ... Mt 3:1
Give me John the **B**-'s head .... Mt 14:8
Some say John the **B**; .... Mt 16:14
John the **B** sent us to ask you, ... Lk 7:20

BAPTIZE

I **b** you with water for .... Mt 3:11
b-ing them in the name of .... Mt 28:19
to be **b-d** with the baptism I .... Mk 10:38
and is **b-d** will be saved, ... Mk 16:16
Tax collectors also came to be **b-d**, ... Lk 3:12
Jesus also was **b-d**. .... Lk 3:21
b-ing more disciples than John .... Jn 4:1
will be **b-d** with the Holy Spirit .... Ac 1:5
Repent and be **b-d**, ... Ac 2:38
there's water. What would keep me
from being **b-d**? .... Ac 8:36
who were **b-d** into Christ Jesus were
b-d into his death? .... Rm 6:3
Christ did not send me to **b**, but 1Co 1:17
all were **b-d** into Moses 1Co 10:2
we were all **b-d** by one Spirit 1Co 12:13
are being **b-d** for the dead? 1Co 15:29

BARABBAS

Insurrectionist released by Pilate instead of Jesus (Mt 27:16-26; Mk 15:7-15; Lk 23:18; Jn 18:40).

BARAK

Reluctantly joined Deborah to fight Canaanites (Jdg 4–5; 1Sm 12:11; Heb 11:32).

BARBARIAN

obligated both to Greeks and **b-s**, ... Rm 1:14
b, Scythian, slave and free; .... Col 3:11

BAREFOOT

he did that, going stripped and **b** .... Is 20:2

BARK

peeled the **b**, exposing white .... Gn 30:37

BARLEY

a loaf of **b** bread came tumbling .... Jdg 7:13
five **b** loaves and two fish .... Jn 6:9

BARN

sow or reap or gather into **b-s**, ... Mt 6:26
but collect the wheat in my **b**. .... Mt 13:30
I'll tear down my **b-s** and build .... Lk 12:18

BARNABAS

Levite from Cyprus, named Joseph (Ac 4:36). Introduced Paul to Jerusalem church (9:26-27). Worked with Paul, initially as leader in Antioch (11:19-30), then on a journey (Ac 13–14), then in Jerusalem (15:1-21). Separated from Paul over whether to bring John Mark with them again (15:36-41).

BARTHOLOMEW

Apostle (Mt 10:3; Mk 3:18; Lk 6:14; Ac 1:13), possibly also called Nathanael (Jn 1:43-51).

BARUCH

Jeremiah's scribe (Jr 36).

BASED

not be **b** on human wisdom 1Co 2:5
the law is not **b** on faith; .... Gl 3:12
righteousness from God **b** on faith. .... Php 3:9
b on the testimony of two .... Heb 10:28
b on what seemed good to them .... Heb 12:10

BASHAN

the rest of Gilead and all B, ... Dt 3:13
strong ones of B encircle me. .... Ps 22:12
against all the oaks of B, ... Is 2:13
you cows of B .... Am 4:1

BASIN

Make a bronze **b** for washing .... Ex 30:18
he made ten bronze **b-s** 1Kg 7:38
poured water into a **b** and began to .... Jn 13:5

BASKET

Three **b-s** . . . were on my head. .... Gn 40:16
she got a papyrus **b** for him .... Ex 2:3
LORD showed me two **b-s** of figs .... Jr 24:1
A **b** of summer fruit. .... Am 8:1
a woman sitting inside the **b**. .... Zch 5:7
a lamp and puts it under a **b**, ... Mt 5:15
they picked up twelve **b-s** full .... Mt 14:20
lowered him in a large **b**. .... Ac 9:25

BATCH

holy, so is the whole **b**. .... Rm 11:16
a little leaven leavens the whole **b**. 1Co 5:6

BATHE

he saw a woman **b-ing** 2Sm 11:2
One who has **b-d**, ... Jn 13:10

BATHSHEBA

Wife of Uriah the Hethite. David committed adultery with her, then married her (2Sm 11). Solomon's mother (2Sm 12; 1Kg 1–2).

BATTLE

the **b** is the LORD's. 1Sm 17:47
the **b** is not yours, but God's. 2Ch 20:15
He smells the **b** from a distance .... Jb 39:25
clothed me with strength for **b**; .... Ps 18:39
the LORD, mighty in **b**. .... Ps 24:8
A horse is prepared for . . . **b**, ... Pr 21:31
or the **b** to the strong, ... Ec 9:11
nations against Jerusalem for **b**. .... Zch 14:2
like horses prepared for **b**. .... Rv 9:7
the **b** on the great day of God, ... Rv 16:14
Magog, to gather them for **b**. .... Rv 20:8

BEAM

b of wood in your own eye? .... Mt 7:3

BEAR (N)

Whenever a lion or a **b** came 1Sm 17:34
two female **b-s** came out 2Kg 2:24
to meet a **b** robbed of her cubs .... Pr 17:12
The cow and the **b** will graze, ... Is 11:7
He is a **b** waiting in ambush, ... Lm 3:10
second one, that looked like a **b**. .... Dn 7:5

BEAR (V)

b children with painful effort. .... Gn 3:16
punishment is too great to **b**! .... Gn 4:13
wife Sarah will **b** you a son, ... Gn 17:19
that **b-s** its fruit in season .... Ps 1:3
a burden too heavy for me to **b**. .... Ps 38:4
he **b-s** our burdens; .... Ps 68:19
They will still **b** fruit in old age, ... Ps 92:14
he himself **bore** our sicknesses, ... Is 53:4
yet he **bore** the sin of many .... Is 53:12
"Blessed is the womb that
bore you .... Lk 11:27
does not **b** his own cross .... Lk 14:27
but you can't **b** them now. .... Jn 16:12
that we may **b** fruit for God. .... Rm 7:4
b the weaknesses of those .... Rm 15:1
so that you may be able to **b** it. 1Co 10:13
b-s all things, believes all 1Co 13:7
b-ing with one another. .... Eph 4:2; Col 3:13
offered once to **b** the sins of .... Heb 9:28
He himself **bore** our sins 1Pt 2:24
tree of life . . . **b-ing** twelve kinds .... Rv 22:2

BEARD

shaved off half their **b-s**, ... 2Sm 10:4
on the **b**, running down Aaron's **b**, ... Ps 133:2

BEAST

Four huge **b-s** came up .... Dn 7:3
b that comes up out of the
abyss .... Rv 11:7
a **b** coming up out of the sea. .... Rv 13:1
calculate the number of the **b**, ... Rv 13:18
who had the mark of the **b** .... Rv 16:2
who accepted the mark of the **b**. .... Rv 19:20

BEAT

gave my back to those who **b** me, ... Is 50:6
will **b** their swords into plows, ... Mc 4:3
they spat in his face and **b** him; .... Mt 26:67
to **b** him, saying, "Prophesy!" .... Mk 14:65
they stopped **b-ing** Paul. .... Ac 21:32
or box like one **b-ing** the air. 1Co 9:26
Three times I was **b-en** 2Co 11:25

BEATING (N)

by **b-s**, by imprisonments, by riots, ... 2Co 6:5

BEAUTIFUL

daughters of mankind were **b**, ... Gn 6:2
know what a **b** woman you are. .... Gn 12:11
Now the girl was very **b**, ... Gn 24:16
Rebekah, for she is a **b** woman. .... Gn 26:7
but Rachel was shapely and **b**. .... Gn 29:17
when she saw that he was **b**, ... Ex 2:2
woman was intelligent and **b**, ... 1Sm 25:3
Let a search be made for **b** young .... Est 2:2
praise from the upright is **b**. .... Ps 33:1
How **b** you are, my darling. .... Sg 1:15; 4:1
How **b** on the mountains are .... Is 52:7
which appear **b** on the outside, ... Mt 23:27
used to sit and beg at the
B Gate .... Ac 3:10

BLAMELESS
b you prove yourself **b**, 2Sm 22:26
happy are those whose way is **b**, Ps 119:1
b in the day of our Lord Jesus 1Co 1:8
to be holy and **b** in love before him. Eph 1:4
so that you may be **b** and pure, Php 2:15
in the law, **b**. Php 3:6
May he make your hearts **b** 1Th 3:13
body be kept sound and **b** 1Th 5:23
b, the husband of one wife, Ti 1:6

BLASPHEME
my name is continually **b-d**. Is 52:5
He has **b-d**! Mt 26:65
He's **b-ing**! Who can forgive sins Mk 2:7
b-s against the Holy Spirit Mk 3:29
tried to make them **b** Ac 26:11
God is **b-d** among the Gentiles Rm 2:24
they may be taught not to **b**. 1Tm 1:20

BLASPHEMER
I was formerly a **b**, 1Tm 1:13

BLASPHEMOUS
We heard him speaking **b** words Ac 6:11
and on its heads were **b** names. Rv 13:1

BLASPHEMY
b against the Spirit will not Mt 12:31
you've heard the **b**. Mt 26:65
stoning you . . . for **b**, Jn 10:33
to utter boasts and **b-ies**. Rv 13:5

BLAZE
fire from the Lord **b-d** among Nm 11:1
mountain was **b-ing** with fire. Dt 5:23
in the morning it **b-s** like Hs 7:6

BLAZING (ADJ)
into the furnace of **b** fire. Dn 3:20

BLEMISH
he is to present one without **b** Lv 3:1
offered himself without **b** to God, Heb 9:14
b in his sight, at peace. 2Pt 3:14
b and with great joy, Jd 24

BLESS
God **b-ed** them: "Be fruitful, Gn 1:22
God **b-ed** the seventh day. Gn 2:3
I will **b** you, Gn 12:2
I will **b** her; indeed, Gn 17:16
b you and make your offspring Gn 22:17
B me too, my father! Gn 27:34
let you go unless you **b** me. Gn 32:26
Lord **b-ed** the Sabbath day Ex 20:11
Lord **b** you and protect you; Nm 6:24
since he has **b-ed**, I cannot Nm 23:20
they curse, you will **b**. Ps 109:28
A generous person will be **b-ed**, Pr 22:9
b-es his neighbor with a loud Pr 27:14
the nations will be **b-ed** by him. Jr 4:2
from this day on I will **b** you. Hg 2:19
took bread, **b-ed** and broke it, Mt 26:26
he **b-ed** and broke the loaves. Mk 6:41
hands on them and **b-ed** them. Mk 10:16
b those who curse you, Lk 6:28
families of the earth will be **b-ed** Ac 3:25
B those who persecute you; **b** Rm 12:14
When we are reviled, we **b**; 1Co 4:12
nations will be **b-ed** through you. Gl 3:8
has **b-ed** us with every spiritual Eph 1:3
inferior is **b-ed** by the superior. Heb 7:7

BLESSED (ADJ)
You will be **b** in the city and **b** in the country. Dt 28:3
May you be **b** by the Lord, Ps 115:15
He who comes in the name of the Lord is **b**. Ps 118:26
Let your fountain be **b**, Pr 5:18
children rise up and call her **b**. Pr 31:28
who trusts in the Lord... is **b**. Jr 17:7
B are the poor in spirit, Mt 5:3
B is he who comes in the name of Mt 21:9
B are you among women, Lk 1:42
B are those who have not seen and Jn 20:29
more **b** to give than to receive. Ac 20:35
while we wait for the **b** hope Ti 2:13
B is the one who endures trials, Jms 1:12
for righteousness, you are **b**. 1Pt 3:14
B is the one who reads aloud the words of this prophecy, and **b** are those Rv 1:3
B is the one who keeps the words of the prophecy of this book. Rv 22:7

BLESSING (N)
you will be a **b**. Gn 12:2
deceitfully and took your **b**. Gn 27:35
set before you a **b** and a curse: Dt 11:26
He turned the curse into a **b** Dt 23:5
these **b-s** will come and overtake Dt 28:2
God turned the curse into a **b**. Neh 13:2
May the Lord's **b** be on you. Ps 129:8
B-s are on the head of the righteous, Pr 10:6
send down . . . showers of **b**. Ezk 34:26
pour out a **b** for you. Mal 3:10
cup of **b** that we bless, 1Co 10:16
b of Abraham . . . to the Gentiles Gl 3:14
blessed us with every spiritual **b** Eph 1:3
so that you may inherit a **b**. 1Pt 3:9
and honor and glory and **b**! Rv 5:12

BLIND (ADJ)
mute or deaf, seeing or **b**? Ex 4:11
When you present a **b** animal Mal 1:8
Woe to you, **b** guides, Mt 23:16
a **b** beggar, was sitting Mk 10:46
I was **b**, and now I can see!. Jn 9:25
are wretched, pitiful, poor, **b**, Rv 3:17

BLIND (N)
block in front of the **b**, Lv 19:14
I was eyes to the **b** Jb 29:15
Lord opens the eyes of the **b**. Ps 146:8
the eyes of the **b** will be opened, Is 35:5
the **b** receive their sight, the lame. Mt 11:5
Can the **b** guide the **b**? Lk 6:39
you are a guide for the **b**, Rm 2:19

BLIND (V)
a bribe **b-s** the clear-sighted Ex 23:8
king of Babylon **b-ed** Zedekiah, 2Kg 25:7
deafen their ears and **b** their eyes; Is 6:10
He has **b-ed** their eyes Jn 12:40
the god of this age has **b-ed** 2Co 4:4
the darkness has **b-ed** his eyes. 1Jn 2:11

BLOCK
I will bow down to a **b** of wood? Is 44:19
became a sinful stumbling **b** Ezk 44:12
Christ crucified, a stumbling **b** 1Co 1:23

BLOOD
Your brother's **b** cries out to me Gn 4:10
Whoever sheds human **b**, by humans his **b** will be shed, Gn 9:6
You are a bridegroom of **b** Ex 4:25
Nile . . . will turn to **b**. Ex 7:17
see the **b**, I will pass over you. Ex 12:13
This is the **b** of the covenant Ex 24:8
must not eat any fat or any **b**. Lv 3:17
life of a creature is in the **b**, Lv 17:11
a man of war and have shed **b**. 1Ch 28:3
or drink the **b** of goats? Ps 50:13
land became polluted with **b**. Ps 106:38
I have no desire for the **b** of bulls, Is 1:11
hold you responsible for his **b**. Ezk 3:18
moon to **b** before the great Jl 2:31
flesh and **b** did not reveal this Mt 16:17
this is my **b** . . . the covenant; Mt 26:28
field has been called "Field of B". Mt 27:8
sweat became like drops of **b**. Lk 22:44
who were born, not of **b**, Jn 1:13
and drinks my **b** has eternal life, Jn 6:54
Hakeldama (that is, "Field of B"). Ac 1:19
and the moon to **b** before the great Ac 2:20
been strangled, and from **b**. Ac 15:20
as the mercy seat by his **b**, Rm 3:25
justified by his **b**, Rm 5:9
is it not a sharing in the **b**. 1Co 10:16
covenant in my **b**. 1Co 11:25
Flesh and **b** cannot inherit 1Co 15:50
redemption through his **b**, Eph 1:7
brought near by the **b** Eph 2:13
struggle is not against flesh and **b**, Eph 6:12
by making peace through the **b** Col 1:20
not by the **b** of goats and calves, but by his own **b**, Heb 9:12
without . . . **b** there is no forgiveness Heb 9:22
with the precious **b** of Christ, 1Pt 1:19
b of Jesus his Son cleanses us 1Jn 1:7
one who came by water and **b**, 1Jn 5:6
set us free from our sins by his **b**, Rv 1:5
purchased people . . . by your **b**. Rv 5:9
the entire moon became like **b**; Rv 6:12
made them white in the **b** Rv 7:14
a third of the sea became **b**, Rv 8:8
conquered . . . by the **b** of the Lamb. Rv 12:11
He wore a robe dipped in **b**, Rv 19:13

BLOODSHED
no one is guilty of **b**. Ex 22:2
b defiles the land, Nm 35:33
responsibility for **b** will be wiped Dt 21:8
Save me from the guilt of **b**, Ps 51:14

BLOSSOM (N)
cups shaped like almond **b-s**, Ex 25:33
has budded, if the **b** has opened, Sg 7:12
their **b-s** will blow away like dust, Is 5:24

BLOSSOM (V)
sprouted, formed buds, **b-ed**, Nm 17:8
the almond tree **b-s**, Ec 12:5
Jacob will take root. Israel will **b** Is 27:6

BLOT
I will destroy them and **b** out Dt 9:14
b out all my guilt. Ps 51:9

Man must not live on **b** alone. Mt 4:4
Give us today our daily **b**. Mt 6:11
if his son asks him for **b**, Mt 7:9
took **b**, blessed and broke it, Mt 26:26
one who is dipping **b** with me Mk 14:20
I am the **b** of life, Jn 6:35
breaking of **b**, and to prayers. Ac 2:42
the Lord Jesus took **b**, 1Co 11:23

BREAK *SEE ALSO* BROKEN (ADJ)

I will **b** down your strong pride. Lv 26:19
I will never **b** my covenant Jdg 2:1
will **b** them with an iron scepter; Ps 2:9
a gentle tongue can **b** a bone. Pr 25:15
three strands is not easily **broken**. Ec 4:12
He will not **b** a bruised reed, Is 42:3
long ago I **broke** your yoke; Jr 2:20
where thieves don't **b** in and Mt 6:19
He will not **b** a bruised reed, Mt 12:20
bread, blessed and **broke** it, Mt 26:26
She **broke** the jar and poured it Mk 14:3
Not only was he **b-ing** the Sabbath Jn 5:18
the Scripture cannot be **broken** Jn 10:35
they did not **b** his legs Jn 19:33
of his bones will be **broken**. Jn 19:36
broke bread from house to house. Ac 2:46
Branches were **broken** off so that. Rm 11:19
given thanks, **broke** it, 1Co 11:24
is guilty of **b-ing** it all. Jms 2:10
to open the scroll and **b** its seals? Rv 5:2
war **broke** out in heaven: Rv 12:7

BREAKERS

b and your billows swept over me. Jnh 2:3

BREAST

let her **b-s** always satisfy you; Pr 5:19
Your **b-s** are like two fawns, Sg 4:5; 7:3

BREATH

breathed the **b** of life into. Gn 2:7
Remember that my life is but a **b**. Jb 7:7
the **b** entered them, Ezk 37:10
gives everyone life and **b** Ac 17:25
b of life from God entered them, Rv 11:11

BREATHE

b-d the breath of life into Gn 2:7
Let everything that **b-s** praise Ps 150:6
b into these slain so that they Ezk 37:9
a loud cry and **b-d** his last. Mk 15:37
He **b-d** on them and said, Jn 20:22

BRIBE

not take a **b**, for a **b** blinds Ex 23:8
no partiality and taking no **b**. Dt 10:17
Do not accept a **b**, for it blinds Dt 16:19
the one who hates **b-s** will live. Pr 15:27
a **b** corrupts the mind. Ec 7:7
love graft and chase after **b-s**. Is 1:23

BRICK

They used **b** for stone. Gn 11:3
require the same quota of **b-s** Ex 5:8

BRIDE

rejoices over his **b**, so your God Is 62:5
I will remove . . . the voices of the
groom and the **b**, Jr 7:34
the **b** her honeymoon chamber. Jl 2:16
He who has the **b** is the groom. Jn 3:29
the **b**, the wife of the Lamb. Rv 21:9

BRIDEGROOM *SEE ALSO* GROOM

You are a **b** of blood to me! Ex 4:25

BRIGHT

B eyes cheer the heart; Pr 15:30
suddenly a **b** cloud covered. Mt 17:5
dressed in pure, **b** linen, Rv 15:6
the **b** morning star. Rv 22:16

BRIGHTER

shining **b** and **b** until midday. Pr 4:18

BRILLIANCE

I did not come with **b** of speech 1Co 2:1

BRING

brought each to the man to see Gn 2:19
b into the ark two of all Gn 6:19
LORD who **brought** you from Ur Gn 15:7
I **brought** you out of Egypt Jdg 2:1
LORD **b-s** death and gives life; 1Sm 2:6
b an offering and enter Ps 96:8
don't know what a day might **b**. Pr 27:1
I **brought** you from the ends of Is 41:9
B my sons from far away, Is 43:6
I have spoken; so I will also **b** it. Is 46:11
anointed me to **b** good news Is 61:1
about to **b** a sword against you, Ezk 6:3
will **b** you into your own land. Ezk 36:24
B the full tenth into the
storehouse. Mal 3:10
I did not come to **b** peace, but Mt 10:34
brought to him all who
were sick. Mt 14:35
I came to **b** fire on the earth, Lk 12:49
b in here the poor, maimed, Lk 14:21
feet of those who **b** good news. Rm 10:15
more will their fullness **b**! Rm 11:12
b them up in the training and Eph 6:4
brought nothing into the
world, 1Tm 6:7

BROAD

b that leads to destruction, Mt 7:13

BROKEN (ADJ) *SEE ALSO* BREAK

sacrifice pleasing to God is a **b** spirit.
You will not despise a **b** and
humbled heart, God. Ps 51:17

BROKENHEARTED

The LORD is near the **b**; Ps 34:18
He heals the **b** and bandages Ps 147:3
He has sent me to heal the **b**, Is 61:1

BRONZE

So Moses made a **b** snake. Nm 21:9
The sky above you will be **b**, Dt 28:23
my arms can bend a bow of **b**. 2Sm 22:35
a third kingdom, of **b**, Dn 2:39

BROOD

B of vipers! Who warned you. Mt 3:7

BROTHER

Am I my **b**-'s guardian? Gn 4:9
His **b-s** were jealous of him, Gn 37:11
When **b-s** . . . and one of them dies
without a son, Dt 25:5
good when **b-s** live together Ps 133:1
a **b** is born for a difficult time. Pr 17:17
offended **b** is harder to reach Pr 18:19
friend who stays closer than a **b**. Pr 18:24
be reconciled with your **b**, Mt 5:24
B will betray **b** to death, Mt 10:21
If your **b** sins against you, Mt 18:15
Whoever does the will of God is my **b**
and sister and mother. Mk 3:35
no one who has left house or **b-s** Mk 10:29
b of yours was dead and is alive Lk 15:32
my **b-s** . . . my own flesh and blood. Rm 9:3
b goes to court against **b**, 1Co 6:6
if food causes my **b** to fall, 1Co 8:13
but warn him as a **b**. 2Th 3:15
not ashamed to call them **b-s**, Heb 2:11
the one who hates his **b** is in the
darkness, 1Jn 2:11
lay down our lives for our **b-s**. 1Jn 3:16

BROTHER-IN-LAW

Perform your duty as her **b**. Gn 38:8
Her **b** is to take her as his wife, Dt 25:5

BROTHERLY

show sincere **b** love for each, 1Pt 1:22

BRUISED

He will not break a **b** reed, Is 42:3; Mt 12:20

BUD

let's see if the vine has **b-ded**, Sg 7:12
Though the fig tree does not **b**. Hab 3:17

BUILD

let's **b** ourselves a city Gn 11:4
cities that you did not **b**, Dt 6:10
So he **built** it in seven years. 1Kg 6:38
who will **b** a house for me, 1Ch 17:12
began to **b** the LORD's temple 2Ch 3:1
appointed me to **b** him a house. Ezr 1:2
Unless the LORD **b-s** a house, Ps 127:1
Wisdom has **built** her house; Pr 9:1
wise woman **b-s** her house, Pr 14:1
to tear down and a time to **b**; Ec 3:3
B houses and live in them. Jr 29:5
who **built** his house on the
rock. Mt 7:24
on this rock I will **b** my church, Mt 16:18
which is able to **b** you up Ac 20:32
for his good, to **b** him up. Rm 15:2
be careful how he **b-s** on it. 1Co 3:10
puffs up, but love **b-s** up. 1Co 8:1
but not everything **b-s** up. 1Co 10:23
Lord gave for **b-ing** you up 2Co 10:8
built on the foundation of the apostles
and prophets, Eph 2:20
to **b** up the body of Christ, Eph 4:12
rooted and **built** up in him Col 2:7
and **b** each other up 1Th 5:11

BUILDING (N)

Do you see these great **b-s**? Mk 13:2
You are God's field, God's **b**. 1Co 3:9
we have a **b** from God, 2Co 5:1
the whole **b**, being put together, Eph 2:21

BUILDER

The stone that the **b-s** rejected .... Ps 118:22
The stone that the **b-s** rejected .... Mt 21:42
whose architect and **b** is God. .... Heb 11:10
The stone that the **b-s** rejected 1Pt 2:7

BULL

their hands on the **b-**'s head. .... Ex 29:10
unblemished **b** as a sin offering .... Lv 4:3
Many **b-s** surround me; .... Ps 22:12
I will not take a **b** from. .... Ps 50:9
Do I eat the flesh of **b-s** .... Ps 50:13
no desire for the blood of **b-s**, ... Is 1:11
impossible for the blood of **b-s** .... Heb 10:4

BULLY

not a **b** but gentle, ... 1Tm 3:3
not a **b**, not greedy for money, ... Ti 1:7

BURDEN (N)

bear the **b** of the people, ... Nm 11:17
Cast your **b** on the LORD, ... Ps 55:22
Day after day he bears our **b-s**; .... Ps 68:19
They have become a **b** to me; .... Is 1:14
no longer refer to the **b**
of the LORD, ... Jr 23:36
yoke is easy and my **b** is light. .... Mt 11:30
You load people with **b-s** .... Lk 11:46
Carry one another's **b-s**; .... Gl 6:2

BURDEN (V)

have **b-ed** me with your sins; .... Is 43:24
you who are weary and **b-ed**, ... Mt 11:28
I will not **b** you, ... 2Co 12:14
Let the church not be **b-ed**, ... 1Tm 5:16

BURIAL

Give me **b** property among you .... Gn 23:4
does not even have a proper **b**, ... Ec 6:3
she has prepared me for **b**. .... Mt 26:12

BURN

Why isn't the bush **b-ing** up? .... Ex 3:3
b for **b**, bruise for bruise, ... Ex 21:25
b-ing on the altar continually; .... Lv 6:13
Israel did not **b** any of the cities .... Jos 11:13
to **b** their sons and daughters .... Jr 7:31
king not to **b** the scroll, ... Jr 36:25
the chaff he will **b** with fire. .... Mt 3:12
into the fire, and they are **b-ed**. .... Jn 15:6
If anyone's work is **b-ed** up, ... 1Co 3:15
better to marry than to **b** 1Co 7:9
a third of the earth was **b-ed** up, ... Rv 8:7
lake of fire that **b-s** with sulfur. .... Rv 19:20

BURNING (ADJ)

turned from his **b** anger. .... Jos 7:26
my insides are full of **b** pain, ... Ps 38:7
in my **b** zeal I speak against. .... Ezk 36:5

BURNT

If his offering is a **b** offering. .... Lv 1:3

BURST

vast watery depths **b** open, ... Gn 7:11
about to **b** like new wineskins. .... Jb 32:19
the new wine will **b** the skins, ... Lk 5:37
He fell headfirst, his body **b** open .... Ac 1:18

BURY

be **b-ied** at a ripe old age. .... Gn 15:15
so that I can **b** my dead. .... Gn 23:4
Joseph's bones, . . . were **b-ied** .... Jos 24:32
first let me go **b** my father. .... Mt 8:21
let the dead **b** their own dead. .... Mt 8:22
were **b-ied** with him by
baptism .... Rm 6:4
was **b-ied**, that he was raised. 1Co 15:4
b-ied with him in baptism, ... Col 2:12

BUSH

the **b** was on fire but was not. .... Ex 3:2
passage about the burning **b**, ... Mk 12:26
in the flame of a burning **b**. .... Ac 7:30

BUSINESS

to mind your own **b**, ... 1Th 4:11
and do **b** and make a profit. .... Jms 4:13

BUSYBODIES

are also gossips and **b**, ... 1Tm 5:13

BUTTER

churning of milk produces **b**, ... Pr 30:33

BUY

B—and do not sell—truth, ... Pr 23:23
She evaluates a field and **b-s** it; .... Pr 31:16
b wine and milk without silver .... Is 55:1
threw out all those **b-ing** and .... Mt 21:12
for you were **bought** at a price. 1Co 6:20
denying the Master who
bought 2Pt 2:1
b from me gold refined .... Rv 3:18
no one can **b** or sell unless. .... Rv 13:17

BUYER

it's worthless!" the **b** says, ... Pr 20:14

C

CAESAREA

came to the region of **C** Philippi, ... Mt 16:13
a man in **C** named Cornelius, ... Ac 10:1
Paul should be kept at **C**, ... Ac 25:4

CAIAPHAS

High priest, along with his father-in-law Annas, who sentenced Jesus (Mt 23:6; Lk 3:2; Jn 18:13). Spoke prophetically (Jn 11:49-52). Threatened Peter and John (Ac 4:6).

CAIN

Firstborn of Adam and Eve; crop farmer; murdered his brother; God marked and banished him (Gn 4:1-25; Heb 11:4; 1Jn 3:12; Jd 11).

CALAMITY

will laugh at your **c**. .... Pr 1:26
your brother in the day of his **c**; .... Ob 12

CALCULATE

first sit down and **c** the cost .... Lk 14:28
c the number of the beast, ... Rv 13:18

CALEB

Judahite who scouted Canaan and, along with Joshua, recommended invasion (Nm 13:30–14:38). Entered the promised land (Dt 1:36); received Hebron (Jos 14:13).

CALF

made it into an image of a **c**. .... Ex 32:4
Then he made two golden **c-ves**, ... 1Kg 12:28
bring the fattened **c** and slaughter .... Lk 15:23
not by the blood of goats
and **c-ves**. .... Heb 9:12

CALL

people began to **c** on the name .... Gn 4:26
I **c** heaven and earth as witnesses .... Dt 4:26
Then the LORD **c-ed** Samuel, ... 1Sm 3:4
I **c-ed** to the LORD in my distress; 2Sm 22:7
c on the name of your god, and I
will **c** on the name of LORD. 1Kg 18:24
C on me in a day of trouble; .... Ps 50:15
I **c** to you from the ends of the earth .... Ps 61:2
is near all who **c** out to him, ... Ps 145:18
Doesn't wisdom **c** out? .... Pr 8:1
Her children rise up and **c** her
blessed. .... Pr 31:28
Woe to those who **c** evil good. .... Is 5:20
c to him while he is near. .... Is 55:6
Even before they **c**, I will answer; .... Is 65:24
everyone who **c-s** on the name of .... Jl 2:32
I didn't come to **c** the righteous, ... Mt 9:13
Why do you **c** me 'Lord, Lord,' .... Lk 6:46
He **c-s** his own sheep by name. .... Jn 10:3
You **c** me Teacher and Lord. .... Jn 13:13
I do not **c** you servants anymore, ... Jn 15:15
those he **c-ed**, he also justified; .... Rm 8:30
everyone who **c-s** on the name of .... Rm 10:13
God's heavenly **c** in Christ Jesus. .... Php 3:14
God has not **c-ed** us to impurity 1Th 4:7

CALLING (N)

God's . . . and **c** are irrevocable. .... Rm 11:29
Brothers and sisters, consider your **c**: 1Co 1:26
walk worthy of the **c** you have. .... Eph 4:1
confirm your **c** and election, ... 2Pt 1:10

CALM (N)

And there was a great **c**. .... Mt 8:26

CALM (V)

I have **c-ed** and quieted myself .... Ps 131:2
one slow to anger **c-s** strife. .... Pr 15:18

CAMEL

she got down from her **c**. .... Gn 24:64
easier for a **c** to go through the eye. .... Mt 19:24
gnat, but gulp down a **c**! .... Mt 23:24

CAMP (N)

Jacob said, "This is God's **c**." .... Gn 32:2
outside the **c** and slaughtered .... Nm 19:3
go to him outside the **c**, ... Heb 13:13

CAMP (V)

c around the tent of meeting .... Nm 2:2

CANA

a wedding took place in **C** of Galilee. .... Jn 2:1

CANAAN

Son of Ham, his descendants, and the land they populated (Gn 9:18-27; 10:15-19). God promised the land to Abraham (12:4-7; 17:8; Ex 6:4; 1Ch 16:15-18).

CANAANITE

"Do not marry a **C** woman." ... Gn 28:6
drive out the **C-s**, Amorites, ... Ex 33:2
so the **C-s** have lived among them ... Jdg 1:30
a **C** woman from that region came ... Mt 15:22

CANAL

among the exiles by the Chebar **C**, ... Ezk 1:1
I was beside the Ulai **C**. ... Dn 8:2

CANCEL

seven years you must **c** debts. ... Dt 15:1

CANOPY

made darkness a **c** around him, ... 2Sm 22:12
spreading out the sky like a **c**, ... Ps 104:2

CAPERNAUM

went to live in **C** by the sea, ... Mt 4:13
teaching in the synagogue in **C**. ... Jn 6:59

CAPITALS

made two **c** of cast bronze ... 1Kg 7:16
Strike the **c** of the pillars ... Am 9:1

CAPTIVE

the king of Babylon took him **c** ... 2Kg 24:12
took many **c-s** to Damascus ... 2Ch 28:5
to the heights, taking away **c-s**; ... Ps 68:18
to proclaim liberty to the **c-s** ... Is 61:1
to proclaim freedom to the **c-s** ... Lk 4:18
take every thought **c** ... 2Co 10:5
took the captives **c**; he gave gifts ... Eph 4:8
Be careful that no one takes you **c** ... Col 2:8
taken **c**, into captivity he goes. ... Rv 13:10

CAPTIVITY

returned to Jerusalem from the **c**, ... Ezr 3:8
those destined for **c**, to **c**. ... Jr 15:2
taken captive, into **c** he goes. ... Rv 13:10

CARCASS

who touches its **c** will be unclean ... Lv 11:39
honey from the lion's **c**. ... Jdg 14:9

CARE (N)

the sheep under his **c**. ... Ps 95:7
I was sick and you took **c** of me; ... Mt 25:36
to an inn, and took **c** of him. ... Lk 10:34
casting all your **c-s** on him, ... 1Pt 5:7

CARE (V)

what is a human that you **c** for him, ... Ps 144:3
son of man that you **c** for him? ... Heb 2:6
because he **c-s** about you. ... 1Pt 5:7

CAREFUL

be **c** not to forget the LORD ... Dt 6:12
Be **c** to obey all these things ... Dt 12:28
c not to practice your righteousness ... Mt 6:1
each one is to be **c** how he builds ... 1Co 3:10
But be **c** that this right of yours ... 1Co 8:9
c attention, then, to how you walk ... Eph 5:15

CARELESS

to account for every **c** word ... Mt 12:36

CARMEL

gathered the prophets at Mount **C** ... 1Kg 18:20

CARMI

Son of Reuben (Gn 46:9; Nm 26:6).

CAROUSING

not in **c** and drunkenness; ... Rm 13:13

CARPENTER

Isn't this the **c-'s** son? ... Mt 13:55
Isn't this the **c**, the son of Mary, ... Mk 6:3

CARRY

I **c-ied** you on eagles' wings ... Ex 19:4
God **c-ied** you as a man **c-ies** his son ... Dt 1:31
No one but the Levites may **c** ... 1Ch 15:2
shepherd them, and **c** them forever. ... Ps 28:9
lambs in his arms and **c-ies** them ... Is 40:11
and he **c-ied** our pains; ... Is 53:4
not **c-ing** a load ... on the Sabbath day .. Jr 17:22
He himself ... **c-ied** our diseases. ... Mt 8:17
Don't **c** a money-bag, traveling bag, ... Lk 10:4
not **c** out the desire of the flesh. ... Gl 5:16
C one another's burdens; ... Gl 6:2

CASE

argue my **c** before God. ... Jb 13:3
The first to state his **c** seems right ... Pr 18:17
Let's argue the **c** together. ... Is 43:26
the LORD has a **c** against his people, ... Mc 6:2

CAST (ADJ)

Do not make **c** images of gods ... Ex 34:17
his **c** images are a lie; ... Jr 10:14; 51:17

CAST (V)

c spells, consult a medium or ... Dt 18:11
Joshua **c** lots for them at Shiloh ... Jos 18:10
He **c** the *pur*—that is, the lot— ... Est 9:24
they **c** lots for my clothing. ... Ps 22:18
C your burden on the LORD, ... Ps 55:22
The lot is **c** into the lap, ... Pr 16:33
who comes to me I will never
  c out. ... Jn 6:37
they **c** lots for my clothing. ... Jn 19:24
Who has **c** a spell on you, ... Gl 3:1
c-ing all your care on him, ... 1Pt 5:7
c their crowns before the throne ... Rv 4:10

CATCH

your sin will **c** up with you. ... Nm 32:23
C the foxes for us—the little foxes ... Sg 2:15
now on you will be **c-ing** people! ... Lk 5:10
brought a woman **caught** in
  adultery, ... Jn 8:3
caught up to the third heaven. ... 2Co 12:2
be **caught** up together with them ... 1Th 4:17
her child was **caught** up to God ... Rv 12:5

CATTLE

is mine, the **c** on a thousand hills. ... Ps 50:10

CAUSE (N)

For you have upheld my just **c**; ... Ps 9:4
have persecuted me without **c**, ... Ps 119:161
upholds the just **c** of the poor, ... Ps 140:12
Don't accuse anyone without **c**, ... Pr 3:30
he will champion their **c**
  against you. ... Pr 23:11

CAUSE (V)

and **c-s** grass to grow on the hills. ... Ps 147:8
Even if he **c-s** suffering, ... Lm 3:32
c you to follow my statutes ... Ezk 36:27
whoever **c-s** ... to fall away— ... Mt 18:6
c one of these little ones to stumble ... Lk 17:2

CAVE

give me the **c** of Machpelah ... Gn 23:9
took refuge in the **c** of Adullam. ... 1Sm 22:1
Then Saul left the **c** and went on. ... 1Sm 24:7
hid them, fifty men to a **c**, ... 1Kg 18:4
hid in the **c-s** and among
  the rocks ... Rv 6:15

CEASE

and day and night will not **c**. ... Gn 8:22
there will never **c** to be poor
  people. ... Dt 15:11
sin ... by **c-ing** to pray for you ... 1Sm 12:23
He makes wars **c** ... Ps 46:9
got into the boat, the wind **c-d**. ... Mt 14:32
otherwise grace **c-s** to be grace. ... Rm 11:6
as for tongues, they will **c**; ... 1Co 13:8

CEDAR

I am living in a **c** house while ... 2Sm 7:2
command that **c-s** from
  Lebanon be ... 1Kg 5:6
and grow like a **c** tree in Lebanon. ... Ps 92:12

CELEBRATE

c it as a festival to the LORD ... Lv 23:41

CENSUS

Take a **c** of the entire ... Nm 1:2; 26:2
he had taken a **c** of the troops. ... 2Sm 24:10

CENTURION

a **c** came to him, pleading with him ... Mt 8:5
When the **c** saw what happened, ... Lk 23:47
in Caesarea named Cornelius, a **c** ... Ac 10:1

CEPHAS

Aramaic for "Rock"; Peter (Jn 1:42; 1Co 1:12; 3:22; 9:5; 15:5; Gl 1:18; 2:9,11,14).

CERTIFICATE

he may write her a divorce **c**, ... Dt 24:1
He erased the **c** of debt, ... Col 2:14

CHAFF

were shattered and became like **c** ... Dn 2:35
But the **c** he will burn up
  with fire. ... Mt 3:12

CHAIN
and broke their **c-s** apart.... Ps 107:14
the **c-s** fell off his wrists.... Ac 12:7
For this I am an ambassador in **c-s**. ... Eph 6:20
in **c-s** of utter darkness 2Pt 2:4
a great **c** in his hand.... Rv 20:1

CHALDEA
Another name for the Babylonian Empire (Jr 51:24; Ezk 12:13; 23:15).

CHALDEAN
Inhabitants of Chaldea (Gn 11:28). Known as sages or magicians (Dn 2:2; 4:7). Took Judah into exile (2Kg 25; 2Ch 36:17-19; Ezr 5:12; Jr 32).

CHAMBER
the king would bring me to his **c-s**.... Sg 1:4

CHAMPION
a **c** named Goliath, from Gath,.... 1Sm 17:4

CHANCE
time and **c** happen to all of them..... Ec 9:11

CHANGE
c-d my wages ten times.... Gn 31:7
or a son of man, that he might **c** his mind. . Nm 23:19
does not lie or **c** his mind, ... 1Sm 15:29
You will **c** them like a garment,.... Ps 102:26
Can the Cushite **c** his skin,.... Jr 13:23
Because I, the LORD, have not **c-d**, ... Mal 3:6
but we will all be **c-d**, ... 1Co 15:51
and they will be **c-d** like clothing. .... Heb 1:12
and will not **c** his mind,.... Heb 7:21

CHANGERS
overturned the tables of the money **c** . . Mt 21:12

CHANNEL
Who cuts a **c** for the flooding rain.... Jb 38:25

CHARACTER
you are a woman of noble **c**.... Ru 3:11
c, and proven **c** produces hope..... Rm 5:4
so that the proven **c** of your faith.... 1Pt 1:7

CHARGE (N)
Joseph was in **c** of the country;.... Gn 42:6
Above his head they put up the **c**.... Mt 27:37
that they could find a **c** against him. .... Lk 6:7
the gospel and offer it free of **c**.... 1Co 9:18

CHARGE (V)
Do not **c** your brother interest.... Dt 23:19
man the Lord will never **c** with sin! .... Rm 4:8
I solemnly **c** you before God.... 1Tm 5:21
c them before God not to fight 2Tm 2:14
c that to my account..... Phm 18

CHARIOT
came back and covered the **c-s**.... Ex 14:28
even though they have iron **c-s**.... Jos 17:18
because those people had
iron **c-s**.... Jdg 1:19
nine hundred iron **c-s**,.... Jdg 4:3
Solomon accumulated 1,400 **c-s** 1Kg 10:26
a **c** of fire with horses of fire 2Kg 2:11
covered with horses and
c-s of fire.... 2Kg 6:17
Some take pride in **c-s**,.... Ps 20:7
God's **c-s** are tens of thousands,.... Ps 68:17
making the clouds his **c**,.... Ps 104:3
saw four **c-s** coming .... Zch 6:1
I will cut off the **c** from Ephraim .... Zch 9:10

CHARITY
doing good works and acts of **c**..... Ac 9:36
your acts of **c** have ascended .... Ac 10:4

CHARM
C is deceptive and beauty is .... Pr 31:30

CHARMED
If the snake bites before it is **c**,.... Ec 10:11

CHASE
whoever **c-s** fantasies lacks sense. .... Pr 12:11

CHEAT
c-ed me and changed my wages.... Gn 31:7
Why not rather be **c-ed**?.... 1Co 6:7

CHEEK
My **c-s** to those who tore out my .... Is 50:6
Let him offer his **c** to the one .... Lm 3:30
if anyone slaps you on your
right **c**, ... Mt 5:39

CHEERFUL
God loves a **c** giver..... 2Co 9:7

CHEMOSH
Moab's god (Jdg 11:24; 1Kg 11:7,33).

CHERUB
Make one **c** at one end and .... Ex 25:19
He rode on a **c** and flew, ... 2Sm 22:11
The first **c-'s** height was 15 feet 1Kg 6:26
one was the face of a **c**, ... Ezk 10:14

CHERUBIM
stationed the **c** and the flaming,.... Gn 3:24
he made two **c** 15 feet high.... 1Kg 6:23
You who sit enthroned between
the **c**, ... Ps 80:1
four wheels beside the **c**, ... Ezk 10:9

CHEST
righteousness like armor on your **c**, ... Eph 6:14

CHICKS
as a hen gathers her **c**..... Mt 23:37; Lk 13:34

CHIEF
the **c-s** of David's warriors.... 1Ch 11:10
rejected by the elders,
the **c** priests, ... Mk 8:31
when the **c** Shepherd appears, ... 1Pt 5:4

CHILD
quieted my soul like a weaned **c**.... Ps 131:2
For a **c** will be born for us,.... Is 9:6
and a **c** will lead them.... Is 11:6
Can a woman forget her nursing **c**,.... Is 49:15
When Israel was a **c**, I loved him,.... Hs 11:1
He called a small **c** and had him .... Mt 18:2
When I was a **c**, I spoke like a **c**,.... 1Co 13:11
give birth it might devour her **c**..... Rv 12:4

CHILDBEARING
But she will be saved through **c**,.... 1Tm 2:15

CHILDISH
a man, I put aside **c** things..... 1Co 13:11

CHILDLESS
I am **c** and the heir of my house is .... Gn 15:2
No woman will miscarry or be **c** .... Ex 23:26
who is **c** gives birth to seven,.... 1Sm 2:5
Rejoice, **c** one,.... Is 54:1
Rejoice, **c** woman,.... Gl 4:27

CHILDREN
you will bear **c** with painful effort.... Gn 3:16
When your **c** ask you,.... Ex 12:26
the consequences of the fathers' iniquity
on the **c**.... Ex 20:5
Teach them to your **c**,.... Dt 11:19
Fathers are not to be put to death for
their **c**, and **c** ... for their fathers;.... Dt 24:16
In the future, when your **c** ask you,.... Jos 4:6
Rachel weeping for her **c**, refusing to
be comforted for her **c** because .... Jr 31:15
and the **c-'s** teeth are set on edge..... Jr 31:29
and the **c-'s** teeth are set on edge .... Ezk 18:2
c for Abraham from these stones..... Mt 3:9
how to give good gifts to your **c**,.... Mt 7:11
you turn and become like little **c**,.... Mt 18:3
Let the little **c** come to me.... Mk 10:14
C will rise up against parents .... Mk 13:12
women without **c**, ... are fortunate! .... Lk 23:29
gave them the right to be **c** of God, ... Jn 1:12
testifies ... that we are God's **c**,.... Rm 8:16
C, obey your parents in the Lord,.... Eph 6:1
C, obey your parents in everything, ... Col 3:20
Fathers, do not exasperate your **c**,.... Col 3:21
managing their **c** and their own.... 1Tm 3:12
that we should be called God's **c**—.... 1Jn 3:1

CHINNERETH
Another name for the Sea of Galilee (Nm 34:11; Jos 13:27) and a city there (Jos 19:35).

CHOICE
I am offering you three **c-s**.... 2Sm 24:12

CHOOSE *SEE ALSO* CHOSEN (ADJ)
Lot **chose** the entire plain of the Jordan . . Gn 13:11
He will let the one he **c-s** come .... Nm 16:5
He **chose** their descendants .... Dt 4:37
LORD ... **chose** you, not because.... Dt 7:7
the place the LORD your God **c-s** .... Dt 12:5
C life so that you .... Dt 30:19
c for yourselves today:.... Jos 24:15
who **chose** me over your father 2Sm 6:21
the LORD has **chosen** Zion;.... Ps 132:13
A good name is to be **chosen** over .... Pr 22:1
servant, Jacob, whom I have **chosen**, ... Is 41:8
I **chose** you before I formed you .... Jr 1:5

are invited, but few are **chosen** Mt 22:14
and he **chose** twelve of them Lk 6:13
You did not **c** me, but I **chose** you Jn 15:16
a remnant **chosen** by grace Rm 11:5
he **chose** us in him, before the Eph 1:4
loved by God, that he has **chosen** you 1Th 1:4

CHOSEN (ADJ)

this is my **c** one; I delight in him. Is 42:1
This is my Son, the **C** One; Lk 9:35
God's **c** ones, holy and dearly Col 3:12
a **c** and honored cornerstone, 1Pt 2:6
you are a **c** race, a royal priesthood, 1Pt 2:9

CHRIST *SEE ALSO* MESSIAH

The birth of Jesus **C** came about Mt 1:18
Messiah is coming" (... called **C**). Jn 4:25
Scriptures that Jesus is the **C**. Ac 18:28
through faith in Jesus **C**, to all Rm 3:22
we were still sinners, **C** died for us. Rm 5:8
if we died with **C**, we believe that Rm 6:8
heirs of God and coheirs with **C** Rm 8:17
can separate us from the love of **C**? Rm 8:35
For **C** is the end of the law Rm 10:4
who are many are one body in **C** Rm 12:5
But put on the Lord Jesus **C**, Rm 13:14
but we preach **C** crucified, 1Co 1:23
and that rock was **C**. 1Co 10:4
Imitate me, as I also imitate **C**. 1Co 11:1
C is the head of every man, 1Co 11:3
you are the body of **C**, 1Co 12:27
C died for our sins according to 1Co 15:3
also in **C** all will be made alive. 1Co 15:22
Jesus **C** as Lord, and ourselves as 2Co 4:5
is in **C**, he is a new creation; 2Co 5:17
I no longer live, but **C** lives in me. Gl 2:20
except the cross of ... Jesus **C**. Gl 6:14
into him who is the head—**C**. Eph 4:15
just as **C** loved the church Eph 5:25
to live is **C** and to die is gain. Php 1:21
considered ... a loss because of **C**. Php 3:7
C is all and in all. Col 3:11
the dead in **C** will rise first. 1Th 4:16
the coming of our Lord Jesus **C**. 2Th 2:1
C ... came into the world to save 1Tm 1:15
salvation, which is in **C** Jesus, 2Tm 2:10
C also suffered for sins once for all, 1Pt 3:18
ridiculed for the name of **C**, 1Pt 4:14
who denies that Jesus is the **C**? 1Jn 2:22
with **C** for a thousand years Rv 20:4

CHRISTIAN

were first called **C-s** at Antioch. Ac 11:26
if anyone suffers as a **C**, 1Pt 4:16

CHURCH

on this rock I will build my **c**, Mt 16:18
pay attention to them, tell the **c**. Mt 18:17
as overseers, to shepherd the **c** Ac 20:28
the **c** that meets in their home. Rm 16:5
one who prophesies builds up the **c**. 1Co 14:4
for a woman to speak in the **c** 1Co 14:35
wife as Christ is the head of the **c**. Eph 5:23
regarding zeal, persecuting the **c**; Php 3:6
the head of the body, the **c**; Col 1:18
are the angels of the seven **c-es**, Rv 1:20
to the angel of the **c** in Ephesus Rv 2:1

CIRCUMCISE

your males must be **c-d**. Gn 17:10
Abraham **c-d** him, Gn 21:4
Therefore, **c** your hearts Dt 10:16
God will **c** your heart Dt 30:6
C yourselves to the LORD; Jr 4:4
they came to **c** the child Lk 1:59
you **c** a man on the Sabbath. Jn 7:22
Unless you are **c-d** according to Ac 15:1
if ... **c-d**, Christ will not benefit you Gl 5:2
c-d the eighth day; Php 3:5

CIRCUMCISION

and **c** is of the heart. Rm 2:29
c and uncircumcision mean nothing; Gl 6:15
we are the **c**, the ones who worship Php 3:3
with a **c** not done with hands, Col 2:11

CIRCUMSTANCES

learned to be content in whatever **c**. Php 4:11

CISTERN

may drink water from his own **c** 2Kg 18:31
Drink water from your own **c**, Pr 5:15
dug **c-s** for themselves, cracked **c-s** Jr 2:13
Jeremiah had been put into the **c**. Jr 38:7

CITIZEN

realized Paul was a Roman **c**. Ac 22:29

CITIZENSHIP

I bought this **c** for a large amount Ac 22:28
Our **c** is in heaven, Php 3:20

CITY

Lot lived in the **c-ies** on the plain Gn 13:12
give **c-ies** ... for the Levites Nm 35:2
will include six **c-ies** of refuge, Nm 35:6
Select your **c-ies** of refuge, Jos 20:2
gave the Levites these **c-ies** Jos 21:3
and **c-ies** you did not build, Jos 24:13
which he named the **c** of David. 2Sm 5:9
unless the LORD watches over a **c**, Ps 127:1
her works praise her at the **c** gates. Pr 31:31
Say to the **c-ies** of Judah, "Here is your God!" Is 40:9
c situated on a hill cannot be hidden. Mt 5:14
I have many people in this **c**. Ac 18:10
he was looking forward to the **c**. Heb 11:10
we do not have an enduring **c** Heb 13:14
saw the holy **c**, the new Jerusalem, Rv 21:2

CLAIM

rose up, **c-ing** to be somebody, Ac 5:36
while **c-ing** to be somebody great. Ac 8:9
C-ing to be wise, ... became fools Rm 1:22

CLAN

small among the **c-s** of Judah; Mc 5:2

CLANGING

a noisy gong or a **c** cymbal. 1Co 13:1

CLAP

C your hands, all you peoples; Ps 47:1
Let the rivers **c** their hands; Ps 98:8
trees of the field will **c** their Is 55:12

CLAY

strength is dried up like baked **c**; Ps 22:15
out of the muddy **c**, and set my feet Ps 40:2
Does **c** say to the one forming it, Is 45:9
we are the **c**, and you are our potter; Is 64:8
Just like **c** in the potter's hand, Jr 18:6
partly iron and partly fired **c**. Dn 2:33
has the potter no right over the **c**, Rm 9:21
Now we have this treasure in **c** jars, 2Co 4:7

CLEAN

of all the **c** animals, and two Gn 7:2
The one who has **c** hands and a Ps 24:4
with hyssop, and I will be **c**; Ps 51:7
create a **c** heart for me and Ps 51:10
You can make me **c**. Mt 8:2
You **c** the outside of the cup and Mt 23:25
he declared all foods **c**). Mk 7:19
You are **c**, but not all of you. Jn 13:10
You are already **c** because of the Jn 15:3
God has made **c**, do not call. Ac 10:15

CLEANSE

my guilt and **c** me from my sin. Ps 51:2
holy, **c-ing** her with the washing Eph 5:26
to **c** for himself a people Ti 2:14
C your hands, sinners, and Jms 4:8
Jesus his Son **c-s** us from all sin. 1Jn 1:7
to **c** us from all unrighteousness. 1Jn 1:9

CLEAR

and he will **c** the way before me Mal 3:1
and he will **c** his threshing Mt 3:12
strive to have a **c** conscience Ac 24:16
the faith with a **c** conscience. 1Tm 3:9
keeping a **c** conscience, 1Pt 3:16

CLIFF

your nest is set in the **c-s**. Nm 24:21

CLIMB

I will **c** the palm tree and take Sg 7:8
he **c-ed** up a sycamore tree to see Lk 19:4
by the door but **c-s** in some other Jn 10:1

CLING

"Don't **c** to me," Jesus told her Jn 20:17
Detest evil; **c** to what is good. Rm 12:9

CLOAK

Put your hand inside your **c**. Ex 4:6
neighbor's **c** as collateral, Ex 22:26
Wrap your **c** around you, Ac 12:8
bring the **c** I left in Troas with 2Tm 4:13
You will roll them up like a **c**, Heb 1:12

CLOSE (ADV)

who stays **c-r** than a brother. Pr 18:24

CLOSE (V)

what he opens, no one can **c**; Is 22:22
who opens and no one will **c**, Rv 3:7

CLOTH

of unshrunk **c** on an old garment. Mk 2:21

him tightly in **c** and laid him. Lk 2:7
he saw the linen **c-s** lying there, Jn 20:5

CLOTHE

and **c-d** me with gladness Ps 30:11
If that's how God **c-s** the grass of Mt 6:30
I was naked and you **c-d** me; Mt 25:36
mortal . . . is **c-d** with immortality, 1Co 15:54
not want to be unclothed but **c-d**, 2Co 5:4
All of you **c** yourselves with humility. 1Pt 5:5
a woman **c-d** with the sun, with the Rv 12:1

CLOTHES

your **c** . . . did not wear out; Dt 29:5
anointed himself, changed his **c**, 2Sm 12:20
fire and his **c** not be burned? Pr 6:27
Tear your hearts, not just your **c**, Jl 2:13
And why do you worry about **c**? Mt 6:28
get in here without wedding **c**? Mt 22:12
in fine **c**, and a poor man dressed in filthy **c** also comes in Jms 2:2

CLOTHING

Your **c** did not wear out, and Dt 8:4
and they cast lots for my **c**. Ps 22:18
Strength and honor are her **c**, Pr 31:25
and the body more than **c**? Mt 6:25
come to you in sheep's **c** Mt 7:15
they cast lots for my **c**. Jn 19:24
If we have food and **c**, 1Tm 6:8

CLOUD

I have placed my bow in the **c-s**, Gn 9:13
a pillar of **c** to lead them Ex 13:21
the mountain, the **c** covered it. Ex 24:15
the **c** filled the LORD's temple, 1Kg 8:10
a **c** as small as a man's hand 1Kg 18:44
your faithfulness reaches the **c-s**. Ps 57:10
making the **c-s** his chariot, Ps 104:3
temple was filled with the **c**, Ezk 10:4
coming with the **c-s** of heaven. Dn 7:13
a bright **c** covered them, and a voice from the **c** said, Mt 17:5
coming on the **c-s** of heaven with Mt 24:30
coming in **c-s** with great power Mk 13:26
of Man coming in a **c** with power Lk 21:27
a **c** took him out of their sight. Ac 1:9
ancestors were all under the **c**, 1Co 10:1
in the **c-s** to meet the Lord in the 1Th 4:17
have such a large **c** of witnesses. Heb 12:1
he is coming with the **c-s**, Rv 1:7

CLOUDLESS

the sun rises on a **c** morning, 2Sm 23:4

COAL

rain burning **c-s** and sulfur Ps 11:6
will heap burning **c-s** on his head, Pr 25:22
a glowing **c** that he had taken Is 6:6
be heaping fiery **c-s** on his head. Rm 12:20

COAT

let him have your **c** as well. Mt 5:40

COFFIN

and placed him in a **c** in Egypt. Gn 50:26

COHEIRS *SEE ALSO* HEIRS

heirs of God and **c** with Christ. Rm 8:17
The Gentiles are **c**, members of Eph 3:6
them honor as **c** of the grace of 1Pt 3:7

COIN

open its mouth you'll find a **c**. Mt 17:27
Show me the **c** used for the tax. Mt 22:19
if she loses one **c**, Lk 15:8
widow dropping in two tiny **c-s**. Lk 21:2

COLD

is like **c** water to a parched throat. Pr 25:25
even a cup of **c** water to one Mt 10:42
the love of many will grow **c**. Mt 24:12
that you are neither **c** nor hot. Rv 3:15

COLLAPSED

a great shout, and the wall **c**. Jos 6:20
pounded that house, and it **c**. Mt 7:27

COLLECTION

Now about the **c** for the saints: 1Co 16:1

COLLECTOR

even the tax **c-s** do the same? Mt 5:46
Thomas and Matthew the tax **c**; Mt 10:3
a friend of tax **c-s** and sinners! Mt 11:19
let him be like . . . a tax **c** to you. Mt 18:17
Tax **c-s** and prostitutes are entering. Mt 21:31
Tax **c-s** also came to be baptized, Lk 3:12
a Pharisee and the other a tax **c**. Lk 18:10
chief tax **c**, and he was rich. Lk 19:2

COLT

on a donkey, on a **c**, the foal of Zch 9:9
a donkey and on a **c**, the foal Mt 21:5
sitting on a donkey's **c**. Jn 12:15

COME

Spirit . . . **c** powerfully on him, Jdg 14:6,19
Spirit . . . **c** powerfully on David. 1Sm 16:13
who **c-s** in the name of the LORD Ps 118:26
Your kingdom **c**. Your will be Mt 6:10
to another, '**C**!' and he **c-s** Mt 8:9
Are you the one who is to **c**, Mt 11:3
who **c-s** in the name of the Lord. Mt 21:9
Father gives me will **c** to me, Jn 6:37
No one **c-s** to the Father except Jn 14:6
who is, who was, and who is **c-ing**; Rv 1:4
Spirit and the bride say, "**C**! Rv 22:17
Let the one who is thirsty **c**. Rv 22:17
Amen! **C**, Lord Jesus! Rv 22:20

COMFORT (N)

This is my **c** in my affliction: Ps 119:50
it is for your **c** and salvation; 2Co 1:6

COMFORT (V)

rod and your staff—they **c** me. Ps 23:4
LORD, have helped and **c-ed** me. Ps 86:17
they have no one to **c** them. Ec 4:1
"**C**, **c** my people," says your God. Is 40:1
For the LORD has **c-ed** his people, Is 49:13
I—I am the one who **c-s** you. Is 51:12
refusing to be **c-ed** for her. Jr 31:15
mourn, for they will be **c-ed**. Mt 5:4
able to **c** those who are in any kind of affliction, through the **c** we. 2Co 1:4

COMFORTERS

You are all miserable **c**. Jb 16:2

COMING

can endure the day of his **c**? Mal 3:2
what is the sign of your **c** and of the. Mt 24:3
still alive at the Lord's **c** 1Th 4:15
Now concerning the **c** of our Lord. 2Th 2:1
be patient until the Lord's **c**. Jms 5:7
"Where is his '**c**' that he promised? 2Pt 3:4

COMMAND (N)

who love him and keep his **c-s**. Dt 7:9
the **c** of the LORD is radiant, Ps 19:8
I love your **c-s** more than gold, Ps 119:127
but let your heart keep my **c-s**; Pr 3:1
who respects a **c** will be rewarded. Pr 13:13
least of these **c-s** and teaches. Mt 5:19
teaching as doctrines human **c-s**. Mt 15:9
the greatest and most important **c**. Mt 22:38
Abandoning the **c** of God, Mk 7:8
I give you a new **c**: Jn 13:34
love me, you will keep my **c-s**. Jn 14:15
If you keep my **c-s** you will remain Jn 15:10
This is my **c**: Love one another. Jn 15:12
I write to you is the Lord's **c**. 1Co 14:37
I am not writing you a new **c** 1Jn 2:7
Now this is his **c**: that we 1Jn 3:23
love for God is: to keep his **c-s**. And his **c-s** are not a burden, 1Jn 5:3
saints, who keep God's **c-s** Rv 14:12

COMMAND (V)

the tree about which I **c-ed** you, Gn 3:17
everything that God had **c-ed** him. Gn 6:22
You must say whatever I **c** you; Ex 7:2
not add anything to what I **c** you Dt 4:2
so that you may **c** your children Dt 32:46
you have **c-ed** us we will do, Jos 1:16
he **c-ed**, and it came into existence. Ps 33:9
for he **c-ed**, and they were created. Ps 148:5
everything I have **c-ed** you. Mt 28:20
I do as the Father **c-ed** me. Jn 14:31
God . . . **c-s** all people everywhere Ac 17:30
love one another as he **c-ed** us. 1Jn 3:23

COMMANDER

I have . . . come as **c** of the LORD's Jos 5:14

COMMANDMENT

He wrote the Ten **C-s**, Ex 34:28
follow the Ten **C-s**, which he wrote. Dt 4:13
the **c** is holy and just and good. Rm 7:12
is the first **c** with a promise Eph 6:2

COMMISSION

and **c** him in their sight. Nm 27:19
The LORD **c-ed** Joshua son of Nun, Dt 31:23

COMMIT

Do not **c** adultery. Ex 20:14; Dt 5:18
C your way to the LORD; Ps 37:5

COMMON

COMPANION

COMPANY

COMPARE

COMPASSION

COMPASSIONATE

COMPELS

COMPETE

COMPETENT

COMPLAIN

COMPLAINT

COMPLETE (ADJ)

COMPLETE (V)

COMPLETION

COMPREHEND

CONCEAL

CONCEIT

CONCEIVE

CONCERN (N)

CONCERN (V)

CONCUBINES

CONDEMN

CONDEMNATION

CONDUCT (N)

CONDUCT (V)

CONFESS

CONFESSION

CONFIDENCE

CONFIRM

CONFLICT

CONFORMED

CONFUSE
down there and **c** their language ... Gn 11:7

CONFUSION
So the city was filled with **c**, ... Ac 19:29

CONGREGATION
sing hymns to you in the **c**. ... Heb 2:12

CONQUER
I have **c-ed** the world. ... Jn 16:33
Do not be **c-ed** by evil, but **c** evil ... Rm 12:21
victory that has **c-ed** the world: ... 1Jn 5:4
as a conqueror in order to **c**. ... Rv 6:2

CONQUEROR
are more than a **c** through him. ... Rm 8:37
I will give the **c** the right to ... Rv 2:7

CONSCIENCE
a clear **c** toward God and men. ... Ac 24:16
Their **c-s** confirm this. ... Rm 2:15
but also because of your **c**. ... Rm 13:5
their **c**, being weak, is defiled. ... 1Co 8:7
of liars whose **c-s** are seared. ... 1Tm 4:2
cleanse our **c-s** from dead works to ... Heb 9:14
sprinkled clean from an evil **c**. ... Heb 10:22
keeping a clear **c**, so that. ... 1Pt 3:16

CONSECRATE
C every firstborn male to me, ... Ex 13:2
c them to serve me as priests. ... Ex 29:1
c it along with all its furnishings ... Ex 40:9
C yourselves and be holy, for I ... Lv 20:7
Joshua told the people, "**C** yourselves ... Jos 3:5
I have **c-d** this temple you have. ... 1Kg 9:3

CONSECRATED (ADJ)
However, there is **c** bread, but ... 1Sm 21:4

CONSIDER
Have you **c-ed** my servant Job? ... Jb 1:8
LORD; **c** my sighing. ... Ps 5:1
Even a fool is **c-ed** wise when he ... Pr 17:28
C how the wildflowers grow: ... Lk 12:27
you too **c** yourselves dead to sin. ... Rm 6:11
Brothers and sisters, **c** your calling: ... 1Co 1:26
but in humility **c** others as more ... Php 2:3
I also **c** everything to be a loss ... Php 3:8
she **c-ed** that the one who had. ... Heb 11:11
C it a great joy, my brothers. ... Jms 1:2

CONSISTENT
produce fruit **c** with repentance ... Mt 3:8

CONSOLATION
Christ, if any **c** of love, if any ... Php 2:1

CONSOLE
refused to be **c-d**, because they ... Mt 2:18

CONSPIRE
all of you have **c-d** against me! ... 1Sm 22:8
and the rulers **c** together ... Ps 2:2
they **c-d** to arrest Jesus ... Mt 26:4

CONSTANTLY
Pray **c**. ... 1Th 5:17

CONSULT
Saul said, "**C** a spirit for me. ... 1Sm 28:8
Rehoboam **c-ed** with the elders ... 1Kg 12:6
even **c-ed** a medium for guidance ... 1Ch 10:13
shouldn't a people **c** their God? ... Is 8:19
not immediately **c** with anyone. ... Gl 1:16

CONSUME
bush was on fire but was not **c-d**. ... Ex 3:2
so I may **c** them instantly. ... Nm 16:21
the LORD your God is a **c-ing** fire, ... Dt 4:24
fire fell and **c-d** the burnt offering ... 1Kg 18:38
zeal for your house has **c-d** me, ... Ps 69:9
For we are **c-d** by your anger; ... Ps 90:7
Zeal for your house will **c** me. ... Jn 2:17
for our God is a **c-ing** fire. ... Heb 12:29

CONTAIN
heaven, cannot **c** you, much less ... 1Kg 8:27
highest heaven cannot **c** him? ... 2Ch 2:6
itself could **c** the books that ... Jn 21:25

CONTEMPT
some to disgrace and eternal **c**. ... Dn 12:2
things and be treated with **c**? ... Mk 9:12
treated him with **c**, mocked him ... Lk 23:11
of God and holding him up to **c**. ... Heb 6:6

CONTEND
Let Baal **c** with him ... Jdg 6:32
Will the one who **c-s** with the ... Jb 40:2
will **c** with the one who **c-s** with you ... Is 49:25
appealing to you to **c** for the faith ... Jd 3

CONTENT
have learned to be **c** in whatever ... Php 4:11
we will be **c** with these. ... 1Tm 6:8

CONTENTMENT
godliness with **c** is a great gain ... 1Tm 6:6

CONTINUE
If you **c** in my word, ... Jn 8:31
urging them to **c** in the grace ... Ac 13:43
Should we **c** in sin so that grace ... Rm 6:1
c in what you have learned ... 2Tm 3:14

CONTRARY
a gospel **c** to what you received, ... Gl 1:9
law therefore **c** to God's promises? ... Gl 3:21
whatever else is **c** to the sound ... 1Tm 1:10

CONTRIVED
we did not follow cleverly **c** myths ... 2Pt 1:16

CONTROL (N)
have his children under **c**. ... 1Tm 3:4

CONTROL (V)
the one who **c-s** his lips is prudent. ... Pr 10:19
person who does not **c** his temper is ... Pr 25:28
able also to **c** the whole body ... Jms 3:2

CONVERT
land and sea to make one **c**. ... Mt 23:15
from Rome (both Jews and **c-s**), ... Ac 2:10
must not be a new **c**, or he might ... 1Tm 3:6

CONVICT
Who among you can **c** me of sin? ... Jn 8:46
He will **c** the world about sin, ... Jn 16:8
he is **c-ed** by all and is judged by ... 1Co 14:24
c all the ungodly ... Jd 15

CONVICTION
same understanding and the same **c** ... 1Co 1:10

CONVINCED
fully **c** that what he had promised ... Rm 4:21
be fully **c** in his own mind ... Rm 14:5

CONVINCING
alive to them by many **c** proofs, ... Ac 1:3

COPING
from foundation to **c** and from ... 1Kg 7:9

COPPER
whose hills you will mine **c**. ... Dt 8:9
and **c** is smelted from ore. ... Jb 28:2
All of them are **c**, tin, iron ... Ezk 22:18
gathers silver, **c**, iron, lead ... Ezk 22:20
it becomes hot and its **c** glows. ... Ezk 24:11
gold, silver, or **c** for your ... Mt 10:9

COPPERSMITH
blacksmiths and **c-s** to repair the ... 2Ch 24:12
Alexander the **c** did great harm ... 2Tm 4:14

COPY
These serve as a **c** and shadow of ... Heb 8:5
c-ies of the things in the heavens ... Heb 9:23

CORBAN
have received from me is **c** ... Mk 7:11

CORD
A **c** of three strands is not ... Ec 4:12
before the silver **c** is snapped, ... Ec 12:6
them with human **c-s**, with ropes ... Hs 11:4

CORINTH
left Athens and went to **C**, ... Ac 18:1

CORNELIUS
Centurion; Christian (Ac 10).

CORNER
cut off the **c** of Saul's robe. ... 1Sm 24:4
on the street **c-s** to be seen by people ... Mt 6:5

DESIRE (N)

Your **d** will be for your husband .... Gn 3:16
will give you your heart's **d-s**. .... Ps 37:4
my heart's **d** and prayer to God. ....Rm 10:1
no provision for the flesh to gratify
its **d-s**. ....Rm 13:14
to marry than to burn with **d**. 1Co 7:9
carry out the **d** of the flesh. ....Gl 5:16
and enticed by his own evil **d**. .... Jms 1:14

DESIRE (V)

or **d** your neighbor's house, ...Dt 5:21
nothing you **d** can equal her. ....Pr 3:15
that we should **d** him. ....Is 53:2
For I **d** loyalty and not .... Hs 6:6
I **d** mercy and not sacrifice .... Mt 9:13; 12:7
I have fervently **d-d** to eat this .... Lk 22:15
But **d** the greater gifts. 1Co 12:31
d-ing to put on our heavenly dwelling . . 2Co 5:2

DESOLATE

your house is left to you **d**. .... Mt 23:38
the children of the **d** woman, ...Gl 4:27

DESOLATION

set up the abomination of **d**. .... Dn 11:31
the abomination of **d**, ...Mt 24:15
abomination of **d** standing where it. . . .Mk 13:14
that its **d** has come near. .... Lk 21:20

DESPAIR (N)

myself over to **d** concerning all. .... Ec 2:20
we are perplexed but not in **d**; 2Co 4:8

DESPAIR (V)

so that we even **d-ed** of life 2Co 1:8

DESPISE

So Esau **d-d** his birthright. .... Gn 25:34
and she **d-d** him in her heart. 2Sm 6:16
fools **d** wisdom and discipline. .... Pr 1:7
He was **d-d** and rejected by men, ...Is 53:3
devoted to one and **d** the other. ....Mt 6:24
Don't let anyone **d** your youth, ...1Tm 4:12
endured a cross, **d-ing** the shame ......Heb 12:2

DESTINED

this child is **d** to cause the fall .... Lk 2:34

DESTITUTE

in goatskins, **d**, afflicted .... Heb 11:37

DESTROY

who is able to **d** both soul and.........Mt 10:28
Have you come to **d** us?................. Mk 1:24
to steal and kill and **d**. ....Jn 10:10
we are struck down but not **d-ed**. 2Co 4:9
our outer person is being **d-ed**, ...2Co 4:16
if our earthly tent . . . is **d-ed**, ... 2Co 5:1
who is able to save and to **d**. ....Jms 4:12

DESTRUCTION

set apart to the LORD for **d**. ....Jos 6:17
Pride comes before **d**, ...Pr 16:18
road broad that leads to **d**, ... Mt 7:13
objects of wrath prepared for **d**? ....Rm 9:22
Their end is **d**; their god is ....Php 3:19

the penalty of eternal **d**. 2Th 1:9
twist them to their own **d**, ...2Pt 3:16

DETERMINE

Since a person's days are **d-d** and ....Jb 14:5
I have **d-d** that my mouth will not ....Ps 17:3
but the LORD **d-s** his steps. ....Pr 16:9
person's steps are **d-d** by the LORD, ... Pr 20:24

DETEST

D evil; cling to what is good. .... Rm 12:9

DETESTABLE

committed all these **d** acts, ... Lv 18:27
imitating the **d** practices 2Kg 16:3

DEVIL

to be tempted by the **d**. .... Mt 4:1
enemy who sowed them is the **d**. ....Mt 13:39
for the **d** and his angels! ....Mt 25:41
Yet one of you is the **d**! .... Jn 6:70
don't give the **d** an opportunity ....Eph 4:27
against the schemes of the **d**. .... Eph 6:11
Resist the **d**, and he will. ....Jms 4:7
adversary the **d** is prowling 1Pt 5:8
who is called the **d** and Satan, ... Rv 12:9

DEVOTED

be **d** to one and despise the other. ....Mt 6:24

DEVOUR

Must the sword **d** forever? 2Sm 2:26
if you bite and **d** one another, ...Gl 5:15
looking for anyone he can **d**. 1Pt 5:8

DEVOUT

This man was righteous and **d**, ... Lk 2:25

DEW

If **d** is only on the fleece, ... Jdg 6:37

DICTATION

At Jeremiah's **d**, Baruch wrote on ....Jr 36:4

DIE

from it, you will certainly **d**. .... Gn 2:17
Where you **d**, I will **d**, and there I ....Ru 1:17
but fools **d** for lack of sense. ....Pr 10:21
him with a rod, he will not **d**. .... Pr 23:13
a time to give birth and a time to **d**; .... Ec 3:2
and drink, for tomorrow we **d**! ....Is 22:13
Even if I have to **d** with you, ... Mt 26:35
believes in me will never **d** ....Jn 11:26
wheat falls to the ground and **d-s**, ... Jn 12:24
time, Christ **d-d** for the ungodly. .... Rm 5:6
How can we who **d-d** to sin still .... Rm 6:2
and if we **d**, we **d** for the Lord. .... Rm 14:8
that Christ **d-d** for our sins 1Co 15:3
the law I **d-d** to the law, ...Gl 2:19
to live is Christ and to **d** is gain. ....Php 1:21
for people to **d** once ....Heb 9:27
The dead who **d** in the Lord. .... Rv 14:13

DIG

cisterns that you did not **d**, ...Dt 6:11
fence around it, **dug** a winepress. ......Mt 21:33

DINAH

Daughter of Jacob and Leah (Gn 30:21). Raped by Shechem; avenged by Simeon and Levi (Gn 34).

DIP

the one who is **d-ping** bread .... Mk 14:20

DIRECT

He **d-s** it wherever he chooses. .... Pr 21:1
May the Lord **d** your hearts to 2Th 3:5

DISAPPOINT

hope will not **d** us, because God's .... Rm 5:5

DISARM

He **d-ed** the rulers and authorities ......Col 2:15

DISASTER

the wicked for the day of **d**. ....Pr 16:4
I make success and create **d**; .... Is 45:7
If a **d** occurs in a city, hasn't .... Am 3:6
No **d** will overtake us. .... Mc 3:11

DISCERN

so that you may **d** what is the. .... Rm 12:2

DISCIPLE

Summoning his twelve **d-s**,
he gave. .... Mt 10:1
A **d** is not above his teacher, ...Mt 10:24
and make **d-s** of all nations, ...Mt 28:19
come after me cannot be my **d**. .... Lk 14:27
and his **d-s** believed in him. .... Jn 2:11
my word, you really are my **d-s**. ....Jn 8:31
and the **d** he loved .... Jn 19:26
d-s were first called Christians at ...... Ac 11:26

DISCIPLINE (N)

Apply yourself to **d** and listen to .... Pr 23:12
Don't withhold **d** from a youth; .... Pr 23:13
No **d** seems enjoyable at the time. ..... Heb 12:11

DISCIPLINE (V)

your anger or **d** me in your
wrath ....Ps 38:1
for the LORD **d-s** the one he loves, ...Pr 3:12
D your son while there is hope; ....Pr 19:18
judged . . . we are **d-d**, so that we. 1Co 11:32
for the Lord **d-s** the one he loves ....Heb 12:6

DISCOURAGED

Do not be afraid or **d**, ...Jos 1:9
stopped walking and looked **d**. ....Lk 18:1

DISCUSS

And they were **d-ing** among
themselves, ... Mt 16:7

DISEASE

all the terrible **d-s** of Egypt that ....Dt 7:15
he heals all your **d-s**. .... Ps 103:3
and healing every **d** and sickness ....Mt 4:23
weaknesses and carried our **d-s**. .... Mt 8:17
demons and to heal **d-s**. ....Lk 9:1

DRAGON
And the **d** stood in front of the ... Rv 12:4
He seized the **d**, that ancient serpent ... Rv 20:2

DRAW
the Father who sent me **d-s** him, ... Jn 6:44
earth I will **d** all people to ... Jn 12:32
let us **d** near with a true heart ... Heb 10:22
D near to God, and he will **d** near ... Jms 4:8

DREAM (N)
Joseph had a **d** ... Gn 37:5
Daniel also understood ... **d-s** ... Dn 1:17
Daniel had a **d** with visions in ... Dn 7:1
your old men will have **d-s**, and ... Jl 2:28
appeared to Joseph in a **d**, ... Mt 2:13
terribly in a **d** because of him ... Mt 27:19
and your old men will dream **d-s** ... Ac 2:17

DREAM (V)
he **d-ed**: A stairway was set on ... Gn 28:12

DRESS
the women are to **d** themselves in ... 1Tm 2:9

DRINK
D water from your own cistern, ... Pr 5:15
eat and **d**, for tomorrow we die! ... Is 22:13
and you gave me something to **d**; ... Mt 25:35
and they all **drank** from it ... Mk 14:23
Do this, as often as you **d** it, ... 1Co 11:25
we were all given one Spirit to **d** ... 1Co 12:13

DRIVE
did not **d** them out completely ... Jos 17:13
He **drove** everyone out of the temple ... Jn 2:15
perfect love **d-s** out fear, ... 1Jn 4:18

DRUNK (ADJ)
And don't get **d** with wine, ... Eph 5:18

DRUNKARD
a glutton and a **d**, a friend of ... Mt 11:19
abusive, a **d** or a swindler ... 1Co 5:11

DRUNKENNESS
not in carousing and **d**; ... Rm 13:13
envy, **d**, carousing, and anything ... Gl 5:21
evil desires, **d**, orgies ... 1Pt 4:3

DRY
and let the **d** land appear ... Gn 1:9
go through the sea on **d** ground ... Ex 14:16
D bones, hear the word of ... Ezk 37:4

DULL
Make the minds of these people **d**; ... Is 6:10

DUST
man out of the **d** from the ground ... Gn 2:7
belly and eat **d** all the days ... Gn 3:14
offspring like the **d** of the earth, ... Gn 13:16
I am **d** and ashes ... Jb 42:6
remembering that we are **d** ... Ps 103:14
all come from **d**, and all return to **d** ... Ec 3:20
shake the **d** off your feet when ... Mt 10:14
The first man was ... a man of **d**; ... 1Co 15:47

DUTY
we've only done our **d** ... Lk 17:10

DWELL
LORD, who can **d** in your tent? ... Ps 15:1
and I will **d** in the house of the ... Ps 23:6
became flesh and **dwelt** among us ... Jn 1:14
that Christ may **d** in your hearts ... Eph 3:17
praiseworthy—**d** on these things ... Php 4:8
all his fullness **d** in him, ... Col 1:19
God's nature **d-s** bodily in Christ, ... Col 2:9

DWELLING
a place for your **d** forever ... 1Kg 8:13; 2Ch 6:2
being built together for
God's **d** ... Eph 2:22

E

EAGLE
I carried you on **e-s'** wings and ... Ex 19:4
youth is renewed like the **e** ... Ps 103:5
they will soar on wings like **e-s**; ... Is 40:31
the left, and the face of an **e** ... Ezk 1:10
creature was like a flying **e** ... Rv 4:7

EAR
One who shaped the **e** not hear, ... Ps 94:9
otherwise they ... hear with
their **e-s**, ... Is 6:10
Let anyone who has **e-s** listen! ... Mt 11:15
servant, and cut off his right **e** ... Jn 18:10
no eye has seen, no **e** has heard, ... 1Co 2:9
And if the **e** should say ... 1Co 12:16
who has **e-s** to hear listen to ... Rv 2:7

EARTH
God created the heavens and the **e** ... Gn 1:1
may know the **e** belongs to LORD ... Ex 9:29
The **e** and everything in it, ... Ps 24:1
whole **e** sing to the LORD ... Ps 96:1
he is coming to judge the **e** ... Ps 96:13
his glory fills the whole **e** ... Is 6:3
they will inherit the **e** ... Mt 5:5
Heaven and **e** will pass away, ... Mt 24:35
and peace on **e** to people he ... Lk 2:14
we wait for ... a new **e**, ... 2Pt 3:13

EARTHLY
if our **e** tent we live in ... 2Co 5:1
they are focused on **e** things ... Php 3:19
not ... above but is **e**, unspiritual, ... Jms 3:15

EARTHQUAKE
but the LORD was not in the **e** ... 1Kg 19:11
be famines and **e-s** in various ... Mt 24:7
There was a violent **e**, ... Mt 28:2
was such a violent **e** that the ... Ac 16:26
A violent **e** occurred; ... Rv 6:12

EASIER
For which is **e**: to say, 'Your ... Mt 9:5
it is **e** for a camel to go ... Mt 19:24
But it is **e** for heaven and earth ... Lk 16:17

EAST
As far as the **e** is from
the west, ... Ps 103:12
wise men from the **e** arrived ... Mt 2:1

EASY
For my yoke is **e** and my burden ... Mt 11:30

EAT
You are free to **e** from any tree ... Gn 2:16
took some of its fruit and **ate** it; ... Gn 3:6
words were found, and I **ate**
them ... Jr 15:16
E this scroll, then go and speak ... Ezk 3:1
of Man came **e-ing** and
drinking, ... Mt 11:19
Everyone **ate** and was satisfied ... Mt 14:20
They all **ate** and were satisfied ... Mt 15:37
and said, "Take and **e** it; ... Mt 26:26
sinners and **e-s** with them! ... Lk 15:2
who **e-s** my flesh and drinks ... Jn 6:54
Get up, Peter; kill and **e**! ... Ac 10:13
believes he may **e** anything, ... Rm 14:2
whether you **e** or drink, or ... 1Co 10:31
work, he should not **e** ... 2Th 3:10
He said to me, "Take and **e** it; ... Rv 10:9

EDEN
LORD God planted a garden in **E**, ... Gn 2:8
You were in **E**, the garden of God ... Ezk 28:13

EDOM
is why he was also named **E** ... Gn 25:30
land of Seir, the territory of **E** ... Gn 32:3

EFFECTIVE
is living and **e** and sharper than ... Heb 4:12

EFFORT
not depend on human will or **e** ... Rm 9:16
then, make every **e** to enter that ... Heb 4:11
make every **e** to supplement your ... 2Pt 1:5

EGYPT
Abram went down to **E** to stay ... Gn 12:10
sold Joseph in **E** to Potiphar, ... Gn 37:36
all his offspring with him
came to **E** ... Gn 46:6
lived in **E** was 430 years ... Ex 12:40
out of **E** I called my son ... Hs 11:1
Out of **E** I called my Son ... Mt 2:15

EHUD
Benjaminite judge (Jdg 3:12-30).

ELAH
1. Valley where David fought Goliath (1Sm 17:2,19; 21:9).
2. Son of Baasha; king of Israel (1Kg 16:6-14).

ELDER
break the tradition of the **e-s**? ... Mt 15:2
appointed **e-s** ... in every church ... Ac 14:23
The **e-s** who are good leaders ... 1Tm 5:17
accusation against an **e** unless ... 1Tm 5:19
call for the **e-s** of the church, ... Jms 5:14
thrones sat twenty-four **e-s** ... Rv 4:4

ELEAZAR
Son of Aaron; high priest (Ex 6:23; Nm 20:25-28). Helped Joshua distribute land (Jos 14:1).

ELECT
if possible, even the **e**. .... Mt 24:24
justice to his **e** who cry out to ....Lk 18:7
but the **e** did find it......................Rm 11:7

ELECTION
purpose according to **e** might stand ....Rm 9:11
to confirm your calling and **e**,...........2Pt 1:10

ELEMENTS
based on the **e** of the world, ... Col 2:8

ELEVEN
appeared to the **E** themselves as ....Mk 16:14

ELI
High priest at Samuel's birth (1Sm 1–4). Blessed Hannah (1:17; 2:20). Failed to discipline his sons (2:12-17,22-36). Died when the ark was captured (4:11-18).

ELÍ
E, E, lemá sabachtháni?...............Mt 27:46

ELIAKIM
1. Son of Hilkiah; Hezekiah's administrator (2Kg 18:18; Is 22:20; 36:3).
2. Son of Josiah; king of Judah. Called Jehoiakim (2Kg 23:34; 2Ch 36:4).

ELIEZER
1. Abraham's servant (Gn 15:2).
2. Son of Moses (Ex 18:4; 1Ch 23:15).
3. Ancestor of Jesus (Lk 3:29).

ELIJAH
Prophet against Ahab and Ahaziah. Predicted famine (1Kg 17:1; Jms 5:17). Fed by ravens (1Kg 17:2-7); fed by widow (17:8-16; Lk 4:26); raised widow's son (1Kg 17:17-24). Defeated prophets of Baal (18:19-40). Fled Jezebel (19:1-3). Chose Elisha to succeed him (19:16,19-21); taken up into heaven (2Kg 2:1-12).

Forerunner to the Messiah, embodied in John the Baptist (Mal 4:5; Mt 11:14; 17:10-13; Lk 1:17). Appeared with Jesus (Mt 17:3-4).

ELISHA
Prophet; successor to Elijah (1Kg 19:16-21; 2Kg 2:1-18). Made bad water good (2Kg 2:19-22); called bears to punish boys (2:23-24); provided water for army (3:13-22). Provided miraculous supply of oil for widow (4:1-7); granted son to barren woman and restored him to life (4:8-37). Healed Naaman and punished Gehazi (5:1-27). Made iron ax head float (6:5-7). Blinded Aramean army (6:8–7:20). A man was revived by touching his dead bones (13:20-21).

Made Hazael king of Aram (2Kg 8:7-15) and Jehu king of Israel (9:1-13).

ELIZABETH
Mother of John the Baptist; Mary's relative (Lk 1).

ELKANAH
Father of Samuel; husband of Hannah (1Sm 1:1).

ELOI
voice, "*E, E, lemá sabachtháni*.........Mk 15:34

EMBRACE
Can a man **e** fire and his clothes..........Pr 6:27

EMMAUS
on their way to a village called **E**,....... Lk 24:13

EMPTY (ADJ)
mouth will not return to me **e**, ... Is 55:11
deceive you with **e** arguments,..........Eph 5:6

EMPTY (V)
cross of Christ will not be **e-ied** 1Co 1:17
he **e-ied** himself by assuming ....Php 2:7

EMPTY-HANDED
No one is to appear before me **e**. .... Ex 23:15

ENCAMPS
of the LORD **e** around those
  who .... Ps 34:7

ENCOURAGE
Therefore **e** one another and........... 1Th 4:18

ENCOURAGEMENT
(which is translated Son of **E**), ...Ac 4:36
through the **e** from the Scriptures ..... Rm 15:4
then, there is any **e** in Christ, ... Php 2:1

END (N)
to put an **e** to every creature,............Gn 6:13
and the **e-s** of the earth your ....Ps 2:8
make me aware of my **e** .... Ps 39:4
but its **e** is the way to death.............Pr 14:12
The **e** of a matter is better than............Ec 7:8
endures to the **e** will be saved..........Mt 10:22
endures to the **e** will be saved..........Mt 24:13
and his kingdom will have no **e**.......... Lk 1:33
He loved them to the **e**. ....Jn 13:1
and to the **e-s** of the earth..................Ac 1:8
Christ is the **e** of the law for .... Rm 10:4
who keeps my works to the **e**:...........Rv 2:26
last, the beginning and the **e**............Rv 22:13

END (V)
Love never **e-s**. But as for 1Co 13:8

ENDURANCE
that affliction produces **e**, ... Rm 5:3
faith, love, **e**, and gentleness. 1Tm 6:11
Let us run with **e** the race that.......... Heb 12:1
the testing of your faith produces **e**. .... Jms 1:3

ENDURE
of the LORD is pure, **e-ing** forever;........Ps 19:9
May they fear you while the sun **e-s**..... Ps 72:5
But who can **e** the day of his.............Mal 3:2
the one who **e-s** to the end will.........Mt 10:22
e-d with much patience
  objects of ....Rm 9:22
hopes all things, **e-s** all things........... 1Co 13:7
if we **e**, we will also reign with 2Tm 2:12
a better and **e-ing** possession......... Heb 10:34
that lay before him, he **e-d** the cross ...Heb 12:2
the word of the Lord **e-s** forever.........1Pt 1:25

ENEMY
an **e** to your **e-ies** and a foe to ....Ex 23:22
me in the presence of my **e-ies**; .... Ps 23:5
do not let my **e-ies** gloat over me. .... Ps 25:2
I make your **e-ies** your footstool......... Ps 110:1
If your **e** is hungry, give him .... Pr 25:21
a man's **e-ies** are the men of his own..... Mc 7:6
love your **e-ies** and pray for those........Mt 5:44
a man's **e-ies** will be the members .....Mt 10:36
e who sowed them is the devil..........Mt 13:39
I put your **e-ies** under your feet ....Mt 22:44
if, while we were **e-ies**, we were......... Rm 5:10
But If your **e** is hungry, feed him......... Rm 12:20
The last **e** he abolishes is death........1Co 15:26
the world becomes the **e** of God.........Jms 4:4

ENGAGED
to a virgin **e** to a man named ....Lk 1:27

ENJOY
to eat, drink, and **e** his work. .... Ec 2:24
provides us with all things to **e**. 1Tm 6:17

ENLIGHTENED
eyes of your heart may be **e** .... Eph 1:18
those who were once **e**,..................Heb 6:4

ENOCH
Father of Methuselah (Gn 5:18-21); prophet (Jd 14); walked with God, and God took him (Gn 5:22-24; Heb 11:5).

ENSLAVE
we may no longer be **e-d** to sin,.......... Rm 6:6
put up with it if someone **e-s** you, ... 2Co 11:20
want to be **e-d** to them all over again? ....Gl 4:9

ENSNARE
the sin that so easily **e-s** us.............. Heb 12:1

ENTANGLE
The ropes of Sheol **e-d** me;............. 2Sm 22:6
soldier gets **e-d** in the concerns 2Tm 2:4
they are again **e-d** in these things 2Pt 2:20

ENTER
anger, "They will not **e** my rest."..........Ps 95:11
E his gates with thanksgiving .... Ps 100:4
you will never **e** the kingdom of.........Mt 5:20
E through the narrow gate............... Mt 7:13
like a little child will never **e** it..........Mk 10:15
he cannot **e** the kingdom of God...........Jn 3:5
just as sin **e-ed** the world through...... Rm 5:12
anger, "They will not **e** my rest."........ Heb 3:11

ENTHRONED
e between the cherubim, ...2Kg 19:15
But the LORD sits **e** forever;.................Ps 9:7
e on the praises of Israel................. Ps 22:3

EXILE

went into **e** from its land....2Kg 25:21
the returned **e-s** were building....Ezr 4:1
I urge you as strangers and **e-s**....1Pt 2:11

EXILED

So Israel has been **e-d** to Assyria....2Kg 17:23

EXIST

who, **e-ing** in the form of God,....Php 2:6
and through whom all things **e**....Heb 2:10
believe that he **e-s** and that he....Heb 11:6
your will they **e** and were....Rv 4:11

EXPECT

coming at an hour you do not **e**....Mt 24:44
and lend, **e-ing** nothing in return....Lk 6:35

EXPECTANTLY

the LORD and wait **e** for him;....Ps 37:7

EXPECTATION

e of the wicked comes will perish....Pr 10:28
but a terrifying **e** of judgment....Heb 10:27

EXPLAIN

He will **e** everything to us....Jn 4:25

EXPOSE

so that his deeds may not be **e-d**....Jn 3:20
darkness, but instead **e** them....Eph 5:11
Everything **e-d** by the light is....Eph 5:13

EXPRESSION

the exact **e** of his nature,....Heb 1:3

EXTEND

would bless me, **e** my border,....1Ch 4:10

EXTINGUISH

you can **e** all the flaming arrows....Eph 6:16

EYE

e for **e**, tooth for tooth....Ex 21:24; Lv 24:20
For the **e-s** of the LORD roam....2Ch 16:9
have made a covenant with my **e-s**....Jb 31:1
Protect me as the pupil of your **e**;....Ps 17:8
I lift my **e-s** toward the....Ps 121:1
they might see with their **e-s** and....Is 6:10
Your **e-s** are too pure to look on....Hab 1:13
If your right **e** causes you to....Mt 5:29
An **e** for an **e** and a tooth for....Mt 5:38
The **e** is the lamp of the body....Mt 6:22
the splinter in your brother's **e** but....Mt 7:3
And their **e-s** were opened....Mt 9:30
see with their **e-s** and hear with....Mt 13:15
and it is wonderful in our **e-s**?....Mt 21:42
Then their **e-s** were opened, and....Lk 24:31
keeping our **e-s** on Jesus,....Heb 12:2
what we have seen with our **e-s**,....1Jn 1:1
clouds, and every **e** will see him....Rv 1:7
away every tear from their **e-s**....Rv 7:17; 21:4

EYEWITNESSES

the original **e** ... handed them down....Lk 1:2
we were **e** of his majesty....2Pt 1:16

EZEKIEL

Hebrew prophet at the time of the exile, writing from Babylon (Ezk 1:1; 2Kg 24:14-16). Wrote about the fall of Jerusalem (Ezk 33:21) and the ultimate restoration of the city and temple (Ezk 40–48).

EZRA

Priest and teacher of the law; leader of the returning exiles, sent by King Artaxerxes of Persia to reestablish worship in the temple (Ezr 7–8). Nehemiah's colleague (Neh 8:2,6; 12:31-37). Made priests stop intermarriage with foreigners (Ezr 9–10).

F

FACE

I have seen God **f** to **f**,....Gn 32:30
LORD would speak ... **f** to **f**,....Ex 33:11
Moses, the skin of his **f** shone!....Ex 34:30
LORD make his **f** shine on you....Nm 6:25
LORD, I will seek your **f**....Ps 27:8
I have set my **f** like flint,....Is 50:7
oil on your head and wash your **f**,....Mt 6:17
and his **f** shone like the sun....Mt 17:2
spat in his **f** and beat him;....Mt 26:67
appearance of his **f** changed,....Lk 9:29
a mirror, but then **f** to **f**....1Co 13:12
with unveiled **f-s** are looking....2Co 3:18
But the **f** of the Lord is against....1Pt 3:12
and his **f** was shining like the sun....Rv 1:16

FACTIONS

it is necessary that there be **f**....1Co 11:19
ambitions, dissensions, **f**,....Gl 5:20

FADE

the flowers **f**, but the word of....Is 40:8
a crown that will never **f** away....1Co 9:25

FAIL

you that your faith may not **f**....Lk 22:32
as though the word of God has **f-ed**....Rm 9:6

FAILURE

and their **f** riches for the....Rm 11:12

FAINT

my body **f-s** for you in a land that....Ps 63:1
they will walk and not **f**....Is 40:31

FAIR

The Lord's way isn't **f**....Ezk 18:25,29; 33:17,20

FAIRLY

He judges the peoples **f**....Ps 96:10
with your slaves justly and **f**,....Col 4:1

FAITH

righteous one will live by his **f**....Hab 2:4
Your **f** has saved you....Mt 9:22
If you have **f** the size of a mustard....Mt 17:20
woman, "Your **f** has saved you....Lk 7:50
to the Lord, "Increase our **f**....Lk 17:5
will he find **f** on earth?....Lk 18:8
that he had **f** to be healed,....Ac 14:9
is justified by **f** apart from....Rm 3:28
been justified by **f**,....Rm 5:1
So **f** comes from what is heard,....Rm 10:17
that is not from **f** is sin....Rm 14:23
if I have all **f** so that I can....1Co 13:2
three remain: **f**, hope, and love....1Co 13:13
stand firm in the **f**, be courageous,....1Co 16:13
For we walk by **f**, not by sight....2Co 5:7
I live by **f** in the Son of God,....Gl 2:20
the righteous will live by **f**....Gl 3:11
patience, kindness, goodness, **f**,....Gl 5:22
you are saved by grace through **f**,....Eph 2:8
one Lord, one **f**, one baptism,....Eph 4:5
situation take up the shield of **f**,....Eph 6:16
righteousness from God based on **f**....Php 3:9
the armor of **f** and love,....1Th 5:8
some will depart from the **f**,....1Tm 4:1
Fight the good fight of the **f**;....1Tm 6:12
finished the race, I have kept the **f**....2Tm 4:7
righteous one will live by **f**;....Heb 10:38
Now **f** is the reality of what is....Heb 11:1
By **f** we understand that the....Heb 11:3
By **f** Abel offered to God a....Heb 11:4
Now without **f** it is impossible....Heb 11:6
pioneer and perfecter of our **f**,....Heb 12:2
f, if it does not have works, is dead....Jms 2:17
supplement your **f** with goodness,....2Pt 1:5

FAITHFUL *SEE ALSO* FAITHFUL LOVE

he is **f** in all my household....Nm 12:7
the **f** God who keeps his gracious....Dt 7:9
With the **f** you prove yourself **f**;....2Sm 22:26
Love the LORD, all his **f** ones....Ps 31:23
Who then is a **f** and wise servant,....Mt 24:45
Well done, good and **f** servant!....Mt 25:21
God is **f**; you were called by him....1Co 1:9
God is **f**, he will not allow you....1Co 10:13
He who calls you is **f**; he will....1Th 5:24
commit to **f** men who will be able....2Tm 2:2
he remains **f**, for he cannot deny....2Tm 2:13
since he who promised is **f**....Heb 10:23
entrust themselves to a **f** Creator....1Pt 4:19
he is **f** and righteous to forgive....1Jn 1:9
Its rider is called **F** and True,....Rv 19:11

FAITHFUL LOVE

goodness and **f** will pursue....Ps 23:6
because your **f** is better....Ps 63:3
will sing about the LORD's **f** forever;....Ps 89:1
to declare your **f** in the morning....Ps 92:2
so great is his **f** toward those....Ps 103:11
For I desire **f** and not sacrifice....Hs 6:6
slow to anger, abounding in **f**,....Jnh 4:2
because he delights in **f**....Mc 7:18

FAITHFULNESS

to heaven, your **f** to the clouds....Ps 36:5
Your **f** reaches the clouds....Ps 57:10
proclaim your **f** to all generations....Ps 89:1
his **f**, through all generations....Ps 100:5
great is your **f**!....Lm 3:23
unfaithfulness nullify God's **f**?....Rm 3:3

FAITHLESS

if we are **f**, he remains faithful,....2Tm 2:13

FALL
How the mighty have f-en! ... 2Sm 1:19
Though he f-s, he will not be ... Ps 37:24
Though a thousand f at your side ... Ps 91:7
an arrogant spirit before a f. ... Pr 16:18
a righteous person f-s seven times, ... Pr 24:16
you have f-en from the heavens ... Is 14:12
Babylon has f-en, has f-en. ... Is 21:9
some seed **fell** along the path, ... Mt 13:4
to cause the f and rise of many ... Lk 2:34
I watched Satan f from heaven ... Lk 10:18
grain of wheat f-s to the ground ... Jn 12:24
have sinned and f short of the ... Rm 3:23
must be careful not to f. ... 1Co 10:12
you have f-en from grace. ... Gl 5:4
and who have f-en away, ... Heb 6:6
thing to f into the hands ... Heb 10:31
a great star . . . **fell** from heaven. ... Rv 8:10
f-en, Babylon the Great has f-en, ... Rv 14:8

FALSE
Do not give f testimony against ... Ex 20:16
Beware of f prophets who come ... Mt 7:15
do not bear f witness; ... Mt 19:18
Many f prophets will rise up and ... Mt 24:11
F messiahs and f prophets will ... Mt 24:24
whether from f motives or true, ... Php 1:18
there will be f teachers among you ... 2Pt 2:1
the mouth of the f prophet ... Rv 16:13

FALSEHOOD
I hate and abhor f, but I love ... Ps 119:163
Keep f and deceitful words far ... Pr 30:8

FALSELY
f say every kind of evil
against you ... Mt 5:11
what is f called knowledge. ... 1Tm 6:20

FAMILY
As for me and my f, we will ... Jos 24:15
All the f-ies of the nations will ... Ps 22:27
makes their f-ies multiply like ... Ps 107:41
All the f-ies of the earth will be ... Ac 3:25
he and all his f were baptized ... Ac 16:33
from whom every f in heaven and ... Eph 3:15

FAMINE
There was a f in the land, ... Gn 12:10
seven years of f will take place ... Gn 41:30
by sword, f, and plague. ... Jr 14:12
not a f of bread or a thirst for ... Am 8:11
There will be f-s and earthquakes ... Mt 24:7
or persecution or f or nakedness ... Rm 8:35

FAR
As f as the east is from the ... Ps 103:12
yet their hearts are f from me, ... Is 29:13
but their heart is f from me. ... Mt 15:8
You are not f from the kingdom ... Mk 12:34
you who were f away have been ... Eph 2:13

FAST (N)
Will the f I choose be like this: ... Is 58:5
Announce a sacred f; ... Jl 1:14; 2:15

FAST (V)
baby was alive, you f-ed ... 2Sm 12:21
After he had f-ed forty days and forty ... Mt 4:2
Whenever you f, don't be
gloomy ... Mt 6:16
but your disciples do not f? ... Mt 9:14
guests cannot f while the groom ... Mk 2:19
I f twice a week; I give a tenth ... Lk 18:12
after they had f-ed, prayed, and ... Ac 13:3

FASTING
so that their f is obvious to people ... Mt 6:16

FAT
is better than the f of rams ... 1Sm 15:22

FATAL
but its f wound was healed. ... Rv 13:3

FATE
there is one f for everyone ... Ec 9:3
and who considered his f? ... Is 53:8

FATHER
a man leaves his f and mother ... Gn 2:24
become the f of many nations ... Gn 17:4
Honor your f and your mother so ... Ex 20:12
Honor your f and your mother ... Dt 5:16
F-s are not to be put to death for ... Dt 24:16
Isn't he your F and Creator? ... Dt 32:6
I will his f, and he ... 2Sm 7:14
today I have become your F ... Ps 2:7
You are my F, my God, the rock ... Ps 89:26
Listen, my son, to your f-'s
instruction ... Pr 1:8
A wise son brings joy to his f, ... Pr 10:1
Eternal F, Prince of Peace ... Is 9:6
not die for his f-'s iniquity. ... Ezk 18:17
Our F in heaven, your name be ... Mt 6:9
who loves a f or mother more ... Mt 10:37
Honor your f and your mother; ... Mt 15:4
will leave his f and mother and ... Mt 19:5
you have one F, who is in heaven ... Mt 23:9
Abba, F! All things are possible ... Mk 14:36
for me to be in my F-'s house? ... Lk 2:49
What f among you, if his son asks ... Lk 11:11
Jesus said, "F, forgive them ... Lk 23:34
Stop turning my F-'s house into ... Jn 2:16
was even calling God his own F, ... Jn 5:18
You are of your f the devil, ... Jn 8:44
snatch them out of the F-'s hand ... Jn 10:29
I and the F are one ... Jn 10:30
the F is in me and I in the F ... Jn 10:38
In my F-'s house are many rooms ... Jn 14:2
comes to the F except through ... Jn 14:6
show us the F, and that's enough ... Jn 14:8
who has seen me has seen the F ... Jn 14:9
you ask the F in my name, ... Jn 15:16
by whom we cry out, "Abba, F!" ... Rm 8:15
I will be a F to you, and you ... 2Co 6:18
one God and F of all, who is ... Eph 4:6
Honor your f and mother, which ... Eph 6:2
F-s, don't stir up anger in ... Eph 6:4
F-s, do not exasperate your ... Col 3:21
I will be his F, and he will be ... Heb 1:5
what son is there that a f does not ... Heb 12:7
down from the F of lights, ... Jms 1:17

FATHERLESS
He executes justice for the f and ... Dt 10:18
You are a helper of the f ... Ps 10:14
a father of the f and a champion ... Ps 68:5
and helps the f and the widow, ... Ps 146:9
don't encroach on the fields of the f ... Pr 23:10

FATTENED
Then bring the f calf and ... Lk 15:23
You have f your hearts ... Jms 5:5

FAULT
Cleanse me from my hidden f-s ... Ps 19:12
Why then does he still find f? ... Rm 9:19
without f or failure until ... 1Tm 6:14

FAULTLESS
who are f in a crooked ... Php 2:15

FAVOR (N)
Noah . . . found f with the LORD ... Gn 6:8
moment, but his f, a lifetime ... Ps 30:5
and obtains f from the LORD, ... Pr 8:35
for you have found f with God ... Lk 1:30
and in f with God and with ... Lk 2:52
God and enjoying the f of all ... Ac 2:47
trying to win the f of people, ... Gl 1:10

FAVOR (V)
peace on earth to people he f-s! ... Lk 2:14

FAVORITISM
that God doesn't show f, ... Ac 10:34
There is no f with God. ... Rm 2:11
and there is no f with him. ... Eph 6:9
doing nothing out of f ... 1Tm 5:21
do not show f as you hold on to ... Jms 2:1

FEAR (N)
The f of the LORD is pure, ... Ps 19:9
and rescued me from all my f-s ... Ps 34:4
f of the LORD is the beginning ... Ps 111:10
The f of the LORD is the beginning ... Pr 1:7
delight will be in the f of the LORD ... Is 11:3
of slavery to fall back into f, ... Rm 8:15
salvation with f and trembling ... Php 2:12
There is no f in love; instead,
perfect love drives out f, ... 1Jn 4:18

FEAR (V)
For now I know that you f God, ... Gn 22:12
F the LORD your God . . .
worship him. ... Dt 6:13
f-ed the LORD, but they also ... 2Kg 17:33
He is f-ed above all gods. ... 1Ch 16:25
f-s God and turns away from ... Jb 1:8; 2:3
darkest valley, I f no danger, for ... Ps 23:4
my salvation—whom
should I f? ... Ps 27:1
To f the LORD is to hate evil ... Pr 8:13
but a woman who f-s the
LORD will ... Pr 31:30
f God and keep his commands, ... Ec 12:13
Do not f, for I am with you; ... Is 41:10
f him who is able to destroy both ... Mt 10:28
town who didn't f God or respect ... Lk 18:2
So the one who f-s is not complete ... 1Jn 4:18

FEARFULNESS
has not given us a spirit of f, ... 2Tm 1:7

FEAST
I hate, I despise your f-s! ... Am 5:21
us observe the f, not with old ... 1Co 5:8
to the marriage f of the Lamb! ... Rv 19:9

FEASTING (N)
than a house full of f with strife. . . . . Pr 17:1
than to go to a house of f, ... Ec 7:2

FEATHERS
He will cover you with his f; . . . . Ps 91:4

FEED
He **fed** you in the wilderness with. . . . . . . Dt 8:16
shepherds f themselves rather than . . . Ezk 34:8
your heavenly Father **f-s** them. . . . . Mt 6:26
so the one who **f-s** on me will live . . . . Jn 6:57
"F my lambs," He told him. . . . . Jn 21:15
If your enemy is hungry, f him. . . . . Rm 12:20

FEEDING
no oxen, the f trough is empty, ... Pr 14:4

FELLOWSHIP
this is the law of the f sacrifice . . . . Lv 7:11
We used to have close f; . . . . Ps 55:14
teaching, to the f, to the breaking . . . . Ac 2:42
Or what f does light have with. 2Co 6:14
and the f of the Holy Spirit be. 2Co 13:13
we say, "We have f with him" 1Jn 1:6

FEMALE
he created them male and f. . . . . Gn 1:27
new . . . a f will shelter a man. . . . . Jr 31:22
beginning made them male and f, ... Mt 19:4
slave or free, male or f; . . . . Gl 3:28

FERVENT
and being f in spirit, he was . . . . Ac 18:25
be f in the Spirit; serve the Lord. . . . . Rm 12:11

FESTIVAL
Celebrate a f in my honor three . . . . Ex 23:14
"Not during the f," they said . . . . Mk 14:2
the matter of a f or a new moon . . . . Col 2:16

FESTIVE
leading the f procession to the . . . . Ps 42:4

FEVER
was lying in bed with a f, ... Mk 1:30

FEW
were f in number, very f indeed . . . . Ps 105:12
Let his days be f; let another . . . . Ps 109:8
but the workers are f. Mt 9:37
are invited, but f are chosen. . . . . Mt 22:14
a f people going to be saved? . . . . Lk 13:23

FEWEST
you were the f of all peoples. . . . . Dt 7:7

FIELD
Let the **f-s** and everything
in them. . . . . Ps 96:12
blooms like a flower of the f; . . . . Ps 103:15
I went by the f of a slacker and . . . . Pr 24:30
how the wildflowers of the f grow: . . . . Mt 6:28
f is the world; and the good seed . . . . Mt 13:38
out in the **f-s** and keeping watch . . . . Lk 2:8
your eyes and look at the **f-s**, ... Jn 4:35
You are God's f, God's building 1Co 3:9

FIERY
surprised when the f ordeal comes 1Pt 4:12

FIG
so they sewed f leaves together . . . . Gn 3:7
Though the f tree does not bud. . . . . Hab 3:17
At once the f tree withered. . . . . Mt 21:19
F-s aren't gathered from thornbushes . . Lk 6:44
Can a f tree produce olives, ... Jms 3:12

FIGHT (N)
Fight the good f of the faith; 1Tm 6:12
I have fought the good f, I have 2Tm 4:7

FIGHT (V)
The LORD will f for you; . . . . Ex 14:14
LORD; f those who f me. Ps 35:1
F the good fight of the faith; 1Tm 6:12
God not to f about words; 2Tm 2:14
I have **fought** the good fight, I have 2Tm 4:7

FILL
Be fruitful, multiply, f the earth, ... Gn 1:28
glory of the LORD **f-ed** the temple. 1Kg 8:11
whole earth is **f-ed** with his glory . . . . Ps 72:19
His glory **f-s** the whole earth. . . . . Is 6:3
Do I not f the heavens and the . . . . Jr 23:24
and I will f this house with glory, ... Hg 2:7
He will be **f-ed** with the Holy . . . . Lk 1:15
"F the jars with water," Jesus . . . . Jn 2:7
you ate the loaves and were **f-ed**. . . . . Jn 6:26
they were all **f-ed** with the Holy . . . . Ac 2:4
Then Peter was **f-ed** with the Holy . . . . Ac 4:8
sight and be **f-ed** with the Holy. . . . . Ac 9:17
called Paul—**f-ed** with the Holy. . . . . Ac 13:9
the God of hope f you with all . . . . Rm 15:13
who **f-s** all things in every way. . . . . Eph 1:23
heavens, to f all things. . . . . Eph 4:10
but be **f-ed** by the Spirit: . . . . Eph 5:18
f-ed with the fruit of. Php 1:11

FILTH
of all moral f and the evil, ... Jms 1:21
removal of the f of the flesh,. 1Pt 3:21

FILTHY
was dressed with f clothes as he . . . . Zch 3:3
and f language from your mouth. . . . . Col 3:8
Let the f still be f; . . . . Rv 22:11

FIND
If I f fifty righteous people. . . . . Gn 18:26
you will f him when you seek . . . . Dt 4:29
those who search for me f me. . . . . Pr 8:17
For the one who **f-s** me **f-s** life. . . . . Pr 8:35
who **f-s** a wife **f-s** a good thing . . . . Pr 18:22
Who can f a wife of noble. . . . . Pr 31:10
the LORD while He may be **found**; . . . . Is 55:6
will seek me and f me when you . . . . Jr 29:13
Seek, and you will f. . . . . Mt 7:7
and you will f rest for. . . . . Mt 11:29
life because of me will f it. . . . . Mt 16:25
whom master **f-s** doing his job . . . . Mt 24:46
I have **found** my lost sheep! . . . . Lk 15:6
he was lost and is **found**! . . . . Lk 15:24
whose name was not **found** written . . . Rv 20:15

FINISH
He said, "It is **f-ed**!". Jn 19:30
to f my course and the ministry . . . . Ac 20:24
I have **f-ed** the race, I have kept. 2Tm 4:7

FIRE
and the pillar of f by night. . . . . Ex 13:22
a chariot of f with horses of f. 2Kg 2:11
their f will never go out, ... Is 66:24
he will be like a refiner's f . . . . Mal 3:2
you with the Holy Spirit and f. . . . . Mt 3:11
burn with f that never goes out. . . . . Mt 3:12
into the eternal f prepared for . . . . Mt 25:41
and the f is not quenched. . . . . Mk 9:44
I came to bring f on the earth, ... Lk 12:49
like flames of f that separated . . . . Ac 2:3
the f will test the quality of 1Co 3:13
for our God is a consuming f. . . . . Heb 12:29
And the tongue is a f. . . . . Jms 3:6
second death, the lake of f. . . . . Rv 20:14

FIRM
Stand f and see the LORD's . . . . Ex 14:13
If you do not stand f in your faith, ... Is 7:9
Be alert, stand f in the faith 1Co 16:13
stand f and hold to the. 2Th 2:15

FIRMLY
The world is f established; . . . . Pss 93:1; 96:10
are like f embedded nails. . . . . Ec 12:11
being rooted and f established . . . . Eph 3:17
if we hold f until the end. . . . . Heb 3:14

FIRST
The f to state his case seems. . . . . Pr 18:17
I and the LORD, the f and with the . . . . Is 41:4
I am the f and I am the last. . . . . Is 44:6
But seek f the kingdom of God . . . . Mt 6:33
F take the beam . . . out of
your eye, ... Mt 7:5
f will be last, and the last f. . . . . Mt 19:30
wants to be f among you must be . . . . . . Mt 20:27
F clean the inside of the cup, ... Mt 23:26
this, the f of his signs, in Cana . . . . Jn 2:11
were f called Christians at Antioch. . . . . . Ac 11:26
who does evil, f to the Jew, and. . . . . Rm 2:9
The f man Adam became a living. 1Co 15:45
the dead in Christ will rise f. 1Th 4:16
We love because he f loved us. 1Jn 4:19
I am the F and the Last, ... Rv 1:17
abandoned the love you had at f. . . . . Rv 2:4
for the f heaven and the f earth had. . . . . . Rv 21:1

FIRSTBORN
LORD struck every f male in . . . . Ex 12:29
Consecrate every f male to me, ... Ex 13:2
He struck all the f in Egypt, ... Ps 78:51
she gave birth to her f son, ... Lk 2:7
the f from the dead and the. . . . . Rv 1:5

FIRSTFRUITS
the f of those who have fallen 1Co 15:20

FISH (N)
will rule the f of the sea, ... Gn 1:26
Jonah was in . . . the f three days. . . . . Jnh 1:17
he asks for a f, will give him . . . . Mt 7:10
have five loaves and two f here, ... Mt 14:17
the seven loaves and the f, ... Mt 15:36
full of large f—153 of them. . . . . Jn 21:11

G

do everything for the g of God ... 1Co 10:31
incomparable eternal weight of g. ... 2Co 4:17
Christ in you, the hope of g. ... Col 1:27
crowned him with g and honor ... Heb 2:7
worthy to receive g and honor ... Rv 4:11

GLUTTON

and the g will become poor ... Pr 23:21
they say, 'Look, a g and a drunkard ... Mt 11:19

GNASH

they **g-ed** their teeth at me ... Ps 35:16
will be weeping and **g-ing** of teeth ... Mt 8:12; 13:12; 25:30
and **g-ed** their teeth at him ... Ac 7:54

GNAT

strain out a g, yet gulp down ... Mt 23:24

GO

Let my people g, ... Ex 5:1
For wherever you g, I will g, ... Ru 1:16
Where can I g to escape your ... Ps 139:7
We all **went** astray like sheep; ... Is 53:6
I say to this one, 'G!' and he **g-es**; ... Mt 8:9
G, therefore, and make disciples ... Mt 28:19
G into all the world and preach ... Mk 16:15
I am **g-ing** to prepare a place ... Jn 14:2

GOAL

I pursue as my g the prize ... Php 3:14
receiving the g of your faith, ... 1Pt 1:9

GOAT

put them on the **g-'s** head and send ... Lv 16:21
bulls or drink the blood of **g-s**? ... Ps 50:13
separates the sheep from the **g-s**. ... Mt 25:32
For if the blood of **g-s** and bulls ... Heb 9:13

GOD

In the beginning G created the ... Gn 1:1
you will be like G, knowing good ... Gn 3:5
the sons of G saw that the ... Gn 6:2
he was a priest to G Most High ... Gn 14:18
saying, "I am G Almighty. ... Gn 17:1
LORD, the Everlasting G. ... Gn 21:33
G planned it for good to bring ... Gn 50:20
I am the G of your father, the G of Abraham, the G of Isaac, and the G of Jacob. ... Ex 3:6
LORD, the G of your ancestors ... Ex 3:15
LORD, the G of the Hebrews, ... Ex 3:18
This is my G, and I will praise him, ... Ex 15:2
Do not have other **g-s** besides me. ... Ex 20:3
I, LORD your G, am a jealous G, ... Ex 20:5
G is not a man, that he might lie, ... Nm 23:19
G is a consuming fire, a jealous G. ... Dt 4:24
the voice of the living G speaking ... Dt 5:26
LORD your G is G, the faithful G ... Dt 7:9
the LORD your G is the G of **g-s** ... Dt 10:17
The G of old is your dwelling ... Dt 33:27
and your G will be my G. ... Ru 1:16
there is no rock like our G. ... 1Sm 2:2
will know that Israel has a G, ... 1Sm 17:46
LORD G of Armies was with him. ... 2Sm 5:10
But will G indeed live on earth ... 1Kg 8:27
G who answers with fire, he is G ... 1Kg 18:24
Their **g-s** are **g-s** of the hill ... 1Kg 20:23
they had worshiped other **g-s**. ... 2Kg 17:7
And G granted his request. ... 1Ch 4:10
Save us, G of our salvation; ... 1Ch 16:35
our G is greater than any of the **g-s**. ... 2Ch 2:5
says in his heart, "There's no G." ... Pss 14:1; 53:1
My G, my G, why have you ... Ps 22:1
the nation whose G is the LORD— ... Ps 33:12
G is our refuge and strength, ... Ps 46:1
Our G is a G of salvation, ... Ps 68:20
What **g** is great like G? ... Ps 77:13
For he is our G, and we are the ... Ps 95:7
Acknowledge that the LORD is G. ... Ps 100:3
Give thanks to the G of **g-s**. ... Ps 136:2
fear G and keep his commands, ... Ec 12:13
Wonderful Counselor, Mighty G, ... Is 9:6
of Judah, "Here is your G!" ... Is 40:9
The LORD is the everlasting G, ... Is 40:28
There is no G but me. ... Is 44:6
I will be their G, and they will ... Jr 31:33
I am the LORD, the G of every ... Jr 32:27
people, and I will be your G. ... Ezk 36:28
Didn't one G create us? ... Mal 2:10
is translated "G is with us." ... Mt 1:23
heart, for they will see G. ... Mt 5:8
Therefore, what G has joined ... Mt 19:6
and to G the things that are **G-'s**. ... Mt 22:21
that is, "My G, My G, why have ... Mt 27:46
Who can forgive sins but G alone? ... Mk 2:7
was with G, and the Word was G. ... Jn 1:1
For G loved the world in this way: ... Jn 3:16
G is spirit, and those who worship ... Jn 4:24
I said, you are **g-s**? ... Jn 10:34
to him, "My Lord and my G!" ... Jn 20:28
We must obey G rather than people ... Ac 5:29
The **g-s** have come down to us in ... Ac 14:11
g-s made by hand are not **g-s**! ... Ac 19:26
Let G be true, even though everyone ... Rm 3:4
If G is for us, who is against ... Rm 8:31
G is the one who justifies. ... Rm 8:33
Be reconciled to G. ... 2Co 5:20
I will be their G, and they will be ... 2Co 6:16
that by nature are not **g-s**. ... Gl 4:8
one G and Father of all, who is ... Eph 4:6
who, existing in the form of G, ... Php 2:6
one G and one mediator between G ... 1Tm 2:5
our great G and Savior, Jesus ... Ti 2:13
for our G is a consuming fire. ... Heb 12:29
G is light, and there is ... 1Jn 1:5
does not know G, because G is love. ... 1Jn 4:8
holy, holy, Lord G, the Almighty, ... Rv 4:8
G-'s dwelling is with humanity, ... Rv 21:3

GODDESS

Ashtoreth, the g of the Sidonians, ... 1Kg 11:5
temple of the great g Artemis ... Ac 19:27

GOD-FEARING

centurion, an upright and G man, ... Ac 10:22

GODLESS

the hope of the g will perish. ... Jb 8:13

GODLESSNESS

heaven against all g and ... Rm 1:18
he will turn g away from Jacob. ... Rm 11:26

GODLINESS

life in all g and dignity. ... 1Tm 2:2
but g is beneficial in every way ... 1Tm 4:8
But g with contentment is ... 1Tm 6:6
holding to the form of g but ... 2Tm 3:5
required for life and g ... 2Pt 1:3
endurance, endurance with g, ... 2Pt 1:6

GODLY

is the one seeking? G offspring ... Mal 2:15
For g grief produces a ... 2Co 7:10
want to live a g life in Christ ... 2Tm 3:12
and g way in the present age, ... Ti 2:12

GOG

the day when G comes against ... Ezk 38:18
G and Magog, to gather them ... Rv 20:8

GOLD

G cannot be exchanged for it, ... Jb 28:15
They are more desirable than g ... Ps 19:10
more than g, even the purest g, ... Ps 119:127
is better than silver and g. ... Pr 22:1
is like g apples in silver settings. ... Pr 25:11
street of the city was pure g, ... Rv 21:21

GOLGOTHA

they came to a place called *G* ... Mt 27:33

GOLIATH

Philistine giant from Gath killed by David (1Sm 17).

GOMER

Hosea's wife (Hs 1:3,8).

GOOD

And God saw that it was g. ... Gn 1:10
God planned it for g to bring about ... Gn 50:20
There is no one who does g. ... Pss 14:1; 53:1
Taste and see that the LORD is g. ... Ps 34:8
withhold the g from those who ... Ps 84:11
How delightfully g when ... Ps 133:1
A joyful heart is g medicine, ... Pr 17:22
who brings news of g things, ... Is 52:7
to do what is g on the Sabbath. ... Mt 12:12
Well done, g and faithful slave! ... Mt 25:21
Why do you call me g? . . . No one is g except God. ... Mk 10:18
I am the g shepherd. ... Jn 10:11
together for the g of those who ... Rm 8:28
by evil, but conquer evil with g. ... Rm 12:21
in Christ Jesus for g works, ... Eph 2:10

GOODNESS

cause all my g to pass in front ... Ex 33:19
Only g and faithful love will ... Ps 23:6
patience, kindness, g, faithfulness, ... Gl 5:22

GOODS

You have many g stored up for ... Lk 12:19
has this world's g and sees ... 1Jn 3:17

GOSHEN

Region of Egypt where Israel settled (Gn 45:10; 46:28-34); the best part of the land (47:6,27); excluded from plagues (Ex 8:22; 9:26).

GOSPEL

and preach the g to all creation ... Mk 16:15
For I am not ashamed of the g, ... Rm 1:16
But if our g is veiled, ... 2Co 4:3
and are turning to a different g ... Gl 1:6
with the eternal g to announce ... Rv 14:6

HAIL

I will rain down the worst **h** that .... Ex 9:18
and mocked him: "H, king of the .... Mt 27:29

HAILSTONES

LORD threw large **h** on them from ...... Jos 10:11
Enormous **h**, each weighing about ..... Rv 16:21

HAIR

is to let the **h** of his head grow .... Nm 6:5
But his **h** began to grow back .... Jdg 16:22
are more than the **h-s** of my head, ... Ps 40:12
make a single **h** white or black .... Mt 5:36
But even the **h-s** of your head have .... Mt 10:30
and wiped his feet with her **h**, ... Jn 11:2
she should have her **h** cut off 1Co 11:6

HAIRSTYLES

with elaborate **h**, gold, pearls, ... 1Tm 2:9
elaborate **h** and wearing gold 1Pt 3:3

HAIRY

A **h** man with a leather belt 2Kg 1:8

HALF

give you, up to **h** my kingdom .... Mk 6:23

HALLELUJAH

H! My soul, praise the LORD .... Ps 146:1
multitude in heaven, saying, H! .... Rv 19:1

HAM

Son of Noah (Gn 5:32; 9:18-27). Ancestor of Cushites, Egyptians, and Canaanites (Gn 9:18-27; 10:6; Pss 78:51; 105:23,27; 106:22).

HAMAN

Nobleman of Persia at the time of Esther (Est 3:1-2); enemy of Jews (3:3-15). Hanged on his own gallows (7:9-10).

HANANIAH

1. False prophet; opposed Jeremiah (Jr 28).
2. Shadrach's original name (Dn 1:6).

HAND (N)

rock and cover you with my **h** .... Ex 33:22
lay their **h-s** on the bull's head .... Lv 4:15
they pierced my **h-s** and my feet .... Ps 22:16
Sit at my right **h** until I make .... Ps 110:1
even there your **h** will lead me; .... Ps 139:10
Whatever your **h-s** find to do, ... Ec 9:10
of the field will clap their **h-s** .... Is 55:12
man's **h** appeared and began writing .... Dn 5:5
if your right **h** causes you to .... Mt 5:30
let your left **h** know what your right .... Mt 6:3
Sit at my right **h** until I put .... Mt 22:44
into your **h-s** I entrust my spirit .... Lk 23:46
he showed them his **h-s** and feet .... Lk 24:40
will snatch them out of my **h** .... Jn 10:28
Because I'm not a **h**, I don't 1Co 12:15
dwelling ... not made with **h-s** 2Co 5:1
lifting up holy **h-s** without anger 1Tm 2:8
to fall into the **h-s** of the living .... Heb 10:31

HAND (V)

h-ed him over to be crucified .... Mt 27:26
when he **h-s** over the kingdom to 1Co 15:24

HANDLE

Don't **h**, don't taste, don't touch"? .... Col 2:21

HANG

anyone **hung** on a tree is under .... Dt 21:23
Then he went and **h-ed** himself .... Mt 27:5
everyone who is **hung** on a tree .... Gl 3:13

HANNAH

Wife of Elkanah; mother of Samuel (1Sm 1–2).

HAPPY

How **h** is the one who does not .... Ps 1:1
H is the nation whose God is .... Ps 33:12
H is the man who has filled his .... Ps 127:5
H is a man who finds wisdom and .... Pr 3:13

HARD

It will be **h** for a rich person .... Mt 19:23
This teaching is **h**! Who can accept .... Jn 6:60
some things **h** to understand 2Pt 3:16

HARDEN

But I will **h** his heart so that .... Ex 4:21
Do not **h** your hearts as at Meribah, ... Ps 95:8
and he **h-s** whom he wants to **h** .... Rm 9:18
elect did find it. The rest were **h-ed** ..... Rm 11:7
A partial **h-ing** has come upon Israel .... Rm 11:25
do not **h** your hearts as in the .... Heb 3:8

HAREM

beautiful young women to the **h** .... Est 2:3

HARM (N)

Don't plan any **h** against your .... Pr 3:29

HARM (V)

But they were planning to **h** me .... Neh 6:2

HARP

praise him with **h** and lyre .... Ps 150:3
Each one had a **h** and golden bowls .... Rv 5:8

HARSH

but a **h** word stirs up wrath .... Pr 15:1

HARVEST

earth endures, seedtime and **h**, ... Gn 8:22
observe the Festival of H with .... Ex 23:16
sleeps during **h** is disgraceful .... Pr 10:5
The **h** is abundant, but the workers .... Mt 9:37
because they are ready for **h** .... Jn 4:35
since the **h** of the earth is ripe .... Rv 14:15

HASTY

Do not be **h** to speak, ... Ec 5:2

HATE

You who love the LORD, **h** evil! .... Ps 97:10
To fear the LORD is to **h** evil .... Pr 8:13
will not use the rod **h-s** his son, ... Pr 13:24
a time to love and a time to **h**; .... Ec 3:8
H evil and love good; .... Am 5:15
I loved Jacob, but I **h-d** Esau .... Mal 1:3
If he **h-s** and divorces .... Mal 2:16
your neighbor and **h** your enemy .... Mt 5:43
do what is good to those who **h** you ..... Lk 6:27
me and does not **h** his own father ...... Lk 14:26
want to do, but I do what I **h**. .... Rm 7:15
loved Jacob, but I have **h-d** Esau. .... Rm 9:13

HATRED

not harbor **h** against your brother .... Lv 19:17

HAY

stones, wood, **h**, or straw, ... 1Co 3:12

HEAD

will strike your **h**, and you will .... Gn 3:15
lay their hands on the bull's **h** .... Lv 4:15
You anoint my **h** with oil; .... Ps 23:5
will heap burning coals on his **h**, ... Pr 25:22
Man has no place to lay his **h**. .... Mt 8:20
His **h** was brought on a platter .... Mt 14:11
Christ is the **h** of every man, and the man is the **h** of the woman, ... 1Co 11:3
her **h** uncovered dishonors her **h**, ... 1Co 11:5
husband is the **h** of the wife as .... Eph 5:23

HEAL

For I am the LORD who **h-s** you .... Ex 15:26
their sin, and **h** their land 2Ch 7:14
He **h-s** the brokenhearted .... Ps 147:3
a time to kill and a time to **h**; .... Ec 3:3
and we are **h-ed** by his wounds .... Is 53:5
H the sick, raise the dead .... Mt 10:8
it lawful to **h** on the Sabbath? .... Mt 12:10
Doctor, **h** yourself. .... Lk 4:23
turn, and I would **h** them .... Jn 12:40
so that you may be **h-ed** .... Jms 5:16
By his wounds you have been **h-ed** 1Pt 2:24

HEALING

will rise with **h** in its wings, ... Mal 4:2
gifts of **h** by the one Spirit, ... 1Co 12:9
the tree are for **h** the nations, ... Rv 22:2

HEALTHY

The **h** don't need a doctor, ... Lk 5:31

HEAR

may you **h** in heaven and forgive 1Kg 8:34
One who shaped the ear not **h**, ... Ps 94:9
with their eyes and **h** with their ears, ... Is 6:10
Have you not **h-d**? Has it not been .... Is 40:21
Dry bones, **h** the word of the LORD ..... Ezk 37:4
You have **h-d** that it was said .... Mt 5:21
longed ... to **h** the things you **h** .... Mt 13:17
Anyone who **h-s** my word and .... Jn 5:24
My sheep **h** my voice, ... Jn 10:27
And how can they **h** without a .... Rm 10:14
So faith comes from what is **h-d**, ... Rm 10:17
no eye has seen, no ear has **h-d**, ... 1Co 2:9
according to his will, he **h-s** us 1Jn 5:14
If anyone **h-s** my voice and opens .... Rv 3:20

HEARERS

For the **h** of the law are not ... Rm 2:13
of the word and not **h** only, ... Jms 1:22

HEARING (N)

works of the law or by **h** with faith? ... Gl 3:2

HEART

I will harden his **h** so that he ... Ex 4:21
when you seek him with all your **h** ... Dt 4:29
LORD your God with all your **h**, ... Dt 6:5
found a man after his own **h** ... 1Sm 13:14
but the LORD sees the **h** ... 1Sm 16:7
meditation of my **h** be acceptable ... Ps 19:14
create a clean **h** for me and ... Ps 51:10
Your word in my **h** so that I may ... Ps 119:11
Search me, God, and know my **h**; ... Ps 139:23
Trust in the LORD with all your **h**, ... Pr 3:5
The **h** is more deceitful than ... Jr 17:9
them and write it on their **h-s** ... Jr 31:33
I will give you a new **h** ... Ezk 36:26
Blessed are the pure in **h**, ... Mt 5:8
there your **h** will be also. ... Mt 6:21
the law is written on their **h-s**. ... Rm 2:15
and circumcision is of the **h** ... Rm 2:29
believe in your **h** that God raised ... Rm 10:9
you do, do it from the **h**,
as done ... Col 3:23

HEAVEN

God created the **h-s** and the earth. ... Gn 1:1
Most High, Creator of **h** and earth, ... Gn 14:19
h, the highest **h**, cannot contain ... 1Kg 8:27
When I observe your **h-s**, the work ... Ps 8:3
The **h-s** declare the glory of God, ... Ps 19:1
Your faithful love reaches to **h**, ... Ps 36:5
Who do I have in **h** but you? ... Ps 73:25
Let the **h-s** be glad and the earth ... Ps 96:11
For as high as the **h-s** are above ... Ps 103:11
time for every activity under **h**: ... Ec 3:1
create new **h-s** and a new earth; ... Is 65:17
coming with the clouds of **h**. ... Dn 7:13
the kingdom of **h** has come near! ... Mt 3:2
The **h-s** suddenly opened for him, ... Mt 3:16
for yourselves treasures in **h**, ... Mt 6:20
H and earth will pass away, ... Mt 24:35
Who will go up to **h**? ... Rm 10:6
to the third **h** fourteen years ago. ... 2Co 12:2
Our citizenship is in **h**, ... Php 3:20
Christ did not enter a sanctuary . . . but
into **h** itself, ... Heb 9:24
that day the **h-s** will pass away ... 2Pt 3:10
I saw a new **h** and a new earth ... Rv 21:1

HEAVENLY

and your **h** Father knows that you ... Mt 6:32
a multitude of the **h** host with ... Lk 2:13
There are **h** bodies and earthly ... 1Co 15:40
by God's **h** call in Christ ... Php 3:14
who share in a **h** calling, ... Heb 3:1

HEBREW

came and told Abram the **H**, ... Gn 14:13
This is one of the **H** boys. ... Ex 2:6
LORD, the God of the **H-s**, ... Ex 3:18
He answered them, "I'm a **H** ... Jnh 1:9
of Benjamin, a **H** born of **H-s**; ... Php 3:5

HEEL

and you will strike his **h** ... Gn 3:15
Esau's **h** with his hand ... Gn 25:26

has raised his **h** against me ... Ps 41:9
has raised his **h** against me ... Jn 13:18

HEIGHT

h nor depth, nor any other ... Rm 8:39
length and width, **h** and depth ... Eph 3:18

HEIR *SEE ALSO* COHEIRS

born in my house will be my **h** ... Gn 15:3
if children, also **h-s**—**h-s** of God ... Rm 8:17
h-s according to the promise. ... Gl 3:29
then God has made you an **h** ... Gl 4:7

HELL *SEE ALSO* HADES, SHEOL

to have two hands and go to **h** ... Mk 9:43
authority to throw people into **h** ... Lk 12:5

HELMET

and a **h** of salvation on his head; ... Is 59:17
Take the **h** of salvation ... Eph 6:17

HELP (N)

He is our **h** and shield ... Ps 33:20
Where will my **h** come from? ... Ps 121:1
gifts of healing, **h-ing**,
leading, ... 1Co 12:28

HELP (V)

LORD has **h-ed** us to this point ... 1Sm 7:12
I do believe; **h** my unbelief! ... Mk 9:24
He is able to **h** those who are ... Heb 2:18

HELPER

I will make a **h** corresponding to him. ... Gn 2:18
You are a **h** of the fatherless ... Ps 10:14
a **h** who is always found in times ... Ps 46:1
Lord is my **h**; I will not be afraid. ... Heb 13:6

HELPLESS

For while we were still **h**, ... Rm 5:6

HEN

as a **h** gathers her chicks under ... Mt 23:37

HERALD

are the feet of the **h**, who proclaims ... Is 52:7

HERB

unleavened bread and bitter **h-s** ... Ex 12:8

HERE

"**H** I am," he answered ... Ex 3:4
ran to Eli and said, "**H** I am; ... 1Sm 3:5
I said: **H** I am. Send me. ... Is 6:8

HERITAGE

Sons are indeed a **h** from the LORD, ... Ps 127:3

HEROD

1. The Great; king in Judea at the time of Jesus's birth; executed male babies (Mt 2).
2. Archelaus; son of 1. (Mt 2:22).
3. Philip; son of 1. (Mk 6:17).
4. Antipas; son of 1.; tetrarch of Galilee; arrested and executed John the Baptist (Mt 14:1-12).
5. Agrippa I; grandson of 1.; persecuted the church; died when he didn't give glory to God (Ac 12).
6. Agrippa II; son of 5. (Ac 25:13). Heard Paul's defense (25:22–26:32).

HERODIAS

Wife of Herod Antipas, formerly of Herod Philip; requested head of John the Baptist (Mt 14:3-11; Mk 6:17-28; Lk 3:19).

HETHITES

Ancient people of the promised land (Gn 10:15-18; 15:20); Abraham lived among them (Gn 23); Esau married them (26:34; 27:46; 36:2). Formerly lived in the hill country (Nm 13:29; Jos 9:1; 11:3; 12:8); dispossessed by Israel (Ex 23:23; Dt 7:1; 20:17; Jos 3:10); some remained (Jdg 3:5; 1Kg 9:20-21); fought alongside Israel (1Sm 26:6).

H-s, Perizzites, Rephaim ... Gn 15:20
and spoke to the **H-s**: ... Gn 23:20
daughter of Beeri the **H** ... Gn 26:34
wife of Uriah the **H**? ... 2Sm 11:3
and your mother a **H** ... Ezk 16:3

HEZEKIAH

Son of Ahaz; king of Judah (2Kg 18–20; 2Ch 29–32; Is 36–39). Reformer (2Kg 18:4; 2Ch 29–31). Healed of fatal illness (2Kg 20:1-11); showed treasures to Babylonians (20:12-19).

HIDDEN (ADJ)

The **h** things belong to the LORD ... Dt 29:29
Cleanse me from my **h** faults ... Ps 19:12
and nothing **h** that won't be made ... Mt 10:26

HIDE

they **hid** from the LORD ... Gn 3:8
she **hid** him for three months ... Ex 2:2
because she **hid** the messengers ... Jos 6:17
h me in the shadow of your wings ... Ps 17:8
hid me in the shadow of his hand. ... Is 49:2
situated on a hill cannot be **h-den**. ... Mt 5:14
and went off and **hid** your talent ... Mt 25:25
your life is **h-den** with Christ ... Col 3:3
Fall on us and **h** us from the ... Rv 6:16

HIDING (ADJ)

You are my **h** place; ... Ps 32:7

HIGH *SEE ALSO* HIGH PLACE, HIGH PRIEST, MOST HIGH

For as **h** as the heavens are ... Ps 103:11
took him to a very **h** mountain ... Mt 4:8

HIGH PLACE

people were sacrificing on the **h-s**, ... 1Kg 3:2
LORD at the **h** in Gibeon ... 1Ch 16:39
They enraged him with their **h-s** ... Ps 78:58

HIGH PRIEST

led him away to Caiaphas the **h**, ... Mt 26:57
become a merciful and
faithful **h** ... Heb 2:17
this is the kind of **h** we need: ... Heb 7:26

I

IGNORANCE
overlooked the times of i,............. Ac 17:30
silence the i of foolish people 1Pt 2:15

IGNORANT
reject foolish and i disputes,........... 2Tm 2:23
those who are i and are going.......... Heb 5:2

ILLEGITIMATE
then you are i children and not......... Heb 12:8

ILLNESSES
stomach and your frequent i. 1Tm 5:23

ILLUMINATE
my God i-s my darkness................. Ps 18:28

IMAGE
Let us make man in our i,................ Gn 1:26
Whose i and inscription is this?....... Mt 22:20
he is the i and glory of God,............. 1Co 11:7
He is the i of the invisible God, ... Col 1:15
an i of the beast......................... Rv 13:14

IMITATE
I urge you to i of me..................... 1Co 4:16
I me, as I also i Christ.................... 1Co 11:1
of their lives, i their faith............... Heb 13:7
do not i what is evil, but what is........... 3Jn 11

IMITATORS
Therefore, be i of God, as .... Eph 5:1
but will be i of those who inherit....... Heb 6:12

IMMANUEL
have a son, and name him I. .... Is 7:14
they will name him I, which is.......... Mt 1:23

IMMORAL
associate with sexually i people......... 1Co 5:9
No sexually i people, idolaters, ... 1Co 6:9
Every sexually i or impure or............ Eph 5:5
there isn't any i or irreverent.......... Heb 12:16
murderers, sexually i, sorcerers......... Rv 21:8

IMMORALITY
except in a case of sexual i,............. Mt 5:32
except for sexual i, and marries .... Mt 19:9
We weren't born of sexual i,............. Jn 8:41
abstain ... from sexual i,................ Ac 15:20
The body is not for sexual i but for 1Co 6:13
Flee sexual i! Every other sin 1Co 6:18
Let us not commit sexual i
as some 1Co 10:8
But sexual i and any impurity or .... Eph 5:3
that you keep away from sexual i,....... 1Th 4:3

IMMORTAL
glory of the i God for images .... Rm 1:23
the King eternal, i, invisible............ 1Tm 1:17

IMMORTALITY
body must be clothed with i. 1Co 15:53
the only One who has i, dwelling 1Tm 6:16
brought life and i to light............... 2Tm 1:10

IMPERISHABLE
into an inheritance that is i, ... 1Pt 1:4

IMPLANTED
humbly receive the i word, ... Jms 1:21

IMPORTANT
have neglected the more i matters .... Mt 23:23
on to you as most i what I also.......... 1Co 15:3
others as more i than yourselves........ Php 2:3

IMPOSSIBLE
Is anything i for the LORD?............. Gn 18:14
It is i for God to do wrong,............. Jb 34:10
Nothing will be i for you................ Mt 17:20
With man this is i, but with
God................................... Mt 19:26

IMPRISONED
For God has i all in disobedience, ... Rm 11:32
Scripture i everything under .... Gl 3:22

IMPURE
immoral or i or greedy person,.......... Eph 5:5

IMPURITY
cleanse you from all your i-ies .... Ezk 36:25
as slaves to moral i,...................... Rm 6:19
and any i or greed should................ Eph 5:3

INCALCULABLE
to the Gentiles the i riches of .... Eph 3:8

INCENSE
an altar for the burning of i;............. Ex 30:1
prayer be set before you as i, ... Ps 141:2

INCITED
against Israel and i David to count 1Ch 21:1

INCORRUPTIBLE
and the dead will be raised i, ... 1Co 15:52

INCORRUPTION
Sown in corruption, raised in i;........ 1Co 15:42

INCREASE
If wealth i-s, don't set your heart
on it.................................. Ps 62:10
said to the Lord, "I our faith."............ Lk 17:5
He must i, but I must decrease........... Jn 3:30

INDICATING
Christ within them was i when he 1Pt 1:11

INEXPRESSIBLE
heard i words, which a human being .. 2Co 12:4
rejoice with i and glorious joy............ 1Pt 1:8

INFANT
mouths of i-s and nursing babies,......... Ps 8:2
mouths of i-s and nursing babies? ..... Mt 21:16
Like newborn i-s,
desire the 1Pt 2:2

INFERIOR
in no way i to those
"super-apostles"....................... 2Co 11:5
the i is blessed by the superior........... Heb 7:7

INFINITE
His understanding is i................... Ps 147:5

INFLATE
Such people are i-d by empty........... Col 2:18

INHERIT
You will i their land, since I............ Lv 20:24
the humble will i the land .... Ps 37:11
his household will i the wind, ... Pr 11:29
blameless will i what is good. .... Pr 28:10
humble, for they will i the earth. .... Mt 5:5
must I do to i eternal life?......... Lk 10:25; 18:18
will not i God's kingdom? 1Co 6:9

INHERITANCE
to be a people for his i,.................. Dt 4:20
Levi has no i among his brothers,
the LORD is his i,...................... Dt 18:2
In him we have also received an i,...... Eph 1:11
and into an i that is imperishable,........ 1Pt 1:4

INIQUITY
you and did not conceal my i. .... Ps 32:5
crushed because of our i-ies;............ Is 53:5
punished him for the i of us all. .... Is 53:6

INJURY
born prematurely but there is no i,..... Ex 21:22

INJUSTICE
Is there i with God?..................... Rm 9:14

INK
don't want to use paper and i............. 2Jn 12

INN
him to an i, and took care............... Lk 10:34

INNER
our i person is being renewed.......... 2Co 4:16
strengthened ... in the i being.......... Eph 3:16

INNKEEPER
two denarii, gave them to the i,......... Lk 10:35

INNOCENCE
wash my hands in i and go
around .... Ps 26:6
will they be incapable of i? .... Hs 8:5

INNOCENT
hands that shed i blood,.................. Pr 6:17
as serpents and as i as doves............ Mt 10:16
sinned by betraying i blood,.............. Mt 27:4

INSANE

pretended to be **i** in their ... 1Sm 21:13

INSCRIBE

tablets **i-d** by the finger of God... Ex 31:18
I have **i-d** you on the palms of my ... Is 49:16

INSCRIPTION

but none could read the **i** ... Dn 5:8
Whose image and **i** is this? ... Mt 22:20

INSENSITIVITY

God gave them a spirit of **i**, ... Rm 11:8

INSIGHT

A man is praised for his **i**,... Pr 12:8
to understand my **i** into the... Eph 3:4

INSIST

I **i** on paying the full price, ... 1Ch 21:24

INSPIRED

then that David, **i** by the Spirit ... Mt 22:43
All Scripture is **i** by God and is... 2Tm 3:16

INSTALL

I have **i-d** my king on Zion,... Ps 2:6

INSTITUTED

those that exist are **i** by God... Rm 13:1

INSTRUCT

Your good Spirit to **i** them... Neh 9:20
I will **i** you and show you the ... Ps 32:8
a wise person **i-s** its mouth; ... Pr 16:23

INSTRUCTION

This book of **i** must not depart ... Jos 1:8
his delight is in the LORD's **i**, ... Ps 1:2
The **i** of the LORD is perfect,... Ps 19:7
see wondrous things from your **i**... Ps 119:18
but I delight in your **i**... Ps 119:70
Listen, my son, to your father's **i**, ... Pr 1:8
Listen to **i** and be wise;... Pr 8:33
who follows divine **i** will be happy... Pr 29:18
For **i** will go out of Zion and ... Is 2:3
For **i** will go out of Zion and ... Mc 4:2
in the past was written for our **i**, ... Rm 15:4
were written for our **i**, ... 1Co 10:11
the goal of our **i** is love... 1Tm 1:5

INSTRUCTOR

may have countless **i-s** in Christ, ... 1Co 4:15

INSULT (N)

whoever ignores an **i** is sensible... Pr 12:16
there began to yell **i-s** at him:... Lk 23:39

INSULT (V)

of those who **i** you have fallen... Ps 69:9
who mocks the poor **i-s** his Maker,... Pr 17:5
blessed when they **i** you and ... Mt 5:11
of those who **i** you have fallen... Rm 15:3
he was **i-ed**, but he did not **i** ... 1Pt 2:23

INTEGRITY

if you walk before me ... with ... **i**... 1Kg 9:4
He still retains his **i**, even though you ... Jb 2:3
You desire **i** in the inner self... Ps 51:6
The **i** of the upright guides them,... Pr 11:3
with **i** and dignity in your teaching... Ti 2:7

INTELLIGENT

The woman was **i** and beautiful,... 1Sm 25:3

INTENSIFY

I will **i** your labor pains; ... Gn 3:16

INTENTION

and reveal the **i-s** of the hearts... 1Co 4:5

INTERCEDE

But Moses **i-d** with the LORD his... Ex 32:11
sins against the LORD, who can **i**... 1Sm 2:25
sin of many and **i-d** for the rebels... Is 53:12
the Spirit himself **i-s** for us with... Rm 8:26
He always lives to **i** for them... Heb 7:25

INTERCESSION

perseverance and **i** for all the ... Eph 6:18
prayers, **i-s**, and thanksgivings... 1Tm 2:1

INTERCOURSE

has sexual **i** with an animal ... Ex 22:19
You are not to have sexual **i** with... Lv 18:9

INTEREST

you must not charge him **i**... Ex 22:25
You may charge a foreigner **i**, ... Dt 23:20
who does not lend his silver at **i**... Ps 15:5
received my money back with **i**... Mt 25:27
not to his own **i-s**, but rather ... Php 2:4
has an unhealthy **i** in disputes... 1Tm 6:4

INTERMARRY

I with us; give your daughters... Gn 34:9
You must not **i** with them, ... Dt 7:3
and **i** with the peoples who... Ezr 9:14

INTERPRET

a dream, and no one can **i** it... Gn 41:15
and the ability to **i** dreams, ... Dn 5:12
in tongues? Do all **i**? ... 1Co 12:30
unless he **i-s** so that the church... 1Co 14:5
and let someone **i**. ... 1Co 14:27

INTERPRETATION

Don't **i-s** belong to God? ... Gn 40:8
tell me the dream and its **i**, ... Dn 2:5
inscription and give me its **i**, ... Dn 5:16
to another, **i** of tongues. ... 1Co 12:10
from the prophet's own **i**, ... 2Pt 1:20

INTERPRETER

But if there is no **i**, that person ... 1Co 14:28

INTIMATE

The man was **i** with his wife Eve,... Gn 4:1

INVADE

king of Assyria **i-d** the whole land,... 2Kg 17:5
For a nation has **i-d** my land, ... Jl 1:6

INVALIDATE

fine way of **i-ing** God's command... Mk 7:9

INVESTIGATE

glory of kings to **i** a matter... Pr 25:2
I have carefully **i-d** everything ... Lk 1:3

INVISIBLE

His **i** attributes, that is, his ... Rm 1:20
He is the image of the **i** God,... Col 1:15
immortal, **i**, the only God,... 1Tm 1:17

INVITE

Then **i** Jesse to the sacrifice, ... 1Sm 16:3
For many are **i-d**, but few are... Mt 22:14
a banquet, **i** those who are poor, ... Lk 14:13

INWARD

was you who created my **i** parts; ... Ps 139:13

INWARDLY

a person is a Jew who is one **i**, ... Rm 2:29

IRON

it there, and made the **i** float... 2Kg 6:6
break them with an **i** scepter; ... Ps 2:9
I sharpens **i**, and one man ... Pr 27:17
legs were **i**, ... feet were partly **i** and... Dn 2:33

IRREVERENT

the unholy and **i**, for those who ... 1Tm 1:9

IRREVOCABLE

gracious gifts and calling are **i**... Rm 11:29

ISAAC

Son of Abraham and Sarah; fulfillment of a promise (Gn 17:17; 21:5). God tested Abraham by asking him to sacrifice Isaac (Gn 22; Heb 11:17-19). Married Rebekah (Gn 24). Heir to Abraham's promise (Gn 25:5,11; Ps 105:9; Rm 9:7). Father of Esau and Jacob (Gn 25:21-26); blessed Jacob (Gn 27). Lied to Abimelech in Gerar about Rebekah (26:7-11). Died in Hebron (35:27-29).

ISAIAH

Son of Amoz; prophet to four kings of Judah (Is 1:1). Called (Is 6). Sons' names were symbolic (7:3; 8:3).

ISH-BOSHETH

Saul's son; tried to become king (2Sm 2:8-17; 3:6-16); was murdered (2Sm 4).

ISHMAEL

Son of Abraham and Hagar (Gn 16:11-15). Received a blessing but not the promise (17:18-21). Descendants are perpetual opponents of Israel (25:18).

ISLAND

the many coasts and **i**-s be glad.......... Ps 97:1

ISRAEL

Name God gave Jacob (Gn 32:28; 35:10). Also his descendants—God's chosen people—and their land (Ex 3:16; 1Sm 13:19; 15:35; 1Kg 4:1; Mt 2:6,20; Php 3:5). In the divided kingdom, the northern (1Kg 12:20).

ISRAELITE

about him, "Here truly is an **I**............ Jn 1:47
They are **I**-s, and to them belong .... Rm 9:4
For I too am an **I**, a descendant.......... Rm 11:1
Are they **I**-s? So am **I**.................... 2Co 11:22

ISSACHAR

Son of Jacob and Leah (Gn 30:18). Tribe with territory from Jezreel to Tabor (Jos 19:17-23); its troops who rallied to David understood the times (1Ch 12:32).

ITCH

have an **i** to hear what they want....... 2Tm 4:3

ITHAMAR

Fourth son of Aaron (Ex 6:23; 28:1; Nm 26:20; 1Ch 6:3; 24:1); took over priesthood when their brothers died (Lv 10:6,12,16; Nm 3:4; 1Ch 24:2); in charge of the Levites (Ex 38:21; Nm 4:28,33; 7:8).

IVORY

from **i** palaces harps bring you.......... Ps 45:8
lie on beds inlaid with **i**,................. Am 6:4

J

JABEZ

Israelite who asked for and received a blessing (1Ch 4:9-10).

JABIN

A king of Canaan, whose commander Sisera was defeated by Israel (Jdg 4–5).

JACOB

Son of Isaac and Rebekah; younger twin brother of Esau (Gn 25:21-26). Took birthright (25:33); fled Esau (27:41–28:5). Received the promise (28:10-22). Worked for his wives (29:1-30). Wrestled with God (32:22-32); God changed his name to Israel (32:28; 49:2). Reconciled with Esau (33:4-16). Fathered the twelve tribes (29:21–30:24; 35:16-18). Went to Egypt (46:1-7). Died there, buried in Hebron (49:29–50:14). Ancestor of Jesus (Mt 1:2).

Even so, I loved **J**, ... Mal 1:2
J-'s well was there, and Jesus............. Jn 4:6
J I have loved, but Esau I have .... Rm 9:13

JAIRUS

Synagogue leader whose daughter Jesus restored (Mk 5:22-43; Lk 8:41-56).

JAMES

1. Apostle; son of Zebedee; brother of John (Mt 4:21; 10:2). At transfiguration (17:1); in Gethsemane (26:36-37). Martyred (Ac 12:2).
2. Apostle; son of Alphaeus (Mt 10:3).
3. Brother of Jesus (Mt 13:55; Gl 1:19). Believed after the resurrection (Jn 7:3; Ac 1:14; 1Co 15:7). Leader of church in Jerusalem (Ac 15; 21:18; Gl 2:9). Author (Jms 1:1).

JAPHETH

Son of Noah (Gn 5:32; 9:18-27).

JAR

in the house except a **j** of oil.............. 2Kg 4:2
an alabaster **j** of very
expensive .... Mk 14:3
an alabaster **j** of perfume................ Lk 7:37
have this treasure in clay **j**-s, ... 2Co 4:7

JAWBONE

He found a fresh **j** of a donkey, ... Jdg 15:15

JEALOUS

His brothers were **j** of him, ... Gn 37:11
Lord your God, am a **j** God, ... Ex 20:5
another god. He is a **j** God............... Ex 34:14
is a consuming fire, a **j** God. .... Dt 4:24
and I will be **j** for my holy
name.............................. Ezk 39:25
I will make you **j** of those who......... Rm 10:19
For I am **j** for you with a
godly................................. 2Co 11:2

JEALOUSY

provoked his **j** with different gods ..... Dt 32:16
For **j** enrages a husband, and he......... Pr 6:34
hatreds, strife, **j**, outbursts of .... Gl 5:20

JEBUSITES

Descendants of Canaan (Gn 10:16; 15:21; Ex 3:8; Dt 7:1; 20:17), inhabitants of Jebus (1Ch 11:4). Defeated by Judah and Benjamin, but not dispossessed (Jos 15:63; Jdg 1:8,21; 3:5); defeated by David (2Sm 5:6 9) and enslaved by Solomon (1Kg 9:20-21).

JEHOAHAZ

1. Son of Jehu; king of Israel (2Kg 13:1-9).
2. Son of Josiah; king of Judah (2Kg 23:30-34). Called Shallum (Jr 22:11).

JEHOASH

1. Alternate name of Joash son of Ahaziah, king of Judah (2Kg 12).
2. Son of Jehoahaz; king of Israel (2Kg 13:10–14:13).

JEHOIACHIN

Son of Jehoiakim; king of Judah (2Kg 24:6). Also called Jeconiah or Coniah (Jr 22:24; 24:1). Exiled (2Kg 24:10-17) but later favored (25:27-30).

JEHOIAKIM

Son of Josiah; king of Judah. Succeeded his brother Jehoahaz; name changed from Eliakim by Neco (2Kg 23:34). Burned Jeremiah's scroll (Jr 36). Became vassal of Babylon; later rebelled and was defeated (2Kg 24:1-6; Dn 1:2).

JEHORAM

1. Alternate form of Joram, son of Ahab; king of Israel (2Kg 3:1).
2. Son of Jehoshaphat; king of Judah (2Kg 8:16-24; 2Ch 21). Ahab's son-in-law (2Kg 8:18). Edom gained independence during his reign (8:20).

JEHOSHAPHAT

1. Son of Asa; king of Judah (1Kg 15:24). Initially faithful, strong, blessed (2Ch 17). Then married Ahab's daughter Athaliah and formed alliances with Ahab and Joram, kings of Israel (1Kg 22; 2Kg 3; 8:26; 2Ch 18; 20).
2. Valley of judgment (Jl 3:2,12).

JEHU

1. Son of Hanani; prophet against Baasha king of Israel (1Kg 16:1-12).
2. Son of Jehoshaphat; king of Israel. Anointed by Elisha's servant; executed Ahaziah king of Judah, Joram, Jezebel and the house of Ahab in Israel, and the worshipers of Baal (2Kg 9–10; cp. 1Kg 19:16-17).

JEPHTHAH

Gileadite judge who made rash vow affecting his daughter (Jdg 11–12; 1Sm 12:11; Heb 11:32).

JEREMIAH

Prophet to Judah in the time leading up to the exile (Jr 1:1-3). Put in stocks (20:1-3), threatened (Jr 26), opposed (Jr 28), imprisoned (32:2; 37), censured (Jr 36), and thrown into a cistern (Jr 38). Taken to Egypt against his will (Jr 43).

JERICHO

City near the Jordan River north of the Dead Sea (Nm 22:1). Spied out (Jos 2) and conquered (Jos 6; Heb 11:30) by Joshua; rebuilt by Hiel (1Kg 16:34). Visited by Jesus (Mt 20:29-34; Mk 10:46-52; Lk 18:35; 19:1-10).

JEROBOAM

1. Son of Nebat; Solomon's servant; rebelled; first king of Israel (1Kg 11:26–12:20). Judged for notorious idolatry (12:25–14:20).
2. Son of Joash, king of Israel (2Kg 14:23-29).

JERUSALEM

Formerly called Salem (Gn 14:18; Ps 76:2) or Jebus (Jos 18:28); 1Ch 11:4. David conquered it and made it his capital (2Sm 5:5-9); Solomon built temple, palace, and fortifications (1Kg 3:1). Conquered by Babylon (2Kg 24:10-12). Rebuilt and resettled after the exile (Ezr 1; Neh 12:27). Jesus visited (Mt 21:1; Jn 2:13); mourned (Mt 23:37). Important city in early church (Ac 15:4). New Jerusalem promised (Rv 3:12; 21:2,10).

in J he reigned thirty-three years 2Sm 5:5
J, the city I chose for myself to put my name there........................ 1Kg 11:36
For a remnant will go out from J, ... 2Kg 19:31
Pray for the well-being of J: .... Ps 122:6
If I forget you, J, may my right...........Ps 137:5
Speak tenderly to J, and announce ....Is 40:2
From ... rebuild J until an Anointed.....Dn 9:25
J! J that kills the prophets and..........Mt 23:37
say that the place to worship is in J...... Jn 4:20
you will be my witnesses in J, in all ....Ac 1:8
holy city, the new J, coming down....... Rv 21:2

JESHUA

Son of Jozadak; high priest; returned with Zerubbabel (Ezr 3:2; Neh 7:7).

JESSE

David's father (Ru 4:17-22; 1Sm 16; 1Ch 2:12-16; Mt 1:5-6; Lk 3:32).

JESUS

Messiah and Lord (Ac 2:36; Eph 3:11; 1Pt 3:15). Born in Bethlehem (Mt 1:18-25; Lk 2:1-7) to a virgin, Mary (Mt 1:20; Lk 1:26-38). Genealogy (Mt 1:1-17; Lk 3:23-38). Raised in Nazareth (Mt 2:19-23; Lk 2:39-40). Visited the temple at age 12 (Lk 2:41-50).

Baptized by John (Mt 3:13-17; Lk 3:21). Tempted in the wilderness (Mt 4:1-11; Lk 4:1-13). Chose apostles (Lk 5:1-11,27-28; 6:12-16; Jn 1:35-51).

Transformation (Mt 17:1-9; Mk 9:2-10). Triumphal entry into Jerusalem (Mt 21:1-11; Lk 19:28-40). Betrayal and arrest (Mt 26:17-25,47-56; Mk 14:17-21,43-50; Lk 22:1-6,47-54), trial (Mt 26:57-66; 27:11-31; Mk 14:53-65; 15:1-20; Lk 22:66–23:25), crucifixion (Mt 27:32-56; Mk 15:21-39; Lk 23:32-49), and resurrection (Mt 28; Mk 16; Lk 24; Jn 20–21).

JETHRO

Priest of Midian; Moses's father-in-law and adviser (Ex 3:1; 4:18; 18). Also called Reuel (2:18).

JEW

He planned to destroy all ... the J-s, ...Est 3:6
has been born king of the J-s? .... Mt 2:2
Are you the king of the J-s?............. Mt 27:11
How is it that you, a J, ask for a ....Jn 4:9
salvation is from the J-s.................. Jn 4:22
first to the J, and also to the ....Rm 1:16
a person is a J who is one inwardly, ... Rm 2:29
the God of J-s only? Is he not .... Rm 3:29
To the J-s I became like a J, ...1Co 9:20
There is no J or Greek, slave or .... Gl 3:28

JEWEL

She is far more precious than j-s..........Pr 3:15

JEZEBEL

Wife of King Ahab of Israel, daughter of the king of Sidon; brought Baal worship to Israel (1Kg 16:31-33). Killed prophets and threatened Elijah (18:4,13; 19:1-2). Killed by Jehu (2Kg 9:30-37) in fulfillment of prophecy (1Kg 21). Name used as a label (Rv 2:20).

JOAB

Son of Zeruiah; David's nephew and commander of his troops (1Ch 2:16; 11:6). Killed Abner (2Sm 3:22-39), Absalom (2Sm 18), Amasa, and Sheba (2Sm 20). Sided with Adonijah (1Kg 1:7,19); David told Solomon to execute him (2:5-6,28-35).

JOASH

1. Son of Ahaziah; king of Judah (2Kg 12). Protected by Jehoiada (2Kg 11). Repaired temple (2Ch 24:4-14).
2. Alternate name of Jehoash son of Jehoahaz, king of Israel (2Kg 13:10).

JOB

Wealthy patriarch. His book tells of his testing (Jb 1–2), perseverance (Jb 3–37), rebuke (Jb 38–41), and vindication (Jb 42; Jms 5:11).

JOEL

1. Dishonest son of Samuel (2Sm 8:2).
2. Son of Pethuel; prophet who urged priests to call Judah to repentance; depicted calamities (Jl 1:1–2:11); predicted the Messiah (2:21-32; Ac 2:16).

JOHANAN

Commander; stayed in Judah and tried to protect Gedaliah (2Kg 25:23); forced Jeremiah to go to Egypt (Jr 40–43).

JOHN

1. The baptizer; Son of Zechariah; prophet. Annunciation and birth (Lk 1:5-25,57-66). Preached repentance, announced the coming Messiah (Mt 3:1-12; Mk 1:1-8; Lk 3:1-18; 7:27-28), and baptized Jesus (Mt 3:13-15; Mk 1:9; Lk 3:21-22). Fulfilled the role of Elijah (Mt 11:13-14; 17:12-13; Mk 9:12-13; Mt 3:4 cp. 2Kg 1:8). Asked Jesus to verify his identity (Mt 11:2-6; Lk 7:18-23). Beheaded by Herod Antipas (Mt 14:1-12; Mk 6:14-29; Lk 3:19-20; 9:7-9).
2. Apostle; Son of Zebedee; brother of James. Call (Mt 4:21-22; Mk 1:19-20). Among the inner three at special occasions (Mk 9:2; 14:32-33). With James, called "Sons of Thunder" (Mk 3:17); asked for places of honor (Mk 10:35-41). Often with Peter (Ac 1:13; 3:1-11; 4:13-20; 8:14); a leader in Jerusalem (Gl 2:9). In his gospel, called the disciple Jesus loved (Jn 13:23; 19:26; 20:2; 21:7,20); also wrote three letters and Revelation.
3. John Mark see MARK, JOHN

JOIN

to house and **j** field to field .... Is 5:8
Then **j** them together into a........... Ezk 37:17
what God has **j-ed** together, ... Mt 19:6

JOINTS

soul and spirit, **j** and marrow. ....Heb 4:12

JOKING

or crude **j** are not suitable ....Eph 5:4

JONAH

Son of Amittai; prophet at the time of Jeroboam II (2Kg 14:23-27). Rejected God's call to preach in Nineveh; swallowed by a great fish (Jnh 1). Prayed (Jnh 2); preached repentance in Nineveh (Jnh 3); scolded by God for his anger (Jnh 4). Used as an example (Mt 12:39-41; 16:4; Lk 11:29-32).

JONATHAN

Son of Saul; friend of David (1Sm 18:1-4; 19:1-7; 20; 23:16-18). Killed in battle (31:1-13); mourned by David (2Sm 1:17-27).

JORAM

1. Son of Ahab; king of Israel (2Kg 3). Succeeded his brother Ahaziah (1:17). Attacked Moab with the help of Judah, Edom, and Elisha (3:4-27). Wounded by Arameans (8:28); killed by Jehu (9:14-26).
2. Alternate form of Jehoram, son of Jehoshaphat; king of Judah (2Kg 8:16-24; 2Ch 21).

JORDAN

Lot chose the entire plain of J .... Gn 13:11
the border will go down to the J....... Nm 34:12
dry ground in the middle of the J, ... Jos 3:17
himself in the J seven times,............ 2Kg 5:14
Jesus came ... to John at the J,........... Mt 3:13

JOSEPH

1. Son of Jacob and Rachel. Sold into slavery in Egypt (Gn 37); imprisoned on false accusations (Gn 39); became Pharaoh's second in command (41:39-45); sold grain to brothers (Gn 42–45); enabled his father and brothers to move to Egypt (Gn 46–47). Sons Ephraim and Manasseh each became tribes (Gn 48). Died in Egypt, buried in Canaan (50:22-26; Ex 13:19; Jos 24:32; Ac 7:16).
2. Husband of Mary; foster father of Jesus (Mt 1:16,20; Lk 2:4; 3:23; 4:22; Jn 1:45; 6:42). Carpenter (Mt 13:55). Told in a dream not to divorce Mary (Mt 1:18-25); told in a dream to flee to Egypt (2:13-23).
3. Of Arimathea; a righteous member of the Sanhedrin who sought the kingdom of God; put Jesus's body in his tomb (Mt 27:57-60; Mk 15:43-46; Lk 23:50-53; Jn 19:38-42).

JOSHUA

Son of Nun; successor to Moses as leader of Israelites. Leader of Moses's army (Ex 17:8-13); Moses's servant on Mt. Sinai (32:17). Scouted Canaan and, along with Caleb, recommended invasion (Nm 13:30–14:38). Chosen, commissioned, and encouraged by God (Nm 27:15-23; Dt 31:14-15,23; Jos 1:1-9).

Conquered Canaan (Jos 2–11) and distributed the land (Jos 12–21). Renewed the covenant and charged the people (Jos 23–24).

JOSIAH

Son of Amon; king of Israel. Became king at age eight (2Kg 21:19–22:2). Found the book of the law and instituted reforms (2Kg 22–23; 2Ch 34–35). Died resisting Pharaoh Neco (2Kg 23:29-30; 2Ch 35:20-25).

JOTHAM

1. Son of Gideon (Jdg 9).
2. Son of Uzziah/Azariah; coregent (2Kg 15:5), then king of Judah (15:32-38).

JOURNEY
like a man on a j, who left his ... Mk 13:34
On frequent j-s, I faced dangers ... 2Co 11:26

JOY
altar of God, to God, my greatest j. ... Ps 43:4
Restore the j of your salvation ... Ps 51:12
A wise son brings j to his father, ... Pr 10:1
crowned with unending j. ... Is 35:10; 51:11
turn their mourning into j, ... Jr 31:13
immediately receives it with j. ... Mt 13:20
Share your master's j!' ... Mt 25:21
news of great j that will be for ... Lk 2:10
will be more j in heaven over ... Lk 15:7
but your sorrow will turn to j. ... Jn 16:20
peace, and j in the Holy Spirit ... Rm 14:17
fruit of the Spirit is love, j, peace ... Gl 5:22
make my j complete by thinking the same ... Php 2:2
For the j that lay before him ... Heb 12:2
Consider it a great j, my brothers ... Jms 1:2
inexpressible and glorious j, ... 1Pt 1:8
I have no greater j than this: ... 3Jn 4

JOYFUL
come before him with j songs. ... Ps 100:2
A j heart is good medicine, ... Pr 17:22
In the day of prosperity be j, ... Ec 7:14
ate their food with a j and sincere ... Ac 2:46

JOYFULLY
Let the whole earth shout j to God! ... Ps 66:1

JUBILEE
It will be your J, when ... Lv 25:10

JUDAH
Son of Jacob and Leah (Gn 29:35); tribe with large territory west and south of Jerusalem (Jos 15:20-63). Tricked by daughter-in-law (Gn 38). Ancestor of David and Jesus (Gn 49:10; 1Sm 17:12; Mt 1:3,6,16; Rv 5:5). Name of the southern part of the divided kingdom (2Kg 12:20; 14:21; 23:27; Ezk 37:15-23) and the Persian province in the restoration (Neh 5:14; Hg 1:1).

JUDAISM
my former way of life in J: ... Gl 1:13

JUDAS
1. Iscariot; apostle (Mt 10:4); treasurer, miser, thief (Jn 12:4-6). Betrayed Jesus (Mt 26:21-25,44-50; Lk 22:3-6; Jn 13:21-30); committed suicide (Mt 27:3-10; Ac 1:16-20).
2. Son of James; apostle; called Thaddaeus (Mt 10:3; Mk 3:18; Lk 6:16; Jn 14:22).
3. Brother of Jesus (Mt 13:55; Mk 6:3); also called Jude.

JUDE
Brother of Jesus; also called Judas; author (Mt 13:55; Jd 1).

JUDEA
Another name for the territory of Judah.
Jesus was born in Bethlehem of J ... Mt 2:1
Pontius Pilate was governor of J, ... Lk 3:1
in Jerusalem, in all J and Samaria, ... Ac 1:8

JUDGE (N)
Won't the J of the whole earth do ... Gn 18:25
LORD raised up j-s, who saved ... Jdg 2:16
a j … who didn't fear God or ... Lk 18:2

JUDGE (V)
May the LORD j between me and ... Gn 16:5
He is coming to j the earth. ... 1Ch 16:33
He j-s the world with righteousness; ... Ps 9:8
There is a God who j-s on earth! ... Ps 58:11
coming to j the earth. He will j the ... Ps 96:13
Do not j, so that you won't be j-d. ... Mt 7:1
rather j according to righteous ... Jn 7:24
I did not come to j the world but ... Jn 12:47
that the saints will j the world? ... 1Co 6:2
who is going to j the living and ... 2Tm 4:1
who are you to j your neighbor? ... Jms 4:12
the dead were j-d according to ... Rv 20:12

JUDGMENT
the wicked will not stand up in the j, ... Ps 1:5
my mouth, for I hope in your j-s. ... Ps 119:43
Teach me good j and discernment, ... Ps 119:66
arrived and a j was given in ... Dn 7:22
Sodom on the day of j than for ... Mt 11:24
not come under j but has passed ... Jn 5:24
his j-s and untraceable ... Rm 11:33
eats and drinks j on himself. ... 1Co 11:29
die once—and after this, j— ... Heb 9:27
has come for j to begin with ... 1Pt 4:17
because his j-s are true and ... Rv 19:2

JUDGMENT SEAT
will all stand before the j of God. ... Rm 14:10
all appear before the j of Christ, ... 2Co 5:10

JUG
and the oil j will not run dry ... 1Kg 17:14

JUST
Judge of the whole earth do what is j? .. Gn 18:25
is holy and j and good. ... Rm 7:12
whatever is j, whatever is pure ... Php 4:8

JUSTICE
must not deny j to a poor person ... Ex 23:6
but he gives j to the oppressed. ... Jb 36:6
The evil do not understand j, ... Pr 28:5
He will bring j to the nations. ... Is 42:1
the LORD, showing faithful love, j, ... Jr 9:24
But let j flow like water, ... Am 5:24
will proclaim j to the nations. ... Mt 12:18
kind of herb, and you bypass j ... Lk 11:42

JUSTIFICATION
and raised for our j. ... Rm 4:25
j leading to life for everyone. ... Rm 5:18

JUSTIFY
he had j-ied himself rather than God. ... Jb 32:2
righteous servant will j many, ... Is 53:11
But wanting to j himself, he ... Lk 10:29
down to his house j-ied rather than ... Lk 18:14
who believes is j-ied through him. ... Ac 13:39
they are j-ied freely by his grace ... Rm 3:24
a person is j-ied by faith apart ... Rm 3:28
and those he called, he also j-ied; ... Rm 8:30
God is the one who j-ies. ... Rm 8:33
no one is j-ied by the works of the ... Gl 2:16
we might be j-ied by faith in Christ ... Gl 2:16
that God would j the Gentiles by ... Gl 3:8
a person is j-ied by works and not ... Jms 2:24

JUSTLY
the LORD requires of you: to act j, ... Mc 6:8

K

KADESH
Oasis, also called Kadesh-barnea. Where Abraham fought the Amalekites (Gn 14:7). Where the Israelites camped, they sent out spies, and Moses struck the rock (Nm 13:26; 20:1,11; 27:14; 32:8; Dt 1:46; 9:23; Jdg 11:16-17). Southern limit of Judah (Nm 34:4; Jos 10:41; 15:3).

KEEP
be with me, and k me from harm ... 1Ch 4:10
and in k-ing them there is an ... Ps 19:11
K your tongue from evil and your ... Ps 34:13
How can a young man k his way pure? By k-ing your word. ... Ps 119:9
K my commands and live ... Pr 4:4; 7:2
fear God and k his commands, ... Ec 12:13
K listening, but do not understand; ... Is 6:9
You will k … in perfect peace ... Is 26:3
"I have **kept** all these," the young ... Mt 19:20
hates his life in this world will k it ... Jn 12:25
loves me, he will k my word. ... Jn 14:23
the race, I have **kept** the faith. ... 2Tm 4:7
whoever k-s the entire law, ... Jms 2:10
and unfading, **kept** in heaven for ... 1Pt 1:4
and those who k the words of ... Rv 22:9

KETURAH
Abraham's second wife (Gn 25:1-4).

KEY
give you the k-s of the kingdom ... Mt 16:19
and I hold the k-s of death and ... Rv 1:18
the One who has the k of David, ... Rv 3:7

KIDNAP
Whoever k-s a person must be put ... Ex 21:16

KILL
his brother Abel and k-ed him. ... Gn 4:8
Am I God, k-ing and giving life ... 2Kg 5:7
a time to k and a time to heal; ... Ec 3:3
Don't fear those who k the body but are not able to k the soul; ... Mt 10:28
k-ed, and be raised the third day. ... Mt 16:21
way to arrest Jesus and k him. ... Mk 14:1
Why are you trying to k me? ... Jn 7:19
You k-ed the source of life, ... Ac 3:15
For the letter k-s, but the Spirit ... 2Co 3:6

KIND (ADJ)
Love is patient, love is k. ... 1Co 13:4
And be k and compassionate to ... Eph 4:32

LAMP

LORD, you light my l; .... Ps 18:28
Your word is a l for my feet and .... Ps 119:105
but the l of the wicked is put out. .... Pr 13:9
No one lights a l and puts it. .... Mt 5:15
The eye is the l of the body. .... Mt 6:22
like ten virgins who took
their l-s .... Mt 25:1
the light of a l will never. .... Rv 18:23

LAMPSTAND

a l out of pure, hammered gold. .... Ex 25:31
but rather on a l, and it gives
light. .... Mt 5:15
seven l-s are the seven churches. .... Rv 1:20
and remove your l from its place. .... Rv 2:5

LAND

God called the dry l "earth," .... Gn 1:10
I will give this l to your .... Gn 12:7
a l flowing with milk and honey .... Ex 3:8
So Joshua took the entire l, ... Jos 11:23
divide this l as an inheritance .... Jos 13:7
Judah went into exile from its l. 2Kg 25:21
forgive their sin, and heal their l. 2Ch 7:14
the humble will inherit the l. .... Ps 37:11
Woe to you, l, when your king is. .... Ec 10:16
My flock from all the l-s where I .... Jr 23:3
and strike the l with a curse. .... Mal 4:6
those who owned l-s or
houses sold .... Ac 4:34
on the sea, his left on the l, ... Rv 10:2

LANGUAGE

The whole earth had the same l .... Gn 11:1
He will speak ... in a foreign l. .... Is 28:11
and filthy l from your mouth. .... Col 3:8
every tribe and l and people. .... Rv 5:9

LAPPED

with the three hundred
men who l .... Jdg 7:7

LASHES

than a hundred l into a fool. .... Pr 17:10
Five times I received forty l 2Co 11:24

LAST (ADJ)

These are the l words of
David: 2Sm 23:1
In the l days the mountain of. .... Is 2:2
are first will be l, and the l first. .... Mt 19:30
he must be l and servant of all. .... Mk 9:35
The l enemy to be abolished is 1Co 15:26
of an eye, at the l trumpet. 1Co 15:52
In these l days, he has spoken .... Heb 1:2
Children, it is the l hour. 1Jn 2:18

LAST (N)

I am the first and I am the l. .... Is 44:6
I am the First and the L, ... Rv 1:17

LAST (V)

For his anger l-s only a moment, ... Ps 30:5

LATER

that in l times some will
depart. 1Tm 4:1

LAUGH

Why did Sarah l, ... Gn 18:13
The one enthroned in heaven l-s; .... Ps 2:4
a time to weep and a time to l; .... Ec 3:4

LAUGHTER

Even in l a heart may be sad, ... Pr 14:13
Let your l be turned to mourning .... Jms 4:9

LAUNDERER

white as no l on earth could .... Mk 9:3

LAW

the stone tablets with the l .... Ex 24:12
Moses wrote down this l and gave it ..... Dt 31:9
L after l, l after l, line after line, ... Is 28:10
think that I came to abolish the L. .... Mt 5:17
All the L and the Prophets depend .... Mt 22:40
stroke of a letter in the l to drop. .... Lk 16:17
the l was given through Moses; .... Jn 1:17
not under the l but under grace .... Rm 6:14
So then, the l is holy, and the. .... Rm 7:12
For Christ is the end of the l .... Rm 10:4
The l, then, was our guardian until. ..... Gl 3:24
For the whole l is fulfilled in .... Gl 5:14
I will put my l-s into their minds .... Heb 8:10
Since the l has only a shadow .... Heb 10:1
For whoever keeps the entire l, ... Jms 2:10

LAWBREAKER

Depart from me, you l-s! .... Mt 7:23

LAWLESS

and then the l one will be. 2Th 2:8

LAWLESSNESS

Because l will multiply, ... Mt 24:12
the mystery of l is already at 2Th 2:7
who commits sin practices l. 1Jn 3:4

LAY

Look, I have **laid** a stone in Zion, ... Is 28:16
Man has no place to l his head. .... Mt 8:20
in cloth and **laid** him in a manger, ... Lk 2:7
I l down my life for the sheep. .... Jn 10:15
through the **l-ing** on of my hands 2Tm 1:6
ritual washings, **l-ing** on of hands ...... Heb 6:2
let us l aside every weight and .... Heb 12:1
He **laid** down his life for us. 1Jn 3:16

LAZARUS

1. Poor man in Jesus's parable (Lk 16:19-31).
2. Brother of Mary and Martha; friend of Jesus (Jn 11:1-5). Died; revived by Jesus (11:3-44). Endangered because of fame (12:9-11,17).

LAZY

A l hunter doesn't roast his game, ... Pr 12:27
and a l person will go hungry. .... Pr 19:15
so that you won't become l .... Heb 6:12

LEAD

of cloud to l them on their way. .... Ex 13:21
way of the wicked l-s to ruin. .... Ps 1:6
He l-s me beside quiet waters. .... Ps 23:2
way, LORD, and l me on a level .... Ps 27:11
L me to a rock that is high
above me. .... Ps 61:2
l me in the everlasting way. .... Ps 139:24
The fear of the LORD l-s to life; .... Pr 19:23
and a child will l them. .... Is 11:6
Like a lamb **led** to the slaughter .... Is 53:7
l astray, if possible, even the elect. ..... Mt 24:24
and **led** him away to crucify him. .... Mt 27:31
sheep by name and l-s them out. .... Jn 10:3
is intended to l you to
repentance? .... Rm 2:4
sin **l-ing** to death or of obedience ...... Rm 6:16
All those **led** by God's Spirit are .... Rm 8:14
But if you are **led** by the Spirit, ... Gl 5:18

LEADER

He chose Judah as l, ... 1Ch 28:4
For the l-s of the earth belong to .... Ps 47:9
of the synagogue l-s,
named Jairus .... Mk 5:22
Obey your l-s and submit. .... Heb 13:17

LEADING (ADJ)

as a number of the l women. .... Ac 17:4

LEAF

they sewed fig **l-ves** together and .... Gn 3:7
and its l does not wither. .... Ps 1:3
becomes tender and sprouts **l-ves**, ... Mt 24:32
The **l-ves** of the tree are for. .... Rv 22:2

LEAH

Wife of Jacob; mother of Reuben, Simeon, Levi, Judah, Issachar, Zebulun, and Dinah (Gn 29:16-35; 30:14-21).

LEAN

temple, so I can l against them. .... Jdg 16:26
So he **l-ed** back against Jesus and ...... Jn 13:25

LEAP

with my God I can l over a wall. .... Ps 18:29
greeting, the baby **l-ed** inside her .... Lk 1:41
walking, **l-ing**, and praising God. .... Ac 3:8

LEARN

will listen and l to fear the LORD. .... Dt 31:13
that I could l your statutes. .... Ps 119:71
and the inexperienced l a lesson; .... Pr 19:25
L to do what is good. .... Is 1:17
take up my yoke and l from me, ... Mt 11:29
for I have **l-ed** to be content in. .... Php 4:11
A woman is to l quietly 1Tm 2:11
He **l-ed** obedience through what he. .... Heb 5:8

LEASE

He **l-d** it to tenant farmers and .... Mt 21:33

LEAST

are by no means l among the. .... Mt 2:6
will be called l in the kingdom .... Mt 5:19
you did for one of the l of these .... Mt 25:40
For I am the l of the apostles, ... 1Co 15:9

LEATHER

man with a l belt around his 2Kg 1:8
garment with a l belt around his .... Mt 3:4

LIFEBLOOD
not eat meat with its l in it. . . . Gn 9:4

LIFE-GIVING
last Adam became a l Spirit. . . . 1Co 15:45

LIFETIME
only a moment, but his favor, a l. . . . Ps 30:5

LIFT
and the One who l-s up my head. . . . Ps 3:3
L up your heads, you gates! . . . Ps 24:7
You have l-**ed** me up and have . . . Ps 30:1
so the Son of Man must be l-**ed** up, . . . Jn 3:14
When you l up the Son of Man, . . . Jn 8:28
if I am l-**ed** up from the earth I . . . Jn 12:32

LIGHT (N)
"Let there be l," and there was l. . . . Gn 1:3
The LORD is my l and my salvation . . . Ps 27:1
for my feet and a l on my path. . . . Ps 119:105
like the l of dawn, shining
brighter . . . Pr 4:18
let's walk in the LORD's l. . . . Is 2:5
in darkness have seen a great l; . . . Is 9:2
people and a l to the nations . . . Is 42:6
Arise, shine, for your l has come, . . . Is 60:1
live in darkness have seen a
great l, . . . Mt 4:16
You are the l of the world. . . . Mt 5:14
a l for revelation to the Gentiles . . . Lk 2:32
I am the l of the world. . . . Jn 8:12
walk in the l as he . . . is in the l . . . 1Jn 1:7

LIGHT (V)
No one l-s a lamp and puts it . . . Mt 5:15
to horizon and l-s up the sky, . . . Lk 17:24

LIGHTNING
was thunder and l, a thick cloud . . . Ex 19:16
he hurled l bolts and routed them. . . . Ps 18:14
For as the l comes from the east . . . Mt 24:27
His appearance was like l, . . . Mt 28:3

LIKE
you will be l God, knowing good . . . Gn 3:5
I am God, and no one is l me. . . . Is 46:9
LORD, there is no one l you. . . . Jr 10:6
What is the kingdom of God l, . . . Lk 13:18
spoke l a child, I thought l a child, . . . 1Co 13:11
He had to be l his brothers . . . Heb 2:17

LIKE-MINDED
have no one else l who will. . . . Php 2:20

LIKENESS
our image, according to our l. . . . Gn 1:26
united with him in the l of his death . . . Rm 6:5
servant, taking on the l of humanity. . . . Php 2:7
curse people who are made in God's l. . . Jms 3:9

LIMIT
when he set a l for the sea so . . . Pr 8:29

LINE
l after l, l after l, a little here . . . Is 28:10

LINEN
on his l robe and l undergarments. . . . Lv 6:10
body, wrapped it in clean, fine l, . . . Mt 27:59
tomb and saw the l cloths lying . . . Jn 20:6

LINTEL
and brush the l and the two . . . Ex 12:22

LION
Judah is a young l. . . . Gn 49:9
and the l will eat straw like cattle. . . . Is 11:7
will be thrown into the l-s' den. . . . Dn 6:7
prowling around like a roaring l, . . . 1Pt 5:8
The l from the tribe of Judah, . . . Rv 5:5

LIPS
His praise will always be on my l. . . . Ps 34:1
a stranger, and not your own l. . . . Pr 27:2
I am a man of unclean l. . . . Is 6:5
people honors me with their l, . . . Mt 15:8
and by the l of foreigners, . . . 1Co 14:21

LIP-SERVICE
honor me with l, yet their hearts . . . Is 29:13

LISTEN
L, Israel: The LORD our God; . . . Dt 6:4
Speak, for your servant is l-**ing**. . . . 1Sm 3:10
LORD, l and be gracious to me; . . . Ps 30:10
For the LORD l-s to the needy and. . . . Ps 69:33
L, sons, to a father's discipline, . . . Pr 4:1
who gives an answer before he l-s . . . Pr 18:13
Keep l-**ing**, but do not understand; . . . Is 6:9
You will l and l, but never. . . . Mt 13:14
whom I am well-pleased. L to him! . . . Mt 17:5
But if he won't l, take one or . . . Mt 18:16
you cannot l to my word. . . . Jn 8:43
and they will l to my voice. . . . Jn 10:16
Everyone should be quick to l, . . . Jms 1:19
not from God does not l to us. . . . 1Jn 4:6

LITTLE
You made him l less than God and . . . Ps 8:5
Better a l with the fear of the . . . Pr 15:16
are you afraid, you of l faith? . . . Mt 8:26
the one who is forgiven l, loves l. . . . Lk 7:47
know how to make do with l, . . . Php 4:12
and he held a l scroll opened in . . . Rv 10:2

LIVE
for humans cannot see me and l. . . . Ex 33:20
man does not l on bread alone . . . Dt 8:3
But I know that my Redeemer l-s, . . . Jb 19:25
The LORD l-s—blessed be my. . . . Ps 18:46
to my God as long as I l. . . . Ps 146:2
Keep my commands and l . . . Pr 4:4; 7:2
on those l-**ing** in the land of
darkness. . . . Is 9:2
listen, so that you will l. . . . Is 55:3
the righteous one will l by
his faith. . . . Hab 2:4
Man must not l on bread alone. . . . Mt 4:4
in me, even if he dies, will l. . . . Jn 11:25
Because I l, you will l too. . . . Jn 14:19
in him we l and move and . . . Ac 17:28
The righteous will l by faith. . . . Rm 1:17
the life he l-s, he l-s to God. . . . Rm 6:10
If we l, we l for the Lord; . . . Rm 14:8
I no longer l, but Christ l-s in me. The
life I now l in the body, I l by faith . . . Gl 2:20
to l is Christ and to
die is gain. . . . Php 1:21

LIVING (ADJ)
and the man became a l being. . . . Gn 2:7
the voice of the l God speaking. . . . Dt 5:26
flesh cry out for the l God. . . . Ps 84:2
let every l thing bless his . . . Ps 145:21
me, the fountain of l water, and dug. . . . Jr 2:13
On that day l water will flow . . . Zch 14:8
Messiah, the Son of the l God! . . . Mt 16:16
and he would give you l water. . . . Jn 4:10
I am the l bread that came down . . . Jn 6:51
your bodies as a l sacrifice, . . . Rm 12:1
word of God is l and effective . . . Heb 4:12
into the hands of the l God. . . . Heb 10:31

LIVING (N)
God of the dead, but of the l. . . . Mt 22:32
to judge the l and the dead. . . . 1Pt 4:5

LOAD (N)
tie up heavy l-s that are hard to . . . Mt 23:4

LOAD (V)
You l people with burdens that. . . . Lk 11:46

LOAF
only have five l-**ves** and two fish . . . Mt 14:17
took the seven l-**ves** and the fish, . . . Mt 15:36

LOAN
to the poor is a l to the LORD, . . . Pr 19:17
Don't . . . put up security for l-s. . . . Pr 22:26

LOCUST
I will bring l-s into your territory. . . . Ex 10:4
fruit of their labor to the l. . . . Ps 78:46
What the devouring l has left, the. . . . Jl 1:4
his food was l-s and wild honey. . . . Mt 3:4

LOFTY
It is l; I am unable to reach it. . . . Ps 139:6
against all that is proud and l, . . . Is 2:12
Lord seated on a high and l throne, . . . Is 6:1

LONG (ADJ)
you may have a l life in the land. . . . Ex 20:12
How l will you waver between . . . 1Kg 18:21
How l will you hide your face . . . Ps 13:1
How l, LORD? Will you hide . . . Ps 89:46
if a man has l hair it is a disgrace. . . . 1Co 11:14

LONG (V)
As a deer l-s for flowing streams, so . . . Ps 42:1
I l for you in the night; . . . Is 26:9
He l-**ed** to eat his fill from the . . . Lk 15:16

LOOK
But Lot's wife l-**ed** back and became . . . Gn 19:26
he was afraid to l at God. . . . Ex 3:6
Do not l at his appearance or. . . . 1Sm 16:7
The LORD l-s down from heaven on . . . Ps 14:2
L down from heaven and see; . . . Ps 80:14
Let your eyes l forward; . . . Pr 4:25
keep l-**ing**, but do not perceive. . . . Is 6:9

that day people will l to their Maker ... Is 17:7
that we should l at him, ... Is 53:2
eyes are too pure to l on evil, ... Hab 1:13
will l at me whom they pierced ... Zch 12:10
everyone who l-s at a woman ... Mt 5:28
because l-ing they do not see, ... Mt 13:13
the plow and l-s back is fit for ... Lk 9:62
L at my hands and my feet, ... Lk 24:39
your eyes and l at the fields, ... Jn 4:35
They will l at the one they ... Jn 19:37
l-ing as in a mirror at the glory ... 2Co 3:18

LOOSE

whatever you l on earth will have ... Mt 16:19

LORD LD = LORD

Ld our God, the **Ld** is one ... Dt 6:4
For the **Ld** your God is the God
of gods and L of l-s, ... Dt 10:17
Ld gives, and the **Ld** takes away ... Jb 1:21
The **Ld** is my shepherd; ... Ps 23:1
declaration of the **Ld** to my L: ... Ps 110:1
Give thanks to the L of l-s ... Ps 136:3
l-s other than you have owned us, ... Is 26:13
who says to me, 'L, L,' will enter ... Mt 7:21
Son of Man is L of the Sabbath ... Mt 12:8
The L declared to my L, ... Mt 22:44
If David calls him 'L,' how, then, ... Mt 22:45
The L our God, the L is one ... Mk 12:29
you call me 'L, L,' and don't do ... Lk 6:46
You call me Teacher and L ... Jn 13:13
Thomas ... "My L and my God!" ... Jn 20:28
crucified, both L and Messiah." ... Ac 2:36
with your mouth, "Jesus is L," ... Rm 10:9
are many "gods" and many "l-s" ... 1Co 8:5
one L, Jesus Christ ... 1Co 8:6
can say, "Jesus is L," except by ... 1Co 12:3
Now the L is the Spirit; ... 2Co 3:17
one L, one faith, one baptism, ... Eph 4:5
confess that Jesus Christ is L, ... Php 2:11
King of kings, and the L of l-s, ... 1Tm 6:15
obeyed Abraham, calling him l ... 1Pt 3:6
but regard Christ the L as holy, ... 1Pt 3:15
was in the Spirit on the L-'s day, ... Rv 1:10
King of Kings and L of L-s ... Rv 19:16

LORDING

not l it over those entrusted to ... 1Pt 5:3

LOSE

who finds his life will l it, ... Mt 10:39
but whoever l-s his life because ... Mt 16:25
a hundred sheep and l-s one ... Lk 15:4
that I should l none of those he ... Jn 6:39

LOSS

everything to be a l in view of ... Php 3:8

LOST (ADJ)

I wander like a l sheep; ... Ps 119:176
and a time to count as l; ... Ec 3:6
My people were l sheep; ... Jr 50:6
go to the l sheep of the house ... Mt 10:6
sent only to the l sheep of the ... Mt 15:24
he was l and is found! ... Lk 15:24
them and not one of them is l, ... Jn 17:12

LOST (N)

I will seek the l, bring back ... Ezk 34:16
will not seek the l or heal the ... Zch 11:16
come to seek and to save
the l ... Lk 19:10

LOT

Abraham's nephew (Gn 11:27). Separated from Abraham; settled in Sodom (13:1-13). Rescued from kings (14:1-16); from Sodom (18:16–19:29; Lk 17:28-29; 2Pt 2:7-9). Fathered Moabites and Ammonites by his daughters (Gn 19:30-38).

LOT

The land is to be divided by l; ... Nm 26:55
Cast the l between me and my ... 1Sm 14:42
pur—that is, the l—was cast ... Est 3:7
and they cast l-s for my clothing ... Ps 22:18
The l is cast into the lap, ... Pr 16:33
cast l-s, and the l singled out Jonah ... Jnh 1:7
His clothes by casting l-s ... Mt 27:35
Let's not tear it, but cast l-s for it, ... Jn 19:24
and the l fell to Matthias ... Ac 1:26

LOUD

neighbor with a l voice early ... Pr 27:14
Jesus cried out with a l voice, ... Mt 27:46
I heard a l voice behind me like ... Rv 1:10

LOVE (N)

showing faithful l to a thousand ... Ex 20:6
abounding in faithful l and truth, ... Ex 34:6
not withdraw my faithful l from ... Ps 89:33
His faithful l endures forever ... Ps 136:1-26
but l covers all offenses ... Pr 10:12
have loved you with an
everlasting l; ... Jr 31:3
with human cords, with ropes of l ... Hs 11:4
No one has greater l than this: ... Jn 15:13
God proves his own l for us in that ... Rm 5:8
Let l must be without hypocrisy ... Rm 12:9
puffs up, but l builds up ... 1Co 8:1
L is patient, l is kind. l does not ... 1Co 13:4
For the l of money is a root of ... 1Tm 6:10
God is l, ... 1Jn 4:16
abandoned the l you had at first ... Rv 2:4

LOVE (V)

but l your neighbor as yourself; ... Lv 19:18
L the LORD your God with all ... Dt 6:5
Your God l-d Israel enough to ... 2Ch 9:8
I l you, LORD, my strength ... Ps 18:1
He l-s righteousness and justice; ... Ps 33:5
I l the LORD because he has ... Ps 116:1
How I l your instruction! ... Ps 119:97
LORD disciplines the one he l-s, ... Pr 3:12
I l those who l me, and those ... Pr 8:17
A friend l-s at all times, ... Pr 17:17
a time to l and a time to hate; ... Ec 3:8
I have l-d you with an everlasting ... Jr 31:3
When Israel was a child, I l-d him, ... Hs 11:1
Hate evil and l good; ... Am 5:15
Even so, I l-d Jacob, ... Mal 1:2
l your enemies and pray for ... Mt 5:44
will hate one and l the other, ... Mt 6:24
L the Lord your God with all ... Mt 22:37
L your neighbor as yourself ... Mt 22:39
is forgiven little, l-s little ... Lk 7:47
For God l-d the world in this way: ... Jn 3:16
a new command: l one another ... Jn 13:34
since God l-s a cheerful giver ... 2Co 9:7
Husbands, l your wives, just as ... Eph 5:25
He who l-s his wife l-s himself ... Eph 5:28
Do not l the world or the things ... 1Jn 2:15
l one another, because l is from God ... 1Jn 4:7
We l because he first l-d us ... 1Jn 4:19
As many as I l, I rebuke and ... Rv 3:19

LOVELY

How l is your dwelling place, ... Ps 84:1
I am dark ... yet l like the
curtains of ... Sg 1:5
whatever is pure, whatever is l, ... Php 4:8

LOVER

will be l-s of self, l-s of money ... 2Tm 3:2

LOW

and hill will be made l; ... Lk 3:5

LOWER

You made him l than the angels ... Heb 2:7

LOWLY

He sets the l on high, ... Jb 5:11
thrones and exalted the l ... Lk 1:52

LOYALTY

keeps his gracious covenant l ... Dt 7:9
He shows l to his anointed, ... 2Sm 22:51
Never let l and faithfulness ... Pr 3:3

LUKE

Companion of Paul (2Tm 4:11; Phm 24); physician (Col 4:14); author of Luke and Acts (note "we" in Ac 16:10; 28:16).

LUKEWARM

because you are l, and neither ... Rv 3:16

LUST (N)

the l of the flesh, the l of the eyes ... 1Jn 2:16

LUST (V)

looks at a woman l has already ... Mt 5:28

LUXURY

L is not appropriate for a fool— ... Pr 19:10

LYDIA

First Philippian convert; seller of purple (Ac 16:12-15,40).

LYING (ADJ)

go and become a l spirit ... 1Kg 22:22
arrogant eyes, a l tongue, hands ... Pr 6:17

LYING (N)

Cursing, l, murder, stealing, ... Hs 4:2
Therefore, putting away l, speak ... Eph 4:25

LYRE

who knows how to play the l ... 1Sm 16:16
Praise the LORD with the l; ... Ps 33:2
we hung up our l-s on the
poplar ... Ps 137:2
flute, zither, l, harp, drum ... Dn 3:5

M

MAACAH
1. David's wife; mother of Absalom (2Sm 3:3; 1Ch 3:2).
2. Mother of Judah's King Abijam (1Kg 15:2); promoted Asherah worship (15:13).

MAD
Too much study is driving you **m**! ...... Ac 26:24

MADMAN
He acted like a **m** around them, ... 1Sm 21:13
I'm talking like a **m**— 2Co 11:23

MADNESS
and knowledge, **m** and folly; .... Ec 1:17

MAGDALENE *SEE* MARY 2.

MAGIC
seems like a **m** stone to its .... Pr 17:8
practiced **m** collected their books ...... Ac 19:19

MAGICIAN
summoned all the **m-s** of Egypt .... Gn 41:8
the **m-s** of Egypt, and they
also did .... Ex 7:11

MAGNIFICENT
our Lord, how **m** is your name .... Ps 8:1
m acts of God in our own tongues .... Ac 2:11

MAGOG
Land ruled by Gog, an apocalyptic foe from the north (Ezk 38:2; 39:6; Rv 20:8).

MAIMED
It is better for you to enter life **m** .... Mt 18:8
invite those who are poor, **m**, lame, ... Lk 14:13

MAJESTIC
All that he does is splendid and **m**; ...... Ps 111:3
came to him from the **M** Glory: 2Pt 1:17

MAJESTY
Splendor and **m** are before him; 1Ch 16:27
and the splendor and the **m** 1Ch 29:11
awesome **m** surrounds him .... Jb 37:22
He is robed in **m**; .... Ps 93:1
right hand of the **M** on high .... Heb 1:3
we were eyewitnesses of his **m** 2Pt 1:16

MAKE
Let us **m** man in our image, ... Gn 1:26
The sea is his; he **made** it .... Ps 95:5
He **made** us, and we are his .... Ps 100:3
is the day the LORD has **made**; .... Ps 118:24
I have been . . . wondrously **made** ...... Ps 139:14
forming it, 'What are you **m-ing**?' .... Is 45:9
when I will **m** a new covenant .... Jr 31:31
and I will **m** you fish for people! .... Mt 4:19
and **m** disciples of all nations, ... Mt 28:19
Sabbath was **made** for man and not ... Mk 2:27
Why did you **m** me like this? .... Rm 9:20
made him lower than the angels .... Heb 2:7

MAKER
a man be more pure than his **M**? .... Jb 4:17
kneel before the LORD our **M** .... Ps 95:6
Indeed, your husband is your **M** .... Is 54:5

MALACHI
Postexilic prophet (Mal 1:1).

MALE
he created them **m** and female .... Gn 1:27
made them **m** and female, ... Mt 19:4
m-s who have sex with **m-s**, ... 1Co 6:9
slave or free, **m** or female; .... Gl 3:28

MALICE
quarrels, deceit, and **m** .... Rm 1:29
anger, wrath, **m**, slander, ... Col 3:8

MAN *SEE ALSO* MAN OF GOD
Let us make **m** in our image, ... Gn 1:26
God formed the **m** out of the dust .... Gn 2:7
Egyptians are **men**, not God; .... Is 31:3
that he did not look like a **m**, ... Is 52:14
One like a son of **m** was coming with ... Dn 7:13
I am God and not **m**, the Holy One .... Hs 11:9
M must not live on bread alone .... Mt 4:4
this reason a **m** will leave his .... Mt 19:5
will see the Son of **M** coming on .... Mt 24:30
for **m** and not **m** for the Sabbath .... Mk 2:27
You—being a **m**—make yourself ...... Jn 10:33
your young **men** will see visions, ... Ac 2:17
Men committed shameless acts .... Rm 1:27
entered the world through one **m**, ... Rm 5:12
Christ is the head of every **m**, and
the **m** is the head of the woman, ... 1Co 11:3
What is **m**, that you remember him ..... Heb 2:6
was one like the Son of **M**, ... Rv 1:13

MAN OF GOD
blessing that Moses, the **m**, gave .... Dt 33:1
She said to Elijah, "**M**, why are 1Kg 17:18
When Elisha the **m** heard 2Kg 5:8
word . . . came to Shemaiah, the **m**: 2Ch 11:2
as David the **m** had prescribed .... Neh 12:24
you, **m**, flee from these things, ... 1Tm 6:11
so that the **m** may be complete, ... 2Tm 3:17

MANAGE
m his own household competently 1Tm 3:4

MANASSEH
1. Son of Joseph and Asenath (Gn 41:50-51). Adopted by Jacob as a tribe (Gn 48); allotted half of its territory east of the Jordan from Gerasa to Mt. Hermon in the far north and half west of the Jordan to the Mediterranean from the Yarkon River to Mt. Carmel (Nm 32:33-42; Jos 13:29-31; 17).
2. Son of Hezekiah; king of Judah (2Kg 21:1-18). Wickedness brought on God's judgment (21:10-15; Jr 15:4).

MANGER
in cloth and lying in a **m**. .... Lk 2:12

MANIFESTATION
A **m** of the Spirit is given to each 1Co 12:7

MANIFESTED
He was **m** in the flesh, vindicated 1Tm 3:16

MANNA
Israel named the substance **m** .... Ex 16:31
The **m** resembled coriander seed, ... Nm 11:7
the land, the **m** ceased .... Jos 5:12
ancestors ate the **m** in the .... Jn 6:31,49

MANSLAUGHTER
could flee there who committed **m**, ... Dt 4:42
for the one who commits **m**, ... Jos 21:13-38

MANTLE
him and threw his **m** over him 1Kg 19:19
picked up the **m** that had
fallen 2Kg 2:13

MANY
give his life as a ransom for **m** .... Mt 20:28
For **m** are invited, but few are .... Mt 22:14
way we who are **m** are one body .... Rm 12:5

MARCH
m around the city seven times, ... Jos 6:4

MARITAL
his **m** duty to his wife, ... 1Co 7:3

MARK, JOHN
Missionary (Ac 12:12,25); Barnabas's cousin (Col 4:10); cause of split between Paul and Barnabas (Ac 15:36-40); later apparently reconciled to Paul (Col 4:10; 2Tm 4:11; Phm 24). Also close to Peter (1Pt 5:13). Wrote the Gospel of Mark.

MARK
he placed a **m** on Cain so that .... Gn 4:15
If I don't see the **m** of the nails .... Jn 20:25
and receives a **m** on his forehead .... Rv 14:9
who accepted the **m** of the beast .... Rv 19:20

MARKET
that is sold in the meat **m** 1Co 10:25

MARKETPLACE
My Father's house into a **m**! .... Jn 2:16

MARRIAGE
nor are given in **m** but are like .... Mt 22:30
and giving in **m**, until the day .... Mt 24:38
M is to be honored by all, ... Heb 13:4
the **m** of the Lamb has come, ... Rv 19:7

MARRIED (ADJ)
a **m** man is concerned about 1Co 7:33

MARROW
soul and spirit, joints and **m**. .... Heb 4:12

from above the **m** seat that was .... Nm 7:89
LORD is waiting to show you **m** .... Is 30:18
for his **m-ies** never end .... Lm 3:22
In your wrath remember **m**! .... Hab 3:2
merciful, for they will be shown **m** ...... Mt 5:7
I desire **m** and not sacrifice .... Mt 9:13
of the law—justice, **m**, and faith ...... Mt 23:23
him as the **m** seat by his blood, ... Rm 3:25
show **m** to whom I will show **m**, ... Rm 9:15
in view of the **m-ies** of God, ... Rm 12:1
the Father of **m-ies** and the
God of 2Co 1:3
But God, who is rich in **m**, ... Eph 2:4
ark overshadowing the **m** seat .... Heb 9:5
M triumphs over judgment .... Jms 2:13

MESSAGE

Their **m** has gone out to all the .... Ps 19:4
because his **m** had authority .... Lk 4:32
Lord, who has believed our **m**? .... Jn 12:38
committed the **m** of reconciliation 2Co 5:19

MESSENGER

or deaf like my **m** I am sending? .... Is 42:19
See, I am going to send my **m**, ... Mal 3:1
am sending my **m** ahead of you; .... Mt 11:10
a **m** of Satan to torment me so 2Co 12:7

MESSIAH *SEE ALSO* CHRIST

false **m-s** and false prophets .... Mt 24:24
was born for you, who is the **M**, ... Lk 2:11
M is coming" (... called Christ) .... Jn 4:25
that you may believe Jesus is the **M** .... Jn 20:31
been appointed for you as the **M** .... Ac 3:20

MICAH

1. Ephraimite idolater (Jdg 17–18).
2. Prophet to Israel and Judah in the days of kings Jotham, Ahaz, and Hezekiah of Judah (Jr 26:18; Mc 1:1).

MICAIAH

Son of Imlah; prophet against Ahab (1Kg 22; 5–28; 2Ch 18:4-27).

MICHAEL

Archangel; guardian of Israel (Dn 10:13,21; 12:1). Disputed with the devil (Jd 9); will fight the dragon (Rv 12:7).

MICHAL

Daughter of Saul (1Sm 14:49); offered to David to endanger him (18:20-29); warned David of a plot (19:11-17). Given to Palti (25:44); taken back (2Sm 3:12-16). Despised David dancing before the Lord (6:14-23; 1Ch 15:29).

MIDDLE

tree in the **m** of the garden, ... Gn 3:3

MIDWIFE

of Egypt said to the Hebrew **m-ves** .... Ex 1:15

MIGHT

and will declare your **m** .... Ps 145:11
Not by strength or by **m**, but by my ..... Zch 4:6
who are greater in **m** and power, ... 2Pt 2:11

MIGHTY

How the **m** have fallen! 2Sm 1:19
strong and **m**, the LORD,
m in battle .... Ps 24:8
and will proclaim your **m** acts .... Ps 145:4
Counselor, **M** God, Eternal Father .... Is 9:6
because the **M** One has done great ...... Lk 1:49
Lord God who judges her is **m** .... Rv 18:8

MILE

if anyone forces you to go one **m**, ... Mt 5:41

MILK

a land flowing with **m** and honey .... Ex 3:8
churning of **m** produces butter .... Pr 30:33
gave you **m** to drink, not
solid food, ... 1Co 3:2
You need **m**, not solid food .... Heb 5:12
desire the pure **m** of the word, ... 1Pt 2:2

MILL

while the sound of the **m** fades; .... Ec 12:4
will be grinding ... with a hand **m**; ..... Mt 24:41

MILLSTONE

the upper **m** as security for a .... Dt 24:6
better for him if a heavy **m** were .... Mt 18:6

MINA

gave them ten **m-s**, and told them .... Lk 19:13

MIND

that he might change his **m** .... Nm 23:19
is not man who changes his **m** 1Sm 15:29
wholeheartedly and a willing **m**, ... 1Ch 28:9
or gave the **m** understanding? .... Jb 38:36
examine my heart and **m** .... Ps 26:2
I applied my **m** to examine .... Ec 1:13
Make the **m-s** of these people
dull; .... Is 6:10
will keep the **m** ... in perfect peace, ... Is 26:3
all your soul, and with all
your **m** .... Mt 22:37
them over to a corrupt **m** .... Rm 1:28
by the renewing of your **m**, ... Rm 12:2
But we have the **m** of Christ 1Co 2:16
has blinded the **m-s** of the 2Co 4:4
renewed in the spirit of your **m-s** ...... Eph 4:23
Set your **m-s** on things above, ... Col 3:2
will put my laws into their **m-s** .... Heb 8:10
One who examines **m-s** and hearts, ... Rv 2:23

MINDSET

Now the **m** of the flesh is death, ... Rm 8:6

MINISTER (N)

Levites to be **m-s** before the ark 1Ch 16:4
speak of you as **m-s** of our God .... Is 61:6
be a **m** of Christ Jesus to the .... Rm 15:16
as God's **m-s**, we commend 2Co 6:4
a **m** of the sanctuary and the .... Heb 8:2

MINISTER (V)

worn by Aaron whenever he **m-s** ...... Ex 28:35

MINISTERING (N)

Are they not all **m** spirits sent .... Heb 1:14

MINISTRY

prayer and to the **m** of the word .... Ac 6:4
given us the **m** of reconciliation: 2Co 5:18
the saints for the work of **m** .... Eph 4:12
an evangelist, fulfill your **m** 2Tm 4:5
has now obtained a superior **m** .... Heb 8:6

MINT

pay a tenth of **m**, dill, and cumin, ... Mt 23:23

MIRACLE

Pharaoh tells you, 'Perform a **m**,' .... Ex 7:9
and do many **m-s** in your name? .... Mt 7:22
For if the **m-s** that were done in .... Mt 11:21
was not able to do a **m** there, ... Mk 6:5
extraordinary **m-s** by Paul's hands ...... Ac 19:11
testified by signs ... various **m-s**, ... Heb 2:4

MIRIAM

Sister of Moses and Aaron; daughter of Jochebed and Amram (Nm 26:59; 1Ch 6:3). Watched over baby Moses (Ex 2:4-8). Prophetess; led dancing at Red Sea (15:20-21). Struck with skin disease for criticizing Moses (Nm 12; Dt 24:9); died in Kadesh (Nm 20:1).

MIRROR

as in a **m**, but then face to face 1Co 13:12
looking at his own face in a **m** .... Jms 1:23

MISERABLE

You are all **m** comforters .... Jb 16:2
Be **m** and mourn and weep .... Jms 4:9

MISERY

I have observed the **m** of my people ...... Ex 3:7

MIST

Your love is like the morning **m** .... Hs 6:4

MISTAKE

do not say ... that it was a **m** .... Ec 5:6

MISTREAT

pray for those who **m** you .... Lk 6:28

MISTRESS

her **m** became contemptible to her ..... Gn 16:4

MISUSE

Do not **m** the name of the LORD .... Ex 20:7

MOABITE

No Ammonite or **M** may enter the ...... Dt 23:3

MOABITESS

her daughter-in-law Ruth the **M** .... Ru 1:22

MOCK

At noon Elijah **m-ed** them 1Kg 18:27
Everyone who sees me **m-s** me; .... Ps 22:7
He **m-s** those who **m** but
gives grace .... Pr 3:34

She has done a **n** thing for me..........Mt 26:10
powerful, not many of **n** birth..........1Co 1:26

NOBLE (N)

Do not trust in **n-s**, in man, who..........Ps 146:3
when your king is a son of **n-s**..........Ec 10:17
slaughtered all Judah's **n-s**..........Jr 39:6

NOISE

Pharaoh king of Egypt was all **n**;..........Jr 46:17
an end to the **n** of your songs,..........Ezk 26:13
from me the **n** of your songs!..........Am 5:23
will pass away with a loud **n**..........2Pt 3:10

NORTH

the king of the **N** will come,..........Dn 11:15

NOSE

and twisting a **n** draws blood,..........Pr 30:33

NOSTRILS

the breath of life into his **n**..........Gn 2:7
from God remains in my **n**..........Jb 27:3
blast of the breath of your **n**..........Ps 18:15

NOTHING

N is too difficult for you!..........Jr 32:17
N will be impossible for you..........Mt 17:20
you can do **n** without me..........Jn 15:5
but do not have love, I am **n**..........1Co 13:2
I didn't run or labor for **n**..........Php 2:16
For we brought **n** into the world,..........1Tm 6:7

NULLIFY

You **n** the word of God by your tradition..Mk 7:13

NUMBER (N)

and grew daily in **n**..........Ac 16:5
it is the **n** of a person. Its **n** is 666..........Rv 13:18

NUMBER (V)

Teach us to **n** our days carefully..........Ps 90:12
God has **n-ed** the days of your..........Dn 5:26
who was **n-ed** among the Twelve..........Lk 22:3

NURSE

that Sarah would **n** children?..........Gn 21:7
woman took the boy and **n-d** him..........Ex 2:9

NURSING (ADJ)

mouths of infants and **n** babies,..........Ps 8:2
a woman forget her **n** child,..........Is 49:15
mouths of infants and **n** babies?..........Mt 21:16

O

OAK

live near the **o-s** of Mamre..........Gn 13:18
and he was as sturdy as the **o-s**;..........Am 2:9

OATH

The LORD swore an **o** to David,..........Ps 132:11
I tell you, don't take an **o** at all:..........Mt 5:34
by earth or with any other **o**..........Jms 5:12

OBADIAH

Prophet against Edom (Ob 1).

OBEDIENCE

through the one man's **o** the many..........Rm 5:19
or of **o** leading to righteousness?..........Rm 6:16
He learned **o** through what he..........Heb 5:8

OBEDIENT

to Nazareth and was **o** to them..........Lk 2:51
becoming **o** to the point of death—..........Php 2:8

OBEY

to **o** is better than sacrifice,..........1Sm 15:22
the winds and the sea **o** him!..........Mt 8:27
unclean spirits, and they **o** him..........Mk 1:27
We must **o** God rather than..........Ac 5:29
Children, **o** your parents as..........Eph 6:1

OBLIGATED

are not **o** to the flesh to..........Rm 8:12

OBSCENE

O and foolish talking..........Eph 5:4

OBSERVE

You must **o** my Sabbaths,..........Ex 31:13
When I **o** your heavens, the work..........Ps 8:3
teaching them to **o** everything I..........Mt 28:20
o-ing special days, months,..........Gl 4:10
they will **o** your good works..........1Pt 2:12

OBTAIN

have **o-ed** righteousness..........Rm 9:30

OBVIOUS

each one's work will become **o**..........1Co 3:13
the works of the flesh are **o**:..........Gl 5:19
good works are **o**, and those that..........1Tm 5:25

OFFEND

one who isn't **o-ed** by me..........Mt 11:6

OFFENSE

but love covers all **o-s**..........Pr 10:12
o-s will inevitably come, but woe to..........Mt 18:7
that case the **o** of the cross has..........Gl 5:11

OFFENSIVE

if there is any **o** way in me;..........Ps 139:24

OFFER

o him there as a burnt offering..........Gn 22:2
if you are **o-ing** your gift on..........Mt 5:23
once for all time when he **o-ed** himself..Heb 7:27
not do this to **o** himself many..........Heb 9:25

OFFERING (N)

take pleasure in burnt **o-s** ... as much as in obeying the LORD?..........1Sm 15:22
You do not delight in sacrifice and **o**..........Ps 40:6
You make him a guilt **o**,..........Is 53:10
of God rather than burnt **o-s**..........Hs 6:6
and fragrant **o** to God..........Eph 5:2
You did not desire sacrifice and **o**,..........Heb 10:5

OFFSPRING

and between your **o** and her **o**..........Gn 3:15
I will give this land to your **o**..........Gn 12:7
said, 'For we are also his **o**.'..........Ac 17:28

OIL

and the **o** jug did not run dry,..........1Kg 17:16
You anoint my head with **o**;..........Ps 23:5
wise ones took **o** in their flasks..........Mt 25:4

OLD

I have been young and now I am **o**,..........Ps 37:25
even when he is **o** he will not..........Pr 22:6
your **o** men will have dreams,..........Jl 2:28
puts new wine into **o** wineskins..........Mt 9:17
and your **o** men will dream dreams..........Ac 2:17
the **o** has passed away,..........2Co 5:17
have put off the **o** self with its..........Col 3:9

OLDER

The **o** will serve the younger..........Rm 9:12

OLIVE *SEE ALSO* MOUNT OF OLIVES

was a plucked **o** leaf in its beak..........Gn 8:11

OMEGA

the Alpha and the **O**..........Rv 1:8; 21:6; 22:13

OMRI

Army commander; king of Israel; founded the city of Samaria (1Kg 16:15-28).

ONCE

He died to sin **o** for all;..........Rm 6:10
appointed for people to die **o**..........Heb 9:27

ONE *SEE ALSO* ONE AND ONLY SON

and then morning: **o** day..........Gn 1:5
the LORD our God, the LORD is **o**..........Dt 6:4
Are you the **o** who is to come,..........Mt 11:3
the two will become **o** flesh?..........Mt 19:5
I and the Father are **o**..........Jn 10:30
they may be **o** as we are **o**..........Jn 17:11
baptized by **o** Spirit into **o** body..........1Co 12:13
you are all **o** in Christ Jesus..........Gl 3:28
o Lord, **o** faith, **o** baptism,..........Eph 4:5
For there is **o** God and **o** mediator..........1Tm 2:5
You believe that God is **o**..........Jms 2:19

ONE AND ONLY SON

glory as the **o** from the Father,..........Jn 1:14
No one has ever seen God. The **o**..........Jn 1:18
He gave his **o**, so that everyone..........Jn 3:16
not believed in the name of the **o**..........Jn 3:18
God sent his **o** into the world..........1Jn 4:9

OPEN

eyes will be **o-ed** and you will be..........Gn 3:5
O my eyes so that I may..........Ps 119:18
what he **o-s**, no one can close;..........Is 22:22

PARTNERSHIP
For what **p** is there between. 2Co 6:14
because of your **p** in the gospel Php 1:5

PASS
see the blood, I will **p** over you. Ex 12:13
When you **p** through the waters, Is 43:2
Heaven and earth will **p** away, but my words will never **p** away. Mt 24:35
let this cup **p** from me. Mt 26:39
he **p-ed** by on the other side. Lk 10:31
but has **p-ed** from death to life. Jn 5:24
God **p-ed** over the sins previously. Rm 3:25
For I **p-ed** on to you as most 1Co 15:3
the old has **p-ed** away, 2Co 5:17
we have **p-ed** from death to life 1Jn 3:14

PASSIONS
them over to disgraceful **p**. Rm 1:26
Flee from youthful **p**, and pursue 2Tm 2:22

PASSOVER
it is the LORD's **P**. Ex 12:11
the **P** lamb had to be sacrificed. Lk 22:7
eat this **P** with you before I suffer. Lk 22:15
For Christ our **P** lamb has been sacrificed. 1Co 5:7

PAST
Do not hold **p** iniquities against us; Ps 79:8
the cleansing from his **p** sins. 2Pt 1:9

PASTORS
some **p** and teachers, Eph 4:11

PASTURE
lets me lie down in green **p-s**; Ps 23:2
His people, the sheep of his **p**. Ps 100:3
come in and go out and find **p**. Jn 10:9

PATCH
No one sews a **p** of unshrunk. Mk 2:21

PATH
the right **p-s** for his name's. Ps 23:3
for my feet and a light on my **p**. Ps 119:105
make his **p-s** straight! Mt 3:3
some seeds fell along the **p**, Mt 13:4
make straight **p-s** for your feet, Heb 12:13

PATIENCE
endured with much **p** objects of Rm 9:22
love, joy, peace, **p**, kindness, Gl 5:22

PATIENT
Rejoice in hope; be **p** in affliction; Rm 12:12
Love is **p**, love is kind. 1Co 13:4
able to teach, and **p**, 2Tm 2:24
but is **p** with you, not wanting any 2Pt 3:9

PATIENTLY
I waited **p** for the LORD, Ps 40:1

PATTERN
according to the **p** you have been shown on the mountain. Ex 25:40
according to the **p** that was shown. Heb 8:5

PAUL
Early church missionary, theologian, and writer. Also called Saul (Ac 13:9). Citizen of Tarsus, a Benjaminite, raised in Jerusalem as a rabbinical student and Pharisee (Ac 21:39; 22:3,28; 26:5; Gl 1:14; Php 3:5). Persecuted Christians, including Stephen (Ac 8:1; 26:9-11); converted on the way to Damascus (9:1-19); began preaching Christ in Arabia and Damascus and was threatened (9:20-22; Gl 1:17; 2Co 11:32-33).

Introduced to the church at Jerusalem by Barnabas (Ac 9:26-30); carried money with Barnabas from Antioch to Judea (11:27-30). Set apart with Barnabas to go through Cyprus and Galatia as missionaries (Ac 13–14); stoned (Ac 14:19-20). Focused on Gentile evangelism (Ac 9:15; Gl 2:7; Eph 3:8). Attended Jerusalem council (Ac 15). Split with Barnabas over John Mark (15:36-39).

Traveled with Silas and Timothy through Asia Minor and Greece (15:39–16:3). Hindered by the Spirit from entering Bithynia; called to Macedonia in a vision (16:7-10). Beaten, imprisoned, and released in Philippi (16:16-40). Spoke at Areopagus in Athens (17:19-34). Preached at Corinth and Ephesus (Ac 18–19). Said farewell in Ephesus (20:17-38).

Arrested at riot in Jerusalem (21:26-36); testified before the Sanhedrin (23:1-10), Governors Felix and Festus (24:10-21; 25:1-12), and King Agrippa (Ac 26); appealed to Caesar (25:11). Shipwrecked on the way to Rome (Ac 27); ministered in Malta, then Rome (Ac 28).

PAY
until you have **paid** the last penny. Mt 5:26
Is it lawful to **p** taxes to Caesar Mt 22:17
P your obligations to everyone: Rm 13:7
not **p-ing** back evil for evil or 1Pt 3:9

PAYMENT
Spirit in our hearts as a down **p**. 2Co 1:22
gave us the Spirit as a down **p**. 2Co 5:5
Spirit is the down **p** of our Eph 1:14

PEACE
favor on you and give you **p**. Nm 6:26
seek **p** and pursue it. Ps 34:14
time for war and a time for **p**. Ec 3:8
Eternal Father, Prince of **P**. Is 9:6
You will keep . . . in perfect **p**. Is 26:3
who proclaims **p**, who brings news Is 52:7
P, **p**, when there is no **p**. Jr 6:14; 8:11
I did not come to bring **p**, Mt 10:34
and **p** on earth to people he favors! Lk 2:14
P I leave with you. My **p** I give Jn 14:27
we have **p** with God through our Rm 5:1
fruit of the Spirit is love, joy, **p**, Gl 5:22
For he is our **p**, who made both Eph 2:14
And the **p** of God, which surpasses Php 4:7
by making **p** through the blood Col 1:20
to take **p** from the earth, Rv 6:4

PEACEMAKERS
Blessed are the **p**, for they Mt 5:9

PEARL
or toss your **p-s** before pigs, Mt 7:6
When he found one priceless **p** Mt 13:46
gate was made of a single **p**. Rv 21:21

PEKAH
King of Israel; assassin (2Kg 15:25-31).

PEKAHIAH
Son of Menahem; king of Israel; assassinated by his captain, Pekah (2Kg 15:22-26).

PENTECOST
When the day of **P** had arrived, Ac 2:1

PEOPLE
your **p** will be my **p**, Ru 1:16
and my **p**, who bear my name 2Ch 7:14
his **p**, the sheep of his pasture. Ps 100:3
but sin is a disgrace to any **p**. Pr 14:34
They will be my **p**, and I will be Jr 24:7
will save his **p** from their sins. Mt 1:21
has God rejected his **p**? Rm 11:1
God, and they will be my **p**. 2Co 6:16
God, and they will be my **p**. Heb 8:10
a holy nation, a **p** for his possession, 1Pt 2:9
and language and **p** and nation. Rv 5:9
will be his **p**, and God himself Rv 21:3

PEOPLE-PLEASERS
Don't work . . . as **p**, Eph 6:6

PERCEIVE
keep looking, but do not **p**. Is 6:9
look and look, but never **p**. Mt 13:14

PERFECT (ADJ)
The instruction of the LORD is **p**, Ps 19:7
You will keep . . . in **p** peace Is 26:3
Be **p**, therefore, as your heavenly Mt 5:48
pleasing, and **p** will of God. Rm 12:2
But when the **p** comes, 1Co 13:10
good and **p** gift is from above, Jms 1:17
instead, **p** love drives out fear, 1Jn 4:18

PERFECT (V)
for my power is **p-ed** in weakness. 2Co 12:9

PERFECTER
the pioneer and **p** of our faith Heb 12:2

PERISH
If I **p**, I **p**. Est 4:16
one of these little ones **p**. Mt 18:14
in him will not **p** but have Jn 3:16
Don't work for the food that **p-es** Jn 6:27
and they will never **p**. Jn 10:28
foolishness to those who are **p-ing** 1Co 1:18
not wanting any to **p** but all to. 2Pt 3:9

PERISHABLE
not of **p** seed but of 1Pt 1:23

PERMISSIBLE
"Everything is **p** for me," 1Co 6:12
"Everything is **p**," but not 1Co 10:23

PERPLEXED
we are **p** but not in despair; 2Co 4:8

PERSECUTE
Princes have **p-d** me without . . . . . Ps 119:161
blessed when they insult you and
p you . . . . . Mt 5:11
and pray for those who **p** you, ... Mt 5:44
they **p-d** me, they will also **p** you . . . . . Jn 15:20
Saul, Saul, why are you **p-ing** me? . . . . . Ac 9:4
Bless those who **p** you; . . . . . Rm 12:14
we are **p-d** but not abandoned; 2Co 4:9
in Christ Jesus will be **p-d** 2Tm 3:12

PERSECUTION
When distress or **p** comes . . . . . Mt 13:21
a severe **p** broke out against . . . . . Ac 8:1
or distress or **p** or famine or . . . . . Rm 8:35

PERSEVERE
p in these things, for in doing 1Tm 4:16

PERSISTENT
be **p** in prayer . . . . . Rm 12:12

PERSUADE
Are you going to **p** me to become . . . . . Ac 26:28
For I am **p-d** that neither death . . . . . Rm 8:38
we seek to **p** people 2Co 5:11
and am **p-d** that he is able 2Tm 1:12

PERVERSION
to mate with it; it is a **p** . . . . . Lv 18:23

PERVERT
Does God **p** justice? . . . . . Jb 8:3

PERVERTED (ADJ)
in a crooked and **p** generation, ... Php 2:15

PESTERING
because this widow keeps **p** me, ... Lk 18:5

PESTILENCE
or the **p** that ravages at noon . . . . . Ps 91:6

PETER
Apostle; originally named Simon; also called Simeon (Ac 15:14) and Cephas. A fisherman in business with James and John (Lk 5:2-3,10); married, lived in Capernaum (Mk 1:21,29-30).

Walked on water (Mt 14:28-31). Confessed Jesus as Messiah (Mt 16:13-20; Mk 8:27-30; Lk 9:18-21). At transfiguration (Mt 17:1-9; Mk 9:2-8; Lk 9:28-36; 2Pt 1:16-18). Jesus predicted he would deny him (Mt 26:31-35; Mk 14:27-31; Lk 22:31-34; Jn 13:36-38); denial (Mt 26:69-75; Mk 14:66-72; Lk 22:54-62; Jn 18:15-18,25-27); restoration to "feed my sheep" (Jn 21:15-19).

Spoke at Pentecost (Ac 2:14-40). Healed people (3:1-10; 5:15; 9:34); raised Tabitha from the dead (9:36-43). Arrested and forbidden to preach (4:1-31; 5:17-41). Saw vision: sent to Cornelius (Ac 10); reported Gentile conversions (Ac 11; 15); confronted by Paul for inconsistency (Gl 2:11-14). Imprisoned by Herod; freed by angel (Ac 12:1-19).

Focused on Jewish evangelism (Gl 2:7). Wrote two letters (1Pt 1:1; 2Pt 1:1).

PETITION
prayer and **p** with thanksgiving, ... Php 4:6
I urge that **p-s**, prayers, ... 1Tm 2:1

PHARAOH
Then **P** sent for Joseph, ... Gn 41:14
when I receive glory through **P**, ... Ex 14:18
For the Scripture tells **P**, ... Rm 9:17

PHARISEE
surpasses that of the scribes and **P-s** . . . . . Mt 5:20
Then the **P-s** went and plotted . . . . . Mt 22:15
woe to you, scribes and **P-s**, ... Mt 23:13
a **P** asked him to dine with him . . . . . Lk 11:37
one a **P** and the other a tax . . . . . Lk 18:10
I am a **P**, a son of **P-s**! . . . . . Ac 23:6
regarding the law, a **P**; . . . . . Php 3:5

PHILIP
1. Apostle (Mt 10:3; Jn 12:21-22). Invited Nathanael to "come and see" (Jn 1:43-51); questioned how to feed the five thousand (6:5-7); asked Jesus to show them the Father (14:8-9).
2. One of the first seven deacons (Ac 6:1-6); evangelized Simon the sorcerer in Samaria (8:5-13) and an Ethiopian eunuch (8:26-39).

PHILIPPI
City in Macedonia where Paul preached (Ac 16:12; 20:6; 1Th 2:2) and to whom he wrote (Php 1:1; 4:15).

PHILISTINES
People of Philistia (Gn 10:14; 26:1). Originated in Caphtor (Jr 47:4; Am 9:7) as the Casluh (Gn 10:14).

Enemies of Israel: Moses and Joshua did not defeat them (Ex 13:17; Jos 13:2; Jdg 3:1-3). In conflict with Shamgar (3:31); with Samson (13–16); with Samuel (1Sm 4–7); with Saul (13–14; 17; 23:27-28; 28:5,15; 31:1-6); with David (17:20-57; 18:20-27; 19:8; 23:1-5; 30:16; 2Sm 5:17-25; 8:1; 21:15-22; 23:9-13); with Jehoram (2Ch 21:16); with Uzziah (26:6-7); with Ahaz (28:18); and with Hezekiah (2Kg 18:8). David hid among them (1Sm 27:1,7,11; 29:11) but did not fight for them (27:8-12; 29:9).

Prophesied against (Is 11:14; 14:29-32; Jr 47; Ezk 25:15-17; Am 1:6-8; Ob 19; Zph 2:4-7; Zch 9:5-7).

PHILOSOPHY
captive through **p** and empty . . . . . Col 2:8

PHYSICIAN
Luke, the dearly loved **p**, ... Col 4:14

PIECE
weighed out thirty **p-s** of silver . . . . . Mt 26:15

PIERCE
they **p-d** my hands and my feet . . . . . Ps 22:16
But he was **p-d** because of our . . . . . Is 53:5
will look at me whom they **p-d** . . . . . Zch 12:10
a sword will **p** your own soul . . . . . Lk 2:35
the soldiers **p-d** his side with . . . . . Jn 19:34
will look at the one they **p-d** . . . . . Jn 19:37

PIG
like a gold ring in a **p**-'s snout . . . . . Pr 11:22
or toss your pearls before **p-s**, ... Mt 7:6
a large herd of **p-s** was feeding . . . . . Mt 8:30
him into his fields to feed **p-s** . . . . . Lk 15:15

PILATE, PONTIUS
Governor of Judea; presided over Jesus's trial and sentencing (Mt 27:11-26; Mk 15:1-15; Lk 23:1-25; Jn 18:28–19:16); warned by his wife (Mt 27:19); gave Jesus's body to Joseph of Arimathea (Mt 27:58; Mk 15:45; Lk 23:52; Jn 19:38); assigned guards to the tomb (Mt 27:65).

PILLAR
back and became a **p** of salt . . . . . Gn 19:26
p of cloud by day and the **p**
of fire . . . . . Ex 13:22
the **p** and foundation of the truth 1Tm 3:15

PINNACLE
stand on the **p** of the temple, ... Mt 4:5; Lk 4:9

PIT
redeems your life from the **P**; . . . . . Ps 103:4
blind, both will fall into a **p** . . . . . Mt 15:14

PITIED (ADJ)
we should be **p** more than anyone 1Co 15:19

PLACE *SEE ALSO* **HIGH PLACE, HOLY**

PLACE
Surely the LORD is in this **p**, ... Gn 28:16
going to prepare a **p** for you? . . . . . Jn 14:2
they now desire a better **p** . . . . . Heb 11:16

PLAGUE
to send all my **p-s** against you, ... Ex 9:14
angels with the seven last **p-s**; . . . . . Rv 15:1
add to him the **p-s** that are . . . . . Rv 22:18

PLAIN
and the rough places, a **p** . . . . . Is 40:4

PLAN
P-s fail when there is no . . . . . Pr 15:22
A man's heart **p-s** his way, but . . . . . Pr 16:9
Many **p-s** are in a man's heart, ... Pr 19:21
I have **p-ned** it; I will also do it . . . . . Is 46:11

PLANT (N)
will eat the **p-s** of the field . . . . . Gn 3:18
grew up before him like a young **p** . . . . . Is 53:2

PLANT (V)

LORD God p-ed a garden in Eden,........Gn 2:8
like a tree p-ed beside flowing..........Ps 1:3
a time to p and a time to uproot;........Ec 3:2
I p-ed, Apollos watered, but God........1Co 3:6

PLATTER

the Baptist's head here on a p!...........Mt 14:8

PLAY

p skillfully on the strings,...............Ps 33:3
An infant will p beside the................Is 11:8
p-ed the flute for you, but you..........Mt 11:17
eat and drink, and got up to p...........1Co 10:7

PLEAD

We p on Christ's behalf,.................2Co 5:20

PLEASANT

have fallen for me in p places;............Ps 16:6

PLEASE

heaven and does whatever
he p-s.................................Ps 115:3
does whatever he p-s in heaven........Ps 135:6
the LORD was p-d to crush him..........Is 53:10
it will accomplish what I p...............Is 55:11
I give it to anyone I p.....................Jr 27:5
The wind blows where it p-s,..............Jn 3:8
in the flesh cannot p God.................Rm 8:8
even Christ did not p himself...........Rm 15:3
—how he may p his wife—.................1Co 7:33
as I also try to p everyone in.........1Co 10:33
am I striving to p people?...................Gl 1:10
God was p-d to have all his..............Col 1:19
obey . . . for this p-s the Lord.............Col 3:20
in order to p men, but......................Col 3:22
it is impossible to p God,..................Heb 11:6

PLEASING (ADJ)

The sacrifice p to God is a..............Ps 51:17
May my meditation be p to him;.......Ps 104:34
living sacrifice, holy and p
to God;.....................................Rm 12:1
acceptable sacrifice, p to God..........Php 4:18

PLEASURE

at your right hand are
eternal p-s...............................Ps 16:11
since he takes p in him.....................Ps 22:8
The one who loves p will become.......Pr 21:17
I take no p in the death of the..........Ezk 18:32
according to his good p.....................Eph 1:9
lovers of p rather than lovers............2Tm 3:4
enjoy the fleeting p of sin................Heb 11:25

PLOT

and the peoples p in vain?...................Ps 2:1

PLOW (N)

swords into p-s and their spears...........Is 2:4
Beat your p-s into swords and..............Jl 3:10
his hand to the p and looks back..........Lk 9:62

PLOW (V)

If you hadn't p-ed with my young.......Jdg 14:18
he who p-s ought to p in hope,...........1Co 9:10

PLUMB LINE

I am setting a p among my people.........Am 7:8

POINT

obedient to the p of death..................Php 2:8
yet stumbles in one p, is guilty..........Jms 2:10

POISON

evil, full of deadly p........................Jms 3:8

POISONOUS

the LORD sent p snakes among.........Nm 21:6

POLLUTED

abstain from things p by idols,.........Ac 15:20

POOL

your eyes like p-s in Heshbon.............Sg 7:4
there is a p, called Bethesda...............Jn 5:2

POOR

there will never cease to be p...........Dt 15:11
He raises the p from the dust............1Sm 2:8
He raises the p from the dust...........Ps 113:7
Idle hands make one p,.....................Pr 10:4
me to bring good news to the p............Is 61:1
Blessed are the p in spirit,..................Mt 5:3
and the p are told the good news........Mt 11:5
You always have the p with you,.......Mt 26:11
for your sake he became p,................2Co 8:9

PORE

You p over the Scriptures..................Jn 5:39

PORTION

But the LORD's p is his people,...........Dt 32:9
strength of my heart, my p
forever....................................Ps 73:26
Jacob's P is not like these.................Jr 10:16
The LORD is my p, therefore I.............Lm 3:24
and brought a p of it and laid...............Ac 5:2

POSSESS

to give you this land to p..................Gn 15:7
nothing yet p-ing everything............2Co 6:10

POSSESSION

Canaan—as a permanent p,...............Gn 17:8
chosen you to be his own p...........Dt 7:6; 14:2
the ends of the earth your p..................Ps 2:8
Honor the LORD with your p-s................Pr 3:9
in the abundance of his p-s................Lk 12:15
sold their p-s and property..................Ac 2:45
a people for his own p,.......................Ti 2:14
a holy nation, a people for his p,..........1Pt 2:9

POSSIBLE

but with God all things are p.............Mt 19:26
If it is p, let this cup pass...............Mt 26:39
Everything is p for the one who..........Mk 9:23
If p, as far as it depends on you,........Rm 12:18

POTTER

we are the clay, and you are our p;.......Is 64:8
Just like clay in the p-'s hand,.............Jr 18:6
and bought the p-'s field with it..........Mt 27:7
Or has the p no right over the clay,......Rm 9:21

POUR

after day they p out speech;...............Ps 19:2
p out your hearts before him...............Ps 62:8
I will p out my Spirit on your...............Is 44:3
I will p out my Spirit on all..................Jl 2:28
of heaven and p out a blessing...........Mal 3:10
that I will p out my Spirit on...............Ac 2:17
even if I am p-ed out as a drink..........Php 2:17

POVERTY

your p will come like a..............Pr 6:11; 24:34
Give me neither p nor wealth;...............Pr 30:8
but she out of her p has put in............Mk 12:44
so that by his p you might...................2Co 8:9

POWER

this purpose: to show you my p..............Ex 9:16
Ascribe p to God...........................Ps 68:34
life are in the p of the tongue,............Pr 18:21
the Scriptures or the p of God............Mt 22:29
right hand of P and coming.................Mt 26:64
the kingdom of God come in p................Mk 9:1
you will receive p when the Holy.............Ac 1:8
the Holy Spirit and with p,..................Ac 10:38
the p of God for salvation to................Rm 1:16
his eternal p and divine nature.............Rm 1:20
or things to come, nor p-s,..................Rm 8:38
for p is perfected in weakness............2Co 12:9
the cosmic p-s of this darkness...........Eph 6:12
know him and the p of his..................Php 3:10
fear, but one of p, love,.....................2Tm 1:7
form of godliness but denying its p.......2Tm 3:5
His divine p has given us.....................2Pt 1:3
glory, and p belong to our God,..............Rv 19:1

POWERFUL

many p, not many of noble..................1Co 1:26
are p through God for the..................2Co 10:4

PRACTICE

they don't p what they teach...............Mt 23:3
those who p such things.........Rm 1:32; Gl 5:21
and are not p-ing the truth....................1Jn 1:6

PRAISE (N)

enthroned on the p-s of Israel..............Ps 22:3
his p will always be on my lips..............Ps 34:1
Sing p to God, sing p;.........................Ps 47:6
and his courts with p........................Ps 100:4
have prepared p from the mouths.........Mt 21:16
For they loved human p more than........Jn 12:43
to the p of his glorious grace................Eph 1:6
up to God a sacrifice of p,..................Heb 13:15

PRAISE (V)

This is my God, and I will p him,...........Ex 15:2
LORD is great and highly p-d;.............1Ch 16:25
that breathes p the LORD....................Ps 150:6
Let another p you, and not your............Pr 27:2
host with the angel, p-ing God..............Lk 2:13

PRAY

against the LORD by ceasing to p.......1Sm 12:23
my name, humble themselves, p..........2Ch 7:14
we p-ed to our God and stationed.........Neh 4:9
P for the well-being of Jerusalem:.......Ps 122:6

and p for those who persecute you, ... Mt 5:44
you should p like this: .... Mt 6:9
the mountain by himself to p. .... Mt 14:23
teach us to p, just as John. .... Lk 11:1
I p for them. I am not p-ing for .... Jn 17:9
know what to p for as we should. .... Rm 8:26
Every man who p-s or prophesies 1Co 11:4
P at all times in the Spirit .... Eph 6:18
p constantly. 1Th 5:17
suffering? He should p. .... Jms 5:13

PRAYER

the LORD accepts my p. .... Ps 6:9
a house of p for all nations. .... Is 56:7
will be called a house of p. .... Mt 21:13
be persistent in p. .... Rm 12:12
everything, through p and petition ...... Php 4:6
which are the p-s of the saints. .... Rv 5:8

PREACH

the world and p the gospel to .... Mk 16:15
how can they p unless they are. .... Rm 10:15
but we p Christ crucified, ... 1Co 1:23
p Christ out of envy and strife .... Php 1:15
seen by angels, p-ed among the 1Tm 3:16

PREACHER

how can they hear without a p? .... Rm 10:14

PRECIOUS

their lives are p in his sight. .... Ps 72:14
She is more p than jewels; .... Pr 3:15
She is far more p than jewels. .... Pr 31:10
a tested stone, a p cornerstone .... Is 28:16
but with the p blood of Christ, ... 1Pt 1:19

PREDESTINED

your will had p to take place. .... Ac 4:28
He also p to be conformed. .... Rm 8:29
a wisdom God p before the ages 1Co 2:7
He p us to be adopted as sons .... Eph 1:5
p according to the plan of the one. ...... Eph 1:11

PREGNANT

and hit a p woman so that her. .... Ex 21:22
that she was p from the Holy .... Mt 1:18
will become p and give birth to. .... Mt 1:23
was engaged to him and was p. .... Lk 2:5

PREPARE

You p a table before me in the .... Ps 23:5
P the way of the LORD in the .... Is 40:3
Israel, p to meet your God! .... Am 4:12
P the way for the Lord; .... Mt 3:3
he will p your way before you. .... Mt 11:10
she has p-d me for burial. .... Mt 26:12
going to p a place for you? .... Jn 14:2
God p-d this for those
    who love 1Co 2:9
which God p-d ahead of time. .... Eph 2:10
but you p-d a body for me. .... Heb 10:5

PRESENCE

the Bread of the P on the table. .... Ex 25:30
in the p of my enemies; .... Ps 23:5
Do not banish me from your p or .... Ps 51:11
Where can I flee from your p? .... Ps 139:7
not only in my p, but now even .... Php 2:12
appear in the p of God for us. .... Heb 9:24

PRESENT (ADJ)

things p nor things to come, ... Rm 8:38
absent in body, I am p
    in spirit, ... 1Co 5:3

PRESENT (V)

I urge you to p your bodies as a .... Rm 12:1
He did this to p the church to. .... Eph 5:27
Be diligent to p yourself 2Tm 2:15

PRESERVE

loses his life will p it. .... Lk 17:33

PRESS

good measure—p-ed down, shaken .... Lk 6:38

PREVIOUSLY

over the sins p committed. .... Rm 3:25
in which you p walked according .... Eph 2:2

PRICE

I insist on paying the full p, ... 1Ch 21:24
the p of him whose p was
    set by. .... Mt 27:9
for you were bought at a p. 1Co 6:20
You were bought at a p; 1Co 7:23

PRICELESS

When he found one p pearl, ... Mt 13:46

PRIDE

P comes before destruction, ... Pr 16:18

PRIEST

he was a p to God Most High. .... Gn 14:18
be my kingdom of p-s and
    my holy .... Ex 19:6
serve me as p—Aaron, his sons. .... Ex 28:1
You are a p forever according to .... Ps 110:4
A p happened to be going .... Lk 10:31
a great high p who has passed .... Heb 4:14
You are a p forever according to .... Heb 5:6
but they will be p-s of
    God and .... Rv 20:6

PRIESTHOOD

a permanent p for them .... Ex 40:15
he holds his p permanently. .... Heb 7:24
race, a royal p, a holy nation. 1Pt 2:9

PRINCE

P-s have persecuted me without .... Ps 119:161
Eternal Father, P of Peace. .... Is 9:6

PRISON

I was in p and you visited me' .... Mt 25:36
Peter was kept in p, but
    the church .... Ac 12:5
saw the doors of the p standing .... Ac 16:27
to the spirits in p. 1Pt 3:19

PRISONER

The LORD frees p-s. .... Ps 146:7
and freedom to the p-s; .... Is 61:1
p of Christ Jesus on behalf .... Eph 3:1

PRIZE

but only one receives the p? 1Co 9:24
as my goal the p promised by .... Php 3:14

PROCLAIM

and I will p the name 'the Lord'. .... Ex 33:19
P his salvation from day to day. 1Ch 16:23
and the expanse p-s the work
    of his .... Ps 19:1
The heavens p his righteousness. .... Ps 50:6
to p liberty to the captives .... Is 61:1
He has sent me to p release. .... Lk 4:18
you p the Lord's death until he 1Co 11:26

PRODUCE

A good tree can't p bad fruit; .... Mt 7:18
of your faith p-s endurance. .... Jms 1:3

PROFANE

Do not p the name of your God; .... Lv 18:21

PROFIT

who hates dishonest p
    prolongs .... Pr 28:16
and do business and make a p. .... Jms 4:13

PROFITABLE

God and is p for teaching. 2Tm 3:16

PROGRESS

for your p and joy in the faith, ... Php 1:25
so that your p may be evident to 1Tm 4:15

PROMINENT

number of the p Greek women. .... Ac 17:12

PROMISCUITY

Go and marry a woman of p. .... Hs 1:2
moral impurity, p, ... Gl 5:19

PROMISE (N)

not one p has failed. .... Jos 23:14
For the p is for you and for .... Ac 2:39
of God's p-s is "Yes" in him. 2Co 1:20
first commandment with a p, ... Eph 6:2
since it holds p for the present 1Tm 4:8
The Lord does not delay his p. 2Pt 3:9

PROMISE (V)

This is the land I p-d Abraham, ... Dt 34:4
since he who p-d is faithful. .... Heb 10:23
did not receive what was p-d, ... Heb 11:39

PROMISED (ADJ)

from the Father the p
    Holy Spirit, ... Ac 2:33

PRONOUNCE

he could not p it correctly, ... Jdg 12:6

PROOF

to them by many
    convincing p-s .... Ac 1:3
the p of what is not seen. .... Heb 11:1

PROPER
Is it p for a woman to pray to ... 1Co 11:13
among you, as is p for saints ... Eph 5:3

PROPERTY
wife Sapphira, sold a piece of p ... Ac 5:1

PROPHECY
miracles, to another, p, ... 1Co 12:10
If I have the gift of p ... 1Co 13:2
But as for p-ies, they will
come to ... 1Co 13:8
it was given to you through p, ... 1Tm 4:14
No p of Scripture comes from ... 2Pt 1:20

PROPHESY
sons and your daughters will p, ... Jl 2:28
Lord, didn't we p in your name, ... Mt 7:22
P to us, Messiah! Who was it ... Mt 26:68
sons and your daughters will p ... Ac 2:17
and especially that you may p ... 1Co 14:1
to p for 1,260 days, dressed in ... Rv 11:3

PROPHET
God will raise up for you a p like ... Dt 18:15
A p is not without honor except ... Mt 13:57
be called a p of the Most High, ... Lk 1:76
No p is accepted in his hometown ... Lk 4:24
"Are you the P?" "No," ... Jn 1:21
first apostles, second p-s, ... 1Co 12:28
apostles, some p-s, some ... Eph 4:11
the beast and the false p are, ... Rv 20:10

PROPHETESS
There was also a p, Anna, ... Lk 2:36

PROPHETIC
known through the p Scriptures, ... Rm 16:26
also have the p word strongly ... 2Pt 1:19

PROSPER
Whatever he does p-s ... Ps 1:3
will p in what I send it to do ... Is 55:11

PROSPERITY
set before you life and p, ... Dt 30:15
I saw the p of the wicked ... Ps 73:3

PROSTITUTE
a p named Rahab, and stayed there ... Jos 2:1
p-s are entering the kingdom ... Mt 21:31
and make it part of a p? ... 1Co 6:15

PROTECT
P me as the pupil of your eye; ... Ps 17:8
He p-s his flock like a shepherd; ... Is 40:11
who is able to p you from ... Jd 24

PROTECTION
lives under the p of the Most High ... Ps 91:1

PROUD
LORD, my heart is not p; ... Ps 131:1
downfall a person's heart is p, ... Pr 18:12
arrogant, p, boastful, inventors ... Rm 1:30
money, boastful, p, demeaning ... 2Tm 3:2
God resists the p but gives ... Jms 4:6

PROVE
But God p-s his own love for us ... Rm 5:8

PROVEN
endurance produces p character, ... Rm 5:4

PROVERB
Solomon spoke 3,000 p-s, ... 1Kg 4:32
The p-s of Solomon son of David, ... Pr 1:1
you will quote this p to me: ... Lk 4:23

PROVIDE
God himself will p the lamb ... Gn 22:8
all these things will be p-d for you ... Mt 6:33
he will also p the way out ... 1Co 10:13
own flesh but p-s and cares for it, ... Eph 5:29
if anyone does not p for his own ... 1Tm 5:8
richly p-s us with all things ... 1Tm 6:17

PROVOKE
tested God and p-d the Holy One ... Ps 78:41

PROWLING
the devil is p around like a ... 1Pt 5:8

PRUNES
and he p every branch that ... Jn 15:2

PSALM
and the P-s must be fulfilled ... Lk 24:44
speaking to one another in p-s, ... Eph 5:19

PUBLIC
your attention to p reading, ... 1Tm 4:13

PUBLICLY
not wanting to disgrace her p ... Mt 1:19
P rebuke those who sin, so that ... 1Tm 5:20

PUNISH
the LORD has p-ed him for the ... Is 53:6
and p-es every son he receives ... Heb 12:6

PUNISHMENT
My p is too great to bear! ... Gn 4:13
p for our peace was on him, ... Is 53:5
son won't suffer p for the
father's ... Ezk 18:20
they will go away into
eternal p, ... Mt 25:46
because fear involves p ... 1Jn 4:18

PUPIL
protected him as the p of his eye ... Dt 32:10
Protect me as the p of
your eye; ... Ps 17:8

PURCHASED
which he p with his own
blood ... Ac 20:28

PURE
The fear of the LORD is p, ... Ps 19:9
can a young man keep his
way p? ... Ps 119:9
eyes are too p to look on evil, ... Hab 1:13
Blessed are the p in heart, ... Mt 5:8
whatever is just, whatever
is p, ... Php 4:8
To the p, everything is p, but to ... Ti 1:15
from a p heart love one another ... 1Pt 1:22

PURIFICATION
After making p for sins, he sat ... Heb 1:3

PURIFY
P me with hyssop, and I will be ... Ps 51:7
he will p the sons of Levi and ... Mal 3:3

PURIM
reason these days are called P, ... Est 9:26

PURITY
by p, by knowledge, by patience, ... 2Co 6:6

PURPLE
crown of thorns and the p robe ... Jn 19:5

PURPOSE
has prepared everything for
his p ... Pr 16:4
because I was sent for this p ... Lk 4:43
are called according to his p ... Rm 8:28
so that God's p according to ... Rm 9:11
and to work out his good p ... Php 2:13

PURSUE
seek peace and p it ... Ps 34:14
who did not p righteousness, ... Rm 9:30
and p righteousness,
godliness ... 1Tm 6:11
P peace with everyone, and ... Heb 12:14
Let him seek peace and p it, ... 1Pt 3:11

PURSUIT
futile, a p of the wind ... Ec 1:14

PUT
But p on the Lord Jesus Christ, ... Rm 13:14
P on the full armor of God so ... Eph 6:11

Q

QUAIL
So at evening q came ... Ex 16:13

QUAKE
earth q-d, and the rocks were split ... Mt 27:51

QUALITY
will test the q of each one's ... 1Co 3:13

QUARREL
The Lord's servant must not q, ... 2Tm 2:24

QUARRELSOME
but gentle, not **q**, not greedy............1Tm 3:3

QUEEN
The **q** of Sheba heard about.............1Kg 10:1
The **q** of the south will rise up..........Mt 12:42

QUICK
Everyone must be **q** to listen,...........Jms 1:19

QUICKLY
What you're doing, do **q**..................Jn 13:27
I am coming **q**. Hold on
to what................................Rv 3:11
Yes, I am coming **q**........................Rv 22:20

R

RABBI
do not be called '**R**,' because you ....Mt 23:8

RABBONI
she said to him in Aramaic, "***R***!" .... Jn 20:16

RACE (N)
the **r** is not to the swift,...................Ec 9:11
I have finished the **r**,
I have kept 2Tm 4:7
endurance the **r** that lies
before ....Heb 12:1
you are a chosen **r**,
a royal..................................1Pt 2:9

RACE (V)
the runners in a stadium all **r**,..........1Co 9:24

RACHEL
Daughter of Laban; wife and cousin of Jacob (Gn 29:10,18-30); mother of Joseph and Benjamin (30:24; 35:16-20); stole her father's household idols (31:19).
R weeping for her children; ....Mt 2:18

RADIANCE
The Son is the **r** of God's glory,...........Heb 1:3

RAGE (N)
king's **r** is like the roaring of a lion,......Pr 19:12

RAGE (V)
Why do the Gentiles **r** and..................Ac 4:25

RAHAB
Prostitute in Jericho who hid the Israelite spies (Jos 2; Heb 11:31); spared by Joshua (Jos 6:17,22-25). Mother of Boaz (Mt 1:5).

RAIN (N)
and the **r** fell on the earth forty.......... Gn 7:12
and sends **r** on the righteous and ....Mt 5:45

RAIN (V)
prayed . . . that it would not **r**,...........Jms 5:17

RAISE
I will **r** up for them a prophet............Dt 18:18
LORD **r-d** up judges, who saved ....Jdg 2:16
God is able to **r** up children for ....Mt 3:9
killed, and be **r-d** the
third day..............................Mt 16:21
and on the third day he
will be **r**..............................Mt 20:19
and I will **r** it up in three days.............Jn 2:19
and I will **r** him up on the last ....Jn 6:40
God has **r** this Jesus. ....Ac 2:32
and **r-d** for our justification..............Rm 4:25
that he was **r-d** on the third..............1Co 15:4
dead will be **r-d** incorruptible,.........1Co 15:52
who **r-d** the Lord Jesus will **r** us 2Co 4:14
He also **r-d** us up with him and..........Eph 2:6

RAM
and saw a **r** caught in the thicket.......Gn 22:13

RANSOM (N)
these cannot . . . pay his **r** to God......... Ps 49:7
to give his life as a **r** for many.......... Mt 20:28
gave himself as a **r** for all,.................1Tm 2:6

RANSOM (V)
r-ed of the LORD will return .... Is 35:10; 51:11
for the LORD has **r-ed** Jacob and..........Jr 31:11

RASHLY
something **r** and later to reconsider . . . Pr 20:25

RAVEN
he sent out a **r**. .... Gn 8:7
The **r-s** kept bringing him bread........ 1Kg 17:6
Consider the **r-s**: They don't sow .... Lk 12:24

READ
Sabbath day and stood up to **r**. .... Lk 4:16
you understand what you're **r-ing**? ..... Ac 8:30
your attention to public **r-ing**,...........1Tm 4:13
Blessed is the one who
r-s aloud ....Rv 1:3

READY
R . . . to give a defense 1Pt 3:15

REALITY
faith is the **r** of what is hoped .... Heb 11:1

REALLY
Did God **r** say, 'You can't
eat from.................................Gn 3:1

REAP
sow in tears will **r** with
shouts................................ Ps 126:5
the wind and **r** the whirlwind............. Hs 8:7
They don't sow or **r** or gather.............Mt 6:26
a person sows he will also **r**,..............Gl 6:7
r, for the time to **r** has come,............Rv 14:15

REASON (N)
They hated me for no **r**.......................Jn 15:25
asks you for a **r** for the hope...............1Pt 3:15

REASON (V)
So he **r-ed** in the synagogue with........Ac 17:17
a child, I **r-ed** like a child. 1Co 13:11

REBEKAH
Sister of Laban; wife of Isaac (Gn 24); mother of Jacob and Esau (25:21-26). Passed off as Isaac's sister (26:6-11). Encouraged Jacob to secure Isaac's blessing (27:1-17).

REBEL
Only don't **r** against the LORD, ... Nm 14:9
but they have **r-led** against me..............Is 1:2

REBELLION
For **r** is like the sin of divination, ...1Sm 15:23
the wicked increase, **r** increases .... Pr 29:16

REBELLIOUS
a stubborn and **r** generation, ... Ps 78:8
unbelieving and **r** generation!.......... Mt 17:17

REBUILD
to go up and **r** the LORD's house ....Ezr 1:5
Come, let's **r** Jerusalem's wall ....Neh 2:17
and the ruins will be **r-t**. ....Ezk 36:33
temple of God and **r** it in three days. . . .Mt 26:61

REBUKE
do not **r** me in your anger;..................Ps 6:1
The LORD **r** you, Satan! ....Zch 3:2
he got up and **r-d** the winds ....Mt 8:26
Don't **r** an older man, ...1Tm 5:1
Publicly **r** those who sin,................ 1Tm 5:20
profitable for teaching,
for **r-ing**, ... 2Tm 3:16
correct, **r**, and encourage with 2Tm 4:2
him but said, "The Lord **r** you!" ....Jd 9
many as I love, I **r** and discipline......... Rv 3:19

RECEIVE
who asks **r-s**, and the one who .... Mt 7:8
But to all who did **r** him, he gave .... Jn 1:12
Ask and you will **r**,............................ Jn 16:24
But you will **r** power when the ....Ac 1:8
is more blessed to give than to **r**. ....Ac 20:35
What do you have that
you didn't **r**? 1Co 4:7
For I **r-d** from the Lord what I 1Co 11:23
as you have **r-d** Christ Jesus .... Col 2:6

RECOGNIZE
r-d his brothers, they did not **r** him......Gn 42:8
opened, and they **r-d** him, but........... Lk 24:31
yet the world did not **r** him. ....Jn 1:10

RECONCILE
First go and be r-d with your . . . . Mt 5:24
Christ's behalf,
"Be r-d to God." 2Co 5:20
that he might r both to God. . . . . Eph 2:16
through him to r everything to. . . . . Col 1:20

RECONCILIATION
we have now received this r . . . . Rm 5:11
if their rejection brings r . . . . Rm 11:15
has given us the ministry of r: 2Co 5:18

RECONSIDER
rashly and later to r his vows. . . . . Pr 20:25

RECORD
does not keep a r of wrongs. 1Co 13:5

RECRUCIFYING
they are r the Son of God . . . . Heb 6:6

RED
Don't gaze at wine because it is r, ... Pr 23:31
they are crimson r, ... Is 1:18
good weather because the sky is r.' . . . . . Mt 16:2
another horse went out,
a fiery r one, ... Rv 6:4

RED SEA
Crossed by Israel (Ex 13:18; 14:15-31; Nm 21:14; Dt 11:4; Jos 2:10; 4:23; 24:6; Neh 9:9; Pss 106:7,9-11,22; 136:13-15; Ac 7:36; Heb 11:29); southern extent of the promised land (Ex 23:31); location of Solomon's fleet (1Kg 9:26).

REDEEM
I will r you with an outstretched
arm . . . . Ex 6:6
to r a people for himself, ... 2Sm 7:23
the price of r-ing him is too
costly, ... Ps 49:8
He r-s your life from the Pit; . . . . Ps 103:4
Christ r-ed us from the curse . . . . Gl 3:13
to r those under the law, ... Gl 4:5

REDEEMED (N)
Let the r of the LORD . . . . Ps 107:2

REDEEMER
I know that my R lives, ... Jb 19:25
LORD, my rock and my R. . . . . Ps 19:14
for their R is strong, ... Pr 23:11
Your R is the Holy One of Israel. . . . . Is 41:14

REDEMPTION
because your r is near! . . . . Lk 21:28
adoption, the r of our bodies . . . . Rm 8:23
In him we have r through his
blood, ... Eph 1:7
We have r, the forgiveness of sins. . . . . Col 1:14
having obtained eternal r . . . . Heb 9:12

REED
He will not break a bruised r, ... Is 42:3
A r swaying in the wind? . . . . Mt 11:7
He will not break a bruised r . . . . Mt 12:20

REFINER
For he will be like a r-'s fire . . . . Mal 3:2

REFRESHING (N)
that seasons of r may come . . . . Ac 3:19

REFUGE
will include six cities of r, ... Nm 35:6
whose wings you have come for r. . . . . . . Ru 2:12
God is our r and strength, ... Ps 46:1
shield to those who take r in him. . . . . Pr 30:5
we who have fled for r might . . . . Heb 6:18

REFUTE
For he vigorously r-d the Jews in . . . . Ac 18:28

REGARD (N)
The LORD had r for Abel and his . . . . Gn 4:4

REGARD (V)
but we in turn r-ed him stricken, ... Is 53:4

REGENERATION
through the washing of r and . . . . Ti 3:5

REGION
In the same r, shepherds were . . . . Lk 2:8

REGISTER
that the whole empire should be r-ed. . . . . Lk 2:1

REGRET
LORD r-ted that he had made man. . . . . Gn 6:6
I r that I made Saul king, ... 1Sm 15:11

REGULATIONS
Why do you submit to r: . . . . Col 2:20

REHOBOAM
Son of Solomon; king of Judah (1Kg 11:43). Answered people harshly; the kingdom was divided (12:1-19; 2Ch 10:1-19).

REIGN
The LORD will r forever and
ever! . . . . Ex 15:18
The LORD r-s! He is robed in . . . . Ps 93:1
The LORD r-s forever; . . . . Ps 146:10
who says to Zion, "Your God r-s!" . . . . Is 52:7
He will r over the house of. . . . . Lk 1:33
death r-ed from Adam to Moses, ... Rm 5:14
do not let sin r in your mortal . . . . Rm 6:12
For he must r until he puts all 1Co 15:25
we will also r with him; 2Tm 2:12
and he will r forever and ever. . . . . Rv 11:15
will r with him a thousand years. . . . . Rv 20:6

REJECT
LORD, he has r-ed you as king. 1Sm 15:23
stone that the builders r-ed has . . . . Ps 118:22
He was despised and r-ed by men, ... Is 53:3
the builders r-ed has become . . . . Mt 21:42
Whoever r-s you r-s me. . . . . Lk 10:16
but the one who r-s the Son . . . . Jn 3:36
has God r-ed his people? . . . . Rm 11:1
r-ed by men but chosen and. 1Pt 2:4

REJOICE
all who take refuge in you r; . . . . Ps 5:11
let's r and be glad in it. . . . . Ps 118:24
R greatly, Daughter Zion! . . . . Zch 9:9
but r that your names are written. . . . . . . Lk 10:20
R with those who r; . . . . Rm 12:15
but r-s in the truth. 1Co 13:6
R in the Lord always. I will say it
again: R!. . . . . Php 4:4
R always, ... 1Th 5:16

RELATIONS
men . . . left natural r with women. . . . . . . Rm 1:27

RELATIVE
The man is a close r. . . . . Ru 2:20
in his hometown, among his r-s, ... Mk 6:4

RELEASE
do you want me to r for you? . . . . Mt 27:21

RELENT
and r concerning this disaster . . . . Ex 32:12
but the LORD r-ed concerning 2Sm 24:16
may turn and r and leave a blessing . . . . . . Jl 2:14
so God r-ed from the disaster . . . . Jnh 3:10

RELIGION
and undefiled r before God. . . . . Jms 1:27

RELIGIOUS
are extremely r in every respect. . . . . Ac 17:22

RELY
He r-ies on the LORD; let him . . . . Ps 22:8
do not r on your own understanding; . . . . . Pr 3:5
What are you r-ing on? . . . . Is 36:4
all who r on the works of the law . . . . Gl 3:10

REMAIN
the word of our God r-s forever. . . . . Is 40:8
R in me, and I in you. Jn 15:4
three r: faith, hope, and love. 1Co 13:13
they would have r-ed with us. 1Jn 2:19

REMARKABLE
and look at this r sight. . . . . Ex 3:3

REMARKABLY
been r and wondrously made. . . . . Ps 139:14

REMEMBER
God r-ed Noah, ... Gn 8:1
R the Sabbath day, to keep it holy: . . . . Ex 20:8
human being that you r him, ... Ps 8:4
made of, r-ing that we are dust. . . . . Ps 103:14
So r your Creator in the days . . . . Ec 12:1
own sake and r your sins no more. . . . . Is 43:25
and never again r their sin. . . . . Jr 31:34
R Lot's wife! . . . . Lk 17:32
asked only that we would r the poor . . . . . Gl 2:10
R my chains. . . . . Col 4:18

REVERE
descendants of Israel, r him! . . . . Ps 22:23

REVERENCE
serve God acceptably, with r. . . . . Heb 12:28
do this with gentleness and r, ... 1Pt 3:16

REVERENT
observe your pure, r lives. 1Pt 3:2

REVILE
When we are **r-d**, we bless; 1Co 4:12

REVIVE
Will you not r us again so that. . . . . Ps 85:6

REWARD (N)
there is a r for the righteous! . . . . Ps 58:11
from the LORD, offspring, a r. . . . . Ps 127:3
and his r accompanies him. . . . . Is 40:10
your r is great in heaven. . . . . Mt 5:12
they have their r. Mt 6:2,5,16
survives, he will receive a r. 1Co 3:14
looking ahead to the r. . . . . Heb 11:26

REWARD (V)
that he **r-s** those who seek him. . . . . Heb 11:6

RIB
God made the r . . . into a woman. . . . . Gn 2:22

RICH
Don't wear yourself out to get r;. . . . . Pr 23:4
in a hurry to get r will not . . . . Pr 28:20
hard for a r person to enter. . . . . Mt 19:23
woe to you who are r,. . . . . Lk 6:24
who want to be r fall into. 1Tm 6:9
r boast in his humiliation. . . . . Jms 1:10

RICHES
and you have not requested r 2Ch 1:11
in her left, r and honor. . . . . Pr 3:16
make known the r of his glory . . . . Rm 9:23
Oh, the depth of the r . . . . Rm 11:33
immeasurable r of his grace. . . . . Eph 2:7

RIDDLE
directly, openly, and not in **r-s**;. . . . . Nm 12:8
"Let me tell you a r," Samson said . . . . . Jdg 14:12
words of the wise, and their **r-s**. . . . . Pr 1:6

RIDE
humble and **r-ing** on a donkey,. . . . . Zch 9:9

RIDER
horse and its r into the sea. . . . . Ex 15:1,21

RIGHT (ADJ)
So you are r when you pass. . . . . Ps 51:4
Sit at my r hand until I make. . . . . Ps 110:1
way that seems r to a person,. . . . . Pr 14:12; 16:25
one on your r and the other on. . . . . Mt 20:21
Sit at my r hand until I put. . . . . Mt 22:44
He will put the sheep on his r. . . . . Mt 25:33
He also is at the r hand of God. . . . . Rm 8:34
Sit at my r hand until I make. . . . . Heb 1:13
sat down at the r hand of God. . . . . Heb 10:12

RIGHT (N)
Defend the **r-s** of the fatherless. . . . . Is 1:17
gave them the r to be children. . . . . Jn 1:12

RIGHTEOUS (ADJ)
no one alive is r in your sight. . . . . Ps 143:2
raise up a R Branch of David. . . . . Jr 23:5
But the r one will live by his faith. . . . . . . Hab 2:4
Joseph, being a r man, and not . . . . Mt 1:19
saying, "This man really was r!" . . . . Lk 23:47
the coming of the R One,. . . . . Ac 7:52
is no one r, not even one. . . . . Rm 3:10
But my r one will live by faith;. . . . . Heb 10:38
Jesus Christ the r one. 1Jn 2:1

RIGHTEOUS (N)
watches over the way of the r . . . . Ps 1:6
I have not seen the r abandoned . . . . Ps 37:25
The r will never be shaken, ... Pr 10:30
the r run to it and are protected. . . . . Pr 18:10
sends rain on the r and the . . . . Mt 5:45
I didn't come to call the r . . . . Mt 9:13
The r will live by faith. . . . . Rm 1:17
because the r will live by faith. . . . . Gl 3:11

RIGHTEOUSLY
He will judge the world r . . . . Ps 98:9

RIGHTEOUSNESS
He credited it to him as r. . . . . Gn 15:6
He judges the world with r;. . . . . Ps 9:8
His r endures forever. . . . . Pss 111:3; 112:3
R exalts a nation, but sin is . . . . Pr 14:34
will be named: The LORD is Our R. . . . . Jr 23:6
those who hunger and thirst for r, ... Mt 5:6
kingdom of God and his r,. . . . . Mt 6:33
apart from the law, the r of God . . . . Rm 3:21
it was credited to him for r. . . . . Rm 4:3
end of the law for r to everyone . . . . Rm 10:4
His r endures forever. 2Co 9:9
r like armor on your chest, ... Eph 6:14
reserved for me the crown of r, ... 2Tm 4:8
was credited to him as r . . . . Jms 2:23

RING
is like a gold r in a pig's snout. . . . . Pr 11:22

RISE
From the **r-ing** of the sun to its. . . . . Ps 113:3
After three days I will r again. . . . . Mt 27:63
For he has r, just as he said. . . . . Mt 28:6
He is **r-n**! He is not here! . . . . Mk 16:6
A great prophet has **r-n**
among us,. . . . . Lk 7:16
that Jesus died and **rose** again,. 1Th 4:14
dead in Christ will r first. 1Th 4:16

RIVALRY
that there is r among you. 1Co 1:11
proclaim Christ out of r . . . . Php 1:17
Do nothing out of r or conceit, ... Php 2:3

RIVER
There is a r—its streams . . . . Ps 46:4
By the **r-s** of Babylon—there we . . . . Ps 137:1
make peace flow to her like a r, ... Is 66:12
were baptized by him in the
Jordan R . . . . Mt 3:6
showed me the r of the water of life, ... Rv 22:1

ROAD
r broad that leads to destruction, ... Mt 7:13

ROAR
though its water **r-s** and foams. . . . . Ps 46:3
The LORD **r-s** from on high; . . . . Jr 25:30
The LORD will r from Zion and. . . . . Jl 3:16

ROARING (ADJ)
prowling around like a r lion, ... 1Pt 5:8

ROAST
they should eat it, **r-ed** over the fire . . . . . Ex 12:8
A lazy hunter doesn't r his game,. . . . . Pr 12:27

ROB
to meet a bear **r-bed** of her cubs. . . . . Pr 17:12
Will a man r God? Yet you are . . . . Mal 3:8

ROBBER
this house . . . become a den of **r-s** . . . . Jr 7:11
and fell into the hands of **r-s**. . . . . Lk 10:30

ROBE
and he made a long-sleeved r . . . . Gn 37:3
cut off the corner of Saul's r. 1Sm 24:4
hem of his r filled the temple. . . . . Is 6:1
If I can just touch his r, ... Mt 9:21
and his r was as white as snow. . . . . Mt 28:3
crown of thorns and the
purple r. . . . . Jn 19:5
He wore a r dipped in blood,. . . . . Rv 19:13

ROBED (V)
He is r in majesty;. . . . . Ps 93:1

ROCK
when you hit the r, water will . . . . Ex 17:6
will put you in the crevice
of the r . . . . Ex 33:22
and struck the r twice with his . . . . Nm 20:11
The LORD is my r,. . . . . Ps 18:2
LORD, my r and my Redeemer. . . . . Ps 19:14
and set my feet on a r, ... Ps 40:2
and a r to trip over,. . . . . Is 8:14
who built his house on the r. . . . . Mt 7:24
on this r I will build my church, ... Mt 16:18
Other seed fell on the r;. . . . . Lk 8:6
and a r to trip over,. . . . . Rm 9:33
drank from a spiritual r that followed
them, and that r was Christ. 1Co 10:4
and a r to trip over. 1Pt 2:8

ROCKY
Other seed fell on r ground, ... Mt 13:5

ROD
your r and your staff—they. . . . . Ps 23:4
not use the r hates his son, ... Pr 13:24
with a r, he will not die. . . . . Pr 23:13

ROLL
The sky will r up like a scroll, ... Is 34:4
Who will r away the stone from ... Mk 16:3
very large—had been
r-ed away. ... Mk 16:4

ROMAN
Tell me, are you a R citizen? ... Ac 22:27

ROME
Italian city, capital of the Roman Empire; represented at Pentecost (Ac 2:10); Jews expelled (18:2); Paul addressed a letter to the church there (Rm 1:7,15) and goes there (Ac 19:21; 23:11; 28:14-16; 2Tm 1:17).

ROOF
From the r he saw a woman ... 2Sm 11:2
went up on the r and lowered him ... Lk 5:19

ROOM
you pray, go into your private r, ... Mt 6:6
there was no guest r available ... Lk 2:7
Father's house are many **r-s**. ... Jn 14:2

ROOSTER
before the r crows, you will ... Mt 26:34

ROOT
On that day the r of Jesse will ... Is 11:10
and like a r out of dry ground. ... Is 53:2
since it had no r, it withered ... Mt 13:6
And if the r is holy, so are the ... Rm 11:16
The r of Jesse will appear, ... Rm 15:12
r-ed and firmly established ... Eph 3:17
r-ed and built up in him and ... Col 2:7
of money is a r of all kinds ... 1Tm 6:10
and that no r of bitterness ... Heb 12:15
of Judah, the R of David, ... Rv 5:5

ROUGH
and the r places, a plain ... Is 40:4
straight, the r ways smooth, ... Lk 3:5

ROYAL
if you fulfill the r law prescribed ... Jms 2:8
a chosen race, a r priesthood, a ... 1Pt 2:9

RUIN (N)
his lips invites his own r ... Pr 13:3
my house still lies in r ... Hg 1:9
desires, which plunge people into r ... 1Tm 6:9
leads to the r of those who listen ... 2Tm 2:14

RUIN (V)
Woe is me for I am **r-ed** ... Is 6:5
and the skins are **r-ed** ... Mt 9:17

RULE (N)
when he abolishes all r and all ... 1Co 15:24
he competes according to the **r-s** ... 2Tm 2:5

RULE (V)
They will r the fish of the sea ... Gn 1:26
He **r-s** forever by his might; ... Ps 66:7
For sin will not r over you, ... Rm 6:14

RULER
and the **r-s** conspire together against ... Ps 2:2
one will come from you to be r ... Mc 5:2
know that the **r-s** of the Gentiles ... Mt 20:25
Now the r of this world will be ... Jn 12:31
death nor life, nor angels nor **r-s**, ... Rm 8:38
but against the **r-s**, against ... Eph 6:12
Remind them to submit to **r-s** ... Ti 3:1

RUMOR
to hear of wars and **r-s** of wars ... Mt 24:6

RUN
his word **r-s** swiftly ... Ps 147:15
righteous **r** to it and are protected ... Pr 18:10
they will r and not become weary, ... Is 40:31
R in such a way to win the prize ... 1Co 9:24
was not **r-ning**, and had not been r ... Gl 2:2
You were **r-ning** well ... Gl 5:7
Let us r with endurance the race ... Heb 12:1

RUNNER
the **r-s** in a stadium all race, but ... 1Co 9:24

RUSH
sound ... of a violent **r-ing** wind ... Ac 2:2

RUST
where moth and r destroy and ... Mt 6:19

RUTH
Moabitess; widowed daughter-in-law of Naomi (Ru 1:1-5); married Boaz; ancestor of David and Christ (Ru 4:1; Mt 1:5-6,16).

RUTHLESSLY
They worked the Israelites r ... Ex 1:13

S

SABBATH
Remember the S day to keep it ... Ex 20:8
through the grainfields on the S ... Mt 12:1
The S was made for man and not ... Mk 2:27
Son of Man is Lord even of the S ... Mk 2:28
whether he would heal him on the S ... Mk 3:2
lawful to do good on the S or ... Mk 3:4
a S rest remains for God's people ... Heb 4:9

SACKCLOTH
with fasting, s, and ashes ... Dn 9:3
proclaimed a fast and dressed in s ... Jnh 3:5
would have repented in s and ashes ... Mt 11:21

SACRED
you have known the s Scriptures, ... 2Tm 3:15

SACRIFICE
is the Passover s to the LORD, ... Ex 12:27
to obey is better than s, ... 1Sm 15:22
You do not delight in s and offering; ... Ps 40:6
You do not want a s, or I would ... Ps 51:16
The s pleasing to God is a broken ... Ps 51:17
faithful love and not s, ... Hs 6:6
I desire mercy and not s ... Mt 9:13
your bodies as a living s, ... Rm 12:1
our Passover lamb has
been **s-d**. ... 1Co 5:7
an acceptable s, pleasing
to God ... Php 4:18
need to offer **s-s** every day, ... Heb 7:27
of sin by the s of himself ... Heb 9:26
offer up to God a s of praise, ... Heb 13:15
offer spiritual **s-s** acceptable to ... 1Pt 2:5

SADDUCEES
of the leaven of the Pharisees
and S ... Mt 16:6
S, who say there is no
resurrection ... Mt 22:23

SAFETY
The horse is a false hope for s; ... Ps 33:17

SAINT
intercedes for the **s-s** according ... Rm 8:27
glorious inheritance in the **s-s**, ... Eph 1:18
Greet every s in Christ Jesus ... Php 4:21
to the **s-s** once for all ... Jd 3
are the prayers of the **s-s** ... Rv 5:8
the righteous acts of the **s-s** ... Rv 19:8

SAKE
right paths for his name's s ... Ps 23:3
not for your s that I will act ... Ezk 36:22,32

SALOME
Wife of Zebedee, mother of James and John (Mk 15:40; 16:1; cp. Mt 27:56); possibly Mary's sister (Jn 19:25).

SALT
back and became a pillar of s ... Gn 19:26
It is a permanent covenant of s ... Nm 18:19
You are the s of the earth ... Mt 5:13
seasoned with s, so that you may ... Col 4:6

SALVATION
Stand firm and see the LORD's s ... Ex 14:13
He has become my s ... Ex 15:2
Proclaim his s from day to day ... 1Ch 16:23
The God of my s is exalted ... Ps 18:46
The LORD is my light and my s ... Ps 27:1
Restore the joy of your s to me, ... Ps 51:12
He has become my s ... Ps 118:14
who proclaims s, who says to ... Is 52:7
For my eyes have seen your s ... Lk 2:30
everyone will see the s of God ... Lk 3:6
There is s in no one else, ... Ac 4:12
now is the day of s ... 2Co 6:2
the helmet of s and the sword ... Eph 6:17
work out your own s with fear ... Php 2:12
if we neglect such a great s? ... Heb 2:3
S belongs to our God, who is ... Rv 7:10

SAMARIA
Capital and namesake of the northern kingdom (1Kg 13:32; 16:24; 2Kg 17:24; Is 7:9; Ezk 16:46; 23:4; Hos 8:5; Ob 19; Mc 1:1); captured by Assyria (2Kg 17:6).

In NT times, region of central hill country between Judah and Galilee (Lk 17:11; Ac 1:8; 8:1,5,14, often shunned by Jews (Jn 4:4-9); home of Samaritans.

SAMARITAN

But a S on his journey came up........Lk 10:33
thanking him. And he was a S...........Lk 17:16
Jews do not associate with S-s..............Jn 4:9

SAME

Jesus Christ is the s yesterday,..........Heb 13:8

SAMSON

Son of Manoah; Danite judge. Birth announced; to be a Nazirite (Jdg 13). Rashly married a Philistine; posed a riddle (Jdg 14). Took revenge on Philistines: set fire to fields; killed one thousand with donkey's jawbone (Jdg 15). Married Delilah; was betrayed (16:4-21). Slaughter in Dagon's temple (16:23-30; Heb 11:32-34).

SAMUEL

Son of Elkanah and Hannah; Ephraimite judge, kingmaker, priest, and prophet. Born in answer to prayer (1Sm 1:1-20); raised at Shiloh by Eli (1:25-28; 2:11); called (3:1-18). Served as military and judicial judge (1Sm 7). Warned people about the nature of a king (8:10-18; 10:25); anointed Saul (10:1); rejected Saul (13:11-14; 15:10-29). Anointed David (16:1-13); protected David from Saul (19:18-24). Death (25:1); appearance to Saul after death (28:3-19).

SANCTIFICATION

which results in s..................Rm 6:19,22
For this is God's will, your s:.............1Th 4:3

SANCTIFY

S them by the truth;........................Jn 17:17
washed, you were s-ied, you were 1Co 6:11
the God of peace himself s you.........1Th 5:23

SANCTUARY

They are to make a s for me ....Ex 25:8
up my hands toward your holy s...........Ps 28:2
Praise God in his s...........................Ps 150:1
and will set my s among them.........Ezk 37:26
not enter a s made with hands ....Heb 9:24

SAND

offspring like the s of the sea, ...Gn 32:12
who built his house on the s..............Mt 7:26

SANDAL

Remove the s-s from your feet, ...Ex 3:5
Remove the s-s from your feet,..........Jos 5:15
not worthy to remove his s-s...............Mt 3:11

SARAH

Wife and half sister of Abraham; originally named Sarai (Gn 11:29-31; 20:12); barren (11:30). Twice passed off as Abraham's sister (12:10-20; 20). Gave Hagar to Abraham, then sent her away (Gn 16; 21:9-21). Laughed when she heard the promise of a son (18:9-15). Bore Isaac (21:1-7; Heb 11:11). Died; buried at Machpelah (Gn 23; 25:10; 49:31).

SATAN

LORD asked S, "Where have you ....Jb 1:7
Jesus told him, "Go away, S!...............Mt 4:10
If S drives out S, he is divided...........Mt 12:26
told Peter, "Get behind me, S!...........Mt 16:23
I watched S fall from heaven ....Lk 10:18
Then S entered Judas, called...............Lk 22:3
and from the power of S to God,..........Ac 26:18
S disguises himself as an angel..........2Co 11:14
messenger of S to torment
me so..2Co 12:7
synagogue of S.........................Rv 2:9; 3:9
who is called the devil and S,.............Rv 12:9
S will be released from his..................Rv 20:7

SATISFY

your wages on what does not s?..........Is 55:2

SAUL

1. First king of united Israel. Son of Kish; tall, handsome Benjaminite (1Sm 9:1-2). Met Samuel while looking for donkeys (9:3-27). Anointed privately (10:1); chosen by lot and announced publicly (10:17-24); delivered Jabesh–gilead (11:1-11); confirmed king at Gilgal (11:12-15). Rebuked and rejected (13:8-15; 15:11-30). Attempted to kill David (18:11,17,25; 19:10-17; 23:8,25; 24:2; 26:2); spared by David (1Sm 24; 26). Among the prophets (10:9-13; 19:18-24). Consulted a medium to inquire of Samuel (1Sm 28). Killed by Philistines (1Sm 31).
2. Paul's Hebrew name. see PAUL

SAVE

and I was s-d from my enemies...........Ps 18:3
and s those stumbling toward............Pr 24:11
Turn to me and be s-d, all the ends ......Is 45:22
on the name of the LORD
will be s-d, ...Jl 2:32
Jesus, because he will s
his people.......................................Mt 1:21
whoever wants to s his life will ....Mt 16:25
asked, "Then who can be s-d?"..........Mt 19:25
cut short, no one would be s-d........ Mt 24:22
and is baptized will be s-d,..............Mk 16:16
come to seek and to s the lost............Lk 19:10
to s the world through him.................Jn 3:17
name of the Lord will be s-d...............Ac 2:21
Sirs, what must I do to be s-d? ....Ac 16:30
on name of the Lord will be s-d..........Rm 10:13
you are s-d by grace
through faith,...............................Eph 2:8
came into the world to s sinners 1Tm 1:15
wants everyone to be s-d..................1Tm 2:4
to this, now s-s you (not as the.........1Pt 3:21

SAVIOR

They forgot God their S,....................Ps 106:21
Besides me, there is no S...................Is 43:11
and no S exists besides me................Hs 13:4
a S ... who is Messiah, the Lord.............Lk 2:11
God, who is the S of all people,..........1Tm 4:10
appearing of our S Christ Jesus,.........2Tm 1:10
glory of our great God and S,..............Ti 2:13
of our Lord and S Jesus Christ. 2Pt 3:18

SAY

"who do you s that I am?"..................Mt 16:15

SCALE

Dishonest s-s are detestable..............Pr 11:1
something like s-s fell from his...........Ac 9:18
had a set of s-s in his hand.................Rv 6:5

SCARLET

Though your sins are s,.........................Is 1:18
dressed him in a s robe......................Mt 27:28

SCATTER

sheep of the flock will be s-ed. ....Mt 26:31
A man s-s seed on the ground; ....Mk 4:26

SCEPTER

s will not depart from Judah ....Gn 49:10
break them with an iron s; ....Ps 2:9

SCHEMES

against the s of the devil.................Eph 6:11

SCOFFERS

S will come in the last days 2Pt 3:3

SCORN

and s-ed the Rock of his salvation...... Dt 32:15
s-ed by mankind and despised by....... Ps 22:6

SCORPION

asks for an egg, will give him a s? ......Lk 11:12

SCOUT

Send men to s out the land ....Nm 13:2

SCRIBE

authority, and not like their s-s.........Mt 7:29
woe to you, s-s and Pharisees,...........Mt 23:13

SCRIPTURE

don't know the S-s or the power....... Mt 22:29
Today ... this S has been fulfilled......... Lk 4:21
concerning himself in all the S-s........Lk 24:27
You pore over the S-s
because you...................................Jn 5:39
and the S cannot be broken................Jn 10:35
you have known the sacred S-s,..........2Tm 3:15
All S is inspired by God and is 2Tm 3:16
No prophecy of S comes from 2Pt 1:20

SCROLL

Eat this s, then go and speak to.......... Ezk 3:1
open the s and break its seals? .... Rv 5:2

SEA

through the s on dry ground,............Ex 14:22
the winds and the s obey him!...........Mt 8:27
toward them walking on the s...........Mt 14:25
Something like a s of glass, ...Rv 4:6

SEAL (N)

Set me as a s on your heart,.............. Sg 8:6
He has also put his s on us and given... 2Co 1:22
the scroll and break its s-s?' .... Rv 5:2

SEAL (V)

s the book until the time of the end...... Dn 12:4
were s-ed with the promised Holy .... Eph 1:13
s-ed with seven seals.........................Rv 5:1
s the servants ... on their
foreheads.....................................Rv 7:3

SEARCH
You have s-ed me and known me........Ps 139:1
S me, God, and know my heart;........Ps 139:23
me when you s for me with all ....Jr 29:13
And he who s-es our hearts
knows..............................Rm 8:27
since the Spirit s-es everything,........1Co 2:10

SEASON
that bears its fruit in its s..................Ps 1:3
days, months, s-s, and years..............Gl 4:10
About the times and the s-s:.............1Th 5:1

SEASONED
be gracious, s with salt, so..................Col 4:6

SEAT (N)
Make a mercy s of pure gold,..........Ex 25:17
love the front s in the.....................Lk 11:43

SEAT (V)
I saw the Lord s-ed on a high and..........Is 6:1
s-ed at the right hand of Power........Mt 26:64
and s-ed us with him the heavens,......Eph 2:6

SECOND
The s is like it: Love your..............Mt 22:39
This is the s death, the lake of ....Rv 20:14

SECRET
He knows the s-s of the heart? ....Ps 44:21
Father who sees in s will
reward you..............................Mt 6:4
things kept s from the ....Mt 13:35
judges what people have kept s,.........Rm 2:16
The s-s of his heart will be............1Co 14:25
I have learned the s of being............Php 4:12

SECRETLY
decided to divorce her s.......................Mt 1:19
but s because of his fear of the ....Jn 19:38

SECURE
anchor for the soul, firm and s.........Heb 6:19

SEE
humans cannot s me and live..............Ex 33:20
They say, "The LORD doesn't s it..........Ps 94:7
they might s with their eyes..............Is 6:10
darkness have s-n a great light,.........Mt 4:16
heart, for they will s God.....................Mt 5:8
because looking they do not s,..........Mt 13:13
No one has ever s-n God.....................Jn 1:18
I was blind, and now I can s!.................Jn 9:25
who has s-n me has s-n the
Father.....................................Jn 14:9
what we have s-n with our eyes, ...1Jn 1:1
because we will s him as he is.............1Jn 3:2

SEED
who sowed good s in his field...........Mt 13:24
like a mustard s that a man
took.......................................Mt 13:31
faith the size of a mustard s,............Mt 17:20
Other s fell on the rock;.......................Lk 8:6
He does not say "and to s-s,"...............Gl 3:16
not of perishable s but of 1Pt 1:23

SEEK
when you s him with all your ....Dt 4:29
If you s him, he will be found...........1Ch 28:9
pray and s my face, and turn 2Ch 7:14
s peace and pursue it.......................Ps 34:14
S the LORD while he may be found;........Is 55:6
But s first the kingdom of God ....Mt 6:33
S, and you will find...............................Mt 7:7
come to s and to save the lost.............Lk 19:10
No one is to s his own good, ...1Co 10:24
he rewards those who s him...........Heb 11:6

SEEM
a way that s-s right to a person... Pr 14:12; 16:25

SEIZE
Then they tried to s him........................Jn 7:30

SELF
put off the old s with its ....Col 3:9
For people will be lovers of s,...........2Tm 3:2

SELF-CONTROL
you because of your lack of s.............1Co 7:5
gentleness, s. The law is not against........Gl 5:23
knowledge with s, s with
endurance,...................................2Pt 1:6

SELF-CONTROLLED
let us stay awake and be s...................1Th 5:6
sensible, righteous, holy, s,.......................Ti 1:8

SELF-INDULGENCE
not of any value in curbing s...........Col 2:23

SELFISH
anger outbursts, s ambitions,
slander.....................................2Co 12:20
envy and s ambition......................Jms 3:14,16

SELL
and do not s—truth, wisdom ....Pr 23:23
"You were **sold** for nothing,
and you ....Is 52:3
joy he goes and s-s everything ....Mt 13:44
s all you have and give to the poor .....Mk 10:21
sold his birthright in exchange ....Heb 12:16
one can buy or s unless he has ....Rv 13:17

SEND
I AM has **sent** me to you....................Ex 3:14
Who will I s? Here I am.
S me...Is 6:8
of the harvest to s out workers..........Mt 9:38
sent out these twelve after giving.......Mt 10:5
me welcomes him who **sent** me...........Mt 10:40
has **sent** me to proclaim release ....Lk 4:18
For God did not s his Son into ....Jn 3:17
the will of him who **sent** me........Jn 5:30; 6:38
If I go, I will s him to you.....................Jn 16:7
Father has **sent** me, I also s you..........Jn 20:21
they preach unless they are **sent**?........Rm 10:15
God **sent** his Son, born of a woman,.........Gl 4:4
he loved us and **sent** his Son to be.........1Jn 4:10

SENSE
who commits adultery lacks s;...........Pr 6:32

SENSIBLE
who accepts correction is s..................Pr 15:5

SEPARATE (ADJ)
out from among them and be s,..........2Co 6:17

SEPARATE (V)
and a gossip s-s close friends..............Pr 16:28
joined together, let no one s...............Mt 19:6
just as a shepherd s-s the sheep ...... Mt 25:32
Who can s us from the love of.............Rm 8:35

SEPARATION
as far as the s of soul and spirit,........Heb 4:12

SERPENT
Now the s was the most cunning.........Gn 3:1
as shrewd as s-s and as innocent.........Mt 10:16
as the s deceived Eve by his...............2Co 11:3
the ancient s, who is called..................Rv 12:9

SERVANT
Speak, for your s is listening.............1Sm 3:10
Give praise, you s-s of the LORD ....Ps 135:1
"This is my s; I strengthen him,............Is 42:1
See, my s will be successful;..................Is 52:13
to my s, 'Do this!' and he does it ....Mt 8:9
Here is my s whom I have chosen,........Mt 12:18
great among you must be your s,.........Mt 20:26
Well done, good and faithful s! ....Mt 25:21
he must be last and s of all.................Mk 9:35
"I am the Lord's s," said Mary. ....Lk 1:38
s-s; we've only done our duty...............Lk 17:10
Where I am, there my s also will be .... Jn 12:26
I do not call you s-s anymore, because
a s doesn't know what..................Jn 15:15
by assuming the form of a s,...............Php 2:7

SERVE
S the LORD with gladness;...................Ps 100:2
No one can s two masters,....................Mt 6:24
did not come to be s-d, but to s,........ Mt 20:28
am among you as the one who s-s......Lk 22:27
but s one another through love.............Gl 5:13
S with a good attitude,.....................Eph 6:7

SERVICE
if s, use it in s; if teaching, in teaching; ..Rm 12:7

SET
S apart for me Barnabas and Saul .... Ac 13:2
instrument, s apart, useful to.......... 2Tm 2:21

SEVEN
march around the city s times,.............Jos 6:4
will be s weeks and sixty-two weeks. ...Dn 9:25
sins against me him? As many as s times?...Mt 18:21
To the s churches in Asia......................Rv 1:4
s angels with the s last plagues; ....Rv 15:1

SEVEN HUNDRED
He had s wives who were...................1Kg 11:3

SEVENTH
On the s day God had completed ....Gn 2:2
the s day is a Sabbath to the LORD ...... Ex 20:10

And on the s day God rested from ... Heb 4:4

SEVENTY

until s years were fulfilled. ... 2Ch 36:21
When s years for Babylon ... Jr 29:10
number of years ... would be s. ... Dn 9:2
S weeks are decreed about your. ... Dn 9:24
but s times seven. ... Mt 18:22

SEVENTY-TWO

The s returned with joy, saying, ... Lk 10:17

SEVERE

and s treatment of the body, ... Col 2:23

SEW

so they s-ed fig leaves together. ... Gn 3:7
No one s-s a patch of unshrunk ... Mk 2:21

SHADE

to provide s for his head. ... Jnh 4:6
birds of the sky can nest in its s. ... Mk 4:32

SHADOW

Our days on earth are like a s, ... 1Ch 29:15
hide me in the s of your wings ... Ps 17:8
person goes about like a mere s. ... Ps 39:6
dwells in the s of the Almighty. ... Ps 91:1
in darkness and the s of death, ... Lk 1:79
least his s might fall on some ... Ac 5:15
as a copy and s of the heavenly ... Heb 8:5

SHAKE

established; it cannot be s-n. ... 1Ch 16:30
of the LORD s-s the wilderness; ... Ps 29:8
The righteous will never be s-n, ... Pr 10:30
s the dust off your feet when you ... Mt 10:14
pressed down, s-n together, ... Lk 6:38
where they were assembled was s-n, ... Ac 4:31
once more I will s not only the ... Heb 12:26

SHALLUM

1. King of Israel; assassinated Zechariah; was assassinated by Menahem (2Kg 15:10-15).
2. Alternate name for Jehoahaz (2Kg 23:30-34; Jr 22:11). see JEHOAHAZ

SHAME

were naked, yet felt no s. ... Gn 2:25
hope in me will not be put to s. ... Is 49:23
some to s and eternal contempt. ... Dn 12:2
on him will not be put to s. ... Rm 9:33
what is foolish ... to s the wise, ... 1Co 1:27
their glory is in their s. ... Php 3:19
the cross, despising the s. ... Heb 12:2
in him will never be put to s. ... 1Pt 2:6

SHAMEFUL

For it is s even to mention what ... Eph 5:12

SHAMELESS

Men committed s acts with men ... Rm 1:27

SHAMGAR

Judge; killed six hundred Philistines with a cattle prod (Jdg 3:31; 5:6).

SHAPHAN

Josiah's court secretary or scribe (2Kg 22:3-14); his sons were friends of Jeremiah (Jr 26:24; 36:10; 39:14).

SHARE

S your master's joy.' ... Mt 25:21
two shirts must s with someone ... Lk 3:11

SHARES

let me inherit two s of your spirit. ... 2Kg 2:9

SHARP

They had such a s disagreement ... Ac 15:39

SHARPEN

s-s iron, and one man s-s another. ... Pr 27:17

SHARPER

s than any double-edged sword, ... Heb 4:12

SHAVE

If I am s-d, my strength will leave ... Jdg 16:17
emissaries, s-d off half their ... 2Sm 10:4
for them to get their heads s-d. ... Ac 21:24
the same as having her head s-d. ... 1Co 11:5

SHEAF

shouts of joy, carrying his s-ves. ... Ps 126:6

SHEARER

a sheep silent before her s-s, ... Is 53:7
a lamb is silent before its s, ... Ac 8:32

SHEBA

Nation whose queen came to see Solomon (1Kg 10; 2Ch 9); also called Sabeans (Jb 1:15; Jl 3:8).

SHECHEM

1. City in the hill country of Ephraim. Simeon and Levi destroyed the city in revenge for the rape of Dinah (Gn 34); Joshua renewed the covenant there (Jos 24:1-28); served as first capital of the northern kingdom (1Kg 12:25).
2. Son of Hamor; raped Dinah (Gn 34).

SHED

Whoever s-s human blood ... Gn 9:6
without the s-ding of blood there ... Heb 9:22

SHEEP

hills like s without a shepherd. ... 1Kg 22:17
people, the s of his pasture. ... Ps 100:3
We all went astray like s; ... Is 53:6
and like a s silent before her. ... Is 53:7
and the s will be scattered; ... Zch 13:7
like s without a shepherd. ... Mt 9:36
go to the lost s of the house of ... Mt 10:6
someone has a hundred s, and ... Mt 18:12
separates the s from the goats. ... Mt 25:32
He calls his own s by name ... Jn 10:3
I lay down my life for the s. ... Jn 10:15
My s hear my voice, I know them, ... Jn 10:27
"Feed my s," Jesus said. ... Jn 21:17
was led like a s to the slaughter, ... Ac 8:32

SHEET

a large s coming down, ... Ac 10:11

SHELTER

The Festival of S-s to the LORD ... Lv 23:34
dwell in s-s during the festival ... Neh 8:14
under the s of your wings. ... Ps 61:4
I will set up three s-s here: ... Mt 17:4
Jewish Festival of S-s was near, ... Jn 7:2

SHEOL

You will not abandon me to S; ... Ps 16:10
make my bed in S, you are there. ... Ps 139:8
Her house is the road to S, ... Pr 7:27
S and Abaddon lie open before ... Pr 15:11
S, where is your sting? ... Hs 13:14

SHEPHERD (N)

hills like sheep without a s. ... 1Kg 22:17
The LORD is my s; I have what ... Ps 23:1
He protects his flock like a s; ... Is 40:11
prophesy against the s-s of Israel. ... Ezk 34:2
establish over them one s, ... Ezk 34:23
Strike the s, and the sheep will ... Zch 13:7
like sheep without a s. ... Mt 9:36
I will strike the s, and the sheep. ... Mt 26:31
s-s were staying out in the fields. ... Lk 2:8
I am the good s. The good s lays ... Jn 10:11
the great S of the sheep ... Heb 13:20
And when the chief S appears, ... 1Pt 5:4

SHEPHERD (V)

You will s my people Israel ... 2Sm 5:2
overseers, to s the church of God, ... Ac 20:28
S God's flock among you, not ... 1Pt 5:2

SHIELD

He is a s to all who take refuge ... 2Sm 22:31
LORD is my strength and my s; ... Ps 28:7
situation take up the s of faith. ... Eph 6:16

SHINE

LORD make his face s on you. ... Nm 6:25
Arise, s, for your light has ... Is 60:1
let your light s before others, ... Mt 5:16
righteous will s like the sun ... Mt 13:43
and his face **shone** like the sun; ... Mt 17:2
glory of the Lord **shone** around them, ... Lk 2:9
That light s-s in the darkness, ... Jn 1:5
and Christ will s on you. ... Eph 5:14

SHIPWRECK

Three times I was s-ed. ... 2Co 11:25
have s-ed the faith. ... 1Tm 1:19

SHIRT

to sue you and take away your s, ... Mt 5:40

SHOOT
a s will grow from the stump.............Is 11:1

SHORE
daybreak came, Jesus stood on the s......Jn 21:4

SHORT
the crowd, since he was a s man.........Lk 19:3
sinned and fall s of the glory ....Rm 3:23

SHOULDERS
government will be on his s................Is 9:6

SHOUT
until the time I say, 'S!' Then you.........Jos 6:10
Let the whole earth s to the LORD;........Ps 98:4
s triumphantly to the LORD, ...Ps 100:1
kept s-ing all the more,
"Crucify him!"..........................Mt 27:23
descend from heaven with a s, ...1Th 4:16

SHOW
for they will be s-n mercy.................Mt 5:7
He s-ed them his hands and feet........Lk 24:40
s us the Father, and that's
enough.................................Jn 14:8
s mercy to whom I will s mercy,.........Rm 9:15
And I will s you an even better 1Co 12:31
S me your faith without works,.........Jms 2:18

SHOWERS
s in ... season—s of blessing. ....Ezk 34:26

SHREWD
crooked you prove yourself s...........Ps 18:26
Therefore be as s as serpents...........Mt 10:16

SHUDDER
demons believe—and they s. ....Jms 2:19

SHUT
and they have s their eyes;..............Mt 13:15
that every mouth may be s ....Rm 3:19

SICK
need a doctor, but those
who are s..............................Mt 9:12
I was s and you took care of me;.......Mt 25:36
is why many are s and ill among 1Co 11:30
Is anyone among you s? ....Jms 5:14

SICKLE
Swing the s because the harvest.........Jl 3:13
and a sharp s in his hand................Rv 14:14

SICKNESS
he himself bore our s-es, ...Is 53:4
healing every disease and every s. ......Mt 9:35

SIDE
Though a thousand fall at your s ....Ps 91:7
the LORD had not been on our s—........Ps 124:1
pierced his s with a spear, ...Jn 19:34
showed them his hands and his s.........Jn 20:20

SIFT
has asked to s you like wheat. ....Lk 22:31

SIGHT
The blind receive their s,.................Lk 7:22
For we walk by faith, not by s 2Co 5:7

SIGN
will give you a s: See, the virgin...........Is 7:14
demands a s, but no s will be given
to it except the s of ... Jonah. ....Mt 12:39
s of your coming and of the end..........Mt 24:3
This will be the s for you:..................Lk 2:12
the first of his s-s, in Cana of Galilee......Jn 2:11
Jesus performed many other s-s ....Jn 20:30
them to do s-s and wonders ....Ac 14:3
Jews ask for s-s and the Greeks 1Co 1:22
tongues, then, is intended as a s, ...1Co 14:22

SILAS
Early church leader and prophet; also called Silvanus. Brought news from Jerusalem to Antioch (Ac 15:22,32); worked with Paul and Peter in missions and writing letters (15:40-41; 16:19-40; 17:10-15; 18:5; 2Co 1:19; 1Th 1:1; 2Th 1:1; 1Pt 5:12).

SILENCE (N)
there was s in heaven for about ....Rv 8:1

SILENCE (V)
that he had s-d the Sadducees, ...Mt 22:34
said to the sea, "S! Be still!"..............Mk 4:39

SILENT
If you keep s at this time, ...Est 4:14
When I kept s, my bones became........Ps 32:3
considered wise when he keeps s, ...Pr 17:28
and like a sheep s before her..............Is 53:7
But Jesus kept s.........................Mt 26:63
and as a lamb is s before its..............Ac 8:32
women should be s in the 1Co 14:34
instead, she is to be s....................1Tm 2:12

SILOAM
Pool in Jerusalem (Jn 9:7,11).

SILVER
return each man's s to his sack, ...Gn 42:25
my instruction instead of s, ...Pr 8:10
like gold apples in s settings.............Pr 25:11
loves s is never satisfied
with s,................................Ec 5:10
you without s, come, buy,
and eat! ....Is 55:1
thirty pieces of s for him.................Mt 26:15
I don't have s or gold, but.................Ac 3:6

SIMEON
1. Son of Jacob and Leah (Gn 29:33); with Levi, avenged Dinah's rape by Shechem (34:25-31; 49:5); held as hostage by Joseph (42:24). Tribe with territory within Judah (Jos 19:1-9; Jdg 1:3,17).
2. Devout Jew who blessed the baby Jesus (Lk 2:25-35).
3. Jewish variation of Simon (Ac 15:14; 2Pt 1:1). see PETER

SIMON
1. Apostle Peter's original name (Mt 4:18). see PETER
2. Apostle; called the Zealot (Mt 10:4; Mk 3:18; Lk 6:15; Ac 1:13).
3. Leper who hosted Jesus (Mt 26:6-13).
4. Cyrenian forced to carry Jesus's cross (Mk 15:21).
5. Sorcerer who wanted to buy the power of the Spirit (Ac 8:9-24).
6. Tanner of Joppa who hosted Peter, where Peter saw the vision (Ac 9:43).

SIN (N)
be sure your s will catch up with......Nm 32:23
forgive their s, and heal their land......2Ch 7:14
and my s is always before me.............Ps 51:3
but s is a disgrace to any people. ....Pr 14:34
yet he bore the s of many ....Is 53:12
authority on earth to forgive s-s ....Mt 9:6
forgive us our s-s, for we ....Lk 11:4
takes away the s of the world!............Jn 1:29
The one without s among you..............Jn 8:7
just as s entered the world ....Rm 5:12
For the wages of s is death,.............Rm 6:23
Christ died for our s-s
according to 1Co 15:3
who did not know s to be s for us,......2Co 5:21
way as we are, yet without s.............Heb 4:15
hindrance and the s that so easily......Heb 12:1
confess our s-s, he is faithful 1Jn 1:9
and s is lawlessness........................1Jn 3:4

SIN (V)
you—you alone—I have s-ned ....Ps 51:4
so that I may not s against you..........Ps 119:11
your right eye causes you to s, ...Mt 5:29
If your brother s-s against you,.........Mt 18:15
If your brother s-s, rebuke him, ...Lk 17:3
And if he s-s against you seven...........Lk 17:4
from now on do not s anymore............Jn 8:11
Rabbi, who s-ned, this man or.............Jn 9:2
For all have s-ned and fall short.........Rm 3:23
say, "We have not s-ned," we.............1Jn 1:10
so that you may not s........................1Jn 2:1

SINAI
Mountain where God revealed the Law (Ex 19:20; 31:18; 34:32; Lv 25:1; Ac 7:38; Gl 4:25). The wilderness region (Ex 19:1; Lv 7:38).

SINCERE
s brotherly love for each other,..........1Pt 1:22

SINFUL
I was s when my mother conceived......Ps 51:5
into the hands of s men, ...Lk 24:7

SING
I will s to the LORD, for he is ....Ex 15:1
Let the whole earth s to the LORD......1Ch 16:23
the morning stars sang together............Jb 38:7
S praise to God, s praise;..................Ps 47:6
S a new song to the LORD ....Pss 96:1; 98:1
After s-ing a hymn, they
went out ....Mt 26:30
praying and s-ing hymns to God,........Ac 16:25
songs, s-ing and making music ....Eph 5:19
s-ing to God with gratitude in...........Col 3:16
cheerful? He should s praises............Jms 5:13
they sang a new song: You are ....Rv 5:9

of his death (8:1; 22:20); start of persecution and dispersion (11:19).

STIFLE
Don't s the Spirit. 1Th 5:19

STILL
reflect in your heart while on your bed and be s. Ps 4:4
Silence! Be s!" The wind ceased. Mk 4:39

STING
Sheol, where is your s? Hs 13:14
Where, death, is your s? 1Co 15:55

STIR
but a harsh word s-s up wrath. Pr 15:1
my compassion is **s-red!** Hs 11:8

STOLEN
S water is sweet, Pr 9:17

STOMACH
passes into the s and is eliminated? Mt 15:17
"Food is for the s and the s for food," 1Co 6:13
their god is their s; Php 3:19
a little wine because of your s 1Tm 5:23

STONE (N)
s tablets inscribed by ... God. Ex 31:18
five smooth s-s from the wadi. 1Sm 17:40
strike your foot against a s. Ps 91:12
The s that the builders rejected. Ps 118:22
a time to throw s-s and a time to Ec 3:5
He will be a s to stumble over. Is 8:14
I have laid a s in Zion, a tested s, Is 28:16
remove your heart of s and give. Ezk 36:26
tell these s-s to become bread." Mt 4:3
strike your foot against a s. Mt 4:6
for bread, will give him a s? Mt 7:9
The s that the builders rejected. Mt 21:42
Who will roll away the s from Mk 16:3
silent, the s-s would cry out! Lk 19:40
be the first to throw a s at her. Jn 8:7
stumbled over the stumbling s. Rm 9:32
not on tablets of s but on tablets. 2Co 3:3
to him, a living s—rejected by 1Pt 2:4

STONE (V)
were **s-ing** Stephen, he called out, Ac 7:59

STORE
Don't s up for yourselves treasures Mt 6:19
have anywhere to s my crops? Lk 12:17

STOREHOUSE
brings the wind from his s-s. Jr 10:13; 51:16
Bring the full tenth into the s Mal 3:10

STOREROOM
brings out of his s treasures new Mt 13:52

STORM
and shelter from s and rain. Is 4:6
such a great s arose on the sea Jnh 1:4
a violent s arose on the sea, Mt 8:24

STRAIGHT
make a s highway for our God in Is 40:3
the crooked will become s, Lk 3:5
Make s the way of the Lord Jn 1:23

STRAIN
You s out a gnat, but gulp down Mt 23:24

STRANGER
I was a s and you took me in; Mt 25:35
no longer foreigners and s-s, Eph 2:19
I urge you as s-s and exiles 1Pt 2:11

STRANGLE
eating anything that has been **s-d**, Ac 15:20

STRAP
whose sandal s I'm not worthy to Jn 1:27

STRAW
go and gather s for themselves. Ex 5:7
costly stones, wood, hay, or s, 1Co 3:12

STREAM
planted beside flowing s-s. Ps 1:3
its s-s delight the city of God, Ps 46:4
s-s of living water flow from Jn 7:38

STREET
Wisdom calls out in the s; Pr 1:20
on the s corners to be seen by people. Mt 6:5
s of the city was pure gold, Rv 21:21

STRENGTH
The LORD is my s and my song; Ex 15:2
all your soul, and with all your s. Dt 6:5
does not prevail by his own s. 1Sm 2:9
I love you, LORD, my s. Ps 18:1
The LORD is my s and my shield; Ps 28:7
God is our refuge and s, a helper Ps 46:1
ascribe to the LORD glory and s. Ps 96:7
in the LORD will renew their s; Is 40:31
strong should not boast in his s; Jr 9:23
Not by s or by might, but by my Zch 4:6
your mind, and with all your s. Mk 12:30

STRENGTHEN
have turned back, s your brothers. Lk 22:32
He will also s you to the end, 1Co 1:8
speaks to people for their **s-ing**, 1Co 14:3
be **s-ed** by the Lord and by his Eph 6:10
things through him who s-s me. Php 4:13
Lord who has **s-ed** me, 1Tm 1:12
Therefore s your tired hands Heb 12:12

STRICKEN
but we in turn regarded him s, Is 53:4

STRIFE
a house full of feasting with s. Pr 17:1
there is envy and s among you, 1Co 3:3
sorcery, hatreds, s, jealousy, Gl 5:20

STRIKE
s your head, and you will s his heel. Gn 3:15
and **struck** the rock twice Nm 20:11
you will not s your foot against Ps 91:12
The sun will not s you by day Ps 121:6
S the shepherd, and the sheep will Zch 13:7
you will not s your foot against Mt 4:6
I will s the shepherd, and the Mt 26:31
struck down but not destroyed. 2Co 4:9

STRIP
They **s-ped** him, beat him up, Lk 10:30

STRIVE
Don't s for what you should eat Lk 12:29
s-ing with his strength that works Col 1:29

STROKE
or one s of a letter will pass from. Mt 5:18
than for one s of a letter ... to drop. Lk 16:17

STRONG
Be s and courageous; Dt 31:6
be s and very courageous. Jos 1:7
LORD, s and mighty, the LORD, Ps 24:8
The name of the LORD is a s tower; Pr 18:10
Redeemer is s, and he will Pr 23:11
Their Redeemer is s; the LORD Jr 50:34
can someone enter a s man's house Mt 12:29
The boy grew up and became s, Lk 2:40
Now we who are s have an Rm 15:1
For when I am weak, then I am s. 2Co 12:10

STRONGER
God's weakness is s than human 1Co 1:25

STRONGHOLD
David did capture the s of Zion, 2Sm 5:7
my salvation, my s, my refuge, 2Sm 22:3
the God of Jacob is our s. Ps 46:7,11
my rock and my salvation, my s; Ps 62:2,6
way of the LORD is a s for the Pr 10:29
for the demolition of s-s. 2Co 10:4

STRUGGLE
our s is not against flesh and blood Eph 6:12
s-ing against sin, you have not Heb 12:4

STUBBORN
a s and rebellious generation, Ps 78:8

STUDY
and much s wearies the body. Ec 12:12
Too much s is driving you mad. Ac 26:24

STUMBLE
nothing makes them s. Ps 119:165
when you run, you will not s. Pr 4:12
be a stone to s over and a rock. Is 8:14
cause one of these little ones to s. Lk 17:2
walks during the day, he doesn't s, Jn 11:9
They **s-d** over the **s-ing** stone. Rm 9:32
for we all s in many ways. Jms 3:2
A stone to s over, 1Pt 2:8
who is able to protect you from **s-ing** Jd 24

should have a s
of authority............................1Co 11:10

SYMPATHIZE
a high priest who is unable to s..........Heb 4:15

SYNAGOGUE
teaching in their s-s,
preaching............................Mt 4:23
He entered the s on the Sabbath......... Lk 4:16
They will ban you from the s-s........... Jn 16:2
taught in the s and in the temple .... Jn 18:20
reasoned in the s every Sabbath.......... Ac 18:4
but are a s of Satan........................ Rv 2:9

T

TABERNACLE
the pattern of the t........................Ex 25:9
glory of the LORD filled the t. ....Ex 40:34
more perfect t not made with ....Heb 9:11

TABLE
construct a t of acacia wood,............Ex 25:23
You prepare a t before me in the .... Ps 23:5
overturned the t-s of the
money changers........................ Mt 21:12
and drink at my t in my kingdom.......Lk 22:30
the Lord's t and the t of demons....... 1Co 10:21

TABLET
that I may give you the stone t-s.........Ex 24:12
them on the t of your heart..............Pr 3:3; 7:3
engraved on the t of their hearts ....Jr 17:1
not on t-s of stone but on t-s..............2Co 3:3

TAKE
or t your Holy Spirit from me.............. Ps 51:11
T up my yoke and learn from me,.........Mt 11:29
deny himself, t up his cross,..............Mt 16:24
one will be **taken** and one left..............Mt 24:40
T and eat it; this is my body..............Mt 26:26
who t-s away the sin of the
world!..................................Jn 1:29
they've **taken** away
my Lord, ... Jn 20:13
t up the full armor of God,...............Eph 6:13

TALENTS
To one he gave five t;.....................Mt 25:15

TALK
T about them when you sit in ....Dt 6:7

TALL
He was nine feet, nine inches t..........1Sm 17:4

TAMAR
1. Judah's daughter-in-law; widow of Er and Onan; mother of Judah's sons (Gn 38).
2. Daughter of David; raped by Amnon; avenged by Absalom (2Sm 13).

TAMBOURINE
Praise him with t and dance;.............. Ps 150:4

TARSHISH
Distant Mediterranean port city known for sea trade (1Kg 10:22; 22:48; Pss 48:7; 72:10; Is 2:16; 23:1,6,10,14; 66:19; Jr 10:9; Ezk 27:12,25; 38:13); Jonah fled toward it (Jnh 1:3).

TASTE
T and see that the LORD is good........... Ps 34:8
if the salt should lose its t,...............Mt 5:13
who will not t death until they ....Mt 16:28
he will never t death—ever!' .... Jn 8:52
handle, don't t, don't touch"? ....Col 2:21
grace he might t death for..................Heb 2:9
who t-d the heavenly gift,.................Heb 6:4
if you have t-d that the Lord 1Pt 2:3

TATTOO
not . . . put t marks on yourselves; ....Lv 19:28

TAUNT
crucified with him t-ed him...............Mt 27:44

TAX *SEE ALSO* **TAX COLLECTOR**
lawful to pay t-es to Caesar
or not? ....Mt 22:17
t-es to those you owe t-es,................Rm 13:7

TAX COLLECTOR
Don't even the t-s do the same? ....Mt 5:46
a friend of t-s and sinners!............. Mt 11:19
like an Gentile and a t to you.............Mt 18:17
T-s and prostitutes are entering..........Mt 21:31
one a Pharisee and the other a t........ Lk 18:10
Zacchaeus who was a chief t,............. Lk 19:2

TEACH
T them to your children ....Dt 4:9; 11:19
t me your paths............................Ps 25:4
T us to number our days...................Ps 90:12
No longer will one t his neighbor ....Jr 31:34
t-ing them to observe
everything ....Mt 28:20
t-ing them as one having
authority.............................. Mk 1:22
He **taught** them many things in......... Mk 4:2
t us to pray, just as John
also **taught** ....Lk 11:1
Holy Spirit . . . will t you all things ....Jn 14:26
allow a woman to t or to have 1Tm 2:12
hospitable, able to t, ...1Tm 3:2
will be able to t others also.................2Tm 2:2
correctly t-ing the word of truth....... 2Tm 2:15
able to t, and patient, ...2Tm 2:24
you don't need anyone to t you. 1Jn 2:27

TEACHER
A disciple is not above his t, ...Mt 10:24
you have one T, and you are all..........Mt 23:8
Are you a t of Israel and don't ....Jn 3:10
if I, your Lord and T, have
washed...................................Jn 13:14
some pastors and t-s, ...Eph 4:11
will be false t-s among you..................2Pt 2:1

TEACHING (N)
I will put my t within them ....Jr 31:33
were astonished at his t .... Mt 7:28; 22:33
is contrary to the sound t...................1Tm 1:10
and is profitable for t, ...2Tm 3:16

TEAR (N)
My t-s have been my food
day and ....Ps 42:3
Put my t-s in your bottle....................Ps 56:8
Those who sow in t-s will reap .... Ps 126:5
to wash his feet with her t-s. .... Lk 7:38
away every t from their eyes ....Rv 7:17; 21:4

TEAR (V)
T your hearts, not just your...................Jl 2:13
high priest **tore** his robes and.......... Mt 26:65

TELL
t about all his wonderful works! .... Ps 105:2
he has **told** each of you
what is good ....Mc 6:8
If it were not so, would I have **told** you... Jn 14:2
I have **told** you now before it .... Jn 14:29

TEMPLE
The LORD is in his holy t;........................Ps 11:4
But the LORD is in his holy t;.................Hab 2:20
will suddenly come to his t,..................Mal 3:1
something greater than
the t is here!.............................Mt 12:6
they found him in the t complex .... Lk 2:46
Destroy this t, and I will raise...............Jn 2:19
that you are God's t 1Co 3:16
your body is a t of the Holy 1Co 6:19
Almighty and the Lamb are its t. .... Rv 21:22

TEMPORARY
what is seen is t, but what is 2Co 4:18

TEMPT
wilderness to be **t-ed** by the devil......... Mt 4:1
allow you to be **t-ed** beyond what 1Co 10:13
and he himself doesn't t anyone.......... Jms 1:13
when he was **t-ed**, he is able............Heb 2:18
who has been **t-ed** in every way........Heb 4:15

TEMPTATION
And do not bring us into t,.................Mt 6:13
pray, so that you won't
enter into t. ....Mt 26:41
No t has come upon you except 1Co 10:13

TEMPTER
Then the t approached him and............Mt 4:3

TEN
He wrote the T Commandments,.........Ex 34:28
will be like t virgins who took...............Mt 25:1
to the one who has t talents............ Mt 25:28
Were not t cleansed?..........................Lk 17:17
The t horns you saw are t kings ....Rv 17:12

TEN THOUSAND
one who owed t talents was...............Mt 18:24
than t words in a tongue. 1Co 14:19

TEND
I will t my flock and let them ....Ezk 34:15

TENDERLY
Speak t to Jerusalem, and.....................Is 40:2

TENT
ark of God sits inside **t** curtains.......... 2Sm 7:2
dwell in your **t** forever and .... Ps 61:4
Enlarge the site of your **t**,................ Is 54:2

TENTH
Abram gave him a **t** of everything...... Gn 14:20
give to you a **t** of all that you give...... Gn 28:22
Bring the full **t** into the storehouse..... Mal 3:10
You pay a **t** of mint, dill, and .... Mt 23:23
I give a **t** of everything I get. .... Lk 18:12

TERRIBLE
great and **t** day of the LORD .... Jl 2:31; Mal 4:5

TERRIFY
around them, and they were **t-ied**........ Lk 2:9
It is a **t-ing** thing to fall into .... Heb 10:31

TERROR
not fear the **t** of the night, ... Ps 91:5
are not a **t** to good conduct .... Rm 13:3

TEST
God **t-ed** Abraham....................... Gn 22:1
Do not **t** the LORD your God.............. Dt 6:16
The LORD left them to **t** Israel, ... Jdg 3:4
t me and know my concerns........... Ps 139:23
but the LORD is the **t-er** of hearts.......... Pr 17:3
stone in Zion, a **t-ed** stone,............... Is 28:16
T me in this way," says the LORD .... Mal 3:10
Do not **t** the Lord your God.............. Mt 4:7
approached him to **t** him. .... Mt 19:3
expert in the law stood up to **t** him..... Lk 10:25
asked this to **t** him, for he . . . knew .... Jn 6:6
did you agree to **t** the Spirit.............. Ac 5:9
t all things. Hold on to what 1Th 5:21
but **t** the spirits to see.................... 1Jn 4:1

TESTIFY
is another who **t-ies** about me, ... Jn 5:32
the Scriptures . . . **t** about me. .... Jn 5:39
the Spirit . . . he will **t** about me.......... Jn 15:26
Spirit himself **t-ies** together .... Rm 8:16
For there are three that **t**:................. 1Jn 5:7

TESTIMONY
Do not give false **t** against your......... Ex 20:16
based on the **t** of one witness.......... Nm 35:30
the **t** of the LORD is trustworthy, ... Ps 19:7
Bind up the **t**. Seal up the .... Is 8:16
looking for false **t** against Jesus .... Mt [illegible]
We know that his **t** is true............... Jn 21:24

THANKS
Give **t** to the LORD; call on............... 1Ch 16:8
Give **t** to the LORD, . . . he is good 1Ch 16:34
Give **t** to him and bless his name........ Ps 100:4
Give **t** to the LORD, for he is good......... Ps 136:1
gave **t**, broke them, and gave .... Mt 15:36
and after giving **t**, he gave it .... Mt 26:27
But **t** be to God, who gives us 1Co 15:57
Give **t** in everything; for this........... 1Th 5:18

THANKSGIVING
Let's enter his presence with **t**; .... Ps 95:2
Enter his gates with **t** and .... Ps 100:4
I will offer you a **t** sacrifice .... Ps 116:17

through prayer and petition with **t**, ... Php 4:6

THIEF
and where **t-ves** don't break in and ..... Mt 6:19
you are making it a den of **t-ves**! .... Mt 21:13
what time the **t** was coming, ... Mt 24:43
other way is a **t** and a robber............. Jn 10:1
Let the **t** no longer steal................. Eph 4:28
come just like a **t** in the night.......... 1Th 5:2
Look, I am coming like a **t**.............. Rv 16:15

THING
all these **t-s** will be provided............. Mt 6:33
with God all **t-s** are possible............. Mt 19:26
kept all these **t-s** in her heart............ Lk 2:51
But one **t** I do: Forgetting .... Php 3:13
praiseworthy—dwell on these **t-s**....... Php 4:8
able to do all **t-s** through him........... Php 4:13

THINK *SEE ALSO* THOUGHT (N)
son of man, that you **t** of him?.......... Ps 144:3
not to **t** of himself more highly than ... Rm 12:3
a child, I **thought** like a child, ... 1Co 13:11
beyond all that we ask or **t**............. Eph 3:20

THIRD
and on the **t** day he will raise............ Hs 6:2
killed, and be raised the **t** day........... Mt 16:21
raised on the **t** day according to......... 1Co 15:4

THIRST
I **t** for God, the living God. .... Ps 42:2
who hunger and **t** for righteousness ..... Mt 5:6
they will no longer **t**;.................... Rv 7:16

THIRSTY
and if he is **t**, give him water........... Pr 25:21
everyone who is **t**, come to the .... Is 55:1
was **t** and you gave me something .... Mt 25:35
this water will get **t** again................. Jn 4:13
in me will ever be **t** again. .... Jn 6:35
If anyone is **t**, let him come .... Jn 7:37
Let the one who is **t** come............... Rv 22:17

THIRTY
my wages, **t** pieces of silver............ Zch 11:12
weighed out **t** pieces of silver .... Mt 26:15
Jesus was about **t** years old and .... Lk 3:23

THISTLES
[illegible] thorns and **t** for you .... Gn 3:18

THOMAS
Apostle; sought evidence of resurrection; made confession of faith (Jn 20:24-29).

THORN
It will produce **t-s** and thistles........... Gn 3:18
fell among **t-s**, and the **t-s** came up...... Mt 13:7
twisted together a crown of **t-s**, ... Mt 27:29
t in the flesh was given to me, ... 2Co 12:7

THOUGHT (N)
The LORD knows the **t-s** of mankind; .... Ps 94:11
You understand my **t-s** from far........ Ps 139:2
My **t-s** are not your **t-s**, ... Is 55:8

Perceiving their **t-s**, Jesus said, ... Mt 9:4
take every **t** captive to obey 2Co 10:5

THOUSAND
his **t-s**, but David his tens of **t-s**. 1Sm 18:7
the cattle on a **t** hills...................... Ps 50:10
in your sight a **t** years are like .... Ps 90:4
one day is like a **t** years,.................... 2Pt 3:8
and bound him for a **t** years.............. Rv 20:2
reign with him for a **t** years.............. Rv 20:6

THREATEN
he suffered, he did not **t** 1Pt 2:23

THREE
cord of **t** strands is not easily............ Ec 4:12
the huge fish **t** days and **t** nights, ... Mt 12:40
For where two or **t** are gathered .... Mt 18:20
you will deny me **t** times." .... Mt 26:34
and rebuild it in **t** days. .... Mt 26:61
killed, and rise after **t** days............. Mk 8:31
Now these **t** remain: faith, hope,....... 1Co 13:13
For there are **t** that testify:................ 1Jn 5:7

THRESHING FLOOR
David bought the **t**........................ 2Sm 24:24

THROAT
their **t** is an open grave;.................... Ps 5:9
Their **t** is an open grave;................. Rm 3:13

THRONE
will establish the **t** of his
kingdom 2Sm 7:13
Your **t**, God, is forever and ever; .... Ps 45:6
seated on a high and lofty **t**, ... Is 6:1
He will reign on the **t** of David............. Is 9:7
Heaven is my **t**, and earth is my........... Is 66:1
heaven, because it is God's **t**; .... Mt 5:34
will also sit on twelve **t-s**,................ Mt 19:28
whether **t-s** or dominions or .... Col 1:16
Your **t**, God, is forever and .... Heb 1:8
let us approach the **t** of grace
with .... Heb 4:16
cast their crowns before the **t**,........... Rv 4:10
great white **t** and one seated on it....... Rv 20:11

THROW
He has **t-n** the horse and its rider .... Ex 15:1
should be the first to **t** a
stone at her................................ Jn 8:7

THUNDERCLOUD
I answered you from the **t**. .... Ps 81:7

TIME
for such a **t** as this........................ Est 4:14
a **t** for every activity under
heaven:..................................... Ec 3:1
for a **t**, **t-s**, and half a **t**............... Dn 7:25; 12:7
Teacher says: My **t** is near;............... Mt 26:18
you will deny me three **t-s**! .... Mt 26:34
My **t** has not yet fully come, ... Jn 7:6
It is not for you to know **t-s** .... Ac 1:7
making the most of the **t**................. Col 4:5
About the **t-s** and the
seasons:.................................... 1Th 5:1
for a **t**, **t-s**, and half a **t**................... Rv 12:14

TIMOTHY
Companion of Paul (Ac 16–20; Rm 16:21; 2Co 1:1; 1Th 1:1; 2Th 1:1; Php 1:1; Phm 1). Sent by Paul to Corinth (1Co 4:17); to Philippi (Php 2:19); to Thessalonica (1Th 3:2). Pastored Ephesian church (1Tm 1:3). Received two letters from Paul (1Tm 1:2; 2Tm 1:2) and a plea to come (4:9).

TIRED
let us not get t of doing good, . . . Gl 6:9

TITUS
Gentile coworker with Paul (Gl 2:1-3; 2Co 8:23). Sent to Corinth (2:1-4; 7:13-15; 8:16-17); in charge of church in Crete (Ti 1:5); went to Dalmatia (2Tm 4:10).

TOBIAH
Adversary against Nehemiah's efforts to rebuild Jerusalem's walls (Neh 2:10,19; 4:1-9; 6; 13:4-9).

TODAY
T, if you hear his voice: . . . Ps 95:7
Give us t our daily bread. . . . Mt 6:11
T you will be with me in paradise. . . . Lk 23:43
t I have become your Father, . . . Heb 1:5; 5:5
while it is still called t, . . . Heb 3:13
T, if you hear his voice, do not . . . Heb 3:15
same yesterday, t, and forever. . . . Heb 13:8

TOLA
Issacharite judge (Jdg 10:1-2).

TOLERABLE
It will be more t on the day of . . . Mt 10:15

TOLERATE
will not t sound doctrine, . . . 2Tm 4:3
and that you cannot t evil people. . . . Rv 2:2

TOMB
You are like whitewashed t-s, . . . Mt 23:27
he laid him in a t cut out of . . . Mk 15:46
stone rolled away from the t. . . . Lk 24:2
already been in the t four days. . . . Jn 11:17

TOMORROW
Don't boast about t, for you don't. . . . Pr 27:1
Let's eat and drink, for t we die! . . . Is 22:13
Therefore don't worry about t, . . . Mt 6:34
us eat and drink, for t we die. . . . 1Co 15:32
do not know what t will bring— . . . Jms 4:14

TONGUE
Before a word is on my t, you. . . . Ps 139:4
death are in the power of the t, . . . Pr 18:21
every t will swear allegiance. . . . Is 45:23
t-s like flames of fire that. . . . Ac 2:3
in t-s and declaring . . . Ac 10:46
in t-s and to prophesy. . . . Ac 19:6
interpretation of t-s. . . . 1Co 12:10
If I speak human or angelic t-s . . . 1Co 13:1
as for t-s, they will cease; . . . 1Co 13:8
person who speaks in a t . . . 1Co 14:2
not forbid speaking in t-s. . . . 1Co 14:39
and every t will confess that. . . . Php 2:11
but no man can tame the t. . . . Jms 3:8

TOOTH
eye for eye, t for t . . . Ex 21:24; Lv 24:20; Dt 19:21
for an eye and a t for a t. . . . Mt 5:38
weeping and gnashing of teeth. . . . Mt 8:12

TOP
was torn in two from t to bottom, . . . Mt 27:51

TORCH
fire pot and a flaming t appeared . . . Gn 15:17

TORMENT
come here to t us before the time? . . . Mt 8:29
those t-ed by unclean spirits . . . Lk 6:18
they will be t-ed day and night . . . Rv 20:10

TORRENT
the t would have swept over us; . . . Ps 124:4

TOSS
driven and t-ed by the wind. . . . Jms 1:6

TOUCH
You must not eat it or t it, . . . Gn 3:3
t-ed my mouth with it and said: . . . Is 6:7
If I can just t his robe, . . . Mt 9:21
in order that he might t them, . . . Mk 10:13
T me and see, because a ghost . . . Lk 24:39
Don't handle, don't taste, don't t"? . . . Col 2:21
and have t-ed with our hands, . . . 1Jn 1:1

TOWEL
took a t, and tied it around himself. . . . Jn 13:4

TOWER
a t with its top in the sky. . . . Gn 11:4
name of the LORD is a strong t; . . . Pr 18:10

TOWN
and from the t of Bethlehem, . . . Jn 7:42

TRADERS
When Midianite t passed by, . . . Gn 37:28

TRADITION
nullify the word of God by your t. . . . Mk 7:13
empty deceit based on human t, . . . Col 2:8
hold to the t-s you were taught, . . . 2Th 2:15

TRAGEDY
a sickening t . . . Ec 5:13,16
Here is a t I have observed . . . Ec 6:1

TRAIN
who t-s my hands for battle and. . . . Ps 144:1
will never again t for war. . . . Is 2:4; Mc 4:3

TRAINING
them up in the t and instruction . . . Eph 6:4
t of the body has a limited benefit, . . . 1Tm 4:8
correcting, for t in righteousness, . . . 2Tm 3:16

TRAITOR
Judas Iscariot, who became a t. . . . Lk 6:16

TRAMPLE
be thrown out and t-d under . . . Mt 5:13
pearls before pigs, or they will t. . . . Mt 7:6
Jerusalem will be t-d by the . . . Lk 21:24
who has t-d on the Son of God, . . . Heb 10:29

TRAMPLING (N)
you—this t of my courts? . . . Is 1:12

TRANSFIGURE
He was t-ed in front of them, . . . Mt 17:2

TRANSFORM
be t-ed by the renewing of your . . . Rm 12:2
are being t-ed into the same image . . . 2Co 3:18
He will t the body of our humble . . . Php 3:21

TRANSGRESSION
is the one whose t is forgiven, . . . Ps 32:1
has he removed our t-s from us. . . . Ps 103:12
I am the one, I sweep away your t-s . . . Is 43:25
where there is no law, there is no t. . . . Rm 4:15

TRANSLATE
law . . . t-ing and giving the meaning . . . Neh 8:8
Immanuel . . . t-d "God is with us." . . . Mt 1:23

TRAP
their gods will be a t for you. . . . Jdg 2:3
to t him by what he said. . . . Mt 22:15
into disgrace and the devil's t. . . . 1Tm 3:7

TREAD
your foot t-s will be yours. . . . Dt 11:24
ox while it t-s out grain. . . . Dt 25:4; 1Co 9:9
ox while it is t-ing out the grain, . . . 1Tm 5:18

TREASURE (N)
for yourselves t-s on earth, . . . Mt 6:19
For where your t is, there your . . . Mt 6:21
The kingdom of heaven is like t, . . . Mt 13:44
and you will have t in heaven. . . . Mt 19:21
Now we have this t in clay jars, . . . 2Co 4:7
the t-s of wisdom and knowledge . . . Col 2:3

TREASURE (V)
I have t-d your word in my heart . . . Ps 119:11
But Mary was t-ing up all these . . . Lk 2:19

TREATY
Make no t with them . . . Dt 7:2
Please make a t with us. . . . Jos 9:6

UNCIRCUMCISED
house of Israel is u in heart. Jr 9:26
A man who is physically u, Rm 2:27
called "the u" by those called Eph 2:11

UNCIRCUMCISION
matter and u does not matter, 1Co 7:19
circumcision nor u accomplishes Gl 5:6
circumcision and u, barbarian, Col 3:11

UNCLEAN
if someone touches anything u. Lv 5:2
I am a man of u lips and live among Is 6:5
gave them authority over u spirits, Mt 10:1
Whenever the u spirits saw him. Mk 3:11
I have never eaten anything ... u! Ac 10:14
am persuaded ... that nothing is u Rm 14:14

UNCLOTHED
do not want to be u but clothed, 2Co 5:4

UNCOVER
go in and u his feet, and lie down. Ru 3:4
with her head u-ed dishonors her. 1Co 11:5

UNDEFILED
and the marriage bed kept u, Heb 13:4

UNDER
no other name u heaven given to. Ac 4:12
you are not u the law but u grace. Rm 6:14

UNDERNEATH
and u are the everlasting arms. Dt 33:27

UNDERSTAND
then you will u the fear of the LORD Pr 2:5
Keep listening, but do not u; Is 6:9
u with their hearts and turn back Mt 13:15
holy place" (let the reader u), Mt 24:15
Then he opened their minds to u Lk 24:45
but u what the Lord's will is. Eph 5:17
some things hard to u in them. 2Pt 3:16

UNDERSTANDING (N)
and do not rely on your own u; Pr 3:5

UNEDUCATED
that they were u and untrained Ac 4:13

UNFADING
and u, kept in heaven 1Pt 1:4
receive the u crown of glory. 1Pt 5:4

UNFRUITFUL
but my understanding is u. 1Co 14:14

UNGODLY
time, Christ died for the u. Rm 5:6

UNINFORMED
We do not want you to be u, 1Th 4:13

UNITED
were continually u in prayer, Ac 1:14

UNITY
until we all reach u in the faith Eph 4:13
the perfect bond of u. Col 3:14

UNJUST
Listen to what the u judge says. Lk 18:6
For God is not u; he will not Heb 6:10

UNKNOWN
'To an U God.' Ac 17:23

UNLEAVENED
observe the Festival of U Bread Ex 12:17
On the first day of U Bread. Mt 26:17

UNMARRIED
I say to the u and to widows: 1Co 7:8

UNNATURAL
natural sexual relations for u ones. Rm 1:26

UNPUNISHED
will not leave the guilty u, Ex 34:7
that the wicked will not go u, Pr 11:21

UNQUENCHABLE
and go to hell, the u fire, Mk 9:43

UNRIGHTEOUS
rain on the righteous and the u. Mt 5:45
whoever is u in very little is also. Lk 16:10
the righteous for the u, 1Pt 3:18

UNRIGHTEOUSNESS
and there is no u in him. Ps 92:15
and to cleanse us from all u. 1Jn 1:9

UNSEARCHABLE
How u his judgments and Rm 11:33

UNSEEN
temporary, but what is u is eternal. 2Co 4:18

UNSHRUNK
an old garment with u cloth, Mt 9:16

UNSTABLE
double-minded and u in all his ways. Jms 1:8
They seduce u people 2Pt 2:14

UNTIE
sandal strap I'm not worthy to u. Jn 1:27

UNTRACEABLE
his judgments and u his ways! Rm 11:33

UNVEILED
We all, with u faces, are looking 2Co 3:18

UNWORTHY
cup of the Lord in an u way. 1Co 11:27

UPRIGHT
The u will see his face. Ps 11:7
God made people u, but they Ec 7:29

UPROOT
Be u-ed and planted in the sea, Lk 17:6

UPSTAIRS
He will show you a large room u, Mk 14:15

UR
City in lower Mesopotamia; birthplace of Abraham (Gn 11:28,31; 15:7; Neh 9:7).

URIAH
Hethite; husband of Bathsheba. One of David's warriors (2Sm 23:39); David arranged his death (2Sm 11).

URIM
Place the U and Thummim in the. Ex 28:30

USEFUL
now he is u both to you and to me. Phm 11

USELESS
that faith without works is u? Jms 2:20

UZZIAH
Son of Amaziah; king of Judah; also known as Azariah (2Kg 15:1-7). Made king by popular acclaim (2Ch 26:1); expanded and fortified Judah (26:6-15); struck with skin disease when he attempted to serve as priest (26:16-21).

V

VAIN
and the peoples plot in v? Ps 2:1
its builders labor over it in v; Ps 127:1
They worship me in v, Mt 15:9
labor in the Lord is not in v. 1Co 15:58
and had not been running, in v. Gl 2:2

VALLEY
when I go through the darkest v, Ps 23:4
Every v will be lifted up, Is 40:4
multitudes in the v of decision! Jl 3:14
Every v will be filled, and every Lk 3:5

VALUE
despised, and we didn't v him. Is 53:3
the surpassing v of knowing Php 3:8
any v in curbing self-indulgence. Col 2:23

WICKED

w men of the city surrounded......... Jdg 19:22
does not walk in the advice of the w ...... Ps 1:1
He was assigned a grave with the w,..... Is 53:9
no pleasure in the death of the w,..... Ezk 33:11

WICKEDNESS

saw that human w was widespread...... Gn 6:5

WIDE

the gate is w and the road broad .... Mt 7:13

WIDOW

Support w-s who are genuinely in need. .1Tm 5:3

WIFE

and mother and bonds with his w,...... Gn 2:24
Do not covet your neighbor's w,....... Ex 20:17
seven hundred w-ves ... turned
his heart 1Kg 11:3
pleasure in the w of your youth. .... Pr 5:18
A man who finds a w finds a good ..... Pr 18:22
Who can find a w of noble
character? .... Pr 31:10
should have ... with his own w,......... 1Co 7:2
W-ves, submit to your .... Eph 5:22
Husbands, love your w-ves, ... Eph 5:25
husband of one w,....................... 1Tm 3:2
the bride, the w of the Lamb. .... Rv 21:9

WILD

Without revelation people run w,...... Pr 29:18
food was locusts and w honey............ Mt 3:4
you, though a w olive branch,........... Rm 11:17
in the same flood of w living 1Pt 4:4

WILDERNESS

Prepare the way of the LORD
in the w;................................ Is 40:3
voice of one crying out in the w: .... Mt 3:3
into the w to be tempted.................. Mt 4:1
ancestors ate the manna in the w,..... Jn 6:31,49

WILDFLOWERS

Consider how the w grow: .... Lk 12:27

WILL (N)

I delight to do your w, my God;.......... Ps 40:8
Your w be done on earth as it is .... Mt 6:10
one who does the w of my Father .... Mt 7:21
Yet not as I w, but as you w............ Mt 26:39
My food is to do the w of him .... Jn 4:34
hand and your w had predestined
to take place .... Ac 4:28
it does not depend on human w........ Rm 9:16
the good, pleasing, and perfect w ...... Rm 12:2
See, I have come to do your w.......... Heb 10:9
ask anything according to his w,........ 1Jn 5:14

WILL (V)

say, "If the Lord w-s, we will .... Jms 4:15

WILLING (ADJ)

giving me a w spirit...................... Ps 51:12
her wings, but you were not w!......... Mt 23:37
The spirit is w, but the flesh .... Mt 26:41
if you are w, take this cup away .... Lk 22:42

WIND

but the LORD was not in the w. 1Kg 19:11
soaring on the wings of the w. .... Ps 18:10
will inherit the w,........................ Pr 11:29
they sow the w and reap the .... Hs 8:7
the w-s and the sea obey him!........... Mt 8:27
The w blows where it pleases,............ Jn 3:8
around by every w of teaching, ... Eph 4:14

WINDSTORM

A great w arose, and the waves......... Mk 4:37

WINE

W is a mocker, beer is a brawler, ... Pr 20:1
and w to one whose life is bitter.......... Pr 31:6
no one puts new w into old............... Mt 9:17
water (after it had become w),............. Jn 2:9
said, "They're drunk on new w!"......... Ac 2:13
And don't get drunk with w,............. Eph 5:18
not drinking a lot of w, ... 1Tm 3:3; Ti 1:7
a little w because of your
stomach................................ 1Tm 5:23

WINESKIN

no one puts new wine into old w-s. ..... Mt 9:17

WING

I carried you on eagles' w-s .... Ex 19:4
under whose w-s you have come .... Ru 2:12
soaring on the w-s of the wind. 2Sm 22:11
hide me in the shadow of
your w-s .... Ps 17:8
soaring on the w-s of the wind. .... Ps 18:10
will soar on w-s like eagles; .... Is 40:31
rise with healing in its w-s,............... Mal 4:2
gathers her chicks under her w-s,...... Mt 23:37

WINTER

Pray it won't happen in w............... Mk 13:18

WIPE

Lord GOD will w away the tears .... Is 25:8
She w-d his feet with the hair .... Lk 7:38
will w away every tear.............. Rv 7:17; 21:4

WISDOM

God gave Solomon w,................... 1Kg 4:29
of the LORD is the beginning of w,........ Pr 9:10
Yet w is vindicated by all her .... Lk 7:35
the w and the knowledge............... Rm 11:33
I will destroy the w of the wise, ... 1Co 1:19
able to give you w for salvation 2Tm 3:15
Now if any of you lacks w,................ Jms 1:5
and riches and w and strength........... Rv 5:12

WISE

making the inexperienced w. .... Ps 19:7
is considered w when he keeps .... Pr 17:28
w men from the east arrived .... Mt 2:1
hidden these things from the w .... Mt 11:25
foolish ... to shame the w,.............. 1Co 1:27

WITHER

and its leaf does not w..................... Ps 1:3
The grass w-s, the flowers fade........... Is 40:7
it had no root, it w-ed away.............. Mt 13:6
At once the fig tree w-ed................ Mt 21:19
grass w-s, and the flower falls, ... 1Pt 1:24

WITHHOLD

have not w-held your only son...... Gn 22:12,16

WITNESS

the testimony of two or three w-es...... Dt 19:15
two or three w-es every fact may ...... Mt 18:16
many false w-es came forward......... Mt 26:60
will be my w-es in Jerusalem,............. Ac 1:8
a good confession ... many w-es. 1Tm 6:12
large cloud of w-es surrounding....... Heb 12:1
from Jesus Christ, the faithful w,.......... Rv 1:5
grant my two w-es authority............. Rv 11:3

WOE

W is me for I am ruined.................... Is 6:5
w to you, scribes and Pharisees,........ Mt 23:13
W to you who are now full,.............. Lk 6:25
And w to me if I do not preach 1Co 9:16
W! W! W to those who live on .... Rv 8:13

WOLF

The w will dwell with the lamb, ... Is 11:6
you out like sheep among w-ves......... Mt 10:16
savage w-ves will come in............. Ac 20:29

WOMAN

this one will be called "w,"............... Gn 2:23
w who fears the LORD ... praised....... Pr 31:30
who looks at a w lustfully .... Mt 5:28
There were also w-en watching....... Mk 15:40
Blessed are you among w-en, ... Lk 1:42
brought a w caught in adultery .... Jn 8:3
for a man not to have sexual relations
with a w." 1Co 7:1
the man is the head of the w,............ 1Co 11:3
w-en should be silent in the........... 1Co 14:34
God sent his Son, born of a w,............. Gl 4:4
I do not allow a w to teach.............. 1Tm 2:12

WOMB

Two nations are in your w;............ Gn 25:23
Naked I came from my mother's w,....... Jb 1:21
me together in my mother's w......... Ps 139:13
me from the w to be his servant,......... Is 49:5
before I formed you in the w;.............. Jr 1:5
his mother's w a second time .... Jn 3:4

WONDERFUL

He will be named W Counselor, ... Is 9:6
and it is w in our eyes?.................. Mt 21:42

WONDERS

God of Israel, who alone does w......... Ps 72:18
I will display w in the heaven............ Ac 2:19

WONDROUS

tell about all his w works! .... Ps 105:2
it is w in our sight....................... Ps 118:23
w things from your instruction.......... Ps 119:18
Your works are w, and I know......... Ps 139:14

WONDROUSLY

been remarkably and w made......... Ps 139:14

WOOD

I bow down to a block of w?" .... Is 44:19
costly stones, w, hay, or straw,.......... 1Co 3:12

YOUTHFUL

Z

ZACCHAEUS

Tax collector who hosted Jesus and was converted (Lk 19:2-9).

ZEAL

ZEBULUN

Son of Jacob and Leah (Gn 30:20). Tribe with territory between the Sea of Galilee and Mount Carmel (Jos 19:10-16).

ZECHARIAH

1. Son of Jeroboam II; king of Israel (2Kg 15:8-12).
2. Prophet after the exile; son of Berechiah; descendant of Iddo (Ezr 5:1; Zch 1:1).
3. Father of John the Baptist (Lk 1:5-23,59-79).

ZEDEKIAH

Son of Josiah; last king of Judah; originally called Mattaniah; sons blinded; exiled (2Kg 24:17–25:7).

ZEPHANIAH

Prophet to Josiah; descendant of Hezekiah (Zph 1:1).

ZERUBBABEL

Leader of those returning from exile to rebuild the temple (Ezr 2:2; 4:2; 5:2; Hg 1:1). Descendant of David and Jehoiachin; ancestor of Jesus (1Ch 3:9-19; Mt 1:13; Lk 3:27).

ZIMRI

Chariot commander; killed Elah king of Israel; reigned seven days (1Kg 16:8-20).

ZION

Specifically, the stronghold in Jerusalem; also refers to the temple, hill, city, people, and heavenly city.

# #

430

666

1,260

144,000

ART CREDITS

Holman Bible Publishers is grateful to the following persons and institutions for the graphics in the *CSB Holy Land Illustrated Bible*. Where we have inadvertently failed to give proper credit for any graphic in the Bible, please contact us (customerservice@lifeway.com), and we will make the required correction in subsequent printings.

BIBLICAL ILLUSTRATOR PHOTOGRAPHS

Biblical Illustrator, Nashville, Tennessee: pp. 41 (top); 629; 631; 689; 692; 693; 702; 974 (top); 1165; 1166; 1300; 1464; 1465; 1511; 1522; 1603; 1631; 1707; 1770 (top).

British Museum, London: pp. 4 (middle left); 7 (bottom); 12 (bottom); 106; 109; 113 (top); 125; 134 (center right); 151 (bottom); 169 (top); 260 (top); 261 (center right); 266 (bottom); 267 (bottom); 288 (top); 319 (bottom right); 320 (top & center right); 321; 333 (bottom); 354; 360 (bottom); 361 (top & bottom); 367; 400; 480; 481 (center left); 512 (bottom); 513 (top); 520 (top); 529; 530 (left & right); 559; 569; 600 (bottom left); 627; 628; 643; 646 (left); 650 (both); 656; 657; 688, 698; 707; 728 (top); 729; 731;746; 801; 843; 849 (center right); 860; 861; 882; 911; 916 (both); 934; 935; 955; 956; 957 (left); 973; 974 (bottom); 975; 984; 1003; 1016; 1017 (top left); 1105; 1147; 1157 (both); 1162; 1175; 1186; 1187 (bottom); 1189; 1193; 1197; 1229; 1230 (both); 1235; 1239; 1240; 1241; 1247; 1250 (both); 1251; 1259; 1260; 1262; 1263 1274; 1275 (top); 1279; 1283; 1284; 1285; 1298; 1346 (bottom); 1361; 1374; 1381 (bottom left); 1384 (bottom); 1389; 1417; 1509; 1518 (both); 1519; 1607; 1620; 1661; 1672; 1673 (top); 1682 (top); 1687; 1730 (left); 1738 (right); 1749 (right); 1764 (right); 1797; 1799 (center left); 1806; 1812; 1825; 1826; 1842; 1862.

FreeIsraelPhotos.com: p. 770.

LifeWay/Fon Scofiled Collection: p. 1257.

Morton-Seats Collection, Midwestern Baptist Theological Seminary: pp. 475 (center right); 957 (right).

Jerry Vardaman Collection: pp. 47; 351; 514 (bottom); 613; 615 (bottom); 625; 638 (center left; Cincinnati Museum); 661; 920 (top); 1381 (bottom right); 1457 (right); 1477; 1502; 1549 (bottom); 1557; 1697.

Anderson, Jeff: pp. 39; 312 (top); 1365; 1845.

Borgan, Joy: pp. 745 (National Museum of Roman Art); 1436 (National Museum of Roman Art); 1686; 1712 (National Museum of Roman Art).

Bruce, Brent: pp. 26 (bottom); 34; 36; 55 (Israel Museum, Jerusalem); 69 (bottom); 72 (center; Oriental Institute Museum, University of Chicago); 78 (Ashmolean Museum, Oxford, England); 83 (bottom; Walters Art Museum, Baltimore); 85 (left & bottom right); 141 (top & bottom); 151 (top right; Lynn H. Wood Archaeological Museum; Southern Adventist University, Collegedale, TN); 159 (Oriental Institute Museum, University of Chicago); 182 (Southern Adventist University, Collegedale, TN); 218; 251 (University of Pennsylvania Museum of Archaeology and Anthropology); 261 (bottom); 268 (bottom left; Ashmolean Museum, Oxford); 279; 284 (right; Oriental Institute Museum, University of Chicago); 284 (left; Walters Art Museum, Baltimore); 292; 293 (bottom); 345; 348; 349; 364 (bottom); 365; 388 (top); 431 (top right); 441; 469; 470 (both); 491; 492 (top & bottom); 521 (top); 522 (top right); 531; 548 (Eretz Israel Museum, Tel Aviv, Israel); 608; 609; 647 (top right; Metropolitan Museum of Art, New York); 665 (University of Pennsylvania Museum of Archaeology and Anthropology); 674; 679 (top); 695 (Southern Adventist University, Collegedale, TN); 709 (Saint Louis Museum of Art); 751; 789; 798; 846; 849 (bottom; Israel Museum, Jerusalem); 889 (Metropolitan Museum of Art); 890 (Eretz Israel Museum, Tel Aviv); 991; 1007; 1017 (top right; Metropolitan Museum of Art, New York); 1085; 1182 (University of Pennsylvania Museum of Archaeology and Anthropology); 1207 (Israel Museum, Jerusalem); 1211; 1225; 1306; 1313 (Museum of the Ancient Orient, Istanbul); 1324 (Metropolitan Museum of Art, New York); 1335 (Metropolitan Museum of Art, New York); 1338; 1342 (Metropolitan Museum of Art, New York); 1348 (Metropolitan Museum of Art, New York); 1357 (University of Pennsylvania Museum of Archaeology and Anthropology); 1360 (bottom; Ashmolean Museum, Oxford); 1396 (Israel Museum); 1399; 1407 (top); 1418; 1444; 1484 (bottom); 1487; 1508 (Metropolitan Museum of Art, New York); 1512; 1516; 1517; 1528; 1594; 1650 (University of Pennsylvania Museum of Archaeology and Anthropology); 1673 (bottom; Ashmolean Museum, Oxford); 1683 (University of Pennsylvania Museum of Archaeology and Anthropology); 1685 (top); 1755 (University of Pennsylvania Museum of Archaeology and Anthropology); 1790 (bottom; Walters Art Museum, Baltimore); 1821 (top; Naples Archaeological Museum, Naples, Italy); 1860 (Naples Archaeological Museum, Naples, Italy); 1861 (Metropolitan Museum of Art, New York).

Eddinger, Terry: pp. 23; 49; 348 (bottom right); 1336; 1398; 1413; 1820.

Gaffney, Philip J.: pp. 20; 21.

Herr, Larry: p. 175.

Hiller, Kristen: pp. 40 (top); 85 (center right); 140; 189; 229; 233; 237; 238; 240 (top & bottom); 267 (top right; Eretz Israel Museum, Tel Aviv University); 293 (top); 315; 319 (top; Eretz Museum, Tel Aviv University); 326; 431 (bottom): 489 (top & bottom); 493; 735; 771; 818; 954 (top right); 999; 1183 (Eretz Israel Museum, Tel Aviv University); 1217; 1221 (both); 1222; 1288 (Eretz Israel Museum, Tel Aviv University); 1322; 1339 (left); 1368; 1372; 1395; 1406; 1415 (both); 1445; 1457 (left); 1470; 1471; 1532; 1553; 1799 (bottom); 1818; 1819.

Hooke, Tom: pp. 51 (top; Archaeological Museum of Piraeus, Greece); 647; 736 (bottom); 1535; 1571;1576 (foreground); 1577; 1638; 1649 (left; Corinth Museum); 1693 (both); 1698; 1699; 1702; 1790 (top); 1835; 1849.

Howell Jr., G.B.: pp. 48; 54 (The Louvre); 71 (The Louvre); 74 (The Louvre); 75 (Chicago Field Museum); 81 (bottom; The Louvre); 82 (Art Institute of Chicago); 83 (The Louvre); 84 (The Louvre); 87 (Cincinnati Museum); 103 (Chicago Field Museum) 113 (bottom; Oriental Institute Museum, University of Chicago); 115 (top right; The Louvre); 122; 133 (top; The Louvre); 134 (top left; The Louvre); 149 (top & bottom); 150 (The Louvre); 169 (bottom left); 205; 247 (bottom left; The Louvre); 260 (bottom right; The Louvre); 289 (left; The Louvre); 313 (The Louvre); 333 (top left; The Louvre); 355 (Oriental Institute Museum, University of Chicago); 364 (top); 372 (The Louvre); 403; 420 (The Louvre); 421 (The Louvre); 439; 448 (The Louvre); 449; 460; 471 (top); 481 (top); 514 (top left); 520 (bottom right); 527 (Chicago Field Museum); 549; 554; 581 (The Louvre); 600 (top); 683; 699 (North Carolina Museum of Art, Raleigh); 701 (The Louvre); 703 (Museum of Fine Arts, Boston); 736 (top left; Oriental Institute Museum, University of Chicago); 747 (both; The Louvre); 769; 776 (Chicago Field Museum); 777; 788 (Oriental Institute Museum, University of Chicago); 823; 842; 903 (Oriental Institute Museum, University of Chicago); 917 (both; Museum of Fine Arts, Boston); 954 (bottom; Athens Airport); 1005; 1017 (bottom; Museum of Fine Arts, Boston); 1096 (The Louvre); 1156 (Oriental Institute Museum, University of Chicago); 1231; 1249; 1276 (The Louvre); 1303; 1310; 1317 (Art Institute of Chicago); 1322 (Oriental Institute Museum, University of Chicago); 1323 (top; Museum of Fine Arts, Boston); 1323 (bottom; Oriental Institute

Museum, University of Chicago); 1343 (top; The Louvre); 1352 (Nof Ginnosar Museum, Israel); 1366 (Thessaloniki Archaeological Museum); 1377; 1391 (The Louvre); 1424; 1427; 1433; 1434; 1448; 1484-1485 (top; Chicago Field Museum); 1501; 1504; 1529; 1545 (Acropolis Museum Athens); 1546 (Dayton Art Institute); 1559; 1560; 1573; 1585; 1616 (Athens Archaeological Museum); 1621 (top); 1626 (Athens Archaeological Museum); 1632; 1636 (Corinth Archaeological Museum); 1642 (Thessaloniki Archaeological Museum); 1662; 1665 (Thessaloniki Archaeological Museum); 1669 (top); 1670; 1686 (bottom; Thessaloniki Archaeological Museum); 1721 (left; Thessaloniki Archaeological Museum/ right; The Louvre); 1726 (bottom left; Corinth Archaeological Museum); 1728 (Corinth Archaeological Museum); 1729 (Corinth Archaeological Museum); 1732 (left; Thessaloniki Archaeological Museum/right; Athens Archaeological Museum); 1733; 1736; 1737; 1763; 1770 (bottom; Thessaloniki Archaeological Museum); 1777 (Museum of Fine Arts, Boston); 1783 (Delphi Archaeological Museum); 1785 (The Louvre); 1789; 1802 (Dayton Art Institute); 1866.

Hughes, Randy: p. 1379.

Kandros, Micah: p. 585.

Maeir, A.: p. 383 (bottom; The Tell es-Safi/Gath Archaelogical Project); 389 (both; The Tell es-Safi/Gath Archaelogical Project).

McLemore, James: pp. 27 (bottom); 31; 37 (bottom); 129; 208 (top); 244; 288 (center right); 299 (top left; Istanbul Archaeological Museum); 341; 392; 466 (bottom); 553; 614; 639; 667; 768; 819; 873 (all); 1179; 1206; 1381 (center right); 1393; 1455; 1590; 1591; 1615 (bottom right); 1706.

Mitchell, Eric: pp. 461; 883.

Nowitz, Richard: pp. 1610; 1751.

Rogers, David: pp. 30 (bottom); 35 (Metropolitan Museum of Art, New York); 40 (bottom; Louvre Museum, Paris); 41 (bottom; Ephesus Museum); 51 (bottom; Joseph A. Callaway Archaeological Museum; The Southern Baptist Theological Seminary, Louisville, KY); 57; 58 (Jewish Museum, New York); David Rogers (British Museum, London); 81 (top; Metropolitan Museum of Art, New York); 93 (bottom; British Museum, London); 95 (Boston Museum of Fine Arts); 115 (bottom; The Louvre); 125 (top right; British Museum, London); 133 (bottom left; Museum of the Ancient Orient, Istanbul); 169 (bottom right; Museum of Art and Archaeology; University of Missouri, Columbia); 183 (Joseph A. Callaway Archaeological Museum; The Southern Baptist Theological Seminary, Louisville, KY); 208 (bottom); 209 (top); 209 (center right; Archaeological Museum, Ankara, Turkey); 218 (bottom right; Archaeological Museum, Ankara, Turkey); 219 (Archaeological Museum, Ankara, Turkey); 247 (right; Joseph A. Callaway Archaeological Museum; The Southern Baptist Theological Seminary, Louisville, KY); 266 (top; Joseph A. Callaway Archaeological Museum; The Southern Baptist Theological Seminary, Louisville, KY); 268 (top right; University Museum, University of Pennsylvania); 283 (center right; Museum of the Ancient Orient, Istanbul); 298 (top right; University Museum, University of Pennsylvania); 299 (center left; Jewish Museum, New York); 299 (bottom right; Adana Archaeological Museum, Adana, Turkey); 306; 312 (bottom right; University Museum, University of Pennsylvania); 332 (top right; Boston Museum of Fine Arts); 332 (bottom left; Joseph A. Callaway Archaeological Museum; The Southern Baptist Theological Seminary, Louisville, KY); 368; 399 (center right; Museum of Art and Archaeology; University of Missouri, Columbia); 416 (bottom right; The Louvre); 426 (University Museum, University of Pennsylvania); 436 (left; University Museum, University of Pennsylvania); 436; 437 (right; University Museum, University of Pennsylvania); 439 (British Museum, London); 467 (top left); 491 (top right; The Louvre); 497; 533 (British Museum, London); 544 (The Louvre); 570 (University Museum, University of Pennsylvania); 646 (right); 673 (Joseph A. Callaway Archaeological Museum; The Southern Baptist Theological Seminary, Louisville, KY); 675; 696 (The Louvre); 707 (Boston Museum of Fine Arts); 713 (Museum of the Ancient Orient); 719; 728 (bottom left; The Archaeological Museum, Ankara, Turkey); 749 (British Museum, London); 758 (University Museum, University of Pennsylvania); 759 (Ephesus Museum); 799 (center; British Museum, London); 800; 815;822 (bottom left; Archaeological Museum, Istanbul); 853 (British Museum, London); 865 (bottom left; Yale University Art Museum, New Haven); 891 (Museum of Fine Arts, Boston); 921 (bottom); 943 (The Louvre); 1030 (bottom); 1031; 1036 (The Louvre); 1037; 1048 (British Museum); 1076 (Oriental Institute Museum, University of Chicago); 1089 (Oriental Institute Museum, University of Chicago); 1090 (Joseph A. Callaway Archaeological Museum; The Southern Baptist Theological Seminary, Louisville, KY); 1115; 1127 (British Museum); 1156 (Metropolitan Museum of Art, New York); 1165 (top right); 1167 (Joseph A. Callaway Archaeological Museum; The Southern Baptist Theological Seminary, Louisville, KY); 1196; 1271; 1272 (University Museum, University of Pennsylvania); 1275 (bottom right); 1277 (The Louvre); 1286 (bottom left); 1321 (top); 1321 (bottom; Jewish Museum, New York); 1334 (bottom; Metropolitan Museum of Art, New York); 1343 (bottom; British Museum, London); 1359 (Jewish Museum, New York); 1360 (top; British Museum, London); 1367 (British Museum, London); 1383 (Joseph A. Callaway Archaeological Museum; The Southern Baptist Theological Seminary, Louisville, KY); 1400; 1450 (Chicago Field Museum); 1460; 1503 (Joseph A. Callaway Archaeological Museum; The Southern Baptist Theological Seminary, Louisville, KY); 1513 (British Museum, London); 1548 (Archaeological Museum, Antakya, Turkey); 1549 (top; The Louvre); 1557 (right); 1558; 1562; 1586 (both; Jewish Museum, New York); 1595 (bottom); 1605 (Museum of Art and Archaeology, University of Missouri, Columbia); 1608 (Metropolitan Museum of Art, New York); 1623 (Metropolitan Museum of Art, New York); 1624 (British Museum); 1645 (top right; Joseph A. Callaway Archaeological Museum; The Southern Baptist Theological Seminary, Louisville, KY); 1680 (left; Archaeological Museum, Ankara, Turkey); 1682 (bottom; British Museum); 1684 (Joseph A. Callaway Archaeological Museum; The Southern Baptist Theological Seminary, Louisville, KY); 1685 (Jewish Museum, New York); 1695 (right); 1700 (top); 1701 (British Museum, London); 1713 (British Museum, London); 1717; 1739; 1744 (right; Archaeological Museum, Ankara, Turkey); 1747 (Museum of Fine Arts, Boston); 1761; 1764 (left; Joseph A. Callaway Archaeological Museum; The Southern Baptist Theological Seminary, Louisville, KY); 1781 (The Louvre); 1801 (Joseph A. Callaway Archaeological Museum; The Southern Baptist Theological Seminary, Louisville, KY); 1803; 1809 (Museum of Art and Archaeology, University of Missouri, Columbia); 1810 (Museum of Fine Arts, Boston); 1813; 1829; 1833; 1855 (bottom; British Museum, London); 1858 (Joseph A. Callaway Archaeological Museum; The Southern Baptist Theological Seminary, Louisville, KY); 1867 (Oriental Institute Museum, University of Chicago).

Rutherford, Mike: pp. 26 (top); 27 (top); 69 (top right); 88; 895; 902; 1340; 1354.

Schatz, Bob: pp. 6; 12 (top, Anatolian Civilizations Museum of Ankara); 13 (top & bottom); 15; 16 (top); 22; 29 (Alaca Huyuk Museum); 30 (top); 37 (top); 38 (Anatolian Civilizations Museum of Ankara); 46 (middle & bottom); 59; 61; 67; 68; 77 (top & bottom); 78 (bottom; Royal Ontario Museum, Toronto); 79; 90; 93 (center right; The Egyptian Museum, Cairo); 94 (both/top left; Aswan Museum); 97; 105; 107 (Greco-Roman Museum, Alexandria, Egypt); 117; 120; 121 (top); 123; 127; 128 (top & bottom); 135; 205; 243; 245; 283; 289 (top right; Hazor Museum, Israel); 295; 299 (top right); 299 (bottom left); 307 (top; The Egyptian Museum, Cairo, Egypt/bottom; Hatay Archaeological Museum); 327; 337; 352; 357; 360 (top); 373; 383 (top); 399 (bottom); 406; 412 (Museum of the Ancient Orient, Istanbul); 417 (top right; (Museum of the Ancient Orient, Istanbul); 417; 427 (Museum at Aphrodite Temple); 437 (left; Hazor Museum, Israel); 447; 453; 466 (top right; Hatay Archaeological Museum); 485; 502; 503 (Istanbul Archaeological Museum); 508; 512 (top); 522 (bottom); 542 (Museum of the Ancient Orient, Istanbul); 543 (top right; Hatay Archaeological Museum); 543 (bottom left; Archaeological Museum, Antakya, Turkey); 560; 571 (Anatolian Civilizations Museum of Ankara); 576; 577; 586; 593 (Istanbul Archaeological Museum); 596; 597 (top & bottom); 605 (Istanbul Archaeological Museum); 634; 637 (top & bottom); 638 (bottom); 653; 659; 660; 669; 680 (bottom left & right); 681 (top & bottom); 682; 730; 737 (Istanbul Archaeological

Museum); 777 (top right; Museum of the Ancient Orient, Istanbul); 799 (top; Museum of the Ancient Orient, Istanbul); 822 (top); 865 (top right); 871; 898; 899 (Cairo Museum); 905 (Oriental Museum, Chicago); 907; 920 (bottom right); 921 (top left); 923; 933; 1029 (Royal Ontario Museum, Toronto); 1058; 1059; 1073 (Coptic Museum, Cairo); 1108 (National Museum of Damascus); 1114 (Archaeological Museum at Pella); 1119; 1120; 1121; 1128; 1163; 1187 (top right; Museum of the Ancient Orient, Istanbul); 1203; 1212; 1213 (Hazor Archaeological Museum); 1220; 1233; 1244; 1245; 1253; 1258; 1261 (Anatolian Civilizations Museum of Ankara); 1265 (National Museum of Damascus); 1269; 1286 (top); 1294; 1299 (Aswan Museum); 1307; 1311 (Museum of the Ancient Orient, Istanbul); 1334 (top; Shahba Museum, Philippopolis, Syria); 1346 (top); 1349; 1350; 1351; 1356 (bottom; Royal Ontario Museum, Toronto); 1362; 1363; 1384 (top); 1403; 1405; 1409; 1410; 1425; 1431; 1437; 1440; 1442 (Cairo Museum); 1456; 1466 (top; Royal Ontario Museum, Toronto); 1466 (bottom); 1467; 1475; 1478 (Department of Antiquities in Jordan Archaeological Museum, Amman, Jordan); 1486; 1493 (top); 1494 (Archaeological Museum at Pella); 1496; 1521 (Hatay Archaeological Museum); 1530; 1539; 1540; 1541; 1550; 1551; 1552; 1556; 1564; 1565 (Hatay Archaeological Museum); 1567; 1568 (Greco-Roman Museum, Cairo); 1572; 1574; 1576 (background); 1578; 1579; 1580; 1581; 1582; 1595 (top); 1596; 1597; 1599; 1604; 1606; 1611; 1612; 1614; 1615 (top left); 1618; 1621; 1625 (Istanbul Archaeological Museum); 1633; 1635; 1637 (The Ancient Corinth Museum); 1639 (top); 1639 (bottom; The Ancient Corinth Museum); 1643 (top); 1645 (bottom left); 1646; 1647 (top); 1647 (bottom; Archaeological Museum in Isthmia); 1648 (Anatolia Civilizations Museum of Ankara); 1652; 1655; 1657; 1658; 1659 (all; Capitoline Museum, Rome); 1660 (Courtesy of Ferrini and Biondi); 1665 (left; Capitoline Museum, Rome); 1666 (Istanbul Archaeological Museum); 1671 (The Ancient Corinth Museum); 1675; 1678 (Anatolia Civilization Museum of Ankara); 1679 (Konya Archaeological Museum); 1680 (right; Capitoline Museum, Rome); 1689; 1692; 1694; 1695 (left); 1700 (bottom; National Museum of Damascus); 1705; 1708; 1709 (bottom); 1710; 1711; 1714 (left); 1718; 1719; 1720 (Istanbul Archaeological Museum); 1726 (top right; Greco-Roman Museum, Alexandria, Egypt); 1727; 1730 (right); 1731; 1738 (left); 1744 (left); 1745; 1748 (center left; Anatolia Civilization Museum of Ankara/bottom); 1749 (left); 1754; 1756; 1757 (Archaeological Museum in Isthmia); 1758 (Istanbul Archaeological Museum); 1762; 1765; 1773; 1776 (The Egyptian Museum, Cairo); 1767; 1778; 1779; 1782; 1784; 1786; 1791; 1793; 1796; 1798; 1811 (right); 1815; 1821 (bottom); 1823; 1828; 1839; 1847; 1848; 1850; 1851; 1852; 1854; 1855 (top); 1856; 1857; 1865; 1869; 1872; 1873.

Severance, Murray: pp. 521; 685; 697; 705; 1291; 1297; 1495; 1668.

Smith, Audrey: pp. 1629; 1643 (bottom); 1664; 1667.

Smith, Louise Kohl: pp. 4 (bottom); 16 (bottom); 17; 73 (bottom); 134 (bottom); 416 (top right); 475 (bottom); 566; 668; 824; 1432; 1441; 1492; 1561; 1649 (right); 1696; 1722; 1788; 1800; 1807; 1808; 1811 (left); 1827.

Tolar, William: p. 1735.

Touchton, Ken: pp. 1; 69 (top left); 121 (bottom; National Maritime Museum, Haifa); 165 (Rockefeller Museum, Jerusalem); 413 (top); 413 (right; Department of Antiquities in Jordan Archaeological Museum, Amman, Jordan); 635; 642; 679 (bottom right); 983; 1200; 1207 (Israel Museum); 1295; 1329; 1333; 1356 (top); 1474; 1483; 1514; 1523; 1542; 1543; 1554; 1644; 1709 (top); 1743 (Vatican Museum, Rome); 1746 (Capitoline Museum, Rome).

Veneman, Justin: pp. 1378; 1386; 1420; 1421 (both); 1499 (both); 1500; 1510.

OTHER PHOTOGRAPHS

iStock Images: pp. 1703; 1715; 1723; 1741; 1759; 1831.

Jupiter Images: pp. 1479

Public Domain Images: pp. 72 (both; Matson Photo Collection, Library of Congress); 91; 755; 847; 1153; 1287 (Matson Photo Collection, Library of Congress); 1347.

Evans, Craig, *Holman QuickSource Guide to the Dead Sea Scrolls*: p. 1843.

Wikimedia Commons: p. 1047 (Chamberi/Israel Museum, Jerusalem)

MAPS, ILLUSTRATIONS, AND RECONSTRUCTIONS

Biblical Illustrator, Nashville, TN: pp. 68 (bottom); 70; 513 (bottom); 615 (top right); 1006.

Cox, Charles: p. 1390.

Holman Bible & Reference: pp. 56; 239; 241; 285; 298 (298); 349 (top); 467 (right); 471 (bottom); 497 (bottom); 509; 515; 523; 555; 651; 690-91; 1401; 1438; 1473; 1525; 1563; 1592; 1853.

Latta, Bill: p. 1030 (top).

Linden Artists, London: pp. 1339 (right); 1407 (bottom); 1493 (bottom); 1569; 1669 (bottom); 1681; 1714 (right).

Maltings Partnership, Derby England: p. 1388.

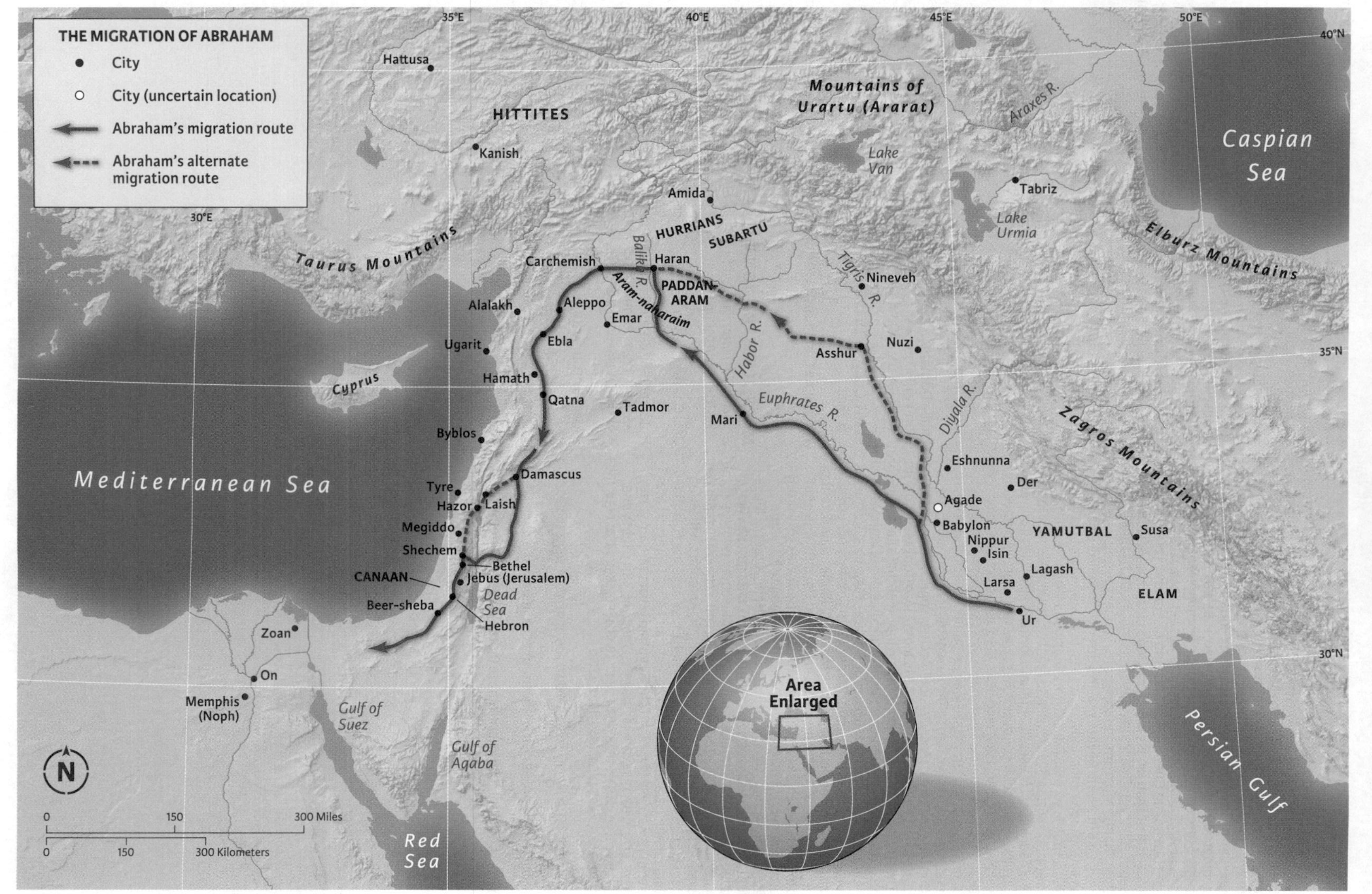
THE MIGRATION OF ABRAHAM
City
City (uncertain location)
Abraham's migration route
Abraham's alternate migration route
35°E
40°E
45°E
50°E
30°E
40°N
35°N
30°N
Hattusa
HITTITES
Kanish
Mountains of Urartu (Ararat)
Araxes R.
Caspian Sea
Lake Van
Tabriz
Lake Urmia
Amida
HURRIANS
SUBARTU
Elburz Mountains
Taurus Mountains
Carchemish
Balikh R.
Haran
PADDAN-ARAM
Aram-naharaim
Tigris R.
Nineveh
Alalakh
Aleppo
Emar
Ebla
Ugarit
Habor R.
Asshur
Nuzi
Cyprus
Hamath
Qatna
Tadmor
Mari
Euphrates R.
Diyala R.
Byblos
Zagros Mountains
Eshnunna
Mediterranean Sea
Damascus
Tyre
Hazor
Laish
Der
Agade
Megiddo
Babylon
YAMUTBAL
Susa
Nippur
Isin
Shechem
Bethel
CANAAN
Jebus (Jerusalem)
Lagash
Larsa
Dead Sea
ELAM
Beer-sheba
Hebron
Ur
Zoan
On
Memphis (Noph)
Gulf of Suez
Area Enlarged
Persian Gulf
Gulf of Aqaba
N
0
150
300 Miles
0
150
300 Kilometers
Red Sea

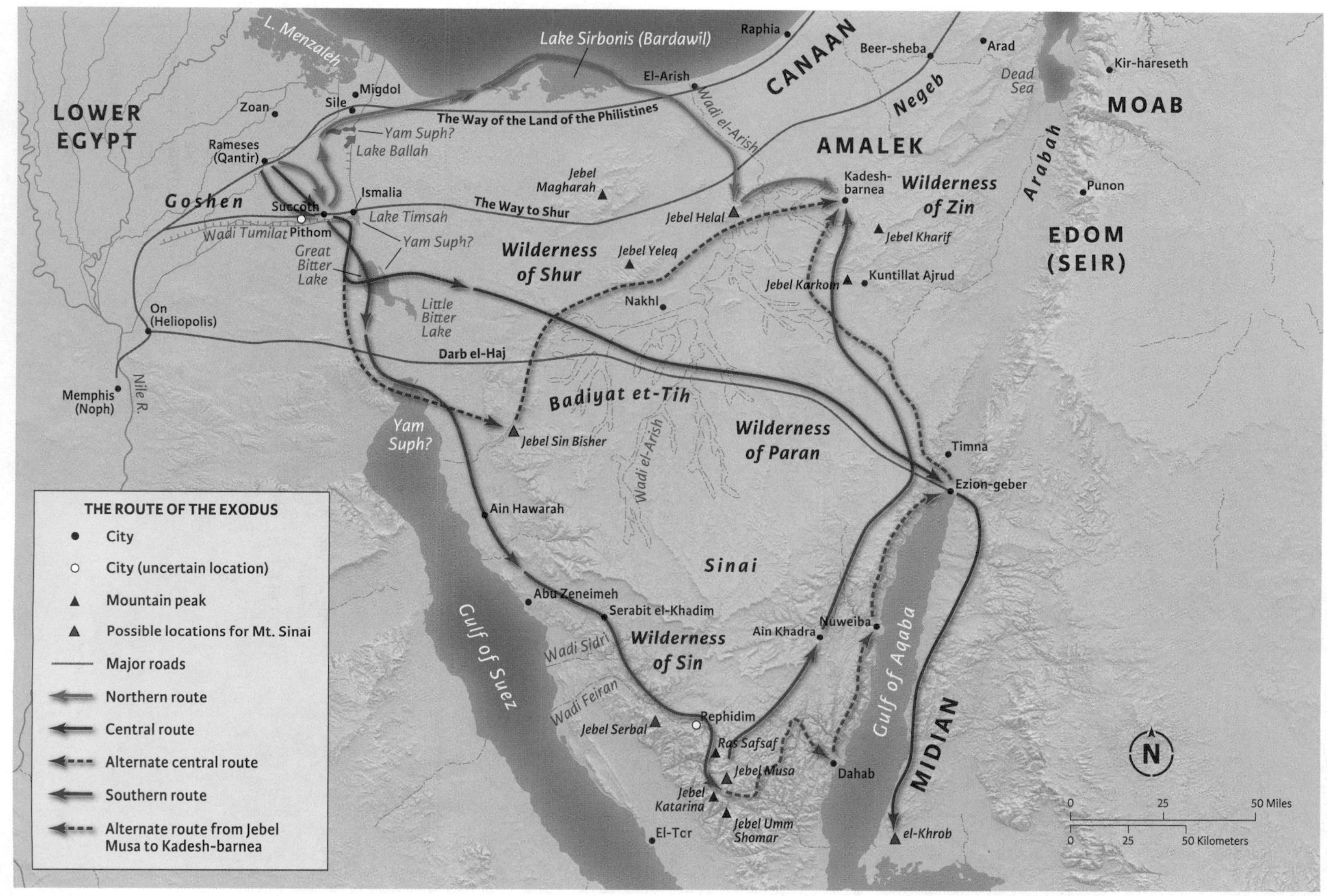
THE ROUTE OF THE EXODUS
City
City (uncertain location)
Mountain peak
Possible locations for Mt. Sinai
Major roads
Northern route
Central route
Alternate central route
Southern route
Alternate route from Jebel Musa to Kadesh-barnea
LOWER EGYPT
L. Menzaleh
Zoan
Rameses (Qantir)
Goshen
Wadi Tumilat
Succoth
Pithom
On (Heliopolis)
Memphis (Noph)
Nile R.
Sile
Migdol
Yam Suph?
Lake Ballah
Ismalia
Lake Timsah
Yam Suph?
Great Bitter Lake
Little Bitter Lake
Lake Sirbonis (Bardawil)
The Way of the Land of the Philistines
The Way to Shur
Darb el-Haj
El-Arish
Wadi el-Arish
Raphia
CANAAN
Beer-sheba
Arad
Negeb
Dead Sea
Kir-hareseth
MOAB
AMALEK
Arabah
Punon
EDOM (SEIR)
Kadesh-barnea
Wilderness of Zin
Jebel Kharif
Jebel Magharah
Jebel Helal
Wilderness of Shur
Jebel Yeleq
Jebel Karkom
Kuntillat Ajrud
Nakhl
Badiyat et-Tih
Wadi el-Arish
Wilderness of Paran
Yam Suph?
Jebel Sin Bisher
Timna
Ezion-geber
Ain Hawarah
Sinai
Abu Zeneimeh
Serabit el-Khadim
Gulf of Suez
Wadi Sidri
Wilderness of Sin
Ain Khadra
Nuweiba
Gulf of Aqaba
Wadi Feiran
Jebel Serbal
Rephidim
Ras Safsaf
Jebel Musa
Dahab
Jebel Katarina
Jebel Umm Shomar
El-Tor
MIDIAN
el-Khrob
N
0
25
50 Miles
0
25
50 Kilometers

THE TRIBAL ALLOTMENTS OF ISRAEL
City
City (uncertain location)
Mountain peak
0 20 40 Miles
0 20 40 Kilometers
34°E
35°E
36°E
33°N
32°N
31°N
Mediterranean Sea
Sidon
Damascus
TYRE
Mt. Hermon
ARAM
Pharpar R.
Ijon
Litani R.
Tyre
Laish (Dan)
Beth-anath
NAPHTALI
ASHER
Kedesh
Lake Huleh
Merom
Iron
Hazor
EAST MANASSEH
Acco
Mishal
Aphek
Cabul
Chinnereth
Sea of Chinnereth
Nahalal
Hannathon
Achshaph
Rimmon
Rakkath
Golan
Ashtaroth
Mt. Carmel
Daberath
Hammath
Kishon R.
ZEBULUN
Jabneel
Yarmuk R.
Helkath
Jokneam
Tabor
En-haddah
Sarid
En-dor
Shunem
Lo-debar
Edrei
Dor
ISSACHAR
Jarmuth
Megiddo
Taanach
Jezreel
Ramoth-gilead
En-gannim
Beth-shean
Dothan
Ibleam
Jabesh-gilead
WEST MANASSEH
Socoh
Tirzah
Jordan R.
Gerasa
Zaphon
Mt. Ebal
Succoth
Penuel
Pirathon
Shechem
AMMON
Yarkon R.
Mahanaim
Jabbok R.
Gath-rimmon
Aphek
Mt. Gerizim
Janoah
EPHRAIM
Shiloh
GAD
Joppa
Upper Beth-horon
Mizpah
Ophrah
Jazer
Jehud
Lod
Gittaim
Shaalbim
Bethel
Beth-nimrah
Amman
DAN
Naaran
Gilgal
Jabneel
Gezer
Gibeon
Aijalon
Jericho
Chephirah
Ramah
Acacia Meadow
Baalath
Bezer
Ashdod
Ekron
Zorah
Jerusalem
Beth-hoglah
Mt. Nebo
Heshbon
Timnah
BENJAMIN
Beth-shemesh
Medeba
Gath
Bethlehem
Ashkelon
Jahaz
Mareshah
Tekoa
Beth-zur
REUBEN
Lachish
Kedemoth
Eglon
Hebron
Dibon
Gaza
Dead Sea
JUDAH
Juttah
Aroer
Gerar
Ziklag
Eshtemoa
Arnon R.
Wadi Besor
Bethul
Jattir
Ashan
Kabzeel
Sharuhen
Beer-sheba
Arad
Hormah
Kir-hareseth
Hazar-shual
Baalah
SIMEON
Eltolad
MOAB
Ezem
Zered R.
Tamar
Arabah
EDOM
Kadesh-barnea

THE KINGDOMS OF ISRAEL AND JUDAH
City
City (uncertain location)
Capital city
Mountain peak
Major roads
Other roads
Israel
Judah
0
20
40 Miles
0
20
40 Kilometers
Mediterranean Sea
PHOENICIA
ARAM
GESHUR
ISRAEL
AMMON
PHILISTIA
JUDAH
MOAB
EDOM
Eastern Desert
Wilderness
Negeb
Arabah
Dead Sea
Beirut
Sidon
Damascus
Mt. Hermon
Pharpar R.
Ijon
Litani R.
Tyre
Abel-beth-maacah
Dan
Jeroboam built a sanctuary
Kedesh
Lake Huleh
Achzib
Hazor
Acco
Chinnereth
Sea of Chinnereth
Mt. Carmel
Gath-hepher
Aphek
Yarmuk R.
Ashtaroth
Kishon R.
Mt. Tabor
Dor
Edrei
Megiddo
Jezreel
Mt. Gilboa
Beth-shean
Ramoth-gilead
Dothan
Ibleam
Pehel
Jabesh-gilead
Political capital of Israel from Omri onward
Socoh
Tirzah
Succoth
Samaria
Mt. Ebal
Jordan R.
Penuel
Shechem
Yarkon R.
Mt. Gerizim
Mahanaim
Jabbok R.
Adam
Aphek
Shiloh
Joppa
Lydda
Upper Beth-horon
Jeroboam built a sanctuary
Rabbah (Amman)
Lower Beth-horon
Bethel
Gezer
Ramah
Geba
Jericho
Aijalon
Jerusalem
Heshbon
Ashdod
Ekron
Mt. Nebo
Gath
Azekah
Bethlehem
Medeba
Ashkelon
Tekoa
Mareshah
Beth-zur
Lachish
Hebron
Ziph
Dibon
Gaza
Adoraim
Carmel
Gerar
Maon
Wadi Besor
Arnon R.
Beer-sheba
Arad
Kir-hareseth
INTERNATIONAL COASTAL HIGHWAY
Zered R.
Tamar
Bozrah
Kadesh-barnea
KING'S HIGHWAY

N
0
20
40 Miles
0
20
40 Kilometers
Mediterranean Sea
ABILENE
Sidon
Damascus
PHOENICIA (TYRE)
Mt. Hermon
Pharpar R.
Litani R.
ITUREA
Tyre
Caesarea-Philippi
(Paneas)
Lake
Huleh
GAULANITIS
Raphana
Cadasa
(Kedesh)
Gischala
(Gush Halav)
BATANEA
Ptolemais
(Acco)
Bethsaida
Capernaum
TRACHONITIS
Jotapata
Gergesa (Kursi)
Mt. Carmel
Tiberias
Gamala
Canatha
Kishon R.
GALILEE
Hippos
Yarmuk R.
Nazareth
Sea of
Galilee
Abila
Adraa
(Edrei)
Mt. Tabor
Gadara
Dora
Dion
Legio
(Megiddo)
Scythopolis
(Beth-shean)
AURANITIS
Caesarea Maritima
(Strato's Tower)
Bostra
Ginae
(Jenin)
Pella
Coponius was named the first prefect
and established the administrative
capital at Caesarea Maritima
Aenon
Salim
Jordan R.
DECAPOLIS
Gerasa
(Jerash)
SAMARIA
Sebaste (Samaria)
Mt. Ebal
Amathus
Apollonia
Neapolis
(Shechem)
Yarkon R.
Jabbok R.
Antipatris
(Aphek)
Alexandrium
Joppa
Ephraim (Ophrah)
Gedor (Gadara)
PEREA
Lydda
Archelais
Philadelphia (Amman)
JUDEA
Jamnia
Jericho
Azotus
(Ashdod)
Emmaus
(Nicopolis)
Jerusalem
Mt. Nebo
Esbus (Heshbon)
Mesad
Hasidim
(Qumran)
Medeba
Ascalon
(Ashkelon)
Hyrcania
Callirrhoe (Zereth-shahar)
Betogabris
(Beth-guvrin)
Hebron
Machaerus
Gaza
Dead
Sea
En-gedi
Arnon R.
Wadi Besor
IDUMEA
Masada
Raphia
Beer-sheba
Arad
NABATEA
INTERNATIONAL
COASTAL HIGHWAY
Malatha
Khirbet
Tannur
Zered R.
Arabah
KING'S HIGHWAY
ISRAEL IN THE TIME OF JESUS
City
City (uncertain location)
Decapolis city
Decapolis city (uncertain location)
Administrative capital
Mountain peak
Major route
Other route
First procuratorship
Territory of Antipas
Territory of Philip
Syrian territory

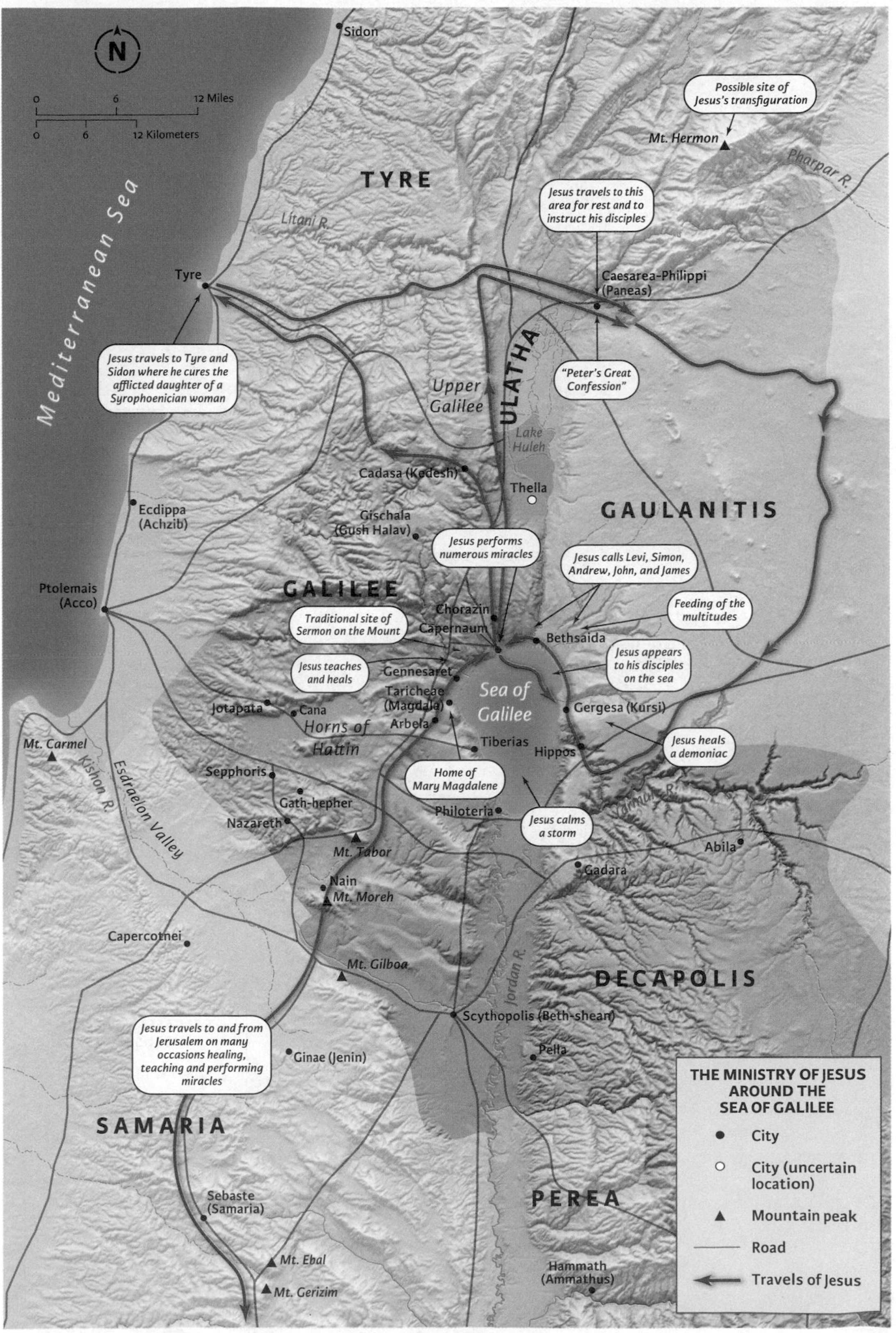

THE MINISTRY OF JESUS AROUND THE SEA OF GALILEE
City
City (uncertain location)
Mountain peak
Road
Travels of Jesus
0 6 12 Miles
0 6 12 Kilometers
N
Sidon
Possible site of Jesus's transfiguration
Mt. Hermon
Pharpar R.
TYRE
Litani R.
Mediterranean Sea
Jesus travels to this area for rest and to instruct his disciples
Tyre
Caesarea-Philippi (Paneas)
ULATHA
Jesus travels to Tyre and Sidon where he cures the afflicted daughter of a Syrophoenician woman
"Peter's Great Confession"
Upper Galilee
Lake Huleh
Cadasa (Kedesh)
Thella
Ecdippa (Achzib)
Gischala (Gush Halav)
GAULANITIS
Jesus performs numerous miracles
Jesus calls Levi, Simon, Andrew, John, and James
Ptolemais (Acco)
GALILEE
Feeding of the multitudes
Chorazin
Traditional site of Sermon on the Mount
Capernaum
Bethsaida
Jesus teaches and heals
Gennesaret
Jesus appears to his disciples on the sea
Taricheae (Magdala)
Sea of Galilee
Jotapata
Cana
Gergesa (Kursi)
Horns of Hattin
Arbela
Tiberias
Hippos
Jesus heals a demoniac
Mt. Carmel
Kishon R.
Esdraelon Valley
Sepphoris
Home of Mary Magdalene
Gath-hepher
Yarmuk R.
Nazareth
Philoteria
Jesus calms a storm
Mt. Tabor
Abila
Gadara
Nain
Mt. Moreh
Capercotnei
Mt. Gilboa
Jordan R.
DECAPOLIS
Scythopolis (Beth-shean)
Jesus travels to and from Jerusalem on many occasions healing, teaching and performing miracles
Ginae (Jenin)
Pella
SAMARIA
Sebaste (Samaria)
PEREA
Mt. Ebal
Hammath (Ammathus)
Mt. Gerizim

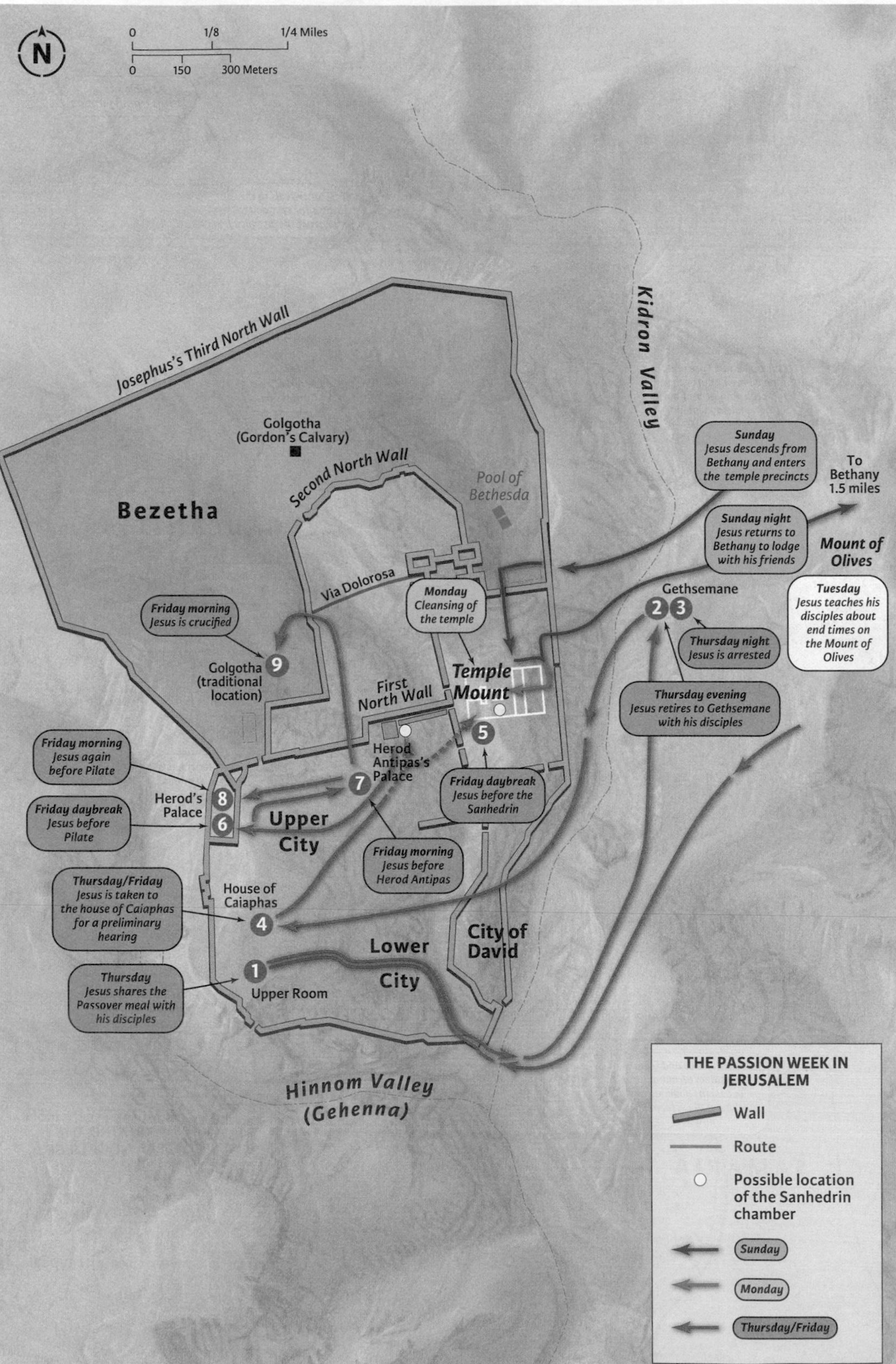
N
0
1/8
1/4 Miles
0
150
300 Meters
Josephus's Third North Wall
Kidron Valley
Golgotha
(Gordon's Calvary)
Second North Wall
Bezetha
Pool of Bethesda
Via Dolorosa
Sunday
Jesus descends from Bethany and enters the temple precincts
To Bethany 1.5 miles
Sunday night
Jesus returns to Bethany to lodge with his friends
Mount of Olives
Monday
Cleansing of the temple
Gethsemane
Tuesday
Jesus teaches his disciples about end times on the Mount of Olives
Friday morning
Jesus is crucified
Thursday night
Jesus is arrested
Golgotha (traditional location)
First North Wall
Temple Mount
Thursday evening
Jesus retires to Gethsemane with his disciples
Friday morning
Jesus again before Pilate
Herod Antipas's Palace
Friday daybreak
Jesus before the Sanhedrin
Herod's Palace
Friday daybreak
Jesus before Pilate
Upper City
Friday morning
Jesus before Herod Antipas
Thursday/Friday
Jesus is taken to the house of Caiaphas for a preliminary hearing
House of Caiaphas
City of David
Lower City
Thursday
Jesus shares the Passover meal with his disciples
Upper Room
Hinnom Valley
(Gehenna)
THE PASSION WEEK IN JERUSALEM
Wall
Route
Possible location of the Sanhedrin chamber
Sunday
Monday
Thursday/Friday

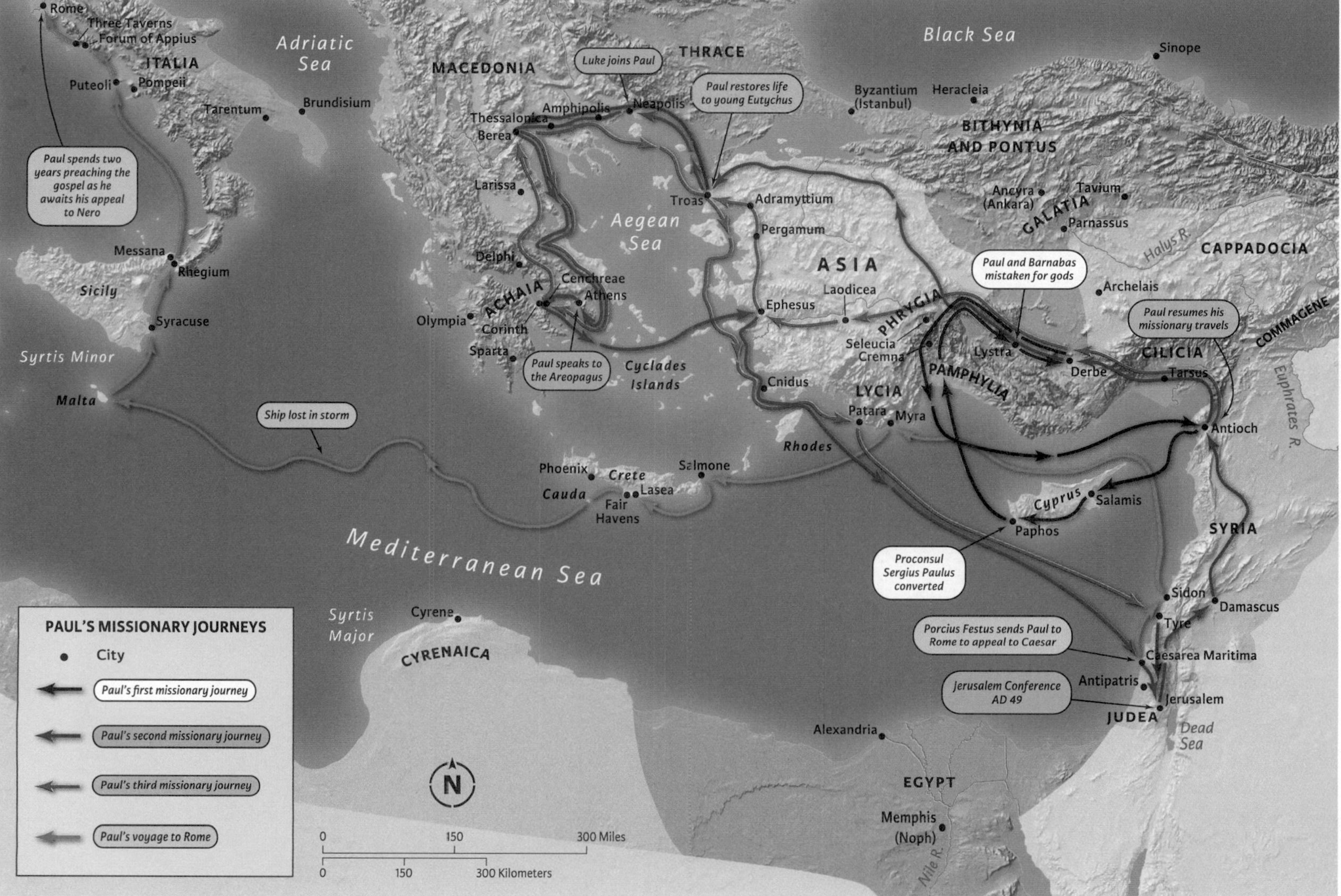
PAUL'S MISSIONARY JOURNEYS
City
Paul's first missionary journey
Paul's second missionary journey
Paul's third missionary journey
Paul's voyage to Rome
Paul spends two years preaching the gospel as he awaits his appeal to Nero
Luke joins Paul
Paul restores life to young Eutychus
Paul speaks to the Areopagus
Ship lost in storm
Paul and Barnabas mistaken for gods
Paul resumes his missionary travels
Proconsul Sergius Paulus converted
Porcius Festus sends Paul to Rome to appeal to Caesar
Jerusalem Conference AD 49
Rome
Three Taverns
Forum of Appius
ITALIA
Puteoli
Pompeii
Tarentum
Brundisium
Adriatic Sea
Messana
Rhegium
Sicily
Syracuse
Syrtis Minor
Malta
MACEDONIA
THRACE
Thessalonica
Berea
Amphipolis
Neapolis
Larissa
Delphi
ACHAIA
Cenchreae
Athens
Olympia
Corinth
Sparta
Aegean Sea
Cyclades Islands
Troas
Adramyttium
Pergamum
ASIA
Ephesus
Laodicea
Cnidus
Rhodes
LYCIA
Patara
Myra
PHRYGIA
Seleucia
Cremna
PAMPHYLIA
Lystra
Derbe
CILICIA
Tarsus
Black Sea
Byzantium (Istanbul)
Heracleia
BITHYNIA AND PONTUS
Sinope
Ancyra (Ankara)
Tavium
GALATIA
Parnassus
Halys R.
CAPPADOCIA
Archelais
COMMAGENE
Euphrates R.
Antioch
SYRIA
Damascus
Sidon
Tyre
Caesarea Maritima
Antipatris
Jerusalem
JUDEA
Dead Sea
Cyprus
Salamis
Paphos
Phoenix
Crete
Salmone
Cauda
Lasea
Fair Havens
Mediterranean Sea
Syrtis Major
Cyrene
CYRENAICA
Alexandria
EGYPT
Memphis (Noph)
Nile R.
N
0
150
300 Miles
0
150
300 Kilometers